THREE CENTURIES OF AMERICAN POETRY AND PROSE

REVISED EDITION

BY

ALPHONSO GERALD NEWCOMER
LATE PROFESSOR OF ENGLISH, STANFORD UNIVERSITY

ALICE E. ANDREWS
TEACHER OF ENGLISH AND HISTORY, HARDING HIGH SCHOOL, ST. PAUL

HOWARD JUDSON HALL
PROFESSOR OF ENGLISH, STANFORD UNIVERSITY

REVISION BY HOWARD JUDSON HALL

SCOTT, FORESMAN & COMPANY

CHICAGO   ATLANTA   DALLAS   NEW YORK

PREFACE

The fact that *Twelve Centuries of English Poetry and Prose* supplied a real need in schools and colleges prompted the editors to compile the present companion volume of American literature. It may be granted that the ideal method of studying literature is through reading authors from complete editions; the mere thumbing through of the author's whole work gives the student a valuable perspective of the particular part he is reading. But every teacher knows that except with the extraordinary coincidence of very small classes and very large libraries that ideal is unattainable. Even in our larger colleges and universities where, if anywhere, the ideal conditions might be found, books of selections representing periods of literary development are being used more and more for general courses in the history of literature, either as the basis of the student's reading or to supplement his reading in the library. The widening scope of the study of literature in kind and form makes necessary a compilation that will represent adequately both the greater authors of an epoch and also those minor authors whose work shows secondary but significant tendencies of their time. All this is the result of that view which takes literature to be not a thing apart from life, but an expression of all life, and would make its study a segment of the ever widening circle of human interests. It may be remarked in passing that the selections of the present book may be used as a valuable supplement in the direct study of American history and society.

In poetry the aim of the editors has been to place between the covers of a single volume the greater part of what will remain permanent in American poetry from its beginnings down to the end of the first great productive period in American literature. The chief poets are represented by selections intended to include much (in some cases all) of enduring worth in their work, and also to show their variety, versatility, and range. To other poets we have tried to accord space according to their importance; and a few appear whose work, though in itself of minor worth, reflects some broad phase of American life that should not be left out of account.

In prose the choice has naturally been more difficult than in poetry. Whenever possible we have used wholes; when this was not possible we have made selections that would show the author's purpose in the whole, and have above all tried to avoid the scrappiness and ineffectiveness of mere fragments. Of fiction it is impossible to represent in a single volume of this kind more than the necessary minimum. In the case of Irving and Hawthorne we have omitted some of the selections easily found in cheap editions, for the sake of others not so common and yet notable in themselves.

The editors have thought it best to give considerable space to colonial writers and thus make the book useful in schools where students do not have access to large libraries, and where colonial authors before Franklin are not to be found. It is safe to say that few high schools have Mather, or Byrd, or Ward, or Sewall. In fact there are colleges and universities of respectable standing that do not afford their students access to these men. We have therefore included from such authors somewhat more proportionately than their artistic worth merits. Our object has been to give young people a chance to know with some degree of adequateness a period of national life that was the seedtime of national ideals. The editors firmly believe that to begin the study of American literature with Franklin is to miss some of the most interesting chapters of American life, interesting not only to mature minds able at once to see their significance in relation to the whole, but fascinating to young people to whom they are a discovery. In working over this literature at a time when the nation is conscious of its inner life as never before, when it is rising to justify that life before the world, we have come to feel more and more strongly that the best of the nineteenth century American literature is no weakling offshoot of English literature. It draws its life-currents from the American spirit of the seventeenth and eighteenth centuries. Emerson and Hawthorne are not to be accounted for fundamentally by the awakening in the Old World. They profited, it is true, by the genial culture of Europe current in their day; but their spiritual foundation was

iii

generations deep in American soil. We hope that these selections will show the unity and continuity of our national spirit as well as its vast changes.

In selecting the material from this early period one primary aim has been to choose what would arouse the student's natural interest. We have chosen units that will tell how the colonists came here, what they came for, of their fights with the Indians, their travails in the founding of a new civil community, of their social life and ideals, and of how at length they became aware of their artistic isolation and began to cultivate grace of expression. As social record these old books need no apology. Young people can scarcely fail to note the difference between the society of Boston as seen in the diary of Sewall, and that of Virginia as the Westover papers show it, nor will they be likely to miss the contrast between the crabbed Puritanism of Ward and the expansive spirit of Williams that was destined to overcome it. We have generally avoided including anything merely because it was an attempt at art. To force upon young students as literature what our Puritan forbears put forward as such is too much like compelling them to admire as pictorial art the illustrations of the *New England Primer*. In the comparative and at times total absence of the aesthetic, we have frankly put before students pictures of social life, trusting that teachers will give them their proper perspective.

For the literature included under the heading From the Revolution to the Civil War, no excuse that it represents the life of an important people in the making is needed. Too long has the tone of the academic expounder of American literature been modeled, unconsciously enough perhaps, on the critical formula provided by Hazlitt in speaking of Irving:

"He [Irving] gives us very good copies of our British essayists and novelists, which may be very well on the other side of the water, or as proof of the capabilities of the national genius, but which might be dispensed with here, where we have to boast of the originals."

American literature, beginning with Irving, is not the product of immaturity, amateurism, and imitation; it has, as an acute American critic (Mr. James Lane Allen) has pointed out, something of the delicacy of outline and clarity of tone that mark French literature; if the possession of aesthetic sense be denied to Anne Bradstreet, it must be admitted in Poe; if our voice is crabbedly provincial and harsh in

Wigglesworth, it is far-reaching and resonant in Emerson; if Charles Brockden Brown is experimental, Hawthorne is finely sure in touch. And even though American literature follows, as Mr. Allen believes, the feminine rather than the masculine model, even if, as compared with the strong and inclusive virility of English letters, it seems somewhat thin, there are compensations and exceptions. Cooper, Mark Twain, and Whitman are no drawing-room products; and a type of insight and envisagement of life peculiarly our own seems to emerge from the collective American writings of the nineteenth century. Lest this be thought literary chauvinism, let it be admitted that American letters lack the scope, the broadly settled solidity of English letters, the penetrating white light of French letters. Still, no need to say "a poor thing but mine own." Kipling's *An American* is rather an identification than an indictment, no matter what its author intended. And it may be noted that our literature, for all "the cynic devil in its blood" has held singularly true to respect for the careful workmanship that if long continued means artistic mastery, and to a veracious presentment of things as they have been—not as one would have wished them to be. Whatever qualifications the cautious critic may wish to urge, it remains true that the American literature of the National Period is independent and important.

The order in which authors appear is in general chronological, in respect to the decade or generation of their greatest influence, or that with which they are most naturally connected. It has seemed best, however, to place the orators and historians as much as possible in groups by themselves, and also to group writers to some extent geographically, as in the case of the southern authors. The individual productions of an author, we have tried to place in the order of writing, feeling that this sequence will be of most interest to the student. Where, however, as in the case of the Dante sonnets of Longfellow, and in the case of authors who wrote both poetry and prose, it has seemed best to violate this order, we have done so.

As far as possible we have attempted to give in italics following each selection the date of writing, and in ordinary numerals the date of publication. In many cases one or both of these dates will fail to appear, though we have used every means at our disposal to find them. We believe that the order is, however, substantially correct.

As in *Twelve Centuries of English Poetry and Prose*, we have placed the notes where they are most accessible, at the bottom of the page, believing that there is no particular virtue, per se, in the hiding of the notes or the search for them, and in thus adding to the temptation not to refer to them at all. We have not attempted to make the notes take the place of the dictionary; but where a word though familiar has an unusual sense, or where even with a dictionary the student might stumble, we have tried to supply the correct gloss. In all cases we have attempted to furnish the student with the condensed and pertinent information necessary to make the text intelligible, and by cross references to coördinate all material in the book. The biographical paragraphs preceding each author's work give only the facts of his life most needed in a study of his work.

In such a book as this, the form that a reprint should take is always a moot question. The old forms are a real bar to the ready apprehension of the thought. On the other hand, emendation and modernizing take from the text the evidence of the lingering medieval that was a real characteristic of the first generation of American life, north and south. We have deemed it best to modernize commonly, but to give a touch of the archaic by retaining the original spelling and punctuation in the selections from Smith, Strachey, Bradford, Mrs. Knight, and Nathaniel Ward. Even in these selections it did not seem best to reproduce such peculiarities of type as the long s's or the abbreviations so fantastic to modern eyes, and so misleading to the inexperienced reader.

In the labor of preparing this book we have had aid from many sources. First of all we would thank Professor Lindsay Todd Damon of Brown University, who as supervising editor has been of invaluable assistance. His criticism and suggestions regarding both subject-matter and notes have been an asset not easily estimated. We would also thank colleagues and friends having access to special information useful in preparing the notes. We would especially thank Mr. Gerould, Librarian of the University of Minnesota; Dr. Solon J. Buck and Miss Jett of the Minnesota State Historical Society; Dr. Dawson Johnston, Mrs. Beals, and Miss Owens of the St. Paul Public Library; Miss Davis of the reference department of the Minneapolis Public Library; Mr. William C. Lane of the Harvard University Library; Mr. W. N. T. Carlton of the Newberry Library. We are indebted to Professor Firkins of the University of Minnesota for his kindness in furnishing the note on page 395; and to other friends who by suggestions and criticisms have aided in the work.

We gratefully acknowledge our indebtedness to the Houghton Mifflin Company for permission to use from Whittier's works "In School-Days," "My Triumph," "John Underhill," "Conductor Bradley," "A Sea Dream," "Sunset on the Bearcamp," "The Trailing Arbutus," "The Lost Occasion," and "The King's Missive"; from Longfellow's poems, "Mezzo Cammin"; from Jones Very's poems "The Soldier," "The Dead," "The War," "The Wild Rose of Plymouth"; from the poems of Oliver Wendell Holmes "Dorothy Q." and "How the Old Horse Won the Bet"; from the works of James Russell Lowell, "After the Burial," "In a Copy of Omar Khayyàm," and "Franciscus de Verulamio Sic Cogitavit"; to the Messrs. B. F. Johnson Publishing Company for permission to print from the poems of Henry Timrod, "I Know Not Why, but All This Weary Day," "Most Men Know Love but as a Part of Life," "Charleston," "Spring," "The Cotton Boll," and "Magnolia Cemetery"; to the Messrs. P. J. Kenedy and Sons for permission to print from the poems of Abram J. Ryan, "The Conquered Banner"; to the Messrs. Lothrop, Lee and Shepard Company for permission to use from the poems of Paul Hamilton Hayne, "Shelley," "Ode to Sleep," "The Mocking-Birds," "Vicksburg," "Aspects of the Pines," "The Rose and Thorn," "The Pine's Mystery," "A Little While I Fain Would Linger Yet," and "In Harbor"; to the Messrs. Little, Brown and Company for permission to use Charles Sumner's "The True Grandeur of Nations," Margaret Junkin Preston's "The Shade of the Trees," Helen Hunt Jackson's poems "Spinning," "October," and "Coronation," and all the poems printed from Emily Dickinson; to Mrs. Janey Hope Marr of Norfolk, Virginia, for permission to print from the poems of her father James Barron Hope, "Our Anglo-Saxon Tongue," "Dreamers," and "Under One Blanket"; to Messrs. Charles Scribner's Sons for permission to print the latest edition of all of Lanier's poems included in this book; to Mr. Horace Traubel for permission to print the poems of Walt Whitman here included.

The present volume was planned and some preliminary work done on it by the authors of *Twelve Centuries of English Poetry and Prose* before the lamented death of Professor Newcomer in 1913. The authorship as it appears on the title page was subsequently agreed upon.

August, 1917

A. E. A.
H. J. H.

PREFACE TO THE REVISED EDITION

The selections used in the first edition of this volume included nothing written after 1886. Since that date American literature has vastly expanded. In the twelve years since the first edition was published, and especially in these years following the World War, the interest in our own literature has increased in proportion as the writings themselves have gained in scope and intensity. No consideration of our literature can ignore this recent development; and the appeal of contemporary American poetry and prose, especially to young people, is so strong as to rekindle an interest in the past record.

In making the revision it was necessary to consider the size of the book for practical class-room purposes. For this reason selections that could best be spared from the old edition were abandoned, and the space thus gained was devoted in the revision to authors of today. The result is that the volume has not been increased unreasonably in size, though nearly one fourth of its material is new. The present volume is therefore of much greater variety than the first and, it is hoped, of correspondingly greater interest. The division of the book into epochs aims to be simple and practical, and is based upon what the student is supposed already to know of American political and social life through American history, and not upon movements seen by literary critics and named in terms beyond the young student's understanding.

In choosing the authors and their writings to fill in the gaps in the old edition between the Civil War and 1886 and to represent the literary development up to the present year the editors have faced a complex task. They cannot have succeeded to the satisfaction of all users of the book even in an element so apparently simple as finding material to represent adequately the literature of the South, East, and West. In choosing selections they have adhered as firmly as they could to their original principle of using wholes rather than extracts, a principle that has shut out some authors from whom no valuable unit short enough to be included might be chosen. Some material, moreover, otherwise excellent had to be rejected because it seemed unfitting for class-room use. From first to last the editors have kept their readers in mind, and without lowering their standards have made, wherever possible, concessions to the tastes of youth.

Instructors who have used the old volume will notice that the headnotes have been considerably expanded in the new volume to include bibliographical material and a few critical hints. These hints are intended to "place" the author in the student's mind; to give the student a starting-point from which he may intelligently read the author's work. They are in no sense to be taken as final critical estimates. In the bibliographical notes and the general bibliography at the end of the volume especial attention has been paid to citing books and articles reflecting recent, but sound, criticism. The assembling of this material and its preparation has been a time-consuming and painstaking task. The editors are especially grateful for the assistance of Dr. Nesta Mary Thompson of La Jolla, and Barbara Merrihew Perkins of Stanford University, California; they also acknowledge the many courtesies extended by George Thomas Clark and Nathan Van Patten, Director Emeritus and Director, respectively, of the Stanford University Libraries.

Copyrights are so jealously guarded by certain publishers that it has been impossible to represent two authors who would otherwise have been included. It was also impossible to print certain pieces of authors here represented; but the editors have spared neither pains nor expense in securing material they wished to include and they have succeeded beyond their first expectations. They therefore gratefully acknowledge the courtesy and coöperation of the great majority of publishers in granting the use of material.

The editors are indebted to the kindness of the following authors or their representatives who have given their express permission for the use of material in this volume:

To Franklin Pierce Adams for "Erring in Company" from *Tobogganing on Parnassus,* and "De Senectute" from *So There!*

vi

To William Rose Benét for Elinor Wylie's "Atavism" from *Nets to Catch the Wind,* and "Castilian" from *Black Armour.*

To Julian Burroughs for selections from *My Boyhood and Youth* by John Burroughs.

To Witter Bynner for "A Fortune-Teller" and "Train-Mates" from *Grenstone Poems,* and "Roofs" from *The Beloved Stranger.*

To Nathalia Crane for "The Flathouse Roof" from *The Janitor's Boy,* and "The Poe Cottage" from *Venus Invisible and Other Poems.*

To Theodosia Garrison Faulks for "Stains" and "April" from *The Joy of Life,* and "The Dreamer" from *The Dreamer and Other Poems.*

To Mary E. Wilkins Freeman for "In Butter-fly Time" from *A Humble Romance.*

To Robert Frost for "Mending Wall" and "The Death of the Hired Man" from *North of Boston,* and "Storm Fear" from *Selected Poems,* and "Not to Keep" from *New Hampshire.*

To Arthur Guiterman for "Afternoon Tea" from *The Mirthful Lyre,* and "Strictly Germ-Proof" from *The Laughing Muse.*

To Du Bose Heyward for "The Mountain Woman" from *Skylines and Horizons,* and "Prodigal," "Dusk in the Low Country," and "The Half Pint Flask" published in *The Bookman.*

To Vachel Lindsay for "Abraham Lincoln Walks at Midnight" from *Collected Poems,* and "These Are the Young" and "The Angel Sons" from *Going-to-the Stars.*

To William McFee for "The Market" from *Harbours of Memory.*

To Edwin Markham for "The Man with the Hoe" and "Lincoln the Man of the People" from *Collected Poems* (in preparation).

To Edgar Lee Masters for "Anne Rutledge" from *Spoon River Anthology,* for "Henry Zoll, the Miller," "Benjamin Franklin Hazard," and "Henry Cogdal" from *The New Spoon River,* and for "Clipper Ships."

To Christopher Morley for "On Unanswering Letters" and "What Men Live By" from *Mince Pie,* "To the Little House" from *Songs for a Little House,* and "Nursery Rhymes for the Tender-Hearted" from *Hide and Seek.*

To Lizette Woodward Reese for "Tears" and "Old Saul" from *Selected Poems,* and "The Lark" from *A Wayside Lute.*

To Edwin Arlington Robinson for "Reuben Bright" and "The House on the Hill" from *The Children of the Night,* "Miniver Cheevy" from *The Town Down the River,* and "Stafford's Cabin" from *Collected Poems.*

To Robert Haven Schauffler for "Scum o' the Earth" from *Scum o' the Earth and Other Poems,* "Helen of Laughing Ledge," "God's-Eye View," and "Trash" from *Hobnails in Eden.*

To Charles L. Seeger for Alan Seeger's "I Have a Rendezvous with Death" from *Poems.*

To Sara Teasdale for "Blue Squills," "August Moonrise," "On the Dunes," and "The Unseen" from *Flame and Shadow,* and "A Star Map," published in *The Bookman.*

To Henry van Dyke for "The Three Best Things" from *Collected Poems.*

To Owen Wister for *Padre Ignacio.*

The editors are further indebted to the following publishers for the use of copyright material as listed:

To D. Appleton and Company for "How Mr. Rabbit Was Too Sharp for Mr. Fox" and "Why Mr. Possum Loves Peace" from *Uncle Remus: His Songs and Sayings,* by Joel Chandler Harris; and for "These Are the Young" and "The Angel Sons" from *Going-to-the-Stars,* by Vachel Lindsay.

To Albert and Charles Boni, Inc., for "The Flathouse Roof" from *The Janitor's Boy,* by Nathalia Crane.

To Boni, Liveright and Company for their concurrence in permission to use "Henry Zoll, the Miller," "Benjamin Franklin Hazard," and "Henry Cogdal," from *The New Spoon River,* by Edgar Lee Masters.

To *The Bookman* for "Dusk in the Low Country," "Prodigal," and "The Half Pint Flask," by Du Bose Heyward; and for "A Star Map," by Sara Teasdale.

To Brandt and Brandt for "God's World" from *Renascence* and "Travel" and "Journey" from *Second April,* by Edna St. Vincent Millay.

To The Century Company for "A Wind-Storm in the Forests" from *The Mountains of California,* by John Muir; and for selections from *Ranch Life and the Hunting Trail,* by Theodore Roosevelt.

To Coward McCann, Inc., for "The Poe Cottage" from *Venus Invisible,* by Nathalia Crane.

To Dodd, Mead and Company for "A Vagabond Song" from *More Songs from Vagabondia,* "Moment Musicale" from *Echoes from Vagabondia,* and "The Joys of the Road" from *Songs from Vagabondia,* by Bliss Carman; and for "The Sea Gypsy" from *More Songs from Vagabondia,* and "The Wander-Lovers" from *Songs from Vagabondia,* by Richard Hovey.

To George H. Doran for "Tears" and "Old Saul" from *Selected Poems,* by Lizette Woodworth Reese; and for "Trees" from *Trees and Other Poems,* by Joyce Kilmer.

To Doubleday, Doran and Company for the use of selections from *My Boyhood,* by John Burroughs; for "The Hiding of Black Bill" from *Options,* by O. Henry; for "The Dreamer" from *The Dreamer and Other Poems,* by Theodosia Garrison; for "Erring in Company" from *Tobogganing on Parnassus,* and "De Senectute" from *So There!,* by Franklin Pierce Adams; for "The Market" from *Harbours of Memory,* by William McFee; for "On Unanswering Letters" and "What Men Live By" from *Mince Pie,* "To the Little House" from *Songs for a Little House,* "Nursery Rhymes for the Tender-Hearted" from *Hide and Seek,* by Christopher Morley; for "Castilian" from *Black Armour,* by Elinor Wylie; and for "The Ballad of William Sycamore" from *Tiger Joy,* by Stephen Vincent Benét.

To Doubleday, Page and Company for concurrence in the use of "The Man With the Hoe" from *The Man With the Hoe and Other Poems,* and for "Lincoln the Man of the People" from *Lincoln and Other Poems,* by Edwin Markham.

To Harcourt, Brace and Company for "Clean Curtains" and "A.E.F." from *Smoke and Steel,* by Carl Sandburg; for "The Buckskin Harness" from *Paul Bunyan,* by Esther Shephard; and for "The Watcher" from *Cross Currents,* by Margaret Widdemer.

To Harper and Brothers for "In Butterfly Time" from *A Humble Romance* by Mary E. Wilkins Freeman; for "Padre Ignacio" from *Padre Ignacio,* by Owen Wister; for "Afternoon Tea" from *The Mirthful Lyre,* and "Strictly Germ-Proof" from *The Laughing Muse,* by Arthur Guiterman; for "A Daring Deed" from *Life on the Mississippi,* and "The Cat and the Pain-killer" from *The Adventures of Tom Sawyer,* by Mark Twain.

To the Harr Wagner Publishing Company for "Exodus for Oregon" from *Complete Poems* by Joaquin Miller.

To Henry Holt and Company for "Mending Wall" and "The Death of the Hired Man" from *North of Boston,* "Storm Fear" from *Selected Poems,* and "Not to Keep" from *New Hampshire,* by Robert Frost; for "Chicago," "Grass," "Lost," "Fog," and "Laughing Corn" from *Selected Poems,* by Carl Sandburg; for "Factories" from *Factories with Other Lyrics,* and "The Modern Woman to Her Lover" from *The Old Road to Paradise,* by Margaret Widdemer; and for selections from *The Edge of the Jungle,* by William Beebe.

The following poems are used by permission of and special arrangement with Houghton Mifflin Company: "Guiliemus Rex" from *Complete Poems,* by Thomas Bailey Aldrich; "The Wild Ride" from *A Roadside Harp,* by Louise Imogen Guiney; "Jim Bludsoe of the Prairie Belle" from *Complete Poetical Works,* by John Hay; "Jim," and "Dickens in Camp" from *Poetical Works,* and "The Outcasts of Poker Flat," from *The Luck of Roaring Camp and Other Tales,* by Bret Harte; "Patterns" from *Men, Women, and Ghosts,* and "Meeting-House Hill" from *What's O'clock,* by Amy Lowell; "Good Friday Night" and "The Menagerie" from *Poems and Poetic Dramas,* by William Vaughan Moody; "The Child" from *A Happy Half-Century,* by Agnes Repplier; "Scum o' the Earth" from *Scum o' the Earth and Other Poems,* by Robert Haven Schauffler; "The Fool's Prayer" and "Opportunity" from *Poetical Works,* by Edward Roland Sill; "The Wreck" from *Irradiations, Sand and Spray,* by John Gould Fletcher.

To Mitchell Kennerley for "Stains" and "April" from *The Joy of Life* by Theodosia Garrison Faulks.

To Alfred A. Knopf, Inc., for "I Explain," "The Black Riders," "The Blades of Grass," "A Newspaper," "The Peaks," "A Slant of Sun," from *The Work of Stephen Crane;* for "The Wagner Matinée from *Youth and the Bright Medusa* by Willa Cather; for "A Fortune-Teller" and "Train-Mates" from *Grenstone Papers,* and "Roofs" from *The Beloved Stranger* by Witter Bynner; and for "Atavism" from *Nets to Catch the Wind,* by Elinor Wylie.

To David McKay for all the selections from the works of Walt Whitman.

To The Macmillan Company for selections from "Down the Mississippi" from *Breakers and Granite,* by John Gould Fletcher; for "Home from the War" from *A Son of the Middle Border,* by Hamlin Garland; for "The Mountain Woman" from *Skylines and Horizons,* by Du Bose Heyward; for "Miss Gunton of Poughkeepsie" from *The Soft Side,* by Henry James; for "Abraham Lincoln Walks at Midnight" from *Collected Poems,* by Vachel Lindsay; for "Anne Rutledge" from *Spoon River Anthology,* by Edgar Lee Masters; for the selection from "The Sowing of the Dragon" from *The Song of the Indian Wars* by John G. Neihardt; for "Stafford's Cabin" from *Collected Poems,* by Edwin Arlington Robinson; and for "Blue Squills," "August Moonrise," "On the Dunes," and "The Unseen" from *Flame and Shadow,* by Sara Teasdale.

To Thomas B. Mosher for "The Lark" from *A Wayside Lute,* by Lizette Woodworth Reese.

To *Poetry: A Magazine of Verse* for its concurrence in permission to use "Atavism" by Elinor Wylie.

To A. M. Robertson for "The Black Vulture" from *The House of Orchids and Other Poems,* and for "The Last Days" and "The Master Mariner" from *Beyond the Breakers and Other Poems,* by George Sterling.

To Charles Scribner's Sons for "The Lady or the Tiger?" from *Novels and Stories* by Frank Stockton; for "Little Boy Blue" from *A Little Book of Western Verse,* "Seein' Things" from *Love Songs of Childhood,* and "Always Right" from *Second Book of Verse,* by Eugene Field; for "The Verdict" from *The Hermit and the Wild Woman,* by Edith Wharton; for "Glory" from *Mr. Dooley Says,* by Finley Peter Dunne;

for "Stains" by Theodosia Garrison Faulks, from *Scribner's Magazine;* for "The Three Best Things" from *Collected Poems,* by Henry van Dyke; for "Reuben Bright" and "The House on the Hill" from *Children of the Night,* and "Miniver Cheevy" from *The Town Down the River,* by Edwin Arlington Robinson; and for "I Have a Rendezvous with Death" from *Poems* by Alan Seeger.

To the Yale University Press for "The Falconer of God" from *The Falconer of God and Other Poems,* and "The Horse Thief" from *The Burglar of the Zodiac and Other Poems,* by William Rose Benét; and for "The Portrait of a Boy" from *Young Adventure,* by Stephen Vincent Benét.

1929

A. E. A.
H. J. H.

CONTENTS

CONTENTS

xiv
CONTENTS

CONTENTS

CONTENTS

THREE CENTURIES OF AMERICAN POETRY AND PROSE

THE COLONIAL PERIOD

AMERICAN writings before the Revolutionary War may be divided into two groups, the Colonial and the Provincial. The break between the two comes after King Philip's War and the Indian wars in Virginia of the same time. It coincides, in general, with the annulment of the colonial charters, and the constituting of the colonies into British provinces. The men who came to North America from 1607 to 1680 brought with them the ideas of the social or religious groups in England from which they sprang; many were tinged with a lingering medievalism. Some were "gentlemen adventurers" touched with the spirit of Elizabethan romance. A large number were ardently attached to religious principles that they felt bound to propagate. All were filled with the wonder of the new world, all intensely occupied with the problems of getting and maintaining a foothold upon a hostile shore. The writers of this period were clergymen, men of affairs, administrators, soldiers. None were skilled writers; yet the simple records they have left show that there was in the colonies a keen intellectual life, sure, sooner or later, to produce a varied and vigorous literature.

JOHN SMITH 1580-1631

John Smith, typical sixteenth-century soldier of fortune, was a man whom Shakespeare might have used as a model for one of his soldiers; indeed, the dramatist may have been sitting by when the none too modest captain was recounting his adventures to eager listeners, over the ale in some London tavern. Smith, a Lincolnshire farm lad, fled an apprenticeship, enlisted under various flags with his share of the spoils for bonus, fought as Christian champion in single-handed duel with heathen warriors, was captured by the Turks and sold into slavery, escaped, suffered shipwreck, and at length made his way back to England, ripe in experience, and joined the Virginia colonists.

In the New World he proved himself indispensable as a resourceful adviser, explorer, and military leader, and was made president of the colony in 1608. He explored the New England coast in 1614-15 and received the title of Admiral of New England. His works include *A True Relation*, etc., 1608; *Description of New England*, 1616; *General History of Virginia and the Summer Isles*, 1624. Despite the quaint manner of Smith's narrative, the reader may perceive in it the joyous spirit of a man to whom the world was full of marvels that might be experienced by one hardy enough to take the risk. An accident forced him back to England, but his heart was in America and we count him one of our first pioneers.

Best edition: Works, ed. by E. Arber, 2 vols., 1895. Criticism: Henry Adams, *Historical Essays*, 1891, an iconoclastic view; same *No. Am.* 95: 1-30; see also A. G. Bradley, "Captain John Smith," *Fortn.* 101:69-82, a vivid appreciation; H. G. Parsons, "A Knight of the Sun," *Blackw.* 174:28-40, emphasizing the sea-roving and piratical side of Smith's life; K. P. Woods, "Captain John Smith and the American Nation," *Harper*, 104:470-75.

From A TRUE RELATION [1]

. . . You shall vnderstand that after many crosses in the downes by tempests, wee arriued safely vppon the Southwest part of the great Canaries: within foure or fiue daies after we set saile for *Dominica,* the 26. of Aprill: the first land we made, wee fell with Cape *Henry,* the verie mouth of the Bay of *Chissiapiacke,* which at that present we little expected, hauing by a cruell storme bene put to the Northward:

Anchoring in this Bay twentie or thirtie went a shore with the Captain, and in comming aboard [2] they were assalted with certaine Indians, which charged them within Pistoll shot: in which conflict, Captaine *Archer* and *Mathew Morton* were shot: whereupon Captaine *Newport* seconding them, made a shot at them, which the Indians little respected, but hauing spent their arrowes, retyred without harme. And in that place was the Box [3] opened, wherin the Counsell for *Virginia* was nominated: and arriuing at the place where wee are now seated, [4] the Counsell was sworn, and the President elected, which for that yeare was Maister *Edm. Maria Wingfield,* where was made choice for our scituation, a verie fit place for the erecting of a great cittie, about which some contention passed betwixt Captaine *Wingfield* and Captaine *Gosnold:* notwithstanding, all our provision was brought a shore, and with as much speede as might bee wee went about our fortification.

The two and twenty day of Aprill, [5] Captain *Newport* and my selfe with diuers others, to the number of twenty two persons, set forward to discouer the Riuer, some fiftie or sixtie miles, finding it in some places broader, and in some narrower, the Countrie (for the moste part) on each side plaine high ground, with many fresh Springes, the people in all places kindely intreating vs, daunsing and feasting vs with strawberries, Mulberies, Bread, Fish, and other their Countrie prouisions wherof we had plenty: for which Captaine *Newport* kindely requited their least fauours with Bels, Pinnes, Needles, beades, or Glasses, which so contented them that his liberallitie made them follow vs from place to place, and euer kindely to respect vs. In the midway staying to refresh our selues in a little Ile, foure or fiue sauages came vnto vs which described vnto vs the course of the Riuer, and after in our iourney, they often met vs, trading with vs for such prouision as wee had, and ariuing at *Arsatecke,* hee whom we supposed to bee the chiefe King of all the rest, moste kindely entertained vs, giuing vs in a guide to go with vs vp the Riuer to *Powhatan,* of which place their great Emperor taketh his name, where he that they honored for King vsed vs kindely. But to finish this discouerie, we passed on further, where within an ile [6] we were intercepted with great craggy stones in the midst of the riuer, where the water falleth so rudely, and with such a violence, as not any boat can possibly passe, and so broad disperseth the streame, as there is not past fiue or sixe Foote at a low water, and to the shore scarce passage with barge, the water floweth [7] foure foote, and the freshes, by reason of the Rockes, haue left markes of the inundations 8. or 9. foote: The south side is plaine low ground, and the north side high mountaines, the rockes being of a grauelly nature, interlaced with many vains of glistring spangles.

That night we returned to *Powhatan:* the next day (being Whitsunday after dinner) we returned to the fals, leauing a mariner in pawn with the Indians for a guide of theirs, hee that they honoured for King followed vs by the riuer. That afternoone we trifled in looking vpon the Rockes and riuer (further he would

---

[1] A band of colonizers, among whom Captain Bartholomew Gosnold was the prime mover and Captain John Smith a leading spirit, having obtained letters patent from King James, set sail from Blackwall for Virginia, December 19, 1606. They were four months on the way, being kept for six weeks in The Downs, in sight of England, and afterwards spending some time in Dominica and other islands of the West Indies. The earliest account of their experiences was Smith's *True Relation,* published at London in black letter in 1608. The original spelling and punctuation are here followed. The title page reads: A true relation of such occurrences and accidents of Noate as hath hapned in Virginia since the first planting of that Collony, which is now resident in the South part thereof, till the last returne from thence. Written by Captain Smith, Coronell of the said Collony, to a worshipfull friend of his in England.

　　Mr. Arber describes the *True Relation* as an "ordinary 'pamphlet of news,' carelessly printed." An example of the careless printing is the first sentence of this selection. It should read somewhat as follows: "Within four or five days after, we set sail for Dominica [where we stayed for some time]. The 26th of April, the first land we made, we fell with Cape Henry," etc.

[2] on land

[3] The proprietors of the colony, all of whom lived in England, had placed in a sealed box, not to be opened until the Company reached Virginia, authoritative directions for the government of the colony.

[4] settled (viz., at Jamestowr)

[5] An error for May (1607). This date marks the beginning of Smith's explorations. As his map, published in 1612, shows, they covered Chesapeake Bay and all the important rivers from the James, "the River" here mentioned, to the Susquehanna, and led him to the future sites of Baltimore, Richmond, and Washington. The places mentioned in the present selection are on or near the James, from Richmond to Point Comfort.

[6] a mile

[7] Rises with the tide; "freshes" are freshets.

not goe) so there we erected a crosse, and that night taking our man at *Powhatans,* Captaine *Newport* congratulated [1] his kindenes with a Gown and a Hatchet: returning to *Arsetecke,* and stayed there the next day to obserue the height [2] therof, and so with many signes of loue we departed.

The next day the Queene of *Agamatack* kindely intreated [3] vs, her people being no lesse contented then the rest, and from thence we went to another place (the name whereof I doe not remember) where the people shewed vs the manner of their diuing for Mussels, in which they finde Pearles.

That night passing by *Weanock* some twentie miles from our Fort, they according to their former churlish condition, seemed little to affect [4] vs, but as wee departed and lodged at the point of *Weanocke,* the people the next morning seemed kindely to content [5] vs, yet we might perceiue many signes of a more Iealousie in them then before, and also the Hinde [6] that the King of *Arseteck* had giuen vs, altered his resolution in going to our Fort, and with many kinde circumstances [7] left us there. This gaue vs some occasion to doubt [8] some mischiefe at the Fort, yet Captaine *Newport* intended to haue visited *Paspahegh* and *Tappahanocke,* but the instant change of the winde being faire for our return we repaired to the fort with all speed, where the first we heard was that 400. Indians the day before had assalted the fort, and supprised it, had not God (beyond al their expectations) by meanes of the shippes (at whom they shot [9] with their Ordinances and Muskets) caused them to retire, they had entred the fort with our own men, which were then busied in setting Corne, their armes beeing then in driefats [10] and few ready but certain Gentlemen of their own, in which conflict, most of the Counsel was hurt, a boy slaine in the Pinnas, and thirteene or fourteene more hurt.

With all speede we pallisadoed our Fort: (each other day) for sixe or seauen daies we had alarums by ambuscadoes, and four or fiue cruelly wounded by being abroad: the Indians losse wee know not, but as they report three were slain and diuers hurt.

Captaine *Newport* hauing set things in order, set saile for England the 22 of June, leauing prouision for 13. or 14 weeks.

The day before the Ships departure, the King of *Pamaunke* [11] sent the Indian that had met vs before in our discouerie, to assure vs peace; our fort being then palisadoed round, and all our men in good health and comfort, albeit, that thro[u]gh some discontented humors, it did not so long continue.

.   .   .   .   .   .

[CONCLUSION]

In all this time, our men being all or the most part well recouered, and we not willing to trifle away more time then necessitie enforced vs vnto: we thought good, for the better content of the aduenturers, in some reasonable sort to fraight home Maister *Nelson,* with Cedar wood. About which, our men going with willing minds, [it] was in very good time effected, and the ship sent for England [on 2nd June, 1608]. Wee now remaining being in good health, all our men wel contented, free from mutinies, in loue one with another, and as we hope in a continuall peace with the Indians: where we doubt not but by Gods gracious assistance, and the aduenturers [12] willing minds and speedie futherance to so honorable an action, in after times to see our Nation to enioy a Country, not onely exceeding pleasant for habitation, but also very profitable for comerce in generall; no doubt pleasing to almightie God, honourable to our gracious Soueraigne, and commodious [13] generally to the whole Kingdome.

1607   1608

From THE GENERAL HISTORY OF VIRGINIA [14]

From BOOK III, CHAPTER II. WHAT HAPPENED TILL THE FIRST SUPPLY

.   .   .   .   .   .

The new President, and *Martin,* [15] being little beloved, of weake iudgement in dangers and

---

[1] gratefully acknowledged   [2] latitude
[3] entertained
[4] seemed somewhat disaffected toward
[5] appeared friendly toward   [7] professions
[6] the guide mentioned before   [8] suspect
[9] *i.e.,* which shot at them
[10] vats or cases, for containing dry articles

[11] King Opechancanough
[12] those who had invested their capital in the colony
[13] profitable
[14] This history was prepared by Smith at the request of the London Virginia Company and printed at London, in 1624, just before the bankruptcy and dissolution of the company. Smith, already subjected to much hostile criticism and anticipating more, vehemently declared: "I thank God I never undertook anything yet [wherein] any could tax me of carelessness or dishonesty; and what is he to whom I am indebted or troublesome?" (Arber's edition of Smith, p. 274.) In regard to the much discussed incident of Pocahontas, Mr. Arber remarks that the story was never questioned in Smith's lifetime, and that to deny the truth of it "is to create more difficulties than are involved in its acceptance" (*ibid.,* p. cxv).
[15] John Ratcliffe, and Captain John Martin, a member of the Council

lesse industrie in peace, committed the managing of all things abroad to Captaine *Smith*: who by his owne example, good words, and faire promises, set some to mow, others to binde thatch, some to build houses, others to thatch them, himselfe alwayes bearing the greatest taske for his owne share, so that in short time, he provided most of them lodgings, neglecting any for himselfe.

This done, seeing the Salvages superfluitie [1] beginne to decrease, [he] (with some of his workemen) shipped himselfe in the Shallop to search the Country for trade. The want of the language, knowledge to mannage his boat without sailes, the want of a sufficient power (knowing the multitude of the Salvages), apparell for his men, and other necessaries, were infinite impediments; yet no discouragement.

Being but six or seauen in company he went downe the river to *Kecoughtan:* where at first they scorned him, as a famished man; and would in derision offer him a handfull of Corne, a peece of bread, for their swords and muskets, and such like proportions also for their apparell. But seeing by trade and courtesie there was nothing to be had, he made bold to try such conclusions as necessitie inforced, though contrary to his Commission: Let fly his muskets, ran his boat on shore; whereat they all fled into the woods.

So marching towards their houses, they might see great heapes of corne: much adoe he had to restraine his hungry souldiers from present taking of it, expecting as it hapned that the Salvages would assault them, as not long after they did with a most hydeous noyse. Sixtie or seaventie of them, some blacke, some red, some white, some party-coloured, came in a square order, singing and dauncing out of the woods, with their *Okee* (which was an Idoll made of skinnes, stuffed with mosse, all painted and hung with chaines and copper) borne before them: and in this manner, being well armed with Clubs, Targets, Bowes, and Arrowes, they charged the English, that so kindly receiued them with their muskets loaden with Pistoll shot, that downe fell their God, and divers lay sprauling on the ground; the rest fled againe to the woods, and ere long sent one of their *Quiyoughkasoucks* [2] to offer peace, and redeeme their *Okee.*

Smith told them, if only six of them would come vnarmed and loade his boat, he would not only be their friend, but restore them their *Okee,* and giue them Beads, Copper, and Hatchets besides: which on both sides was to their contents performed: and then they brought him Venison, Turkies, wild foule, bread, and what they had; singing and dauncing in signe of friendship till they departed.

In his returne, he discovered the Towne and Country of *Warraskoyack.* . . .

And now the winter approaching, the rivers became so covered with swans, geese, duckes, and cranes, that we daily feasted with good bread, Virginia pease, pumpions, [3] and putchamins, [4] fish, fowle, and diverse sorts of wild beasts as fat as we could eate them: so that none of our Tuftaffaty humorists [5] desired to goe for *England.*

But our *Comaedies* never endured long with out a *Tragedie,* some idle exceptions being muttered against Captaine *Smith,* for not discovering the head of *Chickahamania* river, and taxed by the Councell, to be too slow in so worthy an attempt. The next voyage hee proceeded so farre that with much labour by cutting of trees insunder he made his passage; but when his Barge could passe no farther, he left her in a broad bay out of danger of shot, commanding none should goe a shore till his returne: himselfe with two English and two Salvages went vp higher in a Canowe; but hee was not long absent, but his men went a shore, whose want of government gaue both occasion and opportunity to the Salvages to surprise one *George Cassen,* whom they slew, and much failed not to haue cut of[f] the boat and all the rest.

Smith little dreaming of that accident, being got to the marshes at the rivers head, twentie myles in the desert, had his two men slaine (as is supposed) sleeping by the Canowe, whilst himselfe by fowling sought them victuall: who finding he was beset with 200. Salvages, two of them hee slew, still defending himselfe with the ayd of a Salvage his guid, whom he bound to his arme with his garters, and vsed him as a buckler, yet he was shot in his thigh a little, and had many arrowes that stucke in his cloathes but no great hurt, till at last they tooke him prisoner.

When this newes came to *Iames* towne, much was their sorrow for his losse, fewe expecting what ensued.

Sixe or seuen weekes those Barbarians kept him prisoner, many strange triumphes and coniurations [6] they made of him, yet hee so demeaned himselfe amongst them, as he not

---

[1] supplies furnished by the Indians (mentioned earlier in the account)
[2] defined by Smith as "petty gods, and their affinities"

[3] pumpkins   [4] persimmons
[5] fastidious fault-finders (tuft-taffeta, a silk fabric)
[6] religious ceremonies (described later) to avert the evil of his presence

onely diverted them from surprising the Fort, but procured his owne libertie, and got himselfe and his company such estimation amongst them, that those Salvages admired him more then their owne *Quiyouckosucks.*

The manner how they vsed and deliuered him, is as followeth.

The Salvages hauing drawne [1] from *George Cassen* whether Captaine *Smith* was gone, prosecuting that oportunity they followed him with .300. bowmen, conducted by the King of *Pamavnkee,* who in diuisions searching the turnings of the riuer, found *Robinson* and *Emry* by the fire side: those they shot full of arrowes and slew. Then finding the Captaine, as is said, that vsed the Salvage that was his guide as his shield (three of them being slaine and diuers other so gauld) all the rest would not come neere him. Thinking thus to haue returned to his boat, regarding them, as he marched, more then his way, [he] slipped vp to the middle in an oasie creeke and his Salvage with him; yet durst they not come to him till being neere dead with cold, he threw away his armes. Then according to their composition [2] they drew him forth and led him to the fire, where his men were slaine. Diligently they chafed his benummed limbs.

He demanding for their Captaine, they shewed him *Opechankanough,* King of *Pamavnkee,* to whom he gaue a round Ivory double compass Dyall. Much they marvailed at the playing of the Fly and Needle, which they could see so plainely and yet not touch it, because of the glasse that covered them. But when he demonstrated by that Globe-like Iewell, the roundnesse of the earth, and skies, the spheare of the Sunne, Moone, and Starres, and how the Sunne did chase the night round about the world continually; the greatnesse of the Land and Sea, the diversitie of Nations, varietie of complexions, and how we were to them *Antipodes,* and many other such like matters, they all stood as amazed with admiration. [3]

Notwithstanding, within an houre after they tyed him to a tree, and as many as could stand about him prepared to shoot him: but the King holding vp the Compass in his hand, they all laid downe their Bowes and Arrowes, and in a triumphant manner led him to *Orapaks,* where he was after their manner kindly feasted, and well vsed. . . . Not long after, early in a morning a great fire was made in a long house, and a mat spread on the one side, as on the other; on the one they caused him to sit, and all the guard went out of the house, and presently came skipping in a great grim fellow, all painted over with coale, mingled with oyle; and many Snakes and Wesels skins stuffed with mosse, and all their tayles tyed together, so as they met on the crowne of his head in a tassell; and round about the tassell was as a Coronet of feathers, the skins hanging round about his head, backe, and shoulders, and in a manner covered his face; with a hellish voyce, and a rattle in his hand. With most strange gestures and passions he began his invocation, and environed the fire with a circle of meale; which done, three more such like devils came rushing in with the like antique tricks, painted halfe blacke, halfe red: but all their eyes were painted white, and some red stroakes like Mutchato's [4] along their cheekes: round about him those fiends daunced a pretty while, and then came in three more as vgly as the rest; with red eyes, and white stroakes over their blacke faces, at last they all sat downe right against him; three of them on the one hand of the chiefe Priest, and three on the other. Then all with their rattles began a song, which ended, the chiefe Priest layd downe fiue wheat cornes: then strayning his armes and hands with such violence that he sweat, and his veynes swelled, he began a short Oration: at the conclusion they all gaue a short groane; and then layd down three graines more. After that, began their song againe, and then another Oration, ever laying downe so many cornes as before, till they had twice incirculed the fire; that done, they tooke a bunch of little stickes prepared for that purpose, continuing still their devotion, and at the end of every song and Oration, they layd downe a sticke betwixt the divisions of Corne. Till night, neither he nor they did either eate or drinke; and then they feasted merrily, with the best provisions they could make. Three dayes they vsed this Ceremony; the meaning whereof they told him, was to know if he intended them well or no. The circle of meale signified their Country, the circles of corne the bounds of the Sea, and the stickes his Country. They imagined the world to be flat and round, like a trencher; and they in the middest.

After this they brought him a bagge of gunpowder, which they carefully preserved till the next spring, to plant as they did their corne; because they would be acquainted with the nature of that seede.

Opitchapam the Kings brother invited him to his house, where, with as many platters o

---

[1] learned   [2] agreement   [3] wonder   [4] mustachios

bread, foule, and wild beasts, as did environ him, he bid him wellcome; but not any of them would eate a bit with him, but put vp all the remainder in Baskets.

At his return to *Opechancanoughs*, all the Kings women, and their children, flocked about him for their parts; as a due by Custome, to be merry with such fragments.

But his waking mind in hydeous dreames did
oft see wondrous shapes,
Of bodies strange, and huge in growth, and of
stupendious makes.

At last they brought him to *Meronocomoco*, where was *Powhatan*, their Emperor. Here more than two hundred of those grim Courtiers stood wondering at him, as he had beene a monster; till *Powhatan* and his trayne had put themselues in their greatest braveries. Before a fire vpon a seat like a bedsted, he sat covered with a great robe, made of *Rarowcun* skinnes, and all the tayles hanging by. On either hand did sit a young wench of 16 or 18 yeares, and along on each side the house, two rowes of men, and behind them as many women, with all their heads and shoulders painted red: many of their heads bedecked with the white downe of Birds; but every one with something: and a great chayne of white beads about their necks.

At his entrance before the King, all the people gaue a great shout. The Queene of *Appamatuck* was appointed to bring him water to wash his hands, and another brought him a bunch of feathers, in stead of a Towell, to dry them: having feasted him after their best barbarous manner they could, a long consultation was held, but the conclusion was, two great stones were brought before *Powhatan*: then as many as could layd hands on him, dragged him to them, and thereon laid his head, and being ready with their clubs, to beate out his braines, *Pocahontas* the Kings dearest daughter, when no intreaty could prevaile, got his head in her armes, and laid her owne vpon his to saue him from death: whereat the Emperour was contented he should liue to make him hatchets, and her bells, beads, and copper; for they thought him as well of all occupations as themselues. For the King himselfe will make his owne robes, shooes, bowes, arrowes, pots; plant, hunt, or doe any thing so well as the rest.

They say he bore a pleasant shew,
But sure his heart was sad.
For who can pleasant be, and rest,
That liues in feare and dread:
And having life suspected, doth
It still suspected lead.

Two days after, *Powhatan* having disguised himselfe in the most fearefullest manner he could, caused Captain *Smith* to be brought forth to a great house in the woods, and there vpon a mat by the fire to be left alone. Not long after from behinde a mat that divided the house, was made the most dolefullest noyse he ever heard; then *Powhatan* more like a devill then a man, with some two hundred more as blacke as himselfe, came vnto him and told him now they were friends, and presently he should goe to *Iames* towne, to send him two great gunnes, and a gryndstone, for which he would giue him the Country of *Capahowosick*, and for ever esteeme him as his sonne *Nantaquoud*.

So to *Iames* towne with 12 guides *Powhatan* sent him. That night they quarterd in the woods, he still expecting (as he had done all this long time of his imprisonment) every houre to be put to one death or other: for all their feasting. But almightie God (by his divine providence) had mollified the hearts of those sterne *Barbarians* with compassion. The next morning betimes they came to the Fort, where *Smith* having vsed the Salvages with what kindnesse he could, he shewed *Rawhunt*, *Powhatans* trusty servant, two demi-Culverings [1] and a millstone to carry *Powhatan*: they found them somewhat too heavie; but when they did see him discharge them, being loaded with stones, among the boughs of a great tree loaded with Isickles, the yce and branches came so tumbling downe, that the poore Salvages ran away halfe dead with feare. But at last we regained some conference with them, and gaue them such toyes; and sent to *Powhatan*, his women, and children such presents, as gaue them in generall full content.

Now in *Iames* Towne they were all in combustion, the strongest preparing once more to run away with the Pinnace; which with the hazzard of his life, with Sakre falcon [2] and musket shot, *Smith* forced now the third time to stay or sinke.

Some no better then they should be, had plotted with the President, the next day to haue put him to death by the Leviticall law, [3] for the liues of *Robinson* and *Emry;* pretending the fault was his that had led them to their ends: but he quickly tooke such order with such Lawyers, that he layd them by the heeles till he sent some of them prisoners for *England*.

Now ever once in foure or fiue dayes, *Pocahontas* with her attendants, brought him so

[1] a short nine-pound cannon
[2] a very light cannon
[3] *Leviticus* xxiv, 17

much provision, that saved many of their liues, that els for all this had starved with hunger.

Thus from numbe death our good God sent reliefe,
The sweete asswager of all other griefe.

.   .   .   .

1623   1624

WILLIAM STRACHEY

It is not known when or where Strachey was born or died; he was in the prime of life, 1609-1618. He sailed for Virginia in 1609 with Sir Thomas Gates, lieutenant-governor of the Colonization Colony, and Sir George Somers as admiral. The company was wrecked on the Bermudas in July, spent the winter in building boats, and reached Jamestown in the following April. Strachey was secretary and recorder of the Virginia colony, and joint author and editor of several publications concerning the colony—in short a professional writer, a "publicity agent" of the undertaking. Several accounts of this wreck and sojourn were sent back to England. There can be no doubt that some of these were used by Shakespeare as the groundwork of *The Tempest,* in which he speaks of the "still-vex'd Bermoothes" (I, ii, 229).

It is evident that Strachey writes as a man of imagination would concerning a new world not quite, perhaps, under the sway of such natural laws as bound the old world, a place where such wonders as fill the pages of Spenser were not impossible.

From A TRUE REPORTORY [1]

Of the Wracke, and Redemption of Sir Thomas Gates Knight; upon and from the Ilands of the Bermudas: . . .

§. 1

A most dreadfull Tempest . . . . their Wracke on Bermuda, and the Description of those Ilands.

.   .   .   .   .   .

During all this time, the heavens look'd so blacke upon us, that it was not possible the elevation of the Pole [2] might be observed nor a Starre by night, not Sunne beame by day was to be seene. Onely upon the thursday night Sir George Summers being upon the watch, had an apparition of a little round light, like a faint Starre, trembling, and streaming along with a sparkeling blaze, halfe the height upon the Maine Mast, and shooting sometimes

from Shroud to Shroud, tempting to settle as it were upon any of the foure Shrouds: and for three or foure houres together, or rather more, halfe the night it kept with us; running sometimes along the Maine-yard to the very end, and then returning. At which, Sir George Summers called divers about him, and shewed them the same, who observed it with much wonder, and carefulnesse: [3] but upon a sodaine, towards the morning watch, they lost the sight of it, and knew not what way it made. . . .

And surely Madam, it is most true, there was not any houre (a matter of admiration [4]) all these dayes, in which we freed not twelve hundred Barricos [5] of water, the least whereof contained six gallons, and some eight, besides three deepe Pumpes continually going, two beneath at the Capstone, and the other above in the halfe Decke, and at each Pumpe foure thousand stroakes at the least in a watch; so as I may well say, every foure houres, we quitted one hundred tunnes of water: and from tuesday noone till friday noone, we bailed and pumped two thousand tunne, and yet doe what we could, when our Ship held least in her, (after tuesday night second watch) shee bore ten foote deepe, at which stay our extreame working kept her one eight glasses, [6] forbearance whereof had instantly sunke us, and it being now Friday, the fourth morning, it wanted little, but that there had bin a generall determination, to have shut up hatches, and commending our sinfull soules to God, committed the Shippe to the mercy of the Sea: surely, that night we must have done it, and that night had we then perished: but see the goodnesse and sweet introduction of better hope, by our mercifull God given unto us. Sir George Summers, when no man dreamed of such happinesse, had discovered, and cried Land. Indeede the morning now three quarters spent, had wonne a little cleerenesse from the dayes before, and it being better surveyed, the very trees were seene to move with the winde upon the shoare side: whereupon our Governour commanded the Helmeman to beare up, the Boateswaine sounding at the first, found it thirteene fathome, and when we stood a little in seven fatham; and presently heaving his lead the third time, had ground at foure fathome, and by this, we had got her within a mile under the South-east point of the land, where we had somewhat smooth water. But having no hope to save her by comming to an anker in the same, we

---

[1] The *True Reportory* is in the form of a letter addressed to a lady of rank dated 15 July 1610, and was published in *Purchas His Pilgrimes* in 1625. See vol. iv, p. 1734; in the 1905 ed., vol. xix, p. 5.
[2] pole-star

[3] concern   [5] casks
[4] wonder
[6] Eight half-hour glasses (four hours); cf. *The Tempest,* v, i, 223.

were inforced to runne her ashoare, as neere the land as we could, which brought us within three quarters of a mile of shoare, and by the mercy of God unto us, making out our Boates, we had ere night brought all our men, women, and children, about the number of one hundred and fifty, safe into the Iland.

We found it to be the dangerous and dreaded Iland, or rather Ilands of the Bermuda: whereof let mee give your Ladyship a briefe description, before I proceed to my narration. And that the rather, because they be so terrible to all that ever touched on them, and such tempests, thunders, and other fearefull objects are seene and heard about them, that they be called commonly, The Devils Ilands, and are feared and avoyded of all sea travellers alive, above any other place in the world. Yet it pleased our merciful God, to make even this hideous and hated place, both the place of our safetie, and meanes of our deliverance.

.   .   .   .

Sure it is, that there are no Rivers nor running Springs of fresh water to bee found upon any of them: when wee came first wee digged and found certaine gushings and soft bublings, which being either in bottoms, or on the side of hanging ground, were onely fed with raine water, which neverthelesse soone sinketh into the earth and vanisheth away, or emptieth it selfe out of sight into the Sea, without any channell above or upon the superficies of the earth: for according as their raines fell, we had our Wels and Pits (which we digged) either halfe full, or absolute exhausted and dry, howbeit some low bottoms (which the continuall descent from the Hills filled full, and in those flats could have no passage away) we found to continue as fishing Ponds, or standing Pooles, continually Summer and Winter full of fresh water.

.   .   .   .

Fowle there is great store, small Birds, Sparrowes fat and plumpe like a Bunting, bigger then ours, Robbins of divers colours greene and yellow, ordinary and familiar in our Cabbins, and other of lesse sort. White and gray Hernshawes, Bitters, Teale, Snites, Crowes, and Hawkes, of which in March wee found divers Ayres,[1] Goshawkes and Tassells, Oxen-birds, Cormorants, Bald-Cootes, Moore-Hennes, Owls, and Battes in great store. And upon New-yeeres day in the morning, our Governour being walked foorth with another Gentleman Master James Swift, each of them with their Peeces killed a wild Swanne, in a great Sea-

water Bay or Pond in our Iland. A kinde of webbe-footed Fowle there is, of the bignesse of an English greene Plover, or Sea-Meawe, which all the Summer wee saw not, and in the darkest nights of November and December (for in the night they onely feed) they would come forth, but not flye farre from home, and hovering in the ayre, and over the Sea, made a strange hollow and harsh howling. Their colour is inclining to Russet, with white bellies, (as are likewise the long Feathers of their wings Russet and White) these gather themselves together and breed in those Ilands which are high, and so farre alone into the Sea, that the Wilde Hogges cannot swimme over [to] them, and there in the ground they have their Burrowes, like Conyes in a Warren, and so brought in the loose Mould, though not so deepe: which Birds with a light bough in a darke night (as in our Lowbelling[2]) wee caught. I have beene at the taking of three hundred in an houre, and wee might have laden our Boates. Our men found a prettie way to take them, which was by standing on the Rockes or Sands by the Sea side, and hollowing, laughing, and making the strangest out-cry that possibly they could: with the noyse whereof the Birds would come flocking to that place, and settle upon the very armes and head of him that so cryed, and still creepe neerer and neerer, answering the noyse themselves: by which our men would weigh them with their hand, and which weighed heaviest they tooke for the best and let the others alone, and so our men would take twentie dozen in two houres of the chiefest of them; and they were a good and well relished Fowle, fat and full as a Partridge. In January wee had great store of their Egges, which are as great as an Hennes Egge, and so fashioned and white shelled, and have no difference in yolke nor white from an Hennes Egge. There are thousands of these Birds, and two or three Ilands full of their Burrowes, whether at any time (in two houres warning) wee could send our Cock-boat, and bring home as many as would serve the whole Company: which Birds for their blindnesse (for they see weakly in the day) and for their cry and whooting, wee called the Sea Owle:[3] they will bite cruelly with their crooked Bills.

.   .   .   .

[1] aeries, nests

[2] a method of capturing birds by stupefying them with lights and the noise of a bell

[3] In *The Tempest*, II, ii, 176, Caliban says: "Sometimes I'll get thee Young scamels from the rock." If *scamels* be a misprint for *sea-mells* or *sea-mews*, it probably refers to the birds described here; if for *staniels*, it refers to the hawks mentioned earlier.

§. II

ACTIONS AND OCCURRENTS WHILES
THEY CONTINUED
IN THE ILANDS . . . .

So soone as wee were a little setled after our landing, with all the conveniencie wee might, and as the place, and our many wants would give us leave, wee made up our long Boate (as your Ladyship hath heard) in fashion of a Pinnace, fitting her with a little Deck, made of the Hatches of our ruin'd ship, so close that no water could goe in her, gave her Sayles and Oares, and intreating with our Masters Mate Henry Ravens (who was supposed a sufficient Pilot) wee found him easily wonne to make over therewith, as a Barke of Aviso [1] for Virginia, which being in the height of thirtie seven degrees, five degrees from the Iland which we were, might bee some one hundred and fortie leagues from us, or thereabouts (reckoning to every degree that lies North-east, and Westerly twentie eight English leagues) who the twentie eight of August being Munday, with sixe Saylers, and our Cape Merchant Thomas Whittingham departed from us out of Gates his Bay: [2] but to our much wonder returned againe upon the Wednesday night after, having attempted to have got cleere of the Iland, from the North North-east to the South-west, but could not as little water as shee drew, (which might not bee above twentie inches) for shoales and breaches, [3] so as he was faine to go out from Summers Creeks, and the same way we came in on the South South-east of the Ilands, and from thence wee [he] made to Sea the Friday after the first of September, promising if hee lived and arrived safe there, to returne unto us the next new Moone with the Pinnace belonging to the Colony there: according unto which instructions were directed unto the new Leiftenant Governour, and Councell from our Governour here, for which the Ilands were appointed carefully to be watched, and fiers prepared as Beacons to have directed and wafted him in, but two Moones were wasted upon the Promontory before mentioned, and [wee] gave many a long and wished looke round about the Horizon, from the North-east to the South-west, but in vaine, discovering nothing all the while, which way soever we turned our eye, but ayre and sea.

1610   1625

[1] advice-boat, packet-boat
[2] Gates's Bay
[3] breakers

WILLIAM BRADFORD 1590-1657

English laws forbidding people to worship outside established churches did not prevent William Bradford, the young son of a Yorkshire yeoman, from joining the Independent church at Scrooby within the border of Nottingham. When this little congregation was threatened by the sheriffs and its members fled to Holland, Bradford was caught in an unsuccessful attempt to leave the country and imprisoned for several months. In Leyden he became a weaver and silk merchant. He studied much, learning Greek and some Hebrew that he might read the Scriptures in their own tongues.

As the years passed, the Leyden Puritans saw that among the Dutch they would shortly lose their English identity. The congregation therefore divided, and Bradford became a leader among the adventurous spirits who fared forth to a land where they might preserve not only their religious ideals but their English customs and blood. On the death of Governor Carver during the first terrible winter, Bradford was chosen to the office of governor; this office he held by annual election during almost all the rest of his life, serving with the greatest wisdom and self-sacrifice.

His manuscript history, *Of Plimoth Plantation,* lost during the Revolution, found in England, and returned (1897) to this country, is the most important account of the Pilgrims and of the Plymouth colony. It covers the period from 1606 to 1648, was begun about 1630, and was first published by the Massachusetts Historical Society in 1856. Though lacking the picturesqueness of Smith's narrative, its historical accuracy is greater. Its style is that of the Bible.

Bradford and the colony he guided represent the more liberal and primitive type of American Puritanism. After the establishment of the Massachusetts Bay Colony at Boston in 1630, Puritanism in New England took on the aspects of a state religion. The church and the government supported each other; the salaries of the clergy were from the public taxes, and the clergy often sat with the magistrates in the decision of difficult cases. The "Bay Colony" because of its larger population from its founding tended to dominate all the Massachusetts settlements. Plymouth feared that its own milder government in church and civil affairs would be overthrown by Boston. Bradford's tact prevented such a misfortune. He so administered the affairs of the Plymouth Colony that it escaped many of the bitter troubles that befell its stronger neighbor.

Best edition: *History of Plymouth Plantation,* 2 vols., published for the Massachusetts Historical Society, 1912. Bradford's *Of Plimoth Plantation,* published by the State of Massachusetts, 1899, includes a history of the original manuscript, its loss, discovery, and return to the State of Massachusetts. See also: "History of Plimoth Plantation," *Ind.* 52:2219-20; "Governor Bradford's Old Church," *Outlook,* 86:916-921, an interesting account of the church where Bradford was baptized.

From OF PLIMOTH PLANTATION.
BOOK I [1]
The 9. Chap.

Of their vioage, and how they passed the sea, and of their safe arrivall at Cape Codd.

September: 6. These troubles [2] being blowne over, and now all being compacte togeather in one shipe, they put to sea againe with a prosperus winde, which continued diverce days togeather, which was some incouragmente unto them; yet, . . . after they had injoyed faire winds and weather for a season, they were incountred many times with crosse winds, and mette with many feirce stormes, with which the shipe was shroudly shaken, and her upper works made very leakie; and one of the maine beames in the midd ships was bowed and craked, which put them in some fear that the shipe could not be able to performe the vioage. . . . But in examening of all opinions, the master and others affirmed they knew the ship to be stronge and firme under water; and for the buckling [3] of the maine beame, ther was a great iron scrue the passengers brought out of Holland, which would raise the beame into his place; the which being done, the carpenter and master affirmed that with a post put under it, set firme in the lower deck, and otherways bounde, he would make it sufficiente. And as for the decks and uper workes they would calke them as well as they could, and though with the workeing of the ship they would not longe keepe stanch, yet ther would otherwise be no great danger, if they did not overpress her with sails. So they commited them selves to the will of God, and resolved to proseede. . . .

. . . In all this viage ther died but one of the passengers, which was William Butten, a youth, servant to Samuell Fuller, when they drew near the coast. But to omite other things, (that I may be breefe,) after longe beating at sea they fell with that land which is called Cape Cod; [4] the which being made and certainly

knowne to be it, they were not a litle joyfull. After some deliberation had amongst them selves and with the master of the ship, they tacked aboute and resolved to stande for the southward (the wind and weather being faire) to finde some place aboute Hudsons river for their habitation. But after they had sailed that course aboute halfe the day, they fell amongst deangerous shoulds and roring breakers, and they were so farr intangled ther with as [5] they conceived them selves in great danger; and the wind shrinking upon them withall, they resolved to bear up againe for the Cape, and thought them selves hapy to gett out of those dangers before night overtooke them, as by Gods providence they did. And the next day they gott into the Cape-harbor wher they ridd in saftie. A word or too by the way of this cape; it was thus first named by Capten Gosnole and his company, Anno: 1602, and after by Capten Smith was caled Cape James; but it retains the former name amongst seamen. Also that pointe which first shewed those dangerous shoulds unto them, they called Pointe Care, and Tuckers Terrour; but the French and Dutch to this day call it Malabarr, by reason of those perilous shoulds, and the losses they have suffered ther.

Being thus arived in a good harbor and brought safe to land, they fell upon their knees and blessed the God of heaven, who had brought them over the vast and furious ocean, and delivered them from all the periles and miseries therof, againe to set their feete on the firme and stable earth, their proper elemente. And no marvell if they were thus joyefull, seeing wise Seneca was so affected with sailing a few miles on the coast of his owne Italy; as he affirmed, that he had rather remaine twentie years on his way by land, then pass by sea to any place in a short time; so tedious and dreadfull was the same unto him. [6]

But hear I cannot but stay and make a pause, and stand half amased at this poore peoples presente condition; and so I thinke will the reader too, when he well considers the same. Being thus passed the vast ocean, and a sea of troubles before in their preparation (as may be remembred by that which wente before), they had now no freinds to wellcome them, nor inns to entertaine or refresh their weatherbeaten bodys, no houses or much less townes to repaire too, to seeke for succoure. It is recorded in scripture as a mercie to the apostle and his shipwraked company, that the barbarians shewed them no smale kindnes in refreshing them, [7] but these savage barbarians,

---

[1] The Plymouth "Pilgrims" of 1620 were the adventurous spirits from among the Leyden congregation of Puritans which was made up of persons who, like Bradford, had fled from religious persecution in England. These emigrants from Leyden obtained help in fitting out and provisioning the *Mayflower*, in which they sailed, from the merchants of colonization companies in London and Plymouth, and a joint stock company was formed, the merchants imposing rather exacting terms. At the end of seven years, the capital and profits were to be divided between the adventurers (investors) and the planters (colonists).

[2] They had put back once because of the unseaworthiness of their ships.

[3] as for the bending

[4] Because they tooke much of that fishe ther,—Bradford's note.

[5] that   [6] Seneca, *Epistles,* 53   [7] *Acts* xxviii, 2

when they mette with them (as after will appeare) were readier to fill their sids full of arrows then otherwise. And for the season it was winter, and they that know the winters of that cuntrie know them to be sharp and violent, and subjecte to cruell and feirce stormes, deangerous to travill to known places, much more to serch an unknown coast. Besids, what could they see but a hidious and desolate wildernes, full of wild beasts and willd men? and what multituds ther might be of them they knew not. Nether could they, as it were, goe up to the tope of Pisgah,[1] to vew from this willdernes a more goodly cuntrie to feed their hops; for which way soever they turnd their eys (save upward to the heavens) they could have litle solace or content in respecte of any outward objects. For summer being done, all things stand upon them with a wetherbeaten face; and the whole countrie, full of woods and thickets, represented[2] a wild and savage heiw. If they looked behind them, ther was the mighty ocean which they had passed, and was now as a maine barr and goulfe to seperate them from all the civill parts of the world. If it be said they had a ship to sucour them, it is trew; but what heard they daly from the master and company? but that with speede they should looke out a place with their shallop, wher they would be[3] at some near distance; for the season was shuch as he would not stirr from thence till a safe harbor was discovered by them wher they would be, and he might goe without danger; and that victells consumed apace, but he must and would keepe sufficient for them selves[4] and their returne. Yea, it was muttered by some, that if they gott not a place in time, they would turne them and their goods ashore and leave them. Let it also be considred what weake hopes of supply and succoure they left behinde them, that might bear up their minds in this sade condition and trialls they were under; and they could not but be very smale. It is true, indeed, the affections and love of their brethren at Leyden was cordiall and entire towards them, but they had litle power to help them, or them selves; and how the case stode betweene them and the marchants at their coming away, hath allready been declared. What could now sustaine them but the spirite of God and his grace? May not and ought not the children of these fathers rightly say: *Our*

faithers were Englishmen which came over this great ocean, and were ready to perish in this willdernes; but they cried unto the Lord, and he heard their voyce, and looked on their adversitie, etc. Let them therfore praise the Lord, because he is good, and his mercies endure for ever. Yea, let them which have been redeemed of the Lord shew how he hath delivered them from the hand of the oppressour. When they wandered in the deserte willdernes out of the way, and found no citie to dwell in, both hungrie, and thirstie, their sowle was overwhelmed in them. Let them confess before the Lord his loving kindnes, and his wonderfull works before the sons of men.

The 10. Chap.

SHOWING HOW THEY SOUGHT OUT A PLACE OF HABITATION, AND WHAT BEFELL THEM THEREABOUTE.

Being thus arrived at Cap-Codd the 11. of November, and necessitie calling them to looke out a place for habitation, (as well as the maisters and mariners importunitie,) they having brought a large shalop with them out of England, stowed in quarters in the ship, they now gott her out and sett their carpenters to worke to trime her up; but being much brused and shatered in the shipe with foule weather, they saw she would be longe in mending. Wherupon a few of them tendered them selves to goe by land and discoverre those nearest places, whilst the shallop was in mending; and the rather because as they wente into that harbor ther seemed to be an opening some 2. or 3 leagues of, which the maister judged to be a river. It was conceived ther might be some danger in the attempte, yet seeing them resolute, they were permitted to goe, being 16. of them well armed, under the conduct of Captain Standish,[5]

[1] *Deuteronomy* xxxiv, 1
[2] presented
[3] where they wanted to settle
[4] the seamen (In the succeeding sentence also, the pronouns referrıng to the seamen and those referring *to* the passengers are used indiscriminately.)

[5] Longfellow's *Courtship of Miles Standish* makes interesting the following excerpt from Bradford's list of the Pilgrims coming in the *Mayflower:*
"Captin Myles Standish, and Rose, his wife."
"Mr. William Mullines, and his wife, and 2 children, Joseph and Priscila; and a servant, Robart Carter."
"John Alden was hired for a cooper, at South-Hampton, where the ship victuled; and being a hopefull [promising] yong man, was much desired, but left to his owne liking to go or stay when he came here; but he stayed, and maryed here."
Also the following entries, made in 1650:
"Captain Standish his wife died in the first sickness [an epidemic, probably of typhus fever, the first winter], and he married again, and hath four sons living, and some are dead.
"Mr. Molines, and his wife, his sone, and his servant, dyed the first winter. Only his daugter Priscila survived, and maried with John Alden, who are both living and have 11 children. And their eldest daughter is maried and hath five children."

having shuch instructions given them as was thought meete. They sett forth the 15. of November: and when they had marched aboute the space of a mile by the sea side, they espied 5. or 6. persons, with a dogg coming towards them, who were salvages; but they fled from them, and ranne up into the woods, and the English followed them, partly to see if they could speake with them, and partly to discover if ther might not be more of them lying in ambush. But the Indeans seeing them selves thus followed, they againe forsooke the woods, and rane away on the sands as hard as they could, so as they could not come near them, but followed them by the tracte of their feet sundrie miles, and saw that they had come the same way. So, night coming on, they made their randevous and set out their sentinels, and rested in quiete *that night,* and the next morning followed their tracte till they had headed a great creake, and so left the sands, and turned an other way into the woods. But they still followed them by geuss, hopeing to find their dwellings; but they soone lost both them and them selves, falling into shuch thickets as were ready to tear their cloaths and armore in peeces, but were most distresed for wante of drinke. But at length they found water and refreshed them selves, being the first New-England water they drunke of, and was now in thir great thirste as pleasante unto them as wine or bear had been in for-times. Afterwards they directed their course to come to the other shore, for they knew it was a necke of land they were to crosse over, and so at length gott to the seaside, and marched to this supposed river, and by the way found a pond of clear fresh water, and shortly after a good quantitie of clear ground wher the Indeans had formerly set corne, and some of their graves. And proceeding furder, they saw new-stuble wher corne had been set the same year, also they found wher latly a house had been, wher some planks and a great ketle was remaining, and heaps of sand newly padled with their hands, which they, digging up, found in them diverce faire Indean baskets filled with corne, and some in eares, faire and good, of diverce collours, which seemed to them a very goodly sight, (haveing never seen any shuch before). This was near the place of that supposed river they came to seeck; unto which they wente and found it to open it selfe into 2. armes with a high cliffe of sand in the enterance, but more like to be crikes of salte water then any fresh, for ought they saw; and that ther was good harborige for their shalope; leaving it further to be dis-

covered by their shalop when she was ready. So their time [that was] limeted them being expired, they returned to the ship, least they should be in fear of their saftie; and tooke with them parte of the corne and buried up the rest, and so like the men from Eshcoll [1] carried with them of the fruits of the land, and showed their breethren; of which, and their returne, they were marvelusly glad, and their harts incouraged.

.   .   .   .

1630-1650   1856

JOHN WINTHROP 1588-1649

John Winthrop, one of the foremost men in the founding of New England, was a landed gentleman of Suffolk, lord of Groton Manor. He had been educated at Cambridge and was of the Inner Temple. He practiced law in London, and held an administrative office under the crown until his Puritan principles blocked his further progress. Together with other gentlemen he obtained a liberal charter for a new colony overseas whose seat of government should be in the colony, not in London. He was chosen governor and with his assistants (magistrates) and nearly a thousand colonists migrated to Massachusetts Bay in 1630, where they founded Boston.

For twelve of the remaining years of his life Winthrop was chosen governor by annual election. He was a conservative, constructive administrator and statesman, one who believed in fixed creeds and laws, but who also had a large vision of what New England might and should become. His history, written in diary form amid the confusion of pressing affairs, should be read from the point of view of a contemporary, and weighed by the outlook of the seventeenth century, not ours. The style is terse and direct, rarely emotional, the expression of a man of affairs. Its chief social interest is its record of the problems and perplexities that the colonists met; of their ideals, their attitude toward government, education, religion. In all these matters Winthrop shows himself to be not only the wise and patient governor of the rank and file of the colonists, but easily chief among a group of men who were equal or superior to him in training and experience, men of strong, assertive personality. His account of what he considered the most important events in the colony shows how intense was the intellectual and social ferment in the Massachusetts of the first few decades, and indicates how New England came to be the intellectual and spiritual leader of the new world for several generations.

Best edition of Winthrop: Original Narratives series, ed. J. K. Hosmer, New York, 1908. R. C. Winthrop, *Life and Letters of John Winthrop* (authoritative edition), 1869, 1895.

[1] *Numbers* xiii, 24

From HISTORY OF NEW ENGLAND [1]

January, [1631] A house at Dorchester was burnt down.

February 11. Mr. Freeman's house at Watertown was burned down, but, being in the daytime, his goods were saved.

5. The ship *Lyon*, Mr. William Peirce, master, arrived at Nantasket. She brought Mr. Williams, [2] (a godly minister) with his wife, Mr. Throgmorton, ——Perkins, —— Ong, and others, with their wives and children, about twenty passengers, and about two hundred tons of goods. She set sail from Bristol, December 1. She had a very tempestuous passage, yet, through God's mercy, all her people came safe, except Way his son, [3] who fell from the spritsail yard in a tempest, and could not be recovered, though he kept in sight near a quarter of an hour. Her goods also came all in good condition.

8. The governor [4] went aboard the *Lyon*, riding by Long Island. [5]

9. The *Lyon* came to an anchor before Boston, where she rode very well, notwithstanding the great drift of ice.

10. The frost brake up; and after that, though we had many snows and sharp frost, yet they continued not, neither were the waters frozen up as before. It hath been observed, ever since this bay was planted by Englishmen, viz., seven years, that at this day the frost hath broken up every year.

The poorer sort of people (who lay long in tents, etc. [6]) were much afflicted with the scurvy, and many died, especially at Boston and Charlestown; but when this ship came and brought store of juice of lemons, many recovered speedily. It hath been always observed here, that such as fell into discontent, and lingered [7] after their former conditions in England, fell into the scurvy and died.

18. Captain Welden, a hopeful young gentleman, and an experienced soldier, died at Charlestown of a consumption, and was buried at Boston with a military funeral.

Of the old planters, [8] and such as came the year before, there were but two, (and those

servants) which had the scurvy in all the country. At Plymouth not any had it, no not of those, who came this year, whereof there were above sixty. Whereas, at their first planting there, near the half of their people died of it.

A shallop of Mr. Glover's was cast away upon the rocks about Nahant, but the men were saved.

Of those which went back in the ships this summer, for fear of death or famine, etc., many died by the way and after they were landed, and others fell very sick and low, etc.

The *Ambrose*, whereof Capt. Lowe was master, being new masted at Charlton, [9] spent [10] all her masts near Newfoundland, and had perished, if Mr. Peirce, in the *Lyon*, who was her consort, had not towed her home to Bristol. Of the other ships which returned, three, viz., the *Charles*, the *Success*, and the *Whale*, were set upon by Dunkirkers, [11] near Plymouth in England, and after long fight, having lost many men, and being much torn, (especially the *Charles*) they gat into Plymouth.

The provision, which came to us this year, came at excessive rates, in regard of [12] the dearness of corn [13] in England, so as every bushel of wheat-meal stood us in fourteen shillings, peas eleven shillings, etc. Tonnage was at £6.11.

22. We held a day of thanksgiving for this ship's arrival, by order from the governor and council, directed to all the plantations. [14]

[Nov. 1633.] ... The scarcity of workmen had caused them [15] to raise their wages to an excessive rate, so as a carpenter would have three shillings the day, a laborer two shillings and sixpence, etc., and accordingly those who had commodities to sell advanced their prices sometime double to that they cost in England, so as it grew to a general complaint, which the court, taking knowledge of, as also of some further evils which were springing out of the excessive rates of wages, they made an order that carpenters, masons, etc., should take but two shillings the day, and laborers but eighteen pence, and that no commodity should be sold at above four pence in the shilling more than it cost for ready money in England; oil, wine, etc., and cheese, in regard of the hazard of bringing, etc., [excepted]. The evils which were springing, etc., were: 1. Many spent much time

---

[1] The journal covers the period between March, 1630, and January, 1649. The manuscript was used by Cotton Mather in writing his *Magnalia Christi Americana*, and by other historians of New England.
[2] Roger Williams   [3] son of a colonist named Way
[4] Winthrop usually, as here, speaks of himself in the third person.
[5] in the lower Boston harbor
[6] So many had come during the summer before, that houses could not be built at once for all.
[7] longed   [8] founders of the colony

[9] Charlestown   [10] lost
[11] privateers from Dunkirk, a town on the French coast, at that time held by Spain, which was then at war with England.
[12] because of   [13] wheat
[14] all the settlements of the colony under Governor Winthrop's authority
[15] i. e., the workmen

idly, etc., because they could get as much in four days as would keep them a week. *2.* They spent much in tobacco and strong waters, etc., which was a great waste to the commonwealth, which, by reason of so many foreign commodities expended, [1] could not have subsisted to this time, but that it was supplied by the cattle and corn, which were sold to new comers at very dear rates, viz., corn at six shillings the bushel, a cow at £20,—yea, some at £24, some £26,—a mare at £35, an ewe goat at £3 or £4; and yet many cattle were every year brought out of England, and some from Virginia. Soon after order was taken for prices of commodities, viz., not to exceed the rate of four pence in the shilling above the price in England, except cheese and liquors, etc.

. . . .

[July] 20. [1636] John Gallop, with one man more, and two little boys, coming from Connecticut in a bark of twenty tons, intending to put in at Long Island to trade, and being at the mouth of the harbor, were forced, by a sudden change of the wind, to bear up for Block Island or Fisher's Island, lying before Narragansett, where they espied a small pinnace, which, drawing near unto, they found to be Mr. Oldham's (an old planter, and a member of Watertown congregation, who had been long out a-trading, having with him only two English boys, and two Indians of Narragansett). So they hailed him, but had no answer; and the deck was full of Indians, (fourteen in all) and a canoe was gone from her full of Indians and goods. Whereupon they suspected they had killed John Oldham, [2] and the rather, because the Indians let slip and set up sail, being two miles from shore, and the wind and tide being off the shore of the island, whereby they drove towards the main at Narragansett. Whereupon they went ahead of them, and having but two pieces and two pistols, and nothing but duck shot, they bear up near the Indians, (who stood ready armed with guns, pikes, and swords) and let fly among them, and so galled them as they all gate under hatches. Then they stood off again, and returning with a good gale, they stemmed her upon the quarter [3] and almost overset her, which so frighted the Indians, as six of them leaped overboard and were drowned. Yet they durst not board her, but stood off again, and

fitted their anchor, so as, stemming her the second time, they bored her bow through with their anchor, and so sticking fast to her, they made divers shot through her (being but inch board) and so raked her fore and aft, as they must needs kill or hurt some of the Indians; but, seeing none of them come forth, they gate loose from her and stood off again. Then four or five more of the Indians leaped into the sea, and were likewise drowned. So there being now but four left in her, they boarded her; whereupon one Indian came up and yielded; him they bound and put into hold. Then another yielded, whom they bound. But John Gallop, being well acquainted with their skill to untie themselves, if two of them be together, and having no place to keep them asunder, he threw him bound into [the] sea; and, looking about, they found John Oldham under an old seine, stark naked, his head cleft to the brains, and his hand and legs cut as if they had been cutting them off, and yet warm. So they put him into the sea; but could not get to the other two Indians, who were in a little room underneath, with their swords. So they took the goods which were left, and the sails, etc., and towed the boat away; but night coming on, and the wind rising, they were forced to turn her off, and the wind carried her to the Narragansett shore.

. . . .

[September] 4. [1639] At the general court at Boston, one Mr. Nathaniel Eaton, brother to the merchant at Quilipiack, was convented [4] and censured. The occasion was this: He was a schoolmaster, and had many scholars, [5] the sons of gentlemen and others of best note in the country, and had entertained [6] one Nathaniel Briscoe, a gentleman born, to be his usher, [7] and to do some other things for him, which might not be unfit for a scholar. He had not been with him above three days but he fell out with him for a very small occasion, and, with reproachful terms, discharged him, and turned him out of his doors; but, it being then about eight of the clock after the Sabbath, [8] he told him he should stay till next morning, and, some words growing between them, he struck him and pulled him into his house. Briscoe defended himself, and closed with him, and, being

[1] Winthrop seems to mean: foreign luxuries took money out of the colony in payment, and the colony would have been destitute of money, and hence come to naught, had it not been for the local trade in colonial grown cattle and corn.
[2] This murder led to the Pequot War.
[3] struck with their prow aft of the middle

[4] summoned to appear
[5] This school was really Harvard College, or, as Cotton Mather says, the "society of scholars to lodge in the new nests" as soon as the candidates for admission should be prepared for the college, which had been founded three years before.
[6] hired   [7] assistant teacher
[8] The Sabbath began at sunset of Saturday and ended at sunset of Sunday.

parted, he came in and went up to his chamber to lodge there. Mr. Eaton sent for the constable, who advised him first to admonish him, etc., and if he could not, by the power of a master, reform him, then he should complain to the magistrate. But he caused his man to fetch him a cudgel, which was a walnut tree plant, big enough to have killed a horse, and a yard in length, and, taking his two men with him, he went up to Briscoe, and caused his men to hold him till he had given him two hundred stripes about the head and shoulders, etc., and so kept him under blows (with some two or three short intermissions) about the space of two hours, about which time Mr. Shepherd and some others of the town came in at the outcry, and so he gave over. In this distress Briscoe gat out his knife, and struck at the man that held him, but hurt him not. He also fell to prayer, (supposing he should have been murdered) and then Mr. Eaton beat him for taking the name of God in vain. After this Mr. Eaton and Mr. Shepherd (who knew not then of these passages[1]) came to the governor and some other of the magistrates, complaining of Briscoe for his insolent speeches, and for crying out murder and drawing his knife, and desired that he might be enjoined to a public acknowledgment, [2] etc. The magistrates answered that they must first hear him speak, and then they would do as they should see cause. Mr. Eaton was displeased at this, and went away discontented, etc., and, being after called into the court to make answer to the information which had been given by some who knew the truth of the case, and also to answer for his neglect and cruelty, and other ill usage towards his scholars, one of the elders (not suspecting such miscarriages [3] by him) came to the governor, and showed himself much grieved that he should be publicly produced, [4] alleging that it would derogate from his authority and reverence among his scholars, etc. But the cause [5] went on notwithstanding, and he was called, and these things laid to his charge in the open court. His answers were full of pride and disdain, telling the magistrates that they should not need to do any thing herein, for he was intended to leave his employment. And being asked why he used such cruelty to Briscoe his usher, and to other his scholars, (for it was testified by another of his ushers and divers of his scholars that he would give them between twenty and thirty stripes at a time, and would

not leave till they had confessed what he required) his answer was that he had this rule, that he would not give over correcting till he had subdued the party to his will. Being also questioned about the ill and scant diet of his boarders, (for, though their friends gave large allowance, yet their diet was ordinarily nothing but porridge and pudding, and that very homely) he put it off to his wife. So the court dismissed him at present, and commanded him to attend again the next day, when, being called, he was commanded to the lower end of the table, (where all offenders do usually stand) and, being openly convict [6] of all the former offences, by the oaths of four or five witnesses, he yet continued to justify himself; so, it being near night, he was committed to the marshal till the next day. When the court was set in the morning, many of the elders [7] came into the court, (it being then private for matter of consultation) and declared how, the evening before, they had taken pains with him, to convince him of his faults; yet, for divers hours, he had still stood to his justification; but, in the end, he was convinced, and had freely and fully acknowledged his sin, and that with tears; so as they did hope he had truly repented, and therefore desired of the court that he might be pardoned, and continued in his employment, alleging such further reasons as they thought fit. After the elders were departed, the court consulted about it, and sent for him, and there, in the open court, before a great assembly, he made a very solid, wise, eloquent, and serious (seeming) confession, condemning himself in all the particulars, etc. Whereupon, being put aside, the court consulted privately about his sentence, and, though many were taken with his confession, and none but had a charitable opinion of it; yet, because of the scandal of religion, and offence which would be given to such as might intend to send their children hither, they all agreed to censure him, and put him from that employment. So, being called in, the governor, after a short preface, etc., declared the sentence of the court to this effect, viz.: that he should give Briscoe £30, [be] fined 100 marks, [8] and debarred teaching of children within our jurisdiction. A pause being made, and expectation that (according to his former confession) he would have given glory to God, and acknowledged the justice and clemency of the court, the governor giving him occasion, by asking him if he had aught to say,

---

[1] occurrences
[2] induced to confess publicly
[3] misdemeanors
[4] cited to appear
[5] legal proceedings

[6] convicted
[7] ruling officials of the church
[8] about £67

he turned away with a discontented look, saying, "If sentence be passed, then it is to no end to speak." Yet the court remitted his fine to £20, and willed Briscoe to take but £20.

The church at Cambridge, taking notice of these proceedings, intended to deal with him. The pastor moved [1] the governor, if they might, without offence to the court, examine other witnesses. His answer was that the court would leave them to their own liberty; but he saw not to what end they should do it, seeing there had been five already upon oath, and those whom they should examine should speak without oath, and it was an ordinance of God that by the mouths of two or three witnesses every matter should be established. [2] But he soon discovered himself; for, ere the church could come to deal with him, he fled to Pascataquack, and, being pursued and apprehended by the governor there, he again acknowledged his great sin in flying, etc., and promised (as he was a Christian man) he would return with the messengers. But, because his things he carried with him were aboard a bark there, bound to Virginia, he desired leave to go fetch them, which they assented unto, and went with him (three of them) aboard with him. So he took his truss [3] and came away with them in the boat; but, being come to the shore, and two of them going out of the boat, he caused the boatsmen to put off the boat, and because the third man would not go out, he turned him into the water, where he had been drowned, if he had not saved himself by swimming. So he returned to the bark, and presently they set sail and went out of the harbor. Being thus gone, his creditors began to complain; and thereupon it was found that he was run in debt about £1000, and had taken up most of this money upon bills he had charged into England upon his brother's agents, and others whom he had no such relation to. So his estate was seized, and put into commissioners' hands, to be divided among his creditors, allowing somewhat for the present maintenance of his wife and children. And, being thus gone, the church proceeded and cast him out. He had been sometimes [4] initiated among the Jesuits, and, coming into England, his friends drew him from them, but, it was very probable, he now intended to return to them again, being at this time about thirty years of age, and upwards. See after.

[December 1640] ... Mr. Nathaniel Eaton, of whom mention is made before, being come to Virginia, took upon him to be a minister, but was given up of God to extreme pride and sensuality, being usually drunken, as the custom is there. He sent for his wife and children. Her friends here persuaded her to stay awhile, but she went notwithstanding, and the vessel was never heard of after.

.   .   .   .   .   .

[September 22. 1642] The court, with advice of the elders, ordered a general fast. The occasions were, 1. The ill news we had out of England concerning the breach [5] between the King and Parliament. 2. The danger of the Indians. 3. The unseasonable weather, the rain having continued so long, viz. near a fortnight together, scarce one fair day, and much corn and hay spoiled, though indeed it proved a blessing to us, for it being with warm easterly winds, it brought the Indian corn to maturity, which otherwise would not have been ripe, and it pleased God, that so soon as the fast was agreed upon, the weather changed, and proved fair after.

At this court, the propositions sent from Connecticut, about a combination, [6] etc., were read, and referred to a committee to consider of after the court, who meeting, added some few cautions and new articles, and for the taking in of Plymouth, (who were now willing) and Sir Ferdinando Gorges' province, [7] and so returned them back to Connecticut, to be considered upon against the spring, for winter was now approaching, and there could be no meeting before, etc.

The sudden fall of land and cattle, and the scarcity of foreign commodities, and money, etc., with the thin access of people from England, put many into an unsettled frame of spirit, so as they concluded there would be no subsisting here, and accordingly they began to hasten away, some to the West Indies, others to the Dutch, at Long Island, etc., (for the governor there invited them by fair offers) and others back for England. Among others who returned thither, there was one of the magistrates, Mr. Humfrey, and four ministers, and a schoolmaster. These would needs go against all advice, and had a fair and speedy voyage, till they came near England, all which time, three of the ministers, with the schoolmaster, spake reproachfully of the people and of the country, but the wind coming up against them,

---

[1] submitted the proposal to
[2] 2 *Corinthians* xiii, 1
[3] bundle (of effects)
[4] sometime, at one time

[5] the Civil War in England   [7] afterwards Maine
[6] for mutual protection and defense

they were tossed up and down, being in 10ber [1]
so long till their provisions and other necessaries
were near spent, and they were forced to strait
allowance, yet at length the wind coming fair
again, they got into the Sleeve, [2] but then there
arose so great a tempest at S.E. as they could
bear no sail, and so were out of hope of being
saved (being in the night also). Then they
humbled themselves before the Lord, and acknowledged God's hand to be justly out against
them for speaking evil of this good land and the
Lord's people here, etc. Only one of them,
Mr. Phillips of Wrentham, in England, had not
joined with the rest, but spake well of the
people, and of the country; upon this it pleased
the Lord to spare their lives, and when they expected every moment to have been dashed upon
the rocks, (for they were hard by the Needles [3])
he turned the wind so as they were carried
safe to the Isle of Wight by St. Helen's: yet
the Lord followed them on shore. Some were
exposed to great straits and found no entertainment, their friends forsaking them. One
had a daughter that presently ran mad. . . . The
schoolmaster had no sooner hired an house, and
gotten in some scholars, but the plague set in,
and took away two of his own children.

Others who went to other places, upon like
grounds, succeeded no better. They fled for
fear of want, and many of them fell into it, even
to extremity, as if they had hastened into the
misery which they feared and fled from, besides
the depriving themselves of the ordinances [4]
and church fellowship, and those civil liberties
which they enjoyed here; whereas, such as staid
in their places, kept their peace and ease, and
enjoyed still the blessing of the ordinances, and
never tasted of those troubles and miseries
which they heard to have befallen those who
departed. Much disputation there was about
liberty of removing for outward advantages,
and all ways were sought for an open door to
get out at; but it is to be feared many crept
out at a broken wall. For such as come together into a wilderness, where are nothing but
wild beasts and beastlike men, and there confederate together in civil and church estate,
whereby they do, implicitly at least, bind themselves to support each other, and all of them
that society, whether civil or sacred, whereof
they are members, how they can break from
this without free consent, is hard to find, so as
may satisfy a tender or good conscience in time

of trial. Ask thy conscience, if thou wouldst
have plucked up thy stakes, and brought thy
family 3000 miles, if thou hadst expected that
all, or most, would have forsaken thee there.
Ask again, what liberty thou hast towards
others, which thou likest not to allow others
towards thyself; for if one may go, another
may, and so the greater part, and so church and
commonwealth may be left destitute in a wilderness, exposed to misery and reproach, and
all for thy ease and pleasure, whereas these all,
being now thy brethren, as near to thee as the
Israelites were to Moses, it were much safer
for thee, after his example, to choose rather to
suffer affliction with thy brethren, than to enlarge thy ease and pleasure by furthering the
occasion of their ruin. [5]

Nine bachelors commenced [6] at Cambridge;
they were young men of good hope, and performed their acts, [7] so as gave good proof of
their proficiency in the tongues and arts. (8.)
[October] 5. The general court had settled a
government or superintendency over the college, viz., all the magistrates and elders over
the six nearest churches and the president, or
the greatest part of these. Most of them were
now present at this first commencement, and
dined at the college with the scholars' ordinary
commons, which was done of purpose for the
students' encouragement, etc., and it gave good
content to all.

At this commencement, complaint was made
to the governors of two young men, of good
quality, [8] lately come out of England, for foul
misbehavior, in swearing and ribaldry speeches,
etc., for which, though they were *adulti*, [9] they
were corrected [10] in the college, and sequestered,
etc., for a time.

1790; 1825-26

.   .   .   .   .   .

[5] Amid the trials of leadership Winthrop may often
with good reason have felt himself to be the
Moses of the New England people. It is well
to remember that this passage was written by
the same man who recorded in a single line the
death of his son.
[6] graduated
[7] parts; Cotton Mather says, "these exercises were,
besides an oration usually made by the President, orations both salutatory and valedictory,
made by some or other of the commencers,
wherein all persons and orders of any fashion
then present were addressed with proper complements, and reflections were made on the most
remarkable occurrents of the preceding year; and
these orations were made not only in Latin, but
sometimes in Greek and in Hebrew also; and
some of them were in verse, and even in Greek
verse, as well as others in prose."—*Magnalia
Christi Americana*, Book IV; Vol. ii, p. 12, ed
1853.
[8] birth
[9] adults
[10] probably, whipped

[1] Winthrop's usual abbreviation for the month of
December; the year began with March.
[2] *La Manche* (Fr. sleeve), the English Channel
[3] rocks near the Isle of Wight
[4] services of the (Puritan) church, forbidden in England

THE BAY PSALM BOOK [1]

The first English book printed in North America was *The Bay Psalm Book,* published at Cambridge, Massachusetts, 1640. Cotton Mather says of it, "About the year 1639, the New England reformers, considering that their churches enjoyed the other ordinances of Heaven in their scriptural purity, were willing that the ordinance of 'the singing of Psalms' should be restored among them unto a share in that purity." A committee of three ministers did the work.

The attitude of the translators toward artistic excellence is worth noting. In the preface they say: "If therefore the verses are not always so smooth and elegant as some may desire or expect; let them consider that Gods Altar needs not our polishings: *Ex.* 20. for wee have respected rather a plaine translation, then to smooth our verses with the sweetnes of any paraphrase, and soe have attended Conscience rather than Elegance, fidelity rather then poetry, in translating the hebrew words into english language, and Davids poetry into english meetre; that soe wee may sing in Sion the Lords songs of prayse according to his owne will; untill hee take us from hence, and wipe away all our teares, & bid us enter into our masters joye to sing eternall Halleluiahs."

Best edition: facsimile edition edited by Wilberforce Eames, The New England Society, New York, 1903.

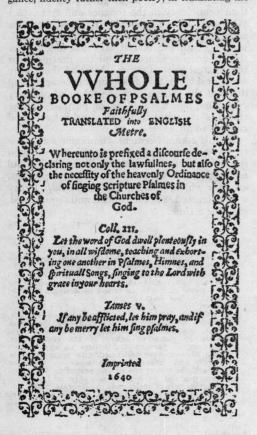

23 *A Pfalme of David.*

The Lord to mee a fhepheard is,
　　want therefore fhall not I.

2　Hee in the folds of tender-graffe,
　　doth caufe mee downe to lie:
　To waters calme me gently leads

3　Reftore my foule doth hee:
　he doth in paths of righteoufnes:
　　for his names fake leade mee.

4　Yea though in valley of deaths fhade
　I walk, none ill I'le feare:
　becaufe thou art with mee, thy rod,
　　and ftaffe my comfort are.

5　For mee a table thou haft fpread,
　in prefence of my foes:
　thou doft annoynt my head with oyle,
　　my cup it over-flowes.

6　Goodnes & mercy furely fhall
　all my dayes follow mee:
　and in the Lords houfe I fhall dwell
　　fo long as dayes fhall bee.

Psalme 24

A psalme of david:

The earth Iehovahs is,
　　and the fulnesse of it :
　the habitable world, & they
　　that there upon doe sit.

2　Because upon the seas,
　　hee hath it firmly layd:
　and it upon the water-floods
　　most sollidly hath stayd.

3　The mountaine of the Lord,
　　who shall thereto ascend?
　and in his place of holynes,
　　who is it that shall stand?

4　The cleane in hands, & pure
　　in heart; to vanity

[1] The selections given follow the spelling and punctuation of the original edition.

who hath not lifted up his soule,
    nor sworne deceitfully.
5 From God he shall receive
    a benediction,
and righteousnes from the strong-God
    of his salvation.
6 This is the progenie
    of them that seek thy face:
of them that doe inquire for him:
    of Iacob 'tis the race.   Selah. [1]
7 Yee gates lift-up your heads,
    and doors everlasting,
be yee lift up: & there into
    shall come the glorious-King
8 Who is this glorious King?
    Iehovah, puissant,
and valiant, Iehovah is
    in battel valiant.
9 Yee gates lift-up your heads,
    and doors everlasting,
doe yee lift-up: & there into
    shall come the glorious-King,
10 Who is this glorious-King?
    loe, it is Iehovah
of warlike armies, hee the King
    of glory is; Selah.

Psalme 121.

A song of degrees.

I TO the hills lift up mine eyes,
    from whence shall come mine aid
2 Mine help doth from Iehovah come,
    which heav'n & earth hath made.
3 Hee will not let thy foot be mov'd,
    nor slumber; that thee keeps.
4 Loe hee that keepeth Israell,
    hee slumbreth not, nor sleeps.
5 The Lord thy keeper is, the Lord
    on thy right hand the shade.
6 The Sun by day, nor Moone by night,
    shall thee by stroke *invade*.
7 The Lord will keep the from all ill:
    thy soule hee keeps alway,
8 Thy going out, & thy income,
    the Lord keeps now & aye.

1640

NATHANIEL WARD 1578-1652

In Ward's writings we get a taste of the controversial satire of the times, not confined to religious discussions within the Puritan church, but marking debate in general throughout Christendom. Discussion, in those days, became personal as it grew

[1] The word perhaps indicated a pause or choral direction in the original singing of the psalm.

in earnestness; good manners in expressing opinion are modern. Ward was born in England, was M.A. of Emanuel College, Cambridge, 1603, studied and practiced law, traveled on the Continent, was rector of Stondon Massey, until excommunicated by Archbishop Laud for Puritan teachings in 1633. He emigrated to New England and was colleague pastor at Agawam, or Ipswich, 1634-36. He compiled the first Massachusetts code of laws, *The Body of Liberties,* 1641. Five years later he returned to England, re-entered the ministry, then controlled by the Puritan Parliament, received the living of Shenfield, Essex, and served until his death. It is interesting that *The Simple Cobbler,* written at Agawam, went through four editions in London within a year.

The book is a satire against any toleration by the Puritans of liberalism in religion, and also against what were thought to be dangerous social customs. Ward with many others of his generation felt that their time was one of tremendous moral crisis; that is that a general judgment was imminent, that Satan would be dethroned, and that the chosen of God would rule the earth. Such an unfolding of the immediate future seemed to them foretold in the persecution of the Puritans in England, the flight to America, and the civil war then in progress in the mother country. To them these events were the fulfillment of ancient prophecies, as the first sentence of the present selection (beginning the book) indicates.

Professor Tyler says: "Upon the whole, *The Simple Cobbler of Agawam* is a droll and pungent bit of early American prose, with many literary offenses upon its head: an excessive fondness for antitheses; an untempered enjoyment of quirks and turns and petty freaks of phraseology; the pursuit of puns and metaphors beyond all decorum; the blurring of its sentences with great daubs and patches of Latin quotation; the willing employment of outlandish and uncouth words belonging to no language at all, sometimes huddled together into combinations that defy syntax and set all readers aghast."

In *The Simple Cobbler* Ward reveals one type of the American Puritan: a man whose face was turned toward the past, toward medievalism and asceticism. In *The Bloody Tenet of Persecution* Williams reveals another type: the man of progressive and tolerant ideas, who faced forward, toward religious enlightenment and freedom. It is well to get clearly in mind the point of view of the Bay Colony Massachusetts Puritans. They had founded a colony not at all in the interests of religious freedom, as we know it, but to promote and to propagate their own religious opinions and practices. Naturally, they did not welcome but often banished those who came to stir up religious dissension among them. They felt that those who were trying to tear down what they themselves were spending their fortunes and their lives in building up should be elsewhere and found, if they wished, their own communities. There was, they felt, plenty of empty space in the New World for everyone.

From THE SIMPLE COBLER OF AGGAV-VAMM IN AMERICA [1]

SUTOR ULTRA CREPIDAM [2]

Either I am in an appoplexie, or that man is in a lethargie, who doth not now sensibly feele God shaking the heavens over his head, and the earth under his feet: the heavens so, as the sun begins to turne into darknesse, the moon into blood,[3] the starres to fall down to the ground; so that little light of comfort or counsell is left to the sonnes of men: the earth so, as the foundations are failing, the righteous scarce know where to finde rest, the inhabitants stagger like drunken men: it is in a manner dissolved both in religions and relations: and no marvell; for, they have defiled it by trans-gressing the lawes, changing the ordinances, and breaking the everlasting covenant. The truths of God are the pillars of the world, wheron states and churches may stand quiet if they will; if they will not, hee can easily shake them off into delusions, and distractions enough.

Sathan is now in his passions, he feeles his passion[4] approaching; hee loves to fish in royled waters. Though that dragon cannot sting the vitals of the elect mortally, yet that Beelzebub[5] can fly-blow their intellectuals mis-erably: the finer religion grows, the finer hee spins his cobwebs, hee will hold pace with Christ so long as his wits will serve him. Hee sees himselfe beaten out of grosse idolatries, heresies, ceremonies, where the light breaks forth with power; he will therefore bestirre him to prevaricate evangelicall truths, and or-dinances, that if they will needs be walking, yet they shall *laborare varicibus*,[6] and not keep their path, he will put them out of time and place; assassinating for his engineers, men of Paracelsian parts; well complexioned for hon-esty; for, such are fittest to mountebanke his chimistry into sicke churches and weake judge-ments.[7]

Nor shall hee need to stretch his strength over-much in this worke: too many men having not laid their foundations sure, nor ballasted their spirits deepe with humility and feare, are prest[8] enough of themselves to evaporate their owne apprehensions. Those that are acquainted with story know, it hath ever beene so in new editions of churches: such as are least able, are most busie to pudder in the rubbish, and to raise dust in the eyes of more steady repayrers. Civill commotions make roome for uncivill prac-tises: religious mutations, for irreligious opin-ions: change of aire, discovers corrupt bodies; reformation of religion, unsound mindes. Hee that hath any well-faced phansy in his crowne, and doth not vent it now, fears the pride of his owne heart will dub him dunce for ever. Such a one will trouble the whole *Israel* of God[9] with his most untimely births, though he makes the bones of his vanity stick up, to the view and griefe of all that are godly wise. The devill desiers no better sport then to see light heads handle their heels, and fetch their carreers in a time, when the roofe of liberty stands open.

The next perplexed question, with pious and ponderous[10] men, will be: what should bee done for the healing of these comfortlesse exulcer-ations. I am the unablest adviser of a thousand, the unworthiest of ten thousand; yet I hope I may presume to assert what follows without just offence.

First, such as have given or taken any un-friendly reports[11] of us *New-English,* should doe well to recollect themselves. Wee have beene reputed a colluvies[12] of wild opinionists, swarmed into a remote wildernes to find elbow-roome for our phanatick doctrines and prac-tises: I trust our diligence past, and constant sedulity against such persons and courses, will plead better things for us. I dare take upon me, to bee the herauld of *New-England* so farre, as to proclaime to the world, in the name of our colony, that all Familists, Antinomians, Ana baptists,[13] and other enthusiasts shall have free

---

[1] The selections from Ward conform in spelling and punctuation with the original volume. The com-plete title is as follows: "The Simple Cobler of Aggavvamm in America. Willing to help 'mend his Native Country, lamentably tattered, both in the upper-Leather and sole, with all the honest stitches he can take. And is willing never to bee paid for his work, by Old English wonted pay. It is his Trade to patch all the year long, gratis. Therefore I pray Gentlemen keep your purses. By Theodore de la Guard." The pseudo-nym is a translation of the author's own name, Theodore meaning "Gift of God" in Greek, as Nathaniel does in Hebrew.

[2] Literally, the cobbler beyond his last; that is, not sticking to his last: appropos of the Latin proverb, *ne sutor supra crepidam judicaret,* let not the cobbler pass judgment on things beyond his last.

[3] *Joel* ii, 31

[4] death throes

[5] prince of demons

[6] be afflicted with an enlarged vein, as in the thigh (hence, walk haltingly)

[7] The passage "assassinating . . . . judgements" may be explained thus: destroying all good within them, so that he can use as his own plotters, these men who are as talented as Paracelsus (a celebrated medieval physician), well balanced in honesty; for such are fittest to introduce by trickery his deception into sick churches and persons of weak judgment.

[8] ready

[9] the entire Christian Church (the chosen ones replacing, in God's favor, the descendents of Israel)

[10] grave, deliberate

[11] See Winthrop's attitude in the same matter, p. 17.

[12] offscourings, rabble

[13] various dissenting sects holding views contrary to those of the Puritans

liberty to keepe away from us, and such as will come to be gone as fast as they can, the sooner the better.

Secondly, I dare averre, that God doth no where in his word tolerate Christian states, to give tolerations to such adversaries of his truth, if they have power in their hands to suppresse them.

Here is lately brought us an extract of a *Magna Charta,* [1] so called, compiled between the sub-planters [2] of a *West-Indian* island; whereof the first article of constipulation, firmly provides free stable-room and litter for all kinde of consciences, be they never so dirty or jadish; making it actionable, yea, treasonable, to disturbe any man in his religion, or to discommend it, whatever it be. Wee are very sorry to see such professed prophanenesse in *English* professors, [3] as industriously to lay their religious foundations on the ruine of true religion; which strictly binds every conscience *to contend earnestly for the truth: to preserve unity of spirit, faith and ordinances, to be all like minded, of one accord; every man to take his brother into his Christian care: to stand fast with one spirit, with one mind, striving together for the faith of the Gospel.* And by no meanes to permit heresies or erronious opinions: but God abhorring such loathsome beverages, hath in his righteous judgement blasted that enterprize, which might otherwise have prospered well, for ought I know; I presume their case is generally knowne ere this. [4]

If the devill might have his free option, I beleeve he would ask nothing else, but liberty to enfranchize all false religions, and to embondage the true; nor should hee need: it is much to be feared, that laxe tolerations upon state-pretences and planting necessities, [5] will be the next subtle stratagem he will spread to distate [6] the truth of God and supplant the peace of the churches. Tolerations in things tolerable, exquisitely drawn out by the lines of the scripture, and pensill of the spirit, are the sacred favours of truth, the due latitudes of love, the faire compartiments of Christian fraternity: but irregular dispensations, dealt forth by the facilities of men, are the frontiers of error, the redoubts of schisme, the perillous irritaments [7] of carnall and spirituall enmity.

My heart hath naturally detested foure things: the standing of the Apocrypha [8] in the Bible; forrainers dwelling in my countrey, to crowd out native subjects into the corners of the earth; alchymized [9] coines; tolerations of divers religions, or of one religion in segregant [10] shapes: he that willingly assents to the last, if he examines his heart by day-light, his conscience will tell him, he is either an atheist, or an heretique, or an hypocrite, or at best a captive to some lust: poly-piety is the greatest impiety in the world. True religion is *ignis probationis,* which doth *congregare homogenea & segregare heterogenea.* [11]

Not to tolerate things meerly indifferent to weak consciences, argues a conscience too strong: pressed uniformity in these, causes much disunity: to tolerate more then indifferents, [12] is not to deale indifferently with God: he that doth it, takes his scepter out of his hand, and bids him stand by. Who hath to doe to institute religion but God. The power of all religion and ordinances, lies in their purity: their purity in their simplicity: then are mixtures pernicious. J lived in a city, where a Papist preached in one church, a Lutheran in another, a Calvinist in a third; a Lutheran one part of the day, a Calvinist the other, in the same pulpit: the religion of that place was but motly and meagre, their affections leopard-like.

If the whole creature should conspire to doe the Creator a mischiefe, or offer him an insolency, it would be in nothing more, than in erecting untruths against his truth, or by sophisticating his truths with humane medleyes: the removing of some one jota in scripture, may draw out all the life, and traverse all the truth of the whole Bible: but to authorise an untruth, by a toleration of state, is to build a sconce against [13] the walls of heaven, to batter God out of his chaire: to tell a practicall lye, is a great sin, but yet transient; but to set up a theoricall untruth, is to warrant every lye that lyes from its root to the top of every branch it hath, which are not a few.

.   .   .   .   .   .

SHOULD I not keepe promise in speaking a little to womens fashions, they would take it unkindly: I was loath to pester better matter with such stuffe; I rather thought it meet to let them stand by themselves like the *Quae Genus*

---

[1] constitution (in reference to the Magna Charta or first written document of the English constitutional liberties)
[2] Settlers, not proprietors; the facts are mentioned in Edward Johnson's *Wonder-Working Providence,* New York, Scribner's, 1910, Book II, Chapter xx.
[3] those professing religion
[4] See Winthrop, p. 16.
[5] necessities arising at the planting of a colony
[6] disstate: lower in position   [7] incentives
[8] books of the Old Testament of doubtful authenticity, retained by the English church, but not as a foundation for doctrine
[9] counterfeit   [10] separated, sectarian
[11] a fire-test which doth bring together the like and scatter the unlike
[12] non-essentials
[13] battlement over against

in the grammer, [1] being deficients, or redundants, not to be brought under any rule: I shall therefore make bold for this once, to borrow a little of their loose tongued liberty, and mispend a word or two upon their long-wasted, but short-skirted patience: a little use of my stirrup will doe no harme.

> *Ridentem dicere verum, quid prohibet?* [2]
> *Gray gravity it selfe can well beteam,* [3]
> *That language be adapted to the theme.*
> *He that to parrots speaks, must parrotise:*
> *He that instructs a foole, may act th' unwise.*

It is known more then enough, that I am neither nigard, nor cinick, to the due bravery of the true gentry: if any man mislikes a bullymong drossock [4] more than I, let him take her for his labour: I honour the woman that can honour her selfe with her attire: a good text alwayes deserves a fair margent; I am not much offended, if I see a trimme, [5] far trimmer than she that weares it: in a word, whatever Christianity or civility will allow, I can afford with *London* measure: [6] but when I heare a nugiperous [7] gentledame inquire what dresse the queen is in this week: what the nudiustertian [8] fashion of the court; with egge [9] to be in it in all haste, whatever it be; I look at her as the very gizzard of a trifle, the product of a quarter of a cypher, the epitome of nothing, fitter to be kickt, if shee were of a kickable substance, than either honour'd or humour'd.

To speak moderately, I truly confesse it is beyond the ken of my understanding to conceive, how those women should have any true grace, or valuable vertue, that have so little wit, as to disfigure themselves with such exotick garbes, as not only dismantles their native lovely lustre, but transclouts [10] them into gant-bar-geese, [11] ill-shapen-shotten [12]-shell-fish, Egyptian hyeroglyphicks, or at the best into French flurts of the pastery, [13] which a proper

English woman should scorne with her heels: it is no marvell they weare drailes [14] on the hinder part of their heads, having nothing as it seems in the fore-part, but a few squirrils brains to help them frisk from one ill-favour'd fashion to another.

> *These whimm-crown'd shees, these fashion-fansying wits,*
> *Are empty thin brain'd shells, and fidling kits.*

The very troublers and impoverishers of mankind, I can hardly forbeare to commend to the world a saying of a lady living sometime with the queen of *Bohemia*, I know not where shee found it, but it is pitty it should be lost.

> *The world is full of care, much like unto a bubble;*
> *Women and care, and care and women, and women*
> *and care and trouble.*

The verses are even enough for such odde pegma's [15] I can make my selfe sicke at any time, with comparing the dazling splender wherewith our gentlewomen were imbellished in some former habits, with the gut-foundred [16] goosdom, wherewith they are now surcingled and debauched. Wee have about five or six of them in our colony: if I see any of them accidentally, I cannot cleanse my phansie of them for a moneth after. I have been a solitary widdower almost twelve years, purposed lately to make a step over to my native country for a yoke-fellow: but when I consider how women there have tripe-wifed [17] themselves with their cladments, [18] I have no heart to the voyage, least their nauseous shapes and the sea, should work too sorely upon my stomach. I speak sadly; me thinkes it should breake the hearts of English-men, to see so many goodly English-women imprisoned in French cages, peering out of their hood-holes for some men of mercy to help them with a little wit, and no body relieves them.

It is a more common then convenient saying, that nine taylors make a man: it were well if nineteene could make a woman to her minde: if taylors were men indeed, well furnished but with meer morall principles, they would disdain to be led about like apes, by such mymick marmosets. It is a most unworthy thing for men that have bones in them, to spend their

[1] The reference is probably to some well-known rule of Latin grammar, known by the catchwords *quae genus.*
[2] *Ridentem dicere verum quid vetat?* What prohibits one speaking the truth in laughter?—Horace, *Satires,* I, i, 24-25.
[3] allow
[4] Bullimong is a variety of grains sown together producing a mixed crop. Drassock is an untidy woman.
[5] ornament
[6] rather more than a full yard, customary among London merchants
[7] trifle-inventing
[8] of the day before yesterday (Latin, *nudius tertius*)
[9] eagerness
[10] To clout is to patch; hence, transform by patchwork.
[11] Misprint: the passage should read: gant [dialect for gaunt] bar-geese [or barnacle geese]. These birds of Arctic origin frequented British waters at some seasons.
[12] thin, from having spawned
[13] the place where pastry is made
[14] trailing head-dresses
[15] A pegma is a framework used in theatrical representations, sometimes bearing an inscription. Here, perhaps, the verses, though uneven, are good enough to apply to such odd frameworks as women make of themselves, in displaying their clothes.
[16] on the point of starvation
[17] A tripe-wife is a woman who dresses tripe; used contemptuously.
[18] garments

lives in making fidle-cases for fatulous [1] womens phansies; which are the very pettitoes [2] of infirmity, the giblets of perquisquilian [3] toyes. I am so charitable to think, that most of that mystery would worke the cheerfuller while they live, if they might bee well discharged of the tyring slavery of mis-tyring women: it is no little labour to be continually putting up English-women into out-landish caskes; who if they be not shifted anew, once in a few months, grow too sowre for their husbands. What this trade will answer for themselves when God shall take measure of taylors consciences is beyond my skill to imagine. There was a time when

The joyning of the red-rose with the white,
Did set our state into a damask plight. [4]

But now our roses are turned to *flore de lices,* [5] our carnations to tulips, our gilliflowers to dayzes, our city-dames, to an indenominable quaemalry [6] of overturcas'd [7] things. Hee that makes coates for the moone, had need to take measure every noone: and he that makes for women, as often, to keepe them from lunacy.

I have often heard divers ladies vent loud feminine complaints of the wearisome varieties and chargable changes of fashions: I marvell themselves preferre not a bill of redresse. I would *Essex* ladies would lead the *chore,* [8] for the honour of their country and persons; or rather the thrice honorable ladies of the court, whom it best beesemes: who may wel presume of a *le roy le veult* [9] from our sober King, a *les seigneurs ont assentus* [10] from our prudent peers, and the like *assentus,* from our considerate, I dare not say wife-worne commons: who I beleeve had much rather passe one such bill, than pay so many taylors bills as they are forced to doe.

Most deare and unparallel'd ladies, be pleased to attempt it: as you have the precellency [11]

of the women of the world for beauty and feature; so assume the honour to give, and not take law from any, in matter of attire: if ye can transact so faire a motion among your selves unanimously, I dare say, they that most renite, [12] will least repent. What greater honour can your honors desire, then to build a promontory president [13] to all foraigne ladies, to deserve so eminently at the hands of all the English gentry present and to come: and to confute the opinion of all the wise men in the world; who never thought it possible for women to doe so good a work?

If any man think I have spoken rather merrily than seriously he is much mistaken, I have written what I write with all the indignation I can, and no more then I ought. I confesse I veer'd my tongue to this kinde of language *de industria* [14] though unwillingly, supposing those I speak to are uncapable of grave and rationall arguments.

I desire all ladies and gentlewomen to understand that all this while I intend not such as through necessary modesty to avoyd morose singularity, follow fashions slowly, a flight shot or two off, shewing by their moderation, that they rather draw countermont [15] with their hearts, then put on by their examples.

I point my pen only against the light-heel'd beagles that lead the chase so fast, that they run all civility out of breath, against these apeheaded pullets, which invent antique foolefangles, meerly for fashion and novelty sake.

.   .   .   .

1645-1646   1647

THE NEW ENGLAND PRIMER [16]

The New England Primer was practically the only textbook used in the primary schools of New England in the seventeenth and eighteenth centuries. Its utility to the Puritans lay in the fact that it combined religious and secular instruction, as the title page announces. The date of the first edition is unknown, but it must have been after 1650; it continued to be printed in varying editions throughout the northern provinces and states until the beginning of the nineteenth century. Six or seven generations of New England men and women grew up knowing this book by heart. Its religious and moral maxims were the essence of Puritan belief and life, and their influence has been incalculable.

See P. L. Ford, *The New England Primer: A History of its Origin and Development,* 1897.

---

[1] foolish
[2] pigs' feet when used for food (contemptuously, trifles)
[3] worthless
[4] Reference is to the "Wars of the Roses" between the rival houses of Lancaster and York, the former taking the red and the latter the white rose as a badge. The houses were joined in Henry VII, 1485. The "damask plight" is a figurative allusion to the happy blending of the houses of York and Lancaster which brought peace.
[5] *fleur de lis* The idea of this and the following figures is that things of natural beauty are turned artificially into things more showy.
[6] perhaps, that which causes qualms: disgusting
[7] covered with turquoises: over-adorned
[8] A dance or company of dancers, or a choir; Ward was an Essex man.
[9] the king wills it
[10] the lords have consented   [11] superiority, pre-eminence

[12] show reluctance   [14] laboriously, not naturally
[13] striking precedent
[15] uphill, against the natural course
[16] The facsimile reprint follows the earliest copy known, a unique copy in the Lenox Library, New York.

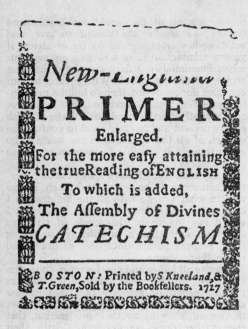

G — As runs the *Glaſs*
Mans life doth paſs.

H — My *Book* and *Heart*
Shall never part.

J — *Job* feels the Rod
Yet bleſſes GOD.

K — Our *KING* the good
No man of blood.

L — The *Lion* bold
The *Lamb* doth hold.

M — The *Moon* gives light
In time of night.

A — In *Adam's* Fall
We Sinned all.

B — Thy Life to Mend
This *Book* Attend.

C — The *Cat* doth play
And after ſlay.

D — A *Dog* will bite
A *Thief* at night.

E — An *Eagles* flight
Is out of ſight.

F — The Idle *Fool*
Is whipt at School.

Nightingales sing,
In time of Spring.

The Royal Oak it was the Tree
That sav'd his Royal Majesty. [1]

Peter denies
His Lord and cries.

Queen Esther comes
In Royal state
To save the Jews
From dismal fate.

Rachel doth mourn
For her first born.

Samuel anoints
Whom God appoints. [2]

Time cuts down all,
Both great and small.

Uriah's beauteous wife,
Made David seek his life. [3]

Whales in the Sea
God's Voice obey.

[1] After the battle of Worcester, Charles II escaped
   from the Parliamentary army by hiding in an
   oak.
[2] See *1 Samuel* x, 1.
[3] See *2 Samuel* xi.

Xerxes the great did die
And so must you and I.

Youth forward slips
Death soonest nips.

Zacheus he
Did climb the Tree
His Lord to see. [1]

ROGER WILLIAMS 1605-1683

To Williams belongs the distinction of being, among American colonial leaders of his time, the man most liberal in respect to religious toleration. He was born in London, and died at Providence, Rhode Island. As a youth he was a protégé of Sir Edward Coke, who sent him to Cambridge, where he graduated, 1627. He was perhaps licensed to preach in the English Church, but came to Massachusetts in 1631. Because of his liberal views he was banished from the colony in 1634; he founded Providence the following year, and later visited England, where he obtained for Rhode Island a charter that allowed freedom of worship. Outside of Holland there were few places in Christendom where religious toleration was then practiced.

The Bloudy Tenent originated, according to Williams's account, as follows: To John Cotton, minister at Boston, had been proposed the question, "Whether persecution for cause of conscience be not against the doctrine of Jesus Christ, the King of Kings." Cotton had replied at some length, maintaining, among other things, "that Christians sinning against light of faith and conscience may justly be censured by the Church with excommunication, and by the civil sword also, in case they shall corrupt others to the perdition of their souls."

It is against this opinion, which may be said to represent the majority opinion of the Massachusetts Puritans, that *The Bloudy Tenent* is directed. The book was written while Williams was in London, and was published there. It is interesting to observe that it appeared in the same year with the more famous *Areopagitica* of John Milton, both of them documents in the long contest for the freedom of the human spirit. Later, Williams came to know Milton personally, and to assist him in the study of the Dutch language.

In reading this selection it is well to compare it with that from Ward, and to note the temperate mood in which it is written, a spirit seldom found in religious controversies of the day. Williams's style is scriptural and figurative like that of much English prose then written. Cotton and Williams do not seem to have been on unfriendly terms, notwithstanding their religious differences. To *The Bloudy Tenent* Cotton published a rejoinder, *The Bloudy Tenent Washed and made White in the Bloude of the Lamb*, London, 1647,

[1] See *Luke* xix, 4.

and Williams replied once more with *The Bloudy Tenent yet more Bloudy by Cotton's Endeavour to Wash it White in the Bloud of the Lambe*, London, 1652.

From THE BLOODY TENET OF PERSECUTION [2]

CHAPTER I

Truth. In what dark corner of the world, sweet Peace, are we two met? [3] How hath this present evil world banished me from all the coasts and quarters of it? And how hath the righteous God in judgment taken thee from the earth, *Rev.* vi. 4.

Peace. 'Tis lamentably true, blessed Truth. The foundations of the world have long been out of course: the gates of earth and hell have conspired together to intercept our joyful meeting and our holy kisses. [4] With what a wearied, tired wing have I flown over nations, kingdoms, cities, towns, to find out precious Truth?

(Truth and Peace rarely and seldom meet.)

Truth. The like inquiries in my flights and travels have I made for Peace and still am told she hath left the earth, and fled to heaven.

Peace. Dear Truth, what is the earth but a dungeon of darkness, where Truth is not?

Truth. And what's the Peace thereof but a fleeting dream, thine ape and counterfeit?

Peace. O where's the promise of the God of heaven, that righteousness and peace shall kiss each other?

Truth. Patience, sweet Peace, these heavens and earth are growing old, and shall be changed like a garment, *Psal.* cii. They shall melt away, and be burnt up with all the works that are therein; and the most high eternal Creator, shall gloriously create new heavens and new earth, wherein dwells righteousness, 2 *Pet.* 3. Our kisses then shall have their endless date [5] of pure and sweetest joys. Till then both thou and I must hope and wait, and bear the fury

[2] The full title is:

THE
BLOVDY TENENT,
OF PERSECUTION, FOR CAUSE OF
CONSCIENCE, DISCUSSED, IN
A Conference betweene
TRVTH and PEACE.
VVho,

In all tender Affection, present to the High Court of Parliament, (as the Result of their Discourse) these, (amongst other Passages) of highest consideration.

As the title page announces, the book is addressed to the British Parliament.

[3] The dialogue form for a discussion of this nature was frequently used during the seventeenth century.

[4] *Psalms* xxxv, 10

[5] duration

of the dragon's wrath, whose monstrous lies and furies shall with himself be cast into the lake of fire, the second death, *Revel*. xx. [1]

Peace. Most precious Truth, thou knowest we are both pursued and laid in wait for. Mine heart is full of sighs, mine eyes with tears. Where can I better vent my full oppressed bosom, than into thine, whose faithful lips may for these few hours revive my drooping wandering spirits, and here begin to wipe tears from mine eyes and the eyes of my dearest children?

Truth. Sweet daughter of the God of Peace, begin; pour out thy sorrows, vent thy complaints. How joyful am I to improve these precious minutes to revive our hearts, both thine and mine, and the hearts of all that love the truth and peace, *Zach*. viii.

Peace. Dear Truth, I know thy birth, thy nature, thy delight. They that know thee will prize thee far above themselves and lives, and sell themselves to buy thee. Well spake that famous Elizabeth to her famous attorney Sir Edward Coke: [2] "Mr. Attorney, go on as thou hast begun and still plead, not *pro domina regina*, but *pro domina veritate*. [3]

Truth. 'Tis true, my crown is high, my scepter's strong to break down strongest holds, to throw down highest crowns of all that plead, though but in thought, against me. Some few there are, but oh! how few, are valiant for the truth, and dare to plead my cause, as my witnesses in sack-cloth, *Revel*. xi., while all men's tongues are bent like bows to shoot out lying words against me.

Peace. O how could I spend eternal days and endless dates at thy holy feet, in listening to the precious oracles of thy mouth! All the words of thy mouth are truth, and there is no iniquity in them; thy lips drop as the honeycomb. But oh! since we must part anon, let us, as thou saidst, improve our minutes and, according as thou promisedst, revive me with thy words, which are sweeter than the honey and the honey-comb.

CHAPTER XLIII

Fourthly, I ask, Were not these elders or ministers of the church of Ephesus sufficiently furnished from the Lord Jesus to drive away these mystical and spiritual wolves? [4]

---

[1] Williams, like many other Puritan thinkers, believed that the second coming of Christ and the final punishment of Satan were at hand.
[2] Sir Edward Coke was the most famous English jurist and legal commentator of his day.
[3] not for sovereign queen but for sovereign truth
[4] Peace is speaking of Paul's warning to the elders or bishops of the church at Ephesus that "wolves" would enter into and not spare the Christian flock he had gathered there. *Acts* xx, 17-35.

Truth. True it is, against the inhuman and uncivil violence of persecutors, they were not, nor are God's children able and provided; but to resist, drive away, expel, and kill spiritual and mystical wolves by the word of the Lord,—none are fit to be Christ's shepherds who are not able, *Tit*. i. 9, 10, 11. The Bishop or overseer must be able by sound doctrine both to exhort and to convince the gainsayers; which gainsayers to be by him convinced, that is, overcome or subdued, though it may be in themselves ever obstinate, they were, I say, as greedy wolves in Crete, as any could be at Ephesus; for so saith Paul, verse 10. They were unruly and vain talkers, deceivers, whose mouths must be stopped, who subverted whole houses; and yet Titus—and every ordinary shepherd of a flock of Christ—had ability sufficient to defend the flock from spiritual and mystical wolves without the help of the civil magistrate.

(Christ Jesus furnisheth his shepherds with power sufficient to drive away wolves.)

Peace. In this respect, therefore, me thinks we may fitly allude to that excellent answer of Job to Bildad, the Shuhite, *Job* xxvi. "How hast thou helped him that is without power? How savest thou the arm that hath no strength? How hast thou counseled him that hath no wisdom? How hast thou plentifully declared the thing as it is?"

(Job xxvi, 1,2.)

5. Lastly, I ask whether, as men deal with wolves, these wolves at Ephesus were intended by Paul to be killed, their brains dashed out with stones, staves, halberts, guns, etc., in the hands of the elders of Ephesus, etc.

Truth. Doubtless, comparing spiritual things with spiritual, all such mystical wolves must spiritually and mystically so be slain. And the witnesses of truth, *Revel*. xi. speak fire, and kill all that hurt them by that fiery word of God, and that two-edged sword in their hand, *Psal*. cxlix.

But oh! what streams of the blood of saints have been and must be shed until the lamb have obtained the victorie, *Revel*. xvii. by this unmerciful—and in the state of the New Testament, when the church is spread all the world over—most bloody doctrine, viz. The wolves, (heretics), are to be driven away, their brains knocked out and killed, the poor sheep to be preserved for whom Christ died, etc.

(Unmerciful and bloody doctrine.)

Is not this to take Christ Jesus, and make him a temporal king by force? *John* vi. 15. Is not this to make his kingdom of this world, to set up a civil and temporal Israel, to bound out new earthly holy lands of Canaan, yea and to set up a Spanish Inquisition in all parts of the world, to the speedy destruction of thousands, yea of millions of souls, and the frustrating of the sweet end of the coming of the Lord Jesus, to wit, to save men's souls—and to that end not to destroy their bodies—by his own blood?

CHAPTER XLIV

Peace. The next scripture produced against such persecution, is *2 Cor.* x. 4.

John vi, 15, *2 Cor.* x, 4, discussed. "The weapons of our warfare are not carnall, but mighty through God to the pulling down of strong holds, casting down imaginations, and every high thing that exalteth itself against the knowledge of God, and bringing into captivity every thought to the obedience of Christ, and having in a readiness to avenge all disobedience," etc.

Unto which it is answered, [1] "When Paul saith, 'The weapons of our warfare are not carnal, but spiritual,' he denieth not civil weapons of justice to the civil magistrate, *Rom.* xiii. but only to church officers; and yet the weapons of church officers he acknowledgeth to be such, as though they be spiritual, yet are ready to take vengeance on all disobedience, *2 Cor.* x. 6. which hath reference, amongst other ordinances, to the censures of the church against scandalous offenders."

Truth. I acknowledge that herein the spirit of God denieth not civil weapons of justice to the civil magistrate, which the scripture he quotes, *Rom.* xiii. abundantly testify.

Yet withal I must ask why he here affirmeth the apostle denies not civil weapons of justice to the civil magistrate? of which there is no question, unless that, according to his scope of proving persecution for conscience, he intends withal that the apostle denies not civil weapons of justice to the civil magistrate in spiritual and religious causes; the contrary whereunto, the Lord assisting, I shall evince, both from this very scripture, and his own observation, and lastly by that xiiith of the *Romans,* by himself quoted.

First, then, from this scripture and his own observation: the weapons of church officers, saith he, are such which, though they be spiritual, are ready to take vengeance on all disobedience; which hath reference, saith he, amongst other ordinances, to the censures of the church against scandalous offenders.

I hence observe that, there being in this scripture held forth a two-fold state, a civil state and a spiritual,

The difference of the

[1] the quotation is from Cotton

civil and spiritual estate.

Civil weapons most improper in spiritual causes: fitly exemplified by that similitude, 2 Cor. x, 4.

civil officers and spiritual, civil weapons and spiritual weapons, civil vengeance and punishment, and a spiritual vengeance and punishment: although the spirit speaks not here expressly of civil magistrates and their civil weapons, yet these states being of different natures and considerations as far differing as spirit from flesh, I first observe that civil weapons are most improper and unfitting in matters of the spiritual state and kingdom, though in the civil state most proper and suitable.

1643-1644   1644

ANNE BRADSTREET 1612-1672

Mrs. Bradstreet is often spoken of by writers upon American literature as the first American poet. This is true only in the sense that she was the first permanent resident of the North American colonies to be known as a poet, and the first to publish a book of poems. Her culture and point of view were wholly English, and her poems are untouched by any atmosphere of the New World.

She was born in Northampton, England, and died in Massachusetts. She was a gentlewoman by birth, her father being Thomas Dudley, steward of the Earl of Lincoln, and afterwards governor of Massachusetts. At the age of sixteen she married Simon Bradstreet, A.B., Emanuel College, Cambridge, who was after her death governor of Massachusetts. She came with her husband to the colony in company with Winthrop in 1630, and finally settled at Andover. In the midst of her domestic duties as mother of eight children she wrote her poems, which first appeared in London, 1650. A second edition was published in Boston, 1678. Among her descendants were Channing, the two Richard H. Danas, Wendell Phillips, and Oliver Wendell Holmes. These selections are full of the frigid conventionality that in her time, even in the old world, often passed for imagination and took the place of real poetic emotion. Her poetry was book-inspired. Her originals were Raleigh's *History of the World* and Du Bartas' *Works and Days* together, of course, with the Geneva translation of the Bible. In reading her poems one should bear in mind that they are the work of an English lady, not a pioneer by choice, who in writing them sought escape from the unloveliness of her surroundings. Some of her lyrics show genuine feeling despite their stilted phrasing.

See introductions to the following: J. H. Ellis, *The Works of Anne Bradstreet in Prose and Verse,* 1867; C. E. Norton, *The Poems of Mrs. Anne Bradstreet* together with her *Prose Remains,* 1897; Helen S. Campbell, *Anne Bradstreet and Her Time,* 1891.

From THE FOUR SEASONS OF THE YEAR
Spring

Another four I've left yet to bring on,
Of four times four the last quaternion; [1]
The winter, summer, autumn, and the spring,
In season all these seasons I shall bring.
Sweet spring, like man in his minority,
At present claimed and had priority.
With smiling face, and garments somewhat
    green,
She trimmed her locks, which late had frosted
    been;
Nor hot nor cold she spake, but with a breath
Fit to revive the numbed earth from death.   10
"Three months," quoth she, "are 'lotted to my
    share—
March, April, May of all the rest most fair.
Tenth of the first, Sol into Aries [2] enters,
And bids defiance to all tedious winters,
Crosseth the line, and equals night and day;
Still adds to the last till after pleasant May;
And now makes glad the darkened northern
    wights
Who for some months have seen but starry
    lights.
Now goes the plowman to his merry toil
He might [3] unloose his winter-locked soil.   20
The seedsman, too, doth lavish out his grain
In hope the more he casts the more to gain.
The gardener now superfluous branches lops,
And poles erects for his young clambering hops;
Now digs, then sows his herbs, his flowers, and
    roots,
And carefully manures [4] his trees of fruits.
The Pleiades their influence [5] now give,
And all that seemed as dead afresh doth live:
The croaking frogs, whom nipping winter killed,
Like birds now chirp and hop about the field.   30
The nightingale, [6] the blackbird, and the thrush

Now tune their lays on sprays of every bush.
The wanton frisking kid and soft-fleeced lambs
Do jump and play before their feeding dams;
The tender tops of budding grass they crop;
They joy in what they have, but more in hope—
For though the frost hath lost his binding
    power,
Yet many a fleece of snow and stormy shower
Doth darken Sol's bright eye, makes us re-
    member
The pinching northwest wind of cold Decem-
    ber.   40
My second month is April, green and fair,
Of longer days, and a more temperate air.
The sun in Taurus [7] keeps his residence,
And with his warmer beams glanceth from
    thence.
This is the month whose fruitful showers pro-
    duces
All set and sown [8] for all delights and uses.
The pear, the plum, and apple-tree now flourish;
The grass grows long the hungry beast to
    nourish.
The primrose pale and azure violet
Among the verdurous grass hath nature set, 50
That when the sun on's love—the earth—doth
    shine
These might as lace set out her garment fine.
The fearful bird his little house now builds
In trees and walls, in cities and in fields;
The outside strong, the inside warm and neat—
A natural artificer complete.
The clucking hen her chirping chickens leads;
With wings and beak defends them from the
    gleads. [9]
My next and last is fruitful pleasant May,
Wherein the earth is clad in rich array.   60
The sun now enters loving Gemini, [10]
And heats us with the glances of his eye;
Our thicker raiment makes us lay aside,
Lest by his fervor we be torrified.
All flowers the sun now with his beams discloses
Except the double pinks and matchless roses.
Now swarms the busy, witty [11] honey-bee,
Whose praise deserves a page from more than
    me.
The cleanly housewife's dairy's now in the
    prime,
Her shelves and firkins filled for winter-time. [70]
The meads with cowslips, honeysuckles, dight, [12]

[1] set of four: The Four Seasons is the fourth poem of
    a series, the first three being The Four Ele-
    ments, The Four Humors of Man, and The
    Four Ages of Man.
[2] The Ram, one of the zodiacal constellations. The
    sun enters Aries, the Ram, on the 21st of March,
    or the 10th of March, O. S. This is the vernal
    equinox, as explained in the next few lines.
[3] The first edition has for to unloose.
[4] The word is probably to be taken as generally in
    Shakespeare in its primitive sense of cultivate,
    till. From OF. manoevrer, manage, handle, work.
[5] The meaning is probably astrological rather than
    general. Power, benign or hurtful, flowed from
    the stars when these were in the ascendant.
    Hence, "to be born under a lucky star." The
    Pleiades, in Taurus, were supposed to exert a
    "sweet" influence. See Job xxxviii, 31. Mrs. Brad-
    street inadvertently places the Pleiades in Aries.
[6] Of course Mrs. Bradstreet heard no nightingale in
    America, but perhaps she is to be excused from
    the charge of insincerity because the whole fauna
    and flora of nature poetry had been convention-
    alized, and because her Puritanism shut her away
    from the most vital Elizabethan poetic models.

[7] the constellation Taurus, the bull
[8] All things set (planted) and sown. Mrs. Bradstreet's
    need for rime interferes with her syntax, as has
    happened with some more famous poets.
[9] kites (used, probably, for hawks)
[10] The third sign of the Zodiac, named from the con-
    stellation Gemini, which it contains. Loving,
    because Castor and Pollux, the Gemini (twins),
    were celebrated for their devotion to each other.
[11] wise, discerning   [12] decked

One hangs his head, the other stands upright;
But both rejoice at th' heaven's clear smiling
    face,
More at her showers, which water them a space.
For fruits my season yields the early cherry,
The hasty peas, and wholesome cool straw-
    berry. [1]
More solid fruits require a longer time;
Each season hath his fruit, so hath each clime—
Each man his own peculiar excellence,
But none in all that hath preëminence.   80

Sweet fragrant spring, with thy short pittance
    fly.
Let some describe thee better than can I.
Yet above all this privilege is thine,
Thy days still lengthen without least decline.
                                         1650

"AS WEARY PILGRIM"

As weary pilgrim, now at rest,
    Hugs with delight his silent nest,
His wasted limbs now lie full soft
    That miry steps have trodden oft;
Blesses himself to think upon
    His dangers past and travails done,
The burning sun no more shall heat,
    Nor stormy rains on him shall beat;
The briars and thorns no more shall scratch,
    Nor hungry wolves at him shall catch;   10
He erring [2] paths no more shall tread,
    Nor wild fruits eat, instead of bread;
For waters cold he doth not long,
    For thirst no more shall parch his tongue;
No rugged stones his feet shall gall,
    Nor stumps nor rocks cause him to fall;
All cares and fears he bids farewell,
    And means in safety now to dwell—
A pilgrim I on earth, perplexed
    With sins, with cares and sorrows vexed,   20
By age and pains brought to decay,
    And my clay house moldering away,
Oh, how I long to be at rest,
    And soar on high among the blest!
This body shall in silence sleep,
    Mine eyes no more shall ever weep;
No fainting fits shall me assail,
    Nor grinding pains my body frail, [3]
With cares and fears ne'er cumbered be,
    Nor losses know, nor sorrows see.   30
What though my flesh shall there consume?
    It is the bed Christ did perfume;
And when a few years shall be gone
    This mortal shall be clothed upon.

[1] The entire flatness of such lines and couplets as these
    admits no defense.
[2] wandering
[3] wear out

A corrupt carcass down it lies,
    A glorious body it shall rise, [4]
In weakness and dishonor sown,
    In power 't is raised by Christ alone.
Then soul and body shall unite,
    And of their maker have the sight;   40
Such lasting joys shall there behold
    As ear ne'er heard nor tongue e'er told.
Lord, make me ready for that day!
    Then come, dear bridegroom, come away.
August 31, 1669   1867

MICHAEL WIGGLESWORTH
1631-1705

Wigglesworth was the most popular versifier of
his day in New England. He was born in England, and died at Malden, Massachusetts. Coming
as a child with his parents to New England, he
graduated at Harvard, 1651, was tutor there, 1652-
1654, and was pastor of the church at Malden
from 1657 until his death. Ill health broke in
upon his preaching and caused him to study and
practice medicine, and from 1686 he carried on
both medicine and the ministry. His published
works are *The Day of Doom*, 1662; *God's Controversy with New England*, 1662, published, 1871;
Meat out of the Eater, 1669. Ten editions of *The
Day of Doom* have been published in America
and two in England.

Of this piece Tyler says, the "shrill reverberating
clatter, that would instantly catch and please the
popular ear, at that time deaf to daintier and
more subtile effects in poetry," made it the best
known American poem in the colonies. The poem
remains a landmark of the poetic taste of the
time and a vigorous and lucid if lurid statement
of Puritan belief in some essential matters. Lowell says, "[*The Day of Doom*] was the solace
of every fireside, the flicker of the pine knots by
which it was conned perhaps adding a livelier
relish to its premonitions of eternal combustion."

The theological tenets and religious attitudes of
the poem were current in New England and to a
large extent in non-conformist England for a hundred years after it was written. Its lilting lines
are easy to remember and, despite the inappropri-
ateness of the meter, they still arrest the attention
with their irresistible vigor and decided picturesqueness of phrasing.

From THE DAY OF DOOM [5]

1

Still was the night, serene and bright,
    when all men sleeping lay;
Calm was the season, and carnal reason
    thought so 't would last for aye.

[4] *2 Corinthians* v, 2-4; *1 Corinthians* xv, 42-43
[5] In Wigglesworth's time the day of doom, or Judg-
    ment Day, was supposed, by many people, to be
    close at hand.

"Soul, take thine ease,[1] let sorrow cease,
  much good thou hast in store:"
This was their song, their cups among,
  the evening before.

2

Wallowing in all kinds of sin,
  vile wretches lay secure:
The best of men had scarcely then
  their lamps kept in good ure.
Virgins unwise,[2] who through disguise
  amongst the best were numbered,
Had closed their eyes; yea and the wise
  through sloth and frailty slumbered;

3

Like as of old,[3] when men grew bold
  God's threatenings to contemn,
Who stopped their ear, and would not hear,
  when mercy warned them:
But took their course, without remorse,
  till God began to pour
Destruction the world upon
  in a tempestuous shower;

4

Who put away the evil day,
  and drowned their cares and fears,
Till drowned were they, and swept away
  by vengeance unawares:
So at the last, whilst men sleep fast
  in their security,
Surprised they are in such a snare
  as cometh suddenly.

5

For at midnight break[4] forth a light,
  which turned the night to day,
And speedily an hideous cry
  did all the world dismay.
Sinners awake, their hearts do ache,
  trembling their loins surpriseth;
Amazed with fear, by what they hear,
  each one of them ariseth.

6

They rush from beds with giddy heads,
  and to their windows run,
Viewing this light, which shines more bright
  than doth the noon-day sun.
Straightway appears (they see't with tears)
  the Son of God most dread;
Who with his train comes on amain
  to judge both quick and dead.

7

Before his face the heavens gave place,
  and skies are rent asunder,
With mighty voice, and hideous noise,
  more terrible than thunder.
His brightness damps heaven's glorious lamps
  and makes them hide their heads;
As if afraid, and quite dismayed,
  they quit their wonted steads.

. . . .

14

The Judge draws nigh, exalted high
  upon a lofty throne,
Amidst the throng of angels strong,
  lo, Israel's Holy One!
The excellence of whose presence
  and awful majesty,
Amazeth nature, and every creature,
  doth more than terrify.

15

The mountains smoke, the hills are shook,
  the earth is rent and torn,
As if she should be clear dissolved,
  or from her center born.[5]
The sea doth roar, forsakes the shore,
  and shrinks away for fear:
The wild beasts flee into the sea,
  so soon as he draws near.

. . . .

20

His winged hosts fly through all coasts,
  together gathering
Both good and bad, both quick and dead
  and all to judgment bring.
Out of their holes those creeping moles,
  that hid themselves for fear,
By force they take, and quickly make
  before the Judge appear.

21

Thus every one before the throne
  of Christ the judge is brought,
Both righteous and impious
  that good or ill hath wrought.
A separation, and differing station
  by Christ appointed is
(To sinners sad) 'twixt good and bad,
  'twixt heirs of woe and bliss.

---

[1] *Luke* xii, 19; the poem is a tissue of Biblical allusions. Only those most necessary to the understanding of the poem are noted.
[2] *Matthew* xxv, 1   [4] brake
[6] The line refers to the destruction of man at the time of the deluge. See *Genesis* vi, 7

[5] borne from the center (According to the old Ptolemaic astronomy the center of the earth is the center of the universe, the one immovable point in all creation. To move fixed objects in their relation to this center means total destruction.)

22

At Christ's right hand the sheep do stand,
  his holy martyrs, who
For his dear name suffering shame,
  calamity and woe
Like champions stood, and with their blood
  their testimony sealed;
Whose innocence without offence,
  to Christ their Judge appealed.

. . . . .

27

At Christ's left hand, the goats do stand,
  all whining hypocrites,
Who for self-ends did seem Christ's friends,
  but fostered guileful sprites:
Who sheep resembled, but they dissembled
  (their hearts were not sincere)
Who once did throng Christ's lambs among
  but now must not come near.

. . . . . .

38

All silence keep both goats and sheep
  before the Judge's throne:
With mild aspect to his elect
  then speaks the holy one;
"My sheep draw near, your sentence hear,
  which is to you no dread,
Who clearly now discern and know,
  your sins are pardoned.

39

" 'Twas meet that ye should judged be,
  that so the world may spy
No cause of grudge, whenas I judge
  and deal impartially.
Know therefore all both great and small,
  the ground and reason why
These men do stand at my right hand,
  and look so cheerfully." [1]

. . . . . .

166

Then to the bar all they drew near
  who died in infancy,
And never had or good or bad
  effected pers'nally;
But from the womb unto the tomb
  were straightway carried,
(Or at the least ere they transgressed)
  who thus began to plead:

167

"If for our own transgression,
  or disobedience,
We here did stand at thy left hand,
  just were the recompense;
But Adam's guilt our souls hath spilt, [2]
  his fault is charged upon us;
And that alone hath overthrown
  and utterly undone us.

168

"Not we, but he ate of the tree,
  whose fruit was interdicted;
Yet on us all of his sad fall
  the punishment's inflicted.
How could we sin that had not been,
  or how is his sin our,
Without consent, which to prevent
  we never had the power?

169

"O great Creator why was our nature
  depraved and forlorn?
Why so defiled, and made so viled,
  whilst we were yet unborn?
If it be just, and needs we must
  transgressors reckoned be,
Thy mercy, Lord, to us afford,
  which sinners hath set free.

170

"Behold we see Adam set free,
  and saved from his trespass,
Whose sinful fall hath spilt us all,
  and brought us to this pass.
Canst thou deny us once to try,
  or grace to us to tender,
When he finds grace before thy face
  who was the chief offender?"

171

Then answered the Judge most dread:
  "God doth such doom forbid,
That men should die eternally
  for what they never did.
But what you call old Adam's fall,
  and only his trespass,
You call amiss to call it his,
  both his and yours it was.

172

"He was designed of all mankind
  to be a public head;
A common root, whence all should shoot
  and stood in all their stead.

---

[1] The stanzas omitted here recount the vain excuses of the heathen and of various classes of enlightened sinners.

[2] ruined

He stood and fell, did ill or well,
    not for himself alone,
But for you all, who now his fall
    and trespass would disown.

173

"If he had stood, then all his brood
    had been established
In God's true love never to move,
    nor once awry to tread;
Then all his race my Father's grace
    should have enjoyed forever,
And wicked sprites [1] by subtile sleights
    could them have harmed never.

174

"Would you have grieved to have received
    through Adam so much good,
As had been your for evermore,
    if he at first had stood?
Would you have said, 'We ne'er obeyed
    nor did thy laws regard;
It ill befits with benefits,
    us, Lord, to so reward?'

175

"Since then to share in his welfare,
    you could have been content,
You may with reason share in his treason,
    and in the punishment.
Hence you were born in state forlorn,
    with natures so depraved;
Death was your due because that you
    had thus yourselves behaved.

176

"You think, 'If we had been as he,
    whom God did so betrust,
We to our cost would ne'er have lost
    all for a paltry lust.'
Had you been made in Adam's stead,
    you would like things have wrought,
And so into the self-same woe,
    yourselves and yours have brought.

177

"I may deny you once to try,
    or grace to you to tender,
Though he finds grace before my face
    who was the chief offender;
Else should my grace cease to be grace,
    for it would not be free,
If to release whom I should please
    I have no liberty.

[1] spirits (often thus in Elizabethan literature)

178

"If upon one what's due to none
    I frankly shall bestow,
And on the rest shall not think best
    compassion's skirts to throw,
Whom injure I? Will you envy
    and grudge at others' weal?
Or me accuse, who do refuse
    yourselves to help and heal?

179

"Am I alone of what's my own,
    no master or no lord?
And if I am, how can you claim
    what I to some afford?
Will you demand grace at my hand,
    and challenge what is mine?
Will you teach me whom to set free,
    and thus my grace confine?

180

"You sinners are, and such a share
    as sinners, may expect;
Such you shall have, for I do save
    none but mine own elect.
Yet to compare your sin with their
    who lived a longer time,
I do confess yours is much less,
    though every sin's a crime.

181

"A crime it is, therefore in bliss
    you may not hope to dwell;
But unto you I shall allow
    the easiest room in hell."
The glorious King thus answering,
    they cease, and plead no longer;
Their consciences must needs confess
    his reasons are the stronger.

182

Thus all men's pleas the Judge with ease
    doth answer and confute.
Until that all, both great and small,
    are silenced and mute.
Vain hopes are cropped, all mouths are stopped,
    sinners have nought to say,
But that 'tis just and equal most
    they should be damned for aye.

    .   .   .   .   .   .

189

O dismal day! whither shall they
    for help and succor flee?
To God above with hopes to move
    their greatest enemy?

His wrath is great, whose burning heat
  no floods of tears can slake;
His word stands fast that they be cast
  into the burning lake.

. . . .

195

Unto the saints with sad complaints
  should they themselves apply?
They're not dejected nor aught affected
  with all their misery.
Friends stand aloof and make no proof
  what prayers or tears can do;
Your godly friends are now more friends
  to Christ than unto you.

196

Where tender love men's hearts did move
  unto a sympathy,
And bearing part of others' smart
  in their anxiety,
Now such compassion is out of fashion,
  and wholly laid aside;
No friends so near, but saints to hear
  their sentence can abide.

197

One natural brother beholds another
  in his astonied fit, [1]
Yet sorrows not thereat a jot,
  nor pities him a whit.
The godly wife conceives no grief,
  nor can she shed a tear
For the sad state of her dear mate,
  when she his doom doth hear.

198

He that was erst a husband pierced
  with sense of wife's distress,
Whose tender heart did bear a part
  of all her grievances,
Shall mourn no more as heretofore,
  because of her ill plight,
Although he see her now to be
  a damned forsaken wight.

199

The tender mother will own no other
  of all her num'rous brood,
But such as stand at Christ's right hand,
  acquitted through his blood.
The pious father had now much rather
  his graceless son should lie
In hell with devils, for all his evils,
  burning eternally,

[1] dazed condition

200

Than God most high should injury
  by sparing him sustain;
And doth rejoice to hear Christ's voice,
  adjudging him to pain.
Thus having all, both great and small,
  convinced and silenced,
Christ did proceed their doom to read,
  and thus it uttered:

201

"Ye sinful wights and cursed sprites,
  that work iniquity,
Depart together from me forever
  to endless misery;
Your portion take in yonder lake,
  where fire and brimstone flameth;
Suffer the smart which your desert, [2]
  as its due wages claimeth."

202

Oh piercing words, more sharp than swords!
  What! to depart from Thee,
Whose face before for evermore
  the best of pleasures be!
What! to depart (unto our smart),
  from thee *eternally!*
To be for aye banished away
  with devils' company!

203

What! to be sent to punishment,
  and flames of burning fire!
To be surrounded, and eke confounded
  with God's revengeful ire!
What! to abide, not for a tide,
  these torments, but forever!
To be released, or to be eased,
  not after years, but never!

204

Oh fearful doom! now there's no room
  for hope or help at all;
Sentence is past which aye shall last;
  Christ will not it recall.
Then might you hear them rend and tear
  the air with their outcries;
The hideous noise of their sad voice
  ascendeth to the skies.

205

They wring their hands, their caitiff-hands,
  and gnash their teeth for terror;
They cry, they roar for anguish sore,
  and gnaw their tongues for horror.

[2] The rime was accurate then.

But get away without delay,
    Christ pities not your cry;
Depart to Hell, there you may yell,
    and roar eternally.

. . . .

1662   1662

BENJAMIN TOMPSON 1642-1714

Benjamin Tompson, first native-born New England poet, was born at Braintree, now Quincy,
Massachusetts, where his father was pastor of the
church. He graduated from Harvard, 1662, was
for two years master of the Boston grammar
school, where he had Cotton Mather as a pupil, and
later taught at Charlestown, Braintree, and at Roxbury, where he died. He also practiced medicine,
a calling that any educated person, at that time,
might assume.

Tompson's verses totally lack beauty, grace, or
imagination, but they are here included because of
their very crudity and the fact that they are a
native New England product, like *The Bay Psalm
Book*. The facts that to his neighbors Tompson
was "the renowned Poet of New-England," and
that Cotton Mather called him "a good poet" and
used one of his poems in his *Magnalia* serve to show
the low standard in poetry then current in New
England. They also indicate how little of literary
grace was then imparted by the study of the classics
at Harvard. It is at once seen that Tompson wrote
of things around him. *New-Englands Crisis*, the
first book of poetry to be published in Boston, is a
versified chronicle of King Philip's War. Its "Prologue" is a picture of Boston in the second generation. The point of view is that the war was sent
as a punishment to the colony which had not, as a
whole, kept the faith of the fathers.

H. J. Hall, *Benjamin Tompson, His Poems*, collected, with an introduction, 1924.

NEW-ENGLANDS CRISIS [1]

From THE PROLOGUE

The times wherein old *Pompion* [2] was a Saint,
When men far'd hardly yet without complaint
On vilest *Cates;* [3] the dainty *Indian Maize*
Was eat with *Clamp-shells* out of wooden
        Trayes
Under thatcht *Hutts* without the cry of *Rent,*
And the best *Sawce* to every Dish, *Content.*
When Flesh was food, & hairy skins made
        coats,
And men as wel as birds had chirping Notes.
When Cimnels [4] were accounted noble bloud
Among the tribes of common herbage food.   10
Of *Ceres* bounty form'd was many a knack

Enough to fill *poor Robins Almanack,* [5]
These golden times (too fortunate to hold)
Were quickly sin'd away for love of gold.
Twas then among the bushes, not the street
If one in place did an inferiour meet,
Good morrow Brother, is there ought you want?
Take freely of me, what I have you ha'nt.
Plain *Tom* and *Dick* would pass as currant now,
As ever since *Your Servant Sir* and bow.   20
Deep-skirted doublets, *puritanick* capes
Which now would render men like upright Apes,
Was comlier wear our wiser Fathers thought
Than the cast fashions from all *Europe* brought.
Twas in those dayes an honest *Grace* would
        hold
Till an hot puddin grew at heart a cold.
And men had better stomachs to religion
Than I to capon, turkey-cock or pigeon.
When honest Sisters met to pray not prate   29
About their own and not their neighbours state.
During *Plain Dealings* Reign, that worthy Stud [6]
Of th' ancient planters race before the flood
These times were good, Merchants car'd not
        a rush
For other fare than *Jonakin and Mush.* [7]
Although men far'd and lodged very hard
Yet Innocence was better than a Guard.
Twas long before spiders & wormes had drawn
Their dungy webs or hid with cheating Lawne
New-Englands beautyes, which stil seem'd to
        me
Illustrious in their own simplicity.   40
Twas ere the neighboring *Virgin-land* [8] had
        broke
The Hogsheads of her worse than hellish
        smoak. [9]
Twas ere the Islands [10] sent their Presents in,
Which but to use was counted next to sin.
Twas ere a *Barge* had made so rich a fraight
As *Chocholatte*, dust-gold and bitts of eight. [11]
Ere wines from *France* and *Moscovadoe* [12] too
Without the which the drink will scarsly doe,
From western Isles, ere fruits and dillicacies,
Did rot maids teeth & spoil their hansome
        faces.   50
Or ere these times did chance the noise of war
Was from our towns and hearts removed far.
No Bugbear Comets [13] in the chrystal air
To drive our christian Planters to despair.

---

[1] The original spelling and punctuation are retained in
    these selections.
[2] pumpion, pumpkin
[3] cakes, delicacies
[4] scalloped summer squashes

[5] the title of an almanac first published in 1661 or 1662
[6] sire
[7] "Johnny-cake"; "mush" is the Indian name for "hasty
    pudding."
[8] Virginia
[9] Tobacco was exported in hogsheads.
[10] the West Indies, then the source of many luxuries
[11] Spanish dollars
[12] unrefined sugar
[13] In the seventeenth and eighteenth centuries comets
    were supposed to be a dire warning of disaster.

No sooner pagan malice [1] peeped forth
But Valour snib'd it; then were men of worth
Who by their prayers slew thousands Angel
    like,
Their weapons are unseen with which they
    strike.
Then had the Churches rest, [2] as yet the coales
Were covered up in most contentious souls.   60
Freeness in Judgment, union in affection,
Dear love, sound truth they were our grand
    protection
These were the twins which in our Councells
    sate,
These gave prognosticks of our future fate,
If these be longer liv'd our hopes increase,
These warrs will usher in a longer peace:
But if *New-Englands* love die in its youth
The grave will open next for blessed Truth.
1676   1676

ON
A FORTIFICATION
AT BOSTON BEGUN BY WOMEN
Dux Foemina Facti

A Grand attempt some Amazonian [3] Dames
Contrive whereby to glorify their names,
A Ruff for *Boston* Neck of mud and turfe,
Reaching from side to side from surfe to surfe, [4]
Their nimble hands spin up like Christmas pyes,
Their pastry by degrees on high doth rise.
The wheel at home counts it an holiday,
Since while the Mistris worketh it may play.
A tribe of female hands, but manly hearts
Forsake at home their pastry-crust and tarts 10
To knead the dirt, the samplers down they
    hurle,
Their undulating silks they closely furle.
The pick-axe one as a Commandress holds,
While t'other at her awkness gently scolds.
One puffs and sweats, the other mutters why
Cant you promove your work so fast as I?
Some dig, some delve, and others hands do feel
The little waggons weight with single wheel.
And least some fainting fits the weak surprize,
They want no sack nor cakes, they are more
    wise.   20
These brave essayes draw forth Male stronger
    hands

[1] The Indians were pagans.
[2] Pious New Englanders thought of the colonies in terms of the churches, centers of the community life.
[3] In Greek mythology the Amazons were female warriors.
[4] Boston was built on a promontory. Its only connection with the mainland was a narrow strip, Boston Neck, sometimes submerged by storm and high tide. The incident told in the verses took place during King Philip's War and probably at the time when the natives came within a few miles of Boston.

More like to Dawbers than to Martial bands:
These do the work, and sturdy bulwarks raise,
But the beginners well deserve the praise.
1676   1676

BENJAMIN CHURCH 1639-1717

Captain Church was one of the first of those frontiersmen who, as farmers, soldiers, scouts, hunters, or adventurers after wealth, have fought with the Indians from Cape Cod to the mountains of Arizona. He was born in England and died at Little Compton, Rhode Island. After settling at Duxbury, Massachusetts, Church was tempted by the fertile lands of Rhode Island and removed to Little Compton, where in the year of the outbreak of King Philip's War, 1675, he became the first white inhabitant. In the struggle with Philip, Church showed himself brave to the point of rashness, resourceful, and a natural leader of men. After recovering from severe wounds, he was placed in command of the Plymouth troops by whom Philip was killed. He was made colonel of militia, but was never fully rewarded for his services.

The *History* was compiled by Thomas Church, son of Benjamin, from full memoranda written by his father, in 1716. It is the unadorned account of a man of action who left the record as a matter of historical importance.

From ENTERTAINING PASSAGES RE-LATING TO PHILIP'S WAR, *which began in the month of June, 1675,—as also of* EXPEDITIONS *more lately made, ... , with some account of the Divine Providence toward Benjamin Church, Esq., by T. C.* [5]

.   .   .   .   .

Their next motion [6] was towards the place where the prisoners told them that they had left their women and children, and surprised them all and some others that were newly come to them. And upon examination they held to one story, that it was hard to tell where to find Annawon, for he never roosted twice in a place.

Now a certain Indian soldier that Captain Church had gained over to be on his side prayed that he might have liberty to go and fetch in his father, who, he said, was about four miles from that place, in a swamp, with no other than one young squaw. Captain Church inclined to go with him, thinking it might be in his way to

[5] The present selection is from the edition of this work by Henry Martyn Dexter, Boston, Wiggin, 1865.
[6] After the death of Philip, a chief, Annawon, remained in arms at the head of a considerable band. It will be seen that Church, who had adopted Indian methods of warfare and was out scouting, away from his main force, led his few men, almost all Indians, and some of them only recently captured from the hostile tribe, into the Indian stronghold in the swamp and captured the chief.

gain some intelligence of Annawon; and so, taking one Englishman and a few Indians with him, leaving the rest there, he went with his new soldier to look [after] his father.

When he came to the swamp, he bid the Indian go see if he could find his father. He was no sooner gone but Captain Church discovered a track coming down out of the woods; upon which he and his little company lay close, some on one side of the track, and some on the other. They heard the Indian soldier make a howling for his father and at length somebody answered him; but while they were listening, they thought they heard somebody coming towards them; presently they saw an old man coming up with a gun on his shoulder, and a young woman following of him in the track which they lay by. They let them come up between them, and then started up and laid hold on them both. Captain Church immediately examined them apart, telling them what they must trust to if they told false stories. He asked the young woman what company they came last from. She said, "From Captain Annawon's." He asked her how many were in company with him when she left him. She said, "Fifty or sixty." He asked her how many miles it was to the place where she left him. She said she did not understand miles, but he was up in Squannaconk [1] swamp.

The old man, who had been one of Philip's council, upon examination gave exactly the same account. Captain Church asked him if they could get there that night. He said if they went presently and traveled stoutly, they might get there by sunset. He asked whither he was going. He answered that Annawon had sent him down to look for some Indians that were gone down into Mount Hope Neck [2] to kill provisions. Captain Church let him know that those Indians were all his prisoners.

By this time came the Indian soldier and brought his father and one Indian more. The Captain was now in great strait of mind what to do next; [he] had a mind to give Annawon a visit, now he knew where to find him. But his company was very small, but half a dozen men beside himself, and [he] was under a necessity to send somebody back to acquaint his lieutenant and company with his proceedings. However, he asked his small company that were with him whether they would willingly go with him and give Annawon a visit. They told him they were always ready to obey his

commands, etc.; but withal told him that they knew this Captain Annawon was a great soldier; that he had been a valiant captain under Asuhmequin, [3] Philip's father; and that he had been Philip's chieftain all this war; a very subtle man, and of great resolution, and had often said that he would never be taken alive by the English. And moreover they knew that the men that were with him were resolute fellows, some of Philip's chief soldiers; and therefore feared whether it was practicable to make an attempt upon him with so small a handful of assailants as now were with him. Told him further that it would be a pity that, after all the great things he had done, he should throw away his life at last, etc. Upon which he replied that he doubted not Annawon was a subtle and valiant man; that he had a long time, but in vain, sought for him, and never till now could find his quarters, and he was very loath to miss of the opportunity; and doubt not but that, if they would cheerfully go with him, the same almighty Providence that had hitherto protected and befriended them would do so still, etc.

Upon this with one consent they said they would go. Captain Church then turned to one Cook of Plymouth (the only Englishman then with him), and asked him what he thought of it. Who replied, "Sir, I am never afraid of going anywhere when you are with me." Then Captain Church asked the old Indian if he could carry his horse with him,—for he conveyed a horse thus far with him. He replied that it was impossible for an horse to pass the swamps. Therefore he sent away his new Indian soldier with his father and the Captain's horse to his lieutenant, and orders for him to move to Taunton with the prisoners, to secure them there, and to come out in the morning in the Rehoboth road in which he might expect to meet him, if he were alive and had success.

The Captain then asked the old fellow if he would pilot him unto Annawon. He answered that he having given him his life, he was obliged to serve him. He bid him move on then, and they followed. The old man would out-travel them so far, sometimes, that they were almost out of sight; looking over his shoulder and seeing them behind he would halt.

Just as the sun was setting, the old man made a full stop and sat down; the company coming up also sat down, being all weary. Captain Church asked, "What news?" He answered, that about that time in the evening, Captain Annawon sent out his scouts to see if

---

[1] In the southeasterly part of the town of Rehoboth, Bristol County, Massachusetts; no scene of colonial history is better preserved today in its original primitive condition.

[2] Philip had just been killed there.

[3] better known as Massasoit, friend of the Pilgrims

the coast were clear, and as soon as it began to grow dark, the scouts return, and then, said he, "we may move again securely." When it began to grow dark, the old man stood up again, and Captain Church asked him if he would take a gun and fight for him. He bowed very low, and prayed him not to impose such a thing upon him as to fight against Captain Annawon, his old friend. "But," says he, "I will go along with you, and be helpful to you, and will lay hands on any man that shall offer to hurt you."

It being now pretty dark, they moved close together;—anon they heard a noise. The Captain stayed the old man with his hand, and asked his own men what noise they thought it might be. They concluded it to be the pounding of a mortar. The old man had given Captain Church a description of the place where Annawon now lay, and of the difficulty of getting at him. Being sensible that they were pretty near them, with two of his Indians he creeps to the edge of the rocks, from whence he could see their camps. He saw three companies of Indians at a little distance from each other; being easy to be discovered by the light of their fires. He saw also the great Annawon and his company, who had formed his camp or kenneling-place by falling a tree under the side of the great clefts of rocks and setting a row of birch bushes up against it; where he himself, and his son, and some of his chiefs had taken up their lodging, and made great fires without them, and had their pots and kettles boiling, and spits roasting. Their arms also he discovered, all set together in a place fitted for the purpose, standing up an-end against a stick lodged in two crotches, and a mat placed over them to keep them from the wet or dew. The old Annawon's feet and his son's head were so near the arms as almost to touch them.

But the rocks were so steep that it was impossible to get down, but as they lowered themselves by the boughs and the bushes that grew in the cracks of the rock. Captain Church creeping back again to the old man asked him if there was no possibility of getting at them some other way. He answered, "No." That he and all that belonged to Annawon, were ordered to come that way, and none could come any other way without difficulty, or danger of being shot.

Captain Church then ordered the old man and his daughter to go down foremost with their baskets at their backs, that when Annawon saw them with their baskets he should not mistrust the intrigue. Captain Church and his handful of soldiers crept down also, under the shadow of these two and their baskets, and the Captain

himself crept close behind the old man, with his hatchet in his hand, and stepped over the young man's head to the arms. The young Annawon discovering of him, whipped his blanket over his head and shrunk up in a heap. The old Captain Annawon started up on his breech and cried out "Howoh." And despairing of escape, threw himself back again, and lay silent until Captain Church had secured all the arms, etc. And having secured that company, he sent his Indian soldiers to the other fires and companies, giving them instructions what to do and say. Accordingly they went into the midst of them. When they discovered themselves who they were, [they] told them that their Captain Annawon was taken, and it would be best for them quietly and peaceably to surrender themselves, which would procure good quarter for them; otherwise, if they should pretend to resist or make their escape, it would be in vain, and they could expect no other but that Captain Church, with his great army, who had now entrapped them, would cut them to pieces. Told them also if they would submit themselves, and deliver up all their arms unto them, and keep every man his place until it was day, they would assure them that their Captain Church, who had been so kind to themselves when they surrendered to him, should be as kind to them. Now they being old acquaintance, and many of them relations, did much the readier give heed to what they said, and complied, and surrendered up their arms unto them, both their guns and hatchets, etc., and were forthwith carried to Captain Church.

Things being so far settled, Captain Church asked Annawon, what he had for supper, "for," said he, "I am come to sup with you." *"Taubut,"* said Annawon with a big voice, and looking about upon his women bid them hasten and get Captain Church and his company some supper; then turned to Captain Church and asked him whether he would eat cow beef or horse beef. The Captain told him cow beef would be most acceptable. It was soon got ready, and pulling his little bag of salt out of his pocket, which was all the provision he brought with him, this seasoned his cow beef. So that with it and the dried green corn, which the old squaw was pounding in the mortar while they were sliding down the rocks, he made a very hearty supper. And this pounding in the mortar proved lucky for Captain Church's getting down the rocks; for when the old squaw pounded they moved, and when she ceased to turn the corn they ceased creeping. The noise of the mortar prevented the enemy's hearing their creeping, and the corn, being now dressed, supplied the want of bread and gave a fine relish with the cow beef.

Supper being over, Captain Church sent two of his men to inform the other companies that he had killed Philip, and had taken their friends in Mount Hope Neck, but had spared their lives, and that he had subdued now all the enemy, he supposed, excepting this company of Annawon's; and now if they would be orderly and keep their places until morning, they should have good quarter, and that he would carry them to Taunton, where they might see their friends again, etc.

The messengers returned and informed that the Indians yielded to his proposals.

Captain Church thought it was now time for him to take a nap, having had no sleep in two days and one night before; told his men that if they would let him sleep two hours, they should sleep all the rest of the night. He laid himself down and endeavored to sleep, but all disposition to sleep departed from him.

After he had lain a little while, he looked up to see how his watch managed, but found them all fast asleep. Now Captain Church had told Captain Annawon's company, as he had ordered his Indians to tell the others, that their lives should all be spared, excepting Captain Annawon's, and it was not in his power to promise him his life, but he must carry him to his masters at Plymouth, and he would entreat them for his life.

Now when Captain Church found not only his own men, but all the Indians fast asleep, Annawon only excepted, who, he perceived, was as broad awake as himself; and so they lay looking one upon the other, perhaps an hour. Captain Church said nothing to him, for he could not speak Indian, and thought Annawon could not speak English.

At length Annawon raised himself up, cast off his blanket, and with no more clothes than his small breeches, walked a little way back from the company. Captain Church thought no other but that he had walked a little distance for some necessary errand, and would very soon return. But by and by he was gone out of sight and hearing, and then Captain Church began to suspect some ill design in him; and got all the guns close to him, and crowded himself close under young Annawon; that if he should anywhere get a gun, he should not make a shot at him, without endangering his son. Lying very still awhile waiting for the event, at length he heard somebody coming the same way that Annawon went. The moon now shining bright, he saw him at a distance coming with something in his hands, and coming up to Captain

Church he fell upon his knees before him, and offered him what he had brought, and speaking in plain English said, "Great Captain, you have killed Philip, and conquered his country; for I believe that I and my company are the last that war against the English, so suppose the war is ended by your means; and therefore these things belong unto you." Then opening his pack, he pulled out Philip's belt, curiously wrought with wampum, being nine inches broad, wrought with black and white wampum in various figures, and flowers and pictures of many birds and beasts. This, when hung upon Captain Church's shoulders, it reached his ankles; and another belt of wampum he presented him with, wrought after the former manner, which Philip was wont to put upon his head. It had two flags on the back part, which hung down on his back, and another small belt with a star upon the end of it, which he used to hang on his breast, and they were all edged with red hair, which Annawon said they got in the Mohogs'[1] country. Then he pulled out two horns of glazed powder, and a red cloth blanket. He told Captain Church these were Philip's royalties[2] which he was wont to adorn himself with when he sat in state; that he thought himself happy that he had an opportunity to present them to Captain Church, who had won them, etc.[3] Spent the remainder of the night in discourse; and Captain Annawon gave an account of what mighty success he had formerly in wars against many nations of Indians, when [he] served Asuhmequin, Philip's father, etc.

In the morning, as soon as it was light, the Captain marched with his prisoners out of that swampy country towards Taunton, met his lieutenant and company about four miles out of town, who expressed a great deal of joy to see him again, and said 't was more than ever they expected. They went into Taunton, were civilly and kindly treated by the inhabitants, refreshed and rested themselves that night.

Early next morning, the Captain took old Annawon and half a dozen of his Indian soldiers, and his own man, and went to Rhode Island; sending the rest of his company, and his prisoners, by his lieutenant to Plymouth. Tarrying two or three days upon the island, he then went to Plymouth, and carried his wife and his two children with him. . . .

Probably 1716   1716

[1] Mohawks'
[2] kingly trappings
[3] Church appreciated the force of this pathetic incident. Throughout the war he showed himself compassionate and honest with the Indians, and it was wholly against his wishes and expectations that the Plymouth authorities put Annawon to death.

THE PROVINCIAL PERIOD

THE grandsons of the first colonists were American-born and educated. Unaided by England they had held their native soil through devastating Indian wars in 1676 both in Virginia and New England. Their victory begot a spirit of self-sufficiency destined to produce momentous results just a century later. In local affairs they claimed and strove stoutly to maintain self-government, the more so because the annulment of their charters had curtailed their political privileges. The provincials often called themselves "New English"; they were loyal British subjects, but their affections were rooted in America. Their relations with England were chiefly commercial, but often their own interests did not coincide with those of England. Immigration from the mother country had practically ceased and the writers of the period were almost without exception born and educated in America. Their writings reflect American points of view in society and in politics, and also a growing care for the art of expression both in prose and poetry. No one of the provincial writers lived by his writing. The chances that a literary genius might arise in so small a population as that of the colonies before the Revolution were small, and the sympathetically stimulating and critical atmosphere necessary to the success of genius was lacking. The mass of fervid political writing toward the close of the period furnished little that is of literary value, for literature thrives best in a time of calm. Nevertheless, one writer, Franklin, has left a fascinating record of self-discipline and attainment in a style that needs no apologies.

COTTON MATHER 1663-1728

Cotton Mather was third in the line of the "Mather dynasty." Increase Mather, his father, was born in Massachusetts, educated at Harvard, and became one of its presidents. Cotton Mather was also Massachusetts bred; it is not known that he ever went a hundred miles from Boston, the place of his birth and death. He has been called the "primate of New England," for no archbishop of an established church ever exercised greater influence than did Mather from his pulpit in the North Church. He was not only a powerful preacher but somewhat of a scientific innovator. He introduced inoculation into New England against much opposition, conspicuously that of the *New England Courant* published by Franklin and his brothers.

Precocious as a youth, Mather was graduated A.B. of Harvard, 1678, A.M. 1681, and became assistant pastor to his father, 1680. A few years later he was in full control of the North Church, his father having been chosen president of Harvard College. He wrote *Memorable Providences Relating to Witchcraft*, 1689; *Wonders of the Invisible World*, 1693; *Magnalia Christi Americana*, 1702; *Essays to do Good*, 1710. His publications, mostly sermons and religious essays, amount to some four hundred titles.

Mather was undoubtedly the most erudite man of his time in the colonies. His library of two or three thousand volumes in many languages was the largest in America north of Mexico. The *Magnalia Christi Americana* (Mighty Works of Christ in America) *or Ecclesiastical History of New England* is the most important literary monument of the colonial seventeenth century. It is written without restraint, is often untrustworthy as to fact, and combines church and political history with biography, anecdote, and legend. The style, consciously adopted by Mather and defended by him, illustrates in its involved sentence-structure, display of learning, and conceits, some of the worst features of the pedantic prose fashionable in England two generations before Mather's time. Of this style, the puns, for example, are characteristic. They are not made with necessarily humorous intent, but for the purpose of extracting from the idea all its suggestiveness, and to show the writer's skill in dressing out a thought in new array. Although a wide gap in style and a wider gap in ideas separates the *Magnalia* from *Treasure Island,* it will be seen that Mather had as keen a relish for a story of mutiny and treasure-trove as did Stevenson.

Biography: B. Wendell, *Cotton Mather,* 1891. See also J. T. Adams, *The Founding of New England;* K. B. Murdock, *Cotton Mather;* same, *Increase Mather, the Foremost American Puritan,* 1925; W. F. Poole, "Cotton Mather and Salem Witchcraft," *No. Am.* 99:337-97.

From MAGNALIA CHRISTI AMERICANA [1]

[SIR WILLIAM PHIPS]

. . . .

. . . For my reader now being satisfied that a person's being obscure in his original [2] is not always a just prejudice to an expectation of considerable matters from him, I shall now inform him that this our Phips was born February 2, A. D. 1650, at a despicable plantation [3] on the river of Kennebec, and almost the furthest village of the eastern settlement of New England. And as the father of that man [4] which was as great a blessing as England had in the age of that man was a smith, so a gun-smith— namely, James Phips, once of Bristol—had the honor of being the father to him whom we shall presently see made by the God of Heaven as great a blessing to New England as that country could have had, if they themselves had pleased. His fruitful mother, yet living, had no less than twenty-six children, whereof twenty-one were sons; but equivalent to them all was William, one of the youngest, whom his father, dying, left young with his mother, and with her he lived, "keeping of sheep in the wilderness," [5] until he was eighteen years old; at which time he began to feel some further dispositions of mind from that providence of God which "took him from the sheepfolds,

from following the ewes great with young, and brought him to feed his people." [6] Reader, inquire no further who was his father. Thou shalt anon see that he was, as the Italians express it, "a son to his own labors!"

His friends earnestly solicited him to settle among them in a plantation of the east; but he had an unaccountable impulse upon his mind, persuading him, as he would privately hint unto some of them, 'that he was born to greater matters.' To come at those 'greater matters' his first contrivance was to bind himself an apprentice unto a ship carpenter for four years; in which time he became a master of the trade that once, in a vessel of more than forty thousand tons, repaired the ruins of the earth: Noah's, I mean; he then betook himself an hundred and fifty miles further afield, even to Boston, the chief town of New England; which being a place of the most business and resort in those parts of the world, he expected there more commodiously to pursue the *Spes majorum et meliorum* [7]—hopes which had inspired him. At Boston, where it was that he now learned first of all to read and write, he followed his trade for about a year; and, by a laudable deportment, so recommended himself, that he married a young gentlewoman [8] of good repute, who was the widow of one Mr. John Hull, a well-bred merchant, but the daughter of one Captain Roger Spencer, a person of good fashion, who, having suffered much damage in his estate, by some unkind and unjust actions, which he bore with such patience, that for fear of thereby injuring the public, he would not seek satisfaction, posterity might afterward see the reward of his patience, in what Providence hath now done for one of his own posterity. Within a little while after his marriage, he indented [9] with several persons in Boston to build them a ship at Sheepscott River, two or three leagues eastward of Kennebec; where having launched the ship, he also provided a lading of lumber to bring with him, which would have been to the advantage of all concerned. But just as the ship was hardly finished, the barbarous Indians on that river broke forth into an open and cruel war upon the English; and the miserable people, surprised by so sudden a storm of blood, had no refuge from the infidels but the ship now finishing in the harbor. Whereupon he left his intended lading behind him, and, instead thereof, carried with

[1] One division of the *Magnalia* comprises the lives of men "that have been Shields unto the churches of New England." The appendix to this division, which is here given in part, is occupied with the life of "Sir William Phips late Governour of New England."

[2] To get under way, Mather has just cited a number of examples of men of obscure origin who have been commanding figures in the world.

[3] small settlement or group of farms

[4] perhaps Bunyan, whose father is said to have been a tinker

[5] *1 Samuel* xvii, 28

[6] *Psalms* lxxviii, 70, 71

[7] hope of greater and better things

[8] Note here and elsewhere the consciousness of social rank in the early New England writers.

[9] contracted

him his old neighbors and their families, free of all charges to Boston; so the first action that he did, after he was his own man, was to save his father's house, with the rest of the neighborhood, from ruin; but the disappointment which befel him from the loss of his other lading, plunged his affairs into greater embarrassments with such as had employed him.

But he was hitherto no more than beginning to make scaffolds for further and higher actions! He would frequently tell the gentlewoman his wife that he should yet be captain of a King's ship;[1] that he should come to have the command of better men than he was now accounted himself; and that he should be owner of a fair brick-house in the Green-lane of North-Boston;[2] and that, it may be, this would not be all that the providence of God would bring him to. She entertained these passages[3] with a sufficient incredulity; but he had so serious and positive an expectation of them, that it is not easy to say what was the original thereof. He was of an enterprising genius, and naturally disdained littleness; but his disposition for business was of the Dutch mold, where, with a little show of wit,[4] there is as much wisdom demonstrated, as can be shown by any nation. His talent lay not in the airs that serve chiefly for the pleasant and sudden turns of conversation; but he might say, as Themistocles,[5] 'Though he could not play upon a fiddle, yet he knew how to make a little city become a great one.' He would prudently contrive a weighty undertaking, and then patiently pursue it unto the end. He was of an inclination cutting rather like a hatchet than like a razor; he would propose very considerable matters to himself, and then so cut through them, that no difficulties could put by the edge of his resolutions. Being thus of the true temper for doing of great things, he betakes himself to the sea, the right scene for such things; and upon advice of a Spanish wreck about the Bahamas, he took a voyage thither; but with little more success than what just served him a little to furnish him for a voyage to England; whither he went in a vessel, not much unlike that which the Dutchmen stamped on their first coin, with these words about it: *Incertum quo Fata ferant.*[6] Having first informed himself that there was another Spanish wreck,

wherein was lost a mighty treasure, hitherto undiscovered, he had a strong impression upon his mind that he must be the discoverer; and he made such representations of his design at Whitehall,[7] that by the year 1683 he became the captain of a King's ship, and arrived at New England commander of the *Algier Rose,* a frigate of eighteen guns and ninety-five men.

To relate all the dangers through which he passed, both by sea and land, and all the tiresome trials of his patience, as well as of his courage, while year after year the most vexing accidents imaginable delayed the success of his design, it would even tire the patience of the reader: for very great was the experiment that Captain Phips made of the Italian observation, "He that cannot suffer both good and evil, will never come to any great preferment." Wherefore I shall supersede all journal of his voyages to and fro, with reciting one instance of his conduct, that showed him to be a person of no contemptible capacity. While he was captain of the *Algier Rose,* his men growing weary of their unsuccessful enterprise, made a mutiny, wherein they approached him on the quarterdeck, with drawn swords in their hands, and required him to join with them in running away with the ship, to drive a trade of piracy on the South Seas. Captain Phips, though he had not so much of a weapon as an ox-goad, or a jawbone in his hands, yet, like another Shamgar or Samson,[8] with a most undaunted fortitude, he rushed in upon them, and with the blows of his bare hands, felled many of them, and quelled all the rest. But this is not the instance which I intended: that which I intend is, that (as it has been related unto me) one day while his frigate lay careening,[9] at a desolate Spanish island, by the side of a rock, from whence they had laid a bridge to the shore, the men, whereof he had about an hundred, went all but about eight or ten to divert themselves, as they pretended, in the woods; where they all entered into an agreement, which they signed in a ring,[10] that about seven o'clock that evening they would seize the captain, and those eight or ten which they knew to be true unto him, and leave them to perish on this island, and so be gone away unto the South Sea to seek their fortune. Will the reader now imagine that Captain Phips, having advice of this plot but about an hour and half before it was to be put

[1] a ship in the English navy
[2] Now Salem Street; North Boston was just coming to be the best residence quarter of the city.
[3] listened to these speeches   [4] ingenuity, skill
[5] According to Plutarch, Themistocles was wont thus to reply to those who twitted him with ignorance of the social graces.
[6] "uncertain whither the fates will lead"

[7] the royal palace in London
[8] Shamgar smote six hundred Philistines with an ox-goad, and Samson one thousand with the jawbone of an ass. See *Judges* iii, 31; xv, 15.
[9] lying far over on one side for repairs to the other
[10] round-robin

in execution, yet within two hours brought all these rogues down upon their knees to beg for their lives? But so it was! for these knaves considering that they should want a carpenter with them in their villainous expedition, sent a messenger to fetch unto them the carpenter, who was then at work upon the vessel; and unto him they showed their articles; telling him what he must look for if he did not subscribe among them. The carpenter being an honest fellow, did with much importunity prevail for one half hour's time to consider of the matter; and returning to work upon the vessel, with a spy by them set upon him, he feigned himself taken with a fit of the colic, for the relief whereof he suddenly run unto the captain in the great cabin for a dram; where, when he came, his business was only, in brief, to tell the captain of the horrible distress which he was fallen into; but the captain bid him as briefly return to the rogues in the woods, and sign their articles, and leave him to provide for the rest. The carpenter was no sooner gone but Captain Phips, calling together the few friends (it may be seven or eight) that were left him aboard, whereof the gunner was one, demanded of them, whether they would stand by him in the extremity which he informed them was now come upon him; whereto they replied, 'They would stand by him, if he could save them'; and he answered, 'By the help of God he did not fear it.' All their provisions had been carried ashore to a tent, made for that purpose there; about which they had placed several great guns to defend it, in case of any assault from Spaniards, that might happen to come that way. Wherefore Captain Phips immediately ordered those guns to be silently drawn [1] and turned; and so pulling up the bridge, he charged his great guns aboard, and brought them to bear on every side of the tent. By this time the army of rebels comes out of the woods; but as they drew near to the tent of provisions, they saw such a change of circumstances, that they cried out, "We are betrayed!" And they were soon confirmed in it, when they heard the captain with a stern fury call to them, "Stand off, ye wretches, at your peril!" He quickly saw them cast into a more than ordinary confusion when they saw him ready to fire his great guns upon them, if they offered one step further than he permitted them: and when he had signified unto them his resolve to abandon them unto all the desolation which they had purposed for him, he caused the bridge to be again laid, and his men begun to take the provisions aboard. When

the wretches beheld what was coming upon them, they fell to very humble entreaties; and at last fell down upon their knees, protesting that they never had anything against him, except only his unwillingness to go away with the King's ship upon the South-Sea design: but upon all other accounts, they would choose rather to live and die with him than with any man in the world: however, since they saw how much he was dissatisfied at it, they would insist upon it no more, and humbly begged his pardon. And when he judged that he had kept them on their knees long enough, he having first secured their arms, received them aboard; but he immediately weighed anchor and, arriving at Jamaica, he turned them off. Now, with a small company of other men he sailed from thence to Hispaniola, [2] where, by the policy of his address, [3] he fished out of a very old Spaniard (or Portuguese) a little advice about the true spot where lay the wreck which he had been hitherto seeking, as unprosperously as the chemists have their aurisick [4] stone: that it was upon a reef of shoals, a few leagues to the northward of Port de la Plata, upon Hispaniola, a port so called, it seems, from the landing of some of the shipwrecked company, with a boat full of plate, [5] saved out of their sinking frigate. Nevertheless, when he had searched very narrowly the spot whereof the old Spaniard had advised him, he had not hitherto exactly lit upon it. Such thorns did vex his affairs while he was in the *Rose* frigate; but none of all these things could retund [6] the edge of his expectations to find the wreck; with such expectations he returned then into England, that he might there better furnish himself to prosecute a new discovery; for though he judged he might, by proceeding a little further, have come at the right spot; yet he found his present company too ill a crew to be confided in.

So proper [7] was his behavior, that the best noblemen in the kingdom now admitted him into their conversation; [8] but yet he was opposed by powerful enemies, that clogged his affairs with such demurrages, [9] and such disappointments, as would have wholly discouraged his designs, if his patience had not been invincible. "He who can wait, hath what he

---

[1] i.e., the powder and shot removed

[2] Haiti, named Española (Little Spain) by Columbus
[3] sagacity and suavity of his manner
[4] Probably a misprint for *aurific* (gold-bearing), the *f* of Mather's manuscript having been mistaken for a long *s;* the reference is to the search of the alchemists for gold.
[5] valuables, generally utensils, of gold and silver
[6] dull
[7] agreeable
[8] intercourse   [9] delays

desireth." [1] Thus his indefatigable patience, with a proportionable diligence, at length overcame the difficulties that had been thrown in his way; and prevailing with the Duke of Albemarle, and some other persons of quality, to fit him out, he set sail for the fishing-ground, which had been so well baited half an hundred years before: and as he had already discovered his capacity for business in many considerable actions, he now added unto those discoveries, by not only providing all, but also by inventing many of the instruments necessary to the prosecution of his intended fishery. Captain Phips arriving with a ship and a tender at Port de la Plata, made a stout canoe of a stately cottontree, so large as to carry eight or ten oars, for the making of which piragua (as they call it) he did, with the same industry that he did everything else, employ his own hand and adz, and endure no little hardship, lying abroad in the woods many nights together. This piragua, with the tender, being anchored at a place convenient, the piragua kept busking to and again, [2] but could only discover a reef of rising shoals thereabouts, called "The Boilers,"— which, rising to be within two or three foot of the surface of the sea, were yet so steep, that a ship striking on them, would immediately sink down, who could say how many fathom? into the ocean. Here they could get no other pay for their long peeping among the boilers, but only such as caused them to think upon returning to their captain with the bad news of their total disappointment. Nevertheless, as they were upon the return, one of the men looking over the side of the piragua, into the calm water, he spied a sea feather, growing, as he judged, out of a rock; whereupon they bade one of their Indians to dive and fetch this feather, that they might, however, carry home something with them, and make, at least, as fair a triumph as Caligula's. [3] The diver bringing up the feather, brought therewithal a surprising story, that he perceived a number of great guns in the watery world where he had found his feather; the report of which great guns exceedingly astonished the whole company; and at once turned their despondencies for their ill success into assurances that they had now lit upon the true spot of ground which

they had been looking for; and they were further confirmed in these assurances, when, upon further diving, the Indian fetched up a sow, as they styled it, or a lump of silver worth perhaps two or three hundred pounds. Upon this they prudently buoyed the place, that they might readily find it again; and they went back unto their captain, whom for some while they distressed with nothing but such bad news as they formerly thought they must have carried him: nevertheless, they so slipped in the sow of silver on one side under the table, where they were now sitting with the captain, and hearing him express his resolutions to wait still patiently upon the providence of God under these disappointments, that when he should look on one side, he might see that odd thing before him. At last he saw it; seeing it, he cried out with some agony, "Why! What is this? whence comes this?" And then, with changed countenances, they told him how and where they got it. "Then," said he, "thanks be to God! we are made"; and so away they went, all hands to work; wherein they had this one further piece of remarkable prosperity, that whereas if they had first fallen upon that part of the Spanish wreck where the pieces of eight [4] had been stowed in bags among the ballast, they had seen a more laborious, and less enriching time of it: now, most happily, they first fell upon that room in the wreck where the bullion had been stored up; and they so prospered in this new fishery, that in a little while they had, without the loss of any man's life, brought up thirty-two tons of silver; for it was now come to measuring of silver by tons. Besides which, one Adderly, of Providence, who had formerly been very helpful to Captain Phips in the search of this wreck, did, upon former agreement, meet him now with a little vessel here; and he, with his few hands, took up about six tons of silver; whereof, nevertheless, he made so little use, that in a year or two he died at Bermudas, and, as I have heard, he ran distracted some while before he died. Thus did there once again come into the light of the sun a treasure which had been half an hundred years groaning under the waters: and in this time there was grown upon the plate a crust like limestone, to the thickness of several inches; which crust being broken open by iron contrived for that purpose, they knocked out whole bushels of rusty pieces of eight which were grown thereinto. Besides that incredible treasure of plate in various forms, thus fetched up, from seven or eight fathom under water, there were vast riches of

[1] possibly an adaptation of such passages as *Proverbs* xxiii, 18; *Hebrews* vi, 15, etc.

[2] scurrying to and fro

[3] Caligula, the mad Roman emperor, wishing to be honored by a military triumph, led an army to the Rhine. Finding no barbarians whom he might fight, he performed some theatrical military movements, and then marched to the sea where he bade his soldiers fill their helmets with shells as trophies of Neptune worthy to adorn the temples of Rome.

[4] a Spanish coin of the value of eight reals, or one dollar

gold, and pearls and jewels, which they also lit upon; and, indeed, for a more comprehensive invoice, I must but summarily say, "All that a Spanish frigate uses to be enriched withal." Thus did they continue fishing till their provisions failing them, 'twas time to be gone; but before they went, Captain Phips caused Adderly and his folk to swear, that they would none of them discover [1] the place of the wreck, or come to the place any more till the next year, when he expected again to be there himself. And it was also remarkable, that though the sows came up still so fast, that on the very last day of their being there they took up twenty, yet it was afterwards found, that they had in a manner wholly cleared that room of the ship where those massy things were stowed.

But there was one extraordinary distress which Captain Phips now found himself plunged into: for his men were come out with him upon seamen's wages, at so much per month; and when they saw such vast litters of silver sows and pigs, as they called them, come on board them at the captain's call, they knew not how to bear it, that they should not share all among themselves, and be gone to lead "a short life and a merry," in a climate where the arrest of those that had hired them should not reach them. In this terrible distress he made his vows unto Almighty God, that if the Lord would carry him safe home to England with what he had now given him, "to suck of the abundance of the seas, and of the treasures hid in the sands," [2] he would for ever devote himself unto the interests of the Lord Jesus Christ and of his people, especially in the country which he did himself originally belong unto. And he then used all the obliging arts imaginable to make his men true unto him, especially by assuring them that, besides their wages, they should have ample requitals made unto them; which if the rest of his employers would not agree unto, he would himself distribute his own share among them. Relying upon the word of one whom they had ever found worthy of their love, and of their trust, they declared themselves content; but still keeping a most careful eye upon them, he hastened back for England with as much money as he thought he could then safely trust his vessel withal; not counting it safe to supply himself with necessary provisions at any nearer port, and so return unto the wreck, by which delays he wisely feared lest all might be lost, more ways than one. Though he also left so much behind him, that many from divers parts made

[1] disclose
[2] *Deuteronomy* xxxiii, 19

very considerable voyages of gleanings after his harvest; which came to pass by certain Bermudians compelling of Adderly's boy, whom they spirited away with them, to tell them the exact place where the wreck was to be found. Captain Phips now coming up to London in the year 1687, with near three hundred thousand pounds sterling aboard him, did acquit himself with such an exemplary honesty, that partly by his fulfilling his assurances to the seamen, and partly by his exact and punctual care to have his employers defrauded of nothing that might conscientiously belong unto them, he had less than sixteen thousand pounds left unto himself; as an acknowledgment of which honesty in him, the Duke of Albemarle made unto his wife, whom he never saw, a present of a golden cup, near a thousand pound in value. The character of an honest man he had so merited in the whole course of his life, and especially in this last act of it, that this, in conjunction with his other serviceable qualities, procured him the favors of the greatest persons in the nation; and "he that had been so diligent in his business, must now stand before kings, and not stand before mean men." [3] There were indeed certain mean men—if base, little, dirty tricks, will entitle men to meanness—who urged the King to seize his whole cargo, instead of the tenths, [4] upon his first arrival; on this pretence, that he had not been rightly informed of the true state of the case when he granted the patent, under the protection whereof these particular men had made themselves masters of all this mighty treasure; but the King replied, that he had been rightly informed by Captain Phips of the whole matter, as it now proved; and that it was the slanders of one then present which had, unto his damage, hindered him from hearkening to the information; wherefore he would give them, he said, no disturbance; they might keep what they had got; but Captain Phips, he saw, was a person of that honesty, fidelity and ability, that he should not want his countenance. [5] Accordingly the King, in consideration of the service done by him, in bringing such a treasure into the nation, conferred upon him the honor of knighthood; and if we now reckon him a knight of the golden fleece, [6] the style might pretend unto some circumstances that would justify it. Or call him, if you please, "the knight of honesty;" for it was honesty with

[3] *Proverbs* xxii, 29
[4] perhaps the usual royal share in treasure thus found, or the royal share agreed upon in the special contract or patent in this case
[5] favor
[6] The Golden Fleece is a Burgundian, not an English order. The allusion is to the story of Jason and the Argonauts, and to Phips's early occupation.

industry that raised him; and he became a mighty river, without the running in of muddy water to make him so. Reader, now make a pause, and behold one raised by God! [1]

.   .   .   .

[WITCHCRAFT]

.   .   .   .

Now, the arrival of Sir William Phips to the government of New England, was at a time when a governor would have had occasion for all the skill in [2] sorcery that was ever necessary to a Jewish counselor; a time when scores of poor people had newly fallen under a prodigious possession of devils, which it was then generally thought had been by witchcrafts introduced. It is to be confessed and bewailed, that many inhabitants of New England, and young people especially, had been led away with little sorceries, wherein they "did secretly those things that were not right against the Lord their God"; [3] they would often cure hurts with spells, and practice detestable conjurations with sieves, and keys, and peas, and nails, and horse-shoes, and other implements, to learn the things for which they had a forbidden and impious curiosity. Wretched books had stolen into the land, wherein fools were instructed how to become able fortune-tellers: among which, I wonder that a blacker brand is not set upon that fortune-telling wheel, which that sham-scribbler that goes under the letters of R. B. has promised in his *Delights for the Ingenious*, [4] as an honest and pleasant recreation: and by these books, the minds of many had been so poisoned, that they studied this finer witch-craft; until 'tis well if some of them were not betrayed into what is grosser, and more sensible and capital. Although these diabolical divinations are more ordinarily committed perhaps all over the whole world, than they are in the country of New England, yet, that being a country devoted unto the worship and service of the Lord Jesus Christ above the rest of the world, He signalized his vengeance against these wickednesses, with such extraordinary dispensations as have not been often seen in other places.

The devils which had been so played withal, [5] and, it may be, by some few criminals more explicitly engaged and employed, now broke in upon the country, after as astonishing a manner as was ever heard of. Some scores of people first about Salem, the center and first-born of all the towns in the colony, and afterwards in several other places, were arrested with many preternatural vexations [6] upon their bodies, and a variety of cruel torments, which were evidently inflicted from the demons of the invisible world. The people that were infected and infested with such demons, in a few days' time arrived unto such a refining alteration upon their eyes, that they could see their tormenters: they saw a devil of a little stature, and of a tawny color, attended still [7] with specters that appeared in more humane circumstances. [8]

These tormenters tendered unto the afflicted a book, requiring them to sign it, or to touch it at least, in token of their consenting to be listed in the service of the devil; which they refusing to do, the specters under the command of that blackman, as they called him, would apply themselves to torture them with prodigious molestations.

The afflicted wretches were horribly distorted and convulsed; they were pinched black and blue: pins would be run everywhere in their flesh; they would be scalded until they had blisters raised on them; and a thousand other things before hundreds of witnesses were done unto them, evidently preternatural: for if it were preternatural to keep a rigid fast for nine, yea, for fifteen days together; or if it were preternatural to have one's hands tied close together with a rope to be plainly seen, and then by unseen hands presently pulled up a great way from the earth before a crowd of people; such preternatural things were endured by them.

But of all the preternatural things which befell these people, there were none more unaccountable than those wherein the prestigious [9] demons would ever now and then cover the most corporeal things in the world with a fascinating mist of invisibility. As now; a person was cruelly assaulted by a specter, that, she said, run at her with a spindle, though nobody else in the room could see either the specter or the spindle: at last, in her agonies, giving a snatch at the specter, she pulled the spindle away; and it was no sooner got into her hand, but the other folks then present beheld that it was indeed a real, proper, iron spindle; which,

---

[1] Here follows an account of Phips's services to the colony as governor, and especially of his staunch support of the church.
[2] wisdom concerning (By old Jewish law and the laws of England witchcraft was punishable by death.)
[3] 2 Kings xvii, 9
[4] probably *Delights for the Ingenious in above Fifty Select and Choice Emblems etc. Collected by R. B.*, London, 1684
[5] played with, used for trivial purposes
[6] physical afflictions of various kinds that might not be accounted for by natural laws
[7] always
[8] appearance, form
[9] juggling

when they locked up very safe, it was never-theless by the demons taken away to do farther mischief.

Again, a person was haunted by a most abusive [1] specter, which came to her, she said, with a sheet about her, though seen to none but herself. After she had undergone a deal of tease from the annoyance of the specter, she gave a violent snatch at the sheet that was upon it; wherefrom she tore a corner, which in her hand immediately was beheld by all that were present, a palpable corner of a sheet: and her father, which was now holding of her, catched, that he might keep what his daughter had so strangely seized; but the specter had like to have wrung his hand off, by endeavoring to wrest it from him; however, he still held it, and several times this odd accident was renewed in the family. There wanted not the oaths of good credible people to these particulars. . . .

1694-1697   1702

From THE DIARY OF COTTON MATHER [2]

. . . .

8 m. Thursday. [October 22, 1702.] This day the Lord graciously carried me, thro' the duties of a fast, which was kept throughout the province.

God helps me, not only on this day, but at other times with great frequency and fervency to commit my children into his merciful hands, now the smallpox is on every side of us.

And being in extreme distress about my poor, feeble, wasted consort, who after more than twenty weeks' languishment, is, for my further trial, fallen into the symptoms of an hopeless consumption, I did the night before the fast, keep, as far as my strength would permit, a vigil. [3] In this vigil after I had, prostrate in the dust, left the case of my consort with the Lord, I repaired unto my bedchamber to take some rest, the latter part of the night. But, before my going to rest, I took my *Psalm-book* into my hand that I might sing something for the quieting of my uneasy mind. And, unto my

surprise, the very first verse that at the opening of the book my eye was carried unto was that: *Psal.* 105:37.

> *And there was not among their tribes,*
> *A feeble person told.*

Lord, thought I! This won't be fulfilled un-til the resurrection of the dead. The tribes of the raised will not have one feeble person among them. And must I resign the condition of my consort, at last, unto what shall be done in the future state? Lord, Thy will be done!

Behold a strange thing! On the night after the fast, my consort had appearing to her, (she supposes, in her sleep) a grave person, who brought with him a woman in the most meager and wretched circumstances imaginable. My consort fell into the praises of God, in that her condition was not yet so miserably circum-stanced as that woman's now before her. The grave person then told her that, inasmuch as there were at this time a couple of symptoms become insupportable to her, he would propose a way wherein she should obtain some help for them. First, for her intolerable pain in her breast, said he, let them cut the warm wool from a living sheep and apply it warm unto the grieved pain. Next, for her salivation, which hitherto nothing had relieved, said he, take a tankard of spring-water, and therein over the fire dissolve an agreeable quantity of mas-tics, and of gum isinglass: drink of this liquor now and then to strengthen the glands, which ought to have been done a great while ago.

She told this on Friday to her principal phy-sician, [4] who mightily encouraged our trying the experiments. We did it; and unto our aston-ishment my consort revived at a most unex-pected rate; insomuch that she came twice on Saturday out of her sick chamber unto me in my study; and there she asked me to give thanks unto God with her, and for her, on the account of the recovery in so surprising a de-gree begun unto her.

After this, my dear consort continued much refreshed and yet feeble. We had great hopes of her becoming a strong person again, and yet great fears, lest some further latent mischief within her prove after all too hard for her.

---

[1] deceptive

[2] Cotton Mather's *Diary*, kept between the years 1681 and 1724, differs in style from his formal writings. It may well be compared in point of self-consciousness with the diary of Sewall. The extracts are taken from that time of his life in which he was at the full height of his physical vigor and personal in-fluence.

[3] This passage is to be taken literally. The religious exercises of Mather were as rigorous as those of many a medieval saint. His diary shows that in one year he kept sixty fasts and twenty vigils. Light on the inner quality of the extreme Puritans is shed by such a biography as that of Saint Cath-erine of Siena.

[4] It is said that as late as 1721 there was but one regu-larly trained physician in Boston. The profession of medicine in America, as in England, was in its infancy; any person who served an apprenticeship to an older practitioner being deemed fit to give medical advice. One Boston surgeon was a butcher. Educated gentlemen trained neither professionally nor by apprenticeship also frequently gave medical advice to their families or friends. Cotton Mather and Michael Wigglesworth were considered good physicians.

8 m. Friday [October 30, 1702.] Yesterday, I first saw my *Church History* since the publication of it. [1] A gentleman arrived here from Newcastle, in England, that had bought it there. Wherefore, I set apart this day for solemn thanksgiving unto God for his watchful and gracious providence over that work, and for the harvest of so many prayers, and cares, and tears, and resignations, as I had employed upon it.

My religious friend, Mr. Bromfield, who had been singularly helpful to the publication of that great book, [2] (of twenty shillings price, at London) came to me at the close of the day, to join with me in some of my praises to God.

On this day my little daughter, Nibby, began to fall sick of the smallpox. [3] The dreadful disease, which is raging in the neighborhood, is now got into my poor family. God prepare me, God prepare me, for what is coming upon me!

The child was favorably visited in comparison of what many are.

It becomes impossible for me to record much in these memorials; the vast numbers of the sick among my neighbors and the duties which I owe to the sick in my own family engrossing my time exceedingly.

It being impossible for me to visit the many scores of sick families in my neighborhood, and yet it being my desire to visit them as far as 'tis possible, I composed a sheet which I entitled, *Wholesome Words, or, A visit of Advice to Families Visited with Sickness*. I put myself to the small expense of printing it; and then dividing my flock into three parts, I singled out three honest men, unto whom I committed the care of lodging a sheet in every family, as fast as they should hear of any falling sick in it. The Lord makes this my poor essay [4] exceeding acceptable and serviceable.

The month of November coming on, I had on my mind a strong impression to look out some agreeable paragraph of scripture to be handled in my public ministry, while the two dreadful and mortal sicknesses of the smallpox and the scarlet fever should be raging among us. After earnest supplications to the Lord for his direction I used an action which I would not encourage ever to be used in any divinatory way. [5] I thought I would observe whether the first place that occurred at my opening of my Bible would prove suitable or no; or such as might carry any intimation of angelical direction in it. Unto my amazement, it proved the history of our Lord's curing the sick son of the nobleman, in the fourth chapter of *John*. I saw that the whole Bible afforded not a more agreeable or profitable paragraph. So I began a course of sermons upon it.

9 m. Saturday. [November 14.] The awful circumstances upon me, (and upon the town) caused me to lie in the dust this day with secret prayer and fasting before the Lord.

In this month, my lovely consort again declines; and some latent mischief within her, brings on a feebleness that gives us great apprehensions of a mortal issue.

9 m. Saturday. [November 21.] I obtained, I compelled, the leisure for another day of prayer with fasting in my study, to carry my distressed family unto the Lord.

Humiliations are coming thick upon me!

My study is though a large, yet a warm chamber, (the hangings [6] whereof are boxes with between two and three thousand books in them); and we are so circumstanced that my house, though none of the smallest, cannot afford a safe hospital now for my sick folks anywhere so well as there. So I resigned my study for an hospital to my little folks that are falling sick of a loathsome disease. God sanctified this to humble me for my not serving him as I should have done in my study; which provokes him to chase me out of it. . . .

9 m. [November 24.] My daughter Nanny was taken sick. She proved full and blind and very sore of the distemper.

9 m. [November 27.] My son Increase was taken sick. He also proved pretty full and blind and sore, though not so bad as his sister.

The little creatures keep calling for me so often to pray with them, that I can scarce do it less than ten or a dozen times in a day; besides what I do with my neighbors.

But the most exquisite of my trials was the condition of my lovely consort. It now began to be hopeless.

---

[1] The force of this paragraph is felt only when we understand that, as Barrett Wendell points out in his *Literary History of America*, Mather undertook the *Magnalia* as an act of religious patriotism. He could see liberalism growing apace and he hoped to stay the scourge by calling to mind the providences through which the Church had passed. Hence his devout thankfulness that the consecrated task was finished.

[2] It was published in London, the only folio in our literature.

[3] Nineteen years later, Mather introduced inoculation to combat the disease, and was so opposed that his life was endangered by a bomb thrown in at his study window.

[4] Attempt, or perhaps with a double meaning of *trial* and *tentative discourse;* see history of the word.

[5] Divination in the manner described was common then and is perhaps not unknown even now. Mather is drawn toward the practice even while intellectually condemning it.

[6] wall coverings

Lord, if thy poor servant have any grace in him, it will now be tried unto the uttermost!

How shall I glorify the Lord in the midst of these distresses and confusions? Truly, after my sorry manner I did set myself to do it.

I spent much time with my lovely consort. I prayed with her as agreeably as I could. I endeavored her most consummate preparation for the heavenly world by suitable questions and proposals. I comforted her with as lively discourses upon the glory of heaven whereto she was going, as I could make unto her. I disposed her and myself, all that I could, unto a glorious resignation.

At last the black day arrives: Tuesday, the first of December. I had never yet seen such a black day in all the time of my pilgrimage. The desire of my eyes is this day to be taken from me. Her death is lingering and painful. All the forenoon of this day she lies in the pangs of death; sensible, until the last minute or two before her final expiration.

I cannot remember the discourses that passed between us. Only her devout soul was full of satisfaction about her going to a state of blessedness with the Lord Jesus Christ, and as far as my distress would permit me, I studied how to confirm her satisfaction and consolation.

This I remember, that a little before she died I asked her to tell me faithfully what fault she had seen in my conversation [1] that she would advise me to rectify. She replied (which I wondered at) that she knew of none, but that God had made what she had observed in my conversation exceedingly serviceable unto her, to bring her much nearer unto himself.

When I saw to what a point of resignation I was now called of the Lord I resolved, with his help therein, to glorify him. So, two hours before my lovely consort expired, I kneeled by her bedside, and I took into my two hands a dear hand, the dearest in the world. With her then in my hands, I solemnly and sincerely gave her up unto the Lord; and in token of my real resignation I gently put her out of my hands, and laid away a most lovely hand, resolving that I would never touch it any more!

This was the hardest and perhaps the bravest action that ever I did. She afterwards told me that she signed and sealed my act of resignation. And though, before that, she called for me continually, she after this never asked for me any more.

She continued until near two o'clock in the afternoon. And the last sensible word that she spoke, was to her weeping father, "Heaven,

[1] behavior, public and private

Heaven will make amends for all."

When she was expired, I immediately prayed with her father, and the other weeping people in the chamber, for the grace to carry it well under the present calamity, and I did consummate my resignation in terms as full of glory to the wisdom and goodness and allsufficiency of the Lord, as I could utter.

She lived with me just as many years as she had lived in the world before she came to me; with an addition of the seven months, wherein her dying languishments were preparing me to part with her. When I had been married unto her just sixteen years, (and as near as I can recollect, on that very week, sixteen years, that I was married unto her) God began to take her from me. I then said unto my father, "I seem to feel in my mind, the bodings of a dark cloud hanging over my family." The cloud came on, and now, see what was in it!

On the Friday following, my lovely consort had a very honorable funeral.

Indeed, I do not know of a gentlewoman who has died in this land, these many years, more generally esteemed and lamented. This was every one's observation. . . .

1702   1911

SARAH KEMBLE KNIGHT
1666-1727

Mrs. Knight was born in Boston, and after the death of her husband was a school teacher there. In consideration of her rank in society, for she belonged to a substantial family, she was known as Madam Knight. For her time, station in life, and sex, she was well educated. Her *Diary* shows that some Puritans were able to take a humorous view of the trivial incidents of life, and to enjoy thoroughly an adventure rather less common in her day than a journey across Africa in ours.

In 1704-5, apparently to secure her interest in the settlement of an estate, Mrs. Knight made the journey from Boston to New York, a distance then estimated at 271 miles, and return. Boston then contained some ten thousand inhabitants, and New York about half as many. Her journey may be followed with tolerable accuracy on any good map. It led along the old "Pequot path," and is approximately the route of the first post road between the two cities. The journal, made for her private satisfaction only, was first printed in 1825. Donald G. Mitchell says of it, "The little book is not perhaps altogether Addisonian: but the vivacious author was very keen of eye, and quick of hearing; and I think has given us the most realistic and vivid account of cross-country journeyings in her time which can anywhere be found." It is well to compare her picture of rural social life in New England with the equally faithful picture of Boston society of the same time in Sewall's *Diary*.

From HER PRIVATE JOURNAL [1]

. . . .

Tuesday, October the third, about 8 in the morning, I with the Post [2] proceeded forward without observing any thing remarkable; And about two, afternoon, Arrived at the Post's second stage, where the western Post mett him and exchanged Letters. Here, having called for something to eat, the woman bro't in a Twisted thing like a cable, but something whiter; and laying it on the bord, tugg'd for life to bring it into a capacity to spread; which having with great pains accomplished, shee serv'd in a dish of Pork and Cabage, I suppose the remains of Dinner. The sause was of a deep Purple, which I tho't was boil'd in her dye Kettle; the bread was Indian, [3] and every thing on the Table service Agreeable to [4] these. I, being hungry, gott a little down; but my stomach was soon cloy'd, and what cabbage I swallowed serv'd me for a Cudd the whole day after.

Having here discharged the Ordnary [5] for self and Guide, (as I understood was the custom,) About Three afternoon went on with my Third Guide, who Rode very hard; and having crossed Providence Ferry, [6] we come to a River [7] which they Generally Ride thro'. But I dare not venture; so the Post got a Ladd and Cannoo to carry me to tother side, and hee rid thro' and Led my hors. The Cannoo was very small and shallow, so that when we were in she seem'd redy to take in water, which greatly terrified mee, and caused me to be very circumspect, sitting with my hands fast on each side, my eyes stedy, not daring so much as to lodg my tongue a hair's breadth more on one side of my mouth then tother, nor so much as think on Lott's wife, [8] for a wry thought would have oversett our wherey: But was soon put out of this pain, by feeling the Cannoo on shore, which I as soon almost saluted with my feet; and Rewarding my sculler, again mounted and made the best of our way forwards. The Rode here was very even and the day pleasant, it being now near Sunsett. But the Post told mee wee had neer 14 miles to Ride to the next Stage, (where we were to Lodg.) I askt him of the rest of the Rode, foreseeing wee must travail in the night. Hee told mee there was a bad River [9] we were to Ride thro', which was so very firce a hors could sometimes hardly stem it: But it was but narrow, and wee should soon be over. I cannot express The concern of mind this relation sett me in: no thoughts but those of the dang'ros River could entertain my Imagination, and they were as formidable as varios, still [10] Tormenting me with blackest Ideas of my Approching fate—Sometimes seing my self drowning, otherwhiles drowned, and at the best like a holy Sister Just come out of a Spiritual Bath in dripping Garments.

Now was the Glorious Luminary, with his swift Coursers arrived at his Stage, [11] leaving poor me with the rest of this part of the lower world in darkness, with which wee were soon Surrounded. The only Glimering we now had was from the spangled Skies, Whose Imperfect Reflections rendered every Object formidable. Each lifeless Trunk, with its shatter'd Limbs, appear'd an Armed Enymie; and every little stump like a Ravenous devourer. Nor could I so much as discern my Guide, when at any distance, which added to the terror.

Thus, absolutely lost in Thought, and dying with the very thoughts of drowning, I come up with the post, who I did not see till even with his Hors: he told mee he stopt for mee; and wee Rode on Very deliberatly a few paces, when we entred a Thickett of Trees and Shrubbs, and I perceived by the Hors's going, we were on the descent of a Hill, which, as wee come neerer the bottom, 'twas totaly dark with the Trees that surrounded it. But I knew by the Going of the Hors wee had entred the water, which my Guide told mee was the hazzardos River he had told me off; and hee, Riding up close to my Side, Bid me not fear—we should be over Imediatly. I now ralyed all the Courage I was mistriss of, Knowing that I must either Venture my fate of drowning, or be left like the Children in the wood. So, as the Post bid me, I gave Reins to my Nagg; and sitting as Stedy as Just before in the Cannoo, in a few minutes got safe to the other side, which hee told mee was the Narragansett country.

Here We found great difficulty in Travailing, the way being very narrow, and on each side the Trees and bushes gave us very unpleasent welcome with their Branches and bow's which wee

[1] The manuscript of Madam Knight's journal is not in her own hand, and contains some evident mistakes. In the extracts here given, the spelling and punctuation follow the manuscript.
[2] postman   [3] of Indian corn
[4] in harmony with
[5] The reckoning, bill; each postman served successively as guide to Mrs. Knight. After a few days she found it so fatiguing to keep the pace, that she hired guides of her own.
[6] This was apparently near the present city of Providence, although the distances given farther on seem to cast this into doubt. The town of Providence is not mentioned, perhaps because of its unimportance, for it had dwindled from 500 to 26 inhabitants during King Philip's War.
[7] probably the Pawtuxet   [8] Genesis xix, 26

[9] perhaps the Potowomut River
[10] always   [11] the end of his journey

could not avoid, it being so exceeding dark. My Guide, as before so now, putt on harder than I, with my weary bones, could follow; so left mee and the way beehind him. Now Returned my distressed aprehensions of the place where I was: the dolesome woods, my Company next to none, Going I knew not whither, and encompased with Terrifying darkness; The least of which was enough to startle a more Masculine courage. Added to which the Reflections, as in the afternoon of the day that my Call [1] was very Questionable, which till then I had not so Prudently as I ought considered. Now, coming to the foot of a hill, I found great difficulty in ascending; But being got to the Top, was there amply recompenced with the friendly Appearance of the Kind Conductress of the night, Just then Advancing above the Horisontall Line. The Raptures which the Sight of that fair Planett produced in mee, caus'd mee, for the Moment to forgett my present wearyness and past toils; and Inspir'd me for most of the remaining way with very divirting tho'ts, some of which, with the other Occurances of the day, I reserved to note down when I should come to my Stage. My tho'ts on the sight of the moon were to this purpose:

Fair Cynthia, [2] all the Homage that I may
Unto a Creature, [3] unto thee I pay;
In Lonesome woods to meet so kind a guide,
To Mee's more worth than all the world beside.
Some Joy I felt just now, when safe got o'er
Yon Surly River to this Rugged shore,
Deeming Rough welcomes from these clownish [4]
    Trees,
Better than Lodgings with Nereidees. [5]
Yet swelling fears surprise; all dark appears—
Nothing but Light can disipate those fears.
My fainting vitals can't lend strength to say,
But softly whisper, O I wish 'twere day.
The murmer hardly warm'd the Ambient air,
E're thy Bright Aspect rescues from dispair:
Makes the old Hagg [6] her sable mantle loose,
And a Bright Joy do's through my Soul diffuse.
The Boistero's [7] Trees now Lend a Passage Free,
And pleasant prospects thou giv'st light to see. [8]

From hence wee kept on, with more ease than before: the way being smooth and even, the night warm and serene, and the Tall and thick Trees at a distance, especially when the moon glar'd light through the branches, fill'd my Imagination with the pleasent delusion of a Sumpteous citty, fill'd with famous Buildings and churches, with their spiring steeples, Balconies, Galleries and I know not what: Granduers which I had heard of, and which the stories of foreign countries had given me the Idea of.

Here stood a Lofty church—there is a steeple,
And there the Grand Parade—O see the people!
That Famouse Castle there, were I but nigh,
To see the mote and Bridg and walls so high—
They'r very fine! sais my deluded eye.

Being thus agreably entertain'd without a thou't of any thing but thoughts themselves, I on a suden was Rous'd from these pleasing Imaginations, by the Post's sounding his horn, which assured mee hee was arrived at the Stage, where we were to Lodg: and that musick was then most musickall and agreeable to mee.

Being come to mr. Havens', I was very civilly Received, and courteously entertained, in a clean comfortable House; and the Good woman was very active in helping off my Riding clothes, and then ask't what I would eat. I told her I had some Chocolett, if shee would prepare it; which with the help of some Milk, and a little clean brass Kettle, she soon effected to my satisfaction. I then betook me to my Apartment, which was a little Room parted from the Kitchen by a single bord partition; where, after I had noted the Occurrances of the past day, I went to bed, which, tho' pretty hard, Yet neet and handsome. But I could get no sleep, because of the Clamor of some of the Town tope-ers in next Room, Who were entred into a strong debate concerning the Signifycation of the name of their Country, (viz.) *Narraganset.* One said it was named so by the Indians, because there grew a Brier there, of a prodigious Highth and bigness, the like hardly ever known, called by the Indians Narragansett; And quotes an Indian of so Barberous a name for his Author, that I could not write it. His Antagonist Replyed no—It was from a Spring it had its name, which hee well knew where it was, which was extreem cold in summer, and as Hott as could be imagined in the winter, which was much resorted too by the natives, and by them called Narragansett, (Hott and Cold,) and that was the originall of their places name—with a thousand Impertinances [9] not worth notice, which He utter'd with such a Roreing voice and Thundering blows with the fist of wickedness on the Table, that it peirced my very head. I heartily fretted, and wish't 'um tongue tyed;

---

[1] errand (perhaps, also, call of duty)
[2] the moon
[3] A created thing; the Puritans and their immediate descendants interpreted the Ten Commandments very strictly.
[4] rustic
[5] The Nereids were the guardian spirits of streams.
[6] spirit of night   [7] strong-growing, massed
[8] the naive amateurishness of these lines is characteristic of early American verse. See, for an English parallel, such bits of verse as Bunyan inserts in *Pilgrim's Progress.*
[9] irrelevant things

but with as little succes as a friend of mine once, who was (as shee said) kept a whole night awake, on a Jorny, by a country Left. [1] and a Sergent, Insigne and a Deacon, contriving how to bring a triangle into a Square. They kept calling for tother Gill, which while they were swallowing, was some Intermission; But presently, like Oyle to fire, encreased the flame. I set my Candle on a Chest by the bed side, and setting up, fell to my old way of composing my Resentments, in the following manner:

I ask thy aid, O Potent Rum!
To Charm these wrangling Topers Dum.
Thou hast their Giddy Brains possest—
The man confounded with the Beast—
And I, poor I, can get no rest.
Intoxicate them with thy fumes:
O still their Tongues till morning comes!

And I know not but my wishes took effect; for the dispute soon ended with 'tother Dram; and so Good night!

Wednesday, October 4th. About four in the morning, we set out for Kingston (for so was the Town called) with a french Docter in our company. Hee and the Post put on very furiously, so that I could not keep up with them, only as now and then they'd stop till they see mee. This Rode was poorly furnished with accommodations for Travellers, so that we were forced to ride 22 miles by the post's account, but neerer thirty by mine, before wee could bait so much as our Horses, which I exceedingly complained of. But the post encourag'd mee, by saying wee should be well accommodated anon at mr. Devills, a few miles further. But I questioned whether we ought to go to the Devil to be helpt out of affliction. However, like the rest of Deluded souls that post to the Infernal denn, Wee made all posible speed to this Devil's Habitation; where alliting, in full assurance of good accommodation, wee were going in. But meeting his two daughters, as I suposed twins, they so neerly resembled each other, both in features and habit, and look't as old as the Divel himselfe, and quite as Ugly, We desired entertainm't, but could hardly get a word out of 'um, till with our Importunity, telling them our necesity, &c. they call'd the old Sophister, who was as sparing of his words as his daughters had bin, and no, or none, was the reply's hee made us to our demands. Hee differed only in this from the old fellow in to'ther Country: hee let us depart. However, I thought it proper to warn poor Travailers to endeavour to Avoid falling into circumstances like ours, which, at our next Stage I sat down and did as followeth:

May all that dread the cruel feind of night
Keep on, and not at this curs't Mansion light.
'Tis Hell; 'tis Hell! and Devills here do dwell:
Here dwells the Devill—surely this's Hell.
Nothing but Wants: [2] a drop to cool yo'r Tongue
Cant be procur'd these cruel Feinds among.
Plenty of horrid Grins and looks sevear,
Hunger and thirst, But pitty's bannish'd here -
The Right hand keep, if Hell on Earth you fear!

Thus leaving this habitation of cruelty, we went forward; and arriving at an Ordinary [3] about two mile further, found tollerable accommodation. But our Hostes, being a pretty full mouth'd old creature, entertain'd our fellow travailer, the french Docter, with Inumirable complaints of her bodily infirmities; and whisperd to him so lou'd, that all the House had as full a hearing as hee; which was very divirting to the company, (of which there was a great many,) as one might see by their sneering. But poor weary I slipt out to enter my mind in my Jornal, and left my Great Landly with her Talkative Guests to themselves.

From hence we proceeded (about ten forenoon) through the Narragansett country, pretty Leisurely; and about one afternoon come to Paukataug [4] River, which was about two hundred paces over, and now very high, and no way over to to'ther side but this. I darid not venture to Ride thro, my courage at best in such cases but small, And now at the Lowest Ebb, by reason of my weary, very weary, hungry, and uneasy Circumstances. So takeing leave of my company, tho' with no little Reluctance, that I could not proceed with them on my Jorny, Stop at a little cottage Just by the River, to wait the Waters falling, which the old man that lived there said would be in a little time, and he would conduct me safe over. This little Hutt was one of the wretchedest I ever saw a habitation for human creatures. It was suported with shores [5] enclosed with Clapbords, laid on Lengthways, and so much asunder, that the Light come throu' every where; the doore tyed on with a cord in the place of hinges; The floor the bear earth; no windows but such as the thin covering afforded, nor any furniture but a Bedd with a glass Bottle hanging at the head on't; an earthan cupp, a small pewter Bason, A Bord with sticks to stand on, instead of a table, and a block or two in the corner instead of chairs. The family were the old man, his wife and two Children; all and

---

[1] leftenant, lieutenant

[2] is lacking
[3] tavern
[4] Pawcatuck
[5] props

every part being the picture of poverty. Notwithstanding both the Hutt and its Inhabitance
were very clean and tydee: to the crossing the
Old Proverb, that bare walls make giddy hows-
wifes.

. . . .

Saturday, Oct. 7th, wee [1] sett out early in the
Morning, and being something unaquainted
with the way, having ask't it of some wee mett,
they told us wee must Ride a mile or tw and
turne down a Lane on the Right hand; and by
their Direction wee Rode on but not Yet come-
ing to the turning, we mett a Young fellow and
ask't him how farr it was to the Lane which
turn'd down towards Guilford. Hee said wee
must Ride a little further, and turn down by
the Corner of uncle Sams Lott. My Guide
vented his Spleen at the Lubber; and we soon
after came into the Rhode, and keeping still
on, without any thing further Remarkabell,
about two a clock afternoon we arrived at New
Haven, where I was received with all Posible
Respects and civility. Here discharged Mr.
Wheeler with a reward to his satisfaction, and
took some time to rest after so long and toilsome a Journey; And Inform'd myselfe of the
manners and customs of the place, and at the
same time employed myselfe in the afair I
went there upon.

They are Govern'd by the same Laws as wee
in Boston, (or little differing,) thr'out this
whole Colony of Conneticot, [2] And much the
same way of Church Government, and many
of them good, Sociable people, and I hope Religious to: but a little too much Independant
in their principalls, and, as I have been told,
were formerly in their Zeal very Riggid in their
Administrations towards such as their Lawes
made Offenders, even to a harmless Kiss or
Innocent merriment among Young people.
Whipping being a frequent and counted an easy
Punishment, about which, as other Crimes, the
Judges were absolute in their Sentances.

. . . Their Diversions in this part of the
Country are on Lecture days [3] and Training
days mostly: on the former there is Riding
from town to town.

And on training dayes The Youth divert
themselves by Shooting at the Target, as they
call it, (but it very much resembles a pillory,)

where hee that hitts neerest the white has some
yards of Red Ribbin presented him, which being
tied to his hattband, the two ends streeming
down his back, he is Led away in Triumph,
with great applause, as the winners of the Olym-
piack Games. [4]. They generally marry very
young: the males oftener as I am told under
twentie than above; they generally make public wedings, and have a way something singular (as they say) in some of them, viz. Just
before Joyning hands the Bridegroom quitts
the place, who is soon followed by the Brides-
men, and as it were, dragg'd back to duty—
being the reverse to the former practice among
us, to steal Mrs. Bride.

There are great plenty of Oysters all along
by the sea side, as farr as I Rode in the Collony, and those very good. And they Generally
lived very well and comfortably in their fame-
lies. But too Indulgent (especially the farmers) to their slaves: sufering too great familiarity from them, permitting them to sit at
Table and eat with them, (as they say to save
time,) and into the dish goes the black hoof as
freely as the white hand. They told me that
there was a farmer lived nere the Town where
I lodgd who had some difference with his
slave, concerning something the master had
promised him and did not punctualy perform;
which caused some hard words between them;
But at length they put the matter to Arbitra-
tion and Bound themselves to stand to the
award of such as they named—which done, the
Arbitrators Having heard the Allegations of
both parties, Order the master to pay 40s to
black face, and acknowledge his fault. And
so the matter ended: the poor master very
honestly standing to the award.

. . . . . .

They give the title of merchant to every
trader; who Rate their Goods according to the
time and spetia [5] they pay in: viz. Pay, mony,
Pay as mony, and trusting. *Pay* is Grain, Pork,
Beef, &c.   the prices sett by the General
Court [6] that year; *mony* is pieces of Eight,
Ryalls, or Boston or Bay shillings [7] (as they
call them,) or Good hard money, as sometimes
silver coin is termed by them; also Wampom,
vizt. Indian beads which serves for change.
Pay as mony is provisions, as aforesaid one
Third cheaper then as the Assembly or General

[1] Mrs. Knight and her guide, Joshua Wheeler; they were now at Killingsworth, Connecticut.
[2] Mrs. Knight feels herself to be in a foreign country, a fact that throws a little light on the feeling of each separate colony for its independence. This led to a certain amount of estrangement quite to the time of the Constitution (1789).
[3] The midweek religious lecture was generally on Thursday afternoon, and the services were less formal than on Sunday.

[4] The Olympic games, held every four years from 776 B.C. at Olympia, constituted the greatest festival of the Greek race.
[5] specie
[6] The General Courts of the colonies were wont to set the prices of staples.
[7] The Spanish dollar or "piece of eight" contained eight reals. The Bay Shilling was coined by the Massachusetts Bay Colony.

Court sets it; and *Trust* as they and the merchant agree for time.

Now, when the buyer comes to ask for a comodity, sometimes before the merchant answers that he has it, he sais, *is Your pay redy?* Perhaps the Chap Reply's Yes: what do You pay in? say's the merchant. The buyer having answered, then the price is set; as suppose he wants a sixpenny knife, in pay it is 12d—in pay as money eight pence, and hard money its own price, viz. 6d. It seems a very Intricate way of trade and what Lex Mercatoria [1] had not thought of.

Being at a merchants house, in come a tall country fellow, with his alfogeos [2] full of Tobacco; for they seldom Loose their Cudd, but keep Chewing and Spitting as long as they'r eyes are open,—he advanc't to the middle of the Room, makes an Awkward Nodd, and spitting a Large deal of Aromatick Tincture, he gave a scrape with his shovel like shoo, leaving a small shovel full of dirt on the floor, made a full stop, Hugging his own pretty Body with his hands under his arms, Stood staring rown'd him, like a Catt let out of a Baskett. At last, like the creature [3] Balamm Rode on, he opened his mouth and said: have You any Ribinen for Hatbands to sell I pray? The Questions and Answers about the pay being past, the Ribin is bro't and opened. Bumpkin Simpers, cryes its confounded Gay I vow; and beckning to the door, in comes Jone Tawdry dropping about 50 curtsees, and stands by him: hee shows her the Ribin. *Law, You,* sais shee, *its right Gent,* [4] do You, take it, *tis dreadfull pretty.* Then she enquires, *have you any hood silk I pray?* which being brought and bought, *Have You any thred silk to sew it with* says shee, which being accommodated with they Departed. They Generaly stand after they come in a great while speachless, and sometimes dont say a word till they are askt what they want, which I impute to the Awe they stand in of the merchants, who they are constantly almost Indebted too; and must take what they bring without Liberty to choose for themselves; but they serve them as well, making the merchants stay long enough for their pay.

We may Observe here the great necessity and bennifitt both of Education and Conversation; [5] for these people have as Large a portion of mother witt, and sometimes a Larger, than those who have bin brought up in Citties; But

for want of emprovements, Render themselves almost Ridiculos, as above. I should be glad if they would leave such follies, and am sure all that Love Clean Houses (at least) would be glad on't too.

They are generaly very plain in their dress, throuout all the Colony, as I saw, and follow one another in their modes; that You may know where they belong, especially the women, meet them where you will.

Their Cheif Red Letter day is St. Election, [6] which is annually Observed according to Charter, to choose their Govenr: a blessing they can never be thankfull enough for, as they will find, if ever it be their hard fortune to loose it. [7] The present Govenor in Conecticott is the Honorable John Winthrop Esq. A Gentleman of an Ancient and Honourable Family, whose Father was Govenor here sometime before, and his Grand father had bin Govr of the Massachusetts. This gentleman is a very curteous and afable person, much Given to Hospitality, and has by his Good services Gain'd the affections of the people as much as any who had bin before him in that post.

Decr. 6th. Being by this time well Recruited and rested after my Journy, my business lying unfinished by some concerns at New York depending thereupon, my Kinsman, Mr. Thomas Trowbridge of New Haven, must needs take a Journy there before it could be accomplished, I resolved to go there in company with him, and a man of the town which I engaged to wait on [8] me there. Accordingly, Dec. 6th we set out from New Haven, and about 11 same morning came to Stratford ferry; which crossing, about two miles on the other side Baited our horses and would have eat a morsell ourselves, But the Pumpkin and Indian mixt Bred had such an Aspect, and the Bare-legg'd Punch [9] so awkerd or rather Awfull a sound, that we left both, and proceeded forward, and about seven at night come to Fairfield, where we met with good entertainment and Lodg'd; and early next morning set forward to Norowalk, from its halfe Indian name *North-walk*, when about 12 at noon we arrived, and Had a Dinner of Fryed Venison, very savoury. Landlady wanting some pepper in the seasoning, bid the Girl hand her the spice in the little *Gay* cupp on the shelfe. From hence we Hasted

---

[1] the law of merchants; trade rules having a certain legal standing
[2] Sp. *alforja*, saddlebags; here, of course, cheeks
[3] *Numbers* xxii, 21-33
[4] elegant
[5] social intercourse
[6] Jocosely: the general election day was celebrated as a holiday, just as a saint's day would be in a Catholic country.
[7] The governor of Massachusetts was at this time appointed by the king, to the general discontent of the colony.
[8] accompany
[9] apparently a local name for some kind of drink

towards Rye, walking and Leading our Horses neer a mile together, up a prodigios high Hill; and so Riding till about nine at night, and there arrived and took up our Lodgings at an ordinary, which a French family kept. Here being very hungry, I desired a fricasee, which the Frenchman undertakeing, mannaged so contrary to my notion of Cookery, that I hastned to Bed superless; And being shewd the way up a pair of stairs which had such a narrow passage that I had almost stopt by the Bulk of my Body; But arriving at my apartment found it to be a little Lento [1] Chamber furnisht amongst other Rubbish with a High Bedd and a Low one, a Long Table, a Bench and a Bottomless chair,—Little Miss went to scratch up my Kennell which Russelled as if shee'd bin in the Barn amongst the Husks, and supose such was the contents of the tickin—nevertheless being exceeding weary, down I laid my poor Carkes (never more tired) and found my Covering as scanty as my Bed was hard. Annon I heard another Russelling noise in The Room— called to know the matter—Little miss said shee was making a bed for the men; who, when they were in Bed, complained their leggs lay out of it by reason of its shortness—my poor bones complained bitterly not being used to such Lodgings, and so did the man who was with us; and poor I made but one Grone, which was from the time I went to bed to the time I Riss, which was about three in the morning, Setting up by the Fire till Light, and having discharged our ordinary which was as dear as if we had had far Better fare—wee took our leave of Monsier and about seven in the morn come to New Rochell a french town, where we had a good Breakfast. And in the strength of that about an how'r before sunsett got to York. Here I applyd myself to Mr. Burroughs, a merchant to whom I was recommended by my Kinsman Capt. Prout, and received great Civilities from him and his spouse, who were now both Deaf but very agreeable in their Conversation, Diverting me with pleasant stories of their knowledge in Brittan from whence they both come. . . .

The Cittie of New York is a pleasant, well compacted place, situated on a Commodious River which is a fine harbour for shipping. The Buildings Brick Generaly, very stately and high, though not altogether like ours in Boston. The Bricks in some of the Houses are of divers Coullers and laid in Checkers, being glazed look very agreeable. The inside of them are neat to admiration, the wooden work, for only the

walls are plasterd, and the Sumers [2] and Gist [3] are plained and kept very white scowr'd as so is all the partitions if made of Bords. The fire places have no Jambs (as ours have) But the Backs run flush with the walls, and the Hearth is of Tyles and is as farr out into the Room at the Ends as before the fire, which is Generally Five foot in the Low'r rooms, and the peice over where the mantle tree should be is made as ours with Joyners work, and as I supose is fasten'd to iron rodds inside. The House where the Vendue [4] was, had Chimney Corners like ours, and they and the hearths were laid with the finest tile that I ever see, and the stair cases laid all with white tile which is ever clean, and so are the walls of the Kitchen which had a Brick floor. They were making Great preparations to Receive their Govenor, Lord Cornbury from the Jerseys, and for that end raised the militia to Gard him on shore to the fort.

They are Generaly of the Church of England and have a New England Gentleman for their minister, and a very fine church set out with all Customary requsites. There are also a Dutch and Divers Conventicles as they call them, viz. Baptist, Quakers, etc. They are not strict in keeping the Sabbath as in Boston and other places where I had bin, But seem to deal with great exactness as farr as I see or Deall with. They are sociable to one another and Curteos and Civill to strangers and fare well in their houses. The English go very fasheonable in their dress. But the Dutch, especially the middling sort, differ from our women, in their habitt [5] go loose, were French muches [6] which are like a Capp and a head band in one, leaving their ears bare, which are sett out with Jewells of a large size and many in number. And their fingers hoop't with Rings, some with large stones in them of many Coullers as were their pendants in their ears, which You should see very old women wear as well as Young.

They have Vendues very frequently and make their Earnings very well by them, for they treat with good Liquor Liberally, and the Customers Drink as Liberally and Generally pay for't as well, by paying for that which they Bidd up Briskly for, after the sack [7] has gone plentifully about, tho' sometimes good penny worths are got there. Their Diversions in the Winter is Riding Sleys about three or four Miles out of Town, where they have Houses of

[1] lean-to
[2] supporting beams   [3] joist(s)
[4] an auction which thrifty Mrs. Knight had just attended
[5] dress
[6] wear French mutches (mutch is Scotch, cap)
[7] a name applied to several sorts of wine

entertainment at a place called the Bowery, and some go to friends Houses who handsomely treat them. Mr. Burroughs carry'd his spouse and Daughter and myself out to one Madame Dowes, a Gentlewoman that lived at a farm House, who gave us a handsome Entertainment of five or six Dishes and choice Beer and metheglin, Cyder, etc., all which she said was the produce of her farm. I believe we mett 50 or 60 slays that day—they fly with great swiftness and some are so furious that they'le turn out of the path for none except a Loaden Cart. Nor do they spare for any diversion the place affords, and sociable to a degree, they'r Tables being as free to their Naybours as to themselves.

Having here transacted the affair I went upon and some other that fell in the way, after about a fortnight's stay there I left New-York with no Little regrett, and Thursday, Dec. 21, set out for New Haven with my Kinsman Trowbridge, and the man that waited on me about one afternoon, and about three come to half-way house about ten miles out of town, where we Baited and went forward, and about 5 come to Spiting Devil, Else [1] Kings bridge, where they pay three pence for passing over with a horse, which the man that keeps the Gate set up at the end of the Bridge receives.

January 6th. Being now well Recruited and fitt for business I discoursed [2] the persons I was concerned with, that we might finnish in order to my return to Boston. They delayd as they had hitherto done hoping to tire my Patience. But I was resolute to stay and see an End of the matter let it be never so much to my disadvantage—So January 9th they come again and promise the Wednesday following to go through with the distribution of the Estate which they delayed till Thursday and then come with new amusements. But at length by the mediation of that holy good Gentleman, the Rev. Mr. James Pierpont, the minister of New Haven, and with the advice and assistance of other our Good friends we come to an accommodation and distribution, which having finished though not till February, the man that waited on me to York taking the charge of me I sit out for Boston. We went from New Haven upon the ice (the ferry being not passable thereby) and the Rev. Mr. Pierpont with Madam Prout Cuzin Trowbridge and divers others were taking leave wee went onward without anything Remarkabl till wee come to New London and Lodged again at Mr. Saltonstalls—

and here I dismist my Guide, and my Generos entertainer provided me Mr. Samuel Rogers of that place to go home with me—I stayed a day here Longer than I intended by the Commands of the Honorable Govenor Winthrop to stay and take a supper with him whose wonderful civility I may not omitt. The next morning I Crossed the Ferry to Groton, having had the Honor of the Company, of Madam Livingston (who is the Govenors Daughter) and Mary Christophers and divers others to the boat— And that night Lodged at Stonington and had Rost Beef and pumpkin sause for supper. The next night at Haven's and had Rost fowle, and the next day wee come to a river which by Reason of The Freshetts coming down was swell'd so high wee feard it impassable and the rapid stream was very terryfying—However we must over and that in a small Cannoo. Mr. Rogers assuring me of his good Conduct. [3] I after a stay of near an how'r on the shore for consultation went into the Cannoo, and Mr. Rogers paddled about 100 yards up the Creek by the shore side, turned into the swift stream and dexterously steering her in a moment wee come to the other side as swiftly passing as an arrow shott out of the Bow by a strong arm. I staid on the shore till Hee returned to fetch our horses, which he caused to swim over himself bringing the furniture [4] in the Cannoo. But it is past my skill to express the Exceeding fright all their [5] transactions formed in me. Wee were now in the colony of the Massachusetts and taking Lodgings at the first Inn we come too had a pretty difficult passage the next day which was the second of March by reason of the sloughy ways when thawed by the Sunn. Here I mett Capt. John Richards of Boston who was going home, So being very glad of his Company we Rode something harder than hitherto, and missing my way in going up a very steep Hill, my horse dropt down under me as Dead; this new surprize no little hurt me meeting it Just at the Entrance into Dedham from whence we intended to reach home that night. But was now obliged to gett another Hors there and leave my own, resolving for Boston that night if possible. But in going over the Causeway at Dedham the Bridge being overflowed by the high waters comming down I very narrowly escaped falling over into the river Hors and all which twas almost a miracle I did not— now it grew late in the afternoon and the people having very much discouraged us about the sloughy way which they said wee should find

---

[1] otherwise   [2] conferred with

[3] skill, dexterity   [5] probably *these* in the original MS.
[4] saddles and other equipment

very difficult and hazardous it so wrought on mee being tired and dispirited and disapointed of my desires of going home that I agreed to Lodg there that night which we did at the house of one Draper, and the next day being March 3d wee got safe home to Boston, where I found my aged and tender mother and my Dear and only Child in good health with open arms redy to receive me, and my kind relations and friends flocking in to welcome mee and hear the story of my transactions and travails I having this day bin five months from home and now I cannot fully express my Joy and Satisfaction. But desire sincearly to adore my Great Benefactor for thus graciously carying forth and returning in safety his unworthy handmaid.

1704-5   1825

SAMUEL SEWALL 1652-1730

The *Diary* that Sewall left, now printed in three large volumes, gives an intimate record of one of the foremost Boston citizens of his time, a man of education, wealth, and position, whose life was built into the social structure of the community. He was born in Hampshire, England, and died in Boston. He came with his parents to Massachusetts in 1661, graduated at Harvard, A.B., 1671, A.M., 1674, studied for the ministry, but entered public life, serving in administrative and judicial offices, and at length as chief justice of Massachusetts, 1718-28. As judge in some of the witchcraft trials he admitted evidence which, years later, he came to consider worthless. For this error he made public confession. In addition to his *Diary,* Sewall wrote *A Description of the New Heaven,* 1697; *The Selling of Joseph,* 1700, the first anti-slavery tract published in America; and several other pamphlets. His writings, consisting of personal memoranda, some of which have been published for their historical importance, are numerous.

The *Diary,* kept in a diary-writing age, when the record of passing events in print was only beginning, has given the author the title of the American Pepys. It is unfortunate that these diarists, Sewall and Pepys, should now, because of the informality and quaintness of their style, and the intimacy of their material, be regarded as almost comic characters. Both were substantial citizens and honest officers highly esteemed by their contemporaries. Diaries equally intimate, written today, will appear equally fantastic two centuries hence. Sewall gives some pictures of colonial life, especially that of the official and higher social circles, that can nowhere be excelled for their vividness. His work is a priceless record of early provincial Massachusetts, as accurate as any such document can humanly be. The parts chosen have been selected for their social picturesqueness.

The Diary of Samuel Sewall, 3 vols., Massachusetts Historical Society, 1882; also *Samuel Sewall's Diary,* (abridged) edited by Mark Van Doren, 1927.

From his DIARY [1]

. . . . . .

October 1, [1720] Saturday. I dine at Mr. Stoddard's: from thence I went to Madam Winthrop's [2] just at three. Spake to her, saying my loving wife died so soon and suddenly, 'twas hardly convenient [3] for me to think of marrying again; however I came to this resolution, that I would not make my court to any person without first consulting with her. Had a pleasant discourse about seven single persons sitting in the fore-seat [4] September 29th, viz. Madam Rebekah Dudley, Catharine Winthrop, [5] Bridget Usher, Deliverance Legg, Rebekah Loyd, Lydia Colman, Elizabeth Bellingham. She propounded one and another for me; but none would do; said Mrs. Loyd was about her age.

October 3. 2. Waited on Madam Winthrop again; 'twas a little while before she came in. Her daughter Noyes being there alone with me, I said I hoped my waiting on her mother would not be disagreeable to her. She answered she should not be against that that might be for her comfort. [6] . . . By and by in came Mr. Airs, Chaplain of the Castle, [7] and hanged up his hat, which I was a little startled at, it seeming as if he was to lodge there. At last Madam Winthrop came too. After a considerable time, I went up to her and said, if it might not be inconvenient I desired to speak with her. She assented, and spake of going into another room; but Mr. Airs and Mrs. Noyes presently [8] rose up, and went out, leaving us there alone. Then I ushered in discourse from the names in the fore-seat; at last I prayed that Katharine [Mrs. Winthrop] might be the person assigned for me. She instantly took it up in the way of denial, as if she had catched at an opportunity to do it, saying she could not do it before she was asked. Said that was her mind unless she should change it, which she believed she should not; could not leave her children. I expressed my sorrow that she should do it so speedily, prayed her consideration, and asked her when

---

[1] The *Diary* covers the period from 1673 to 1729.
[2] Madam Winthrop, who was the mother of twelve children, most of whom died young, was now a second time a widow, and in her fifty-seventh year. Her second husband was Wait Still Winthrop, grandson of the first governor. Judge Sewall's second wife had been dead a little more than four months.
[3] suitable
[4] The front seat of the church was reserved for persons of social rank. Sometimes a place there was voted by the church to a person it wished to honor.
[5] Madam Winthrop
[6] happiness
[7] chaplain of the garrison at the Castle, the fortification on Castle Island in the harbor
[8] at once

I should wait on her again. She setting no time, I mentioned that day sennight. Gave her Mr. Willard's *Fountain Opened* [1] with the little print and verses, saying I hoped, if we did well read that book, we should meet together hereafter, if we did not now. She took the book, and put it in her pocket. Took leave.

October 5. Midweek, I dined with the Court. [2] . . . Although I had appointed to wait upon her, M^m Winthrop, next Monday, yet I went from my Cousin Sewall's thither about three P. M. The nurse told me Madam dined abroad at her daughter Noyes's; they were to go out together. I asked for the maid, who was not within. Gave Katee a penny and a kiss, and came away. Accompanied my son and daughter Cooper in their remove to their new house. Went to tell Joseph, [3] and Mr. Belcher saw me by the South Meetinghouse [4] though 'twas duskish, and said I had been at house-warming [5] (he had been at our house). Invited me to drink a glass of wine at his house at seven and eat part of the pasty provided for the Commissioners' voyage to Casco-Bay. His Excellency, Madam Belcher, S. S. [6] Col. Fitch, Mr. D. Oliver, Mr. Anthony Stoddard, Mr. Welsteed, Mr. White, Mr. Belcher sat down. At coming home gave us of the cake and ginger-bread to carry away. 'Twas about ten before we got home; Mr. Oliver and I waited on the Governor to his gate; and then Mr. Oliver would wait on me home.

October 6. Lecture-day; Mr. Cutler, [7] president of the Connecticut college, [8] preached in Dr. C. Mather's turn. He made an excellent discourse from *Heb.* 11, 14, "For they that say such things, declare plainly that they seek a country." Brother Odlin, Son Sewall of Brookline, and Mary Hirst dine with me. I asked Mary of Madam Lord, Mr. Oliver and wife, and bid her present my service to them.

October 6th. A little after six p.m. I went to Madam Winthrop's. She was not within. I gave Sarah Chickering, the maid, two shillings, Juno, [9] who brought in wood, one shilling. Afterward the nurse came in, I gave her eighteen pence, having no other small bill. After

awhile Dr. Noyes came in with his mother; and quickly after his wife came in. They sat talking, I think, till eight o'clock. I said I feared I might be some interruption to their business. Dr. Noyes replied pleasantly, he feared they might be an interruption to me, and went away. Madam seemed to harp upon the same string. Must take care of her children; could not leave that house and neighborhood where she had dwelt so long. I told her she might do her children as much or more good by bestowing what she laid out in house-keeping, upon them. Said her son would be of age the 7th of August. I said it might be inconvenient for her to dwell with her daughter-in-law, who must be mistress of the house. I gave her a piece of Mr. Belcher's cake and ginger-bread wrapped up in a clean sheet of paper; told her of her father's kindness to me when treasurer, and I constable. My daughter Judith was gone from me and I was more lonesome—might help to forward one another in our journey to Canaan. [10]—Mr. Eyre came within the door; I saluted him, asked how Mr. Clark did, and he went away. I took leave about nine o'clock. I told [her] I came now to refresh her memory as to Monday night; said she had not forgot it. In discourse with her, I asked leave to speak with her sister; I meant to gain Madam Mico's [11] favor to persuade her sister. She seemed surprised and displeased, and said she was in the same condition! [12]

. . . .

October 10. . . . In the evening I visited Madam Winthrop, who treated me with a great deal of courtesy; wine, marmalade. I gave her a *News-Letter* about the Thanksgiving; [13] proposals, for sake of the verses for David Jeffries. [14] She tells me Dr. Increase Mather visited her this day, in Mr. Hutchinson's coach.

It seems Dr. Cotton Mather's chimney fell afire yesterday, so as to interrupt the assembly, A.M. Mr. Cutler ceased preaching a quarter of an hour.

October 11th. I writ a few lines to Madam Winthrop to this purpose: "Madam, these wait on you with Mr. Mayhew's *Sermon* and *Account of the State of the Indians on Martha's Vineyard.* I thank you for your unmerited favors of yesterday; and hope to have the happiness

[1] a sermon entitled *The Fountain Opened* by Samuel Willard, Judge Sewall's former pastor, then dead
[2] Members of the Court (Sewall was now chief justice of Massachusetts) were wont to dine together occasionally at a public house.
[3] one of his sons who would be interested in the sister's moving into the new house
[4] the original Old South Church, on the site of the present, Washington and Milk Streets
[5] festivities attending the opening of the new house
[6] Samuel Sewall
[7] Timothy Cutler, 1684-1765, President of Yale College, 1719-1722
[8] Yale College   [9] probably a negro slave

[10] heaven; in reference to the journey of the Israelites from Egypt to the land of Canaan
[11] Madam Winthrop's sister
[12] state of mind (concerning the marriage)
[13] The *Boston News-Letter* founded 1704; this number perhaps contained notice of the Thanksgiving which was held that year on October 27.
[14] perhaps refers to some proposed printing of memorial verses for David Jeffries, Madam Winthrop's son-in-law, drowned at sea four years before

of waiting on you tomorrow before eight o'clock after noon. I pray God to keep you, and give you a joyful entrance upon the two hundred and twenty-ninth year of Christopher Columbus his [1] discovery; and take leave, who am, madam, your humble servant,   S.S."

Sent this by Deacon Green, who delivered it to Sarah Chickering, her mistress not being at home.

October 12th. . . . Mrs. Anne Cotton came to [the] door ('twas before eight) said Madam Winthrop was within, directed me into the little room, where she was full of work behind a stand; Mrs. Cotton came in and stood. Madam Winthrop pointed to her to set me a chair. Madam Winthrop's countenance was much changed from what 'twas on Monday,— looked dark and lowering. At last, the work, (black stuff or silk) was taken away, I got my chair in place, had some converse, but very cold and indifferent to what 'twas before. Asked her to acquit me of rudeness if I drew off her glove. Inquiring the reason, I told her twas great odds between handling a dead goat, and a living lady. Got it off. I told her I had one petition to ask of her, that was, that she would take off the negative she laid on me the third of October; She readily answered she could not, and enlarged upon it; She told me of it so soon as she could; could not leave her house, children, neighbors, business. I told her she might do some good to help and support me. Mentioning Mrs. Gookin, Nath., [2] the widow Weld was spoken of; said I had visited Mrs. Denison. I told her Yes! Afterward I said, If after a first and second vagary, [3] she would accept of me returning, her victorious kindness and good will would be very obliging. She thanked me for my book, (Mr. Mayhew's Sermon), But said not a word of the letter. When she insisted on the negative, I prayed there might be no more thunder and lightning: I should not sleep all night. I gave her Dr. Preston, The Church's Marriage and the Church's Carriage, which cost me six shillings at the sale. The door standing open, Mr. Airs came in, hung up his hat, and sat down. After awhile, Madam Winthrop moving, he went out. Jno. Eyre looked in, I said How do ye, or Your servant, Mr. Eyre; but heard no word from him. Sarah filled a glass of wine, she drank to me, I to her. She sent Juno home with me with a good lantern; I gave her sixpence and bid her thank her mistress. In some of our discourse, I told her I had rather go to the stone-house adjoining to her, [4] than to come to her against her mind. Told her the reason why I came every other night was lest I should drink too deep draughts of pleasure. She had talked of canary; her kisses were to me better than the best canary. Explained the expression concerning Columbus. . . .

October 19. Midweek, visited Madam Winthrop; Sarah told me she was at Mr. Walley's, would not come home till late. I gave her Hannah three oranges with her duty, [5] not knowing whether I should find her or no. Was ready to go home; but said if I knew she was there, I would go thither. Sarah seemed to speak with pretty good courage, she would be there. I went and found her there, with Mr. Walley and his wife in the little room below. At 7 o'clock I mentioned going home; at 8, I put on my coat, and quickly waited on her home. She found occasion to speak loud to the servant, as if she had a mind to be known. Was courteous to me; but took occasion to speak pretty earnestly about my keeping a coach: I said 'twould cost £100. per annum: she said 'twould cost but £40. Spake much against John Winthrop, [6] his false-heartedness. Mr. Eyre came in and sat awhile; I offered him Dr. Incr. Mather's Sermons, whereof Mr. Appleton's Ordination Sermon was one; said he had them already. I said I would give him another. Exit. Came away somewhat late.

October 20. Mr. Colman preaches from Luke 15. 10. Joy among the Angels: made an excellent discourse.

At Council, Col. Townsend spake to me of my hood: should get a wig. I said 'twas my chief ornament: I wore it for sake of the day. Brother Odlin, and Sam, Mary, and Jane Hirst dine with us. Promised to wait on the Governor about seven. Madam Winthrop not being at lecture, I went thither first; found her very serene with her daughter Noyes, Mrs. Dering, and the widow Shipreev sitting at a little table, she in her armed chair. She drank to me; and I to Mrs. Noyes. After awhile prayed the favor to speak with her. She took one of the candles, and went into the best room, closed the shutters, sat down upon the couch. She told me Madam Usher had been there, and said the coach must be set on wheels, [7] and not by rusting. She spake something of my needing a wig. Asked me what

_____

[1] Columbus's
[2] probably Mrs. Nathaniel Gookin
[3] The Judge was not paying attention to Madam Winthrop only.

[4] The prison; this identifies the site of Madam Winthrop's house with that of the old Court House on Court Street.
[5] compliments (apparently to Hannah's mistress)
[6] Stepson of Madam Winthrop; apparently there had not been cordial feeling between them concerning the settlement of the Winthrop estate.
[7] used, not set by to rust

her sister said to me. I told her, She said, if her sister were for it, she would not hinder it. But I told her, she [1] did not say she would be glad to have me for her brother. Said, I shall keep you in the cold, and asked her if she would be within tomorrow night, for we had had but a running feat. [2] She said she could not tell whether she should, or no. I took leave. As were drinking at the Governor's, he said: In England the ladies minded little more than that they might have money, and coaches to ride in. I said, And New England brooks [3] its name. At which Mr. Dudley smiled. Governor said they were not quite so bad here.

October 21. Friday, my son, the minister, came to me P.M. by appointment and we pray for one another in the old chamber; more especially respecting my courtship. About 6 o'clock I go to Madam Winthrop's; Sarah told me her mistress was gone out, but did not tell me whither she went. She presently ordered me a fire; so I went in, having Dr. Sibb's *Bowels* [4] with me to read. I read the two first sermons, still nobody came in: at last about 9 o'clock Mr. Jno. Eyre came in; I took the opportunity to say to him as I had done to Mrs. Noyes before, that I hoped my visiting his mother would not be disagreeable to him; he answered me with much respect. When 'twas after nine o'clock he of himself said he would go and call her, she was but at one of his brothers: awhile after I heard Madam Winthrop's voice, inquiring something about John. After a good while and clapping the garden door twice or thrice, she came in. I mentioned something of the lateness; she bantered me, and said I was later. She received me courteously. I asked when our proceedings should be made public. She said they were like to be no more public than they were already. Offered me no wine that I remember. I rose up at eleven o'clock to come away, saying I would put on my coat, She offered not to help me. I prayed her that Juno might light me home; she opened the shutter, and said 'twas pretty light abroad; Juno was weary and gone to bed. So I came home by star-light as well as I could. At my first coming in, I gave Sarah five shillings. I writ Mr. Eyre his name in his book with the date October 21, 1720. It cost me eight shillings. Jehovah jireh! [5] Madam told

me she had visited M. Mico, Wendell, and Wm. Clark of the South [Church].

October 22. Daughter Cooper visited me before my going out of town; stayed till about sunset. I brought her going near as far as the Orange Tree. [6] Coming back, near Leg's Corner, little David Jeffries saw me, and looking upon me very lovingly, asked me if I was going to see his grandmother? I said, Not tonight. Gave him a penny, and bid him present my service to his grandmother.

October 24. I went in the hackney coach through the common, stopped at Madam Winthrop's (had told her I would take my departure from thence). Sarah came to the door with Katee in her arms: but I did not think to take notice of the child. Called her mistress. I told her, being encouraged by David Jeffries' loving eyes, and sweet words, I was come to inquire whether she could find in her heart to leave that house and neighborhood, and go and dwell with me at the South-end; I think she said softly, Not yet. I told her it did not lie in my lands to keep a coach. If I should, I should be in danger to be brought to keep company with her Neighbor Brooker, (he was a little before sent to prison for debt). Told her I had an antipathy against those who would pretend to give themselves, but nothing of their estate. I would [7] a portion of my estate with myself. And I supposed she would do so. As to a periwig, my best and greatest Friend, I could not possibly have a greater, began to find me with hair before I was born, and had continued to do so ever since; and I could not find in my heart to go to another. She commended the book I gave her. Dr. Preston, *The Church's Marriage;* quoted him saying 'twas inconvenient keeping out of a fashion commonly used. [8] I said the time and tide did circumscribe my visit. She gave me a dram of black-cherry brandy, and gave me a lump of the sugar that was in it. She wished me a good journey. I prayed God to keep her, and came away. Had a very pleasant journey to Salem. . . .

November 2. Midweek, went again, and found Mrs. Alden there, who quickly went out. Gave her about a half pound of sugar almonds, cost three shillings per pound. Carried them on Monday. She seemed pleased with them, asked what they cost. Spake of giving her a hundred pounds per annum if I died before her. Asked her what sum she would give me, if she should die first? Said I would give her

---

[1] Madam Mico
[2] A vague, neutral word meaning act, deed; here, they had had but a hurried talk, not a deliberate conversation.
[3] bears appropriately
[4] The full title is *Bowels Opened: or A Discovery of the Union between Christ and the Church* by Dr. Sibb, a popular English Puritan minister of the time.
[5] *Genesis* xx, 14—"The Lord will provide."
[6] a tavern
[7] would [give]
[8] The Judge was opposed throughout his life to wearing wigs.

time to consider of it. She said she heard as if I had given all to my children by deeds of gift. I told her 'twas a mistake; Point-Judith was mine, etc. That in England, I owned, my father's desire was that it should go to my eldest son; 'twas £20 per annum; she thought 'twas forty. I think when I seem'd to excuse pressing this, she seemed to think 'twas best to speak of it; a long winter was coming on. Gave me a glass or two of canary.

Nov. 4. Friday. Went again about seven o'clock; found there Mr. John Walley and his wife: sat discoursing pleasantly. I showed them Isaac Moses's[1] writing. Madam W. served comfeits[2] to us. After awhile a table was spread, and supper was set. I urged Mr. Walley to crave a blessing; but he put it upon me. About nine they went away. I asked Madam what fashioned necklace I should present her with. She said, None at all. I asked here whereabout we left off last time; mentioned what I had offered to give her; asked her what she would give me; she said she could not change her condition; she had said so from the beginning; could not be so far from her children, the lecture.[3] Quoted the Apostle Paul affirming that a single life was better than a married. I answered, That was for the present distress.[4] She said she had not pleasure in things of that nature as formerly: I said, you are the fitter to make me a wife. If she held in that mind, I must go home and bewail my rashness in making more haste than good speed. However, considering the supper, I desired her to be within next Monday night, if we lived so long. Assented. She charged me with saying that she must put away Juno, if she came to me: I utterly denied it, it never came in my heart; yet she insisted upon it; saying it came in upon discourse about the Indian woman that obtained her freedom this court. About ten I said I would not disturb the good orders of her house, and came away. She not seeming pleased with my coming away. Spake to her about David Jeffries, had not seen him.

Monday, November 7th. My son prayed in the old chamber. Our time had been taken up by Son and Daughter Cooper's visit; so that I only read the 130th and 143d Psalm. 'Twas on account of my courtship. I went to Mad. Winthrop; found her rocking her little Katee in the cradle. I excused my coming so late (near eight). She set me an armed chair and cushion; and so the cradle was between her armed chair and mine. Gave her the remnant of my almonds; She did not eat of them as before; but laid them away; I said I came to inquire whether she had altered her mind since Friday, or remained of the same mind still. She said, Thereabouts. I told her I loved her, and was so fond as to think that she loved me: she said had a great respect for me. I told her, I had made her an offer, without asking any advice; she had so many to advise with, that 'twas a hindrance. The fire was come to one short brand besides the block, which brand was set up in end; at last it fell to pieces, and no recruit was made: she gave me a glass of wine. I think I repeated again that I would go home and bewail my rashness in making more haste than good speed. I would endeavor to contain myself, and not go on to solicit her to do that which she could not consent to. Took leave of her. As came down the steps she bid me have a care. Treated me courteously. Told her she had entered the fourth year of her widowhood. I had given her the *News-Letter* before: I did not bid her draw off her glove as sometime I had done. Her dress was not so clean as sometime it had been.[5] Jehovah jireh!

Midweek, November 9th. Dine at Brother Stoddard's: were so kind as to inquire of me if they should invite Madam Winthrop; I answered No. Thanked my Sister Stoddard for her courtesy; sat down at the table Simeon Stoddard, Esqr., Madam Stoddard, Samuel Sewall, Mr. Colman, Madam Colman, Mr. Cooper, Mrs. Cooper, Mrs. Hannah Cooper, Mr. Samuel Sewall of Brookline, Mrs. Sewall, Mr. Joseph Sewall, Mrs. Lydia Walley, Mr. William Stoddard. Had a noble treat. At night our meeting was at the Widow Belknap's. Gave each one of the meeting one of Mr. Homes's sermons, 12 in all; she sent her servant home with me with a lantern. Madam Winthrop's shutters were open as I passed by.

·   ·   ·   ·   ·   ·

About the middle of December Madam Winthrop made a treat for her children; Mr. Sewall, Prince, Willoughby: I knew nothing of it; but the same day abode in the council chamber for fear of the rain, and dined alone upon Kilby's pies and good beer.[6]

1673-1729   1882

---

[1] an Indian
[2] preserves (often candied fruits)
[3] The midweek lecture was delivered on Thursday afternoon. The sermon differed little from that of Sunday, but if anything was less formal.
1 Corinthians vii, 26

[5] Other passages, not here quoted, make the meaning clear. She did not dress herself so carefully for his calling as she had sometimes done.
[6] Judge Sewall married Mrs. Mary Gibbs, March 29, 1722.

WILLIAM BYRD 1674-1744

Colonel William Byrd is a striking example of the aristocratic, cultured southern gentleman of the eighteenth century. He was born and he died in the ancestral mansion now standing below Petersburg upon the James River. Byrd was educated in London, admitted to the English bar from the Middle Temple, traveled and studied on the Continent, receiving all the advantages then afforded a person of good birth and wealth. He was a member of the Royal Society to which he contributed a few papers. His life was spent in Virginia as a public official and man of affairs. He founded the cities of Petersburg and Richmond, and extended his estate until it reached some 180,000 acres. His manuscripts, all of them descriptive of the country, *History of the Dividing Line, A Journey to the Land of Eden,* and *A Progress to the Mines,* were published in 1841.

One cannot fail to contrast his view of life, interests, habits, aims, with those of his New England contemporaries. He was one of the wealthiest men in all the colonies, and he lived, as nearly as he could, the life of the English country gentleman. He was abundant in hospitality, free and engaging in manners, pleasure-loving by disposition, but had a keen eye to business. London was to him the center of culture and social enjoyment. His library of four thousand volumes, probably the largest private library in North America in the generation after Cotton Mather, was a well-balanced, carefully selected collection of the classics, and of the best English and Continental history, science, and literature. In urbanity and vivacity of style, Byrd shows a likeness to his friend and correspondent, Richard Steele.

Best edition: ed. John Spencer Bassett, 1901, with biographical and explanatory matter, and a catalogue of his library. Byrd's *Journey to the Land of Eden,* which includes most of the material in Bassett's edition, was edited by Mark Van Doren, 1928. See also J. Fiske, *Old Virginia and her Neighbors,* 1897.

From HISTORY OF THE DIVIDING LINE [1]

. . . .

March 12, [1728]. . . . Our landlord [2] had a tolerable good house and clean furniture, and yet we could not be tempted to lodge in it. We chose rather to lie in the open field, for fear of growing too tender. A clear sky, spangled with stars, was our canopy which, being the last thing we saw before we fell asleep, gave us magnificent dreams. The truth of it is, we took so much pleasure in that natural kind of lodging that I think at the foot of the account mankind are great losers by the luxury of feather-beds and warm apartments.

The curiosity of beholding so new and withal so sweet a method of encamping, brought one of the senators of North Carolina to make us a midnight visit. But he was so very clamorous in his commendations of it that the sentinel, not seeing his quality, [3] either through his habit or behavior, had like to have treated him roughly.

After excusing the unseasonableness of his visit, and letting us know he was a Parliament man, [4] he swore he was so taken with our lodging that he would set fire to his house as soon as he got home, and teach his wife and children to lie, like us, in the open field.

March 13. Early this morning our chaplain repaired to us with the men we had left at Mr. Wilson's. We had sent for them the evening before to relieve those who had the labor-oar [5] from Corotuck Inlet. But to our great surprise they petitioned not to be relieved, hoping to gain immortal reputation by being the first of mankind that ventured through the great Dismal. [6] But the rest being equally ambitious of the same honor, it was but fair to decide their pretensions by lot. After fortune had declared herself, those which she had excluded offered money to the happy persons to go in their stead. But Hercules would have as soon sold the glory of cleansing the Augean stables, [7] which was pretty near the same sort of work.

No sooner was the controversy at an end, but we sent them, unfortunate fellows, back to their quarters, whom chance had condemned to remain upon firm land and sleep in a whole skin. In the mean while the surveyors carried the line three miles, which was no contemptible day's work, considering how cruelly they were entangled with briars and gall bushes. The leaf of this last shrub bespeaks it to be of the *Alaternus* family.

Our work ended within a quarter of a mile of the Dismal above-mentioned, where the ground began to be already full of sunken holes and slashes, which had, here and there, some few reeds growing in them.

[1] Dispute having arisen between Virginia and Carolina concerning the line dividing the two colonies, commissioners from both sides, of whom Byrd was one, were appointed to accompany and oversee the actual work of the surveyors who ran the line 241 miles west from the sea, fixing its location permanently. This part of the diary records Byrd's experiences in executing the commission.

[2] The line had been started from the coast on March 7. The party was now camping at a planter's house some miles inland.

[3] official or social rank
[4] The colonial legislator, apparently tipsy, assumed the title usually applied to a member of the British Parliament. [5] brunt of the work
[6] Dismal Swamp: see any map.
[7] One of the twelve labors of Hercules was to cleanse the stables of King Augeas where three thousand oxen had been stalled for thirty years.

'Tis hardly credible how little the bordering inhabitants were acquainted with this mighty swamp, notwithstanding they had lived their whole lives within smell of it. Yet, as great strangers as they were to it, they pretended to be very exact in their account of its dimensions, and were positive it could not be above seven or eight miles wide, but knew no more of the matter than star-gazers know of the distance of the fixed stars. At the same time, they were simple enough to amuse our men with idle stories of the lions, panthers, and alligators they were like to encounter in that dreadful place.

In short, we saw plainly there was no intelligence of this *terra incognita* [1] to be got, but from our own experience. For that reason it was resolved to make the requisite dispositions to enter it next morning. We allotted every one of the surveyors for this painful enterprise with twelve men to attend them. Fewer than that could not be employed in clearing the way, carrying the chain, marking the trees, and bearing the necessary bedding and provisions. Nor would the commissioners themselves have spared their persons on this occasion, but for fear of adding to the poor men's burthen, while they were certain they could add nothing to their resolution. . . . . .

March 14. Before nine of the clock this morning, the provisions, bedding, and other necessaries were made up into packs for the men to carry on their shoulders into the Dismal. They were victualed for eight days at full allowance, nobody doubting but that would be abundantly sufficient to carry them through that inhospitable place; nor indeed was it possible for the poor fellows to stagger under more. As it was, their loads weighed from 60 to 70 pounds, in just proportion to the strength of those who were to bear them.

'Twould have been unconscionable to have saddled them with burthens heavier than that, when they were to lug them through a filthy bog which was hardly practicable with no burthen at all. Besides this luggage at their backs, they were obliged to measure the distance, mark the trees, and clear the way for the surveyors every step they went. It was really a pleasure to see with how much cheerfulness they undertook, and with how much spirit they went through all this drudgery. For their greater safety, the commissioners took care to furnish them with Peruvian bark, rhubarb, and hipocoacanah, [2] in case they might happen, in that wet journey, to be taken with fevers or fluxes.

Although there was no need of example to inflame persons already so cheerful, yet, to enter the people with better grace, the author and two more of the commissioners accompanied them half a mile into the Dismal. The skirts of it were thinly planted with dwarf reeds and gall-bushes but, when we got into the Dismal itself, we found the reeds grew there much taller and closer and, to mend the matter, was so interlaced with bamboo-briars that there was no scuffling through them without the help of pioneers. At the same time, we found the ground moist and trembling under our feet like a quagmire, insomuch that it was an easy matter to run a ten-foot pole up to the head in it, without exerting any uncommon strength to do it.

Two of the men, whose burthens were the least cumbersome, had orders to march before with their tomahawks and clear the way, in order to make an opening for the surveyors. By their assistance we made a shift to push the line half a mile in three hours, and then reached a small piece of firm land about 100 yards wide standing up above the rest like an island. Here the people were glad to lay down their loads and take a little refreshment, while the happy man whose lot it was to carry the jug of rum began already, like Aesop's bread-carriers, [3] to find it grow a good deal lighter.

After reposing about an hour, the commissioners recommended vigor and constancy to their fellow-travelers, by whom they were answered with three cheerful huzzas in token of obedience. This ceremony was no sooner over but they took up their burthens and attended the motion of the surveyors who, though they worked with all their might, could reach but one mile farther, the same obstacles still attending them which they had met with in the morning.

However small this distance may seem to such as are used to travel at their ease, yet our poor men, who were obliged to work with an unwieldy load at their backs, had reason to think it a long way; especially in a bog where they had no firm footing, but every step made a deep impression, which was instantly filled with water. At the same time they were laboring with their hands to cut down the reeds, which were ten feet high, their legs were hampered with the briars. Besides, the weather happened to be very warm, and the tallness of the reeds

---

[1] unknown land
[2] ipecacuanha

[3] Aesop on asking for the lightest burden, and on being told to choose, chose the bread, the heaviest of all. He was laughed at. But at dinner he distributed to his fellow-servants half the bread, and at supper the remainder. During the rest of the journey Aesop carried only the empty basket.

kept off every friendly breeze from coming to refresh them. And, indeed, it was a little provoking to hear the wind whistling among the branches of the white cedars, which grew here and there amongst the reeds, and at the same time not have the comfort to feel the least breath of it.

In the mean time the three commissioners returned out of the Dismal the same way they went in and, having joined their brethren, proceeded that night as far as Mr. Wilson's.

This worthy person lives within sight of the Dismal, in the skirts whereof his stocks range and maintain themselves all the winter, and yet he knew as little of it as he did of *Terra Australis Incognita.*[1] He told us a Canterbury tale[2] of a North Briton whose curiosity spurred him a long way into this great desert, as he called it, near 20 years ago, but he having no compass, nor seeing the sun for several days together, wandered about till he was almost famished; but at last he bethought himself of a secret his countrymen make use of to pilot themselves in a dark day.

He took a fat louse out of his collar and exposed it to the open day on a piece of white paper which he brought along with him for his journal. The poor insect, having no eye-lids, turned himself about till he found the darkest part of the heavens, and so made the best of his way towards the north. By this direction he steered himself safe out, and gave such a frightful account of the monsters he saw and the distresses he underwent, that no mortal since has been hardy enough to go upon the like dangerous discovery.

March 15. The surveyors pursued their work with all diligence, but still found the soil of the Dismal so spongy that the water oozed up into every footstep they took. To their sorrow, too, they found the reeds and briars more firmly interwoven than they did the day before. But the greatest grievance was from large cypresses which the wind had blown down and heaped upon one another. On the limbs of most of them grew sharp snags, pointing every way like so many pikes, that required much pains and caution to avoid.

.   .   .   .   .   .

March 25. . . . In the mean time, we who stayed behind had nothing to do but to make the best observations we could upon that part of the country. The soil of our landlord's plan-

tation, though none of the best, seemed more fertile than any thereabouts, where the ground is near as sandy as the deserts of Africa, and consequently barren. The road leading from thence to Edenton, being in distance about 27 miles, lies upon a ridge called Sandy Ridge, which is so wretchedly poor that it will not bring potatoes.

The pines in this part of the country are of a different species from those that grow in Virginia: their bearded leaves are much longer and their cones much larger. Each cell contains a seed of the size and figure of a black-eyed pea, which, shedding in November, is very good mast for hogs, and fattens them in a short time.

The smallest of these pines are full of cones, which are eight or nine inches long, and each affords commonly 60 or 70 seeds. This kind of mast has the advantage of all other by being more constant, and less liable to be nipped by the frost or eaten by the caterpillars. The trees also abound more with turpentine, and consequently yield more tar than either the yellow or the white pine; and for the same reason make more durable timber for building. The inhabitants hereabouts pick up knots of lightwood in abundance, which they burn into tar, and then carry it to Norfolk or Nansimond for a market. The tar made in this method is the less valuable because it is said to burn the cordage, though it is full as good for all other uses as that made in Sweden and Muscovy.

Surely there is no place in the world where the inhabitants live with less labor than in North Carolina. It approaches nearer to the description of Lubberland[3] than any other, by the great felicity of the climate, the easiness of raising provisions, and the slothfulness of the people.

Indian corn is of so great increase that a little pains will subsist a very large family with bread, and then they may have meat without any pains at all, by the help of the low grounds, and the great variety of mast that grows on the high-land. The men for their parts, just like the Indians, impose all the work upon the poor women. They make their wives rise out of their beds early in the morning, at the same time that they lie and snore till the sun has run one third of his course and dispersed all the unwholesome damps. Then, after stretching and yawning for half an hour, they light their pipes, and, under the protection of a cloud of smoke, venture out into the open air; though,

[1] unknown southern land
[2] Cock-and-bull story; a humorous tale like Chaucer's *Canterbury Tales;* this tale and another following show Byrd's fashionable London dislike of the Scotch.

[3] A general colloquial term for a sluggard's paradise; local colonial jealousies caused much ill blood, even political danger, till long after the Revolution.

if it happens to be never so little cold, they quickly return shivering into the chimney corner. When the weather is mild, they stand leaning with both their arms upon the cornfield fence, and gravely consider whether they had best go and take a small heat at the hoe: but generally find reasons to put it off till another time.

Thus they loiter away their lives, like Solomon's sluggard,[1] with their arms across, and at the winding up of the year scarcely have bread to eat.

To speak the truth, 'tis a thorough aversion to labor that makes people file off to North Carolina, where plenty and a warm sun confirm them in their disposition to laziness for their whole lives.

March 26. Since we were like to be confined to this place till the people returned out of the Dismal, 'twas agreed that our chaplain might safely take a turn to Edenton to preach the gospel to the infidels there, and christen their children. He was accompanied thither by Mr. Little, one of the Carolina commissioners, who, to show his regard for the church, offered to treat him on the road with a fricassee of rum. They fried half a dozen rashers of very fat bacon in a pint of rum both which, being dished up together, served the company at once for meat and drink.

Most of the rum they get in this country comes from New England and is so bad and unwholesome that it is not improperly called "kill-devil." It is distilled there from foreign molasses which, if skilfully managed, yields near gallon for gallon. Their molasses comes from the same country, and has the name of "long sugar" in Carolina, I suppose from the ropiness of it, and serves all the purposes of sugar both in their eating and drinking.

When they entertain their friends bountifully, they fail not to set before them a capacious bowl of Bombo,[2] so called from the admiral of that name. This is a compound of rum and water in equal parts, made palatable with the said long sugar. As good humor begins to flow and the bowl to ebb, they take care to replenish it with sheer rum, of which there always is a reserve under the table. But such generous doings happen only when that balsam of life is plenty; for they have often such melancholy times that neither Land-graves nor

Cassicks[3] can procure one drop for their wives when they lie in, or are troubled with the colic or vapors. Very few in this country have the industry to plant orchards which, in a dearth of rum, might supply them with much better liquor.

.   .   .   .

November 11.[4] [1728] We had all been so refreshed by our day of rest that we decamped earlier than ordinary, and passed the several fords of Hico River. The woods were thick great part of this day's journey, so that we were forced to scuffle hard to advance seven miles, being equal in fatigue to double that distance of clear and open grounds.

We took up our quarters upon Sugar-tree Creek, in the same camp we had lain in when we came up, and happened to be entertained at supper with a rarity we had never had the fortune to meet with before during the whole expedition.

A little wide of this creek, one of the men had the luck to meet with a young buffalo of two years old. It was a bull which, notwithstanding he was no older, was as big as an ordinary ox. His legs are very thick and very short, and his hoofs exceeding broad. His back rose into a kind of bunch a little above the shoulders, which I believe contributes not a little to that creature's enormous strength. His body is vastly deep from the shoulders to the brisket, sometimes six feet in those that are full grown. The portly figure of this animal is disgraced by a shabby little tail, not above 12 inches long. This he cocks up on end whenever he's in a passion and, instead of lowing or bellowing, grunts with no better grace than a hog.

The hair growing on his head and neck is long and shagged, and so soft that it will spin into thread not unlike mohair, which might be wove into a sort of camlet.[5] Some people have stockings knit of it that would have served an Israelite during his forty years' march through the wilderness.

Its horns are short and strong, of which the Indians make large spoons, which they say will

---

[1] *Proverbs* xix, 24

[2] According to Tobias Smollett, in *Roderick Random*, the liquor is made of rum, sugar, water, and nutmeg. Compare the amusing and important part "Kill-devil Bombo" plays in Owen Wister's *Lady Baltimore*.

[3] Officials of the upper house of the Carolina legislature, and landed proprietors, held these titles of aristocracy as provided by the constitution formed for the colony by John Locke. The separation between the Carolinas was not made till the year following this diary.

[4] After about six weeks' work, "because the rattlesnakes began to crawl out of their winter quarters, and might grow dangerous to the men and their horses, it was determined to proceed no further with the line till fall." The work was resumed in September, and by November 11 had reached high, rolling ground.

[5] an Eastern fabric, perhaps made of camel's hair

split and fall to pieces whenever poison is put into them. Its color is a dirty brown, and its hide so thick that it is scarce penetrable. However, it makes very spongy sole leather by the ordinary method of tanning, though this fault might by good contrivance be mended.

As thick as this poor beast's hide was, a bullet made shift to enter it and fetch him down. It was found all alone, though buffaloes seldom are. They usually range about in herds, like other cattle, and, though they differ something in figure, are certainly of the same species. There are two reasons for this opinion: the flesh of both has exactly the same taste, and the mixed breed betwixt both, they say, will generate. All the difference I could perceive between the flesh of buffalo and common beef was that the flesh of the first was much yellower than that of the other, and the lean something tougher.

The men were so delighted with this new diet, that the gridiron and frying-pan had no more rest all night than a poor husband subject to curtain lectures. Buffaloes may be easily tamed when they are taken young. The best way to catch them is to carry a milch mare into the woods and, when you find a cow and a calf, to kill the cow and then, having catched the calf, to suckle it upon the mare. After once or twice sucking her, it will follow her home and become as gentle as another calf.

If we could get into a breed of them, they might be made very useful not only for the dairy by giving an ocean of milk, but also for drawing vast and cumbersome weights by their prodigious strength. These with the other advantages I mentioned before, would make this sort of cattle more profitable to the owner than any other we are acquainted with, though they would need a world of provender.[1]

1728 1841

. . . . . .

From A PROGRESS TO THE MINES[2]
IN THE YEAR 1732

September 18. For the pleasure of the good company of Mrs. Byrd and her little governor, my son,[3] I went about half way to the falls[4]

in the chariot. There we halted, not far from a purling stream, and upon the stump of a propagate oak picked the bones of a piece of roast beef. By the spirit which that gave me, I was the better able to part with the dear companions of my travels, and to perform the rest of my journey on horseback by myself. I reached Shaccoa's[5] before two o'clock, and crossed the river to the mills. I had the grief to find them both stand as still for the want of water, as a dead woman's tongue for want of breath. It had rained so little for many weeks above the falls, that the Naiades[6] had hardly water enough left to wash their faces. However, as we ought to turn all our misfortunes to the best advantage, I directed Mr. Booker, my first minister[7] there, to make use of the lowness of the water for blowing up the rocks at the mouth of the canal. For that purpose I ordered iron drills to be made about two foot long, pointed with steel, chisel-fashion, in order to make holes, into which we put our cartridges of powder, containing each about three ounces. There wanted skill among my engineers to choose the best parts of the stone for boring, that we might blow to the most advantage. They made all their holes quite perpendicular, whereas they should have humored the grain of the stone for the more effectual execution. I ordered the points of the drills to be made chisel way, rather than the diamond, that they might need to be seldomer repaired, though in stone the diamond points would make the most dispatch. The water now flowed out of the river so slowly that the miller was obliged to pond it up in the canal by setting open the flood-gates at the mouth, and shutting those close at the mill. By this contrivance, he was able at any time to grind two or three bushels, either for his choice customers or for the use of my plantations. Then I walked to the place where they broke[8] the flax, which is wrought with much greater ease than the hemp, and is much better for spinning. From thence I paid a visit to the weaver, who needed a little of Minerva's inspiration[9] to make the most of a piece of fine cloth. Then I looked in upon my Caledonian spinster,[10] who was mended more in her looks than in her humor. However, she promised much, though at the same time

[1] The American bison at this time extended from Tennessee to the Great Slave Lake, and from Oregon to western New York.
[2] situated in Orange and Spottsylvania Counties, Virginia, on or near the Rapidan and Rappahannock Rivers
[3] afterwards a fellow officer of Washington in the defense of Virginia in the French and Indian War
[4] Falls of the James at the site of Richmond; large tracts of land in this vicinity had descended to the Colonel from his father.

[5] At the site of Richmond; a year later Byrd planned the town there, and one at Petersburg.
[6] guardian spirits of brooks and springs
[7] jocularly used: overseer
[8] broke the woody part of the flax stalk from the fiber
[9] Minerva, goddess of wisdom, particularly presided over spinning and weaving.
[10] Scotch woman, perhaps a spinster in both senses of the word: spinner, and unmarried woman

intended to perform little. She is too high-spirited for Mr. Booker, who hates to have his sweet temper ruffled, and will rather suffer matters to go a little wrong sometimes than give his righteous spirit any uneasiness. He is very honest, and would make an admirable over-seer where servants will do as they are bid. But eye-servants,[1] who want abundance of overlooking, are not so proper to be committed to his care. I found myself out of order, and for that reason retired early; yet with all this precaution had a gentle fever in the night, but towards morning nature sat open all her gates, and drove it out in a plentiful perspiration. . . .

Sept. 20. . . . I parted there with my in-tendant,[2] and pursued my journey to Mr. Ran-dolph's, at Tuckahoe, without meeting with any adventure by the way. Here I found Mrs. Fleming, who was packing up her baggage with design to follow her husband the next day, who was gone to a new settlement in Goochland.[3] Both he and she have been about seven years persuading themselves to remove to that retired part of the country, though they had the two strong arguments of health and interest for so doing. The widow[4] smiled graciously upon me, and entertained me very handsomely. Here I learned all the tragical story of her daughter's humble marriage with her uncle's overseer. Be-sides the meanness of this mortal's aspect, the man has not one visible qualification, except impudence, to recommend him to a female's inclinations. But there is sometimes such a charm in that Hibernian endowment that frail woman can't withstand it, though it stand alone without any other recommendation. Had she run away with a gentleman or a pretty fellow, there might have been some excuse for her, though he were of inferior fortune: but to stoop to a dirty plebian without any kind of merit is the lowest prostitution. I found the family justly enraged at it; and though I had more good nature than to join in her condemnation, yet I could devise no excuse for so sense-less a prank as this young gentlewoman had played. . . .

Sept. 21. I was sorry in the morning to find myself stopped in my career by bad weather brought upon us by a north-east wind. This drives a world of raw unkindly vapors upon us from Newfoundland, loaden with blight, coughs, and pleurisies. However, I complained not, lest I might be suspected to be tired of the good company; though Mrs. Fleming was not so much upon her guard, but mutinied

strongly at the rain, that hindered her from pursuing her dear husband. I said what I could to comfort a gentlewoman under so sad a disappointment. I told her a husband that stayed so much at home as hers did, could be no such violent rarity as for a woman to ven-ture her precious health to go daggling through the rain after him, or to be miserable if she hap-pened to be prevented. That it was prudent for married people to fast sometimes from one another, that they might come together again with the better stomach. That the best things in this world, if constantly used, are apt to be cloying, which a little absence would prevent. This was strange doctrine to a fond female, who fancies people should love with as little reason after marriage as before. . . .

September 22. We had another wet day to try both Mrs. Fleming's patience and my good breeding. The northeast wind commonly sticks by us three or four days, filling the atmosphere with damps injurious both to man and beast. The worst of it was, we had no good liquor to warm our blood and fortify our spirits against so strong a malignity. However, I was cheerful under all these misfortunes, and expressed no concern but a decent fear lest my long visit might be troublesome. Since I was like to have thus much leisure, I endeavored to find out what subject a dull married man could intro-duce that might best bring the widow to the use of her tongue. At length I discovered she was a notable quack, and therefore paid that regard to her knowledge as to put some ques-tions to her about the bad distemper that raged then in the country. I mean the bloody flux, that was brought us in the negro-ship consigned to Col. Braxton. She told me she made use of very simple remedies in that case with very good success. She did the business either with hartshorn drink, that had plantain leaves boiled in it, or else with a strong decoction of St. An-drews cross[5] in new milk instead of water. I agreed with her that those remedies might be very good, but would be more effectual after a dose or two of Indian physic. But for fear this conversation might be too grave for a widow, I turned the discourse and began to talk of plays; and finding her taste lay most towards comedy, I offered my service to read one to her, which she kindly accepted. She produced the second part of the *Beggars' Opera*,[6] which had

---

[1] those who will work only under the eye of the master
[2] overseer
[3] Goochland County perpetuates the name.
[4] Byrd does not tell who she is.
[5] a medicinal herb, *Ascyrum hypericoides*
[6] Byrd means that it was the first part of the poet Gay's *Beggars' Opera*, that had run for 40 (really 60) nights in London. The second part, named *Polly* from one of the characters in the first, was pro-hibited upon the stage because of its supposed political bias. The Duchess of Queensbury, an enthusiastic patroness of Gay, solicited subscrip-

diverted the Town for 40 nights successively, and gained four thousand pounds to the author. This was not owing altogether to the wit or humor that sparkled in it, but to some political reflections that seemed to hit the ministry. But the great advantage of the author was, that his interest was solicited by the Duchess of Queensbury, which no man could refuse who had but half an eye in his head, or half a guinea in his pocket. Her Grace, like death, spared nobody, but even took my Lord Selkirk [1] in for two guineas, to repair which extravagance he lived upon Scots herrings two months afterwards. But the best story was, she made a very smart [2] officer in His Majesty's guards give her a guinea, who, swearing at the same time 'twas all he had in the world, she sent him fifty for it the next day, to reward his obedience. After having acquainted my company with the history of the play, I read three acts of it, and left Mrs. Fleming and Mr. Randolph to finish it, who read as well as most actors do at a rehearsal. Thus we killed the time, and triumphed over the bad weather.

. . . . . .

September 27. . . . I took my leave about ten, and drove over a spacious level road ten miles to a bridge built over the river Po, which is one of the four branches of Matopany, about 40 yards wide. Two miles beyond that, we passed by a plantation belonging to the company, of about 500 acres, where they keep a great number of oxen to relieve those that have dragged their loaded carts thus far. Three miles farther we came to the Germanna road, where I quitted the chair, [3] and continued my journey on horseback. I rode eight miles together over a stony road, and had on either side continual poisoned fields, with nothing but saplings growing on them. Then I came into the main county road that leads from Fredericksburgh to Germanna, which last place I reached in ten miles more. This famous town consists of Colonel Spotswood's [4] enchanted castle on one side of the street, and a baker's dozen of ruinous tenements on the other, where so many German families had dwelt some years ago; but are now removed ten miles higher, in the fork of Rappahannock, to land of their own. There had also been a chapel about a bow-shot from the Colonel's house, at the end of an avenue of cherry trees; but some pious people had lately burnt it down with the intent to get another built nearer to their own homes. Here I arrived about three o'clock, and found only Mrs. Spotswood at home, who received her old acquaintance with many a gracious smile. I was carried into a room elegantly set off with pier glasses, the largest of which came soon after to an odd misfortune. Amongst other favorite animals that cheered this lady's solitude, a brace of tame deer ran familiarly about the house, and one of them came to stare at me as a stranger. But unluckily spying his own figure in the glass, he made a spring over the tea table that stood under it, and shattered the glass to pieces and, falling back upon the tea table, made a terrible fracas among the china. This exploit was so sudden, and accompanied with such a noise, that it surprised me, and perfectly frightened Mrs. Spotswood. But 'twas worth all the damage to show the moderation and good humor with which she bore this disaster. In the evening the noble Colonel came home from his mines, who saluted me very civilly; and Mrs. Spotswood's sister, Miss Theky, who had been to meet him *en cavalier,* [5] was so kind too as to bid me welcome. We talked over a legend [6] of old stories, supped about nine, and then prattled with the ladies till 'twas time for a traveler to retire. In the mean time I observed my old friend to be very uxorious and exceedingly fond of his children. This was so opposite to the maxims he used to preach up before he was married, that I could not forbear rubbing up the memory of them. But he gave a very good-natured turn to his change of sentiments by alleging that whoever brings a poor gentlewoman into so solitary a place, from all her friends and acquaintance, would be ungrateful not to use her and all that belongs to her with all possible tenderness.

September 28. We all kept snug in our several apartments till nine, except Miss Theky, who was the housewife of the family. At that hour we met over a pot of coffee, which was not quite strong enough to give us the palsy. After breakfast the Colonel and I left the ladies to their domestic affairs and took a turn in the garden, which has nothing beautiful but three

---

tions even in the royal palace to an edition of *Polly* at a guinea each, and for her partisanship was dismissed from the court. It is interesting to see how closely these Virginians followed London, "The Town," and were alive to the incidents of its gay life that have passed into the literary history of England. Imagine such interest on the part of the Puritan aristocracy of Boston!

[1] a Scotchman; a characteristic English thrust at alleged Scotch penuriousness

[2] finely dressed

[3] Sedan chairs were then sometimes used for rather extensive journeys.

[4] Colonel Spotswood, British army officer and governor of Virginia from 1710-1722, was a prominent figure in the development of Virginia. This residence, built in a wide loop of the Rapidan, commanded a fine view of the country. The local name Germanna Mills remained over a century.

[5] on horseback

[6] It is possible Byrd means legion.

terrace walks that fall in slopes one below another. I let him understand that. besides the
pleasure of paying him a visit, I came to be
instructed by so great a master in the mystery
of making of iron wherein he had led the way,
and was the Tubal Cain [1] of Virginia. He corrected me a little there, by assuring me he was
not only the first in this country, but the first in
North America, who had erected a regular furnace. That they ran altogether upon bloom-
eries [2] in New England and Pennsylvania till
his example had made them attempt greater
works. But, in this last colony, they have so
few ships to carry their iron to Great Britain
that they must be content to make it only for
their own use, and must be obliged to manufacture it when they have done. That he hoped he
had done the country very great service by
setting so good an example. That the four furnaces now at work in Virginia circulated a great
sum of money for provisions and all other necessaries in the adjacent counties. That they took
off a great number of hands from planting tobacco, and employed them in works that produced a large sum of money in England to the
persons concerned, whereby the country is so
much the richer. That they are besides a considerable advantage to Great Britain, because
it lessens the quantity of bar iron imported
from Spain, Holland, Sweden, Denmark and
Muscovy, which used to be no less than 20,000
tons yearly; though at the same time no sow
iron is imported thither from any country but
only from the plantations. For most of this
bar iron they do not only pay silver, but our
friends in the Baltic are so nice, they even
expect to be paid all in crown pieces. On the
contrary, all the iron they receive from the
plantations they pay for it in their own manufactures, and send for it in their own shipping.
Then I inquired after his own mines and hoped,
as he was the first that engaged in this great
undertaking, that he had brought them to the
most perfection. He told me he had iron in
several parts of his great tract of land consisting of 45,000 acres, but that the mine he
was at work upon was thirteen miles below
Germanna. That his ore (which was very rich)
he raised a mile from his furnace, and was
obliged to cart the iron, when it was made,
fifteen miles to Massaponux, a plantation he had
upon Rappahannock River; [3] but that the road

was exceeding good, gently declining all the
way, and had no more than one hill to go up in
the whole journey. For this reason his loaded
carts went it in a day without difficulty. He
said it was true his works were of the oldest
standing: but that his long absence in England,
and the wretched management of Mr. Greame,
whom he had entrusted with his affairs, had put
him back very much. That what with neglect
and severity, above 80 of his slaves were lost
while he was in England, and most of his cattle
starved. That his furnace stood still great
part of the time, and all his plantations ran to
ruin. That indeed he was rightly served for
committing his affairs to the care of a mathematician whose thoughts were always among
the stars. That, nevertheless, since his return
he had applied himself to rectify his steward's
mistakes and bring his business again into order.
That now he had contrived to do everything
with his own people except raising the mine [4]
and running the iron, by which he had contracted his expense very much. Nay, he believed that by his directions he could bring
sensible negroes to perform those parts of the
work tolerably well. But at the same time he
gave me to understand that his furnace had
done no great feats lately, because he had been
taken up in building an air furnace at Massaponux which he had now brought to perfection,
and should be thereby able to furnish the whole
country with all sorts of cast iron as cheap and
as good as ever came from England. I told him
he must do one thing more to have a full vent [5]
for those commodities; he must keep a shallop [6]
running into all the rivers, to carry his wares
home to people's own doors. And, if he would
do that, I would set a good example and take
of a whole ton of them. Our conversation on
this subject continued till dinner, which was
both elegant and plentiful. The afternoon was
devoted to the ladies, who showed me one of
their most beautiful walks. They conducted
me through a shady lane to the landing, and by
the way made me drink some very fine water
that issued from a marble fountain and ran incessantly. Just behind it was a covered bench,
where Miss Theky often sat and bewailed her
virginity. Then we proceeded to the river,
which is the south branch of Rappahanock,
about 50 yards wide, and so rapid that the ferry
boat is drawn over by a chain, and therefore
called the Rapidan. At night we drank prosperity to all the Colonel's projects in a bowl of

[1] The first worker in iron; see *Genesis* iv, 22.
[2] mills for producing wrought iron directly from the
ore without the process of transforming it from
cast iron
[3] There is a confusion in places here hard to reconcile
with modern, or even eighteenth century maps.

[4] ore
[5] sale, market
[6] a boat for shallow water navigation

rack punch, [1] and then retired to our devotions.

September 29. Having employed about two hours in retirement, I sallied out at the first summons to breakfast where our conversation with the ladies, like whip sillabub, [2] was very pretty, but had nothing in it. This it seems was Miss Theky's birthday, upon which I made her my compliments, and wished she might live twice as long a married woman as she had lived a maid. I did not presume to pry into the secret of her age, nor was she forward to disclose it for this humble reason, lest I should think her wisdom fell short of her years. . . . Then the Colonel and I took another turn in the garden, to discourse farther on the subject of iron. He was very frank in communicating all his dear-bought experience to me, and told me very civilly he would not only let me into the whole secret, but would make a journey to James River and give me his faithful opinion of all my conveniences. [3] For his part he wished there were many more iron works in the country, provided the parties concerned would preserve a constant harmony among themselves, and meet and consult frequently what might be for their common advantage. By this they might be better able to manage the workmen, and reduce their wages to what was just and reasonable. After this frank speech, he began to explain the whole charge of an iron-work. He said there ought at least to be an hundred negroes employed in it, and those upon good land would make corn, and raise provisions enough to support themselves and the cattle, and do every other part of the business. That the furnace might be built for £700 and made ready to go to work, if I went the nearest way to do it, especially, since coming after so many, I might correct their errors and avoid their miscarriages. That if I had ore and wood enough, and a convenient stream of water to set the furnace upon, having neither too much nor too little water, I might undertake the affair with a full assurance of success; provided the distance of carting be not too great, which is exceedingly burdensome. That there must be abundance of wheel carriages, shod with iron, and several teams of oxen, provided to transport the wood that is to be coaled, [4] and afterwards the coal and ore to the furnace, and last of all the sow iron to the nearest water carriage, and carry back limestone and other necessaries from thence to the works; and a

sloop also would be useful to carry the iron on board the ships, the masters not being always in the humor to fetch it. Then he enumerated the people that were to be hired, viz.: a founder, a mine-raiser, [5] a collier, a stock-taker, a clerk, a smith, a carpenter, a wheelwright, and several carters. That these altogether will be a standing charge of about £500 a year. That the amount of freight, custom, commission and other charges in England, comes to 27 shillings a ton. But that the merchants yearly find out means to inflame the account with new articles, [6] as they do in those of tobacco. That, upon the whole matter, the expenses here and in England may be computed modestly at £3 a ton. And the rest that the iron sells for will be clear gain, to pay for the land and negroes, which 'tis to be hoped will be £3 more for every ton that is sent over. As this account agreed pretty near with that which Mr. Chiswell had given me, I set it down (notwithstanding it may seem a repetition of the same thing) to prove that both these gentlemen were sincere in their representations. We had a Michaelmas goose for dinner, of Miss Theky's own raising. . . . In the afternoon we walked in a meadow by the river side, which winds in the form of a horseshoe about Germanna, making it a peninsula containing about 400 acres. Rappahanock forks about fourteen miles below this place, the northern branch being the larger, and consequently must be the river that bounds my Lord Fairfax's grant of the northern neck.

September 30. The sun rose clear this morning and so did I, and finished all my little affairs by breakfast. It was then resolved to wait on the ladies on horseback, since the bright sun, the fine air, and the wholesome exercise all invited us to it. We forded the river a little above the ferry and rode six miles up the neck to a fine level piece of rich land where we found about twenty plants of ginseng, [7] with the scarlet berries growing on the top of the middle stalk. The root of this is of wonderful virtue in many cases, particularly to raise the spirits and promote perspiration, which makes it a specific in colds and coughs. The Colonel complimented me with all we found, in return for my telling him the virtues of it. We were all pleased to find so much of this king of plants so near the Colonel's habitation and growing, too, upon his own land; but were, however, surprised to find it upon level ground after we had been told it grew only upon the north side

[1] strictly, punch made with arrack, a liquor distilled from the cocoa palm
[2] wine, ale, or cider whipped with cream
[3] facilities, natural resources
[4] burned into charcoal

[5] skilled mechanic to oversee the hoisting of the ore (?)
[6] increase the account with new stipulations
[7] a plant with an aromatic root much valued as a drug

of stony mountains. I carried home this treasure with as much joy as if every root had been a graft of the tree of life, and washed and dried it carefully. This airing made us hungry as so many hawks so that, between appetite and a very good dinner, 'twas difficult to eat like a philosopher. In the afternoon the ladies walked me about amongst all their little animals, with which they amuse themselves and furnish the table; the worst of it is, they are so tender-hearted they shed a silent tear every time any of them are killed. At night the Colonel and I quitted the threadbare subject of iron, and changed the scene to politics. He told me the Ministry [1] had receded from their demand upon New England to raise a standing salary for all succeeding governors, for fear some curious members of the House of Commons should inquire how the money was disposed of that had been raised in the other American colonies for the support of their governors. And particularly what becomes of the four and one half per cent. paid in the sugar colonies for that purpose. That duty produces near £20,000 a year; but, being remitted into the exchequer, not one of the West India governors is paid out of it; but they, like falcons, are let loose upon the people, who are complaisant enough to settle other revenues upon them, to the great impoverishing of these colonies. In the mean time, 'tis certain the money raised by the four and one half per cent. molders away between the minister's fingers, nobody knows how, like the quitrents [2] of Virginia. And 'tis for this reason that the instructions forbidding all governors to accept of any presents from their assemblies are dispensed with in the Sugar Islands, [3] while 'tis strictly insisted upon everywhere else, where the assemblies were so wise as to keep their revenues among themselves. He said further that, if the assembly in New England would stand bluff, [4] he did not see how they could be forced to raise money against their will; for if they should direct it to be done by act of Parliament, which they have threatened to do, (though it be against the right of Englishmen to be taxed but by their representatives,) yet they would find it no easy matter to put such an act in execution. Then the Colonel read me a lecture upon tar, affirming that it can't be made in this warm climate after the manner they make it in Sweden and Muscovy, by barking the tree two yards from the ground, whereby the turpentine descends all into the stump in a year's time, which is then split in pieces in order for the kiln. But here the sun fries out the turpentine in the branches of the tree, when the leaves are dried, and hinders it from descending. But, on the contrary, those who burn tar of lightwood in the common way, and are careful about it, make as good as that which comes from the east country, nor will it burn the cordage more than that does. Then we entered upon the subject of hemp, which the Colonel told me he never could raise here from foreign seed, but at last sowed the seed of wild hemp, (which is very common in the upper parts of the country) and that came up very thick. That he sent about 500 pounds of it to England, and that the Commissioners of the Navy, after a full trial of it, reported to the Lords of the Admiralty that it was equal in goodness to the best that comes from Riga. [5] I told him if our hemp were never so good it would not be worth the making here, even though they should continue the bounty. And my reason was, because labor is not more than two pence a day in the east country where they produce hemp, and here we can't compute it at less than ten pence which, being five times as much as their labor, and considering besides that our freight is three times as dear as theirs, the price that will make them rich will ruin us, as I have found by woful experience. Besides, if the King, who must have the refusal, [6] buys our hemp, the navy is so long in paying both the price and the bounty that we who live from hand to mouth can't afford to wait so long for it. And then our good friends, the merchants, load it with so many charges that they run away with great part of the profit themselves. Just like the bald eagle which, after the fishing hawk has been at great pains to catch a fish, pounces upon and takes it from him. Our conversation was interrupted by a summons to supper, for the ladies, to show their power, had by this time brought us tamely to go to bed with our bellies full, though we both at first declared positively against it. So very pliable a thing is frail man when women have the bending of him.

·   ·   ·   ·   ·   ·   ·

1732   1841

[1] the English ministry
[2] sums paid to an over-lord or a government in lieu of services that might otherwise be demanded
[3] probably the sugar producing islands of the West Indies, in the commerce of which all the colonies were greatly interested
[4] firm
[5] a Baltic port noted for its trade in hemp
[6] in trade, the right of first buying, or refusing to buy, a commodity

JONATHAN EDWARDS
1703-1758

Just a generation later than Cotton Mather, Edwards was even greater as a pulpit orator than his predecessor, and far outreached him in creative genius. He was born at East Windsor, Connecticut, of an intellectual ancestry, graduated from Yale at the age of seventeen and remained there two years as a tutor. In 1727 he was made colleague pastor with his grandfather of the church at Northampton, Massachusetts. His strictness in church discipline forced his resignation from this pastorate, and he became missionary to the Indians of Stockbridge, Massachusetts, 1750. It was here that he wrote *The Freedom of the Will*, 1754; *The Nature of Virtue*, posthumously published; *Treatise on Original Sin*, 1758; and *A Dissertation Concerning the End for Which God Created the World*. He was elected to the presidency of the College of New Jersey (Princeton College) less than a year before he died. The commanding intellectual figure of New England throughout his day, preacher, missionary, philosopher, educator, he may perhaps be longest known by his philosophical work, *The Freedom of the Will*. This work is remarkable for its originality and for its penetrating psychological conclusions. Edwards believed that there could be no such thing as absolute freedom of the will. Whether the individual realizes it or not, there is some cause disposing him to choose one of several courses of action each of which may seem equally inviting of uninviting. Edwards's diary and sermons, however, are of more popular interest and give a significant glimpse into the Puritan heart absorbed in all-consuming inward struggle. An interesting study might be made of the differences in religious and moral experience between Edwards, Mather, Woolman, and Franklin.

Rather late in Edwards's life a copy of a novel (probably Richardson's *Sir Charles Grandison*) fell into his hands, and he was heard to lament that he himself had not paid much attention to style. Yet he wrote with a vigor and an imaginative touch beyond the reach of most eighteenth century Americans, and showed a great advance in simplicity and directness of style over his New England contemporaries and predecessors, notably Cotton Mather. We can feel the strength of his oratory even today if we bear in mind how seriously his hearers regarded the matters of which he spoke, and how honest his appeal was to their emotions.

The first two pieces following, printed from the writings of Edwards when a boy, show an exceedingly interesting mind, one full of logical, creative curiosity, and capable of great development in the direction of natural science. It is interesting to compare him with his contemporary, Franklin.

Biography: A. V. G. Allen, 1889, 1890. Criticism: Stephen (HL2); More (Shel. 11); E. G. Smythe, "The Flying Spider," etc., *And. Rev.* 13: 1-19; E. G. Smythe, review of Allen's *Jonathan Edwards, And. Rev.* 1:285-304.

THE FLYING SPIDER [1]
OF INSECTS

Of all Insects no one is more wonderfull than the Spider especially with Respect to their sagacity and admirable way of working. these Spiders for the Present shall be Distinguished into those that keep in houses and those that keep in forests upon trees bushes shrubs &c and those that keep in rotten Logs for I take em to be of very Different kinds and natures; there are also other sorts some of which keep in rotten Logs hollow trees swamps and grass. Of these last every One knows the truth of their marching in the air from tree to tree and these sometimes at five or six rods Distanss sometimes, nor Can any one Go out amongst the trees in a Dewey morning towards the latter end of august or at the beginning of september but that he shall see hundreds of webbs made Conspicuous by the Dew that is lodged upon them reaching from one tree & shrub to another that stand at a Considerable Distance, and they may be seen well enough by an observing eye at noon Day by their Glistening against the sun and what is still more wonderfull: i know I have severall times seen in a very Calm and serene Day at that time of year, standing behind some Opake body that shall Just hide the Disk of the sun and keep of his Dazzling rays from my eye and looking close by the side of it, multitudes of little shining webbs and Glistening Strings of a Great Length and at such a height as that one would think they were tack'd to the Sky by one end were it not that they were moving and floating and there Very Often appears at the end of these Webs a Spider floating and sailing in the air with them, which I have Plainly Discerned in those webs that were nearer to my eye and Once saw a very large spider to my surprise swimming in the air in this manner, and Others have assured me that they Often have seen spiders fly, the appearance is truly very Pretty And Pleasing and it was so pleasing as well as surprising to me that I Resolved to endeavour to Satisfy my Curiosity about it by finding Out the way and manner of their Doing of it, being also Persuaded that If I could find out how the[y] flew I could easily find out how they made webs from tree to tree, and accordingly at a time when I was in the

[1] This selection is as far as possible an exact transcript of the original, a closely written, rather obscure ms. As nearly as can be ascertained, it was written when Edwards was about twelve years old, and reveals an analytical keenness of mind and a comprehension of the subject very unusual at any time in a child of that age.

Woods I happened to see one of these spiders on a bush, so I went to the bush and shook it hoping thereby to make him Uneasy upon it and provoke him to leave it by flying and took Good Care that he should not Get of from it any other way, So I Continued Constantly to shake it, which made him severall times let himself fall by his web a little but he would presently creep up again till at last he was pleased ho[w]ever to leave that bush and march along in the air to the next but which way I Did not know nor Could I Concieve but Resolved to watch him more narrowly next time so I brought [him] back to the same bush again and to be sure that there was nothing for him to Go upon the next time I whisked about a stick I had in my hand on all side[s] of the bush that I might breake any web Going from it if there were any and leave nothing else for him to Go on but the Clear air, and then shook the bush as before but it was not long before he again to my surprize went to the next bush. I took [him] of upon my stick and holding of him near my eye shook the stick as I had Done the bush wherupon he let himself Down A little hanging by his web and [I] Presently Perceived a web Out from his tail a Good way into the air. I took hold Of it with my hand and broke it off not knowing but that I might take it out to the Stick with him from the bush, but then I Plainly Percieved another such a string to Proceed Out of his tail I now Concieved I had found out the Whole mystery. I repeated the triall Over and Over again till I was fully satisfied of his way of working which I Dont only Conjecture to be on this wise viz they when they would Go from tree [to] tree or would Sail in the air let themselves hang Down a little way by their webb and then put out a web at their tails which being so Exceeding rare when it first comes from the spider as to be lighter than the air so as of itself it will ascend in it (which I know by Experience) the moving air takes it by the End and by the spiders Permission Pulls it out of his tail to any length and If the further End Of it happens to catch by a tree or anything why there's a web for him to Go over upon and the Spider immediately percieves it and feels when it touches, much after the same manner as the soul in the brain immediately Percieves when any of those little nervous strings that Proceed from it are in the Least Jarred by External things; and this very way I have seen Spiders Go from one thing to another I believe fifty time[s] at least since I first Discovered it: but if nothing is in the way of these webs to hinder their flying out at a sufficient Distance and they Dont catch by any thing, there will be so much of it Drawn out into the air as by its ascending force there will be enough to Carry the spider with it, or which is all one now there is so much of this web which is rarer than the air as that the web taken with the spider shall take up as much or more space than the same quantity of which if it be equall they together will be in a perfect equilibrium or Poise with the air so as that when they are loose therein they will neither ascend nor Descend but only as they are Driven by the wind, but if they together be more will ascend therein, like as a man at the bottom of the sea if he has hold on a stick of wood or any thing that is lighter or takes up more Space for the Quantity of matter than the water, if it be a little piece it may not be enough to Carry him and Cause him to swim therin but if there be enough of it it will Carry him up to the surface of the water if there be so much as that the Greater rarity shall more than Counterballance the Greater Density of the man and if it be Doth but Just Cause to balance, Put the man any where in the water and there he'll keep without ascending or Descending; tis Just so with the Spider in the air as with the man in the water, for what is lighter than the air will swim Or ascend therin as well as that which is lighter than the water swims in that, and If a spider has hold on so much of a web that the Greater Levity of all of it shall more than counterpoise the Greater Gravity of the spider, so that the ascending force of the web shall be more than the Descending force of the spider the web by its ascending will necessarily Carry the Spider up unto such a height as that the air shall be so much thinner and lighter as that the lightness of the web with the Spider shall no longer prevail. Now Perhaps here it will be asked how the spider knows when he has put out web enough and when he Does know how Does he Get himself loose from the web by which he hung to the trees. I answer there is no occasion for the spiders knowing, for their manner is to let out their web untill the ascending force of their web And the force of the wind has upon it together with the weight of the spider shall be enough to break the web by which the spider hung to the tree for the stress of all these Comes upon that and nature has so provided that Just so much web as is sufficient to break that shall be sufficient to carry the spider.

1715?

From A BIT OF AUTOBIOGRAPHY

FOUND IN HIS OWN HANDWRITING

I had a variety of concerns and exercises [1] about my soul from my childhood; but I had two more remarkable seasons of awakening, before I met with that change by which I was brought to those new dispositions, and that new sense of things, that I have since had. The first time was when I was a boy, some years before I went to college, at a time of remarkable awakening in my father's congregation. [2] I was then very much affected for many months, and concerned about the things of religion, and my soul's salvation; and was abundant in religious duties. I used to pray five times a day in secret, and to spend much time in religious conversation with other boys; and used to meet with them to pray together. I experienced I know not what kind of delight in religion. My mind was much engaged in it, and had much self-righteous pleasure; and it was my delight to abound in religious duties. I with some of my schoolmates joined together, and built a booth in a swamp, in a very retired spot, for a place of prayer. And besides, I had particular secret places of my own in the woods, where I used to retire by myself; and was from time to time much affected. My affections seemed to be lively and easily moved, and I seemed to be in my element when engaged in religious duties. And I am ready to think, many are deceived with such affections, and such a kind of delight as I then had in religion, and mistake it for grace. [3]

But in process of time, my convictions and affections wore off and I entirely lost all those affections and delights and left off secret prayer at least as to any constant performance of it; and returned like a dog to his vomit, and went on in the ways of sin. [4] Indeed I was at times very uneasy, especially toward the latter part of my time at college; when it pleased God to seize me with a pleurisy, in which he brought me nigh to the grave, and shook me over the pit of hell. And yet it was not long after my recovery, before I fell again into my old ways of sin. But God would not suffer me to go on with any quietness; I had great and violent inward struggles, till, after many conflicts with wicked inclinations, repeated resolutions, and bonds that I laid myself under by a kind of

[1] distresses
[2] His father was for sixty years pastor at Windsor, Connecticut.
[3] divine favor
[4] not sinful acts, but a perfunctory rather than a positive attitude toward religious matters

vows to God, I was brought wholly to break off all former wicked ways, and all ways of known outward sin; and to apply myself to seek salvation, and practice many religious duties; but without that kind of affection and delight which I had formerly experienced. My concern now wrought more by inward struggles and conflicts, and self reflections. I made seeking my salvation the main business of my life. But yet it seems to me I sought it after a miserable manner; which has made me sometimes since to question, whether ever it issued in that which was saving; being ready to doubt, whether such miserable seeking ever succeeded. I was indeed brought to seek salvation in a manner that I never was before; I felt a spirit to part with all things in the world, for an interest in Christ. My concern continued and prevailed, with many exercising thoughts and inward struggles; but yet it never seemed to be proper to express that concern by the name of terror.

From my childhood up, my mind had been full of objections against the doctrine of God's sovereignty, in choosing whom he would to eternal life, and rejecting whom he pleased; leaving them eternally to perish, and be everlastingly tormented in hell. It used to appear like a horrible doctrine to me. But I remember the time very well, when I seemed to be convinced, and fully satisfied, as to this sovereignty of God, and his justice in thus eternally disposing of men, according to his sovereign pleasure. But I never could give an account how, or by what means, I was thus convinced, not in the least imagining at the time, nor a long time after, that there was any extraordinary influence of God's Spirit in it; but only that now I saw further, and my reason apprehended the justice and reasonableness of it. However my mind rested in it; and it put an end to all those cavils and objections. And there has been a wonderful alteration in my mind, with respect to the doctrine of God's sovereignty, from that day to this; so that I scarce ever have found so much as the rising of an objection against it, in the most absolute sense, in God showing mercy to whom he will show mercy, and hardening [5] whom he will. God's absolute sovereignty and justice, with respect to salvation and damnation, is what my mind seems to rest assured of, as much as of any thing that I see with my eyes; at least it is so at times. But I have often, since that first conviction, had quite another kind of sense of God's sovereignty than I had then. I have often since had not only a conviction, but a

[5] *Romans* ix, 18

delightful conviction. The doctrine has very often appeared exceeding pleasant, bright, and sweet. Absolute sovereignty is what I love to ascribe to God. But my first conviction was not so.

.   .   .   .

Not long after I first began to experience these things, I gave an account to my father of some things that had passed in my mind. I was pretty much affected by the discourse we had together; and when the discourse was ended, I walked abroad alone, in a solitary place in my father's pasture, for contemplation. And as I was walking there, and looking upon the sky and clouds, there came into my mind so sweet a sense of the glorious majesty and grace of God, as I know not how to express. I seemed to see them both in a sweet conjunction; majesty and meekness joined together; it was a sweet, and gentle, and holy majesty; and also a majestic meekness; an awful sweetness; a high, and great, and holy gentleness.

After this my sense of divine things gradually increased, and became more and more lively, and had more of that inward sweetness. The appearance of everything was altered; there seemed to be, as it were, a calm, sweet cast, or appearance of divine glory, in almost everything. God's excellency, his wisdom, his purity and love, seemed to appear in everything; in the sun, moon, and stars; in the clouds and blue sky; in the grass, flowers, trees; in the water, and all nature; which used greatly to fix my mind. I often used to sit and view the moon for a long time; and in the day spent much time in viewing the clouds and sky, to behold the sweet glory of God in these things; in the meantime singing forth, with a low voice, my contemplations of the Creator and Redeemer. And scarce anything, among all the works of nature, was so sweet to me as thunder and lightning; formerly, nothing had been so terrible to me. Before, I used to be uncommonly terrified with thunder, and to be struck with terror when I saw a thunder storm rising; but now, on the contrary, it rejoiced me. I felt God, if I may so speak, at the first appearance of a thunder storm; and used to take the opportunity, at such times, to fix myself in order to view the clouds and see the lightnings play, and hear the majestic and awful voice of God's thunder, which oftentimes was exceedingly entertaining, leading me to sweet contemplations of my great and glorious God. While thus engaged, it always seemed natural to me to sing, or chant forth my meditations; or, to speak my thoughts in soliloquies with a singing voice. [1]

.   .   .   '   .   .   .   .

The heaven I desired was a heaven of holiness; to be with God, and to spend my eternity in divine love, and holy communion with Christ. My mind was very much taken up with contemplations on heaven, and the enjoyments there; and living there in perfect holiness, humility, and love; and it used at that time to appear a great part of the happiness of heaven, that there the saints could express their love to Christ. It appeared to me a great clog and burden that what I felt within, I could not express as I desired. The inward ardor of my soul seemed to be hindered and pent up, and could not freely flame out as it would. I used often to think, how in heaven this principle should freely and fully vent and express itself. Heaven appeared exceedingly delightful, as a world of love; and that all happiness consisted in living in pure, humble, heavenly, divine love.

I remember the thoughts I used then to have of holiness; and said sometimes to myself, "I do certainly know that I love holiness, such as the Gospel prescribes." It appeared to me that there was nothing in it but what was ravishingly lovely; the highest beauty and amiableness—a divine beauty; far purer than anything here upon earth; and that everything else was like mire and defilement, in comparison of it.

Holiness, as I then wrote down some of my contemplations on it, appeared to me to be of a sweet, pleasant, charming, serene, calm nature; which brought an inexpressible purity, brightness, peacefulness, and ravishment to the soul. In other words, that it made the soul like a field or garden of God, with all manner of pleasant flowers; enjoying a sweet calm, and the gentle vivifying beams of the sun. The soul of a true Christian, as I then wrote my meditations, appeared like such a little white flower as we see in the spring of the year; low, and humble on the ground, opening its bosom to receive the pleasant beams of the sun's glory, rejoicing as it were in a calm rapture; diffusing around a sweet fragrancy; standing peacefully and lovingly, in the midst of other flowers round about; all in like manner opening their bosoms, to drink in the light of the sun. There was no part of creature [2] holiness, that I had so great a

---

[1] Edwards's record of his spiritual experiences coincides with that of many other persons of intense devotion from David to St. Francis.
[2] The holiness of a created thing as distinguished from the holiness of God. This sentence structure is now considered incorrect.

sense of its loveliness as humility, brokenness of heart, and poverty of spirit; and there was nothing that I so earnestly longed for. My heart panted after this, to lie low before God, as in the dust; that I might be nothing, and that God might be all, that I might become as a little child. . . .

On Jan. 12, 1723, I made a solemn dedication of myself to God, and wrote it down; giving up myself and all that I had to God to be for the future in no respect my own; to act as one that had no right to himself in any respect. And solemnly vowed to take God for my whole portion and felicity; looking on nothing else as any part of my happiness, nor acting as if it were; and his law for the constant rule of my obedience; engaging to fight with all my might against the world, the flesh, and the devil, to the end of my life. But I have reason to be infinitely humbled, when I consider how much I have failed of answering my obligation.

. . . .

They say there is a young lady [1] in [New Haven] who is beloved of that Great Being, who made and rules the world, and that there are certain seasons in which this Great Being, in some way or other invisible, comes to her and fills her mind with exceeding sweet delight, and that she hardly cares for anything except to meditate on him—that she expects after a while to be received up where he is, to be raised up out of the world and caught up into heaven; being assured that he loves her too well to let her remain at a distance from him always. There she is to dwell with him, and to be ravished with his love and delight forever. Therefore if you present all the world before her, with the richest of its treasures, she disregards it and cares not for it, and is unmindful of any pain or affliction. She has a strange sweetness in her mind and singular purity in her affections; is most just and conscientious in all her conduct; and you could not persuade her to do anything wrong or sinful, if you would give her all the world, lest she should offend this Great Being.

She is of a wonderful sweetness, calmness, and universal benevolence of mind; especially after this great God has manifested himself to her mind. She will sometimes go about from place to place, singing sweetly; and seems to be always full of joy and pleasure; and no one knows for what. She loves to be alone, walking in the fields and groves, and seems to have

[1] This paragraph was found written upon a blank leaf. It is a description of Miss Sarah Pierrepont, whom he married.

someone invisible always conversing with her. [2]
1723

From the sermon SINNERS IN THE HANDS OF AN ANGRY GOD [3]

(Based on the text: "Their foot shall slide in due time." *Deuteronomy* xxxii, 35.)

. . . .

The wrath of God is like great waters that are dammed for the present; they increase more and more and rise higher and higher, till an outlet is given; and the longer the stream is stopped, the more rapid and mighty is its course when once it is let loose. 'Tis true that judgment against your evil work has not been executed hitherto; the floods of God's vengeance have been withheld; but your guilt in the mean time is constantly increasing, and you are every day treasuring up more wrath; the waters are continually rising and waxing more and more mighty; and there is nothing but the mere pleasure of God that holds the waters back, that are unwilling to be stopped, and press hard to go forward. If God should only withdraw his hand from the floodgate it would immediately fly open, and the fiery floods of the fierceness and wrath of God would rush forth with inconceivable fury, and would come upon you with omnipotent power; and if your strength were ten thousand times greater than it is, yea, ten thousand times greater than the strength of the stoutest, sturdiest devil in hell, it would be nothing to withstand or endure it.

The bow of God's wrath is bent, and the arrow made ready on the string, and justice bends the arrow at your heart and strains the bow, and it is nothing but the mere pleasure of God, and that of an angry God, without any promise or obligation at all, that keeps the arrow one moment from being made drunk with your blood.

[2] Thomas Wentworth Higginson, speaking of this paragraph, says in his *History of American Literature*, "This may fairly be called the high-water mark of Puritan prose."

[3] The congregation at Enfield, Connecticut, appears to have remained indifferent during a time of general religious awakening. Edwards, invited from Northampton, preached this sermon as a "lecture," July 8, 1741, to the ministers and people of Enfield and the neighboring towns. Trumbull in his *History of Connecticut* says that before the close "there was heard such a breathing of distress and weeping, that the preacher was obliged to speak to the people and desire silence that he might be heard!" Think as we may concerning the subject-matter of Edwards's sermon, we cannot escape the energy of his imagination and the power of his appeal. This selection is included as one of the most vivid specimens of Puritan imagination and mid-eighteenth century belief. Compare Edwards's oratory with that of the professional orators of a century later.

Thus are all you that never passed under a great change of heart by the mighty power of the Spirit of God upon your souls; all that were never born again and made new creatures, and raised from being dead in sin to a state of new and before altogether unexperienced light and life, (however you may have reformed your life in many things, and may have had religious affections, and may keep up a form of religion in your families and closets and in the house of God, and may be strict in it) you are thus in the hands of an angry God; 'tis nothing but his mere pleasure that keeps you from being this moment swallowed up in everlasting destruction.

However unconvinced you may now be of the truth of what you hear, by and by you will be fully convinced of it. Those that are gone from being in the like circumstances with you, see that it was so with them; for destruction came suddenly upon most of them; when they expected nothing of it, and while they were saying, Peace and safety: now they see that those things that they depended on for peace and safety were nothing but thin air and empty shadows.

The God that holds you over the pit of hell much as one holds a spider or some loathsome insect over the fire, abhors you, and is dreadfully provoked; his wrath towards you burns like fire; he looks upon you as worthy of nothing else but to be cast into the fire; he is of purer eyes than to bear to have you in his sight; you are ten thousand times so abominable in his eyes as the most hateful and venomous serpent is in ours. You have offended him infinitely more than ever a stubborn rebel did his prince: and yet it is nothing but his hand that holds you from falling into the fire every moment. 'Tis ascribed to nothing else, that you did not go to hell the last night; that you was suffered to awake again in this world after you closed your eyes to sleep and there is no other reason to be given why you have not dropped into hell since you arose in the morning, but that God's hand has held you up. There is no other reason to be given why you han't gone to hell since you have sat here in the house of God, provoking his pure eyes by your sinful wicked manner of attending his solemn worship. Yea, there is nothing else that is to be given as a reason why you don't this very moment drop down into hell.

O sinner! Consider the fearful danger you are in. 'Tis a great furnace of wrath, a wide and bottomless pit, full of the fire of wrath, that you are held over in the hand of that God whose wrath is provoked and incensed as much against you as against many of the damned in hell. You hang by a slender thread, with the flames of divine wrath flashing about it, and ready every moment to singe it and burn it asunder; and you have no interest in any Mediator, and nothing to lay hold of to save yourself, nothing to keep off the flames of wrath, nothing of your own, nothing that you ever have done, nothing that you can do, to induce God to spare you one moment. . . .

It is *everlasting* wrath. It would be dreadful to suffer this fierceness and wrath of Almighty God one moment; but you must suffer it to all eternity: there will be no end to this exquisite, horrible misery. When you look forward you shall see a long forever, a boundless duration before you, which will swallow up your thoughts and amaze your soul; and you will absolutely despair of ever having any deliverance, any end, any mitigation, any rest at all; you will know certainly that you must wear out long ages, millions of millions of ages, in wrestling and conflicting with this almighty, merciless vengeance; and then when you have so done, when so many ages have actually been spent by you in this manner, you will know that all is but a point to what remains. So that your punishment will indeed be infinite. Oh, who can express what the state of a soul in such circumstances is! All that we can possibly say about it gives but a very feeble, faint representation of it; it is inexpressible and inconceivable: for "who knows the power of God's anger?"

How dreadful is the state of those that are daily and hourly in danger of this great wrath and infinite misery! But this is the dismal case of every soul in this congregation that has not been born again, however moral and strict, sober and religious, they may otherwise be. Oh, that you would consider it, whether you be young or old! There is reason to think that there are many in this congregation now hearing this discourse, that will actually be the subjects of this very misery to all eternity. We know not who they are, or in what seats they sit, or what thoughts they now have. It may be they are now at ease and hear all these things without much disturbance, and are now flattering themselves that they are not the persons, promising themselves that they shall escape. If we knew that there was one person, and but one, in the whole congregation, that was to be the subject of this misery, what an awful thing it would be to think of! If we knew who it was, what an awful sight would it be to see such a person! How might all the rest of the congregation lift up a lamentable and bitter cry over him! But alas! instead of one, how many is it likely will remember this discourse in hell! And it would be a wonder, if some that are now present should not be in hell in a very short time, before this year is out. And it would be no wonder if some persons that now sit here in some seats of this meeting-house in health, and quiet and secure, should be there before tomorrow morning. Those of you that finally continue in a natural condition, that shall keep out of hell longest, will be there in a little time! Your damnation don't slumber; it will come swiftly and, in all probability, very suddenly upon many of you. You have reason to wonder that you are not already in hell. 'Tis doubtless the case of some that heretofore you have seen and known, that never deserved hell more than you and that heretofore appeared as likely to have been now alive as you. Their case is past all hope; they are crying in extreme misery and perfect despair. But here you are in the land of the living and in the house of God, and have an opportunity to obtain salvation. What would not those poor, damned, hopeless souls give for one day's such opportunity as you now enjoy! ...

Are there not many here that have lived long in the world that are not to this day born again, and so are aliens from the commonwealth of Israel and have done nothing ever since they have lived but treasure up wrath against the day of wrath? Oh, sirs, your case in an especial manner is extremely dangerous; your guilt and hardness of heart is extremely great. Don't you see how generally persons of your years are passed over and left in the present remarkable and wonderful dispensation of God's mercy? You had need to consider yourselves and wake thoroughly out of sleep; you cannot bear the fierceness and the wrath of the infinite God.

And you that are young men and young women, will you neglect this precious season that you now enjoy, when so many others of your age are renouncing all youthful vanities and flocking to Christ? You especially have now an extraordinary opportunity; but if you neglect it, it will soon be with you as it is with those persons that spent away all the precious days of youth in sin and are now come to such a dreadful pass in blindness and hardness.

And you children that are unconverted, don't you know that you are going down to hell to bear the dreadful wrath of that God that is now angry with you every day and every night?

Will you be content to be the children of the devil, when so many other children in the land are converted and are become the holy and happy children of the King of kings?

And let every one that is yet out of Christ and hanging over the pit of hell, whether they be old men and women or middle-aged or young people or little children, now hearken to the loud calls of God's word and providence. This acceptable year of the Lord that is a day of such great favor to some will doubtless be a day of as remarkable vengeance to others. Men's hearts harden and their guilt increases apace at such a day as this, if they neglect their souls. And never was there so great danger of such persons being given up to hardness of heart and blindness of mind. God seems now to be hastily gathering in his elect in all parts of the land; and probably the bigger part of adult persons that ever shall be saved will be brought in now in a little time, and that it will be as it was on that great outpouring of the Spirit upon the Jews in the Apostles' days, the election will obtain and the rest will be blinded. If this should be the case with you, you will eternally curse this day, and will curse the day that ever you was born to see such a season of the pouring out of God's Spirit, and will wish that you had died and gone to hell before you had seen it. Now undoubtedly it is as it was in the days of John the Baptist, the axe is in an extraordinary manner laid at the root of the trees, that every tree that bringeth not forth good fruit may be hewn down and cast into the fire.

Therefore let every one that is out of Christ now awake and fly from the wrath to come. The wrath of Almighty God is now undoubtedly hanging over great part of this congregation. Let every one fly out of Sodom. *"Haste and escape for your lives, look not behind you, escape to the mountain, lest ye be consumed."*

1741   1741

JOHN WOOLMAN 1720-1772

Woolman was exceptional among the eighteenth-century American writers for his gentle sweetness. He was born in the humblest circumstances at Northampton, New Jersey. He was farmer, shopkeeper, tailor, merchant. In 1741 he began to preach as an itinerant evangelist of the Society of Friends, traveling throughout the colonies, and finally to England, where he died at York of smallpox. He wrote a tract, *Some Considerations on the Keeping of Negroes,* 1754. His works, including the *Journal,* were published in 1774-5.

In place of Edwards's gloomy fire of soul, Woolman shows a tolerant, kindly belief in the benevolent intention of the universe. His care for the oppressed, whether bond or free, is the American counterpart of a similar impulse in Wesley, Howard, and Wilberforce, his English contemporaries, which marks the awakening of a broad humanitarianism in Christendom. In his day Quakers· were despised for their unorthodox views and their refusal to do military service. People were yet alive who had seen Quakers hanged. In spite of all Franklin's toleration, Woolman and Franklin, neighbor philanthropists, moved in spheres exclusive each of the other. To understand Woolman, and the beauty of his inner life, one must realize the supreme importance he attaches to the inner voice, and man's duty to heed it.

See *The Journal of John Woolman* with Introduction by J. G. Whittier, 1871.

From A JOURNAL OF JOHN WOOLMAN

From CHAPTER I

[HIS YOUTH]

I have often felt a motion [1] of love to leave some hints in writing of my experience of the goodness of God; and now, in the thirty-sixth year of my age, I begin this work.

I was born in Northampton, in Burlington county, West Jersey, [2] in the year 1720; and before I was seven years old I began to be acquainted with the operations of Divine love. Through the care of my parents, I was taught to read near as soon as I was capable of it; and as I went from school one seventh-day, I remember, while my companions went to play by the way, I went forward out of sight, and sitting down, I read the twenty-second chapter of the *Revelation:* "He showed me a pure river of water of life, clear as crystal, proceeding out of the throne of God and of the lamb," etc.; and in reading it, my mind was drawn to seek after that pure habitation, which, I then believed, God had prepared for his servants. The place where I sat, and the sweetness that attended my mind, remain fresh in my memory. This, and the like gracious visitations, had that effect upon me, that when boys used ill language, it troubled me; and through the continued mercies of God, I was preserved from it.

The pious instructions of my parents were often fresh in my mind when I happened to be among wicked children, and were of use to me. My parents having a large family

[1] prompting
[2] The territory comprising New Jersey was divided into East and West New Jersey in 1676, Quakers becoming proprietors of West New Jersey. Though the colony was reunited in 1702, the old names were long in use.

of children, used frequently, on first-days, [3] after meeting, to put us to read in the Holy Scriptures, or some religious books, one after another, the rest sitting by without much conversation; which I have since often thought was a good practice. From what I had read and heard, I believed there had been, in past ages, people who walked in uprightness before God, in a degree exceeding any that I knew or heard of, now living; and the apprehension of there being less steadiness and firmness amongst people in this age than in past ages, often troubled me while I was a child.

A thing remarkable in my childhood was, that once, going to a neighbor's house, I saw, on the way, a robin sitting on her nest; and as I came near she went off, but, having young ones, flew about, and with many cries expressed her concern for them. I stood and threw stones at her, till one striking her, she fell down dead. At first I was pleased with the exploit; but after a few minutes was seized with horror as having, in a sportive way, killed an innocent creature while she was careful for her young. I beheld her lying dead, and thought those young ones, for which she was so careful, must now perish for want of their dam to nourish them; and after some painful considerations on the subject, I climbed up the tree, took all the young birds, and killed them, supposing that better than to leave them to pine away and die miserably; and believed, in this case, that Scripture proverb was fulfilled, "The tender mercies of the wicked are cruel." I then went on my errand, but for some hours could think of little else but the cruelties I had committed, and was much troubled. Thus He whose tender mercies are over all his works hath placed a principle in the human mind, which incites to exercise goodness toward every living creature; and this being singly attended to, people become tender-hearted and sympathizing; but being frequently and totally rejected, the mind becomes shut up in a contrary disposition.

About the twelfth year of my age, my father being abroad, [4] my mother reproved me for some misconduct; to which I made an undutiful reply; and the next first-day, as I was with my father returning from meeting, he told me he understood I had behaved amiss to my mother, and advised me to be more careful in future. I knew myself blamable, and in shame and confusion remained silent. Being thus awakened to a sense of my wickedness, I felt remorse in

[3] the first day of the week; Quaker terminology
[4] away from home

my mind, and getting home, I retired and prayed to the Lord to forgive me; and do not remember that I ever, after that, spoke unhandsomely to either of my parents, however foolish in some other things.

. . . . .

I kept steadily to meetings, spent first-days afternoon chiefly in reading the Scriptures, and other good books, and was early convinced in my mind that true religion consisted in an inward life wherein the heart doth love and reverence God the Creator, and learns to exercise true justice and goodness, not only toward all men but also toward the brute creatures; that as the mind is moved by an inward principle to love God as an invisible, incomprehensible Being, by the same principle it is moved to love him in all his manifestations in the visible world; that, as by his breath the flame of life was kindled in all animal sensible creatures, to say we love God as unseen, [1] and, at the same time, exercise cruelty toward the least creature moving by his life, or by life derived from him, was a contradiction in itself. I found no narrowness respecting sects and opinions, but believed that sincere upright-hearted people, in every society, [2] who truly love God, were accepted of him.

As I lived under the cross, and simply followed the openings of Truth, my mind, from day to day, was more enlightened; my former acquaintance were left to judge of me as they would, for I found it safest for me to live in private, and to keep these things sealed up in my own breast. While I silently ponder on that change wrought in me, I find no language equal to it, [3] nor any means to convey to another a clear idea of it. I looked upon the works of God in this visible creation, and an awfulness covered me; my heart was tender and often contrite, and universal love to my fellow-creatures increased in me; this will be understood by such who have trodden in the same path.

Some glances of real beauty may be seen in their faces who dwell in true meekness. There is a harmony in the sound of that voice to which Divine love gives utterance, and some appearance of right order in their temper and conduct whose passions are regulated; yet all these do not fully show forth that inward life to such who have not felt it; but this white stone [4] and new name are known rightly to such only who have them. . . .

[1] 1 John iv, 20
[2] sect or religion
[3] to describe it
[4] Revelation ii, 17

From CHAPTER IV

. . . . . .

On the 9th [of May, 1757] breakfasted at a Friend's house, who putting us a little on our way, I had conversation with him in the fear of the Lord, concerning his slaves; in which my heart was tender, and I used much plainness of speech with him, which he appeared to take kindly. We pursued our journey without appointing meetings, being pressed in my mind to be at the Yearly Meeting in Virginia. And in my traveling on the road, I often felt a cry rise from the center of my mind, "O Lord, I am a stranger on the earth, hide not thy face from me." On the 11th day of the fifth month, we crossed the rivers Potomac and Rappahannock, and lodged at Port Royal: and on the way we happening in company with a colonel of the militia, who appeared to be a thoughful man, I took occasion to remark on the difference in general between a people used to labor moderately for their living, training up their children in frugality and business, and those who live on the labor of slaves; the former, in my view, being the most happy life: with which he concurred, and mentioned the trouble arising from the untoward, slothful disposition of the negroes; adding that one of our laborers would do as much in a day as two of their slaves. I replied that free men, whose minds were properly on their business, found a satisfaction in improving, cultivating, and providing for their families; but negroes, laboring to support others, who claim them as their property, and expecting nothing but slavery during life, had not the like inducement to be industrious.

After some further conversation, I said that men having power, too often misapplied it; that though we made slaves of the negroes, and the Turks made slaves of the Christians, I however believed that liberty was the natural right of all men equally; which he did not deny; but said the lives of the negroes were so wretched in their own country, that many of them lived better here than there. I only said, "There is great odds in regard to us, on what principle we act," [5] and so the conversation on that subject ended. I may here add that another person, some time afterward, mentioned the wretchedness of the negroes, occasioned by their intestine wars, as an argument in favor of our fetching them away for slaves; to which I then replied, "If compassion on the Africans, in regard to their domestic troubles, were the real motives of our purchasing them, that spirit

[5] great difference in the principles on which we act (as explained farther on)

of tenderness being attended to, would incite us to use them kindly, that as strangers brought out of affliction, their lives might be happy among us; and as they are human creatures whose souls are as precious as ours, and who may receive the same help and comfort from the holy Scriptures as we do, we could not omit suitable endeavors to instruct them therein. But while we manifest by our conduct, that our views in purchasing them are to advance ourselves; and while our buying captives taken in war, animates those parties to push on that war, and increase desolation amongst them; to say they live unhappy in Africa, is far from being an argument in our favor." I further said, "The present circumstances of these provinces to me appear difficult; that the slaves look like a burthensome stone to such who burthen themselves with them, and if the white people retain a resolution to prefer their outward prospects of gain to all other considerations, and do not act conscientiously toward them as fellow-creatures, I believe that burthen will grow heavier and heavier, until times change in a way disagreeable to us." At this the person appeared very serious, and owned that in considering their condition, and the manner of their treatment in these provinces, he had sometimes thought it might be just in the Almighty so to order it.

.   .   .   .

. . . The prospect of a road lying open to the same degeneracy, [1] in some parts of this newly settled land of America, in respect to our conduct toward the negroes, hath deeply bowed my mind in this journey; and though to briefly relate how these people are treated is no agreeable work, yet, after often reading over the notes I made as I traveled, I find my mind engaged to preserve them. Many of the white people in those provinces take little or no care of negro marriages; and when negroes marry after their own way, some make so little account of those marriages, that, with views of outward interest, they often part men from their wives by selling them far asunder; which is common when estates are sold by executors at vendue. [2] Many whose labor is heavy being followed at their business in the field by a man with a whip, hired for that purpose, have in common little else allowed but one peck of Indian corn and some salt for one week, with a few potatoes; the potatoes they commonly raise by their labor on the first day of the week.

The correction ensuing on their disobedience to overseers, or slothfulness in business, is often very severe, and sometimes desperate.

Men and women have many times scarce clothes enough to hide their nakedness, and boys and girls ten and twelve years old, are often quite naked amongst their master's children. Some of our Society, and some of the society called New Lights, [3] use some endeavors to instruct those they have in reading; but in common this is not only neglected, but disapproved. These are the people by whose labor the other inhabitants are in a great measure supported, and many of them in the luxuries of life; these are the people who have made no agreement to serve us, and who have not forfeited their liberty that we know of; these are the souls for whom Christ died: and for our conduct toward them we must answer before Him who is no respecter of persons.

They who know the only true God, and Jesus Christ, whom he hath sent, and are thus acquainted with the merciful, benevolent, Gospel spirit, will therein perceive that the indignation of God is kindled against oppression and cruelty; and in beholding the great distress of so numerous a people will find cause for mourning. . . .

From CHAPTER VIII

.   .   .   .   .

[A VISIT TO THE INDIANS] [4]

[We] lodged at Bethlehem: [5] parting there with John, William [6] and we went forward on the 9th day of the sixth month, and got lodging on the floor of a house about five miles from Fort Allen. Here we parted with William. At this place we met with an Indian trader, lately come from Wyoming; [7] and in conversation

---

[1] He has just spoken of how the Jews became degenerate through love of dominion.
[2] auction

[3] probably a sect formed in this country in consequence of the preaching of Whitefield, and numerous in Virginia and North Carolina
[4] For many years Woolman had felt love in his heart "towards the natives in this land who dwell far back in the wilderness." Feeling that he might understand them and, as he explains on page 84, bring some message of brotherly sympathy, he resolved to visit them as soon as the way opened. The opportunity came in 1763. The French and Indian War was scarcely over and Pontiac's War was just begun. The journey led him and his companion, Benjamin Parvin, far into the country of the Delaware Indians, many of whom were at the time fighting the English. The selection begins with the first days of the journey. All the places mentioned are in Pennsylvania.
[5] In 1742 the Moravians, a religious sect of the followers of John Huss, founded Bethlehem in Pennsylvania, where the brotherhood still maintains religious and educational establishments.
[6] John Pemberton and William Lightfoot, Quakers
[7] settled in 1762; in 1778 the scene of a massacre by the British and Indians

with him, I perceived that white people often sell rum to the Indians, which I believe is a great evil; first, they being thereby deprived of the use of their reason, and their spirits violently agitated, quarrels often arise which end in mischief; and the bitterness and resentment occasioned hereby are frequently of long continuance. Again, their skins and furs, gotten through much fatigue and hard travels in hunting, with which they intended to buy clothing, when they become intoxicated they often sell at a low rate for more rum; and afterward, when they suffer for want of the necessaries of life, are angry with those who, for the sake of gain, took the advantage of their weakness. Of this their chiefs have often complained, at their treaties with the English. Where cunning people pass counterfeits, and impose that on others which is good for nothing, it is considered as a wickedness; but to sell that to people which we know does them harm, and which often works their ruin, for the sake of gain, manifests a hardened and corrupt heart, and is an evil which demands the care of all true lovers of virtue to suppress. While my mind this evening was thus employed, I also remembered that the people on the frontiers, among whom this evil is too common, are often poor, who venture to the outside of a colony, that they may live more independent of such as are wealthy, who often set high rents on their land. I was renewedly confirmed in a belief, that if all our inhabitants lived according to sound wisdom, laboring to promote universal love and righteousness, and ceased from every inordinate desire after wealth, and from all customs which are tinctured with luxury, the way would be easy for the inhabitants, though much more numerous than at present, to live comfortably on honest employments, without that temptation they are often under of being drawn into schemes to make settlements on lands which have not been purchased of the Indians, or of applying to that wicked practice of selling rum to them.

On the 10th day of the month [June, 1763] we set out early in the morning, and crossed the western branch of the Delaware, called the Great Lehigh, near Fort Allen; the water being high, we went over in a canoe. Here we met an Indian, and had some friendly conversation with him, and gave him some biscuit; and he having killed a deer, gave the Indians with us some of it. Then after traveling some miles, we met several Indian men and women with a cow and horse and some household goods, who were lately come from their dwelling at Wyoming, and going to settle at another place; we made them some small presents; and some of them understanding English, I told them my motive in coming into their country, with which they appeared satisfied. One of our guides talking awhile with an ancient woman concerning us, the poor old woman came to my companion and me, and took her leave of us with an appearance of sincere affection. So going on we pitched our tent near the banks of the same river, having labored hard in crossing some of those mountains called the Blue Ridge; and by the roughness of the stones and the cavities between them, and the steepness of the hills, it appeared dangerous: but we were preserved in safety, through the kindness of Him whose works in these mountainous deserts appeared awful; toward whom my heart was turned during this day's travel.

Near our tent, on the sides of large trees peeled for that purpose, were various representations of men going to and returning from the wars, and of some killed in battle. This being a path heretofore used by warriors, and as I walked about viewing those Indian histories, which were painted mostly in red but some in black, and thinking on the innumerable afflictions which the proud, fierce spirit produceth in the world; thinking on the toils and fatigues of warriors, traveling over mountains and deserts; thinking on their miseries and distresses when wounded far from home by their enemies; and of their bruises and great weariness in chasing one another over the rocks and mountains: and of their restless, unquiet state of mind, who live in this spirit; and of the hatred which mutually grows up in the minds of the children of those nations engaged in war with each other: during these meditations, the desire to cherish the spirit of love and peace amongst these people, arose very fresh in me. [1] This was the first night that we lodged in the woods; and being wet with traveling in the rain, the ground, our tent, and the bushes which we purposed to lay under, our blankets also wet, all looked discouraging; but I believed that it was the Lord who had thus far brought me forward, and that he would dispose of me as he saw good, and therein I felt easy. So we kindled a fire with our tent open to it; and with some bushes next the ground, and then our blankets, we made our bed; and lying down, got some sleep: and in the morning feeling a little unwell, I went into the river; the water was cold, but soon after I felt fresh and well.

[1] One might read long in colonial records for so sympathetic an attitude toward the Indians, and long in any literature of the time for such an attempt to put oneself in the place of the oppressed.

The 11th day of the sixth month, the bushes being wet, we tarried in our tent till about eight o'clock; when going on, crossed a high mountain supposed to be upward of four miles over; the steepness of the north side exceeding all the others: we also crossed two swamps; and it raining near night, we pitched our tent and lodged.

About noon, on our way we were overtaken by one of the Moravian brethren [1] going to Wehaloosing, [2] and an Indian man with him who could talk English; and we being together while our horses eat grass, had some friendly conversation; but they traveling faster than we, soon left us. This Moravian I understood had spent some time this spring at Wehaloosing; and was by some of the Indians invited to come again.

The 12th day of the sixth month, and first of the week, it being a rainy day, we continued in our tent; and here I was led to think on the nature of the exercise which hath attended me. Love was the first motion, [3] and thence a concern arose to spend some time with the Indians, that I might feel and understand their life and the spirit they live in, if haply I might receive some instruction from them, or they be in any degree helped forward by my following the leadings of Truth amongst them. As it pleased the Lord to make way for my going at a time when the troubles of war were increasing, and when by reason of much wet weather, traveling was more difficult than usual at that season, I looked upon it as a more favorable opportunity to season my mind, and bring me into a nearer sympathy with them: and as mine eye was to the great Father of mercies, humbly desiring to learn what his will was concerning me, I was made quiet and content.

Our guide's horse, though hoppled, went away in the night; and after finding our own, and searching some time for him, his footsteps were discovered in the path going back again, whereupon my kind companion went off in the rain, and after about seven hours returned with him; and here we lodged again, tying up our horses before we went to bed, and loosing them to feed about break of day.

On the 13th day of the sixth month, the sun appearing, we set forward; and as I rode over the barren hills, my meditations were on the alteration in the circumstances of the natives of this land since the coming of the English. The lands near the sea are conveniently situated for fishing; the lands near the rivers where the tides flow, and some above, are in many places fertile, and not mountainous, while the running of the tides makes passing up and down easy with any kind of traffic. Those natives have in some places, for trifling considerations, sold their inheritance so favorably situated, and in other places been driven back by superior force; so that in many places as their way of clothing themselves is now altered from what it was, and they are far remote from us, they have to pass over mountains, swamps, and barren deserts where traveling is very troublesome, in bringing their skins and furs to trade with us.

By the extending of English settlements, and partly by English hunters, the wild beasts they chiefly depend on for a subsistence are not so plentiful as they were; and people too often, for the sake of gain, open a door for them to waste their skins and furs in purchasing a liquor which tends to the ruin of them and their families. . . .

We reached the Indian settlement at Wyoming, and here we were told that an Indian runner had been at that place a day or two before us, and brought news of the Indians taking an English fort westward [4] and destroying the people, and that they were endeavoring to take another; and also that another Indian runner came there about the middle of the night before we got there, who came from a town about ten miles from Wehaloosing, and brought news that some Indian warriors from distant parts came to that town with two English scalps, and told the people that it was war with the English.

Our guides took us to the house of a very ancient man; and soon after we had put in our baggage, there came a man from another Indian house some distance off, and I perceiving there was a man near the door, went out; and he having a tomahawk under his matchcoat [5] out of sight, as I approached him he took it in his hand. I however went forward, and speaking to him in a friendly way perceived he understood some English: my companion then coming out, we had some talk with him concerning the nature of our visit in these parts; and then he going into the house with us, and talking with our guides, soon appeared friendly, and sat down and smoked his

---

[1] from Bethlehem

[2] an Indian village, the modern Wyalusing in Bradford County, Pennsylvania

[3] primary inner impulse

[4] This was apparently only a rumor, but four or five days later Forts Presque Isle, Le Boeuf, and Venango, as well as posts at Carlisle and Bedford, all in Pennsylvania, were taken by the Indians.

[5] A mantle or coat, originally of furs, worn by Indians; the word is of Indian origin, but printed and pronounced to appear like an English word.

pipe. Though his taking his hatchet in his hand, at the instant I drew near to him had a disagreeable appearance, I believe he had no other intent than to be in readiness in case any violence was offered to him. . . .

On the 14th day of the sixth month, we sought out and visited all the Indians hereabouts that we could meet with, they being chiefly in one place about a mile from where we lodged, in all perhaps twenty. I expressed the care I had on my mind for their good, and told them that true love had made me willing thus to leave my family to come and see the Indians, and speak with them in their houses. Some of them appeared kind and friendly. So we took our leave of these Indians and went up the river Susquehanna about three miles, to the house of an Indian called Jacob January, who had killed his hog; and the women were making a store of bread, and preparing to move up the river. Here our pilots left their canoe when they came down in the spring, which lying dry, was leaky; so that we being detained some hours, had a good deal of friendly conversation with the family, and eating dinner with them, we made them some small presents. Then putting our baggage in the canoe, some of them pushed slowly up the stream, and the rest of us rode our horses; and swimming them over a creek called Lahawahamunk, we pitched our tent above it, there being a shower in the evening: and in a sense of God's goodness in helping me in my distress, sustaining me under trials and inclining my heart to trust in him, I lay down in an humble, bowed frame of mind, and had a comfortable night's lodging. . . .

On the 17th day, parting from Job Chilaway, [1] we went on and reached Wehaloosing about the middle of the afternoon; and the first Indian we saw was a woman of a modest countenance, with a Bible, who first spake to our guide; and then with a harmonious voice expressed her gladness at seeing us, having before heard of our coming. By the direction of our guide we sat down on a log, and he went to the town to tell the people we were come. My companion and I sitting thus together in a deep inward stillness, the poor woman came and sat near us; and great awfulness coming over us, we rejoiced in a sense of God's love manifested to our poor souls. After a while we heard a conch-shell blow several times, and then came John Curtis [2] and another Indian man, who kindly invited us into a house

near the town, where we found, I suppose, about sixty people sitting in silence. After sitting a short time, I stood up and in some tenderness of spirit acquainted them with the nature of my visit, and that a concern for their good had made me willing to come thus far to see them; all in a few short sentences, which some of them understanding interpreted to the others, and there appeared gladness amongst them. Then I showed them my certificate, [3] which was explained to them; and the Moravian who overtook us on the way, being now here, bade me welcome.

On the 18th day we rested ourselves in this forenoon; and the Indians knowing that the Moravian and I were of different religious societies, and as some of their people had encouraged him to come and stay awhile with them, were, I believe, concerned that no jarring or discord might be in their meetings; and they I suppose, having conferred together, acquainted me that the people at my request, would at any time come together and hold meetings; and also told me, that they expected the Moravian would speak in their settled meetings, which are commonly held morning and near evening. I found a liberty in my heart to speak to the Moravian, and told him of the care I felt on my mind for the good of these people; and that I believed no ill effects would follow if I sometimes spoke in their meetings when love engaged me thereto, without calling them together at times when they did not meet of course: whereupon he expressed his goodwill toward my speaking at any time, all that I found in my heart to say. So near evening I was at their meeting, where the pure Gospel love was felt, to the tendering [4] of some of our hearts; and the interpreters endeavoring to acquaint the people with what I said in short sentences, found some difficulty, as none of them were quite perfect in the English and Delaware tongues, so they helped one another, and we labored along, Divine love attending. Afterward, feeling my mind covered with the spirit of prayer, I told the interpreters that I found it in my heart to pray to God, and believed if I prayed aright, he would hear me, and expressed my willingness for them to omit interpreting; so our meeting ended with a degree of Divine love. Before the people went out, I observed Papunehang, the man who had been zealous in laboring for a reformation in that town, being then very tender, [5] spoke

---
[1] an Indian from Wehaloosing who understood English and had met and befriended them before
[2] an Indian, not mentioned before
[3] his credentials from the Society of Friends; carried by all those sent out by the Quakers
[4] the making tender
[5] much moved

to one of the interpreters; and I was afterward told that he said in substance: "I love to feel where words come from." [1]

On the 19th day and first of the week, this morning in the meeting the Indian who came with the Moravian, being also a member of that society, prayed; and then the Moravian spake a short time to the people. In the afternoon they coming together, and my heart being filled with a heavenly care for their good, I spake to them awhile by interpreters; but none of them being perfect in the work, and I feeling the current of love run strong, told the interpreters that I believed some of the people would understand me, and so I proceeded. In which exercise, I believe the Holy Ghost wrought on some hearts to edification, where all the words were not understood. I looked upon it as a time of divine favor, and my heart was tendered and truly thankful before the Lord; and after I sat down, one of the interpreters seemed spirited [2] to give the Indians the substance of what I had said.

Before our first meeting this morning, I was led to meditate on the manifold difficulties of these Indians, [3] who, by the permission of the Six Nations dwell in these parts; and a near sympathy with them was raised in me, and my heart being enlarged in the love of Christ, I thought that the affectionate care of a good man for his only brother in affliction does not exceed what I then felt for that people. I came to this place through much trouble; and though through the mercies of God, I believed that if I died in the journey, it would be well with me, yet the thoughts of falling into the hands of Indian warriors, were in times of weakness afflicting to me; and being of a tender constitution of body, the thoughts of captivity amongst them were at times grievous; as supposing that they, being strong and hardy, might demand service of me beyond what I could well bear; but the Lord alone was my keeper, and I believed if I went into captivity it would be for some good end; and thus from time to time, my mind was centred in resignation, in which I always found quietness. And now, this day, though I had the same dangerous wilderness between me and home, I was inwardly joyful that the Lord had strengthened me to come on this visit, and manifested a fatherly care

over me in my poor lowly condition, when in mine own eyes I appeared inferior to many amongst the Indians.

When the last-mentioned meeting was ended, it being night, Papunehang went to bed; and one of the interpreters sitting by me, I observed that Papunehang spake with an harmonious voice, I suppose, a minute or two: and asking the interpreter, was told that "he was expressing his thankfulness to God for the favors he had received that day; and prayed that he would continue to favor him with that same which he had experienced in that meeting." Though Papunehang had before agreed to receive the Moravians and join with them, he still appeared kind and loving to us. . . . .

The 21st day. This morning in meeting, my heart was enlarged in pure love amongst them, and in short plain sentences expressed several things that rested upon me, which one of the interpreters gave the people pretty readily; after which the meeting ended in supplication, and I had cause humbly to acknowledge the loving-kindness of the Lord toward us; and then I believed that a door remained open for the faithful disciples of Jesus Christ to labor amongst these people.

I now feeling my mind at liberty to return, took my leave of them in general, at the conclusion of what I said in meeting; and so we prepared to go homeward: but some of their most active men told us, that when we were ready to move, the people would choose to come and shake hands with us; which those who usually came to meeting did; and from a secret draught [4] in my mind, I went amongst some who did not use to go to meeting, and took my leave of them also.

· · · · · ·

From Chapter XI

[voyage to england]

Having been some time under a religious concern [5] to prepare for crossing the seas in order to visit Friends in the northern parts of England, and more particularly in Yorkshire; after weighty consideration, I thought it expedient to inform Friends at our Monthly Meeting at Burlington of it; who having unity with me therein, gave me a certificate. And I afterward communicated the same to our Quarterly Meeting, and they likewise certified their concurrence therewith. Some time after which, at the General Spring Meeting of ministers and elders, I thought it my duty to acquaint them

---

[1] This was significant to Woolman and accorded with his Quaker belief that the divine message comes into man's heart direct from its source—that the spirit may apprehend without words.

[2] inspired, prompted

[3] These were the Delawares, of Algonquin stock, who had been subdued by the Six Nations, or Iroquois, and were allowed by them to live in these parts only upon humiliating terms.

[4] drawing, inclination

[5] solicitude amounting to obligation

of the religious exercise which attended my mind; with which they likewise signified their unity by a certificate, dated the 24th day of the third month, 1772, directed to Friends in Great Britain. . . .

I believe a communication by sea from one part of the world to some other parts of it is at times consistent with the will of our heavenly Father, and to educate some youth in the practice of sailing, I believe may be right. But how lamentable is the present corruption of the world! how impure are the channels through which trade hath a conveyance! how great is that danger to which poor lads are now exposed, when placed on shipboard to learn the art of sailing!

Five lads training up for the seas were now on board this ship, two of them brought up amongst our Society, and one of whom hath a right amongst Friends, by name James Nayler, to whose father, James Nayler, mentioned in Sewel's [1] History appears to have been uncle. I often feel a tenderness of heart toward these poor lads; and at times look at them as though they were my children according to the flesh.

O that all may take heed and beware of covetousness! O that all may learn of Christ, who was meek and low of heart! then in faithfully following him, he will teach us to be content with food and raiment, without respect to the customs or honors of this world. Men thus redeemed, will feel a tender concern for their fellow creatures, and a desire that those in the lowest stations may be assisted and encouraged; and where owners of ships attain to the perfect law of liberty, and are doers of the word, these will be blessed in their deeds.

A ship at sea commonly sails all night, and the seamen take their watches four hours at a time. Rising to work in the night, is not commonly pleasant in any case; but in dark rainy nights it is very disagreeable, even though each man were furnished with all conveniences. But if men must go out at midnight to help manage the ship in the rain, and having small room to sleep and lay their garments in, are often beset to furnish themselves for the watch; their garments or something relating to their business being wanting, and not easily found, when from the urgency occasioned by high winds, they are hastened and called up suddenly,—here is a trial of patience on the poor sailors, and the poor lads their companions.

If after they have been on deck several hours in the night and come down into the steerage soaking wet, and are so closely stowed that proper convenience for change of garment is not easily come at, but for want of proper room their wet garments thrown in heaps, and sometimes, through much crowding, are trodden under foot, in going to their lodgings and getting out of them, and great difficulties at times, each one to find his own,—here are trials on the poor sailors.

Now as I have been with them in my lodge, [2] my heart hath often yearned for them, and tender desires been raised in me, that all owners and masters of vessels may dwell in the love of God, and therein act uprightly; and by seeking less for gain, and looking carefully to their ways, may earnestly labor to remove all cause of provocation from the poor seamen, either to fret or use excess of strong drink; for indeed the poor creatures at times, in the wet and cold, seem to apply to strong drink to supply the want of other conveniences. Great reformation in the world is wanting, and the necessity of it amongst those who do business on great waters, hath at this time been abundantly opened before me.

The 8th day of the fifth month. This morning the clouds gathered, the wind blew strong from the south-eastward, and before noon increased to a degree that made sailing appear dangerous. The seamen then bound up some of their sails and took down some; and the storm increasing, they put the dead lights, so called, into the cabin windows, and lighted a lamp as at night. The wind now blew vehemently, and the sea wrought to such a degree that an awful seriousness prevailed in the cabin, in which I spent, I believe, about seventeen hours; for I believed the poor wet toiling seamen had need of all the room in the crowded steerage, and the cabin passengers had given me frequent invitations. They ceased now from sailing, and put the vessel in the posture called lying-to.

My mind in this tempest, through the gracious assistance of the Lord, was preserved in a good degree of resignation; and I felt at times a few words in his love to my ship-mates, in regard to the all-sufficiency of Him who formed the great deep, and whose care is so extensive that a sparrow falls not without his notice. Thus in a tender frame of mind I spoke to them of the necessity of our yielding, in true obedience, to the instructions of our heavenly Father, who sometimes through adversities intendeth our refinement.

---

[1] Sewel, William: *The History of the Rise, Increase . . . . of the People Called Quakers.* Printed in Dutch, Amsterdam, 1717; in English, London, 1722

[2] He took passage in the forecastle, with the sailors, going on board May 1, 1772.

About eleven o'clock at night I went out on the deck, when the sea wrought exceedingly, and the high foaming waves, all around, had in some sort the appearance of fire, but did not give much, if any, light. The sailor then at the helm said he lately saw a corposant [1] at the head of the mast. About this time I observed the master of the ship ordered the carpenter to keep on the deck; and though he said little, I apprehended his care was that the carpenter with his axe might be in readiness in case of any extremity. Soon after this, the vehemency of the wind abated, and before morning they again put the ship under sail.

. . . .

The 2nd day of the sixth month. Last evening the seamen found bottom at about seventy fathoms. This morning there was a fair wind, and pleasant. And as I sat on deck my heart was overcome with the love of Christ and melted into contrition before him; and in this state, the prospect of that work, to which I have felt my mind drawn when in my native land, being in some degree opened before me, I felt like a little child; and my cries were put up to my heavenly Father for preservation, that in an humble dependence on him, my soul may be strengthened in his love, and kept inwardly waiting for his counsel.

This afternoon we saw that part of England called the Lizard. Some dunghill fowls yet remained of those the passengers took for their sea-store: I believe about fourteen perished in the storms at sea, by the waves breaking over the quarter-deck, and a considerable number with sickness, at different times. I observed the cocks crew coming down the Delaware, and while we were near the land; but afterward, I think I did not hear one of them crow till we came near the land in England, when they again crowed a few times.

In observing their dull appearance at sea, and the pining sickness of some of them, I often remembered the fountain of goodness, who gave being to all creatures, and whose love extends to caring for the sparrows; and I believe where the love of God is verily perfected, and the true spirit of government watchfully attended to, a tenderness toward all creatures made subject to us will be experienced, and a care felt in us that we do not lessen that sweetness of life, in the animal creation, which the great Creator intends for them under our government.

The 4th day of the month. Wet weather,

high winds, and so dark that we could see but a little way. I perceived our seamen were apprehensive of missing the channel which I understood was narrow. In a while it grew lighter, and they saw the land, and they knew where we were. Thus the Father of mercies was pleased to try us with the sight of dangers, and then graciously from time to time deliver from them; thus sparing our lives, that in humility and reverence we may walk before him, and put our trust in him.

About noon a pilot came off from Dover, where my beloved friend Samuel Emlen [2] went on shore, and thence to London, about seventy-two miles by land; but I felt easy in staying in the ship.

The 7th day of the month, and first of the week. . . . Had a head wind up the Thames; sometimes lay at anchor, and saw many ships passing, and some at anchor near, and had large opportunity of feeling the spirit in which the poor bewildered sailors too generally live. That lamentable degeneracy, which so much prevails among the people employed on the seas, so affected my heart that I may not easily convey to another the feeling I have had.

The present state of the sea-faring life in general, appears so opposite to that of a pious education; so full of corruption, and extreme alienation from God; so full of examples the most dangerous to young people, that in looking toward a young generation, I feel a care for them, that they may have an education different from the present education of lads at sea; and that all of us who are acquainted with the pure Gospel spirit, may lay this case to heart, may remember the lamentable corruptions which attend the conveyance of merchandise across the seas, and so abide in the love of Christ, that being delivered from the love of money, from the entangling expenses of a curious, delicate, and luxurious life, we may learn contentment with a little; and promote the sea-faring life no further, than that spirit which leads into all truth attends us in our proceedings.

. . . .

From CHAPTER XII

. . . . . .

[AN EXPERIENCE DURING SICKNESS]

In a time of sickness with the pleurisy, a little upward of two years and a half ago, I was brought so near the gates of death that I forgot my name: being then desirous to know who I was, I saw a mass of matter of a dull

---

[1] a ball of light, sometimes seen during a storm

[2] the friend with whom he had crossed

gloomy color, between the south and the east, and was informed that this mass was human beings in as great misery as they could be, and live; and that I was mixed in with them, and that henceforth I might not consider myself as a distinct or separate being. In this state I remained several hours. I then heard a soft melodious voice, more pure and harmonious than any I had heard before. I believed it was the voice of an angel who spake to the other angels, and the words were these, *John Woolman is dead*. I soon remembered that I once was John Woolman; and being assured that I was alive in the body, I greatly wondered what that heavenly voice could mean. I believed beyond doubting that it was the voice of an holy angel; but as yet it was a mystery to me.

I was then carried in spirit to the mines where poor oppressed people were digging rich treasures for those called Christians; and I heard them blaspheme the name of Christ, at which I was grieved; for his name to me was precious. Then I was informed that these heathens were told that those who oppressed them were the followers of Christ; and they said amongst themselves, "If Christ directed them to use us in this sort, then Christ is a cruel tyrant." All this time the song of the angel remained a mystery; and in the morning, my dear wife and some others coming to my bedside, I asked them if they knew who I was; and they telling me I was John Woolman, thought I was light-headed: for I told them not what the angel said, nor was I disposed to talk much to any one, but was very desirous to get so deep that I might understand this mystery.

My tongue was often so dry that I could not speak till I had moved it about and gathered some moisture, and as I lay still for a time, at length I felt Divine power prepare my mouth that I could speak; and then I said, "I am crucified with Christ, nevertheless I live; yet not I, but Christ liveth in me: and the life that I now live in the flesh, I live by the faith of the Son of God, who loved me, and gave himself for me."

Then the mystery was opened; and I perceived there was joy in heaven over a sinner who had repented; and that that language (John Woolman is dead) meant no more than the death of my own will. [1]

. . . .

[CLEANLINESS]

Having of late traveled [2] often in wet weather through narrow streets in towns and villages where were dirtiness under foot, and the scent arising from that filth which more or less infects the air of all thickly settled towns, and I being but weakly, have felt distress both in body and mind, with that which is impure.

In these journeys I have been where much cloth hath been dyed, and sundry times walked over ground where much of the dye stuffs have drained away. Here I have felt a longing in my mind that people might come into cleanness of spirit, cleanness of person, and cleanness about their houses and garments. Some who are great carry delicacy to a great height themselves, and yet real cleanliness is not generally promoted. Dyes being invented partly to please the eye and partly to hide dirt, I have felt in this weak state, traveling in dirtiness and affected with unwholesome scents, a strong desire that the practice of dyeing cloth to hide dirt may be more fully considered. To hide dirt in our garments appears opposite to real cleanliness. To wash garments and keep them sweet, appears cleanly. Through giving way to hiding dirt in our garments, a spirit which would cover that which is disagreeable is strengthened. Real cleanness becometh a holy people, but hiding that which is not clean by coloring our garments appears contrary to the sweetness of sincerity. Through some sorts of dyes, cloth is less useful; and if the value of dye-stuffs, the expense of dyeing, and the damage done to cloth were all added together, and that expense applied to keep all sweet and clean, how much more cleanly would people be.

1756-1772   1774-5

BENJAMIN FRANKLIN 1706-1790

The first American writer to be read widely abroad, as well as the first to be universally read in America was Franklin, who was born and reared in Boston under strict Puritan influences, but lived much of his life in Philadelphia, London, and Paris, and became the most widely experienced citizen of the nation he helped to form. His services at home and abroad were rendered in the spirit of a practical philanthropist and public servant. His interests extended from the sweeping of streets, the warming of houses, the founding of schools and libraries, to experiments in and application of electric science, and to the affairs of nations. He was

---

[1] However this experience might be explained and classified by psychology, to Woolman it was of vital importance.

[2] In England; these paragraphs are under the last date of entry in his journal. Three weeks later he died of smallpox.

agent in London for the colonies of Pennsylvania, Massachusetts, New Jersey, and Georgia, and general spokesman for America before the British government. He was one of the committee to draft the Declaration of Independence. Almost immediately he was sent as special agent to France, where, largely through his wit, good sense, and personal popularity, he was of inestimable service to the colonies. He was made member and medalist of the Royal Society, 1753, LL.D. of the Universities of Edinburgh and Oxford, 1762, and president (governor) of Pennsylvania, 1785-1788. Franklin wrote his autobiography during short intervals of leisure in the last twenty years of his life. The first parts were intended for his family only. The latter parts were written for possible publication. Though written with no artistic intent, the book is of absorbing interest, truly modern in spirit, and truly native to the soil, the story of the first ambitious, industrious, "self-made" American who has left a record of himself. Franklin's published works consisted of essays, scientific and political pamphlets, monographs, and reports. The most complete edition of these, together with his letters and autobiography, was published in ten volumes, 1910.

Franklin was the first noteworthy American writer to come under Addison's influence. (See p. 92.) The style that he attained is probably more like Defoe's than Addison's, clear, direct, unemotional, lacking the imagination and urbanity of the *Spectator,* but possessing a humor of which Defoe is void, and graced with the mellowness of age and the ripeness of experience that a broad contact with men and affairs alone can give. In the graceful and fanciful "bagatelles" (See p. 112.) written late in life under the influence of French refinement and wit there is an indication of what graces of style Franklin might have acquired had his life been cast in different outward circumstances. But we need not lament Franklin's limitations: his robust directness of speech was tonic to his countrymen. Americans, moreover, will always be debtors to his forward-looking constructive bent of mind, his keenly curious and sagacious intellect, and his gift of humor. His humor is often of the pioneer type reflecting the attitude of one who uses it as a shield, one quite aware that he must meet life cheerfully or else succumb. In this aspect Franklin is the first of a long line of American humorists chief among whom is Mark Twain. Universally read as he was, he doubtless had an influence on American expression of which the epigrammatic terseness of Emerson is perhaps one result.

Biography: P. Russell, *Benjamin Franklin, The First Civilized American,* 1926; J. T. Morse (AS); L. Swift (BB); J. B. McMaster (AML). Criticism: Sherman; More (Shel. 4); Chubb; M. Tudury, "Poor Richard," *Bookm.* 64:580-4; P. Guedalla, "Dr. Ben Franklin," *Forum* 75:37-49; R. Bache, "Apprentice Comes to Philadelphia," *Outlook,* 133:133-135; H. S. Pritchett, "Tale of Two Cities," *Scrib. M.* 76:470-5; A. D. Dickinson, "Benjamin Franklin, Bookman," *Bookm.* 53:197-205.

From his AUTOBIOGRAPHY

Twyford at the Bishop of St. Asaph's, 1771

Dear Son: [1] I have ever had pleasure in obtaining any little anecdotes of my ancestors. You may remember the inquiries I made among the remains of my relations when you were with me in England, and the journey I undertook for that purpose. Imagining it may be equally agreeable to you to know the circumstances of my life, many of which you are yet unacquainted with, and expecting the enjoyment of a week's uninterrupted leisure in my present country retirement, [2] I sit down to write them for you. To which I have besides some other inducements. Having emerged from the poverty and obscurity in which I was born and bred, to a state of affluence and some degree of reputation in the world, and having gone so far through life with a considerable share of felicity, the conducing means I made use of, which with the blessing of God so well succeeded, my posterity may like to know, as they may find some of them suitable to their own situations, and therefore fit to be imitated.

That felicity, when I reflected on it, has induced me sometimes to say, that were it offered to my choice, I should have no objection to a repetition of the same life from its beginning, only asking the advantages authors have in a second edition to correct some faults of the first. So I might, besides correcting the faults, change some sinister accidents and events of it for others more favorable. But though this were denied, I should still accept the offer. Since such a repetition is not to be expected, the next thing most like living one's life over again seems to be a recollection of that life, and to make that recollection as durable as possible by putting it down in writing.

Hereby, too, I shall indulge the inclination so natural in old men, to be talking of themselves and their own past actions; and I shall indulge it without being tiresome to others, who, through respect to age, might conceive themselves obliged to give me a hearing, since this may be read or not as anyone pleases. And, lastly (I may as well confess it, since my denial of it will be believed by nobody), perhaps I shall a good deal gratify my own *vanity.* Indeed, I scarce ever heard or saw the introductory words, *"Without vanity I may say,"* etc., but some vain thing immediately followed. Most people dislike vanity in others, whatever share they have of it themselves; but I give it

[1] William Franklin, royalist governor of New Jersey
[2] as guest of Dr. Jonathan Shipley, bishop of St. Asaph's, at Twyford, Hampshire, England

fair quarter wherever I meet with it, being persuaded that it is often productive of good to the possessor, and to others that are within his sphere of action; and therefore in many cases, it would not be altogether absurd if a man were to thank God for his vanity among the other comforts of life. . . .

Josiah, my father, married young, and carried his wife with three children into New England, about 1682. The conventicles [1] having been forbidden by law, and frequently disturbed, induced some considerable men of his acquaintance to remove to that country, and he was prevailed with to accompany them thither, where they expected to enjoy their mode of religion with freedom. By the same wife he had four children more born there, and by a second wife ten more, in all seventeen; of which I remember thirteen sitting at one time at his table, who all grew up to be men and women, and married; I was the youngest son, and the youngest child but two, and was born in Boston, New England. My mother, the second wife, was Abiah Folger, daughter of Peter Folger, one of the first settlers of New England, of whom honorable mention is made by Cotton Mather, in his church history of that country, entitled *Magnalia Christi Americana,* as *"a godly, learned Englishman,"* if I remember the words rightly. I have heard that he wrote sundry small occasional pieces, but only one of them was printed, which I saw now many years since. It was written in 1675, in the homespun verse of that time and people, and addressed to those then concerned in the government there. It was in favor of liberty of conscience, and in behalf of the Baptists, Quakers, and other sectaries that had been under persecution, ascribing the Indian wars, and other distresses that had befallen the country, to that persecution, as so many judgments of God to punish so heinous an offense, and exhorting a repeal of those uncharitable laws. The whole appeared to me as written with a good deal of decent plainness and manly freedom. The six concluding lines I remember, though I have forgotten the two first of the stanza; but the purport of them was, that his censures proceeded from good-will, and therefore he would be known to be the author.

"Because to be a libeller (says he)
   I hate it with my heart;
From Sherburne town, where now I dwell
   My name I do put here;
Without offense your real friend,
   It is Peter Folgier."

[1] religious meetings, especially of persons dissenting from doctrines of the church of England

My elder brothers were all put apprentices to different trades. I was put to the grammar school at eight years of age, my father intending to devote me, as the tithe [2] of his sons, to the service of the Church. My early readiness in learning to read (which must have been very early, as I do not remember when I could not read), and the opinion of all his friends that I should certainly make a good scholar, encouraged him in this purpose of his. My uncle Benjamin, too, approved of it, and proposed to give me all his short-hand volumes of sermons, I suppose as a stock to set up with, if I would learn his character. [3] I continued, however, at the grammar school not quite one year, though in that time I had risen gradually from the middle of the class of that year to be the head of it, and farther was removed into the next class above it, in order to go with that into the third at the end of the year. But my father, in the mean time, from a view of the expense of a college education, which having so large a family he could not well afford, and the mean living many so educated were afterwards able to obtain—reasons that he gave to his friends in my hearing—altered his first intention, took me from the grammar school, and sent me to a school for writing and arithmetic, kept by a then famous man, Mr. George Brownell, very successful in his profession generally, and that by mild, encouraging methods. Under him I acquired fair writing pretty soon, but I failed in the arithmetic, and made no progress in it. At ten years old I was taken home to assist my father in his business, which was that of a tallow-chandler and soap-boiler; a business he was not bred to, but had assumed on his arrival in New England, and on finding his dyeing trade would not maintain his family, being in little request. Accordingly, I was employed in cutting wick for the candles, filling the dipping mould and the moulds for cast candles, attending the shop, going of errands, etc.

I disliked the trade, and had a strong inclination for the sea, but my father declared against it; however, living near the water, I was much in and about it, learned early to swim well, and to manage boats; and when in a boat or canoe with other boys, I was commonly allowed to govern, especially in any case of difficulty; and upon other occasions I was generally a leader among the boys, and sometimes led them into scrapes, of which I will mention one instance, as it shows an early projecting public spirit, though not then justly conducted.

[2] tenth, or one of ten (in reference to the Jewish custom of giving to Jehovah one tenth of all income)
[3] system of short-hand

There was a salt-marsh that bounded part of the mill-pond, on the edge of which, at high water, we used to stand to fish for minnows. By much trampling, we had made it a mere quagmire. My proposal was to build a wharf there fit for us to stand upon, and I showed my comrades a large heap of stones, which were intended for a new house near the marsh, and which would very well suit our purpose. Accordingly, in the evening, when the workmen were gone, I assembled a number of my playfellows, and working with them diligently, like so many emmets, sometimes two or three to a stone, we brought them all away and built our little wharf. The next morning the workmen were surprised at missing the stones, which were found in our wharf. Inquiry was made after the removers; we were discovered and complained of; several of us were corrected by our fathers; and, though I pleaded the usefulness of the work, mine convinced me that nothing was useful which was not honest.

I think you may like to know something of his person and character. He had an excellent constitution of body, was of middle stature, but well set, and very strong; he was ingenious, could draw prettily, was skilled a little in music, and had a clear, pleasing voice, so that when he played psalm tunes on his violin and sung withal, as he sometimes did in an evening after the business of the day was over, it was extremely agreeable to hear. He had a mechanical genius, too, and, on occasion, was very handy in the use of other tradesmen's tools; but his great excellence lay in a sound understanding and solid judgment in prudential matters, both in private and public affairs. In the latter, indeed, he was never employed, the numerous family he had to educate and the straitness of his circumstances keeping him close to his trade; but I remember well his being frequently visited by leading people, who consulted him for his opinion in affairs of the town or of the church he belonged to, and showed a good deal of respect for his judgment and advice; he was also much consulted by private persons about their affairs when any difficulty occurred, and frequently chosen an arbitrator between contending parties. At his table he liked to have, as often as he could, some sensible friend or neighbor to converse with, and always took care to start some ingenious or useful topic for discourse, which might tend to improve the minds of his children. By this means he turned our attention to what was good, just, and prudent in the conduct of life;

and little or no notice was ever taken of what related to the victuals on the table, whether it was well or ill dressed, in or out of season, of good or bad flavor, preferable or inferior to this or that other thing of the kind, so that I was brought up in such a perfect inattention to those matters as to be quite indifferent what kind of food was set before me, and so unobservant of it, that to this day if I am asked I can scarce tell a few hours after dinner what I dined upon. This has been a convenience to me in traveling, where my companions have been sometimes very unhappy for want of a suitable gratification of their more delicate, because better instructed, tastes and appetites.

My mother had likewise an excellent constitution; she suckled all her ten children. I never knew either my father or mother to have any sickness but that of which they died, he at 89, and she at 85 years of age. They lie buried together at Boston, where I some years since placed a marble over their grave, with this inscription:

JOSIAH FRANKLIN
and
ABIAH his wife,
lie here interred.
They lived lovingly together in wedlock
fifty-five years.
Without an estate, or any gainful employment,
by constant labor and industry,
with God's blessing,
they maintained a large family
comfortably,
and brought up thirteen children
and seven grandchildren
reputably.
From this instance, reader,
be encouraged to diligence in thy calling,
and distrust not Providence.
He was a pious and prudent man;
she, a discreet and virtuous woman.
Their youngest son,
in filial regard to their memory,
places this stone.
J. F. born 1655, died 1744, Ætat 89.
A. F. born 1667, died 1752, —— 85.

By my rambling digressions I perceive myself to be grown old. I used to write more methodically. But one does not dress for private company as for a public ball. 'Tis perhaps only negligence.

To return: I continued thus employed in my father's business for two years, that is, till I was twelve years old; and my brother John, who was bred to that business, having left my father, married, and set up for himself at Rhode Island, there was all appearance that I was destined to supply his place, and become a tallow-chandler. But my dislike to the trade continuing, my father was under apprehensions that if he did not find one for me more agreeable, I should break away and get to sea, as his son Josiah had done, to his great vexation. He therefore sometimes took me to walk with him, and see joiners, bricklayers, turners, braziers, etc., at their work, that he might observe my inclination and endeavor to fix it on some trade or other on land. It has ever since been a pleasure to me to see good workmen handle their tools, and it has been useful to me, having learned so much by it as to be able to do little jobs myself in my house when a workman could not readily be got, and to construct little machines for my experiments, while the intention of making the experiment was fresh and warm in my mind. My father at last fixed upon the cutler's trade, and my uncle Benjamin's son Samuel, who was bred to that business in London, being about that time established in Boston, I was sent to be with him some time on liking. But his expectations of a fee [1] with me displeasing my father, I was taken home again.

From a child I was fond of reading, and all the little money that came into my hands was ever laid out in books. Pleased with the *Pilgrim's Progress*, my first collection was of John Bunyan's works in separate little volumes. I afterward sold them to enable me to buy R. Burton's *Historical Collections*; they were small chapmen's [2] books, and cheap, 40 or 50 in all. My father's little library consisted chiefly of books in polemic divinity, most of which I read, and have since often regretted that, at a time when I had such a thirst for knowledge, more proper books had not fallen in my way, since it was now resolved I should not be a clergyman. Plutarch's *Lives* there was in which I read abundantly, and I still think that time spent to great advantage. There was also a book of Defoe's, called an *Essay on Projects*, and another of Dr. Mather's called *Essays to do Good*, [3] which perhaps gave me a turn of thinking that had an influence on some of the principal future events of my life.

This bookish inclination at length determined my father to make me a printer, though he had already one son (James) of that profession. In 1717 my brother James returned from England with a press and letters to set up his business in Boston. I liked it much better than that of my father, but still had a hankering for the sea. To prevent the apprehended effect of such an inclination, my father was impatient to have me bound to my brother. I stood out some time, but at last was persuaded, and signed the indentures when I was yet but twelve years old. I was to serve as an apprentice till I was twenty-one years of age, only I was to be allowed journeyman's wages during the last year. In a little time I made great proficiency in the business, and became a useful hand to my brother. I now had access to better books. An acquaintance with the apprentices of booksellers enabled me sometimes to borrow a small one, which I was careful to return soon and clean. Often I sat up in my room reading the greatest part of the night, when the book was borrowed in the evening and to be returned early in the morning, lest it should be missed or wanted.

And after some time an ingenious tradesman, [4] Mr. Matthew Adams, who had a pretty [5] collection of books, and who frequented our printing-house, took notice of me, invited me to his library, and very kindly lent me such books as I chose to read. I now took a fancy to poetry, and made some little pieces; my brother, thinking it might turn to account, encouraged me, and put me on composing occasional ballads. One was called *The Lighthouse Tragedy*, and contained an account of the drowning of Captain Worthilake, with his two daughters; the other was a sailor's song, on the taking of Teach [6] (or Blackbeard) the pirate. They were wretched stuff, in the Grub-street-ballad style; [7] and when they were printed he sent me about the town to sell them. The first sold wonderfully, the event being recent, having made a great noise. This flattered my vanity; but my father discouraged me by ridiculing my performances, and telling me verse-makers were generally beggars. So I escaped being a poet, most probably a very bad one; but as prose writing has been of great use to me in the course of my life, and was a principal means of my advancement, I shall tell you how, in such a situation, I acquired what little ability I have in that way.

---

[1] Apprentices or their guardians were often required to pay a fee to the master served, in addition to the services rendered.
[2] peddlers'
[3] The title is *Bonifacius. An Essay*, etc.

[4] intelligent shopkeeper or, perhaps, mechanic
[5] rather fine
[6] Edward Teach or Thatch, "Blackbeard," was trapped and killed on the Carolina coast in 1718.
[7] in the style of the hack writers who lived in Grub Street, London

There was another bookish lad in the town, John Collins by name, with whom I was intimately acquainted. We sometimes disputed, and very fond we were of argument, and very desirous of confuting one another, which disputatious turn, by the way, is apt to become a very bad habit, making people often extremely disagreeable in company by the contradiction that is necessary to bring it into practice; and thence, besides souring and spoiling the conversation, is productive of disgusts and perhaps enmities where you may have occasion for friendship. I had caught it by reading my father's books of dispute about religion. Persons of good sense, I have since observed, seldom fall into it, except lawyers, university men, and men of all sorts that have been bred at Edinburgh.[1]

A question was once, somehow or other, started between Collins and me, of the propriety of educating the female sex in learning, and their abilities for study.[2] He was of opinion that it was improper, and that they were naturally unequal to it. I took the contrary side, perhaps a little for dispute's sake. He was naturally more eloquent, had a ready plenty of words; and sometimes, as I thought, bore me down more by his fluency than by the strength of his reasons. As we parted without settling the point, and were not to see one another again for some time, I sat down to put my arguments in writing, which I copied fair and sent to him. He answered, and I replied. Three or four letters of a side had passed, when my father happened to find my papers and read them. Without entering into the discussion, he took occasion to talk to me about the manner of my writing; observed that, though I had the advantage of my antagonist in correct spelling and pointing (which I owed to the printing-house), I fell far short in elegance of expression, in method, and in perspicuity, of which he convinced me by several instances. I saw the justice of his remarks, and thence grew more attentive to the manner in writing, and determined to endeavor at improvement.

About this time I met with an odd volume of the *Spectator*. It was the third. I had never before seen any of them. I bought it, read it over and over, and was much delighted with it. I thought the writing excellent, and wished, if possible, to imitate it. With this view I took some of the papers, and, making short hints of the sentiment in each sentence, laid them by a few days, and then, without looking at the book, tried to complete the papers again, by expressing each hinted sentiment at length, and as fully as it had been expressed before, in any suitable words that should come to hand. Then I compared my *Spectator* with the original, discovered some of my faults, and corrected them.[3] But I found I wanted[4] a stock of words, or a readiness in recollecting and using them, which I thought I should have acquired before that time if I had gone on making verses; since the continual occasion for words of the same import, but of different length, to suit the measure, or of different sound for the rime, would have laid me under a constant necessity of searching for variety, and also have tended to fix that variety in my mind, and make me master of it. Therefore I took some of the tales and turned them into verse; and, after a time, when I had pretty well forgotten the prose, turned them back again. I also sometimes jumbled my collections of hints into confusion, and after some weeks endeavored to reduce them into the best order, before I began to form the full sentences and complete the paper. This was to teach me method in the arrangement of thoughts. By comparing my work afterwards with the original, I discovered many faults and amended them; but I sometimes had the pleasure of fancying that, in certain particulars of small import, I had been lucky enough to improve the method or the language, and this encouraged me to think I might possibly in time come to be a tolerable English writer, of which I was extremely ambitious. My time for these exercises and for reading was at night, after work, or before it began in the morning, or on Sundays. . . .

And now it was that, being on some occasion made ashamed of my ignorance in figures, which I had twice failed in learning when at school, I took Cocker's book of arithmetic, and went through the whole by myself with great ease. I also read Seller's and Shermy's books of navigation, and became acquainted with the little geometry they contain; but never proceeded far in that science. And I read about this time Locke[5] *On Human Understanding,*

---

[1] Even the good-natured Franklin must have a characteristic eighteenth century fling at the Scotch.

[2] Perhaps Franklin got the idea from Defoe's *Essay on Projects*, London, 1697.

[3] Sixty years later, Samuel Johnson in his life of Addison said, "Whoever wishes to attain an English style, familiar but not coarse, and elegant but not ostentatious, must give his days and nights to the volumes of Addison." Franklin does not attain to the grace and urbanity of Addison; but external polish would ill suit Franklin's material, and the manly vigor and directness of his style are notable.

[4] lacked

[5] John Locke (1632-1704); the *Essay* is fundamental in its analysis of the mind and was the inspirer of modern philosophical method.

and the *Art of Thinking*, by Messrs. du Port Royal. [1]

While I was intent on improving my language, I met with an English grammar (I think it was Greenwood's), at the end of which there were two little sketches of the arts of rhetoric and logic, the latter finishing with a specimen of a dispute in the Socratic method; and soon after I procured Xenophon's *Memorable Things of Socrates,* wherein there are many instances of the same method. I was charmed with it, adopted it, dropped my abrupt contradiction and positive argumentation, and put on the humble inquirer and doubter. And being then, from reading Shaftesbury and Collins, [2] become a real doubter in many points of our religious doctrine, [3] I found this method safest for myself and very embarrassing to those against whom I used it; therefore I took a delight in it, practiced it continually, and grew very artful and expert in drawing people, even of superior knowledge, into concessions, the consequences of which they did not foresee, entangling them in difficulties out of which they could not extricate themselves, and so obtaining victories that neither myself nor my cause always deserved. I continued this method some few years, but gradually left it, retaining only the habit of expressing myself in terms of modest diffidence; never using, when I advanced anything that may possibly be disputed, the words *certainly, undoubtedly,* or any others that give the air of positiveness to an opinion; but rather say, *I conceive or apprehend a thing to be so and so; it appears to me,* or *I should think it so or so, for such and such reasons;* or *I imagine it to be so;* or *it is so, if I am not mistaken.* This habit, I believe, has been of great advantage to me when I have had occasion to inculcate my opinions, and persuade men into measures that I have been from time to time engaged in promoting; and, as the chief ends of conversation are to *inform* or to be *informed,* to *please* or to *persuade,* I wish well-meaning, sensible men would not lessen their power of doing good by a positive, assuming manner, that seldom fails to disgust, tends to create opposition, and to defeat every one of those purposes for which speech was given to us, to wit, giving or receiving information or pleasure. For if you would inform, a positive and dogmatical manner in advancing your sentiments may provoke contradiction and prevent a candid attention. If you wish information and improvement from the knowledge of others, and yet at the same time express yourself as firmly fixed in your present opinions, modest, sensible men who do not love disputation will probably leave you undisturbed in the possession of your error. And by such a manner you can seldom hope to recommend yourself in *pleasing* your hearers, or to persuade those whose concurrence you desire.

. . . .

I have been the more particular in this description of my journey, [4] and shall be so of my first entry into that city, that you may in your mind compare such unlikely beginnings with the figure I have since made there. I was in my working dress, my best clothes being to come round by sea. I was dirty from my journey; my pockets were stuffed out with shirts and stockings, and I knew no soul nor where to look for lodging. I was fatigued with traveling, rowing, and want of rest. I was very hungry; and my whole stock of cash consisted of a Dutch dollar, and about a shilling in copper. The latter I gave the people of the boat for my passage, who at first refused it on account of my rowing; but I insisted on their taking it. A man being sometimes more generous when he has but a little money than when he has plenty, perhaps through fear of being thought to have but little.

Then I walked up the street, gazing about till near the market-house I met a boy with bread. I had made many a meal on bread, and, inquiring where he got it, I went immediately to the baker's he directed me to, in Second Street, and asked for biscuit, intending such as we had in Boston; but they, it seems, were not made in Philadelphia. Then I asked for a

---

[1] The Messrs. du Port Royal were a number of French religious recluses of the seventeenth century whose philosophical works were well known in Europe.

[2] The Earl of Shaftesbury and Anthony Collins, eighteenth century philosophical writers of the rationalistic or deistic school; by the strictly orthodox philosophers they were regarded as little better than infidels.

[3] Even without reading Shaftesbury and Collins, Franklin's mind would doubtless have rejected such religious doctrine as is shown in Michael Wigglesworth's *Day of Doom* (cf. pp. 29-34).

[4] Franklin's printer brother, James, to whom he was bound apprentice and who was a hard master, fell out with the Boston authorities, who ordered "that James Franklin should no longer print the paper called *The New England Courant.*" Releasing Benjamin from his apprenticeship, he continued to print the paper, but in the younger brother's name. He treated Benjamin so severely, however, that the lad, now seventeen years old, ran away by sea to New York to seek his fortune. The city must then have been about as Madam Knight describes it (cf. pp. 48-56). Not finding work here, but hearing of possible employment in Philadelphia, he pushed on afoot across New Jersey. The paragraph finds him just arrived in the Quaker city.

three-penny loaf, and was told they had none such. So not considering or knowing the difference of money, [1] and the greater cheapness nor the names of his bread, I bade him give me three-penny worth of any sort. He gave me, accordingly, three great puffy rolls. I was surprised at the quantity, but took it, and, having no room in my pockets, walked off with a roll under each arm, and eating the other. Thus I went up Market Street as far as Fourth Street, passing by the door of Mr. Read, my future wife's father; when she, standing at the door, saw me, and thought I made, as I certainly did, a most awkward, ridiculous appearance. Then I turned and went down Chestnut Street and part of Walnut Street, eating my roll all the way, and coming round, found myself again at Market Street wharf, near the boat I came in, to which I went for a draught of the river water; and being filled with one of my rolls, gave the other two to a woman and her child that came down the river in the boat with us, and were waiting to go farther.

Thus refreshed, I walked again up the street, which by this time had many clean-dressed people in it, who were all walking the same way. I joined them, and thereby was led into the great meeting-house of the Quakers, near the market. I sat down among them, and after looking round a while and hearing nothing said, being very drowsy through labor and want of rest the preceding night, I fell fast asleep, and continued so till the meeting broke up, when one was kind enough to rouse me. This was, therefore, the first house I was in or slept in, in Philadelphia.

. . . .

I believe I have omitted mentioning that, in my first voyage from Boston, being becalmed off Block Island, our people set about catching cod, and hauled up a great many. Hitherto I had stuck to my resolution of not eating animal food, and on this occasion I considered, with my master Tryon, [2] the taking every fish as a kind of unprovoked murder, since none of them had, or ever could do us any injury that might justify the slaughter. All this seemed very reasonable. But I had formerly been a great lover of fish, and when this came hot out of the frying-pan, it smelt admirably well. I balanced some time between principle and inclination,

till I recollected that, when the fish were opened, I saw smaller fish taken out of their stomachs; then thought I, "If you eat one another, I don't see why we mayn't eat you." So I dined upon cod very heartily, and continued to eat with other people, returning only now and then occasionally to a vegetable diet. So convenient a thing it is to be a *reasonable creature,* since it enables one to find or make a reason for everything one has a mind to do.

. . . .

. . . I now began to think [3] of getting a little money beforehand, and, expecting better work, I left Palmer's to work at Watt's, near Lincoln's Inn Fields, a still greater printing-house. Here I continued all the rest of my stay in London.

At my first admission into this printing-house I took to working at press, imagining I felt a want of the bodily exercise I had been used to in America, where presswork is mixed with composing. I drank only water; the other workmen, near fifty in number, were great guzzlers of beer. On occasion, I carried up and down stairs a large form of types in each hand, when others carried but one in both hands. They wondered to see, from this and several instances, that the *Water-American,* as they called me, was *stronger* than themselves, who drank *strong* beer! We had an ale-house boy who attended always in the house to supply the workmen. My companion at the press drank every day a pint before breakfast, a pint at breakfast with his bread and cheese, a pint between breakfast and dinner, a pint at dinner, a pint in the afternoon about six o'clock, and another when he had done his day's work. I thought it a detestable custom; but it was necessary, he supposed, to drink *strong* beer, that he might be *strong* to labor. I endeavored to convince him that the bodily strength afforded by beer could only be in proportion to the grain or flour of the barley dissolved in the water of which it was made; that there was more flour in a pennyworth of bread; and therefore, if he would eat that with a pint of water, it would give him more strength than a

[1] There was so little English money in colonial circulation that there was no fixed standard of exchange. Bread was dearer in Boston than in Philadelphia, which was surrounded by fertile lands.

[2] a vegetarian propagandist whose system Franklin had been following

[3] Meanwhile Franklin had been befriended by Sir William Keith, governor of the province, a man "who wished to please everybody." He induced Franklin to go to London to procure for himself a new printing outfit on Keith's credit. Arriving in London, Franklin found that Keith had no credit there. He at once turned to his trade, however, earned and saved money, and, boy though he was—he had not yet reached his majority—made the acquaintance of such men as Sir Hans Sloane, afterwards founder of the British Museum, and Dr. Mandeville, author of *The Fable of the Bees.* The whole experience was greatly educative to the lad.

quart of beer. He drank on, however, and had four or five shillings to pay out of his wages every Saturday night for that muddling liquor; an expense I was free from. And thus these poor devils keep themselves always under.

Watts, after some weeks, desiring to have me in the composing-room, I left the pressmen; a new *bien venu* [1] or sum for drink, being five shillings, was demanded of me by the compositors. I thought it an imposition, as I had paid below; the master thought so too, and forbad my paying it. I stood out two or three weeks, was accordingly considered as an excommunicate, and had so many little pieces of private mischief done me, by mixing my sorts, [2] transposing my pages, breaking my matter, [3] etc., etc., if I were ever so little out of the room, and all ascribed to the chapel [4] ghost, which they said ever haunted those not regularly admitted, that, notwithstanding the master's protection, I found myself obliged to comply and pay the money, convinced of the folly of being on ill terms with those one is to live with continually.

I was now on a fair footing with them, and soon acquired considerable influence. I proposed some reasonable alterations in their chapel laws, and carried them against all opposition. From my example, a great part of them left their muddling breakfast of beer, and bread, and cheese, finding they could with me, be supplied from a neighboring house with a large porringer of hot water-gruel, sprinkled with pepper, crumbed with bread, and a bit of butter in it, for the price of a pint of beer, viz., three half-pence. This was a more comfortable as well as cheaper breakfast, and kept their heads clearer. Those who continued sotting with beer all day were often, by not paying, out of credit at the alehouse, and used to make interest with me to get beer; their *light*, as they phrased it, *being out*. I watched the pay-table on Saturday night, and collected what I stood engaged for them, having to pay sometimes near thirty shillings a week on their accounts. This, and my being esteemed a pretty good *riggite*, that is, a jocular verbal satirist, supported my consequence in the society. My constant attendance (I never making a St. Monday [5]) recommended me to the master; and my uncommon quickness at composing occasioned my being put upon all work of dispatch, which was generally better paid. So I went on now very agreeably.

[1] welcome   [2] kinds of type   [3] what he had composed
[4] a printer's cant name for a printing-house
[5] a holiday after a Sunday's drinking spree: jocularly, as if a saint's day

Before I enter upon my public appearance in business, it may be well to let you know the then state of my mind with regard to my principles and morals, that you may see how far those influenced the future events of my life. My parents had early given me religious impressions, and brought me through my childhood piously in the Dissenting way. But I was scarce fifteen when, after doubting by turns of several points, as I found them disputed in the different books I read, I began to doubt of revelation itself. Some books against deism fell into my hands; they were said to be the substance of sermons preached at Boyle's Lectures. It happened that they wrought an effect on me quite contrary to what was intended by them; for the arguments of the deists, which were quoted to be refuted, appeared to me much stronger than the refutations; in short, I soon became a thorough deist. My arguments perverted some others, particularly Collins and Ralph; but each of them having afterwards wronged me greatly without the least compunction, and recollecting Keith's conduct towards me (who was another freethinker), and my own towards Vernon and Miss Read, which at times gave me great trouble, I began to suspect that this doctrine, though it might be true, was not very useful. My London pamphlet, which had for its motto these lines of Dryden:

"Whatever is, is right. Though purblind man
Sees but a part o' the chain, the nearest link:
His eyes not carrying to the equal beam,
That poises all above"; [6]

and from the attributes of God, his infinite wisdom, goodness, and power, concluded that nothing could possibly be wrong in the world, and that vice and virtue were empty distinctions, no such things existing, appeared now not so clever a performance as I once thought it; and I doubted whether some error had not insinuated itself unperceived into my argument, so as to infect all that followed, as is common in metaphysical reasonings.

I grew convinced that *truth, sincerity,* and *integrity* in dealings between man and man were of the utmost importance to the felicity of life; and I formed written resolutions, which still remain in my journal book, to practice them ever while I lived. Revelation had indeed

[6] Franklin quotes inaccurately. The passage is:
   Whatever is, is in its causes just;
   Since all things are by fate. But purblind man
   Sees but a part o' the chain; the nearest links;
   His eyes not carrying to that equal beam,
   That poises above all.
                    Dryden, *Oedipus*, III, i, 284.

no weight with me, as such; but I entertained an opinion that, though certain actions might not be bad *because* they were forbidden by it, or good *because* it commanded them, yet probably these actions might be forbidden *because* they were bad for us, or commanded *because* they were beneficial to us, in their own natures, all the circumstances of things considered. And this persuasion, with the kind hand of Providence, or some guardian angel, or accidental favorable circumstances and situations, or all together, preserved me, through this dangerous time of youth, and the hazardous situations I was sometimes in among strangers, remote from the eye and advice of my father, without any willful gross immorality or injustice, that might have been expected from my want of religion. I say willful, because the instances I have mentioned had something of *necessity* in them, from my youth, inexperience, and the knavery of others. I had, therefore, a tolerable character to begin the world with; I valued it properly, and determined to preserve it.

. . . .

It was about this time [1] I conceived the bold and arduous project of arriving at moral perfection. I wished to live without committing any fault at any time; I would conquer all that either natural inclination, custom, or company might lead me into. As I knew, or thought I knew, what was right and wrong, I did not see why I might not always do the one and avoid the other. But I soon found I had undertaken a task of more difficulty than I had imagined. While my care was employed in guarding against one fault, I was often surprised by another; habit took the advantage of inattention; inclination was sometimes too strong for reason. I concluded, at length, that the mere speculative conviction that it was our interest to be completely virtuous was not sufficient to prevent our slipping; and that the contrary habits must be broken, and good ones acquired and established, before we can have any dependence on a steady, uniform rectitude of conduct. For this purpose I therefore contrived the following method.

In the various enumerations of the moral virtues I had met with in my reading, I found the catalogue more or less numerous, as different writers included more or fewer ideas under the same name. Temperance, for example, was by some confined to eating and drinking, while by others it was extended to mean the moderating every other pleasure, appetite, in-

clination, or passion, bodily or mental, even to our avarice and ambition. I proposed to myself, for the sake of clearness, to use rather more names, with fewer ideas annexed to each, than a few names with more ideas; and I included under thirteen names of virtues all that at any time occurred to me as necessary or desirable, and annexed to each a short precept, which fully expressed the extent I gave to its meaning.

These names of virtues, with their precepts were:

1. TEMPERANCE.
Eat not to dullness; drink not to elevation.

2. SILENCE.
Speak not but what may benefit others or yourself; avoid trifling conversation.

3. ORDER.
Let all your things have their places; let each part of your business have its time.

4. RESOLUTION.
Resolve to perform what you ought; perform without fail what you resolve.

5. FRUGALITY.
Make no expense but to do good to others or yourself; *i.e.*, waste nothing.

6. INDUSTRY.
Lose no time; be always employed in something useful; cut off all unnecessary actions.

7. SINCERITY.
Use no hurtful deceit; think innocently and justly; and, if you speak, speak accordingly.

8. JUSTICE.
Wrong none by doing injuries, or omitting the benefits that are your duty.

9. MODERATION.
Avoid extremes; forbear resenting injuries so much as you think they deserve.

10. CLEANLINESS.
Tolerate no uncleanliness in body, clothes, or habitation.

11. TRANQUILITY.
Be not disturbed at trifles, or at accidents common or unavoidable.

12. CHASTITY.

13. HUMILITY.
Imitate Jesus and Socrates.

---

[1] Franklin was now back in Philadelphia, married, and settled in business.

My intention being to acquire the *habitude* of all these virtues, I judged it would be well not to distract my attention by attempting the whole at once, but to fix it on one of them at a time; and, when I should be master of that, then to proceed to another, and so on, till I should have gone through the thirteen; and as the previous acquisition of some might facilitate the acquisition of certain others, I arranged them with that view, as they stand above. Temperance first, as it tends to procure that coolness and clearness of head, which is so necessary where constant vigilance was to be kept up, and guard maintained against the unremitting attraction of ancient habits, and the force of perpetual temptations. This being acquired and established, Silence would be more easy; and my desire being to gain knowledge at the same time that I improved in virtue, and considering that in conversation it was obtained rather by the use of the ears than of the tongue, and therefore wishing to break a habit I was getting into of prattling, punning, and joking, which only made me acceptable to trifling company, I gave Silence the second place. This and the next, Order, I expected would allow me more time for attending to my project and my studies. Resolution, once become habitual, would keep me firm in my endeavors to obtain all the subsequent virtues; Frugality and Industry freeing me from my remaining debt, and producing affluence and independence, would make more easy the practice of Sincerity and Justice, etc., etc. Conceiving then, that, agreeably to the advice of Pythagoras in his Golden Verses, [1] daily examination would be necessary, I contrived the following method for conducting that examination. [2]

I made a little book, in which I allotted a page for each of the virtues. I ruled each page with red ink, so as to have seven columns, one for each day of the week, marking each column with a letter for the day. I crossed these columns with thirteen red lines, marking the beginning of each line with the first letter of one of the virtues, on which line, and in its proper column, I might mark, by a little black spot, every fault I found upon examination to have been committed respecting that virtue upon that day.

I determined to give a week's strict attention to each of the virtues successively. Thus, in

[1] Pythagoras was a Greek philosopher of the sixth century B.C. The *Golden Verses* may be of a later date.

[2] Franklin, in common with most mid-eighteenth century Englishmen, took an intellectual and utilitarian attitude toward morality, virtue, and religion.

Form of the Pages

TEMPERANCE

EAT NOT TO DULNESS; DRINK NOT TO ELEVATION.

	S.	M.	T.	W.	T.	F.	S.
T.							
S.	*	*		*		*	
O.	* *	*	*		*	*	*
R.			*			*	
F.		*			*		
I.			*				
S.							
J.							
M.							
C.							
T.							
C.							
H.							

the first week, my great guard was to avoid every the least offense against Temperance, leaving the other virtues to their ordinary chance, only marking every evening the faults of the day. Thus, if in the first week I could keep my first line, marked T, clear of spots, I supposed the habit of that virtue so much strengthened, and its opposite weakened, that I might venture extending my attention to include the next, and for the following week keep both lines clear of spots. Proceeding thus to the last, I could go through a course complete in thirteen weeks, and four courses in a year. And like him who, having a garden to weed, does not attempt to eradicate all the bad herbs at once, which would exceed his reach and his strength, but works on one of the beds at a time, and, having accomplished the first, proceeds to a second, so I should have, I hoped, the encouraging pleasure of seeing on my pages the progress I made in virtue, by clearing successively my lines of their spots, till in the end, by a number of courses, I should be happy in viewing a clean book, after a thirteen weeks' daily examination.

This my little book had for its motto these lines from Addison's *Cato:* [3]

"Here will I hold. If there's a power above us
(And that there is, all nature cries aloud
Thro' all her works), He must delight in virtue;
And that which he delights in must be happy."

[3] a tragedy founded on the death of the philosopher and patriot, Cato, 95-46 B.C.

Another from Cicero,

"O vitae Philosophia dux! O virtutum indaga-trix expultrixque vitiorum! Unus dies, bene et ex praeceptis tuis actus, peccanti immortalitati est anteponendus." [1]

Another from the *Proverbs* of Solomon, speaking of wisdom or virtue:

"Length of days is in her right hand, and in her left hand riches and honor. Her ways are ways of pleasantness, and all her paths are peace." iii, 16, 17.

And conceiving God to be the fountain of wisdom, I thought it right and necessary to solicit his assistance for obtaining it; to this end I formed the following little prayer, which was prefixed to my tables of examination, for daily use.

"O powerful Goodness! bountiful Father! merciful Guide! Increase in me that wisdom which discovers my truest interest. Strengthen my resolutions to perform what that wisdom dictates. Accept my kind offices to thy other children as the only return in my power for thy continual favors to me."

I used also sometimes a little prayer which I took from Thomson's [2] poems, viz.:

"Father of light and life, thou Good Supreme!
O teach me what is good; teach me Thyself!
Save me from folly, vanity, and vice,
From every low pursuit; and fill my soul
With knowledge, conscious peace, and virtue pure;
Sacred, substantial, never-fading bliss!"

The precept of Order requiring that *every part of my business should have its allotted time*, one page in my little book contained the following scheme of employment for the twenty-four hours of a natural day.

THE MORNING		
	5	Rise, wash, and address *Powerful Goodness!* Contrive day's business, and take the resolution of the day; prosecute the present study, and breakfast.
Question. What good shall I do this day?	6	
	7	
	8	
	9	Work.
	10	
	11	
NOON	12	Read, or overlook my accounts, and dine.
	1	

[1] O philosophy, guide of life! O searcher-out of virtue and expeller of vice! One day lived well and by thy precepts is to be preferred to an immortality of sin.

[2] James Thomson, 1700-1748, author of *The Seasons*

	2	
	3	Work.
	4	
	5	
EVENING	6	
	7	Put things in their places. Supper. Music or diversion, or conversation. Examination of the day.
Question. What good have I done today?	8	
	9	
	10	
	11	
	12	
NIGHT	1	Sleep.
	2	
	3	
	4	

I entered upon the execution of this plan for self-examination, and continued it with occasional intermissions for some time. I was surprised to find myself so much fuller of faults than I had imagined; but I had the satisfaction of seeing them diminish. To avoid the trouble of renewing now and then my little book, which, by scraping out the marks on the paper of old faults to make room for new ones in a new course, became full of holes, I transferred my tables and precepts to the ivory leaves of a memorandum book, on which the lines were drawn with red ink, that made a durable stain, and on those lines I marked my faults with a black lead-pencil, which marks I could easily wipe out with a wet sponge. After a while I went through one course only in a year, and afterward only one in several years, till at length I omitted them entirely, being employed in voyages and business abroad, with a multiplicity of affairs that interfered; but I always carried my little book with me.

My scheme of ORDER gave me the most trouble; and I found that, though it might be practicable where a man's business was such as to leave him the disposition of his time, that of a journeyman printer, for instance, it was not possible to be exactly observed by a master, who must mix with the world, and often receive people of business at their own hours. *Order*, too, with regard to places for things, papers, etc., I found extremely difficult to acquire. I had not been early accustomed to it, and, having an exceeding good memory, I was not so sensible of the inconvenience attending want of method. This article, therefore, cost me so much painful attention, and my faults in it vexed me so much, and I made so little progress in amendment, and had such frequent relapses, that I was almost ready to give up the attempt, and content myself with a faulty character in that respect, like the man who, in buying an axe of a smith, my neighbor, desired to have the whole of its surface as bright as the edge. The smith consented to grind it bright for him if he would turn the wheel; he turned, while the smith pressed the broad face of the axe hard and heavily on the stone, which made the turning of it very fatiguing. The man came every now and then from the wheel to see how the work went on, and at length would take his axe as it was, without farther grinding. "No," said the smith, "turn on, turn on; we shall have it bright by and by; as yet, it is only speckled." "Yes," says the man, *"but I think I like a speckled axe best."* And I believe this may have been the case with many, who, having, for want of some such means as I have employed, found the difficulty of obtaining good and breaking bad habits in other points of vice and virtue, have given up the struggle, and concluded that *"a speckled axe was best"*;[1] for something, that pretended to be reason, was every now and then suggesting to me that such extreme nicety as I exacted of myself might be a kind of foppery in morals, which, if it were known, would make me ridiculous; that a perfect character might be attended with the inconvenience of being envied and hated; and that a benevolent man should allow a few faults in himself, to keep his friends in countenance.

In truth, I found myself incorrigible with respect to Order; and now I am grown old, and my memory bad, I feel very sensibly the want of it. But, on the whole, though I never arrived at the perfection I had been so ambitious of obtaining, but fell far short of it, yet I was, by the endeavor, a better and a happier man than I otherwise should have been if I had not attempted it; as those who aim at perfect writing by imitating the engraved copies, though they never reach the wished-for excellence of those copies, their hand is mended by the endeavor, and is tolerable while it continues fair and legible.

It may be well my posterity should be informed that to this little artifice, with the blessing of God, their ancestor owed the constant felicity of his life, down to his 79th year, in which this is written. What reverses may attend the remainder is in the hand of Providence; but, if they arrive, the reflection on past happiness enjoyed ought to help his bearing them with more resignation. To Temperance he ascribes his long-continued health, and what is still left to him of a good constitution; to Industry and Frugality, the early easiness of his circumstances and acquisition of his fortune, with all that knowledge that enabled him to be a useful citizen, and obtained for him some degree of reputation among the learned; to Sincerity and Justice, the confidence of his country, and the honorable employs it conferred upon him;.and to the joint influence of the whole mass of the virtues, even in the imperfect state he was able to acquire them, all that evenness of temper, and that cheerfulness in conversation, which makes his company still sought for, and agreeable even to his younger acquaintance. I hope, therefore, that some of my descendants may follow the example and reap the benefit. [2]

It will be remarked that, though my scheme was not wholly without religion, there was in it no mark of any of the distinguishing tenets of any particular sect. I had purposely avoided them; for, being fully persuaded of the utility and excellency of my method, and that it might be serviceable to people in all religions, and intending some time or other to publish it, I would not have anything in it that should prejudice any one, of any sect, against it. I purposed writing a little comment on each virtue, in which I would have shown the advantages of possessing it, and the mischiefs attending its opposite vice; and I should have called my book THE ART OF VIRTUE, because it would have shown the means and manner of obtaining virtue, which would have distinguished it from the mere exhortation to be good, that does not instruct and indicate the means, but is like the apostle's man of verbal charity, who only without showing to the naked and hungry how or where they might get clothes or victuals, exhorted them to be fed and clothed.—*James ii, 15, 16.*

But it so happened that my intention of writing and publishing this comment was never fulfilled. I did, indeed, from time to time, put down short hints of the sentiments, reasonings, etc., to be made use of in it, some of which I have still by me; but the necessary close attention to private business in the earlier part of my life, and public business since, have occasioned my postponing it; for, it being connected in my mind with *a great and extensive*

---

[1] Franklin had a faculty of acquiring and coining sayings like those of Lincoln in their homespun humor and shrewd knowledge of life.

[2] The manly, sincere modesty of such passages as these gives us confidence in all of Franklin's estimates of himself and his fellow men.

project, [1] that required the whole man to execute, and which an unforeseen succession of employs prevented my attending to, it has hitherto remained unfinished.

In this piece it was my design to explain and enforce this doctrine, that vicious actions are not hurtful because they are forbidden, but forbidden because they are hurtful, the nature of man alone considered; that it was, therefore, every one's interest to be virtuous who wished to be happy even in this world; and I should, from this circumstance (there being always in the world a number of rich merchants, nobility, states, and princes, who have need of honest instruments for the management of their affairs, and such being so rare), have endeavored to convince young persons that no qualities were so likely to make a poor man's fortune as those of probity and integrity. [2]

My list of virtues contained at first but twelve; but a Quaker friend having kindly informed me that I was generally thought proud; that my pride showed itself frequently in conversation; that I was not content with being in the right when discussing any point, but was overbearing and rather insolent, of which he convinced me by mentioning several instances; I determined endeavoring to cure myself, if I could, of this vice or folly among the rest, and I added Humility to my list, giving an extensive meaning to the word.

I cannot boast of much success in acquiring the *reality* of this virtue, but I had a good deal with regard to the *appearance* of it. I made it a rule to forbear all direct contradiction to the sentiments of others, and all positive assertion of my own. I even forbid myself, agreeably to the old laws of our Junto, [3] the use of every word or expression in the language that imported a fixed opinion, such as *certainly, undoubtedly,* etc., and I adopted, instead of them, *I conceive, I apprehend,* or *I imagine* a thing to be so or so; or it *so appears to me at present.* When another asserted something that I thought an error I denied myself the pleasure of contradicting him abruptly, and of showing immediately some absurdity in his proposition; and in answering I began by observing that in certain cases or circumstances his opinion would be right, but in the present case there *appeared* or *seemed* to me some difference, etc. I soon found the advantage of this change in my manner; the conversations I engaged in went on more pleasantly. The modest way in which I proposed my opinions procured them a readier reception and less contradiction; I had less mortification when I was found to be in the wrong, and I more easily prevailed with others to give up their mistakes and join with me when I happened to be in the right.

And this mode, which I at first put on with some violence to natural inclination, became at length so easy, and so habitual to me, that perhaps for these fifty years past no one has ever heard a dogmatical expression escape me. And to this habit (after my character of integrity) I think it principally owing that I had early so much weight with my fellow-citizens when I proposed new institutions, or alterations in the old, and so much influence in public councils when I became a member; for I was but a bad speaker, never eloquent, subject to much hesitation in my choice of words, hardly correct in language, and yet I generally carried my points. [4]

In reality, there is, perhaps, no one of our natural passions so hard to subdue as *pride*. Disguise it, struggle with it, beat it down, stifle it, mortify it as much as one pleases, it is still alive, and will every now and then peep out and show itself; you will see it, perhaps, often in this history; for, even if I could conceive that I had completely overcome it, I should probably be proud of my humility.

. . . . . .

In 1732 I first published my *Almanac*, under the name of *Richard Saunders;* it was continued by me about twenty-five years, commonly called *Poor Richard's Almanac.* I endeavored to make it both entertaining and useful; and it accordingly came to be in such demand, that I reaped considerable profit from it, vending annually near ten thousand. And observing that it was generally read, scarce any neighborhood in the province being without it, I considered it as a proper vehicle for conveying instruction among the common people, who bought scarcely any other books; I therefore filled all the little spaces that occurred between the remarkable days in the calendar with proverbial sentences, chiefly such as inculcated industry and frugality as the means of procuring wealth, and thereby securing virtue; it being more difficult for a man in want to act always honestly, as,

---

[1] Franklin, like Bolingbroke and other English deists of the time, had in mind the founding of a new religious sect whose creed was to be much the same as that of the deists.

[2] In this coldly practical view of morality, Franklin is expressing the views of his generation of Englishmen, who valued religion chiefly as a cheap and convenient police force in society.

[3] a debating club that Franklin had organized when a young man.

[4] See what Jefferson says of Franklin's speeches, on page 157.

to use here one of those proverbs, *it is hard for an empty sack to stand upright.*

These proverbs, which contained the wisdom of many ages and nations, I assembled and formed into a connected discourse prefixed to the *Almanac* of 1757, as the harangue of a wise old man to the people attending an auction. The bringing all these scattered counsels thus into a focus enabled them to make greater impression. The piece, being universally approved, was copied in all the newspapers of the continent; reprinted in Britain on a broad side, to be stuck up in houses; two translations were made of it in French, and great numbers bought by the clergy and gentry, to distribute gratis among their poor parishioners and tenants. In Pennsylvania, as it discouraged useless expense in foreign superfluities, some thought it had its share of influence in producing that growing plenty of money which was observable for several years after its publication.

. . . .

In 1739 arrived among us from Ireland the Reverend Mr. Whitefield, [1] who had made himself remarkable there as an itinerant preacher. He was at first permitted to preach in some of our churches; but the clergy, taking a dislike to him, soon refused him their pulpits, and he was obliged to preach in the fields. The multitudes of all sects and denominations that attended his sermons were enormous, and it was matter of speculation to me, who was one of the number, to observe the extraordinary influence of his oratory on his hearers, and how much they admired and respected him, notwithstanding his common abuse of them, by assuring them they were naturally *half beasts and half devils.* It was wonderful to see the change soon made in the manners of our inhabitants. From being thoughtless or indifferent about religion, it seemed as if all the world were growing religious, so that one could not walk through the town in an evening without hearing psalms sung in different families of every street.

And it being found inconvenient to assemble in the open air, subject to its inclemencies, the building of a house to meet in was no sooner proposed, and persons appointed to receive contributions, but sufficient sums were soon received to procure the ground and erect the building, which was one hundred feet long and

seventy broad, about the size of Westminster Hall; [2] and the work was carried on with such spirit as to be finished in a much shorter time than could have been expected. Both house and ground were vested in trustees, expressly for the use of any preacher of any religious persuasion who might desire to say something to the people at Philadelphia; the design in building not being to accommodate any particular sect, but the inhabitants in general; so that even if the Mufti [3] of Constantinople were to send a missionary to preach Mohammedanism to us, he would find a pulpit at his service.

Mr. Whitefield, in leaving us, went preaching all the way through the colonies to Georgia. The settlement of that province had lately been begun, but instead of being made with hardy, industrious husbandmen accustomed to labor, the only people fit for such an enterprise, it was with families of broken shop-keepers and other insolvent debtors, many of indolent and idle habits, taken out of the jails, [4] who, being set down in the woods, unqualified for clearing land, and unable to endure the hardships of a new settlement, perished in numbers, leaving many helpless children unprovided for. The sight of their miserable situation inspired the benevolent heart of Mr. Whitefield with the idea of building an Orphan House there, in which they might be supported and educated. Returning northward, he preached up this charity, and made large collections, for his eloquence had a wonderful power over the hearts and purses of his hearers, of which I myself was an instance.

I did not disapprove of the design, but, as Georgia was then destitute of materials and workmen, and it was proposed to send them from Philadelphia at a great expense, I thought it would have been better to have built the house here, and brought the children to it. This I advised; but he was resolute in his first project, rejected my counsel, and I therefore refused to contribute. I happened soon after to attend one of his sermons, in the course of which I perceived he intended to finish with a collection, and I silently resolved he should get nothing from me. I had in my pocket a handful of copper money, three or four silver dollars,

---

[1] George Whitefield, 1714-70, the celebrated English evangelist and pulpit orator of the Methodist movement in the English church; in religious temperament he was the opposite of Franklin. This was the first of his three tours to America.

[2] a hall famous in English history, adjoining the Houses of Parliament in Westminster; it covers an area 68 by 290 feet.

[3] a high Mohammedan civil official

[4] This passage is not wholly unbiased. Oglethorpe's motives in founding Georgia were philanthropic and his colony may have contained a good many unworthy persons; but the colonists were for the main part chosen with especial care for their usefulness in colonial development.

and five pistoles [1] in gold. As he proceeded I began to soften, and concluded to give the coppers. Another stroke of his oratory made me ashamed of that, and determined me to give the silver; and he finished so admirably, that I emptied my pocket wholly into the collector's dish, gold and all. At this sermon there was also one of our club, who, being of my sentiments respecting the building in Georgia, and suspecting a collection might be intended, had, by precaution, emptied his pockets before he came from home. Towards the conclusion of the discourse, however, he felt a strong desire to give, and applied to a neighbor, who stood near him, to borrow some money for the purpose. The application was unfortunately [made] to perhaps the only man in the company who had the firmness not to be affected by the preacher. His answer was, *"At any other time, Friend Hopkinson, I would lend to thee freely; but not now, for thee seems to be out of thy right senses."*

Some of Mr. Whitefield's enemies affected to suppose that he would apply these collections to his own private emolument; but I, who was intimately acquainted with him (being employed in printing his Sermons and Journals, etc.), never had the least suspicion of his integrity, but am to this day decidedly of opinion that he was in all his conduct a perfectly *honest man;* and methinks my testimony in his favor ought to have the more weight, as we had no religious connection. He used, indeed, sometimes to pray for my conversion, but never had the satisfaction of believing that his prayers were heard. Ours was a mere civil friendship, sincere on both sides, and lasted to his death.

The following instance will show something of the terms on which we stood. Upon one of his arrivals from England at Boston he wrote to me that he should come soon to Philadelphia, but knew not where he could lodge when there, as he understood his old friend and host, Mr. Benezet, was removed to Germantown. My answer was, "You know my house; if you can make shift with its scanty accommodations, you will be most heartily welcome." He replied, that if I made that kind offer for Christ's sake, I should not miss of a reward. And I returned, *"Don't let me be mistaken; it was not for Christ's sake, but for your sake."* One of our common acquaintance jocosely remarked, that, knowing it to be the custom of the saints, when they received any favor, to shift the burden of the obligation from off their own

shoulders, and place it in heaven, I had contrived to fix it on earth.

The last time I saw Mr. Whitefield was in London, when he consulted me about his Orphan House concern, and his purpose of appropriating it to the establishment of a college.

He had a loud and clear voice, and articulated his words and sentences so perfectly, that he might be heard and understood at a great distance, especially as his auditories, however numerous, observed the most exact silence. He preached one evening from the top of the Court-house steps, which are in the middle of Market Street, and on the west side of Second Street, which crosses it at right angles. Both streets were filled with his hearers to a considerable distance. Being among the hindmost in Market Street, I had the curiosity to learn how far he could be heard, by retiring backwards down the street towards the river; and I found his voice distinct till I came near Front Street, when some noise in that street obscured it. Imagining then a semicircle of which my distance should be the radius, and that it were filled with auditors, to each of whom I allowed two square feet, I computed that he might well be heard by more than thirty thousand. This reconciled me to the newspaper accounts of his having preached to twenty-five thousand people in the fields, and to the ancient histories of generals haranguing whole armies, of which I had sometimes doubted.

By hearing him often, I came to distinguish easily between sermons newly composed, and those which he had often preached in the course of his travels. His delivery of the latter was so improved by frequent repetitions that every accent, every emphasis, every modulation of voice was so perfectly well turned and well placed that, without being interested in the subject, one could not help being pleased with the discourse; a pleasure of much the same kind with that received from an excellent piece of music. This is an advantage itinerant preachers have over those who are stationary, as the latter cannot well improve their delivery of a sermon by so many rehearsals.

His writing and printing from time to time gave great advantage to his enemies; unguarded expressions, and even erroneous opinions, delivered in preaching, might have been afterwards explained or qualified by supposing others that might have accompanied them, or they might have been denied; but *litera scripta manet.* [2] Critics attacked his writings violently, and with so much appearance of

---

[1] a Spanish gold coin worth about four dollars

[2] "The written word endures."

reason as to diminish the number of his votaries and prevent their increase; so that I am of the opinion if he had never written anything, he would have left behind him a much more numerous and important sect, and his reputation might in that case have been still growing, even after his death, as there being nothing of his writing on which to found a censure and give him a lower character, his proselytes would be left at liberty to feign for him as great a variety of excellencies as their enthusiastic admiration might wish him to have possessed.

. . . . . .

In order of time, I should have mentioned before, that having, in 1742, invented an open stove for the better warming of rooms, and at the same time saving fuel, as the fresh air admitted was warmed in entering, I made a present of the model to Mr. Robert Grace, one of my early friends, who, having an iron-furnace, found the casting of the plates for these stoves a profitable thing, as they were growing in demand. To promote that demand, I wrote and published a pamphlet, entitled *"An Account of the new-invented Pennsylvania Fireplaces; wherein their Construction and Manner of Operation is particularly explained; their Advantages above every other Method of warming Rooms demonstrated; and all Objections that have been raised against the Use of them answered and obviated,"* etc. This pamphlet had a good effect. Governor Thomas was so pleased with the construction of this stove, as described in it, that he offered to give me a patent for the sole vending of them for a term of years; but I declined it from a principle which has ever weighed with me on such occasions, viz., *That, as we enjoy great advantages from the inventions of others, we should be glad of an opportunity to serve others by any invention of ours; and this we should do freely and generously.*

An ironmonger in London, however, assuming a good deal of my pamphlet, and working it up into his own, and making some small changes in the machine, which rather hurt its operation, got a patent for it there, and made, as I was told, a little fortune by it. And this is not the only instance of patents taken out for my inventions by others, though not always with the same success, which I never contested, as having no desire of profiting by patents myself, and hating disputes. The use of these fireplaces in very many houses, both of this and the neighboring colonies, has been, and is, a great saving of wood to the inhabitants.

. . . . . .

The British government, not choosing to permit the union of the colonies as proposed at Albany; [1] and to trust that union with their defense, lest they should thereby grow too military and feel their own strength, suspicions and jealousies at this time being entertained of them, sent over General Braddock with two regiments of regular English troops for that purpose. He landed at Alexandria, in Virginia, and thence marched to Frederictown, in Maryland, where he halted for carriages. Our Assembly apprehending, from some information, that he had conceived violent prejudices against them, as averse to the service, wished me to wait upon him, not as from them, but as postmaster-general, under the guise of proposing to settle with him the mode of conducting with most celerity and certainty the despatches between him and the governors of the several provinces, with whom he must necessarily have continual correspondence, and of which they proposed to pay the expense. My son accompanied me on this journey.

We found the general at Frederictown, waiting impatiently for the return of those he had sent through the back parts of Maryland and Virginia to collect wagons. I stayed with him several days, dined with him daily, and had full opportunity of removing all his prejudices, by the information of what the Assembly had before his arrival actually done, and were still willing to do, to facilitate his operations. When I was about to depart, the returns of wagons to be obtained were brought in, by which it appeared that they amounted only to twenty-five, and not all of those were in serviceable condition. The general and all the officers were surprised, declared the expedition was then at an end, being impossible, and exclaimed against the ministers for ignorantly landing them in a country destitute of the means of conveying their stores, baggage, etc., not less than one hundred and fifty wagons being necessary.

I happened to say I thought it was pity they had not been landed rather in Pennsylvania, as in that country almost every farmer had his wagon. The general eagerly laid hold of my words, and said, "Then you, sir, who are a man of interest there, can probably procure them for us; and I beg you will under-

[1] At a congress of commissioners from the different colonies, convened in Albany in 1754 to consider ways of defending the colonies against the French and Indians, Franklin had proposed a plan for uniting the colonies in a Federal union. The historian Fiske speaks of the plan as one showing great foresight and wisdom.

take it." I asked what terms were to be offered the owners of the wagons; and I was desired to put on paper the terms that appeared to me necessary. This I did, and they were agreed to, and a commission and instructions accordingly prepared immediately.

. . . . . .

This general was, I think, a brave man, and might probably have made a figure as a good officer in some European war. But he had too much self-confidence, too high an opinion of the validity of regular troops, and too mean a one of both Americans and Indians. George Croghan, our Indian interpreter, joined him on his march with one hundred of those people, who might have been of great use to his army as guides, scouts, etc., if he had treated them kindly; but he slighted and neglected them, and they gradually left him.

In conversation with him one day, he was giving me some account of his intended progress. "After taking Fort Duquesne," says he, "I am to proceed to Niagara; and, having taken that, to Frontenac, if the season will allow time; and I suppose it will, for Duquesne can hardly detain me above three or four days; and then I see nothing that can obstruct my march to Niagara." Having before revolved in my mind the long line his army must make in their march by a very narrow road, to be cut for them through the woods and bushes, and also what I had read of a former defeat of fifteen hundred French, who invaded the Iroquois country, I had conceived some doubts and some fears for the event of the campaign. But I ventured only to say, "To be sure, sir, if you arrive well before Duquesne, with these fine troops, so well provided with artillery, that place not yet completely fortified, and as we hear with no very strong garrison, can probably make but a short resistance. The only danger I apprehend of obstruction to your march is from ambuscades of Indians, who, by constant practice, are dexterous in laying and executing them; and the slender line, near four miles long, which your army must make, may expose it to be attacked by surprise in its flanks, and to be cut like a thread into several pieces, which, from their distance, cannot come up in time to support each other."

He smiled at my ignorance, and replied, "These savages may, indeed, be a formidable enemy to your raw American militia, but upon the king's regular and disciplined troops, sir, it is impossible they should make any impression." I was conscious of an impropriety in my disputing with a military man in matters of his profession, and said no more. The enemy, however, did not take the advantage of his army which I apprehended its long line of march exposed it to, but let it advance without interruption till within nine miles of the place; and then, when more in a body (for it had just passed a river, where the front had halted till all were come over), and in a more open part of the woods than any it had passed, attacked its advanced guard by a heavy fire from behind trees and bushes, which was the first intelligence the general had of an enemy's being near him. This guard being disordered, the general hurried the troops up to their assistance, which was done in great confusion, through wagons, baggage, and cattle; and presently the fire came upon their flank: the officers, being on horseback, were more easily distinguished, picked out as marks, and fell very fast; and the soldiers were crowded together in a huddle, having or hearing no orders, and standing to be shot at till two thirds of them were killed; and then, being seized with a panic, the whole fled with precipitation.

The wagoners took each a horse out of his team and scampered; their example was immediately followed by others; so that all the wagons, provisions, artillery, and stores were left to the enemy. The general, being wounded, was brought off with difficulty; his secretary, Mr. Shirley, was killed by his side; and out of eighty-six officers, sixty-three were killed or wounded, and seven hundred and fourteen men killed out of eleven hundred. These eleven hundred had been picked men from the whole army; the rest had been left behind with Colonel Dunbar, who was to follow with the heavier part of the stores, provisions, and baggage. The flyers, not being pursued, arrived at Dunbar's camp, and the panic they brought with them instantly seized him and all his people; and, though he had now above one thousand men, and the enemy who had beaten Braddock did not at most exceed four hundred Indians and French together, instead of proceeding, and endeavoring to recover some of the lost honor, he ordered all the stores, ammunition, etc., to be destroyed, that he might have more horses to assist his flight towards the settlements, and less lumber to remove. He was there met with requests from the governors of Virginia, Maryland, and Pennsylvania, that he would post his troops on the frontier, so as to afford some protection to the inhabitants; but he continued his hasty march through all the country, not thinking himself safe till he arrived at Philadelphia, where the inhabitants could protect him. This whole transaction gave us Americans the first suspicion that our exalted ideas of the prowess of British regulars had not been well founded.

In their first march, too, from their landing till they got beyond the settlements, they had plundered and stripped the inhabitants, totally ruining some poor families, besides insulting, abusing, and confining the people if they remonstrated. This was enough to put us out of conceit of such defenders, if we had really wanted any. How different was the conduct of our French friends in 1781, who, during a march through the most inhabited part of our country from Rhode Island to Virginia, near seven hundred miles, occasioned not the smallest complaint for the loss of a pig, a chicken, or even an apple.

Captain Orme, who was one of the general's aides-de-camp, and, being grievously wounded, was brought off with him, and continued with him to his death, which happened in a few days, told me that he was totally silent all the first day, and at night only said, *"Who would have thought it?"* That he was silent again the following day, saying only at last, *"We shall better know how to deal with them another time"*; and died in a few minutes after.

. . . .

The next day being fair, we continued our march and arrived at the desolated Gnadenhut.[1] There was a saw-mill near, round which were left several piles of boards, with which we soon hutted ourselves; an operation the more necessary at that inclement season as we had no tents. Our first work was to bury more effectually the dead we found there, who had been half interred by the country people.

The next morning our fort was planned and marked out, the circumference measuring four hundred and fifty-five feet, which would require as many palisades to be made of trees, one with another, of a foot diameter each. Our axes, of which we had seventy, were immediately set to work to cut down trees, and, our men being dexterous in the use of them, great dispatch was made. Seeing the trees

[1] After Braddock's defeat, the governor of Pennsylvania, knowing Franklin to be a man who would carry through what he undertook, gave into his hands the defense of the whole northwestern frontier of the colony, furnishing him with signed blank commissions for this purpose. Franklin raised a force, with one detachment of which he advanced to erect a fort at Gnadenhut, a Moravian village in the wilderness which had been burnt by the Indians.

fall so fast, I had the curiosity to look at my watch when two men began to cut a pine; in six minutes they had it upon the ground, and I found it of fourteen inches diameter. Each pine made three palisades of eighteen feet long, pointed at one end. While these were preparing, our other men dug a trench all round, of three feet deep, in which the palisades were to be planted; and our wagons, the bodies being taken off, and the fore and hind wheels separated by taking out the pin which united the two parts of the perch, we had ten carriages, with two horses each, to bring the palisades from the woods to the spot. When they were set up, our carpenters built a stage of boards all round within, about six feet high, for the men to stand on when to fire through the loopholes. We had one swivel gun, which we mounted on one of the angles, and fired it as soon as fixed, to let the Indians know, if any were within hearing, that we had such pieces; and thus our fort, if such a magnificent name may be given to so miserable a stockade, was finished in a week, though it rained so hard every other day that the men could not work.

This gave me occasion to observe, that, when men are employed they are best contented; for on the days they worked they were good-natured and cheerful, and, with the consciousness of having done a good day's work, they spent the evening jollily; but on idle days they were mutinous and quarrelsome, finding fault with their pork, the bread, etc., and in continual ill-humor, which put me in mind of a sea-captain, whose rule it was to keep his men constantly at work; and when his mate once told him that they had done everything, and there was nothing further to employ them about, *"Oh,"* says he, *"make them scour the anchor."*

This kind of fort, however contemptible, is a sufficient defense against Indians, who have no cannon. Finding ourselves now posted securely, and having a place to retreat to on occasion, we ventured out in parties to scour the adjacent country. We met with no Indians, but we found the places on the neighboring hills where they had lain to watch our proceedings. There was an art in their contrivance of those places that seems worth mention. It being winter, a fire was necessary for them; but a common fire on the surface of the ground would by its light have discovered their position at a distance. They had therefore dug holes in the ground about three feet diameter and somewhat deeper; we saw where they had with their hatchets cut off the charcoal from the sides of burnt logs lying in the woods. With these coals they had made small fires in the bottom of the holes, and we observed among the weeds and grass the prints of their bodies, made by their laying all round, with their legs hanging down in the holes to keep their feet warm, which with them is an essential point. This kind of fire, so managed, could not discover them, either by its light, flame, sparks, or even smoke: it appeared that their number was not great, and it seems they saw we were too many to be attacked by them with prospect of advantage.

We had for our chaplain a zealous Presbyterian minister, Mr. Beatty, who complained to me that the men did not generally attend his prayers and exhortations. When they enlisted, they were promised, besides pay and provisions, a gill of rum a day, which was punctually served out to them, half in the morning and the other half in the evening; and I observed they were as punctual in attending to receive it; upon which I said to Mr. Beatty, "It is, perhaps, below the dignity of your profession to act as steward of the rum, but if you were to deal it out and only just after prayers, you would have them all about you." He liked the thought, undertook the office, and, with the help of a few hands to measure out the liquor, executed it to satisfaction, and never were prayers more generally and more punctually attended; so that I thought this method preferable to the punishment inflicted by some military laws for non-attendance on divine service.

Before I proceed in relating the part I had in public affairs under this new governor's [1] administration, it may not be amiss here to give some account of the rise and progress of my philosophical reputation.

In 1746, being at Boston, I met there with a Dr. Spence, who was lately arrived from Scotland, and showed me some electric experiments. They were imperfectly performed, as he was not very expert; but, being on a subject quite new to me, they equally surprised and pleased me. Soon after my return to Philadelphia, our library company received from Mr. P. Collinson, Fellow of the Royal Society of London, a present of a glass tube, [2] with some account of the use of it in making such experiments.

I eagerly seized the opportunity of repeating what I had seen at Boston; and, by much practice, acquired great readiness in performing those, also, which we had an account of from England, adding a number of new ones. I say much practice, for my house was continually full, for some time, with people who came to see these new wonders.

To divide a little this incumbrance among my friends, I caused a number of similar tubes to be blown at our glass-house, with which they furnished themselves, so that we had at length several performers. Among these, the principal was Mr. Kinnersley, an ingenious neighbor, who, being out of business, I encouraged to undertake showing the experiments for money, and drew up for him two lectures, in which the experiments were ranged in such order, and accompanied with such explanations in such method, as that the foregoing should assist in comprehending the following. He procured an elegant apparatus for the purpose, in which all the little machines that I had roughly made for myself were nicely formed by instrument-makers. His lectures were well attended, and gave great satisfaction; and after some time he went through the colonies, exhibiting them in every capital town, and picked up some money. In the West India islands, indeed, it was with difficulty the experiments could be made, from the general moisture of the air.

Obliged as we were to Mr. Collinson for his present of the tube, etc., I thought it right he should be informed of our success in using it, and wrote him several letters containing accounts of our experiments. He got them read in the Royal Society, where they were not at first thought worth so much notice as to be printed in their Transactions. One paper, which I wrote for Mr. Kinnersley, on the sameness of lightning with electricity, I sent to Dr. Mitchel, an acquaintance of mine, and one of the members also of that society, who wrote me word that it had been read but was laughed at by the connoisseurs. The papers, however, being shown to Dr. Fothergill, [3] he thought them of too much value to be stifled, and advised the printing of them. Mr. Collinson then gave them to Cave [4] for publication in his *Gentleman's Magazine;* but he chose to print them separately in a pamphlet, and Dr. Fothergill wrote the preface. Cave, it seems, judged

[1] Captain Denny
[2] Franklin had been influential in founding the Philadelphia Public Library some twenty-five years before. The Royal Society, founded in 1660, was the oldest scientific association in England. The glass tubes used in these primitive but important electrical experiments for producing frictional electricity were some two feet and a half long and three inches in diameter.

[3] John Fothergil, M.D., F.R.S., ever afterward a warm friend, especially during Franklin's residence in London as agent of the colonies
[4] Edward Cave founded the *Gentleman's Magazine* in 1731. This monthly was devoted to politics, literature, science, and art, and was the most influential publication of the day in Great Britain.

rightly for his profit, for by the additions that arrived afterward, they swelled to a quarto volume, which has had five editions, and cost him nothing for copy-money.

It was, however, some time before those papers were much taken notice of in England. A copy of them happening to fall into the hands of the Count de Buffon, [1] a philosopher deservedly of great reputation in France, and, indeed, all over Europe, he prevailed with M. Dalibard to translate them into French, and they were printed at Paris. The publication offended the Abbé Nollet, preceptor in Natural Philosophy to the royal family, and an able experimenter, who had formed and published a theory of electricity, which then had the general vogue. He could not at first believe that such a work came from America, and said it must have been fabricated by his enemies at Paris, to decry his system. Afterwards, having been assured that there really existed such a person as Franklin at Philadelphia, which he had doubted, he wrote and published a volume of Letters, chiefly addressed to me, defending his theory, and denying the verity of my experiments, and of the positions deduced from them.

I once purposed answering the Abbé, and actually began the answer; but, on consideration that my writings contained a description of experiments which any one might repeat and verify, and if not to be verified, could not be defended; or of observations offered as conjectures, and not delivered dogmatically, therefore not laying me under any obligation to defend them; and reflecting that a dispute between two persons, writing in different languages, might be lengthened greatly by mistranslations, and thence misconceptions of one another's meaning, much of one of the Abbé's letters being founded on an error in the translation, I concluded to let my papers shift for themselves, believing it was better to spend what time I could spare from public business in making new experiments, than in disputing about those already made. I therefore never answered M. Nollet, and the event gave me no cause to repent my silence; for my friend M. le Roy, of the Royal Academy of Sciences, took up my cause and refuted him; my book was translated into the Italian, German, and Latin languages; and the doctrine it contained was by degrees universally adopted by the philosophers of Europe, in preference to that of the Abbé; so that he lived to see himself the last of his sect, except Monsieur B——,

of Paris, his *élève* [2] and immediate disciple.

What gave my book the more sudden and general celebrity, was the success of one of its proposed experiments, made by Messrs. Dalibard and De Lor at Marly, for drawing lightning from the clouds. This engaged the public attention everywhere. M. De Lor, who had an apparatus for experimental philosophy, and lectured in that branch of science, undertook to repeat what he called the *Philadelphia Experiments;* and, after they were performed before the king and court, all the curious of Paris flocked to see them. I will not swell this narrative with an account of that capital experiment, nor of the infinite pleasure I received in the success of a similar one I made soon after with a kite at Philadelphia, as both are to be found in the histories of electricity.

Dr. Wright, an English physician, when at Paris, wrote to a friend, who was of the Royal Society, an account of the high esteem my experiments were in among the learned abroad, and of their wonder that my writings had been so little noticed in England. The society, on this, resumed the consideration of the letters that had been read to them; and the celebrated Dr. Watson [3] drew up a summary account of them, and of all I had afterwards sent to England on the subject, which he accompanied with some praise of the writer. This summary was then printed in their Transactions; and some members of the society in London, particularly the very ingenious Mr. Canton, having verified the experiment of procuring lightning from the clouds by a pointed rod, and acquainting them with the success, they soon made me more than amends for the slight with which they had before treated me. Without my having made any application for that honor, they chose me a member, and voted that I should be excused the customary payments, which would have amounted to twenty-five guineas; and ever since have given me their Transactions gratis. They also presented me with the gold medal of Sir Godfrey Copley for the year 1753, the delivery of which was accompanied by a very handsome speech of the president, Lord Macclesfield, wherein I was highly honored. [4]

.   .   .   .   .   .

1771-1789   1791, 1817, 1868

[2] pupil
[3] Sir William Watson, 1715-1787, F.R.S., physician and scientist
[4] The remainder of the *Autobiography* includes a brief account of Franklin's further services to Pennsylvania at home, and the beginning of his career as agent for the colony in London, closing with the year 1757.

[1] a celebrated French scientist, 1707-1788

THE WAY TO WEALTH

PREFACE TO POOR RICHARD IMPROVED: [1]

1758

Courteous Reader: I have heard that nothing gives an author so great pleasure as to find his works respectfully quoted by other learned authors. This pleasure I have seldom enjoyed, for, though I have been, if I may say it without vanity, an eminent author (of almanacs) annually now a full quarter of a century, my brother authors in the same way, for what reason I know not, have ever been very sparing in their applauses and no other author has taken the least notice of me; so that, did not my writings produce me some solid pudding, the great deficiency of praise would have quite discouraged me.

I concluded at length that the people were the best judges of my merit, for they buy my works; and, besides, in my rambles where I am not personally known, I have frequently heard one or other of my adages repeated with "As Poor Richard says" at the end on 't; this gave me some satisfaction, as it showed not only that my instructions were regarded, but discovered likewise some respect for my authority; and I own that, to encourage the practice of remembering and repeating those wise sentences, I have sometimes *quoted myself* with great gravity.

Judge then how much I must have been gratified by an incident I am going to relate to you. I stopped my horse lately where a great number of people were collected at a vendue [2] of merchant goods. The hour of sale not being come, they were conversing on the badness of the times, and one of the company called to a plain, clean old man with white locks, "Pray, Father Abraham, what think you of the times? Won't these heavy taxes quite ruin

the country? How shall we be ever able to pay them? What would you advise us to?" Father Abraham stood up and replied, "If you'd have my advice, I'll give it you in short; for A word to the wise is enough, and Many words won't fill a bushel, as Poor Richard says." They joined in desiring him to speak his mind, and gathering round him, he proceeded as follows:

"Friends," says he, "and neighbors, the taxes are indeed very heavy, and if those laid on by the government were the only ones we had to pay, we might more easily discharge them; but we have many others, and much more grievous to some of us. We are taxed twice as much by our idleness, three times as much by our pride, and four times as much by our folly; and from these taxes the commissioners cannot ease or deliver us by allowing an abatement. However, let us hearken to good advice, and something may be done for us; God helps them that help themselves, as Poor Richard says in his almanac of 1733.

"It would be thought a hard government that should tax its people one tenth part of their time, to be employed in its service; but idleness taxes many of us much more if we reckon all that is spent in absolute sloth, or doing of nothing, with that which is spent in idle employments or amusements, that amount to nothing. Sloth, by bringing on diseases, absolutely shortens life. Sloth, like rust, consumes faster than labor wears, while the used key is always bright, as Poor Richard says. But dost thou love life? Then do not squander time, for that's the stuff life is made of, as Poor Richard says. How much more than is necessary do we spend in sleep, forgetting that The sleeping fox catches no poultry, and that There will be sleeping enough in the grave, as Poor Richard says. If time be of all things the most precious, wasting time must be, as Poor Richard says, the greatest prodigality; since, as he elsewhere tells us, Lost time is never found again, and what we call time enough always proves little enough. Let us, then, up and be doing, and doing to the purpose; so by diligence shall we do more with less perplexity. Sloth makes all things difficult, but industry, all things easy, as Poor Richard says; and, He that riseth late must trot all day and shall scarce overtake his business at night; while Laziness travels so slowly that Poverty soon overtakes him, as we read in Poor Richard, who adds, Drive thy business, let not that drive thee; and, Early to bed, and early to rise, makes a man healthy, wealthy, and wise.

---

[1] *Poor Richard's Almanac*, first issued for the year 1733 by Franklin under the pseudonym of "Richard Saunders," continued to appear regularly until 1758. The witty and philosophic maxims which were inserted to fill spaces at the top or bottom of the pages, though by no means all original with Franklin (see p. 100), were so well chosen to fit the tastes of the average reader of the time that the almanac came to have the unprecedented sale of ten thousand annually. The death of a rival almanac-maker in 1748 gave Franklin the opportunity of imitating "his well-known Method, of giving two pages to each Month," and so of changing the title to *Poor Richard Improved*. In the preface to the last number, that of 1758, Franklin gathered together the most striking of the sayings of the earlier twenty-five issues. This preface has been reprinted (so Paul Leicester Ford reckons) at least four hundred times, under such various headings as "Father Abraham's Speech" and "The Way to Wealth," and has been translated into thirteen languages, including the Chinese.

[2] auction

"So what signifies wishing and hoping for better times? We may make these times better if we bestir ourselves. Industry need not wish, as Poor Richard says, and he that lives upon hope will die fasting. There are no gains without pains; then help, hands, for I have no lands; or, if I have, they are smartly taxed. And as Poor Richard likewise observes, He that hath a trade hath an estate; and he that hath a calling, hath an office of profit and honor; but then the trade must be worked at and the calling well followed, or neither the estate nor the office will enable us to pay our taxes. If we are industrious, we shall never starve; for, as Poor Richard says, At the workingman's house hunger looks in, but dares not enter. Nor will the bailiff or the constable enter; for Industry pays debts, while despair increaseth them, says Poor Richard.—What though you have found no treasure, nor has any rich relation left you a legacy; Diligence is the mother of good luck, as Poor Richard says, and God gives all things to Industry. Then plow deep while sluggards sleep, and you shall have corn to sell and to keep, says Poor Dick. Work while it is called today, for you know not how much you may be hindered tomorrow, which makes Poor Richard say, One today is worth two tomorrows; and farther, Have you somewhat to do tomorrow, do it today. If you were a servant, would you not be ashamed that a good master should catch you idle? Are you, then, your own master? Be ashamed to catch yourself idle, as Poor Dick says. When there is so much to be done for yourself, your family, your country, and your gracious King, be up by peep of day. Let not the sun look down and say, Inglorious here he lies. Handle your tools without mittens; remember that The cat in gloves catches no mice, as Poor Richard says. 'Tis true there is much to be done, and perhaps you are weak-handed; but stick to it steadily, and you will see great effects; for, Constant dropping wears away stones; and, By diligence and patience the mouse ate in two the cable; and, Little strokes fell great oaks, as Poor Richard says in his almanac, the year I cannot just now remember.

"Methinks I hear some of you say, Must a man afford himself no leisure? I will tell thee, my friend, what Poor Richard says: Employ thy time well, if thou meanest to gain leisure; and since thou art not sure of a minute, throw not away an hour. Leisure is time for doing something useful; this leisure the diligent man will obtain, but the lazy man never; so that, as Poor Richard says, A life of leisure and a life of laziness are two things. Do you imagine that sloth will afford you more comfort than labor? No, for as Poor Richard says, Trouble springs from idleness, and grievous toil from needless ease. Many, without labor, would live by their wits only, but they break for want of stock. Whereas industry gives comfort and plenty and respect. Fly pleasures and they'll follow you. The diligent spinner has a large shift; and now I have a sheep and a cow, everybody bids me good morrow. All which is well said by Poor Richard.

"But with our industry we must likewise be steady, settled, and careful, and oversee our own affairs with our own eyes, and not trust too much to others; for, as Poor Richard says:

> I never saw an oft-removed tree,
> Nor yet an oft-removed family,
> That throve so well as those that
> settled be.

And again, Three removes is as bad as a fire; and again, Keep thy shop, and thy shop will keep thee; and again, If you would have your business done, go; if not, send. And again,

> He that by the plow would thrive,
> Himself must either hold or drive.

And again, The eye of a master will do more work than both his hands; and again, Want of care does us more damage than want of knowledge; and again, Not to oversee workmen is to leave them your purse open. Trusting too much to others' care is the ruin of many; for, as the *Almanac* says, In the affairs of this world men are saved, not by faith, but by the want of it. But a man's own care is profitable; for, saith Poor Dick, Learning is to the studious, and riches to the careful, as well as Power to the bold, and heaven to the virtuous. And, farther, If you would have a faithful servant and one that you like, serve yourself. And again, he adviseth to circumspection and care, even in the smallest matters, because sometimes, A little neglect may breed great mischief; adding, For want of a nail the shoe was lost, for want of a shoe the horse was lost, and for want of a horse the rider was lost, being overtaken and slain by the enemy; all for want of care about a horseshoe nail.

"So much for industry, friends, and attention to one's own business; but to these we must add frugality, if we would make our industry more certainly successful. A man may, if he knows not how to save as he gets, keep his nose all his life to the grindstone, and die not worth a groat at last. A fat kitchen makes a lean will, as Poor Richard says; and

Many estates are spent in the getting,
Since women for tea forsook spinning and knitting,
And men for punch forsook hewing and splitting.

If you would be wealthy, says he, in another *Almanac*, Think of saving as well as of getting. The Indies have not made Spain rich, because her outgoes are greater than her incomes.

"Away, then, with your expensive follies, and you will not then have so much cause to complain of hard times, heavy taxes, and chargeable families; for, as Poor Dick says,

Women and wine, game and deceit,
Make the wealth small, and the wants great.

And farther, What maintains one vice would bring up two children. You may think, perhaps that a *little* tea or a *little* punch now and then, diet a *little* more costly, clothes a *little* finer, and a *little* entertainment now and then, can be no *great* matter; but remember what Poor Richard says, Many a little makes a mickle; and farther, Beware of little expenses; A small leak will sink a great ship; and again, Who dainties love shall beggars prove; and moreover, Fools make feasts and wise men eat them.

"Here you are all got together at this vendue of fineries and knick knacks. You call them goods; but, if you do not take care, they will prove evils to some of you. You expect they will be sold cheap, and perhaps they may for less than they cost; but, if you have no occasion for them, they must be dear to you. Remember what Poor Richard says; Buy what thou hast no need of, and ere long thou shalt sell thy necessaries. And again, At a great pennyworth pause awhile. He means that perhaps the cheapness is *apparent* only, and not *real;* or, the bargain, by straitening thee in thy business, may do thee more harm than good. For in another place he says, Many have been ruined by buying good pennyworths. Again, Poor Richard says, 'Tis foolish to lay out money in a purchase of repentance; and yet this folly is practiced every day at vendues for want of minding the *Almanac.* Wise men, as Poor Dick says, learn by others' harms, fools scarcely by their own; but *Felix quem facirent aliena pericula cautum.* [1] Many a one, for the sake of finery on the back have gone with a hungry belly, and half-starved their families. Silks and satins, scarlet and velvets, as Poor Richard says, put out the kitchen fire.

"These are not the necessaries of life; they can scarcely be called the conveniences; and yet, only because they look pretty, how many

[1] "Happy the man whom the experiences of others make cautious."

want to have them. The artificial wants of mankind thus become more numerous than the natural; and as Poor Dick says, For one poor person there are an hundred indigent. By these and other extravagancies the genteel are reduced to poverty, and forced to borrow of those whom they formerly despised, but who, through industry and frugality, have maintained their standing; in which case it appears plainly that, A plowman on his legs is higher than a gentleman on his knees, as Poor Richard says. Perhaps they have had a small estate left them which they knew not the getting of; they think, 'Tis day and will never be night; that a little to be spent out of so much is not worth minding; a child and a fool, as Poor Richard says, imagine twenty shillings and twenty years can never be spent, but, Always take out of the meal tub and never putting in, soon comes to the bottom; then as Poor Dick says, When the well's dry, they know the worth of water. But this they might have known before, if they had taken his advice. If you would know the value of money, go and try to borrow some; for, he that goes a borrowing goes a sorrowing; and, indeed, so does he that lends to such people, when he goes to get it in again. Poor Dick farther advises and says:

Fond pride of dress is sure a very curse;
Ere fancy you consult, consult your purse.

And again, Pride is as loud a beggar as want, and a great deal more saucy. When you have bought one fine thing, you must buy ten more, that your appearance may be all of a piece; but Poor Dick says, 'Tis easier to suppress the first desire than to satisfy all that follow it. And 'tis as truly folly for the poor to ape the rich, as for the frog to swell in order to equal the ox.

Great estates may venture more,
But little boats should keep near shore.

'Tis, however, a folly soon punished; for, Pride that dines on vanity, sups on contempt, as Poor Richard says. And in another place, Pride breakfasted with Plenty, dined with Poverty, and supped with Infamy. And, after all, of what use is this pride of appearance, for which so much is risked, so much is suffered? It cannot promote health or ease pain; it makes no increase of merit in the person, it creates envy, it hastens misfortune.

What is a butterfly? At best
He's but a caterpillar dressed.
The gaudy fop's his picture just.

as Poor Richard says.

"But what madness must it be to run in debt for these superfluities! We are offered by the terms of this vendue six months' credit; and that, perhaps, has induced some of us to attend it, because we cannot spare the ready money, and hope now to be fine without it. But ah, think what you do when you run in debt; you give to another power over your liberty. If you cannot pay at the time, you will be ashamed to see your creditor; you will be in fear when you speak to him; you will make poor, pitiful, sneaking excuses, and by degrees come to lose your veracity, and sink into base, downright lying; for, as Poor Richard says, The second vice is lying, the first is running in debt. And again to the same purpose, Lying rides upon debt's back; whereas a freeborn Englishman ought not to be ashamed or afraid to see or speak to any man living. But poverty often deprives a man of all spirit and virtue. 'Tis hard for an empty bag to stand upright, as Poor Richard truly says.

"What would you think of that prince, or that government, who should issue an edict forbidding you to dress like a gentleman or a gentlewoman, on pain of imprisonment or servitude? Would you not say that you are free, have a right to dress as you please, and that such an edict would be a breach of your privileges and such a government tyrannical? And yet you are about to put yourself under that tyranny, when you run in debt for such dress. Your creditor has authority, at his pleasure, to deprive you of your liberty by confining you in jail for life, or to sell you for a servant, if you should not be able to pay him. When you have got your bargain, you may, perhaps, think little of payment! But, Creditors, Poor Richard tells us, have better memories than debtors; and in another place says, Creditors are a superstitious sect, great observers of set days and times. The day comes round before you are aware, and the demand is made before you are prepared to satisfy it; or, if you bear your debt in mind, the term, which at first seemed so long, will, as it lessens, appear extremely short. Time will seem to have added wings to his heels as well as shoulders. Those have a short Lent, saith Poor Richard, who owe money to be paid at Easter. Then, since as he says, The borrower is a slave to the lender, and the debtor to the creditor, disdain the chain, preserve your freedom; and maintain your independency; be industrious and free; be frugal and free. At present, perhaps, you may think yourself in thriving circumstances, and that you can bear a little extravagance without injury; but

For age and want save while you may;
No morning sun lasts a whole day,

1757

as Poor Richard says. Gain may be temporary and uncertain, but ever, while you live, expense is constant and certain; and, 'Tis easier to build two chimneys than to keep one in fuel, as Poor Richard says. So Rather go to bed supperless than rise in debt.

Get what you can, and what you get, hold;
'Tis the stone that will turn all your lead into gold,

as Poor Richard says. And when you have got the philosopher's stone, sure you will no longer complain of bad times or the difficulty of paying taxes.

"This doctrine, my friends, is reason and wisdom; but, after all, do not depend too much upon your own industry and frugality and prudence, though excellent things; for they may all be blasted, without the blessing of Heaven; and, therefore, ask that blessing humbly, and be not uncharitable to those that at present seem to want it, but comfort and help them. Remember Job suffered, and was afterward prosperous.

"And now, to conclude, Experience keeps a dear school, but fools will learn in no other, and scarce in that; for, it is true, We may give advice, but we cannot give conduct, as Poor Richard says. However, remember this: They that won't be counseled can't be helped, as Poor Richard says; and farther that, If you will not hear Reason, she'll surely rap your knuckles."

Thus the old gentleman ended his harangue. The people heard it, and approved the doctrine, and immediately practiced the contrary, just as if it had been a common sermon; for the vendue opened and they began to buy extravagantly notwithstanding his cautions, and their own fear of taxes. I found the good man had thoroughly studied my almanacs, and digested all I had dropped on these topics during the course of five-and-twenty years. The frequent mention he made of me must have tired any one else; but my vanity was wonderfully delighted with it, though I was conscious that not a tenth part of the wisdom was my own which he ascribed to me, but rather the gleanings I had made of the sense of all ages and nations. However, I resolved to be the better for the echo of it; and, though I had at first determined to buy stuff for a new coat, I went away resolved to wear my old one a little longer. Reader, if thou wilt do the same, thy profit will be as great as mine. I am, as ever, thine to serve thee.

RICHARD SAUNDERS.

1757

DIALOGUE BETWEEN FRANKLIN AND THE GOUT [1]

Midnight, October 22, 1780.

Franklin. Eh! Oh! Eh! What have I done to merit these cruel sufferings?

Gout. Many things; you have ate and drank [2] too freely, and too much indulged those legs of yours in their indolence.

Franklin. Who is it that accuses me?

Gout. It is I, even I, the Gout.

Franklin. What! my enemy in person?

Gout. No, not your enemy.

Franklin. I repeat it; my enemy; for you would not only torment my body to death, but ruin my good name; you reproach me as a glutton and a tippler; now all the world, that knows me, will allow that I am neither the one nor the other.

Gout. The world may think as it pleases; it is always very complaisant to itself, and sometimes to its friends; but I very well know that the quantity of meat and drink proper for a man who takes a reasonable degree of exercise, would be too much for another who never takes any.

Franklin. I take—Eh! Oh!—as much exercise—Eh!—as I can, Madam Gout. You know my sedentary state, and on that account, it would seem, Madam Gout, as if you might spare me a little, seeing it is not altogether my own fault.

Gout. Not a jot; your rhetoric and your politeness are thrown away; your apology avails nothing. If your situation in life is a sedentary one, your amusements, your recreations, at least, should be active. You ought to walk or ride; or, if the weather prevents that, play at billiards. But let us examine your course of life. While the mornings are long, and you have leisure to go abroad, what do you do? Why, instead of gaining an appetite for breakfast by salutary exercise, you amuse yourself with books, pamphlets, or newspapers, which commonly are not worth the reading. Yet you eat an inordinate breakfast, four dishes of tea with cream, and one or two buttered toasts, with slices of hung beef, which I fancy are not things the most easily digested. Immediately afterward you sit down to write at your desk, or converse with persons who apply to you on business. Thus the time passes till one, without any kind of bodily exercise. But all this I could pardon in regard, as you say, to your sedentary condition. But what is your practice after dinner? Walking in the beautiful gardens of those friends with whom you have dined would be the choice of men of sense; yours is to be fixed down to chess, where you are found engaged for two or three hours! This is your perpetual recreation, which is the least eligible of any for a sedentary man, because, instead of accelerating the motion of the fluids, [3] the rigid attention it requires helps to retard the circulation and obstruct internal secretions. Wrapt in the speculations of this wretched game, you destroy your constitution. What can be expected from such a course of living, but a body replete with stagnant humors, ready to fall a prey to all kinds of dangerous maladies, if I, the Gout, did not occasionally bring you relief by agitating those humors, and so purifying or dissipating them? If it was in some nook or alley in Paris, deprived of walks, that you played awhile at chess after dinner, this might be excusable; but the same taste prevails with you in Passy, Auteuil, Montmartre, or Sanoy, [4] places where there are the finest gardens and walks, a pure air, beautiful women, and most agreeable and instructive conversation; all which you might enjoy by frequenting the walks. But these are rejected for this abominable game of chess. Fie, then, Mr. Franklin! But amidst my instructions, I had almost forgot to administer my wholesome corrections; so take that twinge,—and that.

Franklin. Oh! Eh! Oh! Ohhh! As much instruction as you please, Madam Gout, and as many reproaches; but pray, madam, a truce with your corrections!

Gout. No, sir, no,—I will not abate a particle of what is so much for your good,—therefore—

Franklin. Oh! Ehhh!—It is not fair to say I take no exercise, when I do very often, going out to dine and returning in my carriage.

Gout. That, of all imaginable exercises, is the most slight and insignificant, if you allude to the motion of a carriage suspended on springs. By observing the degree of heat obtained by different kinds of motion, we may form an estimate of the quantity of exercise given by each. Thus, for example, if you turn out to walk in winter with cold feet, in an hour's

---

[1] It is an interesting indication of the flexibility of Franklin's mind and the buoyancy of his spirit that he could in old age, with the fate of a nation often balancing in his hand, compose this playful little essay.

[2] These forms were not incorrect in Franklin's time.

[3] Any of the animal fluids: an echo of an old theory of medicine that the human body contained four humors, or fluids—blood, phlegm, yellow bile (choler), and black bile (melancholy); health depended upon keeping these active, and in the right proportions.

[4] places in which Franklin resided or which he visited

time you will be in a glow all over; ride on horseback, the same effect will scarcely be perceived by four hours' round trotting; but if you loll in a carriage, such as you have mentioned, you may travel all day, and gladly enter the last inn to warm your feet by a fire. Flatter yourself then no longer, that half an hour's airing in your carriage deserves the name of exercise. Providence has appointed few to roll in carriages, while he has given to all a pair of legs, which are machines infinitely more commodious and serviceable. Be grateful, then, and make a proper use of yours. Would you know how they forward the circulation of your fluids, in the very action of transporting you from place to place; observe when you walk, that all your weight is alternately thrown from one leg to the other; this occasions a great pressure on the vessels of the foot, and repels their contents; when relieved, by the weight being thrown on the other foot, the vessels of the first are allowed to replenish, and by a return of this weight, this repulsion again succeeds; thus accelerating the circulation of the blood. The heat produced in any given time, depends on the degree of this acceleration; the fluids are shaken, the humors attenuated, the secretions facilitated, and all goes well; the cheeks are ruddy, and health is established. Behold your fair friend [1] at Auteuil, a lady who received from bounteous nature more really useful science, than half a dozen such pretenders to philosophy as you have been able to extract from all your books. When she honors you with a visit, it is on foot. She walks all hours of the day, and leaves indolence, and its concomitant maladies, to be endured by her horses. In this see at once the preservative of her health and personal charms. But when you go to Auteuil, you must have your carriage, though it is no further from Passy to Auteuil than from Auteuil to Passy.

Franklin. Your reasonings grow very tiresome.

Gout. I stand corrected. I will be silent and continue my office; take that, and that.

Franklin. Oh! Ohh! Talk on, I pray you!

Gout. No, no; I have a good number of twinges for you tonight, and you may be sure of some more tomorrow.

Franklin. What, with such a fever! I shall go distracted. Oh! Eh! Can no one bear it for me?

Gout. Ask that of your horses; they have served you faithfully.

Franklin. How can you so cruelly sport with my torments?

Gout. Sport! I am very serious. I have here a list of offences against your own health distinctly written, and can justify every stroke inflicted on you.

Franklin. Read it then.

Gout. It is too long a detail; but I will briefly mention some particulars.

Franklin. Proceed. I am all attention.

Gout. Do you remember how often you have promised yourself, the following morning, a walk in the grove of Boulogne, in the garden de la Muette, or in your own garden, and have violated your promise, alleging at one time it was too cold, at another too warm, too windy, too moist, or what else you pleased; when in truth it was too nothing, but your insuperable love of ease?

Franklin. That I confess may have happened occasionally, probably ten times in a year.

Gout. Your confession is very far short of the truth; the gross amount is one hundred and ninety-nine times.

Franklin. Is it possible?

Gout. So possible, that it is fact; you may rely on the accuracy of my statement. You know M. Brillon's [2] gardens, and what fine walks they contain; you know the handsome flight of an hundred steps, which lead from the terrace above to the lawn below. You have been in the practice of visiting this amiable family twice a week, after dinner, and it is a maxim of your own, that "a man may take as much exercise in walking a mile, up and down stairs, as in ten on level ground." What an opportunity was here for you to have had exercise in both these ways! Did you embrace it, and how often?

Franklin. I cannot immediately answer that question.

Gout. I will do it for you; not once.

Franklin. Not once?

Gout. Even so. During the summer you went there at six o'clock. You found the charming lady with her lovely children and friends eager to walk with you, and entertain you with their agreeable conversation; and what has been your choice? Why, to sit on the terrace, satisfying yourself with the fine prospect, and passing your eye over the beauties of the garden below, without taking one step to descend and walk about in them. On the contrary, you call for tea and the chessboard; and lo! you are occupied in your seat

[1] Madam Helvetius, one of Franklin's intimate circle

[2] a French neighbor of Franklin's

till nine o'clock, and that besides two hours' play after dinner; and then, instead of walking home, which would have bestirred you a little, you step into your carriage. How absurd to suppose that all this carelessness can be reconcilable with health, without my interposition!

Franklin. I am convinced now of the justness of Poor Richard's remark, that "Our debts and our sins are always greater than we think for."

Gout. So it is. You philosophers are sages in your maxims, and fools in your conduct.

Franklin. But do you charge among my crimes, that I return in a carriage from Mr. Brillon's?

Gout. Certainly; for, having been seated all the while, you cannot object the fatigue of the day, and cannot want therefore the relief of a carriage.

Franklin. What then would you have me do with my carriage?

Gout. Burn it if you choose; you would at least get heat out of it once in this way; or, if you dislike that proposal, here's another for you; observe the poor peasants, who work in the vineyards and grounds about the villages of Passy, Auteuil, Chaillot, etc.; you may find every day, among these deserving creatures, four or five old men and women, bent and perhaps crippled by weight of years, and too long and too great labor. After a most fatiguing day, these people have to trudge a mile or two to their smoky huts. Order your coachman to set them down. This is an act that will be good for your soul; and, at the same time, after your visit to the Brillons', if you return on foot, that will be good for your body.

Franklin. Ah! how tiresome you are!

Gout. Well, then, to my office; it should not be forgotten that I am your physician. There.

Franklin. Ohhh! what a devil of a physician!

Gout. How ungrateful you are to say so! Is it not I who, in the character of your physician, have saved you from the palsy, dropsy, and apoplexy? one or other of which would have done for you long ago, but for me.

Franklin. I submit, and thank you for the past, but entreat the discontinuance of your visits for the future; for, in my mind, one had better die than be cured so dolefully. Permit me just to hint, that I have also not been unfriendly to *you.* I never feed physician or quack of any kind, to enter the list against you; if then you do not leave me to my repose, it may be said you are ungrateful too.

Gout. I can scarcely acknowledge that as any objection. As to quacks, I despise them; they may kill you indeed, but cannot injure me. And, as to regular physicians, they are at last convinced that the gout, in such a subject as you are, is no disease, but a remedy; and wherefore cure a remedy?—but to our business, —there.

Franklin. Oh! oh!—for Heaven's sake leave me! and I promise faithfully never more to play at chess, but to take exercise daily, and live temperately.

Gout. I know you too well. You promise fair; but, after a few months of good health, you will return to your old habits; your fine promises will be forgotten like the forms of last year's clouds. Let us then finish the account, and I will go. But I leave you with an assurance of visiting you again at a proper time and place; for my object is your good, and you are sensible now that I am your *real friend.*

1780   1780

HECTOR ST. JOHN DE CRÈVE-COEUR 1735-1812

Crèvecoeur was born of a good family in Caen, Normandy. At the age of eighteen or nineteen he came to America and entered the service of Montcalm in New France. As a surveyor and maker of maps, he apparently explored and mapped regions about the Great Lakes, and became acquainted with Upper Canada and the Ohio country. After about five years he came to New York, was naturalized, married, and settled in the forest region of Orange county, New York, about sixty miles from the city and twenty miles from West Point. In the Revolution he tried to remain neutral but, inclining toward the Royalist party, he retired to New York City. The British there thought him a spy, and after imprisoning him sent him to England where he was exchanged for a British prisoner and deported to France. After the war he returned to New York as French consul, serving for ten years. He died in France.

Though details of his early American life are uncertain, we may accept his own words: "I was never but a simple Surveyor of lands, a cultivator of my own grounds, or a wanderer through the forests of this country, in company with some of the natives." Evidently, few men of his day knew so much of French and British America from Lake Huron to the West Indies. His accounts of rural America, generally optimistic, sometimes tragic, show him to have been a close observer, with a love for the picturesque. He was touched with but not wholly won by Rousseau's doctrine that man is inherently good, was born free, but is corrupted by society. He never wholly mastered the English language, and his writings have been a good deal edited. But despite this fact, and despite his tendency to idealize too greatly rural provincial life, his observations give us the best picture of this life extant. His *Letters from an American Farmer* were published in London, 1782, and with additions from his manuscripts and variations by different editors, have been issued in many editions in America and upon the Continent. His *Sketches of Eighteenth Century America* were published from manuscripts in the hands of his French descendants, 1925.

For extracts from Crèvecoeur manuscripts, see the following, edited by H. L. Bourdin and S. T. Williams: "Crèvecoeur the Loyalist," *Nation* 121: 328-30, and "Crèvecoeur on the Susquehanna," *Yale R.* ns 14:552-84.

Biography: Julia Post Mitchell, 1916. Comment and criticism: H. L. Bourdin and S. T. Williams, "The American Farmer Returns," *No. Am.* 222:135-40; P. H. Boynton, "A Colonial Farmer's Letters," *New Repub.* 3:168-70; W. B. Blake, "Some Eighteenth Century Travelers in America," *Dial* 52:5-9; H. W. Boynton, "Letters from an American Farmer," *Atlan.* 94:847-8.

From LETTERS FROM AN AMERICAN FARMER

LETTER III.   WHAT IS AN AMERICAN

I wish I could be acquainted with the feelings and thoughts which must agitate the heart and present themselves to the mind of an enlightened Englishman when he first lands on this continent. He must greatly rejoice that he lived at a time to see this fair country discovered and settled; he must necessarily feel a share of national pride when he views the chain of settlements which embellishes these extended shores. When he says to himself, this is the work of my countrymen who, when convulsed by factions, afflicted by a variety of miseries and wants, restless and impatient, took refuge here. They brought along with them their national genius, to which they principally owe what liberty they enjoy and what substance they possess. Here he sees the industry of his native country displayed in a new manner, and traces in their works the embryos of all the arts, sciences, and ingenuity which flourish in Europe. Here he beholds fair cities, substantial villages, extensive fields, an immense country filled with decent houses, good roads, orchards, meadows, and bridges, where an hundred years ago all was wild, woody and uncultivated! What a train of pleasing ideas this fair spectacle must suggest; it is a prospect which must inspire a good citizen with the most heartfelt pleasure. The difficulty consists in the manner of viewing so extensive a scene. He is arrived on a new continent; a modern

society offers itself to his contemplation, different from what he had hitherto seen. It is not composed, as in Europe, of great lords who possess everything, and of a herd of people who have nothing. Here are no aristocratical families, no courts, no kings, no bishops, no ecclesiastical dominion, no invisible power giving to a few a very visible one; no great manufacturers employing thousands, no great refinements of luxury. The rich and the poor are not so far removed from each other as they are in Europe. Some few towns excepted, we are all tillers of the earth, from Nova Scotia to West Florida. We are a people of cultivators, scattered over an immense territory, communicating with each other by means of good roads and navigable rivers, united by the silken bands of mild government, all respecting the laws, without dreading their power, because they are equitable. We are all animated with the spirit of an industry which is unfettered and unrestrained, because each person works for himself. If he travels through our rural districts he views not the hostile castle, and the haughty mansion, contrasted with the clay-built hut and miserable cabin, where cattle and men help to keep each other warm, and dwell in meanness, smoke, and indigence. A pleasing uniformity of decent competence appears throughout our habitations. The meanest of our loghouses is a dry and comfortable habitation. Lawyer or merchant are the fairest titles our towns afford; that of a farmer is the only appellation of the rural inhabitants of our country. It must take some time ere he can reconcile himself to our dictionary, which is but short in words of dignity, and names of honor. There, on a Sunday, he sees a congregation of respectable farmers and their wives, all clad in neat homespun, well mounted, or riding in their own humble wagons. There is not among them an esquire, saving the unlettered magistrate. There he sees a parson as simple as his flock, a farmer who does not riot on the labor of others. We have no princes, for whom we toil, starve, and bleed: we are the most perfect society now existing in the world. Here man is free as he ought to be; nor is this pleasing equality so transitory as many others are. Many ages will not see the shores of our great lakes replenished with inland nations, nor the unknown bounds of North America entirely peopled. Who can tell how far it extends? Who can tell the millions of men whom it will feed and contain? for no European foot has as yet traveled half the extent of this mighty continent! . . .

In this great American asylum, the poor of Europe have by some means met together, and in consequence of various causes; to what purpose should they ask one another what countrymen they are? Alas, two thirds of them had no country. Can a wretch who wanders about, who works and starves, whose life is a continual scene of sore affliction or pinching penury; can that man call England or any other kingdom his country? A country that had no bread for him, whose fields procured him no harvest, who met with nothing but the frowns of the rich, the severity of the laws, with jails and punishments; who owned not a single foot of the extensive surface of this planet? No! urged by a variety of motives, here they came. Everything has tended to regenerate them; new laws, a new mode of living, a new social system; here they are become men: in Europe they were as so many useless plants, wanting vegetative mould, and refreshing showers; they withered, and were mowed down by want, hunger, and war; but now by the power of transplantation, like all other plants they have taken root and flourished! Formerly they were not numbered in any civil lists of their country, except in those of the poor; here they rank as citizens. . . . . What then is the American, this new man? He is either an European, or the descendant of an European, hence that strange mixture of blood, which you will find in no other country. I could point out to you a family whose grandfather was an Englishman, whose wife was Dutch, whose son married a French woman, and whose present four sons have now four wives of different nations. *He* is an American, who leaving behind him all his ancient prejudices and manners, receives new ones from the new mode of life he has embraced, the new government he obeys, and the new rank he holds. He becomes an American by being received in the broad lap of our great *Alma Mater*. Here individuals of all nations are melted into a new race of men, whose labors and posterity will one day cause great changes in the world. Americans are the western pilgrims, who are carrying along with them that great mass of arts, sciences, vigor, and industry which began long since in the East; they will finish the great circle. The Americans were once scattered all over Europe; here they are incorporated into one of the finest systems of population which has ever appeared, and which will hereafter become distinct by the power of the different climates they inhabit. The American ought therefore to love this country much better than that wherein he or his forefathers

were born. Here the rewards of his industry follow with equal steps the progress of his labor; his labor is founded on the basis of nature, *self-interest*; can it want a stronger allurement? Wives and children, who before in vain demanded of him a morsel of bread, now, fat and frolicsome, gladly help their father to clear those fields whence exuberant crops are to arise to feed and to clothe them all; without any part being claimed, either by a despotic prince, a rich abbot, or a mighty lord. Here religion demands but little of him; a small voluntary salary to the minister, and gratitude to God; can he refuse these? The American is a new man, who acts upon new principles; he must therefore entertain new ideas, and form new opinions. From involuntary idleness, servile dependence, penury, and useless labor, he has passed to toils of a very different nature, rewarded by ample subsistence.—This is an American.

From SKETCHES OF EIGHTEENTH CENTURY AMERICA

[VARIOUS RURAL SUBJECTS]

. . . . . . I think we have made most rapid strides, considering that the country was but a huge wilderness fifty years ago without a path. You'd be astonished, were I to tell you the extent of its cleared ground, of its meadows, the number of its houses, inhabitants, etc. I have often amused myself with making an estimate of the sum of labor and then comparing it with the original and present value of the land. This fair estimate would be the strongest proof of our industry, an industry which the people of the South cannot boast of, for the evenness and fertility of their land are very superior to ours. There they labor with slaves; here we do everything ourselves. There they enjoy a variety of pleasures and pastimes; here we know of none except our frolics and going to the meeting on a Sunday.

The name "frolic" may perhaps scandalize you and make you imagine that we meet to riot together. Lest you should misunderstand me, give me leave to explain myself. I really know among us of no custom which is so useful and tends so much to establish the union and the little society which subsists among us. Poor as we are, if we have not the gorgeous balls, the harmonious concerts, and the shrill horn of Europe, yet we dilate our hearts as well with the simple negro fiddle, and with our rum and water, as you do with your delicious wines. In the summer it often happens that either through sickness or accident some families are not able to do all they must do. Are we afraid, for instance, that we shall not be able to break up our summer fallow? In due time we invite a dozen neighbors, who will come with their teams and finish it all in one day. At dinner we give them the best victuals our farm affords; these are feasts the goodness of which greatly depends on the knowledge and ability of our wives. Pies, puddings, fowls, roasted and boiled—nothing is spared that can evince our gratitude. In the evening the same care is repeated, after which young girls and lads generally come from all parts to unite themselves to the assembly. As they have done no work, they generally come after supper and partake of the general dance. I have never been so happy in my life as when I have assisted at these simple merriments, and indeed they are the only ones I know. Each returns home happy and is satisfied, and our work is done.

If any of our wives are unable to spin that quantity of flax which was intended, they give out one pound to every one of their acquaintances. The youngsters take the same quantity, which they get spun by their sweethearts. The day is fixed when they all bring home the yarn to the house and receive in return a hearty supper and a dance. Can there be anything more harmless or more useful? The same is done for every species of labor. When my father[1] built his house he had had the stones previously pitched in large heaps, and the winter following he invited upwards of thirty people who came with their sleighs and horses, and brought him in one day upwards of five hundred loads. Had he been obliged to have done that himself, or to have hired it done, it would have cost him more than the house. We generally invite the minister of the precinct who partakes of the pleasures of the day, and who sanctifies by his presence the well-meant labors of our people. Thus we help one another; thus by our single toils at home and our collective strength we remove many obstacles which no single family could do. Many swamps have been cleared in this manner to the great joy of the possessors who were not able to hire the work done.

. . . . Would you believe that the great electrical discoveries of Mr. Franklin have not only preserved our barns and our houses from the fire of heaven but have even taught our wives to multiply their chickens? The invisible effects of thunder are powerfully felt in the egg.

[1] perhaps father-in-law

If, when a hen is hatching, there happens a great storm, not one chicken will appear. (I can express myself but very imperfectly.) To prevent this electrical mischief our wives, without going through a course of lectures, have been taught to place a piece of iron in the bottom of their hens' nests in such a manner that it touches the ground. By what magic I know not, but all the mischief is prevented, and the eggs bring prosperous chickens. Can the name of that distinguished, useful citizen be mentioned by an American without feeling a double sentiment: that of pleasure inspired by our calling him our countryman, and that of gratitude? Before the erection of his iron conductors, the mischiefs occasioned in Pennsylvania and everywhere else by the thunder annually amounted to a great sum. Now everyone may rest secure. These rods fetch from the clouds (strange to tell) that powerful fire and convey it into the earth alongside the very house which it would have consumed, had it accidentally fallen on the roof. Happy Pennsylvania! Thou Queen of Provinces! Among the many useful citizens thou hast already produced, Benjamin Franklin is one of the most eminent of thy sons.

You have often admired our two-horse wagons. They are extremely well-contrived and executed with a great deal of skill; and they answer with ease and dispatch all the purposes of a farm. A well-built wagon, when loaded, will turn in a very few more feet than its length, which is sixteen feet including the length of the tongue. We have room in what is called their bodies to carry five barrels of flour. We commonly put in them a ton of hay and often more. The load is built on shelvings fixed on their sides. A ladder of ⅝ [sic] stands erect in the front. [The hay is held in place] by means of a boom, one end of which passes through the ladder, and the other end [of which] is brought tight down and fastened to a staple in the hindmost axle-tree. Thus the whole is secured. We can carry twenty-five green oak rails, two thirds of a cord of wood, three thousand pounds of dung. In short there is no operation that ought to be performed on a farm but what is easily accomplished with one of these. We can lengthen them as we please, and bring home the body of a tree twenty or thirty feet long. We commonly carry with them thirty bushels of wheat and at sixty pounds to the bushel this makes a weight of eighteen hundred pounds, with which we can go forty miles a day with two horses.

On a Sunday it becomes the family coach. We then take off the common, plain sides and fix on it others which are handsomely painted. The after-part, on which either our names or ciphers are delineated, hangs down back, suspended by neat chains. If it rains, flat hoops made on purpose are placed in mortises, and a painted cloth is spread and tied over the whole. Thus equipped, the master of the family can carry six persons either to church or to meetings. When roads are good we can travel seven miles an hour. In order to prevent too great shakings, our seats are suspended on wooden springs—a simple but very useful mechanism. These inventions and [this] neatness we owe to the original Dutch settlers. I do not know where an American farmer can possibly enjoy more dignity as a father or as a citizen than when he thus carries with him his wife and family all clad in good, neat homespun clothes, manufactured within his own house, and trots along with a neat pair of fat horses of his own raising. The single-horse Irish car, with wheels not above two feet high, must appear very inferior to our wagons, and yet several people from that country have told me that the whole internal trade of that kingdom is effected with no other carriages. Exclusive of these middle-sized wagons there are many public ones, driven by six horses, which carry great burthens. In the southern provinces, where the roads are level, they use no other. We generally pay for ours from fifty to sixty dollars. The Dutch build them with timber which has been previously three years under water and then gradually seasoned. . . .

. . . . It is in this [the winter] season that the hospitality of the Americans is most conspicuous. The severity of the climate requires that all our doors should be opened to the frozen traveler, and indeed we shut them not by night or by day at any time of the year. The traveler when cold has a right to stop and warm himself at the first house he sees. He freely goes to the fire, which is kept a-burning all night. There he forgets the keenness of the cold; he smokes his pipe; drinks of the cider which is often left on the hearth; and departs in peace. We always sleep in these rooms; at least I do, and have often seen mine full when I was in my bed. On waking I have sometimes spoken to them; at other times it was a silent meeting. The reasons which force these people to travel in these dreadful nights is that they may be able to return home the same day. They are farmers carrying their produce to the market, and their great distance

from it obliges them to set out sometimes at twelve o'clock. Far from being uneasy at seeing my house thus filled while my wife and I are abed, I think it, on the contrary, a great compliment, when I consider that by thus stopping they convince me that they have thought my house and my fire better than that of my neighbors.

THOMAS GODFREY 1736-1765

Godfrey, the first American dramatist, was born in Philadelphia. His father, a friend of Franklin, was a glazier and mathematician who died when the son was thirteen years old, leaving him to be a watchmaker's apprentice. After a short experience as a soldier, Godfrey removed to North Carolina, where, about 1759, he wrote *The Prince of Parthia*, a blank verse tragedy, the first drama written in America. This with his poems was printed in Philadelphia, 1765, but was not acted until 1767.

Godfrey's lyrics, though conventional and imitative, following the eighteenth century models, are quite as good as many of their type produced at the same time by poets of reputation in England. They show America awakening to artistic self-consciousness.

For *Prince of Parthia*, see A. H. Quinn, *Representative American Plays*, 1917.

THE INVITATION

Damon. [1] Haste, Sylvia, haste, my charming
        maid!
  Let's leave these fashionable toys:
Let's seek the shelter of some shade,
  And revel in ne'er fading joys.
See, Spring in livery gay appears,
  And winter's chilly blasts are fled;
Each grove its leafy honors rears,
  And meads their lovely verdure spread.

Sylvia. Yes, Damon, glad I'll quit the town;
  Its gayeties now languid seem: 10
Then sweets to luxury unknown
  We'll taste, and sip the untainted stream.
In Summer's sultry noon-tide heat
  I'll lead thee to the shady grove,
There hush thy cares, or pleased repeat
  Those vows that won my soul to love.

Damon. When o'er the mountain peeps the
        dawn,
  And round her ruddy beauties play,
I'll wake my love to view the lawn,
  Or hear the warblers hail the day.   20
But without thee the rising morn
  In vain awakes the cooling breeze;

[1] Damon and Sylvia are conventional pastoral names for shepherd and shepherdess.

In vain does nature's face adorn—
  Without my Sylvia nought can please.

Sylvia. At night, when universal gloom
  Hides the bright prospects from our view,
When the gay groves give up their bloom
  And verdant meads their lovely hue,
Though fleeting specters round me move,
  When in thy circling arms I'm prest, 30
I'll hush my rising fears with love,
  And sink in slumber on thy breast.

Damon. The new-blown rose, whilst on its
    leaves
  Yet the bright scented dew-drop's found,
Pleased on thy bosom whilst it heaves,
  Shall shake its heavenly fragrance round.
Then mingled sweets the sense shall raise,
  Then mingled beauties catch the eye:
What pleasure on such charms to gaze,
  What rapture 'mid such sweets to lie! 40

Sylvia. How sweet thy words! But, Damon,
    cease,
  Nor strive to fix me ever here;
Too well you know these accents please,
  That oft have filled my ravished ear.
Come, lead me to these promised joys
  That dwelt so lately on thy tongue;
Direct me by thy well-known voice,
  And calm my transports with thy song!

1758   1758

A DITHYRAMBIC ON WINE

I

Come! let Mirth our hours employ,
The jolly God inspires;
The rosy juice our bosom fires,
And tunes our souls to joy.
See, great Bacchus [1] now descending,
Gay, with blushing honors crowned;
Sprightly Mirth and Love attending,
    Around him wait,
    In smiling state—
    Let Echo resound   10
    Let Echo resound
    The joyful news all around.

II

Fond Mortals come, if love perplex,
In wine relief you'll find;
Who'd whine for woman's giddy sex
More fickle than the wind?

[1] god of wine and revelry

If beauty's bloom thy fancy warms,
Here see her shine,
Clothed in superior charms;
More lovely than the blushing morn, 20
When first the opening day
Bedecks the thorn,
And makes the meadows gay.
Here see her in her crystal shrine;
See and adore; confess her all divine,
The Queen of Love and Joy
Heed not thy Chloe's [2] scorn—
    This sparkling glass,
    With winning grace,
Shall ever meet thy fond embrace, 30
And never, never, never cloy,
    No never, never cloy.

III

Here, Poet, see, Castalia's [3] spring—
Come, give me a bumper, I'll mount to the
    skies,
Another, another—'Tis done! I arise;
    On fancy's wing,
    I mount, I sing,
    And now, sublime,
Parnassus' lofty top I climb—
But hark! what sounds are these I hear, 40
Soft as the dream of her in love,
Or zephyrs whispering through the grove?
And now, more solemn far than funeral woe,
The heavy numbers flow!
    And now again,
    The varied strain,
Grown louder and bolder, strikes quick on the
    ear,
And thrills through every vein.

IV

'Tis Pindar's [4] song!
His softer notes the fanning gales 50
Waft across the spicy vales,
    While through the air,
    Loud whirlwinds bear
The harsher notes along.
    Inspired by wine,
He leaves the lazy crowd below,
Who never dared to peep abroad,
And, mounting to his native sky,
For ever there shall shine.
    No more I'll plod 60
    The beaten road;

[2] conventional pastoral name for a young woman
[3] A spring upon Mount Parnassus; it was sacred to
  Apollo, god of poetry, and to the Muses.
[4] Pindar, a Greek lyric poet of the fifth century, B.C.,
  wrote hymns in honor of Dionysus, the Greek
  god of wine. Pindar's poetry is not, however,
  characteristically bacchanalian.

Like him inspired, like him I'll mount high;
  Like his my strain shall flow.

V

Haste, ye mortals! leave your sorrow;
Let pleasure crown today—tomorrow
  Yield to fate.
Join the universal chorus,
  Bacchus reigns
    Ever great;
  Bacchus reigns   70
    Ever glorious—
Hark! the joyful groves rebound,
Sporting breezes catch the sound,
And tell to hill and dale around—
  "Bacchus reigns"—
    While far away,
    The busy echoes die away. [1]

PHILLIS WHEATLEY
c. [2] 1754-1784

Phillis, a negro slave just from Africa, was bought in Boston in 1761 by John Wheatley, a resident of the city. She was about seven years old. Showing remarkable precocity, she was encouraged in study and made much of for her ability to write verses. She went with the family to London in 1773, where in the same year her poems were published, dedicated to the Countess of Huntingdon. She died in Boston. It is interesting that one in her situation could so far master the verse form and appropriate the literary vocabulary and phraseology of the day that her work will bear not unfavorable comparison with much of the poetry then current in England and America.

TO THE RIGHT HONORABLE WILLIAM,

EARL OF DARTMOUTH, [3] HIS MAJESTY'S
PRINCIPAL SECRETARY OF STATE FOR
NORTH AMERICA, ETC.

Hail, happy day, when, smiling like the
    morn,
Fair freedom rose New England to adorn;
The northern clime beneath her genial ray,
Dartmouth, congratulates thy blissful sway;
Elate with hope her race no longer mourns,

Each soul expands, each grateful bosom burns,
While in thine hand with pleasure we behold
The silken reins, and freedom's charms unfold.
Long lost to realms beneath the northern skies
She shines supreme, while hated faction dies:
Soon as appeared the goddess long desired,   11
Sick at the view, she languished and expired;
Thus from the splendors of the morning light
The owl in sadness seeks the caves of night.

No more, America, in mournful strain
Of wrongs, and grievances unredressed complain;
No longer shall thou dread the iron chain,
Which wanton tyranny with lawless hand
Had made, and with it meant to enslave the
    land.

Should you, my lord, while you peruse my
    song,   20
Wonder from whence my love of freedom
    sprung,
Whence flow the wishes for the common good,
By feeling hearts alone best understood,
I, young in life, by seeming cruel fate
Was snatched from Afric's fancied happy seat:
What pangs excruciating must molest,
What sorrows labor in my parents' breast?
Steeled was that soul, and by no misery moved,
That from a father seized his babe beloved;
Such such my case. And can I then but pray
Others may never feel tyrannic sway?   31

For favors past, great sir, our thanks are
    due,
And thee we ask thy favors to renew,
Since in thy power, as in thy will before,
To soothe the griefs, which thou didst once
    deplore.
May heavenly grace the sacred sanction give
To all thy works, and thou forever live
Not only on the wings of fleeting fame,
Though praise immortal crowns the patriot's
    name,
But to conduct to heaven's refulgent fane,   40
May fiery coursers sweep the ethereal plain,
And bear thee upwards to that blest abode,
Where, like the prophet, thou shalt find thy
    God.

                                              1773

HIS EXCELLENCY GENERAL
WASHINGTON

Celestial Choir! [4] enthroned in realms of light,
Columbia's scenes of glorious toils I write.
While freedom's cause her anxious breast
    alarms,

---

[1] "As our Poet appears so warm on his subject it may not be amiss to remark here, that he never drank any wine, and that his bumpers are all ideal, which may serve, perhaps, as a refutation of that noted adage, that a water drinker can never be a good Dithyrambic Poet." Duyckinck's note in his *Cyclopaedia of American Literature.*

[2] L. *circa,* about

[3] The people of Boston, in the commercial distress brought upon them by the repressive measures of the English government, hoped much from the Earl of Dartmouth, who was a man of great integrity and piety. He had before this been president of the Board of Trade and Foreign Plantations in London, the organization that had controlled the colonies.

[4] the Muses

She flashes dreadful in refulgent arms.
See mother earth her offspring's fate bemoan,
And nations gaze at scenes before unknown!
See the bright beams of heaven's revolving
　　light
Involved in sorrows and the veil of night!
　　The goddess comes, she moves divinely fair,
Olive and laurel binds her golden hair:　　10
Wherever shines this native of the skies,
Unnumbered charms and recent graces rise.
　　Muse! bow propitious while my pen relates
How pour her armies through a thousand
　　gates,
As when Aeolus [1] heaven's fair face deforms,
Enwrapped in tempest and a night of storms;
Astonished ocean feels the wild uproar,
The refluent surges beat the sounding shore;
Or thick as leaves in autumn's golden reign, [19]
Such, and so many, moves the warrior's train.
In bright array they seek the work of war,
Where high unfurled the ensign waves in air.
Shall I to Washington their praise recite?
Enough thou knowest them in the fields of
　　fight.
Thee, first in place and honors,—we demand
The grace and glory of thy martial band.
Famed for thy valor, for thy virtues more,
Hear every tongue thy guardian aid implore!
　　One century scarce performed its destined
　　round,　　29
When Gallic powers [2] Columbia's fury found;
And so may you, whoever dares disgrace
The land of freedom's heaven-defended race!
Fixed are the eyes of nations on the scales,
For in their hopes Columbia's arm prevails.
Anon Britannia droops the pensive head,
While round increase the rising hills of dead.
Ah! cruel blindness to Columbia's state!
Lament thy thirst of boundless power too late.
　　Proceed, great chief, with virtue on thy side,
Thy every action let the goddess guide.　　40
A crown, a mansion, and a throne that shine
With gold unfading, Washington! be thine.

1776

TIMOTHY DWIGHT 1752-1817

Dwight, Trumbull, and Barlow were among a
group of young men living in or near Hartford,
Yale graduates, and known as the "Hartford Wits"
(intellectuals). Some of them had been tutors at
Yale, and were aware of the shortcomings of the
infant United States in educational methods and in
literature. They instituted some reforms in the
Yale courses of study, and in their writings sought
mostly to develop an energetic style and to write
upon American subjects.

[1] god of the winds
[2] The forces of France (ancient Gaul) in America were
　　overcome in the French and Indian War.

Dwight was born at Northampton, Massachusetts, a grandson of Jonathan Edwards. Although
he is said to have been able to pass the Yale entrance examinations at the age of seven, he did not
enter until the maturer age of thirteen. He was
chosen tutor at nineteen. He entered the ministry
in 1777 and served as chaplain in the American
army. From 1795 until his death at New Haven
he was president of Yale College and one of the
most influential men in its history. His published
works include *The Conquest of Canaan*, 1785; *The
Triumph of Infidelity*, 1788; *Greenfield Hill*, 1794;
Travels in New England and New York, 1821-
1822.

Perhaps Dwight wished to be remembered for
his poetry. Though some of Dwight's verse consists of social satire, and his themes are often
American, he was less successful in poetry than
Trumbull and Barlow. He will be known to
students of American social history through his
Travels, which are painstaking, accurate, and still
readable, containing valuable observations and statistics.

L. Hayward, "An Early Writer of New England
Travels," *New Eng. M.* ns 23:256-62.

COLUMBIA [3]

Columbia, Columbia, to glory arise,
The queen of the world, and the child of the
　　skies;
Thy genius commands thee; with rapture be-
　　hold,
While ages on ages thy splendors unfold.
Thy reign is the last and the noblest of time;
Most fruitful thy soil, most inviting thy clime;
Let the crimes of the East ne'er encrimson thy
　　name;
Be freedom and science and virtue thy fame.

To conquest and slaughter let Europe aspire,
Whelm nations in blood, and wrap cities in
　　fire:　　10
Thy heroes the rights of mankind shall defend,
And triumphs pursue them, and glory attend.
A world is thy realm: for a world be thy laws,
Enlarged as thine empire, and just as thy
　　cause;
On Freedom's broad basis that empire shall
　　rise.
Extend with the main, and dissolve with the
　　skies.

Fair Science her gates to thy sons shall unbar,
And the east see thy morn hide the beams of
　　her star;
New bards and new sages, unrivaled, shall soar
To fame unextinguished when time is no more;
To thee, the last refuge of virtue designed,　　21
Shall fly from all nations the best of mankind;

[3] composed when Dwight was stationed, as chaplain in
　　the Revolutionary army, at West Point

Here, grateful to Heaven, with transport shall
bring
Their incense, more fragrant than odors of
spring.
Nor less shall thy fair ones to glory ascend,
And genius and beauty in harmony blend;
The graces of form shall awake pure desire,
And the charms of the soul ever cherish the
fire;
Their sweetness unmingled, [1] their manners re-
fined,
And virtue's bright image instamped on the
mind,   30
When peace and soft rapture shall teach life
to glow,
And light up a smile in the aspect of woe.

Thy fleets to all regions thy power shall dis-
play,
The nations admire, and the ocean obey;
Each shore to thy glory its tribute unfold,
And the East and the South yield their spices
and gold.
As the day-spring abounded, thy splendor shall
flow,
And earth's little kingdoms before thee shall
bow;
While the ensigns of union, in triumph unfurled,
Hush the tumult of war, and give peace to the
world.   40

Thus, as down a lone valley, with cedars o'er-
spread,
From war's dread confusion I pensively
strayed—
The gloom from the face of fair heaven retired,
The winds ceased to murmur, the thunders
expired;
Perfumes, as of Eden, flowed sweetly along,
And a voice, as of angels, enchantingly sung:
"Columbia, Columbia, to glory arise,
The queen of the world, and the child of the
skies."
1777

From THE TRIUMPH OF INFIDELITY
[THE SMOOTH DIVINE [2]]

There smiled the smooth Divine, unused to
wound

The sinner's heart with hell's alarming sound.
No terrors on his gentle tongue attend;
No grating truths the nicest ear offend.
That strange new-birth, that methodistic
grace, [3]
Nor in his heart nor sermons found a place.
Plato's fine tales he clumsily retold,
Trite, fireside, moral seesaws, dull as old;
His Christ and Bible placed at good remove,
Guilt hell-deserving, and forgiving love.   10
'T was best, he said, mankind should cease to
sin:
Good fame required it; so did peace within.
Their honors, well he knew, would ne'er be
driven;
But hoped they still would please to go to
heaven.
Each week he paid his visitation dues; [4]
Coaxed, jested, laughed; rehearsed the private
news;
Smoked with each goody, thought her cheese
excelled;
Her pipe he lighted, [5] and her baby held.
Or placed in some great town, with lacquered
shoes,
Trim wig, and trimmer gown, and glistening
hose,   20
He bowed, talked politics, learned manners
mild,
Most meekly questioned, and most smoothly
smiled;
At rich men's jests laughed loud, their stories
praised;
Their wives' new patterns gazed, and gazed, and
gazed;
Most daintily on pampered turkeys dined;
Nor shrunk with fasting, nor with study pined:
Yet from their churches saw his brethren
driven,
Who thundered truth, and spoke the voice of
heaven,
Chilled trembling guilt in Satan's headlong path,
Charmed the feet back, and roused the ear of
death.   30
"Let fools," he cried, "starve on, while pru-
dent I
Snug in my nest shall live, and snug shall die."

.   .   .   .

1788

---

[1] unalloyed
[2] This selection is part of a long poetical satire called
The Triumph of Infidelity, 1788, dedicated to
M. Voltaire. Professor Wendell points out that
the poem is directed specifically against the new
liberalism of belief already growing up in Boston,
centering in the worship at King's Chapel with its
liturgy newly modified in 1785.

[3] The doctrines of the necessity of the new birth or
conversion and of the presence in the heart of
divine grace were fundamental with Methodism,
and Methodism was held somewhat in contempt
by the most liberal persons of other sects.
[4] pastoral calls due
[5] Smoking was not unusual among women of the common people.

LOVE TO THE CHURCH [1]

I love thy kingdom, Lord,
  The house of thine abode,
The church our blest Redeemer saved
  With his own precious blood.

I love thy church, O God!
  Her walls before thee stand,
Dear as the apple of thine eye,
  And graven on thy hand.

If e'er to bless thy sons
  My voice or hands deny,   10
These hands let useful skill forsake,
  This voice in silence die.

For her my tears shall fall,
  For her my prayers ascend;
To her my cares and toils be given
  Till toils and cares shall end.

If e'er my heart forget
  Her welfare or her woe,
Let every joy this heart forsake,
  And every grief o'erflow.   20

Beyond my highest joy
  I prize her heavenly ways,
Her sweet communion, solemn vows,
  Her hymns of love and praise.

Jesus, thou friend divine,
  Our Saviour and our King,
Thy hand from every snare and foe
  Shall great deliverance bring.

Sure as thy truth shall last,
  To Zion shall be given   30
The brightest glories earth can yield,
  And brighter bliss of heaven.
                 1800

JOHN TRUMBULL 1750-1831

Trumbull, a wide-awake educator and politician, seeing faults in the education and government of his day, was one of the first and ablest of American satirists. He was born in an intellectual and prominent Connecticut family at Watertown, entered Yale in his fourteenth year, and was appointed tutor in 1771. He studied law with John Adams in Boston, was a member of the Connecticut legislature, and judge of the Connecticut Superior Court 1801-1825. His chief poems are *The Progress of Dulness*, 1772, and *M'Fingal*, 1775-83. Throughout

[1] This hymn, founded on *Psalm* cxxxvii, is perhaps the best of the Puritan hymns.

his life he was a contributor of political articles to the press. His *Poems* were published in 1820.

It is by the political and social satire *M'Fingal* that Trumbull will long have a place in American literature. This poem was undertaken, the author says, "with a political view, at the instigation of some of the leading members of the first Congress, who urged him to compose a satirical poem on the events of the campaign in the year 1775." He aimed to express, "in a poetical manner, a general account of the American contest, . . . and with as much impartiality as possible satirize the follies and extravagances of my countrymen as well as of their enemies." The first three cantos were published in Philadelphia in 1775 during the session of Congress. The indebtedness of Trumbull to Samuel Butler's *Hudibras* (1663), a satire upon the English Puritans, is very evident, both in form and manner, yet Trumbull's wit is quite his own. Thirty editions were printed within a few years. Tyler thinks *M'Fingal* "one of the world's masterpieces in political badinage," and also "a genuine embodiment of the spirit and life of a people."

M. C. Tyler, *Three Men of Letters*, 1895.

From M'FINGAL [2]

Canto I

THE TOWN-MEETING, A. M.

When Yankees, skilled in martial rule, [3]
First put the British troops to school;
Instructed them in warlike trade,
And new maneuvers of parade,
The true war-dance of Yankee reels,
And manual exercise of heels;
Made them give up, like saints complete,
The arm of flesh, and trust the feet,
And work, like Christians undissembling,
Salvation out, by fear and trembling;   10
Taught Percy fashionable races, [4]
And modern modes of Chevy Chases:
From Boston, in his best array,
Great 'Squire M'Fingal took his way,
And graced with ensigns of renown,
Steered homeward to his native town.
His high descent our heralds trace

[2] M'Fingal represents the typical loyalist magistrate, assiduous in his support of law lest his office be taken from him. The mock epic or mock heroic of which this poem is a type, burlesques the heroic epic in structure, phrase, and diction, often producing its best effects by a mingling of the lofty and the commonplace.

[3] This opening passage refers especially to the flight of the British regular troops before the colonial minute men from Concord to Boston, April 19, 1775.

[4] Sir Hugh Percy, in command of the British forces on this retreat, was said to be descended from the chieftain who led the English against the Scotch in the battle of Otterburn or, as it is often called, Chevy Chase, in 1388.

From Ossian's famed Fingalian race : [1]
For though their name some part may lack,
Old Fingal spelled it with a Mac;   20
Which great Macpherson, with submission,
We hope will add the next addition.

  His fathers flourished in the Highlands
Of Scotia's fog-benighted islands;
Whence gained our 'Squire two gifts by right,
Rebellion and the second-sight. [2]
Of these, the first, in ancient days,
Had gained the noblest palm of praise,
'Gainst kings stood forth and many a crowned
    head
With terror of its might confounded;   30
Till rose a king with potent charm [3]
His foes by meekness to disarm,
Whom every Scot and Jacobite
Strait fell in love with at first sight;
Whose gracious speech with aid of pensions,
Hushed down all murmurs of dissensions,
And with the sound of potent metal
Brought all their buzzing swarms to settle;
Who rained his ministerial manna, [4]
Till loud Sedition sung hosanna;   40
The grave lords-bishops and the kirk
United in the public work;
Rebellion, from the northern regions,
With Bute and Mansfield [5] swore allegiance,
All hands combined to raze, as nuisance,
Of church and state the constitutions, [6]
Pull down the empire, on whose ruins
They meant to edify their new ones;
Enslave the American wildernesses,
And rend the provinces in pieces.   50
With these our 'Squire, among the valiant'st,

Employed his time, and tools, and talents,
And found this new rebellion pleasing
As his old king-destroying treason.

  .   .   .   .

  The Town, our hero's scene of action,
Had long been torn by feuds of faction,   110
And as each party's strength prevails,
It turned up different, heads or tails;
With constant rattling, in a trice,
Showed various sides, as oft as dice.
As that famed weaver, wife to Ulysses, [7]
By night her day's-work picked in pieces,
And though she stoutly did bestir her,
Its finishing was ne'er the nearer:
So did this town with ardent zeal
Weave cobwebs for the public weal,   120
Which when completed, or before,
A second vote in pieces tore.
They met, made speeches full long-winded,
Resolved, protested and rescinded;
Addresses signed; then chose committees
To stop all drinking of Bohea teas; [8]
With winds of doctrine veered about,
And turned all Whig committees out. [9]
Meanwhile our hero, as their head,
In pomp the Tory faction led,   130
Still following, as the 'Squire should please,
Successive on, like files of geese.
  And now the town was summoned, greeting,
To grand parading of town-meeting;
A show, that strangers might appall,
As Rome's grave senate did the Gaul. [10]
High o'er the rout, on pulpit stairs,
Mid den of thieves in house of prayers,
(That house, which loth a rule to break
Served heaven but one day in the week,   140
Open the rest for all supplies
Of news, and politics, and lies)
Stood forth the constable; and bore
His staff, like Mercury's wand of yore, [11]
Waved potent round, the peace to keep,
As that laid dead men's souls to sleep.
Above and near the hermetic staff,
The moderator's [12] upper half
In grandeur o'er the cushion bowed,
Like Sol half seen behind a cloud.   150

[1] James Macpherson, a Scotchman, published in 1762 an epic poem, *Fingal*, which he said was the work of Ossian, son of Fingal, a Celtic chieftain. The poem, though founded on epic fragments, is probably a forgery, the work of Macpherson or his friends. According to Scotch custom, Ossian should properly be called Ossian Mac Fingal (son of Fingal). The last word in l. 22 should probably read *edition* in reference to the great popularity of Macpherson's work.

[2] The Highlanders had supported the Stuarts against the established kings of the House of Hanover. Second-sight, a kind of clairvoyance, was long believed in among them. The fourth canto of *M'Fingal* is the vision of the squire.

[3] George III had begun his reign in the hope of reducing parties and leaders to his own will by means of royal patronage. By the Whigs he was thought too favorably inclined toward the Scotch, who had generally supported the Jacobites, followers of James (Jacobus) Stuart and his heirs, in their endeavor to put back the Stuarts on the English throne.

[4] offices and pensions

[5] John Stuart, Earl of Bute, was prime minister in 1762-3. James Mansfield, solicitor-general, was greatly disliked by the colonists, since his official duties often bore against them; and since they also suspected him of favoring the Catholics.

[6] The English ministers had proposed to "reform the American charters," an interference the colonists greatly dreaded.

[7] Penelope, in the twenty years' absence of her husband, Ulysses, was courted by many suitors. To these she declared that she would not marry until she had finished weaving a certain rich robe. Each night she would unravel what she had woven by day until she had delayed her suitors for three years. *Odyssey*, xix, 140.

[8] until the tax on tea should be abolished

[9] The colonial Whigs stood for more liberal ideas than the colonial Tories.

[10] There is a legend that when in 390 B.C. the victorious Gauls entered Rome, they were for a moment overawed by the sight of the Roman senators seated in their official seats in the Forum.

[11] See any classical encyclopedia.

[12] chairman's

Beneath stood voters of all colors,
Whigs, Tories, orators, and brawlers;
With every tongue in either faction
Prepared like minute-men for action;
Where truth and falsehood, wrong and right,
Draw all their legions forth to fight.
With equal uproar scarcely rave
Opposing winds in Aeolus' cave;
Such dialogues with earnest face
Held never Balaam with his ass.   160

. . . .

CANTO II

THE TOWN-MEETING, P. M. [1]

The Sun, who never stops to dine,
Two hours had passed the mid-way line,
And driving at his usual rate,
Lashed on his downward car of state.
And now expired the short vacation,
And dinner o'er in epic fashion,
While all the crew, beneath the trees,
Eat pocket-pies, or bread and cheese,
(Nor shall we, like old Homer, [2] care
To versify their bill of fare)   10
Each active party, feasted well,
Thronged in, like sheep, at sound of bell;
With equal spirit took their places,
And meeting oped with three *Oh Yesses:* [3]
When first, the daring Whigs to oppose,
Again the great M'Fingal rose,
Stretched magisterial arm amain,
And thus resumed the accusing strain.
"Ye Whigs attend, and hear affrighted
The crimes whereof ye stand indicted;   20
The sins and follies past all compass,
That prove you guilty, or *non compos*.
I leave the verdict to your senses,
And jury of your consciences;
Which though they're neither good nor true,
Must yet convict you and your crew.
"Ungrateful sons! a factious band,
That rise against your parent land!
Ye viper race, that burst in strife
The genial womb that gave you life,   30
Tear with sharp fangs and forked tongue
The indulgent bowels whence ye sprung;
And scorn the debt and obligation,
You justly owe the British nation,

Which since you cannot pay, your crew
Affect to swear was never due.
"Did not the deeds of England's primate [4]
First drive your fathers to this climate,
Whom jails and fines and every ill
Forced to their good against their will?   40
Ye owe to their obliging temper
The peopling your new-fangled empire,
While every British act and canon
Stood forth your *causa sine qua non.* [5]
Who'd seen, except for these restraints,
Your witches, Quakers, Whigs, and saints,
Or heard of Mather's famed *Magnalia*, [6]
If Charles and Laud had chanced to fail you? [7]
Did they not send your charters o'er,
And give you lands you owned before, [8]   50
Permit you all to spill your blood,
And drive out heathen where you could;
On these mild terms, that, conquest won,
The realm you gained should be their own?
And when of late attacked by those,
Whom her connection made your foes,
Did they not then, distressed by war,
Send generals to your help from far, [9]
Whose aid you owned, in terms less haughty,
And thankfully o'er paid your quota?   60
Say, at what period did they grudge
To send you governor or judge,
With all their missionary crew, [10]
To teach you law and gospel too?
They brought all felons in the nation
To help you on in population;
Proposed their bishops to surrender,
And made their priests a legal tender,
Who only asked, in surplice clad,
The simple tithe [11] of all you had: 70
And now, to keep all knaves in awe,
Have sent their troops to establish law,
And with gunpowder, fire and ball,
Reform your people, one, and all.

[1] The assembling of the voters of the township for an all-day's session or "town meeting" with an hour's interval for luncheon is a custom still observed in some states.
[2] Homer sometimes particularizes carefully the kinds and abundance of food at the feasts of his heroes.
[3] "Oyez," or "Oyes," meaning "Hear ye!" from the French verb *ouir*, hear, is the call of the crier for attention at the beginning of a session of court or town meeting.

[4] William Laud, primate of England 1633-40, by his rigorous policy toward nonconformists caused thousands of them to settle in the colonies.
[5] indispensable cause or condition
[6] Cotton Mather's *Magnalia Christi Americana;* or *Ecclesiastical History of New England.* See p. 40 ff.
[7] Charles I was very slow to grant political rights to the colonists.
[8] The colonists felt that they had fully won their domain by force of conquest and that they held it more rightfully thus than by grace of the English sovereign.
[9] The generals sent over by England were often, like Braddock, incompetent to face the situations of colonial warfare. The colonies, nevertheless, supplied more than their quota of troops.
[10] There were now some two hundred and fifty Episcopal clergymen in the colonies, all missionaries under charge of the bishop of London. The colonists greatly feared that a bishop would be sent to America, with authority over the churches and having temporal as well as spiritual powers, as in England.
[11] A tenth part; in England the church was supported by a tax of one-tenth the produce of the soil.

Yet when their insolence and pride
Have angered all the world beside;
When fear and want at once invade,
Can you refuse to lend them aid,
And rather risk your heads in fight,
Than gratefully throw in your mite?   80
Can they for debts make satisfaction,
Should they dispose their realm at auction,
And sell off Britain's goods and land all
To France and Spain, by inch of candle? [1]
Shall good King George, with want oppressed,
Insert his name in bankrupt list,
And shut up shop, like failing merchant,
That fears the bailiffs should make search in't;
With poverty shall princes strive,
And nobles lack whereon to live?   90
Have they not racked their whole inventions
To feed their brats on posts and pensions; [2]
Made their Scotch friends with taxes groan,
And picked poor Ireland to the bone:
Yet have on hand, as well deserving,
Ten thousand bastards, left for starving?
And can you now, with conscience clear,
Refuse them an asylum here,
And not maintain, in manner fitting,
These genuine sons of mother Britain?"   100

.   .   .   .

Canto III

THE LIBERTY POLE [3]

Now warm with ministerial ire,
Fierce sallied forth our loyal 'Squire,
And on his striding steps attends
His desperate clan of Tory friends.
When sudden met his wrathful eye
A pole ascending through the sky,
Which numerous throngs of Whiggish race
Were raising in the market-place.
Not higher school-boy's kites aspire,
Or royal mast, or country spire;   10
Like spears at Brobdignagian [4] tilting,
Or Satan's walking-staff in Milton.
And on its top, the flag unfurled
Waved triumph o'er the gazing world;
Inscribed with inconsistent types
Of liberty and thirteen stripes. [5]

[1] By auction; a custom at auctions was to receive bids while a small section of candle burned, the highest offer before the falling of the wick being accepted.
[2] This refers to the creation of offices for the illegitimate offspring of the British aristocracy.
[3] Meanwhile, just when the debate between M'Fingal and the Whigs had waxed so hot as almost to lead to blows, a shouting from without had caused a sudden adjournment of the assembly.
[4] Brobdingnag, or Brobdignag, was a land of giants described in Swift's *Gulliver's Travels*; Satan's staff, taller than a "pine hewn on Norwegian hills," is mentioned in *Paradise Lost*, i, 292.
[5] a satirical allusion to slavery

Beneath, the crowd without delay
The dedication-rites essay,
And gladly pay, in ancient fashion,
The ceremonies of libation;   20
While briskly to each patriot lip
Walks eager round the inspiring flip: [6]
Delicious draught! whose powers inherit
The quintessence of public spirit;
Which whoso tastes, perceives his mind
To nobler politics refined;
Or roused to martial controversy,
As from transforming cups of Circe; [7]
Or warmed with Homer's nectared liquor,
That filled the veins of gods with ichor.   30
At hand for new supplies in store,
The tavern opes its friendly door,
Whence to and fro the waiters run,
Like bucket-men at fires in town.
Then with three shouts that tore the sky,
'Tis consecrate to Liberty.
To guard it from the attacks of Tories,
A grand committee culled of four is;
Who foremost on the patriot spot,
Had brought the flip, and paid the shot.   40
By this, M'Fingal with his train
Advanced upon the adjacent plain,
And full with loyalty possessed,
Poured forth the zeal that fired his breast.
"What mad-brained rebel gave commission,
To raise this May-pole of sedition?
Like Babel, reared by bawling throngs,
With like confusion too of tongues,
To point at heaven and summon down
The thunders of the British crown?   50
Say, will this paltry pole secure
Your forfeit heads from Gage's power?
Attacked by heroes brave and crafty,
Is this to stand your ark of safety;
Or driven by Scottish laird and laddie,
Think ye to rest beneath its shadow?
When bombs, like fiery serpents, fly,
And balls rush hissing through the sky,
Will this vile pole, devote to freedom,
Save like the Jewish pole in Edom; [8]   60
Or like the brazen snake of Moses,
Cure your cracked skulls and battered noses?
"Ye dupes to every factious rogue
And tavern-prating demagogue,
Whose tongue but rings, with sound more full,

[6] a liquor made of spirits sweetened and mixed with beer, and heated by stirring with a hot iron
[7] By means of an enchanted liquor and other charms, Circe changed the companions of Ulysses into swine: *Odyssey* x. Nectar was the drink of the Homeric gods, ichor the liquid that filled their veins.
[8] When the fugitive Israelites, encamped in Edom, were bitten by serpents, Moses raised on a standard a serpent of brass upon which those who had been bitten might look and be saved from death. *Numbers* xxi, 6-9.

On the empty drumhead of his skull;
Behold you not what noisy fools
Use you, worse simpletons, for tools?
For liberty, in your own by-sense, [1]
Is but for crimes a patent license,   70
To break of law the Egyptian yoke, [2]
And throw the world in common stock; [3]
Reduce all grievances and ills
To Magna Charta of your wills;
Establish cheats and frauds and nonsense,
Framed to the model of your conscience;
Cry justice down, as out of fashion,
And fix its scale of depreciation; [4]
Defy all creditors to trouble ye,
And keep new years of Jewish jubilee; [5]   80
Drive judges out, like Aaron's calves, [6]
By jurisdiction of white staves, [7]
And make the bar and bench and steeple
Submit to our sovereign lord, the people;
By plunder rise to power and glory,
And brand all property, as Tory;
Expose all wares to lawful seizures
By mobbers or monopolizers;
Break heads and windows and the peace,
For your own interest and increase;   90
Dispute and pray and fight and groan
For public good, and mean your own;
Prevent the law by fierce attacks
From quitting scores upon your backs;
Lay your old dread, the gallows, low,
And seize the stocks, [8] your ancient foe,
And turn them to convenient engines
To wreak your patriotic vengeance;
While all, your rights who understand,
Confess them in their owner's hand;   100
And when by clamors and confusions,
Your freedom's grown a public nuisance,
Cry "Liberty," with powerful yearning,
As he does "Fire!" whose house is burning;
Though he already has much more
Than he can find occasion for.
While every clown, that tills the plains,
Though bankrupt in estate and brains,
By this new light transformed to traitor,
Forsakes his plow to turn dictator,   110

[1] A coined word meaning, apparently, nonsense; cf. by-path.
[2] the law, which all must bear as the Israelites bore the yoke of Egyptian slavery
[3] reduce all ranks to a common level
[4] Congress ascertained the course of the depreciation of the Continental currency by what was called the scale of depreciation.
[5] Every fiftieth year was by Jewish law a year of jubilee in which all slaves were set free, debts canceled, and all property was returned to its original owners.
[6] Moses destroyed—he did not drive out—the calf made by Aaron and worshiped by the idolators.
[7] In some cases, the colonists armed with white staves, symbols of order, had driven the King's judges from the bench.
[8] instruments of punishment

Starts an haranguing chief of Whigs,
And drags you by the ears, like pigs.
All bluster, armed with factious license,
New-born at once to politicians.
Each leather-aproned dunce, grown wise,
Presents his forward face to advise,
And tattered legislators meet,
From every workshop through the street.
His goose the tailor finds new use in,
To patch and turn the Constitution;   120
The blacksmith comes with sledge and grate
To iron-bind the wheels of state;
The quack forbears his patients' souse, [9]
To purge the Council and the House;
The tinker quits his molds and doxies,
To cast [10] assembly-men and proxies,
From dunghills deep of blackest hue,
Your dirt-bred patriots spring to view,
To wealth and power and honors rise,
Like new-winged maggots changed to flies,   130
And fluttering round in high parade,
Strut in the robe, or gay cockade.

. . . .

For in this ferment of the stream
The dregs have worked up to the brim,
And by the rule of topsy-turvies,
The scum stands foaming on the surface.
You've caused your pyramid to ascend,
And set it on the little end.
Like Hudibras, your empire's made,
Whose crupper had o'ertopped his head, [11]
You've pushed and turned the whole world up-
Side down, and got yourselves at top,   150
While all the great ones of your state
Are crushed beneath the popular weight;
Nor can you boast, this present hour,
The shadow of the form of power.
For what's your Congress or its end?
A power, to advise and recommend;
To call forth troops, adjust your quotas—
And yet no soul is bound to notice;
To pawn your faith to the utmost limit,
But cannot bind you to redeem it;   160
And when in want no more in them lies,
Than begging from your state-assemblies; [12]
Can utter oracles of dread,
Like Friar Bacon's brazen head, [13]
But when a faction dares dispute 'em,
Has ne'er an arm to execute 'em:

[9] apparently a copious draught of medicine
[10] Perhaps, to add up votes; legislative votes were often cast by proxy.
[11] The reference is to the grotesque figure of the knight, Hudibras. See *Hudibras*, I, i, 294.
[12] Under the Articles of Confederation, Congress could advise but could not enforce its wishes.
[13] Roger Bacon, a Franciscan monk of the thirteenth century, was said to have made a brazen head that could utter oracles.

As though you chose supreme dictators,
And put them under conservators.
You've but pursued the self-same way
With Shakspere's Trinculo in the play; [1]   170
"You shall be viceroys here, 'tis true,
But we'll be viceroys over you."
What wild confusion hence must ensue?
Though common danger yet cements you:
So some wrecked vessel, all in shatters,
Is held up by surrounding waters,
But stranded, when the pressure ceases,
Falls by its rottenness to pieces.

.   .   .   .

Such is the government you chose;
For this you bade the world be foes;
For this, so marked for dissolution,
You scorn the British constitution,
That constitution formed by sages,
The wonder of all modern ages;
Which owns no failure in reality,
Except corruption and venality;
And merely proves the adage just,
That best things spoiled corrupt to worst: 200
So man supreme in earthly station,
And mighty lord of this creation,
When once his corse is dead as herring,
Becomes the most offensive carrion,
And sooner breeds the plague, 'tis found,
Than all beasts rotting on the ground.

.   .   .   .

Rise then, my friends, in terror rise,
And sweep this scandal from the skies.   290
You'll see their Dagon, [2] though well jointed,
Will shrink before the Lord's anointed;
And like old Jericho's proud wall, [3]
Before our ram's-horns prostrate fall."
     This said, our 'Squire, yet undismayed,
Called for the constable to aid,
And bade him read, in nearer station,
The riot-act and proclamation,
He swift advancing to the ring,   299
Began, "Our Sovereign Lord, the King"—
When thousand clamorous tongues he hears,
And clubs and stones assail his ears.
To fly was vain; to fight was idle;
By foes encompassed in the middle,
His hope, in stratagems, he found,
And fell right craftily to ground;
Then crept to seek an hiding place,
'Twas all he could, beneath a brace;

Where soon the conquering crew espied him,
And where he lurked, they caught and tied
     him.   310
     At once with resolution fatal,
Both Whigs and Tories rushed to battle.
Instead of weapons, either band
Seized on such arms as came to hand.
And as famed Ovid paints the adventures
Of wrangling Lapithae and Centaurs, [4]
Who at their feast, by Bacchus led,
Threw bottles at each other's head;
And these arms failing in their scuffles,
Attacked with andirons, tongs and shovels: 320
So clubs and billets, staves and stones
Met fierce, encountering every sconce,
And covered o'er with knobs and pains
Each void receptacle for brains;
Their clamors rend the skies around,
The hills rebellow to the sound; [5]
And many a groan increased the din
From battered nose and broken shin.
M'Fingal, rising at the word,
Drew forth his old militia sword;   330
Thrice cried "King George," as erst in distress,
Knights of romance invoked a mistress;
And brandishing the blade in air,
Struck terror through the opposing war.
The Whigs, unsafe within the wind
Of such commotion, shrunk behind.
With whirling steel around addressed,
Fierce through their thickest throng he pressed,
(Who rolled on either side in arch,
Like Red Sea waves in Israel's march)   340
And like a meteor rushing through,
Struck on their pole a vengeful blow.
Around, the Whigs, of clubs and stones
Discharged whole volleys, in platoons,
That o'er in whistling fury fly;
But not a foe dares venture nigh.
And now perhaps with glory crowned
Our 'Squire had felled the pole to ground,
Had not some Power, a Whig at heart,
Descended down and took their part;   350
(Whether 'twere Pallas, Mars or Iris, [6]
'Tis scarce worth while to make inquiries)
Who at the nick of time alarming,
Assumed the solemn form of Chairman,
Addressed a Whig, in every scene
The stoutest wrestler on the green,
And pointed where the spade was found,

[1] The drunken Stephano proposes to make the monster, Caliban, and Trinculo, the jester, viceroys. *Tempest*, III, ii, 102.

[2] The idol of Dagon, chief god of the Philistines, had the figure of a man joined to the tail of a fish. *1 Samuel* v, 1-5.

[3] The walls of the heathen city Jericho fell at the blast of the trumpets of the besieging army of Israelites. *Joshua* vi, 20.

[4] At the marriage of Pirithous, king of the Lapithae, to Hippodamia, the Centaurs, who were guests, attempted violence to the bride, and a battle ensued.

[5] Cf. Pope's *Rape of the Lock*, Canto v, 49-51.

[6] The passage is strongly reminiscent of *The Iliad* and other epics where the gods and goddesses take personal part in the contests of men. As mock-epic the poem is at its best here, and compares favorably with *Hudibras* or with Pope's *Rape of the Lock*.

Late used to set their pole in ground,
And urged, with equal arms and might,
To dare our 'Squire to single fight.   360
The Whig thus armed, untaught to yield,
Advanced tremendous to the field:
Nor did M'Fingal shun the foe,
But stood to brave the desperate blow;
While all the party gazed, suspended
To see the deadly combat ended;
And Jove in equal balance weighed
The sword against the brandished spade.
He weighed; but lighter than a dream,
The sword flew up, and kicked the beam.   370
Our 'Squire on tiptoe rising fair
Lifts high a noble stroke in air,
Which hung not, but like dreadful engines,
Descended on his foe in vengeance.
But ah! in danger, with dishonor
The sword perfidious fails its owner;
That sword, which oft had stood its ground,
By huge trainbands encircled round;
And on the bench, with blade [1] right loyal,
Had won the day at many a trial,   380
Of stones and clubs had braved the alarms,
Shrunk from these new Vulcanian arms. [2]
The spade so tempered from the sledge,
Nor keen nor solid harmed its edge,
Now met it, from his arm of might,
Descending with steep force to smite;
The blade snapped short—and from his hand,
With rust embrowned the glittering sand.
Swift turned M'Fingal at the view,
And called to aid the attendant crew,   390
In vain; the Tories all had run,
When scarce the fight was well begun;
Their setting wigs he saw decreased
Far in the horizon toward the west.
Amazed he viewed the shameful sight,
And saw no refuge, but in flight:
But age unwieldy checked his pace,
Though fear had winged his flying race;
For not a trifling prize at stake;
No less than great M'Fingal's back.   400
With legs and arms he worked his course,
Like rider that outgoes his horse,
And labored hard to get away, as
Old Satan struggling on through chaos; [3]
Till looking back, he spied in rear
The spade-armed chief advanced too near:
Then stopped and seized a stone, that lay
An ancient landmark near the way;

Nor shall we as old bards have done,
Affirm it weighed an hundred ton;   410
But such a stone, as at a shift
A modern might suffice to lift,
Since men, to credit their enigmas,
Are dwindled down to dwarfs and pigmies,
And giants exiled with their cronies
To Brobdignags and Patagonias.
But while our hero turned him round,
And tugged to raise it from the ground,
The fatal spade discharged a blow
Tremendous on his rear below: 420
His bent knee failed, and void of strength
Stretched on the ground his manly length.
Like ancient oak o'erturned, he lay,
Or tower to tempests fallen a prey,
Or mountain sunk with all his pines,
Or flower the plow to dust consigns,
And more things else—but all men know 'em,
If slightly versed in epic poem.
At once the crew, at this dread crisis,
Fall on, and bind him, ere he rises;   430
And with loud shouts and joyful soul,
Conduct him prisoner to the pole.
When now the mob in lucky hour
Had got their enemies in their power,
They first proceed, by grave command,
To take the constable in hand.
Then from the pole's sublimest top
The active crew let down the rope,
At once its other end in haste bind,
And make it fast upon his waistband;   440
Till like the earth, as stretched on tenter, [4]
He hung self-balanced on his center.
Then upwards, all hands hoisting sail,
They swung him, like a keg of ale,
Till to the pinnacle in height
He vaulted, like balloon or kite.
As Socrates of old at first did
To aid philosophy get hoisted,
And found his thoughts flow strangely clear,
Swung in a basket in mid air: [5]   450
Our culprit thus, in purer sky,
With like advantage raised his eye,
And looking forth in prospect wide,
His Tory errors clearly spied,
And from his elevated station,
With bawling voice began addressing.
    "Good gentlemen and friends and kin,
For Heaven's sake hear, if not for mine!
I here renounce the Pope, the Turks,
The King, the Devil and all their works;   460

[1] In New England, judges wore swords when presiding
    on the bench.
[2] The arms of Achilles were forged by Vulcan. From
    the shield, the spear of Hector recoiled. *Iliad*,
    xviii; xxii, 290.
[3] on his journey from the gates of hell through chaos
    to the bounds of the starry universe: *Paradise
    Lost*, ii, 880-1055

[4] Cloth when first woven or after dying is stretched on
    tenters or tenter-hooks to preserve the shape.
[5] In his comedy *The Clouds* Aristophanes figures Soc-
    rates suspended in a basket above the earth in
    order to enjoy a finer and clearer atmosphere for
    philosophic speculation.

And will, set me but once at ease,
Turn Whig or Christian, what you please;
And always mind your rules so justly,
Should I live long as old Methuselah,
I'll never join in British rage,
Nor help Lord North, nor General Gage;
Nor lift my gun in future fights,
Nor take away your charter-rights;
Nor overcome your new-raised levies,
Destroy your towns, nor burn your navies; 470
Nor cut your poles down while I've breath,
Though raised more thick than hatchel-teeth: [1]
But leave King George and all his elves
To do their conquering work themselves."

This said, they lowered him down in state,
Spread at all points, like falling cat;
But took a vote first on the question,
That they'd accept this full confession,
And to their fellowship and favor,
Restore him on his good behavior. 480

Not so our 'Squire submits to rule,
But stood, heroic as a mule.
"You'll find it all in vain," quoth he,
"To play your rebel tricks on me.
All punishments the world can render,
Serve only to provoke the offender;
The will gains strength from treatment horrid,
As hides grow harder when they're curried.
No man e'er felt the halter draw,
With good opinion of the law; 490
Or held in method orthodox
His love of justice, in the stocks;
Or failed to lose by sheriff's shears
At once his loyalty and ears. [2]
Have you made Murray [3] look less big,
Or smoked old Williams to a Whig?
Did our mobbed Oliver quit his station,
Or heed his vows of resignation?
Has Rivington, in dread of stripes,
Ceased lying since you stole his types? 500
And can you think my faith will alter,
By tarring, whipping or the halter?
I'll stand the worst; for recompense
I trust King George and Providence.
And when with conquest gained I come,
Arrayed in law and terror home,
Ye'll rue this inauspicious morn,
And curse the day when ye were born,
In Job's high style of imprecations, [4]

[1] an implement consisting of a board thickly set with sharp spikes, used in separating the fibers of flax or hemp
[2] Cropping the ears was a punishment not unknown in New England.
[3] The men mentioned here were all prominent loyalists of Boston or New York, most of whom were mobbed. Oliver was "smoked" in a room with a covered chimney. Rivington, a New York printer and publisher, was mobbed and his press destroyed.
[4] Job cursed the day in which he was born. Job iii, 2 ff.

With all his plagues, without his patience." 510
Meanwhile beside the pole, the guard
A bench of justice had prepared.
Where sitting round in awful sort
The grand committee hold their court;
While all the crew, in silent awe,
Wait from their lips the lore of law.
Few moments with deliberation
They hold the solemn consultation;
When soon in judgment all agree,
And clerk proclaims the dread decree; 520
"That 'Squire M'Fingal having grown
The vilest Tory in the town,
And now in full examination
Convicted by his own confession,
Finding no tokens of repentance,
This court proceeds to render sentence:
That first the mob a slip-knot single
Tie round the neck of said M'Fingal,
And in due form do tar him next,
And feather, as the law directs; 530
Then through the town attendant ride him
In cart with constable beside him,
And having held him up to shame,
Bring to the pole, from whence he came."

Forthwith the crowd proceed to deck
With haltered noose M'Fingal's neck,
While he in peril of his soul
Stood tied half-hanging to the pole;
Then lifting high the ponderous jar,
Poured o'er his head the smoking tar. 540
With less profusion once was spread
Oil on the Jewish monarch's head, [5]
That down his beard and vestments ran,
And covered all his outward man.
As when (so Claudian sings) the gods
And earth-born giants fell at odds,
The stout Enceladus [6] in malice
Tore mountains up to throw at Pallas;
And while he held them o'er his head,
The river, from their fountains fed, 550
Poured down his back its copious tide,
And wore its channels in his hide:
So from the high-raised urn the torrents
Spread down his side their various currents;
His flowing wig, as next the brim,
First met and drank the sable stream;
Adown his visage stern and grave
Rolled and adhered the viscid wave;
With arms depending as he stood,
Each cuff capacious holds the flood; 560
From nose and chin's remotest end,
The tarry icicles descend;
Till all o'erspread, with colors gay,

[5] Perhaps the author has in mind Psalms cxxxiii, 2. If so the reference is not exact.
[6] Enceladus was one of the giants who disputed the sovereignty of Zeus, and Athene (Pallas).

He glittered to the western ray,
Like sleet-bound trees in wintry skies,
Or Lapland idol carved in ice.
And now the feather-bag displayed
Is waved in triumph o'er his head,
And clouds him o'er with feathers missive,
And down, upon the tar, adhesive: 570
Not Maia's son, [1] with wings for ears,
Such plumage round his visage wears;
Nor Milton's six-winged angel [2] gathers
Such superfluity of feathers.
Now all complete appears our 'Squire,
Like gorgon or chimaera dire; [3]
Nor more could boast on Plato's plan [4]
To rank among the race of man,
Or prove his claim to human nature,
As a two-legged, unfeathered creature.   580
    Then on the fatal cart, in state
They raised our grand Duumvirate.
And as at Rome a like committee,
Who found an owl within their city,
With solemn rites and grave processions
At every shrine performed lustrations, [5]
And, lest infection might take place
From such grim fowl with feathered face,
All Rome attends him through the street
In triumph to his country seat: 590
With like devotion all the choir
Paraded round our awful 'Squire;
In front the martial music comes
Of horns and fiddles, fifes and drums,
With jingling sound of carriage bells,
And treble creak of rusted wheels.
Behind, the crowd, in lengthened row
With proud procession, closed the show.
And at fit periods every throat
Combined in universal shout;   600
And hailed great Liberty in chorus,
Or bawled "Confusion to the Tories."
Not louder storm the welkin braves
From clamors of conflicting waves;
Less dire in Lybian wilds the noise
When ravening lions lift their voice;
Or triumphs at town-meetings made,
On passing votes to regulate trade. [6]
    Thus having borne them round the town,
Last at the pole they set them down;   610
And to the tavern take their way
To end in mirth the festal day.

[1] Mercury of the winged cap
[2] Raphael: *Paradise Lost*, v, 277
[3] *Paradise Lost*, ii, 628
[4] Plato described man as a featherless biped.
[5] An owl found in Rome was regarded as a prodigy of
    evil omen and, after being taken from temple to
    temple where sacrifices were performed, was re-
    leased in a wood outside the city.
[6] In early colonial days, prices were regulated by town-
    meetings or the "general court" of the colony.

    And now the mob, dispersed and gone,
Left 'Squire and constable alone.
The constable with rueful face
Leaned sad and solemn o'er a brace;
And fast beside him, cheek by jowl,
Stuck 'Squire M'Fingal 'gainst the pole,
Glued by the tar to his rear applied,
Like barnacle on vessel's side.   620
But though his body lacked physician,
His spirit was in worse condition.
He found his fears of whips and ropes
By many a dram outweighed his hopes.
As men in jail without mainprize [7]
View everything with other eyes,
And all goes wrong in church and state,
Seen through perspective of the grate:
So now M'Fingal's second-sight
Beheld all things in gloomier light;   630
His visual nerve, well purged with tar,
Saw all the coming scenes of war.
As his prophetic soul grew stronger,
He found he could hold in no longer.
First from the pole, as fierce he shook,
His wig from pitchy durance broke,
His mouth unglued, his feathers fluttered
His tarred skirts cracked, and thus he uttered.
    "Ah, Mr. Constable, in vain
We strive 'gainst wind and tide and rain!   640
Behold my doom! this feathery omen
Portends what dismal times are coming.
Now future scenes, before my eyes,
And second-sighted forms arise.
I hear a voice, that calls away,
And cries 'The Whigs will win the day.'
My beckoning genius gives command,
And bids me fly the fatal land;
Where changing name and constitution,
Rebellion turns to revolution,   650
While loyalty, oppressed, in tears,
Stands trembling for its neck and ears.
    "Go, summon all our brethren, greeting,
To muster at our usual meeting;
There my prophetic voice shall warn 'em
Of all things future that concern 'em,
And scenes disclose on which, my friend,
Their conduct and their lives depend.
There I—but first 'tis more of use,
From this vile pole to set me loose;   660
Then go with cautious steps and steady,
While I steer home and make all ready." [8]

1775   1775

[7] surety, bail
[8] The fourth and last canto tells of a secret meeting
    of Tories at night in M'Fingal's cellar, at which
    the squire recounts visions that have come to
    him, and prophesies the Revolution and the com-
    plete triumph of the Whigs. See notes 3. p. 123,
    and 2, p. 124.

JOEL BARLOW 1755-1812

Barlow was born at Reading, Connecticut, and was educated at Dartmouth, and at Yale, where he graduated in 1778 and was for a brief period tutor. He then for a time studied law, but was soon in the army as chaplain. After the war he led the life of a lawyer, agitator, and officeholder, actively supported the principles of the French Revolution in France and in London. He was later consul at Algiers. At the time of his death he was minister plenipotentiary to France and on a special mission to Poland to treat with Napoleon, then on his Russian campaign. His chief literary works are *The Vision of Columbus,* 1787, expanded into *The Columbiad,* 1807, and *The Hasty Pudding,* 1796.

Barlow's heavier pieces fall lamentably short of the true epic stride that they attempted. Like Dwight's they are but imitations of an imitation, following pseudo-classic models. *The Hasty Pudding* is more successful. It expresses Barlow's serious desire to promote simplicity of diet and manners among his countrymen; wishing to make his appeal popular, he put it in the playful form of the mock-heroic. The poem was written when Barlow was on a mission from the French government to Savoy in 1792-3, and was dedicated to Mrs. Washington.

Life and Letters of Joel Barlow by C. B. Todd, 1886; see also *Three Men of Letters,* M. C. Tyler, 1895.

THE HASTY PUDDING

Canto I

Ye Alps audacious, through the heavens that
    rise,
To cramp the day and hide me from the skies;
Ye Gallic flags, that o'er their heights unfurled,
Bear death to kings and freedom to the world, [1]
I sing not you. A softer theme I choose,
A virgin theme, unconscious of the muse,
But fruitful, rich, well suited to inspire
The purest frenzy of poetic fire.

Despise it not, ye bards to terror steeled,
Who hurl your thunders round the epic field; [10]
Nor ye who strain your midnight throats to
    sing
Joys that the vineyard and the stillhouse bring;
Or on some distant fair your notes employ,
And speak of raptures that you ne'er enjoy. [2]
I sing the sweets I know, the charms I feel,
My morning incense, and my evening meal,—
The sweets of Hasty Pudding. Come dear
    bowl,
Glide o'er my palate, and inspire my soul.
The milk beside thee, smoking from the kine,

---

[1] France was at this time the exponent of liberty, standing alone against the rest of Europe.
[2] Barlow asks consideration from epic, convivial, and lyric poets.

Its substance mingled, married in with thine, [20]
Shall cool and temper thy superior heat,
And save the pains of blowing while I eat.
    Oh! could the smooth, the emblematic song
Flow like thy genial juices o'er my tongue,
Could those mild morsels in my numbers chime,
And, as they roll in substance, roll in rime,
No more thy awkward, unpoetic name
Should shun the muse or prejudice thy fame;
But, rising grateful to the accustomed ear, [29]
All bards should catch it, and all realms revere!
    Assist me first with pious toil to trace
Through wrecks of time, thy lineage and thy
    race;
Declare what lovely squaw, in days of yore,
(Ere great Columbus sought thy native shore)
First gave thee to the world; her works of fame
Have lived indeed, but lived without a name.
Some tawny Ceres, [3] goddess of her days,
First learned with stones to crack the well-
    dried maize,
Through the rough sieve to shake the golden
    · shower,
In boiling water stir the yellow flour: [40]
The yellow flour, bestrewed and stirred with
    haste,
Swells in the flood and thickens to a paste,
Then puffs and wallops, rises to the brim,
Drinks the dry knobs that on the surface swim;
The knobs at last the busy ladle breaks,
And the whole mass its true consistence takes.
    Could but her sacred name, unknown so long,
Rise, like her labors, to the son of song,
To her, to them I'd consecrate my lays,
And blow her pudding with the breath of
    praise. [50]
If 'twas Oella whom I sang before, [4]
I here ascribe her one great virtue more.
Not through the rich Peruvian realms alone
The fame of Sol's sweet daughter should be
    known,
But o'er the world's wide climes should live
    secure,
Far as his rays extend, as long as they endure.
    Dear Hasty Pudding, what unpromised joy
Expands my heart, to meet thee in Savoy! [5]
Doomed o'er the world through devious paths to
    roam,
Each clime my country, and each house my
    home, [60]
My soul is soothed, my cares have found an
    end;

---

[3] goddess of agriculture and harvest
[4] Oella, imagined to be the daughter of a Peruvian chief, had been celebrated by Barlow in *The Vision of Columbus* as the inventor of spinning.
[5] Indian corn was then, as now, grown on the southern slopes of Savoy.

I greet my long-lost, unforgotten friend.
   For thee through Paris, that corrupted town,
How long in vain I wandered up and down,
Where shameless Bacchus, [1] with his drenching
    board,
Cold from his cave usurps the morning board.
London is lost in smoke and steeped in tea;
No Yankee there can lisp the name of thee;
The uncouth word, a libel on the town,
Would call a proclamation from the crown.   70
For climes oblique, that fear the sun's full
    rays,
Chilled in their fogs, exclude the generous
    maize:
A grain whose rich, luxuriant growth requires
Short, gentle showers, and bright, ethereal fires.
   But here, though distant from our native
    shore,
With mutual glee, we meet and laugh once
    more.
The same! I know thee by that yellow face,
That strong complexion of true Indian race,
Which time can never change, nor soil impair,
Nor Alpine snows, nor Turkey's morbid air;   80
For endless years, through every mild domain,
Where grows the maize, there thou art sure to
    reign.

   But man, more fickle, the bold licence
    claims,
In different realms to give thee different names.
Thee the soft nations round the warm Levant
Polanta call; the French, of course, *Polante*.
E'en in thy native regions, how I blush
To hear the Pennsylvanians call thee *Mush!*
On Hudson's banks, while men of Belgic [2]
    spawn   89
Insult and eat thee by the name *Suppawn*.
All spurious appellations, void of truth;
I've better known thee from my earliest youth:
Thy name is *Hasty Pudding!* thus my sire
Was wont to greet the fuming from his fire;
And while he argued in thy just defense
With logic clear he thus explained the sense:
"In haste the boiling caldron, o'er the blaze,
Receives and cooks the ready powdered maize;
In haste 'tis served, and then in equal haste,
With cooling milk, we make the sweet re-
    past.   100
No carving to be done, no knife to grate
The tender ear and wound the stony plate;
But the smooth spoon, just fitted to the lip,
And taught with art the yielding mass to dip,
By frequent journeys to the bowl well stored,

Performs the hasty honors of the board."
Such is thy name, significant and clear,
A name, a sound to every Yankee dear,
But most to me, whose heart and palate chaste
Preserve my pure, hereditary taste.   110
   There are who strive to stamp with dis-
    repute
The luscious food, because it feeds the brute;
In tropes of high-strained wit, while gaudy
    prigs
Compare thy nursling, man, to pampered pigs;
With sovereign scorn I treat the vulgar jest,
Nor fear to share thy bounties with the beast.
What though the generous cow gives me to
    quaff
The milk nutritious: am I then a calf?
Or can the genius of the noisy swine,
Though nursed on pudding, thence lay claim
    to mine?   120
Sure the sweet song I fashion to thy praise,
Runs more melodious than the notes they raise.

   My song, resounding in its grateful glee,
No merit claims: I praise myself in thee.
My father loved thee through his length of
    days!
For thee his fields were shaded o'er with maize;
From thee what health, what vigor he pos-
    sessed,
Ten sturdy freemen from his loins attest;
Thy constellation ruled my natal morn,   129
And all my bones were made of Indian corn.
Delicious grain, whatever form it take,
To roast or boil, to smother or to bake,
In every dish 'tis welcome still to me,
But most, my Hasty Pudding, most in thee.

   Let the green succotash with thee contend;
Let beans and corn their sweetest juices blend;
Let butter drench them in its yellow tide,
And a long slice of bacon grace their side;
Not all the plate, how famed soe'er it be,
Can please my palate like a bowl of thee.   140
Some talk of hoe-cake, fair Virginia's pride!
Rich johnny-cake this mouth has often tried;
Both please me well, their virtues much the
    same,
Alike their fabric, as allied their fame,
Except in dear New England, where the last
Receives a dash of pumpkin in the paste,
To give it sweetness and improve the taste.
But place them all before me, smoking hot,
The big, round dumpling, rolling from the pot;
The pudding of the bag, whose quivering breast,
With suet lined, leads on the Yankee feast;   151
The charlotte brown, within whose crusty sides
A belly soft the pulpy apple hides;

[1] god of wine and revelry
[2] referring to the Dutch settlers of New York, from
    the Low Countries, indeed, but not from Belgium

The yellow bread whose face like amber glows,
And all of Indian that the bakepan knows,—
You tempt me not; my favorite greets my
    eyes,
To that loved bowl my spoon by instinct flies.

CANTO II

To mix the food by vicious rules of art,
To kill the stomach and to sink the heart,
To make mankind to social virtue sour,
Cram o'er each dish, and be what they devour;
For this the kitchen muse first framed her book,
Commanding sweats to stream from every
    cook;
Children no more their antic gambols tried,
And friends to physic wondered why they died.

Not so the Yankee: his abundant feast,
With simples furnished and with plainness
    dressed,   10
A numerous offspring gathers round the board,
And cheers alike the servant and the lord;
Whose well-bought hunger prompts the joyous
    taste,
And health attends them from the short repast.

. While the full pail rewards the milkmaid's
    toil,
The mother sees the morning caldron boil;
To stir the pudding next demands their care;
To spread the table and the bowls prepare;
To feed the household as their portions cool
And send them all to labor or to school.   20

Yet may the simplest dish some rules impart,
For nature scorns not all the aids of art.
E'en Hasty Pudding, purest of all food,
May still be bad, indifferent, or good,
As sage experience the short process guides,
Or want of skill, or want of care presides.
Whoe'er would form it on the surest plan,
To rear the child and long sustain the man;
To shield the morals while it mends the size,
And all the powers of every food supplies,— 30
Attend the lesson that the muse shall bring,
Suspend your spoons, and listen while I sing.

But since, O man! thy life and health de-
    mand
Not food alone, but labor from thy hand,
First, in the field, beneath the sun's strong rays,
Ask of thy mother earth the needful maize;
She loves the race that courts her yielding soil,
And gives her bounties to the sons of toil.

When now the ox, obedient to thy call,
Repays the loan that filled the winter stall,   40
Pursue his traces o'er the furrowed plain,

And plant in measured hills the golden grain.
But when the tender germ begins to shoot,
And the green spire declares the sprouting root,
Then guard your nursling from each greedy foe,
The insidious worm, the all-devouring crow.
A little ashes sprinkled round the spire,
Soon steeped in rain, will bid the worm retire;
The feathered robber with his hungry maw
Swift flies the field before your man of straw, 50
A frightful image, such as schoolboys bring
When met to burn the Pope or hang the King.

Thrice in the season, through each verdant
    row,
Wield the strong plowshare and the faithful
    hoe;
The faithful hoe, a double task that takes,
To till the summer corn and roast the winter
    cakes.

Slow springs the blade, while checked by
    chilling rains,
Ere yet the sun the seat of Cancer [1] gains;
But when his fiercest fires emblaze the land,
Then start the juices, then the roots expand;   60
Then, like a column of Corinthian mold,
The stalk struts upward and the leaves unfold;
The bushy branches all the ridges fill,
Entwine their arms, and kiss from hill to hill.
Here cease to vex them; all your cares are
    done:
Leave the last labors to the parent sun;
Beneath his genial smiles, the well-dressed field,
When autumn calls, a plenteous crop shall yield.

Now the strong foliage bears the standards
    high,
And shoots the tall top-gallants to the sky;   70
The suckling ears their silky fringes bend,
And pregnant grown, their swelling coats dis-
    tend;
The loaded stalk, while still the burden grows,
O'erhangs the space that runs between the rows;
High as a hop-field waves the silent grove,
A safe retreat for little thefts of love,
When the pledged roasting-ears invite the maid
To meet her swain beneath the new-formed
    shade;
His generous hand unloads the cumbrous hill,
And the green spoils her ready basket fill;   80
Small compensation for the twofold bliss,
The promised wedding, and the present kiss.

Slight depredations these; but now the moon
Calls from his hollow tree the sly raccoon;
And while by night he bears his prize away,

[1] The sun enters the zodiacal sign of Cancer on June 2L

The bolder squirrel labors through the day.
Both thieves alike, but provident of time,
A virtue rare, that almost hides their crime.
Then let them steal the little stores they can,
And fill their granaries from the toils of man; 90
We've one advantage where they take no part—
With all their wiles, they ne'er have found the
   art
To boil the Hasty Pudding; here we shine
Superior far to tenants of the pine;
This envied boon to man shall still belong,
Unshared by them in substance or in song.

At last the closing season browns the plain,
And ripe October gathers in the grain;
Deep-loaded carts the spacious corn-house fill;
The sack distended marches to the mill;   100
The laboring mill beneath the burden groans,
And showers the future pudding from the
   stones;
Till the glad housewife greets the powdered
   gold,
And the new crop exterminates the old.
Ah who can sing what every wight must feel,
The joy that enters with the bag of meal,
A general jubilee pervades the house,
Wakes every child and gladdens every mouse.

CANTO III

The days grow short; but though the falling
   sun
To the glad swain proclaims his day's work
   done,
Night's pleasing shades his various tasks pro-
   long,
And yield new subjects to my various song.
For now, the corn-house filled, the harvest
   home,
The invited neighbors to the husking come;
A frolic scene, where work, and mirth, and play,
Unite their charms to chase the hours away.

Where the huge heap lies centered in the hall,
The lamp suspended from the cheerful wall,   10
Brown, corn-fed nymphs, and strong, hard-
   handed beaux,
Alternate ranged, extend in circling rows,
Assume their seats, the solid mass attack;
The dry husks rustle, and the corncobs crack;
The song, the laugh, alternate notes resound,
And the sweet cider trips in silence round.

The laws of husking every wight can tell;
And sure no laws he ever keeps so well:
For each red ear a general kiss he gains,
With each smut ear she smuts the luckless   20
   swains;

But when to some sweet maid a prize is cast,
Red as her lips and taper as her waist,
She walks the round and culls one favored
   beau,
Who leaps the luscious tribute to bestow.
Various the sport, as are the wits and brains
Of well-pleased lasses and contending swains;
Till the vast mound of corn is swept away,
And he that gets the last ear wins the day.

Meanwhile, the housewife urges all her care,
The well-earned feast to hasten and prepare. 30
The sifted meal already waits her hand,
The milk is strained, the bowls in order stand,
The fire flames high; and as a pool—that takes
The headlong stream that o'er the milldam
   breaks—
Foams, roars, and rages with incessant toils,
So the vexed caldron rages, roars, and boils.

First with clean salt she seasons well the
   food,
Then strews the flour, and thickens all the
   flood.
Long o'er the simmering fire she lets it stand;
To stir it well demands a stronger hand;   40
The husband takes his turn: and round and
   round
The ladle flies; at last the toil is crowned;
When to the board the thronging huskers pour,
And take their seats as at the corn before.

I leave them to their feast.   There still
   belong
More useful matters to my faithful song.
For rules there are, though ne'er unfolded yet,
Nice rules and wise, how pudding should be ate.

Some with molasses line the luscious treat, 49
And mix, like bards, the useful with the sweet.
A wholesome dish, and well deserving praise,
A great resource in those bleak wintry days,
When the chilled earth lies buried deep in snow,
And raging Boreas [1] dries the shivering cow.

Blest cow! thy praise shall still my notes
   employ,
Great source of health, the only source of joy;
Mother [2] of Egypt's god,—but sure, for me,
Were I to leave my God, I'd worship thee.
How oft thy teats these pious hands have
   pressed!
How oft thy bounties proved my only feast! 60
How oft I've fed thee with my favorite grain!
And roared, like thee, to see thy children slain!

[1] the north wind
[2] Barlow is perhaps a little confused in his Egyptian
   mythology.   The cow was consecrated to Isis, the
   goddess of beauty and fertility.

Ye swains who know her various worth to prize,
Ah! house her well from winter's angry skies.
Potatoes, pumpkins, should her sadness cheer,
Corn from your crib, and mashes from your beer;
When spring returns, she'll well acquit the loan,
And nurse at once your infants and her own.
Milk then with pudding I should always choose;
To this in future I confine my muse,　　70
Till she in haste some further hints unfold,
Well for the young, nor useless to the old.
First in your bowl the milk abundant take,
Then drop with care along the silver lake
Your flakes of pudding; these at first will hide
Their little bulk beneath the swelling tide;
But when their growing mass no more can sink,
When the soft island looms above the brink,
Then check your hand; you've got the portion due;
So taught our sires, and what they taught is true.　　80

There is a choice in spoons. Though small appear
The nice distinction, yet to me 'tis clear.
The deep-bowled Gallic spoon, contrived to scoop
In ample draughts the thin, diluted soup,
Performs not well in those substantial things,
Whose mass adhesive to the metal clings;
Where the strong labial muscles must embrace
The gentle curve, and sweep the hollow space
With ease to enter and discharge the freight,
A bowl less concave, but still more dilate,　　90
Becomes the pudding best. The shape, the size,
A secret rests, unknown to vulgar eyes.
Experienced feeders can alone impart
A rule so much above the lore of art.
These tuneful lips that thousand spoons have tried,
With just precision could the point decide,
Though not in song; the muse but poorly shines
In cones, and cubes, and geometric lines;
Yet the true form, as near as she can tell,
Is that small section of a goose-egg shell,　　100
Which in two equal portions shall divide
The distance from the center to the side.

Fear not to slaver; 'tis no deadly sin.
Like the free Frenchman, from your joyous chin
Suspend the ready napkin; or, like me,
Poise with one hand your bowl upon your knee;
Just in the zenith your wise head project,

Your full spoon, rising in a line direct,
Bold as a bucket, heeds no drops that fall;
The wide-mouthed bowl will surely catch them all!　　110

1792-93　　　　　　　　　　　　　1796

[ANONYMOUS]

HALE IN THE BUSH [1]

The breezes went steadily through the tall pines,
　A-saying "Oh! hu-ush!" a-saying "Oh! hu-ush!"
As stilly stole by a bold legion of horse,
　For Hale in the bush, for Hale in the bush.

"Keep still!" said the thrush, as she nestled her young
　In a nest by the road, in a nest by the road;
"For the tyrants are near, and with them appear
　What bodes us no good, what bodes us no good."

The brave captain heard it, and thought of his home
　In a cot by the brook, in a cot by the brook;
With mother and sister and memories dear,　11
　He so gaily forsook, he so gaily forsook.

Cooling shades of the night were coming apace,
　The tattoo had beat, the tattoo had beat:
The noble one sprang from his dark lurking-place
　To make his retreat, to make his retreat.

He warily trod on the dry rustling leaves,
　As he passed through the wood, as he passed through the wood,
And silently gained his rude launch on the shore,
　As she played with the flood, as she played with the flood.　20

The guards of the camp on that dark dreary night,
　Had a murderous will, had a murderous will:
They took him and bore him afar from the shore,
　To a hut on the hill, to a hut on the hill.

No mother was there, nor a friend who could cheer,
　In that little stone cell, in that little stone cell;

---

[1] This anonymous ballad is a tribute to Nathan Hale, hanged as a spy Sept. 22, 1776. Hale's last words were, "I regret that I have but one life to lose for my country."

But he trusted in love from his Father above—
  In his heart all was well, in his heart all was
    well.

An ominous owl with his solemn bass voice
  Sat moaning hard by, sat moaning hard by:
"The tyrant's proud minions most gladly re-
    joice,   31
  For he must soon die, for he must soon die."

The brave fellow told them, no thing he re-
    strained,—
  The cruel gen'ral; the cruel gen'ral!—
His errand from camp, of the ends to be gained,
  And said that was all, and said that was all.

They took him and bound him and bore him
    away,
  Down the hill's grassy side, down the hill's
    grassy side.
'T was there the base hirelings, in royal array,
  His cause did deride, his cause did deride.   40

Five minutes were given, short moments, no
    more,
  For him to repent, for him to repent.
He prayed for his mother—he asked not an-
    other,—
  To heaven he went, to heaven he went.

The faith of a martyr the tragedy showed,
  As he trod the last stage, as he trod the last
    stage.
And Britons will shudder at gallant Hale's
    blood,
  As his words do presage, as his words do
    presage:

"Thou pale king of terrors, thou life's gloomy
    foe,   49
Go frighten the slave, go frighten the slave;
Tell tyrants, to you their allegiance they owe—
  No fears for the brave, no fears for the
    brave!"

                    1776

FRANCIS HOPKINSON 1737-1791

Hopkinson, the writer of essays, poems, and much Revolutionary satire, was born in Philadelphia and attended the school that has become the University of Pennsylvania. He had the advantage of residence in England for two years where he saw much of social life. He studied law, rose in his profession, was a member of the Continental Congress from New Jersey, and a signer of the Declaration of Independence; and later was judge of the admiralty court of Pennsylvania.

Hopkinson was a man of much versatility and vivacity, an artist and a musician-composer. He was the author of some didactic poetry, and of lyrics that followed the conventional English fashion of the time. During the Revolution he was active in writing newspaper articles, partisan verse, and all kinds of satire both in prose and verse for the cause of independence. Of these pieces, "The Battle of the Kegs" is most worth preservation. Among the titles of his works are *A Pretty Story*, 1774; *The Prophecy*, 1776; *The Political Catechism*, 1777. His writings were collected in three volumes, 1792.

Biography and criticism: G. E. Hastings, *Life and Works of F. Hopkinson*, 1926. See also A. R. Marble, *Heralds of American Literature*.

THE BATTLE OF THE KEGS [1]

Gallants, attend, and hear a friend
  Trill forth harmonious ditty:
Strange things I'll tell, which late befell
  In Philadelphia city.

'Twas early day, as poets say,
  Just when the sun was rising,
A soldier stood on a log of wood
  And saw a thing surprising.

As in amaze he stood to gaze,
  The truth can't be denied, sir,   10
He spied a score of kegs or more
  Come floating down the tide, sir.

A sailor, too, in jerkin blue,
  This strange appearance viewing,
First damned his eyes, in great surprise,
  Then said, "Some mischief's brewing:

"These kegs, I'm told, the rebels hold,
  Packed up like pickled herring;
And they're come down to attack the town,
  In this new way of ferrying."   20

The soldier flew, the sailor too,
  And scared almost to death, sir,
Wore out their shoes to spread the news,
  And ran till out of breath, sir.

Now up and down throughout the town
  Most frantic scenes were acted;

[1] The incident on which the ballad was founded took place during Sir William Howe's occupation of Philadelphia (1777-1778) while Washington was at Valley Forge.

"The ballad was occasioned by a real incident. Certain machines, in the form of kegs, charged with gunpowder, were sent down the river to annoy the British shipping then at Philadelphia. The danger of these machines being discovered, the British manned the wharfs and shipping, and discharged their small arms and cannons at everything they saw floating in the river during the ebb tide."—Hopkinson's note.

And some ran here and others there,
  Like men almost distracted.

Some fire cried, which some denied,
  But said the earth had quaked;   30
And girls and boys, with hideous noise,
  Ran through the streets half naked.

Sir William, he, snug as a flea,
  Lay all this time a snoring,
Nor dreamed of harm, as he lay warm,

Now in a fright he starts upright,
  Awaked by such a clatter;
He rubs his eyes and boldly cries,
  "For God's sake, what's the matter?"   40

At his bedside he then espied
  Sir Erskine at command, sir:
Upon one foot he had one boot,
  And t'other in his hand, sir.

"Arise, arise!" Sir Erskine cries;
  "The rebels, more 's the pity,
Without a boat are all afloat
  And ranged before the city.

"The motley crew, in vessels new,
  With Satan for their guide, sir,   50
Packed up in bags, or wooden kegs, [1]
  Come driving down the tide, sir,

"Therefore prepare for bloody war:
  These kegs must all be routed,
Or surely we despised shall be,
  And British courage doubted."

The royal band now ready stand,
  All ranged in dread array, sir,
With stomachs stout, to see it out,
  And make a bloody day, sir.   60

The cannons roar from shore to shore,
  The small arms make a rattle;
Since wars began, I'm sure no man
  Ere saw so strange a battle.

The rebel dales, the rebel vales,
  With rebel trees surrounded,
The distant woods, the hills and floods,
  With rebel echoes sounded.

The fish below swam to and fro,
  Attacked from every quarter: 70
"Why sure," thought they, "the devil's to pay
  'Mongst folks above the water"

[1] Note the pronunciation of *keg*.

The kegs, 't is said, though strongly made
  Of rebel staves and hoops, sir,
Could not oppose their powerful foes,
  The conquering British troops, sir.

From morn till night these men of might
  Displayed amazing courage,
And when the sun was fairly down
  Retired to sup their porridge.   80

An hundred men, with each a pen,
  Or more, upon my word, sir,
It is most true would be too few
  Their valor to record, sir.

Such feats did they perform that day
  Against those wicked kegs, sir,
That years to come, if they get home,
  They'll make their boasts and brags, sir.

1778

PATRICK HENRY 1736-1799

Henry, a native Virginian, was unsuccessful in business, but rose quickly into prominence when at twenty-four he entered upon the practice of law. He was a member of the Virginia legislature, and of the Continental Congress, 1774; and a delegate to the Virginia Revolutionary Convention at Richmond, 1775. There he introduced the resolution, opposed by influential delegates, that the colony of Virginia "be immediately put into a posture of defense," and made the speech given below in its support. Few Americans felt at that date that such a step was necessary or advisable. Henry had for months believed it to be inevitable.

This speech was extemporaneous. Those who heard it were struck with the powerful effect that it had upon the assembly. When frequent reading or declamation of such a piece has made us deaf to its appeal, we should exert the imagination and read it as for the first time, calling up the circumstances that brought it forth. Such a fresh, unprejudiced attitude should reveal in this speech the terse brevity, the absence of turgid phrases, the fineness and elevation of spirit that belong to great oratory.

Henry was Governor of Virginia 1776-1779, and 1784-1786. He refused office after 1791 and retired from the practice of law.

M. C. Tyler, *Patrick Henry* (AS), 1890.

SPEECH IN THE VIRGINIA CONVENTION, 1775 [2]

Mr. President:—

No man thinks more highly than I do of the patriotism, as well as abilities, of the very worthy gentlemen who have just addressed the house. [3] But different men often see the same

[2] The convention met March 20-26.
[3] the convention assembled

LOVE TO THE CHURCH [1]

I love thy kingdom, Lord,
  The house of thine abode,
The church our blest Redeemer saved
  With his own precious blood.

I love thy church, O God!
  Her walls before thee stand,
Dear as the apple of thine eye,
  And graven on thy hand.

If e'er to bless thy sons
  My voice or hands deny,   10
These hands let useful skill forsake,
  This voice in silence die.

For her my tears shall fall,
  For her my prayers ascend;
To her my cares and toils be given
  Till toils and cares shall end.

If e'er my heart forget
  Her welfare or her woe,
Let every joy this heart forsake,
  And every grief o'erflow.   20

Beyond my highest joy
  I prize her heavenly ways,
Her sweet communion, solemn vows,
  Her hymns of love and praise.

Jesus, thou friend divine,
  Our Saviour and our King,
Thy hand from every snare and foe
  Shall great deliverance bring.

Sure as thy truth shall last,
  To Zion shall be given   30
The brightest glories earth can yield,
  And brighter bliss of heaven.

                     1800

JOHN TRUMBULL 1750-1831

Trumbull, a wide-awake educator and politician, seeing faults in the education and government of his day, was one of the first and ablest of American satirists. He was born in an intellectual and prominent Connecticut family at Watertown, entered Yale in his fourteenth year, and was appointed tutor in 1771. He studied law with John Adams in Boston, was a member of the Connecticut legislature, and judge of the Connecticut Superior Court 1801-1825. His chief poems are *The Progress of Dulness*, 1772, and *M'Fingal*, 1775-83. Throughout

[1] This hymn, founded on *Psalm* cxxxvii, is perhaps the best of the Puritan hymns.

his life he was a contributor of political articles to the press. His *Poems* were published in 1820.

It is by the political and social satire *M'Fingal* that Trumbull will long have a place in American literature. This poem was undertaken, the author says, "with a political view, at the instigation of some of the leading members of the first Congress, who urged him to compose a satirical poem on the events of the campaign in the year 1775." He aimed to express, "in a poetical manner, a general account of the American contest, . . . and with as much impartiality as possible satirize the follies and extravagances of my countrymen as well as of their enemies." The first three cantos were published in Philadelphia in 1775 during the session of Congress. The indebtedness of Trumbull to Samuel Butler's *Hudibras* (1663), a satire upon the English Puritans, is very evident, both in form and manner, yet Trumbull's wit is quite his own. Thirty editions were printed within a few years. Tyler thinks *M'Fingal* "one of the world's masterpieces in political badinage," and also "a genuine embodiment of the spirit and life of a people."

    M. C. Tyler, *Three Men of Letters*, 1895.

From M'FINGAL [2]

CANTO I

THE TOWN-MEETING, A. M.

When Yankees, skilled in martial rule, [3]
First put the British troops to school;
Instructed them in warlike trade,
And new maneuvers of parade,
The true war-dance of Yankee reels,
And manual exercise of heels;
Made them give up, like saints complete,
The arm of flesh, and trust the feet,
And work, like Christians undissembling,
Salvation out, by fear and trembling;   10
Taught Percy fashionable races, [4]
And modern modes of Chevy Chases:
From Boston, in his best array,
Great 'Squire M'FINGAL took his way,
And graced with ensigns of renown,
Steered homeward to his native town.
His high descent our heralds trace

[2] M'Fingal represents the typical loyalist magistrate, assiduous in his support of law lest his office be taken from him. The mock epic or mock heroic of which this poem is a type, burlesques the heroic epic in structure, phrase, and diction, often producing its best effects by a mingling of the lofty and the commonplace.

[3] This opening passage refers especially to the flight of the British regular troops before the colonial minute men from Concord to Boston, April 19, 1775.

[4] Sir Hugh Percy, in command of the British forces on this retreat, was said to be descended from the chieftain who led the English against the Scotch in the battle of Otterburn or, as it is often called, Chevy Chase, in 1388.

From Ossian's famed Fingalian race : [1]
For though their name some part may lack,
Old Fingal spelled it with a MAC;   20
Which great Macpherson, with submission,
We hope will add the next addition.
   His fathers flourished in the Highlands
Of Scotia's fog-benighted islands;
Whence gained our 'Squire two gifts by right,
Rebellion and the second-sight. [2]
Of these, the first, in ancient days,
Had gained the noblest palm of praise,
'Gainst kings stood forth and many a crowned
      head
With terror of its might confounded;   30
Till rose a king with potent charm [3]
His foes by meekness to disarm,
Whom every Scot and Jacobite
Strait fell in love with at first sight;
Whose gracious speech with aid of pensions,
Hushed down all murmurs of dissensions,
And with the sound of potent metal
Brought all their buzzing swarms to settle;
Who rained his ministerial manna, [4]
Till loud Sedition sung hosanna;   40
The grave lords-bishops and the kirk
United in the public work;
Rebellion, from the northern regions,
With Bute and Mansfield [5] swore allegiance,
All hands combined to raze, as nuisance,
Of church and state the constitutions, [6]
Pull down the empire, on whose ruins
They meant to edify their new ones;
Enslave the American wildernesses,
And rend the provinces in pieces.   50
With these our 'Squire, among the valiant'st,

Employed his time, and tools, and talents,
And found this new rebellion pleasing
As his old king-destroying treason.

      .   .   .   .   .   .

   The Town, our hero's scene of action,
Had long been torn by feuds of faction,   110
And as each party's strength prevails,
It turned up different, heads or tails;
With constant rattling, in a trice,
Showed various sides, as oft as dice.
As that famed weaver, wife to Ulysses, [7]
By night her day's-work picked in pieces,
And though she stoutly did bestir her,
Its finishing was ne'er the nearer:
So did this town with ardent zeal
Weave cobwebs for the public weal,   120
Which when completed, or before,
A second vote in pieces tore.
They met, made speeches full long-winded,
Resolved, protested and rescinded;
Addresses signed; then chose committees
To stop all drinking of Bohea teas; [8]
With winds of doctrine veered about,
And turned all Whig committees out. [9]
Meanwhile our hero, as their head,
In pomp the Tory faction led,   130
Still following, as the 'Squire should please,
Successive on, like files of geese.
   And now the town was summoned, greeting,
To grand parading of town-meeting;
A show, that strangers might appall,
As Rome's grave senate did the Gaul. [10]
High o'er the rout, on pulpit stairs,
Mid den of thieves in house of prayers,
(That house, which loth a rule to break
Served heaven but one day in the week,   140
Open the rest for all supplies
Of news, and politics, and lies)
Stood forth the constable; and bore
His staff, like Mercury's wand of yore, [11]
Waved potent round, the peace to keep,
As that laid dead men's souls to sleep.
Above and near the hermetic staff,
The moderator's [12] upper half
In grandeur o'er the cushion bowed,
Like Sol half seen behind a cloud.   150

[1] James Macpherson, a Scotchman, published in 1762 an epic poem, *Fingal*, which he said was the work of Ossian, son of Fingal, a Celtic chieftain. The poem, though founded on epic fragments, is probably a forgery, the work of Macpherson or his friends. According to Scotch custom, Ossian should properly be called Ossian Mac Fingal (son of Fingal). The last word in l. 22 should probably read *edition* in reference to the great popularity of Macpherson's work.
[2] The Highlanders had supported the Stuarts against the established kings of the House of Hanover. Second-sight, a kind of clairvoyance, was long believed in among them. The fourth canto of *M'Fingal* is the vision of the squire.
[3] George III had begun his reign in the hope of reducing parties and leaders to his own will by means of royal patronage. By the Whigs he was thought too favorably inclined toward the Scotch, who had generally supported the Jacobites, followers of James (Jacobus) Stuart and his heirs, in their endeavor to put back the Stuarts on the English throne.
[4] offices and pensions
[5] John Stuart, Earl of Bute, was prime minister in 1762-3. James Mansfield, solicitor-general, was greatly disliked by the colonists, since his official duties often bore against them; and since they also suspected him of favoring the Catholics.
[6] The English ministers had proposed to "reform the American charters," an interference the colonists greatly dreaded.

[7] Penelope, in the twenty years' absence of her husband, Ulysses, was courted by many suitors. To these she declared that she would not marry until she had finished weaving a certain rich robe. Each night she would unravel what she had woven by day until she had delayed her suitors for three years. *Odyssey*, xix, 140.
[8] until the tax on tea should be abolished
[9] The colonial Whigs stood for more liberal ideas than the colonial Tories.
[10] There is a legend that when in 390 B.C. the victorious Gauls entered Rome, they were for a moment overawed by the sight of the Roman senators seated in their official seats in the Forum.
[11] See any classical encyclopedia.
[12] chairman's

subject in different lights; and, therefore, I hope it will not be thought disrespectful to those gentlemen, if, entertaining as I do opinions of a character very opposite to theirs, I shall speak forth my sentiments freely, and without reserve. This is no time for ceremony. The question before the house is one of awful moment to this country. For my own part, I consider it as nothing less than a question of freedom or slavery. And in proportion to the magnitude of the subject ought to be the freedom of the debate. It is only in this way that we can hope to arrive at truth, and fulfill the great responsibility which we hold to God and our country. Should I keep back my opinions at such a time, through fear of giving offense, I should consider myself as guilty of treason towards my country, and of an act of disloyalty toward the Majesty of Heaven, which I revere above all earthly kings.

Mr. President, it is natural to man to indulge in the illusions of hope. We are apt to shut our eyes against a painful truth, and listen to the song of that siren till she transforms us into beasts. Is this the part of wise men, engaged in a great and arduous struggle for liberty? Are we disposed to be of the number of those who having eyes see not, and having ears hear not, the things which so nearly concern their temporal salvation? For my part, whatever anguish of spirit it may cost, I am willing to know the whole truth; to know the worst and to provide for it.

I have but one lamp by which my feet are guided, and that is the lamp of experience. I know of no way of judging of the future but by the past. And judging by the past, I wish to know what there has been in the conduct of the British ministry for the last ten years, to justify those hopes with which gentlemen have been pleased to solace themselves and the house? Is it that insidious smile with which our petition has been lately received? Trust it not, sir: it will prove a snare to your feet. Suffer not yourselves to be betrayed with a kiss. Ask yourselves how this gracious reception of our petition comports with those warlike preparations which cover our waters and darken our land.¹ Are fleets and armies necessary to a work of love and reconciliation? Have we shown ourselves so unwilling to be reconciled that force must be called in to win back our love? Let us not deceive ourselves, sir. These are the implements of war and subjugation—the

last arguments to which kings resort. I ask gentlemen, sir, What means this martial array, if its purpose be not to force us to submission? Can gentlemen assign any other possible motive for it? Has Great Britain any enemy in this quarter of the world, to call for all this accumulation of navies and armies? No, sir, she has none. They are meant for us: they can be meant for no other. They are sent over to bind and rivet upon us those chains which the British ministry have been so long forging. And what have we to oppose to them? Shall we try argument? Sir, we have been trying that for the last ten years. Have we anything new to offer upon the subject? Nothing. We have held the subject up in every light of which it is capable; but it has been all in vain. Shall we resort to entreaty and humble supplication? What terms shall we find which have not been already exhausted? Let us not, I beseech you, sir, deceive ourselves longer.

Sir, we have done everything that could be done to avert the storm which is now coming on. We have petitioned; we have remonstrated; we have supplicated; we have prostrated ourselves before the throne, and have implored its interposition to arrest the tyrannical hands of the ministry and Parliament. Our petitions have been slighted; our remonstrances have produced additional violence and insult; our supplications have been disregarded; and we have been spurned with contempt from the foot of the throne! In vain, after these things, may we indulge the fond hope of peace and reconciliation. There is no longer any room for hope. If we wish to be free, if we mean to preserve inviolate those inestimable privileges for which we have been so long contending, if we mean not basely to abandon the noble struggle in which we have been so long engaged, and which we have pledged ourselves never to abandon until the glorious object of our contest shall be obtained —we must fight! I repeat it, sir, we must fight! An appeal to arms and to the God of Hosts is all that is left us!

They tell us, sir, that we are weak—unable to cope with so formidable an adversary. But when shall we be stronger? Will it be the next week, or the next year? Will it be when we are totally disarmed, and when a British guard shall be stationed in every house? Shall we gather strength by irresolution and inaction? Shall we acquire the means of effectual resistance by lying supinely on our backs, and hugging the delusive phantom of hope until our enemies shall have bound us hand and foot? Sir, we are not weak, if we make a proper use of those

¹ The Boston garrison was constantly being augmented, and war vessels were gathering in constantly increasing numbers in Boston harbor, the chief British naval rendezvous for North America.

means which the God of nature hath placed in our power. Three millions of people, armed in the holy cause of liberty, and in such a country as that which we possess, are invincible by any force which our enemy can send against us. Besides, sir, we shall not fight our battles alone. There is a just God who presides over the destinies of nations, and who will raise up friends to fight our battles for us. The battle, sir, is not to the strong alone; it is to the vigilant, the active, the brave. Besides, sir, we have no election. [1] If we were base enough to desire it, it is now too late to retire from the contest. There is no retreat but in submission and slavery! Our chains are forged! their clanking may be heard on the plains of Boston! The war is inevitable—and let it come! I repeat it, sir, let it come!

It is in vain, sir, to extenuate the matter. Gentlemen may cry, Peace, Peace—but there is no peace. [2] The war is actually begun! The next gale that sweeps from the north will bring to our ears the clash of resounding arms! Our brethren are already in the field! Why stand we here idle? What is it that gentlemen wish? What would they have? Is life so dear, or peace so sweet, as to be purchased at the price of chains and slavery? Forbid it, Almighty God! I know not what course others may take; but as for me, give me liberty or give me death!

1775

THOMAS PAINE 1737-1809

Born in England, Paine entered business after having received a common-school education, and was afterwards appointed to the British excise service. In 1774 he came to America and enlisted as a volunteer under Washington. His service to the Revolutionary cause was as a pamphleteer rather than as a soldier; but since this was of inestimable value, he was rewarded for it both by Congress and by the states of Pennsylvania and New York. He returned to Europe, was engaged in the French Revolution, and became a citizen of France; but disagreeing with the faction in power he was obliged to return to America. He arrived in this country greatly reduced in circumstances, shattered in health and, because of his deistic views, under suspicion of being an atheist. Aside from some verse, Paine wrote *Common Sense*, 1776; *The Crisis* (a periodical), 1776-1783; *The Rights of Man*, 1791; *The Age of Reason*, 1794.

Paine may be considered as an agitator born, in opposition to things that are, eager for a contest, negative and destructive. There is no proof that he possessed any faculty of constructive statesmanship or any skill in social organization. But he was a man of vision, a maker of phrases and a coiner

of watchwords. Though his arguments were often absurdly unsound, he appealed to the American populace so directly and was so easily understood that he made thousands of converts to the cause of independence.

See G. Bradford, *Damaged Souls*, 1923; same, *Harper* 146:369-78; E. F. Wyatt, "Our First Internationalist," *New Repub.* 48:90-92; *Outlook* 94:334-5, 608.

From COMMON SENSE [3]

THOUGHTS ON THE PRESENT STATE OF THE AMERICAN AFFAIRS

In the following pages I offer nothing more than simple facts, plain arguments, and common sense; and have no other preliminaries to settle with the reader, than that he will divest himself of prejudice and prepossession, and will suffer his reason and his feelings to determine for themselves; that he will put on, or rather that he will not put off the true character of a man, and generously enlarge his views beyond the present day.

Volumes have been written on the subject of the struggle between England and America. Men of all ranks have embarked in the controversy, from different motives, and with various designs: but all have been ineffectual, and the period of debate is closed. Arms, as the last resource, must decide the contest; the appeal was the choice of the king, and the continent hath accepted the challenge.

It has been reported of the late Mr. Pelham [4] (who, though an able minister was not without his faults) that on his being attacked in the house of commons, on the score that his measures were only of a temporary kind, replied, "they will last my time." Should a thought so fatal and unmanly possess the colonies in the present contest, the name of ancestors will be remembered by future generations with detestation.

The sun never shone on a cause of greater worth. 'Tis not the affair of a city, a county, a province, or a kingdom, but of a continent—of at least one eighth part of the habitable globe. 'Tis not the concern of a day, a year, or an age; posterity are virtually involved in the contest, and will be more or less affected even to the end of time, by the proceedings now. Now is the seedtime of continental union, faith and honor. The least fracture now will be like a name engraved with the point of a pin on the tender rind of a young oak; the

---

[1] choice   [2] *Jeremiah* vi, 14

[3] Paine had been in the colonies scarcely two years when he wrote *Common Sense*.
[4] Thomas Pelham, Duke of Newcastle, 1693-1768, member of various English ministries

wound will enlarge with the tree, and posterity read it in full grown characters.

By referring the matter from argument to arms, a new area for politics is struck; a new method of thinking hath arisen. All plans, proposals, etc., prior to the nineteenth of April, i.e., to the commencement of hostilities, are like the almanacs of last year; which, though proper then, are superseded and useless now. Whatever was advanced by the advocates on either side of the question then, terminated in one and the same point, viz., a union with Great Britain; the only difference between the parties was the method of effecting it; the one proposing force, the other friendship; but it hath so far happened that the first has failed, and the second has withdrawn her influence.

As much hath been said of the advantages of reconciliation, which, like an agreeable dream, hath passed away and left us as we were, it is but right that we should examine the contrary side of the argument, and inquire into some of the many material injuries which these colonies sustain, and always will sustain, by being connected with and dependent on Great Britain. To examine that connection and dependence, on the principles of nature and common sense, to see what we have to trust to, if separated, and what we are to expect, if dependent.

I have heard it asserted by some, that as America has flourished under her former connection with Great Britain, the same connection is necessary towards her future happiness, and will always have the same effect. Nothing can be more fallacious than this kind of argument. We may as well assert that because a child has thrived upon milk, that it is never to have meat, or that the first twenty years of our lives is to become a precedent for the next twenty. But even this is admitting more than is true, for I answer roundly that America would have flourished as much, and probably much more, had no European power had anything to do with her. The articles of commerce by which she has enriched herself, are the necessaries of life, and will always have a market while eating is the custom of Europe.

But she has protected us, say some. That she hath engrossed us is true, and defended the continent at our expense as well as her own, is admitted, and she would have defended Turkey from the same motives, viz., for the sake of trade and dominion.

Alas! we have been long led away by ancient prejudices, and made large sacrifices to superstition. We have boasted the protection of Great Britain, without considering that her motive was interest not attachment; and that she did not protect us from our enemies on our account, but from her enemies on her own account, from those who had no quarrel with us on any other account, and who will always be our enemies on the same account. Let Britain waive her pretensions to the continent, or the continent throw off the dependence, and we should be at peace with France and Spain, were they at war with Britain. The miseries of Hanover's last war ought to warn us against connections. [1]

It hath lately been asserted in Parliament, that the colonies have no relation to each other But through the parent country, i.e., that Pennsylvania and the Jerseys, and so on for the rest, are sister colonies by the way of England; this is certainly a very roundabout way of proving relationship, but it is the nearest and only true way of proving enemyship, if I may so call it. France and Spain never were, nor perhaps ever will be, our enemies as Americans, but as our being the subjects of Great Britain.

But Britain is the parent country, say some. Then the more shame upon her conduct. Even brutes do not devour their young, nor savages make war upon their families; wherefore, the assertion, if true, turns to her reproach; but it happens not to be true, or only partly so, and the phrase parent or mother country hath been jesuitically adopted by the King and his parasites, with a low papistical design of gaining an unfair bias on the credulous weakness of our minds. Europe, and not England, is the parent country of America. This new world hath been the asylum for the persecuted lovers of civil and religious liberty from every part of Europe. Hither have they fled, not from the tender embraces of the mother, but from the cruelty of the monster; and it is so far true of England, that the same tyranny which drove the first emigrants from home, pursues their descendants still.

In this extensive quarter of the globe, we forget the narrow limits of three hundred and sixty miles (the extent of England [2]) and carry our friendship on a larger scale; we claim brotherhood with every European Christian, and triumph in the generosity of the sentiment.

It is pleasant to observe by what regular

---

[1] From 1714 to 1837 Hanover was ruled by the sovereigns of England (the House of Hanover). In 1756 George II allied himself with Frederick the Great in the Seven Years' War. The next year, after the defeat of his son, the Duke of Cumberland, he gave Hanover to the French and made no attempt to recover it, though it was restored by the treaty of 1763.

[2] the distance from north to south of England proper

gradations we surmount local prejudices, as we enlarge our acquaintance with the world. A man born in any town in England divided into parishes, will naturally associate most with his fellow parishioners (because their interests in many cases will be common) and distinguish him by the name of neighbor; if he meet him but a few miles from home, he drops the narrow idea of a street, and salutes him by the name of townsman; if he travel out of the county, and meets him in any other, he forgets the minor divisions of street and town, and calls him countryman, i.e., county-man; but if in their foreign excursions they should associate in France or any other part of Europe, their local remembrance would be enlarged into that of Englishmen. And by a just parity of reasoning, all Europeans meeting in America, or any other quarter of the globe, are countrymen; for England, Holland, Germany, or Sweden, when compared with the whole, stand in the same places on the larger scale which the divisions of street, town, and county do on the smaller one; distinctions too limited, for continental minds. Not one third of the inhabitants, even of this province, are of English descent. [1] Wherefore, I reprobate the phrase of parent or mother country applied to England only, as being false, selfish, narrow and ungenerous.

But, admitting that we were all of English descent, what does it amount to? Nothing. Britain, being now an open enemy, extinguishes every other name and title: and to say that reconciliation is our duty, is truly farcical. The first king of England, of the present line (William the Conqueror) was a Frenchman, and half the peers of England are descendents from the same country; wherefore, by the same method of reasoning, England ought to be governed by France.

Much hath been said of the united strength of Britain and the colonies, that in conjunction they might bid defiance to the world. But this is mere presumption; the fate of war is uncertain, neither do the expressions mean any-

thing; for this continent would never suffer itself to be drained of inhabitants, to support the British arms in either Asia, Africa, or Europe. [2]

Besides, what have we to do with setting the world at defiance? Our plan is commerce, and that, well attended to, will secure us the peace and friendship of all Europe; because it is the interest of all Europe to have America a free port. Her trade will always be a protection, and her barrenness of gold and silver secure her from invaders.

I challenge the warmest advocate for reconciliation, to show a single advantage that this continent can reap, by being connected with Great Britain. I repeat the challenge; not a single advantage is derived. Our corn will fetch its price in any market in Europe, and our imported goods must be paid for, buy them where we will.

But the injuries and disadvantages which we sustain by that connection, are without number; and our duty to mankind at large, as well as to ourselves, instructs us to renounce the alliance; because any submission to or dependence on Great Britain tends directly to involve this continent in European wars and quarrels; and sets us at variance with nations, who would otherwise seek our friendship, and against whom we have neither anger nor complaint. As Europe is our market for trade, we ought to form no partial connection with any part of it. It is the true interest of America to steer clear of European contentions, which she never can do, while, by her dependence on Britain, she is made the make-weight in the scale of British politics.

Europe is too thickly planted with kingdoms to be long at peace, and whenever a war breaks out between England and any foreign power, the trade of America goes to ruin, because of her connection with Britain. The next war may not turn out like the last, and should it not, the advocates for reconciliation now will be wishing for separation then, because neutrality, in that case, would be a safer convoy than a man-of-war. Everything that is right or natural pleads for separation. The blood of the slain, the weeping voice of nature cries, " 'Tis time to part." Even the distance at which the Almighty hath placed England and America, is a strong and natural proof that the authority of the one over the other was never the design of Heaven. The time likewise at which the

---

[1] John Fiske says of *Common Sense:* "The pamphlet is full of scurrilous abuse of the English people, and resorts to such stupid arguments as the denial of the English origin of the Americans. Not one third of the people, *even* of Pennsylvania, are of English descent, argues Paine, as if Pennsylvania had been pre-eminent among the colonies for its English blood, and not, as in reality, perhaps the least English of all the thirteen save New York. But along with all this stuff there was a sensible and striking statement of the practical state of the case between England and the colonies. The reasons were shrewdly and vividly set forth for looking upon reconciliation as hopeless, and for seizing the present moment to declare to the world what the logic of events was already fast making an accomplished fact." *The American Revolution*, i, 174.

[2] The World War of 1914-1918 shows Paine's forecast to be untrue, but we must remember that after our Revolution England took pains to endear herself to her remaining colonies.

continent was discovered, adds weight to the argument, and the manner in which it was peopled increases the force of it. The Reformation [1] was preceded by the discovery of America, as if the Almighty graciously meant to open a sanctuary to the persecuted in future years, when home should afford neither friendship nor safety.

The authority of Great Britain over this continent, is a form of government which sooner or later must have an end: and a serious mind can draw no true pleasure by looking forward, under the painful and positive conviction that what he calls "the present constitution," is merely temporary. As parents, we can have no joy, knowing that this government is not sufficiently lasting to insure anything which we may bequeathe to posterity; and by a plain method of argument, as we are running the next generation into debt, we ought to do the work of it; otherwise we use them meanly and pitifully. In order to discover the line of our duty rightly, we should take our children in our hand, and fix our station a few years farther into life; that eminence will present a prospect which a few present fears and prejudices conceal from our sight. . . .

It is repugnant to reason, and the universal order of things, to all examples from former ages, to suppose that this continent can longer remain subject to any external power. The most sanguine in Britain do not think so. The utmost stretch of human wisdom cannot, at this time, compass a plan short of separation, which can promise the continent even a year's security. Reconciliation is now a fallacious dream. Nature hath deserted the connection, and art cannot supply her place. For, as Milton wisely expresses, "never can true reconcilement grow, where wounds of deadly hate have pierced so deep." [2]

Every quiet method for peace hath been ineffectual. Our prayers have been rejected with disdain; and only tended to convince us that nothing flatters vanity, or confirms obstinacy in kings more than repeated petitioning—nothing hath contributed more than this very measure to make the kings of Europe absolute: witness Denmark and Sweden. Wherefore, since nothing but blows will do, for God's sake let us come to a final separation, and not leave the next generation to be cutting throats, under the violated unmeaning names of parent and child.

To say they will never attempt it again, is idle and visionary; we thought so at the repeal of the Stamp Act, yet a year or two undeceived us: as well may we suppose that nations which have been once defeated, will never renew the quarrel.

As to government matters, it is not in the power of Britain to do this continent justice: the business of it will soon be too weighty and intricate to be managed with any tolerable degree of convenience by a power so distant from us, and so very ignorant of us; for if they cannot conquer us, they cannot govern us. To be always running three or four thousand miles with a tale or a petition, waiting four or five months for an answer, which when obtained, requires five or six more to explain it in, will in a few years be looked upon as folly and childishness—there was a time when it was proper, and there is a proper time for it to cease.

Small islands, not capable of protecting themselves, are the proper objects for kingdoms to take under their care; but there is something absurd in supposing a continent to be perpetually governed by an island. In no instance hath nature made the satellite larger than its primary planet; and as England and America, with respect to each other, reverses the common order of nature, it is evident that they belong to different systems: England to Europe —America to itself.

I am not induced by motives of pride, party, or resentment, to espouse the doctrine of separation and independence; I am clearly, positively, and conscientiously persuaded that it is the true interest of this continent to be so; that everything short of that is mere patchwork; that it can afford no lasting felicity,— that it is leaving the sword to our children, and shrinking back at a time when going a little further would have rendered this continent the glory of the earth.

.   .   .   .   .   .

A government of our own is our natural right: and when a man seriously reflects on the precariousness of human affairs, he will become convinced that it is infinitely wiser and safer to form a constitution of our own in a cool, deliberate manner, while we have it in our power, than to trust such an interesting event to time and chance. If we omit it now, some Masaniello [3] may hereafter arise, who,

---

[1] the movement in the sixteenth century against the authority of the Roman Catholic church
[2] *Paradise Lost,* iv, 98

[3] Masaniello (Tomaso Aniello), 1622-1647, a Neapolitan fisherman, led a revolt against the Spanish viceroy of Naples which was successful in bringing relief from oppressive taxation.

laying hold of popular disquietudes, may collect together the desperate and the discontented, and by assuming to themselves the powers of government, finally sweep away the liberties of the continent like a deluge. Should the government of America return again into the hands of Britain, the tottering situation of things will be a temptation for some desperate adventurer to try his fortune; and in such a case, what relief can Britain give? Ere she could hear the news, the fatal business might be done; and ourselves suffering like the wretched Britons under the oppression of the Conqueror. Ye that oppose independence now, ye know not what ye do; ye are opening a door to eternal tyranny, by keeping vacant the seat of government. There are thousands and tens of thousands who would think it glorious to expel from the continent that barbarous and hellish power which hath stirred up the Indians and negroes to destroy us [1]—the cruelty hath a double guilt: it is dealing brutally by us, and treacherously by them.

To talk of friendship with those in whom our reason forbids us to have faith, and our affections, wounded through a thousand pores, instruct us to detest, is madness and folly. Every day wears out the little remains of kindred between us and them; and can there be any reason to hope that as the relationship expires the affection will increase, or that we shall agree better when we have ten times more and greater concerns to quarrel over than ever?

Ye that tell us of harmony and reconciliation, can ye restore to us the time that is past? Can ye give to prostitution its former innocence? Neither can ye reconcile Britain and America. The last cord now is broken, the people of England are presenting addresses against us. There are injuries which nature cannot forgive; she would cease to be nature if she did. As well can the lover forgive the ravisher of his mistress, as the continent forgive the murders of Britain. The Almighty hath implanted in us these unextinguishable feelings, for good and wise purposes. They are the guardians of his image in our hearts, and distinguish us from the herd of common animals. The social compact would dissolve, and justice be extirpated from the earth, or have only a casual existence were we callous to the touches of affection. The robber and the murderer would often escape unpunished, did not the injuries which our tempers sustain provoke us into justice.

O! ye that love mankind! Ye that dare oppose, not only the tyranny, but the tyrant, stand forth! Every spot of the old world is overrun with oppression. Freedom hath been haunted round the globe. Asia, and Africa, have long expelled her. Europe regards her like a stranger, and England hath given her warning to depart. O receive the fugitive, and prepare in time an asylum for mankind.

1775   1776

---

[1] In the Revolution, Great Britain employed Indian tribes to attack and ravage outlying settlements. Some renegade negro slaves may also have been thus employed.

FROM THE REVOLUTION
TO THE CIVIL WAR

IN THE period between the Revolution and the Civil War the new nation grew rapidly, at first into a body of loosely-joined and ever-expanding geographical units, then into two great sections with sharply divergent interests, to be brought together only after the pain of civil war. In literature the line separating the sections was fainter than in political and social life; North and South alike were prevailingly romantic in tone and technique. Poe, the great genius of the South, and in Europe the most widely acclaimed of American poets before Whitman, was at one with the New England poets in avoiding realism; he is apart from them in his insistent pursuit of beauty as an end in itself, and in his shunning moral themes so strongly characteristic of Emerson and Longfellow. Cooper, the Northerner, and Simms, the Southerner, alike stress the picturesque in narrative, the conflict of savage and settler.

There is a division to be noted in the literature of the period; but it is one of time, not of geography. The independence secured by the Revolution at first showed only faintly in our literature. The scenes of Brown and Cooper and Irving and Bryant were American scenes; but Brown was inspired by the English "Gothic" novel then in vogue, especially by the tales of Mrs. Radcliffe; Cooper, giving a vigorous picture of the contact and conflict between Indian and White, yet followed closely the method of his great forerunner in the historical novel, Sir Walter Scott; Irving, in style, took Addison and Goldsmith as his models; and Bryant was especially stimulated by Wordsworth's veneration of nature. What this first great group of American writers did was to give body and dignity to American literature.

In the group that followed, the New England writers of the middle of the century, Longfellow, Emerson, Whittier, Hawthorne, Thoreau, Holmes, and Lowell, the native undercurrent mounted. That it was in some sense a local current—Emerson and Thoreau and Hawthorne are New England to the core— made for the sharper distinctness of the native element: even Longfellow, who frankly followed in the footsteps of Irving as a reporter of European culture to the New World, is distinctly American in point of view: to Holmes, "Boston was the hub of the Universe." Lacking, perhaps, the many-hued vitality that springs only from such a depth of subsoil as the long ages have given to European literature, the new American literature, nevertheless, showed a fine elevation, a carefulness of standards, a clarity that compensated for lack of complexity; its voice was distinct and clear-toned if not deep or richly resonant. In spirit, the New England literature of this period showed an odd combination of Puritanism and Romance.

In the fifties the shadow of the coming of the Civil War and of approaching social changes affected our literature deeply; the outstanding Puritan theme of individual righteousness receded before the questions forced on the nation by the division between North and South; and as the era closed, the growing democracy of America and the world, the emergence to prominence of the "common man," produced the prophet of the new order in Whitman, breaker of molds and acclaimer of the worker and the crowd. Whitman is deeply symbolical of the changes to come in the sixty-odd years after 1865.

GEORGE WASHINGTON
1732-1799

Although Washington has impressed himself upon the world's imagination as a personality and an administrator rather than as a writer, his political maxims are worthy of thoughtful consideration, and are admirable examples of the style of much political literature of his day. Notwithstanding his advantages as son of a well-to-do planter, he received but a meager schooling, mostly in mathematics and surveying. His services in the French and Indian War gave him excellent experience, especially in the discipline and organization of the British army. Afterwards he lived for ten years the life of a Virginia planter, modeled on that of the English country gentleman of the time, engaged in the rotation of crops, the improvement of stock, and the development of plantation industries. He was the wealthiest man in the colonies. In the Revolution he was the principal commander on the American side. After the Revolution, during which his estate had suffered neglect, he resumed the life in which he most delighted. Soon, however, he was called to preside over the Constitutional Convention, and in 1789 became the first President under the Constitution. His administration was marked by violent political controversies, sometimes engendered and always intensified by the French Revolution, then in progress. Washington's policy favored a strong central government free from foreign alliances, for the United States was in his day a weak nation amply secure in its geographical isolation.

The Farewell Address is the most carefully written of all Washington's papers. The President consulted Madison and Hamilton in its preparation, and to the latter is largely due its style, as a comparison of the formality of its manner with the simplicity of that of Washington's other papers will show. Washington's mode of expression, though involved, is dignified, strong, and to the point, especially in such letters as that written to Congress from Valley Forge appealing for relief.

Biography: H. C. Lodge (AS); recent: *Diaries of G. Washington*, 4 vols., 1925; R. Hughes, *G. Washington, the Human Being and the Hero*, 2 vols., 1926, 1927. Criticism: J. C. Fitzpatrick, "The George Washington Scandals," *Scrib. M.* 81: 389-95; W. N. Brigance, "Bible of the Isolationists," *Ind.* 118:213-15; "Washington Dismounted from his High Horse," *Lit. Digest* 87:50-52, Dec. 12, 1925.

TO THE PRESIDENT OF CONGRESS

Valley Forge, 23 December, 1777.

SIR,

Full as I was in my representation of the matters in the commissary's department yesterday, fresh and more powerful reasons oblige me to add that I am now convinced beyond a doubt, that, unless some great and capital change suddenly takes [place] in that line, this army must inevitably be reduced to one or other of these three things: starve, dissolve, or disperse in order to obtain subsistence in the best manner they can. Rest assured, Sir, this is not an exaggerated picture, and that I have abundant reason to suppose what I say.

Yesterday afternoon, receiving information that the enemy in force had left the city, and were advancing toward Derby with the apparent design to forage, and draw subsistence from that part of the country, I ordered the troops to be in readiness, that I might give every opposition in my power; when behold, to my great mortification, I was not only informed but convinced that the men were unable to stir on account of provision, and that a dangerous mutiny, begun the night before, and which with difficulty was suppressed by the spirited exertions of some officers, was still much to be apprehended for want of this article. This brought forth the only commissary in the purchasing line in this camp; and, with him, this melancholy and alarming truth, that he had not a single hoof of any kind to slaughter, and not more than twenty-five barrels of flour! From hence form an opinion of our situation when I add that he could not tell when to expect any.

All I could do under these circumstances, was to send out a few light parties to watch and harass the enemy, whilst other parties were instantly detached different ways to collect, if possible, as much provision as would satisfy the present pressing wants of the soldiery. But will this answer? No, Sir; three or four days of bad weather would prove our destruction. What then is to become of the army this winter? And if we are so often without provisions now, what is to become of us in the spring, when our force will be collected, with the aid perhaps of militia to take advantage of an early campaign, before the enemy can be reinforced? These are considerations of great magnitude, meriting the closest attention; and they will, when my own reputation is so intimately connected with the event and to be affected by it, justify my saying that the present commissaries are by no means equal to the execution of the office, or that the disaffection of the people is past all belief. The misfortune, however, does in my opinion proceed from both causes; and, though I have been tender heretofore of giving any opinion, or lodging complaints, as the change in that department took place contrary to my judgment, and the consequences thereof were predicted; yet, finding that the inactivity of the army, whether for want of provisions, clothes, or other essentials, is charged to my account, not only by the common vulgar but by those in power, it is time to speak plain in exculpation of myself. With truth, then, I can declare that no man in my opinion ever had his measures more impeded than I have, by every department of the army.

Since the month of July we have had no assistance from the quartermaster-general, and to want of assistance from this department the commissary-general charges great part of his deficiency. To this I am to add that, notwithstanding it is a standing order, and often repeated, that the troops shall always have two days' provisions by them, that they might be ready at any sudden call; yet an opportunity has scarcely ever offered, of taking an advantage of the enemy, that has not been either totally obstructed, or greatly impeded, on this account. And this, the great and crying evil, is not all. The soap, vinegar, and other articles allowed by Congress, we see none of, nor have we seen them, I believe, since the battle of Brandywine.[1] The first, indeed, we have now little occasion for; few men having more than one shirt, many only the moiety of one, and some none at all. In addition to which, as a proof of the little benefit received from a clothier-general, and as a further proof of the inability of an army, under the circumstances of this, to perform the common duties of soldiers (besides a number of men confined to hospitals for want of shoes, and others in farmers' houses on the same account) we have, by a field-return this day made, no less than two thousand eight hundred and ninety-eight men now in camp unfit for duty, because they are barefoot and otherwise naked. By the same return it appears that our whole strength in Continental troops, including the eastern brigades, which have joined us since the surrender of General Burgoyne, exclusive of the Maryland troops sent to Wilmington, amounts to no more than eight thousand two hundred in camp fit for duty; notwithstanding which, and that since the 4th instant our numbers fit for duty, from the hardships and exposures they have undergone, particularly on account of blankets (numbers having been obliged, and still are, to sit up all night by fires, instead of taking comfortable rest in a natural and common way), have decreased near two thousand men.

We find gentlemen, without knowing whether the army was really going into winter-quarters or not (for I am sure no resolution of mine would warrant the Remonstrance[2]), reprobating the measure as much as if they thought the soldiers were made of stocks or stones, and equally insensible of frost and snow; and moreover, as if they conceived it easily practicable for an inferior army, under the disadvantages I have described ours to be, which are by no means exaggerated, to confine a superior one, in all respects well-appointed and provided for a winter's campaign, within the city of Philadelphia, and to cover from depredation and waste the States of Pennsylvania and Jersey.

[1] Sept. 11, 1777
[2] alluding to the Memorial, or Remonstrance, of the legislature of Pennsylvania, respecting his going into winter-quarters

But what makes this matter still more extraordinary in my eye is that these very gentlemen—who were well apprized of the nakedness of the troops from ocular demonstration, who thought their own soldiers worse clad than others, and who advised me near a month ago to postpone the execution of a plan I was about to adopt, in consequence of a resolve of Congress for seizing clothes, under strong assurances that an ample supply would be collected in ten days agreeably to a decree of the State (not one article of which, by the by, is yet come to hand)—should think a winter's campaign, and the covering of these States from the invasion of an enemy, so easy and practicable a business. I can assure those gentlemen that it is a much easier and less distressing thing to draw remonstrances in a comfortable room by a good fireside, than to occupy a cold bleak hill, and sleep under frost and snow, without clothes or blankets. However, although they seem to have little feeling for the naked and distressed soldiers, I feel superabundantly for them, and, from my soul, I pity those miseries, which it is neither in my power to relieve or prevent.

It is for these reasons, therefore, that I have dwelt upon the subject; and it adds not a little to my other difficulties and distress to find that much more is expected of me than is possible to be performed, and that upon the ground of safety and policy I am obliged to conceal the true state of the army from public view, and thereby expose myself to detraction and calumny. The honorable committee of Congress went from camp fully possessed of my sentiments respecting the establishment of this army, the necessity of auditors of accounts, the appointment of officers, and new arrangements. I have no need, therefore, to be prolix upon these subjects, but I refer to the committee. I shall add a word or two to show, first, the necessity of some better provision for binding the officers by the tie of interest to the service, as no day nor scarce an hour passes without the offer of a resigned commission [1] (otherwise I much doubt the practicability of holding the army together much longer, and in this I shall probably be thought the more sincere when I freely declare that I do not myself expect to derive the smallest benefit from any establishment that Congress may adopt, otherwise than as a member of the community at large in the good which I am persuaded will result from

[1] The House of Commons of North Carolina passed a resolution that any officer resigning at such a critical period without "good and sufficient reasons" should never again hold office in the state.

the measure, by making better officers and better troops); and, secondly, to point out the necessity of making the appointments and arrangements without loss of time. We have not more than three months in which to prepare a great deal of business. If we let these slip or waste, we shall be laboring under the same difficulties all next campaign as we have been this, to rectify mistakes and bring things to order.

Military arrangement, and movements in consequence, like the mechanism of a clock, will be imperfect and disordered by the want of a part. In a very sensible degree have I experienced this in the course of the last summer, several brigades having no brigadiers appointed to them till late, and some not at all; by which means it follows that an additional weight is thrown upon the shoulders of the Commander-in-chief, to withdraw his attention from the great line of his duty. The gentlemen of the committee, when they were at camp, talked of an expedient for adjusting these matters, which I highly approved and wish to see adopted; namely, that two or three members of the Board of War, or a committee of Congress, should repair immediately to camp, where the best aid can be had, and with the commanding officer, or a committee of his appointment, prepare and digest the most perfect plan that can be devised for correcting all abuses and making new arrangements; considering what is to be done with the weak and debilitated regiments, if the States to which they belong will not draft men to fill them, for as to enlisting soldiers it seems to me to be totally out of the question; together with many other things that would occur in the course of such a conference; and, after digesting matters in the best manner they can, to submit the whole to the ultimate determination of Congress.

If this measure is approved, I would earnestly advise the immediate execution of it, and that the commissary-general of purchases, whom I rarely see, may be directed to form magazines without a moment's delay in the neighborhood of this camp, in order to secure provisions for us in case of bad weather. The quartermaster-general ought also to be busy in his department. In short, there is as much to be done in preparing for a campaign, as in the active part of it. Everything depends upon the preparation that is made in the several departments, and the success or misfortunes of the next campaign will more than probably originate with our activity or supineness during this winter. I have the honor to be, &c.

FAREWELL ADDRESS

To the People of the United States [1]

Friends and Fellow-Citizens,

The period for a new election of a citizen to administer the executive government of the United States being not far distant, and the time actually arrived when your thoughts must be employed in designating the person who is to be clothed with that important trust, it appears to me proper, especially as it may conduce to a more distinct expression of the public voice, that I should now apprise you of the resolution I have formed, to decline being considered among the number of those out of whom a choice is to be made.

I beg you, at the same time, to do me the justice to be assured that this resolution has not been taken without a strict regard to all the considerations appertaining to the relation which binds a dutiful citizen to his country;— and that, in withdrawing the tender of service, which silence in my situation might imply, I am influenced by no diminution of zeal for your future interest, no deficiency of grateful respect for your past kindness; but act under am supported by [2] a full conviction that the step is compatible with both.

The acceptance of, and continuance hitherto in, the office to which your suffrages have twice called me, have been a uniform sacrifice of inclination to the opinion of duty, and to a deference for what appeared to be your desire. I constantly hoped that it would have been much earlier in my power, consistently with motives which I was not at liberty to disregard, to return to that retirement from which I had been reluctantly drawn. [3] The strength of my inclination to do this previous to the last election, had even led to the preparation of an address to declare it to you; but mature reflection on the then perplexed and critical posture of our affairs with foreign nations, and the unanimous advice of persons entitled to my confidence, impelled me to abandon the idea.

I rejoice that the state of your concerns, external as well as internal, no longer renders the pursuit of inclination incompatible with the sentiment of duty or propriety; and am persuaded, whatever partiality may be retained for my services, that in the present circumstances of our country you will not disapprove my determination to retire.

The impressions with which I first undertook the arduous trust were explained on the proper occasion. [4] In the discharge of this trust I will only say that I have, with good intentions, contributed towards the organization and administration of the government the best exertions of which a very fallible judgment was capable. Not unconscious, in the outset, of the inferiority of my qualifications, experience in my own eyes, perhaps still more in the eyes of others, has strengthened the motives to diffidence of myself; and every day the increasing weight of years admonishes me more and more that the shade of retirement is as necessary to me as it will be welcome. Satisfied that if any circumstances have given peculiar value to my services they were temporary, I have the consolation to believe that while choice and prudence invite me to quit the political scene, patriotism does not forbid it.

In looking forward to the moment which is intended to terminate the career of my public life, my feelings do not permit me to suspend the deep acknowledgment of that debt of gratitude which I owe to my beloved country for the many honors it has conferred upon me; still more for the steadfast confidence with which it has supported me; and for the opportunities I have thence enjoyed of manifesting my inviolable attachment by services faithful and persevering, though in usefulness unequal to my zeal. If benefits have resulted to our country from these services, let it always be remembered to your praise and as an instructive example in our annals, that under circumstances in which the passions agitated in every direction were liable to mislead, amidst appearances sometimes dubious, vicissitudes of fortune often discouraging, in situations in which not unfrequently want of success has countenanced the spirit of criticism, the constancy of your support was the essential prop of the efforts, and a guarantee of the plans by which they were effected. Profoundly penetrated with this idea, I shall carry it with me to the grave as a strong incitement to unceasing vows that Heaven may continue to you the choicest tokens of its beneficence; that your union and brotherly affection may be perpetual; that the free Constitution which is the work of your hands may be sacredly maintained; that its administration in every department may be stamped with wisdom and virtue; that, in fine, the happiness of the

---

[1] This address, delivered September 17, 1796, has, in common regard, a place beside the Monroe Doctrine and the Declaration of Independence, second only to the Constitution.

[2] This should probably read "but am supported by" or "but act under and supported by." The text is from the copy in Washington's letter book.

[3] Washington was deeply sincere in his reluctance to hold office.

[4] upon his first inauguration

people of these States under the auspices of liberty may be made complete, by so careful a preservation and so prudent a use of this blessing as will acquire to them the glory of recommending it to the applause, the affection, and adoption, of every nation which is yet a stranger to it.

Here, perhaps, I ought to stop. But a solicitude for your welfare, which cannot end but with my life, and the apprehension of danger, natural to that solicitude, urge me on an occasion like the present, to offer to your solemn contemplation, and to recommend to your frequent review, some sentiments which are the result of much reflection, of no inconsiderable observation, and which appear to me all-important to the permanency of your felicity as a people. These will be offered to you with the more freedom, as you can only see in them the disinterested warnings of a parting friend, who can possibly have no personal motive to bias his counsels. Nor can I forget, as an encouragement to it, your indulgent reception of my sentiments on a former and not dissimilar occasion. [1]

Interwoven as is the love of liberty with every ligament of your hearts, no recommendation of mine is necessary to fortify or confirm the attachment.

The unity of government which constitutes you one people, is also now dear to you. It is justly so, for it is a main pillar in the edifice of your real independence; the support of your tranquillity at home, your peace abroad, of your safety, of your prosperity in every shape, of that very liberty which you so highly prize. But as it is easy to foresee that from different causes, and from different quarters, much pains will be taken, many artifices employed, to weaken in your minds the conviction of this truth; as this is the point in your political fortress against which the batteries of internal and external enemies will be most constantly and actively (though often covertly and insidiously) directed, it is of infinite moment that you should properly estimate the immense value of your national union to your collective and individual happiness; that you should cherish a cordial, habitual, and immovable attachment to it; accustoming yourselves to think and speak of it as of the Palladium [2] of your political safety and prosperity; watching for its preservation with jealous anxiety; discountenancing whatever may suggest even a suspicion that it

can in any event be abandoned, and indignantly frowning upon the first dawning of every attempt to alienate any portion of our country from the rest, or to enfeeble the sacred ties which now link together the various parts. [3]

For this you have every inducement of sympathy and interest. Citizens by birth or choice of a common country, that country has a right to concentrate your affections. The name of AMERICAN, which belongs to you in your national capacity, must always exalt the just pride of patriotism more than any appellation derived from local discriminations. With slight shades of difference you have the same religion, manners, habits, and political principles. You have in a common cause fought and triumphed together. The independence and liberty you possess are the work of joint councils and joint efforts, of common dangers, sufferings and successes.

But these considerations, however powerfully they address themselves to your sensibility, are greatly outweighed by those which apply more immediately to your interest. Here every portion of our country finds the most commanding motives for carefully guarding and preserving the union of the whole.

The North in an unrestrained intercourse [4] with the South, protected by the equal laws of a common government, finds in the productions of the latter great additional resources of maritime and commercial enterprise and precious materials of manufacturing industry. The South, in the same intercourse, benefiting by the agency of the North, sees its agriculture grow and its commerce expand. Turning partly into its own channels the seamen of the North, it finds its particular navigation envigorated; and while it contributes in different ways to nourish and increase the general mass of the national navigation, it looks forward to the protection of a maritime strength to which itself is

---

[1] when he took farewell of the army

[2] Safeguard: the image of Pallas, the Palladium, fell from heaven, and so long as it was preserved in the citadel, protected Troy from destruction.

[3] During the last days of the Confederation it seemed probable that New England would form a separate union. It is difficult today to comprehend the state of public opinion toward government in Washington's time. The masses were intensely democratic; the aristocracy felt that government should be chiefly in their own hands; and there was little desire in either class to sacrifice rights or privileges to the common good. There was no experience in more than local self-government; and few but Washington and his immediate associates grasped the idea of national unity or clearly saw what the relations of our nation to others should be. The marvel is that these few men held their own till a new generation with larger ideas than those of their fathers made the compact secure.

[4] After the Revolution and before the adoption of the Constitution, some of the states had enacted tariffs against others. Local commercial interests were leading to disruption.

unequally adapted. The East, in a like intercourse with the West, already finds, and in the progressive improvement of interior communications by land and water will more and more find, a valuable vent for the commodities which it brings from abroad or manufactures at home. The West derives from the East supplies requisite to its growth and comfort, and what is perhaps of still greater consequence, it must of necessity owe the secure enjoyment of indispensable outlets for its own productions to the weight, influence, and the future maritime strength of the Atlantic side of the Union, directed by an indissoluble community of interest, as one nation. Any other tenure by which the West can hold this essential advantage, whether derived from its own separate strength, or from an apostate and unnatural connection with any foreign power,[1] must be intrinsically precarious.

While, then, every part of our country thus feels an immediate and particular interest in union, all the parts combined in the united mass of means and efforts cannot fail to find greater strength, greater resource, proportionably greater security from external danger, a less frequent interruption of their peace by foreign nations; and what is of inestimable value, they must derive from union an exemption from those broils and wars between themselves, which so frequently afflict neighboring countries not tied together by the same government, which their own rivalships alone would be sufficient to produce, but which opposite foreign alliances, attachments, and intrigues would stimulate and embitter. Hence, likewise, they will avoid the necessity of those overgrown military establishments which under any form of government are inauspicious to liberty, and which are to be regarded as particularly hostile to republican liberty. In this sense it is that your union ought to be considered as a main prop of your liberty, and that the love of the one ought to endear to you the preservation of the other.

These considerations speak a persuasive language to every reflecting and virtuous mind, and exhibit the continuance of the UNION as a primary object of patriotic desire. Is there a doubt whether a common government can embrace so large a sphere?[2] Let experience solve it. To listen to mere speculation in such a case were criminal. We are authorized to hope that a proper organization of the whole, with the auxiliary agency of governments for the respective subdivisions, will afford a happy issue to the experiment. It is well worth a fair and full experiment. With such powerful and obvious motives to union affecting all parts of our country, while experience shall not have demonstrated its impracticability, there will always be reason to distrust the patriotism of those who in any quarter may endeavor to weaken its bands.

In contemplating the causes which may disturb our Union, it occurs as matter of serious concern that any ground should have been furnished for characterizing parties by geographical discriminations, Northern and Southern, Atlantic and Western; whence designing men may endeavor to excite a belief that there is a real difference of local interests and views. One of the expedients of party to acquire influence within particular districts, is to misrepresent the opinions and aims of other districts. You cannot shield yourselves too much against the jealousies and heart burnings which spring from these misrepresentations; they tend to render alien to each other those who ought to be bound together by fraternal affection. The inhabitants of our western country have lately had a useful lesson on this head; they have seen, in the negotiation by the executive and in the unanimous ratification by the Senate, of the treaty with Spain,[3] and in the universal satisfaction at that event throughout the United States a decisive proof how unfounded were the suspicions propagated among them of a policy in the General Government and in the Atlantic States unfriendly to their interests in regard to the Mississippi; they have been witnesses to the formation of two treaties, that with Great Britain[4] and that with Spain, which secure to them everything they could desire in respect to our foreign relations, towards confirming their prosperity. Will it not be their wisdom to rely for the preservation of these advantages on the Union by which they were procured? Will they not henceforth be deaf to those advisers, if such there are, who would sever them from their brethren, and connect them with aliens?

[1] The United States government had failed for years to secure from Spain the right to navigate the Mississippi, a privilege indispensable to Tennessee and Kentucky. These communities, feeling deeply the neglect of their interests in the East, secretly intrigued with Spain and were with difficulty kept within the union.

[2] Much as Washington strove for power in the central government, he could scarcely have foreseen the scope of the central government of today, with an oversight not merely regulative, but also scientific and industrial.

[3] signed at Madrid, October, 1795, and allowing the free navigation of the Mississippi

[4] Jay's famous treaty with England brought about, in June, 1796, the surrender of the remaining posts of the British in the Northwest.

To the efficacy and permanency of your Union, a government for the whole is indispensable. No alliances, however strict, between the parts can be an adequate substitute. They must inevitably experience the infractions and interruptions which all alliances in all times have experienced. Sensible of this momentous truth, you have improved upon your first essay,[1] by the adoption of a constitution of government better calculated than your former for an intimate union, and for the efficacious management of your common concerns. This Government, the offspring of our own choice, uninfluenced and unawed, adopted upon full investigation and mature deliberation, completely free in its principles, in the distribution of its powers, uniting security with energy, and containing within itself a provision for its own amendment, has a just claim to your confidence and your support. Respect for its authority, compliance with its laws, acquiescence in its measures, are duties enjoined by the fundamental maxims of true liberty. The basis of our political systems is the right of the people to make and to alter their constitutions of government. But the constitution which at any time exists, till changed by an explicit and authentic act of the whole people, is sacredly obligatory upon all. The very idea of the power and the right of the people to establish government, presupposes the duty of every individual to obey the established government.

All obstructions to the execution of the laws, all combinations and associations,[2] under whatever plausible character, with the real design to direct, control, counteract, or awe the regular deliberation and action of the constituted authorities, are destructive of this fundamental principle, and of fatal tendency. They serve to organize faction, to give it an artificial and extraordinary force; to put in the place of the delegated will of the nation, the will of a party;[3] often a small but artful and enterprising minority of the community, and, according to the alternate triumphs of different parties, to make the public administration the mirror of the ill-concerted and incongruous projects of faction, rather than the organ of consistent and wholesome plans digested by common councils, and modified by mutual interests. However combinations or associations of the above description may now and then answer popular ends, they are likely in the course of time and things, to become potent engines by which cunning, ambitious, and unprincipled men will be enabled to subvert the power of the people and to usurp for themselves the reins of government; destroying afterwards the very engines which have lifted them to unjust dominion.

Towards the preservation of your Government and the permanency of your present happy state it is requisite, not only that you steadily discountenance irregular oppositions to its acknowledged authority, but also that you resist with care the spirit of innovation upon its principles, however specious the pretexts. One method of assault may be to effect in the forms of the Constitution alterations which will impair the energy of the system, and thus to undermine what cannot be directly overthrown. In all the changes to which you may be invited, remember that time and habit are at least as necessary to fix the true character of governments, as of other human institutions; that experience is the surest standard by which to test the real tendency of the existing constitution of a country; that facility in changes, upon the credit of mere hypothesis and opinion exposes to perpetual change, from the endless variety of hypothesis and opinion; and remember especially, that for the efficient management of your common interests, in a country so extensive as ours, a government of as much vigor as is consistent with the perfect security of liberty is indispensable. Liberty itself will find in such a government, with powers properly distributed and adjusted, its surest guardian. It is, indeed, little else than a name, where the government is too feeble to withstand the enterprises of faction, to confine each member of the society within the limits prescribed by the laws, and to maintain all in the secure and tranquil enjoyment of the rights of person and property.

I have already intimated to you the danger of parties in the state, with particular reference to the founding of them on geographical discriminations. Let me now take a more comprehensive view, and warn you in the most solemn manner against the baneful effects of the spirit of party generally.

This spirit, unfortunately, is inseparable from our nature, having its root in the strongest passions of the human mind. It exists under different shapes in all governments, more or less stifled, controlled, or repressed; but in those

[1] the Articles of Confederation

[2] Clubs of citizens framed on the model of the Jacobin Club of Paris had been formed throughout the country to propagate the ideas of the French Revolution and to express sympathy with France in her struggle with the nations of Europe allied against her.

[3] Notwithstanding Washington's strong feeling, party had already gained permanent foothold in the country.

of the popular form it is seen in its greatest rankness, and is truly their worst enemy.

The alternate domination of one faction over another, sharpened by the spirit of revenge natural to party dissension, which in different ages and countries has perpetrated the most horrid enormities, is itself a frightful despotism. But this leads at length to a more formal and permanent despotism. The disorders and miseries which result, gradually incline the minds of men to seek security and repose in the absolute power of an individual; and sooner or later the chief of some prevailing faction, more able or more fortunate than his competitors, turns this disposition to the purposes of his own elevation on the ruins of public liberty.

Without looking forward to an extremity of this kind (which nevertheless ought not to be entirely out of sight), the common and continual mischiefs of the spirit of party are sufficient to make it the interest and duty of a wise people to discourage and restrain it.

It serves always to distract the public councils and enfeeble the public administration. It agitates the community with ill-founded jealousies and false alarms, kindles the animosity of one part against another, foments occasionally riot and insurrection. It opens the doors to foreign influence and corruption which find a facilitated access to the government itself through the channels of party passions. Thus the policy and the will of one country are subjected to the policy and will of another.[1]

There is an opinion that parties in free countries are useful checks upon the administration of the government, and serve to keep alive the spirit of liberty. This within certain limits is probably true; and in governments of a monarchical cast, patriotism may look with indulgence if not with favor upon the spirit of party. But in those of the popular character, in governments purely elective, it is a spirit not to be encouraged. From their natural tendency it is certain there will always be enough of that spirit for every salutary purpose. And there being constant danger of excess, the effort ought to be by force of public opinion to mitigate and assuage it. A fire not to be quenched, it demands a uniform vigilance to prevent its bursting into a flame, lest, instead of warming, it should consume.

It is important, likewise, that the habits of thinking in a free country should inspire caution in those entrusted with its administration, to confine themselves within their respective constitutional spheres, avoiding in the exercise of the powers of one department to encroach upon another. The spirit of encroachment tends to consolidate the powers of all the departments in one, and thus to create, whatever the form of government, a real despotism. A just estimate of that love of power and proneness to abuse it which predominates in the human heart, is sufficient to satisfy us of the truth of this position. The necessity of reciprocal checks in the exercise of political power, by dividing and distributing it into different depositories, and constituting each the guardian of the public weal against invasions by the others, has been evinced by experiments ancient and modern; some of them in our country and under our own eyes.[2] To preserve them must be as necessary as to institute them. If in the opinion of the people the distribution or modification of the constitutional powers be in any particular wrong, let it be corrected by an amendment in the way which the Constitution designates. But let there be no change by usurpation; for though this, in one instance may be the instrument of good, it is the customary weapon by which free governments are destroyed. The precedent must always greatly overbalance in permanent evil any partial or transient benefit which the use can at any time yield.

Of all the dispositions and habits which lead to political prosperity, religion and morality are indispensable supports. In vain would that man claim the tribute of patriotism who should labor to subvert these great pillars of human happiness, these firmest props of the duties of men and citizens. The mere politician, equally with the pious man, ought to respect and to cherish them. A volume could not trace all their connections with private and public felicity. Let it simply be asked, where is the security for property, for reputation, for life, if the sense of religious obligation desert the oaths which are the instruments of investigation in courts of justice? And let us with caution indulge the supposition that morality can be maintained without religion. Whatever may be conceded to the influence of refined education on minds of peculiar structure, reason and experience both forbid us to expect that national morality can prevail in exclusion of religious principle.

It is substantially true that virtue or morality is a necessary spring of popular government.

---

[1] War had almost been thrust upon the country through the imprudence of Genet, minister from France, who through the press appealed directly to the party in America favoring alliance with his country.

[2] The proper division of the government into legislative, executive, and judicial departments, so that one should not encroach upon another, had been a most difficult task.

The rule indeed extends with more or less force to every species of free government. Who that is a sincere friend to it can look with indifference upon attempts to shake the foundation of the fabric?

Promote then, as an object of primary importance, institutions for the general diffusion of knowledge. In proportion as the structure of a government gives force to public opinion, it is essential that public opinion should be enlightened.

As a very important source of strength and security, cherish public credit. One method of preserving it is to use it as sparingly as possible; avoiding occasions of expense by cultivating peace, but remembering also that timely disbursements to prepare for danger frequently prevent much greater disbursements to repel it; avoiding likewise the accumulation of debt, not only by shunning occasions of expense, but by vigorous exertions in time of peace to discharge the debts which unavoidable wars may have occasioned, not ungenerously throwing upon posterity the burden which we ourselves ought to bear. The execution of these maxims belongs to your representatives, but it is necessary that public opinion should coöperate. To facilitate to them the performance of their duty, it is essential that you should practically bear in mind that towards the payment of debts there must be revenue; that to have revenue there must be taxes; that no taxes can be devised which are not more or less inconvenient and unpleasant; that the intrinsic embarrassment inseparable from the selection of the proper objects (which is always a choice of difficulties) ought to be a decisive motive for a candid construction of the conduct of the government in making it, and for a spirit of acquiescence in the measures for obtaining revenue which the public exigencies may at any time dictate. [1]

Observe good faith and justice towards all nations; cultivate peace and harmony with all. Religion and morality enjoin this conduct; and can it be that good policy does not equally enjoin it? It will be worthy of a free, enlightened, and, at no distant period, a great nation, to give to mankind the magnanimous and too novel example of a people always guided by an exalted justice and benevolence. Who can doubt that in the course of time and things the fruits of such a plan would richly repay any temporary advantages which might be lost by a steady adherence to it? Can it be that Provi-

dence has not connected the permanent felicity of a nation with its virtue? The experiment, at least, is recommended by every sentiment which ennobles human nature. Alas! is it rendered impossible by its vices?

In the execution of such a plan nothing is more essential than that permanent, inveterate antipathies against particular nations, and passionate attachments for others, should be excluded; and that in place of them, just and amicable feelings towards all should be cultivated. The nation which indulges towards another an habitual hatred or an habitual fondness is in some degree a slave. It is a slave to its animosity or to its affection, either of which is sufficient to lead it astray from its duty and its interest. Antipathy in one nation against another disposes each more readily to offer insult and injury, to lay hold of slight causes of umbrage, and to be haughty and intractable when accidental or trifling occasions of dispute occur. Hence frequent collisions, obstinate, envenomed and bloody contests. The nation prompted by ill-will and resentment sometimes impels to war the government, contrary to the best calculations of policy. The government sometimes participates in the national propensity and adopts through passion what reason would reject; at other times it makes the animosity of the nation subservient to projects of hostility instigated by pride, ambition, and other sinister and pernicious motives. The peace often, sometimes perhaps the liberty, of nations has been the victim.

So likewise a passionate attachment of one nation for another produces a variety of evils. Sympathy for the favorite nation, facilitating the illusion of an imaginary common interest, in cases where no real common interest exists, and infusing into one the enmities of the other, betrays the former into a participation in the quarrels and wars of the latter, without adequate inducement or justification. It leads also to concessions to the favorite nation of privileges denied to others, which is apt doubly to injure the nation making the concessions; by unnecessarily parting with what ought to have been retained, and by exciting jealousy, ill-will, and a disposition to retaliate, in the parties from whom equal privileges are withheld. And it gives to ambitious, corrupted, or deluded citizens (who devote themselves to the favorite nation), facility to betray, or sacrifice the interests of their own country, without odium, sometimes even with popularity; gilding with the appearances of a virtuous sense of obligation, a commendable deference for public

---

[1] The "Whisky Rebellion" of 1794 was an insurrection caused by a tax levied by Congress.

opinion, or a laudable zeal for public good, the base or foolish compliances of ambition, corruption or infatuation.

As avenues to foreign influence in innumerable ways, such attachments are particularly alarming to the truly enlightened and independent patriot. How many opportunities do they afford to tamper with domestic factions, to practice the arts of seduction, to mislead public opinion, to influence or awe the public councils! Such an attachment of a small or weak, towards a great and powerful nation, dooms the former to be the satellite of the latter.

Against the insidious wiles of foreign influence, I conjure you to believe me, fellow-citizens, the jealousy of a free people ought to be constantly awake, since history and experience prove that foreign influence is one of the most baneful foes of republican government. But that jealousy, to be useful, must be impartial; else it becomes the instrument of the very influence to be avoided, instead of a defense against it. Excessive partiality for one foreign nation and excessive dislike of another, cause those whom they actuate to see danger only on one side, and serve to veil and even second the arts of influence on the other. Real patriots, who may resist the intrigues of the favorite, are liable to become suspected and odious; while its tools and dupes usurp the applause and confidence of the people, to surrender their interests.

The great rule of conduct for us in regard to foreign nations is, in extending our commercial relations, to have with them as little political connection as possible. So far as we have already formed engagements, let them be fulfilled with perfect good faith. Here let us stop.

Europe has a set of primary interests, which to us have none, or a very remote relation. Hence she must be engaged in frequent controversies, the causes of which are essentially foreign to our concerns. Hence therefore it must be unwise in us to implicate ourselves by artificial ties in the ordinary vicissitudes of her politics, or the ordinary combinations and collisions of her friendships, or enmities.

Our detached and distant situation invites and enables us to pursue a different course. If we remain one people, under an efficient government, the period is not far off when we may defy material injury from external annoyance; when we may take such an attitude as will cause the neutrality we may at any time resolve upon, to be scrupulously respected; when belligerent nations, under the impossibility of

making acquisitions upon us, will not lightly hazard the giving us provocation; when we may choose peace or war, as our interest guided by our justice shall counsel.

Why forego the advantages of so peculiar a situation? Why quit our own to stand upon foreign ground? Why, by interweaving our destiny with that of any part of Europe, entangle our peace and prosperity in the toils of European ambition, rivalship, interest, humor, or caprice?

It is our true policy to steer clear of permanent alliances with any portion of the foreign world; so far as I mean as we are now at liberty to do it; for let me not be understood as capable of patronizing infidelity to existing engagements. I hold the maxim no less applicable to public than to private affairs, that honesty is always the best policy. I repeat it therefore, let those engagements be observed in their genuine sense. But in my opinion it is unnecessary and would be unwise to extend them.

Taking care always to keep ourselves by suitable establishments on a respectable defensive posture, we may safely trust to temporary alliances for extraordinary emergencies.

Harmony, liberal intercourse with all nations, are recommended by policy, humanity, and interest. But even our commercial policy should hold an equal and impartial hand; neither seeking nor granting exclusive favors or preferences; consulting the natural course of things; diffusing and diversifying by gentle means the streams of commerce, but forcing nothing; establishing with powers so disposed, in order to give trade a stable course, to define the rights of our merchants, and to enable the government to support them, conventional rules of intercourse, the best that present circumstances and mutual opinion will permit, but temporary, and liable to be from time to time abandoned or varied, as experience and circumstances shall dictate; constantly keeping in view that it is folly in one nation to look for disinterested favors from another; that it must pay with a portion of its independence for whatever it may accept under that character; that by such acceptance it may place itself in the condition of having given equivalents for nominal favors, and yet of being reproached with ingratitude for not giving more. There can be no greater error than to expect or calculate upon real favors from nation to nation. It is an illusion which experience must cure, which a just pride ought to discard.

In offering to you, my countrymen, these counsels of an old and affectionate friend, I dare not hope they will make the strong and lasting impression I could wish; that they will control the usual current of the passions, or prevent our nation from running the course which has hitherto marked the destiny of nations. But if I may even flatter myself that they may be productive of some partial benefit, some occasional good; that they may now and then recur to moderate the fury of party spirit, to warn against the mischiefs of foreign intrigue, to guard against the impostures of pretended patriotism; this hope will be a full recompense for the solicitude for your welfare, by which they have been dictated.

How far in the discharge of my official duties I have been guided by the principles which have been delineated, the public records and other evidences of my conduct must witness to you, and to the world. To myself the assurance of my own conscience is, that I have at least believed myself to be guided by them.

In relation to the still subsisting war in Europe,[1] my proclamation of the 22d of April 1793 is the index to my plan. Sanctioned by your approving voice and by that of your representatives in both Houses of Congress, the spirit of that measure has continually governed me, uninfluenced by any attempts to deter or divert me from it.

After deliberate examination with the aid of the best lights I could obtain, I was well satisfied that our country, under all the circumstances of the case, had a right to take and was bound in duty and interest to take a neutral position. Having taken it, I determined as far as should depend upon me, to maintain it, with moderation, perseverance, and firmness.

The considerations which respect the right to hold this conduct, it is not necessary on this occasion to detail. I will only observe that, according to my understanding of the matter, that right, so far from being denied by any of the belligerent powers has been virtually admitted by all.

The duty of holding a neutral conduct may be inferred without anything more, from the obligation which justice and humanity impose on every nation, in cases in which it is free to act, to maintain inviolate the relations of peace and amity towards other nations.

The inducements of interest for observing that conduct will best be referred to your own reflections and experience. With me a predominant motive has been to endeavor to gain

[1] The war between France and the nations of Europe ending with Napoleon in control of France; Washington's proclamation of neutrality was a severe blow to American sympathizers with France.

time to our country to settle and mature its yet recent institutions, and to progress without interruption to that degree of strength and consistency which is necessary to give it, humanly speaking, the command of its own fortunes.

Though in reviewing the incidents of my administration I am unconscious of intentional error, I am nevertheless too sensible of my defects not to think it probable that I may have committed many errors. Whatever they may be I fervently beseech the Almighty to avert or mitigate the evils to which they may tend. I shall also carry with me the hope that my country will never cease to view them with indulgence; and that after forty-five years of my life dedicated to its service with an upright zeal, the faults of incompetent abilities will be consigned to oblivion, as myself must soon be to the mansions of rest.

Relying on its kindness in this as in other things, and actuated by that fervent love towards it which is so natural to a man who views in it the native soil of himself and his progenitors for several generations, I anticipate with pleasing expectation that retreat, in which I promise myself to realize without alloy the sweet enjoyment of partaking in the midst of my fellow-citizens the benign influence of good laws under a free government, the ever favorite object of my heart, and the happy reward, as I trust, of our mutual cares, labors, and dangers.

GEORGE WASHINGTON

United States, September 19th, 1796

THOMAS JEFFERSON 1743-1826

Perhaps more than any other American of his day, not excepting even Franklin, Jefferson was a world-citizen, responsive to the ideas and forces most active in European life before and during the French Revolution. He was born at Shadwell, Albemarle County, Virginia, and died at his estate, Monticello, near Charlottesville, Virginia. He had a good classical schooling, was two years at William and Mary College, studied and practiced law, and early entered public life in the Virginia legislature. He was member of the Continental Congress, governor of Virginia, 1779-81, United States minister to France, 1785-1789, vice president under Adams, and President, 1801-1809. Jefferson's political faith rested in the people as a directly active governing force, a faith opposed to that of Washington, who placed greater reliance on a strong central government. His writings are nearly all political, though his intellectual interests were of great range. He was a student of the classics, of modern languages, Indian dialects, Anglo-Saxon, geology, the sciences, and architecture. He was the founder of the University of Virginia. It is interesting that

Jefferson's style, like that of his friend Paine, and his English contemporary Godwin—all three leaders in liberal thought—is one of plain, direct simplicity. Biography: J. T. Morse (AS). Recent: F. W. Hirst, *Life and Letters of T. Jefferson*, 1926; P. Wilstach, *Jefferson at Monticello*, 1926. Also, for an interesting contemporary picture, G. Ticknor, *Life, Letters and Correspondence*, 2 vols. 1909, vol. 1, p. 34 ff.

From his AUTOBIOGRAPHY [1]

· · · · · · · ·

[CONGRESS UNDER THE CONFEDERATION [2]]

Our body was little numerous but very contentious. Day after day was wasted on the most unimportant questions. My colleague Mercer was one of those afflicted with the morbid rage of debate, of an ardent mind, prompt imagination, and copious flow of words; he heard with impatience any logic which was not his own. Sitting near me on some occasion of a trifling but wordy debate, he asked how I could sit in silence hearing so much false reasoning which a word should refute. I observed to him that to refute indeed was easy, but to silence impossible. That in measures brought forward by myself I took the laboring oar, as was incumbent on me; but that in general I was willing to listen. If every sound argument or objection was used by some one or other of the numerous debaters it was enough: if not, I thought it sufficient to suggest the omission without going into a repetition of what had been already said by others. That this was a waste and abuse of the time and patience of the house which could not be justified. And I believe that if the members of deliberative bodies were to observe this course generally, they would do in a day what takes them a week; and it is really more questionable than may at first be thought whether Bonaparte's dumb legislature [3] which said nothing and did much may not be preferable to one which talks much and does nothing. I served with General Washington in the legislature of Virginia before the Revolution, and during it with Dr. Franklin in Congress. I never heard either of them speak ten minutes at a time, nor to any but the main point which was to decide the question. They laid their shoulders

to the great points, knowing that the little ones would follow of themselves. If the present Congress errs in too much talking, how can it be otherwise in a body to which the people send one hundred and fifty lawyers whose trade it is to question everything, yield nothing, and talk by the hour? That one hundred and fifty lawyers should do business together ought not to be expected. But to return again to our subject.

· · · · · · · ·

[THE FRENCH REVOLUTION [4]]

[July 12, 1789] The King [5] was now completely in the hands of men [6] the principal among whom had been noted through their lives for the Turkish despotism of their characters, and who were associated around the King as proper instruments for what was to be executed. The news of this change began to be known at Paris about one or two o'clock. In the afternoon a body of about one hundred German cavalry [7] were advanced and drawn up in the Place Louis XV. and about two hundred Swiss posted at a little distance in their rear. This drew people to the spot, who thus accidentally found themselves in front of the troops, merely at first as spectators; but as their numbers increased their indignation rose. They retired a few steps and posted themselves on and behind large piles of stones, large and small, collected in that Place for a bridge which was to be built adjacent to it. In this position, happening to be in my carriage on a visit, I passed through the lane they had formed, without interruption. But the moment after I had passed, the people attacked the cavalry with stones. They charged, but the advantageous position of the people, and the showers of stones, obliged the horse to retire and quit the field altogether, leaving one of their number on the ground, and the Swiss in their rear not moving to their aid. This was the signal for universal insurrection, and this body of cavalry, to avoid being massacred, retired towards Versailles. [8] The people now armed themselves with such weapons as they could find in armorers' shops and private houses, and with bludgeons, and were roaming all night through all parts of the city, without any decided object.

---

[1] The autobiography is a condensed narrative written when Jefferson was seventy-seven years of age, and comes down only to the death of Franklin in 1790.

[2] the Congress under the Articles of Confederation, session of 1784

[3] When Bonaparte obtained control of France the national assembly voted without debate the decrees he proposed.

[4] Jefferson was minister to France, 1785-1789, and, as may be inferred from his account, strongly sympathized with the revolution there.

[5] Louis XVI

[6] the newly formed reactionary ministry appointed at the dismissal of Necker whom the people trusted

[7] The king, distrusting French troops, had surrounded himself with mercenaries.

[8] royal residence and military headquarters ten miles from Paris

The next day (13th.) the Assembly pressed on the King to send away the troops, to permit the *bourgeoisie* [1] of Paris to arm for the preservation of order in the city, and offered to send a deputation from their body to tranquilize them; but their propositions were refused. A committee of magistrates and electors of the city are appointed by those bodies to take upon them its government. The people now openly joined by the French guards force the prison of St. Lazare, release all the prisoners, and take a great store of corn, which they carry to the Corn-market. [2] Here they get some arms, and the French guards [3] begin to form and train them. The City-committee determined to raise forty-eight thousand *bourgeoisie,* or rather to restrain their numbers to forty-eight thousand. On the 14th. they send one of their members (Mons. de Corny) to the Hôtel des Invalides, [4] to ask arms for their Garde-Bourgeoisie. [5] He was followed by, and he found there a great collection of people. The Governor of the Invalides came out and represented the impossibility of his delivering arms without the orders of those from whom he received them. De Corny advised the people then to retire, and retired himself; but the people took possession of the arms. It was remarkable that not only the Invalides themselves made no opposition, but that a body of five thousand foreign troops within four hundred yards never stirred. M. de Corny and five others were then sent to ask arms of M. de Launay, governor of the Bastile. [6] They found a great collection of people already before the place, and they immediately planted a flag of truce, which was answered by a like flag hoisted on the parapet. The deputation prevailed on the people to fall back a little, advanced themselves to make their demand of the Governor, and in that instant a discharge from the Bastile killed four persons, of those nearest to the deputies. The deputies retired. I happened to be at the house of M. de Corny when he returned to it, and received from him a narrative of these transactions. On the retirement of the deputies, the people rushed forward and almost in an instant were in possession of a fortification defended by one hundred men, of infinite strength, which in other times had stood several regular sieges, and had never been taken. How they forced their entrance has never been explained. [7] They took all the arms, discharged the prisoners, and such of the garrison as were not killed in the first moment of fury, carried the Governor and Lt. Governor to the Place de Grève (the place of public execution), cut off their heads, and sent them through the city in triumph to the Palais Royal. [8] About the same instant a treacherous correspondence having been discovered in M. de Flesselles, Prévôt des Marchands, [9] they seized him in the Hôtel de Ville where he was in the execution of his office, and cut off his head. These events carried imperfectly to Versailles were the subject of two successive deputations from the Assembly to the King, to both of which he gave dry and hard answers, for nobody had as yet been permitted to inform him truly and fully of what had passed at Paris. But at night the Duke de Liancourt forced his way into the King's bed chamber and obliged him to hear a full and animated detail of the disasters of the day in Paris. He went to bed fearfully impressed. The decapitation of de Launay worked powerfully through the night on the whole aristocratic party insomuch that in the morning those of the greatest influence on the Count d'Artois [10] represented to him the absolute necessity that the King should give up everything to the Assembly. This according with the depositions of the King, he went about eleven o'clock, accompanied only by his brothers, to the Assembly and there read to them a speech in which he asked their interposition to re-establish order. Although couched in terms of some caution yet the manner in which it was delivered made it evident that it was meant as a surrender at discretion. He returned to the Chateau [11] afoot accompanied by the Assembly. They sent off a deputation to quiet Paris, at the head of which was the Marquis de la Fayette who had the same morning been named Commandant en chef of the Milice Bourgeoise, and Mons. Bailly, former President of the States General, [12] was called for as Prévôt des Marchands. The demolition of the Bastile was now ordered and begun. A body

---

[1] the middle classes
[2] The people were starving.
[3] The Gardes Françaises, native French soldiers, sympathized with the revolutionists.
[4] Originally a home for disabled soldiers; arms were stored there.
[5] citizen-guard, forming at first a kind of city militia
[6] an ancient fortress, then used like the Tower of London, as the state prison: the visible sign of tyranny
[7] Compare this matter-of-fact account with that of Carlyle's *French Revolution,* I, v, 6.
[8] residence of the Duc d'Orléans, Louis Philippe, nicknamed "Egalité," representative of one branch of the Bourbon family, who at first sided with the revolutionists but later fell a victim to the Jacobins
[9] the chief city official
[10] brother of Louis XVI; king as Charles X, 1824-1830
[11] The royal residence at Versailles; the new national Assembly was in session near at hand.
[12] the national legislature before the Revolution

of the Swiss guards of the regiment of Venti-mille, and the city horse guards joined the people. The alarm at Versailles increased. The foreign troops were ordered off instantly. Every minister resigned. The King confirmed Bailly as Prévôt des Marchands, wrote to Mr. Necker to recall him, sent his letter open to the Assembly to be forwarded by them, and invited them to go with him to Paris the next day to satisfy the city of his dispositions; and that night, and the next morning the Count d'Artois and M. de Montesson, a deputy connected with him, Madame de Polignac, Madame de Guiche, and the Count de Vaudreuil, favorites of the Queen, the Abbé de Vermont her confessor, the Prince of Condé and Duke of Bourbon [1] fled. The King came to Paris, leaving the Queen in consternation for his return. Omitting the less important figures of the procession, the King's carriage was in the center, on each side of it the Assembly in two ranks afoot, at their head the M. de la Fayette as Commander-in-chief on horseback, and Bourgeoise guards before and behind. About sixty thousand citizens of all forms and conditions, armed with the muskets of the Bastile and Invalides, as far as they would go, the rest with pistols, swords, pikes, pruning hooks, scythes etc. lined all the streets through which the procession passed, and with the crowds of people in the streets, doors and windows, saluted them everywhere with cries of *"Vive la nation,"* but not a single *"Vive le roy"* was heard. The King landed at the Hôtel de Ville. There M. Bailly presented and put into his hat the popular cockade, [2] and addressed him. The King being unprepared and unable to answer, Bailly went to him, gathered from him some scraps of sentences, and made out an answer, which he delivered to the audience as from the King. On their return the popular cries were *"Vive le roy et la nation."* He was conducted by a *garde bourgeoise* to his palace at Versailles, and thus concluded an *amende honorable* as no sovereign ever made, and no people ever received.

And here again was lost another precious occasion of sparing to France the crimes and cruelties through which she has since passed, and to Europe, and finally America the evils which flowed on them also from this mortal source. The King was now become a passive machine in the hands of the National Assembly, and had he been left to himself, he would have willingly acquiesced in whatever they should

devise as best for the nation. A wise constitution would have been formed, hereditary in his line, himself placed at its head, with powers so large as to enable him to do all the good of his station, and so limited as to restrain him from its abuse. This he would have faithfully administered, and more than this I do not believe he ever wished. But he had a Queen of absolute sway over his weak mind, and timid virtue; and of a character the reverse of his in all points. This angel, as gaudily painted in the rhapsodies of the Rhetor Burke, [3] with some smartness of fancy but no sound sense, was proud, disdainful of restraint, indignant at all obstacles to her will, eager in the pursuit of pleasure, and firm enough to hold to her desires or perish in their wreck. Her inordinate gambling and dissipations, with those of the Count d'Artois and others of her clique, had been a sensible item in the exhaustion of the treasury, which called into action the reforming hand of the nation; and her opposition to it, her inflexible perverseness, and dauntless spirit, led herself to the guillotine, and drew the King on with her, and plunged the world into crimes and calamities which will forever stain the pages of modern history. I have ever believed that had there been no Queen, there would have been no revolution. No force would have been provoked nor exercised. The King would have gone hand in hand with the wisdom of his sounder counselors, who, guided by the increased lights of the age, wished only, with the same pace, to advance the principles of their social institution. The deed which closed the mortal course of these sovereigns, I shall neither approve nor condemn. I am not prepared to say that the first magistrate of a nation cannot commit treason against his country, or is unamenable to its punishment: nor yet that where there is no written law, no regulated tribunal, there is not a law in our hearts, and a power in our hands, given for righteous employment in maintaining right, and redressing wrong. Of those who judged the King, many thought him wilfully criminal, many that his existence would keep the nation in perpetual conflict with the horde of kings who would war against a regeneration which might come home to themselves, and that it were better that one should die than all. I should not have voted with this portion of the legislature. I should have shut up the Queen

---

[1] father and son, representing the Condé branch of the Bourbon family

[2] the tri-colored rosette, the emblem of the Revolution

[3] The student should by all means compare Jefferson's view with that of Edmund Burke in *Reflections on the Revolution in France.* Jefferson feels that Burke was in this case more a rhetorician than a historian.

in a convent, putting harm out of her power, and placed the King in his station, investing him with limited powers, which I verily believe he would have honestly exercised, according to the measure of his understanding. In this way no void would have been created, courting the usurpation of a military adventurer, nor occasion given for those enormities which demoralized the nations of the world, and destroyed, and is yet to destroy millions and millions of its inhabitants. There are three epochs in history signalized by the total extinction of national morality. The first was of the successors of Alexander, not omitting himself. The next the successors of the first Caesar, the third our own age. This was begun by the partition of Poland,[1] followed by that of the treaty of Pilnitz,[2] next the conflagration of Copenhagen;[3] then the enormities of Bonaparte partitioning the earth at his will, and devastating it with fire and sword; now the conspiracy of kings, the successors of Bonaparte, blasphemously calling themselves the Holy Alliance,[4] and treading in the footsteps of their incarcerated leader,[5] not yet indeed usurping the government of other nations avowedly and in detail, but controlling by their armies the forms in which they will permit them to be governed; and reserving *in petto*[6] the order and extent of the usurpations further meditated. But I will return from a digression, anticipated too in time, into which I have been led by reflection on the criminal passions which refused to the world a favorable occasion of saving it from the afflictions it has since suffered.

1821   1829

FIRST INAUGURAL ADDRESS
March 4, 1801 [7]

Friends and Fellow-Citizens :—

Called upon to undertake the duties of the first executive office of our country, I avail myself of the presence of that portion of my fellow-citizens which is here assembled, to express my grateful thanks for the favor with which they have been pleased to look towards me, to declare a sincere consciousness that the task is above my talents, and that I approach it with those anxious and awful presentiments which the greatness of the charge and the weakness of my powers so justly inspire. A rising nation spread over a wide and fruitful land, traversing all the seas with the rich productions of their industry, engaged in commerce with nations who feel power and forget right, advancing rapidly to destinies beyond the reach of mortal eye; when I contemplate these transcendant objects, and see the honor, the happiness, and the hopes of this beloved country committed to the issue and the auspices of this day, I shrink from the contemplation, and humble myself before the magnitude of the undertaking.

Utterly, indeed, should I despair, did not the presence of many whom I here see remind me that in the other high authorities provided by our constitution I shall find resources of wisdom, of virtue, and of zeal on which to rely under all difficulties. To you, then, gentlemen, who are charged with the sovereign functions of legislation, and to those associated with you, I look with encouragement for that guidance and support which may enable us to steer with safety the vessel in which we are all embarked, amidst the conflicting elements of a troubled sea.[8]

During the contest of opinion through which we have passed, the animation of discussions and of exertions has sometimes worn an aspect which might impose on strangers unused to think freely and to speak and to write what they think. But this being now decided by the voice of the nation, announced according to the rules of the Constitution, all will, of course, arrange themselves under the will of the law, and unite in common efforts for the common good. All too will bear in mind this sacred principle, that though the will of the majority is in all cases to prevail, that will, to be rightful, must be reasonable; that the minority possess their equal rights, which equal laws must protect, and to violate would be oppression. Let us then, fellow-citizens, unite with one heart and one mind; let us restore to social intercourse that harmony and affection without which liberty, and even life itself, are but dreary things. And let us reflect that having

---

[1] in 1772 between Russia, Austria, and Prussia
[2] by which the Emperor of Austria and the King of Prussia agreed, in 1792, to support in arms the cause of the French king
[3] The victory of Nelson over the Danes in 1801, and the bombardment and partial destruction of Copenhagen in 1807, marked the ruthless driving of Denmark by the allies from a position of neutrality in the great European struggle.
[4] a compact formed by the sovereigns of Russia, Austria, and Prussia in 1815, and joined later by nearly all the monarchs of Europe, for the avowed purpose of perpetuating the Christian religion, but really to perpetuate their own respective dynasties
[5] Bonaparte, exiled to St. Helena
[6] in the breast
[7] Jefferson took the presidency as a Republican, or liberal, after the Federalists, or conservatives, had been in office for the first twelve years under the Constitution. His inaugural address is frequently entitled "Democracy Defined."

[8] Jefferson wrote it: "I look wth encorgm^t for y^t guid^{ce} & supp^{rt} wch m enable us to steer wth safety ye vess^l in wch w'r all mb^{kd} am^{dst} ye confl^{ctg} elem^{ts} of a troubl^d sea."

banished from our land that religious intolerance under which mankind so long bled and suffered, we have yet gained little if we countenance a political intolerance as despotic, as wicked, and capable of as bitter and bloody persecutions. During the throes and convulsions of the ancient world, during the agonizing spasms of infuriated man, seeking through blood and slaughter his long-lost liberty, it was not wonderful that the agitation of the billows should reach even this distant and peaceful shore; that this should be more felt and feared by some and less by others; and should divide opinions as to measures of safety. But every difference of opinion is not a difference of principle. We have called by different names brethren of the same principle. We are all Republicans; we are all Federalists. [1] If there be any among us who would wish to dissolve this Union, or to change its republican form, let them stand undisturbed as monuments of the safety with which error of opinion may be tolerated, where reason is left free to combat it. I know, indeed, that some honest men have feared that a republican government cannot be strong; that this Government is not strong enough. But would the honest patriot, in the full tide of successful experiment, abandon a government which has so far kept us free and firm, on the theoretic and visionary fear that this Government, the world's best hope, may by possibility want energy to preserve itself? I trust not. I believe this, on the contrary, the strongest government on earth. I believe it the only one where every man, at the call of the law would fly to the standard of the law; would meet invasions of the public order as his own personal concern. Sometimes it is said that man cannot be trusted with the government of himself. Can he then, be trusted with the government of others? Or have we found angels in the form of kings to govern him? Let history answer this question.

Let us then, pursue with courage and confidence our own federal and republican principles, our attachment to union and representative government. Kindly separated by nature and a wide ocean from the exterminating havoc of one quarter of the globe; too high-minded to endure the degradations of the others; possessing a chosen country, with room enough for our descendants to the hundredth and thousandth generation; entertaining a due sense of our equal right to the use of our own faculties, to the acquisitions of our own industry, to honor

and confidence from our fellow-citizens, resulting not from birth, but from our actions and their sense of them; enlightened by a benign religion, professed indeed and practiced in various forms yet all of them inculcating honesty, truth, temperance, gratitude, and the love of man, acknowledging and adoring an overruling Providence, which by all its dispensations proves that it delights in the happiness of man here and his greater happiness hereafter: with all these blessings, what more is necessary to make us a happy and a prosperous people? Still one thing more, fellow-citizens—a wise and frugal government, which shall restrain men from injuring one another, shall leave them otherwise free to regulate their own pursuits of industry and improvement, and shall not take from the mouth of labor the bread it has earned. This is the sum of good government; and this is necessary to close the circle of our felicities.

About to enter, fellow-citizens, on the exercise of duties which comprehend everything dear and valuable to you, it is proper you should understand what I deem the essential principle of this government, and consequently those which ought to shape its administration. I will compress them in the narrowest compass they will bear, stating the general principle but not all its limitations. Equal and exact justice to all men of whatever state or persuasion, religious or political; peace, commerce and honest friendship with all nations, entangling alliances with none; [2] the support of the state governments in all their rights, as the most competent administrations for our domestic concerns, and the surest bulwarks against anti-republican tendencies; the preservation of the general government in its whole constitutional vigor, as the sheet-anchor of our peace at home and safety abroad; a jealous care of the right of election by the people; a mild and safe corrective of abuses which are lopped by the sword of revolution, where peaceable remedies are unprovided; absolute acquiescence in the decisions of the majority, the vital principle of republics, from which is no appeal but to force, the vital principle and immediate parent of despotism; a well-disciplined militia, our best reliance in peace and for the first moments of war, till regulars may relieve them; the supremacy of the civil over the military authority—economy in the public expense, that labor may be lightly burdened; the honest payment of our debts, and sacred preservation of the public faith; encouragement of agriculture, and of commerce as its handmaid; the diffusion of information and arraignment of all abuses at the bar of the

---

[1] Jefferson's tact, and his moderation as President, gradually softened the prejudice of the great minority opposed to his theoretical principles of government.

[2] Cf. Washington's words, p. 155.

public reason; freedom of religion, freedom of the press, and freedom of person, under the protection of the habeas corpus; and trial by juries impartially selected. These principles form the bright constellation which has gone before us, and guided our steps through an age of revolution and reformation. The wisdom of our sages and blood of our heroes have been devoted to their attainment; they should be the creed of our political faith; the text of civic instruction; the touchstone by which to try the services of those we trust; and should we wander from them in moments of error or alarm, let us hasten to retrace our steps and to regain the road which alone leads to peace, liberty, and safety.

I repair then, fellow-citizens, to the post which you have assigned me. With experience enough in subordinate stations to know the difficulties of this, the greatest of all, I have learned to expect that it will rarely fall to the lot of imperfect man to retire from this station with the reputation and the favor which bring him into it. Without pretensions to that high confidence you reposed in our first and greatest revolutionary character, whose preëminent services had entitled him to the first place in his country's love, and had destined for him the fairest page in the volume of faithful history, I ask so much confidence only as may give firmness and effect to the legal administration of your affairs. I shall often go wrong through defect of judgment. When right, I shall often be thought wrong by those whose positions will not command a view of the whole ground. I ask your indulgence for my own errors, which will never be intentional; and your support against the errors of others, who may condemn what they would not, if seen in all its parts. The approbation implied by your suffrage is a great consolation to me for the past; and my future solicitude will be to retain the good opinion of those who have bestowed it in advance, to conciliate that of others by doing them all the good in my power, and to be instrumental to the happiness and freedom of all.

Relying then on the patronage of your goodwill, I advance with obedience to the work, ready to retire from it whenever you become sensible how much better choice it is in your power to make. And may that Infinite Power which rules the destinies of the universe lead our councils to what is best, and give them a favorable issue for your peace and prosperity.

1801

PHILIP FRENEAU 1752-1832

Freneau was the first American of our national period who showed any particular gift for poetic expression. He was born of Huguenot parentage in New York City. After graduating from Princeton College in 1771, he was often at sea between Philadelphia and the West Indies, and in 1780 was captured by the British and confined for a time in a prison ship. During the Revolution he wrote many patriotic lyrics and satires. Newspaper work and journalism in New York and Philadelphia occupied most of his active years, though in 1790 he was translator for the Department of State. He published volumes of poetry from 1786 to 1815, notably an edition from his own press at Monmouth, New Jersey, 1795, where he lived until his death.

Freneau was versatile and vivacious and was one of the first poets writing in English to express the new "romantic" attitude toward nature. Nothing like it had appeared before in America and little in England; for his first volume appeared in the same year with Burns's poems, and twelve years before the publication of Wordsworth and Coleridge's *Lyrical Ballads*. We may, therefore, well wish that his outward circumstances had been less turbulent, and that he had been favored with friends who were also stimulating and sympathetic critics of poetry. Some of his shorter pieces have a finish and a harmony between thought and form worthy of all praise. *The House of Night*, longer and more pretentious, lacks these qualities, but it shows genuine power of original imagination, and some passages are gorgeous beyond anything previous in American literature. The poem is uneven and in places crude; but we must remember that it was written when standards in American literature were not yet formed.

Works: F. L. Pattee, ed. 3 vols., 1902-7. See P. E. More (Shel. 5).

From THE HOUSE OF NIGHT [1]

A VISION

Trembling I write my dream, and recollect
A fearful vision at the midnight hour;
So late, Death o'er me spread his sable wings,
Painted with fancies of malignant power!

[1] In explaining the poem Freneau says:
    ADVERTISEMENT—This Poem is founded upon the authority of Scripture, inasmuch as these sacred books assert that "the last enemy that shall be conquered is Death." For the purposes of poetry he is here personified, and represented as on his dying bed. The scene is laid at a solitary palace (the time midnight), which, tho' before beautiful and joyous, is now become sad and gloomy, as being the abode and receptacle of Death. Its owner, an amiable, majestic youth, who had lately lost a beloved consort, nevertheless with a noble philosophical fortitude and humanity, entertains him in a friendly manner, and by employing Physicians, endeavors to restore him to health, altho' an enemy; convinced of the excellence and

Such was the dream the sage Chaldean saw
Disclosed to him that felt heaven's vengeful
    rod,
Such was the ghost, who through deep silence
    cried,
Shall mortal man—be juster than his God? [1]

Let others draw from smiling skies their theme,
And tell of climes that boast unfading light, 10
I draw a darker scene, replete with gloom,
I sing the horrors of the House of Night.

Stranger, believe the truth experience tells,
Poetic dreams are of a finer cast
Than those which o'er the sober brain diffused,
Are but a repetition of some action past.

Fancy, I own thy power—when sunk in sleep
Thou play'st thy wild delusive part so well
You lift me into immortality,   19
Depict new heavens, or draw the scenes of hell.

By some sad means, when reason holds no
    sway,
Lonely I roved at midnight o'er a plain
Where murmuring streams and mingling rivers
    flow
Far to their springs, or seek the sea again.

Sweet vernal May! though then thy woods in
    bloom
Flourished, yet nought of this could fancy see,
No wild pinks blessed the meads, no green the
    fields,
And naked seemed to stand each lifeless tree:

Dark was the sky, and not one friendly star
Shone from the zenith or horizon, clear, 80
Mist sat upon the woods, and darkness rode
In her black chariot, with a wild career.

And from the woods the late resounding note
Issued of the loquacious whippoorwill,
Hoarse, howling dogs, and nightly roving wolves
Clamored from far-off cliffs invisible.

Rude, from the wide extended Chesapeake
I heard the winds the dashing waves assail,
And saw from far, by picturing fancy formed,
The black ship traveling through the noisy
    gale. 40

At last, by chance and guardian fancy led,
I reached a noble dome, [2] raised fair and high,
And saw the light from upper windows flame,
Presage of mirth and hospitality.

And by that light around the dome appeared
A mournful garden of autumnal hue,
Its lately pleasing flowers all drooping stood
Amidst high weeds that in rank plenty grew.

The primrose there, the violet darkly blue,
Daisies and fair narcissus ceased to rise, 50
Gay spotted pinks their charming bloom with-
    drew,
And polyanthus quenched its thousand dyes.

No pleasant fruit or blossom gaily smiled,
Nought but unhappy plants or trees were seen,
The yew, the myrtle, and the church-yard elm,
The cypress, with its melancholy green. [3]

There cedars dark, the osier, and the pine,
Shorn tamarisks, and weeping willows grew.
The poplar tall, the lotus, and the lime,
And pyracantha did her leaves renew. 60

The poppy there, companion to repose,
Displayed her blossoms that began to fall,
And here the purple amaranthus rose
With mint strong-scented, for the funeral.

And here and there with laurel shrubs between
A tombstone lay, inscribed with strains of woe,
And stanzas sad, throughout the dismal green,
Lamented for the dead that slept below. [4]

---

propriety of that divine precept, "If thine enemy
hunger, feed him; if he thirst, give him drink."
He nevertheless, as if by a spirit of prophecy,
informs this (fictitiously) wicked being of the
certainty of his doom, and represents to him in a
pathetic manner, the vanity of his expectations,
either of a reception into the abodes of the just,
or continuing longer to make havock of mankind
upon earth.   The patient finding his end approaching, composes his epitaph, and orders it to be engraved on his tombstone, hinting to us thereby
that even Death and Distress have vanity; and
would be remembered with honour after he is no
more, altho' his whole life has been spent in
deeds of devastation and murder.   He dies at
last in the utmost agonies of despair, after agreeing with an avaricious Undertaker to intomb his
bones.   This reflects upon the inhumanity of those
men, who, not to mention an enemy, would scarcely
cover a departed friend with a little dust, without
certainty of reward for so doing.   The circumstances of his funeral are then recited, and the
visionary and fabulous part of the poem disappears.   It concludes with a few reflexions on
the impropriety of a too great attachment to the
present life, and incentives to such moral virtue
as may assist in conducting us to a better.
[1] Eliphaz told Job what he had seen and heard in a
   vision—of a spirit that said, "Shall mortal man
   be more just than God?" *Job* iv, 17.

[2] the home of the "majestic youth" spoken of in the
   "advertisement"
[3] characteristic eighteenth century graveyard trees
[4] There follows the consultation of Death's physicians.

Then up three winding stairs my feet were
  brought   89
To a high chamber, hung with mourning sad;
The unsnuffed candles glared with visage dim,
'Midst grief, in ecstasy of woe run mad.

A wide leafed table stood on either side,
Well fraught with phials, half their liquids
  spent,
And from a couch, behind the curtain's veil,
I heard a hollow voice of loud lament.

Turning to view the object whence it came,
My frighted eyes a horrid form surveyed;
Fancy, I own thy power—Death on the couch,
With fleshless limbs, at rueful length, was laid.

And o'er his head flew jealousies and cares,   101
Ghosts, imps, and half the black Tartarian [1]
  crew,
Archangels damned, nor was their Prince re-
  mote,
Borne on the vaporous wings of Stygian [2] dew.

Around his bed, by the dull flambeaux' glare,
I saw pale phantoms—rage to madness vexed,
Wan, wasting grief, and ever musing care,
Distressful pain, and poverty perplexed.

Sad was his countenance, if we can call   109
That countenance, where only bones were seen
And eyes sunk in their sockets, dark and low,
And teeth, that only showed themselves to grin.

Reft was his skull of hair, and no fresh bloom
Of cheerful mirth sat on his visage hoar:
Sometimes he raised his head, while deep-drawn
  groans
Were mixed with words that did his fate de-
  plore.

Oft did he wish to see the daylight spring,
And often toward the window leaned to hear,
Fore-runner of the scarlet-mantled morn,
The early note of wakeful chanticleer. [3]   120

. . . .

"Death in this tomb his weary bones hath laid,
"Sick of dominion o'er the human kind—   390
"Behold what devastations he hath made,
"Survey the millions by his arm confined.

"Six thousand years [4] has sovereign sway been
  mine,
"None, but myself, can real glory claim;
"Great Regent of the world I reigned alone,
"And princes trembled when my mandate came.

"Vast and unmatched throughout the world,
  my fame
"Takes place of gods, and asks no mortal
  date— [5]
"No; by myself, and by the heavens, I swear,
"Not Alexander's name is half so great.   400

"Nor swords nor darts my prowess could with-
  stand,
"All quit their arms, and bowed to my decree,
"Even mighty Julius died beneath my hand,
"For slaves and Caesars were the same to me!

"Traveler, wouldst thou his noblest trophies
  seek,
"Search in no narrow spot obscure for those;
"The sea profound, the surface of all land
"Is molded with the myriads of his foes."

Scarce had he spoke, when on the lofty dome
Rushed from the clouds a hoarse resounding
  blast—   410
Round the four eaves so loud and sad it played
As though all music were to breathe its last.

Warm was the gale, and such as travelers say
Sport with the winds on Zaara's [6] barren waste;
Black was the sky, a mourning carpet spread,
Its azure blotted, and its stars o'ercast!

Lights in the air like burning stars were hurled,
Dogs howled, heaven muttered, and the tempest
  blew,
The red half-moon peeped from behind a cloud
As if in dread the amazing scene to view.   420

The mournful trees that in the garden stood
Bent to the tempest as it rushed along,
The elm, the myrtle, and the cypress sad
More melancholy tuned its bellowing song.

No more that elm its noble branches spread,
The yew, the cypress, or the myrtle tree,
Rent from the roots the tempest tore them
  down,
And all the grove in wild confusion lay.

---

[1] pertaining to Tartarus, the abode of the wicked in
    Hades
[2] Styx was one of the rivers of the lower world.
[3] There follow a description of the mortal sickness
    and agony of Death, and the directions he gives
    for his burial, ending with his epitaph in lines
    389 ff.

[4] According to Jewish chronology, the creation and fall
    of man, and with it the beginning of the reign
    of death, took place four thousand years before
    the Christian era.
[5] Death can scarcely conceive that he is not immortal,
    dateless, like the gods.
[6] Sahara's

Yet, mindful of his dread command I part   429
Glad from the magic dome—nor found relief;
Damps from the dead hung heavier round my
    heart,
While sad remembrance roused her stores of
    grief.

O'er a dark field I held my dubious way
Where Jack-a-lanthorn walked his lonely round,
Beneath my feet substantial darkness lay,
And screams were heard from the distempered
    ground.

Nor looked I back, till to a far-off wood,
Trembling with fear, my weary feet had sped—
Dark was the night, but at the enchanted dome
I saw the infernal windows flaming red.   440

And from within the howls of Death I heard,
Cursing the dismal night that gave him birth,
Damning his ancient sire, and mother sin,
Who at the gates of hell, accursed, brought him
    forth. [1]

For fancy gave to my enraptured soul
An eagle's eye, with keenest glance to see,
And bade those distant sounds distinctly roll,
Which, waking, never had affected me.

Oft his pale breast with cruel hand he smote,
And tearing from his limbs a winding sheet,   450
Roared to the black skies, while the woods
    around
As wicked as himself, his words repeat.

Thrice toward the skies his meager arms he
    reared,
Invoked all hell, and thunders on his head,
Bid lightnings fly, earth yawn, and tempests
    roar,
And the sea wrap him in its oozy bed.

"My life for one cool draught!—O, fetch your
    springs,
Can one unfeeling to my woes be found!
No friendly visage comes to my relief,   459
But ghosts impend, and specters hover round.

"Though humbled now, disheartened and dis-
    tressed,
Yet when admitted to the peaceful ground,
With heroes, kings, and conquerors I shall rest,
Shall sleep as safely, and perhaps as sound."

Dim burnt the lamp, and now the phantom
    Death

[1] Cf. *Paradise Lost*, ii, 749-790.

Gave his last groans in horror and despair—
"All hell demands me hence,"—he said, and
    threw
The red lamp hissing through the midnight air.

Trembling, across the plain my course I held,
And found the graveyard, loitering through the
    gloom,   470
And in the midst, a hell-red, wandering light,
Walking in fiery circles round the tomb.

Among the graves a spiry building stood,
Whose tolling bell, resounding through the
    shade,
Sung doleful ditties to the adjacent wood,
And many a dismal drowsy thing it said.

This fabric tall, with towers and chancels
    graced,
Was raised by sinners' hands in ages fled;
The roof they painted, and the beams they
    braced,
And texts from scripture o'er the walls they
    spread: 480

But wicked were their hearts, for they refused
To aid the helpless orphan, when distressed,
The shivering, naked stranger they misused,
And banished from their doors the starving
    guest.

By laws protected, cruel and profane,
The poor man's ox these monsters drove
    away;—
And left Distress to attend her infant train,
No friend to comfort, and no bread to stay.

But Heaven looked on with keen, resentful eye,
And doomed them to perdition and the grave,
That as they felt not for the wretch dis-
    tressed,   491
So Heaven no pity on their souls would have.

In pride they raised this building tall and fair,
Their hearts were on perpetual mischief bent,
With pride they preached, and pride was in
    their prayer,
With pride they were deceived, and so to hell
    they went.

At distance far approaching to the tomb,
By lamps and lanthorns guided through the
    shade,
A coal-black chariot hurried through the gloom,
Specters attending, in black weeds arrayed,   500

Whose woeful forms yet chill my soul with
    dread,
Each wore a vest in Stygian chambers wove,
Death's kindred all—Death's horses they be-
    strode.
And galloped fiercely, as the chariot drove.

Each horrid face a grisly mask concealed,
Their busy eyes shot terror to my soul
As now and then, by the pale lanthorn's glare,
I saw them for their parted friend condole.

Before the hearse Death's chaplain seemed to
    go,
Who strove to comfort, what he could, the
    dead;   510
Talked much of Satan, and the land of woe,
And many a chapter from the Scriptures read.

At last he raised the swelling anthem high,
In dismal numbers seemed he to complain;
The captive tribes that by Euphrates wept, [1]
Their song was jovial to his dreary strain.

That done, they placed the carcass in the tomb,
To dust and dull oblivion now resigned,
Then turned the chariot toward the House of
    Night,   519
Which soon flew off, and left no trace behind.

But as I stooped to write the appointed verse,
Swifter than thought the airy scene decayed;
Blushing the morn arose, and from the east
With her gay streams of light dispelled the
    shade.

What is this Death, ye deep read Sophists,
    say?—
Death is no more than one unceasing change;
New forms arise, while other forms decay,
Yet all is Life throughout creation's range.

The towering Alps, the haughty Appenine,
The Andes, wrapped in everlasting snow,   530
The Apalachian and the Ararat
Sooner or later must to ruin go.

Hills sink to plains, and man returns to dust,
That dust supports a reptile or a flower;
Each changeful atom by some other nursed
Takes some new form, to perish in an hour.

Too nearly joined to sickness, toils, and pains,
(Perhaps for former crimes imprisoned here)

[1] the Israelites, *Psalms* cxxxvii, 1

True to itself the immortal soul remains,   539
And seeks new mansions in the starry sphere.

When Nature bids thee from the world retire,
With joy thy lodging leave, a fated guest;
In Paradise, the land of thy desire,
Existing always, always to be blessed.
1776?   1779, 1786

TO THE MEMORY OF THE BRAVE AMERICANS

Under General Greene, in South Caro-lina, Who Fell in the Action of September 8, 1781

At Eutaw Springs the valiant died;
    Their limbs with dust are covered o'er—
Weep on, ye springs, your tearful tide;
    How many heroes are no more!

If in this wreck of ruin, they
    Can yet be thought to claim a tear,
O smite your gentle breast, and say
    The friends of freedom slumber here!

Thou, who shalt trace this bloody plain,
    If goodness rules thy generous breast,   10
Sigh for the wasted rural reign;
    Sigh for the shepherds sunk to rest!

Stranger, their humble graves adorn;
    You too may fall, and ask a tear:
'T is not the beauty of the morn
    That proves the evening shall be clear.—

They saw their injured country's woe,
    The flaming town, the wasted field;
Then rushed to meet the insulting foe;
    They took the spear—but left the shield.   20

Led by thy conquering genius, Greene,
    The Britons they compelled to fly;
None distant viewed the fatal plain,
    None grieved in such a cause to die—

But, like the Parthians famed of old,
    Who, flying, still their arrows threw,
These routed Britons, full as bold,
    Retreated, and retreating slew.

Now rest in peace our patriot band;
    Though far from nature's limits thrown,
We trust they find a happier land,   31
    A brighter sunshine of their own.
1781   1781

STANZAS

OCCASIONED BY THE RUINS OF A COUNTRY INN,
UNROOFED AND BLOWN DOWN IN A STORM

Where now these mingled ruins lie
    A temple once to Bacchus [1] rose,
Beneath whose roof, aspiring high,
    Full many a guest forgot his woes.

No more this dome, by tempests torn,
    Affords a social safe retreat;
But ravens here, with eye forlorn,
    And clustering bats henceforth will meet.

The priestess of this ruined shrine,
    Unable to survive the stroke,   10
Presents no more the ruddy wine,
    Her glasses gone, her china broke.

The friendly host, whose social hand
    Accosted strangers at the door,
Has left at length his wonted stand,
    And greets the weary guest no more.

Old creeping Time, that brings decay,
    Might yet have spared these moldering walls,
Alike beneath whose potent sway
    A temple or a tavern falls.   20

Is this the place where mirth and joy,
    Coy nymphs, and sprightly lads were found?
Indeed! no more the nymphs are coy,
    No more the flowing bowls go round.

Is this the place where festive song
    Deceived the wintry hours away?
No more the swains the tune prolong,
    No more the maidens join the lay:

Is this the place where Nancy slept
    In downy beds of blue and green?—   30
Dame Nature here no vigils kept,
    No cold unfeeling guards were seen.

'T is gone!—and Nancy tempts no more,
    Deep, unrelenting silence reigns;
Of all that pleased, that charmed before,
    The tottering chimney scarce remains!

Ye tyrant winds, whose ruffian blast
    Through doors and windows blew too strong,
And all the roof to ruin cast,—
    The roof that sheltered us so long,—   40

[1] god of conviviality

Your wrath appeased, I pray be kind
    If Mopsus [2] should the dome renew;
That we again may quaff his wine,
    Again collect our jovial crew.

1782

THE WILD HONEYSUCKLE

Fair flower, that dost so comely grow,
    Hid in this silent, dull retreat,
Untouched thy honied blossoms blow,
    Unseen thy little branches greet:
        No roving foot shall crush thee here,
        No busy hand provoke a tear.

By Nature's self in white arrayed,
    She bade thee shun the vulgar eye,
And planted here the guardian shade,
    And sent soft waters murmuring by;   10
        Thus quietly thy summer goes,
        Thy days declining to repose.

Smit with those charms, that must decay,
    I grieve to see your future doom;
They died—nor were those flowers more gay,
    The flowers that did in Eden bloom;
        Unpitying frosts and Autumn's power
        Shall leave no vestige of this flower.

From morning suns and evening dews
    At first thy little being came: 20
If nothing once, you nothing lose,
    For when you die you are the same;
        The space between is but an hour,
        The frail duration of a flower.

1786   1786

THE INDIAN BURYING GROUND

In spite of all the learned have said,
    I still my old opinion keep;
The posture that we give the dead
    Points out the soul's eternal sleep.

Not so the ancients of these lands;—
    The Indian, when from life released,
Again is seated with his friends,
    And shares again the joyous feast.

His imaged birds, and painted bowl,
    And venison, for a journey dressed,   10
Bespeak the nature of the soul,
    Activity, that knows no rest.

[2] perhaps, as in idyllic poetry, used for the name of a
countryman

His bow for action ready bent,
   And arrows with a head of stone,
Can only mean that life is spent,
   And not the old ideas gone.

Thou, stranger, that shalt come this way,
   No fraud upon the dead commit,—
Observe the swelling turf, and say
   They do not lie, but here they sit.   20

Here still a lofty rock remains,
   On which the curious eye may trace
(Now wasted half by wearing rains)
   The fancies of a ruder race.

Here still an aged elm aspires,
   Beneath whose far-projecting shade
(And which the shepherd still admires)
   The children of the forest played.

There oft a restless Indian queen
   (Pale Shebah [1] with her braided hair)   30
And many a barbarous form is seen
   To chide the man that lingers there.

By midnight moons, o'er moistening dews,
   In habit for the chase arrayed,
The hunter still the deer pursues,
   The hunter and the deer, a shade!

And long shall timorous fancy see
   The painted chief, and pointed spear,
And reason's self shall bow the knee
   To shadows and delusions here.   40
                    1788

THE PARTING GLASS

The man that joins in life's career
And hopes to find some comfort here,
To rise above this earthly mass,—
The only way's to drink his glass.

But still, on this uncertain stage
Where hopes and fears the soul engage,
And while, amid the joyous band,
Unheeded flows the measured sand,
Forget not as the moments pass
That time shall bring the parting glass!   10

In spite of all the mirth I've heard,
This is the glass I always feared,
The glass that would the rest destroy,
The farewell cup, the close of joy!

[1] *1 Kings*, x

With you, whom reason taught to think,
I could for ages sit and drink;
But with the fool, the sot, the ass,
I haste to take the parting glass.

The luckless wight, that still delays
His draught of joys to future days,   20
Delays too long—for then, alas!
Old age steps up, and—breaks the glass!

The nymph who boasts no borrowed charms,
Whose sprightly wit my fancy warms,
What though she tends this country inn,
And mixes wine, and deals out gin?
With such a kind, obliging lass,
I sigh to take the parting glass.

With him who always talks of gain
(Dull Momus, [2] of the plodding train),   30
The wretch who thrives by others' woes,
And carries grief where'er he goes,—
With people of this knavish class
The first is still my parting glass,

With those that drink before they dine,
With him that apes the grunting swine,
Who fills his page with low abuse,
And strives to act the gabbling goose
Turned out by fate to feed on grass—
Boy, give me quick, the parting glass.   40

The man whose friendship is sincere,
Who knows no guilt, and feels no fear,—
It would require a heart of brass
With him to take the parting glass!

With him who quaffs his pot of ale,
Who holds to all an even scale,
Who hates a knave in each disguise,
And fears him not—whate'er his size—
With him, well pleased my days to pass,
May Heaven forbid the Parting Glass!   50
                    1790

ON A HONEY BEE

DRINKING FROM A GLASS OF WINE AND DROWNED THEREIN

Thou, born to sip the lake or spring,
   Or quaff the waters of the stream,
Why hither come, on vagrant wing?
   Does Bacchus tempting seem,

[2] Momus, a god personifying mockery and ridicule

Did he for you this glass prepare?
Will I admit you to a share?

Did storms harass or foes perplex,
  Did wasps or king-birds bring dismay,
Did wars distress, or labors vex,
  Or did you miss your way?   10
    A better seat you could not take
    Than on the margin of this lake.

Welcome!—I hail you to my glass:
  All welcome here you find;
Here let the cloud of trouble pass,
  Here be all care resigned.
    This fluid never fails to please,
    And drown the griefs of men or bees.

What forced you here we cannot know,
  And you will scarcely tell,—   20
But cheery we would have you go
  And bid a glad farewell:
    On lighter wings we bid you fly, —
    Your dart will now all foes defy.

Yet take not, oh! too deep a drink,
  And in this ocean die;
Here bigger bees than you might sink,
  Even bees full six feet high.
    Like Pharaoh, then, you would be said
    To perish in a sea of red.   30

Do as you please, your will is mine;
  Enjoy it without fear,
And your grave will be this glass of wine,
  Your epitaph—a tear;
    Go, take your seat in Charon's [1] boat;
    We'll tell the hive, you died afloat.
                                    1809

TO A CATY-DID

In a branch of willow hid
Sings the evening Caty-did:
From the lofty locust bough
Feeding on a drop of dew,
In her suit of green arrayed
Hear her singing in the shade
  Caty-did, Caty-did, Caty-did!

While upon a leaf you tread,
Or repose your little head,
On your sheet of shadows laid,   10
All the day you nothing said:
Half the night your cheery tongue

[1] the ferryman who carried the souls of the dead across
  the rivers of the underworld

Reveled out its little song,
  Nothing else but Caty-did.

From your lodgings on the leaf
Did you utter joy or grief?—
Did you only mean to say,
I have had my summer's day,
And am passing, soon, away
To the grave of Caty-did:—   20
  Poor, unhappy Caty-did!

But you would have uttered more
Had you known of nature's power—
From the world when you retreat,
And a leaf's your winding sheet,
Long before your spirit fled,
Who can tell but nature said,
Live again, my Caty-did!
  Live and chatter, Caty-did.

Tell me, what did Caty do?   30
Did she mean to trouble you?
Why was Caty not forbid
To trouble little Caty-did?
Wrong indeed at you to fling,
Hurting no one while you sing
  Caty-did! Caty-did! Caty-did!

Why continue to complain?
Caty tells me, she again
Will not give you plague or pain:—
Caty says you may be hid   40
Caty will not go to bed
While you sing us Caty-did.
  Caty-did! Caty-did! Caty-did!

But while singing, you forgot
To tell us what did Caty not:
Caty did not think of cold,
Flocks retiring to the fold,
Winter, with his wrinkles old,
Winter, that yourself foretold
  When you gave us Caty-did.   50

Stay securely in your nest;
Caty now, will do her best,
All she can to make you blest;
But, you want no human aid—
Nature, when she formed you, said,
"Independent you are made,
My dear little Caty-did:
Soon yourself must disappear
With the verdure of the year,—"
And to go, we know not where,   60
  With your song of Caty-did.

                                    1815

JOSEPH HOPKINSON 1770-1842

Joseph Hopkinson, who was born and died in Philadelphia, was the son of Francis Hopkinson, author of *The Battle of the Kegs* and other poems, page 137. He was educated at the University of Pennsylvania, studied and practiced law, was a member of Congress, 1815-1819, and from 1828 Judge of the United States District Court. He was chiefly influential in founding the Philadelphia Academy of Fine Arts. His most popular song, "Hail Columbia," was written in 1798 when war with France was urged by a large party in America and was expected by all. The song, appealing to patriotic rather than party feelings, was immediately accepted by all factions.

HAIL COLUMBIA [1]

Hail, Columbia! happy land!
Hail, ye heroes! heaven-born band!
  Who fought and bled in freedom's cause,
  Who fought and bled in freedom's cause,
And when the storm of war was gone,
Enjoyed the peace your valor won.
    Let independence be our boast,
    Ever mindful what it cost;
    Ever grateful for the prize,
    Let its altar reach the skies.   10

    Firm, united, let us be,
    Rallying round our liberty;
    As a band of brothers joined, [2]
    Peace and safety we shall find.

Immortal patriots! rise once more:
Defend your rights, defend your shore:
  Let no rude foe, with impious hand,
  Let no rude foe, with impious hand,
Invade the shrine where sacred lies
Of toil and blood the well-earned prize. 20
    While offering peace sincere and just,
    In Heaven we place a manly trust,
    That truth and justice will prevail,
    And every scheme of bondage fail.

    Firm, united, etc.

Sound, sound, the trump of fame!
Let WASHINGTON's great name
  Ring through the world with loud applause;
  Ring through the world with loud applause;
Let every clime to freedom dear,
Listen with a joyful ear. 30
    With equal skill, and godlike power,
    He governed in the fearful hour

---

[1] Hopkinson wrote the song to a popular piece of music "President's March."
[2] Throughout the eighteenth century *joined* and many other words of similar *oi* formation were pronounced to rime with *find*.

Of horrid war; or guides, with ease,
The happier times of honest peace.

    Firm, united, etc.

Behold the chief who now commands, [3]
Once more to serve his country, stands—
  The rock on which the storm will beat,
  The rock on which the storm will beat;
But, armed in virtue firm and true,
His hopes are fixed on Heaven and you. 40
    When hope was sinking in dismay,
    And glooms obscured Columbia's day,
    His steady mind, from changes free,
    Resolved on death or liberty.

    Firm, united, let us be,
    Rallying round our liberty;
    As a band of brothers joined,
    Peace and safety we shall find.

1798   1798

CHARLES BROCKDEN BROWN 1771-1810

To Brown belongs the distinction of being the first American novelist. He was born in Philadelphia and died there of consumption in his fortieth year. He received a good classical schooling, studied law, but soon took up literary work in verse and prose; he was the first American to make imaginative literature his calling. He was the editor of several literary magazines, but his name is remembered for his novels, of which he wrote seven between 1797 and 1801. Of these the foremost are *Wieland*, 1798, and *Arthur Mervyn*, 1799, the latter being founded upon the actual experience of Brown in the yellow fever scourge in New York City.

Brown was a man of sensitive spirit, shy and dreamy, but a pleasing companion. He had high ideals in fiction which, from lack of first-class ability and robust health, he could never reach. In his day the "Gothic" novel was in vogue. A leading characteristic of this type of fiction was the portrayal of horror for horror's sake. Brown, in following Mrs. Radcliffe and "Monk" Lewis, English novelists of the "Gothic" vogue, went even beyond them in picturing how the senses and the intellect respond to situations of the utmost horror. He was, however, in some respects, a realist; the scenes of his novels and the incidents worked into them are American and in many cases record fact, or incidents taken for fact, as well as beliefs and superstitions current in the country in his time. The terrible tragedy in *Wieland* was doubtless suggested by a tale told in an American newspaper (See *Nation* 99:577-8) of the murder of a family by the father, a religious maniac. This novel, the best of Brown's, is formed of extraordinary incidents cast into a highly exciting plot. This plot too often depends on the chance coincidence of events,

---

[3] Congress had voted an army for the expected war and had placed Washington in command.

but shows great ingenuity on the author's part. The effects it produces are sometimes highly dramatic, and sometimes decidedly stagy. Woven into the story is an element of mystery on a higher plane than the merely ghastly, and never wholly solved. The atmosphere of the occult and the horrible in Brown may profitably be compared in detail with the like elements in the work of Hawthorne and Poe.

J. Erskine, *Leading American Novelists*, 1910; A. R. Marble, "Centenary of America's First Novelist," *Dial* 48:109-10; C. Van Doren, "Early American Realism," *Nation* 99:577-8.

From WIELAND [1]
OR
THE TRANSFORMATION
CHAPTER XVI

As soon as I arrived in sight of the front of the house, my attention was excited by a light from the window of my own chamber. No appearance could be less explicable. A meeting was expected with Carwin; but that he preoccupied my chamber, and had supplied himself with light, was not to be believed. What motive could influence him to adopt this conduct? Could I proceed until this was explained? Perhaps, if I should proceed to a distance in front, someone would be visible. A sidelong but feeble beam from the window fell upon the piny copse which skirted the bank. As I eyed it, it suddenly became mutable, [2] and, after flitting to and fro for a short time, it vanished. I turned my eye again towards the window, and per-

---

[1] The Wieland family is beset with mysterious phenomena. The first group of these, accompanied with the appearance of fire and attending the death of the father, are never fully explained, and lead the younger Wieland and his sister Clara to regard as connected with these and equally inexplicable, a second series consisting of mysterious voices. The latter are, in fact, produced by Carwin, a ventriloquist, who in wanton mischief imposes upon the family. Clara Wieland has every reason to fear Carwin as a villain in whose presence she is unsafe. Wieland, inheriting insanity, is played upon by Carwin through the voices until his mind suddenly gives way. In a religious mania he kills his wife, Catharine, who happens to be in his sister's house, and immediately goes home and destroys his own children.

The extract begins at this point. Clara, who tells the tale throughout, is returning late at night to her own home, where she lives with a single servant. She is expecting yet fearing to meet Carwin there. It is actually his face that she sees and his voice that she hears. Though she is really in no physical danger from Carwin, and he in fact tries to prevent her by means of his ventriloquial voice from entering the room where her sister-in-law lies murdered, she immediately concludes upon discovering the body that he has planned her own death, but by some mistake has killed her sister-in-law.

[2] Brown's pages abound in such indirect, sometimes quite obscure, phrasings.

ceived that the light was still there; but the change which I had noticed was occasioned by a change in the position of the lamp or candle within. Hence, that some person was there was an unavoidable inference.

I paused to deliberate on the propriety of advancing. Might I not advance cautiously, and, therefore, without danger? Might I not knock at the door, or call, and be apprised of the nature of my visitant before I entered? I approached and listened at the door, but could hear nothing. I knocked at first timidly, but afterwards with loudness. My signals were unnoticed. I stepped back and looked, but the light was no longer discernible. Was it suddenly extinguished by a human agent? What purpose but concealment was intended? Why was the illumination produced, to be thus suddenly brought to an end? And why, since someone was there, had silence been observed?

These were questions the solution of which may be readily supposed to be entangled with danger. Would not this danger, when measured by a woman's fears, expand into gigantic dimensions? Menaces of death; the stunning exertions of a warning voice; the known and unknown attributes of Carwin; our recent interview in this chamber; the preappointment of a meeting at this place and hour,—all thronged into my memory. What was to be done?

Courage is no definite or steadfast principle. Let that man who shall purpose to assign motives to the actions of another blush at his folly and forbear. Not more presumptuous would it be to attempt the classification of all nature and the scanning of supreme intelligence. I gazed for a minute at the window, and fixed my eyes, for a second minute, on the ground. I drew forth from my pocket, and opened, a penknife. "This," said I, "be my safeguard and avenger. The assailant shall perish, or myself shall fall."

I had locked up the house in the morning, but had the key of the kitchen door in my pocket. I therefore determined to gain access behind. Thither I hastened, unlocked, and entered. All was lonely, darksome, and waste. Familiar as I was with every part of my dwelling, I easily found my way to a closet, drew forth a taper, a flint, tinder, and steel, and in a moment, as it were, gave myself the guidance and protection of light.

What purpose did I meditate? Should I explore my way to my chamber, and confront the being who had dared to intrude into this recess and had labored for concealment? By putting out the light did he seek to hide himself, or mean only to circumvent my incautious steps? Yet was it not more probable that he desired my absence by thus encouraging the supposition that the house was unoccupied? I would see this man in spite of all impediments; ere I died, I would see his face, and summon him to penitence and retribution; no matter at what cost an interview was purchased. Reputation and life might be wrested from me by another, but my rectitude and honor were in my own keeping, and were safe.

I proceeded to the foot of the stairs. At such a crisis my thoughts may be supposed at no liberty to range; yet vague images rushed into my mind of the mysterious interposition which had been experienced on the last night. [1] My case at present was not dissimilar; and, if my angel were not weary of fruitless exertions to save, might not a new warning be expected? Who could say whether his silence were ascribable to the absence of danger, or to his own absence?

In this state of mind, no wonder that a shivering cold crept through my veins; that my pause was prolonged; and that a fearful glance was thrown backward.

Alas! My heart droops, and my fingers are enervated; my ideas are vivid, but my language is faint: now know I what it is to entertain incommunicable sentiments. The chain of subsequent incidents is drawn through my mind, and, being linked with those which forewent, by turns rouse [2] up agonies and sink me into hopelessness.

Yet I will persist to the end. My narrative may be invaded by inaccuracy and confusion; but, if I live no longer, I will, at least, live to complete it. What but ambiguities, abruptnesses, and dark transitions, can be expected from the historian who is, at the same time, the sufferer of these disasters?

I have said that I cast a look behind. Some object was expected to be seen, or why should I have gazed in that direction? Two senses were at once assailed. The same piercing exclamation of "Hold! hold!" was uttered within the same distance of my ear. This it was that I heard. The airy undulation, and the shock given to my nerves, were real. Whether the spectacle which I beheld existed in my fancy or without might be doubted.

I had not closed the door of the apartment I had just left. The staircase, at the foot of which I stood, was eight or ten feet from the door, and attached to the wall through which the door led. My view, therefore, was sidelong, and took in no part of the room.

Through this aperture was a head thrust and drawn back with so much swiftness that the immediate conviction was, that thus much of a form ordinarily invisible had been unshrouded. The face was turned towards me. Every muscle was tense; the forehead and brows were drawn into vehement expression; the lips were stretched as in the act of shrieking, and the eyes emitted sparks, which, no doubt, if I had been unattended by a light, would have illuminated like the coruscations of a meteor. The sound and the vision were present, and departed together at the same instant; but the cry was blown into my ear, while the face was many paces distant.

This face was well suited to a being whose performances exceeded the standard of humanity; and yet its features were akin to those I had before seen. The image of Carwin was blended in a thousand ways with the stream of my thoughts. This visage was, perhaps, portrayed by my fancy. If so, it will excite no surprise that some of his lineaments were now discovered. Yet affinities were few and inconspicuous, and were lost amidst the blaze of opposite qualities.

What conclusion could I form? Be the face human or not, the intimation was imparted from above. [3] Experience had evinced the benignity of that being who gave it. Once he had interposed to shield me from harm, and subsequent events demonstrated the usefulness of that interposition. Now was I again warned to forbear. I was hurrying to the verge of the same gulf, and the same power was exerted to recall my steps. Was it possible for me not to obey? Was I capable of holding on in the same perilous career? Yes. Even of this I was capable!

The intimation was imperfect; it gave no form to my danger and prescribed no limits to my caution. I had formerly neglected it, and yet escaped. Might I not trust to the same issue? This idea might possess, though imperceptibly, some influence. I persisted; but it was not merely on this account. I cannot delineate the motives that led me on. I now speak as if no remnant of doubt existed in my mind as to the supernatural origin of these sounds; but this is owing to the imperfection of my language, for I only mean that the belief was more permanent and visited more frequently my sober meditations than its opposite.

---

[1] when the mysterious voice, apparently of a guardian presence, had held her back from danger
[2] Brown's sentences are often, as here, loose and incorrect.

[3] as if by her good angel

The immediate effects served only to undermine the foundations of my judgment and precipitate my resolutions. [1]

I must either advance or return. I chose the former, and began to ascend the stairs. The silence underwent no second interruption. My chamber door was closed, but unlocked, and, aided by vehement efforts of my courage, I opened and looked in.

No hideous or uncommon object was discernible. The danger, indeed, might easily have lurked out of sight, have sprung upon me as I entered, and have rent me with his iron talons; but I was blind to this fate, and advanced, though cautiously, into the room.

Still, everything wore its accustomed aspect. Neither lamp nor candle was to be found. Now, for the first time, suspicions were suggested as to the nature of the light which I had seen. Was it possible to have been the companion of that supernatural visage; a meteorous refulgence producible at the will of him to whom that visage belonged, and partaking of the nature of that which accompanied my father's death?

The closet was near, and I remembered the complicated horrors of which it had been productive. [2] Here, perhaps, was enclosed the source of my peril and the gratification of my curiosity. Should I adventure once more to explore its recesses? This was a resolution not easily formed. I was suspended in thought when, glancing my eye on the table, I perceived a written paper. Carwin's hand was instantly recognized, and, snatching up the paper, I read as follows:—

"There was folly in expecting your compliance with my invitation. Judge how I was disappointed in finding another in your place. I have waited, but to wait any longer would be perilous. I shall still seek an interview, but it must be at a different time and place; meanwhile, I will write this—How will you bear— how inexplicable will be this transaction!—An event so unexpected,—a sight so horrible!"

Such was this abrupt and unsatisfactory script. The ink was yet moist; the hand was that of Carwin. Hence it was to be inferred that he had this moment left the apartment, or was still in it. I looked back, on the sudden expectation of seeing him behind me.

What other did he mean? What transaction had taken place adverse to my expectations? What sight was about to be exhibited? I looked around me once more, but saw nothing which indicated strangeness. Again I remembered the closet, and was resolved to seek in that the solution of these mysteries. Here, perhaps, was enclosed the scene destined to awaken my horrors and baffle my foresight.

I have already said that the entrance into this closet was beside my bed, which, on two sides, was closely shrouded by curtains. On that side nearest the closet the curtain was raised. As I passed along I cast my eye thither. I started, and looked again. I bore a light in my hand, and brought it nearer my eyes, in order to dispel any illusive mists that might have hovered before them. Once more I fixed my eyes upon the bed, in hope that this more steadfast scrutiny would annihilate the object which before seemed to be there.

This, then, was the sight which Carwin had predicted! This was the event which my understanding was to find inexplicable! This was the fate which had been reserved for me, but which, by some untoward chance, had befallen another!

I had not been terrified by empty menaces. Violation and death awaited my entrance into this chamber. Some inscrutable chance had led *her* hither before me, and the merciless fangs of which I was designed to be the prey had mistaken their victim, and had fixed themselves in *her* heart. But where was my safety? Was the mischief exhausted or flown? The steps of the assassin had just been here; they could not be far off; in a moment he would rush into my presence, and I should perish under the same polluting and suffocating grasp!

My frame shook, and my knees were unable to support me. I gazed alternately at the closet door and at the door of my room. At one of these avenues would enter the exterminator of my honor and my life. I was prepared for defense; but, now that danger was imminent, my means of defense and my power to use them were gone. I was not qualified by education and experience to encounter perils like these; or perhaps I was powerless because I was again assaulted by surprise, and had not fortified my mind by foresight and previous reflection against a scene like this.

Fears for my own safety again yielded place to reflections on the scene before me. I fixed my eyes upon her countenance. My sister's [3] well-known and beloved features could not be

---

[1] Such situations are the joy of the modern psychological novelist. Brown merely states the real or supposed facts, without analysis, and gives the conclusion. Compare Poe and Hawthorne.

[2] Before this, Carwin had concealed himself there and terrified Clara by means of the mysterious voice.

[3] sister-in-law's

concealed by convulsion or lividness. What direful illusion led thee hither? Bereft of thee, what hold on happiness remains to thy off-spring and thy spouse? To lose thee by a common fate would have been sufficiently hard; but thus suddenly to perish,—to become the prey of this ghastly death! How will a spectacle like this be endured by Wieland? To die beneath his grasp would not satisfy thy enemy. This was mercy to the evils which he previously made thee suffer! After these evils death was a boon which thou besoughtest him to grant. He entertained no enmity against thee; I was the object of his treason; but by some tremendous mistake his fury was misplaced. But how comest thou hither? and where was Wieland in thy hour of distress?

I approached the corpse; I lifted the still flexible hand, and kissed the lips which were breathless. Her flowing drapery was discomposed. I restored it to order, and, seating myself on the bed, again fixed steadfast eyes upon her countenance. I cannot distinctly recollect the ruminations of that moment. I saw confusedly, but forcibly, that every hope was extinguished with the life of Catharine. All happiness and dignity must henceforth be banished from the house and name of Wieland; all that remained was to linger out in agonies a short existence and leave to the world a monument of blasted hopes and changeable fortune. Pleyel [1] was already lost to me; yet, while Catharine lived, life was not a destestable possession. But now, severed from the companion of my infancy, the partaker of all my thoughts, my cares, and my wishes, I was like one set afloat upon a stormy sea and hanging his safety upon a plank; night was closing upon him, and an unexpected surge had torn him from his hold and overwhelmed him forever. [2]

CHAPTER XXV

. . . . "Sister," said he, [3] in an accent mournful and mild, "I have acted poorly my part in this world. What thinkest

[1] Catharine's brother, whom Clara loved but who had been turned against Clara by Carwin
[2] The scene in its possibilities of physical terror is scarcely equaled elsewhere by Brown. Contrast his handling of it with that of the usual treatment of such scenes a century later.
[3] In the interval, Wieland has been confined in a mad-house, possessed now with the idea that he must add Clara to his quota of religious sacrifices. Carwin, unaware of the tragedy for which he is partly responsible, comes to explain himself to Clara in her own house. He confesses the source of the voices but honestly disavows any criminal intent. At this moment Wieland himself appears, wild and tattered, just escaped from his keepers, and bent upon the death of Clara. At intervals he appears lucid. It is he who speaks.

thou? Shall I not do better in the next?"

I could make no answer. The mildness of his tone astonished and encouraged me. I continued to regard him with wistful and anxious looks.

"I think," resumed he, "I will try. My wife and my babes have gone before. Happy wretches! I have sent you to repose, and ought not to linger behind."

These words had a meaning sufficiently intelligible. I looked at the open knife in his hand and shuddered, but knew not how to prevent the deed which I dreaded. He quickly noticed my fears, and comprehended them. Stretching towards me his hand, with an air of increasing mildness, "Take it," said he; "fear not for thy own sake, nor for mine. The cup is gone by, and its transient inebriation is succeeded by the soberness of truth.

"Thou angel whom I was wont to worship! Fearest, thou, my sister, for thy life? Once it was the scope of my labors to destroy thee, but I was prompted to the deed by heaven; such, at least, was my belief. Thinkest thou that thy death was sought to gratify malevolence? No. I am pure from all stain. I believed that my God was my mover!

"Neither thee nor myself have I cause to injure. I have done my duty; and surely there is merit in having sacrificed to that all that is dear to the heart of man. If a devil has deceived me, he came in the habit of an angel. If I erred, it was not my judgment that deceived me, but my senses. In thy sight, Being of beings! I am still pure. Still will I look for my reward in thy justice!"

Did my ears truly report these sounds? If I did not err, my brother was restored to just perceptions. He knew himself to have been betrayed to the murder of his wife and children, to have been the victim of infernal artifice; yet he found consolation in the rectitude of his motives. He was not devoid of sorrow, for this was written on his countenance; but his soul was tranquil and sublime.

Perhaps this was merely a transition of his former madness into a new shape. Perhaps he had not yet awakened to the memory of the horrors which he had perpetrated. Infatuated wretch that I was! To set myself up as a model by which to judge of my heroic brother! My reason taught me that his conclusions were right; but, conscious of the impotence of reason over my own conduct, conscious of my cowardly rashness and my criminal despair, I doubted whether anyone could be steadfast and wise.

Such was my weakness, that even in the midst of these thoughts my mind glided into abhorrence of Carwin, and I uttered, in a low voice. "O Carwin! Carwin! what hast thou to answer for?"

My brother immediately noticed the involuntary exclamation. "Clara!" said he, "be thyself. Equity used to be a theme for thy eloquence. Reduce its lessons to practice, and be just to that unfortunate man. The instrument has done its work, and I am satisfied.

"I thank thee, my God, for this last illumination! My enemy is thine also. I deemed him to be man,—the man with whom I have often communed; but now thy goodness has unveiled to me his true nature. As the performer of thy behests, he is my friend."

My heart began now to misgive me. His mournful aspect had gradually yielded place to a serene brow. A new soul appeared to actuate his frame, and his eyes to beam with preternatural luster. These symptoms did not abate, and he continued:—

"Clara, I must not leave thee in doubt. I know not what brought about thy interview with the being whom thou callest Carwin. For a time I was guilty of thy error, and deduced from his incoherent confessions that I had been made the victim of human malice. He left us at my bidding, and I put up a prayer that my doubts should be removed. Thy eyes were shut and thy ears sealed to the vision that answered my prayer.

"I was indeed deceived. The form thou hast seen was the incarnation of a demon. The visage and voice which urged me to the sacrifice of my family were his. Now he personates a human form; then he was environed with the luster of heaven.

"Clara," he continued, advancing closer to me, "thy death must come. This minister is evil, but he from whom his commission was received is God. Submit then with all thy wonted resignation to a decree that cannot be reversed or resisted. Mark the clock. Three minutes are allowed to thee, in which to call up thy fortitude and prepare thee for thy doom." There he stopped.

Even now, when this scene exists only in memory, when life and all its functions have sunk into torpor, my pulse throbs, and my hairs uprise; my brows are knit, as then, and I gaze around me in distraction. I was unconquerably averse to death; but death, imminent and full of agony as that which was threatened, was nothing. This was not the only or chief inspirer of my fears.

For him, not for myself, was my soul tormented. I might die, and no crime, surpassing the reach of mercy, would pursue me to the presence of my Judge; but my assassin would survive to contemplate his deed, and that assassin was Wieland!

Wings to bear me beyond his reach I had not. I could not vanish with a thought. The door was open, but my murderer was interposed between that and me. Of self-defense I was incapable. The frenzy that lately prompted me to blood was gone: my state was desperate; my rescue was impossible.

The weight of these accumulated thoughts could not be borne. My sight became confused; my limbs were seized with convulsions; I spoke, but my words were half formed:—

"Spare me, my brother! Look down, righteous Judge! snatch me from this fate! take away this fury from him, or turn it elsewhere!"

Such was the agony of my thoughts that I noticed not steps entering my apartment. Supplicating eyes were cast upward; but when my prayer was breathed I once more wildly gazed at the door. A form met my sight; I shuddered as if the God whom I invoked were present. It was Carwin that again intruded, and who stood before me, erect in attitude and steadfast in look!

The sight of him awakened new and rapid thoughts. His recent tale was remembered; his magical transitions and mysterious energy of voice. Whether he were infernal or miraculous or human, there was no power and no need to decide. Whether the contriver or not of this spell, he was able to unbind it, and to check the fury of my brother. He had ascribed to himself intentions not malignant. Here now was afforded a test of his truth. Let him interpose, as from above; revoke the savage decree which the madness of Wieland has assigned to heaven, and extinguish forever this passion for blood!

My mind detected at a glance this avenue to safety. The recommendations it possessed thronged as it were together, and made but one impression on my intellect. Remoter effects and collateral dangers I saw not. Perhaps the pause of an instant had sufficed to call them up. The improbability that the influence which governed Wieland was external or human; the tendency of this stratagem to sanction so fatal an error or substitute a more destructive rage in place of this; the insufficiency of Carwin's mere muscular forces to counteract the efforts and restrain the fury of Wieland, might, at a second glance, have been discovered; but no second glance was allowed. My first thought hurried me to action, and, fixing my eyes upon Carwin, I exclaimed,—

"O wretch! once more hast thou come? Let it be to abjure thy malice; to counterwork this hellish stratagem; to turn from me and from my brother this desolating rage!

"Testify thy innocence or thy remorse; exert the powers which pertain to thee, whatever they be, to turn aside this ruin. Thou art the author of these horrors! What have I done to deserve thus to die? How have I merited this unrelenting persecution? I adjure thee, by that God whose voice thou hast dared to counterfeit, to save my life!

"Wilt thou then go?—leave me! Succorless!"

Carwin listened to my entreaties unmoved, and turned from me. He seemed to hesitate a moment,—then glided through the door. Rage and despair stifled my utterance. The interval of respite was past; the pangs reserved for me by Wieland were not to be endured; my thoughts rushed again into anarchy. Having received the knife from his hand, I held it loosely and without regard; but now it seized again my attention, and I grasped it with force.

He seemed to notice not the entrance or exit of Carwin. My gesture and the murderous weapon appeared to have escaped his notice. His silence was unbroken; his eye, fixed upon the clock for a time, was now withdrawn; fury kindled in every feature; all that was human in his face gave way to an expression supernatural and tremendous. I felt my left arm within his grasp.

Even now I hesitated to strike. I shrunk from his assault, but in vain.

Here let me desist. Why should I rescue this event from oblivion? Why should I paint this detestable conflict? Why not terminate at once this series of horrors?—Hurry to the verge of the precipice, and cast myself forever beyond remembrance and beyond hope?

Still I live; with this load upon my breast; with this phantom to pursue my steps; with adders lodged in my bosom, and stinging me to madness; still I consent to live!

Yes! I will rise above the sphere of mortal passions; I will spurn at the cowardly remorse that bids me seek impunity in silence, or comfort in forgetfulness. My nerves shall be new-strung to the task. Have I not resolved? I will die. The gulf before me is inevitable and near. I will die, but then only when my tale is at an end.

Chapter XXVI

My right hand, grasping the unseen knife, was still disengaged. It was lifted to strike. All my strength was exhausted but what was sufficient to the performance of this deed. Already was the energy awakened and the impulse given that should bear the fatal steel to his heart, when—Wieland shrunk back; his hand was withdrawn. Breathless with affright and desperation, I stood, freed from his grasp; unassailed; untouched.

Thus long had the power which controlled the scene forborne to interfere: but now his might was irresistible; and Wieland in a moment was disarmed of all his purposes. A voice, louder than human organs could produce, shriller than language can depict, burst from the ceiling and commanded him—*to hold!*

Trouble and dismay succeeded to the steadfastness that had lately been displayed in the looks of Wieland. His eyes roved from one quarter to another, with an expression of doubt. He seemed to wait for a further intimation.

Carwin's agency was here easily recognized. I had besought him to interpose in my defense. He had flown. I had imagined him deaf to my prayer, and resolute to see me perish; yet he disappeared merely to devise and execute the means of my relief.

Why did he not forbear when this end was accomplished. Why did his misjudging zeal and accursed precipitation overpass that limit? Or meant he thus to crown the scene, and conduct his inscrutable plots to this consummation?

Such ideas were the fruit of subsequent contemplation. This moment was pregnant with fate. I had no power to reason. In the career of my tempestuous thoughts, rent into pieces as my mind was by accumulating horrors, Carwin was unseen and unsuspected. I partook of Wieland's credulity, shook with his amazement, and panted with his awe.

Silence took place for a moment: so much as allowed the attention to recover its post. Then new sounds were uttered from above:—

"Man of errors! cease to cherish thy delusion; not heaven or hell, but thy senses, have misled thee to commit these acts. Shake off thy frenzy, and ascend into rational and human. Be lunatic no longer."

My brother opened his lips to speak. His tone was terrific [1] and faint. He muttered an appeal to heaven. It was difficult to comprehend the theme of his inquiries. They

---

[1] terror-struck (loosely used)

implied doubt as to the nature of the impulse that hitherto had guided him, and questioned whether he had acted in consequence of insane perceptions.

To these interrogatories the voice, which now seemed to hover at his shoulder, loudly answered in the affirmative. Then uninterrupted silence ensued.

Fallen from his lofty and heroic station; now finally restored to the perception of truth; weighed to earth by the recollection of his own deeds; consoled no longer by a consciousness of rectitude for the loss of offspring and wife,— a loss for which he was indebted to his own misguided hand,—Wieland was transformed [1] at once into the *man of sorrows!*

He reflected not that credit should be as reasonably denied to the last as to any former intimation; that one might as justly be ascribed to erring or diseased senses as the other. He saw not that this discovery in no degree affected the integrity of his conduct; that his motives had lost none of their claims to the homage of mankind; that the preference of supreme good, and the boundless energy of duty, were undiminished in his bosom.

It is not for me to pursue him through the ghastly changes of his countenance. Words he had none. Now he sat upon the floor, motionless in all his limbs, with his eyes glazed and fixed, a monument of woe.

Anon a spirit of tempestuous but undesigning activity seized him. He rose from his place and strode across the floor, tottering and at random. His eyes were without moisture, and gleamed with the fire that consumed his vitals. The muscles of his face were agitated by convulsions. His lips moved, but no sound escaped him.

That nature should long sustain this conflict was not to be believed. My state was little different from that of my brother. I entered, as it were, into his thoughts. My heart was visited and rent by his pangs. "Oh that thy frenzy had never been cured! that thy madness, with its blissful visions, would return! or, if that must not be, that thy scene would hasten to a close!—that death would cover thee with his oblivion!

"What can I wish for thee? Thou who hast vied with the great Preacher of thy faith in sanctity of motives, and in elevation above sensual and selfish? Thou whom thy fate has changed into parricide and savage! Can I wish for the continuance of thy being? No."

---

[1] See the sub-title at the head of the selection.

For a time his movements seemed destitute of purpose. If he walked; if he turned; if his fingers were entwined with each other; if his hands were pressed against opposite sides of his head with a force sufficient to crush it into pieces; it was to tear his mind from self-contemplation; to waste his thoughts on external objects.

Speedily this train was broken. A beam appeared to be darted into his mind which gave a purpose to his efforts. An avenue to escape presented itself; and now he eagerly gazed about him. When my thoughts became engaged by his demeanor, my fingers were stretched as by a mechanical force, and the knife, no longer heeded or of use, escaped from my grasp and fell unperceived on the floor. His eye now lighted upon it; he seized it with the quickness of thought.

I shrieked aloud, but it was too late. He plunged it to the hilt in his neck; and his life instantly escaped with the stream that gushed from the wound. He was stretched at my feet and my hands were sprinkled with his blood as he fell.

Such was thy last deed, my brother! For a spectacle like this was it my fate to be reserved! Thy eyes were closed—thy face ghastly with death—thy arms, and the spot where thou lyedst, [2] floated in thy life's blood! These images have not for a moment forsaken me. Till I am breathless and cold, they must continue to hover in my sight. . . .

1788   1798

WASHINGTON IRVING 1783-1859

Little that is new can be said regarding Irving, whose youthful wit softened into grace, and whose graciousness ripened into benignity; who gained the first continental recognition given an American author; and who was made by his government first of a long line of "literary diplomats" to represent it abroad. He was born of parents in comfortable circumstances, was privately educated, studied law but inclined toward literature. He traveled in Europe, 1805-1806, and was in journalism and business in New York until 1815, when he went to England on business, and remained in Europe for seventeen years. He was (1826-1832) attaché of the American legation at Madrid and secretary to that at London. He then settled at "Sunnyside," his little estate on the Hudson, but was United States minister to Spain, 1842-1846. His chief works are *Knickerbocker's History of New York,* 1809; *Sketch-Book,* 1819; *Bracebridge Hall,* 1822; *Tales of a Traveller,* 1824; *History of Columbus,* 1828; *A*

---

[2] The form of the verb should be "layest."

Chronicle of the Conquest of Granada, 1829; *The Alhambra*, 1832; *Crayon Miscellanies*, 1835; *Astoria*, 1836; *Life of Goldsmith*, 1849; *Life of Washington*, 1855-1859.

The qualities of Irving's style are obvious. In it are found the grace of Addison, humor and kindliness that reach the mark set by Goldsmith, and a zest born of new adventure.

Irving was fortunate in his ability to become a citizen of the world, to see the fineness in English life and to interpret it to Americans; and to give his fellow countrymen such an account of the lands overseas as to make them eager to find in the culture of Europe what he had discovered. In this service Irving's work was greatly fruitful, for it came forth in all its popularity in a period when many Americans were inclined to be jealous of other peoples, and to be filled with national self-conceit. But American literature owes an even greater debt to Irving's original and imaginative treatment of American themes.

C. D. Warner (AML), 1888; G. S. Hellman, *W. Irving, Esq.*, 1925; Tuckerman (LJ); Macy; Payne; Chubb; H. S. Canby, "Irving as a Federalist," *Sat. R. Lit.* 3:461-3.

From A HISTORY OF NEW YORK, [1]

BY DIEDRICH KNICKERBOCKER

Book III

IN WHICH IS RECORDED THE GOLDEN REIGN OF WOUTER VAN TWILLER

CHAPTER I

OF THE RENOWNED WOUTER VAN TWILLER, [2] HIS UNPARALLELED VIRTUES—AS LIKEWISE HIS UNUTTERABLE WISDOM IN THE LAW-CASE OF WANDLE SCHOONHOVEN AND BARENT BLEECKER—AND THE GREAT ADMIRATION OF THE PUBLIC THEREAT.

Grievous and very much to be commiserated is the task of the feeling historian, who writes the history of his native land. If it fall to his lot to be the recorder of calamity or crime, the mournful page is watered with his tears; nor can he recall the most prosperous and blissful era, without a melancholy sigh at the reflection that it has passed away forever! I know not whether it be owing to an immoderate love for the simplicity of former times, or to that certain tenderness of heart incident to all sentimental historians; but I candidly confess that I cannot look back on the happier days of our city, which I now describe, without great dejection of spirit. With faltering hand do I withdraw the curtain of oblivion that veils the modest merit of our venerable ancestors, and as their figures rise to my mental vision, humble myself before their mighty shades.

Such are my feelings when I revisit the family mansion of the Knickerbockers, and spend a lonely hour in the chamber where hang the portraits of my forefathers, shrouded in dust, like the forms they represent. With pious reverence do I gaze on the countenances of those renowned burghers, who have preceded me in the steady march of existence,—whose sober and temperate blood now meanders through my veins, flowing slower and slower in its feeble conduits, until its current shall soon be stopped forever!

These, I say to myself, are but frail memorials of the mighty men who flourished in the days of the patriarchs; but who, alas, have long since moldered in that tomb towards which my steps are insensibly and irresistibly hastening! As I pace the darkened chamber and lose myself in melancholy musings, the shadowy images around me almost seem to steal once more into existence,—their countenances to assume the animation of life,—their eyes to pursue me in every movement! Carried away by the delusions of fancy, I almost imagine myself surrounded by the shades of the departed, and holding sweet converse with the worthies of antiquity! Ah, hapless Diedrich! born in a degenerate age, abandoned to the buffetings of fortune,—a stranger and a weary pilgrim in thy native land,—blest with no weeping wife, nor family of helpless children, but doomed to wander neglected through those crowded streets, and elbowed by foreign upstarts from those fair abodes where once thine ancestors held sovereign empire!

Let me not, however, lose the historian in the man, nor suffer the doting recollections of age to overcome me, while dwelling with fond garrulity on the virtuous days of the patriarchs, —on those sweet days of simplicity and ease, which never more will dawn on the lovely island of Manna-hata. [3]

---

[1] The Knickerbocker *History of New York* "from the beginning of the world to the end of the Dutch dynasty" was written and published, Irving says, as a "temporary *jeu d'esprit*" (play of wit). Its nominal author, Diedrich Knickerbocker, disappeared and left behind a manuscript which his landlord seized and sold and which was finally published as the *History*. The old Dutch aristocracy of New York, or New Amsterdam as it was formerly called, at first felt itself scandalized at the free treatment of its ancestors, but for the most part soon forgave the author because of the sheer good humor of the whole work. See Irving's introduction to *Rip Van Winkle*, p. 188.

[2] born in Holland about 1580; governor of New Netherlands 1633-1637

[3] Manhattan, the Indian name of the island on which New York stands

These melancholy reflections have been forced from me by the growing wealth and importance of New Amsterdam, which, I plainly perceive, are to involve it in all kinds of perils and disasters. Already, as I observed at the close of my last book, they had awakened the attentions of the mother-country. The usual mark of protection shown by mother-countries to wealthy colonies was forthwith manifested; a governor being sent out to rule over the province, and squeeze out of it as much revenue as possible. The arrival of a governor of course put an end to the protectorate of Oloffe the Dreamer. [1] He appears, however, to have dreamt to some purpose during his sway, as we find him afterwards living as a patroon [2] on a great landed estate on the banks of the Hudson; having virtually forfeited all right to his ancient appellation of Kortlandt or Lackland.

It was in the year of our Lord 1629 [3] that Mynheer Wouter Van Twiller was appointed governor of the province of Nieuw Nederlandts, under the commission and control of their High Mightinesses the Lords States General of the United Netherlands, and the privileged West India Company.

This renowned old gentleman arrived at New Amsterdam in the merry month of June, the sweetest month in all the year; when dan Apollo [4] seems to dance up the transparent firmament,—when the robin, the thrush, and a thousand other wanton songsters, make the woods to resound with amorous ditties, and the luxurious little boblincon [5] revels among the clover blossoms of the meadows,—all which happy coincidence persuaded the old dames of New Amsterdam, who were skilled in the art of foretelling events, that this was to be a happy and prosperous administration.

The renowned Wouter (or Walter) Van Twiller was descended from a long line of Dutch burgomasters, who had successively dozed away their lives, and grown fat upon the bench of magistracy in Rotterdam; and who had comported themselves with such singular wisdom and propriety, that they were never either heard or talked of—which, next to being universally applauded, should be the object of ambition of all magistrates and rulers. There are two opposite ways by which some men make a figure in the world: one, by talking faster than they think, and the other, by holding their tongues and not thinking at all. By the first, many a smatterer acquires the reputation of a man of quick parts; by the other, many a dunderpate, like the owl, the stupidest of birds, comes to be considered the very type of wisdom. This, by the way, is a casual remark, which I would not, for the universe, have it thought I apply to Governor Van Twiller. It is true he was a man shut up within himself, like an oyster, and rarely spoke, except in monosyllables; but then it was allowed he seldom said a foolish thing. So invincible was his gravity that he was never known to laugh or even to smile through the whole course of a long and prosperous life. Nay, if a joke were uttered in his presence, that set light-minded hearers in a roar, it was observed to throw him into a state of perplexity. Sometimes he would deign to inquire into the matter, and when, after much explanation, the joke was made as plain as a pike-staff, he would continue to smoke his pipe in silence, and at length, knocking out the ashes, would exclaim, "Well! I see nothing in all that to laugh about."

With all his reflective habits, he never made up his mind on a subject. His adherents accounted for this by the astonishing magnitude of his ideas. He conceived every subject on so grand a scale that he had not room in his head to turn it over and examine both sides of it. Certain it is, that, if any matter were propounded to him on which ordinary mortals would rashly determine at first glance, he would put on a vague, mysterious look, shake his capacious head, smoke some time in profound silence, and at length observe, that 'he had his doubts about the matter'; which gained him the reputation of a man slow of belief and not easily imposed upon. What is more, it gained him a lasting name; for to this habit of the mind has been attributed his surname of Twiller; which is said to be a corruption of the original Twijfler, or, in plain English, Doubter.

The person of this illustrious old gentleman was formed and proportioned as though it had been molded by the hands of some cunning Dutch statuary, as a model of majesty and lordly grandeur. He was exactly five feet six inches in height, and six feet five inches in circumference. His head was a perfect sphere, and of such stupendous dimensions that Dame Nature, with all her sex's ingenuity, would have been puzzled to construct a neck capable of supporting it; wherefore she wisely declined the attempt, and settled it firmly on the top of his backbone, just between the shoulders.

---

[1] Oloffe Van Kortland (Shortland or Lackland), leader of the Dutch in their first settlement of Manhattan
[2] landed proprietor
[3] Irving's date is incorrect; see note 2, p. 178.
[4] Apollo, the sun-god; dan, from Latin, dominus (cf. Don), lord
[5] bobolink

His body was oblong and particularly capacious at bottom; which was wisely ordered by Providence, seeing that he was a man of sedentary habits, and very averse to the idle labor of walking. His legs were short, but sturdy in proportion to the weight they had to sustain; so that when erect he had not a little the appearance of a beer-barrel on skids. His face, that infallible index of the mind, presented a vast expanse, unfurrowed by any of those lines and angles which disfigure the human countenance with what is termed expression. Two small gray eyes twinkled feebly in the midst, like two stars of lesser magnitude in a hazy firmament, and his full-fed cheeks, which seemed to have taken toll of everything that went into his mouth, were curiously mottled and streaked with dusky red, like a spitzenburgh apple.

His habits were as regular as his person. He daily took his four stated meals, appropriating exactly an hour to each; he smoked and doubted eight hours, and he slept the remaining twelve of the four-and-twenty. Such was the renowned Wouter Van Twiller,—a true philosopher, for his mind was either elevated above, or tranquilly settled below, the cares and perplexities of this world. He had lived in it for years, without feeling the least curiosity to know whether the sun revolved round it, or it round the sun; and he had watched, for at least half a century, the smoke curling from his pipe to the ceiling, without once troubling his head with any of those numerous theories by which a philosopher would have perplexed his brain, in accounting for its rising above the surrounding atmosphere.

In his council he presided with great state and solemnity. He sat in a huge chair of solid oak, hewn in the celebrated forest of the Hague, fabricated by an experienced timmerman [1] of Amsterdam, and curiously carved about the arms and feet, into exact imitations of gigantic eagle's claws. Instead of a scepter he swayed a long Turkish pipe, wrought with jasmin and amber, which had been presented to a stadtholder [2] of Holland at the conclusion of a treaty with one of the petty Barbary powers. In this stately chair would he sit, and this magnificent pipe would he smoke, shaking his right knee with a constant motion, and fixing his eye for hours together upon a little print of Amsterdam, which hung in a black frame against the opposite wall of the council-chamber. Nay, it has even been said, that when any deliberation of

extraordinary length and intricacy was on the carpet, the renowned Wouter would shut his eyes for full two hours at a time, that he might not be disturbed by external objects; and at such times the internal commotion of his mind was evinced by certain regular guttural sounds, which his admirers declared were merely the noise of conflict made by his contending doubts and opinions.

It is with infinite difficulty I have been enabled to collect these biographical anecdotes of the great man under consideration. The facts respecting him were so scattered and vague, and divers of them so questionable in point of authenticity, that I have had to give up the search after many, and decline the admission of still more, which would have tended to heighten the coloring of his portrait.

I have been the more anxious to delineate fully the person and habits of Wouter Van Twiller, from the consideration that he was not only the first, but also the best governor that ever presided over this ancient and respectable province; and so tranquil and benevolent was his reign, that I do not find throughout the whole of it a single instance of any offender being brought to punishment,—a most indubitable sign of a merciful governor, and a case unparalleled, excepting in the reign of the illustrious King Log, [3] from whom, it is hinted, the renowned Van Twiller was a lineal descendant.

The very outset of the career of this excellent magistrate was distinguished by an example of legal acumen that gave flattering presage of a wise and equitable administration. The morning after he had been installed in office, and at the moment that he was making his breakfast from a prodigious earthen dish filled with milk and Indian pudding, he was interrupted by the appearance of Wandle Schoonhoven, a very important old burgher of New Amsterdam, who complained bitterly of one Barent Bleecker, inasmuch as he refused to come to a settlement of accounts, seeing that there was a heavy balance in favor of the said Wandle. Governor Van Twiller, as I have already observed, was a man of few words; he was likewise a mortal enemy to multiplying writings—or being disturbed at his breakfast. Having listened attentively to the statement of Wandle Schoonhoven, giving an occasional grunt as he shoveled a spoonful of Indian pudding into his mouth,—

---

[1] carpenter (Dutch)
[2] governor

[3] A phlegmatic monarch; from the story of Aesop that the frogs, wishing a king, were given by Jove a log of wood. When they complained, they were given for monarch a stork, who ate them up.

either as a sign that he relished the dish, or comprehended the story,—he called unto him his constable, and pulling out of his breeches-pocket a huge jack-knife, dispatched it after the defendant as a summons, accompanied by his tobacco-box as a warrant.

This summary process was as effectual in those simple days as was the seal-ring of the great Haroun Alraschid [1] among the true believers. The two parties being confronted before him, each produced a book of accounts, written in a language and character that would have puzzled any but a High-Dutch commentator, or a learned decipherer of Egyptian obelisks. The sage Wouter took them one after the other, and having poised them in his hands, and attentively counted over the number of leaves, fell straightway into a very great doubt, and smoked for half an hour without saying a word; at length, laying his finger beside his nose, and shutting his eyes for a moment, with the air of a man who has just caught a subtle idea by the tail, he slowly took his pipe from his mouth, puffed forth a column of tobacco smoke, and with marvelous gravity and solemnity pronounced, that, having carefully counted over the leaves and weighed the books, it was found, that one was just as thick and as heavy as the other: therefore, it was the final opinion of the court that the accounts were equally balanced: therefore, Wandle should give Barent a receipt, and Barent should give Wandle a receipt, and the constable should pay the costs.

This decision, being straightway made known, diffused general joy throughout New Amsterdam, for the people immediately perceived that they had a very wise and equitable magistrate to rule over them. But its happiest effect was, that not another lawsuit took place throughout the whole of his administration; and the office of constable fell into such decay, that there was not one of those losel scouts [2] known in the province for many years. I am the more particular in dwelling on this transaction, not only because I deem it one of the most sage and righteous judgments on record, and well worthy the attention of modern magistrates, but because it was a miraculous event in the history of the renowned Wouter—being the only time he was ever known to come to a decision in the whole course of his life.

[1] or "Aaron the Just," a celebrated Calif of Bagdad of the eighth century, well known through the *Arabian Nights*
[2] worthless sleuths

Chapter II

CONTAINING SOME ACCOUNT OF THE GRAND COUNCIL OF NEW AMSTERDAM, AS ALSO DIVERS ESPECIAL GOOD PHILOSOPHICAL REASONS WHY AN ALDERMAN SHOULD BE FAT—WITH OTHER PARTICULARS TOUCHING THE STATE OF THE PROVINCE.

In treating of the early governors of the province, I must caution my readers against confounding them, in point of dignity and power, with those worthy gentlemen who are whimsically denominated governors in this enlightened republic,—a set of unhappy victims of popularity, who are, in fact, the most dependent, henpecked beings in the community; doomed to bear the secret goadings and corrections of their own party, and the sneers and revilings of the whole world beside; set up, like geese at Christmas holidays, to be pelted and shot at by every whipster and vagabond in the land. On the contrary, the Dutch governors enjoyed that uncontrolled authority vested in all commanders of distant colonies or territories. They were, in a manner, absolute despots in their little domains, lording it, if so disposed, over both law and gospel, and accountable to none but the mother-country; which it is well known is astonishingly deaf to all complaints against its governors, provided they discharge the main duty of their station—squeezing out a good revenue. This hint will be of importance, to prevent my readers from being seized with doubt and incredulity, whenever, in the course of this authentic history, they encounter the uncommon circumstance of a governor acting with independence, and in opposition to the opinions of the multitude.

To assist the doubtful Wouter in the arduous business of legislation, a board of magistrates was appointed, which presided immediately over the police. This potent body consisted of a schout or bailiff, with powers between those of the present mayor and sheriff; five burgermeesters, who were equivalent to aldermen; and five schepens, who officiated as scrubs, subdevils, or bottle-holders to the burgermeesters, in the same manner as do assistant aldermen to their principals at the present day,—it being their duty to fill the pipes of the lordly burgermeesters, hunt the markets for delicacies for corporation dinners, and to discharge such other little offices of kindness as were occasionally required. It was, moreover, tacitly understood, though not specifically enjoined, that they should consider themselves as butts for the blunt wits of the burgermeesters, and should laugh most heartily at all their jokes; but this last was a duty as rarely called in action in those days as it is at present, and was shortly remitted, in consequence of the tragical death of a fat little schepen, who actually died of suffocation in an unsuccessful effort to force a laugh at one of burgermeester Van Zandt's best jokes.

In return for these humble services, they were permitted to say *yes* and *no* at the council-board, and to have that enviable privilege, the run of the public kitchen,—being graciously permitted to eat, and drink, and smoke, at all those snug junketings and public gormandizings for which the ancient magistrates were equally famous with their modern successors. The post of schepen, therefore, like that of assistant alderman, was eagerly coveted by all your burghers of a certain description, who have a huge relish for good feeding, and an humble ambition to be great men in a small way,—who thirst after a little brief authority, that shall render them the terror of the alms-house and the bridewell, [1]—that shall enable them to lord it over obsequious poverty, vagrant vice, outcast prostitution, and hunger-driven dishonesty, —that shall give to their beck a houndlike pack of catchpolls and bumbailiffs [2]—tenfold greater rogues than the culprits they hunt down! My readers will excuse this sudden warmth, which I confess is unbecoming of a grave historian,— but I have a mortal antipathy to catchpolls, bumbailiffs, and little-great men.

The ancient magistrates of this city corresponded with those of the present time no less in form, magnitude, and intellect, than in prerogative and privilege. The burgomasters, like our aldermen, were generally chosen by weight, —and not only the weight of the body, but likewise the weight of the head. It is a maxim practically observed in all honest, plain-thinking, regular cities, that an alderman should be fat,—and the wisdom of this can be proved to a certainty. That the body is in some measure an image of the mind, or rather that the mind is molded to the body, like melted lead to the clay in which it is cast, has been insisted on by many philosophers, who have made human nature their peculiar study; for, as a learned gentleman of our own city observes, "there is a constant relation between the moral character of all intelligent creatures and their physical constitution, between their habits and the structure of their bodies." Thus we see

that a lean, spare, diminutive body is generally accompanied by a petulant, restless, meddling mind: either the mind wears down the body, by its continual motion, or else the body, not affording the mind sufficient house-room, keeps it continually in a state of fretfulness, tossing and worrying about from the uneasiness of its situation. Whereas your round, sleek, fat, unwieldy periphery [3] is ever attended by a mind like itself, tranquil, torpid, and at ease; and we may always observe, that your well-fed, robustious [4] burghers are in general very tenacious of their ease and comfort, being great enemies to noise, discord, and disturbance,—and surely none are more likely to study the public tranquillity than those who are so careful of their own. Who ever hears of fat men heading a riot, or herding together in turbulent mobs?— no—no; it is your lean, hungry men who are continually worrying society, and setting the whole community by the ears.

The divine Plato, [5] whose doctrines are not sufficiently attended to by philosophers of the present age, allows to every man three souls: one, immortal and rational, seated in the brain, that it may overlook and regulate the body; a second, consisting of the surly and irascible passions which, like belligerent powers, lie encamped around the heart; a third, mortal and sensual, destitute of reason, gross and brutal in its propensities, and enchained in the belly, that it may not disturb the divine soul by its ravenous howlings. Now, according to this excellent theory, what can be more clear than that your fat alderman is most likely to have the most regular and well-conditioned mind. His head is like a huge spherical chamber, containing a prodigious mass of soft brains, whereon the rational soul lies softly and snugly couched, as on a feather-bed; and the eyes, which are the windows of the bed-chamber, are usually half closed, that its slumberings may not be disturbed by external objects. A mind thus comfortably lodged, and protected from disturbance, is manifestly most likely to perform its functions with regularity and ease. By dint of good feeding, moreover, the mortal and malignant soul, which is confined in the belly, and which, by its raging and roaring, puts the irritable soul in the neighborhood of the heart in an intolerable passion, and thus renders men crusty and quarrelsome when hungry, is completely pacified, silenced, and put to rest,— whereupon a host of honest, good-fellow quali-

[1] The Bridewell prison, named from St. Bride's Well or spring near by, was a famous jail of London.
[2] contemptuous terms for sheriffs' officers, constables

[3] circumference
[4] robust (rather than boisterous and violent, the usual meaning)
[5] in the *Phoedrus*

ties, and kind-hearted affections, which had lain perdu, [1] slyly peeping out of the loop-holes of the heart, finding this Cerberus [2] asleep, do pluck up their spirits, turn out one and all in their holiday suits, and gambol up and down the diaphragm,—disposing their possessor to laughter, good-humor, and a thousand friendly offices toward his fellow-mortals.

As a board of magistrates, formed on this principle, think but very little, they are the less likely to differ and wrangle about favorite opinions; and as they generally transact business upon a hearty dinner, they are naturally disposed to be lenient and indulgent in the administration of their duties. Charlemagne was conscious of this, and therefore ordered in his cartularies, [3] that no judge should hold a court of justice, except in the morning, on an empty stomach.—A pitiful rule, which I can never forgive, and which I warrant bore hard upon all the poor culprits in the kingdom. The more enlightened and humane generation of the present day have taken an opposite course, and have so managed that the aldermen are the best-fed men in the community; feasting lustily on the fat things of the land, and gorging so heartily on oysters and turtles, that in process of time they acquire the activity of the one, and the form, the waddle, and the green fat of the other. The consequence is, as I have just said, these luxurious feastings do produce such a dulcet equanimity and repose of the soul, rational and irrational, that their transactions are proverbial for unvarying monotony; and the profound laws which they enact in their dozing moments, amid the labors of digestion, are quietly suffered to remain as dead letters, and never enforced when awake. In a word, your fair, round-bellied burgomaster, like a full-fed mastiff, dozes quietly at the house-door, always at home, and always at hand, to watch over its safety; but as to electing a lean, meddling candidate to the office, as has now and then been done, I would as lief put a greyhound to watch the house, or a race-horse to draw an ox-wagon.

The burgomasters, then, as I have already mentioned, were wisely chosen by weight, and the schepens, or assistant aldermen, were appointed to attend upon them and help them eat; but the latter, in the course of time, when they had been fed and fattened into sufficient bulk of body and drowsiness of brain, became very eligible candidates for the burgomasters' chairs,

having fairly eaten themselves into office, as a mouse eats his way into a comfortable lodgment in a goodly, blue-nosed, skimmed-milk, New England cheese.

Nothing could equal the profound deliberations that took place between the renowned Wouter and these his worthy compeers, unless it be the sage divans [4] of some of our modern corporations. They would sit for hours, smoking and dozing over public affairs, without speaking a word to interrupt that perfect stillness so necessary to deep reflection. Under the sober sway of Wouter Van Twiller and these his worthy coadjutors, the infant settlement waxed vigorous apace, gradually emerging from the swamps and forests, and exhibiting that mingled appearance of town and country, customary in new cities, and which at this day may be witnessed in the city of Washington,— that immense metropolis, which makes so glorious an appearance on paper. [5]

It was a pleasing sight, in those times, to behold the honest burgher, like a patriarch of yore, seated on the bench at the door of his whitewashed house, under the shade of some gigantic sycamore or overhanging willow. Here would he smoke his pipe of a sultry afternoon, enjoying the soft southern breeze, and listening with silent gratulation to the clucking of his hens, the cackling of his geese, and the sonorous grunting of his swine,—that combination of farmyard melody which may truly be said to have a silver sound, inasmuch as it conveys a certain assurance of profitable marketing.

The modern spectator, who wanders through the streets of this populous city, can scarcely form an idea of the different appearance they presented in the primitive days of the Doubter. The busy hum of multitudes, the shouts of revelry, the rumbling equipages of fashion, the rattling of accursed carts, and all the spirit-grieving sounds of brawling commerce, were unknown in the settlement of New Amsterdam. The grass grew quietly in the highways; the bleating sheep and frolicsome calves sported about the verdant ridge where now the Broadway loungers take their morning stroll; the cunning fox or ravenous wolf skulked in the woods where now are to be seen the dens of Gomez [6] and his righteous fraternity of money-brokers; and flocks of vociferous geese cackled about the fields where now the great Tammany

---

[1] lost to sight, hidden
[2] the watch-dog of the infernal regions
[3] records (here used as if law codes)

[4] Turkish, diwan; council of state
[5] When the *History* was published, jealousy was still rife between New York, the first capital under the Constitution, and Washington, which had been the seat of government but nine years.
[6] probably a money lender

wigwam [1] and the patriotic tavern of Martling [2] echo with the wranglings of the mob.

In these good times did a true and enviable equality of rank and property prevail, equally removed from the arrogance of wealth, and the servility and heart-burnings of repining poverty; and, what in my mind is still more conducive to tranquillity and harmony among friends, a happy equality of intellect was likewise to be seen. The minds of the good burghers of New Amsterdam seemed all to have been cast in one mold, and to be those honest, blunt minds, which, like certain manufactures, are made by the gross, and considered as exceedingly good for common use.

Thus it happens that your true dull minds are generally preferred for public employ, and especially promoted to city honors; your keen intellects, like razors, being considered too sharp for common service. I know that it is common to rail at the unequal distribution of riches, as the great source of jealousies, broils, and heart-breakings; whereas, for my part, I verily believe it is the sad inequality of intellect that prevails, that embroils communities more than anything else; and I have remarked that your knowing people, who are so much wiser than anybody else, are eternally keeping society in a ferment. Happily for New Amsterdam, nothing of the kind was known within its walls; the very words of learning, education, taste, and talents were unheard of; a bright genius was an animal unknown, and a blue-stocking lady [3] would have been regarded with as much wonder as a horned frog or a fiery dragon. No man, in fact, seemed to know more than his neighbor, nor any man to know more than an honest man ought to know, who has nobody's business to mind but his own; the parson and the council clerk were the only men that could read in the community, and the sage Van Twiller always signed his name with a cross.

Thrice happy and ever to be envied little Burgh! existing in all the security of harmless insignificance,—unnoticed and unenvied by the world, without ambition, without vainglory, without riches, without learning, and all their train of carking cares;—and as of yore, in the better days of man, the deities were wont to visit him on earth and bless his rural habitations; so, we are told, in the sylvan days of New Amsterdam, the good St. Nicholas [4] would often make his appearance in his beloved city, of a holiday afternoon, riding jollily among the tree-tops, or over the roofs of the houses, now and then drawing forth magnificent presents from his breeches pockets, and dropping them down the chimneys of his favorites. Whereas, in these degenerate days of iron and brass, he never shows us the light of his countenance, nor ever visits us, save one night in the year, when he rattles down the chimneys of the descendants of patriarchs, confining his presents merely to the children, in token of the degeneracy of the parents.

Such are the comfortable and thriving effects of a fat government. The province of the New Netherlands, destitute of wealth, possessed a sweet tranquillity that wealth could never purchase. There were neither public commotions, nor private quarrels; neither parties, nor sects, nor schisms; neither persecutions, nor trials, nor punishments; nor were there counselors, attorneys, catchpolls, or hangmen. Every man attended to what little business he was lucky enough to have, or neglected it if he pleased, without asking the opinion of his neighbor. In those days nobody meddled with concerns above his comprehension; nor thrust his nose into other people's affairs; nor neglected to correct his own conduct, and reform his own character, in his zeal to pull to pieces the characters of others;—but, in a word, every respectable citizen ate when he was not hungry, drank when he was not thirsty, and went regularly to bed when the sun set and the fowls went to roost, whether he was sleepy or not; all which tended so remarkably to the population of the settlement, that I am told every dutiful wife throughout New Amsterdam made a point of enriching her husband with at least one child a year, and very often a brace,—this superabundance of good things clearly constituting the true luxury of life, according to the favorite Dutch maxim, that, "more than enough constitutes a feast." Everything, therefore, went on exactly as it should do, and in the usual words employed by historians to express the welfare of a country, "the profoundest *tranquillity* and *repose* reigned throughout the province."

[1] The home of the ostensibly fraternal and benevolent order of the Tammany Society or Columbian Order, an organization already in 1809 of much political influence; its views were opposite to those of Irving.
[2] landlord of the tavern at the corner of Nassau and Spruce Streets, New York, where the Tammany political meetings were held
[3] a woman of intellectual ambition

[4] Irving has previously made him the patron saint of New York.

CHAPTER IX

HOW THE FORT GOED HOOP WAS FEARFULLY BE-
LEAGUERED—HOW THE RENOWNED WOUTER
FELL INTO A PROFOUND DOUBT, AND HOW HE
FINALLY EVAPORATED.

. . . .

I have already noticed, in a former chapter of my history, that the territories of the Nieuw Nederlandts extended on the east, quite to the Varsche or fresh, or Connecticut river. Here, at an early period, had been established a frontier post on the bank of the river, and called Fort Goed Hoop, not far from the site of the present fair city of Hartford. It was placed under the command of Jacobus Van Curlet, or Curlis, as some historians will have it,—a doughty soldier, of that stomachful class famous for eating all they kill. He was long in the body and short in the limb, as though a tall man's body had been mounted on a little man's legs. He made up for this turnspit construction by striding to such an extent that you would have sworn he had on the seven-leagued boots of Jack the Giant-killer; and so high did he tread on parade, that his soldiers were sometimes alarmed lest he should trample himself under foot.

But notwithstanding the erection of this fort and the appointment of this ugly little man of war as commander, the Yankees continued the interlopings hinted at in my last chapter, and at length had the audacity to *squat* themselves down within the jurisdiction of Fort Goed Hoop. [1]

The long-bodied Van Curlet protested with great spirit against these unwarrantable encroachments, couching his protest in Low Dutch, by way of inspiring more terror, and forthwith dispatched a copy of the protest to the governor at New Amsterdam, together with a long and bitter account of the aggressions of the enemy. This done, he ordered his men, one and all, to be of good cheer, shut the gate of the fort, smoked three pipes, went to bed, and awaited the result with a resolute and intrepid tranquillity that greatly animated his adherents, and no doubt struck sore dismay and affright into the hearts of the enemy.

Now it came to pass that about this time the renowned Wouter Van Twiller, full of years and honors, and council-dinners, had reached that period of life and faculty which, according to the great Gulliver, entitles a man to admission into the ancient order of Struldbruggs. [2]

He employed his time in smoking his Turkish pipe, amid an assemblage of sages, equally enlightened and nearly as venerable as himself, and who, for their silence, their gravity, their wisdom, and their cautious averseness to coming to any conclusion in business are only to be equaled by certain profound corporations which I have known in my time. Upon reading the protest of the gallant Jacobus Van Curlet, therefore, His Excellency fell straightway into one of the deepest doubts that ever he was known to encounter; his capacious head gradually drooped on his chest, he closed his eyes, and inclined his ear to one side, as if listening with great attention to the discussion that was going on in his belly,—and which all who knew him declared to be the huge court-house or council-chamber of his thoughts, forming to his head what the House of Representatives does to the Senate. An inarticulate sound, very much resembling a snore, occasionally escaped him; but the nature of this internal cogitation was never known, as he never opened his lips on the subject to man, woman, or child. In the mean time, the protest of Van Curlet lay quietly on the table, where it served to light the pipes of the venerable sages assembled in council; and in the great smoke which they raised, the gallant Jacobus, his protest, and his mighty Fort Goed Hoop were soon as completely beclouded and forgotten as is a question of emergency swallowed up in the speeches and resolutions of a modern session of Congress.

There are certain emergencies when your profound legislators and sage deliberative councils are mightily in the way of a nation, and when an ounce of hare-brained decision is worth a pound of sage doubt and cautious discussion. Such, at least, was the case at present; for, while the renowned Wouter Van Twiller was daily battling with his doubts, and his resolution growing weaker and weaker in the contest, the enemy pushed farther and farther into his territories, and assumed a most formidable appearance in the neighborhood of Fort Goed Hoop. Here they founded the mighty town of Pyquag, or, as it has since been called, Weathersfield, a place which, if we may credit the assertions of that worthy historian, John Josselyn, Gent., [3] "hath been infamous by reason of the witches therein." And so daring did these men of Pyquag become, that they extended those plantations of onions, for which their town is illustrious, under the very noses

---

[1] The paragraph is substantially true history.
[2] in the third part of *Gulliver's Travels,* beings gifted with bodily immortality, but nothing else

[3] John Josselyn, born in England about 1600, wrote three books giving accounts of early voyages to New England, and descriptions of the country.

of the garrison of Fort Goed Hoop, insomuch that the honest Dutchmen could not look toward that quarter without tears in their eyes.

This crying injustice was regarded with proper indignation by the gallant Jacobus Van Curlet. He absolutely trembled with the violence of his choler and the exacerbations [1] of his valor, which were the more turbulent in their workings from the length of the body in which they were agitated. He forthwith proceeded to strengthen his redoubts, heighten his breastworks, deepen his fosse, [2] and fortify his position with a double row of abatis; [3] after which he dispatched a fresh courier with accounts of his perilous situation.

The courier chosen to bear the despatches was a fat, oily, little man, as being less liable to be worn out, or to lose leather on the journey; and to insure his speed, he was mounted on the fleetest wagon-horse in the garrison, remarkable for length of limb, largeness of bone, and hardness of trot, and so tall, that the little messenger was obliged to climb on his back by means of his tail and crupper. Such extraordinary speed did he make, that he arrived at Fort Amsterdam in a little less than a month, though the distance was full two hundred pipes, or about one hundred and twenty miles.

With an appearance of great hurry and business, and smoking a short traveling-pipe, he proceeded on a long swing-trot through the muddy lanes of the metropolis, demolishing whole batches of dirt-pies which the little Dutch children were making in the road; and for which kind of pastry the children of this city have ever been famous. On arriving at the governor's house, he climbed down from his steed, roused the gray-headed door-keeper, old Skaats, who, like his lineal descendant and faithful representative, the venerable crier of our court, was nodding at his post, rattled at the door of the council-chamber, and startled the members as they were dozing over a plan for establishing a public market.

At that very moment a gentle grunt, or rather a deep-drawn snore, was heard from the chair of the governor; a whiff of smoke was at the same instant observed to escape from his lips, and a light cloud to ascend from the bowl of his pipe. The council, of course, supposed him engaged in deep sleep, for the good of the community, and according to

[1] irritations, exasperations   [2] ditch, moat
[3] a military defense of stakes or tree-tops planted in the earth with sharpened ends protruding toward the enemy

custom in all such cases established, every man bawled out silence, when, of a sudden, the door flew open, and the little courier straddled into the apartment, cased to the middle in a pair of Hessian boots, which he had got into for the sake of expedition. In his right hand he held forth the ominous dispatches, and with his left he grasped firmly the waistband of his galligaskins, [4] which had unfortunately given way in the exertion of descending from his horse. He stumped resolutely up to the governor, and with more hurry than perspicuity delivered his message. But fortunately his ill tidings came too late to ruffle the tranquillity of this most tranquil of rulers. His venerable Excellency had just breathed and smoked his last,—his lungs and his pipe having been exhausted together, and his peaceful soul having escaped in the last whiff that curled from his tobacco pipe. In a word, the renowned Walter the Doubter, who had so often slumbered with his contemporaries, now slept with his fathers, and Wilhelmus Kieft [5] governed in his stead.

1808-09   *1809*

From THE SKETCH-BOOK
THE AUTHOR'S ACCOUNT OF HIMSELF

I am of this mind with Homer, that as the snaile that crept out of her shel was turned eftsoons into a toad, and thereby was forced to make a stoole to sit on; so the traveller that stragleth from his owne country is in a short time transformed into so monstrous a shape, that he is faine to alter his mansion with his manners, and to live where he can, not where he would.

                              LYLY'S *Euphues.*

I was always fond of visiting new scenes, and observing strange characters and manners. Even when a mere child I began my travels, and made many tours of discovery into foreign parts and unknown regions of my native city, to the frequent alarm of my parents, and the emolument of the town-crier. As I grew into boyhood, I extended the range of my observations. My holiday afternoons were spent in rambles about the surrounding country. I made myself familiar with all its places famous in history or fable. I knew every spot where a murder or robbery had been committed, or a ghost seen. I visited the neighboring villages, and added greatly to my stock of knowledge by noting their habits and customs, and conversing with their sages and great men.

[4] loose breeches
[5] third Dutch governor of New York

I even journeyed one long summer's day to the summit of the most distant hill, whence I stretched my eye over many a mile of *terra incognita,* [1] and was astonished to find how vast a globe I inhabited.

This rambling propensity strengthened with my years. Books of voyages and travels became my passion, and in devouring their contents, I neglected the regular exercises of the school. How wistfully would I wander about the pier-heads in fine weather, and watch the parting ships, bound to distant climes—with what longing eyes would I gaze after their lessening sails, and waft myself in imagination to the ends of the earth!

Further reading and thinking, though they brought this vague inclination into more reasonable bounds, only served to make it more decided. I visited various parts of my own country; and had I been merely a lover of fine scenery, I should have felt little desire to seek elsewhere its gratification, for on no country have the charms of nature been more prodigally lavished. Her mighty lakes, like oceans of liquid silver; her mountains, with their bright aërial tints; her valleys, teeming with wild fertility; her tremendous cataracts, thundering in their solitudes; her boundless plains, waving with spontaneous verdure; her broad, deep rivers, rolling in solemn silence to the ocean; her trackless forests, where vegetation puts forth all its magnificence; her skies, kindling with the magic of summer clouds and glorious sunshine;—no, never need an American look beyond his own country for the sublime and beautiful of natural scenery.

But Europe held forth the charms of storied and poetical association. There were to be seen the masterpieces of art, the refinements of highly cultivated society, the quaint peculiarities of ancient and local custom. My native country was full of youthful promise: Europe was rich in the accumulated treasures of age. Her very ruins told the history of times gone by, and every moldering stone was a chronicle. I longed to wander over the scenes of renowned achievement—to tread, as it were, in the footsteps of antiquity—to loiter about the ruined castle—to meditate on the falling tower—to escape, in short, from the commonplace realities of the present, and lose myself among the shadowy grandeurs of the past.

I had, beside all this, an earnest desire to see the great men of the earth. We have, it is true, our great men in America: not a city

[1] unknown land

but has an ample share of them. I have mingled among them in my time, and been almost withered by the shade into which they cast me; for there is nothing so baleful to a small man as the shade of a great one, particularly the great man of a city. But I was anxious to see the great men of Europe; for I had read in the works of various philosophers, that all animals degenerated in America, and man among the number. A great man of Europe, thought I, must therefore be as superior to a great man of America as a peak of the Alps to a highland of the Hudson; and in this idea I was confirmed by observing the comparative importance and swelling magnitude of many English travelers among us, who, I was assured, were very little people in their own country. I will visit this land of wonders, thought I, and see the gigantic race from which I am degenerated.

It has been either my good or evil lot to have my roving passion gratified. I have wandered through different countries, and witnessed many of the shifting scenes of life. I cannot say that I have studied them with the eye of a philosopher; but rather with the sauntering gaze with which humble lovers of the picturesque stroll from the window of one print-shop to another, caught sometimes by the delineations of beauty, sometimes by the distortions of caricature, and sometimes by the loveliness of landscape. As it is the fashion for modern tourists to travel pencil in hand, and bring home their portfolios filled with sketches, I am disposed to get up a few for the entertainment of my friends. When, however, I look over the hints and memorandums I have taken down for the purpose, my heart almost fails me at finding how my idle humor has led me aside from the great objects studied by every regular traveler who would make a book. I fear I shall give equal disappointment with an unlucky landscape painter, who had traveled on the continent, but, following the bent of his vagrant inclination, had sketched in nooks, and corners, and by-places. His sketch-book was accordingly crowded with cottages, and landscapes, and obscure ruins; but he had neglected to paint St. Peter's, or the Coliseum; the cascade of Terni, [2] or the bay of Naples; [3] and had not a single glacier or volcano in his whole collection.

1818-19   1819

[2] A series of waterfalls near Terni, Italy, called Cascate delle Marmore; the total fall is nearly six hundred feet.

[3] considered one of the most beautiful in the world

RIP VAN WINKLE

A Posthumous Writing of Diedrich Knickerbocker [1]

By Woden, God of Saxons,
From whence comes Wensday, that is Wodensday,
Truth is a thing that ever I will keep
Unto thylke day in which I creep into
My sepulcher—

CARTWRIGHT.

[The following Tale was found among the papers of the late Diedrich Knickerbocker, an old gentleman of New York, who was very curious in the Dutch history of the province, and the manners of the descendants from its primitive settlers. His historical researches, however, did not lie so much among books as among men; for the former are lamentably scanty on his favorite topics; whereas he found the old burghers, and still more their wives, rich in that legendary lore so invaluable to true history. Whenever, therefore, he happened upon a genuine Dutch family, snugly shut up in its low-roofed farmhouse under a spreading sycamore, he looked upon it as a little clasped volume of black-letter, [2] and studied it with the zeal of a book-worm.

The result of all these researches was a history of the province during the reign of the Dutch governors, which he published some years since. There have been various opinions as to the literary character of his work, and, to tell the truth, it is not a whit better than it should be. Its chief merit is its scrupulous accuracy, which indeed was a little questioned on its first appearance, but has since been completely established; and it is now admitted into all historical collections, as a book of unquestionable authority.

The old gentleman died shortly after the publication of his work, and now that he is dead and gone, it cannot do much harm to his memory to say that his time might have been much better employed in weightier labors. He, however, was apt to ride his hobby his own way; and though it did now and then kick up the dust a little in the eyes of his neighbors, and grieve the spirit of some

friends, for whom he felt the truest deference and affection; yet his errors and follies are remembered "more in sorrow than in anger," and it begins to be suspected that he never intended to injure or offend. But however his memory may be appreciated by critics, it is still held dear by many folks whose good opinion is well worth having; particularly by certain biscuit-bakers, who have gone so far as to imprint his likeness on their new-year cakes; and have thus given him a chance for immortality, almost equal to the being stamped on a Waterloo Medal or a Queen Anne's Farthing. [3]]

Whoever has made a voyage up the Hudson must remember the Kaatskill Mountains. They are a dismembered branch of the great Appalachian family, and are seen away to the west of the river, swelling up to a noble height, and lording it over the surrounding country. Every change of season, every change of weather, indeed, every hour of the day, produces some change in the magical hues and shapes of these mountains, and they are regarded by all the good wives, far and near, as perfect barometers. When the weather is fair and settled, they are clothed in blue and purple, and print their bold outlines on the clear evening sky; but sometimes when the rest of the landscape is cloudless, they will gather a hood of gray vapors about their summits, which, in the last rays of the setting sun, will glow and light up like a crown of glory.

At the foot of these fairy mountains, the voyager may have descried the light smoke curling up from a village, whose shingle-roofs gleam among the trees, just where the blue tints of the upland melt away into the fresh green of the nearer landscape. It is a little village of great antiquity, having been founded by some of the Dutch colonists in the early times of the province, just about the beginning of the government of the good Peter Stuyvesant, [4] (may he rest in peace!) and there were some of the houses of the original settlers standing within a few years, built of small yellow bricks brought from Holland, having latticed windows and gable fronts, surmounted with weather-cocks.

In that same village, and in one of these very houses (which, to tell the precise truth, was sadly time-worn and weather-beaten) there lived many years since, while the country was yet a province of Great Britain, a simple good-

[1] Continuing the very transparent fiction of Diedrich Knickerbocker, as author of the tales here printed, as well as of the *History of New York*, Irving takes occasion to disavow any ill-natured intent in the ridicule they contain. Although the staid Dutch aristocracy had taken Irving's freedom with their ancestors somewhat unkindly, his readers in general relished the *History* all the more because of its satirical flavor; and as he hints, the growing frequency of the name Knickerbocker, not only on biscuits, but in other trade connections, showed the popularity of the vein he was working. Irving is not wholly original in the germ-idea of the twenty years' sleep, for it had appeared in old-world literature several times in the twenty-four hundred years before Irving's day. Irving, however, adapts the idea completely to the characters and the time of which he writes, making it not only local in scene, but distinctly American in tone.
[2] the print characteristic of fourteenth century Latin manuscripts and books

[3] Waterloo medals were given regardless of rank to all British survivors of the battle of Waterloo. Queen Anne's farthing was a coin of Queen Anne's reign, supposed to be, but not in fact, excessively rare.
[4] the last Dutch governor of New York

natured fellow, of the name of Rip Van Winkle. He was a descendant of the Van Winkles who figured so gallantly in the chivalrous days of Peter Stuyvesant, and accompanied him to the siege of Fort Christina. [1] He inherited, however, but little of the martial character of his ancestors. I have observed that he was a simple good-natured man; he was, moreover, a kind neighbor, and an obedient henpecked husband. Indeed, to the latter circumstance might be owing that meekness of spirit which gained him such universal popularity; for those men are most apt to be obsequious and conciliating abroad, who are under the discipline of shrews at home. Their tempers, doubtless, are rendered pliant and malleable in the fiery furnace of domestic tribulation; and a curtain lecture is worth all the sermons in the world for teaching the virtues of patience and long-suffering. A termagant wife may, therefore, in some respects be considered a tolerable blessing; and if so, Rip Van Winkle was thrice blessed.

Certain it is, that he was a great favorite among all the good wives of the village, who, as usual with the amiable sex, took his part in all family squabbles; and never failed, whenever they talked those matters over in their evening gossipings, to lay all the blame on Dame Van Winkle. The children of the village, too, would shout with joy whenever he approached. He assisted at their sports, made their playthings, taught them to fly kites and shoot marbles, and told them long stories of ghosts, witches, and Indians. Whenever he went dodging about the village, he was surrounded by a troop of them, hanging on his skirts, clambering on his back, and playing a thousand tricks on him with impunity; and not a dog would bark at him throughout the neighborhood.

The great error in Rip's composition was an insuperable aversion to all kinds of profitable labor. It could not be from the want of assiduity or perseverance; for he would sit on a wet rock, with a rod as long and heavy as a Tartar's lance, and fish all day without a murmur even though he should not be encouraged by a single nibble. He would carry a fowling-piece on his shoulder for hours together, trudging through woods and swamps, and up hill and down dale, to shoot a few squirrels or wild pigeons. He would never refuse to assist a neighbor, even in the roughest toil, and was a foremost man at all country frolics for husking Indian corn, or building stone-fences; the women of the village, too, used to employ him

to run their errands, and to do such little odd jobs as their less obliging husbands would not do for them. In a word, Rip was ready to attend to anybody's business but his own; but as to doing any family duty, and keeping his farm in order, he found it impossible.

In fact, he declared it was of no use to work on his farm; it was the most pestilent little piece of ground in the whole country; everything about it went wrong, and would go wrong, in spite of him. His fences were continually falling to pieces; his cow would either go astray or get among the cabbages; weeds were sure to grow quicker in his fields than anywhere else; the rain always made a point of setting in just as he had outdoor work to do; so that though his patrimonial estate had dwindled away under his management, acre by acre, until there was little more left than a mere patch of Indian corn and potatoes, yet it was the worst-conditioned farm in the neighborhood.

His children, too, were as ragged and wild as if they belonged to nobody. His son Rip, an urchin begotten in his own likeness, promised to inherit the habits, with the old clothes of his father. He was generally seen trooping like a colt at his mother's heels, equipped in a pair of his father's cast-off galligaskins, [2] which he had much ado to hold up with one hand, as a fine lady does her train in bad weather.

Rip Van Winkle, however, was one of those happy mortals, of foolish, well-oiled dispositions, who take the world easy, eat white bread or brown, whichever can be got with least thought or trouble, and would rather starve on a penny than work for a pound. If left to himself, he would have whistled life away in perfect contentment; but his wife kept continually dinning in his ears about his idleness, his carelessness, and the ruin he was bringing on his family. Morning, noon, and night, her tongue was incessantly going, and everything he said or did was sure to produce a torrent of household eloquence. Rip had but one way of replying to all lectures of the kind, and that, by frequent use, had grown into a habit. He shrugged his shoulders, shook his head, cast up his eyes, but said nothing. This, however, always provoked a fresh volley from his wife; so that he was fain to draw off his forces, and take to the outside of the house—the only side which, in truth, belongs to a henpecked husband.

Rip's sole domestic adherent was his dog Wolf, who was as much henpecked as his master; for Dame Van Winkle regarded them as

---

[1] a Swedish fort on the Delaware captured by the Dutch in 1655 after a bloodless siege

[2] large, loose knee-breeches

companions in idleness, and even looked upon Wolf with an evil eye, as the cause of his master's going so often astray. True it is, in all points of spirit befitting an honorable dog, he was as courageous an animal as ever scoured the woods—but what courage can withstand the ever-during and all-besetting terrors of a woman's tongue? The moment Wolf entered the house his crest fell, his tail drooped to the ground, or curled between his legs, he sneaked about with a gallows air, casting many a side-long glance at Dame Van Winkle, and at the least flourish of a broomstick or ladle, he would fly to the door with yelping precipitation.

Times grew worse and worse with Rip Van Winkle as years of matrimony rolled on; a tart temper never mellows with age, and a sharp tongue is the only edged tool that grows keener with constant use. For a long while he used to console himself, when driven from home, by frequenting a kind of perpetual club of the sages, philosophers, and other idle personages of the village; which held its sessions on a bench before a small inn, designated by a rubicund portrait of His Majesty George the Third. Here they used to sit in the shade through a long lazy summer's day, talking listlessly over village gossip, or telling endless sleepy stories about nothing. But it would have been worth any statesman's money to have heard the profound discussions that sometimes took place, when by chance an old newspaper fell into their hands from some passing traveler. How solemnly they would listen to the contents, as drawled out by Derrick Van Bummel, the schoolmaster, a dapper learned little man, who was not to be daunted by the most gigantic word in the dictionary; and how sagely they would deliberate upon public events some months after they had taken place.

The opinions of this junto were completely controlled by Nicholas Vedder, a patriarch of the village, and landlord of the inn, at the door of which he took his seat from morning till night, just moving sufficiently to avoid the sun and keep in the shade of a large tree; so that the neighbors could tell the hour by his movements as accurately as by a sun-dial. It is true he was rarely heard to speak, but smoked his pipe incessantly. His adherents, however (for every great man has his adherents) perfectly understood him, and knew how to gather his opinions. When anything that was read or related displeased him, he was observed to smoke his pipe vehemently, and to send forth short, frequent, and angry puffs; but when pleased, he would inhale the smoke slowly and tranquilly, and emit it in light and placid clouds; and sometimes, taking the pipe from his mouth, and letting the fragrant vapor curl about his nose, would gravely nod his head in token of perfect approbation.

From even this stronghold the unlucky Rip was at length routed by his termagant wife, who would suddenly break in upon the tranquillity of the assemblage and call the members all to naught; nor was that august personage, Nicholas Vedder himself, sacred from the daring tongue of this terrible virago, who charged him outright with encouraging her husband in habits of idleness.

Poor Rip was at last reduced almost to despair; and his only alternative, to escape from the labor of the farm and clamor of his wife, was to take gun in hand and stroll away into the woods. Here he would sometimes seat himself at the foot of a tree, and share the contents of his wallet with Wolf, with whom he sympathized as a fellow-sufferer in persecution. "Poor Wolf," he would say, "thy mistress leads thee a dog's life of it; but never mind, my lad, whilst I live thou shalt never want a friend to stand by thee!" Wolf would wag his tail, look wistfully in his master's face, and if dogs can feel pity I verily believe he reciprocated the sentiment with all his heart.

In a long ramble of the kind on a fine autumnal day, Rip had unconsciously scrambled to one of the highest parts of the Kaatskill Mountains. He was after his favorite sport of squirrel shooting, and the still solitudes had echoed and reëchoed with the reports of his gun. Panting and fatigued, he threw himself, late in the afternoon, on a green knoll, covered with mountain herbage, that crowned the brow of a precipice. From an opening between the trees he could overlook all the lower country for many a mile of rich woodland. He saw at a distance the lordly Hudson, far, far below him, moving on its silent but majestic course, with the reflection of a purple cloud, or the sail of a lagging bark, here and there sleeping on its glassy bosom, and at last losing itself in the blue highlands.

On the other side he looked down into a deep mountain glen, wild, lonely, and shagged, the bottom filled with fragments from the impending cliffs, and scarcely lighted by the reflected rays of the setting sun. For some time Rip lay musing on this scene; evening was gradually advancing; the mountains began to throw their long blue shadows over the valleys; he saw that it would be dark long before he could reach the village, and he heaved a heavy sigh when he thought of encountering the terrors of Dame Van Winkle.

As he was about to descend, he heard a voice from a distance, hallooing, "Rip Van Winkle! Rip Van Winkle!" He looked round, but could see nothing but a crow winging its solitary flight across the mountain. He thought his fancy must have deceived him, and turned again to descend, when he heard the same cry ring through the still evening air; "Rip Van Winkle! Rip Van Winkle!"—at the same time Wolf bristled up his back, and giving a low growl, skulked to his master's side, looking fearfully down into the glen. Rip now felt a vague apprehension stealing over him; he looked anxiously in the same direction, and perceived a strange figure slowly toiling up the rocks, and bending under the weight of something he carried on his back. He was surprised to see any human being in this lonely and unfrequented place; but supposing it to be someone of the neighborhood in need of his assistance, he hastened down to yield it.

On nearer approach he was still more surprised at the singularity of the stranger's appearance. He was a short, square-built old fellow, with thick bushy hair, and a grizzled beard. His dress was of the antique Dutch fashion: a cloth jerkin [1] strapped round the waist, several pairs of breeches, the outer one of ample volume, decorated with rows of buttons down the sides, and bunches at the knees. He bore on his shoulder a stout keg, that seemed full of liquor, and made signs for Rip to approach and assist him with the load. Though rather shy and distrustful of this new acquaintance, Rip complied with his usual alacrity; and mutually relieving one another, they clambered up a narrow gully, apparently the dry bed of a mountain torrent. As they ascended, Rip every now and then heard long rolling peals, like distant thunder, that seemed to issue out of a deep ravine, or rather cleft, between lofty rocks, toward which their rugged path conducted. He paused for an instant, but supposing it to be the muttering of one of those transient thunder-showers which often take place in mountain heights, he proceeded. Passing through the ravine, they came to a hollow, like a small amphitheater, surrounded by perpendicular precipices, over the brinks of which impending trees shot their branches, so that you only caught glimpses of the azure sky and the bright evening cloud. During the whole time Rip and his companion had labored on in silence; for though the former marveled greatly what could be the object of carrying a keg of liquor up this wild mountain, yet there was something strange and incomprehensible about the unknown, that inspired awe and checked familiarity.

On entering the amphitheater, new objects of wonder presented themselves. On a level spot in the center was a company of odd-looking personages playing at ninepins. They were dressed in a quaint outlandish fashion; some wore short doublets, [2] others jerkins, with long knives in their belts, and most of them had enormous breeches of similar style with that of the guide's. Their visages, too, were peculiar: one had a large beard, broad face, and small piggish eyes: the face of another seemed to consist entirely of nose, and was surmounted by a white sugar-loaf hat, set off with a little red cock's tail. They all had beards, of various shapes and colors. There was one who seemed to be the commander. He was a stout old gentleman, with a weather-beaten countenance; he wore a laced doublet, broad belt and hanger, [3] high-crowned hat and feather, red stockings, and high-heeled shoes, with roses in them. The whole group reminded Rip of the figures in an old Flemish painting in the parlor of Dominie Van Shaick, the village parson, and which had been brought over from Holland at the time of the settlement.

What seemed particularly odd to Rip was, that though these folks were evidently amusing themselves, yet they maintained the gravest faces, the most mysterious silence, and were, withal, the most melancholy party of pleasure he had ever witnessed. Nothing interrupted the stillness of the scene but the noise of the balls, which, whenever they rolled, echoed along the mountains like rumbling peals of thunder.

As Rip and his companion approached them, they suddenly desisted from their play, and stared at him with such fixed, statue-like gaze, and such strange, uncouth, lack-luster countenances, that his heart turned within him, and his knees smote together. His companion now emptied the contents of the keg into large flagons, and made signs to him to wait upon the company. He obeyed with fear and trembling; they quaffed the liquor in profound silence, and then returned to their game.

By degrees Rip's awe and apprehension subsided. He even ventured, when no eye was fixed upon him, to taste the beverage, which he found had much of the flavor of excellent Hollands. [4] He was naturally a thirsty soul,

[1] short coat

[2] closely-fitting jackets   [4] gin made in Holland
[3] sword

and was soon tempted to repeat the draught. One taste provoked another; and he reiterated his visits to the flagon so often that at length his senses were overpowered, his eyes swam in his head, his head gradually declined, and he fell into a deep sleep.

On waking, he found himself on the green knoll whence he had first seen the old man of the glen. He rubbed his eyes—it was a bright, sunny morning. The birds were hopping and twittering among the bushes, and the eagle was wheeling aloft, and breasting the pure mountain breeze. "Surely," thought Rip, "I have not slept here all night." He recalled the occurrences before he fell asleep. The strange man with a keg of liquor—the mountain ravine—the wild retreat among the rocks—the woe-begone party at ninepins—the flagon—"Oh! that flagon! that wicked flagon!" thought Rip—"what excuse shall I make to Dame Van Winkle!"

He looked round for his gun, but in place of the clean, well-oiled fowling-piece, he found an old firelock lying by him, the barrel incrusted with rust, the lock falling off, and the stock worm-eaten. He now suspected that the grave roisters of the mountain had put a trick upon him, and, having dosed him with liquor, had robbed him of his gun. Wolf, too, had disappeared, but he might have strayed after a squirrel or partridge. He whistled after him, and shouted his name, but all in vain; the echoes repeated his whistle and shout, but no dog was to be seen.

He determined to revisit the scene of the last evening's gambol, and if he met with any of the party, to demand his dog and gun. As he rose to walk, he found himself stiff in the joints, and wanting in his usual activity. "These mountain beds do not agree with me," thought Rip, "and if this frolic should lay me up with a fit of the rheumatism, I shall have a blessed time with Dame Van Winkle." With some difficulty he got down into the glen: he found the gully up which he and his companion had ascended the preceding evening; but to his astonishment a mountain stream was now foaming down it, leaping from rock to rock, and filling the glen with babbling murmurs. He, however, made shift to scramble up its sides, working his toilsome way through thickets of birch, sassafras, and witch-hazel, and sometimes tripped up or entangled by the wild grapevines that twisted their coils or tendrils from tree to tree, and spread a kind of network in his path.

At length he reached to where the ravine had opened through the cliffs to the amphitheater; but no traces of such opening remained. The rocks presented a high, impenetrable wall, over which the torrent came tumbling in a sheet of feathery foam, and fell into a broad, deep basin, black from the shadows of the surrounding forest. Here, then, poor Rip was brought to a stand. He again called and whistled after his dog; he was only answered by the cawing of a flock of idle crows, sporting high in air about a dry tree that overhung a sunny precipice; and who, secure in their elevation, seemed to look down and scoff at the poor man's perplexities. What was to be done? the morning was passing away, and Rip felt famished for want of his breakfast. He grieved to give up his dog and gun; he dreaded to meet his wife; but it would not do to starve among the mountains. He shook his head, shouldered the rusty firelock, and, with a heart full of trouble and anxiety, turned his steps homeward.

As he approached the village he met a number of people, but none whom he knew, which somewhat surprised him, for he had thought himself acquainted with everyone in the country round. Their dress, too, was of a different fashion from that to which he was accustomed. They all stared at him with equal marks of surprise, and whenever they cast their eyes upon him, invariably stroked their chins. The constant recurrence of this gesture induced Rip, involuntarily, to do the same, when, to his astonishment, he found his beard had grown a foot long!

He had now entered the skirts of the village. A troop of strange children ran at his heels, hooting after him, and pointing at his gray beard. The dogs, too, not one of which he recognized for an old acquaintance, barked at him as he passed. The very village was altered; it was larger and more populous. There were rows of houses which he had never seen before, and those which had been his familiar haunts had disappeared. Strange names were over the doors—strange faces at the windows—everything was strange. His mind now misgave him; he began to doubt whether both he and the world around him were not bewitched. Surely this was his native village, which he had left but the day before. There stood the Kaatskill Mountains—there ran the silver Hudson at a distance—there was every hill and dale precisely as it had always been—Rip was sorely perplexed—"That flagon last night," thought he, "has addled my poor head sadly!"

It was with some difficulty that he found the way to his own house, which he approached with silent awe, expecting every moment to hear the shrill voice of Dame Van Winkle. He found the house gone to decay—the roof fallen in, the windows shattered, and the doors off the hinges. A half-starved dog that looked like Wolf was skulking about it. Rip called him by name, but the cur snarled, showed his teeth, and passed on. This was an unkind cut indeed—"My very dog," sighed poor Rip, "has forgotten me!"

He entered the house, which, to tell the truth, Dame Van Winkle had always kept in neat order. It was empty, forlorn, and apparently abandoned. This desolateness overcame all his connubial fears—he called loudly for his wife and children—the lonely chambers rang for a moment with his voice, and then all again was silence.

He now hurried forth, and hastened to his old resort, the village inn—but it, too, was gone. A large, rickety wooden building stood in its place, with great gaping windows, some of them broken and mended with old hats and petticoats, and over the door was painted, "The Union Hotel, by Jonathan Doolittle." Instead of the great tree that used to shelter the quiet little Dutch inn of yore, there now was reared a tall naked pole, with something on the top that looked like a red night-cap, [1] and from it was fluttering a flag, on which was a singular assemblage of stars and stripes—all this was strange and incomprehensible. He recognized on the sign, however, the ruby face of King George, under which he had smoked so many a peaceful pipe; but even this was singularly metamorphosed. The red coat was changed for one of blue and buff, a sword was held in the hand instead of a scepter, the head was decorated with a cocked hat, and underneath was painted in large characters, GENERAL WASHINGTON.

There was, as usual, a crowd of folk about the door, but none that Rip recollected. The very character of the people seemed changed. There was a busy, bustling, disputatious tone about it, instead of the accustomed phlegm and drowsy tranquillity. He looked in vain for the sage Nicholas Vedder, with his broad face, double chin, and fair long pipe, uttering clouds of tobacco smoke instead of idle speeches; or Van Bummel, the schoolmaster, doling forth the contents of an ancient newspaper. In place of these, a lean, bilious-looking fellow, with his pockets full of hand bills was haranguing vehemently about rights of citizens—elections—members of Congress—liberty—Bunker's Hill—heroes of seventy-six—and other words, which were a perfect Babylonish jargon to the bewildered Van Winkle.

The appearance of Rip, with his long grizzled beard, his rusty fowling-piece, his uncouth dress, and an army of women and children at his heels, soon attracted the attention of the tavern-politicians. They crowded round him, eyeing him from head to foot with great curiosity. The orator bustled up to him, and, drawing him partly aside, inquired on which side he voted?' Rip stared in vacant stupidity. Another short but busy little fellow pulled him by the arm, and, rising on tiptoe, inquired in his ear, 'Whether he was Federal or Democrat?' Rip was equally at a loss to comprehend the question; when a knowing, self-important old gentleman, in a sharp cocked hat, made his way through the crowd, putting them to the right and left with his elbows as he passed, and planting himself before Van Winkle, with one arm akimbo, the other resting on his cane, his keen eyes and sharp hat penetrating, as it were, into his very soul, demanded in an austere tone, 'what brought him to the election with a gun on his shoulder, and a mob at his heels, and whether he meant to breed a riot in the village?'—"Alas! gentlemen," cried Rip, somewhat dismayed, "I am a poor quiet man, a native of the place, and a loyal subject of the King, God bless him!"

Here a general shout burst from the bystanders—"A tory! a tory! a spy! a refugee! hustle him! away with him!" It was with great difficulty that the self-important man in the cocked hat restored order; and, having assumed a tenfold austerity of brow, demanded again of the unknown culprit what he came there for, and whom he was seeking? The poor man humbly assured him that he meant no harm, but merely came there in search of some of his neighbors, who used to keep about the tavern.

"Well—who are they?—name them."

Rip bethought himself a moment, and inquired, "Where's Nicholas Vedder?"

There was a silence for a little while, when an old man replied, in a thin, piping voice, "Nicholas Vedder! why, he is dead and gone these eighteen years! There was a wooden tombstone in the churchyard that used to tell all about him, but that's rotten and gone too."

"Where's Brom Dutcher?"

"Oh, he went off to the army in the beginning of the war; some say he was killed at the storming of Stony Point—others say he was drowned

---

[1] the *bonnet rouge*, red cap, an emblem borrowed from the French revolutionists of the most extreme views

in a squall at the foot of Antony's Nose. [1] I don't know—he never came back again."

"Where's Van Bummel, the schoolmaster?"

"He went off to the wars too, was a great militia general, and is now in Congress."

Rip's heart died away at hearing of these sad changes in his home and friends, and finding himself thus alone in the world. Every answer puzzled him too, by treating of such enormous lapses of time, and of matters which he could not understand : war—Congress—Stony Point; he had no courage to ask after any more friends, but cried out in despair, "Does nobody here know Rip Van Winkle?"

"Oh, Rip Van Winkle!" exclaimed two or three, "Oh, to be sure! that's Rip Van Winkle yonder, leaning against the tree."

Rip looked, and beheld a precise counterpart of himself, as he went up the mountain: apparently as lazy, and certainly as ragged. The poor fellow was now completely confounded. He doubted his own identity, and whether he was himself or another man. In the midst of his bewilderment, the man in the cocked hat demanded who he was, and what was his name?

"God knows," exclaimed he, at his wit's end; "I'm not myself—I'm somebody else—that's me yonder—no—that's somebody else got into my shoes—I was myself last night, but I fell asleep on the mountain, and they've changed my gun, and everything's changed, and I'm changed, and I can't tell what's my name, or who I am!"

The bystanders began now to look at each other, nod, wink significantly, and tap their fingers against their foreheads. There was a whisper, also, about securing the gun, and keeping the old fellow from doing mischief, at the very suggestion of which the self-important man in the cocked hat retired with some precipitation. At this critical moment a fresh, comely woman pressed through the throng to get a peep at the gray-bearded man. She had a chubby child in her arms, which, frightened at his looks, began to cry. "Hush, Rip," cried she, "hush, you little fool; the old man won't hurt you." The name of the child, the air of the mother, the tone of her voice, all awakened a train of recollections in his mind. "What is your name, my good woman?" asked he.

"Judith Gardenier."

"And your father's name?"

"Ah, poor man, Rip Van Winkle was his name, but it's twenty years since he went away from home with his gun, and never has been heard of since—his dog came home without

him; but whether he shot himself, or was carried away by the Indians, nobody can tell. I was then but a little girl."

Rip had but one question more to ask; but he put it with a faltering voice:—

"Where's your mother?"

"Oh, she too had died but a short time since; she broke a blood-vessel in a fit of passion at a New England peddler."

There was a drop of comfort, at least, in this intelligence. The honest man could contain himself no longer. He caught his daughter and her child in his arms. "I am your father!" cried he—"Young Rip Van Winkle once—old Rip Van Winkle now!—Does nobody know poor Rip Van Winkle?"

All stood amazed, until an old woman, tottering out from among the crowd, put her hand to her brow, and peering under it in his face for a moment, exclaimed, "Sure enough! it is Rip Van Winkle—it is himself! Welcome home again, old neighbor—Why, where have you been these twenty long years?".

Rip's story was soon told, for the whole twenty years had been to him but as one night. The neighbors stared when they heard it; some were seen to wink at each other, and put their tongues in their cheeks; and the self-important man in the cocked hat, who, when the alarm was over, had returned to the field, screwed down the corners of his mouth, and shook his head—upon which there was a general shaking of the head throughout the assemblage.

It was determined, however, to take the opinion of old Peter Vanderdonk, who was seen slowly advancing up the road. He was a descendant of the historian of that name, [2] who wrote one of the earliest accounts of the province. Peter was the most ancient inhabitant of the village, and well versed in all the wonderful events and traditions of the neighborhood. He recollected Rip at once, and corroborated his story in the most satisfactory manner. He assured the company that it was a fact, handed down from his ancestor the historian, that the Kaatskill Mountains had always been haunted by strange beings. That it was affirmed that the great Hendrick Hudson, the first discoverer of the river and country, kept a kind of vigil there every twenty years, with his crew of the *Half-moon;* being permitted in this way to revisit the scenes of his enterprise, and keep a guardian eye upon the river and the

[1] a point of land on the Hudson, near West Point

[2] Adrian Van der Donck, a prominent Dutch colonist who died in 1655, wrote a *Description of New Netherland*, a source of authentic information.

great city called by his name. [1] That his father had seen them in their old Dutch dresses playing at ninepins in a hollow of the mountain; and that he himself had heard, one summer afternoon, the sound of their balls, like distant peals of thunder.

To make a long story short, the company broke up, and returned to the more important concerns of the election. Rip's daughter took him home to live with her; she had a snug well-furnished house, and a stout cheery farmer for a husband, whom Rip recollected for one of the urchins that used to climb upon his back. As to Rip's son and heir, who was the ditto of himself, seen leaning against the tree, he was employed to work on the farm; but evinced an hereditary disposition to attend to anything else but his business.

Rip now resumed his old walks and habits; he soon found many of his former cronies, though all rather the worse for the wear and tear of time; and preferred making friends among the rising generation, with whom he soon grew into great favor.

Having nothing to do at home, and being arrived at that happy age when a man can be idle with impunity, he took his place once more on the bench at the inn door, and was reverenced as one of the patriarchs of the village, and a chronicle of the old times "before the war." It was some time before he could get into the regular track of gossip, or could be made to comprehend the strange events that had taken place during his torpor. How that there had been a revolutionary war—that the country had thrown off the yoke of old England —and that, instead of being a subject of His Majesty George the Third, he was now a free citizen of the United States. Rip, in fact, was no politician; the changes of states and empires made but little impression on him; but there was one species of despotism under which he had long groaned, and that was—petticoat government. Happily that was at an end; he had got his neck out of the yoke of matrimony, and could go in and out whenever he pleased, without dreading the tyranny of Dame Van Winkle. Whenever her name was mentioned, however, he shook his head, shrugged his shoulders, and cast up his eyes; which might pass either for an expression of resignation to his fate, or joy at his deliverance.

He used to tell his story to every stranger that arrived at Mr. Doolittle's hotel. He was observed, at first, to vary on some points every time he told it, which was, doubtless, owing to his having so recently awaked. It at last settled down precisely to the tale I have related, and not a man, woman, or child in the neighborhood but knew it by heart. Some always pretended to doubt the reality of it, and insisted Rip had been out of his head, and that this was one point on which he always remained flighty. The old Dutch inhabitants, however, almost universally gave it full credit. Even to this day they never hear a thunderstorm of a summer afternoon about the Kaatskill, but they say Hendrick Hudson and his crew are at their game of ninepins; and it is a common wish of all henpecked husbands in the neighborhood, when life hangs heavy on their hands, that they might have a quieting draught out of Rip Van Winkle's flagon.

NOTE

The foregoing Tale, one would suspect, had been suggested to Mr. Knickerbocker by a little German superstition about the Emperor Frederick *der Rothbart*,[2] and the Kypphäuser Mountain; the subjoined note, however, which he had appended to the tale, shows that it is an absolute fact, narrated with his usual fidelity:

"The story of Rip Van Winkle may seem incredible to many, but nevertheless I give it my full belief, for I know the vicinity of our old Dutch settlements to have been very subject to marvelous events and appearances. Indeed, I have heard many stranger stories than this, in the villages along the Hudson; all of which were too well authenticated to admit of a doubt. I have even talked with Rip Van Winkle myself, who, when last I saw him, was a very venerable old man, and so perfectly rational and consistent on every other point, that I think no conscientious person could refuse to take this into the bargain; nay, I have seen a certificate on the subject taken before a country justice and signed with a cross, in the justice's own handwriting. The story, therefore, is beyond the possibility of doubt.

"D. K."

POSTSCRIPT

The following are traveling notes from a memorandum-book of Mr. Knickerbocker:

The Kaatsberg, or Catskill Mountains, have always been a region full of fable. The Indians considered them the abode of spirits, who influenced

---

[1] The city of Hudson, twenty-eight miles south of Albany, has now only about twelve thousand inhabitants, but may have been relatively much larger in Irving's time; or, Irving may be joking.

[2] Frederick Barbarossa (red-beard), 1123-1190, emperor of the Holy Roman Empire, according to old legend sits asleep beside a marble table in the interior of the Kyffhäuser Mountain in Thuringia, Germany, surrounded by his knights and awaiting the day when he shall lead the Germans against their enemies.

the weather, spreading sunshine or clouds over the landscape, and sending good or bad hunting seasons. They were ruled by an old squaw spirit, said to be their mother. She dwelt on the highest peak of the Catskills, and had charge of the doors of day and night to open and shut them at the proper hour. She hung up the new moons in the skies, and cut up the old ones into stars. In times of drought, if properly propitiated, she would spin light summer clouds out of cobwebs and morning dew, and send them off from the crest of the mountain, flake after flake, like flakes of carded cotton, to float in the air; until, dissolved by the heat of the sun, they would fall in gentle showers, causing the grass to spring, the fruits to ripen, and the corn to grow an inch an hour. If displeased, however, she would brew up clouds black as ink, sitting in the midst of them like a bottle-bellied spider in the midst of its web; and when these clouds broke, woe betide the valleys!

In old times, say the Indian traditions, there was a kind of Manitou or Spirit, who kept about the wildest recesses of the Catskill Mountains, and took a mischievous pleasure in wreaking all kinds of evils and vexations upon the red men. Sometimes he would assume the form of a bear, a panther, or a deer, lead the bewildered hunter a weary chase through tangled forests and among ragged rocks; and then spring off with a loud ho! ho! leaving him aghast on the brink of a beetling precipice or raging torrent.

The favorite abode of this Manitou is still shown. It is a great rock or cliff on the loneliest part of the mountains, and, from the flowering vines which clamber about it, and the wild flowers which abound in its neighborhood, is known by the name of the Garden Rock. Near the foot of it is a small lake, the haunt of the solitary bittern, with water-snakes basking in the sun on the leaves of the pond-lilies which lie on the surface. This place was held in great awe by the Indians, insomuch that the boldest hunter would not pursue his game within its precincts. Once upon a time, however, a hunter, who had lost his way, penetrated to the Garden Rock, where he beheld a number of gourds placed in the crotches of trees. One of these he seized and made off with it, but in the hurry of his retreat he let it fall among the rocks when a great stream gushed forth, which washed him away and swept him down precipices, where he was dashed to pieces, and the stream made its way to the Hudson, and continues to flow to the present day; being the identical stream known by the name of the Kaaters-kill.

1818-19   1819

CHRISTMAS EVE

Saint Francis and Saint Benedight
Blesse this house from wicked wight;
From the night-mare and the goblin,
That is hight good fellow Robin;
Keep it from all evil spirits,

Fairies, weezels, rats, and ferrets:
From curfew time
To the next prime.
                                    CARTWRIGHT.

It was a brilliant moonlight night, but extremely cold; our chaise whirled rapidly over the frozen ground; the postboy smacked his whip incessantly, and a part of the time his horses were on a gallop. "He knows where he is going," said my companion, [1] laughing, "and is eager to arrive in time for some of the merriment and good cheer of the servants' hall. My father, you must know, is a bigoted devotee of the old school, and prides himself upon keeping up something of old English hospitality. He is a tolerable specimen of what you will rarely meet with nowadays in its purity, the old English country gentleman; for our men of fortune spend so much of their time in town, and fashion is carried so much into the country, that the strong rich peculiarities of ancient rural life are almost polished away. My father, however, from early years took honest Peacham [2] for his text-book, instead of Chesterfield; [3] he determined in his own mind that there was no condition more truly honorable and enviable than that of a country gentleman on his paternal lands, and therefore passes the whole of his time on his estate. He is a strenuous advocate for the revival of the old rural games and holiday observances, and is deeply read in the writers, ancient and modern, who have treated on the subject. Indeed his favorite range of reading is among the authors who flourished at least two centuries since; who, he insists, wrote and thought more like true Englishmen than any of their successors. He even regrets sometimes that he had not been born a few centuries earlier, when England was itself, and had its peculiar manners and customs. As he lives at some distance from the main road, in rather a lonely part of the country, without any rival gentry near him, he has that most enviable of all blessings to an Englishman, an opportunity of indulging the bent of his own humor without molestation. Being representative of the oldest family in the neighborhood, and a great part of the peasantry being his tenants, he is much looked up to, and, in general, is known simply by the appellation of

[1] Irving by chance had met at an inn his former traveling acquaintance, Frank Bracebridge, who had invited him to spend the Christmas at Bracebridge Hall.
[2] author of *The Complete Gentleman*, 1622
[3] Philip Stanhope, fourth Earl of Chesterfield, 1694-1773, the "mirror of politeness"

'The Squire'; a title which has been accorded to the head of the family since time immemorial. I think it best to give you these hints about my worthy old father, to prepare you for any eccentricities that might otherwise appear absurd."

We had passed for some time along the wall of a park, and at length the chaise stopped at the gate. It was in a heavy magnificent old style, of iron bars, fancifully wrought at top into flourishes and flowers. The huge square columns that supported the gate were surmounted by the family crest. Close adjoining was the porter's lodge, sheltered under dark fir trees, and almost buried in shrubbery.

The postboy rang a large porter's bell, which resounded through the still, frosty air, and was answered by the distant barking of dogs, with which the mansion-house seemed garrisoned. An old woman immediately appeared at the gate. As the moonlight fell strongly upon her, I had a full view of a little primitive dame, dressed very much in the antique taste, with a neat kerchief and stomacher, and her silver hair peeping from under a cap of snowy whiteness. She came courtseying forth, with many expressions of simple joy at seeing her young master. Her husband, it seemed, was up at the house keeping Christmas eve in the servants' hall; they could not do without him, as he was the best hand at a song and story in the household.

My friend proposed that we should alight and walk through the park to the hall, which was at no great distance, while the chaise should follow on. Our road wound through a noble avenue of trees, among the naked branches of which the moon glittered, as she rolled through the deep vault of a cloudless sky. The lawn beyond was sheeted with a slight covering of snow, which here and there sparkled as the moonbeams caught a frosty crystal; and at a distance might be seen a thin transparent vapor, stealing up from the low grounds, and threatening gradually to shroud the landscape.

My companion looked around him with transport: "How often," said he, "have I scampered up this avenue, on returning home on school vacations! How often have I played under these trees when a boy! I feel a degree of filial reverence for them, as we look up to those who have cherished us in childhood. My father was always scrupulous in exacting our holidays, and having us around him on family festivals. He used to direct and superintend our games with the strictness that some parents do the studies of their children. He was very particular that we should play the old English games according to their original form; and consulted old books for precedent and authority for every 'merrie disport'; yet I assure you there never was pedantry so delightful. It was the policy of the good old gentleman to make his children feel that home was the happiest place in the world; and I value this delicious home-feeling as one of the choicest gifts a parent could bestow."

We were interrupted by the clamor of a troop of dogs of all sorts and sizes, "mongrel, puppy, whelp, and hound, and curs of low degree," [1] that, disturbed by the ring of the porter's bell and the rattling of the chaise, came bounding, open-mouthed, across the lawn.

————The little dogs and all,
Tray, Blanch, and Sweetheart, see, they bark at me! [2]

cried Bracebridge, laughing. At the sound of his voice, the bark was changed into a yelp of delight, and in a moment he was surrounded and almost overpowered by the caresses of the faithful animals.

We had now come in full view of the old family mansion, partly thrown in deep shadow, and partly lit up by the cool moonshine. It was an irregular building, of some magnitude, and seemed to be of the architecture of different periods. One wing was evidently very ancient, with heavy stone-shafted bow windows jutting out and overrun with ivy, from among the foliage of which the small diamond-shaped panes of glass glittered with the moonbeams. The rest of the house was in the French taste of Charles the Second's time, having been repaired and altered, as my friend told me, by one of his ancestors, who returned with that monarch at the Restoration. The grounds about the house were laid out in the old formal manner of artificial flower-beds, clipped shrubberies, raised terraces, and heavy stone balustrades, ornamented with urns, a leaden statue or two, and a jet of water. The old gentleman, I was told, was extremely careful to preserve this obsolete finery in all its original state. He admired this fashion in gardening; it had an air of magnificence, was courtly and noble, and befitting good old family style. The boasted imitation of nature in modern gardening had sprung up with modern republican notions, but did not suit a monarchical government; it

---

[1] from "Elegy on a Mad Dog" in Goldsmith's *The Vicar of Wakefield*
[2] Shakespeare, *King Lear*, III, vi, 60

smacked of the leveling system.—I could not help smiling at this introduction of politics into gardening, though I expressed some apprehension that I should find the old gentleman rather intolerant in his creed.—Frank assured me, however, that it was almost the only instance in which he had ever heard his father meddle with politics; and he believed that he got this notion from a member of Parliament who once passed a few weeks with him. The Squire was glad of any argument to defend his clipped yew-trees and formal terraces, which had been occasionally attacked by modern landscape gardeners.

As we approached the house, we heard the sound of music, and now and then a burst of laughter, from one end of the building. This, Bracebridge said, must proceed from the servants' hall, where a great deal of revelry was permitted, and even encouraged by the Squire, throughout the twelve days of Christmas, provided everything was done conformably to ancient usage. Here were kept up the old games of hoodman blind, shoe the wild mare, hot cockles, steal the white loaf, bob apples, and snap dragon: the Yule clog [1] and Christmas candle were regularly burnt, and the mistletoe, with its white berries, hung up, to the imminent peril of all the pretty housemaids.

So intent were the servants upon their sports that we had to ring repeatedly before we could make ourselves heard. On our arrival being announced, the Squire came out to receive us, accompanied by his two other sons: one a young officer in the army, home on leave of absence; the other an Oxonian, just from the university. The Squire was a fine, healthy-looking old gentleman, with silver hair curling lightly round an open florid countenance; in which the physiognomist, with the advantage, like myself, of a previous hint or two, might discover a singular mixture of whim and benevolence.

The family meeting was warm and affectionate: as the evening was far advanced, the Squire would not permit us to change our traveling dresses, but ushered us at once to the company, which was assembled in a large old-fashioned hall. It was composed of different branches of a numerous family connection, where there were the usual proportion of old uncles and aunts, comfortable married dames, superannuated spinsters, blooming country cousins, half-fledged striplings, and bright-eyed boarding-school hoydens. They were variously

[1] the log which must be kept burning all through Christmas night or ill-luck will come upon the house

occupied: some at a round game of cards; others conversing around the fireplace; at one end of the hall was a group of the young folks, some nearly grown up, others of a more tender and budding age, fully engrossed by a merry game; and a profusion of wooden horses, penny trumpets, and tattered dolls, about the floor, showed traces of a troop of little fairy beings who, having frolicked through a happy day, had been carried off to slumber through a peaceful night.

While the mutual greetings were going on between young Bracebridge and his relatives, I had time to scan the apartment. I have called it a hall, for so it had certainly been in old times, and the Squire had evidently endeavored to restore it to something of its primitive state. Over the heavy projecting fireplace was suspended a picture of a warrior in armor, standing by a white horse, and on the opposite wall hung a helmet, buckler, and lance. At one end an enormous pair of antlers were inserted in the wall, the branches serving as hooks on which to suspend hats, whips, and spurs; and in the corners of the apartment were fowling-pieces, fishing-rods, and other sporting implements. The furniture was of the cumbrous workmanship of former days, though some articles of modern convenience had been added, and the oaken floor had been carpeted; so that the whole presented an odd mixture of parlor and hall.

The grate had been removed from the wide overwhelming fireplace, to make way for a fire of wood, in the midst of which was an enormous log glowing and blazing, and sending forth a vast volume of light and heat: this I understood was the Yule clog, which the Squire was particular in having brought in and illumined on a Christmas eve, according to ancient custom.

It was really delightful to see the old Squire seated in his hereditary elbow-chair, by the hospitable fireside of his ancestors, and looking around him like the sun of a system, beaming warmth and gladness to every heart. Even the very dog that lay stretched at his feet, as he lazily shifted his position and yawned, would look fondly up in his master's face, wag his tail against the floor, and stretch himself again to sleep, confident of kindness and protection. There is an emanation from the heart in genuine hospitality which cannot be described, but is immediately felt, and puts the stranger at once at his ease. I had not been seated many minutes by the comfortable hearth of the worthy old cavalier, before I found myself as much at home as if I had been one of the family.

Supper was announced shortly after our arrival. It was served up in a spacious oaken chamber, the panels of which shone with wax, and around which were several family portraits decorated with holly and ivy. Besides the accustomed lights, two great wax tapers, called Christmas candles, wreathed with greens, were placed on a highly-polished beaufet among the family plate. The table was abundantly spread with substantial fare; but the Squire made his supper of frumenty, a dish made of wheatcakes boiled in milk, with rich spices, being a standing dish in old times for Christmas eve.

I was happy to find my old friend, minced pie, in the retinue of the feast; and finding him to be perfectly orthodox, and that I need not be ashamed of my predilection, I greeted him with all the warmth wherewith we usually greet an old and very genteel acquaintance.

The mirth of the company was greatly promoted by the humors of an eccentric personage whom Mr. Bracebridge always addressed with the quaint appellation of Master Simon. He was a tight brisk little man, with the air of an arrant old bachelor. His nose was shaped like the bill of a parrot; his face slightly pitted with the smallpox, with a dry perpetual bloom on it, like a frost-bitten leaf in autumn. He had an eye of great quickness and vivacity, with a drollery and lurking waggery of expression that was irresistible. He was evidently the wit of the family, dealing very much in sly jokes and innuendoes with the ladies, and making infinite merriment by harping upon old themes; which, unfortunately, my ignorance of the family chronicles did not permit me to enjoy. It seemed to be his great delight during supper to keep a young girl next him in a continual agony of stifled laughter, in spite of her awe of the reproving looks of her mother, who sat opposite. Indeed, he was the idol of the younger part of the company, who laughed at everything he said or did, and at every turn of his countenance; I could not wonder at it, for he must have been a miracle of accomplishments in their eyes. He could imitate Punch and Judy; make an old woman of his hand, with the assistance of a burnt cork and pockethandkerchief; and cut an orange into such a ludicrous caricature, that the young folks were ready to die with laughing.

I was let briefly into his history by Frank Bracebridge. He was an old bachelor, of a small independent income, which, by careful management, was sufficient for all his wants.

He revolved through the family system like a vagrant comet in its orbit; sometimes visiting one branch, and sometimes another quite remote; as is often the case with gentlemen of extensive connections and small fortunes in England. He had a chirping buoyant disposition, always enjoying the present moment; and his frequent change of scene and company prevented his acquiring those rusty unaccommodating habits, with which old bachelors are so uncharitably charged. He was a complete family chronicle, being versed in the genealogy, history, and intermarriages of the whole house of Bracebridge, which made him a great favorite with the old folks; he was a beau of all the elder ladies and superannuated spinsters, among whom he was habitually considered rather a young fellow, and he was master of the revels among the children; so that there was not a more popular being in the sphere in which he moved than Mr. Simon Bracebridge. Of late years, he had resided almost entirely with the Squire, to whom he had become a factotum, and whom he particularly delighted by jumping with his humor in respect to old times, and by having a scrap of an old song to suit every occasion. We had presently a specimen of his last-mentioned talent; for no sooner was supper removed, and spiced wines and other beverages peculiar to the season introduced, than Master Simon was called on for a good old Christmas song. He bethought himself for a moment, and then, with a sparkle of the eye, and a voice that was by no means bad, excepting that it ran occasionally into a falsetto, like the notes of a split reed, he quavered forth a quaint old ditty.

> Now Christmas is come,
> Let us beat up the drum,
> And call all our neighbors together,
> And when they appear,
> Let us make them such cheer,
> As will keep out the wind and the weather, etc.

The supper had disposed everyone to gayety, and an old harper was summoned from the servants' hall, where he had been strumming all the evening, and to all appearance comforting himself with some of the Squire's homebrewed. He was a kind of hanger-on, I was told, of the establishment, and, though ostensibly a resident of the village, was oftener to be found in the Squire's kitchen than his own home, the old gentleman being fond of the sound of "harp in hall."

The dance, like most dances after supper, was a merry one; some of the older folks joined in it, and the Squire himself figured down several couple with a partner, with whom he affirmed he had danced at every Christmas for nearly half a century. Master Simon, who seemed to be a kind of connecting link between the old times and the new, and to be withal a little antiquated in the taste of his accomplishments, evidently piqued himself on his dancing, and was endeavoring to gain credit by the heel and toe, rigadoon, and other graces of the ancient school; but he had unluckily assorted himself with a little romping girl from boarding-school, who, by her wild vivacity, kept him continually on the stretch, and defeated all his sober attempts at elegance:—such are the ill-assorted matches to which antique gentlemen are unfortunately prone!

The young Oxonian, on the contrary, had led out one of his maiden aunts, on whom the rogue played a thousand little knaveries with impunity: he was full of practical jokes, and his delight was to tease his aunts and cousins; yet, like all madcap youngsters, he was a universal favorite among the women. The most interesting couple in the dance was the young officer and a ward of the Squire's, a beautiful blushing girl of seventeen. From several shy glances which I had noticed in the course of the evening, I suspected there was a little kindness growing up between them; and, indeed, the young soldier was just the hero to captivate a romantic girl. He was tall, slender, and handsome, and, like most young British officers of late years, had picked up various small accomplishments on the continent;—he could talk French and Italian—draw landscapes—sing very tolerably—dance divinely; but, above all, he had been wounded at Waterloo:—what girl of seventeen, well read in poetry and romance, could resist such a mirror of chivalry and perfection!

The moment the dance was over, he caught up a guitar and, lolling against the old marble fireplace, in an attitude which I am half inclined to suspect, was studied, began the little French air of the Troubadour. [1] The Squire, however, exclaimed against having anything on Christmas eve but good old English; upon which the young minstrel, casting up his eye for a moment, as if in an effort of memory, struck into another strain, and, with a charming air of gallantry, gave Herrick's [2] *Night-piece, to Julia*.

[1] The Troubadours were poets of the twelfth and thirteenth centuries who used the Langue d'Oc, the language of southern France.
[2] Robert Herrick, 1591-1674, an English poet

Her eyes the glow-worm lend thee;
The shooting stars attend thee,
  And the elves also,
  Whose little eyes glow
Like the sparks of fire, befriend thee.

No Will-o'-the-Wisp mislight thee;
Nor snake nor slow-worm bite thee;
  But on, on thy way,
  Not making a stay,
Since ghost there is none to affright thee.

Then let not the dark thee cumber;
What though the moon does slumber,
  The stars of the night
  Will lend thee their light,
Like tapers clear without number.

Then, Julia, let me woo thee,
Thus, thus to come unto me:
  And when I shall meet
  Thy silvery feet,
My soul I'll pour into thee.

The song might or might not have been intended in compliment to the fair Julia, for so I found his partner was called; she, however, was certainly unconscious of any such application, for she never looked at the singer, but kept her eyes cast upon the floor. Her face was suffused, it is true, with a beautiful blush, and there was a gentle heaving of the bosom, but all that was doubtless caused by the exercise of the dance; indeed, so great was her indifference, that she amused herself with plucking to pieces a choice bouquet of hot-house flowers, and by the time the song was concluded the nosegay lay in ruins on the floor.

The party now broke up for the night with the kind-hearted old custom of shaking hands. As I passed through the hall, on my way to my chamber, the dying embers of the Yule clog still sent forth a dusky glow, and had it not been the season when "no spirit dares stir abroad," I should have been half tempted to steal from my room at midnight, and peep whether the fairies might not be at their revels about the hearth.

My chamber was in the old part of the mansion, the ponderous furniture of which might have been fabricated in the days of the giants. The room was paneled with cornices of heavy carved work, in which flowers and grotesque faces were strangely intermingled; and a row of black-looking portraits stared mournfully at me from the walls. The bed was of rich, though faded damask, with a lofty tester, [3] and stood in a niche opposite a bow window. I had scarcely got into bed when a strain of music

[3] canopy

seemed to break forth in the air just below the window. I listened, and found it proceeded from a band, which I concluded to be the waits [1] from some neighboring village. They went round the house, playing under the windows. I drew aside the curtains to hear them more distinctly. The moonbeams fell through the upper part of the casement, partially lighting up the antiquated apartment. The sounds, as they receded, became more soft and aërial, and seemed to accord with the quiet and moonlight. I listened and listened,—they became more and more tender and remote, and, as they gradually died away, my head sunk upon the pillow, and I fell asleep.

1819

From THE ALHAMBRA [2]
From PALACE OF THE ALHAMBRA

To the traveler imbued with a feeling for the historical and poetical, so inseparably intertwined in the annals of romantic Spain, the Alhambra is as much an object of devotion as is the Caaba [3] to all true Moslems. How many legends and traditions, true and fabulous,—how many songs and ballads, Arabian and Spanish, of love and war and chivalry, are associated with this Oriental pile! It was the royal abode of the Moorish kings, where, surrounded with the splendors and refinements of Asiatic luxury, they held dominion over what they vaunted as a terrestrial paradise, and made their last stand for empire in Spain. The royal palace forms but a part of a fortress, the walls of which, studded with towers, stretch irregularly round the whole crest of a hill, a spur of the Sierra Nevada or Snowy Mountains, and overlook the city; externally it is a rude congregation of towers and battlements, with no regularity of plan nor grace of architecture, and giving little promise of the grace and beauty which prevail within.

[1] Christmas serenaders
[2] The Alhambra, a fortress begun by Moorish kings in the twelfth century on a hill overlooking Granada, was the last foothold of the Moors in Spain, and still stands as the visible emblem of the former Moslem empire in Europe. The Moors entered Spain in the eighth century, quickly overcame the Gothic kingdom of some three centuries' standing, and maintained a civilization that in many respects was the most enlightened in medieval Europe. Science, literature, and philosophy were encouraged. From the twelfth century the Moorish power declined until in the fifteenth century Granada, which had attained great influence and splendor, was the only remaining city of the Moors; and this, rent by internal feuds, at length fell to Ferdinand and Isabella in 1492.
  Irving, while attaché of the American legation at Madrid, lived during some months of 1829 in the Alhambra, as *The Alhambra* narrates.
[3] the Kaaba at Mecca, the most sacred Moslem shrine

In the time of the Moors the fortress was capable of containing within its outward precincts an army of forty thousand men, and served occasionally as a stronghold of the sovereigns against their rebellious subjects. After the kingdom had passed into the hands of the Christians, the Alhambra continued to be a royal demesne, and was occasionally inhabited by the Castilian monarchs. The emperor Charles V [4] commenced a sumptuous palace within its walls, but was deterred from completing it by repeated shocks of earthquakes. The last royal residents were Philip V. and his beautiful queen, Elizabetta of Parma, early in the eighteenth century. Great preparations were made for their reception. The palace and gardens were placed in a state of repair, and a new suite of apartments erected, and decorated by artists brought from Italy. The sojourn of the sovereigns was transient, and after their departure the palace once more became desolate. Still the place was maintained with some military state. The governor held it immediately from the crown; its jurisdiction extended down into the suburbs of the city, and was independent of the captain-general of Granada. [5] A considerable garrison was kept up; the governor had his apartments in the front of the old Moorish palace, and never descended into Granada without some military parade. The fortress, in fact, was a little town of itself, having several streets of houses within its walls, together with a Franciscan convent and a parochial church.

The desertion of the court, however, was a fatal blow to the Alhambra. Its beautiful halls became desolate, and some of them fell to ruin; the gardens were destroyed, and the fountains ceased to play. By degrees the dwellings became filled with a loose and lawless population: contrabandistas, [6] who availed themselves of its independent jurisdiction to carry on a wide and daring course of smuggling, and thieves and rogues of all sorts, who made this their place of refuge whence they might depredate upon Granada and its vicinity. The strong arm of government at length interfered; the whole community was thoroughly sifted; none were suffered to remain but such as were of honest character, and had legitimate right to a

[4] Charles V, 1500-1558, grandson of Ferdinand and Isabella, ruler of the Holy Roman Empire, Spain, The Netherlands, Mexico, and Peru, was the most powerful monarch of his time in Europe. In 1555 he gave up Spain and Netherlands to his son Philip; and in 1557 he abdicated the throne in favor of his brother Ferdinand. His equestrian portrait by Titian is famous.
[5] chief official of the province of Granada
[6] smugglers

residence; the greater part of the houses were demolished and a mere hamlet left, with the parochial church and the Franciscan convent. During the recent troubles in Spain, when Granada was in the hands of the French,[1] the Alhambra was garrisoned by their troops, and the palace was occasionally inhabited by the French commander. With that enlightened taste which has ever distinguished the French nation in their conquests, this monument of Moorish elegance and grandeur was rescued from the absolute ruin and desolation that were overwhelming it. The roofs were repaired, the saloons and galleries protected from the weather, the gardens cultivated, the water courses restored, the fountains once more made to throw up their sparkling showers; and Spain may thank her invaders for having preserved to her the most beautiful and interesting of her historical monuments.

On the departure of the French they blew up several towers of the outer wall, and left the fortifications scarcely tenable. Since that time the military importance of the post is at an end. The garrison is a handful of invalid soldiers, whose principal duty is to guard some of the outer towers, which serve occasionally as a prison of state; and the governor, abandoning the lofty hill of the Alhambra, resides in the center of Granada, for the more convenient dispatch of his official duties. I cannot conclude this brief notice of the state of the fortress without bearing testimony to the honorable exertions of its present commander,[2] Don Francisco de Serna, who is tasking all the limited resources at his command to put the palace in a state of repair, and by his judicious precautions has for some time arrested its too certain decay. Had his predecessors discharged the duties of their station with equal fidelity, the Alhambra might yet have remained in almost its pristine beauty; were government to second him with means equal to his zeal, this relic of it might still be preserved for many generations to adorn the land, and attract the curious and enlightened of every clime.

Our first object of course, on the morning after our arrival, was a visit to this time-honored edifice; it has been so often, however, and so minutely described by travelers, that I shall not undertake to give a comprehensive and elaborate account of it, but merely occasional sketches of parts, with the incidents and associations connected with them.

．　　．　　．　　．　　．　　．　　．

While waiting for admittance, our self-imposed cicerone,[3] Mateo Ximenes, informed us that the royal palace was intrusted to the care of a worthy old maiden dame called Doña Antonia-Molina, but who, according to Spanish custom, went by the more neighborly appellation of Tia Antonia (Aunt Antonia), who maintained the Moorish halls and gardens in order and showed them to strangers. While we were talking, the door was opened by a plump little black-eyed Andalusian damsel, whom Mateo addressed as Dolores, but who from her bright looks and cheerful disposition evidently merited a merrier name.[4] Mateo informed me in a whisper that she was the niece of Tia Antonia, and I found she was the good fairy who was to conduct us through the enchanted palace. Under her guidance we crossed the threshold, and were at once transported, as if by magic wand, into other times and an oriental realm, and were treading the scenes of Arabian story. Nothing could be in greater contrast than the unpromising exterior of the pile with the scene now before us. We found ourselves in a vast patio or court, one hundred and fifty feet in length, and upwards of eighty feet in breadth, paved with white marble, and decorated at each end with light Moorish peristyles,[5] one of which supported an elegant gallery of fretted architecture. Along the moldings of the cornices and on various parts of the walls were escutcheons and ciphers, and cufic[6] and Arabic characters in high relief, repeating the pious mottoes of the Moslem monarchs, the builders of the Alhambra, or extolling their grandeur and munificence. Along the center of the court extended an immense basin or tank (estanque), a hundred and twenty-four feet in length, twenty-seven in breadth, and five in depth, receiving its water from two marble vases. Hence it is called the Court of the Alberca (from al Beerkah, the Arabic for a pond or tank). Great numbers of gold-fish were to be seen gleaming through the waters of the basin, and it was bordered by hedges of roses.

Passing from the court of the Alberca under a Moorish archway, we entered the renowned court of Lions. No part of the edifice gives a more complete idea of its original beauty than this, for none has suffered so little from the ravages of time. In the center stands the fountain famous in song and story. The alabaster basins still shed their diamond drops; the

[1] during the Napoleonic wars
[2] in 1829

[3] Mateo was born within the old palace and called himself a legitimate son of the Alhambra.
[4] Dolores means "sorrows."   [5] rows of columns
[6] from Cufa or Kufa, an old city on the Euphrates noted for expert reproductions of the Koran

twelve lions which support them, and give the court its name, still cast forth crystal streams as in the days of Boabdil. [1] The lions, however, are unworthy of their fame, being of miserable sculpture, the work probably of some Christian captive. The court is laid out in flower-beds, instead of its ancient and appropriate pavement of tiles or marble; the alteration, an instance of bad taste, was made by the French when in possession of Granada. Round the four sides of the court are light Arabian arcades of open filigree work, supported by slender pillars of white marble, which it is supposed were originally gilded. The architecture, like that in most parts of the interior of the palace, is characterized by elegance rather than grandeur, bespeaking a delicate and graceful taste, and a disposition to indolent enjoyment. When one looks upon the fairy traces of the peristyles, and the apparently fragile fretwork of the walls, it is difficult to believe that so much has survived the wear and tear of centuries, the shocks of earthquakes, the violence of war, and the quiet, though no less baneful, pilferings of the tasteful traveler: it is almost sufficient to excuse the popular tradition, that the whole is protected by a magic charm.

On one side of the court a rich portal opens into the Hall of the Abencerrages: [2] so called from the gallant cavaliers of that illustrious line who were here perfidiously massacred. There are some who doubt the whole story, but our humble cicerone Mateo pointed out the very wicket of the portal through which they were introduced one by one into the court of Lions, and the white marble fountain in the center of the hall beside which they were beheaded. He showed us also certain broad ruddy stains on the pavement, traces of their blood, which, according to popular belief, can never be effaced.

. . . .

Immediately opposite the hall of the Abencerrages, a portal, richly adorned, leads into a hall of less tragical associations. It is light and lofty, exquisitely graceful in its architecture, paved with white marble, and bears the suggestive name of the Hall of the Two Sisters. Some destroy the romance of the name by attributing it to two enormous slabs of alabaster which lie side by side, and form a great part of the pavement: an opinion strongly supported by Mateo Ximenes. Others are disposed to

give the name a more poetical significance, as the vague memorial of Moorish beauties who once graced this hall, which was evidently a part of the royal harem. This opinion I was happy to find entertained by our little bright-eyed guide, Dolores, who pointed to a balcony over an inner porch; which gallery, she had been told, belonged to the women's apartment. "You see, señor," said she, "it is all grated and latticed, like the gallery in a convent chapel where the nuns hear mass; for the Moorish kings," added she, indignantly, "shut up their wives just like nuns."

The latticed "jalousies," in fact, still remain, whence the dark-eyed beauties of the harem might gaze unseen upon the zambras [3] and other dances and entertainments of the hall below.

On each side of this hall are recesses or alcoves for ottomans and couches, on which the voluptuous lords of the Alhambra indulged in that dreamy repose so dear to the Orientalists. A cupola or lantern admits a tempered light from above and a free circulation of air; while on one side is heard the refreshing sound of waters from the fountain of the lions, and on the other side the soft plash from the basin in the garden of Lindaraxa.

It is impossible to contemplate this scene, so perfectly Oriental, without feeling the early associations of Arabian romance, and almost expecting to see the white arm of some mysterious princess beckoning from the gallery, or some dark eye sparkling through the lattice. The abode of beauty is here as if it had been inhabited but yesterday; but where are the two sisters, where the Zoraydas and Lindaraxas! [4]

An abundant supply of water, brought from the mountains by old Moorish aqueducts, circulates throughout the palace, supplying its baths and fish-pools, sparkling in jets within its halls or murmuring in channels along the marble pavements. When it has paid its tribute to the royal pile, and visited its gardens and parterres, it flows down the long avenue leading to the city, tinkling in rills, gushing in fountains, and maintaining a perpetual verdure in those groves that embower and beautify the whole hill of the Alhambra.

Those only who have sojourned in the ardent climates of the South can appreciate the delights of an abode combining the breezy coolness of the mountain with the freshness and verdure of the valley. While the city below

---

[1] Boabdil (called El Chico, the little) was the last Moorish sovereign of Granada.
[2] A Moorish tribal family of Granada at feud with the Zegrys; its warriors are supposed to have been massacred under King Abu Hassan toward the close of the Moorish dynasty.

[3] feasts, merrymakings
[4] Legendary beauties of the Moorish court; see *The Mysterious Chambers*, p. 205.

pants with the noontide heat, and the parched Vega [1] trembles to the eye, the delicate airs from the Sierra Nevada play through these lofty halls, bringing with them the sweetness of the surrounding gardens. Everything invites to that indolent repose, the bliss of southern climes; and while the half-shut eye looks out from shaded balconies upon the glittering landscape, the ear is lulled by the rustling of groves and the murmur of running streams.

.   .   .   .

From THE HALL OF AMBASSADORS

In one of my visits to the old Moorish chamber where the good Tia Antonia cooks her dinner and receives her company, I observed a mysterious door in one corner, leading apparently into the ancient part of the edifice. My curiosity being aroused, I opened it, and found myself in a narrow, blind corridor, groping along which I came to the head of a dark winding staircase, leading down an angle of the tower of Comares. [2] Down this staircase I descended darkling, guiding myself by the wall, until I came to a small door at the bottom, throwing which open, I was suddenly dazzled by emerging into the brilliant antechamber of the Hall of Ambassadors; with the fountain of the court of the Alberca sparkling before me. The antechamber is separated from the court by an elegant gallery, supported by slender columns with spandrels [3] of open work in the Morisco style. At each end of the antechamber are alcoves, and its ceiling is richly stuccoed and painted. Passing through a magnificent portal, I found myself in the far-famed Hall of Ambassadors, the audience chamber of the Moslem monarchs. It is said to be thirty-seven feet square, and sixty feet high; occupies the whole interior of the Tower of Comares; and still bears the traces of past magnificence. The walls are beautifully stuccoed and decorated with Morisco fancifulness; the lofty ceiling was originally of the same favorite material, with the usual frostwork and pensile [4] ornaments or stalactites; which, with the embellishments of vivid coloring and gilding, must have been gorgeous in the extreme. Unfortunately it gave way during an earthquake, and brought down with it an immense arch which traversed the hall. It was replaced by the present vault or

[1] plain, lowland
[2] A heavy tower of the fortress; it contains the Hall of the Ambassadors.
[3] in a wall pierced by arches, as here, the flat spaces between the arches themselves; or the wall just outside the curve of an arch piercing it
[4] hanging

dome of larch or cedar, with intersecting ribs, the whole curiously wrought and richly colored; still Oriental in its character, reminding one of "those ceilings of cedar and vermilion that we read of in the Prophets and the Arabian Nights."

From the great height of the vault above the windows, the upper part of the hall is almost lost in obscurity; yet there is a magnificence as well as solemnity in the gloom, as through it we have gleams of rich gilding and the brilliant tints of the Moorish pencil.

The royal throne was placed opposite the entrance in a recess, which still bears an inscription intimating that Yusef I [5] (the monarch who completed the Alhambra) made this the throne of his empire. Everything in this noble hall seems to have been calculated to surround the throne with impressive dignity and splendor; there is none of the elegant voluptuousness which reigns in other parts of the palace. The tower is of massive strength, domineering over the whole edifice and overhanging the steep hillside. On three sides of the Hall of Ambassadors are windows cut through the immense thickness of the walls, and commanding extensive prospects. The balcony of the central window especially looks down upon the verdant valley of the Darro, with its walks, its groves, and gardens. To the left it enjoys a distant prospect of the Vega; while directly in front rises the rival height of the Albaycin, with its medley of streets, and terraces, and gardens, and once crowned by a fortress that vied in power with the Alhambra. "Ill fated the man who lost all this!" exclaimed Charles V., as he looked forth from his window upon the enchanting scenery it commands.

The balcony of the window where this royal exclamation was made, has of late become one of my favorite resorts. I have just been seated there, enjoying the close of a long brilliant day. The sun, as he sank behind the purple mountains of Alhama, sent a stream of effulgence up the valley of the Darro, that spread a melancholy pomp over the ruddy towers of the Alhambra; while the Vega, covered with a slight sultry vapor that caught the setting ray, seemed spread out in the distance like a golden sea. Not a breath of air disturbed the stillness of the hour, and though the faint sound of music and merriment now and then rose from the gardens of the Darro, it but rendered more impressive the monumental silence of the pile which overshadowed me. It was one of those hours and scenes in which memory asserts an

[5] Yusef succeeded to the throne in 1333.

almost magical power; and, like the evening sun beaming on these moldering towers, sends back her retrospective rays to light up the glories of the past.

*   *   *   *   *

THE MYSTERIOUS CHAMBERS

As I was rambling one day about the Moorish halls, my attention was, for the first time, attracted to a door in a remote gallery, communicating apparently with some part of the Alhambra which I had not yet explored. I attempted to open it, but it was locked. I knocked, but no one answered, and the sound seemed to reverberate through empty chambers. Here then was a mystery. Here was the haunted wing of the castle. How was I to get at the dark secrets here shut up from the public eye? Should I come privately at night with lamp and sword, according to the prying custom of heroes of romance; or should I endeavor to draw the secret from Pépe the stuttering gardener; or the ingenuous Dolores, or the loquacious Mateo? Or should I go frankly and openly to Dame Antonia the chatelaine, and ask her about it? I chose the latter course, as being the simplest though the least romantic; and found, somewhat to my disappointment, that there was no mystery in the case. I was welcome to explore the apartment, and there was the key.

Thus provided, I returned forthwith to the door. It opened, as I had surmised, to a range of vacant chambers; but they were quite different from the rest of the palace. The architecture, though rich and antiquated, was European. There was nothing Moorish about it. The first two rooms were lofty; the ceilings, broken in many places, were of cedar, deeply paneled and skilfully carved with fruits and flowers, intermingled with grotesque masks or faces.

The walls had evidently in ancient times been hung with damask; but now were naked, and scrawled over by that class of aspiring travelers who defile noble monuments with their worthless names. The windows, dismantled and open to wind and weather, looked out into a charming little secluded garden, where an alabaster fountain sparkled among roses and myrtles, and was surrounded by orange and citron trees, some of which flung their branches into the chambers. Beyond these rooms were two saloons, longer but less lofty, looking also into the garden. In the compartments of the paneled ceilings were baskets of fruit and garlands of flowers, painted by no mean hand, and in tolerable preservation. The walls also had been painted in fresco in the Italian style, but the paintings were nearly obliterated; the windows were in the same shattered state with those of the other chambers. This fanciful suite of rooms terminated in an open gallery with balustrades, running at right angles along another side of the garden. The whole apartment, so delicate and elegant in its decorations, so choice and sequestered in its situation along this retired little garden, and so different in architecture from the neighboring halls, awakened an interest in its history. I found on inquiry that it was an apartment fitted up by Italian artists in the early part of the last century, at the time when Philip V. and his second wife, the beautiful Elizabetta of Farnese, daughter of the Duke of Parma, were expected at the Alhambra. It was destined for the queen and the ladies of her train. One of the loftiest chambers had been her sleeping-room. A narrow staircase, now walled up, led up to a delightful belvidere, originally a mirador [1] of the Moorish sultanas, communicating with the harem; but which was fitted up as a boudoir for the fair Elizabetta, and still retains the name of *el tocador de la reyna,* or the queen's toilette.

One window of the royal sleeping-room commanded a prospect of the Generalife [2] and its embowered terraces; another looked out into the little secluded garden I have mentioned, which was decidedly Moorish in its character, and also had its history. It was in fact the garden of Lindaraxa, so often mentioned in descriptions of the Alhambra; but who this Lindaraxa was I had never heard explained. A little research gave me the few particulars known about her. She was a Moorish beauty who flourished in the court of Muhamed the Left-Handed, [3] and was the daughter of his loyal adherent, the alcayde of Malaga, who sheltered him in his city when driven from the throne. On regaining his crown, the alcayde was rewarded for his fidelity. His daughter had her apartment in the Alhambra, and was given by the king in marriage to Nasar, a young Cetimerien prince descended from Aben Hud the Just. Their espousals were doubtless celebrated in the royal palace, and their honeymoon may have passed among these very bowers.

Four centuries had elapsed since the fair Lindaraxa passed away, yet how much of the fragile beauty of the scenes she inhabited remained! The garden still bloomed in which

---

[1] Belvidere and mirador have the same meaning, a roofed but open chamber affording a view.
[2] a Moorish palace east of the Alhambra
[3] Muhamed Nasar El Hayzare, or left-handed, ascended the throne in 1423.

she delighted; the fountain still presented the crystal mirror in which her charms may once have been reflected; the alabaster, it is true, had lost its whiteness, the basin beneath, over-run with weeds, had become the lurking-place of the lizard, but there was something in the very decay that enhanced the interest of the scene, speaking as it did of that mutability, the irrevocable lot of man and all his works.

The desolation too of these chambers, once the abode of the proud and elegant Elizabetta, had a more touching charm for me than if I had beheld them in their pristine splendor, glittering with the pageantry of a court.

When I returned to my quarters, in the governor's apartment, everything seemed tame and commonplace after the poetic region I had left. The thought suggested itself: Why could I not change my quarters to these vacant chambers? that would indeed be living in the Alhambra, surrounded by its gardens and fountains, as in the time of the Moorish sovereigns. I proposed the change to Dame Antonia and her family, and it occasioned vast surprise. They could not conceive any rational inducement for the choice of an apartment so forlorn, remote, and solitary. Dolores exclaimed at its frightful loneliness; nothing but bats and owls flitting about,—and then a fox and wildcat kept in the vaults of the neighboring baths, and roamed about at night. The good Tia had more reasonable objections. The neighborhood was infested by vagrants; gipsies swarmed in the caverns of the adjacent hills; the palace was ruinous and easy to be entered in many places; the rumor of a stranger quartered alone in one of the rooms and ruined apartments, out of the hearing of the rest of the inhabitants, might tempt unwelcome visitors in the night, especially as foreigners were always supposed to be well stocked with money. I was not to be diverted from my humor, however, and my will was law with these good people. So, calling in the assistance of a carpenter, and the ever officious Mateo Ximenes, the doors and windows were soon placed in a state of tolerable security, and the sleeping-room of the stately Elizabetta prepared for my reception. Mateo kindly volunteered as a body-guard to sleep in my ante-chamber; but I did not think it worth while to put his valor to the proof.

With all the hardihood I had assumed and all the precautions I had taken, I must confess the first night passed in these quarters was inexpressibly dreary. I do not think it was so much the apprehension of dangers from without that affected me, as the character of the place

itself, with all its strange associations: the deeds of violence committed there; the tragical ends of many of those who had once reigned there in splendor. As I passed beneath the fated halls of the tower of Comares on the way to my chamber, I called to mind a quotation, that used to thrill me in the days of boyhood:

Fate sits on these dark battlements and frowns;
And, as the portal opens to receive me,
A voice in sullen echoes through the courts
Tells of a nameless deed! [1]

The whole family escorted me to my chamber, and took leave of me as of one engaged on a perilous enterprise; and when I heard their retreating steps die away along the waste ante-chambers and echoing galleries, and turned the key of my door, I was reminded of those hob-goblin stories, where the hero is left to accomplish the adventure of an enchanted house.

Even the thoughts of the fair Elizabetta and the beauties of her court, who had once graced these chambers, now, by a perversion of fancy, added to the gloom. Here was the scene of their transient gayety and loveliness; here were the very traces of their elegance and enjoyment; but what and where were they? Dust and ashes! tenants of the tomb! phantoms of the memory! . . . .

In the course of a few evenings a thorough change took place in the scene and its associations. The moon, which when I took possession of my new apartments was invisible, gradually gained each evening upon the darkness of the night, and at length rolled in full splendor above the towers, pouring a flood of tempered light into every court and hall. The garden beneath my window, before wrapped in gloom, was gently lighted up, the orange and citron trees were tipped with silver; the fountain sparkled in the moonbeams, and even the blush of the rose was faintly visible.

I now felt the poetic merit of the Arabic inscription on the walls,—"How beauteous is this garden; where the flowers of the earth vie with the stars of heaven. What can compare with the vase of yon alabaster fountain filled with crystal water? nothing but the moon in her fulness, shining in the midst of an unclouded sky!"

On such heavenly nights I would sit for hours at my window inhaling the sweetness of the garden, and musing on the checkered fortunes of those whose history was dimly shadowed out in the elegant memorials around. Sometimes,

[1] This is the motto on the title-page of Mrs. Anne Radcliffe's *Mysteries of Udolpho*, an English romantic novel of 1794.

when all was quiet, and the clock from the distant cathedral of Granada struck the midnight hour, I have sallied out on another tour and wandered over the whole building; but how different from my first tour! No longer dark and mysterious; no longer peopled with shadowy foes; no longer recalling scenes of violence and murder; all was open, spacious, beautiful; everything called up pleasing and romantic fancies; Lindaraxa once more walked in her garden; the gay chivalry of Moslem Granada once more glittered about the Court of Lions! Who can do justice to a moonlight night in such a climate and such a place? The temperature of a summer midnight in Andalusia is perfectly ethereal. We seem lifted up into a purer atmosphere; we feel a serenity of soul, a buoyancy of spirits, an elasticity of frame, which render mere existence happiness. But when moonlight is added to all this, the effect is like enchantment. Under its plastic sway the Alhambra seems to regain its pristine glories. Every rent and chasm of time; every moldering tint and weather-stain is gone; the marble resumes its original whiteness; the long colonnades brighten in the moonbeams; the halls are illuminated with a softened radiance, —we tread the enchanted palace of an Arabian tale!

What a delight at such a time, to ascend to the little airy pavilion of the queen's toilet (*el tocador de la reyna*), which, like a birdcage, overhangs the valley of the Darro, and gaze from its light arcades upon the moonlight prospect! To the right, the swelling mountains of the Sierra Nevada, robbed of their ruggedness and softened into a fairy land, with their snowy summits gleaming like silver clouds against the deep blue sky. And then to lean over the parapet of the Tocador and gaze down upon Granada and the Albaycin [1] spread out like a map below; all buried in deep repose; the white palaces and convents sleeping in the moonshine, and beyond all these the vapory Vega fading away like a dreamland in the distance.

Sometimes the faint click of castanets rises from the Alameda, where some gay Andalusians are dancing away the summer night. Sometimes the dubious tones of a guitar and the notes of an amorous voice, tell perchance the whereabout of some moonstruck lover serenading his lady's window.

Such is a faint picture of the moonlight nights I have passed loitering about the courts and halls and balconies of this most suggestive pile; "feeding my fancy with sugared suppositions," and enjoying that mixture of reverie and sensation which steal away existence in a southern climate; so that it has been almost morning before I have retired to bed, and been lulled to sleep by the falling waters of the fountain of Lindaraxa.

LEGEND OF THE MOOR'S LEGACY [2]

Just within the fortress of the Alhambra, in front of the royal palace, is a broad open esplanade, called the Place or Square of the Cisterns, (*la Plaza de los Algibes*) so called from being undermined by reservoirs of water, hidden from sight, and which have existed from the time of the Moors. At one corner of this esplanade is a Moorish well, cut through the living rock to a great depth, the water of which is cold as ice and clear as crystal. The wells made by the Moors are always in repute, for it is well known what pains they took to penetrate to the purest and sweetest springs and fountains. The one of which we now speak is famous throughout Granada, insomuch that water-carriers, some bearing great water-jars on their shoulders, others driving asses before them laden with earthen vessels, are ascending and descending the steep woody avenues of the Alhambra, from early dawn until a late hour of the night.

Fountains and wells, ever since the scriptural days, have been noted gossiping-places in hot climates; and at the well in question there is a kind of perpetual club kept up during the livelong day, by the invalids, old women, and other curious do-nothing folk of the fortress, who sit here on the stone benches, under an awning spread over the well to shelter the toll-gatherer from the sun, and dawdle over the gossip of the fortress, and question every water-carrier that arrives about the news of the city, and make long comments on everything they hear and see. Not an hour of the day but loitering housewives and idle maid-servants may be seen, lingering, with pitcher on head or in hand, to hear the last of the endless tattle of these worthies.

Among the water-carriers who once resorted to this well, there was a sturdy, strong-backed, bandy-legged little fellow, named Pedro Gil, but called Peregil for shortness. Being a water-carrier, he was a Gallego, or native of Gallicia, of course. Nature seems to have

---

[1] a quarter of Granada north of the Alhambra just across the Darro

[2] To this tale Irving has imparted much of the racy flavor of the medieval tale.

formed races of men, as she has of animals, for different kinds of drudgery. In France the shoeblacks are all Savoyards, the porters of hotels all Swiss, and in the days of hoops and hair-powder in England, [1] no man could give the regular swing to a sedan-chair but a bog-trotting Irishman. So in Spain, the carriers of water and bearers of burdens are all sturdy little natives of Gallicia. No man says, "Get me a porter," but, "Call a Gallego."

To return from this digression, Peregil the Gallego had begun business with merely a great earthen jar which he carried upon his shoulder; by degrees he rose in the world, and was enabled to purchase an assistant of a correspondent class of animals, being a stout shaggy-haired donkey. On each side of this his long-eared aide-de-camp, in a kind of pannier, were slung his water-jars, covered with fig-leaves to protect them from the sun. There was not a more industrious water-carrier in all Granada, nor one more merry withal. The streets rang with his cheerful voice as he trudged after his donkey, singing forth the usual summer note that resounds through the Spanish towns: *"Quien quiere agua—agua mas fria que la nieve?"*—"who wants water—water colder than snow? Who wants water from the well of the Alhambra, cold as ice and clear as crystal?" When he served a customer with a sparkling glass, it was always with a pleasant word that caused a smile; and if, perchance, it was a comely dame or dimpling damsel, it was always with a sly leer and a compliment to her beauty that was irresistible. Thus Peregil the Gallego was noted throughout all Granada for being one of the civilest, pleasantest, and happiest of mortals. Yet it is not he who sings loudest and jokes most that has the lightest heart. Under all this air of merriment, honest Peregil had his cares and troubles. He had a large family of ragged children to support, who were hungry and clamorous as a nest of young swallows, and beset him with their outcries for food whenever he came home of an evening. He had a helpmate, too, who was anything but a help to him. She had been a village beauty before her marriage, noted for her skill at dancing the bolero [2] and rattling the castanets; and she still retained her early propensities, spending the hard earnings of honest Peregil in frippery, and laying the very donkey under requisition for junketing parties into the country on Sundays and saints' days, and those innumerable holidays which are rather more numerous in Spain than the days of the week. With all this she was a little of a slattern, something more of a lie-abed, and, above all, a gossip of the first water; neglecting house, household, and everything else, to loiter slip-shod in the houses of her gossip neighbors.

He, however, who tempers the wind to the shorn lamb, accommodates the yoke of matrimony to the submissive neck. Peregil bore all the heavy dispensations of wife and children with as meek a spirit as his donkey bore the water-jars; and, however he might shake his ears in private, never ventured to question the household virtues of his slattern spouse.

He loved his children, too, even as an owl loves its owlets, seeing in them his own image multiplied and perpetuated; for they were a sturdy, long-backed, bandy-legged little brood. The great pleasure of honest Peregil was, whenever he could afford himself a scanty holiday, and had a handful of maravedis [3] to spare, to take the whole litter forth with him, some in his arms, some tugging at his skirts, and some trudging at his heels, and to treat them to a gambol among the orchards of the Vega, while his wife was dancing with her holiday friends in the Angosturas of the Darro. [4]

It was a late hour one summer night, and most of the water-carriers had desisted from their toils. The day had been uncommonly sultry; the night was one of those delicious moonlights which tempt the inhabitants of southern climes to indemnify themselves for the heat and inaction of the day, by lingering in the open air, and enjoying its tempered sweetness until after midnight. Customers for water were therefore still abroad. Peregil, like a considerate, painstaking father, thought of his hungry children. "One more journey to the well," said he to himself, "to earn a Sunday's puchero [5] for the little ones." So saying, he trudged manfully up the steep avenue of the Alhambra, singing as he went, and now and then bestowing a hearty thwack with a cudgel on the flanks of his donkey, either by way of cadence to the song, or refreshment to the animal; for dry blows serve in lieu of provender in Spain for all beasts of burden.

When arrived at the well, he found it deserted by everyone except a solitary stranger in Moorish garb, seated on a stone bench in the moonlight. Peregil paused at first and

---

[1] the eighteenth century
[2] A Spanish dance representing the progress of love from shyness to passion; it is accompanied with the voice and castanets.
[3] Spanish copper coins of less than one cent in value
[4] perhaps a local name for the part of Granada close to the river Darro before it was covered over as it now is within the city
[5] pot (of food)

regarded him with surprise, not unmixed with awe, but the Moor feebly beckoned him to approach. "I am faint and ill," said he; "aid me to return to the city, and I will pay thee double what thou couldst gain by thy jars of water."

The honest heart of the little water-carrier was touched with compassion at the appeal of the stranger. "God forbid," said he, "that I should ask fee or reward for doing a common act of humanity." He accordingly helped the Moor on his donkey, and set off slowly for Granada, the poor Moslem being so weak that it was necessary to hold him on the animal to keep him from falling to the earth.

When they entered the city, the water-carrier demanded whither he should conduct him. "Alas!" said the Moor, faintly, "I have neither home nor habitation; I am a stranger in the land. Suffer me to lay my head this night beneath thy roof, and thou shalt be amply repaid."

Honest Peregil thus saw himself unexpectedly saddled with an infidel guest, but he was too humane to refuse a night's shelter to a fellow-being in so forlorn a plight; so he conducted the Moor to his dwelling. The children, who had sallied forth open-mouthed as usual on hearing the tramp of the donkey, ran back with affright when they beheld the turbaned stranger, and hid themselves behind their mother. The latter stepped forth intrepidly, like a ruffling hen before her brood when a vagrant dog approaches.

"What infidel companion," cried she, "is this you have brought home at this late hour, to draw upon us the eyes of the inquisition?"

"Be quiet, wife," replied the Gallego, "here is a poor sick stranger, without friend or home; wouldst thou turn him forth to perish in the streets?"

The wife would still have remonstrated, for although she lived in a hovel, she was a furious stickler for the credit of her house; the little water-carrier, however, for once was stiff necked, and refused to bend beneath the yoke. He assisted the poor Moslem to alight, and spread a mat and a sheepskin for him on the ground, in the coolest part of the house; being the only kind of bed that his poverty afforded.

In a little while the Moor was seized with violent convulsions, which defied all the ministering skill of the simple water-carrier. The eye of the poor patient acknowledged his kindness. During an interval of his fits he called him to his side, and addressing him in a low voice, "My end," said he, "I fear is at hand.

If I die, I bequeath you this box as a reward for your charity:" so saying, he opened his albornoz, or cloak, and showed a small box of sandal-wood, strapped round his body. "God grant, my friend," replied the worthy little Gallego, "that you may live many years to enjoy your treasure, whatever it may be." The Moor shook his head; he laid his hand upon the box, and would have said something more concerning it, but his convulsions returned with increasing violence, and in a little while he expired.

The water-carrier's wife was now as one distracted. "This comes," said she, "of your foolish good-nature, always running into scrapes to oblige others. What will become of us when this corpse is found in our house? We shall be sent to prison as murderers; and if we escape with our lives, shall be ruined by notaries and alguazils." [1]

Poor Peregil was in equal tribulation, and almost repented himself of having done a good deed. At length a thought struck him. "It is not yet day," said he; "I can convey the dead body out of the city, and bury it in the sands on the banks of the Xenil. No one saw the Moor enter our dwelling, and no one will know anything of his death."

So said, so done. The wife aided him; they rolled the body of the unfortunate Moslem in the mat on which he had expired, laid it across the ass, and Peregil set out with it for the banks of the river.

As ill luck would have it, there lived opposite to the water-carrier a barber named Pedrillo Pedrugo, one of the most prying, tattling, and mischief-making of his gossip tribe. He was a weasel-faced, spider-legged varlet, supple and insinuating; the famous barber of Seville [2] could not surpass him for his universal knowledge of the affairs of others, and he had no more power of retention than a sieve. It was said that he slept but with one eye at a time, and kept one ear uncovered, so that even in his sleep he might see and hear all that was going on. Certain it is, he was a sort of scandalous chronicle for the quidnuncs [3] of Granada, and had more customers than all the rest of his fraternity.

This meddlesome barber heard Peregil arrive at an unusual hour at night, and the exclamations of his wife and children. His head was instantly popped out of a little window which served him as a look-out, and he saw his neighbor assist a man in Moorish garb into

[1] constables
[2] Figaro, in *The Barber of Seville*, a comic opera by Beaumarchais, written in 1772
[3] one always asking "What now?" a gossip

his dwelling. This was so strange an occurrence, that Pedrillo Pedrugo slept not a wink that night. Every five minutes he was at his loophole watching the lights that gleamed through the chinks of his neighbor's door, and before daylight he beheld Peregil sally forth with his donkey unusually laden.

The inquisitive barber was in a fidget; he slipped on his clothes, and, stealing forth silently followed the water-carrier at a distance, until he saw him dig a hole in the sandy bank of the Xenil, and bury something that had the appearance of a dead body.

The barber hied him home, and fidgeted about his shop, setting everything upside down, until sunrise. He then took a basin under his arm, and sallied forth to the house of his daily customer the alcalde. [1]

The alcalde was just risen. Pedrillo Pedrugo seated him in a chair, threw a napkin round his neck, put a basin of hot water under his chin, and began to mollify his beard with his fingers.

"Strange doings!" said Pedrugo, who played barber and newsmonger at the same time,— "strange doings! Robbery, and murder, and burial all in one night!"

"Hey!—how!—what is that you say?" cried the alcalde.

"I say," replied the barber rubbing a piece of soap over the nose and mouth of the dignitary, for a Spanish barber disdains to employ a brush, —"I say that Peregil the Gallego has robbed and murdered a Moorish Mussulman, and buried him, this blessed night. *Maldita sea la noche;*—Accursed be the night for the same!"

"But how do you know all this?" demanded the alcalde.

"Be patient, Señor, and you shall hear all about it," replied Pedrillo, taking him by the nose and sliding a razor over his cheek. He then recounted all that he had seen, going through both operations at the same time, shaving his beard, washing his chin, and wiping him dry with a dirty napkin, while he was robbing, murdering, and burying the Moslem.

Now it so happened that this alcalde was one of the most overbearing, and at the same time most griping and corrupt curmudgeons in all Granada. It could not be denied, however, that he set a high value upon justice, for he sold it at its weight in gold. He presumed the case in point to be one of murder and robbery; doubtless there must be a rich spoil; how was it to be secured into the legitimate hands of the law? for as to merely entrapping

[1] mayor-magistrate

the delinquent—that would be feeding the gallows; but entrapping the booty—that would be enriching the judge, and such, according to his creed, was the great end of justice. So thinking, he summoned to his presence his trustiest alguazil—a gaunt, hungry-looking varlet, clad according to the custom of his order, in the ancient Spanish garb, a broad black beaver turned up at its sides; a quaint ruff; a small black coat dangling from his shoulders; rusty black under clothes that set off his spare wiry frame, while in his hands he bore a slender white wand, the dreaded insignia of his office. Such was the legal bloodhound of the ancient Spanish breed, that he put upon the traces of the unlucky water-carrier, and such was his speed and certainty, that he was upon the haunches of poor Peregil before he had returned to his dwelling, and brought both him and his donkey before the dispenser of justice.

The alcalde bent upon him one of the most terrific frowns. "Hark ye, culprit," roared he, in a voice that made the knees of the little Gallego smite together,—"hark ye, culprit! there is no need of denying thy guilt, everything is known to me. A gallows is the proper reward for the crime thou hast committed, but I am merciful, and readily listen to reason. The man that has been murdered in thy house was a Moor, an infidel, the enemy of our faith. It was doubtless in a fit of religious zeal that thou hast slain him. I will be indulgent, therefore; render up the property of which thou hast robbed him, and we will hush the matter up."

The poor water-carrier called upon all the saints to witness his innocence; alas! not one of them appeared; and if they had, the alcalde would have disbelieved the whole calendar. The water-carrier related the whole story of the dying Moor with the straightforward simplicity of truth, but it was all in vain. "Wilt thou persist in saying," demanded the judge, "that this Moslem had neither gold nor jewels, which were the object of thy cupidity?"

"As I hope to be saved, your worship," replied the water-carrier, "he had nothing but a small box of sandal-wood which he bequeathed to me in reward for my services."

"A box of sandal-wood! a box of sandal-wood!" exclaimed the alcalde, his eyes sparkling at the idea of precious jewels. "And where is this box? where have you concealed it?"

"An' it please your grace," replied the water-carrier, "it is in one of the panniers of my mule, and heartily at the service of your worship."

He had hardly spoken the words, when the keen alguazil darted off, and reappeared in an instant with the mysterious box of sandal-wood. The alcalde opened it with an eager and trembling hand; all pressed forward to gaze upon the treasure it was expected to contain; when, to their disappointment, nothing appeared within, but a parchment scroll, covered with Arabic characters, and an end of a waxen taper.

When there is nothing to be gained by the conviction of a prisoner, justice, even in Spain, is apt to be impartial. The alcalde, having recovered from his disappointment, and found that there was really no booty in the case, now listened dispassionately to the explanation of the water-carrier, which was corroborated by the testimony of his wife. Being convinced, therefore, of his innocence, he discharged him from arrest; nay more, he permitted him to carry off the Moor's legacy, the box of sandal-wood and its contents, as the well-merited reward of his humanity; but he retained his donkey in payment of costs and charges.

Behold the unfortunate little Gallego reduced once more to the necessity of being his own water-carrier, and trudging up to the well of the Alhambra with a great earthen jar upon his shoulder.

As he toiled up the hill in the heat of a summer noon, his usual good-humor forsook him. "Dog of an alcalde!" would he cry, "to rob a poor man of the means of his subsistence, of the best friend he had in the world!" And then at the remembrance of the beloved companion of his labors, all the kindness of his nature would break forth. "Ah, donkey of my heart!" would he exclaim, resting his burden on a stone, and wiping the sweat from his brow, —"ah, donkey of my heart! I warrant me thou thinkest of thy old master! I warrant me thou missest the water-jars—poor beast."

To add to his afflictions, his wife received him, on his return home, with whimperings and repinings; she had clearly the vantage-ground of him, having warned him not to commit the egregious act of hospitality which had brought on him all these misfortunes; and, like a knowing woman, she took every occasion to throw her superior sagacity in his teeth. If her children lacked food, or needed a new garment, she could answer with a sneer, "Go to your father—he is heir to king Chico of the Alhambra: ask him to help you out of the Moor's strong box."

Was ever poor mortal so soundly punished for having done a good action? The unlucky Peregil was grieved in flesh and spirit, but still he bore meekly with the railings of his spouse. At length, one evening, when, after a hot day's toil, she taunted him in the usual manner, he lost all patience. He did not venture to retort upon her, but his eye rested on the box of sandal-wood, which lay on a shelf with lid half open, as if laughing in mockery at his vexation. Seizing it up, he dashed it with indignation to the floor. "Unlucky was the day that I ever set eyes on thee," he cried, "or sheltered thy master beneath my roof!"

As the box struck the floor, the lid flew wide open, and the parchment scroll rolled forth.

Peregil sat regarding the scroll for some time in moody silence. At length rallying his ideas, "Who knows," thought he, "but this writing may be of some importance, as the Moor seems to have guarded it with such care?" Picking it up therefore, he put it in his bosom, and the next morning, as he was crying water through the streets, he stopped at the shop of a Moor, a native of Tangiers, who sold trinkets and perfumery in the Zacatin, [1] and asked him to explain the contents.

The Moor read the scroll attentively, then stroked his beard and smiled. "This manuscript," said he, "is a form of incantation for the recovery of hidden treasure that is under the power of enchantment. It is said to have such virtue that the strongest bolts and bars, nay the adamantine rock itself, will yield before it!"

"Bah!" cried the little Gallego, "what is all that to me? I am no enchanter, and know nothing of buried treasure." So saying, he shouldered his water-jar, left the scroll in the hands of the Moor, and trudged forward on his daily rounds.

That evening, however, as he rested himself about twilight at the well of the Alhambra, he found a number of gossips assembled at the place, and their conversation, as is not unusual at that shadowy hour, turned upon old tales and traditions of a supernatural nature. Being all poor as rats, they dwelt with peculiar fondness upon the popular theme of enchanted riches left by the Moors in various parts of the Alhambra. Above all, they concurred in the belief that there were great treasures buried deep in the earth under the tower of the seven floors.

These stories made an unusual impression on the mind of the honest Peregil, and they sank deeper and deeper into his thoughts as he returned alone down the darkling avenues. "If, after all, there should be treasure hid beneath

[1] a narrow market-street of Granada

that tower; and if the scroll I left with the Moor should enable me to get at it!" In the sudden ecstasy of the thought he had wellnigh let fall his water-jar.

That night he tumbled and tossed, and could scarcely get a wink of sleep for the thoughts that were bewildering his brain. Bright and early he repaired to the shop of the Moor, and told him all that was passing in his mind. "You can read Arabic," said he; "suppose we go together to the tower, and try the effect of the charm; if it fails, we are no worse off than before; but if it succeeds, we will share equally all the treasure we may discover."

"Hold," replied the Moslem; "this writing is not sufficient of itself; it must be read at midnight, by the light of a taper singularly compounded and prepared, the ingredients of which are not within my reach. Without such a taper the scroll is of no avail."

"Say no more!" cried the little Gallego; "I have such a taper at hand, and will bring it here in a moment." So saying, he hastened home, and soon returned with the end of yellow wax taper that he had found in the box of sandal-wood.

The Moor felt it and smelt of it. "Here are rare and costly perfumes," said he, "combined with this yellow wax. This is the kind of taper specified in the scroll. While this burns, the strongest walls and most secret caverns will remain open. Woe to him, however, who lingers within it until it be extinguished. He will remain enchanted with the treasure."

It was now agreed between them to try the charm that very night. At a late hour, therefore, when nothing was stirring but bats and owls, they ascended the woody hill of the Alhambra, and approached that awful tower, shrouded by trees and rendered formidable by so many traditionary tales. By the light of a lantern they groped their way through bushes, and over fallen stones, to the door of a vault beneath the tower. With fear and trembling they descended a flight of steps cut into the rock. It led to an empty chamber, damp and drear, from which another flight of steps led to a deeper vault. In this way they descended four several flights, leading into as many vaults, one below the other, but the floor of the fourth was solid; and though, according to tradition, there remained three vaults still below, it was said to be impossible to penetrate further, the residue being shut up by strong enchantment. The air of this vault was damp and chilly, and had an earthy smell, and the light scarce cast

forth any rays. They paused here for a time, in breathless suspense, until they faintly heard the clock of the watch-tower strike midnight; upon this they lit the waxen taper, which diffused an odor of myrrh and frankincense and storax. [1]

The Moor began to read in a hurried voice. He had scarce finished when there was a noise as of subterraneous thunder. The earth shook, and the floor, yawning open, disclosed a flight of steps. Trembling with awe, they descended, and by the light of the lantern found themselves in another vault covered with Arabic inscriptions. In the center stood a great chest, secured with seven bands of steel, at each end of which sat an enchanted Moor in armor, but motionless as a statue, being controlled by the power of the incantation. Before the chest were several jars filled with gold and silver and precious stones. In the largest of these they thrust their arms up to the elbow, and at every dip hauled forth handfuls of broad yellow pieces of Moorish gold, or bracelets and ornaments of the same precious metal, while occasionally a necklace of Oriental pearl would stick to their fingers. Still they trembled and breathed short while cramming their pockets with the spoils; and cast many a fearful glance at the two enchanted Moors, who sat grim and motionless, glaring upon them with unwinking eyes. At length, struck with a sudden panic at some fancied noise, they both rushed up the staircase, tumbled over one another into the upper apartment, overturned and extinguished the waxen taper, and the pavement again closed with a thundering sound.

Filled with dismay, they did not pause until they had groped their way out of the tower, and beheld the stars shining through the trees. Then seating themselves upon the grass, they divided the spoil, determining to content themselves for the present with this mere skimming of the jars, but to return on some future night and drain them to the bottom. To make sure of each other's good faith, also, they divided the talismans between them, one retaining the scroll and the other the taper; this done, they set off with light hearts and well-lined pockets for Granada.

As they wended their way down the hill, the shrewd Moor whispered a word of counsel in the ear of the simple little water-carrier.

"Friend Peregil," said he, "all this affair must be kept a profound secret until we have

[1] Myrrh, frankincense, and storax are all gums or resins much used in the making of perfumes.

secured the treasure, and conveyed it out of harm's way. If a whisper of it gets to the ear of the alcalde, we are undone!"

"Certainly," replied the Gallego, "nothing can be more true."

"Friend Peregil," said the Moor, "you are a discreet man, and I make no doubt can keep a secret; but you have a wife."

"She shall not know a word of it," replied the little water-carrier sturdily.

"Enough," said the Moor, "I depend upon thy discretion and thy promise."

Never was promise more positive and sincere; but, alas! what man can keep a secret from his wife? Certainly not such a one as Peregil the water-carrier, who was one of the most loving and tractable of husbands. On his return home, he found his wife moping in a corner. "Mighty well," cried she as he entered, "you've come at last, after rambling about until this hour of the night. I wonder you have not brought home another Moor as a house-mate." Then bursting into tears, she began to wring her hands and smite her breast. "Unhappy woman that I am!" exclaimed she, "what will become of me? My house stripped and plundered by lawyers and alguazils; my husband a do-no-good, that no longer brings home bread to his family, but goes rambling about day and night, with infidel Moors! O my children! my children! what will become of us? We shall all have to beg in the streets!"

Honest Peregil was so moved by the distress of his spouse, that he could not help whimpering also. His heart was as full as his pockets, and not to be restrained. Thrusting his hand into the latter he hauled forth three or four broad gold pieces, and slipped them into her bosom. The poor woman stared with astonishment, and could not understand the meaning of this golden shower. Before she could recover her surprise, the little Gallego drew forth a chain of gold and dangled it before her, capering with exultation, his mouth distended from ear to ear.

"Holy Virgin protect us!" exclaimed the wife. "What hast thou been doing Peregil? surely thou hast not been committing murder and robbery!"

The idea scarce entered the brain of the poor woman, than it became a certainty with her. She saw a prison and a gallows in the distance, and a little bandy-legged Gallego hanging pendent from it; and, overcome by the horrors conjured up by her imagination, fell into violent hysterics.

What could the poor man do? He had no other means of pacifying his wife, and dispelling the phantoms of her fancy, than by relating the whole story of his good fortune. This, however, he did not do until he had exacted from her the most solemn promise to keep it a profound secret from every living being.

To describe her joy would be impossible. She flung her arms round the neck of her husband, and almost strangled him with her caresses. "Now, wife," exclaimed the little man with honest exultation, "what say you now to the Moor's legacy? Henceforth never abuse me for helping a fellow-creature in distress."

The honest Gallego retired to his sheepskin mat, and slept as soundly as if on a bed of down. Not so his wife; she emptied the whole contents of his pockets upon the mat, and sat counting gold pieces of Arabic coin, trying on necklaces and earrings, and fancying the figure she should one day make when permitted to enjoy her riches.

On the following morning the honest Gallego took a broad golden coin, and repaired with it to a jeweler's shop in the Zacatin to offer it for sale, pretending to have found it among the ruins of the Alhambra. The jeweler saw that it had an Arabic inscription and was of the purest gold; he offered, however, but a third of its value, with which the water-carrier was perfectly content. Peregil now bought new clothes for his little flock, and all kinds of toys, together with ample provisions for a hearty meal, and returning to his dwelling, set all his children dancing around him, while he capered in the midst, the happiest of fathers.

The wife of the water-carrier kept her promise of secrecy with surprising strictness. For a whole day and a half she went about with a look of mystery and a heart swelling almost to bursting, yet she held her peace, though surrounded by her gossips. It is true, she could not help giving herself a few airs, apologized for her ragged dress, and talked of ordering a new basquina [1] all trimmed with gold lace and bugles, and a new lace mantilla. She threw out hints of her husband's intention of leaving off his trade of water-carrying, as it did not altogether agree with his health. In fact she thought they should all retire to the country for the summer, that the children might have the benefit of the mountain air, for there was no living in the city in this sultry season.

The neighbors stared at each other, and thought the poor woman had lost her wits; and

[1] under petticoat

her airs and graces and elegant pretentions were the theme of universal scoffing and merriment among her friends, the moment her back was turned.

If she restrained herself abroad, however, she indemnified herself at home, and putting a string of rich Oriental pearls round her neck, Moorish bracelets on her arms, and an aigrette of diamonds on her head, sailed backwards and forwards in her slattern rags about the room, now and then stopping to admire herself in a broken mirror. Nay, in the impulse of her simple vanity, she could not resist, on one occasion, showing herself at the window to enjoy the effect of her finery on the passers-by.

As the fates would have it, Pedrillo Pedrugo, the meddlesome barber, was at this moment sitting idly in his shop on the opposite side of the street, when his ever-watchful eye caught the sparkle of a diamond. In an instant he was at his loophole reconnoitering the slattern spouse of the water-carrier, decorated with the splendor of an eastern bride. No sooner had he taken an accurate inventory of her ornaments, than he posted off with all speed to the alcalde. In a little while the hungry alguazil was again on the scent, and before the day was over the unfortunate Peregil was once more dragged into the presence of the judge.

"How is this, villain!" cried the alcalde, in a furious voice. "You told me that the infidel who died in your house left nothing behind but an empty coffer, and now I hear of your wife flaunting in her rags decked out with pearls and diamonds. Wretch that thou art! prepare to render up the spoils of thy miserable victim, and to swing on the gallows that is already tired of waiting for thee."

The terrified water-carrier fell on his knees, and made a full relation of the marvelous manner in which he had gained his wealth. The alcalde, the alguazil, and the inquisitive barber listened with greedy ears to this Arabian tale of enchanted treasure. The alguazil was dispatched to bring the Moor who had assisted in the incantation. The Moslem entered half frightened out of his wits at finding himself in the hands of the harpies of the law. When he beheld the water-carrier standing with sheepish looks and downcast countenance, he comprehended the whole matter. "Miserable animal," said he, as he passed near him, "did I not warn thee against babbling to thy wife?"

The story of the Moor coincided exactly with that of his colleague; but the alcalde affected to be slow of belief, and threw out menaces of imprisonment and rigorous investigation.

"Softly, good señor Alcalde," said the Mussulman, who by this time had recovered his usual shrewdness and self-possession. "Let us not mar fortune's favors in the scramble for them. Nobody knows anything of this matter but ourselves; let us keep the secret. There is wealth enough in the cave to enrich us all. Promise a fair division, and all shall be produced; refuse, and the cave shall remain forever closed."

The alcalde consulted apart with the alguazil. The latter was an old fox in his profession. "Promise anything," said he, "until you get possession of the treasure. You may then seize upon the whole, and if he and his accomplice dare to murmur, threaten them with the fagot and stake as infidels and sorcerers."

The alcalde relished the advise. Smoothing his brow and turning to the Moor, "This is a strange story," said he, "and may be true, but I must have ocular proof of it. This very night you must repeat the incantation in my presence. If there be really such treasure, we will share it amicably between us, and say nothing further of the matter; if ye have deceived me, expect no mercy at my hands. In the mean time you must remain in custody."

The Moor and the water-carrier cheerfully agreed to these conditions, satisfied that the event would prove the truth of their words.

Towards midnight the alcalde sallied forth secretly, attended by the alguazil and the meddlesome barber, all strongly armed. They conducted the Moor and the water-carrier as prisoners, and were provided with the stout donkey of the latter to bear off the expected treasure. They arrived at the tower without being observed, and tying the donkey to a fig-tree, descended into the fourth vault of the tower.

The scroll was produced, the yellow waxen taper lighted, and the Moor read the form of incantation. The earth trembled as before, and the pavement opened with a thundering sound, disclosing the narrow flight of steps. The alcalde, the alguazil, and the barber were struck aghast, and could not summon courage to descend. The Moor and the water-carrier entered the lower vault, and found the two Moors seated as before, silent and motionless. They removed two of the great jars, filled with golden coin and precious stones. The water-carrier bore them up one by one upon his shoulders, but though a strong-backed little man, and accustomed to carry burdens, he staggered beneath their weight, and found, when slung on each side of his donkey, they were as much as the animal could bear.

"Let us be content for the present," said the Moor; "here is as much treasure as we can carry off without being perceived, and enough to make us all wealthy to our heart's desire."

"Is there more treasure remaining behind?" demanded the alcalde.

"The greatest prize of all," said the Moor, "a huge coffer bound with bands of steel, and filled with pearls and precious stones."

"Let us have up the coffer by all means," cried the grasping alcalde.

"I will descend for no more," said the Moor, doggedly; "enough is enough for a reasonable man—more is superfluous."

"And I," said the water-carrier, "will bring up no further burden to break the back of my poor donkey."

Finding commands, threats, and entreaties equally vain, the alcalde turned to his two adherents. "Aid me," said he, "to bring up the coffer, and its contents shall be divided between us." So saying, he descended the steps, followed with trembling reluctance by the alguazil and the barber.

No sooner did the Moor behold them fairly earthed than he extinguished the yellow taper; the pavement closed with its usual crash, and the three worthies remained buried in its womb.

He then hastened up the different flights of steps, nor stopped until in the open air. The little water-carrier followed him as fast as his short legs would permit.

"What hast thou done?" cried Peregil, as soon as he could recover breath. "The alcalde and the other two are shut up in the vault."

"It is the will of Allah!" said the Moor, devoutly.

"And will you not release them?" demanded the Gallego.

"Allah forbid!" replied the Moor, smoothing his beard. "It is written in the book of fate that they shall remain enchanted until some future adventurer arrive to break the charm. The will of God be done!" so saying, he hurled the end of the waxen taper far among the gloomy thickets of the glen.

There was now no remedy; so the Moor and the water-carrier proceeded with the richly laden donkey toward the city, nor could honest Peregil refrain from hugging and kissing his long-eared fellow-laborer, thus restored to him from the clutches of the law; and, in fact, it is doubtful which gave the simple-hearted little man most joy at the moment, the gaining of the treasure, or the recovery of the donkey.

The two partners in good luck divided their spoil amicably and fairly, except that the Moor, who had a little taste for trinketry, made out to get into his heap the most of the pearls and precious stones and other baubles, but then he always gave the water-carrier in lieu magnificent jewels of massy gold, of five times the size, with which the latter was heartily content. They took care not to linger within reach of accidents, but made off to enjoy their wealth undisturbed in other countries. The Moor returned to Africa, to his native city of Tangiers, and the Gallego, with his wife, his children, and his donkey made the best of his way to Portugal. Here, under the admonition and tuition of his wife, he became a personage of some consequence, for she made the worthy little man array his long body and short legs in doublet and hose, with a feather in his hat and a sword by his side, and laying aside his familiar appellation of Peregil, assume the more sonorous title of Don Pedro Gil: his progeny grew up a thriving and merry-hearted, though short and bandy-legged generation, while Señora Gil, befringed, belaced, and betasseled from her head to her heels, with glittering rings on every finger, became a model of slattern fashion and finery.

As to the alcalde and his adjuncts, they remained shut up under the great tower of the seven floors, and there they remain spellbound at the present day. Whenever there shall be a lack in Spain of gossiping barbers, sharking alguazils, and corrupt alcaldes, they may be sought after; but if they have to wait until such time for their deliverance, there is danger of their enchantment enduring until doomsday.

SPANISH ROMANCE

In the latter part of my sojourn in the Alhambra, I made frequent descents into the Jesuit's Library of the University; and relished more and more the old Spanish chronicles, which I found there bound in parchment. I delight in those quaint histories which treat of the times when the Moslems maintained a foothold in the Peninsula. With all their bigotry and occasional intolerance, they are full of noble acts and generous sentiments, and have a high, spicy, oriental flavor, not to be found in other records of the times, which were merely European. In fact, Spain, even at the present day, is a country apart; severed in history, habits, manners, and modes of thinking, from all the rest of Europe. It is a romantic country; but its romance has none of the sentimentality of modern European romance; it is chiefly derived from the brilliant regions of the East, and from the high-minded school of Saracenic chivalry.

The Arab invasion and conquest brought a higher civilization, and a nobler style of thinking, into Gothic Spain. The Arabs were a quick-witted, sagacious, proud-spirited, and poetical people, and were imbued with oriental science and literature. Wherever they established a seat of power, it became a rallying-place for the learned and ingenious; and they softened and refined the people whom they conquered. By degrees, occupancy seemed to give them an hereditary right to their foothold in the land; they ceased to be looked upon as invaders, and were regarded as rival neighbors. The Peninsula, broken up into a variety of states, both Christian and Moslem, became, for centuries, a great campaigning-ground, where the art of war seemed to be the principal business of man, and was carried to the highest pitch of romantic chivalry. The original ground of hostility, a difference of faith, gradually lost its rancor. Neighboring states, of opposite creeds, were occasionally linked together in alliances, offensive and defensive; so that the cross and crescent were to be seen side by side, fighting against some common enemy. In times of peace, too, the noble youth of either faith resorted to the same cities, Christian or Moslem, to school themselves in military science. Even in the temporary truces of sanguinary wars, the warriors who had recently striven together in the deadly conflicts of the field, laid aside their animosity, met at tournaments, jousts, and other military festivities, and exchanged the courtesies of gentle and generous spirits. Thus the opposite races became frequently mingled together in peaceful intercourse, or if any rivalry took place, it was in those high courtesies and nobler acts, which bespeak the accomplished cavalier. Warriors of opposite creeds became ambitious of transcending each other in magnanimity as well as valor. Indeed, the chivalric virtues were refined upon to a degree sometimes fastidious and constrained, but at other times inexpressibly noble and affecting. The annals of the times teem with illustrious instances of high-wrought courtesy, romantic generosity, lofty disinterestedness, and punctilious honor, that warm the very soul to read them. These have furnished themes for national plays and poems, or have been celebrated in those all-pervading ballads, which are as the life-breath of the people, and thus have continued to exercise an influence on the national character, which centuries of vicissitude and decline have not been able to destroy;

so that, with all their faults, and they are many, the Spaniards, even at the present day, are, on many points, the most high-minded and proud-spirited people of Europe. It is true, the romance of feeling derived from the sources I have mentioned, has, like all other romance, its affectations and extremes. It renders the Spaniard at times pompous and grandiloquent; prone to carry the *pundonor*, or point of honor, beyond the bounds of sober sense and sound morality; disposed, in the midst of poverty, to affect the *grande caballero*, [1] and to look down with sovereign disdain upon "arts mechanical," and all the gainful pursuits of plebeian life; but this very inflation of spirit, while it fills his brain with vapors, lifts him above a thousand meannesses; and though it often keeps him in indigence, ever protects him from vulgarity.

In the present day, when popular literature is running into the low levels of life, and luxuriating on the vices and follies of mankind; and when the universal pursuit of gain is trampling down the early growth of poetic feeling, and wearing out the verdure of the soul, I question whether it would not be of service for the reader occasionally to turn to these records of prouder times and loftier modes of thinking; and to steep himself to the very lips in old Spanish romance.

1829-1832   1832

. . . .

JAMES FENIMORE COOPER
1789-1851

The first American novelist to attract wide attention in the Old World was James Fenimore Cooper, born at Burlington, New Jersey, of English and Swedish Quaker ancestry. He was brought up on his father's vast wilderness estate at Otsego Lake, New York, educated in the local schools and in the home of an Episcopal clergyman at Albany, was three years at Yale, went to sea, secured a midshipman's commission, and served in the navy until 1811. He took up literature by chance in 1820 and soon achieved success. From 1826 until 1833 he lived abroad, and then settled at Cooperstown, New York, where he spent the remainder of his life, and died. A rather irritable disposition and tactless criticism of his fellow countrymen involved him in frequent local and public controversies. His works include some forty titles, chief among which are *The Spy,* 1821; *The Pioneers,* and *The Pilot,* 1823; *The Last of the Mohicans,* 1826; *The Prairie,* 1827; *History of the Navy of the United States,* 1839; *The Pathfinder,* 1840; *The Deerslayer,* 1841. Cooper has been translated into nearly all European languages.

[1] great gentleman

It was Cooper's privilege to write into American literature the prose epic of the white man's struggle with natives not yet emerged from a Stone Age civilization, and of the conquest of a continent. No such event had taken place before in modern history, and Cooper was its witness and recorder. He pictured that part of the conflict extending in time from the French and Indian War well into the nineteenth century, and in space from the Hudson to west of the Mississippi. The story is told in the life of one hero who figures under five different names in five books: *Deerslayer, The Last of the Mohicans, The Pathfinder, The Pioneers,* and *The Prairie.* Many parallels can be discovered between the work of Cooper and that of his contemporary and fellow romanticist, Scott. Where their fields overlapped in tales of the sea, Cooper was superior, for he wrote from a first-hand knowledge of the subject. In details Cooper is often inaccurate, the story not infrequently drags, the diction is often remote from life, and the characters sometimes pose. Nevertheless, Cooper was deeply original. He seized the opportunity of organizing into picturesque form the details of a large racial movement of which none of his contemporaries seem to have been aware. In more recent times, Harte, Mark Twain, Neihardt, and Garland have continued the story in the West.

T. R. Lounsbury, *J. F. Cooper,* (AML) 1889; W. B. S. Clymer (BB); Macy; Chubb; B. Matthews, "Fenimore Cooper," *Atlan.* 100:329-341; W. C. Brownell, "Cooper," *Scrib. M.* 39:455-468; "A Century of Fenimore Cooper," *Nation* 112: 255-56; S. F. Cooper, "A Glance Backward," *Atlan.* 59:199-206; "Chronicle and Comment," *Bookm.* 10:102-5.

THE PILOT [3]

CHAPTER IV

Behold the threaden [1] sails,
Borne with the invisible and creeping winds
Draw the huge bottoms through the furrowed sea,
Breasting the lofty surge.

SHAKESPEARE [2]

It has been already explained to the reader, that there were threatening symptoms in the appearance of the weather to create serious forebodings of evil in the breast of a seaman. When removed from the shadows of the cliffs, the night was not so dark but objects could be discerned at some little distance, and in the eastern horizon there was a streak of fearful light impending over the gloomy waters, in which the swelling outline formed by the rising waves was becoming each moment more distinct, and consequently, more alarming. Several dark clouds overhung the vessel, whose towering masts apparently propped the black vapor, while a few stars were seen twinkling with a sickly flame in the streak of clear sky that skirted the ocean. Still, light currents of air occasionally swept across the bay, bringing with them the fresh odor from the shore, but their flitting irregularity too surely foretold them to be the expiring breath of the land-breeze. The roaring

[1] of thread, fabric
[2] *Henry V,* Act III (Prologue)
[3] Cooper, in his preface to *The Pilot,* says: "The Pilot was published in 1823. This was not long after the appearance of *The Pirate,* a work which, it is hardly necessary to remind the reader, has a direct connection with the sea. In a conversation with a friend, a man of polished taste and extensive reading, the authorship of the Scottish novels came under discussion. The claims of Sir Walter were a little distrusted, on account of the peculiar and minute information that the romances were then very generally thought to display. *The Pirate* was cited as a very marked instance of this universal knowledge, and it was wondered where a man of Scott's habits and associations could have become so familiar with the sea. The writer had frequently observed that there was much looseness in this universal knowledge, and that the secret of its success was to be traced to the power of creating that *vraisemblance,* which is so remarkably exhibited in those world-renowned fictions, rather than to any very accurate information on the part of their author. It would have been hypercritical to object to *The Pirate,* that it was not strictly nautical, or true in its details; but, when the reverse was urged as a proof of what, considering the character of other portions of the work, would have been most extraordinary attainments, it was a sort of provocation to dispute the seamanship of *The Pirate,* a quality to which the book has certainly very little just pretension. The result of this conversation was a sudden determination to produce a work which, if it had no other merit, might present truer pictures of the ocean and ships than any that are to be found in *The Pirate.* To this unpremeditated decision, purely an impulse, is not only *The Pilot* due, but a tolerably numerous school of nautical romances that have succeeded it."

The Pilot introduces, in the character of the pilot, John Paul Jones, famous in American naval battles of the Revolution. Jones, a native of the British sea coast, performed many daring feats in English and Irish harbors and waters as commander of American ships of war, and is perhaps the only commander of a foreign military force to land and capture a fortified place on English soil from the time of William the Conqueror to the present. His daring was so great that a plan was really undertaken for his landing in England and capturing the persons of several English officials to be held in exchange for American officers in British prisons. The plan was not carried out, but Cooper uses it as the germ idea of the plot of *The Pilot.*

When the extract here given opens, Captain Munson, commander of a squadron consisting of an unnamed frigate and the schooner *Ariel,* has worked his two ships into a narrow and dangerous bay on the Northumberland coast. Here the pilot, Gray (Jones), has just been taken aboard after some delay. This, in combination with the state of the tide, the darkness, and the eastern gale, would have made the task of working the ships out to sea impossible to one lacking the pilot's perfect knowledge of the channel and the currents. The pilot is in disguise (his rank and dangerous mission being known only to Captain Munson), and is treated with some contempt by Griffith, first officer of the frigate.

In the following notes, no attempt will be made to explain the nautical terms further than for a bare understanding of the text.

of the surf, as it rolled on the margin of the bay, produced a dull, monotonous sound, that was only interrupted, at times, by a hollow bellowing, as a larger wave than usual broke violently against some cavity in the rock. Everything, in short, united to render the scene gloomy and portentous, without creating instant terror, for the ship rose easily on the long billows, without even straightening the heavy cable that held her to her anchor.

The higher officers were collected around the capstan, engaged in earnest discourse about their situation and prospects, while some of the oldest and most favored seamen would extend their short walk to the hallowed precincts of the quarter-deck, to catch with greedy ears the opinions that fell from their superiors. Numberless were the uneasy glances that were thrown from both officers and men at their commander and the Pilot, who still continued their secret communion in a distant part of the vessel. Once, an ungovernable curiosity, or the heedlessness of his years, led one of the youthful midshipmen near them, but a stern rebuke from his captain sent the boy, abashed and cowering, to hide his mortification among his fellows. This reprimand was received by the elder officers as an intimation that the consultation which they beheld was to be strictly inviolate; and, though it by no means suppressed the repeated expressions of their impatience, it effectually prevented an interruption to the communications which all, however, thought were unreasonably protracted for the occasion.

"This is no time to be talking over bearings and distances," observed the officer next in rank to Griffith; "but we should call the hands up, and try to kedge [1] her off while the sea will suffer a boat to live."

" 'Twould be a tedious and bootless job to attempt warping a ship for miles against a head-beating sea," returned the first lieutenant; "but the land-breeze yet flutters aloft, and if our light sails would draw, with the aid of this ebb tide we might be able to shove her from the shore."

"Hail the tops, Griffith," said the other, "and ask if they feel the air above; 'twill be a hint at least to set the old man and that lubberly Pilot in motion."

Griffith laughed as he complied with the request, and when he received the customary reply to his call, he demanded in a loud voice,—

"Which way have you the wind, aloft?"

"We feel a light cat's-paw, now and then, from the land, sir," returned the sturdy captain of the top; "but our top-sail hangs in the clew-lines, sir, without winking."

Captain Munson and his companion suspended their discourse while this question and answer were exchanged, and then resumed their dialogue as earnestly as if it had received no interruption.

"If it did wink, the hint would be lost on our betters," said the officer of the marines, whose ignorance of seamanship added greatly to his perception of the danger, but who, from pure idleness, made more jokes than any other man in the ship. "That Pilot would not receive a delicate intimation through his ears, Mr. Griffith; suppose you try him by the nose."

"Faith, there was a flash of gunpowder between us in the barge," returned the first lieutenant, "and he does not seem a man to stomach such hints as you advise. Although he looks so meek and quiet, I doubt whether he has paid much attention to the book of Job."

"Why should he?" exclaimed the chaplain, whose apprehensions at least equaled those of the marine, and with a much more disheartening effect; "I am sure it would have been a great waste of time: there are so many charts of the coast, and books on the navigation of these seas, for him to study, that I sincerely hope he has been much better employed." [2]

A loud laugh was created at this speech among the listeners, and it apparently produced the effect that was so long anxiously desired, by putting an end to the mysterious conference between their captain and the pilot. As the former came forward towards his expecting crew, he said, in the composed, steady manner that formed the principal trait in his character,—

"Get the anchor, Mr. Griffith, and make sail on the ship; the hour has arrived when we must be moving."

The cheerful "Aye, aye, sir!" of the young lieutenant was hardly uttered, before the cries of half a dozen midshipmen were heard summoning the boatswain and his mates to their duty.

There was a general movement in the living masses that clustered around the mainmast, on the booms, and in the gangways, though their habits of discipline held the crew a moment longer in suspense. The silence was first broken by the sound of the boatswain's whistle,

---

[1] to move a ship against wind or current by means of light kedge anchors carried ahead in boats and dropped, the ship being worked up to these successively by cable and capstan

[2] Cooper is generally, as here, laborious and awkward in his attempts at humor.

followed by the hoarse cry of "All hands, up anchor, ahoy!" the former rising on the night air from its first low mellow notes to a piercing shrillness that gradually died away on the waters and the latter bellowing through every cranny of the ship, like the hollow murmurs of distant thunder.

The change produced by the customary summons was magical. Human beings sprang out from between the guns, rushed up the hatches, threw themselves with careless activity from the booms, and gathered from every quarter so rapidly, that in an instant, the deck of the frigate was alive with men. The profound silence that had hitherto been only interrupted by the low dialogue of the officers was now changed for the stern orders of the lieutenants, mingled with the shriller cries of the midshipmen, and the hoarse bawling of the boatswain's crew, rising above the tumult of preparation and general bustle.

The captain and the Pilot alone remained passive, in this scene of general exertion; for apprehension had even stimulated that class of officers which is called "idlers" to unusual activity, though frequently reminded by their more experienced messmates that, instead of aiding, they retarded the duty of the vessel. The bustle, however, gradually ceased, and in a few minutes, the same silence pervaded the ship as before.

"We are brought-to,[1] sir," said Griffith, who stood overlooking the scene, holding in one hand a short speaking-trumpet, and grasping with the other one of the shrouds of the ship, to steady himself in the position he had taken on a gun.

"Heave round, sir," was the calm reply.

"Heave round!" repeated Griffith, aloud.

"Heave round!" echoed a dozen eager voices at once, and the lively strains of a fife struck up a brisk air, to enliven the labor. The capstan was instantly set in motion, and the measured tread of the seamen was heard, as they stamped the deck in the circle of their march. For a few minutes no other sounds were heard, if we except the voice of an officer, occasionally cheering the sailors, when it was announced that they "were short"; or, in other words, that the ship was nearly over her anchor.

"Heave and pawl,"[2] cried Griffith; when the quivering notes of the whistle were again succeeded by a general stillness in the vessel.

"What is to be done now, sir?" continued the lieutenant; "shall we trip[3] the anchor? There seems not a breath of air; and as the tide runs slack, I doubt whether the sea do not heave the ship ashore."

There was so much obvious truth in this conjecture, that all eyes turned from the light and animation afforded by the decks of the frigate, to look abroad on the waters, in a vain desire to pierce the darkness, as if to read the fate of their apparently devoted ship, from the aspect of nature.

"I leave all to the Pilot," said the captain, after he had stood a short time by the side of Griffith, anxiously studying the heavens and the ocean. "What say you, Mr. Gray?"

The man who was thus addressed by name was leaning over the bulwarks, with his eyes bent in the same direction as the others; but as he answered he turned his face towards the speaker, and the light from the deck fell full upon his quiet features, which exhibited a calmness bordering on the supernatural, considering his station and responsibility.

"There is much to fear from this heavy ground-swell," he said, in the same unmoved tones as before; "but there is certain destruction to us, if the gale that is brewing in the east finds us waiting its fury in this wild anchorage. All the hemp that ever was spun into cordage would not hold a ship an hour, chafing on these rocks, with a northeaster pouring its fury on her. If the powers of man can compass it, gentlemen, we must get an offing, and that speedily."

"You say no more, sir, than the youngest boy in the ship can see for himself," said Griffith; "ha! here comes the schooner!"

The dashing of the long sweeps in the water was now plainly audible, and the little *Ariel*[4] was seen through the gloom, moving heavily under their feeble impulse. As she passed slowly under the stern of the frigate, the cheerful voice of Barnstable was first heard, opening the communications between them.

"Here's a night for spectacles, Captain Munson!" he cried; "but I thought I heard your fife, sir. I trust in God, you do not mean to ride it out here till morning?"

"I like the berth as little as yourself, Mr. Barnstable," returned the veteran seaman, in his calm manner, in which anxiety was, however, beginning to grow evident. "We are short; but are afraid to let go our hold of the bottom, lest the sea cast us ashore. How make you out the wind?"

[1] the slack of the cable taken up
[2] heave on the capstan and let what is gained be secured by means of the pawls working in the ratchet at its base
[3] lift from the bottom
[4] The schooner *Ariel* in command of Lieutenant Barnstable was so light that it could be moved by oars.

"Wind!" echoed the other; "there is not enough to blow a lady's curl aside. If you wait, sir, till the land-breeze fills your sails, you will wait another moon. I believe I've got my egg-shell out of that nest of gray-caps; but how it has been done in the dark, a better man than myself must explain."

"Take your directions from the Pilot, Mr. Barnstable," returned his commanding officer, "and follow them strictly and to the letter."

A deathlike silence, in both vessels, succeeded this order; for all seemed to listen eagerly to catch the words that fell from the man on whom, even the boys now felt, depended their only hopes for safety. A short time was suffered to elapse, before his voice was heard, in the same low but distinct tones as before:—

"Your sweeps will soon be of no service to you," he said, "against the sea that begins to heave in; but your light sails will help them to get you out. So long as you can head east-and-by-north, you are doing well, and you can stand on till you open [1] the light from that northern headland, when you can heave to, and fire a gun; but if, as I dread, you are struck aback [2] before you open the light, you may trust to your lead on the larboard tack; but beware, with your head to the southward, for no lead will serve you there."

"I can walk over the same ground on one tack as on the other," said Barnstable, "and make both legs of a length." [3]

"It will not do," returned the Pilot. "If you fall off a point to starboard from east-and-by-north, in going large, [4] you will find both rocks and points of shoals to bring you up; and beware, as I tell you, of the starboard tack."

"And how shall I find my way? you will let me trust to neither time, lead, nor log."

"You must trust to a quick eye and a ready hand. The breakers only will show you the dangers, when you are not able to make out the bearings of the land. Tack in season, sir, and don't spare the lead when you head to port."

"Aye, aye," returned Barnstable, in a low, muttering voice. "This is a sort of blind navigation with a vengeance, and all for no purpose that I can see—see! damme, eyesight is of about as much use now as a man's nose would be in reading the Bible."

[1] come in view of, past some obstruction, as a headland
[2] struck with a wind which blows upon the side of the sails opposite to that on which it blew at first, and tends to stop the ship
[3] make both courses of a ship, to starboard or port (larboard), as she tacks, of equal length
[4] not sailing so closely as possible toward the direction of the wind

"Softly, softly, Mr. Barnstable," interrupted his commander,—for such was the anxious stillness in both vessels that even the rattling of the schooner's rigging was heard, as she rolled in the trough of the sea,—"the duty on which Congress has sent us must be performed, at the hazard of our lives."

"I don't mind my life, Captain Munson," said Barnstable, "but there is a great want of conscience in trusting a vessel in such a place as this. However, it is a time to do, and not to talk. But if there be such danger to an easy draught of water, what will become of the frigate? had I not better play jackal and try to feel the way for you?"

"I thank you," said the Pilot; "the offer is generous, but would avail us nothing. I have the advantage of knowing the ground well, and must trust to my memory, and God's good favor. Make sail, make sail, sir, and if you succeed, we will venture to break ground."

The order was promptly obeyed, and in a very short time the *Ariel* was covered with canvas. Though no air was perceptible on the decks of the frigate, the little schooner was so light, that she succeeded in stemming her way over the rising waves, aided a little by the tide; and in a few minutes her low hull was just discernible in the streak of light along the horizon, with the dark outline of her sails rising above the sea, until their fanciful summits were lost in the shadows of the clouds.

Griffith had listened to the foregoing dialogue like the rest of the junior officers, in profound silence; but when the *Ariel* began to grow indistinct to the eye, he jumped lightly from the gun to the deck, and cried,—

"She slips off, like a vessel from the stocks! shall I trip the anchor, sir, and follow?"

"We have no choice," replied his captain. "You hear the question, Mr. Gray? shall we let go the bottom?"

"It must be done, Captain Munson; we may want more drift than the rest of this tide to get us into a place of safety," said the Pilot. "I would give five years from a life that I know will be short, if the ship lay one mile further seaward."

This remark was unheard by all, except the commander of the frigate, who again walked aside with the Pilot, where they resumed their mysterious communications. The words of assent were no sooner uttered, however, than Griffith gave forth from his trumpet the command to "Heave away!" Again the strains of the fife were followed by the tread of the men at the capstan. At the same time that the anchor was heaving up, the sails were loosened from the yards, and opened to invite the breeze. In effecting this duty, orders were thundered through the trumpet of the first lieutenant, and executed with the rapidity of thought. Men were to be seen, like spots in the dim light from the heavens, lying on every yard, or hanging as in air, while strange cries were heard issuing from every part of the rigging, and each spar of the vessel. "Ready the fore-royal," cried a shrill voice, as if from the clouds; "Ready the fore-yard," uttered the hoarser tones of a seaman beneath him; "All ready aft, sir," cried a third, from another quarter; and in a few minutes the order was given to "Let fall."

The little light which fell from the sky was now excluded by the falling canvas, and a deeper gloom was cast athwart the decks of the ship, that served to render the brilliancy of the lanterns even vivid, while it gave to objects outboard a more appalling and dreary appearance than before.

Every individual, excepting the commander and his associate, was now earnestly engaged in getting the ship under way. The sounds of "We're away," were repeated by a burst from fifty voices, and the rapid evolutions of the capstan announced that nothing but the weight of the anchor was to be lifted. The hauling of cordage, the rattling of blocks, blended with the shrill calls of the boatswain and his mates, succeeded; and though to a landsman all would have appeared confusion and hurry, long practice and strict discipline enabled the crew to exhibit their ship under a cloud of canvas, from her deck to her trucks, in less time than we have consumed in relating it.

For a few minutes, the officers were not disappointed by the result; for though the heavy sails flapped lazily against the masts, the light duck on the loftier spars swelled outwardly, and the ship began sensibly to yield to their influence.

"She travels! she travels!" exclaimed Griffith, joyously; "ah, the hussy! she has as much antipathy to the land as any fish that swims: it blows a little gale aloft, yet!"

"We feel its dying breath," said the Pilot, in low, soothing tones, but in a manner so sudden as to startle Griffith, at whose elbow they were unexpectedly uttered. "Let us forget, young man, everything but the number of lives that depend, this night, on your exertions and my knowledge."

"If you be but half as able to exhibit the one, as I am willing to make the other, we shall do well," returned the lieutenant, in the same tone. "Remember, whatever may be your feelings, that we are on an enemy's coast, and love it not enough to wish to lay our bones there."

With this brief explanation they separated, the vessel requiring the constant and close attention of the officer to her movements.

The exultation produced in the crew by the progress of their ship through the water was of short duration; for the breeze that had seemed to await their motions, after forcing the vessel for a quarter of a mile, fluttered for a few minutes amid their light canvas, and then left them entirely. The quartermaster, whose duty it was to superintend the helm, soon announced that he was losing the command of the vessel, as she was no longer obedient to her rudder. This ungrateful intelligence was promptly communicated to his commander by Griffith, who suggested the propriety of again dropping an anchor.

"I refer you to Mr. Gray," returned the captain; "he is the pilot, sir, and with him rests the safety of the vessel."

"Pilots sometimes lose ships as well as save them," said Griffith: "know you the man well, Captain Munson, who holds all our lives in his keeping, and so coolly as if he cared but little for the venture?"

"Mr. Griffith, I do know him; he is, in my opinion, both competent and faithful. Thus much I tell you, to relieve your anxiety; more you must not ask; but is there not a shift of wind?"

"God forbid!" exclaimed his lieutenant; "if that northeaster catches us within the shoals, our case will be desperate indeed!"

The heavy rolling of the vessel caused an occasional expansion, and as sudden a reaction, in their sails, which left the oldest seaman in the ship in doubt which way the currents of air were passing, or whether there existed any that were not created by the flapping of their own canvas. The head of the ship, however, began to fall off from the sea, and notwithstanding the darkness, it soon became apparent that she was driving in, bodily, towards the shore.

During these few minutes of gloomy doubt, Griffith, by one of those sudden revulsions of the mind that connect the opposite extremes of feeling, lost his animated anxiety, and relapsed into the listless apathy that so often came over him, even in the most critical moments of trial and danger. He was standing with one elbow resting on his capstan, shading his eyes from the light of the battle-lantern that stood near him with one hand, when he felt a gentle pressure of the other that recalled his recollection. Looking affectionately, though still recklessly, at the boy who stood at his side, he said,—

"Dull music, Mr. Merry."

"So dull, sir, that I can't dance to it," returned the midshipman. "Nor do I believe there is a man in the ship who would not rather hear 'The Girl I left Behind me,' than those execrable sounds."

"What sounds, boy? The ship is as quiet as the Quaker meetings in the Jerseys, before your good old grandfather used to break the charm of silence with his sonorous voice."

"Ah! laugh at my peaceable blood, if thou wilt, Mr. Griffith," said the arch youngster; "but remember, there is a mixture of it in all sorts of veins. I wish I could hear one of the old gentleman's chants now, sir; I could always sleep to them like a gull in the surf. But he that sleeps tonight with that lullaby, will make a nap of it."

"Sounds! I hear no sounds, boy, but the flapping aloft; even that Pilot, who struts the quarter-deck like an admiral, has nothing to say."

"Is not that a sound to open a seaman's ear?"

"It is in truth a heavy roll of the surf, lad, but the night air carries it heavily to our ears. Know you not the sound of the surf yet, younker?"

"I know it too well, Mr. Griffith, and do not wish to know it better. How fast are we tumbling in-towards that surf, sir?"

"I think we hold our own," said Griffith, rousing again; "though we had better anchor. Luff, fellow, luff; you are broadside to the sea!"

The man at the wheel repeated his former intelligence, adding a suggestion, that he thought the ship 'was gathering stern-way.'

"Haul up your courses,[1] Mr. Griffith," said Captain Munson, "and let us feel the wind."

The rattling of the blocks was soon heard, and the enormous sheets of canvas that hung from the lower yards were instantly suspended "in the brails." When this change was effected, all on board stood silent and breathless, as if expecting to learn their fate by the result. Several contradictory opinions were at length hazarded among the officers, when Griffith seized the candle from the lantern, and springing on one of the guns, held it on high, exposed to the action of the air. The little flame waved, with uncertain glimmering, for a moment, and

then burned steadily, in a line with the masts. Griffith was about to lower his extended arm, when, feeling a slight sensation of coolness on his hand, he paused, and the light turned slowly towards the land, flared, flickered, and finally deserted the wick.

"Lose not a moment, Mr. Griffith," cried the Pilot aloud; "clew up and furl everything but your three topsails, and let them be double-reefed. Now is the time to fulfill your promise."

The young man paused one moment, in astonishment, as the clear, distinct tones of the stranger struck his ears so unexpectedly; but turning his eyes to seaward, he sprang on the deck, and proceeded to obey the order, as if life and death depended on his dispatch.

CHAPTER V

She rights! she rights, boys! wear[2] off shore.
                                        Song.

The extraordinary activity of Griffith, which communicated itself with promptitude to the crew, was produced by a sudden alteration in the weather. In place of the well defined streak along the horizon, that has been already described, an immense body of misty light appeared to be moving in, with rapidity, from the ocean, while a distinct but distant roaring announced the sure approach of the tempest that had so long troubled the waters. Even Griffith, while thundering his orders through the trumpet and urging the men by his cries to expedition, would pause, for instants, to cast anxious glances in the direction of the coming storm; and the faces of the sailors who lay on the yards were turned, instinctively, towards the same quarter of the heavens, while they knotted the reef-points, or passed the gaskets that were to confine the unruly canvas to the prescribed limits.

The Pilot alone, in that confused and busy throng, where voice rose above voice, and cry echoed cry in quick succession, appeared as if he held no interest in the important stake. With his eyes steadily fixed on the approaching mist, and his arms folded together in composure, he stood calmly waiting the result.

The ship had fallen off with her broadside to the sea, and was become unmanageable, and the sails were already brought into the folds necessary to her security, when the quick and heavy fluttering of canvas was thrown across the water with all the gloomy and chilling sensations that such sounds produce, where darkness and danger unite to appall the seaman.

[1] Haul up the lower fore and main sails to the yards; the sails prevented the officers on deck from judging the direction of the very slight breeze.

[2] when beating against the wind, to change the ship to the other course by steering away from the wind and turning the ship around

"The schooner has it!" cried Griffith. "Barnstable has held on, like himself, to the last moment. God send that the squall leave him cloth enough to keep him from the shore!"

"His sails are easily handled," the commander observed, "and she must be over the principal danger. We are falling off before it, Mr. Gray; shall we try a cast of the lead?"

The Pilot turned from his contemplative posture, and moved slowly across the deck before he returned any reply to this question, like a man who not only felt that everything depended on himself, but that he was equal to the emergency.

" 'Tis unnecessary," he at length said; " 'twould be certain destruction to be taken aback; and it is difficult to say, within several points, how the wind may strike us."

" 'Tis difficult no longer," cried Griffith; "for here it comes, and in right earnest!"

The rushing sounds of the wind were now, indeed, heard at hand; and the words were hardly past the lips of the young lieutenant, before the vessel bowed down heavily to one side, and then, as she began to move through the water, rose again majestically to her upright position, as if saluting, like a courteous champion, the powerful antagonist with which she was about to contend. Not another minute elapsed before the ship was throwing the water aside, with a lively progress, and, obedient to her helm, was brought as near to the desired course as the direction of the wind would allow. The hurry and bustle on the yards gradually subsided, and the men slowly descended to the deck, all straining their eyes to pierce the gloom in which they were enveloped, and some shaking their heads, in melancholy doubt, afraid to express the apprehensions they really entertained. All on board anxiously waited for the fury of the gale; for there were none so ignorant or inexperienced in that gallant frigate, as not to know that as yet they only felt the infant efforts of the wind. Each moment, however, it increased in power, though so gradual was the alteration that the relieved mariners began to believe that all their gloomy forebodings were not to be realized. During this short interval of uncertainty, no other sounds were heard than the whistling of the breeze as it passed quickly through the mass of rigging that belonged to the vessel, and the dashing of the spray that began to fly from her bows like the foam of a cataract.

"It blows fresh," cried Griffith, who was the first to speak in that moment of doubt and anxiety; "but it is no more than a capful of wind after all. Give us elbow-room, and the right canvas, Mr. Pilot, and I'll handle the ship like a gentleman's yacht, in this breeze."

"Will she stay, think ye, under this sail?" said the low voice of the stranger.

"She will do all that man, in reason, can ask of wood and iron," returned the lieutenant; "but the vessel don't float the ocean that will tack under double-reefed topsails alone, against a heavy sea. Help her with the courses,[1] Pilot, and you shall see her come round like a dancing-master."

"Let us feel the strength of the gale first," returned the man who was called Mr. Gray, moving from the side of Griffith to the weather gangway of the vessel, where he stood in silence, looking ahead of the ship, with an air of singular coolness and abstraction.

All the lanterns had been extinguished on the deck of the frigate, when her anchor was secured, and as the first mist of the gale had passed over, it was succeeded by a faint light that was a good deal aided by the glittering foam of the waters, which now broke in white curls around the vessel in every direction. The land could be faintly discerned, rising like a heavy bank of black fog, above the margin of the waters, and was only distinguishable from the heavens by its deeper gloom and obscurity. The last rope was coiled and deposited in its proper place by the seamen, and for several minutes the stillness of death pervaded the crowded decks. It was evident to everyone that their ship was dashing at a prodigious rate through the waves and as she was approaching, with such velocity, the quarter of the bay where the shoals and dangers were known to be situated, nothing but the habits of the most exact discipline could suppress the uneasiness of the officers and men within their own bosoms. At length the voice of Captain Munson was heard, calling to the Pilot.

"Shall I send a hand into the chains, Mr. Gray," he said, "and try our water?"

Although this question was asked aloud, and the interest it excited drew many of the officers and men around him in eager impatience for his answer, it was unheeded by the man to whom it was addressed. His head rested on his hand, as he leaned over the hammock-cloths[2] of the vessel, and his whole air was that of one whose thoughts wandered from the pressing necessity of their situation. Griffith was among those who had approached the Pilot; and after waiting a moment, from respect, to hear the answer to his commander's question, he presumed on

[1] lower fore and main sails
[2] tarpaulins covering the hammocks which were stowed, when not in use, in the bulwarks of the old men-of-war

his own rank, and leaving the circle that stood at a little distance, stepped to the side of the mysterious guardian of their lives.

"Captain Munson desires to know whether you wish a cast of the lead," said the young officer, with a little impatience of manner. No immediate answer was made to this repetition of the question, and Griffith laid his hand unceremoniously on the shoulder of the other, with an intent to rouse him before he made another application for a reply, but the convulsive start of the Pilot held him silent in amazement.

"Fall back there," said the lieutenant, sternly, to the men who were closing around them in a compact circle; "away with you to your stations, and see all clear for stays."[1] The dense mass of heads dissolved, at this order, like the water of one of the waves commingling with the ocean, and the lieutenant and his companion were left by themselves.

"This is not a time for musing, Mr. Gray," continued Griffith; "remember our compact, and look to your charge; is it not time to put the vessel in stays? Of what are you dreaming?"

The Pilot laid his hand on the extended arm of the lieutenant and grasped it with a convulsive pressure, as he answered,—

"'Tis a dream of reality. You are young, Mr. Griffith, nor am I past the noon of life; but should you live fifty years longer, you never can see and experience what I have encountered in my little period of three-and-thirty years!"

A good deal astonished at this burst of feeling, so singular at such a moment, the young sailor was at a loss for a reply; but as his duty was uppermost in his thoughts he still dwelt on the theme that most interested him.

"I hope much of your experience has been on this coast, for the ship travels lively," he said, "and the daylight showed us so much to dread that we do not feel over valiant in the dark. How much longer shall we stand on, upon this tack?"

The Pilot turned slowly from the side of the vessel, and walked towards the commander of the frigate, as he replied, in a tone that seemed deeply agitated by his melancholy reflections,—

"You have your wish, then; much, very much of my early life was passed on this dreaded coast. What to you is all darkness and gloom, to me is light as if a noon-day sun shone upon it. But tack your ship, sir, tack your ship; I would see how she works before we reach the point where she *must* behave well or we perish."

[1] ready for executing the maneuver of tacking

Griffith gazed after him in wonder, while the Pilot slowly paced the quarter-deck, and then, rousing from his trance, gave forth the cheering order that called each man to his station to perform the desired evolution. The confident assurances which the young officer had given to the pilot respecting the qualities of his vessel, and his own ability to manage her, were fully realized by the result. The helm was no sooner put a-lee, than the huge ship bore up gallantly against the wind, and, dashing directly through the waves, threw the foam high into the air as she looked boldly into the very eye of the wind; and then, yielding gracefully to its power, she fell off on the other tack, with her head pointed from those dangerous shoals that she had so recently approached with such terrifying velocity. The heavy yards swung round, as if they had been vanes to indicate the currents of air; and in a few moments the frigate again moved, with stately progress, through the water, leaving the rocks and shoals behind her on one side of the bay, but advancing towards those that offered equal danger on the other.

During this time the sea was becoming more agitated, and the violence of the wind was gradually increasing. The latter no longer whistled amid the cordage of the vessel, but it seemed to howl, surlily, as it passed the complicated machinery that the frigate obtruded on its path. An endless succession of white surges rose above the heavy billows, and the very air was glittering with the light that was disengaged from the ocean. The ship yielded, each moment, more and more before the storm, and in less than half an hour from the time that she had lifted her anchor, she was driven along with tremendous fury by the full power of a gale of wind. Still, the hardy and experienced mariners who directed her movements held her to the course that was necessary to their preservation, and still Griffith gave forth, when directed by their unknown Pilot, those orders that turned her in the narrow channel where alone safety was to be found.

So far, the performance of his duty appeared easy to the stranger, and he gave the required directions in those still, calm tones, that formed so remarkable a contrast to the responsibility of his situation. But when the land was becoming dim, in distance as well as darkness, and the agitated sea alone was to be discovered as it swept by them in foam, he broke in upon the monotonous roaring of the tempest with the sounds of his voice, seeming to shake off his apathy and rouse himself to the occasion.

"Now is the time to watch her closely, Mr. Griffith," he cried; "here we get the true tide and the real danger. Place the best quarter-master of your ship in those chains, and let an officer stand by him, and see that he gives us the right water."

"I will take that office on myself," said the captain, "pass a light into the weather main-chains."

"Stand by your braces!"[1] exclaimed the Pilot, with startling quickness. "Heave away that lead!"

These preparations taught the crew to expect the crisis, and every officer and man stood in fearful silence, at his assigned station, awaiting the issue of the trial. Even the quartermaster at the con[2] gave out his orders to the men at the wheel, in deeper and hoarser tones than usual, as if anxious not to disturb the quiet and order of the vessel.

While this deep expectation pervaded the frigate, the piercing cry of the leadsman, as he called "By the mark seven," rose above the tempest, crossed over the decks, and appeared to pass away to leeward, borne on the blast like the warnings of some water spirit.

" 'Tis well," returned the Pilot calmly; "try it again."

The short pause was succeeded by another cry, "And a half-five!"

"She shoals! she shoals!" exclaimed Griffith; "keep her a good full."[3]

"Aye! you must hold the vessel in command, now," said the Pilot, with those cool tones that are most appalling in critical moments, because they seem to denote most preparation and care.

The third call, "By the deep four!" was followed by a prompt direction from the stranger to tack.

Griffith seemed to emulate the coolness of the Pilot, in issuing the necessary orders to execute this maneuver.

The vessel rose slowly from the inclined position into which she had been forced by the tempest, and the sails were shaking vio-lently, as if to release themselves from their confinement, while the ship stemmed the bil-lows, when the well-known voice of the sailing-master was heard shouting from the fore-castle,—

"Breakers! breakers, dead ahead!"

This appalling sound seemed yet to be lin-gering about the ship, when a second voice cried,—

"Breakers on our lee-bow!"

"We are in the bight of the shoals, Mr. Gray,"

cried the commander. "She loses her way; perhaps an anchor might hold her."

"Clear away that best bower!"[4] shouted Griffith through his trumpet.

"Hold on!" cried the Pilot, in a voice that reached the very hearts of all who heard him; "hold on everything."

The young man turned fiercely to the daring stranger who thus defied the discipline of his vessel, and at once demanded,—

"Who is it that dares to countermand my orders? is it not enough that you run the ship into danger, but you must interfere to keep her there? If another word"—

"Peace, Mr. Griffith," interrupted the captain, bending from the rigging, his gray locks blow-ing about in the wind, and adding a look of wildness to the haggard care that he exhibited by the light of the lantern; "yield the trumpet to Mr. Gray; he alone can save us."

Griffith threw his speaking-trumpet on the deck, and as he walked proudly away, mut-tered in bitterness of feeling,—

"Then all is lost, indeed! and among the rest, the foolish hopes with which I visited this coast."

There was, however, no time for reply; the ship had been rapidly running into the wind, and as the efforts of the crew were paralyzed by the contradictory orders they had heard, she gradually lost her way, and in a few seconds all her sails were taken aback.

Before the crew understood their situation, the Pilot had applied the trumpet to his mouth, and in a voice that rose above the tempest, he thundered forth his orders. Each command was given distinctly, and with a precision that showed him to be master of his profession. The helm was kept fast, the head yards swung up heavily against the wind, and the vessel was soon whirling round on her heel, with a retro-grade movement.

Griffith was too much of a seaman not to perceive that the Pilot had seized, with a per-ception almost intuitive, the only method that promised to extricate the vessel from her situ-ation. He was young, impetuous, and proud—but he was also generous. Forgetting his re-sentment and his mortification, he rushed for-ward among the men, and, by his presence and example, added certainty to the experiment. The ship fell off slowly before the gale, and bowed her yards nearly to the water, as she felt the blast pouring its fury on her broadside, while the surly waves beat violently against her stern, as if in reproach at departing from her usual manner of moving.

---

[1] ropes from the yards to the deck, holding the yards in a given direction

[2] any station taken by the officer giving orders to the men at the wheel

[3] keep all sails full by sailing not too close to the wind

[4] largest anchor

The voice of the Pilot, however, was still heard, steady and calm, and yet so clear and high as to reach every ear; and the obedient seamen whirled the yards at his bidding, in despite of the tempest, as if they handled the toys of their childhood. When the ship had fallen off dead before the wind, her head-sails were shaken, her after-yards trimmed, and her helm shifted, before she had time to run upon the danger that had threatened, as well to leeward as to windward. The beautiful fabric, obedient to her government, threw her bows up gracefully towards the wind again; and, as her sails were trimmed, moved out from amongst the dangerous shoals in which she had been embayed, as steadily and swiftly as she had approached them.

A moment of breathless astonishment succeeded the accomplishment of this nice maneuver, but there was no time for the usual expressions of surprise. The stranger still held the trumpet, and continued to lift his voice amid the howlings of the blast, whenever prudence or skill required any change in the management of the ship. For an hour longer there was a fearful struggle for their preservation, the channel becoming at each step more complicated, and the shoals thickening around the mariners on every side. The lead was cast rapidly, and the quick eye of the Pilot seemed to pierce the darkness with a keenness of vision that exceeded human power. It was apparent to all in the vessel that they were under the guidance of one who understood the navigation thoroughly, and their exertions kept pace with their reviving confidence. Again and again the frigate appeared to be rushing blindly on shoals where the sea was covered with foam, and where destruction would have been as sudden as it was certain, when the clear voice of the stranger was heard warning them of the danger and inciting them to their duty. The vessel was implicitly yielded to his government; and during those anxious moments when she was dashing the waters aside, throwing the spray over her enormous yards, each ear would listen eagerly for those sounds that had obtained a command over the crew, that can only be acquired, under such circumstances, by great steadiness and consummate skill. The ship was recovering from the inaction of changing her course, in one of those critical tacks that she had made so often, when the Pilot, for the first time, addressed the commander of the frigate, who still continued to superintend the all-important duty of the leadsman."

"Now is the pinch," he said, "and if the ship behaves well, we are safe; but if otherwise, all we have yet done will be useless."

The veteran seaman whom he addressed, left the chains at this portentous notice, and calling to his first lieutenant, required of the stranger an explanation of his warning.

"See you yon light on the southern headland?" returned the Pilot; "you may know it from the star near it, by its sinking, at times, in the ocean. Now observe the hummock a little north of it, looking like a shadow in the horizon; 'tis a hill far inland. If we keep that light open from the hill, we shall do well; but if not, we surely go to pieces."

"Let us tack again!" exclaimed the lieutenant.

The Pilot shook his head as he replied,—

"There is no more tacking or box-hauling [1] to be done tonight. We have barely room to pass out of the shoals on this course; and if we can weather the 'Devil's Grip,' we clear their outermost point; but if not, as I said before, there is but an alternative."

"If we had beaten out the way we entered," exclaimed Griffith, "we should have done well."

"Say, also, if the tide would have let us do so," returned the Pilot, calmly. "Gentlemen, we must be prompt; we have but a mile to go, and the ship appears to fly. That topsail is not enough to keep her up to the wind; we want both jib and mainsail."

"'Tis a perilous thing to loosen canvas in such a tempest!" observed the doubtful captain.

"It must be done," returned the collected stranger; "we perish without it; see! the light already touches the edge of the hummock; the sea casts us to leeward!"

"It shall be done!" cried Griffith, seizing the trumpet from the hand of the Pilot.

The orders of the lieutenant were executed almost as soon as issued; and, everything being ready, the enormous folds of the mainsail were trusted loose to the blast. There was an instant when the result was doubtful; the tremendous threshing of the heavy sail seemed to bid defiance to all restraint, shaking the ship to her center; but art and strength prevailed, and gradually the canvas was distended, and bellying as it filled, was drawn down to its usual place by the power of a hundred men. The vessel yielded to this immense addition of force, and bowed before it like a reed bending to a breeze. But the success of the measure was announced by a joyful cry from the stranger, that seemed to burst from his inmost soul.

[1] a method of coming upon the other tack by steering the ship into the wind and then backing away from the wind in turning

"She feels it! she springs her luff! [1] observe," he said, "the light opens from the hummock already: if she will only bear her canvas, we shall go clear!"

A report, like that of a cannon, interrupted his exclamation, and something resembling a white cloud was seen drifting before the wind from the head of the ship, till it was driven into the gloom far to leeward.

" 'Tis the jib, blown from the bolt-ropes," said the commander of the frigate. "This is no time to spread light duck—but the mainsail may stand it yet."

"The sail would laugh at a tornado," returned the lieutenant; "but the mast springs like a piece of steel."

"Silence all!" cried the Pilot. "Now, gentlemen, we shall soon know our fate. Let her luff—luff you can!" [2]

This warning effectually closed all discourse, and the hardy mariners, knowing that they had already done all in the power of man to insure their safety, stood in breathless anxiety awaiting the result. At a short distance ahead of them the whole ocean was white with foam, and the waves instead of rolling on in regular succession, appeared to be tossing about in mad gambols. A single streak of dark billows, not half a cable's length in width, could be discerned running into this chaos of water; but it was soon lost to the eye amid the confusion of the disturbed element. Along this narrow path the vessel moved more heavily than before, being brought so near the wind as to keep her sails touching. The Pilot silently proceeded to the wheel, and, with his own hands, he undertook the steerage of the ship. No noise proceeded from the frigate to interrupt the horrid tumult of the ocean; and she entered the channel among the breakers, with the silence of a desperate calmness. Twenty times, as the foam rolled away to leeward, the crew were on the eve of uttering their joy, as they supposed the vessel past the danger; but breaker after breaker would still heave up before them, following each other into the general mass, to check their exultation. Occasionally, the fluttering of the sails would be heard; and when the looks of the startled seamen were turned to the wheel, they beheld the stranger grasping its spokes, with his quick eye glancing from the water to the canvas. At length the ship reached a point where she appeared to be rushing directly into the jaws of destruction, when suddenly her course was changed, and her head

[1] sails closer to the wind
[2] come nearer the wind, as close as you can

receded rapidly from the wind. At the same instant the voice of the Pilot was heard shouting,—

"Square away the yards!—in mainsail!"

A general burst from the crew echoed, "Square away the yards!" and, quick as thought, the frigate was seen gliding along the channel before the wind. The eye had hardly time to dwell on the foam, which seemed like clouds driving in the heavens, and directly the gallant vessel issued from her perils, and rose and fell on the heavy waves of the sea.

The seamen were yet drawing long breaths, and gazing about them like men recovered from a trance, when Griffith approached the man who had so successfully conducted them through their perils. The lieutenant grasped the hand of the other, as he said,—

"You have this night proved yourself a faithful pilot and such a seaman as the world cannot equal."

The pressure of the hand was warmly returned by the unknown mariner, who replied,—

"I am no stranger to the seas, and I may yet find my grave in them. But you, too, have deceived me; you have acted nobly, young man, and Congress—"

"What of Congress?" asked Griffith, observing him to pause.

"Why, Congress is fortunate if it has many such ships as this," said the stranger, coldly, walking away towards the commander.

Griffith gazed after him a moment in surprise; but, as his duty required his attention, other thoughts soon engaged his mind.

The vessel was pronounced to be in safety. The gale was heavy and increasing, but there was a clear sea before them; and, as she slowly stretched out into the bosom of the ocean, preparations were made for her security during its continuance. Before midnight, everything was in order.

A gun from the *Ariel* soon announced the safety of the schooner also, which had gone out by another and an easier channel that the frigate had not dared to attempt; when the commander directed the usual watch to be set, and the remainder of the crew to seek their necessary repose.

The captain withdrew with the mysterious pilot to his own cabin. Griffith gave his last order; and renewing his charge to the officer instructed with the care of the vessel, he wished him a pleasant watch, and sought the refreshment of his own cot. For an hour the young lieutenant lay musing on the events of the day. The remark of Barnstable would occur to him, in connection with the singular comment of the boy; and then his thoughts would recur to the Pilot, who, taken from the hostile shores of Britain, and with her accent on his tongue, had served them so faithfully and so well. He remembered the anxiety of Captain Munson to procure this stranger, at the very hazard from which they had just been relieved, and puzzled himself with conjecturing why a pilot was to be sought at such a risk. His more private feelings would then resume their sway, and the recollection of America, his mistress, his home, mingled with the confused images of the drowsy youth. The dashing of the billows against the side of the ship, the creaking of guns and bulkheads, with the roaring of the tempest, however, became gradually less and less distinct, until nature yielded to necessity, and the young man forgot even the romantic images of his love, in the deep sleep of a seaman.

·   ·   ·   ·   ·   ·

1823

From THE DEERSLAYER [1]
Chapter XXVII

Thou hast been busy, Death, this day, and yet
But half thy work is done! The gates of hell
Are thronged, yet twice ten thousand spirits more,
Who, from their warm and healthful tenements,
Fear no divorce, must, ere the sun go down,
Enter the world of woe!

SOUTHEY

One experienced in the signs of the heavens would have seen that the sun wanted but two or three minutes of the zenith, when Deerslayer landed on the point where the Hurons were now encamped, nearly abreast of the castle. This spot was similar to the one already described, with the exception that the surface of the land was less broken and less crowded with trees.

[1] *The Deerslayer* is placed before *The Prairie* because, though last in date of composition, it is first in epic order of the Leatherstocking Tales. These tales vary in scene and in characters, but they work out a unified theme, the contact of the red man with the white, at the shifting border of American settlement, from the Mohawk to the Platte. One character, Natty Bumppo, or Leatherstocking, or Deerslayer, as he is variously called, runs through all the tales. He has been brought up among the Delaware Indians, and has, at the beginning of the present tale, come to Otsego Lake in the central part of the present state of New York. The time is the beginning of the French and Indian War and the region is a wilderness. Here he is to meet a young Delaware chief, Chingachgook, or The Serpent, of the renowned Uncas family, whose betrothed, Hist, or Wah-ta-Wah, has been, through the connivance of the traitor Briarthorn, stolen away and adopted by the Hurons, a tribe of the Iroquois or Mingo Confederacy. The only settlers at the lake are the old trapper, Hutter, and his two daughters,

Owing to these two circumstances, it was all the better suited to the purpose for which it had been selected, the space beneath the branches bearing some resemblance to a densely-wooded lawn. Favored by its position and its spring, it had been much resorted to by savages and hunters, and the natural grasses has succeeded their fires, leaving an appearance of sward in places, a very unusual accompaniment of the virgin forest. Nor was the margin of water fringed with bushes as on so much of its shore, but the eye penetrated the woods immediately on reaching the strand, commanding nearly the whole area of the projection.

If it was a point of honor with the Indian warrior to redeem his word, when pledged to return and meet his death at a given hour, so was it a point of characteristic pride to show no womanish impatience but to reappear as nearly as possible at the appointed moment. It was well not to exceed the grace accorded by the generosity of the enemy, but it was better to meet it to a minute. Something of this dramatic effect mingles with most of the graver usages of the American aborigines, and no doubt —like the prevalence of a similar feeling among people more sophisticated and refined—may be referred to a principle of nature. We all love the wonderful, and when it comes attended by chivalrous self-devotion and a rigid regard to honor, it presents itself to our admiration in a shape doubly attractive. As respects Deerslayer, though he took a pride in showing his

the beautiful Judith and the feeble-minded Hester. This family, for protection from the Indians, lives in the "castle," a lake-dwelling on piles, or sometimes in the "ark," a rude house-boat. Just as Deerslayer arrives at the lake in the company of Harry Hurry, a reckless frontiersman, a party of Hurons attempts to surprise the lake-dwellers. Hutter and Hurry, against the protest of Deerslayer, risk a night attack on these Indians for the sake of the scalp-bounty. They are themselves captured, but Deerslayer manages to negotiate their release in exchange for four curiously carved ivory chess-men in the form of elephants, that he finds, together with rich articles of dress, in a mysterious chest of Hutter's. A day or two later the Hurons attack the "castle" and kill and scalp Hutter. Deerslayer and Chingachgook, finding that Hist is captive in the same camp of Hurons, steal upon the camp at night, and snatch Hist away; but Deerslayer is himself made captive. The following day the Hurons release him on twenty-four hours' furlough: if Hist is returned to the Hurons and Judith and Hester will also go with the Hurons, Deerslayer is to be free. These conditions none will accept, much less will Deerslayer advise them; and he himself, true to his word, returns to the Huron camp at the edge of the lake to undergo, as he has every reason to expect, death by torture as a captive enemy. The selection above begins as he sets foot among the savages. These have just begun to suspect that their presence may be known at the frontier posts, and are in some haste to set out on their return to Canada.

white blood, by often deviating from the usages of the red men, he frequently dropped into their customs, and oftener into their feelings, unconsciously to himself, in consequence of having no other arbiters to appeal to than their judgments and tastes. On the present occasion, he would have abstained from betraying a feverish haste by a too speedy return, since it would have contained a tacit admission that the time asked for was more than had been wanted; but, on the other hand, had the idea occurred to him, he would have quickened his movements a little, in order to avoid the dramatic appearance of returning at the precise instant set as the utmost limit of his absence. Still, accident had interfered to defeat the last intention, for when the young man put his foot on the point, and advanced with a steady tread toward the group of chiefs that was seated in grave array on a fallen tree, the oldest of their number cast his eye upward at an opening in the trees, and pointed out to his companions the startling fact that the sun was just entering a space that was known to mark the zenith. A common but low exclamation of surprise and admiration escaped every mouth, and the grim warriors looked at each other; some with envy and disappointment, some with astonishment at the precise accuracy of their victim, and others with a more generous and liberal feeling. The American Indian always deemed his moral victories the noblest, prizing the groans and yielding of his victim under torture more than the trophy of his scalp; and the trophy itself more than his life. To slay, and not to bring off the proof of victory, indeed, was scarcely deemed honorable; even these rude and fierce tenants of the forest, like their more nurtured brethren of the court and the camp, having set up for themselves imaginary and arbitrary points of honor, to supplant the conclusions of the right and the decisions of reason.

The Hurons had been divided in their opinions concerning the probability of their captive's return. Most among them, indeed, had not expected it possible for a paleface to come back voluntarily, and meet the known penalties of an Indian torture; but a few of the seniors expected better things from one who had already shown himself so singularly cool, brave, and upright. The party had come to its decision, however, less in the expectation of finding the pledge redeemed, than in the hope of disgracing the Delawares by casting into their teeth the delinquency of one bred in their villages. They would have greatly preferred that Chingachgook should be their prisoner, and

prove the traitor; but the paleface scion of the hated stock was no bad substitute for their purposes, failing in their designs against the ancient stem. With a view to render the triumph as signal as possible, in the event of the hour's passing without the reappearance of the hunter, all the warriors and scouts of the party had been called in; and the whole band, men, women and children, was now assembled at this single point, to be a witness of the expected scene. As the castle was in plain view, and by no means distant, it was easily watched by daylight; and it being thought that its inmates were now limited to Hurry, the Delaware, and the two girls, no apprehensions were felt of their being able to escape unseen. A large raft, having a breastwork of logs, had been prepared, and was in actual readiness to be used against either ark or castle, as occasion might require, as soon as the fate of Deerslayer was determined; the seniors of the party having come to the opinion that it was getting to be hazardous to delay their departure for Canada beyond the coming night. In short, the band waited merely to dispose of this single affair, ere it brought matters to a crisis, and prepared to commence its retreat towards the distant waters of Ontario.

It was an imposing scene into which Deerslayer now found himself advancing. All the older warriors were seated on the trunk of the fallen tree, waiting his approach with grave decorum. On the right stood the young men, armed, while the left was occupied by the women and children. In the center was an open space of considerable extent, always canopied by leaves, but from which the underbrush, dead wood, and other obstacles had been carefully removed. The more open area had probably been much used by former parties, for this was the place where the appearance of a sward was the most decided. The arches of the woods, even at high noon, cast their somber shadows on the spot, which the brilliant rays of the sun that struggled through the leaves contributed to mellow, and, if such an expression can be used, to illuminate. It was probably from a similar scene that the mind of man first got its idea of the effects of Gothic tracery and churchly hues; [1] this temple of nature producing some such effect, so far as light and shadows were concerned, as the well-known offspring of human invention.

As was not unusual among the tribes and wandering bands of the aborigines, two chiefs

[1] More recent investigation renders untenable this theory of the origin of Gothic architecture.

shared, in nearly equal degrees, the principal and primitive authority that was wielded over these children of the forest. There were several who might claim the distinction of being chief men, but the two in question were so much superior to all the rest in influence, that when they agreed, no one disputed their mandates; and when they were divided, the band hesitated, like men who had lost their governing principle of action. It was also in conformity with practice—perhaps we might add, in conformity with nature—that one of the chiefs was indebted to his mind for his influence, whereas the other owed his distinction altogether to qualities that were physical. One was a senior well known for eloquence in debate, wisdom in council, and prudence in measures; while his great competitor, if not his rival, was a brave,—distinguished in war, notorious for ferocity, and remarkable, in the way of intellect, for nothing but the cunning and expedients of the warpath. The first was Rivenoak, who has already been introduced to the reader, while the last was called Le Panthère, in the language of the Canadas; or the Panther, to resort to the vernacular of the English colonies. The appellation of the fighting chief was supposed to indicate the qualities of the warrior, agreeably to a practice of the red man's nomenclature; ferocity, cunning, and treachery being, perhaps, the distinctive features of his character. The title had been received from the French, and was prized so much the more from that circumstance, the Indian submitting profoundly to the greater intelligence of his paleface allies in most things of this nature. How well the *sobriquet* was merited will be seen in the sequel.

Rivenoak and the Panther sat side by side, awaiting the approach of their prisoner, as Deerslayer put his moccasined foot on the strand; nor did either move or utter a syllable until the young man had advanced into the center of the area, and proclaimed his presence with his voice. This was done firmly, though in the simple manner that marked the character of the individual.

"Here I am, Mingos," he said, in the dialect of the Delawares, a language that most present understood; "here I am, and there is the sun. One is not more true to the laws of natur' than the other has proved true to his word. I am your prisoner; do with me what you please. My business with man and 'arth is settled; nothing remains now but to meet the white man's God; accordin' to a white man's duties and gifts."

A murmur of approbation escaped even the women at this address, and, for an instant, there was a strong and pretty general desire to adopt into the tribe one who owned so brave a spirit. Still there were dissenters from this wish, among the principal of whom might be classed the Panther, and his sister, Le Sumach, so called from the number of her children, who was the widow of Le Loup Cervier,[1] now known to have fallen by the hand of the captive. Native ferocity held one in subjection, while the corroding passion of revenge prevented the other from admittting any gentler feeling at the moment. Not so with Rivenoak. This chief arose, stretched his arm before him, in a gesture of courtesy, and paid his compliments with an ease and dignity that a prince might have envied. As, in that band, his wisdom and eloquence were confessedly without rivals, he knew that on himself would properly fall the duty of first replying to the speech of the paleface.

"Paleface, you are honest," said the Huron orator. "My people are happy in having captured a man, and not a skulking fox. We now know you; we shall treat you like a brave. If you have slain one of our warriors, and helped to kill others, you have a life of your own ready to give away in return. Some of my young men thought that the blood of a paleface was too thin; that it would refuse to run under the Huron knife. You will show them it is not so; your heart is stout as well as your body. It is a pleasure to make such a prisoner; should my warriors say that the death of Le Loup Cervier ought not to be forgotten, and that he cannot travel towards the land of spirits alone, that his enemy must be sent to overtake him, they will remember that he fell by the hand of a brave, and send you after him with such signs of our friendship as shall not make him ashamed to keep your company. I have spoken: you know what I have said."

"True enough, Mingo, all true as the gospel," returned the simple-minded hunter; "you *have* spoken, and I *do* know, not only what you have *said*, but, what is still more important, what you *mean*. I dare say your warrior, the Lynx, was a stout-hearted brave, and worthy of your fri'ndship and respect, but I do not feel unworthy to keep his company, without any passport from your hands. Nevertheless, here I am, ready to receive judgment from your council, if, indeed, the matter was not determained among you afore I got back."

"My old men would not sit in council over a paleface until they saw him among them,"

[1] Deerslayer had killed The Lynx or Le Loup Cervier, in a skirmish a few days before.

answered Rivenoak, looking around him a little ironically; "they said it would be like sitting in council over the winds; they go where they will, and come back as they see fit, and not otherwise. There was one voice that spoke in your favor, Deerslayer, but it was alone, like the song of the wren whose mate has been struck by the hawk."

"I thank that voice, whosoever it may have been, Mingo, and will say it was as true a voice as the rest were lying voices. A furlough is as binding on a paleface, if he be honest, as it is on a redskin; and was it not so, I would never bring disgrace on the Delawares, among whom I may be said to have received my edication. But words are useless, and lead to braggin' feelin's; here I am; act your will on me."

Rivenoak made a sign of acquiescence, and then a short conference was privately held among the chiefs. As soon as the latter ended, three or four young men fell back from among the armed group, and disappeared. Then it was signified to the prisoner that he was at liberty to go at large on the point, until a council was held concerning his fate. There was more of seeming than of real confidence, however, in this apparent liberality, inasmuch as the young men mentioned already formed a line of sentinels across the breadth of the point, inland, and escape from any other part was out of the question. Even the canoe was removed beyond this line of sentinels, to a spot where it was considered safe from any sudden attempt. These precautions did not proceed from a failure of confidence, but from the circumstance that the prisoner had now complied with all the required conditions of his parole, and it would have been considered a commendable and honorable exploit to escape from his foes. So nice, indeed, were the distinctions drawn by the savages, in cases of this nature, that they often gave their victims a chance to evade the torture, deeming it as creditable to the captors to overtake, or to outwit a fugitive, when his exertions were supposed to be quickened by the extreme jeopardy of his situation, as it was for him to get clear from so much extraordinary vigilance.

Nor was Deerslayer unconscious of, or forgetful of, his rights and his opportunities. Could he now have seen any probable opening for an escape, the attempt would not have been delayed a minute. But the case seemed desperate. He was aware of the line of sentinels, and felt the difficulty of breaking through it unharmed. The lake offered no advantages, as the canoe would have given his foes the greatest facilities for overtaking him; else would he have found it no difficult task to swim as far as the castle. As he walked about the point, he even examined the spot to ascertain if it offered no place of concealment; but its openness, its size, and the hundred watchful glances that were turned towards him, even while those who made them affected not to see him, prevented any such expedient from succeeding. The dread and disgrace of failure had no influence on Deerslayer, who deemed it ever a point of honor to reason and feel like a white man, rather than as an Indian, and who felt it a sort of duty to do all he could that did not involve a dereliction from principle, in order to save his life. Still he hesitated about making the effort, for he also felt that he ought to see the chance of success before he committed himself.

In the mean time the business of the camp appeared to proceed in its regular train. The chiefs consulted apart, admitting no one but the Sumach to their councils; for she, the widow of the fallen warrior, had an exclusive right to be heard on such an occasion. The young men strolled about in indolent listlessness, awaiting the result with Indian impatience, while the females prepared the feast that was to celebrate the termination of the affair, whether it proved fortunate or otherwise for our hero. No one betrayed feeling; and an indifferent observer, beyond the extreme watchfulness of the sentinels, would have detected no extraordinary movement or sensation to denote the real state of things. Two or three old women put their heads together, and it appeared unfavorably to the prospect of Deerslayer, by their scowling looks and angry gestures; but a group of Indian girls were evidently animated by a different impulse, as was apparent by stolen glances that expressed pity and regret. In this condition of the camp, an hour soon glided away.

Suspense is, perhaps, the feeling of all others, that is most difficult to be supported. When Deerslayer landed, he fully expected in the course of a few minutes to undergo the tortures of an Indian revenge, and he was prepared to meet his fate manfully; but the delay proved far more trying than the nearer approach of suffering, and the intended victim began seriously to meditate some desperate effort at escape, as it might be from sheer anxiety to terminate the scene, when he was suddenly summoned to appear, once more, in front of his judges, who had already arranged the band in its former order, in readiness to receive him.

"Killer of the Deer," commenced Rivenoak,

as soon as his captive stood before him, "my aged men have listened to wise words; they are ready to speak. You are a man whose fathers came from beyond the rising sun; we are children of the setting sun; we turn our faces towards the Great Sweet Lakes when we look towards our villages. It may be a wise country and full of riches towards the morning, but it is very pleasant towards the evening. We love most to look in that direction. When we gaze at the east we feel afraid, canoe after canoe bringing more and more of your people in the track of the sun, as if their land was so full as to run over. The red men are few already; they have need of help. One of our best lodges has lately been emptied by the death of its master; it will be a long time before his son can grow big enough to sit in his place. There is his widow! she will want venison to feed her and her children, for her sons are yet like the young of the robin before they quit the nest. By your hand has this great calamity befallen her. She has two duties: one to Le Loup Cervier, and one to his children. Scalp for scalp, life for life, blood for blood, is one law; to feed her young another. We know you, Killer of the Deer. You are honest; when you say a thing it is so. You have but one tongue, and that is not forked like a snake's. Your head is never hid in the grass; all can see it. What you say that will you do. You are just. When you have done wrong, it is your wish to do right again as soon as you can. Here is the Sumach; she is alone in her wigwam, with children crying around her for food; yonder is a rifle, it is loaded and ready to be fired. Take the gun; go forth and shoot a deer; bring the venison and lay it before the widow of Le Loup Cervier; feed her children; call yourself her husband. After which your heart will no longer be Delaware, but Huron; Le Sumach's ears will not hear the cries of her children; my people will count the proper number of warriors.

"I feared this, Rivenoak," answered Deerslayer, when the other had ceased speaking; "yes, I did dread that it would come to this. Hows'ever, the truth is soon told, and that will put an end to all expectations on this head. Mingo, I'm white, and Christian-born; 'twould ill become me to take a wife, under redskin forms, from among heathen. That which I wouldn't do in peaceable times, and under a bright sun, still less would I do behind clouds, in order to save my life. I may never marry; most likely Providence, in putting me up here in the woods, has intended I should live single, and without a lodge of my own; but should such a thing come to pass, none but a woman of my own color and gifts shall darken the door of my wigwam. As for feeding the young of your dead warrior, I would do that cheerfully, could it be done without discredit; but it cannot, seeing that I can never live in a Huron village. Your own young men must find the Sumach in venison, and the next time she marries, let her take a husband whose legs are not long enough to overrun territory that don't belong to him. We fou't a fair battle, and he fell,—in this there is nothin' but what a brave expects, and should be ready to meet. As for getting a Mingo heart, as well might you expect to see gray hairs on a boy, or the blackberry growing on the pine. No, no, Huron; my gifts are white so far as wives are consarned; it is Delaware in all things touchin' Injins."

These words were scarcely out of the mouth of Deerslayer before a common murmur betrayed the dissatisfaction with which they had been heard. The aged women, in particular, were loud in their expressions of disgust; and the gentle Sumach herself, a woman quite old enough to be our hero's mother, was not the least pacific in her denunciations. But all the other manifestations of disappointment and discontent were thrown into the background by the fierce resentment of the Panther. This grim chief had thought it a degradation to permit his sister to become the wife of a paleface of the Yengeese,[1] at all, and had only given a reluctant consent to the arrangement—one by no means unusual among the Indians, however —at the earnest solicitations of the bereaved widow; and it goaded him to the quick to find his condescension slighted, the honor he with so much regret had been persuaded to accord, contemned. The animal from which he got his name does not glare on his intended prey with more frightful ferocity than his eyes gleamed on the captive; nor was his arm backward in seconding the fierce resentment that almost consumed his breast.

"Dog of the palefaces!" he exclaimed, in Iroquois, "go yell among the curs of your own evil hunting-grounds!"

The denunciation was accompanied by an appropriate action. Even while speaking, his arm was lifted and the tomahawk hurled. Luckily the loud tones of the speaker had drawn the eye of Deerslayer towards him, else would that moment have probably closed his career. So great was the dexterity with which this dangerous weapon was thrown, and so deadly the intent, that it would have riven the skull of the

[1] Yankees, English

prisoner had he not stretched forth an arm and caught the handle in one of its turns, with a readiness quite as remarkable as the skill with which the missile had been hurled. The projectile force was so great, notwithstanding, that when Deerslayer's arm was arrested, his hand was raised above and behind his own head, and in the very attitude necessary to return the attack. It is not certain whether the circumstance of finding himself unexpectedly in this menacing posture and armed, tempted the young man to retaliate, or whether sudden resentment overcame his forbearance and prudence. His eye kindled, however, and a small red spot appeared on each cheek, while he cast all his energy into the effort of his arm, and threw back the weapon at his assailant. The unexpectedness of this blow contributed to its success—the Panther neither raising an arm nor bending his head to avoid it. The keen little axe struck the victim in a perpendicular line with the nose, directly between the eyes, literally braining him on the spot. Sallying forward, as the serpent darts at its enemy even while receiving its own death-wound, this man of powerful frame fell his length into the open area formed by the circle, quivering in death. A common rush to his relief left the captive for a single instant, quite without the crowd; and, willing to make one desperate effort for his life, he bounded off with the activity of a deer. There was but a breathless instant, when the whole band, old and young, women and children, abandoning the lifeless body of the Panther where it lay, raised the yell of alarm and followed in pursuit.

Sudden as had been the event which induced Deerslayer to make this desperate trial of speed, his mind was not wholly unprepared for the fearful emergency. In the course of the past hour, he had pondered well on the chances of such an experiment, and had shrewdly calculated all the details of success and failure. At the first leap, therefore, his body was completely under the direction of an intelligence that turned all its efforts to the best account, and prevented everything like hesitation or indecision at the important instant of the start. To this alone was he indebted for the first great advantage, that of getting through the line of sentinels unharmed. The manner in which this was done, though sufficiently simple, merits a description.

Although the shores of the point were not fringed with bushes, as was the case with most of the others on the lake, it was owing altogether to the circumstance that the spot had been so much used by hunters and fishermen. This fringe commenced on what might be termed the mainland, and was as dense as usual, extending in long lines both north and south. In the latter direction, then, Deerslayer held his way; and, as the sentinels were a little without the commencement of this thicket before the alarm was clearly communicated to them, the fugitive had gained its cover. To run among the bushes, however, was out of the question, and Deerslayer held his way for some forty or fifty yards in the water, which was barely knee-deep, offering as great an obstacle to the speed of his pursuers as it did to his own. As soon as a favorable spot presented, he darted through the line of bushes, and issued into the open woods.

Several rifles were discharged at Deerslayer while in the water, and more followed as he came out into the comparative exposure of the clear forest. But the direction of his line of flight, which partially crossed that of the fire, the haste with which the weapons had been aimed, and the general confusion that prevailed in the camp, prevented any harm from being done. Bullets whistled past him, and many cut twigs from the branches at his side, but not one touched even his dress. The delay caused by these fruitless attempts was of great service to the fugitive, who had gained more than a hundred yards on even the leading men of the Hurons, ere something like concert and order had entered into the chase. To think of following with rifle in hand was out of the question; and, after emptying their pieces in vague hope of wounding their captive, the best runners of the Indians threw them aside, calling out to the women and boys to recover and load them again as soon as possible.

Deerslayer knew too well the desperate nature of the struggle in which he was engaged to lose one of the precious moments. He also knew that his only hope was to run in a straight line, for as soon as he began to turn or double the greater number of his pursuers would put escape out of the question. He held his way, therefore, in a diagonal direction, up the acclivity, which was neither very high nor very steep, in this part of the mountain, but which was sufficiently toilsome for one contending for life, to render it painfully oppressive. There, however, he slackened his speed to recover breath, proceeding even at a quick walk, or slow trot, along the more difficult parts of the way. The Hurons were whooping and leaping behind him; but this he disregarded, well knowing they must overcome the difficulties he had surmounted ere they could reach the elevation to which he had attained. The summit of the first hill was now quite near him, and he saw, by the formation of the land, that a deep glen intervened before the base of a second hill could be reached. Walking deliberately to the summit, he glanced eagerly about him in every direction, in quest of a cover. None offered in the ground; but a fallen tree lay near him, and desperate circumstances required desperate remedies. This tree lay in a line parallel to the glen at the brow of the hill; to leap on it, and then to force his person as close as possible under its lower side, took but a moment. Previously to disappearing from his pursuers, however, Deerslayer stood on the height and gave a cry of triumph, as if exulting at the sight of the descent that lay before him. In the next instant he was stretched beneath the tree.

No sooner was this expedient adopted, than the young man ascertained how desperate had been his own efforts, by the violence of the pulsation in his frame. He could hear his heart beat, and his breathing was like the action of a bellows in quick motion. Breath was gained, however, and the heart soon ceased to throb as if about to break through its confinement. The footsteps of those who toiled up the opposite side of the acclivity were now audible, and presently voices and treads announced the arrival of the pursuers. The foremost shouted as they reached the height; then, fearful that their enemy would escape under favor of the descent, each leaped upon the fallen tree, and plunged into the ravine, trusting to get a sight of the pursued, ere he reached the bottom. In this manner Huron followed Huron, until Natty began to hope the whole had passed. Others succeeded, however, until quite forty had leaped over the tree; and then he counted them, as the surest mode of ascertaining how many could be behind. Presently all were in the bottom of the glen, quite a hundred feet below him, and some had even ascended part of the opposite hill, when it became evident an inquiry was making as to the direction he had taken. This was the critical moment; and one of nerves less steady, or of a training that had been neglected, would have seized it to rise and fly. Not so with Deerslayer. He still lay quiet, watching with jealous vigilance every movement below, and fast regaining his breath.

The Hurons now resembled a pack of hounds at fault. Little was said, but each man ran about, examining the dead leaves, as the hound hunts for the lost scent. The great number of moccasins that had passed made the examination difficult, though the in-toe of an Indian was easily to be distinguished from the freer and wider step of a white man. Believing that no more pursuers remained behind, and hoping to steal away unseen, Deerslayer suddenly threw himself over the tree, and fell on the upper side. This achievement appeared to be effected successfully, and hope beat high in the bosom of the fugitive. Rising to his hands and feet, after a moment lost in listening to the sounds in the glen, in order to ascertain if he had been seen, the young man next scrambled to the top of the hill, a distance of only ten yards, in the expectation of getting its brow between him and his pursuers, and himself so far under cover. Even this was effected, and he rose to his feet, walking swiftly but steadily along the summit, in a direction opposite to that in which he had first fled. The nature of the calls in the glen, however, soon made him uneasy, and he sprang upon the summit again, in order to reconnoiter. No sooner did he reach the height, than he was seen, and the chase renewed. As it was better footing on the level ground, Deerslayer now avoided the side-hill, holding his flight along the ridge; while the Hurons, judging from the general formation of the land, saw that the ridge would soon melt into the hollow, and kept to the latter, as the easiest mode of heading the fugitive. A few at the same time turned south, with a view to prevent his escaping in that direction; while some crossed his trail towards the water, in order to prevent his retreat by the lake, running southerly.

The situation of Deerslayer was now more critical than it ever had been. He was virtually surrounded on three sides, having the lake on the fourth. But he had pondered well on all the chances, and took his measures with coolness, even while at the top of his speed. As is generally the case with the vigorous border-men, he could outrun any single Indian among his pursuers, who were principally formidable to him on account of their numbers, and the advantages they possessed in position; and he would not have hesitated to break off, in a straight line, at any spot, could he have got the whole band again fairly behind him. But no such chance did, or indeed could, now offer; and when he found that he was descending towards the glen, by the melting away of the ridge, he turned short, at right angles to his previous course, and went down the declivity with tremendous velocity, holding his way towards the shore. Some of his pursuers came panting up the hill, in direct chase, while most still kept on, in the ravine, intending to head him at its termination.

Deerslayer had now a different though a desperate project in view. Abandoning all thoughts of escape by the woods, he made the best of his way towards the canoe. He knew where it lay: could it be reached, he had only to run the gauntlet of a few rifles, and success would be certain. None of the warriors had kept their weapons, which would have retarded their speed, and the risk would come either from the uncertain hands of the women, or from those of some well-grown boy; though most of the latter were already out in hot pursuit. Everything seemed propitious to the execution of this plan, and the course being a continued descent, the young man went over the ground at a rate that promised a speedy termination to his toil.

As Deerslayer approached the point, several women and children were passed, but, though the former endeavored to cast dried branches between his legs, the terror inspired by his bold retaliation on the redoubted Panther was so great that none dared come near enough seriously to molest him. He went by all triumphantly, and reached the fringe of bushes. Plunging through these, our hero found himself once more in the lake and within fifty feet of the canoe. Here he ceased to run, for he well understood that his breath was now all-important to him. He even stooped, as he advanced, and cooled his parched mouth by scooping up water in his hand to drink. Still the moments pressed, and he soon stood at the side of the canoe. The first glance told him that the paddles had been removed! This was a sore disappointment after all his efforts, and, for a single moment, he thought of turning and of facing his foes by walking with dignity into the center of the camp again. But an infernal yell, such as the American savage alone can raise, proclaimed the quick approach of the nearest of his pursuers, and the instinct of life triumphed. Preparing himself duly, and giving a right direction to its bows, he ran off into the water bearing the canoe before him, threw all his strength and skill into a last effort, and cast himself forward so as to fall into the bottom of the light craft, without materially impeding its way. Here he remained on his back, both to regain his breath and to cover his person from the deadly rifle. The lightness, which was such an advantage in paddling the canoe, now operated unfavorably. The material was so like a feather that the boat had no momentum; else would the impulse in that smooth and placid sheet have impelled it to a distance from the shore, that would have rendered paddling with the hands safe. Could such a point once be reached, Deerslayer thought he might get far enough out to attract the attention of Chingachgook and Judith, who would not fail to come to his relief with other canoes,—a circumstance that promised everything. As the young man lay in the bottom of the canoe he watched its movements by studying the tops of the trees on the mountain-side, and judged of his distance by the time and the motion. Voices on the shore were now numerous, and he heard something said about manning the raft, which fortunately for the fugitive lay at a considerable distance on the other side of the point.

Perhaps the situation of Deerslayer had not been more critical that day than it was at this moment. It certainly had not been one half as tantalizing. He lay perfectly quiet for two or three minutes, trusting to the single sense of hearing, confident that the noise on the lake would reach his ears, did any one venture to approach by swimming. Once or twice he fancied that the element was stirred by the cautious movement of an arm, and then he perceived it was the wash of the water on the pebbles of the strand; for, in mimicry of the ocean, it is seldom that those little lakes are so totally tranquil as not to possess a slight heaving and setting on their shores. Suddenly all the voices ceased, and a death-like stillness pervaded the spot, a quietness as profound as if all lay in the repose of inanimate life. By this time the canoe had drifted so far as to render nothing visible to Deerslayer, as he lay on his back, except the blue void of space, and a few of those brighter rays that proceed from the effulgence of the sun, marking his proximity. It was not possible to endure this uncertainty long. The young man well knew that the profound stillness foreboded evil, the savages never being so silent as when about to strike a blow— resembling the stealthy foot of the panther ere he takes his leap. He took out a knife, and was about to cut a hole through the bark in order to get a view of the shore, when he paused from a dread of being seen in the operation, which would direct the enemy where to aim their bullets. At this instant a rifle *was* fired, and the ball pierced both sides of the canoe, within eighteen inches of the spot where his head lay. This was close work, but our hero had too lately gone through that which was closer, to be appalled. He lay still half a minute longer, and then he saw the summit of an oak coming slowly within his narrow horizon.

Unable to account for this change, Deerslayer could restrain his impatience no longer. Hitching his body along with the utmost caution, he got his eye at the bullet-hole and fortunately commanded a very tolerable view of the point. The canoe, by one of those imperceptible impulses that so often decide the fate of men, as well as the course of things, had inclined southerly, and was slowly drifting down the lake. It was lucky that Deerslayer had given it a shove sufficiently vigorous to send it past the end of the point ere it took this inclination, or it must have gone ashore again. As it was, it drifted so near it as to bring the tops of two or three trees within the range of the young man's view, as has been mentioned, and, indeed, to come in quite as close proximity with the extremity of the point as was at all safe. The distance could not much have exceeded a hundred feet, though fortunately a light current of air from the southwest began to set it slowly off shore.

Deerslayer now felt the urgent necessity of resorting to some expedient to get farther from his foes, and if possible, to apprise his friends of his situation. The distance rendered the last difficult, while the proximity to the point rendered the first indispensable. As was usual in such craft, a large, round, smooth stone was in each end of the canoe, for the double purpose of seats and ballast; one of these was within reach of his feet. The stone he contrived to get so far between his legs as to reach it with his hands, and then he managed to roll it to the side of its fellow in the bows, where the two served to keep the trim of the light boat, while he worked his own body as far aft as possible. Before quitting the shore, and as soon as he perceived that the paddles were gone, Deerslayer had thrown a bit of dead branch into the canoe, and this was within reach of his arm. Removing the cap he wore, he put it on the end of this stick, and just let it appear over the edge of the canoe, as far as possible from his own person. This ruse was scarcely adopted before the young man had a proof how much he had underrated the intelligence of his enemies. In contempt of an artifice so shallow and commonplace, a bullet was fired directly through another part of the canoe, which actually grazed his skin. He dropped the cap and instantly raised it immediately over his head, as a safeguard. It would seem that this second artifice was unseen,—or what was more probable, the Hurons, feeling certain of recovering their captive, wished to take him alive.

Deerslayer lay passive a few minutes longer,

his eye at the bullet-hole, however, and much did he rejoice at seeing that he was drifting gradually farther and farther from the shore. When he looked upwards the treetops had disappeared, but he soon found that the canoe was slowly turning, so as to prevent his getting a view of anything at his peep-hole but of the two extremities of the lake. He now bethought him of the stick, which was crooked, and offered some facilities for rowing without the necessity of rising. The experiment succeeded, on trial, better even that he had hoped, though his great embarrassment was to keep the canoe straight. That his present maneuver was seen soon became apparent by the clamor on the shore, and a bullet entering the stern of the canoe, traversed its length, whistling between the arms of our hero, passed out at the head. This satisfied the fugitive that he was getting away with tolerable speed, and induced him to increase his efforts. He was making a stronger push than common, when another messenger from the point broke the stick out-board, and at once deprived him of his oar. As the sound of voices seemed to grow more and more distant, however, Deerslayer determined to leave all to the drift, until he believed himself beyond the reach of bullets. This was nervous work, but it was the wisest of all the expedients that offered; and the young man was encouraged to persevere in it by the circumstance that he felt his face fanned by the air, a proof that there was a little more wind.

Chapter XXVIII

Nor widows' tears, nor tender orphans' cries
  Can stop th' invaders' force;
Nor swelling seas, nor threatening skies,
  Prevent the pirate's course:
Their lives to selfish ends decreed,
Through blood and rapine they proceed;
No anxious thoughts of ill-repute
Suspend the impetuous and unjust pursuit;
But power and wealth obtained, guilty and great,
Their fellow-creatures' fears they raise, or urge
  their hate.

                        Congreve

By this time Deerslayer had been twenty minutes in the canoe, and he began to grow a little impatient for some signs of relief from his friends. The position of the boat still prevented his seeing in any direction, unless it were up or down the lake; and, though he knew that his line of sight must pass within a hundred yards of the castle, it, in fact, passed that distance to the westward of the buildings. The profound stillness troubled him also, for he knew not whether to ascribe it to the increasing space between him and the Indians, or to some new artifice. At length, wearied with fruitless watchfulness, the young man turned himself on his back, closed his eyes, and awaited the result in determined acquiescence. If the savages could so completely control their thirst for revenge, he was resolved to be as calm as themselves, and to trust his fate to the interposition of the currents and air.

Some additional ten minutes may have passed in this quiescent manner, on both sides, when Deerslayer thought he heard a slight noise, like a low rubbing against the bottom of his canoe. He opened his eyes of course, in expectation of seeing the face or arm of an Indian rising from the water, and found that a canopy of leaves was impending directly over his head. Starting to his feet, the first object that met his eye was Rivenoak, who had so far aided the slow progress of the boat as to draw it on the point, the grating on the strand being the sound that had first given our hero the alarm. The change in the drift of the canoe had been altogether owing to the baffling nature of the light currents of air, aided by some eddies in the water.

"Come," said the Huron, with a quiet gesture of authority to order his prisoner to land; "my young friend has sailed about till he is tired; he will forget how to run again, unless he uses his legs." [1]

· · · · · · ·

Chapter XXX

So deem'st thou—so each mortal deems
Of that which is from that which seems;
    But other harvest here
Than that which peasant's scythe demands,
Was gathered in by sterner hands,
    With bayonet, blade and spear.

SCOTT

It exceeded Deerslayer's power to ascertain what had produced the sudden pause in the movements of his enemies, until the fact was revealed in the due course of events. He perceived that much agitation prevailed among the women in particular, while the warriors rested on their arms, in a sort of dignified expectation. It was plain no alarm was excited, though it was not equally apparent that a friendly occurrence produced the delay. Rivenoak was evidently apprised of all, and by a gesture of his arm he appeared to direct the circle to remain unbroken, and for each person to await the issue in the situation he or she

[1] In what is here omitted the Indians begin torturing Deerslayer, and Hetty comes to the Indian camp in a vain attempt to rescue him.

then occupied. It required but a minute or two to bring an explanation of this singular and mysterious pause, which was soon terminated by the appearance of Judith, on the exterior of the line of bodies, and her ready admission within its circle.

If Deerslayer was startled by this unexpected arrival, well knowing that the quick-witted girl could claim none of that exemption from the penalties of captivity that was so cheerfully accorded to her feeble-minded sister, he was equally astonished at the guise in which she came. All her ordinary forest attire, neat and becoming as this usually was, had been already laid aside for the brocade that has been already mentioned, and which had once before wrought so great and magical an effect in her appearance. Nor was this all. Accustomed to see the ladies of the garrison in the formal gala attire of the day, and familiar with the more critical niceties of these matters, the girl had managed to complete her dress in a way to leave nothing strikingly defective in its details, or even to betray an incongruity that would have been detected by one practiced in the mysteries of the toilet. Head, feet, arms, hands, bust, and drapery, were all in harmony, as female attire was then deemed attractive and harmonious; and the end she aimed at, that of imposing on the uninstructed senses of the savages, by causing them to believe their guest was a woman of rank and importance, might well have succeeded with those whose habits had taught them to discriminate between persons. Judith, in addition to her rare native beauty, had a singular grace of person, and her mother had imparted enough of her own deportment to prevent any striking or offensive vulgarity of manner; so that, sooth to say, the gorgeous dress might have been worse bestowed in nearly every particular. Had it been displayed in a capital, a thousand might have worn it before one could have been found to do more credit to its gay colors, glossy satins, and rich laces than the beautiful creature whose person it now aided to adorn.

The effect of such an apparition had not been miscalculated. The instant Judith found herself within the circle, she was in a degree compensated for the fearful personal risk she ran, by the unequivocal sensation of surprise and admiration produced by her appearance. The grim old warriors uttered their favorite exclamation, "Hugh!" The younger men were still more sensibly overcome, and even the women were not backward in letting open manifestations of pleasure escape them. It was seldom that these untutored children of the forest had ever seen any white female above the commonest sort, and as to dress, never before had so much splendor shone before their eyes. The gayest uniforms of both French and English seemed dull compared with the luster of the brocade; and while the rare personal beauty of the wearer added to the effect produced by its hues, the attire did not fail to adorn that beauty in a way which surpassed even the hopes of its wearer. Deerslayer himself was astounded, and this quite as much by the brilliant picture the girl presented as at the indifference to consequences with which she had braved the danger of the step she had taken. Under such circumstances, all waited for the visitor to explain her object, which to most of the spectators seemed as inexplicable as her appearance.

"Which of these warriors is the principal chief?" demanded Judith of Deerslayer, as soon as she found it was expected that she should open the communication; "my errand is too important to be delivered to any of inferior rank. First explain to the Hurons what I say: then give an answer to the question I have put."

Deerslayer quietly complied, his auditors greedily listening to the interpretation of the first words that fell from so extraordinary a vision. The demand seemed perfectly in character for one who had every appearance of an exalted rank herself. Rivenoak gave an appropriate reply, by presenting himself before his fair visitor in a way to leave no doubt that he was entitled to all the consideration he claimed.

"I can believe this, Huron," resumed Judith, enacting her assumed part with a steadiness and dignity that did credit to her powers of imitation, for she strove to impart to her manner the condescending courtesy she had once observed in the wife of a general officer, at a similar, though a more amicable, scene—"I can believe you to be the principal person of this party; I see in your countenance the marks of thought and reflection. To you, then, I must make my communication."

"Let the Flower of the Woods speak," returned the old chief, courteously, as soon as her address had been translated, so that all might understand it. "If her words are as pleasant as her looks, they will never quit my ears; I shall hear them long after the winter in Canada has killed the flowers, and frozen all the speeches of summer."

This admiration was grateful to one constituted like Judith, and contributed to aid her self-possession quite as much as it fed her vanity. Smiling involuntarily, or in spite of her wish to seem reserved, she proceeded in her plot.

"Now, Huron," she continued, "listen to my words. Your eyes tell you that I am no common woman. I will not say I am queen of this country; *she* is afar off, in a distant land; but under our gracious monarchs there are many degrees of rank; one of these I fill. What that rank is precisely it is unnecessary for me to say, since you would not understand it. For that information you must trust your eyes. You *see* what I am; you must *feel* that in listening to my words you listen to one who can be your friend or your enemy, as you treat her."

This was well uttered, with a due attention to manner and a steadiness of tone that was really surprising, considering all the circumstances of the case. It was well though simply rendered into the Indian dialect, too, and it was received with a respect and gravity that augured favorably for the girl's success. But Indian thought is not easily traced to its sources. Judith waited with anxiety to hear the answer, filled with hope even while she doubted. Rivenoak was a ready speaker, and he answered as promptly as comported with the notions of Indian decorum; that peculiar people seeming to think a short delay respectful, inasmuch as it manifests that the words already heard have been duly weighed.

"My daughter is handsomer than the wild roses of Ontario; her voice is pleasant to the ear as the song of the wren," answered the cautious and wily chief, who of all the band stood alone in not being fully imposed on by the magnificent and unusual appearance of Judith, but who distrusted even while he wondered; "the humming-bird is not much larger than the bee; yet its feathers are as gay as the tail of the peacock. The Great Spirit sometimes puts very bright clothes on very little animals. Still, he covers the moose with coarse hair. These things are beyond the understanding of poor Indians, who can only comprehend what they see and hear. No doubt my daughter has a very large wigwam somewhere about the lake; the Hurons have not found it on account of their ignorance!"

"I have told you, chief, that it would be useless to state my rank and residence, inasmuch as you would not comprehend them. You must trust to your eyes for this knowledge; what red man is there that cannot see? This blanket that I wear is not the blanket of a common squaw; these ornaments are such as the wives and daughters of chiefs only appear in. Now listen and hear why I have come alone among your people, and hearken to the errand that has brought me here. The Yengeese have young men as well as the Hurons; and plenty of them, too; this you well know."

"The Yengeese are as plenty as the leaves on the trees! This every Huron knows and feels."

"I understand you, chief. Had I brought a party with me it might have caused trouble. My young men and your young men would have looked angrily at each other, especially had my young men seen that paleface bound for the tortures. He is a great hunter, and is much loved by all the garrisons, far and near. There would have been blows about him, and the trail of the Iroquois back to the Canadas would have been marked with blood."

"There is so much blood on it now," returned the chief, gloomily, "that it blinds our eyes. My young men see that it is all Huron."

"No doubt; and more Huron blood would be spilt, had I came surrounded with palefaces. I have heard of Rivenoak, and have thought it would be better to send him back in peace to his village, that he might leave his women and children behind him. If he then wished to come for our scalps, we would meet him. He loves animals made of ivory and little rifles. See; I have brought some with me to show him. I am his friend. When he has packed up these things among his goods, he will start for his village, before any of my young men can overtake him; and then he will show his people in Canada what riches they can come to seek, now that our great fathers, across the salt lake, have sent each other the war-hatchet. I will lead back with me this great hunter, of whom I have need to keep my house in venison."

Judith, who was sufficiently familiar with Indian phraseology, endeavored to express her ideas in the sententious manner common to those people; and she succeeded even beyond her own expectations. Deerslayer did her full justice in the translation, and this so much the more readily since the girl carefully abstained from uttering any direct untruth; a homage she paid to the young man's known aversion to falsehood, which he deemed a meanness altogether unworthy of a white man's gifts. The offering of the two remaining elephants, and of the pistols already mentioned, one of which was all the worse for the recent accident, produced a lively sensation among the Hurons generally, though Rivenoak received it coldly, notwithstanding the delight with which he had first discovered the probable existence of a creature

with two tails. In a word, this cool and sagacious savage was not so easily imposed on as his followers; and with a sentiment of honor that half the civilized world would have deemed supererogatory, he declined the acceptance of a bribe that he felt no disposition to earn by a compliance with the donor's wishes.

"Let my daughter keep her two-tailed hog to eat when venison is scarce," he dryly answered; "and the little gun which has two muzzles. The Hurons will kill deer when they are hungry; and they have long rifles to fight with. This hunter cannot quit my young men now; they wish to know if he is as stout-hearted as he boasts himself to be."

"That I deny, Huron," interrupted Deerslayer, with warmth; "yes, that I downright deny as agin truth and reason. No man has heard me *boast* and no man shall, though ye flay me alive, and then roast the quivering flesh with your own infarnal devices and cruelties! I may be humble, and misfortunate, and your prisoner; but I'm no boaster, by my very gifts."

"My young paleface *boasts* he is *no* boaster," returned the crafty chief; "he *must* be right. I hear a strange bird singing. It has very rich feathers. No Huron ever before saw such feathers. They will be ashamed to go back to their village and tell their people that they let their prisoner go on account of the song of this strange bird, and not be able to give the *name* of the bird. They do not know how to say whether it is a wren or a cat-bird. This would be a great disgrace; my young men would not be allowed to travel in the woods without taking their mothers with them to tell them the names of the birds."

"You can ask my name of your prisoner," returned the girl. "It is Judith; and there is a great deal of the history of Judith in the palefaces' best book, the Bible. If I am a bird of fine feathers, I have also my name."

"No," answered the wily Huron, betraying the artifice he had so long practised by speaking in English with tolerable accuracy; "I not ask prisoner. He tired; he want rest. I ask my daughter with feeble mind. She speak truth. Come here, daughter; you answer. *Your* name Hetty?"

"Yes, that's what they call me," returned the girl; "though it's written Esther in the Bible."

"He write *him* in Bible, too? All write in Bible. No matter—what *her* name?"

"That's Judith, and it's so written in the Bible, though father sometimes called her Jude. That's my sister Judith, Thomas Hutter's daughter—Thomas Hutter, whom you called the Muskrat [1]; though he was *no* muskrat, but a man, like yourself—he lived in a house on the water, and that was enough for *you*."

A smile of triumph gleamed on the hard-wrinkled countenance of the chief when he found how completely his appeal to the truth-loving Hetty had succeeded. As for Judith herself, the moment her sister was questioned, she saw that all was lost; for no sign, or even entreaty, could have induced the right-feeling girl to utter a falsehood. To attempt to impose a daughter of the Muskrat on the savages as a princess or a great lady she knew would be idle; and she saw her bold and ingenious expedient for liberating the captive fail through one of the simplest and most natural causes that could be imagined. She turned her eye on Deerslayer, therefore, as if imploring him to interfere to save them both.

"It will not do, Judith," said the young man, in answer to this appeal, which he understood, though he saw its uselessness; "it will not do. 'Twas a bold idee, and fit for a general's lady; but yonder Mingo"—Rivenoak had withdrawn to a little distance, and was out of ear-shot—"but yonder Mingo is an uncommon man, and not to be deceived by any unnat'ral sarcum-ventions. Things must come afore him in their right order to draw a cloud afore *his* eyes! 'Twas too much to attempt making him fancy that a queen or a great lady lived in these mountains; and no doubt he thinks the fine clothes you wear are some of the plunder of your own father—or, at least, of him who once passed for your father; as quite likely it was, if all they say is true!"

"At all events, Deerslayer, my presence here will save you for a time. They will hardly attempt torturing you before my face!"

"Why not, Judith? Do you think they will treat a woman of the palefaces more tenderly than they treat their own? It's true that your sex will most likely save you from the torments, but it will not save your liberty, and may not save your scalp. I wish you hadn't come, my good Judith; it can do no good to me, while it may do great harm to yourself."

"I can share your fate," the girl answered with generous enthusiasm. "They shall not injure you while I stand by, if in my power to prevent it; besides—"

"Besides what, Judith? What means have you to stop Injin cruelties, or to avart Injin deviltries?"

[1] the name of the Indians for Hutter

"None, perhaps, Deerslayer," answered the girl, with firmness; "but I can suffer with my friends—die with them if necessary."

"Ah! Judith—suffer you may; but die you will not until the Lord's time shall come. It's little likely that one of your sex and beauty will meet with a harder fate than to become the wife of a chief, if indeed your white inclinations can stoop to match with an Injin. 'Twould have been better had you stayed in the ark or the castle; but what has been done is done. You was about to say something, when you stopped at 'besides'?"

"It might not be safe to mention it here, Deerslayer," the girl hurriedly answered, moving past him carelessly, that she might speak in a low tone; "half an hour is all in all to us. None of your friends are idle."

The hunter replied merely by a grateful look. Then he turned toward his enemies, as if ready again to face the torments. A short consultation had passed among the elders of the band, and by this time they also were prepared with their decision. The merciful purpose of Rivenoak had been much weakened by the artifice of Judith, which, failing of its real object, was likely to produce results the very opposite of those she had anticipated. This was natural; the feeling being aided by the resentment of an Indian, who found how near he had been to becoming the dupe of an inexperienced girl. By this time Judith's real character was fully understood—the wide-spread reputation of her beauty contributed to the exposure. As for the unusual attire, it was confounded with the profound mystery of the animals with two tails, and, for the moment, lost its influence.

When Rivenoak, therefore, faced the captive again, it was with an altered countenance. He had abandoned the wish of saving him, and was no longer disposed to retard the more serious part of the torture. This change of sentiment was, in effect, communicated to the young men, who were already eagerly engaged in making their preparations for the contemplated scene. Fragments of dried wood were rapidly collected near the sapling, the splinters which it was intended to thrust into the flesh of the victim previously to lighting were all collected, and the thongs were already produced that were again to bind him to the tree. All this was done in profound silence, Judith watching every movement with breathless expectation, while Deerslayer himself stood seemingly as unmoved as one of the pines of the hills. When the warriors advanced to bind him, however, the young man glanced at Judith, as if to inquire whether resistance or submission were most advisable. By a significant gesture she counseled the last; and in a minute, he was once more fastened to the tree, a helpless object of any insult or wrong that might be offered. So eagerly did every one now act, that nothing was said. The fire was immediately lighted in the pile, and the end of all was anxiously expected.

It was not the intention of the Hurons absolutely to destroy the life of their victim by means of fire. They designed merely to put his physical fortitude to the severest proofs it could endure, short of that extremity. In the end, they fully intended to carry his scalp with them into their village, but it was their wish first to break down his resolution, and to reduce him to the level of a complaining sufferer. With this view, the pile of brush and branches had been placed at a proper distance, or one at which it was thought the heat would soon become intolerable, though it might not be immediately dangerous. As often happened, however, on these occasions, this distance had been miscalculated, and the flames began to wave their forked tongues in a proximity to the face of the victim that would have proved fatal, in another instant, had not Hetty rushed through the crowd, armed with a stick, and scattered the blazing pile in a dozen directions. More than one hand was raised to strike the presumptuous intruder to the earth; but the chiefs prevented the blows by reminding their irritated followers of the state of her mind. Hetty, herself, was insensible to the risk she ran; but, as soon as she had performed this bold act, she stood looking about her in frowning resentment, as if to rebuke the crowd of attentive savages for their cruelty.

"God bless you, dearest sister, for that brave and ready act!" murmured Judith, herself unnerved so much as to be incapable of exertion; "Heaven itself has sent you on its holy errand."

" 'Twas well meant, Judith," rejoined the victim; " 'twas excellently meant, and 'twas timely, though it may prove ontimely in the ind! What is to come to pass must come to pass soon, or 'twill quickly be too late. Had I drawn in one mouthful of that flame in breathing, the power of man couldn't save my life; and you see that this time they've so bound my forehead as not to leave my head the smallest chance. 'Twas well meant; but it might have been more marciful to let the flames act their part."

"Cruel, heartless Hurons!" exclaimed the still indignant Hetty; "would you burn a man and a Christian as you would burn a log of wood! Do you never read your Bibles? or do you think God will forget such things?"

A gesture from Rivenoak caused the scattered brands to be collected; fresh wood was brought, even the women and children busying themselves eagerly in the gathering of dried sticks. The flame was just kindling a second time, when an *Indian* female pushed through the circle, advanced to the heap, and with her foot dashed aside the lighted twigs in time to prevent the conflagration. A yell followed this second disappointment; but when the offender turned towards the circle, and presented the countenance of Hist, it was succeeded by a common exclamation of pleasure and surprise. For a minute, all thought of pursuing the business in hand was forgotten, and young and old crowded around the girl, in haste to demand an explanation of her sudden and unlooked-for return. It was at this critical instant that Hist spoke to Judith in a low voice, placed some small object, unseen, in her hand, and then turned to meet the salutations of the Huron girls, with whom she was personally a great favorite. Judith recovered her self-possession and acted promptly. The small, keen-edged knife, that Hist had given to the other, was passed by the latter into the hands of Hetty, as the safest and least-suspected medium of transferring it to Deerslayer. But the feeble intellect of the last defeated the well-grounded hopes of all three. Instead of first cutting loose the hands of the victim, and then concealing the knife in his clothes, in readiness for action at the most available instant, she went to work herself, with earnestness and simplicity, to cut the thongs that bound his head, that he might not again be in danger of inhaling flames. Of course this deliberate procedure was seen, and the hands of Hetty were arrested ere she had more than liberated the upper portion of the captive's body, not including his arms, below the elbows. This discovery at once pointed distrust towards Hist; and, to Judith's surprise, when questioned on the subject, that spirited girl was not disposed to deny her agency in what had passed.

"Why should I not help the Deerslayer?" the girl demanded, in the tones of a firm-minded woman. "He is the brother of a Delaware chief; my heart is all Delaware. Come forth, miserable Briarthorn, and wash the Iroquois paint from your face,—stand before the Hurons, the crow that you are; you would eat the carrion of your own dead rather than starve. Put him face to face with Deerslayer, chiefs and warriors; I will show you how great a knave you have been keeping in your tribe."

This bold language, uttered in their own dialect, and with a manner full of confidence, produced a deep sensation among the Hurons. Treachery is always liable to distrust; and though the recreant Briarthorn had endeavored to serve the enemy well, his exertions and assiduities had gained for him little more than toleration. His wish to obtain Hist for a wife had first induced him to betray her and his own people; but serious rivals to his first project had risen up among his new friends, weakening still more their sympathies with treason. In a word, Briarthorn had been barely permitted to remain in the Huron encampment, where he was as closely and as jealously watched as Hist herself; seldom appearing before the chiefs, and sedulously keeping out of view of Deerslayer, who, until this moment, was ignorant even of his presence. Thus summoned, however, it was impossible to remain in the background. "Wash the Iroquois paint from his face" he did not; for when he stood in the center of the circle, he was so disguised in these new colors, that at first the hunter did not recognize him. He assumed an air of defiance, notwithstanding, and haughtily demanded what any could say against "Briarthorn."

"Ask yourself that," continued Hist, with spirit, though her manner grew less concentrated, and there was a slight air of abstraction that became observable to Deerslayer and Judith, if to no others. "Ask that of your own heart, sneaking woodchuck of the Delawares; come not here with the face of an innocent man. Go look in the spring; see the colors of your enemies on your lying skin,—and then come back and boast how you ran from your tribe, and took the blanket of the French for your covering. Paint yourself as bright as a humming-bird, you will still be as black as the crow."

Hist had been so uniformly gentle while living with the Hurons, that they now listened to her language with surprise. As for the delinquent, his blood boiled in his veins; and it was well for the pretty speaker that it was not in his power to execute the revenge he burned to inflict on her, in spite of his pretended love.

"Who wishes Briarthorn?" he sternly asked. "If this paleface is tired of life; if afraid of Indian torments, speak, Rivenoak; I will send him after the warriors we have lost."

"No, chief,—no, Rivenoak," eagerly interrupted Hist. "The Deerslayer fears nothing;

least of all a crow! Unbind him—cut his withes—place him face to face with this cawing bird; then let us see which is tired of life."

Hist made a forward movement, as if to take a knife from a young man, and perform the office she had mentioned in person; but an aged warrior interposed, at a sign from Rivenoak. This chief watched all the girl did with distrust; for, even while speaking in her most boastful language and in the steadiest manner, there was an air of uncertainty and expectation about her that could not escape so close an observer. She acted well; but two or three of the old men were equally satisfied that it was merely acting. Her proposal to release Deerslayer, therefore, was rejected; and the disappointed Hist found herself driven back from the sapling at the very moment she fancied herself about to be successful. At the same time the circle, which had got to be crowded and confused, was enlarged, and brought once more into order. Rivenoak now announced the intention of the old men again to proceed; the delay having been continued long enough, and leading to no result.

"Stop, Huron; stay, chiefs!" exclaimed Judith, scarcely knowing what she said, or why she interposed, unless to obtain time; "for God's sake, a single minute longer—"

The words were cut short by another and still more extraordinary interruption. A young Indian came bounding through the Huron ranks, leaping into the very center of the circle, in a way to denote the utmost confidence, or a temerity bordering on foolhardiness. Five or six sentinels were still watching the lake at different and distant points; and it was the first impression of Rivenoak that one of these had come in with tidings of import. Still, the movements of the stranger were so rapid, and his war-dress, which scarcely left him more drapery than an antique statue, had so little distinguishing about it, that, at the first moment, it was impossible to ascertain whether he were friend or foe. Three leaps carried this warrior to the side of Deerslayer, whose withes were cut in the twinkling of an eye with a quickness and precision that left the prisoner perfect master of his limbs. Not till this was effected did the stranger bestow a glance on any other object; then he turned and showed the astonished Hurons the noble brow, fine person, and eagle eye of a young warrior, in the paint and panoply of a Delaware. He held a rifle in each hand, the butts of both resting on the earth, while from one dangled its proper pouch and horn. This was Killdeer, which even as he looked boldly and in defiance on the crowd around him, he suffered to fall back into the hands of its proper owner. The presence of two armed men, though it was in their midst, startled the Hurons. Their rifles were scattered about against the different trees, and their only weapons were their knives and tomahawks. Still, they had too much self-possession to betray fear. It was little likely that so small a force would assail so strong a band; and each man expected some extraordinary proposition to succeed so decisive a step. The stranger did not seem disposed to disappoint them; he prepared to speak.

"Hurons," he said, "this earth is very big. The great lakes are big, too; there is room beyond them for the Iroquois, there is room for the Delawares on this side. I am Chingachgook, the son of Uncas, the kinsman of Tamenund. This is my betrothed; that paleface is my friend. My heart was heavy when I missed him. All the Delaware girls are waiting for Wah; they wonder that she stays away so long. Come, let us say farewell, and go on our path."

"Hurons, this is your mortal enemy, the Great Serpent of them you hate!" cried Briarthorn. "If he escape, blood will be in your moccasin-prints from this spot to the Canadas. I am all Huron."

As the last words were uttered, the traitor cast his knife at the naked breast of the Delaware. A quick movement of the arm on the part of Hist, who stood near, turned aside the blow, the dangerous weapon burying its point in a pine. At the next instant a similar weapon glanced from the hand of the Serpent, and quivered in the recreant's heart. A minute had scarcely elapsed from the moment in which Chingachgook bounded into the circle, and that in which Briarthorn fell, like a dog, dead in his tracks. The rapidity of events prevented the Hurons from acting; but this catastrophe permitted no further delay. A common exclamation followed, and the whole party was in motion. At this instant a sound unusual to the woods was heard, and every Huron, male and female, paused to listen, with ears erect, and faces filled with expectation. The sound was regular and heavy, as if the earth were struck with beetles. Objects became visible among the trees of the background, and a body of troops was seen advancing with measured tread. They came upon the charge, the scarlet of the king's livery shining among the bright green foliage of the forest.

The scene that followed is not easily described. It was one in which wild confusion, despair, and frenzied efforts were so blended as to destroy the unity and distinctness of the action. A general yell burst from the enclosed Hurons; it was succeeded by the hearty cheers of England. Still not a musket or rifle was fired, though that steady, measured tramp continued, and the bayonet was seen gleaming in advance of a line that counted nearly sixty men. The Hurons were taken at a fearful disadvantage. On three sides was the water, while their formidable and trained foes cut them off from flight on the fourth. Each warrior rushed for his arms, and then all on the point, man, woman, and child, eagerly sought the covers. In this scene of confusion and dismay, however, nothing could surpass the discretion and coolness of Deerslayer. His first care was to place Judith and Hist behind trees, and he looked for Hetty; but she had been hurried away in the crowd of Huron women. This effected, he threw himself on a flank of the retiring Hurons, who were inclining off towards the southern margin of the point, in the hope of escaping through the water. Deerslayer watched his opportunity, and finding two of his recent tormenters in a range, his rifle first broke the silence of the terrific scene. The bullet brought down both at one discharge. This drew a general fire from the Hurons, and the rifle and war cry of the Serpent were heard in the clamor. Still the trained men returned no answering volley, the whoop and piece of Hurry alone being heard on their side, if we except the short, prompt word of authority, and that heavy, measured, and menacing tread. Presently, however, the shrieks, groans, and denunciations that usually accompany the use of the bayonet followed. That terrible and deadly weapon was glutted in vengeance. The scene that succeeded was one of those of which so many have occurred in our own times in which neither age nor sex forms an exemption to the lot of a savage warfare. . . .

1841

From THE PRAIRIE [1]
CHAPTER XXXIV

•   •   •   •   •   •   •   •   •

The trapper was placed on a rude seat, which had been made, with studied care, to support his frame in an upright and easy attitude. The

---

[1] In The Prairie we find Natty Bumppo, driven from the borders of the eastern states by the tide of civilization, spending his last days as a trapper west of the Mississippi among the Pawnees. Suddenly the old man's physical strength fails him, and his Indian friends, who have held him in

first glance of the eye told his former friends that the old man was at length called upon to pay the last tribute of nature. His eye was glazed, and apparently as devoid of sight as of expression. His features were a little more sunken and strongly marked than formerly; but there all change, so far as exterior was concerned, might be said to have ceased. His approaching end was not to be ascribed to any positive disease, but had been a gradual and mild decay of the physical powers. Life, it is true, still lingered in his system; but it was as if at times entirely ready to depart, and then it would appear to reanimate the sinking form, reluctant to give up the possession of a tenement that had never been corrupted by vice or undermined by disease. It would have been no violent fancy to have imagined that the spirit fluttered about the placid lips of the old woodsman, reluctant to depart from a shell that had so long given it an honest and honorable shelter.

His body was placed so as to let the light of the setting sun fall full upon the solemn features. His head was bare, the long, thin, locks of gray fluttering lightly in the evening breeze. His rifle lay upon his knee, and the other accouterments of the chase were placed at his side, within reach of his hand. Between his feet lay the figure of a hound, with its head crouching to the earth, as if it slumbered; and so perfectly easy and natural was its position that a second glance was necessary to tell Middleton he saw only the skin of Hector, stuffed, by Indian tenderness and ingenuity, in a manner to represent the living animal. His own dog was playing at a distance with the child of Tachechana and Mahtoree. The mother herself stood at hand, holding in her arms a second offspring, that might boast of a parentage no less honorable than that which belonged

great veneration because of his wise counsel and his perfect integrity, perceiving that his spirit is about to pass, gather solemnly at his side. Just at this hour Middleton, an officer of the United States army, whom the old man had greatly befriended and who is a descendant of one of the early patrons of the hunter, comes to the Pawnee village to visit his aged friend. The scene described is what opens before him as he enters the Indian camp. Of the Indian characters, Le Balafré is an aged chief; Hard-Heart, the friend and filial support of the old trapper, is war-chief of the tribe; and Tachechana, the former wife of Mahtoree, a Sioux chief whom Hard-Heart had killed in combat, is now the wife of Hard-Heart.

In this scene Cooper puts the final touches upon a character wholly his own creation, one full of impossibilities when viewed realistically, yet painted with such brilliance, and such a sense for basal truth, as to stand after many literary generations as the type of the virtues of the class Natty Bumppo represents.

to the son of Hard-Heart. Le Balafré was seated nigh the dying trapper, with every mark about his person that the hour of his own departure was not far distant. The rest of those immediately in the center were aged men, who had apparently drawn near in order to observe the manner in which a just and fearless warrior would depart on the greatest of his journeys.

The old man was reaping the rewards of a life remarkable for temperance and activity, in a tranquil and placid death. His vigor in a manner endured to the very last. Decay, when it did occur, was rapid, but free from pain. He had hunted with the tribe in the spring, and even throughout most of the summer, when his limbs suddenly refused to perform their customary offices. A sympathizing weakness took possession of all his faculties; and the Pawnees believed that they were going to lose, in this unexpected manner, a sage and counselor whom they had begun both to love and respect. But, as we have already said, the immortal occupant seemed unwilling to desert its tenement. The lamp of life flickered, without becoming extinguished. On the morning of the day on which Middleton arrived, there was a general reviving of the powers of the whole man. His tongue was again heard in wholesome maxims, and his eye from time to time recognized the persons of his friends. It merely proved to be a brief and final intercourse with the world on the part of one who had already been considered, as to mental communion, to have taken his leave of it forever.

When he had placed his guests in front of the dying man, Hard-Heart, after a pause that proceeded as much from sorrow as decorum, leaned a little forward, and demanded:

"Does my father hear the words of his son?"

"Speak," returned the trapper, in tones that issued from his chest, but which were rendered awfully distinct by the stillness that reigned in the place. "I am about to depart from the village of the Loups, and shortly shall be beyond the reach of your voice."

"Let the wise chief have no cares for his journey," continued Hard-Heart, with an earnest solicitude that led him to forget, for the moment, that others were waiting to address his adopted parent; "a hundred Loups shall clear his path from briers."

"Pawnee, I die, as I have lived, a Christian man!" resumed the trapper, with a force of voice that had the same startling effect on his hearers as is produced by the trumpet, when its blast rises suddenly and freely on the air after its obstructed sounds have been heard struggling in the distance; "as I came into life so will I leave it.   Horses and arms are not needed to stand in the presence of the Great Spirit of my people. He knows my color, and according to my gifts will he judge my deeds."

"My father will tell my young men how many Mingos [1] he has struck, and what acts of valor and justice he has done, that they may know how to imitate him."

"A boastful tongue is not heard in the heaven of a white man!" solemnly returned the old man. "What I have done, He has seen. His eyes are always open. That which has been well done will He remember; wherein I have been wrong will He not forget to chastise, though He will do the same in mercy. No, my son; a paleface may not sing his own praises, and hope to have them acceptable before his God!"

A little disappointed, the young partisan stepped modestly back, making way for the recent comers to approach. Middleton took one of the meager hands of the trapper, and struggling to command his voice, he succeeded in announcing his presence.

The old man listened like one whose thoughts were dwelling on a very different subject; but when the other had succeeded in making him understand that he was present, an expression of joyful recognition passed over his faded features.

"I hope you have not so soon forgotten those whom you so materially served!" Middleton concluded. "It would pain me to think my hold on your memory was so light."

"Little that I have ever seen is forgotten," returned the trapper. "I am at the close of many weary days, but there is not one among them all that I could wish to overlook. I remember you, with the whole of your company; aye, and your gran'ther that went before you. I am glad that you have come back upon these plains, for I had need of one who speaks the English, since little faith can be put in the traders [2] of these regions. Will you do a favor to an old and dying man?"

"Name it," said Middleton; "it shall be done."

"It is a far journey to send such trifles," resumed the old man, who spoke at short intervals, as strength and breath permitted; "a far and weary journey is the same; but kindnesses and friendships are things not to be forgotten.

There is a settlement among the Otsego hills"— [3]

"I know the place," interrupted Middleton, observing that he spoke with increasing difficulty; "proceed to tell me what you would have done."

"Take this rifle, and pouch, and horn, and send them to the person whose name is graven on the plates of the stock,—a trader cut the letters with his knife—for it is long that I have intended to send him such a token of my love!"

"It shall be so. Is there more that you could wish?"

"Little else have I to bestow. My traps I give to my Indian son; [4] for honestly and kindly has he kept his faith. Let him stand before me."

Middleton explained to the chief what the trapper had said, and relinquished his own place to the other.

"Pawnee," continued the old man, always changing his language to suit the person he addressed, and not infrequently according to the ideas he expressed, "it is a custom of my people for the father to leave his blessing with the son before he shuts his eyes forever. This blessing I give to you; take it; for the prayers of a Christian man will never make the path of a just warrior to the blessed prairies either longer or more tangled. May the God of a white man look on your deeds with friendly eyes, and may you never commit an act that shall cause him to darken his face. I know not whether we shall ever meet again. There are many traditions concerning the place of Good Spirits. It is not for one like me, old and experienced though I am, to set up my opinion against a nation's. You believe in the blessed prairies, and I have faith in the sayings of my fathers. If both are true, our parting will be final; but if it should prove that the same meaning is hid under different words, we shall yet stand together, Pawnee, before the face of your Wahcondah, [5] who will then be no other than my God. There is much to be said in favor of both religions, for each seems suited to its own people, and no doubt it was so intended. I fear I have not altogether followed the gifts of my color, inasmuch as I find it a little painful to give up forever the use of the rifle and the comforts of the chase. But then the fault has been my own, seeing that it could not have been His. Aye, Hector," he continued, leaning

---

[1] Iroquois; see note introducing the selection from *The Deerslayer*, p. 228.
[2] The traders of the West were mostly French Canadians.
[3] The next few lines refer to the old man's youth among the forests of central New York and to the persons who had befriended him there.
[4] Hard-Heart, his son by adoption
[5] The Great Spirit

forward a little, and feeling for the ears of the hound, "our parting has come at last, dog, and it will be a long hunt. You have been an honest, and a bold, and a faithful hound. Pawnee, you cannot slay the pup on my grave, for where a Christian dog falls there he lies forever; but you can be kind to him after I am gone, for the love you bear his master."

"The words of my father are in my ears," returned the young partisan, making a grave and respectful gesture of assent.

"Do you hear what the chief has promised, dog?" demanded the trapper, making an effort to attract the notice of the insensible effigy of his hound. Receiving no answering look, nor hearing any friendly whine, the old man felt for the mouth, and endeavored to force his hand between the cold lips. The truth then flashed upon him, although he was far from perceiving the whole extent of the deception. Falling back in his seat, he hung his head, like one who felt a severe and unexpected shock. Profiting by this momentary forgetfulness, two young Indians removed the skin with the same delicacy of feeling that had induced them to attempt the pious fraud.

"The dog is dead!" muttered the trapper, after a pause of many minutes; "a hound has his time as well as a man; and well has he filled his days! Captain," he added, making an effort to wave his hand for Middleton, "I am glad you have come; for though kind, and well-meaning according to the gifts of their color, these Indians are not the men to lay the head of a white man in his grave. I have been thinking, too, of this dog at my feet; it will not do to set forth the opinion that a Christian can expect to meet his hound again; still there can be little harm in placing what is left of so faithful a servant nigh the bones of his master."

"It shall be as you desire."

"I'm glad you think with me in this matter. In order, then, to save labor, lay the pup at my feet; or for that matter, put him side by side. A hunter need never be ashamed to be found in company with his dog!"

"I charge myself with your wish."

The old man made a long and apparently a musing pause. At times he raised his eyes wistfully, as if he would again address Middleton, but some innate feeling appeared always to suppress his words. The other, who observed his hesitation, inquired in a way most likely to encourage him to proceed, whether there was aught else that he could wish to have done.

"I am without kith or kin in the wide world!" the trapper answered; "when I am gone there will be an end of my race. We have never been chiefs; but honest, and useful in our way, I hope it cannot be denied we have always proved ourselves. My father lies buried near the sea, and the bones of his son will whiten on the prairies"—

"Name the spot, and your remains shall be placed by the side of your father," interrupted Middleton.

"Not so, not so, captain. Let me sleep where I have lived,—beyond the din of the settlements! Still I see no need why the grave of an honest man should be hid, like a redskin in his ambushment. I paid a man in the settlements to make and put a graven stone at the head of my father's resting-place. It was of the value of twelve beaver-skins, and cunningly and curiously was it carved! Then it told to all comers that the body of such a Christian lay beneath; and it spoke of his manner of life, of his years, and of his honesty. When we had done with the Frenchers in the old war [1] I made a journey to the spot, in order to see that all was rightly performed, and glad I am to say, the workman had not forgotten his faith."

"And such a stone you would have at your grave?"

"I! no, no; I have no son but Hard-Heart, and it is little that an Indian knows of white fashions and usages. Besides, I am his debtor already, seeing it is so little I have done since I have lived in his tribe. The rifle might bring the value of such a thing—but then I know it will give the boy pleasure to hang the piece in his hall, for many is the deer and the bird that he has seen it destroy. No, no, the gun must be sent to him whose name is graven on the lock!"

"But there is one who would gladly prove his affection in the way you wish,—he who owes you not only his own deliverance from so many dangers, but who inherits a heavy debt of gratitude from his ancestors. The stone shall be put at the head of your grave."

The old man extended his emaciated hand, and gave the other a squeeze of thanks.

"I thought you might be willing to do it, but I was backward in asking the favor," he said, "seeing that you are not of my kin. Put no boastful words on the same, but just the name, the age, and the time of death, with something from the Holy Book; no more, no more. My

[1] the French and Indian War

name will then not be altogether lost on 'arth; I need no more."

Middleton intimated his assent, and then followed a pause that was only broken by distant and broken sentences from the dying man. He appeared now to have closed his accounts with the world, and to await merely for the final summons to quit it. Middleton and Hard-Heart placed themselves on the opposite sides of his seat, and watched with melancholy solicitude the variations of his countenance. For two hours there was no very sensible alteration. The expression of his faded and time-worn features was that of a calm and dignified repose. From time to time he spoke, uttering some brief sentence in the way of advice, or asking some simple questions concerning those in whose fortunes he still took a friendly interest. During the whole of that solemn and anxious period each individual of the tribe kept his place, in the most self-restrained patience. When the old man spoke, all bent their heads to listen; and when his words were uttered, they seemed to ponder on their wisdom and usefulness.

As the flame drew nigher to the socket his voice was hushed, and there were moments when his attendants doubted whether he still belonged to the living. Middleton, who watched each wavering expression of his weather-beaten visage with the interest of a keen observer of human nature, softened by the tenderness of personal regard, fancied he could read the workings of the old man's soul in the strong lineaments of his countenance. Perhaps what the enlightened soldier took for the delusion of mistaken opinion did actually occur—for who has returned from that unknown world to explain by what forms, and in what manner, he was introduced into its awful precincts? Without pretending to explain what must ever be a mystery to the quick, we shall simply relate facts as they occurred.

The trapper had remained nearly motionless for an hour. His eyes alone had occasionally opened and shut. When opened, his gaze seemed fastened on the clouds which hung around the western horizon, reflecting the bright colors, and giving form and loveliness to the glorious tints of an American sunset. The hour—the calm beauty of the season—the occasion, all conspired to fill the spectators with solemn awe. Suddenly, while musing on the remarkable position in which he was placed, Middleton felt the hand which he held grasp his own with incredible power, and the old man, supported on either side by his friends, rose upright to his feet. For a moment he looked about him, as if to invite all in presence to listen (the lingering remnant of human frailty), and then, with a fine military elevation of the head, and with a voice that might be heard in every part of that numerous assembly, he pronounced the word—

"Here!" [1]

A movement so entirely unexpected, and the air of grandeur and humility which were so remarkably united in the mien of the trapper, together with the clear and uncommon force of his utterance, produced a short period of confusion in the faculties of all present. When Middleton and Hard-Heart, each of whom had involuntarily extended a hand to support the form of the old man, turned to him again, they found that the subject of their interest was removed forever beyond the necessity of their care. They mournfully placed the body in its seat, and Le Balafré arose to announce the termination of the scene to the tribe. The voice of the old Indian seemed a sort of echo from that invisible world to which the meek spirit of the trapper had just departed.

"A valiant, a just, and a wise warrior has gone on the path which will lead him to the blessed grounds of his people!" he said. "When the voice of the Wahcondah called him, he was ready to answer. Go, my children; remember the just chief of the palefaces, and clear your own tracks from briers!"

The grave was made beneath the shade of some noble oaks. It has been carefully watched to the present hour by the Pawnees of the Loup, [2] and is often shown to the traveler and the trader as a spot where a just white man sleeps. In due time the stone was placed at its head, with the simple inscription which the trapper had himself requested. The only liberty taken by Middleton was to add, "May no wanton hand ever disturb his remains!"

1827

[1] It is worthy of note that this passage was written some thirty years before Thackeray conceived a somewhat similar final scene in the life of the beloved Colonel Newcome, the aged pensioner at the school he had attended as a boy: "At the usual evening hour, the chapel bell began to toll, and Thomas Newcome's hands outside the bed feebly beat time. And just as the last bell struck, a peculiar sweet smile shone over his face, and he lifted up his head a little, and quickly said, 'Adsum!' and fell back. It was the word we used at school, when our names were called; and lo, he whose heart was as that of a little child, had answered to his name, and stood in the presence of The Master." *The Newcomes*, vol. ii.

[2] the Pawnee Indians living on the Loup River in Nebraska

WILLIAM CULLEN BRYANT
1794-1878

The eldest of the "six great American poets," as the phrase once went (Bryant, Emerson, Longfellow, Whittier, Holmes, Lowell), was born at Cummington, Massachusetts, the son of a poor but able country doctor. He was sent after meager preparation to Williams College, where he remained seven months; then, giving up hope of a college training, he studied law. After a few years' practice, during which his poetry was beginning to attract attention, he entered journalism in New York City, and from 1828 was editor-in-chief of the *Evening Post*. He traveled extensively abroad and was active till his death by sunstroke. Aside from frequent volumes of poems from 1821 to 1863, he wrote *Letters of a Traveller*, 1852; *Letters from Spain*, 1859; *Letters from the East*, 1869. His translation of the *Iliad* appeared in 1870, and that of the *Odyssey* in 1871-1872.

American literature was fortunate in the fact that at the outset of its first really productive period it had, in Bryant and Irving, writers of taste who knew the value of form in poetry and prose respectively. Bryant's work is enveloped in a "cold, thin atmosphere," lacks passion and spontaneity, and personal charm; yet has high value because of its elemental dignity, its correctness, its sobriety, and the fact that it transmuted into art some spiritual forces strong in America a hundred years ago. Bryant's culture was essentially classic, and his art is based upon the classical tradition of the eighteenth century; this shows itself much as it does in Gray. But Bryant is also sensitive to nature and shows a joy in natural objects akin to that of Wordsworth.

Biography and criticism: J. Bigelow, *William C. Bryant* (AML), 1890; W. A. Bradley, *W. C. Bryant* (EML), 1905; C. H. Kirkland (LJ); Stedman (Poets); Chubb; W. L. Phelps, *No. Am.* 201: 224-7; J. L. Hervey, *Dial* 59:361-3.

THANATOPSIS [1]

To him who in the love of Nature holds
Communion with her visible forms, she speaks
A various language; for his gayer hours
She has a voice of gladness, and a smile

[1] The word thanatopsis is made up of two Greek words, θάνατος , death, and ὄψις, view, hence a view of death. Bryant wrote most of the poem ("Yet a few days" to "As the long train") when he was seventeen or eighteen years old, and then placed the verses in a pigeon-hole of his father's desk, where they remained, apparently untouched, for several years. When at last Richard Henry Dana, one of the editors of the *North American Review*, read the lines in 1817 he could not at first believe that the author was an American, and agreed finally to publish them only on the supposition that they had been written by Bryant's father, then a senator in the Massachusetts legislature. See Parke Godwin's *Life of Bryant*, i, 150. The poem was completed in 1821.

And eloquence of beauty, and she glides
Into his darker musings, with a mild
And healing sympathy, that steals away
Their sharpness, ere he is aware. When thoughts
Of the last bitter hour come like a blight
Over thy spirit, and sad images   10
Of the stern agony, and shroud, and pall,
And breathless darkness, and the narrow house,
Make thee to shudder and grow sick at heart;—
Go forth, under the open sky, and list
To Nature's teachings, while from all around—
Earth and her waters, and the depths of air—
Comes a still voice—
                    Yet a few days, and thee
The all-beholding sun shall see no more
In all his course; nor yet in the cold ground,
Where thy pale form was laid with many tears,
Nor in the embrace of ocean, shall exist   21
Thy image.   Earth, that nourished thee, shall claim
Thy growth, to be resolved to earth again,
And, lost each human trace, surrendering up
Thine individual being, shalt thou go
To mix forever with the elements,
To be a brother to the insensible rock
And to the sluggish clod, which the rude swain
Turns with his share, and treads upon. The oak
Shall send his roots abroad, and pierce thy mold.   30

Yet not to thine eternal resting-place
Shalt thou retire alone, nor couldst thou wish
Couch more magnificent. Thou shalt lie down
With patriarchs of the infant world—with kings,
The powerful of the earth—the wise, the good,
Fair forms, and hoary seers of ages past,
All in one mighty sepulcher. The hills
Rock-ribbed and ancient as the sun,—the vales
Stretching in pensive quietness between;
The venerable woods—rivers that move   40
In majesty, and the complaining brooks
That make the meadows green; and, poured round all,
Old Ocean's gray and melancholy waste,— [2]
Are but the solemn decorations all
Of the great tomb of man. The golden sun,
The planets, all the infinite host of heaven,
Are shining on the sad abodes of death
Through the still lapse of ages. All that tread
The globe are but a handful to the tribes

[2] Bryant is particularly notable in such phrasings as these, which would be remarkable in the work of even a much greater poet. It is in such felicities that his greatest merit lies, for though the literary vistas opened by his work are meager, his eye for nature is correct and inspires him often to the faultless stroke.

That slumber in its bosom.—Take the wings   50
Of morning, pierce the Barcan [1] wilderness,
Or lose thyself in the continuous woods
Where rolls the Oregon, and hears no sound,
Save his own dashings—yet the dead are there;
And millions in those solitudes, since first
The flight of years began, have laid them down
In their last sleep—the dead reign there alone.
So shalt thou rest, and what if thou withdraw
In silence from the living, and no friend   59
Take note of thy departure? All that breathe
Will share thy destiny. The gay will laugh
When thou art gone, the solemn brood of care
Plod on, and each one as before will chase
His favorite phantom; yet all these shall leave
Their mirth and their employments, and shall
    come
And make their bed with thee. As the long
    train
Of ages glides away, the sons of men,
The youth in life's green spring, and he who
    goes
In the full strength of years, matron and maid,
The speechless babe, and the gray-headed
    man—   70
Shall one by one be gathered to thy side,
By those, who in their turn shall follow them.

   So live, that when thy summons comes to join
The innumerable caravan, which moves
To that mysterious realm, where each shall take
His chamber in the silent halls of death,
Thou go not, like the quarry-slave at night,
Scourged to his dungeon, but, sustained and
    soothed
By an unfaltering trust, approach thy grave,
Like one who wraps the drapery of his couch   80
About him, and lies down to pleasant dreams.
1811   *1817*

TO A WATERFOWL [2]

Whither, midst falling dew,
While glow the heavens with the last steps of
    day,
Far, through their rosy depths, dost thou pursue
    Thy solitary way?

Vainly the fowler's eye
Might mark thy distant flight to do thee wrong,
As, darkly seen against the crimson sky,
    Thy figure floats along.

[1] The Barcan desert is northwest of Egypt.
[2] Bryant wrote the poem at a time of peculiar anxiety
when away from home, seeking a place where he
might find work in his profession. The picture
is what he saw as he walked over the Massachusetts hills at sunset.

   Seek'st thou the plashy brink
Of weedy lake, or marge of river wide,   10
Or where the rocking billows rise and sink
    On the chafed ocean-side?

There is a Power whose care
Teaches thy way along that pathless coast—
The desert and illimitable air—
    Lone wandering, but not lost.

All day thy wings have fanned,
At that far height, the cold, thin atmosphere,
Yet stoop not, weary, to the welcome land,
    Though the dark night is near.   20

And soon that toil shall end;
Soon shalt thou find a summer home, and rest,
And scream among thy fellows; reeds shall
    bend,
    Soon, o'er thy sheltered nest.

Thou'rt gone, the abyss of heaven
Hath swallowed up thy form; yet, on my heart
Deeply hath sunk the lesson thou has given,
    And shall not soon depart.

He who, from zone to zone,
Guides through the boundless sky thy certain
    flight,   30
In the long way that I must tread alone
    Will lead my steps aright.
1815   *1818*

GREEN RIVER

When breezes are soft and skies are fair,
I steal an hour from study and care,
And hie me away to the woodland scene,
Where wanders the stream with waters of green,
As if the bright fringe of herbs on its brink
Had given their stain to the wave they drink;
And they, whose meadows it murmurs through,
Have named the stream from its own fair hue.

Yet pure its waters—its shallows are bright
With colored pebbles and sparkles of light,   10
And clear the depths where its eddies play,
And dimples deepen and whirl away,
And the plane-tree's speckled arms o'ershoot
The swifter current that mines its root,
Through whose shifting leaves, as you walk
    the hill,
The quivering glimmer of sun and rill
With a sudden flash on the eye is thrown,
Like the ray that streams from the diamond-
    stone.
Oh, loveliest there the spring days come,   19
With blossoms, and birds, and wild-bees' hum;
The flowers of summer are fairest there,

And freshest the breath of the summer air;
And sweetest the golden autumn day
In silence and sunshine glides away.

Yet, fair as thou art, thou shunnest to glide,
Beautiful stream! by the village side;
But windest away from haunts of men,
To quiet valley and shaded glen;
And forest, and meadow, and slope of hill,
Around thee, are lonely, lovely, and still,   30
Lonely—save when by thy rippling tides,
From thicket to thicket the angler glides;
Or the simpler [1] comes, with basket and book,
For herbs of power on thy banks to look;
Or haply, some idle dreamer, like me,
To wander, and muse, and gaze on thee,
Still—save the chirp of birds that feed
On the river cherry and seedy reed,
And thy own wild music gushing out
With mellow murmur and fairy shout,   40
From dawn to the blush of another day,
Like a traveler singing along his way.

That fairy music I never hear,
Nor gaze on those waters so green and clear,
And mark them winding away from sight,
Darkened with shade or flashing with light,
While o'er them the vine to its thicket clings,
And the zephyr stoops to freshen his wings,
But I wish that fate had left me free
To wander these quiet haunts with thee,   50
Till the eating cares of earth should depart,
And the peace of the scene pass into my heart;
And I envy thy stream, as it glides along
Through its beautiful banks in a trance of
    song.

Though forced to drudge for the dregs of
    men,
And scrawl strange words with the barbarous
    pen,
And mingle among the jostling crowd,
Where the sons of strife are subtle and loud—
I often come to this quiet place,
To breathe the airs that ruffle thy face,   60
And gaze upon thee in silent dream,
For in thy lonely and lovely stream
An image of that calm life appears
That won my heart in my greener years.
1819   *1821*

SUMMER WIND [2]

It is a sultry day; the sun has drunk
The dew that lay upon the morning grass;
There is no rustling in the lofty elm

[1] one who collects simples, herbs
[2] It may be noted that wind is the element most influential in Bryant's poetic moods.

That canopies my dwelling, and its shade
Scarce cools me. All is silent, save the faint
And interrupted murmur of the bee,
Settling on the sick flowers, and then again
Instantly on the wing. The plants around
Feel the too potent fervors: the tall maize
Rolls up its long green leaves; the clover droops
Its tender foliage, and declines its blooms.   11
But far in the fierce sunshine tower the hills,
With all their growth of woods, silent and stern,
As if the scorching heat and dazzling light
Were but an element they loved. Bright clouds,
Motionless pillars of the brazen heaven—
Their bases on the mountains—their white tops
Shining in the far ether—fire the air
With a reflected radiance, and make turn
The gazer's eye away. For me, I lie   20
Languidly in the shade, where the thick turf,
Yet virgin from the kisses of the sun,
Retains some freshness, and I woo the wind
That still delays his coming. Why so slow,
Gentle and voluble spirit of the air?
Oh, come and breathe upon the fainting earth
Coolness and life. Is it that in his caves
He hears me? See, on yonder woody ridge,
The pine is bending his proud top, and now
Among the nearer groves, chestnut and oak   30
Are tossing their green boughs about. He
    comes;
Lo, where the grassy meadow runs in waves!
The deep distressful silence of the scene
Breaks up with mingling of unnumbered sounds
And universal motion. He is come,
Shaking a shower of blossoms from the shrubs,
And bearing on their fragrance; and he brings
Music of birds, and rustling of young boughs,
And sound of swaying branches, and the voice
Of distant waterfalls. All the green herbs   40
Are stirring in his breath; a thousand flowers,
By the road-side and the borders of the brook,
Nod gayly to each other; glossy leaves
Are twinkling in the sun, as if the dew
Were on them yet, and silver waters break
Into small waves and sparkle as he comes.
1824   *1824*

THE DEATH OF THE FLOWERS

The melancholy days are come, the saddest of
    the year,
Of wailing winds, and naked woods, and mead-
    ows brown and sere.
Heaped in the hollows of the grove, the autumn
    leaves lie dead;
They rustle to the eddying gust, and to the
    rabbit's tread;
The robin and the wren are flown, and from
    the shrubs the jay,

And from the wood-top calls the crow through
all the gloomy day.

Where are the flowers, the fair young flowers,
that lately sprang and stood
In brighter light and softer airs, a beauteous
sisterhood?
Alas! they all are in their graves, the gentle
race of flowers
Are lying in their lowly beds, with the fair and
good of ours.   10
The rain is falling where they lie, but the cold
November rain
Calls not from out the gloomy earth the lovely
ones again. [1]

The wind-flower and the violet, they perished
long ago,
And the brier-rose and the orchis died amid the
summer glow;
But on the hill the golden-rod, and the aster in
the wood,
And the yellow sun-flower by the brook, in
autumn beauty stood,
Till fell the frost from the clear cold heaven,
as falls the plague on men,
And the brightness of their smile was gone,
from upland, glade, and glen.

And now, when comes the calm mild day, as
still such days will come,
To call the squirrel and the bee from out their
winter home;   20
When the sound of dropping nuts is heard,
though all the trees are still,
And twinkle in the smoky light the waters of
the rill,
The south wind searches for the flowers whose
fragrance late he bore,
And sighs to find them in the wood and by the
stream no more.

And then I think of one who in her youthful
beauty died,
The fair meek blossom that grew up and faded
by my side.
In the cold moist earth we laid her, when the
forest cast the leaf,
And we wept that one so lovely should have a
life so brief:
Yet not unmeet it was that one, like that young
friend of ours,   29
So gentle and so beautiful, should perish with
the flowers.

1825   1825

---

[1] Bryant's work contains a good deal of eighteenth century poetic diction, the realism in his pictures ridding them of artificiality. "The Death of the Flowers" may well be compared with Tennyson's "Song," "A spirit haunts the year's last hours."

"O, FAIREST OF THE RURAL MAIDS" [2]

O, fairest of the rural maids!
Thy birth was in the forest shades;
Green boughs, and glimpses of the sky,
Were all that met thine infant eye.

Thy sports, thy wanderings, when a child,
Were ever in the sylvan wild;
And all the beauty of the place
Is in thy heart and on thy face.

The twilight of the trees and rocks
Is in the light shade of thy locks;   10
Thy step is as the wind, that weaves
Its playful way among the leaves.

Thy eyes are springs, in whose serene
And silent waters heaven is seen;
Their lashes are the herbs that look
On their young figures in the brook.

The forest depths, by foot unpressed,
Are not more sinless than thy breast;
The holy peace, that fills the air
Of those calm solitudes, is there.   20

1820   1832

A FOREST HYMN

The groves were God's first temples. Ere
man learned
To hew the shaft, and lay the architrave,
And spread the roof above them—ere he framed
The lofty vault, to gather and roll back
The sound of anthems; in the darkling wood,
Amid the cool and silence, he knelt down,
And offered to the Mightiest solemn thanks
And supplication. For his simple heart
Might not resist the sacred influences
Which, from the stilly twilight of the place,   10
And from the gray old trunks that high in
heaven
Mingled their mossy boughs, and from the
sound
Of the invisible breath that swayed at once
All their green tops, stole over him, and bowed
His spirit with the thought of boundless power
And inaccessible majesty. Ah, why
Should we, in the world's riper years, neglect
God's ancient sanctuaries, and adore
Only among the crowd, and under roofs
That our frail hands have raised? Let me, at
least,   20
Here, in the shadow of this aged wood,
Offer one hymn—thrice happy, if it find
Acceptance in His ear.

---

[2] These verses Bryant addressed to his wife. Comparison with "She was a phantom of delight," written by Wordsworth to his own wife, is illuminating.

                    Father, thy hand
Hath reared these venerable columns, thou
Didst weave this verdant roof. Thou didst look
        down
Upon the naked earth, and, forthwith, rose
All these fair ranks of trees. They, in thy sun,
Budded, and shook their green leaves in thy
        breeze,
And shot toward heaven. The century-living
        crow,
Whose birth was in their tops, grew old and
        died   30
Among their branches, till, at last, they stood,
As now they stand, massy, and tall, and dark,
Fit shrine for humble worshiper to hold
Communion with his Maker. These dim vaults,
These winding aisles, of human pomp or pride
Report not. No fantastic carvings show
The boast of our vain race to change the form
Of thy fair works. But thou art here—thou
        fill'st
The solitude. Thou art in the soft winds
That run along the summit of these trees   40
In music; thou art in the cooler breath
That from the inmost darkness of the place
Comes, scarcely felt; the barky trunks, the
        ground,
The fresh moist ground, are all instinct with
        thee.
Here is continual worship;—Nature, here,
In the tranquillity that thou dost love,
Enjoys thy presence. Noiselessly, around,
From perch to perch, the solitary bird
Passes; and yon clear spring, that, midst its
        herbs,
Wells softly forth and wandering steeps the
        roots   50
Of half the mighty forest, tells no tale
Of all the good it does. Thou hast not left
Thyself without a witness, in these shades,
Of thy perfections. Grandeur, strength, and
        grace
Are here to speak of thee. This mighty oak—
By whose immovable stem I stand and seem
Almost annihilated—not a prince,
In all that proud old world beyond the deep,
E'er wore his crown as loftily as he   59
Wears the green coronal of leaves with which
Thy hand has graced him. Nestled at his root
Is beauty, such as blooms not in the glare
Of the broad sun. That delicate forest flower,
With scented breath and look so like a smile,
Seems, as it issues from the shapeless mold,
An emanation of the indwelling Life,
A visible token of the upholding Love,
That are the soul of this wide universe.

    My heart is awed within me when I think
Of the great miracle that still goes on,   70
In silence, round me—the perpetual work
Of thy creation, finished, yet renewed
Forever. Written on thy works I read
The lesson of thy own eternity.
Lo! all grow old and die—but see again,
How on the faltering footsteps of decay
Youth presses—ever gay and beautiful youth
In all its beautiful forms. These lofty trees
Wave not less proudly that their ancestors   79
Molder beneath them. [1] Oh, there is not lost
One of earth's charms: upon her bosom yet,
After the flight of untold centuries,
The freshness of her far beginning lies
And yet shall lie. Life mocks the idle hate
Of his arch enemy Death—yea, seats himself
Upon the tyrant's throne—the sepulcher,
And of the triumphs of his ghastly foe
Makes his own nourishment. For he came forth
From thine own bosom, and shall have no end.

    There have been holy men who hid them-
        selves   90
Deep in the woody wilderness, and gave
Their lives to thought and prayer, till they
        outlived
The generation born with them, nor seemed
Less aged than the hoary trees and rocks
Around them;—and there have been holy men
Who deemed it were not well to pass life thus.
But let me often to these solitudes
Retire, and in thy presence reassure
My feeble virtue. Here its enemies,   99
The passions, at thy plainer footsteps shrink
And tremble and are still. Oh, God! when thou
Dost scare the world with tempests, set on fire
The heavens with falling thunderbolts, or fill,
With all the waters of the firmament,
The swift dark whirlwind that uproots the
        woods
And drowns the villages; when, at thy call,
Uprises the great deep and throws himself
Upon the continent, and overwhelms
Its cities—who forgets not, at the sight   109
Of these tremendous tokens of thy power,
His pride, and lays his strifes and follies by?
Oh, from these sterner aspects of thy face
Spare me and mine, nor let us need the wrath
Of the mad unchained elements to teach

---

[1] Bryant's method of treating this idea is pointedly in
    contrast with that of Omar Khayyám, *Rubáiyát*,
    xx:

    "And this delightful herb of tender Green
    Fledges the River's Lip on which we lean—
        Ah, lean upon it lightly! for who knows
    From what once lovely lip it springs unseen!"

Who rules them. Be it ours to meditate,
In these calm shades, thy milder majesty,
And to the beautiful order of thy works
Learn to conform the order of our lives.
1825   1825

JUNE

I gazed upon the glorious sky
 And the green mountains round,
And thought that when I came to lie
 At rest within the ground,
'T were pleasant, that in flowery June,
When brooks send up a cheerful tune,
 And groves a joyous sound,
The sexton's hand, my grave to make,
The rich, green mountain-turf should break. [1]

A cell within the frozen mold,   10
 A coffin borne through sleet,
And icy clods above it rolled,
 While fierce the tempests beat—
Away!—I will not think of these—
Blue be the sky and soft the breeze,
 Earth green beneath the feet,
And be the damp mold gently pressed
Into my narrow place of rest.

There through the long, long summer hours,
 The golden light should lie,   20
And thick young herbs and groups of flowers
 Stand in their beauty by.
The oriole should build and tell
His love-tale close beside my cell;
 The idle butterfly
Should rest him there, and there be heard
The housewife bee and humming-bird.

And what if cheerful shouts at noon
 Come, from the village sent,
Or songs of maids, beneath the moon   30
 With fairy laughter blent?
And what if, in the evening light,
Betrothed lovers walk in sight
 Of my low monument?
I would the lovely scene around
Might know no sadder sight nor sound.

I know that I no more should see
 The season's glorious show,
Nor would its brightness shine for me,
 Nor its wild music flow;   40
But if, around my place of sleep,
The friends I love should come to weep,
 They might not haste to go.

[1] Bryant died June 12th, 1878.

Soft airs, and song, and light, and bloom
Should keep them lingering by my tomb.

These to their softened hearts should bear
 The thought of what has been,
And speak of one who cannot share
 The gladness of the scene;
Whose part, in all the pomp that fills   50
 The circuit of the summer hills,
 Is that his grave is green;
And deeply would their hearts rejoice
To hear again his living voice.
1825   1826

THE PAST

Thou unrelenting Past! [2]
Strong are the barriers round thy dark domain,
 And fetters, sure and fast,
Hold all that enter thy unbreathing reign.

Far in thy realm withdrawn
Old empires sit in sullenness and gloom,
 And glorious ages gone
Lie deep within the shadow of thy womb.

Childhood, with all its mirth,
Youth, Manhood, Age that draws us to the
  ground,   10
 And last, Man's Life on earth,
Glide to thy dim dominions, and are bound.

Thou hast my better years;
Thou hast my earlier friends, the good, the
  kind,
 Yielded to thee with tears;
The venerable form, the exalted mind.

My spirit yearns to bring
The lost ones back—yearns with desire intense,
 And struggles hard to wring   19
Thy bolts apart, and pluck thy captives thence.

In vain; thy gates deny
All passage save to those who hence depart;
 Nor to the streaming eye
Thou giv'st them back—nor to the broken
  heart.

In thy abysses hide
Beauty and excellence unknown; to thee

[2] The theme of this poem is the same as that of the
Rubàiyàt of Omar Khayyàm, lxxi,

 "The Moving Finger writes; and having writ,
 Moves on: nor all thy Piety nor Wit
  Shall lure it back to cancel half a Line,
 Nor all thy Tears wash out a Word of it."

Earth's wonder and her pride
Are gathered, as the waters to the sea;

Labors of good to man,
Unpublished charity, unbroken faith,   30
   Love, that midst grief began,
And grew with years, and faltered not in death.

Full many a mighty name
Lurks in thy depths, unuttered, unrevered;
   With thee are silent fame,
Forgotten arts, and wisdom disappeared.

Thine for a space are they—
Yet shalt thou yield thy treasures up at last:
   Thy gates shall yet give way,
Thy bolts shall fall, inexorable Past!   40

All that of good and fair
Has gone into thy womb from earliest time,
   Shall then come forth to wear
The glory and the beauty of its prime.

They have not perished—no!
Kind words, remembered voices once so sweet,
   Smiles, radiant, long ago,
And features, the great soul's apparent seat.

All shall come back; each tie
Of pure affection shall be knit again;   50
   Alone shall Evil die,
And Sorrow dwell a prisoner in thy reign.

And then shall I behold
Him, by whose kind paternal side I sprung,
   And her, who, still and cold,
Fills the next grave—the beautiful and young.
1828   1829

THE EVENING WIND

Spirit that breathest through my lattice, thou
   That cool'st the twilight of the sultry day,
Gratefully flows thy freshness round my brow;
   Thou hast been out upon the deep at play,
Riding all day the wild blue waves till now,
   Roughening their crests, and scattering high
      their spray,
And swelling the white sail. I welcome thee
To the scorched land, thou wanderer of the sea!

Nor I alone; a thousand bosoms round
   Inhale thee in the fulness of delight;   10
And languid forms rise up, and pulses bound
   Livelier, at coming of the wind of night;
And, languishing to hear thy grateful sound,
   Lies the vast inland stretched beyond the
      sight.

Go forth into the gathering shade; go forth,
God's blessing breathed upon the fainting earth!

Go, rock the little wood-bird in his nest,
   Curl the still waters, bright with stars, and
      rouse
The wide old wood from his majestic rest,   19
   Summoning from the innumerable boughs
The strange, deep harmonies that haunt his
      breast:
   Pleasant shall be thy way where meekly bows
The shutting flower, and darkling waters pass,
And where the o'ershadowing branches sweep
      the grass.

The faint old man shall lean his silver head
   To feel thee; thou shalt kiss the child asleep,
And dry the moistened curls that overspread
   His temples, while his breathing grows more
      deep;
And they who stand about the sick man's bed
   Shall joy to listen to thy distant sweep.   30
And softly part his curtains to allow
Thy visit, grateful to his burning brow.

Go—but the circle of eternal change,
   Which is the life of Nature, shall restore,
With sounds and scents from all thy mighty
      range,
   Thee to thy birthplace of the deep once more;
Sweet odors in the sea-air, sweet and strange,
   Shall tell the homesick mariner of the shore;
And, listening to thy murmur, he shall deem   39
He hears the rustling leaf and running stream.
1829   1830

TO THE FRINGED GENTIAN

Thou blossom bright with autumn dew,
And colored with the heaven's own blue,
That openest when the quiet light
Succeeds the keen and frosty night,

Thou comest not when violets lean
O'er wandering brooks and springs unseen,
Or columbines, in purple dressed,
Nod o'er the ground-bird's hidden nest.

Thou waitest late and com'st alone,
When woods are bare and birds are flown,   10
And frosts and shortening days portend
The aged year is near his end.

Then doth thy sweet and quiet eye
Look through its fringes to the sky,
Blue—blue—as if that sky let fall
A flower from its cerulean wall.

I would that thus, when I shall see
The hour of death draw near to me,
Hope, blossoming within my heart,   19
May look to heaven as I depart.
1829   1832

SONG OF MARION'S MEN [1]

Our band is few but true and tried,
  Our leader frank and bold;
The British soldier trembles
  When Marion's name is told.
Our fortress is the good greenwood,
  Our tent the cypress-tree;
We know the forest round us,
  As seamen know the sea.
We know its walls of thorny vines
  Its glades of reedy grass,   10
Its safe and silent islands
  Within the dark morass.

Woe to the English soldiery
  That little dread us near!
On them shall light at midnight
  A strange and sudden fear:
When, waking to their tents on fire,
  They grasp their arms in vain,
And they who stand to face us
  Are beat to earth again;   20
And they who fly in terror deem
  A mighty host behind,
And hear the tramp of thousands
  Upon the hollow wind.

Then sweet the hour that brings release
  From danger and from toil:
We talk the battle over,
  And share the battle's spoil.
The woodland rings with laugh and shout,
  As if a hunt were up,   30
And woodland flowers are gathered
  To crown the soldier's cup.
With merry songs we mock the wind
  That in the pine-top grieves,
And slumber long and sweetly
  On beds of oaken leaves.

Well knows the fair and friendly moon
  The band that Marion leads—
The glitter of their rifles,
  The scampering of their steeds.   40
'Tis life to guide the fiery barb
  Across the moonlight plain;

[1] General Francis Marion, 1732-95, was the brilliant
commander of a force of irregular cavalry that
did much to annoy large bodies of British troops
and prevent them from concerted movements
against the colonists.

'Tis life to feel the night-wind
  That lifts the tossing mane
A moment in the British camp—
  A moment—and away
Back to the pathless forest,
  Before the peep of day.

Grave men there are by broad Santee,
  Grave men with hoary hairs;   50
Their hearts are all with Marion,
  For Marion are their prayers.
And lovely ladies greet our band
  With kindliest welcoming,
With smiles like those of summer,
  And tears like those of spring.
For them we wear these trusty arms,
  And lay them down no more
Till we have driven the Briton,   59
  Forever, from our shore.
1831   1831

THE PRAIRIES [2]

These are the gardens of the Desert, these
The unshorn fields, boundless and beautiful,
For which the speech of England has no name—
The Prairies. I behold them for the first,
And my heart swells while the dilated sight
Takes in the encircling vastness. Lo! they
    stretch
In airy undulations, far away,
As if the ocean, in his gentlest swell,
Stood still, with all his rounded billows fixed,
And motionless forever.—Motionless?—   10
No—they are all unchained again. The clouds
Sweep over with their shadows, and, beneath,
The surface rolls and fluctuates to the eye;
Dark hollows seem to glide along and chase
The sunny ridges. Breezes of the South!
Who toss the golden and the flame-like flowers,
And pass the prairie-hawk that, poised on high,
Flaps his broad wings, yet moves not—ye have
    played
Among the palms of Mexico and vines
Of Texas, and have crisped the limpid brooks
That from the fountains of Sonora glide   21
Into the calm Pacific—have ye fanned
A nobler or a lovelier scene than this?
Man hath no part in all this glorious work:
The hand that built the firmament hath heaved
And smoothed these verdant swells, and sown
    their slopes
With herbage, planted them with island groves,
And hedged them round with forests. Fitting
    floor

[2] Written when Bryant visited the prairies of Illinois in
1832; the word prairie is the French *prairie*,
meadow.

For this magnificent temple of the sky—   29
With flowers whose glory and whose multitude
Rival the constellations! The great heavens
Seem to stoop down upon the scene in love,—
A nearer vault, and of a tenderer blue,
Than that which bends above our eastern hills.

As o'er the verdant waste I guide my steed,
Among the high rank grass that sweeps his
          sides
The hollow beating of his footsteps seems
A sacrilegious sound. I think of those
Upon whose rest he tramples. Are they here—
The dead of other days?—and did the dust   40
Of these fair solitudes once stir with life
And burn with passion? Let the mighty
          mounds
That overlook the rivers, or that rise
In the dim forest crowded with old oaks,
Answer: A race that long has passed away
Built them;—a disciplined and populous race [1]
Heaped, with long toil, the earth, while yet the
          Greek
Was hewing the Pentelicus to forms
Of symmetry, and rearing on its rock   49
The glittering Parthenon. [2] These ample fields
Nourished their harvests, here their herds were
          fed,
When haply by their stalls the bison lowed,
And bowed his maned shoulder to the yoke.
All day this desert murmured with their toils,
Till twilight blushed, and lovers walked, and
          wooed
In a forgotten language, and old tunes,
From instruments of unremembered form,
Gave the soft winds a voice. The red man
          came—
The roaming hunter tribes, warlike and fierce,
And the mound-builders vanished from the
          earth.   60
The solitude of centuries untold
Has settled where they dwelt. The prairie-
          wolf
Hunts in their meadows, and his fresh-dug den
Yawns by my path. The gopher mines the
          ground
Where stood their swarming cities. All is gone;
All—save the piles of earth that hold their
          bones,
The platforms where they worshiped unknown
          gods,
The barriers which they builded from the soil

---

[1] The mound builders, to whom Bryant here refers, are
   now generally supposed by archaeologists to have
   been of the same general race as the Indians of
   more modern times.
[2] The Parthenon, situated on the acropolis of Athens,
   the highest point of the city, was built from marble
   quarried at Mount Pentelicus.

To keep the foe at bay—till o'er the walls
The wild beleaguerers broke, and, one by one,
The strongholds of the plain were forced and
          heaped   71
With corpses. The brown vultures of the wood
Flocked to those vast uncovered sepulchers,
And sat, unscared and silent, at their feast.
Haply some solitary fugitive,
Lurking in marsh and forest, till the sense
Of desolation and of fear became
Bitterer than death, yielded himself to die.
Man's better nature triumphed then. Kind
          words
Welcomed and soothed him; the rude conquer-
          ors   80
Seated the captive with their chiefs; he chose
A bride among their maidens, and at length
Seemed to forget—yet ne'er forgot—the wife
Of his first love, and her sweet little ones,
Butchered amid their shrieks, with all his race.

Thus change the forms of being. Thus arise
Races of living things, glorious in strength,
And perish, as the quickening breath of God
Fills them, or is withdrawn. The red man,
          too,
Has left the blooming wilds he ranged so long,
And, nearer to the Rocky Mountains, sought   91
A wider hunting-ground. The beaver builds
No longer by these streams, but far away,
On waters whose blue surface ne'er gave back
The white man's face — among Missouri's
          springs,
And pools whose issues swell the Oregon—
He rears his little Venice. In these plains
The bison feeds no more. Twice twenty leagues
Beyond remotest smoke of hunter's camp,   99
Roams the majestic brute, in herds that shake
The earth with thundering steps—yet here I
          meet
His ancient footprints stamped beside the pool.

Still this great solitude is quick with life.
Myriads of insects, gaudy as the flowers
They flutter over, gentle quadrupeds,
And birds, that scarce have learned the fear of
          man,
Are here, and sliding reptiles of the ground,
Startlingly beautiful. The graceful deer
Bounds to the wood at my approach. The bee,
A more adventurous colonist than man,   110
With whom he came across the eastern deep,
Fills the savannas with his murmurings,
And hides his sweets, as in the golden age,
Within the hollow oak. I listen long
To his domestic hum, and think I hear
The sound of that advancing multitude

Which soon shall fill these deserts. From the
    ground
Comes up the laugh of children, the soft voice
Of maidens, and the sweet and solemn hymn
Of Sabbath worshipers; the low of herds   120
Blends with the rustling of the heavy grain
Over the dark-brown furrows. All at once
A fresher wind sweeps by, and breaks my
    dream,
And I am in the wilderness alone.
1832   1833

THE BATTLE-FIELD

Once this soft turf, this rivulet's sands,
  Were trampled by a hurrying crowd,
And fiery hearts and armed hands
  Encountered in the battle-cloud.

Ah! never shall the land forget
  How gushed the life-blood of her brave;
Gushed, warm with hope and valor yet,
  Upon the soil they fought to save.

Now all is calm, and fresh, and still;
  Alone the chirp of flitting bird,   10
And talk of children on the hill,
  And bell of wandering kine, are heard.

No solemn host goes trailing by
  The black-mouthed gun and staggering wain;
Men start not at the battle-cry,
  Oh, be it never heard again!

Soon rested those who fought; but thou
  Who minglest in the harder strife
For truths which men receive not now,
  Thy warfare only ends with life.   20

A friendless warfare! lingering long
  Through weary day and weary year,
A wild and many-weaponed throng
  Hang on thy front, and flank, and rear.

Yet nerve thy spirit to the proof,
  And blench not at thy chosen lot.
The timid good may stand aloof,
  The sage may frown—yet faint thou not.

Nor heed the shaft too surely cast,
  The foul and hissing bolt of scorn;   30
For with thy side shall dwell, at last,
  The victory of endurance born.

Truth, crushed to earth, shall rise again;
  Th' eternal years of God are hers;
But Error, wounded, writhes in pain,
  And dies among his worshipers. [1]

[1] probably Bryant's best known stanza

Yea, though thou lie upon the dust,
  When those who helped thee flee in fear,
Die full of hope and manly trust,
  Like those who fell in battle here.   40

Another hand thy sword shall wield,
  Another hand the standard wave,
Till from the trumpet's mouth is pealed
  The blast of triumph o'er thy grave.

                                     1837

ROBERT OF LINCOLN

Merrily swinging on brier and weed,
  Near to the nest of his little dame,
Over the mountain-side or mead
  Robert of Lincoln is telling his name:
    Bob-o'-link, bob-o'-link,
    Spink, spank, spink;
Snug and safe is that nest of ours,
Hidden among the summer flowers.
          Chee, chee, chee.

Robert of Lincoln is gayly drest,   10
  Wearing a bright black wedding-coat;
White are his shoulders and white his crest.
  Hear him call his merry note:
    Bob-o'-link, bob-o'-link,
    Spink, spank, spink;
Look what a nice new coat is mine,
Sure there was never a bird so fine.
          Chee, chee, chee.

Robert of Lincoln's Quaker wife,
  Pretty and quiet, with plain brown wings,   20
Passing at home a patient life,
  Broods in the grass while her husband sings:
    Bob-o'-link, bob-o'-link,
    Spink, spank, spink;
Brood, kind creature; you need not fear
Thieves and robbers while I am here.
          Chee, chee, chee.

Modest and shy as a nun is she;
  One weak chirp is her only note.
Braggart and prince of braggarts is he,   30
  Pouring boasts from his little throat:
    Bob-o'-link, bob-o'-link,
    Spink, spank, spink;
Never was I afraid of man;
Catch me, cowardly knaves, if you can!
          Chee, chee, chee.

Six white eggs on a bed of hay,
  Flecked with purple, a pretty sight!
There as the mother sits all day,
  Robert is singing with all his might: 40

Bob-o'-link, bob-o'-link,
Spink, spank, spink;
Nice good wife, that never goes out,
Keeping house while I frolic about.
      Chee, chee, chee.

Soon as the little ones chip the shell
  Six wide mouths are open for food;
Robert of Lincoln bestirs him well,
  Gathering seeds for the hungry brood.
  Bob-o'-link, bob-o'-link,   50
  Spink, spank, spink;
This new life is likely to be
Hard for a gay young fellow like me.
      Chee, chee, chee.

Robert of Lincoln at length is made
  Sober with work, and silent with care;
Off is his holiday garment laid,
  Half forgotten that merry air:
  Bob-o'-link, bob-o'-link,
  Spink, spank, spink;   60
Nobody knows but my mate and I
Where our nest and our nestlings lie.
      Chee, chee, chee.

Summer wanes; the children are grown;
  Fun and frolic no more he knows;
Robert of Lincoln's a humdrum crone;
  Off he flies, and we sing as he goes:
  Bob-o'-link, bob-o'-link,
  Spink, spank, spink;
When you can pipe that merry old strain,   70
Robert of Lincoln, come back again.
      Chee, chee, chee.
1855   *1855*

WAITING BY THE GATE [1]

Beside a massive gateway built up in years
  gone by,
Upon whose top the clouds in eternal shadow
  lie,
While streams the evening sunshine on quiet
  wood and lea,
I stand and calmly wait till the hinges turn
  for me.

The tree-tops faintly rustle beneath the breeze's
  flight,
A soft and soothing sound, yet it whispers of the
  night;
I hear the wood-thrush piping one mellow
  descant more,
And scent the flowers that blow when the heat
  of day is o'er.

[1] Cf. Tennyson's *Crossing the Bar*, and Browning's *Prospice*.

Behold, the portals open, and o'er the threshold,
  now,
There steps a weary one with a pale and furrowed brow;   10
His count of years is full, his allotted task is
  wrought;
He passes to his rest from a place that needs
  him not.

In sadness then I ponder how quickly fleets the
  hour
Of human strength and action, man's courage
  and his power.
I muse while still the wood-thrush sings down
  the golden day,
And as I look and listen the sadness wears
  away.

Again the hinges turn, and a youth, departing,
  throws
A look of longing backward, and sorrowfully
  goes;
A blooming maid, unbinding the roses from
  her hair,
Moves mournfully away from amid the young
  and fair.   20

O glory of our race that so suddenly decays!
O crimson flush of morning that darkens as we
  gaze!
O breath of summer blossoms that on the restless air
Scatters a moment's sweetness, and flies we
  know not where!

I grieve for life's bright promise, just shown
  and then withdrawn;
But still the sun shines round me: the evening bird sings on,
And I again am soothed, and, beside the ancient
  gate,
In this soft evening sunlight, I calmly stand
  and wait.

Once more the gates are opened; an infant
  group go out,
The sweet smile quenched forever, and stilled
  the sprightly shout.   30
O frail, frail tree of Life, that upon the greensward strows
Its fair young buds unopened, with every wind
  that blows!

So come from every region, so enter, side by
  side,
The strong and faint of spirit, the meek and
  men of pride.

Steps of earth's great and mighty, between
    those pillars gray,
And prints of little feet, mark the dust along
    the way.

And some approach the threshold whose looks
    are blank with fear,
And some whose temples brighten with joy in
    drawing near,
As if they saw dear faces, and caught the gra-
    cious eye
Of Him, the Sinless Teacher, who came for us
    to die.   40

I mark the joy, the terror; yet these, within
    my heart,
Can neither wake the dread nor the longing to
    depart;
And, in the sunshine streaming on quiet wood
    and lea,
I stand and calmly wait till the hinges turn
    for me.

1860   *1864*

JOSEPH RODMAN DRAKE
1796-1820

Outward circumstances in the lives of Drake and Keats have sometimes made the American poet remembered in terms of the more famous English-man. They were born in the same year, and the death of both was by consumption within the same six months. Drake was born and died in New York City. After obtaining a good schooling which cost him much in effort against adverse cir-cumstances, he was for a time employed in business and then took up the study of medicine, in which he received a degree. Shortly after, he married a woman of means and visited Europe; but less than two years after his return he died. With Halleck he contributed in 1819 to the New York *Evening Post* a series of poems over the signature of "Croaker & Co.," satirizing local persons and local political and social occurrences.

Like Keats, Drake is lamented because of the brilliant promise that he showed. "The Culprit Fay," his finest poem, was written in two days and shows a degree of inventive imagination lacking in American poetry of his time. Very likely it was inspired in style by Coleridge's "Christabel"; but the poem is original and natively American in set-ting and details. It will be noticed that the flora, and the animals and insects of the tale, belong to the Hudson River region where the narrative begins. The poem depends for its success upon genuine poetic gifts, and upon a sprightliness of fancy ex-actly in keeping with the airy subject.

Criticism: J. G. Wilson, "The Author of 'The American Flag,'" *Cent.* 80:439-44; A. E. Corning, "Joseph Rodman Drake," *Bookm.* 41:574-6.

THE AMERICAN FLAG

When Freedom from her mountain height
    Unfurled her standard to the air,
She tore the azure robe of night,
    And set the stars of glory there;
She mingled with its gorgeous dyes
The milky baldric of the skies,
And striped its pure, celestial white
With streakings of the morning light;
Then from his mansion in the sun
She called her eagle bearer down,   10
And gave into his mighty hand
The symbol of her chosen land.

Majestic monarch of the cloud,
    Who rear'st aloft thy regal form,
To hear the tempest-trumpings loud
And see the lightning-lances driven,
    When strive the warriors of the storm,
And rolls the thunder-drum of heaven—
Child of the sun! to thee 'tis given
To guard the banner of the free,   20
To hover in the sulphur smoke
To ward away the battle-stroke,
And bid its blendings shine afar,
Like rainbows on the cloud of war,
    The harbingers of victory!

Flag of the brave! thy folds shall fly,
The sign of hope and triumph high,
When speaks the signal-trumpet tone,
And the long line comes gleaming on.
Ere yet the life-blood, warm and wet,   30
Has dimmed the glistening bayonet,
Each soldier eye shall brightly turn
Where thy sky-born glories burn,
And, as his springing steps advance,
Catch war and vengeance from the glance.
And when the cannon-mouthings loud
Heave in wild wreaths the battle shroud,
And gory sabers rise and fall
Like shoots of flame on midnight's pall,
    Then shall thy meteor-glances glow,   40
And cowering foes shall shrink beneath
    Each gallant arm that strikes below
That lovely messenger of death.

Flag of the seas! on ocean wave
Thy stars shall glitter o'er the brave;
When death, careering on the gale,
Sweeps darkly round the bellied sail,
And frighted waves rush wildly back
Before the broadside's reeling rack,
Each dying wanderer of the sea   50
Shall look at once to heaven and thee,
And smile to see thy splendors fly
In triumph o'er his closing eye.

Flag of the free heart's hope and home!
  By angel hands to valor given;
The stars have lit the welkin dome,
  And all thy hues were born in heaven.
Forever float that standard sheet!
  Where breathes the foe but falls before us,
With Freedom's soil beneath our feet,   60
  And Freedom's banner streaming o'er us? [1]

1819   1819

THE CULPRIT FAY [2]

I

'Tis the middle watch of a summer's night—
The earth is dark, but the heavens are bright;
Naught is seen in the vault on high
But the moon, and the stars, and the cloudless
    sky,
And the flood which rolls its milky hue,
A river of light on the welkin blue.
The moon looks down on old Cronest,
She mellows the shades on his shaggy breast,
And seems his huge gray form to throw
In a silver cone on the wave below;   10
His sides are broken by spots of shade,
By the walnut bough and the cedar made,
And through their clustering branches dark
Glimmers and dies the fire-fly's spark—
Like starry twinkles that momently break,
Through the rifts of the gathering tempest's
    rack.

II

The stars are on the moving stream,
  And fling, as its ripples gently flow,
A burnished length of wavy beam
  In an eel-like, spiral line below;   20
The winds are whist, and the owl is still,
  The bat in the shelvy rock is hid,
And naught is heard on the lonely hill
But the cricket's chirp, and the answer shrill
  Of the gauze-winged katy-did;
And the plaint of the wailing whip-poor-will,
Who moans unseen, and ceaseless sings,
  Ever a note of wail and woe,
Till morning spreads her rosy wings,
  And earth and sky in her glances glow.   30

III

'Tis the hour of fairy ban and spell;
The wood-tick has kept the minutes well;
He has counted them all with click and stroke
Deep in the heart of the mountain oak,

And he has awakened the sentry elve
  Who sleeps with him in the haunted tree,
To bid him ring the hour of twelve,
  And call the fays to their revelry;
Twelve small strokes on his tinkling bell—
('Twas made of the white snail's pearly shell;)
"Midnight comes, and all is well!   41
Hither, hither, wing your way!
'Tis the dawn of the fairy-day."

IV

They come from beds of lichen green,
They creep from the mullein's velvet screen;
Some on the backs of beetles fly
  From the silver tops of moon-touched trees,
Where they swung in their cobweb hammocks
    high,
  And rocked about in the evening breeze;
Some from the hum-bird's downy nest—   50
  They had driven him out by elfin power,
And pillowed on plumes of his rainbow breast,
  Had slumbered there till the charmed hour;
Some had lain in the scoop of the rock,
  With glittering ising-stars [3] inlaid;
And some had opened the four-o'clock,
  And stole within its purple shade.
And now they throng the moonlight glade,
Above—below—on every side,
  Their little minim [4] forms arrayed   60
In the tricksy pomp of fairy pride!

V

They come not now to print the lea,
In freak and dance around the tree,
Or at the mushroom board to sup,
And drink the dew from the buttercup;
A scene of sorrow waits them now,
For an Ouphe [5] has broken his vestal vow;
He has loved an earthly maid,
And left for her his woodland shade;
He has lain upon her lip of dew,   70
And sunned him in her eye of blue,
Fanned her cheek with his wing of air,
Played in the ringlets of her hair,
And, nestling on her snowy breast,
Forgot the lily-king's behest.
For this the shadowy tribes of air
  To the elfin court must haste away:—
And now they stand expectant there,
  To hear the doom of the culprit Fay.

VI

The throne was reared upon the grass,   80
Of spice-wood and the sassafras;

---

[1] The last four lines were written by Halleck.
[2] The poem was written by Drake, perhaps as early as 1816, as an answer to one of his friends who remarked that it would be difficult to write a fairy poem without the aid of human characters.

[3] a word irregularly compounded from *isinglass*
[4] very least; smallest
[5] oaf; strictly, a changeling left by fairies; here a recalcitrant fairy

On pillars of mottled tortoise-shell
  Hung the burnished canopy—
And over it gorgeous curtains fell
  Of the tulip's crimson drapery.
The monarch sat on his judgment-seat,
  On his brow the crown imperial shone,
The prisoner Fay was at his feet,
  And his peers were ranged around the throne.
He waved his scepter in the air,   90
  He looked around and calmly spoke;
His brow was grave and his eye severe,
  But his voice in a softened accent broke:

VII

"Fairy! Fairy! list and mark:
  Thou hast broke thine elfin chain; [1]
Thy flame-wood lamp is quenched and dark,
  And thy wings are dyed with a deadly stain—
Thou hast sullied thine elfin purity
  In the glance of a mortal maiden's eye,
Thou hast scorned our dread decree,   100
  And thou shouldst pay the forfeit high.
But well I know her sinless mind
  Is pure as the angel forms above,
Gentle and meek, and chaste and kind,
  Such as a spirit well might love;
Fairy! had she spot or taint,
  Bitter had been thy punishment.
Tied to the hornet's shardy wings;
  Tossed on the pricks of nettle's stings;
Or seven long ages doomed to dwell   110
  With the lazy worm in the walnut-shell;
Or every night to writhe and bleed
  Beneath the tread of the centipede;
Or bound in a cobweb dungeon dim,
  Your jailer a spider huge and grim,
Amid the carrion bodies to lie,
  Of the worm, and the bug, and the murdered
    fly;
These it had been your lot to bear,
  Had a stain been found on the earthly fair.
Now list, and mark our mild decree—   120
  Fairy, this your doom must be:

VIII

"Thou shalt seek the beach of sand
  Where the water bounds the elfin land;
Thou shalt watch the oozy brine
  Till the sturgeon leaps in the bright moonshine,
Then dart the glistening arch below,
  And catch a drop from his silver bow.
The water-sprites will wield their arms
  And dash around, with roar and rave,
And vain are the woodland spirits' charms,
  They are the imps that rule the wave.   131

[1] possibly the mystic bond of purity that bound him to
    the other fays

Yet trust thee in thy single might:
  If thy heart be pure and thy spirit right,
Thou shalt win the warlock [2] fight.

IX

"If the spray-bead gem be won,
  The stain of thy wing is washed away:
But another errand must be done
  Ere thy crime be lost for aye;
Thy flame-wood lamp is quenched and dark;
  Thou must reillume its spark.   140
Mount thy steed and spur him high
  To the heaven's blue canopy;
And when thou seest a shooting star,
  Follow it fast, and follow it far—
The last faint spark of its burning train
  Shall light the elfin lamp again.
Thou hast heard our sentence, Fay;
  Hence! to the water-side, away!"

X

The goblin marked his monarch well;
  He spake not, but he bowed him low,   150
Then plucked a crimson colen-bell, [3]
  And turned him round in act to go.
The way is long, he cannot fly,
  His soiled wing has lost its power,
And he winds adown the mountain high,
  For many a sore and weary hour.
Through dreary beds of tangled fern,
Through groves of nightshade dark and dern, [4]
Over the grass and through the brake,
  Where toils the ant and sleeps the snake;
Now over the violet's azure flush   161
He skips along in lightsome mood;
  And now he thrids [5] the bramble-bush,
Till its points are dyed in fairy blood.
He has leaped the bog, he has pierced the brier,
He has swum the brook, and waded the mire,
Till his spirits sank, and his limbs grew weak,
And the red waxed fainter in his cheek.
He had fallen to the ground outright,
  For rugged and dim was his onward track,
But there came a spotted toad in sight,   171
  And he laughed as he jumped upon her back:
He bridled her mouth with a silkweed twist,
  He lashed her sides with an osier thong;
And now through evening's dewy mist,
  With leap and spring they bound along,
Till the mountain's magic verge is past,
And the beach of sand is reached at last.

XI

Soft and pale is the moony beam,
Moveless still the glassy stream;   180

[2] wizard
[3] perhaps the columbine
[4] secret
[5] threads

The wave is clear, the beach is bright
  With snowy shells and sparkling stones;
The shore-surge comes in ripples light,
  In murmurings faint, and distant moans;
And ever afar in the silence deep
Is heard the splash of the sturgeon's leap,
And the bend of his graceful bow is seen—
A glittering arch of silver sheen,
Spanning the wave of burnished blue,
And dripping with gems of the river-dew.

XII

The elfin cast a glance around,   191
  As he lighted down from his courser toad,
Then round his breast his wings he wound,
  And close to the river's brink he strode;
He sprang on a rock, he breathed a prayer,
  Above his head his arms he threw,
Then tossed a tiny curve in air,
  And headlong plunged in the waters blue.

XIII

Up sprung the spirits of the waves,   199
From the sea-silk beds in their coral caves,
With snail-plate armor snatched in haste,
They speed their way through the liquid waste;
Some are rapidly borne along
On the mailed shrimp or the prickly prong, [1]
Some on blood-red leeches glide,
Some on the stony star-fish ride,
Some on the back of the lancing squab, [2]
Some on the sideling soldier-crab;
And some on the jellied quarl, [3] that flings
At once a thousand streamy stings;   210
They cut the wave with the living oar,
And hurry on to the moonlight shore,
To guard their realms and chase away
The footsteps of the invading Fay.

XIV

Fearlessly he skims along,
His hope is high, and his limbs are strong,
He spreads his arms like the swallow's wing,
And throws his feet with a frog-like fling;
His locks of gold on the waters shine,
  At his breast the tiny foam-beads rise,   220
His back gleams bright above the brine,
  And the wake-line foam behind him lies,
But the water-sprites are gathering near
  To check his course along the tide;
Their warriors come in swift career
  And hem him round on every side;
On his thigh the leech has fixed his hold,
The quarl's long arms are round him rolled,
The prickly prong has pierced his skin,

[1] perhaps prawn, a small crustacean
[2] squid   [3] jellyfish

And the squab has thrown his javelin,   230
The gritty star has rubbed him raw,
And the crab has struck with his giant claw,
He howls with rage, and he shrieks with pain,
He strikes around, but his blows are vain;
Hopeless is the unequal fight,
Fairy! naught is left but flight.

XV

He turned him round, and fled amain
With hurry and dash to the beach again.
He twisted over from side to side,
And laid his cheek to the cleaving tide;   240
The strokes of his plunging arms are fleet,
And with all his might he flings his feet,
But the water-sprites are round him still,
To cross his path and work him ill.
They bade the waves before him rise,
They flung the sea-fire in his eyes,
And they stunned his ears with the scallop-
          stroke,
With the porpoise heave—and the drum-fish
          croak.
Oh! but a weary wight was he
When he reached the foot of the dog-wood tree.
Gashed and wounded, and stiff and sore,   251
He laid him down on the sandy shore;
He blessed the force of the charmed line,
  And he banned the water-goblins' spite,
For he saw around in the sweet moonshine
  Their little wee faces above the brine,
    Giggling and laughing with all their might
    At the piteous hap of the Fairy wight.

XVI

Soon he gathered the balsam dew   259
From the sorrel-leaf and the henbane bud;
Over each wound the balm he drew,
And with cobweb lint he stanched the blood.
The mild west wind was soft and low,
It cooled the heat of his burning brow,
And he felt new life in his sinews shoot,
As he suck'd the juice of the calamus [4] root;
And now he treads the fatal shore,
As fresh and vigorous as before.

XVII

Wrapped in musing stands the sprite;
  'Tis the middle wane of night;   270
His task is hard, his way is far,
  But he must do his errand right,
Ere dawning mounts her beamy car,
  And rolls her chariot wheels of light;
And vain are the spells of fairy-land:
He must work with a human hand.

[4] sweetflag

XVIII

He cast a saddened look around,
  But he felt new joy his bosom swell,
When glittering on the shadowed ground,
  He saw a purple mussel-shell;   280
Thither he ran, and he bent him low,
He heaved at the stern and he heaved at the
        bow,
And he pushed her over the yielding sand,
Till he came to the verge of the haunted land.
She was as lovely a pleasure-boat
  As ever fairy had traveled in,
For she glowed with purple paint without,
  And shone with silvery pearl within;
A sculler's notch in the stern he made,
An oar he shaped of the bootle-blade; [1]   290
Then sprung to his seat with a lightsome leap,
And launched afar, on the calm, blue deep.

XIX

The imps of the river yell and rave;
They had no power above the wave,
But they heaved the billow before the prow,
  And they dashed the surge against her side,
And they struck her keel with jerk and blow,
  Till the gunwale bent to the rocking tide.
She wimpled [2] about to the pale moon-beam,
Like a feather that floats on a wind-tossed
        stream;   300
And momently athwart her track
The quarl upreared his island back,
And the fluttering scallop behind would float,
And spatter the water about the boat;
But he bailed her out with his colen-bell,
  And he kept her trimmed with a wary tread,
While on every side like lightning fell
  The heavy strokes of his bootle-blade.

XX

Onward still he held his way,
Till he came where the column of moonshine
        lay,   310
And saw beneath the surface dim
The brown-backed sturgeon slowly swim;
Around him were the goblin train—
But he sculled with all his might and main,
And followed wherever the sturgeon led,
Till he saw him upward point his head;
Then he dropped his paddle-blade,
And held his colen-goblet up
To catch the drop in its crimson cup.

XXI

With sweeping tail and quivering fin,   320
  Through the wave the sturgeon flew,

[1] perhaps coined for its alliteration
[2] literally, rippled

And, like the heaven-shot javelin,
  He sprung above the waters blue.
Instant as the star-fall light
  He plunged him in the deep again,
But left an arch of silver bright,
  The rainbow of the moony main.
It was a strange and lovely sight [3]
  To see the puny goblin there;
He seemed an angel form of light,   330
  With azure wings and sunny hair,
Throned on a cloud of purple fair,
Circled with blue and edged with white,
And sitting at the fall of even
Beneath the bow of summer heaven.

XXII

A moment, and its luster fell;
  But ere it met the billow blue,
He caught within his crimson bell
  A droplet of its sparkling dew—
Joy to thee, Fay! thy task is done,   340
Thy wings are pure, for the gem is won—
Cheerly ply thy dripping oar,
And haste away to the elfin shore.

XXIII

He turns, and lo! on either side
The ripples on his path divide;
And the track o'er which his boat must pass
Is smooth as a sheet of polished glass,
Around, their limbs the sea-nymphs lave,
  With snowy arms half swelling out,
While on the glossed and gleamy wave   350
  Their sea-green ringlets loosely float;
They swim around with smile and song;
  They press the bark with pearly hand,
And gently urge her course along,
  Toward the beach of speckled sand;
And, as he lightly leaped to land,
They bade adieu with nod and bow,
  Then gaily kissed each little hand,
And dropped in the crystal deep below.

XXIV

A moment stayed the fairy there;   360
He kissed the beach and breathed a prayer;
Then spread his wings of gilded blue,
And on to the elfin court he flew;
As ever he saw a bubble rise,
And shine with a thousand changing dyes,
Till, lessening far, through ether driven,
It mingles with the hues of heaven;
As, at the glimpse of morning pale,
The lance-fly spreads his silken sail,   369
And gleams with blendings soft and bright,
Till lost in the shades of fading night;

[3] apparently an echo of Coleridge's "Christabel," i, 280

So rose from earth the lovely Fay—
So vanished, far in heaven away!

———

Up, Fairy! quit thy chick-weed bower,
The cricket has called the second hour,
Twice again, and the lark will rise
To kiss the streaking of the skies—
Up! thy charmed armor don,
Thou'lt need it ere the night be gone.

XXV

He put his acorn helmet on;   380
It was plumed of the silk of the thistle down;
The corselet plate that guarded his breast
Was once the wild bee's golden vest;
His cloak, of a thousand mingled dyes,
Was formed of the wings of butterflies;
His shield was the shell of a lady-bug queen,
Studs of gold on a ground of green;
And the quivering lance, which he brandished
    bright,
Was the sting of a wasp he had slain in fight.
Swift he bestrode his fire-fly steed;   390
    He bared his blade of the bent grass blue;
He drove his spurs of the cockle-seed,
    And away like a glance of thought he flew,
To skim the heavens and follow far
The fiery trail of the rocket-star.

XXVI

The moth-fly, as he shot in air,
Crept under the leaf, and hid her there;
The katy-did forgot its lay,
The prowling gnat fled fast away,
The fell mosquito checked his drone   400
And folded his wings till the Fay was gone,
And the wily beetle dropped his head,
And fell on the ground as if he were dead;
They crouched them close in the darksome
    shade,
    They quaked all o'er with awe and fear,
For they had felt the blue-bent blade,
    And writhed at the prick of the elfin spear;
Many a time, on a summer's night,
When the sky was clear and the moon was
    bright,
They had been roused from the haunted ground
By the yelp and bay of the fairy hound,   411
They had heard the tiny bugle-horn,
    They had heard the twang of the maize-silk
        string,
When the vine-twig bows were tightly drawn,
And the nettle-shaft through air was borne,
    Feathered with down of the hum-bird's wing.
And now they deemed the courier Ouphe
    Some hunter-sprite of the elfin ground;

And they watched till they saw him mount the
    roof
    That canopies the world around;   420
Then glad they left their covert lair,
And freaked about in the midnight air.

XXVII

Up to the vaulted firmament
His path the fire-fly courser bent,
And at every gallop on the wind,
He flung a glittering spark behind;
He flies like a feather in the blast
Till the first light cloud in heaven is past,
    But the shapes of air have begun their work,
And a drizzly mist is round him cast,   430
    He cannot see through the mantle murk,
He shivers with cold, but he urges fast,
    Through storm and darkness, sleet and shade;
He lashes his steed and spurs amain,
For shadowy hands have twitched the rein,
    And flame-shot tongues around him played,
And near him many a fiendish eye
Glared with a fell malignity,
And yells of rage, and shrieks of fear,
Came screaming on his startled ear.   440

XXVIII

His wings are wet around his breast,
The plume hangs dripping from his crest,
His eyes are blurred by the lightning's glare,
And his ears are stunned with the thunder's
    blare,
But he gave a shout, and his blade he drew,
    He thrust before and he struck behind,
Till he pierced their cloudy bodies through,
    And gashed their shadowy limbs of wind;
Howling the misty specters flew,
    They rend the air with frightful cries,   450
For he has gained the welkin blue,
    And the land of clouds beneath him lies.

XXIX

Up to the cope,[1] careering swift
    In breathless motion fast,
Fleet as the swallow cuts the drift,
    Or the sea-roc rides the blast,
The sapphire sheet of eve is shot,
    The sphered moon is past,
The earth but seems a tiny blot
    On a sheet of azure cast.   460
O! it was sweet in the clear moonlight,
    To tread the starry plain of even,
To meet the thousand eyes of night,
    And feel the cooling breath of heaven!
But the elfin made no stop or stay
Till he came to the bank of the milky-way;

[1] vault of heaven

Then he checked his courser's foot,
And watched for the glimpse of the planet-
　　shoot.

XXX

Sudden along the snowy tide　　　469
　　That swelled to meet their footsteps' fall,
The sylphs of heaven were seen to glide,
　　Attired in sunset's crimson pall;
Around the Fay they weave the dance,
　　They skip before him on the plain,
And one has taken his wasp-sting lance,
　　And one upholds his bridle-rein;
With warblings wild they lead him on
　　To where, through clouds and amber seen,
Studded with stars, resplendent shone
　　The palace of the sylphid queen.　　480
Its spiral columns, gleaming bright,
Were streamers of the northern light;
Its curtains light and lovely flush
Was of the morning's rosy blush,
And the ceiling fair, that rose aboon, [1]
The white and feathery fleece of noon.

XXXI

But, O! how fair the shape that lay
　　Beneath a rainbow bending bright;
She seemed to the entranced Fay
　　The loveliest of the forms of light;　　490
Her mantle was the purple rolled
　　At twilight in the west afar;
'Twas tied with threads of dawning gold
　　And buttoned with a sparkling star.
Her face was like the lily roon [2]
　　That veils the vestal planet's hue;
Her eyes, two beamlets from the moon,
　　Set floating in the welkin blue.
Her hair is like the sunny beam,
And the diamond gems which round it gleam
Are the pure drops of dewey even　　501
That ne'er have left their native heaven.

XXXII

She raised her eyes to the wondering sprite,
　　And they leaped with smiles, for well I ween
Never before in the bowers of light
　　Had the form of an earthly Fay been seen.
Long she looked in his tiny face;
　　Long with his butterfly cloak she played;
She smoothed his wings of azure lace,
　　And handled the tassel of his blade;　　510
And as he told in accents low
The story of his love and woe,
She felt new pains in her bosom rise,
And the tear-drop started in her eyes.
And "O! sweet spirit of earth," she cried,

[1] above　　　[2] border

"Return no more to your woodland height,
But ever here with me abide
　　In the land of everlasting light!
Within the fleecy drift we'll lie,
　　We'll hang upon the rainbow's rim;　　520
And all the jewels of the sky
　　Around thy brow shall brightly beam!
And thou shalt bathe thee in the stream
　　That rolls its whitening foam aboon,
And ride upon the lightning's gleam,
　　And dance upon the orbed moon!
We'll sit within the Pleiad ring,
　　We'll rest on Orion's starry belt,
And I will bid my sylphs to sing
　　The song that makes the dew-mist melt;
Their harps are of the umber shade　　531
　　That hides the blush of waking day,
And every gleamy string is made
　　Of silvery moonshine's lengthened ray;
And thou shalt pillow on my breast,
　　While heavenly breathings float around,
And, with the sylphs of ether blest,
　　Forget the joys of fairy ground."

XXXIII

She was lovely and fair to see,
And the elfin's heart beat fitfully;　　540
But lovelier far, and still more fair,
The earthly form imprinted there;
Naught he saw in the heavens above
Was half so dear as his mortal love,
For he thought upon her look so meek,
And he thought of the light flush on her cheek;
Never again might he bask and lie
On that sweet cheek and moonlight eye,
But in his dreams her form to see,
To clasp her in his revery,　　550
To think upon his virgin bride,
Was worth all heaven, and earth beside.

XXXIV

"Lady," he cried, "I have sworn tonight,
On the word of a fairy-knight,
To do my sentence-task aright;
My honor scarce is free from stain,
I may not soil its snows again;
Betide me weal, betide me wo,
Its mandate must be answered now."
Her bosom heaved with many a sigh,　　560
The tear was in her drooping eye;
But she led him to the palace-gate,
　　And called the sylphs who hovered there
And bade them fly and bring him straight
　　Of clouds condensed a sable car.
With charm and spell she blessed it there,
From all the fiends of upper air;
Then round him cast the shadowy shroud,

And tied his steed behind the cloud;
And pressed his hand as she bade him fly
Far to the verge of the northern sky,   571
For by its wan and wavering light
There was a star would fall tonight.

XXXV

Borne afar on the wings of the blast,
Northward away, he speeds him fast,
And his courser follows the cloudy wain
Till the hoof-strokes fall like pattering rain.
The clouds roll backward as he flies,
Each flickering star behind him lies,
And he has reached the northern plain,   580
And backed his fire-fly steed again,
Ready to follow in its flight
The streaming of the rocket-light.

XXXVI

The star is yet in the vault of heaven,
But it rocks in the summer gale;
And now 'tis fitful and uneven,
And now 'tis deadly pale;
And now 'tis wrapped in sulphur-smoke,
And quenched in its rayless beam,   589
And now with a rattling thunder-stroke
It burst in flash and flame.
As swift as the glance of the arrowy lance
That the storm-spirit flings from high,
The star-shot flew o'er the welkin blue,
As it fell from the sheeted sky.
As swift as the wind in its trail behind
The elfin gallops along,
The fiends of the cloud are bellowing loud,
But the sylphid charm is strong;
He gallops unhurt in the shower of fire,   600
While the cloud-fiends fly from the blaze;
He watches each flake till its sparks expire,
And rides in the light of its rays.
But he drove his steed to the lightning's speed,
And caught a glimmering spark;
Then wheeled around to the fairy ground,
And sped through the midnight dark.

Ouphe and Goblin! Imp and Sprite!
Elf of eve! and starry Fay!
Ye that love the moon's soft light,   610
Hither, hither wend your way;
Twine ye in a jocund ring,
Sing and trip it merrily,
Hand to hand, and wing to wing,
Round the wild witch-hazel tree.

Hail the wanderer again,
With dance and song, and lute and lyre.
Pure his wing and strong his chain, [1]

[1] perhaps, here, armor

And doubly bright his fairy fire.
Twine ye in an airy round.   620
Brush the dew and print the lea;
Skip and gambol, hop and bound,
Round the wild witch-hazel tree.

XXXVII

The beetle guards our holy ground,
He flies about the haunted place,
And if mortal there be found,
He hums in his ears and flaps his face;
The leaf-harp sounds our roundelay,
The owlet's eyes our lanterns be;
Thus we sing, and dance, and play,   630
Round the wild witch-hazel tree.

But, hark! from tower on tree-top high
The sentry-elf his call has made:
A streak is in the eastern sky,
Shapes of moonlight! flit and fade!
The hill-tops gleam in morning's spring,
The skylark shakes his dabbled wing,
The day-glimpse glimmers on the lawn,
The cock has crowed, and the Fays are gone.

1816?-1819?   1835

FITZ-GREENE HALLECK
1790-1867

The present estimate of Halleck as one of the minor poets of the nineteenth century shows the fickleness of literary fame; for he was one of the most popular poets of his day, and was by Poe placed among the foremost writers of American verse. His statue in bronze was erected in Central Park, New York, ten years after his death. Halleck was educated in the public schools of Guilford, Connecticut, his birthplace, was clerk and book-keeper there and removed to New York in 1811, where until 1848 he remained as a bookkeeper and accountant. He met Drake in 1813 and the friendship and collaboration of the two is one of the pleasing relationships in American literary biography. Drake's death was the occasion of one of Halleck's best poems, at the same time one of the best American elegies. Halleck's poems were published at various dates from 1819 to 1858, chief among them being the "Croaker" poems with Drake, 1819; *Fanny,* 1819; *Alnwick Castle,* 1827. He had a gift for manly, somewhat rhetorical poems, following the lead of Byron. He was especially fortunate in his occasional verse, for he was fortunate in being able to grasp vigorously the elements of a dramatic situation and phrase them in popular if not enduring lines.

Biography and criticism: J. G. Wilson, *Life and Letters of Halleck,* 1869; Chubb; S. M. Ward, "A Romantic Episode in the Life of the Poet, Fitz-Greene Halleck," *Bookm.* 47:499-502.

ON THE DEATH OF JOSEPH RODMAN DRAKE [1]

OF NEW YORK, SEPTEMBER, 1820

The good die first,
And they whose hearts are dry
    as summer dust,
Burn to the socket.
                    WORDSWORTH

Green be the turf above thee,
    Friend of my better days!
None knew thee but to love thee,
    Nor named thee but to praise.

Tears fell when thou wert dying,
    From eyes unused to weep,
And long where thou art lying,
    Will tears the cold turf steep.

When hearts, whose truth was proven,
    Like thine, are laid in earth,   10
There should a wreath be woven
    To tell the world their worth;

And I, who woke each morrow
    To clasp thy hand in mine,
Who shared thy joy and sorrow,
    Whose weal and woe were thine:

It should be mine to braid it
    Around thy faded brow,
But I've in vain essayed it,
    And feel I cannot now.   20

While memory bids me weep thee,
    Nor thoughts nor words are free,
The grief is fixed too deeply
    That mourns a man like thee.

1820

BURNS

TO A ROSE, BROUGHT FROM NEAR ALLOWAY
KIRK, [2] IN AYRSHIRE, IN THE AUTUMN OF
1822

Wild Rose of Alloway! my thanks;
    Thou 'mindst me of that autumn noon
When first we met upon "the banks
    And braes o' bonny Doon."

Like thine, beneath the thorn-tree's bough,
    My sunny hour was glad and brief,

[1] Drake died at the age of twenty-five.
[2] Alloway Kirk is the scene of Tam O'Shanter's adventure; near it are Burns's birthplace and the monument referred to later; and all are near the banks of the River Doon, familiar from Burns's song, "The Banks o' Doon."

We've crossed the winter sea, and thou
    Art withered—flower and leaf.

And will not thy death-doom be mine—
    The doom of all things wrought of clay—
And withered my life's leaf like thine,   11
    Wild rose of Alloway?

Not so his memory, for whose sake
    My bosom bore thee far and long,
His—who a humbler flower could make
    Immortal as his song, [3]

The memory of Burns—a name
    That calls, when brimmed her festal cup,
A nation's glory and her shame,
    In silent sadness up.   20

A nation's glory—be the rest
    Forgot—she's canonized his mind;
And it is joy to speak the best
    We may of human kind.

I've stood beside the cottage-bed
    Where the Bard-peasant first drew breath;
A straw-thatched roof above his head,
    A straw-wrought couch beneath.

And I have stood beside the pile,
    His monument—that tells to Heaven   30
The homage of earth's proudest isle
    To that Bard-peasant given!

Bid thy thoughts hover o'er that spot,
    Boy-minstrel, in thy dreaming hour;
And know, however low his lot,
    A Poet's pride and power:

The pride that lifted Burns from earth,
    The power that gave a child of song
Ascendency o'er rank and birth,
    The rich, the brave, the strong;   40

And if despondency weigh down
    Thy spirit's fluttering pinions then,
Despair—thy name is written on
    The roll of common men.

There have been loftier themes than his,
    And longer scrolls, and louder lyres,
And lays lit up with Poesy's
    Purer and holier fires:

Yet read the names that know not death;
    Few nobler ones than Burns are there;   50

[3] referring to Burns's "To a Mountain Daisy"

And few have won a greener wreath
  Than that which binds his hair.

His is that language of the heart,
  In which the answering heart would speak,
Thought, word, that bids the warm tear start,
  Or the smile light the cheek;

And his that music, to whose tone
  The common pulse of man keeps time,
In cot or castle's mirth or moan,
  In cold or sunny clime.   60

And who hath heard his song, nor knelt
  Before its spell with willing knee,
And listened, and believed, and felt
  The Poet's mastery

O'er the mind's sea, in calm and storm,
  O'er the heart's sunshine and its showers,
O'er Passion's moments bright and warm,
  O'er Reason's dark, cold hours;

On field's where brave men "die or do,"
  In halls where rings the banquet's mirth,   70
Where mourners weep, where lovers woo,
  From throne to cottage hearth?

What sweet tears dim the eye unshed,
  What wild vows falter on the tongue,
When "Scots wha hae wi' Wallace bled,"
  Or "Auld Lang Syne" is sung!

Pure hopes, that lift the soul above,
  Come with his Cotter's hymn of praise,
And dreams of youth, and truth, and love,
  With "Logan's" banks and braes.   80

And when he breathes his master-lay
  Of Alloway's witch-haunted wall,
All passions in our frames of clay
  Come thronging at his call.

Imagination's world of air,
  And our own world, its gloom and glee,
Wit, pathos, poetry, are there,
  And death's sublimity.

And Burns—though brief the race he ran,
  Though rough and dark the path he trod,   90
Lived—died—in form and soul a Man,
  The image of his God.

Through care and pain, and want, and woe,
  With wounds that only death could heal,
Tortures—the poor alone can know,
  The proud alone can feel;

He kept his honesty and truth,
  His independent tongue and pen,
And moved, in manhood as in youth,
  Pride of his fellow-men.   100

Strong sense, deep feeling, passions strong,
  A hate of tyrant and of knave,
A love of right, a scorn of wrong,
  Of coward and of slave;

A kind, true heart, a spirit high,
  That could not fear and would not bow,
Were written in his manly eye
  And on his manly brow.

Praise to the bard! his words are driven,
  Like flower-seeds by the far winds sown,
Where'er, beneath the sky of heaven,   111
  The birds of fame have flown.

Praise to the man! a nation stood
  Beside his coffin with wet eyes,—
Her brave, her beautiful, her good,
  As when a loved one dies.

And still, as on his funeral day,
  Men stand his cold earth-couch around,
With the mute homage that we pay
  To consecrated ground.   120

And consecrated ground it is,
  The last, the hallowed home of one
Who lives upon all memories,
  Though with the buried gone.

Such graves as his are pilgrim shrines,
  Shrines to no code nor creed confined—
The Delphian vales, [1] the Palestines,
  The Meccas of the mind.

Sages with wisdom's garland wreathed,
  Crowned kings, and mitered priests of power,
And warriors with their bright swords sheathed,
  The mightiest of the hour;   132

And lowlier names, whose humble home
  Is lit by fortune's dimmer star,
Are there—o'er wave and mountain come,
  From countries near and far;

Pilgrims whose wandering feet have pressed
  The Switzer's snow, the Arab's sand,
Or trod the piled leaves of the West,
  My own green forest-land.   140

[1] At Delphi in Greece was the oracle of the Pythian
  Apollo, the most famous shrine of the ancient
  world.

All ask the cottage of his birth,
  Gaze on the scenes he loved and sung,
And gather feelings not of earth
  His fields and streams among.

They linger by the Doon's low trees,
  And pastoral Nith, and wooded Ayr,
And round thy sepulchers, Dumfries!
  The poet's tomb is there.

But what to them the sculptor's art,
  His funeral columns, wreaths and urns?   150
Wear they not graven on the heart
  The name of Robert Burns?

1822   1827

MARCO BOZZARIS [1]

At midnight, in his guarded tent,
  The Turk was dreaming of the hour
When Greece, her knee in suppliance bent,
  Should tremble at his power:
In dreams, through camp and court, he bore
The trophies of a conqueror;
  In dreams his song of triumph heard;
Then wore his monarch's signet ring:
Then pressed that monarch's throne—a king;
As wild his thoughts, and gay of wing,   10
  As Eden's garden bird.

At midnight, in the forest shades,
  Bozzaris ranged his Suliote [2] band,
True as the steel of their tried blades,
  Heroes in heart and hand.
There had the Persian's thousands stood,
There had the glad earth drunk their blood
  On old Plataea's [3] day;
And now there breathed that haunted air
The sons of sires who conquered there,   20
With arm to strike, and soul to dare,
  As quick, as far as they.

An hour passed on—the Turk awoke;
  That bright dream was his last;
He woke—to hear his sentries shriek,
"To arms! they come! the Greek! the Greek!"
He woke—to die midst flame, and smoke,
And shout, and groan, and saber-stroke,
  And death shots falling thick and fast
As lightnings from the mountain cloud;   30
And heard, with voice as trumpet loud,
  Bozzaris cheer his band:

[1] a patriot of the Greek war for independence from
  the Turks, 1821-29
[2] The Suliotes, a Greco-Albanian tribe, driven from
  their own territory in Albania, took active part
  in the war against the Turks.
[3] At Plataea the Greeks overcame the Persians, 479 B.C.

"Strike—till the last armed foe expires;
Strike—for your altars and your fires;
Strike—for the green graves of your sires;
  God—and your native land!"

They fought—like brave men, long and well;
  They piled that ground with Moslem slain,
They conquered—but Bozzaris fell,
  Bleeding at every vein.   40
His few surviving comrades saw
His smile when rang their proud hurrah,
  And the red field was won;
Then saw in death his eyelids close
Calmly, as to a night's repose,
  Like flowers at set of sun.

Come to the bridal-chamber, Death!
  Come to the mother's, when she feels,
For the first time, her first-born's breath;
  Come when the blessed seals   50
That close the pestilence are broke, [4]
And crowded cities wail its stroke;
Come in consumption's ghastly form,
The earthquake shock, the ocean storm;
Come when the heart beats high and warm
  With banquet song, and dance, and wine;
And thou art terrible—the tear,
The groan, the knell, the pall, the bier;
And all we know, or dream, or fear
  Of agony are thine.   60

But to the hero, when his sword
  Has won the battle for the free,
Thy voice sounds like a prophet's word;
And in its hollow tones are heard
  The thanks of millions yet to be.
Come, when his task of fame is wrought—
Come, with her laurel-leaf, blood-bought—
  Come in her crowning hour—and then
Thy sunken eye's unearthly light
To him is welcome as the sight   70
  Of sky and stars to prisoned men;
Thy grasp is welcome as the hand
Of brother in a foreign land;
Thy summons welcome as the cry
That told the Indian isles were nigh
  To the world-seeking Genoese,
When the land wind, from woods of palm,
And orange groves, and fields of balm,
  Blew o'er the Haytian seas.

Bozzaris! with the storied brave   80
  Greece nurtured in her glory's time,
Rest thee—there is no prouder grave,
  Even in her own proud clime.
She wore no funeral-weeds for thee,

[4] apparently in allusion to the opening of the fourth
  seal, *Revelation*, vi, 1-8

Nor bade the dark hearse wave its plume
Like torn branch from death's leafless tree
In sorrow's pomp and pageantry,
　The heartless luxury of the tomb:
But she remembers thee as one
Long loved and for a season gone;　　　90
For thee her poet's lyre is wreathed,
Her marble wrought, her music breathed;
For thee she rings the birthday bells;
Of thee her babes' first lisping tells;
For thine her evening prayer is said
At palace couch and cottage bed;
Her soldier, closing with the foe,
Gives for thy sake a deadlier blow;
His plighted maiden, when she fears
For him the joy of her young years,　　100
Thinks of thy fate, and checks her tears:
　And she, the mother of thy boys,
Though in her eye and faded cheek
Is read the grief she will not speak,
　The memory of her buried joys,
And even she who gave thee birth,
Will, by their pilgrim-circled hearth,
　Talk of thy doom without a sigh:
For thou art Freedom's now, and Fame's;
One of the few, the immortal names,　　110
　That were not born to die.

　　　　　　　　　　　　　　1825

NATHANIEL PARKER WILLIS
1806-1867

Willis was born of staid New England ancestry.
His father was the founder of the first religious
newspaper in the world, the *Boston Recorder,* and
later established the *Youth's Companion.* Willis
graduated from Yale, 1827, established the *American Monthly Magazine,* in New York, in 1829, and
later merged it with the *Mirror,* to which he was
a frequent contributor. His published works include *Pencilings by the Way,* 1835; *A l'Abri, or the
Tent Pitched,* 1839; *Loiterings of Travel,* 1840;
Sacred Poems, 1843; *Poems of Passion,* 1843;
Lady Jane and Humorous Poems, 1844.

Willis belongs to that self-conscious period of
American mental and social development when the
resources of the country were being developed with
a speed that made some Americans obnoxiously
boastful. At the same time increasing intelligence
was showing other Americans their lack of cul-
tural background, and the absence of the fixed institutions that nourish solid intellectual and artistic
growth. Willis found these congenial conditions in
Europe, and all that he reported of European society was absorbed by Americans with almost pathetic
eagerness. His essays were popular. His poetry was
intimately known; it was varied in range, sometimes deeply religious, often vivacious, but usually
marked with the sentimentality and didacticism
characteristic of much poetry of his time.

Biography: H. A. Beers, *N. P. Willis* (AML),
1885.

UNSEEN SPIRITS

The shadows lay along Broadway—
　'T was near the twilight-tide—
And slowly there a lady fair
　Was walking in her pride.
Alone walked she; but viewlessly
　Walked spirits at her side.

Peace charmed the street beneath her feet,
　And Honor charmed the air;
And all astir looked kind on her,
　And called her good as fair；　　10
For all God ever gave to her
　She kept with chary care.

She kept with care her beauties rare
　From lovers warm and true;
For her heart was cold to all but gold,
　And the rich came not to woo—
But honored well are charms to sell
　If priests the selling do.

Now walking there was one more fair,—
　A slight girl, lily-pale;　　20
And she had unseen company
　To make the spirit quail:
'Twixt Want and Scorn she walked forlorn,
　And nothing could avail.

No mercy now can clear her brow
　For this world's peace to pray;
For, as love's wild prayer dissolved in air,
　Her woman's heart gave way!—　　28
But the sin forgiven by Christ in heaven
　By man is cursed alway!

　　　　　　　　　　　　　　1843

From PENCILINGS BY THE WAY
From LETTER LXX [1]
[A BREAKFAST WITH CHARLES LAMB]

Invited to breakfast with a gentleman in the
Temple [2] to meet Charles Lamb and his sister,
—"Elia, and Bridget Elia." I never in my life
had an invitation more to my taste. The essays
of Elia are certainly the most charming things
in the world, and it has been for the last ten
years my highest compliment to the literary
taste of a friend to present him with a copy.
Who has not smiled over the humorous description of Mrs. Battle? [3] Who that has read Elia

[1] *Pencilings by the Way* (1835) first appeared in the
　form of letters written for the *Mirror.* The essays
　relate Willis's first experiences of foreign society
　with a gusto that allows the reader at home to lose
　none of the deliciousness of the event to the writer.
[2] the lodgings and offices of barristers in London, in
　buildings occupying the site of the medieval es-
　tablishment of the Knights Templar.
[3] "Mrs. Battle's Opinions on Whist" is one of the
　Essays of Elia.

would not give more to see him than all the other authors of his time put together?

Our host was rather a character. I had brought a letter of introduction to him from Walter Savage Landor, the author of *Imaginary Conversations*, living at Florence, with a request that he would put me in a way of seeing one or two men about whom I had a curiosity, Lamb more particularly. I could not have been recommended to a better person. Mr. R. [1] is a gentleman who, everybody says, *should have been* an author, but who never wrote a book. He is a profound German scholar, has traveled much, is the intimate friend of Southey, Coleridge, and Lamb, has breakfasted with Goethe, traveled with Wordsworth through France and Italy, and spends part of every summer with him, and knows everything and everybody that is distinguished,—in short, is, in his bachelor's chambers in the Temple, the friendly nucleus of a great part of the talent of England.

I arrived a half-hour before Lamb, and had time to learn some of his peculiarities. He lives a little out of London, and is very much of an invalid. Some family circumstances have tended to depress him very much of late years, and unless excited by convivial intercourse, he scarce shows a trace of what he was. He was very much pleased with the American reprint of his Elia, though it contains several things which are not his—written so in his style, however, that it is scarce a wonder the editor should mistake them. If I remember right, they were *Valentine's Day*, the *Nuns of Caverswell*, and *Twelfth Night*. He is excessively given to mystifying his friends, and is never so delighted as when he has persuaded some one into the belief of one of his grave inventions. His amusing biographical sketch of Liston [2] was in this vein, and there was no doubt in anybody's mind that it was authentic, and written in perfectly good faith. Liston was highly enraged with it, and Lamb was delighted in proportion.

There was a rap at the door at last, and enter a gentleman in black small-clothes and gaiters, short and very slight in his person, his head set on his shoulders with a thoughtful forward bent, his hair just sprinkled with gray, a beautiful deep-set eye, aquiline nose, and a very indescribable mouth. Whether it expressed most humor or feeling, good-nature or a kind of whimsical peevishness, or twenty other things which passed over it by turns, I cannot in the least be certain.

His sister, whose literary reputation is associated very closely with her brother's, and who, as the original of "Bridget Elia," is a kind of object for literary affection, came in after him. She is a small, bent figure, evidently a victim to illness, and hears with difficulty. Her face has been, I should think, a fine and handsome one, and her bright gray eye is still full of intelligence and fire. They both seemed quite at home in our friend's chambers, and as there was to be no one else, we immediately drew round the breakfast-table. I had set a large arm-chair for Miss Lamb. "Don't take it, Mary," said Lamb, pulling it away from her very gravely: "it appears as if you were going to have a tooth drawn."

The conversation was very local. Our host and his guest had not met for some weeks, and they had a great deal to say of their mutual friends. Perhaps in this way, however, I saw more of the author; for his manner of speaking of them, and the quaint humor with which he complained of one, and spoke well of another, was so in the vein of his inimitable writings, that I could have fancied myself listening to an audible composition of a new Elia. Nothing could be more delightful than the kindness and affection between the brother and the sister, though Lamb was continually taking advantage of her deafness to mystify her with the most singular gravity upon every topic that was started. "Poor Mary!" said he, "she hears all of an epigram but the point."—"What are you saying of me, Charles?" she asked. "Mr. Willis," said he, raising his voice, "admires *your Confessions of a Drunkard very much;* and I was saying that it was no merit of yours, that you understood the subject." We had been speaking of this admirable essay (which is his own) half an hour before.

The conversation turned upon literature after a while; and our host, the Templar, could not express himself strongly enough in admiration of Webster's speeches, which he said were exciting the greatest attention among the politicians and lawyers of England. Lamb said, "I don't know much of American authors. Mary, there, devours Cooper's novels with a ravenous appetite, with which I have no sympathy. The only American book I ever read twice was the *Journal* of Edward Woolman, a Quaker preacher and tailor, whose character is one of the finest I ever met with. He tells a story or two [3] about negro slaves, that brought the tears into my eyes. I can read no prose now, though Hazlitt [4] sometimes, to be sure—but then, Hazlitt is

---

[1] Henry Crabb Robinson, 1775-1867
[2] John Liston, 1776-1846; Lamb's nonsensically grave article certainly did not long interrupt the friendship of the two men.

[3] Lamb's memory was perhaps playing him false. The stories are not in Woolman's *Journal*.
[4] William Hazlitt, English essayist and critic, 1778-1830

worth all modern prose-writers put together."

Mr. R. spoke of buying a book of Lamb's a few days before; and I mentioned my having bought a copy of *Elia* the last day I was in America, to send as a parting gift to one of the most lovely and talented women in our country.

"What did you give for it?" said Lamb.

"About seven and sixpence."

"Permit me to pay you that," said he, and with the utmost earnestness he counted out the money upon the table.

"I never yet wrote anything that would sell," he continued. "I am the publisher's ruin. My last poem won't sell a copy. Have you seen it, Mr. Willis?"

I had not.

"It's only eighteen pence, and I'll give you sixpence toward it"; and he described to me where I should find it sticking up in a shop-window in the Strand.

Lamb ate nothing, and complained in a querulous tone of the veal-pie. There was a kind of potted fish (of which I forget the name at this moment) which he had expected our friend would procure for him. He inquired whether there was not a morsel left perhaps in the bottom of the last pot. Mr. R. was not sure.

"Send and see," said Lamb; "and if the pot has been cleaned, bring me the cover. I think the sight of it would do me good."

The cover was brought, upon which there was a picture of the fish. Lamb kissed it with a reproachful look at his friend, and then left the table, and began to wander round the room with a broken, uncertain step, as if he almost forgot to put one leg before the other. His sister rose after a while, and commenced walking up and down very much in the same manner on the opposite side of the table; and in the course of half an hour they took their leave.

To any one who loves the writings of Charles Lamb with but half my own enthusiasm, even these little particulars of an hour passed in his company will have an interest. To him who does not, they will seem dull and idle. Wreck as he certainly is, and must be, however, of what he was, I would rather have seen him for that single hour, than the hundred and one sights of London put together.

1835

JOHN HOWARD PAYNE
1792-1852

To Payne belongs the honor of writing a song that is by far the most widely-known piece of American verse. He was of a good New York City family, was sent to Union College but gave up college for the stage. He appeared in New York in 1809, and in London four years later, remaining abroad as a player and playwright for nineteen years. His song, *Home, Sweet Home,* was sung in an opera, *Clari, the Maid of Milan,* at Covent Garden, in 1823. Payne produced, adapted, or re-wrote some sixty plays and operas, among which *Brutus,* 1819, *Therese,* adapted from the French, 1821, and *Charles the Second,* 1824, were particularly well received. He retired from the stage in 1832, and from 1841 to 1845, and again in 1851-1852 was American consul at Tunis, where he died. His remains were brought back to America amid much ceremony in 1883 and interred in Washington.

Although Payne was reasonably successful in his work as actor and dramatist he is today virtually a poet of one lyric. This owes its popularity to its appeal to sentiment, and to the music, an Italian melody that Payne had heard in Italy, afterwards adapted by an English composer.

HOME, SWEET HOME!

Mid pleasures and palaces though we may roam,
Be it ever so humble, there's no place like
    home;
A charm from the sky seems to hallow us there,
Which, seek through the world, is ne'er met
    with elsewhere.
    Home, Home, sweet, sweet Home!
There's no place like Home! there's no place
    like Home!

An exile from home, splendor dazzles in vain;
Oh, give me my lowly thatched cottage again!
The birds singing gayly, that came at my call,—
Give me them,—and the peace of mind, dearer
    than all!   10
    Home! Home! sweet, sweet Home!
There's no place like Home! there's no place
    like Home!

How sweet 't is to sit 'neath a fond father's
    smile,
And the cares of a mother to soothe and be-
    guile!
Let others delight mid new pleasures to roam,
But give me, oh, give me, the pleasures of
    home!
    Home! Home! sweet, sweet Home!
There's no place like Home! there's no place
    like Home!

To thee I'll return, overburdened with care;
The heart's dearest solace will smile on me
    there;   20
No more from that cottage again will I roam;

Be it ever so humble, there's no place like home.
  Home! Home! sweet, sweet Home!
There's no place like Home! there's no place
    like Home!
1823?   1823

GEORGE POPE MORRIS
1802-1864

Though born in Philadelphia, Morris lived in
New York from boyhood. In 1823 he founded
with Samuel Woodworth the *New York Mirror*
and conducted it successfully for twenty years,
after which he engaged in a number of other journalistic enterprises. His most successful sustained
work was *Brier Cliff*, a drama of the Revolution.

Morris represents a small group of journalistic
song writers, of whom his partner, Woodward,
author of "The Old Oaken Bucket," was another
member, who essayed to do in America what
Thomas Moore was doing for the popular song of
England during the same time.

WOODMAN, SPARE THAT TREE!

Woodman, spare that tree!
  Touch not a single bough!
In youth it sheltered me,
  And I'll protect it now.
'T was my forefather's hand
  That placed it near his cot;
There, woodman, let it stand,
  Thy axe shall harm it not.

That old familiar tree,
  Whose glory and renown   10
Are spread o'er land and sea,—
  And wouldst thou hew it down?
Woodman, forbear thy stroke!
  Cut not its earth-bound ties;
Oh, spare that aged oak
  Now towering to the skies!

When but an idle boy,
  I sought its grateful shade;
In all their gushing joy
  Here, too, my sisters played.   20
My mother kissed me here;
  My father pressed my hand—
Forgive this foolish tear,
  But let that old oak stand!

My heart-strings round thee cling,
  Close as thy bark, old friend!
Here shall the wild-bird sing,
  And still thy branches bend.
Old tree! the storm still brave!
  And, woodman, leave the spot;   30
While I've a hand to save,
  Thy axe shall harm it not.

FRANCIS SCOTT KEY 1779-1843

Key was not a professional writer, and except
for the one stirring poem which may outlast any
other memorial of our "Second War of Independence" he would not be remembered as a poet. He
was born in Maryland. After graduating at St.
John's College, Annapolis, Key studied law and
practiced in Frederick, and in Washington, where he
became district attorney, and where he died. A
volume of his poems was published in 1857.

THE STAR-SPANGLED BANNER [1]

O say, can you see, by the dawn's early light,
  What so proudly we hailed at the twilight's
    last gleaming?
Whose broad stripes and bright stars, through
    the perilous fight,
  O'er the ramparts we watched were so gal-
    lantly streaming!
And the rockets' red glare, the bombs bursting
    in air,
Gave proof through the night that our flag was
    still there;
  O say, does that star-spangled banner yet
    wave
  O'er the land of the free, and the home of the
    brave?

On the shore dimly seen through the mists of
    the deep,
  Where the foe's haughty host in dread silence
    reposes,   10
What is that which the breeze, o'er the towering
    steep,
  As it fitfully blows, now conceals, now dis-
    closes?
Now it catches the gleam of the morning's first
    beam,
In full glory reflected now shines on the
    stream;
  'T is the star-spangled banner; O long may
    it wave
  O'er the land of the free, and the home of the
    brave.

And where is that band who so vauntingly
    swore
That the havoc of war and the battle's con-
    fusion
A home and a country should leave us no
    more?
  Their blood has washed out their foul foot-
    steps' pollution.   20

[1] During the War of 1812 a British fleet unsuccessfully
    bombarded Fort McHenry, a defense of Baltimore.
    Key, aboard one of the British vessels as a pris-
    oner of war, watched the battle from that point
    of vantage and wrote the song immediately after.

No refuge could save the hireling and slave
From the terror of flight, or the gloom of the
          grave;
     And the star-spangled banner in triumph
          doth wave
     O'er the land of the free, and the home of the
          brave.

O! thus be it ever, when freemen shall stand
     Between their loved homes and the war's
          desolation!
Blest with victory and peace, may the heaven-
          rescued land
     Praise the power that hath made and pre-
          served us a nation.
Then conquer we must, for our cause it is just,
And this be our motto—*"In God is our trust."*
     And the star-spangled banner in triumph
          shall wave   31
     O'er the land of the free, and the home of the
          brave.
1814

SOUTHERN LYRICS

Of WILDE, PINKNEY, and DICKSON it may be
said that they represent in their poetry the literary
tastes and activities of southern gentlemen, who
often made literature their avocation. In their
poetry is the graciousness of fine breeding mingled
with strains of melody that seem to come out of
the courtly manners of the seventeenth and the
eighteenth centuries, made vital by an appreciation
of nature that is more modern.

RICHARD HENRY WILDE
1789-1872

Wilde was born in Ireland. Coming with his
parents to Augusta, Georgia, as a child, he studied
and practiced law, became attorney-general for the
state, served for three terms in Congress, and in
1844 was appointed professor of law in the University of Louisiana. He resided abroad from 1835
to 1840, and should be remembered as influential in
the discovery and restoration of a fresco portrait
of Dante in the Bargello at Florence. He was
greatly interested in the Italian poet Tasso, and in
1842 published his *Conjectures and Researches Concerning Torquinato Tasso.*

"MY LIFE IS LIKE THE SUMMER
ROSE"

My life is like the summer rose,
     That opens to the morning sky,
But, ere the shades of evening close,
     Is scattered on the ground—to die!
Yet on the rose's humble bed
The sweetest dews of night are shed,

As if she wept the waste to see—
But none shall weep a tear for me!

My life is like the autumn leaf
     That trembles in the moon's pale ray: 10
Its hold is frail—its date is brief,
     Restless—and soon to pass away!
Yet, ere that leaf shall fall and fade,
The parent tree will mourn its shade,
The winds bewail the leafless tree,—
But none shall breathe a sigh for me!

My life is like the prints, which feet
     Have left on Tampa's desert strand;
Soon as the rising tide shall beat,
     All trace will vanish from the sand;   20
Yet, as if grieving to efface
All vestige of the human race,
On that lone shore loud moans the sea,—
But none, alas! shall mourn for me!
                                   c. 1815

TO THE MOCKING-BIRD

Winged mimic of the woods! thou motley fool!
Who shall thy gay buffoonery describe?
Thine ever-ready notes of ridicule
Pursue thy fellows still with jest and gibe:
Wit, sophist, songster, Yorick [1] of thy tribe,
Thou sportive satirist of Nature's school,
To thee the palm of scoffing we ascribe,
Arch-mocker and mad Abbot of Misrule! [2]
For such thou art by day—but all night long
Thou pourest a soft, sweet, pensive, solemn
          strain,   10
As if thou didst in this thy moonlight song
Like to the melancholy Jacques [3] complain,
Musing on falsehood, folly, vice, and wrong,
And sighing for thy motley coat again.

EDWARD COATE PINKNEY
1802-1828

Pinkney was born in London, England, son of
William Pinkney, United States agent and minister
to Great Britain. He was in the United States
navy, 1816-1824, and later became a lawyer and a
journalist. His best-known work is *Rodolph and
Other Poems,* 1825.

A HEALTH

I fill this cup to one made up
     Of loveliness alone,
A woman, of her gentle sex

[1] Jester; see *Hamlet*, V, i, 195.
[2] the chief character in the medieval English Christmas
     revels
[3] a character in Shakespeare's *As You Like It*

The seeming paragon;
To whom the better elements
And kindly stars have given
A form so fair, that, like the air,
'T is less of earth than heaven.

Her every tone is music's own,
Like those of morning birds,   10
And something more than melody
Dwells ever in her words;
The coinage of her heart are they,
And from her lips each flows
As one may see the burdened bee
Forth issue from the rose.

Affections are as thoughts to her,
The measures of her hours;
Her feelings have the fragrancy,
The freshness of young flowers;   20
And lovely passions, changing oft,
So fill her, she appears
The image of themselves by turns,—
The idol of past years!

Of her bright face one glance will trace
A picture on the brain,
And of her voice in echoing hearts
A sound must long remain;
But memory, such as mine of her,
So very much endears,   30
When death is nigh my latest sigh
Will not be life's, but hers.

I fill this cup to one made up
Of loveliness alone,
A woman, of her gentle sex
The seeming paragon—
Her health! and would on earth there stood
Some more of such a frame,
That life might be all poetry,   39
And weariness a name.

                                      1825

SAMUEL HENRY DICKSON
1798-1872

Dickson was born in Charleston, South Carolina. After graduating at Yale in 1814 and receiving his degree in medicine at the University of Pennsylvania in 1819, Dr. Dickson was professor of medicine successively at the medical school at Charleston, 1824, at the University of the City of New York, 1847, and at Jefferson College, Philadelphia, 1858. He was the author of several medical works.

"I SIGH FOR THE LAND OF THE CYPRESS AND PINE"

I sigh for the land of the cypress and pine,
Where the jessamine blooms, and the gay woodbine;
Where the moss droops low from the green oak tree,—
Oh, that sun-bright land is the land for me!

The snowy flower of the orange there
Sheds its sweet fragrance through the air;
And the Indian rose delights to twine
Its branches with the laughing vine.

There the deer leaps light through the open glade,
Or hides him far in the forest shade,   10
When the woods resound in the dewy morn
With the clang of the merry hunter's horn.

There the humming-bird, of rainbow plume,
Hangs over the scarlet creeper's bloom;
While 'midst the leaves his varying dyes
Sparkle like half-seen fairy eyes.

There the echoes ring through the livelong day
With the mock-bird's changeful roundelay;
And at night, when the scene is calm and still,
With the moan of the plaintive whip-poor-will.   20

Oh! I sigh for the land of the cypress and pine,
Of the laurel, the rose, and the gay woodbine,
Where the long, gray moss decks the rugged oak tree,—
That sun-bright land is the land for me.

WILLIAM GILMORE SIMMS
1806-1870

Simms, leading novelist and miscellaneous writer of the South before the Civil War, was born and died in Charleston, South Carolina. After a meager schooling, he studied law, was admitted to the bar, but soon turned to journalism and literature. He lived for a short time in Massachusetts, but supported the South during the Civil War, and suffered as a victim of fire and pillage through Sherman's "march to the sea." His writings include *Lyrical and Other Poems*, 1827; *Atalantis*, poem, 1832; *The Yemassee*, 1835; *Areytos, or Songs and Ballads of the South*, 1846. He produced poetry, fiction, biography, and drama under more than eighty titles, besides a mass of journalistic work. His narrative is headlong and stirring, inclining toward the melodramatic. Some of his novels have been dramatized. His strong affection for the South—especially for its customs, history, and legends—is manifest in all his work; and for his treatment of the Indian characters he describes, he has been called the Cooper of the South; some critics hold him to be a truer painter of Indian life than Cooper himself, and also more perfect in his women characters. *The Yemassee,* which is considered the best of his novels, describes his native state in 1815 when it was still inhabited by the great tribe of the Yemassee Indians.

Criticism: J. Erskine, *Leading American Novelists,* 1910; W. P. Trent, *W. G. Simms* (AML), 1892; see also W. C. Bryant (LJ).

THE SWAMP FOX [1]

We follow where the Swamp Fox guides,
  His friends and merry men are we;
And when the troop of Tarleton [2] rides,
  We burrow in the cypress tree.
The turfy hammock [3] is our bed,
  Our home is in the red deer's den,
Our roof, the tree-top overhead,
  For we are wild and hunted men.

We fly by day and shun its light,
  But, prompt to strike the sudden blow, 10
We mount and start with early night,
  And through the forest track our foe.
And soon he hears our chargers leap,
  The flashing saber blinds his eyes,
And ere he drives away his sleep,
  And rushes from his camp, he dies.

Free bridle-bit, good gallant steed,
  That will not ask a kind caress
To swim the Santee at our need,
  When on his heels the foemen press— 20
The true heart and the ready hand,
  The spirit stubborn to be free,
The twisted bore, the smiting brand—
  And we are Marion's men, you see.

Now light the fire and cook the meal,
  The last perhaps that we shall taste;
I hear the Swamp Fox round us steal,
  And that's a sign we move in haste.
He whistles to the scouts, and hark!
  You hear his order calm and low. 30
Come, wave your torch across the dark,
  And let us see the boys that go.

[1] The nickname given to General Francis Marion, the noted South Carolina partisan, or independent leader, of the Revolutionary War; with but a handful of men (he seldom had over seventy) he performed valiant and valuable service. He was said to be as courteous and honest as he was brave. See Fiske, *The American Revolution,* ii, 183. Cf. Bryant's "The Song of Marion's Men," p. 255.
[2] a noted British cavalry officer
[3] hummock, a low elevation especially in swampy ground

We may not see their forms again,
  God help 'em, should they find the strife!
For they are strong and fearless men,
  And make no coward terms for life;
They'll fight as long as Marion bids,
  And when he speaks the word to shy,
Then, not till then, they turn their steeds, 39
  Through thickening shade and swamp to fly.

Now stir the fire and lie at ease—
  The scouts are gone, and on the brush
I see the Colonel bend his knees,
  To take his slumbers too. But hush!
He's praying, comrades; 'tis not strange;
  The man that's fighting day by day
May well, when night comes, take a change,
  And down upon his knees to pray.

Break up that hoe-cake, boys, and hand
  The sly and silent jug that's there 50
I love not it should idly stand
  When Marion's men have need of cheer.
'Tis seldom that our luck affords
  A stuff like this we just have quaffed,
And dry potatoes on our boards
  May always call for such a draught.

Now pile the brush and roll the log;
  Hard pillow, but a soldier's head
That's half the time in brake and bog
  Must never think of softer bed. 60
The owl is hooting to the night,
  The cooter [4] crawling o'er the bank,
And in that pond the flashing light
  Tells where the alligator sank.

What! 'tis the signal! start so soon,
  And through the Santee swamp so deep,
Without the aid of friendly moon,
  And we, Heaven help us! half asleep!
But courage, comrades! Marion leads,
  The Swamp Fox takes us out tonight; 70
So clear your swords and spur your steeds,
  There's goodly chance, I think, of fight.

We follow where the Swamp Fox guides,
  We leave the swamp and cypress tree,
Our spurs are in our coursers' sides,
  And ready for the strife are we.
The Tory camp is now in sight,
  And there he cowers within his den;
He hears our shouts, he dreads the fight, 79
  He fears, and flies from Marion's men.

1832

[4] terrapin

From THE YEMASSEE [1]
CHAPTER XXV

The pain of death is nothing. To the chief,
The forest warrior, it is good to die!
To die as he has lived, battling and hoarse,
Shouting a song of triumph. But to live
Under such doom as this, were far beyond
Even his stoic, cold philosophy.

It was a gloomy amphitheater in the deep forests to which the assembled multitude bore the unfortunate Occonestoga. The whole scene was unique in that solemn grandeur, that somber hue, that deep spiritual repose, in which the human imagination delights to invest the region which has been rendered remarkable for the deed of punishment or crime. A small swamp or morass hung upon one side of the wood, from the rank bosom of which, in numberless millions, the flickering firefly perpetually darted upwards, giving a brilliance and animation to the spot, which at that moment no assemblage of light or life could possibly enliven. The ancient oak, a bearded Druid, was there to contribute to the due solemnity of all associations—the green but gloomy cedar, the ghostly cypress, and here and there, the overgrown pine,—all rose up in their primitive strength, and with an undergrowth around them of shrub and flower that scarcely at any time, in that sheltered and congenial habitation, had found it necessary to shrink from winter. In the center of the area thus invested rose a high and venerable mound, the tumulus of many preceding ages, from the washed sides of which might now and then be seen protruding the bleached bones of some ancient warrior or sage. A circle of trees at a little distance hedged it in, made secure and sacred by the performance there of many of their religious rites and offices, —themselves, as they bore the broad arrow of the Yemassee, being free from all danger of overthrow or desecration by Indian hands.

Amid the confused cries of the multitude, they bore the captive to the foot of the tumulus, and bound him backward, half reclining upon a tree. An hundred warriors stood around, armed according to the manner of the nation, each with a tomahawk and knife and bow. They stood up as for battle, but spectators simply, and took no part in a proceeding which belonged entirely to the priesthood. In a wider and denser circle gathered hundreds more—not the warriors, but the people—the old, the young, the women and the children, all fiercely excited, and anxious to see a ceremony so awfully exciting to an Indian imagination; involving as it did not only the perpetual loss of human caste and national consideration, but the eternal doom, the degradation, the denial of and the exile from their simple forest heaven. Interspersed with this latter crowd, seemingly at regular intervals, and with an allotted labor assigned them, came a number of old women, not unmeet representatives, individually, for either of the weird sisters of the Scottish thane,

So withered and so wild in their attire— [2]

and regarding their cries and actions, of whom we may safely affirm that they looked like anything but inhabitants of earth! In their hands they bore, each of them, a flaming torch of the rich and gummy pine; and these they waved over the heads of the multitude in a thousand various evolutions, accompanying each movement with a fearful cry, which at regular periods was chorused by the assembled mass. A bugle, a native instrument of sound, five feet or more in length hollowed out from the commonest timber—the cracks and breaks of which were carefully sealed up with the resinous gum oozing from their burning torches, and which to this day, borrowed from the natives, our negroes employ on the Southern waters with a peculiar compass and variety of note—was carried by one of the party, and gave forth at intervals timed with much regularity, a long protracted, single blast, adding greatly to the wild and picturesque character of the spectacle. At the articulation of these sounds, the circles continued to contract, though slowly; until at length but a brief space lay between the armed warriors, the crowd, and the unhappy victim.

The night grew dark of a sudden, and the sky was obscured by one of the brief tempests that usually usher in the summer, and mark the transition, in the South, of one season to another. A wild gust rushed along the wood. The leaves were whirled over the heads of the

[1] The hero of the story is Sanutee, one of the most revered and most beloved chiefs of the tribe. His wisdom has foreseen the final victory of the whites and the doom of the Indians. Stung into action by the fact that his son Occonestoga has been given the strong drink of the English, he raises a rebellion intended to exterminate the settlers. A few of the other chiefs, who have been tempted by gifts to side with the English, suffer the punishment of having the yellow arrow, the symbol of their common ancestry, cut and burned from the arm and breast, and of being sent forth exiles from the tribe forever—not only on earth, but in the hereafter. Occonestoga, the son of Sanutee, has also, while intoxicated, taken sides with the English. He has been captured and is to suffer the doom of exile. Matiwan, his mother, has believed in him to the last, but she is loyal to her husband Sanutee, the accuser.

[2] *Macbeth*, I, iii, 40

assemblage, and the trees bent downwards until they cracked and groaned again beneath the wind. A feeling of natural superstition crossed the minds of the multitude, as the hurricane, though common enough in that region, passed hurriedly along; and a spontaneous and universal voice of chanted prayer rose from the multitude, in their own wild and emphatic language, to the evil deity whose presence they beheld in its progress:

Thy wing, Opitchi-Manneyto, [1]
It o'erthrows the tall trees—
Thy breath, Opitchi-Manneyto,
Makes the waters tremble—
Thou art in the hurricane,
When the wigwam tumbles—
Thou art in the arrow-fire,
When the pine is shivered—
But upon the Yemassee,
Be thy coming gentle—
Are they not thy well-beloved?
Bring they not a slave to thee?
Look! the slave is bound for thee,
'Tis the Yemassee that brings him.
Pass, Opitchi-Manneyto—
Pass, black spirit, pass from us—
Be thy passage gentle.

And as the uncouth strain rose at the conclusion into a diapason of unanimous and contending voices, of old and young, male and female, the brief summer tempest had gone by. A shout of self-gratulation, joined with warm acknowledgments, testified the popular sense and confidence in that especial Providence, which even the most barbarous nations claim as forever working in their behalf.

At this moment, surrounded by the chiefs, and preceded by the great prophet or high-priest, Enoree-Mattee, came Sanutee, the well-beloved of the Yemassee, to preside over the destinies of his son. There was a due and becoming solemnity, but nothing of the peculiar feelings of the father, visible in his countenance. Blocks of wood were placed around as seats for the chiefs; but Sanutee and the prophet threw themselves, with more of imposing veneration in the proceeding, upon the edge of the tumulus, just where an overcharged spot, bulging out with the crowding bones of its inmates, had formed an elevation answering the purpose of couch or seat. They sat directly looking upon the prisoner; who reclined, bound securely upon his back to a decapitated tree, at a little distance before them. A signal having been given, the women ceased their clamors; and approaching him they waved their torches

[1] Manneyto is spirit, and Opitchi-Manneyto the evil spirit.

so closely above his head as to make all his features distinctly visible to the now watchful and silent multitude. He bore the examination with stern, unmoved features, which the sculptor in brass or marble might have been glad to transfer to his statue in the block. While the torches waved, one of the women now cried aloud, in a barbarous chant, above him:—

Is not this a Yemassee?
Wherefore is he bound thus—
Wherefore with the broad arrow
On his right arm growing?
Wherefore is he bound thus?
Is not this a Yemassee?

A second woman now approached him, waving her torch in like manner, seeming closely to inspect his features, and actually passing her fingers over the emblem upon his shoulder, as if to ascertain more certainly the truth of the image. Having done this, she turned about to the crowd, and in the same barbarous sort of strain with the preceding, replied as follows:—

It is not the Yemassee,
But a dog that runs away.
From his right arm take the arrow,
He is not the Yemassee.

As these words were uttered, the crowd of women and children around cried out for the execution of the judgment thus given; and once again flamed the torches wildly, and the shoutings were general among the multitude. When they had subsided, a huge Indian came forward and sternly confronted the prisoner. This man was Malatchie, the executioner; and he looked the horrid trade which he professed. His garments were stained and smeared with blood, and covered with scalps, which, connected together by slight strings, formed a loose robe over his shoulders. In one hand he carried a torch, in the other a knife. He came forward, under the instructions of Enoree-Mattee, the prophet, to claim the slave of Opitchi-Manneyto,—that is, in our language, the slave of hell. This he did in the following strain:—

'Tis Opitchi-Manneyto
In Malatchie's ear that cries:—
"This is not the Yemassee,—
And the woman's word is true,—
He's a dog that should be mine:
I have hunted for him long.
From his master he had run,
With the stranger made his home;
Now I have him, he is mine:
Hear Opitchi-Manneyto."

And as the besmeared and malignant executioner howled his fierce demand in the very ears of his victim, he hurled the knife which he carried, upwards with such dexterity into the air, that it rested point downward and sticking fast, on its descent, into the tree and just above the head of the doomed Occonestoga. With his hand, the next instant, he laid a resolute gripe upon the shoulder of the victim, as if to confirm and strengthen his claim by actual possession; while at the same time, with a sort of malignant pleasure, he thrust his besmeared and distorted visage close into the face of his prisoner. Writhing against the ligaments which bound him fast, Occonestoga strove to turn his head aside from the disgusting and obtrusive presence; and the desperation of his effort, but that he had been too carefully secured, might have resulted in the release of some of his limbs; for the breast heaved and labored, and every muscle of his arms and legs was wrought, by his severe action, into so many ropes,—hard, full, and indicative of prodigious strength.

There was one person in that crowd who sympathized with the victim. This was Hiwassee, the maiden in whose ears he had uttered a word, which in her thoughtless scream and subsequent declaration of the event, when she had identified him, had been the occasion of his captivity. Something of self-reproach for her share in his misfortune, and an old feeling of regard for Occonestoga,—who had once been a favorite with the young of both sexes among his people, —was at work in her bosom; and turning to Echotee, her newly accepted lover, as soon as the demand of Malatchie had been heard, she prayed him to resist the demand.

In such cases, all that a warrior had to do was simply to join issue upon the claim, and the popular will then determined the question. Echotee could not resist an application so put to him, and by one who had just listened to a prayer of his own so all-important to his own happiness; and being himself a noble youth— one who had been a rival of the captive in his better days,—a feeling of generosity combined with the request of Hiwassee, and he boldly leaped forward. Seizing the knife of Malatchie, which stuck in the tree, he drew it forth and threw it upon the ground; thus removing the sign of property which the executioner had put up in behalf of the evil deity.

"Occonestoga is the brave of the Yemassee," exclaimed the young Echotee, while the eyes of the captive looked what his lips could not have said. "Occonestoga is a brave of Yemassee: he is no dog of Malatchie. Wherefore is the cord upon the limbs of a free warrior? Is not Occonestoga a free warrior of Yemassee?

The eyes of Echotee have looked upon a warrior like Occonestoga when he took many scalps. Did not Occonestoga lead the Yemassee against the Savannahs? The eyes of Echotee saw him slay the red-eyed Suwannee, the great chief of the Savannahs. Did not Occonestoga go on the war-path with our young braves against the Edistoes,—the brown foxes that came out of the swamp? The eyes of Echotee beheld him. Occonestoga is a brave, and a hunter of Yemassee: he is not the dog of Malatchie. He knows not fear. He hath an arrow with wings, and the panther he runs down in the chase. His tread is the tread of a sly serpent, that comes so that he hears him not upon the track of the red deer feeding down in the valley. Echotee knows the warrior; Echotee knows the hunter; he knows Occonestoga,—but he knows no dog of Opitchi-Manneyto."

"He hath drunk of the poison drink of the pale-faces; his feet are gone from the good path of the Yemassee; he would sell his people to the English for a painted bird. He is the slave of Opitchi-Manneyto," cried Malatchie in reply. Echotee was not satisfied to yield the point so soon, and he responded accordingly.

"It is true; the feet of the young warrior have gone away from the good paths of the Yemassee; but I see not the weakness of the chief when my eye looks back upon the great deeds of the warrior. I see nothing but the shrinking body of Suwannee under the knee— under the knife of the Yemassee. I hear nothing but the war-whoop of the Yemassee, when he broke through the camp of the brown foxes, and scalped them where they skulked in the swamp. I see this Yemassee strike the foe and take the scalp, and I know Occonestoga,— Occonestoga, the son of the well-beloved, the great chief of the Yemassee."

"It is good; Occonestoga has thanks for Echotee; Echotee is a brave warrior!" murmured the captive to his champion, in tones of melancholy acknowledgment. The current of public feeling began to set somewhat in behalf of the victim, and an occasional whisper to that effect might be heard here and there among the multitude. Even Malatchie himself looked for a moment as if he thought it not improbable that he might be defrauded of his prey; and while a free shout from many attested the compliment which all were willing to pay to Echotee for his magnanimous defense of one who had once been a rival—and not always successful—in the general estimation, the executioner turned to the prophet and to Sanutee, as if doubtful whether or not to proceed farther in his claim. But all doubt was soon quieted, as the stern father rose before the assembly. Every sound was stilled in expectation of his words on this so momentous an occasion to himself. They waited not long. The old man had tasked all the energies of the patriot, not less than of the stoic; and having once determined upon the necessity of the sacrifice, he had no hesitating fears or scruples palsying his determination. He seemed not to regard the imploring glance of his son, seen and felt by all besides in the assembly, but with a voice entirely unaffected by the circumstances of his position, he spoke forth the doom of the victim in confirmation with that originally expressed.

"Echotee has spoken like a brave warrior with a tongue of truth and a soul that has birth with the sun. But he speaks out of his own heart, and does not speak to the heart of the traitor. The Yemassee will all say for Echotee, but who can say for Occonestoga when Sanutee himself is silent? Does the Yemassee speak with a double tongue? Did not the Yemassee promise Occonestoga to Opitchi-Manneyto with the other chiefs? Where are they? They are gone into the swamp, where the sun shines not, and the eyes of Opitchi-Manneyto are upon them. He knows them for his slaves. The arrow is gone from their shoulders and the Yemassee knows them no longer. Shall the dog escape who led the way to the English—who brought the poison drink to the chiefs, which made them dogs to the English and slaves to Opitchi-Manneyto? Shall he escape the doom the Yemassee hath put upon them? Sanutee speaks the voice of the Manneyto. Occonestoga is a dog, who would sell his father —who would make our women to carry water for the palefaces. He is not the son of Sanutee—Sanutee knows him no more. Look, Yemassees,—the Well-beloved has spoken!"

He paused, and turning away, sank down silently upon the little bank on which he had before rested; while Malatchie, without further opposition,—for the renunciation of his own son, by one so highly esteemed as Sanutee, was conclusive against the youth,—advanced to execute the terrible judgment upon his victim.

"O father, chief, Sanutee the Well-beloved!" was the cry that now, for the first time, burst convulsively from the lips of the prisoner; "hear me, father,—Occonestoga will go on the warpath with thee and with the Yemassee against the Edisto, against the Spaniard; hear, Sanutee,—he will go with thee against the English." But the old man bent not, yielded not,

and the crowd gathered nigher in the intensity of their interest.

"Wilt thou have no ear, Sanutee? It is Occonestoga, it is the son of Matiwan, that speaks to thee." Sanutee's head sank as the reference was made to Matiwan, but he showed no other sign of emotion. He moved not, he spoke not; and bitterly and hopelessly the youth exclaimed:—

"Oh! thou art colder than the stone house of the adder, and deafer than his ears. Father, Sanutee, wherefore wilt thou lose me, even as the tree its leaf, when the storm smites it in summer? Save me, my father."

And his head sank in despair as he beheld the unchanging look of stern resolve with which the unbending sire regarded him. For a moment he was unmanned; until a loud shout of derision from the crowd, as they beheld the show of his weakness, came to the support of his pride. The Indian shrinks from humiliation, where he would not shrink from death; and as the shout reached his ears, he shouted back his defiance, raised his head loftily in air, and with the most perfect composure commenced singing his song of death,—the song of many victories.

"Wherefore sings he his death-song?" was the cry from many voices: "he is not to die!"

"Thou art the slave of Opitchi-Manneyto," cried Malatchie to the captive; "thou shalt sing no lie of thy victories in the ear of Yemassee. The slave of Opitchie-Manneyto has no triumph"; and the words of the song were effectually drowned, if not silenced in the tremendous clamor which they raised about him.

It was then that Malatchie claimed his victim. The doom had been already given, but the ceremony of expatriation and outlawry was yet to follow, and under the direction of the prophet, the various castes and classes of the nation prepared to take a final leave of one who could no longer be known among them. First of all came a band of young marriageable women, who, wheeling in a circle three times about him, sang together a wild apostrophe containing a bitter farewell, which nothing in our language could perfectly embody:—

Go; thou hast no wife in Yemassee—thou hast given no lodge to the daughter of Yemassee—thou hast slain no meat for thy children. Thou hast no name—the women of Yemassee know thee no more. They know thee no more.

And the final sentence was reverberated from the entire assembly:—

They know thee no more—they know thee no more.

Then came a number of the ancient men, the patriarchs of the nation, who surrounded him in circular mazes three several times, singing as they did so a hymn of like import:—

Go: thou sittest not in the council of Yemassee—thou shalt not speak wisdom to the boy that comes. Thou hast no name in Yemassee—the fathers of Yemassee, they know thee no more.

And again the whole assembly cried out, as with one voice:—

They know thee no more—they know thee no more.

These were followed by the young warriors, his old associates, who now in a solemn band approached him to go through a like performance. His eyes were shut as they came, his blood was chilled in his heart, and the articulated farewell of their wild chant failed seemingly to reach his ear. Nothing but the last sentence he heard:—

> Thou that wast a brother,
> Thou art nothing now—
> The young warriors of Yemassee,
> They know thee no more.

And the crowd cried with them:—

They know thee no more.

"Is no hatchet sharp for Occonestoga?" moaned forth the suffering savage.

But his trials were only then begun. Enoree-Mattee now approached him with the words with which, as the representative of the good Manneyto, he renounced him—with which he denied him access to the Indian heaven, and left him a slave and an outcast, a miserable wanderer amid the shadows and the swamps, and liable to all the dooms and terrors which come with the service of Opitchi-Manneyto.

> Thou wast a child of Manneyto—

sung the high priest in a solemn chant, and with a deep-toned voice that thrilled strangely amid the silence of the scene.

> Thou wast a child of Manneyto—
> He gave thee arrows and an eye;
> Thou wast the strong son of Manneyto—
> He gave thee the feathers and a wing;
> Thou wast a young brave of Manneyto—
> He gave thee scalps and a war-song:
> But he knows thee no more—he knows thee no
>   more.

And the clustering multitude again gave back the last line in wild chorus. The prophet continued his chant:—

> That Opitchi-Manneyto!
> He commands thee for his slave—
> And the Yemassee must hear him,

> Hear, and give thee for his slave:
> They will take from thee the arrow,
> The broad arrow of thy people;
> Thou shalt see no blessed valley,
> Where the plum-groves always bloom;
> Thou shalt hear no song of valor
> From the ancient Yemassee;
> Father, mother, name, and people,
> Thou shalt lose with that broad arrow.
> Thou art lost to the Manneyto—
> He knows thee no more, he knows thee no more.

The despair of hell was in the face of the victim, and he howled forth in a cry of agony—that for a moment silenced the wild chorus of the crowd around—the terrible consciousness in his mind of that privation which the doom entailed upon him. Every feature was convulsed with emotion; and the terrors of Opitchi-Manneyto's dominion seemed already in strong exercise upon the muscles of his heart, when Sanutee, the father, silently approached him, and with a pause of a few moments, stood gazing upon the son from whom he was to be separated eternally—whom not even the uniting, the restoring, hand of death could possibly restore to him. And he, his once noble son,—the pride of his heart, the gleam of his hope, the triumphant warrior, who was even to increase his own glory, and transmit the endearing title of Well-beloved, which the Yemassee had given him, to a succeeding generation—he was to be lost forever! These promises were all blasted; and the father was now present to yield him up eternally—to deny him—to forfeit him, in fearful penalty, to the nation whose genius he had wronged, and whose rights he had violated. The old man stood for a moment,—rather, we may suppose, for the recovery of his resolution, than with any desire for the contemplation of the pitiable form before him. The pride of the youth came back to him—the pride of the strong mind in its desolation—as his eye caught the inflexible gaze of his unswerving father; and he exclaimed bitterly and loud:—

"Wherefore art thou come? Thou hast been my foe, not my father! Away—I would not behold thee!" and he closed his eyes after the speech, as if to relieve himself from a disgusting presence.

"Thou hast said well, Occonestoga; Sanutee is thy foe; he is not thy father. To say this in thy ears has he come. Look on him, Occonestoga—look up and hear thy doom. The young and the old of the Yemassee, the warrior and the chief—they have all denied thee—all given thee up to Opitchi-Manneyto! Occonestoga is no name for the Yemassee. The Yemassee gives it to his dog. The prophet of Manneyto has forgotten thee; thou art unknown to those who were thy people. And I, thy father—with this speech, I yield thee to Opitchi-Manneyto. Sanutee is no longer thy father—thy father knows thee no more."

And once more came to the ears of the victim melancholy chorus of the multitude:

He knows thee no more, he knows thee no more.

Sanutee turned quickly away as he had spoken; and as if he suffered more than he was willing to show, the old man rapidly hastened to the little mound where he had been previously sitting, his eyes averted from the further spectacle. Occonestoga, goaded to madness by these several incidents, shrieked forth the bitterest execrations, until Enoree-Mattee, preceding Malatchie, again approached. Having given some directions in an under-tone to the latter, he retired, leaving the executioner alone with his victim. Malatchie then, while all was silence in the crowd,—a thick silence, in which even respiration seemed to be suspended,—proceeded to his duty; and lifting the feet of Occonestoga carefully from the ground, he placed a log under them; then addressing him, as he again bared his knife, which he stuck in the tree above his head, he sung:—

I take from thee the earth of Yemassee—
I take from thee the water of Yemassee—
I take from thee the arrow of Yemassee—
Thou art no longer a Yemassee—
The Yemassee knows thee no more.

"The Yemassee knows thee no more," cried the multitude; and their universal shout was deafening upon the ear. Occonestoga said no word now; he could offer no resistance to the unnerving hands of Malatchie, who now bared the arm more completely of its covering. But his limbs were convulsed with the spasms of that dreadful terror of the future which was racking and raging in every pulse of his heart. He had full faith in the superstitions of his people. His terrors acknowledged the full horrors of their doom. A despairing agony, which no language could describe, had possession of his soul. Meanwhile the silence of all indicated the general anxiety; and Malatchie prepared to seize the knife and perform the operation, when a confused murmur arose from the crowd around: the mass gave way and parted; and rushing wildly into the area came Matiwan, his mother—the long black hair streaming—the features, an astonishing likeness to his own, convulsed like his; and her action that of one reckless of all things in the way of the forward progress she was making to the person of her child. She cried aloud as she

came, with a voice that rang like a sudden death-bell through the ring:—

"Would you keep the mother from her boy, and he be lost to her for ever? Shall she have no parting with the young brave she bore in her bosom? Away, keep me not back—I will look upon, I will love him. He shall have the blessing of Matiwan, though the Yemassee and the Manneyto curse."

The victim heard; and a momentary renovation of mental life, perhaps a renovation of hope, spoke out in the simple exclamation which fell from his lips:—

"Oh Matiwan—Oh mother!"

She rushed towards the spot where she heard his appeal; and thrusting the executioner aside, threw her arms desperately about his neck.

"Touch him not, Matiwan," was the general cry from the crowd. "Touch him not, Matiwan: Manneyto knows him no more."

"But Matiwan knows him; the mother knows her child, though the Manneyto denies him. O boy—O boy, boy, boy!" And she sobbed like an infant on his neck.

"Thou art come, Matiwan, thou art come; but wherefore? To curse like the father—to curse like the Manneyto?" mournfully said the captive.

"No, no, no! Not to curse—not to curse! When did mother curse the child she bore? Not to curse but to bless thee. To bless thee and forgive."

"Tear her away," cried the prophet; "let Opitchi-Manneyto have his slave."

"Tear her away, Malatchie," cried the crowd, now impatient for the execution. Malatchie approached.

"Not yet—not yet," appealed the woman. "Shall not the mother say farewell to the child she shall see no more?" and she waved Malatchie back, and in the next instant drew hastily from the drapery of her dress a small hatchet, which she had there carefully concealed.

"What wouldst thou do, Matiwan?" asked Occonestoga, as his eye caught the glare of the weapon.

"Save thee, my boy—save thee for thy mother, Occonestoga—save thee for the happy valley."

"Wouldst thou slay me, mother? Wouldst strike the heart of thy son?" he asked, with a something of reluctance to receive death from the hands of a parent.

"I strike thee but to save thee, my son; since they cannot take the totem from thee after the life is gone. Turn away from me thy head; let me not look upon thine eyes as I strike, lest my hands grow weak and tremble. Turn thine eyes away—I will not lose thee."

His eyes closed; and the fatal instrument, lifted above her head, was now visible in the sight of all. The executioner rushed forward to interpose, but he came too late. The tomahawk was driven deep into the skull, and but a single sentence from his lips preceded the final insensibility of the victim.

"It is good, Matiwan, it is good; thou hast saved me—the death is in my heart." And back he sank as he spoke; while a shriek of mingled joy and horror from the lips of the mother announced the success of her effort to defeat the doom, the most dreadful in the imagination of the Yemassee.

"He is not lost—he is not lost! They may not take the child from his mother. They may not keep him from the valley of Manneyto. He is free—he is free!" And she fell back in a deep swoon into the arms of Sanutee, who by this time had approached. She had defrauded Opitchi-Manneyto of his victim, for they may not remove the badge of the nation from any but the living victim.

1835

EDGAR ALLAN POE 1809-1849

As the years recede and with them sinks many a figure that once seemed of prime importance, the interest in Poe looms ever greater. Poe's mother was of English birth; his father was from a distinguished Maryland family. Both were actors playing in Boston when their son was born. They died in 1811 and Poe was adopted by John Allan of Richmond, Virginia. He had good educational opportunities in Richmond, in England, and at the University of Virginia. There he ran into debt so heavily that Mr. Allan withdrew him from the institution, whereupon Poe enlisted in the United States Army. After two years' service he was given a cadetship at West Point but was dismissed a few months later. After 1831 he lived by journalism. He became editor of *The Southern Library Messenger*, 1835, and from then until 1845 was editor or associate editor of *The Gentleman's Magazine, Graham's Magazine,* and *The Broadway Journal*, to which in succession he contributed his tales, poems, and criticisms. His death, in Baltimore, was under distressing circumstances. Important titles in Poe's works are *Tamerlane and Other Poems*, 1827; *Tales of the Grotesque and Arabesque*, 1839; *The Raven and Other Poems*, 1845.

The reading of American verse in chronological order from the beginning strongly impresses the fact that Poe is the first American poet whose work needs no apology. In melody, imagery, and the haunting spell laid on the emotions, Poe's verse more than makes up for its comparative lack of substance. We may use it as a standard by which we may measure our lyric poetry.

Poe was the first American poet to be received with enthusiasm by Europeans, who even today give him and Whitman the honor of being the greatest poetical geniuses that have come from the New World. But the grounds for the European acceptance of Poe and Whitman are very different. Whitman is bizarrely American; Poe belongs to no era or culture. His incentive is to express the emotion that all men feel in the presence of beauty. He has a wizardry of words that no analysis can explain; yet the melody of lines and individual words, and the association between the mere sound of the words and the images they convey, are some of its elements. In his prose, the use of the elements of sound is much the same; though in the detective story and the pseudo-scientific tale he drops the poetic coloring for an intellectual ingenuity. He is the virtual creator of the detective story as practiced by Conan Doyle and a host of others.

Poe's literary criticism, though sometimes hasty and ill-timed, was stimulating, and ranked among the best of its day in this country.

Works: 10 vols. ed. E. C. Stedman and G. E. Woodberry, 1914; 17 vols. ed. J. A. Harrison, 1902.

Biography and criticism: J. Macy (BB), 1907; G. E. Woodberry, *Life of E. A. Poe, Personal and Literary, with his Chief Correspondence*, 2 vols. 1909; also (AML); H. Allen, *Israfel*, 2 vols. 1926; J. W. Krutch, *Edgar Allan Poe: a Study in Genius*, 1926; C. A. Smith (HKA); More (Shel. 1); Stedman (Poets); Chubb; M. S. Yewdale, "Edgar Allan Poe, Pathologically," *No. Am.* 212:686-96; B. Matthews, "Poe's Cosmopolitan Fame," *Cent.* 81:271-5; J. Macy, *Atlan.* 102:835-43; L. Melville, "The Centenary of Edgar Allan Poe," *19th Cent.* 65:140-52.

TO HELEN [1]

Helen, thy beauty is to me
  Like those Nicaean [2] barks of yore,
That gently, o'er a perfumed sea,
  The weary, wayworn wanderer bore
    To his own native shore. [3]

On desperate seas long wont to roam,
  Thy hyacinth hair, thy classic face,
Thy Naiad airs, have brought me home
  To the glory that was Greece
    And the grandeur that was Rome. [4]   10

[1] The poem was written, Poe says, "to the first purely ideal love of my soul—to Helen Stannard . . ." See Harrison's *Life and Letters of Poe*, ii, 294.
[2] The word, as here used, is not in ancient geography.
[3] Nothing but an intelligent reading of Poe aloud can bring out the music of such lines.
[4] It is concerning an equally famous expression in Keats that Kipling in "Wireless" says "Remember that in all the millions permitted there are no more than five—five little lines of which one can say: 'These are the Vision. The rest is only poetry.'"

Lo! in yon brilliant window-niche
  How statue-like I see thee stand,
The agate lamp within thy hand!
  Ah, Psyche, [1] from the regions which
  Are Holy Land!

1823?   1831

ISRAFEL

And the angel Israfel, whose heart-strings are a
lute, and who has the sweetest voice of all God's
creatures.—KORAN. [2]

In Heaven a spirit doth dwell
  Whose heart-strings are a lute;
None sing so wildly well
As the angel Israfel,
And the giddy stars (so legends tell),
Ceasing their hymns [3] attend the spell
  Of his voice, all mute.

Tottering above
  In her highest noon,
  The enamoured moon   10
Blushes with love,
  While, to listen, the red levin
  (With the rapid Pleiads, even,
  Which were seven)
Pauses in Heaven.

And they say (the starry choir [3]
  And the other listening things)
That Israfeli's fire
Is owing to that lyre
  By which he sits and sings,   20
The trembling living wire
  Of those unusual strings.

But the skies that angel trod, [4]
  Where deep thoughts are a duty,
Where Love's a grown-up God,
Where the Houri glances are
  Imbued with all the beauty
Which we worship in a star.

Therefore thou art not wrong,
  Israfeli, who despisest   30
An unimpassioned song;
To thee the laurels belong,
  Best bard, because the wisest:
Merrily live, and long!

[1] the Greek word for soul, often, as here, personified
[2] The motto comes, through Moore's *Lalla Rookh*, from
Sale's *Introduction to the Koran.* It is inexact,
for Poe added "whose heartstrings are a lute."
[3] According to an ancient theory, the fixed stars were
set in a crystalline sphere. The planets were also
thus set, each in its sphere. These spheres, moving on one another, made music that might be
heard by celestial beings.
[4] "But that angel trod skies where," etc.

The ecstasies above
  With thy burning measures suit:
Thy grief, thy joy, thy hate, thy love,
  With the fervor of thy lute:
  Well may the stars be mute!

Yes, Heaven is thine; but this   40
  Is a world of sweets and sours;
  Our flowers are merely—flowers,
And the shadow of thy perfect bliss
  Is the sunshine of ours.

If I could dwell
  Where Israfel
  Hath dwelt, and he where I,
He might not sing so wildly well
  A mortal melody,   49
While a bolder note than this might swell
  From my lyre within the sky.

                                         1831

THE CITY IN THE SEA

Lo! Death has reared himself a throne
In a strange city lying alone
Far down within the dim West,
Where the good and the bad and the worst and
      the best
Have gone to their eternal rest.
There shrines and palaces and towers
(Time-eaten towers that tremble not)
Resemble nothing that is ours.
Around, by lifting winds forgot,
Resignedly beneath the sky   10
The melancholy waters lie.

No rays from the holy heaven come down
On the long night-time of that town;
But light from out the lurid sea
Streams up the turrets silently,
Gleams up the pinnacles far and free:
Up domes, up spires, up kingly halls,
Up fanes, up Babylon-like walls,
Up shadowy long-forgotten bowers
Of sculptured ivy and stone flowers,   20
Up many and many a marvelous shrine
Whose wreathed friezes intertwine
The viol, the violet, and the vine.

Resignedly beneath the sky
The melancholy waters lie.
So blend the turrets and shadows there
That all seem pendulous in air,
While from a proud tower in the town
Death looks gigantically down.

There open fanes and gaping graves   30
Yawn level with the luminous waves;

But not the riches there that lie
In each idol's diamond eye,—
Not the gayly-jeweled dead,
Tempt the waters from their bed;
For no ripples curl, alas,
Along that wilderness of glass;
No swellings tell that winds may be
Upon some far-off happier sea;
No heavings hint that winds have been   40
On seas less hideously serene!

But lo, a stir is in the air!
The wave—there is a movement there!
As if the towers had thrust aside,
In slightly sinking, the dull tide;
As if their tops had feebly given
A void within the filmy Heaven!
The waves have now a redder glow,
The hours are breathing faint and low;
And when, amid no earthly moans,   50
Down, down that town shall settle hence,
Hell, rising from a thousand thrones,
Shall do it reverence.

                                                    1831

THE SLEEPER

At midnight, in the month of June,
I stand beneath the mystic moon.
An opiate vapor, dewy, dim,
Exhales from out her golden rim,
And, softly dripping, drop by drop,
Upon the quiet mountain-top,
Steals drowsily and musically
Into the universal valley.
The rosemary nods upon the grave;
The lily lolls upon the wave;   10
Wrapping the fog about its breast,
The ruin molders into rest;
Looking like Lethe, see! the lake
A conscious slumber seems to take,
And would not, for the world, awake.
All beauty sleeps!—and lo! where lies
Irene, with her destinies!

O lady bright! can it be right,
This window open to the night?
The wanton airs, from the tree-top,   20
Laughingly through the lattice drop;
The bodiless airs, a wizard rout,
Flit through thy chamber in and out,
And wave the curtain canopy
So fitfully, so fearfully,
Above the closed and fringed lid
'Neath which thy slumb'ring soul lies hid,
That, o'er the floor and down the wall,
Like ghosts the shadows rise and fall.

O lady dear, hast thou no fear?   30
Why and what art thou dreaming here?
Sure thou art come o'er far-off seas,
A wonder to these garden trees!
Strange is thy pallor: strange thy dress:
Strange, above all, thy length of tress,
And this all solemn silentness!

The lady sleeps. Oh, may her sleep,
Which is enduring, so be deep!
Heaven have her in its sacred keep!
This chamber changed for one more holy,
This bed for one more melancholy,   41
I pray to God that she may lie
Forever with unopened eye,
While the pale sheeted ghosts go by.

My love, she sleeps. Oh, may her sleep,
As it is lasting, so be deep!
Soft may the worms about her creep!
Far in the forest, dim and old,
For her may some tall vault unfold:
Some vault that oft hath flung its black   50
And winged panels fluttering back,
Triumphant, o'er the crested palls
Of her grand family funerals:
Some sepulcher, remote, alone,
Against whose portal she hath thrown,
In childhood many an idle stone:
Some tomb from out whose sounding door
She ne'er shall force an echo more,
Thrilling to think, poor child of sin,   59
It was the dead who groaned within!
1831, 1845   *1831, 1845*

THE COLISEUM [1]

Type of the antique Rome! Rich reliquary
Of lofty contemplation left to Time
By buried centuries of pomp and power!
At length—at length—after so many days
Of weary pilgrimage and burning thirst,
(Thirst for the springs of lore that in thee
      lie)
I kneel, an altered and an humble man,
Amid thy shadows, and so drink within
My very soul thy grandeur, gloom, and glory.

Vastness, and Age, and Memories of Eld!   10
Silence, and Desolation, and dim Night!
I feel ye now, I feel ye in your strength,
O spells more sure than e'er Judaean king

[1] Poe never visited Rome. The poem may have been
suggested by Byron's well-known lines:
    "While stands the Coliseum, Rome shall stand;
    When falls the Coliseum, Rome shall fall";
                Childe Harold's Pilgrimage, iv, 145.

Taught in the gardens of Gethsemane!
O charms more potent than the rapt Chaldee [1]
Ever drew down from out the quiet stars!

Here, where a hero fell, a column falls;
Here, where the mimic eagle glared in gold,
A midnight vigil holds the swarthy bat;
Here, where the dames of Rome their gilded
    hair   20
Waved to the wind, now wave the reed and
    thistle;
Here, where on golden throne the monarch
    lolled,
Glides, specter-like, unto his marble home,
Lit by the wan light of the horned moon,
The swift and silent lizard of the stones.

But stay! these walls, these ivy-clad arcades,
These moldering plinths, these sad and black-
    ened shafts,
These vague entablatures, this crumbling frieze,
These shattered cornices, this wreck, this ruin,
These stones—alas! these gray stones—are they
    all,   30
All of the famed and the colossal left
By the corrosive Hours to Fate and me?

"Not all"—the Echoes answer me—"not all!
Prophetic sounds and loud, arise forever
From us, and from all Ruin, unto the wise,
As melody from Memnon [2] to the Sun.
We rule the hearts of mightiest men—we rule
With a despotic sway all giant minds.
We are not impotent, we pallid stones:
Not all our power is gone, not all our fame,   40
Not all the magic of our high renown,
Not all the wonder that encircles us,
Not all the mysteries that in us lie,
Not all the memories that hang upon
And cling around about us as a garment,
Clothing us in a robe of more than glory."
1833   1833

TO ONE IN PARADISE [3]

Thou wast all that to me, love,
  For which my soul did pine:
A green isle in the sea, love,
  A fountain and a shrine
All wreathed with fairy fruits and flowers,
  And all the flowers were mine.

[1] The Chaldeans were famous as astrologers.
[2] A colossal statue near Thebes, in Egypt, supposed to be
    that of Memnon, a solar hero-divinity, was said
    to give forth a musical note when struck by the
    rays of the rising sun.
[3] from Poe's tale, "The Assignation"

Ah, dream too bright to last!
  Ah, starry Hope, that didst arise
But to be overcast!
  A voice from out the Future cries,   10
"On! on!"—but o'er the Past
  (Dim gulf!) my spirit hovering lies
Mute, motionless, aghast.

For, alas! alas! with me
  The light of Life is o'er!
No more—no more—no more—
  (Such language holds the solemn sea
  To the sands upon the shore)
Shall bloom the thunder-blasted tree,
  Or the stricken eagle sore.   20

And all my days are trances,
  And all my nightly dreams
Are where thy gray eye glances,
  And where thy footstep gleams —
In what ethereal dances,
  By what eternal streams.
                        1834, 1845

TO FRANCES S. OSGOOD [4]

Thou wouldst be loved?—then let thy heart
  From its present pathway part not:
Being everything which now thou art,
  Be nothing which thou art not.
So with the world thy gentle ways,
  Thy grace, thy more than beauty,
Shall be an endless theme of praise,
  And love—a simple duty.
1835, 1845   1835, 1845

THE CONQUEROR WORM [5]

Lo! 't is a gala night
  Within the lonesome latter years.
An angel throng, bewinged, bedight
  In veils, and drowned in tears,
Sit in a theater to see
  A play of hopes and fears,
While the orchestra breathes fitfully
  The music of the spheres.

Mimes, in the form of God on high,
  Mutter and mumble low,   10
And hither and thither fly;
  Mere puppets they, who come and go
At bidding of vast formless things
  That shift the scenery to and fro,
Flapping from out their condor wings
  Invisible Woe.

[4] Mrs. Osgood belonged to Poe's literary circle.
[5] from Poe's tale, "Ligeia"

That motley drama—oh, be sure
    It shall not be forgot!
With its Phantom chased for evermore
    By a crowd that seize it not,   20
Through a circle that ever returneth in
    To the self-same spot;
And much of Madness, and more of Sin,
    And Horror the soul of the plot.

But see amid the mimic rout
    A crawling shape intrude:
A blood-red thing that writhes from out
    The scenic solitude!
It writhes—it writhes!—with mortal pangs
    The mimes become its food,   30
And seraphs sob at vermin fangs
    In human gore imbued.

Out—out are the lights—out all!
    And over each quivering form
The curtain, a funeral pall,
    Comes down with the rush of a storm,
While the angels, all pallid and wan,
    Uprising, unveiling, affirm
That the play is the tragedy, "Man,"   39
    And its hero, the Conqueror Worm.

                                        1843

THE RAVEN [1]

Once upon a midnight dreary, while I pon-
    dered, weak and weary,
Over many a quaint and curious volume of
    forgotten lore,—
While I nodded, nearly napping, suddenly there
    came a tapping,
As of some one gently rapping, rapping at my
    chamber door.
" 'T is some visitor," I muttered, "tapping at
    my chamber door:
    Only this and nothing more."

[1] "In 'The Philosophy of Composition,' Poe gives an account of the manner in which he constructed 'The Raven,' saying that he did it as he would work out a mathematical problem, by reasoning beforehand upon the nature of poetry, determining that beauty should be the essence of a poem, that sadness is the tone of the highest manifestation of beauty, that the refrain is the most effective of artistic devices, and that the refrain should be composed of sonorous and protractible sounds. The account may be taken for what it is worth. The present editor is inclined to regard it merely as part of a defense which Poe had been moved to make against an insinuation that in 'The Raven' he had imitated the repetitions of phrases in Coleridge's 'Ancient Mariner.' . . . At any rate, against his peculiar explanation of the composition of 'The Raven' should be set a sentence from his own preface to the 1845 edition of his poems: 'With me poetry has been not a purpose, but a passion, and the passions should be held in reverence.' " *Poems and Tales of Edgar Allan Poe,* edited by Alphonso G. Newcomer, *The Lake English Classics.*

Ah, distinctly I remember it was in the bleak
    December,
And each separate dying ember wrought its
    ghost upon the floor.
Eagerly I wished the morrow;—vainly I had
    sought to borrow
From my books surcease of sorrow—sorrow for
    the lost Lenore,   10
For the rare and radiant maiden whom the
    angels name Lenore:
    Nameless here for evermore.

And the silken sad uncertain rustling of each
    purple curtain
Thrilled me—filled me with fantastic terrors
    never felt before;
So that now, to still the beating of my heart,
    I stood repeating
" 'T is some visitor entreating entrance at my
    chamber door,
Some late visitor entreating entrance at my
    chamber door:
    This it is and nothing more."

Presently my soul grew stronger; hesitating
    then no longer,
"Sir," said I, "or Madam, truly your forgive-
    ness I implore;   20
But the fact is I was napping, and so gently
    you came rapping,
And so faintly you came tapping, tapping at my
    chamber door,
That I scarce was sure I heard you"—here I
    opened wide the door:—
    Darkness there and nothing more.

Deep into that darkness peering, long I stood
    there wondering, fearing,
Doubting, dreaming dreams no mortals ever
    dared to dream before;
But the silence was unbroken, and the stillness
    gave no token,
And the only word there spoken was the whis-
    pered word, "Lenore?"
This I whispered, and an echo murmured back
    the word, "Lenore!"
    Merely this and nothing more.   30

Back into the chamber turning, all my soul
    within me burning,
Soon again I heard a tapping somewhat louder
    than before.
"Surely," said I, "surely that is something at
    my window lattice;
Let me see, then, what thereat is, and this
    mystery explore;

Let my heart be still a moment and this mystery explore:
'T is the wind and nothing more."

Open here I flung the shutter, when, with many
a flirt and flutter,
In there stepped a stately Raven of the saintly
days of yore.
Not the least obeisance made he; not a minute
stopped or stayed he;
But, with mien of lord or lady, perched above
my chamber door,   40
Perched upon a bust of Pallas just above my
chamber door:
Perched, and sat, and nothing more.

Then this ebony bird beguiling my sad fancy
into smiling
By the grave and stern decorum of the counte-
nance it wore,—
"Though thy crest be shorn and shaven, thou,"
I said, "art sure no craven,
Ghastly grim and ancient Raven wandering
from the Nightly shore:
Tell me what thy lordly name is on the Night's
Plutonian [1] shore!"
Quoth the Raven, "Nevermore."

Much I marveled this ungainly fowl to hear discourse so plainly,
Though its answer little meaning—little rele-
vancy bore;   50
For we cannot help agreeing that no living
human being
Ever yet was blessed with seeing bird above his
chamber door,
Bird or beast upon the sculptured bust above
his chamber door,
With such name as "Nevermore."

But the Raven, sitting lonely on the placid bust,
spoke only
That one word, as if his soul in that one word
he did outpour.
Nothing further then he uttered, not a feather
then he fluttered,
Till I scarcely more than muttered,—"Other
friends have flown before;
On the morrow *he* will leave me, as my Hopes
have flown before."
Then the bird said, "Nevermore."   60

Startled at the stillness broken by reply so
aptly spoken,
"Doubtless," said I, "what it utters is its only
stock and store,

[1] Pluto, in the Roman mythology, was ruler of the dead.

Caught from some unhappy master whom unmerciful Disaster
Followed fast and followed faster till his songs
one burden bore:
Till the dirges of his Hope that melancholy
burden bore
Of 'Never—nevermore.' "

But the Raven still beguiling all my fancy into
smiling,
Straight I wheeled a cushioned seat in front of
bird and bust and door;
Then, upon the velvet sinking, I betook myself
to linking
Fancy unto fancy, thinking, what this ominous
bird of yore,   70
What this grim, ungainly, ghastly, gaunt, and
ominous bird of yore
Meant in croaking "Nevermore."

This I sat engaged in guessing, but no syllable
expressing
To the fowl whose fiery eyes now burned into
my bosom's core;
This and more I sat divining, with my head at
ease reclining
On the cushion's velvet lining that the lamp-
light gloated o'er,
But whose velvet violet lining with the lamp-
light gloating o'er
She shall press, ah, nevermore!

Then, methought, the air grew denser, perfumed
from an unseen censer
Swung by seraphim whose foot-falls tinkled on
the tufted floor.   80
"Wretch," I cried, "thy God hath lent thee—
by these angels he hath sent thee
Respite—respite and nepenthe [2] from thy memories of Lenore!
Quaff, oh quaff this kind nepenthe, and forget
this lost Lenore!"
Quoth the Raven, "Nevermore."

"Prophet!" said I, "thing of evil! prophet still,
if bird or devil!
Whether Tempter sent, or whether tempest
tossed thee here ashore,
Desolate yet all undaunted, on this desert land
enchanted—
On this home by Horror haunted—tell me truly,
I implore:
Is there—*is* there balm in Gilead? [3] tell me—
tell me, I implore!"
Quoth the Raven, "Nevermore."   90

[2] a draft producing forgetfulness of pain
[3] a region in eastern Palestine where a balm was produced; *Jeremiah* viii, 22

"Prophet!" said I, "thing of evil—prophet still,
    if bird or devil!
By that Heaven that bends above us, by that
    God we both adore,
Tell this soul with sorrow laden if, within the
    distant Aidenn, [1]
It shall clasp a sainted maiden whom the angels
    name Lenore:
Clasp a rare and radiant maiden whom the
    angels name Lenore!"
    Quoth the Raven, "Nevermore."

"Be that word our sign of parting, bird or
    fiend!" I shrieked, upstarting:
"Get thee back into the tempest and the Night's
    Plutonian shore!
Leave no black plume as a token of that lie
    thy soul hath spoken!
Leave my loneliness unbroken! quit the bust
    above my door! 100
Take thy beak from out my heart, and take
    thy form from off my door!"
    Quoth the Raven, "Nevermore."

And the Raven, never flitting, still is sitting,
    still is sitting
On the pallid bust of Pallas just above my
    chamber door;
And his eyes have all the seeming of a demon's
    that is dreaming,
And the lamp-light o'er him streaming throws
    his shadow on the floor:
And my soul from out that shadow that lies
    floating on the floor
    Shall be lifted—nevermore!

                1845

ULALUME [2]

The skies they were ashen and sober;
    The leaves they were crisped and sere,
    The leaves they were withering and sere;
It was night in the lonesome October
    Of my most immemorial year;
It was hard by the dim lake of Auber,
    In the misty mid region of Weir:
It was down by the dank tarn of Auber,
    In the ghoul-haunted woodland of Weir.

Here once, through an alley Titanic 10
    Of cypress, I roamed with my Soul—
    Of cypress, with Psyche, my Soul.
These were days when my heart was volcanic
    As the scoriac rivers that roll,
    As the lavas that restlessly roll
Their sulphurous currents down Yaanek
    In the ultimate climes of the pole,
That groan as they roll down Mount Yaanek
    In the realms of the boreal pole.

Our talk had been serious and sober, 20
    But our thoughts they were palsied and
    sere,
    Our memories were treacherous and sere,
For we knew not the month was October,
    And we marked not the night of the year,
    (Ah, night of all nights in the year!)
We noted not the dim lake of Auber
    (Though once we had journeyed down
    here),
Remembered not the dank tarn of Auber,
    Nor the ghoul-haunted woodland of Weir.

And now, as the night was senescent 30
    And star-dials pointed to morn,
    As the star-dials hinted of morn,
At the end of our path a liquescent
    And nebulous luster was born,
Out of which a miraculous crescent
    Arose with a duplicate horn,
Astarte's [3] bediamonded crescent
    Distinct with its duplicate horn.

And I said—"She is warmer than Dian:
    She rolls through an ether of sighs, 40
    She revels in a region of sighs:
She has seen that the tears are not dry on
    These cheeks, where the worm never dies,
And has come past the stars of the Lion [4]
    To point us the path to the skies,
    To the Lethean peace of the skies:
Come up, in despite of the Lion,
    To shine on us with her bright eyes:
Come up through the lair of the Lion,
    With love in her luminous eyes." 50

[1] from Arabic *adn*, Eden, Paradise
[2] "The appeal of Poe's poetry is to the sentiment of Beauty—the one appeal which, according to Poe's theory, is the final justification of any poem. Language is made to yield its utmost of melody. From words, even from letters, one might say—for Poe actually fabricated words whose sounds would suit his purpose—effects were wrested such as had never been wrested before." . . . "This fantasy ['Ulalume'] is perhaps the supreme test of one's power to enjoy the strange music and imagery of Poe's verse without demanding any intellectual basis for the enjoyment. It is about as idle to search for a meaning in 'Ulalume' as it would be to search in an atlas for the geographical names, and criticism will most safely keep silence." *Poems and Tales of Edgar Allan Poe*, edited by Alphonso G. Newcomer, *The Lake English Classics*. Perhaps, however, as one reader suggests, this poem portrays a slight rising of hope in a gloomy soul, the gloom coming back when the soul sinks again to its normal level. If so, it may have some definite biographical significance.
[3] Astarte, the Greek form of the Hebrew Ashtoreth, moon-goddess of the Phoenicians, corresponding to Diana (Dian) of the Greeks
[4] the constellation Leo

But Psyche, uplifting her finger,
 Said—"Sadly this star I mistrust,
 Her pallor I strangely mistrust:
Oh, hasten!—oh, let us not linger!
 Oh, fly!—let us fly!—for we must."
In terror she spoke, letting sink her
 Wings until they trailed in the dust;
In agony sobbed, letting sink her
 Plumes till they trailed in the dust,
 Till they sorrowfully trailed in the dust.

I replied—"This is nothing but dreaming: 61
 Let us on by this tremulous light!
 Let us bathe in this crystalline light!
Its sibyllic splendor is beaming
 With hope and in beauty tonight:
 See, it flickers up the sky through the
  night!
Ah, we safely may trust to its gleaming,
 And be sure it will lead us aright:
We safely may trust to a gleaming
 That cannot but guide us aright,   70
 Since it flickers up to Heaven through the
  night."

Thus I pacified Psyche and kissed her,
 And tempted her out of her gloom,
 And conquered her scruples and gloom;
And we passed to the end of the vista,
 But were stopped by the door of a tomb,
 By the door of a legended tomb;
And I said—"What is written, sweet sister,
 On the door of this legended tomb?"
 She replied—"Ulalume—Ulalume—   80
 'T is the vault of thy lost Ulalume!"

Then my heart it grew ashen and sober
 As the leaves that were crisped and sere,
 As the leaves that were withering and sere,
And I cried—"It was surely October
 On this very night of last year
 That I journeyed—I journeyed down here,
 That I brought a dread burden down here:
 On this night of all nights in the year,
 Ah, what demon has tempted me here?   90
Well I know, now, this dim lake of Auber,
 This misty mid region of Weir:
Well I know, now, this dank tarn of Auber,
 This ghoul-haunted woodland of Weir."
            1847

THE BELLS

I

Hear the sledges with the bells,
 Silver bells!
What a world of merriment their melody fore-
 tells!

How they tinkle, tinkle, tinkle,
 In the icy air of night!
While the stars, that oversprinkle
All the heavens, seem to twinkle
 With a crystalline delight;
 Keeping time, time, time,
 In a sort of Runic [1] rime,   10
To the tintinnabulation that so musically
 wells
From the bells, bells, bells, bells,
 Bells, bells, bells—
From the jingling and the tinkling of the
 bells.

II

Hear the mellow wedding bells,
 Golden bells!
What a world of happiness their harmony fore-
 tells!
 Through the balmy air of night
 How they ring out their delight!
 From the molten-golden notes,   20
  And all in tune,
 What a liquid ditty floats
To the turtle-dove that listens, while she
  gloats
  On the moon!
Oh, from out the sounding cells,
What a gush of euphony voluminously wells!
  How it swells!
  How it dwells
 On the Future! how it tells
 Of the rapture that impels   30
To the swinging and the ringing
 Of the bells, bells, bells,
Of the bells, bells, bells, bells,
 Bells bells, bells—
To the riming and the chiming of the bells!

III

Hear the loud alarum bells,
 Brazen bells!
What a tale of terror, now, their turbulency
 tells!
 In the startled ear of night
 How they scream out their affright!   40
 Too much horrified to speak,
 They can only shriek, shriek,
  Out of tune,
In a clamorous appealing to the mercy of the
 fire,
In a mad expostulation with the deaf and fran-
 tic fire,
 Leaping higher, higher, higher,
 With a desperate desire,
 And a resolute endeavor

[1] secret, mysterious, as the ancient inscriptions or runes of northern Europe were secret to all but the initiated

Now—now to sit or never,
By the side of the pale-faced moon.   50
    Oh, the bells, bells, bells!
    What a tale their terror tells
        Of Despair!
How they clang, and clash, and roar!
What a horror they outpour
On the bosom of the palpitating air!
    Yet the ear it fully knows,
        By the twanging
        And the clanging,
    How the danger ebbs and flows;   60
    Yet the ear distinctly tells,
        In the jangling
        And the wrangling,
How the danger sinks and swells,—
By the sinking or the swelling in the anger
        of the bells,
        Of the bells,
    Of the bells, bells, bells, bells,
        Bells, bells, bells—
In the clamor and the clangor of the bells!

IV

    Hear the tolling of the bells,   70
        Iron bells!
What a world of solemn thought their monody
        compels!
    In the silence of the night
    How we shiver with affright
At the melancholy menace of their tone!
    For every sound that floats
    From the rust within their throats
        Is a groan.
    And the people—ah, the people,
    They that dwell up in the steeple,   80
        All alone,
    And who tolling, tolling, tolling
    In that muffled monotone,
    Feel a glory in so rolling
    On the human heart a stone—
They are neither man nor woman,
They are neither brute nor human,
        They are Ghouls:
    And their king it is who tolls;
    And he rolls, rolls, rolls,   90
        Rolls
    A paean from the bells;
    And his merry bosom swells
        With the paean of the bells,
    And he dances, and he yells:
    Keeping time, time, time,
In a sort of Runic rime,
    To the paean of the bells,
        Of the bells:
    Keeping time, time, time,   100
    In a sort of Runic rime,

    To the throbbing of the bells,
    Of the bells, bells, bells—
        To the sobbing of the bells;
    Keeping time, time, time,
        As he knells, knells, knells,
    In a happy Runic rime,
        To the rolling of the bells,
    Of the bells, bells, bells:
        To the tolling of the bells,   110
    Of the bells, bells, bells, bells,
        Bells, bells, bells—
To the moaning and the groaning of the bells.
1848-49   1849

ANNABEL LEE [1]

It was many and many a year ago,
    In a kingdom by the sea,
That a maiden there lived whom you may know
    By the name of Annabel Lee;
And this maiden she lived with no other thought
    Than to love and be loved by me.

I was a child and she was a child,
    In this kingdom by the sea,
But we loved with a love that was more than
    love,
    I and my Annabel Lee;   10
With a love that the winged seraphs of heaven
    Coveted her and me.

And this was the reason that, long ago,
    In this kingdom by the sea,
A wind blew out of a cloud, chilling
    My beautiful Annabel Lee;
So that her highborn kinsmen came
    And bore her away from me,
To shut her up in a sepulcher
    In this kingdom by the sea.   20

The angels, not half so happy in heaven,
    Went envying her and me;
Yes! that was the reason (as all men know,
    In this kingdom by the sea)
That the wind came out of the cloud by night,
    Chilling and killing my Annabel Lee.

But our love it was stronger by far than the
    love
    Of those who were older than we,
    Of many far wiser than we;   29
And neither the angels in heaven above,
    Nor the demons down under the sea,
Can ever dissever my soul from the soul
    Of the beautiful Annabel Lee:

[1] Stedman in his introduction to the poems of Poe says
that this poem was doubtless inspired by the
memory of Poe's wife, Virginia Clemm.

For the moon never beams, without bringing
  me dreams
    Of the beautiful Annabel Lee;
And the stars never rise, but I feel the bright
  eyes
    Of the beautiful Annabel Lee;
And so, all the night-tide, I lie down by the side
Of my darling—my darling—my life and my
  bride,
    In her sepulcher there by the sea,   40
    In her tomb by the sounding sea.

1849   1849

ELDORADO [1]

  Gayly bedight,
  A gallant knight,
In sunshine and in shadow,
  Had journeyed long,
  Singing a song,
In search of Eldorado.

  But he grew old,
  This knight so bold,
And o'er his heart a shadow
  Fell as he found   10
  No spot of ground
That looked like Eldorado.

  And, as his strength
  Failed him at length,
He met a pilgrim shadow;
  "Shadow," said he,
  "Where can it be,
This land of Eldorado?"

  "Over the Mountains
  Of the Moon,   20
Down the Valley of the Shadow,
  Ride, boldly ride,"
  The shade replied,
"If you seek for Eldorado!"

                                          1850

THE FALL OF THE HOUSE OF USHER [2]

  Son coeur est un luth suspendu;
  Sitôt qu'on le touche il résonne.
                      BÉRANGER. [3]

During the whole of a dull, dark, and soundless day in the autumn of the year, when the

[1] Spanish, golden; here, the land of the ideal
[2] Poe's purely imaginative tales move in a land that no
man has ever visited, under clouds or sunshine
such as none have ever seen. It is not a little
pathetic, and it shows, if proof were needed, the
essential poetry of his nature, that amid all the
misfortunes and wretchedness of his actual life
he could still live in this all-enveloping realm of
his own creation.
[3] "His heart is a lute suspended; as soon as it is
touched it resounds." Béranger was a French
lyric poet contemporary with Poe, but the lines
quoted have not been found in his work.

clouds hung oppressively low in the heavens,
I had been passing alone, on horseback, through
a singularly dreary tract of country, and at
length found myself, as the shades of the evening drew on, within view of the melancholy
House of Usher. I know not how it was—but,
with the first glimpse of the building, a sense of
insufferable gloom pervaded my spirit. I say
insufferable; for the feeling was unrelieved by
any of that half-pleasurable, because poetic,
sentiment with which the mind usually receives
even the sternest natural images of the desolate or terrible. I looked upon the scene before
me—upon the mere house, and the simple landscape features of the domain, upon the bleak
walls, upon the vacant eye-like windows, upon
a few rank sedges, and upon a few white trunks
of decayed trees—with an utter depression of
soul which I can compare to no earthly sensation more properly than to the after-dream of
the reveler upon opium: the bitter lapse into
every-day life, the hideous dropping off of the
veil. There was an iciness, a sinking, a sickening of the heart, an unredeemed dreariness of
thought which no goading of the imagination
could torture into aught of the sublime. What
was it—I paused to think—what was it that so
unnerved me in the contemplation of the House
of Usher? It was a mystery all insoluble; nor
could I grapple with the shadowy fancies that
crowded upon me as I pondered. I was forced
to fall back upon the unsatisfactory conclusion,
that while, beyond doubt, there *are* combinations of very simple natural objects which have
the power of thus affecting us, still the analysis
of this power lies among considerations beyond
our depth. It was possible, I reflected, that a
mere different arrangement of the particulars
of the scene, of the details of the picture, would
be sufficient to modify, or perhaps to annihilate,
its capacity for sorrowful impression; and acting upon this idea, I reined my horse to the precipitous brink of a black and lurid tarn that lay
in unruffled luster by the dwelling, and gazed
down—but with a shudder even more thrilling
than before—upon the remodeled and inverted
images of the gray sedge, and the ghastly tree-
stems, and the vacant and eye-like windows.

Nevertheless, in this mansion of gloom I now
proposed to myself a sojourn of some weeks.
Its proprietor, Roderick Usher, had been one of
my boon companions in boyhood; but many
years had elapsed since our last meeting. A
letter, however, had lately reached me in a
distant part of the country—a letter from him
—which in its wildly importunate nature had
admitted of no other than a personal reply.

The MS. gave evidence of nervous agitation. The writer spoke of acute bodily illness, of a mental disorder which oppressed him, and of an earnest desire to see me, as his best and indeed his only personal friend, with a view of attempting, by the cheerfulness of my society, some alleviation of his malady. It was the manner in which all this, and much more, was said— it was the apparent *heart* that went with his request—which allowed me no room for hesitation; and I accordingly obeyed forthwith what I still considered a very singular summons.

Although as boys we had been even intimate associates, yet I really knew little of my friend. His reserve had been always excessive and habitual. I was aware, however, that his very ancient family had been noted, time out of mind, for a peculiar sensibility of temperament, displaying itself, through long ages, in many works of exalted art, and manifested of late in repeated deeds of munificent yet unobtrusive charity, as well as in a passionate devotion to the intricacies, perhaps even more than to the orthodox and easily recognizable beauties, of musical science. I had learned, too, the very remarkable fact that the stem of the Usher race, all time-honored as it was, had put forth at no period any enduring branch; in other words, that the entire family lay in the direct line of descent, and had always, with very trifling and very temporary variation, so lain. It was this deficiency, I considered, while running over in thought the perfect keeping of the character of the premises with the accredited character of the people, and while speculating upon the possible influence which the one, in the long lapse of centuries, might have exercised upon the other—it was this deficiency, perhaps, of collateral issue, and the consequent undeviating transmission from sire to son of the patrimony with the name, which had, at length, so identified the two as to merge the original title of the estate in the quaint and equivocal appellation of the "House of Usher"—an appellation which seemed to include, in the minds of the peasantry who used it, both the family and the family mansion.

I have said that the sole effect of my somewhat childish experiment, that of looking down within the tarn, had been to deepen the first singular impression. There can be no doubt that the consciousness of the rapid increase of my superstition—for why should I not so term it?—served mainly to accelerate the increase itself. Such, I have long known, is the paradoxical law of all sentiments having terror as a basis. And it might have been for this reason only, that, when I again uplifted my eyes to the house itself, from its image in the pool, there grew in my mind a strange fancy—a fancy so ridiculous, indeed, that I but mention it to show the vivid force of the sensations which oppressed me. I had so worked upon my imagination as really to believe that about the whole mansion and domain there hung an atmosphere peculiar to themselves and their immediate vicinity: an atmosphere which had no affinity with the air of heaven, but which had reeked up from the decayed trees, and the gray wall, and the silent tarn: a pestilent and mystic vapor, dull, sluggish, faintly discernible, and leaden-hued.

Shaking off from my spirit what *must* have been a dream, I scanned more narrowly the real aspect of the building. Its principal feature seemed to be that of an excessive antiquity. The discoloration of ages had been great. Minute fungi overspread the whole exterior, hanging in a fine tangled web-work from the eaves. Yet all this was apart from any extraordinary dilapidation. No portion of the masonry had fallen; and there appeared to be a wild inconsistency between its still perfect adaptation of parts and the crumbling condition of the individual stones. In this there was much that reminded me of the specious totality of old wood-work which has rotted for long years in some neglected vault, with no disturbance from the breath of the external air. Beyond this indication of extensive decay, however, the fabric gave little token of instability. Perhaps the eye of a scrutinizing observer might have discovered a barely perceptible fissure, which, extending from the roof of the building in front, made its way down the wall in a zig-zag direction, until it became lost in the sullen waters of the tarn.

Noticing these things, I rode over a short causeway to the house. A servant in waiting took my horse, and I entered the Gothic archway of the hall. A valet, of stealthy step, thence conducted me, in silence, through many dark and intricate passages in my progress to the studio of his master. Much that I encountered on the way contributed, I know not how, to heighten the vague sentiments of which I have already spoken. While the objects around me—while the carvings of the ceilings, the somber tapestries of the walls, the ebon blackness of the floors, and the phantasmagoric armorial trophies which rattled as I strode, were but matters to which, or to such as which, I had been accustomed from my infancy—while I hesitated not to acknowledge how familiar was all this—I still wondered to find how unfamiliar were the fancies which ordinary images were stirring up. On one of the staircases, I met the physician of the family. His countenance, I thought, wore a mingled expression of low cunning and perplexity. He accosted me with trepidation and passed on. The valet now threw open a door and ushered me into the presence of his master.

The room in which I found myself was very large and lofty. The windows were long, narrow, and pointed, and at so vast a distance from the black oaken floor as to be altogether inaccessible from within. Feeble gleams of encrimsoned light made their way through the trellised panes, and served to render sufficiently distinct the more prominent objects around; the eye, however, struggled in vain to reach the remoter angles of the chamber, or the recesses of the vaulted and fretted ceiling. Dark draperies hung upon the walls. The general furniture was profuse, comfortless, antique, and tattered. Many books and musical instruments lay scattered about, but failed to give any vitality to the scene. I felt that I breathed an atmosphere of sorrow. An air of stern, deep, and irredeemable gloom hung over and pervaded all.

Upon my entrance, Usher arose from a sofa on which he had been lying at full length, and greeted me with a vivacious warmth which had much in it, I at first thought, of an overdone cordiality—of the constrained effort of the ennuyé [1] man of the world. A glance, however, at his countenance convinced me of his perfect sincerity. We sat down; and for some moments, while he spoke not, I gazed upon him with a feeling half of pity, half of awe. Surely man had never before so terribly altered, in so brief a period, as had Roderick Usher! It was with difficulty that I could bring myself to admit the identity of the wan being before me with the companion of my early boyhood. Yet the character of his face had been at all times remarkable. A cadaverousness of complexion; an eye large, liquid, and luminous beyond comparison; lips somewhat thin and very pallid, but of a surpassingly beautiful curve; a nose of a delicate Hebrew model, but with a breadth of nostril unusual in similar formations; a finely molded chin, speaking, in its want of prominence, of a want of moral energy; hair of a more than web-like softness and tenuity; these features, with an inordinate expansion above the regions of the temple, made up altogether a countenance not easily to be forgotten. And

[1] bored

now in the mere exaggeration of the prevailing character of these features, and of the expression they were wont to convey, lay so much of change that I doubted to whom I spoke. The now ghostly pallor of the skin, and the now miraculous luster of the eye, above all things startled and even awed me. The silken hair, too, had been suffered to grow all unheeded, and as, in its wild gossamer texture, it floated rather than fell about the face, I could not, even with effort, connect its arabesque [2] expression with any idea of simple humanity.

In the manner of my friend I was at once struck with an incoherence, an inconsistency; and I soon found this to arise from a series of feeble and futile struggles to overcome an habitual trepidancy, an excessive nervous agitation. For something of this nature I had indeed been prepared, no less by his letter than by reminiscences of certain boyish traits, and by conclusions deduced from his peculiar physical conformation and temperament. His action was alternately vivacious and sullen. His voice varied rapidly from a tremulous indecision (when the animal spirits seemed utterly in abeyance) to that species of energetic concision—that abrupt, weighty, unhurried, and hollow-sounding enunciation—that leaden, self-balanced and perfectly modulated guttural utterance—which may be observed in the lost drunkard, or the irreclaimable eater of opium, during the periods of his most intense excitement.

It was thus that he spoke of the object of my visit, of his earnest desire to see me, and of the solace he expected me to afford him. He entered, at some length, into what he conceived to be the nature of his malady. It was, he said, a constitutional and a family evil, and one for which he despaired to find a remedy—a mere nervous affection, he immediately added, which would undoubtedly soon pass off. It displayed itself in a host of unnatural sensations. Some of these, as he detailed them, interested and bewildered me; although, perhaps, the terms and the general manner of the narration had their weight. He suffered much from a morbid acuteness of the senses; the most insipid food was alone endurable; he could wear only garments of certain texture; the odors of all flowers were oppressive; his eyes were tortured by even a faint light; and there were but peculiar sounds, and these from stringed instruments, which did not inspire him with horror.

To an anomalous species of terror I found him a bounden slave. "I shall perish," said he,

[2] fantastic; unusual in this sense

"I *must* perish in this deplorable folly. Thus, thus, and not otherwise, shall I be lost. I dread the events of the future, not in themselves, but in their results. I shudder at the thought of any, even the most trivial, incident, which may operate upon this intolerable agitation of soul. I have, indeed, no abhorrence of danger, except in its absolute effect—in terror. In this unnerved—in this pitiable condition, I feel that the period will sooner or later arrive when I must abandon life and reason together, in some struggle with the grim phantasm, FEAR."

I learned moreover at intervals, and through broken and equivocal hints, another singular feature of his mental condition. He was enchained by certain superstitious impressions in regard to the dwelling which he tenanted, and whence, for many years, he had never ventured forth—in regard to an influence whose supposititious force was conveyed in terms too shadowy here to be restated—an influence which some peculiarities in the mere form and substance of his family mansion, had, by dint of long sufferance, he said, obtained over his spirit—an effect which the physique of the gray walls and turrets, and of the dim tarn into which they all looked down, had, at length, brought about upon the morale of his existence.

He admitted, however, although with hesitation, that much of the peculiar gloom which thus afflicted him could be traced to a more natural and far more palpable origin—to the severe and long-continued illness, indeed to the evidently approaching dissolution, of a tenderly beloved sister—his sole companion for long years, his last and only relative on earth. 'Her decease,' he said, with a bitterness which I can never forget, 'would leave him (him the hopeless and the frail) the last of the ancient race of the Ushers.' While he spoke the lady Madeline (for so was she called) passed slowly through a remote portion of the apartment, and, without having noticed my presence, disappeared. I regarded her with an utter astonishment not unmingled with dread, and yet I found it impossible to account for such feelings. A sensation of stupor oppressed me, as my eyes followed her retreating steps. When a door, at length, closed upon her, my glance sought instinctively and eagerly the countenance of the brother; but he had buried his face in his hands, and I could only perceive that a far more than ordinary wanness had overspread the emaciated fingers through which trickled many passionate tears.

The disease of the lady Madeline had long baffled the skill of her physicians. A settled apathy, a gradual wasting away of the person, and frequent although transient affections of a partially cataleptical character, were the unusual diagnosis. Hitherto she had steadily borne up against the pressure of her malady, and had not betaken herself finally to bed; but, on the closing in of the evening of my arrival at the house, she succumbed (as her brother told me at night with inexpressible agitation) to the prostrating power of the destroyer; and I learned that the glimpse I had obtained of her person would thus probably be the last I should obtain—that the lady, at least while living, would be seen by me no more.

For several days ensuing, her name was unmentioned by either Usher or myself; and during this period I was busied in earnest endeavors to alleviate the melancholy of my friend. We painted and read together; or I listened, as if in a dream, to the wild improvisations of his speaking guitar. And thus, as a closer and still closer intimacy admitted me more unreservedly into the recesses of his spirit, the more bitterly did I perceive the futility of all attempt at cheering a mind from which darkness, as if an inherent positive quality, poured forth upon all objects of the moral and physical universe, in one unceasing radiation of gloom.

I shall ever bear about me a memory of the many solemn hours I thus spent alone with the master of the House of Usher. Yet I should fail in any attempt to convey an idea of the exact character of the studies, or of the occupations, in which he involved me, or led the way. An excited and highly distempered ideality threw a sulphurous luster over all. His long improvised dirges will ring forever in my ears. Among other things, I hold painfully in mind a certain singular perversion and amplification of the wild air of the last waltz of Von Weber. [1] From the paintings over which his elaborate fancy brooded, and which grew, touch by touch, into vaguenesses at which I shuddered the more thrillingly because I shuddered knowing not why;—from these paintings (vivid as their images now are before me) I would in vain endeavor to educe more than a small portion which should lie within the compass of merely written words. By the utter simplicity, by the nakedness of his designs, he arrested and overawed attention. If ever mortal painted an idea, that mortal was Roderick Usher. For me at least, in the circumstances then surrounding me, there arose, out of the pure abstractions which the hypochondriac contrived to throw upon his canvas, an intensity of intolerable

[1] a German composer, 1786-1826

awe, no shadow of which felt I ever yet in the contemplation of the certainly glowing yet too concrete reveries of Fuseli. [1]

One of the phantasmagoric conceptions of my friend, partaking not so rigidly of the spirit of abstraction, may be shadowed forth, although feebly, in words. A small picture presented the interior of an immensely long and rectangular vault or tunnel, with low walls, smooth, white, and without interruption or device. Certain accessory points of the design served well to convey the idea that this excavation lay at an exceeding depth below the surface of the earth. No outlet was observed in any portion of its vast extent, and no torch or other artificial source of light was discernible; yet a flood of intense rays rolled throughout, and bathed the whole in a ghastly and inappropriate splendor.

I have just spoken of that morbid condition of the auditory nerve which rendered all music intolerable to the sufferer, with the exception of certain effects of stringed instruments. It was, perhaps, the narrow limits to which he thus confined himself upon the guitar, which gave birth, in great measure, to the fantastic character of his performances. But the fervid *facility* of his impromptus could not be so accounted for. They must have been, and were, in the notes, as well as in the words of his wild fantasias (for he not unfrequently accompanied himself with rimed verbal improvisations), the result of that intense mental collectedness and concentration to which I have previously alluded as observable only in particular moments of the highest artificial excitement. The words of one of these rhapsodies I have easily remembered. I was, perhaps, the more forcibly impressed with it, as he gave it, because, in the under or mystic current of its meaning, I fancied that I perceived, and for the first time, a full consciousness, on the part of Usher, of the tottering of his lofty reason upon her throne. The verses, which were entitled "The Haunted Palace," ran very nearly, if not accurately, thus :—

I

In the greenest of our valleys
  By good angels tenanted,
Once a fair and stately palace—
  Radiant palace—reared its head.
In the monarch Thought's dominion,
  It stood there;
Never seraph spread a pinion
  Over fabric half so fair.

[1] A Swiss-English painter, 1741-1825; his work is noted for its fantastic intensity.

II

Banners yellow, glorious, golden,
  On its roof did float and flow,
(This—all this—was in the olden
  Time long ago)
And every gentle air that dallied,
  In that sweet day,
Along the ramparts plumed and pallid,
  A wingéd odor went away.

III

Wanderers in that happy valley
  Through two luminous windows saw
Spirits moving musically
  To a lute's well-tunéd law,
Round about a throne where, sitting,
  Porphyrogene, [2]
In state his glory well befitting,
  The ruler of the realm was seen.

IV

And all with pearl and ruby glowing
  Was the fair palace door,
Through which came flowing, flowing, flowing,
  And sparkling evermore,
A troop of Echoes whose sweet duty
  Was but to sing,
In voices of surpassing beauty,
  The wit and wisdom of their king.

V

But evil things, in robes of sorrow,
  Assailed the monarch's high estate;
(Ah, let us mourn, for never morrow
  Shall dawn upon him, desolate!)
And round about his home the glory
  That blushed and bloomed
Is but a dim-remembered story
  Of the old time entombed.

VI

And travelers now within that valley
  Through the red-litten windows see
Vast forms that move fantastically
  To a discordant melody;
While, like a ghastly rapid river,
  Through the pale door
A hideous throng rush out forever,
  And laugh—but smile no more.

I well remember that suggestions arising from this ballad led us into a train of thought, wherein there became manifest an opinion of Usher's which I mention not so much on account of its novelty, (for other men [3] have thought

[2] "Born to the purple"; said of a son born to a reigning monarch
[3] "Watson, Dr. Percival, Spallanzini, and especially the Bishop of Landaff.—See *Chemical Essays, Vol. V*" (Poe's note). Richard Watson, Bishop of Landaff. friend of Franklin, 1737-1816; Spallanzini, an Italian scientist, 1729-1799; Percival, an American scientist and poet, 1795-1856.

thus), as on account of the pertinacity with which he maintained it. This opinion, in its general form, was that of the sentience of all vegetable things. But in his disordered fancy the idea had assumed a more daring character, and trespassed, under certain conditions, upon the kingdom of inorganization. [1] I lack words to express the full extent, or the earnest *abandon* of his persuasion. The belief, however, was connected (as I have previously hinted) with the gray stones of the home of his forefathers. The conditions of the sentience had been here, he imagined, fulfilled in the method of collocation of these stones—in the order of their arrangement, as well as in that of the many fungi which overspread them, and of the decayed trees which stood around—above all, in the long undisturbed endurance of this arrangement, and in its reduplication in the still waters of the tarn. Its evidence—the evidence of the sentience—was to be seen, he said (and I here started as he spoke), in the gradual yet certain condensation of an atmosphere of their own about the waters and the walls. The result was discoverable, he added, in that silent, yet importunate and terrible influence which for centuries had molded the destinies of his family, and which made *him* what I now saw him— what he was. Such opinions need no comment, and I will make none.

Our books, the books which, for years, had formed no small portion of the mental existence of the invalid—were, as might be supposed, in strict keeping with this character of phantasm. We pored together over such works as the *Ververt* and *Chartreuse* of Gresset; the *Belphegor* of Machiavelli; the *Heaven and Hell* of Swedenborg; the *Subterranean Voyage of Nicholas Klimm* by Holberg; the *Chiromancy* of Robert Flud, of Jean d'Indaginé, and of De la Chambre; the *Journey into the Blue Distance* of Tieck; and the *City of the Sun* of Campanella. One favorite volume was a small octavo edition of the *Directorium Inquisitorum* by the Dominican Eymeric de Gironne, and there were passages in Pomponius Mela, about the old African Satyrs and Aegipans, over which Usher would sit dreaming for hours. His chief delight, however, was found in the perusal of an exceedingly rare and curious book in quarto Gothic—the manual of a forgotten church—the *Vigiliae Mortuorum secundum Chorum Ecclesiae Maguntinae.* [2]

[1] inorganic matter
[2] One may reasonably infer that Poe in marshaling this array of rather out-of-the-way books, most of which are tinged with mysticism or the occult, wishes to deepen the atmosphere of horror as well

I could not help thinking of the wild ritual of this work, and of its probable influence upon the hypochondriac, when one evening, having informed me abruptly that the lady Madeline was no more, he stated his intention of preserving her corpse for a fortnight, (previously to its final interment) in one of the numerous vaults within the main walls of the building. The worldly reason, however, assigned for this singular proceeding, was one which I did not feel at liberty to dispute. The brother had been led to his resolution (so he told me) by consideration of the unusual character of the malady of the deceased, of certain obtrusive and eager inquiries on the part of her medical men, and of the remote and exposed situation of the burial-ground of the family. I will not deny that when I called to mind the sinister countenance of the person whom I met upon the staircase, on the day of my arrival at the house, I had no desire to oppose what I regarded as at best but a harmless, and by no means an unnatural precaution.

At the request of Usher, I personally aided him in the arrangements for the temporary entombment. The body having been encoffined, we two alone bore it to its rest. The vault in which we placed it (and which had been so long unopened that our torches, half smothered in its oppressive atmosphere, gave us little opportunity for investigation) was small, damp, and entirely without means of admission for light; lying, at great depth, immediately beneath that portion of the building in which was my own sleeping apartment. It had been used, apparently, in remote feudal times, for the worst purposes of a donjon-keep, and in later days as a place of deposit for powder, or some other highly combustible substance, as a portion of its floor, and the whole interior of a long archway through which we reached it, were carefully sheathed with copper. The door, of massive iron, had been, also, similarly protected. Its immense weight caused an unusually sharp grating sound, as it moved upon its hinges.

Having deposited our mournful burden upon tressels within this region of horror, we partially turned aside the yet unscrewed lid of the coffin, and looked upon the face of the tenant. A striking similitude between the brother and sister now first arrested my attention; and Usher, divining, perhaps, my thoughts, murmured out some few words from which I

as to impress us with the width of his reading. The last mentioned book, *Vigils for the Dead According to the Choir of the Church of Mayence,* has not been traced. Poe did not scruple to invent when actual material failed.

learned that the deceased and himself had been twins, and that sympathies of a scarcely intelligible nature had always existed between them. Our glances, however, rested not long upon the dead—for we could not regard her unawed. The disease which had thus entombed the lady in the maturity of youth, had left, as usual in all maladies of a strictly cataleptical character, the mockery of a faint blush upon the bosom and the face, and that suspiciously lingering smile upon the lip which is so terrible in death. We replaced and screwed down the lid, and, having secured the door of iron, made our way, with toil, into the scarcely less gloomy apartments of the upper portions of the house.

And now, some days of bitter grief having elapsed, an observable change came over the features of the mental disorder of my friend. His ordinary manner had vanished. His ordinary occupations were neglected or forgotten. He roamed from chamber to chamber with hurried, unequal, and objectless step. The pallor of his countenance had assumed, if possible, a more ghastly hue—but the luminousness of his eye had utterly gone out. The once occasional huskiness of his tone was heard no more; and a tremulous quaver, as if of extreme terror, habitually characterized his utterance. There were times, indeed, when I thought his unceasingly agitated mind was laboring with some oppressive secret, to divulge which he struggled for the necessary courage. At times, again, I was obliged to resolve all into the mere inexplicable vagaries of madness, for I beheld him gazing upon vacancy for long hours, in an attitude of the profoundest attention, as if listening to some imaginary sound. It was no wonder that his condition terrified—that it infected me. I felt creeping upon me, by slow yet certain degrees, the wild influences of his own fantastic yet impressive superstitions.

It was, especially, upon retiring to bed late in the night of the seventh or eighth day after the placing of the lady Madeline within the donjon, that I experienced the full power of such feelings. Sleep came not near my couch, while the hours waned and waned away. I struggled to reason off the nervousness which had dominion over me. I endeavored to believe that much, if not all, of what I felt was due to the bewildering influence of the gloomy furniture of the room—of the dark and tattered draperies which, tortured into motion by the breath of a rising tempest, swayed fitfully to and fro upon the walls, and rustled uneasily about the decorations of the bed. But my efforts were fruitless. An irrepressible tremor gradually pervaded my frame; and at length there sat upon my very heart an incubus of utterly causeless alarm. Shaking this off with a gasp and a struggle, I uplifted myself upon the pillows, and, peering earnestly within the intense darkness of the chamber, hearkened—I know not why, except that an instinctive spirit prompted me—to certain low and indefinite sounds which came, through the pauses of the storm, at long intervals, I knew not whence. Overpowered by an intense sentiment of horror, unaccountable yet unendurable, I threw on my clothes with haste (for I felt that I should sleep no more during the night) and endeavored to arouse myself from the pitiable condition into which I had fallen, by pacing rapidly to and fro through the apartment.

I had taken but few turns in this manner, when a light step on an adjoining staircase arrested my attention. I presently recognized it as that of Usher. In an instant afterward he rapped with a gentle touch at my door, and entered, bearing a lamp. His countenance was, as usual, cadaverously wan—but, moreover, there was a species of mad hilarity in his eyes—an evidently restrained hysteria in his whole demeanor. His air appalled me—but anything was preferable to the solitude which I had so long endured, and I even welcomed his presence as a relief.

"And you have not seen it?" he said abruptly, after having stared about him for some moments in silence—"you have not then seen it?—but, stay! you shall." Thus speaking, and having carefully shaded his lamp, he hurried to one of the casements, and threw it freely open to the storm.

The impetuous fury of the entering gust nearly lifted us from our feet. It was, indeed, a tempestuous yet sternly beautiful night, and one wildly singular in its terror and its beauty. A whirlwind had apparently collected its force in our vicinity; for there were frequent and violent alterations in the direction of the wind; and the exceeding density of the clouds (which hung so low as to press upon the turrets of the house) did not prevent our perceiving the lifelike velocity with which they flew careering from all points against each other, without passing away into the distance. I say that even their exceeding density did not prevent our perceiving this; yet we had no glimpse of the moon or stars, nor was their any flashing forth of the lightning. But the under surfaces of the huge masses of agitated vapor, as well as all terrestrial objects immediately around us, were glowing in the unnatural light of a faintly luminous and distinctly visible gaseous exhalation which hung about and enshrouded the mansion.

"You must not—you shall not behold this!" said I, shudderingly, to Usher, as I led him with a gentle violence from the window to a seat. "These appearances which bewilder you, are merely electrical phenomena not uncommon —or it may be that they have their ghastly origin in the rank miasma of the tarn. Let us close this casement; the air is chilling and dangerous to your frame. Here is one of your favorite romances. I will read, and you shall listen;—and so we will pass away this terrible night together."

The antique volume which I had taken up was the *Mad Trist* of Sir Launcelot Canning, [1] but I had called it a favorite of Usher's more in sad jest than in earnest; for, in truth, there is little in its uncouth and unimaginative prolixity which could have had interest for the lofty and spiritual ideality of my friend. It was, however, the only book immediately at hand; and I indulged a vague hope that the excitement which now agitated the hypochondriac might find relief (for the history of mental disorder is full of similar anomalies) even in the extremeness of the folly which I should read. Could I have judged, indeed, by the wild overstrained air of vivacity with which he hearkened, or apparently hearkened, to the words of the tale, I might well have congratulated myself upon the success of my design.

I had arrived at that well-known portion of the story where Ethelred, the hero of the *Trist*, having sought in vain for peaceable admission into the dwelling of the hermit, proceeds to make good an entrance by force. Here, it will be remembered, the words of the narrative run thus:—

And Ethelred, who was by nature of a doughty heart, and who was now mighty withal, on account of the powerfulness of the wine which he had drunken, waited no longer to hold parley with the hermit, who, in sooth, was of an obstinate and maliceful turn, but, feeling the rain upon his shoulders, and fearing the rising of the tempest, uplifted his mace outright, and with blows made quickly room in the plankings of the door for his gauntleted hand and now pulling therewith sturdily, he so cracked, and ripped, and tore all asunder, that the noise of the dry and hollow-sounding wood alarumed and reverberated throughout the forest.

At the termination of this sentence I started, and for a moment paused; for it appeared to me (although I at once concluded that my excited fancy had deceived me)—it appeared to me that from some very remote portion of the mansion there came, indistinctly, to my ears, what might have been, in its exact similarity of character, the echo (but a stifled and dull one certainly) of the very cracking and ripping sound which Sir Launcelot had so particularly described. It was, beyond doubt, the coincidence alone which had arrested my attention; for, amid the rattling of the sashes of the casements, and the ordinary commingled noises of the still increasing storm, the sound, in itself, had nothing, surely, which should have interested or disturbed me. I continued the story:—

But the good champion Ethelred, now entering within the door, was sore enraged, and amazed to perceive no signal of the maliceful hermit; but, in the stead thereof, a dragon of a scaly and prodigious demeanor, and of a fiery tongue, which sate in guard before a palace of gold, with a floor of silver; and upon the wall there hung a shield of shining brass with this legend enwritten—

Who entereth herein, a conqueror
    hath bin;
Who slayeth the dragon, the shield
    he shall win.

And Ethelred uplifted his mace, and struck upon the head of the dragon, which fell before him, and gave up his pesty breath, with a shriek so horrid and harsh, and withal so piercing, that Ethelred had fain to close his ears with his hands against the dreadful noise of it, the like whereof was never before heard.

Here again I paused abruptly, and now with a feeling of wild amazement; for there could be no doubt whatever that, in this instance, I did actually hear (although from what direction it proceeded I found it impossible to say) a low and apparently distant, but harsh, protracted, and most unusual screaming or grating sound—the exact counterpart of what my fancy had already conjured up for the dragon's unnatural shriek as described by the romancer.

Oppressed, as I certainly was, upon the occurrence of this second and most extraordinary coincidence, by a thousand conflicting sensations, in which wonder and extreme terror were predominant, I still retained sufficient presence of mind to avoid exciting, by any observation, the sensitive nervousness of my companion. I was by no means certain that he had noticed the sounds in question; although, assuredly, a strange alteration had during the last few minutes taken place in his demeanor. From a position fronting my own, he had gradually brought round his chair, so as to sit with his face to the door of the chamber; and thus I could but partially perceive his features, although I saw that his lips trembled as if he were murmuring inaudibly. His head had dropped

---

[1] Since no one has identified author or book, both are probably the invention of Poe.

upon his breast—yet I knew that he was not asleep, from the wide and rigid opening of the eye as I caught a glance of it in profile. The motion of his body, too, was at variance with this idea—for he rocked from side to side with a gentle yet constant and uniform sway. Having rapidly taken notice of all this, I resumed the narrative of Sir Launcelot, which thus proceeded:—

And now, the champion, having escaped from the terrible fury of the dragon, bethinking himself of the brazen shield, and of the breaking up of the enchantment, which was upon it, removed the carcass from out of the way before him, and approached valorously over the silver pavement of the castle to where the shield was upon the wall, which in sooth tarried not for his full coming, but fell down at his feet upon the silver floor, with a mighty great and terrible ringing sound.

No sooner had these syllables passed my lips, than—as if a shield of brass had indeed, at the moment, fallen heavily upon a floor of silver— I became aware of a distinct, hollow, metallic and clangorous yet apparently muffled reverberation. Completely unnerved, I leaped to my feet; but the measured rocking movement of Usher was undisturbed. I rushed to the chair in which he sat. His eyes were bent fixedly before him, and throughout his whole countenance there reigned a stony rigidity. But as I placed my hand upon his shoulder, there came a strong shudder over his whole person; a sickly smile quivered about his lips; and I saw that he spoke in a low, hurried, and gibbering murmur, as if unconscious of my presence. Bending closely over him, I at length drank in the hideous import of his words.

"Not hear it?—yes, I hear it, and *have* heard it. Long—long—long—many minutes, many hours, many days, have I heard it—yet I dared not—oh, pity me, miserable wretch that I am! —I dared not—I *dared* not speak! *We have put her living in the tomb!* Said I not that my senses were acute? I *now* tell you that I heard her first feeble movements in the hollow coffin. I heard them—many, many days ago—yet I dared not—*I dared not speak!* And now tonight—Ethelred—ha! ha!—the breaking of the hermit's door, and the death-cry of the dragon, and the clangor of the shield!—say, rather, the rending of her coffin, and the grating of the iron hinges of her prison, and her struggles within the coppered archway of the vault! Oh, whither shall I fly? Will she not be here anon? Is she not hurrying to upbraid me for my haste? Have I not heard her footstep on the stair? Do I not distinguish that heavy and horrible beating

of her heart? Madman!"—here he sprang furiously to his feet, and shrieked out his syllables, as if in the effort he were giving up his soul— *"Madman! I tell you that she now stands without the door!"*

As if in the superhuman energy of his utterance there had been found the potency of a spell, the huge antique panels to which the speaker pointed threw slowly back, upon the instant, their ponderous and ebony jaws. It was the work of the rushing gust [1]—but then without those doors there *did* stand the lofty and enshrouded figure of the lady Madeline of Usher. There was blood upon her white robes, and the evidence of some bitter struggle upon every portion of her emaciated frame. For a moment she remained trembling and reeling to and fro upon the threshold—then, with a low moaning cry, fell heavily inward upon the person of her brother, and, in her violent and now final death-agonies, bore him to the floor a corpse, and a victim to the terrors he had anticipated.

From that chamber, and from that mansion, I fled aghast. The storm was still abroad in all its wrath as I found myself crossing the old causeway. Suddenly there shot along the path a wild light, and I turned to see whence a gleam so unusual could have issued; for the vast house and its shadows were alone behind me. The radiance was that of the full, setting, and blood-red moon, which now shone vividly through that once barely discernible fissure, of which I have before spoken as extending from the roof of the building, in a zigzag direction, to the base. While I gazed, this fissure rapidly widened—there came a fierce breath of the whirlwind—the entire orb of the satellite burst at once upon my sight—my brain reeled as I saw the mighty walls rushing asunder—there was a long tumultuous shouting sound like the voice of a thousand waters—and the deep and dank tarn at my feet closed sullenly and silently over the fragments of the *"House of Usher."* [2]

1839

[1] "Perhaps this is the finest touch in the tale. The reader is fully prepared for the apparition of the lady Madeline. Then, for the briefest possible moment, with the natural explanation of the opening of the doors, his expectation is disappointed, to the great intensifying of the thrill that follows when, after all, the apparition is revealed." *Poems and Tales of Edgar Allan Poe*, edited by Alphonso G. Newcomer, *The Lake English Classics.*

[2] If the student does not at first see the perfection of plan in this story he should re-read it until he understands how ingeniously part answers to part. Poe himself in reviewing Hawthorne's *Twice-Told Tales* said: "A skilful literary artist has constructed a tale. If wise, he has not fashioned his thoughts to accommodate his incidents;

A DESCENT INTO THE MAELSTROM [1]

The ways of God in Nature, as in Providence, are not as our *ways; nor are the models that we frame any way commensurate to the vastness, profundity, and unsearchableness of His works, which have a depth in them greater than the well of Democritus.*

JOSEPH GLANVILL [2]

We had now reached the summit of the loftiest crag. For some minutes the old man seemed too much exhausted to speak.

"Not long ago," said he at length, "and I could have guided you on this route as well as the youngest of my sons; but, about three years past, there happened to me an event such as never happened before to mortal man— or at least such as no man ever survived to tell of—and the six hours of deadly terror which I then endured have broken me up body and soul. You suppose me a *very* old man— but I am not. It took less than a single day to change these hairs from a jetty black to white, to weaken my limbs, and to unstring my nerves, so that I tremble at the least exertion, and am frightened at a shadow. Do you know I can scarcely look over this little cliff without getting giddy?"

The "little cliff," upon whose edge he had so carelessly thrown himself down to rest that the weightier portion of his body hung over it, while he was only kept from falling by the tenure of his elbow on its extreme and slippery edge—this "little cliff" arose, a sheer unobstructed precipice of black shining rock, some fifteen or sixteen hundred feet from the world of crags beneath us. Nothing would have tempted me to within half a dozen yards of its brink. In truth so deeply was I excited by the perilous position of my companion, that I fell at full length upon the ground, clung to the shrubs around me, and dared not even glance upward at the sky—while I struggled in vain to divest myself of the idea that the very foundations of the mountain were in danger from the fury of the winds. It was long before I could reason myself into sufficient courage to sit up and look out into the distance.

"You must get over these fancies," said the guide, "for I have brought you here that you might have the best possible view of the scene of that event I mentioned—and to tell you the whole story with the spot just under your eye.

"We are now," he continued, in that particularizing manner which distinguished him—"we are now close upon the Norwegian coast—in the sixty-eighth degree of latitude—in the great province of Nordland—and in the dreary district of Lofoden. The mountain upon whose top we sit is Helseggen, the Cloudy. Now raise yourself up a little higher—hold on to the grass if you feel giddy—so—and look out, beyond the belt of vapor beneath us, into the sea."

I looked dizzily, and beheld a wide expanse of ocean, whose waters wore so inky a hue as to bring at once to my mind the Nubian geographer's account of the *Mare Tenebrarum.* [3] A panorama more deplorably desolate no human imagination can conceive. To the right and left, as far as the eye could reach, there lay outstretched, like ramparts of the world, lines of horridly black and beetling cliff, whose character of gloom was but the more forcibly illustrated by the surf which reared high up against it its white and ghastly crest, howling and shrieking forever. Just opposite the promontory upon whose apex we were placed, and at a distance of some five or six miles out at sea, there was visible a small, bleak-looking island; or, more properly, its position was discernible through the wilderness of surge in which it was enveloped. About two miles nearer the land arose another of smaller size, hideously craggy and barren, and encompassed at various intervals by a cluster of dark rocks.

The appearance of the ocean, in the space between the more distant island and the shore, had something very unusual about it. Although, at the time, so strong a gale was blowing landward that a brig in the remote offing lay to under a double-reefed trysail, and constantly plunged her whole hull out of sight, still, there was here nothing like a regular swell, but only

---

but having conceived, with deliberate care, a certain unique or single *effect* to be wrought out, he then invents such incidents—he then combines such events as may best aid him in establishing this preconceived effect. If his very initial sentence tend not to the outbringing of this effect, then he has failed in his first step. In the whole composition there should be no word written, of which the tendency, direct or indirect, is not to the one preëstablished design. And by such means, with such care and skill, a picture is at length painted which leaves in the mind of him who contemplates it with a kindred art, a sense of the fullest satisfaction. The idea of the tale has been presented unblemished, because undisturbed."

[1] A strong and dangerous tidal current, not literally a whirlpool, really exists on the coast of Norway. Although Poe had never been there, he is fairly correct in his references to actual places.

[2] Joseph Glanvill was an English divine of the seventeenth century. Democritus of Abdera was a contemporary of Socrates and one of the founders of the atomic philosophy. The "well" is perhaps the infinite void through which he conceived atoms, the ultimate material of all things, to be moving.

[3] The sea of darkness, the outer ocean unexplored by the dwellers about the Mediterranean; "the Nubian geographer" is Ptolemy Chennus, an Alexandrian of the time of Trajan. There is no proof that he was a Nubian.

a short, quick, angry cross-dashing of water in every direction—as well in the teeth of the wind as otherwise. Of foam there was little except in the immediate vicinity of the rocks.

"The island in the distance," resumed the old man, "is called by the Norwegians Vurrgh. The one midway is Moskoe. That a mile to the northward is Ambaaren. Yonder are Iflesen, Hoeyholm, Kieldholm, Suarven, and Buckholm. Farther off—between Moskoe and Vurrgh—are Otterholm, Flimen, Sandflesen, and Skarholm. These are the true names of the places—but why it has been thought necessary to name them at all is more than either you or I can understand. Do you hear anything? Do you see any change in the water?"

We had now been about ten minutes upon the top of Helseggen, to which we had ascended from the interior of Lofoden, so that we had caught no glimpse of the sea until it had burst upon us from the summit. As the old man spoke, I became aware of a loud and gradually increasing sound, like the moaning of a vast herd of buffaloes upon an American prairie; and at the same moment I perceived that what seamen term the *chopping* character of the ocean beneath us, was rapidly changing into a current which set to the eastward. Even while I gazed, this current acquired a monstrous velocity. Each moment added to its speed—to its headlong impetuosity. In five minutes the whole sea, as far as Vurrgh, was lashed into ungovernable fury; but it was between Moskoe and the coast that the main uproar held its sway. Here the vast bed of the waters, seamed and scarred into a thousand conflicting channels, burst suddenly into frenzied convulsion—heaving, boiling, hissing—gyrating in gigantic and innumerable vortices, and all whirling and plunging on to the eastward with a rapidity which water never elsewhere assumes, except in precipitous descents.

In a few minutes more, there came over the scene another radical alteration. The general surface grew somewhat more smooth, and the whirlpools, one by one, disappeared, while prodigious streaks of foam became apparent where none had been seen before. These streaks, at length, spreading out to a great distance, and entering into combination, took unto themselves the gyratory motion of the subsided vortices, and seemed to form the germ of another more vast. Suddenly—very suddenly—this assumed a distinct and definite existence, in a circle of more than a mile in diameter. The edge of the whirl was represented by a broad belt of gleaming spray; but no particle of this slipped into the mouth of the terrific funnel, whose interior, as far as the eye could fathom it, was a smooth, shining, and jet-black wall of water, inclined to the horizon at an angle of some forty-five degrees, speeding dizzily round and round with a swaying and sweltering motion, and sending forth to the winds an appalling voice, half shriek, half roar, such as not even the mighty cataract of Niagara ever lifts up in its agony to Heaven.

The mountain trembled to its very base, and the rock rocked. I threw myself upon my face, and clung to the scant herbage in an excess of nervous agitation.

"This," said I at length, to the old man— "this *can* be nothing else than the great whirlpool of the Maelström."

"So it is sometimes termed," said he. "We Norwegians call it the Moskoe-ström, from the island of Moskoe in the midway."

The ordinary accounts of this vortex had by no means prepared me for what I saw. That of Jonas Ramus, [1] which is perhaps the most circumstantial of any, cannot impart the faintest conception either of the magnificence or the horror of the scene—or of the wild bewildering sense of *the novel* which confounds the beholder. I am not sure from what point of view the writer in question surveyed it, nor at what time; but it could neither have been from the summit of Helseggen, nor during a storm. There are some passages of his description, nevertheless, which may be quoted for their details, although their effect is exceedingly feeble in conveying an impression of the spectacle.

"Between Lofoden and Moskoe," he says, "the depth of the water is between thirty-six and forty fathoms; but on the other side, toward Ver (Vurrgh), this depth decreases so as not to afford a convenient passage for a vessel, without the risk of splitting on the rocks, which happens even in the calmest weather. When it is flood, the stream runs up the country between Lofoden and Moskoe with a boisterous rapidity; but the roar of its impetuous ebb to the sea is scarce equaled by the loudest and most dreadful cataracts, the noise being heard several leagues off; and the vortices or pits are of such an extent and depth, that if a ship comes within its attraction, it is inevitably absorbed and carried down to the bottom, and there beat to pieces against the rocks; and when the water relaxes, the fragments thereof are thrown up again. But these intervals of tranquillity are only at the turn of the ebb and flood, and in calm weather, and last but a quarter of an hour, its violence gradually returning. When the stream is most boisterous, and its fury heightened by a storm, it is

[1] a Norse historian of the seventeenth century

dangerous to come within a Norway mile of it. Boats, yachts, and ships have been carried away by not guarding against it before they were within its reach. It likewise happens frequently that whales come too near the stream, and are overpowered by its violence; but then it is impossible to describe their howlings and bellowings in their fruitless struggles to disengage themselves. A bear once, attempting to swim from Lofoden to Moskoe, was caught by the stream and borne down, while he roared terribly, so as to be heard on shore. Large stocks of firs and pine trees, after being absorbed by the current, rise again broken and torn to such a degree as if bristles grew upon them. This plainly shows the bottom to consist of craggy rocks, among which they are whirled to and fro. This stream is regulated by the flux and reflux of the sea—it being constantly high and low water every six hours. In the year 1645, early in the morning of Sexagesima Sunday, it raged with such noise and impetuosity that the very stones of the houses on the coast fell to the ground."

In regard to the depth of the water, I could not see how this could have been ascertained at all in the immediate vicinity of the vortex. The "forty fathoms" must have reference only to portions of the channel close upon the shore either of Moskoe or Lofoden. The depth in the center of the Moskoe-ström must be immeasurably greater; and no better proof of this fact is necessary than can be obtained from even the sidelong glance into the abyss of the whirl which may be had from the highest crag of Helseggen. Looking down from this pinnacle upon the howling Phlegethon [1] below, I could not help smiling at the simplicity with which the honest Jonas Ramus records, as a matter difficult of belief, the anecdotes of the whales and the bears; for it appeared to me, in fact, a self-evident thing that the largest ships of the line in existence, coming within the influence of that deadly attraction, could resist it as little as a feather the hurricane, and must disappear bodily and at once.

The attempts to account for the phenomenon —some of which, I remember, seemed to me sufficiently plausible in perusal—now wore a very different and unsatisfactory aspect. The idea generally received is that this, as well as three smaller vortices among the Feroe Islands, "have no other cause than the collision of waves rising and falling, at flux and reflux, against a ridge of rocks and shelves, which confines the water so that it precipitates itself like a cataract; and thus the higher the flood rises, the deeper must the fall be, and the natural result of all is a whirlpool or vortex, the prodigious suction of which is sufficiently known by lesser

[1] the flaming river of the lower world

experiments."—These are the words of the *Encyclopedia Britannica.* Kircher [2] and others imagine that in the center of the channel of the Maelström is an abyss penetrating the globe, and issuing in some very remote part—the Gulf of Bothnia being somewhat decidedly named in one instance. This opinion, idle in itself, was the one to which, as I gazed, my imagination most readily assented; and, mentioning it to the guide, I was rather surprised to hear him say that, although it was the view almost universally entertained of the subject by the Norwegians, it nevertheless was not his own. As to the former notion he confessed his inability to comprehend it; and here I agreed with him— for, however conclusive on paper, it becomes altogether unintelligible, and even absurd, amid the thunder of the abyss.

"You have had a good look at the whirl now," said the old man, " and if you will creep round this crag, so as to get in its lee, and deaden the roar of the water, I will tell you a story that will convince you I ought to know something of the Moskoe-ström."

I placed myself as desired, and he proceeded.

"Myself and my two brothers once owned a schooner-rigged smack of about seventy tons burden, with which we were in the habit of fishing among the islands beyond Moskoe, nearly to Vurrgh. In all violent eddies at sea there is good fishing, at proper opportunities, if one has only the courage to attempt it; but among the whole of the Lofoden coastmen we three were the only ones who made a regular business of going out to the islands, as I tell you. The usual grounds are a great way lower down to the southward. There fish can be got at all hours, without much risk, and therefore these places are preferred. The choice spots over here among the rocks, however, not only yield the finest variety, but in far greater abundance; so that we often got in a single day what the more timid of the craft could not scrape together in a week. In fact, we made it a matter of desperate speculation—the risk of life standing instead of labor, and courage answering for capital.

"We kept the smack in a cove about five miles higher up the coast than this; and it was our practice, in fine weather, to take advantage of the fifteen minutes' slack to push across the main channel of the Moskoe-ström, far above the pool, and then drop down upon anchorage somewhere near Otterholm, or Sandflesen, where the eddies are not so violent as elsewhere. Here we used to remain until nearly

[2] a seventeenth century German mathematician

time for slack water again, when we weighed and made for home. We never set out upon this expedition without a steady side wind for going and coming—one that we felt sure would not fail us before our return—and we seldom made a miscalculation upon this point. Twice, during six years, we were forced to stay all night at anchor on account of a dead calm, which is a rare thing indeed just about here; and once we had to remain on the grounds nearly a week, starving to death, owing to a gale which blew up shortly after our arrival, and made the channel too boisterous to be thought of. Upon this occasion we should have been driven out to sea in spite of everything (for the whirlpools threw us round and round so violently that, at length, we fouled our anchor and dragged it) if it had not been that we drifted into one of the innumerable cross currents—here today and gone tomorrow—which drove us under the lee of Flimen, where, by good luck, we brought up.

"I could not tell you the twentieth part of the difficulties we encountered 'on the ground'— it is a bad spot to be in, even in good weather —but we made shift always to run the gauntlet of the Moskoe-ström itself without accident; although at times my heart has been in my mouth when we happened to be a minute or so behind or before the slack. The wind sometimes was not as strong as we thought it at starting, and then we made rather less way than we could wish, while the current rendered the smack unmanageable. My eldest brother had a son eighteen years old, and I had two stout boys of my own. These would have been of great assistance at such times, in using the sweeps, [1] as well as afterward in fishing—but, somehow, although we ran the risk ourselves, we had not the heart to let the young ones get into the danger—for, after all said and done, it *was* a horrible danger, and that is the truth.

"It is now within a few days of three years since what I am going to tell you occurred. It was on the tenth of July, 18—, a day which the people of this part of the world will never forget—for it was one in which blew the most terrible hurricane that ever came out of the heavens. And yet all the morning, and indeed until late in the afternoon, there was a gentle and steady breeze from the southwest, while the sun shone brightly, so that the oldest seaman among us could not have foreseen what was to follow.

"The three of us—my two brothers and myself—had crossed over to the islands about two o'clock P.M., and soon nearly loaded the smack with fine fish, which, we all remarked, were more plenty that day than we had ever known them. It was just seven, *by my watch,* when we weighed and started for home, so as to make the worst of the Ström at slack water, which we knew would be at eight.

"We set out with a fresh wind on our starboard quarter, and for some time spanked along at a great rate, never dreaming of danger, for indeed we saw not the slightest reason to apprehend it. All at once we were taken aback [2] by a breeze from over Helseggen. This was most unusual—something that had never happened to us before—and I began to feel a little uneasy, without exactly knowing why. We put the boat on the wind, but could make no headway at all for the eddies, and I was upon the point of proposing to return to the anchorage, when, looking astern, we saw the whole horizon covered with a singular copper-colored cloud that rose with the most amazing velocity.

"In the mean time the breeze that had headed us off fell away, and we were dead becalmed, drifting about in every direction. This state of things, however, did not last long enough to give us time to think about it. In less than a minute the storm was upon us—in less than two the sky was entirely overcast—and what with this and the driving spray, it became suddenly so dark that we could not see each other in the smack.

"Such a hurricane as then blew it is folly to attempt describing. The oldest seaman in Norway never experienced anything like it. We had let our sails go by the run before it cleverly [3] took us; but, at the first puff, both our masts went by the board as if they had been sawed off—the mainmast taking with it my youngest brother, who had lashed himself to it for safety.

"Our boat was the lightest feather of a thing that ever sat upon water. It had a complete flush deck, with only a small hatch near the bow, and this hatch it had always been our custom to batten down when about to cross the Ström, by way of precaution against the chopping seas. But for this circumstance we should have foundered at once—for we lay entirely buried for some moments. How my elder brother escaped destruction I cannot say, for I never had an opportunity of ascertaining. For my part, as soon as I had let the foresail run, I threw myself flat on deck, with my feet against the narrow gunwale of the bow, and with my hands grasping a ringbolt near the foot of the foremast. It was mere instinct that prompted me to do this—which was undoubt-

[1] large oars used in guiding or propelling a vessel

[2] See note 2, Cooper, *The Pilot*, p. 220.
[3] actually

edly the very best thing I could have done—for I was too much flurried to think.

"For some moments we were completely deluged, as I say, and all this time I held my breath, and clung to the bolt. When I could stand it no longer I raised myself upon my knees, still keeping hold with my hands, and thus got my head clear. Presently our little boat gave herself a shake, just as a dog does in coming out of the water, and thus rid herself, in some measure, of the seas. I was now trying to get the better of the stupor that had come over me, and to collect my senses so as to see what was to be done, when I felt somebody grasp my arm. It was my elder brother, and my heart leaped for joy, for I had made sure that he was overboard—but the next moment all this joy was turned into horror—for he put his mouth close to my ear, and screamed out the word 'Moskoe-ström!'

"No one will ever know what my feelings were at that moment. I shook from head to foot as if I had had the most violent fit of the ague. I knew what he meant by that one word well enough—I knew what he wished to make me understand. With the wind that now drove us on, we were bound for the whirl of the Ström, and nothing could save us!

"You perceive that in crossing the Ström channel, we always went a long way up above the whirl, even in the calmest weather, and then had to wait and watch carefully for the slack—but now we were driving right upon the pool itself, and in such a hurricane as this! 'To be sure,' I thought, 'we shall get there just about the slack—there is some little hope in that'—but in the next moment I cursed myself for being so great a fool as to dream of hope at all. I knew very well that we were doomed, had we been ten times a ninety-gun ship.

"By this time the first fury of the tempest had spent itself, or perhaps we did not feel it so much as we scudded before it; but at all events the seas, which at first had been kept down by the wind, and lay flat and frothing, now got up into absolute mountains. A singular change, too, had come over the heavens. Around in every direction it was still as black as pitch, but nearly overhead there burst out, all at once, a circular rift of clear sky—as clear as I ever saw—and of a deep bright blue—and through it there blazed forth the full moon with a luster that I never before knew her to wear. She lit up everything about us with the greatest distinctness—but, oh God, what a scene it was to light up!

"I now made one or two attempts to speak to my brother—but, in some manner which I could not understand, the din had so increased that I could not make him hear a single word, although I screamed at the top of my voice in his ear. Presently he shook his head, looking as pale as death, and held up one of his fingers, as if to say listen!

"At first I could not make out what he meant—but soon a hideous thought flashed upon me. I dragged my watch from its fob. It was not going. I glanced at its face by the moonlight, and then burst into tears as I flung it far away into the ocean. It had run down at seven o'clock! We were behind the time of the slack, and the whirl of the Ström was in full fury!

"When a boat is well built, properly trimmed, and not deep laden, the waves in a strong gale, when she is going large, [1] seem always to slip from beneath her—which appears very strange to a landsman—and this is what is called riding, in sea phrase.

"Well, so far we had ridden the swells very cleverly; but presently a gigantic sea happened to take us right under the counter, and bore us with it as it rose—up—up—as if into the sky. I would not have believed that any wave could rise so high. And then down we came with a sweep, a slide, and a plunge, that made me feel sick and dizzy, as if I was falling from some lofty mountain-top in a dream. But while we were up I had thrown a quick glance around—and that one glance was all-sufficient. I saw our exact position in an instant. The Moskoe-ström whirlpool was about a quarter of a mile dead ahead—but no more like the everyday Moskoe-ström, than the whirl as you now see it is like a mill-race. If I had not known where we were, and what we had to expect, I should not have recognized the place at all. As it was, I involuntarily closed my eyes in horror. The lids clenched themselves together as if in a spasm.

"It could not have been more than two minutes afterwards until we suddenly felt the waves subside, and were enveloped in foam. The boat made a sharp half turn to larboard, and then shot off in its new direction like a thunderbolt. At the same moment the roaring noise of the water was completely drowned in a kind of shrill shriek—such a sound as you might imagine given out by the water-pipes of many thousand steam vessels, letting off their steam all together. We were now in the belt of surf that always surrounds the whirl; and I thought, of course, that another moment would plunge us into the abyss—down which we could only see indistinctly on account of the amazing velocity with which we were borne along. The

[1] See note 4, Cooper, The Pilot, p. 220.

boat did not seem to sink into the water at all, but to skim like an air-bubble upon the surface of the surge. Her starboard side was next the whirl, and on the larboard arose the world of ocean we had left. It stood like a huge writhing wall between us and the horizon.

"It may appear strange, but now, when we were in the very jaws of the gulf, I felt more composed than when we were only approaching it. Having made up my mind to hope no more, I got rid of a great deal of that terror which unmanned me at first. I suppose it was despair that strung my nerves.

"It may look like boasting—but what I tell you is truth—I began to reflect how magnificent a thing it was to die in such a manner, and how foolish it was in me to think of so paltry a consideration as my own individual life, in view of so wonderful a manifestation of God's power. I do believe that I blushed with shame when this idea crossed my mind. After a little while I became possessed with the keenest curiosity about the whirl itself. I positively felt a *wish* to explore its depths, even at the sacrifice I was going to make; and my principal grief was that I should never be able to tell my old companions on shore about the mysteries I should see. These, no doubt, were singular fancies to occupy a man's mind in such extremity—and I have often thought since, that the revolutions of the boat around the pool might have rendered me a little light-headed.

"There was another circumstance which tended to restore my self-possession; and this was the cessation of the wind, which could not reach us in our present situation—for, as you saw yourself, the belt of surf is considerably lower than the general bed of the ocean, and this latter now towered above us, a high, black, mountainous ridge. If you have never been at sea in a heavy gale, you can form no idea of the confusion of mind occasioned by the wind and spray together. They blind, deafen, and strangle you, and take away all power of action or reflection. But we were now, in a great measure, rid of these annoyances—just as death-condemned felons in prisons are allowed petty indulgences, forbidden them while their doom is yet uncertain.

"How often we made the circuit of the belt it is impossible to say. We careered round and round for perhaps an hour, flying rather than floating, getting gradually more and more into the middle of the surge, and then nearer and nearer to its horrible inner edge. All this time I had never let go of the ring-bolt. My brother was at the stern, holding on to a small empty water-cask which had been securely lashed under the coop of the counter, and was the only thing on deck that had not been swept overboard when the gale first took us. As we approached the brink of the pit he let go his hold upon this, and made for the ring, from which, in the agony of his terror, he endeavored to force my hands, as it was not large enough to afford us both a secure grasp. I never felt deeper grief than when I saw him attempt this act—although I knew he was a madman when he did it—a raving maniac through sheer fright. I did not care, however, to contest the point with him. I knew it could make no difference whether either of us held on at all; so I let him have the bolt, and went astern to the cask. This there was no great difficulty in doing; for the smack flew round steadily enough, and upon an even keel—only swaying to and fro, with the immense sweeps and swelters of the whirl. Scarcely had I secured myself in my new position, when we gave a wild lurch to starboard, and rushed headlong into the abyss. I muttered a hurried prayer to God, and thought all was over.

"As I felt the sickening sweep of the descent, I had instinctively tightened my hold upon the barrel, and closed my eyes. For some seconds I dared not open them—while I expected instant destruction, and wondered that I was not already in my death-struggles with the water. But moment after moment elapsed. I still lived. The sense of falling had ceased; and the motion of the vessel seemed much as it had been before, while in the belt of foam, with the exception that she now lay more along.[1] I took courage and looked once again upon the scene.

"Never shall I forget the sensations of awe, horror, and admiration with which I gazed about me. The boat appeared to be hanging, as if by magic, midway down, upon the interior surface of a funnel vast in circumference, prodigious in depth, and whose perfectly smooth sides might have been mistaken for ebony, but for the bewildering rapidity with which they spun around, and for the gleaming and ghastly radiance they shot forth, as the rays of the full moon, from that circular rift amid the clouds, which I have already described, streamed in a flood of golden glory along the black walls, and far away down into the inmost recesses of the abyss.

"At first I was too much confused to observe anything accurately. The general burst of terrific grandeur was all that I beheld. When I recovered myself a little, however, my gaze fell instinctively downward. In this direction I was

[1] lay more over, as if under a side wind

able to obtain an unobstructed view, from the manner in which the smack hung on the inclined surface of the pool. She was quite upon an even keel—that is to say, her deck lay in a plane parallel with that of the water—but this latter sloped at an angle of more than forty-five degrees, so that we seemed to be lying upon our beam-ends. I could not help observing, nevertheless, that I had scarcely more difficulty in maintaining my hold and footing in this situation, than if we had been upon a dead level; and this, I suppose, was owing to the speed at which we revolved.

"The rays of the moon seemed to search the very bottom of the profound gulf; but still I could make out nothing distinctly, on account of a thick mist in which everything there was enveloped, and over which there hung a magnificent rainbow, [1] like that narrow and tottering bridge which Mussulmen say is the only pathway between Time and Eternity. This mist, or spray, was no doubt occasioned by the clashing of the great walls of the funnel, as they all met together at the bottom—but the yell that went up to the heavens from out of that mist, I dare not attempt to describe.

"Our first slide into the abyss itself, from the belt of foam above, had carried us to a great distance down the slope; but our farther descent was by no means proportionate. Round and round we swept—not with any uniform movement, but in dizzying swings and jerks, that sent us sometimes only a few hundred yards—sometimes nearly the complete circuit of the whirl. Our progress downward, at each revolution, was slow, but very perceptible.

"Looking about me upon the wide waste of liquid ebony on which we were thus borne, I perceived that our boat was not the only object in the embrace of the whirl. Both above and below us were visible fragments of vessels, large masses of building timber and trunks of trees, with many smaller articles, such as pieces of house furniture, broken boxes, barrels, and staves. I have already described the unnatural curiosity which had taken the place of my original terrors. It appeared to grow upon me as I drew nearer and nearer to my dreadful doom. I now began to watch, with a strange interest, the numerous things that floated in our company. I *must* have been delirious—for I even sought *amusement* in speculating upon the

[1] Poe exaggerates here; a rainbow by moonlight is really very faint. But this error need not prejudice us against the imaginative vigor of the scene. The bridge Al Sirat, no broader than the edge of a scimitar, conducts the faithful across the gulf of hell, to paradise.

relative velocities of their several descents toward the foam below. 'This fir tree,' I found myself at one time saying, 'will certainly be the next thing that takes the awful plunge and disappears,'—and then I was disappointed to find that the wreck of a Dutch merchant ship overtook it and went down before. At length, after making several guesses of this nature, and being deceived in all—this fact—the fact of my invariable miscalculation, set me upon a train of reflection that made my limbs again tremble, and my heart beat heavily once more.

"It was not a new terror that thus affected me, but the dawn of a more exciting *hope*. This hope arose partly from memory, and partly from present observation. I called to mind the great variety of buoyant matter that strewed the coast of Lofoden, having been absorbed and then thrown forth by the Moskoe-ström. By far the greater number of the articles were shattered in the most extraordinary way—so chafed and roughened as to have the appearance of being stuck full of splinters—but then I distinctly recollected that there were *some* of them which were not disfigured at all. Now I could not account for this difference except by supposing that the roughened fragments were the only ones which had been *completely absorbed*—that the others had entered the whirl at so late a period of the tide, or, from some reason, had descended so slowly after entering, that they did not reach the bottom before the turn of the flood came, or of the ebb, as the case might be. I conceived it possible, in either instance, that they might thus be whirled up again to the level of the ocean, without undergoing the fate of those which had been drawn in more early or absorbed more rapidly. I made, also, three important observations. The first was, that as a general rule, the larger the bodies were, the more rapid their descent; the second, that, between two masses of equal extent, the one spherical, and the other *of any other shape*, the superiority in speed of descent was with the sphere; the third, that, between two masses of equal size, the one cylindrical, and the other of any other shape, the cylinder was absorbed the more slowly. Since my escape, I have had several conversations on this subject with an old schoolmaster of the district; and it was from him that I learned the use of the words 'cylinder' and 'sphere.' He explained to me—although I have forgotten the explanation—how what I observed was, in fact, the natural consequence of the forms of the floating fragments, and showed me how it happened that a cylinder, swimming in a vortex, offered more resistance to its suction, and was drawn in with greater difficulty, than an equally bulky body, of any form whatever. [1]

"There was one startling circumstance which went a great way in enforcing these observations, and rendering me anxious to turn them to account, and this was that, at every revolution, we passed something like a barrel, or else the yard or the mast of a vessel, while many of these things, which had been on our level when I first opened my eyes upon the wonders of the whirlpool, were now high up above us, and seemed to have moved but little from their original station.

"I no longer hesitated what to do. I resolved to lash myself securely to the water cask upon which I now held, to cut it loose from the counter, and to throw myself with it into the water. I attracted my brother's attention by signs, pointed to the floating barrels that came near us, and did everything in my power to make him understand what I was about to do. I thought at length that he comprehended my design—but, whether this was the case or not, he shook his head despairingly, and refused to move from his station by the ring-bolt. It was impossible to reach him; the emergency admitted of no delay; and so, with a bitter struggle, I resigned him to his fate, fastened myself to the cask by means of the lashings which secured it to the counter, and precipitated myself with it into the sea, without another moment's hesitation.

"The result was precisely what I had hoped it might be. As it is myself who now tell you this tale—as you see that I *did* escape—and as you are already in possession of the mode in which this escape was effected, and must therefore anticipate all that I have farther to say—I will bring my story quickly to conclusion. It might have been an hour, or thereabout, after my quitting the smack, when, having descended to a vast distance beneath me, it made three or four wild gyrations in rapid succession, and, bearing my loved brother with it, plunged headlong, at once and forever, into the chaos of foam below. The barrel to which I was attached sunk very little farther than half the distance between the bottom of the gulf and the spot at which I leaped overboard, before a great change took place in the character of the whirlpool. The slope of the sides of the vast funnel became momently less and less steep. The gyrations of the whirl grew, gradually, less and less violent. By degrees, the

froth and the rainbow disappeared, and the bottom of the gulf seemed slowly to uprise. The sky was clear, the winds had gone down, and the full moon was setting radiantly in the west, when I found myself on the surface of the ocean, in full view of the shores of Lofoden, and above the spot where the pool of the Moskoe-ström *had been*. It was the hour of the slack, but the sea still heaved in mountainous waves from the effects of the hurricane. I was borne violently into the channel of the Ström, and in a few minutes was hurried down the coast into the 'grounds' of the fishermen. A boat picked me up—exhausted from fatigue—and (now that the danger was removed) speechless from the memory of its horror. Those who drew me on board were my old mates and daily companions, but they knew me no more than they would have known a traveler from the spirit-land. My hair, which had been raven-black the day before, was as white as you see it now. They say, too, that the whole expression of my countenance had changed. I told them my story—they did not believe it. I now tell it to you—and I can scarcely expect you to put more faith in it than did the merry fishermen of Lofoden."

1841

THE MASQUE OF THE RED DEATH [2]

(NORTHERN ITALY)

The "Red Death" had long devastated the country. No pestilence had ever been so fatal, or so hideous. Blood was its avatar and its seal—the redness and the horror of blood. There were sharp pains, and sudden dizziness, and then profuse bleeding at the pores, with dissolution. The scarlet stains upon the body, and especially upon the face, of the victim were the pest ban which shut him out from the aid and from the sympathy of his fellow-men. And the whole seizure, progress, and termination of the disease were the incidents of half an hour.

But the Prince Prospero was happy and dauntless and sagacious. When his dominions

---

[1] "See Archimedes, *De iis Quae Humido Vehuntur,* lib. ii," Poe's note.

[2] "In this tale are to be found again all those properties of ultra-Gothic romance of which Poe was the final master. As a work of art it stands quite apart from the more or less famous realistic descriptions of actual pestilence by Boccaccio, Manzoni, Defoe, and Charles Brockden Brown, though at the outset it is not a little like Boccaccio's account (see the *Decameron,* Introduction). [It is] allegorical, but without moral significance—the fear it symbolizes is purely physical. But this is another of Poe's most successful fantasies, at once gorgeous and spectral, ridiculously impossible, yet awfully real." *Poems and Tales of Edgar Allan Poe,* edited by Alphonso G. Newcomer, *The Lake English Classics.*

were half depopulated, he summoned to his presence a thousand hale and light-hearted friends from among the knights and dames of his court, and with these retired to the deep seclusion of one of his castellated abbeys. This was an extensive and magnificent structure, the creation of the Prince's own eccentric yet august taste. A strong and lofty wall girdled it in. This wall had gates of iron. The courtiers, having entered, brought furnaces and massy hammers, and welded the bolts. They resolved to leave means neither of ingress or egress to the sudden impulses of despair or of frenzy from within. The abbey was amply provisioned. With such precautions the courtiers might bid defiance to contagion. The external world could take care of itself. In the mean time it was folly to grieve, or to think. The Prince had provided all the appliances of pleasure. There were buffoons, there were improvisatori, [1] there were ballet-dancers, there were musicians, there was Beauty, there was wine. All these and security were within. Without was the "Red Death."

It was toward the close of the fifth or sixth month of his seclusion, and while the pestilence raged most furiously abroad, that the Prince Prospero entertained his thousand friends at a masked ball of the most unusual magnificence.

It was a voluptuous scene, that masquerade. But first let me tell of the rooms in which it was held. There were seven—an imperial suite. In many palaces, however, such suites form a long and straight vista, while the folding-doors slide back nearly to the walls on either hand, so that the view of the whole extent is scarcely impeded. Here the case was very different, as might have been expected from the Prince's love of the bizarre. The apartments were so irregularly disposed that the vision embraced but little more than one at a time. There was a sharp turn at every twenty or thirty yards, and at each turn a novel effect. To the right and left, in the middle of each wall, a tall and narrow Gothic window looked out upon a closed corridor which pursued the windings of the suite. These windows were of stained glass, whose color varied in accordance with the prevailing hue of the decorations of the chamber into which it opened. That at the eastern extremity was hung, for example, in blue—and vividly blue were its windows. The second chamber was purple in its ornaments and tapestries, and here the panes were purple. The third was green throughout, and so were the casements. The fourth was furnished and lighted with orange, the fifth with white, the

[1] those who improvise: poets

sixth with violet. The seventh apartment was closely shrouded in black velvet tapestries that hung all over the ceiling and down the walls, falling in heavy folds upon a carpet of the same material and hue. But, in this chamber only, the color of the windows failed to correspond with the decorations. The panes here were scarlet—a deep blood-color. Now in no one of the seven apartments was there any lamp or candelabrum, amid the profusion of golden ornaments that lay scattered to and fro or depended from the roof. There was no light of any kind emanating from lamp or candle within the suite of chambers. But in the corridors that followed the suite there stood, opposite to each window, a heavy tripod, bearing a brazier of fire, that projected its rays through the tinted glass and so glaringly illumined the room. And thus were produced a multitude of gaudy and fantastic appearances. But in the western or black chamber the effect of the firelight that streamed upon the dark hangings through the blood-tinted panes was ghastly in the extreme, and produced so wild a look upon the countenances of those who entered that there were few of the company bold enough to set foot within its precincts at all.

It was in this apartment, also, that there stood against the western wall a gigantic clock of ebony. Its pendulum swung to and fro with a dull, heavy, monotonous clang; and when the minute-hand made the circuit of the face, and the hour was to be stricken, there came from the brazen lungs of the clock a sound which was clear and loud and deep and exceedingly musical, but of so peculiar a note and emphasis that, at each lapse of an hour, the musicians of the orchestra were constrained to pause, momentarily, in their performance, to hearken to the sound; and thus the waltzers perforce ceased their evolutions; and there was a brief disconcert of the whole gay company; and, while the chimes of the clock yet rang, it was observed that the giddiest grew pale, and the more aged and sedate passed their hands over their brows as if in confused revery or meditation. But when the echoes had fully ceased, a light laughter at once pervaded the assembly; the musicians looked at each other and smiled as if at their own nervousness and folly, and made whispering vows, each to the other, that the next chiming of the clock should produce in them no similar emotion; and then, after the lapse of sixty minutes (which embrace three thousand and six hundred seconds of the Time that flies) there came yet another chiming of the clock, and then were the same disconcert and tremulousness and meditation as before.

But, in spite of these things, it was a gay and magnificent revel. The tastes of the Prince were peculiar. He had a fine eye for colors and effects. He disregarded the *decora* of mere fashion. His plans were bold and fiery, and his conceptions glowed with barbaric luster. There are some who would have thought him mad. His followers felt that he was not. It was necessary to hear and see and touch him to be *sure* that he was not.

He had directed, in great part, the movable embellishments of the seven chambers, upon occasion of this great *fête;* and it was his own guiding taste which had given character to the masqueraders. Be sure they were grotesque. There were much glare and glitter and piquancy and phantasm—much of what has been since seen in *Hernani.* [1] There were arabesque figures with unsuited limbs and appointments. There were delirious fancies such as the madman fashions. There was much of the beautiful, much of the wanton, much of the bizarre, something of the terrible, and not a little of that which might have excited disgust. To and fro in the seven chambers there stalked, in fact, a multitude of dreams. And these—the dreams —writhed in and about, taking hue from the rooms, and causing the wild music of the orchestra to seem as the echo of their steps. And, anon, there strikes the ebony clock which stands in the hall of the velvet. And then, for a moment, all is still, and all is silent save the voice of the clock. The dreams are stiff-frozen as they stand. But the echoes of the chime die away—they have endured but an instant—and a light, half-subdued laughter floats after them as they depart. And now again the music swells, and the dreams live, and writhe to and fro more merrily than ever, taking hue from the many tinted windows through which stream the rays from the tripods. But to the chamber which lies most westwardly of the seven, there are now none of the maskers who venture; for the night is waning away, and there flows a ruddier light through the blood-colored panes; and the blackness of the sable drapery appalls; and to him whose foot falls upon the sable carpet, there comes from the near clock of ebony a muffled peal more solemnly emphatic than any which reaches *their* ears who indulge in the more remote gayeties of the other apartments.

But these other apartments were densely crowded, and in them beat feverishly the heart of life. And the revel went whirlingly on, until at length there commenced the sounding of midnight upon the clock. And then the music ceased, as I have told; and the evolutions of the waltzers were quieted; and there was an uneasy cessation of all things as before. But now there were twelve strokes to be sounded by the bell of the clock; and thus it happened, perhaps, that more of thought crept, with more of time, into the meditations of the thoughtful among those who reveled. And thus, too, it happened, perhaps, that before the last echoes of the last chime had utterly sunk into silence, there were many individuals in the crowd who had found leisure to become aware of the presence of a masked figure which had arrested the attention of no single individual before. And the rumor of this new presence having spread itself whisperingly around, there arose at length from the whole company a buzz, or murmur, expressive of disapprobation and surprise—then, finally, of terror, of horror, and of disgust.

In an assembly of phantasms such as I have painted, it may well be supposed that no ordinary appearance could have excited such sensation. In truth the masquerade license of the night was nearly unlimited; but the figure in question had out-Heroded Herod, [2] and gone beyond the bounds of even the Prince's indefinite decorum. There are chords in the hearts of the most reckless which cannot be touched without emotion. Even with the utterly lost, to whom life and death are equally jests, there are matters of which no jest can be made. The whole company, indeed, seemed now deeply to feel that in the costume and bearing of the stranger neither wit nor propriety existed. The figure was tall and gaunt, and shrouded from head to foot in the habiliments of the grave. The mask which concealed the visage was made so nearly to resemble the countenance of a stiffened corpse that the closest scrutiny must have had difficulty in detecting the cheat. And yet all this might have been endured, if not approved, by the mad revelers around. But the mummer had gone so far as to assume the type of the Red Death. His vesture was dabbled in *blood*—and his broad brow, with all the features of the face, was besprinkled with the scarlet horror.

When the eyes of Prince Prospero fell upon this spectral image (which with a slow and solemn movement, as if more fully to sustain its *rôle*, stalked to and fro among the waltzers) he was seen to be convulsed, in the first

---

[1] a tragedy by Victor Hugo, 1830: the beginning of the modern romantic drama in France

[2] Herod, a character in the old Mystery Plays, was usually over-acted. See *Hamlet* III, ii, 15.

moment, with a strong shudder, either of terror or distaste; but, in the next, his brow reddened with rage.

"Who dares?" he demanded hoarsely of the courtiers who stood near him—"who dares insult us with this blasphemous mockery? Seize him and unmask him—that we may know whom we have to hang at sunrise, from the battlements!"

It was in the eastern or blue chamber in which stood the Prince Prospero as he uttered these words. They rang throughout the seven rooms loudly and clearly—for the Prince was a bold and robust man, and the music had become hushed at the waving of his hand.

It was in the blue room where stood the Prince, with a group of pale courtiers by his side. At first, as he spoke, there was a slight rushing movement of this group in the direction of the intruder, who at the moment was also near at hand, and now, with deliberate and stately step, made closer approach to the speaker. But from a certain nameless awe with which the mad assumptions of the mummer had inspired the whole party, there were found none who put forth hand to seize him; so that, unimpeded, he passed within a yard of the Prince's person; and while the vast assembly, as if with one impulse, shrank from the centers of the rooms to the wall, he made his way uninterruptedly, but with the same solemn and measured step which had distinguished him from the first, through the blue chamber to the purple—through the purple to the green—through the green to the orange—through this again to the white—and even thence to the violet, ere a decided movement had been made to arrest him. It was then, however, that the Prince Prospero, maddening with rage and the shame of his own momentary cowardice, rushed hurriedly through the six chambers, while none followed him, on account of a deadly terror that had seized upon all. He bore aloft a drawn dagger, and had approached, in rapid impetuosity, to within three or four feet of the retreating figure, when the latter, having attained the extremity of the velvet apartment, turned suddenly and confronted his pursuer. There was a sharp cry—and the dagger dropped gleaming upon the sable carpet, upon which, instantly afterwards, fell prostrate in death the Prince Prospero. Then, summoning the wild courage of despair, a throng of the revelers at once threw themselves into the black apartment, and, seizing the mummer, whose tall figure stood erect and motionless within the shadow of the ebony clock, gasped in unutterable horror at finding the grave cerements and corpse-like mask, which they handled with so violent a rudeness, untenanted by any tangible form.

And now was acknowledged the presence of the Red Death. He had come like a thief in the night. And one by one dropped the revelers in the blood-bedewed halls of their revel, and died each in the despairing posture of his fall. And the life of the ebony clock went out with that of the last of the gay. And the flames of the tripods expired. And Darkness and Decay and the Red Death held illimitable dominion over all.

1845

THE PURLOINED LETTER [1]

Nil sapientiae odiosius acumine nimio. [2]

SENECA.

At Paris, just after dark one gusty evening in the autumn of 18—, I was enjoying the twofold luxury of meditation and a meerschaum, in company with my friend, C. Auguste Dupin, in his little back library, or book closet, *au troisième*, [3] No. 33 Rue Dunôt, Faubourg St. Germain. For one hour at least we had maintained a profound silence; while each, to any casual observer, might have seemed intently and exclusively occupied with the curling eddies of smoke that oppressed the atmosphere of the chamber. For myself, however, I was mentally discussing certain topics which had formed matter for conversation between us at an earlier period of the evening; I mean the affair of the Rue Morgue, and the mystery attending the murder of Marie Rogêt. I looked upon it, therefore, as something of a coincidence, when the door of our apartment was thrown open and admitted our old acquaintance, Monsieur G——, the Prefect of the Parisian police.

We gave him a hearty welcome; for there was nearly half as much of the entertaining as of the contemptible about the man, and we had not seen him for several years. We had been sitting in the dark, and Dupin now arose for the purpose of lighting a lamp, but sat down again, without doing so, upon G——'s saying that he had called to consult us, or rather to ask the opinion of my friend, about some official

---

[1] One realm of Poe's genius was that of logical or psychological analysis. "The Gold Bug," "The Murders in the Rue Morgue," "The Mystery of Marie Roget," and the present tale belong to this class. This type of fiction lies close to journalism, which was, indeed, Poe's occupation, and in the hands of a person of less skill and creative power degenerates into the ordinary detective story.

[2] "nothing more hateful to wisdom than over-acuteness"

[3] on the third floor, really the fourth, since the first, usually occupied in Paris by shops, is not counted

business which had occasioned a great deal of trouble.

"If it is any point requiring reflection," observed Dupin, as he forbore to enkindle the wick, "we shall examine it to better purpose in the dark."

"That is another of your odd notions," said the Prefect, who had a fashion of calling everything "odd" that was beyond his comprehension, and thus lived amid an absolute legion of "oddities."

"Very true," said Dupin, as he supplied his visitor with a pipe, and rolled towards him a comfortable chair.

"And what is the difficulty now?" I asked. "Nothing more in the assassination way, I hope?"

"Oh, no; nothing of that nature. The fact is, the business is *very* simple indeed, and I make no doubt that we can manage it sufficiently well ourselves; but then I thought Dupin would like to hear the details of it, because it is so excessively *odd*."

"Simple and odd," said Dupin.

"Why, yes; and not exactly that, either. The fact is, we have all been a good deal puzzled because the affair *is* so simple, and yet baffles us altogether."

"Perhaps it is the very simplicity of the thing which puts you at fault," said my friend.

"What nonsense you *do* talk!" replied the Prefect, laughing heartily.

"Perhaps the mystery is a little *too* plain," said Dupin.

"Oh, good heavens! who ever heard of such an idea?"

"A little *too* self evident."

"Ha! ha! ha!—ha! ha! ha!—ho! ho! ho!" roared our visitor, profoundly amused, "oh, Dupin, you will be the death of me yet!"

"And what, after all, *is* the matter on hand?" I asked.

"Why, I will tell you," replied the Prefect, as he gave a long, steady, and contemplative puff, and settled himself in his chair. "I will tell you in a few words; but, before I begin, let me caution you that this is an affair demanding the greatest secrecy, and that I should most probably lose the position I now hold were it known that I confided it to any one."

"Proceed," said I.

"Or not," said Dupin.

"Well, then; I have received personal information from a very high quarter that a certain document of the last importance has been purloined from the royal apartments. The individual who purloined it is known; this beyond a doubt; he was seen to take it. It is known, also, that it still remains in his possession."

"How is this known?" asked Dupin.

"It is clearly inferred," replied the Prefect, "from the nature of the document, and from the non-appearance of certain results which would at once arise from its passing *out* of the robber's possession; that is to say, from his employing it as he must design in the end to employ it."

"Be a little more explicit," I said.

"Well, I may venture so far as to say that the paper gives its holder a certain power in a certain quarter where such power is immensely valuable." The Prefect was fond of the cant of diplomacy.

"Still I do not quite understand," said Dupin.

"No? Well; the disclosure of the document to a third person, who shall be nameless, would bring in question the honor of a personage of most exalted station; and this fact gives the holder of the document an ascendancy over the illustrious personage whose honor and peace are so jeopardized."

"But this ascendancy," I interposed, "would depend upon the robber's knowledge of the loser's knowledge of the robber. Who would dare"—

"The thief," said G——, "is the Minister D——, who dares all things, those unbecoming as well as those becoming a man. The method of the theft was not less ingenious than bold. The document in question—a letter, to be frank—had been received by the personage robbed while alone in the royal *boudoir*. During its perusal she was suddenly interrupted by the entrance of the other exalted personage, from whom especially it was her wish to conceal it. After a hurried and vain endeavor to thrust it in a drawer, she was forced to place it, open as it was, upon a table. The address, however, was uppermost, and, the contents thus unexposed, the letter escaped notice. At this juncture enters the Minister D——. His lynx eye immediately perceives the paper, recognizes the handwriting of the address, observes the confusion of the personage addressed, and fathoms her secret. After some business transactions, hurried through in his ordinary manner, he produces a letter somewhat similar to the one in question, opens it, pretends to read it, and then places it in close juxtaposition to the other. Again he converses for some fifteen minutes upon the public affairs. At length in taking leave he takes also from the table the letter to which he had no claim. Its rightful owner saw, but of course dared not call attention to the act, in the presence of the third personage, who stood at her elbow. The Minister decamped, leaving his own letter—one of no importance—upon the table.''

"Here, then," said Dupin to me, "you have precisely what you demand to make the ascendancy complete—the robber's knowledge of the loser's knowledge of the robber.''

"Yes," replied the Prefect; "and the power thus attained has, for some months past, been wielded, for political purposes, to a very dangerous extent. The personage robbed is more thoroughly convinced, every day, of the necessity of reclaiming her letter. But this, of course, cannot be done openly. In fine, driven to despair, she has committed the matter to me.''

"Than whom," said Dupin, amid a perfect whirlwind of smoke, "no more sagacious agent could, I suppose, be desired, or even imagined.''

"You flatter me," replied the Prefect; "but it is possible that some such opinion may have been entertained.''

"It is clear," said I, "as you observe, that the letter is still in possession of the Minister; since it is this possession, and not any employment of the letter, which bestows the power. With the employment the power departs.''

"True," said G——; "and upon this conviction I proceeded. My first care was to make thorough search of the Minister's Hotel; [1] and here my chief embarrassment lay in the necessity of searching without his knowledge. Beyond all things, I have been warned of the danger which would result from giving him reason to suspect our design.''

"But," said I, "you are quite *au fait* [2] in these investigations. The Parisian police have done this thing often before.''

"Oh, yes; and for this reason I did not despair. The habits of the Minister gave me, too, a great advantage. He is frequently absent from home all night. His servants are by no means numerous. They sleep at a distance from their master's apartment, and, being chiefly Neapolitans, are readily made drunk. I have keys, as you know, with which I can open any chamber or cabinet in Paris. For three months a night has not passed, during the greater part of which I have not been engaged, personally, in ransacking the D—— Hotel. My honor is interested, and, to mention a great secret, the reward is enormous. So I did not abandon the search until I had become fully satisfied that the thief is a more astute man than myself. I fancy that I have investigated

[1] residence, mansion
[2] expert

every nook and corner of the premises in which it is possible that the paper can be concealed.''

"But is it not possible," I suggested, "that although the letter may be in possession of the Minister, as it unquestionably is, he may have concealed it elsewhere than upon his own premises?''

"This is barely possible," said Dupin. "The present peculiar condition of affairs at court, and especially of those intrigues in which D—— is known to be involved, would render the instant availability of the document—its susceptibility of being produced at a moment's notice—a point of nearly equal importance with its possession.''

"Its susceptibility of being produced?" said I.

"That is to say, of being *destroyed*," said Dupin.

"True," I observed; "the paper is clearly then upon the premises. As for its being upon the person of the Minister, we may consider that as out of the question.''

"Entirely," said the Prefect. "He has been twice waylaid, as if by footpads, and his person rigorously searched under my own inspection.''

"You might have spared yourself this trouble," said Dupin. "D——, I presume, is not altogether a fool, and, if not, must have anticipated these waylayings as a matter of course.''

"Not *altogether* a fool," said G——, "but then he's a poet, which I take to be only one remove from a fool.''

"True," said Dupin, after a long and thoughtful whiff from his meerschaum, "although I have been guilty of certain doggerel myself.''

"Suppose you detail," said I, "the particulars of your search.''

"Why, the fact is, we took our time, and we searched *everywhere*. I have had long experience in these affairs. I took the entire building, room by room, devoting the nights of a whole week to each. We examined, first, the furniture of each apartment. We opened every possible drawer; and I presume you know that, to a properly trained police agent, such a thing as a *secret* drawer is impossible. Any man is a dolt who permits a 'secret' drawer to escape him in a search of this kind. The thing is *so* plain. There is a certain amount of bulk—of space—to be accounted for in every cabinet. Then we have accurate rules. The fiftieth part of a line could not escape us. After the cabinets we took the chairs. The cushions we probed with the fine long needles you have seen me employ. From the tables we removed the tops.''

"Why so?"

"Sometimes the top of a table, or other similarly arranged piece of furniture, is removed by the person wishing to conceal an article; then the leg is excavated, the article deposited within the cavity, and the top replaced. The bottoms and tops of bed-posts are employed in the same way."

"But could not the cavity be detected by sounding?" I asked.

"By no means, if, when the article is deposited, a sufficient wadding of cotton be placed around it. Besides, in our case we were obliged to proceed without noise."

"But you could not have removed—you could not have taken to pieces all articles of furniture in which it would have been possible to make a deposit in the manner you mention. A letter may be compressed into a thin spiral roll, not differing much in shape or bulk from a large knitting-needle, and in this form it might be inserted into the rung of a chair, for example. You did not take to pieces all the chairs?"

"Certainly not; but we did better—we examined the rungs of every chair in the Hotel, and indeed, the jointings of every description of furniture, by the aid of a most powerful microscope. Had there been any traces of recent disturbance we should not have failed to detect it instantly. A single grain of gimlet-dust, for example, would have been as obvious as an apple. Any disorder in the gluing—any unusual gaping in the joints—would have sufficed to insure detection."

"I presume you looked to the mirrors, between the boards and the plates, and you probed the beds and the bedclothes, as well as the curtains and carpets?"

"That, of course; and when we had absolutely completed every particle of the furniture in this way, then we examined the house itself. We divided its entire surface into compartments, which we numbered, so that none might be missed; then we scrutinized each individual square inch throughout the premises, including the two houses immediately adjoining, with the microscope, as before."

"The two houses adjoining!" I exclaimed; "you must have had a great deal of trouble."

"We had; but the reward offered is prodigious."

"You include the *grounds* about the houses?"

"All the grounds are paved with brick. They gave us comparatively little trouble. We examined the moss between the bricks, and found it undisturbed."

"You looked among D——'s papers, of course, and into the books of the library?"

"Certainly; we opened every package and parcel; we not only opened every book, but we turned over every leaf in each volume, not contenting ourselves with a mere shake, according to the fashion of some of our police officers. We also measured the thickness of every book-*cover,* with the most accurate admeasurement, [1] and applied to each the most jealous scrutiny of the microscope. Had any of the bindings been recently meddled with, it would have been utterly impossible that the fact should have escaped observation. Some five or six volumes, just from the hands of the binder, we carefully probed, longitudinally, with the needles."

"You explored the floors beneath the carpets?"

"Beyond doubt. We removed every carpet, and examined the boards with the microscope."

"And the paper on the walls?"

"Yes."

"You looked into the cellars?"

"We did."

"Then," I said, "you have been making a miscalculation, and the letter is *not* upon the premises, as you suppose."

"I fear you are right, there," said the Prefect. "And now, Dupin, what would you advise me to do?"

"To make a thorough re-search of the premises."

"That is absolutely needless," replied G——. "I am not more sure that I breathe than I am that the letter is not at the Hotel."

"I have no better advice to give you," said Dupin. "You have, of course, an accurate description of the letter?"

"Oh, yes!"—And here the Prefect, producing a memorandum-book, proceeded to read aloud a minute account of the internal, and especially of the external appearance of the missing document. Soon after finishing the perusal of this description, he took his departure, more entirely depressed in spirits than I had ever known the good gentleman before.

In about a month afterwards he paid us another visit, and found us occupied very nearly as before. He took a pipe and a chair, and entered into some ordinary conversation. At length I said,—

"Well, but G——, what of the purloined letter? I presume you have at last made up your mind that there is no such thing as over-reaching the Minister?"

"Confound him, say I—yes; I made the reexamination, however, as Dupin suggested— but it was all labor lost, as I knew it would be."

[1] measurement that determines the capacity or the comparative size

"How much was the reward offered, did you say?" asked Dupin.

"Why, a very great deal—a *very* liberal reward—I don't like to say how much precisely; but one thing I *will* say, that I wouldn't mind giving my individual check for fifty thousand francs to any one who could obtain me that letter. The fact is, it is becoming of more and more importance every day; and the reward has been lately doubled. If it were trebled, however, I could do no more than I have done."

"Why, yes," said Dupin, drawlingly, between the whiffs of his meerschaum, "I really—think, G——, you have not exerted yourself—to the utmost in this matter. You might—do a little more, I think, eh?"

"How?—in what way?"

"Why—puff, puff—you might—puff, puff—employ counsel in the matter, eh?—puff, puff, puff—Do you remember the story they tell of Abernethy?" [1]

"No; hang Abernethy!"

"To be sure! hang him and welcome. But, once upon a time, a certain rich miser conceived the design of sponging upon this Abernethy for a medical opinion. Getting up, for this purpose, an ordinary conversation in a private company, he insinuated his case to the physician, as that of an imaginary individual.

" 'We will suppose,' said the miser, 'that his symptoms are such and such; now, doctor, what would *you* have directed him to take?' "

" 'Take!' said Abernethy, 'why, take *advice*, to be sure.' "

"But," said the Prefect, a little discomposed, "*I* am *perfectly* willing to take advice, and to pay for it. I would *really* give fifty thousand francs to any one who would aid me in the matter."

"In that case," replied Dupin, opening a drawer, and producing a check-book, "you may as well fill me up a check for the amount mentioned. When you have signed it, I will hand you the letter."

I was astounded. The Prefect appeared absolutely thunderstricken. For some minutes he remained speechless and motionless, looking incredulously at my friend with open mouth, and eyes that seemed starting from their sockets; then, apparently recovering himself in some measure, he seized a pen, and after several pauses and vacant stares, finally filled up and signed a check for fifty thousand francs, and handed it across the table to Dupin. The latter examined it carefully and deposited it in his pocketbook; then, unlocking an escritoire, took

thence a letter and gave it to the Prefect. This functionary grasped it in a perfect agony of joy, opened it with a trembling hand, cast a rapid glance at its contents, and then, scrambling and struggling to the door, rushed at length unceremoniously from the room and from the house, without having uttered a syllable since Dupin had requested him to fill up the check.

When he had gone, my friend entered into some explanations.

"The Parisian police," he said, "are exceedingly able in their way. They are persevering, ingenious, cunning, and thoroughly versed in the knowledge which their duties seem chiefly to demand. Thus, when G—— detailed to us his mode of searching the premises at the Hotel D——, I felt entire confidence in his having made a satisfactory investigation—so far as his labors extended."

"So far as his labors extended?" said I.

"Yes," said Dupin. "The measures adopted were not only the best of their kind, but carried out to absolute perfection. Had the letter been deposited within the range of their search, these fellows would, beyond a question, have found it."

I merely laughed—but he seemed quite serious in all that he said.

"The measures, then," he continued, "were good in their kind, and well executed; their defect lay in their being inapplicable to the case, and to the man. A certain set of highly ingenious resources are, with the Prefect, a sort of Procrustean [2] bed to which he forcibly adapts his designs. But he perpetually errs by being too deep or too shallow, for the matter in hand; and many a schoolboy is a better reasoner than he. I knew one about eight years of age, whose success at guessing in the game of 'even and odd' attracted universal admiration. This game is simple, and is played with marbles. One player holds in his hand a number of these toys, and demands of another whether that number is even or odd. If the guess is right, the guesser wins one; if wrong, he loses one. The boy to whom I allude won all the marbles of the school. Of course he had some principle of guessing; and this lay in mere observation and admeasurement of the astuteness of his opponents. For example, an arrant simpleton is his opponent, and, holding up his closed hand, asks, 'Are they even or odd?' Our schoolboy replies, 'Odd,' and loses; but upon the second trial he wins, for he then says to himself, 'The simpleton had them even upon

[1] a celebrated and rather eccentric English surgeon, 1764-1831

[2] Procrustes, a legendary Attic robber, tortured his victims by stretching or lopping them to fit a certain bed.

the first trial, and his amount of cunning is just sufficient to make him have them odd upon the second; I will therefore guess odd;' he guesses odd, and wins. Now, with a simpleton a degree above the first he would have reasoned thus: 'This fellow finds that in the first instance I guessed odd, and in the second he will propose to himself, upon the first impulse, a simple variation from even to odd, as did the first simpleton; but then a second thought will suggest that this is too simple a variation, and finally he will decide upon putting it even as before. I will therefore guess even'; he guesses even, and wins. Now, this mode of reasoning in the schoolboy, whom his fellows termed 'lucky'—what, in its last analysis, is it?"

"It is merely," I said, "an identification of the reasoner's intellect with that of his opponent."

"It is," said Dupin; "and, upon inquiring of the boy by what means he effected the *thorough* identification in which his success consisted, I received answer as follows: 'When I wish to find out how wise, or how stupid, or how good, or how wicked is any one, or what are his thoughts at the moment, I fashion the expression of my face, as accurately as possible, in accordance with the expression of his, and then wait to see what thoughts or sentiments arise in my mind or heart, as if to match or correspond with the expression.' This response of the schoolboy lies at the bottom of all the spurious profundity which has been attributed to Rochefoucauld, to La Bruyère, to Machiavelli, and to Campanella." [1]

"And the identification," I said, "of the reasoner's intellect with that of his opponent, depends, if I understand you aright, upon the accuracy with which the opponent's intellect is admeasured."

"For its practical value it depends upon this," replied Dupin, "and the Prefect and his cohort fail so frequently, first, by default of this identification, and secondly, by ill-admeasurement, or rather through non-admeasurement, of the intellect with which they are engaged. They consider only their *own* ideas of ingenuity; and, in searching for anything hidden, advert only to the modes in which *they* would have hidden it. They are right in this much—that their own ingenuity is a faithful representative of that of *the mass:* but when the cunning of the individual felon is diverse in character from

their own, the felon foils them, of course. This always happens when it is above their own, and very usually when it is below. They have no variation of principle in their investigations; at best, when urged by some unusual emergency—by some extraordinary reward—they extend or exaggerate their old modes of *practice,* without touching their principles. What, for example, in this case of D——, has been done to vary the principle of action? What is all this boring, and probing, and sounding, and scrutinizing with the microscope, and dividing the surface of the building into registered square inches— what is it all but an exaggeration *of the application* of the one principle or set of principles of search, which are based upon the one set of notions regarding human ingenuity, to which the Prefect, in the long routine of his duty, has been accustomed? Do you not see he has taken it for granted that *all* men proceed to conceal a letter,—not exactly in a gimlet-hole bored in a chair-leg—but, at least, in *some* out-of-the-way hole or corner suggested by the same tenor of thought which would urge a man to secrete a letter in a gimlet-hole bored in a chair leg? And do you not see, also, that such *recherchés* [2] nooks for concealment are adapted only for ordinary occasions and would be adopted only by ordinary intellects; for, in all cases of concealment, a disposal of the article concealed— a disposal of it in this *recherché* manner—is, in the very first instance, presumable and presumed; and thus its discovery depends, not at all upon the acumen, but altogether upon the mere care, patience, and determination of the seekers; and where the case is of importance— or, what amounts to the same thing in the policial eyes, when the reward is of magnitude —the qualities in question have *never* been known to fail. You will now understand what I meant in suggesting that, had the purloined letter been hidden anywhere within the limits of the Prefect's examination—in other words, had the principle of its concealment been comprehended within the principles of the Prefect— its discovery would have been a matter altogether beyond question. This functionary, however, has been thoroughly mystified; and the remote source of his defeat lies in the supposition that the Minister is a fool because he has acquired renown as a poet. All fools are poets; this the Prefect *feels;* and he is merely guilty of a *non distributio medii* [3] in thence inferring that all poets are fools."

---

[1] Rochefoucauld and La Bruyère, French moralists of the seventeenth century; Machiavelli, an Italian statesman of the sixteenth century, celebrated for his open cynicism concerning the morals of statecraft; Campanella, Italian philosopher, born 1568

[2] carefully sought out, hidden
[3] undistributed middle term (of a logical syllogism), causing a fallacious conclusion

"But is this really the poet?" I asked. "There are two brothers, I know; and both have attained reputation in letters. The Minister, I believe, has written learnedly on the Differential Calculus. He is a mathematician and no poet."

"You are mistaken; I know him well; he is both. As poet *and* mathematician he would reason well; as mere mathematician he could not have reasoned at all, and thus would have been at the mercy of the Prefect."

"You surprise me," I said, "by these opinions, which have been contradicted by the voice of the world. You do not mean to set at naught the well-digested idea of centuries. The mathematical reason has long been regarded as *the* reason *par excellence*." [1]

" '*Il y a à parier*,' " replied Dupin, quoting from Chamfort, " '*que toute idée publique, toute convention reçue, est une sottise, car elle a convenu au plus grand nombre*.' [2] The mathematicians, I grant you, have done their best to promulgate the popular error to which you allude, and which is none the less an error for its promulgation as truth. With an art worthy a better cause, for example, they have insinuated the term 'analysis' into application to algebra. The French are the originators of this particular deception; but if a term is of any importance— if words derive any value from applicability— then 'analysis' conveys 'algebra,' about as much as, in Latin, '*ambitus*' implies 'ambition,' '*religio*,' 'religion,' or '*homines honesti*,' a set of honorable men." [3]

"You have a quarrel on hand, I see," said I, "with some of the algebraists of Paris; but proceed."

"I dispute the availability, and thus the value of that reason which is cultivated in any especial form other than the abstractly logical. I dispute, in particular, the reason educed by mathematical study. The mathematics are the science of form and quantity; mathematical reasoning is merely logic applied to observation upon form and quantity. The great error lies in supposing that even the truths of what is called *pure* algebra are abstract or general truths. And this error is so egregious that I am confounded at the universality with which it has been received. Mathematical axioms are *not* axioms of general truth. What is true of rela-

tion—of form and quantity—is often grossly false in regard to morals, for example. In this latter science it is very usually *un*true that the aggregated parts are equal to the whole. In chemistry, also, the axiom fails. In the consideration of motive it fails; for two motives, each of a given value, have not, necessarily, a value, when united, equal to the sum of their values apart. There are numerous other mathematical truths which are only truths within the limits of *relation*. But the mathematician argues, from his *finite truths*, through habit, as if they were of an absolutely general applicability —as the world indeed imagines them to be. Bryant, [4] in his very learned '*Mythology*,' mentions an analogous source of error, when he says that 'although the Pagan fables are not believed, yet we forget ourselves continually, and make inferences from them as existing realities.' With the algebraists, however, who are Pagans themselves, the 'Pagan fables' *are* believed and the inferences are made, not so much through lapse of memory as through an unaccountable addling of the brains. In short I never yet encountered the mere mathematician who could be trusted out of equal roots, or one who did not clandestinely hold it as a point of his faith that x^2+px was absolutely and unconditionally equal to q. Say to one of these gentlemen, by way of experiment, if you please, that you believe occasions may occur where x^2+px is *not* altogether equal to q, and, having made him understand what you mean, get out of his reach as speedily as convenient, for, beyond doubt, he will endeavor to knock you down.

"I mean to say," continued Dupin, while I merely laughed at his last observations, "that if the Minister had been no more than a mathematician, the Prefect would have been under no necessity of giving me this check. I knew him, however, as both mathematician and poet, and my measures were adapted to his capacity with reference to the circumstances by which he was surrounded. I knew him as courtier, too, and as a bold *intriguant*. [5] Such a man, I considered, could not fail to be aware of the ordinary policial modes of action. He could not have failed to anticipate—and events have proved that he did not fail to anticipate—the waylayings to which he was subjected. He must have foreseen, I reflected, the secret investigations of his premises. His frequent absences from home at night, which were hailed by the Prefect as certain aids to his success, I regarded only as ruses, to afford opportunity for

[1] above all others
[2] "It is safe to wager that every common notion, every received convention, is a piece of stupidity, since it has found favor with the majority." Nicholas Chamfort, 1741-1794, was a French writer of maxims.
[3] *Ambitus* really means "a going round, office-seeking"; *religio* may mean "punctiliousness," and *homines honesti*, "distinguished men."

[4] Jacob Bryant, 1715-1804, an English antiquary
[5] intriguer

thorough search to the police, and thus the sooner to impress them with the conviction to which G——, in fact, did finally arrive,—the conviction that the letter was not upon the premises. I felt, also, that the whole train of thought, which I was at some pains in detailing to you just now, concerning the invariable principle of policial action in searches for articles concealed—I felt that this whole train of thought would necessarily pass through the mind of the Minister. It would imperatively lead him to despise all the ordinary *nooks* of concealment. *He* could not, I reflected, be so weak as not to see that the most intricate and remote recess of his Hotel would be as open as his commonest closets to the eyes, to the probes, to the gimlets, and to the microscopes of the Prefect. I saw, in fine, that he would be driven, as a matter of course, to *simplicity*, if not deliberately induced to it as a matter of choice. You will remember, perhaps, how desperately the Prefect laughed when I suggested, upon our first interview, that it was just possible this mystery troubled him so much on account of its being so *very* self-evident."

"Yes," said I, "I remember his merriment well. I really thought he would have fallen into convulsions."

"The material world," continued Dupin, "abounds with very strict analogies to the immaterial; and thus some color of truth has been given to the rhetorical dogma, that metaphor, or simile, may be made to strengthen an argument, as well as to embellish a description. The principle of the *vis inertiae*,[1] for example, seems to be identical in physics and metaphysics. It is not more true in the former, that a large body is with more difficulty set in motion than a smaller one, and that its subsequent momentum is commensurate with this difficulty, than it is, in the latter, that intellects of the vaster capacity, while more forcible, more constant, and more eventful in their movements than those of inferior grade, are yet the less readily moved, and more embarrassed and full of hesitation in the first few steps of their progress. Again: have you ever noticed which of the street signs over the shop doors are the most attractive of attention?"

"I have never given the matter a thought," I said.

"There is a game of puzzles," he resumed, "which is played upon a map. One party playing requires another to find a given word,—the name of town, river, state, or empire,—any word, in short, upon the motley and perplexed

[1] force of inertia

surface of the chart. A novice in the game generally seeks to embarrass his opponents by giving them the most minutely lettered names; but the adept selects such words as stretch in large characters, from one end of the chart to the other. These, like the over-largely lettered signs and placards of the street, escape observation by dint of being excessively obvious; and here the physical oversight is precisely analogous with the moral inapprehension by which the intellect suffers to pass unnoticed those considerations which are too obtrusively and too palpably self-evident. But this is a point, it appears, somewhat above or beneath the understanding of the Prefect. He never once thought it probable, or possible, that the Minister had deposited the letter immediately beneath the nose of the whole world by way of best preventing any portion of that world from perceiving it.

"But the more I reflected upon the daring, dashing, and discriminating ingenuity of D——; upon the fact that the document must always have been *at hand*, if he intended to use it to good purpose; and upon the decisive evidence, obtained by the Prefect, that it was not hidden within the limits of that dignitary's ordinary search—the more satisfied I became that, to conceal this letter, the Minister had resorted to the comprehensive and sagacious expedient of not attempting to conceal it at all.

"Full of these ideas, I prepared myself with a pair of green spectacles, and called one fine morning, quite by accident, at the Ministerial Hotel. I found D—— at home, yawning, lounging, and dawdling, as usual, and pretending to be in the last extremity of *ennui*. He is, perhaps, the most really energetic human being now alive—but that is only when nobody sees him.

"To be even with him, I complained of my weak eyes, and lamented the necessity of the spectacles, under cover of which I cautiously and thoroughly surveyed the whole apartment, while seemingly intent only upon the conversation of my host.

"I paid especial attention to a large writing-table near which he sat, and upon which lay confusedly some miscellaneous letters and other papers, with one or two musical instruments and a few books. Here, however, after a long and very deliberate scrutiny, I saw nothing to excite particular suspicion.

"At length my eyes, in going the circuit of the room, fell upon a trumpery filigree card-rack of paste-board, that hung, dangling, by a dirty blue ribbon, from a little brass knob just beneath the middle of the mantelpiece. In this rack, which had three or four compartments, were five or six visiting cards and a solitary letter. This last was much soiled and crumpled. It was torn nearly in two, across the middle— as if a design, in the first instance, to tear it entirely up as worthless had been altered, or stayed, in the second. It had a large black seal, bearing the D—— cipher *very* conspicuously, and was addressed, in a diminutive female hand, to D——, the Minister himself. It was thrust carelessly, and even, as it seemed, contemptuously, into one of the upper divisions of the rack.

"No sooner had I glanced at this letter than I concluded it to be that of which I was in search. To be sure, it was, to all appearance, radically different from the one of which the Prefect had read us so minute a description. Here the seal was large and black, with the D—— cipher; there it was small and red, with the ducal arms of the S—— family. Here, the address, to the Minister, was diminutive and feminine; there, the superscription, to a certain royal personage, was markedly bold and decided; the size alone formed a point of correspondence. But, then, the *radicalness* of these differences, which was excessive; the dirt; the soiled and torn condition of the paper, so inconsistent with the *true* methodical habits of D——, and so suggestive of a design to delude the beholder into an idea of the worthlessness of the document; these things, together with the hyper-obtrusive situation of this document, full in the view of every visitor, and thus exactly in accordance with the conclusions to which I had previously arrived; these things, I say, were strongly corroborative of suspicion, in one who came with the intention to suspect.

"I protracted my visit as long as possible, and while I maintained a most animated discussion with the Minister, upon a topic which I knew well had never failed to interest and excite him, I kept my attention really riveted upon the letter. In this examination, I committed to memory its external appearance and arrangement in the rack; and also fell, at length, upon a discovery which set at rest whatever trivial doubt I might have entertained. In scrutinizing the edges of the paper, I observed them to be more *chafed* than seemed necessary. They presented the *broken* appearance which is manifested when a stiff paper, having been once folded and pressed with a folder, is refolded in a reversed direction, in the same creases or edges which had formed the original fold. This discovery was sufficient. It was clear to me that the letter had been turned, as

a glove, inside out, re-directed, and re-sealed. I bade the Minister good-morning, and took my departure at once, leaving a gold snuff-box upon the table.

"The next morning I called for the snuff-box, when we resumed, quite eagerly, the conversation of the preceding day. While thus engaged, however, a loud report, as if of a pistol, was heard immediately beneath the windows of the Hotel, and was succeeded by a series of fearful screams, and the shoutings of a terrified mob. D—— rushed to a casement, threw it open, and looked out. In the meantime, I stepped to the card-rack, took the letter, put it in my pocket, and replaced it by a facsimile (so far as regards externals) which I had carefully prepared at my lodgings—imitating the D—— cipher very readily by means of a seal formed of bread.

"The disturbance in the street had been occasioned by the frantic behavior of a man with a musket. He had fired it among a crowd of women and children. It proved, however, to have been without ball, and the fellow was suffered to go his way as a lunatic or a drunkard. When he had gone, D—— came from the window, whither I had followed him immediately upon securing the object in view. Soon afterwards I bade him farewell. The pretended lunatic was a man in my own pay."

"But what purpose had you," I asked, "in replacing the letter by a facsimile? Would it not have been better, at the first visit, to have seized it openly and departed?"

"D——," replied Dupin, "is a desperate man, and a man of nerve. His Hotel, too, is not without attendants devoted to his interest. Had I made the wild attempt you suggest, I might never have left the Ministerial presence alive. The good people of Paris might have heard of me no more. But I had an object apart from these considerations. You know my political prepossessions. In this matter I act as a partisan of the lady concerned. For eighteen months the Minister has had her in his power. She has now him in hers—since, being unaware that the letter is not in his possession, he will proceed with his exactions as if it was. Thus will he inevitably commit himself at once to his political destruction. His downfall, too, will not be more precipitate than awkward. It is all very well to talk about the *facilis descensus Averni;* [1] but in all kinds of climbing, as Catalani [2] said of singing, it is far more easy to get up than to come down. In the present instance I have no

[1] "Easy is the descent into Avernus" (the lower regions). Vergil, *Aeneid*, vi, 126.
[2] Angelica Catalani, a celebrated Italian singer of Poe's time

sympathy—at least no pity—for him who descends. He is that *monstrum horrendum*,[1] an unprincipled man of genius. I confess, however, that I should like very well to know the precise character of his thoughts, when, being defied by her whom the Prefect terms 'a certain personage,' he is reduced to opening the letter which I left for him in the card-rack."

"How? Did you put anything particular in it?"

"Why—it did not seem altogether right to leave the interior blank—that would have been insulting. D——, at Vienna once, did me an evil turn, which I told him, quite good-humoredly, that I should remember. So, as I knew he would feel some curiosity in regard to the identity of the person who had outwitted him, I thought it a pity not to give him a clew. He is well acquainted with my MS., and I just copied into the middle of the blank sheet the word:—

'——Un dessein si funeste,
S'il n'est digne d'Atrée, est digne de Thyeste.[2]

They are to be found in Crébillon's[3] *Atrée*."

1845

THE CASK OF AMONTILLADO
(ROME)

The thousand injuries of Fortunato I had borne as I best could; but when he ventured upon insult, I vowed revenge. You, who so well know the nature of my soul, will not suppose, however, that I gave utterance to a threat. *At length* I would be avenged; this was a point definitively settled—but the very definitiveness with which it was resolved precluded the idea of risk. I must not only punish, but punish with impunity. A wrong is unredressed when retribution overtakes its redresser. It is equally unredressed when the avenger fails to make himself felt as such to him who has done the wrong.

It must be understood that neither by word nor deed had I given Fortunato cause to doubt my good-will. I continued, as was my wont, to smile in his face, and he did not perceive that my smile *now* was at the thought of his immolation.

He had a weak point—this Fortunato—although in other regards he was a man to be respected and even feared. He prided himself

on his connoisseurship in wine. Few Italians have the true virtuoso spirit. For the most part their enthusiasm is adopted to suit the time and opportunity—to practice imposture upon the British and Austrian millionaires. In painting and gemmary, Fortunato, like his countrymen, was a quack—but in the matter of old wines he was sincere. In this respect I did not differ from him materially: I was skilful in the Italian vintages myself, and bought largely whenever I could.

It was about dusk, one evening during the supreme madness of the carnival season, that I encountered my friend. He accosted me with excessive warmth, for he had been drinking much. The man wore motley. He had on a tight-fitting parti-striped dress, and his head was surmounted by the conical cap and bells. I was so pleased to see him that I thought I should never have done wringing his hand.

I said to him, "My dear Fortunato, you are luckily met. How remarkably well you are looking today! But I have received a pipe of what passes for Amontillado, and I have my doubts."

"How?" said he. "Amontillado? A pipe? Impossible. And in the middle of the carnival!"

"I have my doubts," I replied; "and I was silly enough to pay the full Amontillado price without consulting you in the matter. You were not to be found, and I was fearful of losing a bargain."

"Amontillado!"

"I have my doubts."

"Amontillado!"

"And I must satisfy them."

"Amontillado!"

"As you are engaged, I am on my way to Luchesi. If any one has a critical turn, it is he. He will tell me—"

"Luchesi cannot tell Amontillado from Sherry."

"And yet some fools will have it that his taste is a match for your own."

"Come, let us go."

"Whither?"

"To your vaults."

"My friend, no; I will not impose upon your good-nature. I perceive you have an engagement. Luchesi—"

"I have no engagement;—come."

"My friend, no. It is not the engagement, but the severe cold with which I perceive you are afflicted. The vaults are insufferably damp. They are incrusted with niter."

"Let us go, nevertheless. The cold is merely nothing. Amontillado! You have been imposed upon. And as for Luchesi, he cannot distinguish Sherry from Amontillado."

Thus speaking, Fortunato possessed himself of my arm. Putting on a mask of black silk, and drawing a roquelaire [1] closely about my person, I suffered him to hurry me to my palazzo. [2]

There were no attendants at home; they had absconded to make merry in honor of the time. I had told them that I should not return until the morning, and had given them explicit orders not to stir from the house. These orders were sufficient, I well knew, to insure their immediate disappearance, one and all, as soon as my back was turned.

I took from their sconces two flambeaus, and giving one to Fortunato, bowed him through several suites of rooms to the archway that led into the vaults. I passed down a long and winding staircase, requesting him to be cautious as he followed. We came at length to the foot of the descent, and stood together on the damp ground of the catacombs of the Montresors.

The gait of my friend was unsteady, and the bells upon his cap jingled as he strode.

"The pipe," said he.

"It is farther on," said I; "but observe the white web-work which gleams from these cavern walls."

He turned towards me, and looked into my eyes with two filmy orbs that distilled the rheum of intoxication.

"Niter?" he asked at length.

"Niter," I replied. "How long have you had that cough?"

"Ugh! ugh! ugh!—ugh! ugh! ugh!—ugh! ugh! ugh!—ugh! ugh! ugh!—ugh! ugh! ugh!"

My poor friend found it impossible to reply for many minutes.

"It is nothing," he said, at last.

"Come," I said, with decision, "we will go back; your health is precious. You are rich, respected, admired, beloved; you are happy, as once I was. You are a man to be missed. For me it is no matter. We will go back; you will be ill, and I cannot be responsible. Besides, there is Luchesi—"

"Enough," he said; "the cough is a mere nothing; it will not kill me. I shall not die of a cough."

"True—true," I replied; "and, indeed, I had no intention of alarming you unnecessarily—but you should use all proper caution. A draught of this Medoc will defend us from the damps."

Here I knocked off the neck of a bottle which I drew from a long row of its fellows that lay upon the mold.

"Drink," I said, presenting him the wine.

He raised it to his lips with a leer. He paused and nodded to me familiarly, while his bells jingled.

"I drink," he said, "to the buried that repose around us."

"And I to your long life."

He again took my arm, and we proceeded.

"These vaults," he said, "are extensive."

"The Montresors," I replied, "were a great and numerous family."

"I forget your arms."

"A huge human foot d'or, in a field azure; [3] the foot crushes a serpent rampant whose fangs are embedded in the heel."

"And the motto?"

"Nemo me impune lacessit." [4]

"Good!" he said.

The wine sparkled in his eyes and the bells jingled. My own fancy grew warm with the Medoc. We had passed through walls of piled bones, with casks and puncheons intermingling, into the inmost recesses of the catacombs. I paused again, and this time I made bold to seize Fortunato by an arm above the elbow.

"The niter!" I said; "see, it increases. It hangs like moss upon the vaults. We are below the river's bed. The drops of moisture trickle among the bones. Come, we will go back ere it is too late. Your cough—"

"It is nothing," he said; "let us go on. But first, another draught of the Medoc."

I broke and reached him a flagon of De Grâve. He emptied it at a breath. His eyes flashed with a fierce light. He laughed and threw the bottle upwards with a gesticulation I did not understand.

I looked at him in surprise. He repeated the movement—a grotesque one.

"You do not comprehend?" he said.

"Not I," I replied.

"Then you are not of the brotherhood."

"How?"

"You are not of the masons."

"Yes, yes," I said, "yes, yes."

"You? Impossible! A mason?"

"A mason," I replied.

"A sign," he said.

"It is this," I answered, producing a trowel from beneath the folds of my roquelaire.

"You jest," he exclaimed, recoiling a few paces. "But let us proceed to the Amontillado."

[1] short cloak
[2] literally, palace; residence of a person of wealth
[3] golden foot in a blue field
[4] "No one challenges me in safety."

"Be it so," I said, replacing the tool beneath the cloak, and again offering him my arm. He leaned upon it heavily. We continued our route in search of the Amontillado. We passed through a range of low arches, descended, passed on, and, descending again, arrived at a deep crypt, in which the foulness of the air caused our flambeaus rather to glow than flame.

At the most remote end of the crypt there appeared another less spacious. Its walls had been lined with human remains, piled to the vault overhead, in the fashion of the great catacombs of Paris. Three sides of this interior crypt were still ornamented in this manner. From the fourth the bones had been thrown down, and lay promiscuously upon the earth, forming at one point a mound of some size. Within the wall thus exposed by the displacing of the bones, we perceived a still interior recess, in depth about four feet, in width three, in height six or seven. It seemed to have been constructed for no especial use within itself, but formed merely the interval between two of the colossal supports of the roof of the catacombs, and was backed by one of their circumscribing walls of solid granite.

It was in vain that Fortunato, uplifting his dull torch, endeavored to pry into the depth of the recess. Its termination the feeble light did not enable us to see.

"Proceed," I said; "herein is the Amontillado. As for Luchesi—"

"He is an ignoramus," interrupted my friend, as he stepped unsteadily forward, while I followed immediately at his heels. In an instant he had reached the extremity of the niche, and finding his progress arrested by the rock, stood stupidly bewildered. A moment more and I had fettered him to the granite. In its surface were two iron staples, distant from each other about two feet, horizontally. From one of these depended a short chain, from the other a padlock. Throwing the links about his waist, it was but the work of a few seconds to secure it. He was too much astounded to resist. Withdrawing the key, I stepped back from the recess.

"Pass your hand," I said, "over the wall; you cannot help feeling the niter. Indeed it is very damp. Once more let me implore you to return. No? Then I must positively leave you. But I must first render you all the little attentions in my power."

"The Amontillado!" ejaculated my friend, not yet recovered from his astonishment.

"True," I replied; "the Amontillado."

As I said these words I busied myself among the pile of bones of which I have before spoken. Throwing them aside, I soon uncovered a quantity of building stone and mortar. With these materials and with the aid of my trowel, I began vigorously to wall up the entrance of the niche.

I had scarcely laid the first tier of the masonry when I discovered that the intoxication of Fortunato had in a great measure worn off. The earliest indication I had of this was a low moaning cry from the depth of the recess. It was not the cry of a drunken man. There was then a long and obstinate silence. I laid the second tier, and the third, and the fourth; and then I heard the furious vibrations of the chain. The noise lasted for several minutes, during which, that I might hearken to it with the more satisfaction, I ceased my labors and sat down upon the bones. When at last the clanking subsided, I resumed the trowel, and finished without interruption the fifth, the sixth, and the seventh tier. The wall was now nearly upon a level with my breast. I again paused, and holding the flambeaus over the mason work, threw a few feeble rays upon the figure within.

A succession of loud and shrill screams, bursting suddenly from the throat of the chained form, seemed to thrust me violently back. For a brief moment I hesitated—I trembled. Unsheathing my rapier, I began to grope with it about the recess; but the thought of an instant reassured me. I placed my hand upon the solid fabric of the catacombs, and felt satisfied. I reapproached the wall. I replied to the yells of him who clamored. I reëchoed—I aided—I surpassed them in volume and in strength. I did this, and the clamorer grew still.

It was now midnight, and my task was drawing to a close. I had completed the eighth, the ninth, and the tenth tier. I had finished a portion of the last and the eleventh; there remained but a single stone to be fitted and plastered in. I struggled with its weight; I placed it partially in its destined position. But now there came from out the niche a low laugh that erected the hairs upon my head. It was succeeded by a sad voice, which I had difficulty in recognizing as that of the noble Fortunato. The voice said—

"Ha! ha! ha!—he! he! he!—a very good joke indeed—an excellent jest. We will have many a rich laugh about it at the palazzo—he! he! he—over our wine—he! he! he!"

"The Amontillado!" I said.

"He! he! he!—he! he! he!—yes, the Amontillado. But is it not getting late? Will not they be awaiting us at the palazzo,—the Lady Fortunato and the rest? Let us be gone."

"Yes," I said, "let us be gone."

"For the love of God, Montresor!"

"Yes," I said, "for the love of God!"

But to these words I hearkened in vain for a reply. I grew impatient. I called aloud—

"Fortunato!"

No answer. I called again—

"Fortunato!"

No answer still. I thrust a torch through the remaining aperture and let it fall within. There came forth in return only a jingling of the bells. My heart grew sick—on account of the dampness of the catacombs. I hastened to make an end of my labor. I forced the last stone into its position; I plastered it up. Against the new masonry I reërected the old rampart of bones. For the half of a century no mortal has disturbed them. *In pace requiescat.* [1]

1846

NATHANIEL HAWTHORNE
1804-1864

Hawthorne was born in Salem, Massachusetts, of an old New England family prominent in the witchcraft days but for some generations afterwards in obscurity. He graduated in 1825 with Longfellow from Bowdoin College, one year later than his friend Franklin Pierce. After the appearance of his first work of fiction, *Fanshawe,* 1828, he spent several years writing short stories. From 1839 to 1841 he was weigher at the Salem custom house; the following year he spent at Brook Farm, a community of idealists; and in 1842 he married. From 1853 to 1857 he was consul at Liverpool. His home was at various places in Massachusetts, notably at Concord. He died while on a journey with ex-President Pierce, at Plymouth, New Hampshire. His principal works are *Twice-Told Tales,* 1837; *Mosses from an Old Manse,* 1846; *The Scarlet Letter,* 1850; *The House of the Seven Gables,* 1851; *The Blithedale Romance,* 1852; *The Marble Faun,* 1860.

Hawthorne's work is the finest literary expression of New England Puritanism. To give it expression Hawthorne was well prepared, for his ancestry and experience had steeped him in its ideas, its superstitions as well as its vital spirit. No outsider could so sympathize with it and comprehend it, for its psychology was as familiar to him as its severe, solid architecture. The deepest problem with which Puritanism wrestled was also Hawthorne's problem—the mystery, in a world divinely ordered, of the presence and the results of sin. This problem he faced earnestly and continuously throughout his life, ever examining it in some new light, but reaching no conclusion.

[1] "May he rest in peace."

Hawthorne stands with Poe high above all previous American writers. His work is original in material and in theme; it is American in scene and in spirit. As a stylist Hawthorne bears comparison with any of his contemporaries writing in English. He is rich and satisfying in suggestion; a robust, though refined humor keeps him in balance; and a constant play of fancy, often whimsical and tantalizing and sometimes serious, fills his work. Above all, his work is made vital by an imagination so rich and penetrating as to be a positive, constructive force.

Biography and criticism: J. Hawthorne, *N. Hawthorne and His Wife,* 1893; H. James, Jr., (EML) 1889; G. E. Woodberry (HKA), (AML), 1902; M. D. Conway (GW); G. W. Curtis (LJ); L. Morris, *The Rebellious Puritan,* 1927; Stephen (HL 1); More (Shel. 1 and 2); Sherman; C. Van Doren, "The Flower of Puritanism," *Nation* 111:649-50; W. C. Brownell, "Hawthorne," *Scrib. M.* 43:69-84; B. Perry, "The Centenary of Hawthorne," *Atlan.* 94:195-206; see also *Sat. R. Lit.* 3:727-8, 866, 916.

From TWICE-TOLD TALES
DR. HEIDEGGER'S EXPERIMENT

That very singular man, old Dr. Heidegger, once invited four venerable friends to meet him in his study. There were three white-bearded gentlemen, Mr. Medbourne, Colonel Killigrew, and Mr. Gascoigne, and a withered gentlewoman, whose name was the Widow Wycherly. They were all melancholy old creatures, who had been unfortunate in life, and whose greatest misfortune it was that they were not long ago in their graves. Mr. Medbourne, in the vigor of his age, had been a prosperous merchant, but had lost his all by a frantic speculation, and was now little better than a mendicant. Colonel Killigrew had wasted his best years, and his health and substance, in the pursuit of sinful pleasures which had given birth to a brood of pains, such as the gout, and divers other torments of soul and body. Mr. Gascoigne was a ruined politician, a man of evil fame, or at least had been so, till time had buried him from the knowledge of the present generation, and made him obscure instead of infamous. As for the Widow Wycherly, tradition tells us that she was a great beauty in her day; but, for a long while past, she had lived in deep seclusion, on account of certain scandalous stories which had prejudiced the gentry of the town against her. It is a circumstance worth mentioning, that each of these three old gentlemen, Mr. Medbourne, Colonel Killigrew, and Mr. Gascoigne, were early lovers of the Widow Wycherly, and had once been on the point of cutting each other's throats for her sake. And, before proceeding farther, I will merely hint that Dr. Heidegger and all his four guests were sometimes thought to be a little beside themselves; as is not unfrequently the case with old people, when worried either by present troubles or woful recollections.

"My dear old friends," said Dr. Heidegger, motioning them to be seated, "I am desirous of your assistance in one of those little experiments with which I amuse myself here in my study."

If all stories were true, Dr. Heidegger's study must have been a very curious place. It was a dim, old-fashioned chamber, festooned with cobwebs, and besprinkled with antique dust. Around the walls stood several oaken bookcases, the lower shelves of which were filled with rows of gigantic folios and black-letter quartos, and the upper with little parchment-covered duodecimos. Over the central bookcase was a bronze bust of Hippocrates, [1] with which, according to some authorities, Dr. Heidegger was accustomed to hold consultations in all difficult cases of his practice. In the obscurest corner of the room stood a tall and narrow oaken closet, with its door ajar, within which doubtfully appeared a skeleton. Between two of the bookcases hung a looking-glass, presenting its high and dusty plate within a tarnished gilt frame. Among many wonderful stories related of this mirror, it was fabled that the spirits of all the doctor's deceased patients dwelt within its verge, and would stare him in the face whenever he looked thitherward. The opposite side of the chamber was ornamented with the full-length portrait of a young lady, arrayed in the faded magnificence of silk, satin, and brocade, and with a visage as faded as her dress. Above half a century ago, Dr. Heidegger had been on the point of marriage with this young lady; but, being affected with some slight disorder, she had swallowed one of her lover's prescriptions, and died on the bridal evening. The greatest curiosity of the study remains to be mentioned; it was a ponderous folio volume, bound in black leather, with massive silver clasps. There were no letters on the back and nobody could tell the title of the book. But it was well known to be a book of magic; and once, when a chambermaid had lifted it, merely to brush away the dust, the skeleton had rattled in its closet, the picture of the young lady had stepped one foot upon the floor, and several ghastly faces had peeped forth from the mirror;

[1] a Greek physician, 460-377 B.C., called the Father of Medicine

while the brazen head of Hippocrates frowned, and said,—"Forbear."

Such was Dr. Heidegger's study. On the summer afternoon of our tale, a small round table, as black as ebony, stood in the center of the room, sustaining a cut-glass vase of beautiful form and elaborate workmanship. The sunshine came through the window, between the heavy festoons of two faded damask curtains, and fell directly across this vase; so that a mild splendor was reflected from it on the ashen visages of the five old people who sat around. Four champagne glasses were also on the table.

"My dear old friends," repeated Dr. Heidegger, "may I reckon on your aid in performing an exceedingly curious experiment?"

Now Dr. Heidegger was a very strange old gentleman, whose eccentricity had become the nucleus for a thousand fantastic stories. Some of these fables, to my shame be it spoken, might possibly be traced back to mine own veracious self; and if any passages of the present tale should startle the reader's faith, I must be content to bear the stigma of a fiction-monger.

When the doctor's four guests heard him talk of his proposed experiment, they anticipated nothing more wonderful than the murder of a mouse in an air-pump, or the examination of a cobweb by the microscope, or some similar nonsense, with which he was constantly in the habit of pestering his intimates. But without waiting for a reply, Dr. Heidegger hobbled across the chamber, and returned with the same ponderous folio, bound in black leather, which common report affirmed to be a book of magic. Undoing the silver clasps, he opened the volume, and took from among its black-letter pages a rose, or what was once a rose, though now the green leaves and crimson petals had assumed one brownish hue, and the ancient flower seemed ready to crumble to dust in the doctor's hands.

"This rose," said Dr. Heidegger, with a sigh, "this same withered and crumbling flower, blossomed five-and-fifty years ago. It was given me by Sylvia Ward, whose portrait hangs yonder; and I meant to wear it in my bosom at our wedding. Five-and-fifty years it has been treasured between the leaves of this old volume. Now, would you deem it possible that this rose of half a century could ever bloom again?"

"Nonsense!" said the Widow Wycherly, with a peevish toss of her head. "You might as well ask whether an old woman's wrinkled face could ever bloom again."

"See!" answered Dr. Heidegger.

He uncovered the vase, and threw the faded rose into the water which it contained. At first, it lay lightly on the surface of the fluid, appearing to imbibe none of its moisture. Soon, however, a singular change began to be visible. The crushed and dried petals stirred, and assumed a deepening tinge of crimson, as if the flower were reviving from a deathlike slumber; the slender stalk and twigs of foliage became green; and there was the rose of half a century, looking as fresh as when Sylvia Ward had first given it to her lover. It was scarcely full blown; for some of its delicate red leaves curled modestly around its moist bosom, within which two or three dewdrops were sparkling.

"That is certainly a very pretty deception," said the doctor's friends; carelessly, however, for they had witnessed greater miracles at a conjurer's show; "pray how was it effected?"

"Did you never hear of the 'Fountain of Youth?'" asked Dr. Heidegger, "which Ponce De Leon,[1] the Spanish adventurer, went in search of two or three centuries ago?"

"But did Ponce De Leon ever find it?" said the Widow Wycherly.

"No," answered Dr. Heidegger, "for he never sought it in the right place. The famous Fountain of Youth, if I am rightly informed, is situated in the southern part of the Floridian peninsula, not far from Lake Macaco. Its source is overshadowed by several gigantic magnolias, which, though numberless centuries old, have been kept as fresh as violets by the virtues of this wonderful water. An acquaintance of mine, knowing my curiosity in such matters, has sent me what you see in the vase."

"Ahem!" said Colonel Killigrew, who believed not a word of the doctor's story; "and what may be the effect of this fluid on the human frame?"

"You shall judge for yourself, my dear Colonel," replied Dr. Heidegger; "and all of you, my respected friends, are welcome to so much of this admirable fluid as may restore to you the bloom of youth. For my own part, having had much trouble in growing old, I am in no hurry to grow young again. With your permission, therefore, I will merely watch the progress of the experiment."

While he spoke, Dr. Heidegger had been filling the four champagne glasses with the water of the Fountain of Youth. It was apparently impregnated with an effervescent gas,

for little bubbles were continually ascending from the depths of the glasses, and bursting in silvery spray at the surface. As the liquor diffused a pleasant perfume, the old people doubted not that it possessed cordial and comfortable properties; and, though utter skeptics as to its rejuvenescent power, they were inclined to swallow it at once. But Dr. Heidegger besought them to stay a moment.

"Before you drink, my respectable old friends," said he, "it would be well that, with the experience of a lifetime to direct you, you should draw up a few general rules for your guidance, in passing a second time through the perils of youth. Think what a sin and a shame it would be, if with your peculiar advantages, you should not become patterns of virtue and wisdom to all the young people of the age!"

The doctor's four venerable friends made him no answer, except by a feeble and tremulous laugh; so very ridiculous was the idea, that, knowing how closely repentance treads behind the steps of error, they should ever go astray again.

"Drink, then," said the doctor, bowing: "I rejoice that I have so well selected the subjects of my experiment."

With palsied hands, they raised the glasses to their lips. The liquor, if it really possessed such virtues as Dr. Heidegger imputed to it, could not have been bestowed on four human beings who needed it more wofully. They looked as if they had never known what youth or pleasure was, but had been the offspring of Nature's dotage, and always the gray, decrepit, sapless, miserable creatures, who now sat stooping round the doctor's table, without life enough in their souls or bodies to be animated even by the prospect of growing young again. They drank off the water, and replaced their glasses on the table.

Assuredly there was an almost immediate improvement in the aspect of the party, not unlike what might have been produced by a glass of generous wine, together with a sudden glow of cheerful sunshine brightening over all their visages at once. There was a healthful suffusion on their cheeks, instead of the ashen hue that had made them look so corpse-like. They gazed at one another, and fancied that some magic power had really begun to smooth away the deep and sad inscriptions which Father Time had been so long engraving on their brows. The Widow Wycherly adjusted her cap, for she felt almost like a woman again.

"Give us more of this wondrous water!" cried they, eagerly. "We are younger—but we are

[1] the Spanish explorer who discovered Florida, March 27, 1513, while in search of the island wherein was the Fountain of Youth

still too old! Quick—give us more!"

"Patience, patience!" quoth Dr. Heidegger, who sat watching the experiment with philosophic coolness. "You have been a long time growing old. Surely you might be content to grow young in half an hour! But the water is at your service."

Again he filled their glasses with the liquor of youth, enough of which still remained in the vase to turn half the old people in the city to the age of their own grandchildren. While the bubbles were yet sparkling on the brim, the doctor's four guests snatched their glasses from the table, and swallowed the contents at a single gulp. Was it delusion? Even while the draught was passing down their throats, it seemed to have wrought a change on their whole systems. Their eyes grew clear and bright; a dark shade deepened among their silvery locks, they sat around the table, three gentlemen of middle age, and a woman hardly beyond her buxom prime.

"My dear widow, you are charming!" cried Colonel Killigrew, whose eyes had been fixed upon her face, while the shadows of age were flitting from it like darkness from the crimson daybreak.

The fair widow knew, of old, that Colonel Killigrew's compliments were not always measured by sober truth; so she started up and ran to the mirror, still dreading that the ugly visage of an old woman would meet her gaze. Meanwhile, the three gentlemen behaved in such a manner as proved that the water of the Fountain of Youth possessed some intoxicating qualities; unless, indeed, their exhilaration of spirits were merely a lightsome dizziness caused by the sudden removal of the weight of years. Mr. Gascoigne's mind seemed to run on political topics, but whether relating to the past, present, or future, could not easily be determined, since the same ideas and phrases have been in vogue these fifty years. Now he rattled forth full-throated sentences about patriotism, national glory, and the people's right; now he muttered some perilous stuff or other, in a sly and doubtful whisper, so cautiously that even his own conscience could scarcely catch the secret; and now again he spoke in measured accents, and a deeply deferential tone, as if a royal ear were listening to his well-turned periods. Colonel Killigrew all this time had been trolling forth a jolly bottle-song, and ringing his glass in symphony with the chorus, while his eyes wandered towards the buxom figure of the Widow Wycherly. On the other side of the table, Mr. Medbourne was involved in a calculation of dollars and cents, with which was strangely intermingled a project for supplying the East Indies with ice, by harnessing a team of whales to the polar icebergs.

As for the Widow Wycherly, she stood before the mirror curtsying and simpering to her own image, and greeting it as the friend whom she loved better than all the world beside. She thrust her face close to the glass, to see whether some long-remembered wrinkle or crow's-foot had indeed vanished. She examined whether the snow had so entirely melted from her hair, that the venerable cap could be safely thrown aside. At last, turning briskly away, she came with a sort of dancing step to the table.

"My dear old doctor," cried she, "pray favor me with another glass!"

"Certainly, my dear madam, certainly!" replied the complaisant doctor; "see! I have already filled the glasses."

There, in fact, stood the four glasses, brimful of this wonderful water, the delicate spray of which, as it effervesced from the surface, resembled the tremulous glitter of diamonds. It was now so nearly sunset that the chamber had grown duskier than ever; but a mild and moonlike splendor gleamed from within the vase, and rested alike on the four guests, and on the doctor's venerable figure. He sat in a high-backed, elaborately carved, oaken arm-chair, with a gray dignity of aspect that might have well befitted that very Father Time whose power had never been disputed save by this fortunate company. Even while quaffing the third draught of the Fountain of Youth, they were almost awed by the expression of his mysterious visage.

But, the next moment, the exhilarating gush of young life shot through their veins. They were now in the happy prime of youth. Age, with its miserable train of cares, and sorrows, and diseases, was remembered only as the trouble of a dream from which they had joyously awoke. The fresh gloss of the soul, so early lost, and without which the world's successive scenes had been but a gallery of faded pictures, again threw its enchantment over all their prospects. They felt like new-created beings in a new-created universe.

"We are young! We are young!" they cried exultingly.

Youth, like the extremity of age, had effaced the strongly-marked characteristics of middle life, and mutually assimilated them all. They were a group of merry youngsters, almost maddened with the exuberant frolicsomeness of their years. The most singular effect of their gayety was an impulse to mock the infirmity and decrepitude of which they had so lately been the victims. They laughed loudly at their old-fashioned attire, the wide-skirted coats and flapped waistcoats of the young men, and the ancient cap and gown of the blooming girl. One limped across the floor like a gouty grandfather; one set a pair of spectacles astride of his nose, and pretended to pore over the black-letter pages of the book of magic; a third seated himself in an arm-chair, and strove to imitate the venerable dignity of Dr. Heidegger. Then all shouted mirthfully, and leaped about the room. The Widow Wycherly—if so fresh a damsel could be called a widow—tripped up to the doctor's chair, with a mischievous merriment in her rosy face.

"Doctor, you dear old soul," cried she, "get up and dance with me!" And then the four young people laughed louder than ever, to think what a queer figure the poor old doctor would cut.

"Pray excuse me," answered the doctor quietly. "I am old and rheumatic, and my dancing days were over long ago. But either of these gay young gentlemen will be glad of so pretty a partner."

"Dance with me, Clara!" cried Colonel Killigrew.

"No, no, I will be her partner!" shouted Mr. Gascoigne.

"She promised me her hand, fifty years ago!" exclaimed Mr. Medbourne.

They all gathered round her. One caught both her hands in his passionate grasp—another threw his arm about her waist—the third buried his hand among the glossy curls that clustered beneath the widow's cap. Blushing, panting, struggling, chiding, laughing, her warm breath fanning each of their faces by turns, she strove to disengage herself, yet still remained in their triple embrace. Never was there a livelier picture of youthful rivalship, with bewitching beauty for the prize. Yet, by a strange deception, owing to the duskiness of the chamber, and the antique dresses which they still wore, the tall mirror is said to have reflected the figures of the three old, gray, withered grandsires, ridiculously contending for the skinny ugliness of a shriveled grandam.

But they were young: their burning passions proved them so. Inflamed to madness by the coquetry of the girl-widow, who neither granted nor quite withheld her favors, the three rivals began to interchange threatening glances. Still keeping hold of the fair prize, they grappled fiercely at one another's throats. As they struggled to and fro, the table was overturned, and the vase dashed into a thousand fragments. The precious Water of Youth flowed in a bright stream across the floor, moistening the wings of a butterfly, which, grown old in the decline of summer, had alighted there to die. The insect fluttered lightly through the chamber, and settled on the snowy head of Dr. Heidegger.

"Come, come, gentlemen!—come, Madame Wycherly," exclaimed the doctor, "I really must protest against this riot."

They stood still, and shivered; for it seemed as if gray Time were calling them back from their sunny youth, far down into the chill and darksome vale of years. They looked at old Dr. Heidegger, who sat in his carved arm-chair, holding the rose of half a century, which he had rescued from among the fragments of the shattered vase. At the motion of his hand, the four rioters resumed their seats; the more readily, because their violent exertions had wearied them, youthful though they were.

"My poor Sylvia's rose!" ejaculated Dr. Heidegger, holding it in the light of the sunset clouds; "it appears to be fading again."

And so it was. Even while the party were looking at it, the flower continued to shrivel up, till it became as dry and fragile as when the doctor had first thrown it into the vase. He shook off the few drops of moisture which clung to its petals.

"I love it as well thus as in its dewy freshness," observed he, pressing the withered rose to his withered lips. While he spoke, the butterfly fluttered down from the doctor's snowy head, and fell upon the floor.

His guests shivered again. A strange chilliness, whether of the body or spirit they could not tell, was creeping gradually over them all. They gazed at one another, and fancied that each fleeting moment snatched away a charm, and left a deepening furrow where none had been before. Was it an illusion? Had the changes of a lifetime been crowded into so brief a space, and were they now four aged people, sitting with their old friend, Dr. Heidegger?

"Are we grown old again, so soon?" cried they, dolefully.

In truth they had. The Water of Youth possessed merely a virtue more transient than that of wine. The delirium which it created had effervesced away. Yes! they were old again. With a shuddering impulse, that showed her a woman still, the widow clasped her skinny hands before her face, and wished that the coffin lid were over it, since it could be no longer beautiful.

"Yes, friends, ye are old again," said Dr. Heidegger, "and lo! the Water of Youth is all lavished on the ground. Well—I bemoan it not; for if the fountain gushed at my very doorstep, I would not stoop to bathe my lips in it— no, though its delirium were for years instead of moments. Such is the lesson ye have taught me!"

But the doctor's four friends had taught no such lesson to themselves. They resolved forthwith to make a pilgrimage to Florida, and quaff at morning, noon, and night, from the Fountain of Youth. 1837

NOTE.—In an English review, not long since, I have been accused of plagiarizing the idea of this story from a chapter in one of the novels of Alexandre Dumas. There has undoubtedly been a plagiarism on one side or the other; but as my story was written a good deal more than twenty years ago, and as the novel is of considerably more recent date, I take pleasure in thinking that M. Dumas has done me the honor to appropriate one of the fanciful conceptions of my earlier days. He is heartily welcome to it; nor is it the only instance, by many, in which the great French romancer has exercised the privilege of commanding genius by confiscating the intellectual property of less famous people to his own use and behoof.

September, 1860.

From TWICE-TOLD TALES
LEGENDS OF THE PROVINCE HOUSE [1]

III

LADY ELEANORE'S MANTLE

Mine excellent friend, the landlord of the Province House, was pleased, the other evening, to invite Mr. Tiffany and myself to an oyster supper. This slight mark of respect and gratitude, as he handsomely observed, was far less than the ingenious tale-teller, and I, the humble note-taker of his narratives, had fairly earned, by the public notice which our joint lucubrations [2] had attracted to his establishment. Many a cigar had been smoked within his premises—many a glass of wine, or more potent *aqua vitae,* [3] had been quaffed—many a

[1] The first four stories of the second series of the *Twice-Told Tales* have their setting in the old Boston Province House, which stood nearly opposite the Old South Church on Washington Street. This old three-story brick building built by Peter Sergeant, third husband of Sir W. Phipps's widow, was bought in 1716 to be the home of the royal governors of Massachusetts, but in Hawthorne's time was used as an inn. Mr. Thomas Waite, the landlord, and Mr. Bela Tiffany, the elderly lodger, are supposed to have told Hawthorne the legends connected with the place.
[2] the *Twice-Told Tales*
[3] any kind of distilled spirits

dinner had been eaten by curious strangers, who, save for the fortunate conjunction of Mr. Tiffany and me, would never have ventured through that darksome avenue which gives access to the historic precincts of the Province House. In short, if any credit be due to the courteous assurances of Mr. Thomas Waite, we had brought his forgotten mansion almost as effectually into public view as if we had thrown down the vulgar range of shoe shops and dry goods stores which hides its aristocratic front from Washington Street. It may be unadvisable, however, to speak too loudly of the increased custom of the house, lest Mr. Waite should find it difficult to renew the lease on so favorable terms as heretofore.

Being thus welcomed as benefactors, neither Mr. Tiffany nor myself felt any scruple in doing full justice to the good things that were set before us. If the feast were less magnificent than those same paneled walls had witnessed, in a by-gone century,—if mine host presided with somewhat less of state than might have befitted a successor of the royal governors,— if the guests made a less imposing show than the bewigged, and powdered, and embroidered dignitaries, who erst banqueted at the gubernatorial table, and now sleep within their armorial tombs on Copp's Hill, [4] or round King's Chapel [5]—yet never, I may boldly say, did a more comfortable little party assemble in the Province House, from Queen Anne's days to the Revolution. The occasion was rendered more interesting by the presence of a venerable personage, whose own actual reminiscences went back to the epoch of Gage and Howe, [6] and even supplied him with a doubtful anecdote or two of Hutchinson. [7] He was one of that small, and now all but extinguished class, whose attachment to royalty, and to the colonial institutions and customs that were connected with it, had never yielded to the democratic heresies of after times. The young queen of Britain has not a more loyal subject in her realm— perhaps not one who would kneel before her throne with such reverential love—as this old grandsire, whose head has whitened beneath the mild sway of the republic, which still, in his mellower moments, he terms a usurpation. Yet prejudices so obstinate have not made him an ungentle or impracticable companion. If the truth must be told, the life of the aged loyalist

[4] The Copp's Hill burying ground, at the north end of Boston, dates from 1660.
[5] The first King's Chapel on Tremont Street was built by Andros in 1689; but the present one, on the same site, dates from 1754.
[6] British generals in the Revolutionary War
[7] governor of Massachusetts 1771-1774

has been of such a scrambling and unsettled character,—he has had so little choice of friends, and been so often destitute of any,—that I doubt whether he would refuse a cup of kindness [1] with either Oliver Cromwell or John Hancock;—to say nothing of any democrat now upon the stage. In another paper of this series, I may perhaps give the reader a closer glimpse of his portrait.

Our host, in due season, uncorked a bottle of Madeira, of such exquisite perfume and admirable flavor, that he surely must have discovered it in an ancient bin, down deep beneath the deepest cellar, where some jolly old butler stored away the Governor's choicest wine, and forgot to reveal the secret on his deathbed. Peace to his red-nosed ghost, and a libation to his memory! This precious liquor was imbibed by Mr. Tiffany with peculiar zest; and after sipping the third glass, it was his pleasure to give us one of the oddest legends which he had yet raked from the storehouse where he keeps such matters. With some suitable adornments from my own fancy, it ran pretty much as follows.

Not long after Colonel Shute [2] had assumed the government of Massachusetts Bay, now nearly a hundred and twenty years ago, a young lady of rank and fortune arrived from England, to claim his protection as her guardian. He was her distant relative, but the nearest who had survived the gradual extinction of her family; so that no more eligible shelter could be found for the rich and high-born Lady Eleanore Rochcliffe than within the Province House of a transatlantic colony. The consort of Governor Shute, moreover, had been as a mother to her childhood, and was now anxious to receive her, in the hope that a beautiful young woman would be exposed to infinitely less peril from the primitiv society of New England than amid the artifices and corruptions of a court. If either the Governor or his lady had especially consulted their own comfort, they would probably have sought to devolve the responsibility on other hands; since, with some noble and splendid traits of character, Lady Eleanore was remarkable for a harsh, unyielding pride, a haughty consciousness of her hereditary and personal advantages, which made her almost incapable of control. Judging from many traditionary anecdotes, this peculiar temper was hardly less than a monomania; or, if the acts which it inspired were those of a sane person,

it seemed due from Providence that pride so sinful should be followed by as severe a retribution. That tinge of the marvelous, which is thrown over so many of these half-forgotten legends, has probably imparted an additional wildness to the strange story of Lady Eleanore Rochcliffe.

The ship in which she came passenger had arrived at Newport, whence Lady Eleanore was conveyed to Boston in the Governor's coach, attended by a small escort of gentlemen on horseback. The ponderous equipage, with its four black horses, attracted much notice as it rumbled through Cornhill, [3] surrounded by the prancing steeds of half a dozen cavaliers, with swords dangling to their stirrups and pistols at their holsters. Through the large glass windows of the coach, as it rolled along, the people could discern the figure of Lady Eleanore, strangely combining an almost queenly stateliness with the grace and beauty of a maiden in her teens. A singular tale had gone abroad among the ladies of the province, that their fair rival was indebted for much of the irresistible charm of her appearance to a certain article of dress—an embroidered mantle—which had been wrought by the most skilful artist in London, and possessed even magical properties of adornment. On the present occasion, however, she owed nothing to the witchery of dress, being clad in a riding habit of velvet, which would have appeared stiff and ungraceful on any other form.

The coachman reined in his four black steeds, and the whole cavalcade came to a pause in front of the contorted iron balustrade that fenced the Province House from the public street. It was an awkward coincidence that the bell of the Old South [4] was just then tolling for a funeral; so that, instead of a gladsome peal with which it was customary to announce the arrival of distinguished strangers, Lady Eleanore Rochcliffe was ushered by a doleful clang, as if calamity had come embodied in her beautiful person.

"A very great disrespect!" exclaimed Captain Langford, an English officer, who had recently brought dispatches to Governor Shute. "The funeral should have been deferred, lest Lady Eleanore's spirits be affected by such a dismal welcome."

"With your pardon, sir," replied Doctor Clarke, a physician, and a famous champion of

[1] Cf. Burns's "Auld Lang Syne."
[2] Samuel Shute, governor of Massachusetts, 1716-1727

[3] Hawthorne is here perhaps slightly mistaken. Cornhill was the part of Washington Street north of the Old South Church and of the Province House; not the south part, over which Lady Eleanore would have entered Boston. See Bonner's Map of Boston, 1722.
[4] the Old South Church

the popular party, "whatever the heralds may pretend, a dead beggar must have precedence of a living queen. King Death confers high privileges."

These remarks were interchanged while the speakers waited a passage through the crowd, which had gathered on each side of the gateway, leaving an open avenue to the portal of the Province House. A black slave in livery now leaped from behind the coach, and threw open the door; while at the same moment, Governor Shute descended the flight of steps from his mansion, to assist Lady Eleanore in alighting. But the Governor's stately approach was anticipated in a manner that excited general astonishment. A pale young man, with his black hair all in disorder, rushed from the throng, and prostrated himself beside the coach, thus offering his person as a footstool for Lady Eleanore Rochcliffe to tread upon. She held back an instant, yet with an expression as if doubting whether the young man were worthy to bear the weight of her footstep, rather than dissatisfied to receive such awful reverence from a fellow-mortal.

"Up, sir," said the Governor, sternly, at the same time lifting his cane over the intruder. "What means the bedlamite [1] by this freak?"

"Nay," answered Lady Eleanore playfully, but with more scorn than pity in her tone, "Your Excellency shall not strike him. When men seek only to be trampled upon, it were a pity to deny them a favor so easily granted— and so well deserved!"

Then, though as lightly as a sunbeam on a cloud, she placed her foot upon the cowering form, and extended her hand to meet that of the Governor. There was a brief interval, during which Lady Eleanore retained this attitude; and never, surely, was there an apter emblem of aristocracy and hereditary pride, trampling on human sympathies and the kindred of nature, than these two figures presented at that moment. Yet the spectators were so smitten with her beauty, and so essential did pride seem to the existence of such a creature, that they gave a simultaneous exclamation of applause.

"Who is this insolent young fellow?" inquired Captain Langford, who still remained beside Doctor Clarke. "If he be in his senses, his impertinence demands the bastinado. If mad, Lady Eleanore should be secured from further inconvenience by his confinement."

"His name is Jervase Helwyse," answered

[1] lunatic (originally an inmate of the hospital of St. Mary of Bethlehem in London where lunatics were confined)

the doctor, "a youth of no birth or fortune, or other advantages, save the mind and soul that nature gave him; and being secretary to our colonial agent in London, it was his misfortune to meet this Lady Eleanore Rochcliffe. He loved her—and her scorn has driven him mad."

"He was mad so to aspire," observed the English officer.

"It may be so," said Doctor Clarke, frowning as he spoke. "But I tell you, sir, I could well-nigh doubt the justice of the Heaven above us, if no signal humiliation overtake this lady, who now treads so haughtily into yonder mansion. She seeks to place herself above the sympathies of our common nature, which envelops all human souls. See if that nature do not assert its claim over her in some mode that shall bring her level with the lowest!"

"Never!" cried Captain Langford, indignantly; "neither in life, nor when they lay her with her ancestors."

Not many days afterward the Governor gave a ball in honor of Lady Eleanore Rochcliffe. The principal gentry of the colony received invitations, which were distributed to their residences, far and near, by messengers on horseback, bearing missives sealed with all the formality of official dispatches. In obedience to the summons, there was a general gathering of rank, wealth, and beauty; and the wide door of the Province House had seldom given admittance to more numerous and honorable guests than on the evening of Lady Eleanore's ball. Without much extravagance of eulogy, the spectacle might even be termed splendid; for, according to the fashion of the times, the ladies shone in rich silks and satins, outspread over wide projecting hoops; and the gentlemen glittered in gold embroidery, laid unsparingly upon the purple, or scarlet, or sky-blue velvet, which was the material of their coats and waistcoats. The latter article of dress was of great importance, since it enveloped the wearer's body nearly to the knees, and was perhaps bedizened with the amount of his whole year's income, in golden flowers and foliage. The altered taste of the present day—a taste symbolic of a deep change in the whole system of society—would look upon almost any of those gorgeous figures as ridiculous; although that evening the guests sought their reflections in the pier-glasses, and rejoiced to catch their own glitter amid the glittering crowd. What a pity that one of the stately mirrors has not preserved a picture of the scene, which, by the very traits that were so transitory, might have taught us much that would be worth knowing and remembering!

Would, at least, that either painter or mirror could convey to us some faint idea of a garment, already noticed in this legend,—the Lady Eleanore's embroidered mantle,—which the gossips whispered was invested with magic properties, so as to lend a new and untried grace to her figure each time that she put it on! Idle fancy as it is, this mysterious mantle has thrown an awe around my image of her, partly from its fabled virtues, and partly because it was the handiwork of a dying woman, and, perchance, owed the fantastic grace of its conception to the delirium of approaching death.

After the ceremonial greetings had been paid, Lady Eleanore Rochcliffe stood apart from the mob of guests, insulating herself within a small and distinguished circle, to whom she accorded a more cordial favor than to the general throng. The waxen torches threw their radiance vividly over the scene, bringing out its brilliant points in strong relief; but she gazed carelessly, and with now and then an expression of weariness or scorn, tempered with such feminine grace that her auditors scarcely perceived the moral deformity of which it was the utterance. She beheld the spectacle not with vulgar ridicule, as disdaining to be pleased with the provincial mockery of a court festival, but with the deeper scorn of one whose spirit held itself too high to participate in the enjoyment of other human souls. Whether or no the recollections of those who saw her that evening were influenced by the strange events with which she was subsequently connected, so it was that her figure ever after recurred to them as marked by something wild and unnatural, although at the time the general whisper was of her exceeding beauty, and of the indescribable charm which her mantle threw around her. Some close observers, indeed, detected a feverish flush and alternate paleness of countenance, with a corresponding flow and revulsion of spirits, and once or twice, a painful and helpless betrayal of lassitude, as if she were on the point of sinking to the ground. Then, with a nervous shudder, she seemed to arouse her energies, and threw some bright and playful, yet half-wicked sarcasm, into the conversation. There was so strange a characteristic in her manners and sentiments, that it astonished every right-minded listener; till looking in her face, a lurking and incomprehensible glance and smile perplexed them with doubts both as to her seriousness and sanity. Gradually, Lady Eleanore Rochcliffe's circle grew smaller, till only four gentlemen remained in it. These were Captain Langford, the English

officer before mentioned; a Virginian planter, who had come to Massachusetts on some political errand; a young Episcopal clergyman, the grandson of a British earl; and, lastly, the private secretary of Governor Shute, whose obsequiousness had won a sort of tolerance from Lady Eleanore.

At different periods of the evening the liveried servants of the Province House passed among the guests, bearing huge trays of refreshments, and French and Spanish wines. Lady Eleanore Rochcliffe, who refused to wet her beautiful lips even with a bubble of champagne, had sunk back into a large damask chair, apparently overwearied either with the excitement of the scene or its tedium; and while, for an instant, she was unconscious of voices, laughter, and music, a young man stole forward, and knelt down at her feet. He bore a salver in his hand, on which was a chased silver goblet, filled to the brim with wine, which he offered as reverentially as to a crowned queen, or rather with the awful devotion of a priest doing sacrifice to his idol. Conscious that some one touched her robe, Lady Eleanore started, and unclosed her eyes upon the pale, wild features and disheveled hair of Jervase Helwyse.

"Why do you haunt me thus?" said she, in a languid tone, but with a kindlier feeling than she ordinarily permitted herself to express. "They tell me that I have done you harm."

"Heaven knows if that be so," replied the young man, solemnly. "But, Lady Eleanore, in requital of that harm, if such there be, and for your own earthly and heavenly welfare, I pray you to take one sip of this holy wine, and then to pass the goblet round among the guests. And this shall be a symbol that you have not sought to withdraw yourself from the chain of human sympathies—which whoso would shake off must keep company with fallen angels."

"Where has this mad fellow stolen that sacramental vessel?" exclaimed the Episcopal clergyman.

This question drew the notice of the guests to the silver cup, which was recognized as appertaining to the communion plate of the Old South Church; and, for aught that could be known, it was brimming over with the consecrated wine.

"Perhaps it is poisoned," half whispered the Governor's secretary.

"Pour it down the villain's throat!" cried the Virginian, fiercely.

"Turn him out of the house!" cried Captain Langford, seizing Jervase Helwyse so roughly by the shoulder that the sacramental cup was overturned, and its contents sprinkled upon

Lady Eleanore's mantle. "Whether knave, fool, or bedlamite, it is intolerable that the fellow should go at large."

"Pray, gentlemen, do my poor admirer no harm," said Lady Eleanore, with a faint and weary smile. "Take him out of my sight, if such be your pleasure; for I can find in my heart to do nothing but laugh at him; whereas, in all decency and conscience, it would become me to weep for the mischief I have wrought!"

But while the bystanders were attempting to lead away the unfortunate young man, he broke from them, and with a wild, impassioned earnestness, offered a new and equally strange petition to Lady Eleanore. It was no other than that she should throw off the mantle, which, while he pressed the silver cup of wine upon her, she had drawn more closely around her form, so as almost to shroud herself within it.

"Cast it from you!" exclaimed Jervase Helwyse, clasping his hands in an agony of entreaty. "It may not yet be too late! Give the accursed garment to the flames!"

But Lady Eleanore, with a laugh of scorn, drew the rich folds of the embroidered mantle over her head in such a fashion as to give a completely new aspect to her beautiful face, which—half hidden, half revealed—seemed to belong to some being of mysterious character and purposes.

"Farewell, Jervase Helwyse!" said she. "Keep my image in your remembrance as you behold it now."

"Alas, lady!" he replied, in a tone no longer wild, but sad as a funeral bell. "We must meet shortly, when your face may wear another aspect—and that shall be the image that must abide within me."

He made no more resistance to the violent efforts of the gentlemen and servants, who almost dragged him out of the apartment, and dismissed him roughly from the iron gate of the Province House. Captain Langford, who had been very active in this affair, was returning to the presence of Lady Eleanore Rochcliffe, when he encountered the physician, Doctor Clarke, with whom he had held some casual talk on the day of her arrival. The Doctor stood apart, separated from Lady Eleanore by the width of the room, but eyeing her with such keen sagacity that Captain Langford involuntarily gave him credit for the discovery of some deep secret.

"You appear to be smitten, after all, with the charms of this queenly maiden," said he, hoping thus to draw forth the physician's hidden knowledge.

"God forbid!" answered Doctor Clarke, with a grave smile; "and if you be wise, you will put up the same prayer for yourself. Woe to those who shall be smitten by this beautiful Lady Eleanore! But yonder stands the Governor—and I have a word or two for his private ear. Good night!"

He accordingly advanced to Governor Shute, and addressed him in so low a tone that none of the bystanders could catch a word of what he said; although the sudden change of His Excellency's hitherto cheerful visage betokened that the communication could be of no agreeable import. A very few moments afterwards, it was announced to the guests that an unforeseen circumstance rendered it necessary to put a premature close to the festival.

The ball at the Province House supplied a topic of conversation for the colonial metropolis for some days after its occurrence, and might still longer have been the general theme, only that a subject of all-engrossing interest thrust it, for a time, from the public recollection. This was the appearance of a dreadful epidemic, which, in that age, and long before and afterwards, was wont to slay its hundreds and thousands on both sides of the Atlantic. On the occasion of which we speak it was distinguished by a peculiar virulence, insomuch that it has left its traces—its pitmarks, to use an appropriate figure—on the history of the country, the affairs of which were thrown into confusion by its ravages. [1] At first, unlike its ordinary course, the disease seemed to confine itself to the higher circles of society, selecting its victims from among the proud, the well-born, and the wealthy, entering unabashed into stately chambers, and lying down with the slumberers in silken beds. Some of the most distinguished guests of the Province House—even those whom the haughty Lady Eleanore Rochcliffe had deemed not unworthy of her favor—were stricken by this fatal scourge. It was noticed, with an ungenerous bitterness of feeling, that the four gentlemen—the Virginian, the British officer, the young clergyman, and the Governor's secretary—who had been her most devoted attendants on the evening of the ball were the foremost on whom the plague-stroke fell. But the disease, pursuing its onward progress, soon ceased to be exclusively a prerogative of aristocracy. Its red brand was no longer conferred like a noble's star, or an order of knighthood. It threaded its way through the narrow and crooked streets, and entered the low, mean, darksome dwellings, and laid its hand of death

[1] See Cotton Mather's *Diary*, pp. 46-48.

upon the artisans and laboring classes of the town. It compelled rich and poor to feel themselves brethren then; and stalking to and fro across the Three Hills, [1] with a fierceness which made it almost a new pestilence, there was that mighty conqueror—that scourge and horror of our forefathers—the Smallpox!

We cannot estimate the affright which this plague inspired of yore, by contemplating it as the fangless monster of the present day. We must remember, rather, with what awe we watched the gigantic footsteps of the Asiatic cholera striding from shore to shore of the Atlantic, and marching like destiny upon cities far remote, which flight had already half depopulated. There is no other fear so horrible and unhumanizing as that which makes man dread to breathe heaven's vital air, lest it be poison, or to grasp the hand of a brother or friend, lest the gripe of the pestilence should clutch him. Such was the dismay that now followed in the track of the disease, or ran before it throughout the town. Graves were hastily dug, and the pestilential relics as hastily covered, because the dead were enemies of the living, and strove to draw them headlong, as it were, into their own dismal pit. The public councils were suspended, as if mortal wisdom might relinquish its devices now that an unearthly usurper had found his way into the ruler's mansion. Had an enemy's fleet been hovering on the coast, or his armies trampling on our soil, the people would probably have committed their defense to that same direful conqueror who had wrought their own calamity, and would permit no interference with his sway. This conqueror had a symbol of his triumphs. It was a blood-red flag, that fluttered in the tainted air over the door of every dwelling into which the smallpox had entered.

Such a banner was long since waving over the portal of Province House; for thence, as was proved by tracking its footsteps back, had all this dreadful mischief issued. It had been traced back to a lady's luxurious chamber— to the proudest of the proud—to her that was so delicate, and hardly owned herself of earthly mold—to the haughty one who took her stand above human sympathies—to Lady Eleanore! There remained no room for doubt that the contagion had lurked in that gorgeous mantle, which threw so strange a grace around her at the festival. Its fantastic splendor had been conceived in the delirious brain of a woman on her deathbed, and was the last toil of her stiffening fingers, which had interwoven fate and misery with its golden threads. This dark tale, whispered at first, was now bruited far and wide. The people raved against the Lady Eleanore, and cried out that her pride and scorn had evoked a fiend, and that between them both this monstrous evil had been born. At times their rage and despair took the semblance of grinning mirth; and whenever the red flag of the pestilence was hoisted over another, and yet another door, they clapped their hands and shouted through the streets, in bitter mockery: "Behold a new triumph for the Lady Eleanore!"

One day, in the midst of these dismal times, a wild figure approached the portal of the Province House, and folding his arms, stood contemplating the scarlet banner, which a passing breeze shook fitfully as if to fling abroad the contagion that it typified. At length, climbing one of the pillars by means of the iron balustrade, he took down the flag and entered the mansion, waving it above his head. At the foot of the staircase he met the Governor, booted and spurred, with his cloak drawn around him, evidently on the point of setting forth upon a journey.

"Wretched lunatic, what do you seek here?" exclaimed Shute, extending his cane to guard himself from contact. "There is nothing here but Death. Back—or you will meet him!"

"Death will not touch me, the banner-bearer of the pestilence!" cried Jervase Helwyse, shaking the red flag aloft. "Death and the Pestilence, who wears the aspect of the Lady Eleanore, will walk through the streets tonight, and I must march before them with this banner!"

"Why do I waste words on the fellow?" muttered the governor, drawing his cloak across his mouth. "What matters his miserable life, when none of us are sure of twelve hours' breath? On, fool, to your own destruction!"

He made way for Jervase Helwyse, who immediately ascended the staircase, but on the first landing-place was arrested by the firm grasp of a hand upon his shoulder. Looking fiercely up, with a madman's impulse to struggle with and rend asunder his opponent, he found himself powerless beneath a calm, stern eye, which possessed the mysterious property of quelling frenzy at its height. The person whom he had now encountered was the physician, Doctor Clarke, the duties of whose sad profession had led him to the Province House, where he was an infrequent guest in more prosperous times.

"Young man, what is your purpose?" demanded he.

[1] Trimountaine was the early name given Boston (Cf. Tremont) because of its conspicuous three-topped hill afterwards named Beacon Hill.

"I seek the Lady Eleanore," answered Jervase Helwyse, submissively.

"All have fled from her," said the physician. "Why do you seek her now? I tell you, youth, her nurse fell death-stricken on the threshold of that fatal chamber. Know ye not that never came such a curse to our shores as this lovely Lady Eleanore?—that her breath has filled the air with poison?—that she has shaken pestilence and death upon the land from the folds of her accursed mantle?"

"Let me look upon her!" rejoined the mad youth, more wildly. "Let me behold her, in her awful beauty, clad in the regal garments of the pestilence! She and Death sit on a throne together. Let me kneel down before them!"

"Poor youth!" said Doctor Clarke; and, moved by a deep sense of human weakness, a smile of caustic humor curled his lip even then. "Wilt thou still worship the destroyer, and surround her image with fantasies the more magnificent the more evil she has wrought? Thus man doth ever to his tyrants. Approach, then! Madness, as I have noted, has that good efficacy that it will guard you from contagion—and perchance its own cure may be found in yonder chamber."

Ascending another flight of stairs, he threw open a door and signed to Jervase Helwyse that he should enter. The poor lunatic, it seems probable, had cherished a delusion that his haughty mistress sat in state, unharmed herself by the pestilential influence which, as by enchantment, she scattered round about her. He dreamed, no doubt, that her beauty was not dimmed, but brightened into superhuman splendor. With such anticipations he stole reverentially to the door at which the physician stood, but paused upon the threshold, gazing fearfully into the gloom of the darkened chamber.

"Where is the Lady Eleanore?" whispered he.

"Call her," replied the physician.

"Lady Eleanore!—Princess!—Queen of Death!" cried Jervase Helwyse, advancing three steps into the chamber. "She is not here! There, on yonder table, I behold the sparkle of a diamond which once she wore upon her bosom. There"—and he shuddered—"there hangs her mantle, on which a dead woman embroidered a spell of dreadful potency. But where is the Lady Eleanore?"

Something stirred within the silken curtains of a canopied bed; and a low moan was uttered, which, listening intently, Jervase Helwyse began to distinguish as a woman's voice, complaining dolefully of thirst. He fancied even that he recognized its tones.

"My throat!—my throat is scorched," murmured the voice. "A drop of water!"

"What thing art thou?" said the brain-stricken youth, drawing near the bed and tearing asunder its curtains. "Whose voice hast thou stolen for thy murmurs and miserable petitions, as if Lady Eleanore could be conscious of mortal infirmity? Fie! Heap of diseased mortality, why lurkest thou in my lady's chamber?"

"Oh, Jervase Helwyse," said the voice—and as it spoke the figure contorted itself, struggling to hide its blasted face—"look not now on the woman you once loved! The curse of Heaven hath stricken me, because I would not call man my brother, nor woman sister. I wrapt myself in PRIDE as in a MANTLE, and scorned the sympathies of nature; and therefore has nature made this wretched body the medium of a dreadful sympathy. You are avenged—they are all avenged—nature is avenged—for I am Eleanore Rochcliffe!"

The malice of his mental disease, the bitterness lurking at the bottom of his heart, mad as he was, for a blighted and ruined life, and love that had been paid with cruel scorn, awoke within the breast of Jervase Helwyse. He shook his finger at the wretched girl, and the chamber echoed, the curtains of the bed were shaken, with his outburst of insane merriment.

"Another triumph for the Lady Eleanore!" he cried. "All have been her victims! Who so worthy to be the final victim as herself?"

Impelled by some new fantasy of his crazed intellect, he snatched the fatal mantle, and rushed from the chamber and the house. That night a procession passed by torch-light through the streets, bearing in the midst the figure of a woman enveloped with a richly embroidered mantle; while in advance stalked Jervase Helwyse, waving the red flag of the pestilence. Arriving opposite the Province House, the mob burned the effigy, and a strong wind came and swept away the ashes. It was said that from that very hour the pestilence abated, as if its sway had some mysterious connection, from the first plague-stroke to the last, with Lady Eleanore's mantle. A remarkable uncertainty broods over that unhappy lady's fate. There is a belief, however, that, in a certain chamber of this mansion, a female form may sometimes be duskily discerned, shrinking into the darkest corner, and muffling her face within an embroidered mantle. Supposing the legend true, can this be other than the once proud Lady Eleanore?

Mine host, and the old loyalist, and I, bestowed no little warmth of applause upon this narrative, in which we had all been deeply interested; for the reader can scarcely conceive how unspeakably the effect of such a tale is heightened when, as in the present case, we may repose perfect confidence in the veracity of him who tells it. For my own part, knowing how scrupulous is Mr. Tiffany to settle the foundation of his facts, I could not have believed him one whit the more faithfully had he professed himself an eye-witness of the doings and sufferings of poor Lady Eleanore. Some skeptics, it is true, might demand documentary evidence, or even require him to produce the embroidered mantle, forgetting that—Heaven be praised—it was consumed to ashes. But now the old loyalist, whose blood was warmed by the good cheer, began to talk, in his turn, about the traditions of the Province House, and hinted that he, if it were agreeable, might add a few reminiscences to our legendary stock. Mr. Tiffany, having no cause to dread a rival, immediately besought him to favor us with a specimen; my own entreaties, of course, were urged to the same effect; and our venerable guest, well pleased to find willing auditors, awaited only the return of Mr. Thomas Waite, who had been summoned forth to provide accommodation for several new arrivals. Perchance the public—but be this as its own caprice and ours shall settle the matter—may read the result in another Tale of the Province House.

1842

From MOSSES FROM AN OLD MANSE

THE OLD MANSE [1]

Between two tall gateposts of rough-hewn stone (the gate itself having fallen from its hinges at some unknown epoch) we beheld the gray front of the old parsonage terminating

[1] Back some distance from the street, and surrounded by great elms, there still stands, in Concord, Mass., the Old Manse, or parsonage, first built by the Rev. William Emerson in 1765, and occupied by Emerson during one year (1834-35) and by Hawthorne during the first three years (1842-45) of his married life. The friends that occasionally entered this "Paradise," as the Hawthornes named it, included George S. Hillard, the Boston lawyer and journalist; William Ellery Channing, a poet and journalist, the nephew of the more famous William Ellery Channing; Margaret Fuller; Horatio Bridge, of the U. S. navy, whose Journal of an African Cruiser Hawthorne edited; Franklin Pierce, later President of the United States; and Thoreau and Emerson. From the upstairs study at the rear, in which Emerson had written Nature, and where Hawthorne wrote the Mosses, there can be seen the river where Hawthorne and Emerson skated together, and the Concord Bridge, where was shed almost the first blood in the Revolution. The essay descriptive of the manse was written last to introduce the stories and essays—some of them written much earlier—which make up the book called Mosses from an Old Manse.

the vista of an avenue of black ash trees. It was now a twelvemonth since the funeral procession of the venerable clergyman, its last inhabitant, had turned from that gateway towards the village burying ground. The wheel-track leading to the door as well as the whole breadth of the avenue, was almost overgrown with grass, affording dainty mouthfuls to two or three vagrant cows, and an old white horse who had his own living to pick up along the roadside. The glimmering shadows that lay half asleep between the door of the house and the public highway were a kind of spiritual medium, seen through which the edifice had not quite the aspect of belonging to the material world. Certainly it had little in common with those ordinary abodes which stand so imminent upon the road that every passer-by can thrust his head, as it were, into the domestic circle. From these quiet windows the figures of passing travelers looked too remote and dim to disturb the sense of privacy. In its near retirement and accessible seclusion it was the very spot for the residence of a clergyman,—a man not estranged from human life, yet enveloped, in the midst of it, with a veil woven of intermingled gloom and brightness. It was worthy to have been one of the time-honored parsonages of England in which, through many generations, a succession of holy occupants pass from youth to age, and bequeath each an inheritance of sanctity to pervade the house and hover over it as with an atmosphere.

Nor, in truth, had the Old Manse ever been profaned by a lay occupant until that memorable summer afternoon when I entered it as my home. A priest had built it; a priest had succeeded to it; other priestly men from time to time had dwelt in it; and children born in its chambers had grown up to assume the priestly character. It was awful to reflect how many sermons must have been written there. The latest inhabitant alone—he by whose translation to paradise the dwelling was left vacant—had penned nearly three thousand discourses, besides the better, if not the greater, number that gushed living from his lips. How often, no doubt, had he paced to and fro along the avenue, attuning his meditations to the sighs and gentle murmurs and deep and solemn peals of the wind among the lofty tops of the trees! In that variety of natural utterances he could find something accordant with every passage of his sermon, were it of tenderness or reverential fear. The boughs over my head seemed shadowy with solemn thoughts as well as with rustling leaves. I took shame to myself for having been so long a writer of idle stories, and ventured to hope that wisdom would descend upon me with the falling leaves of the avenue, and that I should light upon an intellectual treasure in the Old Manse well worth those hoards of long-hidden gold which people seek for in moss-grown houses. Profound treatises of morality; a layman's unprofessional, and therefore unprejudiced, views of religion; histories (such as Bancroft [1] might have written had he taken up his abode here as he once proposed) bright with picture, gleaming over a depth of philosophic thought,—these were the works that might fitly have flowed from such a retirement. In the humblest event, I resolved at least to achieve a novel that should evolve some deep lesson and should possess physical substance enough to stand alone.

In furtherance of my design, and as if to leave me no pretext for not fulfilling it, there was in the rear of the house the most delightful little nook of a study that ever afforded its snug seclusion to a scholar. It was here that Emerson wrote *Nature;* for he was then an inhabitant of the Manse, and used to watch the Assyrian dawn and Paphian sunset [2] and moonrise from the summit of our eastern hill. When I first saw the room its walls were blackened with the smoke of unnumbered years and made still blacker by the grim prints of Puritan ministers that hung around. These worthies looked strangely like bad angels, or at least like men who had wrestled so continually and so sternly with the devil that somewhat of his sooty fierceness had been imparted to their own visages. They had all vanished now; a cheerful coat of paint and golden tinted paper-hangings lighted up the small apartment; while the shadow of a willow tree that swept against the overhanging eaves attempered the cheery western sunshine. In place of the grim prints there was the sweet and lovely head of one of Raphael's Madonnas and two pleasant little pictures of the Lake of Como. The only other decorations were a purple vase of flowers, always fresh, and a bronze one containing graceful ferns. My books (few, and by no means choice; for they were chiefly such waifs as chance had thrown in my way) stood in order about the room, seldom to be disturbed.

The study had three windows, set with little old-fashioned panes of glass, each with a crack across it. The two on the western side looked,

[1] George Bancroft, American historian, 1800-1891

[2] Emerson says in *Nature,* "Give me health and a day, and I will make the pomp of emperors ridiculous. The dawn is my Assyria; the sunset and moonrise my Paphos, and unimaginable realms of faerie." Paphos was a city in western Cyprus notable as a site of the worship of Venus.

or rather peeped between the willow branches, down into the orchard, with glimpses of the river through the trees. The third, facing northward, commanded a broader view of the river, at a spot where its hitherto obscure waters gleam forth into the light of history. It was at this window that the clergyman who then dwelt in the Manse stood watching the outbreak of a long and deadly struggle between two nations; he saw the irregular array of his parishioners on the farther side of the river and the glittering line of the British on the hither bank. He awaited, in an agony of suspense, the rattle of the musketry. It came; and there needed but a gentle wind to sweep the battle smoke around this quiet house.

Perhaps the reader, whom I cannot help considering as my guest in the Old Manse and entitled to all courtesy in the way of sight-showing,—perhaps he will choose to take a nearer view of the memorable spot. We stand now on the river's brink. It may well be called the Concord, the river of peace and quietness; for it is certainly the most unexcitable and sluggish stream that ever loitered imperceptibly towards its eternity—the sea. Positively I had lived three weeks beside it before it grew quite clear to my perception which way the current flowed. It never has a vivacious aspect except when a northwestern breeze is vexing its surface on a sunshiny day. From the incurable indolence of its nature, the stream is happily incapable of becoming the slave of human ingenuity, as is the fate of so many a wild, free mountain torrent. While all things else are compelled to subserve some useful purpose, it idles its sluggish life away in lazy liberty, without turning a solitary spindle or affording even water power enough to grind the corn that grows upon its banks. The torpor of its movement allows it nowhere a bright, pebbly shore, nor so much as a narrow strip of glistening sand, in any part of its course. It slumbers between broad prairies, kissing the long meadow grass, and bathes the overhanging boughs of elder bushes and willows or the roots of elms and ash trees and clumps of maples. Flags and rushes grow along its plashy shore; the yellow water lily spreads its broad, flat leaves on the margin; and the fragrant white pond-lily abounds, generally selecting a position just so far from the river's brink that it cannot be grasped save at the hazard of plunging in.

It is a marvel whence this perfect flower derives its loveliness and perfume, springing as it does from the black mud over which the river sleeps, and where lurk the slimy eel, and speckled frog, and the mud turtle, whom continual washing cannot cleanse. It is the very same black mud out of which the yellow lily sucks its obscene life and noisome odor. Thus we see, too, in the world that some persons assimilate only what is ugly and evil from the same moral circumstances which supply good and beautiful results—the fragrance of celestial flowers—to the daily life of others.

The reader must not, from any testimony of mine, contract a dislike towards our slumberous stream. In the light of a calm and golden sunset it becomes lovely beyond expression; the more lovely for the quietude that so well accords with the hour, when even the wind, after blustering all day long, usually hushes itself to rest. Each tree and rock and every blade of grass is distinctly imaged, and, however unsightly in reality, assumes ideal beauty in the reflection. The minutest things of earth and the broad aspect of the firmament are pictured equally without effort and with the same felicity of success. All the sky glows downward at our feet; the rich clouds float through the unruffled bosom of the stream like heavenly thoughts through a peaceful heart. We will not, then, malign our river as gross and impure while it can glorify itself with so adequate a picture of the heaven that broods above it; or, if we remember its tawny hue and the muddiness of its bed, let it be a symbol that the earthliest human soul has an infinite spiritual capacity and may contain the better world within its depths. But, indeed, the same lesson might be drawn out of any mud puddle in the streets of a city; and, being taught us everywhere, it must be true.

Come, we have pursued a somewhat devious track in our walk to the battle-ground. Here we are, at the point where the river was crossed by the old bridge, the possession of which was the immediate object of the contest. On the hither side grow two or three elms, throwing a wide circumference of shade, but which must have been planted at some period within the threescore years and ten that have passed since the battle day. On the farther shore, overhung by a clump of elder bushes, we discern the stone abutment of the bridge. Looking down into the river, I once discovered some heavy fragments of the timbers, all green with half a century's growth of water moss; for during that length of time the tramp of horses and human footsteps have ceased along this ancient highway. The stream has here about the breadth of twenty strokes of a swimmer's arm—a space not too wide when the bullets were whistling across. Old people who dwell hereabouts will point out the very spots on the western bank where our countrymen fell down and died; and on this side of the river an obelisk of granite has grown up from the soil that was fertilized with British blood. The monument, not more than twenty feet in height, is such as it befitted the inhabitants of a village to erect in illustration of a matter of local interest rather than what was suitable to commemorate an epoch of national history. Still, by the fathers of the village this famous deed was done; and their descendants might rightfully claim the privilege of building a memorial.

A humbler token of the fight, yet a more interesting one than the granite obelisk, may be seen close under the stone wall which separates the battle-ground from the precincts of the parsonage. It is the grave—marked by a small, mossgrown fragment of stone at the head and another at the foot—the grave of two British soldiers who were slain in the skirmish, and have ever since slept peacefully where Zechariah Brown and Thomas Davis buried them. Soon was their warfare ended; a weary night march from Boston, a rattling volley of musketry across the river, and then these many years of rest. In the long procession of slain invaders who passed into eternity from the battle-fields of the Revolution, these two nameless soldiers led the way.

Lowell, the poet, as we were once standing over this grave, told me a tradition in reference to one of the inhabitants below. The story has something deeply impressive, though its circumstances cannot altogether be reconciled with probability. A youth in the service of the clergyman happened to be chopping wood, that April morning, at the back door of the Manse, and when the noise of battle rang from side to side of the bridge he hastened across the intervening field to see what might be going forward. It is rather strange, by the way, that this lad should have been so diligently at work when the whole population of town and country were startled out of their customary business by the advance of the British troops. Be that as it might, the tradition says that the lad now left his task and hurried to the battle-field with the axe still in his hand. The British had by this time retreated, the Americans were in pursuit; and the late scene of strife was thus deserted by both parties. Two soldiers lay on the ground —one was a corpse; but, as the young New Englander drew nigh, the other Briton raised himself painfully upon his hands and knees and gave a ghastly stare into his face. The boy,—it must have been a nervous impulse, without purpose, without thought, and betokening a sensitive and impressible nature rather than a hardened one,—the boy uplifted his axe and dealt the wounded soldier a fierce and fatal blow upon the head.

I could wish that the grave might be opened; for I would fain know whether either of the skeleton soldiers has the mark of an axe in his skull. The story comes home to me like truth. Oftentimes, as an intellectual and moral exercise, I have sought to follow that poor youth through his subsequent career, and observe how his soul was tortured by the blood stain, contracted as it had been before the long custom of war had robbed human life of its sanctity and while it still seemed murderous to slay a brother man. This one circumstance has borne more fruit for me than all that history tells us of the fight.

Many strangers come in the summer time to view the battle-ground. For my own part, I have never found my imagination much excited by this or any other scene of historic celebrity; nor would the placid margin of the river have lost any of its charm for me had men never fought and died there. There is a wilder interest in the tract of land—perhaps a hundred yards in breadth—which extends between the battle-field and the northern face of our Old Manse with its contiguous avenue and orchard. Here, in some unknown age, before the white man came, stood an Indian village, convenient to the river, whence its inhabitants must have drawn so large a part of their subsistence. The site is identified by the spear and arrow heads, the chisels, and other implements of war, labor, and the chase, which the plow turns up from the soil. You see a splinter of stone, half hidden beneath a sod; it looks like nothing worthy of note; but, if you have faith enough to pick it up, behold a relic! Thoreau, who has a strange faculty of finding what the Indians have left behind them, first set me on the search; and I afterwards enriched myself with some very perfect specimens, so rudely wrought that it seemed almost as if chance had fashioned them. Their great charm consists in this rudeness and in the individuality of each article, so different from the productions of civilized machinery, which shapes everything on one pattern. There is exquisite delight, too, in picking up for one's self an arrow head that was dropped centuries ago and has never been handled since, and which we thus receive directly from the hand of the red hunter, who purposed to shoot it at his game or at an enemy. Such an incident builds up again the Indian village and its

encircling forest, and recalls to life the painted chiefs and warriors, the squaws at their household toil, and the children sporting among the wigwams, while the little wind-rocked papoose swings from the branch of a tree. It can hardly be told whether it is a joy or a pain, after such a momentary vision, to gaze around in the broad daylight of reality and see stone fences, white houses, potato fields, and men doggedly hoeing in their shirt sleeves and homespun pantaloons. But this is nonsense. The Old Manse is better than a thousand wigwams.

The Old Manse! We had almost forgotten it, but will return thither through the orchard. This was set out by the last clergyman, in the decline of his life, when the neighbors laughed at the hoary-headed man for planting trees from which he could have no prospect of gathering fruit. Even had that been the case, there was only so much the better motive for planting them, in the pure and unselfish hope of benefiting his successors,—an end so seldom achieved by more ambitious efforts. But the old minister, before reaching his patriarchal age of ninety, ate the apples from this orchard during many years, and added silver and gold to his annual stipend by disposing of the superfluity. It is pleasant to think of him walking among the trees in the quiet afternoons of early autumn and picking up here and there a windfall, while he observes how heavily the branches are weighed down, and computes the number of empty flour barrels that will be filled by their burden. He loved each tree, doubtless, as if it had been his own child. An orchard has a relation to mankind, and readily connects itself with matters of the heart. The trees possess a domestic character; they have lost the wild nature of their forest kindred, and have grown humanized by receiving the care of man as well as by contributing to his wants. There is so much individuality of character, too, among apple trees that it gives them an additional claim to be the objects of human interest. One is harsh and crabbed in its manifestations; another gives us fruit as mild as charity. One is churlish and illiberal, evidently grudging the few apples that it bears; another exhausts itself in freehearted benevolence. The variety of grotesque shapes into which apple trees contort themselves has its effect on those who get acquainted with them: they stretch out their crooked branches, and take such hold of the imagination that we remember them as humorists and odd fellows. And what is more melancholy than the old apple trees that linger about the spot where once stood a homestead, but where there is now only a ruined chimney rising out of a grassy and weedgrown cellar? They offer their fruit to every wayfarer,—apples that are bitter sweet with the moral of Time's vicissitude.

I have met with no other such pleasant trouble in the world as that of finding myself, with only the two or three mouths which it was my privilege to feed, the sole inheritor of the old clergyman's wealth of fruits. Throughout the summer there were cherries and currants; and then came autumn, with his immense burden of apples, dropping them continually from his overladen shoulders as he trudged along. In the stillest afternoon, if I listened, the thump of a great apple was audible, falling without a breath of wind, from the mere necessity of perfect ripeness. And, besides, there were pear trees, that flung down bushels upon bushels of heavy pears; and peach trees, which, in a good year, tormented me with peaches, neither to be eaten nor kept, nor, without labor and perplexity, to be given away. The idea of an infinite generosity and exhaustless bounty on the part of our mother Nature was well worth obtaining through such cares as these. That feeling can be enjoyed in perfection only by the natives of summer islands where the breadfruit, the cocoa, the palm and the orange grow spontaneously and hold forth the ever-ready meal; but likewise almost as well by a man long habituated to city life, who plunges into such a solitude as that of the Old Manse, where he plucks the fruit of trees that he did not plant, and which therefore, to my heterodox taste, bear the closest resemblance to those that grew in Eden. It has been an apothegm these five thousand years, that toil sweetens the bread it earns. For my part, (speaking from hard experience, acquired while belaboring the rugged furrows of Brook Farm [1]), I relish best the free gifts of Providence.

Not that it can be disputed that the light toil requisite to cultivate a moderately-sized garden imparts such zest to kitchen vegetables as is never found in those of the market gardener. Childless men, if they would know something of the bliss of paternity, should plant a seed,—be it squash, bean, Indian corn, or perhaps a mere flower or worthless weed,—should plant it with their own hands, and nurse it from infancy to maturity altogether by their own care. If there

be not too many of them, each individual plant becomes an object of separate interest. My garden, that skirted the avenue of the Manse, was of precisely the right extent. An hour or two of morning labor was all that it required. But I used to visit and revisit it a dozen times a day, and stand in deep contemplation over my vegetable progeny with a love that nobody could share or conceive of, who had never taken part in the process of creation. It was one of the most bewitching sights in the world to observe a hill of beans thrusting aside the soil, or a row of early peas just peeping forth sufficiently to trace a line of delicate green. Later in the season the humming-birds were attracted by the blossoms of a peculiar variety of bean; and they were a joy to me, those little spiritual visitants, for deigning to sip airy food out of my nectar cups. Multitudes of bees used to bury themselves in the yellow blossoms of the summer squashes. This, too, was a deep satisfaction; although, when they had laden themselves with sweets, they flew away to some unknown hive, which would give back nothing in requital of what my garden had contributed. But I was glad thus to fling a benefaction upon the passing breeze with the certainty that somebody must profit by it, and that there would be a little more honey in the world to allay the sourness and bitterness which mankind is always complaining of. Yes, indeed; my life was the sweeter for that honey.

Speaking of summer squashes, I must say a word of their beautiful and varied forms. They presented an endless diversity of urns and vases, shallow or deep, scalloped or plain, moulded in patterns which a sculptor would do well to copy, since Art has never invented any thing more graceful. A hundred squashes in the garden were worthy, in my eyes at least, of being rendered indestructible in marble. If ever Providence (but I know it never will) should assign me a superfluity of gold, part of it shall be expended for a service of plate, or most delicate porcelain, to be wrought into the shapes of summer squashes gathered from vines which I will plant with my own hands. As dishes for containing vegetables, they would be peculiarly appropriate.

But not merely the squeamish love of the beautiful was gratified by my toil in the kitchen garden. There was a hearty enjoyment, likewise, in observing the growth of the crooknecked winter squashes, from the first little bulb, with the withered blossom adhering to it, until they lay strewn upon the soil, big, round fellows, hiding their heads beneath the leaves,

---

[1] Brook Farm in West Roxbury, Mass., was the scene of an attempt on the part of a group of philosophers to solve the problems of life by the establishment of an ideal community. Hawthorne remained there some months, and like the other enthusiasts did hard manual work on the farm.

but turning up their great yellow rotundities to the noontide sun. Gazing at them, I felt that by my agency something worth living for had been done. A new substance was born into the world. They were real and tangible existences, which the mind could seize hold of and rejoice in. A cabbage, too,—especially the early Dutch cabbage, which swells to a monstrous circumference, until its ambitious heart often bursts asunder,—is a matter to be proud of when we can claim a share with the earth and sky in producing it. But, after all, the hugest pleasure is reserved until these vegetable children of ours are smoking on the table, and we, like Saturn, make a meal of them.

What with the river, the battle-field, the orchard and the garden, the reader begins to despair of finding his way back into the Old Manse. But, in agreeable weather, it is the truest hospitality to keep him out of doors. I never grew quite acquainted with my habitation till a long spell of sulky rain had confined me beneath its roof. There could not be a more somber aspect of external nature than as then seen from the windows of my study. The great willow tree had caught and retained among its leaves a whole cataract of water, to be shaken down at intervals by the frequent gusts of wind. All day long, and for a week together, the rain was drip-drip-dripping and splash-splash-splashing from the eaves and bubbling and foaming into the tubs beneath the spouts. The old, unpainted shingles of the house and out buildings were black with moisture; and the mosses of ancient growth upon the walls looked green and fresh, as if they were the newest things and afterthought of Time. The usually mirrored surface of the river was blurred by an infinity of raindrops; the whole landscape had a completely water-soaked appearance, conveying the impression that the earth was wet through like a sponge; while the summit of a wooded hill, about a mile distant, was enveloped in a dense mist, where the demon of the tempest seemed to have his abiding-place and to be plotting still direr inclemencies.

Nature has no kindness, no hospitality, during a rain. In the fiercest heat of sunny days she retains a secret mercy, and welcomes the wayfarer to shady nooks of the woods whither the sun cannot penetrate; but she provides no shelter against her storms. It makes us shiver to think of those deep, umbrageous recesses, those overshadowing banks, where we found such enjoyment during the sultry afternoons. Not a twig of foliage there but would dash a little shower into our faces. Looking reproachfully towards the impenetrable sky,—if sky there be above that dismal uniformity of cloud, —we are apt to murmur against the whole system of the universe, since it involves the extinction of so many summer days in so short a life by the hissing and spluttering rain. In such spells of weather—and it is to be supposed such weather came—Eve's bower in paradise must have been but a cheerless and aguish kind of shelter, nowise comparable to the old parsonage, which had resources of its own to beguile the week's imprisonment. The idea of sleeping on a couch of wet roses!

Happy the man who in a rainy day can betake himself to a huge garret, stored, like that of the Manse with lumber that each generation has left behind it from a period before the revolution. Our garret was an arched hall, dimly illuminated through small and dusty windows; it was but a twilight at the best, and there were nooks, or rather caverns, of deep obscurity, the secrets of which I never learned, being too reverent of their dust and cobwebs. The beams and rafters roughly hewn and with strips of bark still on them and the rude masonry of the chimneys, made the garret look wild and uncivilized,—an aspect unlike what was seen elsewhere in the quiet and decorous old house. But on one side there was a little whitewashed apartment, which bore the traditionary title of the Saint's Chamber, because holy men in their youth had slept, and studied, and prayed there. With its elevated retirement, its one window, its small fireplace, and its closet convenient for an oratory,[1] it was the very spot where a young man might inspire himself with solemn enthusiasm and cherish saintly dreams. The occupants, at various epochs, had left brief records and ejaculations inscribed upon the walls. There, too, hung a tattered and shriveled roll of canvas, which on inspection proved to be the forcibly wrought picture of a clergyman, in wig, band, and gown, holding a Bible in his hand. As I turned his face towards the light he eyed me with an air of authority such as men of his profession seldom assume in our days. The original[2] had been pastor of the parish more than a century ago, a friend of Whitefield, and almost his equal in fervid eloquence. I bowed before the effigy of the dignified divine, and felt as if I had now met face to face with the ghost by whom, as there was reason to apprehend, the Manse was haunted.

Houses of any antiquity in New England are

[1] a small private chapel for prayer
[2] Very possibly Dr. Bliss, predecessor to Rev. William Emerson, grandfather of Ralph Waldo Emerson; George Whitefield, 1714-1770, was one of the founders of Methodism.

so invariably possessed with spirits that the matter seems hardly worth alluding to. Our ghost used to heave deep sighs in a particular corner of the parlor, and sometimes rustled paper, as if he were turning over a sermon in the long upper entry—where nevertheless he was invisible, in spite of the bright moonshine that fell through the eastern window. Not improbably he wished me to edit and publish a selection from a chest full of manuscript discourses that stood in the garret. Once, while Hillard and other friends sat talking with us in the twilight, there came a rustling noise as of a minister's silk gown, sweeping through the very midst of the company, so closely as almost to brush against the chairs. Still there was nothing visible. A yet stranger business was that of a ghostly servant maid, who used to be heard in the kitchen at deepest midnight, grinding coffee, cooking, ironing,—performing, in short, all kinds of domestic labor,—although no traces of anything accomplished could be detected the next morning. Some neglected duty of her servitude—some ill-starched ministerial band—disturbed the poor damsel in her grave and kept her at work without any wages.

But to return from this digression. A part of my predecessor's library was stored in the garret,—no unfit receptacle indeed for such dreary trash as comprised the greater number of volumes. The old books would have been worth nothing at an auction. In this venerable garret, however, they possessed an interest, quite apart from their literary value, as heirlooms, many of which had been transmitted down through a series of consecrated hands from the days of the mighty Puritan divines. Autographs of famous names were to be seen in faded ink on some of their flyleaves; and there were marginal observations or interpolated pages closely covered with manuscript in illegible shorthand, perhaps concealing matter of profound truth and wisdom. The world will never be the better for it. A few of the books were Latin folios, written by Catholic authors; others demolished Papistry, as with a sledgehammer, in plain English. A dissertation on the book of Job—which only Job himself could have had patience to read—filled at least a score of small, thickset quartos, at the rate of two or three volumes to a chapter. Then there was a vast folio body of divinity—too corpulent a body, it might be feared, to comprehend the spiritual element of religion. Volumes of this form dated back two hundred years or more, and were generally bound in black leather, exhibiting precisely such an appearance as we should attribute to books of

enchantment. Others equally antique were of a size proper to be carried in the large waistcoat pockets of old times,—diminutive, but as black as their bulkier brethren, and abundantly interfused with Greek and Latin quotations. These little old volumes impressed me as if they had been intended for very large ones, but had been unfortunately blighted at an early stage of their growth.

The rain pattered upon the roof and the sky gloomed through the dusty garret windows, while I burrowed among these venerable books in search of any living thought which should burn like a coal of fire, or glow like an inextinguishable gem, beneath the dead trumpery that had long hidden it. But I found no such treasure; all was dead alike; and I could not but muse deeply and wonderingly upon the humiliating fact that the works of man's intellect decay like those of his hands. Thought grows moldy. What was good and nourishing food for the spirits of one generation affords no sustenance for the next. Books of religion, however, cannot be considered a fair test of the enduring and vivacious properties of human thought, because such books so seldom really touch upon their ostensible subject, and have, therefore, so little business to be written at all. So long as an unlettered soul can attain to saving grace there would seem to be no deadly error in holding theological libraries to be accumulations of, for the most part, stupendous impertinence.

Many of the books had accrued in the latter years of the last clergyman's lifetime. These threatened to be of even less interest than the elder works a century hence to any curious inquirer who should then rummage them as I was doing now. Volumes of the *Liberal Preacher* and *Christian Examiner,* occasional sermons, controversial pamphlets, tracts, and other productions of a like fugitive nature took the place of the thick and heavy volumes of past time. In a physical point of view, there was much the same difference as between a feather and a lump of lead; but, intellectually regarded, the specific gravity of old and new was about upon a par. Both also were alike frigid. The elder books nevertheless seemed to have been earnestly written, and might be conceived to have possessed warmth at some former period; although, with the lapse of time, the heated masses had cooled down even to the freezing point. The frigidity of the modern productions, on the other hand, was characteristic and inherent, and evidently had little to do with the writer's qualities of mind and heart. In fine, of this whole dusty heap of literature I tossed aside all the sacred part, and felt myself none the less a Christian for eschewing it. There appeared no hope of either mounting to the better world on a Gothic staircase of ancient folios or of flying thither on the wings of a modern tract. [1]

Nothing, strange to say, retained any sap except what had been written for the passing day and year without the remotest pretension or idea of permanence. There were a few old newspapers, and still older almanacs, which reproduced to my mental eye the epochs when they had issued from the press with a distinctness that was altogether unaccountable. It was as if I had found bits of magic looking-glass among the books with the images of a vanished century in them. I turned my eyes towards the tattered picture above mentioned, and asked of the austere divine wherefore it was that he and his brethren, after the most painful rummaging and groping into their minds, had been able to produce nothing half so real as these newspaper scribblers and almanac makers had thrown off in the effervescence of a moment. The portrait responded not; so I sought an answer for myself. It is the age itself that writes newspapers and almanacs, which therefore have a distinct purpose and meaning at the time, and a kind of intelligible truth for all times; whereas most other works—being written by men who, in the very act, set themselves apart from their age—are likely to possess little significance when new, and none at all when old. Genius, indeed, melts many ages into one, and thus effects something permanent, yet still with a similarity of office to that of the more ephemeral writer. A work of genius is but the newspaper of a century, or perchance of a hundred centuries.

Lightly as I have spoken of these old books, there yet lingers with me a superstitious reverence for literature of all kinds. A bound volume has a charm in my eyes similar to what scraps of manuscript possess for the good Mussulman. He imagines that those wind-wafted records are perhaps hallowed by some sacred verse; and I, that every new book or antique one may contain the "open sesame,"—the spell to disclose treasures hidden in some unsuspected cave of Truth. Thus it was not without sadness that I turned away from the library of the Old Manse.

Blessed was the sunshine when it came again at the close of another stormy day, beaming from the edge of the western horizon; while

the massive firmament of clouds threw down all the gloom it could, but served only to kindle the golden light into a more brilliant glow by the strongly contrasted shadows. Heaven smiled at the earth, so long unseen, from beneath its heavy eyelid. Tomorrow for the hill tops and the wood paths.

Or it might be that Ellery Channing came up the avenue to join me in a fishing excursion on the river. Strange and happy times were those when we cast aside all irksome forms and strait-laced habitudes and delivered ourselves up to the free air, to live like the Indians or any less conventional race during one bright semicircle of the sun. Rowing our boats against the current, between wide meadows, we turned aside into the Assabeth. A more lovely stream than this, for a mile above its junction with the Concord, has never flowed on earth,— nowhere, indeed, except to lave the interior regions of a poet's imagination. It is sheltered from the breeze by woods and a hillside; so that elsewhere there might be a hurricane, and here scarcely a ripple across the shaded water. The current lingers along so gently that the mere force of the boatman's will seems sufficient to propel his craft against it. It comes flowing softly through the midmost privacy and deepest heart of a wood which whispers it to be quiet; while the stream whispers back again from its sedgy borders, as if river and wood were hushing one another to sleep. Yes; the river sleeps along its course and dreams of the sky and of the clustering foliage, amid which fall showers of broken sunlight, imparting specks of vivid cheerfulness, in contrast with the quiet depth of the prevailing tint. Of all this scene, the slumbering river has a dream picture in its bosom. Which, after all, was the most real—the picture, or the original?—the objects palpable to our grosser senses, or their apotheosis in the stream beneath? Surely the disembodied images stand in closer relation to the soul. But both the original and the reflection had here an ideal charm; and, had it been a thought more wild, I could have fancied that this river had strayed forth out of the rich scenery of my companion's inner world; only the vegetation along its banks should then have had an Oriental character.

Gentle and unobtrusive as the river is, yet the tranquil woods seem hardly satisfied to allow it passage. The trees are rooted on the very verge of the water, and dip their pendent branches into it. At one spot there is a lofty bank, on the slope of which grow some hemlocks, declining across the stream with out-

[1] Hawthorne seems to contrast medieval and modern theology.

stretched arms, as if resolute to take the plunge. In other places the banks are almost on a level with the water; so that the quiet congregation of trees set their feet in the flood, and are fringed with foliage down to the surface. Cardinal flowers kindle their spiral flames and illuminate the dark nooks among the shrubbery. The pond-lily grows abundantly along the margin—that delicious flower, which, as Thoreau tells me, opens its virgin bosom to the first sunlight and perfects its being through the magic of that genial kiss. He has beheld beds of them unfolding in due succession as the sunrise stole gradually from flower to flower—a sight not to be hoped for unless when a poet adjusts his inward eye to a proper focus with the outward organ. Grapevines here and there twine themselves around shrub and tree and hang their clusters over the water within reach of the boatman's hand. Oftentimes they unite two trees of alien race in an inextricable twine, marrying the hemlock and the maple against their will and enriching them with a purple offspring of which neither is the parent. One of these ambitious parasites has climbed into the upper branches of a tall white pine, and is still ascending from bough to bough, unsatisfied till it shall crown the tree's airy summit with a wreath of its broad foliage and a cluster of its grapes.

The winding course of the stream continually shut out the scene behind us and revealed as calm and lovely a one before. We glided from depth to depth and breathed new seclusion at every turn. The shy kingfisher flew from the withered branch close at hand to another at a distance, uttering a shrill cry of anger or alarm. Ducks that had been floating there since the preceding eve were startled at our approach and skimmed along the glassy river, breaking its dark surface with a bright streak. The pickerel leaped from among the lily pads. The turtle, sunning itself upon a rock or at the root of a tree, slid suddenly into the water with a plunge. The painted Indian who paddled his canoe along the Assabeth three hundred years ago could hardly have seen a wilder gentleness displayed upon its banks and reflected in its bosom than we did. Nor could the same Indian have prepared his noontide meal with more simplicity. We drew up our skiff at some point where the overarching shade formed a natural bower, and there kindled a fire with the pine cones and decayed branches that lay strewn plentifully around. Soon the smoke ascended among the trees, impregnated with a savory incense, not heavy, dull, and surfeiting, like the

steam of cookery within doors, but sprightly and piquant. The smell of our feast was akin to the woodland odors with which it mingled: there was no sacrilege committed by our intrusion there: the sacred solitude was hospitable, and granted us free leave to cook and eat in the recess that was at once our kitchen and banqueting hall. It is strange what humble offices may be performed in a beautiful scene without destroying its poetry. Our fire, red-gleaming among the trees, and we beside it, busied with culinary rites and spreading out our meal on a mossgrown log, all seemed in unison with the river gliding by and the foliage rustling over us. And, what was strangest, neither did our mirth seem to disturb the propriety of the solemn woods; although the hobgoblins of the old wilderness and the will-of-the-wisps that glimmered in the marshy places might have come trooping to share our table talk and have added their shrill laughter to our merriment. It was the very spot in which to utter the extremest nonsense or the profoundest wisdom, or that ethereal product of the mind which partakes of both, and may become one or the other, in correspondence with the faith and insight of the auditor.

So, amid sunshine and shadow, rustling leaves and sighing waters, up gushed our talk like the babble of a fountain. The evanescent spray was Ellery's; and his, too, the lumps of golden thought that lay glimmering in the fountain's bed and brightened both our faces by the reflection. Could he have drawn out that virgin gold, and stamped it with the mint mark that alone gives currency, the world might have had the profit, and he the fame. My mind was the richer merely by the knowledge that it was there. But the chief profit of those wild days, to him and me, lay, not in any definite idea, not in any angular or rounded truth, which we dug out of the shapeless mass of problematical stuff, but in the freedom which we thereby won from all custom and conventionalism and fettering influences of man on man. We were so free today that it was impossible to be slaves again tomorrow. When we crossed the threshold of the house or trod the thronged pavements of a city, still the leaves of the trees that overhang the Assabeth were whispering to us, "Be free! be free!" Therefore along that shady river bank there are spots, marked with a heap of ashes and half-consumed brands, only less sacred in my remembrance than the hearth of a household fire.

And yet how sweet, as we floated homeward adown the golden river at sunset,—how sweet was it to return within the system of human society, not as to a dungeon and a chain, but as to a stately edifice, whence we could go forth at will into statelier simplicity! How gently, too, did the sight of the Old Manse, best seen from the river, overshadowed with its willow, and all environed about with the foliage of its orchard and avenue,—how gently did its gray, homely aspect rebuke the speculative extravagances of the day! It had grown sacred in connection with the artificial life against which we inveighed; it had been a home for many years in spite of all; it was my home too; and, with these thoughts, it seemed to me that all the artifice and conventionalism of life was but an impalpable thinness upon its surface, and that the depth below was none the worse for it. Once, as we turned our boat to the bank, there was a cloud, in the shape of an immensely gigantic figure of a hound, couched above the house, as if keeping guard over it. Gazing at this symbol, I prayed that the upper influences might long protect the institutions that had grown out of the heart of mankind.

If ever my readers should decide to give up civilized life, cities, houses, and whatever moral or material enormities in addition to these the perverted ingenuity of our race has contrived, let it be in the early autumn. Then Nature will love him better than at any other season, and will take him to her bosom with a more motherly tenderness. I could scarcely endure the roof of the old house above me in those first autumnal days. How early in the summer, too, the prophecy of autumn comes! Earlier in some years than in others; sometimes even in the first weeks of July. There is no other feeling like what is caused by this faint, doubtful, yet real perception—if it be not rather a foreboding—of the year's decay, so blessedly sweet and sad in the same breath.

Did I say that there was no feeling like it? Ah, but there is a half-acknowledged melancholy like to this when we stand in the perfected vigor of our life and feel that Time has now given us all his flowers, and that the next work of his never idle fingers must be to steal them one by one away.

I have forgotten whether the song of the cricket be not as early a token of autumn's approach as any other,—that song which may be called an audible stillness; for though very loud and heard afar, yet the mind does not take note of it as a sound, so completely is its individual existence merged among the accompanying characteristics of the season. Alas for the pleasant summer time! In August the grass is still verdant on the hills and in the valleys; the foliage of the trees is as dense as ever and as green; the flowers gleam forth in richer abundance along the margin of the river and by the stone walls and deep among the woods; the days, too, are as fervid now as they were a month ago; and yet in every breath of wind and in every beam of sunshine we hear the whispered farewell and behold the parting smile of a dear friend. There is a coolness amid all the heat, a mildness in the blazing noon. Not a breeze can stir but it thrills us with the breath of autumn. A pensive glory is seen in the far golden gleams, among the shadows of the trees. The flowers—even the brightest of them, and they are the most gorgeous of the year—have this gentle sadness wedded to their pomp, and typify the character of the delicious time each within itself. The brilliant cardinal flower has never seemed gay to me.

Still later in the season Nature's tenderness waxes stronger. It is impossible not to be fond of our mother now; for she is so fond of us! At other periods she does not make this impression on me, or only at rare intervals; but in those genial days of autumn, when she has perfected her harvests and accomplished every needful thing that was given her to do, then she overflows with a blessed superfluity of love. She has leisure to caress her children now. It is good to be alive at such times. Thank Heaven for breath—yes, for mere breath—when it is made up of a heavenly breeze like this! It comes with a real kiss upon our cheeks; it would linger fondly around us if it might; but, since it must be gone, it embraces us with its whole kindly heart and passes onward to embrace likewise the next thing that it meets. A blessing is flung abroad and scattered far and wide over the earth, to be gathered up by all who choose. I recline upon the still unwithered grass and whisper to myself, "O perfect day! O beautiful world! O beneficent God!" And it is the promise of a blessed eternity; for our Creator would never have made such lovely days and have given us the deep hearts to enjoy them, above and beyond all thought, unless we were meant to be immortal. This sunshine is the golden pledge thereof. It beams through the gates of paradise and shows us glimpses far inward.

By and by, in a little time, the outward world puts on a drear austerity. On some October morning there is a heavy hoarfrost on the grass and along the tops of the fences; and at sunrise the leaves fall from the trees of our avenue without a breath of wind, quietly descending by their own weight. All summer long they have murmured like the noise of waters; they have roared loudly while the branches were wrestling with the thunder gust; they have made music both glad and solemn; they have attuned my thoughts by their quiet sound as I paced to and fro beneath the arch of intermingling boughs. Now they can only rustle under my feet. Henceforth the gray parsonage begins to assume a larger importance, and draws to its fireside,— for the abomination of the air-tight stove is reserved till wintry weather,—draws closer and closer to its fireside the vagrant impulses that had gone wandering about through the summer.

When summer was dead and buried the Old Manse became as lonely as a hermitage. Not that ever—in my time at least—it had been thronged with company; but, at no rare intervals, we welcomed some friend out of the dusty glare and tumult of the world and rejoiced to share with him the transparent obscurity that was floating over us. In one respect our precincts were like the Enchanted Ground through which the pilgrim traveled on his way to the Celestial City.[1] The guests, each and all, felt a slumberous influence upon them; they fell asleep in chairs, or took a more deliberate siesta on the sofa, or were seen stretched among the shadows of the orchard, looking up dreamily through the boughs. They could not have paid a more acceptable compliment to my abode nor to my own qualities as a host. I held it as a proof that they left their cares behind them as they passed between the stone gateposts at the entrance of our avenue, and that the so powerful opiate was the abundance of peace and quiet within and all around us. Others could give them pleasure and amusement or instruction—these could be picked up anywhere; but it was for me to give them rest— rest in a life of trouble. What better could be done for those weary and world-worn spirits?— for him whose career of perpetual action was impeded and harassed by the rarest of his powers and the richest of his acquirements?— for another who had thrown his ardent heart from earliest youth into the strife of politics, and now, perchance, began to suspect that one lifetime is too brief for the accomplishment of any lofty aim?—for her on whose feminine nature had been imposed the heavy gift of intellectual power, such as a strong man might have staggered under, and with it the necessity to act upon the world?[2]—in a word, not to multiply instances, what better could be done for anybody who came within our magic circle than to throw the spell of a tranquil spirit over him? And when it had wrought its full effect, then we dismissed him, with but misty reminiscences, as if he had been dreaming of us.

Were I to adopt a pet idea as so many people do and fondle it in my embraces to the exclusion of all others, it would be, that the great want which mankind labors under at this present period is sleep. The world should recline its vast head on the first convenient pillow and take an age-long nap. It has gone distracted through a morbid activity, and, while preternaturally wide awake, is nevertheless tormented by visions that seem real to it now, but would assume their true aspect and character were all things once set right by an interval of sound repose. This is the only method of getting rid of old delusions and avoiding new ones; of regenerating our race, so that it might in due time awake as an infant out of dewy slumber; of restoring to us the simple perception of what is right and the single-hearted desire to achieve it, both of which have long been lost in consequence of this weary activity of brain and torpor or passion of the heart that now afflict the universe. Stimulants, the only mode of treatment hitherto attempted, cannot quell the disease; they do but heighten the delirium.

Let not the above paragraph ever be quoted against the author; for, though tinctured with its modicum of truth, it is the result and expression of what he knew, while he was writing, to be but a distorted survey of the state and prospects of mankind. There were circumstances around me which made it difficult to view the world precisely as it exists; for, severe and sober as was the Old Manse, it was necessary to go but a little way beyond its threshold before meeting with stranger moral shapes of men than might have been encountered elsewhere in a circuit of a thousand miles.

These hobgoblins of flesh and blood were attracted thither by the widespreading influence of a great original thinker, who had his earthly abode at the opposite extremity of our village. His mind acted upon other minds of a certain constitution with wonderful magnetism, and drew many men upon long pilgrimages to speak with him face to face. Young visionaries—to whom just so much of insight had been imparted as to make life all a labyrinth around

---

[1] Cf. Bunyan, *The Pilgrim's Progress*. The shepherds in the Delectable Mountains warned Christian of the enchanted ground, "whose air naturally tended to make one sleepy."

[2] Hawthorne probably refers respectively to Horatio Bridge, Franklin Pierce, and Margaret Fuller. See note 1, p. 335.

them—came to seek the clew that should guide them out of their self-involved bewilderment. Grayheaded theorists—whose systems, at first air, had finally imprisoned them in an iron framework—traveled painfully to his door, not to ask deliverance, but to invite the free spirit into their own thraldom. People that had lighted on a new thought, or a thought that they fancied new, came to Emerson, as the finder of a glittering gem hastens to a lapidary, to ascertain its quality and value. Uncertain, troubled, earnest wanderers through the midnight of the moral world beheld his intellectual fire as the beacon burning on a hill-top, and, climbing the difficult ascent, looked forth into the surrounding obscurity more hopefully than hitherto. The light revealed objects unseen before,—mountains, gleaming lakes, glimpses of a creation among the chaos; but also, as was unavoidable, it attracted bats and owls and the whole host of night birds, which flapped their dusky wings against the gazer's eyes, and sometimes were mistaken for fowls of angelic feather. Such delusions always hover nigh whenever a beacon fire of truth is kindled.

For myself, there had been epochs of my life when I, too, might have asked of this prophet the master word that should solve me the riddle of the universe, but now, being happy, I felt as if there were no question to be put, and therefore admired Emerson as a poet of deep beauty and austere tenderness, but sought nothing from him as a philosopher. It was good, nevertheless, to meet him in the woodpaths, or sometimes in our avenue, with that pure, intellectual gleam diffused about his presence like the garment of a shining one; and he, so quiet, so simple, so without pretension, encountering each man alive as if expecting to receive more than he could impart. And, in truth, the heart of many an ordinary man had, perchance, inscriptions which he could not read. But it was impossible to dwell in his vicinity without inhaling more or less the mountain atmosphere of his lofty thought, which, in the brains of some people, wrought a singular giddiness,—new truth being as heady as new wine. Never was a poor little country village infested with such a variety of queer, strangely-dressed, oddly-behaved mortals, most of whom took upon themselves to be important agents of the world's destiny, yet were simply bores of a very intense water. Such, I imagine, is the invariable character of persons who crowd so closely about an original thinker as to draw in his unuttered breath and thus become imbued with a false originality. This triteness of novelty is enough to make any man of common sense blaspheme at all ideas of less than a century's standing, and pray that the world may be petrified and rendered immovable in precisely the worst moral and physical state that it ever yet arrived at, rather than be benefited by such schemes of such philosophers.

And now I begin to feel—and perhaps should have sooner felt—that we have talked enough of the Old Manse. Mine honored reader, it may be, will vilify the poor author as an egotist for babbling through so many pages about a mossgrown country parsonage, and his life within its walls and on the river and in the woods, and the influences that wrought upon him, from all these sources. My conscience, however, does not reproach me with betraying anything too sacredly individual to be revealed by a human spirit to its brother or sister spirit. How narrow—how shallow and scanty too—is the stream of thought that has been flowing from my pen, compared with the broad tide of dim emotions, ideas, and associations which swell around me from that portion of my existence! How little have I told! and of that little, how almost nothing is even tinctured with any quality that makes it exclusively my own! Has the reader gone wandering, hand in hand with me, through the inner passages of my being? and have we groped together into all its chambers and examined their treasures or their rubbish? Not so. We have been standing on the greensward, but just within the cavern's mouth, where the common sunshine is free to penetrate, and where every footstep is therefore free to come. I have appealed to no sentiment or sensibilities save such as are diffused among us all. So far as I am a man of really individual attributes I veil my face; nor am I, nor have I ever been, one of those supremely hospitable people who serve up their own hearts, delicately fried, with brain sauce, as a tidbit for their beloved public.

Glancing back over what I have written, it seems but the scattered reminiscences of a single summer. In fairyland there is no measurement of time; and, in a spot so sheltered from the turmoil of life's ocean, three years hastened away with a noiseless flight, as the breezy sunshine chases the cloud shadows across the depths of a still valley. Now came hints, growing more and more distinct, that the owner of the old house was pining for his native air. Carpenters next appeared making a tremendous racket among the out-buildings, strewing the green grass with pine shavings and chips of chestnut joists, and vexing the whole antiquity of the place with their discordant renovations. Soon, moreover, they divested our abode of the veil of woodbine which had crept over a large portion of its southern face. All the aged mosses were cleared unsparingly away; and there were horrible whispers about brushing up the external walls with a coat of paint—a purpose as little to my taste as might be that of rouging the venerable cheeks of one's grandmother. But the hand that renovates is always more sacrilegious than that which destroys. In fine, we gathered up our household goods, drank a farewell cup of tea in our pleasant little breakfast room,—delicately fragrant tea, an unpurchasable luxury, one of the many angel gifts that had fallen like dew upon us,—and passed forth between the tall stone gate-posts as uncertain as the wandering Arabs where our tent might next be pitched. Providence took me by the hand, and—an oddity of dispensation which, I trust, there is no irreverence in smiling at—has led me, as the newspapers announce while I am writing, from the Old Manse into a custom house.[1] As a story teller, I have often contrived strange vicissitudes for my imaginary personages, but none like this.

The treasure of intellectual gold which I had hoped to find in our secluded dwelling had never come to light. No profound treatise of ethics, no philosophic history, no novel even, that could stand unsupported on its edges. All that I had to show, as a man of letters, were these few tales and essays, which had blossomed out like flowers in the calm summer of my heart and mind. Save editing (an easy task) the journal of my friend of many years, the African Cruiser, I had done nothing else. With these idle weeds and withering blossoms I have intermixed some that were produced long ago,—old, faded things, reminding me of flowers pressed between the leaves of a book,—and now offer the bouquet, such as it is, to any whom it may please. These fitful sketches, with so little of external life about them, yet claiming no profundity of purpose,—so reserved, even while they sometimes seem so frank,—often but half in earnest, and never, even when most so, expressing satisfactorily the thoughts which they profess to image, —such trifles, I truly feel, afford no solid basis for a literary reputation. Nevertheless, the public—if my limited number of readers, whom I venture to regard rather as a circle of friends, may be termed a public—will receive them the more kindly, as the last offering, the last collection, of this nature which it is my purpose ever to put forth. Unless I could do better, I have done enough in this kind. For myself the

book will always retain one charm—as reminding me of the river, with its delightful solitudes, and of the avenue, the garden, and the orchard, and especially the dear Old Manse, with the little study on its western side, and the sunshine glimmering through the willow branches while I wrote.

Let the reader, if he will do me so much honor, imagine himself my guest, and that, having seen whatever may be worthy of notice within and about the Old Manse, he has finally been ushered into my study. There, after seating him in an antique elbow-chair, an heirloom of the house, I take forth a roll of manuscript and entreat his attention to the following tales —an act of personal inhospitality, however, which I never was guilty of, nor ever will be, even to my worst enemy.

1846

From THE SCARLET LETTER [2]

I

THE PRISON DOOR

A throng of bearded men, in sad-colored garments and gray steeple-crowned hats, intermixed with women, some wearing hoods, and others bareheaded, was assembled in front of a wooden edifice, the door of which was heavily timbered with oak, and studded with iron spikes.

The founders of a new colony, whatever Utopia [3] of human virtue and happiness they might originally project, have invariably recognized it among their earliest practical necessities to allot a portion of the virgin soil as a cemetery, and another portion as the site of a prison. In accordance with this rule, it may safely be assumed that the forefathers of Boston had built the first prison-house somewhere in the vicinity of Cornhill,[4] almost as seasonably as they marked out the first burial-ground, on Isaac Johnson's [5] lot, and round about his grave, which subsequently became the nucleus of all the congregated sepulchers in the old churchyard of King's Chapel. Certain it is that, some fifteen or twenty years after the settlement of the town, the wooden jail was already marked with weather-stains and other indications of age, which gave a yet darker aspect to its beetle-browed and gloomy front. The rust on the

[2] In the introduction to this novel Hawthorne relates how he found in the attic of the Salem Custom House a parchment roll containing an embroidered scarlet letter A and its history briefly written out.

[3] an ideal commonwealth described in a work published by Sir Thomas More in 1516

[4] See note 3, page 329.

[5] He came to Massachusetts with Winthrop in 1630 and died the same year. His lot was bounded by the present School, Tremont, Court, and Washington Streets.

---

[1] Hawthorne, whose literary work had as yet paid him but poorly, had obtained the position of Surveyor in the Salem Custom House.

ponderous iron-work of its oaken door looked more antique than anything else in the New World. Like all that pertains to crime, it seemed never to have known a youthful era. Before this ugly edifice, and between it and the wheel-track of the street, was a grass-plot, much overgrown with burdock, pig-weed, apple-peru, and such unsightly vegetation, which evidently found something congenial in the soil that had so early borne the black flower of civilized society, a prison. But on one side of the portal, and rooted almost at the threshold, was a wild rose-bush, covered, in this month of June, with its delicate gems, which might be imagined to offer their fragrance and fragile beauty to the prisoner as he went in, and to the condemned criminal as he came forth to his doom, in token that the deep heart of Nature could pity and be kind to him.

This rose-bush, by a strange chance, has been kept alive in history; but whether it had merely survived out of the stern old wilderness, so long after the fall of the gigantic pines and oaks that originally overshadowed it,—or whether, as there is fair authority for believing, it had sprung up under the footsteps of the sainted Ann Hutchinson [1] as she entered the prison-door,—we shall not take upon us to determine. Finding it so directly on the threshold of our narrative, which is now about to issue from that inauspicious portal, we could hardly do otherwise than pluck one of its flowers, and present it to the reader. It may serve, let us hope, to symbolize some sweet moral blossom that may be found along the track, or relieve the darkening close of a tale of human frailty and sorrow.

II

THE MARKET PLACE

The grass-plot before the jail, in Prison Lane, on a certain summer morning, not less than two centuries ago, was occupied by a pretty large number of the inhabitants of Boston, all with their eyes intently fastened on the iron-clamped oaken door. Amongst any other population, or at a later period in the history of New England, the grim rigidity that petrified the bearded physiognomies of these good people would have augured some awful business in hand. It could have betokened nothing short of the anticipated execution of some noted culprit, on whom the sentence of a legal tribunal had but confirmed the verdict of public sentiment. But, in that

early severity of the Puritan character, an inference of this kind could not so indubitably be drawn. It might be that a sluggish bond-servant, or an undutiful child, whom his parents had given over to the civil authority, was to be corrected at the whipping-post. It might be that an Antinomian, [2] a Quaker, or other heterodox religionist, was to be scourged out of the town, or an idle and vagrant Indian, whom the white man's firewater had made riotous about the streets, was to be driven with stripes into the shadow of the forest. It might be, too, that a witch, like old Mistress Hibbins, [3] the bitter-tempered widow of the magistrate, was to die upon the gallows. In either case, there was very much the same solemnity of demeanor on the part of the spectators, as befitted a people amongst whom religion and law were almost identical, and in whose character both were so thoroughly interfused, that the mildest and severest acts of public discipline were alike made venerable and awful. Meager, indeed, and cold, was the sympathy that a transgressor might look for, from such bystanders, at the scaffold. On the other hand, a penalty which, in our days, would infer a degree of mocking infamy and ridicule, might then be invested with almost as stern a dignity as the punishment of death itself.

It was a circumstance to be noted on the summer morning when our story begins its course, that the women, of whom there were several in the crowd, appeared to take a peculiar interest in whatever penal infliction might be expected to ensue. The age had not so much refinement, that any sense of impropriety restrained the wearers of petticoat and farthingale [4] from stepping forth into the public ways, and wedging their not unsubstantial persons, if occasion were, into the throng nearest to the scaffold at an execution. Morally, as well as materially, there was a coarser fiber in those wives and maidens of old English birth and breeding than in their fair descendants, separated from them by a series of six or seven

---

[1] Mrs. Hutchinson, one of the most intellectual women of early Boston, was placed on trial and finally banished for her unorthodox views.

[2] Christians who held that the moral law of the Old Testament was not binding

[3] "Mrs. Ann Hibbins was the widow of an immigrant of special distinction. He had been agent for the colony in England, and one of the Assistants (magistrates). He had lost his property, and the melancholy and ill-temper to which his disappointed wife gave way appear to have exposed her to misconstructions and hatred, in the sequel of which she was convicted as a witch, and after some opposition on the part of the magistrates was hanged." Palfrey, *History of New England*. IV, 98. John Norton, teacher of the First Church, said she was hanged only for having more wit than her neighbors.

[4] hoop-petticoat

generations; for, throughout that chain of ancestry, every successive mother had transmitted to her child a fainter bloom, a more delicate and briefer beauty, and a slighter physical frame, if not a character of less force and solidity than her own. The women who were now standing about the prison-door stood within less than half a century of the period when the man-like Elizabeth had been the not altogether unsuitable representative of the sex. They were her countrywomen; and the beef and ale of their native land, with a moral diet not a whit more refined, entered largely into their composition. The bright morning sun, therefore, shown on broad shoulders and well-developed busts, and on round and ruddy cheeks, that had ripened in the far-off island, and had hardly yet grown paler or thinner in the atmosphere of New England. There was, moreover, a boldness and rotundity of speech among these matrons, as most of them seemed to be, that would startle us at the present day, whether in respect to its purport or its volume of tone.

"Goodwives," said a hard-featured dame of fifty, "I'll tell ye a piece of my mind. It would be greatly for the public behoof, if we women, being of mature age and church-members in good repute, should have the handling of such malefactresses as this Hester Prynne. What think ye, gossips? If the hussy stood up for judgment before us five, that are now here in a knot together, would she come off with such a sentence as the worshipful magistrates have awarded? Marry, I trow not!"

"People say," said another, "that the Reverend Master Dimmesdale, her godly pastor, takes it very grievously to heart that such a scandal should have come upon his congregation."

"The magistrates are God-fearing gentlemen, but merciful overmuch,—that is a truth," added a third autumnal matron. "At the very least, they should have put the brand of a hot iron on Hester Prynne's forehead. Madam Hester would have winced at that, I warrant me. But she,—the naughty baggage,—little will she care what they put upon the bodice of her gown! Why, look you, she may cover it with a brooch, or such like heathenish adornment, and so walk the streets as brave as ever!"

"Ah, but," interposed more softly a young wife, holding a child by the hand, "let her cover the mark as she will, the pang of it will be always in her heart."

"What do we talk of marks and brands, whether on the bodice of her gown or the flesh of her forehead?" cried another female, the ugliest as well as the most pitiless of these self-constituted judges. "This woman has brought shame upon us all, and ought to die. Is there not a law for it? Truly there is, both in the Scripture and the statute-book. Then let the magistrates, who have made it of no effect, thank themselves if their own wives and daughters go astray!"

"Mercy on us, goodwife!" exclaimed a man in the crowd, "is there no virtue in woman, save what springs from a wholesome fear of the gallows? That is the hardest word yet! Hush, now, gossips! for the lock is turning in the prison-door, and here comes Mistress Prynne herself."

The door of the jail being flung open from within, there appeared, in the first place, like a black shadow emerging into sunshine, the grim and grisly presence of the town-beadle, with a sword by his side, and his staff of office in his hand. This personage prefigured and represented in his aspect the whole dismal severity of the Puritanic code of law, which it was his business to administer in its final and closest application to the offender. Stretching forth the official staff in his left hand, he laid his right upon the shoulder of a young woman, whom he thus drew forward, until, on the threshold of the prison-door, she repelled him, by an action marked with natural dignity and force of character, and stepped into the open air as if by her own free will. She bore in her arms a child, a baby of some three months old, who winked and turned aside its little face from the too vivid light of day; because its existence, heretofore, had brought it acquaintance only with the gray twilight of a dungeon, or other darksome apartment of the prison.

When the young woman—the mother of this child—stood fully revealed before the crowd, it seemed to be her first impulse to clasp the infant closely to her bosom; not so much by an impulse of motherly affection, as that she might thereby conceal a certain token, which was wrought or fastened into her dress. In a moment, however, wisely judging that one token of her shame would but poorly serve to hide another, she took the baby on her arm, and with a burning blush, and yet a haughty smile, and a glance that would not be abashed, looked around at her townspeople and neighbors. On the breast of her gown, in fine red cloth, surrounded with an elaborate embroidery and fantastic flourishes of gold thread, appeared the letter A. It was so artistically done, and with so much fertility and gorgeous luxuriance of fancy, that it had all the effect of a last and fitting decoration to the apparel which she wore; and which was of a splendor in accordance with the taste of the age, but greatly beyond what was allowed by the sumptuary regulations of the colony.

The young woman was tall, with a figure of perfect elegance on a large scale. She had dark and abundant hair, so glossy that it threw off the sunshine with a gleam and a face which, besides being beautiful from regularity of feature and richness of complexion, had the impressiveness belonging to a marked brow and deep black eyes. She was ladylike, too, after the manner of the feminine gentility of those days; characterized by a certain state and dignity, rather than by the delicate, evanescent, and indescribable grace which is now recognized as its indication. And never had Hester Prynne appeared more ladylike, in the antique interpretation of the term, than as she issued from the prison. Those who had before known her, and had expected to behold her dimmed and obscured by a disastrous cloud, were astonished, and even startled, to perceive how her beauty shone out, and made a halo of the misfortune and ignominy in which she was enveloped. It may be true that, to a sensitive observer, there was something exquisitely painful in it. Her attire, which indeed, she had wrought for the occasion in prison, and had modeled much after her own fancy, seemed to express the attitude of her spirit, the desperate recklessness of her mood, by its wild and picturesque peculiarity. But the point which drew all eyes, and, as it were, transfigured the wearer—so that both men and women who had been familiarly acquainted with Hester Prynne were now impressed as if they beheld her for the first time— was that SCARLET LETTER, so fantastically embroidered and illuminated upon her bosom. It had the effect of a spell, taking her out of the ordinary relations with humanity, and enclosing her in a sphere by herself.

"She hath good skill at her needle, that's certain," remarked one of her female spectators; "but did ever a woman, before this brazen hussy, contrive such a way of showing it! Why, gossips, what is it but to laugh in the faces of our godly magistrates, and make a pride out of what they, worthy gentlemen, meant for a punishment?"

"It were well," muttered the most iron-visaged of the old dames, "if we stripped Madame Hester's rich gown off her dainty shoulders; and as for the red letter which she hath stitched so curiously, I'll bestow a rag of mine own rheumatic flannel to make a fitter one!"

"Oh, peace, neighbors, peace!" whispered their youngest companion; "do not let her hear you! Not a stitch in that embroidered letter but she has felt it in her heart."

The grim beadle now made a gesture with his staff.

"Make way, good people, make way, in the King's name!" cried he. "Open a passage; and, I promise ye, Mistress Prynne shall be set where man, woman, and child may have a fair sight of her brave apparel from this time till an hour past meridian. A blessing on the righteous colony of the Massachusetts, where iniquity is dragged out into the sunshine! Come along, Madam Hester, and show your scarlet letter in the market-place!"

A lane was forthwith opened through the crowd of spectators. Preceded by the beadle, and attended by an irregular procession of stern-browed men and unkindly visaged women, Hester Prynne set forth towards the place appointed for her punishment. A crowd of eager and curious schoolboys, understanding little of the matter in hand, except that it gave them a half-holiday, ran before her progress, turning their heads continually to stare into her face and at the winking baby in her arms, and at the ignominious letter on her breast. It was no great distance, in those days, from the prison door to the market-place. Measured by the prisoner's experience, however, it might be reckoned a journey of some length; for haughty as her demeanor was, she perchance underwent an agony from every footstep of those that thronged to see her, as if her heart had been flung into the street for them all to spurn and trample upon. In our nature, however, there is a provision, alike marvelous and merciful, that the sufferer should never know the intensity of what he endures by its present torture, but chiefly by the pang that rankles after it. With almost a serene deportment, therefore, Hester Prynne passed through this portion of her ordeal, and came to a sort of scaffold, at the western extremity of the market-place. It stood nearly beneath the eaves of Boston's earliest church, and appeared to be a fixture there.

In fact, this scaffold constituted a portion of a penal machine, which now, for two or three generations past, has been merely historical and traditionary among us, but was held, in the old time, to be as effectual an agent, in the promotion of good citizenship, as ever was the guillotine among the terrorists of France. It was, in short, the platform of the pillory; and above it rose the framework of that instrument of discipline, so fashioned as to confine the human head in its tight grasp, and thus hold it up to the public gaze. The very ideal of ignominy was embodied and made manifest in this contrivance of wood and iron. There can be no outrage, methinks, against our common nature, —whatever be the delinquencies of the individual,—no outrage more flagrant than to forbid the culprit to hide his face for shame; as it was the essence of this punishment to do. In Hester Prynne's instance, however, as not unfrequently in other cases, her sentence bore that she should stand a certain time upon the platform, but without undergoing that gripe about the neck and confinement of the head, the proneness to which was the most devilish characteristic of this ugly engine. Knowing well her part, she ascended a flight of wooden steps, and was thus displayed to the surrounding multitude, at about the height of a man's shoulders above the street.

Had there been a Papist among the crowd of Puritans, he might have seen in this beautiful woman, so picturesque in her attire and mien, and with the infant at her bosom, an object to remind him of the image of Divine Maternity, which so many illustrious painters have vied with one another to represent; something which should remind him, indeed, but only by contrast, of that sacred image of sinless motherhood, whose infant was to redeem the world. Here, there was the taint of deepest sin in the most sacred quality of human life, working such effect, that the world was only the darker for this woman's beauty, and the more lost for the infant that she had borne.

The scene was not without a mixture of awe, such as must always invest the spectacle of guilt and shame in a fellow-creature, before society shall have grown corrupt enough to smile, instead of shuddering at it. The witnesses of Hester Prynne's disgrace had not yet passed beyond their simplicity. They were stern enough to look upon her death, had that been the sentence, without a murmur at its severity, but had none of the heartlessness of another social state, which would find only a theme for jest in an exhibition like the present. Even had there been a disposition to turn the matter into ridicule, it must have been repressed and overpowered by the solemn presence of men no less dignified than the Governor, and several of his counsellors, a judge, a general, and the ministers of the town, all of whom sat or stood in a balcony of the meeting-house, looking down upon the platform. When such personages could constitute a part of the spectacle, without risking the majesty, or reverence of rank and office, it was safely to be inferred that the infliction of a legal sentence would have

an earnest and effectual meaning. Accordingly, the crowd was somber and grave. The unhappy culprit sustained herself as best a woman might, under the heavy weight of a thousand unrelenting eyes, all fastened upon her, and concentrated at her bosom. It was almost intolerable to be borne. Of an impulsive and passionate nature, she had fortified herself to encounter the stings and venomous stabs of public contumely, wreaking itself in every variety of insult; but there was a quality so much more terrible in the solemn mood of the popular mind, that she longed rather to behold all those rigid countenances contorted with scornful merriment, and herself the object. Had a roar of laughter burst from the multitude,—each man, each woman, each little shrill-voiced child, contributing their individual parts,—Hester Prynne might have repaid them all with a bitter and disdainful smile. But, under the leaden infliction which it was her doom to endure, she felt, at moments, as if she must needs shriek out with the full power of her lungs, and cast herself from the scaffold down upon the ground, or else go mad at once.

Yet there were intervals when the whole scene, in which she was the most conspicuous object, seemed to vanish from her eyes, or, at least, glimmered indistinctly before them, like a mass of imperfectly shaped and spectral images. Her mind, and especially her memory, was preternaturally active, and kept bringing up other scenes than this roughly hewn street of a little town, on the edge of the western wilderness: other faces than were lowering upon her from beneath the brims of those steeple-crowned hats. Reminiscences, the most trifling and immaterial, passages of infancy and school days, sports, childish quarrels, and the little domestic traits of her maiden years, came swarming back upon her, intermingled with recollections of whatever was gravest in her subsequent life; one picture precisely as vivid as another; as if all were of similar importance, or all alike a play. Possibly, it was an instinctive device of her spirit to relieve itself, by the exhibition of these phantasmagoric forms, from the cruel weight and hardness of the reality.

Be that as it might, the scaffold of the pillory was a point of view that revealed to Hester Prynne the entire track along which she had been treading, since her happy infancy. Standing on that miserable eminence, she saw her native village, in Old England, and her paternal home: a decayed house of gray stone, with a poverty-stricken aspect, but retaining a half obliterated shield of arms over the portal, in token of antique gentility. She saw her father's face, with its bald brow, and reverend white beard, that flowed over the old-fashioned Elizabethan ruff; her mother's, too, with the look of heedful and anxious love which it always wore in her remembrance, and which, even since her death, had so often laid the impediment of a gentle remonstrance in her daughter's pathway. She saw her own face, glowing with girlish beauty, and illuminating all the interior of the dusky mirror in which she had been wont to gaze at it. There she beheld another countenance, of a man well stricken in years, a pale, thin, scholar-like visage, with eyes dim and bleared by the lamplight that had served them to pore over many ponderous books. Yet those same bleared optics had a strange, penetrating power, when it was their owner's purpose to read the human soul. This figure of the study and the cloister, as Hester Prynne's womanly fancy failed not to recall, was slightly deformed, with the left shoulder a trifle higher than the right. Next rose before her, in memory's picture-gallery, the intricate and narrow thoroughfares, the tall, gray houses, the huge cathedrals, and the public edifices, ancient in date and quaint in architecture, of a Continental city; where new life had awaited her, still in connection with the misshapen scholar: a new life, but feeding itself on time-worn materials, like a tuft of green moss on a crumbling wall. Lastly, in lieu of these shifting scenes, came back the rude market-place of the Puritan settlement, with all the townspeople assembled, and leveling their stern regards at Hester Prynne,—yes, at herself,—who stood on the scaffold of the pillory, an infant on her arm, and the letter A, in scarlet, fantastically embroidered with gold thread, upon her bosom!

Could it be true? She clutched the child so fiercely to her breast that it sent forth a cry; she turned her eyes downward at the scarlet letter, and even touched it with her finger to assure herself that the infant and the shame were real. Yes!—these were her realities—all else had vanished!

III

THE RECOGNITION

From this intense consciousness of being the object of severe and universal observation, the wearer of the scarlet letter was at length relieved, by discerning, on the outskirts of the crowd, a figure which irresistibly took possession of her thoughts. An Indian in his native garb was standing there; but the red men were not so infrequent visitors of the English settlements that one of them would have attracted any notice from Hester Prynne at such a time; much less would he have excluded all other objects and ideas from her mind. By the Indian's side, and evidently sustaining a companionship with him, stood a white man, clad in a strange disarray of civilized and savage costume.

He was small in stature, with a furrowed visage, which as yet could hardly be termed aged. There was a remarkable intelligence in his features, as of a person who had so cultivated his mental part that it could not fail to mold the physical to itself, and become manifest by unmistakable tokens. Although, by a seemingly careless arrangement of his heterogeneous garb, he had endeavoured to conceal or abate the peculiarity, it was sufficiently evident to Hester Prynne that one of this man's shoulder's rose higher than the other. Again, at the first instant of perceiving that thin visage, and the slight deformity of the figure, she pressed her infant to her bosom with so convulsive a force that the poor babe uttered another cry of pain. But the mother did not seem to hear it.

At his arrival in the market-place, and some time before she saw him, the stranger had bent his eyes on Hester Prynne. It was carelessly at first, like a man chiefly accustomed to look inward, and to whom external matters are of little value and import, unless they bear relation to something within his mind. Very soon, however, his look became keen and penetrative. A writhing horror twisted itself across his features, like a snake gliding swiftly over them, and making one little pause, with all its wreathed intervolutions in open sight. His face darkened with some powerful emotion, which, nevertheless, he so instantaneously controlled by an effort of his will, that, save at a single moment, its expression might have passed for calmness. After a brief space, the convulsion grew almost imperceptible, and finally subsided into the depths of his nature. When he found the eyes of Hester Prynne fastened on his own, and saw that she appeared to recognize him, he slowly and calmly raised his finger, made a gesture with it in the air, and laid it on his lips.

Then touching the shoulder of a townsman who stood next to him, he addressed him in a formal and courteous manner.

"I pray you, good Sir," said he, "who is this woman?—and wherefore is she here set up to public shame?"

"You must needs be a stranger in this region, friend," answered the townsman, looking curiously at the questioner and his savage companion, "else you would surely have heard of

Mistress Hester Prynne and her evil doings. She hath raised a great scandal, I promise you, in godly Master Dimmesdale's church."

"You say truly," replied the other. "I am a stranger, and have been a wanderer, sorely against my will. I have met with grievous mishaps by sea and land, and have been long held in bonds among the heathen-folk to the southward; and am now brought hither by this Indian to be redeemed out of my captivity. Will it please you, therefore, to tell me of Hester Prynne's—have I her name rightly?—of this woman's offences, and what has brought her to yonder scaffold?"

"Truly, friend; and methinks it must gladden your heart, after your troubles and sojourn in the wilderness," said the townsman, "to find yourself at length in a land where iniquity is searched out and punished in the sight of rulers and people, as here in our godly New England. Yonder woman, sir, you must know, was the wife of a certain learned man, English by birth, but who had long dwelt in Amsterdam, whence some good time agone he was minded to cross over and cast in his lot with us of the Massachusetts. To this purpose he sent his wife before him, remaining himself to look after some necessary affairs. Marry, good sir, in some two years, or less, that the woman has been a dweller here in Boston, no tidings have come of this learned gentleman, Master Prynne; and his young wife, look you, being left to her own misguidance"—

"Ah!—aha!—I conceive you," said the stranger with a bitter smile. "So learned a man as you speak of should have learned this too in his books. And who, by your favor, sir, may be the father of yonder babe—it is some three or four months old, I should judge—which Mistress Prynne is holding in her arms?"

"Of a truth, friend, that matter remaineth a riddle; and the Daniel who shall expound it is yet a-wanting," answered the townsman. "Madame Hester absolutely refuseth to speak, and the magistrates have laid their heads together in vain. Peradventure the guilty one stands looking on at this sad spectacle, unknown of man, and forgetting that God sees him."

"The learned man," observed the stranger with another smile, "should come himself to look into the mystery."

"It behooves him well if he be still in life," responded the townsman. "Now, good sir, our Massachusetts magistracy, bethinking themselves that this woman is youthful and fair, and doubtless was strongly tempted to her fall, and that, moreover, as is most likely, her hus-

band may be at the bottom of the sea, they have not been bold to put in force the extremity of our righteous law against her. The penalty thereof is death. But in their great mercy and tenderness of heart they have doomed Mistress Prynne to stand only a space of three hours on the platform of the pillory, and then and thereafter, for the remainder of her natural life, to wear a mark of shame upon her bosom."

"A wise sentence!" remarked the stranger, gravely bowing his head. "Thus she will be a living sermon against sin, until the ignominious letter be engraved upon her tombstone. It irks me, nevertheless, that the partner of her iniquity should not, at least, stand on the scaffold by her side. But he will be known!—he will be known!—he will be known!"

He bowed courteously to the communicative townsman, and whispering a few words to his Indian attendant, they both made their way through the crowd.

While this passed, Hester Prynne had been standing on her pedestal, still with a fixed gaze towards the stranger—so fixed a gaze that, at moments of intense absorption, all other objects in the visible world seemed to vanish, leaving only him and her. Such an interview, perhaps, would have been more terrible than even to meet him as she now did, with the hot mid-day sun burning down upon her face, and lighting up its shame; with the scarlet token of infamy on her breast; with the sin-born infant in her arms; with a whole people, drawn forth as to a festival, staring at the features that should have been seen only in the quiet gleam of the fireside, in the happy shadow of a home, or beneath a matronly veil at church. Dreadful as it was, she was conscious of a shelter in the presence of these thousand witnesses. It was better to stand thus, with so many betwixt him and her, than to greet him face to face, they two alone. She fled for refuge, as it were, to the public exposure, and dreaded the moment when its protection should be withdrawn from her. Involved in these thoughts, she scarcely heard a voice behind her until it had repeated her name more than once, in a loud and solemn tone, audible to the whole multitude.

"Hearken unto me, Hester Prynne!" said the voice.

It has already been noticed that directly over the platform on which Hester Prynne stood was a kind of balcony, or open gallery, appended to the meeting-house. It was the place whence proclamations were wont to be made, amidst an assemblage of the magistracy, with all the ceremonial that attended such public observances in those days. Here, to witness the scene which we are describing, sat Governor Bellingham [1] himself with four sergeants about his chair, bearing halberds, as a guard of honor. He wore a dark feather in his hat, a border of embroidery on his cloak, and a black velvet tunic beneath; a gentleman advanced in years, with a hard experience written in his wrinkles. He was not ill fitted to be the head and representative of a community which owed its origin and progress, and its present state of development, not to the impulses of youth, but to the stern and tempered energies of manhood and the somber sagacity of age; accomplishing so much, precisely because it imagined and hoped so little. The other eminent characters by whom the chief ruler was surrounded were distinguished by a dignity of mien, belonging to a period when the forms of authority were felt to possess the sacredness of divine institutions. They were, doubtless, good men, just and sage. But, out of the whole human family, it would not have been easy to select the same number of wise and virtuous persons, who should be less capable of sitting in judgment on an erring woman's heart, and disentangling its mesh of good and evil, than the sages of rigid aspect towards whom Hester Prynne now turned her face. She seemed conscious, indeed, that whatever sympathy she might expect lay in the larger and warmer heart of the multitude; for, as she lifted her eyes towards the balcony, the unhappy woman grew pale, and trembled.

The voice which had called her attention was that of the reverend and famous John Wilson, [2] the eldest clergyman of Boston, a great scholar, like most of his contemporaries in the profession, and withal a man of kind and genial spirit. This last attribute, however, had been less carefully developed than his intellectual gifts, and was, in truth, rather a matter of shame than self-congratulation with him. There he stood, with a border of grizzled locks beneath his skullcap; while his gray eyes, accustomed to the shaded light of his study, were winking, like those of Hester's infant, in the unadulterated sunshine. He looked like the darkly engraved portraits which we see prefixed to old volumes of sermons, and had no more right than one of those portraits would have to step forth, as he now did, and meddle with a question of human guilt, passion, and anguish.

[1] governor of Massachusetts in 1641, 1654, and 1665-72
[2] John Wilson, pastor of the First Church, Boston, from 1632 till 1667

"Hester Prynne," said the clergyman, "I have striven with my young brother here, under whose preaching of the Word you have been privileged to sit"—here Mr. Wilson laid his hand on the shoulder of a pale young man beside him—"I have sought, I say, to persuade this godly youth, that he should deal with you, here in the face of Heaven, and before these wise and upright rulers, and in hearing of all the people, as touching the vileness and blackness of your sin. Knowing your natural temper better than I, he could the better judge what arguments to use, whether of tenderness or terror, such as might prevail over your hardness and obstinacy; insomuch that you should no longer hide the name of him who tempted you to this grievous fall. But he opposes to me (with a young man's over-softness, albeit wise beyond his years), that it were wronging the very nature of woman to force her to lay open her heart's secrets in such broad daylight, and in presence of so great a multitude. Truly, as I sought to convince him, the shame lay in the commission of the sin, and not in the showing of it forth. What say you to it, once again, Brother Dimmesdale? Must it be thou, or I, that shall deal with this poor sinner's soul?"

There was a murmur among the dignified and reverend occupants of the balcony; and Governor Bellingham gave expression to its purport, speaking in an authoritative voice, although tempered with respect towards the youthful clergyman whom he addressed.

"Good Master Dimmesdale," said he, "the responsibility of this woman's soul lies greatly with you. It behooves you, therefore, to exhort her to repentance and to confession, as a proof and consequence thereof."

The directness of this appeal drew the eyes of the whole crowd upon the Reverend Mr. Dimmesdale—a young clergyman, who had come from one of the great English universities, bringing all the learning of the age into our wild forest land. His eloquence and religious fervor had already given the earnest of high eminence in his profession. He was a person of very striking aspect, with a white, lofty, and impending brow, large, brown, melancholy eyes, and a mouth which, unless when he forcibly compressed it, was apt to be tremulous, expressing both nervous sensibility and a vast power of self-restraint. Notwithstanding his high native gifts and scholar-like attainments, there was an air about this young minister—an apprehensive, a startled, a half-frightened look, as of a being who felt himself quite astray, and at a loss in the pathway of human existence, and could only be at ease in some seclusion of his own. Therefore, so far as his duties would permit, he trod in the shadowy by-paths, and thus kept himself simple and childlike; coming forth, when occasion was, with a freshness, and fragrance, and dewy purity of thought, which, as many people said, affected them like the speech of an angel.

Such was the young man whom the Reverend Mr. Wilson and the Governor had introduced so openly to the public notice, bidding him speak, in the hearing of all men, to that mystery of a woman's soul, so sacred even in its pollution. The trying nature of his position drove the blood from his cheek, and made his lips tremulous.

"Speak to the woman, my brother," said Mr. Wilson. "It is of moment to her soul, and, therefore, as the worshipful Governor says, momentous to thine own, in whose charge hers is. Exhort her to confess the truth!"

The Reverend Mr. Dimmesdale bent his head, in silent prayer, as it seemed, and then came forward.

"Hester Prynne," said he, leaning over the balcony and looking down steadfastly into her eyes, "thou hearest what this good man says, and seest the accountability under which I labor. If thou feelest it to be for thy soul's peace, and that thy earthly punishment will thereby be made more effectual to salvation, I charge thee to speak out the name of thy fellow-sinner and fellow-sufferer! Be not silent from any mistaken pity and tenderness for him; for, believe me, Hester, though he were to step down from a high place, and stand there beside thee, on thy pedestal of shame, yet better were it so than to hide a guilty heart through life. What can thy silence do for him, except it tempt him—yea, compel him, as it were—to add hypocrisy to sin? Heaven hath granted thee an open ignominy, that thereby thou mayest work out an open triumph over the evil within thee, and the sorrow without. Take heed how thou deniest to him—who, perchance, hath not the courage to grasp it for himself— the bitter, but wholesome, cup that is now presented to thy lips!"

The young pastor's voice was tremulously sweet, rich, deep, and broken. The feeling that it so evidently manifested, rather than the direct purport of the words, caused it to vibrate within all hearts, and brought the listeners into one accord of sympathy. Even the poor baby at Hester's bosom was affected by the same influence, for it directed its hitherto vacant gaze towards Mr. Dimmesdale, and held up its little

arms with a half-pleased, half-plaintive murmur. So powerful seemed the minister's appeal that the people could not believe but that Hester Prynne would speak out the guilty name; or else that the guilty one himself, in whatever high or lowly place he stood, would be drawn forth by an inward and inevitable necessity, and compelled to ascend the scaffold.

Hester shook her head.

"Woman, transgress not beyond the limits of Heaven's mercy!" cried the Reverend Mr. Wilson, more harshly than before. "That little babe hath been gifted with a voice, to second and confirm the counsel which thou hast heard. Speak out the name! That, and thy repentance, may avail to take the scarlet letter off thy breast."

"Never!" replied Hester Prynne, looking, not at Mr. Wilson, but into the deep and troubled eyes of the younger clergyman. "It is too deeply branded. Ye cannot take it off. And would that I might endure his agony as well as mine!"

"Speak, woman!" said another voice, coldly and sternly, proceeding from the crowd about the scaffold. "Speak; and give your child a father!"

"I will not speak!" answered Hester, turning pale as death, but responding to this voice, which she too surely recognized. "And my child must seek a heavenly Father; she shall never know an earthly one!"

"She will not speak!" murmured Mr. Dimmesdale, who, leaning over the balcony, with his hand upon his heart, had awaited the result of his appeal. He now drew back with a long respiration. "Wondrous strength and generosity of a woman's heart! She will not speak!"

Discerning the impracticable state of the poor culprit's mind, the elder clergyman, who had carefully prepared himself for the occasion, addressed to the multitude a discourse on sin, in all its branches, but with continual reference to the ignominious letter. So forcibly did he dwell upon this symbol, for the hour or more during which his periods were rolling over the people's heads, that it assumed new terrors in their imagination, and seemed to derive its scarlet hue from the flames of the infernal pit. Hester Prynne, meanwhile, kept her place upon the pedestal of shame, with glazed eyes, and an air of weary indifference. She had borne that morning all that nature could endure; and as her temperament was not of the order that escapes from too intense suffering by a swoon, her spirit could only shelter itself beneath a stony crust of insensibility, while the faculties of animal life remained entire. In this state, the voice of the preacher thundered remorselessly, but unavailingly, upon her ears. The infant, during the latter portion of her ordeal, pierced the air with its wailings and screams; she strove to hush it, mechanically, but seemed scarcely to sympathize with its trouble. With the same hard demeanor, she was led back to prison, and vanished from the public gaze within its iron-clamped portal. It was whispered by those who peered after her, that the scarlet letter threw a lurid gleam along the dark passageway of the interior.

1849-1850   1850

From THE HOUSE OF THE SEVEN GABLES

XVIII

GOVERNOR PYNCHEON

Judge Pyncheon,[1] while his two relatives have fled away with such ill-considered haste, still sits in the old parlor, keeping house, as the familiar phrase is, in the absence of its ordinary occupants. To him, and to the venerable House of the Seven Gables, does our story

[1] In Hawthorne's novel, Col. Pyncheon in about 1660 had laid apparently unlawful claim to a piece of land belonging to Matthew Maule, a man of humble station. The dispute had ended when Matthew Maule—some said at the instigation of Col. Pyncheon—had been hanged as a wizard. His last words on the scaffold, as he pointed his finger at the Colonel had been, "God will give him blood to drink." The prophecy was remembered some years later, on the occasion of the Colonel's great house-warming in the new seven-gabled mansion erected on the site of Maule's hut and garden-spot, when, after the guests had all assembled, Col. Pyncheon was found dead at his desk in his library, with blood on his ruff and beard. Maule's curse was again remembered one hundred years later when another Pyncheon died under similar circumstances. In the mid-nineteenth century the violent death of one member of the Pyncheon family at the hands of another had aroused the memories of the superstitious. The owner of the estate was then a rich Judge Pyncheon who allowed his very poor cousin Hepzibah Pyncheon to inhabit the house of the seven gables. Her rather simple-minded brother Clifford, who had been accused of the murder of the former heir, his bachelor uncle, had after about thirty years of imprisonment returned to Hepzibah, his mind almost a blank, and more like a gentle child than a man. Happy, cheerful little Phoebe Pyncheon, the daughter of another cousin, had also come to live with Hepzibah.

In the two preceding chapters Judge Pyncheon has announced to Hepzibah that he must see Clifford to get from him the secret of where the documents or deeds conveying vast estates of the Pyncheons lie hid. When Hepzibah insists that Clifford does not know, Judge Pyncheon states the alternative: Clifford must either tell or go to an insane asylum. Hepzibah, after resisting the demand as bravely as she can, has at last gone to call her brother. She does not find him until returning she meets him at the door of the parlor. Frightened by what they both see within, they hastily leave the house.

now betake itself, like an owl, bewildered in the daylight, and hastening back to his hollow tree.

The Judge has not shifted his position for a long while now. He has not stirred hand or foot, nor withdrawn his eyes so much as a hair's breadth from their fixed gaze towards the corner of the room, since the footsteps of Hepzibah and Clifford creaked along the passage, and the outer door was closed cautiously behind their exit. He holds his watch in his left hand, but clutched in such a manner that you cannot see the dial-plate. How profound a fit of meditation! Or, supposing him asleep, how infantile a quietude of conscience, and what wholesome order in the gastric region, are betokened by slumber so entirely undisturbed with starts, cramp, twitches, muttered dream-talk, trumpet-blasts through the nasal organ, or any the slightest irregularity of breath! You must hold your own breath, to satisfy yourself whether he breathes at all. It is quite inaudible. You hear the ticking of his watch; his breath you do not hear. A most refreshing slumber, doubtless! And yet, the Judge cannot be asleep. His eyes are open! A veteran politician, such as he, would never fall asleep with wide-open eyes, lest some enemy or mischief-maker, taking him thus at unawares, should peep through these windows into his consciousness, and make strange discoveries among the reminiscences, projects, hopes, apprehensions, weaknesses, and strong points, which he has heretofore shared with nobody. A cautious man is proverbially said to sleep with one eye open. That may be wisdom. But not with both; for this were heedlessness! No, no! Judge Pyncheon cannot be asleep.

It is odd, however, that a gentleman so burdened with engagements—and noted, too, for punctuality, should linger thus in an old lonely mansion, which he has never seemed very fond of visiting. The oaken chair, to be sure, may tempt him with its roominess. It is, indeed, a spacious, and, allowing for the rude age that fashioned it, a moderately easy seat, with capacity enough, at all events, and offering no restraint to the Judge's breadth of beam. A bigger man might find ample accommodation in it. His ancestor, now pictured upon the wall, with all his English beef about him, used hardly to present a front extending from elbow to elbow of this chair, or a base that would cover its whole cushion. But there are better chairs than this,—mahogany, black walnut, rosewood, spring-seated and damask-cushioned, with varied slopes, and innumerable artifices to make them easy, and obviate the irksomeness of too tame an ease,—a score of such might be at Judge Pyncheon's service. Yes! in a score of drawing-rooms he would be more than welcome. Mamma would advance to meet him, with outstretched hand; the virgin daughter, elderly as he has now got to be,—an old widower, as he smilingly describes himself,—would shake up the cushion for the Judge, and do her pretty little utmost to make him comfortable. For the Judge is a prosperous man. He cherishes his schemes, moreover, like other people, and reasonably brighter than most others; or did so, at least, as he lay abed, this morning, in an agreeable half-drowse, planning the business of the day, and speculating on the probabilities of the next fifteen years. With his firm health, and the little inroad that age has made upon him, fifteen years or twenty—yes, or perhaps five-and-twenty!—are no more than he may fairly call his own. Five-and-twenty years for the enjoyment of his real estate in town and country, his railroad, bank, and insurance shares, his United States stock,—his wealth, in short, however invested, now in possession, or soon to be acquired; together with the public honors that have fallen upon him, and the weightier ones that are yet to fall! It is good! It is excellent! It is enough!

Still lingering in the old chair! If the Judge has a little time to throw away, why does not he visit the insurance office, as is his frequent custom, and sit awhile in one of their leathern-cushioned arm-chairs, listening to the gossip of the day, and dropping some deeply-designed chance-word, which will be certain to become the gossip of tomorrow! And have not the bank directors a meeting, at which it was the Judge's purpose to be present, and his office to preside? Indeed they have; and the hour is noted on a card, which is, or ought to be, in Judge Pyncheon's right vest-pocket. Let him go thither, and loll at ease upon his money-bags! He has lounged long enough in the old chair!

This was to have been such a busy day! In the first place, the interview with Clifford. Half an hour, by the Judge's reckoning, was to suffice for that; it would probably be less, but,—taking into consideration that Hepzibah was first to be dealt with, and that these women are apt to make many words where a few would do much better—it might be safest to allow half an hour. Half an hour? Why, Judge, it is already two hours, by your own undeviatingly accurate chronometer! Glance your eye down at it, and see! Ah! he will not give himself the trouble either to bend his head, or elevate his hand, so as to

bring the faithful time-keeper within his range of vision! Time, all at once, appears to have become a matter of no moment with the Judge!

And has he forgotten all the other items of his memoranda? Clifford's affair arranged, he was to meet a State Street [1] broker, who has undertaken to procure a heavy percentage, and the best of paper, for a few loose thousands which the Judge happens to have by him, uninvested. The wrinkled note-shaver [2] will have taken his railroad trip in vain. Half an hour later, in the street next to this, there was to be an auction of real estate, including a portion of the old Pyncheon property, originally belonging to Maule's garden-ground. It has been alienated from the Pyncheons these fourscore years; but the Judge had kept it in his eye, and had set his heart on reannexing it to the small demesne still left around the Seven Gables; and now, during this odd fit of oblivion, the fatal hammer must have fallen, and transferred our ancient patrimony to some alien possessor! Possibly, indeed, the sale may have been postponed till fairer weather. If so, will the Judge make it convenient to be present, and favor the auctioneer with his bid, on the proximate occasion?

The next affair was to buy a horse for his own driving. The one heretofore his favorite stumbled, this very morning, on the road to town, and must be at once discarded. Judge Pyncheon's neck is too precious to be risked on such a contingency as a stumbling steed. Should all the above business be seasonably got through with, he might attend the meeting of a charitable society; the very name of which, however, in the multiplicity of his benevolence, is quite forgotten; so that this engagement may pass unfulfilled, and no great harm done. And if he have time, amid the press of more urgent matters, he must take measures for the renewal of Mrs. Pyncheon's tombstone, which, the sexton tells him, has fallen on its marble face, and is cracked quite in twain. She was a praiseworthy woman enough, thinks the Judge, in spite of her nervousness, and the tears that she was so oozy with, and her foolish behavior about the coffee; and as she took her departure so seasonably, he will not grudge the second tombstone. It is better, at least, than if she had never needed any! The next item on his list was to give orders for some fruit-trees, of a rare variety, to be deliverable at his country-seat in the ensuing autumn. Yes, buy them,

[1] a business street in Boston
[2] one who buys promissory notes at a higher rate of discount than is current

by all means; and may the peaches be luscious in your mouth, Judge Pyncheon! After this comes something more important. A committee of his political party has besought him for a hundred or two of dollars, in addition to his previous disbursements, towards carrying on the fall campaign. The Judge is a patriot; the fate of the country is staked on the November election; and besides, as will be shadowed forth in another paragraph, he has no trifling stake of his own in the same great game. He will do what the committee asks; nay, he will be liberal beyond their expectations; they shall have a check for five hundred dollars, and more anon, if it be needed. What next? A decayed widow, whose husband was Judge Pyncheon's early friend, has laid her case of destitution before him, in a very moving letter. She and her fair daughter have scarcely bread to eat. He partly intends to call on her, today,—perhaps so— perhaps not,—accordingly as he may happen to have leisure, and a small bank note.

Another business, which, however, he puts no great weight on—(it is well, you know, to be heedful, but not over anxious, as respects one's personal health)—another business, then, was to consult his family physician. About what, for Heaven's sake? Why, it is rather difficult to describe the symptoms. A mere dimness of sight and dizziness of brain, was it?—or a disagreeable choking, or stifling, or gurgling, or bubbling, in the region of the thorax, as the anatomists say?—or was it a pretty severe throbbing and kicking of the heart, rather creditable to him than otherwise, as showing that the organ had not been left out of the Judge's physical contrivance? No matter what it was. The doctor, probably, would smile at the statement of such trifles to his professional ear; the Judge would smile, in his turn; and meeting one another's eyes, they would enjoy a hearty laugh together! But a fig for medical advice. The Judge will never need it!

Pray, pray, Judge Pyncheon, look at your watch, now! What—not a glance! It is within ten minutes of the dinner-hour! It surely cannot have slipped your memory that the dinner of today is to be the most important, in its consequences, of all the dinners you ever ate. Yes, precisely the most important; although, in the course of your somewhat eminent career, you have been placed high towards the head of the table, at splendid banquets, and have poured out your festive eloquence to ears yet echoing with Webster's mighty organ-tones. No public dinner this, however. It is merely a gathering of some dozen or so of friends from several districts of the state; men of distin-guished character and influence, assembling, almost casually, at the house of a common friend, likewise distinguished, who will make them welcome to a little better than his ordinary fare. Nothing in the way of French cookery, but an excellent dinner nevertheless. Real turtle, we understand, and salmon, tautog, canvas-backs, pig, English mutton, good roast beef, or dainties of that serious kind, fit for substantial country gentlemen, as these honorable persons mostly are. The delicacies of the season, in short, and flavored by a brand of old Madeira which has been the pride of many seasons. It is the Juno brand; a glorious wine, fragrant, and full of gentle might; a bottled-up happiness, put by for use; a golden liquid, worth more than liquid gold; so rare and admirable, that veteran wine-bibbers count it among their epochs to have tasted it! It drives away the heart-ache, and substitutes no head-ache! Could the Judge but quaff a glass, it might enable him to shake off the unaccountable lethargy which (for the ten intervening minutes, and five to boot, are already past) has made him such a laggard at this momentous dinner. It would all but revive a dead man! Would you like to sip it now, Judge Pyncheon?

Alas, this dinner! Have you really forgotten its true object? Then let us whisper it, that you may start at once out of the oaken chair, which really seems to be enchanted, like the one in *Comus*, or that in which Moll Pitcher imprisoned your own grandmother. [1] But ambition is a talisman more powerful than witchcraft. Start up, then, and hurrying through the streets, burst in upon the company, that they may begin before the fish is spoiled! They wait for you; and it is little for your interest that they should wait. These gentlemen—need you be told it?—have assembled, not without purpose, from every quarter of the state. They are practiced politicians, every man of them, and skilled to adjust those preliminary measures which steal from the people, without its knowledge, the power of choosing its own rulers. The popular voice, at the next gubernatorial election, though loud as thunder, will be really

---

[1] Comus, the evil spirit in Milton's masque, by his enchantment, prevents the lady from arising from the chair in which he has seated her. Moll Pitcher was a fortune-teller of Lynn, Massachusetts, who died in 1813. C. W. Upham, in his *Lectures on Witchcraft*, says: ". . . She derived her mysterious gifts by inheritance, her grandfather having practiced them before in Marblehead. Sailors, merchants, and adventurers of every kind visited her residence, and placed confidence in her predictions." According to Whittier, she foretold by consulting tea-leaves. See Whittier's suppressed poem, "Moll Pitcher"; also Alonzo Lewis's *History of Lynn*. Hawthorne apparently invents the story of her rivaling Comus.

but an echo of what these gentlemen shall speak, under their breath, at your friend's festive board. They meet to decide upon their candidate. This little knot of subtle schemers will control the convention, and, through it, dictate to the party. And what worthier candidate—more wise and learned, more noted for philanthropic liberality, truer to safe principles, tried oftener by public trusts, more spotless in private character, with a larger stake in the common welfare, and deeper grounded, by hereditary descent, in the faith and practice of the Puritans,—what man can be presented for the suffrage of the people, so eminently combining all these claims to the chief-rulership as Judge Pyncheon here before us?

Make haste, then! Do your part! The meed for which you have toiled, and fought, and climbed, and crept, is ready for your grasp! Be present at this dinner!—drink a glass or two of that noble wine!—make your pledges in as low a whisper as you will!—and you rise up from table virtually governor of the glorious old state! Governor Pyncheon, of Massachusetts!

And is there no potent and exhilarating cordial in a certainty like this? It has been the grand purpose of half your lifetime to obtain it. Now, when there needs little more than to signify your acceptance, why do you sit so lumpishly in your great-great-grandfather's oaken chair, as if preferring it to the gubernatorial one? We have all heard of King Log; [1] but, in these jostling times, one of that royal kindred will hardly win the race for an elective chief-magistracy.

Well! it is absolutely too late for dinner! Turtle, salmon, tautog, woodcock, boiled turkey, South-Down mutton, pig, roast beef, have vanished, or exist only in fragments, with lukewarm potatoes, and gravies crusted over with cold fat. The Judge, had he done nothing else, would have achieved wonders with his knife and fork. It was he, you know, of whom it used to be said, in reference to his ogre-like appetite, that his creator made him a great animal, but that the dinner hour made him a great beast. Persons of his large sensual endowments must claim indulgence, at their feeding-time. But, for once, the Judge is entirely too late for dinner! Too late, we fear, even to join the party at their wine! The guests are warm and merry; they have given up the Judge; and, concluding that the Free-Soilers [2] have him, they will fix upon another candidate. Were

our friend now to stalk in among them, with that wide-open stare, at once wild and stolid, his ungenial presence would be apt to change their cheer. Neither would it be seemly in Judge Pyncheon, generally so scrupulous in his attire, to show himself at a dinner-table with that crimson stain upon his shirt-bosom. By the bye, how came it there? It is an ugly sight, at any rate; and the wisest way for the judge is to button his coat closely over his breast, and, taking his horse and chaise from the livery-stable, to make all speed to his own house. There, after a glass of brandy and water, and a mutton chop, a beef steak, a broiled fowl, or some such hasty little dinner and supper all in one, he had better spend the evening by the fireside. He must toast his slippers a long while, in order to get rid of the chilliness which the air of this vile old house has sent curdling through his veins.

Up, therefore, Judge Pyncheon, up! You have lost a day. But tomorrow will be here anon. Will you rise, betimes, and make the most of it? Tomorrow! Tomorrow! Tomorrow! We, that are alive, may rise betimes tomorrow. As for him that has died today, his morrow will be the resurrection morn.

Meanwhile the twilight is glooming upward out of the corners of the room. The shadows of the tall furniture grow deeper, and at first become more definite; then, spreading wider, they lose their distinctness of outline in the dark gray tide of oblivion, as it were, that creeps slowly over the various objects, and the one human figure sitting in the midst of them. The gloom has not entered from without; it has brooded here all day, and now, taking its own inevitable time, will possess itself of everything. The Judge's face, indeed, rigid, and singularly white, refuses to melt into this universal solvent. Fainter and fainter grows the light. It is as if another double handful of darkness had been scattered through the air. Now it is no longer gray, but sable. There is still a faint appearance at the window; neither a glow, nor a gleam, nor a glimmer,—any phase of light would express something far brighter than this doubtful perception, or sense, rather, that there is a window there. Has it yet vanished? No!—yes!—not quite! And there is still the swarthy whiteness,—we shall venture to marry these ill-agreeing words,—the swarthy whiteness of Judge Pyncheon's face. The features are all gone: there is only the paleness of them left. And how looks it now? There is no window! There is no face! An infinite, inscrutable blackness has annihilated sight! Where is our universe? All crumbled away

[1] See note 3. p. 180.
[2] The Free-Soil party, organized in 1848, believed in stipulating, on the admission of a state or territory, that slavery should not exist within its boundaries.

from us; and we, adrift in chaos, may hearken to the gusts of homeless wind, that go sighing and murmuring about, in quest of what was once a world!

Is there no other sound? One other, and a fearful one. It is the ticking of the Judge's watch, which, ever since Hepzibah left the room in search of Clifford, he has been holding in his hand. Be the cause what it may, this little, quiet, never-ceasing throb of Time's pulse, repeating its small strokes with such busy regularity, in Judge Pyncheon's motionless hand, has an effect of terror, which we do not find in any other accompaniment of the scene. [1]

But, listen! That puff of the breeze was louder; it had a tone unlike the dreary and sullen one which has bemoaned itself, and afflicted all mankind with miserable sympathy, for five days past. The wind has veered about! It now comes boisterously from the northwest, and, taking hold of the aged frame-work of the Seven Gables, gives it a shake, like a wrestler that would try strength with his antagonist. Another and another sturdy tussle with the blast! The old house creaks again, and makes a vociferous but somewhat unintelligible bellowing in its sooty throat (the big flue, we mean, of its wide chimney) partly in complaint at the rude wind, but rather, as befits their century and a half of hostile intimacy, in tough defiance. A rumbling kind of a bluster roars behind the fire-board. [2] A door has slammed above-stairs. A window, perhaps, has been left open, or else is driven in by an unruly gust. It is not to be conceived, beforehand, what wonderful wind-instruments are these old timber mansions, and how haunted with the strangest noises, which immediately begin to sing, and sigh, and sob, and shriek,—and to smite with sledge-hammers, airy, but ponderous, in some distant chamber,—and to tread along the entries as with stately footsteps, and rustle up and down the staircase, as with silks miraculously stiff,—whenever the gale catches the house with a window open, and gets fairly into it. Would that we were not an attendant spirit here! It is too awful! This clamor of the wind through the lonely house; the Judge's quietude, as he sits invisible; and that pertinacious ticking of his watch!

As regards Judge Pyncheon's invisibility, however, that matter will soon be remedied.

The northwest wind has swept the sky clear. The window is distinctly seen. Through its panes, moreover, we dimly catch the sweep of the dark, clustering foliage, outside, fluttering with a constant irregularity of movement, and letting in a peep of starlight, now here, now there. Oftener than any other object, these glimpses illuminate the Judge's face. But here comes more effectual light. Observe that silvery dance upon the upper branches of the pear tree, and now a little lower, and now on the whole mass of boughs, while, through their shifting intricacies, the moonbeams fall aslant into the room. They play over the Judge's figure, and show that he has not stirred throughout the hours of darkness. They follow the shadows, in changeful sport, across his unchanging features. They gleam upon his watch. His grasp conceals the dial-plate; but we know that the faithful hands have met; for one of the city clocks tells midnight.

A man of sturdy understanding, like Judge Pyncheon, cares no more for twelve o'clock at night than for the corresponding hour of noon. However just the parallel drawn, in some of the preceding pages, between his Puritan ancestor and himself, it fails in this point. The Pyncheon of two centuries ago, in common with most of his contemporaries, professed his full belief in spiritual ministrations, although reckoning them chiefly of a malignant character. The Pyncheon of tonight, who sits in yonder arm-chair, believes in no such nonsense. Such, at least, was his creed, some few hours since. His hair will not bristle, therefore, at the stories which—in times when chimney-corners had benches in them, where old people sat poking into the ashes of the past, and raking out traditions like live coals—used to be told about this very room of his ancestral house. In fact, these tales are too absurd to bristle even childhood's hair. What sense, meaning, or moral, for example, such as even ghost-stories should be susceptible of, can be traced in the ridiculous legend, that, at midnight, all the dead Pyncheons are bound to assemble in this parlor? And, pray, for what? Why, to see whether the portrait of their ancestor still keeps its place upon the wall, in compliance with his testamentary directions! [3] Is it worth while to come out of their graves for that?

We are tempted to make a little sport with the idea. Ghost-stories are hardly to be treated seriously, any longer. The family-party of the

---

[1] The same effect is produced in Stevenson's "Markheim" by the ticking of innumerable clocks in the antique shop.
[2] the wooden screen for the fireplace formerly used when there was no fire

[3] The portrait of the first Colonel Pyncheon, who built the house, was, according to the supposed terms of his will, to remain fixed to the wall.

defunct Pyncheons, we presume, goes off in this wise.

First comes the ancestor himself, in his black cloak, steeple-hat, and trunk-breeches, girt about the waist with a leathern belt, in which hangs his steel-hilted sword; he has a long staff in his hand, such as gentlemen in advanced life used to carry, as much for the dignity of the thing as for the support to be derived from it. He looks up at the portrait; a thing of no substance, gazing at its own painted image! All is safe. The picture is still there. The purpose of his brain has been kept sacred thus long after the man himself has sprouted up in graveyard grass. See! he lifts his ineffectual hand, and tries the frame. All safe! But is that a smile?—is it 'not, rather, a frown of deadly import, that darkens over the shadow of his features? The stout Colonel is dissatisfied! So decided is his look of discontent as to impart additional distinctness to his features; through which, nevertheless, the moonlight passes, and flickers on the wall beyond. Something has strangely vexed the ancestor! With a grim shake of the head, he turns away. Here come other Pyncheons, the whole tribe, in their half a dozen generations, jostling and elbowing one another, to reach the picture. We behold aged men and grandames, a clergyman with the Puritanic stiffness still in his garb and mien, and a red-coated officer of the old French war; [1] and there comes the shop-keeping Pyncheon of a century ago, with the ruffles turned back from his wrists; and there the periwigged and brocaded gentleman of the artist's legend, [2] with the beautiful and pensive Alice, who brings no pride out of her virgin grave. All try the picture frame. What do these ghostly people seek? A mother lifts her child, that his little hands may touch it! There is evidently a mystery about the picture, that perplexes these poor Pyncheons when they ought to be at rest. In a corner, meanwhile, stands the figure of an elderly man, [3] in a leather jerkin and breeches, with a carpenter's rule sticking out of his side pocket; he points his finger at the bearded Colonel and his descendants,

nodding, jeering, mocking, and finally bursting into obstreperous, though inaudible laughter.

Indulging our fancy in this freak, we have partly lost the power of restraint and guidance. We distinguish an unlooked-for figure in our visionary scene. Among those ancestral people there is a young man, dressed in the very fashion of today: he wears a dark frock-coat, almost destitute of skirts, gray pantaloons, gaiter boots of patent leather, and has a finely wrought gold chain across his breast, and a little silver-headed whalebone stick in his hand. Were we to meet this figure at noonday, we should greet him as young Jaffrey Pyncheon, the Judge's only surviving child, who has been spending the last two years in foreign travel. If still in life, how comes his shadow hither? If dead, what a misfortune! The old Pyncheon property, together with the great estate acquired by the young man's father, would devolve on whom? On poor, foolish Clifford, gaunt Hepzibah, and rustic little Phoebe! But another and a greater marvel greets us! Can we believe our eyes? A stout, elderly gentleman has made his appearance; he has an aspect of eminent respectability, wears a black coat and pantaloons, of roomy width, and might be pronounced scrupulously neat in his attire, but for a broad crimson stain across his snowy neckcloth and down his shirt-bosom. Is it the Judge, or no? How can it be Judge Pyncheon? We discern his figure, as plainly as the flickering moonbeams can show us anything, still seated in the oaken chair! Be the apparition whose it may, it advances to the picture, seems to seize the frame, tries to peep behind it, and turns away, with a frown as black as the ancestral one.

The fantastic scene just hinted at must by no means be considered as forming an actual portion of our story. We were betrayed into this brief extravagance by the quiver of the moonbeams; they dance hand-in-hand with shadows, and are reflected in the looking-glass, which, you are aware, is always a kind of window or doorway into the spiritual world. We needed relief, moreover, from our too long and exclusive contemplation of that figure in the chair. This wild wind, too, has tossed our thoughts into strange confusion, but without tearing them away from their one determined center. Yonder leaden Judge sits immovably upon our soul. Will he never stir again? We shall go mad, unless he stirs! You may the better estimate his quietude by the fearlessness of a little mouse, which sits on its hind legs, in a streak of moonlight, close by Judge

[1] the French and Indian War, 1754-1763
[2] Holgrave, the daguerreotype artist, a minor character, tells the story of Gervayse Pyncheon, who in his effort to find the missing deed, allowed his daughter, Alice, to fall under the spell of one of the Maules, who was thought to have inherited the art of witchcraft. Neither then nor later did the Pyncheons discover the secret, but Holgrave, a descendant of the Maules', at the end of the story finds the deed hidden in a recess behind the picture of Colonel Pyncheon.
[3] Matthew Maule's son: he had built the house and hidden away the deed.

Pyncheon's foot, and seems to meditate a journey of exploration over this great black bulk. Ha! what has startled the nimble little mouse? It is the visage of grimalkin, outside of the window, where he appears to have posted himself for a deliberate watch. This grimalkin has a very ugly look. Is it a cat watching for a mouse, or the devil for a human soul? Would we could scare him from the window!

Thank Heaven, the night is well-nigh past! The moonbeams have no longer so silvery a gleam, nor contrast so strongly with the blackness of the shadows among which they fall. They are paler, now; the shadows look gray, not black. The boisterous wind is hushed. What is the hour? Ah! the watch has at last ceased to tick; for the Judge's forgetful fingers neglected to wind it up, as usual, at ten o'clock, being half an hour or so before his ordinary bed-time,—and it has run down, for the first time in five years. But the great world-clock of Time still keeps its beat. The dreary night— for, oh, how dreary seems its haunted waste, behind us!—gives place to a fresh, transparent, cloudless morn. Blessed, blessed radiance! The daybeam—even what little of it finds its way into this always dusky parlor—seems part of the universal benediction, annulling evil, and rendering all goodness possible, and happiness attainable. Will Judge Pyncheon now rise up from his chair? Will he go forth, and receive the early sunbeams on his brow? Will he begin this new day,—which God has smiled upon, and blessed, and given to mankind,— will he begin it with better purposes than the many that have been spent amiss? Or are all the deep-laid schemes of yesterday as stubborn in his heart, and as busy in his brain, as ever?

In this latter case, there is much to do. Will the Judge still insist with Hepzibah on the interview with Clifford? Will he buy a safe, elderly gentleman's horse? Will he persuade the purchaser of the old Pyncheon property to relinquish the bargain in his favor? Will he see his family physician, and obtain a medicine that shall preserve him, to be an honor and blessing to his race, until the utmost term of patriarchal longevity? Will Judge Pyncheon, above all, make due apologies to that company of honorable friends, and satisfy them that his absence from the festive board was unavoidable, and so fully retrieve himself in their good opinion that he shall yet be Governor of Massachusetts? And, all these great purposes accomplished, will he walk the streets again, with that dog-day smile of elaborate benevolence, sultry enough to tempt flies to come and buzz in it? Or will he, after the tomb-like seclusion of the past day and night, go forth a humbled and repentant man, sorrowful, gentle, seeking no profit, shrinking from worldly honor, hardly daring to love God, but bold to love his fellowman, and to do him what good he may? Will he bear about with him,—no odious grin of feigned benignity, insolent in its pretence, and loathsome in its falsehood,—but the tender sadness of a contrite heart, broken, at last, beneath its own weight of sin? For it is our belief, whatever show of honor he may have piled upon it, that there was heavy sin at the base of this man's being.

Rise up, Judge Pyncheon! The morning sunshine glimmers through the foliage, and, beautiful and holy as it is, shuns not to kindle up your face. Rise up, thou subtle, worldly, selfish, iron-hearted hypocrite, and make thy choice whether still to be subtle, worldly, selfish, iron-hearted, and hypocritical, or to tear these sins out of thy nature, though they bring the life-blood with them! The Avenger is upon thee! Rise up, before it be too late!

What! Thou art not stirred by this last appeal? No, not a jot! And there we see a fly,—one of your common house-flies, such as are always buzzing on the window-pane,—which has smelt out Governor Pyncheon, and alights, now on his forehead, now on his chin, and now, Heaven help us! is creeping over the bridge of his nose, towards the would-be chief-magistrate's wide-open eyes! Canst thou not brush the fly away? Art thou too sluggish? Thou man, that hadst so many busy projects, yesterday! Art thou too weak, that wast so powerful? Not brush away a fly? Nay, then, we give thee up!

And hark! the shop-bell rings. After hours like these latter ones, through which we have borne our heavy tale, it is good to be made sensible that there is a living world, and that even this old, lonely mansion retains some manner of connection with it. We breathe more freely, emerging from Judge Pyncheon's presence into the street before the Seven Gables.

1850-51   1851

RALPH WALDO EMERSON
1803-1882

Foremost among American didactic essayists and poets is Emerson, who expresses the awakened spiritual consciousness of his generation in New England. He was born in Boston of ministerial ancestry, graduated at Harvard, 1821, studied theology, and in 1829 was made minister in the pulpit held by Cotton Mather a century before, but which now had become Unitarian. Four years later he left the formal ministry, though he continued occasionally to preach. After a tour abroad he settled at Concord in 1834 where he spent the remainder of his life, and where he died. Collections of his poems were published in 1846, 1865, 1878. Conspicuous among his prose works are: *The American Scholar*, 1837; *Divinity College Address*, 1838; *Essays*, first series, 1841, second series, 1844; *Representative Men*, 1850; *The Conduct of Life*, 1860; *Letters and Social Aims*, 1875.

Two general views are held concerning Emerson's place as a poet. Some feel in him a manifest deficiency in artistic sense. This appears in thin and imperfect rimes, unnatural inversions in word order, lack of melody, inability to use verse forms suitable to his subjects, and general carelessness of artistic technique. Other critics stress his high-spirited presentation of Nature; he held it to be at one and the same time a part of the Divine Idea and a constant object of beauty for everyday men. He is also ranked high for the glow of moral enthusiasm that illuminates his verse, and for the frequent flashes of insight expressed in lines that cannot be forgotten or surpassed.

His prose has many of the qualities of his poetry, good and bad. Like Carlyle, he had faith in the inner vision and consciousness; he believed that the highest truth comes not from reasoning and experience, but from intuition. This belief, one of the tenets of Transcendentalism, caused him to be classed as a New England Transcendentalist, though he was not formally of that cult. His prose, like his poetry, may lack constructive skill, but like his poetry, it is full of a passionate earnestness pointed by wit, wisdom, and paradox. Of our greater nineteenth century writers, no other has produced so vital an effect on the minds and lives of his readers. Lowell speaks of him as a "fecundating" energy.

Biography and criticism: B. Perry, *The Heart of Emerson's Journals*, 1926; Richard Garnett, *Life of Emerson*, (GW) 1888; O. W. Firkins, same, 1915; G. E. Woodberry, *R. W. Emerson*, (EML) 1907; Sanborn (BB); Holmes (AML); Curtis (JL); Crothers (HKA); Sherman; P. E. More, "The Influence of Emerson," *Ind.* 55:1183-8 and (Shel. 1 and 11); Van Wyck Brooks, "Congenial Concord: An Emersonian Episode," *Harper* 153: 767-72, and "Emerson and the Reformers," *Harper* 154:114-19; J. M. Sloan, "Carlyle and Emerson," *Liv. Age* 309:486-9; "Emerson," *Liv. Age* 292: 674-9.

SELF RELIANCE [1]

"Ne te quaesiveris extra." [2]

Man is his own star and the soul that can
Render an honest and a perfect man,
Commands all light, all influence, all fate;
Nothing to him falls early or too late.
Our acts our angels are, or good or ill,
Our fatal shadows that walk by us still.

Epilogue to Beaumont and Fletcher's *Honest Man's Fortunes*.

[1] This essay of Emerson's can be profitably compared with Carlyle's *Sartor Resartus*.
[2] "Seek not beyond thyself."

I read the other day some verses written by an eminent painter which were original and not conventional. The soul always hears an admonition in such lines, let the subject be what it may. The sentiment they instill is of more value than any thought they may contain. To believe your own thought, to believe that what is true for you in your private heart is true for all men,—that is genius. Speak your latent conviction, and it shall be the universal sense; for the inmost in due time becomes the outmost,—and our first thought is rendered back to us by the trumpets of the Last Judgment. Familiar as the voice of the mind is to each, the highest merit we ascribe to Moses, Plato, and Milton is, that they set at naught books and traditions, and spoke not what men but what they thought. A man should learn to detect and watch that gleam of light which flashes across his mind from within, more than the luster of the firmament of bards and sages. Yet he dismisses without notice his thought, because it is his. In every work of genius we recognize our own rejected thoughts: they come back to us with a certain alienated majesty. [3] Great works of art have no more affecting lesson for us than this. They teach us to abide by our spontaneous impression with good-humored inflexibility then most when the whole cry of voices is on the other side. Else, tomorrow a stranger will say with masterly good sense precisely what we have thought and felt all the time, and we shall be forced to take with shame our own opinion from another.

There is a time in every man's education when he arrives at the conviction that envy is ignorance; that imitation is suicide; that he must take himself for better, for worse, as his portion; that though the wide universe is full of good, no kernel of nourishing corn can come to him but through his toil bestowed on that plot of ground which is given to him to till. The power which resides in him is new in nature, and none but he knows what that is which he can do, nor does he know until he has tried. Not for nothing one face, one character, one fact, makes much impression on him, and another none. This sculpture in the memory is not without pre-established harmony. The eye was placed where one ray should fall, that it might testify of that particular ray. We

[3] It is such perfect molding of form to thought that sets apart the maker of literature from the mere maker of phrases. Compare Browning,

"we love
First when we see them painted, things we have passed
Perhaps a hundred times nor cared to see;
. . . Art was given for that;"
"Fra Lippo Lippi," 1, 299.

but half express ourselves, and are ashamed of that divine idea which each of us represents. It may be safely trusted as proportionate and of good issues, [1] so it be faithfully imparted, but God will not have his work made manifest by cowards. A man is relieved and gay when he has put his heart into his work and done his best; but what he has said or done otherwise shall give him no peace. It is a deliverance which does not deliver. In the attempt his genius deserts him; no muse befriends; no invention, no hope.

Trust thyself: every heart vibrates to that iron string. Accept the place the divine providence has found for you, the society of your contemporaries, the connection of events. Great men have always done so, and confided themselves childlike to the genius of their age, betraying their perception that the absolutely trustworthy was seated at their heart, working through their hands, predominating in all their being. And we are now men, and must accept in the highest mind the same transcendent destiny; and not minors and invalids in a protected corner, not cowards fleeing before a revolution, but guides, redeemers, and benefactors, obeying the Almighty effort, and advancing on Chaos and the Dark.

What pretty oracles nature yields us on this text, in the face and behavior of children, babes, and even brutes! That divided and rebel mind, that distrust of a sentiment because our arithmetic has computed the strength and means opposed to our purpose, these have not. Their mind being whole, their eye is as yet unconquered, and when we look in their faces, we are disconcerted. Infancy conforms to nobody; all conform to it, so that one babe commonly makes four or five out of the adults who prattle and play to it. So God has armed youth and puberty and manhood no less with its own piquancy and charm, and made it enviable and gracious and its claims not to be put by, if it will stand by itself. Do not think the youth has no force, because he cannot speak to you and me. Hark! in the next room his voice is sufficiently clear and emphatic. It seems he knows how to speak to his contemporaries. Bashful or bold, then, he will know how to make us seniors very unnecessary.

The nonchalance of boys who are sure of a dinner, and would disdain as much as a lord to do or say aught to conciliate one, is the healthy attitude of human nature. A boy is in the parlor what the pit is in the playhouse;

[1] well proportioned to our needs or abilities and fitted to bring forth good

independent, irresponsible, looking out from his corner on such people and facts as pass by, he tries and sentences them on their merits, in the swift, summary way of boys, as good, bad, interesting, silly, eloquent, troublesome. He cumbers himself never about consequences, about interests; he gives an independent, genuine verdict. You must court him: he does not court you. But the man is as it were clapped into jail by his consciousness. As soon as he has once acted or spoken with *éclat* he is a committed person, watched by the sympathy or the hatred of hundreds, whose affections must now enter into his account. There is no Lethe [2] for this. Ah, that he could pass again into his neutrality! Who can thus avoid all pledges and having observed, observe again from the same unaffected, unbiased, unbribable, unaffrighted innocence, must always be formidable. He would utter opinions on all passing affairs, which being seen to be not private, but necessary, would sink like darts into the ear of men and put them in fear.

These are the voices which we hear in solitude, but they grow faint and inaudible as we enter into the world. Society everywhere is in conspiracy against the manhood of every one of its members. Society is a joint-stock company, in which the members agree, for the better securing of his bread to each shareholder, to surrender the liberty and culture of the eater. The virtue in most request is conformity. Self-reliance is its aversion. It loves not realities and creators, but names and customs.

Whoso would be a man, must be a nonconformist. He who would gather immortal palms must not be hindered by the name of goodness, but must explore if it be goodness. Nothing is at last sacred but the integrity of your own mind. Absolve you to yourself, and you shall have the suffrage of the world. I remember an answer which when quite young I was prompted to make to a valued adviser, who was wont to importune me with the dear old doctrines of the church. On my saying, What have I to do with the sacredness of traditions, if I live wholly from within? my friend suggested,—"But these impulses may be from below, not from above." I replied, "They do not seem to me to be such; but if I am the Devil's child, I will live then from the Devil." No law can be sacred to me but that of my nature. Good and bad are but names very readily transferable to that or this; the only right is what is after my constitution, the only

[2] the river of forgetfulness in Hades

wrong what is against it. A man is to carry himself in the presence of all opposition, as if every thing were titular and ephemeral but he. I am ashamed to think how easily we capitulate to badges and names, to large societies and dead institutions. Every decent and well-spoken individual affects and sways me more than is right. I ought to go upright and vital, and speak the rude truth in all ways. If malice and vanity wear the coat of philanthropy, shall that pass? If an angry bigot assumes this bountiful cause of Abolition, and comes to me with his last news from Barbadoes,[1] why should I not say to him, 'Go love thy infant; love thy wood-chopper; be good-natured and modest; have that grace; and never varnish your hard, uncharitable ambition with this incredible tenderness for black folk a thousand miles off. Thy love afar is spite at home.' Rough and graceless would be such greeting, but truth is handsomer than the affectation of love. Your goodness must have some edge to it,—else it is none. The doctrine of hatred must be preached as the counteraction of the doctrine of love when that pules and whines. I shun father and mother and wife and brother, when my genius calls me. I would write on the lintels of the door-post, *Whim.* I hope it is somewhat better than whim at last, but we cannot spend the day in explanation. Expect me not to show cause why I seek or why I exclude company. Then, again, do not tell me, as a good man did today, of my obligation to put all poor men in good situations. Are they *my* poor? I tell thee, thou foolish philanthropist, that I grudge the dollar, the dime, the cent, I give to such men as do not belong to me and to whom I do not belong. There is a class of persons to whom by all spiritual affinity I am bought and sold; for them I will go to prison, if need be; but your miscellaneous popular charities; the education at college of fools; the building of meeting-houses to the vain end to which many now stand; alms to sots; and the thousand-fold Relief Societies;—though I confess with shame I sometimes succumb and give the dollar, it is a wicked dollar which by and by I shall have the manhood to withhold.

Virtues are, in the popular estimate, rather the exception than the rule. There is the man *and* his virtues. Men do what is called a good action, as some piece of courage or charity, much as they would pay a fine in expiation of daily non-appearance on parade. Their works are done as an apology or extenuation of

their living in the world,—as invalids and the insane pay a high board. Their virtues are penances. I do not wish to expiate, but to live. My life is for itself and not for a spectacle. I much prefer that it should be of a lower strain, so it be genuine and equal, than that it should be glittering and unsteady. I wish it to be sound and sweet, and not to need diet and bleeding. I ask primary evidence that you are a man, and refuse this appeal from the man to his actions. I know that for myself it makes no difference whether I do or forbear those actions which are reckoned excellent. I cannot consent to pay for a privilege where I have intrinsic right. Few and mean as my gifts may be, I actually am, and do not need for my own assurance or the assurance of my fellows any secondary testimony.

What I must do is all that concerns me, not what the people think. This rule, equally arduous in actual and in intellectual life, may serve for the whole distinction between greatness and meanness. It is the harder because you will always find those who think they know what is your duty better than you know it. It is easy in the world to live after the world's opinion; it is easy in solitude to live after our own; but the great man is he who in the midst of the crowd keeps with perfect sweetness the independence of solitude.[2]

The objection to conforming to usages that have become dead to you is that it scatters your force. It loses your time and blurs the impression of your character. If you maintain a dead church, contribute to a dead Bible-society, vote with a great party either for the government or against it, spread your table like base housekeepers,—under all these screens I have difficulty to detect the precise man you are. And of course so much force is withdrawn from your proper life. But do your work,[3] and I shall know you. Do your work, and you shall reinforce yourself. A man must consider what a blind-man's-buff is this game of conformity. If I know your sect I anticipate your argument. I hear a preacher announce for his text and topic the expediency of one of the institutions of his church. Do I not know beforehand that not possibly can he say a new and spontaneous word? Do I not know that with all this ostentation of examining the grounds of the institution he will do no such

---

[1] One of the British West India Islands; slavery was abolished there in 1834.

[2] Emerson shaped his own life by this bracing maxim.

[3] Cf. Carlyle: "Cast forth thy Act, thy Word, into the ever-living, ever-working Universe: it is a seed grain that cannot die; unnoticed today (says one), it will be found flourishing as a Banyan-grove (perhaps, alas, as a Hemlock-forest!) after a thousand years." *Sartor Resartus*, Bk. i, Ch. 5.

thing? Do I not know that he is pledged to himself not to look but at one side, the permitted side, not as a man, but as a parish minister? He is a retained attorney, and these airs of the bench are the emptiest affectation. Well, most men have bound their eyes with one or another handkerchief, and attached themselves to some one of these communities of opinion. This conformity makes them not false in a few particulars, authors of a few lies, but false in all particulars. Their every truth is not quite true. Their two is not the real two, their four not the real four; so that every word they say chagrins us and we know not where to begin to set them right. Meantime nature is not slow to equip us in the prison-uniform of the party to which we adhere. We come to wear one cut of face and figure, and acquire by degrees the gentlest asinine expression. There is a mortifying experience in particular, which does not fail to wreak itself also in the general history; I mean "the foolish face of praise," the forced smile which we put on in company where we do not feel at ease in answer to conversation which does not interest us. The muscles, not spontaneously moved, but moved by a low usurping willfulness, grow tight about the outline of the face with the most disagreeable sensation.

For nonconformity the world whips you with its displeasure. And therefore a man must know how to estimate a sour face. The bystanders look askance on him in the public street or in the friend's parlor. If this aversation [1] had its origin in contempt and resistance like his own he might well go home with a sad countenance; but the sour faces of the multitude, like their sweet faces, have no deep cause, but are put on and off as the wind blows and a newspaper directs. Yet is the discontent of the multitude more formidable than that of the senate and the college. It is easy enough for a firm man who knows the world to brook the rage of the cultivated classes. Their rage is decorous and prudent, for they are timid, as being very vulnerable themselves. But when to their feminine rage the indignation of the people is added, when the ignorant and the poor are aroused, when the unintelligent brute force that lies at the bottom of society is made to growl and mow, it needs the habit of magnanimity and religion to treat it godlike as a trifle of no concernment.

The other terror that scares us from selftrust is our consistency; a reverence for our past act or word because the eyes of others

[1] hatred, aversion

have no other data for computing our orbit than our past acts, and we are loath to disappoint them.

But why should you keep your head over your shoulder? Why drag about this corpse of your memory, lest you contradict somewhat you have stated in this or that public place? Suppose you should contradict yourself; what then? It seems to be a rule of wisdom never to rely on your memory alone, scarcely even in acts of pure memory, but to bring the past for judgment into the thousand-eyed present, and live ever in a new day. In your metaphysics you have denied personality to the Deity: yet when the devout motions of the soul come, yield to them heart and life, though they should clothe God with shape and color. Leave your theory, as Joseph [2] his coat in the hand of the harlot, and flee.

A foolish consistency is the hobgoblin of little minds, adored by little statesmen and philosophers and divines. With consistency a great soul has simply nothing to do. He may as well concern himself with his shadow on the wall. Speak what you think now in hard words, and tomorrow speak what tomorrow thinks in hard words again, though it contradict every thing you said today.—"Ah, so you shall be sure to be misunderstood."—Misunderstood. Is it so bad, then, to be misunderstood? Pythagoras was misunderstood, and Socrates and Jesus, and Luther and Copernicus, and Galileo, and Newton, and every pure and wise spirit that ever took flesh. [3] To be great is to be misunderstood.

I suppose no man can violate his nature. All the sallies of his will are rounded in by the law of his being, as the inequalities of Andes and Himmaleh are insignificant in the curve of the sphere. Nor does it matter how you gauge and try him. A character is like an acrostic or Alexandrian stanza, [4]—read it forward, backward, or across, it still spells the same thing. In this pleasing, contrite woodlife which God allows me, let me record day by day my honest thought without prospect or

[2] *Genesis* xxxix
[3] Pythagoras, a Greek philosopher, was banished; Socrates because of his advanced views was given poison; Luther was imprisoned; Copernicus, who first proved that the sun, not the earth, is the center of the solar system, was doubted; Galileo, for his astronomical views, was condemned, and by being menaced with the torture of the Inquisition was made to abjure the Copernican theory; Sir Isaac Newton, who discovered the law of gravitation, waited years for recognition; all these like Christ dared to face disbelief.
[4] A mistake; Emerson means a palindrome, which is the same read backwards or forwards: for example, "Madam, I'm Adam."

retrospect, and, I cannot doubt, it will be found symmetrical, though I mean it not and see it not. My book should smell of pines and resound with the hum of insects. The swallow over my window should interweave that thread or straw he carries in his bill into my web also. We pass for what we are. Character teaches above our wills. Men imagine that they communicate their virtue or vice only by overt actions, and do not see that virtue or vice emit a breath every moment.

There will be an agreement in whatever variety of actions, so they be each honest and natural in their hour. For of one will, the actions will be harmonious, however unlike they seem. These varieties are lost sight of at a little distance, at a little height of thought. One tendency unites them all. The voyage of the best ship is a zigzag line of a hundred tacks. See the line from a sufficient distance, and it straightens itself to the average tendency. Your genuine action will explain itself and will explain your other genuine actions. Your conformity explains nothing. Act singly, and what you have already done singly will justify you now. Greatness appeals to the future. If I can be firm enough today to do right, and scorn eyes, I must have done so much right before as to defend me now. Be it how it will, do right now. Always scorn appearances, and you always may. The force of character is cumulative. All the foregone days of virtue work their health into this. What makes the majesty of the heroes of the senate and the field, which so fills the imagination? The consciousness of a train of great days and victories behind. They shed an united light on the advancing actor. He is attended as by a visible escort of angels. That is it which throws thunder into Chatham's [1] voice, and dignity into Washington's port, [2] and America into Adams's [3] eye. Honor is venerable to us because it is no ephemeris. It is always ancient virtue. We worship it today because it is not of today. We love it and pay it homage, because it is not a trap for our love and homage, but is self-dependent, self-derived, and therefore of an old immaculate pedigree, even if shown in a young person.

I hope in these days we have heard the last of conformity and consistency. Let the words be gazetted and ridiculous henceforward. Instead of the gong for dinner, let us hear a whistle from the Spartan fife. Let us never bow and apologize more. A great man is coming to eat at my house. I do not wish to please him; I wish that he should wish to please me. I will stand here for humanity, and though I would make it kind, I would make it true. Let us affront and reprimand the smooth mediocrity and squalid contentment of the times, and hurl in the face of custom and trade and office, the fact which is the upshot of all history, that there is a great responsible Thinker and Actor working wherever a man works; that a true man belongs to no other time or place, but is the center of things. Where he is, there is nature. He measures you and all men and all events. Ordinarily, everybody in society reminds us of somewhat else, or of some other person. Character, reality, reminds you of nothing else; it takes place of the whole creation. The man must be so much that he must make all circumstances indifferent. Every true man is a cause, a country, and an age; requires infinite spaces and numbers and time fully to accomplish his design;—and posterity seem to follow his steps as a train of clients. A man Caesar is born, and for ages after we have a Roman Empire. Christ is born, and millions of minds so grow and cleave to his genius that he is confounded with virtue and the possible of man. An institution is the lengthened shadow of one man; as, Monachism, of the Hermit Anthony; the Reformation, of Luther; Quakerism, of Fox; Methodism, of Wesley; Abolition, of Clarkson. Scipio, [4] Milton called "the height of Rome"; and all history resolves itself very easily into the biography of a few stout and earnest persons. [5]

Let a man then know his worth, and keep things under his feet. [6] Let him not peep or steal, or skulk up and down with the air of a charity-boy, a bastard, or an interloper in the world which exists for him. But the man in

---

[1] It is to the bold, imaginative energy of William Pitt, a brilliant orator, one of the greatest English prime ministers, that England owes her largest accessions in empire.

[2] bearing

[3] Samuel Adams, one of the earliest and boldest leaders of the American Revolution

[4] Saint Anthony, or Anthony the Great, an Egyptian of the third century A.D., the founder of asceticism; George Fox, 1624-1691, founder of the Society of Friends; John Wesley, 1703-1791, one of the first "Methodists," so called from their strict methods of living; Thomas Clarkson, 1760-1846, worker for the abolition of slavery; Publius Cornelius Scipio Africanus Major, the great Roman general who defeated Hannibal in 202 B.C.

[5] Cf. Carlyle: "Universal history, the history of what man has accomplished in this world, is at bottom the history of the great men who have worked here." "In all epochs of the world's history we shall find the great man to have been the indispensable savior of his epoch: the lightning without which the fuel never would have burnt." *Heroes and Hero Worship*

[6] Cf. the old lama of Thibet, in Kipling's *Kim*, whose aim was to get free from the Wheel of Things, upon which most men are bound.

the street, finding no worth in himself which corresponds to the force which built a tower or sculptured a marble god, feels poor when he looks on these. To him a palace, a statue, or a costly book have an alien and forbidding air, much like a gay equipage, and seem to say like that, "Who are you, Sir?" Yet they all are his, suitors for his notice, petitioners to his faculties that they will come out and take possession. The picture waits for my verdict: it is not to command me, but I am to settle its claims to praise. That popular fable of the sot who was picked up dead drunk in the street, carried to the duke's house, washed and dressed and laid in the duke's bed, [1] and, on his waking, treated with all obsequious ceremony like the duke, and assured that he had been insane, owes its popularity to the fact that it symbolizes so well the state of man, who is in the world a sort of sot, but now and then wakes up, exercises his reason, and finds himself a true prince.

Our reading is mendicant and sycophantic. In history our imagination plays us false. Kingdom and lordship, power and estate, are a gaudier vocabulary than private John and Edward in a small house and common day's work; but the things of life are the same to both; the sum total of both is the same. Why all this deference to Alfred and Scanderbeg and Gustavus? [2] Suppose they were virtuous; did they wear out virtue? As great a stake depends on your private act today as followed their public and renowned steps. When private men shall act with original views, the luster will be transferred from the actions of kings to those of gentlemen.

The world has been instructed by its kings, who have so magnetized the eyes of nations. It has been taught by this colossal symbol the mutual reverence that is due from man to man. The joyful loyalty with which men have everywhere suffered the king, the noble, or the great proprietor to walk among them by a law of his own, make his own scale of men and things and reverse theirs, pay for benefits not with money but with honor, and represent the law in his person, was the hieroglyphic by which they obscurely signified their consciousness of their own right and comeliness, the right of every man.

[1] The oldest version is probably "The Story of The Sleeper Awakened" in *The Arabian Nights*. See also *The Taming of the Shrew*, induction.
[2] Alfred the Great was King of England, 871-901; Scanderbeg Bey, in the 15th century, bravely defended his principality of Albania against the encroachments of Turkey; Gustavus Adolphus, King of Sweden, 1611-32, was a great Protestant leader in the Thirty Years' War.

The magnetism which all original action exerts is explained when we inquire the reason of self-trust. Who is the Trustee? What is the aboriginal Self, on which a universal reliance may be grounded? What is the nature and power of that science-baffling star, without parallax, [3] without calculable elements, which shoots a ray of beauty even into trivial and impure actions, if the least mark of independence appear? The inquiry leads us to that source, at once the essence of genius, of virtue, and of life, which we call Spontaneity or Instinct. We denote this primary wisdom as Intuition, whilst all later teachings are tuitions. In that deep force, the last fact behind which analysis cannot go, all things find their common origin. For the sense of being which in calm hours rises, we know not how, in the soul, is not diverse from things, from space, from light, from time, from man, but one with them, and proceeds obviously from the same source whence their life and being also proceeds. We first share the life by which things exist, and afterwards see them as appearances in nature, and forget that we have shared their cause. Here is the fountain of action and of thought. Here are the lungs of that inspiration which giveth man wisdom, and which cannot be denied without impiety and atheism. We lie in the lap of immense intelligence, which makes us receivers of its truth and organs of its activity. When we discern justice, when we discern truth we do nothing of ourselves, but allow a passage to its beams. If we ask whence this comes, if we seek to pry into the soul that causes, all philosophy is at fault. Its presence or its absence is all we can affirm. Every man discriminates between the voluntary acts of his mind, and his involuntary perceptions, and knows that to his involuntary perceptions a perfect faith is due. He may err in the expression of them, but he knows that these things are so, like day and night, not to be disputed. My wilful actions and acquisitions are but roving;—the idlest reverie, the faintest native emotion, command my curiosity and respect. Thoughtless people contradict as readily the statement of perceptions as of opinions, or rather much more readily; for, they do not distinguish between perception and notion. They fancy that I choose to see this or that thing. But perception is not whimsical, but fatal. If I see a trait, my children will see it after me, and in course of time all mankind,—

[3] without apparent displacement as seen from two different stations and hence too far distant to be measured by ordinary means

although it may chance that no one has seen it before me. For my perception of it is as much a fact as the sun.

The relations of the soul to the divine spirit are so pure that it is profane to seek to interpose helps. It must be that when God speaketh he should communicate, not one thing, but all things; should fill the world with his voice; should scatter forth light, nature, time, souls, from the center of the present thought; and new date and new create the whole. Whenever a mind is simple and receives a divine wisdom, old things pass away,—means, teachers, texts, temples fall; it lives now, and absorbs past and future into the present hour. All things are made sacred by relation to it,—one as much as another. All things are dissolved to their center by their cause, and in the universal miracle petty and particular miracles disappear. If, therefore, a man claims to know and speak of God and carries you backward to the phraseology of some old moldered nation in another country, in another world, believe him not. Is the acorn better than the oak which is its fulness and completion? Is the parent better than the child into whom he has cast his ripened being? Whence then this worship of the past? The centuries are conspirators against the sanity and authority of the soul. Time and space are but physiological colors which the eye makes, but the soul is light; where it is, is day; where it was, is night; and history is an impertinence and an injury if it be any thing more than a cheerful apologue or parable of my being and becoming. [1]

Man is timid and apologetic; he is no longer upright; he dares not say 'I think,' 'I am,' but quotes some saint or sage. He is ashamed before the blade of grass or the blowing rose. These roses under my window make no reference to former roses or to better ones; they are for what they are; they exist with God today. There is no time to them. There is simply the rose; it is perfect in every moment of its existence. Before a leaf-bud has burst, its whole life acts; in the full-blown flower there is no more; in the leafless root there is no less. Its nature is satisfied and it satisfies nature in all moments alike. But man postpones or remembers; he does not live in the present, but with reverted eye laments the past, or, heedless of the riches that surround him, stands on tiptoe to foresee the future. He

cannot be happy and strong until he too lives with nature in the present, above time.

This should be plain enough. Yet see what strong intellects dare not yet hear God himself unless he speaks the phraseology of I know not what David, or Jeremiah, or Paul. We shall not always set so great a price on a few texts, on a few lives. We are like children who repeat by rote the sentences of grandames and tutors, and, as they grow older, of the men of talents and character they chance to see,—painfully recollecting the exact words they spoke; afterwards, when they come into the point of view which those had who uttered these sayings, they understand them and are willing to let the words go; for at any time they can use words as good when occasion comes. If we live truly, we shall see truly. It is as easy for the strong man to be strong, as it is for the weak to be weak. When we have new perception, we shall gladly disburden the memory of its hoarded treasures as old rubbish. When a man lives with God, his voice shall be as sweet as the murmur of the brook and the rustle of the corn.

And now at last the highest truth on this subject remains unsaid; probably cannot be said; for all that we say is the far-off remembering of the intuition. That thought, by what I can now nearest approach to say it, is this. When good is near you, when you have life in yourself, it is not by any known or accustomed way; you shall not discern the footprints of any other; you shall not see the face of man; you shall not hear any name;—the way, the thought, the good, shall be wholly strange and new. It shall exclude example and experience. You take the way from man, not to man. All persons that ever existed are its forgotten ministers. Fear and hope are alike beneath it. There is somewhat low even in hope. In the hour of vision there is nothing that can be called gratitude, nor properly joy. The soul raised over passion beholds identity and eternal causation, perceives the self-existence of Truth and Right, and calms itself with knowing that all things go well. Vast spaces of nature, the Atlantic Ocean, the South Sea, —long intervals of time, years, centuries,—are of no account. This which I think and feel underlay every former state of life and circumstances, as it does underlie my present, and what is called life, and what is called death.

Life only avails, not the having lived. Power ceases in the instant of repose; it resides in the moment of transition from a past to a new state, in the shooting of the gulf, in the darting

[1] Cf. Carlyle: "Think well, thou too wilt find that Space is but a mode of our human sense, so likewise Time; there *is* no Space and no Time: WE are— we know not what;—light—sparkles floating in the aether of Deity!" *Sartor Resartus*, Bk. i, Ch. 8.

to an aim. This one fact the world hates, that the soul *becomes;* for that forever degrades the past, turns all riches to poverty, all reputation to a shame, confounds the saint with the rogue, shoves Jesus and Judas [1] equally aside. Why then do we prate of self-reliance? Inasmuch as the soul is present, there will be power not confident but agent. [2] To talk of reliance is a poor external way of speaking. Speak rather of that which relies, because it works and is. Who has more obedience than I masters me, though he should not raise his finger. Round him I must revolve by the gravitation of spirits. We fancy it rhetoric when we speak of eminent virtue. We do not yet see that virtue is Height and that a man or a company of men, plastic and permeable to principles, by the law of nature must overpower and ride all cities, nations, kings, rich men, poets, who are not.

This is the ultimate fact which we so quickly reach on this, as on every topic, the resolution of all into the ever-blessed ONE. Self-existence is the attribute of the Supreme Cause, and it constitutes the measure of good by the degree in which it enters into all lower forms. All things real are so by so much virtue as they contain. Commerce, husbandry, hunting, whaling, war, eloquence, personal weight, are somewhat and engage my respect as examples of its presence and impure action. I see the same law working in nature for conservation and growth. Power is in nature the essential measure of right. Nature suffers nothing to remain in her kingdoms which cannot help itself. The genesis and maturation of a plant, its poise and orbit, the bended tree recovering itself from the wind, the vital resources of every animal and vegetable, are strong demonstrations of the self-sufficing, and therefore self-relying soul.

Thus all concentrates: let us not rove; let us sit at home with the cause. Let us stun and astonish the intruding rabble of men and books and institutions by a simple declaration of the divine fact. Bid the invaders take the shoes from off their feet, [3] for God is here within. Let our simplicity judge them, and our docility to our own law demonstrate the poverty of nature and fortune beside our native riches.

But now we are a mob. Man does not stand in awe of man, nor is the soul admonished to stay at home, to put itself in communication with the internal ocean, but it goes abroad to beg a cup of water of the urns of other men.

We must go alone. Isolation must precede true society. I like the silent church before the service begins, better than any preaching. How far off, how cool, how chaste the persons look, begirt each one with a precinct or sanctuary! So let us always sit. Why should we assume the faults of our friend, or wife, or father, or child, because they sit around our hearth, or are said to have the same blood? All men have my blood and I have all men's. Not for that will I adopt their petulance or folly, even to the extent of being ashamed of it. But your isolation must not be mechanical, but spiritual, that is, must be elevation. At times the whole world seems to be in conspiracy to importune you with emphatic trifles. Friend, client, child, sickness, fear, want, charity, all knock at once at thy closet door and say,—"Come out unto us." But keep thy state; come not into their confusion. The power men possess to annoy me I give them by a weak curiosity. No man can come near me but through my act. "What we love that we have, but by desire we bereave ourselves of the love."

If we cannot at once rise to the sanctities of obedience and faith, let us at least resist our temptations; let us enter into the state of war, and wake Thor and Woden, [4] courage and constancy, in our Saxon breasts. This is to be done in our smooth times by speaking the truth. Check this lying hospitality and lying affection. Live no longer to [5] the expectation of these deceived and deceiving people with whom we converse. Say to them, O father, O mother, O wife, O brother, O friend, I have lived with you after appearances hitherto. Henceforward I am the truth's. Be it known unto you that henceforward I obey no law less than the eternal law. I will have no covenants but proximities. [6] I shall endeavor to nourish my parents, to support my family, to be the chaste husband of one wife,—but these relations I must fill after a new and unprecedented way. I appeal from your customs. I must be myself. I cannot break myself any longer for you, or you. If you can love me for what I am, we shall be the happier. If you cannot, I will still seek to deserve that you should. I will not hide my tastes or aversions. I will so trust that what is deep is holy, that I will do strongly before the sun and moon whatever inly rejoices me and the heart appoints.

---

[1] i. e., the highest and the lowest
[2] active   [3] *Exodus* iii, 5

[4] In Teutonic mythology Thor is the god of thunder and Woden or Odin the supreme father.
[5] according to
[6] I will make no promises for the future, but will do the nearest duty only.

If you are noble, I will love you; if you are not, I will not hurt you and myself by hypocritical attentions. If you are true, but not in the same truth with me, cleave to your companions; I will seek my own. I do this not selfishly but humbly and truly. It is alike your interest, and mine, and all men's, however long we have dwelt in lies, to live in truth. Does this sound harsh today? You will soon love what is dictated by your nature as well as mine, and if we follow the truth it will bring us out safe at last.—But so may you give these friends pain. Yes, but I cannot sell my liberty and my power, to save their sensibility. Besides, all persons have their moments of reason, when they look out into the region of absolute truth; then will they justify me and do the same thing.

The populace think that your rejection of popular standards is a rejection of all standard, and mere antinomianism; [1] and the bold sensualist will use the name of philosophy to gild his crimes. But the law of consciousness abides. There are two confessionals, in one or the other of which we must be shriven. You may fulfil your round of duties by clearing yourself in the *direct,* or in the *reflex* way. Consider whether you have satisfied your relations to father, mother, cousin, neighbor, town, cat, and dog; whether any of these can upbraid you. But I may also neglect this reflex standard and absolve me to myself. I have my own stern claims and perfect circle. It denies the name of duty to many offices that are called duties. But if I can discharge its debts it enables me to dispense with the popular code. If any one imagines that this law is lax, let him keep its commandment one day.

And truly it demands something godlike in him who has cast off the common motives of humanity and has ventured to trust himself for a taskmaster. High be his heart, faithful his will, clear his sight, that he may in good earnest be doctrine, society, law, to himself, that a simple purpose may be to him as strong as iron necessity is to others!

If any man consider the present aspects of what is called by distinction *society,* he will see the need of these ethics. The sinew and heart of man seem to be drawn out, and we are become timorous, desponding whimperers. We are afraid of truth, afraid of fortune, afraid of death, and afraid of each other. Our age yields no great and perfect persons. We want

men and women who shall renovate life and our social state, but we see that most natures are insolvent, cannot satisfy their own wants, have an ambition out of all proportion to their practical force and do lean and beg day and night continually. Our housekeeping is mendicant, our arts, our occupations, our marriages, our religion, we have not chosen, but society has chosen for us. We are parlor soldiers. We shun the rugged battle of fate, where strength is born.

If our young men miscarry in their first enterprises they lose all heart. If the young merchant fails, men say he is *ruined.* If the finest genius studies at one of our colleges, and is not installed in an office within one year afterwards in the cities or suburbs of Boston or New York, it seems to his friends and to himself that he is right in being disheartened and in complaining the rest of his life. A sturdy lad from New Hampshire or Vermont, who in turn tries all the professions, who *teams it, farms it, peddles,* keeps a school, preaches, edits a newspaper, goes to Congress, buys a township, and so forth, in successive years, and always like a cat falls on his feet, is worth a hundred of these city dolls. He walks abreast with his days and feels no shame in not 'studying a profession,' for he does not postpone his life, but lives already. He has not one chance, but a hundred chances. Let a Stoic [2] open the resources of man and tell men they are not leaning willows, but can and must detach themselves; that with the exercise of self-trust, new powers shall appear; that a man is the word [3] made flesh, born to shed healing to the nations, that he should be ashamed of our compassion, and that the moment he acts from himself, tossing the laws, the books, idolatries, and customs out of the window, we pity him no more but thank and revere him,—and that teacher shall restore the life of man to splendor and make his name dear to all history.

It is easy to see that a greater self-reliance must work a revolution in all the offices and relations of men; in their religion; in their education; in their pursuits; their modes of living; their association; in their property; in their speculative views.

1. In what prayers do men allow [4] themselves! That which they call a holy office [5] is not so much as brave and manly. Prayer

---

[1] opposition to law; from the Greek ἀντί, against, and νόμος, law

[2] The Greek Stoics suppressed outward emotion of joy or grief, and held that virtue, not happiness, is the aim of life.
[3] The spirit of God; see *John* i, 1.
[4] justify, sanction   [5] an act of worship

looks abroad and asks for some foreign addition to come through some foreign virtue, and loses itself in endless mazes of natural and supernatural, and mediatorial and miraculous. Prayer that craves a particular commodity,—anything less than all good,—is vicious. Prayer is the contemplation of the facts of life from the highest point of view. It is the soliloquy of a beholding and jubilant soul. It is the spirit of God pronouncing his works good. But prayer as a means to effect a private end is theft and meanness. It supposes dualism and not unity in nature and consciousness. As soon as the man is at one with God, he will not beg. He will then see prayer in all action. The prayer of the farmer kneeling in his field to weed it, the prayer of the rower kneeling with the stroke of his oar, are true prayers heard throughout nature, though for cheap ends. Caratach, in Fletcher's *Bonduca,* [1] when admonished to inquire the mind of the god Audate, replies,—

> His hidden meaning lies in our endeavors;
> Our valors are our best gods.

Another sort of false prayers are our regrets. Discontent is the want of self-reliance: it is infirmity of will. Regret calamities if you can thereby help the sufferer; if not, attend your own work and already the evil begins to be repaired. Our sympathy is just as base. We come to them who weep foolishly and sit down and cry for company, instead of imparting to them truth and health in rough electric shocks, putting them once more in communication with their own reason. The secret of fortune is joy in our hands. Welcome evermore to gods and men is the self-helping man. For him all doors are flung wide: him all tongues greet, all honors crown, all eyes follow with desire. Our love goes out to him and embraces him because he did not need it. We solicitously and apologetically caress and celebrate him because he held on his way and scorned our disapprobation. The gods love him because men hated him. "To the persevering mortal," said Zoroaster, [2] "the blessed Immortals are swift."

As men's prayers are a disease of the will, so are their creeds a disease of the intellect. They say with those foolish Israelites, "Let not God speak to us, lest we die. Speak thou, speak any man with us, and we will obey."

Everywhere I am hindered of meeting God in my brother, because he has shut his own temple doors, and recites fables merely of his brother's, or his brother's brother's God. Every new mind is a new classification. If it prove a mind of uncommon activity and power, a Locke, a Lavoisier, a Hutton, a Bentham, a Fourier, [3] it imposes its classification on other men, and lo! a new system. In proportion to the depth of the thought, and so to the number of the objects it touches and brings within reach of the pupil, is his complacency. But chiefly is this apparent in creeds and churches, which are also classifications of some powerful mind acting on the great elemental thought of duty and man's relation to the Highest. Such is Calvinism, Quakerism, Swedenborgism. The pupil takes the same delight in subordinating every thing to the new terminology as a girl does who has just learned botany in seeing a new earth and new seasons thereby. It will happen for a time that the pupil will find his intellectual power has grown by the study of his master's mind. But in all unbalanced minds the classification is idolized, passes for the end and not for a speedily exhaustible means, so that the walls of the system blend to their eye in the remote horizon with the walls of the universe; the luminaries of heaven seem to them hung on the arch their master built. They cannot imagine how you aliens have any right to see,—how you can see; "It must be somehow that you stole the light from us." They do not yet perceive that light, unsystematic, indomitable, will break into any cabin, even into theirs. Let them chirp awhile and call it their own. If they are honest and do well, presently their neat new pinfold [4] will be too strait and low, will crack, will lean, will rot and vanish, and the immortal light, all young and joyful, million-orbed, million-colored, will beam over the universe as on the first morning.

2. It is for want of self-culture that the superstition of Traveling, whose idols are Italy, England, Egypt, retains its fascination for all educated Americans. They who made England, Italy, or Greece venerable in the imagination did so by sticking fast where they were, like an axis of the earth. In manly hours we feel that duty is our place. The soul is no traveler; the wise man stays at home, and when his necessities, his duties, on any occasion call him from his house, or into foreign lands, he is

---

[1] John Fletcher, the Elizabethan dramatist, used the older names for Caractacus, the leader, and for Boadicea, the queen, of the Britons about 50 A.D. Audate was the Druid god of war.
[2] Zarathustra, the reputed founder of the ancient Persian religion

[3] Locke and Bentham were English philosophers; Lavoisier was a French chemist, the chief founder of modern chemistry; Fourier was a French socialist; Hutton was a celebrated Scotch geologist.
[4] a pound or enclosure for beasts

at home still, and shall make men sensible by the expression of his countenance that he goes the missionary of wisdom and virtue, and visits cities and men like a sovereign and not like an interloper or a valet.

I have no churlish objection to the circumnavigation of the globe, for the purposes of art, of study, and benevolence, so that the man is first domesticated, or does not go abroad with the hope of finding somewhat greater than he knows. He who travels to be amused, or to get somewhat which he does not carry, travels away from himself, and grows old, even in youth among old things. In Thebes, in Palmyra, his will and mind have become old and dilapidated as they. He carries ruins to ruins.

Traveling is a fool's paradise. Our first journeys discover to us the indifference of places. At home I dream that at Naples, at Rome, I can be intoxicated with beauty and lose my sadness. I pack my trunk, embrace my friends, embark on the sea, and at last wake up in Naples, and there beside me is the stern fact, the sad self, unrelenting, identical, that I fled from. I seek the Vatican [1] and the palaces. I affect to be intoxicated with sights and suggestions, but I am not intoxicated. My giant goes with me wherever I go.

3. But the rage of traveling is a symptom of a deeper unsoundness affecting the whole intellectual action. The intellect is vagabond, and our system of education fosters restlessness. Our minds travel when our bodies are forced to stay at home. We imitate; and what is imitation but the traveling of the mind? Our houses are built with foreign taste; our shelves are garnished with foreign ornaments; our opinions, our tastes, our faculties, lean, and follow the Past and the Distant. The soul created the arts wherever they have flourished. It was in his own mind that the artist sought his model. It was an application of his own thought to the thing to be done and the conditions to be observed. And why need we copy the Doric or the Gothic [2] model? Beauty, convenience, grandeur of thought, and quaint expression are as near to us as to any, and if the American artist will study with hope and love the precise thing to be done by him, considering the climate, the soil, the length of the day, the wants of the people, the habit and form of the government, he will create a house in which all these will find themselves fitted, and taste and sentiment will be satisfied also.

Insist on yourself; never imitate. Your own gift you can present every moment with the cumulative force of a whole life's cultivation; but of the adopted talent of another you have only an extemporaneous, half possession. That which each can do best, none but his Maker can teach him. No man yet knows what it is, nor can, till that person has exhibited it. Where is the master who could have taught Shakespeare? Where is the master who could have instructed Franklin, or Washington, or Bacon, or Newton? Every great man is a unique. The Scipionism [3] of Scipio is precisely that part he could not borrow. Shakespeare will never be made by the study of Shakespeare. Do that which is assigned you and you cannot hope too much or dare too much. There is at this moment, for you an utterance brave and grand as that of the colossal chisel of Phidias, [4] or trowel of the Egyptians, or the pen of Moses, or Dante, but different from all these. Not possibly will the soul, all rich, all eloquent, with thousand-cloven tongue, deign to repeat itself; but if you can hear what these patriarchs say, surely you can reply to them in the same pitch of voice; for the ear and the tongue are two organs of one nature. Abide in the simple and noble regions of thy life, obey thy heart, and thou shalt reproduce the Foreworld again.

4. As our Religion, our Education, our Art look abroad, so does our spirit of society. All men plume themselves on the improvement of society, and no man improves.

Society never advances. It recedes as fast on one side as it gains on the other. It undergoes continual changes; it is barbarous, it is civilized, it is christianized, it is rich, it is scientific; but this change is not amelioration. For every thing that is given something is taken. Society acquires new arts and loses old instincts. What a contrast between the well-clad, reading, writing, thinking American, with a watch, a pencil, and a bill of exchange in his pocket, and the naked New Zealander, whose property is a club, a spear, a mat, and an undivided twentieth of a shed to sleep under! But compare the health of the two men, and you shall see that the white man has lost his aboriginal strength. If the traveler tell us truly, strike the savage with a broad axe and in a day or two the flesh shall unite and heal as if you struck the blow into soft pitch, and the same blow shall send the white to his grave.

[1] the Pope's palace, which contains famous art galleries and libraries rich in ancient manuscripts
[2] classic or medieval

[3] Scipio's daring resourcefulness often turned defeat into victory; see note 4, p. 367.
[4] A Greek sculptor; see The Problem, note 1, p. 386.

The civilized man has built a coach, but has lost the use of his feet. He is supported on crutches, but lacks so much support of muscle. He has a fine Geneva watch, but he fails of the skill to tell the hour by the sun. A Greenwich nautical almanac he has, and so being sure of the information when he wants it, the man in the street does not know a star in the sky. The solstice he does not observe; the equinox he knows as little; and the whole bright calendar of the year is without a dial in his mind. His notebooks impair his memory; his libraries overload his wit; the insurance-office increases the number of accidents; and it may be a question whether machinery does not encumber; whether we have not lost by refinement some energy, by a Christianity entrenched in establishments and forms, some vigor of wild virtue. For every Stoic was a Stoic; but in Christendom where is the Christian?

There is no more deviation in the moral standard than in the standard of height or bulk. No greater men are now than ever were. A singular equality may be observed between the great men of the first and of the last ages; nor can all the science, art, religion, and philosophy of the nineteenth century avail to educate greater men than Plutarch's [1] heroes, three or four and twenty centuries ago. Not in time is the race progressive. Phocion, Socrates, Anaxagoras, Diogenes, are great men, but they leave no class. He who is really of their class will not be called by their name, but will be his own man, and in his turn the founder of a sect. The arts and inventions of each period are only its costume, and do not invigorate men. The harm of the improved machinery may compensate its good. Hudson and Behring accomplished so much in their fishing-boats as to astonish Parry and Franklin, [2] whose equipment exhausted the resources of science and art. Galileo, with an opera-glass, discovered a more splendid series of celestial phenomena than any one since. Columbus found the New World in an undecked [3] boat. It is curious to see the periodical disuse and perishing of means and machinery which were introduced with loud laudation a few years or centuries before. The great genius returns to essential man. We reckoned the improvements of the art of war among the triumphs of science, and yet Napoleon conquered Europe by the bivouac, which consisted of falling back on naked valor and disencumbering it of all aids. The Emperor held it impossible to make a perfect army, says Las Casas, [4] "without abolishing our arms, magazines, commissaries, and carriages, until, in imitation of the Roman custom, the soldier should receive his supply of corn, grind it in his hand-mill, and bake his bread himself."

Society is a wave. The wave moves onward, but the water of which it is composed does not. The same particle does not rise from the valley to the ridge. Its unity is only phenomenal. [5] The persons who make up a nation today, next year die, and their experience with them.

And so the reliance on Property, including the reliance on governments which protect it, is the want of self-reliance. Men have looked away from themselves and at things so long that they have come to esteem the religious, learned, and civil institutions as guards of property, and they deprecate assaults on these, because they feel them to be assaults on property. They measure their esteem of each other by what each has, and not by what each is. But a cultivated man becomes ashamed of his property, out of new respect for his nature. Especially he hates what he has if he see that it is accidental,—came to him by inheritance, or gift, or crime; then he feels that it is not having; it does not belong to him, has no root in him, and merely lies there because no revolution or no robber takes it away. But that which a man is, does always by necessity acquire, and what the man acquires, is living property, which does not wait the beck of rulers, or mobs, or revolutions, or fire, or storm, or bankruptcies, but perpetually renews itself wherever the man breathes. "Thy lot or portion of life," said the Caliph Ali, [6] "is seeking after thee; therefore be at rest from seeking after it." Our dependence on these foreign goods leads us to our slavish respect for numbers. The political parties meet in numerous conventions; the greater the concourse and with each new uproar of announcement, The delegation from Essex! The Democrats from New Hampshire! The Whigs of Maine! the young patriot feels himself stronger than before by a new thousand of eyes and arms. In like

---

[1] Plutarch was a Greek historian whose *Parallel Lives* of forty-six Greeks and Romans is a classic; Phocion, an Athenian statesman put to death on a false charge of treason; Socrates, a Greek philosopher given poison because of his beliefs; Anaxagoras, a Greek philosopher, exiled on the charge of heresy; Diogenes, a Greek cynic philosopher famous for his eccentricities.

[2] Henry Hudson was a navigator of the seventeenth century; Vitus Bering, a Danish explorer of the eighteenth century; Sir William Edward Parry and Sir John Franklin, English navigators of the nineteenth century.

[3] a mistake of Emerson's

[4] a voluntary exile with Napoleon at St. Helena, to whom the emperor dictated part of his memoirs
[5] apparent
[6] fourth caliph or successor of Mohammed, 600-661, and supposed writer of a collection of proverbs

manner the reformers summon conventions and vote and resolve in multitude. Not so, O friends! will the God deign to enter and inhabit you, but by a method precisely the reverse. It is not only as a man puts off all foreign support, and stands alone, that I see him to be strong and to prevail. He is weaker by every recruit to his banner. Is not a man better than a town? Ask nothing of men, and in the endless mutation, thou only firm column must presently appear the upholder of all that surrounds thee. He who knows that power is inborn, that he is weak because he has looked for good out of him and elsewhere, and so perceiving throws himself unhesitatingly on his thought, instantly rights himself, stands in the erect position, commands his limbs, works miracles; just as a man who stands on his feet is stronger than a man who stands on his head.

So use all that is called Fortune. Most men gamble with her, and gain all, and lose all, as her wheel rolls. But do thou leave as unlawful these winnings, and deal with Cause and Effect, the chancellors of God. In the Will work and acquire, and thou hast chained the wheel of Chance, and shalt sit hereafter out of fear from her rotations. A political victory, a rise of rents, the recovery of your sick, or the return of your absent friend, or some other favorable event raises your spirits, and you think good days are preparing for you. Do not believe it. Nothing can bring you peace but yourself. Nothing can bring you peace but the triumph of principles.

1841

COMPENSATION

The wings of Time are black and white,
Pied with morning and with night.
Mountain tall and ocean deep
Trembling balance duly keep.
In changing moon, in tidal wave,
Glows the feud of Want and Have.
Gauge of more and less through space
Electric star and pencil plays.
The lonely Earth amid the balls
That hurry through the eternal halls,
A makeweight flying to the void,
Supplemental asteroid,
Or compensatory spark,
Shoots across the neutral Dark.

Man's the elm, and Wealth the vine;
Stanch and strong the tendrils twine:
Though the frail ringlets thee deceive,
None from its stock that vine can reave.
Fear not, then, thou child infirm,
There's no god dare wrong a worm.
Laurel crowns cleave to deserts

And power to him who power exerts;
Hast not thy share? On winged feet,
Lo! it rushes thee to meet;
And all that Nature made thy own,
Floating in air or pent in stone,
Will rive the hills and swim the sea
And, like thy shadow, follow thee.

Ever since I was a boy I have wished to write a discourse on Compensation: for it seemed to me when very young that on this subject life was ahead of theology and the people knew more than the preachers taught. The documents too from which the doctrine is to be drawn, charmed my fancy by their endless variety, and lay always before me, even in sleep; for they are the tools in our hands, the bread in our basket, the transactions of the street, the farm, and the dwelling-house, the greetings, the relations, the debts and credits, the influence of character, the nature and endowment of all men. It seemed to me, also, that in it might be shown men a ray of divinity, the present action of the soul of this world, clean from all vestige of tradition, and so the heart of man might be bathed by an inundation of eternal love, conversing with that which he knows was always and always must be, because it really is now. It appeared, moreover, that if this doctrine could be stated in terms with any resemblance to those bright intuitions in which this truth is sometimes revealed to us, it would be a star in many dark hours and crooked passages in our journey that would not suffer us to lose our way.

I was lately confirmed in these desires by hearing a sermon at church. The preacher, a man esteemed for his orthodoxy, unfolded in the ordinary manner the doctrine of the Last Judgment. He assumed that judgment is not executed in this world; that the wicked are successful; that the good are miserable; and then urged from reason and from Scripture a compensation to be made to both parties in the next life. No offense appeared to be taken by the congregation at this doctrine. As far as I could observe, when the meeting broke up they separated without remark on the sermon.

Yet what was the import of this teaching? What did the preacher mean by saying that the good are miserable in the present life? Was it that houses and lands, offices, wine, horses, dress, luxury, are had by unprincipled men, whilst the saints are poor and despised; and that a compensation is to be made to these last hereafter, by giving them the like gratifications another day,—bank-stock and doubloons, venison and champagne? This must be the compensation intended: for what else? Is it that they are to have leave to pray and praise? to love and serve men? Why, that they can do now. The legitimate inference the disciple would draw was,—"We are to have *such* a good time as the sinners have now";—or, to push it to its extreme import, "You sin now; we shall sin by and by; we would sin now, if we could; not being successful we expect our revenge tomorrow."

The fallacy lay in the immense concession that the bad are successful; that justice is not done now. The blindness of the preacher consisted in deferring to the base estimate of the market of what constitutes a manly success, instead of confronting and convicting the world from the truth; announcing the presence of the soul; the omnipotence of the will: and so establishing the standard of good and ill, of success and falsehood.

I find a similar base tone in the popular religious works of the day and the same doctrines assumed by the literary men when occasionally they treat the related topics. I think that our popular theology has gained in decorum, and not in principle, over the superstitions it has displaced. But·men are better than this theology. Their daily life gives it the lie. Every ingenuous and aspiring soul leaves the doctrine behind him in his own experience; and all men feel sometimes the falsehood which they cannot demonstrate. For men are wiser than they know. That which they hear in schools and pulpits without afterthought, if said in conversation would probably be questioned in silence. If a man dogmatize in a mixed company on Providence and the divine laws, he is answered by a silence which conveys well enough to an observer the dissatisfaction of the hearer, but his incapacity to make his own statement.

I shall attempt in this and the following chapter [1] to record some facts that indicate the path of the law of Compensation; happy beyond my expectation if I shall truly draw the smallest arc of this circle.

POLARITY, or action and reaction, we meet in every part of nature; in darkness and light; in heat and cold; in the ebb and flow of waters; in male and female; in the inspiration and expiration of plants and animals; equation of quantity and quality in the fluids of the animal body; in the systole and diastole of the heart; in the undulations of fluids, and of sound; in the centrifugal and centripetal gravity; in electricity, galvanism, and chemical affinity. Superinduce magnetism at one end of a needle;

[1] the essay entitled "Spiritual Laws"

the opposite magnetism takes place at the other end. If the south attracts, the north repels. To empty here, you must condense there. An inevitable dualism bisects nature, so that each thing is a half, and suggests another thing to make it whole; as, spirit, matter; man, woman; odd, even; subjective, objective; in, out; upper, under; motion, rest; yea, nay.

Whilst the world is thus dual, so is every one of its parts. The entire system of things gets represented in every particle. There is somewhat that resembles the ebb and flow of the sea, day and night, man and woman, in a single needle of the pine, in a kernel of corn, in each individual of every animal tribe. The reaction, so grand in the elements, is repeated within these small boundaries. For example, in the animal kingdom the physiologist has observed that no creatures are favorites, but a certain compensation balances every gift and every defect. A surplusage given to one part is paid out of a reduction from another part of the same creature. If the head and neck are enlarged, the trunk and extremities are cut short.

The theory of the mechanic forces is another example. What we gain in power is lost in time; [2] and the converse. The periodic or compensating errors of the planets is another instance. [3] The influences of climate and soil in political history are another. The cold climate invigorates. The barren soil does not breed fevers, crocodiles, tigers, or scorpions.

The same dualism underlies the nature and condition of man. Every excess causes a defect; every defect an excess. Every sweet hath its sour; every evil its good. Every faculty which is a receiver of pleasure has an equal penalty put on its abuse. It is to answer for its moderation with its life. For every grain of wit there is a grain of folly. For every thing you have missed, you have gained something else; and for every thing you gain, you lose something. If riches increase, they are increased that use them. If the gatherer gathers too much, nature takes out of the man what she puts into his chest; swells the estate, but kills the owner. Nature hates monopolies and exceptions. The waves of the sea do not more speedily seek a level from their loftiest tossing than the varieties of condition tend to equalize themselves. There is always some leveling circumstance that puts down the over-

[2] a law of mechanics
[3] "The periodic inequalities of the planets are so small, because as a rule there is a nearly complete compensation effected at every few revolutions, so that the accelerations balance the retardations." Young, *General Astronomy*, p. 312.

bearing, the strong, the rich, the fortunate, substantially on the same ground with all others. Is a man too strong and fierce for society, and by temper and position a bad citizen,—a morose ruffian, with a dash of the pirate in him;—nature sends him a troop of pretty sons and daughters who are getting along in the dame's classes at the village school, and love and fear for them smooths his grim scowl to courtesy. Thus she contrives to intenerate[1] the granite and felspar, takes the boar out and puts the lamb in, and keeps her balance true.

The farmer imagines power and place are fine things. But the President has paid dear for his White House. It has commonly cost him all his peace, and the best of his manly attributes. To preserve for a short time so conspicuous an appearance before the world, he is content to eat dust before the real masters who stand erect behind the throne. Or, do men desire the more substantial and permanent grandeur of genius? Neither has this an immunity. He who by force of will or of thought is great, and overlooks thousands, has the charges of that eminence. With every influx of light comes new danger. Has he light? he must bear witness to the light, and always outrun that sympathy which gives him such keen satisfaction, by his fidelity to new revelations of the incessant soul. He must hate father and mother, wife and child. Has he all that the world loves and admires and covets? —he must cast behind him their admiration, and afflict them by faithfulness to his truth, and become a byword and a hissing.[2]

This law writes the laws of cities and nations. It is in vain to build or plot or combine against it. Things refuse to be mismanaged long. *Res nolunt diu male administrari.*[3] Though no checks to a new evil appear, the checks exist, and will appear. If the government is cruel, the governor's life is not safe. If you tax too high, the revenue will yield nothing. If you make the criminal code sanguinary, juries will not convict. If the law is too mild, private vengeance comes in. If the government is a terrific democracy, the pressure is resisted by an overcharge of energy in the citizen, and life glows with a fierce flame. The true life and satisfactions of man seem to elude the utmost rigors or felicities of condition, and to establish themselves with great indifference under all varieties of circumstances. Under all governments the influence of character remains the same,—in Turkey and in New England about alike. Under the primeval despots of Egypt, history honestly confesses that man must have been as free as culture could make him.

These appearances indicate the fact that the universe is represented in every one of its particles. Every thing in nature contains all the powers of nature. Every thing is made of one hidden stuff; as the naturalist sees one type under every metamorphosis, and regards a horse as a running man, a fish as a swimming man, a bird as a flying man, a tree as a rooted man. Each new form repeats not only the main character of the type, but part for part all the details, all the aims, furtherances, hindrances, energies, and whole system of every other. Every occupation, trade, art, transaction is a compend of the world and a correlative of every other. Each one is an entire emblem of human life; of its good and ill, its trials, its enemies, its course and its end. And each one must somehow accommodate the whole man, and recite all his destiny.

The world globes itself in a drop of dew. The microscope cannot find the animalcule which is less perfect for being little.[4] Eyes, ears, taste, smell, motion, resistance, appetite, and organs of reproduction that take hold on eternity,—all find room to consist in the small creature. So do we put our life into every act. The true doctrine of omnipresence is, that God reappears with all his parts in every moss and cobweb. The value of the universe contrives to throw itself into every point. If the good is there, so is the evil; if the affinity, so the repulsion; if the force, so the limitation.

Thus is the universe alive. All things are moral. That soul, which within us is a sentiment, outside of us is a law. We feel its inspirations; out there in history we can see its fatal strength. "It is in the world, and the world was made by it." Justice is not postponed. A perfect equity adjusts its balance in all parts of life. Οἱ κύβοι Διὸς ἀεὶ εὐπίπτουσι,[5] The dice of God are always loaded. The world looks like a multiplication table, or a mathematical equation, which, turn it how you will, balances itself. Take what figure you will, its

[1] soften

[2] Emerson was himself twice hissed: once when making a political speech in favor of his friend Dr. Palfrey; and again when in 1861 at Wendell Phillips's request he addressed an Anti-Slavery Society. He wrote in his Journal, "The mob roared and hissed whenever I attempted to speak, and after several attempts I withdrew." From *A Memoir of Ralph Waldo Emerson*, by James Elliott Cabot, Vol. ii, p. 598-9.

[3] translated in the preceding sentence

[4] The amoebas, though they cannot be said to have eyes, ears, taste, and smell, are nevertheless sensitive to light, sound, and odors, and distinguish between food and other substances.

[5] translated in the following sentence

exact value, nor more nor less, still returns to you. Every secret is told, every crime is punished, every virtue rewarded, every wrong redressed, in silence and certainty. What we call retribution is the universal necessity by which the whole appears wherever a part appears. If you see smoke, there must be fire. If you see a hand or a limb, you know that the trunk to which it belongs is there behind.

Every act rewards itself, or in other words integrates [1] itself, in a twofold manner; first in the thing, or in real nature; and secondly in the circumstance, or in apparent nature. Men call the circumstance the retribution. The causal retribution is in the thing, and is seen by the soul. The retribution in the circumstance is seen by the understanding; it is inseparable from the thing, but is often spread over a long time, and so does not become distinct until after many years. The specific stripes may follow late after the offense, but they follow because they accompany it. Crime and punishment grow out of one stem. Punishment is a fruit that unsuspected ripens within the flower of the pleasure which concealed it. Cause and effect, means and ends, seed and fruit, cannot be severed; for the effect already blooms in the cause, the end preëxists in the means, the fruit in the seed.

Whilst thus the world will be whole, and refuses to be disparted, we seek to act partially, to sunder, to appropriate; for example,—to gratify the senses, we sever the pleasure of the senses from the needs of the character. The ingenuity of man has always been dedicated to the solution of one problem,—how to detach the sensual sweet, the sensual strong, the sensual bright, etc., from the moral sweet, the moral deep, the moral fair; that is, again, to contrive to cut clean off this upper surface so thin as to leave it bottomless; to get a *one end*, without an *other end*. The soul says, "Eat"; the body would feast. The soul says, "The man and woman shall be one flesh and one soul"; the body would join the flesh only. The soul says, "Have dominion over all things to the ends of virtue"; the body would have the power over things to its own ends.

The soul strives amain to live and work through all things. It would be the only fact. All things shall be added unto it,—power, pleasure, knowledge, beauty. The particular man aims to be somebody; to set up for himself; to truck and higgle for a private good; and, in particulars, to ride that he may ride; to dress that he may be dressed; to eat that

he may eat; and to govern, that he may be seen. Men seek to be great; they would have offices, wealth, power, and fame. They think that to be great is to possess one side of nature,—the sweet, without the other side,—the bitter.

This dividing and detaching is steadily counteracted. Up to this day, it must be owned, no projector has had the smallest success. The parted water reunites behind our hand. Pleasure is taken out of pleasant things, profit out of profitable things, power out of strong things, as soon as we seek to separate them from the whole. We can no more halve things and get the sensual good, by itself, than we can get an inside that shall have no outside, or a light without a shadow. "Drive out nature with a fork, she comes running back." [2]

Life invests itself with inevitable conditions, which the unwise seek to dodge, which one and another brags that he does not know; brags that they do not touch him;—but the brag is on his lips, the conditions are in his soul. If he escapes them in one part they attack him in another more vital part. If he has escaped them in form and in the appearance, it is because he has resisted his life, and fled from himself, and the retribution is so much death. So signal is the failure of all attempts to make this separation of the good from the tax, that the experiment would not be tried,—since to try it is to be mad,—but for the circumstance that when the disease began in the will, of rebellion and separation, the intellect is at once infected, so that the man ceases to see God whole in each object, but is able to see the sensual allurement of an object and not see the sensual hurt; he sees the mermaid's head but not the dragon's tail; and thinks he can cut off that which he would have, from that which he would not have. "How secret art thou who dwellest in the highest heavens in silence, O thou only great God, sprinkling with an unwearied Providence certain penal blindnesses upon such as have unbridled desires!" [3]

The human soul is true to these facts in the painting of fable, of history, of law, of proverbs, of conversation. It finds a tongue in literature unawares. Thus the Greeks called Jupiter, Supreme Mind; but having traditionally ascribed to him many base actions, they involuntarily made amends to reason by tying up the hands of so bad a god. He is made as helpless as a king of England. [4] Prometheus knows one secret which Jove must bargain

---

[1] makes a whole of

[2] Horace, *Epistles*, i, 10, 24
[3] from St. Augustine's *Confessions*, I, xviii
[4] dependent upon Parliament

for; [1] Minerva, another. He cannot get his own thunders; Minerva keeps the key of them.

> Of all the gods, I only know the keys
> That ope the solid doors within whose vaults
> His thunders sleep. [2]

A plain confession of the in-working of the All and of its moral aim. The Indian mythology ends in the same ethics; [3] and it would seem impossible for any fable to be invented and get any currency which was not moral. Aurora forgot to ask youth for her lover, and though Tithonus [4] is immortal, he is old. Achilles is not quite invulnerable; the sacred waters did not wash the heel by which Thetis held him. Siegfried, in the Niebelungen, [5] is not quite immortal, for a leaf fell on his back whilst he was bathing in the dragon's blood, and that spot which it covered is mortal. And so it must be. There is a crack in every thing God has made. It would seem there is always this vindictive circumstance stealing in at unawares even into the wild poesy in which the human fancy attempted to make bold holiday and to shake itself free of the old laws,—this backstroke, this kick of the gun, certifying that the law is fatal; that in nature nothing can be given, all things are sold.

This is that ancient doctrine of Nemesis, [6] who keeps watch in the universe and lets no offense go unchastised. The Furies, [7] they said, are attendants on justice, and if the sun in heaven should transgress his path they would punish him. The poets related that stone walls and iron swords and leathern thongs had an occult sympathy with the wrongs of their owners; that the belt which Ajax gave Hector dragged the Trojan hero over the field at the wheels of the car of Achilles, and the sword which Hector gave Ajax was that on whose point Ajax fell. [8] They recorded that when the Thasians [9] erected a statue to Theogenes, a victor in the games, one of his rivals went to it by night, and endeavored to throw it down by repeated blows, until at last he moved it from its pedestal and was crushed to death beneath its fall.

This voice of fable has in it somewhat divine. It came from thought above the will of the writer. That is the best part of each writer which has nothing private in it; that which he does not know; that which flowed out of his constitution and not from his too active invention; that which in the study of a single artist you might not easily find, but in the study of many you would abstract as the spirit of them all. Phidias [10] it is not, but the work of man in that early Hellenic world that I would know. The name and circumstances of Phidias, however convenient for history, embarrass when we come to the highest criticism. We are to see that which man was tending to do in a given period, and was hindered, or, if you will, modified in doing, by the interfering volitions of Phidias, of Dante, of Shakespeare, the organ whereby man at the moment wrought.

Still more striking is the expression of this fact in the proverbs of all nations, which are always the literature of reason, or the statements of an absolute truth, without qualification. Proverbs, like the sacred books of each nation, are the sanctuary of the intuitions. That which the droning world, chained to appearances, will not allow the realist to say in his own words, it will suffer him to say in proverbs without contradiction. And this law of laws, which the pulpit, the senate, and the college deny, is hourly preached in all markets and workshops by flights of proverbs, whose teaching is as true and as omnipresent as that of birds and flies.

All things are double, one against another. —Tit for tat; an eye for an eye; a tooth for a tooth; blood for blood; measure for measure; love for love.—Give, and it shall be given you.—He that watereth shall be watered himself.—What will you have? quoth God; pay for it and take it.—Nothing venture, nothing have.—Thou shalt be paid exactly for what thou hast done, no more, no less.—Who doth not work shall not eat.—Harm watch, harm catch.—Curses always recoil on the head of him who imprecates them.—If you put a chain around the neck of a slave, the other end fastens itself around your own.—Bad counsel confounds the adviser.—The Devil is an ass. [11]

It is thus written, because it is thus in life. Our action is overmastered and characterized above our will by the law of nature. We aim at a petty end quite aside from the public good,

---

[1] Jupiter tried unsuccessfully to extort the secret of his own doom from Prometheus. See the *Prometheus* of Aeschylus, and Shelley's *Prometheus Unbound.*
[2] Aeschylus, *The Eumenides,* 830
[3] God in everything, and everything leading to God
[4] Cf. Tennyson, "Tithonus."
[5] an ancient Teutonic epic
[6] Greek goddess of retribution who allotted to each mortal his exact share of good and evil
[7] the Erinyes, or Eumenides, or Furies—the avengers of iniquity
[8] See *Iliad,* vii, 303; and Sophocles's *Ajax,* 865, 1029.
[9] inhabitants of Thasos, an island off the coast of Thrace

[10] See note 1, page, 386.
[11] very probably Emerson's own thought, though possibly suggested by the title of Ben Jonson's play, *The Devil Is an Ass*

but our act arranges itself by irresistible magnetism in a line with the poles of the world.

A man cannot speak but he judges himself. With his will, or against his will, he draws his portrait to the eye of his companions by every word. Every opinion reacts on him who utters it. It is a thread-ball thrown at a mark, but the other end remains in the thrower's bag. Or, rather, it is a harpoon thrown at the whale, unwinding, as it flies, a coil of cord in the boat, and if the harpoon is not good, or not well thrown, it will go nigh to cut the steersman in twain or to sink the boat.

You cannot do wrong without suffering wrong. "No man had ever a point of pride that was not injurious to him," said Burke. The exclusive in fashionable life does not see that he excludes himself from enjoyment, in the attempt to appropriate it. The exclusionist in religion does not see that he shuts the door of heaven on himself, in striving to shut out others. Treat men as pawns and ninepins and you shall suffer as well as they. If you leave out their heart, you shall lose your own. The senses would make things of all persons; of women, of children, of the poor. The vulgar proverb, "I will get it from his purse or get it from his skin," is sound philosophy.

All infractions of love and equity in our social relations are speedily punished. They are punished by fear. Whilst I stand in simple relations to my fellow-man, I have no displeasure in meeting him. We meet as water meets water, or as two currents of air mix, with perfect diffusion and interpenetration of nature. But as soon as there is any departure from simplicity and attempt at halfness, or good for me that is not good for him, my neighbor feels the wrong; he shrinks from me as far as I have shrunk from him; his eyes no longer seek mine; there is war between us; there is hate in him and fear in me.

All the old abuses in society, universal and particular, all unjust accumulations of property and power, are avenged in the same manner. Fear is an instructor of great sagacity, and the herald of all revolutions. One thing he teaches, that there is rottenness where he appears. He is a carrion crow, and though you see not well what he hovers for, there is death somewhere. Our property is timid, our laws are timid, our cultivated classes are timid. Fear for ages has boded and mowed and gibbered over government and property. That obscene bird is not there for nothing. He indicates great wrongs which must be revised.

Of the like nature is that expectation of change which instantly follows the suspension of our voluntary activity. The terror of cloudless noon, the emerald of Polycrates, [1] the awe of prosperity, the instinct which leads every generous soul to impose on itself tasks of a noble asceticism and vicarious virtue, are the tremblings of the balance of justice through the heart and mind of man.

Experienced men of the world know very well that it is best to pay scot and lot [2] as they go along, and that a man often pays dear for a small frugality. The borrower runs in his own debt. Has a man gained any thing who has received a hundred favors and rendered none? Has he gained by borrowing, through indolence or cunning, his neighbor's wares, or horses, or money? There arises on the deed the instant acknowledgment of benefit on the one part and of debt on the other; that is, of superiority and inferiority. The transaction remains in the memory of himself and his neighbor; and every new transaction alters according to its nature their relation to each other. He may soon come to see that he had better have broken his own bones than to have ridden in his neighbor's coach, and that "the highest price he can pay for a thing is to ask for it."

A wise man will extend this lesson to all parts of life, and know that it is the part of prudence to face every claimant and pay every just demand on your time, your talents, or your heart. Always pay; for, first or last, you must pay your entire debt. Persons and events may stand for a time between you and justice, but it is only a postponement. You must pay at last your own debt. If you are wise you will dread a prosperity which only loads you with more. Benefit is the end of nature. But for every benefit which you receive, a tax is levied. He is great who confers the most benefits. He is base—and that is the one base thing in the universe—to receive favors and render none. In the order of nature we cannot render benefits to those from whom we receive them, or only seldom. But the benefit we receive must be rendered again, line for line, deed for deed, cent for cent, to somebody. Beware of too much good staying in your hand. It will fast corrupt and worm worms. [3] Pay it away quickly in some sort.

---

[1] Polycrates, tyrant of Samos, fearing, because of his great good fortune, to incur the envy of the gods, threw away a ring. But it was found in a fish and returned to him.

[2] taxes   [3] breed worms

Labor is watched over by the same pitiless laws. Cheapest, say the prudent, is the dearest labor. What we buy in a broom, a mat, a wagon, a knife, is some application of good sense to a common want. It is best to pay in your land a skilful gardener, or to buy good sense applied to gardening; in your sailor, good sense applied to navigation; in the house, good sense applied to cooking, sewing, serving; in your agent, good sense applied to accounts and affairs. So do you multiply your presence, or spread yourself throughout your estate. But because of the dual constitution of things, in labor as in life there can be no cheating. The thief steals from himself. The swindler swindles himself. For the real price of labor is knowledge and virtue, whereof wealth and credit are signs. These signs, like paper money, may be counterfeited or stolen, but that which they represent, namely, knowledge and virtue, cannot be counterfeited or stolen. These ends of labor cannot be answered but by real exertions of the mind, and in obedience to pure motives. The cheat, the defaulter, the gambler, cannot extort the knowledge of material and moral nature which his honest care and pains yield to the operative. The law of nature is, Do the thing, and you shall have the power: but they who do not the thing have not the power.

Human labor, through all its forms, from the sharpening of a stake to the construction of a city or an epic, is one immense illustration of the perfect compensation of the universe. The absolute balance of Give and Take, the doctrine that every thing has its price,—and if that price is not paid, not that thing but something else is obtained, and that it is impossible to get any thing without its price,— is not less sublime in the columns of a ledger than in the budgets of states, in the laws of light and darkness, in all the action and reaction of nature. I cannot doubt that the high laws which each man sees ever implicated in those processes with which he is conversant, the stern ethics which sparkle on his chisel-edge, which are measured out by his plumb and foot-rule, which stand as manifest in the footing of the shop-bill as in the history of a state, —do recommend to him his trade, and though seldom named, exalt his business to his imagination.

The league between virtue and nature engages all things to assume a hostile front to vice. The beautiful laws and substances of the world persecute and whip the traitor. He finds that things are arranged for truth and benefit, but there is no den in the wide world to hide a rogue. Commit a crime, and the earth is made of glass. Commit a crime, and it seems as if a coat of snow fell on the ground, such as reveals in the woods the track of every partridge and fox and squirrel and mole. You cannot recall the spoken word, you cannot wipe out the foot-track, you cannot draw up the ladder, so as to leave no inlet or clew. Some damning circumstance always transpires. The laws and substances of nature—water, snow, wind, gravitation—become penalties to the thief.

On the other hand, the law holds with equal sureness for all right action. Love, and you shall be loved. All love is mathematically just, as much as the two sides of an algebraic equation. The good man has absolute good, which like fire turns every thing to its own nature, so that you cannot do him any harm; but as the royal armies sent against Napoleon, [1] when he approached cast down their colors and from enemies became friends, so disasters of all kinds, as sickness, offense, poverty, prove benefactors:—

> Winds blow and waters roll
> Strength to the brave, and Power and Deity;
> Yet in themselves are nothing! [2]

The good are befriended even by weakness and defect. As no man had ever a pint of pride that was not injurious to him, so no man had ever a defect that was not somewhere made useful to him. The stag in the fable admired his horns and blamed his feet, but when the hunter came, his feet saved him, and afterwards, caught in the thicket, his horns destroyed him. Every man in his lifetime needs to thank his faults. As no man thoroughly understands a truth until he has contended against it, so no man has a thorough acquaintance with the hindrances or talents of men, until he has suffered from the one, and seen the triumph of the other over his own want of the same. Has he a defect of temper that unfits him to live in society? Thereby he is driven to entertain himself alone, and acquire habits of self-help; and thus, like the wounded oyster, he mends his shell with pearl. Our strength grows out of our weakness. The indignation which arms itself with secret

[1] Troops were sent by the Bourbon government against Napoleon, on his escape from Elba, but at sight of him they shouted "Vive l'Empereur" and joined his ranks.
[2] Wordsworth's sonnet, "Near Dover, September, 1802," "Inland, within a hollow vale, I stood."

forces does not awaken until we are pricked and stung, and sorely assailed. A great man is always willing to be little. Whilst he sits on the cushion of advantages, he goes to sleep. When he is pushed, tormented, defeated, he has a chance to learn something; he has been put on his wits, on his manhood; he has gained facts; learns his ignorance; is cured of the insanity of conceit; has got moderation and real skill. The wise man throws himself on the side of his assailants. It is more his interest than it is theirs to find his weak point. The wound cicatrizes and falls off from him like a dead skin, and when they would triumph, lo! he has passed on invulnerable. Blame is safer than praise. I hate to be defended in a newspaper. As long as all that is said is said against me, I feel a certain assurance of success. But as soon as honeyed words of praise are spoken for me, I feel as one that lies unprotected before his enemies. In general, every evil to which we do not succumb is a benefactor. As the Sandwich Islander believes that the strength and valor of the enemy he kills passes into himself, so we gain the strength of the temptation we resist.

The same guards which protect us from disaster, defect, and enmity, defend us, if we will, from selfishness and fraud. Bolts and bars are not the best of our institutions, nor is shrewdness in trade a mark of wisdom. Men suffer all their life long under the foolish superstition that they can be cheated. But it is as impossible for a man to be cheated by any one but himself, as for a thing to be and not to be at the same time. There is a third silent party to all our bargains. The nature and soul of things takes on itself the guaranty of the fulfilment of every contract, so that honest service cannot come to loss. If you serve an ungrateful master, serve him the more. Put God in your debt. Every stroke shall be repaid. The longer the payment is withholden, the better for you; for compound interest on compound interest is the rate and usage of this exchequer.

The history of persecution is a history of endeavors to cheat nature, to make water run up hill, to twist a rope of sand. It makes no difference whether the actors be many or one, a tyrant or a mob. A mob is a society of bodies voluntarily bereaving themselves of reason and traversing its work. The mob is man voluntarily descending to the nature of the beast. Its fit hour of activity is night. Its actions are insane, like its whole constitution. It persecutes a principle; it would whip a right; it would tar and feather justice, by inflicting fire and outrage upon the houses

and persons of those who have these. It resembles the prank of boys, who run with fire-engines to put out the ruddy aurora streaming to the stars. The inviolate spirit turns their spite against the wrongdoers. The martyr cannot be dishonored. Every lash inflicted is a tongue of fame; every prison, a more illustrious abode; every burned book or house enlightens the world; every suppressed or expunged word reverberates through the earth from side to side. Hours of sanity and consideration are always arriving to communities as to individuals, when the truth is seen, and the martyrs are justified.

Thus do all things preach the indifference of circumstances. The man is all. Every thing has two sides, a good and an evil. Every advantage has its tax. I learn to be content. But the doctrine of compensation is not the doctrine of indifference. The thoughtless say, on hearing these representations,—What boots it to do well? there is one event to good and evil; if I gain any good I must pay for it; if I lose any good I gain some other; all actions are indifferent.

There is a deeper fact in the soul than compensation, to wit, its own nature. The soul is not a compensation, but a life. The soul *is*. Under all this running sea of circumstance, whose waters ebb and flow with perfect balance, lies the aboriginal abyss of real Being. Essence, or God, is not a relation, or a part, but the whole. Being is the vast affirmative, excluding negation, self-balanced, and swallowing up all relations, parts, and times within itself. Nature, truth, virtue, are the influx from thence. Vice is the absence or departure of the same. Nothing, Falsehood, may indeed stand as the great Night or shade, on which, as a background, the living universe paints itself forth; but no fact is begotten by it; it cannot work; for it is not."[1] It cannot work any good; it cannot work any harm. It is harm inasmuch as it is worse not to be than to be.

We feel defrauded of the retribution due to evil acts, because the criminal adheres to his vice and contumacy and does not come to a crisis or judgment anywhere in visible nature. There is no stunning confutation of his nonsense before men and angels. Has he therefore outwitted the law? Inasmuch as he carries

[1] Cf. "A false man found a religion? Why, a false man cannot build a brick house! If he do not know and follow *truly* the properties of mortar, burnt clay, and what else he works in, it is no house that he makes, but a rubbish-heap." Carlyle, *Heroes and Hero Worship*: "The Hero as Prophet."

the malignity and the lie with him he so far deceases from nature. In some manner there will be a demonstration of the wrong to the understanding also; but should we not see it, this deadly deduction makes square the eternal account.

Neither can it be said, on the other hand, that the gain of rectitude must be bought by any loss. There is no penalty to virtue; no penalty to wisdom; they are proper additions of being. In a virtuous action, I properly *am;* in a virtuous act I add to the world; I plant into deserts conquered from Chaos and Nothing and see the darkness receding on the limits of the horizon. There can be no excess to love; none to knowledge; none to beauty, when these attributes are considered in the purest sense. The soul refuses limits, and always affirms an Optimism, never a Pessimism.

His life is a progress, and not a station. His instinct is trust. Our instinct uses "more" and "less" in application to man, of the *presence of the soul,* and not of its absence; the brave man is greater than the coward; the true, the benevolent, the wise, is more a man and not less, than the fool and knave. There is no tax on the good of virtue; for that is the incoming of God himself, or absolute existence, without any comparative. Material good has its tax, and if it came without desert or sweat, has no root in me, and the next wind will blow it away. But all the good of nature is the soul's, and may be had, if paid for in nature's lawful coin, that is, by labor which the heart and the head allow. I no longer wish to meet a good I do not earn, for example to find a pot of buried gold, knowing that it brings with it new burdens. I do not wish more external goods,—neither possessions, nor honors, nor powers, nor persons. The gain is apparent; the tax is certain. But there is no tax on the knowledge that the compensation exists and that it is not desirable to dig up treasure. Herein I rejoice with a serene eternal peace. I contract the boundaries of possible mischief. I learn the wisdom of St. Bernard, [1]—"Nothing can work me damage except myself; the harm that I sustain I carry about with me, and never am a real sufferer but by my own fault."

In the nature of the soul is the compensation for the inequalities of condition. The radical tragedy of nature seems to be the distinction of More and Less. How can Less not feel the pain; how not feel indignation or malevolence towards More? Look at those who have less faculty, and one feels sad, and knows not well

what to make of it. He almost shuns their eye; he fears they will upbraid God. What should they do? It seems a great injustice. But see the facts nearly and these mountainous inequalities vanish. Love reduces them as the sun melts the iceberg in the sea. The heart and soul of all men being one, this bitterness of *His* and *Mine* ceases. His is mine. I am my brother, and my brother is me. If I feel overshadowed and outdone by great neighbors, I can yet love; I can still receive; and he that loveth maketh his own the grandeur he loves. Thereby I make the discovery that my brother is my guardian, acting for me with the friendliest designs, and the estate I so admired and envied is my own. It is the nature of the soul to appropriate all things. Jesus and Shakespeare are fragments of the soul, and by love I conquer and incorporate them in my own conscious domain. His virtue,—is not that mine? His wit,—if it cannot be made mine, it is not wit.

Such also is the natural history of calamity. The changes which break up at short intervals the prosperity of men are advertisements of a nature whose law is growth. Every soul is by this intrinsic necessity quitting its whole system of things, its friends and home and laws and faith, as the shell-fish crawls out of its beautiful but stony case, because it no longer admits of its growth, and slowly forms a new house. [2] In proportion to the vigor of the individual, these revolutions are frequent, until in some happier mind they are incessant and all worldly relations hang very loosely about him, becoming, as it were, a transparent fluid membrane through which the living form is always seen, and not, as in most men, an indurated heterogeneous fabric of many dates, and of no settled character, in which the man is imprisoned. Then there can be enlargement, and the man of today scarcely recognizes the man of yesterday. And such should be the outward biography of man in time, a putting off of dead circumstances day by day, as he renews his raiment day by day. But to us, in our lapsed estate, resting, not advancing, resisting, not coöperating with the divine expansion, this growth comes by shocks.

We cannot part with our friends. We cannot let our angels go. We do not see that they only go out that archangels may come in. We are idolators of the old. We do not believe in the riches of the soul, in its proper eternity and omnipresence. We do not believe there is any force in today to rival or recreate that beautiful yesterday. We linger in the ruins of

---

[1] a French monk of the twelfth century, who preached the Second Crusade

[2] Cf. Holmes, "The Chambered Nautilus," p. 565.

the old tent where once we had bread and shelter and organs, nor believe that the spirit can feed, cover, and nerve us again. We cannot again find aught so dear, so sweet, so graceful. But we sit and weep in vain. The voice of the Almighty saith, "Up and onward for evermore!" We cannot stay amid the ruins. Neither will we rely on the new; and so we walk ever with reverted eyes, like those monsters who look backwards.

And yet the compensations of calamity are made apparent to the understanding also, after long intervals of time. A fever, a mutilation, a cruel disappointment, a loss of wealth, a loss of friends, seems at the moment unpaid loss, and unpayable. But the sure years reveal the deep remedial force that underlies all facts. The death of a dear friend, wife, brother, lover, which seemed nothing but privation, somewhat later assumes the aspect of a guide or genius; for it commonly operates revolutions in our way of life, terminates an epoch of infancy or of youth which was waiting to be closed, breaks up a wonted occupation, or a household, or style of living, and allows the formation of new ones more friendly to the growth of character. It permits or constrains the formation of new acquaintances and the reception of new influences that prove of the first importance to the next years; and the man or woman who would have remained a sunny garden-flower, with no room for its roots and too much sunshine for its head, by the falling of the walls and the neglect of the gardener is made the banian [1] of the forest, yielding shade and fruit to wide neighborhoods of men.

1841

THE RHODORA:

ON BEING ASKED, WHENCE IS THE FLOWER?

In May, when sea-winds pierced our solitudes,
I found the fresh Rhodora in the woods,
Spreading its leafless blooms in a damp nook,
To please the desert and the sluggish brook.
The purple petals, fallen in the pool,
Made the black water with their beauty gay;
Here might the red-bird come his plumes to cool,
And court the flower that cheapens his array.
Rhodora! if the sages ask thee why   9
This charm is wasted on the earth and sky,
Tell them, dear, that if eyes were made for seeing,

[1] A fig tree of India which sends down from its branches roots that in turn become trunks. One tree group may become 1500 feet in circumference; see note 3, p. 365.

Then Beauty is its own excuse for being:
Why thou wert there, O rival of the rose!
I never thought to ask, I never knew;
But, in my simple ignorance, suppose
The self-same Power that brought me there
    brought you.
1834   1839

EACH AND ALL

Little thinks, in the field, yon red-cloaked clown,
Of thee from the hill-top looking down;
The heifer that lows in the upland farm,
Far-heard, lows not thine ear to charm;
The sexton, tolling his bell at noon,
Deems not that great Napoleon
Stops his horse, and lists with delight,
Whilst his files sweep round yon Alpine height;
Nor knowest thou what argument
Thy life to thy neighbor's creed has lent.   10
All are needed by each one,
Nothing is fair or good alone.
I thought the sparrow's note from heaven,
Singing at dawn on the alder bough;
I brought him home, in his nest, at even;
He sings the song, but it pleases not now,
For I did not bring home the river and sky;—
He sang to my ear,—they sang to my eye.
The delicate shells lay on the shore;
The bubbles of the latest wave   20
Fresh pearls to their enamel gave;
And the bellowing of the savage sea
Greeted their safe escape to me.
I wiped away the weeds and foam,
I fetched my sea-born treasures home;
But the poor, unsightly, noisome things
Had left their beauty on the shore
With the sun, and the sand, and the wild uproar.
The lover watched his graceful maid,
As 'mid the virgin train she strayed,   30
Nor knew her beauty's best attire
Was woven still by the snow-white choir.
At last she came to his hermitage,
Like the bird from the woodlands to the cage;—
The gay enchantment was undone,
A gentle wife, but fairy none.
Then I said, "I covet truth;
Beauty is unripe childhood's cheat;
I leave it behind with the games of youth"—
As I spoke, beneath my feet   40
The ground-pine curled its pretty wreath,
Running over the club-moss burrs;
I inhaled the violet's breath;
Around me stood the oaks and firs;
Pine-cones and acorns lay on the ground;

Over me soared the eternal sky,
Full of light and of deity;
Again I saw, again I heard,
The rolling river, the morning bird;—
Beauty through my senses stole;   50
I yielded myself to the perfect whole.
1834?   1839

HYMN

SUNG AT THE COMPLETION OF THE CONCORD MONUMENT

By the rude bridge that arched the flood,
  Their flag to April's breeze unfurled,
Here once the embattled farmers stood,
  And fired the shot heard round the world.

The foe long since in silence slept;
  Alike the conqueror silent sleeps;
And Time the ruined bridge has swept
  Down the dark stream which seaward creeps.

On this green bank, by this soft stream,
  We set today a votive stone;   10
That memory may their deed redeem,
  When, like our sires, our sons are gone.

Spirit, that made those heroes dare
  To die and leave their children free,
Bid Time and Nature gently spare
  The shaft we raise to them and thee.
1836   1837

THE HUMBLEBEE

Burly, dozing humblebee,
Where thou art is clime for me.
Let them sail for Porto Rique,
Far-off heats through seas to seek;
I will follow thee alone,
Thou animated torrid-zone!
Zigzag steerer, desert cheerer,
Let me chase thy waving lines;
Keep me nearer, me thy hearer,
Singing over shrubs and vines.   10

Insect lover of the sun,
Joy of thy dominion!
Sailor of the atmosphere;
Swimmer through the waves of air;
Voyager of light and noon;
Epicurean of June;
Wait, I prithee, till I come
Within earshot of thy hum,—
All without is martyrdom.

When the south wind, in May days,   20
With a net of shining haze
Silvers the horizon wall,
And, with softness touching all,
Tints the human countenance
With the color of romance,
And, infusing subtle heats,
Turns the sod to violets,
Thou, in sunny solitudes,
Rover of the underwoods,
The green silence dost displace   30
With thy mellow, breezy bass.

Hot midsummer's petted crone,
Sweet to me thy drowsy tone
Tells of countless sunny hours,
Long days, and solid banks of flowers;
Of gulfs of sweetness without bound
In Indian wildernesses found;
Of Syrian peace, immortal leisure,
Firmest cheer, and bird-like pleasure.

Aught unsavory or unclean   40
Hath my insect never seen;
But violets and bilberry bells,
Maple-sap and daffodels,
Grass with green flag half-mast high,
Succory to match the sky,
Columbine with horn of honey,
Scented fern, and agrimony,
Clover, catchfly, adder's-tongue
And brier-roses, dwelt among;
All beside was unknown waste,   50
All was picture as he passed.
Wiser far than human seer,
Yellow-breeched philosopher!
Seeing only what is fair,
Sipping only what is sweet,
Thou dost mock at fate and care,
Leave the chaff and take the wheat.
When the fierce northwestern blast
Cools sea and lands so far and fast,
Thou already slumberest deep;   60
Woe and want thou canst outsleep;
Want and woe, which torture us,
Thy sleep makes ridiculous.
1837   1839

THE PROBLEM

I like a church; I like a cowl;
I love a prophet of the soul;
And on my heart monastic aisles
Fall like sweet strains, or pensive smiles;
Yet not for all his faith can see
Would I that cowled churchman be.

Why should the vest on him allure,
Which I could not on me endure?

Not from a vain or shallow thought   9
His awful Jove young Phidias [1] brought;
Never from lips of cunning fell
The thrilling Delphic oracle; [2]
Out from the heart of nature rolled
The burdens of the Bible old;
The litanies of nations came,
Like the volcano's tongue of flame,
Up from the burning core below,—
The canticles of love and woe;
The hand that rounded Peter's dome,   19
And groined the aisles of Christian Rome,
Wrought in a sad sincerity;
Himself from God he could not free;
He builded better than he knew;—
The conscious stone to beauty grew.

Know'st thou what wove yon woodbird's nest
Of leaves, and feathers from her breast?
Or how the fish outbuilt her shell,
Painting with morn each annual cell?
Or how the sacred pine-tree adds
To her old leaves new myriads?   30
Such and so grew these holy piles,
Whilst love and terror laid the tiles.

Earth proudly wears the Parthenon, [3]
As the best gem upon her zone;
And Morning opes with haste her lids
To gaze upon the Pyramids;
O'er England's abbeys bends the sky,
As on its friends, with kindred eye;
For, out of Thought's interior sphere,
These wonders rose to upper air;   40
And Nature gladly gave them place,
Adopted them into her race,
And granted them an equal date
With Andes and with Ararat.

These temples grew as grows the grass;
Art might obey, but not surpass.
The passive Master lent his hand
To the vast soul that o'er him planned;
And the same power that reared the shrine,
Bestrode the tribes that knelt within.   50
Ever the fiery Pentecost [4]

Girds with one flame the countless host,
Trances the heart through chanting choirs,
And through the priest the mind inspires.

The word unto the prophet spoken
Was writ on tables yet unbroken;
The word by seers or sibyls [5] told,
In groves of oak, [6] or fanes of gold,
Still floats upon the morning wind,
Still whispers to the willing mind.   60
One accent of the Holy Ghost
The heedless world hath never lost.
I know what say the fathers wise,—
The Book itself before me lies,
Old *Chrysostom,* [7] best *Augustine,* [8]
And he who blent both in his line,
The younger *Golden Lips* or mines,
Taylor, [9] the Shakespeare of divines.
His words are music in my ear,
I see his cowled portrait dear;   70
And yet, for all his faith could see,
I would not the good bishop be.

1839   1840

THE SNOW-STORM

Announced by all the trumpets of the sky
Arrives the snow, and, driving o'er the fields,
Seems nowhere to alight: the whited air
Hides hills and woods, the river, and the
          heaven,
And veils the farm-house at the garden's end.
The sled and traveler stopped, the courier's
          feet
Delayed, all friends shut out, the housemates
          sit
Around the radiant fireplace, enclosed
In a tumultuous privacy of storm.

Come see the north wind's masonry.   10
Out of an unseen quarry evermore
Furnished with tile, the fierce artificer
Curves his white bastions with projected roof
Round every windward stake, or tree, or door.
Speeding, the myriad-handed, his wild work
So fanciful, so savage, naught cares he
For number or proportion. Mockingly,
On coop or kennel he hangs Parian [10] wreaths;

[1] Phidias, the greatest Greek sculptor; one of his masterpieces was a colossal statue of Zeus, or Jove, at Olympia; his work was highly regarded by the ancients for its moral value.
[2] The utterances of the oracle of the Pythian Apollo at Delphi, the greatest of all the Greek oracles, were not, Emerson implies, the mere whims of priestcraft, but the voice of morality and justice.
[3] This temple of Pallas Athene at Athens is the purest example of Greek architecture.
[4] The fiftieth day after the Passover and the crucifixion, when the Holy Spirit appeared as tongues of flame upon the Christians assembled in Jerusalem; see *Acts* ii, 1 ff.

[5] prophetesses
[6] The Druid priests of early Britain are supposed to have worshiped in oak groves.
[7] Saint John Chrysostom (golden mouthed), so named because of his eloquence, was a celebrated prelate of the Greek church in the fourth century A.D.
[8] Saint Augustine, 354-430 A.D., a great ecclesiastic of the Latin church, whose autobiography is found in his *Confessions*
[9] Jeremy Taylor, a seventeenth century bishop of the English church, whose *Holy Living* and *Holy Dying* are rich in poetic imagination
[10] i. e., as of Parian marble, from Paros, in the Aegean Sea

A swan-like form invests the hidden thorn; 19
Fills up the farmer's lane from wall to wall,
Maugre the farmer's sighs; and, at the gate
A tapering turret overtops the work.
And when his hours are numbered, and the
    world
Is all his own, retiring, as he were not,
Leaves, when the sun appears, astonished Art
To mimic in slow structures, stone by stone,
Built in an age, the mad wind's night-work,
The frolic architecture of the snow.
                                        1841

COMPENSATION

Why should I keep holiday
    When other men have none?
Why but because, when these are gay,
    I sit and mourn alone?

And why, when mirth unseals all tongues
    Should mine alone be dumb?
Ah! late I spoke to silent throngs,
    And now their hour is come.

1834   1841

FORBEARANCE

Hast thou named all the birds without a gun?
Loved the wood-rose, and left it on its stalk?
At rich men's tables eaten bread and pulse?
Unarmed, faced danger with a heart of trust?
And loved so well a high behavior,
In man or maid, that thou from speech re-
    frained,
Nobility more nobly to repay?
O, be my friend, and teach me to be thine!
                                        1842

TO RHEA [1]

Thee, dear friend, a brother soothes,
Not with flatteries, but truths,
Which tarnish not, but purify
To light which dims the morning's eye.
I have come from the spring-woods.
From the fragrant solitudes;—
Listen what the poplar-tree
And murmuring waters counseled me.

If with love thy heart has burned;
If thy love is unreturned;   10
Hide thy grief within thy breast,

[1] Rhea, recognized by the ancients as a deity of the
earth, seems in this poem to typify men and
women of earthly mold. The gods, or the higher
sort of humanity, escape the pangs of human passion and mere earthly love by heaping gifts on
those who have rejected their devotion. Emerson
would point the contrast between ordinary human
passion and love of a more ethereal nature. See
his essay "Love."

Though it tear thee unexpressed;
For when love has once departed
From the eyes of the false-hearted,
And one by one has torn off quite
The bandages of purple light;
Though thou wert the loveliest
Form the soul had ever dressed,
Thou shalt seem, in each reply,
A vixen to his altered eye;   20
Thy softest pleadings seem too bold,
Thy praying lute shall seem to scold;
Though thou kept the straightest road,
Yet thou errest far and broad.

But thou shalt do as do the gods
In their cloudless periods;
For of this lore be thou sure,—
Though thou forget, the gods, secure,
Forget never their command,
But make the statute of this land.   30
As they lead, so follow all,
Ever have done, ever shall.
Warning to the blind and deaf,
'Tis written on the iron leaf, [2]
*Who drinks of Cupid's nectar cup
Loveth downward, and not up;*
Therefore, who loves, of gods or men,
Shall not by the same be loved again;
His sweetheart's idolatry
Falls, in turn, a new degree.   40
When a god is once beguiled
By beauty of a mortal child,
And by her radiant youth delighted,
He is not fooled, but warily knoweth
His love shall never be requited.
And thus the wise Immortal doeth.—
'Tis his study and delight
To bless that creature day and night;
From all evils to defend her;
In her lap to pour all splendor;   50
To ransack earth for riches rare,
And fetch her stars to deck her hair:
He mixes music with her thoughts,
And saddens her with heavenly doubts:
All grace, all good his great heart knows,
Profuse in love, the king bestows:
Saying, "Hearken! Earth, Sea, Air!
This monument of my despair
Build I to the All-Good, All-Fair.
Not for a private good,   60
But I, from my beatitude,
Albeit scorned as none was scorned,
Adorn her as was none adorned.
I make this maiden an ensample
To Nature, through her kingdoms ample,
Whereby to model newer races,
Statelier forms, and fairer faces;

[2] i. e., inexorably

To carry man to new degrees
Of power, and of comeliness.
These presents be the hostages   70
Which I pawn for my release.
See to thyself, O Universe!
Thou art better, and not worse."—
And the god, having given all,
Is freed forever from his thrall.

                                        1843

EROS [1]

The sense of the world is short, —
Long and various the report,—
    To love and be beloved;
Men and gods have not outlearned it;
And, how oft soe'er they've turned it,
    'Tis not to be improved.

                                        1844

EXPERIENCE

The lords of life, the lords of life,—
I saw them pass,
In their own guise,
Like and unlike,
Portly and grim,—
Use and Surprise,
Surface and Dream,
Succession swift, and spectral Wrong,
Temperament without a tongue,
And the inventor of the game   10
Omnipresent without name;—
Some to see, some to be guessed,
They march from east to west:
Little man, least of all,
Among the legs of his guardians tall,
Walked about with puzzled look.
Him by the hand dear Nature took,
Dearest Nature, strong and kind,
Whispered, "Darling never mind!   19
Tomorrow they will wear another face,
The founder thou; these are thy race!"

                                    1844, 1867

FORERUNNERS

Long I followed happy guides,
I could never reach their sides;
Their step is forth, and, ere the day,
Breaks up their leaguer, [2] and away.
Keen my sense, my heart was young,
Right good-will my sinews strung,
But no speed of mine avails
To hunt upon their shining trails.
On and away, their hasting feet
Make the morning proud and sweet;   10
Flowers they strew,—I catch the scent;
Or tone of silver instrument

[1] god of love
[2] camp

Leaves on the wind melodious trace;
Yet I could never see their face.
On eastern hills I see their smokes,
Mixed with mist by distant lochs.
I met many travelers
Who the road had surely kept;
They saw not my fine revelers,—   19
These had crossed them while they slept.
Some had heard their fair report,
In the country or the court.
Fleetest couriers alive
Never yet could once arrive,
As they went or they returned,
At the house where these sojourned.
Sometimes their strong speed they slacken,
Though they are not overtaken;
In sleep their jubilant troop is near,—
I tuneful voices overhear;   30
It may be in wood or waste,—
At unawares 'tis come and past.
Their near camp my spirit knows
By signs gracious as rainbows.
I thenceforward, and long after,
Listen for their harp-like laughter,
And carry in my heart, for days,
Peace that hallows rudest ways.

                                        1846

FABLE

The mountain and the squirrel
Had a quarrel;
And the former called the latter "Little Prig;"
Bun replied,
"You are doubtless very big;
But all sorts of things and weather
Must be taken in together,
To make up a year
And a sphere.
And I think it no disgrace   10
To occupy my place.
If I'm not so large as you,
You are not so small as I,
And not half so spry.
I'll not deny you make
A very pretty squirrel track;
Talents differ; all is well and wisely put;
If I cannot carry forests on my back,
Neither can you crack a nut."

                                        1846

MITHRIDATES [3]

I cannot spare water or wine,
    Tobacco-leaf, or poppy, or rose;
From the earth-poles to the line,

[3] Mithridates, 132-63 B.C., was King of Pontus, a country on the Black Sea. He was said so to have filled his system with poisons, by magic, as to be immune to them.

All between that works or grows,
Everything is kin of mine.

Give me agates for my meat;
Give me cantharids [1] to eat;
From air and ocean bring me foods,
From all zones and altitudes;—

From all natures, sharp and slimy,   10
  Salt and basalt, wild and tame:
Tree and lichen, ape, sea-lion,
  Bird, and reptile, be my game.

Ivy for my fillet band;
Blinding dog-wood in my hand;
Hemlock for my sherbet cull me,
And the prussic juice to lull me;
Swing me in the upas [2] boughs,
Vampyre-fanned, when I carouse.

Too long shut in strait and few,   20
Thinly dieted on dew,
I will use the world, and sift it,
To a thousand humors shift it,
As you spin a cherry.
O doleful ghosts, and goblins merry!
O all you virtues, methods, mights,
Means, appliances, delights,
Reputed wrongs and braggart rights,
Smug routine, and things allowed,
Minorities, things under cloud!   30
Hither! take me, use me, fill me,
Vein and artery, though ye kill me;
God! I will not be an owl,
But sun me in the Capitol.

                                  1847

ASTRAEA [3]

Each the herald is who wrote
His rank, and quartered [4] his own coat.
There is no king nor sovereign state
That can fix a hero's rate;
Each to all is venerable,
Cap-a-pie invulnerable,
Until he write, where all eyes rest,
Slave or master on his breast.

I saw men go up and down,
In the country and the town,   10
With this tablet on their neck,—
"Judgment and a judge we seek."
Not to monarchs they repair,
Nor to learned jurist's chair;
But they hurry to their peers,

[1] a kind of poisonous beetle
[2] a poisonous tree
[3] the Greek goddess of justice
[4] added an heraldic sign to a coat of arms; hence, set-
    tled his own rank

To their kinsfolk and their dears;
Louder than with speech they pray,—
"What am I? companion, say."
And the friend not hesitates
To assign just place and mates;   20
Answers not in word or letter,
Yet is understood the better;
Each to each a looking-glass,
Reflects his figure that doth pass.
Every wayfarer he meets
What himself declared repeats,
What himself confessed records,
Sentences him in his words;
The form is his own corporal form,
And his thought the penal worm.   30

Yet shine forever virgin minds,
Loved by stars and purest winds,
Which, o'er passion throned sedate,
Have not hazarded their state;
Disconcert the searching spy,
Rendering to a curious eye
The durance of a granite ledge
To those who gaze from the sea's edge.
It is there for benefit;
It is there for purging light;   40
There for purifying storms;
And its depths reflect all forms;
It cannot parley with the mean,—
Pure by impure is not seen.
For there's no sequestered grot,
Lone mountain tarn, [5] or isle forgot,
But Justice, journeying in the sphere,
Daily stoops to harbor there.

                                  1847

GIVE ALL TO LOVE

Give all to love;
Obey thy heart;
Friends, kindred, days,
Estate, good-fame,
Plans, credit, and the Muse,—
Nothing refuse.

'Tis a brave master;
Let it have scope:
Follow it utterly,
Hope beyond hope: 10
High and more high
It dives into noon,
With wing unspent,
Untold intent;
But it is a god,
Knows its own path,
And the outlets of the sky.

It was not for the mean;
It requireth courage stout,

[5] lake

Souls above doubt,   20
Valor unbending;
Such 'twill reward,—
They shall return
More than they were,
And ever ascending.

Leave all for love;
Yet, hear me, yet,
One word more thy heart behoved,
One pulse more of firm endeavor,—
Keep thee today,   30
Tomorrow, forever,
Free as an Arab
Of thy beloved.

Cling with life to the maid;
But when the surprise,
First vague shadow of surmise
Flits across her bosom young
Of a joy apart from thee,
Free be she, fancy-free;
Nor thou detain her vesture's hem,   40
Nor the palest rose she flung
From her summer diadem.

Though thou loved her as thyself,
As a self of purer clay,
Though her parting dims the day,
Stealing grace from all alive;
Heartily know,
When half-gods go,
The gods arrive.

                                              1847

MERLIN[1]

I

Thy trivial harp will never please
Or fill my craving ear;
Its chords should ring as blows the breeze,
Free, peremptory, clear.
No jingling serenader's art,
Nor tinkle of piano strings,
Can make the wild blood start
In its mystic springs.
The kingly bard
Must smite the chords rudely and hard,   10
As with hammer or with mace;
That they may render back
Artful thunder, which conveys
Secrets of the solar track,
Sparks of the supersolar blaze.
Merlin's blows are strokes of fate,

Chiming with the forest tone,
When boughs buffet boughs in the wood;
Chiming with the gasp and moan
Of the ice-imprisoned flood;   20
With the pulse of manly hearts;
With the voice of orators;
With the din of city arts;
With the cannonade of wars;
With the marches of the brave;
And prayers of might from martyrs' cave.

Great is the art,
Great be the manners, of the bard.
He shall not his brain encumber
With the coil of rhythm and number;   30
But, leaving rule and pale forethought,
He shall aye climb
For his rime.
"Pass in, pass in," the angels say,
"In to the upper doors,
Nor count compartments of the floors.
But mount to paradise
By the stairway of surprise."

Blameless master of the games,
King of sport that never shames,   40
He shall daily joy dispense
Hid in song's sweet influence.
Things more cheerly live and go.
What time the subtle mind
Sings aloud the tune whereto
Their pulses beat,
And march their feet,
And their members are combined.

By Sybarites[2] beguiled,
He shall no task decline;   50
Merlin's mighty line
Extremes of nature reconciled,—
Bereaved a tyrant of his will,
And made the lion mild.
Songs can the tempest still,
Scattered on the stormy air,
Mold the year to fair increase
And bring in poetic peace.

He shall not seek to weave,
In weak, unhappy times,   60
Efficacious rimes;
Wait his returning strength.
Bird, that from the nadir's[3] floor
To the zenith's top can soar,
The soaring orbit of the muse exceeds that
            journey's length.

[1] A half-legendary poet of perhaps the sixth century; the name is also that of the great magician of the Arthurian legends.

[2] The inhabitants of the city of Sybaris, an ancient city of Italy, were known for their great luxury.
[3] the point just opposite the zenith or directly below our feet

Nor profane affect to hit
Or compass that, by meddling wit,
Which only the propitious mind
Publishes when 'tis inclined.
There are open hours   70
When the God's will sallies free,
And the dull idiot might see
The flowing fortunes of a thousand years;—
Sudden, at unawares,
Self-moved, fly-to the doors,
Nor sword of angels could reveal
What they conceal.

II

The rime of the poet
Modulates the king's affairs;
Balance-loving Nature   80
Made all things in pairs.
To every foot its antipode;
Each color with its counter glowed;
To every tone beat answering tones,
Higher or graver;.
Flavor gladly blends with flavor;
Leaf answers leaf upon the bough;
And match the paired cotyledons.
Hands to hands, and feet to feet,
In one body grooms and brides;   90
Eldest rite, two married sides
In every mortal meet.
Light's far furnace shines,
Smelting balls and bars,
Forging double stars,
Glittering twins and trines.
The animals are sick with love,
Lovesick with rime;
Each with all propitious time
Into chorus wove.   100

Like the dancer's ordered band,
Thoughts come also hand in hand;
In equal couples mated,
Or else alternated;
Adding by their mutual gage,
One to other, health and age.
Solitary fancies go
Short-lived wandering to and fro,
Most like to bachelors,
Or an ungiven maid,   110
Not ancestors,
With no posterity to make the lie afraid,
Or keep truth undecayed.
Perfect-paired as eagle's wings,
Justice is the rime of things;
Trade and counting use
The self-same tuneful muse;
And Nemesis, [1]

[1] goddess of retribution, and allotter of divine justice

Who with even matches odd,
Who athwart space redresses   120
The partial wrong,
Fills the just period,
And finishes the song.

Subtle rimes, with ruin rife,
Murmur in the house of life,
Sung by the Sisters [2] as they spin;
In perfect time and measure they
Build and unbuild our echoing clay,
As the two twilights of the day   129
Fold us music-drunken in.

1847

THRENODY [3]

The South-wind brings
Life, sunshine, and desire,
And on every mount and meadow
Breathes aromatic fire;
But over the dead he has no power,
The lost, the lost, he cannot restore;
And, looking over the hills, I mourn
The darling who shall not return.

I see my empty house,
I see my trees repair their boughs;   10
And he, the wondrous child,
Whose silver warble wild
Outvalued every pulsing sound
Within the air's cerulean round,—
The hyacinthine boy, for whom
Morn well might break and April bloom,—
The gracious boy, who did adorn
The world whereinto he was born,
And by his countenance repay
The favor of the loving Day, —   20
Has disappeared from the Day's eye;
Far and wide she cannot find him;
My hopes pursue, they cannot bind him.
Returned this day, the south wind searches,
And finds young pines and budding birches;
But finds not the budding man;
Nature, who lost, cannot remake him;
Fate let him fall, Fate can't retake him;
Nature, Fate, men, him seek in vain.

And whither now, my truant wise and sweet,
O, whither tend thy feet?   31
I had the right, few days ago,
Thy steps to watch, thy place to know;
How have I forfeited the right?

[2] the Fates, who spin, weave, and cut the thread of human life

[3] From θρῆνος, wailing, and ὠδή, song: the poem was written in 1842, just after the death of Emerson's oldest son Waldo, "a perfect little boy of five years and three months," as Emerson wrote Carlyle.

Hast thou forgot me in a new delight?
I hearken for thy household cheer,
O eloquent child!
Whose voice, an equal messenger,
Conveyed thy meaning mild.
What though the pains and joys   40
Whereof it spoke were toys
Fitting his age and ken,
Yet fairest dames and bearded men,
Who heard the sweet request,
So gentle, wise, and grave,
Bended with joy to his behest,
And let the world's affairs go by,
Awhile to share his cordial game,
Or mend his wicker wagon-frame,
Still plotting how their hungry ear   50
That winsome voice again might hear;
For his lips could well pronounce
Words that were persuasions.

Gentlest guardians marked serene
His early hope, his liberal mien;
Took counsel from his guiding eyes
To make this wisdom earthly wise,
Ah, vainly do these eyes recall
The school-march, each day's festival,
When every morn my bosom glowed   60
To watch the convoy on the road;
The babe in willow wagon closed,
With rolling eyes and face composed;
With children forward and behind,
Like Cupids studiously inclined;
And he the chieftain paced beside,
The center of the troop allied,
With sunny face of sweet repose,
To guard the babe from fancied foes.
The little captain innocent   70
Took the eye with him as he went,
Each village senior paused to scan
And speak the lovely caravan.
From the window I look out
To mark thy beautiful parade,
Stately marching in cap and coat
To some tune by fairies played;—
A music heard by thee alone
To works as noble led thee on.

Now Love and Pride, alas! in vain,   80
Up and down their glances strain.
The painted sled stands where it stood;
The kennel by the corded wood;
The gathered sticks to stanch the wall
Of the snow-tower, when snow should fall;
The ominous hole he dug in the sand,
And childhood's castles built or planned;
His daily haunts I well discern,—
The poultry-yard, the shed, the barn,—

And every inch of garden ground   90
Paced by the blessed feet around,
From the roadside to the brook
Whereinto he loved to look.
Step the meek birds where erst they ranged;
The wintry garden lies unchanged;
The brook into the stream runs on;
But the deep-eyed boy is gone.

On that shaded day,
Dark with more clouds than tempests are,
When thou didst yield thy innocent breath
In birdlike heavings unto death,   101
Night came, and Nature had not thee;
I said, "We are mates in misery."
The morrow dawned with needless glow;
Each snowbird chirped, each fowl must crow;
Each tramper started; but the feet
Of the most beautiful and sweet
Of human youth had left the hill
And garden,—they were bound and still.
There's not a sparrow or a wren,   110
There's not a blade of autumn grain,
Which the four seasons do not tend,
And tides of life and increase lend;
And every chick of every bird,
And weed and rock-moss is preferred.
O ostrich-like forgetfulness!
O loss of larger in the less!
Was there no star that could be sent,
No watcher in the firmament,
No angel from the countless host   120
That loiters round the crystal coast,
Could stoop to heal that only child,
Nature's sweet marvel undefiled,
And keep the blossom of the earth,
Which all her harvests were not worth?
Not mine,—I never called thee mine,
But Nature's heir,—if I repine,
And seeing rashly torn and moved
Not what I made, but what I loved,
Grow early old with grief that thou   130
Must to the wastes of Nature go,—
'T is because a general hope
Was quenched, and all must doubt and grope.
For flattering planets seemed to say
This child should ills of ages stay,
By wondrous tongue, and guided pen,
Bring the flown Muses back to men.
Perchance not he but Nature ailed,
The world and not the infant failed.
It was not ripe yet to sustain   140
A genius of so fine a strain,
Who gazed upon the sun and moon
As if he came unto his own,
And, pregnant with his grander thought,
Brought the old order into doubt.

His beauty once their beauty tried;
They could not feed him, and he died.
And wandered backward as in scorn,
To wait an aeon to be born.
Ill day which made this beauty waste,   150
Plight broken, this high face defaced!
Some went and came about the dead;
And some in books of solace read;
Some to their friends the tidings say;
Some went to write, some went to pray;
One tarried here, there hurried one;
But their heart abode with none.
Covetous death bereaved us all,
To aggrandize one funeral.
The eager fate which carried thee   160
Took the largest part of me:
For this losing is true dying;
This is lordly man's down-lying;
This his slow but sure reclining,
Star by star his world resigning.

O child of paradise,
Boy who made dear his father's home,
In whose deep eyes
Men read the welfare of the times to come,
I am too much bereft.   170
The world dishonored thou hast left.
O truth's and nature's costly lie!
O trusted broken prophecy!
O richest fortune sourly crossed!
Born for the future, to the future lost!
The deep Heart answered, "Weepest thou?
Worthier cause for passion wild
If I had not taken the child.
And deemest thou as those who pore,
With aged eyes, short way before,—   180
Think'st Beauty vanished from the coast
Of matter, and thy darling lost?
Taught he not thee—the man of eld,
Whose eyes within his eyes beheld
Heaven's numerous hierarchy span
The mystic gulf from God to man?
To be alone wilt thou begin
When worlds of lovers hem thee in?
Tomorrow, when the masks shall fall
That dizen Nature's carnival,   190
The pure shall see by their own will,
Which overflowing Love shall fill,
'T is not within the force of fate
The fate-conjoined to separate.
But thou, my votary, weepest thou?
I gave thee sight—where is it now?
I taught thy heart beyond the reach
Of ritual, bible, or of speech;
Wrote in thy mind's transparent table,
As far as the incommunicable;   200
Taught thee each private sign to raise

Lit by the supersolar blaze.
Past utterance, and past belief,
And past the blasphemy of grief,
The mysteries of Nature's heart;
And though no Muse can these impart,
Throb thine with Nature's throbbing breast,
And all is clear from east to west.

"I came to thee as to a friend;
Dearest, to thee I did not send   210
Tutors, but a joyful eye,
Innocence that matched the sky,
Lovely locks, a form of wonder,
Laughter rich as woodland thunder,
That thou mightst entertain apart
The richest flowering of all art:
And, as the great all-loving Day
Through smallest chambers takes its way,
That thou mightst break thy daily bread
With prophet, savior and head;   220
That thou mightst cherish for thine own
The riches of sweet Mary's Son,
Boy-Rabbi, Israel's paragon.
And thoughtest thou such guest
Would in thy hall take up his rest?
Would rushing life forget her laws,
Fate's glowing revolution pause?
High omens ask diviner guess;
Not to be conned to tediousness.
And know my higher gifts unbind   230
The zone that girds the incarnate mind.
When the scanty shores are full
With Thought's perilous, whirling pool;
When frail Nature can no more,
Then the Spirit strikes the hour:
My servant Death, with solving rite,
Pours finite into infinite.

"Wilt thou freeze love's tidal flow,
Whose streams through nature circling go?
Nail the wild star to its track   240
On the half-climbed zodiac?
Light is light which radiates,
Blood is blood which circulates,
Life is life which generates,
And many-seeming life is one,—
Wilt thou transfix and make it none?
Its onward force too starkly pent
In figure, bone, and lineament?
Wilt thou, uncalled, interrogate,
Talker! the unreplying Fate?   250
Nor see the genius of the whole
Ascendant in the private soul,
Beckon it when to go and come,
Self-announced its hour of doom?
Fair the soul's recess and shrine,
Magic-built to last a season;

Masterpiece of love benign,
Fairer that expansive reason
Whose omen 't is, and sign.
Wilt thou not ope thy heart to know   260
What rainbows teach, and sunsets show?
Verdict which accumulates
From lengthening scroll of human fates,
Voice of earth to earth returned,
Prayers of saints that inly burned,—
Saying, *What is excellent,*
As God lives, is permanent;
Hearts are dust, hearts' loves remain;
Heart's love will meet thee again.
Revere the Maker; fetch thine eye   270
Up to his style, and manners of the sky.
Not of adamant and gold
Built he heaven stark and cold;
No, but a nest of bending reeds,
Flowering grass and scented weeds;
Or like a traveler's fleeing tent,
Or bow above the tempest bent;
Built of tears and sacred flames,
And virtue reaching to its aims;
Built of furtherance and pursuing,   280
Not of spent deeds, but of doing.
Silent rushes the swift Lord
Through ruined systems still restored,
Broadsowing, bleak and void to bless,
Plants with worlds the wilderness;
Waters with tears of ancient sorrow
Apples of Eden ripe tomorrow.
House and tenant go to ground,
Lost in God, in Godhead found."
1842   1847

ODE

SUNG IN THE TOWN HALL, CONCORD, JULY 4,
1857

Oh tenderly the haughty day
   Fills his blue urn with fire;
One morn is in the mighty heaven,
   And one in our desire.

The cannon booms from town to town,
   Our pulses are not less,
The joy-bells chime their tidings down,
   Which children's voices bless.

For He that flung the broad blue fold
   O'er-mantling land and sea,   10
One third part of the sky unrolled
   For the banner of the free.

The men are ripe of Saxon kind
   To build an equal state,—
To take the statute from the mind
   And make of duty fate.

United States! the ages plead,—
   Present and Past in under-song,—
Go put your creed into your deed,
   Nor speak with double tongue.   20

For sea and land don't understand
   Nor skies without a frown
See rights for which the one hand fights
   By the other cloven down.

Be just at home; then write your scroll
   Of honor o'er the sea,
And bid the broad Atlantic roll
   A ferry of the free.

And henceforth there shall be no chain,
   Save underneath the sea   30
The wires shall murmur through the main [1]
   Sweet songs of liberty.

The conscious stars accord above,
   The waters wild below,
And under, through the cable wove,
   Her fiery errands go.

For He that worketh high and wise,
   Nor pauses in his plan,
Will take the sun out of the skies   39
   Ere freedom out of man.
1857   1867

THE ROMANY [2] GIRL

The sun goes down, and with him takes
The coarseness of my poor attire;
The fair moon mounts, and aye the flame
Of gypsy beauty blazes higher.

Pale northern girls! you scorn our race;
You captives of your air-tight halls,
Wear out in-doors your sickly days,
But leave us the horizon walls.

And if I take you, dames, to task,
And say it frankly without guile,   10
Then you are gypsies in a mask,
And I the lady all the while.

If, on the heath, below the moon,
I court and play with paler blood,
Me false to mine dare whisper none,—
One sallow horseman knows me good.

----

[1] Although submarine telegraphy had already been established between Nova Scotia and Newfoundland,
and the transatlantic line had been projected, the
laying of the great Atlantic cable was not completed until 1866.
[2] gypsy

Go, keep your cheek's rose from the rain,
For teeth and hair with shopmen deal;
My swarthy tint is in the grain,
The rocks and forest know it real.   20

The wild air bloweth in our lungs,
The keen stars twinkle in our eyes,
The birds gave us our wily tongues,
The panther in our dances flies.

You doubt we read the stars on high,
Nathless we read your fortunes true;
The stars may hide in the upper sky,
But without glass we fathom you.
1855   *1857*

BRAHMA [1]

If the red slayer think he slays,
  Or if the slain think he is slain,
They know not well the subtle ways
  I keep, and pass, and turn again.

Far or forgot to me is near;
  Shadow and sunlight are the same;
The vanished gods to me appear;
  And one to me are shame and fame.

They reckon ill who leave me out;
  When me they fly, I am the wings;   10
I am the doubter and the doubt,
  And I the hymn the Brahmin sings.

The strong gods pine for my abode,
  And pine in vain the sacred Seven;
But thou, meek lover of the good!
  Find me, and turn thy back on heaven.
1857   *1857*

WORSHIP

This is he, who, felled by foes,
Sprung harmless up, refreshed by blows:
He to captivity was sold,
But him no prison-bars would hold:

[1] Brahma was the personal god of the Hindus, "the
original source and ultimate goal of all that exists."
Oscar W. Firkins, of the University of Minnesota, author of *Ralph Waldo Emerson* (Houghton
Mifflin Company, 1915), has kindly furnished
the following interpretation of the poem:
  "In the poem Brahma stands for the cosmic
force which is the ultimatum of science, and
which in Emerson's mind was identical with the
divine spirit, the spirit of truth, goodness, and
beauty, the ultimatum of religion. As Brahma,
this force is here viewed with special reference
to its unending and manifold transformations."
  Emerson, hearing that the poem was not always
understood, said that the meaning might be easily
grasped if "Jehovah" were substituted for
"Brahma." See *Centenary Edition* of Emerson's
Poems, page 464, 7.

Though they sealed him in a rock,
Mountain chains he can unlock:
Thrown to lions for their meat,
The crouching lion kissed his feet:
Bound to the stake, no flames appalled,
But arched o'er him an honoring vault.   10
This is he men miscall Fate,
Threading dark ways, arriving late,
But ever coming in time to crown
The truth, and hurl wrong-doers down.
He is the oldest, and best known,
More near than aught thou call'st thy own,
Yet, greeted in another's eyes,
Disconcerts with glad surprise.
This is Jove, who, deaf to prayers,
Floods with blessings unawares.   20
Draw, if thou canst, the mystic line
Severing rightly his from thine,
Which is human, which divine.
1859-1860   *1860*

BOSTON HYMN

READ IN MUSIC HALL, JANUARY 1, 1863

The word of the Lord by night
To the watching Pilgrims came,
As they sat by the seaside,
And filled their hearts with flame.

God said, I am tired of kings,
I suffer them no more;
Up to my ear the morning brings
The outrage of the poor.

Think ye I made this ball
A field of havoc and war,   10
Where tyrants great and tyrants small
Might harry the weak and poor?

My angel, his name is Freedom,—
Choose him to be your king;
He shall cut pathways east and west,
And fend you with his wing.

Lo! I uncover the land
Which I hid of old time in the West,
As the sculptor uncovers the statue
When he has wrought his best;   20

I show Columbia, of the rocks
Which dip their foot in the seas,
And soar to the air-borne flocks
Of clouds, and the boreal fleece.

I will divide my goods;
Call in the wretch and slave:
None shall rule but the humble,
And none but Toil shall have.

I will have never a noble,
No lineage counted great;   30
Fishers and choppers and plowmen
Shall constitute a state.

Go, cut down trees in the forest,
And trim the straightest boughs;
Cut down the trees in the forest,
And build me a wooden house.

Call the people together,
The young men and the sires,
The digger in the harvest field,
Hireling, and him that hires;   40

And here in a pine state-house
They shall choose men to rule
In every needful faculty,
In church, and state, and school.

Lo, now! if these poor men
Can govern the land and sea,
And make just laws below the sun,
As planets faithful be.

And ye shall succour men;
'T is nobleness to serve;   50
Help them who cannot help again:
Beware from right to swerve.

I break your bonds and masterships,
And I unchain the slave:
Free be his heart and hand henceforth
As wind and wandering wave.

I cause from every creature
His proper good to flow:
As much as he is and doeth,
So much he shall bestow.   60

But laying hands on another
To coin his labor and sweat,
He goes in pawn to his victim
For eternal years in debt.

Today unbind the captive
So only are ye unbound;
Lift up a people from the dust,
Trump of their rescue, sound!

Pay ransom to the owner,
And fill the bag to the brim.   70
Who is the owner? The slave is owner,
And ever was. Pay him.

O North! give him beauty for rags,
And honor, O South! for his shame;

Nevada! coin thy golden crags
With Freedom's image and name. [1]

Up! and the dusky race
That sat in darkness long,—
Be swift their feet as antelopes,
And as behemoth [2] strong.   80

Come, East and West and North,
By races, as snow-flakes,
And carry my purpose forth,
Which neither halts nor shakes.

My will fulfilled shall be,
For, in daylight or in dark,
My thunderbolt has eyes to see
His way home to the mark.

               1863

VOLUNTARIES

I

Low and mournful be the strain,
Haughty thought be far from me;
Tones of penitence and pain,
Moanings of the tropic sea;
Low and tender in the cell
Where a captive sits in chains,
Crooning ditties treasured well
From his Afric's torrid plains.
Sole estate his sire bequeathed—
Hapless sire to hapless son—   10
Was the wailing song he breathed,
And his chain when life was done.
  What his fault, or what his crime?
Or what ill planet crossed his prime?
Heart too soft and will too weak
To front the fate that crouches near,—
Dove beneath the vulture's beak;—
Will song dissuade the thirsty spear?
Dragged from his mother's arms and breast,
Displaced, disfurnished here,   20
His wistful toil to do his best
Chilled by a ribald jeer,
Great men in the Senate sate,
Sage and hero, side by side,
Building for their sons the State,
Which they shall rule with pride.
They forbore to break the chain
Which bound the dusky tribe,
Checked by the owners' fierce disdain,
Lured by "Union" as the bribe.   30
Destiny sat by, and said,
"Pang for pang your seed shall pay,

---

[1] Nevada was admitted in 1864 chiefly to add one more
    loyal state to the Union.
[2] an animal described in *Job* xl, 15-24; possibly the hip-
    popotamus

Hide in false peace your coward head,
I bring round the harvest-day."

II

Freedom all winged expands,
Nor perches in a narrow place;
Her broad van seeks unplanted lands;
She loves a poor and virtuous race.
Clinging to a colder zone   39
Whose dark sky sheds the snow-flake down,
The snow-flake is her banner's star,
Her stripes the boreal streamers are.
Long she loved the Northman well:
Now the iron age is done,
She will not refuse to dwell
With the offspring of the Sun;
Foundling of the desert far,
Where palms, plume, siroccos blaze,
He roves unhurt the burning ways
In climates of the summer star.   50
He has avenues to God
Hid from men of Northern brain,
Far beholding, without cloud,
What these with slowest steps attain
If once the generous chief arrive
To lead him willing to be led,
For freedom he will strike and strive,
And drain his heart till he be dead.

III

In an age of fops and toys,
Wanting wisdom, void of right,   60
Who shall nerve heroic boys
To hazard all in Freedom's fight,—
Break sharply off their jolly games,
Forsake their comrades gay,
And quit proud homes and youthful dames
For famine, toil, and fray?
Yet on the nimble air benign
Speed nimbler messages,
That waft the breath of grace divine
To hearts in sloth and ease.   70
So nigh is grandeur to our dust,
So near is God to man,
When Duty whispers low, *Thou must,*
The youth replies, *I can.*

IV

O, well for the fortunate soul
Which music's wings infold,
Stealing away the memory
Of sorrows new and old!
Yet happier he whose inward sight,
Stayed on his subtile thought,   80
Shuts his sense on toys of time,
To vacant bosoms brought.

But best befriended of the God
He who, in evil times,
Warned by an inward voice,
Heeds not the darkness and the dread,
Biding by his rule and choice,
Feeling only the fiery thread
Leading over heroic ground,
Walled with mortal terror round,   90
To the aim which him allures,
And the sweet heaven his deed secures.

Stainless soldier on the walls,
Knowing this,—and knows no more,—
Whoever fights, whoever falls,
Justice conquers evermore,
Justice after as before,—
And he who battles on her side,
God, though he were ten times slain,
Crowns him victor glorified,   100
Victor over death and pain;
Forever: but his erring foe,
Self-assured that he prevails,
Looks from his victim lying low,
And sees aloft the red right arm
Redress the eternal scales.
He, the poor foe, whom angels foil,
Blind with pride, and fooled by hate,
Writhes within the dragon coil,
Reserved to a speechless fate.   110

V

Blooms the laurel which belongs
To the valiant chief who fights;
I see the wreath, I hear the songs
Lauding the Eternal Rights,
Victors over daily wrongs:
Awful victors, they misguide
Whom they will destroy,
And their coming triumph hide
In our downfall, or our joy:
They reach no term, they never sleep,   120
In equal strength through space abide;
Though, feigning dwarfs, they crouch and
    creep,
The strong they slay, the swift outstride:
Fate's grass grows rank in valley clods,
And rankly on the castled steep,—
Speak it firmly, these are gods,
All are ghosts beside.

1863

LETTERS

Every day brings a ship,
Every ship brings a word;
Well for those who have no fear,

Looking seaward well assured
That the word the vessel brings
Is the word they wish to hear.

1867

THE PAST

The debt is paid,
The verdict said,
The Furies [1] laid,
The plague is stayed,
All fortunes made;
Turn the key and bolt the door,
Sweet is death forevermore.
Nor haughty hope, nor swart chagrin,
Nor murdering hate, can enter in.
All is now secure and fast;   10
Not the gods can shake the Past;
Flies-to the adamantine door
Bolted down forevermore.
None can re-enter there,—
No thief so politic,
No Satan with a royal trick
Steal in by window, chink, or hole,
To bind or unbind, add what lacked,
Insert a leaf, or forge a name,
New-face or finish what is packed,   20
Alter or mend eternal Fact.

1867

HENRY DAVID THOREAU
1817-1862

Thoreau, who was of mingled French and New
England blood, was born and died at Concord,
Massachusetts. He graduated at Harvard, 1837,
returned to Concord, lived for a while with
Emerson, and intermittently taught school, surveyed, or worked at lead-pencil making, carpentry,
or other day-labor, long enough to meet the necessities of his simple life. He expressed his independent mind in social and ethical essays, and strongly
upheld the cause of anti-slavery. His chief delight
was in the first-hand study of nature. Foremost
among his works are *A Week on the Concord and
Merrimac Rivers*, 1849; *Walden*, 1854; *Excursions*,
1863; *The Maine Woods*, 1864; *Cape Cod*, 1865.
Thoreau is the most conspicuous convert and
disciple of Emerson, the sage. He follows his
master somewhat in style, but more particularly in
his attitude toward nature and the spiritual values
of life. Yet Thoreau was individual. Although,
like Emerson, he interpreted nature with spiritual
insight, he also loved it for its own sake with the
instinct of a naturalist. He was the foremost of his
generation to live and preach the simple life, withdrawing for awhile to the woods of Walden Pond
where he lived alone. Doubtless much more has

[1] the Eumenides, female divinities and the avengers of iniquity

been made of this "hermit life" than the facts warrant; but the scenes from nature that it brought
into his writings are exact, permanent, tonic. As a
member of society he tried to put into practice such
principles as Emerson preached; he was once jailed
because he refused to pay taxes to support a government that he thought to be iniquitous. He embodied so strongly the shrewd, gnarled phases of
Yankeeism that Lowell, for one, felt that his sense
of social and spiritual values was warped and his
spiritual vision distorted. However we approach
him, Thoreau remains one of the most picturesque
figures in American literature of the nineteenth
century.

Biography and criticism: H. S. Salt, (GW) 1890,
1896; B. F. Sanborn, (AML) 1882, 1910; same,
The Life of Henry David Thoreau, 1917; L. Bazal-
gette, *H. Thoreau, Bachelor of Nature*, 1924; More
(Shel. 1 and 2); Payne; Macy; Chubb; N. Foer-
ster, "Thoreau and 'The Wild,'" *Dial* 63:8-11;
H. S. Canby, "The Modern Thoreau," *Dial* 59:
54-55; N. Foerster, "The Humanism of Thoreau,"
Nation 105:9-12; O. Shepard, "The Paradox of
Thoreau," *Scrib. M.* 68:335-42; J. Burroughs, "A
Critical Glance into Thoreau," *Atlan.* 123:777-86.
See also J. R. Lowell, *My Study Windows*, 1871;
R. L. Stevenson, *Familiar Studies in Men and
Books*, 1882.

From WALDEN [2]
From I. ECONOMY

When I wrote the following pages, or rather
the bulk of them, I lived alone, in the woods,
a mile from any neighbor, in a house which I
had built myself, on the shore of Walden Pond,
in Concord, Massachusetts, and earned my living by the labor of my hands only. I lived
there two years and two months. At present I
am a sojourner in civilized life again.

I should not obtrude my affairs so much on
the notice of my readers if very particular
inquiries had not been made by my townsmen
concerning my mode of life, which some would
call impertinent, though they do not appear to
me at all impertinent, but, considering the
circumstances, very natural and pertinent.
Some have asked what I got to eat; if I did
not feel lonesome; if I was not afraid; and the
like. Others have been curious to learn what
portion of my income I devoted to charitable
purposes; and some, who have large families,
how many poor children I maintained. I will
therefore ask those of my readers who feel no
particular interest in me to pardon me if I
undertake to answer some of these questions in
this book. In most books, the *I*, or first person, is omitted; in this it will be retained;

[2] Walden Pond is a small lake one and one-half miles south of Concord, Massachusetts.

that, in respect to egotism, is the main difference. We commonly do not remember that it is, after all, always the first person that is speaking. I should not talk so much about myself if there were anybody else whom I knew as well. Unfortunately, I am confined to this theme by the narrowness of my experience. Moreover, I, on my side, require of every writer, first or last, a simple and sincere account of his own life, and not merely what he has heard of other men's lives; some such account as he would send to his kindred from a distant land; for if he has lived sincerely, it must have been in a distant land to me. Perhaps these pages are more particularly addressed to poor students. As for the rest of my readers, they will accept such portions as apply to them. I trust that none will stretch the seams in putting on the coat, for it may do good service to him whom it fits.

I would fain say something, not so much concerning the Chinese and Sandwich Islanders, as you who read these pages, who are said to live in New England; something about your condition, especially your outward condition or circumstances in this world, in this town, what it is, whether it is necessary that it be as bad as it is, whether it cannot be improved as well as not. I have traveled a good deal in Concord; and everywhere, in shops, and offices, and fields, the inhabitants have appeared to me to be doing penance in a thousand remarkable ways. What I have heard of Brahmans sitting exposed to four fires and looking in the face of the sun; or hanging suspended, with their heads downward, over flames; or looking at the heavens over their shoulders "until it becomes impossible for them to resume their natural position, while from the twist of the neck nothing but liquids can pass into the stomach"; or dwelling, chained for life, at the foot of a tree; or measuring with their bodies, like caterpillars, the breadth of vast empires; or standing on one leg on the tops of pillars,—even these forms of conscious penance are hardly more incredible and astonishing than the scenes which I daily witness. The twelve labors of Hercules [1] were trifling in comparison with those which my neighbors have undertaken; for they were only twelve, and had an end; but I could never see that these men slew or captured any monster or finished any labor. They

have no friend Iolas [2] to burn with a hot iron the root of the hydra's head, but as soon as one head is crushed, two spring up.

I see young men, my townsmen, whose misfortune it is to have inherited farms, houses, barns, cattle, and farming tools; for these are more easily acquired than got rid of. Better if they had been born in the open pasture and suckled by a wolf, that they might have seen with clearer eyes what field they were called to labor in. Who made them serfs of the soil? Why should they eat their sixty acres, when man is condemned to eat only his peck of dirt? Why should they begin digging their graves as soon as they are born? They have got to live a man's life, pushing all these things before them, and get on as well as they can. How many a poor immortal soul have I met well nigh crushed and smothered under its load, creeping down the road of life, pushing before it a barn seventy-five feet by forty, its Augean stables [3] never cleansed, and one hundred acres of land tillage, mowing, pasture, and wood-lot! The portionless, who struggle with no such unnecessary inherited encumbrances, find it labor enough to subdue and cultivate a few cubic feet of flesh.

. . . . . .

Near the end of March, 1845, I borrowed an axe and went down to the woods by Walden Pond, nearest to where I intended to build my house, and began to cut down some tall arrowy white pines, still in their youth, for timber. It it difficult to begin without borrowing, but perhaps it is the most generous course thus to permit your fellow-men to have an interest in your enterprise. The owner of the axe, as he released his hold on it, said that it was the apple of his eye; but I returned it sharper than I received it. It was a pleasant hillside where I worked, covered with pine woods, through which I looked out on the pond, and a small open field in the woods where pines and hickories were springing up. The ice in the pond was not yet dissolved, though there were some open spaces, and it was all dark colored and saturated with water. There were some slight flurries of snow during the days that I worked there; but for the most part when I came out on to the railroad, on my way home, its yellow sand heap stretched away gleaming in the hazy atmosphere, and the rails shone in

[1] Hercules, to obtain immortality, had to perform twelve great tasks; he cleansed the Augean stables, strangled the Nemean lion, killed the Lernean hydra, procured the golden apples from the Hesperides, brought to earth Cerberus, the dog that guarded Hades, and did other superhuman deeds.

[2] the companion and charioteer of Hercules, without whose help the hydra might scarcely have been overcome

[3] Hercules cleansed the stables of Augeas, in which three thousand oxen had been stabled for thirty years, in one day by turning the rivers Alpheus and Peneus through them.

the spring sun, and I heard the lark and pewee and other birds already come to commence another year with us. They were pleasant spring days, in which the winter of man's discontent [1] was thawing as well as the earth, and the life that had lain torpid began to stretch itself. One day, when my axe had come off and I had cut a green hickory for a wedge, driving it with a stone, and had placed the whole to soak in a pond hole in order to swell the wood, I saw a striped snake run into the water, and he lay on the bottom, apparently without inconvenience, as long as I stayed there, or more than a quarter of an hour; perhaps because he had not yet fairly come out of the torpid state. It appeared to me that for a like reason men remain in their present low and primitive condition; but if they should feel the influence of the spring of springs arousing them, they would of necessity rise to a higher and more ethereal life. I had previously seen the snakes in frosty mornings in my path with portions of their bodies still numb and inflexible, waiting for the sun to thaw them. On the 1st of April it rained and melted the ice, and in the early part of the day, which was very foggy, I heard a stray goose groping about over the pond and cackling as if lost, or like the spirit of the fog.

So I went on for some days cutting and hewing timber, and also studs and rafters, all with my narrow axe, not having many communicable or scholar-like thoughts, singing to myself,—

> Men say they know many things;
> But lo! they have taken wings,—
> The arts and sciences,
> And a thousand appliances;
> The wind that blows
> Is all that anybody knows.

I hewed the main timbers six inches square, most of the studs on two sides only, and the rafters and floor timbers on one side, leaving the rest of the bark on, so that they were just as straight and much stronger than sawed ones. Each stick was carefully mortised or tenoned by its stump, for I had borrowed other tools by this time. My days in the woods were not very long ones; yet I usually carried my dinner of bread and butter, and read the newspaper in which it was wrapped, at noon, sitting amid the green pine boughs which I had cut off, and to my bread was imparted some of their fragrance, for my hands were covered with a thick coat of pitch. Before I had done I was more the friend than the foe of the pine tree, though I had cut down some of them,

[1] Cf. *Richard III*, I, i, 1, 2.

having become better acquainted with it. Sometimes a rambler in the wood was attracted by the sound of my axe, and we chatted pleasantly over the chips which I had made.

By the middle of April, for I made no haste in my work, but rather made the most of it, my house was framed and ready for the raising. I had already bought the shanty of James Collins, an Irishman who worked on the Fitchburg Railroad, for boards. James Collins' shanty was considered an uncommonly fine one. When I called to see it he was not at home. I walked about the outside, at first unobserved from within, the window was so deep and high. It was of small dimensions, with a peaked cottage roof, and not much else to be seen, the dirt being raised five feet all around as if it were a compost heap. The roof was the soundest part, though a good deal warped and made brittle by the sun. Door-sill there was none, but a perennial passage for the hens under the door board. Mrs. C. came to the door and asked me to view it from the inside. The hens were driven in by my approach. It was dark, and had a dirt floor for the most part, dank, clammy, and aguish, only here a board and there a board which would not bear removal. She lighted a lamp to show me the inside of the roof and the walls, and also that the board floor extended under the bed, warning me not to step into the cellar, a sort of dust hole two feet deep. In her own words, they were "good boards overhead, good boards all around, and a good window,"—of two whole squares originally, only the cat had passed out that way lately. There was a stove, a bed, and a place to sit, an infant in the house where it was born, a silk parasol, gilt-framed looking-glass, and a patent new coffeemill nailed to an oak sapling, all told. The bargain was soon concluded, for James had in the mean while returned. I to pay four dollars and twenty-five cents tonight, he to vacate at five tomorrow morning, selling to nobody else meanwhile: I to take possession at six. It were well, he said, to be there early, and anticipate certain indistinct but wholly unjust claims on the score of ground rent and fuel. This he assured me was the only encumbrance. At six I passed him and his family on the road. One large bundle held their all,—bed, coffeemill, looking-glass, hens,—all but the cat; she took to the woods and became a wild cat, and, as I learned afterward, trod in a trap set for woodchucks, and so became a dead cat at last.

I took down this dwelling the same morning, drawing the nails, and removed it to the pond side by small cart-loads, spreading the boards on the grass there to bleach and warp back again in the sun. One early thrush gave me a note or two as I drove along the woodland path. I was informed treacherously by a young Patrick that neighbor Seeley, an Irishman, in the intervals of the carting, transferred the still tolerable straight, and drivable nails, staples, and spikes to his pocket, and then stood when I came back to pass the time of day, and look freshly up, unconcerned, with spring thoughts, at the devastation; there being a dearth of work, as he said. He was there to represent spectatordom, and help make this seemingly insignificant event one with the removal of the gods of Troy. [1]

I dug my cellar in the side of a hill sloping to the south, where a woodchuck had formerly dug his burrow, down through sumach and blackberry roots, and the lowest stain of vegetation, six feet square by seven deep, to a fine sand where potatoes would not freeze in any winter. The sides were left shelving, and not stoned; but the sun having never shone on them, the sand still keeps its place. It was but two hours' work. I took particular pleasure in this breaking of ground, for in almost all latitudes men dig into the earth for an equable temperature. Under the most splendid house in the city is still to be found the cellar where they store their roots as of old, and long after the superstructure has disappeared posterity remark its dent in the earth. The house is still but a sort of porch at the entrance of a burrow.

At length, in the beginning of May, with the help of some of my acquaintances, [2] rather to improve so good an occasion for neighborliness than from any necessity, I set up the frame of my house. No man was ever more honored in the character of his raisers than I. They are destined, I trust, to assist at the raising of loftier structures one day. I began to occupy my house on the 4th of July, as soon as it was boarded and roofed, for the boards were carefully feather-edged and lapped, so that it was perfectly impervious to rain; but before boarding I laid the foundation of a chimney at one end, bringing two cartloads of stones up the hill from the pond in my arms. I built the chimney after my hoeing in the fall, before a

fire became necessary for warmth, doing my cooking in the mean while out of doors on the ground, early in the morning: which mode I still think is in some respects more convenient and agreeable than the usual one. When it stormed before my bread was baked, I fixed a few boards over the fire, and sat under them to watch my loaf, and passed some pleasant hours in that way. In those days, when my hands were much employed, I read but little, but the least scraps of paper which lay on the ground, my holder, or tablecloth, afforded me as much entertainment, in fact answered the same purpose as the Iliad.

. . . .

Before winter I built a chimney, and shingled the sides of my house, which were already impervious to rain, with imperfect and sappy shingles made of the first slice of the log, whose edges I was obliged to straighten with a plane.

I have thus a tight shingled and plastered house, ten feet wide by fifteen long, and eight-feet posts, with a garret and a closet, a large window on each side, two trap doors, one door at the end, and a brick fireplace opposite. The exact cost of my house, paying the usual price for such materials as I used, but not counting the work, all of which was done by myself, was as follows; and I give the details because very few are able to tell exactly what their houses cost, and fewer still, if any, the separate cost of the various materials which compose them:—

Boards	$8.03½,	mostly shanty boards.
Refuse shingles for roof and sides. .	4.00	
Laths	1.25	
Two second-hand windows with glass	2.43	
One thousand old brick	4.00	
Two casks of lime	2.40	That was high.
Hair	.31	More than I needed.
Mantle-tree iron.	.15	
Nails	3.90	
Hinges and screws	.14	
Latch	.10	
Chalk	.01	
Transportation	1.40	I carried a good part on my back.
In all	$28.12½	

These are all the materials excepting the timber, stones, and sand, which I claimed by squatter's right. I have also a small woodshed adjoining, made chiefly of the stuff which was left after building the house.

[1] The spirit of Hector commanded Aeneas to build a new city, Rome, to shelter the Lares and Penates —household gods—of fallen Troy. Vergil, *Aeneid* ii, 248-311.

[2] These helpers included Emerson, Ellery Channing, Bronson Alcott, and George William Curtis, then a Harvard student of twenty-one who was working on a farm near by.

I intend to build me a house which will surpass any on the main street in Concord in grandeur and luxury, as soon as it pleases me as much and will cost me no more than my present one.

I thus found that the student who wishes for a shelter can obtain one for a lifetime at an expense not greater than the rent which he now pays annually. If I seem to boast more than is becoming, my excuse is that I brag for humanity rather than for myself; and my shortcomings and inconsistencies do not affect the truth of my statement. Notwithstanding much cant and hypocrisy,—chaff which I find it difficult to separate from my wheat, but for which I am as sorry as any man,—I will breathe freely and stretch myself in this respect, it is such a relief to both the moral and physical system; and I am resolved that I will not through humility become the devil's attorney. I will endeavor to speak a good word for the truth. At Cambridge College the mere rent of a student's room, which is only a little larger than my own, is thirty dollars each year, though the corporation had the advantage of building thirty-two side by side and under one roof, and the occupant suffers the inconvenience of many and noisy neighbors, and perhaps a residence in the fourth story. I cannot but think that if we had more true wisdom in these respects, not only less education would be needed, because, forsooth, more would already have been acquired, but the pecuniary expense of getting an education would in a great measure vanish. Those conveniences which the student requires at Cambridge or elsewhere cost him or somebody else ten times as great a sacrifice of life as they would with proper management on both sides. Those things for which the most money is demanded are never the things which the student most wants. Tuition, for instance, is an important item in the term bill, while for the far more valuable education which he gets by associating with the most cultivated of his contemporaries no charge is made. The mode of founding a college is, commonly, to get up a subscription of dollars and cents, and then following blindly the principles of a division of labor to its extreme, a principle which should never be followed but with circumspection,—to call in a contractor who makes this a subject of speculation, and he employs Irishmen or other operatives actually to lay the foundations, while the students that are to be are said to be fitting themselves for it; and for these oversights successive generations have to pay. I think that it would be *better than this,* for the students, or those

who desire to be benefited by it, even to lay the foundation themselves. The student who secures his coveted leisure and retirement by systematically shirking any labor necessary to man obtains but an ignoble and unprofitable leisure, defrauding himself of the experience which alone can make leisure fruitful. "But," says one, "you do not mean that the students should go to work with their hands instead of their heads?" I do not mean that exactly, but I mean something which he might think a good deal like that; I mean that they should not *play* life, or *study* it merely, while the community supports them at this expensive game, but earnestly *live* it from beginning to end. How could youths better learn to live than by at once trying the experiment of living? [1] Methinks this would exercise their minds as much as mathematics. If I wished a boy to know something about the arts and sciences, for instance, I would not pursue the common course, which is merely to send him into the neighborhood of some professor, where anything is professed and practiced but the art of life;—to survey the world through a telescope or a microscope, and never with his natural eye; to study chemistry, and not learn how his bread is made, or mechanics, and not learn how it is earned; to discover new satellites to Neptune, and not detect the motes in his eyes, or to what vagabond he is a satellite himself; or to be devoured by the monsters that swarm all around him, while contemplating the monsters in a drop of vinegar. Which would have advanced the most at the end of a month,—the boy who had made his own jackknife from the ore which he had dug and smelted, reading as much as would be necessary for this,—or the boy who had attended the lectures on metallurgy at the Institute in the meanwhile, and had received a Rogers' penknife from his father? Which would be most likely to cut his fingers? . . . To my astonishment I was informed on leaving college that I had studied navigation! —why, if I had taken one turn down the harbor I should have known more about it. Even the *poor* student studies and is taught only *political* economy, while that economy of living which is synonymous with philosophy is not even sincerely professed in our colleges. The consequence is that while he is reading Adam Smith, Ricardo, and Say, [2] he runs his father in debt irretrievably.

. . . .

[1] This shows the seriousness of Thoreau's own experiment.

[2] These three men were prominent students of and writers on economics; the first two were English, the third was French.

Before I finished my house, wishing to earn ten or twelve dollars by some honest and agreeable method, in order to meet my unusual expenses, I planted about two acres and a half of light and sandy soil near it chiefly with beans, but also a small part with potatoes, corn, peas, and turnips. The whole lot contains eleven acres, mostly growing up to pines and hickories, and was sold the preceding season for eight dollars and eight cents an acre. One farmer said that it was "good for nothing but to raise cheeping squirrels on." I put no manure whatever on this land, not being the owner, but merely a squatter, and not expecting to cultivate so much again, and I did not quite hoe it all once. I got out several cords of stumps in plowing, which supplied me with fuel for a long time, and left small circles of virgin mold, easily distinguishable through the summer by the greater luxuriance of the beans there. The dead and for the most part unmerchantable wood behind my house, and the driftwood from the pond, have supplied the remainder of my fuel. I was obliged to hire a team and a man for the plowing, though I held the plow myself. My farm outgoes for the first season were, for implements, seed, work, etc., $14.72½. The seed corn was given me. This never costs anything to speak of, unless you plant more than enough. I got twelve bushels of beans, and eighteen bushels of potatoes, besides some peas and sweet corn. The yellow corn and turnips were too late to come to anything. My whole income from the farm was

$23.44

Deducting the outgoes 14.72½

There are left .... $ 8.71½

besides produce consumed and on hand at the time this estimate was made of the value of $4.50,—the amount on hand much more than balancing a little grass which I did not raise. All things considered, that is, considering the importance of a man's soul and of today, notwithstanding the short time occupied by my experiment, nay, partly even because of its transient character, I believe that that was doing better than any farmer in Concord did that year.

The next year I did better still, for I spaded up all the land which I required, about a third of an acre, and I learned from the experience of both years, not being in the least awed by many celebrated works on husbandry, Arthur Young [1] among the rest, that if one would live

[1] a noted English writer on agriculture and social economy

simply and eat only the crop which he raised, and raise no more than he ate, and not exchange it for an insufficient quantity of more luxurious and expensive things, he would need to cultivate only a few rods of ground, and that it would be cheaper to spade up that than to use oxen to plow it, and to select a fresh spot from time to time than to manure the old, and he could do all his necessary farm work as it were with his left hand at odd hours in the summer; and thus he would not be tied to an ox, or horse, or cow, or pig, as at present. I desire to speak impartially on this point, and as one not interested in the success or failure of the present economical and social arrangements. I was more independent than any farmer in Concord, for I was not anchored to a house or farm, but could follow the bent of my genius, which is a very crooked one, every moment. Besides being better off than they already, if my house had been burned or my crops had failed, I should have been nearly as well off as before.

. . . . . .

By surveying, carpentry, and day-labor of various other kinds in the village in the meanwhile, for I have as many trades as fingers, I had earned $13.34. The expense of food for eight months, namely, from July 4th to March 1st, the time when these estimates were made, though I lived there more than two years,— not counting potatoes, a little green corn, and some peas, which I had raised, nor considering the value of what was on hand at the last date, was

Rice $1.73½
Molasses .... 1.73 Cheapest form of the saccharine.
Rye meal 1.04¾
Indian meal ..... .99¾ Cheaper than rye.
Pork .... .22

Flour .... .88 { Costs more than Indian meal, both money and trouble.

Sugar .... .80
Lard .... .65
Apples .... .25
Dried apples .... .22
Sweet potatoes .. .10
One pumpkin ... .06
One watermelon . .02
Salt .... .03

All experiments which failed.

Yes, I did eat $8.74, all told; but I should not thus unblushingly publish my guilt, if I did not know that most of my readers were equally guilty with myself, and that their deeds would look no better in print. The next year I sometimes caught a mess of fish for my dinner, and once I went so far as to slaughter a woodchuck which ravaged my beanfield,—effect his transmigration, as a Tartar would say,—and devour him, partly for experiment's sake; but though it afforded me a momentary enjoyment, notwithstanding a musky flavor, I saw that the longest use would not make that a good practice, however it might seem to have your woodchucks ready dressed by the village butcher.

Clothing and some incidental expenses within the same dates, though little can be inferred from this item, amounted to. .$8.40¾
Oil and some household utensils 2.00

So that all the pecuniary outgoes, excepting for washing and mending, which for the most part were done out of the house, and their bills have not yet been received,—and these are all and more than all the ways by which money necessarily goes out in this part of the world,—were

House $28.12½
Farm, one year 14.72½
Food, eight months 8.74
Clothing, etc., eight months 8.40¾
Oil, etc., eight months 2.00

    In all $61.99¾

I address myself now to those of my readers who have a living to get. And to meet this I have for farm produce sold

                          $23.44
Earned by day-labor 13.34

    In all $36.78

which subtracted from the sum of the outgoes leaves a balance of $25.21¾ on the one side,—this being very nearly the means with which I started, and the measure of expenses to be incurred,—and on the other, besides the leisure and independence and health thus secured, a comfortable house for me as long as I choose to occupy it.

These statistics, however accidental and therefore uninstructive they may appear, as they have a certain completeness, have a certain value also. Nothing was given me of which I have not rendered some account. It appears from the above estimate, that my food alone cost me in money about twenty-seven cents a week. It was for nearly two years after this, rye and Indian meal, without yeast, potatoes, rice, a very little salt pork, molasses, and salt, and my drink, water. It was fit that I should live on rice, mainly, who loved so well the philosophy of India. To meet the

objections of some inveterate cavilers, I may as well state that if I dined out occasionally, as I always had done, and I trust shall have opportunities to do again, it was frequently to the detriment of my domestic arrangements. But the dining out, being, as I have stated, a constant element, does not in the least effect a comparative statement like this.

I learned from my two years' experience that it would cost incredibly little trouble to obtain one's necessary food, even in this latitude; that a man may use as simple a diet as the animals, and yet retain health and strength.

   .   .   .   .   .   .

From II. WHERE I LIVED AND WHAT I LIVED FOR

   .   .   .   .   .   .

When first I took up my abode in the woods, that is, began to spend my nights as well as days there, which, by accident, was on Independence day, or the fourth of July, 1845, my house was not finished for winter, but was merely a defense against the rain, without plastering or chimney, the walls being of rough weather-stained boards, with wide chinks, which made it cool at night. The upright white hewn studs and freshly planed door and window casings gave it a clean and airy look, especially in the morning, when its timbers were saturated with dew, so that I fancied that by noon some sweet gum would exude from them. To my imagination it retained throughout the day more or less of this auroral character, reminding me of a certain house on a mountain which I had visited the year before. This was an airy and unplastered cabin, fit to entertain a traveling god, and where a goddess might trail her garments. The winds which passed over my dwelling were such as sweep over the ridges of mountains, bearing the broken strains, or celestial parts only, of terrestrial music. The morning wind forever blows, the poem of creation is uninterrupted; but few are the ears that hear it. Olympus is but the outside of the earth everywhere.

The only house I had been the owner of before, if I except a boat, was a tent, which I used occasionally when making excursions in the summer, and this is still rolled up in my garret; but the boat, after passing from hand to hand, has gone down the stream of time. With this more substantial shelter about me, I had made some progress toward settling in the world. This frame, so slightly clad, was a sort of crystallization around me, and reacted on the builder. It was suggestive somewhat as a picture in outlines. I did not need to go out doors to take the air, for the atmosphere within had lost none of its freshness. It was not so much within doors as behind a door where I sat, even in the rainiest weather. The Harivansa [1] says, "An abode without birds is like a meat without seasoning." Such was not my abode, for I found myself suddenly neighbor to the birds; not by having imprisoned one, but having caged myself near them. I was not only nearer to some of those which commonly frequent the garden and the orchard, but to those wilder and more thrilling songsters of the forest which never, or rarely, serenade a villager,—the wood-thrush, the veery, the scarlet tanager, the field-sparrow, the whippoorwill, and many others.

I was seated by the shore of a small pond, about a mile and a half south of the village of Concord and somewhat higher than it, in the midst of an extensive wood between that town and Lincoln, and about two miles south of that our only field known to fame, Concord Battle Ground; but I was so low in the woods that the opposite shore, half a mile off, like the rest, covered with wood, was my most distant horizon. For the first week, whenever I looked out on the pond it impressed me like a tarn high up on the side of a mountain, its bottom far above the surface of other lakes, and, as the sun arose, I saw it throwing off its nightly clothing of mist, and here and there, by degrees, its soft ripples or its smooth reflecting surface was revealed, while the mists, like ghosts, were stealthily withdrawing in every direction into the woods, as at the breaking up of some nocturnal conventicle. The very dew seemed to hang upon the trees later into the day than usual, as on the sides of mountains.

This small lake was of most value as a neighbor in the intervals of a gentle rain storm in August, when, both air and water being perfectly still, but the sky overcast, mid-afternoon had all the serenity of evening, and the wood-thrush sang around, and was heard from shore to shore. A lake like this is never smoother than at such a time; and the clear portion of the air above it being shallow and darkened by clouds, the water, full of light and reflections, becomes a lower heaven itself so much the more important. From a hill top near by, where the wood had been recently cut off, there was a pleasing vista southward across the pond, through a wide indentation in the hills which form the shore there, where their oppo-

site sides sloping toward each other suggested a stream flowing out in that direction through a wooded valley, but stream there was none. That way I looked between and over the near green hills to some distant and higher ones in the horizon, tinged with blue. Indeed, by standing on tiptoe I could catch a glimpse of some of the peaks of the still bluer and more distant mountain ranges in the northwest, those true-blue coins from heaven's own mint, and also of some portion of the village. But in other directions, even from this point, I could not see over or beyond the woods which surrounded me. It is well to have some water in your neighborhood, to give buoyancy to and float the earth. One value even of the smallest well is, that when you look into it you see that earth is not continent but insular. This is as important as that it keeps butter cool. When I looked across the pond from this peak toward the Sudbury meadows, which in time of flood I distinguished elevated perhaps by a mirage in their seething valley, like a coin in a basin, all the earth beyond the pond appeared like a thin crust insulated and floated even by this small sheet of intervening water, and I was reminded that this on which I dwelt was but *dry land*.

Though the view from my door was still more contracted, I did not feel crowded or confined in the least. There was pasture enough for my imagination. The low shrub-oak plateau to which the opposite shore arose, stretched away toward the prairies of the West and the steppes of Tartary, affording ample room for all the roving families of men. "There are none happy in the world but beings who enjoy freely a vast horizon,"—said Damodara, [2] when his herds required new and larger pastures.

Both place and time were changed, and I dwelt nearer to those parts of the universe and to those eras in history which had most attracted me. Where I lived was as far off as many a region viewed nightly by astronomers. We are wont to imagine rare and delectable places in some remote and more celestial corner of the system, behind the constellation of Cassiopeia's Chair, far from noise and disturbance. I discovered that my house actually had its site in such a withdrawn, but forever new and unprofaned, part of the universe. If it were worth the while to settle in those parts near to the Pleiades or the Hyades, [3] to Aldebaran or Altair, [4] then I was really there, or at an equal remoteness from the life which I

[1] an ancient Sanskrit poem

[2] a name for Krishna, a Hindoo divinity
[3] star groups   [4] stars

had left behind, dwindled and twinkling with as fine a ray to my nearest neighbor, and to be seen only in moonless nights by him. Such was that part of creation where I had squatted:

There was a shepherd that did live,
  And held his thoughts as high
As were the mounts whereon his flocks
  Did hourly feed him by.

What should we think of the shepherd's life if his flocks always wandered to higher pastures than his thoughts?

Every morning was a cheerful invitation to make my life of equal simplicity, and I may say innocence, with Nature herself. I have been as sincere a worshiper of Aurora as the Greeks. I got up early and bathed in the pond; that was a religious exercise, and one of the best things which I did. They say that characters were engraven on the bathing tub of king Tching-thang to this effect: "Renew thyself completely each day; do it again, and again, and forever again." I can understand that. Morning brings back the heroic ages. I was as much affected by the faint hum of a mosquito making its invisible and unimaginable tour through my apartment at earliest dawn, when I was sitting with door and windows open, as I could be by any trumpet that ever sang of fame. It was Homer's requiem; itself an Iliad and Odyssey in the air, singing its own wrath and wanderings. There was something cosmical about it; a standing advertisement, till forbidden, of the everlasting vigor and fertility of the world. The morning, which is the most memorable season of the day, is the awakening hour. Then there is least somnolence in us; and for an hour, at least, some part of us awakes which slumbers all the rest of the day and night. Little is to be expected of that day, if it can be called a day, to which we are not awakened by our Genius, but by the mechanical nudgings of some servitor, are not awakened by our own newly-acquired force and aspirations from within, accompanied by the undulations of celestial music, instead of factory bells, and a fragrance filling the air— to a higher life than we fell asleep from; and thus the darkness bear its fruit, and prove itself to be good, no less than the light. That man who does not believe that each day contains an earlier, more sacred, and auroral hour than he has yet profaned, has despaired of life, and is pursuing a descending and darkening way. After a partial cessation of his sensuous life, the soul of man, or its organs rather, are reinvigorated each day, and his Genius tries again what noble life it can make. All mem-

orable events, I should say, transpire in morning time and in a morning atmosphere. The Vedas [1] say, "All intelligences awake with the morning." Poetry and art, and the fairest and most memorable of the actions of men, date from such an hour. All poets and heroes, like Memnon, are the children of Aurora, and emit their music at sunrise. [2] To him whose elastic and vigorous thought keeps pace with the sun, the day is a perpetual morning. It matters not what the clocks say or the attitudes and labors of men. Morning is when I am awake and there is a dawn in me. Moral reform is the effort to throw off sleep. Why is it that men give so poor an account of their day if they have not been slumbering? They are not such poor calculators. If they had not been overcome with drowsiness they would have performed something. The millions are awake enough for physical labor; but only one in a million is awake enough for effective intellectual exertion, only one in a hundred millions to a poetic or divine life. To be awake is to be alive. I have never yet met a man who was quite awake. How could I have looked him in the face?

We must learn to reawaken and keep ourselves awake, not by mechanical aids, but by an infinite expectation of the dawn, which does not forsake us in our soundest sleep. I know of no more encouraging fact than the unquestionable ability of man to elevate his life by a conscious endeavor. It is something to be able to paint a particular picture, or to carve a statue, and so to make a few objects beautiful; but it is far more glorious to carve and paint the very atmosphere and medium through which we look, which morally we can do. To affect the quality of the day, that is the highest of arts. Every man is tasked to make his life, even in its details, worthy of the contemplation of his most elevated and critical hour. If we refused, or rather used up, such paltry information as we get, the oracles would distinctly inform us how this might be done.

I went to the woods because I wished to live deliberately, to front only the essential facts of life, and see if I could not learn what it had to teach, and not, when I came to die, discover that I had not lived. [3] I did not wish to live

---

[1] These are ancient writings of India dating before 1500 B.C.

[2] The colossal statue at Thebes, when struck by the rays of the morning sun, gave forth, it was believed, a musical sound; it was supposed to represent Memnon, a solar hero who fought in the Trojan war, who thus greeted his mother Aurora, the Dawn.

[3] Cf. Stevenson's more suavely stated but similar thought in "Aes Triplex" and "El Dorado."

what was not life, living is so dear; nor did I wish to practice resignation, unless it was quite necessary. I wanted to live deep and suck out all the marrow of life, to live so sturdily and Spartan-like as to put to rout all that was not life, to cut a broad swath and shave close, to drive life into a corner, and reduce it to its lowest terms, and, if it proved to be mean, why then to get the whole and genuine meanness of it, and publish its meanness to the world; or if it were sublime, to know it by experience, and be able to give a true account of it in my next excursion. For most men, it appears to me, are in a strange uncertainty about it, whether it is of the devil or of God, and have *somewhat hastily* concluded that it is the chief end of man here to "glorify God and enjoy him forever."

Still we live meanly, like ants; though the fable tells us that we were long ago changed into men; like pygmies we fight with cranes; [1] it is error upon error, and clout upon clout, and our best virtue has for its occasion a superfluous and evitable wretchedness. Our life is frittered away by detail. An honest man has hardly need to count more than his ten fingers or in extreme cases he may add his ten toes, and lump the rest. Simplicity, simplicity, simplicity! I say, let your affairs be as two or three, and not a hundred or a thousand; instead of a million count half a dozen, and keep your accounts on your thumb nail. In the midst of this chopping sea of civilized life, such are the clouds and storms and quicksands and thousand-and-one items to be allowed for, that a man has to live, if he would not founder and go to the bottom and not make his port at all, by dead reckoning, and he must be a great calculator indeed who succeeds. Simplify, simplify. Instead of three meals a day, if it be necessary eat but one; instead of a hundred dishes, five; and reduce other things in proportion. Our life is like a German Confederacy, made up of petty states, with its boundary forever fluctuating, so that even a German cannot tell you how it is bounded at any moment. The nation itself, with all its so-called internal improvements, which, by the way are all external and superficial, is just such an unwieldy and overgrown establishment, cluttered with furniture and tripped up by its own traps, ruined by luxury and heedless expense, by want of calculation and a worthy aim, as the million households in the land;

and the only cure for it as for them is in a rigid economy, a stern and more than Spartan simplicity of life and elevation of purpose. It lives too fast. Men think that it is essential that the *Nation* have commerce, and export ice, and talk through a telegraph, and ride thirty miles an hour, without a doubt, whether *they* do or not; but whether we should live like baboons or like men, is a little uncertain. If we do not get out sleepers, and forge rails, and devote days and nights to the work, but go to tinkering upon our *lives* to improve *them*, who will build railroads? And if railroads are not built, how shall we get to heaven in season? But if we stay at home and mind our business, who will want railroads? We do not ride on the railroad; it rides upon us. [2] Did you ever think what those sleepers are that underlie the railroad? Each one is a man, an Irishman, or a Yankee man. The rails are laid on them, and they are covered with sand, and the cars run smoothly over them. They are sound sleepers, I assure you. And every few years a new lot is laid down and run over; so that, if some have the pleasure of riding on a rail, others have the misfortune to be ridden upon. And when they run over a man that is walking in his sleep, a supernumary sleeper in the wrong position, and wake him up, they suddenly stop the cars, and make a hue and cry about it, as if this were an exception. I am glad to know that it takes a gang of men for every five miles to keep the sleepers down and level in their beds as it is, for this is a sign that they may sometime get up again.

Why should we live with such hurry and waste of life? We are determined to be starved before we are hungry. Men say that a stitch in time saves nine, and so they take a thousand stitches today to save nine tomorrow. As for *work*, we haven't any of any consequence. We have the Saint Vitus' dance, and cannot possibly keep our heads still. If I should only give a few pulls at the parish bell-rope, as for a fire, that is, without setting the bell, [3] there is hardly a man on his farm in the outskirts of Concord, notwithstanding that press of engagements which was his excuse so many times

[1] According to Homer, the pygmies, or dwarfs, were obliged each autumn to defend themselves against the cranes on the shores of the ocean. See *Iliad*, iii, 6.

[2] Cf. Ruskin, *Fors Clavigera*, Letter v. "You Enterprised a Railroad through the valley—you blasted its rock away, heaped thousands of tons of shale into its lovely stream. The valley is gone and the Gods with it; and now, every fool in Buxton can be in Bakewell in half an hour, and every fool in Bakewell at Buxton; which you think a lucrative process of exchange—you Fools Everywhere."

[3] Making it stand upside down; but any careless jerk of the rope would draw the crowd, Thoreau thought.

this morning, nor a boy, nor a woman, I might almost say, but would forsake all and follow that sound, not mainly to save property from the flames, but, if we will confess the truth, much more to see it burn, since burn it must, and we, be it known, did not set it on fire,— or to see it put out, and have a hand in it, if that is done as handsomely; yes, even if it were the parish church itself. Hardly a man takes a half hour's nap after dinner, but when he wakes he holds up his head and asks, "What's the news?" as if the rest of mankind had stood his sentinels. Some give directions to be waked every half hour, doubtless for no other purpose; and then, to pay for it, they tell what they have dreamed. After a night's sleep the news is as indispensable as the breakfast. "Pray tell me anything new that has happened to a man anywhere on this globe,"— and he reads it over his coffee and rolls, that a man has had his eyes gouged out this morning on the Wachito River; never dreaming the while that he lives in the dark unfathomed mammoth cave of this world, and has but the rudiment of an eye himself.

From IV. SOUNDS

Sometimes, on Sundays, I heard the bells, the Lincoln, Acton, Bedford, or Concord bell, when the wind was favorable, a faint, sweet, and, as it were, natural melody, worth importing into the wilderness. At a sufficient distance over the woods this sound acquires a certain vibratory hum, as if the pine needles in the horizon were the strings of a harp which it swept. All sound heard at the greatest possible distance produces one and the same effect, a vibration of the universal lyre, just as the intervening atmosphere makes a distant ridge of earth interesting to our eyes by the azure tint it imparts to it. There came to me in this case a melody which the air had strained, and which had conversed with every leaf and needle of the wood, that portion of the sound which the elements had taken up and modulated and echoed from vale to vale. The echo is, to some extent, an original sound, and therein is the magic and charm of it. It is not merely a repetition of what was worth repeating in the bell, but partly the voice of the wood; the same trivial words and notes sung by a wood-nymph.

At evening, the distant lowing of some cow in the horizon beyond the woods sounded sweet and melodious, and at first I would mistake it for the voices of certain minstrels by whom I was sometimes serenaded, who might be straying over hill and dale; but soon I was not unpleasantly disappointed when it was prolonged into the cheap and natural music of the cow. I do not mean to be satirical, but to express my appreciation of those youths' singing, when I state that I perceived clearly that it was akin to the music of the cow, and they were at length one articulation of Nature.

Regularly at half past seven, in one part of the summer, after the evening train had gone by, the whippoorwills chanted their vespers for half an hour, sitting on a stump by my door, or upon the ridgepole of the house. They would begin to sing almost with as much precision as a clock, within five minutes of a particular time, referred to the setting of the sun, every evening. I had a rare opportunity to become acquainted with their habits. Sometimes I heard four or five at once in different parts of the wood, by accident one a bar behind another, and so near me that I distinguished not only the cluck after each note, but often that singular buzzing sound like a fly in a spider's web, only proportionately louder. Sometimes one would circle round and round me in the woods a few feet distant as if tethered by a string, when probably I was near its eggs. They sang at intervals throughout the night, and were again as musical as ever just before and about dawn.

From XVII. SPRING

One attraction in coming to the woods to live was that I should have leisure and opportunity to see the spring come in. The ice in the pond at length begins to be honey-combed, and I can set my heel in it as I walk. Fogs and rains and warmer suns are gradually melting the snow; the days have grown sensibly longer; and I see how I shall get through the winter without adding to my wood-pile, for large fires are no longer necessary. I am on the alert for the first signs of spring, to hear the chance note of some arriving bird, or the striped squirrel's chirp, for his stores must be now nearly exhausted, or see the woodchuck venture out of his winter quarters. On the 13th of March, after I had heard the bluebird, song-sparrow, and red-wing, the ice was still nearly a foot thick. As the weather grew warmer, it was not sensibly worn away by the water, nor broken up and floated off as in rivers, but, though it was completely melted for half a rod in width about the shore, the middle was merely honey-combed and saturated with water, so that you could put your foot through it when six inches thick; but by the next day evening, perhaps, after a warm rain followed by fog, it would have wholly disappeared, all gone off with the fog, spirited away. One year I went across the middle only five days before it disappeared entirely.

. . . .

When the ground was partially bare of snow, and a few warm days had dried its surface somewhat, it was pleasant to compare the first tender signs of the infant year just peeping forth, with the stately beauty of the withered vegetation which had withstood the winter, —life-everlasting, golden-rods, pinweeds, and graceful wild grasses, more obvious and interesting frequently than in summer even, as if their beauty was not ripe till then; even cotton-grass, cat-tails, mulleins, johnswort, hardhack, meadow-sweet, and other strong-stemmed plants, those unexhausted granaries which entertain the earliest birds,—decent weeds, at least, which widowed Nature wears. I am particularly attracted by the arching and sheaf-like top of the wool-grass; it brings back the summer to our winter memories, and is among the forms which art loves to copy, and which, in the vegetable kingdom, have the same relation to types already in the mind of man that astronomy has. It is an antique style, older than Greek or Egyptian. Many of the phenomena of Winter are suggestive of an inexpressible tenderness and fragile delicacy. We are accustomed to hear this king described as a rude and boisterous tyrant; but with the gentleness of a lover he adorns the tresses of Summer.

At the approach of spring the red squirrels got under my house, two at a time, directly under my feet as I sat reading or writing, and kept up the queerest chuckling and chirruping and vocal pirouetting and gurgling sounds that ever were heard; and when I stamped they only chirruped the louder, as if past all fear and respect in their mad pranks, defying humanity to stop them. No you don't—chickaree —chickaree. They were wholly deaf to my arguments, or failed to perceive their force, and fell into a strain of invective that was irresistible.

The first sparrow of spring! The year beginning with younger hope than ever! The faint silvery warblings heard over the partially bare and moist fields from the bluebird, the song-sparrow, and the red-wing, as if the last flakes of winter tinkled as they fell! What at such a time are histories, chronologies, traditions, and all written revelations? The brooks sing carols and glees to the spring. The marsh-hawk sailing low over the meadow is already seeking the first slimy life that awakes. The sinking sound of melting snow is heard in all dells, and the ice dissolves apace in the ponds. The grass flames up on the hillsides like a spring fire,—"*et primitus oritur herba imbribus primoribus evocata,*" [1]—as if the earth sent forth an inward heat to greet the returning sun; not yellow but green is the color of its flame;—the symbol of perpetual youth, the grass-blade, like a long green ribbon, streams from the sod into the summer, checked indeed by the frost, but anon pushing on again, lifting its spear of last year's hay with the fresh life below. It grows as steadily as the rill oozes out of the ground. It is almost identical with that, for in the growing days of June, when the rills are dry, the grass-blades are their channels, and from year to year the herds drink at this perennial green stream, and the mower draws from it betimes their winter supply. So our human life but dies down to its root, and still puts forth its green blade to eternity.

Walden is melting apace. There is a canal two rods wide along the northerly and westerly sides, and wider still at the east end. A great field of ice has cracked off from the main body. I hear a song-sparrow singing from the bushes on the shore,—*olit, olit, olit,—chip, chip, chip, che, char,—che wiss, wiss, wiss.* He too is helping to crack it. How handsome the great sweeping curves in the edge of the ice, answering somewhat to those of the shore, but more regular! It is unusually hard, owing to the recent severe but transient cold, and all watered or waved like a palace floor. But the wind slides eastward over its opaque surface in vain, till it reaches the living surface beyond. It is glorious to behold this ribbon of water sparkling in the sun, the bare face of the pond full of glee and youth, as if it spoke the joy of the fishes within it, and of the sands on its shore,—a silvery sheen as from the scales of a *leuciscus,* [2] as it were all one active fish. Such is the contrast between winter and spring. Walden was dead and is alive again. But this spring it broke up more steadily, as I have said.

[1] "And first the grass appears, called forth by the early rains."

Varro, *Rerum Rusticarum* ii, 2.

[2] a genus of fish including the dace and the roach

The change from storm and winter to serene and mild weather, from dark and sluggish hours to bright and elastic ones, is a memorable crisis which all things proclaim. It is seemingly instantaneous at last. Suddenly an influx of light filled my house, though the evening was at hand, and the clouds of winter still overhung it, and the eaves were dripping with sleety rain. I looked out of the window, and lo! where yesterday was cold gray ice there lay the transparent pond already calm and full of hope as in a summer evening, reflecting a summer evening sky in its bosom, though none was visible overhead, as if it had intelligence with some remote horizon. I heard a robin in the distance, the first I had heard for many a thousand years, methought, whose note I shall not forget for many a thousand more,—the same sweet and powerful song as of yore. O the evening robin, at the end of a New England summer day! If I could ever find the twig he sits upon! I mean *he;* I mean *the twig.* This at least is not the *Turdus* [1] *migratorius.* The pitch-pines and shrub-oaks about my house, which had so long drooped, suddenly resumed their several characters, looked brighter, greener, and more erect and alive, as if effectually cleansed and restored by the rain. I knew that it would not rain any more. You may tell by looking at any twig of the forest, ay, at your very woodpile, whether its winter is past or not. As it grew darker, I was startled by the *honking* of geese flying low over the woods, like weary travelers getting in late from southern lakes, and indulging at last in unrestrained complaint and mutual consolation. Standing at my door, I could hear the rush of their wings; when, driving toward my house, they suddenly spied my light, and with hushed clamor wheeled and settled in the pond. So I came in, and shut the door, and passed my first spring night in the woods.

In the morning I watched the geese from the door through the mist, sailing in the middle of the pond, fifty rods off, so large and tumultuous that Walden appeared like an artificial pond for their amusement. But when I stood on the shore they at once rose up with a great flapping of wings at the signal of their commander, and when they had got into rank circled about over my head, twenty-nine of them, and then steered straight to Canada, with a regular *honk* from the leader at intervals, trusting to break their fast in muddier pools. A "plump" of ducks rose at the same time and took the route to the north in the wake of their noisier cousins.

For a week I heard the circling groping clangor of some solitary goose in the foggy mornings, seeking its companion, and still peopling the woods with the sound of a larger life than they could sustain. In April the pigeons were seen again flying express in small flocks, and in due time I heard the martins twittering over my clearing, though it had not seemed that the township contained so many that it could afford me any, and I fancied that they were peculiarly of the ancient race that dwelt in hollow trees ere white men came. In almost all climes the tortoise and the frog are among the precursors and heralds of this season, and birds fly with song and glancing plumage, and plants spring and bloom, and winds blow, to correct this slight oscillation of the poles and preserve the equilibrium of Nature.

As every season seems best to us in its turn, so the coming in of spring is like the creation of Cosmos [2] out of Chaos and the realization of the Golden Age.—

"Eurus ad Auroram, Nabathacaque regna recessit, Persidaque, et radiis juga subdita matutinis."

The East-Wind withdrew to Aurora and the
    Nabathaean kingdom,
And the Persian, and the ridges placed under the
    morning rays.

Man was born. Whether that Artificer of things,
The origin of a better world, made him from the
    divine seed;
Or the earth being recent and lately sundered from
    the high
Ether, retained some seeds of cognate heaven.

A single gentle rain makes the grass many shades greener. So our prospects brighten on the influx of better thoughts. We should be blessed if we lived in the present always, and took advantage of every accident that befell us, like the grass which confesses the influence of the slightest dew that falls on it; and did not spend our time in atoning for the neglect of past opportunities, which we call doing our duty. We loiter in winter while it is already spring. In a pleasant spring morning all men's sins are forgiven. Such a day is a truce to vice. While such a sun holds out to burn, the vilest sinner may return. Through our own recovered innocence we discern the innocence of our neighbors. You may have known your neighbor yesterday for a thief, a drunkard, or a sensualist, and merely pitied or despised him, and despaired of the world; but the sun shines bright and warm this first spring morning, recreating the world, and you meet him at some

[1] or *Merula migratoria,* the American robin

[2] a world

serene work, and see how his exhausted and debauched veins expand with still joy and bless the new day, feel the spring influence with the innocence of infancy, and all his faults are forgotten. There is not only an atmosphere of good will about him, but even a savor of holiness groping for expression, blindly and ineffectually perhaps, like a new-born instinct, and for a short hour the south hillside echoes to no vulgar jest. You see some innocent fair shoots preparing to burst from his gnarled rind and try another year's life, tender and fresh as the youngest plant. Even he has entered into the joy of his Lord. Why the jailer does not leave open his prison doors,—why the judge does not dismiss his case,—why the preacher does not dismiss his congregation! It is because they do not obey the hint which God gives them, nor accept the pardon which he freely offers to all.

.   .   .   .

From XVIII. CONCLUSION

I left the woods for as good a reason as I went there. Perhaps it seemed to me that I had several more lives to live, and could not spare any more time for that one. It is remarkable how easily and insensibly we fall into a particular route, and make a beaten track for ourselves. I had not lived there a week before my feet wore a path from my door to the pond-side; and though it is five or six years since I trod it, it is still quite distinct. It is true, I fear that others may have fallen into it, and so helped to keep it open. The surface of the earth is soft and impressible by the feet of men; and so with the paths which the mind travels. How worn and dusty, then, must be the highways of the world, how deep the ruts of tradition and conformity! I did not wish to take a cabin passage, but rather to go before the mast and on the deck of the world, for there I could best see the moonlight amid the mountains. I do not wish to go below now.

I learned this, at least, by my experiment; that if one advances confidently in the direction of his dreams, and endeavors to live the life which he has imagined, he will meet with a success unexpected in common hours. He will put some things behind, will pass an invisible boundary; new, universal, and more liberal laws will begin to establish themselves around and within him; or the old laws be expanded, and interpreted in his favor in a more liberal sense, and he will live with the license of a higher order of beings. In proportion as he simplifies his life, the laws of the universe will appear less complex, and solitude will not be solitude, nor poverty poverty, nor weakness weakness. If you have built castles in the air, your work need not be lost; that is where they should be. Now put the foundations under them.

.   .   .   .

1845-1847   1854

PRAYER

Great God! I ask thee for no meaner pelf,
Than that I may not disappoint myself;
That in my action I may soar as high
As I can now discern with this clear eye.

And next in value, which thy kindness lends,
That I may greatly disappoint my friends,
Howe'er they think or hope that it may be
They may not dream how thou'st distinguished me.

That my weak hand may equal my firm faith,
And my life practice more than my tongue saith;   10
That my low conduct may not show,
Nor my relenting lines,
That I thy purpose did not know
Or overrated thy designs.

1842

THE FISHER'S BOY

My life is like a stroll upon the beach,
    As near the ocean's edge as I can go;
My tardy steps its waves sometimes o'erreach,
    Sometimes I stay to let them overflow.

My sole employment 'tis, and scrupulous care,
    To place my gains beyond the reach of tides,—
Each smoother pebble, and each shell more rare,
    Which Ocean kindly to my hand confides.

I have but few companions on the shore;
    They scorn the strand who sail upon the sea;   10
Yet oft I think the ocean they've sailed o'er
    Is deeper known upon the strand to me.

The middle sea contains no crimson dulse,
    Its deeper waves cast up no pearls to view;
Along the shore my hand is on its pulse,
    And I converse with many a shipwrecked crew.

1849

INSPIRATION

If with light head erect I sing,
Though all the Muses lend their force,
From my poor love of anything,
The verse is weak and shallow as its source.

But if with bended neck I grope
Listening behind me for my wit,
With faith superior to hope,
More anxious to keep back than forward it,—

Making my soul accomplice there
Unto the flame my heart hath lit,   10
Then will the verse forever wear,—
Time cannot bend the line which God has writ.

I hearing get, who had but ears,
And sight, who had but eyes before;
I moments live, who lived but years,
And truth discern, who knew but learning's
    lore.

Now chiefly is my natal hour,
And only now my prime of life;
Of manhood's strength it is the flower,
'Tis peace's end and war's beginning strife. 20

It comes in summer's broadest noon,
By a gray wall, or some chance place,
Unseasoning time, insulting June,
And vexing day with its presuming face.

I will not doubt the love untold
Which not my worth nor want hath bought,
Which wooed me young, and wooes me old,
And to this evening hath me brought.

                  1863

MINOR LYRIC POETS

WOODWORTH, DANA, FURNESS, and SMITH are prominent among the minor American poets and popular in the middle of the nineteenth century. They are each famous for one or two lyrics, some of which still retain their first appeal.

SAMUEL WOODWORTH, 1785-1842, born at Scituate, Massachusetts, was primarily a journalist. After an apprenticeship in printing, he removed to New York in 1809, and in 1823, with George P. Morris, founded the *New York Mirror*. He produced a volume of poems in 1818, and in 1825 a play, *The Forest Rose*, which was popular for twenty years.

RICHARD HENRY DANA, 1787-1879, was born at Cambridge, and after three years at Harvard he entered upon the study and practice of law. He was connected with the *North American Review*

for five years from its founding in 1815. Although ill-health hindered his work, he published poems in 1827, 1833, and 1849, and occasionally lectured upon Shakespeare. Richard Henry Dana Jr. was his son.

WILLIAM HENRY FURNESS, 1802-1896, was born in Boston, graduated from Harvard, 1820, and was in 1825 installed pastor of the First Congregational Unitarian Church of Philadelphia, where he remained pastor for fifty years, and died. In addition to many theological works he published translations from German prose and poetry, and *Verses: Translations and Hymns*, 1886.

SAMUEL FRANCIS SMITH, 1808-1895, was born and died in Boston. He graduated from Harvard in the class with Holmes and entered the Baptist ministry. He wrote many hymns, *The Morning Light Is Breaking* being, aside from *America*, probably the best known. See Holmes, *The Boys*, p. 558, l. 29.

SAMUEL WOODWORTH

THE BUCKET

How dear to this heart are the scenes of my
    childhood,
  When fond recollection presents them to
    view!
The orchard, the meadow, the deep-tangled
    wild-wood,
  And every loved spot which my infancy
    knew!
The wide-spreading pond, and the mill that
    stood by it,
  The bridge, and the rock where the cataract
    fell,
The cot of my father, the dairy-house nigh it,
  And e'en the rude bucket that hung in the
    well—
The old oaken bucket, the iron-bound bucket,
The moss-covered bucket which hung in the
    well.   10

That moss-covered vessel I hailed as a treasure,
  For often at noon, when returned from the
    field,
I found it the source of an exquisite pleasure,
  The purest and sweetest that nature can
    yield.
How ardent I seized it, with hands that were
    glowing,
  And quick to the white-pebbled bottom it
    fell;
Then soon, with the emblem of truth overflow-
    ing,
  And dripping with coolness, it rose from the
    well—
The old oaken bucket, the iron-bound bucket,
The moss-covered bucket arose from the well.

How sweet from the green mossy brim to re-
    ceive it,   21
As poised on the curb it inclined to my lips!
Not a full blushing goblet could tempt me to
    leave it,
The brightest that beauty or revelry sips.
And now, far removed from the loved hab-
    itation,
The tear of regret will intrusively swell,
As fancy reverts to my father's plantation,
    And sighs for the bucket that hangs in the
    well—   28
The old oaken bucket, the iron-bound bucket,
The moss-covered bucket that hangs in the
    well!

                    1826

RICHARD HENRY DANA

THE LITTLE BEACH-BIRD

Thou little bird, thou dweller by the sea,
    Why takest thou its melancholy voice,
        And with that boding cry
        Why o'er the waves dost fly?
O, rather, bird, with me
    Through the fair land rejoice!

Thy flitting form comes ghostly dim and pale,
    As driven by a beating storm at sea;
        Thy cry is weak and scared,
        As if thy mates had shared   10
The doom of us. Thy wail,—
    What doth it bring to me?

Thou call'st along the sand, and haunt'st the
    surge,
    Restless, and sad; as if, in strange accord
        With the motion and the roar
        Of waves that drive to shore,
One spirit did ye urge—
    The Mystery—the Word.

Of thousands, thou, both sepulcher and pall,
    Old Ocean, art! A requiem o'er the dead,
        From out thy gloomy cells   21
        A tale of mourning tells,—
Tells of man's woe and fall,
    His sinless glory fled.

Then turn thee, little bird, and take thy flight
    Where the complaining sea shall sadness
    bring
        Thy spirit never more.
        Come, quit with me the shore,
For gladness and the light,   29
    Where birds of summer sing.

                    1853

WILLIAM HENRY FURNESS

EVENING HYMN

Slowly by God's hand unfurled,
Down around the weary world
Falls the darkness; oh, how still
Is the working of Thy will!

Mighty Maker! Here am I,—
Work in me as silently,
Veil the day's distracting sights,
Show me heaven's eternal lights.

From the darkened sky come forth
Countless stars, a wondrous birth!   10
So may gleams of glory dart,
Through the dim abyss, my heart;

Living worlds to view he brought
In the boundless realms of thought,
High and infinite desires,
Burning like those upper fires.

Holy truth, eternal right,
Let them break upon my sight.
Let them shine unclouded, still,
And with light my being fill.   20

Thou art there. Oh, let me know,
Thou art here within me too;
Be the perfect peace of God
Here as there now shed abroad.

May my soul attuned be
To that perfect harmony,
Which, beyond the power of sound,
Fills the universe around.

                    1886

SAMUEL FRANCIS SMITH

AMERICA [1]

My country,—'tis of thee,
Sweet land of liberty,
    Of thee I sing;
Land where my fathers died,
Land of the pilgrims' pride,
    From every mountain side
        Let freedom ring.

My native country,—thee,
Land of the noble, free,
    Thy name I love;   10
I love thy rocks and rills,
Thy woods and templed hills,
    My heart with rapture thrills
        Like that above.

[1] The poem is printed from an autograph version dated
May, 1894, in the Stanford University Library.

Let music swell the breeze,
And ring from all the trees
   Sweet freedom's song;
Let mortal tongues awake,
Let all that breathe partake,
Let rocks their silence break,—   20
   The sound prolong.

Our fathers' God,—to Thee,
Author of liberty,
   To Thee we sing;
Long may our land be bright
With freedom's holy light,
Protect us by Thy might,
   Great God, our King.

1832   1832

WILLIAM HICKLING PRESCOTT
1796-1859

With Prescott a comparatively new type of prose, history written with the intent to give pleasure, enters American literature. Prescott was born of distinguished ancestry, graduated from Harvard in 1814, and entered upon the study of law. An accident at college had left him with greatly impaired eyesight, which rapidly grew worse. He turned from law to literature and, carefully saving his strength, settled down to the study of Spanish-American history as his life work. His chief essays and books are *Italian Narrative Poetry,* 1824; *The History of Ferdinand and Isabella,* 1837; *The Conquest of Mexico,* 1843; *The Conquest of Peru,* 1847; *Philip the Second,* 1855-1858.

Prescott's choice of subjects connected with Spanish history was most natural. Possibly because American historians had at hand a topic so picturesque as the discovery and occupation of America, we find in American literature a group of writers who have with unusual charm developed the romance of history. His style was to some extent modified by the limitations of his eyesight, for Prescott was obliged to compose and memorize whole chapters at a time before having them written out. His work, therefore, has some of the qualities of eloquence—flow, formal grace, and appeal through the ear. In company with other literary historians, he has the gift of selecting the dramatic moments in history and fixing them in unforgettable panoramic scenes. Though many discoveries have since his time been made in Spanish-American history, his method of taking documentary evidence for his foundation made his work as accurate as the documents then accessible to him would permit. The charm of his style has kept his books alive.

Biography: G. Ticknor, *Life of Prescott,* 1864; Rollo Ogden, *W. H. Prescott,* (AML) 1905; H. T. Peck, *W. H. Prescott,* (EML) 1905; Hilliard, (LJ). Criticism: R. Ogden, "Prescott the Man," *Atlan.* 93:320-37.

From HISTORY OF THE CONQUEST OF MEXICO
Book III. Chapter VIII
March Resumed.—Ascent of the Great Volcano.—Valley of Mexico.—Impression on the Spaniards.—Conduct of Montezuma.—They Descend Into the Valley.
1519

Everything being now restored to quiet in Cholula,[1] the allied army of Spaniards and Tlascalans set forward in high spirits and resumed the march on Mexico.[2] The road lay through the beautiful savannas and luxuriant plantations that spread out for several leagues in every direction. On the march they were met occasionally by embassies from the neighboring places, anxious to claim the protection of the white men and to propitiate them by gifts, especially of gold, for which their appetite was generally known throughout the country.

Some of these places were allies of the Tlascalans, and all showed much discontent with the oppressive rule of Montezuma. The natives cautioned the Spaniards against putting themselves in his power by entering his capital; and they stated, as evidence of his hostile disposition, that he had caused the direct road to it to be blocked up that the strangers might be compelled to choose another which, from its narrow passes and strong positions, would enable him to take them at great disadvantage.

The information was not lost on Cortés, who kept a strict eye on the movements of the Mexican envoys and redoubled his own precautions against surprise. Cheerful and active, he was ever where his presence was needed, sometimes in the van, at others in the rear, encouraging the weak, stimulating the sluggish, and striving to kindle in the breasts of others the same courageous spirit which glowed in his own. At night he never omitted to go the rounds to see that every man was at his post. On one occasion his vigilance had well nigh proved fatal to him. He approached so near

[1] near the modern city of Puebla
[2] Cortés had landed at Vera Cruz in April, 1519, and had in August begun his march to Mexico City, seat of the great Montezuma, the so-called emperor of Mexico. The inhabitants of the town of Tlascala, capital of the small republic of that name, had at first opposed Cortés but later submitted to him, and six thousand had joined him as allies in a march upon their rivals, the Cholulans. The Cholulans made a conspiracy against Cortés, which he avenged by a massacre of the inhabitants, which is a blot upon Spanish history. He is, as the selection begins, just leaving Cholula.

a sentinel that the man, unable to distinguish his person in the dark, leveled his crossbow at him, when fortunately an exclamation of the general, who gave the watchword of the night, arrested a movement which might else have brought the campaign to a close and given a respite for some time longer to the empire of Montezuma.

The army came at length to the place mentioned by the friendly Indians, where the road forked, and one arm of it was found, as they had foretold, obstructed with large trunks of trees and huge stones which had been strewn across it. Cortés inquired the meaning of this from the Mexican ambassadors. They said it was done by the emperor's orders, to prevent their taking a route which after some distance they would find nearly impracticable for the cavalry. They acknowledged, however, that it was the most direct road; and Cortés, declaring that this was enough to decide him in favor of it, as the Spaniards made no account of obstacles, commanded the rubbish to be cleared away. Some of the timber might still be seen by the roadside, as Bernal Diaz [1] tells us, many years after. The event left little doubt in the general's mind of the meditated treachery of the Mexicans. But he was too politic to betray his suspicions.

They were now leaving the pleasant champaign country, as the road wound up the bold sierra which separates the great plateaus of Mexico and Puebla. The air, as they ascended, became keen and piercing; and the blasts sweeping down the frozen sides of the mountains made the soldiers shiver in their thick harness of cotton, [2] and benumbed the limbs of both men and horses.

They were passing between two of the highest mountains on the North American continent—Popocatepetl, [3] "the hill that smokes," and Iztaccihuatl, [4] or "white woman," a name suggested doubtless by the bright robe of snow spread over its broad and broken surface. A puerile superstition of the Indians regarded these celebrated mountains as gods, and Iztaccihuatl as the wife of her more formidable neighbor. A tradition of a higher character described the northern volcano as the abode of

the departed spirits of wicked rulers, whose fiery agonies in their prison-house caused the fearful bellowings and convulsions in times of eruption. It was the classic fable of Antiquity. [5] These superstitious legends had invested the mountain with a mysterious horror that made the natives shrink from attempting its ascent, which, indeed, was from natural causes a work of incredible difficulty.

The great *volcan,* as Popocatepetl was called, rose to the enormous height of 17,852 feet above the level of the sea—more than two thousand feet above the "monarch of mountains," the highest elevation in Europe. [6] During the present century it has rarely given evidence of its volcanic origin, and "the hill that smokes" has almost forfeited its claim to the appellation. But at the time of the Conquest it was frequently in a state of activity and raged with uncommon fury while the Spaniards were at Tlascala—an evil omen, it was thought, for the natives of Anahuac. [7] Its head, gathered into a regular cone by the deposits of successive eruptions, wore the usual form of volcanic mountains when not disturbed by the falling in of the crater. Soaring towards the skies, with its silver sheet of everlasting snow, it was seen far and wide over the broad plains of Mexico and Puebla—the first object which the morning sun greeted in his rising, and the last where his evening rays were seen to linger, shedding a glorious effulgence over its head that contrasted strikingly with the ruinous waste of sand and lava immediately below and the fringe of funereal pines that shrouded its base.

The mysterious terrors which hung over the spot and the wild love of adventure, made some of the Spanish cavaliers desirous to attempt the ascent which the natives declared no man could accomplish and live. Cortés encouraged them in the enterprise, willing to show the Indians that no achievement was above the dauntless daring of his followers. One of his captains, accordingly, Diego Ordaz, with nine Spaniards and several Tlascalans, encouraged by their example, undertook the ascent. It was attended with more difficulty than had been anticipated.

The lower region was clothed with a dense forest, so thickly matted that in some places

---

[1] A soldier with Cortés; he later wrote a history of the conquest, published in 1632.

[2] The Mexicans wore "a close vest of quilted cotton so thick as to be impenetrable to the light missiles of Indian warfare. This garment was so light and serviceable that it was adopted by the Spaniards." Bk. I, Ch. 2.

[3] This volcano, forty miles southeast of Mexico City, is 17,876 feet high and has a crater 2000 feet in width.

[4] north of Popocatepetl, and 16,705 feet high

[5] Enceladus, one of the hundred-armed giants that made war on the gods, was overcome by Zeus and buried under Mt. Aetna.

[6] Mt. Blanc, the highest mountain of the Alps, is 15,781 feet. Mt. Elbruz, the highest peak of the Caucasus, is 18,526 feet.

[7] pronounced a-na'wak—a name given to that part of the central tableland near Mexico City

it was scarcely possible to penetrate it. It grew thinner, however, as they advanced, dwindling by degrees into a straggling, stunted vegetation till, at the height of somewhat more than thirteen thousand feet, it faded away altogether. The Indians who had held on thus far, intimidated by the strange subterranean sounds of the volcano, even then in a state of combustion, now left them. The track opened on a black surface of glazed volcanic sand and of lava, the broken fragments of which, arrested in its boiling progress in a thousand fantastic forms, opposed continual impediments to their advance. Amidst these one huge rock, the *Pico del Fraile,* a conspicuous object from below, rose to the perpendicular height of a hundred and fifty feet, compelling them to take a wide circuit. They soon came to the limits of perpetual snow, where new difficulties presented themselves, as the treacherous ice gave an imperfect footing, and a false step might precipitate them into the frozen chasms that yawned around. To increase their distress, respiration in these aërial regions became so difficult that every effort was attended with sharp pains in the head and limbs. Still they pressed on, till, drawing nearer the crater, such volumes of smoke, sparks, and cinders were belched forth from its burning entrails and driven down the sides of the mountain, as nearly suffocated and blinded them. It was too much even for their hardy frames to endure, and, however reluctantly, they were compelled to abandon the attempt on the eve of its completion. They brought back some huge icicles —a curious sight in these tropical regions—as a trophy of their achievement, which, however imperfect, was sufficient to strike the minds of the natives with wonder by showing that with the Spaniards the most appalling and mysterious perils were only as pastimes. The undertaking was eminently characteristic of the bold spirit of the cavalier of that day, who, not content with the dangers that lay in his path, seemed to court them from the mere Quixotic love of adventure. A report of the affair was transmitted to the Emperor Charles the Fifth, and the family of Ordaz was allowed to commemorate the exploit by assuming a burning mountain on their escutcheon.

The general was not satisfied with the result. Two years after, he sent up another party, under Francisco Montaño, a cavalier of determined resolution. The object was to obtain sulphur to assist in making gunpowder for the army. The mountain was quiet at this time, and the expedition was attended with better success. The Spaniards, five in number, climbed to the very edge of the crater, which presented an irregular ellipse at its mouth, more than a league in circumference. Its depth might be from eight hundred to a thousand feet. A lurid flame burned gloomily at the bottom, sending up a sulphureous steam, which, cooling as it rose, was precipitated on the sides of the cavity. The party cast lots, and it fell on Montaño himself to descend in a basket into this hideous abyss, into which he was lowered by his companions to the depth of four hundred feet! This was repeated several times till the adventurous cavalier had collected a sufficient quantity of sulphur for the wants of the army. This doughty enterprise excited general admiration at the time. Cortés concludes his report of it to the emperor with the judicious reflection that it would be less inconvenient, on the whole, to import their powder from Spain.

But it is time to return from our digression, which may, perhaps, be excused as illustrating in a remarkable manner the chimerical spirit of enterprise—not inferior to that in his own romances of chivalry [1]—which glowed in the breast of the Spanish cavalier in the sixteenth century.

The army held on its march through the intricate gorges of the sierra. The route was nearly the same as that pursued at the present day by the courier from the capital to Puebla, by the way of Mecameca. It was not that usually taken by travelers from Vera Cruz, who follow the more circuitous road round the northern base of Iztaccihuatl, as less fatiguing than the other, though inferior in picturesque scenery and romantic points of view. The icy winds that now swept down the sides of the mountains brought with them a tempest of arrowy sleet and snow, from which the Christians suffered even more than the Tlascalans reared from infancy among the wild solitudes of their own native hills. As night came on, their sufferings would have been intolerable, but they luckily found a shelter in the commodious stone buildings which the Mexican government had placed at stated intervals along the roads for the accommodation of the traveler and their own couriers. It little dreamed it was providing a protection for its enemies.

The troops, refreshed by a night's rest, succeeded, early on the following day, in gaining the crest of the sierra of Ahualco, which

---

[1] The romances clustering about the Cid (the great Spanish hero), Don Roderic, Charlemagne, Amadis, and others were most fanciful and chimerical.

stretches like a curtain between the two great mountains on the north and south. Their progress was now comparatively easy, and they marched forward with a buoyant step, as they felt they were treading the soil of Montezuma.

They had not advanced far when, turning an angle of the sierra, they suddenly came on a view which more than compensated the toils of the preceding day. It was that of the Valley of Mexico, or Tenochtitlan, as more commonly called by the natives; which, with its picturesque assemblage of water, woodland, and cultivated plains, its shining cities [1] and shadowy hills, was spread out like some gay and gorgeous panorama before them. In the highly rarefied atmosphere of these upper regions even remote objects have a brilliancy of coloring and a distinctness of outline which seem to annihilate distance. Stretching far away at their feet were seen noble forests of oak, sycamore, and cedar, and beyond, yellow fields of maize and the towering maguey, intermingled with orchards and blooming gardens; for flowers, in such demand for their religious festivals, were even more abundant in this populous valley than in other parts of Anahuac. In the center of the great basin were beheld the lakes, occupying then a much larger portion of its surface than at present; their borders thickly studded with towns and hamlets, and in the midst, like some Indian empress with her coronal of pearls, the fair city of Mexico with her white towers and pyramidal temples, reposing, as it were, on the bosom of the waters—the far-famed "Venice of the Aztecs." High over all rose the royal hill of Chapoltepec, the residence of the Mexican monarchs, crowned with the same grove of gigantic cypresses, which at this day fling their broad shadows over the land. In the distance, beyond the blue waters of the lake and nearly screened by intervening foliage, was seen a shining speck, the rival capital of Tezcuco, [2] and still further on, the dark belt of porphyry, girdling the valley around like a rich setting which nature had devised for the fairest of her jewels.

Such was the beautiful vision which broke on the eyes of the conquerors. And even now, when so sad a change has come over the scene;

when the stately forests have been laid low, and the soil, unsheltered from the fierce radiance of a tropical sun, is in many places abandoned to sterility; when the waters have retired, leaving a broad and ghastly margin white with the incrustation of salts, while the cities and hamlets on their borders have moldered into ruins—even now that desolation broods over the landscape, so indestructible are the lines of beauty which nature has traced on its features that no traveler, however cold, can gaze on them with any other emotions than those of astonishment and rapture.

What, then, must have been the emotions of the Spaniards when, after working their toilsome way into the upper air, the cloudy tabernacle parted before their eyes and they beheld these fair scenes in all their pristine magnificence and beauty! It was like the spectacle which greeted the eyes of Moses from the summit of Pisgah, [3] and in the warm glow of their feelings they cried out, "It is the promised land!"

But these feelings of admiration were soon followed by others of a very different complexion, as they saw in all this the evidences of a civilization and power far superior to anything they had yet encountered. The more timid, disheartened by the prospect, shrunk from a contest so unequal, and demanded, as they had done on some former occasions, to be led back again to Vera Cruz. Such was not the effect produced on the sanguine spirit of the general. His avarice was sharpened by the display of the dazzling spoil at his feet, and if he felt a natural anxiety at the formidable odds, his confidence was renewed as he gazed on the lines of his veterans, whose weather-beaten visages and battered armor told of battles won and difficulties surmounted, while his bold barbarians, with appetites whetted by the view of their enemies' country, seemed like eagles on the mountains, ready to pounce upon their prey. By argument, entreaty, and menace, he endeavored to restore the faltering courage of the soldiers, urging them not to think of retreat, now that they had reached the goal for which they had panted and the golden gates were opened to receive them. In these efforts he was well seconded by the brave cavaliers, who held honor as dear to them as fortune; until the dullest spirits caught somewhat of the enthusiasm of their leaders, and the general had the satisfaction to see his hesitating

---

[1] Prescott placed more confidence in the statements of the early Spanish and Mexican writers than do later historians. Some of these descriptions are perhaps somewhat exaggerated, but they are fundamentally true. See *Encyclopedia Britannica*, "Mexico"—Civilization.

[2] The Tezcucans, who had been independent but were now subject to Montezuma, joined Cortés during the following year in his siege and capture of Mexico City.

[3] a mountain, also called Mt. Nebo, northeast of the Dead Sea, from which Moses viewed Canaan, *Deuteronomy* iii, 27; xxxiv, 1

columns, with their usual buoyant step, once more on their march down the slopes of the sierra.

With every step of their progress the woods became thinner; patches of cultivated land more frequent; and hamlets were seen in the green and sheltered nooks, the inhabitants of which coming out to meet them gave the troops a kind reception. Everywhere they heard complaints of Montezuma, especially of the unfeeling manner in which he carried off their young men to recruit his armies and their maidens for his harem. These symptoms of discontent were noticed with satisfaction by Cortés, who saw that Montezuma's "mountain throne," as it was called, was indeed seated on a volcano with the elements of combustion so active within that it seemed as if any hour might witness an explosion. He encouraged the disaffected natives to rely on his protection, as he had come to redress their wrongs. He took advantage, moreover, of their favorable dispositions to scatter among them such gleams of spiritual light as time and the preaching of father Olmedo could afford.

He advanced by easy stages, somewhat retarded by the crowd of curious inhabitants gathered on the highways to see the strangers, and halting at every spot of interest or importance. On the road he was met by another embassy from the capital. It consisted of several Aztec lords, freighted, as usual, with a rich largess of gold and robes of delicate furs and feathers. The message of the emperor was couched in the same deprecatory terms as before. He even condescended to bribe the return of the Spaniards by promising in that event four loads of gold to the general and one to each of the captains, with a yearly tribute to their sovereign. So effectually had the lofty and naturally courageous spirit of the barbarian monarch been subdued by the influence of superstition! [1]

But the man whom the hostile array of armies could not daunt was not to be turned from his purpose by a woman's [2] prayers. He received the embassy with his usual courtesy, declaring, as before, that he could not answer it to his own sovereign if he were now to return without visiting the emperor in his capital. It would be much easier to arrange matters by a personal interview than by distant negotiation. The Spaniards came in the spirit of peace. Montezuma would so find it; but should their presence prove burdensome to him, it would be easy for them to relieve him of it.

The Aztec monarch meanwhile was a prey to the most dismal apprehensions. It was intended that the embassy above noticed should reach the Spaniards before they crossed the mountains. When he learned that this was accomplished and that the dread strangers were on their march across the Valley, the very threshold of his capital, the last spark of hope died away in his bosom. Like one who suddenly finds himself on the brink of some dark and yawning gulf, he was too much bewildered to be able to rally his thoughts or even to comprehend his situation. He was the victim of an absolute destiny, against which no foresight or precautions could have availed. It was as if the strange beings who had thus invaded his shores had dropped from some distant planet, so different were they from all he had ever seen, in appearance and manners; so superior—though a mere handful in numbers—to the banded nations of Anahuac in strength and science and all the fearful accompaniments of war! They were now in the Valley. The huge mountain screen which nature had so kindly drawn around it for its defense had been overleaped. The golden visions of security and repose in which he had so long indulged, the lordly sway descended from his ancestors, his broad imperial domain, were all to pass away. It seemed like some terrible dream—from which he was now, alas! to awake to a still more terrible reality.

In a paroxysm of despair he shut himself up in his palace, refused food, and sought relief in prayer and in sacrifice. But the oracles were dumb. He then adopted the more sensible expedient of calling a council of his principal and oldest nobles. Here was the same division of opinion which had before prevailed. Cacama, the young king of Tezcuco, his nephew, counseled him to receive the Spaniards courteously, as ambassadors, so styled by themselves, of a foreign prince. Cuitlahua, Montezuma's more warlike brother, urged him to muster his forces on the instant and drive back the invaders from his capital, or die in its defense. But the monarch found it difficult to rally his spirits for this final struggle. With downcast eye and dejected mien he exclaimed, "Of what avail is resistance when the gods have

---

[1] Several things unnerved the monarch: the activity of Popocatepetl, an evil omen; the apparently superhuman daring of the Spaniards in crossing the mountains as they had done; the tradition that Quetzalcoatl, a white god, was to send his brethren from the east to rule Mexico; and a prophecy made when Montezuma became king, that the empire would be desolated and the people enslaved.

[2] Montezuma had lost all manly courage.

declared themselves against us! Yet I mourn most for the old and infirm, the women and children, too feeble to fight or to fly. For myself and the brave men around me, we must bare our breasts to the storm and meet it as we may!" Such are the sorrowful and sympathetic tones in which the Aztec emperor is said to have uttered the bitterness of his grief. He would have acted a more glorious part had he put his capital in a posture of defense and prepared, like the last of the Palaeologi, [1] to bury himself under its ruins.

He straightway prepared to send a last embassy to the Spaniards, with his nephew, the lord of Tezcuco, at its head, to welcome them to Mexico.

The Christian army meanwhile had advanced as far as Amaquemecan, a well built town of several thousand inhabitants. They were kindly received by the cacique, [2] lodged in large, commodious stone buildings, and at their departure presented, among other things, with gold to the amount of three thousand *castellanos*. [3] Having halted there a couple of days, they descended among flourishing plantations of maize and of maguey, the latter of which might be called the Aztec vineyards, towards the lake of Chalco. Their first resting-place was Ajotzinco, a town of considerable size, with a great part of it then standing on piles in the water. It was the first specimen which the Spaniards had seen of this maritime architecture. The canals which intersected the city instead of streets presented an animated scene from the number of barks which glided up and down freighted with provisions and other articles for the inhabitants. The Spaniards were particularly struck with the style and commodious structure of the houses, built chiefly of stone, and with the general aspect of wealth and even elegance which prevailed there.

Though received with the greatest show of hospitality, Cortés found some occasion for distrust in the eagerness manifested by the people to see and approach the Spaniards. Not content with gazing at them in the roads, some even made their way stealthily into their quarters, and fifteen or twenty unhappy Indians were shot down by the sentinels as spies. Yet there appears, as well as we can judge at this distance of time, to have been no real ground

for such suspicion. The undisguised jealousy of the Court, and the cautions he had received from his allies, while they very properly put the general on his guard, seem to have given an unnatural acuteness, at least in the present instance, to his perceptions of danger.

Early on the following morning, as the army was preparing to leave the place, a courier came, requesting the general to postpone his departure till after the arrival of the king of Tezcuco, who was advancing to meet him. It was not long before he appeared, borne in a palanquin, or litter, richly decorated with plates of gold and precious stones, having pillars curiously wrought, supporting a canopy of green plumes, a favorite color with the Aztec princes. He was accompanied by a numerous suite of nobles and inferior attendants. As he came into the presence of Cortés, the lord of Tezcuco descended from his palanquin, and the obsequious officers swept the ground before him as he advanced. He appeared to be a young man of about twenty-five years of age, with a comely presence, erect and stately in his deportment. He made the Mexican salutation usually addressed to persons of high rank, touching the earth with his right hand and raising it to his head. Cortés embraced him as he rose, when the young prince informed him that he came as the representative of Montezuma to bid the Spaniards welcome to his capital. He then presented the general with three pearls of uncommon size and luster. Cortés in return threw over Cacama's neck a chain of cut glass, which, where glass was as rare as diamonds, might be admitted to have a value as real as the latter. After this interchange of courtesies and the most friendly and respectful assurances on the part of Cortés, the Indian prince withdrew, leaving the Spaniards strongly impressed with the superiority of his state and bearing over anything they had hitherto seen in the country.

Resuming its march, the army kept along the southern borders of the lake of Chalco, overshadowed at that time by noble woods and by orchards glowing with autumnal fruits of unknown names, but rich and tempting hues. More frequently it passed through cultivated fields waving with the yellow harvest and irrigated by canals introduced from the neighboring lake, the whole showing a careful and economical husbandry essential to the maintenance of a crowded population.

Leaving the main land, the Spaniards came on the great dike, or causeway, which stretches some four or five miles in length, and divides

---

[1] the family of most of the rulers of the Eastern Roman Empire from 1261 to the time of Constantine XII, the last emperor, who dièd with his troops when the Turks broke through the walls of Constantinople in 1453
[2] chief
[3] a Spanish coin of the fourteenth century, worth about one-sixth of an ounce of gold, or about $2.50

lake Chalco from Xochicalco on the west. It was a lance in breadth in the narrowest part, and in some places wide enough for eight horsemen to ride abreast. It was a solid structure of stone and lime, running directly through the lake, and struck the Spaniards as one of the most remarkable works which they had seen in the country.

As they passed along they beheld the gay spectacle of multitudes of Indians darting up and down in their light pirogues,[1] eager to catch a glimpse of the strangers or bearing the products of the country to the neighboring cities. They were amazed, also, by the sight of the *chinampas,* or floating gardens—those wandering islands of verdure, to which we shall have occasion to return hereafter—teeming with flowers and vegetables and moving like rafts over the waters. All round the margin and occasionally far in the lake they beheld little towns and villages which, half concealed by the foliage and gathered in white clusters round the shore, looked in the distance like companies of wild swans riding quietly on the waves. A scene so new and wonderful filled their rude hearts with amazement. It seemed like enchantment; and they could find nothing to compare it with but the magical pictures in the *Amadis de Gaula.*[2] Few pictures, indeed, in that or any other legend of chivalry could surpass the realities of their own experience. The life of the adventurer in the New World was romance put into action. What wonder, then, if the Spaniard of that day, feeding his imagination with dreams of enchantment at home and with its realities abroad, should have displayed a Quixotic enthusiasm, a romantic exaltation of character not to be comprehended by the colder spirits of other lands!

Midway across the lake the army halted at the town of Cuitlahuac, a place of moderate size but distinguished by the beauty of the buildings—the most beautiful, according to Cortés, that he had yet seen in the country. After taking some refreshment at this place they continued their march along the dike. Though broader in this northern section, the troops found themselves much embarrassed by the throng of Indians, who not content with gazing on them from the boats, climbed up the causeway and lined the sides of the road. The general, afraid that his ranks might be disordered and that too great familiarity might diminish a salutary awe in the natives, was obliged to resort not merely to command but

menace to clear a passage. He now found as he advanced a considerable change in the feelings shown towards the government. He heard only of the pomp and magnificence, nothing of the oppressions, of Montezuma. Contrary to the usual fact, it seemed that the respect for the court was greatest in its immediate neighborhood.

From the causeway the army descended on that narrow point of land which divides the waters of the Chalco from the Tezcucan lake, but which in those days was overflowed for many a mile now laid bare. Traversing this peninsula, they entered the royal residence of Iztapalapan, a place containing twelve or fifteen thousand houses, according to Cortés. It was governed by Cuitlahua, the emperor's brother, who, to do greater honor to the general, had invited the lords of some neighboring cities, of the royal house of Mexico like himself, to be present at the interview. This was conducted with much ceremony, and after the usual present of gold and delicate stuffs, a collation was served to the Spaniards in one of the great halls of the palace. The excellence of the architecture here also excited the admiration of the general, who does not hesitate, in the glow of his enthusiasm, to pronounce some of the buildings equal to the best in Spain. They were of stone, and the spacious apartments had roofs of odorous cedar-wood, while the walls were tapestried with fine cottons stained with brilliant colors.

But the pride of Iztapalapan, on which its lord had freely lavished his care and his revenues, was its celebrated gardens. They covered an immense tract of land, were laid out in regular squares, and the paths intersecting them were bordered with trellises supporting creepers and aromatic shrubs that loaded the air with their perfumes. The gardens were stocked with fruit trees imported from distant places and with the gaudy family of flowers which belong to Mexican flora, scientifically arranged and growing luxuriant in the equable temperature of the tableland. The natural dryness of the atmosphere was counteracted by means of aqueducts and canals that carried water into all parts of the grounds.

In one quarter was an aviary filled with numerous kinds of birds remarkable in this region both for brilliancy of plumage and of song. The gardens were intersected by a canal communicating with the lake of Tezcuco and of sufficient size for barges to enter from the latter. But the most elaborate piece of work was a huge reservoir of stone filled to a considerable height with water well supplied with

[1] dug-out canoes
[2] one of the great legendary heroes of the medieval romances of the fifteenth and sixteenth centuries

different sorts of fish. This basin was sixteen hundred paces in circumference, and was surrounded by a walk, made also of stone, wide enough for four persons to go abreast. The sides were curiously sculptured, and a flight of steps led to the water below, which fed the aqueducts above noticed or, collected into fountains, diffused a perpetual moisture.

Such are the accounts transmitted of these celebrated gardens at a period when similar horticultural establishments were unknown in Europe; and we might well doubt their existence in this semi-civilized land were it not a matter of such notoriety at the time and so explicitly attested by the invaders. [1] But a generation had scarcely passed after the Conquest before a sad change came over these scenes so beautiful. The town itself was deserted and the shore of the lake was strewed with the wreck of buildings which once were its ornament and its glory. The gardens shared the fate of the city. The retreating waters withdrew the means of nourishment, converting the flourishing plains into a foul and unsightly morass, the haunt of loathsome reptiles; and the water-fowl built her nest in what had once been the palaces of princes!

In the city of Iztapalapan, Cortés took up his quarters for the night. We may imagine what a crowd of ideas must have pressed on the mind of the Conqueror as, surrounded by these evidences of civilization, he prepared with his handful of followers to enter the capital of a monarch who, as he had abundant reason to know, regarded him with distrust and aversion. This capital was now but a few miles distant, distinctly visible from Iztapalapan. And as its long lines of glittering edifices struck by the rays of the evening sun, trembled on the dark-blue waters of the lake, it looked like a thing of fairy creation rather than the work of mortal hands. Into this city of enchantment Cortés prepared to make his entry on the following morning. [2]

1838-1843   1843

---

[1] Prescott here refers in a note to five Spanish records of the conquest.
[2] Nov. 8, 1519. There follows a detailed account of the City of Mexico, the people, gods, customs, etc. Montezuma is persuaded to become the guest—really the prisoner—of Cortés. Learning too late of the Spanish desire for conquest and booty, and overcome with humiliation at his failure to maintain his people's supremacy, he refuses medicine, and dies. The Aztecs unite, and drive Cortés, with the small remnant of his army, out of the city; but, weakened by tribal jealousies, the natives are later, after some terrible battles, defeated. In May, 1521, Cortés for the second time marches upon and successfully besieges Mexico City.

JOHN LOTHROP MOTLEY
1814-1877

Born at Dorchester, Massachusetts, and graduating from Harvard in 1831, Motley followed the few ambitious American youths who were studying abroad, and found inspiration in Germany. He came home, practiced law, but entered public life. He was secretary of the American legation at St. Petersburg (now Leningrad) for a few months in 1841. In 1851 he went to Holland to gather materials for the *History of the Rise of the Dutch Republic,* published in 1856. Four years later came the first part of *The History of the United Netherlands,* completed in 1868. *John van Barneveld* appeared in 1874. From 1861 to 1867 Motley was United States Minister to Austria, and 1869-1870, Minister to England. Motley was a worthy representative of his country abroad, but becoming the victim of party politics with which he was in no way connected, he was recalled from England after about a year's service.

Motley's histories are fine examples of scholarly history made interesting. His style is vigorous and picturesque, and many of his narrative passages have almost the plot interest of a novel. Nearly all his work deals with the struggles of the Dutch against the oppression of Spain.

Biography and criticism: O. W. Holmes, *J. L. Motley, a Memoir,* 1898; Chubb; J. P. Grund, "Bismarck and Motley," *No. Am.* 167: 360-76, 481-96, 569-72; J. T. Morse Jr., "Centenary of the Historian," *Nation* 98:425-7; H. A. Bruce, "John Lothrop Motley—American," *Outlook,* 95:891-4.

From THE RISE OF THE DUTCH REPUBLIC [3]
PART IV. CHAPTER II.
[The Relief of Leyden]

The invasion of Louis of Nassau had, as already stated, effected the raising of the first siege of Leyden. That leaguer had lasted from the 31st of October 1573, to the 21st of March 1574, when the soldiers were summoned away to defend the frontier. By an extraordinary and culpable carelessness, the citizens, neglecting the advice of the Prince, had not taken

---

[3] The Netherlands under Charles V of Austria and his son Philip II of Spain revealed the unnatural situation of a people of democratic instincts held in political servitude by a foreign power of different religious principles. They suffered all the terrors of the Inquisition at the hands of the cruel Spanish governor-general, the Duke of Alva, until in 1570, led by William the Silent, Prince of Orange, they rose in rebellion. The heroic endurance of the city of Leyden in resisting the Spanish siege is famous in history. Count Louis, of the house of Nassau—the reigning family in the Netherlands—a brother of the Prince of Orange, with help from France, made a successful counter attack from the French side and thus temporarily caused the siege of Leyden to be raised. He was killed in the battle of Mookerheyde, April, 1574.

advantage of the breathing time thus afforded them to victual the city and strengthen the garrison. They seemed to reckon more confidently upon the success of Count Louis than he had even done himself; for it was very probable that, in case of his defeat, the siege would be instantly resumed. This natural result was not long in following the battle of Mookerheyde.

On the 26th of May, Valdez [1] reappeared before the place, at the head of eight thousand Walloons and Germans, and Leyden was now destined to pass through a fiery ordeal. This city was one of the most beautiful in the Netherlands. Placed in the midst of broad and fruitful pastures, which had been reclaimed by the hand of industry from the bottom of the sea, it was fringed with smiling villages, blooming gardens, fruitful orchards. The ancient and, at last, decrepit Rhine, flowing languidly towards its sandy death-bed, had been multiplied into innumerable artificial currents, by which the city was completely interlaced. These watery streets were shaded by lime trees, poplars, and willows, and crossed by one hundred and forty-five bridges, mostly of hammered stone. The houses were elegant, the squares and streets spacious, airy, and clean, the churches and public edifices imposing, while the whole aspect of the place suggested thrift, industry, and comfort. Upon an artificial elevation, in the center of the city, rose a ruined tower of unknown antiquity. By some it was considered to be of Roman origin, while others preferred to regard it as a work of the Anglo-Saxon Hengist, raised to commemorate his conquest of England. [2] Surrounded by fruit trees, and overgrown in the center with oaks, it afforded, from its moldering battlements, a charming prospect over a wide expanse of level country, with the spires of neighboring cities rising in every direction. It was from this commanding height, during the long and terrible summer days which were approaching, that many an eye was to be strained anxiously seaward, watching if yet the ocean had begun to roll over the land.

Valdez lost no time in securing himself in the possession of Maeslandsluis, Vlaardingen, and The Hague. Five hundred English, under command of Colonel Edward Chester, abandoned the fortress of Valkenburg, and fled towards Leyden. Refused admittance by the citizens, who now, with reason, distrusted

them, [3] they surrendered to Valdez, and were afterwards sent back to England. In the course of a few days, Leyden was thoroughly invested, no less than sixty-two redoubts, some of them having remained undestroyed from the previous siege, now girdling the city, while the besiegers already numbered nearly eight thousand, a force to be daily increased. On the other hand, there were no troops in the town, save a small corps of "freebooters," and five companies of the burgher guard. John Van der Does, Seigneur [4] of Nordwyck, a gentleman of distinguished family, but still more distinguished for his learning, his poetical genius, and his valor, had accepted the office of military commandant.

The main reliance of the city, under God, was on the stout hearts of its inhabitants within the walls, and on the sleepless energy of William the Silent without. The Prince, hastening to comfort and encourage the citizens, although he had been justly irritated by their negligence in having omitted to provide more sufficiently against the emergency while there had yet been time, now reminded them that they were not about to contend for themselves alone, but that the fate of their country and of unborn generations would, in all human probability, depend on the issue about to be tried. Eternal glory would be their portion if they manifested a courage worthy of their race and of the sacred cause of religion and liberty. He implored them to hold out at least three months, assuring them that he would, within that time, devise the means of their deliverance. The citizens responded, courageously and confidently, to these missives, and assured the Prince of their firm confidence in their own fortitude and his exertions.

And truly they had a right to rely on that calm and unflinching soul, as on a rock of adamant. All alone, without a being near him to consult, his right arm struck from him by the death of Louis, with no brother left to him but the untiring and faithful John, [5] he prepared without delay for the new task imposed upon him. France, since the defeat and death of Louis, and the busy intrigues which had followed the accession of Henry III, [6] had but small sympathy for the Netherlands. The

[1] Leader of the Spanish forces; Walloons were inhabitants of French Flanders.
[2] In the sixteenth century it was thought by some antiquarians that the Saxon conquerors of Britain came from Holland.

[3] The relations between England and Spain had been very close. Philip II had been the husband of Queen Mary of England, and after her death had become suitor to Elizabeth. On the other hand, England depended greatly upon the Flemish trade, so that it was to her interest to remain neutral. Some of her soldiers were helping the Dutch, rather as soldiers of fortune than officially; often, as in this case, they were considered untrustworthy.

[4] Lord   [6] King of France, 1551-1589
[5] Count John of Nassau

English government, relieved from the fear of France, was more cold and haughty than ever. An Englishman, employed by Requesens [1] to assassinate the Prince of Orange, had been arrested in Zeeland, who impudently pretended that he had undertaken to perform the same office for Count John, with the full consent and privity of Queen Elizabeth. The provinces of Holland and Zeeland were stanch and true, but the inequality of the contest between a few brave men, upon that handsbreadth of territory, and the powerful Spanish Empire, seemed to render the issue hopeless.

Moreover, it was now thought expedient to publish the amnesty which had been so long in preparation, and this time the trap was more liberally baited. The pardon, which had passed the seals upon the 8th of March, was formally issued by the Grand Commander on the 6th of June. By the terms of this document the King [2] invited all his erring and repentant subjects to return to his arms, and to accept a full forgiveness for their past offences, upon the sole condition that they should once more throw themselves upon the bosom of the Mother Church. There were but few exceptions to the amnesty, a small number of individuals, all mentioned by name, being alone excluded; but although these terms were ample, the act was liable to a few stern objections. It was easier now for the Hollanders to go to their graves than to mass, for the contest, in its progress, had now entirely assumed the aspect of a religious war. Instead of a limited number of heretics in a state which, although constitutional, was Catholic, there was now hardly a Papist to be found among the natives. To accept the pardon then was to concede the victory, and the Hollanders had not yet discovered that they were conquered. They were resolved, too, not only to be conquered, but annihilated, before the Roman Church should be reëstablished on their soil, to the entire exclusion of the Reformed worship. They responded with steadfast enthusiasm to the sentiment expressed by the Prince of Orange, after the second siege of Leyden had been commenced: "As long as there is a living man left in the country, we will contend for our liberty and our religion." The single condition of the amnesty assumed, in a phrase, what Spain had fruitlessly striven to establish by a hundred battles, and the Hollanders had not faced their enemy on land and sea for seven years to succumb to a phrase at last.

[1] the new Spanish governor-general of the Netherlands successor to Alva
[2] Philip II

Moreover, the pardon came from the wrong direction. The malefactor gravely extended forgiveness to his victims. Although the Hollanders had not yet disembarrassed their minds of the supernatural theory of government, and felt still the reverence of habit for regal divinity, they naturally considered themselves outraged by the trick now played before them. The man who had violated all his oaths, trampled upon all their constitutional liberties, burned and sacked their cities, confiscated their wealth, hanged, beheaded, burned, and buried alive their innocent brethren, now came forward, not to implore, but to offer forgiveness. Not in sackcloth, but in royal robes; not with ashes, but with a diadem upon his head, did the murderer present himself vicariously upon the scene of his crimes. It may be supposed that, even in the sixteenth century, there were many minds which would revolt at such blasphemy. Furthermore, even had the people of Holland been weak enough to accept the pardon, it was impossible to believe that the promise would be fulfilled. It was sufficiently known how much faith was likely to be kept with heretics, notwithstanding that the act was fortified by a papal bull, dated on the 30th of April, by which Gregory XIII promised forgiveness to those Netherland sinners who duly repented and sought absolution for their crimes, even although they had sinned more than seven times seven.

For a moment the Prince had feared lest the pardon might produce some effect upon men wearied by interminable suffering, but the event proved him wrong. It was received with universal and absolute contempt. No man came forward to take advantage of its conditions, save one brewer in Utrecht, and the son of a refugee peddler from Leyden. With these exceptions, the only ones recorded, Holland remained deaf to the royal voice. The city of Leyden was equally cold to the messages of mercy, which were especially addressed to its population by Valdez and his agents. Certain Netherlanders, belonging to the King's party, and familiarly called "Glippers," despatched from the camp many letters to their rebellious acquaintances in the city. In these epistles the citizens of Leyden were urgently and even pathetically exhorted to submission by their loyal brethren, and were implored "to take pity upon their poor old fathers, their daughters, and their wives." But the burghers of Leyden thought that the best pity which they could show to those poor old fathers, daughters, and wives was to keep them from the clutches of the Spanish soldiery; so they made no answer to the Glippers, save by this single line, which they wrote on a sheet of paper, and forwarded, like a letter, to Valdez:—

Fistula dulce canit, volucrem cum decipit auceps. [1]

According to the advice early given by the Prince of Orange, the citizens had taken an account of their provisions of all kinds, including the live stock. By the end of June, the city was placed on a strict allowance of food, all the provisions being purchased by the authorities at an equitable price. Half a pound of meat and half a pound of bread was allotted to a full grown man, and to the rest, a due proportion. The city being strictly invested, no communication, save by carrier pigeons, and by a few swift and skilful messengers, called jumpers, was possible. Sorties and fierce combats were, however, of daily occurrence, and a handsome bounty was offered to any man who brought into the city gates the head of a Spaniard. The reward was paid many times, but the population was becoming so excited and so apt, that the authorities felt it dangerous to permit the continuance of these conflicts. Lest the city, little by little, should lose its few disciplined defenders, it was now proclaimed, by sound of church bell, that in future no man should leave the gates.

The Prince had his headquarters at Delft and at Rotterdam. Between those two cities, an important fortress, called Polderwaert, secured him in the control of the alluvial quadrangle, watered on two sides by the Yssel and the Meuse. On the 29th June, the Spaniards, feeling its value, had made an unsuccessful effort to carry this fort by storm. They had been beaten off, with the loss of several hundred men, the Prince remaining in possession of the position, from which alone he could hope to relieve Leyden. He still held in his hand the keys with which he could unlock the ocean gates, and let the waters in upon the land, and he had long been convinced that nothing could save the city but to break the dikes. Leyden was not upon the sea, but he could send the sea to Leyden, although an army fit to encounter the besieging force under Valdez could not be levied. The battle of Mookerheyde had, for the present, quite settled the question of land relief, but it was possible to besiege the besiegers with the waves of the ocean. The Spaniards occupied the coast from the Hague to Vlaardingen, but the dikes along the Meuse and Yssel were in possession of the Prince. He determined that these should be pierced, while, at the same time, the great sluices at Rotterdam, Schiedam, and Delftshaven should be opened. The damage to the fields, villages, and growing crops would be enormous, but he felt that no other course could rescue Leyden, and with it the whole of Holland from destruction. His clear expositions and impassioned eloquence at last overcame all resistance. By the middle of July the estates fully consented to his plan, and its execution was immediately undertaken. "Better a drowned land than a lost land," cried the patriots, with enthusiasm, as they devoted their fertile fields to desolation. The enterprise for restoring their territory, for a season, to the waves, from which it had been so patiently rescued, was conducted with as much regularity as if it had been a profitable undertaking. A capital was formally subscribed, for which a certain number of bonds were issued, payable at a long date. In addition to this preliminary fund, a monthly allowance of forty-five guldens [2] was voted by the estates, until the work should be completed, and a large sum was contributed by the ladies of the land, who freely furnished their plate, jewelry, and costly furniture to the furtherance of the scheme.

Meantime, Valdez, on the 30th July, issued most urgent and ample offers of pardon to the citizens, if they would consent to open their gates and accept the King's authority, but his overtures were received with silent contempt, notwithstanding that the population was already approaching the starvation point. Although not yet fully informed of the active measures taken by the Prince, yet they still chose to rely upon his energy and their own fortitude, rather than upon the honied words which had formerly been heard at the gates of Harlem and Naarden. [3] On the 3d of August, the Prince, accompanied by Paul Buys, chief of the commission appointed to execute the enterprise, went in person along the Yssel, as far as Kappelle, and superintended the rupture of the dikes in sixteen places. The gates at Schiedam and Rotterdam were opened, and the ocean began to pour over the land. While waiting for the waters to rise, provisions were rapidly collected, according to an edict of the

[1] "The pipe sounds sweetly while the fowler beguiles the bird." Ovid.

[2] A gulden was worth about forty cents of American money.

[3] Naarden and Haarlem, which had endured terrible sieges, finally, after receiving pledges of safety, surrendered, only to suffer worse atrocities.

Prince, in all the principal towns of the neighborhood, and some two hundred vessels, of various sizes, had also been got ready at Rotterdam, Delfthaven, and other ports.

The citizens of Leyden were, however, already becoming impatient, for their bread was gone, and of its substitute malt-cake, they had but slender provision. On the 12th of August they received a letter from the Prince, encouraging them to resistance, and assuring them of a speedy relief, and on the 21st they addressed a despatch to him in reply, stating that they had now fulfilled their original promise, for they had held out two months with food, and another month without food. If not soon assisted, human strength could do no more; their malt-cake would last but four days, and after that was gone, there was nothing left but starvation. Upon the same day, however, they received a letter, dictated by the Prince, who now lay in bed at Rotterdam with a violent fever, assuring them that the dikes were all pierced, and that the water was rising upon the "Land-scheiding," the great outer barrier which separated the city from the sea. He said nothing however of his own illness, which would have cast a deep shadow over the joy which now broke forth among the burghers.

The letter was read publicly in the market-place; and to increase the cheerfulness, burgomaster Van der Werf, knowing the sensibility of his countrymen to music, ordered the city musicians to perambulate the streets, playing lively melodies and martial airs. Salvos of cannon were likewise fired, and the starving city for a brief space put on the aspect of a holiday, much to the astonishment of the besieging forces, who were not yet aware of the Prince's efforts. They perceived very soon, however, as the water everywhere about Leyden had risen to the depth of ten inches, that they stood in a perilous position. It was no trifling danger to be thus attacked by the waves of the ocean, which seemed about to obey with docility the command of William the Silent. Valdez became anxious and uncomfortable at the strange aspect of affairs; for the besieging army was now in its turn beleaguered, and by a stronger power than man's. He consulted with the most experienced of his officers, with the country people, with the most distinguished among the Glippers, and derived encouragement from their views concerning the Prince's plan. They pronounced it utterly futile and hopeless. The Glippers knew the country well, and ridiculed the desperate project in unmeasured terms.

Even in the city itself, a dull distrust had succeeded to the first vivid gleam of hope, while the few royalists among the population boldly taunted their fellow-citizens to their faces with the absurd vision of relief which they had so fondly welcomed. "Go up to the tower, ye beggars," [1] was the frequent and taunting cry, "go up to the tower, and tell us if ye can see the ocean coming over the dry land to your relief"—and day after day they did go up to the ancient tower of Hengist, with heavy heart and anxious eye, watching, hoping, praying, fearing, and at last almost despairing of relief by God or man. On the 27th they addressed a desponding letter to the estates, [2] complaining that the city had been forgotten in its utmost need, and on the same day a prompt and warm-hearted reply was received, in which the citizens were assured that every human effort was to be made for their relief. "Rather," said the estates, "will we see our whole land and all our possessions perish in the waves, than forsake thee, Leyden. We know full well, moreover, that with Leyden, all Holland must perish also." They excused themselves for not having more frequently written, upon the ground that the whole management of the measures for their relief had been intrusted to the Prince, by whom alone all the details had been administered, and all the correspondence conducted.

The fever of the Prince had, meanwhile, reached its height. He lay at Rotterdam, utterly prostrate in body, and with mind agitated nearly to delirium, by the perpetual and almost unassisted schemes which he was constructing. Relief, not only for Leyden, but for the whole country, now apparently sinking into the abyss, was the vision which he pursued as he tossed upon his restless couch. Never was illness more unseasonable. His attendants were in despair, for it was necessary that his mind should for a time be spared the agitation of business. The physicians who attended him agreed, as to his disorder, only in this, that it was the result of mental fatigue and melancholy, and could be cured only by removing all distressing and perplexing subjects from his thoughts, but all the physicians in the world could not have succeeded in turning his attention for an instant from the great cause of his country. Leyden lay, as it were, anxious and despairing at his feet, and it was impossible

[1] The Dutch patriots had been nicknamed Sea-beggars or Water-beggars.
[2] the government, i. e., the representatives of the three estates or orders of society: the clergy, the nobility, and the common people

for him to close his ears to her cry. Therefore, from his sick bed he continued to dictate words of counsel and encouragement to the city; to Admiral Boisot, commanding the fleet, minute directions and precautions. Towards the end of August a vague report had found its way into his sick chamber that Leyden had fallen, and although he refused to credit the tale, yet it served to harass his mind, and to heighten fever. Cornelius Van Mierop, Receiver-General of Holland, had occasion to visit him at Rotterdam, and strange to relate, found the house almost deserted. Penetrating, unattended, to the Prince's bed-chamber, he found him lying quite alone. Inquiring what had become of all his attendants, he was answered by the Prince, in a very feeble voice, that he had sent them all away. The Receiver-General seems, from this, to have rather hastily arrived at the conclusion that the Prince's disorder was the pest, and that his servants and friends had all deserted him from cowardice. This was very far from being the case. His private secretary and his maître d'hôtel [1] watched, day and night, by his couch, and the best physicians of the city were in constant attendance. By a singular accident, all had been despatched on different errands, at the express desire of their master, but there had never been a suspicion that his disorder was the pest, or pestilential. Nerves of steel, and a frame of adamant could alone have resisted the constant anxiety and the consuming fatigue to which he had so long been exposed. His illness had been aggravated by the rumor of Leyden's fall, a fiction which Cornelius Mierop was now enabled flatly to contradict. The Prince began to mend from that hour. By the end of the first week of September, he wrote a long letter to his brother, assuring him of his convalescence, and expressing, as usual, a calm confidence in the divine decrees—"God will ordain for me," said he, "all which is necessary for my good and my salvation. He will load me with no more afflictions than the fragility of this nature can sustain."

The preparations for the relief of Leyden, which, notwithstanding his exertions, had grown slack during his sickness, were now vigorously resumed. On the 1st of September, Admiral Boisot arrived out of Zeeland with a small number of vessels, and with eight hundred veteran sailors. A wild and ferocious crew were those eight hundred Zeelanders. Scarred, hacked, and even maimed, in the unceasing conflicts in which their lives had passed; wearing

[1] steward or superintendent (of his household)

crescents in their caps, with the inscription "Rather Turkish than Popish"; renowned far and wide, as much for their ferocity as for their nautical skill; the appearance of these wildest of the "Sea-beggars" was both eccentric and terrific. They were known never to give nor to take quarter, for they went to *mortal* combat only, and had sworn to spare neither noble nor simple, neither king, kaiser, nor pope, should they fall into their power.

More than two hundred vessels had been now assembled, carrying generally ten pieces of cannon, with from ten to eighteen oars, and manned with twenty-five hundred veterans, experienced both on land and water. The work was now undertaken in earnest. The distance from Leyden to the outer dike, over whose ruins the ocean had already been admitted, was nearly fifteen miles. This reclaimed territory, however, was not maintained against the sea by these external barriers alone. The flotilla made its way with ease to the Land-scheiding, a strong dike within five miles of Leyden, but here its progress was arrested. The approach to the city was surrounded by many strong ramparts, one within the other, by which it was defended against its ancient enemy, the ocean, precisely like the circumvallations by means of which it was now assailed by its more recent enemy, the Spaniard. To enable the fleet, however, to sail over the land, it was necessary to break through this twofold series of defenses. Between the Land-scheiding and Leyden were several dikes, which kept out the water; upon the level territory, thus encircled, were many villages, together with a chain of sixty-two forts which completely occupied the land. All these villages and fortresses were held by the veteran troops of the King; the besieging force being about four times as strong as that which was coming to the rescue.

The Prince had given orders that the Land-scheiding, which was still one-and-a-half foot above water, should be taken possession of at every hazard. On the night of the 10th and 11th of September this was accomplished, by surprise, and in a masterly manner. The few Spaniards who had been stationed upon the dike were all despatched or driven off, and the patriots fortified themselves upon it, without the loss of a man. As the day dawned the Spaniards saw the fatal error which they had committed in leaving this bulwark so feebly defended, and from two villages which stood close to the dike, the troops now rushed in considerable force to recover what they had lost. A hot action succeeded, but the patriots had too securely established themselves. They completely defeated the enemy, who retired, leaving hundreds of dead on the field, and the patriots in complete possession of the Land-scheiding. This first action was sanguinary and desperate. It gave an earnest of what these people, who came to relieve their brethren, by sacrificing their property and their lives, were determined to effect. It gave a revolting proof, too, of the intense hatred which nerved their arms. A Zeelander, having struck down a Spaniard on the dike, knelt on his bleeding enemy, tore his heart from his bosom, fastened his teeth in it for an instant, and then threw it to a dog, with the exclamation, " 'Tis too bitter." The Spanish heart was, however, rescued, and kept for years, with the marks of the soldier's teeth upon it, a sad testimonial of the ferocity engendered by this war for national existence.

The great dike having been thus occupied, no time was lost in breaking it through in several places, a work which was accomplished under the very eyes of the enemy. The fleet sailed through the gaps; but, after their passage had been effected in good order, the Admiral found, to his surprise, that it was not the only rampart to be carried. The Prince had been informed, by those who claimed to know the country, that, when once the Land-scheiding had been passed, the water would flood the country as far as Leyden, but the "Green-way," another long dike, three-quarters of a mile farther inward, now rose at least a foot above the water, to oppose their further progress. Fortunately, by a second and still more culpable carelessness, this dike had been left by the Spaniards in as unprotected a state as the first had been. Promptly and audaciously Admiral Boisot took possession of this barrier also, leveled it in many places, and brought his flotilla, in triumph, over its ruins. Again, however, he was doomed to disappointment. A large mere, called the Fresh-water Lake, was known to extend itself directly in his path about midway between the Land-scheiding and the city. To this piece of water, into which he expected to have instantly floated, his only passage lay through one deep canal. The sea, which had thus far borne him on, now diffusing itself over a very wide surface, and under the influence of an adverse wind, had become too shallow for his ships. The canal alone was deep enough, but it led directly towards a bridge, strongly occupied by the enemy. Hostile troops, moreover, to the amount of three thousand, occupied both sides of the canal. The bold Boisot, nevertheless, determined to force his passage, if possible. Selecting a few of his strongest vessels, his heaviest artillery, and his bravest sailors, he led the van himself, in a desperate attempt to make his way to the mere. He opened a hot fire upon the bridge, then converted into a fortress, while his men engaged in hand-to-hand combat with a succession of skirmishers from the troops along the canal. After losing a few men, and ascertaining the impregnable position of the enemy, he was obliged to withdraw, defeated, and almost despairing.

A week had elapsed since the great dike had been pierced, and the flotilla now lay motionless in shallow water, having accomplished less than two miles. The wind, too, was easterly, causing the sea rather to sink than to rise. Everything wore a gloomy aspect, when, fortunately, on the 18th, the wind shifted to the northwest, and for three days blew a gale. The waters rose rapidly, and before the second day was closed the armada was afloat again. Some fugitives from Zoetermeer village now arrived, and informed the Admiral that, by making a detour to the right, he could completely circumvent the bridge and the mere. They guided him, accordingly, to a comparatively low dike, which led between the villages of Zoetermeer and Benthuyzen. A strong force of Spaniards was stationed in each place, but seized with a panic, instead of sallying to defend the barrier, they fled inwardly towards Leyden, and halted at the village of North Aa. It was natural that they should be amazed. Nothing is more appalling to the imagination than the rising ocean tide, when man feels himself within its power; and here were the waters, hourly deepening and closing around them, devouring the earth beneath their feet, while on the waves rode a flotilla, manned by a determined race, whose courage and ferocity were known throughout the world. The Spanish soldiers, brave as they were on land, were not sailors, and in the naval contests which had taken place between them and the Hollanders, had been almost invariably defeated. It was not surprising in these amphibious skirmishes, where discipline was of little avail, and habitual audacity faltered at the vague dangers which encompassed them, that the foreign troops should lose their presence of mind.

Three barriers, one within the other, had now been passed, and the flotilla, advancing with the advancing waves, and driving the enemy steadily before it, was drawing nearer to the beleaguered city. As one circle after another was passed, the besieging army found itself compressed within a constantly contracting field. The *Ark of Delft,* an enormous vessel, with shot-proof bulwarks, and moved by paddle-wheels turned by a crank, now arrived at Zoetermeer, and was soon followed by the whole fleet. After a brief delay, sufficient to allow the few remaining villagers to escape, both Zoetermeer and Benthuyzen, with the fortifications, were set on fire, and abandoned to their fate. The blaze lighted up the desolate and watery waste around, and was seen at Leyden, where it was hailed as the beacon of hope. Without further impediment, the armada proceeded to North Aa; the enemy retreating from this position also, and flying to Zoeterwoude, a strongly fortified village but a mile and three quarters from the city walls. It was now swarming with troops, for the bulk of the besieging army had gradually been driven into a narrow circle of forts, within the immediate neighborhood of Leyden. Besides Zoeterwoude, the two posts where they were principally established, were Lammen and Leyderdorp, each within three hundred rods of the town. At Leyderdorp, were the headquarters of Valdez; Colonel Borgia commanded in the very strong fortress of Lammen.

The fleet was, however, delayed at North Aa by another barrier, called the "Kirk-way." The waters, too, spreading once more over a wider space, and diminishing under an east wind, which had again arisen, no longer permitted their progress, so that very soon the whole armada was stranded anew. The waters fell to the depth of nine inches, while the vessels required eighteen and twenty. Day after day the fleet lay motionless upon the shallow sea. Orange, rising from his sick bed as soon as he could stand, now came on board the fleet. His presence diffused universal joy; his words inspired his desponding army with fresh hope. He rebuked the impatient spirits, who, weary of their compulsory idleness, had shown symptoms of ill-timed ferocity; and those eight hundred mad Zeelanders, so frantic in their hatred to the foreigners who had so long profaned their land, were as docile as children to the Prince. He reconnoitered the whole ground, and issued orders for the immediate destruction of the Kirk-way, the last important barrier which separated the fleet from Leyden. Then, after a long conference with Admiral Boisot, he returned to Delft.

Meantime, the besieged city was at its last gasp. The burghers had been in a state of uncertainty for many days; being aware that the fleet had set forth for their relief, but knowing full well the thousand obstacles which it had to surmount. They had guessed its progress by the illumination from the blazing villages; they had heard its salvos of artillery on its arrival at North Aa; but since then, all had been dark and mournful again, hope and fear, in sickening alternation, distracting every breast. They knew that the wind was unfavorable, and, at the dawn of each day, every eye was turned wistfully to the vanes of the steeples. So long as the easterly breeze prevailed, they felt, as they anxiously stood on towers and house-tops, that they must look in vain for the welcome ocean. Yet, while thus patiently waiting, they were literally starving; for even the misery endured at Harlem had not reached that depth and intensity of agony to which Leyden was now reduced. Bread, malt-cake, horse-flesh, had entirely disappeared; dogs, cats, rats, and other vermin, were esteemed luxuries. A small number of cows, kept as long as possible, for their milk, still remained; but a few were killed from day to day, and distributed in minute proportions, hardly sufficient to support life among the famishing population. Starving wretches swarmed daily around the shambles where these cattle were slaughtered, contending for any morsel which might fall, and lapping eagerly the blood as it ran along the pavement; while the hides, chopped and boiled, were greedily devoured. Women and children, all day long, were seen searching gutters and dunghills for morsels of food, which they disputed fiercely with the famishing dogs. The green leaves were stripped from the trees, every living herb was converted into human food, but these expedients could not avert starvation. The daily mortality was frightful—infants starved to death on the maternal breasts, which famine had parched and withered; mothers dropped dead in the streets, with their dead children in their arms. In many a house the watchmen, in their rounds, found a whole family of corpses,—father, mother, and children, side by side, for a disorder called the plague, naturally engendered of hardship and famine, now came, as if in kindness, to abridge the agony of the people. The pestilence stalked at noonday through the city, and the doomed inhabitants fell like grass beneath its scythe. From six thousand to eight thousand human beings sank before this scourge alone, yet the people resolutely held out—women and men mutually encouraging each other to resist the entrance of their foreign foe—an evil more horrible than pest or famine.

The missives from Valdez, who saw more vividly than the besieged could do, the uncertainty of his own position, now poured daily into the city, the enemy becoming more prodigal of his vows, as he felt that the ocean might yet save the victims from his grasp. The inhabitants, in their ignorance, had gradually abandoned their hopes of relief, but they spurned the summons to surrender. Leyden was sublime in its despair. A few murmurs were, however, occasionally heard at the steadfastness of the magistrates, and a dead body was placed at the door of the burgomaster, as a silent witness against his inflexibility. A party of the more faint-hearted even assailed the heroic Adrian Van der Werf [1] with threats and reproaches as he passed through the streets. A crowd had gathered around him, as he reached a triangular place in the center of the town, into which many of the principal streets emptied themselves, and upon one side of which stood the church of Saint Pancras, with its high brick tower surmounted by two pointed turrets, and with two ancient lime-trees at its entrance. There stood the burgomaster, a tall, haggard, imposing figure, with dark visage, and a tranquil but commanding eye. He waved his broad-leaved felt hat for silence, and then exclaimed, in language which has been almost literally preserved, "What would ye, my friends? Why do ye murmur that we do not break our vows and surrender the city to the Spaniards?—a fate more horrible than the agony which she now endures. I tell you I have made an oath to hold the city, and may God give me strength to keep my oath! I can die but once; whether by your hands, the enemy's, or by the hand of God. My own fate is indifferent to me, not so that of the city intrusted to my care. I know that we shall starve if not soon relieved; but starvation is preferable to the dishonored death which is the only alternative. Your menaces move me not; my life is at your disposal; here is my sword, plunge it into my breast, and divide my flesh among you. Take my body to appease your hunger, but expect no surrender so long as I remain alive."

The words of the stout burgomaster inspired a new courage in the hearts of those who heard him, and a shout of applause and defiance arose from the famishing but enthusiastic crowd. They left the place, after exchanging new vows of fidelity with their magistrate, and again ascended tower and battlement to watch for the coming fleet. From the ramparts they hurled renewed defiance at the enemy. "Ye call us rat-eaters and dog-eaters," they cried, "and it is true. So long, then, as ye hear dog bark or cat mew within the walls, ye may know that the city holds out. And when all has perished but ourselves, be sure that we will each devour our left arms, retaining our right to defend our women, our liberty, and our religion against the foreign tyrant. Should God, in his wrath, doom us to destruction, and deny us all relief, even then will we maintain ourselves for ever against your entrance. When the last hour has come, with our own hands we will set fire to the city, and perish, men, women, and children together in the flames, rather than suffer our homes to be polluted, and our liberties to be crushed." Such words of defiance, thundered daily from the battlements, sufficiently informed Valdez as to his chance of conquering the city, either by force or fraud, but at the same time he felt comparatively relieved by the inactivity of Boisot's fleet, which still lay stranded at North Aa. "As well," shouted the Spaniards, derisively, to the citizens, "as well can the Prince of Orange pluck the stars from the sky as bring the ocean to the walls of Leyden for your relief."

On the 28th of September, a dove flew into the city, bringing a letter from Admiral Boisot. In this despatch, the position of the fleet at North Aa was described in encouraging terms, and the inhabitants were assured that, in a very few days at furthest, the long-expected relief would enter their gates. The letter was read publicly upon the market-place, and the bells were rung for joy. Nevertheless, on the morrow, the vanes pointed to the east, the waters, so far from rising, continued to sink, and Admiral Boisot was almost in despair. He wrote to the Prince, that if the spring-tide, now to be expected, should not, together with a strong and favorable wind, come immediately to their relief, it would be in vain to attempt anything further, and that the expedition would of necessity be abandoned. The tempest came to their relief. A violent equinoctial gale, on the night of the 1st and 2nd of October, came storming from the northwest, shifting after a few hours full eight points and then blowing still more violently from the southwest. The waters of the North Sea were piled in vast masses upon the southern coast of Holland,

[1] the burgomaster (mayor).

and then dashed furiously landward, the ocean rising over the earth, and sweeping with unrestrained power across the ruined dikes.

In the course of twenty-four hours, the fleet at North Aa, instead of nine inches, had more than two feet of water. No time was lost. The Kirk-way, which had been broken through, according to the Prince's instructions, was now completely overflowed, and the fleet sailed at midnight, in the midst of the storm and darkness. A few sentinel vessels of the enemy challenged them as they steadily rowed towards Zoeterwoude. The answer was a flash from Boisot's cannon, lighting up the black waste of waters. There was a fierce naval midnight battle; a strange spectacle among the branches of those quiet orchards, and with the chimney-stacks of half-submerged farm houses rising around the contending vessels. The neighboring village of Zoeterwoude shook with the discharges of the Zeelanders' cannon, and the Spaniards assembled in that fortress knew that the rebel Admiral was at last afloat, and on his course. The enemy's vessels were soon sunk, their crews hurled into the waves. On went the fleet, sweeping over the broad waters which lay between Zoeterwoude and Zwieten. As they approached some shallows, which led into the great mere, the Zeelanders dashed into the sea, and with sheer strength shouldered every vessel through. Two obstacles lay still in their path—the forts of Zoeterwoude and Lammen, distant from the city five hundred and two hundred and fifty yards respectively. Strong redoubts, both well supplied with troops and artillery, they were likely to give a rough reception to the light flotilla; but the panic, which had hitherto driven their foes before the advancing patriots, had reached Zoeterwoude. Hardly was the fleet in sight, when the Spaniards, in the early morning, poured out from the fortress, and fled precipitately to the left, along a road which led in a westerly direction towards The Hague. Their narrow path was rapidly vanishing in the waves, and hundreds sank beneath the constantly deepening and treacherous flood. The wild Zeelanders, too, sprang from their vessels upon the crumbling dike, and drove their retreating foes into the sea. They hurled their harpoons at them, with an accuracy acquired in many a polar chase; they plunged into the waves in the keen pursuit, attacking them with boat-hook and dagger. The numbers who thus fell beneath these corsairs, who neither gave nor took quarter, were never counted, but probably not less than a thousand perished. The rest effected their escape to The Hague.

The first fortress was thus seized, dismantled, set on fire, and passed, and a few strokes of the oars brought the whole fleet close to Lammen. This last obstacle rose formidable and frowning directly across their path. Swarming as it was with soldiers, and bristling with artillery, it seemed to defy the armada either to carry it by storm or to pass under its guns into the city. It appeared that the enterprise was, after all, to founder within sight of the long expecting and expected haven. Boisot anchored his fleet within a respectful distance, and spent what remained of the day in carefully reconnoitering the fort, which seemed only too strong. In conjunction with Leyderdorp, the headquarters of Valdez, a mile and a half distant on the right, and within a mile of the city, it seemed so insuperable an impediment that Boisot wrote in despondent tone to the Prince of Orange. He announced his intention of carrying the fort, if it were possible, on the following morning, but if obliged to retreat, he observed, with something like despair, that there would be nothing for it but to wait for another gale of wind. If the waters should rise sufficiently to enable them to make a wide detour, it might be possible—if, in the meantime, Leyden did not starve or surrender—to enter its gates from the opposite side.

Meantime, the citizens had grown wild with expectation. A dove had been despatched by Boisot, informing them of his precise position, and a number of citizens accompanied the burgomaster, at nightfall, toward the tower of Hengist—"Yonder," cried the magistrate, stretching out his hand towards Lammen, "yonder, behind that fort, are bread and meat, and brethren in thousands. Shall all this be destroyed by the Spanish guns, or shall we rush to the rescue of our friends?" "We will tear the fortress to fragments with our teeth and nails," was the reply, "before the relief, so long expected, shall be wrested from us." It was resolved that a sortie, in conjunction with the operations of Boisot, should be made against Lammen with the earliest dawn. Night descended upon the scene, a pitch-dark night, full of anxiety to the Spaniards, to the armada, to Leyden. Strange sights and sounds occurred at different moments to bewilder the anxious sentinels. A long procession of lights issuing from the fort was seen to flit across the black face of the waters, in the dead of night, and the whole of the city wall, between the Cow-gate and the Tower of Burgundy, fell with a loud crash. The horror-struck citizens thought that the Spaniards were upon them at last; the Spaniards imagined the noise to indicate a desperate sortie of the citizens. Everything was vague and mysterious.

Day dawned at length, after the feverish night, and the Admiral prepared for the assault. Within the fortress reigned a death-like stillness, which inspired a sickening suspicion. Had the city, indeed, been carried in the night; had the massacre already commenced; had all this labor and audacity been expended in vain? Suddenly a man was descried, wading breast-high through the water from Lammen towards the fleet, while at the same time, one solitary boy was seen to wave his cap from the summit of the fort. After a moment of doubt, the happy mystery was solved. The Spaniards had fled, panic-struck, during the darkness. Their position would still have enabled them, with firmness, to frustrate the enterprise of the patriots, but the hand of God, which had sent the ocean and the tempest to the deliverance of Leyden, had struck her enemies with terror likewise. The lights which had been seen moving during the night were the lanterns of the retreating Spaniards, and the boy who was now waving his triumphant signal from the battlements had alone witnessed the spectacle. So confident was he in the conclusion to which it led him, that he had volunteered at daybreak to go thither all alone. The magistrates, fearing a trap, hesitated for a moment to believe the truth, which soon, however, became quite evident. Valdez, flying himself from Leyderdorp, had ordered Colonel Borgia to retire with all his troops from Lammen. Thus, the Spaniards had retreated at the very moment that an extraordinary accident had laid bare a whole side of the city for their entrance. The noise of the wall, as it fell, only inspired them with fresh alarm; for they believed that the citizens had sallied forth in the darkness to aid the advancing flood in the work of destruction. All obstacles being now removed, the fleet of Boisot swept by Lammen, and entered the city on the morning of the 3d of October. Leyden was relieved.

The quays were lined with the famishing population, as the fleet rowed through the canals, every human being who could stand, coming forth to greet the preservers of the city. Bread was thrown from every vessel among the crowd. The poor creatures who for two months had tasted no wholesome human food, and who had literally been living within the jaws of death, snatched eagerly the blessed gift, at last too liberally bestowed. Many choked themselves to death, in the greediness with which they devoured their bread; others became ill with the effects of plenty thus suddenly succeeding starvation;—but these were isolated cases, a repetition of which was prevented. The Admiral, stepping ashore, was welcomed by the magistracy, and a solemn procession was immediately formed. Magistrates and citizens, wild Zeelanders, emaciated burgher guards, sailors, soldiers, women, children,—nearly every living person within the walls, all repaired without delay to the great church, stout Admiral Boisot leading the way. The starving and heroic city, which had been so firm in its resistance to an earthly king, now bent itself in humble gratitude before the King of kings. After prayers, the whole vast congregation joined in the thanksgiving hymn. Thousands of voices raised the song, but few were able to carry it to its conclusion, for the universal emotion, deepened by the music, became too full for utterance. The hymn was abruptly suspended, while the multitude wept like children. This scene of honest pathos terminated, the necessary measures for distributing the food and for relieving the sick were taken by the magistracy. A note dispatched to the Prince of Orange, was received by him at two o'clock, as he sat in church at Delft. It was of somewhat different purport from that of the letter which he had received early in the same day from Boisot—the letter in which the admiral had informed him that the success of the enterprise depended, after all, upon the desperate assault upon a nearly impregnable fort. The joy of the Prince may be easily imagined, and so soon as the sermon was concluded, he handed the letter just received to the minister, to be read to the congregation. Thus, all participated in his joy, and united with him in thanksgiving.

The next day, notwithstanding the urgent entreaties of his friends, who were anxious lest his life should be endangered by breathing, in his scarcely convalescent state, the air of the city where so many thousands had been dying of the pestilence, the Prince repaired to Leyden. He, at least, had never doubted his own or his country's fortitude. They could, therefore, most sincerely congratulate each other, now that the victory had been achieved. "If we are doomed to perish," he had said a little before the commencement of the siege, "in the name of God, be it so! At any rate, we shall have the honor to have done what no nation ever did before us, that of having defended and maintained ourselves, unaided, in so small a country, against the tremendous efforts of such powerful enemies. . . ."

1851-1855

1856

FRANCIS PARKMAN 1823-1893

Pre-eminent among American historians who have written of their native land is Parkman. He was born in Boston and died near there. After he had graduated at Harvard and for a while studied law, his mind turned toward American life on the border in the previous century. Wishing to know Indians in their primitive state, he spent a summer with a Sioux tribe in the Black Hills and on the eastern Rocky Mountain slopes, impairing his health for the remainder of his life. He made many visits to Europe for documentary materials, and traveled much in America visiting the scenes of his narratives. His works include *The Conspiracy of Pontiac*, 1851; *Pioneers of France in the New World*, 1865; *The Jesuits in North America*, 1867; *La Salle and the Discovery of the Great West*, 1869; *The Old Régime in Canada*, 1874; *Count Frontenac and New France under Louis XIV*, 1877; *Montcalm and Wolfe*, 1884; *A Half-Century of Conflict*, 1892.

Parkman was pre-eminently the historian of the French in America. *The Conspiracy of Pontiac* was said by John Fiske to be "one of the most brilliant and fascinating books that has ever been written by any historian since the days of Herodotus." The book deals with relations between Englishmen and Indians, after France in 1760 had practically yielded Canada to England.

Parkman's histories present not only the romance of New World colonization but the conflict of two civilizations. The triumph of England resulted in making the North American continent, to the Rio Grande, an area for the extension of those free institutions that had been developing for a thousand years among Englishmen. His success came from exact knowledge gained in research, acquaintance with the topography of the scenes he describes, an understanding of the Indian mind, and a love, like Cooper's, for American themes. These elements led to the swift vividness of his style.

Biography and criticism: Henry Dwight Sedgwick, *Francis Parkman*, (AML) 1904; C. H. Farnham, *Life*, 1900; L. F. Abbott, "Francis Parkman," *Outlook*, 135:212-4; C. W. Alvord, *Nation* 117: 394-6; E. F. Wyatt, *No. Am.* 218:484-96.

From THE CONSPIRACY OF PONTIAC [1]
Chapter XVI
MICHILLIMACKINAC

In the spring of the year 1763, before the war broke out, several English traders went up to Michillimackinac, some adopting the old route of the Ottawa, and others that of Detroit and the lakes. We will follow one of the latter

[1] Great dissatisfaction prevailed among the Indians: the French had tactfully been their friends; the English were haughty; it was rumored that the English would seize all the Indian land. Making use of the Indian feeling thus aroused, French traders gradually aroused the Indians to oppose the English, and vaguely promised to help them.

on his adventurous progress. Passing the fort and settlement of Detroit, he soon enters Lake St. Clair, which seems like a broad basin filled to overflowing, while, along its far distant verge, a faint line of forest separates the water from the sky. He crosses the lake, and his voyageurs [2] next urge his canoe against the current of the great river above. At length, Lake Huron opens before him, stretching its liquid expanse, like an ocean, to the farthest horizon. His canoe skirts the eastern shore of Michigan, where the forest rises like a wall from the water's edge; and as he advances northward, an endless line of stiff and shaggy fir trees, hung with long mosses, fringes the shore with an aspect of monotonous desolation. In the space of two or three weeks, if his Canadians labor well, and no accident occur, the trader approaches the end of his voyage. Passing on his right the extensive Island of Bois Blanc, he sees, nearly in front, the beautiful Mackinaw, rising, with its white cliffs and green foliage, from the broad breast of the waters. He does not steer towards it, for at that day the Indians were its only tenants, but keeps along the main shore to the left, while his voyageurs raise their song and chorus. Doubling a point, he sees before him the red flag of England swelling lazily in the wind, and the palisades and wooden bastions of Fort Michillimackinac standing close upon the margin of the lake. On the beach, canoes are drawn up, and Canadians and Indians are idly lounging. A little beyond the fort is a cluster of the white Canadian houses, roofed with bark, and protected by fences of strong round pickets.

The trader enters at the gate, and sees before him an extensive square area, surrounded by high palisades. Numerous houses, barracks, and other buildings form a smaller square within, and in the vacant space which they enclose, appear the red uniforms of British

A prophet, too, appeared among the Indians who urged them to rise up against the English outposts. All these things influenced Pontiac, the chief of the Ottawas, whose home was a village near Detroit. He was a man of such unusual intellect, courage, and strength of character, that his influence was felt far and wide among the Indian tribes. He foresaw the fate of the Indians if the English were left in control, and determined to make one great effort to restore the power of his race. Accordingly a plot was formed to attack at the same time all the scattered English forts of the western frontier, the combined garrisons of which numbered not more than five or six hundred men. In the spring and summer of 1763, therefore, a force made up of Delawares, Wyandottes, Shawnees, Mingoes, Chippewas, and other tribes, besieged Detroit, and in June made the attack here described on Fort Michilimackinac (pronounced mĭsh'ĭ-lĭ-măk'ĭ-nô).

[2] Canadian river-boatmen

soldiers, the gray coats of Canadians, and the gaudy Indian blankets, mingled in picturesque confusion, while a multitude of squaws, with children of every hue, stroll restlessly about the place. Such was Fort Michillimackinac in 1763. Its name, which, in the Algonquin tongue, signifies the Great Turtle, was first, from a fancied resemblance, applied to the neighboring island, and thence to the fort.

Though buried in a wilderness, Michillimackinac was still of no recent origin. As early as 1671, the Jesuits had established a mission near the place, and a military force was not long in following; for, under the French dominion, the priest and the soldier went hand in hand. Neither toil, nor suffering, nor all the terrors of the wilderness, could damp the zeal of the undaunted missionary; and the restless ambition of France was always on the alert to seize every point of vantage, and avail itself of every means to gain ascendency over the forest tribes. Besides Michillimackinac, there were two other posts in this northern region, Green Bay, and the Sault Ste. Marie. Both were founded at an early period, and both presented the same characteristic features, a mission-house, a fort, and a cluster of Canadian dwellings. They had been originally garrisoned by small parties of militia, who, bringing their families with them, settled on the spot, and were founders of these little colonies. Michillimackinac, much the largest of the three, contained thirty families within the palisades of the fort, and about as many more without. Besides its military value, it was important as a center of the fur trade; for it was here that the traders engaged their men, and sent out their goods in canoes, under the charge of subordinates, to the more distant regions of the Mississippi and the northwest.

During the greater part of the year, the garrison and the settlers were completely isolated —cut off from all connection with the world; and, indeed, so great was the distance, and so serious the perils, which separated the three sister posts of the northern lakes, that often, through the whole winter all intercourse was stopped between them.

It is difficult for the imagination adequately to conceive the extent of these fresh-water oceans, and vast regions of forest, which, at the date of our narrative, were the domain of nature, a mighty hunting and fishing ground, for the sustenance of a few wandering tribes. One might journey among them for days, and even weeks together, without beholding a human face. The Indians near Michillimackinac were the Ojibwas and Ottawas, the former of whom claimed the eastern section of Michigan, and the latter the western, their respective portions being separated by a line drawn southward from the fort itself. The principal village of the Ojibwas contained about a hundred warriors, and stood upon the Island of Michillimackinac, now called Mackinaw. There was another smaller village near the head of Thunder Bay. The Ottawas, to the number of two hundred and fifty warriors, lived at the settlement of L'Arbe Croche, on the shores of Lake Michigan, some distance west of the fort. This place was then the seat of the old Jesuit mission of St. Ignace, originally placed by Father Marquette [1] on the northern side of the straits. Many of the Ottawas were nominal Catholics. They were all somewhat improved from their original savage condition, living in log houses, and cultivating corn and vegetables to such an extent as to supply the fort with provision, besides satisfying their own wants. The Ojibwas, on the other hand, were not in the least degree removed from their primitive barbarism.

These two tribes, with most of the other neighboring Indians, were strongly hostile to the English. Many of their warriors had fought against them in the late war, for France had summoned allies from the farthest corners of the wilderness, to aid her in her desperate struggle. This feeling of hostility was excited to a higher pitch by the influence of the Canadians, who disliked the English, not merely as national enemies, but also as rivals in the fur trade, and were extremely jealous of their intrusion upon the lakes. The following incidents, which occurred in the autumn of the year 1761, will illustrate the state of feeling which prevailed:—

At that time, although Michillimackinac had been surrendered, and the French garrison removed, no English troops had yet arrived to supply their place, and the Canadians were the only tenants of the fort. An adventurous trader, Alexander Henry, who, with one or two others, was the pioneer of the English fur trade in this region, came to Michillimackinac by the route of the Ottawa. On the way, he was several times warned to turn back, and assured of death if he proceeded, and, at length, was compelled for safety to assume the disguise of a Canadian voyageur. When his canoes, laden with goods, reached the fort, he was very coldly received by its inhabitants, who did all in their power to alarm and discourage

---

[1] Jacques Marquette, 1637-1675, a Jesuit missionary and explorer, established the mission at St. Ignace about 1671.

him. Soon after his arrival, he received the very unwelcome information that a large number of Ojibwas, from the neighboring villages, were coming, in their canoes, to call upon him. Under ordinary circumstances such a visitation, though disagreeable enough, would excite neither anxiety nor surprise; for the Indians, when in their villages, lead so monotonous an existence, that they are ready to snatch at the least occasion of excitement, and the prospect of a few trifling presents, and a few pipes of tobacco, is often a sufficient inducement for a journey of several days. But in the present instance, there was serious cause of apprehension, since Canadians and Frenchmen were alike hostile to the solitary trader. The story could not be better told than in his own graphic and truthful words.

"At two o'clock in the afternoon, the Chippewas (Ojibwas) came to the house, about sixty in number, and headed by Minavavana, their chief. They walked in single file, each with his tomahawk in one hand and scalping-knife in the other. Their bodies were naked from the waist upward, except in a few examples, where blankets were thrown loosely over the shoulders. Their faces were painted with charcoal, worked up with grease, their bodies with white clay, in patterns of various fancies. Some had feathers thrust through their noses, and their heads decorated with the same. It is unnecessary to dwell on the sensations with which I beheld the approach of this uncouth, if not frightful assemblage.

"The chief entered first, and the rest followed without noise. On receiving a sign from the former, the latter seated themselves on the floor.

"Minavavana appeared to be about fifty years of age. He was six feet in height, and had in his countenance an indescribable mixture of good and evil. Looking steadfastly at me, where I sat in ceremony, with an interpreter on either hand, and several Canadians behind me, he entered, at the same time, into conversation with Campion,[1] inquiring how long it was since I left Montreal, and observing, that the English, as it would seem, were brave men, and not afraid of death, since they dared to come, as I had done, fearlessly among their enemies.

"The Indians now gravely smoked their pipes, while I inwardly endured the tortures of suspense. At length, the pipes being finished, as well as a long pause, by which they were succeeded, Minavavana, taking a few strings of

[1] probably an interpreter

wampum [2] in his hand, began the following speech:—

" 'Englishman, it is to you that I speak, and I demand your attention.

" 'Englishman, you know that the French King is our father. He promised to be such; and we, in return, promised to be his children. This promise we have kept.

" 'Englishman, it is you that have made war with this our father. You are his enemy; and how, then, could you have the boldness to venture among us, his children? You know that his enemies are ours.

" 'Englishman, we are informed that our father, the King of France, is old and infirm; and that, being fatigued with making war upon your nation, he is fallen asleep. During his sleep, you have taken advantage of him, and possessed yourselves of Canada. But his nap is almost at an end. I think I hear him already stirring, and inquiring for his children, the Indians; and when he does awake, what must become of you? He will destroy you utterly.

" 'Englishman, although you have conquered the French, you have not yet conquered us. We are not your slaves. These lakes, these woods and mountains, were left to us by our ancestors. They are our inheritance; and we will part with them to none. Your nation supposes that we, like the white people, cannot live without bread, and pork, and beef! But you ought to know that He, the Great Spirit and Master of Life, has provided food for us in these spacious lakes, and on these woody mountains.

" 'Englishman, our father, the King of France, employed our young men to make war upon your nation. In this warfare, many of them have been killed; and it is our custom to retaliate until such time as the spirits of the slain are satisfied. But the spirits of the slain are to be satisfied in either of two ways; the first is, by the spilling of the blood of the nation by which they fell; the other, by *covering the bodies of the dead*, and thus allaying the resentment of their relations. This is done by making presents.

" 'Englishman, your King has never sent us any presents, nor entered into any treaty with us; wherefore he and we are still at war; and, until he does these things, we must consider that we have no other father nor friend, among the white men, than the King of France; but for you, we have taken into consideration that you have ventured your life among us, in the

[2] shells or strings of shells used by the Indians as money and for ceremonial purposes

expectation that we should not molest you. You do not come armed, with an intention to make war; you come in peace, to trade with us, and supply us with necessaries, of which we are in much want. We shall regard you, therefore, as a brother; and you may sleep tranquilly, without fear of the Chippewas. As a token of our friendship, we present you this pipe to smoke.'

"As Minavavana uttered these words, an Indian presented me with a pipe, which, after I had drawn the smoke three times, was carried to the chief, and after him to every person in the room. This ceremony ended, the chief arose, and gave me his hand, in which he was followed by all the rest."

These tokens of friendship were suitably acknowledged by the trader, who made a formal reply to Minavavana's speech. To this succeeded a request for whisky on the part of the Indians, with which Henry unwillingly complied; and, having distributed several small additional presents, he beheld, with profound satisfaction, the departure of his guests. Scarcely had he ceased to congratulate himself on having thus got rid of the Ojibwas, or, as he calls them, the Chippewas, when a more formidable invasion once more menaced him with destruction. Two hundred L'Arbre Croche Ottawas came in a body to the fort, and summoned Henry, together with Goddard and Solomons, two other traders, who had just arrived, to meet them in council. Here they informed their startled auditors that they must distribute their goods among the Indians, adding a worthless promise to pay them in the spring, and threatening force in case of a refusal. Being allowed until the next morning to reflect on what they had heard, the traders resolved on resistance, and, accordingly, arming about thirty of their men, with muskets, they barricaded themselves in the house occupied by Henry, and kept strict watch all night. The Ottawas, however, did not venture an attack. On the following day, the Canadians, with pretended sympathy, strongly advised compliance with the demand; but the three traders resolutely held out, and kept possession of their stronghold till night, when, to their surprise and joy, the news arrived that the body of troops known to be on their way towards the fort were, at that moment, encamped within a few miles of it. Another night of watching and anxiety succeeded; but at sunrise, the Ottawas launched their canoes and departed, while, immediately after, the boats of the English detachment were seen to approach the landing-place. Michillimackinac received a strong garrison, and for a time, at least, the traders were safe.

Time passed on, and the hostile feelings of the Indians towards the English did not diminish. It necessarily follows, from the extremely loose character of Indian government,—if indeed the name government be applicable at all, —that the separate members of the same tribe have little political connection, and are often united merely by the social tie of totemship. [1] Thus the Ottawas at L'Arbre Croche were quite independent of those at Detroit. They had a chief of their own, who by no means acknowledged the authority of Pontiac, though the high reputation of this great warrior everywhere attached respect and influence to his name. The same relations subsisted between the Ojibwas of Michillimackinac and their more southern tribesmen; and the latter might declare war and make peace without at all involving the former.

The name of the Ottawa chief at L'Arbre Croche has not survived in history or tradition. The chief of the Ojibwas, however, is still remembered by the remnants of his people, and was the same whom Henry calls Minavavana, or, as the Canadians, entitled him, by way of distinction, *Le Grand Sauteur*, [2] or the Great Ojibwa. He lived in the little village of Thunder Bay, though his power was acknowledged by the Indians of the neighboring islands. That his mind was of no common order is sufficiently evinced by his speech to Henry; but he had not the commanding spirit of Pontiac. His influence seems not to have extended beyond his own tribe. He could not, or, at least, he did not, control the erratic forces of an Indian community, and turn them into one broad current of steady and united energy. Hence, in the events about to be described, the natural instability of the Indian character was abundantly displayed.

In the spring of the year 1763, Pontiac, in compassing his grand scheme of hostility, sent, among the rest, to the Indians of Michillimackinac, inviting them to aid him in the war. His messengers, bearing in their hands the war-belt of black and purple wampum, appeared before the assembled warriors, flung at their feet a hatchet painted red and delivered the speech with which they had been charged. The warlike auditory answered with deep ejacula-

---

[1] Tribal or clan relationship in a common ancestry was usually signified by an animal or object, a totem, to which the tribe believed themselves to be peculiarly or even sacredly related.

[2] "The Great Leaper"

tions of applause, and, taking up the blood-red hatchet, pledged themselves to join in the contest. Before the end of May, news reached the Ojibwas that Pontiac had already struck the English at Detroit. This wrought them up to a high pitch of excitement and emulation, and they resolved that peace should last no longer. Their numbers were at this time more than doubled, by several bands of their wandering people, who had gathered at Michillimackinac, from far and near, attracted probably by rumors of impending war. Being, perhaps, jealous of the Ottawas, or willing to gain all the glory and plunder to themselves, they determined to attack the fort, without communicating the design to their neighbors at L'Arbre Croche.

At this time there were about thirty-five men, with their officers, in garrison at Michillimackinac. Warning of the tempest that impended had been clearly given; enough, had it been heeded, to have averted the fatal disaster. Several of the Canadians least hostile to the English had thrown out hints of approaching danger, and one of them had even told Captain Etherington, the commandant, that the Indians had formed a design to destroy, not only his garrison, but all the English on the lakes. With a folly, of which, at this period, there were several parallel instances among the British officers in America, Etherington not only turned a deaf ear to what he heard, but threatened to send prisoner to Detroit the next person who should disturb the fort with such tidings. Henry, the trader, who was at this time in the place, had also seen occasion to distrust the Indians; but on communicating his suspicions to the commandant, the latter treated them with total disregard. Henry accuses himself of sharing this officer's infatuation. That his person was in danger, had been plainly intimated to him, under the following curious circumstances:—

An Ojibwa chief, named Wawatam, had conceived for him one of those strong friendly attachments which often form so pleasing a feature in the Indian character. It was about a year since Henry had first met with this man. One morning, Wawatam had entered his house, and placing before him on the ground a large present of furs and dried meat, delivered a speech to the following effect: Early in life, after the ancient usage of his people, he had withdrawn to fast and pray in solitude, that he might propitiate the Great Spirit, and learn the future career marked out for him. In the course of his dreams and visions on this occa-

sion it was revealed to him that, in after years, he should meet a white man, who should be to him a friend and brother. No sooner had he seen Henry, than the irrepressible conviction rose up within him, that he was the man whom the Great Spirit had indicated, and that the dream was now fulfilled. Henry replied to the speech with suitable acknowledgments of gratitude, made a present in his turn, smoked a pipe with Wawatam, and, as the latter soon after left the fort, speedily forgot his Indian friend and brother altogether. Many months had elapsed since the occurrence of this very characteristic incident when, on the second of June, Henry's door was pushed open without ceremony, and the dark figure of Wawatam glided silently in. He said that he was just returned from his wintering ground. Henry, at length recollecting him, inquired after the success of his hunt; but the Indian, without replying, sat down with a dejected air, and expressed his surprise and regret at finding his brother still in the fort. He said that he was going on the next day to the Sault Ste. Marie, and that he wished Henry to go with him. He then asked if the English had heard no bad news, and said that through the winter he himself had been much disturbed by the singing of evil birds. Seeing that Henry gave little attention to what he said, he at length went away with a sad and mournful face. One the next morning, he came again, together with his squaw, and, offering the trader a present of dried meat, again pressed him to go with him, in the afternoon, to the Sault Ste. Marie. When Henry demanded his reason for such urgency, he asked if his brother did not know that many bad Indians, who had never shown themselves at the fort, were encamped in the woods around it. Tomorrow, he said, they are coming to ask for whisky, and would all get drunk, so that it would be dangerous to remain. Wawatam let fall, in addition, various other hints, which, but for Henry's imperfect knowledge of the Algonquin language, could hardly have failed to draw his attention. As it was, however, his friend's words were spoken in vain; and at length, after long and persevering efforts, he and his squaw took their departure, but not, as Henry declares, before each had let fall some tears. Among the Indian women, the practice of weeping and wailing is universal upon all occasions of sorrowful emotion; and the kind-hearted squaw, as she took down her husband's lodge, and loaded his canoe for departure, did not cease to sob and moan aloud.

On this same afternoon, Henry remembers

that the fort was full of Indians, moving about among the soldiers with a great appearance of friendship. Many of them came to his house, to purchase knives and small hatchets, often asking to see silver bracelets, and other ornaments, with the intention, as afterwards appeared, of learning their places of deposit, in order the more easily to lay hand on them at the moment of pillage. As the afternoon drew to a close, the visitors quietly went away; and many of the unhappy garrison saw for the last time the sun go down behind the waters of Lake Michigan.

CHAPTER XVII

THE MASSACRE

The following morning was warm and sultry. It was the fourth of June, the birthday of King George. The discipline of the garrison was relaxed, and some license allowed to the soldiers. Encamped in the woods, not far off, were a large number of Ojibwas, lately arrived; while several bands of the Sac Indians from the River Wisconsin had also erected their lodges in the vicinity. Early in the morning, many Ojibwas came to the fort, inviting officers and soldiers to come out and see a grand game of ball, which was to be played between their nation and the Sacs. In consequence, the place was soon deserted by half its tenants. An outline of Michillimackinac, as far as tradition has preserved its general features, has already been given; and it is easy to conceive, with sufficient accuracy, the appearance it must have presented on this eventful morning. The houses and barracks were so ranged as to form a square, enclosing an extensive area, upon which their doors all opened, while behind rose the tall palisades, forming a large external square. The picturesque Canadian houses, with their rude porticoes, and projecting roofs of bark, sufficiently indicated the occupations of their inhabitants; for birch canoes were lying near many of them, and fishing nets were stretched to dry in the sun. Women and children were moving about the doors; knots of Canadian voyageurs reclined on the ground, smoking and conversing; soldiers were lounging listlessly at the doors and windows of the barracks, or strolling in a careless undress about the area.

Without the fort, the scene was of a very different character. The gates were wide open, and the soldiers were collected in groups under the shadow of the palisades, watching the Indian ball play. Most of them were without arms, and mingled among them were a great number of Canadians, while a multitude of Indian squaws, wrapped in blankets, were conspicuous in the crowd.

Captain Etherington and Lieutenant Leslie stood near the gate, the former indulging his inveterate English propensity; for, as Henry informs us, he had promised the Ojibwas that he would bet on their side against the Sacs. Indian chiefs and warriors were also among the spectators, intent, apparently, on watching the game, but with thoughts, in fact, far otherwise employed.

The plain in front was covered by the ball players. The game in which they were engaged, called *baggattaway* [1] by the Ojibwas, is still, as it always has been, a favorite with many Indian tribes. At either extremity of the ground, a tall post was planted, marking the stations of the rival parties. The object of each was to defend its own post, and drive the ball to that of its adversary. Hundreds of lithe and agile figures were leaping and bounding upon the plain. Each was nearly naked, his loose black hair flying in the wind, and each bore in his hand a bat of a form peculiar to this game. At one moment the whole were crowded together, a dense throng of combatants, all struggling for the ball; at the next, they were scattered again, and running over the ground like hounds in full cry. Each, in his excitement, yelled and shouted at the height of his voice. Rushing and striking, tripping their adversaries, or hurling them to the ground, they pursued the animating contest amid the laughter and applause of the spectators. Suddenly, from the midst of the multitude, the ball soared into the air, and, descending in a wide curve, fell near the pickets of the fort. This was no chance stroke. It was part of a preconcerted stratagem to insure the surprise and destruction of the garrison. As if in pursuit of the ball, the players turned and came rushing, a maddened and tumultuous throng, towards the gate. In a moment they had reached it. The amazed English had no time to think or act. The shrill cries of the ball players were changed to the ferocious warwhoop. The warriors snatched from the squaws the hatchets, which the latter, with this design, had concealed beneath their blankets. Some of the Indians assailed the spectators without, while others rushed into the fort, and all was carnage and confusion. At the outset, several strong hands had fastened their gripe upon Etherington and Leslie, and led them away from the scene of massacre towards the woods.

[1] lacrosse

Within the area of the fort, the men were slaughtered without mercy. But here the task of description may well be resigned to the simple and manly pen of the trader Henry.

"I did not go myself to see the match which was now to be played without the fort, because, there being a canoe prepared to depart on the following day for Montreal, I employed myself in writing letters to my friends, and even when a fellow-trader, Mr. Tracy, happened to call upon me, saying that another canoe had just arrived from Detroit, and proposing that I should go with him to the beach, to inquire the news, it so happened that I still remained to finish my letters; promising to follow Mr. Tracy in the course of a few minutes. Mr. Tracy had not gone more than twenty paces from my door, when I heard an Indian war-cry, and a noise of general confusion.

"Going instantly to my window, I saw a crowd of Indians within the fort, furiously cutting down and scalping every Englishman they found: in particular, I witnessed the fate of Lieutenant Jamette.

"I had, in the room in which I was, a fowling-piece, loaded with swan shot. This I immediately seized, and held it for a few minutes, waiting to hear the drum beat to arms. In this dreadful interval, I saw several of my countrymen fall, and more than one struggling between the knees of an Indian, who, holding him in this manner, scalped him while yet living.

"At length, disappointed in the hope of seeing resistance made to the enemy, and sensible, of course, that no effort of my own unassisted arm could avail against four hundred Indians, I thought only of seeking shelter amid the slaughter which was raging. I observed many of the Canadian inhabitants of the fort calmly looking on, neither opposing the Indians nor suffering injury; and from this circumstance, I conceived a hope of finding security in their houses.

"Between the yard door of my own house and that of M. Langlade, my next neighbor, there was only a low fence, over which I easily climbed. At my entrance, I found the whole family at the windows, gazing at the scene of blood before them. I addressed myself immediately to M. Langlade, begging that he would put me into some place of safety, until the heat of the affair should be over; an act of charity by which he might, perhaps, preserve me from the general massacre; but while I uttered my petition, M. Langlade, who had looked for a moment at me, turned again to the window, shrugging his shoulders, and intimating that he could do nothing for me—'*Que voudriez-vous que j'en ferais?*'[1]

"This was a moment for despair; but the next a Pani[2] woman, a slave of M. Langlade's, beckoned me to follow her. She brought me to a door, which she opened, desiring me to enter, and telling me that it led to the garret, where I must go and conceal myself. I joyfully obeyed her directions; and she, having followed me up to the garret door, locked it after me, and, with great presence of mind, took away the key.

"This shelter obtained, if shelter I could hope to find it, I was naturally anxious to know what might still be passing without. Through an aperture, which afforded me a view of the area of the fort, I beheld, in shapes the foulest and most terrible, the ferocious triumphs of barbarian conquerors. The dead were scalped and mangled; the dying were writhing and shrieking under the unsatiated knife and tomahawk; and from the bodies of some, ripped open, their butchers were drinking the blood, scooped up in the hollow of joined hands, and quaffed amid shouts of rage and victory. I was shaken not only with horror, but with fear. The sufferings which I witnessed I seemed on the point of experiencing. No long time elapsed before, every one being destroyed who could be found, there was a general cry of 'All is finished.' At the same instant, I heard some of the Indians enter the house where I was.

"The garret was separated from the room below only by a layer of single boards, at once the flooring of the one and the ceiling of the other. I could, therefore, hear everything that passed; and the Indians no sooner came in than they inquired whether or not any Englishmen were in the house. M. Langlade replied that 'he could not say, he did not know of any,' answers in which he did not exceed the truth; for the Pani woman had not only hidden me by stealth, but kept my secret and her own. M. Langlade was, therefore, as I presume, as far from a wish to destroy me as he was careless about saving me, when he added to these answers, that 'they might examine for themselves, and would soon be satisfied as to the object of their question.' Saying this, he brought them to the garret door.

"The state of my mind will be imagined. Arrived at the door, some delay was occasioned by the absence of the key; and a few moments were thus allowed me, in which to look around

[1] "What would you like to have me do about it?"
[2] Pawnee, a tribe of western Indians

for a hiding-place. In one corner of the garret was a heap of those vessels of birch bark used in maple sugar making.

"The door was unlocked and opening, and the Indians ascending the stairs, before I had completely crept into a small opening which presented itself at one end of the heap. An instant after, four Indians entered the room, all armed with tomahawks, and all besmeared with blood, upon every part of their bodies.

"The die appeared to be cast. I could scarcely breathe; but I thought the throbbing of my heart occasioned a noise loud enough to betray me. The Indians walked in every direction about the garret; and one of them approached me so closely, that, at a particular moment, had he put forth his hand, he must have touched me. Still I remained undiscovered; a circumstance to which the dark color of my clothes, and the want of light, in a room which had no window in the corner in which I was, must have contributed. In a word, after taking several turns in the room, during which they told M. Langlade how many they had killed, and how many scalps they had taken, they returned downstairs, and I, with sensations not to be expressed, heard the door, which was the barrier between me and my fate, locked for the second time.

"There was a feather bed on the floor; and on this, exhausted as I was by the agitation of my mind, I threw myself down and fell asleep. In this state I remained till the dusk of the evening, when I was awakened by a second opening of the door. The person that now entered was M. Langlade's wife, who was much surprised at finding me, but advised me not to be uneasy, observing that the Indians had killed most of the English, but that she hoped that I might myself escape. A shower of rain having begun to fall, she had come to stop a hole in the roof. On her going away, I begged her to send me a little water to drink, which she did.

"As night was now advancing, I continued to lie on the bed, ruminating on my condition, but unable to discover a resource from which I could hope for life. A flight to Detroit had no probable chance of success. The distance from Michillimackinac was four hundred miles; I was without provisions and the whole length of the road lay through Indian countries, countries of an enemy in arms, where the first man whom I should meet would kill me. To stay where I was, threatened nearly the same issue. As before, fatigue of mind, and not tranquillity,

suspended my cares, and procured me farther sleep.

"The respite which sleep afforded me during the night was put an end to by the return of morning. I was again on the rack of apprehension. At sunrise, I heard the family stirring; and, presently after, Indian voices, informing M. Langlade that they had not found my hapless self among the dead, and they supposed be to be somewhere concealed. M. Langlade appeared, from what followed, to be, by this time, acquainted with the place of my retreat; of which, no doubt, he had been informed by his wife. The poor woman, as soon as the Indians mentioned me, declared to her husband, in the French tongue, that he should no longer keep me in his house, but deliver me up to my pursuers; giving as a reason for this measure, that should the Indians discover his instrumentality in my concealment, they might revenge it on her children, and that it was better that I should die than they. M. Langlade resisted, at first, this sentence of his wife, but soon suffered her to prevail, informing the Indians that he had been told I was in his house; that I had come there without his knowledge, and that he would put me into their hands. This was no sooner expressed than he began to ascend the stairs, the Indians following upon his heels.

"I now resigned myself to the fate with which I was menaced; and regarding every effort at concealment as vain, I arose from the bed, and presented myself full in view to the Indians, who were entering the room. They were all in a state of intoxication, and entirely naked, except about the middle. One of them, named Wenniway, whom I had previously known, and who was upwards of six feet in height, had his entire face and body covered with charcoal and grease, only that a white spot, of two inches in diameter, encircled either eye. This man, walking up to me, seized me, with one hand, by the collar of the coat, while in the other he held a large carving-knife, as if to plunge it into my breast; his eyes, meanwhile, were fixed steadfastly on mine. At length, after some seconds of the most anxious suspense, he dropped his arm, saying, 'I won't kill you!' To this he added, that he had been frequently engaged in wars against the English, and had brought away many scalps; that, on a certain occasion, he had lost a brother, whose name was Musinignon, and that I should be called after him.

"A reprieve, upon any terms, placed me

among the living, and gave me back the sustaining voice of hope; but Wenniway ordered me downstairs, and there informing me that I was to be taken to his cabin, where, and indeed everywhere else, the Indians were all mad with liquor, death again was threatened, and not as possible only, but as certain. I mentioned my fears on this subject to M. Langlade, begging him to represent the danger to my master. M. Langlade, in this instance, did not withhold his compassion, and Wenniway immediately consented that I should remain where I was, until he found another opportunity to take me away."

Scarcely, however, had he been gone an hour, when an Indian came to the house, and directed Henry to follow him to the Ojibwa camp. Henry knew this man, who was largely in his debt, and some time before, on the trader's asking him for payment the Indian had declared in a significant tone, that he would pay him soon. There seemed at present good ground to suspect his intention; but, having no choice, Henry was obliged to follow him. The Indian led the way out of the gate; but, instead of going towards the camp, he moved with a quick step in the direction of the bushes and sandhills behind the fort. At this, Henry's suspicions were confirmed. He refused to proceed farther, and plainly told his conductor that he believed he meant to kill him. The Indian coolly replied that he was quite right in thinking so, and at the same time, seizing the prisoner by the arm, raised his knife to strike him in the breast. Henry parried the blow, flung the Indian from him, and ran for his life. He gained the gate of the fort, his enemy close at his heels, and, seeing Wenniway standing in the center of the area, called upon him for protection. The chief ordered the Indian to desist; but the latter, who was foaming at the mouth with rage, still continued to pursue Henry, vainly striking at him with his knife. Seeing the door of Langlade's house wide open, the trader darted in, and at length found himself in safety. He retired once more to his garret, and lay down, feeling, as he declares, a sort of conviction that no Indian had power to harm him.

This confidence was somewhat shaken when, early in the night, he was startled from sleep by the opening of the door. A light gleamed in upon him, and he was summoned to descend. He did so, when, to his surprise and joy, he found, in the room below, Captain Etherington, Lieutenant Leslie, and Mr. Bostwick, a trader, together with Father Jonois, the Jesuit priest from L'Arbre Croche. The Indians were bent on enjoying that night a grand debauch upon the liquor they had seized; and the chiefs, well knowing the extreme danger to which the prisoners would be exposed during these revels, had conveyed them all into the fort, and placed them in charge of the Canadians.

Including officers, soldiers, and traders, they amounted to about twenty men, this handful being all that had escaped the massacre.

When Henry entered the room, he found his three companions in misfortune engaged in earnest debate. These men had supped full of horrors; yet they were almost on the point of risking a renewal of the bloodshed from which they had just escaped. The temptation was a strong one. The fort was this evening actually in the hands of the white men. The Indians, with their ordinary recklessness and improvidence, had neglected even to place a guard within the palisades. They were now, one and all, in their camp, mad with liquor, and the fort was occupied by twenty Englishmen, and about three hundred Canadians, principally voyageurs. To close the gates, and set the Indians at defiance, seemed no very difficult matter. It might have been attempted, but for the dissuasions of the Jesuit, who had acted throughout the part of a true friend of humanity, and who now strongly represented the probability that the Canadians would prove treacherous, and the certainty that a failure would involve destruction to every Englishman in the place. The idea was therefore abandoned, and Captain Etherington, with his companions, that night shared Henry's garret, where they passed the time in condoling with each other on their common misfortune.

A party of Indians came to the house in the morning, and ordered Henry to follow them out. The weather had changed, and a cold storm had set in. In the dreary and forlorn area of the fort were a few of the Indian conquerors, though the main body were still in their camp, not yet recovered from the effects of their last night's carouse. Henry's conductors led him to a house, where, in a room almost dark, he saw two traders and a soldier imprisoned. They were released, and directed to follow the party. The whole then proceeded together to the lake shore, where they were to embark for the Isles du Castor. [1] A chilling wind blew strongly from the northeast, and the lake was covered with mists, and tossing angrily. Henry stood shivering on the beach, with no other upper garment than a shirt, drenched with the cold rain. He asked Langlade, who was near him, for a blanket, which

[1] Beaver Islands in Lake Michigan

the latter, with cold-blooded inhumanity, refused to furnish unless security was given for payment. Another Canadian proved more merciful, and Henry received a covering from the weather. With his three companions, guarded by seven Indians, he embarked in the canoe, the soldier being tied by his neck to one of the cross-bars of the vessel. The thick mists and the tempestuous weather compelled them to keep along the shore, close beneath the wet dripping forests. In this manner they had proceeded about eighteen miles, and were approaching L'Arbre Croche, when an Ottawa Indian came out of the woods, and called to them from the beach, inquiring the news, and asking who were their prisoners. Some conversation followed, in the course of which the canoe approached the shore, where the water was quite shallow. All at once, a loud yell was heard, and a hundred Ottawas, rising from among the trees and bushes, rushed into the water, and seized upon the canoe and prisoners. The astonished Ojibwas remonstrated in vain. The four Englishmen were taken from them, and led in safety to the shore. Good will to the prisoners, however, had by no means prompted the Ottawas to this very unexpected proceeding. They were jealous and angry that the Ojibwas should have taken the fort without giving them an opportunity to share in the plunder; and they now chose this summary mode of asserting their rights.

The chiefs, however, shook Henry and his companions by the hand, professing great good will, assuring them, at the same time, that the Ojibwas were carrying them to the Isles du Castor merely to kill and eat them. The four prisoners, the sport of so many changing fortunes, soon found themselves embarked in an Ottawa canoe, and on their way back to Michillimackinac. They were not alone. A flotilla of canoes accompanied them, bearing a great number of Ottawa warriors; and before the day was over, the whole had arrived at the fort. At this time, the principal Ojibwa encampment was near the woods, in full sight of the landing-place. Its occupants, astonished at this singular movement on the part of their rivals, stood looking on in silent amazement, while the Ottawa warriors, well armed, filed into the fort, and took possession of it.

This conduct is not difficult to explain, when we take into consideration the peculiarities of the Indian character. Pride and jealousy are always strong and active elements in it. The Ottawas deemed themselves grossly insulted because the Ojibwas had undertaken an enterprise of such importance without consulting

them, or asking their assistance. It may be added, that the Indians of L'Arbre Croche were somewhat less hostile to the English than the neighboring tribes; for the great influence of the priest Jonois seems always to have been exerted on the side of peace and friendship.

The English prisoners looked upon the new comers as champions and protectors, and conceived hopes from their interference not destined to be fully realized. On the morning after their arrival, the Ojibwa chiefs invited the principal men of the Ottawas to hold a council with them in a building within the fort. They placed upon the floor a valuable present of goods, which were part of the plunder they had taken; and their great war-chief Minavavana, who had conducted the attack, rose and addressed the Ottawas.

Their conduct, he said, had greatly surprised him. They had betrayed the common cause, and opposed the will of the Great Spirit, who had decreed that every Englishman must die. Excepting them, all the Indians had raised the hatchet. Pontiac had taken Detroit, and every other fort had also been destroyed. The English were meeting with destruction throughout the whole world, and the King of France was awakened from his sleep. He exhorted them, in conclusion, no longer to espouse the cause of the English, but, like their brethren, to lift the hatchet against them.

When Minavavana had concluded his speech, the council adjourned until the next day; a custom common among Indians, in order that the auditors may have time to ponder with due deliberation upon what they have heard. At the next meeting, the Ottawas expressed a readiness to concur with the views of the Ojibwas. Thus the difference between the two tribes was at length amicably adjusted. The Ottawas returned to the Ojibwas some of the prisoners whom they had taken from them, still, however, retaining the officers and several of the soldiers. These they soon after carried to L'Arbre Croche, where they were treated with kindness, probably owing to the influence of Father Jonois. The priest went down to Detroit with a letter from Captain Etherington, acquainting Major Gladwyn with the loss of Michillimackinac and entreating that a force might be sent immediately to his aid. [1] The letter, as we have seen, was safely delivered; but Gladwyn was, of course, unable to render the required assistance.

[1] Major Gladwyn in command of Fort Detroit, at this time—June, 1763—was resisting with about one hundred men, a siege by over eight hundred Indians. Detroit was the only western fort that had not fallen a prey to Indian massacres.

Though the Ottawas and Ojibwas had come to terms, they still looked on each other with distrust, and it is said that the former never forgot the slight that had been put upon them. The Ojibwas took the prisoners who had been returned to them from the fort, and carried them to one of their small villages, which stood near the shore, at no great distance to the southeast. Among the other lodges was a large one, of the kind often seen in Indian villages, erected for use on public occasions, such as dances, feasts, or councils. It was now to serve as a prison. The soldiers were bound together, two and two, and farther secured by long ropes tied round their necks, and fastened to the pole which supported the lodge in the center. Henry and the other traders escaped this rigorous treatment. The spacious lodge was soon filled with Indians, who came to look at their captives, and gratify themselves by deriding and jeering at them. At the head of the lodge sat the great war-chief Minavavana, side by side with Henry's master, Wenniway. Things had remained for some time in this position, when Henry observed an Indian stooping to enter at the low aperture which served for a door, and, to his great joy, recognized his friend and brother, Wawatam, whom he had last seen on the day before the massacre. Wawatam said nothing; but, as he passed the trader, he shook him by the hand, in token of encouragement, and, proceeding to the head of the lodge, sat down with Wenniway and the war-chief. After he had smoked with them for a while in silence, he rose and went out again. Very soon he came back, followed by his squaw, who brought in her hands a valuable present, which she laid at the feet of the two chiefs. Wawatam then addressed them in the following speech: —

"Friends and relations, what is it that I shall say? You know what I feel. You all have friends, and brothers, and children, whom as yourselves you love; and you,—what would you experience, did you, like me, behold your dearest friend—your brother—in the condition of a slave; a slave, exposed every moment to insult, and to menaces of death? This case, as you all know, is mine. See there [pointing to Henry], my friend and brother among slaves,—himself a slave!

"You all well know that, long before the war began, I adopted him as my brother. From that moment, he became one of my family, so that no change of circumstances could break the cord which fastened us together.

"He is my brother; and because I am your relation, he is therefore your relation too; and how, being your relation, can he be your slave?

"On the day on which the war began, you were fearful lest, on this very account, I should reveal your secret. You requested, therefore, that I would leave the fort, and even cross the lake. I did so; but I did it with reluctance. I did it with reluctance, notwithstanding that you, Minavavana, who had the command in this enterprise, gave me your promise that you would protect my friend, delivering him from all danger, and giving him safely to me.

"The performance of this promise I now claim. I come not with empty hands to ask it. You, Minavavana, best know whether or not, as it respects yourself, you have kept your word; but I bring these goods to buy off every claim which any man among you all may have on my brother as his prisoner."

To this speech the war-chief returned a favorable answer. Wawatam's request was acceded to, the present was accepted, and the prisoner released. Henry soon found himself in the lodge of his friend, where furs were spread for him to lie upon, food and drink brought for his refreshment, and everything done to promote his comfort that Indian hospitality could suggest. As he lay in the lodge, on the day after his release, he heard a loud noise from within the prison-house, which stood close at hand, and, looking through a crevice in the bark, he saw the dead bodies of seven soldiers dragged out. It appeared that a noted chief had just arrived from his wintering ground. Having come too late to take part in the grand achievement of his countrymen, he was anxious to manifest to all present his entire approval of what had been done, and with this design he had entered the lodge and despatched seven of the prisoners with his knife.

The Indians are not habitual cannibals. After a victory, however, it often happens that the bodies of their enemies are consumed at a formal war-feast—a superstitious rite, adapted, as they think, to increase their courage and hardihood. Such a feast took place on the present occasion, and most of the chiefs partook of it, though some of them, at least, did so with repugnance.

About a week had now elapsed since the massacre, and a revulsion of feeling began to take place among the Indians. Up to this time all had been triumph and exultation; but they now began to fear the consequences of their conduct. Indefinite and absurd rumors of an approaching attack from the English were afloat at the camp, and, in their growing uneasiness, they thought it expedient to shift their position to some point more capable of defense. Three hundred and fifty warriors, with their families and household effects, embarked in canoes for the Island of Michillimackinac, seven or eight miles distant. Wawatam, with his friend Henry, was of the number. Strong gusts of wind came from the north, and when the fleet of canoes were half way to the island, it blew a gale, the waves pitching and tossing with such violence, that the frail and heavy-laden vessels were much endangered. Many voices were raised in prayer to the Great Spirit, and a dog was thrown into the lake, as a sacrifice to appease the angry manitou [1] of the waters. The canoes weathered the storm, and soon drew near the island. Two squaws, in the same canoe with Henry, raised their voices in mournful wailing and lamentation. Late events had made him sensible to every impression of horror, and these dismal cries seemed ominous of some new disaster, until he learned that they were called forth by the recollection of dead relatives, whose graves were visible upon a neighboring point of the shore.

The Island of Michillimackinac or Mackinaw, owing to its situation, its beauty, and the fish which the surrounding waters supplied, had long been a favorite resort of Indians. It is about three miles wide. So clear are the waters of Lake Huron, which wash its shores, that one may count the pebbles at an incredible depth. The island is fenced round by white limestone cliffs, beautifully contrasting with the green foliage that half covers them, and in the center the land rises in woody heights. The rock which forms its foundation assumes fantastic shapes—natural bridges, caverns, or sharp pinnacles, which, at this day, are pointed out as the curiosities of the region. In many of the caves have been found quantities of human bones, as if, at some period, the island had served as a grand depository for the dead; yet of these remains the present race of Indians can give no account. Legends and superstitions attached a mysterious celebrity to the place, and here it was said the fairies of Indian tradition might often be seen dancing upon the white rocks, or basking in the moonlight.

The Indians landed at the margin of a little bay. Unlading their canoes, and lifting them

[1] spirit (Indian)

high and dry upon the beach, they began to erect their lodges, and before night had completed their work. Messengers arrived on the next day from Pontiac, informing them that he was besieging Detroit, and urging them to come to his aid. But their warlike ardor had well-nigh died out. A senseless alarm prevailed among them, and they now thought more of securing their own safety than of injuring the enemy. A vigilant watch was kept up all day, and the unusual precaution taken of placing guards at night. Their fears, however, did not prevent them from seizing two English trading canoes, which had come from Montreal by way of the Ottawa. Among the booty found in them was a quantity of whisky, and a general debauch was the immediate result. As night closed in, the dolorous chanting of drunken songs was heard from within the lodges, the prelude of a scene of riot; and Wawatam, knowing that his friend Henry's life would be in danger, privately led him out of the camp to a cavern in the hills, towards the interior of the island. Here the trader spent the night, in a solitude made doubly dreary by a sense of his forlorn and perilous situation. On waking in the morning, he found that he had been lying on human bones, which covered the floor of the cave. The place had anciently served as a charnel-house. Here he spent another solitary night, before his friend came to apprise him that he might return with safety to the camp.

Famine soon began to be felt among the Indians, who were sometimes without food for days together. No complaints were heard; but with faces blackened, in sign of sorrow, they patiently endured the privation with that resignation, under inevitable suffering, which distinguishes the whole Indian race. They were at length compelled to cross over to the north shore of Lake Huron, where fish were more abundant, and here they remained until the end of summer, when they gradually dispersed, each family repairing to its winter hunting-grounds. Henry, painted and attired like an Indian, followed his friend Wawatam, and spent a lonely winter among the frozen forests, hunting the bear and moose for subsistence.

The posts of Green Bay and the Sault Ste. Marie did not share the fate of Michillimackinac. During the preceding winter, Ste. Marie had been partially destroyed by an accidental fire, and was therefore abandoned, the garrison withdrawing to Michillimackinac, where many of them perished in the massacre. The fort at

Green Bay first received an English garrison in the year 1761, at the same time with the other posts of this region. The force consisted of seventeen men, commanded by Lieutenant Gorell. Though so few in number, their duties were of a very important character. In the neighborhood of Green Bay were numerous and powerful Indian tribes. The Menomonies lived at the mouth of Fox River, close to the fort. The Winnebagoes had several villages on the lake which bears their name, and the Sacs and Foxes were established on the River Wisconsin, in a large village composed of houses neatly built of logs and bark, and surrounded by fields of corn and vegetables. West of the Mississippi was the powerful nation of the Dahcotah, whose strength was loosely estimated at thirty thousand fighting men, and who, in the excess of their haughtiness, styled the surrounding tribes their dogs and slaves. The commandant of Green Bay was the representative of the British government, in communication with all these tribes. It devolved upon him to secure their friendship, and keep them at peace; and he was also intrusted, in a great measure, with the power of regulating the fur trade among them. In the course of each season, parties of Indians, from every quarter, would come to the fort, each expecting to be received with speeches and presents.

Gorell seems to have acquitted himself with great judgment and prudence. On first arriving at the fort, he had found its defenses decayed and ruinous, the Canadian inhabitants unfriendly, and many of the Indians disposed to hostility. His good conduct contributed to allay their irritation, and he was particularly successful in conciliating his immediate neighbors, the Menomonies. They had taken an active part in the late war between France and England, and their spirits were humbled by the losses they had sustained, as well as by recent ravages of the smallpox. Gorell summoned them to a council, and delivered a speech, in which he avoided wounding their pride, but at the same time assumed a tone of firmness and decision, such as can alone command an Indian's respect. He told them that the King of England had heard of their ill conduct, but that he was ready to forget all that had passed. If, however, they should again give him cause of complaint, he would send an army, numerous as the trees of the forest, and utterly destroy them. Flattering expressions of confidence and esteem succeeded, and the whole was enforced by the distribution of a few presents. The Menomonies replied by assurances of friendship, more sincerely made and faithfully kept than could have been expected. As Indians of the other tribes came from time to time to the fort, they met with a similar reception, and, in his whole intercourse with them, the constant aim of the commandant was to gain their good will. The result was most happy for himself and his garrison.

On the fifteenth of June, 1763, an Ottawa Indian brought to Gorell the following letter from Captain Etherington:—

"Michillimackinac, June 11, 1763.
"Dear Sir:
"This place was taken by surprise, on the fourth instant, by the Chippeways, [Ojibwas,] at which time Lieutenant Jamet and twenty [fifteen] more were killed, and all the rest taken prisoners; but our good friends, the Ottawas, have taken Lieutenant Lesley, me, and eleven men, out of their hands, and have promised to reinstate us again. You'll therefore, on the receipt of this, which I send by a canoe of Ottawas, set out with all your garrison, and what English traders you have with you, and come with the Indian who gives you this, who will conduct you safe to me. You must be sure to follow the instruction you receive from the bearer of this, as you are by no means to come to this post before you see me at the village, twenty miles from this. . . . I must once more beg you'll lose no time in coming to join me; at the same time, be very careful, and always be on your guard. I long much to see you, and am, dear sir,
"Your most humble serv't.
"Geo. Etherington.
"J. Gorell,
"Royal Americans."

On receiving this letter, Gorell summoned the Menomonies to a council, told them what the Ojibwas had done, and said that he and his soldiers were going to Michillimackinac to restore order, adding, that during his absence he commended the fort to their care. Great numbers of the Winnebagoes and of the Sacs and Foxes afterwards arrived, and Gorell addressed them in nearly the same words. Presents were given them, and it soon appeared that the greater part were well disposed towards the English, though a few were inclined to prevent their departure, and even to threaten hostility. At this juncture, a fortunate incident occurred. A Dahcotah chief arrived with a message from his people to the following import: They had heard, he said, of the bad conduct of the Ojibwas. They hoped that the tribes of Green Bay would not follow their example, but, on the contrary, would protect the English garrison. Unless they did so, the Dahcotah would fall upon them, and take ample revenge. This auspicious interference must, no doubt, be ascribed to the hatred with which the Dahcotah had long regarded the Ojibwas. That the latter should espouse one side of the quarrel, was abundant reason to the Dahcotah for adopting the other.

Some of the Green Bay Indians were also at enmity with the Ojibwas, and all opposition to the departure of the English was now at an end. Indeed, some of the more friendly offered to escort the garrison on its way; and on the twenty-first of June, Gorell's party embarked in several bateaux, [1] accompanied by ninety warriors in canoes. Approaching Isle du Castor, near the mouth of Green Bay, an alarm was given that the Ojibwas were lying there in ambush; on which the Menomonies raised the war-song, stripped themselves, and prepared to do battle in behalf of the English. The alarm, however, proved false; and, having crossed Lake Michigan in safety, the party arrived at the village of L'Arbre Croche on the thirtieth. The Ottawas came down to the beach to salute them with a discharge of guns, and, on landing, they were presented with the pipe of peace. Captain Etherington and Lieutenant Leslie, with eleven men, were in the village, detained as prisoners, though treated with kindness. It was thought that the Ottawas intended to disarm the party of Gorell also; but the latter gave out that he would resist such an attempt, and his soldiers were permitted to retain their weapons.

Several succeeding days were occupied by the Indians in holding councils. Those from Green Bay requested the Ottawas to set their prisoners at liberty, and the latter, at length, assented. A difficulty still remained, as the Ojibwas had declared that they would prevent the English from passing down to Montreal. Their chiefs were therefore summoned; and being at this time, as we have seen, in a state of much alarm, they at length reluctantly yielded the point. On the eighteenth of July, the English, escorted by a fleet of Indian canoes, left L'Arbre Croche, and reaching, without interruption, the portage of the River Ottawa, descended to Montreal, where they all arrived in safety, on the thirteenth day of August. Except the garrison of Detroit, not a British soldier now remained in the region of the lakes.

1848-1850　　　　　　　　　　　　　1851

[1] boats (Fr.)

JOHN CALDWELL CALHOUN
1782-1850

Born in Abbeville District, South Carolina, Calhoun was brought up in all the customs and traditions of Southern society. He was graduated from Yale in 1804, studied and practiced law and soon entered politics. He was in Congress from South Carolina, 1811-1817, secretary of war, 1817-1825, vice-president of the United States, 1825-1832. He served in the Senate from 1832 to 1843, was secretary of state, 1844-1845, and from 1845 until his death was the chief spokesman for the South before the Civil War. His *Works,* consisting of state papers and orations, were first published in 1853.

Calhoun's theories of government and of our constitution rest upon his belief that sovereignty cannot be divided; that the nation is the servant of communities and not their coercer; and that minorities have rights that should not be overthrown by majorities. These theories he explained and defended with great skill both in writing and in his public speeches. These speeches appeal less to the emotions than Webster's, and less to popular interest; but to the student of government they present considerations that cannot be overlooked.

W. E. Dodd, "John C. Calhoun," in *Statesmen of the Old South,* 1911; W. M. Meigs, *The Life of J. C. Calhoun,* 2 vols. 1917; H. E. von Holst, (AS).

SPEECH ON THE FORCE BILL [2]
FEBRUARY 15TH AND 16TH, 1833

. . . .

Having made these remarks, the great question is now presented, Has Congress the right to pass this bill? which I will next proceed to consider. The decision of this question involves an inquiry into the provisions of the bill. What are they? It puts at the disposal of the President the army and navy, and the entire militia of the country; it enables him, at his pleasure, to subject every man in the

[2] In this speech, Calhoun was defending the action of his state in resisting the tariff act of Congress of July 14th, 1832, imposing, for revenue and protection, duties upon various articles of imported merchandise. As agriculture was the chief resource of the South and manufacture that of the North, tariff for protection would especially benefit the North. Opposition in South Carolina to this act brought before Congress what was called the Force Bill, authorizing the President to use military force if necessary to enforce the tariff act. It was upon this bill that Calhoun was speaking. He had discussed at some length the tariff laws of 1816 and 1828, had said that South Carolina was loyal to the Union, that it did not deny the right of the Federal Government to lay duties on imports for revenue, but did deny its right to lay them for the protection of manufactures: that the public debt had been paid; and that this new impost duty would cause a large and dangerous surplus in the treasury. He then continued as above.

United States, not exempt from militia duty, to martial law; to call him from his ordinary occupation to the field, and under the penalty of fine and imprisonment, inflicted by a court martial, to imbrue his hand in his brother's blood. There is no limitation on the power of the sword;—and that over the purse is equally without restraint; for among the extraordinary features of the bill, it contains no appropriation, which, under existing circumstances, is tantamount to an unlimited appropriation. The President may, under its authority, incur any expenditure, and pledge the national faith to meet it. He may create a new national debt, at the very moment of the termination of the former—a debt of millions, to be paid out of the proceeds of the labor of that section of the country whose dearest constitutional rights this bill prostrates! Thus exhibiting the extraordinary spectacle, that the very section of the country which is urging this measure, and carrying the sword of devastation against us, is, at the same time, incurring a new debt, to be paid by those whose rights are violated; while those who violate them are to receive the benefits, in the shape of bounties and expenditures.

And for what purpose is the unlimited control of the purse and of the sword thus placed at the disposition of the Executive? To make war against one of the free and sovereign members of this confederation, which the bill proposes to deal with, not as a State, but as a collection of banditti or outlaws. Thus exhibiting the impious spectacle of this Government, the creature of the States, making war against the power to which it owes its existence.

The bill violates the Constitution, plainly and palpably, [1] in many of its provisions, by authorizing the President at his pleasure, to place the different ports of this Union on an unequal footing, [2] contrary to that provision of the Constitution which declares that no preference shall be given to one port over another. It also violates the Constitution by authorizing him, at his discretion, to impose cash duties on one port, while credit is allowed in others; by enabling the President to regulate commerce, a power vested in Congress alone;

and by drawing within the jurisdiction of the United States courts, powers never intended to be conferred on them. As great as these objections are, they become insignificant in the provisions of a bill which, by a single blow—by treating the States as a mere lawless mass of individuals—prostrates all the barriers of the Constitution. I will pass over the minor considerations, and proceed directly to the great point. This bill proceeds on the ground that the entire sovereignty of this country belongs to the American people, as forming one great community, and regards the States as mere fractions or counties, and not as integral parts of the Union; having no more right to resist the encroachments of the Government than a county has to resist the authority of a State; and treating such resistance as the lawless acts of so many individuals, without possessing sovereignty or political rights. It has been said that the bill declares war against South Carolina. No. It decrees a massacre of her citizens! War has something ennobling about it, and, with all its horrors, brings into action the highest qualities, intellectual and moral. It was, perhaps, in the order of Providence that it should be permitted for that very purpose. But this bill declares no war, except, indeed, it be that which savages wage—a war, not against the community, but the citizens of whom that community is composed. But I regard it as worse than savage warfare—as an attempt to take away life under the color of law, without the trial by jury, or any other safeguard which the Constitution has thrown around the life of the citizen! It authorizes the President, or even his deputies, when they may suppose the law to be violated, without the intervention of a court or jury, to kill without mercy or discrimination!

It has been said by the Senator from Tennessee [Mr. Grundy] to be a measure of peace! Yes, such peace as the wolf gives to the lamb—the kite to the dove! Such peace as Russia gives to Poland, [3] or death to its victim! A peace, by extinguishing the political existence of the State, by awing her into an abandonment of the exercise of every power which constitutes her a sovereign community. It is to South Carolina a question of self-preservation; and I proclaim it, that, should this bill pass, and an attempt be made to enforce it, it will be resisted, at every hazard—even that of

---

[1] Those interested in the arguments on the other side may read Webster's speech in reply, which follows this. It should be remembered that the doctrines of nullification and secession were not uncommon. New England had thought of the possibility of seceding at the time of the war with Mexico. Cf. Lowell, *Biglow Papers*, First Series, I, last stanza.

[2] The bill authorized the President, in case of unlawful obstruction, to move a customhouse to a secure port.

[3] in 1772, 1793, 1795, and again in 1814, Prussia, Austria, and Russia partitioned Poland among themselves. A Polish revolution in 1830-31 was put down by a large Russian army, and in 1832 Poland was declared a Russian province.

death itself. Death is not the greatest calamity: there are others still more terrible to the free and brave, and among them may be placed the loss of liberty and honor. There are thousands of her brave sons who, if need be, are prepared cheerfully to lay down their lives in defense of the State, and the great principles of constitutional liberty for which she is contending. God forbid that this should become necessary! It never can be, unless this Government is resolved to bring the question to extremity, when her gallant sons will stand prepared to perform the last duty—to die nobly.

I go on the ground that this Constitution was made by the States; that it is a federal union of the States, in which the several States still retain their sovereignty. If these views be correct, I have not characterized the bill too strongly; and the question is, whether they be or be not. I will not enter into the discussion of this question now. I will rest it, for the present, on what I have said on the introduction of the resolutions now on the table, [1] under a hope that another opportunity will be afforded for more ample discussion. I will, for the present, confine my remarks to the objections which have been raised to the views which I presented when I introduced them. The authority of Luther Martin [2] has been adduced by the Senator from Delaware, to prove that the citizens of a state, acting under the authority of a state, are liable to be punished as traitors by this government. Eminent as Mr. Martin was as a lawyer, and high as his authority may be considered on a legal point, I cannot accept it in determining the point at issue. The attitude which he occupied, if taken into view, would lessen, if not destroy, the weight of his authority. He had been violently opposed in convention to the Constitution, and the very letter from which the Senator has quoted was intended to dissuade Maryland from its adoption. With this view, it was to be expected that every consideration calculated to effect that object should be urged; that real objections should be exaggerated; and that those having no foundation, except mere plausible deductions, should be presented. It is to this spirit that I attribute the opinion of Mr. Martin in reference to the point under consider-

ation. But if his authority be good on one point, it must be admitted to be equally so on another. If his opinion be sufficient to prove that a citizen of a State may be punished as a traitor when acting under allegiance to the State, it is also sufficient to show that no authority was intended to be given in the Constitution for the protection of manufactures by the general Government, and that the provisions in the Constitution permitting a State to lay an impost duty, [3] with the consent of Congress, was intended to reserve the right of protection to the States themselves, and that each State should protect its own industry. Assuming his opinion to be of equal authority on both points, how embarrassing would be the attitude in which it would place the Senator from Delaware, and those with whom he is acting—that of using the sword and bayonet to enforce the execution of an unconstitutional act of Congress. I must express my surprise that the slightest authority in favor of *power* should be received as the most conclusive evidence, while that which is, at least, equally strong in favor of right and *liberty,* is wholly overlooked or rejected.

Notwithstanding all that has been said, I may say that neither the Senator from Delaware [Mr. Clayton], nor any other who has spoken on the same side, has directly and fairly met the great questions at issue: Is this a federal union? a union of States, as distinct from that of individuals? Is the sovereignty in the several States, or in the American people in the aggregate? The very language which we are compelled to use when speaking of our political institutions, affords proof conclusive as to its real character. The terms union, federal, united, all imply a combination of sovereignties, a confederation of States. They are never applied to an association of individuals. Who ever heard of the United State of New York, of Massachusetts, or of Virginia? Who ever heard the term federal or union applied to the aggregation of individuals into one community? Nor is the other point less clear—that the sovereignty is in the several States, and that our system is a union of twenty-four sovereign powers, under a constitutional compact, and not of a divided sovereignty between the States severally and the United States. In spite of all that has been said, I maintain that sovereignty is in its nature indivisible. It is

[1] Calhoun had submitted, on Jan. 22, 1833, a series of resolutions against the Force Bill, and he had, in the first part of his speech here quoted, and in other speeches, discussed the relation of the Federal Government to the states.

[2] a member of the Constitutional Convention of 1787 from Maryland, who had strongly opposed the centralization of power in the Federal Government and had even refused to sign the Constitution

[3] "No State shall, without consent of the Congress, lay any imposts or duties on imports or exports except what may be absolutely necessary for executing its inspection laws." Art. 1, Section 10 of the Constitution.

the supreme power in a State, and we might just as well speak of half a square, or half a triangle, as of half a sovereignty. It is a gross error to confound the *exercise* of sovereign powers with *sovereignty* itself, or the *delegation* of such powers with the *surrender* of them. A sovereign may delegate his powers to be exercised by as many agents as he may think proper, under such conditions and with such limitations as he may impose; but to surrender any portion of his sovereignty to another is to annihilate the whole. The Senator from Delaware [Mr. Clayton] calls this metaphysical reasoning, which he says he cannot comprehend. If by metaphysics he means that scholastic refinement which makes distinctions without difference, no one can hold it in more utter contempt that I do; but if, on the contrary, he means the power of analysis and combination—that power which reduces the most complex idea into its elements, which traces causes to their first principle, and, by the power of generalization and combination, unites the whole in one harmonious system—then, so far from deserving contempt, it is the highest attribute of the human mind. It is the power which raises man above the brute—which distinguishes his faculties from mere sagacity, which he holds in common with inferior animals. It is this power which has raised the astronomer from being a mere gazer at the stars to the high intellectual eminence of a Newton or a Laplace, [1] and astronomy itself from a mere observation of insulated facts into that noble science which displays to our admiration the system of the universe. And shall this high power of the mind, which has effected such wonders when directed to the laws which control the material world, be for ever prohibited, under a senseless cry of metaphysics, from being applied to the high purpose of political science and legislation? I hold them to be subject to laws as fixed as matter itself, and to be as fit a subject for the application of the highest intellectual power. Denunciation may, indeed, fall upon the philosophical inquirer into these first principles, as it did upon Galileo and Bacon [2] when they first unfolded the great discoveries which have immortalized their names; but the time will come when truth will prevail in spite of prejudice and denunciation, and when politics and

legislation will be considered as much a science as astronomy and chemistry.

In connection with this part of the subject, I understood the Senator from Virginia [Mr. Rives] to say that sovereignty was divided, and that a portion remained with the States severally, and that the residue was vested in the Union. By Union, I suppose the Senator meant the United States. If such be his meaning—if he intended to affirm that the sovereignty was in the twenty-four States, in whatever light he may view them, our opinions will not disagree; but according to my conception, the whole sovereignty is in the several States, while the exercise of sovereign powers is divided—a part being exercised under compact, through this general Government, and the residue through the separate State Governments. But if the Senator from Virginia [Mr. Rives] means to assert that the twenty-four States form but one community, with a single sovereign power as to the objects of the Union, it will be but the revival of the old question, of whether the Union is a union between States, or distinct communities, or a mere aggregate of the American people, as a mass of individuals; and in this light his opinions would lead directly to consolidation.

But to return to the bill. It is said that the bill ought to pass, because the law must be enforced. The law must be enforced! The imperial edict must be executed! It is under such sophistry, couched in general terms, without looking to the limitations which must ever exist in the practical exercise of power, that the most cruel and despotic acts ever have been covered. It was such sophistry as this that cast Daniel into the lion's den, and the three Innocents into the fiery furnace. [3] Under the same sophistry the bloody edicts of Nero and Caligula [4] were executed. The law must be enforced. Yes, the act imposing the "tea-tax must be executed." This was the very argument which impelled Lord North and his administration to that mad career which forever separated us from the British crown. Under a similar sophistry, "that religion must be protected," how many massacres have been perpetrated? and how many martyrs have been tied to the stake? What! acting on this vague abstraction, are you prepared to enforce a law without considering whether it be just or unjust, constitutional or unconstitutional? Will you collect money when it is acknowledged that it is not wanted? He who earns the money, who digs it from the earth with the sweat of his

---

[1] Sir Isaac Newton, 1642-1727, discovered the law of gravitation. Laplace, 1749-1827, was a noted French astronomer.

[2] Galileo, 1564-1642, the great Italian astronomer, was threatened with torture by the Inquisition. Sir Francis Bacon, 1561-1626, who was one of the first exponents of the inductive or experimental method of reasoning as opposed to the deductive, was ridiculed by many learned men.

[3] *Daniel* iii, 20; vi, 16

[4] two of the most cruel of the Roman emperors

brow, has a just title to it against the universe. No one has a right to touch it without his consent except his government, and this only to the extent of its legitimate wants; to take more is robbery, and you propose by this bill to enforce robbery by murder. Yes: to this result you must come, by this miserable sophistry, this vague abstraction of enforcing the law, without a regard to the fact whether the law be just or unjust, constitutional or unconstitutional.

In the same spirit, we are told that the Union must be preserved, without regard to the means. And how is it proposed to preserve the Union? By force! Does any man in his senses believe that this beautiful structure—this harmonious aggregate of States, produced by the joint consent of all—can be preserved by force? Its very introduction will be certain destruction to this Federal Union. No, no. You cannot keep the States united in their constitutional and federal bonds by force. Force may, indeed, hold the parts together, but such union would be the bond between master and slave—a union of exaction on one side and of unqualified *obedience* on the other. That *obedience* which, we are told by the Senator from Pennsylvania [Mr. Wilkins], is the Union! Yes, exaction on the side of the master; for this very bill is intended to collect what can be no longer called taxes— the voluntary contribution of a free people— but tribute—tribute to be collected under the mouths of the cannon! Your custom-house is already transferred to a garrison, and that garrison with its batteries turned, not against the enemy of your country, but on subjects (I will not say citizens), on whom you propose to levy contributions. Has reason fled from our borders? Have we ceased to reflect? It is madness to suppose that the Union can be preserved by force. I tell you plainly, that the bill, should it pass, cannot be enforced. It will prove only a blot upon your statute-book, a reproach to the year, and a disgrace to the American Senate. I repeat, it will not be executed; it will rouse the dormant spirit of the people, and open their eyes to the approach of despotism. The country has sunk into avarice and political corruption, from which nothing can arouse it but some measure, on the part of the Government, of folly and madness, such as that now under consideration. [1]

[SECOND DAY]

• • • • •

Having supplied the omissions of yesterday, I now resume the subject at the point where my remarks then terminated. The Senate will remember that I stated, at their close, that the great question at issue is, whether ours is a federal or a consolidated system of government; a system in which the parts, to use the emphatic language of Mr. Palgrave, [2] are the integers, and the whole the multiple, or in which the whole is an unit and the parts the fractions. I stated, that on the decision of this question, I believed, depend not only the liberty and prosperity of this country, but the place which we are destined to hold in the intellectual and moral scale of nations. I stated, also, in my remarks on this point, that there is a striking analogy between this and the great struggle between Persia and Greece, which was decided by the battles of Marathon, Plataea, and Salamis, and which immortalized the names of Miltiades and Themistocles. I illustrated this analogy by showing that centralism or consolidation, with the exception of a few nations along the eastern borders of the Mediterranean, has been the pervading principle in the Asiatic governments, while the federal system, or what is the same in principle, that system which organizes a community in reference to its parts, has prevailed in Europe. [3] . . .

But to return to the point immediately under consideration. I know that it is not only the opinion of a large majority of our country, but it may be said to be the opinion of the age, that the very beau ideal of a perfect government is the government of a majority, acting through a representative body, without check or limitation on its power; yet, if we may test this theory by experience and reason, we shall find that, so far from being perfect, the necessary tendency of all governments, based upon the will of an absolute majority, without constitutional check or limitation of power, is to faction, corruption, anarchy, and despotism; and this, whether the will of the majority be expressed directly through an assembly of the people themselves, or by their representatives. I know that, in venturing this assertion, I utter what is unpopular both within and without these walls; but where truth and liberty are con-

---

[1] Calhoun, in closing his speech of the first day, criticized the stand taken by several senators, repeated the statement that the question was whether there was to be power or liberty, a federal government or a "consolidated one." On the second day, after reiterating that the action of South Carolina was not directed against revenue, but against protection, but that the two were so blended that it was impossible to discriminate between them, Calhoun proceeded as above.

[2] Sir Francis Palgrave, 1788-1861, an English historian

[3] In the omitted paragraph the government of the twelve tribes of Israel is used as an illustration of the evils of a too centralized government.

cerned, such considerations should not be regarded. I will place the decision of this point
on the fact that no government of the kind,
among the many attempts which have been
made, has ever endured for a single generation,
but, on the contrary has invariably experienced
the fate which I have assigned to it. Let a
single instance be pointed out, and I will surrender my opinion. But, if we had not the
aid of experience to direct our judgment, reason
itself would be a certain guide. The view which
considers the community as an unit, and all
its parts as having a similar interest, is radically
erroneous. However small the community
may be, and however homogeneous its interests, the moment that government is put into
operation—as soon as it begins to collect taxes
and to make appropriations, the different portions of the community must, of necessity,
bear different and opposing relations in reference to the action of the government. There
must inevitably spring up two interests—a direction and a stockholder interest—an interest
profiting by the action of the government, and
interested in increasing its powers and action;
and another, at whose expense the political machine is kept in motion. I know how difficult
it is to communicate distinct ideas on such a
subject, through the medium of general propositions, without particular illustration; and in
order that I may be distinctly understood,
though at the hazard of being tedious, I will
illustrate the important principle which I have
ventured to advance, by examples.

Let us, then, suppose a small community of
five persons, separated from the rest of the
world; and, to make the example strong, let
us suppose them all to be engaged in the same
pursuit, and to be of equal wealth. Let us
further suppose that they determine to govern
the com/muity by the will of a majority; and,
to make the case as strong as possible, let us
suppose that the majority, in order to meet the
expenses of the government, lay an equal tax,
say of one hundred dollars on each individual
of this little community. Their treasury would
contain five hundred dollars. Three are a
majority; and they, by supposition, have contributed three hundred as their portion, and the
other two (the minority), two hundred. The
three have the right to make the appropriations
as they may think proper. The question is,
How would the principle of the absolute and
unchecked majority operate, under these circumstances, in this little community? If the
three be governed by a sense of justice—if they
should appropriate the money to the objects
for which it was raised, the common and equal

benefit of the five, then the object of the
association would be fairly and honestly effected, and each would have a common interest
in the government. But, should the majority
pursue an opposite course—should they appropriate the money in a manner to benefit their
own particular interest, without regard to the
interest of the two (and that they will so act,
unless there be some efficient check, he who
best knows human nature will least doubt), who
does not see that the three and the two would
have directly opposite interests in reference to
the action of the government? The three who
contribute to the common treasury but three
hundred dollars, could, in fact, by appropriating the five hundred to their own use, convert
the action of the government into the means of
making money, and, of consequence, would
have a direct interest in increasing the taxes.
They put in three hundred and take out five;
that is, they take back to themselves all that
they put in, and, in addition, that which was
put in by their associates; or, in other words,
taking taxation and appropriation together,
they have gained, and their associates have lost,
two hundred dollars by the fiscal action of the
government. Opposite interests, in reference
to the action of the government, are thus
created between them: the one having an interest in favor, and the other against the taxes;
the one to increase, and the other to decrease
the taxes; the one to retain the taxes when the
money is no longer wanted, and the other to
repeal them when the objects for which they
were levied have been secured.

Let us now suppose this community of five to
be raised to twenty-four individuals, to be
governed, in like manner, by the will of a majority: it is obvious that the same principle
would divide them into two interests—into a
majority and a minority, thirteen against
eleven, or in some other proportion; and that
all the consequences which I have shown to be
applicable to the small community of five would
be applicable to the greater, the cause not
depending upon the number, but resulting necessarily from the action of the government
itself. Let us now suppose that, instead of
governing themselves directly in an assembly
of the whole, without the intervention of agents,
they should adopt the representative principle;
and that, instead of being governed by a majority of themselves, they should be governed
by a majority of their representatives. It is
obvious that the operation of the system would
not be affected by the change: the representatives being responsible to those who chose them,
would conform to the will of their constituents,

and would act as they would do were they present and acting for themselves; and the same conflict of interest, which we have shown would exist in one case, would equally exist in the other. In either case, the inevitable result would be a system of hostile legislation on the part of the majority, or the stronger interest, against the minority, or the weaker interest; the object of which, on the part of the former, would be to exact as much as possible from the latter, which would necessarily be resisted by all the means in their power. Warfare, by legislation, would thus be commenced between the parties, with the same object, and not less hostile than that which is carried on between distinct and rival nations —the only distinction would be in the instruments and the mode. Enactments, in the one case, would supply what could only be effected by arms in the other; and the inevitable operation would be to engender the most hostile feelings between the parties, which would merge every feeling of patriotism—that feeling which embraces the whole—and substitute in its place the most violent party attachment; and instead of having one common center of attachment, around which the affections of the community might rally, there would in fact be two—the interests of the majority, to which those who constitute that majority would be more attached than they would be to the whole,—and that of the minority, to which they, in like manner, would also be more attached than to the interests of the whole. Faction would thus take the place of patriotism; and, with the loss of patriotism, corruption must necessarily follow, and in its train, anarchy, and, finally, despotism, or the establishment of absolute power in a single individual, as a means of arresting the conflict of hostile interests; on the principle that it is better to submit to the will of a single individual, who by being made lord and master of the whole community, would have an equal interest in the protection of all the parts.

Let us next suppose that, in order to avert the calamitous train of consequences, this little community should adopt a written constitution, with limitations restricting the will of the majority, in order to protect the minority against the oppression which I have shown would necessarily result without such restrictions. It is obvious that the case would not be in the slightest degree varied, if the majority be left in possession of the right of judging exclusively of the extent of its powers, without any right on the part of the minority to enforce the restrictions imposed by the constitution on the will of the majority. The point is almost too clear for illustration. Nothing can be more certain than that, when a constitution grants power, and imposes limitations on the exercise of that power, whatever interests may obtain possession of the government, will be in favor of extending the power at the expense of the limitation; and that, unless those in whose behalf the limitations were imposed have, in some form or mode, the right of enforcing them, the power will ultimately supersede the limitation, and the government must operate precisely in the same manner as if the will of the majority governed without constitution or limitation of power.

I have thus presented all possible modes in which a government founded upon the will of an absolute majority will be modified; and have demonstrated that, in all its forms, whether in a majority of the people, as in a mere democracy, or in a majority of their representatives, without a constitution or with a constitution, to be interpreted as the will of the majority, the result will be the same: two hostile interests will inevitably be created by the action of the government, to be followed by hostile legislation, and that by faction, corruption, anarchy, and despotism.

The great and solemn question here presents itself, Is there any remedy for these evils? on the decision of which depends the question, whether the people can govern themselves, which has been so often asked with so much skepticism and doubt. There is a remedy, and but one,—the effect of which, whatever may be the form, is to organize society in reference to this conflict of interests, which springs out of the action of government; and which can only be done by giving to each part the right of self-protection; which, in a word, instead of considering the community of twenty-four a single community, having a common interest, and to be governed by the single will of an entire majority, shall upon all questions tending to bring the parts into conflict, the thirteen against the eleven, take the will, not of the twenty-four as a unit, but that of the thirteen and that of the eleven separately,—the majority of each governing the parts, and where they concur, governing the whole,—and where they disagree, arresting the action of the government. This I will call the concurring, as distinct from the absolute majority. It would not be, as was generally supposed, a minority governing a majority. In either way the number would be the same, whether taken as the absolute or as the concurring majority. Thus, the majority of the thirteen is seven, and of the eleven six; and the two together make thirteen, which is the majority of twenty-four. But, though the number is the same, the mode of counting is essentially different: the one representing the strongest interest, and the other, the entire interests of the community. The first mistake is, in supposing that the government of the absolute majority is the government of this people—that beau ideal of a perfect government which has been so enthusiastically entertained in every age by the generous and patriotic, where civilization and liberty have made the smallest progress. There can be no greater error: the government of the people is the government of the whole community—of the twenty-four—the self-government of all the parts—too perfect to be reduced to practice in the present, or any past stage of human society. The government of the absolute majority, instead of being the government of the people, is but the government of the strongest interests, and, when not efficiently checked, is the most tyrannical and oppressive that can be devised. Between this ideal perfection on one side, and despotism on the other, no other system can be devised but that which considers society in reference to its parts, as differently affected by the action of the government, and which takes the sense of each part separately, and thereby the sense of the whole, in the manner already illustrated.

These principles, as I have already stated, are not affected by the number of which the community may be composed, and are just as applicable to one of thirteen millions—the number which composes ours—as of the small community of twenty-four, which I have supposed for the purpose of illustration; and are not less applicable to the twenty-four States united in one community, than to the case of the twenty-four individuals. There is, indeed, a distinction between a large and a small community, not affecting the principle, but the violence of the action. In the former, the similarity of the interests of all the parts will limit the oppression from the hostile action of the parts, in a great degree, to the fiscal action of the government merely; but in the large community, spreading over a country of great extent, and having a great diversity of interests, with different kinds of labor, capital, and production, the conflict and oppression will extend not only to a monopoly of the appropriations on the part of the stronger interests, but will end in unequal taxes, and a general conflict between the entire interests of conflicting sections, which, if not arrested by the most powerful checks, will terminate in the most oppressive tyranny that can be conceived, or in the destruction of the community itself.

If we turn our attention from these supposed cases, and direct it to our Government and its actual operation, we shall find a practical confirmation of the truth of what has been stated, not only of the oppressive operation of the system of an absolute majority, but also a striking and beautiful illustration, in the formation of our system, of the principle of the concurring majority, as distinct from the absolute, which I have asserted to be the only means of efficiently checking the abuse of power, and, of course, the only solid foundation of constitutional liberty. That our Government, for many years, has been gradually verging to consolidation; that the Constitution has gradually become a dead letter; and that all restrictions upon the power of government have been virtually removed, so as practically to convert the general Government into a government of an absolute majority, without check or limitation, cannot be denied by any one who has impartially observed its operation.

It is not necessary to trace the commencement and gradual progress of the causes which have produced this change in our system; it is sufficient to state that the change has taken place within the last few years. What has been the result? Precisely that which might have been anticipated: the growth of faction, corruption, anarchy, and, if not despotism itself, its near approach, as witnessed in the provisions of this bill. And from what have these consequences sprung? We have been involved in no war. We have been at peace with all the world. We have been visited with no national calamity. Our people have been advancing in general intelligence, and, I will add, as great and alarming as has been the advance of political corruption among the mercenary corps who look to government for support, the morals and virtue of the community at large have been advancing in improvement. What, I again repeat, is the cause? No other can be assigned but a departure from the fundamental principles of the Constitution, which has converted the Government into the will of an absolute and irresponsible majority, and which, by the laws that must inevitably govern in all such majorities, has placed in conflict the great interests of the country, by a system of hostile legislation, by an oppressive and unequal imposition of taxes, by unequal and profuse appropriations, and by rendering the entire labor and capital of the weaker interest subordinate to the stronger. [1]

To maintain the ascendency of the Constitution over the law-making majority is the great and essential point, on which the success of the system must depend. Unless that ascendency can be preserved, the necessary consequence must be, that the laws will supersede the Constitution; and, finally, the will of the Executive, by the influence of his patronage, will supersede the laws—indications of which are already perceptible. This ascendency can only be preserved through the action of the States as organized bodies, having their own separate governments, and possessed of the right, under the structure of our system, of judging of the extent of their separate powers, and of interposing their authority to arrest the unauthorized enactments of the general Government within their respective limits. I will not enter, at this time, into the discussion of this important point, as it has been ably and fully presented by the Senator from Kentucky [Mr. Bibb], and others who preceded him in this debate on the same side, whose arguments not only remain unanswered, but are unanswerable. It is only by this power of interposition that the reserved rights of the States can be peacefully and efficiently protected against the encroachments of the general Government—that the limitations imposed upon its authority can be enforced, and its movements confined to the orbit allotted to it by the Constitution. [2]

But, to return to the general Government. We have now sufficient experience to ascertain that the tendency to conflict in its action is between the southern and other sections. The latter having a decided majority, must habitually be possessed of the powers of the Government, both in this and in the other House; and, being governed by that instinctive love of power so natural to the human breast, they must become the advocates of the power of Government, and in the same degree opposed to the limitations; while the other and weaker section is as necessarily thrown on the side of the limitations. One section is the natural guardian of the delegated powers, and the other of the reserved; and the struggle on the side of the former will be to enlarge the powers,

while that on the opposite side will be to restrain them within their constitutional limits. The contest will, in fact, be a contest between power and liberty, and such I consider the present—a contest in which the weaker section, with its peculiar labor, productions, and institutions, has at stake all that can be dear to freemen. Should we be able to maintain in their full vigor our reserved rights, liberty and prosperity will be our portion; but if we yield, and permit the stronger interest to concentrate within itself all the powers of the Government, then will our fate be more wretched than that of the aborigines whom we have expelled. In this great struggle between the delegated and reserved powers, so far from repining that my lot, and that of those whom I represent, is cast on the side of the latter, I rejoice that such is the fact; for, though we participate in but few of the advantages of the Government, we are compensated, and more than compensated, in not being so much exposed to its corruption. Nor do I repine that the duty, so difficult to be discharged, of defending the reserved powers against apparently such fearful odds, has been assigned to us. To discharge successfully requires the highest qualities, moral and intellectual; and should we perform it with a zeal and ability in proportion to its magnitude, instead of being mere planters, our section will become distinguished for its patriots and statesmen. But, on the other hand, if we prove unworthy of the trust—if we yield to the steady encroachment of power, the severest calamity and most debasing corruption will overspread the land. Every Southern man, true to the interests of his section, and faithful to the duties which Providence has allotted him, will be forever excluded from the honors and emoluments of this Government, which will be reserved for those only who have qualified themselves, by political prostitution, for admission into the *Magdalen* Asylum.

1833   1833

DANIEL WEBSTER 1782-1852

To millions of American youth Webster has stood with Lincoln as an example of how men may rise from untoward circumstances to positions of national importance. He was born in poverty at Franklin, New Hampshire, the son of a farmer, but graduated from Dartmouth, 1801. He studied and practiced law, entered politics in Massachusetts, was congressman and senator, 1823-1841, and 1845-1850. He was twice secretary of state, and

---

[1] There follows a more definite summary of the political corruption of the time, and a reiteration of the statement that the rule of the absolute majority is the cause of this corruption.
[2] Calhoun here draws a parallel from Roman history.

would undoubtedly have been made President had not his "compromise stand" displeased both North and South. His massive and commanding figure and his sonorous voice added greatly to the convincingness of his speeches. Webster's chief orations were on the Dartmouth College case in the Supreme Court of the United States, 1818; the Bunker Hill Monument oration, 1825; the speech in reply to Senator Hayne, 1830; the speech maintaining that the Constitution is not a compact, 1833; and the speech for the Constitution and the Union, March, 1850.

It is hard to estimate the literary value of Webster's work. Its substance is weighty, but its sonorous, orotund phrases are in a style of speech now gone out of fashion. He was doubtless a close, if not a widely-trained student of written style, but it is as an orator that he is remembered. He was also the foremost interpreter of a constitutional theory that became, through the final test of arms, the will of the nation.

Biography and criticism: H. E. Scudder, (AML); Norman Hapgood, *Daniel Webster*, (BB) 1899; H. C. Lodge, (AS) 1899; J. B. McMaster, 1902; same, *Cent.* 61:103-119,763-76; 62:228-46, 719-41; S. W. McCall, "Daniel Webster," *Atlan.* 88:600-614.

THE CONSTITUTION NOT A COMPACT BETWEEN SOVEREIGN STATES [1]

And now sir, against all these theories and opinions, I maintain,—

1. That the Constitution of the United States is not a league, confederacy, or compact between the people of the several States in their sovereign capacities; but a government proper, founded on the adoption of the people, and creating direct relations between itself and individuals.

2. That no State authority has power to dissolve these relations; that nothing can dissolve them but revolution; and that, consequently, there can be no such thing as secession without revolution.

3. That there is a supreme law, consisting of the Constitution of the United States, and acts of Congress passed in pursuance of it, and treaties; and that, in cases not capable of assuming the character of a suit in law or equity, Congress must judge of, and finally interpret, this supreme law so often as it has occasion to pass acts of legislation; and in cases

[1] This speech was delivered on Feb. 16, 1833, in answer to Calhoun's speech of the same day. (See p. 445.) Since it is very long, the elaboration of the argument has been omitted whenever possible, the main points, however, being kept. After reviewing and briefly answering the resolutions and arguments brought forward by Calhoun, Webster proceeded as above.

capable of assuming, and actually assuming, the character of a suit, the Supreme Court of the United States is the final interpreter.

4. That an attempt by a State to abrogate, annul, or nullify an act of Congress, or to arrest its operation within her limits, on the ground that, in her opinion, such law is unconstitutional, is a direct usurpation on the just powers of the general Government, and on the equal rights of other States; a plain violation of the Constitution, and a proceeding essentially revolutionary in its character and tendency.

Whether the Constitution be a compact between States in their sovereign capacities, is a question which must be mainly argued from what is contained in the instrument itself. We all agree that it is an instrument which has been in some way clothed with power. We all admit that it speaks with authority. The first question then is, What does it say of itself? What does it purport to be? Does it style itself a league, confederacy, or compact between sovereign States? It is to be remembered, sir, that the Constitution began to speak only after its adoption. Until it was ratified by nine States, it was but a proposal, the mere draught of an instrument. It was like a deed drawn, but not executed. The Convention had framed it; sent it to Congress, then sitting under the Confederation; Congress had transmitted it to the State legislatures; and by these last it was laid before conventions of the people in the several States. All this while it was inoperative paper. It had received no stamp of authority, no sanction; it spoke no language. But when ratified by the people in their respective conventions, then it had a voice, and spoke authentically. Every word in it had then received the sanction of the popular will, and was to be received as the expression of that will. What the Constitution says of itself, therefore, is as conclusive as what it says on any other point. Does it call itself a "compact"? Certainly not. It uses the word *compact* but once, and that is when it declares that the States shall enter into no compact. Does it call itself a "league," a "confederacy," a "subsisting treaty between the States"? Certainly not. There is not a particle of such language in all its pages. But it declares itself a CONSTITUTION. What is a *constitution*? Certainly not a league, compact, or confederacy, but a *fundamental law*. That fundamental regulation which determines the manner in which the public authority is to be executed, is what forms the *constitution* of a state. Those primary rules which concern the body itself, and the very being of the political society, the form of government, and the manner in which power is to be exercised,—all, in a word, which form together the *constitution of a state*,—these are the fundamental laws. This, sir, is the language of the public writers. But do we need to be informed, in this country, what a *constitution* is? Is it not an idea perfectly familiar, definite, and well settled? We are at no loss to understand what is meant by the constitution of one of the States; and the Constitution of the United States speaks of itself as being an instrument of the same nature. It says, this *Constitution* shall be the law of the land, anything in any State *constitution* to the contrary notwithstanding. And it speaks of itself, too, in plain contradistinction from a confederation; for it says that all debts contracted, and all engagements entered into, by the United States, shall be as valid under this *Constitution* as under the *Confederation*. It does not say, as valid under this *compact*, or this league, or this confederation, as under the former confederation, but as valid under this *Constitution*.

This, then, sir, is declared to be a *constitution*. A constitution is the fundamental law of the state; and this is expressly declared to be the supreme law. It is as if the people had said "We prescribe this fundamental law," or "this supreme law," for they do say that they establish this Constitution, and that it shall be the supreme law. They say that they *ordain and establish* it. Now, sir, what is the common application of these words? We do not speak of *ordaining* leagues and compacts. If this was intended to be a compact or league, and the States to be parties to it, why was it not so said? Why is there found no one expression in the whole instrument indicating such intent? The old Confederation was expressly called a *league*, and into this league it was declared that the States, as States, severally entered. Why was not similar language used in the Constitution, if a similar intention had existed? Why was it not said, "the States enter into this new league," "the States form this new confederation," or "the States agree to this new compact"? Or why was it not said, in the language of the gentleman's resolution, that the people of the several States acceded to this compact in their sovereign capacities? What reason is there for supposing that the framers of the Constitution rejected expressions appropriate to their own meaning, and adopted others wholly at war with that meaning?

Again, sir, the Constitution speaks of that political system which is established as "the government of the United States." Is it not doing strange violence to language to call a league or a compact between sovereign powers a *government?* The government of a state is that organization in which the political power resides. It is the political being created by the constitution or fundamental law. The broad and clear difference between a government and a league or compact is, that a government is a body politic; it has a will of its own; and it possesses powers and faculties to execute its own purposes. Every compact looks to some power to enforce its stipulations. Even in a compact between sovereign communities, there always exists this ultimate reference to a power to insure its execution; although, in such case, this power is but the force of one party against the force of another; that is to say, the power of war. But a *government* executes its decisions by its own supreme authority. Its use of force in compelling obedience to its own enactments is not war. It contemplates no opposing party having a right of resistance. It rests on its own power to enforce its own will; and when it ceases to possess this power, it is no longer a government.

Mr. President, I concur so generally in the very able speech of the gentleman from Virginia near me,[1] that it is not without diffidence and regret that I venture to differ with him on any point. His opinions, sir, are redolent of the doctrines of a very distinguished school, for which I have the highest regard, of whose doctrines I can say, what I can also say of the gentleman's speech, that, while I concur in the results, I must be permitted to hesitate about some of the premises. I do not agree that the Constitution is a compact between States in their sovereign capacities. I do not agree that in strictness of language, it is a compact at all. But I do agree that it is founded on consent or agreement, or on compact, if the gentleman prefers that word, and means no more by it than voluntary consent or agreement. The Constitution, sir, is not a contract, but the result of a contract; meaning by contract no more than assent. Founded on consent, it is a government proper. Adopted by the agreement of the people of the United States, when adopted, it has become a Constitution. The people have agreed to make a Constitution; but when made, that Constitution becomes what its name imports. It is no longer a mere agreement. Our laws, sir, have their foundation in the agreement or consent of the two houses

[1] Mr. Rives [Webster's note]

of Congress. We say, habitually, that one house proposes a bill, and the other agrees to it; but the result of this agreement is not a compact but a law. The law, the statute, is not the agreement, but something created by the agreement; and something which, when created, has a new character, and acts by its own authority. So the Constitution of the United States, founded in or on the consent of the people, may be said to rest on compact or consent; but it is not itself the compact, but its result. When the people agree to erect a government, and actually erect it, the thing is done, and the agreement is at an end. The compact is executed, and the end designed by it attained. Henceforth, the fruit of the agreement exists, but the agreement itself is merged in its own accomplishment; since there can be no longer a subsisting agreement or compact *to form* a constitution or government, after that constitution or government has been actually formed and established.

It appears to me, Mr. President, that the plainest account of the establishment of this Government presents the most just and philosophical view of its foundation. The people of the several States had their separate State governments; and between the States there also existed a Confederation. With this condition of things the people were not satisfied, as the Confederation had been found not to fulfill its intended objects. It was *proposed,* therefore, to erect a new, common government, which should possess certain definite powers, such as regarded the prosperity of the people of all the States, and to be formed upon the general model of American constitutions. This proposal was assented to, and an instrument was presented to the people of the several States for their consideration. They approved it, and agreed to adopt it, as a Constitution. They executed that agreement; they adopted the Constitution as a Constitution, and henceforth it must stand as a Constitution until it shall be altogether destroyed. Now, sir, is not this the truth of the whole matter? And is not all that we have heard of compact between sovereign States the mere effect of a theoretical and artificial mode of reasoning upon the subject? a mode of reasoning which disregards plain facts for the sake of hypothesis? [1]

.   .   .   .   .   .

Looking still further to the provisions of the Constitution itself, in order to learn its true character, we find its great apparent purpose to be, to unite the people of all the States under one general government, for certain definite objects, and, to the extent of this union, to restrain the separate authority of the States. Congress only can declare war; therefore, when one State is at war with a foreign nation, all must be at war. The President and the Senate only can make peace; when peace is made for one State, therefore, it must be made for all.

Can anything be conceived more preposterous, than that any State should have power to nullify the proceedings of the general government respecting peace and war? When war is declared by a law of Congress, can a single State nullify that law, and remain at peace? And yet she may nullify that law as well as any other. If the President and Senate make peace, may one State, nevertheless, continue the war? And yet, if she can nullify a law, she may quite as well nullify a treaty.

The truth is, Mr. President, and no ingenuity of argument, no subtilty of distinction can evade it, that, as to certain purposes, the people of the United States are one people. They are one in making war, and one in making peace; they are one in regulating commerce, and one in laying duties of imposts. The very end and purpose of the Constitution was, to make them one people in these particulars; and it has effectually accomplished its object. All this is apparent on the face of the Constitution itself. I have already said, sir, that to obtain a power of direct legislation over the people, especially in regard to imposts, was always prominent as a reason for getting rid of the Confederation, and forming a new Constitution. Among innumerable proofs of this, before the assembling of the Convention, allow me to refer only to the report of the committee of the old Congress, July, 1785.

But, sir, let us go to the actual formation of the Constitution; let us open the journal of the Convention itself, and we shall see that the very first resolution which the Convention adopted was, "THAT A NATIONAL GOVERNMENT OUGHT TO BE ESTABLISHED, CONSISTING OF A SUPREME LEGISLATURE, JUDICIARY, AND EXECUTIVE."

This itself completely negatives all idea of league, and compact, and confederation. Terms could not be chosen more fit to express an intention to establish a national government, and to banish forever all notion of a compact between sovereign States.

This resolution was adopted on the 30th of May, 1787. Afterwards, the style was altered,

[1] The six short paragraphs omitted emphasize the idea that the sovereignty of the United States government is a sovereignty of the people.

and, instead of being called a national government, it was called the government of the United States; but the substance of this resolution was retained, and was at the head of that list of resolutions which was afterwards sent to the committee who were to frame the instrument. [1]

.   .   .   .

Indeed, sir, if we look to all contemporary history, to the numbers of *The Federalist*, to the debates in the conventions, to the publications of friends and foes, they all agree, that a change had been made from a confederacy of States, to a different system; they all agree, that the Convention had formed a constitution for a national government. With this result some were satisfied, and some were dissatisfied; but all admitted that the thing had been done. In none of these various productions and publications did anyone intimate that the new Constitution was but another compact between States in their sovereign capacities. I do not find such an opinion advanced in a single instance. Everywhere, the people were told that the old Confederation was to be abandoned, and a new system to be tried; that a proper government was proposed, to be founded in the name of the people, and to have a regular organization of its own. Everywhere, the people were told that it was to be a government with direct powers to make laws over individuals, and to lay taxes and imposts without the consent of the States. Everywhere, it was understood to be a popular constitution. It came to the people for their adoption, and was to rest on the same deep foundation as the State constitutions themselves. Its most distinguished advocates, who had been themselves members of the Convention, declared that the very object of submitting the Constitution to the people was, to preclude the possibility of its being regarded as a mere compact. "However gross a heresy," say the writers [2] of *The Federalist*, "it may be to maintain that a party to a *compact* has a right to revoke that *compact*, the doctrine itself has had respectable advocates. The possibility of a question of this nature proves the necessity of laying the foundations of our national government deeper than in the mere sanction of delegated authority. The fabric of American empire ought to rest

on the solid basis of THE CONSENT OF THE PEOPLE." [3]

.   .   .   .   .   .

Finally, sir, how can any man get over the words of the Constitution itself?—"WE, THE PEOPLE OF THE UNITED STATES, DO ORDAIN AND ESTABLISH THIS CONSTITUTION." These words must cease to be a part of the Constitution, they must be obliterated from the parchment on which they are written, before any human ingenuity or human argument can remove the popular basis on which that Constitution rests, and turn the instrument into a mere compact between sovereign States.

The second proposition, sir, which I propose to maintain, is, that no State authority can dissolve the relations subsisting between the Government of the United States and individuals; that nothing can dissolve these relations but revolution; and that, therefore, there can be no such thing as *secession* without revolution. All this follows, as it seems to me, as a just consequence, if it be first proved that the Constitution of the United States is a government proper, owing protection to individuals, and entitled to their obedience.

The people, sir, in every State, live under two governments. They owe obedience to both. These governments, though distinct, are not adverse. Each has its separate sphere, and its peculiar powers and duties. It is not a contest between two sovereigns for the same power, like the wars of the rival houses in England; nor is it a dispute, between a government *de facto* [4] and a government *de jure*. It is the case of a division of powers between two governments, made by the people, to whom both are responsible. Neither can dispense with the duty which individuals owe to the other; neither can call itself master of the other: the people are masters of both. This division of power, it is true, is in a great measure unknown in Europe. It is the peculiar system of America; and though new and singular, it is not incomprehensible. The State constitutions are established by the people of the States. This Constitution is established by the people of all the States. How, then, can a State secede? How can a State undo what the whole people have done? How can she absolve her citizens from their obedience to the laws of the United States? How can she annul their obligations and oaths? How can the members of her legislature renounce their own oaths? Sir, secession,

---

[1] There follows the explanation that though the Constitutional Convention debated whether to continue the Confederacy, they finally decided to reject the idea of a compact and instead to form a strong national government. Webster quotes from the speeches made in the convention.

[2] See *The Federalist*, No. XXII (by Alexander Hamilton).

[3] There follows proof that the states in ratifying the Constitution recognized that it was a government of the people.

[4] "in reality," as opposed to *de jure*, "by law"

as a revolutionary right, is intelligible; as a right to be proclaimed in the midst of civil commotions, and asserted at the head of armies, I can understand it. But as a practical right, existing under the Constitution, and in conformity with its provisions, it seems to me to be nothing but a plain absurdity; for it supposes resistance to government, under the authority of government itself; it supposes dismemberment, without violating the principles of union; it supposes opposition to law, without crime; it supposes the violation of oaths, without responsibility; it supposes the total overthrow of government, without revolution.

The Constitution, sir, regards itself as perpetual and immortal. It seeks to establish a union among the people of the States, which shall last through all time. Or, if the common fate of things human must be expected at some period to happen to it, yet that catastrophe is not anticipated.

The instrument contains ample provisions for its amendment, at all times; none for its abandonment, at any time. It declares that new States may come into the Union, but it does not declare that old States may go out. The Union is not a temporary partnership of States. It is the association of the people, under a constitution of government, uniting their power, joining together their highest interests, cementing their present enjoyments, and blending, in one indivisible mass, all their hopes for the future. Whatsoever is steadfast in just political principles; whatsoever is permanent in the structure of human society; whatsoever there is which can derive an enduring character from being founded on deep-laid principles of constitutional liberty and on the broad foundations of the public will,—all these unite to entitle this instrument to be regarded as a permanent constitution of government.

In the next place, Mr. President, I contend that there is a supreme law of the land, consisting of the Constitution, acts of Congress passed in pursuance of it, and the public treaties. This will not be denied, because such are the very words of the Constitution. But I contend, further, that it rightfully belongs to Congress, and to the courts of the United States, to settle the construction of this supreme law, in doubtful cases. This is denied; and here arises the great practical question, *Who is to construe finally the Constitution of the United States?* We all agree that the Constitution is the supreme law; but who shall interpret that law? In our system of the division of powers between different governments,

controversies will necessarily sometimes arise, respecting the extent of the powers of each. Who shall decide these controversies? Does it rest with the general government, in all or any of its departments, to exercise the office of final interpreter? Or may each of the States, as well as the general government, claim this right of ultimate decision? The practical result of this whole debate turns on this point. The gentleman contends that each State may judge for itself of any alleged violation of the Constitution, and may finally decide for itself, and may execute its own decisions by its own power. All the recent proceedings in South Carolina are founded on this claim of right. Her convention has pronounced the revenue laws of the United States unconstitutional; and this decision she does not allow any authority of the United States to overrule or reverse. Of course she rejects the authority of Congress, because the very object of the ordinance is to reverse the decision of Congress; and she rejects, too, the authority of the courts of the United States, because she expressly prohibits all appeal to those courts. It is in order to sustain this asserted right of being her own judge, that she pronounces the Constitution of the United States to be but a compact, to which she is a party, and a sovereign party. If this be established, then the inference is supposed to follow, that, being sovereign, there is no power to control her decision; and her own judgment on her own compact is, and must be, conclusive. [1]

. . . .

But, Mr. President, the Constitution has not left this cardinal point without full and explicit provisions. First, as to the authority of Congress. Having enumerated the specific powers conferred on Congress, the Constitution adds, as a distinct and substantive clause, the following, viz.: "To make all laws which shall be necessary and proper for carrying into execution the foregoing powers, and all other powers vested by this Constitution in the Government of the United States, or in any department or officer thereof." If this means anything, it means that Congress may judge of the true extent and just interpretation of the specific powers granted to it, and may judge also of what is necessary and proper for executing those powers. If Congress is to judge of what is necessary for the execution of its powers, it must, of necessity, judge of the extent and interpretation of those powers.

[1] The truism is then emphasized that the whole cannot govern the parts if one part can govern the whole.

And in regard, sir, to the judiciary, the Constitution is still more express and emphatic. It declares that the judicial power shall extend to all *cases* in law or equity arising under the Constitution, laws of the United States, and treaties; that there shall be *one* Supreme Court, and that this Supreme Court shall have appellate jurisdiction [1] of all these cases, subject to such exceptions as Congress may make. It is impossible to escape from the generality of these words. If a case arises under the Constitution, that is, if a case arises depending on the construction of the Constitution, the judicial power of the United States extends to it. It reaches *the case, the question;* it attaches the power of the national judicature to the *case* itself, in whatever court it may arise or exist; and in this *case* the Supreme Court has appellate jurisdiction over all courts whatever. No language could provide with more effect and precision than is here done, for subjecting constitutional questions to the ultimate decision of the Supreme Court. And, sir, this is exactly what the Convention found it necessary to provide for, and intended to provide for. It is, too, exactly what the people were universally told was done when they adopted the Constitution. One of the first resolutions adopted by the Convention was in these words, viz.: "That the jurisdiction of the national judiciary shall extend to cases which respect *the collection of the national revenue,* and questions which involve the national peace and harmony." Now, sir, this either had no sensible meaning at all, or else it meant that the jurisdiction of the national judiciary should extend to these questions, *with a paramount authority.* It is not to be supposed that the Convention intended that the power of the national judiciary should extend to these questions, and that the power of the judicatures of the States should also extend to them, with *equal power of final decision.* This would be to defeat the whole object of the provision. There were thirteen judicatures already in existence. The evil complained of, or the danger to be guarded against, was contradiction and repugnance in the decisions of these judicatures. If the framers of the Constitution meant to create a fourteenth, and yet not to give it power to revise and control the decisions of the existing thirteen, then they only intended to augment the existing evil and the apprehended danger by increasing still further the chances of discordant judgments. Why, sir, has it become a settled axiom in politics that every

government must have a judicial power coextensive with its legislative power? Certainly, there is only this reason, namely, that the laws may receive a uniform interpretation and a uniform execution. This object cannot be otherwise attained. A statute is what it is judicially interpreted to be; and if it be construed one way in New Hampshire, and another way in Georgia, there is no uniform law. One supreme court, with appellate and final jurisdiction, is the natural and only adequate means, in any government, to secure this uniformity. The Convention saw all this clearly; and the resolution which I have quoted, never afterwards rescinded, passed through various modifications, till it finally received the form which the article now bears in the Constitution. [2]

Gentlemen appear to me, sir, to look at but one side of the question. They regard only the supposed danger of trusting a government with the interpretation of its own powers. But will they view the question in its other aspect? Will they show us how it is possible for a government to get along with four-and-twenty interpreters of its laws and powers? Gentlemen argue, too, as if, in these cases, the State would be always right, and the general government always wrong. But suppose the reverse; suppose the State wrong (and, since they differ, some of them must be wrong); are the most important and essential operations of the government to be embarrassed and arrested, because one State holds the contrary opinion? Mr. President, every argument which refers the constitutionality of acts of Congress to State decision appeals from the majority to the minority; it appeals from the common interest to a particular interest; from the counsels of all to the counsel of one; and endeavors to supersede the judgment of the whole by the judgment of a part. [3]

Sir, those who espouse the doctrines of nullification reject, as it seems to me, the first great principle of all republican liberty; that is, that the majority *must* govern. In matters of common concern, the judgment of a majority *must* stand as the judgment of the whole. This is

---

[1] Shall hear appeals.

[2] Webster then shows that different methods of strengthening the central government were suggested in the Federal Convention, some of which were not approved, but all of which aimed at the same end. Of what use would be a supreme court if the judiciary of each state were supreme?

[3] Webster goes on to say that as the supreme court is constituted the highest judicial body, so Congress is constituted the supreme legislative body.

a law imposed on us by the absolute necessity of the case; and if we do not act upon it, there is no possibility of maintaining any government but despotism. We hear loud and repeated denunciations against what is called *majority government*. It is declared, with much warmth, that a majority government cannot be maintained in the United States. What, then, do gentlemen wish? Do they wish to establish a *minority government?* Do they wish to subject the will of the many to the will of the few? The honorable gentleman from South Carolina has spoken of absolute majorities and majorities concurrent; language wholly unknown to our Constitution, and to which it is not easy to affix definite ideas. As far as I understand it, it would teach us that the absolute majority may be found in Congress, but the majority concurrent must be looked for in the States; that is to say, sir, stripping the matter of this novelty of phrase, that the dissent of one or more States, as States, renders void the decision of a majority of Congress, so far as that State is concerned. And so this doctrine, running but a short career, like other dogmas of the day, terminates in nullification. [1]

.   .   .   .   .   .

Does not the gentleman perceive, sir, how his argument against majorities might here be retorted upon him? Does he not see how cogently he might be asked, whether it be the character of nullification to practice what it preaches? Look to South Carolina, at the present moment. How far are the rights of minorities there respected? I confess, sir, I have not known, in peaceable times, the power of the majority carried with a higher hand, or upheld with more relentless disregard of the rights, feelings, and principles of the minority; —a minority embracing, as the gentleman himself will admit, a large portion of the worth and respectability of the State; [2] a minority comprehending in its numbers men who have been associated with him, and with us, in these halls of legislation; men who have served their country at home and honored it abroad; men who would cheerfully lay down their lives for their native State, in any cause which they could regard as the cause of honor and duty; men above fear, and above reproach; whose

[1] Here Webster emphasizes the fact that the Constitution of the United States, by means of the President's veto power and the Senate, where states have equal representation without regard to size, furnishes checks upon mere majorities.
[2] The leader of this strong minority, which opposed nullification, was the statesman Joel Roberts Poinsett.

deepest grief and distress spring from the conviction, that the present proceedings of the State must ultimately reflect discredit upon her. How is this minority, how are these men, regarded? They are enthralled and disfranchised by ordinances and acts of legislation; subjected to tests and oaths, incompatible, as they conscientiously think, with oaths already taken, and obligations already assumed, they are proscribed and denounced, as recreants to duty and patriotism, and slaves to a foreign power. Both the spirit which pursues them, and the positive measures which emanate from that spirit, are harsh and proscriptive beyond all precedent within my knowledge, except in periods of professed revolution.

It is not, sir, one would think, for those who would approve these proceedings to complain of the power of majorities.

Mr. President, all popular governments rest on two principles, or two assumptions:—

First, That there is so far a common interest among those over whom the government extends, as that it may provide for the defense, protection, and good government of the whole, without injustice or oppression to parts; and

Secondly, That the representatives of the people, and especially the people themselves, are secure against general corruption, and may be trusted, therefore, with the exercise of power.

Whoever argues against these principles argues against the practicability of all free governments. And whoever admits these, must admit, or cannot deny, that power is as safe in the hands of Congress as in those of other representative bodies. Congress is not irresponsible. Its members are agents of the people, elected by them, answerable to them, and liable to be displaced or superseded, at their pleasure; and they possess as fair a claim to the confidence of the people, while they continue to deserve it, as any other public political agents.

If, then, sir, the manifest intention of the Convention, and the contemporary admission of both friends and foes, prove anything; if the plain text of the instrument itself, as well as the necessary implication from other provisions, prove anything; if the early legislation of Congress, the course of judicial decisions, acquiesced in by all the States for forty years, prove anything,—then it is proved that there is a supreme law and a final interpreter.

My fourth and last proposition, Mr. President, was, that any attempt by a State to abrogate or nullify acts of Congress is a usurpation on the powers of the general government and on the equal rights of other States, a violation of the Constitution, and a proceeding essentially revolutionary. This is undoubtedly true, if the preceding propositions be regarded as proved. If the Government of the United States be trusted with the duty, in any department, of declaring the extent of its own powers, then a State ordinance, or act of legislation, authorizing resistance to an act of Congress, on the alleged ground of its unconstitutionality, is manifestly a usurpation upon its powers. If the States have equal rights in matters concerning the whole, then for one State to set up her judgment against the judgment of the rest, and to insist on executing that judgment by force, is also a manifest usurpation on the rights of other States. If the Constitution of the United States be a government proper, with authority to pass laws, and to give them a uniform interpretation and execution, then the interposition of a State, to enforce her own construction, and to resist, as to herself, that law which binds the other States, is a violation of the Constitution.

If that be revolutionary which arrests the legislative, executive, and judicial power of government, dispenses with existing oaths and obligations of obedience, and elevates another power to supreme dominion, then nullification is revolutionary. Or if that be revolutionary the natural tendency and practical effect of which are to break the Union into fragments, to sever all connection among the people of the respective States, and to prostrate this general government in the dust, then nullification is revolutionary.

Nullification, sir, is as distinctly revolutionary as secession; but I cannot say that the revolution which it seeks is one of so respectable a character. Secession would, it is true, abandon the Constitution altogether; but then it would profess to abandon it. Whatever other inconsistencies it might run into, one, at least, it would avoid. It would not belong to a government, while it rejected its authority. It would not repel the burden, and continue to enjoy the benefits. It would not aid in passing laws which others are to obey, and yet reject their authority as to itself. It would not undertake to reconcile obedience to public authority with an asserted right of command over that same authority. It would not be in the Government, and above the Government, at the same time. But though secession may be a more respectable mode of attaining the object than nullification, it is not more truly

revolutionary. Each, and both, resist the constitutional authorities; each, and both, would sever the Union, and subvert the government. [1]

.   .   .   .

Mr. President, if the friends of nullification should be able to propagate their opinions, and to give them practical effect, they would, in my judgment, prove themselves the most skilful "architects of ruin," the most effectual extinguishers of high-raised expectation, the greatest blasters of human hopes, that any age has produced. They would stand up to proclaim, in tones which would pierce the ears of half the human race, that the last great experiment of representative government had failed. They would send forth sounds, at the hearing of which the doctrine of the divine right of kings would feel, even in its grave, a returning sense of vitality and resuscitation. Millions of eyes, of those who now feed their inherent love of liberty on the success of the American example, would turn away from beholding our dismemberment, and find no place on earth whereon to rest their gratified sight. Amidst the incantations and orgies of nullification, secession, disunion, and revolution, would be celebrated the funeral rites of constitutional and republican liberty.

But, sir, if the government do its duty, if it act with firmness and with moderation, these opinions cannot prevail. Be assured, sir, be assured that, among the political sentiments of this people, the love of union is still uppermost. They will stand fast by the Constitution, and by those who defend it. I rely on no temporary expedients, on no political combination; but I rely on the true American feeling, the genuine patriotism of the people, and the imperative decision of the public voice. Disorder and confusion, indeed, may arise; scenes of commotion and contest are threatened, and perhaps may come. With my whole heart I pray for the continuance of the domestic peace and quiet of the country. I desire, most ardently, the restoration of affection and harmony to all its parts. I desire that every citizen of the whole country may look to this Government with no other sentiments than those of grateful respect and attachment. But I cannot yield even to kind feelings the cause of the Constitution, the true glory of the country, and the great trust which we hold in our

[1] There follows a minute exposition of the ordinance and resolutions (see note 2, p. 445) of South Carolina and of their necessary result, and the proof that in the first Congress representatives from South Carolina were among the foremost to suggest the laying of impost duties.

hands for succeeding ages. If the Constitution cannot be maintained without meeting these scenes of commotion and contest, however unwelcome, they must come. We cannot, we must not, we dare not, omit to do that which, in our judgment, the safety of the Union requires. Not regardless of consequences, we must yet meet consequences; seeing the hazards which surround the discharge of public duty, it must yet be discharged. For myself, sir, I shun no responsibility justly devolving on me, here or elsewhere, in attempting to maintain the cause. I am bound to it by indissoluble ties of affection and duty, and I shall cheerfully partake in its fortunes and its fate. I am ready to perform my own appropriate part, whenever and wherever the occasion may call on me, and to take my chance among those upon whom blows may fall first and fall thickest. I shall exert every faculty I possess in aiding to prevent the Constitution from being nullified, destroyed, or impaired; and even should I see it fall, I will still, with a voice feeble perhaps, but earnest as ever issued from human lips, and with fidelity and zeal which nothing shall extinguish, call on the PEOPLE to come to its rescue.

1833   1833

CHARLES SUMNER 1811-1874

Sumner was born in Boston, graduated from Harvard in 1830 and for ten years studied and practiced law, wrote upon legal subjects, and traveled abroad. His career as a high-minded politician and official filled nearly all his public life. Though independent of strict party lines, he was active in the anti-slavery cause. From 1851 until his death in Washington he was United States senator from Massachusetts. His speeches in the Senate and elsewhere constitute his best-known literary work.

The selection here given from an early oration of Sumner's shows the bent of his idealism. The speech represents the type of oratory in vogue in Sumner's day, but its attitude toward war and military glory is more common now than in Sumner's time.

Moorfield Storey, *Charles Sumner,* (AS) 1900.

From THE TRUE GRANDEUR OF NATIONS [1]

In accordance with uninterrupted usage, on this Sabbath of the nation, we have put aside our daily cares, and seized a respite from the

never-ending toils of life, to meet in gladness and congratulation, mindful of the blessings transmitted from the past, mindful also, I trust, of our duties to the present and the future.

All hearts turn first to the Fathers of the Republic. Their venerable forms rise before us, in the procession of successive generations. They come from the frozen rock of Plymouth, from the wasted bands of Raleigh, from the heavenly companionship of Penn, from the anxious councils of the Revolution,—from all those fields of sacrifice, where, in obedience to the spirit of their age, they sealed their devotion to duty with their blood. They say to us, their children, "Cease to vaunt what you do, and what has been done for you. Learn to walk meekly and to think humbly. Cultivate habits of self-sacrifice. Never aim at what is not RIGHT, persuaded that without this every possession and all knowledge will become an evil and a shame. And may these words of ours be ever in your minds! Strive to increase the inheritance we have bequeathed to you,—bearing in mind always, that, if we excel you in virtue, such a victory will be to us a mortification, while defeat will bring happiness. In this way you may conquer us. Nothing is more shameful for a man than a claim to esteem, not on his own merits, but on the fame of his ancestors. The glory of the fathers is doubtless to their children a most precious treasure; but to enjoy it without transmission to the next generation, and without addition, is the extreme of ignominy. Following these counsels, when your days on earth are finished, you will come to join us, and we shall receive you as friend receives friend; but if you neglect our words, expect no happy greeting from us."

Honor to the memory of our fathers! May the turf lie lightly on their sacred graves! Not in words only, but in deeds also, let us testify our reverence for their name, imitating what in them was lofty, pure, and good, learning from them to bear hardship and privation. May we, who now reap in strength what they sowed in weakness, augment the inheritance we have received! To this end, we must not fold our hands in slumber, nor abide content with the past. To each generation is appointed its peculiar task; nor does the heart which responds to the call of duty find rest except in the grave.

Be ours the task now in the order of Providence cast upon us. And what is this duty? What can we do to make our coming welcome to our fathers in the skies, and draw to our

[1] This, Sumner's first great oration, was delivered July 4, 1845, in the Old South Church, Boston, before the authorities of the city. Sumner had in mind the aggressive policy of the United States toward Mexico just before the Mexican War.

memory hereafter the homage of a grateful posterity? How add to the inheritance received? The answer must interest all, particularly on this festival, when we celebrate the nativity of the Republic. It well becomes the patriot citizen, on this anniversary, to consider the national character, and how it may be advanced,—as the good man dedicates his birthday to meditation on his life, and to resolutions of improvement.

Avoiding, then, all exultation in the abounding prosperity of the land, and in that freedom whose influence is widening to the uttermost circles of the earth, I would turn attention to the character of our country, and humbly endeavor to learn what must be done that the Republic may best secure the welfare of the people committed to its care,—that it may perform its part in the world's history,—that it may fulfil the aspirations of generous hearts, —and, practicing that righteousness which exalteth a nation, attain to the elevation of true grandeur.

With this aim, and believing that I can in no other way so fitly fulfil the trust reposed in me today, I purpose to consider *what, in our age, are the true objects of national ambition,—what is truly national honor, national glory,—*WHAT IS THE TRUE GRANDEUR OF NATIONS. I would not depart from the modesty that becomes me, yet I am not without hope that I may do something to rescue these terms, now so powerful over the minds of men, from mistaken objects, especially from deeds of war, and the extension of empire, that they may be applied to works of justice and beneficence, which are better than war or empire.

The subject may be novel, on an occasion like the present; but it is comprehensive, and of transcendent importance. It raises us to the contemplation of things not temporary or local, but belonging to all ages and countries, —things lofty as truth, universal as humanity. Nay, more; it practically concerns the general welfare, not only of our own cherished Republic, but of the whole federation of nations. It has an urgent interest from transactions in which we are now unhappily involved. By an act of unjust legislation, extending our power over Texas, peace with Mexico is endangered,— while, by petulant assertion of a disputed claim to a remote territory beyond the Rocky Mountains,[1] ancient fires of hostile strife are kindled

anew on the hearth of our mother country. Mexico and England both avow the determination to vindicate what is called the *national honor;* and our Government calmly contemplates the dread arbitrament of war, provided it cannot obtain what is called an honorable peace.

Can there be in our age any peace that is not honorable, any war that is not dishonorable? The true honor of a nation is conspicuous only in deeds of justice and beneficence, securing and advancing human happiness. In the clear eye of that Christian judgment which must yet prevail, vain are the victories of war, infamous its spoils. He is the benefactor, and worthy of honor, who carries comfort to wretchedness, dries the tear of sorrow, relieves the unfortunate, feeds the hungry, clothes the naked, does justice, enlightens the ignorant, unfastens the fetters of the slave, and finally, by virtuous genius, in art, literature, science, enlivens and exalts the hours of life, or, by generous example, inspires a love for God and man. This is the Christian hero; this is the man of honor in a Christian land. He is no benefactor, nor worthy of honor, whatever his worldly renown, whose life is absorbed in feats of brute force, who renounces the great law of Christian brotherhood, whose vocation is blood. Well may the modern poet exclaim, "The world knows nothing of its greatest men!" [2]—for thus far it has chiefly honored the violent brood of battle, armed men springing up from the dragon's teeth sown by hate, and cared little for the truly good men, children of love, guiltless of their country's blood, whose steps on earth are noiseless as an angel's wing.

It will not be disguised that this standard differs from that of the world even in our day. The voice of man is yet given to martial praise, and the honors of victory are chanted even by the lips of woman. The mother, rocking the infant on her knee, stamps the images of war upon his tender mind, at that age more impressible than wax; she nurses his slumber with

[1] The annexation of Texas to the United States in 1845, increasing, as it did, the slave territory, was strongly opposed by the Free-Soilers, of whom Sumner was one, who favored admitting new states or territories only on condition that slavery should be excluded. Mexico strongly opposed the admission of Texas to the United States because it had been Mexican territory previous to its independence. The "Oregon Country," which both England and the United States claimed, included all Pacific coast territory between 42° and 54°40'—that is most of our Pacific Northwest and much of British Columbia. Concession on both sides resulted in the adoption in 1846 of 49° as the boundary line.

[2] Sir Henry Taylor, 1800-1886, in his drama *Philip Van Arteveld*, I, 1-5

its music, pleases his waking hours with its stories, and selects for his playthings the plume and the sword. From the child is formed the man; and who can weigh the influence of a mother's spirit on the opinions of his life? The mind which trains the child is like the hand at the end of a long lever; a gentle effort suffices to heave the enormous weight of succeeding years. As the boy advances to youth, he is fed like Achilles, not only on honey and milk only, but on bears' marrow and lions' hearts.[1] He draws the nutriment of his soul from a literature whose beautiful fields are moistened by human blood. Fain would I offer my tribute to the Father of Poetry, standing with harp of immortal melody on the misty mountain-top of distant antiquity,—to those stories of courage and sacrifice which emblazon the annals of Greece and Rome,—to the fulminations of Demosthenes and the splendors of Tully,—to the sweet verse of Virgil and the poetic prose of Livy; fain would I offer my tribute to the new literature, which shot up in modern times as a vigorous forest from the burnt side of ancient woods,—to the passionate song of the Troubadour in France and the Minnesinger in Germany,[2]—to the thrilling ballad of Spain and the delicate music of the Italian lyre: but from all these has breathed the breath of war, that has swept the heart-strings of men in all the thronging generations.

And when the youth becomes a man, his country invites his service in war, and holds before his bewildered imagination the prizes of worldly honor. For him the pen of the historian and the verse of the poet. His soul is taught to swell at the thought that he, too, is a soldier,—that his name shall be entered on the list of those who have borne arms for their country; and perhaps he dreams that he, too, may sleep, like the Great Captain of Spain,[3] with a hundred trophies over his grave. The law of the land throws its sanction over this frenzy. The contagion spreads beyond those subject to positive obligation. Peaceful citizens volunteer to appear as soldiers, and affect, in dress, arms, and deportment, what is called the "pride, pomp, and circumstance of glorious war." The ear-piercing fife has today filled our streets, and we have come to this church, on this National Sabbath, by the thump of drum and with the parade of bristling bayonets.[4]

.   .   .   .   .   .

From prejudices engendered by the Church I pass to prejudices engendered by the army itself, having their immediate origin in military life, but unfortunately diffusing themselves throughout the community, in widening, though less apparent circles. I allude directly to what is called *the Point of Honor,* early child of Chivalry, living representative of its barbarism. It is difficult to define what is so evanescent, so impalpable, so chimerical, so unreal, and yet which exercises such fiendish power over many men, and controls the intercourse of nations. As a little water, fallen into the crevice of a rock, under the congelation of winter, swells till it bursts the thick and stony fibers, so a word or slender act, dropping into the heart of man, under the hardening influence of this pernicious sentiment, dilates till it rends in pieces the sacred depository of human affection, and the demons of hate and strife are left to rage. The musing Hamlet saw this sentiment in its strange and unnatural potency, when his soul pictured to his contemplations an

> army of such mass and charge,
> Led by a delicate and tender prince, . . .
> Exposing what is mortal and unsure
> To all that fortune, death, and danger dare,
> *Even for an egg-shell;*

and when, again, giving to the sentiment its strongest and most popular expression, he exclaims,—

> Rightly to be great
> Is not to stir without great argument,
> *But greatly to find quarrel in a straw,*
> *When honor's at the stake.*[5]

And when is honor at stake? This inquiry opens again the argument with which I commenced, and with which I hope to close. Honor can be at stake only where justice and beneficence are at stake; it can never depend on egg-shell or straw; it can never depend on any hasty word of anger or folly, not even if followed by vulgar violence. True honor appears in the dignity of the human soul, in that highest moral and intellectual excellence which is the nearest approach to qualities we reverence as attributes of God. Our community frowns with indignation upon the profaneness of the duel, having its rise in this irrational *point of honor.* Are you aware that you indulge the same sentiment on a gigantic scale, when you recognize

---

[1] Tradition later than Homer, the "Father of Poetry," relates that Achilles was fed by Thetis, his mother, upon milk and honey, but by Chiron, his centaur-tutor, upon lions' hearts and bears' meat.

[2] The Troubadours and the Minnesingers were medieval lyric poets of France and Germany, respectively.

[3] Probably the Cid, the great national hero of Spanish romance; see note 1, p. 416.

[4] The vigorous explanation of what war is and of the obstacles to peace, which follows, is too long to include.

[5] *Hamlet,* IV, iv, 47-55.

this very point of honor as a proper apology for war? We have already seen that justice is in no respect promoted by war. Is true honor promoted where justice is not?

The very word honor, as used by the world, fails to express any elevated sentiment. How immeasurably below the sentiment of duty! It is a word of easy virtue, that has been prostituted to the most opposite characters and transactions. From the field of Pavia, [1] where France suffered one of the worst reverses in her annals, the defeated king writes to his mother, "All is lost, except honor." At a later day, the renowned French cook, Vatel, [2] in a paroxysm of grief and mortification at the failure of two dishes for the table, exclaims, "I have lost my *honor!*" and stabs himself to the heart. Montesquieu, [3] whose writings are constellations of epigrams, calls honor a prejudice only, which he places in direct contrast with virtue,—the former being the animating principle of monarchy, and the latter the animating principle of a republic; but he reveals the inferiority of honor, as a principle, when he adds, that, in a well-governed monarchy, almost everybody is a good citizen, while it is rare to meet a really good man. The man of honor is not the man of virtue. By an instinct pointing to the truth, we do not apply this term to the high columnar qualities which sustain and decorate life,—parental affection, justice, benevolence, the attributes of God. He would seem to borrow a feebler phrase, showing a slight appreciation of the distinctive character to whom reverence is accorded, who should speak of father, mother, judge, angel, or finally of God, as *persons of honor.* In such sacred connections, we feel, beyond the force of any argument, the mundane character of the sentiment which plays such a part in history and even in common life.

The rule of honor is founded in the imagined necessity of resenting by force a supposed injury, whether of word or act. Admit the injury received, seeming to sully the character; is it wiped away by any force, and descent to the brutal level of its author? "Could I wipe your blood from my conscience as easily as this insult from my face," said a Marshal of France, greater on this occasion than on any field of battle, "I would lay you dead at my feet." Plato, reporting the angelic wisdom of Socrates,

declares, in one of those beautiful dialogues shining with stellar light across the ages, that *to do a wrong is more shameful than to receive a wrong.* And this benign sentiment commends itself alike to the Christian, who is bid to render good for evil, and to the enlightened soul of man. But who confessing its truth will resort to force on any point of *honor?*

. . . .

And now, if it be asked, why, in considering the TRUE GRANDEUR OF NATIONS, I dwell thus singly and exclusively on war, it is because war is utterly and irreconcilably inconsistent with true greatness. Thus far, man has worshiped in military glory a phantom idol, compared with which the colossal images of ancient Babylon or modern Hindostan are but toys; and we, in this favored land of freedom, in this blessed day of light, are among the idolators. The Heaven-descended injunction, *Know thyself,* still speaks to an unheeding world from the far-off letters of gold at Delphi: [4] *Know thyself; know that the moral is the noblest part of man,* transcending far that which is the seat of passion, strife, and war,—nobler than the intellect itself. And the human heart, in its untutored, spontaneous homage to the virtues of peace, declares the same truth,—admonishing the military idolator that it is not the bloody combats, even of bravest chiefs, even of gods themselves, as they echo from the resounding lines of the great poet of war, which receive the warmest admiration, but those two scenes where are painted the gentle, unwarlike affections of our nature, the parting of Hector from Andromache, and the supplication of Priam. In the definitive election of these peaceful pictures, the soul of man, inspired by a better wisdom than that of books, and drawn unconsciously by the heavenly attraction of what is truly great, acknowledges, in touching instances, the vanity of military glory. The beatitudes of Christ, which shrink from saying, "Blessed are the war-makers," inculcate the same lesson. Reason affirms and repeats what the heart has prompted and Christianity proclaimed. Suppose war decided by *force,* where is the glory? Suppose it decided by *chance,* where is the glory? Surely, in other ways true greatness lies. Nor is it difficult to tell where.

True greatness consists in imitating, as nearly as possible for finite man, the perfections of an infinite Creator,—above all, in cultivating those highest perfections, justice and love:

---

[1] The French under Francis I were defeated at Pavia, in 1525, by the armies of Emperor Charles V.
[2] steward of the Prince of Condé, a seventeenth century French nobleman
[3] The French philosophical historian; see *L'Esprit des Lois,* iii, 3-8.

[4] In the vestibule of the temple at Delphi were written in golden letters sayings of the mythical Seven Wise Men of Greece.

justice, which, like that of St. Louis, does not swerve to the right hand or to the left; love, which, like that of William Penn, regards all mankind as of kin. "God is angry," says Plato, "when any one censures a man like Himself, *or praises a man of an opposite character: and the godlike man is the good man*." Again, in another of those lovely dialogues precious with immortal truth: "Nothing resembles God more than that man among us who has attained to the highest degree of justice." The true greatness of nations is in those qualities which constitute the true greatness of the individual. It is not in extent of territory, or vastness of population, or accumulation of wealth,—not in fortifications, or armies, or navies,—not in the sulphurous blaze of battle,— not in Golgothas, [1] though covered by monuments that kiss the clouds; for all these are creatures and representatives of those qualities in our nature which are unlike anything in God's nature. Nor is it in triumphs of the intellect alone,—in literature, learning, science, or art. The polished Greeks, our masters in the delights of art, and the commanding Romans, overawing the earth with their power, were little more than splendid savages. And the age of Louis the Fourteenth [2] of France, spanning so long a period of ordinary worldly magnificence, thronged by marshals bending under military laurels, enlivened by the unsurpassed comedy of Moliere, dignified by the tragic genius of Corneille, illumined by the splendors of Bossuet, [3] is degraded by immoralities that cannot be mentioned without a blush, by a heartlessness in comparison with which the ice of Nova Zembla is warm, and by a succession of deeds of injustice not to be washed out by the tears of all the recording angels of Heaven.

The true greatness of a nation cannot be in triumphs of the intellect alone. Literature and art may enlarge the sphere of its influence; they may adorn it; but in their nature they are but accessories. *The true grandeur of humanity is in moral elevation, sustained, enlightened, and decorated by the intellect of man.* The surest tokens of this grandeur in a nation are that Christian beneficence which diffuses the greatest happiness among all, and that passionless, godlike justice which controls the relations of the nation to other nations, and to all the people committed to its charge.

But war crushes with bloody heel all beneficence, all happiness, all justice, all that is god-like in man,—suspending every commandment of the decalogue, setting at naught every principle of the Gospel, and silencing all law, human as well as divine, except only that impious code of its own, the *Laws of War*. If in its dismal annals there is any cheerful passage, be assured it is not inspired by a martial fury. Let it not be forgotten, let it be ever borne in mind, as you ponder this theme, that the virtues which shed their charm over its horrors are all borrowed of peace,—that they are emanations from the spirit of love, which is so strong in the heart of man that it survives the rudest assault. The flowers of gentleness, kindliness, fidelity, humanity, which flourish unregarded in the rich meadows of peace, receive unwonted admiration when we discern them in war,—like violets shedding their perfume on the perilous edge of the precipice, beyond the smiling borders of civilization. [4] God be praised for all the examples of magnanimous virtue which he has vouchsafed to mankind! God be praised, that the Roman Emperor, [5] about to start on a distant expedition of war, encompassed by squadrons of cavalry, and by golden eagles swaying in the wind, stooped from his saddle to hear the prayer of a humble widow, demanding justice for the death of her son! God be praised, that Sidney, [6] on the field of battle, gave with dying hand the cup of cold water to the dying soldier! That single act of self-forgetful sacrifice has consecrated the deadly field of Zutphen, far, oh, far beyond its battle; it has consecrated thy name, gallant Sidney, beyond any feat of thy sword, beyond any triumph of thy pen! But there are lowly supplicants in other places than the camp; there are hands outstretched elsewhere than on fields of blood. Everywhere is opportunity for deeds of like charity. Know well that these are not the product of war. They do not spring from enmity, hatred, and strife, but from those benign sentiments whose natural and ripened fruit of joy and blessing are found only in peace. If at any time they appear in the soldier, it is less *because* than *notwithstanding* he is the hireling of battle. Let me not be told, then, of the virtues of war. Let not the acts of generosity and sacrifice sometimes blossoming on its fields be invoked in its defense. From such a giant root of bitterness no true good can spring. The poisonous tree, [7] in Oriental

---

[1] Golgotha was the place of the crucifixion.
[2] The material wealth, extravagance, and luxury of his reign, 1643-1715, was equaled only by its selfishness, absolutism, and tyranny.
[3] a prelate and orator
[4] Note the ornateness of the oratory of Sumner's time as compared with that of the present.
[5] Trajan, whose kind deed Dante has made immortal in his *Purgatorio*, x, 76
[6] Sir Philip Sidney, 1554-1586, was mortally wounded on the battlefield of Zutphen in the Netherlands.
[7] possibly the upas tree, concerning which many fabulous tales have been told

imagery, though watered by nectar and covered with roses, produces only the fruit of death.

Casting our eyes over the history of nations, with horror we discern the succession of murderous slaughters by which their progress is marked. Even as the hunter follows the wild beast to his lair by the drops of blood on the ground, so we follow man, faint, weary, staggering with wounds, through the Black Forest of the past, which he has reddened with his gore. Oh, let it not be in the future ages as in those we now contemplate! Let the grandeur of man be discerned, not in bloody victory or ravenous conquest, but in the blessings he has secured, in the good he has accomplished, in the triumphs of justice and beneficence, in the establishment of perpetual peace!

As ocean washes every shore, and with all-embracing arms clasps every land, while on its heaving bosom it bears the products of various climes, so peace surrounds, protects, and upholds all other blessings. Without it, commerce is vain, the order of industry is restrained, justice is arrested, happiness is blasted, virtue sickens and dies.

. . . .

Far be from us, fellow citizens, on this festival, the pride of national victory, and the illusion of national freedom, in which we are too prone to indulge! None of you make rude boast of individual prosperity or prowess. And here I end as I began. Our country cannot do what an individual cannot do. Therefore it must not vaunt or be puffed up. Rather bend to unperformed duties. Independence is not all. We have but half done, when we have made ourselves free. The scornful taunt wrung from bitter experience of the great Revolution in France must not be leveled at us: "They wish to be *free,* but know not how to be *just.*"[1] Nor is priceless freedom an end in itself, but rather the means of justice and beneficence, where alone is enduring concord, with that attendant happiness which is the final end and aim of nations, as of every human heart. It is not enough to be free. There must be peace which cannot fail, and other nations must share the great possession. For this good must we labor, bearing ever in mind two special objects, complements of each other: first, the arbitrament of war must end; and, secondly, disarmament must begin. With this ending and this beginning the great gates of the future will be opened, and the guardian virtues will assert a new empire. Alas! until this is done, national

honor and national glory will yet longer flaunt in blood, and there can be no true grandeur of nations.

To this great work let me summon you. That future, which filled the lofty visions of sages and bards in Greece and Rome, which was foretold by prophets and heralded by evangelists, when man, in happy isles or in a new paradise, shall confess the loveliness of peace, may you secure, if not for yourselves, at least for your children! *Believe* that you can do it, and you *can* do it. The true golden age is before, not behind. If man has once been driven from paradise, while an angel with flaming sword forbade his return, there is another paradise, even on earth, which he may make for himself, by the cultivation of knowledge, religion, and the kindly virtues of life, where the confusion of tongues shall be dissolved in the union of hearts, and joyous nature, borrowing prolific charms from prevailing harmony, shall spread her lap with unimagined bounty, and there shall be perpetual jocund Spring, and sweet strains borne on "the odoriferous wing of gentle gales," through valleys of delight, more pleasant than the Vale of Tempe, [2] richer than the garden of the Hesperides, with no dragon to guard its golden fruit.

It is said that the age does not demand this work. The robber conqueror of the past, from fiery sepulcher demands it; the precious blood of millions unjustly shed in war, crying from the ground, demands it; the heart of the good man demands it, the conscience, even of the soldier, whispers, "Peace." There are considerations, springing from our situation and condition, which fervently invite us to take the lead. Here should join the patriotic ardor of the land, the ambition of the statesman, the effort of the scholar, the pervasive influence of the press, the mild persuasion of the sanctuary, the early teaching of the school. Here, in ampler ether and diviner air, are untried fields for exalted triumph, more truly worthy the American name than any snatched from rivers of blood. War is known as the *last reason of kings.* Let it be no reason of our Republic. Let us renounce and throw off forever the yoke of tyranny most oppressive of all in the world's annals. As those standing on the mountain-top first discern the coming beams of morning, so may we from the vantage-ground of liberal institutions, first recognize the ascending sun of a new era! Lift high the gates, and let the King of Glory in,—the King of true Glory,—of Peace! I catch the last words of music from the lips of innocence and beauty:—

[1] a saying of Abbé Sieyès, a French statesman, 1748-1836

[2] a valley in Greece famed for its beauty

"And let the whole earth be filled with His glory!"

It is a beautiful picture in Grecian story, that there was at least one spot, the small island of Delos, dedicated to the gods, and kept at all times sacred from war. No hostile foot ever pressed this kindly soil, and citizens of all countries met here, in common worship, beneath the aegis of inviolable peace. So let us dedicate our beloved country; and may the blessed consecration be felt, in all its parts, everywhere throughout its ample domain! The Temple of Honor shall be enclosed by the Temple of Concord, that it may never more be entered through any portal of war; the horn of abundance shall overflow at its gates; the angel of religion shall be the guide over its steps of flashing adamant; while within its happy courts, purged of violence and wrong, JUSTICE, returned to the earth from long exile in the skies, with equal scales for nations as for men, shall rear her serene and majestic front; and by her side, greatest of all, CHARITY, sublime in meekness, hoping all and enduring all, shall divinely temper every righteous decree, and with words of infinite cheer inspire to those deeds that cannot vanish away. And the future chief of the Republic, destined to uphold the glories of a new era, unspotted by human blood, shall be first in peace, first in the hearts of his countrymen.

While seeking these fruitful glories for ourselves, let us strive for their extension to other lands. Let the bugles sound the *Truce of God* [1] to the whole world forever. Not to one people, but to every people, let the glad tidings go. The selfish boast of the Spartan women, that they never saw the smoke of an enemy's camp, must become the universal chorus of mankind, while the iron belt of war, now encompassing the globe, is exchanged for the golden cestus of peace, clothing all with celestial beauty. History dwells with fondness on the reverent homage bestowed by massacring soldiers, upon the spot occupied by the sepulcher of the Lord; vain man! Why confine regard to a few feet of sacred mold? The whole earth is the sepulcher of the Lord; nor can any righteous man profane any part thereof. Confessing this truth let us now, on this Sabbath of the Nation, lay a new and living stone in the grand Temple of Universal Peace, whose dome shall be lofty as the firmament of heaven, broad and comprehensive as earth itself.

1845   1845

[1] a suspension of private feuds from Thursday evening to Monday morning for the celebration of church festivals, common in the 11th and 12th centuries

ABRAHAM LINCOLN 1809-1865

Lincoln's immediate ancestors were frontiersmen in straightened circumstances, woodsmen, farmers. Removing with his father from Hardin County, Kentucky, where he was born, to Indiana and then to Illinois, he obtained in the aggregate perhaps a year's schooling, helped clear a pioneer farm, was flat-boat hand on the Mississippi, soldier in the Black Hawk War, postmaster, surveyor, member of the legislature, lawyer, and at length member of Congress in 1846. In 1858, as Republican candidate for the United States Senate from Illinois, he met his opponent, Douglas, in a series of debates that made him more than locally known. In 1860 and 1864 he was elected President of the United States. He was assassinated April 14, 1865, a few days after the downfall of the Confederacy.

In the present generation Lincoln has become almost a cult. His leadership in the greatest crisis of the nation's history and the circumstances of his tragic death make it still difficult to see the man in true perspective. Nevertheless, it is easy to feel in his best speeches and writings the evidence of a great spirit, great in emotion, and masterful in expression. Upon the English Bible and other masterpieces of English literature he formed a style of such directness, simplicity, terseness, and strength as is granted only to genius. It is not through the anecdotes and biographies of such a man that we can get the truest measure of his character and his greatness, but through his own words; these are the man himself.

Biography and criticism: (Articles and books upon Lincoln are so numerous that only a few, mostly recent, are noted.) J. T. Morse, *Abraham Lincoln* (AS), 2 vols. 1893; F. F. Browne, *The Every-day Life of Abraham Lincoln*, 1913; Lord Charnwood, *Abraham Lincoln*, 1916; J. G. Nicolay and John Hay, *Abraham Lincoln, a History*, 10 vols. 1890; Ida Tarbell, *Life of Abraham Lincoln*, 2 vols. 1900; Brand Whitlock, *Abraham Lincoln*, (BB) 1916; same, Carl Sandburg, 2 vols. 1926; A. J. Beveridge, *Abraham Lincoln, 1809-1858*, 2 vols. 1928. See also John Drinkwater, *Abraham Lincoln* (play), 1919; Mary R. S. Andrews, *The Perfect Tribute*, 1906; same, *Scrib. M.* 40:17-24.

FAREWELL ADDRESS AT SPRINGFIELD, ILLINOIS [2]

My Friends: No one, not in my situation, can appreciate my feeling of sadness at this parting. To this place, and the kindness of these people, I owe everything. Here I have lived a quarter of a century, and have passed from a young to an old man. Here my children have been born, and one is buried. I now leave, not knowing when or whether ever I may return, with a task before me greater than that which rested upon Washington. Without the

[2] delivered Feb. 11, 1861, on Lincoln's departure from Springfield to assume the Presidency

assistance of that Divine Being who ever attended him, I cannot succeed. With that assistance, I cannot fail. Trusting in Him who can go with me, and remain with you, and be everywhere for good, let us confidently hope that all will yet be well. To His care commending you, as I hope in your prayers you will commend me, I bid you an affectionate farewell.

1861   1861

ADDRESS IN INDEPENDENCE HALL, PHILADELPHIA [1]

Mr. Cuyler: I am filled with deep emotion at finding myself standing in this place, where were collected together the wisdom, the patriotism, the devotion to principle, from which sprang the institutions under which we live. You have kindly suggested to me that in my hands is the task of restoring peace to our distracted country. I can say in return, sir, that all the political sentiments I entertain have been drawn, so far as I have been able to draw them, from the sentiments which originated in and were given to the world from this hall. I have never had a feeling, politically, that did not spring from the sentiments embodied in the Declaration of Independence. I have often pondered over the dangers which were incurred by the men who assembled here and framed and adopted that Declaration. I have pondered over the toils that were endured by the officers and soldiers of the army who achieved that independence. I have often inquired of myself what great principle or idea it was that kept this Confederacy so long together. It was not the mere matter of separation of the colonies from the motherland, but that sentiment in the Declaration of Independence which gave liberty not alone to the people of this country, but hope to all the world, for all future time. It was that which gave promise that in due time the weights would be lifted from the shoulders of all men, and that all should have an equal chance. This is the sentiment embodied in the Declaration of Independence. Now, my friends, can this country be saved on that basis? If it can, I will consider myself one of the happiest men in the world if I can help to save it. If it cannot be saved upon that principle, it will be truly awful. But if this country cannot be saved without giving

up that principle, I was about to say I would rather be assassinated on this spot than surrender it. Now, in my view of the present aspect of affairs, there is no need of bloodshed and war. There is no necessity for it. I am not in favor of such a course; and I may say in advance that there will be no bloodshed unless it is forced upon the government. The government will not use force, unless force is used against it.

My friends, this is wholly an unprepared speech. I did not expect to be called on to say a word when I came here. I supposed I was merely to do something toward raising a flag. I may, therefore, have said something indiscreet. But I have said nothing but what I am willing to live by, and, if it be the pleasure of Almighty God, to die by.

1861   1861

THE GETTYSBURG ADDRESS [2]

Four score and seven years ago our fathers brought forth on this continent a new nation, conceived in liberty, and dedicated to the proposition that all men are created equal.

Now we are engaged in a great civil war, testing whether that nation, or any nation so conceived and so dedicated, can long endure. We are met on a great battlefield of that war. We have come to dedicate a portion of that field as a final resting-place for those who here gave their lives that that nation might live. It is altogether fitting and proper that we should do this.

But in a larger sense we cannot dedicate, we cannot consecrate, we cannot hallow this ground. The brave men, living and dead, who struggled here have consecrated it, far above our poor power to add or detract. The world will little note, nor long remember what we say here, but it can never forget what they did here. It is for us, the living, rather, to be dedicated here to the unfinished work which they who fought here have thus far so nobly advanced. It is rather for us to be here dedicated to the great task remaining before us,— that from these honored dead we take increased devotion to that cause for which they gave the last full measure of devotion; that we here highly resolve that these dead shall not have

[1] Delivered Feb. 22, 1861; Theodore Cuyler, who presided at the meeting, was a prominent lawyer of Philadelphia and a War-Democrat; that is, a Democrat who believed that the Union should be maintained even at the cost of war. He therefore favored Lincoln's Republican administration.

[2] Delivered November 19, 1863, at the dedication of the National Cemetery at Gettysburg; the battle of Gettysburg, July 1-3, 1863, one of the bloodiest in American history, is generally conceded to have been the turning point in the Civil War. This speech has passed into the permanent literature of the English tongue, while the long, formal address which preceded it, delivered by Edward Everett, the orator of the occasion, is forgotten.

died in vain; that this nation, under God, shall have a new birth of freedom; and that government of the people, by the people, and for the people, shall not perish from the earth.

1863   1863

LETTER TO MRS. BIXBY

Executive Mansion, Washington,
November 21, 1864.

Mrs. Bixby, Boston, Massachusetts.

Dear Madam: I have been shown in the files of the War Department a statement of the Adjutant-General of Massachusetts that you are the mother of five sons who have died gloriously on the field of battle. I feel how weak and fruitless must be any words of mine which should attempt to beguile you from the grief of a loss so overwhelming. But I cannot refrain from tendering to you the consolation that may be found in the thanks of the Republic they died to save. I pray that our heavenly Father may assuage the anguish of your bereavement, and leave you only the cherished memory of the loved and lost, and the solemn pride that must be yours to have laid so costly a sacrifice upon the altar of freedom.

Yours very sincerely and respectfully,
ABRAHAM LINCOLN.

THE SECOND INAUGURAL ADDRESS [1]

Fellow-countrymen: At this second appearing to take the oath of the presidential office, there is less occasion for an extended address than there was at the first. Then a statement, somewhat in detail, of a course to be pursued, seemed fitting and proper. Now, at the expiration of four years, during which public declarations have been constantly called forth on every point and phase of the great contest which still absorbs the attention and engrosses the energies of the nation, little that is new could be presented. The progress of our arms, upon which all else chiefly depends, is as well known to the public as to myself; and it is, I trust, reasonably satisfactory and encouraging to all. With high hope for the future, no prediction in regard to it is ventured.

On the occasion corresponding to this four years ago, all thoughts were anxiously directed to an impending civil war. All dreaded it—all sought to avert it. While the inaugural address was being delivered from this place, devoted altogether to saving the Union without war, insurgent agents were in the city seeking to destroy it without war—seeking to dissolve the Union, and divide effects, by negotiation. Both parties deprecated war; but one of them would make war rather than let the nation survive; and the other would accept war rather than let it perish. And the war came.

One eighth of the whole population were colored slaves, not distributed generally over the Union, but localized in the southern part of it. These slaves constituted a peculiar and powerful interest. All knew that this interest was, somehow, the cause of the war. To strengthen, perpetuate, and extend this interest was the object for which the insurgents would rend the Union, even by war; while the government claimed no right to do more than to restrict the territorial enlargement of it.

Neither party expected for the war the magnitude or the duration which it has already attained. Neither anticipated that the cause of the conflict might cease with, or even before, the conflict itself should cease. Each looked for an easier triumph and a result less fundamental and astounding. Both read the same Bible, and pray to the same God; and each invokes his aid against the other. It may seem strange that any men should dare to ask a just God's assistance in wringing their bread from the sweat of other men's faces; but let us judge not, that we be not judged. The prayers of both could not be answered—that of neither has been answered fully.

The Almighty has his own purposes. "Woe unto the world because of offenses! for it must needs be that offenses come; but woe to that man by whom the offense cometh." [2] If we shall suppose that American slavery is one of those offenses which in the providence of God, must needs come, but which, having continued through his appointed time, he now wills to remove, and that he gives to both North and South this terrible war, as the woe due to those by whom the offense came, shall we discern therein any departure from those divine attributes which the believers in a living God always ascribe to him? Fondly do we hope—fervently do we pray—that this mighty scourge of war may speedily pass away. Yet, if God wills that it continue until all the wealth piled by the bondman's two hundred and fifty years of unrequited toil shall be sunk, and until every drop of blood drawn with the lash shall be paid by another drawn with the sword, as was said three thousand years ago, so still it must be said, "The judgments of the Lord are true and righteous altogether." [3]

[1] delivered March 4, 1865

[2] *Matthew* xviii, 7   [3] *Psalms* xix, 9

With malice toward none; with charity for all; with firmness in the right, as God gives us to see the right, let us strive on to finish the work we are in; to bind up the nation's wounds; to care for him who shall have borne the battle, and for his widow and his orphan—to do all which may achieve and cherish a just and lasting peace among ourselves, and with all nations.
1865   1865

JOHN GREENLEAF WHITTIER
1807–1892

Of the "six great American poets" of the nineteenth century Whittier sprang most closely from the soil. He was born at Haverhill, Massachusetts, of Quaker parents in the humblest circumstances. He lived the life of a typical farm boy; he attended the country schools and an academy; he worked at various trades and taught school. His life before the Civil War was that of an active anti-slavery reformer, and he suffered personal violence for his opinions. From 1830–1836 he engaged in journalism, beginning with the *Haverhill Gazette,* and ending with the *Pennsylvania Freeman;* and he continued until the Civil War closed, an earnest contributor to reform journals. Whittier's poems and collections of poetry date from 1831 to 1892; some of his best poetical work was done toward the close of his life, and no American poet save Bryant has had so long a career of productive literary activity. The collected and revised edition of his works in verse and prose occupies seven volumes.

Whittier's poems fall into two general divisions, those relating to the anti-slavery cause, and those relating to New England. Those of the first division, controversial and of temporary interest, do not now concern us. Those relating to the history and legends of his region, and especially those descriptive of the life and spirit of the New England of Whittier's day—now gone forever—are of great interest. The style may be in places diffuse, and there may be faults in versification and diction; but the picture of the simple, unified life of the New England home with its labor, self-sacrifice, and piety, its devotion to truth and honor, its intellectual and spiritual ambition, is final; for the life that produced it will never return. It is the humble but deep-rooted flower of Puritanism—less brilliant and less imaginative than Hawthorne's —photographic in its realism.

Biography and criticism: G. R. Carpenter, (AML) 1903; T. W. Higginson, (EML) 1902; R. Burton, (BB) 1901; W. J. Linton, (GW) 1893; Macy; Chubb; More (Shel. 3); B. Perry, "Whittier for Today," *Atlan.* 100:851-9; E. C. Stedman, "Whittier," *Cent.* 30:38-50; G. E. Woodberry, "John Greenleaf Whittier," *Atlan.* 70:642-8; L. Abbott, "John Greenleaf Whittier, Mystic," *Outlook,* 127:96-8; N. Foerster, "Nature in Whittier," *Nation* 104:15-17.

MEMORIES [1]

A beautiful and happy girl,
  With step as light as summer air,
Eyes glad with smiles, and brow of pearl,
Shadowed by many a careless curl
  Of unconfined and flowing hair;
A seeming child in everything,
  Save thoughtful brow and ripening charms,
As Nature wears the smile of Spring
  When sinking into Summer's arms.

A mind rejoicing in the light   10
  Which melted through its graceful bower,
Leaf after leaf, dew-moist and bright,
And stainless in its holy white,
  Unfolding like a morning flower:
A heart, which, like a fine-toned lute,
  With every breath of feeling woke,
And, even when the tongue was mute,
  From eye and lip in music spoke.

How thrills once more the lengthening chain
  Of memory, at the thought of thee!   20
Old hopes which long in dust have lain,
Old dreams, come thronging back again,
  And boyhood lives again in me;
I feel its glow upon my cheek,
  Its fulness of the heart is mine,
As when I leaned to hear thee speak,
  Or raised my doubtful eye to thine.

I hear again thy low replies,
  I feel thy arm within my own,
And timidly again uprise   30
The fringed lids of hazel eyes,
  With soft brown tresses overblown.
Ah! memories of sweet summer eves,
  Of moonlit wave and willowy way,
Of stars and flowers, and dewy leaves,
  And smiles and tones more dear than they!

Ere this, thy quiet eye hath smiled
  My picture of thy youth to see,
When, half a woman, half a child,
Thy very artlessness beguiled,   40
  And folly's self seemed wise in thee;
I too can smile, when o'er that hour
  The lights of memory backward stream,
Yet feel the while that manhood's power
  Is vainer than my boyhood's dream.

Years have passed on, and left their trace
  Of graver care and deeper thought;

[1] This poem, as well as "My Playmate" and others, was doubtless founded upon the memories and affections of Whittier's youth.

And unto me the calm, cold face
Of manhood, and to thee the grace
    Of woman's pensive beauty brought.   50
More wide, perchance, for blame than praise,
    The schoolboy's humble name has flown;
Thine, in the green and quiet ways
    Of unobtrusive goodness known.

And wider yet in thought and deed
    Diverge our pathways, one in youth;
Thine the Genevan's [1] sternest creed,
While answers to my spirit's need
    The Derby dalesman's [2] simple truth.
For thee, the priestly rite and prayer,   60
    And holy day, and solemn psalm;
For me, the silent reverence where
    My brethren gather, slow and calm.

Yet hath thy spirit left on me
    An impress Time has worn not out,
And something of myself in thee,
A shadow from the past, I see,
    Lingering, even yet, thy way about;
Not wholly can the heart unlearn
    That lesson of its better hours,   70
Nor yet has Time's dull footstep worn
    To common dust that path of flowers.

Thus, while at times before our eyes
    The shadows melt, and fall apart,
And, smiling through them, round us lies
    The warm light of our morning skies,—
    The Indian Summer of the heart!—
In secret sympathies of mind,
    In founts of feeling which retain
Their pure, fresh flow, we yet may find   80
    Our early dreams not wholly vain!
1841   1850

PROEM [3]

I love the old melodious lays
Which softly melt the ages through,
    The songs of Spenser's golden days,
    Arcadian Sidney's [4] silvery phrase,
Sprinkling our noon of time with freshest morn-
    ing dew.

    Yet, vainly in my quiet hours
To breathe their marvelous notes I try;
    I feel them, as the leaves and flowers

[1] John Calvin, 1509-1564, a prominent theologian of the
    Protestant Reformation, lived in Geneva, Switzer-
    land.
[2] The implication is wrong. George Fox, the founder
    of the Society of Friends, came from Leicester-
    shire, though some of his hardest experiences as
    an evangelist took place in Derbyshire.
[3] written to introduce the first general collection of
    Whittier's poems
[4] The reference is to Sir Philip Sidney's *Arcadia*
    (1590).

In silence feel the dewy showers,
And drink with glad, still lips the blessing of
    the sky.   10

    The rigor of a frozen clime,
The harshness of an untaught ear,
    The jarring words of one whose rime
    Beat often Labor's hurried time,
Or Duty's rugged march through storm and
    strife, are here.

    Of mystic beauty, dreamy grace,
No rounded art the lack supplies;
    Unskilled the subtle lines to trace,
    Or softer shades of Nature's face,
I view her common forms with unanointed
    eyes.   20

    Nor mine the seer-like power to show
The secrets of the heart and mind;
    To drop the plummet-line below
    Our common world of joy and woe,
A more intense despair or brighter hope to find.

    Yet here at least an earnest sense
Of human right and weal is shown;
    A hate of tyranny intense,
    And hearty in its vehemence,
As if my brother's pain and sorrow were my
    own.   30

    O Freedom! if to me belong
Nor mighty Milton's gift divine,
    Nor Marvell's [5] wit and graceful song,
    Still with a love as deep and strong
As theirs, I lay like them, my best gifts on thy
    shrine!
1847   1849

BARCLAY OF URY [6]

Up the streets of Aberdeen,
By the kirk and college green,
    Rode the Laird of Ury;
Close behind him, close beside,
Foul of mouth and evil-eyed,
    Pressed the mob in fury.

Flouted him the drunken churl,
Jeered at him the serving-girl,
    Prompt to please her master;
And the begging carlin, late   10
Fed and clothed at Ury's gate,
    Cursed him as he passed her.

[5] Andrew Marvell, 1621-1678, a satirical and lyric
    Puritan poet
[6] Barclay, a distinguished Scotch soldier, was one of
    the earliest converts to Quakerism in Scotland.

Yet, with calm and stately mien,
Up the streets of Aberdeen
   Came he slowly riding;
And, to all he saw and heard,
Answering not with bitter word,
   Turning not for chiding.

Came a troop with broadswords swinging,
Bits and bridles sharply ringing,   20
   Loose and free and froward;
Quoth the foremost, "Ride him down!
Push him! prick him! through the town
   Drive the Quaker coward!"

But from out the thickening crowd
Cried a sudden voice and loud:
   "Barclay! Ho! a Barclay!"
And the old man at his side
Saw a comrade, battle tried,
   Scarred and sunburned darkly;   30

Who with ready weapon bare,
Fronting to the troopers there,
   Cried aloud: "God save us,
Call ye coward him who stood
Ankle deep in Lützen's [1] blood,
   With the brave Gustavus?"

"Nay, I do not need thy sword,
Comrade mine," said Ury's lord;
   "Put it up, I pray thee:
Passive to his holy will,   40
Trust I in my Master's still,
   Even though he slay me.

"Pledges of thy love and faith,
Proved on many a field of death,
   Not by me are needed."
Marveled much that henchman bold,
That his laird, so stout of old,
   Now so meekly pleaded.

"Woe's the day!" he sadly said,
With a slowly shaking head,   50
   And a look of pity;
"Ury's honest lord reviled,
Mock of knave and sport of child,
   In his own good city!

"Speak the word, and, master mine,
As we charged on Tilly's [2] line,
   And his Walloon lancers,

---

[1] During the Thirty Years' War, Gustavus Adolphus,
king of Sweden, gained a victory in 1632 at
Lützen, Prussia, over Wallenstein, the great general of Ferdinand II, emperor of Austria.
[2] Tilly, a Belgian, another of Ferdinand's great generals, had in his army many Walloons—Celtic
people of southern Belgium.

Smiting through their midst we'll teach
Civil look and decent speech
   To these boyish prancers!"   60

"Marvel not, mine ancient friend,
Like beginning, like the end,"
   Quoth the Laird of Ury;
"Is the sinful servant more
Than his gracious Lord who bore
   Bonds and stripes in Jewry?

"Give me joy that in his name
I can bear, with patient frame,
   All these vain ones offer;
While for them he suffereth long,   70
Shall I answer wrong with wrong,
   Scoffing with the scoffer?

"Happier I, with loss of all,
Hunted, outlawed, held in thrall,
   With few friends to greet me,
Than when reeve [3] and squire were seen,
Riding out from Aberdeen,
   With bared heads to meet me.

"When each goodwife, o'er and o'er,
Blessed me as I passed her door;   80
   And the snooded daughter,
Through her casement glancing down,
Smiled on him who bore renown
   From red fields of slaughter.

"Hard to feel the stranger's scoff,
Hard the old friend's falling off,
   Hard to learn forgiving;
But the Lord his own rewards,
And his love with theirs accords,
   Warm and fresh and living.   90

"Through this dark and stormy night
Faith beholds a feeble light
   Up the blackness streaking;
Knowing God's own time is best,
In a patient hope I rest
   For the full day-breaking!"

So the Laird of Ury said,
Turning slow his horse's head
   Towards the Tolbooth [4] prison,
Where, through iron grates, he heard   100
Poor disciples of the Word
   Preach of Christ arisen!

Not in vain, Confessor old,
Unto us the tale is told

---

[3] an officer of justice
[4] a prison or jail, particularly the prison at Edinburgh

Of thy day of trial;
Every age on him who strays
From its broad and beaten ways
    Pours its sevenfold vial.

Happy he whose inward ear
Angel comfortings can hear,   110
    O'er the rabble's laughter;
And, while Hatred's fagots burn,
Glimpses through the smoke discern
    Of the good hereafter.

Knowing this, that never yet
Share of Truth was vainly set
    In the world's wide fallow;
After hands shall sow the seed,
After hands from hill and mead
    Reap the harvests yellow.   120

Thus, with somewhat of the Seer,
Must the moral pioneer
    From the Future borrow;
Clothe the waste with dreams of grain,
And, on midnight's sky of rain,
    Paint the golden morrow!
1847

THE ANGELS OF BUENA VISTA [1]

Speak and tell us, our Ximena, [2] looking north-
    ward far away,
O'er the camp of the invaders, o'er the Mexican
    array,
Who is losing? who is winning? are they far or
    come they near?
Look abroad, and tell us, sister, whither rolls
    the storm we hear.

"Down the hills of Angostura [3] still the storm
    of battle rolls;
Blood is flowing, men are dying; God have
    mercy on their souls!"
Who is losing? who is winning?—"Over hill
    and over plain,
I see but smoke of cannon clouding through
    the mountain rain."

Holy Mother! keep our brothers! Look,
    Ximena, look once more.
"Still I see the fearful whirlwind rolling darkly
    as before,   10
Bearing on, in strange confusion, friend and
    foeman, foot and horse,

[1] At the battle of Buena Vista, in 1847, during the
    Mexican War, Mexican women aided the wounded
    of both armies.
[2] pronounced Hē-māy'-nä
[3] a range of mountains near Buena Vista

Like some wild and troubled torrent sweeping
    down its mountain course."

Look forth once more, Ximena! "Ah! the
    smoke has rolled away;
And I see the Northern rifles gleaming down
    the ranks of gray.
Hark! that sudden blast of bugles! there the
    troop of Miñon [4] wheels;
There the Northern horses thunder, with the
    cannon at their heels.

"Jesu, pity! how it thickens! now retreat and
    now advance!
Right against the blazing cannon shivers
    Puebla's charging lance!
Down they go, the brave young riders; horse
    and foot together fall;
Like a plowshare in the fallow through them
    plows the Northern ball."   20

Nearer came the storm and nearer, rolling fast
    and frightful on;
Speak, Ximena, speak and tell us, who has
    lost, and who has won?
"Alas! alas! I know not; friend and foe to-
    gether fall,
O'er the dying rush the living: pray, my sis-
    ters, for them all!

"Lo! the wind the smoke is lifting: Blessed
    Mother, save my brain!
I can see the wounded crawling slowly out
    from heaps of slain.
Now they stagger, blind and bleeding; now
    they fall, and strive to rise;
Hasten, sisters, haste and save them, lest they
    die before our eyes!

"O my heart's love! O my dear one! lay thy
    poor head on my knee:
Dost thou know the lips that kiss thee? Canst
    thou hear me? canst thou see?   30
O my husband, brave and gentle! O my Ber-
    nal, look once more
On the blessed cross before thee! Mercy!
    mercy! all is o'er!"

Dry thy tears, my poor Ximena; lay thy dear
    one down to rest;
Let his hands be meekly folded, lay the cross
    upon his breast;
Let his dirge be sung hereafter, and his funeral
    masses said:
Today, thou poor bereaved one, the living ask
    thy aid.

[4] Miñon was a Mexican general under Santa Anna.

Close beside her, faintly moaning, fair and
    young, a soldier lay,
Torn with shot and pierced with lances, bleed-
    ing slow his life away;
But, as tenderly before him, the lorn Ximena
    knelt,
She saw the Northern eagle shining on his
    pistol-belt.   40

With a stifled cry of horror straight she turned
    away her head;
With a sad and bitter feeling looked she back
    upon her dead;
But she heard the youth's low moaning, and his
    struggling breath of pain,
And she raised the cooling water to his parch-
    ing lips again.

Whispered low the dying soldier, pressed her
    hand and faintly smiled:
Was that pitying face his mother's? did she
    watch beside her child?
All his stranger words with meaning her wom-
    an's heart supplied;
With her kiss upon his forehead, "Mother!"
    murmured he, and died!

"A bitter curse upon them, poor boy, who
    led thee forth,
From some gentle, sad-eyed mother, weeping,
    lonely, in the North!"   50
Spake the mournful Mexic woman, as she laid
    him with her dead,
And turned to soothe the living, and bind the
    wounds which bled.

Look forth once more, Ximena! "Like a cloud
    before the wind
Rolls the battle down the mountains, leaving
    blood and death behind;
Ah! they plead in vain for mercy; in the dust
    the wounded strive;
Hide your faces, holy angels! oh thou Christ
    of God, forgive!"

Sink, O Night, among thy mountains! let the
    cool, gray shadows fall;
Dying brothers, fighting demons, drop thy cur-
    tain over all!
Through the thickening winter twilight, wide
    apart the battle rolled,
In its sheath the saber rested, and the cannon's
    lips grew cold.   60

But the noble Mexic women still their holy
    task pursued,

Through that long, dark night of sorrow, worn
    and faint and lacking food;
Over weak and suffering brothers, with a tender
    care they hung,
And the dying foeman blessed them in a strange
    and Northern tongue.

Not wholly lost, O Father! is this evil world
    of ours;
Upward, through its blood and ashes, spring
    afresh the Eden flowers;
From its smoking hell of battle, Love and Pity
    send their prayer,
And still thy white-winged angels hover dimly
    in our air!
1847

THE POOR VOTER ON ELECTION DAY

The proudest now is but my peer,
    The highest not more high;
Today, of all the weary year,
    A king of men am I.
Today, alike are great and small,
    The nameless and the known;
My palace is the people's hall,
    The ballot-box my throne!

Who serves today upon the list
    Beside the served shall stand;   10
Alike the brown and wrinkled fist,
    The gloved and dainty hand!
The rich is level with the poor,
    The weak is strong today;
And sleekest broadcloth counts no more
    Than homespun frock of gray.

Today let pomp and vain pretence
    My stubborn right abide;
I set a plain man's common sense
    Against the pedant's pride.   20
Today shall simple manhood try
    The strength of gold and land;
The wide world has not wealth to buy
    The power in my right hand!

While there's a grief to seek redress,
    Or balance to adjust,
Where weighs our living manhood less
    Than Mammon's vilest dust,—
While there's a right to need my vote,
    A wrong to sweep away,   30
Up! clouted knee and ragged coat!
    A man's a man today! [1]
1848

[1] Cf. Burns's "Is There for Honest Poverty," the sentiment of which is similar to that of this poem.

ICHABOD![1]

So fallen! so lost! the light withdrawn
    Which once he wore!
The glory from his gray hairs gone
    Forevermore!

Revile him not,—the Tempter hath
    A snare for all;
And pitying tears, not scorn and wrath,
    Befit his fall!

Oh, dumb be passion's stormy rage,
    When he who might   10
Have lighted up and led his age,
    Falls back in night.

Scorn! would the angels laugh, to mark
    A bright soul driven,
Fiend-goaded, down the endless dark,
    From hope and heaven!

Let not the land once proud of him
    Insult him now,
Nor brand with deeper shame his dim,
    Dishonored brow.   20

But let its humbled sons, instead,
    From sea to lake,
A long lament, as for the dead,
    In sadness make.

Of all we loved and honored, naught
    Save power remains,—
A fallen angel's pride of thought,
    Still strong in chains.

All else is gone; from those great eyes
    The soul has fled: 30
When faith is lost, when honor dies,
    The man is dead!

Then, pay the reverence of old days
    To his dead fame;
Walk backward, with averted gaze,
    And hide the shame!

1850

[1] Hebrew, "the glory is departed"; see *1 Samuel* iv, 21. Whittier thus characterizes Webster, whose Seventh of March Speech in 1850 had made the Abolitionists of his time feel that he had compromised his conscience in an endeavor to win the presidency. Recent historians, however, believe Webster to have been influenced solely by a desire to save the Union. The degree of tenderness, dignity, and strength shown here does not appear elsewhere in Whittier's political poetry. Cf. Browning's "The Lost Leader," written five years before.

BURNS[2]

ON RECEIVING A SPRIG OF HEATHER IN BLOSSOM

No more these simple flowers belong
    To Scottish maid and lover;
Sown in the common soil of song,
    They bloom the wide world over.

In smiles and tears, in sun and showers,
    The minstrel and the heather,
The deathless singer and the flowers
    He sang of live together.

Wild heather-bells and Robert Burns!
    The moorland flower and peasant!   10
How, at their mention, memory turns
    Her pages old and pleasant!

The gray sky wears again its gold
    And purple of adorning,
And manhood's noonday shadows hold
    The dews of boyhood's morning.

The dews that washed the dust and soil
    From off the wings of pleasure,
The sky, that flecked the ground of toil
    With golden threads of leisure.   20

I call to mind the summer day,
    The early harvest mowing,
The sky with sun and clouds at play,
    And flowers with breezes blowing.

I hear the blackbird in the corn,
    The locust in the haying;
And, like the fabled hunter's horn,
    Old tunes my heart is playing.

How oft that day, with fond delay,
    I sought the maple's shadow,   30
And sang with Burns the hours away,
    Forgetful of the meadow!

Bees hummed, birds twittered, overhead
    I heard the squirrels leaping,
The good dog listened while I read,
    And wagged his tail in keeping.

I watched him while in sportive mood
    I read *The Twa Dogs'* story,
And half believed he understood
    The poet's allegory.   40

Sweet day, sweet songs! The golden hours
    Grew brighter for that singing,

[2] The poem is in one of Burns's favorite ballad forms.

1850

From brook and bird and meadow flowers
A dearer welcome bringing.

New light on home-seen Nature beamed,
New glory over Woman;
And daily life and duty seemed
No longer poor and common.

I woke to find the simple truth
Of fact and feeling better 50
Than all the dreams that held my youth
A still repining debtor:

That Nature gives her handmaid, Art,
The themes of sweet discoursing;
The tender idyls of the heart
In every tongue rehearsing.

Why dream of lands of gold and pearl,
Of loving knight and lady,
When farmer boy and barefoot girl
Were wandering there already? 60

I saw through all familiar things
The romance underlying;
The joys and griefs that plume the wings
Of Fancy skyward flying.

I saw the same blithe day return,
The same sweet fall of even,
That rose on wooded Craigie-burn, [1]
And sank on crystal Devon.

I matched with Scotland's heathery hills
The sweet-brier and the clover; 70
With Ayr and Doon, my native rills,
Their wood-hymns chanting over.

O'er rank and pomp, as he had seen,
I saw the Man uprising;
No longer common or unclean,
The child of God's baptizing!

With clearer eyes I saw the worth
Of life among the lowly;
The Bible at his Cotter's hearth [2]
Had made my own more holy. 80

And if at times an evil strain,
To lawless love appealing,
Broke in upon the sweet refrain
Of pure and healthful feeling,

It died upon the eye and ear,
No inward answer gaining;

[1] The Craigie Burn (stream), the Devon, Ayr, and Doon are all rivers of Scotland.
[2] See Burns's "The Cotter's Saturday Night."

No heart had I to see or hear
The discord and the staining.

Let those who never erred forget
His worth, in vain bewailings; 90
Sweet Soul of Song! I own my debt
Uncanceled by his failings!

Lament who will the ribald line
Which tells his lapse from duty,
How kissed the maddening lips of wine
Or wanton ones of beauty;

But think, while falls that shade between
The erring one and Heaven,
That he who loved like Magdalen,
Like her may be forgiven. 100

Not his the song whose thunderous chime
Eternal echoes render,—
The mournful Tuscan's [3] haunted rime,
And Milton's starry splendor!

But who his human heart has laid
To Nature's bosom nearer?
Who sweetened toil like him, or paid
To love a tribute dearer?

Through all his tuneful art, how strong [4]
The human feeling gushes! 110
The very moonlight of his song
Is warm with smiles and blushes!

Give lettered pomp to teeth of Time,
So "Bonnie Doon" but tarry;
Blot out the Epic's stately rime,
But spare his Highland Mary!
1854

MAUD MULLER [5]

Maud Muller on a summer's day
Raked the meadow sweet with hay.

[3] Dante
[4] Cf. Wordsworth's "At the Grave of Burns" and "Thoughts Suggested The Day Following."
[5] Whittier wrote regarding this poem: "The poem had no real foundation in fact, though a hint of it may have been found in recalling an incident, trivial in itself, of a journey on the picturesque Maine seaboard with my sister some years before it was written. We had stopped to rest our tired horse under the shade of an apple-tree, and refresh him with water from a little brook which rippled through the stone wall across the road. A very beautiful young girl in scantest summer attire was at work in the hayfield, and as we talked with her we noticed that she strove to hide her bare feet by raking hay over them, blushing as she did so, through the tan of her cheek and neck." See Whittier's Poems, Cambridge Edition, p. 47, The Houghton Mifflin Company.

Beneath her torn hat glowed the wealth
Of simple beauty and rustic health.

Singing, she wrought, and her merry glee
The mock-bird echoed from his tree.

But when she glanced to the far-off town,
White from its hill-slope looking down,

The sweet song died, and a vague unrest
And a nameless longing filled her breast,— 10

A wish that she hardly dared to own,
For something better than she had known.

The Judge rode slowly down the lane,
Smoothing his horse's chestnut mane.

He drew his bridle in the shade
Of the apple-trees, to greet the maid,

And ask a draught from the spring that flowed
Through the meadow across the road.

She stooped where the cool spring bubbled up,
And filled for him her small tin cup, 20

And blushed as she gave it, looking down
On her feet so bare, and her tattered gown.

"Thanks!" said the Judge; "a sweeter draught
From a fairer hand was never quaffed."

He spoke of the grass and flowers and trees,
Of the singing birds and the humming bees;

Then talked of the haying, and wondered
       whether
The cloud in the west would bring foul weather.

And Maud forgot her brier-torn gown
And her graceful ankles bare and brown; 30

And listened, while a pleased surprise
Looked from her long-lashed hazel eyes.

At last, like one who for delay
Seeks a vain excuse, he rode away.

Maud Muller looked and sighed: "Ah me!
That I the Judge's bride might be!

"He would dress me up in silks so fine,
And praise and toast me at his wine.

"My father should wear a broadcloth coat;
My brother should sail a painted boat. 40

"I'd dress my mother so grand and gay,
And the baby should have a new toy each day.

"And I'd feed the hungry and clothe the poor,
And all should bless me who left our door."

The Judge looked back as he climbed the hill,
And saw Maud Muller standing still.

"A form more fair, a face more sweet,
Ne'er hath it been my lot to meet.

"And her modest answer and graceful air
Show her wise and good as she is fair. 50

"Would she were mine, and I today,
Like her, a harvester of hay;

"No doubtful balance of rights and wrongs,
Nor weary lawyers with endless tongues,

"But low of cattle and song of birds,
And health and quiet and loving words."

But he thought of his sisters, proud and cold,
And his mother, vain of her rank and gold.

So, closing his heart, the Judge rode on,
And Maud was left in the field alone. 60

But the lawyers smiled that afternoon,
When he hummed in court an old love-tune;

And the young girl mused beside the well
Till the rain on the unraked clover fell.

He wedded a wife of richest dower,
Who lived for fashion, as he for power.

Yet oft in his marble hearth's bright glow,
He watched a picture come and go;

And sweet Maud Muller's hazel eyes
Looked out in their innocent surprise. 70

Oft, when the wine in his glass was red,
He longed for the wayside well instead;

And closed his eyes on his garnished rooms
To dream of meadows and clover-blooms.

And the proud man sighed, with a secret pain,
"Ah, that I were free again!

"Free as when I rode that day,
Where the barefoot maiden raked her hay."

She wedded a man unlearned and poor,   79
And many children played round her door.

But care and sorrow, and childbirth pain,
Left their traces on heart and brain.

And oft, when the summer sun shone hot
On the new-mown hay in the meadow lot,

And she heard the little spring brook fall
Over the roadside, through the wall,

In the shade of the apple-tree again
She saw a rider draw his rein.

And, gazing down with timid grace,
She felt his pleased eyes read her face.   90

Sometimes her narrow kitchen walls
Stretched away into stately halls;

The weary wheel to a spinnet turned,
The tallow candle an astral [1] burned,

And for him who sat by the chimney lug,
Dozing and grumbling o'er pipe and mug,

A manly form at her side she saw,
And joy was duty and love was law.

Then she took up her burden of life again,
Saying only, "It might have been." [2]   100

Alas for maiden, alas for Judge,
For rich repiner and household drudge!

God pity them both! and pity us all,
Who vainly the dreams of youth recall.

For of all sad words of tongue or pen,
The saddest are these: "It might have been!"

Ah, well! for us all some sweet hope lies
Deeply buried from human eyes;   108

And, in the hereafter, angels may
Roll the stone from its grave away!

                                          1854

THE BAREFOOT BOY

Blessings on thee, little man,
Barefoot boy, with cheeks of tan!
With thy turned-up pantaloons,
And thy merry whistled tunes;

[1] an old-fashioned parlor lamp
[2] Note the rustic pronunciation of *been* to rime with
again and below with *pen*. Whittier defended
these rimes when they were objected to.

With thy red lip, redder still
Kissed by strawberries on the hill;
With the sunshine on thy face,
Through thy torn brim's jaunty grace;
From my heart I give thee joy,—
I was once a barefoot boy!   10
Prince thou art,—the grown-up man
Only is republican.
Let the million-dollared ride!
Barefoot, trudging at his side,
Thou hast more than he can buy
In the reach of ear and eye,—
Outward sunshine, inward joy:
Blessings on thee, barefoot boy!

Oh for boyhood's painless play,
Sleep that wakes in laughing day,   20
Health that mocks the doctor's rules,
Knowledge never learned of schools,
Of the wild bee's morning chase,
Of the wild-flower's time and place,
Flight of fowl and habitude
Of the tenants of the wood;
How the tortoise bears his shell,
How the woodchuck digs his cell,
And the ground-mole sinks his well;
How the robin feeds her young,   30
How the oriole's nest is hung;
Where the whitest lilies blow,
Where the freshest berries grow,
Where the groundnut trails its vine,
Where the wood-grape's clusters shine;
Of the black wasp's cunning way,
Mason of his walls of clay,
And the architectural plans
Of gray hornet artisans!
For, eschewing books and tasks,   40
Nature answers all he asks;
Hand in hand with her he walks,
Face to face with her he talks,
Part and parcel of her joy,—
Blessings on the barefoot boy!

Oh for boyhood's time of June,
Crowding years in one brief moon,
When all things I heard or saw
Me, their master, waited for.
I was rich in flowers and trees,   50
Humming-birds and honey-bees;
For my sport the squirrel played,
Plied the snouted mole his spade;
For my taste the blackberry cone
Purpled over hedge and stone;
Laughed the brook for my delight
Through the day and through the night,
Whispering at the garden wall,
Talked with me from fall to fall;

Mine the sand-rimmed pickerel pond,   60
Mine the walnut slopes beyond,
Mine, on bending orchard trees,
Apples of Hesperides!
Still as my horizon grew,
Larger grew my riches too;
All the world I saw or knew
Seemed a complex Chinese toy,
Fashioned for a barefoot boy!

Oh for festal dainties spread,
Like my bowl of milk and bread,—   70
Pewter spoon and bowl of wood,
On the door-stone, gray and rude!
O'er me, like a regal tent,
Cloudy-ribbed, the sunset bent,
Purple-curtained, fringed with gold
Looped in many a wind-swung fold;
While for music came the play
Of the pied frogs' orchestra;
And, to light the noisy choir,
Lit the fly his lamp of fire.   80
I was monarch: pomp and joy
Waited on the barefoot boy!

Cheerily, then, my little man,
Live and laugh, as boyhood can!
Though the flinty slopes be hard,
Stubble-speared the new-mown sward,
Every morn shall lead thee through
Fresh baptisms of the dew;
Every evening from thy feet
Shall the cool wind kiss the heat: 90
All too soon these feet must hide
In the prison cells of pride,
Lose the freedom of the sod,
Like a colt's for work be shod,
Made to tread the mills of toil,
Up and down in ceaseless moil:
Happy if their track be found
Never on forbidden ground;
Happy if they sink not in
Quick and treacherous sands of sin.   100
Ah! that thou couldst know thy joy,
Ere it passes, barefoot boy!
1855   1856

SKIPPER IRESON'S RIDE [1]

Of all the rides since the birth of time,
Told in story or sung in rime,—

[1] Whittier based this poem on a bit of rime he had
heard a schoolmate from Marblehead repeat. He
supposed the incident to be a century old, but it
was really of 1807. The fact was that Skipper
Ireson was blameless, for his men compelled him
to leave the sinking crew. He was, however,
tarred and feathered. See *History of Marblehead*,
by Samuel Roads, Jr., p. 232-234.

On Apuleius's Golden Ass, [2]
Or one-eyed Calendar's horse of brass, [3]
Witch astride of a human hack,
Islam's prophet on Al-Borák, [4]
The strangest ride that ever was sped
Was Ireson's out from Marblehead!
  Old Floyd Ireson, for his hard heart,
    Tarred and feathered and carried in a cart
      By the women of Marblehead!   11

Body of Turkey, head of owl,
Wings a-droop like a rained-on fowl,
Feathered and ruffled in every part,
Skipper Ireson stood in the cart.
Scores of women, old and young,
Strong of muscle, and glib of tongue,
Pushed and pulled up the rocky lane,
Shouting and singing the shrill refrain:
  "Here's Flud Oirson, fur his horrd horrt,   20
    Torr'd an' futherr'd an' corr'd in a corrt
      By the women o' Morble'ead!"

Wrinkled scolds with hands on hips,
Girls in bloom of cheek and lips,
Wild-eyed, free-limbed, such as chase
Bacchus round some antique vase,
Brief of skirt, with ankles bare,
Loose of kerchief and loose of hair,
With conch-shells blowing and fish-horns'
        twang,
Over and over the Maenads [5] sang: 30
  "Here's Flud Oirson, fur his horrd horrt,
    Torr'd an' futherr'd an' corr'd in a corrt
      By the women o' Morble'ead!"

Small pity for him!—He sailed away
From a leaking ship in Chaleur Bay,—
Sailed away from a sinking wreck,
With his own town's-people on her deck!
"Lay by! lay by!" they called to him.
Back he answered, "Sink or swim!
Brag of your catch of fish again!"   40
And off he sailed through the fog and rain!
  Old Floyd Ireson, for his hard heart,

[2] Apuleius, a Roman philosopher of the second century,
in his *Metamorphoses*, or, as it was popularly
termed, *The Golden Ass*, tells the story of a young
man who was turned into an ass and met many
adventures before regaining human form. The
book was heavily drawn upon by the makers of
medieval narrative compilations like Boccaccio's
Decameron.

[3] A calendar, or dervish, was a begging saint. Whittier
is confusing two of the *Arabian Nights* stories,
that of the "Royal Mendicants," who were one-
eyed, and that of "The Magic Horse," which was
of brass but which soared into the sky at the
rider's will.

[4] Al Borák (Arabic, the lightning), a winged animal
with the face of a man, that carried Mahomet
to the seventh heaven

[5] the frenzied priestesses of Bacchus

Tarred and feathered and carried in a cart
By the women of Marblehead!

Fathoms deep in dark Chaleur
That wreck shall lie forevermore.
Mother and sister, wife and maid,
Looked from the rocks of Marblehead
Over the moaning and rainy sea,—
Looked for the coming that might not be!   50
What did the winds and the sea-birds say
Of the cruel captain who sailed away?—
  Old Floyd Ireson, for his hard heart,
  Tarred and feathered and carried in a cart
    By the women of Marblehead.

Through the street, on either side,
Up flew windows, doors swung wide;
Sharp-tongued spinsters, old wives gray,
Treble lent the fish-horn's bray.
Sea-worn grandsires, cripple-bound,   60
Hulks of old sailors run aground,
Shook head, and fist, and hat, and cane,
And cracked with curses the hoarse refrain:
  "Here's Flud Oirson, fur his horrd horrt,
  Torr'd an' futherr'd an' corr'd in a corrt
    By the women o' Morble'ead!"

Sweetly along the Salem road
Bloom of orchard and lilac showed.
Little the wicked skipper knew
Of the fields so green and the sky so blue.   70
Riding there in his sorry trim,
Like an Indian idol glum and grim,
Scarcely he seemed the sound to hear
Of voices shouting far and near:
  "Here's Flud Oirson, fur his horrd horrt,
  Torr'd an' futherr'd an' corr'd in a corrt
    By the women o' Morble'ead!"

"Hear me, neighbors!" at last he cried,—
"What to me is this noisy ride?
What is the shame that clothes the skin   80
To the nameless horror that lives within?
Waking or sleeping, I see a wreck,
And hear a cry from a reeling deck!
Hate me and curse me,—I only dread
The hand of God and the face of the dead!"
  Said old Floyd Ireson, for his hard heart,
  Tarred and feathered and carried in a cart
    By the women of Marblehead!

Then the wife of the skipper lost at sea   89
Said, "God has touched him! why should we?"
Said an old wife mourning her only son,
"Cut the rogue's tether and let him run!"
So with soft relentings and rude excuse,
Half scorn, half pity, they cut him loose,

And gave him a cloak to hide him in,
And left him alone with his shame and sin.
  Poor Floyd Ireson, for his hard heart,
  Tarred and feathered and carried in a cart
    By the women of Marblehead!

1828, 1857   1857

TELLING THE BEES

Here is the place; right over the hill
  Runs the path I took;
You can see the gap in the old wall still,
  And the stepping-stones in the shallow brook.

There is the house, with the gate red-barred,
  And the poplars tall;
And the barn's brown length, and the cattle-
    yard,
  And the white horns tossing above the wall.

There are the beehives ranged in the sun;
  And down by the brink   10
Of the brook are her poor flowers, weed-o'errun,
  Pansy and daffodil, rose and pink.

A year has gone, as the tortoise goes,
  Heavy and slow;
And the same rose blows, and the same sun
    glows,
  And the same brook sings of a year ago.

There's the same sweet clover-smell in the
    breeze;
  And the June sun warm
Tangles his wings of fire in the trees,
  Setting, as then, over Fernside farm.   20

I mind me how with a lover's care
  From my Sunday coat
I brushed off the burrs, and smoothed my hair,
  And cooled at the brookside my brow and
    throat.

Since we parted, a month had passed,—
  To love, a year;
Down through the beeches I looked at last
  On the little red gate and the well-sweep near.

I can see it all now,—the slantwise rain
  Of light through the leaves,   30
The sundown's blaze on her window-pane,
  The bloom of her roses under the eaves.

Just the same as a month before,—
  The house and the trees,
The barn's brown gable, the vine by the door,—
  Nothing changed but the hives of bees.

Before them, under the garden wall,
  Forward and back,
Went drearily singing the chore-girl small,
  Draping each hive with a shred of black. [1]

Trembling, I listened: the summer sun   41
  Had the chill of snow;
For I knew she was telling the bees of one
  Gone on the journey we all must go!

Then I said to myself, "My Mary weeps
  For the dead today:
Haply her blind old grandsire sleeps
  The fret and the pain of his age away."

But her dog whined low; on the doorway sill
  With his cane to his chin,   50
The old man sat; and the chore-girl still
  Sung to the bees stealing out and in.

And the song she was singing ever since
  In my ear sounds on:—
"Stay at home, pretty bees, fly not hence!
  Mistress Mary is dead and gone!"
1858   *1858*

MY PLAYMATE [2]

The pines were dark on Ramoth hill, [3]
  Their song was soft and low;
The blossoms in the sweet May wind
  Were falling like the snow.

The blossoms drifted at our feet,
  The orchard birds sang clear;
The sweetest and the saddest day
  It seemed of all the year.

For, more to me than birds or flowers,
  My playmate left her home,   10
And took with her the laughing spring,
  The music and the bloom.

She kissed the lips of kith and kin,
  She laid her hand in mine:
What more could ask the bashful boy
  Who fed her father's kine?

[1] "A remarkable custom, brought from the Old Country,
formerly prevailed in the rural districts of New
England. On the death of a member of the
family, the bees were at once informed of the
event, and their hives dressed in mourning. This
ceremonial was supposed to be necessary to prevent the swarms from leaving their hives and
seeking a new home." (Cambridge edition of
Whittier, The Houghton Mifflin Company.) The
scenery of the poem is that of Whittier's homestead.
[2] See note 1, p. 471.
[3] A hill about two miles from Whittier's Amesbury
home; the neighboring woods of Follymill were
"famous for their mayflowers or ground laurel."
Pickard, *Life of Whittier*, ii, 427.

She left us in the bloom of May:
  The constant years told o'er
Their seasons with as sweet May morns,
  But she came back no more.   20

I walk, with noiseless feet, the round
  Of uneventful years;
Still o'er and o'er I sow the spring
  And reap the autumn ears.

She lives where all the golden year
  Her summer roses blow;
The dusky children of the sun
  Before her come and go.

There haply with her jeweled hands
  She smooths her silken gown,—   30
No more the homespun lap wherein
  I shook the walnuts down.

The wild grapes wait us by the brook,
  The brown nuts on the hill,
And still the May-day flowers make sweet
  The woods of Follymill.

The lilies blossom in the pond,
  The bird builds in the tree,
The dark pines sing on Ramoth hill
  The slow song of the sea.   40

I wonder if she thinks of them,
  And how the old time seems,—
If ever the pines of Ramoth wood
  Are sounding in her dreams.

I see her face, I hear her voice.
  Does she remember mine?
And what to her is now the boy
  Who fed her father's kine?

What cares she that the orioles build
  For other eyes than ours,—   50
That other hands with nuts are filled,
  And other laps with flowers?

O playmate in the golden time!
  Our mossy seat is green,
Its fringing violets blossom yet,
  The old trees o'er it lean.

The winds so sweet with birch and fern
  A sweeter memory blow;
And there in spring the veeries sing
  The song of long ago.   60

And still the pines of Ramoth wood
  Are moaning like the sea,—
The moaning of the sea of change
  Between myself and thee !

1859-60   1860

SNOW-BOUND [1]

A WINTER IDYL

As the Spirits of Darkness be stronger in the
dark, so Good Spirits which be Angels of Light
are augmented not only by the Divine light of the
Sun, but also by our common VVood Fire: and as
the Celestial Fire drives away dark spirits, so also
this our Fire of VVood doth the same.—COR.
AGRIPPA, *Occult Philosophy*, Book I, ch. v.

Announced by all the trumpets of the sky,
Arrives the snow, and, driving o'er the fields,
Seems nowhere to alight: the whited air
Hides hills and woods, the river, and the heaven,
And veils the farm-house at the garden's end.
The sled and traveler stopped, the courier's feet
Delayed, all friends shut out, the housemates sit
Around the radiant fireplace, enclosed
In a tumultuous privacy of storm.
        EMERSON, *The Snow Storm.*

The sun that brief December day
Rose cheerless over hills of gray,
And, darkly circled, gave at noon
A sadder light than waning moon.
Slow tracing down the thickening sky
Its mute and ominous prophecy,
A portent seeming less than threat,
It sank from sight before it set.
A chill no coat, however stout,
Of homespun stuff could quite shut out,   10
A hard, dull bitterness of cold,
  That checked, mid-vein, the circling race
  Of life-blood in the sharpened face,
The coming of the snow-storm told.
The wind blew east : we heard the roar
Of Ocean on his wintry shore,
And felt the strong pulse throbbing there
Beat with low rhythm our inland air.

Meanwhile we did our nightly chores,—
Brought in the wood from out of doors,   20
Littered the stalls, and from the mows
Raked down the herd's-grass for the cows;
Heard the horse whinnying for his corn;
And, sharply clashing horn on horn,
Impatient down the stanchion rows
The cattle shake their walnut bows;

[1] In this poem, which pictures his own boyhood home,
Whittier gives poetic warmth and significance to
the homely details of the New England farm-life
of the early nineteenth century. For contemporary
treatment of the New England country, see Robert
Frost's *North of Boston*, etc.

While, peering from his early perch
Upon the scaffold's pole of birch,
The cock his crested helmet bent
And down his querulous challenge sent.   30

Unwarmed by any sunset light
The gray day darkened into night,
A night made hoary with the swarm
And whirl-dance of the blinding storm,
As zigzag wavering to and fro,
Crossed and recrossed the winged snow:
And ere the early bedtime came
The white drift piled the window-frame,
And through the glass the clothes-line posts
Looked in like tall and sheeted ghosts.   40

So all night long the storm roared on:
The morning broke without a sun;
In tiny spherule traced with lines
Of Nature's geometric signs,
In starry flake and pellicle,
All day the hoary meteor fell;
And, when the second morning shone,
We looked upon a world unknown,
On nothing we could call our own.
Around the glistening wonder bent   50
The blue walls of the firmament,
No cloud above, no earth below,—
A universe of sky and snow!
The old familiar sights of ours
Took marvelous shapes; strange domes and
      towers
Rose up where sty or corn-crib stood,
Or garden-wall, or belt of wood;
A smooth white mound the brush-pile showed,
A fenceless drift what once was road;
The bridle-post an old man sat   60
With loose-flung coat and high cocked hat;
The well-curb had a Chinese roof;
And even the long sweep, high aloof,
In its slant splendor, seemed to tell
Of Pisa's leaning miracle.

A prompt, decisive man, no breath
Our father wasted: "Boys, a path!"
Well pleased, (for when did farmer boy
Count such a summons less than joy?)
Our buskins on our feet we drew;   70
  With mittened hands, and caps drawn low,
  To guard our necks and ears from snow,
We cut the solid whiteness through.
And, where the drift was deepest, made
A tunnel walled and overlaid
With dazzling crystal: we had read
Of rare Aladdin's wondrous cave,
And to our own his name we gave,
With many a wish the luck were ours

To test his lamp's supernal powers.   80
We reached the barn with merry din,
And roused the prisoned brutes within.
The old horse thrust his long head out,
And grave with wonder gazed about;
The cock his lusty greeting said,
And forth his speckled harem led;
The oxen lashed their tails, and hooked,
And mild reproach of hunger looked;
The hornéd patriarch of the sheep,
Like Egypt's Amun [1] roused from sleep,   90
Shook his sage head with gesture mute,
And emphasized with stamp of foot.

All day the gusty north-wind bore
The loosening drift its breath before;
Low circling round its southern zone,
The sun through dazzling snow-mist shone.
No church-bell lent its Christian tone
To the savage air, no social smoke
Curled over woods of snow-hung oak.
A solitude made more intense   100
By dreary-voicéd elements,
The shrieking of the mindless wind,
The moaning tree-boughs swaying blind,
And on the glass the unmeaning beat
Of ghostly finger-tips of sleet.
Beyond the circle of our hearth
No welcome sound of toil or mirth
Unbound the spell, and testified
Of human life and thought outside.
We minded that the sharpest ear   110
The buried brooklet could not hear,
The music of whose liquid lip
Had been to us companionship,
And, in our lonely life, had grown
To have an almost human tone.

As night drew on, and, from the crest
Of wooded knolls that ridged the west,
The sun, a snow-blown traveler, sank
From sight beneath the smothering bank,
We piled with care our nightly stack   120
Of wood against the chimney-back,—
The oaken log, green, huge, and thick,
And on its top the stout backstick;
The knotty forestick laid apart,
And filled between with curious art
The ragged brush; then, hovering near,
We watched the first red blaze appear,
Heard the sharp crackle, caught the gleam
On whitewashed wall and sagging beam,
Until the old, rude-furnished room   130
Burst, flower-like, into rosy bloom;
While radiant with a mimic flame

[1] one of the chief deities of ancient Egypt, usually represented as a ram with great horns

Outside the sparkling drift became,
And through the bare-boughed lilac-tree
Our own warm hearth seemed blazing free.
The crane and pendent trammels showed,
The Turks' heads on the andirons glowed;
While childish fancy, prompt to tell
The meaning of the miracle,
Whispered the old rime: *"Under the tree*   140
When fire outdoors burns merrily,
There the witches are making tea."

The moon above the eastern wood
Shone at its full; the hill-range stood
Transfigured in the silver flood,
Its blown snows flashing cold and keen,
Dead white, save where some sharp ravine
Took shadow, or the somber green
Of hemlocks turned to pitchy black
Against the whiteness at their back.   150
For such a world and such a night
Most fitting that unwarming light,
Which only seemed where'er it fell
To make the coldness visible.

Shut in from all the world without,
We sat the clean-winged hearth about,
Content to let the north-wind roar
In baffled rage at pane and door,
While the red logs before us beat
The frost-line back with tropic heat;   160
And ever, when a louder blast
Shook beam and rafter as it passed,
The merrier up its roaring draught
The great throat of the chimney laughed;
The house-dog on his paws outspread
Laid to the fire his drowsy head,
The cat's dark silhouette on the wall
A couchant tiger's seemed to fall;
And, for the winter fireside meet,
Between the andirons' straddling feet,   170
The mug of cider simmered slow,
The apples sputtered in a row,
And, close at hand, the basket stood
With nuts from brown October's wood.

What matter how the night behaved?
What matter how the north-wind raved?
Blow high, blow low, not all its snow
Could quench out hearth-fire's ruddy glow.
O Time and Change!—with hair as gray
As was my sire's that winter day,   180
How strange it seems, with so much gone
Of life and love, to still live on!
Ah, brother! only I and thou
Are left of all that circle now,—
The dear home faces whereupon
That fitful firelight paled and shone.

Henceforward, listen as we will,
The voices of that hearth are still;
Look where we may, the wide earth o'er,
Those lighted faces smile no more.   190
We tread the paths their feet have worn,
  We sit beneath their orchard-trees,
  We hear, like them, the hum of bees
And rustle of the bladed corn;
We turn the pages that they read,
  Their written words we linger o'er,
But in the sun they cast no shade,
No voice is heard, no sign is made,
  No step is on the conscious floor!
Yet Love will dream, and Faith will trust,   200
(Since He who knows our need is just,)
That somehow, somewhere, meet we must.
Alas for him who never sees
The stars shine through his cypress-trees! [1]
Who, hopeless, lays his dead away,
Nor looks to see the breaking day
Across the mournful marbles play!
Who hath not learned, in hours of faith,
  The truth to flesh and sense unknown,
That Life is ever lord of Death,   210
  And Love can never lose its own!

We sped the time with stories old,
Wrought puzzles out, and riddles told,
Or stammered from our school-book lore
"The chief of Gambia's golden shore." [2]
How often since, when all the land
Was clay in Slavery's shaping hand,
As if a trumpet called, I've heard,
Dame Mercy Warren's rousing word:
"Does not the voice of reason cry,   220
  Claim the first right which Nature gave,
From the red scourge of bondage fly,
  Nor deign to live a burdened slave!"
Our father rode again his ride
On Memphremagog's [3] wooded side;
Sat down again to moose and samp
In trapper's hut and Indian camp;
Lived o'er the old idyllic ease
Beneath St. François' hemlock trees;
Again for him the moonlight shone   230
On Norman cap and bodiced zone; [4]
Again he heard the violin play
Which led the village dance away,
And mingled in its merry whirl

---

[1] The cypress tree is a symbol of mourning.
[2] "The African Chief," a poem in *The American Preceptor*, edited by Caleb Bingham; Mercy Otis Warren (mentioned below), 1728-1814, a daughter of James Otis the elder, was a dramatist and historian.
[3] A lake in Vermont and Quebec; samp, in the next line, is a kind of hominy.
[4] Whittier's father had made trading trips into Canada, where he had seen French girls in Norman cap and bodice.

The grandam and the laughing girl.
Or, nearer home, our steps he led
Where Salisbury's [5] level marshes spread
  Mile-wide as flies the laden bee;
Where merry mowers, hale and strong,
Swept, scythe on scythe, their swaths along
  The low green prairies of the sea.   241
We shared the fishing off Boar's Head, [6]
  And round the rocky Isles of Shoals [6]
  The hake-broil on the driftwood coals;
The chowder on the sand-beach made,
Dipped by the hungry, steaming hot,
With spoons of clam-shell from the pot.
We heard the tales of witchcraft old,
And dream and sign and marvel told
To sleepy listeners as they lay   250
Stretched idly on the salted hay
Adrift along the winding shores,
When favoring breezes deigned to blow
The square sail of the gundalow,
And idle lay the useless oars.

Our mother, while she turned her wheel
Or run the new-knit stocking-heel,
Told how the Indian hordes came down
At midnight on Cocheco town, [7]
And how her own great-uncle bore   260
His cruel scalp-mark to fourscore.
Recalling, in her fitting phrase,
  So rich and picturesque and free,
  (The common unrimed poetry
Of simple life and country ways)
The story of her early days,—
She made us welcome to her home;
Old hearths grew wide to give us room;
We stole with her a frightened look
At the gray wizard's conjuring-book,   270
The fame whereof went far and wide
Through all the simple country-side;
We heard the hawks at twilight play,
The boat-horn on Piscataqua, [8]
The loon's weird laughter far away;
We fished her little trout-brook, knew
What flowers in wood and meadow grew,
What sunny hillsides autumn-brown
She climbed to shake the ripe nuts down,
Saw where in sheltered cove and bay   280
The ducks' black squadron anchored lay,
And heard the wild-geese calling loud
Beneath the gray November cloud.

Then, haply, with a look more grave,
And soberer tone, some tale she gave
From painful Sewel's [9] ancient tome,

---

[5] a town in Massachusetts   [7] Dover, New Hampshire
[6] on the New Hampshire coast
[8] Note the rustic pronunciation of this rime.
[9] William Sewel, 1654-1720, a Quaker see n. 1, p. 85.

Beloved in every Quaker home,
Of faith fire-winged by martyrdom,
Or Chalkley's [1] Journal, old and quaint,—
Gentlest of skippers, rare sea-saint !—   290
Who, when the dreary calms prevailed,
And water-butt and bread-cask failed,
And cruel, hungry eyes pursued
His portly presence, mad for food,
With dark hints muttered under breath
Of casting lots for life or death,
Offered, if Heaven withheld supplies,
To be himself the sacrifice.
Then, suddenly, as if to save
The good man from his living grave,   300
A ripple on the water grew,
A school of porpoise flashed in view.
"Take, eat," he said, "and be content;
These fishes in my stead are sent
By Him who gave the tangled ram
To spare the child of Abraham."

Our uncle, innocent of books,
Was rich in lore of fields and brooks,
The ancient teachers never dumb
Of Nature's unhoused lyceum.   310
In moons and tides and weather wise,
He read the clouds as prophecies,
And foul or fair could well divine,
By many an occult hint and sign,
Holding the cunning-warded keys
To all the woodcraft mysteries;
Himself to Nature's heart so near
That all her voices in his ear
Of beast or bird had meanings clear,
Like Apollonius [2] of old,   320
Who knew the tales the sparrows told,
Or Hermes, [3] who interpreted
What the sage cranes of Nilus said;
A simple, guileless, childlike man,
Content to live where life began;
Strong only on his native grounds,
The little world of sights and sounds
Whose girdle was the parish bounds,
Whereof his fondly partial pride
The common features magnified,   330
As Surrey hills to mountains grew
In White [4] of Selborne's loving view,—
He told how teal and loon he shot,
And how the eagle's eggs he got,

[1] an English Quaker preacher, 1675-1741
[2] a Greek philosopher and reputed magician, 4 B.C.-97 A.D.
[3] Hermes Trismegistus, thrice greatest, the Greek name of the Egyptian god Thoth, reputed writer of much scientific and magic lore
[4] Gilbert White, 1720-1793, whose careful description, in *The Natural History of Selborne*, of natural objects about his home in the parish of Selborne, in Hampshire, England, has made his work a classic

The feats on pond and river done,
The prodigies of rod and gun;
Till, warming with the tales he told,
Forgotten was the outside cold,
The bitter wind unheeded blew,
From ripening corn the pigeons flew,   340
The partridge drummed i' the wood, the mink
Went fishing down the river-brink.
In fields with bean or clover gay,
The woodchuck, like a hermit gray,
Peered from the doorway of his cell;
The muskrat plied the mason's trade,
And tier by tier his mud-walls laid;
And from the shagbark overhead
The grizzled squirrel dropped his shell.

Next, the dear aunt, whose smile of cheer
And voice in dreams I see and hear,—   351
The sweetest woman ever Fate
Perverse denied a household mate,
Who, lonely, homeless, not the less
Found peace in love's unselfishness,
And welcome whereso'er she went,
A calm and gracious element,
Whose presence seemed the sweet income
And womanly atmosphere of home,—
Called up her girlhood memories,   360
The huskings and the apple-bees,
The sleigh-rides and the summer sails,
Weaving through all the poor details
And homespun warp of circumstance
A golden woof-thread of romance.
For well she kept her genial mood
And simple faith of maidenhood;
Before her still a cloud-land lay,
The mirage loomed across her way;
The morning dew, that dries so soon   370
With others, glistened at her noon;
Through years of toil and soil and care,
From glossy tress to thin gray hair,
All unprofaned she held apart
The virgin fancies of the heart.
Be shame to him of woman born
Who hath for such but thought of scorn.

There, too, our elder sister plied
Her evening task the stand beside;
A full, rich nature, free to trust,   380
Truthful and almost sternly just,
Impulsive, earnest, prompt to act,
And make her generous thought a fact,
Keeping with many a light disguise
The secret of self-sacrifice.
O heart sore-tried ! thou hast the best
That Heaven itself could give thee,—rest,
Rest from all bitter thoughts and things !
How many a poor one's blessing went

With thee beneath the low green tent 390
Whose curtain never outward swings!

As one who held herself a part
Of all she saw, and let her heart
　Against the household bosom lean,
Upon the motley-braided mat
Our youngest and our dearest [1] sat,
Lifting her large, sweet, asking eyes,
　Now bathed within the fadeless green
And holy peace of Paradise.
Oh, looking from some heavenly hill, 400
　Or from the shade of saintly palms,
　Or silver reach of river calms,
Do those large eyes behold me still?
With me one little year ago:—
The chill weight of the winter snow
　For months upon her grave has lain;
And now, when summer south-winds blow
　And brier and harebell bloom again,
I tread the pleasant paths we trod,
I see the violet-sprinkled sod 410
Whereon she leaned, too frail and weak
The hillside flowers she loved to seek,
Yet following me where'er I went
With dark eyes full of love's content.
The birds are glad; the brier-rose fills
The air with sweetness; all the hills
Stretch green to June's unclouded sky;
But still I wait with ear and eye
For something gone which should be nigh,
A loss in all familiar things, 420
In flower that blooms, and bird that sings.
And yet, dear heart! remembering thee,
　Am I not richer than of old?
Safe in thy immortality,
　What change can reach the wealth I hold?
　What chance can mar the pearl and gold
Thy love hath left in trust with me?
And while in life's late afternoon,
　Where cool and long the shadows grow,
I walk to meet the night that soon 430
　Shall shape and shadow overflow,
I cannot feel that thou art far,
Since near at need the angels are;
And when the sunset gates unbar,
　Shall I not see thee waiting stand,
And, white against the evening star,
　The welcome of thy beckoning hand?

Brisk wielder of the birch and rule,
The master of the district school
Held at the fire his favored place, 440
Its warm glow lit a laughing face
Fresh-hued and fair, where scarce appeared
The uncertain prophecy of beard.

[1] Elizabeth, Whittier's much beloved younger sister

He teased the mitten-blinded cat,
Played cross-pins on my uncle's hat,
Sang songs, and told us what befalls
In classic Dartmouth's college halls.
Born the wild Northern hills among,
From whence his yeoman father wrung
By patient toil subsistence scant, 450
Not competence and yet not want,
He early gained the power to pay
His cheerful, self-reliant way;
Could doff at ease his scholar's gown
To peddle wares from town to town;
Or through the long vacation's reach
In lonely lowland districts teach,
Where all the droll experience found
At stranger hearths in boarding round,
The moonlit skater's keen delight, 460
The sleigh-drive through the frosty night,
The rustic party, with its rough
Accompaniment of blind-man's-buff,
And whirling plate, and forfeits paid,
His winter task a pastime made.
Happy the snow-locked homes wherein
He tuned his merry violin,
Or played the athlete in the barn,
Or held the good dame's winding yarn,
Or mirth-provoking versions told 470
Of classic legends rare and old,
Wherein the scenes of Greece and Rome
Had all the commonplace of home,
And little seemed at best the odds
'Twixt Yankee pedlers and old gods;
Where Pindus-born Araxes [2] took
The guise of any grist-mill brook,
And dread Olympus at his will
Became a huckleberry hill.

A careless boy that night he seemed; 480
　But at his desk he had the look
And air of one who wisely schemed,
　And hostage from the future took
　In trained thought and lore of book.
Large-brained, clear-eyed,—of such as he
Shall Freedom's young apostles be,
Who, following in War's bloody trail,
Shall every lingering wrong assail;
All chains from limb and spirit strike,
Uplift the black and white alike; 490
Scatter before their swift advance
The darkness and the ignorance,
The pride, the lust, the squalid sloth,
Which nurtured Treason's monstrous growth,
Made murder pastime, and the hell
Of prison-torture possible;

[2] A river which flows down from the Pindus mountains
in Greece; Mt. Olympus was the home of the
gods.

The cruel lie of caste refute,
Old forms remold, and substitute
For Slavery's lash the freeman's will,
For blind routine, wise-handed skill;   500
A school-house plant on every hill,
Stretching in radiate nerve-lines thence
The quick wires of intelligence;
Till North and South together brought
Shall own the same electric thought,
In peace a common flag salute,
And, side by side in labor's free
And unresentful rivalry,
Harvest the fields wherein they fought.

Another guest [1] that winter night   510
Flashed back from lustrous eyes the light.
Unmarked by time, and yet not young,
The honeyed music of her tongue
And words of meekness scarcely told
A nature passionate and bold,
Strong, self-concentered, spurning guide,
Its milder features dwarfed beside
Her unbent will's majestic pride.
She sat among us, at the best,
A not unfeared, half-welcome guest,   520
Rebuking with her cultured phrase
Our homeliness of words and ways.
A certain pard-like, treacherous grace
    Swayed the lithe limbs and drooped the
      lash,
    Lent the white teeth their dazzling flash;
    And under low brows, black with night,
    Rayed out at times a dangerous light;
The sharp heat-lightnings of her face
    Presaging ill to whom Fate
Condemned to share her love or hate.   530
A woman tropical, intense
In thought and act, in soul and sense,

[1] Whittier's own explanatory note is interesting: "The
not unfeared, half-welcome guest was Harriet
Livermore, daughter of Judge Livermore, of New
Hampshire, a young woman of fine natural ability,
enthusiastic, eccentric, with slight control over her
violent temper, which sometimes made her religious profession doubtful. She was equally ready
to exhort in schoolhouse, prayer-meeting and dance
in a Washington ballroom while her father was
a member of Congress. She early embraced the
doctrine of the Second Advent and felt it her
duty to proclaim the Lord's speedy coming. With
this message she crossed the Atlantic and spent
the greater part of a long life in traveling over
Europe and Asia. She lived some time with Lady
Hester Stanhope, a woman as fantastic and mentally strained as herself, on the slope of Mt. Lebanon, but finally quarreled with her. . . . A friend
of mine found her, when quite an old woman,
wandering in Syria with a tribe of Arabs, who,
with the Oriental notion that madness is inspiration, accepted her as their prophetess and leader.
At the time referred to in *Snow-Bound* she was
boarding at the Rocks Village, about two miles
from us." *Riverside Classics* edition of Whittier's poems, p. ix.

She blended in a like degree
The vixen and the devotee,
Revealing with each freak or feint
    The temper of Petruchio's Kate, [2]
The raptures of Siena's saint. [3]
Her tapering hand and rounded wrist
Had facile power to form a fist;
The warm, dark languish of her eyes   540
Was never safe from wrath's surprise.
Brows saintly calm and lips devout
Knew every change of scowl and pout;
And the sweet voice had notes more high
And shrill for social battle-cry.

Since then what old cathedral town
Has missed her pilgrim staff and gown,
What convent-gate has held its lock
Against the challenge of her knock!
Through Smyrna's plague-hushed thorough-
      fares,   550
Up sea-set Malta's rocky stairs,
Gray olive slopes of hills that hem
Thy tombs and shrines, Jerusalem,
Or startling on her desert throne
The crazy Queen of Lebanon
With claims fantastic as her own,
Her tireless feet have held their sway;
And still, unrestful, bowed, and gray,
She watches under Eastern skies,   559
    With hope each day renewed and fresh,
    The Lord's quick coming in the flesh,
Whereof she dreams and prophesies!

Where'er her troubled path may be,
    The Lord's sweet pity with her go!
The outward wayward life we see,
    The hidden springs we may not know.
Nor is it given us to discern
    What threads the fatal sisters spun,
    Through what ancestral years has run
The sorrow with the woman born,   570
What forged her cruel chain of moods,
What set her feet in solitudes,
    And held the love within her mute,
What mingled madness in the blood,
    A life-long discord and annoy,
    Water of tears with oil of joy,
And hid within the folded bud
    Perversities of flower and fruit.
It is not ours to separate
The tangled skein of will and fate,   580
To show what metes and bounds should stand
Upon the soul's debatable land,
And between choice and Providence

[2] Shakespeare's *The Taming of the Shrew*
[3] Saint Catherine of Siena, a famous saint, experienced many trances and visions.

Divide the circle of events;
But he who knows our frame is just,
  Merciful and compassionate,
And full of sweet assurances
And hope for all the language is,
That He remembereth we are dust!

At last the great logs, crumbling low,
Sent out a dull and duller glow,   591
The bull's-eye watch that hung in view,
Ticking its weary circuit through,
Pointed with mutely-warning sign
Its black hand to the hour of nine.
That sign the pleasant circle broke:
My uncle ceased his pipe to smoke,
Knocked from its bowl the refuse gray
And laid it tenderly away,
Then roused himself to safely cover   600
The dull red brands with ashes over.
And while, with care, our mother laid
The work aside, her steps she stayed
One moment, seeking to express
Her grateful sense of happiness
For food and shelter, warmth and health,
And love's contentment more than wealth,
With simple wishes (not the weak,
Vain prayers which no fulfilment seek,
But such as warm the generous heart,   610
O'er-prompt to do with Heaven its part)
That none might lack, that bitter night,
For bread and clothing, warmth and light.

Within our beds awhile we heard
The wind that round the gables roared,
With now and then a ruder shock,
Which made our very bedsteads rock.
We heard the loosened clapboards tost,
The board-nails snapping in the frost;
And on us, through the unplastered wall,
Felt the light-sifted snow-flakes fall;   621
But sleep stole on, as sleep will do
When hearts are light and life is new;
Faint and more faint the murmurs grew,
Till in the summer-land of dreams
They softened to the sound of streams,
Low stir of leaves, and dip of oars,
And lapsing waves on quiet shores.

Next morn we wakened with the shout
Of merry voices high and clear;   630
And saw the teamsters drawing near
To break the drifted highways out.
Down the long hillside treading slow
We saw the half-buried oxen go,
Shaking the snow from heads uptost,
Their straining nostrils white with frost.
Before our door the straggling train

Drew up, an added team to gain.
The elders threshed their hands a-cold,
  Passed, with the cider-mug, their jokes
  From lip to lip; the younger folks   641
Down the loose snow-banks, wrestling, rolled,
Then toiled again the cavalcade
  O'er windy hill, through clogged ravine,
  And woodland paths that wound between
Low drooping pine-boughs winter-weighed.
From every barn a team afoot,
At every house a new recruit,
Where, drawn by Nature's subtlest law,
Haply the watchful young men saw   650
Sweet doorway pictures of the curls
And curious eyes of merry girls,
Lifting their hands in mock defense
Against the snow-ball's compliments,
And reading in each missive tost
The charm with Eden never lost.

We heard once more the sleigh-bells' sound;
  And, following where the teamsters led,
The wise old Doctor went his round,
Just pausing at our door to say,   660
In the brief autocratic way
Of one who, prompt at Duty's call,
Was free to urge her claim on all,
  That some poor neighbor sick abed
At night our mother's aid would need.
For, one in generous thought and deed,
  What mattered in the sufferer's sight
  The Quaker matron's inward light,
The Doctor's mail of Calvin's creed?
All hearts confess the saints elect   670
  Who, twain in faith, in love agree,
And melt not in an acid sect
  The Christian pearl of charity!

So days went on: a week had passed
Since the great world was heard from last.
The almanac we studied o'er,
Read and reread our little store
Of books and pamphlets, scarce a score;
One harmless novel, mostly hid
From younger eyes, a book forbid,   680
And poetry, (or good or bad,
A single book was all we had,)
Where Ellwood's [1] meek, drab-skirted Muse,
  A stranger to the heathen Nine,
  Sang, with a somewhat nasal whine,
The wars of David and the Jews.
At last the floundering carrier bore
The village paper to our door.

[1] Thomas Ellwood, an English Quaker, 1639-1713, and
a friend of Milton's, wrote a long poem in five
books about the life of King David, which, as
Whittier intimates, was not inspired by the Greek
Muses.

Lo! broadening outward as we read,
To warmer zones the horizon spread; 690
In panoramic length unrolled
We saw the marvels that it told.
Before us passed the painted Creeks, [1]
    And daft McGregor on his raids
    In Costa Rica's everglades.
And up Taygetos winding slow
Rode Ypsilanti's Mainote Greeks,
A Turk's head at each saddle bow!
Welcome to us its week-old news,
Its corner for the rustic Muse, 700
    Its monthly gauge of snow and rain,
Its record, mingling in a breath
The wedding bell and dirge of death;
Jest, anecdote, and love-lorn tale,
The latest culprit sent to jail;
Its hue and cry of stolen and lost,
Its vendue sales and goods at cost,
    And traffic calling loud for gain.
We felt the stir of hall and street,
The pulse of life that round us beat; 710
The chill embargo of the snow
Was melted in the genial glow;
Wide swung again our ice-locked door,
And all the world was ours once more!

Clasp, Angel of the backward look
    And folded wings of ashen gray
    And voice of echoes far away,
The brazen covers of thy book;
The weird palimpsest [2] old and vast,
Wherein thou hid'st the spectral past; 720
Where, closely mingling, pale and glow
The characters of joy and woe;
The monographs of outlived years,
Or smile-illumed or dim with tears,
    Green hills of life that slope to death, .
And haunts of home, whose vistaed trees
Shade off to mournful cypresses
    With the white amaranths [3] underneath.
Even while I look, I can but heed
    The restless sands' incessant fall, 730
Importunate hours that hours succeed,
Each clamorous with its own sharp need,
    And duty keeping pace with all.
Shut down and clasp the heavy lids;
I hear again the voice that bids
The dreamer leave his dream midway
For larger hopes and graver fears:

[1] They read of the war with the Seminole or Creek
    Indians in Georgia, 1817-18; of the Scotch Sir
    Gregor McGregor, who tried to establish a colony
    in Costa Rica; of Ypsilanti, a Greek who, in the
    war for Greek independence, gathered his cavalry-
    men from the province of Maina, near Mt. Tay-
    getus, a locality inhabited by robbers and pirates.
[2] a parchment from which one writing has been erased
    to make room for another
[3] an immortal flower

Life greatens in these later years,
The century's aloe flowers today!

Yet, haply, in some lull of life, 740
Some Truce of God [4] which breaks its strife
The worldling's eyes shall gather dew,
    Dreaming in throngful city ways
Of winter joys his boyhood knew;
And dear and early friends—the few
Who yet remain—shall pause to view
    These Flemish pictures [5] of old days;
Sit with me by the homestead hearth,
And stretch the hands of memory forth
    To warm them at the wood-fire's blaze!
And thanks untraced to lips unknown 751
Shall greet me like the odors blown
From unseen meadows newly mown,
Or lilies floating in some pond,
Wood-fringed, the wayside gaze beyond;
The traveler owns the grateful sense
Of sweetness near, he knows not whence,
And, pausing, takes with forehead bare
The benediction of the air.
1865   1866

THE ETERNAL GOODNESS

O friends! with whom my feet have trod
    The quiet aisles of prayer,
Glad witness to your zeal for God
    And love of man I bear.

I trace your lines of argument;
    Your logic linked and strong
I weigh as one who dreads dissent,
    And fears a doubt as wrong.

But still my human hands are weak
    To hold your iron creeds; 10
Against the words ye bid me speak
    My heart within me pleads.

Who fathoms the Eternal Thought?
    Who talks of scheme and plan?
The Lord is God! He needeth not
    The poor device of man.

I walk with bare, hushed feet the ground
    Ye tread with boldness shod;
I dare not fix with mete and bound
    The love and power of God. 20

Ye praise his justice; even such
    His pitying love I deem:

[4] in medieval times a cessation of private hostilities
    from Thursday evening to Monday morning
[5] The Flemish painters of the 15th century were among
    the first to depict homely, domestic life.

Ye seek a king; I fain would touch
 The robe that hath no seam.

Ye see the curse which overbroods
 A world of pain and loss;
I hear our Lord's beatitudes
 And prayer upon the cross.

More than your schoolmen teach, within
 Myself, alas! I know: 30
Too dark ye cannot paint the sin,
 Too small the merit show.

I bow my forehead to the dust,
 I veil mine eyes for shame,
And urge, in trembling self-distrust,
 A prayer without a claim.

I see the wrong that round me lies,
 I feel the guilt within;
I hear, with groan and travail-cries,
 The world confess its sin.   40

Yet, in the maddening maze of things,
 And tossed by storm and flood,
To one fixed trust my spirit clings;
 I know that God is good!

Not mine to look where cherubim
 And seraphs may not see,
But nothing can be good in him
 Which evil is in me.

The wrong that pains my soul below
 I dare not throne above,   50
I know not of his hate,—I know
 His goodness and his love.

I dimly guess from blessings known
 Of greater out of sight,
And, with the chastened Psalmist, own
 His judgments too are right. [1]

I long for household voices gone,
 For vanished smiles I long,
But God hath led my dear ones on,
 And he can do no wrong.   60

I know not what the future hath
 Of marvel or surprise,
Assured alone that life and death
 His mercy underlies.

And if my heart and flesh are weak
 To bear an untried pain,
The bruised reed he will not break,
 But strengthen and sustain.

[1] Cf. David, *Psalms* xix, 9.

No offering of my own I have,
 Nor works my faith to prove;   70
I can but give the gifts he gave,
 And plead his love for love.

And so beside the Silent Sea
 I wait the muffled oar;
No harm from him can come to me
 On ocean or on shore.

I know not where his islands lift
 Their fronded palms in air;
I only know I cannot drift
 Beyond his love and care.   80

O brothers! if my faith is vain,
 If hopes like these betray,
Pray for me that my feet may gain
 The sure and safer way.

And Thou, O Lord! by whom are seen
 Thy creatures as they be,
Forgive me if too close I lean
 My human heart on thee!
1865   1867

IN SCHOOL-DAYS

Still sits the school-house by the road,
 A ragged beggar sleeping;
Around it still the sumachs grow,
 And blackberry vines are creeping.

Within, the master's desk is seen,
 Deep scarred by raps official;
The warping floor, the battered seats,
 The jack-knife's carved initial;

The charcoal frescoes on its wall;
 Its door's worn sill, betraying   10
The feet that, creeping slow to school,
 Went storming out to playing!

Long years ago a winter sun
 Shone over it at setting;
Lit up its western window-panes,
 And low eaves' icy fretting.

It touched the tangled golden curls,
 And brown eyes full of grieving,
Of one who still her steps delayed
 When all the school were leaving.

For near her stood the little boy
 Her childish favor singled:
His cap pulled low upon a face
 Where pride and shame were mingled.

Pushing with restless feet the snow
　To right and left, he lingered;—
As restlessly her tiny hands
　The blue-checked apron fingered.

He saw her lift her eyes; he felt
　The soft hand's light caressing,　　　　30
And heard the tremble of her voice,
　As if a fault confessing.

"I'm sorry that I spelt the word:
　I hate to go above you,
Because,"—the brown eyes lower fell,—
　"Because, you see, I love you!"

Still memory to a gray-haired man
　That sweet child-face is showing.
Dear girl! the grasses on her grave
　Have forty years been growing!　　　　40

He lives to learn, in life's hard school,
　How few who pass above him
Lament their triumph and his loss,
　Like her,—because they love him.
1870　　　　　　　　　　　　　　*1870*

MY TRIUMPH

The autumn-time has come;
On woods that dream of bloom,
And over purpling vines,
The low sun fainter shines.

The aster-flower is failing,
The hazel's gold is paling;
Yet overhead more near
The eternal stars appear!

And present gratitude
Insures the future's good,　　　　10
And for the things I see
I trust the things to be;

That in the paths untrod,
And the long days of God,
My feet shall still be led,
My heart be comforted.

O living friends who love me!
O dear ones gone above me!
Careless of other fame,
I leave to you my name.　　　　20

Hide it from idle praises,
Save it from evil phrases:
Why, when dear lips that spake it
Are dumb, should strangers wake it?

Let the thick curtain fall;
I better know than all
How little I have gained,
How vast the unattained.

Not by the page word-painted
Let life be banned or sainted:　　　　30
Deeper than written scroll
The colors of the soul.

Sweeter than any sung
My songs that found no tongue;
Nobler than any fact
My wish that failed of act. [1]

Others shall sing the song,
Others shall right the wrong,—
Finish what I begin,
And all I fail of win.　　　　40

What matter, I or they?
Mine or another's day,
So the right word be said
And life the sweeter made?

Hail to the coming singers!
Hail to the brave light-bringers!
Forward I reach and share
All that they sing and dare.

The airs of heaven blow o'er me;
A glory shines before me　　　　50
Of what mankind shall be,—
Pure, generous, brave and free.

A dream of man and woman
Diviner but still human,
Solving the riddle old,
Shaping the Age of Gold! [2]

The love of God and neighbor;
An equal-handed labor;
The richer life, where beauty
Walks hand in hand with duty.　　　　60

Ring, bells in unreared steeples,
The joy of unborn peoples!
Sound, trumpets far off blown,
Your triumph is my own!

[1] Cf. Browning's "Rabbi Ben Ezra."
　　"What I aspired to be,
　　And was not comforts me";
　　. . . . .
　　"All I could never be,
　　All, men ignored in me,
　　This, I was worth to God, whose wheel the pitcher
　　　shaped."
[2] the fabled primeval age of innocence and happiness

Parcel and part of all,
I keep the festival,
Fore-reach the good to be,
And share the victory.

I feel the earth move sunward,
I join the great march onward,   70
And take, by faith, while living,
My freehold of thanksgiving.

1870   1871

JOHN UNDERHILL [1]

A score of years had còme and gone
Since the Pilgrims landed on Plymouth stone,
When Captain Underhill, bearing scars
From Indian ambush and Flemish wars,
Left three-hilled Boston and wandered down,
East by north, to Cocheco [2] town.

With Vane the younger, [3] in council sweet,
He had sat at Anna Hutchinson's feet,
And, when the bolt of banishment fell
On the head of his saintly oracle,   10
He had shared her ill as her good report,
And braved the wrath of the General Court.

He shook from his feet as he rode away
The dust of the Massachusetts Bay.
The world might bless and the world might ban,
What did it matter the perfect man,
To whom the freedom of earth was given,
Proof against sin, and sure of heaven?

He cheered his heart as he rode along
With screed [4] of Scripture and holy song,   20
Or thought how he rode with his lances free
By the Lower Rhine and the Zuyder-Zee.

[1] Captain Underhill, c. 1600-1672, after having served in the Netherlands and in Spain, came to Massachusetts in 1630. Here he was a member of the Massachusetts Assembly and aided valiantly in putting down the Pequot rebellion. Being disfranchised by the Massachusetts court, and fearing to face a charge of adultery, he fled to Cocheco (Dover, New Hampshire), where he was chosen governor. Later he returned to Massachusetts, publicly confessed his sins, and was reinstated. After this he lived in the New Haven colony and among the Dutch in New Netherlands, doing excellent service as an Indian fighter. His career, which shows a strange mixture of courage, passion, humility, integrity, and hypocrisy, is pretty thoroughly set forth in Winthrop's *History*, even to his "taking" [smoking] of tobacco. His life is a most interesting sidelight upon the trials of those who administered law and formal religion in the New England colonies.
[2] Dover, New Hampshire
[3] Sir Harry Vane, governor of the Massachusetts Bay Colony 1636-37, whose independence and breadth of view were unusual in his time; he sympathized with Mrs. Hutchinson, a religious extremist who was banished from the Massachusetts Bay Colony in 1637 because of her views.
[4] quotation

Till his wood-path grew to a trodden road,
And Hilton Point [5] in the distance showed.

He saw the church with the blockhouse nigh,
The two fair rivers, the flakes thereby,
And, tacking to windward, low and crank,
The little shallop from Strawberry Bank; [5]
And he rose in his stirrups and looked abroad
Over land and water, and praised the Lord.

Goodly and stately and grave to see,   31
Into the clearing's space rode he,
With the sun on the hilt of his sword in sheath,
And his silver buckles and spurs beneath,
And the settlers welcomed him, one and all,
From swift Quampeagan to Gonic Fall. [5]

And he said to the elders: "Lo, I come
As the way seemed open to seek a home.
Somewhat the Lord hath wrought by my hands
In the Narragansett and Netherlands,   40
And if here ye have work for a Christian man,
I will tarry, and serve ye as best I can.

"I boast not of gifts, but fain would own
The wonderful favor God hath shown,
The special mercy vouchsafed one day
On the shore of Narragansett Bay,
As I sat, with my pipe, from the camp aside,
And mused like Isaac at eventide.

"A sudden sweetness of peace I found,
A garment of gladness wrapped me round;   50
I felt from the law of works released,
The strife of the flesh and the spirit ceased,
My faith to a full assurance grew,
And all I had hoped for myself I knew.

"Now as God appointeth, I keep my way,
I shall not stumble, I shall not stray;
He hath taken away my fig-leaf dress,
I wear the robe of His righteousness;
And the shafts of Satan no more avail
Than Pequot arrows on Christian mail."

"Tarry with us," the settler cried,   61
Thou man of God, as our ruler and guide."
And Captain Underhill bowed his head.
"The will of the Lord be done!" he said.
And the morrow beheld him sitting down
In the ruler's seat in Cocheco town.

And he judged therein as a just man should;
His words were wise and his rule was good;
He coveted not his neighbor's land,
From the holding of bribes he shook his hand;

[5] near Dover

And through the camps of the heathen ran   71
A wholesome fear of the valiant man.

But the heart is deceitful, the good Book saith,
And life hath ever a savor of death.
Through hymns of triumph the tempter calls,
And whoso thinketh he standeth falls.
Alas! ere their round the seasons ran,
There was grief in the soul of the saintly man.

The tempter's arrows that rarely fail
Had found the joints of his spiritual mail;   80
And men took note of his gloomy air,
The shame in his eye, the halt in his prayer,
The signs of a battle lost within,
The pain of a soul in the coils of sin.

Then a whisper of scandal linked his name
With broken vows and a life of blame;
And the people looked askance on him
As he walked among them sullen and grim,
Ill at ease, and bitter of word,
And prompt of quarrel with hand or sword.   90

None knew how, with prayer and fasting still,
He strove in the bonds of his evil will;
But he shook himself like Samson at length,
And girded anew his loins of strength,
And bade the crier go up and down
And call together the wondering town.

Jeer and murmur and shaking of head
Ceased as he rose in his place and said:
"Men, brethren, and fathers, well ye know
How I came among you a year ago,   100
Strong in the faith that my soul was freed
From sin of feeling, or thought, or deed.

"I have sinned, I own it with grief and shame,
But not with a lie on my lips I came.
In my blindness I verily thought my heart
Swept and garnished in every part.
He chargeth His angels with folly; He sees
The heavens unclean. Was I more than these?

"I urge no plea. At your feet I lay
The trust you gave me, and go my way.   110
Hate me or pity me, as you will,
The Lord will have mercy on sinners still;
And I, who am chiefest, say to all,
Watch and pray, lest ye also fall."

No voice made answer; a sob so low
That only his quickened ear could know
Smote his heart with a bitter pain,
As into the forest he rode again,
And the veil of its oaken leaves shut down
On his latest glimpse of Cocheco town.   120

Crystal-clear on the man of sin
The streams flashed up, and the sky shone in;
On his cheek of fever the cool wind blew,
The leaves dropped on him their tears of dew,
And angels of God, in the pure, sweet guise
Of flowers, looked on him with sad surprise.

Was his ear at fault that brook and breeze
Sang in their saddest of minor keys?
What was it the mournful wood-thrush said?
What whispered the pine-trees overhead?   130
Did he hear the Voice on his lonely way
That Adam heard in the cool of day?

Into the desert alone rode he,
Alone with the Infinite Purity;
And, bowing his soul to its tender rebuke,
As Peter did to the Master's look,
He measured his path with prayers of pain
For peace with God and nature again.

And in after years to Cocheco came
The bruit of a once familiar name;   140
How among the Dutch of New Netherlands,
From wild Danskamer to Haarlem sands,
A penitent soldier preached the Word,
And smote the heathen with Gideon's sword! [1]

And the heart of Boston was glad to hear
How he harried the foe on the long frontier,
And heaped on the land against him barred
The coals of his generous watch and ward.
Frailest and bravest! the Bay State still   149
Counts with her worthies John Underhill.
1873   1873

CONDUCTOR BRADLEY [2]

Conductor Bradley, (always may his name
Be said with reverence!) as the swift doom
          came,
Smitten to death, a crushed and mangled frame,

Sank, with the brake he grasped just where he
          stood
To do the utmost that a brave man could,
And die, if needful, as a true man should.

Men stooped above him; women dropped their
          tears
On that poor wreck beyond all hopes or fears,
Lost in the strength and glory of his years.

What heard they? Lo! the ghastly lips of
          pain,   10

---

[1] *Judges* vii, 18
[2] "A railway conductor who lost his life in an accident on a Connecticut railway, May 9, 1873." (Cambridge Edition of Whittier's poems, p. 117.)

Dead to all thought save duty's, moved again:
  "Put out the signals for the other train!"

No nobler utterance since the world began
From lips of saint or martyr ever ran,
Electric, through the sympathies of man.

Ah me! how poor and noteless seem to this
The sick-bed dramas of self-consciousness,
Our sensual fears of pain and hopes of bliss!

Oh, grand supreme endeavor! Not in vain   19
That last brave act of failing tongue and brain!
Freighted with life the downward rushing train,

Following the wrecked one, as wave follows
      wave,
Obeyed the warning which the dead lips gave.
Others he saved, himself he could not save.

Nay, the lost life *was* saved. He is not dead
Who, in his record still the earth shall tread
With God's clear aureole shining round his
      head.

We bow as in the dust, with all our pride
Of virtue dwarfed the noble deed beside.   29
God give us grace to live as Bradley died!
1873

A SEA DREAM

We saw the slow tides go and come,
  The curving surf-lines lightly drawn,
The gray rocks touched with tender bloom
  Beneath the fresh-blown rose of dawn.

We saw in richer sunsets lost
  The somber pomp of showery noons;
And signaled spectral sails that crossed
  The weird, low light of rising moons.

On stormy eves from cliff and head   9
  We saw the white spray tossed and spurned;
While over all, in gold and red,
  Its face of fire the lighthouse turned.

The rail-car brought its daily crowds,
  Half curious, half indifferent,
Like passing sails or floating clouds,
  We saw them as they came and went.

But, one calm morning, as we lay
  And watched the mirage-lifted wall
Of coast, across the dreamy bay,
  And heard afar the curlew call,   20

And nearer voices, wild or tame,
  Of airy flocks and childish throng,

Up from the water's edge there came
  Faint snatches of familiar song.

Careless we heard the singer's choice
  Of old and common airs; at last
The tender pathos of his voice
  In one low chanson held us fast.

A song that mingled joy and pain,
  And memories old and sadly sweet;   30
While, timing to its minor strain,
  The waves in lapsing cadence beat.

———

The waves are glad in breeze and sun;
  The rocks are fringed with foam;
I walk once more a haunted shore,
  A stranger, yet at home,
  A land of dreams I roam.

Is this the wind, the soft sea-wind
  That stirred thy locks of brown?
Are these the rocks whose mosses knew   40
  The trail of thy light gown,
  Where boy and girl sat down?

I see the gray fort's broken wall,
  The boats that rock below;
And, out at sea, the passing sails
  We saw so long ago
  Rose-red in morning's glow.

The freshness of the early time
  On every breeze is blown;
As glad the sea, as blue the sky,—   50
  The change is ours alone;
  The saddest is my own.

A stranger now, a world-worn man,
  Is he who bears my name;
But thou, methinks, whose mortal life
  Immortal youth became,
  Art evermore the same.

Thou art not here, thou art not there,
  Thy place I cannot see;
I only know that where thou art   60
  The blessed angels be,
  And heaven is glad for thee.

Forgive me if the evil years
  Have left on me their sign;
Wash out, O soul so beautiful,
  The many stains of mine
  In tears of love divine!

I could not look on thee and live,
　　If thou wert by my side;
The vision of a shining one,　　　　　　　70
　　The white and heavenly bride,
　　Is well to me denied.

But turn to me thy dear girl-face
　　Without the angel's crown,
The wedded roses of thy lips,
　　Thy loose hair rippling down
　　In waves of golden brown.

Look forth once more through space and time,
　　And let thy sweet shade fall
In tenderest grace of soul and form　　　　80
　　On memory's frescoed wall,
　　A shadow, and yet all!

Draw near, more near, forever dear!
　　Where'er I rest or roam,
Or in the city's crowded streets,
　　Or by the blown sea foam,
　　The thought of thee is home!

At breakfast hour the singer read
　　The city news, with comment wise,
Like one who felt the pulse of trade　　　90
　　Beneath his finger fall and rise.

His look, his air, his curt speech, told
　　The man of action, not of books,
To whom the corners made in gold
　　And stocks were more than seaside nooks.

Of life beneath the life confessed
　　His song had hinted unawares;
Of flowers in traffic's ledgers pressed,
　　Of human hearts in bulls and bears.

But eyes in vain were turned to watch　　　100
　　That face so hard and shrewd and strong;
And ears in vain grew sharp to catch
　　The meaning of that morning song.

In vain some sweet-voiced querist sought
　　To sound him, leaving as she came;
Her baited album only caught
　　A common, unromantic name.

No word betrayed the mystery fine,
　　That trembled on the singer's tongue;
He came and went, and left no sign　　　　110
　　Behind him save the song he sung.

1874

SUNSET ON THE BEARCAMP [1]

A gold fringe on the purpling hem
　　Of hills the river runs,
As down its long, green valley falls
　　The last of summer's suns.
Along its tawny gravel-bed
　　Broad-flowing, swift, and still,
As if its meadow levels felt
　　The hurry of the hill.
Noiseless between its banks of green
　　From curve to curve it slips;　　　　10
The drowsy maple-shadows rest
　　Like fingers on its lips.

A waif from Carroll's [2] wildest hills,
　　Unstoried and unknown;
The ursine legend of its name
　　Prowls on its banks alone.
Yet flowers as fair its slopes adorn
　　As ever Yarrow [3] knew,
Or, under rainy Irish skies,
　　By Spenser's Mulla [4] grew;　　　　20
And through the gaps of leaning trees
　　Its mountain cradle shows:
The gold against the amethyst,
　　The green against the rose.

Touched by a light that hath no name,
　　A glory never sung,
Aloft on sky and mountain wall
　　Are God's great pictures hung.
How changed the summits vast and old!
　　No longer granite-browed,　　　　30
They melt in rosy mist; the rock
　　Is softer than the cloud;
The valley holds its breath; no leaf
　　Of all its elms is twirled;
The silence of eternity
　　Seems falling on the world.

The pause before the breaking seals
　　Of mystery is this;
Yon miracle-play of night and day
　　Makes dumb its witnesses.　　　　40
What unseen altar crowns the hills
　　That reach up stair on stair?
What eyes look through, what white wings fan
　　These purple veils of air?
What Presence from the heavenly heights
　　To those of earth stoops down?

[1] Whittier was very fond of the scenery near Ossipee,
　　N.H., on the Bearcamp River.
[2] Carroll County, New Hampshire
[3] the Scotch stream and valley made famous by Words-
　　worth's "Yarrow Unvisited," and other poems
[4] Edmund Spenser lived for a time in Kilcolman
　　Castle near the Mulla River in Ireland.

Not vainly Hellas dreamed of gods
  On Ida's snowy crown! [1]

Slow fades the vision of the sky,
  The golden water pales,   50
And over all the valley-land
  A gray-winged vapor sails.
I go the common way of all;
  The sunset fires will burn,
The flowers will blow, the river flow,
  When I no more return.
No whisper from the mountain pine
  Nor lapsing stream shall tell
The stranger, treading where I tread,
  Of him who loved them well.   60

But beauty seen is never lost,
  God's colors all are fast;
The glory of this sunset heaven
  Into my soul has passed,
A sense of gladness unconfined
  To mortal date or clime;
As the soul liveth, it shall live
  Beyond the years of time.
Beside the mystic asphodels [2]
  Shall bloom the home-born flowers, 70
And new horizons flush and glow
  With sunset hues of ours.

Farewell! these smiling hills must wear
  Too soon their wintry frown,
And snow-cold winds from off them shake
  The maple's red leaves down.
But I shall see a summer sun
  Still setting broad and low;
The mountain slopes shall blush and bloom,
  The golden water flow.   80
A lover's claim is mine on all
  I see to have and hold,—
The rose-light of perpetual hills,
  And sunsets never cold!

1876   1876

THE TRAILING ARBUTUS

I wandered lonely where the pine-trees made
Against the bitter East their barricade,
  And, guided by its sweet
Perfume, I found, within a narrow dell,
The trailing spring flower tinted like a shell
  Amid dry leaves and mosses at my feet.

[1] The Greeks naturally peopled the beautiful Mt. Ida
  with gods.
[2] A flower of the lily order; in Greek mythology the
  asphodel covered the meadows of the underworld
  and was associated with the dead.

From under dead boughs, for whose loss the
    pines
Moaned ceaseless overhead, the blossoming
    vines
  Lifted their glad surprise,
While yet the bluebird smoothed in leafless
    trees   10
His feathers ruffled by the chill sea-breeze,
  And snow-drifts lingered under April skies.

As, pausing o'er the lonely flower I bent,
I thought of lives thus lowly, clogged and pent,
  Which yet find room,
Through care and cumber, coldness and decay,
To lend a sweetness to the ungenial day,
  And make the sad earth happier for their
    bloom.

1879

THE LOST OCCASION [3]

Some die too late and some too soon,
At early morning, heat of noon,
Or the chill evening twilight. Thou,
Whom the rich heavens did so endow
With eyes of power and Jove's [4] own brow,
With all the massive strength that fills
Thy home-horizon's granite hills,
With rarest gifts of heart and head
From manliest stock inherited,
New England's stateliest type of man,   10
In port and speech Olympian;
Whom no one met, at first, but took
A second awed and wondering look
(As turned, perchance the eyes of Greece
On Phidias' unveiled masterpiece); [5]
Whose words in simplest homespun clad,
The Saxon strength of Caedmon's [6] had,
With power reserved at need to reach
The Roman forum's loftiest speech,
Sweet with persuasion, eloquent   20
In passion, cool in argument,
Or, ponderous, falling on thy foes

[3] This poem, written thirty years after "Ichabod," shows
Whittier's softened feeling regarding Webster,
but it is still tinged by strong Abolition sentiment.
See note 1, p. 476.
[4] Carlyle, who once saw Webster, described his eyes
as: "dull black eyes under their precipice of brows
like dull anthracite furnaces needing only to be
blown"; Webster's large head and great forehead
made him seem indeed Olympian. The remark
of Richard Brinsley Sheridan concerning Lord
Thurlow, that "no man was ever so wise as Lord
Thurlow looked," might well have been made of
Webster.
[5] the colossal statue of Zeus at Olympia
[6] an old English poet who died about 680; his life is
narrated in Bede's *Ecclesiastical History of England*. See note 7, p. 713.

As fell the Norse god's [1] hammer blows,
Crushing as if with Talus' [2] flail
Through Error's logic-woven mail,
And failing only when they tried
The adamant of the righteous side,—
Thou, foiled in aim and hope, bereaved
Of old friends, by the new deceived,
Too soon for us, too soon for thee,　　30
Beside thy lonely Northern sea,
Where long and low the marsh-lands spread,
Laid wearily down thy august head.

Thou shouldst have lived to feel below
Thy feet Disunion's fierce upthrow;
The late-sprung mine that underlaid
Thy sad concessions vainly made.
Thou shouldst have seen from Sumter's wall
The star-flag of the Union fall,
And armed rebellion pressing on　　40
The broken lines of Washington!
No stronger voice than thine had then
Called out the utmost might of men,
To make the Union's charter free
And strengthen law by liberty.
How had that stern arbitrament
To thy gray age youth's vigor lent,
Shaming ambition's paltry prize
Before thy disillusioned eyes;
Breaking the spell about thee wound　　50
Like the green withes that Samson bound; [3]
Redeeming in one effort grand,
Thyself and thy imperiled land!
Ah, cruel fate, that closed to thee,
O sleeper by the Northern sea,
The gates of opportunity!
God fills the gaps of human need,
Each crisis brings its word and deed.
Wise men and strong we did not lack;
But still, with memory turning back,　　60
In the dark hours we thought of thee,
And thy lone grave beside the sea.

Above that grave the east winds blow,
And from the marsh-lands drifting slow
The sea-fog comes, with evermore
The wave-wash of a lonely shore,
And sea-bird's melancholy cry,
As Nature fain would typify
The sadness of a closing scene,
The loss of that which should have been.
But, where thy native mountains bare　　71

Their foreheads to diviner air,
Fit emblem of enduring fame,
One lofty summit keeps thy name. [4]
For thee the cosmic forces did
The rearing of that pyramid,
The prescient ages shaping with
Fire, flood, and frost thy monolith.
Sunrise and sunset lay thereon
With hands of light their benison,　　80
The stars of midnight pause to set
Their jewels in its coronet.
And evermore that mountain mass
Seems climbing from the shadowy pass
To light, as if to manifest
Thy nobler self, thy life at best!
1880

THE KING'S MISSIVE [5]
1661

Under the great hill sloping bare
　　To cove and meadow and Common lot,
In his council chamber and oaken chair,
　　Sat the worshipful Governor Endicott.
A grave, strong man, who knew no peer
In the pilgrim land, where he ruled in fear
Of God, not man, and for good or ill
Held his trust with an iron will.

He had shorn with his sword the cross [6] from
　　out
　　The flag, and cloven the May-pole down,　　10
Harried the heathen round about,
　　And whipped the Quakers from town to town.
Earnest and honest, a man at need
To burn like a torch for his own harsh creed,
He kept with the flaming brand of his zeal
The gate of the holy common weal.

His brow was clouded, his eye was stern,
　　With a look of mingled sorrow and wrath;

[1] Thor, the Scandinavian god of thunder, who carried
　　a mighty hammer
[2] An iron man who carried an iron flail with which
　　he threshed out falsehood; see Spenser's *Faerie
　　Queene* V, i, 12.
[3] I. e., that bound Samson; see *Judges* xvi, 6-9.

[4] Mount Webster, in the White Mountains
[5] This poem was based on a historic incident. Endicott,
　　governor of Massachusetts from 1649-1665, except
　　during 1650 and 1654 when he was deputy gover-
　　nor, had been very harsh in his persecution of the
　　Quakers. They had been imprisoned or driven
　　out of the colony, but had persisted in returning
　　until finally a law was passed punishing with death
　　any Quaker that returned after having been sent
　　away. In October, 1659, two men were hanged,
　　and in the spring of 1660 Mrs. Mary Dyer
　　suffered death for her faith. Meantime a petition
　　in behalf of the Quakers had been sent to Charles
　　II, who in May, 1660, had been restored to the
　　throne of England. The poem tells, with con-
　　siderable poetic license Whittier says, how the
　　King's letter demanding toleration of the Quakers
　　was received.
[6] Apparently thinking of it only as a mark of Catholi-
　　cism, he had cut the royal red cross of St. George
　　out of the flag of a Salem company of militia. See
　　in Hawthorne's *Twice-Told Tales*, "Endicott and
　　the Red Cross." For the maypole story see, in the
　　same book, "The Maypole of Merry Mount."

"Woe's me!" he murmured: "at every turn
  The pestilent Quakers are in my path!   20
Some we have scourged, and banished some,
Some hanged, more doomed, and still they
    come,
Fast as the tide of yon bay sets in,
Sowing their heresy's seed of sin.

"Did we count on this? Did we leave behind
  The graves of our kin, the comfort and ease
Of our English hearths and homes, to find
  Troublers of Israel such as these?
Shall I spare? Shall I pity them? God forbid!
I will do as the prophet to Agag did: [1]   30
They come to poison the wells of the Word,
I will hew them in pieces before the Lord!"

The door swung open, and Rawson the clerk
  Entered, and whispered under breath,
"There waits below for the hangman's work
  A fellow banished on pain of death—
Shattuck of Salem, unhealed of the whip,
Brought over in Master Goldsmith's ship
At anchor here in a Christian port,   39
With freight of the devil and all his sort!"

Twice and thrice on the chamber floor
  Striding fiercely from wall to wall,
"The Lord do so to me and more,"
  The Governor cried, "if I hang not all!
Bring hither the Quaker." Calm, sedate,
With the look of a man at ease with fate,
Into that presence grim and dread
Came Samuel Shattuck, with hat on head.

"Off with the knave's hat!" An angry hand
  Smote down the offence; but the wearer said,
With a quiet smile, "By the King's command
  I bear his message and stand in his stead."
In the governor's hand a missive he laid   53
With the royal arms on its seal displayed,
And the proud man spake as he gazed thereat,
Uncovering, "Give Mr. Shattuck his hat."

He turned to the Quaker, bowing low,—
  "The King commandeth your friends' release;
Doubt not he shall be obeyed, although
  To his subjects' sorrow and sin's increase.   60
What he here enjoineth, John Endicott,
His loyal servant, questioneth not.
You are free! God grant the spirit you own
May take you from us to parts unknown."

So the door of the jail was open cast,
  And, like Daniel, out of the lion's den [2]
Tender youth and girlhood passed,

[1] *1 Samuel* xv, 8   [2] *Daniel* vi, 23

With age-bowed women and gray-locked men.
And the voice of one appointed to die
Was lifted in praise and thanks on high,   70
And the little maid from New Netherlands
Kissed, in her joy, the doomed man's hands.

And one, whose call was to minister
  To the souls in prison, beside him went,
An ancient woman, bearing with her
  The linen shroud for his burial meant.
For she, not counting her own life dear,
In the strength of a love that cast out fear,
Had watched and served where her brethren
    died,
Like those who waited the cross beside.   80

One moment they paused on their way to look
  On the martyr graves by the Common side,
And much scourged Wharton of Salem took
  His burden of prophecy up and cried:
"Rest, souls of the valiant! Not in vain
Have ye borne the Master's cross of pain;
Ye have fought the fight, ye are victors crowned,
With a fourfold chain ye have Satan bound!"

The autumn haze lay soft and still   89
  On wood and meadow and upland farms;
On the brow of Snow Hill the great windmill
  Slowly and lazily swung its arms;
Broad in the sunshine stretched away,
With its capes and islands, the turquoise bay;
And over water and dusk of pines
Blue hills lifted their faint outlines.

The topaz leaves of the walnut glowed,
  The sumach added its crimson fleck,
And double in air and water showed   99
  The tinted maples along the Neck; [3]
Through frost flower clusters of pale star-mist,
And gentian fringes of amethyst,
And royal plumes of golden-rod,
The grazing cattle on Centry [4] trod.

But as they who see not, the Quakers saw
  The world about them; they only thought
With deep thanksgiving and pious awe
  On the great deliverance God had wrought.
Through lane and alley the gazing town
Noisily followed them up and down;   110
Some with scoffing and brutal jeer,
Some with pity and words of cheer.

[3] the name in early times for the narrow strip of land
    that connected the peninsula of Boston with the
    mainland
[4] Beacon Hill in early times, because it was a point of
    observation, was frequently called Sentry or
    Centry Hill.

One brave voice rose above the din.
　Upsall, gray with his length of days,
Cried from the door of his Red Lion Inn:
　"Men of Boston, give God the praise!
No more shall innocent blood call down
The bolts of wrath on your guilty town.
The freedom of worship, dear to you,
Is dear to all, and to all is due.　　　　120

"I see the vision of days to come,
　When your beautiful City of the Bay,
Shall be Christian liberty's chosen home,
　And none shall his neighbor's rights gainsay.
The varying notes of worship shall blend
And as one great prayer to God ascend,
And hands of mutual charity raise
Walls of salvation and gates of praise."

So passed the Quakers through Boston town,
　Whose painful [1] ministers sighed to see　　130
The walls of their sheep-fold falling down,
　And wolves of heresy prowling free.
But the years went on, and brought no wrong;
With milder counsels the State grew strong,
At outward Letter and inward Light [2]
Kept the balance of truth aright.

The Puritan spirit perishing not,
　To Concord's yeomen the signal sent,
And spake in the voice of the cannon-shot
　That severed the chains of a continent.　140
With its gentler mission of peace and good-will
The thought of the Quaker is living still,
And the freedom of soul he prophesied
Is gospel and law where the martyrs died.
1880　　　　　　　　　　　　　　　　1881

HENRY WADSWORTH LONG-
FELLOW 1807-1882

　Tennyson was above all others the representative
poet of England during the nineteenth century;
Longfellow, of this country. Outward circumstances could scarcely have been more favorable
to one who was to occupy such a place. He was
born in Portland, Maine, of a family high in social,
professional, and political standing, and steeped
in New England tradition. His life was that of
a teacher and scholar shielded by circumstances
from the hard blows of the world, and having
an abundance of all that makes life comfortable
and profitable. He was graduated from Bowdoin
College in 1825, traveled and studied in Europe
1826-1829, was professor of modern languages at
Bowdoin 1829-1835, and at Harvard College 1836-

[1] diligent, painstaking
[2] The Quaker faith is based largely on the revelations
　　to each of the Inward Light.

1854. He published in prose *Outre-Mer, A Pilgrimage beyond the Sea,* 1833, and *Hyperion,* 1839.
The publication of his poems runs from 1826 to
1883, chief landmarks being *Evangeline,* 1847, *Hiawatha,* 1855, *Tales of a Wayside Inn,* 1863. The
most serious work of his life was the translation of
the *Divina Comedia,* completed in 1867. Into this
difficult task, which has been the despair of many
translators, Longfellow put not only long years of
toil and the fruits of ripe scholarship, but religious
enthusiasm and devotion.

　It is useless to expect in Longfellow the force
of Byron or the mystic insight of Wordsworth.
He was one of a generation whose grandfathers
regarded imaginative literature as a possible snare
of the devil, but who were appealed to by sentiment and didacticism. These we must expect to
find in his poetry. But we must also notice that
whatever he touched he handled in the spirit of the
artist and with all the skill that his own careful
workmanship could achieve; that his work brought
home to America the best of the continental spirit
of his day; that it nourished the affections and
stimulated the intelligence of his readers here; and
that to millions of Europeans as well his poems
were an inspiration and a solace. Longfellow is
perhaps the best story-teller in verse that America
has produced. He was a skillful experimenter in
versification, and the perfection of some of his sonnets is worthy of all praise.

　Biography: G. R. Carpenter, (BB) 1901; T. W.
Higginson, (AML) 1902; S. Longfellow, with ex-
tracts from journal and correspondence, 2 vols.
1886; E. S. Robertson, (GW); G. W. Curtis, (LJ);
Macy. Criticism: P. E. More, (Shel. 5); J. L.
Hervey, "The 'Distinction' of Longfellow." *Dial*
60:49-51; G. Bradford, "Portraits of American
Authors," *Bookm.* 42:248-61; W. D. Howells, "The
Art of Longfellow," *No. Am.* 184:472-85; B. Perry,
"The Centenary of Longfellow," *Atlan.* 99:379-88.

A PSALM OF LIFE

WHAT THE HEART OF THE YOUNG MAN SAID
TO THE PSALMIST [3]

Tell me not, in mournful numbers,
　Life is but an empty dream!—
For the soul is dead that slumbers,
　And things are not what they seem.

Life is real! Life is earnest!
　And the grave is not its goal;
Dust thou art, to dust returnest,
　Was not spoken of the soul.

Not enjoyment, and not sorrow,
　Is our destined end or way;　　　　　10
But to act, that each tomorrow
　Find us farther than today.

[3] King David, whose psalms are among the greatest
　　poems of Hebrew literature

Art is long, and Time is fleeting, [1]
   And our hearts, though stout and brave,
Still, like muffled drums, are beating
   Funeral marches to the grave.

In the world's broad field of battle,
   In the bivouac of Life,
Be not like dumb, driven cattle!
   Be a hero in the strife!   20

Trust no Future, howe'er pleasant!
   Let the dead Past bury its dead!
Act,—act in the living Present!
   Heart within, and God o'erhead!

Lives of great men all remind us
   We can make our lives sublime,
And, departing, leave behind us,
   Footprints on the sands of time;

Footprints, that perhaps another,
   Sailing o'er life's solemn main,   30
A forlorn and shipwrecked brother,
   Seeing, shall take heart again.

Let us, then, be up and doing,
   With a heart for any fate;
Still achieving, still pursuing,
   Learn to labor and to wait.
1838   *1839*

THE REAPER AND THE FLOWERS

There is a Reaper whose name is Death,
   And, with his sickle keen,
He reaps the bearded grain at a breath,
   And the flowers that grow between.

"Shall I have nought that is fair?" saith he;
   "Have nought but the bearded grain?
Though the breath of these flowers is sweet to
     me,
   I will give them all back again."

He gazed at the flowers with tearful eyes,
   He kissed their drooping leaves;   10
It was for the Lord of Paradise
   He bound them in his sheaves.

"My Lord has need of these flowerets gay,"
   The Reaper said, and smiled;
"Dear tokens of the earth are they,
   Where he was once a child.

"They shall all bloom in fields of light,
   Transplanted by my care,
And saints, upon their garments white,
   These sacred blossoms wear."   20

And the mother gave, in tears and pain,
   The flowers she most did love;
She knew she could find them all again
   In the fields of light above.

O, not in cruelty, not in wrath,
   The Reaper came that day;
'Twas an angel visited the green earth,
   And took the flowers away.
1838   *1839*

THE WRECK OF THE HESPERUS [2]

It was the schooner Hesperus,
   That sailed the wintry sea;
And the skipper had taken his little daughtèr,
   To bear him company.

Blue were her eyes as the fairy-flax,
   Her cheeks like the dawn of day,
And her bosom white as the hawthorn buds,
   That ope in the month of May.

The skipper he stood beside the helm,
   His pipe was in his mouth,   10
And he watched how the veering flaw did blow
   The smoke now West, now South.

Then up and spake an old Sailòr,
   Had sailed to the Spanish Main, [3]
"I pray thee, put into yonder port,
   For I fear a hurricane.

"Last night the moon had a golden ring,
   And tonight no moon we see!"
The skipper, he blew a whiff from his pipe,
   And a scornful laugh laughed he.   20

Colder and louder blew the wind,
   A gale from the Northeast,
The snow fell hissing in the brine,
   And the billows frothed like yeast.

Down came the storm, and smote amain
   The vessel in its strength;

---

[1] "Vita brevis, ars longa," a thought probably expressed first by Hippocrates, the Greek Philosopher, 460-377 B.C., and later by Seneca, in *De Brevitate Vitae* I

[2] This is an unusually good imitation of the ancient English popular ballad. Note the similarity of the fourth and fifth stanzas to the second, sixth, and seventh of "Sir Patrick Spens," and compare the concluding invocation with that of "The Hunting of the Cheviot."

[3] a common name for the northern coast of South America or more especially the waters north of that coast

She shuddered and paused, like a frighted steed,
  Then leaped her cable's length.

"Come hither! come hither! my little daughtèr,
  And do not tremble so;   30
For I can weather the roughest gale
  That ever wind did blow."

He wrapped her warm in his seaman's coat
  Against the stinging blast;
He cut a rope from a broken spar,
  And bound her to the mast.

"O father! I hear the church-bells ring, [1]
  Oh say, what may it be?"
" 'Tis a fog-bell on a rock-bound coast!"—
  And he steered for the open sea.   40

"O father! I hear the sound of guns,
  Oh say, what may it be?"
"Some ship in distress, that cannot live
  In such an angry sea!"

"O father! I see a gleaming light,
  Oh say, what may it be?"
But the father answered never a word,
  A frozen corpse was he.

Lashed to the helm, all stiff and stark,
  With his face turned to the skies,   50
The lantern gleamed through the gleaming snow,
  On his fixed and glassy eyes.

Then the maiden clasped her hands and prayed
  That savèd she might be;
And she thought of Christ who stilled the wave,
  On the Lake of Galilee.

And fast through the midnight dark and drear,
  Through the whistling sleet and snow,
Like a sheeted ghost, the vessel swept
  Tow'rds the reef of Norman's Woe. [2]

And ever the fitful gusts between   61
  A sound came from the land;
It was the sound of the trampling surf
  On the rocks and the hard sea-sand.

The breakers were right beneath her bows,
  She drifted a dreary wreck,
And a whooping billow swept the crew
  Like icicles from her deck.

She struck where the white and fleecy waves
  Looked soft as carded wool,   70
But the cruel rocks, they gored her side
  Like the horns of an angry bull.

Her rattling shrouds, all sheathed in ice,
  With the masts went by the board;
Like a vessel of glass, she stove and sank,
  Ho! ho! the breakers roared!

At daybreak, on the bleak sea-beach,
  A fisherman stood aghast,
To see the form of a maiden fair,
  Lashed close to a drifting mast.   80

The salt sea was frozen on her breast,
  The salt tears in her eyes;
And he saw her hair, like the brown sea-weed,
  On the billows fall and rise.

Such was the wreck of the Hesperus,
  In the midnight and the snow!
Christ save us all from a death like this,
  On the reef of Norman's Woe!
1839   1840

THE VILLAGE BLACKSMITH

Under a spreading chestnut-tree
  The village smithy stands;
The smith, a mighty man is he,
  With large and sinewy hands;
And the muscles of his brawny arms
  Are strong as iron bands.

His hair is crisp, and black, and long,
  His face is like the tan;
His brow is wet with honest sweat,
  He earns whate'er he can,   10
And looks the whole world in the face,
  For he owes not any man.

Week in, week out, from morn till night,
  You can hear his bellows blow;
You can hear him swing his heavy sledge
  With measured beat and slow,
Like a sexton ringing the village bell,
  When the evening sun is low.

And children coming home from school
  Look in at the open door;   20
They love to see the flaming forge,
  And hear the bellows roar,
And catch the burning sparks that fly
  Like chaff from a threshing-floor.

[1] The suggestion of impending woe is in the manner
    of the ancient ballads.
[2] a dangerous reef just outside Gloucester harbor, Mass-
    achusetts

He goes on Sunday to the church,
　And sits among his boys;
He hears the parson pray and preach,
　He hears his daughter's voice,
Singing in the village choir,
　And it makes his heart rejoice. 30

It sounds to him like her mother's voice,
　Singing in Paradise!
He needs must think of her once more,
　How in the grave she lies;
And with his hard, rough hand he wipes
　A tear out of his eyes.

Toiling,—rejoicing,—sorrowing,
　Onward through life he goes;
Each morning sees some task begin,
　Each evening sees its close; 40
Something attempted, something done,
　Has earned a night's repose.

Thanks, thanks to thee, my worthy friend,
　For the lesson thou hast taught!
Thus at the flaming forge of life
　Our fortunes must be wrought;
Thus on its sounding anvil shaped
　Each burning deed and thought!
1839　　　　　　　　　　　　　1841

HYMN TO THE NIGHT

'Ασπάσίη, τρίλλιστος[1]

I heard the trailing garments of the Night
　Sweep through her marble halls!
I saw her sable skirts all fringed with light
　From the celestial walls!

I felt her presence, by its spell of might,
　Stoop o'er me from above;
The calm, majestic presence of the Night,
　As of the one I love.

I heard the sounds of sorrow and delight,
　The manifold, soft chimes, 10
That fill the haunted chambers of the Night,
　Like some old poet's rimes.

From the cool cisterns of the midnight air
　My spirit drank repose;
The fountain of perpetual peace flows there,—
　From those deep cisterns flows.

O holy Night! from thee I learn to bear
　What man has borne before!
Thou layest thy finger on the lips of Care,
　And they complain no more. 20

[1] ". . . Welcome, thrice prayed for . . ." Iliad, viii, 488.

Peace! Peace! Orestes-like I breathe this
　prayer![2]
Descend with broad-winged flight,
The welcome, the thrice-prayed for, the most
　fair,
　The best-beloved Night!
1839　　　　　　　　　　　　　1839

THE SKELETON IN ARMOR [3]

"Speak! speak! thou fearful guest!
Who, with thy hollow breast,
Still in rude armor drest,
　Comest to daunt me!
Wrapt not in Eastern balms,[4]
But with thy fleshless palms
Stretched, as if asking alms,
　Why dost thou haunt me?"

Then from those cavernous eyes
Pale flashes seemed to rise, 10
As when the Northern skies
　Gleam in December;
And, like the water's flow
Under December's snow,
Came a dull voice of woe
　From the heart's chamber.

"I was a Viking[5] old!
My deeds, though manifold,
No Skald[6] in song has told,
　No Saga[7] taught thee! 20
Take heed that in thy verse
Thou dost the tale rehearse,
Else dread a dead man's curse;
　For this I sought thee.

"Far in the Northern Land,
By the wild Baltic's strand,
I, with my childish hand,
　Tamed the gerfalcon;[8]
And, with my skates fast-bound,

[2] Orestes, in Aeschylus's drama The Eumenides, when seeking peace from the Furies, prays to the goddess Athena for righteous judgment.
[3] "A skeleton had been dug up at Fall River clad in broken and corroded armor; and the idea occurred to me of connecting it with the Round Tower at Newport."—Longfellow's note. The tower was once thought to be of Norse origin, but has been proved modern. Longfellow is here using the meter and stanza of Michael Drayton's famous ballad "Agincourt."
[4] as the Egyptian dead were wrapped in spices
[5] Scandinavian sea-rover
[6] bard (Scandinavian)
[7] ancient Norse heroic legend
[8] an Arctic falcon of unusual fierceness

Skimmed the half-frozen Sound,   30
That the poor whimpering hound
   Trembled to walk on.

"Oft to his frozen lair
Tracked I the grisly bear,
While from my path the hare
   Fled like a shadow;
Oft through the forest dark
Followed the were-wolf's [1] bark
Until the soaring lark
   Sang from the meadow.   40

"But when I older grew,
Joining a corsair's crew,
O'er the dark sea I flew
   With the marauders.
Wild was the life we led;
Many the souls that sped,
Many the hearts that bled,
   By our stern orders.

"Many a wassail-bout [2]
Wore the long winter out;   50
Often our midnight shout
   Set the cocks crowing,
As we the Berserk's [3] tale
Measured in cups of ale,
Draining the oaken pail
   Filled to o'erflowing.

"Once as I told in glee
Tales of the stormy sea,
Soft eyes did gaze on me,
   Burning yet tender;   60
And as the white stars shine
On the dark Norway pine,
On that dark heart of mine
   Fell their soft splendor.

"I wooed the blue-eyed maid,
Yielding, yet half afraid,
And in the forest's shade
   Our vows were plighted.
Under its loosened vest
Fluttered her little breast,   70
Like birds within their nest
   By the hawk frighted.

"Bright in her father's hall
Shields gleamed upon the wall,
Loud sang the minstrels all,

Chanting his glory;
When of old Hildebrand
I asked his daughter's hand,
Mute did the minstrels stand
   To hear my story.   80

"While the brown ale he quaffed,
Loud then the champion laughed,
And as the wind-gusts waft
   The sea-foam brightly,
So the loud laugh of scorn
Out of those lips unshorn,
From the deep drinking-horn
   Blew the foam lightly.

"She was a Prince's child,
I but a Viking wild,   90
And though she blushed and smiled,
   I was discarded!
Should not the dove so white
Follow the sea-mew's flight?
Why did they leave that night
   Her nest unguarded?

"Scarce had I put to sea,
Bearing the maid with me,
Fairest of all was she
   Among the Norsemen!   100
When on the white sea-strand,
Waving his armèd hand,
Saw we old Hildebrand,
   With twenty horsemen.

"Then launched they to the blast,
Bent like a reed each mast,
Yet we were gaining fast,
   When the wind failed us;
And with a sudden flaw   109
Came round the gusty Skaw, [4]
So that our foe we saw
   Laugh as he hailed us.

"And as to catch the gale
Round veered the flapping sail,
'Death!' was the helmsman's hail,
   'Death without quarter!'
Midships with iron keel
Struck we her ribs of steel;
Down her black hulk did reel
   Through the black water!   120

"As with his wings aslant,
Sails the fierce cormorant,
Seeking some rocky haunt,
   With his prey laden,—
So toward the open main,

---

[1] a man-wolf; one who can turn himself into a wolf, or has been turned into a wolf, still retaining human intelligence
[2] carouse
[3] a wild Scandinavian warrior of barbaric times; probably one who fought "bear-sark," i.e., clad in a bear-skin shirt

[4] Cape Skagen in northeastern Denmark

Beating to sea again,
Through the wild hurricane,
  Bore I the maiden.

"Three weeks we westward bore,
And when the storm was o'er,   130
Cloud-like we saw the shore
  Stretching to leeward;
There for my lady's bower
Built I the lofty tower,
Which, to this very hour,
  Stands looking seaward.

"There lived we many years;
Time dried the maiden's tears;
She had forgot her fears,
  She was a mother;   140
Death closed her mild blue eyes;
Under that tower she lies;
Ne'er shall the sun arise
  On such another!

"Still grew my bosom then,
Still as a stagnant fen!
Hateful to me were men,
  The sunlight hateful!
In the vast forest here,
Clad in my warlike gear,   150
Fell I upon my spear,
  Oh, death was grateful!

"Thus, seamed with many scars,
Bursting these prison bars
Up to its native stars
  My soul ascended!
There from the flowing bowl
Deep drinks the warrior's soul,   158
Skoal! to the Northland! *skoal!*" [1]
  Thus the tale ended.

1840   1841

ENDYMION [2]

The rising moon has hid the stars;
Her level rays, like golden bars,
  Lie on the landscape green,
  With shadows brown between.

And silver white the river gleams,
As if Diana, in her dreams,

[1] "In Scandinavia this was the customary salutation when drinking a health. I have slightly changed the orthography of the word, in order to preserve the correct pronunciation."—Longfellow's note.
[2] The legendary Greek youth who, in some legends, was said to have asked Zeus for immortality, eternal youth, and lasting slumber; he was beloved by Selene, the moon (Roman Diana), as he lay sleeping on Mt. Latmos. See Keats's *Endymion*.

  Had dropt her silver bow
  Upon the meadows low.

On such a tranquil night as this,
She woke Endymion with a kiss,   10
  When, sleeping in the grove,
  He dreamed not of her love.

Like Dian's kiss, unasked, unsought,
Love gives itself, but is not bought;
  Nor voice, nor sound betrays
  Its deep, impassioned gaze.

It comes,—the beautiful, the free,
The crown of all humanity,—
  In silence and alone
  To seek the elected one.   20

It lifts the boughs, whose shadows deep
Are Life's oblivion, the soul's sleep,
  And kisses the closed eyes
  Of him, who slumbering lies.

O weary hearts! O slumbering eyes!
O drooping souls, whose destinies
  Are fraught with fear and pain,
  Ye shall be loved again!

No one is so accursed by fate,
No one so utterly desolate,   30
  But some heart, though unknown,
  Responds unto his own.

Responds,—as if with unseen wings,
An angel touched its quivering strings;
  And whispers, in its song,
  "Where hast thou stayed so long?"

1841   1841

MAIDENHOOD

Maiden! with the meek, brown eyes,
In whose orbs a shadow lies
Like the dusk in evening skies!

Thou whose locks outshine the sun,
Golden tresses, wreathed in one,
As the braided streamlets run!

Standing, with reluctant feet,
Where the brook and river meet,
Womanhood and childhood fleet!

Gazing, with a timid glance,   10
On the brooklet's swift advance,
On the river's broad expanse!

Deep and still, that gliding stream
Beautiful to thee must seem,
As the river of a dream.

Then why pause with indecision
When bright angels in thy vision
Beckon thee to fields Elysian? [1]

Seest thou shadows sailing by,
As the dove, with startled eye,   20
Sees the falcon's shadow fly?

Hearest thou voices on the shore,
That our ears perceive no more,
Deafened by the cataract's roar?

O, thou child of many prayers!
Life hath quicksands,—Life hath snares!
Care and age come unawares!

Like the swell of some sweet tune,
Morning rises into noon,
May glides onward into June.   30

Childhood is the bough, where slumbered
Birds and blossoms many-numbered;—
Age, that bough with snows encumbered.

Gather, then, each flower that grows,
When the young heart overflows,
To embalm that tent of snows.

Bear a lily in thy hand;
Gates of brass cannot withstand
One touch of that magic wand.

Bear through sorrow, wrong, and ruth,   40
In thy heart the dew of youth,
On thy lips the smile of truth.

O, that dew, like balm, shall steal
Into wounds, that cannot heal,
Even as sleep our eyes doth seal;

And that smile, like sunshine, dart
Into many a sunless heart,
For a smile of God thou art.

1841   1841

EXCELSIOR [2]

The shades of night were falling fast,
As through an Alpine village passed

A youth, who bore, 'mid snow and ice,
A banner with the strange device,
　　　Excelsior!

His brow was sad; his eye beneath,
Flashed like a falchion from its sheath,
And like a silver clarion rung
The accents of that unknown tongue,
　　　Excelsior!   10

In happy homes he saw the light
Of household fires gleam warm and bright;
Above, the spectral glaciers shone,
And from his lips escaped a groan,
　　　Excelsior!

"Try not the Pass!" the old man said;
"Dark lowers the tempest overhead,
The roaring torrent is deep and wide!"
And loud that clarion voice replied,
　　　Excelsior!   20

"O stay," the maiden said, "and rest
Thy weary head upon this breast!"
A tear stood in his bright blue eye,
But still he answered, with a sigh,
　　　Excelsior!

"Beware the pine tree's withered branch!
Beware the awful avalanche!"
This was the peasant's last Good-night;
A voice replied far up the height,
　　　Excelsior!   30

At break of day, as heavenward
The pious monks of Saint Bernard [3]
Uttered the oft-repeated prayer,
A voice cried through the startled air,
　　　Excelsior!

A traveler, by the faithful hound,
Half-buried in the snow was found,
Still grasping in his hand of ice
That banner with the strange device,
　　　Excelsior!   40

There in the twilight cold and gray,
Lifeless, but beautiful, he lay,
And from the sky, serene and far,
A voice fell, like a falling star,
　　　Excelsior!

1841   1841

[1] heavenly
[2] Longfellow described his purpose in writing the poem as "to display, in a series of pictures, the life of a man of genius, resisting all temptations, laying aside all fears, heedless of all warnings, and pressing right on to accomplish his purpose. His motto is Excelsior—'higher.'"

[3] The great monastery, 8108 feet above the sea in the St. Bernard Pass leading from Switzerland to Italy, was founded in the tenth or eleventh century. Many lives have been saved by the monks and their faithful dogs.

MEZZO CAMMIN [1]

WRITTEN AT BOPPARD ON THE RHINE AUGUST 25, 1842, JUST BEFORE LEAVING FOR HOME

Half of my life is gone, and I have let
The years slip from me and have not fulfilled
The aspiration of my youth, to build
Some tower of song with lofty parapet.
Not indolence, nor pleasure, nor the fret
Of restless passions that would not be stilled,
But sorrow, and a care that almost killed, [2]
Kept me from what I may accomplish yet;
Though, half-way up the hill, I see the Past
Lying beneath me with its sounds and sights,—
A city in the twilight dim and vast,   11
With smoking roofs, soft bells, and gleaming
    lights,—
And hear above me on the autumnal blast
The cataract of Death far thundering from the
    heights.

1842   1887

THE ARSENAL AT SPRINGFIELD [3]

This is the Arsenal. From floor to ceiling,
  Like a huge organ, rise the burnished arms;
But from their silent pipes no anthem pealing
  Startles the villages with strange alarms.

Ah! what a sound will rise, how wild and
    dreary,
  When the death-angel touches those swift
    keys!
What loud lament and dismal Miserere [4]
  Will mingle with their awful symphonies!

I hear even now the infinite fierce chorus,
  The cries of agony, the endless groan,   10
Which, through the ages that have gone before
    us,
  In long reverberations reach our own.

On helm and harness rings the Saxon hammer,
  Through Cimbric forest roars the Norseman's
    song, [5]
And loud, amid the universal clamor,
  O'er distant deserts sounds the Tartar gong.

I hear the Florentine, who from his palace
  Wheels out his battle-bell [6] with dreadful din,
And Aztec priests upon their teocallis [7]
  Beat the wild war-drum made of serpent's
    skin;   20

The tumult of each sacked and burning vil-
    lage:
  The shout that every prayer for mercy
    drowns;
The soldiers' revels in the midst of pillage;
  The wail of famine in beleaguered towns;

The bursting shell, the gateway wrenched
    asunder,
  The rattling musketry, the clashing blade;
And ever and anon, in tones of thunder,
  The diapason of the cannonade.

Is it, O man, with such discordant noises,
  With such accursed instruments as these,
Thou drownest Nature's sweet and kindly
    voices,   31
  And jarrest the celestial harmonies?

Were half the power, that fills the world with
    terror,
  Were half the wealth, bestowed on camps
    and courts,
Given to redeem the human mind from error,
  There were no need of arsenals nor forts:

The warrior's name would be a name ab-
    horrèd!
  And every nation, that should lift again
Its hand against a brother, on its forehead
  Would wear forevermore the curse of Cain!

Down the dark future, through long gener-
    ations,   41
  The echoing sounds grow fainter and then
    cease;
And like a bell, with solemn, sweet vibrations,
  I hear once more the voice of Christ say,
    "Peace!"

Peace! and no longer from its brazen portals
  The blast of War's great organ shakes the
    skies!
But beautiful as songs of the immortals,
  The holy melodies of love arise.

1844   1844

---

[1] "The middle of the journey"; the title was suggested by the first line of *The Inferno*, begun in the thirty-fifth year of Dante's life. See Milton's sonnet "On His Having Arrived at the Age of Twenty-three."
[2] Longfellow's wife had died in November, 1835.
[3] Massachusetts
[4] the Latin Vulgate version of the 51st Psalm (50th in the Vulgate), beginning "Miserere mei Domine,"—"Have mercy upon me, O Lord!"
[5] The reference is probably to Jutland, supposed by the ancients to have been the first home of the Cimbri, a Teutonic tribe who invaded Roman territory and were destroyed in Piedmont 101 B.C.
[6] In time of war, the Florentines of the 13th century wheeled out the Martinella, the battle bell, upon the battlefield itself, close by the battle standard.
[7] flat-topped pyramids for Aztec worship

THE BRIDGE

I stood on the bridge at midnight,
    As the clocks were striking the hour,
And the moon rose o'er the city,
    Behind the dark church-tower.

I saw her bright reflection
    In the waters under me,
Like a golden goblet falling
    And sinking into the sea.

And far in the hazy distance
    Of that lovely night in June,   10
The blaze of the flaming furnace
    Gleamed redder than the moon.

Among the long, black rafters
    The wavering shadows lay,
And the current that came from the ocean
    Seemed to lift and bear them away;

As, sweeping and eddying through them,
    Rose the belated tide,
And, streaming into the moonlight,
    The seaweed floated wide.   20

And like those waters rushing
    Among the wooden piers,
A flood of thoughts came o'er me
    That filled my eyes with tears.

How often, oh how often,
    In the days that had gone by,
I had stood on that bridge at midnight
    And gazed on that wave and sky!

How often, oh how often,
    I had wished that the ebbing tide   30
Would bear me away on its bosom
    O'er the ocean wild and wide!

For my heart was hot and restless,
    And my life was full of care,
And the burden laid upon me
    Seemed greater than I could bear.

But now it has fallen from me,
    It is buried in the sea;
And only the sorrow of others
    Throws its shadow over me.   40

Yet whenever I cross the river
    On its bridge with wooden piers,
Like the odor of brine from the ocean
    Comes the thought of other years.

And I think how many thousands
    Of care-encumbered men,
Each bearing his burden of sorrow,
    Have crossed the bridge since then.

I see the long procession
    Still passing to and fro,   50
The young heart hot and restless,
    And the old subdued and slow!

And forever and forever,
    As long as the river flows,
As long as the heart has passions,
    As long as life has woes;

The moon and its broken reflection
    And its shadows shall appear,
As the symbol of love in heaven,   59
    And its wavering image here.

1845   1845

THE OLD CLOCK ON THE STAIRS

L'éternité est une pendule, dont le balancier dit
et redit sans cesse ces deux mots seulement, dans
le silence des tombeaux, "Toujours, jamais! Jamais, toujours!"

—JACQUES BRIDAINE.[1]

Somewhat back from the village street
Stands the old-fashioned country-seat.[2]
Across its antique portico
Tall poplar-trees their shadows throw,
And from its station in the hall
An ancient timepiece says to all,—
    "Forever—never!
    Never—forever!"

Half-way up the stairs it stands,
And points and beckons with its hands   10
From its case of massive oak,
Like a monk, who, under his cloak,
Crosses himself, and sighs, alas!
With sorrowful voice to all who pass,—
    "Forever—never!
    Never—forever!"

By day its voice is low and light;
But in the silent dead of night,
Distinct as a passing footstep's fall
It echoes along the vacant hall,   20
Along the ceiling, along the floor,
And seems to say, at each chamber-door,—

[1] "Eternity is a clock whose pendulum utters and re-
    peats without ceasing these two words only, in
    the silence of the tomb—'Forever, never! Never,
    forever!'" Bridaine was a famous Catholic
    preacher in France (1710-1767).
[2] a house in Pittsfield, Mass., in which Mrs. Long-
    fellow's grandfather lived

"Forever—never!
Never—forever!"

Through days of sorrow and of mirth,
Through days of death and days of birth,
Through every swift vicissitude
Of changeful time, unchanged it has stood,
And as if, like God, it all things saw,
It calmly repeats those words of awe,—   30
"Forever—never!
Never—forever!"

In that mansion used to be
Free-hearted Hospitality;
His great fires up the chimney roared;
The stranger feasted at his board;
But, like the skeleton at the feast,
That warning timepiece never ceased,—   1845
"Forever—never!
Never—forever!"   40

There groups of merry children played,
There youths and maidens dreaming strayed.
O precious hours! O golden prime,
And affluence of love and time!
Even as a miser counts his gold,
Those hours the ancient timepiece told,—
"Forever—never!
Never—forever!"

From that chamber, clothed in white,
The bride came forth on her wedding night;
There, in that silent room below,   51
The dead lay in his shroud of snow;
And in the hush that followed the prayer,
Was heard the old clock on the stair,—
"Forever—never!
Never—forever!"

All are scattered now and fled,
Some are married, some are dead;
And when I ask, with throbs of pain,
"Ah! when shall they all meet again?"   60
As in the days long since gone by,
The ancient timepiece makes reply,—
"Forever—never!
Never—forever!"

Never here, forever there,
Where all parting, pain, and care,
And death, and time, shall disappear,—
Forever there, but never here!
The horologe of Eternity
Sayeth this incessantly,—   70
"Forever—never!
Never—forever!"

1845   1845

THE ARROW AND THE SONG

I shot an arrow into the air,
It fell to earth, I knew not where;
For, so swiftly it flew, the sight
Could not follow it in its flight.

I breathed a song into the air,
It fell to earth, I knew not where;
For who has sight so keen and strong
That it can follow the flight of song?

Long, long afterward, in an oak
I found the arrow, still unbroke;   10
And the song, from beginning to end,
I found again in the heart of a friend.

1845

THE BUILDERS

All are architects of Fate,
Working in these walls of Time;
Some with massive deeds and great,
Some with ornaments of rime.

Nothing useless is, or low;
Each thing in its place is best;
And what seems but idle show
Strengthens and supports the rest.

For the structure that we raise,
Time is with materials filled;   10
Our todays and yesterdays
Are the blocks with which we build.

Truly shape and fashion these;
Leave no yawning gaps between;
Think not, because no man sees,
Such things will remain unseen.

In the elder days of Art,
Builders wrought with greatest care
Each minute and unseen part;
For the Gods see everywhere.   20

Let us do our work as well,
Both the unseen and the seen;
Make the house, where Gods may dwell,
Beautiful, entire, and clean.

Else our lives are incomplete,
Standing in these walls of Time,
Broken stairways where the feet
Stumble as they seek to climb.

Build today, then, strong and sure,
With a firm and ample base;   30

And ascending and secure
  Shall tomorrow find its place.

Thus alone can we attain
  To those turrets, where the eye
Sees the world as one vast plain,
  And one boundless reach of sky.

1846

TEGNER'S DRAPA [1]

I heard a voice that cried,
"Balder [2] the Beautiful
Is dead, is dead!"
And through the misty air
Passed like the mournful cry
Of sunward sailing cranes.

I saw the pallid corpse
Of the dead sun
Borne through the Northern sky.
Blasts from Niffelheim [3]   10
Lifted the sheeted mists
Around him as he passed.

And the voice forever cried,
"Balder the Beautiful
Is dead, is dead!"
And died away
Through the dreary night,
In accents of despair.

Balder the Beautiful,
God of the summer sun,   20
Fairest of all the Gods!
Light from his forehead beamed,
Runes were upon his tongue,
As on the warrior's sword.

All things in earth and air
Bound were by magic spell

Never to do him harm;
Even the plants and stones;
All save the mistletoe,
The sacred mistletoe!   30

Höder, the blind old God,
Whose feet are shod with silence,
Pierced through that gentle breast
With his sharp spear, by fraud
Made of the mistletoe,
The accursed mistletoe!

They laid him in his ship,
With horse and harness,
As on a funeral pyre.
Odin placed   40
A ring upon his finger,
And whispered in his ear.

They launched the burning ship!
It floated far away
Over the misty sea,
Till like the sun it seemed,
Sinking beneath the waves.
Balder returned no more!

So perish the old Gods!
But out of the sea of Time   50
Rises a new land of song,
Fairer than the old.
Over its meadows green
Walk the young bards and sing.

Build it again,
O ye bards,
Fairer than before!
Ye fathers of the new race,
Feed upon morning dew,
Sing the new Song of Love!   60

The law of force is dead!
The law of love prevails!
Thor, [4] the thunderer,
Shall rule the earth no more,
No more, with threats,
Challenge the meek Christ.

Sing no more,
O ye bards of the North,
Of Vikings and of Jarls! [5]
Of the days of Eld   70
Preserve the freedom only,
Not the deeds of blood.

1847   1850

[1] Tegner's Death Song or Dirge; Esaias Tegnér (těg-när'), 1782-1846, was an eminent Swedish poet. Longfellow translated several of his poems, "Frithiof's Saga," "The Children of the Lord's Supper," etc.

[2] The sun-god Balder (*baldr*, foremost), the son of Odin and Freya, was the wisest, purest, most beautiful, and most beloved of the Scandinavian gods. Evil dreams having come to Baldur, Freya, his mother, persuaded all things on earth, vegetable, mineral, and animal, to take oath that they would not hurt him. As he was therefore believed invulnerable, the gods amused themselves by shooting at him. But Loki the evil god, discovering that the mistletoe had been too young to take the oath, made an arrow out of that plant. This, as if in sport, he helped the blind god Höder (night), Balder's brother, to aim. Höder shot and killed Balder. Great was the mourning in heaven. However, according to Scandinavian myth, Balder will return, as the sun returns in summer, to a newly created heaven and earth. Cf. Matthew Arnold's "Balder Dead" and Gray's "The Descent of Odin."

[3] in Norse mythology, the northern land of fog and cold

[4] the Norse God of thunder

[5] Scandinavian noblemen; cf. earl; Vikings were sea-rovers.

From EVANGELINE [1]

A TALE OF ACADIE

This is the forest primeval. The murmuring
    pines and the hemlocks,
Bearded with moss, and in garments green,
    indistinct in the twilight,
Stand like Druids [2] of eld, with voices sad and
    prophetic,
Stand like harpers hoar, with beards that rest
    on their bosoms.
Loud from its rocky caverns, the deep-voiced
    neighboring ocean
Speaks, and in accents disconsolate answers the
    wail of the forest.

This is the forest primeval; but where are
    the hearts that beneath it
Leaped like the roe, when he hears in the
    woodland the voice of the huntsman?
Where is the thatch-roofed village, the home
    of Acadian farmers,—
Men whose lives glided on like rivers that
    water the woodlands,   10
Darkened by shadows of earth, but reflecting
    an image of heaven?
Waste are those pleasant farms, and the farmers
    forever departed!
Scattered like dust and leaves, when the mighty
    blasts of October
Seize them, and whirl them aloft, and sprinkle
    them far o'er the ocean.
Naught but tradition remains of the beautiful
    village of Grand-Pré.

Ye who believe in affection that hopes, and
    endures, and is patient,
Ye who believe in the beauty and strength of
    woman's devotion,
List to the mournful tradition, still sung by the
    pines of the forest;
List to a Tale of Love in Acadie, home of the
    happy.

PART THE FIRST

I

In the Acadian land, on the shores of the Basin
    of Minas,   20
Distant, secluded, still, the little village of
    Grand-Pré
Lay in the fruitful valley. Vast meadows
    stretched to the eastward,
Giving the village its name, and pasture to
    flocks without number.
Dikes, that the hands of the farmers had raised
    with labor incessant,
Shut out the turbulent tides; but at stated
    seasons the flood-gates
Opened, and welcomed the sea to wander at
    will o'er the meadows.
West and south there were fields of flax, and
    orchards and cornfields
Spreading afar and unfenced o'er the plain;
    and away to the northward
Blomidon [3] rose, and the forests old, and aloft
    on the mountains
Sea-fogs pitched their tents, and mists from
    the mighty Atlantic   30
Looked on the happy valley, but ne'er from
    their station descended.
There, in the midst of its farms, reposed the
    Acadian village.
Strongly built were the houses, with frames of
    oak and of hemlock,
Such as the peasants of Normandy built in the
    reign of the Henries. [4]
Thatched were the roofs, with dormer-windows;
    and gables projecting
Over the basement below protected and shaded
    the doorway.
There in the tranquil evenings of summer, when
    brightly the sunset
Lighted the village street, and gilded the vanes
    on the chimneys,
Matrons and maidens sat in snow-white caps
    and in kirtles
Scarlet and blue and green, with distaffs spin-
    ning the golden   40
Flax for the gossiping looms, whose noisy shut-
    tles within doors
Mingled their sound with the whir of the wheels
    and the songs of the maidens.
Solemnly down the street came the parish
    priest, and the children
Paused in their play to kiss the hand he ex-
    tended to bless them.

---

[1] In Hawthorne's *American Note-Books* occurs this passage: "H. L. C. (Reverend H. L. Conolly) heard from a French Canadian a story of a young couple in Acadie. On their marriage day all the men of the Province were summoned to assemble in the church to hear a proclamation. When assembled, they were all seized and shipped off to be distributed throughout New England,—among them the new bridegroom. His bride set off in search of him—wandered about New England all her life-time, and at last, when she was old, found her bridegroom on his death-bed. The shock was so great that it killed her likewise." Since Hawthorne, however, did not wish to use the incident for a story, Longfellow asked permission to develop it.

[2] The Druids or priests of the early Celts in Britain worshiped in forests.

[3] Cape Blomidon, one of the northern extremities of the precipitous ridge lying along the Bay of Fundy

[4] Probably Henry III and Henry IV, kings of France 1574-1610; Acadia was colonized in 1604.

Reverend walked he among them; and up rose
    matrons and maidens,
Hailing his slow approach with words of affec-
    tionate welcome.
Then came the laborers home from the field,
    and serenely the sun sank
Down to his rest, and twilight prevailed. Anon
    from the belfry
Softly the Angelus [1] sounded, and over the
    roofs of the village
Columns of pale blue smoke, like clouds of
    incense ascending,   50
Rose from a hundred hearts, the homes of peace
    and contentment.
Thus dwelt together in love these simple Aca-
    dian farmers,—
Dwelt in the love of God and of man. Alike
    were they free from
Fear, that reigns with the tyrant, and envy, the
    vice of republics.
Neither locks had they to their doors, nor bars
    to their windows;
But their dwellings were open as day and the
    hearts of the owners;
There the richest was poor, and the poorest
    lived in abundance.

Somewhat apart from the village, and nearer
    the Basin of Minas,
Benedict Bellefontaine, the wealthiest farmer
    of Grand-Pré,
Dwelt on his goodly acres; and with him, di-
    recting his household,   60
Gentle Evangeline lived, his child, and the pride
    of the village.
Stalwart and stately in form was the man of
    seventy winters;
Hearty and hale was he, an oak that is covered
    with snow-flakes;
White as the snow were his locks, and his
    cheeks as brown as the oak-leaves.
Fair was she to behold, that maiden of seven-
    teen summers;
Black were the eyes as the berry that grows on
    the thorn by the wayside,
Black, yet how softly they gleamed beneath
    the brown shade of her tresses!
Sweet was her breath as the breath of kine that
    feed in the meadows.
When in the harvest heat she bore to the reapers
    at noontide
Flagons of home-brewed ale, ah! fair in sooth
    was the maiden.   70
Fairer was she when on Sunday morn, while
    the bell from its turret

Sprinkled with holy sounds the air, as the priest
    with his hyssop [2]
Sprinkles the congregation, and scatters bless-
    ings upon them,
Down the long street she passed, with her
    chaplet of beads and her missal,
Wearing her Norman cap and her kirtle of blue,
    and the ear-rings
Brought in the olden time from France, and
    since, as an heirloom,
Handed down from mother to child, through
    long generations.
But a celestial brightness—a more ethereal
    beauty—
Shone on her face and encircled her form, when,
    after confession,
Homeward serenely she walked with God's
    benediction upon her.   80
When she had passed, it seemed like the ceas-
    ing of exquisite music.

Firmly builded with rafters of oak, the house
    of the farmer
Stood on the side of a hill commanding the
    sea; and a shady
Sycamore grew by the door, with a woodbine
    wreathing around it.
Rudely carved was the porch, with seats be-
    neath; and a footpath
Led through an orchard wide, and disappeared
    in the meadow.
Under the sycamore-tree were hives overhung
    by a penthouse,
Such as the traveler sees in regions remote by
    the roadside,
Built o'er a box for the poor, or the blessed
    image of Mary.
Farther down, on the slope of the hill, was the
    well with its moss-grown   90
Bucket, fastened with iron, and near it a trough
    for the horses.
Shielding the house from storms, on the north,
    were the barns and the farmyard.
There stood the broad-wheeled wains and the
    antique plows and the harrows;
There were the folds for the sheep; and there,
    in his feathered seraglio,
Strutted the lordly turkey, and crowed the cock,
    with the selfsame
Voice that in ages of old had startled the peni-
    tent Peter. [3]
Bursting with hay were the barns, themselves
    a village. In each one
Far o'er the gable projected a roof of thatch;
    and a staircase,

[1] a bell rung at morning, noon, and night as a call to devotion; named the Angelus in commemoration of the annunciation by the angel Gabriel, of the Incarnation

[2] an herb, the twigs of which were used by Jewish priests in ceremonial purifications by sprinkling; in Catholic churches the holy water sprinkler
[3] *Matthew* xxvi, 74, 75

Under the sheltering eaves, led up to the odorous corn-loft.
There too the dove-cot stood, with its meek and innocent inmates   100
Murmuring ever of love; while above in the variant breezes
Numberless noisy weathercocks rattled and sang of mutation.

Thus, at peace with God and the world, the farmer of Grand-Pré
Lived on his sunny farm, and Evangeline governed his household.
Many a youth, as he knelt in the church and opened his missal,
Fixed his eyes upon her as the saint of his deepest devotion;
Happy was he who might touch her hand or the hem of her garment!
Many a suitor came to her door, by the darkness befriended,
And, as he knocked and waited to hear the sound of her footsteps,
Knew not which beat the louder, his heart or the knocker of iron;   110
Or, at the joyous feast of the Patron Saint of the village,
Bolder grew, and pressed her hand in the dance as he whispered
Hurried words of love, that seemed a part of the music.
But among all who came young Gabriel only was welcome;
Gabriel Lajeunesse, the son of Basil the blacksmith,
Who was a mighty man in the village, and honored of all men;
For, since the birth of time, throughout all ages and nations,
Has the craft of the smith been held in repute by the people.
Basil was Benedict's friend. Their children from earliest childhood
Grew up together as brother and sister; and Father Felician,   120
Priest and pedagogue both in the village, had taught them their letters
Out of the selfsame book, with the hymns of the church and the plain-song. [1]
But when the hymn was sung, and the daily lesson completed,
Swiftly they hurried away to the forge of Basil the blacksmith.
There at the door they stood, with wondering eyes to behold him
Take in his leathern lap the hoof of the horse as a plaything,

Nailing the shoe in its place; while near him the tire of the cart-wheel
Lay like a fiery snake, coiled round in a circle of cinders.
Oft on autumnal eves, when without in the gathering darkness
Bursting with light seemed the smithy, through every cranny and crevice,   130
Warm by the forge within they watched the laboring bellows,
And as its panting ceased, and the sparks expired in the ashes,
Merrily laughed, and said they were nuns going into the chapel.
Oft on sledges in winter, as swift as the swoop of the eagle,
Down the hillside bounding, they glided away o'er the meadow.
Oft in the barns they climbed to the populous nests on the rafters,
Seeking with eager eyes that wondrous stone, which the swallow
Brings from the shore of the sea to restore the sight of its fledglings; [2]
Lucky was he who found that stone in the nest of the swallow!
Thus passed a few swift years, and they no longer were children.   140
He was a valiant youth, and his face, like the face of the morning,
Gladdened the earth with its light, and ripened thought into action.
She was a woman now, with the heart and hopes of a woman.
"Sunshine of St. Eulalie," [3] was she called; for that was the sunshine
Which, as the farmers believed, would load their orchards with apples;
She too would bring to her husband's house delight and abundance,
Filling it with love and the ruddy faces of children.

II

Now had the season returned, when the nights grow colder and longer,
And the retreating sun the sign of the Scorpion [4] enters.

[1] the simple liturgical music required in Catholic services

[2] "If the eyes of one of the young of a swallow be put out, the mother bird will bring from the seashore a little stone, which will immediately restore its sight." Pluquet, *Contes Populaires;* quoted by Wright, *Literature and Superstitions of England in the Middle Ages.*

[3] Pluquet gives the rime:
"Si le soleil rit le jour Sainte Eulalie
Il y aura pommes et cidre à folie."
i. e., "If the sun laughs on Saint Eulalie's day There will be apples and cider a-plenty."

[4] the eighth of the signs of the zodiac, that which the sun enters Oct. 20

Birds of passage sailed through the leaden air,
from the ice-bound,   150
Desolate northern bays to the shores of tropical islands.
Harvests were gathered in; and wild with the
winds of September
Wrestled the trees of the forest, as Jacob of
old with the angel. [1]
All the signs foretold a winter long and inclement.
Bees, with prophetic instinct of want, had
hoarded their honey
Till the hives overflowed; and the Indian hunters asserted
Cold would the winter be, for thick was the
fur of the foxes.
Such was the advent of autumn. Then followed
that beautiful season,
Called by the pious Acadian peasants the Sum-
mer of All-Saints! [2]
Filled was the air with a dreamy and magical
light; and the landscape   160
Lay as if new-created in all the freshness of
childhood.
Peace seemed to reign upon earth, and the
restless heart of the ocean
Was for a moment consoled. All sounds were
in harmony blended.
Voices of children at play, the crowing of cocks
in the farm-yards,
Whir of wings in the drowsy air, and the cooing
of pigeons,
All were subdued and low as the murmurs of
love, and the great sun
Looked with the eye of love through the golden
vapors around him;
While arrayed in its robes of russet and scarlet
and yellow,
Bright with the sheen of the dew, each glittering tree of the forest
Flashed like the plane-tree the Persian adorned
with mantles and jewels. [3]

Now recommenced the reign of rest and
affection and stillness.   171
Day with its burden and heat had departed,
and twilight descending
Brought back the evening star to the sky, and
the herds to the homestead.
Pawing the ground they came, and resting their
necks on each other,
And with their nostrils distended inhaling the
freshness of evening.

[1] *Genesis* xxxii, 24-30
[2] about the first of November, that day being All Saints'
Day, corresponding to our Indian summer
[3] Xerxes found a plane tree so beautiful that he "presented it with golden ornaments" and put it in
the care of a soldier of his chosen legion. See
Herodotus vii, 31.

Foremost, bearing the bell, Evangeline's beautiful heifer,
Proud of her snow-white hide, and the ribbon
that waved from her collar,
Quietly paced and slow, as if conscious of human affection.
Then came the shepherd back with his bleating
flocks from the seaside,
Where was their favorite pasture. Behind them
followed the watch-dog,   180
Patient, full of importance, and grand in the
pride of his instinct,
Walking from side to side with a lordly air,
and superbly
Waving his bushy tail, and urging forward the
stragglers;
Regent of flocks was he when the shepherd
slept; their protector,
When from the forest at night, through the
starry silence, the wolves howled.
Late, with the rising moon, returned the wains
from the marshes,
Laden with briny hay, that filled the air with
its odor.
Cheerily neighed the steeds, with dew on their
manes and their fetlocks,
While aloft on their shoulders the wooden and
ponderous saddles,
Painted with brilliant dyes, and adorned with
tassels of crimson,   190
Nodded in bright array, like hollyhocks heavy
with blossoms.
Patiently stood the cows meanwhile, and yielded
their udders
Unto the milkmaid's hand; whilst loud and in
regular cadence
Into the sounding pails the foaming streamlets
descended.
Lowing of cattle and peals of laughter were
heard in the farm-yard,
Echoed back by the barns. Anon they sank
into stillness;
Heavily closed, with a jarring sound, the valves
of the barn-doors,
Rattled the wooden bars, and all for a season
was silent.

In-doors, warm by the wide-mouthed fire-
place, idly the farmer
Sat in his elbow-chair, and watched how the
flames and the smoke-wreaths   200
Struggled together like foes in a burning city.
Behind him,
Nodding and mocking along the wall, with ges-
tures fantastic,
Darted his own huge shadow, and vanished
away into darkness.

Faces, clumsily carved in oak, on the back of
    his arm-chair
Laughed in the flickering light, and the pewter
    plates on the dresser
Caught and reflected the flame, as shields of
    armies the sunshine:
Fragments of song the old man sang, and carols
    of Christmas,
Such as at home, in the olden time, his fathers
    before him
Sang in their Norman orchards and bright
    Burgundian vineyards.
Close at her father's side was the gentle Evan-
    geline seated,   210
Spinning flax for the loom that stood in the
    corner behind her.
Silent awhile were its treadles, at rest was its
    diligent shuttle,
While the monotonous drone of the wheel, like
    the drone of a bagpipe,
Followed the old man's song, and united the
    fragments together.
As in a church, when the chant of the choir at
    intervals ceases,
Footfalls are heard in the aisles, or words of
    the priest at the altar,
So, in each pause of the song, with measured
    motion the clock clicked.

Thus as they sat, there were footsteps heard,
    and, suddenly lifted,
Sounded the wooden latch, and the door swung
    back on its hinges.
Benedict knew by the hob-nailed shoes it was
    Basil the blacksmith,   220
And by her beating heart Evangeline knew who
    was with him.
"Welcome!" the farmer exclaimed, as their
    footsteps paused on the threshold,
"Welcome, Basil, my friend! Come, take thy
    place on the settle
Close by the chimney-side, which is always
    empty without thee;
Take from the shelf overhead thy pipe and the
    box of tobacco;
Never so much thyself art thou as when,
    through the curling
Smoke of the pipe or the forge, thy friendly
    and jovial face gleams
Round and red as the harvest moon through the
    mist of the marshes."
Then, with a smile of content, thus answered
    Basil the blacksmith,
Taking with easy air the accustomed seat by
    the fireside:—   230
"Benedict Bellefontaine, thou hast ever thy
    jest and thy ballad!

Ever in cheerfullest mood art thou, when others
    are filled with
Gloomy forebodings of ill, and see only ruin
    before them.
Happy art thou, as if every day thou hadst
    picked up a horseshoe."
Pausing a moment, to take the pipe that Evan-
    geline brought him,
And with a coal from the embers had lighted,
    he slowly continued:—
"Four days now are passed since the English
    ships at their anchors
Ride in the Gaspereau's mouth, with their can-
    non pointed against us.
What their design may be is unknown; but all
    are commanded
On the morrow to meet in the church, where
    his Majesty's mandate   240
Will be proclaimed as law in the land. Alas!
    in the mean time
Many surmises of evil alarm the hearts of the
    people."
Then made answer the farmer:—"Perhaps
    some friendlier purpose
Brings these ships to our shores. Perhaps the
    harvests in England
By untimely rains or untimelier heat have been
    blighted,
And from our bursting barns they would feed
    their cattle and children."
"Not so thinketh the folk in the village," said
    warmly the blacksmith,
Shaking his head as in doubt; then, heaving a
    sigh, he continued: —
"Louisburg is not forgotten, nor Beau Séjour,
    nor Port Royal. [1]
Many already have fled to the forest, and lurk
    on its outskirts,   250
Waiting with anxious hearts the dubious fate
    of tomorrow.
Arms have been taken from us, and warlike
    weapons of all kinds;
Nothing is left but the blacksmith's sledge and
    the scythe of the mower."
Then with a pleasant smile made answer the
    jovial farmer:—
"Safer are we unarmed, in the midst of our
    flocks and our cornfields,
Safer within these peaceful dikes besieged by
    the ocean,
Than our fathers in forts, besieged by the
    enemy's cannon.
Fear no evil, my friend, and tonight may no
    shadow of sorrow

[1] Louisburg, capital of Cape Breton Island, had been captured by the English in 1745 and 1758; Beau Séjour, on the neck connecting Acadia with the mainland, in 1755; and Port Royal, in Acadia, in 1690 and 1710.

Fall on this house and hearth; for this is the
    night of the contract.
Built are the house and the barn. The merry
    lads of the village   260
Strongly have built them and well; and break-
    ing the glebe round about them, [1]
Filled the barn with hay, and the house with
    food for a twelvemonth.
René Leblanc will be here anon, with his papers
    and inkhorn.
Shall we not then be glad, and rejoice in the
    joy of our children?"
As apart by the window she stood, with her
    hand in her lover's,
Blushing Evangeline heard the words that her
    father had spoken,
And, as they died on his lips, the worthy notary
    entered.

III

Bent like a laboring oar, that toils in the
    surf of the ocean,
Bent, but not broken, by age was the form of
    the notary public;
Shocks of yellow hair, like the silken floss of
    the maize, hung   270
Over his shoulders; his forehead was high; and
    glasses with horn bows
Sat astride on his nose, with a look of wisdom
    supernal.
Father of twenty children was he, and more
    than a hundred
Children's children rode on his knee, and heard
    his great watch tick.
Four long years in the times of the war [2] had
    he languished a captive,
Suffering much in an old French fort as the
    friend of the English.
Now, though warier grown, without all guile or
    suspicion,
Ripe in wisdom was he, but patient, and simple,
    and childlike.
He was beloved by all, and most of all by the
    children;
For he told them tales of the Loup-garou [3] in
    the forest,   280

And of the goblin that came in the night to
    water the horses,
And of the white Létiche, the ghost of a child
    who unchristened
Died, and was doomed to haunt unseen the
    chambers of 'children;
And how on Christmas eve the oxen talked in
    the stable,
And how the fever was cured by a spider shut
    up in a nutshell,
And of the marvelous powers of four-leafed
    clover and horseshoes,
With whatsoever else was writ in the lore of
    the village.
Then up rose from his seat by the fireside
    Basil the blacksmith,
Knocked from his pipe the ashes, and slowly
    extending his right hand,
"Father Leblanc," he exclaimed, "thou hast
    heard the talk in the village,   290
And, perchance, canst tell us some news of
    these ships and their errand."
Then with modest demeanor made answer the
    notary public,—
"Gossip enough have I heard, in sooth, yet am
    never the wiser;
And what their errand may be I know not
    better than others.
Yet am I not of those who imagine some evil
    intention
Brings them here, for we are at peace; and why
    then molest us?"
"God's name!" shouted the hasty and some-
    what irascible blacksmith;
"Must we in all things look for the how, and
    the why, and the wherefore?
Daily injustice is done, and might is the right
    of the strongest!"
But, without heeding his warmth, continued
    the notary public,—   300
"Man is unjust, but God is just; and finally
    justice
Triumphs; and well I remember a story [4] that
    often consoled me,
When as a captive I lay in the old French fort
    at Port Royal."
This was the old man's favorite tale, and he
    loved to repeat it
When his neighbors complained that any in-
    justice was done them.
"Once in an ancient city, whose name I no
    longer remember,

---

[1] "As soon as a young man arrived to the proper age,
    the community built him a house, broke up the
    lands about it, and supplied him with all the
    necessaries of life for a twelve-month. There
    he received the partner whom he had chosen,
    and who brought him her portion in flocks." See
    Haliburton's *History of Nova Scotia*, I, 172.
[2] Probably King George's War, 1744-1748, between
    England and her colonies on the one side and
    France and the Indians on the other; in Europe
    it was known as the War of the Austrian Suc-
    cession, 1741-1748.
[3] The man-wolf; cf. "Skeleton in Armor," note 1, p. 504.
    Belief in the Létiche was perhaps based on
    glimpses of the white ermine. It was said that on

Christmas eve the cattle knelt to worship Christ;
a spider sealed up in a goose-quill and hung about
a person's neck would cure the ague, etc. For
these and similar beliefs see Pluquet.
[4] A version of the same story is found in Rossini's
    opera *The Thieving Magpie*, 1817.

Raised aloft on a column, a brazen statue of
    Justice
Stood in the public square, upholding the scales
    in its left hand,
And in its right a sword, as an emblem that
    justice presided
Over the laws of the land, and the hearts and
    homes of the people.   310
Even the birds had built their nests in the scales
    of the balance,
Having no fear of the sword that flashed in the
    sunshine above them.
But in the course of time the laws of the land
    were corrupted;
Might took the place of right, and the weak
    were oppressed, and the mighty
Ruled with an iron rod. Then it chanced in a
    nobleman's palace
That a necklace of pearls was lost, and ere long
    a suspicion
Fell on an orphan girl who lived as maid in the
    household.
She, after form of trial condemned to die on
    the scaffold,
Patiently met her doom at the foot of the statue
    of Justice.
As to her Father in heaven her innocent spirit
    ascended,   320
Lo! o'er the city a tempest rose; and the bolts
    of the thunder
Smote the statue of bronze, and hurled in wrath
    from its left hand
Down on the pavement below the clattering
    scales of the balance,
And in the hollow thereof was found the nest
    of a magpie,
Into whose clay-built walls the necklace of
    pearls was inwoven."
Silenced, but not convinced, when the story was
    ended, the blacksmith
Stood like a man who fain would speak, but
    findeth no language;
All his thoughts were congealed into lines on
    his face, as the vapors
Freeze in fantastic shapes on the window panes
    in the winter.

Then Evangeline lighted the brazen lamp on
    the table,   330
Filled, till it overflowed, the pewter tankard
    with home-brewed
Nut-brown ale, that was famed for its strength
    in the village of Grand-Pré;
While from his pocket the notary drew his
    papers and inkhorn,
Wrote with a steady hand the date and the age
    of the parties,

Naming the dower of the bride in flocks of
    sheep and in cattle.
Orderly all things proceeded, and duly and well
    were completed,
And the great seal of the law was set like a
    sun on the margin.
Then from his leathern pouch the farmer threw
    on the table
Three times the old man's fee in solid pieces
    of silver;
And the notary rising, and blessing the bride
    and the bridegroom,   340
Lifted aloft the tankard of ale and drank to
    their welfare.
Wiping the foam from his lip, he solemnly
    bowed and departed,
While in silence the others sat and mused by
    the fireside,
Till Evangeline brought the draught-board out
    of its corner.
Soon was the game begun. In friendly con-
    tention the old men
Laughed at each lucky hit, or unsuccessful
    maneuver,
Laughed when a man was crowned, or a breach
    was made in the king-row.
Meanwhile apart, in the twilight gloom of a
    window's embrasure,
Sat the lovers and whispered together, behold-
    ing the moon rise
Over the pallid sea and the silvery mist of the
    meadows.   350
Silently one by one, in the infinite meadows of
    heaven,
Blossomed the lovely stars, the forget-me-nots
    of the angels.

Thus was the evening passed. Anon the bell
    from the belfry
Rang out the hour of nine, the village curfew,
    and straightway
Rose the guests and departed; and silence
    reigned in the household.
Many a farewell word and sweet good-night on
    the door-step
Lingered long in Evangeline's heart, and filled
    it with gladness.
Carefully then were covered the embers that
    glowed on the hearth-stone,
And on the oaken stairs resounded the tread of
    the farmer.
Soon with a soundless step the foot of Evange-
    line followed.   360
Up the staircase moved a luminous space in
    the darkness,
Lighted less by the lamp than the shining face
    of the maiden.

Silent she passed the hall, and entered the door of her chamber.

Simple that chamber was, with its curtains of white, and its clothes-press

Ample and high, on whose spacious shelves were carefully folded

Linen and woollen stuffs, by the hand of Evangeline woven.

This was the precious dower she would bring to her husband in marriage,

Better than flocks and herds, being proofs of her skill as a housewife.

Soon she extinguished her lamp, for the mellow and radiant moonlight

Streamed through the windows, and lighted the room, till the heart of the maiden

Swelled and obeyed its power, like the tremulous tides of the ocean.   371

Ah! she was fair, exceeding fair to behold, as she stood with

Naked snow-white feet on the gleaming floor of her chamber!

Little she dreamed that below, among the trees of the orchard,

Waited her lover and watched for the gleam of her lamp, and her shadow.

Yet were her thoughts of him, and at times a feeling of sadness

Passed o'er her soul, as the sailing shade of clouds in the moonlight

Flitted across the floor and darkened the room for a moment.

And, as she gazed from the window, she saw serenely the moon pass

Forth from the folds of a cloud, and one star follow her footsteps,   380

As out of Abraham's tent young Ishmael wandered with Hagar! [1]

IV

Pleasantly rose next morn the sun on the village of Grand-Pré.

Pleasantly gleamed in the soft, sweet air the Basin of Minas,

Where the ships, with their wavering shadows, were riding at anchor.

Life had long been astir in the village, and clamorous labor

Knocked with its hundred hands at the golden gates of the morning.

Now from the country around, from the farms and neighboring hamlets,

Came in their holiday dresses the blithe Acadian peasants.

Many a glad good-morrow and jocund laugh from the young folk

Made the bright air brighter, as up from the numerous meadows,   390

Where no path could be seen but the track of wheels in the greensward,

Group after group appeared, and joined, or passed on the highway.

Long ere noon, in the village all sounds of labor were silenced.

Thronged were the streets with people; and noisy groups at the house-doors

Sat in the cheerful sun, and rejoiced and gossiped together.

Every house was an inn, where all were welcomed and feasted;

For with this simple people, who lived like brothers together,

All things were held in common, and what one had was another's.

Yet under Benedict's roof hospitality seemed more abundant:

For Evangeline stood among the guests of her father;   400

Bright was her face with smiles, and words of welcome and gladness

Fell from her beautiful lips, and blessed the cup as she gave it.

Under the open sky, in the odorous air of the orchard,

Stript of its golden fruit, was spread the feast of betrothal.

There in the shade of the porch were the priest and the notary seated;

There good Benedict sat, and sturdy Basil the blacksmith.

Not far withdrawn from these, by the cider-press and the beehives,

Michael the fiddler was placed, with the gayest of hearts and of waistcoats.

Shadow and light from the leaves alternately played on his snow-white

Hair, as it waved in the wind; and the jolly face of the fiddler   410

Glowed like a living coal when the ashes are blown from the embers.

Gayly the old man sang to the vibrant sound of his fiddle,

Tous les Bourgeois de Chartres, and *Le Carillon de Dunkerque*. [2]

And anon with his wooden shoes beat time to the music.

Merrily, merrily whirled the wheels of the dizzying dances

Under the orchard-trees and down the path to the meadows;

---

[1] *Genesis* xxi, 14-21

[2] "All the Citizens of Chartres," and "The Chime of Dunkirk"—popular French songs

Old folk and young together, and children
    mingled among them.
Fairest of all the maids was Evangeline, Bene-
    dict's daughter!
Noblest of all the youths was Gabriel, son of
    the blacksmith!

So passed the morning away. And lo! with
    a summons sonorous   420
Sounded the bell from its tower, and over the
    meadows a drum beat.
Thronged ere long was the church with men.
    Without, in the churchyard,
Waited the women. They stood by the graves,
    and hung on the headstones
Garlands of autumn-leaves and evergreens fresh
    from the forest.
Then came the guard from the ships, and
    marching proudly among them
Entered the sacred portal. With loud and dis-
    sonant clangor
Echoed the sound of their brazen drums from
    ceiling and casement,—
Echoed a moment only, and slowly the ponder-
    ous portal
Closed, and in silence the crowd awaited the
    will of the soldiers.
Then uprose their commander, and spake from
    the steps of the altar,   430
Holding aloft in his hands, with its seals, the
    royal commission.
"You are convened this day," he said, "by His
    Majesty's orders.
Clement and kind has he been; but how you
    have answered his kindness
Let your own hearts reply! To my natural
    make and my temper
Painful the task is I do, which to you I know
    must be grievous.
Yet must I bow and obey, and deliver the will
    of our monarch:
Namely, that all your lands, and dwellings, and
    cattle of all kinds
Forfeited be to the crown; and that you your-
    selves from this province
Be transported to other lands. God grant you
    may dwell there
Ever as faithful subjects, a happy and peace-
    able people!   440
Prisoners now I declare you, for such is His
    Majesty's pleasure!"
As, when the air is serene in the sultry solstice
    of summer,
Suddenly gathers a storm, and the deadly sling
    of the hailstones
Beats down the farmer's corn in the field, and
    shatters his windows,

Hiding the sun, and strewing the ground with
    thatch from the house-roofs,
Bellowing fly the herds, and seek to break their
    enclosures;
So on the hearts of the people descended the
    words of the speaker.
Silent a moment they stood in speechless won-
    der, and then rose
Louder and ever louder a wail of sorrow and
    anger,
And, by one impulse moved, they madly rushed
    to the doorway.   450
Vain was the hope of escape; and cries and
    fierce imprecations
Rang through the house of prayer; and high
    o'er the head of the others
Rose, with his arms uplifted, the figure of Basil
    the blacksmith,
As, on a stormy sea, a spar is tossed by the
    billows.
Flushed was his face and distorted with passion;
    and wildly he shouted,—
"Down with the tyrants of England! we never
    have sworn them allegiance!
Death to these foreign soldiers, who seize on
    our homes and our harvests!"
More he fain would have said, but the merciless
    hand of a soldier
Smote him upon the mouth, and dragged him
    down to the pavement.

In the midst of the strife and tumult of angry
    contention,   460
Lo! the door of the chancel opened, and Father
    Felician
Entered, with serious mien, and ascended the
    steps of the altar.
Raising his reverend hand, with a gesture he
    awed into silence
All that clamorous throng; and thus he spake
    to his people.
Deep were his tones and solemn; in accents
    measured and mournful
Spake he, as, after the tocsin's alarum, dis-
    tinctly the clock strikes.
"What is this that ye do, my children? what
    madness has seized you?
Forty years of my life have I labored among
    you, and taught you,
Not in word alone, but in deed, to love one
    another!
Is this the fruit of my toils, of my vigils and
    prayers and privations?   470
Have you so soon forgotten all lessons of love
    and forgiveness?
This is the house of the Prince of Peace, and
    would you profane it

Thus with violent deeds and hearts overflowing
    with hatred?
Lo! where the crucified Christ from his cross
    is gazing upon you!
See! in those sorrowful eyes what meekness
    and holy compassion!
Hark! how those lips still repeat the prayer,
    'O Father, forgive them!'
Let us repeat that prayer in the hour when the
    wicked assail us,
Let us repeat it now, and say, 'O Father, for-
    give them!' " [1]
Few were his words of rebuke, but deep in the
    hearts of his people
Sank they, and sobs of contrition succeeded
    the passionate outbreak,   480
While they repeated his prayer, and said, "O
    Father, forgive them!"

Then came the evening service. The tapers
    gleamed from the altar;
Fervent and deep was the voice of the priest,
    and the people responded,
Not with their lips alone, but their hearts; and
    the Ave Maria
Sang they, and fell on their knees, and their
    souls, with devotion translated,
Rose on the ardor of prayer, like Elijah ascend-
    ing to heaven. [2]

Meanwhile had spread in the village the tid-
    ings of ill, and on all sides
Wandered, wailing, from house to house the
    women and children.
Long at her father's door Evangeline stood,
    with her right hand
Shielding her eyes from the level rays of the
    sun, that, descending,   490
Lighted the village street with mysterious splen-
    dor, and roofed each
Peasant's cottage with golden thatch, and em-
    blazoned its windows.
Long within had been spread the snow-white
    cloth on the table;
There stood the wheaten loaf, and the honey
    fragrant with wild flowers;
There stood the tankard of ale, and the cheese
    fresh brought from the dairy:
And, at the head of the board, the great arm-
    chair of the farmer.
Thus did Evangeline wait at her father's door,
    as the sunset
Threw the long shadows of trees o'er the broad
    ambrosial meadows.
Ah! on her spirit within a deeper shadow had
    fallen,

And from the fields of her soul a fragrance
    celestial ascended,—   500
Charity, meekness, love, and hope, and for-
    giveness, and patience!
Then, all forgetful of self, she wandered into
    the village,
Cheering with looks and words the mournful
    hearts of the women,
As o'er the darkening fields with lingering steps
    they departed,
Urged by their household cares, and the weary
    feet of their children.
Down sank the great red sun, and in golden,
    glimmering vapors
Veiled the light of his face, like the Prophet
    descending from Sinai. [3]
Sweetly over the village the bell of the Ange-
    lus sounded.

Meanwhile amid the gloom, by the church
    Evangeline lingered.
All was silent within; and in vain at the door
    and the windows   510
Stood she, and listened and looked, until, over-
    come by emotion,
"Gabriel!" cried she aloud with tremulous
    voice; but no answer
Came from the graves of the dead, nor the
    gloomier grave of the living.
Slowly at length she returned to the tenantless
    house of her father.
Smoldered the fire on the hearth, on the board
    was the supper untasted.
Empty and drear was each room, and haunted
    with phantoms of terror.
Sadly echoed her step on the stair and the floor
    of her chamber.
In the dead of the night she heard the disconso-
    late rain fall
Loud on the withered leaves of the sycamore-
    tree by the window.
Keenly the lightning flashed; and the voice of
    the echoing thunder   520
Told her that God was in heaven, and governed
    the world he created!
Then she remembered the tale she had heard
    of the justice of Heaven;
Soothed was her troubled soul, and she peace-
    fully slumbered till morning.

v

Four times the sun had risen and set; and
    now on the fifth day
Cheerily called the cock to the sleeping maids
    of the farm-house.

---

[1] *Luke* xxiii, 34   [2] *2 Kings* ii, 11   [3] *Exodus* xxxiv, 29-35

Soon o'er the yellow fields, in silent and mournful procession,
Came from the neighboring hamlets and farms the Acadian women,
Driving in ponderous wains their household goods to the seashore,
Pausing and looking back to gaze once more on their dwellings,
Ere they were shut from sight by the winding road and the woodland.   530
Close at their sides their children ran, and urged on the oxen,
While in their little hands they clasped some fragments of playthings.

Thus to the Gaspereau's mouth they hurried; and there on the sea-beach
Piled in confusion lay the household goods of the peasants.
All day long between the shore and the ships did the boats ply;
All day long the wains came laboring down from the village.
Late in the afternoon, when the sun was near to his setting,
Echoed far o'er the fields came the roll of drums from the churchyard.
Thither the women and children thronged. On a sudden the church-doors
Opened, and forth came the guard, and marching in gloomy procession   540
Followed the long-imprisoned, but patient, Acadian farmers.
Even as pilgrims, who journey afar from their homes and their country,
Sing as they go, and in singing forget they are weary and wayworn,
So with songs on their lips the Acadian peasants descended
Down from the church to the shore, amid their wives and their daughters.
Foremost the young men came; and, raising together their voices,
Sang with tremulous lips a chant of the Catholic Missions:—
"Sacred heart of the Saviour! O inexhaustible fountain!
Fill our hearts this day with strength and submission and patience!"
Then the old men, as they marched, and the women that stood by the wayside
Joined in the sacred psalm, and the birds in the sunshine above them   551
Mingled their notes therewith, like voices of spirits departed.

Half-way down to the shore Evangeline waited in silence,

Not overcome with grief, but strong in the hour of affliction,—
Calmly and sadly she waited, until the procession approached her,
And she beheld the face of Gabriel pale with emotion.
Tears then filled her eyes, and, eagerly running to meet him,
Clasped she his hands, and laid her head on his shoulder, and whispered,—
"Gabriel, be of good cheer! for if we love one another,
Nothing, in truth, can harm us, whatever mischances may happen!"   560
Smiling she spake these words; then suddenly paused, for her father
Saw she, slowly advancing. Alas! how changed was his aspect!
Gone was the glow from his cheek, and the fire from his eye, and his footstep
Heavier seemed with the weight of the heavy heart in his bosom.
But with a smile and a sigh, she clasped his neck and embraced him,
Speaking words of endearment where words of comfort availed not.
Thus to the Gaspereau's mouth moved on that mournful procession.

There disorder prevailed, and the tumult and stir of embarking.
Busily plied the freighted boats; and in the confusion
Wives were torn from their husbands, and mothers, too late, saw their children
Left on the land, extending their arms, with wildest entreaties.   571
So unto separate ships were Basil and Gabriel carried,
While in despair on the shore Evangeline stood with her father.
Half the task was not done when the sun went down, and the twilight
Deepened and darkened around; and in haste the refluent ocean
Fled away from the shore, and left the line of the sand-beach
Covered with waifs of the tide, with kelp and the slippery seaweed.
Farther back in the midst of the household goods and the wagons,
Like to a gypsy camp, or a leaguer [1] after a battle,
All escape cut off by the sea, and the sentinels near them,   580
Lay encamped for the night the houseless Acadian farmers.

[1] camp

Back to its nethermost caves retreated the
    bellowing ocean,
Dragging adown the beach the rattling pebbles,
    and leaving
Inland and far up the shore the stranded boats
    of the sailors.
Then, as the night descended, the herds re-
    turned from their pastures;
Sweet was the moist still air with the odor of
    milk from their udders;
Lowing they waited, and long, at the well-
    known bars of the farm-yard,—
Waited and looked in vain for the voice and
    the hand of the milkmaid.
Silence reigned in the streets; from the church
    no Angelus sounded,
Rose no smoke from the roofs, and gleamed
    no lights from the windows.   590

    But on the shores meanwhile the evening fires
    had been kindled,
Built of the drift-wood thrown on the sands
    from wrecks in the tempest.
Round them shapes of gloom and sorrowful
    faces were gathered,
Voices of women were heard, and of men, and
    the crying of children.
Onward from fire to fire, as from hearth to
    hearth in his parish,
Wandered the faithful priest, consoling and
    blessing and cheering,
Like unto shipwrecked Paul on Melita's deso-
    late seashore. [1]
Thus he approached the place where Evange-
    line sat with her father,
And in the flickering light beheld the face of
    the old man,
Haggard and hollow and wan, and without
    either thought or emotion,   600
E'en as the face of a clock from which the
    hands have been taken.
Vainly Evangeline strove with words and ca-
    resses to cheer him,
Vainly offered him food; yet he moved not, he
    looked not, he spake not,
But, with a vacant stare, ever gazed at the
    flickering fire-light.
"Benedicite!" [2] murmured the priest, in tones
    of compassion.
More he fain would have said, but his heart
    was full, and his accents
Faltered and paused on his lips, as the feet of
    a child on a threshold,
Hushed by the scene he beholds, and the awful
    presence of sorrow.

Silently, therefore, he laid his hand on the head
    of the maiden,
Raising his tearful eyes to the silent stars that
    above them   610
Moved on their way, unperturbed by the
    wrongs and sorrows of mortals.
Then sat he down at her side, and they wept
    together in silence.

    Suddenly rose from the south a light, as in
    autumn the blood-red
Moon climbs the crystal walls of heaven, and
    o'er the horizon
Titan-like stretches its hundred hands [3] upon
    mountain and meadow,
Seizing the rocks and the rivers, and piling huge
    shadows together.
Broader and ever broader it gleamed on the
    roofs of the village,
Gleamed on the sky and the sea, and the ships
    that lay in the roadstead.
Columns of shining smoke uprose, and flashes
    of flame were   619
Thrust through their folds and withdrawn, like
    the quivering hands of a martyr.
Then as the wind seized the gleeds [4] and the
    burning thatch, and, uplifting,
Whirled them aloft through the air, at once
    from a hundred house-tops
Started the sheeted smoke with flashes of flame
    intermingled.

    These things beheld in dismay the crowd on
    the shore and on shipboard.
Speechless at first they stood, then cried aloud
    in their anguish,
"We shall behold no more our homes in the
    village of Grand-Pré!"
Loud on a sudden the cocks began to crow in
    the farm-yards,
Thinking the day had dawned; and anon the
    lowing of cattle
Came on the evening breeze, by the barking of
    dogs interrupted.
Then rose a sound of dread, such as startles the
    sleeping encampments   630
Far in the western prairies or forests that skirt
    the Nebraska,
When the wild horses affrighted sweep by with
    the speed of the whirlwind,
Or the loud bellowing herds of buffaloes rush
    to the river.

[3] The Titans, here apparently confused with their hun-
dred-handed brothers, the Uranids, of whom
Briareus was one of the chief, represent convulsive
forces of nature.
[4] burning coals

[1] Acts xxviii, 1-10   [2] "Blessing upon you"

Such was the sound that arose on the night, as
the herds and the horses
Broke through their folds and fences, and madly
rushed o'er the meadows.

Overwhelmed with the sight, yet speechless,
the priest and the maiden
Gazed on the scene of terror that reddened and
widened before them;
And as they turned at length to speak to their
silent companion,
Lo! from his seat he had fallen, and stretched
abroad on the seashore
Motionless lay his form, from which the soul
had departed. 640
Slowly the priest uplifted the lifeless head, and
the maiden
Knelt at her father's side, and wailed aloud in
her terror.
Then in a swoon she sank, and lay with her
head on his bosom.
Through the long night she lay in deep, obliv-
ious slumber;
And when she woke from the trance, she beheld
a multitude near her.
Faces of friends she beheld, that were mourn-
fully gazing upon her,
Pallid, with tearful eyes, and looks of saddest
compassion.
Still the blaze of the burning village illumined
the landscape,
Reddened the sky overhead, and gleamed on
the faces around her,
And like the day of doom it seemed to her
wavering senses. 650
Then a familiar voice she heard, as it said to
the people,—
"Let us bury him here by the sea. When a
happier season
Brings us again to our homes from the unknown land of our exile,
Then shall his sacred dust be piously laid in the
churchyard."
Such were the words of the priest. And there
in haste by the seaside,
Having the glare of the burning village for
funeral torches,
But without bell or book,[1] they buried the
farmer of Grand-Pré.
And as the voice of the priest repeated the
service of sorrow,
Lo! with a mournful sound like the voice of
a vast congregation,
Solemnly answered the sea, and mingled its
roar with the dirges. 660

[1] without religious ceremony

'Twas the returning tide, that afar from the
waste of the ocean,
With the first dawn of the day, came heaving
and hurrying landward.
Then recommenced once more the stir and noise
of embarking;
And with the ebb of the tide the ships sailed
out of the harbor,
Leaving behind them the dead on the shore,
and the village in ruins.

1845-1847   1847

[End of Part the First]

THE SECRET OF THE SEA [2]

Ah! what pleasant visions haunt me
  As I gaze upon the sea!
All the old romantic legends,
  All my dreams, come back to me.

Sails of silk and ropes of sendal,[3]
  Such as gleam in ancient lore;
And the singing of the sailors,
  And the answer from the shore!

Most of all, the Spanish ballad
  Haunts me oft, and tarries long,   10
Of the noble Count Arnaldos
  And the sailor's mystic song.

Like the long waves on a sea-beach,
  Where the sand as silver shines,
With a soft, monotonous cadence,
  Flow its unrimed lyric lines;—

Telling how the Count Arnaldos,
  With his hawk upon his hand,
Saw a fair and stately galley,
  Steering onward to the land;—   20

How he heard the ancient helmsman
  Chant a song so wild and clear,
That the sailing sea-bird slowly
  Poised upon the mast to hear,

Till his soul was full of longing,
  And he cried, with impulse strong,—
"Helmsman! for the love of heaven,
  Teach me, too, that wondrous song!"

[2] This poem is based upon and in places is almost a
literal translation of a Spanish ballad, the "Romance del Conde Arnaldo." It may be found in
Primavera y Flor de Romance collected by Wolf
and Hofman, 1856.
[3] a kind of thin silk material

"Wouldst thou,"—so the helmsman answered,
"Learn the secret of the sea?   30
Only those who brave its dangers
Comprehend its mystery!"

In each sail that skims the horizon,
In each landward-blowing breeze,
I behold that stately galley,
Hear those mournful melodies;

Till my soul is full of longing
For the secret of the sea,
And the heart of the great ocean   39
Sends a thrilling pulse through me.

1848

SIR HUMPHREY GILBERT [1]

Southward with fleet of ice
Sailed the corsair Death;
Wild and fast blew the blast,
And the east-wind was his breath.

His lordly ships of ice
Glistened in the sun;
On each side, like pennons wide,
Flashing crystal streamlets run.

His sails of white sea-mist
Dripped with silver rain;   10
But where he passed there were cast
Leaden shadows o'er the main.

Eastward from Campobello [2]
Sir Humphrey Gilbert sailed;
Three days or more seaward he bore,
Then, alas! the land-wind failed.

Alas! the land-wind failed,
And ice-cold grew the night;
And never more, on sea or shore,
Should Sir Humphrey see the light.   20

[1] An English adventurer, a half brother of Sir Walter
Raleigh; he established the first English colony
in North America at St. Johns, Newfoundland,
where he landed Aug. 5, 1583. On his return
to England, after disastrous experiences, he was
one tempestuous day seen by those of an accompanying vessel, the *Golden Hind,* sitting at the
stern of his little pinnace of ten tons, the *Squirrel,*
reading a book, and as often as the two ships
drew near was heard to exclaim, "We are as
near heaven by sea as by land." That night,
Sept. 9, 1583, the lights of the *Squirrel* suddenly
disappeared and no trace of the vessel was ever
found. See Hakluyt, *The Principal Navigations,
Voyages, and Discoveries of the English Nation,*
vol. viii, p. 174, Edinburgh, 1904. Hakluyt
makes no suggestion of the ice as incidental to
the disaster.
[2] Campobello Island, probably mentioned because of its
musical name, is in the Bay of Fundy.

He sat upon the deck,
The Book was in his hand;
"Do not fear! Heaven is as near,"
He said, "by water as by land!"

In the first watch of the night,
Without a signal's sound,
Out of the sea, mysteriously,
The fleet of Death rose all around.

The moon and the evening star
Were hanging in the shrouds;   30
Every mast, as it passed,
Seemed to rake the passing clouds.

They grappled with their prize,
At midnight black and cold!
As of a rock was the shock;
Heavily the ground-swell rolled.

Southward through day and dark,
They drift in close embrace,
With mist and rain, to the Spanish Main; [3]
Yet there seems no change of place.   40

Southward, forever southward,
They drift through dark and day;
And like a dream, in the Gulf-Stream
Sinking, vanish all away.

1848   *1848*

RESIGNATION [4]

There is no flock, however watched and tended,
But one dead lamb is there!
There is no fireside, howsoe'er defended,
But has one vacant chair!

The air is full of farewells to the dying,
And mournings for the dead;
The heart of Rachel, for her children crying,
Will not be comforted! [5]

Let us be patient! These severe afflictions
Not from the ground arise,   10
But oftentimes celestial benedictions
Assume this dark disguise.

We see but dimly through the mists and vapors;
Amid these earthly damps
What seem to us but sad funeral tapers
May be heaven's distant lamps.

[3] the seas north of South America
[4] written after the death of his little daughter Fanny
[5] *Jeremiah* xxxi, 15

There is no Death! What seems so is tran-
    sition;
  This life of mortal breath
Is but a suburb of the life elysian,
  Whose portal we call Death.   20

She is not dead,—the child of our affection,—
  But gone unto that school
Where she no longer needs our poor protection,
  And Christ himself doth rule.

In that great cloister's stillness and seclusion,
  By guardian angels led,
Safe from temptation, safe from sin's pollution,
  She lives, whom we call dead.

Day after day we think what she is doing
  In those bright realms of air;   30
Year after year, her tender steps pursuing,
  Behold her grown more fair.

Thus do we walk with her, and keep unbroken
  The bond which nature gives,
Thinking that our remembrance, though un-
    spoken,
  May reach her where she lives.

Not as a child shall we again behold her;
  For when with raptures wild
In our embraces we again enfold her,
  She will not be a child;   40

But a fair maiden, in her Father's mansion, [1]
  Clothed with celestial grace;
And beautiful with all the soul's expansion
  Shall we behold her face.

And though at times impetuous with emotion
  And anguish long suppressed,
The swelling heart heaves moaning like the
    ocean,
  That cannot be at rest,—

We will be patient, and assuage the feeling
  We may not wholly stay;   50
By silence sanctifying, not concealing,
  The grief that must have way.

1848

KING WITLAF'S DRINKING HORN

Witlaf, [2] a king of the Saxons,
  Ere yet his last he breathed,

[1] *John* xiv. 2
[2] Witlaf, King of Mercia, once took refuge for four
  months at the Abbey of Croyland, which he rewarded with gifts and privileges. In his will

To the merry monks of Croyland
  His drinking-horn bequeathed,—

That, whenever they sat at their revels
  And drank from the golden bowl,
They might remember the donor,
  And breathe a prayer for his soul.

So sat they once at Christmas,
  And bade the goblet pass;   10
In their beards the red wine glistened
  Like dew-drops in the grass.

They drank to the soul of Witlaf,
  They drank to Christ the Lord,
And to each of the Twelve Apostles,
  Who had preached his holy word.

They drank to the Saints and Martyrs
  Of the dismal days of yore,
And as soon as the horn was empty
  They remembered one Saint more.   20

And the reader droned from the pulpit,
  Like the murmur of many bees,
The legend of good Saint Guthlac, [3]
  And Saint Basil's [4] homilies;

Till the great bells of the convent,
  From their prison in the tower,
Guthlac and Bartholomaeus, [5]
  Proclaimed the midnight hour.

And the Yule-log cracked in the chimney,
  And the Abbot bowed his head,   30
And the flamelets flapped and flickered,
  But the Abbot was stark and dead.

Yet still in his pallid fingers
  He clutched the golden bowl,
In which, like a pearl dissolving,
  Had sunk and dissolved his soul.

But not for this their revels
  The jovial monks forbore,   38
For they cried, "Fill high the goblet!
  We must drink to one Saint more!"

1848

was found this bequest: "I also offer to the
refectory . . . the horn of my table, that the
elders of the monastery may drink out of it on
the festivals of the saints; and may sometimes
amid their benedictions remember the soul of the
donor, Witlaf."
[3] Saint Guthlac the English hermit, 673?-714, died at
  Croyland, where he had lived for fifteen years.
[4] one of the early fathers of the Greek Church
[5] Bartholomew, one of the twelve apostles

THE BUILDING OF THE SHIP [1]

"Build me straight, O worthy Master!
  Stanch and strong, a goodly vessel,
That shall laugh at all disaster,
  And with wave and whirlwind wrestle!"

The merchant's word
Delighted the Master heard;
For his heart was in his work, and the heart
Giveth grace unto every Art.
A quiet smile played round his lips,
As the eddies and dimples of the tide   10
Play round the bows of ships,
That steadily at anchor ride.
And with a voice that was full of glee,
He answered, "Ere long we will launch
A vessel as goodly, and strong, and stanch,
As ever weathered a wintry sea!"

And first with nicest skill and art,
Perfect and finished in every part,
A little model the Master wrought,
Which should be to the larger plan   20
What the child is to the man,
Its counterpart in miniature;
That with a hand more swift and sure
The greater labor might be brought
To answer to his inward thought.
And as he labored, his mind ran o'er
The various ships that were built of yore,
And above them all, and strangest of all,
Towered the Great Harry, [2] crank and tall,
Whose picture was hanging on the wall,   30
With bows and stern raised high in air,
And balconies hanging here and there,
And signal lanterns and flags afloat,
And eight round towers, like those that frown
From some old castle, looking down
Upon the drawbridge and the moat.
And he said, with a smile, "Our ship, I wis,
Shall be of another form than this!"

It was of another form, indeed;
Built for freight, and yet for speed,   40
A beautiful and gallant craft;
Broad in the beam, that the stress of the blast,
Pressing down upon sail and mast,
Might not the sharp bows overwhelm;
Broad in the beam, but sloping aft
With graceful curve and slow degrees,
That she might be docile to the helm,

And that the currents of parted seas,
Closing behind, with mighty force,
Might aid and not impede her course.   50

In the ship-yard stood the Master,
  With the model of the vessel
That should laugh at all disaster,
  And with wave and whirlwind wrestle!

Covering many a rood of ground,
Lay the timber piled around;
Timber of chestnut, and elm, and oak,
And scattered here and there, with these,
The knarred and crooked cedar knees;
Brought from regions far away,   60
From Pascagoula's sunny bay, [3]
And the banks of the roaring Roanoke! [4]
Ah! what a wondrous thing it is
To note how many wheels of toil
One thought, one word, can set in motion!
There's not a ship that sails the ocean,
But every climate, every soil,
Must bring its tribute, great or small,
And help to build the wooden wall! [5]

The sun was rising o'er the sea,   70
And long the level shadows lay,
As if they, too, the beams would be
Of some great, airy argosy, [6]
Framed and launched in a single day.
That silent architect, the sun,
Had hewn and laid them every one,
Ere the work of man was yet begun.
Beside the Master, when he spoke,
A youth, against an anchor leaning,
Listened, to catch his slightest meaning.   80
Only the long waves, as they broke
In ripples on the pebbly beach,
Interrupted the old man's speech.

Beautiful they were, in sooth,
The old man and the fiery youth!
The old man, in whose busy brain
Many a ship that sailed the main
Was modeled o'er and o'er again;—
The fiery youth, who was to be
The heir of his dexterity,   90
The heir of his house, and his daughter's hand,
When he had built and launched from land
What the elder head had planned.

[1] This poem is comparable with Schiller's "Song of the Bell," in which the changes of meter are adapted to the changes in thought. Note the occasional use of the meter which Longfellow later used in "Hiawatha."
[2] a three-masted English war-ship, huge for its day, built in 1488

[3] on the southern coast of Mississippi
[4] in North Carolina
[5] The answer of the Delphic oracle to the Greeks who asked how they were to meet Xerxes was:
  "Zeus the sire of all
  Hath safety promised in a wooden wall."
Accordingly, by using well their ships the Greeks overthrew the Persians in the naval battle of Salamis.
[6] a richly laden merchant vessel

"Thus," said he, "will we build this ship!
Lay square the blocks upon the slip, [1]
And follow well this plan of mine.
Choose the timbers with greatest care;
Of all that is unsound beware;
For only what is sound and strong
To this vessel shall belong.   100
Cedar of Maine and Georgia pine
Here together shall combine.
A goodly frame, and a goodly fame,
And the UNION [2] be her name!
For the day that gives her to the sea
Shall give my daughter unto thee!"

The Master's word
Enraptured the young man heard;
And as he turned his face aside,
With a look of joy and a thrill of pride,   110
Standing before
Her father's door,
He saw the form of his promised bride.
The sun shone on her golden hair,
And her cheek was glowing fresh and fair,
With the breath of morn and the soft sea air,
Like a beauteous barge was she,
Still at rest on the sandy beach,
Just beyond the billow's reach;
But he   120
Was the restless, seething, stormy sea!

Ah, how skilful grows the hand
That obeyeth Love's command!
It is the heart, and not the brain,
That to the highest doth attain,
And he who followeth Love's behest
Far excelleth all the rest!

Thus with the rising of the sun
Was the noble task begun,
And soon throughout the ship-yard's bounds
Were heard the intermingled sounds   131
Of axes and of mallets, plied
With vigorous arms on every side;
Plied so deftly and so well,
That, ere the shadows of evening fell,
The keel of oak for a noble ship,
Scarfed [3] and bolted, straight and strong,
Was lying ready, and stretched along
The blocks, well placed upon the slip.
Happy, thrice happy, every one   140
Who sees his labor well begun,
And not perplexed and multiplied,
By idly waiting for time and tide!

And when the hot, long day was o'er,
The young man at the Master's door
Sat with the maiden calm and still.
And, within the porch, a little more
Removed beyond the evening chill,
The father sat, and told them tales   149
Of wrecks in the great September gales, [4]
Of pirates upon the Spanish Main, [5]
And ships that never came back again,
The chance and change of a sailor's life,
Want and plenty, rest and strife,
His roving fancy, like the wind,
That nothing can stay and nothing can bind,
And the magic charm of foreign lands,
With shadows of palms, and shining sands,
Where the tumbling surf,
O'er the coral reefs of Madagascar,   160
Washes the feet of the swarthy Lascar, [6]
As he lies alone and asleep on the turf.
And the trembling maiden held her breath
At the tales of that awful, pitiless sea,
With all its terror and mystery,
The dim, dark sea, so like unto Death,
That divides and yet unites mankind!
And whenever the old man paused, a gleam
From the bowl of his pipe would awhile illume
The silent group in the twilight gloom,   170
And thoughtful faces, as in a dream;
And for a moment one might mark
What had been hidden by the dark,
That the head of the maiden lay at rest,
Tenderly, on the young man's breast!

Day by day the vessel grew,
With timbers fashioned strong and true,
Stemson and keelson and sternson-knee, [7]
Till, framed with perfect symmetry,
A skeleton ship rose up to view!   180
And around the bows and along the side
The heavy hammers and mallets plied,
Till after many a week, at length,
Wonderful for form and strength,
Sublime in its enormous bulk,
Loomed aloft the shadowy hulk!
And around it columns of smoke, upwreathing,
Rose from the boiling, bubbling, seething
Caldron, that glowed,
And overflowed   190
With the black tar, heated for the sheathing.
And amid the clamors
Of clattering hammers,
He who listened heard now and then
The song of the Master and his men:—

[1] an inclined plane on which a vessel is built or repaired
[2] The poem was written during the great secession agitation.
[3] spliced lengthwise
[4] A great gale in 1815 was long known as the great September gale.
[5] the waters north of South America
[6] an East Indian sailor
[7] bracings at the stern of a wooden ship's hull

"Build me straight, O worthy Master,
  Stanch and strong, a goodly vessel,
That shall laugh at all disaster,
  And with wave and whirlwind wrestle!"

With oaken brace and copper band,   200
Lay the rudder on the sand,
That, like a thought, should have control
Over the movement of the whole;
And near it the anchor, whose giant hand
Would reach down and grapple with the land,
And immovable and fast
Hold the great ship against the bellowing blast!
And at the bows an image stood,
By a cunning artist carved in wood,
With robes of white, that far behind   210
Seemed to be fluttering in the wind.
It was not shaped in a classic mold,
Not like a nymph or Goddess of old,
Or naiad [1] rising from the water,
But modeled from the Master's daughter!
On many a dreary and misty night,
'Twill be seen by the rays of the signal light,
Speeding along through the rain and the dark,
Like a ghost in its snow-white sark, [2]
The pilot of some phantom bark,   220
Guiding the vessel, in its flight,
By a path none other knows aright!

Behold, at last,
Each tall and tapering mast
Is swung into its place;
Shrouds and stays
Holding it firm and fast!

Long ago,
In the deer-haunted forests of Maine,
When upon mountain and plain   230
Lay the snow,
They fell,—those lordly pines!
Those grand, majestic pines!
'Mid shouts and cheers
The jaded steers,
Panting beneath the goad,
Dragged down the weary, winding road
Those captive kings so straight and tall,
To be shorn of their streaming hair,
And, naked and bare,   240
To feel the stress and the strain
Of the wind and the reeling main,
Whose roar
Would remind them forevermore
Of their native forests they should not see again.

And everywhere
The slender, graceful spars

[1] sea nymph   [2] shirt

Poise aloft in the air,
And at the masthead,
White, blue, and red,   250
A flag unrolls the stripes and stars.
Ah! when the wanderer, lonely, friendless,
In foreign harbors shall behold
That flag unrolled,
'Twill be as a friendly hand
Stretched out from his native land,
Filling his heart with memories sweet and end-
      less.

All is finished! and at length
Has come the bridal day
Of beauty and of strength.   260
Today the vessel shall be launched!
With fleecy clouds the sky is blanched,
And o'er the bay,
Slowly, in all his splendors dight,
The great sun rises to behold the sight.

The ocean old,
Centuries old,
Strong as youth, and as uncontrolled,
Paces restless to and fro,
Up and down the sands of gold.   270
His beating heart is not at rest;
And far and wide,
With ceaseless flow,
His beard of snow
Heaves with the heaving of his breast.

He waits impatient for his bride.
There she stands,
With her foot upon the sands,
Decked with flags and streamers gay,
In honor of her marriage day,   280
Her snow-white signals fluttering, blending,
Round her like a veil descending,
Ready to be
The bride of the gray, old sea.

On the deck another bride
Is standing by her lover's side.
Shadows from the flags and shrouds,
Like the shadows cast by clouds,
Broken by many a sunny fleck,
Fall around them on the deck.   290

The prayer is said,
The service read,
The joyous bridegroom bows his head;
And in tears the good old Master
Shakes the brown hand of his son,
Kisses his daughter's glowing cheek
In silence, for he cannot speak,
And ever faster
Down his own the tears begin to run.

The worthy pastor—   300
The shepherd of that wandering flock,
That has the ocean for its wold,
That has the vessel for its fold,
Leaping ever from rock to rock—
Spake, with accents mild and clear,
Words of warning, words of cheer,
But tedious to the bridegroom's ear.
He knew the chart
Of the sailor's heart,
All its pleasures and its griefs,   310
All its shallows and rocky reefs,
All those secret currents, that flow
With such resistless undertow,
And lift and drift, with terrible force,
The will from its moorings and its course.
Therefore he spake, and thus said he:—
"Like unto ships far off at sea,
Outward or homeward bound are we.
Before, behind, and all around,
Floats and swings the horizon's bound,   320
Seems at its distant rim to rise
And climb the crystal wall of the skies,
And then again to turn and sink,
As if we could slide from its outer brink.
Ah! it is not the sea,
It is not the sea that sinks and shelves,
But ourselves
That rock and rise
With endless and uneasy motion,
Now touching the very skies,   330
Now sinking into the depths of ocean.
Ah! if our souls but poise and swing
Like the compass in its brazen ring,
Ever level and ever true
To the toil and the task we have to do,
We shall sail securely, and safely reach
The Fortunate Isles, [1] on whose shining beach
The sights we see, and the sounds we hear,
Will be those of joy and not of fear!"

Then the Master,   340
With a gesture of command,
Waved his hand;
And at the word,
Loud and sudden there was heard,
All around them and below,
The sound of hammers, blow on blow,
Knocking away the shores and spurs.
And see! she stirs!
She starts,—she moves,—she seems to feel
The thrill of life along her keel,   350
And, spurning with her foot the ground,
With one exulting, joyous bound,
She leaps into the ocean's arms!

[1] or Isles of the Blest—the last home of the favorites
of the gods

And lo! from the assembled crowd
There rose a shout, prolonged and loud,
That to the ocean seemed to say,
"Take her, Oh bridegroom, old and gray,
Take her to thy protecting arms,
With all her youth and all her charms!"

How beautiful she is! How fair   360
She lies within those arms, that press
Her form with many a soft caress
Of tenderness and watchful care!
Sail forth into the sea, O ship!
Through wind and wave, right onward steer!
The moistened eye, the trembling lip,
Are not the signs of doubt or fear.

Sail forth into the sea of life,
O gentle, loving, trusting wife,
And safe from all adversity   370
Upon the bosom of that sea
Thy comings and thy goings be!
For gentleness and love and trust
Prevail o'er angry wave and gust;
And in the wreck of noble lives
Something immortal still survives!

Thou, too, sail on, O Ship of State!
Sail on, O UNION, strong and great!
Humanity with all its fears,
With all the hopes of future years,   380
Is hanging breathless on thy fate!
We know what Master laid thy keel,
What Workmen wrought thy ribs of steel,
Who made each mast, and sail, and rope,
What anvils rang, what hammers beat,
In what a forge, and what a heat
Were shaped the anchors of thy hope!
Fear not each sudden sound and shock,
'Tis of the wave and not the rock;
'Tis but the flapping of the sail,   390
And not a rent made by the gale!
In spite of rock and tempest's roar,
In spite of false lights on the shore,
Sail on, nor fear to breast the sea!
Our hearts, our hopes, are all with thee,
Our hearts, our hopes, our prayers, our tears,
Our faith triumphant o'er our fears,
Are all with thee,—are all with thee!
1849   1849

CHILDREN

Come to me, O ye children!
For I hear you at your play,
And the questions that perplexed me
Have vanished quite away.

Ye open the eastern windows,
 That look towards the sun,
Where thoughts are singing swallows,
 And the brooks of morning run.

In your hearts are the birds and the sunshine,
 In your thoughts the brooklet's flow, 10
But in mine is the wind of Autumn
 And the first fall of the snow.

Ah! what would the world be to us
 If the children were no more?
We should dread the desert behind us
 Worse than the dark before.

What the leaves are to the forest,
 With light and air for food,
Ere their sweet and tender juices
 Have been hardened into wood,— 20

That to the world are children;
 Through them it feels the glow
Of a brighter and sunnier climate
 Than reaches the trunks below.

Come to me, O ye children!
 And whisper in my ear
What the birds and the winds are singing
 In your sunny atmosphere.

For what are all our contrivings,
 And the wisdom of our books, 30
When compared with your caresses,
 And the gladness of your looks?

Ye are better than all the ballads
 That ever were sung or said;
For ye are living poems,
 And all the rest are dead.

1849

THE LADDER OF SAINT AUGUSTINE [1]

Saint Augustine! well hast thou said,
 That of our vices we can frame
A ladder, if we will but tread
 Beneath our feet each deed of shame!

All common things, each day's events,
 That with the hour begin and end,
Our pleasures and our discontents,
 Are rounds by which we may ascend.

[1] Saint Augustine (354-430) said, *"De vitiis nostris scalam nobis facimus, si vitia ipsa calcamus"*— We make a ladder for ourselves from our faults if we tread upon the faults themselves. *Sermon III, De Ascensione.*

The low desire, the base design,
 That makes another's virtues less; 10
The revel of the ruddy wine,
 And all occasions of excess;

The longing for ignoble things;
 The strife for triumph more than truth;
The hardening of the heart, that brings
 Irreverence for the dreams of youth;

All thoughts of ill; all evil deeds,
 That have their root in thoughts of ill;
Whatever hinders or impedes
 The action of the nobler will;— 20

All these must first be trampled down
 Beneath our feet, if we would gain
In the bright fields of fair renown
 The right of eminent domain.

We have not wings, we cannot soar;
 But we have feet to scale and climb
By slow degrees, by more and more,
 The cloudy summits of our time.

The mighty pyramids of stone
 That wedge-like cleave the desert airs, 30
When nearer seen, and better known,
 Are but gigantic flights of stairs.

The distant mountains that uprear
 Their solid bastions [2] to the skies,
Are crossed by pathways, that appear
 As we to higher levels rise.

The heights by great men reached and kept
 Were not attained by sudden flight,
But they, while their companions slept,
 Were toiling upward in the night. 40

Standing on what too long we bore
 With shoulders bent and downcast eyes,
We may discern—unseen before—
 A path to higher destinies.

Nor deem the irrevocable Past,
 As wholly wasted, wholly vain,
If, rising on its wrecks, at last
 To something nobler we attain.

1850

[2] earthworks

THE WARDEN OF THE CINQUE PORTS [1]

A mist was driving down the British Channel,
  The day was just begun,
And through the window-panes, on floor and
    panel,
  Streamed the red autumn sun.

It glanced on flowing flag and rippling pennon,
  And the white sails of ships;
And from the frowning rampart, the black
    cannon
  Hailed it with feverish lips.

Sandwich and Romney, Hastings, Hithe, and
    Dover
  Were all alert that day,   10
To see the French war-steamers speeding over, [2]
  When the fog cleared away.

Sullen and silent, and like couchant lions,
  Their cannon, through the night,
Holding their breath, had watched, in grim de-
    fiance,
  The sea-coast opposite.

And now they roared at drum-beat from their
    stations
  On every citadel;
Each answering each, with morning salutations,
  That all was well.   20

And down the coast, all taking up the burden,
  Replied the distant forts,
As if to summon from his sleep the Warden
  And Lord of the Cinque Ports.

Him shall no sunshine from the fields of azure,
  No drum-beat from the wall,
No morning gun from the black fort's embra-
    sure,
  Awaken with its call!

No more, surveying with an eye impartial
  The long line of the coast,   30
Shall the gaunt figure of the old Field Marshal
  Be seen upon his post!

For in the night, unseen, a single warrior,
  In somber harness mailed,
Dreaded of man, and surnamed the Destroyer,
  The rampart wall had scaled.

He passed into the chamber of the sleeper,
  The dark and silent room,
And as he entered, darker grew, and deeper,
  The silence and the gloom.   40

He did not pause to parley or dissemble,
  But smote the Warden hoar;
Ah! what a blow! that made all England
    tremble
  And groan from shore to shore.

Meanwhile, without, the surly cannon waited,
  The sun rose bright o'erhead;
Nothing in Nature's aspect intimated
  That a great man was dead.
1852   1853

From THE SONG OF HIAWATHA [3]

INTRODUCTION

Should you ask me, whence these stories?
Whence these legends and traditions,
With the odors of the forest,
With the dew and damp of meadows,
With the curling smoke of wigwams,
With the rushing of great rivers,
With their frequent repetitions,
And their wild reverberations,
As of thunder in the mountains?
  I should answer, I should tell you,   10
"From the forests and the prairies,
From the great lakes of the Northland,
From the land of the Ojibways, [4]
From the land of the Dacotahs, [5]
From the mountains, moors, and fenlands,

---

[1] This poem was written in October, 1852, in honor of
  Field Marshal the Duke of Wellington, England's
  great general, who had died Sept. 14th, and who
  in 1829 had been given the very honorable title of
  Warden of the Cinque (Fr. *five*) Ports—the ports
  mentioned in the third stanza. These had once,
  because of their strength in ships, been considered
  the defense of England from continental invasion.
[2] out of respect to the memory of Wellington

[3] Longfellow in a note that accompanied the poem wrote:
  "This Indian Edda—if I may so call it—is
  founded on a tradition prevalent among the North
  American Indians, of a person of miraculous
  birth, who was sent among them to clear their
  rivers, forests, and fishing grounds, and to teach
  them the arts of peace. He was known among
  the different tribes by the several names of Micha-
  bou, Chiabo, Manabozo, Tarenyawagon, and Hiawatha. . . . Into this old tradition I have woven
  other curious Indian legends, drawn chiefly from
  the various and valuable writings of Mr. School-
  craft, to whom the literary world is greatly indebted for his indefatigable zeal in rescuing from
  oblivion so much of the legendary lore of the
  Indians." The meter was copied from that of
  the Finnish epic *Kalevala*.
[4] or Chippewas, a tribe of Algonquins who lived on
  the south shore of Lakes Superior and Huron
  and in northern Minnesota and Dakota
[5] A branch of the Sioux: they lived where now are
  North and South Dakota.

Where the heron, the Shuh-shuh-gah,
Feeds among the reeds and rushes.
I repeat them as I heard them
From the lips of Nawadaha
The musician, the sweet singer."   20
      Should you ask where Nawadaha
Found these songs so wild and wayward,
Found these legends and traditions,
I should answer, I should tell you,
"In the birds'-nests of the forest,
In the lodges of the beaver,
In the hoof-prints of the bison,
In the eyry of the eagle!
      "All the wild-fowl sang them to him,
In the moorlands and the fenlands,   30
In the melancholy marshes;
Chetowaik, the plover sang them,
Mahng, the loon, the wild-goose, Wawa,
The blue heron, the Shuh-shuh-gah,
And the grouse, the Mushkodasa!"
      If still further you should ask me,
Saying, "Who was Nawadaha?
Tell us of this Nawadaha,"
I should answer your inquiries
Straightway in such words as follow.   40
      "In the vale of Tawasentha, [1]
In the green and silent valley,
By the pleasant water-courses,
Dwelt the singer Nawadaha.
Round about the Indian village
Spread the meadows and the corn-fields,
And beyond them stood the forest,
Stood the groves of singing pine-trees,
Green in summer, white in winter,
Ever sighing, ever singing.   50
      "And the pleasant water-courses,
You could trace them through the valley,
By the rushing in the spring-time,
By the alders in the summer,
By the white fog in the autumn,
By the black line in the winter;
And beside them dwelt the singer,
In the vale of Tawasentha,
In the green and silent valley.
      "There he sang of Hiawatha,   60
Sang the Song of Hiawatha,
Sang his wondrous birth and being,
How he prayed and how he fasted,
How he lived, and toiled, and suffered,
That the tribes of men might prosper,
That he might advance his people!"
      Ye who love the haunts of nature,
Love the sunshine of the meadow,
Love the shadow of the forest,
Love the wind among the branches,   70

And the rain-shower and the snow-storm,
And the rushing of great rivers
Through their palisades of pine-trees,
And the thunder in the mountains,
Whose innumerable echoes
Flap like eagles in their eyries;—
Listen to these wild traditions,
To this Song of Hiawatha!
      Ye who love a nation's legends,
Love the ballads of a people,   80
That like voices from afar off
Call to us to pause and listen,
Speak in tones so plain and childlike,
Scarcely can the ear distinguish
Whether they are sung or spoken;—
Listen to this Indian Legend,
To this Song of Hiawatha!
      Ye whose hearts are fresh and simple,
Who have faith in God and Nature,
Who believe, that in all ages   90
Every human heart is human,
That in even savage bosoms
There are longings, yearnings, strivings
For the good they comprehend not,
That the feeble hands and helpless,
Groping blindly in the darkness,
Touch God's right hand in that darkness
And are lifted up and strengthened;—
Listen to this simple story,
To this Song of Hiawatha!   100
      Ye, who sometimes in your rambles
Through the green lanes of the country,
Where the tangled barberry-bushes
Hang their tufts of crimson berries
Over stone walls gray with mosses,
Pause by some neglected graveyard,
For a while to muse, and ponder
On a half-effaced inscription,
Written with little skill of song-craft,
Homely phrases, but each letter   110
Full of hope and yet of heart-break,
Full of all the tender pathos
Of the Here, and the Hereafter;—
Stay and read this rude inscription,
Read this Song of Hiawatha!

IV

HIAWATHA AND MUDJEKEEWIS [2]

Out of childhood into manhood
Now had grown my Hiawatha,
Skilled in all the craft of hunters,

---

[1] a valley in Albany County, New York, now known
    as Norman's Kill

[2] Hiawatha is the son of Mudjekeewis the West Wind
    and Wenonah, daughter of Nokomis, the child
    of the Moon. Wenonah, deserted by Mudje-
    keewis, has died of sorrow, and Hiawatha is cared
    for by his grandmother, near the shores of Gitche
    Gumee—Lake Superior.

Learned in all the lore of old men,
In all youthful sports and pastimes,
In all manly arts and labors.
　　Swift of foot was Hiawatha;
He could shoot an arrow from him,
And run forward with such fleetness,
That the arrow fell behind him!　　　10
Strong of arm was Hiawatha;
He could shoot ten arrows upward,
Shoot them with such strength and swiftness,
That the tenth had left the bow-string
Ere the first to earth had fallen!
　　He had mittens, Minjekahwun,
Magic mittens made of deer-skin;
When upon his hands he wore them,
He could smite the rocks asunder,
He could grind them into powder,　　　20
He had moccasins enchanted,
Magic moccasins of deer-skin;
When he bound them round his ankles,
When upon his feet he tied them,
At each stride a mile he measured!
　　Much he questioned old Nokomis
Of his father Mudjekeewis;
Learned from her the fatal secret
Of the beauty of his mother,
Of the falsehood of his father;　　　30
And his heart was hot within him,
Like a living coal his heart was.
　　Then he said to old Nokomis,
"I will go to Mudjekeewis,
See how fares it with my father,
At the doorways of the West-Wind,
At the portals of the Sunset!"
　　From his lodge went Hiawatha,
Dressed for travel, armed for hunting;
Dressed in deer-skin shirt and leggings,　　40
Richly wrought with quills and wampum; [1]
On his head his eagle feathers,
Round his waist his belt of wampum,
In his hand his bow of ash-wood,
Strung with sinews of the reindeer;
In his quiver oaken arrows,
Tipped with jasper, winged with feathers;
With his mittens, Minjekahwun,
With his moccasins enchanted.
　　Warning said the old Nokomis,　　　50
"Go not forth, O Hiawatha!
To the kingdom of the West-Wind,
To the realms of Mudjekeewis,
Lest he harm you with his magic,
Lest he kill you with his cunning!"
　　But the fearless Hiawatha
Heeded not her woman's warning;
Forth he strode into the forest,

[1] small shells strung together like beads and used for decoration and sometimes as money

At each stride a mile he measured;
Lurid seemed the sky above him,　　　60
Lurid seemed the earth beneath him,
Hot and close the air around him,
Filled with smoke and fiery vapors,
As of burning woods and prairies,
For his heart was hot within him,
Like a living coal his heart was.
　　So he journeyed westward, westward,
Left the fleetest deer behind him,
Left the antelope and bison;
Crossed the rushing Esconaba,　　　70
Crossed the mighty Mississippi,
Passed the Mountains of the Prairie,
Passed the land of Crows and Foxes,
Passed the dwellings of the Blackfeet,
Came unto the Rocky Mountains,
To the kingdom of the West-Wind,
Where upon the gusty summits
Sat the ancient Mudjekeewis,
Ruler of the winds of heaven.
　　Filled with awe was Hiawatha　　　80
At the aspect of his father.
On the air about him wildly
Tossed and streamed his cloudy tresses,
Gleamed like drifting snow his tresses,
Glared like Ishkoodah, the comet,
Like the star with fiery tresses.
　　Filled with joy was Mudjekeewis
When he looked on Hiawatha,
Saw his youth rise up before him
In the face of Hiawatha,　　　90
Saw the beauty of Wenonah
From the grave rise up before him.
　　"Welcome!" said he, "Hiawatha,
To the kingdom of the West-Wind!
Long have I been waiting for you!
Youth is lovely, age is lonely,
Youth is fiery, age is frosty;
You bring back the days departed,
You bring back my youth of passion,
And the beautiful Wenonah!"　　　100
　　Many days they talked together,
Questioned, listened, waited, answered;
Much the mighty Mudjekeewis
Boasted of his ancient prowess,
Of his perilous adventures,
His indomitable courage,
His invulnerable body.
　　Patiently sat Hiawatha,
Listening to his father's boasting;
With a smile he sat and listened,　　　110
Uttered neither threat nor menace,
Neither word nor look betrayed him,
But his heart was hot within him,
Like a living coal his heart was.

Then he said, "O Mudjekeewis,
Is there nothing that can harm you?
Nothing that you are afraid of?"
And the mighty Mudjekeewis,
Grand and gracious in his boasting,
Answered, saying, "There is nothing,   120
Nothing but the black rock yonder,
Nothing but the fatal Wawbeek!"
    And he looked at Hiawatha
With a wise look and benignant,
With a countenance paternal,
Looked with pride upon the beauty
Of his tall and graceful figure,
Saying, "O my Hiawatha!
Is there anything can harm you?
Anything you are afraid of?"   130
    But the wary Hiawatha
Paused awhile, as if uncertain,
Held his peace, as if resolving,
And then answered, "There is nothing,
Nothing but the bulrush yonder,
Nothing but the great Apukwa!"
    And as Mudjekeewis, rising,
Stretched his hand to pluck the bulrush,
Hiawatha cried in terror,
Cried in well-dissembled terror,   140
"Kago![1] kago! do not touch it!"
"Ah, kaween!" said Mudjekeewis,
"No indeed, I will not touch it!"
    Then they talked of other matters;
First of Hiawatha's brothers,
First of Wabun, of the East-Wind,
Of the South-Wind, Shawondasee,
Of the North, Kabibonokka;
Then of Hiawatha's mother,
Of the beautiful Wenonah,   150
Of her birth upon the meadow,
Of her death, as old Nokomis
Had remembered and related.
    And he cried, "O Mudjekeewis,
It was you who killed Wenonah,
Took her young life and her beauty,
Broke the Lily of the Prairie,
Trampled it beneath your footsteps;
You confess it! you confess it!"
And the mighty Mudjekeewis   160
Tossed upon the wind his tresses,
Bowed his hoary head in anguish,
With a silent nod assented.
    Then up started Hiawatha,
And with threatening look and gesture
Laid his hand upon the black rock,
On the fatal Wawbeek laid it,
With his mittens, Minjekahwun,
Rent the jutting crag asunder,
Smote and crushed it into fragments,   170

[1] *Kago* meant, "do not touch it"; *Kaw*, "no"; and *Kaween*, "no indeed."

Hurled them madly at his father,
The remorseful Mudjekeewis,
For his heart was hot within him,
Like a living coal his heart was.
    But the ruler of the West-Wind,
Blew the fragments backward from him,
With the breathing of his nostrils,
With the tempest of his anger,
Blew them back at his assailant;
Seized the bulrush, the Apukwa,   180
Dragged it with its roots and fibers
From the margin of the meadow,
From its ooze, the giant bulrush;
Long and loud laughed Hiawatha!
    Then began the deadly conflict,
Hand to hand among the mountains;
From his eyry screamed the eagle,
The Keneu, the great war-eagle,
Sat upon the crags around them,
Wheeling flapped his wings above them.   190
    Like a tall tree in the tempest
Bent and lashed the giant bulrush;
And in masses huge and heavy
Crashing fell the fatal Wawbeek;
Till the earth shook with the tumult
And confusion of the battle,
And the air was full of shoutings,
And the thunder of the mountains,
Starting, answered, "Baim-wawa!"[2]
    Back retreated Mudjekeewis,   200
Rushing westward o'er the mountains,
Stumbling westward down the mountains,
Three whole days retreated fighting,
Still pursued by Hiawatha
To the doorways of the West-Wind,
To the portals of the Sunset,
To the earth's remotest border,
Where into the empty spaces
Sinks the sun, as a flamingo
Drops into her nest at nightfall   210
In the melancholy marshes.
    "Hold!" at length cried Mudjekeewis,
"Hold, my son, my Hiawatha!
'Tis impossible to kill me,
For you cannot kill the immortal.
I have put you to this trial,
But to know and prove your courage;
Now receive the prize of valor!
    "Go back to your home and people,
Live among them, toil among them,   220
Cleanse the earth from all that harms it,
Clear the fishing-grounds and rivers,
Slay all monsters and magicians,
All the Wendigoes, the giants,
All the serpents, the Kenabeeks,
As I slew the Mishe-Mokwa,
Slew the Great Bear of the mountains.

[2] the sound of the thunder

"And at last when Death draws near you,
When the awful eyes of Pauguk
Glare upon you in the darkness, 230
I will share my kingdom with you,
Ruler shall you be thenceforward
Of the Northwest-Wind, Keewaydin,
Of the home-wind, the Keewaydin."
    Thus was fought that famous battle
In the dreadful days of Shah-shah, [1]
In the days long since departed,
In the kingdom of the West-Wind.
Still the hunter sees its traces
Scattered far o'er hill and valley; 240
Sees the giant bulrush growing
By the ponds and water-courses,
Sees the masses of the Wawbeek
Lying still in every valley.
    Homeward now went Hiawatha;
Pleasant was the landscape round him,
Pleasant was the air above him,
For the bitterness of anger
Had departed wholly from him, 249
From his brain the thought of vengeance,
From his heart the burning fever.
    Only once his pace he slackened,
Only once he paused or halted,
Paused to purchase heads of arrows
Of the ancient Arrow-maker,
In the land of the Dacotahs,
Where the Falls of Minnehaha [2]
Flash and gleam among the oak-trees,
Laugh and leap into the valley.
    There the ancient Arrow-maker 260
Made his arrow-heads of sandstone,
Arrow-heads of chalcedony,
Arrow-heads of flint and jasper,
Smoothed and sharpened at the edges,
Hard and polished, keen and costly.
    With him dwelt his dark-eyed daughter,
Wayward as the Minnehaha,
With her moods of shade and sunshine,
Eyes that smiled and frowned alternate,
Feet as rapid as the river, 270
Tresses flowing like the water,
And as musical a laughter;
And he named her from the river,
From the water-fall he named her,
Minnehaha, Laughing Water.
    Was it then for heads of arrows,
Arrow-heads of chalcedony,
Arrow-heads of flint and jasper,
That my Hiawatha halted
In the land of the Dacotahs? 280
    Was it not to see the maiden,
See the face of Laughing Water

[1] long ago
[2] The beautiful Falls of Minnehaha (*laughing water*) are in Minnesota, near St. Paul and Minneapolis, in a small tributary to the Mississippi.

Peeping from behind the curtain,
Hear the rustling of her garments
From behind the waving curtain,
As one sees the Minnehaha
Gleaming, glancing through the branches,
As one hears the Laughing Water
From behind its screen of branches?
    Who shall say what thoughts and visions
Fill the fiery brains of young men? 291
Who shall say what dreams of beauty
Filled the heart of Hiawatha?
All he told to old Nokomis,
When he reached the lodge at sunset,
Was the meeting with his father,
Was his fight with Mudjekeewis;
Not a word he said of arrows,
Not a word of Laughing Water.
1854-55   1855

VICTOR GALBRAITH [3]

Under the walls of Monterey
At daybreak the bugles began to play,
        Victor Galbraith!
In the mist of the morning damp and gray,
These were the words they seemed to say:
        "Come forth to thy death,
        Victor Galbraith!"

Forth he came, with a martial tread;
Firm was his step, erect his head;
        Victor Galbraith, 10
He who so well the bugle played,
Could not mistake the words it said:
        "Come forth to thy death,
        Victor Galbraith!"

He looked at the earth, he looked at the sky,
He looked at the files of musketry,
        Victor Galbraith!
And he said, with a steady voice and eye,
"Take good aim; I am ready to die!"
        Thus challenges death 20
        Victor Galbraith.

Twelve fiery tongues flashed straight and red,
Six leaden balls on their errand sped;
        Victor Galbraith
Falls to the ground, but he is not dead;
His name was not stamped on those balls of
        lead, [4]
        And they only scath
        Victor Galbraith.

[3] He was a bugler in a regiment of cavalry in Mexico, and was sentenced to death for some breach of discipline.
[4] According to superstition a bullet will not kill a soldier unless his name is written on it.

Three balls are in his breast and brain,
But he rises out of the dust again,   30
        Victor Galbraith!
The water he drinks has a bloody stain;
"O kill me, and put me out of my pain!"
        In his agony prayeth
        Victor Galbraith.

Forth dart once more those tongues of flame,
And the bugler has died a death of shame,
        Victor Galbraith!
His soul has gone back to whence it came,
And no one answers to the name,   40
        When the Sergeant saith,
        "Victor Galbraith!"

Under the walls of Monterey
By night a bugle is heard to play,
        Victor Galbraith!
Through the mist of the valley damp and gray
The sentinels hear the sound, and say,
        "That is the wraith
        Of Victor Galbraith!"

1855

MY LOST YOUTH

Often I think of the beautiful town [1]
    That is seated by the sea;
Often in thought go up and down
The pleasant streets of that dear old town,
    And my youth comes back to me.
        And a verse of a Lapland song
        Is haunting my memory still:
        "A boy's will is the wind's will,
And the thoughts of youth are long, long
        thoughts." [2]

I can see the shadowy lines of its trees,   10
    And catch, in sudden gleams,
The sheen of the far-surrounding seas,
And islands that were the Hesperides [3]
    Of all my boyish dreams.
        And the burden of that old song,
        It murmurs and whispers still:
        "A boy's will is the wind's will,
And the thoughts of youth are long, long
        thoughts."

I remember the black wharves and the slips,
    And the sea-tides tossing free;   20
And Spanish sailors with bearded lips,

And the beauty and mystery of the ships,
    And the magic of the sea.
        And the voice of that wayward song
        Is singing and saying still:
        "A boy's will is the wind's will,
And the thoughts of youth are long, long
        thoughts."

I remember the bulwarks by the shore,
    And the fort upon the hill;
The sunrise gun, with its hollow roar,   30
The drum-beat repeated o'er and o'er,
    And the bugle wild and shrill.
        And the music of that old song
        Throbs in my memory still:
        "A boy's will is the wind's will,
And the thoughts of youth are long, long
        thoughts."

I remember the sea-fight far away, [4]
    How it thundered o'er the tide!
And the dead captains, as they lay
In their graves, o'erlooking the tranquil bay   41
    Where they in battle died.
        And the sound of that mournful song
        Goes through me with a thrill:
        "A boy's will is the wind's will,
And the thoughts of youth are long, long
        thoughts."

I can see the breezy dome of groves,
    The shadows of Deering's Woods;
And the friendships old and the early loves
Come back with a Sabbath sound, as of doves
    In quiet neighborhoods.   50
        And the verse of that sweet old song,
        It flutters and murmurs still:
        "A boy's will is the wind's will,
And the thoughts of youth are long, long
        thoughts."

I remember the gleams and glooms that dart
    Across the school-boy's brain;
The song and the silence in the heart,
That in part are prophecies, and in part
    Are longings wild and vain.
        And the voice of that fitful song   60
        Sings on, and is never still:
        "A boy's will is the wind's will,
And the thoughts of youth are long, long
        thoughts."

---

[1] Portland, Maine, Longfellow's birthplace
[2] The lines are in a nuptial song in a Latin treatise on Lapland, published in 1674, by Johannes Scheffer, Professor at Upsala.
[3] mythological maidens, guardians of the golden apples of the sunset; hence, loosely, the western islands where they lived

[4] The reference is to an engagement, between the American brig *Enterprise* and the English brig *Boxer*, which occurred off Portland in 1813. The *Enterprise* conquered, but the captains of both ships were killed and were buried side by side on shore.

There are things of which I may not speak;
　There are dreams that cannot die;
There are thoughts that make the strong heart
　　weak,
And bring a pallor into the cheek,
　And a mist before the eye.
　　And the words of that fatal song
　　Come over me like a chill: 70
And the thoughts of youth are long, long
　　thoughts."
"A boy's will is the wind's will,

Strange to me now are the forms I meet
　When I visit the dear old town;
But the native air is pure and sweet,
And the trees that o'ershadow each well-known
　　street,
　As they balance up and down,
　　Are singing the beautiful song,
　　Are sighing and whispering still:
　　"A boy's will is the wind's will, 80
And the thoughts of youth are long, long
　　thoughts."

And Deering's Woods are fresh and fair,
　And with joy that is almost pain
My heart goes back to wander there,
And among the dreams of the days that were,
　I find my lost youth again.
　　And the strange and beautiful song,
　　The groves are repeating it still:
　　"A boy's will is the wind's will, 89
And the thoughts of youth are long, long
　　thoughts."

1855 1855

THE DISCOVERER OF THE NORTH CAPE

A LEAF FROM KING ALFRED'S *Orosius* [1]

Othere, the old sea-captain,
　Who dwelt in Helgoland, [2]
To King Alfred, the Lover of Truth,
Brought a snow-white walrus-tooth,
　Which he held in his brown right hand.

His figure was tall and stately,
　Like a boy's his eye appeared;

[1] Alfred, king of the West Saxons 871-901 and a lover of learning, not only translated the history of the world written by Orosius, a Spanish monk of the fifth century, but also added to it. He relates among other things what was told him by Ohthere (or Ottar), a Norwegian sailor who about 870 rounded the North Cape and discovered the White Sea.
[2] evidently not Helgoland, the island off the coast of Schleswig-Holstein (cf. ll. 26, 27), but possibly Helgo Island on the Norway coast southwest of North Cape

His hair was yellow as hay,
　But threads of a silvery gray
　　Gleamed in his tawny beard. 10

Hearty and hale was Othere,
　His cheek had the color of oak;
With a kind of laugh in his speech,
Like the sea-tide on a beach,
　As unto the King he spoke.

And Alfred, King of the Saxons,
　Had a book upon his knees,
And wrote down the wondrous tale
Of him who was first to sail
　Into the Arctic seas. 20

"So far I live to the northward,
　No man lives north of me:
To the east are wild mountain-chains,
And beyond them meres and plains;
　To the westward all is sea.

"So far I live to the northward,
　From the harbor of Skeringes-hale, [3]
If you only sailed by day,
With a fair wind all the way,
　More than a month would you sail. 30

"I own six hundred reindeer,
　With sheep and swine beside;
I have tribute from the Finns,
Whalebone and reindeer-skins,
　And ropes of walrus-hide.

"I plowed the land with horses,
　But my heart was ill at ease,
For the old seafaring men
Came to me now and then,
　With their sagas of the seas;— 40

"Of Iceland and of Greenland,
　And the stormy Hebrides,
And the undiscovered deep;—
Oh, I could not eat nor sleep
　For thinking of those seas.

"To the northward stretched the desert,
　How far I fain would know;
So at last I sallied forth,
And three days sailed due north,
　As far as the whale-ships go. 50

"To the west of me was the ocean,
　To the right the desolate shore,
But I did not slacken sail
For the walrus or the whale,
　Till after three days more.

[3] in the Gulf of Christiania

"The days grew longer and longer,
  Till they became as one,
And northward through the haze
I saw the sullen blaze
  Of the red midnight sun.   60

"And then uprose before me,
  ` Upon the water's edge,
The huge and haggard shape
Of that unknown North Cape,
  Whose form is like a wedge.

"The sea was rough and stormy,
  The tempest howled and wailed,
And the sea-fog, like a ghost,
Haunted that dreary coast,
  But onward still I sailed.   70

"Four days I steered to eastward,
  Four days without a night:
Round in a fiery ring
Went the great sun, O King,
  With red and lurid light."

Here Alfred, King of the Saxons,
  Ceased writing for a while;
And raised his eyes from his book,
With a strange and puzzled look,
  And an incredulous smile.   80

But Othere, the old sea-captain,
  He neither paused nor stirred,
Till the King listened, and then
Once more took up his pen,
  And wrote down every word.

"And now the land," said Othere,
  "Bent southward suddenly,
And I followed the curving shore
And ever southward bore
  Into a nameless sea.   90

"And there we hunted the walrus,
  The narwhale, [1] and the seal;
Ha! 'twas a noble game!
And like the lightning's flame
  Flew our harpoons of steel.

"There were six of us all together,
  Norsemen of Helgoland;
In two days and no more
We killed of them threescore,
  And dragged them to the strand!"   100

[1] an animal resembling a small whale and having a
  tusk projecting horizontally forward from its
  upper jaw

Here Alfred the Truth-Teller
  Suddenly closed his book,
And lifted his blue eyes
With doubt and strange surmise
  Depicted in their look.

And Othere the old sea-captain
  Stared at him wild and weird,
Then smiled, till his shining teeth
Gleamed white from underneath
  His tawny, quivering beard.   110

And to the King of the Saxons,
  In witness of the truth,
Raising his noble head,
He stretched his brown hand, and said,
  "Behold this walrus-tooth!"
1857

SANDALPHON [2]

Have you read in the Talmud [3] of old,
In the Legends the Rabbins have told
  Of the limitless realms of the air,
Have you read it,—the marvelous story
Of Sandalphon, the Angel of Glory,
  Sandalphon, the Angel of Prayer?

How, erect, at the outermost gates
Of the City Celestial he waits,
  With his feet on the ladder of light,
That, crowded with angels unnumbered,   10
By Jacob was seen as he slumbered [4]
  Alone in the desert at night?

The Angels of Wind and of Fire
Chant only one hymn, and expire
  With the song's irresistible stress;
Expire in their rapture and wonder,
As harp-strings are broken asunder
  By music they throb to express.

But serene in the rapturous throng,
Unmoved by the rush of the song,   20
  With eyes unimpassioned and slow,
Among the dead angels, the deathless
Sandalphon stands listening breathless
  To sounds that ascend from below;—

From the spirits on earth that adore,
From the souls that entreat and implore

[2] In Jewish tradition, Sandalphon, who stands on earth
  but whose head reaches heaven, is an angel who
  weaves into garlands the prayers of the Israelites.
  He is not one of the multitudes of angels created
  each day who sing one song and then perish,
  but has existed since the first creation. Cf.
  Poe's "Israfel," p. 284.
[3] the book of Jewish commentary upon the Old Testament
[4] *Genesis* xxviii, 12

In the fervor and passion of prayer;
From the hearts that are broken with losses,
And weary with dragging the crosses
    Too heavy for mortals to bear.   30

And he gathers the prayers as he stands,
And they change into flowers in his hands,
    Into garlands of purple and red;
And beneath the great arch of the portal,
Through the streets of the City Immortal
    Is wafted the fragrance they shed.

It is but a legend, I know,—
A fable, a phantom, a show,
    Of the ancient Rabbinical lore;
Yet the old medieval tradition,   40
The beautiful, strange superstition,
    But haunts me and holds me the more.

When I look from my window at night,
And the welkin above is all white,
    All throbbing and panting with stars,
Among them majestic is standing
Sandalphon the angel, expanding
    His pinions in nebulous bars.

And the legend, I feel, is a part
Of the hunger and thirst of the heart,   50
    The frenzy and fire of the brain,
That grasps at the fruitage forbidden,
The golden pomegranates of Eden,
    To quiet its fever and pain.
1857

THE CHILDREN'S HOUR

Between the dark and the daylight,
    When the night is beginning to lower,
Comes a pause in the day's occupations,
    That is known as the Children's Hour.

I hear in the chamber above me
    The patter of little feet,
The sound of a door that is opened,
    And voices soft and sweet.

From my study I see in the lamplight,
    Descending the broad hall stair,   10
Grave Alice, and laughing Allegra,
    And Edith with golden hair.

A whisper, and then a silence:
    Yet I know by their merry eyes
They are plotting and planning together
    To take me by surprise.

A sudden rush from the stairway,
    A sudden raid from the hall!
By three doors left unguarded
    They enter my castle wall!   20

They climb up into my turret
    O'er the arms and back of my chair;
If I try to escape, they surround me;
    They seem to be everywhere.

They almost devour me with kisses,
    Their arms about me entwine,
Till I think of the Bishop of Bingen
    In his Mouse-Tower on the Rhine! [1]

Do you think, O blue-eyed banditti,
    Because you have scaled the wall,   30
Such an old mustache as I am
    Is not a match for you all!

I have you fast in my fortress,
    And will not let you depart,
But put you down into the dungeon
    In the round-tower of my heart.

And there will I keep you forever,
    Yes, forever and a day,
Till the walls shall crumble to ruin,   39
    And molder in dust away.
1859   1860

A DAY OF SUNSHINE

O gift of God! O perfect day:
Whereon shall no man work, but play;
Whereon it is enough for me,
Not to be doing, but to be!

Through every fiber of my brain,
Through every nerve, through every vein,
I feel the electric thrill, the touch
Of life, that seems almost too much.

I hear the wind among the trees
Playing celestial symphonies;   10
I see the branches downward bent,
Like keys of some great instrument.

And over me unrolls on high
The splendid scenery of the sky,
Where through a sapphire sea the sun
Sails like a golden galleon, [2]

[1] Legend says that Archbishop Hatto of the 10th century, because in time of famine he had burned poor people caught stealing grain, was eaten by mice, although he had tried to escape them by building a high tower. Cf. Southey's poem "God's Judgment on a Wicked Bishop."

[2] an ancient Spanish ship often carrying treasure

Towards yonder cloud-land in the West,
Towards yonder Islands of the Blest,
Whose steep sierra far uplifts
Its craggy summits white with drifts.   20

Blow, winds! and waft through all the rooms
The snow-flakes of the cherry-blooms!
Blow, winds! and bend within my reach
The fiery blossoms of the peach!

O Life and Love! O happy throng
Of thoughts, whose only speech is song!
O heart of man! canst thou not be
Blithe as the air is, and as free?
1860

From TALES OF A WAYSIDE INN [1]

PART FIRST

PRELUDE

THE WAYSIDE INN

One autumn night, in Sudbury town,
Across the meadows bare and brown,
The windows of the wayside inn
Gleamed red with fire-light through the leaves
Of woodbine, hanging from the eaves
Their crimson curtains rent and thin.

As ancient is this hostelry
As any in the land may be,
Built in the old Colonial day,
When men lived in a grander way,   10
With ampler hospitality;
A kind of old Hobgoblin Hall,
Now somewhat fallen to decay,
With weather-stains upon the wall,
And stairways worn, and crazy doors,
And creaking and uneven floors,
And chimneys huge, and tiled and tall.

A region of repose it seems,
A place of slumber and of dreams,
Remote among the wooded hills!   20
For there no noisy railway speeds,
Its torch-race scattering smoke and gleeds; [2]
But noon and night, the panting teams
Stop under the great oaks, that throw
Tangles of light and shade below,
On roofs and doors and window-sills.

[1] Longfellow, grouping the tellers of his tales after the
   manner of Boccaccio and Chaucer, brings them
   together in the Red-Horse Inn of Sudbury, Mass.,
   about twenty miles west of Boston. The same
   family, the Howes, had kept the inn for one
   hundred and seventy-five years. In stage-coaching
   times it had been the regular stopping place for
   all travelers going westward.
[2] burning coals

Across the road the barns display
Their lines of stalls, their mows of hay,
Through the wide doors the breezes blow,
The wattled cocks strut to and fro,   30
And, half effaced by rain and shine,
The Red Horse prances on the sign.
Round this old-fashioned, quaint abode
Deep silence reigned, save when a gust
Went rushing down the county road,
And skeletons of leaves, and dust,
A moment quickened by its breath,
Shuddered and danced their dance of death,
And through the ancient oaks o'erhead
Mysterious voices moaned and fled.   40

But from the parlor of the inn
A pleasant murmur smote the ear,
Like water rushing through a weir:
Oft interrupted by the din
Of laughter and of loud applause,
And, in each intervening pause,
The music of a violin.
The fire-light, shedding over all
The splendor of its ruddy glow,
Filled the whole parlor large and low;   50
It gleamed on wainscot and on wall,
It touched with more than wonted grace
Fair Princess Mary's pictured face;
It bronzed the rafters overhead,
On the old spinet's ivory keys
It played inaudible melodies,
It crowned the somber clock with flame,
The hands, the hours, the maker's name,
And painted with a livelier red
The Landlord's coat-of-arms again;   60
And, flashing on the window-pane,
Emblazoned with its light and shade
The jovial rimes, that still remain,
Writ near a century ago
By the great Major Molineaux,
Whom Hawthorne has immortal made. [3]

Before the blazing fire of wood
Erect the rapt musician [4] stood;
And ever and anon he bent
His head upon his instrument,   70
And seemed to listen, till he caught
Confessions of its secret thought,—

[3] In his tale "My Kinsman, Major Molineux," in *The
   Snow Image and Other Twice-Told Tales;* the
   lines on the window with the name Wm. Molineux, Jr., Esq., June 24, 1774, are:

>   What do you think?
>   Here is a good drink
>   Perhaps you may not know it;
>   If not in haste
>   Do stop and taste!
>   You very merry folk will show it.

[4] Ole Bull, 1810-1880, the Norwegian violinist

The joy, the triumph, the lament,
The exultation and the pain;
Then, by the magic of his art,
He soothed the throbbings of its heart,
And lulled it into peace again.

Around the fireside at their ease
There sat a group of friends, entranced
With the delicious melodies;   80
Who from the far-off noisy town
Had to the wayside inn come down,
To rest beneath its old oak trees.
The fire-light on their faces glanced,
Their shadows on the wainscot danced,
And, though of different lands and speech,
Each had his tale to tell, and each
Was anxious to be pleased and please.
And while the sweet musician plays,
Let me in outline sketch them all,   90
Perchance uncouthly as the blaze
With its uncertain touch portrays
Their shadowy semblance on the wall.

But first the Landlord will I trace;
Grave in his aspect and attire;
A man of ancient pedigree,
A Justice of the Peace was he,
Known in all Sudbury as "The Squire."
Proud was he of his name and race,
Of old Sir William and Sir Hugh,   100
And in the parlor, full in view,
His coat-of-arms, well framed and glazed,
Upon the wall in colors blazed;
He beareth gules [1] upon his shield,
A chevron argent [2] in the field,
With three wolf's heads, and for the crest [3]
A Wyvern part-per-pale addressed
Upon a helmet barred; below
The scroll reads, "By the name of Howe."
And over this, no longer bright,   110
Though glimmering with a latent light,
Was hung the sword his grandsire bore
In the rebellious days of yore,
Down there at Concord in the fight. [4]

A youth was there, of quiet ways,
A Student [5] of old books and days,
To whom all tongues and lands were known,
And yet a lover of his own;

With many a social virtue graced,
And yet a friend of solitude;   120
A man of such a genial mood
The heart of all things he embraced,
And yet of such fastidious taste,
He never found the best too good.
Books were his passion and delight,
And in his upper room at home
Stood many a rare and sumptuous tome,
In vellum bound, with gold bedight,
Great volumes garmented in white,
Recalling Florence, Pisa, Rome.   130
He loved the twilight that surrounds
The border-land of old romance;
Where glitter hauberk, helm, and lance,
And banner waves, and trumpet sounds,
And ladies ride with hawk on wrist,
And mighty warriors sweep along,
Magnified by the purple mist,
The dusk of centuries and of song.
The chronicles of Charlemagne,
Of Merlin and the Mort d'Arthure,   140
Mingled together in his brain
With tales of Flores and Blanchefleur,
Sir Ferumbras, Sir Eglamour,
Sir Launcelot, Sir Morgadour,
Sir Guy, Sir Bevis, Sir Gawain. [6]

A young Sicilian, [7] too was there;
In sight of Etna born and bred,
Some breath of its volcanic air
Was glowing in his heart and brain,
And, being rebellious to his liege,   150
After Palermo's fatal siege,
Across the western seas he fled,
In good King Bomba's [8] happy reign.
His face was like a summer night,
All flooded with a dusky light;
His hands were small; his teeth shone white
As sea-shells, when he smiled or spoke;
His sinews supple and strong as oak;
Clean shaven was he as a priest,
Who at the mass on Sunday sings,   160
Save that upon his upper lip
His beard, a good palm's length at least,
Level and pointed at the tip,
Shot sideways, like a swallow's wings.
The poets read he o'er and o'er,
And most of all the Immortal Four [9]

---

[1] red   [2] silver chevron
[3] "A device supported by a wreath or coronet displayed above the shield; the description of the crest here is that of a helmet surmounted by a winged dragon (Wyvern), the whole appearing in a vertical bar through the middle of the shield (part-per-pale)." Quoted from *The Lake Classics* edition of the *Tales*, edited by J. R. Powell.
[4] April 19, 1775
[5] Henry Ware Wales, a scholar and traveler

[6] All these are heroes or heroines of medieval romance.
[7] Luigi Monti, an intimate friend of Longfellow's; Palermo fell into the hands of the French in 1849.
[8] a nickname given Ferdinand II, king of the Two Sicilies, because of his bombardment of Messina
[9] Dante, 1265-1321; Petrarch, 1304-1374; Tasso, 1544-1595; Ariosto, 1474-1533; Boccaccio, 1313-1375, laid the scene of his group of stories, the *Decameron*, in Florence and its environs. Fiesole is a town three miles from Florence.

Of Italy; and next to those,
The story-telling bard of prose,
Who wrote the joyous Tuscan tales
Of the *Decameron*, that make   170
Fiesole's green hills and vales
Remembered for Boccaccio's sake.
Much too of music was his thought;
The melodies and measures fraught
With sunshine and the open air,
Of vineyards and the singing sea
Of his beloved Sicily;
And much it pleased him to peruse
The songs of the Sicilian muse,—
Bucolic songs by Meli sung [1]   180
In the familiar peasant tongue,
That made men say, "Behold! once more
The pitying gods to earth restore
Theocritus of Syracuse!" [2]

A Spanish Jew [3] from Alicant
With aspect grand and grave was there;
Vender of silks and fabrics rare,
And attar of rose from the Levant.
Like an old Patriarch he appeared,
Abraham or Isaac, or at least   190
Some later Prophet or High-Priest;
With lustrous eyes, and olive skin,
And, wildly tossed from cheeks and chin,
The tumbling cataract of his beard.
His garments breathed a spicy scent
Of cinnamon and sandal blent,
Like the soft aromatic gales
That meet the mariner, who sails
Through the Moluccas and the seas
That wash the shores of Celebes. [4]   200
All stories that recorded are
By Pierre Alphonse [5] he knew by heart,
And it was rumored he could say
The parables of Sandabar, [6]
And all the Fables of Pilpay, [7]
Or if not all, the greater part!
Well versed was he in Hebrew books
Talmud and Targum, and the lore
Of Kabala; [8] and evermore
There was a mystery in his looks;   210
His eyes seemed gazing far away,

As if in vision or in trance
He heard the solemn sackbut [9] play,
And saw the Jewish maidens dance.

A Theologian, [10] from the school
Of Cambridge, on the Charles was there;
Skilful alike with tongue and pen,
He preached to all men everywhere
The Gospel of the Golden Rule,
The New Commandment given to men,   220
Thinking the deed, and not the creed,
Would help us in our utmost need.
With reverent feet the earth he trod,
Nor banished nature from his plan,
But studied still with deep research
To build the Universal Church,
Lofty as in the love of God,
And ample as the wants of man.

A Poet, [11] too, was there, whose verse
Was tender, musical, and terse;   230
The inspiration, the delight,
The gleam, the glory, the swift flight,
Of thoughts so sudden, that they seem
The revelations of a dream,
All these were his; but with them came
No envy of another's fame;
He did not find his sleep less sweet
For music in some neighboring street,
Nor rustling hear in every breeze
The laurels of Miltiades. [12]   240
Honor and blessings on his head
While living, good report when dead,
Who, not too eager for renown,
Accepts, but does not clutch, the crown!

Last the Musician, as he stood
Illumined by that fire of wood;
Fair-haired, blue-eyed, his aspect blithe,
His figure tall and straight and lithe,
And every feature of his face
Revealing his Norwegian race;   250
A radiance, streaming from within,
Around his eyes and forehead beamed,
The Angel with the violin,
Painted by Raphael, [13] he seemed.
He lived in that ideal world
Whose language is not speech, but song;
Around him evermore the throng
Of elves and sprites their dances whirled;

---

[1] The Sicilian, Meli, 1740-1815, wrote poetry that was genuinely pastoral (bucolic) in its reflection of simple shepherd life.
[2] a pastoral poet of Sicily in the third century B.C.
[3] A Boston merchant, Israel Edrehi; Alicante is a province in Spain.
[4] islands of the Dutch East Indies
[5] a learned Spanish Jew of the 12th century
[6] Hebrew tales of the middle ages
[7] or more correctly *Kalilah and Dimnah*, a Sanskrit work of the 4th century B.C.
[8] The Talmud contains the Jewish traditional law; the Targum is the Chaldaic version of the Old Testament; the Kabbala, of the tenth century, is a mystic explanation of the Hebrew religion.

[9] a musical instrument
[10] Daniel Treadwell, a professor at Harvard
[11] Thomas William Parsons, 1819-1892, an American poet and translator of parts of Dante
[12] The Greek general Themistocles was jealous of Miltiades who won the battle of Marathon. Plutarch says "the trophies of Miltiades robbed Themistocles of sleep."
[13] the great Italian painter, 1483-1520

The Strömkarl [1] sang, the cataract hurled
Its headlong waters from the height;   260
And mingled in the wild delight
The scream of sea-birds in their flight,
The rumor of the forest trees,
The plunge of the implacable seas,
The tumult of the wind at night,
Voices of eld, like trumpets blowing,
Old ballads, and wild melodies
Through mist and darkness pouring forth,
Like Elivagar's [2] river flowing
Out of the glaciers of the North.   270

The instrument on which he played
Was in Cremona's [3] workshop's made,
By a great master of the past,
Ere yet was lost the art divine;
Fashioned of maple and of pine,
That in Tyrolian forests vast
Had rocked and wrestled with the blast:
Exquisite was it in design,
Perfect in each minutest part,
A marvel of the lutist's art;   280
And in its hollow chamber, thus,
The maker from whose hands it came
Had written his unrivaled name,—
"Antonius Stradivarius."

And when he played, the atmosphere
Was filled with magic, and the ear
Caught echoes of that Harp of Gold, [4]
Whose music had so weird a sound,
The hunted stag forgot to bound,
The leaping rivulet backward rolled,   290
The birds came down from bush and tree,
The dead came from beneath the sea,
The maiden to the harper's knee!

The music ceased; the applause was loud,
The pleased musician smiled and bowed;
The wood-fire clapped its hands of flame,
The shadows on the wainscot stirred,
And from the harpsichord there came
A ghostly murmur of acclaim,
A sound like that sent down at night   300
By birds of passage in their flight,
From the remotest distance heard.

Then silence followed; then began
A clamor for the Landlord's tale,—

The story promised them of old,
They said, but always left untold;
And he, although a bashful man,
And all his courage seemed to fail,
Finding excuse of no avail,   309
Yielded; and thus the story ran.
1862   1863

THE LANDLORD'S TALE

PAUL REVERE'S RIDE [5]

Listen, my children, and you shall hear
Of the midnight ride of Paul Revere,
On the eighteenth of April, in Seventy-five;
Hardly a man is now alive
Who remembers that famous day and year.

He said to his friend, "If the British march
By land or sea from the town tonight,
Hang a lantern aloft in the belfry arch
Of the North Church tower as a signal light,—
One, if by land, and two, if by sea;   10
And I on the opposite shore will be,
Ready to ride and spread the alarm
Through every Middlesex village and farm,
For the country folk to be up and to arm."

Then he said, "Good night!" and with muffled
    oar
Silently rowed to the Charlestown shore,
Just as the moon rose over the bay,
Where swinging wide at her moorings lay
The *Somerset*, British man-of-war;
A phantom ship, with each mast and spar   20
Across the moon like a prison bar,
And a huge black hulk that was magnified
By its own reflection in the tide.

Meanwhile, his friend, through alley and street,
Wanders and watches with eager ears,
Till in the silence around him he hears
The muster of men at the barrack door,
The sound of arms, and the tramp of feet,
And the measured tread of the grenadiers,
Marching down to their boats on the shore.

Then he climbed the tower of the Old North
    Church,   31
By the wooden stairs, with stealthy tread,

---

[1] In Norse mythology, the spirit of a river; he plays on a five-stringed viol and sometimes teaches his art to mortals.

[2] Ten rivers, the Elivagar, flowed from the spring Hvergelmir in the midst of Niflheim, the world of fog and cold in Norse mythology.

[3] a city of Lombardy, Italy, noted for its violin makers, among them Stradivarius, 1644?-1737

[4] Orpheus, the Greek, by the music of his golden lyre enticed even trees and stones to follow him.

[5] Paul Revere, 1735-1818, rode from Boston to Lexington, in Middlesex county, on the night of April 18, 1775, to summon the militia. Longfellow believed that the lanterns—signals indicating that the British had left Boston for Concord—were hung in Christ Church, popularly called North Church, which still stands. Possibly they were hung, rather, in the North Meeting House in North Square, destroyed in the siege of Boston, 1775-1776.

To the belfry chamber overhead,
And startled the pigeons from their perch
On the somber rafters, that round him made
Masses and moving shapes of shade,—
By the trembling ladder, steep and tall,
To the highest window in the wall,
Where he paused to listen and look down
A moment on the roofs of the town,   40
And the moonlight flowing over all.

Beneath, in the churchyard, lay the dead,
In their night-encampment on the hill,
Wrapped in silence so deep and still
That he could hear, like a sentinel's tread,
The watchful night-wind, as it went
Creeping along from tent to tent,
And seeming to whisper, "All is well!"
A moment only he feels the spell
Of the place and the hour, and the secret
        dread   50
Of the lonely belfry and the dead;
For suddenly all his thoughts are bent
On a shadowy something far away,
Where the river widens to meet the bay,—
A line of black that bends and floats
On the rising tide, like a bridge of boats.

Meanwhile, impatient to mount and ride,
Booted and spurred, with a heavy stride
On the opposite shore walked Paul Revere.
Now he patted his horse's side,   60
Now gazed at the landscape far and near,
Then, impetuous, stamped the earth,
And turned and tightened his saddle-girth;
But mostly he watched with eager search
The belfry-tower of the Old North Church,
As it rose above the graves on the hill,
Lonely and spectral and somber and still.
And lo! as he looks, on the belfry's height
A glimmer, and then a gleam of light!   69
He springs to the saddle, the bridle he turns,
But lingers and gazes, till full on his sight
A second lamp in the belfry burns!

A hurry of hoofs in a village street,
A shape in the moonlight, a bulk in the dark,
And beneath, from the pebbles, in passing, a
        spark
Struck out by a steed flying fearless and fleet:
That was all! And yet, through the gloom and
        the light,
The fate of a nation was riding that night;
And the spark struck out by that steed, in his
        flight,
Kindled the land into flame with its heat.   80

He has left the village and mounted the steep,
And beneath him, tranquil and broad and deep,

Is the Mystic,[1] meeting the ocean tides;
And under the alders, that skirt its edge,
Now soft on the sand, now loud on the ledge,
Is heard the tramp of his steed as he rides.

It was twelve by the village clock
When he crossed the bridge into Medford
        town.
He heard the crowing of the cock,
And the barking of the farmer's dog,   90
And felt the damp of the river fog,
That rises after the sun goes down.

It was one by the village clock
When he galloped into Lexington.
He saw the gilded weathercock
Swim in the moonlight as he passed,
And the meeting-house windows, blank and
        bare,
Gaze at him with a spectral glare,
As if they already stood aghast   99
At the bloody work they would look upon.

It was two by the village clock
When he came to the bridge in Concord town.
He heard the bleating of the flock,
And the twitter of birds among the trees,
And felt the breath of the morning breeze
Blowing over the meadows brown.
And one[2] was safe and asleep in his bed
Who at the bridge would be first to fall,
Who that day would be lying dead,
Pierced by a British musket-ball.   110

You know the rest. In the books you have
        read,
How the British Regulars fired and fled,—
How the farmers gave them ball for ball,
From behind each fence and farm-yard wall,
Chasing the red-coats down the lane,
Then crossing the fields to emerge again
Under the trees at the turn of the road,
And only pausing to fire and load.

So through the night rode Paul Revere;
And so through the night went his cry of
        alarm   120
To every Middlesex village and farm,—
A cry of defiance and not of fear,
A voice in the darkness, a knock at the door,
And a word that shall echo forevermore!
For, borne on the night-wind of the Past,
Through all our history, to the last,
In the hour of darkness and peril and need,

[1] The Mystic River separates Charlestown from Chelsea.
[2] Captain Isaac Davis of Acton, a town near Concord,
        was said to be the first killed in the Concord fight.

The people will waken and listen to hear
The hurrying hoof-beats of that steed, 129
And the midnight message of Paul Revere.
1860   1861

THE SICILIAN'S TALE

KING ROBERT OF SICILY [1]

Robert of Sicily, brother of Pope Urbane [2]
And Valmond, Emperor of Allemaine, [3]
Appareled in magnificent attire,
With retinue of many a knight and squire,
On St. John's eve, [4] at vespers, proudly sat
And heard the priests chant the Magnificat. [5]
And as he listened, o'er and o'er again
Repeated, like a burden or refrain,
He caught the words, "*Deposuit potentes
De sede, et exaltavit humiles;*" [5]   10
And slowly lifting up his kingly head
He to a learned clerk [6] beside him said,
"What mean these words?" The clerk made
    answer meet,
"He has put down the mighty from their seat,
And has exalted them of low degree."
Thereat King Robert muttered scornfully,
" 'Tis well that such seditious words are sung
Only by priests and in the Latin tongue;
For unto priests and people be it known,
There is no power can push me from my
    throne!"   20
And leaning back, he yawned and fell asleep,
Lulled by the chant monotonous and deep.

When he awoke, it was already night;
The church was empty, and there was no light,
Save where the lamps, that glimmered few and
    faint,
Lighted a little space before some saint.
He started from his seat and gazed around,
But saw no living thing and heard no sound.
He groped towards the door, but it was locked;
He cried aloud, and listened, and then knocked,
And uttered awful threatenings and complaints,
And imprecations upon men and saints.   32
The sounds reëchoed from the roof and walls
As if dead priests were laughing in their stalls!

[1] This old legend is said to date back as far as the time of Solomon, and is found in Hindu myths, in the *Gesta Romanorum*, a collection of medieval tales, and also in modern poetry. See Morris's *The Earthly Paradise* and Leigh Hunt's *A Jar of Honey from Mount Hybla*—the last probably being the source of Longfellow's poem.
[2] There were seven popes named Urban during the 11th-17th centuries, but no emperor Valmond.
[3] Germany   [4] the eve of June 23d
[5] "*Magnificat anima mea Dominum*" the Vulgate version of the song of the Virgin Mary (*Luke* i, 46-55). "My soul doth magnify the Lord. . . . He hath put down the mighty from their seats, and exalted them of low degree."
[6] scholar

At length the sexton, hearing from without
The tumult of the knocking and the shout,
And thinking thieves were in the house of
    prayer,
Came with his lantern, asking, "Who is there?"
Half choked with rage, King Robert fiercely
    said,   39
"Open: 'tis I, the King! Art thou afraid?"
The frightened sexton, muttering, with a curse,
"This is some drunken vagabond, or worse!"
Turned the great key and flung the portal wide;
A man rushed by him at a single stride,
Haggard, half naked, without hat or cloak,
Who neither turned, nor looked at him, nor
    spoke,
But leaped into the blackness of the night,
And vanished like a specter from his sight.

Robert of Sicily, brother of Pope Urbane
And Valmond, Emperor of Allemaine,   50
Despoiled of his magnificent attire,
Bareheaded, breathless, and besprent with mire,
With sense of wrong and outrage desperate,
Strode on and thundered at the palace gate;
Rushed through the courtyard, thrusting in his
    rage
To right and left each seneschal [7] and page,
And hurried up the broad and sounding stair,
His white face ghastly in the torches' glare,
From hall to hall he passed with breathless
    speed;   59
Voices and cries he heard, but did not heed,
Until at last he reached the banquet-room,
Blazing with light, and breathing with perfume.

There on the dais sat another king,
Wearing his robes, his crown, his signet-ring,
King Robert's self in features, form, and height,
But all transfigured with angelic light!
It was an Angel; and his presence there
With a divine effulgence filled the air,
An exaltation, piercing the disguise,
Though none the hidden Angel recognize.   70

A moment speechless, motionless, amazed,
The throneless monarch on the Angel gazed,
Who met his looks of anger and surprise
With the divine compassion of his eyes;
Then said, "Who art thou? and why com'st
    thou here?"
To which King Robert answered with a sneer,
"I am the King, and come to claim my own
From an impostor, who usurps my throne!"
And suddenly, at these audacious words,
Up sprang the angry guests, and drew their
    swords;   80

[7] high steward

The Angel answered, with unruffled brow,
"Nay, not the King, but the King's Jester, thou
Henceforth shalt wear the bells and scalloped cape,
And for thy counselor shalt lead an ape;
Thou shalt obey my servants when they call,
And wait upon my henchmen in the hall!"

Deaf to King Robert's threats and cries and prayers,
They thrust him from the hall and down the stairs;
A group of tittering pages ran before,   89
And as they opened wide the folding-door,
His heart failed, for he heard, with strange alarms,
The boisterous laughter of the men-at-arms,
And all the vaulted chamber roar and ring
With the mock plaudits of "Long live the King!"

Next morning, waking with the day's first beam,
He said within himself, "It was a dream!"
But the straw rustled as he turned his head,
There were the cap and bells beside his bed,
Around him rose the bare, discolored walls,
Close by, the steeds were champing in their stalls,   100
And in the corner, a revolting shape,
Shivering and chattering sat the wretched ape.
It was no dream; the world he loved so much
Had turned to dust and ashes at his touch!

Days came and went; and now returned again
To Sicily the old Saturnian[1] reign;
Under the Angel's governance benign
The happy island danced with corn and wine,
And deep within the mountain's burning breast
Enceladus,[2] the giant, was at rest.   110

Meanwhile King Robert yielded to his fate,
Sullen and silent and disconsolate.
Dressed in the motley garb that Jesters wear,
With look bewildered and a vacant stare,
Close shaven above the ears, as monks are shorn,
By courtiers mocked, by pages laughed to scorn,
His only friend the ape, his only food   117
What others left,—he still was unsubdued.
And when the Angel met him on his way,

[1] According to Roman mythology, Saturn was one of the most ancient of the gods; deposed by Jupiter, he went to Italy, where he reigned as king. His age was termed golden because as god of harvest he taught the people agriculture and raised them from barbarism to civilization. His wife was Ops, plenty.
[2] One of the hundred-armed giants who made war upon the gods; according to some he was buried by Zeus under Mt. Aetna, in Sicily. His movements caused earthquakes.

And half in earnest, half in jest, would say,
Sternly, though tenderly, that he might feel
The velvet scabbard held a sword of steel,
"Art thou the King?" the passion of his woe
Burst from him in resistless overflow,
And, lifting high his forehead, he would fling
The haughty answer back, "I am, I am the King!"

Almost three years were ended; when there came
Ambassadors of great repute and name
From Valmond, Emperor of Allemaine,   129
Unto King Robert, saying that Pope Urbane
By letter summoned them forthwith to come
On Holy Thursday to his city of Rome.
The Angel with great joy received his guests,
And gave them presents of embroidered vests,
And velvet mantles with rich ermine lined,
And rings and jewels of the rarest kind.
Then he departed with them o'er the sea
Into the lovely land of Italy,
Whose loveliness was more resplendent made
By the mere passing of that cavalcade,   140
With plumes, and cloaks, and housings, and the stir
Of jeweled bridle and of golden spur.
And lo! among the menials, in mock state,
Upon a piebald steed, with shambling gait,
His cloak of fox-tails flapping in the wind,
The solemn ape demurely perched behind,
King Robert rode, making huge merriment
In all the country towns through which they went.

The Pope received them with great pomp, and blare
Of bannered trumpets, on Saint Peter's square,
Giving his benediction and embrace   151
Fervent, and full of apostolic grace.
While with congratulations and with prayers
He entertained the Angel unawares,
Robert, the Jester, bursting through the crowd,
Into their presence rushed, and cried aloud,
"I am the King! Look, and behold in me
Robert, your brother, King of Sicily!
This man, who wears my semblance to your eyes,
Is an impostor in a King's disguise.   160
Do you not know me? does no voice within
Answer my cry, and say we are akin?"
The Pope in silence, but with troubled mien,
Gazed at the Angel's countenance serene;
The Emperor, laughing, said, "It is strange sport
To keep a madman for thy Fool at court!"
And the poor, baffled Jester in disgrace
Was hustled back among the populace.

In solemn state the Holy Week went by,   169
And Easter Sunday gleamed upon the sky;
The presence of the Angel, with its light,
Before the sun rose, made the city bright,
And with new fervor filled the hearts of men,
Who felt that Christ indeed had risen again.
Even the Jester, on his bed of straw,
With haggard eyes the unwonted splendor saw,
He felt within a power unfelt before,
And, kneeling humbly on his chamber floor,
He heard the rushing garments of the Lord
Sweep through the silent air, ascending heaven-
     ward.   180

And now the visit ending, and once more
Valmond returning to the Danube's shore,
Homeward the Angel journeyed, and again
The land was made resplendent with his train,
Flashing along the towns of Italy
Unto Salerno, and from there by sea.
And when once more within Palermo's wall,
And, seated on the throne in his great hall,
He heard the Angelus from convent towers,
As if the better world conversed with ours,   190
He beckoned to King Robert to draw nigher,
And with a gesture bade the rest retire;
And when they were alone, the Angel said,
"Art thou the King?" Then bowing down his
     head,
King Robert crossed both hands upon his
     breast,
And meekly answered him: "Thou knowest
     best!
My sins as scarlet are; let me go hence,
And in some cloister's school of penitence,
Across those stones, that pave the way to
     heaven,   199
Walk barefoot, till my guilty soul is shriven!"

The Angel smiled, and from his radiant face
A holy light illumined all the place,
And through the open window, loud and clear,
They heard the monks chant in the chapel near,
Above the stir and tumult of the street:
"He has put down the mighty from their seat,
And has exalted them of low degree!"
And through the chant a second melody
Rose like the throbbing of a single string:
"I am an Angel, and thou art the King!"   210

King Robert, who was standing near the throne,
Lifted his eyes, and lo! he was alone!
But all appareled as in days of old,
With ermined mantle and with cloth of gold;
And when his courtiers came, they found him
     there
Kneeling upon the floor, absorbed in silent
     prayer.
1862

HAWTHORNE

MAY 23, 1864 [1]

How beautiful it was, that one bright day
  In the long week of rain!
Though all its splendor could not chase away
  The omnipresent pain.

The lovely town was white with apple-blooms,
  And the great elms o'erhead
Dark shadows wove on their aërial looms,
  Shot through with golden thread.

Across the meadows, by the gray old manse,
  The historic river flowed: 10
I was as one who wanders in a trance,
  Unconscious of his road.

The faces of familiar friends seemed strange;
  Their voices I could hear,
And yet the words they uttered seemed to
     change
  Their meaning to my ear.

For the one face I looked for was not there,
  The one low voice was mute;
Only an unseen presence filled the air,
  And baffled my pursuit.   20

Now I look back, and meadow, manse, and
     stream
  Dimly my thought defines;
I only see—a dream within a dream—
  The hill-top hearsed with pines. [2]

I only hear above his place of rest
  Their tender undertone,
The infinite longings of a troubled breast,
  The voice so like his own.

There in seclusion and remote from men
  The wizard hand lies cold,   30
Which at its topmost speed let fall the pen,
  And left the tale half told.

Ah! who shall lift that wand of magic power,
  And the lost clew regain?
The unfinished window in Aladdin's [3] tower
  Unfinished must remain!

1864

[1] This was the date of the burial of Hawthorne.
[2] the Sleepy Hollow Cemetery in Concord, where Haw-
    thorne is buried
[3] Aladdin, by means of his magic lamp, had a palace
    built for his bride in one night, but one window
    was left unfinished. Hawthorne left two romances
    unfinished, *Septimius Felton* and *Dr. Grimshaw's
    Secret.*

FLOWER-DE-LUCE [1]

Beautiful lily, dwelling by still rivers,
 Or solitary mere,
Or where the sluggish meadow-brook delivers
 Its waters to the weir! [2]

Thou laughest at the mill, the whirr and worry
 Of spindle and of loom,
And the great wheel that toils amid the hurry
 And rushing of the flume.

Born in the purple, born to joy and pleasance,
 Thou dost not toil nor spin,   10
But makest glad and radiant with thy presence
 The meadow and the lin. [3]

The wind blows, and uplifts thy drooping
  banner,
 And round thee throng and run
The rushes, the green yeomen of thy manor,
 The outlaws of the sun.

The burnished dragon-fly is thine attendant,
 And tilts against the field,
And down the listed sunbeam rides resplendent
 With steel-blue mail and shield.   20

Thou art the Iris, fair among the fairest,
 Who, armed with golden rod
And winged with the celestial azure, bearest
 The message of some God.

Thou art the Muse, who far from crowded cities
 Hauntest the sylvan streams,
Playing on pipes of reed the artless ditties
 That come to us as dreams.

O flower-de-luce, bloom on, and let the river
 Linger to kiss thy feet!   30
O flower of song, bloom on, and make forever
 The world more fair and sweet.
1866   1867

KILLED AT THE FORD

He is dead, the beautiful youth,
The heart of honor, the tongue of truth,
He, the life and light of us all,
Whose voice was blithe as a bugle-call,
Whom all eyes followed with one consent,
The cheer of whose laugh, and whose pleasant
  word,
Hushed all murmurs of discontent.

[1] The fleur-de-lis or lily of France—the iris; this selection is the title poem of a small collection published in 1867.
[2] dam or other obstruction to check the flow of a stream
[3] waterfall, or the pool below it

Only last night, as we rode along
Down the dark of the mountain gap,
To visit the picket-guard at the ford, 10
Little dreaming of any mishap,
He was humming the words of some old song:
"Two red roses he had on his cap
And another he bore at the point of his sword."

Sudden and swift a whistling ball
Came out of a wood, and the voice was still;
Something I heard in the darkness fall,
And for a moment my blood grew chill;
I spake in a whisper, as one who speaks
In a room where some one is lying dead; 20
But he made no answer to what I said.

We lifted him up to his saddle again,
And through the mire and the mist and the rain
Carried him back to the silent camp,
And laid him as if asleep on his bed;
And I saw by the light of the surgeon's lamp
Two white roses upon his cheeks,
And one, just over his heart, blood-red!

And I saw in a vision how far and fleet
That fatal bullet went speeding forth, 30
Till it reached a town in the distant North,
Till it reached a house in a sunny street,
Till it reached a heart that ceased to beat
Without a murmur, without a cry;
And a bell was tolled, in that far-off town,
For one who had passed from cross to crown,
And the neighbors wondered that she should die.
1866   1867

GIOTTO'S TOWER [4]

How many lives, made beautiful and sweet
 By self-devotion and by self-restraint,
 Whose pleasure is to run without complaint
 On unknown errands of the Paraclete, [5]
Wanting the reverence of unshodden feet,
 Fail of the nimbus which the artists paint
 Around the shining forehead of the saint,
 And are in their completeness incomplete!
In the old Tuscan town stands Giotto's tower,
 The lily of Florence blossoming in stone,—
 A vision, a delight, and a desire,— 11
The builder's perfect and centennial flower,
 That in the night of ages bloomed alone, [6]
 But wanting still the glory of the spire.
1866   1866

[4] Giotto, 1276-1337, the painter, architect, and sculptor,
  who designed and began the campanile or bell-
  tower at Florence, intended that it should have
  a spire one hundred feet high, but Gaddi who
  completed the structure after Giotto's death, gave
  up that plan.
[5] intercessor—used especially of the Holy Spirit
[6] in allusion to the flowering after a supposed hundred
  years' growth, of the century plant

DANTE [1]

Tuscan, that wanderest through the realms of
 gloom,
  With thoughtful pace, and sad, majestic eyes,
  Stern thoughts and awful from thy soul arise,
  Like Farinata from his fiery tomb.
Thy sacred song is like the trump of doom;
  Yet in thy heart what human sympathies,
  What soft compassion glows; as in the skies
  The tender stars their clouded lamps relume!
Methinks I see thee stand with pallid cheeks
  By Fra Hilario in his diocese,   10
  As up the convent-walls, in golden streaks,
The ascending sunbeams mark the day's de-
 crease;
  And, as he asks what there the stranger seeks,
  Thy voice along the cloister whispers,
   "Peace!"

1843   *1845*

DIVINA COMMEDIA [2]

I

Oft have I seen at some cathedral door
  A laborer, pausing in the dust and heat,
  Lay down his burden, and with reverent feet
  Enter, and cross himself, and on the floor
Kneel to repeat his paternoster [3] o'er;
  Far off the noises of the world retreat;
  The loud vociferations of the street
  Become an undistinguishable roar.
So, as I enter here from day to day,   9
  And leave my burden at this minster gate,
  Kneeling in prayer, and not ashamed to pray,

[1] From 1842, the year in which, according to one biographer, "he had been steeping his soul in Dante"
to the close of his life, Longfellow was a student
of the Italian poet. He translated the *Divina
Commedia*, 1867-1870. In this sonnet he sees
Dante in two aspects, first as the passionate
exile resentful of his political wrongs even in the
realms of the lost where he meets Farinata, leader
of his ancestral enemies, enduring fiery punishment, and returns to him scorn for scorn (*Inferno*, x); secondly, as the world-worn pilgrim
seeking peace. A letter whose authenticity has
been questioned, written by "Frate Ilario, a
humble monk of Corvo," relates that when Dante,
unknown, visited the monastery, "I questioned
him of what he wanted . . . thereat he looked
round at me and the brethren who were with me
and answered, 'Peace.'" Longfellow's six sonnets relating to Dante have been placed together
here without regard to chronology.
[2] Longfellow wrote these sonnets while translating the
Divina Commedia into English verse, and prefixed them to different divisions of the translation.
The student will note the extended figure beginning in the first sonnet and running through the
whole sequence: Dante's work, in spirit and in
intellect, is a reflection, like the cathedral, of the
intense religious life of the Middle Ages. It is
significant that Longfellow, whose creed was fundamentally so different from Dante's, should have
been influenced, like all deep students of the great
Tuscan, to a feeling of profound veneration for
Dante's beliefs.
[3] The Lord's Prayer—"Our Father"

The tumult of the time disconsolate
  To inarticulate murmurs dies away,
  While the eternal ages watch and wait.

1864   1864

II

How strange the sculptures that adorn these
 towers!
  This crowd of statues, in whose folded sleeves
  Birds build their nests; while canopied with
   leaves
  Parvis [4] and portal bloom like trellised
   bowers,
And the vast minster seems a cross of flowers!
  But fiends and dragons on the gargoyled [5]
   eaves
  Watch the dead Christ between the living
   thieves,
  And, underneath, the traitor Judas lowers!
Ah! from what agonies of heart and brain,
  What exultations trampling on despair,   10
  What tenderness, what tears, what hate of
   wrong,
What passionate outcry of a soul in pain,
  Uprose this poem of the earth and air,
  This medieval miracle of song!

1864

III

I enter, and I see thee in the gloom
  Of the long aisles, O poet saturnine!
  And strive to make my steps keep pace with
   thine. [6]
  The air is filled with some unknown perfume;
The congregation of the dead make room
  For thee to pass; the votive tapers shine;
  Like rooks that haunt Ravenna's groves of
   pine
  The hovering echoes fly from tomb to tomb.
From the confessionals I hear arise
  Rehearsals of forgotten tragedies,   10
  And lamentations from the crypts below;
And then a voice celestial that begins
  With the pathetic words, "Although your sins
  As scarlet be," and ends with "as the snow."

1865

V

I lift mine eyes, and all the windows blaze
  With forms of Saints and holy men who died,

[4] church-porch
[5] Furnished with gargoyles, that is, water-spouts gro-
tesquely carved; see Ruskin, *Stones of Venice*
(Vol. II, Chap. iv, St. Mark's) on the imagery
and symbolism of Gothic art.
[6] As Vergil conducted Dante through Hell and part of
Purgatory, so Dante seems to be conducting Longfellow. The sonnet is full of echoes from Dante.

Here martyred and hereafter glorified;
And the great Rose [1] upon its leaves displays
Christ's triumph, and the angelic roundelays,
  With splendor upon splendor multiplied;
  And Beatrice again at Dante's side
  No more rebukes, but smiles her words of
    praise.
And then the organ sounds, and unseen choirs
  Sing the old Latin hymns of peace and love,
  And benedictions of the Holy Ghost;   11
And the melodious bells among the spires
  O'er all the house-tops and through heaven
    above
  Proclaim the elevation of the Host! [2]

1866

VI

O star of morning and of liberty! [3]
  O bringer of the light, whose splendor shines
  Above the darkness of the Apennines,
  Forerunner of the day that is to be!
The voices of the city and the sea,
  The voices of the mountains and the pines,
  Repeat thy song, till the familiar lines
  Are footpaths for the thought of Italy!
Thy fame is blown abroad from all the heights,
  Through all the nations, and a sound is heard,
  As of a mighty wind, and men devout,   11
Strangers of Rome, and the new proselytes,
  In their own language hear thy wondrous
    word,
  And many are amazed, and many doubt.

1866

OLIVER WENDELL HOLMES
1809-1894

In Holmes we have a Boston New Englander conscious of a distinguished American ancestry, loyal to his city, to Harvard, to his profession, and to the literary and social circle of which he was one of the most brilliant members. He was born at Cambridge, Massachusetts, son of a clergyman, a descendant of Anne Bradstreet and of several persons prominent in colonial and Revolutionary New England. He was educated at

[1] A circular window of tracery and stained glass in conventionalized rose design generally placed in the western gable of a Gothic church; see also the Heavenly Rose, as described by Dante, *Paradiso,* xxx, xxxi.

[2] At the elevation, or lifting from the altar by the priest, of the host, or elements of the Lord's Supper, bells are rung and the worshipers adore the elements as the body and blood of Christ.

[3] Although Dante was a strict adherent of the medieval Church, he so constantly inveighed against its abuses and proclaimed the cause of liberty, that his name has been a rallying cry through the centuries in the struggle for the unification of Italy. This union was taking place when Longfellow wrote.

Phillips Academy, Andover, and at Harvard, graduating in 1829. He studied medicine in Boston and Paris, was made professor of anatomy and physiology at Dartmouth in 1839, and at Harvard in 1847, retaining his connection with Harvard until 1882. His poems, written at various dates from 1836, are included in the volumes *Songs in Many Keys,* 1861, *Humorous Poems,* 1865, *Songs of Many Seasons,* 1874, and *Before the Curfew,* 1888. His chief prose works were: *The Autocrat of the Breakfast Table,* 1858; *The Professor at the Breakfast Table,* 1860; *Elsie Venner* (novel), 1861; *The Guardian Angel* (novel), 1867. To these should be added notable reviews, memorials, essays, and important scientific publications.

Holmes had the most facile brain of any major American writer of his day. This is seen in his essays and in his humorous and satirical poems. The discursive essay form seems especially made for the type of mind like his, a mind that expresses itself most congenially in conversation in which it has liberty to handle ideas as it will, lightly or gravely, with what brilliancy or spontaneity is native to it. The salient feature of Holmes's essays is their vivacity; they show a mind intensely interested in whatever occupies it, especially its own workings, a mind not so profound as scintillating, one that can touch the varied scenes of life with a flash of wit that places the picture forever in memory. His poetry, by reason of its incisiveness, is unique in American literature. No other American has equaled him in the perfection of his *vers de société.*

Biography and criticism: J. T. Morse, *Life and Letters of O. W. Holmes,* 2 vols. 1896; L. Stephen, "Life and Literary Work of Holmes," *Studies of a Biographer,* 2:149-82; Burton; Macy; Chubb; S. M. Crothers, "The Autocrat and his Fellow Boarders," *Atlan.* 104:237-44; "Oliver Wendell Holmes," *Liv. Age* 263:99-103; W. G. Ballantine, "Oliver Wendell Holmes as a Poet and as a Man," *No. Am.* 190:178-93.

OLD IRONSIDES [4]

Ay, tear her tattered ensign down!
  Long has it waved on high,
And many an eye has danced to see
  That banner in the sky;
Beneath it rung the battle shout,
  And burst the cannon's roar;—
The meteor of the ocean air
  Shall sweep the clouds no more.

[4] In this poem, written September 15, 1830, and printed next day in the *Boston Daily Advertiser,* Holmes voiced the indignation of the American people over the proposal made by the secretary of the navy and printed in the *Advertiser* on September 14, 1830, that the naval ship *Constitution,* familiarly known as *Old Ironsides,* which had survived several thrilling engagements in the War of 1812, be dismantled and sold. As a result of the popular feeling aroused, the old frigate was used instead as a school-ship, and later as a receiving ship.

Her deck, once red with heroes' blood,
  Where knelt the vanquished foe,   10
When winds were hurrying o'er the flood,
  And waves were white below,
No more shall feel the victor's tread,
  Or know the conquered knee;—
The harpies of the shore shall pluck
  The eagle of the sea!

Oh, better that her shattered hulk
  Should sink beneath the wave;
Her thunders shook the mighty deep,
  And there should be her grave;   20
Nail to the mast her holy flag,
  Set every threadbare sail,
And give her to the god of storms,
  The lightning and the gale!
1830   1830

TO AN INSECT

I love to hear thine earnest voice,
  Wherever thou art hid,
Thou testy little dogmatist,
  Thou pretty Katydid! [1]
Thou mindest me of gentlefolks,—
  Old gentlefolks are they,—
Thou say'st an undisputed thing
  In such a solemn way.

Thou art a female, Katydid!
  I know it by the trill   10
That quivers through thy piercing notes,
  So petulant and shrill;
I think there is a knot of you
  Beneath the hollow tree,—
A knot of spinster Katydids,—
  Do Katydids drink tea?

Oh, tell me where did Katy live,
  And what did Katy do?
And was she very fair and young,
  And yet so wicked, too?   20
Did Katy love a naughty man,
  Or kiss more cheeks than one?
I warrant Katy did no more
  Than many a Kate has done.

Dear me! I'll tell you all about
  My fuss with little Jane,
And Ann, with whom I used to walk
  So often down the lane,
And all that tore their locks of black,
  Or wet their eyes of blue,—   30
Pray tell me, sweetest Katydid,
  What did poor Katy do?

[1] Cf. Freneau's poem, p. 169.

Ah, no! the living oak shall crash,
  That stood for ages still,
The rock shall rend its mossy base
  And thunder down the hill,
Before the little Katydid
  Shall add one word, to tell
The mystic story of the maid
  Whose name she knows so well.   40

Peace to the ever-murmuring race!
  And when the latest one
Shall fold in death her feeble wings
  Beneath the autumn sun,
Then shall she raise her fainting voice
  And lift her drooping lid,
And then the child of future years
  Shall hear what Katy did.
1831   1831

MY AUNT

My aunt! my dear unmarried **aunt**!
  Long years have o'er her flown;
Yet still she strains the aching clasp
  That binds her virgin zone;
I know it hurts her,—though she looks
  As cheerful as she can;
Her waist is ampler than her life,
  For life is but a span.

My aunt! my poor deluded aunt!
  Her hair is almost gray;   10
Why will she train that winter curl
  In such a spring-like way?
How can she lay her glasses down,
  And say she reads as well,
When, through a double convex **lens**,
  She just makes out to spell?

Her father—grandpapa! forgive
  This erring lip its smiles—
Vowed she should make the finest **girl**
  Within a hundred miles;   20
He sent her to a stylish school;
  'Twas in her thirteenth June;
And with her, as the rules required,
  "Two towels and a spoon."

They braced my aunt against a board,
  To make her straight and tall;
They laced her up, they starved her down,
  To make her light and small;
They pinched her feet, they singed her hair,
  They screwed it up with pins;—   30
Oh, never mortal suffered more
  In penance for her sins.

So, when my precious aunt was done,
  My grandsire brought her back;
(By daylight, lest some rabid youth
  Might follow on the track;)
"Ah!" said my grandsire, as he shook
  Some powder in his pan, [1]
"What could this lovely creature do
  Against a desperate man!"   40

Alas! nor chariot, nor barouche,
  Nor bandit cavalcade,
Tore from the trembling father's arms
  His all-accomplished maid.
For her how happy had it been!
  And heaven had spared to me
To see one sad, ungathered rose
  On my ancestral tree.

1831   1831

THE LAST LEAF [2]

I saw him once before,
As he passed by the door,
    And again
The pavement stones resound
As he totters o'er the ground
    With his cane.

They say that in his prime,
Ere the pruning-knife of Time
    Cut him down,
Not a better man was found   10
By the Crier on his round
    Through the town.

But now he walks the streets,
And he looks at all he meets
    Sad and wan,
And he shakes his feeble head,
That it seems as if he said,
    "They are gone."

[1] Just before shooting the old flint-lock fire-arms, the
pan, a small spoon-shaped receptacle outside the
lock, had to be replenished with fresh powder,
which, when ignited by flint and steel, would fire
the charge inside.

[2] Major Thomas Melville, an ancestor of Herman
Melville, and "the last of the cocked hats,"
was a familiar sight in Boston in 1831-32. "His
aspect among the crowds of a later generation
reminded me of a withered leaf which has held
to its stem through the storms of autumn and
winter, and finds itself still clinging to its bough
while the new growths of spring are bursting their
buds and spreading their foliage all around it. I
make this explanation for the benefit of those who
have been puzzled by the lines,
    "The last leaf upon the tree
        In the spring."
[Holmes's note in the *Cambridge Edition* of his
poems, published by The Houghton Mifflin Company.]

The mossy marbles rest
On the lips that he has prest   20
    In their bloom,
And the names he loved to hear
Have been carved for many a year
    On the tomb.

My grandmamma has said—
Poor old lady, she is dead
    Long ago—
That he had a Roman nose,
And his cheek was like a rose
    In the snow.   30

But now his nose is thin,
And it rests upon his chin
    Like a staff,
And a crook is in his back,
And a melancholy crack
    In his laugh.

I know it is a sin
For me to sit and grin
    At him here;
But the old three-cornered hat,   40
And the breeches, and all that,
    Are so queer!

And if I should live to be
The last leaf upon the tree
    In the spring,
Let them smile, as I do now,
At the old forsaken bough
    Where I cling.

1831   1831

A SONG

FOR THE CENTENNIAL CELEBRATION OF HARVARD
COLLEGE, 1836

When the Puritans came over
  Our hills and swamps to clear,
The woods were full of catamounts,
  And Indians red as deer,
With tomahawks and scalping-knives,
  That make folks' heads look queer;
Oh the ship from England used to bring
  A hundred wigs a year!

The crows came cawing through the air
  To pluck the Pilgrims' corn,   10
The bears came snuffing round the door
  Whene'er a babe was born,
The rattlesnakes were bigger round
  Than the butt of the old ram's horn
The deacon blew at meeting time
  On every "Sabbath" morn.

But soon they knocked the wigwams down,
  And pine-tree trunk and limb
Began to sprout among the leaves
  In shape of steeples slim;   20
And out the little wharves were stretched
  Along the ocean's rim,
And up the little school-house shot
  To keep the boys in trim.

And when at length the College rose,
  The sachem cocked his eye
At every tutor's meager ribs
  Whose coat-tails whistled by:
But when the Greek and Hebrew words
  Came tumbling from their jaws,   30
The copper-colored children all
  Ran screaming to the squaws.

And who was on the Catalogue
  When college was begun?
Two nephews of the President,
  And *the* Professor's son;
(They turned a little Indian boy,
  As brown as any bun;)
Lord! how the seniors knocked about
  The freshman class of one!   40

They had not then the dainty things
  That commons now afford,
But *succotash* and *hominy*
  Were smoking on the board;
They did not rattle round in gigs,
  Or dash in long-tail blues,
But always on Commencement days
  The tutors blacked their shoes.

God bless the ancient Puritans!
  Their lot was hard enough;   50
But honest hearts make iron arms,
  And tender maids are tough;
So love and faith have formed and fed
  Our true-born Yankee stuff,
And keep the kernel in the shell
  The British found so rough!

1836   1849

ON LENDING A PUNCH-BOWL

This ancient silver bowl of mine, it tells of
    good old times,
Of joyous days, and jolly nights, and merry
    Christmas chimes;
They were a free and jovial race, but honest,
    brave, and true,
That dipped their ladle in the punch when this
    old bowl was new.

A Spanish galleon brought the bar;[1] so runs the
    ancient tale;
'T was hammered by an Antwerp smith, whose
    arm was like a flail;
And now and then beneath the strokes, for fear
    his strength should fail,
He wiped his brow, and quaffed a cup of good
    old Flemish ale.

'T was purchased by an English squire to please
    his loving dame,
Who saw the cherubs, and conceived a longing
    for the same;   10
And oft as on the ancient stock another twig
    was found,
'T was filled with caudle[2] spiced and hot, and
    handed smoking round.

But, changing hands, it reached at length a
    Puritan divine,
Who used to follow Timothy, and take a little
    wine,[3]
But hated punch and prelacy; and so it was,
    perhaps,
He went to Leyden,[4] where he found conventi-
    cles[5] and schnapps.[6]

And then, of course, you know what's next,—it
    left the Dutchman's shore
With those that in the *Mayflower* came,—a
    hundred souls and more,—
Along with all the furniture, to fill their new
    abodes,—
To judge by what is still on hand, at least a
    hundred loads.   20

'T was on a dreary winter's eve, the night was
    closing dim,
When brave Miles Standish took the bowl, and
    filled it to the brim;
The little Captain stood and stirred the posset
    with his sword,
And all his sturdy men-at-arms were ranged
    about the board.

He poured the fiery Hollands in,—the man that
    never feared,—
He took a long and solemn draught, and wiped
    his yellow beard;
And one by one the musketeers—the men that
    fought and prayed—
All drank as 't were their mother's milk, and
    not a man afraid.

[1] bar silver   [3] *1 Timothy* v, 23
[2] a hot drink made of wines, eggs, etc.
[4] The Pilgrims went to Leyden, Holland, from England
    before coming to America.
[5] Dissenters' religious meetings   [6] Holland gin

That night, affrighted from his nest, the scream-
    ing eagle flew,
He heard the Pequot's ringing whoop, the sol-
    dier's wild halloo;   30
And there the sachem [1] learned the rule he
    taught to kith and kin,
"Run from the white man when you find he
    smells of Hollands gin!"

A hundred years, and fifty more, had spread
    their leaves and snows,
A thousand rubs had flattened down each little
    cherub's nose;
When once again the bowl was filled, but not
    in mirth or joy,
'T was mingled by a mother's hand to cheer her
    parting boy.

"Drink, John," she said, " 't will do you good,
    —poor child, you'll never bear
This working in the dismal trench, out in the
    midnight air;
And if—God bless me!—you were hurt, 't would
    keep away the chill";
So John *did* drink,—and well he wrought that
    night at Bunker's Hill!   40

I tell you, there was generous warmth in good
    old English cheer;
I tell you, 't was a pleasant thought to bring
    its symbol here.
'T is but the fool that loves excess; hast thou
    a drunken soul?
Thy bane is in thy shallow skull, not in my
    silver bowl!

I love the memory of the past,—its pressed yet
    fragrant flowers,—
The moss that clothes its broken walls,—the
    ivy on its towers;—
Nay, this poor bauble it bequeathed,—my eyes
    grow moist and dim,
To think of all the vanished joys that danced
    around its brim.

Then fill a fair and honest cup, and bear it
    straight to me;
The goblet hallows all it holds, whate'er the
    liquid be;   50
And may the cherubs on its face protect me
    from the sin,
That dooms one to those dreadful words,—
"My dear, where *have* you been?"

                              1849

[1] tribal chief

NON-RESISTANCE [2]

Perhaps too far in these considerate days
Has patience carried her submissive ways;
Wisdom has taught us to be calm and meek,
To take one blow, and turn the other cheek;
It is not written what a man shall do
If the rude caitiff smite the other too!

Land of our fathers, in thine hour of need
God help thee, guarded by the passive creed!
As the lone pilgrim trusts to beads and cowl,
When through the forest ring's the gray wolf's
    howl;   10
As the deep galleon trusts her gilded prow
When the black corsair slants athwart her bow;
As the poor pheasant, with his peaceful mien,
Trusts to his feathers, shining golden-green,
When the dark plumage with the crimson beak
Has rustled shadowy from its splintered peak,—
So trust thy friends, whose babbling tongues
    would charm
The lifted saber from thy foeman's arm,
Thy torches ready for the answering peal   19
From bellowing fort and thunder-freighted
    keel!
1850   1862

THE OLD MAN DREAMS

Oh for one hour of youthful joy! [3]
    Give back my twentieth spring!
I'd rather laugh a bright-haired boy
    Than reign a gray-beard king!

Off with the spoils of wrinkled age!
    Away with Learning's crown!
Tear out life's Wisdom-written page,
    And dash its trophies down!

One moment let my life-blood stream
    From boyhood's fount of flame!   10
Give me one giddy, reeling dream
    Of life all love and fame!

        ———

My listening angel heard the prayer,
    And calmly smiling, said,
"If I but touch thy silvered hair,
    Thy hasty wish hath sped.

[2] This poem may have been called forth by some lines
of Whittier's revealing Quaker sentiment at the
beginning of the agitation that led to the Civil
War.
[3] Cf. Byron, "Oh, talk not to me of a name great in
story," etc., in "Stanzas Written on the Road
between Florence and Pisa."

"But is there nothing in thy track
  To bid thee fondly stay,
While the swift seasons hurry back
  To find the wished-for day?"   20

"Ah, truest soul of womankind!
  Without thee, what were life?
One bliss I cannot leave behind:
  I'll take—my—precious—wife!"

The angel took a sapphire pen
  And wrote in rainbow dew,
The man would be a boy again,
  And be a husband too!

"And is there nothing yet unsaid
  Before the change appears?   30
Remember, all their gifts have fled
  With those dissolving years!"

"Why, yes"; for memory would recall
  My fond paternal joys;
"I could not bear to leave them all—
  I'll take—my—girl—and—boys."

The smiling angel dropped his pen,—
  "Why, this will never do;
The man would be a boy again,
  And be a father, too!"   40

And so I laughed,—my laughter woke
  The household with its noise,—
And wrote my dream, when morning broke,
  To please the gray-haired boys.
1854   1858

THE TWO ARMIES

As Life's unending column pours,
  Two marshaled hosts are seen,—
Two armies on the trampled shores
  That Death flows black between.

One marches to the drum-beat's roll,
  The wide-mouthed clarion's bray,
And bears upon a crimson scroll,
  "Our glory is to slay."

One moves in silence by the stream,
  With sad, yet watchful eyes,   10
Calm as the patient planet's gleam
  That walks the clouded skies.

Along its front no sabers shine,
  No blood-red pennons wave;

Its banner bears the single line,
  "Our duty is to save."

For those no death-bed's lingering shade;
  At Honor's trumpet-call,
With knitted brow and lifted blade
  In Glory's arms they fall.   20

For these no clashing falchions bright,
  No stirring battle-cry;
The bloodless stabber calls by night,—
  Each answers, "Here am I!"

For those the sculptor's laureled bust,
  The builder's marble piles,
The anthems pealing o'er their dust
  Through long cathedral aisles.

For these the blossom-sprinkled turf
  That floods the lonely graves   30
When Spring rolls in her sea-green surf
  In flowery-foaming waves.

Two paths lead upward from below,
  And angels wait above,
Who count each burning life-drop's flow,
  Each falling tear of Love.

Though from the Hero's bleeding breast
  Her pulses Freedom drew,
Though the white lilies in her crest
  Sprang from that scarlet dew,—   40

While Valor's haughty champions wait
  Till all their scars are shown,
Love walks unchallenged through the gate,
  To sit beside the Throne!
1858   1858

THE DEACON'S MASTERPIECE;[1]

OR, THE WONDERFUL "ONE-HOSS-SHAY."
A LOGICAL STORY

Have you heard of the wonderful one-hoss-shay,
That was built in such a logical way
It ran a hundred years to a day,
And then, of a sudden, it—ah, but stay,
I'll tell you what happened without delay,
Scaring the parson into fits,
Frightening people out of their wits,—
Have you ever heard of that, I say?

Seventeen hundred and fifty-five.
Georgius Secundus was then alive,—   10

----

[1] Professor Barrett Wendell sees in this poem a satire
  in which the "shay" is the extreme Puritan doctrine of the eighteenth century.

Snuffy old drone from the German hive! [1]
That was the year when Lisbon-town
Saw the earth open and gulp her down,
And Braddock's army was done so brown,
Left without a scalp to its crown.
It was on the terrible Earthquake-day
That the Deacon finished the one-hoss-shay.

Now in building of chaises, I tell you what,
There is always *somewhere* a weakest spot,—
In hub, tire, felloe, in spring or thill,   20
In panel, or crossbar, or floor, or sill,
In screw, bolt, thoroughbrace,—lurking still,
Find it somewhere you must and will,—
Above or below, or within or without,—
And that's the reason, beyond a doubt,
That a chaise *breaks down*, but doesn't *wear
    out.*

But the Deacon swore (as Deacons do,
With an "I dew vum," or an "I tell *yeou*,")
He would build one shay to beat the taown
'N' the keounty 'n' all the kentry raoun';   30
It should be so built that it *couldn'* break
    daown:
—"Fur," said the Deacon, " 't's mighty plain
Thut the weakes' place mus' stan' the strain;
'N' the way t' fix it, uz I maintain,
    Is only jest
T' make that place uz strong uz the rest."

So the Deacon inquired of the village folk
Where he could find the strongest oak,
That couldn't be split nor bent nor broke,—
That was for spokes and floor and sills;   40
He sent for lancewood to make the thills;
The crossbars were ash, from the straightest
    trees;
The panels of white-wood, that cuts like cheese,
But lasts like iron for things like these;
The hubs of logs from the "Settler's ellum,"—
Last of its timber,—they couldn't sell 'em,
Never an axe had seen their chips,
And the wedges flew from between their lips,
Their blunt ends frizzled like celery-tips;
Step and prop-iron, bolt and screw,   50
Spring, tire, axle, and linchpin too,
Steel of the finest, bright and blue;
Thoroughbrace bison-skin, thick and wide;
Boot, top, dasher, from tough old hide
Found in the pit when the tanner died.
That was the way he "put her through."—
"There!" said the Deacon, "naow she'll dew !"

Do ! I tell you, I rather guess
She was a wonder, and nothing less !
Colts grew horses, beards turned gray,   60

[1] The Hanoverian kings of England—the four Georges
    —were of German descent.

Deacon and deaconess dropped away,
Children and grandchildren—where were they?
But there stood the stout old one-hoss-shay
As fresh as on Lisbon-earthquake-day !

EIGHTEEN HUNDRED;—it came and found
The Deacon's masterpiece strong and sound.
Eighteen hundred increased by ten;—
"Hahnsum kerridge" they called it then.
Eighteen hundred and twenty came;—
Running as usual; much the same.   70
Thirty and forty at last arrive,
And then come fifty, and FIFTY-FIVE.

Little of all we value here
Wakes on the morn of its hundredth year
Without both feeling and looking queer.
In fact, there's nothing that keeps its youth,
So far as I know, but a tree and truth.
(This is a moral that runs at large;
Take it.—You're welcome.—No extra charge.)

FIRST OF NOVEMBER,—the Earthquake-day.—
There are traces of age in the one-hoss-shay,
A general flavor of mild decay,   82
But nothing local, as one may say.
There couldn't be,—for the Deacon's art
Had made it so like in every part
That there wasn't a chance for one to start.
For the wheels were just as strong as the thills,
And the floor was just as strong as the sills,
And the panels just as strong as the floor,
And the whippletree neither less nor more,   90
And the back crossbar as strong as the fore,
And spring and axle and hub *encore*.
And yet, *as a whole*, it is past a doubt
In another hour it will be *worn out !*

First of November, 'Fifty-five !
This morning the parson takes a drive.
Now, small boys, get out of the way!
Here comes the wonderful one-horse-shay,
Drawn by a rat-tailed, ewe-necked bay.   99
"Huddup !" said the parson.—Off went they.

The parson was working his Sunday's text,—
Had got to *fifthly*, and stopped perplexed
At what the—Moses—was coming next.
All at once the horse stood still,
Close by the meet'n'-house on the hill.
—First a shiver, and then a thrill,
Then something decidedly like a spill,—
And the parson was sitting upon a rock,
At half-past nine by the meet'n'-house clock,—
Just the hour of the Earthquake shock !   110
—What do you think the parson found,
When he got up and stared around?

The poor old chaise in a heap or mound,
As if it had been to the mill and ground!
You see, of course, if you're not a dunce,
How it went to pieces all at once,—
All at once and nothing first,—
Just as bubbles do when they burst. 118

End of the wonderful one-hoss-shay.
Logic is logic. That's all I say.
1858 1858

THE VOICELESS

We count the broken lyres that rest
　Where the sweet wailing singers slumber,
But o'er their silent sister's breast
　The wild flowers who will stoop to number?
A few can touch the magic string,
　And noisy Fame is proud to win them:—
Alas for those that never sing,
　But die with all their music in them!

Nay, grieve not for the dead alone
　Whose song has told their hearts' sad story,—
Weep for the voiceless, who have known 11
　The cross without the crown of glory!
Not where Leucadian [1] breezes sweep
　O'er Sappho's memory-haunted billow,
But where the glistening night-dews weep
　On nameless sorrow's churchyard pillow.

O hearts that break and give no sign
　Save whitening lip and fading tresses,
Till Death pours out his longed-for wine
　Slow-dropped from Misery's crushing
　　presses,— 20
If singing breath or echoing chord
　To every hidden pang were given,
What endless melodies were poured,
　As sad as earth, as sweet as heaven!
1858 1858

BOSTON COMMON.—THREE PICTURES

FOR THE FAIR IN AID OF THE FUND TO PROCURE
BALL'S STATUE OF WASHINGTON [2]

1630

All overgrown with bush and fern,
　And straggling clumps of tangled trees,
With trunks that lean and boughs that turn,
　Bent eastward by the mastering breeze,—

With spongy bogs that drip and fill
　A yellow pond with muddy rain,
Beneath the shaggy southern hill
　Lies wet and low the Shawmut plain.
And hark! the trodden branches crack;
　A crow flaps off with startled scream; 10
A straying woodchuck canters back;
　A bittern rises from the stream;
Leaps from his lair a frightened deer;
　An otter plunges in the pool;—
Here comes old Shawmut's pioneer, [3]
　The parson on his brindled bull!

1774

The streets are thronged with trampling feet,
　The northern hill is ridged with graves,
But night and morn the drum is beat
　To frighten down the "rebel knaves." 20
The stones of King Street [4] still are red,
　And yet the bloody red-coats come:
I hear their pacing sentry's tread,
　The click of steel, the tap of drum,
And over all the open green,
　Where grazed of late the harmless kine,
The cannon's deepening ruts are seen,
　The war-horse stamps, the bayonets shine.
The clouds are dark with crimson rain
　Above the murderous hirelings' den, 30
And soon their whistling showers shall stain
　The pipe-clayed [5] belts of Gage's men.

186–

Around the green, in morning light,
　The spired and palaced summits blaze,
And, sunlike, from her Beacon-height [6]
　The dome-crowned city spreads her rays;
They span the waves, they belt the plains,
　They skirt the roads with bands of white,
Till with a flash of gilded panes
　Yon farthest hillside bounds the sight. 40
Peace, Freedom, Wealth! no fairer view,
　Though with the wild-bird's restless wings
We sailed beneath the noontide's blue
　Or chased the moonlight's endless rings!
Here, fitly raised by grateful hands
　His holiest memory to recall,
The Hero's, Patriot's image stands;
　He led our sires who won them all!
1859 1859

[1] Leucadia is one of the Ionian islands. Sappho
(c. 600 B.C.), the Greek poet, is said, but without
confirmation, to have thrown herself into the sea
from one of its southwestern cliffs.

[2] Thomas Ball, 1819-1911, was an American sculptor.
His equestrian statue of Washington is in the
Boston Public Gardens.

[3] The Reverend William Blackstone (or Blaxton) was
the first settler, in 1623, of Shawmut (Boston).
Later he sold his land for cattle and became the
first white settler of Rhode Island. In his old
age, being too poor to own a horse, he frequently
rode a bull to town.

[4] The scene of the "Boston Massacre," 1770, which led
to the withdrawing from Boston of General Gates's
two regiments; see Fiske, *American Revolution*,
i, 66.

[5] whitened with pipe-clay　　　[6] Beacon Hill

THE BOYS [1]

Has there any old fellow got mixed with the boys?
If there has, take him out, without making a noise.
Hang the Almanac's cheat and the Catalogue's spite!
Old Time is a liar! We're twenty tonight!

We're twenty! We're twenty! Who says we are more?
He's tipsy,—young jackanapes!—show him the door!
"Gray temples at twenty?"—Yes! *white,* if we please;
Where the snow-flakes fall thickest there's nothing can freeze!

Was it snowing I spoke of? Excuse the mistake!
Look close,—you will see not a sign of a flake;
We want some new garlands for those we have shed,— [11]
And these are white roses in place of the red!

We've a trick, we young fellows, you may have been told,
Of talking (in public) as if we were old:—
That boy we call "Doctor," [2] and this we call "Judge"; [3]—
It's a neat little fiction,—of course it's all fudge.

That fellow's the "Speaker," [4]—the one on the right;
"Mr. Mayor," [5] my young one, how are you tonight?
That's our "Member of Congress," [6] we say when we chaff;
There's the "Reverend" [7] What's his name?—don't make me laugh. [20]

The boy with the grave mathematical look [8]
Made believe he had written a wonderful book,
And the ROYAL SOCIETY thought it was *true!*
So they chose him right in; a good joke it was, too!

There's a boy, we pretend, with a three-decker-brain, [9]
That could harness a team with a logical chain;
When he spoke for our manhood in syllabled fire,
We called him "The Justice," but now he's "The Squire."

And there's a nice youngster of excellent pith,—
Fate tried to conceal him by naming him Smith; [10] [30]
But he shouted a song for the brave and the free,—
Just read on his medal, "My country, of thee!"

You hear that boy laughing?—You think he's all fun;
But the angels laugh, too, at the good he has done;
The children laugh loud as they troop to his call,
And the poor man that knows him laughs loudest of all!

Yes, we're boys,—always playing with tongue or with pen,
And I sometimes have asked,—Shall we ever be men?
Shall we always be youthful and laughing and gay,
Till the last dear companion drops smiling away? [40]

Then here's to our boyhood, its gold and its gray!
The stars of its winter, the dews of its May!
And when we have done with our life-lasting toys,
Dear Father, take care of thy children, THE BOYS!

1859   1859

INTERNATIONAL ODE [11]

OUR FATHERS' LAND

God bless our Fathers' Land!
Keep her in heart and hand
    One with our own!
From all her foes defend,
Be her brave People's Friend,
On all her realms descend,
    Protect her Throne!

[1] This poem was written for the meeting of the Harvard class of 1829 held on January 6, 1859.
[2] Francis Thomas
[3] George Tyler Bigelow, Chief Justice of the Supreme Court of Massachusetts
[4] Francis B. Crowninshield, Speaker of the Massachusetts House of Representatives
[5] G. W. Richardson of Worcester, Massachusetts
[6] George T. Davis
[7] James Freeman Clarke, a Unitarian minister
[8] Benjamin Peirce, an eminent mathematician, was associate member of the Royal Astronomical Society of London and honorary member of the Royal Society of London.
[9] Benjamin R. Curtis, Judge of the Supreme Court of the United States 1851-1857
[10] Samuel Francis Smith, author of "America"
[11] Sung in unison by twelve hundred children of the public schools, at the visit of the Prince of Wales to Boston, October 18, 1860; air, "God Save the Queen" [Holmes's note]

Father, with loving care,
Guard Thou her kingdom's Heir,
 Guide all his ways: 10
Thine arm his shelter be,
From him by land and sea
Bid storm and danger flee,
 Prolong his days!

Lord, let War's tempest cease,
Fold the whole Earth in peace
 Under Thy wings!
Make all Thy nations one,
All hearts beneath the sun,
Till Thou shalt reign alone,   20
 Great King of kings!

1860   1860

TO MY READERS

Nay, blame me not; I might have spared
 Your patience many a trivial verse,
Yet these my earlier welcome shared,
 So, let the better shield the worse.

And some might say, "Those ruder songs
 Had freshness which the new have lost;
To spring the opening leaf belongs,
 The chestnut-burs await the frost."

When those I wrote, my locks were brown,
 When these I write—ah, well-a-day! 10
The autumn thistle's silvery down
 Is not the purple bloom of May!

Go, little book, whose pages hold
 Those garnered years in loving trust;
How long before your blue and gold [1]
 Shall fade and whiten in the dust?

O sexton of the alcoved tomb,
 Where souls in leathern cerements lie,
Tell me each living poet's doom!
 How long before his book shall die?

It matters little, soon or late,   21
 A day, a month, a year, an age,—
I read oblivion in its date,
 And Finis on its title-page.

Before we sighed, our griefs were told;
 Before we smiled, our joys were sung;
And all our passions shaped of old
 In accents lost to mortal tongue.

In vain a fresher mold we seek,—
 Can all the varied phrases tell   30

<hr>

[1] This poem was written to introduce the "Blue and
Gold" edition of Holmes's poems.

That Babel's wandering children [2] speak
 How thrushes sing or lilacs smell?

Caged in the poet's lonely heart,
 Love wastes unheard its tenderest tone;
The soul that sings must dwell apart,
 Its inward melodies unknown.

Deal gently with us, ye who read!
 Our largest hope is unfulfilled,—
The promise still outruns the deed,—
 The tower, but not the spire, we build. [3]

Our whitest pearl we never find;   41
 Our ripest fruit we never reach;
The flowering moments of the mind
 Drop half their petals in our speech.

These are my blossoms; if they wear
 One streak of morn or evening's glow,
Accept them; but to me more fair
 The buds of song that never blow.

1862   1862

DOROTHY Q.

A FAMILY PORTRAIT [4]

Grandmother's mother: her age, I guess,
Thirteen summers, or something less;
Girlish bust, but womanly air;
Smooth, square forehead with uprolled hair;
Lips that lover has never kissed;
Taper fingers and slender wrist;
Hanging sleeves of stiff brocade;
So they painted the little maid.

On her hand a parrot green
Sits unmoving and broods serene.   10
Hold up the canvas full in view,—
Look! there's a rent the light shines through,
Dark with a century's fringe of dust,—
That was a Red-Coat's rapier-thrust!
Such is the tale the lady old,
Dorothy's daughter's daughter, told.

Who the painter was none may tell,—
One whose best was not over well;
Hard and dry, it must be confessed,
Flat as a rose that has long been pressed;
Yet in her cheek the hues are bright, 21
Dainty colors of red and white,

<hr>

[2] *Genesis* xi, 9.   [3] See note 4, p. 548.
[4] Dorothy Quincy, Holmes's great-grandmother, was
 a niece of Josiah Quincy, a patriot of pre-Revo-
 lutionary times, whose son, the distinguished
 Josiah Quincy, was statesman, orator, and historian. The name came into England with the
 Norman Conquest as De or de Quincey, the form
 used by the English essayist.

And in her slender shape are seen
Hint and promise of stately mien.

Look not on her with eyes of scorn,—
Dorothy Q. was a lady born!
Ay! since the galloping Normans came,
England's annals have known her name;
And still to the three-hilled rebel town [1]
Dear is that ancient name's renown,   30
For many a civic wreath they won,
The youthful sire and the gray-haired son.

O Damsel Dorothy! Dorothy Q.!
Strange is the gift that I owe to you;
Such a gift as never a king
Save to daughter or son might bring,—
All my tenure of heart and hand,
All my title to house and land;
Mother and sister and child and wife
And joy and sorrow and death and life!   40

What if a hundred years ago
Those close-shut lips had answered No,
When forth the tremulous question came
That cost the maiden her Norman name,
And under the folds that look so still
The bodice swelled with the bosom's thrill?
Should I be I, or would it be
One tenth another, to nine tenths me?

Soft is the breath of a maiden's YES:
Not the light gossamer stirs with less;   50
But never a cable that holds so fast
Through all the battles of wave and blast,
And never an echo of speech or song
That lives in the babbling air so long!
There were tones in the voice that whispered
        then
You may hear today in a hundred men.

O lady and lover, how faint and far
Your images hover,—and here we are,
Solid and stirring in flesh and bone,—
Edward's [2] and Dorothy's—all their own,—
A goodly record for Time to show   61
Of a syllable spoken so long ago!—
Shall I bless you, Dorothy, or forgive
For the tender whisper that bade me live?

It shall be a blessing, my little maid!
I will heal the stab of the Red-Coat's blade,
And freshen the gold of the tarnished frame,
And gild with a rime your household name
So you shall smile on us brave and bright

As first you greeted the morning's light,   70
And live untroubled by woes and fears
Through a second youth of a hundred years.
1871   1871

HOW THE OLD HORSE WON THE BET

DEDICATED BY A CONTRIBUTOR TO THE COL-
LEGIAN, 1830, TO THE EDITORS OF THE
HARVARD ADVOCATE, 1876.

'T was on the famous trotting-ground,
The betting men were gathered round
From far and near; the "cracks" were there
Whose deeds the sporting prints declare:
The swift g. m., [3] Old Hiram's nag,
The fleet s. h., [4] Dan Pfeiffer's brag,
With these a third—and who is he
That stands beside his fast b. g.? [5]
Budd Doble, whose catarrhal name
So fills the nasal trump of fame.   10
There too stood many a noted steed
Of Messenger and Morgan breed;
Green horses also, not a few;
Unknown as yet what they could do;
And all the hacks that know so well
The scourgings of the Sunday swell.

Blue are the skies of opening day;
The bordering turf is green with May;
The sunshine's golden gleam is thrown
On sorrel, chestnut, bay, and roan;   20
The horses paw and prance and neigh,
Fillies and colts like kittens play,
And dance and toss their rippled manes
Shining and soft as silken skeins;
Wagons and gigs are ranged about,
And fashion flaunts her gay turn-out;
Here stands—each youthful Jehu's dream—
The jointed tandem, ticklish team!
And there in ampler breadth expand
The splendors of the four-in-hand;   30
On faultless ties and glossy tiles
The lovely bonnets beam their smiles;
(The style's the man, so books avow;
The style's the woman, anyhow);
From flounces frothed with creamy lace
Peeps out the pug-dog's smutty face,
Or spaniel rolls his liquid eye,
Or stares the wiry pet of Skye,—
O woman, in your hours of ease
So shy with us, so free with these! [6]   40

---

[1] Boston was originally called Trimountaine because it
        was built on the three-topped hill afterwards
        called Beacon Hill.
[2] Dorothy Quincy married Edward Jackson.

[3] gray mare   [4] sorrel horse
[5] bay gelding (Budd Doble was a man well known in
        racing circles as was probably Dan Pfeiffer.)
[6] a parody on the lines in Scott's *Marmion* vi, 30:
        "O, woman! in our hours of ease
        Uncertain, coy, and hard to please"

"Come on! I'll bet you two to one
I'll make him do it!" "Will you?
    Done!"

What was it who was bound to do?
I did not hear and can't tell you,—
Pray listen till my story's through.
Scarce noticed, back behind the rest,
By cart and wagon rudely prest,
The parson's lean and bony bay
Stood harnessed in his one-horse shay—
Lent to his sexton for the day;   50
(A funeral—so the sexton said;
His mother's uncle's wife was dead).

Like Lazarus bid to Dives' feast, [1]
So looked the poor forlorn old beast;
His coat was rough, his tail was bare,
The gray was sprinkled in his hair;
Sportsmen and jockeys knew him not
And yet they say he once could trot
Among the fleetest of the town,
Till something cracked and broke him down,—
The steed's, the statesman's, common lot!   61
"And are we then so soon forgot?"
Ah me! I doubt if one of you
Has ever heard the name "Old Blue,"
Whose fame through all this region rung
In those old days when I was young!

"Bring forth the horse!" [2] Alas! he showed
Not like the one Mazeppa rode;
Scant-maned, sharp-backed, and shaky-kneed,
The wreck of what was once a steed,   70
Lips thin, eyes hollow, stiff in joints;
Yet not without his knowing points.
The sexton laughing in his sleeve,
As if 't were all a make-believe,
Led forth the horse, and as he laughed
Unhitched the breeching from a shaft,
Unclasped the rusty belt beneath,
Drew forth the snaffle from his teeth,
Slipped off his head-stall, set him free
From strap and rein,—a sight to see!   80

So worn, so lean, in every limb,
It can't be they are saddling him!
It is! his back the pig-skin strides
And flaps his lank, rheumatic sides;
With look of mingled scorn and mirth
They buckle round the saddle-girth;

[1] Lazarus ate only the crumbs from Dives' table. *Luke* xvi, 21.
[2] Byron's *Mazeppa*, 9:
    " 'Bring forth the horse!'—the horse was brought;
    In truth, he was a noble steed . . .
    Who looked as though the speed of thought
    Were in his limbs";

With horsy wink and saucy toss
A youngster throws his leg across,
And so, his rider on his back,
They lead him, limping, to the track,   90
Far up behind the starting-point,
To limber out each stiffened joint.

As through the jeering crowd he past,
One pitying look old Hiram cast;
"Go it, ye cripple, while ye can!"
Cried out unsentimental Dan;
"A Fast-Day dinner for the crows!"
Budd Doble's scoffing shout arose.

Slowly, as when the walking-beam
First feels the gathering head of steam,   100
With warning cough and threatening wheeze
The stiff old charger crooks his knees;
At first with cautious step sedate,
As if he dragged a coach of state;
He's not a colt; he knows full well
That time is weight and sure to tell;
No horse so sturdy but he fears
The handicap of twenty years.

As through the throng on either hand
The old horse nears the judges' stand,   110
Beneath his jockey's feather-weight
He warms a little to his gait,
And now and then a step is tried
That hints of something like a stride.

"Go!"—Through his ear the summons stung
As if a battle-trump had rung;
The slumbering instincts long unstirred
Start at the old familiar word;
It thrills like flame through every limb—
What means his twenty years to him?   120
The savage blow his rider dealt
Fell on his hollow flanks unfelt;
The spur that pricked his staring hide
Unheeded tore his bleeding side;
Alike to him are spur and rein,—
He steps a five-year-old again!

Before the quarter pole was past,
Old Hiram said, "He's going fast."
Long ere the quarter was a half,
The chuckling crowd had ceased to laugh;   130
Tighter his frightened jockey clung
As in a mighty stride he swung,
The gravel flying in his track,
His neck stretched out, his ears laid back,
His tail extended all the while
Behind him like a rat-tail file!
Off went a shoe,—away it spun,
Shot like a bullet from a gun;

The quaking jockey shapes a prayer
From scraps of oaths he used to swear;
He drops his whip, he drops his rein,   141
He clutches fiercely for a mane;
He'll lose his hold—he sways and reels—
He'll slide beneath those trampling heels!
The knees of many a horseman quake,
The flowers on many a bonnet shake,
And shouts arise from left and right,
"Stick on! Stick on!" "Hould tight! Hould
        tight!"

"Cling round his neck and don't let go—
That pace can't hold—there! steady! whoa!"
But like the sable steed that bore   151
The spectral lover of Lenore, [1]
His nostrils snorting foam and fire,
No stretch his bony limbs can tire;
And now the stand he rushes by,
And "Stop him!—stop him!" is the cry.
Stand back! he's only just begun—
He's having out three heats in one!

"Don't rush in front! he'll smash your brains;
But follow up and grab the reins!"   160
Old Hiram spoke. Dan Pfeiffer heard,
And sprang impatient at the word;
Budd Doble started on his bay,
Old Hiram followed on his gray,
And off they spring, and round they go,
The fast ones doing "all they know."
Look! twice they follow at his heels,
As round the circling course he wheels,
And whirls with him that clinging boy
Like Hector round the walls of Troy; [2]   170
Still on, and on, the third time round!
They're tailing off! they're losing ground!
Budd Doble's nag begins to fail!
Dan Pfeiffer's sorrel whisks his tail!
And see! in spite of whip and shout,
Old Hiram's mare is giving out!
Now for the finish! at the turn,
The old horse—all the rest astern—
Comes swinging in, with easy trot;
By Jove! he's distanced all the lot!   180

That trot no mortal could explain;
Some said, "Old Dutchman [3] come again!"
Some took his time,—at least they tried,
But what it was could none decide;
One said he couldn't understand
What happened to his second hand;
One said 2:10; *that* couldn't be—

[1] In the ballad "Lenore" by the German poet Bürger (1748-1794) the heroine is borne away by a specter lover on a specter steed. The same story is told in Scott's "William and Helen."
[2] *Iliad* xxii
[3] a champion American trotter

More like two twenty-two or -three;
Old Hiram settled it at last;
"The time was two—too dee-vel-ish fast!"

The parson's horse had won the bet;   191
It cost him something of a sweat;
Back in the one-horse shay he went;
The parson wondered what it meant,
And murmured, with a mild surprise
And pleasant twinkle of the eyes,
"That funeral must have been a trick,
Or corpses drive at double-quick;
I shouldn't wonder, I declare,
If brother Jehu made the prayer!"   200

And this is all I have to say
About the parson's poor old bay,
The same that drew the one-hoss shay.

Moral for which this tale is told:
A horse *can* trot, for all he's old.
1876   1876

From THE AUTOCRAT OF THE BREAK-FAST-TABLE [4]

EVERY MAN HIS OWN BOSWELL [5]

From I

I was just going to say, when I was interrupted, that one of the many ways of classifying minds is under the heads of arithmetical and algebraical intellects. All economical and practical wisdom is an extension or variation of the following arithmetical formula: $2 + 2 = 4$. Every philosophical proposition has the more general character of the expression $a + b = c$. We are mere operatives, empirics, and egotists, until we learn to think in letters instead of figures.

They all stared. There is a divinity student lately come among us to whom I commonly

[4] Holmes in his introduction wrote: "The interruption referred to in the first sentence of the first of these papers was just a quarter of a century in duration. Two articles entitled *The Autocrat of the Breakfast Table* will be found in *The New England Magazine*, formerly published in Boston by J. T. and E. Buckingham. The date of the first of these articles is November, 1831, and that of the second February, 1832. When *The Atlantic Monthly* was begun, twenty-five years afterwards, and the author was asked to write for it, the recollection of these crude products of his uncombed literary boyhood suggested the thought that it would be a curious experiment to shake the same bough again, and see if the ripe fruit were better or worse than the early windfalls. So began this series of papers, ..."
[5] Biographer of Dr. Samuel Johnson; his success lay largely in the minuteness of detail with which he recorded Johnson's life, especially his conversation.

address remarks like the above, allowing him to take a certain share in the conversation, so far as assent or pertinent questions are involved. He abused his liberty on this occasion by presuming to say that Leibnitz [1] had the same observation.—No, sir, I replied, he has not. But he said a mighty good thing about mathematics, that sounds something like it, and you found it, *not in the original*, but quoted by Dr. Thomas Reid. [2] I will tell the company what he did say, one of these days.

——If I belong to a Society of Mutual Admiration? [3]—I blush to say that I do not at this present moment. I once did, however. It was the first association to which I ever heard the term applied; a body of scientific young men in a great foreign city [4] who admired their teacher, and to some extent each other. Many of them deserved it; they have become famous since. It amuses me to hear the talk of one of those beings described by Thackeray—

Letters four do form his name [5]

about a social development which belongs to the very noblest stage of civilization. All generous companies of artists, authors, philanthropists, men of science, are, or ought to be, Societies of Mutual Admiration. A man of genius, or any kind of superiority, is not debarred from admiring the same quality in another, nor the other from returning his admiration. They may even associate together and continue to think highly of each other. And so of a dozen such men, if any one place is fortunate enough to hold so many. The being referred to above assumes several false premises. First, that men of talent necessarily hate each other. Secondly, that intimate knowledge or habitual association destroys our admiration of persons whom we esteemed highly at a distance. Thirdly, that a circle of clever fellows, who meet together to dine and have

a good time, have signed a constitutional compact to glorify themselves and to put down him and the fraction of the human race not belonging to their number. Fourthly, that it is an outrage that he is not asked to join them.

Here the company laughed a good deal, and the old gentleman who sits opposite said: "That's it! that's it!"

I continued, for I was in the talking vein. As to clever people's hating each other, I think *a little* extra talent does sometimes make people jealous. They become irritated by perpetual attempts and failures, and it hurts their tempers and dispositions. Unpretending mediocrity is good, and genius is glorious; but a weak flavor of genius in an essentially common person is detestable. It spoils the grand neutrality of a commonplace character, as the rinsings of an unwashed wineglass spoil a draught of fair water. No wonder the poor fellow we spoke of, who always belongs to this class of slightly flavored mediocrities, is puzzled and vexed by the strange sight of a dozen men of capacity working and playing together in harmony. He and his fellows are always fighting. With them familiarity naturally breeds contempt. If they ever praise each other's bad drawings, or broken-winded novels, or spavined verses, nobody ever supposed it was from admiration; it was simply a contract between themselves and a publisher or dealer.

If the Mutuals have really nothing among them worth admiring, that alters the question. But if they are men with noble powers and qualities, let me tell you, that, next to youthful love and family affections, there is no human sentiment better than that which unites the Societies of Mutual Admiration. And what would literature or art be without such associations? Who can tell what we owe to the Mutual Admiration Society of which Shakespeare, and Ben Jonson, and Beaumont and Fletcher were members? [6] Or to that of which Addison and Steele formed the center, and which gave us the Spectator? Or to that where Johnson, and Goldsmith, and Burke, and Reynolds, and Beauclerk, and Boswell, most admiring among all admirers, met together? Was there any great harm in the fact that the Irvings and Paulding wrote in company? or any unpardonable cabal in the literary union of

---

[1] a German philosopher and mathematician (1646-1716)
[2] a Scottish philosopher (1710-1796)
[3] This term was sometimes applied to the Saturday Club in existence in Boston when the *Autocrat* was being written. It was a dinner-club including as members Holmes, Emerson, Agassiz, Longfellow, Lowell, and other prominent writers and scientists.
[4] "The 'body of scientific young men in a great foreign city' was the Société d'Observation Medicale, of Paris, of which M. Louis was president, and MM. Barth, Grisotte, and our own Dr. Bowditch were members. They agreed in admiring their justly-honored president, and thought highly of some of their associates, who have since made good their promise of distinction." [Holmes's note in *Riverside Literature Series* edition.]
[5] Thackeray satirizes the snob in his *Book of Snobs*. The line Holmes quotes was originally from a political satire by Coleridge upon William Pitt the younger, "Fire, Famine and Slaughter."

[6] The Elizabethan dramatists met frequently at the Mermaid Tavern; Addison, Steele, and their friends met at Button's Coffee House; Dr. Samuel Johnson, Oliver Goldsmith, Edmund Burke, Sir Joshua Reynolds the painter, Beauclerk, the friend of Johnson, and Boswell, Johnson's biographer, were all members of The Literary Club in London during the last half of the eighteenth century.

Verplanck and Bryant and Sands, [1] and as many more as they chose to associate with them?

The poor creature does not know what he is talking about when he abuses this noblest of institutions. Let him inspect its mysteries through the knot-hole he has secured, but not use that orifice as a medium for his pop-gun. Such a society is the crown of a literary metropolis; if a town has not material for it, and spirit and good feeling enough to organize it, it is a mere caravansary, fit for a man of genius to lodge in, but not to live in. Foolish people hate and dread and envy such an association of men of varied powers and influence, because it is lofty, serene, impregnable, and, by the necessity of the case, exclusive. Wise ones are prouder of the title M. S. M. A. than of all their other honors put together.

. . . . . .

From IV

. . . . .

No, no!—give me a chance to talk to you, my fellow-boarders, and you need not be afraid that I shall have any scruples about entertaining you, if I can do it, as well as giving you some of my serious thoughts, and perhaps my sadder fancies. I know nothing in English or any other literature more admirable than that sentiment of Sir Thomas Browne: [2] "EVERY MAN TRULY LIVES, SO LONG AS HE ACTS HIS NATURE, OR SOME WAY MAKES GOOD THE FACULTIES OF HIMSELF."

I find the great thing in this world is not so much where we stand, as in what direction we are moving. To reach the port of heaven, we must sail sometimes with the wind and sometimes against it,—but we must sail, and not drift, nor lie at anchor. There is one very sad thing in old friendships, to every mind that is really moving onward. It is this: that one cannot help using his early friends as the seaman uses the log, to mark his progress. Every now and then we throw an old schoolmate over the stern with a string of thought tied to him, and look—I am afraid with a kind of luxurious and sanctimonious compassion—to see the rate at which the string reels off, while he lies there bobbing up and down, poor fellow! and we are dashing along with the white foam and bright sparkle at our bows;—the ruffled bosom of

prosperity and progress, with a sprig of diamonds stuck in it! But this is only the sentimental side of the matter; for grow we must, if we outgrow all that we love.

Don't misunderstand that metaphor of heaving the log, I beg you. It is merely a smart way of saying that we cannot avoid measuring our rate of movement by those with whom we have long been in the habit of comparing ourselves; and when they once become stationary, we can get our reckoning from them with painful accuracy. We see just what we were when they were our peers, and can strike the balance between that and whatever we may feel ourselves to be now. No doubt we may sometimes be mistaken. If we change our last simile to that very old and familiar one of a fleet leaving the harbor and sailing in company, for some distant region, we can get what we want out of it. There is one of our companions;—her streamers were torn into rags before she had got into the open sea, then by-and-by her sails blew out of the ropes one after another, the waves swept her deck, and as night came on we left her a seeming wreck, as we flew under our pyramid of canvas. But lo! at dawn she is still in sight,—it may be in advance of us. Some deep ocean-current has been moving her on, strong, but silent,—yes, stronger than these noisy winds that puff our sails until they are swollen as the cheeks of jubilant cherubim. And when at last the black steam-tug with the skeleton arms, which comes out of the mist sooner or later and takes us all in tow, grapples her and goes off panting and groaning with her, it is to that harbor where all wrecks are refitted, and where, alas! we, towering in our pride, may never come.

So you will not think I mean to speak lightly of old friendships, because we cannot help instituting comparisons between our present and former selves by the aid of those who were what we were, but are not what we are. Nothing strikes one more, in the race of life, than to see how many give out in the first half of the course. "Commencement day" always reminds me of the start for the "Derby," [3] when the beautiful highbred three-year olds of the season are brought up for trial. That day is the start, and life is the race. Here we are at Cambridge, and a class is just "graduating." Poor Harry! he was to have been there too, but he has paid forfeit; step out here into the grass back of the church; ah! there it is:—

[1] Washington Irving, his brother William, and their brother-in-law, James K. Paulding, together edited *Salmagundi* in New York in 1807-1808. Gulian C. Verplanck, Robert C. Sands, and William Cullen Bryant issued an annual called *The Talisman*, in 1827-30.
[2] an English physician and author (1605-1682)

[3] the annual horse race held in May or June at Epsom, southwest of London, and named for its founder, the 12th Earl of Derby

"HUNC LAPIDEM POSUERUNT SOCII MOERENTES."[1]

But this is the start, and here they are,—coats bright as silk, and manes as smooth as *eau lustrale*[2] can make them. Some of the best of the colts are pranced round, a few minutes each, to show their paces. What is that old gentleman crying about? and the old lady by him, and the three girls, what are they all covering their eyes for? Oh, that is *their* colt which has just been trotted up on the stage. Do they really think those little thin legs can do anything in such a slashing sweepstakes as is coming off in these next forty years? Oh, this terrible gift of second-sight that comes to some of us when we begin to look through the silvered rings of the *arcus senilis!*[3]

Ten years gone. First turn in the race. A few broken down; two or three bolted. Several show in advance of the ruck. *Cassock,* a black colt, seems to be ahead of the rest; those black colts commonly get the start, I have noticed, of the others, in the first quarter. *Meteor* has pulled up.

Twenty years. Second corner turned. *Cassock* has dropped from the front, and *Judex,* an iron-gray, has the lead. But look! how they have thinned out? Down flat,—five,—six,—how many? They lie still enough! they will not get up again in this race, be very sure! And the rest of them, what a "tailing off!" Anybody can see who is going to win,—perhaps.

Thirty years. Third corner turned. *Dives,* bright sorrel, ridden by the fellow in a yellow jacket, begins to make play fast; is getting to be the favorite, with many. But who is that other one that has been lengthening his stride from the first, and now shows close up to the front? Don't you remember the quiet brown colt *Asteroid,* with the star in his forehead? That is he; he is one of the sort that lasts; look out for him! The black "colt," as we used to call him, is in the background, taking it easily in a gentle trot. There is one they used to call *the Filly,* on account of a certain feminine air he had; well up, you see; the Filly is not to be despised, my boy!

Forty years. More dropping off,—but places much as before.

Fifty years. Race over. All that are on the course are coming in at a walk; no more running. Who is ahead? Ahead? What! and the

winning-post a slab of white or gray stone standing out from that turf where there is no more jockeying or straining for victory! Well, the world marks their places in its betting-book; but be sure that these matter very little, if they have run as well as they knew how!

——Did I not say to you a little while ago that the universe swam in an ocean of similitudes and analogies? I will not quote Cowley,[4] or Burns, or Wordsworth, just now, to show you what thoughts were suggested to them by the simplest natural objects, such as a flower or a leaf; but I will read you a few lines, if you do not object, suggested by looking at a section of one of those chambered shells to which is given the name of Pearly Nautilus. We need not trouble ourselves about the distinction between this and the Paper Nautilus, the *Argonauta*[5] of the ancients. The name applied to both shows that each has long been compared to a ship, as you may see more fully in Webster's Dictionary, or the "Encyclopedia," to which he refers. If you will look into Roget's Bridgewater Treatise,[6] you will find a figure of one of these shells and a section of it. The last will show you the series of enlarging compartments successively dwelt in by the animal that inhabits the shell, which is built in a widening spiral. Can you find no lesson in this?

THE CHAMBERED NAUTILUS

This is the ship of pearl, which, poets feign,
　　Sails the unshadowed main,—
　　The venturous bark that flings
On the sweet summer wind its purpled wings
In gulfs enchanted, where the siren sings,
　　And coral reefs lie bare,
Where the cold sea-maids rise to sun their streaming hair.

Its webs of living gauze no more unfurl;
　　Wrecked is the ship of pearl!
　　And every chambered cell,
Where its dim dreaming life was wont to dwell,
As the frail tenant shaped his growing shell,
　　Before thee lies revealed,—
Its irised ceiling rent, its sunless crypt unsealed!

Year after year beheld the silent toil
　　That spread his lustrous coil;
　　Still, as the spiral grew,
He left the past year's dwelling for the new,

[1] "Mourning friends have erected this stone."
[2] water used in ceremonies of purification
[3] bow of old age; opaqueness of the edge of the cornea usual in old age

[4] Abraham Cowley, an English poet, 1618-1667
[5] a species of mollusk
[6] The Earl of Bridgewater (1758-1829) bequeathed £8,000 for the publishing of works "on the Goodness of God as manifested in the Creation." Dr. P. M. Roget, 1779-1869, wrote on *Animal and Vegetable Physiology.*

Stole with soft step its shining archway through,
    Built up its idle door,
Stretched in his last-found home, and knew the old
    no more.

Thanks for the heavenly message brought by thee,
    Child of the wandering sea,
    Cast from her lap forlorn!
From thy dead lips a clearer note is born
Than ever Triton blew from wreathed horn![1]
    While on mine ear it rings,
Through the deep caves of thought I hear a voice
    that sings:—

Build thee more stately mansions, O my soul,
    As the swift seasons roll!
    Leave thy low-vaulted past!
Let each new temple, nobler than the last,
Shut thee from heaven with a dome more vast,
    Till thou at length art free,
Leaving thine outgrown shell by life's unresting
    sea!

From VI

. . . .

——Every person's feelings have a front-door and a side-door by which they may be entered. The front-door is on the street. Some keep it always open; some keep it latched; some, locked; some, bolted,—with a chain that will let you peep in, but not get in; and some nail it up, so that nothing can pass its threshold. This front-door leads into a passage which opens into an ante-room and this into the interior apartments. The side-door opens at once into the sacred chambers.

There is almost always at least one key to this side-door. This is carried for years hidden in a mother's bosom. Fathers, brothers, sisters, and friends, often, but by no means so universally, have duplicates of it. The wedding-ring conveys a right to one; alas, if none is given with it!

If nature or accident has put one of these keys into the hands of a person who has the torturing instinct, I can only solemnly pronounce the words that Justice utters over its doomed victim,—*The Lord have mercy on your soul!* You will probably go mad within a reasonable time,—or, if you are a man, run off and die with your head on a curb-stone, in Melbourne or San Francisco,—or, if you are a woman, quarrel and break your heart, or turn into a pale, jointed petrifaction that moves about as if it were alive, or play some real life-tragedy or other.

Be very careful to whom you trust one of these keys of the side-door. The fact of possessing one renders those even who are dear to you very terrible at times. You can keep the world out from your front-door, or receive visitors only when you are ready for them; but those of your own flesh and blood, or of certain grades of intimacy, can come in at the side-door, if they will, at any hour and in any mood. Some of them have a scale of your whole nervous system, and can play all the gamut of your sensibilities in semitones,—touching the naked nerve-pulps as a pianist strikes the keys of his instrument. I am satisfied that there are as great masters of this nerve-playing, as Vieuxtemps[2] or Thalberg in their lines of performance. Married life is the school in which the most accomplished artists in this department are found. A delicate woman is the best instrument; she has such a magnificent compass of sensibilities! From the deep inward moan which follows pressure on the great nerves of right, to the sharp cry as the filaments of taste are struck with a crashing sweep, is a range which no other instrument possesses. A few exercises on it daily at home fit a man wonderfully for his habitual labors, and refresh him immensely as he returns from them. No stranger can get a great many notes of torture out of a human soul; it takes one that knows it well,—parent, child, brother, sister, intimate. Be very careful to whom you give a side-door key; too many have them already.

——You remember the old story of the tender-hearted man, who placed a frozen viper in his bosom, and was stung by it when it became thawed? If we take a cold-blooded creature into our bosom, better that it should sting us and we should die than that its chill should slowly steal into our hearts; warm it we never can! I have seen faces of women that were fair to look upon, yet one could see that the icicles were forming round these women's hearts. I knew what freezing image lay on the white breasts beneath the laces!

A very simple *intellectual* mechanism answers the necessities of friendship, and even of the most intimate relations of life. If a watch tells us the hour and the minute, we can be content to carry it about with us for a lifetime, though it has no second-hand, and is not a repeater, nor a musical watch,—though it is not enameled nor jeweled,—in short, though it has little beyond the wheels required for a

---

[1] See the last line of Wordsworth's sonnet "The World
Is Too Much With Us:"

    "Or hear old Triton blow his wreathéd horn."

[2] A Belgian violinist and composer, 1820-1881; Thalberg
    was a Swiss composer for the piano, 1812-1871.

trustworthy instrument, added to a good face and a pair of useful hands. The more wheels there are in a watch or a brain, the more trouble they are to take care of. The movements of exaltation which belong to genius are egotistic by their very nature. A calm, clear mind, not subject to the spasms and crises which are so often met with in creative or intensely perceptive natures, is the best basis for love or friendship.—Observe, I am talking about *minds*. I won't say, the more intellect, the less capacity for loving; for that would do wrong to the understanding and reason;—but, on the other hand, that the brain often runs away with the heart's best blood, which gives the world a few pages of wisdom or sentiment or poetry, instead of making one other heart happy, I have no question.

If one's intimate in love or friendship cannot or does not share all one's intellectual tastes or pursuits, that is a small matter. Intellectual companions can be found easily in men and books. After all, if we think of it, most of the world's loves and friendships have been between people that could not read nor spell.

But to radiate the heat of the affections into a clod, which absorbs all that is poured into it, but never warms beneath the sunshine of smiles or the pressure of hand or lip,—this is the great martyrdom of sensitive beings,—most of all in that perpetual *auto da fé* [1] where young womanhood is the sacrifice.

From VII [2]

. . . . . .

As to *giving up* because the almanac or the Family Bible says that it is about time to do it, I have no intention of doing any such thing. I grant you that I burn less carbon than some years ago. I see people of my standing really good for nothing, decrepit, effete, *la lèvre inférieure dejà pendante*, [3] with what little life they have left mainly concentrated in their epigastrium. But as the disease of old age is epidemic, endemic, and sporadic, and everybody who lives long enough is sure to catch it, I am going to say, for the encouragement of such as need it, how I treat the malady in my own case.

First. As I feel, that, when I have anything to do, there is less time for it than when I was younger, I find that I give my attention more thoroughly, and use my time more economically than ever before; so that I can learn anything twice as easily as in my earlier days. I am not, therefore, afraid to attack a new study. I took up a difficult language a very few years ago with good success, and think of mathematics and metaphysics by-and-by.

Secondly. I have opened my eyes to a good many neglected privileges and pleasures within my reach, and requiring only a little courage to enjoy them. You may well suppose it pleased me to find that old Cato was thinking of learning to play the fiddle, when I had deliberately taken it up in my old age, [4] and satisfied myself that I could get much comfort, if not much music, out of it.

Thirdly. I have found that some of those active exercises, which are commonly thought to belong to young folks only, may be enjoyed at a much later period.

A young friend has lately written an admirable article in one of the journals, entitled, *Saints and their Bodies*. [5] Approving of his general doctrines, and grateful for his records of personal experience, I cannot refuse to add my own experimental confirmation of his eulogy of one particular form of active exercise and amusement, namely, *boating*. For the past nine years, I have rowed about, during a good part of the summer, on fresh or salt water. My present fleet on the river Charles consists of three row-boats. 1. A small flat-bottomed skiff of the shape of a flat-iron, kept mainly to lend to boys. 2. A fancy "dory" for two pairs of sculls, in which I sometimes go out with my young folks. 3. My own particular watersulky, a "skeleton" or "shell" race-boat, twenty-two feet long, with huge outriggers, which boat I pull with ten-foot sculls,—alone, of course, as it holds but one, and tips him out, if he doesn't mind what he is about. In this I glide around the Back Bay, down the stream, up the Charles to Cambridge and Watertown, up the Mystic, round the wharves, in the wake of steamboats, which leave a swell after them delightful to rock upon; I linger under the bridges,—those "caterpillar bridges" as my brother professor so happily called them; rub against the black sides of old wood-schooners; cool down under the overhanging stern of some tall Indiaman;

---

[1] Spanish, literally "act of faith"; the sentence pronounced at a public solemnity by the courts of the Spanish Inquisition, ecclesiastical courts for detecting and trying heretics. Since in capital cases the execution of the offender followed immediately, the phrase came to apply to the execution as well as to the sentence itself.

[2] What follows is part of the Professor's paper on "Old Age," the first part of which is omitted.

[3] "the lower lip already drooping"

[4] Cicero in *De Senectute* (8) represents Cato as saying, "When I heard what Socrates had done about the lyre, I should have liked for my part to have done that too." Holmes was at this time forty-nine.

[5] Col. Thomas Wentworth Higginson in the *Atlantic Monthly*, March, 1858

stretch across to the Navy-Yard, where the sentinel warns me off from the *Ohio*,—just as if I should hurt her by lying in her shadow; then strike out into the harbor, where the water gets clear and the air smells of the ocean,—till all at once I remember, that, if a west wind blows up of a sudden, I shall drift along past the islands, out of sight of the dear old State-house,—plate, tumbler, knife and fork all waiting at home, but no chair drawn up at the table,—all the dear people waiting, waiting, waiting, while the boat is sliding, sliding, sliding into the great desert, where there is no tree and no fountain. As I don't want my wreck to be washed up on one of the beaches in company with devil's-aprons, bladder-weeds, dead horse-shoes, and bleached crab-shells, I turn about and flap my long, narrow wings for home. When the tide is running out swiftly, I have a splendid fight to get through the bridges, but always make it a rule to beat,—though I have been jammed up into pretty tight places at times, and was caught once between a vessel swinging round and the pier, until our bones (the boat's that is) cracked as if we had been in the jaws of Behemoth. Then back to my moorings at the foot of the Common, off with the rowing-dress, dash under the green translucent wave, return to the garb of civilization, walk through my Garden, take a look at my elms on the Common, and, reaching my habitat, in consideration of my advanced period of life, indulge in the Elysian abandonment of a huge recumbent chair.

When I have established a pair of well-pronounced feathering-calluses on my thumbs, when I am in training so that I can do my fifteen miles at a stretch without coming to grief in any way, when I can perform my mile in eight minutes or a little less, then I feel as if I had old Time's head in chancery,[1] and could give it to him at my leisure.

I do not deny the attraction of walking. I have bored this ancient city through and through in my daily travels, until I know it as an old inhabitant of a Cheshire knows his cheese. Why, it was I who, in the course of these rambles discovered that remarkable avenue called *Myrtle Street*, stretching in one long line from east of the Reservoir to a precipitous and rudely paved cliff which looks down on the grim abode of Science,[2] and beyond it to the far hills; a

promenade so delicious in its repose, so cheerfully varied with glimpses down the northern slope into busy Cambridge Street with its iron river of the horse-railroad, and wheeled barges gliding back and forward over it,—so delightfully closing at its western extremity in sunny courts and passages where I know peace, and beauty, and virtue, and serene old age must be perpetual tenants,—so alluring to all who desire to take their daily stroll, in the words of Dr. Watts,—

Alike unknowing and unknown—

that nothing but a sense of duty would have prompted me to reveal the secret of its existence. I concede, therefore, that walking is an immeasurably fine invention, of which old age ought constantly to avail itself.

Saddle-leather is in some respects even preferable to sole-leather. The principal objection to it is of a financial character. But you may be sure that Bacon and Sydenham[3] did not recommend it for nothing. One's *hepar*, or in vulgar language, liver,—a ponderous organ, weighing some three or four pounds,—goes up and down like the dasher of a churn in the midst of the other vital arrangements, at every step of a trotting horse. The brains also are shaken up like coppers in a money-box. Riding is good, for those that are born with a silver-mounted bridle in their hand, and can ride as much and as often as they like, without thinking all the time they hear that steady grinding sound as the horse's jaws triturate with calm lateral movement the bank-bills and promises to pay upon which it is notorious that the profligate animal in question feeds day and night.

Instead, however, of considering these kinds of exercise in this empirical way, I will devote a brief space to an examination of them in a more scientific form.

The pleasure of exercise is due first to a purely physical impression, and secondly to a sense of power in action. The first source of pleasure varies of course with our condition and the state of the surrounding circumstances; the second with the amount and kind of power, and the extent and kind of action. In all forms of active exercise there are three powers simultaneously in action,—the will, the muscles, and the intellect. Each of these predominates in different kinds of exercise. In walking, the will and muscles are so accustomed to work together and perform their task with so little

---

[1] "In boxing, said of the head caught and securely held under the arm of an opponent."—*New Standard Dictionary.*

[2] At the extremity of Myrtle St., which runs west from back of the State House, stood the Harvard Medical School of Holmes's day.

[3] See Bacon *Of Studies;* Sydenham, 1624-1689, was an English physician and writer on medicine.

expenditure of force, that the intellect is left comparatively free. The mental pleasure in walking, as such, is in the sense of power over all our moving machinery. But in riding, I have the additional pleasure of governing another will, and my muscles extend to the tips of the animal's ears and to his four hoofs, instead of stopping at my hands and feet. Now in this extension of my volition and my physical frame into another animal, my tyrannical instincts and my desire for heroic strength are at once gratified. When the horse ceases to have a will of his own and his muscles require no special attention on your part, then you may live on horseback as Wesley did, [1] and write sermons or take naps, as you like. But you will observe, that, in riding on horseback, you always have a feeling, that, after all, it is not you that do the work, but the animal, and this prevents the satisfaction from being complete.

Now let us look at the conditions of rowing. I won't suppose you to be disgracing yourself in one of those miserable tubs, tugging in which is to rowing the true boat what riding a cow is to bestriding an Arab. You know the Esquimaux *kayak*, (if that is the name of it), don't you? Look at that model of one over my door. Sharp, rather?—On the contrary, it is a lubber to the one you and I must have; a Dutch fishwife to Psyche, [2] contrasted with what I will tell you about. Our boat, then, is something of the shape of a pickerel, as you look down upon his back, he lying in the sunshine just where the sharp edge of the water cuts in among the lily-pads. It is a kind of giant *pod,* as one may say,—tight everywhere, except in a little place in the middle, where you sit. Its length is from seven to ten yards, and as it is only from sixteen to thirty inches wide in its widest part, you understand why you want those "outriggers," or projecting iron frames with the rowlocks in which the oars play. My rowlocks are five feet apart; double the greatest width of the boat.

Here you are, then, afloat with a body a rod and a half long, with arms, or wings, as you may choose to call them, stretching more than twenty feet from tip to tip; every volition of yours extending as perfectly into them as if your spinal cord ran down the center strip of your boat, and the nerves of your arms tingled as far as the broad blades of your oars,—oars of spruce, balanced, leathered, and ringed under your own special direction. This, in sober earnest, is the nearest approach to flying that man has ever made or perhaps ever will make. As the hawk sails without flapping his pinions, so you drift with the tide when you will, in the most luxurious form of locomotion indulged to an embodied spirit. But if your blood wants rousing, turn round that stake in the river, which you see a mile from here; and when you come in in sixteen minutes (if you do, for we are old boys, and not champion scullers, you remember), then say if you begin to feel a little warmed up or not! You can row easily and gently all day, and you can row yourself blind and black in the face in ten minutes, just as you like. It has been long agreed that there is no way in which a man can accomplish so much labor with his muscles as in rowing. It is in the boat, then, that man finds the largest extension of his volitional and muscular existence; and yet he may tax both of them so slightly, in that most delicious of exercises, that he shall mentally write his sermon, or his poem, or recall the remarks he has made in company and put them in form for the public, as well as in his easy-chair.

I dare not publicly name the rare joys, the infinite delights, that intoxicate me on some sweet June morning, when the river and bay are smooth as a sheet of beryl-green silk, and I run along ripping it up with my knife-edged shell of a boat, the rent closing after me like those wounds of angels which Milton tells of, [3] but the seam still shining for many a long rood behind me. To lie still over the Flats, where the waters are shallow, and see the crabs crawling and the sculpins gliding busily and silently beneath the boat,—to rustle in through the long harsh grass that leads up some tranquil creek,—to take shelter from the sunbeams under one of the thousand-footed bridges, and look down its interminable colonnades, crusted with green and oozy growths, studded with minute barnacles, and belted with rings of dark muscles, while overhead streams and thunders that other river whose every wave is a human soul flowing to eternity as the river below flows to the ocean, —lying there moored unseen, in loneliness so profound that the columns of Tadmor in the Desert [4] could not seem more remote from life,—the cool breeze on one's forehead, the stream whispering against the half-sunken pillars,—why should I tell of these things, that I should live to see my beloved haunts invaded and the waves blackened with boats as with

---

[1] during his work as itinerant preacher
[2] the personification of the soul, generally represented as a sylph-like figure

[3] *Paradise Lost,* vi, 330, 331
[4] Tadmor or Palmyra, an ancient city situated in an oasis in the desert of Syria, was famous for its temples and colonnaded streets.

a swarm of water-beetles? What a city of idiots we must be not to have covered this glorious bay with gondolas and wherries, as we have just learned to cover the ice in winter with skaters!

I am satisfied that such a set of black-coated, stiff-jointed, soft-muscled, paste-complexioned youth as we can boast in our Atlantic cities never before sprang from loins of Anglo-Saxon lineage. Of the females that are the mates of these males I do not here speak. I preached my sermon from the lay-pulpit on this matter a good while ago. Of course, if you heard it, you know my belief is that the total climatic influences here are getting up a number of new patterns of humanity, some of which are not an improvement on the old model. Clipper-built, sharp in the bows, long in the spars, slender to look at, and fast to go, the ship, which is the great organ of our national life of relation, is but a reproduction of the typical form which the elements impress upon its builder. All this we cannot help; but we can make the best of these influences, such as they are. We have a few good boatmen,—no good horsemen that I hear of,—I cannot speak for cricketing,—but as for any great athletic feat performed by a gentleman in these latitudes, society would drop a man who should run round the Common in five minutes. Some of our amateur fencers, single-stick players, and boxers, we have no reason to be ashamed of. Boxing is rough play, but not too rough for a hearty young fellow. Anything is better than this white-blooded degeneration to which we all tend.

I dropped into a gentlemen's sparring exhibition only last evening. It did my heart good to see that there were a few young and youngish youths left who could take care of their own heads in case of emergency. It is a fine sight, that of a gentleman resolving himself into the primitive constituents of his humanity. Here is a delicate young man now, with an intellectual countenance, a slight figure, a sub-pallid complexion, a most unassuming deportment, a mild adolescent in fact, that any Hiram or Jonathan from between the plowtails would of course expect to handle with perfect ease. Oh, he is taking off his gold-bowed spectacles! Ah, he is divesting himself of his cravat! Why, he is stripping off his coat! Well, here he is, sure enough, in a tight silk shirt, and with two things that look like batter puddings in the place of his fists. Now see that other fellow with another pair of batter puddings,—the big one with the broad shoulders; he will certainly

knock the little man's head off, if he strikes him. Feinting, dodging, stopping, hitting, countering,—little man's head not off yet. You might as well try to jump upon your own shadow as to hit the little man's intellectual features. He needn't have taken off the gold-bowed spectacles at all. Quick, cautious, shifty, nimble, cool, he catches all the fierce lunges or gets out of their reach, till his turn comes, and then whack goes one of the batter puddings against the big one's ribs, and bang goes the other into the big one's face, and, staggering, shuffling, slipping, tripping, collapsing, sprawling, down goes the big one in a miscellaneous bundle.—If my young friend, whose excellent article I have referred to, could only introduce the manly art of self-defense among the clergy, I am satisfied that we should have better sermons and an infinitely less quarrelsome church-militant. A bout with the gloves would let off the ill-nature, and cure the indigestion, which, united, have embroiled their subject in a bitter controversy. We should then often hear that a point of difference between an infallible and a heretic, instead of being vehemently discussed in a series of newspaper articles, had been settled by a friendly contest in several rounds, at the close of which the parties shook hands and appeared cordially reconciled.

But boxing you and I are too old for, I am afraid. I was for a moment tempted, by the contagion of muscular electricity last evening, to try the gloves with the Benicia Boy, who looked in as a friend to the noble art; but remembering that he had twice my weight and half my age, besides the advantage of his training, I sat still and said nothing.

There is one other delicate point I wish to speak of with reference to old age. I refer to the use of *dioptric media* which correct the diminished refracting power of the humors of the eye,—in other words, spectacles. I don't use them. All I ask is a large, fair type, a strong daylight or gas-light, and one yard of focal distance, and my eyes are as good as ever. But if *your* eyes fail, I can tell you something encouraging. There is now living in New York State an old gentleman who, perceiving his sight to fail, immediately took to exercising it on the finest print, and in this way fairly bullied Nature out of her foolish habit of taking liberties at five-and-forty, or thereabout. And now this old gentleman, performs the most extraordinary feats with his pen, showing that his eyes must be a pair of microscopes. I should be afraid to say to you how much he writes in the compass of a half-dime,—whether the Psalms or the Gospels, or the Psalms *and* the Gospels, I won't be positive.

But now let me tell you this. If the time comes when you must lay down the fiddle and the bow, because your fingers are too stiff, and drop the ten-foot sculls, because your arms are too weak, and after dallying awhile with eye-glasses, come at last to the undisguised reality of spectacles,—if the time comes when that fire of life we spoke of has burned so low that where its flames reverberated there is only the somber stain of regret, and where its coals glowed, only the white ashes that cover the embers of memory,—don't let your heart grow cold, and you may carry cheerfulness and love with you into the teens of your second century, if you can last so long. As our friend, the Poet, once said, in some of those old-fashioned heroics of his which he keeps for his private reading,—

Call him not old, whose visionary brain
Holds o'er the past its undivided reign.
For him in vain the envious seasons roll
Who bears eternal summer in his soul.
If yet the minstrel's song, the poet's lay,
Spring with her birds, or children with their play,
Or maiden's smile, or heavenly dream of art
Stir the few life-drops creeping round his heart,—
Turn to the record where his years are told,—
Count his gray hairs,—they cannot make him old!

End of the Professor's paper.

.   .   .   .

From IX

[*Aquí está encerrada el alma del licenciado Pedro Garcias.*

If I should ever make a little book out of these papers, which I hope you are not getting tired of, I suppose I ought to save the above sentence for a motto on the title-page. But I want it now, and must use it. I need not say to you that the words are Spanish, nor that they are to be found in the short Introduction to *Gil Blas,* nor that they mean, "Here lies buried the soul of the licentiate [1] Pedro Garcias."

I warned all young people off the premises when I began my notes referring to old age. I must be equally fair with old people now. They are earnestly requested to leave this paper to young persons from the age of twelve to that of fourscore years and ten, at which latter period of life I am sure that I shall have

at least one youthful reader. You know well enough what I mean by youth and age;—something in the soul, which has no more to do with the color of the hair than the vein of gold in a rock has to do with the grass a thousand feet above it.

I am growing bolder as I write. I think it requires not only youth, but genius, to read this paper. I don't mean to imply that it required any whatsoever to talk what I have here written down. It did demand a certain amount of memory, and such command of the English tongue as is given by a common school education. So much I do claim. But here I have related, at length, a string of trivialities. You must have the imagination of a poet to transfigure them. These little colored patches are stains upon the windows of a human soul; stand on the outside, they are but dull and meaningless spots of color; seen from within, they are glorified shapes with empurpled wings and sunbright aureoles.

My hand trembles when I offer you this. Many times I have come bearing flowers such as my garden grew; but now I offer you this poor, brown, homely growth, you may cast it away as worthless. And yet—and yet—it is something better than flowers; it is a *seed-capsule.* Many a gardener will cut you a bouquet of his choicest blossoms for small fee, but he does not love to let the seeds of his rarest varieties go out of his own hands.

It is by little things that we know ourselves; a soul would very probably mistake itself for another, when once disembodied, were it not for individual experiences which differ from those of others only in details seemingly trifling. All of us have been thirsty thousands of times, and felt, with Pindar, that water was the best of things. [2] I alone, as I think, of all mankind, remember one particular pailful of water, flavored with the white-pine of which the pail was made, and the brown mug out of which one Edmund, a red-faced and curly-haired boy, was averred to have bitten a fragment in his haste to drink; it being then high summer, and little full-blooded boys feeling very warm and porous in the low-"studded" school-room where Dame Prentiss, dead and gone, ruled over young children, many of whom are old ghosts now, and have known Abraham for twenty or thirty years of our mortal time.

Thirst belongs to humanity, everywhere, in all ages; but that white-pine pail and that brown mug belong to me in particular; and just so

[1] a person licensed to perform the offices of the church

[2] "Best of all things is water." *Olympian Odes,* i, 1.

of my special relationships with other things and with my race. One could never remember himself in eternity by the mere fact of having loved or hated any more than by that of having thirsted; love and hate have no more individuality in them than single waves in the ocean; —but the accidents or trivial marks which distinguished those whom we loved or hated make their memory our own forever, and with it that of our own personality also.

Therefore, my aged friend of five-and-twenty, or thereabouts, pause at the threshold of this particular record, and ask yourself seriously whether you are fit to read such revelations as are to follow. For observe, you have here no splendid array of petals such as poets offer you, —nothing but a dry shell, containing, if you will get out what is in it, a few small seeds of poems. You may laugh at them, if you like. I shall never tell you what I think of you for so doing. But if you can read into the heart of these things, in the light of other memories as slight, yet as dear to your soul, then you are neither more nor less than a POET, and can afford to write no more verses during the rest of your natural life,—which abstinence I take to be one of the surest marks of your meriting the divine name I have just bestowed upon you.

May I beg of you who have begun this paper, nobly trusting to your own imagination and sensibilities to give it the significance which it does not lay claim to without your kind assistance,—may I beg of you, I say, to pay particular attention to the *brackets* which enclose certain paragraphs? I want my "asides," you see, to whisper loud to you who read my notes, and sometimes I talk a page or two to you without pretending that I said a word of it to our boarders. You will find a very long "aside" to you almost as soon as you begin to read. And so, dear young friend, fall to at once, taking such things as I have provided for you; and if you turn them, by the aid of your powerful imagination, into a fair banquet, why, then, peace be with you, and a summer by the still waters of some quiet river, or by some yellow beach, where, as my friend, the Professor, says, you can sit with Nature's wrist in your hand and count her ocean-pulses.]

I should like to make a few intimate revelations relating especially to my early life, if I thought you would like to hear them.

[The schoolmistress turned a little in her chair, and sat with her face directed partly towards me.—Half-mourning now;—purple ribbon. That breastpin she wears has *gray*

hair in it; her mother's no doubt;—I remember our landlady's daughter telling me, soon after the schoolmistress came to board with us, that she had lately "buried a payrent." That's what made her look so pale,—kept the poor dying thing alive with her own blood. Ah! long illness is the real vampyrism; think of living a year or two after one is dead, by sucking the life-blood out of a frail young creature at one's bedside! Well, souls grow white, as well as cheeks, in these holy duties; one that goes in a nurse may come out an angel. —God bless all good women!—to their soft hands and pitying hearts we must all come at last!——The schoolmistress has a better color than when she came.—Too late!—"It might have been."—Amen!—How many thoughts go to a dozen heartbeats, sometimes! There was no long pause after my remark addressed to the company, but in that time I had the train of ideas and feelings I have just given flash through my consciousness sudden and sharp as the crooked red streak that springs out of its black sheath like the creese of a Malay in his death-race, and stabs the earth right and left in its blind rage.

I don't deny that there was a pang in it,— yes, a stab; but there was a prayer, too,—the "Amen" belonged to that.—Also, a vision of a four-story brick house, nicely furnished,—I actually saw many specific articles—curtains, sofas, tables, and others, and could draw the patterns of them at this moment,—a brick house, I say, looking out on the water, with a fair parlor, and books and busts and pots of flowers and bird-cages, all complete; and at the window, looking on the water, two of us.— "Male and female created He them."—These two were standing at the window, when a smaller shape that was playing near them looked up at me with such a look that I——poured out a glass of water, drank it all down, and then continued.]

I said I should like to tell you some things, such as people commonly never tell, about my early recollections. Should you like to hear them?

Should we *like* to hear them?—said the schoolmistress;—no, but we should *love* to.

[The voice was a sweet one, naturally, and had something very pleasant in its tone, just then.—The four-story brick house, which had gone out like a transparency when the light behind it is quenched, glimmered again for a moment; parlor, books, busts, flower-pots, bird-cages, all complete,—and the figures as before.]

We are waiting with eagerness, sir,—said the divinity-student.

[The transparency went out as if a flash of black lightning had struck it.]

If you want to hear my confessions, the next thing—I said—is to know whether I can trust you with them. It is only fair to say that there are a great many people in the world that laugh at such things. *I* think they are fools, but perhaps you don't all agree with me.

Here are children of tender age talked to as if they were capable of understanding Calvin's *Institutes,*[1] and nobody has honesty or sense enough to tell the plain truth about the little wretches: that they are as superstitious as naked savages, and such miserable spiritual cowards—that is, if they have any imagination —that they will believe anything which is taught them, and a great deal more which they teach themselves.

I was born and bred, as I have told you twenty times, among books and those who knew what was in books. I was carefully instructed in things temporal and spiritual. But up to a considerable maturity of childhood I believed Raphael and Michael Angelo[2] to have been superhuman beings. The central doctrine of the prevalent religious faith of Christendom was utterly confused and neutralized in my mind for years by one of those too common stories of actual life, which I overheard repeated in a whisper.—Why did I not ask? you will say.—You don't remember the rosy pudency of sensitive children. The first instinctive movement of the little creatures is to make a *cache,* and bury in it beliefs, doubts, dreams, hopes, and terrors. I am uncovering one of these *caches.* Do you think I was necessarily a greater fool and coward than another?

I was afraid of ships. Why, I could never tell. The masts looked frightfully tall,—but they were not so tall as the steeple of our old yellow meeting-house. At any rate, I used to hide my eyes from the sloops and schooners that were wont to lie at the end of the bridge, and I confess that traces of this undefined terror lasted very long.—One other source of alarm had a still more fearful significance. There was a great wooden HAND,—a glove-maker's sign, which used to swing and creak in the blast, as it hung from a pillar before a certain shop a mile or two outside of the city. Oh, the dreadful hand! Always hanging there ready to catch up a little boy, who would come home to

supper no more, nor yet to bed,—whose porringer would be laid away empty thenceforth, and his half-worn shoes wait until his small brother grew to fit them.

As for all manner of superstitious observances, I used once to think I must have been peculiar in having such a list of them, but I now believe that half the children of the same age go through the same experiences. No Roman soothsayer ever had such a catalogue of *omens* as I found in the Sibylline leaves[3] of my childhood. That trick of throwing a stone at a tree and attaching some mighty issue to hitting or missing, which you will find mentioned in one or more biographies, I well remember. Stepping on or over certain particular things or spots—Dr. Johnson's especial weakness—I got the habit of at a very early age.—I won't swear that I have not some tendency to these not wise practices even at this present date. [How many of you that read these notes can say the same thing!]

With these follies mingled sweet delusions, which I loved so well I would not outgrow them, even when it required a voluntary effort to put a momentary trust in them. Here is one which I cannot help telling you.

The firing of the great guns at the Navy-Yard is easily heard at the place where I was born and lived. "There is a ship of war come in," they used to say, when they heard them. Of course, I supposed that such vessels came in unexpectedly, after indefinite years of absence,— suddenly as falling stones; and that the great guns roared in their astonishment and delight at the sight of the old war-ship splitting the bay with her cutwater. Now, the sloop-of-war the *Wasp,*[4] Captain Blakely, after gloriously capturing the *Reindeer* and the *Avon,* had disappeared from the face of the ocean, and was supposed to be lost. But there was no proof of it, and, of course, for a time, hopes were entertained that she might be heard from. Long after the last real chance had utterly vanished, I pleased myself with the fond illusion that somewhere on the waste of waters she was still floating, and there were *years* during which I never heard the sound of the great gun booming inland from the Navy-Yard without saying to myself, "The *Wasp*

[1] *Institutes* [foundations] *of the Christian Religion,* by John Calvin, Basel, 1536
[2] the most famous Italian painter and sculptor respectively
[3] The sybils were said to have written their prophecies and omens on separate leaves. Once the order was lost the meaning could scarcely be unraveled, though none the less momentous. See *Aeneid,* iii, 444; vi, 74.
[4] an American warship, built in 1814, which overcame the *Reindeer* June 28, and the *Avon* Sept. 1, then hailed another vessel Oct. 9, but was never heard from again

has come!" and almost thinking I could see her, as she rolled in, crumpling the water before her, weather-beaten, barnacled, with shattered spars and threadbare canvas, welcomed by the shouts and tears of thousands. This was one of those dreams that I nursed and never told. Let me make a clean breast of it now, and say, that, so late as to have outgrown childhood, perhaps to have got far on towards manhood, when the roar of the cannon has struck suddenly on my ear, I have started with a thrill of vague expectation and tremulous delight, and the long-unspoken words have articulated themselves in the mind's dumb whisper, *The Wasp has come!*

——Yes, children believe plenty of queer things. I suppose all of you have had the pocketbook fever when you were little?— What do I mean? Why, ripping up old pocketbooks in the firm belief that bank-bills to an immense amount were hidden in them.—So, too, you must all remember some splendid unfulfilled promise of somebody or other, which fed you with hopes perhaps for years, and which left a blank in your life which nothing has ever filled up.—O. T.[1] quitted our household carrying with him the passionate regrets of the more youthful members. He was an ingenious youngster; wrote wonderful copies, and carved the two initials given above with great skill on all available surfaces. I thought, by the way, they were all gone; but the other day I found them on a certain door which I will show you some time. How it surprised me to find them so near the ground! I had thought the boy of no trivial dimensions. Well, O. T., when he went, made a solemn promise to two of us. I was to have a ship, and the other a mar*tin*-house (last syllable pronounced as in the word *tin*). Neither ever came; but, oh, how many and many a time I have stolen to the corner,—the cars pass close by it at this time,—and looked up that long avenue, thinking that he must be coming now, almost sure, as I turned to look northward, that there he would be, trudging towards me, the ship in one hand and the mar*tin*-house in the other!

[You must not suppose that all I am going to say, as well as all I have said, was told to the whole company. The young fellow whom they call John was in the yard, sitting on a barrel and smoking a cheroot, the fumes of which came in, not ungrateful, through the open window. The divinity-student disappeared in the midst of our talk. The poor relation in

[1] possibly some youthful chore-boy

black bombazine, who looked and moved as if all her articulations were elbow-joints, had gone off to her chamber, after waiting with a look of soul-subduing decorum at the foot of the stairs until one of the male sort had passed her and ascended into the upper regions. This is a famous point of etiquette in our boarding-house; in fact, between ourselves, they make such an awful fuss about it, that I, for one, had a great deal rather have them simple enough not to think of such matters at all. Our landlady's daughter said, the other evening, that she was going to "retire"; whereupon the young fellow called John took up a lamp and insisted on lighting her to the foot of the staircase. Nothing would induce her to pass by him, until the schoolmistress, saying in good plain English that it was her bedtime, walked straight by them both, not seeming to trouble herself about either of them.

I have been led away from what I meant the portion included in these brackets to inform my readers about. I say, then, most of the boarders had left the table about the time when I began telling some of these secrets of mine,—all of them, in fact, but the old gentleman opposite and the schoolmistress. I understand why a young woman should like to hear these simple but genuine experiences of early life, which are, as I have said, the little brown seeds of what may yet grow to be poems with leaves of azure and gold; but when the old gentleman pushed up his chair nearer to me, and slanted round his best ear, and once, when I was speaking of some trifling, tender reminiscence, drew a long breath, with such a tremor in it that a little more and it would have been a sob, why, then, I felt there must be something of nature in them which redeemed their seeming insignificance. Tell me, man or woman with whom I am whispering, have you not a small store of recollections, such as these I am uncovering, buried beneath the dead leaves of many summers, perhaps under the unmelting snows of fast-returning winters,—a few such recollections, which, if you should write them all out, would be swept into some careless editor's drawer, and might cost a scanty half-hour's lazy reading to his subscribers,—and yet, if Death should cheat you out of them, you would not know yourself in eternity?]

——I made three acquaintances at a very early period of life, my introduction to whom was never forgotten. The first unequivocal act of wrong that has left its trace in my memory was this: refusing a small favor asked of me,— nothing more than telling what had happened at school one morning. No matter who asked it; but there were circumstances which saddened and awed me. I had no heart to speak;—I faltered some miserable, perhaps petulant excuse, stole away, and the first battle of life was lost. What remorse followed I need not tell. Then and there, to the best of my knowledge, I first consciously took Sin by the hand and turned my back on Duty. Time has led me to look upon my offense more leniently; I do not believe it or any other childish wrong is infinite, as some have pretended, but infinitely finite. Yet, oh, if I had but won that battle!

The great Destroyer, whose awful shadow it was that had silenced me, came near me,—but never, so as to be distinctly seen and remembered, during my tender years. There flits dimly before me the image of a little girl, whose name even I have forgotten, a schoolmate, whom we missed one day, and were told that she had died. But what death was I never had any very distinct idea, until one day I climbed the low stone wall of the old burial-ground and mingled with a group that were looking into a very deep, long, narrow hole, dug down through the green sod, down through the brown loam, down through the yellow gravel, and there at the bottom was an oblong red box, and a still, sharp, white face of a young man seen through an opening at one end of it. When the lid was closed, and the gravel and stones rattled down pell-mell, and the woman in black, who was crying and wringing her hands, went off with the other mourners, and left him, then I felt that I had seen Death, and should never forget him.

One other acquaintance I made at an earlier period of life than the habit of romancers authorizes.—Love, of course.—She was a famous beauty afterwards.—I am satisfied that many children rehearse their parts in the drama of life before they have shed all their milk-teeth.—I think I won't tell the story of the golden blonde.—I suppose everybody has had his childish fancies; but sometimes they are passionate impulses, which anticipate all the tremulous emotions belonging to a later period. Most children remember seeing and adoring an angel before they were a dozen years old.

[The old gentleman had left his chair opposite and taken a seat by the schoolmistress and myself, a little way from the table.—It's true, it's true,—said the old gentleman.—He took hold of a steel watch-chain, which carried a large, square gold key at one end and was supposed to have some kind of timekeeper at the other. With some trouble he dragged up an ancient-looking, thick, silver, bull's-eye watch. He looked at it for a moment,—hesitated,—touched the inner corner of his right eye with the pulp of his middle finger,—looked at the face of the watch,—said it was getting into the forenoon,—then opened the watch and handed me the loose outside case without a word.—The watch-paper had been pink once, and had a faint tinge still, as if all its tender life had not yet quite faded out. Two little birds, a flower, and, in small school-girl letters, a date,—17..—no matter.—Before I was thirteen years old,—said the old gentleman.—I don't know what was in that young schoolmistress's head, nor why she should have done it; but she took out the watch-paper and put it softly to her lips, as if she were kissing the poor thing that made it so long ago. The old gentleman took the watch-paper carefully from her, replaced it, turned away and walked out, holding the watch in his hand. I saw him pass the window a moment after with that foolish white hat on his head; he couldn't have been thinking of what he was about when he put it on. So the schoolmistress and I were left alone. I drew my chair a shade nearer to her, and continued.]

And since I am talking of early recollections, I don't know why I shouldn't mention some others that still cling to me,—not that you will attach any very particular meaning to these same images so full of significance to me, but that you will find something parallel to them in your own memory. You remember, perhaps, what I said one day about smells. There were certain *sounds* also which had a mysterious suggestiveness to me,—not so intense, perhaps, as that connected with the other sense, but yet peculiar, and never to be forgotten.

The first was the creaking of the wood-sleds, bringing their loads of oak and walnut from the country, as the slow-swinging oxen trailed them along over the complaining snow, in the cold, brown light of early morning. Lying in bed and listening to their dreary music had a pleasure in it akin to the Lucretian luxury, [1] or that which Byron speaks of as to be enjoyed in looking on at a battle by one "who hath no friend, no brother there." [2]

There was another sound, in itself so sweet, and so connected with one of those simple and curious superstitions of childhood of which I have spoken, that I can never cease to cherish

[1] Later editions of the *Autocrat* read: "Akin to that which Lucretius describes in witnessing a ship toiling through the waves while we sit at ease on shore." Cf. Lucretius, *De Rerum Natura*, Bk. II, i, 1.

[2] *Childe Harold* i, 40

a sad sort of love for it. Let me tell the superstitious fancy first. The Puritan "Sabbath," as everybody knows, began at "sundown" on Saturday evening. To such observance of it I was born and bred. As the large, round disk of day declined, a stillness, a solemnity, a somewhat melancholy hush came over us all. It was time for work to cease, and for playthings to be put away. The world of active life passed into the shadow of an eclipse, not to emerge until the sun should sink again beneath the horizon.

It was in this stillness of the world without and of the soul within that the pulsating lullaby of the evening crickets used to make itself most distinctly heard,—so that I well remember I used to think that the purring of these little creatures, which mingled with the batrachian hymns [1] from the neighboring swamp, *was peculiar to Saturday evenings.* I don't know that anything could give a clearer idea of the quieting and subduing effect of the old habit of observance of what was considered holy time, than this strange, childish fancy.

Yes, and there was still another sound which mingled its solemn cadences with the waking and sleeping dreams of my boyhood. It was heard only at times,—a deep, muffled roar, which rose and fell, not loud, but vast,—a whistling boy would have drowned it for his next neighbor, but it must have been heard over the space of a hundred square miles. I used to wonder what this might be. Could it be the roar of the thousand wheels and the ten thousand footsteps jarring and trampling along the stones of the neighboring city? That would be continuous; but this, as I have said, rose and fell in regular rhythm. I remember being told, and I suppose this to have been the true solution, that it was the sound of the waves, after a high wind, breaking on the long beaches many miles distant. I should really like to know whether any observing people living ten miles, more or less, inland from long beaches,—in such a town, for instance, as Cantabridge, in the eastern part of the Territory of the Massachusetts,—have ever observed any such sound, and whether it was rightly accounted for as above.

Mingling with these inarticulate sounds in the low murmur of memory, are the echoes of certain voices I have heard at rare intervals. I grieve to say it, but our people, I think, have not generally agreeable voices. The marrowy organisms, with skins that shed water like the backs of ducks, with smooth surfaces neatly

[1] frog choruses

padded beneath, and velvet linings to their singing-pipes, are not so common among us as that other pattern of humanity with angular outlines and plane surfaces, arid integuments, hair like the fibrous covering of a cocoa-nut in gloss and suppleness as well as color, and voices at once thin and strenuous;—acidulous enough to produce effervescence with alkalis, and stridulous enough to sing duets with the katydids. I think our conversational soprano, as sometimes overheard in the cars, arising from a group of young persons, who may have taken the train at one of our great industrial centers, for instance,—young persons of the female sex, we will say, who have bustled in, full-dressed, engaged in loud strident speech, and who, after free discussion, have fixed on two or more double seats, which having secured, they proceed to eat apples and hand round daguerreotypes,—I say, I think the conversational soprano, heard under these circumstances, would not be among the allurements the old Enemy would put in requisition, were he getting up a new temptation of St. Anthony. [2]

There are sweet voices among us, we all know, and voices not musical, it may be, to those who hear them for the first time, yet sweeter to us than any we shall hear until we listen to some warbling angel in the overture to that eternity of blissful harmonies we hope to enjoy. But why should I tell lies? If my friends love me, it is because I try to tell the truth. I never heard but two voices in my life that frightened me by their sweetness.

——Frightened you?—said the schoolmistress.—Yes, frightened me. They made me feel as if there might be constituted a creature with such a chord in her voice to some string in another's soul, that, if she but spoke, he would leave all and follow her, though it were into the jaws of Erebus. [3] Our only chance to keep our wits is, that there are so few natural chords between others' voices and this string in our souls, and that those which at first may have jarred a little, by-and-by come into harmony with it.—But I tell you this is no fiction. You may call the story of Ulysses and the Sirens a fable, but what will you say to Mario and the poor lady who followed him? [4]

[2] Anthony the Great 251-356, an ascetic, was often sorely tempted by the devil who, he said, appeared to him in the shape of beautiful women.

[3] hell

[4] The sirens by their sweet music tempted sailors to turn aside from their course only to be dashed upon treacherous rocks. Mario, 1810-1883, was an Italian opera singer. A lady, whose name is not given and who never spoke to him nor sought to win his favor, was, throughout thirty years, present at all but three performances of his.

——Whose were those two voices that bewitched me so?—They both belonged to German women. One was a chambermaid, not otherwise fascinating. The key of my room at a certain great hotel was missing, and this Teutonic maiden was summoned to give information respecting it. The simple soul was evidently not long from her motherland, and spoke with sweet uncertainty of dialect. But to hear her wonder and lament and suggest, with soft, liquid inflections, and low, sad murmurs, in tones as full of serious tenderness for the fate of the lost key as if it had been a child that had strayed from its mother, was so winning, that, had her features and figure been as delicious as her accents,—if she had looked like the marble Clytie, [1] for instance,—why, all I can say is——

[The schoolmistress opened her eyes so wide, that I stopped short.]

I was only going to say that I should have drowned myself. For Lake Erie was close by and it is so much better to accept asphyxia, which takes only three minutes by the watch, than a *mésalliance,* that lasts fifty years to begin with, and then passes along down the line of descent, (breaking out in all manner of boorish manifestations of feature and manner, which, if men were only as short-lived as horses, could be readily traced back through the square-roots and the cube-roots of the family stem on which you have hung the armorial bearings of the De Champignons or the De la Morues, [2] until one came to beings that ate with knives and said "Haow?"), that no person of right feeling could have hesitated for a single moment.

The second of the ravishing voices I have heard, was, as I have said, that of another German woman.—I suppose I shall ruin myself by saying that such a voice could not have come from any Americanized human being.

——What was there in it?—said the schoolmistress,—and, upon my word, her tones were so very musical, that I almost wished I had said three voices instead of two, and not made the unpatriotic remark above reported.—Oh, I said, it had so much *woman* in it,—*muliebrity,* [3] as well as *femineity;*—no self-assertion, such as free suffrage introduces into every word and movement; large, vigorous nature, running back to those huge-limbed Germans of Tacitus, [4] but

subdued by the reverential training and tuned by the kindly culture of fifty generations. Sharp business habits, a lean soil, independence, enterprise, and east winds, are not the best things for the larynx. Still, you hear noble voices among us,—I have known families famous for them,—but ask the first person you meet a question, and ten to one there is a hard, sharp, metallic, matter-of-business clink in the accents of the answer, that produces the effect of one of those bells which small trades-people connect with their shop-doors, and which spring upon your ear with such vivacity, as you enter, that your first impulse is to retire at once from the precincts.

——Ah, but I must not forget that dear little child I saw and heard in a French hospital. Between two and three years old. Fell out of her chair and snapped both thigh-bones. Lying in bed, patient, gentle. Rough students round her, some in white aprons, looking fearfully business-like; but the child placid, perfectly still. I spoke to her, and the blessed little creature answered me in a voice of such heavenly sweetness, with that reedy thrill in it which you have heard in the thrush's even-song, that I hear it at this moment, while I am writing, so many, many years afterwards.—*C'est tout comme un serin* [5] said the French student at my side.

These are the voices which struck the keynote of my conceptions as to what the sounds we are to hear in heaven will be, if we shall enter through one of the twelve gates of pearl. There must be other things besides aërolites that wander from their own spheres to ours; and when we speak of celestial sweetness or beauty, we may be nearer the literal truth than we dream. If mankind generally are the ship-wrecked survivors of some pre-Adamitic cataclysm, set adrift in these little open boats of humanity to make one more trial to reach the shore,—as some grave theologians have maintained,—if, in plain English, men are the ghosts of dead devils who have "died into life," (to borrow an expression from Keats), and walk the earth in a suit of living rags which lasts three or four score summers,—why, there must have been a few good spirits sent to keep them company, and these sweet voices I speak of must belong to them.

——I wish you could once hear my sister's voice,—said the schoolmistress.

If it is like yours, it must be a pleasant one,—said I.

I never thought mine was anything,—said the schoolmistress.

[1] A nymph beloved by Apollo; a Clytie in marble was a frequent New England parlor decoration in Holmes's day.
[2] the De Mushrooms and De la Codfishes: the newly rich
[3] *Mulier* is Latin for *woman.*
[4] Roman historian, 55-117, author of *De Germania,* the first systematic description of the Germans

[5] "It is quite like a canary."

How should you know?—said I.—People never hear their own voices,—any more than they see their own faces. There is not even a looking-glass for the voice. Of course, there is something audible to us when we speak; but that something is not our own voice as it is known to all our acquaintances. I think, if an image spoke to us in our own tones, we should not know them in the least.—How pleasant it would be, if in another state of being we could have shapes like our former selves for play-things,—we standing outside or inside of them, as we liked, and they being to us just what we used to be to others!

——I wonder if there will be nothing like what we call "play," after our earthly toys are broken,—said the schoolmistress.

Hush,—said I,—what will the divinity-student say?

[I thought she was hit, that time;—but the shot must have gone over her, or on one side of her; she did not flinch.]

Oh,—said the schoolmistress,—he must look out for my sister's heresies; I am afraid he will be too busy with them to take care of mine.

Do you mean to say,—said I,—that it is *your sister* whom that student——

[The young fellow commonly known as John, who had been sitting on the barrel, smoking, jumped off just then, kicked over the barrel, gave it a push with his foot that set it rolling, and stuck his saucy-looking face in at the window so as to cut my question off in the middle; and the schoolmistress leaving the room a few minutes afterwards, I did not have a chance to finish it.

The young fellow came in and sat down in a chair, putting his heels on the top of another.

Pooty girl,—said he.

A fine young lady,—I replied.

Keeps a fust-rate school, according to accounts,—said he,—teaches all sorts of things,—Latin and Italian and music. Folks rich once,—smashed up. She went right ahead as smart as if she'd been born to work. That's the kind o' girl I go for. I'd marry her, only two or three other girls would drown themselves, if I did.

I think the above is the longest speech of this young fellow's which I have put on record. I do not like to change his peculiar expressions, for this is one of those cases in which the style is the man, as M. de Buffon[1] says. The fact is, the young fellow is a good-hearted creature

[1] Count de Buffon, 1707-1788, a French naturalist celebrated in literature for his essay on style which contains the words quoted, "Le style est l'homme même."

enough, only too fond of his jokes,—and if it were not for those heat-lightning winks on one side of his face, I should not mind his fun much.]

· · · · · ·

From XI

· · · · · ·

——Should you like to hear what moderate wishes life brings one to at last? I used to be very ambitious,—wasteful, extravagant, and luxurious in all my fancies. Read too much in the *Arabian Nights*. Must have the lamp,—couldn't do without the ring. Exercise every morning on the brazen horse. Plump down into castles as full of little milk-white princesses as a nest is of young sparrows. All love me dearly at once.—Charming idea of life, but too high-colored for the reality. I have outgrown all this; my tastes have become exceedingly primitive,—almost, perhaps, ascetic. We carry happiness into our condition, but must not hope to find it there. I think you will be willing to hear some lines which embody the subdued and limited desires of my maturity.

CONTENTMENT

"Man wants but little here below."[2]

Little I ask; my wants are few;
  I only wish a hut of stone,
(A *very plain* brown stone will do,)
    That I may call my own;—
And close at hand is such a one,
In yonder street that fronts the sun.

Plain food is quite enough for me;
  Three courses are as good as ten;—
If Nature can subsist on three,
    Thank Heaven for three. Amen!   10
I always thought cold victual nice;—
My *choice* would be vanilla-ice.

I care not much for gold or land;—
  Give me a mortgage here and there,—
Some good bank-stock,—some note of hand,
    Or trifling railroad share;—
I only ask that Fortune send
A *little* more than I shall spend.

Honors are silly toys, I know,
  And titles are but empty names;—   20
I would, *perhaps*, be Plenipo,—[3]

[2] Goldsmith, *The Hermit*, stanza eight, but probably taken by Goldsmith from Young's *Night Thoughts*, iv, 118, "Man wants but little, nor that little long."
[3] Minister Plenipotentiary—a representative of a country sent to a foreign state

But only near St. James;—
I'm very sure I should not care
To fill our Gubernator's chair.

Jewels are baubles; 'tis a sin
    To care for such unfruitful things;—
One good-sized diamond in a pin,—
        Some, *not so large*, in rings,—
A ruby, and a pearl, or so,
Will do for me;—I laugh at show.   30

My dame should dress in cheap attire;
    (Good, heavy silks are never dear;)
I own perhaps I *might* desire
        Some shawls of true cashmere,—
Some marrowy crapes of China silk,
Like wrinkled skins on scalded milk.

I would not have the horse I drive
    So fast that folks must stop and stare;
An easy gait—two, forty-five,—
        Suits me; I do not care;—   40
Perhaps, for just a *single spurt*,
Some seconds less would do no hurt.

Of pictures, I should like to own
    Titians and Raphaels three or four.—
I love so much their style and tone,—
        One Turner, and no more,—[1]
(A landscape,—foreground golden dirt,—
The sunshine painted with a squirt.)

Of books but few,—some fifty score
    For daily use, and bound for wear;   50
The rest upon an upper floor;—
        Some *little* luxury *there*
Of red morocco's gilded gleam,
And vellum rich as country cream.

Busts, cameos, gems,—such things as these,
    Which others often show for pride,
I value, for their power to please,
        And selfish churls deride;—
One Stradivarius, I confess,
Two Meerschaums, I would fain possess.   60

Wealth's wasteful tricks I will not learn,
    Nor ape the glittering upstart fool;—
Shall not carved tables serve my turn,
        But *all* must be of buhl?[2]
Give grasping pomp its double share,—
I ask but *one* recumbent chair.

[1] The paintings of the Italians Titian (1477-1576) and Raphael (1483-1520) and of the English Turner (1775-1851) are of priceless value.
[2] inlaid work of tortoise shell, mother of pearl, and **metal**

Thus humble let me live and die,
    Nor long for Midas' golden touch;[3]
If Heaven more generous gifts deny,
        I shall not miss them *much*,—   70
Too grateful for the blessing lent
Of simple tastes and mind content!

MY LAST WALK WITH THE SCHOOL-MISTRESS

(*A Parenthesis*)

I can't say just how many walks she and I had taken together before this one. I found the effect of going out every morning was decidedly favorable on her health. Two pleasing dimples, the places for which were just marked when she came, played, shadowy, in her freshening cheeks when she smiled and nodded good-morning to me from the school-house-steps.

I am afraid I did the greater part of the talking. At any rate, if I should try to report all that I said during the first half-dozen walks we took together, I fear that I might receive a gentle hint from my friends the publishers, that a separate volume, at my own risk and expense, would be the proper method of bringing them before the public.

——I would have a woman as true as Death. At the first real lie which works from the heart outward, she should be tenderly chloroformed into a better world, where she can have an angel for a governess, and feed on strange fruits which will make her all over again, even to her bones and marrow.—Whether gifted with the accident of beauty or not, she should have been molded in the rose-red clay of Love, before the breath of life made a moving mortal of her. Love-capacity is a congenital endowment; and I think, after a while, one gets to know the warm-hued natures it belongs to from the pretty pipe-clay counterfeits of them.—Proud she may be, in the sense of respecting herself; but pride, in the sense of contemning others less gifted than herself, deserves the two lowest circles of a vulgar woman's Inferno, where the punishments are Smallpox and Bankruptcy.—She who nips off the end of a brittle courtesy, as one breaks the tip of an icicle, to bestow upon those whom she ought cordially and kindly to recognize, proclaims the fact that she comes not merely of low blood, but of bad blood. Consciousness of unquestioned position makes people gracious in proper measure to all; but if a woman puts on airs with her real equals, she has something about herself or her family she

[3] In the Greek myth, everything King Midas touched turned to gold—even his food.

is ashamed of, or ought to be. Middle, and more than middle-aged people, who know family histories, generally see through it. An official of standing was rude to me once. Oh, that is the maternal grandfather,—said a wise old friend to me,—he was a boor.—Better too few words, from the woman we love, than too many: while she is silent, Nature is working for her; while she talks, she is working for herself.—Love is sparingly soluble in the words of men; therefore they speak much of it; but one syllable of woman's speech can dissolve more of it than a man's heart can hold.

——Whether I said any or all of these things to the schoolmistress, or not,—whether I stole them out of Lord Bacon,—whether I cribbed them from Balzac,[1] whether I dipped them from the ocean of Tupperian wisdom,—or whether I have just found them in my head, laid there by that solemn fowl, Experience (who, according to my observation, cackles oftener than she drops real live eggs), I cannot say. Wise men have said more foolish things,—and foolish men, I don't doubt, have said as wise things. Anyhow, the schoolmistress and I had pleasant walks and long talks, all of which I do not feel bound to report.

——You are a stranger to me, Ma'am.—I don't doubt you would like to know all I said to the schoolmistress.—I sha'n't do it;—I had rather get the publishers to return the money you have invested in this. Besides, I have forgotten a good deal of it. I shall tell only what I like of what I remember.

——My idea was, in the first place, to search out the picturesque spots which the city affords a sight of, to those who have eyes. I know a good many, and it was a pleasure to look at them in company with my young friend. There were the shrubs and flowers in the Franklin-Place front-yards or borders. Commerce is just putting his granite foot upon them. Then there are certain small seraglio-gardens, into which one can get a peep through the crevices of high fences,—one in Myrtle Street, or backing on it,—here and there one at the North and South Ends. Then the great elms in Essex Street. Then the stately horse-chestnuts in that vacant lot in Chambers Street, which hold their outspread hands over your head, (as I said in my poem the other day,) and look as if they were whispering, "May grace, mercy, and peace be with you!"—and the rest of that benediction. Nay, there are certain patches of ground, which,

having lain neglected for a time, Nature, who always has her pockets full of seeds, and holes in all her pockets, has covered with hungry plebeian growths, which fight for life with each other, until some of them get broad-leaved and succulent, and you have a coarse vegetable tapestry which Raphael would not have disdained to spread over the foreground of his masterpiece. The Professor pretends that he found such a one in Charles Street, which, in its daredevil impudence of rough-and-tumble vegetation, beat the pretty-behaved flower-beds of the Public Garden as ignominiously as a group of young tatterdemalions playing pitch-and-toss beats a row of Sunday-school-boys with their teacher at their head.

But then the Professor has one of his burrows in that region, and puts everything in high colors relating to it. This is his way about everything——I hold any man cheap,—he said, —of whom nothing stronger can be uttered than that all his geese are swans.——How is that, Professor?—said I;—I should have set you down for one of that sort.——Sir,—said he,—I am proud to say, that Nature has so far enriched me, that I cannot own so much as a *duck* without seeing in it as pretty a swan as ever swam the basin in the garden of the Luxembourg.[2] And the Professor showed the whites of his eyes devoutly, like one returning thanks after a dinner of many courses.

I don't know anything sweeter than this leaking in of Nature through all the cracks in the walls and floors of cities. You heap up a million tons of hewn rocks on a square mile or two of earth which was green once. The trees look down from the hill-sides and ask each other, as they stand on tiptoe,—"What are these people about?" And the small herbs at their feet look up and whisper back,—"We will go and see." So the small herbs pack themselves up in the least possible bundles, and wait until the wind steals to them at night and whispers, —"Come with me." Then they go softly with it into the great city,—one to a cleft in the pavement, one to a spout on the roof, one to a seam in the marbles over a rich gentleman's bones, and one to the grave without a stone where nothing but a man is buried,—and there they grow, looking down on the generations of men from moldy roofs, looking up from between the less-trodden pavements, looking out through iron cemetery-railings. Listen to them, when there is only a light breath stirring, and you will hear them saying to each other,—

---

[1] The great French novelist, 1799-1850; Martin Farquhar Tupper, 1810-1889, an inferior English didactic poet, at one time was very popular.

[2] The palace of the Luxembourg in Paris has beautiful formal gardens surrounding an artificial lake.

"Wait awhile!" The words run along the telegraph of those narrow green lines that border the roads leading from the city, until they reach the slope of the hills, and the trees repeat in low murmurs to each other,—"Wait awhile!" By-and-by the flow of life in the streets ebbs and the old leafy inhabitants—the smaller tribes always in front—saunter in, one by one, very careless, seemingly, but very tenacious, until they swarm so that the great stones gape from each other with the crowding of their roots, and the feldspar begins to be picked out of the granite to find them food. At last the trees take up their solemn line of march, and never rest until they have encamped in the market-place. Wait long enough and you will find an old doting oak hugging a huge worn block in its yellow underground arms; that was the cornerstone of the State-House. Oh, so patient is she, this imperturbable Nature!

——Let us cry!——

But all this has nothing to do with my walks and talks with the schoolmistress. I did not say that I would not tell you something about them. Let me alone, and I shall talk to you more than I ought to, probably. We never tell our secrets to people that pump for them.

Books we talked about, and education. It was her duty to know something of these, and of course she did. Perhaps I was somewhat more learned than she, but I found that the difference between her reading and mine was like that of a man's and a woman's dusting a library. The man flaps about with a bunch of feathers; the woman goes to work softly with a cloth. She does not raise half the dust, nor fill her own eyes and mouth with it,—but she goes into all the corners and attends to the leaves as much as to the covers.—Books are the *negative* pictures of thought, and the more sensitive the mind that receives their images, the more nicely the finest lines are reproduced. A woman (of the right kind), reading after a man, follows him as Ruth followed the reapers of Boaz, [1] and her gleanings are often the finest of the wheat.

But it was in talking of Life that we came most nearly together. I thought I knew something about that,—that I could speak or write about it somewhat to the purpose.

To take up this fluid earthly being of ours as a sponge sucks up water,—to be steeped and soaked in its realities as a hide fills its pores lying seven years in a tan-pit,—to have winnowed every wave of it as a mill-wheel works up the stream that runs through the flume

upon its float-boards,—to have curled up in the keenest spasms and flattened out in the laxest languors of this breathing-sickness, which keeps certain parcels of matter uneasy for three or four score years,—to have fought all the devils and clasped all the angels of its delirium,—and then, just at the point when the white-hot passions have cooled down to cherry-red, plunge our experience into the ice-cold stream of some human language or other, one might think would end in a rhapsody with something of spring and temper in it. All this I thought my power and province.

The schoolmistress had tried life, too. Once in a while one meets with a single soul greater than all the living pageant which passes before it. As the pale astronomer sits in his study with sunken eyes and thin fingers, and weighs Uranus or Neptune as in a balance, so there are meek, slight women who have weighed all which this planetary life can offer, and hold it like a bauble in the palm of their slender hands. This was one of them. Fortune had left her, sorrow had baptized her; the routine of labor and the loneliness of almost friendless city-life were before her. Yet, as I looked upon her tranquil face, gradually regaining a cheerfulness which was often sprightly, as she became interested in the various matters we talked about and places we visited, I saw that eye and lip and every shifting lineament were made for love,—unconscious of their sweet office as yet, and meeting the cold aspect of Duty with the natural graces which were meant for the reward of nothing less than the Great Passion.

——I never addressed one word of love to the schoolmistress in the course of these pleasant walks. It seemed to me that we talked of everything but love on that particular morning. There was, perhaps, a little more timidity and hesitancy on my part than I have commonly shown among our people at the boarding-house. In fact, I considered myself the master at the breakfast-table; but, somehow, I could not command myself just then so well as usual. The truth is, I had secured a passage to Liverpool in the steamer which was to leave at noon, —with the condition, however, of being released in case circumstances occurred to detain me. The schoolmistress knew nothing about all this, of course, as yet.

It was on the Common that we were walking. The *mall* or boulevard of our Common, you know, has various branches leading from it in different directions. One of these runs down from opposite Joy Street southward across the whole length of the Common to Boylston

[1] *Ruth* ii, 2

Street. We called it the long path, and were fond of it.

I felt very weak indeed (though of a tolerably robust habit) as we came opposite the head of this path on that morning. I think I tried to speak twice without making myself distinctly audible. At last I got out the question,—Will you take the long path with me?——Certainly, —said the schoolmistress,—with much pleasure. ——Think,—I said,—before you answer: if you take the long path with me now, I shall interpret it that we are to part no more!—— The schoolmistress stepped back with a sudden movement, as if an arrow had struck her.

One of the long granite blocks used as seats was hard by,—the one you may still see close by the Gingko-tree.—Pray, sit down,—I said. ——No, no, she answered, softly,—I will walk the *long path* with you!

——The old gentleman who sits opposite met us walking, arm in arm, about the middle of the long path, and said, very charmingly,— "Good-morning, my dears!"

1858

JAMES RUSSELL LOWELL
1819-1891

None other of the major American writers of the nineteenth century was so closely connected with Cambridge and Harvard as Lowell. The old colonial mansion in which he was born, where he did his most important literary work and where he died, still stands in Cambridge; almost in sight, in Mount Auburn, is the plain gravestone beneath which he is buried. Yet no American man of letters had more varied interests and wider experiences. Lowell was of intellectual ancestry. He was graduated from Harvard, 1838, studied law, but soon gave this over for literature. He became professor of modern languages at Harvard, 1855, and was editor of the *Atlantic Monthly*, 1857-1862, and of the *North American Review*, 1863-1872. He was minister to Spain, 1877-1880, and to England, 1880-1885. His poems appeared at various dates from 1841 to 1888. His most notable prose works are *Conversations on Some Old Poets*, 1845; *Among my Books*, 1870, 1876; *My Study Windows*, 1871; *Democracy and Other Addresses*, 1886; *The Old English Dramatists*, 1892.

In breadth of experience and the variety of his interests, Lowell differs from Longfellow, whom he followed in the chair of languages at Harvard. Lowell was not only a teacher and a poet, but an editor, an essayist, a publicist, and a successful foreign minister. Some of his early poetry has many of the characteristics of Longfellow's, though it is more personal and appealing. The Bigelow papers and the odes occasioned by the Civil War

outrank in their kind the work of any of his contemporaries, for they have a virility and a largeness of view characteristically Lowell's own. In his essays we find sound judgment, wisdom, and a humor that sweetens and keeps all in balance.

Biography: It was expected by Lowell that his letters edited by C. E. Norton, 2 vols. 1894, 3 vols. 1904, would sufficiently tell the story of his life. See also H. E. Scudder, 1901; E. E. Hale (BB); F. Greenslet (AML); F. Briggs (LJ). Recent criticism: Burton; Macy; Chubb; R. E. Roberts, "James Russell Lowell: a British Estimate," *Liv. Age* 301:231-5; W. B. Cairns, "James Russell Lowell: A Centenary View," *Nation* 108: 274-7; W. R. Thayer, "James Russell Lowell as a Teacher," *Scrib. M.* 68:473-80.

RHOECUS [1]

God sends his teachers unto every age,
To every clime, and every race of men,
With revelations fitted to their growth
And shape of mind, nor gives the realm of Truth
Into the selfish rule of one sole race:
Therefore each form of worship that hath
    swayed
The life of man, and given it to grasp
The master-key of knowledge, reverence,
Enfolds some germs of goodness and of right;
Else never had the eager soul, which loathes
The slothful down of pampered ignorance,   11
Found in it even a moment's fitful rest.

There is an instinct in the human heart
Which makes that all the fables it hath coined,
To justify the reign of its belief
And strengthen it by beauty's right divine,
Veil in their inner cells a mystic gift,
Which, like the hazel twig, in faithful hands,
Points surely to the hidden springs of truth.
For, as in nature naught is made in vain,   20
But all things have within their hull of use
A wisdom and a meaning which may speak
Of spiritual secrets to the ear
Of spirit; so, in whatsoe'er the heart
Hath fashioned for a solace to itself,
To make its inspirations suit its creed,
And from the niggard hands of falsehood wring
Its needful food of truth, there ever is
A sympathy with Nature, which reveals,
Not less than her own works, pure gleams of
    light   30
And earnest parables of inward lore.
Hear now this fairy legend of old Greece,
As full of gracious youth, and beauty still
As the immortal freshness of that grace
Carved for all ages on some Attic frieze.

[1] Another treatment of the theme of Rhoecus is found in Walter Savage Landor's "Hamadryad."

A youth named Rhoecus, wandering in the
    wood,
Saw an old oak just trembling to its fall,
And, feeling pity of so fair a tree,
He propped its gray trunk with admiring care,
And with a thoughtless footstep loitered on. 40
But, as he turned, he heard a voice behind
That murmured "Rhoecus!" 'T was as if the
    leaves,
Stirred by a passing breath, had murmured it,
And, while he paused bewildered, yet again
It murmured "Rhoecus!" softer than a breeze.
He started and beheld with dizzy eyes
What seemed the substance of a happy dream
Stand there before him, spreading a warm glow
Within the green glooms of the shadowy oak,
It seemed a woman's shape, yet far too fair   50
To be a woman, and with eyes too meek
For any that were wont to mate with gods.
All naked like a goddess stood she there,
And like a goddess all too beautiful
To feel the guilt-born earthliness of shame.
"Rhoecus, I am the Dryad of this tree,"
Thus she began, dropping her low-toned words
Serene, and full, and clear, as drops of dew,
"And with it I am doomed to live and die;
The rain and sunshine are my caterers,   60
Nor have I other bliss than simple life;
Now ask me what thou wilt, that I can give,
And with a thankful joy it shall be thine."

Then Rhoecus, with a flutter at the heart,
Yet, by the prompting of such beauty, bold,
Answered: "What is there that can satisfy
The endless craving of the soul but love?
Give me thy love, or but the hope of that
Which must be evermore my spirit's goal."
After a little pause she said again,   70
But with a glimpse of sadness in her tone,
"I give it, Rhoecus, though a perilous gift;
An hour before the sunset meet me here."
And straightway there was nothing he could see
But the green glooms beneath the shadowy oak,
And not a sound came to his straining ears
But the low trickling rustle of the leaves,
And far away upon an emerald slope
The falter of an idle shepherd's pipe.   79

Now, in those days of simpleness and faith,
Men did not think that happy things were
    dreams
Because they overstepped the narrow bourne
Of likelihood, but reverently deemed
Nothing too wondrous or too beautiful
To be the guerdon of a daring heart.
So Rhoecus made no doubt that he was blest,
And all along unto the city's gate

Earth seemed to spring beneath him as he
    walked,
The clear, broad sky looked bluer than its wont,
And he could scarce believe he had not wings,
Such sunshine seemed to glitter through his
    veins   91
Instead of blood, so light he felt and strange.

Young Rhoecus had a faithful heart enough,
But one that in the present dwelt too much,
And, taking with blithe welcome whatsoe'er
Chance gave of joy, was wholly bound in that,
Like the contented peasant of a vale,
Deemed it the world, and never looked beyond.
So, haply meeting in the afternoon
Some comrades who were playing at the dice,
He joined them and forgot all else beside.   101

The dice were rattling at the merriest,
And Rhoecus, who had met but sorry luck,
Just laughed in triumph at a happy throw,
When through the room there hummed a yellow
    bee
That buzzed about his ear with down-dropped
    legs
As if to light. And Rhoecus laughed and said,
Feeling how red and flushed he was with loss,
"By Venus! does he take me for a rose?"
And brushed him off with rough, impatient
    hand.   110
But still the bee came back, and thrice again
Rhoecus did beat him off with growing wrath.
Then through the window flew the wounded bee,
And Rhoecus, tracking him with angry eyes,
Saw a sharp mountain-peak of Thessaly
Against the red disc of the setting sun,—
And instantly the blood sank from his heart,
As if its very walls had caved away.
Without a word he turned, and, rushing forth,
Ran madly through the city and the gate,   120
And o'er the plain, which now the wood's long
    shade,
By the low sun thrown forward broad and dim,
Darkened wellnigh unto the city's wall.

Quite spent and out of breath he reached the
    tree,
And, listening fearfully, he heard once more
The low voice murmur "Rhoecus!" close at
    hand:
Whereat he looked around him, but could see
Naught but the deepening glooms beneath the
    oak.
Then sighed the voice, "O Rhoecus! nevermore
Shalt thou behold me or by day or night,   130
Me, who would fain have blessed thee with a
    love

More ripe and bounteous than ever yet
Filled up with nectar any mortal heart:
But thou didst scorn my humble messenger,
And sent'st him back to me with bruised wings.
We spirits only show to gentle eyes.
We ever ask an undivided love,
And he who scorns the least of Nature's works
Is thenceforth exiled and shut out from all. 139
Farewell! for thou canst never see me more."

Then Rhoecus beat his breast, and groaned
    aloud,
And cried, "Be pitiful! forgive me yet
This once, and I shall never need it more!"
"Alas!" the voice returned, "'tis thou art
    blind, [1]
Not I unmerciful; I can forgive,
But have no skill to heal thy spirit's eyes;
Only the soul hath power o'er itself."
With that again there murmured "Nevermore!"
And Rhoecus after heard no other sound,
Except the rattling of the oak's crisp leaves,
Like the long surf upon a distant shore, 151
Raking the sea-worn pebbles up and down.
The night had gathered round him: o'er the
    plain
The city sparkled with its thousand lights,
And sounds of revel fell upon his ear
Harshly and like a curse; above, the sky,
With all its bright sublimity of stars,
Deepened, and on his forehead smote the
    breeze; 158
Beauty was all around him and delight,
But from that eve he was alone on earth.
                         1843

A CONTRAST

Thy love thou sentest oft to me,
  And still as oft I thrust it back;
Thy messengers I could not see
  In those who everything did lack,
  The poor, the outcast, and the black.

Pride held his hand before mine eyes,
  The world with flattery stuffed mine ears;
I looked to see a monarch's guise,
  Nor dreamed thy love would knock for
    years,
  Poor, naked, fettered, full of tears. 10

Yet, when I sent my love to thee,
  Thou with a smile didst take it in,
And entertain'dst it royally,
  Though grimed with earth, with hunger thin,
  And leprous with the taint of sin.

[1] In one version of the legend the dryad in anger deprived Rhoecus of his eyesight.

Now every day thy love I meet,
  As o'er the earth it wanders wide,
With weary step and bleeding feet,
  Still knocking at the heart of pride 19
  And offering grace, though still denied.
1845   *1845*

TO THE DANDELION

Dear common flower, that grow'st beside the
    way,
Fringing the dusty road with harmless gold,
  First pledge of blithesome May,
Which children pluck, and, full of pride, up-
    hold,
High-hearted buccaneers, o'erjoyed that they
An Eldorado in the grass have found,
  Which not the rich earth's ample round
  May match in wealth,—thou art more dear
    to me
Than all the prouder summer-blooms may
    be.

Gold such as thine ne'er drew the Spanish
    prow 10
Through the primeval hush of Indian seas,
  Nor wrinkled the lean brow
Of age, to rob the lover's heart of ease;
  'Tis the spring's largess, which she scatters
    now
To rich and poor alike, with lavish hand,
  Though most hearts never understand
To take it at God's value, but pass by
The offered wealth with unrewarded eye.

Thou art my tropics and mine Italy;
To look at thee unlocks a warmer clime; 20
  The eyes thou givest me
Are in the heart, and heed not space or time:
  Not in mid June the golden-cuirassed bee
Feels a more summer-like warm ravishment
  In the white lily's breezy tent,
  His fragrant Sybaris, [2] than I, when first
From the dark green thy yellow circles burst.

Then think I of deep shadows on the grass,
Of meadows where in sun the cattle graze,
  Where, as the breezes pass, 30
The gleaming rushes lean a thousand ways,
  Of leaves that slumber in a cloudy mass,
Or whiten in the wind, of waters blue
  That from the distance sparkle through
Some woodland gap, and of a sky above,
  Where one white cloud like a stray lamb
    doth move.

[2] an ancient Grecian city of southern Italy noted for its luxury

My childhood's earliest thoughts are linked
    with thee;
The sight of thee calls back the robin's song,
    Who, from the dark old tree
Beside the door, sang clearly all day long,
    And I, secure in childish piety,   41
Listened as if I heard an angel sing
    With news from heaven, which he could
        bring
    Fresh every day to my untainted ears,
When birds and flowers and I were happy
    peers.

How like a prodigal doth nature seem,
When thou, for all thy gold, so common art!
    Thou teachest me to deem
More sacredly of every human heart,   49
    Since each reflects in joy its scanty gleam
Of heaven, and could some wondrous secret
    show
    Did we but pay the love we owe,
And with a child's undoubting wisdom look
On all these living pages of God's book.
1845   1845

HEBE [1]

I saw the twinkle of white feet,
I saw the flash of robes descending;
    Before her ran an influence fleet,
That bowed my heart like barley bending.

As, in bare fields, the searching bees
Pilot to blooms beyond our finding,
    It led me on, by sweet degrees,
Joy's simple honey-cells unbinding.

Those Graces were that seemed grim Fates;
With nearer love the sky leaned o'er me;   10
    The long-sought Secret's golden gates
On musical hinges swung before me.

I saw the brimmed bowl in her grasp
Thrilling with godhood; like a lover
    I sprang the proffered life to clasp;—
The beaker fell; the luck was over.

The Earth has drunk the vintage up;
What boots it patch the goblet's splinters?
    Can summer fill the icy cup,
Whose treacherous crystal is but winter's?

O spendthrift, haste! await the Gods;   21
Their nectar crowns the lips of Patience;
    Haste scatters on unthankful sods
The immortal gift in vain libations.

[1] the personification of youth and spring; the cupbearer of the gods

Coy Hebe flies from those that woo,
And shuns the hands would seize upon her,
    Follow thy life, and she will sue
To pour for thee the cup of honor.

             1847

AMBROSE

Never, surely, was holier man
Than Ambrose, since the world began;
With diet spare and raiment thin,
He shielded himself from the father of sin;
With bed of iron and scourgings oft,
His heart to God's hand as wax made soft.

Through earnest prayer and watchings long
He sought to know 'twixt right and wrong,
Much wrestling with the blessed Word
To make it yield the sense of the Lord,   10
That he might build a storm-proof creed
To fold the flock in at their need.

At last he builded a perfect faith,
Fenced round about with *The Lord thus saith,*
To himself he fitted the doorway's size,
Meted the light to the need of his eyes,
And knew, by a sure and inward sign,
That the work of his fingers was divine.

Then Ambrose said, "All those shall die
The eternal death who believe not as I";   20
And some were boiled, some burned in fire,
Some sawn in twain, that his heart's desire,
For the good of men's souls might be satisfied,
By the drawing of all to the righteous side.

One day, as Ambrose was seeking the truth
In his lonely walk, he saw a youth
Resting himself in the shade of a tree;
It had never been given him to see
So shining a face, and the good man thought
'Twere pity he should not believe as he ought.

So he sat himself by the young man's side,   31
And the state of his soul with questions tried;
But the heart of the stranger was hardened
    indeed
Nor received the stamp of the one true creed.
And the spirit of Ambrose waxed sore to find
Such face the porch of so narrow a mind.

"As each beholds in cloud and fire
The shape that answers his own desire,
So each," said the youth, "in the Law shall find
The figure and features of his mind;   40
And to each in his mercy hath God allowed
His several pillar of fire and cloud." [2]

[2] *Exodus* xiii, 21

The soul of Ambrose burned with zeal
And holy wrath for the young man's weal:
"Believest thou then, most wretched youth,"
Cried he, "a dividual essence in Truth?
I fear me thy heart is too cramped with sin
To take the Lord in his glory in."

Now there bubbled beside them where they
          stood,
A fountain of waters sweet and good;   50
The youth to the streamlet's brink drew near
Saying, "Ambrose, thou maker of creeds, look
          here!"
Six vases of crystal then he took,
And set them along the edge of the brook.

"As into these vessels the water I pour,
There shall one hold less, another more,
And the water unchanged, in every case,
Shall put on the figure of the vase;
O thou, who wouldst unity make through strife,
Canst thou fit this sign to the Water of Life?"

When Ambrose looked up, he stood alone,   61
The youth and the stream and the vases were
          gone;
But he knew, by a sense of humbled grace,
He had talked with an angel face to face,
And felt his heart change inwardly,
As he fell on his knees beneath the tree.
1848   1848

THE VISION OF SIR LAUNFAL

PRELUDE TO PART FIRST

Over his keys the musing organist,
    Beginning doubtfully and far away,
First lets his fingers wander as they list,
    And builds a bridge from Dreamland for his
          lay:
Then, as the touch of his loved instrument
    Gives hope and fervor, nearer draws his
          theme,
First guessed by faint auroral flushes sent
Along the wavering vista of his dream.

Not only around our infancy [1]
    Doth heaven with all its splendors lie;   10
Daily, with souls that cringe and plot,
    We Sinais [2] climb and know it not.

Over our manhood bend the skies;
    Against our fallen and traitor lives

[1] Cf. Wordsworth's "Ode, Intimations of Immortality"
          . . . .l. 67.
[2] Moses ascended Sinai to talk with God. *Exodus* iii,
    1; xix, 20.

The great winds utter prophecies;
    With our faint hearts the mountain strives;
Its arms outstretched, the druid [3] wood
    Waits with its benedicite; [4]
And to our age's drowsy blood
    Still shouts the inspiring sea.   20
Earth gets its price for what Earth gives us;
    The beggar is taxed for a corner to die in,
The priest hath his fee who comes and shrives
          us,
We bargain for the graves we lie in;
At the devil's booth are all things sold,
Each ounce of dross costs its ounce of gold;
    For a cap and bells [5] our lives we pay,
Bubbles we buy with a whole soul's tasking:
'Tis heaven alone that is given away,
'Tis only God may be had for the asking;   30
No price is set on the lavish summer;
June may be had by the poorest comer.

And what is so rare as a day in June? [6]
    Then, if ever, come perfect days;
Then Heaven tries earth if it be in tune,
    And over it softly her warm ear lays:
Whether we look, or whether we listen,
We hear life murmur, or see it glisten;
Every clod feels a stir of might,
    An instinct within it that reaches and towers,
And, groping blindly above it for light,   41
    Climbs to a soul in grass and flowers;
The flush of life may well be seen
    Thrilling back over hills and valleys;
The cowslip startles in meadows green,
The buttercup catches the sun in its chalice,
And there's never a leaf nor a blade too mean
    To be some happy creature's palace;
The little bird sits at his door in the sun,
    Atilt like a blossom among the leaves,   50
And lets his illumined being o'errun
    With the deluge of summer it receives;
His mate feels the eggs beneath her wings,
And the heart in her dumb breast flutters and
          sings;
He sings to the wide world, and she to her
          nest,—
In the nice ear of Nature which song is the
          best?

Now is the high-tide of the year,
    And whatever of life hath ebbed away
Comes flooding back with a ripply cheer,
    Into every bare inlet and creek and bay;   60

[3] The druids, ancient Celtic priests, held the oak sacred
          and worshiped in the forests.
[4] blessing (literally, *be ye blessed*)
[5] the regalia of the king's jester
[6] Cf. Lowell's less familiar description of June in
          Biglow Papers Second Series, No. vi.

Now the heart is so full that a drop overfills it,
We are happy now because God wills it;
No matter how barren the past may have been,
'Tis enough for us now that the leaves are
     green;
We sit in the warm shade and feel right well
How the sap creeps up and the blossoms swell;
We may shut our eyes but we cannot help
     knowing
That skies are clear and grass is growing;
The breeze comes whispering in our ear,
That dandelions are blossoming near,   70
    That maize has sprouted, that streams are
        flowing,
That the river is bluer than the sky,
That the robin is plastering his house hard by;
And if the breeze kept the good news back,
For other couriers we should not lack;
    We could guess it all by yon heifer's lowing,—
And hark! how clear bold chanticleer,
Warmed with the new wine of the year,
    Tells all in his lusty crowing!

Joy comes, grief goes, we know not how;   80
Everything is happy now,
    Everything is upward striving;
'Tis as easy now for the heart to be true
As for grass to be green or skies to be blue,—
    'Tis the natural way of living:
Who knows whither the clouds have fled?
    In the unscarred heavens they leave no wake;
And the eyes forget the tears they have shed,
    The heart forgets its sorrow and ache;
The soul partakes the season's youth,   90
    And the sulphurous rifts of passion and woe
Lie deep 'neath a silence pure and smooth,
    Like burnt-out craters healed with snow.
What wonder if Sir Launfal now
Remembered the keeping of his vow?

PART FIRST

I

"My golden spurs now bring to me,
    And bring to me my richest mail,
For tomorrow I go over land and sea
    In search of the Holy Grail; [1]
Shall never a bed for me be spread,
Nor shall a pillow be under my head,
    Till I begin my vow to keep;

Here on the rushes will I sleep,
And perchance there may come a vision true
Ere day create the world anew."   10
    Slowly Sir Launfal's eyes grew dim,
    Slumber fell like a cloud on him,
And into his soul the vision flew.

II

The crows flapped over by twos and threes,
In the pool drowsed the cattle up to their
     knees,
    The little birds sang as if it were
    The one day of summer in all the year,
And the very leaves seemed to sing on the
     trees:
The castle alone in the landscape lay
Like an outpost of winter, dull and gray;   20
'Twas the proudest hall in the North Countree,
And never its gates might opened be,
Save to lord or lady of high degree;
Summer besieged it on every side,
But the churlish stone her assaults defied;
She could not scale the chilly wall,
Though round it for leagues her pavilions tall
Stretched left and right,
Over the hills and out of sight;
    Green and broad was every tent,   30
    And out of each a murmur went
Till the breeze fell off at night.

III

The drawbridge dropped with a surly clang,
And through the dark arch a charger sprang,
Bearing Sir Launfal, the maiden [2] knight,
In his gilded mail, that flamed so bright
It seemed the dark castle had gathered all
Those shafts the fierce sun had shot over its
     wall
In his siege of three hundred summers long,
And, binding them all in one blazing sheaf,   40
    Had cast them forth: so, young and strong,
And lightsome as a locust-leaf,
Sir Launfal flashed forth in his maiden mail,
To seek in all climes for the Holy Grail.

---

[1] "According to the mythology of the Romancers, the San Greal, or Holy Grail, was the cup out of which Jesus Christ partook of the Last Supper with his disciples. It was brought into England by Joseph of Arimathea, and remained there, an object of pilgrimage and adoration, for many years in the keeping of his lineal descendants. It was incumbent upon those who had charge of it to be chaste in thought, word, and deed; but one of the keepers having broken this condition, the Holy Grail disappeared. From that time it was a favorite enterprise of the knights of Arthur's court to go in search of it. . . .
    "The plot (if I may give that name to anything so slight) of the following poem is my own, and, to serve its purposes, I have enlarged the circle of competition in search of the miraculous cup in such a manner as to include not only other persons than the heroes of the Round Table, but also a period of time subsequent to the date of King Arthur's reign."—LOWELL.

[2] untried

IV

It was morning on hill and stream and tree,
　And morning in the young knight's heart;
Only the castle moodily
Rebuffed the gifts of the sunshine free,
　And gloomed by itself apart;
The season brimmed all other things up　　50
Full as the rain fills the pitcher-plant's cup.

V

As Sir Launfal made morn through the dark-
　　　some gate,
　He was 'ware of a leper, crouched by the
　　　same,
Who begged with his hand and moaned as he
　　　sate;
　And a loathing over Sir Launfal came;
The sunshine went out of his soul with a thrill,
　The flesh 'neath his armor 'gan shrink and
　　　crawl,
And midway its leap his heart stood still
　Like a frozen waterfall;
For this man, so foul and bent of stature,　　60
Rasped harshly against his dainty nature,
And seemed the one blot on the summer
　　　morn,—
So he tossed him a piece of gold in scorn.

VI

The leper raised not the gold from the dust:
"Better to me the poor man's crust,
Better the blessing of the poor,
Though I turn me empty from his door;
That is no true alms which the hand can hold;
He gives nothing but worthless gold
　Who gives from a sense of duty;　　70
But he who gives but a slender mite,
And gives to that which is out of sight,
　That thread of the all-sustaining Beauty
Which runs through all and doth all unite,—
The hand cannot clasp the whole of his alms,
The heart outstretches its eager palms,
For a god goes with it and makes it store
To the soul that was starving in darkness
　　　before."

PRELUDE TO PART SECOND

Down swept the chill wind from the mountain
　　　peak,
　From the snow five thousand summers old;
On open wold and hill-top bleak
　It had gathered all the cold,
And whirled it like sleet on the wanderer's
　　　cheek;
It carried a shiver everywhere

From the unleafed boughs and pastures bare;
The little brook heard it and built a roof
'Neath which he could house him, winterproof;
All night by the white stars' frosty gleams　　10
He groined his arches and matched his beams;
Slender and clear were his crystal spars
As the lashes of light that trim the stars:
He sculptured every summer delight
In his halls and chambers out of sight;
Sometimes his tinkling waters slipt
Down through a frost-leaved forest-crypt,
Long, sparkling aisles of steel-stemmed trees
Bending to counterfeit a breeze;
Sometimes the roof no fretwork knew　　20
But silvery mosses that downward grew;
Sometimes it was carved in sharp relief
With quaint arabesques of ice-fern leaf;
Sometimes it was simply smooth and clear
For the gladness of heaven to shine through,
　　　and here
He had caught the nodding bulrush-tops
And hung them thickly with diamond drops,
That crystaled the beams of moon and sun,
And made a star of every one:
No mortal builder's most rare device　　30
Could match this winter-palace of ice;
'Twas as if every image that mirrored lay
In his depths serene through the summer day,
Each fleeting shadow of earth and sky,
　Lest the happy model should be lost,
Had been mimicked in fairy masonry
　By the elfin builders of the frost.

Within the hall are song and laughter,
　The cheeks of Christmas glow red and jolly,
And sprouting is every corbel [1] and rafter　　40
　With lightsome green of ivy and holly;
Through the deep gulf of the chimney wide
Wallows the Yule-log's roaring tide;
The broad flame-pennons droop and flap
　And belly and tug as a flag in the wind;
Like a locust shrills the imprisoned sap,
　Hunted to death in its galleries blind;
And swift little troops of silent sparks,
　Now pausing, now scattering away as in fear,
Go threading the soot-forest's tangled darks
　Like herds of startled deer.　　51

But the wind without was eager and sharp,
Of Sir Launfal's gray hair it makes a harp,
　And rattles and wrings
　The icy strings,
Singing, in dreary monotone,
A Christmas carol of its own,
Whose burden still, as he might guess,
Was—"Shelterless, shelterless, shelterless!"

[1] bracket

The voice of the seneschal flared like a torch
As he shouted the wanderer away from the
    porch, 61
And he sat in the gateway and saw all night
  The great hall-fire, so cheery and bold,
  Through the window-slits of the castle old,
Build out its piers of ruddy light
Against the drift of the cold.

PART SECOND

I

There was never a leaf on bush or tree,
The bare boughs rattled shudderingly;
The river was dumb and could not speak,
  For the weaver Winter its shroud had spun;
A single crow on the tree-top bleak
  From his shining feathers shed off the cold
    sun.
Again it was morning, but shrunk and cold,
As if her veins were sapless and old,
And she rose up decrepitly
For a last dim look at earth and sea. 10

II

Sir Launfal turned from his own hard gate,
For another heir in his earldom sate;
An old, bent man, worn out and frail,
He came back from seeking the Holy Grail;
Little he recked of his earldom's loss,
No more on his surcoat was blazoned the cross,
But deep in his soul the sign he wore,
The badge of the suffering and the poor.

III

Sir Launfal's raiment thin and spare
Was idle mail 'gainst the barbed air, 20
For it was just at the Christmas time;
So he mused, as he sat, of a sunnier clime,
And sought for a shelter from cold and snow
In the light and warmth of long-ago;
He sees the snake-like caravan crawl
O'er the edge of the desert, black and small,
Then nearer and nearer, till, one by one,
He can count the camels in the sun,
As over the red-hot sands they pass
To where, in its slender necklace of grass, 30
The little spring laughed and leapt in the shade,
And with its own self like an infant played,
And waved its signal of palms.

IV

"For Christ's sweet sake, I beg an alms;"—
The happy camels may reach the spring,
But Sir Launfal sees only the grewsome thing,
The leper, lank as the rain-blanched bone,

That cowers beside him, a thing as lone
And white as the ice-isles of Northern seas
In the desolate horror of his disease. 40

V

And Sir Launfal said,—"I behold in thee
An image of Him who died on the tree;
Thou also hast had thy crown of thorns,—
Thou also hast had the world's buffets and
    scorns,—
And to thy life were not denied
The wounds in the hands and feet and side:
Mild Mary's Son, acknowledge me;
Behold, through him, I give to thee!"

VI

Then the soul of the leper stood up in his eyes
  And looked at Sir Launfal, and straightway
    he 50
Remembered in what a haughtier guise
  He had flung an alms to leprosie,
When he girt his young life up in gilded mail
And set forth in search of the Holy Grail.
The heart within him was ashes and dust;
He parted in twain his single crust,
He broke the ice on the streamlet's brink,
And gave the leper to eat and drink,
'Twas a moldy crust of coarse brown bread,
  'Twas water out of a wooden bowl,— 60
Yet with fine wheaten bread was the leper fed,
  And 'twas red wine he drank with his thirsty
    soul.

VII

As Sir Launfal mused with a downcast face,
A light shone round about the place;
The leper no longer crouched at his side,
But stood before him glorified,
Shining and tall and fair and straight
As the pillar that stood by the Beautiful
    Gate,— [1]
Himself the Gate whereby men can
Enter the temple of God in Man. 70

VIII

His words were shed softer than leaves from the
    pine,
And they fell on Sir Launfal as snows on the
    brine,
That mingle their softness and quiet in one
With the shaggy unrest they float down upon;
And the voice that was softer than silence said,
"Lo, it is I, be not afraid!
In many climes, without avail,
Thou hast spent thy life for the Holy Grail;

[1] *Acts* iii, 2

Behold it is here,—this cup which thou
Didst fill at the streamlet for me but now;   80
This crust is my body broken for thee,
This water His blood that died on the tree:
The Holy Supper is kept, indeed,
In whatso we share with another's need;
Not what we give, but what we share,
For the gift without the giver is bare;
Who gives himself with his alms feeds three,
Himself, his hungering neighbor, and me."

IX

Sir Launfal awoke as from a swound:
"The Grail in my castle here is found!   90
Hang my idle armor upon the wall,
Let it be the spider's banquet hall;
He must be fenced with stronger mail
Who would seek and find the Holy Grail."

X

The castle gate stands open now,
    And the wanderer is welcome to the hall
As the hangbird [1] is to the elm-tree bough;
No longer scowl the turrets tall,
The Summer's long siege at last is o'er;
When the first poor outcast went in at the door,
She entered with him in disguise,   101
And mastered the fortress by surprise;
There is no spot she loves so well on ground,
She lingers and smiles there the whole year
    round;
The meanest serf on Sir Launfal's land
Has hall and bower at his command;
And there's no poor man in the North Countree
But is lord of the earldom as much as he.
1848   1848

From A FABLE FOR CRITICS [2]

. . . .

"There comes Emerson first, whose rich
    words, every one,
Are like gold nails in temples to hang trophies
    on,
Whose prose is grand verse, while his verse,
    the Lord knows,

---

[1] the oriole, or any bird building a hanging nest
[2] A few lines from Lowell's humorous preface will explain the spirit in which this piece of penetrating banter was written: "To the Reader: This trifle, begun to please only myself and my own private fancy, was laid on the shelf. But some friends, who had seen it, induced me, by dint of saying they liked it, to put it in print. . . . Having scrawled at full gallop (as far as that goes) in a style that is neither good verse nor bad prose, and being a person whom nobody knows, some people will say I am rather more free with my readers than it is becoming to be. . . . All the characters sketched in this slight *jeu d'esprit*,

Is some of it pr—— No, 'tis not even prose;
I'm speaking of meters; some poems have
    welled
From those rare depths of soul that have ne'er
    been excelled;   530
They're not epics, but that doesn't matter a pin,
In creating, the only hard thing's to begin;
A grass-blade's no easier to make than an oak,
If you've once found the way, you've achieved
    the grand stroke;
In the worst of his poems are mines of rich
    matter,
But thrown in a heap with a crash and a clatter;
Now it is not one thing nor another alone
Makes a poem, but rather the general tone,
The something pervading, uniting the whole,
The before unconceived, unconceivable soul,
So that just in removing this trifle or that,
    you   541
Take away, as it were, a chief limb of the
    statue;
Roots, wood, bark, and leaves, singly perfect
    may be,
But, clapt hodge-podge together, they don't
    make a tree.

"But to come back to Emerson (whom by
    the way,
I believe we left waiting),—his is, we may
    say,
A Greek head on right Yankee shoulders, whose
    range
Has Olympus [3] for one pole, for t'other the
    Exchange; [4]
He seems, to my thinking, (although I'm afraid
The comparison must, long ere this, have been
    made),   550
A Plotinus-Montaigne, [5] where the Egyptian's
    gold mist
And the Gascon's shrewd wit cheek-by-jowl co-
    exist;
All admire, and yet scarcely six converts he's
    got
To I don't (nor they either) exactly know
    what;
For though he builds glorious temples, 'tis odd

---

though, it may be, they seem, here and there, rather free, and drawn from a Mephistophelian standpoint, are *meant* to be faithful, and that is the grand point, and none but an owl would feel sore at a rub from a jester who tells you, without any subterfuge, that he sits in Diogenes' tub."
[3] the home of the gods
[4] the mart of business
[5] Plotinus was an idealistic Greek philosopher born in Egypt c. 204 A.D. Montaigne, 1533-1592, a French essayist whose work is marked by shrewd worldliness, lived in Bordeaux in what was once the old duchy of Guienne and Gascony.

He leaves never a doorway to get in a god.
'Tis refreshing to old-fashioned people like me
To meet such a primitive Pagan as he,
In whose mind all creation is duly respected
As parts of himself—just a little projected;
And who's willing to worship the stars and the sun, 561
A convert to—nothing but Emerson.
So perfect a balance there is in his head,
That he talks of things sometimes as if they were dead;
Life, nature, love, God, and affairs of that sort,
He looks at as merely ideas; in short,
As if they were fossils stuck round in a cabinet,
Of such vast extent that our earth's a mere dab in it;
Composed just as he is inclined to conjecture her,
Namely, one part pure earth, ninety-nine parts pure lecturer; 570
You are filled with delight at his clear demonstration,
Each figure, word, gesture, just fits the occasion,
With the quiet precision of science he'll sort 'em,
But you can't help suspecting the whole a *post mortem.*

"There are persons, mole-blind to the soul's make and style,
Who insist on a likeness 'twixt him and Carlyle;
To compare him with Plato would be vastly fairer,
Carlyle's the more burly, but E. is the rarer;
He sees fewer objects, but clearlier, truelier,
If C.'s as original, E.'s more peculiar; 580
That he's more of a man you might say of the one,
Of the other he's more of an Emerson;
C.'s the Titan, [1] as shaggy of mind as of limb,—
E. the clear-eyed Olympian, rapid and slim;
The one's two-thirds Norseman, the other half Greek,
Where the one's most abounding, the other's to seek;
C.'s generals require to be seen in the mass—
E.'s specialties gain if enlarged by the glass;
C. gives nature and God his own fits of the blues,
And rims common-sense things with mystical hues,— 590
E. sits in a mystery calm and intense,
And looks coolly around him with sharp common sense;
C. shows you how every-day matters unite

With the dim transdiurnal [2] recesses of night,—
While E., in a plain, preternatural way,
Makes mysteries matters of mere every day;
C. draws all his characters quite *à la* Fuseli, [3]—
Not sketching their bundles of muscles and thews illy, [4]
But he paints with a brush so untamed and profuse,
They seem nothing but bundles of muscles and thews; 600
E. is rather like Flaxman, [5] lines straight and severe,
And a colorless outline, but full, round, and clear;—
To the men he thinks worthy he frankly accords
The design of a white marble statue in words.
C. labors to get at the center, and then
Take a reckoning from there of his actions and men;
E. calmly assumes the said center as granted,
And, given himself, has whatever is wanted.

"He has imitators in scores, who omit 609
No part of the man but his wisdom and wit,—
Who go carefully o'er the sky-blue of his brain,
And when he has skimmed it once, skim it again;
If at all they resemble him, you may be sure it is
Because their shoals mirror his mists and obscurities,
As a mud-puddle seems deep as heaven for a minute,
While a cloud that floats o'er is reflected within it.

"There comes ——, [6] for instance; to see him's rare sport,
Tread in Emerson's tracks with legs painfully short;
How he jumps, how he strains, and gets red in the face,
To keep step with the mystagogue's natural pace! 620
He follows as close as a stick to a rocket,
His fingers exploring the prophet's each pocket,
Fie, for shame, brother bard; with good fruit of your own,
Can't you let Neighbor Emerson's orchards alone?

---

[1] the giant race, descended from Uranus and Gaea (Heaven and Earth)
[2] beyond the confines of the day
[3] John Henry Fuseli, 1741-1825, a Swiss-English painter of powerful imagination rather than technical excellence
[4] This line at first read, "He don't sketch . . ." Notice the great liberties Lowell takes. Cf. lines 620 and 817.
[5] John Flaxman, 1755-1826, an English sculptor.
[6] Thoreau?

Besides, 'tis no use, you'll not find e'en a core,—
——[1] has picked up all the windfalls before.
They might strip every tree, and E. never
    would catch 'em,
His Hesperides[2] have no rude dragon to watch
    'em,
When they send him a dishful, and ask him
    to try 'em,
He never suspects how the sly rogues came
    by 'em;   630
He wonders why 'tis there are none such his
    trees on,
And thinks 'em the best he has tasted this
    season.

"There is Bryant, as quiet, as cool, and as
    dignified,
As a smooth, silent iceberg, that never is ig-
    nified,
Save when by reflection 'tis kindled o' nights
With a semblance of flame by the chill Northern
    Lights.
He may rank (Griswold[3] says so) first bard of
    your nation,
(There's no doubt that he stands in supreme
    ice-olation),
Your topmost Parnassus[4] he may set his heel
    on,
But no warm applauses come, peal following
    peal on,—
He's too smooth and too polished to hang any
    zeal on: 820
Unqualified merits, I'll grant, if you choose, he
    has 'em,
But he lacks the one merit of kindling en-
    thusiasm;
If he stir you at all, it is just, on my soul,
Like being stirred up with the very North Pole.

"He is very nice reading in summer, but
    inter
Nos,[5] we don't want extra freezing in winter;
Take him up in the depth of July, my advice is,
When you feel an Egyptian devotion to ices,[6]
But, deduct all you can, there's enough that's
    right good in him,
He has a true soul for field, river, and wood
    in him;   830
And his heart, in the midst of brick walls, or
    where'er it is,

Glows, softens, and thrills with the tenderest
    charities—
To you mortals that delve in this trade-ridden
    planet?
No, to old Berkshire's hills, with their limestone
    and granite.
If you're one who in loco (add foco here)
    desipis,[7]
You will get of his outermost heart (as I
    guess) a piece;
But you'd get deeper down if you came as a
    precipice,
And would break the last seal of its inwardest
    fountain,
If you only could palm yourself off for a
    mountain.   839
Mr. Quivis,[8] or somebody quite as discerning,
Some scholar who's hourly expecting his learn-
    ing,
Calls B. the American Wordsworth; but Words-
    worth
May be rated at more than your whole tuneful
    herd's worth.
No, don't be absurd, he's an excellent Bryant;
But, my friends, you'll endanger the life of
    your client,
By attempting to stretch him up into a giant:
If you choose to compare him, I think there are
    two per-
sons fit for a parallel—Thomson and Cowper;[9]
I don't mean exactly,—there's something of
    each,
There's T.'s love of nature, C.'s penchant to
    preach;   850
Just mix up their minds so that C.'s spice of
    craziness
Shall balance and neutralize T.'s turn for lazi-
    ness,
And it gives you a brain cool, quite frictionless,
    quiet,
Whose internal police nips the buds of all
    riot,—
A brain like a permanent strait-jacket put on
The heart which strives vainly to burst off a
    button,—
A brain which, without being slow or mechanic,
Does more than a larger less drilled, more
    volcanic;
He's a Cowper condensed, with no craziness
    bitten,

---

[1] Alcott?
[2] the golden apples of the mythical gardens
[3] Rufus Wilmot Griswold compiled the anthologies
    Poets and Poetry of America (1842) and Prose
    Writers of America (1846).
[4] a mountain ridge northwest of Athens, supposed to be
    the haunt of Apollo and the Muses; hence the
    source of music and poetry
[5] between ourselves
[6] Note the pun on Isis, the chief goddess of the Egyp-
    tians.

[7] "If you're one who in a place (by the fire) can be
    foolish."
[8] Mr. Anyone
[9] English poets of the 18th century

    "To demonstrate quickly and easily how perversely
       absurd 'tis to sound this name Cowper,
    As people in general call him named super,
    I remark that he rimes it himself with horse-
       trooper."—(Lowell's note.)

And the advantage that Wordsworth before him
    had written. 860

"But, my dear little bardlings, don't prick up
    your ears
Nor suppose I would rank you and Bryant as
    peers;
If I call him an iceberg, I don't mean to say
There is nothing in that which is grand, in its
    way;
He is almost the one of your poets that knows
How much grace, strength, and dignity lie in
    Repose;
If he sometimes fall short, he is too wise to
    mar
His thought's modest fulness by going too far;
'Twould be well if your authors should all make
    a trial 869
Of what virtue there is in severe self-denial,
And measure their writings by Hesiod's staff, [1]
Which teaches that all has less value than
    half.

"There is Whittier, whose swelling and vehe-
    ment heart
Strains the strait-breasted drab of the Quaker
    apart,
And reveals the live Man, still supreme and
    erect,
Underneath the bemummying wrappers of sect;
There was ne'er a man born who had more of
    the swing
Of the true lyric bard and all that kind of
    thing;
And his failures arise (though perhaps he don't
    know it)
From the very same cause that has made him
    a poet,— 880
A fervor of mind which knows no separation
'Twixt simple excitement and pure inspira-
    tion,
As my Pythoness [2] erst sometimes erred from
    not knowing
If 'twere I or mere wind through her tripod
    was blowing;
Let his mind once get head in its favorite
    direction
And the torrent of verse bursts the dams of
    reflection,
While, borne with the rush of the meter along,
The poet may chance to go right or go wrong,
Content with the whirl and delirium of song;

Then his grammar's not always correct, nor
    his rimes, [3] 890
And he's prone to repeat his own lyrics some-
    times,
Not his best, though, for those are struck off
    at white-heats
When the heart in his breast like a trip-hammer
    beats,
And can ne'er be repeated again any more
Than they could have been carefully plotted
    before:
Like old what's-his-name [4] there at the battle
    of Hastings
(Who, however, gave more than mere rhythmi-
    cal bastings),
Our Quaker leads off metaphorical fights
For reform and whatever they call human
    rights, 899
Both singing and striking in front of the war
And hitting his foes with the mallet of Thor; [5]
Anne haec, one exclaims, on beholding his
    knocks,
Vestis filii tui, [6] O, leather-clad Fox?
Can that be thy son, in the battle's mid din,
Preaching brotherly love and then driving it in
To the brain of the tough old Goliah [7] of sin,
With the smoothest of pebbles from Castaly's
    spring, [8]
Impressed on his hard moral sense with a
    sling?

"All honor and praise to the right-hearted
    bard
Who was true to The Voice when such service
    was hard, 910
Who himself was so free he dared sing for the
    slave
When to look but a protest in silence was
    brave;
All honor and praise to the women and men

[1] The poems of Hesiod, who is noted for his sententious philosophy, were not recited to the accompaniment of a harp as were those of Homer, but the reciter held in his hand a laurel branch or staff.
[2] a woman having power of divination as the priestess at Delphi.

[3] Cf. "Maud Muller":
    "For of all sad words of tongue or pen,
    The saddest are these: 'It might have been!' "
[4] Taillefer, Norman juggler and minstrel, who struck the first blow at the battle of Hastings, 1066, rode at the head of the Norman army singing songs of Roland and Charlemagne and throwing in the air and catching again his sword; before he fell he used his sword in earnest.
[5] The hammer Mjöllnir, the Crusher, of Thor, the Scandinavian god of thunder, returned to his hand of itself when he had hurled it.
[6] "Is this indeed the dress of thy son?" *Genesis* xxxvii, 32. George Fox, 1624-1691, a shoemaker, said to have worn leather breeches, was the founder of The Society of Friends, or Quakers. They were always known for their love of peace. Carlyle's rhapsody over Fox's costume (*Sartor Resartus*), which Lowell apparently follows, is probably ill-founded.
[7] *1 Samuel* xvii
[8] Castalia, or Castaly, was an ancient spring on Mt. Parnassus sacred to the Muses and to Apollo.

Who spoke out for the dumb and the down-
    trodden then!
It needs not to name them, already for each
I see History preparing the statue and niche;
They were harsh, but shall *you* be so shocked
    at hard words
Who have beaten your pruning-hooks up into
    swords, [1]
Whose rewards and hurrahs men are surer to
    gain
By the reaping of men and of women than
    grain?   920
Why should *you* stand aghast at their fierce
    wordy war, if
You scalp one another for Bank or for Tariff? [2]
Your calling them cut-throats and knaves all
    day long
Doesn't prove that the use of hard language
    is wrong;
While the World's heart beats quicker to think
    of such men
As signed Tyranny's doom with a bloody steel-
    pen,
While on Fourth-of-Julys beardless orators
    fright one
With hints at Harmodius and Aristogeiton, [3]
You need not look shy at your sisters and
    brothers
Who stab with sharp words for the freedom of
    others;—   930
No, a wreath, twine a wreath for the loyal and
    true
Who, for sake of the many, dared stand with
    the few,
Not of blood-spattered laurel for enemies
    braved,
But of broad, peaceful oak-leaves for citizens
    saved!

.   .   .   .   .   .

"There is Hawthorne, with genius so shrink-
    ing and rare
That you hardly at first see the strength that
    is there;
A frame so robust, with a nature so sweet,
So earnest, so graceful, so solid, so fleet,
Is worth a descent from Olympus [4] to meet;
'Tis as if a rough oak that for ages had stood,
With his gnarled bony branches like ribs of the
    wood,   1001

[1] *Joel* iii, 10
[2] The question as to the constitutionality of establishing
    a National Bank had agitated the country since
    1787, and had not been finally settled until 1846.
    The tariff question had also caused much feeling.
    See Calhoun's and Webster's speeches, p. 445 and
    p. 454.
[3] two Athenians, who killed Hipparchus, tyrant of
    Athens, and were executed 514 B.C.
[4] the home of the gods

Should bloom, after cycles of struggle and
    scathe,
With a single anemone trembly and rathe; [5]
His strength is so tender, his wildness so meek,
That a suitable parallel sets one to seek,—
He's a John Bunyan Fouqué, a Puritan Tieck; [6]
When Nature was shaping him, clay was not
    granted
For making so full-sized a man as she wanted,
So, to fill out her model, a little she spared
From some finer-grained stuff for a woman
    prepared,   1010
And she could not have hit a more excellent
    plan
For making him fully and perfectly man.
The success of her scheme gave her so much
    delight,
That she tried it again, shortly after, in
    Dwight; [7]
Only, while she was kneading and shaping the
    clay,
She sang to her work in her sweet childish way,
And found, when she'd put the last touch to
    his soul,
That the music had somehow got mixed with
    the whole.

"Here's Cooper, who's written six volumes
    to show
He's as good as a lord: [8] well, let's grant that
    he's so;   1020
If a person prefer that description of praise,
Why, a coronet's certainly cheaper than bays;
But he need take no pains to convince us he's
    not
(As his enemies say) the American Scott.
Choose any twelve men, and let C. read aloud
That one of his novels of which he's most
    proud,
And I'd lay any bet that without ever quitting
Their box, they'd be all, to a man, for ac-
    quitting.
He has drawn you one character, though, that
    is new,
One wildflower he's plucked that is wet with
    the dew   1030
Of this fresh Western world, and, the thing
    not to mince,

[5] early; cf. "rather" (sooner)
[6] i. e., a union of the allegorical vision of Bunyan with
    the romantic imagination of Baron de La Motte
    Fouqué, 1777-1843, the German author of *Undine;*
    or the union of the soberness of the Puritan with
    the romanticism of Ludwig Tieck (1773-1853), a
    German novelist
[7] John Sullivan Dwight, 1813-1893, a musical critic of
    Boston
[8] Cooper's display of ancestry annoyed as well as
    amused his countrymen. Poets were in ancient
    times crowned with bay leaves. See l. 1022.

He has done naught but copy it ill ever since;
His Indians, with proper respect be it said,
Are just Natty Bumppo [1] daubed over with
    red,
And his very Long Toms [2] are the same useful
    Nat,
Rigged up in duck pants and a sou'-wester hat,
(Though once in a Coffin, a good chance was
    found
To have slipt the old fellow away under-
    ground).
All his other men-figures are clothes upon
    sticks,
The *dernière chemise* [3] of a man in a fix,
(As a captain besieged, when his garrison's
    small,   1041
Sets up caps upon poles to be seen o'er the
    wall);
And the women he draws from one model don't
    vary,
All sappy as maples and flat as a prairie.
When a character's wanted, he goes to the task
As a cooper would do in composing a cask;
He picks out the staves, of their qualities
    heedful,
Just hoops them together as tight as is needful,
And, if the best fortune should crown the
    attempt, he
Has made at the most something wooden and
    empty.   1050

"Don't suppose I would underrate Cooper's
    abilities,
If I thought you'd do that, I should feel very
    ill at ease;
The men who have given to *one* character life
And objective existence, are not very rife,
You may number them all, both prose-writers
    and singers,
Without overrunning the bounds of your fin-
    gers,
And Natty won't go to oblivion quicker
Than Adams the parson or Primrose the vicar. [4]

"There is one thing in Cooper I like, too,
    and that is
That on manners he lectures his countrymen
    gratis,   1060
Not precisely so either, because, for a rarity,
He is paid for his tickets in unpopularity. [5]

[1] in the Leather-stocking Tales
[2] Long Tom Coffin, a sailor in *The Pilot*
[3] last shirt
[4] Parson Abraham Adams is a whimsical but manly
    character in Henry Fielding's novel *Joseph An-
    drews* (1742). Mr. Primrose is the title character
    of *The Vicar of Wakefield* (1766) by Goldsmith.
[5] Cooper, with most loyal intentions but with little
    tact, on his return after seven years abroad
    criticized Americans very severely and aroused
    much antagonism.

Now he may overcharge his American pictures,
But you'll grant there's a good deal of truth
    in his strictures;
And I honor the man who is willing to sink
Half his present repute for the freedom to
    think,
And, when he has thought, be his cause strong
    or weak,
Will risk t'other half for the freedom to speak,
Caring naught for what vengeance the mob has
    in store,
Let that mob be the upper ten thousand or
    lower.   1070

"There are truths you Americans need to be
    told,
And it never'll refute them to swagger and
    scold;
John Bull, looking o'er the Atlantic, in choler
At your aptness for trade, says you worship
    the dollar;
But to scorn such eye-dollar-try's what very
    few do,
And John goes to that church as often as you
    do.
No matter what John says, don't try to out-
    crow him,
'Tis enough to go quietly on and outgrow him;
Like most fathers, Bull hates to see Number
    One
Displacing himself in the mind of his son,
And detests the same faults in himself he'd
    neglected   1081
When he sees them again in his child's glass
    reflected;
To love one another you're too like by half.
If he is a bull, you're a pretty stout calf,
And tear your own pasture for naught but to
    show
What a nice pair of horns you're beginning to
    grow.

"There are one or two things I should just
    like to hint,
For you don't often get the truth told you in
    print;
The most of you (this is what strikes all be-
    holders)
Have a mental and physical stoop in the
    shoulders;   1090
Though you ought to be free as the winds and
    the waves,
You've the gait and the manners of run-away
    slaves;
Tho' you brag of your New World, you don't
    half believe in it,
And as much of the Old as is possible weave
    in it;

Your goddess of freedom, a tight, buxom girl,
With lips like a cherry and teeth like a pearl,
With eyes bold as Herè's, and hair floating free,
And full of the sun as the spray of the sea,
Who can sing at a husking or romp at a
    shearing,
Who can trip through the forests alone without
    fearing,   1100
Who can drive home the cows with a song
    through the grass,
Keeps glancing aside into Europe's cracked
    glass,
Hides her red hands in gloves, pinches up her
    lithe waist,
And makes herself wretched with transmarine
    taste;
She loses her fresh country charm when she
    takes
Any mirror except her own rivers and lakes.

"You steal Englishmen's books [1] and think
    Englishmen's thought,
With their salt on her tail your wild eagle is
    caught;
Your literature suits its each whisper and mo-
    tion
To what will be thought of it over the ocean;
The cast clothes of Europe your statesmanship
    tries   1111
And mumbles again the old blarneys and lies;—
Forget Europe wholly, your veins throb with
    blood,
To which the dull current in hers is but mud;
Let her sneer, let her say your experiment fails,
In her voice there's a tremble e'en now while
    she rails,
And your shore will soon be in the nature of
    things
Covered thick with gilt driftwood of run-away
    kings,
Where alone, as it were in a Longfellow's Waif,
Her fugitive pieces will find themselves safe. [2]
O, my friends, thank your god, if you have
    one, that he   1121
'Twixt the Old World and you set the gulf of
    a sea;
Be strong-backed, brown-handed, upright as
    your pines,
By the scale of a hemisphere shape your de-
    signs,
Be true to yourselves and this new nineteenth
    age,

As a statue by Powers, [3] or a picture by Page,
Plow, sail, forge, build, carve, paint, all things
    make new,
To your own New-World instincts contrive to
    be true,
Keep your ears open wide to the Future's first
    call,
Be whatever you will, but yourselves first of
    all,   1130
Stand fronting the dawn on Toil's heaven-
    scaling peaks,
And become my new race of more practical
    Greeks.—
Hem! your likeness at present I shudder to
    tell o't,
Is that you have your slaves, and the Greek
    had his helot."

   .   .   .   .   .

"There comes Poe, with his raven, like Barn-
    aby Rudge, [4]
Three fifths of him genius and two fifths sheer
    fudge,
Who talks like a book of iambs and pentam-
    eters, [5]
In a way to make people of common-sense
    damn meters,
Who has written some things quite the best of
    their kind,
But the heart somehow seems all squeezed out
    by the mind,   1300
Who—but hey-dey! What's this? Messieurs
    Mathews and Poe, [6]
You mustn't fling mud-balls at Longfellow so,
Does it make a man worse that his character's
    such
As to make his friends love him (as you think)
    too much?
Why, there is not a bard at this moment alive
More willing than he that his fellows should
    thrive,
While you are abusing him thus, even now
He would help either one of you out of a
    slough;
You may say that he's smooth and all that till
    you're hoarse,   1309
But remember that elegance also is force;
After polishing granite as much as you will,
The heart keeps its tough old persistency still;
Deduct all you can *that* still keeps you at bay;

---

[1] The proposal for an international copyright law between England and the United States was long a
matter of somewhat bitter discussion.
[2] Longfellow's collection of scattered prose pieces,
Driftwood, though projected in 1852 was not
published until 1857.

[3] Hiram Powers, 1805-1873; William Page, 1811-1885
[4] In Dickens's *Barnaby Rudge* a raven figures prominently.
[5] Poe in his critical essay "The Philosophy of Composition" had explained with great technical detail
how he wrote "The Raven."
[6] Poe in a review of *Voices of the Night* in *Burton's
Gentleman's Magazine,* "Mr. Longfellow and
Other Plagiarists," had accused Longfellow of
plagiarism. The Mr. Mathews is probably Cornelius Mathews, a New York writer.

Why, he'll live till men weary of Collins and
     Gray. [1]
I'm not overfond of Greek meters in English,
To me rime's a gain, so it be not too jinglish,
And your modern hexameter verses are no
     more
Like Greek ones than sleek Mr. Pope is like
     Homer; [2]
As the roar of the sea to the coo of a pigeon is,
So, compared to your moderns, sounds old
     Melesigenes; [3]   1320
I may be too partial, the reason, perhaps, o't is
That I've heard the old blind man recite his
     own rhapsodies,
And my ear with that music impregnate may
     be,
Like the poor exiled shell with the soul of the
     sea,
Or as one can't bear Strauss [4] when his nature
     is cloven
To its deeps within deeps by the stroke of
     Beethoven;
But, set that aside, and 'tis truth that I speak,
Had Theocritus [5] written in English, not Greek,
I believe that his exquisite sense would scarce
     change a line
In that rare, tender, virgin-like pastoral Evan-
     geline.   1330
That's not ancient nor modern, its place is
     apart
Where time has no sway, in the realm of pure
     Art,
'Tis a shrine of retreat from Earth's hubbub
     and strife
As quiet and chaste as the author's own life.

          .   .   .   .   .   .

"What! Irving? thrice welcome, warm heart
     and fine brain,
You bring back the happiest spirit from
     Spain, [6]
And the gravest sweet humor, that ever were
     there
Since Cervantes [7] met death in his gentle de-
     spair;   1440

[1] English poets of the 18th century
[2] *Evangeline* was written in dactyllic hexameters unrimed, the meter corresponding to that of Homer's
Iliad. Pope's translation of the latter is so free
as to be hardly Homeric.
[3] Meles-born, a name used occasionally for Homer, who,
tradition relates, composed some of his poems in a
cave near the source of the river Meles in Ionia
near the ancient Smyrna
[4] Johann Strauss, an Austrian composer (1804-1849),
famous for his waltz music
[5] the great Sicilian-Greek pastoral poet of the third
century B.C.
[6] Irving returned to America in 1846 from his second
residence in Spain.
[7] Spanish poet and novelist, 1547-1616, author of *Don
Quixote;* three years before his death he entered
the order of the Franciscan friars.

Nay, don't be embarrassed, nor look so be-
     seeching,—
I shan't run directly against my own preaching,
And, having just laughed at their Raphaels
     and Dantes, [8]
Go to setting you up beside matchless Cer-
     vantes;
But allow me to speak what I honestly feel,—
To a true poet-heart add the fun of Dick
     Steele,
Throw in all of Addison, *minus* the chill, [9]
With the whole of that partnership's stock and
     good-will,
Mix well, and while stirring, hum o'er, as a
     spell,   1449
The fine *old* English Gentleman, simmer it well,
Sweeten just to your own private liking, then
     strain,
That only the finest and clearest remain,
Let it stand out of doors till a soul it receives
From the warm lazy sun loitering down through
     green leaves,
And you'll find a choice nature, not wholly
     deserving
A name either English or Yankee,—just Irving.

          .   .   .   .   .   .

"There's Holmes, who is matchless among
     you for wit;
A Leyden-jar [10] always full-charged, from which
     flit
The electrical tingles of hit after hit;
In long poems 'tis painful sometimes and in-
     vites
A thought of the way the new Telegraph
     writes, [11]
Which pricks down its little sharp sentences
     spitefully   1560
As if you got more than you'd title to rightfully,
And you find yourself hoping its wild father
     Lightning
Would flame in for a second and give you a
     fright'ning.
He has perfect sway of what *I* call a sham
     meter,
But many admire it, the English pentameter,
And Campbell, I think, wrote most commonly
     worse,
With less nerve, swing, and fire in the same
     kind of verse,

[8] Raphael the greatest painter and Dante the greatest
poet of Italy; cf. lines 1618-1635, which apparently
were written earlier.
[9] The warm-hearted Steele and the decorous Addison
wrote *The Spectator* together.
[10] a glass jar used in condensing electricity and capable
of giving a strong shock
[11] The first telegraph line was set up between Washington and Baltimore in 1844. The primitive instruments of the first lines pricked messages upon
moving strips of paper.

Nor e'er achieved aught in't so worthy of
  praise
As the tribute of Holmes to the grand *Mar-
  seillaise.* [1]
You went crazy last year over Bulwer's New
  Timon;— [2]   1570
Why, if B. to the day of his dying, should
  rime on,
Heaping verses on verses and tomes upon
  tomes,
He could ne'er reach the best point and vigor
  of Holmes.
His are just the fine hands, too, to weave you
  a lyric
Full of fancy, fun, feeling, or spiced with
  satyric
In a measure so kindly, you doubt if the toes
That are trodden upon are your own or your
  foes'.

"There is Lowell, who's striving Parnassus [3]
  to climb
With a whole bale of *isms* tied together with
  rime,
He might get on alone, spite of brambles and
  boulders,   1580
But he can't with that bundle he has on his
  shoulders,
The top of the hill he will ne'er come nigh
  reaching
Till he learns the distinction 'twixt singing and
  preaching;
His lyre has some chords that would ring pretty
  well,
But he'd rather by half make a drum of the
  shell,
And rattle away till he's old as Methusalem,
At the head of a march to the last new Jerusalem."

.   .   .   .   .   .

1848   **1848**

BEAVER BROOK [4]

Hushed with broad sunlight lies the hill,
And, minuting [5] the long day's loss,
The cedar's shadow, slow and still,
Creeps o'er its dial of gray moss.

[1] in "A Metrical Essay": read before the Phi Beta
  Kappa Society, Harvard, 1836
[2] a satire published by Bulwer Lytton in 1846
[3] See note 8, p. 593.
[4] Originally called "The Mill." "The little mill stands
  in a valley between one of the spurs of Wellington Hill and the main summit, just on the edge
  of Waltham. It is surely one of the loveliest spots
  in the world. It is one of my lions, and if you
  will make me a visit this spring I will take you
  up to hear it roar . . ." *Letters of James Russell
  Lowell*, i, 149.
[5] measuring by minutes

Warm noon brims full the valley's cup,
The aspen's leaves are scarce astir,
Only the little mill sends up
Its busy, never-ceasing burr.

Climbing the loose-piled wall that hems
The road along the mill-pond's brink,   10
From 'neath the arching barberry-stems,
My footstep scares the sly chewink.

Beneath a bony buttonwood
The mill's red door lets forth the din;
The whitened miller, dust-imbued,
Flits past the square of dark within.

No mountain torrent's strength is here;
Sweet Beaver, child of forest still,
Heaps its small pitcher to the ear,
And gently waits the miller's will.   20

Swift slips Undine [6] along the race
Unheard, and then, with flashing bound,
Floods the dull wheel with light and grace,
And, laughing, hunts the loath drudge round.

The miller dreams not at what cost
The quivering mill stones hum and whirl,
Nor how for every turn, are tost
Armfuls of diamonds and of pearl.

But summer cleared my happier eyes
With drops of some celestial juice,   30
To see how Beauty underlies
For evermore each form of Use.

And more; methought I saw that flood,
Which now so dull and darkling steals,
Thick, here and there, with human blood,
To turn the world's laborious wheels.

No more than doth the miller there,
Shut in our several cells, do we
Know with what waste of beauty rare
Moves every day's machinery.   40

Surely the wiser time shall come
When this fine overplus of might,
No longer sullen, slow, and dumb,
Shall leap to music and to light.

In that new childhood of the Earth
Life of itself shall dance and play,
Fresh blood in Time's shrunk veins make mirth,
And labor meet delight half-way.
1848   **1848**

[6] the water spirit in *Undine* (1811) by Fouqué, Baron
  de la Motte

THE FIRST SNOW-FALL [1]

The snow had begun in the gloaming,
  And busily all the night
Had been heaping field and highway
  With a silence deep and white.

Every pine and fir and hemlock
  Wore ermine too dear for an earl,
And the poorest twig on the elm-tree
  Was ridged inch deep with pearl.

From sheds new-roofed with Carrara [2]
  Came Chanticleer's muffled crow,   10
The stiff rails softened to swan's-down
  And still fluttered down the snow.

I stood and watched by the window
  The noiseless work of the sky,
And the sudden flurries of snow-birds,
  Like brown leaves whirling by.

I thought of a mound in sweet Auburn
  Where a little headstone stood;
How the flakes were folding it gently,
  As did robins the babes in the wood.   20

Up spoke our own little Mabel,
  Saying, "Father, who makes it snow?"
And I told of the good All-father
  Who cares for us here below.

Again I looked at the snow-fall,
  And thought of the leaden sky
That arched o'er our first great sorrow,
  When that mound was heaped so high.

I remembered the gradual patience
  That fell from that cloud like snow,   30
Flake by flake, healing and hiding
  The scar that renewed our woe.

And again to the child I whispered,
  "The snow that husheth all,
Darling, the merciful Father
  Alone can make it fall!"

Then, with eyes that saw not, I kissed her;
  And she, kissing back, could not know
That *my* kiss was given to her sister,   39
  Folded close under deepening snow.
1849   1849

[1] In memory of Lowell's first child, Blanche, who had died in 1847 when but fourteen months old; she was buried in Mt. Auburn cemetery, Cambridge, very near Lowell's home.
[2] a very beautiful white Italian marble quarried at Carrara

SHE CAME AND WENT

As a twig trembles, which a bird
  Lights on to sing, then leaves unbent,
So is my memory thrilled and stirred;—
  I only know she came and went.

As clasps some lake, by gusts unriven,
  The blue dome's measureless content,
So my soul held that moment's heaven;—
  I only know she came and went.

As, at one bound, our swift spring heaps
  The orchards full of bloom and scent,   10
So clove her May my wintry sleeps;—
  I only know she came and went.

An angel stood and met my gaze,
  Through the low doorway of my tent;
The tent is struck, the vision stays;—
  I only know she came and went.

Oh, when the room grows slowly dim,
  And life's last oil is nearly spent,
One gush of light these eyes will brim,   19
  Only to think she came and went.
1847?   1849

AUF WIEDERSEHEN [3]

SUMMER

The little gate was reached at last,
  Half hid in lilacs down the lane;
She pushed it wide, and, as she past,
A wistful look she backward cast,
  And said,—*"Auf wiedersehen!"*

With hand on latch, a vision white
  Lingered reluctant, and again
Half doubting if she did aright,
Soft as the dews that fell that night,
  She said,—*"Auf wiedersehen!"*   10

The lamp's clear gleam flits up the stair;
  I linger in delicious pain;
Ah, in that chamber, whose rich air
To breathe in thought I scarcely dare,
  Thinks she,—*"Auf wiedersehen!"*

'Tis thirteen years; once more I press
  The turf that silences the lane;
I hear the rustle of her dress,
I smell the lilacs, and—ah, yes,
  I hear,—*"Auf wiedersehen!"*   20

Sweet piece of bashful maiden art!
  The English words had seemed too fain,

[3] "May we meet again."

But these—they drew us heart to heart,
Yet held us tenderly apart;
  She said,—*"Auf wiedersehen!"*
1854   1854

DAS EWIG-WEIBLICHE [1]

How was I worthy so divine a loss,
  Deepening my midnights, kindling all my
      morns?
Why waste such precious wood to make my
      cross,
  Such far-sought roses for my crown of
      thorns?

And when she came, how earned I such a gift?
  Why spend on me, a poor earth-delving
      mole,
The fireside sweetnesses, the heavenward lift,
  The hourly mercy, of a woman's soul?

Ah, did we know to give her all her right,
  What wonders even in our poor clay were
      done!   10
It is not Woman leaves us to our night,
  But our brute earth that grovels from her
      sun.

Our nobler cultured fields and gracious domes
We whirl too oft from her who still shines on
To light in vain our caves and clefts, the homes
Of night-bird instincts pained till she be gone.

Still must this body starve our souls with
      shade;
  But when Death makes us what we were
      before,   18
Then shall her sunshine all our depths invade,
  And not a shadow stain heaven's crystal
      floor.
1858   1858

From THE BIGLOW PAPERS [2]

[*First Series, 1846-1848*]

No. I—A LETTER

FROM MR. EZEKIEL BIGLOW OF JAALAM TO THE
HON. JOSEPH T. BUCKINGHAM, EDITOR OF
THE BOSTON COURIER, INCLOSING A POEM.

JAYLEM, june 1846.

MISTER EDDYTER:—Our Hosea wuz down to
Boston last week, and he see a cruetin Sarjunt
a struttin round as popler as a hen with 1

chicking, with 2 fellers a drummin and fifin
arter him like all nater. the sarjunt he thout
Hosea hedn't gut his i teeth cut cos he looked
a kindo's though he'd jest com down, so he
cal'lated to hook him in, but Hosy woodn't
take none o' his sarse for all he hed much as 20
Rooster's tales stuck onto his hat and eenamost
enuf brass a bobbin up and down on his shoulders and figureed onto his coat and trousis, let
alone wut nater hed sot in his featers, to make
a 6 pounder out on.

wal, Hosea he com home considerabal riled,
and arter I'd gone to bed I heern Him a thrashin
round like a short-tailed Bull in fli-time. The
old Woman ses she to me ses she, Zekle, ses
she, our Hosee's gut the chollery or suthin
anuther ses she, don't you Bee skeered, ses I,
he's oney amakin pottery [*Aut insanit, aut
versos facit.*—H. W. [3]]ses i, he's ollers on hand
at that ere busynes like Da & martin, [4] and
shure enuf, cum mornin, Hosy he cum down
stares full chizzle, hare on eend and cote tales
flyin, and sot rite of to go reed his varses to
Parson Wilbur bein he haint aney grate shows
o' book larnin himself, bimeby he cum back
and sed the parson wuz dreffle tickled with 'em
as i hoop you will Be, and said they wuz True
grit.

Hosea ses taint hardly fair to call 'em hisn
now, cos the parson kind o' slicked off sum o'
the last varses, but he told Hosee he didn't
want to put his ore in to tetch to the Rest on
'em, bein they wuz verry well As thay wuz, and
then Hosy ses he sed suthin a nuther about
Simplex Mundishes [5] or sum sech feller, but I
guess Hosea kind o' didn't hear him, for I
never hearn o' nobody o' that name in this
villadge, and I've lived here man and boy 76
year cum next tater diggin, and thair aint no
wheres a kitting spryer'n I be.

If you print 'em I wish you'd jest let folks
know who hosy's father is, cos my ant Keziah
used to say it's nater to be curus ses she, she
aint livin though and he's a likely kind o' lad.

                          EZEKIEL BIGLOW.

---

[1] The eternally feminine; Lowell's first wife, Maria
White, had died five years before.

[2] In these satires, which came out at intervals—the
first series during the Mexican War, and the

second series during the Civil War—Lowell, often
with stinging force, puts into the mouth of the
Yankee farmer the ideas current in New England
at the time. Many believed that the Mexican
War was begun with a view to increasing slave
territory. At its close Mexico yielded to the
United States much of what is now California,
Nevada, Utah, Arizona, New Mexico, Colorado,
and Wyoming. H. W. or Homerus Wilbur, Esq.,
a pedantic minister, purports to edit the poems of
his parishioner, Hosea Biglow.

[3] "Either he raves or he composes verses." Horace,
Satires, II, vii, 117.

[4] Messrs. Day and Martin's shoe blacking came in
earthen (pottery) jars.

[5] *Simplex munditiis;* "plain in thy neatness." Horace,
Carmina, I, v, 5

Thrash away, you'll *hev* to rattle
  On them kittle-drums o' yourn,—
'Taint a knowin' kind o' cattle
  Thet is ketched with moldy corn;
Put in stiff, you fifer feller,
  Let folks see how spry you be,—
Guess you'll toot till you are yeller
  'Fore you git ahold o' me!

Thet air flag's a leetle rotten,
  Hope it aint your Sunday's best;—   10
Fact! it takes a sight o' cotton
  To stuff out a soger's chest:
Sence we farmers hev to pay fer't,
  Ef you must wear humps like these,
Sposin' you should try salt hay fer't,
  It would du ez slick ez grease.

'Twouldn't suit them Southun fellers,
  They're a dreffle graspin' set,
We must ollers blow the bellers
  Wen they want their irons het;   20
May be it's all right ez preachin',
  But *my* narves it kind o' grates,
Wen I see the overreachin'
  O' them nigger-drivin' States.

Them thet rule us, them slave-traders,
  Haint they cut a thunderin' swarth,
(Helped by Yankee renegaders),
  Thru the vartu o' the North!
We begin to think it's nater
  To take sarse an' not be riled;—   30
Who'd expect to see a tater
  All on eend at bein' biled?

Ez fer war, I call it murder,—
  There you hev it plain an' flat;
I don't want to go no furder
  Than my Testament fer that;
God hez sed so plump an' fairly,
  It's ez long ez it is broad,
An' you've gut to git up airly
  Ef you want to take in God.   40

'Taint your eppyletts an' feathers
  Make the thing a grain more right;
'Taint afollerin' your bell-wethers
  Will excuse ye in His sight;
Ef you take a sword an' dror it,
  An' go stick a feller thru,
Guv'ment aint to answer for it,
  God'll send the bill to you.

Wut's the use o' meetin'-goin'
  Every Sabbath, wet or dry,   50
Ef it's right to go amowin'

Feller-men like oats an' rye?
  I dunno but wut it's pooty
    Trainin' round in bobtail coats,—
But it's curus Christian dooty
    This 'ere cuttin' folks's throats.

They may talk o' Freedom's airy [1]
  Tell they're pupple in the face,—
It's a grand gret cemetary
  Fer the barthrights of our race;   60
They jest want this Californy
  So's to lug new slave-states in
To abuse ye, an' to scorn ye,
  An' to plunder ye like sin.

Aint it cute to see a Yankee
  Take sech everlastin' pains,
All to git the Devil's thankee,
  Helpin' on 'em weld their chains?
Wy, it's jest ez clear ez figgers,
  Clear ez one an' one make two,   70
Chaps thet make black slaves o' niggers
  Want to make wite slaves o' you.

Tell ye jest the eend I've come to
  Arter cipherin' plaguy smart,
An' it makes a handy sum, tu,
  Any gump could larn by heart;
Laborin' man an' laborin' woman
  Hev one glory an' one shame,
Ev'y thin' thet's done inhuman
  Injers all on 'em the same.   80

'Taint by turnin' out to hack folks
  You're agoin' to git your right,
Nor by lookin' down on black folks
  Coz you're put upon by wite;
Slavery aint o' nary color,
  'Taint the hide thet makes it wus,
All it keers fer in a feller
  'S jest to make him fill its pus.

Want to tackle *me* in, du ye?
  I expect you'll hev to wait;   90
Wen cold lead puts daylight thru ye
  You'll begin to kal'late;
'Spose the crows wun't fall to pickin'
  All the carkiss from your bones,
Coz you helped to give a lickin'
  To them poor half-Spanish drones?

Jest go home an' ask our Nancy
  Wether I'd be sech a goose
Ez to jine ye,—guess you'd fancy
  The etarnal bung was loose!   100
She wants me fer home consumption,
  Let alone the hay's to mow,—

[1] area; or possibly aerie (eagle-nest)

Ef you're arter folks o' gumption,
  You've a darned long row to hoe.

Take them editors thet's crowin'
  Like a cockerel three months old,—
Don't ketch any on 'em goin',
  Though they *be* so blasted bold;
Aint they a prime lot o' fellers?
  'Fore they think on't guess they'll sprout,
(Like a peach thet's got the yellers)   111
  With the meanness bustin' out.

Wal, go 'long to help 'em stealin'
  Bigger pens to cram with slaves,
Help the men thet's ollers dealin'
  Insults on your fathers' graves;
Help the strong to grind the feeble,
  Help the many agin the few,
Help the men thet call your people
  Witewashed slaves an' peddlin' crew !

Massachusetts, God forgive her,   121
  She's akneelin' with the rest,
She thet ough' to ha' clung ferever
  In her grand old eagle-nest;
She thet ough' to stand so fearless
  Wile the wracks are round her hurled,
Holdin' up a beacon peerless
  To the oppressed of all the world!

Ha'n't they sold your colored seamen?
  Ha'n't they made your env'ys w'iz? [1]
Wut'll make ye act like free men?   131
  Wut'll git your dander riz?
Come, I'll tell ye wut I'm thinkin'
  Is our dooty in this fix,
They'd ha' done 't ez quick ez winkin'
  In the days o' seventy-six.

Clang the bells in every steeple,
  Call all true men to disown
The tradoocers of our people,
  The enslavers o' their own;   140
Let our dear old Bay State proudly
  Put the trumpet to her mouth,
Let her ring this messidge loudly
  In the ears of all the South:—

"I'll return ye good for evil
  Much ez we frail mortils can,
But I won't go help the Devil
  Makin' man the cus o' man;

Call me coward, call me traiter,
  Jest ez suits your mean idees,—   150
Here I stand a tyrant-hater,
  An' the friend o' God an' Peace !"

Ef I'd *my* way.I hed ruther
  We should go to work an' part,— [2]
They take one way, we take t'other,—
  Guess it wouldn't break my heart;
Man hed ough' to put asunder
  Them thet God has noways jined;
An' I shouldn't gretly wonder
  Ef there's thousands o' my mind.   160

[The first recruiting sergeant on record I conceive to have been that individual who is mentioned in the Book of Job as *going to and fro in the earth, and walking up and down in it.* Bishop Latimer will have him to have been a bishop, but to me that other calling would appear more congenial. The sect of Cainites is not yet extinct, who esteemed the first-born of Adam to be the most worthy, not only because of that privilege of primogeniture, but inasmuch as he was able to overcome and slay his younger brother. That was a wise saying of the famous Marquis Pescara to the Papal Legate, that *it was impossible for men to serve Mars and Christ at the same time.* Yet in time past the profession of arms was judged to be κατ ἐξοχήν [3] that of a gentleman, nor does this opinion want for strenuous upholders even in our day. Must we suppose, then, that the profession of Christianity was only intended for losels, or, at best, to afford an opening for plebeian ambition? Or shall we hold with that nicely metaphysical Pomeranian, Captain Vratz, who was Count Königsmark's chief instrument in the murder of Mr. Thynne, that the Scheme of Salvation had been arranged with an especial eye to the necessities of the upper classes, and that "God would consider a *gentleman* and deal with him suitably to the condition and profession he had placed him in"? It may be said of us all, *Exemplo plus quam ratione vivimus.* [4]—H. W.]

[*Second Series, 1862-1866*]

THE COURTIN'

God makes sech nights, all white an' still
  Fur'z you can look or listen,
Moonshine an' snow on field an' hill,
  All silence an' all glisten.

[1] Several southern states had laws forbidding colored freemen to enter their territory. Black sailors had been imprisoned and even sold as slaves in some southern ports. Mr. Samuel Hoar of Massachusetts, who had been sent to Charleston in the interests of black sailors, was expelled from South Carolina, and Mr. Hubbard, who had been sent to New Orleans, was made to leave Louisiana.

[2] The idea of secession was not confined to the South.
[3] "par excellence"
[4] "we live more by example than by reason"

Zekle crep' up quite unbeknown
  An' peeked in thru' the winder,
An' there sot Huldy all alone,
  'ith no one nigh to hender.

A fireplace filled the room's one side
  With half a cord o' wood in—   10
There warn't no stoves (tell comfort died)
  To bake ye to a puddin'.

The wa'nut logs shot sparkles out
  Towards the pootiest, bless her,
An' leetle flames danced all about
  The chiny on the dresser.

Agin the chimbley crook-necks ¹ hung,
  An' in amongst 'em rusted
The ole queen's-arm ² thet gran'ther Young
  Fetched back f'om Concord busted.   20

The very room, coz she was in,
  Seemed warm from floor to ceilin',
An' she looked full ez rosy agin
  Ez the apples she was peelin'.

'Twas kin' o' kingdom-come to look
  On sech a blessed cretur,
A dogrose blushin' to a brook
  Ain't modester nor sweeter.

He was six foot o' man, A 1,
  Clear grit an' human natur';   30
None couldn't quicker pitch a ton
  Nor dror a furrer straighter.

He'd sparked it with full twenty gals,
  He'd squired 'em, danced 'em, druv 'em,
Fust this one, an' then thet, by spells—
  All is, he couldn't love 'em.

But long o' her his veins 'ould run
  All crinkly like curled maple,
The side she breshed felt full o' sun
  Ez a south slope in Ap'il.   40

She thought no v'ice hed sech a swing
  Ez hisn in the choir;
My! when he made Ole Hunderd ring,
  She *knowed* the Lord was nigher.

An' she'd blush scarlit, right in prayer,
  When her new meetin'-bunnet
Felt somehow thru' its crown a pair
  O' blue eyes sot upun it.

Thet night, I tell ye, she looked *some!*
  She seemed to 've gut a new soul,   50

For she felt sartin-sure he'd come,
  Down to her very shoe-sole.

She heered a foot, an' knowed it tu,
  A-raspin' on the scraper,—
All ways to once her feelin's flew
  Like sparks in burnt-up paper.

He kin' o' l'itered on the mat
  Some doubtfle o' the sekle,
His heart kep' goin' pity-pat,
  But hern went pity Zekle.   60

An' yit she gin her cheer a jerk
  Ez though she wished him furder,
An' on her apples kep' to work,
  Parin' away like murder.

"You want to see my Pa, I s'pose?"
  "Wal . . . no . . . I come dasignin' "—
"To see my Ma? She's sprinklin' clo'es
  Agin to-morrer's i'nin'."

To say why gals acts so or so,
  Or don't, 'ould be presumin';   70
Mebby to mean *yes* an' say *no*
  Comes nateral to women.

He stood a spell on one foot fust,
  Then stood a spell on t'other,
An' on which one he felt the wust
  He couldn't ha' told ye nuther.

Says he, "I'd better call agin";
  Says she, "Think likely, Mister":
Thet last word pricked him like a pin,
  An' . . . Wal, he up an' kist her.   80

When Ma bimeby upon 'em slips,
  Huldy sot pale ez ashes,
All kin' o' smily roun' the lips
  An' teary roun' the lashes.

For she was jes' the quiet kind
  Whose naturs never vary,
Like streams that keep a summer mind
  Snowhid in Jenooary.

The blood clost roun' her heart felt glued
  Too tight for all expressin',   90
Tell mother see how metters stood,
  And gin 'em both her blessin'.

Then her red come back like the tide
  Down to the Bay o' Fundy,
An' all I know is they was cried ³
  In meetin' come nex' Sunday.

¹ squashes   ² musket

³ The marriage bans were published.

THE WASHERS OF THE SHROUD [1]
OCTOBER, 1861

Along a river-side, I know not where,
I walked one night in mystery of dream;
A chill creeps curdling yet beneath my hair,
To think what chanced me by the pallid gleam
Of a moon-wraith that waned through haunted
air.

Pale fireflies pulsed within the meadow-mist
Their halos, wavering thistle-downs of light;
The loon, that seemed to mock some goblin
tryst,
Laughed; and the echoes, huddling in affright,
Like Odin's hounds, fled baying down the
night. 10

Then all was silent, till there smote my ear
A movement in the stream that checked my
breath:
Was it the slow plash of a wading deer?
But something said, "This water is of Death!
The Sisters [2] wash a shroud,—ill thing to hear!"

I, looking then, beheld the ancient Three
Known to the Greeks and to the Norseman's
creed,
That sit in shadow of the mystic Tree,
Still crooning, as they weave their endless
brede, [3]
One song: "Time was, Time is, and Time shall
be." 20

No wrinkled crones were they, as I had deemed,
But fair as yesterday, today, tomorrow,
To mourner, lover, poet, ever seemed:
Something too deep for joy, too high for
sorrow,
Thrilled in their tones, and from their faces
gleamed.

"Still men and nations reap as they have
strawn,"
So sang they, working at their task the while,—
"The fatal raiment must be cleansed ere dawn:

For Austria? Italy? The Sea-Queen's isle?
O'er what quenched grandeur must our shroud
be drawn? 30

"Or is it for a younger, fairer corse,
That gathered States like children round his
knees,
That tamed the wave to be his posting-horse,
Feller of forests, linker of the seas,
Bridge-builder, hammerer, youngest son of
Thor's?

"What make we, murmur'st thou? and what
are we?
When empires must be wound, we bring the
shroud,
The time-old web of the implacable Three:
Is it too coarse for him, the young and proud?
Earth's mightiest deigned to wear it,—why not
he?" 40

"Is there no hope?" I moaned, "so strong, so
fair!
Our Fowler whose proud bird would brook
erewhile
No rival's swoop in all our western air! [4]
Gather the ravens, then, in funeral file
For him, life's morn yet golden in his hair?

"Leave me not hopeless, ye unpitying dames!
I see, half seeing. Tell me, ye who scanned
The stars, Earth's elders, still must noblest
aims
Be traced upon oblivious ocean-sands?
Must Hesper [5] join the wailing ghosts of
names?" 50

"When grass-blades stiffen with red battle-dew,
Ye deem we choose the victor and the slain:
Say, choose we them that shall be leal and true
To the heart's longing, the high faith of brain?
Yet there the victory lies, if ye but knew.

"Three roots bear up Dominion: Knowledge,
Will,—
These twain are strong, but stronger yet the
third,
Obedience,—'tis the great tap-root that still,
Knit round the rock of Duty, is not stirred,
Though Heaven-loosed tempests spend their
utmost skill. 60

[1] In a letter to Charles Eliot Norton, Lowell wrote: "the hint [for the poem] came to me from one of those books of Souvestre's you lent me—the Breton legends." *Letters of James Russell Lowell*, i, 317. From the date of the poem and its imagery it is evident that Lowell greatly feared the breaking up of the Union.

[2] The Three Sisters or Fates; in classic mythology Clotho spun the thread of life, Lachesis measured it, and Atropos cut it. In Norse mythology the three Fates or Norns are Udur, Verdandi, and Skuld. They sit tending that root of the ash tree Yggdrasil, the supporter of the universe, which penetrates Asgard, the home of the gods.

[3] braid

[4] France and Spain had, by 1803 and 1819 respectively, withdrawn from what is now the United States. Moreover, the "Monroe Doctrine" declared that the American continents must not be considered as subject to future colonization by European nations.

[5] Hesperus, son of Eos, Dawn, is the evening (and so the western) star; it was regarded by the ancients as also the morning star—the bringer of light.

"Is the doom sealed for Hesper? 'Tis not we
Denounce it, but the Law before all time:
The brave makes danger opportunity;
The waverer, paltering with the chance sub-
    lime,
Dwarfs it to peril: which shall Hesper be?

"Hath he let vultures climb his eagle's seat
To make Jove's bolts purveyors of their maw?
Hath he the Many's plaudits found more sweet
Than Wisdom? held Opinion's wind for law?
Then let him hearken for the doomster's feet!

"Rough are the steps, slow-hewn in flintiest
    rock,   71
States climb to power by; slippery those with
    gold
Down which they stumble to eternal mock:
No chafferer's hand shall long the scepter hold,
Who, given a Fate to shape, would sell the
    block.

"We sing old sagas, songs of weal and woe,
Mystic because too cheaply understood;
Dark sayings are not ours: men hear and know,
See Evil weak, see strength alone in Good,
Yet hope to stem God's fire with walls of
    tow.   80

"Time Was unlocks the riddle of Time Is,
That offers choice of glory or of gloom;
The solver makes Time Shall Be surely his.
But hasten, Sisters! for even now the tomb
Grates its slow hinge and calls from the abyss."

"But not for him," I cried, "not yet for him,
Whose large horizon, westering, star by star
Wins from the void to where on ocean's rim
The sunset shuts the world with golden bar,—
Not yet his thews shall fail, his eye grow
    dim!   90

"His shall be larger manhood, saved for those
That walk unblenching through the trial-fires;
Not suffering, but faint heart, is worst of woes,
And he no base-born son of craven sires,
Whose eye need blench confronted with his
    foes.

"Tears may be ours, but proud, for those who
    win
Death's royal purple in the foeman's lines;
Peace, too, brings tears; and mid the battle-din,
The wiser ear some text of God divines;
For the sheathed blade may rust with darker
    sin.   100

"God, give us peace! not such as lulls to sleep,
But sword on thigh, and brow with purpose
    knit!
And let our Ship of State to harbor sweep,
Her ports all up, her battle-lanterns lit,
And her leashed thunders gathering for their
    leap!"

So said I with clenched hands and passionate
    pain,
Thinking of dear ones by Potomac's side;
Again the loon laughed mocking, and again
The echoes bayed far down the night and
    died,   109
While, waking, I recalled my wandering brain.
1861   1861

ODE RECITED AT THE HARVARD COMMEMORATION [1]

I

Weak-winged is song,
Nor aims at that clear-ethered height
Whither the brave deed climbs for light:
    We seem to do them wrong,
Bringing our robin's-leaf to deck their hearse
Who in warm life-blood wrote their nobler
    verse,
Our trivial song to honor those who come
With ears attuned to strenuous trump and
    drum,
And shaped in squadron-strophes [2] their desire,
Live battle-odes whose lines were steel and
    fire.   10
    Yet sometimes feathered words are strong
A gracious memory to buoy up and save
From Lethe's [3] dreamless ooze, the common
    grave
    Of the unventurous throng.

II

Today our Reverend Mother welcomes back
    Her wisest Scholars, those who understood
The deeper teaching of her mystic tome
    And offered their fresh lives to make it good.
    No lore of Greece or Rome,
No science peddling with the names of things,
Or reading stars to find inglorious fates,   21

[1] The ode was read at Harvard College on July 21, 1865, at a solemn commemoration held in memory of the sons of the College who had fallen during the Civil War.

[2] The strophe, or turn, was a division of the Greek choral ode, sung by one part of the Greek chorus; the response or anti-strophe was sung by the other part of the chorus.

[3] the river of oblivion in Hades

Can lift our life with wings
Far from Death's idle gulf that for the many
   waits,
 And lengthen out our dates
With that clear fame whose memory sings
In manly hearts to come; and nerves them and
   dilates:
Nor such thy teaching, Mother of us all!
  Not such the trumpet-call
  Of thy diviner mood,
  That could thy sons entice   30
From happy homes and toils, the fruitful nest
Of those half-virtues which the world calls best,
  Into War's tumult rude;
  But rather far that stern device
The sponsors chose that round thy cradle stood
  In the dim, unventured wood,
  The VERITAS [1] that lurks beneath
  The letter's unprolific sheath,
 Life of whate'er makes life worth living,
Seed-grain of high emprise, immortal food, 40
 One heavenly thing whereof earth hath the
   giving.

III

Many loved Truth, and lavished life's best oil
 Amid the dust of books to find her,
Content at last, for guerdon of their toil,
 With the cast mantle she hath left behind
   her; [2]
  Many in sad faith sought for her,
  Many with crossed hands sighed for her.
 But these, our brothers, fought for her,
  At life's dear peril wrought for her,
  So loved her that they died for her, 50
  Tasting the raptured fleetness
  Of her divine completeness:
   Their higher instinct knew
Those love her best who to themselves are true,
And what they dare to dream of dare to do:
  They followed her and found her
  Where all may hope to find,
 Not in the ashes of the burnt-out mind,
 But beautiful, with danger's sweetness round
   her:
  Where faith, made whole with deed, 60
  Breathes its awakening breath
  Into the lifeless creed,
  They saw her, plumed and mailed,
  With sweet, stern face unveiled,
And all-repaying eyes, look proud on them in
   death.

IV

Our slender life runs rippling by, and glides
 Into the silent hollow of the past;

What is there that abides
To make the next age better for the last?
 Is earth too poor to give us   70
Something to live for here that shall out-
   live us?
 Some more substantial boon
Than such as flows and ebbs with Fortune's
   fickle moon?
  The little that we see
  From doubt is never free; [3]
  The little that we do
  Is but half-nobly true;
  With our laborious hiving
What men call treasure, and the gods call dross,
  Life seems a jest of Fate's contriving, 80
  Only secure in every one's conniving,
A long account of nothings paid with loss,
Where we poor puppets, jerked by unseen
   wires,
 After our little hour of strut and rave, [4]
With all our pasteboard passions and desires,
Loves, hates, ambitions, and immortal fires,
 Are tossed pell-mell together in the grave.
  Ah, there is something here
 Unfathomed by the cynic's sneer;
  Something that gives our feeble light 90
  A high immunity from Night;
  Something that leaps life's narrow bars
To claim its birthright with the hosts of
   heaven: [5]
 A seed of sunshine that doth leaven
 Our earthly dulness with the beams of stars,
  And glorify our clay
With light from fountains elder than the Day;
 A conscience more divine than we,
 A gladness fed with secret tears,
 A vexing, forward-reaching sense 100
 Of some more noble permanence;
  A light across the sea,
 Which haunts the soul and will not let it be,
Still glimmering from the heights of undegen-
   erate years.

V

  Whither leads the path
  To ampler fates that leads?
  Not down through flowery meads,
  To reap an aftermath
  Of youth's vainglorious weeds;
  But up the steep, amid the wrath 110
And shock of deadly-hostile creeds,

[1] Veritas (L. truth) motto on Harvard University seal
[2] knowledge of the past

[3] Cf. Browning in "Bishop Blougram's Apology," ll. 100-
 112:
  "All we have gained then by our unbelief
  Is a life of doubt diversified by faith,
  For one of faith diversified by doubt:
  We called the chess-board white,—we call it
   black."
[4] Cf. Macbeth V, v, 25.
[5] Cf. Wordsworth's "Ode, Intimations of Immortality
 from Recollections of Early Childhood," ix.

Where the world's best hope and stay
By battle's flashes grope a desperate way,
And every turf the fierce foot clings to bleeds.
    Peace hath her not ignoble wreath,
    Ere yet the sharp, decisive word
Lights the black lips of cannon, and the sword
    Dreams in its easeful sheath:
But some day the live coal behind the thought,
    Whether from Baäl's [1] stone obscene, 120
    Or from the shrine serene
    Of God's pure altar brought,
Bursts up in flame; the war of tongue and pen
Learns with what deadly purpose it was fraught,
And, helpless in the fiery passion caught,
Shakes all the pillared state with shock of men.
Some day the soft Ideal that we wooed
Confronts us fiercely, foe-beset, pursued,
And cries reproachful: Was it, then, my
    praise,
And not myself was loved? Prove now thy
    truth!   130
I claim of thee the promise of thy youth;
Give me thy life, or cower in empty phrase,
The victim of thy genius, not its mate!"
    Life may be given in many ways,
    And loyalty to Truth be sealed
As bravely in the closet as the field,
    So generous is Fate;
    But then to stand beside her,
    When craven churls deride her,
To front a lie in arms and not to yield,   140
    This shows, methinks, God's plan
    And measure of a stalwart man,
    Limbed like the old heroic breeds,
Who stands self-poised on manhood's solid
    earth,
Not forced to frame excuses for his birth,
    Fed from within with all the strength he
    needs.

VI

Such was he, our Martyr-Chief, [2]
    Whom late the Nation he had led,
    With ashes on her head,   149
Wept with the passion of an angry grief:
Forgive me, if from present things I turn
To speak what in my heart will beat and burn,
And hang my wreath on his world-honored urn.
    Nature, they say, doth dote,
    And cannot make a man
    Save on some worn-out plan,
    Repeating us by rote:
For him her Old-World mold aside she threw,
    And, choosing sweet clay from the breast

    Of the unexhausted West,   160
With stuff untainted shaped a hero new,
Wise, steadfast in the strength of God, and
    true.
    How beautiful to see
Once more a shepherd of mankind indeed,
Who loved his charge but never loved to lead;
One whose meek flock the people joyed to be,
    Not lured by any cheat of birth,
    But by his clear-grained human worth,
And brave old wisdom of sincerity!
    They knew that outward grace is dust; 170
    They could not choose but trust
In that sure-footed mind's unfaltering skill,
    And supple-tempered will
That bent like perfect steel to spring again and
    thrust.
    Nothing of Europe here—
Or, then, of Europe fronting mornward still,
    Ere any names of Serf and Peer
    Could Nature's equal scheme deface:
    Here was a type of the true elder race,
And one of Plutarch's men [3] talked with us
    face to face.   180
    I praise him not: it were too late;
And some innative weakness there must be
In him who condescends to victory
Such as the Present gives, and cannot wait,
    Safe in himself as in a fate.
    So always firmly he:
    He knew to bide his time,
    And can his fame abide,
Still patient in his simple faith sublime,
    Till the wise years decide.   190
    Great captains, with their guns and drums,
    Disturb our judgment for the hour,
    But at last silence comes;
These all are gone, and, standing like a tower,
Our children shall behold his fame,
The kindly-earnest, brave, foreseeing man,
Sagacious, patient, dreading praise, not blame,
New birth of our new soil, the first American.

VII

Long as man's hope insatiate can discern
    Or only guess some more inspiring goal
    Outside of Self, enduring as the pole, 201
Along whose course the flying axles burn
Of spirits bravely-pitched, earth's manlier
    brood;
    Long as below we cannot find
    The meed that stills the inexorable mind;
So long this faith to some ideal Good,
Under whatever mortal names it masks—
Freedom, Law, Country,—this ethereal mood

---

[1] A Canaanitish deity, god of abundance and fertility;
his worship, attended with wild orgies, was introduced among the Israelites during the time of the
kings.
[2] Abraham Lincoln, assassinated April 14, 1865

[3] Plutarch, a Greek historian of the first century, wrote
the lives of forty-six of the most famous Greeks
and Romans.

That thanks the Fates for their severer tasks,
  Feeling its challenged pulses leap   210
While others skulk in subterfuges cheap,
And, set in Danger's van, has all the boon it
      asks,
  Shall win man's praise and woman's love,
  Shall be a wisdom that we set above
All other skills and gifts to culture dear,
  A virtue round whose forehead we enwreathe
  Laurels that with a living passion breathe
When other crowns are cold and soon grow
      sear.
  What brings us thronging these high rites to
      pay,
And seal these hours the noblest of our year,
  Save that our brothers found this better
      way?   221

VIII

We sit here in the Promised Land [1]
That flows with Freedom's honey and milk;
  But 't was they won it, sword in hand,
Making the nettle danger [2] soft for us as silk.
  We welcome back our bravest and our best—
  Ah me! not all! some come not with the
      rest,
Who went forth brave and bright as any here!
I strive to mix some gladness with my strain,
  But the sad strings complain,   230
  And will not please the ear:
I sweep them for a paean, [3] but they wane
  Again and yet again
Into a dirge and die away in pain.
In these brave ranks I only see the gaps,
Thinking of dear ones whom the dumb turf
      wraps,
Dark to the triumph which they died to gain:
  Fitlier may others greet the living,
  For me the past is unforgiving;
  I with uncovered head   240
  Salute the sacred dead,
Who went, and who return not.—Say not so!
'T is not the grapes of Canaan [4] that repay,
But the high faith that failed not by the way;
Virtue treads paths that end not in the grave;
No ban of endless night exiles the brave;
  And to the saner mind
We rather seem the dead that stayed behind.
Blow, trumpets, all your exultations blow!
For never shall their aureoled presence lack:
I see them muster in a gleaming row,   251
With ever-youthful brows that nobler show;
We find in our dull road their shining track;

[1] Cf. the land of Canaan promised to the Israelites, *Exodus* iii, 8.
[2] "Out of this nettle, danger, we pluck this flower, safety." Shakespeare, 1 *Henry* IV, II, iii.
[3] song of triumph   [4] See *Numbers* xiii, 17, ff.

In every nobler mood
We feel the orient of their spirit glow,
Part of our life's unalterable good,
  Of all our saintlier aspiration;
  They come transfigured back,
Secure from change in their high-hearted ways,
Beautiful evermore, and with the rays   260
Of morn on their white Shields of Expectation!

IX

  Who now shall sneer?
  Who dare again to say we trace
  Our lines to a plebeian race?
  Roundhead and Cavalier! [5]
Dreams are those names erewhile in battle
      loud;
Forceless as is the shadow of a cloud,
  They live but in the ear:
That is best blood that hath most iron in 't
To edge resolve with, pouring without stint
  For what makes manhood dear.   271
  Tell us not of Plantagenets,
Hapsburgs, and Guelfs, [6] whose thin bloods
      crawl
Down from some victor in a border-brawl!
  How poor their outworn coronets,
Matched with one leaf of that plain civic
      wreath
Our brave for honor's blazon shall bequeath,
  Through whose desert a rescued Nation sets
Her heel on treason, and the trumpet hears
Shout victory, tingling Europe's sullen ears
  With vain resentments and more vain re-
      grets!   281

X

  Not in anger, not in pride,
  Pure from passion's mixture rude
  Ever to base earth allied,
  But with far-heard gratitude,
  Still with heart and voice renewed,
To heroes living and dear martyrs dead,
The strain should close that consecrates our
      brave.
  Lift the heart and lift the head!
  Lofty be its mood and grave,   290
  Not without a martial ring,
  Not without a prouder tread
  And a peal of exultation:
  Little right has he to sing
Through whose heart in such an hour

[5] The Roundheads, or Puritans, and the Cavaliers, or monarchists, were the two parties in the Puritan Revolution, 1642-1646, in England.
[6] The Plantagenets were the rulers of England from 1154 to 1399; the Hapsburgs were sovereigns of the Holy Roman Empire, Austria, and Spain for many centuries, and still rule Spain; and the Guelphs were ancestors of the House of Hanover, the present ruling family in England.

Beats no march of conscious power,
Sweeps no tumult of elation!
'T is no Man we celebrate,
By his country's victories great,
A hero half, and half the whim of Fate,   300
  But the pith and marrow of a Nation
  Drawing force from all her men,
  Highest, humblest, weakest, all,
  Pulsing it again through them,
Till the basest can no longer cower,
  Feeling his soul spring up divinely tall,
  Touched but in passing by her mantle-hem.
Come back, then, noble pride, for 't is her
    dower!
  How could poet ever tower,
  If his passions, hopes, and fears,   310
  If his triumphs and his tears,
  Kept not measure with his people?
Boom, cannon, boom to all the winds and
    waves!
Clash out, glad bells, from every rocking
    steeple!
Banners, advance with triumph, bend your
    staves!
  And from every mountain-peak
  Let beacon-fire to answering beacon speak,
Katahdin tell Monadnock, Whiteface[1] he,
And so leap on in light from sea to sea,
  Till the glad news be sent   320
  Across a kindling continent,
Making earth feel more firm and air breathe
    braver:
"Be proud! for she is saved, and all have
    helped to save her!
She that lifts up the manhood of the poor,
She of the open soul and open door,
With room about her hearth for all mankind!
The helm from her bold front she doth un-
    bind,
Sends all her handmaid armies back to spin,
And bids her navies hold their thunders in.
No challenge sends she to the elder world,
That looked askance and hated; a light
    scorn   331
Plays on her mouth, as round her mighty
    knees
She calls her children back, and waits the
    morn
Of nobler day, enthroned between her subject
    seas."

XI

Bow down, dear Land, for thou hast found
    release!
  Thy God, in these distempered days,

[1] Mount Katahdin is the highest mountain in Maine;
Monadnock and Whiteface are mountains in New
Hampshire.

Hath taught thee the sure wisdom of His ways,
  And through thine enemies hath wrought thy
    peace.
  Bow down in prayer and praise!   339
O Beautiful! my Country! ours once more!
  Smoothing thy gold of war-dishevelled hair
O'er such sweet brows as never other wore,
  And letting thy set lips,
  Freed from wrath's pale eclipse,
The rosy edges of their smile lay bare,
What words divine of lover or of poet
Could tell our love and make thee know it,
Among the Nations bright beyond compare?
  What were our lives without thee?
  What all our lives to save thee;   350
  We reck not what we gave thee;
  We will not dare to doubt thee;
But ask whatever else, and we will dare!
1865   1865

AFTER THE BURIAL

YES, faith is a goodly anchor;[2]
  When skies are sweet as a psalm,
At the bows it lolls so stalwart,
  In its bluff, broad-shouldered calm.

And when over breakers to leeward
  The tattered surges are hurled,
It may keep our head to the tempest,
  With its grip on the base of the world.

But, after the shipwreck, tell me
  What help in its iron thews,   10
Still true to the broken hawser,
  Deep down among sea-weed and ooze?

In the breaking gulfs of sorrow,
  When the helpless feet stretch out
And find in the deeps of darkness
  No footing so solid as doubt.

Then better one spar of Memory,
  One broken plank of the Past,
That our human heart may cling to,
  Though hopeless of shore at last!   20

To the spirit its splendid conjectures,
  To the flesh its sweet despair,
Its tears o'er the thin-worn locket
  With its anguish of deathless hair!

Immortal? I feel it and know it,
  Who doubts it of such as she?

[2] The first draft of the first six stanzas of "After the
Burial" was written at the death of Lowell's
second little infant, Rose, in 1850. Before the
poem was finished he had lost a little son and
his wife, Maria White.

But that is the pang's very secret,—
Immortal away from me.

There's a narrow ridge in the graveyard
  Would scarce stay a child in his race,   30
But to me and my thought it is wider
  Than the star-sown vague of Space.

Your logic, my friend, is perfect,
  Your moral most drearily true;
But, since the earth clashed on *her* coffin,
  I keep hearing that, and not you.

Console if you will, I can bear it;
  'T is a well-meant alms of breath;
But not all the preaching since Adam
  Has made Death other than Death.   40

It is pagan; but wait till you feel it,—
  That jar of our earth, that dull shock
When the plowshare of deeper passion
  Tears down to our primitive rock.

Communion in spirit! Forgive me,
  But I, who am earthly and weak,
Would give all my incomes from dreamland
  For a touch of her hand on my cheek.

That little shoe in the corner,
  So worn and wrinkled and brown,   50
With its emptiness confutes you,
  And argues your wisdom down.

1868   1868

IN A COPY OF OMAR KHAYYÁM

THESE pearls of thought in Persian gulfs were
    bred,
Each softly lucent as a rounded moon;
The diver Omar plucked them from their bed,
Fitzgerald strung them on an English thread.

Fit rosary for a queen, in shape and hue,
When Contemplation tells her pensive beads
Of mortal thoughts, forever old and new.
Fit for a queen? Why, surely then for you!

The moral? Where Doubt's eddies toss and
    twirl
Faith's slender shallop till her footing reel,   10
Plunge: if you find not peace beneath the
    whirl,
Groping, you may like Omar grasp a pearl.

                       1888

[1] *The Rubáiyát* (quatrains) by Omar Khayyàm, the Persian poet of the 11th and 12th centuries, is one of the world's great poems. The best translation is that of Edward Fitzgerald, 1859.

"FRANCISCUS DE VERULAMIO SIC COGITAVIT" [2]

THAT'S a rather bold speech, my Lord Bacon,
  For, indeed, is't so easy to know
Just how much we from others have taken,
  And how much our own natural flow?

Since your mind bubbled up at its fountain,
  How many streams made it elate,
While it calmed to the plain from the moun-
    tain,
  As every mind must that grows great?

While you thought 't was You thinking as
    newly
  As Adam still wet with God's dew,   10
You forgot in your self-pride that truly
  The whole Past was thinking through you.

Greece, Rome, nay, your namesake, old
    Roger, [3]
  With Truth's nameless delvers who wrought
In the dark mines of Truth, helped to prod
    your
  Fine brain with the goad of their thought.

As mummy [4] was prized for a rich hue
  The painter no elsewhere could find,
So't was buried men's thinking with which you
  Gave the ripe mellow tone to your mind.   20

I heard the proud strawberry saying,
  "Only look what a ruby I've made!"
It forgot how the bees in their maying
  Had brought it the stuff for its trade.

And yet there's the half of a truth in it,
  And my Lord might his copyright sue;
For a thought's his who kindles new youth
    in it,
  Or so puts it as makes it more true.

The birds but repeat without ending
  The same old traditional notes,   30
Which some, by more happily blending,
  Seem to make over new in their throats;

[2] The heading to the preface of Bacon's great philosophical work, the *Instauratio Magna*, is:

  Franciscus de Verulamio sic cogitavit, talemque apud se rationem instituit; quam viventibus et posteris notam fieri, ipsorum interesse putavit.

  [Francis Bacon thought as follows and reached conclusions such as these, which he thought when made known to the living and their descendants would be of concern to them.]

[3] Roger Bacon, 1214-1294, an English philosopher and scientist

[4] an oil-painters' color that was made from asphalt taken from mummies

And we men through our old bit of song run,
  Until one just improves on the rest,
And we call a thing his, in the long run,
  Who utters it clearest and best.
                                        1888

JONES VERY 1813-1880

Very was the son of a sea captain with whom he made several voyages to Europe. He was graduated from Harvard in 1836 and was for two years afterwards tutor in Greek there. He was licensed to preach as a Unitarian clergyman but was never a pastor. After his Harvard experience he lived a retired life at Salem, where he was born and where, also, he died, preaching occasionally and engaged in literary work. *Essays and Poems* appeared in 1839 and again in a completed edition under the same title in 1886. It is easy to see that the idealism of these sonnets carries out, on a different plane, the spirit of Emerson and Thoreau.

THE SOLDIER

He was not armed like those of eastern clime,
Whose heavy axes [1] felled their heathen foe;
Nor was he clad like those of later time,
Whose breast-worn cross betrayed no cross
    below; [2]
Nor was he of the tribe of Levi [3] born,
Whose pompous rites proclaim how vain their
    prayer;
Whose chilling words are heard at night and
    morn,
Who rend their robes, but still their hearts
    would spare;
But he nor steel nor sacred robe had on,   9
Yet went he forth in God's almighty power,
And spake the word whose will is ever done
From day's first dawn till earth's remotest
    hour;
And mountains melted from his presence down,
And hell affrighted fled before his frown.

THE DEAD [4]

I see them,—crowd on crowd they walk the
    earth,
Dry leafless trees no autumn wind laid bare;
And in their nakedness find cause for mirth,
And all unclad would winter's rudeness dare;
No sap doth through their clattering branches
    flow,

[1] Battle-axes were used in war by the Jews.
[2] Some of the Crusaders were prompted quite as much by personal ambition as by religious devotion.
[3] The Levites, originally attendants and assistants of the Jewish priests, in later times assumed the offices of priesthood.
[4] This strange sonnet characterizes those who, though alive in body, are really dead to all that is best.

Whence springing leaves and blossoms bright
    appear;
Their hearts the living God have ceased to
    know
Who gives the spring time to th' expectant
    year;
They mimic life, as if from him to steal
His glow of health to paint the livid cheek;   10
They borrow words for thoughts they cannot
    feel,
That with a seeming heart their tongue may
    speak;
And in their show of life more dead they live
Than those that to the earth with many tears
    they give.

THE WAR [5]

I saw a war, yet none the trumpet blew,
Nor in their hands the steel-wrought weapons
    bare;
And in that conflict armed there fought but
    few,
And none that in the world's loud tumults
    share;
They fought against their wills,—the stubborn
    foe
That mail-clad warriors left unfought within,
And wordy champions left unslain below,—
The ravening wolf though drest in fleecy skin;
They fought for peace,—not that the world
    can give,
Whose tongue proclaims the war its hands have
    ceased,   10
And bids us as each other's neighbor live,
Ere haughty Self within us has deceased;
They fought for him whose kingdom must in-
    crease,
Good will to men, on earth forever peace.

THE WILD ROSE OF PLYMOUTH

Upon the Plymouth shore the wild rose blooms
As when the Pilgrims lived beside the bay,
And scents the morning air with sweet per-
    fumes,
Though new this hour, more ancient far than
    they;
More ancient than the wild yet friendly race
That roved the land before the Pilgrims came,
And here for ages found a dwelling-place,
Of whom our histories tell us but the name!
Though new this hour, out from the past it
    springs,
Telling this summer morning of earth's prime;
And happy visions of the future brings   11

[5] the battle in the heart between right and wrong

That reach beyond, e'en to the verge of time;
Wreathing earth's children in one flowery chain
Of love and beauty, ever to remain.

RICHARD HENRY DANA, JR.
1815-1882

Interest in ships and the sea may rise or fall, but such an account as Dana's of a phase of sea life that has passed away will last for its sheer narrative interest. Dana was born at Cambridge, Massachusetts, son of Richard Henry Dana. His Harvard career was interrupted by ill-health which occasioned a sea voyage to California, the basis of his classic of sea life, *Two Years Before the Mast*, 1840. He was graduated in 1837, studied and practiced law, contributed to legal and political periodicals, and was pursuing the study of international law abroad at the time of his death at Rome.

Thousands of sailors have been through all that Dana experienced and more, but the narrative of this Boston lad is unique. It is the crude stuff of life handled with unforced, spontaneous vigor. Dana leans hard on his facts, makes these tell their own story. Masefield has done much the same thing in verse.

"Dana and our Literature of the Sea," *Nation* 101:487-8; J. London, "A Classic of the Sea," *Ind.* 71:1297-9; *Outlook* 99:928-9.

From TWO YEARS BEFORE THE MAST [1]
CHAPTER XXXI

There began now to be a decided change in the appearance of things. The days became shorter and shorter; the sun running lower in its course each day, and giving less and less heat, and the nights so cold as to prevent our sleeping on deck; the Magellan Clouds [2] in sight, of a clear night; the skies looking cold and angry; and, at times, a long, heavy, ugly sea, setting in from the southward, told us what we were coming to. Still, however, we had a fine, strong breeze, and kept on our way, under as much sail as our ship would bear. Toward the middle of the week, the wind hauled to the southward, which brought us upon a taut bowline, made the ship meet, nearly head-on, the heavy swell which rolled from that direction; and there was something not at all encouraging in the manner in which she met it. Being so deep and heavy, she wanted the buoyancy which should have carried her over the seas, and she dropped heavily into them, the water washing over the decks; and every now and then, when an unusually large sea met her fairly upon the bows, she struck it with a sound as dead and heavy as that with which a sledge-hammer falls upon the pile, and took the whole of it in upon the forecastle, and, rising, carried it aft in the scuppers, [3] washing the rigging off the pins, and carrying along with it everything which was loose on deck. She had been acting in this way all of our forenoon watch below; as we could tell by the washing of the water over our heads, and the heavy breaking of the seas against her bows, (with a sound as though she were striking against a rock,) only the thickness of the plank from our heads, as we lay in our berths, which are directly against the bows. At eight bells, [4] the watch was called, and we came on deck, one hand going aft to take the wheel, and another going to the galley to get the grub for dinner. I stood on the forecastle, looking at the seas, which were rolling high, as far as the eye could reach, their tops white with foam, and the body of them of a deep indigo blue, reflecting the bright rays of the sun. Our ship rose slowly over a few of the largest of them, until one immense fellow came rolling on, threatening to cover her, and which I was sailor enough to know, by the "feeling of her" under my feet, she would not rise over. I sprang upon the knight-heads, [5] and, seizing hold of the forestay, drew myself up upon it. My feet were just off the stanchion when she struck fairly into the middle of the sea, and it washed her fore and aft, burying her in the water. As soon as she rose out of it, I looked aft, and everything forward of the mainmast, except the

---

[1] Dana gives in this book an account of a voyage he took, at the age of nineteen, because of weakness of eyesight, just after his junior year at Harvard. Shipping as an ordinary sailor, he left Boston in the *Pilgrim*, August 14, 1834, for California via Cape Horn. The cargo consisted, as Dana says, "of everything under the sun—spirits of all kinds, tea, coffee, sugar, spices, raisins, molasses, hardware, crockery, tinware, cutlery, clothing . . . in fact everything that can be imagined from Chinese fireworks to English cart-wheels." See Chap. XIII. On May 8, 1836, Dana started from San Diego on the return trip in the *Alert*, which carried a cargo of forty thousand hides. The crew of the *Alert* consisted of fourteen sailors, a carpenter, cook, steward, three mates, and the captain. They were, at the opening of Chapter XXXI, eighteen hundred miles northwest of Cape Horn. Only those nautical terms have been annotated which are needed for a general understanding of the narrative, most explanations of rigging and of sailing directions being therefore omitted. For more detailed explanations see the *Lake English Classics* edition of *Two Years Before the Mast*.

[2] three cloud-like nebulae in the southern heavens discovered by Magellan, 1480-1541

[3] holes at the side of the deck, to let water run off, and the channels leading to them

[4] Noon: a bell is rung for every half hour that has elapsed, beginning with twelve, four, and eight o'clock, day and night.

[5] Upright timbers placed to hold the bowsprit; they come up through the forward deck and extend a few feet above it.

long-boat, which was griped and double-lashed down to the ring-bolts, was swept off clear. The galley, [1] the pigsty, the hencoop, and a large sheep-pen which had been built upon the fore-hatch, were all gone in the twinkling of an eye,—leaving the deck as clean as a chin new-reaped,—and not a stick left to show where they had stood. In the scuppers lay the galley, bottom up, and a few boards floating about,—the wreck of the sheep-pen,—and half a dozen miserable sheep floating among them, wet through, and not a little frightened at the sudden change that had come upon them. As soon as the sea had washed by, all hands sprang up out of the forecastle to see what had become of the ship; and in a few moments the cook and Old Bill crawled out from under the galley, where they had been lying in the water, nearly smothered, with the galley over them. Fortunately, it rested against the bulwarks, or it would have broken some of their bones. When the water ran off, we picked the sheep up, and put them in the long-boat, got the galley back in its place, and set things a little to rights; but, had not our ship had uncommonly high bulwarks and rail, everything must have been washed overboard, not excepting Old Bill and the cook. Bill had been standing at the galley-door, with the kid [2] of beef in his hand for the forecastle mess, when away he went, kid, beef, and all. He held on to the kid till the last, like a good fellow, but the beef was gone, and when the water had run off we saw it lying high and dry, like a rock at low tide—nothing could hurt *that*. We took the loss of our beef very easily, consoling ourselves with the recollection that the cabin had more to lose than we; and chuckled not a little at seeing the remains of the chicken-pie and pancakes floating in the scuppers. "This will never do!" was what some said, and every one felt. Here we were, not yet within a thousand miles of the latitude of Cape Horn, and our decks swept by a sea not one half so high as we must expect to find there. Some blamed the captain for loading his ship so deep when he knew what he must expect; while others said that the wind was always southwest, off the Cape, in the winter; and that, running before it, we should not mind the seas so much. When we got down into the forecastle, Old Bill, who was somewhat of a croaker,—having met with a great many accidents at sea,—said that if that was the way she was going to act, we might as well make our wills, and balance the books at once, and put on a clean shirt. " 'Vast there, you

bloody old owl! you're always hanging out blue lights! You're frightened by the ducking you got in the scuppers, and can't take a joke! What's the use in being always on the lookout for Davy Jones?" [3] "Stand by!" says another, "and we'll get an afternoon watch below, by this scrape"; but in this they were disappointed, for at two bells [4] all hands were called and set to work, getting lashings upon everything on deck; and the captain talked of sending down the long topgallant masts; but as the sea went down toward night, and the wind hauled abeam, we left them standing, and set the studding sails.

The next day all hands were turned-to upon unbending the old sails, and getting up the new ones; for a ship, unlike people on shore, puts on her best suit in bad weather. The old sails were sent down, and three new topsails, and new fore and main courses, jib, and fore-top-mast staysail, which were made on the coast, and never had been used, were bent, with a complete set of new earings, robands, and reef-points; and reef-tackles were rove to the courses, and spilling-lines to the topsails. These, with new braces and clew-lines fore and aft, gave us a good suit of running rigging.

The wind continued westerly, and the weather and sea less rough since the day on which we shipped the heavy sea, and we were making great progress under studding-sails, with our light sails all set, keeping a little to the eastward of south; for the captain, depending upon westerly winds off the Cape, had kept so far to the westward that, though we were within about five hundred miles of the latitude of Cape Horn, we were nearly seventeen hundred miles to the westward of it. Through the rest of the week we continued on with a fair wind, gradually, as we got more to the southward, keeping a more easterly course, and bringing the wind on our larboard quarter, until—

Sunday, June 26th; when, having a fine, clear day, the captain got a lunar observation, as well as his meridian altitude, which made us in lat. 47° 50′ S., long. 113° 49′ W.; Cape Horn bearing, according to my calculation, E. S. E. $\frac{1}{2}$ E., and distant eighteen hundred miles.

Monday, June 27th. During the first part of this day the wind continued fair, and, as we were going before it, it did not feel very cold, so that we kept at work on deck in our common clothes and round jackets. Our watch had an afternoon watch below for the first time since leaving San Diego; and, having inquired of the third mate what the latitude was at noon,

---

[1] ship's kitchen   [2] wooden dish   [3] the evil spirit of the sea   [4] one o'clock

and made our usual guesses as to the time she would need to be up with the Horn, we turned-in for a nap. We were sleeping away "at the rate of knots," when three knocks on the scuttle [1] and "All hands, ahoy!" started us from our berths. What could be the matter? It did not appear to be blowing hard, and, looking up through the scuttle, we could see that it was a clear day overhead; yet the watch were taking in sail. We thought there must be a sail in sight, and that we were about to heave-to and speak her; and were just congratulating ourselves upon it,—for we had seen neither sail nor land since we left port,—when we heard the mate's voice on deck (he turned-in "all standing," and was always on deck the moment he was called) singing out to the men who were taking in the studding-sails, and asking where his watch [2] were. We did not wait for a second call, but tumbled up the ladder; and there, on the starboard bow, was a bank of mist, covering sea and sky, and driving directly for us. I had seen the same before, in my passage round in the *Pilgrim*, and knew what it meant, and that there was no time to be lost. We had nothing on but thin clothes, yet there was not a moment to spare, and at it we went.

The boys of the other watch were in the tops, taking in the topgallant studding sails and the lower and topmast studding sails were coming down by the run. It was nothing but "haul down and clew up," until we got all the studding-sails in, and the royals, flying jib, and mizzen topgallant sail furled, and the ship kept off a little, to take the squall. The fore and main topgallant sails were still on her, for the "old man" did not mean to be frightened in broad daylight, and was determined to carry sail till the last minute. We all stood waiting for its coming, when the first blast showed us that it was not to be trifled with. Rain, sleet, snow, and wind enough to take our breath from us, and make the toughest turn his back to windward! The ship lay nearly over upon her beam-ends; the spars and rigging snapped and cracked; and her topgallant-masts bent like whipsticks. "Clew up the fore and main topgallant sails!" shouted the captain, and all hands sprang to the clew lines. The decks were standing nearly at an angle of forty-five degrees, and the ship going like a mad steed

[1] hatchway
[2] "The crew are divided into two divisions as equally as may be, called the watches. . . . They divide the time between them, being on and off duty, or as it is called, on deck and below, every other four hours." [Dana's note.]

through the water, the whole forward part of her in a smother of foam. The halyards were let go and the yard clewed down, and the sheets started, and in a few minutes the sails smothered and kept in by clewlines and buntlines. "Furl 'em, sir?" asked the mate. "Let go the topsail halyards, fore and aft!" shouted the captain in answer, at the top of his voice. Down came the topsail yards, the reef-tackles were manned and hauled out, and we climbed up to windward, and sprang into the weather rigging. The violence of the wind, and the hail and sleet, driving nearly horizontally across the ocean, seemed actually to pin us down to the rigging. It was hard work making head against them. One after another we got out upon the yards. And here we had work to do; for our new sails which had hardly been bent long enough to get the starch out of them, and the new earings and reef-points, stiffened with the sleet, knotted like pieces of iron wire. Having only our round jackets and straw hats on, we were soon wet through, and it was every moment growing colder. Our hands were soon stiffened and numbed, which, added to the stiffness of everything else, kept us a good while on the yard. After we had got the sail hauled upon the yard, we had to wait a long time for the weather earing to be passed; but there was no fault to be found, for French John was at the earing, and a better sailor never laid out on a yard; so we leaned over the yard and beat our hands upon the sail to keep them from freezing. At length the word came—"Haul out to leeward,"—and we seized the reef points and hauled the band taut for the lee earing. "Taut band—Knot away," and we got the first reef fast, and were just going to lay down, when— "Two reefs—two reefs!" shouted the mate, and we had a second reef to take, in the same way. When this was fast we laid down on deck, manned the halyards to leeward, nearly up to our knees in water, set the topsail, and then laid aloft on the main topsail yard, and reefed that sail in the same manner; for, as I have before stated, we were a good deal reduced in numbers, and, to make it worse, the carpenter, only two days before, had cut his leg with an axe, so that he could not go aloft. This weakened us so that we could not well manage more than one topsail at a time, in such weather as this, and, of course, our labor was doubled. From the main topsail yard, we went upon the main yard, and took a reef in the mainsail. No sooner had we got on deck than—"Lay aloft there, mizzen-top-men, and close-reef mizzen topsail!" This called me; and being nearest the rigging, I got first aloft, and out to the weather earing. English Ben was on the yard just after me, and took the lee earing, and the rest of our gang were soon on the yard, and began to fist the sail, when the mate considerately sent up the cook and steward to help us. I could now account for the long time it took to pass the other earings, for, to do my best, with a strong hand to help me at the dog's-ear, I could not get it passed until I heard them beginning to complain in the bunt. One reef after another we took in, until the sail was close-reefed, when we went down and hoisted away at the halyards. In the mean time, the jib had been furled and the staysail set, and the ship, under her reduced sail had got more upright, and was under management; but the two topgallant sails were still hanging in the buntlines, and slatting and jerking as though they would take the masts out of her. We gave a look aloft, and knew that our work was not done yet; and sure enough, no sooner did the mate see that we were on deck than —"Lay aloft there, four of you, and furl the topgallant sails!" This called me again, and two of us went aloft up the fore rigging, and two more up the main, upon the topgallant yards. The shrouds were now iced over, the sleet having formed a crust or cake round all the standing rigging, and on the weather side of the masts and yards. When we got upon the yard, my hands were so numb that I could not have cast off the knot of the gasket to have saved my life. We both lay over the yard for a few seconds, beating our hands upon the sail, until we started the blood into our fingers' ends, and at the next moment our hands were in a burning heat. My companion on the yard was a lad, who came out in the ship a weak, puny boy, from one of the Boston schools,— "no larger than a spritsail-sheet knot," nor "heavier than a paper of lamp-black," and "not strong enough to haul a shad off a gridiron," but who was now "as long as a spare topmast, strong enough to knock down an ox, and hearty enough to eat him." We fisted the sail together, and, after six or eight minutes of hard hauling and pulling and beating down the sail which was as stiff as sheet iron, we managed to get it furled; and snugly furled it must be, for we knew the mate well enough to be certain that if it got adrift again, we should be called up from our watch below, at any hour of the night, to furl it.

I had been on the lookout for a chance to jump below and clap on a thick jacket and southwester; but when we got on deck we found that eight bells had been struck, and the other watch gone below, so that there were two hours of dog watch for us, and a plenty of work to do. It had now set in for a steady gale from the southwest; but we were not yet far enough to the southward to make a fair wind of it, for we must give Terra del Fuego a wide berth. The decks were covered with snow, and there was a constant driving of sleet. In fact, Cape Horn had set in with good earnest. In the midst of all this, and before it became dark, we had all the studding-sails to make up and stow away, and then to lay aloft and rig in all the booms, fore and aft, and coil away the tacks, sheets, and halyards. This was pretty tough work for four or five hands, in the face of a gale which almost took us off the yards, and with ropes so stiff with ice that it was almost impossible to bend them. I was nearly half an hour out on the end of the fore yard, trying to coil away and stop down the topmast studding sail tack and lower halyards. It was after dark when we got through, and we were not a little pleased to hear four bells [1] struck, which sent us below for two hours, and gave us each a pot of hot tea with our cold beef and bread, and, what was better yet, a suit of thick, dry clothing, fitted for the weather, in place of our thin clothes, which were wet through and now frozen stiff.

This sudden turn, for which we were so little prepared, was as unacceptable to me as to any of the rest; for I had been troubled for several days with a slight toothache, and this cold weather and wetting and freezing were not the best things in the world for it. I soon found that it was getting strong hold, and running over all parts of my face; and before the watch was out I went aft to the mate, who had charge of the medicine chest, to get something for it. But the chest showed like the end of a long voyage, for there was nothing that would answer but a few drops of laudanum, which must be saved for any emergency; so I had only to bear the pain as well as I could.

When we got on deck at eight bells, [2] it had stopped snowing, and there were a few stars out, but the clouds were still black, and it was blowing a steady gale. Just before midnight, I went aloft and sent down the mizzen royal yard, and had the good luck to do it to the satisfaction of the mate, who said it was done "out of hand and shipshape." The next four hours below were but little relief to me, for I lay awake in my berth the whole time,

[1] six o'clock   [2] eight o'clock

from the pain in my face, and heard every bell strike, and, at four o'clock, turned out with the watch, feeling little spirit for the hard duties of the day. Bad weather and hard work at sea can be borne up against very well if one only has spirit and health; but there is nothing brings a man down, at such a time, like bodily pain and want of sleep. There was, however, too much to do to allow time to think; for the gale of yesterday, and the heavy seas we met with a few days before, while we had yet ten degrees more southing to make, had convinced the captain that we had something before us which was not to be trifled with, and orders were given to send down the long topgallant masts. The topgallant and royal yards were accordingly struck, the flying jib-boom rigged in, and the topgallant masts sent down on deck, and all lashed together by the side of the long-boat. The rigging was then sent down and coiled away below, and everything made snug aloft. There was not a sailor in the ship who was not rejoiced to see these sticks come down; for, so long as the yards were aloft, on the least sign of a lull, the topgallant sails were loosed, and then we had to furl them again in a snow-squall, and shin up and down single ropes caked with ice, and send royal yards down in the teeth of a gale coming right from the south pole. It was an interesting sight, too, to see our noble ship, dismantled of all her top-hamper of long tapering masts and yards, and boom pointed with spear-head, which ornamented her in port; and all that canvas, which a few days before had covered her like a cloud, from the truck to the water's edge, spreading far out beyond her hull on either side, now gone; and she stripped, like a wrestler for the fight. It corresponded, too, with the desolate character of her situation,—alone, as she was, battling with storms, wind, and ice, at this extremity of the globe, and in almost constant night.

Friday, July 1st. We were now nearly up to the latitude of Cape Horn, and having over forty degrees of easting to make, we squared away the yards before a strong westerly gale, shook a reef out of the fore-top sail, and stood on our way, east-by-south, with the prospect of being up with the Cape in a week or ten days. As for myself, I had had no sleep for forty-eight hours; and the want of rest, together with constant wet and cold, had increased the swelling, so that my face was nearly as large as two, and I found it impossible to get my mouth open wide enough to eat. In this state, the steward applied to the captain for some rice to boil for me, but he only got

a—"No! d—— you! Tell him to eat salt junk and hard bread, like the rest of them." For this, of course, I was much obliged to him, and in truth it was just what I expected. However, I did not starve, for the mate, who was a man as well as a sailor, and had always been a good friend to me, smuggled a pan of rice into the galley, and told the cook to boil it for me, and not let the "old man" see it. Had it been fine weather, or in port, I should have gone below and lain by until my face got well; but in such weather as this, and short-handed as we were, it was not for me to desert my post; so I kept on deck, and stood my watch and did my duty as well as I could.

Saturday, July 2d. This day the sun rose fair, but it ran too low in the heavens to give any heat, or thaw out our sails and rigging; yet the sight of it was pleasant; and we had a steady "reef-topsail breeze" from the westward. The atmosphere, which had previously been clear and cold, for the last few hours grew damp, and had a disagreeable, wet chilliness in it; and the man who came from the wheel said he heard the captain tell "the passenger" that the thermometer had fallen several degrees since morning, which he could not account for in any other way than by supposing that there must be ice near us; though such a thing had never been heard of in this latitude at this season of the year. At twelve o'clock we went below, and had just got through dinner, when the cook put his head down the scuttle and told us to come on deck and see the finest sight that we had ever seen. "Where away, cook?" asked the first man who was up. "On the larboard bow." And there lay, floating in the ocean, several miles off, an immense, irregular mass, its top and points covered with snow, and its center of a deep indigo color. This was an iceberg, and of the largest size, as one of our men said who had been in the Northern ocean. As far as the eye could reach, the sea in every direction was of a deep blue color, the waves running high and fresh, and sparkling in the light, and in the midst lay this immense mountain-island, its cavities and valleys thrown into deep shade, and its points and pinnacles glittering in the sun. All hands were soon on deck, looking at it, and admiring in various ways its beauty and grandeur. But no description can give any idea of the strangeness, splendor, and, really, the sublimity, of the sight. Its great size,—for it must have been from two to three miles in circumference, and several hundred feet in height,—its slow motion, as its base rose and sank in the water, and its high points nodded against the clouds; the dashing of the waves upon it, which, breaking high with foam, lined its base with a white crust; and the thundering sound of the cracking of the mass, and the breaking and tumbling down of huge pieces; together with its nearness and approach, which added a slight element of fear,—all combined to give to it the character of true sublimity. The main body of the mass was, as I have said, of an indigo color, its base crusted with frozen foam; and as it grew thin and transparent toward the edges and top, its color shaded off from a deep blue to the whiteness of snow. It seemed to be drifting slowly toward the north, so that we kept away and avoided it. It was in sight all the afternoon; and when we got to leeward of it the wind died away, so that we lay-to quite near it for a greater part of the night. Unfortunately, there was no moon, but it was a clear night, and we could plainly mark the long, regular heaving of the stupendous mass, as its edges moved slowly against the stars. Several times in our watch loud cracks were heard, which sounded as though they must have run through the whole length of the iceberg, and several pieces fell down with a thundering crash, plunging heavily into the sea. Toward morning a strong breeze sprang up, and we filled away, and left it astern, and at daylight it was out of sight. The next day, which was—

Sunday, July 3rd, the breeze continued strong, the air exceedingly chilly, and the thermometer low. In the course of the day we saw several icebergs of different sizes, but none so near as the one which we saw the day before. Some of them, as well as we could judge, at the distance at which we were, must have been as large as that, if not larger. At noon we were in latitude 55° 12′ south, and supposed longitude 89° 5′ west. Toward night the wind hauled to the southward, and headed us off our course a little, and blew a tremendous gale; but this we did not mind, as there was no rain nor snow, and we were already under close sail.

Monday, July 4th. This was "Independence Day" in Boston. What firing of guns, and ringing of bells, and rejoicings of all sorts, in every part of our country! The ladies (who have not gone down to Nahant, for a breath of cool air, and sight of the ocean) walking the streets with parasols over their heads, and the dandies in their white pantaloons and silk stockings! What quantities of ice-cream have been eaten, and what quantities of ice brought into the city from a distance, and sold out by the lump and the pound! The smallest of the islands which we saw today would have made the

fortune of poor Jack, [1] if he had had it in Boston; and I dare say he would have had no objection to being there with it. This, to be sure, was no place to keep the Fourth of July. To keep ourselves warm, and the ship out of the ice, was as much as we could do. Yet no one forgot the day; and many were the wishes and conjectures and comparisons, both serious and ludicrous, which were made among all hands. The sun shone bright as long as it was up, only that a scud of black clouds was ever and anon driving across it. At noon we were in lat. 54° 27′ S., and long. 85° 5′ W., having made a good deal of easting, but having lost in our latitude by the heading of the wind. Between daylight and dark—that is, between nine o'clock and three—we saw thirty-four ice islands of various sizes; some no bigger than the hull of our vessel, and others apparently nearly as large as the one that we first saw; though, as we went on, the islands became smaller and more numerous; and, at sundown of this day, a man at the mast-head saw large tracts of floating ice, called "field-ice," at the southeast. This kind of ice is much more dangerous than the large islands, for those can be seen at a distance, and kept away from; but the field-ice, floating in great quantities, and covering the ocean for miles and miles, in pieces of every size,—large, flat, and broken cakes, with here and there an island rising twenty and thirty feet, and as large as the ship's hull,—this it is very difficult to sheer clear of. A constant lookout was necessary; for any of these pieces, coming with the heave of the sea, were large enough to have knocked a hole in the ship, and that would have been the end of us; for no boat (even if we could have got one out) could have lived in such a sea; and no man could have lived in a boat in such weather. To make our condition still worse, the wind came out due east, just after sundown, and it blew a gale dead ahead, with hail and sleet and a thick fog, so that we could not see half the length of the ship. Our chief reliance, the prevailing westerly gales, was thus cut off; and here we were, nearly seven hundred miles to the westward of the Cape, with a gale dead from the eastward, and the weather so thick that we could not see the ice with which we were surrounded, until it was directly under our bows. At four P. M. (it was then quite dark) all hands were called, and sent aloft in a violent squall of hail and rain, to take in sail. We had now all got on our "Cape Horn rig"—thick boots, southwesters coming down over our necks and ears, thick trousers and jackets, and some with

[1] the usual nickname for sailors

oil-cloth suits over all. Mittens, too, we wore on deck, but it would not do to go aloft with them on, for it was impossible to work with them, and, being wet and stiff, they might let a man slip overboard, for all the hold he could get upon a rope; so we were obliged to work with bare hands, which, as well as our faces, were often cut with the hail-stones, which fell thick and large. Our ship was now all cased with ice,—hull, spars, and standing rigging;—and the running rigging so stiff that we could hardly bend it so as to belay it, or, still worse, take a knot with it; and the sails nearly as stiff as sheet iron. One at a time (for it was a long piece of work and required many hands) we furled the courses, mizzen topsail, and fore topmast staysail, and close-reefed the fore and main topsails, and hove the ship to under the fore, with the main hauled up by the clew lines and bunt lines, and ready to be sheeted home, if we found it necessary to make sail to get to windward of an island. A regular lookout was then set, and kept by each watch in turn, until the morning. It was a tedious and anxious night. It blew hard the whole time, and there was an almost constant driving of either rain, hail, or snow. In addition to this, it was "as thick as muck," and the ice was all about us. The captain was on deck nearly the whole night, and kept the cook in the galley, with a roaring fire, to make coffee for him, which he took every few hours, and once or twice gave a little to his officers; but not a drop of anything was there for the crew. The captain, who sleeps all the day-time, and comes and goes at night as he chooses, can have his brandy-and-water in the cabin, and his hot coffee at the galley; while Jack, who has to stand through everything, and work in wet and cold, can have nothing to wet his lips or warm his stomach. This was a "temper-ance ship," and, like too many such ships, the temperance was all in the forecastle. The sailor, who only takes his one glass as it is dealt out to him, is in danger of being drunk; while the captain, who has all under his hand, and can drink as much as he chooses, and upon whose self-possession and cool judgment the lives of all depend, may be trusted with any amount, to drink at his will. Sailors will never be convinced that rum is a dangerous thing, by taking it away from them and giving it to the officers; nor that that temperance is their friend which takes from them what they have always had, and gives them nothing in the place of it. By seeing it allowed to their officers, they will not be convinced that it is taken from them for their good; and by receiving nothing

in its place they will not believe that it is done in kindness. On the contrary, many of them look upon the change as a new instrument of tyranny. Not that they prefer rum. I never knew a sailor, in my life, who would not prefer a pot of hot coffee or chocolate, in a cold night, to all the rum afloat. They all say that rum only warms them for a time; yet, if they can get nothing better, they will miss what they have lost. The momentary warmth and glow from drinking it; the break and change which is made in a long, dreary watch by the mere calling all hands aft and serving of it out; and the simply having some event to look forward to and to talk about,—all give it an impor-tance and a use which no one can appreciate who has not stood his watch before the mast. On my passage round Cape Horn before, the vessel that I was in was not under temperance articles, and grog was served out every middle and morning watch, and after every reefing of topsails; and though I had never drunk rum before, and never intend to again, I took my allowance then at the capstan, as the rest did, merely for the momentary warmth it gave the system, and the change in our feelings and as-pect of our duties on the watch. At the same time, as I have stated, there was not a man on board who would not have pitched the rum to the dogs, (I had heard them say so a dozen times), for a pot of coffee, or chocolate; or even for our common beverage,—"water be-witched and tea begrudged," as it was. [1] The temperance reform is the best thing that ever was undertaken for the sailor; but when the grog is taken from him, he ought to have some-thing in its place. As it is now, in most vessels, it is a mere saving to the owners; and this accounts for the sudden increase of temperance ships, which surprised even the best friends of the cause. If every merchant, when he struck grog from the list of the expenses of his ship, had been obliged to substitute as much coffee, or chocolate, as would give each man a pot-full when he came off the topsail yard, on a stormy night,—I fear Jack might have gone to ruin on the old road. [2]

[1] "The proportions of the ingredients of the tea that was made for us (and ours, as I have before stated, was a favorable specimen of American merchantmen) were a pint of tea and a pint and a half of molasses to about three gallons of water. These are all boiled down together in the "cop-pers," and, before serving it out, the mess is stirred up with a stick, so as to give each man his fair share of sweetening and tea-leaves. The tea for the cabin is, of course, made in the usual way, in a teapot, and drunk with sugar." [Dana's note.]

[2] "I do not wish these remarks, so far as they relate to the saving of expense in the outfit, to be ap-

But this is not doubling Cape Horn. Eight hours of the night our watch was on deck, and during the whole of that time we kept a bright lookout; one man on each bow, another in the bunt of the fore yard, the third mate on the scuttle, one on each quarter, and a man always standing by the wheel. The chief mate was everywhere, and commanded the ship when the captain was below. When a large piece of ice was seen in our way, or drifting near us, the word was passed along, and the ship's head turned one way and another; and sometimes, the yards squared or braced up. There was little else to do than to look out; and we had the sharpest eyes in the ship on the forecastle. The only variety was the monotonous voice of the lookout forward,—"Another island!" "Ice ahead!" "Ice on the lee bow!" "Hard up the helm!" "Keep her off a little!" "Stead-y!"

In the mean time the wet and cold had brought my face into such a state that I could neither eat nor sleep; and though I stood it out all night, yet, when it became light, I was in such a state that all hands told me I must go below, and lie-by for a day or two, or I should be laid up for a long time, and perhaps have the lock-jaw. When the watch was changed I went into the steerage, and took off my hat and comforter, and showed my face to the mate, who told me to go below at once, and stay in my berth until the swelling went down, and gave the cook orders to make a poultice for me, and said he would speak to the captain.

I went below and turned-in, covering myself over with blankets and jackets, and lay in my berth nearly twenty-four hours, half asleep and half awake, stupid from the dull pain. I heard the watch called, and the men going up and down, and sometimes a noise on deck, and a cry of "ice," but I gave little attention to anything. At the end of twenty-four hours the pain went down, and I had a long sleep, which brought me back to my proper state; yet my

face was so swollen and tender that I was obliged to keep to my berth for two or three days longer. During the two days I had been below, the weather was much the same that it had been,—head winds, and snow and rain; or, if the wind came fair, too foggy, and the ice too thick, to run. At the end of the third day the ice was very thick; a complete fog-bank covered the ship. It blew a tremendous gale from the eastward, with sleet and snow, and there was every promise of a dangerous and fatiguing night. At dark, the captain called all hands aft, and told them that not a man was to leave the deck that night; that the ship was in the greatest danger; any cake of ice might knock a hole in her, or she might run on an island and go to pieces. No one could tell whether she would be a ship the next morning. The lookouts were then set, and every man was put in his station. When I heard what was the state of things, I began to put on my clothes to stand it out with the rest of them, when the mate came below, and looking at my face, ordered me back to my berth, saying that if we went down, we should all go down together, but if I went on deck I might lay myself up for life. This was the first word I had heard from aft; for the captain had done nothing, nor inquired how I was, since I went below.

In obedience to the mate's orders, I went back to my berth; but a more miserable night I never wish to spend. I never felt the curse of sickness so keenly in my life. If I could only have been on deck with the rest, where something was to be done and seen and heard, where there were fellow-beings for companions in duty and danger; but to be cooped up alone in a black hole, in equal danger, but without the power to do, was the hardest trial. Several times, in the course of the night, I got up, determined to go on deck; but the silence which showed that there was nothing doing, and the knowledge that I might make myself seriously ill, for nothing, kept me back. It was not easy to sleep, lying as I did with my head directly against the bows, which might be dashed in by an island of ice, brought down by the very next sea that struck her. This was the only time I had been ill since I left Boston, and it was the worst time it could have happened. I felt almost willing to bear the plagues of Egypt for the rest of the voyage, if I could but be well and strong for that one night. Yet it was a dreadful night for those on deck. A watch of eighteen hours, with wet and cold and constant anxiety, nearly wore them out; and when they came below at nine o'clock for breakfast, they

---

plied to the owners of our ship, for she was supplied with an abundance of stores of the best kind that are given to seamen; though the dispensing of them is necessarily left to the captain. And I learned, on our return, that the captain withheld many of the stores from us, from mere ugliness. He brought several barrels of flour home, but would not give us the usual twice-a-week duff, and so as to other stores. Indeed, so high was the reputation of 'the employ' among men and officers for the character and outfit of their vessels, and for their liberality in conducting their voyages, that when it was known that they had the *Alert* fitting out for a long voyage, and that hands were to be shipped at a certain time,— a half hour before the time, as one of the crew told me, sailors were steering down the wharf, hopping over the barrels, like a drove of sheep." [Dana's note.]

almost dropped asleep on their chests, and some of them were so stiff that they could with difficulty sit down. Not a drop of anything had been given them during the whole time, (though the captain, as on the night that I was on deck, had his coffee every four hours), except that the mate stole a pot-full of coffee for two men to drink behind the galley, while he kept a lookout for the captain. Every man had his station, and was not allowed to leave it; and nothing happened to break the monotony of the night, except once setting the main topsails, to run clear of a large island to leeward, which they were drifting fast upon. Some of the boys got so sleepy and stupefied that they actually fell asleep at their posts; and the young third mate, whose station was the exposed one of standing on the fore scuttle, was so stiff, when he was relieved, that he could not bend his knees to get down. By a constant lookout, and a quick shifting of the helm, as the islands and pieces came in sight, the ship went clear of everything but a few small pieces, though daylight showed the ocean covered for miles. At daybreak it fell a dead calm, and with the sun the fog cleared a little, and a breeze sprang up from the westward, which soon grew into a gale. We had now a fair wind, daylight, and comparatively clear weather; yet, to the surprise of every one, the ship continued hove-to. "Why does not he run?" "What is the captain about?" was asked by everyone; and from questions it soon grew into complaints and murmurings. When the daylight was so short, it was too bad to lose it, and a fair wind, too, which every one had been praying for. As hour followed hour, and the captain showed no sign of making sail, the crew became impatient, and there was a good deal of talking and consultation together on the forecastle. They had been beaten out with the exposure and hardship, and impatient to get out of it, and this unaccountable delay was more than they could bear in quietness, in their excited and restless state. Some said that the captain was frightened,—completely cowed by the dangers and difficulties that surrounded us, and was afraid to make sail; while others said that in his anxiety and suspense he had made a free use of brandy and opium, and was unfit for his duty. The carpenter, who was an intelligent man, and a thorough seaman, and had great influence with the crew, came down into the forecastle, and tried to induce the crew to go aft and ask the captain why he did not run, or request him, in the name of all hands, to make sail. This appeared to be a very reasonable request, and the crew agreed that if he did not make sail before noon they would go aft. Noon came, and no sail was made. A consultation was held again, and it was proposed to take the ship from the captain and give the command of her to the mate, who had been heard to say that if he could have his way the ship would have been half the distance to the Cape before night,—ice or no ice. And so irritated and impatient had the crew become, that even this proposition, which was open mutiny, punishable with state prison, was entertained, and the carpenter went to his berth, leaving it tacitly understood that something serious would be done if things remained as they were many hours longer. When the carpenter left, we talked it over, and I gave my advice strongly against it. Another of the men, too, who had known something of the kind attempted in another ship by a crew who were dissatisfied with their captain, and which was followed with serious consequences, was opposed to it. Stimson, who soon came down, joined us, and we determined to have nothing to do with it. By these means, they were soon induced to give it up for the present, though they said they would not lie where they were much longer without knowing the reason.

The affair remained in this state until four o'clock, when an order came forward for all hands to come aft upon the quarter-deck. In about ten minutes they came forward again, and the whole affair had been blown. The carpenter, very prematurely, and without any authority from the crew, had sounded the mate as to whether he would take command of the ship, and intimated an intention to displace the captain; and the mate, as in duty bound, had told the whole to the captain, who immediately sent for all hands aft. Instead of violent measures, or, at least, an outbreak of quarter-deck bravado, threats, and abuse, which they had every reason to expect, a sense of common danger and common suffering seemed to have tamed his spirit, and begotten something like a humane fellow-feeling; for he received the crew in a manner quiet, and even almost kind. He told them what he had heard, and said that he did not believe that they would try to do any such thing as was intimated; that they had always been good men,—obedient, and knew their duty, and he had no fault to find with them, and asked them what they had to complain of; said that no one could say that he was slow to carry sail (which was true enough), and that, as soon as he thought it was safe and proper, he should make sail. He added a few words about their duty in their present situation, and sent them forward, saying that he should take no further notice of the matter; but, at the same time, told the carpenter to recollect whose power he was in, and that if he heard another word from him he would have cause to remember him to the day of his death.

This language of the captain had a very good effect upon the crew, and they returned quietly to their duty.

For two days more the wind blew from the southward and eastward; or in the short intervals when it was fair, the ice was too thick to run; yet the weather was not so dreadfully bad, and the crew had watch and watch. I still remained in my berth, fast recovering, yet still not well enough to go safely on deck. And I should have been perfectly useless; for, from having eaten nothing for nearly a week, except a little rice which I forced into my mouth the last day or two, I was as weak as an infant. To be sick in a forecastle is miserable indeed. It is the worst part of a dog's life, especially in bad weather. The forecastle, shut up tight to keep out the water and cold air; the watch either on deck or asleep in their berths; no one to speak to; the pale light of the single lamp, swinging to and fro from the beam, so dim that one can scarcely see, much less read, by it; the water dropping from the beams and carlines and running down the sides, and the forecastle so wet and dark and cheerless, and so lumbered up with chests and wet clothes, that sitting up is worse than lying in the berth! These are some of the evils. Fortunately, I needed no help from any one, and no medicine; and if I had needed help I don't know where I should have found it. Sailors are willing enough, but it is true, as is often said, no one ships for nurse on board a vessel. Our merchant ships are always undermanned, and if one man is lost by sickness, they cannot spare another to take care of him. A sailor is always presumed to be well, and if he's sick he's a poor dog. One has to stand his wheel, and another his lookout, and the sooner he gets on deck again the better.

Accordingly, as soon as I could possibly go back to my duty, I put on my thick clothes and boots and southwester, and made my appearance on deck. Though I had been but a few days below, yet everything looked strangely enough. The ship was cased in ice,—decks, sides, masts, yards, and rigging. Two close-reefed top-sails were all the sail she had on, and every sail and rope was frozen so stiff in

its place that it seemed as though it would be impossible to start anything. Reduced, too, to her topmasts, she had altogether a most forlorn and crippled appearance. The sun had come up brightly; the snow was swept off the decks and ashes thrown upon them so that we could walk, for they had been as slippery as glass. It was, of course, too cold to carry on any ship's work, and we had only to walk the deck and keep ourselves warm. The wind was still ahead, and the whole ocean, to the eastward, covered with islands and field-ice. At four bells the order was given to square away the yards; and the man who came from the helm said that the captain had kept her off to N.N.E. What could this mean? Some said that he was going to put into Valparaiso and winter, and others that he was going to run out of the ice and cross the Pacific, and go home round the Cape of Good Hope. Soon, however, it leaked out, and we found that we were running for the Straits of Magellan. The news soon spread through the ship, and all tongues were at work talking about it. No one on board had been through the straits; but I had in my chest an account of the passage of the ship *A. J. Donelson*, of New York, through those straits a few years before. The account was given by the captain, and the representation was as favorable as possible. It was soon read by every one on board, and various opinions pronounced. The determination of our captain had at least this good effect; it gave us something to think and talk about, made a break in our life, and diverted our minds from the monotonous dreariness of the prospect before us. Having made a fair wind of it, we were going off at a good rate, and leaving the thickest of the ice behind us. This, at least, was something.

Having been long enough below to get my hands well warmed and softened, the first handling of the ropes was rather tough; but a few days hardened them, and as soon as I got my mouth open wide enough to take in a piece of salt beef and hard bread, I was all right again.

Sunday, July 10th. Lat. 54° 10′, long. 79° 07′. This was our position at noon. The sun was out bright; the ice was all left behind, and things had quite a cheering appearance. We brought our wet pea-jackets and trousers on deck, and hung them up in the rigging, that the breeze and the few hours of sun might dry them a little; and, by the permission of the cook, the galley was nearly filled with stockings and mittens, hung round to be dried.

Boots, too, were brought up; and, having got a little tar and slush from below, we gave them a thick coat. After dinner all hands were turned-to, to get the anchors over the bows, bend on the chains, etc. The fish-tackle was got up, the fish davit [1] rigged out, and, after two or three hours of hard and cold work, both the anchors were ready for instant use, a couple of kedges got up, a hawser coiled away upon the fore-hatch, and the deep-sea lead-line overhauled and got ready. Our spirits returned with having something to do; and when the tackle was manned to bowse the anchor home, notwithstanding the desolation of the scene, we struck up "Cheerly, ho!" in full chorus. This pleased the mate, who rubbed his hands and cried out, "That's right, my boys; never say die! That sounds like the old crew!" and the captain came up, on hearing the song, and said to the passenger, within hearing of the man at the wheel, "That sounds like a lively crew. They'll have their song so long as there're enough left for a chorus!"

This preparation of the cable and anchors was for the passage of the straits; for, being very crooked, and with a variety of currents, it is necessary to come frequently to anchor. This was not, by any means, a pleasant prospect; for, of all the work that a sailor is called upon to do in cold weather, there is none so bad as working the ground-tackle. The heavy chain-cables to be hauled and pulled about decks with bare hands; wet hawsers, slip-ropes, and buoy-ropes to be hauled aboard dripping in water, which is running up your sleeves, and freezing; clearing hawse under the bows; getting under way and coming-to at all hours of the night and day, and a constant lookout for rocks and sands and turns of tides,—these are some of the disagreeables of such a navagation to a common sailor. Fair or foul, he wants to have nothing to do with the ground-tackle between port and port. One of our hands, too, had unluckily fallen upon a half of an old newspaper which contained an account of the passage, through the straits, of a Boston brig, called, I think, the *Peruvian*, in which she lost every cable and anchor she had, got aground twice, and arrived at Valparaiso in distress. This was set off against the account of the *A. J. Donelson*, and led us to look forward with less confidence to the passage, especially as no one on board had ever been through, and the captain had no very perfect charts. However,

[1] "A short spar with a sheave at the end used as a crane to hoist the flukes of the anchor to the top of the bow." Worcester.

we were spared any further experience on the point; for the next day, when we must have been near the Cape of Pillars, which is the southwest point of the mouth of the straits, a gale set in from the eastward, with a heavy fog, so that we could not see half of the ship's length ahead. This, of course, put an end to the project for the present; for a thick fog and a gale blowing dead ahead are not the most favorable circumstances for the passage of difficult and dangerous straits. This weather, too, seemed likely to last for some time, and we could not think of beating about the mouth of the straits for a week or two, waiting for a favorable opportunity; so we braced up on the larboard tack, put the ship's head due south, and struck her off for Cape Horn again.

1834-1840   1840

JULIA WARD HOWE 1819-1910

Though Mrs. Howe was engaged in many social and philanthropic activities, and composed several small volumes of verse, she will be most remembered for the stirring patriotic song of the Civil War here printed. She was born in New York City in a family of high standing. Marrying a physician whose chief professional interest was in the blind and the mentally deficient, she was led by circumstances to adopt philanthropy almost as a career. She was active in the anti-slavery movement and later in the work for woman suffrage. She died in South Portsmouth, Rhode Island. Her best known writings aside from collections of poems published in 1854, 1857, and 1866 are *Life of Margaret Fuller*, 1883; *Reminiscences*, 1899.

BATTLE HYMN OF THE REPUBLIC

Mine eyes have seen the glory of the coming of the Lord:
He is trampling out the vintage where the grapes of wrath are stored;
He hath loosed the fateful lightning of his terrible swift sword:
His truth is marching on.

I have seen him in the watch-fires of a hundred circling camps;
They have builded him an altar in the evening dews and damps;
I can read his righteous sentence by the dim and flaring lamps:
His day is marching on.

I have read a fiery gospel, writ in burnished rows of steel:
"As ye deal with my contemners, so with you my grace shall deal;   10

Let the Hero, born of woman, crush the ser-
    pent with his heel,
Since God is marching on."

He has sounded forth the trumpet that shall
    never call retreat;
He is sifting out the hearts of men before his
    judgment-seat;
Oh, be swift, my soul, to answer him! be jubi-
    lant, my feet!
Our God is marching on.

In the beauty of the lilies Christ was born
    across the sea,
With a glory in his bosom that transfigures you
    and me:
As he died to make men holy, let us die to
    make men free,   19
While God is marching on.

1861   1862

EDWARD EVERETT HALE
1822-1909

Born in Boston, spending his life there, and dying in the suburbs, Hale was an embodiment of the New England spirit of his generation, especially in its higher aspects. He graduated at Harvard, 1839, studied theology, entered the Unitarian ministry in 1846, and from 1856 until his death was pastor and pastor emeritus of the South Congregational (Unitarian) Church, Boston. He was a frequent contributor to magazines and newspapers, and to historical compilations. Among his books are *Sketches of Christian History*, 1850; *The Man Without a Country and Other Tales*, 1868; *Ten Times One is Ten*, 1870; *In His Name*, 1873; *Philip Nolan's Friends*, 1876; *Life of George Washington*, 1888; *James Russell Lowell and his Friends*, 1899; *A New England Boyhood*, 1893.

Almost all of Hale's writing was done with a didactic purpose. In the present story the "moral," strong as it is, does not spoil the narrative. The reason perhaps lies in the amazing air of truth Hale gives to his invention; by thousands of readers of the day the story was taken to be a record of fact.

See *Cur. Opinion* 64:343; *Outlook* 104:273-4.

THE MAN WITHOUT A COUNTRY [1]

I suppose that very few casual readers of the *New York Herald* of August 13th [1863] observed, in an obscure corner, among the

---

[1] This story was written "in the darkest period of the Civil War to show what love of country is." Philip Nolan was an entirely fictitious character. "Frederic Ingham, the 'I' of the narrative, is supposed to be a retired officer of the United States Navy." (See Hale's note in the edition copyrighted by Messrs. Little, Brown and Company, 1898.)

"Deaths," the announcement,—

"NOLAN. Died on board U. S. Corvette *Levant*, Lat. 2° 11′ S., Long. 131° W., on the 11th of May, PHILIP NOLAN."

I happened to observe it, because I was stranded at the old Mission House in Mackinac, waiting for a Lake Superior steamer which did not choose to come, and I was devouring to the very stubble all the current literature I could get hold of, even down to the deaths and marriages in the *Herald*. My memory for names and people is good, and the reader will see, as he goes on, that I had reason enough to remember Philip Nolan. There are hundreds of readers who would have paused at that announcement, if the officer of the *Levant* who reported it had chosen to make it thus: "Died, May 11th, THE MAN WITHOUT A COUNTRY." For it was as "The Man without a Country" that poor Philip Nolan had generally been known by the officers who had him in charge during some fifty years, as, indeed, by all the men who sailed under them. I dare say there is many a man who has taken wine with him once a fortnight, in a three years' cruise, who never knew that his name was "Nolan," or whether the poor wretch had any name at all.

There can now be no possible harm in telling this poor creature's story. Reason enough there has been till now, ever since Madison's administration went out in 1817, for very strict secrecy, the secrecy of honor itself, among the gentlemen of the navy who have had Nolan in successive charge. And certainly it speaks well for the *esprit de corps* of the profession, and the personal honor of its members, that to the press this man's story has been wholly unknown,—and, I think, to the country at large also. I have reason to think, from some investigations I made in the Naval Archives when I was attached to the Bureau of Construction, that every official report relating to him was burned when Ross [2] burned the public buildings at Washington. One of the Tuckers, or possibly one of the Watsons, had Nolan in charge at the end of the war; and when, on returning from his cruise, he reported at Washington to one of the Crowninshields,—who was in the Navy Department when he came home, —he found that the Department ignored the whole business. Whether they really knew nothing about it, or whether it was a *"Non mi ricordo,"* [3] determined on as a piece of policy, I do not know. But this I do know, that since

---

[2] Robert Ross, 1766-1814, a British general, captured Washington in 1814 and before evacuating the city burned the public buildings.
[3] "I do not remember."

1817, and possibly before, no naval officer has mentioned Nolan in his report of a cruise.

But, as I say, there is no need for secrecy any longer. And now the poor creature is dead, it seems to me worth while to tell a little of his story, by way of showing young Americans of today what it is to be A MAN WITHOUT A COUNTRY.

PHILIP NOLAN was as fine a young officer as there was in the "Legion of the West," as the Western division of our army was then called. When Aaron Burr [1] made his first dashing expedition down to New Orleans in 1805, at Fort Massac, or somewhere above on the river, he met, as the Devil would have it, this gay, dashing, bright young fellow; at some dinner-party, I think. Burr marked him, talked to him, walked with him, took him a day or two's voyage in his flat-boat, and, in short, fascinated him. For the next year, barrack-life was very tame to poor Nolan. He occasionally availed himself of the permission the great man had given him to write to him. Long, high-worded, stilted letters the poor boy wrote and rewrote and copied. But never a line did he have in reply from the gay deceiver. The other boys in the garrison sneered at him, because he sacrificed in this unrequited affection for a politician the time which they devoted to Monongahela, sledge, and high-low-jack. Bourbon, euchre, and poker were still unknown. But one day Nolan had his revenge. This time Burr came down the river, not as an attorney seeking a place for his office, but as a disguised conqueror. He had defeated I know not how many district-attorneys; he had dined at I know not how many public dinners; he had been heralded in I know not how many *Weekly Arguses,* and it was rumored that he had an army behind him and an empire before him. It was a great day —his arrival—to poor Nolan. Burr had not been at the fort an hour before he sent for him. That evening he asked Nolan to take him out in his skiff to show him a cane-brake or a cotton-wood tree, as he said,—really to seduce

him; and by the time the sail was over, Nolan was enlisted body and soul. From that time, though he did not yet know it, he lived as A MAN WITHOUT A COUNTRY.

What Burr meant to do I know no more than you, dear reader. It is none of our business just now. Only, when the grand catastrophe came, and Jefferson and the House of Virginia [2] of that day undertook to break on the wheel all the possible Clarences of the then House of York, by the great treason trial at Richmond, some of the lesser fry in that distant Mississippi Valley, which was farther from us than Puget's Sound is today, introduced the like novelty on their provincial stage; and, to while away the monotony of the summer at Fort Adams, got up, for *spectacles,* a string of court-martials on the officers there. One and another of the colonels and majors were tried, and, to fill out the list, little Nolan, against whom, Heaven knows, there was evidence enough,—that he was sick of the service, had been willing to be false to it, and would have obeyed any order to march any-whither with any one who would follow him had the order only been signed, "By command of His Exc. A. Burr." The courts dragged on. The big flies escaped,—rightly for all I know. Nolan was proved guilty enough, as I say; yet you and I would never have heard of him, reader, but that, when the president of the court asked him at the close whether he wished to say anything to show that he had always been faithful to the United States, he cried out, in a fit of frenzy,—

"D—n the United States! I wish I may never hear of the United States again!"

I suppose he did not know how the words shocked old Colonel Morgan, [3] who was holding the court. Half the officers who sat in it had served through the Revolution, and their lives, not to say their necks, had been risked for the very idea which he so cavalierly cursed in his madness. He, on his part, had grown up in the West of those days, in the midst of "Spanish plot," "Orleans plot," and all the rest. [4] He had been educated on a plantation where the finest company was a Spanish officer or a French

---

[1] Aaron Burr, who had been elected vice-president of the United States in 1800, had lost his influence by 1804, and was then defeated in his effort to become Governor of New York. Angered by Alexander Hamilton's open stand against him, he challenged Hamilton to duel and killed him. His reputation ruined, Burr, now desperate, conceived the idea of founding a republic of which he himself should be president, which should include Texas and perhaps Mexico, and have New Orleans as its capital. He visited the West, secured a large tract of land on the Washita River, and was known to have been in correspondence with the British and Spanish ministers at Washington. He was indicted for treason at Richmond, Virginia, May, 1807, but from lack of sufficient evidence he was acquitted.

[2] As in the Wars of the Roses the houses of York and Lancaster were rivals, so, Hale implies, the Virginia statesmen regarded the statesmen of the North as their natural enemies. George, Duke of Clarence, a Yorkist, was imprisoned for treason in the Tower of London and there murdered.

[3] "Colonel Morgan is a fictitious character, like all the others in this book except Aaron Burr." (Hale's note, in the edition copyrighted 1898 by Messrs. Little, Brown and Company.)

[4] The years following our Revolution were marked by plots of the Mississippi Valley settlers to gain possession of the mouth of the Mississippi, then held by Spain.

merchant from Orleans. His education, such as it was, had been perfected in commercial expeditions to Vera Cruz, and I think he told me his father once hired an Englishman to be a private tutor for a winter on the plantation. He had spent half his youth with an older brother, hunting horses in Texas; and, in a word, to him "United States" was scarcely a reality. Yet he had been fed by "United States" for all the years since he had been in the army. He had sworn on his faith as a Christian to be true to "United States." It was "United States" which gave him the uniform he wore, and the sword by his side. Nay, my poor Nolan, it was only because "United States" had picked you out first as one of her own confidential men of honor that "A. Burr" cared for you a straw more than for the flat-boat men who sailed his ark for him. I do not excuse Nolan; I only explain to the reader why he damned his country, and wished he might never hear her name again.

He never did hear her name but once again. From that moment, September 23, 1807, till the day he died, May 11, 1863, he never heard her name again. For that half century and more he was a man without a country.

Old Morgan, as I said, was terribly shocked. If Nolan had compared George Washington to Benedict Arnold, or had cried "God save King George," Morgan would not have felt worse. He called the court into his private room, and returned in fifteen minutes, with a face like a sheet, to say,—

"Prisoner, hear the sentence of the Court! The Court decides, subject to the approval of the President, that you never hear the name of the United States again."

Nolan laughed. But nobody else laughed. Old Morgan was too solemn, and the whole room was hushed dead as night for a minute. Even Nolan lost his swagger in a moment. Then Morgan added,—

"Mr. Marshal, take the prisoner to Orleans in an armed boat, and deliver him to the naval commander there."

The marshal gave his orders and the prisoner was taken out of court.

"Mr. Marshal," continued old Morgan, "see that no one mentions the United States to the prisoner. Mr. Marshal, make my respects to Lieutenant Mitchell at Orleans, and request him to order that no one shall mention the United States to the prisoner while he is on board ship. You will receive your written orders from the officer on duty here this evening. The Court is adjourned without day."

I have always supposed that Colonel Morgan himself took the proceedings of the court to Washington City, and explained them to Mr. Jefferson. Certain it is that the President approved them,—certain, that is, if I may believe the men who say they have seen his signature. Before the *Nautilus* got round from New Orleans to the northern Atlantic coast with the prisoner on board, the sentence had been approved, and he was a man without a country.

The plan then adopted was substantially the same which was necessarily followed ever after. Perhaps it was suggested by the necessity of sending him by water from Fort Adams and Orleans. The Secretary of the Navy—it must have been the first Crowninshield, though he is a man I do not remember—was requested to put Nolan on board a government vessel bound on a long cruise, and to direct that he should be only so far confined there as to make it certain that he never saw or heard of the country. We had few long cruises then, and the navy was very much out of favor; and as almost all of this story is traditional, as I have explained, I do not know certainly what his first cruise was. But the commander to whom he was entrusted, —perhaps it was Tingey or Shaw, though I think it was one of the younger men,—we are all old enough now,—regulated the etiquette and the precautions of the affair, and according to his scheme they were carried out, I suppose, till Nolan died.

When I was second officer of the *Intrepid*, some thirty years after, I saw the original paper of instructions. I have been sorry ever since that I did not copy the whole of it. It ran, however, much in this way:—

"WASHINGTON (with a date, which must have been late in 1807).

"Sir,—You will receive from Lieutenant Neale the person of Philip Nolan, late a lieutenant in the United States army.

"This person on his trial by court-martial expressed, with an oath, the wish that he might 'never hear of the United States again.'

"The Court sentenced him to have his wish fulfilled.

"For the present, the execution of the order is entrusted by the President to this Department.

"You will take the prisoner on board your ship, and keep him there with such precautions as shall prevent his escape.

"You will provide him with such quarters, rations, and clothing as would be proper for an officer of his late rank, if he were a passenger on your vessel on the business of his Government.

"The gentlemen on board will make any arrangements agreeable to themselves regarding his society.

He is to be exposed to no indignity of any kind, nor is he ever unnecessarily to be reminded that he is a prisoner.

"But under no circumstances is he ever to hear of his country or to see any information regarding it; and you will specially caution all the officers under your command to take care, that, in the various indulgences which may be granted, this rule, in which his punishment is involved, shall not be broken.

"It is the intention of the Government that he shall never again see the country which he has disowned. Before the end of your cruise you will receive orders which will give effect to this intention.

"Respectfully yours,
"W. SOUTHARD, for the
"Secretary of the Navy."

If I had only preserved the whole of this paper, there would be no break in the beginning of my sketch of this story. For Captain Shaw, if it was he, handed it to his successor in the charge, and he to his, and I suppose the commander of the *Levant* has it today as his authority for keeping this man in this mild custody.

The rule adopted on board the ships on which I have met "the man without a country" was, I think, transmitted from the beginning. No mess liked to have him permanently, because his presence cut off all talk of home or of the prospect of return, of politics or letters, of peace or of war,—cut off more than half the talk men like to have at sea. But it was always thought too hard that he should never meet the rest of us, except to touch hats, and we finally sank into one system. He was not permitted to talk with the men, unless an officer was by. With officers he had unrestrained intercourse, as far as they and he chose. But he grew shy, though he had favorites: I was one. Then the captain always asked him to dinner on Monday. Every mess in succession took up the invitation in its turn. According to the size of the ship, you had him at your mess more or less often at dinner. His breakfast he ate in his own state-room,—he always had a state-room,—which was where a sentinel or somebody on the watch could see the door. And whatever else he ate or drank, he ate or drank alone. Sometimes, when the marines or sailors had any special jollification, they were permitted to invite "Plain-Buttons," as they called him. Then Nolan was sent with some officer, and the men were forbidden to speak of home while he was there. I believe the theory was that the sight of his punishment did them good. They called him "Plain-Buttons," because, while he always chose to wear a regulation army-uniform, he was not permitted to wear the army-button, for the reason that it bore either the initials or the insignia of the country he had disowned.

I remember, soon after I joined the navy, I was on shore with some of the older officers from our ship and from the *Brandywine,* which we had met at Alexandria. We had leave to make a party and go up to Cairo and the Pyramids. As we jogged along (you went on donkeys then), some of the gentlemen (we boys called them "Dons," but the phrase was long since changed) fell to talking about Nolan, and some one told the system which was adopted from the first about his books and other reading. As he was almost never permitted to go on shore, even though the vessel lay in port for months, his time at the best hung heavy; and everybody was permitted to lend him books, if they were not published in America and made no allusion to it. These were common enough in the old days, when people in the other hemisphere talked of the United States as little as we do of Paraguay. He had almost all the foreign papers that came into the ship, sooner or later; only somebody must go over them first, and cut out any advertisement or stray paragraph that alluded to America. This was a little cruel sometimes, when the back of what was cut out might be as innocent as Hesiod.[1] Right in the midst of one of Napoleon's battles, or one of Canning's[2] speeches, poor Nolan would find a great hole, because on the back of the page of that paper there had been an advertisement of a packet for New York, or a scrap from the President's message. I say this was the first time I ever heard of this plan, which afterwards I had enough and more than enough to do with. I remember it, because poor Phillips, who was of the party, as soon as the allusion to reading was made, told a story of something which happened at the Cape of Good Hope on Nolan's first voyage; and it is the only thing I ever knew of that voyage. They had touched at the Cape, and had done the civil thing with the English Admiral and the fleet, and then, leaving for a long cruise up the Indian Ocean, Phillips had borrowed a lot of English books from an officer, which, in those days, as indeed in these, was quite a windfall. Among them, as the Devil would order, was the *Lay of the Last Minstrel,* which they had all of them heard of, but which most of them had never seen. I think it could

[1] a Greek poet of probably the eighth century B.C.
[2] George Canning, 1770-1827, was a celebrated English statesman and orator.

not have been published long. Well, nobody thought there could be any risk of anything national in that, though Phillips swore old Shaw had cut out *The Tempest* from Shakespeare before he let Nolan have it, because he said "the Bermudas ought to be ours, and, by Jove, should be one day." So Nolan was permitted to join the circle one afternoon when a lot of them sat on deck smoking and reading aloud. People do not do such things so often now; but when I was young we got rid of a great deal of time so. Well, so it happened that in his turn Nolan took the book and read to the others; and he read very well, as I know. Nobody in the circle knew a line of the poem, only it was all magic and Border chivalry, and was ten thousand years ago. Poor Nolan read steadily through the fifth canto, stopped a minute and drank something, and then began, without a thought of what was coming,—

Breathes there a man, with soul so dead,
Who never to himself hath said,—

It seems impossible to us that anybody ever heard this for the first time; but all these fellows did then, and poor Nolan himself went on, still unconsciously or mechanically,—

This is my own, my native land!

Then they all saw something was to pay; but he expected to get through, I suppose, turned a little pale, but plunged on,—

Whose heart hath ne'er within him burned,
As home his footsteps he hath turned
From wandering on a foreign strand?—
If such there breathe, go, mark him well,—

By this time the men were all beside themselves, wishing there was any way to make him turn over two pages; but he had not quite presence of mind for that; he gagged a little, colored crimson, and staggered on,—

For him no minstrel raptures swell;
High though his titles, proud his name,
Boundless his wealth as wish can claim,
Despite these titles, power, and pelf,
The wretch, concentered all in self,—

and here the poor fellow choked, could not go on, but started up, swung the book into the sea, and vanished into his state-room, "And by Jove," said Phillips, "we did not see him for two months again. And I had to make up some beggarly story to that English surgeon why I did not return his Walter Scott to him."

That story shows about the time when Nolan's braggadocio must have broken down. At first, they said, he took a very high tone,

considered his imprisonment a mere farce, effected to enjoy the voyage, and all that; but Phillips said that after he came out of his state-room he never was the same man again. He never read aloud again, unless it was the Bible or Shakespeare, or something else he was sure of. But it was not that merely. He never entered in with the other young men exactly as a companion again. He was always shy afterwards, when I knew him,—very seldom spoke, unless he was spoken to, except to a very few friends. He lighted up occasionally, —I remember late in his life hearing him fairly eloquent on something which had been suggested to him by one of Fléchier's [1] sermons,— but generally he had the nervous, tired look of a heart-wounded man.

When Captain Shaw was coming home,—if, as I say, it was Shaw,—rather to the surprise of everybody they made one of the Windward Islands, and lay off and on for nearly a week. The boys said the officers were sick of salt-junk, and meant to have turtle-soup before they came home. But after several days the *Warren* came to the same rendezvous; they exchanged signals; she sent to Phillips and these homeward-bound men letters and papers, and told them she was outward-bound, perhaps to the Mediterranean, and took poor Nolan and his traps on the boat back to try his second cruise. He looked very blank when he was told to get ready to join her. He had known enough of the signs of the sky to know that till that moment he was going "home." But this was a distinct evidence of something he had not thought of, perhaps,—that there was no going home for him, even to a prison. And this was the first of some twenty such transfers, which brought him sooner or later into half our best vessels, but which kept him all his life at least some hundred miles from the country he had hoped he might never hear of again.

It may have been on that second cruise,—it was once when he was up the Mediterranean,— that Mrs. Graff, the celebrated Southern beauty of those days, danced with him. They had been lying a long time in the Bay of Naples, and the officers were very intimate in the English fleet, and there had been great festivities, and our men thought they must give a great ball on board the ship. How they ever did it on board the *Warren* I am sure I do not know. Perhaps it was not the *Warren*, or perhaps ladies did not take up so much room as they do now. They wanted to use Nolan's state-

---

[1] Esprit Fléchier, 1632-1710, a French bishop, noted for his pulpit eloquence

room for something, and they hated to do it without asking him to the ball; so the captain said they might ask him, if they would be responsible that he did not talk with the wrong people, "who would give him intelligence." So the dance went on, the finest party that had ever been known, I dare say; for I never heard of a man-of-war ball that was not. For ladies they had the family of the American consul, one or two travelers who had adventured so far, and a nice bevy of English girls and matrons, perhaps Lady Hamilton [1] herself.

Well, different officers relieved each other in standing and talking with Nolan in a friendly way, so as to be sure that nobody else spoke to him. The dancing went on with spirit, and after a while even the fellows who took this honorary guard of Nolan ceased to fear any *contretemps*. [2] Only when some English lady —Lady Hamilton, as I said, perhaps—called for a set of "American dances," an odd thing happened. Everybody then danced contra-dances. The black band, nothing loath, conferred as to what "American dances" were, and started off with "Virginia Reel," which they followed with "Money-Musk," which, in its turn in those days, should have been followed by "The Old Thirteen." But just as Dick, the leader, tapped for his fiddles to begin, and bent forward, about to say, in true negro state, " 'The Old Thirteen,' gentlemen and ladies!" as he had said " 'Virginny Reel,' if you please!" and " 'Money-Musk,' if you please!" the captain's boy tapped him on the shoulder, whispered to him, and he did not announce the name of the dance; he merely bowed, began on the air, and they all fell to,—the officers teaching the English girls the figure, but not telling them why it had no name.

But that is not the story I started to tell.— As the dancing went on, Nolan and our fellows all got at ease, as I said,—so much so, that it seemed quite natural for him to bow to that splendid Mrs. Graff, and say,—

"I hope you have not forgotten me, Miss Rutledge. Shall I have the honor of dancing?"

He did it so quickly, that Shubrick, who was with him, could not hinder him. She laughed and said,—

"I am not Miss Rutledge any longer, Mr. Nolan; but I will dance all the same," just nodded to Shubrick, as if to say he must leave Mr. Nolan to her, and led him off to the place where the dance was forming.

Nolan thought he had got his chance. He had known her at Philadelphia, and at other places had met her, and this was a godsend. You could not talk in contra-dances, as you do in cotillions, or even in the pauses of waltzing; but there were chances for tongues and sounds, as well as for eyes and blushes. He began with her travels, and Europe, and Vesuvius, and the French; and then, when they had worked down, and had that long talking time at the bottom of the set, he said boldly,—a little pale, she said, as she told me the story years after,—

"And what do you hear from home, Mrs. Graff?"

And that splendid creature looked through him. Jove! how she must have looked through him!

"Home!! Mr. Nolan!!! I thought you were the man who never wanted to hear of home again!"—and she walked directly up the deck to her husband, and left poor Nolan alone, as he always was.—He did not dance again.

I cannot give any history of him in order; nobody can now; and, indeed, I am not trying to. These are the traditions, which I sort out, as I believe them, from the myths which have been told about this man for forty years. The lies that have been told about him are legion. The fellows used to say he was the "Iron Mask"; [3] and poor George Pons went to his grave in the belief that this was the author of "Junius," [4] who was being punished for his celebrated libel on Thomas Jefferson. Pons was not very strong in the historical line. A happier story than either of these I have told is of the war. [5] That came along soon after. I have heard this affair told in three or four ways,—and, indeed, it may have happened more than once. But which ship it was on I cannot tell. However, in one, at least, of the great frigate-duels with the English, in which the navy was really baptized, it happened that a round shot from the enemy entered one of our ports square, and took right down the officer of the gun himself, and almost every man of the gun's crew. Now you may say what you choose about courage, but that is not a nice thing to see. But, as the men who were not killed picked themselves up, and as they and the surgeon's people were carrying off the bodies, there appeared Nolan, in his shirt-sleeves, with

---

[1] a celebrated beauty and diplomatic intriguer, wife of Sir William Hamilton, the diplomatist and archeologist, who was ambassador at Naples, 1764-1800
[2] mishap, mischance

[3] a French prisoner of state in the Bastile who from 1673 (?) until his death in 1703 wore a mask which tradition made iron
[4] the unknown writer of a series of letters against the English Government, which appeared in London papers from November, 1768, to January, 1772
[5] of 1812

the rammer in his hand, and, just as if he had been the officer, told them off with authority,—who should go to the cock-pit with the wounded men, who should stay with him,—perfectly cheery, and with that way which makes men feel sure all is right and is going to be right. And he finished loading the gun with his own hands, aimed it, and bade the men fire. And there he stayed, captain of that gun, keeping those fellows in spirits, till the enemy struck,—sitting on the carriage while the gun was cooling, though he was exposed all the time,—showing them easier ways to handle heavy shot, —making the raw hands laugh at their own blunders,—and when the gun cooled again, getting it loaded and fired twice as often as any other gun on the ship. The captain walked forward by way of encouraging the men, and Nolan touched his hat and said,—

"I am showing them how we do this in the artillery, sir."

And this is the part of the story where all the legends agree: that Commodore said,—

"I see you do, and I thank you, sir; and I shall never forget this day, sir, and you never shall, sir."

And after the whole thing was over, and he had the Englishman's sword, in the midst of the state and ceremony of the quarter-deck, he said,—"Where is Mr. Nolan? Ask Mr. Nolan to come here."

And when Nolan came, the captain said,—

"Mr. Nolan, we are all very grateful to you today; you are one of us today; you will be named in the despatches."

And then the old man took off his own sword of ceremony, and gave it to Nolan, and made him put it on. The man told me this who saw it. Nolan cried like a baby, and well he might. He had not worn a sword since that infernal day at Fort Adams. But always afterwards on occasions of ceremony, he wore that quaint old French sword of the Commodore's.

The captain did mention him in the despatches. It was always said he asked that he might be pardoned. He wrote a special letter to the Secretary of War. But nothing ever came of it. As I said, that was about the time when they began to ignore the whole transaction at Washington, and when Nolan's imprisonment began to carry itself on because there was nobody to stop it without any new orders from home.

I have heard it said that he was with Porter [1] when he took possession of the Nukahiwa Islands. Not this Porter, you know, but old Porter, his father, Essex Porter,—that is, the old *Essex* Porter, not this *Essex*. As an artillery officer, who had seen service in the West, Nolan knew more about fortifications, embrasures, ravelins, [2] stockades, and all that, than any of them did; and he worked with a right good-will in fixing that battery all right. I have always thought it was a pity Porter did not leave him in command there with Gamble. That would have settled all the question about his punishment. We should have kept the islands, and at this moment we should have one station in the Pacific Ocean. Our French friends, too, when they wanted this little watering-place, would have found it was preoccupied. [3] But Madison and the Virginians, of course, flung all that away.

All that was near fifty years ago. If Nolan was thirty then, he must have been near eighty when he died. He looked sixty when he was forty. But he never seemed to me to change a hair afterwards. As I imagine his life, from what I have seen and heard of it, he must have been in every sea, and yet almost never on land. He must have known, in a formal way, more officers in our service than any man living knows. He told me once, with a grave smile, that no man in the world lived so methodical a life as he. "You know the boys say I am the Iron Mask, and you know how busy he was." He said it did not do for any one to try to read all the time, more than to do anything else all the time; and that he read just five hours a day. "Then," he said, "I keep up my notebooks, writing in them at such and such hours from what I have been reading; and I include in these my scrap-books." These were very curious indeed. He had six or eight, of different subjects. There was one of History, one of Natural Science, one which he called "Odds and Ends." But they were not merely books of extracts from newspapers. They had bits of plants and ribbons, shells tied on, and carved scraps of bone and wood, which he had taught the men to cut for him, and they were beautifully illustrated. He drew admirably. He had some of the funniest drawings

---

[1] David Porter, 1780-1843, commanded the American man-of-war *Essex* in the War of 1812; in 1813 he took formal possession of the Marquesas Islands, in the Pacific, the largest of which is Nukahiva. These, however, the American Government did not seem to consider worth endeavoring to hold. David Porter's son, David Dixon Porter, "this Porter," 1813-1891, was an admiral in the Civil War. Or, reference may be to Commodore William David Porter, who commanded the gunboat *Essex* in the Civil War.

[2] an A-shaped outwork of a fortification

[3] The French took possession of the Marquesas Islands in 1842.

there, and some of the most pathetic, that I have ever seen in my life. I wonder who will have Nolan's scrap-books.

Well, he said his reading and his notes were his profession, and that they took five hours and two hours respectively of each day. "Then," said he, "every man should have a diversion as well as a profession. My Natural History is my diversion." That took two hours a day more. The men used to bring him birds and fish, but on a long cruise he had to satisfy himself with centipedes and cockroaches and such small game. He was the only naturalist I ever met who knew anything about the habits of the house-fly and the mosquito. All those people can tell you whether they are *Lepidoptera* or *Steptopotera;* [1] but as for telling how you can get rid of them, or how they get away from you when you strike them,—why Linnaeus [2] knew as little of that as John Foy the idiot did. These nine hours made Nolan's regular daily "occupation." The rest of the time he talked or walked. Till he grew very old, he went aloft a great deal. He always kept up his exercise; and I never heard that he was ill. If any other man was ill, he was the kindest nurse in the world; and he knew more than half the surgeons do. Then if anybody was sick or died, or if the captain wanted him to, on any other occasion, he was always ready to read prayers. I have remarked that he read beautifully.

My own acquaintance with Philip Nolan began six or eight years after the war, on my first voyage after I was appointed a midshipman. It was in the first days after our Slave-Trade treaty, [3] while the Reigning House, which was still the House of Virginia, had still a sort of sentimentalism about the suppression of the horrors of the Middle Passage, and something was sometimes done that way. We were in the South Atlantic on that business. From the time I joined, I believe I thought Nolan was a sort of lay chaplain,—a chaplain with a blue coat. I never asked about him. Everything in the ship was strange to me. I knew it was green

to ask questions, and I suppose I thought there was a "Plain-Buttons" on every ship. We had him to dine in our mess once a week, and the caution was given that on that day nothing was to be said about home. But if they had told us not to say anything about the planet Mars or the book of *Deuteronomy,* I should not have asked why; there were a great many things which seemed to me to have as little reason. I first came to understand anything about "the man without a country" one day when we overhauled a dirty little schooner which had slaves on board. An officer was sent to take charge of her, and, after a few minutes, he sent back his boat to ask that some one might be sent him who could speak Portuguese. We were all looking over the rail when the message came, and we all wished we could interpret, when the captain asked who spoke Portuguese. But none of the officers did; and just as the captain was sending forward to ask if any of the people could, Nolan stepped out and said he should be glad to interpret, if the captain wished, as he understood the language. The captain thanked him, fitted out another boat with him, and in this boat it was my luck to go.

When we got there, it was such a scene as you seldom see, and never want to. Nastiness beyond account, and chaos run loose in the midst of the nastiness. There were not a great many of the negroes; but by way of making what there were understand that they were free, Vaughan had had their hand-cuffs and ankle-cuffs knocked off, and, for convenience' sake, was putting them upon the rascals of the schooner's crew. The negroes were, most of them, out of the hold, and swarming all round the dirty deck, with a central throng surrounding Vaughan and addressing him in every dialect and *patois* of a dialect, from the Zulu click up to the Parisian of Beledeljereed. [4]

As we came on deck, Vaughan looked down from a hogshead, on which he had mounted in desperation, and said:—

"For God's love, is there anybody who can make these wretches understand something? The men gave them rum, and that did not quiet them. I knocked that big fellow down twice, and that did not soothe him. And then I talked Choctaw to all of them together; and I'll be hanged if they understand that as well as they understood the English."

---

[1] *Lepidoptera* are insects distinguished primarily by their having four membranous wings covered with overlapping scales. *Steptopotera:* Hale has, perhaps, coined the word for the occasion.

[2] The famous Swedish naturalist, 1707-1778; John Foy is the chief character in Wordsworth's poem, *The Idiot Boy.*

[3] By the Treaty of Ghent, 1814, Great Britain and the United States agreed to abolish the slave traffic. In 1820 slave-trade was made piracy punishable by death. Washington, Jefferson, Madison, and Monroe were all from Virginia. The "Middle Passage" was that part of the Atlantic between the west African coast and the West Indies most traversed by slave ships.

[4] Beled el Jerid, "country of dates," a region in the northern Sahara; Hale probably implies that its language is Parisian in comparison to the Zulu dialect; or he may refer in irony to its actual commercial language, which is corrupt French, mixed with other tongues.

Nolan said he could speak Portuguese, and one or two fine-looking Kroomen [1] were dragged out, who, as it had been found already, had worked for the Portuguese on the coast at Fernando Po.

"Tell them they are free," said Vaughan; "and tell them that these rascals are to be hanged as soon as we can get rope enough."

Nolan "put that into Spanish,"—that is, he explained it in such Portuguese as the Kroomen could understand, and they in turn to such of the negroes as could understand them. Then there was such a yell of delight, clinching of fists, leaping and dancing, kissing of Nolan's feet, and a general rush made to the hogshead by way of spontaneous worship of Vaughan, as the *deus ex machina* [2] of the occasion.

"Tell them," said Vaughan, well pleased, "that I will take them all to Cape Palmas."

This did not answer so well. Cape Palmas was practically as far from the homes of most of them as New Orleans, or Rio Janeiro was; that is, they would be eternally separated from home there. And their interpreters, as we could understand, instantly said, *"Ah, non Palmas,"* and began to propose infinite other expedients in most voluble language. Vaughan was rather disappointed at this result of his liberality, and asked Nolan eagerly what they said. The drops stood on poor Nolan's white forehead, as he hushed the men down, and said:—

"He says, 'Not Palmas.' He says, 'Take us home, take us to our own country, take us to our own house, take us to our own pickaninnies and our own women.' He says he has an old father and mother who will die if they do not see him. And this one says he left his people all sick, and paddled down to Fernando to beg the white doctor to come and help them, and that these devils caught him in the bay just in sight of home, and that he has never seen anybody from home since then. And this one says," choked out Nolan, "that he has not heard a word from his home in six months, while he has been locked up in an infernal barracoon." [3]

Vaughan always said he grew gray himself while Nolan struggled through this interpretation. I, who did not understand anything of the passion involved in it, saw that the very elements were melting with fervent heat, and

that something was to pay somewhere. Even the negroes themselves stopped howling, as they saw Nolan's agony, and Vaughan's almost equal agony of sympathy. As quick as he could get words, he said:—

"Tell them yes, yes, yes; tell them they shall go to the Mountains of the Moon, if they will. If I sail the schooner through the Great White Desert, they shall go home!"

And after some fashion Nolan said so. And then they all fell to kissing him again, and wanted to rub his nose with theirs.

But he could not stand it long; and getting Vaughan to say he might go back, he beckoned me down into our boat. As we lay back in the stern-sheets and the men gave way, he said to me: "Youngster, let that show you what it is to be without a family, without a home, and without a country. And if you are ever tempted to say a word or to do a thing that shall put a bar between you and your family, your home, and your country, pray God in his mercy to take you that instant home to his own heaven. Stick by your family, boy; forget you have a self, while you do everything for them. Think of your home, boy; write and send, and talk about it. Let it be nearer and nearer to your thought, the farther you have to travel from it; and rush back to it when you are free, as that poor black slave is doing now. And for your country, boy," and the words rattled in his throat, "and for that flag," and he pointed to the ship, "never dream a dream but of serving her as she bids you, though the service carry you through a thousand hells. No matter what happens to you, no matter who flatters you or who abuses you, never look at another flag, never let a night pass but you pray God to bless that flag. Remember, boy, that behind all these men you have to do with, behind officers, and government, and people even, there is the Country Herself, your Country, and that you belong to Her as you belong to your own mother. Stand by Her, boy, as you would stand by your mother, if those devils there had got hold of her today!"

I was frightened to death by his calm, hard passion; but I blundered out that I would, by all that was holy, and that I had never thought of doing anything else. He hardly seemed to hear me; but he did, almost in a whisper, say,— "Oh, if anybody had said so to me when I was of your age!"

I think it was this half-confidence of his, which I never abused, for I never told this story till now, which afterward made us great friends. He was very kind to me. Often he sat up, or

[1] an industrious tribe, never enslaved, living in Liberia
[2] "A god from a machine"; this expression means the person who, at a critical moment, solves a difficulty or hastens a dénouement; it refers to the device used in ancient drama of letting a god down from above by machinery when divine intervention was needed.
[3] slave pen

even got up, at night, to walk the deck with me, when it was my watch. He explained to me a great deal of my mathematics, and I owe to him my taste for mathematics. He lent me books, and helped me about my reading. He never alluded so directly to his story again; but from one and another officer I have learned, in thirty years, what I am telling. When we parted from him in St. Thomas harbor, at the end of our cruise, I was more sorry than I can tell. I was very glad to meet him again in 1830; and later in life, when I thought I had some influence in Washington, I moved heaven and earth to have him discharged. But it was like getting a ghost out of prison. They pretended there was no such man, and never was such a man. They will say so at the Department now! Perhaps they do not know. It will not be the first thing in the service of which the Department appears to know nothing!

There is a story that Nolan met Burr once on one of our vessels, when a party of Americans came on board in the Mediterranean. But this I believe to be a lie; or rather, it is a myth, *ben trovato*,[1] involving a tremendous blowing-up with which he sunk Burr,—asking him how he liked to be "without a country." But it is clear from Burr's life, that nothing of the sort could have happened; and I mention this only as an illustration of the stories which get a-going where there is the least mystery at bottom.

For him, poor fellow, he repented of his folly, and then, like a man, submitted to the fate he had asked for. He never intentionally added to the difficulty or delicacy of the charge of those who had him in hold. Accidents would happen; but they never happened from his fault. Lieutenant Truxton told me that, when Texas was annexed, there was a careful discussion among the officers, whether they should get hold of Nolan's handsome set of maps and cut Texas out of it,—from the map of the world and the map of Mexico. The United States had been cut out when the atlas was bought for him. But it was voted, rightly enough, that to do this would be virtually to reveal to him what had happened, or, as Harry Cole said, to make him think Old Burr had succeeded. So it was from no fault of Nolan's that a great botch happened at my own table, when, for a short time, I was in command of the *George Washington* corvette, on the South American station. We were lying in the La Plata, and some of the officers, who had been on shore and had just

joined again, were entertaining us with accounts of their misadventures in riding the half-wild horses of Buenos Ayres. Nolan was at table, and was in an unusually bright and talkative mood. Some story of a tumble reminded him of an adventure of his own when he was catching wild horses in Texas with his brother Stephen, at a time when he must have been quite a boy. He told the story with a good deal of spirit,—so much so, that the silence which often follows a good story hung over the table for an instant, to be broken by Nolan himself. For he asked perfectly unconsciously, —"Pray, what has become of Texas? After the Mexicans got their independence, I thought that province of Texas would come forward very fast. It is really one of the finest regions on earth; it is the Italy of this continent. But I have not seen or heard a word of Texas for near twenty years."

There were two Texan officers at the table. The reason he had never heard of Texas was that Texas and her affairs had been painfully cut out of his newspapers since Austin[2] began his settlements; so that, while he read of Honduras and Tamaulipas,[3] and, till quite lately, of California,—this virgin province, in which his brother had traveled so far, and, I believe, had died, had ceased to be to him. Waters and Williams, the two Texas men, looked grimly at each other and tried not to laugh. Edward Morris had his attention attracted by the third link in the chain of the captain's chandelier. Watrous was seized with a convulsion of sneezing. Nolan himself saw that something was to pay, he did not know what. And I, as master of the feast, had to say,— "Texas is out of the map, Mr. Nolan. Have you seen Captain Back's curious account of Sir Thomas Roe's Welcome?"[4]

After that cruise I never saw Nolan again. I wrote to him at least twice a year, for in that voyage we became even confidentially intimate; but he never wrote to me. The other men tell me that in those fifteen years he *aged* very fast, as well he might indeed, but that he was still the same gentle, uncomplaining, silent sufferer that he ever was, bearing as best he could his self-

[1] well invented (For some years Burr was virtually an exile from the United States; was expelled from England, and rebuffed by Napoleon.)

[2] Stephen Fuller Austin in 1821 first led a colony of settlers from the United States into Texas, thus carrying out the purpose of his father, Moses Austin.

[3] a Mexican state that borders on Texas

[4] Captain Back was a famous English Arctic explorer of Hale's time. Sir Thomas Roe was a traveler and English diplomat of the seventeenth century. He was a patron of an exploring expedition under Captain Luke Fox, who in 1631 named an island north of Hudson's Bay "Sir Thomas Roe's Welcome Island." The name "Welcome" is now confined to the straits surrounding the island.

appointed punishment,—rather less social, perhaps, with new men whom he did not know, but more anxious, apparently, than ever to serve and befriend and teach the boys, some of whom fairly seemed to worship him. And now it seems the dear old fellow is dead. He has found a home at last, and a country.

Since writing this, and while considering whether or no I would print it, as a warning to the young Nolans and Vallandighams [1] and Tatnalls of today of what it is to throw away a country, I have received from Danforth, who is on board the *Levant,* a letter which gives an account of Nolan's last hours. It removes all my doubts about telling this story.

To understand the first words of the letter, the non-professional reader should remember that after 1817, the position of every officer who had Nolan in charge was one of the greatest delicacy. The government had failed to renew the order of 1807 regarding him. What was a man to do? Should he let him go? What, then, if he were called to account by the Department for violating the order of 1807? Should he keep him? What, then, if Nolan should be liberated some day, and should bring an action for false imprisonment or kidnapping against every man who had had him in charge? I urged and pressed this upon Southard, and I have reason to think that other officers did the same thing. But the Secretary always said, as they often do at Washington, that there were no special orders to give, and that we must act on our own judgment. That means, "if you succeed, you will be sustained; if you fail, you will be disavowed." Well, as Danforth says, all that is over now, though I do not know but I expose myself to a criminal prosecution on the evidence of the very revelation I am making.

Here is the letter:—

Levant, 2° 2′ S. @ 131° W.

"DEAR FRED:—I try to find heart and life to tell you that it is all over with dear old Nolan. I have been with him on this voyage more than I ever was, and I can understand wholly now the way in which you used to speak of the dear old fellow. I could see that he was not strong, but I had no idea the end was so near. The

[1] Clement Vallandigham, leader of the "Copper-heads," i.e., Northerners who were believed to sympathize unduly with the South in the Civil War, was once arrested by the Federal troops and banished to the Confederate lines. Commodore Josiah Tattnall, a gallant naval officer, resigned from the Federal navy to join the Confederate navy. It must be remembered that Hale's partisanship belonged to the times.

doctor has been watching him very carefully, and yesterday morning came to me and told me that Nolan was not so well, and had not left his state-room,—a thing I never remember before. He had let the doctor come and see him as he lay there,—the first time the doctor had been in the state-room,—and he said he should like to see me. Oh, dear! do you remember the mysteries we boys used to invent about his room in the old *Intrepid* days? Well, I went in, and there, to be sure, the poor fellow lay in his berth, smiling pleasantly as he gave me his hand, but looking very frail. I could not help a glance round, which showed me what a little shrine he had made of the box he was lying in. The stars and stripes were triced up above and around a picture of Washington, and he had painted a majestic eagle, with lightnings blazing from his beak and his foot just clasping the whole globe, which his wings over-shadowed. The dear old boy saw my glance, and said, with a sad smile, 'Here, you see, I have a country!' And then he pointed to the foot of his bed, where I had not seen before a great map of the United States, as he had drawn it from memory, and which he had there to look upon as he lay. Quaint, queer old names were on it, in large letters: 'Indiana Territory,' 'Mississippi Territory,' and 'Louisiana Territory,' as I suppose our fathers learned such things: but the old fellow had patched in Texas, too; he had carried his western boundary all the way to the Pacific, but on that shore he had defined nothing.

" 'O Danforth,' he said, 'I know I am dying. I cannot get home. Surely you will tell me something now?—Stop! stop. Do not speak till I say what I am sure you know, that there is not in this ship, that there is not in America, —God bless her!—a more loyal man than I. There cannot be a man who loves the old flag as I do, or prays for it as I do, or hopes for it as I do. There are thirty-four stars in it now, Danforth. I thank God for that, though I do not know what their names are. There has never been one taken away: I thank God for that. I know by that that there has never been any successful Burr. O Danforth, Danforth,' he sighed out, 'how like a wretched night's dream a boy's idea of personal fame or of separate sovereignty seems, when one looks back on it after such a life as mine! But tell me,—tell me something,—tell me everything, Danforth, before I die!'

"Ingham, I swear to you that I felt like a monster that I had not told him everything before. Danger or no danger, delicacy or no delicacy, who was I, that I should have been acting the tyrant all this time over this dear, sainted old man, who had years ago expiated, in his whole manhood's life, the madness of a boy's treason? 'Mr. Nolan,' said I, 'I will tell you everything you ask about. Only, where shall I begin?'

"Oh, the blessed smile that crept over his white face! and he pressed my hand and said, 'God bless you! Tell me their names,' he said, and he pointed to the stars on the flag. 'The last I know is Ohio. My father lived in Kentucky. But I have guessed Michigan and Indiana and Mississippi,—that was where Fort Adams is,—they make twenty. But where are your other fourteen? You have not cut up any of the old ones, I hope?'

"Well, that was not a bad text, and I told him the names in as good order as I could, and he bade me take down his beautiful map and draw them in as I best could with my pencil. He was wild with delight about Texas, told me how his brother died there; he had marked a gold cross where he supposed his brother's grave was; and he had guessed at Texas. Then he was delighted as he saw California and Oregon;— that, he said, he had suspected partly, because he had never been permitted to land on that shore, though the ships were there so much. 'And the men,' said he, laughing, 'brought off a good deal besides furs.' Then he went back— heavens, how far!—to ask about the *Chesapeake*,[1] and what was done to Barron for surrendering her to the *Leopard*, and whether Burr ever tried again,—and he ground his teeth with the only passion he showed. But in a moment that was over, and he said, 'God forgive me, for I am sure I forgive him.' Then he asked about the old war,—told me the true story of his serving the gun the day we took the *Java*,—asked about dear old David Porter, as he called him. Then he settled down more quietly, and very happily, to hear me tell in an hour the history of fifty years.

"How I wished it had been somebody who knew something! But I did as well as I could. I told him of the English war. I told him about Fulton and the steamboat beginning. I told him about old Scott, and Jackson; told him all I

could think about the Mississippi, and New Orleans, and Texas, and his own old Kentucky. And do you think, he asked me who was in command of the 'Legion of the West.' I told him it was a very gallant officer named Grant, and that, by our last news, he was about to establish his headquarters at Vicksburg. Then, 'Where was Vicksburg?' I worked that out on the map; it was about a hundred miles, more or less, above his old Fort Adams; and I thought Fort Adams must be a ruin now. 'It must be at old Vick's plantation,' said he: 'well, that is a change!'

"I tell you, Ingham, it was a hard thing to condense the history of half a century into that talk with a sick man. And I do not now know what I told him,—of emigration, and the means of it,—of steamboats, and railroads, and telegraphs,—of inventions, and books, and literature,—of the colleges, and West Point, and the Naval School,—but with the queerest interruptions that ever you heard. You see it was Robinson Crusoe asking all the accumulated questions of fifty-six years!

"I remember he asked, all of a sudden, who was President now; and when I told him, he asked if Old Abe was General Benjamin Lincoln's[2] son. He said he met old General Lincoln, when he was quite a boy himself, at some Indian treaty. I said no, that Old Abe was a Kentuckian like himself, but I could not tell him of what family; he had worked up from the ranks. 'Good for him!' cried Nolan; 'I am glad of that. As I have brooded and wondered, I have thought our danger was in keeping up those regular successions in the first families.' Then I got talking about my visit to Washington. I told him of meeting the Oregon Congressman, Harding; I told him about the Smithsonian, and the Exploring Expedition;[3] I told him about the Capitol, and the statues for the pediment, and Crawford's Liberty,[4] and Greenough's Washington: Ingham, I told him everything I could think of that would show the grandeur of his country and its prosperity; but I could not make up my mouth to tell him a word about this infernal rebellion!

"And he drank it in and enjoyed it as I cannot tell you. He grew more and more silent,

---

[1] In 1807 the American frigate *Chesapeake*, commanded by James Barron, was pursued by the English frigate *Leopard*, whose commander demanded the delivery of four men, three of whom were native Americans. Barron refused and the *Leopard* opened fire. The *Chesapeake* was unprepared, and after three of her men had been killed and sixteen wounded she was boarded from the *Leopard* and the four men were seized. One was hanged, one died in prison, and two were not returned for five years. The incident aroused strong feeling.

[2] a Revolutionary general, secretary of war 1781-84
[3] John C. Frémont in 1842 explored parts of the Rocky Mountains, and in 1843-44 and 1845 the Pacific slope; in 1853 he discovered a route to California.
[4] Thomas Crawford, 1814-1857, an American sculptor, designed the Statue of Liberty surmounting the Capitol at Washington, and the bronze doors depicting the life of Washington. The statue of Washington near the Capitol is by another American sculptor, Horatio Greenough, 1805-1852.

yet I never thought he was tired or faint. I gave him a glass of water, but he just wet his lips, and told me not to go away. Then he asked me to bring the Presbyterian 'Book of Public Prayer' which lay there, and said, with a smile, that it would open at the right place,—and so it did. There was his double red mark down the page; and I knelt down and read, and he repeated with me, 'For ourselves and our country, O gracious God, we thank Thee, that, notwithstanding our manifold transgressions of Thy holy laws, Thou hast continued to us Thy marvelous kindness,'—and so to the end of that thanksgiving. Then he turned to the end of the same book, and I read the words more familiar to me: 'Most heartily we beseech Thee with Thy favor to behold and bless Thy servant, the President of the United States, and all others in authority,'—and the rest of the Episcopal collect. 'Danforth,' said he, 'I have repeated those prayers night and morning, it is now fifty-five years.' And then he said he would go to sleep. He bent me down over him and kissed me; and he said, 'Look in my Bible, Danforth, when I am gone.' And I went away.

"But I had no thought it was the end. I thought he was tired and would sleep. I knew he was happy, and I wanted him to be alone.

"But in an hour, when the doctor went in gently, he found Nolan had breathed his life away with a smile. He had something pressed close to his lips. It was his father's badge of the Order of Cincinnati.[1]

"We looked in his Bible, and there was a slip of paper at the place where he had marked the text:—

"'They desire a country, even a heavenly: wherefore God is not ashamed to be called their God: for He hath prepared for them a city.'

"On this slip of paper he had written:

"'Bury me in the sea; it has been my home, and I love it. But will not some one set up a stone for my memory at Fort Adams or at Orleans, that my disgrace may not be more than I ought to bear? Say on it:—

'In Memory of
'PHILIP NOLAN,
'Lieutenant in the Army of the United States.

'He loved his country as no other man has loved her; but no man deserved less at her hands.'"

1865

[1] An association of the regular officers of the American Army of the Revolution; Washington was its first president.

HERMAN MELVILLE 1819-1891

Although he was born in the city of New York and died there, the leading traits of Melville's character were derived from his New England ancestors. After a good schooling he went to sea at the age of nineteen, and at the age of twenty-two signed articles for a whaling voyage. Deserting on the Marquesas, he spent several years in the Pacific islands. On his return home he rapidly produced several narratives of sea adventure, the most notable being *Typee*, 1846; *Omoo*, 1847; *Mardi*, 1849; *White-Jacket*, 1850; *Moby Dick*, 1851.

Much interest and a revived study of Melville about the time of his centenary has brought him the understanding criticism and the fame that he seems to have lacked during his lifetime. Recent estimates point out that he first discovered the romance of the South Seas, later developed by Stevenson and minor writers, and that together with Dana he showed for the first time the real life of the sailor in the forecastle of the merchant ship and the whaler. His style cannot be characterized in a word: *Typee* is idyllic; *Moby Dick*, now considered Melville's masterpiece, is, to Augustine Birrell, notable for "its most amazing eloquence and its mingling an ever-present romanticism of style with an almost savage reality of narrative."

Biography and criticism: J. Freeman, (EML); C. Van Doren, "Lucifer from Nantucket," *Cent.* 110:494-501; "Rediscovering the Genius of Herman Melville," *Cur. Opinion* 72:101-3; R. M. Weaver, "The Centennial of Herman Melville," *Nation* 109:145-6; A. Birrell, "The Immortal White Whale," *Liv. Age* 308:659-61.

From TYPEE[2]

CHAPTER X

Midnight Reflections—Morning Visitors—A Warrior in Costume—A Savage Aesculapius —Practice of the Healing Art—Body Servant—A Dwelling-house of the Valley described—Portraits of its Inmates.

Various and conflicting were the thoughts which oppressed me during the silent hours that followed the events related in the preceding chapter. Toby, wearied with the fatigues of the day, slumbered heavily by my side; but the pain under which I was suffering effectually prevented my sleeping, and I remained distressingly alive to all the fearful circumstances of our present situation. Was it possible that after

[2] On his whaling voyage, Melville found conditions so intolerable that with a single companion, Toby, he deserted at the Marquesas, the two sailors hiding ashore till the ship had sailed. To avoid arrest they plunged into the jungle, but lost their way while seeking the friendly Happar tribe, and found themselves, after four days, captive among the dreaded cannibal tribe of Typee, Melville himself disabled by exposure.

all our vicissitudes we were really in the terrible valley of Typee, and at the mercy of its inmates, a fierce and unrelenting tribe of savages?

Typee or Happar? I shuddered when I reflected that there was no longer any room for doubt; and that, beyond all hope of escape, we were now placed in those very circumstances from the bare thought of which I had recoiled with such abhorrence but a few days before. What might not be our fearful destiny? To be sure, as yet we had been treated with no violence; nay, had been even kindly and hospitably entertained. But what dependence could be placed upon the fickle passions which sway the bosom of a savage? His inconstancy and treachery are proverbial. Might it not be that beneath these fair appearances the islanders covered some perfidious design, and that their friendly reception of us might only precede some horrible catastrophe? How strongly did these forebodings spring up in my mind as I lay restlessly upon a couch of mats, surrounded by the dimly revealed forms of those whom I so greatly dreaded.

From the excitement of these fearful thoughts I sank towards morning into an uneasy slumber; and on awaking, with a start, in the midst of an appalling dream, looked up into the eager countenances of a number of the natives, who were bending over me.

It was broad day; and the house was nearly filled with young females, fancifully decorated with flowers, who gazed upon me as I rose with faces in which childish delight and curiosity were vividly portrayed. After waking Toby, they seated themselves round us on the mats, and gave full play to that prying inquisitiveness which time out of mind has been attributed to the adorable sex.

As these unsophisticated young creatures were attended by no jealous duennas, their proceedings were altogether informal, and void of artificial restraint. Long and minute was the investigation with which they honored us, and so uproarious their mirth, that I felt infinitely sheepish; and Toby was immeasurably outraged at their familiarity.

These lively young ladies were at the same time wonderfully polite and humane; fanning aside the insects that occasionally lighted on our brows; presenting us with food; and compassionately regarding me in the midst of my afflictions. But in spite of all their blandishments, my feelings of propriety were exceedingly shocked, for I could not but consider them as having overstepped the due limits of female decorum.

Having diverted themselves to their hearts' content, our young visitants now withdrew, and gave place to successive troops of the other sex, who continued flocking towards the house until near noon; by which time I have no doubt that the greater part of the inhabitants of the valley had bathed themselves in the light of our benignant countenances.

At last, when their numbers began to diminish, a superb-looking warrior stooped the towering plumes of his head-dress beneath the low portal, and entered the house. I saw at once that he was some distinguished personage, the natives regarding him with the utmost deference, and making room for him as he approached. His aspect was imposing. The splendid long drooping tail-feathers of the tropical bird, thickly interspersed with the gaudy plumage of the cock, were disposed in an immense upright semicircle upon his head, their lower extremities being fixed in a crescent of guinea-beads which spanned the forehead. Around his neck were several enormous necklaces of boar's tusks, polished like ivory, and disposed in such a manner as that the longest and largest were upon his capacious chest. Thrust forward through the large apertures in his ears were two small and finely-shaped sperm whale teeth, presenting their cavities in front, stuffed with freshly-plucked leaves, and curiously wrought at the other end into strange little images and devices. These barbaric trinkets, garnished in this manner at their open extremities, and tapering and curving round to a point behind the ear, resembled not a little a pair of cornucopias.

The loins of the warrior were girt about with heavy folds of a dark-colored tappa,[1] hanging before and behind in clusters of braided tassels, while anklets and bracelets of curling human hair completed his unique costume. In his right hand he grasped a beautifully carved paddle-spear, nearly fifteen feet in length, made of the bright koarwood,[2] one end sharply pointed and the other flattened like an oar-blade. Hanging obliquely from his girdle by a loop of sinnate,[3] was a richly decorated pipe; the slender reed forming its stem was colored with a red pigment, and round it, as well as the idol-bowl, fluttered little streamers of the thinnest tappa.

But that which was most remarkable in the appearance of this splendid islander was the elaborate tattooing displayed on every noble

[1] tapa (cloth made of bark fibers soaked in water and then pounded together)
[2] perhaps koa, a handsome acacia wood of the Pacific islands
[3] sennit: flat, loosely-braided cordage

limb. All imaginable lines and curves and figures were delineated over his whole body, and in their grotesque variety and infinite profusion I could only compare them to the crowded groupings of quaint patterns we sometimes see in costly pieces of lacework. The most simple and remarkable of all these ornaments was that which decorated the countenance of the chief. Two broad stripes of tattooing, diverging from the center of his shaven crown, obliquely crossed both eyes—staining the lids—to a little below either ear, where they united with another stripe which swept in a straight line along the lips and formed the base of the triangle. The warrior, from the excellence of his physical proportions, might certainly have been regarded as one of Nature's noblemen, and the lines drawn upon his face may possibly have denoted his exalted rank.

This warlike personage, upon entering the house, seated himself at some distance from the spot where Toby and myself reposed, while the rest of the savages looked alternately from us to him, as if in expectation of something they were disappointed in not perceiving. Regarding the chief attentively, I thought his lineaments appeared familiar to me. As soon as his full face was turned upon me, and I again beheld its extraordinary embellishment, and met the strange gaze to which I had been subjected the preceding night, I immediately, in spite of the alteration in his appearance, recognized the noble Mehevi. [1] On addressing him, he advanced at once in the most cordial manner, and greeting me warmly, seemed to enjoy not a little the effect his barbaric costume had produced upon me.

I forthwith determined to secure, if possible, the good will of this individual, as I easily perceived he was a man of great authority in his tribe, and one who might exert a powerful influence upon our subsequent fate. In the endeavor I was not repulsed; for nothing could surpass the friendliness he manifested towards both my companion and myself. He extended his sturdy limbs by our side, and endeavored to make us comprehend the full extent of the kindly feelings by which he was actuated. The almost insuperable difficulty in communicating to one another our ideas affected the chief with no little mortification. He evinced a great desire to be enlightened with regard to the customs and peculiarities of the far-off country we had left behind us, and to which under the name of Maneeka [2] he frequently alluded.

But that which more than any other subject engaged his attention was the late proceedings of the "Franee," as he called the French, in the neighboring bay of Nukuheva. [3] This seemed a never-ending theme with him, and one concerning which he was never weary of interrogating us. All the information we succeeded in imparting to him on this subject was little more than that we had seen six men-of-war lying in the hostile bay at the time we had left it. When he received this intelligence, Mehevi, by the aid of his fingers, went through a long numerical calculation, as if estimating the number of Frenchmen the squadron might contain.

It was just after employing his faculties in this way that he happened to notice the swelling in my limb. He immediately examined it with the utmost attention, and after doing so, despatched a boy who happened to be standing by, with some message.

After the lapse of a few moments the stripling reëntered the house with an aged islander, who might have been taken for old Hippocrates [4] himself. His head was as bald as the polished surface of a cocoa-nut shell, which article it precisely resembled in smoothness and color, while a long silvery beard swept almost to his girdle of bark. Encircling his temples was a bandeau of the twisted leaves of the omoo tree, pressed closely over the brows to shield his feeble vision from the glare of the sun. His tottering steps were supported by a long slim staff, resembling the wand with which a theatrical magician appears on the stage, and in one hand he carried a freshly plaited fan of the green leaflets of the cocoa-nut tree. A flowing robe of tappa, knotted over the shoulder, hung loosely round his stooping form, and heightened the venerableness of his aspect.

Mehevi, saluting this old gentleman, motioned him to a seat between us, and then uncovering my limb, desired him to examine it. The leech gazed intently from me to Toby, and then proceeded to business. After diligently observing the ailing member, he commenced manipulating it; and on the supposition probably that the complaint had deprived the leg of all sensation, began to pinch and hammer it in such a manner that I absolutely roared with the pain. Thinking that I was as capable of making an application of thumps and pinches to the part as any one else, I endeavored to resist this species of medical treatment. But it was not so easy a matter to get out of the clutches

[1] a chieftain who had greeted them the evening before
[2] America
[3] The French had lately taken possession of the Marquesas.
[4] The Greek physician, called the "Father of Medicine"; he died about 377 B.C.

of the old wizard; he fastened on the unfortunate limb as if it were something for which he had been long seeking, and muttering some kind of incantation continued his discipline, pounding it after a fashion that set me well nigh crazy; while Mehevi, upon the same principle which prompts an affectionate mother to hold a struggling child in a dentist's chair, restrained me in his powerful grasp, and actually encouraged the wretch in this infliction of torture.

Almost frantic with rage and pain, I yelled like a bedlamite; while Toby, throwing himself into all the attitudes of a posture-master, vainly endeavored to expostulate with the natives by signs and gestures. To have looked at my companion, as, sympathizing with my sufferings, he strove to put an end to them, one would have thought that he was the deaf and dumb alphabet incarnated. Whether my tormentor yielded to Toby's entreaties, or paused from sheer exhaustion, I do not know; but all at once he ceased his operations, and at the same time the chief relinquishing his hold upon me, I fell back, faint and breathless with the agony I had endured.

My unfortunate limb was now left much in the same condition of a rump-steak after undergoing the castigating process which precedes cooking. My physician, having recovered from the fatigues of his exertions, as if anxious to make amends for the pain to which he had subjected me, now took some herbs out of a little wallet that was suspended from his waist, and moistening them in water, applied them to the inflamed part, stooping over it at the same time, and either whispering a spell, or having a little confidential chat with some imaginary demon located in the calf of my leg. My limb was now swathed in leafy bandages, and grateful to Providence for the cessation of hostilities, I was suffered to rest.

Mehevi shortly after rose to depart; but before he went he spoke authoritatively to one of the natives whom he addressed as Kory-Kory; and from the little I could understand of what took place, pointed him out to me as a man whose peculiar business thenceforth would be to attend upon my person. I am not certain that I comprehended as much as this at the time, but the subsequent conduct of my trusty body-servant fully assured me that such must have been the case.

I could not but be amused at the manner in which the chief addressed me upon this occasion, talking to me for at least fifteen or twenty minutes as calmly as if I could understand every word that he said. I remarked this peculiarity very often afterwards in many other of the islanders.

Mehevi having now departed, and the family physician having likewise made his exit, we were left about sunset with the ten or twelve natives, who by this time I had ascertained composed the household of which Toby and I were members. As the dwelling to which we had been first introduced was the place of my permanent abode while I remained in the valley, and as I was necessarily placed upon the most intimate footing with its occupants, I may as well here enter into a little description of it and its inhabitants. This description will apply also to nearly all the other dwelling-places in the vale, and will furnish some idea of the generality of the natives.

Near one side of the valley, and about midway up the ascent of a rather abrupt rise of ground waving with the richest verdure, a number of large stones were laid in successive courses, to the height of nearly eight feet, and disposed in such a manner that their level surface corresponded in shape with the habitation which was perched upon it. A narrow space, however, was reserved in front of the dwelling, upon the summit of this pile of stones (called by the natives a "pi-pi"), which being enclosed by a little picket of canes, gave it somewhat the appearance of a veranda. The frame of the house was constructed of large bamboos planted uprightly, and secured together at intervals by transverse stalks of the light wood of the hibiscus, lashed with thongs of bark. The rear of the tenement—built up with successive ranges of cocoa-nut boughs bound one upon another, with their leaflets cunningly woven together—inclined a little from the vertical, and extended from the extreme edge of the "pi-pi" to about twenty feet from its surface; whence the shelving roof—thatched with the long tapering leaves of the palmetto—sloped steeply off to within about five feet of the floor; leaving the eaves drooping with tassel-like appendages over the front of the habitation. This was constructed of light and elegant canes, in a kind of open screen-work, tastefully adorned with bindings of variegated sinnate, which served to hold together its various parts. The sides of the house were similarly built; thus presenting three quarters for the circulation of the air, while the whole was impervious to the rain.

In length this picturesque building was perhaps twelve yards, while in breadth it could not have exceeded as many feet. So much for the exterior; which, with its wire-like reed-twisted sides, not a little reminded me of an immense aviary.

Stooping a little, you passed through a narrow aperture in its front; and facing you, on entering, lay two long, perfectly straight, and well-polished trunks of the cocoa-nut tree, extending the full length of the dwelling; one of them placed closely against the rear, and the other lying parallel with it some two yards distant, the interval between them being spread with a multitude of gaily-worked mats, nearly all of a different pattern. This space formed the common couch and lounging place of the natives, answering the purpose of a divan in Oriental countries. Here would they slumber through the hours of the night, and recline luxuriously during the greater part of the day. The remainder of the floor presented only the cool shining surfaces of the large stones of which the "pi-pi" was composed.

From the ridge-pole of the house hung suspended a number of large packages enveloped in coarse tappa; some of which contained festival dresses, and various other matters of the wardrobe, held in high estimation. These were easily accessible by means of a line, which, passing over the ridge-pole, had one end attached to a bundle, while with the other, which led to the side of the dwelling and was there secured, the package could be lowered or elevated at pleasure.

Against the farther wall of the house were arranged in tasteful figures a variety of spears and javelins, and other implements of savage warfare. Outside of the habitation, and built upon the piazza-like area in its front, was a little shed used as a sort of larder or pantry, and in which were stored various articles of domestic use and convenience. A few yards from the pi-pi was a large shed built of cocoa-nut boughs, where the process of preparing the "poee-poee" [1] was carried on, and all culinary operations attended to.

Thus much for the house, and its appurtenances; and it will be readily acknowledged that a more commodious and appropriate dwelling for the climate and the people could not possibly be devised. It was cool, free to admit the air, scrupulously clean, and elevated above the dampness and impurities of the ground.

But now to sketch the inmates; and here I claim for my tried servitor and faithful valet Kory-Kory the precedence of a first description. As his character will be gradually unfolded in the course of my narrative, I shall for the present content myself with delineating his personal appearance. Kory-Kory,

though the most devoted and best natured serving-man in the world, was, alas! a hideous object to look upon. He was some twenty-five years of age, and about six feet in height, robust and well made, and of the most extraordinary aspect. His head was carefully shaven, with the exception of two circular spots, about the size of a dollar, near the top of the cranium, where the hair, permitted to grow of an amazing length, was twisted up in two prominent knots, that gave him the appearance of being decorated with a pair of horns. His beard, plucked out by the root from every other part of his face, was suffered to droop in hairy pendants, two of which garnished his upper lip, and an equal number hung from the extremity of his chin.

Kory-Kory, with a view of improving the handiwork of nature, and perhaps prompted by a desire to add to the engaging expression of his countenance, had seen fit to embellish his face with three broad longitudinal stripes of tattooing, which, like those country roads that go straight forward in defiance of all obstacles, crossed his nasal organ, descended into the hollow of his eyes, and even skirted the borders of his mouth. Each completely spanned his physiognomy; one extending in a line with his eyes, another crossing the face in the vicinity of the nose, and the third sweeping along his lips from ear to ear. His countenance thus triply hooped, as it were, with tattooing, always reminded me of those unhappy wretches whom I have sometimes observed gazing out sentimentally from behind the grated bars of a prison window; whilst the entire body of my savage valet, covered all over with representations of birds and fishes, and a variety of most unaccountable-looking creatures, suggested to me the idea of a pictorial museum of natural history, or an illustrated copy of Goldsmith's *Animated Nature*. [2]

But it seems really heartless in me to write thus of the poor islander, when I owe perhaps to his unremitting attentions the very existence I now enjoy. Kory-Kory, I mean thee no harm in what I say in regard to thy outward adornings; but they were a little curious to my unaccustomed sight, and therefore I dilate upon them. But to underrate or forget thy faithful services is something I could never be guilty of, even in the giddiest moment of my life.

The father of my attached follower was a native of gigantic frame, and had once possessed prodigious physical powers; but the lofty form was now yielding to the inroads of time, though the hand of disease seemed never to have been

---

[1] A starchy food prepared from taro root or breadfruit variously compounded; it is fermented and forms a glutinous paste.

[2] a compilation produced by Oliver Goldsmith in 1774

laid upon the aged warrior. Marheyo—for such was his name—appeared to have retired from all active participation in the affairs of the valley, seldom or never accompanying the natives in their various expeditions; and employing the greater part of his time in throwing up a little shed just outside the house, upon which he was engaged to my certain knowledge for four months, without appearing to make any sensible advance. I suppose the old gentleman was in his dotage, for he manifested in various ways the characteristics which mark this particular stage of life.

I remember in particular his having a choice pair of ear-ornaments, fabricated from the teeth of some sea-monster. These he would alternately wear and take off at least fifty times in the course of the day, going and coming from his little hut on each occasion with all the tranquillity imaginable. Sometimes slipping them through the slits in his ears, he would seize his spear—which in length and slightness resembled a fishing-pole—and go stalking beneath the shadows of the neighboring groves, as if about to give a hostile meeting to some cannibal knight. But he would soon return again, and hiding his weapon under the projecting eaves of the house, and rolling his clumsy trinkets carefully in a piece of tappa, would resume his more pacific operations as quietly as if he had never interrupted them.

But despite his eccentricities, Marheyo was a most paternal and warm-hearted old fellow, and in this particular not a little resembled his son Kory-Kory. The mother of the latter was the mistress of the family, and a notable housewife, and a most industrious old lady she was. If she did not understand the art of making jellies, jams, custards, tea-cakes, and such like trashy affairs, she was profoundly skilled in the mysteries of preparing "amar," "poee-poee," and "kokoo,"[1] with other substantial matters. She was a genuine busy-body; bustling about the house like a country landlady at an unexpected arrival; forever giving the young girls tasks to perform, which the little hussies as often neglected; poking into every corner, and rummaging over bundles of old tappa, and making a prodigious clatter among the calabashes. Sometimes she might have been seen squatting upon her haunches in front of a huge wooden basin, and kneading poee-poee with terrific vehemence, dashing the stone pestle about as if she would shiver the vessel into fragments; on other occasions, galloping about the valley in search of a particular kind of leaf, used in

some of her recondite operations, and returning home, toiling and sweating, with a bundle, under which most women would have sunk.

To tell the truth, Kory-Kory's mother was the only industrious person in all the valley of Typee; and she could not have employed herself more actively had she been left an exceedingly muscular and destitute widow, with an inordinate supply of young children, in the bleakest part of the civilized world. There was not the slightest necessity for the greater portion of the labor performed by the old lady: but she seemed to work from some irresistible impulse; her limbs continually swaying to and fro, as if there were some indefatigable engine concealed within her body which kept her in perpetual motion.

Never suppose that she was a termagant or a shrew for all this; she had the kindliest heart in the world, and acted towards me in particular in a truly maternal manner, occasionally putting some little morsel of choice food into my hand, some outlandish kind of savage sweetmeat or pastry, like a doting mother petting a sickly urchin with tarts and sugar plums. Warm indeed are my remembrances of the dear, good, affectionate old Tinor!

Besides the individuals I have mentioned, there belonged to the household three young men, dissipated, good-for-nothing, roystering blades of savages, who were either employed in prosecuting love affairs with the maidens of the tribe, or grew boozy on "arva"[2] and tobacco in the company of congenial spirits, the scapegraces of the valley.

Among the permanent inmates of the house were likewise several lovely damsels, who instead of thrumming pianos and reading novels, like more enlightened young ladies, substituted for these employments the manufacture of a fine species of tappa; but for the greater portion of the time were skipping from house to house, gadding and gossiping with their acquaintances.

From the rest of these, however, I must except the beauteous nymph Fayaway, who was my peculiar favorite. Her free, pliant figure was the very perfection of female grace and beauty. Her complexion was a rich and mantling olive, and when watching the glow upon her cheeks I could almost swear that beneath the transparent medium there lurked the blushes of a faint vermilion. The face of this girl was a rounded oval, and each feature as perfectly formed as the heart or imagination of man could desire. Her full lips, when parted with a smile, disclosed teeth of a dazzling whiteness;

[1] articles of food

[2] a fermented drink made from green cocoa-nut juice

and when her rosy mouth opened with a burst of merriment, they looked like the milk-white seeds of the "arta," a fruit of the valley, which, when cleft in twain, shows them reposing in rows on either side, imbedded in the red and juicy pulp. Her hair of the deepest brown, parted irregularly in the middle, flowed in natural ringlets over her shoulders, and whenever she chanced to stoop, fell over and hid from view her lovely bosom. Gazing into the depths of her strange blue eyes, when she was in a contemplative mood, they seemed most placid yet unfathomable; but when illuminated by some lively emotion, they beamed upon the beholder like stars. The hands of Fayaway were as soft and delicate as those of any countess; for an entire exemption from rude labor marks the girlhood and even prime of a Typee woman's life. Her feet, though wholly exposed, were as diminutive and fairly shaped as those which peep from beneath the skirts of a Lima lady's dress. The skin of this young creature, from continual ablutions and the use of mollifying ointments, was inconceivably smooth and soft.

I may succeed, perhaps, in particularizing some of the individual features of Fayaway's beauty, but that general loveliness of appearance which they all contributed to produce I will not attempt to describe. The easy unstudied graces of a child of nature like this, breathing from infancy an atmosphere of perpetual summer, and nurtured by the simple fruits of the earth; enjoying a perfect freedom from care and anxiety, and removed effectually from all injurious tendencies, strike the eye in a manner which cannot be portrayed. This picture is no fancy sketch; it is drawn from the most vivid recollections of the person delineated.

Were I asked if the beauteous form of Fayaway was altogether free from the hideous blemish of tattooing, I should be constrained to answer that it was not. But the practitioners of this barbarous art, so remorseless in their inflictions upon the brawny limbs of the warriors of the tribe, seem to be conscious that it needs not the resources of their profession to augment the charms of the maidens of the vale. The females are very little embellished in this way, and Fayaway, and all the other young girls of her age, were even less so than those of their sex more advanced in years. The reason of this peculiarity will be alluded to hereafter. All the tattooing that the nymph in question exhibited upon her person may be easily described. Three minute dots, no bigger than pin-heads, decorated either lip, and at a little distance were not at all discernible. Just upon the fall of the shoulder were drawn two parallel lines half an inch apart, and perhaps three inches in length, the interval being filled with delicately executed figures. These narrow bands of tattooing, thus placed, always reminded me of those stripes of gold lace worn by officers in undress, and which are in lieu of epaulettes to denote their rank.

Thus much was Fayaway tattooed. The audacious hand which had gone so far in its desecrating work stopping short, apparently wanting the heart to proceed.

But I have omitted to describe the dress worn by this nymph of the valley.

Fayaway—I must avow the fact—for the most part clung to the primitive and summer garb of Eden. But how becoming the costume! It showed her fine figure to the best possible advantage; and nothing could have been better adapted to her peculiar style of beauty. On ordinary occasions she was habited precisely as I have described the two youthful savages whom we had met on first entering the valley. At other times, when rambling among the groves, or visiting at the houses of her acquaintances, she wore a tunic of white tappa, reaching from her waist to a little below the knees; and when exposed for any length of time to the sun, she invariably protected herself from its rays by a floating mantle of the same material, loosely gathered about the person. Her gala dress will be described hereafter.

As the beauties of our own land delight in bedecking themselves with fanciful articles of jewelry, suspending them from their ears, hanging them about their necks, and clasping them around their wrists; so Fayaway and her companions were in the habit of ornamenting themselves with similar appendages.

Flora was their jeweler. Sometimes they wore necklaces of small carnation flowers, strung like rubies upon a fiber of tappa, or displayed in their ears a single white bud, the stem thrust backward through the aperture, and showing in front the delicate petals folded together in a beautiful sphere, and looking like a drop of the purest pearl. Chaplets too, resembling in their arrangement the strawberry coronal worn by an English peeress, and composed of intertwined leaves and blossoms, often crowned their temples; and bracelets and anklets of the same tasteful pattern were frequently to be seen. Indeed, the maidens of the island were passionately fond of flowers, and never wearied of decorating their persons with them; a lovely trait in their character, and one that ere long will be more fully alluded to.

Though in my eyes, at least, Fayaway was indisputably the loveliest female I saw in Typee, yet the description I have given of her will in some measure apply to nearly all the youthful portion of her sex in the valley. Judge ye then, reader, what beautiful creatures they must have been.

1846

BAYARD TAYLOR 1825-1878

Taylor was born in Chester County, Pennsylvania, apprenticed as a printer, and began early to contribute to newspapers. He went to Europe as a special writer for the New York *Tribune*, traveling afoot all over western Europe, 1844-1846, visited California during the gold excitement, and later nearly all the countries of the civilized world. He had a diplomatic post at Petrograd, 1862-1863, and had but recently been appointed minister to Germany when he died. Aside from many books of travel between 1846 and 1869, notably *Views Afoot,* 1846; *El Dorado,* 1850; and *Greece and Russia,* 1859, Taylor produced *Ximena* (poem), 1844; *Rhymes of Travel,* 1848; *Translation of Faust,* 1870-1871; *Lars: A Pastoral of Norway,* 1873; *Studies in German Literature,* 1879.

His appeal to his countrymen was first as a traveler and lecturer. His journeys were eagerly followed in newspapers and books by isolated men and women hungry for news of countries and peoples of the modern world; and though it is said that he traveled farther and saw less than any other American wanderer, his lectures upon his travels were everywhere crowded. A second appeal, made to another class of people, was through his excellent translation of *Faust,* in which he aided in the introduction of German literature to America. Taylor was too versatile and worked too rapidly for lasting results. His poetry though vigorous is diffuse and lacks high imagination. Changes in literary reputation are well illustrated in Taylor's case, for many of his contemporaries ranked him among the foremost American men of letters.

Biography and criticism: A. H. Smythe, *Bayard Taylor* (AML); M. Hansen and H. Scudder, *Life and Letters of Bayard Taylor,* 2 vols. 1884; H. W. Mabie, "Bayard Taylor: Adventurer," *Bookm.* 43: 51-9; R. Armstrong, "Bayard Taylor's Romance," *Bookm.* 42:270-5; "Memories of Bayard Taylor," *Dial* 39:200-2.

From VIEWS A-FOOT

CHAPTER XXX

PASSAGE OF THE ST. GOTHARD

Leaving Amstegg, I passed the whole day among snowy, sky-piercing Alps, torrents, chasms, and clouds! The clouds appeared to be breaking up as we set out, and the white top of the Reussberg was now and then visible in the sky. Just above the village are the remains of Zwing Uri, the castle begun by the tyrant Gessler,[1] for the complete subjugation of the canton. Following the Reuss up through a narrow valley, we passed the Bristenstock, which lifts its jagged crags nine thousand feet in the air, while on the other side stand the snowy summits which lean towards the Rhone Glacier and St. Gothard. From the deep glen where the Reuss foamed down towards the Lake of the Forest Cantons, the mountains rose with a majestic sweep so far into the sky that the brain grew dizzy in following their outlines. Woods, chalets, and slopes of herbage covered their bases, where the mountain cattle and goats were browsing, while the herd-boys sang their native melodies or woke the ringing echoes with the loud, sweet sounds of their wooden horns; higher up, the sides were broken into crags and covered with stunted pines; then succeeded a belt of bare rock with a little snow lying in the crevices, and the summits of dazzling white looked out from the clouds half-way to the zenith. Sometimes when the vale was filled with clouds it was startling to see them parting around a solitary summit, apparently isolated in the air at an immense height, for the mountain to which it belonged was hidden to the very base!

The road passed from one side of the valley to the other, crossing the Reuss on bridges sometimes ninety feet high. After three or four hours' walking, we reached a frightful pass called the Schöllenen. So narrow is the defile that before reaching it, the road seemed to enter directly into the mountain. Precipices a thousand feet high tower above, and the stream roars and boils in the black depth below. The road is a wonder of art; it winds around the edge of horrible chasms or is carried on lofty arches across, with sometimes a hold apparently so frail that one involuntarily shudders. At a place called the Devil's Bridge, the Reuss leaps about seventy feet in three or four cascades, sending up a continual cloud of spray, while a wind created by the fall, blows and whirls around, with a force that nearly lifts one from his feet.

Beyond the Devil's Bridge, the mountains which nearly touched before, interlock into each other, and a tunnel three hundred and seventy-five feet long leads through the rock into the vale of Urseren, surrounded by the Upper Alps. The little town of Andermatt lies in the middle

[1] The tyrant whom William Tell defied; the story is now thought to be legendary.

of this valley, which with the peaks around is covered with short, yellowish-brown grass. We met near Amstegg a little Italian boy walking home from Germany, quite alone and without money, for we saw him give his last kreutzer to a blind beggar along the road. We therefore took him with us, as he was afraid to cross the St. Gothard alone.

After refreshing ourselves at Andermatt, we started, five in number, including a German student, for the St. Gothard. Behind the village of Hospiz, which stands at the bottom of the valley leading to Realp and the Furca pass, the way commences winding backwards and forwards, higher and higher, through a valley covered with rocks, with the mighty summits of the Alps around, untenanted save by the chamois and mountain eagle. Not a tree was to be seen. The sides of the mountains were covered with loose rocks waiting for the next rain to wash them down, and the tops were robed in eternal snow. A thick cloud rolled over us as we went on, following the diminishing brooks to their snowy source in the peak of St. Gothard. We cut off the bends of the road by footpaths up the rocks, which we ascended in single file, little Pietro with his staff and bundle bringing up the rear. The rarefied air we breathed, seven thousand feet above the sea, was like exhilarating gas. We felt no fatigue, but ran and shouted and threw snowballs, in the middle of August!

After three hours' walk we reached the two clear and silent lakes which send their waters to the Adriatic and the North Sea. Here, as we looked down on the Italian side, the sky became clear; we saw the top of St. Gothard many thousand feet above, and stretching to the south the summits of the mountains which guard the vales of the Ticino and the Adda. The former monastery [1] has been turned into an inn; there is, however, a kind of church attached, attended by a single monk. It was so cold that although late, we determined to descend to the first village. The Italian side is very steep, and the road, called the Via Trimola, is like a thread dropped down and constantly doubling back upon itself. The deep chasms were filled with snow, although exposed to the full force of the sun, and for a long distance there was scarcely a sign of vegetation.

I thought as we went down, that every step was bringing me nearer to a sunnier land—that the glories of Italy, which had so long lain in the airy background of the future, would soon spread themselves before me in their real or imagined beauty. Reaching at dusk the last height above the vale of the Ticino, we saw the little village of Airolo with its musical name, lying in a hollow of the mountains. A few minutes of leaping, sliding, and rolling, took us down the grassy declivity, and we found we had descended from the top in an hour and a half, although the distance by the road is nine miles! I need not say how glad we were to relieve our trembling knees and exhausted limbs.

When, at night, I looked out of my chamber-window, the silver moon of Italy, (for we fancied that her light was softer and that the skies were already bluer) hung trembling above the fields of snow that stretched in their wintry brilliance along the mountains around. I heard the roar of the Ticino and the deepened sound of falling cascades, and thought, if I were to take those waters for my guide, to what glorious places they would lead me!

We left Airolo early the next morning, to continue our journey down the valley of the Ticino. The mists and clouds of Switzerland were exchanged for a sky of the purest blue, and we felt, for the first time in ten days, uncomfortably warm. The mountains which flank the Alps on this side, are still giants—lofty and bare, and covered with snow in many places. The limit of the German dialect is on the summit of St. Gothard, and the peasants saluted us with a *"buon giorno,"* [2] as they passed. This, with the clearness of the skies and the warmth of the air, made us feel that Italy was growing nearer.

On our first day's journey we passed through two terrific mountain gorges, almost equaling in grandeur the defile of the Devil's Bridge. The Ticino, in its course to Lago Maggiore, has to make a descent of nearly three thousand feet, passing through three valleys, which lie like terraces, one below the other. In passing from one to the other, it forces its way in twenty cataracts through a cleft in the mountains. The road, constructed with the umost labor, threads these dark chasms, sometimes carried in a tunnel through the rock, sometimes passing on arches above the boiling flood. I here noticed a very beautiful effect of the water, perhaps attributable to some mineral substance it contained. The spray and foam thrown up in the dashing of the vexed current, was of a light, delicate pink, although the stream itself was a soft blue; and the contrast of these two colors was very remarkable.

As we kept on, however, there was a very perceptible change in the scenery. The gloomy

---

[1] The hospice there dates from the fourteenth century.

[2] "Good day."

pines disappeared and the mountains were covered in their stead, with picturesque chestnut trees, with leaves of a shining green. The grass and vegetation were much more luxuriant than on the other side of the Alps, and fields of maize and mulberry orchards covered the valley. We saw the people busy at work reeling silk in the villages. Every mile we advanced made a sensible change in the vegetation. The chestnuts were larger, the maize higher, the few straggling grapevines increased into bowers and vineyards, while the gardens were filled with plum, pear, and fig-trees, and the display of delicious fruit which we saw in the villages, gave us promise of the luxuriance that was to come.

The vineyards are much more beautiful than the German fields of stakes. [1] The vines are not trimmed, but grow from year to year over a frame higher than the head, supported through the whole field on stone pillars. They interlace and form a complete leafy screen, while the clusters hang below. The light came dimly through the green, transparent leaves, and nothing was wanting to make them real bowers of Arcadia. Although we were still in Switzerland, the people began to have that lazy indolent look which characterizes the Italians; most of the occupations were carried on in the open air, and brown-robed, sandaled friars were going about from house to house, collecting money and provisions for their support.

We passed Faido and Giornico, near which last village are the remains of an old castle, supposed to have been built by the ancient Gauls, and stopped for the night at Cresciano, which being entirely Italian, we had an opportunity to put in practice the few words we had picked up from Pietro. The little fellow had parted from us with regret a few hours before, at Biasco, where he had relations. The rustic landlord at Cresciano was an honest young fellow, who tried to serve us as well as he could, but we made some ludicrous mistakes through our ignorance of the language.

Three hours' walk brought us to Bellinzona, the capital of the canton. Before reaching it, our road joined that of the Splügen which comes down through the valley of Bernardino. From the bridge where the junction takes place we had a triple view, the grandeur of which took me by surprise, even after coming from Switzerland. We stood at the union of three valleys—that leading to St. Gothard, terminated by the glaciers of the Bernese Oberland, that running off obliquely to the Splügen, and

[1] stakes for supporting the vines

finally the broad vale of the Ticino, extending to Lago Maggiore, whose purple mountains closed the vista. Each valley was perhaps two miles broad and from twenty to thirty long, and the mountains that enclosed them from five to seven thousand feet in height, so you may perhaps form some idea what a view down three such avenues in this Alpine temple would be.

We left Bellinzona at noon, and saw, soon after, from an eminence, the blue line of Lago Maggiore stretched across the bottom of the valley. We saw sunset fade away over the lake, but it was clouded, and did not realize my ideal of such a scene in Italy. A band of wild Italians paraded up and down the village, drawing one of their number in a hand-cart. They made a great noise with a drum and trumpet, and were received everywhere with shouts of laughter. A great jug of wine was not wanting, and the whole seemed to me a very characteristic scene.

We were early awakened at Magadino, at the head of Lago Maggiore, and after swallowing a hasty breakfast, went on board the steamboat *San Carlo*, for Sesto Calende. We got under way at six o'clock, and were soon in motion over the crystal mirror. The water is of the loveliest green hue, and so transparent that we seemed to be floating in mid-air. Another heaven arched far below us; other chains of mountains joined their bases to those which surrounded the lake, and the mirrored cascades leaped upward to meet their originals at the surface. It may be because I have seen it more recently, that the water of Lago Maggiore appears to me the most beautiful in the world. I was delighted with the Scotch lakes, and enraptured with the Traunsee and "Zurich's waters," but this last exceeds them both. I am now incapable of any stronger feeling, until I see the Egean from the Grecian Isles.

The morning was cloudy, and the white wreaths hung low on the mountains, whose rocky sides were covered everywhere with the rank and luxuriant growth of this climate. As we advanced further over this glorious mirror, the houses became more Italian-like; the lower stories rested on arched passages, and the windows were open, without glass, while in the gardens stood the solemn, graceful cypress, and vines, heavy with ripening grapes, hung from bough to bough through the mulberry orchards. Half-way down, in a broad bay, which receives the waters of a stream that descends with the Simplon, are the celebrated Borromean Islands. They are four in number, and seem to float like fairy creations on the water, while the lofty hills form a background whose grandeur enhances by contrast their exquisite beauty.

On passing by Isola Madre, we could see the roses in its terraced gardens and the broad-leaved aloes clinging to the rocks. Isola Bella, the loveliest of them all, as its name denotes, was farther off; it rose like a pyramid from the water, terrace above terrace to the summit, and its gardens of never fading foliage, with the glorious panorama around, might make it a paradise, if life were to be dreamed away. On the northern side of the bay lies a large town with a lofty Romanesque tower, and noble mountains sweep around as if to shut out the world from such a scene. The lake was perfectly calm, and groves and gardens slept mirrored in the dark green wave, while the Alps rose afar through the dim, cloudy air. Towards the other end the hills sink lower, and slope off into the plains of Lombardy. Near Arona, on the western side, is a large monastery, overlooking the lower part of the lake. Beside it, on a hill, is a colossal statue of San Carlo Borromeo, who gave his name to the lovely islands above.

After a seven hours' passage, we ran into Sesto Calende, at the foot of the lake. Here passengers and baggage were tumbled promiscuously on shore, the latter gathered into the office to be examined, and the former left at liberty to ramble about an hour until their passports could be signed. We employed the time in trying the flavor of the grapes and peaches of Lombardy, and in looking at the groups of travelers who had come down from the Alps with the annual avalanche at this season. The custom house officers were extremely civil and obliging, as they did not think it necessary to examine our knapsacks, and our passports being soon signed, we were at liberty to enter again into the dominions of His Majesty of Austria. Our companion, the German, whose feet could carry him no further, took a seat on the top of a diligence for Milan; we left Sesto Calende on foot, and plunged into the cloud of dust which was whirling towards the capital of Northern Italy.

We spent the night at the little village of Casina, about sixteen miles from Milan, and here made our first experience of the honesty of Italian inns. We had taken the precaution to inquire beforehand the price of a bed; but it seemed unnecessary and unpleasant, as well as evincing a mistrustful spirit, to do the same with every article we asked for, so we decided

to leave it to the host's conscience not to overcharge us. Imagine our astonishment, however, when at starting, a bill was presented to us, in which the smallest articles were set down at three or four times their value. We remonstrated, but to little purpose; the fellow knew scarcely any French, and we as little Italian, so rather than lose time and temper, we paid what he demanded and went on, leaving him to laugh at the successful imposition.

About noon, the road turned into a broad and beautiful avenue of poplars, down which we saw, at a distance, the triumphal arch terminating the Simplon road, which we had followed from Sesto Calende. Beyond it rose the slight and airy pinnacle of the Duomo. [1] We passed by the exquisite structure, gave up our passports at the gates, traversed the broad Piazzi d'Armi, and found ourselves at liberty to choose one of the dozen streets that led into the heart of the city.

1846

BEDOUIN SONG

From the Desert I come to thee
  On a stallion shod with fire;
And the winds are left behind
  In the speed of my desire.
Under thy window I stand,
  And the midnight hears my cry:
I love thee, I love but thee,
  With a love that shall not die
    Till the sun grows cold,
    And the stars are old,   10
    And the leaves of the Judgment
      Book unfold!

Look from thy window and see
  My passion and my pain;
I lie on the sands below,
  And I faint in thy disdain.
Let the night-winds touch thy brow
With the heat of my burning sigh,
And melt thee to hear the vow
  Of a love that shall not die   20
    Till the sun grows cold,
    And the stars are old,
    And the leaves of the Judgment
      Book unfold!

My steps are nightly driven,
  By the fever in my breast,
To hear from thy lattice breathed
  The word that shall give me rest.
Open the door of thy heart,

[1] the Gothic cathedral of Milan

And open thy chamber door, 30
And my kisses shall teach thy lips
The love that shall fade no more
    Till the sun grows cold,
    And the stars are old,
    And the leaves of the Judgment
        Book unfold!
1853   1855

TO THE NILE

Mysterious flood,—that through the silent sands
Hast wandered, century on century,
Watering the length of great Egyptian lands,
    Which were not, but for thee,—

Art thou the keeper of that eldest lore,
    Written ere yet thy hieroglyphs began,
When dawned upon thy fresh, untrampled shore
    The earliest life of man?

Thou guardest temple and vast pyramid,
    Where the gray past records its ancient
        speech;   10
But in thine unrevealing breast lies hid
    What they refuse to teach.

All other streams with human joys and fears
    Run blended, o'er the plains of history:
Thou tak'st no note of man; a thousand years
    Are as a day to thee.

What were to thee the Osirian[1] festivals?
    Or Memnon's[2] music on the Theban plain?
The carnage, when Cambyses[3] made thy halls
    Ruddy with royal slain?   20

Even then thou wast a God, and shrines were
        built
    For worship of thine own majestic flood;
For thee the incense burned,—for thee was spilt
    The sacrificial blood.

And past the bannered pylons[4] that arose
    Above thy palms, the pageantry and state,
Thy current flowed, calmly as now it flows,
    Unchangeable as fate.

Thou givest blessings as a God might give,
    Whose being is his bounty: from the slime 30

[1] Osiris was an Egyptian deity.
[2] Memnon was a Greek solar hero, son of the dawn.
    The Greeks gave his name to a colossal statue near
    Thebes that was said to give forth a musical note
    when struck by the rays of the rising sun.
[3] Cambyses III, King of Persia, conquered Egypt
    525 B.C. and is said to have caused the murder of
    the king Psammetichus III.
[4] massive gateways

Shaken from off thy skirts the nations live,
    Through all the years of time.

In thy solemnity, thine awful calm,
    Thy grand indifference of destiny,
My soul forgets its pain, and drinks the balm
    Which thou dost proffer me.

Thy godship is unquestioned still: I bring
    No doubtful worship to thy shrine su-
        preme;
But thus my homage as a chaplet fling,
    To float upon thy stream!   40
                                            1855

ARIEL IN THE CLOVEN PINE[5]

Now the frosty stars are gone:
I have watched them one by one,
Fading on the shores of Dawn.
Round and full the glorious sun
Walks with level step the spray,
Through his vestibule of Day,
While the wolves that late did howl
Slink to dens and coverts foul,
Guarded by the demon owl,
Who, last night, with mocking croon,   10
Wheeled athwart the chilly moon,
And with eyes that blankly glared
On my direful torment stared.

The lark is flickering in the light;
Still the nightingale doth sing;—
All the isle, alive with spring,
Lies, a jewel of delight,
On the blue sea's heaving breast:
Not a breath from out the west,
But some balmy smell doth bring   20
From the sprouting myrtle buds,
Or from meadowy vales that lie
Like a green inverted sky,
Which the yellow cowslip stars,
And the bloomy almond woods,
Cloud-like, cross with roseate bars.
All is life that I can spy,
To the farthest sea and sky,
And my own the only pain
Within this ring of Tyrrhene[6] main.   30

[5] Ariel, the spirit of the air in Shakespeare's *Tempest,*
    had been imprisoned in a pine by the witch
    Sycorax.
    "Thou . . . wast then her servant;
    And, for thou wast a spirit too delicate
    To act her earthy and abhorr'd commands,
    Refusing her grand hests, she did confine thee,
    By help of her more potent ministers
    And in her most unmitigable rage,
    Into a cloven pine; within which rift
    Imprison'd thou didst painfully remain
    A dozen years";
                        The Tempest I, ii, 270
[6] that part of the Mediterranean west of Italy

In the gnarled and cloven Pine
Where the hell-born hag did chain me,
All this orb of cloudless shine,
All this youth in Nature's veins
Tingling with the season's wine,
With a sharper torment pain me.
Pansies in soft April rains
Fill their stalks with honeyed sap
Drawn from Earth's prolific lap;
But the sluggish blood she brings   40
To the tough Pine's hundred rings,
Closer locks their cruel hold,
Closer draws the scaly bark
Round the crevice, damp and cold,
Where my useless wings I fold,—
Sealing me in iron dark.
By this coarse and alien state
Is my dainty essence wronged;
Finer senses that belonged
To my freedom, chafe at Fate,   50
Till the happier elves I hate,
Who in moonlight dances turn
Underneath the palmy fern,
Or in light and twinkling bands
Follow on with linked hands
To the Ocean's yellow sands.

Primrose-eyes each morning ope
In their cool, deep beds of grass;
Violets make the airs that pass
Telltales of their fragrant slope.   60
I can see them where they spring
Never brushed by fairy wing.
All those corners I can spy
In the island's solitude,
Where the dew is never dry,
Nor the miser bees intrude.
Cups of rarest hue are there,
Full of perfumed wine undrained,—
Mushroom banquets, ne'er profaned,
Canopied by maiden-hair.   70
Pearls I see upon the sands,
Never touched by other hands,
And the rainbow bubbles shine
On the ridged and frothy brine,
Tenantless of voyager
Till they burst in vacant air.
O, the songs that sung might be,
And the mazy dances woven,
Had that witch ne'er crossed the sea
And the Pine been never cloven!   80

Many years my direst pain
Has made the wave-rocked isle complain
Winds, that from the Cyclades [1]
Came, to blow in wanton riot

[1] islands in the Aegean Sea

Round its shore's enchanted quiet,
Bore my wailings on the seas:
Sorrowing birds in autumn went
Through the world with my lament.
Still the bitter fate is mine,
All delight unshared to see,   90
Smarting in the cloven Pine,
While I wait the tardy axe
Which, perchance, shall set me free
From the damned Witch Sycorax.

THE SONG OF THE CAMP

"Give us a song!" the soldiers cried,
    The outer trenches guarding,
When the heated guns of the camps allied [2]
    Grew weary of bombarding.

The dark Redan, [3] in silent scoff,
    Lay, grim and threatening, under;
And the tawny mound of Malakoff
    No longer belched its thunder.

There was a pause. A guardsman said,
    "We storm the forts tomorrow;   10
Sing while we may, another day
    Will bring enough of sorrow."

They lay along the battery's side,
    Below the smoking cannon:
Brave hearts, from Severn and from Clyde,
    And from the banks of Shannon.

They sang of love, and not of fame;
    Forgot was Britain's glory:
Each heart recalled a different name,
    But all sang "Annie Lawrie."   20

Voice after voice caught up the song,
    Until its tender passion
Rose like an anthem, rich and strong,—
    Their battle-eve confession.

Dear girl, her name he dared not speak,
    But, as the song grew louder,
Something upon the soldier's cheek
    Washed off the stains of powder.

Beyond the darkening ocean burned
    The bloody sunset's embers,   30
While the Crimean valleys learned
    How English love remembers.

[2] In the Crimean war, 1853-1856, to which the poem refers, France and England were allied with Turkey and Sardinia against Russia.
[3] The Redan and the Malakoff were fortifications of Sebastopol finally captured by the allies.

And once again a fire of hell
  Rained on the Russian quarters,
With scream of shot, and burst of shell,
  And bellowing of the mortars!

And Irish Nora's eyes are dim
  For a singer, dumb and gory;
And English Mary mourns for him
  Who sang of "Annie Lawrie."   40

Sleep, soldiers! still in honored rest
  Your truth and valor wearing:
The bravest are the tenderest,—
  The loving are the daring.

THOMAS BUCHANAN READ
1822-1872

Born in Chester County, Pennsylvania, Read died in New York City. After working at various handicrafts, he studied art, settling for a while at Rome, and making portrait painting a specialty. He published poems at various dates from 1847 to 1867, including *The House by the Sea*, 1855, and *The Wagoner of the Alleghanies*, 1862. Today Read is chiefly known as the author of the popular ballad-lyric that follows.

SHERIDAN'S RIDE

Up from the south, at break of day,
Bringing to Winchester [1] fresh dismay,
The affrighted air with a shudder bore,
Like a herald in haste, to the chieftain's door,
The terrible grumble and rumble and roar,
Telling the battle was on once more,
And Sheridan twenty miles away.

And wider still those billows of war
Thundered along the horizon's bar,
And louder yet into Winchester rolled   10
The roar of that red sea, uncontrolled,
Making the blood of the listener cold
As he thought of the stake in that fiery fray,
And Sheridan twenty miles away.

But there is a road from Winchester town,
A good broad highway leading down;
And there, through the flush of the morning
    light,
A steed as black as the steeds of night
Was seen to pass as with eagle flight,
As if he knew the terrible need: 20
He stretched away with his utmost speed;

[1] Although the poem is not historically accurate, it is true that Sheridan's presence saved the day at the battle of Winchester (or Opequan), September 19-20, 1864. See Sheridan's *Memoirs*, Vol. II, Ch. 3.

Hills rose and fell, but his heart was gay,
With Sheridan fifteen miles away.

Still sprung from those swift hoofs, thundering
    south,
The dust, like smoke from the cannon's mouth
Or the trail of a comet, sweeping faster and
    faster,
Foreboding to traitors the doom of disaster;
The heart of the steed and the heart of the
    master
Were beating like prisoners assaulting their
    walls,
Impatient to be where the battlefield calls:
Every nerve of the charger was strained to full
    play,   31
With Sheridan only ten miles away.

Under his spurning feet the road
Like an arrowy Alpine river flowed;
And the landscape sped away behind
Like an ocean flying before the wind;
And the steed, like a bark fed with furnace ire,
Swept on with his wild eye full of fire.
But lo, he is nearing his heart's desire;
He is snuffing the smoke of the roaring fray,   40
With Sheridan only five miles away.

The first that the general saw were the groups
Of stragglers, and then the retreating troops,
What was done? what to do? a glance told him
    both;
Then striking his spurs, with a terrible oath,
He dashed down the line 'mid a storm of
    huzzas,
And the wave of retreat checked its course
    there, because
The sight of the master compelled it to pause.
With foam and with dust the black charger
    was gray;
By the flash of his eye and the red nostril's
    play   50
He seemed to the whole great army to say,
"I have brought you Sheridan, all the way
From Winchester, down to save the day!"

Hurrah, hurrah, for Sheridan!
Hurrah, hurrah, for horse and man!
And when their statues are placed on high,
Under the dome of the Union sky
(The American soldiers' Temple of Fame),
There with the glorious general's name,
Be it said, in letters both bold and bright,   60
  "Here is the steed that saved the day
By carrying Sheridan into the fight,
  From Winchester, twenty miles away!"

    1865

GEORGE HENRY BOKER
1823-1890

Boker was born and died in Philadelphia. He was graduated from Princeton College in 1842 and then studied law, but did not practice. From 1871 to 1875 he was minister to Turkey, and from 1875 to 1879 minister to Russia. From 1848 to 1886 he was engaged in literary work, producing many poems and plays.

DIRGE FOR A SOLDIER [1]

Close his eyes; his work is done!
  What to him is friend or foeman,
Rise of moon, or set of sun,
  Hand of man, or kiss of woman?
    Lay him low, lay him low,
    In the clover or the snow!
    What cares he? he cannot know:
    Lay him low!

As man may, he fought his fight,
  Proved his truth by his endeavor;   10
Let him sleep in solemn night,
  Sleep forever and forever.
    Lay him low, lay him low,
    In the clover or the snow!
    What cares he? he cannot know:
    Lay him low!

Fold him in his country's stars,
  Roll the drum and fire the volley!
What to him are all our wars?
  What but death bemocking folly?   20
    Lay him low, lay him low,
    In the clover or the snow!
    What cares he? he cannot know:
    Lay him low!

Leave him to God's watching eye;
  Trust him to the hand that made him.
Mortal love weeps idly by;
  God alone has power to aid him.
    Lay him low, lay him low,
    In the clover or the snow!   30
    What cares he? he cannot know:
    Lay him low!
1862

RICHARD HENRY STODDARD
1825-1903

For an intimate account of Stoddard's early struggles, varied experiences, and numerous friends, one should turn to his *Recollections Personal and Literary*, 1903. He was born in Hingham, Massachusetts, son of a sea captain lost at sea. He went

[1] General Philip Kearney, killed at Chantilly, Va., September 1, 1862

as a boy to New York, attended public schools for a time, and at twenty-one was molder in a foundry. All this time he was also serving his literary apprenticeship, reading widely and writing much.

Before long this self-made man was intimate with Taylor, Read, Hawthorne, and other influential men of letters, wrote for magazines and newspapers, and was literary editor of the New York *World* and the *Mail and Express*. He died in New York. Stoddard was essayist, biographer, and critic, but was best known for his lyric poetry. Though he was not a major poet, his verse is characterized by spontaneity, freshness, melody, and simplicity of diction.

Criticism: E. C. Stedman, *Genius and Other Essays*, 141-53; 166-73; also *Putnam's* 1:18-21; S. W. Halsey, *American Authors*, 17-27; S. H. Ward, "The Last of the Stoddards," *Ind.* 55: 1202-5; "Richard Henry Stoddard," *Outlook* 74: 216-8. See also *Dial* 35:299-301; *Atlan.* 93:82-3; *Harpers* 108:479-81.

SILENT SONGS

If I could ever sing the songs
  Within me day and night,
The only fit accompaniment
  Would be a lute of light!

A thousand dreamy melodies,
  Begot with pleasant pain,
Like incantations float around
  The chambers of my brain!

But when I strive to utter one,
  It mocks my feeble art,   10
And leaves me silent, with the thorns
  Of Music in my heart!
                    1852

THE SEA
[STORM]

Through the night, through the night,
  In the saddest unrest,
Wrapt in white, all in white,
  With her babe on her breast,
Walks the mother so pale,
Staring out on the gale,
  Through the night!

Through the night, through the night,
  Where the sea lifts the wreck,
Land in sight, close in sight,   10
  On the surf-flooded deck
Stands the father so brave,
Driving on to his grave,
  Through the night!
                    1852

OUT TO SEA

The wind is blowing east,
  And the waves are running free;
Let's hoist the sail at once,
  And stand out to sea,
    (You and me.)
I am growing more and more
  A-weary of the shore;
It was never so before—
    Out to sea!

The wind is blowing east,   10
  How it swells the straining sail!
A little further out
  We shall have a jolly gale.
    (Cling to me.)
The waves are running high,
  And the gulls, how they fly!
We shall only see the sky
    Out to sea.

The wind is blowing east
  From the dark and bloody shore,   20
Where flash a million swords,
  And the dreadful cannon roar.
    (Woe is me.)
There's a curse upon the land,
  (Is that blood upon my hand?)
What *can* we do but stand
    Out to sea?

1854

BIRDS

Birds are singing round my window,
  Tunes the sweetest ever heard,
And I hang my cage there daily,
  But I never catch a bird.

So with thoughts my brain is peopled,
  And they sing there all day long;
But they will not fold their pinions
  In the little cage of song!

1857

THE SKY

The sky is a drinking cup,
  That was overturned of old,
And it pours in the eyes of men
  Its wine of airy gold!

We drink that wine all day,
  Till the last drop is drained up,
And are lighted off to bed
  By the jewels in the cup!

1857

THERE ARE GAINS FOR ALL OUR LOSSES [1]

There are gains for all our losses,
  There are balms for all our pain:
But when youth, the dream, departs,
It takes something from our hearts,
  And it never comes again.

We are stronger, and are better,
  Under manhood's sterner reign:
Still we feel that something sweet
Followed youth, with flying feet,
  And will never come again.   10

Something beautiful is vanished,
  And we sigh for it in vain:
We behold it everywhere,
On the earth, and in the air,
  But it never comes again!

1857

ADSUM [2]

DECEMBER 23-24, 1863

I

The Angel came by night,
  (Such angels still come down),
And like a winter cloud
  Passed over London town;
Along its lonesome streets,
  Where Want had ceased to weep,
Until it reached a house
  Where a great man lay asleep:
The man of all his time
  Who knew the most of men,   10
The soundest head and heart,
  The sharpest, kindest pen.
It paused beside his bed,
  And whispered in his ear;
He never turned his head,
  But answered, "I am here."

II

Into the night they went.
  At morning, side by side,
They gained the sacred Place
  Where the greatest Dead abide.   20
Where grand old Homer sits
  In godlike state benign;
Where broods in endless thought
  The awful Florentine;
Where sweet Cervantes walks,
  A smile on his grave face;

[1] This poem was later entitled "The Flight of Youth."
[2] "I am here"; an answer to a roll-call; the poem refers to the death of Thackeray. See note 1, p. 247.

Where gossips quaint Montaigne,
The wisest of his race;
Where Goethe looks through all
With that calm eye of his;   30
Where—little seen but Light—
The only Shakespeare is!
When the new Spirit came,
They asked him, drawing near,
"Art thou become like us?"
He answered, "I am here."
1863

GEORGE WILLIAM CURTIS
1824-1892

On account of his generous, whole-hearted devotion to the service of literature and his country, Curtis deserves a twofold recognition. He was born in Providence, Rhode Island, of a family in good circumstances, and was privately educated. He was for a time at the Brook Farm community. Then he lived in Concord, on terms of intimacy with its famous men, and influenced by the theories of Emerson and Thoreau. He helped Thoreau build his hut at Walden Pond. Proving unsuited to commercial life, he roamed for four years through Europe and the East, preserving his impressions in *Nile Notes of a Howadji*, 1851, and *Lotus Eating*, 1852.

After 1852 he was connected with New York periodicals—*The Tribune, Putnam's Monthly, Harpers Magazine*, and *Harpers Weekly*—and was an influential shaper of public opinion, writing and lecturing widely against slavery and for Civil Service reform. His writing is a delightful mingling of humorous effects and exquisite ideals; the chief titles are *Potiphar Papers*, 1853; *Prue and I*, 1856; *From the Easy Chair*, 1891-1894; *Orations and Addresses*, 1893-1894. His friend William Winter characterized him as "the illustrious orator, the wise and gentle philosopher, the serene and delicate artist, the incorruptible patriot, the supreme gentleman."

Biography: E. Cary, (AML) 1894. Criticism: W. Winter, *G. W. Curtis, a Eulogy*, 1893; in *Old Friends*, 223-74; E. E. Hale, in *Five Prophets of Today*, 1892; Payne; L. H. Vincent, in *American Literary Masters*, 417-35; C. Schurz, "George William Curtis, Friend of the Republic," *McClure* 23: 614-23; H. M. Alden, *Cur. Lit.* 36:237-8; "Some Early Letters of George William Curtis," *Atlan.* 114:363-76; "War-time Letters of Charles Eliot Norton to George William Curtis," *Atlan.* 110: 597-614.

From PRUE AND I

A WORD TO THE GENTLE READER

An old bookkeeper, who wears a white cravat and black trousers in the morning, who rarely goes to the opera, and never dines out, is clearly a person of no fashion and of no superior sources of information. His only journey is from his house to his office; his only satisfaction is in doing his duty; his only happiness is in his Prue and his children.

What romance can such a life have? What stories can such a man tell?

Yet I think, sometimes, when I look up from the parquet at the opera, and see Aurelia smiling in the boxes, and holding her court of love, and youth, and beauty, that the historians have not told of a fairer queen, nor the travelers seen devouter homage. And when I remember that it was in misty England that quaint old George Herbert sang of the—

Sweet day so cool, so calm, so bright
The bridall of the earth and skie. [1]

I am sure that I see days as lovely in our clearer air, and do not believe that Italian sunsets have a more gorgeous purple or a softer gold.

So, as the circle of my little life revolves, I console myself with believing, what I cannot help believing, that a man need not be a vagabond to enjoy the sweetest charm of travel, but that all countries and all times repeat themselves in his experience. This is an old philosophy, I am told, and much favored by those who have traveled; and I cannot but be glad that my faith has such a fine name and such competent witnesses. I am assured, however, upon the other hand, that such a faith is only imagination. But, if that be true, imagination is as good as many voyages—and how much cheaper! —a consideration which an old bookkeeper can never afford to forget.

I have not found, in my experience, that travelers always bring back with them the sunshine of Italy or the elegance of Greece. They tell us that there are such things, and that they have seen them; but, perhaps, they saw them, as the apples in the garden of the Hesperides [2] were sometimes seen—over the wall. I prefer the fruit which I can buy in the market to that which a man tells me he saw in Sicily, but of which there is no flavor in his story. Others, like Moses Primrose, [3] bring us a gross of such spectacles as we prefer not to see; so that I begin to suspect a man must have Italy and Greece in his heart and mind, if he would ever see them with his eyes.

[1] from "Virtue," by the English poet Herbert, 1593-1633
[2] maidens who guarded the golden apples that Earth had caused to grow as a wedding gift for Hera
[3] A character in Goldsmith's novel *The Vicar of Wakefield;* he goes to the county fair to sell a horse, and brings back nothing in exchange but a gross of green spectacles the mountings of which are of copper.

I know that this may be only a device of that compassionate imagination designed to comfort me, who shall never take but one other journey than my daily beat. Yet there have been wise men who taught that all scenes are but pictures upon the mind; and if I can see them as I walk the street that leads to my office, or sit at the office-window looking into the court, or take a little trip down the bay or up the river, why are not my pictures as pleasant and as profitable as those which men travel for years, at great cost of time, and trouble, and money, to behold?

For my part, I do not believe that any man can see softer skies than I see in Prue's eyes; nor hear sweeter music than I hear in Prue's voice; nor find a more heaven-lighted temple than I know Prue's mind to be. And when I wish to please myself with a lovely image of peace and contentment, I do not think of the plain of Sharon, nor of the valley of Enna, nor of Arcadia, nor of Claude's pictures; [1] but, feeling that the fairest fortune of my life is the right to be named with her, I whisper gently, to myself, with a smile—for it seems as if my very heart smiled within me, when I think of her— "Prue and I."

SEA FROM SHORE

Come unto these yellow sands.
            —*The Tempest*
            Argosies of magic sails,
Pilots of the purple twilight, dropping down with
      costly bales.
                                 —TENNYSON

In the month of June, Prue and I like to walk upon the Battery [2] toward sunset, and watch the steamers, crowded with passengers, bound for the pleasant places along the coast where people pass the hot months. Sea-side lodgings are not very comfortable, I am told; but who would not be a little pinched in his chamber, if his windows looked upon the sea?

In such praises of the ocean do I indulge at such times, and so respectfully do I regard the sailors who may chance to pass, that Prue often says, with her shrewd smiles, that my mind is a kind of Greenwich Hospital, [3] full of abortive marine hopes and wishes, broken-legged intentions, blind regrets, and desires, whose hands have been shot away in some hard battle

of experience, so that they cannot grasp the results towards which they reach.

She is right, as usual. Such hopes and intentions do lie, ruined and hopeless now, strewn about the placid contentment of my mental life, as the old pensioners sit about the grounds at Greenwich, maimed and musing in the quiet morning sunshine. Many a one among them thinks what a Nelson he would have been if both his legs had not been prematurely carried away; or in what a Trafalgar [4] of triumph he would have ended, if, unfortunately, he had not happened to have been blown blind by the explosion of that unlucky magazine.

So I dream, sometimes, of a straight scarlet collar, stiff with gold lace, around my neck, instead of this limp white cravat; and I have even brandished my quill at the office so cutlass-wise, that Titbottom [5] has paused in his additions and looked at me as if he doubted whether I should come out quite square in my petty cash. Yet he understands it. Titbottom was born in Nantucket.

That is the secret of my fondness for the sea; I was born by it. Not more surely do Savoyards pine for the mountains, nor Cockneys for the sound of Bow bells, [6] than those who are born within sight and sound of the ocean to return to it and renew their fealty. In dreams the children of the sea hear its voice.

I have read in some book of travels that certain tribes of Arabs have no name for the ocean, and that when they came to the shore for the first time, they asked with eager sadness, as if penetrated by the conviction of a superior beauty, "what is that desert of water more beautiful than the land?" And in the translations of German stories which Adoniram and the other children read, and into which I occasionally look in the evening when they are gone to bed—for I like to know what interests my children—I find that the Germans, who do not live near the sea, love the fairy lore of water, and tell the sweet stories of Undine and Melusina, [7] as if they had especial charm for them, because their country is inland.

We who know the sea have less fairy feeling about it, but our realities are romance. My

---

[1] The plain of Sharon in Palestine was noted for its fertility. Enna is not a valley but a mountain in central Sicily, once rich in luxuriant gardens. Arcadia is the mythical home of ideal simplicity. Claude Lorrain was a great French landscape painter.
[2] a once fashionable park at the south end of New York City
[3] a seamen's hospital and pensioners' home in Greenwich, England

[4] the great naval victory over the French won by Admiral Nelson off Cape Trafalgar, southern Spain, in 1805
[5] an assistant bookkeeper in the office, who drew only $900.00 a year but also had castles in Spain
[6] Savoyards, inhabitants of the former duchy of Savoy, a mountainous district of eastern France; Cockneys, traditionally, dwellers within the sound of the bells of St. Mary le Bow, a church in London
[7] Undine is a water-spirit in a romance (1811) by Fouqué, Baron de la Motte, 1777-1843; Melusina, another water-spirit, is a character in an ancient French legend.

earliest remembrances are of a long range of old, half dilapidated stores; red brick stores with steep wooden roofs, and stone window-frames and door-frames, which stood upon docks built as if for immense trade with all quarters of the globe. [1]

Generally there were only a few sloops moored to the tremendous posts, which I fancied could easily hold fast a Spanish Armada in a tropical hurricane. But sometimes a great ship, an East Indiaman, with rusty, seamed, blistered sides, and dingy sails, came slowly moving up the harbor, with an air of indolent self-importance and consciousness of superiority, which inspired me with profound respect. If the ship had ever chanced to run down a row-boat, or a sloop, or any specimen of smaller craft, I should only have wondered at the temerity of any floating thing in crossing the path of such supreme majesty. The ship was leisurely chained and cabled to the old dock, and then came the disembowelling.

How the stately monster had been fattening upon foreign spoils! How it had gorged itself (such galleons did never seem to me of the feminine gender) with the lucious treasures of the tropics! It had lain its lazy length along the shores of China, and sucked in whole flowery harvests of tea. The Brazilian sun flashed through the strong wicker prisons, bursting with bananas and nectarean fruits that eschew the temperate zone. Steams of camphor, of sandal-wood, arose from the hold. Sailors chanting cabalistic strains, that had to my ear a shrill and monotonous pathos, like the uniform rising and falling of an autumn wind, turned cranks that lifted the bales, and boxes, and crates, and swung them ashore.

But to my mind, the spell of their singing raised the fragrant freight, and not the crank. Madagascar and Ceylon appeared at the mystic bidding of the song. The placid sunshine of the docks was perfumed with India. The universal calm of southern seas poured from the bosom of the ship over the quiet, decaying, old northern port.

Long after the confusion of unloading was over, and the ship lay as if all voyages were ended, I dared to creep timorously along the edge of the dock, and at great risk of falling in the black water of its huge shadow, I placed my hand upon the hot hulk, and so established a mystic and exquisite connection with Pacific islands, with palm groves and all the passionate beauties they embower; with jungles, Bengal

tigers, pepper, and the crushed feet of Chinese fairies. I touched Asia, the Cape of Good Hope, and the Happy Islands. [2] I would not believe that the heat I felt was of our northern sun; to my finer sympathy it burned with equatorial fervors.

The freight was piled in the old stores. I believe that many of them remain, but they have lost their character. When I knew them, not only was I younger, but partial decay had overtaken the town; at least the bulk of its India trade had shifted to New York and Boston. But the appliances remained. There was no throng of busy traffickers, and after school, in the afternoon, I strolled by and gazed into the solemn interiors.

Silence reigned within,—silence, dimness, and piles of foreign treasure. Vast coils of cable, like tame boa-constrictors, served as seats for men with large stomachs, and heavy watch-seals, and nankeen trousers, who sat looking out of the door toward the ships, with little other sign of life than an occasional low talking, as if in their sleep. Huge hogsheads perspiring brown sugar and oozing slow molasses, as if nothing tropical could keep within bounds, but must continually expand, and exude, and overflow, stood against the walls, and had an architectural significance, for they darkly reminded me of Egyptian prints, and in the duskiness of the low-vaulted store seemed cyclopean columns incomplete. Strange festoons and heaps of bags, square piles of square boxes cased in mats, bales of airy summer stuffs, which, even in winter, scoffed at cold, and shamed it by audacious assumptions of eternal sun, little specimen boxes of precious dyes that even now shine through my memory, like old Venetian schools unpainted, [3]—these were all there in rich confusion.

The stores had a twilight of dimness, the air was spicy with mingled odors. I liked to look suddenly in from the glare of sunlight outside, and then the cool sweet dimness was like the palpable breath of the far-off island-groves; and if only some parrot or macaw hung within, would flaunt with glistening plumage in his cage, and as the gay hue flashed in a chance sunbeam, call in his hard, shrill voice, as if thrusting sharp sounds upon a glistening wire from out that grateful gloom, then the enchantment was complete, and without moving, I was circumnavigating the globe.

---

[1] Curtis's boyhood was passed in Providence, which then had a large sea-trade.

[2] The Isles of the Blest or The Fortunate Islands were imaginary lands in the western ocean; later, the names were applied to the Canary and Madeira Is.

[3] perhaps paintings (never done) in the rich manner of the Venetian school

From the old stores and the docks slowly crumbling, touched, I know not why or how, by the pensive air of past prosperity, I rambled out of town on those well-remembered afternoons, to the fields that lay upon hillsides over the harbor, and there sat, looking out to sea, fancying some distant sail proceeding to the glorious ends of the earth, to be my type and image, who would so sail, stately and successful, to all the glorious ports of the Future. Going home, I returned by the stores, which black porters were closing. But I stood long looking in, saturating my imagination, and as it appeared, my clothes, with the spicy suggestion. For when I reached home my thrifty mother—another Prue—came snuffing and smelling about me.

"Why! my son (*snuff, snuff,*) where have you been (*snuff, snuff*)? Has the baker been making (*snuff*) ginger-bread? You smell as if you'd been in (*snuff, snuff,*) a bag of cinnamon."

"I've only been on the wharves, mother."

"Well, my dear, I hope you haven't stuck up your clothes with molasses. Wharves are dirty places, and dangerous. You must take care of yourself, my son. Really this smell is (*snuff, snuff,*) very strong."

But I departed from the maternal presence, proud and happy. I was aromatic. I bore about me the true foreign air. Whoever smelt me smelt distant countries. I had nutmeg, spices, cinnamon, and cloves, without the jolly red nose. I pleased myself with being the representative of the Indies. I was in good odor with myself and all the world.

I do not know how it is, but surely Nature makes kindly provision. An imagination so easily excited as mine could not have escaped disappointment if it had had ample opportunity and experience of the lands it so longed to see. Therefore, although I made the India voyage, I have never been a traveler, and saving the little time I was ashore in India, I did not lose the sense of novelty and romance, which the first sight of foreign lands inspires.

That little time was all my foreign travel. I am glad of it. I see now that I should never have found the country from which the East Indiaman of my early days arrived. The palm groves do not grow, with which that hand laid upon the ship placed me in magic conception. As for the lovely Indian maid whom the palmy arches bowered, she has long since clasped some native lover to her bosom, and, ripened into mild maternity, how should I know her now?

"You would find her quite as easily now as then," says my Prue, when I speak of it.

She is right again, as usual, that precious woman; and it is therefore I feel that if the chances of life have moored me fast to a book-keeper's desk, they have left all the lands I longed to see fairer and fresher in my mind than they could ever be in my memory. Upon my only voyage I used to climb into the top and search the horizon for the shore. But now in a moment of calm thought I see a more Indian India than ever mariner discerned, and do not envy the youths who go there and make fortunes, who wear grass-cloth jackets, drink iced beer, and eat curry; whose minds fall asleep, and whose bodies have liver complaints.

Unseen by me forever, nor ever regretted shall wave the Egyptian palms and the Italian pines. Untrodden by me, the Forum shall still echo with the footfall of imperial Rome, and the Parthenon unrifled of its marbles, look, perfect, across the Aegean blue.

My young friends return from their foreign tours elate with the smiles of a nameless Italian or Parisian belle. I know not such cheap delights; I am suitor of Vittoria Colonna;[1] I walk with Tasso[2] along the terraced garden of the Villa d'Este, and look to see Beatrice smiling down the rich gloom of the cypress shade. You stayed at the *Hôtel Europa* in Venice, at *Danielli's,* or the *Leone bianco;*[3] I am the guest of Marino Faliero, and I whisper to his wife as we climb the giant staircase in the summer moonlight,

Ah! senza amare
Andare sul mare,
Col sposo del mare,
Non puo consolare.[4]

It is for the same reason that I did not care to dine with you and Aurelia, that I am content not to stand in St. Peter's. Alas! if I could see the end of it, it would not be St. Peter's. For those of us whom Nature means to keep at home, she provides entertainment. One man goes four thousand miles to Italy, and does not see it, he is so short-sighted. Another is so far-sighted that he stays in his room and sees more than Italy.

[1] an Italian poet,—the only woman known to have been beloved by Michael Angelo

[2] One of the four greatest Italian poets; he served the family of Este, whose seat of power was Ferrara. He is said to have loved the princess Leonora d'Este. Curtis may have confused Tasso's experiences there with those of the poet Boiardo, of a century before, who was patronized by Duke Hercules d'Este, whose daughter Beatrice was one of the most beautiful and accomplished women of Italy. Later, as Duchess of Milan she was herself a patron of art and letters.

[3] "The White Lion," a hotel in Venice; Marino Faliero, doge (ruler) of Venice, died 1355.

[4] "Ah, without love to put forth to sea with the consort of the sea,—for that there is no solace."

But for this very reason that it washes the shores of my possible Europe and Asia, the sea draws me constantly to itself. Before I came to New York, while I was still a clerk in Boston, courting Prue, and living out of town, I never knew of a ship sailing for India or even for England and France, but I went up to the State House cupola or to the observatory on some friend's house in Roxbury, where I could not be interrupted, and there watched the departure.

The sails hung ready; the ship lay in the stream; busy little boats and puffing steamers darted about it, clung to its sides, paddled away for it, or led the way to sea, as minnows might pilot a whale. The anchor was slowly swung at the bow; I could not hear the sailors' song, but I knew they were singing. I could not see the parting friends, but I knew farewells were spoken. I did not share the confusion, although I knew what bustle there was, what hurry, what shouting, what creaking, what fall of ropes and iron, what sharp oaths, low laughs, whispers, sobs. But I was cool, high, separate. To me it was

a painted ship
Upon a painted ocean. [1]

The sails were shaken out, and the ship began to move. It was a fair breeze, perhaps, and no steamer was needed to tow her away. She receded down the bay. Friends turned back—I could not see them—and waved their hands, and wiped their eyes, and went home to dinner. Farther and farther from the ships at anchor, the lessening vessel became single and solitary upon the water. The sun sank in the west; but I watched her still. Every flash of her sails, as she tacked and turned, thrilled my heart.

Yet Prue was not on board. I had never seen one of the passengers or the crew. I did not know the consignees, nor the name of the vessel. I had shipped no adventure, nor risked any insurance, nor made any bet, but my eyes clung to her as Ariadne's to the fading sail of Theseus. [2] The ship was freighted with more than appeared upon her papers, yet she was not a smuggler. She bore all there was of that nameless lading, yet the next ship would carry as much. She was freighted with fancy. My hopes, and wishes, and vague desires, were all on board. It seemed to me a treasure not less rich than that which filled the East Indiaman at the old dock in my boyhood.

When, at length, the ship was a sparkle upon the horizon, I waved my hand in last farewell, I strained my eyes for a last glimpse. My mind had gone to sea, and had left noise behind. But now I heard again the multitudinous murmur of the city, and went down rapidly, and threaded the short, narrow streets to the office. Yet, believe it, every dream of that day, as I watched the vessel, was written at night to Prue. She knew my heart had not sailed away.

Those days are long past now, but still I walk upon the Battery and look towards the Narrows, and know that beyond them, separated only by the sea, are many of whom I would so gladly know, and so rarely hear. The sea rolls between us like the lapse of dusky ages. They trusted themselves to it, and it bore them away far and far as if into the past. Last night I read of Antony, but I have not heard from Christopher these many months, and by so much farther away is he, so much older and more remote than Antony. As for William, he is as vague as any of the shepherd kings of ante-Pharaonic dynasties.

It is the sea that has done it, it has carried them off and put them away upon its other side. It is fortunate the sea did not put them upon its under-side. Are they hale and happy still? Is their hair gray, and have they mustachios? Or have they taken to wigs and crutches? Are they popes or cardinals yet? Do they feast with Lucrezia Borgia, [3] or preach red republicanism to the Council of Ten? [4] Do they sing, *Behold how brightly breaks the morning* with Masaniello? [5] Do they laugh at Ulysses and skip ashore to the Sirens? [6] Has Mesrour, chief of the Eunuchs, caught them with Zobeide [7] in the Caliph's garden, or have they made cheese cakes without pepper? Friends of my youth, where in your wanderings have you tasted the blissful Lotus, [8] that you neither come nor send us tidings?

Across the sea also came idle rumors, as false reports steal into history and defile fair fames. Was it longer ago than yesterday that I walked

[1] from Coleridge's "Ancient Mariner," Part II
[2] All the various myths concerning the loves of Theseus and Ariadne, although differing as to the cause, agree that Theseus left Ariadne on the island of Naxos.
[3] Lucrezia, 1480-1519, one of the famous Italian family of Borgia, a patron of learning and art.
[4] a powerful secret tribunal instituted when Venice was a republic
[5] a song in the opera *La Muette de Portici*, better known as *Masaniello*, produced in 1828 by Auber, the French composer
[6] The sirens were sea-nymphs who by their songs tempted seamen passing their island to turn aside from their course, and then destroyed them. Ulysses filled the ears of his companions with wax so that they could not hear the music.
[7] wife of the caliph Harun al Raschid in the *Arabian Nights*
[8] A plant of northern Africa whose fruit, it was said, caused travelers to wish no longer to return to their native land; see Tennyson's "The Lotus Eaters."

with my cousin, then recently a widow, and talked with her of the countries to which she meant to sail? She was young, and dark-eyed, and wore great hoops of gold, barbaric gold, in her ears. The hope of Italy, the thought of living there, had risen like a dawn in the darkness of her mind. I talked and listened by rapid turns.

Was it longer ago than yesterday that she told me of her splendid plans, how palaces tapestried with gorgeous paintings should be cheaply hired, and the best of teachers lead her children to the completest and most various knowledge; how,—and with her slender pittance!—she should have a box at the opera, and a carriage, and liveried servants, and in perfect health and youth, lead a perfect life in a perfect climate?

And now what do I hear? Why does a tear sometimes drop so audibly upon my paper, that Titbottom looks across with a sort of mild rebuking glance of inquiry, whether it is kind to let even a single tear fall, when an ocean of tears is pent up in hearts that would burst and overflow if but one drop should force its way out? Why across the sea came faint gusty stories, like low voices in the wind, of a cloistered garden and sunny seclusion—and a life of unknown and unexplained luxury. What is this picture of a pale face showered with streaming black hair, and large sad eyes looking upon lovely and noble children playing in the sunshine—and a brow pained with thought straining into their destiny? Who is this figure, a man tall and comely, with melting eyes and graceful motion, who comes and goes at pleasure, who is not a husband, yet has the key of the cloistered garden?

I do not know. They are secrets of the sea. The pictures pass before my mind suddenly and unawares, and I feel the tears rising that I would gladly repress. Titbottom looks at me, then stands by the window of the office and leans his brow against the cold iron bars, and looks down into the little square paved court. I take my hat and steal out of the office for a few minutes, and slowly pace the hurrying streets. Meek-eyed Alice! magnificent Maud! sweet baby Lilian! why does the sea imprison you so far away, when will you return, where do you linger? The water laps idly about the docks,— lies calm, or gaily heaves. Why does it bring me doubts and fears now, that brought such bounty of beauty in the days long gone?

I remember that the day when my dark-haired cousin, with hoops of barbaric gold in her ears, sailed for Italy, was quarter-day, and we balanced the books at the office. It was

nearly noon, and in my impatience to be away, I had not added my columns with sufficient care. The inexorable hand of the office clock pointed sternly towards twelve, and the remorseless pendulum ticked solemnly to noon.

To a man whose pleasures are not many, and rather small, the loss of such an event as saying farewell and wishing God-speed to a friend going to Europe, is a great loss. It was so to me, especially, because there was always more to me, in every departure, than the parting and the farewell. I was gradually renouncing this pleasure, as I saw small prospect of ending before noon, when Titbottom, after looking at me a moment, came to my side of the desk, and said:

"I should like to finish that for you."

I looked at him: poor Titbottom! he had no friends to wish God-speed upon any journey. I quietly wiped my pen, took down my hat, and went out. It was in the days of sail packets and less regularity, when going to Europe was more of an epoch in life. How gaily my cousin stood upon the deck and detailed to me her plan! How merrily the children shouted and sang! How long I held my cousin's little hand in mine, and gazed into her great eyes, remembering that they would see and touch the things that were invisible to me for ever, but all the more precious and fair! She kissed me—I was younger then—there were tears, I remember, and prayers, and promises, a waving handkerchief,—a fading sail.

It was only the other day that I saw another parting of the same kind. I was not a principal, only a spectator; but so fond am I of sharing, afar off, as it were, and unseen, the sympathies of human beings, that I cannot avoid often going to the dock upon steamer-days and giving myself to that pleasant and melancholy observation. There is always a crowd, but this day it was almost impossible to advance through the masses of people. The eager faces hurried by; a constant stream poured up the gangway into the steamer, and the upper deck, to which I gradually made my way, was crowded with the passengers and their friends.

There was one group upon which my eyes first fell, and upon which my memory lingers. A glance, brilliant as daybreak,—a voice,

Her voice's music,—call it the well's bubbling, the
    bird's warble,

a goddess girdled with flowers, and smiling farewell upon a circle of worshipers, to each one of whom that gracious calmness made the smile sweeter, and the farewell more sad—other figures, other flowers, an angel face—all these I saw in that group as I was swayed up and down the deck by the eager swarm of people. The hour came, and I went on shore with the rest. The plank was drawn away—the captain raised his hand—the huge steamer slowly moved—a cannon was fired—the ship was gone.

The sun sparkled upon the water as they sailed away. In five minutes the steamer was as much separated from the shore as if it had been at sea a thousand years.

I leaned against a post upon the dock and looked around. Ranged upon the edge of the wharf stood that band of worshipers, waving handkerchiefs and straining their eyes to see the last smile of farewell—did any eager selfish eye hope to see a tear? They to whom the handkerchiefs were waved stood high upon the stern, holding flowers. Over them hung the great flag, raised by the gentle wind into the graceful folds of a canopy,—say rather a gorgeous gonfalon waved over the triumphant departure, over that supreme youth, and bloom, and beauty, going out across the mystic ocean to carry a finer charm and more human splendor into those realms of my imagination beyond the sea.

"You will return, O youth and beauty!" I said to my dreaming and foolish self, as I contemplated those fair figures, "richer than Alexander with Indian spoils. [1] All that historic association, that copious civilization, those grandeurs and graces of art, that variety and picturesqueness of life, will mellow and deepen your experience even as time silently touches those old pictures into a more persuasive and pathetic beauty, and as this increasing summer sheds ever softer lustre upon the landscape. You will return conquerors and not conquered. You will bring Europe, even as Aurelian brought Zenobia captive, [2] to deck your homeward triumph. I do not wonder that these clouds break away, I do not wonder that the sun presses out and floods all the air, and land, and water, with light that graces with happy omens your stately farewell."

But if my faded face looked after them with such earnest and longing emotion,—I, a solitary old man, unknown to those fair beings, and standing apart from that band of lovers, yet in that moment bound more closely to them than they knew,—how was it with those whose hearts sailed away with that youth and beauty? I watched them closely from behind my post. I knew that life had paused with them; that the

[1] Alexander the Great in 327 B.C. invaded India.
[2] Aurelian, Roman Emperor from 270 to 275, having conquered Palmyra, east of Syria, took Zenobia, Queen of Palmyra, to Rome.

world stood still. I knew that the long, long summer would be only a yearning regret. I knew that each asked himself the mournful question, "Is this parting typical—this slow, sad, sweet, recession?" And I knew that they did not care to ask whether they should meet again, nor dare to contemplate the chances of the sea.

The steamer swept on, she was near Staten Island, and a final gun boomed far and low across the water. The crowd was dispersing, but the little group remained. Was it not all Hood had sung?

> I saw thee, lovely Inez,
> Descend along the shore,
> With bands of noble gentlemen,
> And banners waved before;
> And gentle youths and maidens gay,
> And snowy plumes they wore;—
> It would have been a beauteous dream,—
> If it had been no more! [3]

"O youth!" I said to them without speaking, "be it gently said, as it is solemnly thought, should they return no more, yet in your memories the high hour of their loveliness is for ever enshrined. Should they come no more they never will be old, nor changed, to you. You will wax and wane, you will suffer, and struggle, and grow old; but this summer vision will smile, immortal, upon your lives, and those fair faces shall shed, forever, from under that slowly waving flag, hope and peace."

It is so elsewhere; it is the tenderness of Nature. Long, long ago we lost our first-born, Prue and I. Since then, we have grown older and our children with us. Change comes, and grief, perhaps, and decay. We are happy, our children are obedient and gay. But should Prue live until she has lost us all, and laid us, gray and weary, in our graves, she will have always one babe in her heart. Every mother who has lost an infant, has gained a child of immortal youth. Can you find comfort here, lovers, whose mistress has sailed away?

I did not ask the question aloud, I thought it only, as I watched the youths, and turned away while they still stood gazing. One, I observed, climbed a post and waved his black hat before the white-washed side of the shed over the dock, whence I supposed he would tumble into the water. Another had tied a handkerchief to the end of a somewhat baggy umbrella, and in the eagerness of gazing, had forgotten to wave it, so that it hung mournfully down, as if overpowered with grief it could not express. The entranced youth still held the umbrella

[3] from Hood's "Fair Ines"

aloft. It seemed to me as if he had struck his flag; or as if one of my cravats were airing in that sunlight. A negro carter was joking with an apple-woman at the entrance of the dock. The steamer was out of sight.

I found that I was belated and hurried back to my desk. Alas! poor lovers; I wonder if they are watching still? Has he fallen exhausted from the post into the water? Is that handkerchief, bleached and rent, still pendant upon that somewhat baggy umbrella?

"Youth and beauty went to Europe today," said I to Prue, as I stirred my tea at evening.

As I spoke, our youngest daughter brought me the sugar. She is just eighteen, and her name should be Hebe. [1] I took a lump of sugar and looked at her. She had never seemed so lovely, and as I dropped the lump in my cup, I kissed her. I glanced at Prue as I did so. The dear woman smiled, but did not answer my exclamation.

Thus, without traveling, I travel, and share the emotions of those I do not know. But sometimes the old longing comes over me as in the days when I timidly touched the huge East Indiaman, and magnetically sailed around the world.

It was but a few days after the lovers and I waved farewell to the steamer, and while the lovely figures standing under the great gonfalon were as vivid in my mind as ever, that a day of premature sunny sadness, like those of the Indian summer, drew me away from the office early in the afternoon: for fortunately it is our dull season now, and even Titbottom sometimes leaves the office by five o'clock. Although why he should leave it, or where he goes, or what he does, I do not well know. Before I knew him, I used sometimes to meet him with a man whom I was afterwards told was Bartleby, the scrivener. [2] Even then it seemed to me that they rather clubbed their loneliness than made society for each other. Recently I have not seen Bartleby; but Titbottom seems no more solitary because he is alone.

I strolled into the Battery as I sauntered about. Staten Island looked so alluring, tender-hued with summer and melting in the haze, that I resolved to indulge myself in a pleasure-trip. It was a little selfish, perhaps, to go alone, but I looked at my watch, and saw that if I should hurry home for Prue the trip would be lost; then I should be disappointed, and she would be grieved.

Ought I not rather (I like to begin questions, which I am going to answer affirmatively, with *ought*,) to take the trip and recount my adventures to Prue upon my return, whereby I should actually enjoy the excursion and the pleasure of telling her; while she would enjoy my story and be glad that I was pleased? Ought I wilfully to deprive us both of this various enjoyment by aiming at a higher, which, in losing, we should lose all?

Unfortunately, just as I was triumphantly answering "Certainly not!" another question marched into my mind, escorted by a very defiant *ought*.

"Ought I to go when I have such a debate about it?"

But while I was perplexed, and scoffing at my own scruples, the ferry-bell suddenly rang, and answered all my questions. Involuntarily I hurried on board. The boat slipped from the dock. I went up on deck to enjoy the view of the city from the bay, but just as I sat down, and meant to have said "how beautiful!" I found myself asking:

"Ought I to have come?"

Lost in perplexing debate, I saw little of the scenery of the bay; but the remembrance of Prue and the gentle influence of the day plunged me into a mood of pensive reverie which nothing tended to destroy, until we suddenly arrived at the landing.

As I was stepping ashore, I was greeted by Mr. Bourne, [3] who passes the summer on the island and who hospitably asked if I were going his way. His way was toward the southern end of the island, and I said yes. His pockets were full of papers and his brow of wrinkles; so when we reached the point where he should turn off, I asked him to let me alight, although he was very anxious to carry me wherever I was going.

"I am only strolling about," I answered, as I clambered carefully out of the wagon.

"Strolling about?" asked he, in a bewildered manner; "do people stroll about, now-a-days?"

"Sometimes," I answered, smiling, as I pulled my trousers down over my boots, for they had dragged up, as I stepped out of the wagon, "and beside, what can an old bookkeeper do better in the dull season than stroll about this pleasant island, and watch the ships at sea?"

Bourne looked at me with his weary eyes.

"I'd give five thousand dollars a year for a dull season," said he, "but as for strolling, I've forgotten how."

As he spoke, his eyes wandered dreamily across the fields and woods, and were fastened upon the distant sails.

---

[1] goddess of youth and spring, cupbearer of the gods
[2] copyist

[3] a millionaire, once in love with Prue, and still unmarried

"It is pleasant," he said musingly, and fell into silence. But I had no time to spare, so I wished him good-afternoon.

"I hope your wife is well," said Bourne to me, as I turned away. Poor Bourne! He drove on alone in his wagon.

But I made haste to the most solitary point upon the southern shore, and there sat, glad to be so near the sea. There was that warm, sympathetic silence in the air, that gives to Indian-summer days almost a human tenderness of feeling. A delicate haze, that seemed only the kindly air made visible, hung over the sea. The water lapped languidly among the rocks, and the voices of children in the boat beyond, rang musically, and gradually receded, until they were lost in the distance.

It was some time before I was aware of the outline of a large ship, drawn vaguely upon the mist, which I supposed, at first, to be only a kind of mirage. But the more steadfastly I gazed, the more distinct it became, and I could no longer doubt that I saw a stately ship lying at anchor, not more than half a mile from the land.

"It is an extraordinary place to anchor," I said to myself, "or can she be ashore?"

There were no signs of distress; the sails were carefully clewed up, and there were no sailors in the tops, nor upon the shrouds. A flag, of which I could not see the device or the nation, hung heavily at the stern, and looked as if it had fallen asleep. My curiosity began to be singularly excited. The form of the vessel seemed not to be permanent; but within a quarter of an hour, I was sure that I had seen half a dozen different ships. As I gazed, I saw no more sails nor masts, but a long range of oars, flashing like a golden fringe, or straight and stiff, like the legs of a sea-monster.

"It is some bloated crab, or lobster, magnified by the mist," I said to myself, complacently.

But, at the same moment, there was a concentrated flashing and blazing in one spot among the rigging, and it was as if I saw a beatified ram, or, more truly, a sheep-skin, splendid as the hair of Berenice.[1]

"Is that the golden fleece?" I thought. "But, surely, Jason and the Argonauts have gone

[1] Wife of Ptolemy Euergetes, King of Egypt 247-222 B.C.; to insure the safe return of her husband from a military expedition, she sacrificed to the gods her beautiful hair. It was later believed to have been turned into the constellation Coma Berenices. Jason, a mythical Greek, sailed with other heroes in the ship Argo to Cholchis to obtain the golden fleece. Medea, the daughter of Aëtes, king of that land, enabled Jason to fulfil her father's conditions and to overcome the dragon that guarded the fleece.

home long since. Do people go on gold-fleecing expeditions now?" I asked myself, in perplexity. "Can this be a California steamer?"

How could I have thought it a steamer? Did I not see those sails, "thin and sere"?[2] Did I not feel the melancholy of that solitary bark? It had a mystic aura; a boreal brilliancy shimmered in its wake, for it was drifting seaward. A strange fear curdled along my veins. That summer sun shone cool. The weary, battered ship was gashed, as if gnawed by ice. There was terror in the air, as a "skinny hand so brown" waved to me from the deck. I lay as one bewitched. The hand of the ancient mariner seemed to be reaching for me, like the hand of death.

Death? Why, as I was inly praying Prue's forgiveness for my solitary ramble and consequent demise, a glance like the fulness of summer splendor gushed over me; the odor of flowers and of eastern gums made all the atmosphere. I breathed the orient, and lay drunk with balm, while that strange ship, a golden galley now, with glittering draperies festooned with flowers, paced to the measured beat of oars along the calm, and Cleopatra smiled alluringly from the great pageant's heart.[3]

Was this a barge for summer waters, this peculiar ship I saw? It had a ruined dignity, a cumbrous grandeur, although its masts were shattered, and its sails rent. It hung preternaturally still upon the sea, as if tormented and exhausted by long driving and drifting. I saw no sailors, but a great Spanish ensign floated over, and waved, a funereal plume. I knew it then. The armada was long since scattered; but, floating far

> on desolate rainy seas,

lost for centuries, and again restored to sight, here lay one of the fated ships of Spain. The huge galleon seemed to fill all the air, built up against the sky, like the gilded ships of Claude Lorrain[4] against the sunset.

But it fled, for now a black flag fluttered at the mast-head—a long low vessel darted swiftly where the vast ship lay; there came a shrill piping whistle, the clash of cutlasses, fierce ringing oaths, sharp pistol cracks, the thunder of command, and over all the gusty yell of a demoniac chorus,

> My name was Robert Kidd, when I sailed.

—There were no clouds longer, but under a serene sky I saw a bark moving with festal

[2] Coleridge's "Ancient Mariner," Part V
[3] Shakespeare's Antony and Cleopatra, II, ii, 196, ff.
[4] a French landscape painter

pomp thronged with grave senators in flowing robes, and one with ducal bonnet in the midst, holding a ring. The smooth bark swam upon a sea like that of southern latitudes. I saw the *Bucentoro* and the nuptials of Venice and the Adriatic.[1]

Who were those coming over the side? Who crowded the boats, and sprang into the water, men in old Spanish armor, with plumes and swords, and bearing a glittering cross? Who was he standing upon the deck with folded arms and gazing towards the shore, as lovers on their mistresses and martyrs upon heaven? Over what distant and tumultuous seas had this small craft escaped from other centuries and distant shores? What sounds of foreign hymns, forgotten now, were these, and what solemnity of debarkation? Was this grave form Columbus?

Yet these were not so Spanish as they seemed just now. This group of stern-faced men with high peaked hats, who knelt upon the cold deck and looked out upon a shore which, I could see by their joyless smile of satisfaction, was rough, and bare, and forbidding. In that soft afternoon, standing in mournful groups upon the small deck, why did they seem to me to be seeing the sad shores of wintry New England? That phantom ship could not be the *Mayflower!*

I gazed long upon the shifting illusion.

"If I should board this ship," I asked myself, "where should I go? whom should I meet? what should I see? Is not this the vessel that shall carry me to my Europe, my foreign countries, my impossible India, the Atlantis[2] that I have lost?"

As I sat staring at it I could not but wonder whether Bourne had seen this sail when he looked upon the water? Does he see such sights every day, because he lives down here? Is it not perhaps a magic yacht of his; and does he slip off privately after business hours to Venice, and Spain, and Egypt, perhaps to El Dorado? Does he run races with Ptolemy Philopater, and Hiero of Syracuse, rare regattas on fabulous seas?[3]

[1] In the ceremony of wedding the Adriatic, the doge, from the *Bucentaur,* the Venetian state galley, dropped a ring into the sea, saying, "We espouse thee, Sea, in token of true and lasting dominion." This was to commemorate the victory of the Venetians over Frederick Barbarossa, Emperor of the Holy Roman Empire, 1155-1189.

[2] A legendary island situated, according to ancient tradition, in the Atlantic Ocean just beyond the Straits of Gibraltar, and believed to have been swallowed up in a cataclysm; it was first mentioned by Plato, who makes it the seat of an ideal commonwealth.

[3] Ptolemy Philopator was king of Egypt, 221-204 B.C.; Hiero, Tyrant of Syracuse, 478 B.C., maintained a great fleet.

Why not? He is a rich man, too, and why should not a New York merchant do what a Syracuse tyrant and an Egyptian prince did? Has Bourne's yacht those sumptuous chambers, like Philopater's galley, of which the greater part was made of split cedar, and of Milesian cypress; and has he twenty doors put together with beams of citronwood with many ornaments? Has the roof of his cabin a carved golden face, and is his sail linen with a purple fringe?

"I suppose it is so," I said to myself, as I looked wistfully at the ship, which began to glimmer and melt in the haze.

"It certainly is not a fishing-smack?" I asked, doubtfully.

No, it must be Bourne's magic yacht; I was sure of it. I could not help laughing at poor old Hiero, whose cabins were divided into many rooms, with floors composed of mosaic work, of all kinds of stones tessellated. And, on this mosaic, the whole story of the Iliad was depicted in a marvelous manner. He had gardens "of all sorts of most wonderful beauty, enriched with all sorts of plants, and shadowed by roofs of lead or tiles. And, besides this, there were tents roofed with boughs of white ivy and of the vine—the roots of which derived their moisture from casks full of earth, and were watered in the same manner as the gardens. There were temples, also, with doors of ivory and citronwood, furnished in the most exquisite manner, with pictures and statues, and with goblets and vases of every form and shape imaginable."

"Poor Bourne!" I said. "I suppose his is finer than Hiero's, which is a thousand years old. Poor Bourne! I don't wonder that his eyes are weary, and that he would pay so dearly for a day of leisure. Dear me! is it one of the prices that must be paid for wealth, the keeping of a magic yacht?"

Involuntarily, I had asked the question aloud.

"The magic yacht is not Bourne's," answered a familiar voice. I looked up, and Titbottom stood by my side. "Do you not know that all Bourne's money would not buy the yacht?" asked he. "He cannot even see it. And if he could, it would be no magic yacht to him, but only a battered and solitary hulk."

The haze blew gently away, as Titbottom spoke, and there lay my Spanish galleon, my *Bucentoro,* my Cleopatra's galley, Columbus's *Santa María,* and the Pilgrims' *Mayflower,* an old bleaching wreck upon the beach.

"Do you suppose any true love is in vain?" asked Titbottom solemnly, as he stood bareheaded, and the soft sunset wind played with his few hairs. "Could Cleopatra smile upon Antony, and the moon upon Endymion, [1] and the sea not love its lovers?"

The fresh air breathed upon our faces as he spoke. I might have sailed in Hiero's ship, or in Roman galleys, had I lived long centuries ago, and been born a nobleman. But would it be so sweet a remembrance, that of lying on a marble couch, under a golden-faced roof, and within doors of citron-wood and ivory, and sailing in that state to greet queens who are mummies now, as that of seeing those fair figures, standing under the great gonfalon, themselves as lovely as Egyptian belles, and going to see more than Egypt dreamed?

The yacht was mine, then, and not Bourne's. I took Titbottom's arm, and we sauntered toward the ferry. What sumptuous sultan was I, with this sad vizier? My languid odalisque, [2] the sea, lay at my feet as we advanced, and sparkled all over with a sunset smile. Had I trusted myself to her arms, to be borne to the realms that I shall never see, or sailed long voyages towards Cathay, [3] I am not sure I should have brought a more precious present to Prue, than the story of that afternoon.

"Ought I to have gone alone?" I asked her, as I ended.

"I ought not to have gone with you," she replied, "for I had work to do. But how strange that you should see such things at Staten Island. I never did, Mr. Titbottom," said she, turning to my deputy, whom I had asked to tea.

"Madam," answered Titbottom, with a kind of wan and quaint dignity, so that I could not help thinking he must have arrived in that stray ship from the Spanish armada, "neither did Mr. Bourne."

1856

SOUTHERN LYRICS OF THE CIVIL WAR

Almost all of the lyrics of the present group arose from the war between the states. They vary much in tone and attitude, from those charged with the fierce passion of conflict to those suffused with the more sustained mood of pathos and heroism. As a whole they represent the spirit of the South at the time of its greatest crisis.

ALBERT PIKE, 1809-1891, though a Bostonian and a graduate of Harvard, is claimed by the South.

---

[1] He fell in love with Selene, the moon, who kissed him as he lay sleeping on Mt. Latmos. Cf. Keats's *Endymion.*
[2] female slave
[3] ancient name for northern China, and, by extension, the Orient

After teaching school, emigrating to Arkansas, editing and publishing *The Arkansas Advocate,* and practicing law, he served in the Mexican War as a captain of cavalry, and during the Civil War he was a brigadier general in the Confederate service. He died at Washington. His *Hymns to the Gods* was published in *Blackwood's* in 1839, and *Poems* appeared in 1873 and 1881.

THEODORE O'HARA, 1820-1867, was a Kentuckian, born in Danville and educated at St. Joseph's College, Bardstown. He gave up his law practice for an appointment as captain in the United States army in the Mexican War, and was brevetted colonel. During the Civil War he served as colonel in the Confederate army. He died at Guerrytown, Alabama.

MARGARET PRESTON, 1820-1897, the daughter of a Presbyterian clergyman, was born in Milton, Pennsylvania, was educated in private schools, married Colonel J. T. L. Preston of the Virginia Military Institute, and died in Baltimore. She wrote *Silverwood* (novel), 1856; *Beechenbrook* (verse), 1865; *Old Songs and New,* 1870; *Colonial Ballads,* 1887.

FRANCIS ORRAY TICKNOR, 1822-1874, though born in Baldwin County, Georgia, was educated in Massachusetts and studied medicine in New York and Philadelphia. He became a practicing physician at Columbus, Georgia, and died in that vicinity. His *Poems* were published in 1879.

JOHN R. THOMPSON, 1823-1873, was born in Richmond, Virginia, and was a graduate of the state university. He studied law, but turned to literature and was editor of *The Southern Literary Messenger,* 1847-1860. In 1864 he went to London, where for some time he contributed to *Blackwood's Magazine.* Afterwards he was literary editor of the New York *Evening Post* and a frequent contributor to American literary magazines. His death took place in New York.

THADDEUS OLIVER, 1826-1864, was born at Jeffersonville, Georgia, was a lawyer by profession, served in the Confederate army, and died at Charleston, South Carolina, of a wound received in battle. He was the author of several pleasing lyrics, and is supposed, for good reasons, to have written "All Quiet Along the Potomac Tonight," though there are other claimants to the authorship.

JAMES BARRON HOPE, 1827-1887, was born in Norfolk, Virginia, was educated at William and Mary College, and was a frequent contributor to *The Southern Literary Messenger.* After serving as captain in the Confederate army during the Civil War, he engaged in education and in newspaper work at Norfolk, where he died. Among his books are *Elegiac Ode and Other Poems,* 1875; *Under the Empire,* 1878.

ABRAM JOSEPH RYAN, 1839-1886, was born in Norfolk, Virginia, studied from youth for the

Roman Catholic priesthood, was ordained, and soon became chaplain to a Confederate regiment with which he served, sometimes in the ranks, until the close of the war. Afterwards he engaged in religious newspaper work in New Orleans and in Augusta, Georgia, as well as in pastoral duties. He died in Louisville, Kentucky. His *Poems* were published in 1880.

ALBERT PIKE

DIXIE

Southrons, hear your country call you!
Up, lest worse than death befall you!
  To arms! To arms! To arms, in Dixie!
Lo! all the beacon-fires are lighted,—
Let all hearts be now united!
  To arms! To arms! To arms, in Dixie!
  Advance the flag of Dixie!
    Hurrah! Hurrah!
For Dixie's land we take our stand,
  And live or die for Dixie! 10
  To arms! To arms!
  And conquer peace for Dixie!
  To arms! To arms!
  And conquer peace for Dixie!

Hear the Northern thunders mutter,
Northern flags in South winds flutter:
Send them back your fierce defiance!
Stamp upon the accursed alliance!

Fear no danger! Shun no labor!
Lift up rifle, pike, and saber! 20
Shoulder pressing close to shoulder,
Let the odds make each heart bolder!

How the South's great heart rejoices
At your cannons' ringing voices,
For faith betrayed, and pledges broken,
Wrongs inflicted, insults spoken!

Strong as lions, swift as eagles,
Back to their kennels hunt these beagles!
Cut the unequal bonds asunder:
Let them hence each other plunder! 30

Swear upon your country's altar
Never to submit or falter,
Till the spoilers are defeated,
Till the Lord's work is completed.

Halt not till our Federation
Secures among earth's powers its station:
Then at peace, and crowned with glory,
Hear your children tell the story!

If the loved ones weep in sadness, 39
Victory soon shall bring them gladness,—

To arms!
Exultant pride soon banish sorrow,
Smiles chase tears away tomorrow.
  To arms! To arms! To arms, in Dixie!
  Advance the flag of Dixie!
    Hurrah! hurrah!
For Dixie's land we take our stand,
  And live or die for Dixie!
  To arms! To arms!
  And conquer peace for Dixie! 50
  To arms! To arms!
  And conquer peace for Dixie!

1861   1861?

THEODORE O'HARA

THE BIVOUAC OF THE DEAD [1]

The muffled drum's sad roll has beat
  The soldier's last tattoo; [2]
No more on life's parade shall meet
  That brave and fallen few.
On Fame's eternal camping-ground
  Their silent tents are spread,
And Glory guards, with solemn round,
  The bivouac of the dead.

No rumor of the foe's advance
  Now swells upon the wind; 10
No troubled thought at midnight haunts
  Of loved ones left behind;
No vision of the morrow's strife
  The warrior's dream alarms;
No braying horn nor screaming fife
  At dawn shall call to arms.

Their shivered swords are red with rust;
  Their plumed heads are bowed;
Their haughty banner, trailed in dust,
  Is now their martial shroud. 20
And plenteous funeral tears have washed
  The red stains from each brow,
And the proud forms, by battle gashed,
  Are free from anguish now.

The neighing troop, the flashing blade,
  The bugle's stirring blast,
The charge, the dreadful cannonade,
  The din and shout, are past;
Nor war's wild note nor glory's peal
  Shall thrill with fierce delight 30
Those breasts that never more may feel
  The rapture of the fight.

[1] This poem was written in memory of Kentucky comrades killed in the Mexican War and buried in Frankfort, Ky.
[2] A drum call to repair to quarters for the night; "taps" is "lights out."

Like a fierce northern hurricane
  That sweeps this great plateau,
Flushed with triumph yet to gain,
  Came down the serried foe. [1]
Who heard the thunder of the fray
  Break o'er the field beneath,
Knew well the watchword of that day
  Was "Victory or Death."   40

Long had the doubtful conflict raged
  O'er all that stricken plain,
For never fiercer fight had waged
  The vengeful blood of Spain;
And still the storm of battle blew,
  Still swelled the gory tide;
Not long, our stout old chieftain [2] knew,
  Such odds his strength could bide.

'Twas in that hour his stern command
  Called to a martyr's grave   50
The flower of his beloved land
  The nation's flag to save.
By rivers of their fathers' gore
  His first-born laurels grew,
And well he deemed the sons would pour
  Their lives for glory too.

Full many a norther's breath has swept
  O'er Angostura's plain [3]—
And long the pitying sky has wept
  Above its moldered slain.   60
The raven's scream, or eagle's flight,
  Or shepherd's pensive lay,
Alone awakes each sullen height
  That frowned o'er that dread fray.

Sons of the Dark and Bloody Ground, [4]
  Ye must not slumber there,
Where stranger steps and tongues resound
  Along the heedless air.
Your own proud land's heroic soil
  Shall be your fitter grave;   70
She claims from War his richest spoil—
  The ashes of her brave.

Thus 'neath their parent turf they rest,
  Far from the gory field;
Borne to a Spartan mother's breast
  On many a bloody shield;
The sunlight of their native sky
  Smiles sadly on them here,
And kindred eyes and hearts watch by
  The heroes' sepulcher.   80

[1] The Mexican forces numbered over twenty thousand.
[2] General Zachary Taylor
[3] a ridge or tableland near Buena Vista where on February 22-23, 1847, General Taylor won a great victory
[4] the meaning of the Indian word *Kentucky*

Rest on, embalmed and sainted dead,
  Dear as the blood ye gave;
No impious footstep here shall tread
  The herbage of your grave;
Nor shall your glory be forgot
  While Fame her record keeps,
Or Honor points the hallowed spot
  Where Valor proudly sleeps.

Yon marble minstrel's voiceless stone
  In deathless song shall tell,   90
When many a vanished age hath flown,
  The story how ye fell;
Nor wreck, nor change, nor winter's blight,
  Nor Time's remorseless doom,
Shall dim one ray of glory's light
  That gilds your glorious tomb.
1847

MARGARET JUNKIN PRESTON

THE SHADE OF THE TREES

What are the thoughts that are stirring his
      breast?
  What is the mystical vision he sees?
"Let us pass over the river and rest
  Under the shade of the trees." [5]

Has he grown sick of his toils and his tasks?
  Sighs the worn spirit for respite or ease?
Is it a moment's cool halt that he asks
  Under the shade of the trees?

Is it the gurgle of waters whose flow
  Ofttime has come to him borne on the breeze,
Memory listens to, lapsing so low,   11
  Under the shade of the trees?

Nay—though the rasp of the flesh was so sore,
  Faith, that had yearnings far keener than
      these,
Saw the soft sheen of the Thitherward Shore,
  Under the shade of the trees;—

Caught the high psalms of ecstatic delight,
  Heard the harps harping like soundings of
      seas,
Watched earth's assoiled ones walking in white
  Under the shade of the trees.   20

O, was it strange he should pine for release,
  Touched to the soul with such transports as
      these,
He who so needed the balsam of peace,
  Under the shade of the trees?

[5] These were the last words of General Thomas Jonathan Jackson, better known as Stonewall Jackson, who was mortally wounded at the battle of Chancellorsville, May, 1863.

Yes, it was noblest for him—it was best
  (Questioning naught of our Father's decrees)
There to pass over the river and rest
  Under the shade of the trees!
1863

FRANCIS ORRAY TICKNOR

LITTLE GIFFEN [1]

Out of the focal and foremost fire,
Out of the hospital walls as dire,
Smitten of grapeshot and gangrene,
Eighteenth battle and he sixteen—
Specter such as you seldom see,
Little Giffen of Tennessee.

"Take him and welcome," the surgeon said;
"Not the doctor can help the dead!"
So we took him and brought him where
The balm was sweet in our summer air;   10
And we laid him down on a wholesome bed;
Utter Lazarus, heel to head!

And we watched the war with abated breath,
Skeleton boy against skeleton death!
Months of torture, how many such!
Weary weeks of the stick and crutch,—
And still a glint in the steel-blue eye
Told of a spirit that wouldn't die,

And didn't! Nay! more! in death's despite
The crippled skeleton learned to write—   20
"Dear mother!" at first, of course, and then
"Dear Captain!" inquiring about the men.
Captain's answer: "Of eighty and five,
Giffen and I are left alive."

"Johnston [2] pressed at the front," they say;—
Little Giffen was up and away!
A tear, his first, as he bade good-by,
Dimmed the glint of his steel-blue eye.
"I'll write, if spared!" There was news of fight,
But none of Giffen—he did not write!   30

I sometimes fancy that were I King
Of the courtly Knights of Arthur's ring,
With the voice of the minstrel in mine ear
And the tender legend that trembles here,
I'd give the best on his bended knee—
The whitest soul of my chivalry—
For Little Giffen of Tennessee.

[1] "Little Giffen" is "A true story of a boy whom Dr.
  Ticknor nursed back to life at Torch Hill,
  Georgia." (Quoted from Riverside Classics,
  "*Southern Poems*," Houghton Mifflin Company.)
[2] General Joseph E. Johnston of Virginia

THE VIRGINIANS OF THE VALLEY

The Knightliest of the Knightly race,
That since the days of old,
Have kept the lamp of chivalry
Alive in hearts of gold.
The kindliest of the kindly band
That, rarely hating ease,
Yet rode with Raleigh round the land,
With Smith around the seas.

Who climbed the blue embattled hills   10
Against uncounted foes,
And planted there, in valleys fair,
The Lily and the Rose!
Whose fragrance lives in many lands,
Whose beauty stars the earth;
And lights the hearths of happy homes
With loveliness and worth!

We thought they slept! the sons who kept
The names of noble sires,
And slumbered, while the darkness crept
Around their vigil fires!   20
But aye! the "Golden Horseshoe" Knights
Their Old Dominion keep,
Whose foes have found enchanted ground
But not a knight asleep.

JOHN R. THOMPSON

MUSIC IN CAMP

Two armies covered hill and plain,
  Where Rappahannock's waters
Ran deeply crimsoned with the stain
  Of battle's recent slaughters. [3]

The summer clouds lay pitched like tents
  In meads of heavenly azure;
And each dread gun of the elements
  Slept in its hid embrasure.

The breeze so softly blew it made
  No forest leaf to quiver,   10
And the smoke of the random cannonade
  Rolled slowly from the river.

And now, where circling hills looked down
  With cannon grimly planted,
O'er listless camp and silent town
  The golden sunset slanted.

When on the fervid air there came
  A strain, now rich, now tender;

[3] After the battle of Fredericksburg on the Rappahannock River, one of the severest battles of the
  Civil War, December 13, 1862, the Union and
  Confederate armies remained all winter encamped
  on the opposite banks of the river.

The music seemed itself aflame
  With day's departing splendor.   20

A Federal band, which, eve and morn,
  Played measures brave and nimble,
Had just struck up, with flute and horn
  And lively clash of cymbal.

Down flocked the soldiers to the banks,
  Till, margined by its pebbles,
One wooded shore was blue with "Yanks,"
  And one was gray with "Rebels."

Then all was still, and then the band,
  With movement light and tricksy,   30
Made stream and forest, hill and strand,
  Reverberate with "Dixie."

The conscious stream with burnished glow
  Went proudly o'er its pebbles,
But thrilled throughout its deepest flow
  With yelling of the Rebels.

Again a pause, and then again
  The trumpets pealed sonorous,
And "Yankee Doodle" was the strain
  To which the shore gave chorus.   40

The laughing ripple shoreward flew,
  To kiss the shining pebbles;
Loud shrieked the swarming Boys in Blue
  Defiance to the Rebels.

And yet once more the bugle sang
  Above the stormy riot;
No shout upon the evening rang—
  There reigned a holy quiet.

The sad, slow stream its noiseless flood
  Poured over the glistening pebbles;   50
All silent now the Yankees stood,
  And silent stood the Rebels.

No unresponsive soul had heard
  That plaintive note's appealing,
So deeply "Home, Sweet Home" had stirred
  The hidden founts of feeling.

Or Blue, or Gray, the soldier sees,
  As by the wand of fairy,
The cottage 'neath the live-oak trees,
  The cabin by the prairie.   60

Or cold, or warm, his native skies
  Bend in their beauty o'er him;
Seen through the tear mist in his eyes,
  His loved ones stand before him.

As fades the iris after rain
  In April's tearful weather,
The vision vanished, as the strain
  And daylight died together.

But Memory, waked by Music's art,
  Expressed in simplest numbers,   70
Subdued the sternest Yankee's heart,
  Made light the Rebel's slumbers.

And fair the form of Music shines,
  That bright celestial creature,
Who still, 'mid war's embattled lines,
  Gave this one touch of Nature.
1863

THADDEUS OLIVER

ALL QUIET ALONG THE POTOMAC TONIGHT

"All quiet along the Potomac," they say,
  "Except now and then a stray picket
Is shot, as he walks on his beat to and fro,
  By a rifleman hid in the thicket.
'Tis nothing—a private or two now and then
  Will not count in the news of the battle;
Not an officer lost—only one of the men,
  Moaning out, all alone, the death-rattle."

All quiet along the Potomac tonight,
  Where the soldiers lie peacefully dreaming;
Their tents in the rays of the clear autumn
      moon,   11
  Or the light of the watch-fires, are gleaming.
A tremulous sigh as the gentle night-wind
  Through the forest-leaves softly is creeping;
While stars up above, with their glittering eyes,
  Keep guard, for the army is sleeping.

There's only the sound of the lone sentry's
      tread,
  As he tramps from the rock to the fountain,
And thinks of the two in the low trundlebed
  Far away in the cot on the mountain.   20
His musket falls slack; his face, dark and grim,
  Grows gentle with memories tender,
As he mutters a prayer for the children asleep,
  For their mother—may Heaven defend her!

The moon seems to shine just as brightly as
      then,
  That night, when the love yet unspoken
Leaped up to his lips—when low-murmured
      vows
  Were pledged to be ever unbroken.
Then drawing his sleeve roughly over his eyes,
  He dashes off tears that are welling,   80
And gathers his gun closer up to its place
  As if to keep down the heart-swelling.

He passes the fountain, the blasted pine tree,
    The footstep is lagging and weary;
Yet onward he goes, through the broad belt of
    light,
    Toward the shades of the forest so dreary.
Hark! was it the night-wind that rustled the
    leaves?
    Was it moonlight so wondrously flashing?
It looked like a rifle. . . "Ha! Mary, good-bye!"
    The red life-blood is ebbing and plashing.   40

All quiet along the Potomac tonight,
    No sound save the rush of the river;
While soft falls the dew on the face of the
    dead—
    The picket's off duty forever.
                                        1861

JAMES BARRON HOPE

Our Anglo-Saxon Tongue

Good is the Saxon speech! clear, short, and
    strong,
Its clean-cut words, fit both for prayer and
    song;
Good is this tongue for all the needs of life;
Good for sweet words with friend, or child, or
    wife.
Seax—short sword—and like a sword its sway
Hews out a path 'mid all the forms of speech,
For in itself it hath the power to teach
Itself, while many tongues slow fade away.

'Tis good for laws; for vows of youth and
    maid;
Good for the preacher; or shrewd folk in
    trade;   10
Good for sea-calls when loud the rush of
    spray;
Good for war-cries where men meet hilt to
    hilt,
And man's best blood like new-trod wine is
    spilt,—
Good for all times, and good for what thou
    wilt!

Dreamers

Fools laugh at dreamers, and the dreamers
    smile
In answer, if they any answer make:
They know that Saxon Alfred could not
    bake
The oaten cakes, but that he snatched his
    Isle
Back from the fierce and bloody-handed
    Dane.

And so, they leave the plodders to their
    gains—
Quit money-changing for the student's
    lamp,
And tune the harp to gain thereby some
    camp,
Where what they learn is worth a king-
    dom's crown;
They fashion bows and arrows to bring
    down   10
The mighty truths which sail the upper air;
To them the facts which make the fools
    despair
Become familiar, and a thousand things
Tell them the secrets they refuse to kings.

Under One Blanket

The sun went down in flame and smoke,
    The cold night passed without alarms,
And when the bitter morning broke
    Our men stood to their arms.

But not a foe in front was found
    After the long and stubborn fight.
The enemy had left the ground
    Where we had lain that night.

In hollows where the sun was lost
    Unthawed still lay the shining snow,   10
And on the rugged ground the frost
    In slender spears did grow.

Close to us, where our final rush
    Was made at closing in of day,
We saw, amid an awful hush,
    The rigid shapes of clay:

Things, which but yesterday had life,
    And answered to the trumpet's call,
Remained as victims of the strife,
    Clods of the Valley all!   20

Then, the grim detail marched away
    A grave from the hard soil to wrench
Wherein should sleep the Blue and Gray
    All in a ghastly trench!

A thicket of young pines arose,
    Midway upon that frosty ground;
A shelter from the winds and snows,
    And by its edge I found

Two stiffened forms, where they had died,
    As sculptured marble white and cold,   30
Lying together side by side
    Beneath one blanket's fold.

My heart already touched and sad
   The blanket down I gently drew
And saw a sturdy form, well clad
   From head to heel in Blue.

Beside him, gaunt from a many a fast,
   A pale and boyish "rebel" lay,
Free of all pangs of life, at last,
   In tattered suit of Gray.   40

There side by side those soldiers slept
   Each for the cause that he thought good,
And bowing down my head I wept
   Through human brotherhood.

Oh, sirs! it was a piteous thing
   To see how they had vainly tried
With strips of shirts, and bits of string
   To stay life's ebbing tide!

The story told itself aright;
   (Print scarce were plainer to the eye) 50
How they together in the night
   Had laid them down to die.

The story told itself, I say,
   How smitten by their wounds and cold
They'd nestled close, the Blue and Gray,
   Beneath one blanket's fold.

All their poor surgery could do
   They did to stop their wounds so deep,
Until at last the Gray and Blue
   Like comrades fell asleep.   60

We dug for them a generous grave,
   Under that somber thicket's lee,
And there we laid the sleeping brave
   To wait God's reveillé.

That grave by many a tear was graced
   From ragged heroes ranged around
As in one blanket they were placed
   In consecrated ground.

Aye! consecrated, without flaw,
   Because upon that bloody sod,   70
My soul uplifted stood and saw
   Where CHRIST had lately trod!

ABRAM JOSEPH RYAN

THE CONQUERED BANNER

Furl that Banner, for 'tis weary;
Round its staff 'tis drooping dreary;
   Furl it, fold it,—it is best;

For there's not a man to wave it,
And there's not a sword to save it,
And there's not one left to lave it
In the blood which heroes gave it;
And its foes now scorn and brave it;
   Furl it, hide it,—let it rest!

Take that Banner down! 'tis tattered;   10
Broken is its staff and shattered;
And the valiant hosts are scattered,
   Over whom it floated high.
Oh, 'tis hard for us to fold it,
Hard to think there's none to hold it,
Hard that those who once unrolled it
   Now must furl it with a sigh!

Furl that Banner—furl it sadly!
Once ten thousands hailed it gladly,
And ten thousands wildly, madly,   20
   Swore it should forever wave—
Swore that foeman's sword should never
Hearts like theirs entwined dissever,
Till that flag should float forever
   O'er their freedom or their grave!

Furl it! for the hands that grasped it,
And the hearts that fondly clasped it,
   Cold and dead are lying low;
And that Banner—it is trailing,
While around it sounds the wailing   30
   Of its people in their woe.

For, though conquered, they adore it—
Love the cold, dead hands that bore it,
Weep for those who fell before it,
Pardon those who trailed and tore it—
But oh, wildly they deplore it,
   Now who furl and fold it so!

Furl that Banner! True, 'tis gory,
Yet 'tis wreathed around with glory,
And 'twill live in song and story   40
   Though its folds are in the dust!
For its fame on brightest pages,
Penned by poets and by sages,
Shall go sounding down the ages—
   Furl its folds though now we must.

Furl that Banner, softly, slowly,
Treat it gently—it is holy,
   For it droops above the dead.
Touch it not—unfold it never,   49
Let it droop there, furled forever,—
   For its people's hopes are fled!

1865

HENRY TIMROD 1829-1867

Timrod was the first of three Southern poets who are linked by a similarity in their tragic lives and in their work. He belonged to a family of fighters and poets. He received a good education in a private school in Charleston, South Carolina, the place of his birth, and at seventeen entered the University of Georgia. Lack of funds cut short his attendance after two years, and he turned to law, but soon found himself unfit for that profession. For ten years he taught, and contributed to *Russell's Magazine* and *The Southern Literary Messenger.* Denied active service during the Civil War by his delicate physique, he engaged in journalism as correspondent and editor of South Carolina newspapers, rallying the Confederacy by his splendid battle lyrics. The war took the little property he had possessed, and the rest of his short life, spent in Columbia, South Carolina, was a losing fight against destitution and disease.

Timrod's poems were published in 1859, again in 1873, when they were edited by his friend Hayne, and also in a memorial edition, 1899. They fall into three groups: like Wordsworth he interpreted the world of nature with simplicity and restrained emotion; as a poet of love he did some of his best work; his war lyrics include his most notable verse.

Poems (memorial edition), with memoir and portrait, 1899. Criticism: G. A. Wauchope, *Henry Timrod: Man and Poet, a Critical Study,* 1915; "A Southern Poet," *Outlook* 68:107-8; Holliday.

I KNOW NOT WHY, BUT ALL THIS WEARY DAY

I know not why, but all this weary day,
Suggested by no definite grief or pain,
Sad fancies have been flitting through my brain;
Now it has been a vessel losing way,
Rounding a stormy headland; now a gray
Dull waste of clouds above a wintry main;
And then, a banner, drooping in the rain,
And meadows beaten into bloody clay.
Strolling at random with this shadowy woe
At heart, I chanced to wander hither! Lo!   10
A league of desolate marsh-land, with its lush,
Hot grasses in a noisome, tide-left bed,
And faint, warm airs that rustle in the hush,
Like whispers round the body of the dead.

MOST MEN KNOW LOVE BUT AS A PART OF LIFE

Most men know love but as a part of life;
They hide it in some corner of the breast,
Even from themselves; and only when they rest
In the brief pauses of that daily strife,
Wherewith the world might else be not so rife,
They draw it forth (as one draws forth a toy

To soothe some ardent, kiss-exacting boy)
And hold it up to sister, child, or wife.
Ah me! why may not love and life be one?
Why walk we thus alone, when by our side,   10
Love, like a visible God, might be our guide?
How would the marts grow noble! and the street,
Worn like a dungeon floor by weary feet,
Seem then a golden court-way of the Sun!

1859

CHARLESTON [1]

Calm as that second summer which precedes
    The first fall of the snow,
In the broad sunlight of heroic deeds,
    The city bides the foe.

As yet, behind their ramparts stern and proud,
    Her bolted thunders sleep,—
Dark Sumter, like a battlemented cloud,
    Looms o'er the solemn deep.

No Calpe [2] frowns from lofty cliff or scar
    To guard the holy strand;   10
But Moultrie holds in leash her dogs of war
    Above the level sand.

And down the dunes a thousand guns lie couched,
    Unseen, beside the flood,—
Like tigers in some Orient jungle crouched,
    That wait and watch for blood.

Meanwhile, through streets still echoing with trade,
    Walk grave and thoughtful men,
Whose hands may one day wield the patriot's blade
    As lightly as the pen.   20

And maidens, with such eyes as would grow dim
    Over a bleeding hound,
Seem each one to have caught the strength of him
    Whose sword she sadly bound.

Thus girt without and garrisoned at home,
    Day patient following day,
Old Charleston looks from roof and spire and dome,
    Across her tranquil bay.

[1] Timrod, "the laureate of the Confederacy," here voices the war feeling so strong in Charleston, where the first engagement of the Civil War took place at Fort Sumter, April, 1861. When he wrote the poem, both Sumter and Moultrie were in the hands of the Confederates.
[2] the ancient name for the rock of Gibraltar

Ships, through a hundred foes, from Saxon [1]
    lands
  And spicy Indian ports,   30
Bring Saxon steel and iron to her hands,
  And summer to her courts.

But still, along yon dim Atlantic line,
  The only hostile smoke
Creeps like a harmless mist above the brine,
  From some frail floating oak.

Shall the spring dawn, and she, still clad in
    smiles,
  And with an unscathed brow,
Rest in the strong arms of her palm-crowned
    isles,
  As fair and free as now?   40

We know not; in the temple of the Fates
  God has inscribed her doom;
And, all untroubled in her faith, she waits
  The triumph or the tomb.

1861-62?   1862

SPRING

Spring, with that nameless pathos in the air
Which dwells with all things fair,
Spring, with her golden suns and silver rain,
Is with us once again.

Out in the lonely woods the jasmine burns
Its fragrant lamps, and turns
Into a royal court with green festoons
The banks of dark lagoons.

In the deep heart of every forest tree
The blood is all aglee,   10
And there's a look about the leafless bowers
As if they dreamed of flowers.

Yet still on every side we trace the hand
Of winter in the land,
Save where the maple reddens on the lawn,
Flushed by the season's dawn;

Or where, like those strange semblances we find
That age to childhood bind,
The elm puts on, as if in Nature's scorn,
The brown of autumn corn.   20

As yet the turf is dark, although you know
That, not a span below,
A thousand germs are groping through the
    gloom,
And soon will burst their tomb.

Already, here and there, on frailest stems
Appear some azure gems,
Small as might deck, upon a gala day,
The forehead of a fay.

In gardens you may note amid the dearth
The crocus breaking earth;   30
And near the snowdrop's tender white and green,
The violet in its screen.

But many gleams and shadows need must pass
Along the budding grass,
And weeks go by, before the enamored South
Shall kiss the rose's mouth.

Still there's a sense of blossoms yet unborn
In the sweet airs of morn;
One almost looks to see the very street
Grow purple at his feet.   40

At times a fragrant breeze comes floating by,
And brings, you know not why,
A feeling as when eager crowds await
Before a palace gate

Some wondrous pageant; and you scarce would
    start,
If from a beech's heart,
A blue-eyed Dryad, [2] stepping forth, should
    say,
"Behold me! I am May!"

Ah! who would couple thoughts of war [3] and
    crime
With such a blessed time!   50
Who in the west wind's aromatic breath
Could hear the call of Death!

Yet not more surely shall the spring awake
The voice of wood and brake,
Than she shall rouse, for all her tranquil charms,
A million men to arms.

There shall be deeper hues upon her plains
Than all her sunlit rains,
And every gladdening influence around,
Can summon from the ground.   60

Oh! standing on this desecrated mold,
Methinks that I behold,
Lifting her bloody daisies up to God,
Spring kneeling on the sod,

And calling, with the voice of all her rills,
Upon the ancient hills

---

[1] British supplies came to the South in English ships.
[2] wood nymph
[3] the Civil War

To fall and crush the tyrants and the slaves
Who turn her meads to graves.
1862   *1862?*

THE COTTON BOLL

While I recline
At ease beneath
This immemorial pine,
Small sphere!
(By dusky fingers brought this morning here
And shown with boastful smiles),
I turn thy cloven sheath,
Through which the soft white fibers peer,
That, with their gossamer bands,
Unite, like love, the sea-divided lands,   10
And slowly, thread by thread,
Draw forth the folded strands,
Than which the trembling line,
By whose frail help yon startled spider fled
Down the tall spear-grass from his swinging
          bed,
Is scarce more fine;
And as the tangled skein
Unravels in my hands,
Betwixt me and the noonday light,   19
A veil seems lifted, and for miles and miles
The landscape broadens on my sight,
As, in the little boll, there lurked a spell
Like that which, in the ocean shell,
With mystic sound,
Breaks down the narrow walls that hem us
          round,
And turns some city lane
Into the restless main,
With all his capes and isles!

Yonder bird,
Which floats, as if at rest,   30
In those blue tracts above the thunder, where
No vapors cloud the stainless air,
And never sound is heard,
Unless at such rare time
When, from the City of the Blest,
Rings down some golden chime,
Sees not from his high place
So vast a cirque of summer space
As widens round me in one mighty field,
Which, rimmed by seas and sands,   40
Doth hail its earliest daylight in the beams
Of gray Atlantic dawns;
And, broad as realms made up of many lands,
Is lost afar
Behind the crimson hills and purple lawns
Of sunset, among plains which roll their streams
Against the Evening Star!
And lo!

To the remotest point of sight,
Although I gaze upon no waste of snow,   50
The endless field is white;
And the whole landscape glows,
For many a shining league away,
With such accumulated light
As Polar lands would flash beneath a tropic
          day!
Nor lack there (for the vision grows,
And the small charm within my hands—
More potent even than the fabled one,
Which oped whatever golden mystery
Lay hid in fairy wood or magic vale,   60
The curious ointment of the Arabian tale [1]—
Beyond all mortal sense
Doth stretch my sight's horizon, and I see,
Beneath its simple influence,
As if, with Uriel's [2] crown,
I stood in some great temple of the Sun,
And looked, as Uriel, down!)
Nor lack there pastures rich and fields all green
With all the common gifts of God,
For temperate airs and torrid sheen   70
Weave Edens of the sod;
Through lands which look one sea of billowy
          gold
Broad rivers wind their devious ways;
A hundred isles in their embraces fold
A hundred luminous bays;
And through yon purple haze
Vast mountains lift their plumed peaks cloud-
          crowned;
And, save where up their sides the plowman
          creeps,
An unhewn forest girds them grandly round,
In whose dark shades a future navy sleeps!
Ye Stars, which, though unseen, yet with me
          gaze   81
Upon this loveliest fragment of the earth!
Thou Sun, that kindlest all thy gentlest rays
Above it, as to light a favorite hearth!
Ye Clouds, that in your temples in the West
See nothing brighter than its humblest flowers!
And you, ye Winds, that on the ocean's breast
Are kissed to coolness ere ye reach its bowers!
Bear witness with me in my song of praise,
And tell the world that, since the world be-
          gan,   90
No fairer land hath fired a poet's lays,
Or given a home to man!

[1] In the story of the Blind Baba, Abdalla, the magic
     ointment if applied to the left eye caused one to
     behold all the treasures of the earth, but if ap-
     plied to the right eye destroyed the sight. Ab-
     dalla, doubting, applied it to both and lost both
     treasures and sight.
[2] One of the seven archangels mentioned in the *Books
     of Esdras* and by Milton; he is generally thought
     of as an angel of light.

But these are charms already widely blown!
His be the meed whose pencil's trace
Hath touched our very swamps with grace,
And round whose tuneful way
All Southern laurels bloom;
The Poet of "The Woodlands," [1] unto whom
Alike are known
The flute's low breathing and the trumpets'
    tone,   100
And the soft west wind's sighs;
But who shall utter all the debt,
O Land wherein all powers are met
That bind a people's heart,
The world doth owe thee at this day,
And which it never can repay,
Yet scarcely deigns to own!
Where sleeps the poet who shall fitly sing
The source wherefrom doth spring
That mighty commerce which, confined   110
To the mean channels of no selfish mart,
Goes out to every shore
Of this broad earth, and throngs the sea with
    ships
That bear no thunders; hushes hungry lips
In alien lands;
Joins with a delicate web remotest strands;
And gladdening rich and poor,
Doth gild Parisian domes,
Or feed the cottage-smoke of English homes,
And only bounds its blessings by mankind! 120
In offices like these, thy mission lies,
My Country! and it shall not end
As long as rain shall fall and heaven bend
In blue above thee; though thy foes be hard
And cruel as their weapons, it shall guard
Thy hearth-stones as a bulwark; make thee
    great
In white and bloodless state;
And haply, as the years increase—
Still working through its humbler reach
With that large wisdom which the ages
    teach—   130
Revive the half-dead dream of universal peace!
As men who labor in that mine
Of Cornwall, hollowed out beneath the bed
Of ocean, when a storm rolls overhead,
Hear the dull booming of the world of brine
Above them, and a mighty muffled roar
Of winds and waters, yet toil calmly on,
And split the rock, and pile the massive ore,
Or carve a niche, or shape the arched roof;
So I, as calmly, weave my woof   140
Of song, chanting the days to come,
Unsilenced, though the quiet summer air
Stirs with the bruit of battles, and each dawn
Wakes from its starry silence to the hum

[1] the home of William Gilmore Simms

Of many gathering armies. Still,
In that we sometimes hear,
Upon the Northern winds, the voice of woe
Not wholly drowned in triumph, though I know
The end must crown us, and a few brief years
Dry all our tears,   150
I may not sing too gladly. To Thy will
Resigned, O Lord! we cannot all forget
That there is much even Victory must regret.
And, therefore, not too long
From the great burthen of our country's wrong
Delay our just release!
And, if it may be, save
These sacred fields of peace
From stain of patriot or of hostile blood!
Oh, help us, Lord! to roll the crimson flood
Back on its course, and, while our banners
    wing   161
Northward, strike with us! till the Goth [2] shall
    cling
To his own blasted altar-stones, and crave
Mercy; and we shall grant it, and dictate
The lenient future of his fate
There, where some rotting ships and crumbling
    quays
Shall one day mark the Port which ruled the
    Western seas.

1861-65

AT MAGNOLIA CEMETERY [3]

Sleep sweetly in your humble graves,
    Sleep, martyrs of a fallen cause;
Though yet no marble column craves
    The pilgrim here to pause.

In seeds of laurel in the earth
    The blossom of your fame is blown,
And somewhere, waiting for its birth,
    The shaft is in the stone!

Meanwhile, behalf the tardy years   9
    Which keep in trust your storied tombs,
Behold! your sisters bring their tears,
    And these memorial blooms.

Small tributes! but your shades will smile
    More proudly on these wreaths today,
Than when some cannon-molded pile
    Shall overlook this bay.

Stoop, angels, hither from the skies!
    There is no holier spot of ground

[2] Timrod thought of the Northern soldiers as like the Goths and Vandals who came down upon Rome.
[3] This poem, written for Memorial Day, 1867, in honor of the Confederate soldiers buried in Magnolia Cemetery, Charleston, was Timrod's last work.

Than where defeated valor lies, 19
By mourning beauty crowned.
1867

PAUL HAMILTON HAYNE
1830-1886

Hayne, often called "the poet of the pine," was born in Charleston, South Carolina; he came of good old Southern stock, and was a nephew of Senator Hayne of South Carolina. After graduating from the University of South Carolina he devoted himself to literature. He edited in succession several periodicals and contributed to *The Southern Literary Messenger.* Volumes of his poems appeared from 1855 to 1882: separate titles are *Avolio and Other Poems,* 1857; *Legends and Lyrics,* 1872; *The Mountain of the Lovers,* 1875.

After serving through the Civil War on General Pickett's staff, Hayne retired, ruined in fortune and health, to "Copse Hill," a humble cottage in the pine barrens near Augusta, Georgia, where for fifteen years he struggled courageously to support himself and his family. Hamilton Mabie says: "He touched the two themes which lay deepest in his heart, love of nature and love of the personal ideals of the old South, with perfect sincerity, with deep tenderness, and with lyric sweetness." But it is as a poet of nature that he excelled.

Poems, complete ed. with biographical sketch by Margaret J. Preston, 1882. "Last of the Literary Cavaliers," *Ind.* 87:92, a short sketch by his son. "Some Unpublished Letters of Wilkie Collins," *Bookm.* 37:66-71; Holliday.

SHELLEY

Because they thought his doctrines were not just, 1
Mankind assumed for him the chastening rod,
And tyrants reared in pride, and strong in lust,
Wounded the noblest of the sons of God;
The heart's most cherished benefactions riven,
Basely they strove to humble and malign
A soul whose charities were wide as heaven,
Whose *deeds,* if not his *doctrines,* were divine;
And in the name of Him, whose sunshine warms
The evil as the righteous, deemed it good 10
To wreak their bigotry's relentless storms
On one whose nature was not understood.
Ah, well! God's ways are wondrous; it may be
His seal hath not been set to man's decree.
1857

ODE TO SLEEP

Beyond the sunset and the amber sea
To the lone depths of ether, cold and bare,

1 Percy Bysshe Shelley, 1792-1822, was criticized for his extreme political and social views.

Thy influence, soul of all tranquillity,
Hallows the earth and awes the reverent air;
Yon laughing rivulet quells its silvery tune;
The pines, like priestly watchers tall and grim,
Stand mute against the pensive twilight dim,
Breathless to hail the advent of the moon;
From the white beach the ocean falls away
Coyly, and with a thrill; the sea-birds dart 10
Ghostlike from out the distance, and depart
With a gray fleetness, moaning the dead day;
The wings of Silence, overfolding space,
Droop with dusk grandeur from the heavenly steep,
And through the stillness gleams thy starry face,—
Serenest Angel—Sleep!

Come! woo me here, amid these flowery charms,
Breathe on my eyelids; press thy odorous lips
Close to mine own, enwreathe me in thine arms,
And cloud my spirit with thy sweet eclipse; 20
No dreams! no dreams! keep back the motley throng,—
For such are girded round with ghastly might,
And sing low burdens of despondent song,
Decked in the mockery of a lost delight;
I ask oblivion's balsam! the mute peace
Toned to still breathings, and the gentlest sighs;
Not music woven of rarest harmonies
Could yield me such elysium of release:
The tones of earth are weariness,—not only
'Mid the loud mart, and in the walks of trade, 30
But where the mountain Genius broodeth lonely,
In the cool pulsing of the sylvan shade;
Then bear me far into thy noiseless land;
Surround me with thy silence, deep on deep,
Until serene I stand
Close by a duskier country, and more grand,
Mysterious solitude, than thine, O Sleep!

As he whose veins a feverous frenzy burns,
Whose life-blood withers in the fiery drouth,
Feebly and with a languid longing turns
To the spring breezes gathering from the South, 41
So, feebly and with languid longing, I
Turn to thy wishes nepenthe, 2 and implore
The golden dimness, the purpureal gloom
Which haunt thy poppied realm, and make the shore

2 originally an Egyptian drug—possibly opium: poetically, anything that causes sleep

Of thy dominion balmy with all bloom:
In the clear gulfs of thy serene profound,
Worn passions sink to quiet, sorrows pause,
　Suddenly fainting to still-breathèd rest;
Thou own'st a magical atmosphere, which
　　awes　　　　　　　　　　　　　　　50
　　The memories seething in the turbulent
　　breast;
Which, muffling up the sharpness of all sound
Of mortal lamentations,—solely bears
　The silvery minor toning of our woe,
　All mellowed to harmonious underflow,
Soft as the sad farewells of dying years,—
　　Lulling as sunset showers that veil the west,
　　And sweet as Love's last tears
When over-welling hearts do mutely weep:
　O griefs! O wailings! your tempestuous mad-
　　ness,　　　　　　　　　　　　　　　60
　Merged in a regal quietude of sadness,
Wins a strange glory by the streams of sleep!

Then woo me here, amid these flowery charms,
　Breathe on my eyelids, press thy odorous lips
Close to mine own,—enfold me in thine arms,
　And cloud my spirit with thy sweet eclipse;
And while from waning depth to depth I fall,
Down lapsing [1] to the utmost depths of all,
　Till wan forgetfulness obscurely stealing,
Creeps like an incantation on the soul,
And o'er the slow ebb of my conscious life
　Dies the thin flush of the last conscious feel-
　　ing,　　　　　　　　　　　　　　　72
　　And like abortive thunder, the dull roll
　Of sullen passions ebbs far, far away,—
O Angel! loose the chords which cling to strife,
Sever the gossamer bondage of my breath,
　And let me pass, gently as winds in May,
　　From the dim realm which owns thy
　　shadowy sway,
To thy diviner sleep, O sacred Death!
　　　　　　　　　　　　　　　　　1857

THE MOCKING-BIRDS

Oh, all day long they flood with song
　The forest shades, the fields of light;
Heaven's heart is stilled and strangely thrilled
　By ecstasies of lyric might;
From flower-crowned nooks of splendid dyes,
　Lone dells a shadowy quiet girds;
Far echoes, wakening, gently rise,
And o'er the woodland track send back
　Soft answers to the mocking-birds.

The winds, in awe, no gusty flaw　　　　10
　Dare breathe in rhythmic Beauty's face;

[1] gliding

Nearer the pale-gold cloudlets draw
　Above a charmed, melodious place:
Entrancèd Nature listening knows
　No music set to mortal words,
Nor nightingales that woo the rose,
　Can vie with these deep harmonies
　　Poured from the minstrel mocking-birds.

But, vaguely seen through gulfs of green,
　We glimpse the plumed and choral throng—
Sole poets born whose instincts scorn　　21
　To do Song's lowliest utterance wrong:
Whate'er they sing, a sylvan art,
　On each wild, wood-born note conferred,
Guides the hot brain and hurtling heart.
Oh magical flame, whence pulsing came
　This passion of the mocking-bird?

Aye—pause and hark—be still, and mark
　What countless grades of voice and tone
From bosk and tree, from strand and sea,
　These small, winged genii make their
　　own:　　　　　　　　　　　　　　31
Fine lyric memories live again,
　From tuneful burial disinterred,
To magnify the fiery strain
Which quivering trills and smites the hills
　With rapture of the mocking-bird.

Aye—pause and hark—be still, and mark
　How downward borne from Song's high clime
(No loftier haunts the English lark)
　They revel, each a jocund mime: [2]　　40
Their glad sides shake in bush and brake;
　And farm-girls, bowed o'er cream and curd,
Glance up to smile, and think the while
Of all blithe things that flit on wings
　None match the jovial mocking-bird.

When fun protrudes gay interludes
　Of blissful, glorious unrestraint,
They run, all wild with motley moods,
　Thro' Mirth's rare gamut, sly and quaint:
Humors grotesque and arabesque　　　　50
　Flash up from spirits brightly stirred;
And even the pedant at his desk,
Feeling in turn his spirit burn,
　Laughs with the loudest mocking-bird.

Oh, all day long the world with song
　Is flooded, till the twilight dim;
What time its whole mysterious soul
　Seems rippling to the conscious brim:
Arcadian Eve through tranquil skies
　Pastures her stars in radiant herds;　　60
And still the unwearied echoes rise,

[2] mimic

And down a silvery track send back
  Fond greeting to the mocking-birds.

At last, fair boon, the summer moon,
  Beyond the hazed horizon shines;
Ah, soon through night they wing their flight
  To coverts of Aeolian pines:
A tremulous hush—then sweet and grand,
  From depths the dense, fair foliage girds,
Their love notes fill the enchanted land; 70
Through leaf-wrought bars they storm the stars,
  These love songs of the mocking-birds.

VICKSBURG [1]

For sixty days and upwards,
  A storm of shell and shot
Rained round us in a flaming shower,
  But still we faltered not.
"If the noble city perish,"
  Our grand young leader said,
"Let the only walls the foe shall scale
  Be ramparts of the dead!"

For sixty days and upwards,
  The eye of heaven waxed dim; 10
And even throughout God's holy morn,
  O'er Christian prayer and hymn,
Arose a hissing tumult,
  As if the fiends in air
Strove to engulf the voice of faith
  In the shrieks of their despair.

There was wailing in the houses,
  There was trembling on the marts,
While the tempest raged and thundered,
  'Mid the silent thrill of hearts; 20
But the Lord, our shield, was with us,
  And ere a month had sped,
Our very women walked the streets
  With scarce one throb of dread.

And the little children gamboled,
  Their faces purely raised,
Just for a wondering moment,
  As the huge bombs whirled and blazed;
Then turned with silvery laughter
  To the sports which children love, 30
Thrice-mailed in the sweet, instinctive
    thought
  That the good God watched above.

Yet the hailing bolts fell faster,
  From scores of flame-clad ships,

[1] Vicksburg was besieged from May 18 until July 4, 1863, and then fell into the hands of the Union forces.

And about us, denser, darker,
  Grew the conflict's wild eclipse,
Till a solid cloud closed o'er us,
  Like a type of doom and ire,
Whence shot a thousand quivering tongues
  Of forked and vengeful fire. 40

But the unseen hands of angels
  Those death-shafts warned aside,
And the dove of heavenly mercy
  Ruled o'er the battle tide;
In the houses ceased the wailing,
  And through the war-scarred marts
The people strode, with step of hope,
  To the music in their hearts.

ASPECTS OF THE PINES

Tall, somber, grim, against the morning sky
  They rise, scarce touched by melancholy airs,
Which stir the fadeless foliage dreamfully,
  As if from realms of mystical despairs.

Tall, somber, grim, they stand with dusky
    gleams
  Brightening to gold within the woodland's
    core,
Beneath the gracious noontide's tranquil
    beams,—
  But the weird winds of morning sigh no more.

A stillness, strange, divine, ineffable,
  Broods round and o'er them in the wind's sur-
    cease, 10
And on each tinted copse and shimmering dell
  Rests the mute rapture of deep-hearted peace.

Last, sunset comes—the solemn joy and might
  Borne from the west when cloudless day de-
    clines—
Low, flute-like breezes sweep the waves of light,
  And, lifting dark green tresses of the pines,

Till every lock is luminous—gently float,
  Fraught with hale odors up the heavens afar,
To faint when twilight on her virginal throat
  Wears for a gem the tremulous vesper
    star. 20

THE ROSE AND THORN

She's loveliest of the festal throng
  In delicate form and Grecian face,—
A beautiful, incarnate song,
  A marvel of harmonious grace,
And yet I know the truth I speak:
  From those gay groups she stands apart,

A rose upon her tender cheek,
  A thorn within her heart.

Though bright her eyes' bewildering gleams,
  Fair tremulous lips and shining hair,   10
A something born of mournful dreams
  Breathes round her sad enchanted air;
No blithesome thoughts at hide and seek
  From out her dimples smiling start;
If still the rose be on her cheek,
  A thorn is in her heart.

Young lover, tossed 'twixt hope and fear,
  Your whispered vow and yearning eyes
Yon marble Clytie [1] pillared near
  Could move as soon to soft replies;   20
Or, if she thrill at words you speak,
  Love's memory prompts the sudden start;
The rose has paled upon her cheek,
  The thorn has pierced her heart.

THE PINE'S MYSTERY

Listen! the somber foliage of the Pine
  A swart Gitana [2] of the woodland trees,
Is answering what we may but half divine,
  To those soft whispers of the twilight breeze!

Passion and mystery murmur through the
    leaves,
  Passion and mystery, touched by deathless
    pain,
Whose monotone of long, low anguish grieves
  For something lost that shall not live again!

A LITTLE WHILE I FAIN WOULD
LINGER YET [3]

A little while (my life is almost set!)
  I fain would pause along the downward way,
  Musing an hour in this sad sunset-ray,
While, Sweet! our eyes with tender tears are
    wet:
A little hour I fain would linger yet.

A little while I fain would linger yet,
  All for love's sake, for love that cannot tire;
  Though fervid youth be dead, with youth's
    desire,
And hope has faded to a vague regret,
A little while I fain would linger yet.   10

A little while I fain would linger here:

[1] a nymph loved by Apollo
[2] gypsy maiden
[3] This and the following poem were written shortly before the death of Hayne.

Behold! who knows what strange, mysterious
    bars
  'Twixt souls that love may rise in other
    stars?
Nor can love deem the face of death is fair:
A little while I still would linger here.

A little while I yearn to hold thee fast,
  Hand locked in hand, and loyal heart to
    heart;
  (O pitying Christ! those woeful words, *"We
    part!"*)
So ere the darkness fall, the light be past,
A little while I fain would hold thee fast.

A little while, when night and twilight
    meet: 21
  Behind, our broken years! before, the deep
  Weird wonder of the last unfathomed sleep,—
A little while I still would clasp thee Sweet;
A little while, when night and twilight meet.

A little while I fain would linger here;
  Behold! who knows what soul-dividing bars
  Earth's faithful loves may part in other
    stars?
Nor can love deem the face of death is fair:
A little while I still would linger here.   30

IN HARBOR

I think it is over, over,
  I think it is over at last:
Voices of foeman and lover,
  The sweet and the bitter have passed:
Life, like a tempest of ocean
  Hath outblown its ultimate blast:
There's but a faint sobbing seaward
While the calm of the tide deepens leeward,
And behold! like the welcoming quiver   9
Of heart-pulses throbbed through the river,
  Those lights in the harbor at last,
  The heavenly harbor at last!

I feel it is over! over!
  For the winds and the waters surcease;
Ah, few were the days of the rover
  That smiled in the beauty of peace!
And distant and dim was the omen
  That hinted redress or release!
From the ravage of life, and its riot,
What marvel I yearn for the quiet   20
  Which bides in the harbor at last,—
For the lights, with their welcoming quiver
That throbs through the sanctified river,
  Which girdles the harbor at last,
  This heavenly harbor at last?

I *know* it is over, over,
  I know it is over at last!
Down sail! the sheathed anchor uncover,
  For the stress of the voyage has passed:
Life, like a tempest of ocean   30
  Hath outbreathed its ultimate blast:

There's but a faint sobbing to seaward,
  While the calm of the tide deepens leaward;
And behold! like the welcoming quiver
  Of heart-pulses throbbed through the river,
Those lights in the harbor at last,
  The heavenly harbor at last!

FROM THE CIVIL WAR TO THE
END OF THE CENTURY

THE thirty-five years between 1865 and 1900 produced in the United States a greater amount of writing than the previous two and a half centuries. The tremendous growth of these years in population, native and immigrant, the increase in wealth following the push westward to the Pacific, and the development of eastern manufactures to meet the demands of a richer and more thickly settled America combined to give both desire and means for literary expression. Newspapers and magazines grew apace; great numbers of schools and colleges sprang up; the popular imagination was stirred by life upon the advancing border; the scientific discoveries of the middle of the century were already quickening thought and enlarging its borders. All these facts made for the growth of an extensive and many-sided literature.

During this period regional writings developed; "local color" came out of South, East, and West—Harris, Miss Wilkins, Bret Harte may stand as examples. A new romance came into being from the life of ranch and mine and the Pacific seaboard, a romance growing directly out of the conditions of American life, and founded upon a realism quite in line with the spread of scientific consciousness. This mingling of the real and the romantic is found even in the growing body of "nature essays" as in seen in the writings of Muir and Burroughs.

During these years the influence of Whitman was strengthening. His inroads upon existing literary forms and vogues did not produce wide-spread results before 1900; but his worship of "the man on the street" stimulated the literary imagination from the first: the continent, it seemed, might be conquered by and for a truly democratic population, and the abstract equality and brotherhood of man implied in the Declaration of Independence and the Revolution might be realized. Despite Whitman's rough and raucous utterance there was in his view of American life a largeness that approached majesty and began to give color to the writings of the period. Gradually through these years, American literature was becoming recognizable as such, not by virtue of the local color in Southern streams and Western hills, but by virtue of a national tone that proclaimed a distinctive way of thought.

WALT WHITMAN 1819-1892

Contemporary with the New England poets—for he was born in the same year with Lowell and died in the year after Lowell's death—Whitman stands as much apart from them as if he belonged to a different world of art and of thought. His ancestry was partly Dutch, partly English Quaker; his father was a farmer-carpenter and building contractor at Westhills, Long Island, where his son was born. Whitman received some education in the public schools of Brooklyn and New York, and learned the trades of carpentry and typesetting; but though at times he followed these, his life was more or less wandering and experimental. His most significant employment was the editing of newspapers in Brooklyn and New Orleans. For these papers he wrote some conventional verse. *Leaves of Grass* appeared in 1855, but because it abandoned traditional poetic forms attracted little favorable attention except from Emerson. In 1862 Whitman became a nurse in the Union Army and remained in this service until after the close of the war. Afterwards he was made clerk in the Treasury Department, where he worked until he suffered a stroke of paralysis in 1873. Aside from *Leaves of Grass,* which appeared in eleven editions during his life, his chief works are *Drum Taps,* 1865; *Specimen Days and Collect,* prose, 1882; *Good-bye, My Fancy,* 1891.

Since the publication of *Leaves of Grass,* Whitman has been the most discussed American poet both at home and abroad. His poems, daring in their rejection of established poetic form, were—largely for that very reason—hailed by Europeans as a product that revealed, at length, the real American art. For that same reason, too, he was largely repudiated at home. He exalted the common people, yet he was received joyfully only by the sophisticated and enlightened.

Whitman's poetry and formal poetry are at one in spirit and substance. Both come from and touch the emotions; both are full of image and picture; both suggest rather than explain the idea. The body is the same. It is the garb that differs. In form and method of expression Whitman has been followed by poets of genuine worth; he has also been copied by many poetasters without message or imagination, or patience to master the technique of an art. His rather confused utterances concerning democracy may fade in importance, but his services to poetry remain: he awakened it from a too complacent faith in its conventional forms, and he showed the limitless possibilities of the commonplace in arousing emotions.

Even respecting democracy, Whitman's sober opinions were less visionary than may commonly be supposed. He knew that democracy could be attained only through the slow development of social forces. In "Democratic Vistas" (1871) he says:

"The purpose of democracy—supplanting old belief in the necessary absoluteness of establish'd dynastic rulership, temporal, ecclesiastical, and scholastic, as furnishing the only security against chaos, crime, and ignorance—is, through many transmigrations, and amid endless ridicules, arguments, and ostensible failures, to illustrate, at all hazards, this doctrine or theory that man, properly train'd in sanest, highest freedom, may and must become a law, and series of laws, unto himself . . ."

(And:)

"In short, and to sum up, America, betaking herself to formative action (as it is about time for more solid achievement, and less windy promise,) must, for her purposes, cease to recognize a theory of character grown of feudal aristocracies, or form'd by merely literary standards, or from any ultramarine, full-dress formulas of culture, polish, caste, etc., and must sternly promulgate her own new standard, yet old enough, and accepting the old, the perennial elements, and combining them into groups, unities, appropriate to the modern, the democratic, the West, and to the practical occasions and needs of our own cities, and of the agricultural regions."

Biography and criticism: The Whitman bibliography is enormous. The following items are standard, and some are of recent date: J. Burroughs, *Whitman: a Study,* 1896; B. Perry, *W. Whitman: His Life and Works,* (AML) 1906; G. R. Carpenter, *W. Whitman,* (EML) 1909; J. Bailey (EML ns) 1925; I. H. Platt, (BB) 1904; E. Hubbard, (LJ) 1896; H. Traubel, *With Walt Whitman in Camden,* 3 vols. 1906-1914; E. Holloway, *Whitman, an Interpretation in Narrative,* 1926; C. Rogers, *The Magnificent Idler,* (imaginative, based on fact) 1926; Sherman; More (Shel. 4); C. E. Stedman, "Walt Whitman," *Scrib. M.* (now *Cent.*) 21:47-64; same, *Poets of America,* 1885; G. Bradford, "Portraits of American Authors," *Bookm.* 42: 533-48; W. R. Thayer, "Personal Recollections of Walt Whitman," *Scrib. M.* 65:674-87; W. B. Cairns, "Walt Whitman," *Yale R.* ns 8:737-54; N. Foerster, "Whitman and the Cult of Confusion," *No. Am.* 213:799-812.

From SONG OF MYSELF

I

I celebrate myself, and sing myself,
And what I assume you shall assume,
For every atom belonging to me as good belongs
    to you.

I loafe and invite my soul,
I lean and loafe at my ease observing a spear of
    summer grass.

My tongue, every atom of my blood, form'd
    from this soil, this air,
Born here of parents born here from parents
    the same, and their parents the same,
Hoping to cease not till death.

Creeds and schools in abeyance,
Retiring back a while sufficed at what they are,
    but never forgotten,
I harbor for good or bad, I permit to speak at
    every hazard,
Nature without check with original energy.
1855

From *LEAVES OF GRASS*

CROSSING BROOKLYN FERRY

1

Flood-tide below me! I see you face to face!
Clouds of the west—sun there half an hour
    high—I see you also face to face.

Crowds of men and women attired in the usual
    costumes, how curious you are to me!
On the ferry-boats the hundreds and hundreds
    that cross, returning home, are more
    curious to me than you suppose,
And you that shall cross from shore to shore
    years hence are more to me, and more
    in my meditations, than you might sup-
    pose.

2

The impalpable sustenance of me from all
    things at all hours of the day,
The simple, compact, well-join'd scheme, my-
    self disintegrated, every one disinte-
    grated yet part of the scheme,
The similitudes of the past and those of the
    future,
The glories strung like beads on my smallest
    sights and hearings, on the walk in the
    street and the passage over the river,
The current rushing so swiftly and swimming
    with me far away,   10
The others that are to follow me, the ties be-
    tween me and them,
The certainty of others, the life, love, sight,
    hearing of others.

Others will enter the gates of the ferry and
    cross from shore to shore,
Others will watch the run of the flood-tide,
Others will see the shipping of Manhattan north
    and west, and the heights of Brooklyn
    to the south and east,
Others will see the islands large and small;
Fifty years hence, others will see them as they
    cross, the sun half an hour high,
A hundred years hence, or ever so many hun-
    dred years hence, others will see them,

Will enjoy the sunset, the pouring-in of the
    flood-tide, the falling-back to the sea of
    the ebb-tide.

3

It avails not, time nor place—distance avails
    not,   20
I am with you, you men and women of a gen-
    eration, or ever so many generations
    hence,
Just as you feel when you look on the river
    and sky, so I felt,
Just as any of you is one of a living crowd, I
    was one of a crowd,
Just as you are refresh'd by the gladness of
    the river and the bright flow, I was re-
    fresh'd,
Just as you stand and lean on the rail, yet hurry
    with the swift current, I stood yet was
    hurried,
Just as you look on the numberless masts of
    ships and the thick-stemm'd pipes of
    steamboats, I look'd.
I too many and many a time cross'd the river
    of old,
Watched the Twelfth-month [1] sea-gulls, saw
    them high in the air floating with motion-
    less wings, oscillating their bodies,
Saw how the glistening yellow lit up parts of
    their bodies and left the rest in strong
    shadow,
Saw the slow-wheeling circles and the gradual
    edging toward the south,   30
Saw the reflection of the summer sky in the
    water,
Had my eyes dazzled by the shimmering track
    of beams,
Look'd at the fine centrifugal spokes of light
    round the shape of my head in the sunlit
    water,
Look'd on the haze on the hills southward and
    south-westward,
Look'd on the vapor as it flew in fleeces tinged
    with violet,
Look'd toward the lower bay to notice the ves-
    sels arriving,
Saw their approach, saw aboard those that were
    near me,
Saw the white sails of schooners and sloops,
    saw the ships at anchor,
The sailors at work in the rigging or out astride
    the spars,
The round masts, the swinging motion of the
    hulls, the slender serpentine pennants,

---

[1] December in Quaker terminology: cf. "Ninth-month
midnight" l. 3, p. 681 and "Fifth-month grass,"
l. 24, p. 682, in "Out of the Cradle Endlessly
Rocking."

The large and small steamers in motion, the
     pilots in their pilot-houses,   41
The white wake left by the passage, the quick
     tremulous whirl of the wheels,
The flags of all nations, the falling of them at
     sunset,
The scallop-edged waves in the twilight, the
     ladled cups, the frolicsome crests and
     glistening,
The stretch afar growing dimmer and dimmer,
     the gray walls of the granite storehouses
     by the docks,
On the river the shadowy group, the big steam-
     tug closely flank'd on each side by the
     barges, the hay-boat, the belated lighter,
On the neighboring shore the fires from the
     foundry chimneys burning high and glar-
     ingly into the night,
Casting their flicker of black contrasted with
     wild red and yellow light over the tops of
     houses, and down into the clefts of
     streets.

4

These and all else were to me the same as they
     are to you,
I loved well those cities, loved well the stately
     and rapid river,   50
The men and women I saw were all near to me,
Others the same—others who look back on me
     because I look'd forward to them,
(The time will come, though I stop here today
     and tonight.)

5

What is it then between us?
What is the count of the scores or hundreds
     of years between us?

Whatever it is, it avails not—distance avails
     not, and place avails not,
I too lived, Brooklyn of ample hills was mine,
I too walk'd the streets of Manhattan island,
     and bathed in the waters around it,
I too felt the curious abrupt questionings stir
     within me,
In the day among crowds of people sometimes
     they came upon me,   60
In my walks home late at night or as I lay
     in my bed they came upon me,
I too had been struck from the float forever
     held in solution,
I too had receiv'd identity by my body,
That I was I knew was of my body, and what
     I should be I knew I should be of my
     body.

6

It is not upon you alone the dark patches fall,
The dark threw its patches down upon me also,
The best I had done seem'd to me blank and
     suspicious,
My great thoughts as I supposed them, were
     they not in reality meager?
Nor is it you alone who know what it is to be
     evil,
I am he who knew what it was to be evil,   70
I too knitted the old knot of contrariety,
Blabb'd, blush'd, resented, lied, stole, grudg'd,
Had guile, anger, lust, hot wishes I dared not
     speak,
Was wayward, vain, greedy, shallow, sly, cow-
     ardly, malignant,
The wolf, the snake, the hog, not wanting in me,
The cheating look, the frivolous word, the adul-
     terous wish, not wanting,
Refusals, hates, postponements, meanness, lazi-
     ness, none of these wanting,
Was one with the rest, the days and haps of the
     rest,
Was call'd by my nighest name by clear loud
     voices of young men as they saw me
     approaching or passing,
Felt their arms on my neck as I stood, or the
     negligent leaning of their flesh against
     me as I sat,   80
Saw many I loved in the street or ferry-boat or
     public assembly, yet never told them a
     word,
Lived the same life with the rest, the same old
     laughing, gnawing, sleeping,
Play'd the part that still looks back on the
     actor or actress,
The same old role, the role that is what we
     make it, as great as we like,
Or as small as we like, or both great and small.

7

Closer yet I approach you,
What thought you have of me now, I had as
     much of you—I laid in my stores in ad-
     vance,
I consider'd long and seriously of you before
     you were born.

Who was to know what should come home to
     me?
Who knows but I am enjoying this?   90
Who knows, for all the distance, but I am as
     good as looking at you now, for all you
     cannot see me?

8

Ah, what can ever be more stately and admirable to me than mast-hemm'd Manhattan?
River and sunset and scallop-edg'd waves of flood-tide?
The sea-gulls oscillating their bodies, the hay-boat in the twilight, and the belated lighter?

What gods can exceed these that clasp me by the hand, and with voices I love call me promptly and loudly by my nighest name as I approach?
What is more subtle than this which ties me to the woman or man that looks in my face?
Which fuses me into you now, and pours my meaning into you?

We understand then do we not?
What I promis'd without mentioning it, have you not accepted?
What the study could not teach—what the preaching could not accomplish is accomplish'd, is it not?   100

9

Flow on, river! flow with the flood-tide, and ebb with the ebb-tide!
Frolic on, crested and scallop-edg'd waves!
Gorgeous clouds of the sunset! drench with your splendor me, or the men and women generations after me!
Cross from shore to shore, countless crowds of passengers!
Stand up, tall masts of Mannahatta! stand up, beautiful hills of Brooklyn!
Throb, baffled and curious brain! throw out questions and answers!
Suspend here and everywhere, eternal float of solution!
Gaze, loving and thirsting eyes, in the house or street or public assembly!
Sound out, voices of young men! loudly and musically call me by my nighest name!
Live, old life! play the part that looks back on the actor or actress!   110
Play the old role, the role that is great or small according as one makes it!
Consider, you who peruse me, whether I may not in unknown ways be looking upon you;
Be firm, rail over the river, to support those who lean idly, yet haste with the hasting current;

Fly on, sea-birds! fly sideways, or wheel in large circles high in the air;
Receive the summer sky, you water, and faithfully hold it till all downcast eyes have time to take it from you!
Diverge, fine spokes of light, from the shape of my head, or any one's head, in the sunlit water!
Come on, ships from the lower bay! pass up or down, white-sail'd schooners, sloops, lighters!
Flaunt away, flags of all nations! be duly lower'd at sunset!
Burn high your fires, foundry chimneys! cast black shadows at nightfall! cast red and yellow light over the tops of the houses!
Appearances, now or henceforth, indicate what you are,   120
You necessary film, continue to envelop the soul,
About my body for me, and your body for you, be hung our divinest aromas,
Thrice, cities—bring your freight, bring your shows, ample and sufficient rivers,
Expand, being than which none else is perhaps more spiritual,
Keep your places, objects than which none else is more lasting.

You have waited, you always wait, you dumb, beautiful ministers,
We receive you with free sense at last, and are insatiate henceforward,
Not you any more shall be able to foil us, or withhold yourselves from us,
We use you, and do not cast you aside—we plant you permanently within us,
We fathom you not—we love you—there is perfection in you also,   130
You furnish your parts toward eternity,
Great or small, you furnish your parts toward the soul.

1856

OUT OF THE CRADLE ENDLESSLY ROCKING

Out of the cradle endlessly rocking,
Out of the mocking-bird's throat, the musical shuttle,
Out of the Ninth-month midnight,
Over the sterile sands and the fields beyond, where the child leaving his bed wander'd alone, bareheaded, barefoot,
Down from the shower'd halo,
Up from the mystic play of shadows twining and twisting as if they were alive,

Out from the patches of briers and black-
     berries,
From the memories of the bird that chanted
     to me,
From your memories sad brother, from the fit-
     ful risings and fallings I heard,
From under that yellow half-moon late-risen
     and swollen as if with tears,   10
From those beginning notes of yearning and
     love there in the mist,
From the thousand responses of my heart never
     to cease,
From the myriad thence-arous'd words,
From the word stronger and more delicious than
     any,
From such as now they start the scene revisiting,
As a flock, twittering, rising, or overhead pass-
     ing,
Borne hither, ere all eludes me, hurriedly,
A man, yet by these tears a little boy again,
Throwing myself on the sand, confronting the
     waves,
I, chanter of pains and joys, uniter of here and
     hereafter,   20
Taking all hints to use them, but swiftly leap-
     ing beyond them,
A reminiscence sing.

Once Paumanok, [1]
When the lilac-scent was in the air and Fifth-
     month grass was growing,
Up this seashore in some briers,
Two feather'd guests from Alabama, two to-
     gether,
And their nest, and four light-green eggs spotted
     with brown,
And every day the he-bird to and fro near at
     hand,
And every day the she-bird crouch'd on her
     nest, silent, with bright eyes,
And every day I, a curious boy, never too close,
     never disturbing them,   30
Cautiously peering, absorbing, translating.

Shine! shine! shine!
Pour down your warmth, great sun!
While we bask, we two together.

Two together!
Winds blow south, or winds blow north,
Day come white, or night come black,
Home, or rivers and mountains from home,
Singing all time, minding no time,
While we two keep together.   40

[1] The Indian name for Long Island; Whitman used it
     at first as a pseudonym.

Till of a sudden,
May-be kill'd, unknown to her mate,
One forenoon the she-bird crouch'd not on the
     nest,
Nor return'd that afternoon, nor the next,
Nor ever appear'd again.

And thenceforward all summer in the sound of
     the sea,
And at night under the full of the moon in
     calmer weather,
Over the hoarse surging of the sea,
Or flitting from brier to brier by day,
I saw, or heard at intervals the remaining one,
     the he-bird,   50
The solitary guest from Alabama.

Blow! blow! blow!
Blow up sea-winds along Paumanok's shore;
I wait and I wait till you blow my mate to me.

Yes, when the stars glisten'd,
All night long on the prong of a moss-scallop'd
     stake,
Down almost amid the slapping waves,
Sat the lone singer wonderful causing tears.

He call'd on his mate,
He pour'd forth the meanings which I of all
     men know.   60

Yes my brother I know,
The rest might not, but I have treasur'd every
     note,
For more than once dimly down to the beach
     gliding,
Silent, avoiding the moonbeams, blending my-
     self with the shadows,
Recalling now the obscure shapes, the echoes,
     the sounds and sights after their sorts,
The white arms out in the breakers tirelessly
     tossing,
I, with bare feet, a child, the wind wafting my
     hair,
Listen'd long and long.

Listen'd to keep, to sing, now translating the
     notes,
Following you my brother.   70

Soothe! soothe! soothe!
Close on its wave soothes the wave behind,
And again another behind embracing and lap-
     ping, every one close,
But my love soothes not me, not me.

Low hangs the moon, it rose late,
It is lagging—O I think it is heavy with love,
    with love.

O madly the sea pushes upon the land,
With love, with love.

O night! do I not see my love fluttering out
    among the breakers?
What is that little black thing I see there in
    the white?   80

Loud! loud! loud!
Loud I call to you, my love!
High and clear I shoot my voice over the waves,
Surely you must know who is here, is here,
You must know who I am, my love.

Low-hanging moon!
What is that dusky spot in your brown yellow?
O it is the shape, the shape of my mate!
O moon do not keep her from me any longer.

Land! land! O land!   90
Whichever way I turn, O I think you could give
    me my mate back again if you only
    would,
For I am almost sure I see her dimly whichever
    way I look.

O rising stars!
Perhaps the one I want so much will rise, will
    rise with some of you.

O throat! O trembling throat!
Sound clearer through the atmosphere!
Pierce the woods, the earth,
Somewhere listening to catch you must be the
    one I want.

Shake out carols!
Solitary here, the night's carols!   100
Carols of lonesome love! death's.carols!
Carols under that lagging, yellow, waning moon!
O under that moon where she droops almost
    down into the sea!
O reckless despairing carols.

But soft! sink low!
Soft! let me just murmur,
And do you wait a moment you husky-nois'd
    sea,
For somewhere I believe I heard my mate re-
    sponding to me,
So faint, I must be still, be still to listen,
But not altogether still, for then she might not
    come immediately to me.   110

Hither my love!
Here I am! here!
With this just-sustain'd note I announce my-
    self to you,
This gentle call is for you my love, for you.

Do not be decoy'd elsewhere,
That is the whistle of the wind, it is not my
    voice,
That is the fluttering, the fluttering of the
    spray,
Those are the shadows of leaves.

O darkness! O in vain!
O I am very sick and sorrowful.   120

O brown halo in the sky near the moon, droop-
    ing upon the sea!
O troubled reflection in the sea!
O throat! O throbbing heart!
And I singing uselessly, uselessly all the night.

O past! O happy life! O songs of joy!
In the air, in the woods, over fields,
Loved! loved! loved! loved! loved!
But my mate no more, no more with me!
We two together no more.

The aria sinking,   130
All else continuing, the stars shining,
The winds blowing, the notes of the bird con-
    tinuous echoing,
With angry moans the fierce old mother inces-
    santly moaning,
On the sands of Paumanok's shore gray and
    rustling,
The yellow half-moon enlarged, sagging down,
    drooping, the face of the sea almost
    touching,
The boy ecstatic, with his bare feet the waves,
    with his hair the atmosphere dallying,
The love in the heart long pent, now loose, now
    at last tumultuously bursting,
The aria's meaning, the ears, the soul, swiftly
    depositing,
The strange tears down the cheeks coursing,
The colloquy there, the trio, each uttering,
The undertone, the savage old mother inces-
    santly crying,   141
To the boy's soul's questions sullenly timing,
    some drown'd secret hissing,
To the outsetting bard.

Demon or bird! (said the boy's soul),
Is it indeed toward your mate you sing? or is
    it really to me?
For I, that was a child, my tongue's use sleep-
    ing, now I have heard you,

Now in a moment I know what I am for, I
    awake,
And already a thousand singers, a thousand
    songs, clearer, louder and more sorrow-
    ful than yours,
A thousand warbling echoes have started to life
    within me, never to die.

O you singer solitary, singing by yourself, pro-
    jecting me,   150
O solitary me listening, never more shall I
    cease perpetuating you,
Never more shall I escape, never more the re-
    verberations,
Never more the cries of unsatisfied love be
    absent from me,
Never again leave me to be the peaceful child
    I was before what there in the night,
By the sea under the yellow and sagging moon,
The messenger there arous'd, the fire, the sweet
    hell within,
The unknown want, the destiny of me.

O give me the clew! (it lurks in the night here
    somewhere),
O if I am to have so much, let me have more!

A word then, (for I will conquer it),   160
The word final, superior to all,
Subtle, sent up—what is it?—I listen;
Are you whispering it, and have been all the
    time, you sea-waves?
Is that it from your liquid rims and wet sands?

Whereto answering, the sea,
Delaying not, hurrying not,
Whisper'd me through the night, and very
    plainly before daybreak,
Lisp'd to me the low and delicious word death
And again death, death, death, death,
Hissing melodious, neither like the bird nor like
    my arous'd child's heart,   170
But edging near as privately for me rustling
    at my feet,
Creeping thence steadily up to my ears and
    laving me softly all over,
Death, death, death, death, death.

Which I do not forget,
But fuse the song of my dusky demon and
    brother,
That he sang to me in the moonlight on Pauma-
    nok's gray beach,
With the thousand responsive songs at random,
My own songs awaked from that hour,
And with them the key, the word up from the
    waves,

The word of the sweetest song and all songs,
That strong and delicious word which, creeping
    to my feet,   181
(Or like some old crone rocking the cradle,
    swathed in sweet garments, bending
    aside)
The sea whisper'd me.

                                       1859

ME IMPERTURBE [1]

Me imperturbe, standing at ease in Nature,
Master of all or mistress of all, aplomb in
    the midst of irrational things,
Imbued as they, passive, receptive, silent as
    they,
Finding my occupation, poverty, notoriety,
    foibles, crimes, less important than I
    thought,
Me toward the Mexican sea, or in the Manna-
    hatta or the Tennessee, or far north or
    inland,
A river man, or a man of the woods or of any
    farm-life of these States or of the coast,
    or the lakes or Kanada,
Me wherever my life is lived, O to be self-
    balanced for contingencies,
To confront night, storms, hunger, ridicule,
    accidents, rebuffs, as the trees and ani-
    mals do.

                                       1860

POETS TO COME

Poets to come! orators, singers, musicians to
    come!
Not today is to justify me and answer what I
    am for,
But you, a new brood, native, athletic, conti-
    nental, greater than before known,
Arouse! for you must justify me.

I myself but write one or two indicative words
    for the future,
I but advance a moment only to wheel and
    hurry back in the darkness.

I am a man who, sauntering along without fully
    stopping, turns a casual look upon you
    and then averts his face,
Leaving it to you to prove and define it,
Expecting the main things from you.

                                       1860

---

[1] As here, Whitman often coins words to fit his purpose
the correct Latin form being *me imperturbato*,
"I undisturbed." It is interesting to note the
extreme range of Whitman's vocabulary, which
includes such quasi-learned words as "fetor,"
"libertad," the "parturient earth," and such
phrases as "so long."

I HEAR AMERICA SINGING

I hear America singing, the varied carols I hear,
Those of mechanics, each one singing his as
it should be blithe and strong,
The carpenter singing his as he measures his
plank or beam,
The mason singing his as he makes ready for
work, or leaves off work,
The boatman singing what belongs to him in his
boat, the deck-hand singing on the steamboat deck,
The shoemaker singing as he sits on his bench,
the hatter singing as he stands,
The wood-cutter's song, the plowboy's on his
way in the morning, or at noon intermission or at sundown,
The delicious singing of the mother, or of the
young wife at work, or of the girl sewing or washing,
Each singing what belongs to him or her and
to none else,   9
The day what belongs to the day—at night the
party of young fellows, robust, friendly,
Singing with open mouths their strong melodious songs.
                                          1860

I SAW IN LOUISIANA A LIVE-OAK GROWING

I saw in Louisiana a live-oak growing,
All alone stood it and the moss hung down from
the branches,
Without any companion it grew there uttering
joyous leaves of dark green,
And its look, rude, unbending, lusty, made me
think of myself,
But I wonder'd how it could utter joyous leaves
standing alone there without its friend
near, for I knew I could not,
And I broke off a twig with a certain number
of leaves upon it, and twined around it
a little moss,
And brought it away, and I have placed it in
sight in my room,
It is not needed to remind me as of my own
dear friends,
(For I believe lately I think of little else than
of them,)
Yet it remains to me a curious token, it makes
me think of manly love;   10
For all that, and though the live-oak glistens
there in Louisiana solitary in a wide flat
space,
Uttering joyous leaves all its life without a
friend, a lover near,
I know very well I could not.
                                          1860

AS AT THY PORTALS ALSO DEATH

As at thy portals also death,
Entering thy sovereign, dim, illimitable grounds,
To memories of my mother, to the divine blend-
ing, maternity,
To her, buried and gone, yet buried not, gone
not from me,
(I see again the calm benignant face fresh and
beautiful still,
I sit by the form in the coffin,
I kiss and kiss convulsively again the sweet
old lips, the cheeks, the closed eyes in
the coffin;)
To her, the ideal woman, practical, spiritual, of
all of earth, life, love, to me the best,
I grave a monumental line, before I go, amid
these songs,
And set a tombstone here.   10

FOR YOU, O DEMOCRACY

Come, I will make the continent indissoluble,
I will make the most splendid race the sun ever
shone upon,
I will make divine magnetic lands,
   With the love of comrades,
   With the life-long love of comrades.

I will plant companionship thick as trees along
all the rivers of America, and along the
shores of the great lakes, and all over
the prairies,
I will make inseparable cities with their arms
about each other's necks,
   By the love of comrades,
   By the manly love of comrades.   9

For you these from me, O Democracy, to serve
you *ma femme!* [1]
For you, for you I am trilling these songs.
                                          1860

SO LONG!

To conclude, I announce what comes after me.

I remember I said before my leaves sprang at
all,
I would raise my voice jocund and strong with
reference to consummations.

When America does what was promis'd,
When through these States walk a hundred millions of superb persons,
When the rest part away for superb persons
and contribute to them,

[1] my wife

When breeds of the most perfect mothers denote America,
Then to me and mine our due fruition.

I have press'd through in my own right,
I have sung the body and the soul, war and
peace have I sung, and the songs of life
and death, 10
And the songs of birth, and shown that there
are many births.

I have offer'd my style to every one, I have
journey'd with confident step;
While my pleasure is yet at the full I whisper
So long!
And take the young woman's hand and the
young man's hand for the last time.

I announce natural persons to arise,
I announce justice triumphant,
I announce uncompromising liberty and equal-
ity,
I announce the justification of candor and the
justification of pride.

I announce that the identity of these States is
a single identity only,
I announce the Union more and more compact,
indissoluble, 20
I announce splendors and majesties to make all
the previous politics of the earth insignificant.

I announce adhesiveness, I say it shall be limitless, unloosen'd,
I say you shall yet find the friend you were
looking for.

I announce a man or woman coming, perhaps
you are the one, (*So long!*)
I announce the great individual, fluid as Nature, chaste, affectionate, compassionate,
fully arm'd.

I announce a life that shall be copious, vehement, spiritual, bold,
I announce an end that shall lightly and joyfully meet its translation.

I announce myriads of youths, beautiful, gigantic, sweet-blooded,
I announce a race of splendid and savage old
men.

O thicker and faster—(*So long!*) 30
O crowding too close upon me,

I foresee too much, it means more than I
thought,
It appears to me I am dying.

Hasten throat and sound your last,
Salute me—salute the days once more. Peal
the old cry once more.

Screaming electric, the atmosphere using,
At random glancing, each as I notice absorb-
ing,
Swiftly on, but a little while alighting,
Curious envelop'd messages delivering,
Sparkles hot, seed ethereal down in the dirt
dropping, 40
Myself unknowing, my commission obeying, to
question it never daring,
To ages and ages yet the growth of the seed
leaving,
To troops out of the war arising, they the
tasks I have set promulging,
To women certain whispers of myself bequeath-
ing, their affection me more clearly explaining,
To young men my problems offering—no dal-
lier I—I the muscle of their brains trying,
So I pass, a little time vocal, visible, contrary,
Afterward a melodious echo, passionately bent
for, (death making me really undying)
The best of me then when no longer visible, for
toward that I have been incessantly preparing.

What is there more, that I lag and pause and
crouch extended with unshut mouth?
Is there a single final farewell? 50

My songs cease, I abandon them,
From behind the screen where I hid I advance
personally solely to you.

Camerado, this is no book,
Who touches this touches a man,
(Is it night? are we here together alone?)
It is I you hold and who holds you,
I spring from the pages into your arms—decease
calls me forth.

O how your fingers drowse me,
Your breath falls around me like dew, your
pulse lulls the tympans of my ears,
I feel immerged from head to foot, 60
Delicious, enough.

Enough O deed impromptu and secret,
Enough O gliding present—enough O summ'd-
up past.

Dear friend whoever you are take this kiss,
I give it especially to you, do not forget me,
I feel like one who has done work for the day
    to retire awhile,
I receive now again of my many translations,
    from my avataras [1] ascending, while
    others doubtless await me,
An unknown sphere more real than I dream'd,
    more direct, darts awakening rays about
    me, *So long!*
Remember my words, I may again return,
I love you, I depart from materials,   70
I am as one disembodied, triumphant, dead.

                                            1860

PIONEERS! O PIONEERS!

Come my tan-faced children,
Follow well in order, get your weapons ready,
Have you your pistols? have you your sharp-
    edged axes?
    Pioneers! O pioneers!

For we cannot tarry here,
We must march my darlings, we must bear the
    brunt of danger,
We the youthful sinewy races, all the rest on
    us depend.
    Pioneers! O pioneers!

O you youths, Western youths,
So impatient, full of action, full of manly pride
    and friendship,   10
Plain I see you Western youths, see you tramp-
    ing with the foremost,
    Pioneers! O pioneers!

Have the elder races halted?
Do they droop and end their lesson, wearied
    over there beyond the seas?
We take up the task eternal, and the burden
    and the lesson,
    Pioneers! O pioneers!

All the past we leave behind,
We debouch upon a newer mightier world,
    varied world,
Fresh and strong the world we seize, world of
    labor and the march,
    Pioneers! O pioneers!   20

We detachments steady throwing,
Down the edges, through the passes, up the
    mountains steep,
Conquering, holding, daring, venturing as we
    go the unknown ways,
    Pioneers! O pioneers!

[1] previous incarnations

We primeval forests felling,
We the rivers stemming, vexing we and pierc-
    ing deep the mines within,
We the surface broad surveying, we the virgin
    soil upheaving,
    Pioneers! O pioneers!

Colorado men are we,
From the peaks gigantic, from the great sierras
    and the high plateaus,   30
From the mine and from the gully, from the
    hunting trail we come,
    Pioneers! O pioneers!

From Nebraska, from Arkansas,
Central inland race are we, from Missouri, with
    the continental blood intervein'd,
All the hands of comrades clasping, all the
    Southern, all the Northern,
    Pioneers! O pioneers!

O resistless restless race!
O beloved race in all! O my breast aches with
    tender love for all!
O I mourn and yet exult, I am rapt with love
    for all,
    Pioneers! O pioneers!   40

Raise the mighty mother mistress,
Waving high the delicate mistress, over all the
    starry mistress, (bend your heads all)
Raise the fang'd and warlike mistress, stern,
    impassive, weapon'd mistress,
    Pioneers! O pioneers!

See my children, resolute children,
By those swarms upon our rear we must never
    yield or falter,
Ages back in ghostly millions frowning there
    behind us urging,
    Pioneers! O pioneers!

On and on the compact ranks,
With accessions ever waiting, with the places
    of the dead quickly fill'd,   50
Through the battle, through defeat, moving
    yet and never stopping,
    Pioneers! O pioneers!

O to die advancing on!
Are there some of us to droop and die? has
    the hour come?
Then upon the march we fittest die, soon and
    sure the gap is fill'd,
    Pioneers! O pioneers!

All the pulses of the world,
Falling in they beat for us, with the Western
     movement beat,
Holding single or together, steady moving to the
     front, all for us,
Pioneers! O pioneers!   60

Life's involv'd and varied pageants,
All the forms and shows, all the workmen at
     their work,
All the seamen and the landsmen, all the mas-
     ters with their slaves,
Pioneers! O pioneers!

All the hapless silent lovers,
All the prisoners in the prisons, all the right-
     eous and the wicked,
All the joyous, all the sorrowing, all the living,
     all the dying,
Pioneers! O pioneers!

I too with my soul and body,
We, a curious trio, picking, wandering on our
     way,   70
Through these shores amid the shadows, with
     the apparitions pressing,
Pioneers! O pioneers!

Lo, the darting bowling orb!
Lo, the brother orbs around, all the clustering
     suns and planets,
All the dazzling days, all the mystic nights with
     dreams,
Pioneers! O pioneers!

These are of us, they are with us,
All for primal needed work, while the followers
     there in embryo wait behind,
We today's procession heading, we the route
     for travel clearing,
Pioneers! O pioneers!   80

O you daughters of the West!
O you young and elder daughters! O you moth-
     ers and you wives!
Never must you be divided, in our ranks you
     move united,
Pioneers! O pioneers!

Minstrels latent on the prairies!
(Shrouded bards of other lands, you may rest,
     you have done your work)
Soon I hear you coming warbling, soon you rise
     and tramp amid us,
Pioneers! O pioneers!

Not for delectations sweet,
Not the cushion and the slipper, not the peace-
     ful and the studious,   90
Not the riches safe and palling, not for us the
     tame enjoyment,
Pioneers! O pioneers!

Do the feasters gluttonous feast?
Do the corpulent sleepers sleep? have they
     lock'd and bolted doors?
Still be ours the diet hard, and the blanket on
     the ground,
Pioneers! O pioneers!

Has the night descended?
Was the road of late so toilsome? did we stop
     discouraged nodding on our way?
Yet a passing hour I yield you in your tracks to
     pause oblivious,
Pioneers! O pioneers!   100

Till with sound of trumpet,
Far, far off the daybreak call—hark! how loud
     and clear I hear it wind,
Swift! to the head of the army!—swift! spring
     to your places,
Pioneers! O pioneers!
     1865

EIGHTEEN SIXTY-ONE [1]

Arm'd year—year of the struggle,
No dainty rimes or sentimental love verses for
     you terrible year,
Not you as some pale poetling seated at a desk
     lisping cadenzas piano,
But as a strong man erect, clothed in blue
     clothes, advancing, carrying a rifle on
     your shoulder,
With well-gristled body and sunburnt face and
     hands, with a knife in the belt at your
     side,
As I heard you shouting loud, your sonorous
     voice ringing across the continent,
Your masculine voice O year, as rising amid
     the great cities,
Amid the men of Manhattan I saw you as one
     of the workmen, the dwellers in Man-
     hattan,
Or with large steps crossing the prairies out of
     Illinois and Indiana,
Rapidly crossing the West with springy gait and
     descending the Alleghanies,   10

[1] One of the most noble phases of Whitman's life was
his work in the hospitals of Washington during
the entire Civil War. He so gave of his strength
and spirit to the suffering and dying soldiers
that they came to look upon him as almost an
angel of mercy. See Edith Wharton's striking
story, "The Spark."

Or down from the great lakes or in Pennsylvania, or on deck along the Ohio river,
Or southward along the Tennessee or Cumberland rivers, or at Chattanooga on the
  mountain top,
Saw I your gait and saw I your sinewy limbs
  clothed in blue, bearing weapons, robust
  year,

Heard your determin'd voice launch'd forth
  again and again,
Year that suddenly sang by the mouths of the
  round-lipp'd cannon,
I repeat you, hurrying, crashing, sad, distracted
  year.

1865

CAVALRY CROSSING A FORD

A line in long array where they wind betwixt
  green islands,
They take a serpentine course, their arms flash
  in the sun—hark to the musical clank,
Behold the silvery river, in it the splashing
  horses loitering stop to drink,
Behold the brown-faced men, each group, each
  person a picture, the negligent rest on
  the saddles,
Some emerge on the opposite bank, others are
  just entering the ford—while,
Scarlet and blue and snowy white,
The guidon [1] flags flutter gayly in the wind.

1865

BIVOUAC ON A MOUNTAIN SIDE

I see before me now a traveling army halting,
Below a fertile valley spread, with barns and
  the orchards of summer,
Behind, the terraced sides of a mountain,
  abrupt, in places rising high,
Broken, with rocks, with clinging cedars, with
  tall shapes dingily seen,
The numerous camp-fires scatter'd near and far,
  some away up on the mountain,
The shadowy forms of men and horses, loom
  ing, large-sized, flickering,
And over all the sky—the sky! far, far out of
  reach, studded, breaking out, the eternal
  stars.

1865

COME UP FROM THE FIELDS FATHER

Come up from the fields father, here's a letter
  from our Pete,

[1] a pennant-like guide flag used especially by mounted
  troops

And come to the front door mother, here's a
  letter from thy dear son.

Lo, 'tis autumn,
Lo, where the trees, deeper green, yellower and
  redder,
Cool and sweeten Ohio's villages with leaves
  fluttering in the moderate wind,
Where apples ripe in the orchards hang and
  grapes on the trellis'd vines,
(Smell you the smell of the grapes on the
  vines?
Smell you the buckwheat where the bees were
  lately buzzing?)

Above all, lo, the sky so calm, so transparent
  after the rain, and with wondrous clouds,
Below too, all calm, all vital and beautiful, and
  the farm prospers well.   10

Down in the fields all prospers well,
But now from the fields come father, come at
  the daughter's call,
And come to the entry mother, to the front
  door come right away.

Fast as she can she hurries, something ominous,
  her steps trembling,
She does not tarry to smooth her hair nor adjust her cap.

Open the envelope quickly,—
O this is not our son's writing, yet his name is
  sign'd,
O a strange hand writes for our dear son, O
  stricken mother's soul!
All swims before her eyes, flashes with black,
  she catches the main words only,
Sentences broken, *gunshot wound in the breast,
  cavalry skirmish, taken to hospital,*   20
At present low, but will soon be better.

Ah now the single figure to me,
Amid all teeming and wealthy Ohio with all its
  cities and farms,
Sickly white in the face and dull in the head,
  very faint,
By the jamb of a door leans.

Grieve not so, dear mother, (the just-grown
  daughter speaks through her sobs,
The little sisters huddle around speechless and
  dismay'd)
*See, dearest mother, the letter says Pete will
  soon be better.*

Alas poor boy, he will never be better, (nor
    may-be needs to be better, that brave
    and simple soul,)
While they stand at home at the door he is dead
    already,   30
The only son is dead.

But the mother needs to be better,
She with thin form presently drest in black,
By day her meals untouch'd, then at night fit-
    fully sleeping, often waking,
In the midnight waking, weeping, longing with
    one deep longing,
O that she might withdraw unnoticed, silent
    from life escape and withdraw,
To follow, to seek, to be with her dear dead son.
                                             1865

A MARCH IN THE RANKS HARD-
PREST, AND THE ROAD
UNKNOWN [1]

A march in the ranks hard-prest, and the road
    unknown,
A route through a heavy wood with muffled
    steps in the darkness,
Our army foil'd with loss severe, and the sullen
    remnant retreating,
Till after midnight glimmer upon us the lights
    of a dim-lighted building,
We come to an open space in the woods, and
    halt by the dim-lighted building,
'Tis a large old church at the crossing roads,
    now an impromptu hospital,
Entering but for a minute I see a sight beyond
    all the pictures and poems ever made,
Shadows of deepest, deepest black, just lit by
    moving candles and lamps,
And by one great pitchy torch stationary with
    wild red flame and clouds of smoke,
By these, crowds, groups of forms vaguely I
    see on the floor, some in the pews laid
    down,   10
At my feet more distinctly a soldier, a mere lad,
    in danger of bleeding to death, (he is
    shot in the abdomen)
I stanch the blood temporarily, (the young-
    ster's face is white as a lily)
Then before I depart I sweep my eyes o'er the
    scene fain to absorb it all,
Faces, varieties, postures beyond description,
    most in obscurity, some of them dead,

[1] Is Whitman's unflinching realism in his war poetry as
    shown in this poem and also in "The Wound-
    dresser," due to lack of delicacy or to a fuller
    and more exact sense of the horrors of war than
    most poets have had the means of acquiring?

Surgeons operating, attendants holding lights,
    the smell of ether, the odor of blood,
The crowd, O the crowd of the bloody forms,
    the yard outside also fill'd,
Some on the bare ground, some on planks or
    stretchers, some in the death-spasm
    sweating,
An occasional scream or cry, the doctor's
    shouted orders or calls,
The glisten of the little steel instruments catch-
    ing the glint of the torches,
These I resume as I chant, I see again the
    forms, I smell the odor,   20
Then hear outside the orders given, *Fall in,
    my men, fall in;*
But first I bend to the dying lad, his eyes open,
    a half-smile gives he me,
Then the eyes close, calmly close, and I speed
    forth to the darkness,
Resuming, marching, ever in darkness march-
    ing, on in the ranks,
The unknown road still marching.
                                             1865

A SIGHT IN CAMP IN THE DAYBREAK
GRAY AND DIM

A sight in camp in the daybreak gray and dim,
As from my tent I emerge so early sleepless,
As slow I walk in the cool fresh air the path
    near by the hospital tent,
Three forms I see on stretchers lying, brought
    out there untended lying,
Over each the blanket spread, ample brownish
    woolen blanket,
Gray and heavy blanket, folding, covering all.

Curious I halt and silent stand,
Then with light fingers I from the face of the
    nearest the first just lift the blanket;
Who are you elderly man so gaunt and grim,
    with well-gray'd hair, and flesh all sunken
    about the eyes?
Who are you my dear comrade?   10

Then to the second I step—and who are you my
    child and darling?
Who are you sweet boy with cheeks yet bloom-
    ing?

Then to the third—a face nor child nor old, very
    calm, as of beautiful yellow-white ivory;
Young man I think I know you—I think this
    face is the face of the Christ himself,
Dead and divine and brother of all, and here
    again he lies.
                                             1865

AS TOILSOME I WANDER'D VIRGINIA'S WOODS

As toilsome I wander'd Virginia's woods,
To the music of rustling leaves kick'd by my
    feet, (for 'twas autumn),
I mark'd at the foot of a tree the grave of a
    soldier;
Mortally wounded he and buried on the re-
    treat, (easily all could I understand),
The halt of a mid-day hour, when up! no time
    to lose—yet this sign left,
On a tablet scrawl'd and nail'd on the tree by
    the grave,
Bold, cautious, true, and my loving comrade.

Long, long I muse, then on my way go wander-
    ing,
Many a changeful season to follow, and many
    a scene of life,
Yet at times through changeful season and
    scene, abrupt, alone, or in the crowded
    street,   10
Comes before me the unknown soldier's grave,
    comes the inscription rude in Virginia's
    woods,
Bold, cautious, true, and my loving comrade.
            1865

THE WOUND-DRESSER

1

An old man bending I come among new faces,
Years looking backward resuming in answer to
    children,
Come tell us old man, as from young men and
    maidens that love me,
(Arous'd and angry, I'd thought to beat the
    alarum, and urge relentless war,
But soon my fingers fail'd me, my face droop'd
    and I resign'd myself,
To sit by the wounded and soothe them, or
    silently watch the dead;)
Years hence of these scenes, of these furious
    passions, these chances,
Of unsurpass'd heroes, (was one side so brave?
    the other was equally brave;)
Now be witness again, paint the mightiest
    armies of earth,
Of those armies so rapid so wondrous what saw
    you to tell us?   10
What stays with you latest and deepest? of
    curious panics,
Of hard-fought engagements or sieges tremen-
    dous what deepest remains?

2

O maidens and young men I love and that
    love me,
What you ask of my days those the strangest
    and sudden your talking recalls,
Soldier alert I arrive after a long march cover'd
    with sweat and dust,
In the nick of time I come, plunge in the fight,
    loudly shout in the rush of successful
    charge,
Enter the captur'd works—yet lo, like a swift-
    running river they fade,
Pass and are gone, they fade—I dwell not on
    soldiers' perils or soldiers' joys,
(Both I remember well—many the hardships,
    few the joys, yet I was content.)

But in silence, in dreams' projections,   20
While the world of gain and appearance and
    mirth goes on,
So soon what is over forgotten, and waves wash
    the imprints off the sand,
With hinged knees returning I enter the doors,
    (while for you up there,
Whoever you are, follow without noise and be
    of strong heart.)

Bearing the bandages, water and sponge,
Straight and swift to my wounded I go,
Where they lie on the ground after the battle
    brought in,
Where their priceless blood reddens the grass
    the ground,
Or to the rows of the hospital tent, or under the
    roof'd hospital,
To the long rows of cots up and down each side
    I return,   30
To each and all one after another I draw near,
    not one do I miss,
An attendant follows holding a tray, he carries
    a refuse pail,
Soon to be fill'd with clotted rags and blood,
    emptied, and fill'd again.

I onward go, I stop,
With hinged knees and steady hand to dress
    wounds,
I am firm with each, the pangs are sharp yet
    unavoidable,
One turns to me his appealing eyes—poor boy!
    I never knew you,
Yet I think I could not refuse this moment to
    die for you, if that would save you.

3

On, on I go, (open doors of time! open hospital doors!)
The crush'd head I dress, (poor crazed hand tear not the bandage away,)   40
The neck of the cavalry-man with the bullet through and through I examine,
Hard the breathing rattles, quite glazed already the eye, yet life struggles hard,
(Come sweet death! be persuaded O beautiful death!
In mercy come quickly.)

From the stump of the arm, the amputated hand,
I undo the clotted lint, remove the slough, wash off the matter and blood,
Back on his pillow the soldier bends with curv'd neck and side-falling head,
His eyes are closed, his face is pale, he dares not look on the bloody stump,
And has not yet look'd on it.

I dress a wound in the side, deep, deep,   50
But a day or two more, for see the frame all wasted and sinking,
And the yellow-blue countenance see.

I dress the perforated shoulder, the foot with the bullet-wound,
Cleanse the one with a gnawing and putrid gangrene, so sickening, so offensive,
While the attendant stands behind aside me holding the tray and pail.

I am faithful, I do not give out,
The fractur'd thigh, the knee, the wound in the abdomen,
These and more I dress with impassive hand, (yet deep in my breast a fire, a burning flame).

4

Thus in silence in dreams' projections,
Returning, resuming, I thread my way through the hospitals,   60
The hurt and wounded I pacify with soothing hand,
I sit by the restless all the dark night, some are so young,
Some suffer so much, I recall the experience sweet and sad,
(Many a soldier's loving arms about this neck have cross'd and rested,
Many a soldier's kiss dwells on these bearded lips).

1865

GIVE ME THE SPLENDID SILENT SUN

1

Give me the splendid silent sun with all his beams full-dazzling,
Give me juicy autumnal fruit ripe and red from the orchard,
Give me a field where the unmow'd grass grows,
Give me an arbor, give me the trellis'd grape,
Give me fresh corn and wheat, give me serene-moving animals teaching content,
Give me nights perfectly quiet as on high plateaus west of the Mississippi, and I looking up at the stars,
Give me odorous at sunrise a garden of beautiful flowers where I can walk undisturb'd,
Give me for marriage a sweet-breath'd woman of whom I should never tire,
Give me a perfect child, give me away aside from the noise of the world a rural domestic life,   9
Give me to warble spontaneous songs recluse by myself, for my own ears only,
Give me solitude, give me Nature, give me again O Nature your primal sanities!

These demanding to have them, (tired with ceaseless excitement, and rack'd by the war-strife,)
These to procure incessantly asking, rising in cries from my heart,
While yet incessantly asking still I adhere to my city,
Day upon day and year upon year O city, walking your streets,
Where you hold me enchain'd a certain time refusing to give me up,
Yet giving to make me glutted, enrich'd of soul, you give me forever faces;
(O I see what I sought to escape, confronting, reversing my cries,
I see my own soul trampling down what it ask'd for.)

2

Keep your splendid silent sun,   20
Keep your woods O Nature, and the quiet places by the woods,
Keep your fields of clover and timothy, and your corn-fields and orchards,
Keep the blossoming buckwheat fields where the Ninth-month bees hum;
Give me faces and streets—give me these phantoms incessant and endless along the trottoirs! [1]

[1] side-walks

Give me interminable eyes—give me women—
    give me comrades and lovers by the thou-
    sand!
Let me see new ones every day—let me hold
    new ones by the hand every day!
Give me such shows—give me the streets of
    Manhattan!
Give me Broadway, with the soldiers marching
    —give me the sound of the trumpets
    and drums!
(The soldiers in companies or regiments—some
    starting away, flush'd and reckless,
Some, their time up, returning with thinn'd
    ranks, young, yet very old, worn, march-
    ing, noticing nothing;)   30
Give me the shores and wharves heavy-fringed
    with black ships!
O such for me! O an intense life, full to reple-
    tion and varied!
The life of the theater, bar-room, huge hotel,
    for me!
The saloon of the steamer! the crowded excur-
    sion for me! the torchlight procession!
The dense brigade bound for the war, with high
    piled military wagons following;
People, endless, streaming, with strong voices,
    passions, pageants,
Manhattan streets with their powerful throbs,
    with beating drums as now,
The endless and noisy chorus, the rustle and
    clank of muskets, (even the sight of the
    wounded,)
Manhattan crowds, with their turbulent musical
    chorus!   39
Manhattan faces and eyes forever for me.
                                        1865

O TAN-FACED PRAIRIE-BOY!

O tan-faced prairie-boy,
Before you came to camp came many a welcome
    gift,
Praises and presents came and nourishing food,
    till at last among the recruits,
You came, taciturn, with nothing to give—we
    but look'd on each other,
When lo! more than all the gifts of the world
    you gave me.
                                        1865

LOOK DOWN, FAIR MOON

Look down, fair moon, and bathe this scene,
Pour softly down night's nimbus floods on faces
    ghastly, swollen, purple,
On the dead on their backs with arms toss'd
    wide,
Pour down your unstinted nimbus sacred moon.
                                        1865

RECONCILIATION

Word over all, beautiful as the sky,
Beautiful that war and all its deeds of carnage
    must in time be utterly lost,
That the hands of the sisters Death and Night
    incessantly softly wash again, and ever
    again, this soil'd world;
For my enemy is dead, a man divine as myself
    is dead,
I look where he lies white-faced and still in the
    coffin—I draw near,
Bend down and touch lightly with my lips the
    white face in the coffin.
                                        1865

WEAVE IN, MY HARDY LIFE

Weave in, weave in, my hardy life,
Weave yet a soldier strong and full for great
    campaigns to come,
Weave in red blood, weave sinews in like ropes,
    the senses, sight weave in,
Weave lasting sure, weave day and night the
    weft, the warp, incessant weave, tire not,
(We know not what the use O life, nor know
    the aim, the end, nor really aught we
    know,
But know the work, the need goes on and shall
    go on, the death envelop'd march of
    peace as well as war goes on,)
For great campaigns of peace the same the wiry
    threads to weave,
We know not why or what, yet weave, forever
    weave.
                                        1865

OUT OF THE ROLLING OCEAN THE CROWD

Out of the rolling ocean the crowd came a drop
    gently to me,
Whispering, *I love you, before long I die,*
I have travel'd a long way merely to look on
    you, to touch you,
For I could not die till I once look'd on you,
For I fear'd I might afterward lose you.

Now we have met, we have look'd, we are safe,
Return in peace to the ocean my love,
I too am part of that ocean my love, we are not
    so much separated,
Behold the great rondure, the cohesion of all,
    how perfect!
But as for me, for you, the irresistible sea is
    to separate us,   10
As for an hour carrying us diverse, yet cannot
    carry us diverse forever;

Be not impatient—a little space—know you I
    salute the air, the ocean and the land,
Every day at sundown for your dear sake my
    love.
                      1865

TO A CERTAIN CIVILIAN

Did you ask dulcet rimes from me?
Did you seek the civilian's peaceful and lan-
    guishing rimes?
Did you find what I sang erewhile so hard to
    follow?
Why I was not singing erewhile for you to
    follow, to understand—nor am I now;
(I have been born of the same as the war was
    born,
The drum-corps' rattle is ever to me sweet
    music, I love well the martial dirge,
With slow wail and convulsive throb leading
    the officer's funeral;)
What to such as you anyhow such a poet as I?
    therefore leave my works,
And go lull yourself with what you can under-
    stand, and with piano tunes,   9
For I lull nobody, and you will never under-
    stand me.
                      1865

QUICKSAND YEARS

Quicksand years that whirl me I know not
    whither,
Your schemes, politics, fail, lines give way, sub-
    stances mock and elude me,
Only the theme I sing, the great and strong-
    possess'd soul, eludes not,
One's-self must never give way—that is the final
    substance—that out of all is sure,
Out of politics, triumphs, battles, life, what at
    last finally remains?
When shows break up what but One's-Self is
    sure?
                      1865

ASHES OF SOLDIERS

Ashes of soldiers South or North,
As I muse retrospective murmuring a chant in
    thought,
The war resumes, again to my sense your
    shapes,
And again the advance of the armies.

Noiseless as mists and vapors,
From their graves in the trenches ascending,
From cemeteries all through Virginia and Ten-
    nessee,

From every point of the compass out of the
    countless graves,
In wafted clouds, in myriads large, or squads of
    twos or threes or single ones they come,
And silently gather round me.   10

Now sound no note O trumpeters,
Not at the head of my cavalry parading on
    spirited horses,
With sabers drawn and glistening, and carbines
    by their thighs, (ah my brave horse-
    men!
My handsome tan-faced horsemen! what life,
    what joy and pride,
With all the perils were yours.)

Nor you drummers, neither at reveillé at dawn,
Nor the long roll alarming the camp, nor even
    the muffled beat for a burial,
Nothing from you this time O drummers bear-
    ing my warlike drums.

But aside from these and the marts of wealth
    and the crowded promenade,
Admitting around me comrades close unseen by
    the rest and voiceless,   20
The slain elate and alive again, the dust and
    debris alive,
I chant this chant of my silent soul in the name
    of all dead soldiers.

Faces so pale with wondrous eyes, very dear,
    gather closer yet,
Draw close, but speak not.
Phantoms of countless lost,
Invisible to the rest henceforth become my
    companions,
Follow me ever—desert me not while I live.

Sweet are the blooming cheeks of the living—
    sweet are the musical voices sounding,
But sweet, ah sweet, are the dead with their
    silent eyes.   29

Dearest comrades, all is over and long gone,
But love is not over—and what love, O com-
    rades!
Perfume from battlefields rising, up from the
    foetor arising.

Perfume therefore my chant, O love, immortal
    love,
Give me to bathe the memories of all dead sol-
    diers,
Shroud them, embalm them, cover them all over
    with tender pride.

Perfume all—make all wholesome,
Make these ashes to nourish and blossom,
O love, solve all, fructify all with the last chem-
    istry.

Give me exhaustless, make me a fountain,
That I exhale love from me wherever I go like
    a moist perennial dew,   40
For the ashes of all dead soldiers South or North.
                                                1865

PENSIVE ON HER DEAD GAZING

Pensive on her dead gazing I heard the Mother
    of All,
Desperate on the torn bodies, on the forms cov-
    ering the battlefields gazing,
(As the last gun ceased, but the scent of the
    powder-smoke linger'd,)
As she called to her earth with mournful voice
    while she stalk'd,
Absorb them well O my earth, she cried, I
    charge you lose not my sons, lose not
    an atom,
And you streams absorb them well, taking their
    dear blood,
And you local spots, and you airs that swim
    above lightly impalpable,
And all you essences of soil and growth, and
    you my rivers' depths,
And you mountain sides, and the woods where
    my dear children's blood trickling red-
    den'd,
And you trees down in your roots to bequeath
    to all future trees,   10
My dead absorb or South or North—my young
    men's bodies absorb, and their precious
    precious blood,
Which holding in trust for me faithfully back
    again give me many a year hence,
In unseen essence and odor of surface and
    grass, centuries hence,
In blowing airs from the fields back again give
    me my darlings, give my immortal
    heroes,
Exhale me them centuries hence, breathe me
    their breath, let not an atom be lost,
O years and graves! O air and soil! O my dead,
    an aroma sweet!
Exhale them perennial sweet death, years, cen-
    turies hence.
                                                1865

HUSH'D BE THE CAMPS TODAY [1]
(May 4, 1865)

Hush'd be the camps today,
And soldiers let us drape our war-worn weapons,

[1] This poem and the three following have reference to
    the death and burial of Abraham Lincoln. His

And each with musing soul retire to celebrate,
Our dear commander's death.

No more for him life's stormy conflicts,
Nor victory, nor defeat—no more time's dark
    events,
Charging like ceaseless clouds across the sky.

But sing poet in our name,
Sing of the love we bore him—because you,
    dweller in camps, know it truly.

As they invault the coffin there,   10
Sing—as they close the doors of earth upon him
    —one verse,
For the heavy hearts of soldiers.
                                                1865

BEAT! BEAT! DRUMS!

Beat! beat! drums!—blow! bugles! blow!
Through the windows—through doors—burst
    like a ruthless force,
Into the solemn church, and scatter the congre-
    gation,
Into the school where the scholar is studying;
Leave not the bridegroom quiet—no happiness
    must he have now with his bride,
Nor the peaceful farmer any peace, plowing
    his field or gathering his grain,
So fierce you whirr and pound you drums—so
    shrill you bugles blow.

Beat! beat! drums!—blow! bugles! blow!
Over the traffic of cities—over the rumble of
    wheels in the streets;
Are beds prepared for sleepers at night in the
    houses? no sleepers must sleep in those
    beds,   10
No bargainers' bargains by day—no brokers or
    speculators—would they continue?
Would the talkers be talking? would the singer
    attempt to sing?
Would the lawyer rise in the court to state his
    case before the judge?
Then rattle quicker, heavier drums—you bugles
    wilder blow.

Beat! beat! drums!—blow! bugles! blow!
Make no parley—stop for no expostulation,
Mind not the timid—mind not the weeper or
    prayer,

body was taken to his home at Springfield, Illinois,
with pauses and sometimes funeral sermons at the
principal cities along the route. The entombment
took place May 5, 1865.

Mind not the old man beseeching the young
man,
Let not the child's voice be heard, nor the
mother's entreaties,
Make even the trestles to shake the dead where
they lie awaiting the hearses, 20
So strong you thump O terrible drums—so loud
you bugles blow.

1865

WHEN LILACS LAST IN THE DOOR-
YARD BLOOM'D

1

When lilacs last in the dooryard bloom'd,
And the great star early droop'd in the western
sky in the night,
I mourn'd, and yet shall mourn with ever-
returning spring.

Ever-returning spring, trinity sure to me you
bring,
Lilac blooming perennial and drooping star in
the west,
And thought of him I love.

2

O powerful western fallen star!
O shades of night—O moody, tearful night!
O great star disappear'd—O the black murk
that hides the star!
O cruel hands that hold me powerless—O help-
less soul of me! 10
O harsh surrounding cloud that will not free my
soul.

3

In the dooryard fronting an old farmhouse
near the white-wash'd palings,
Stands the lilac-bush tall-growing with heart-
shaped leaves of rich green,
With many a pointed blossom rising delicate,
with the perfume strong I love,
With every leaf a miracle—and from this bush
in the dooryard,
With delicate-color'd blossoms and heart-shaped
leaves of rich green,
A sprig with its flower I break.

4

In the swamp in secluded recesses,
A shy and hidden bird is warbling a song.

Solitary the thrush, 20
The hermit withdrawn to himself, avoiding the
settlements,
Sings by himself a song.

Song of the bleeding throat,
Death's outlet song of life, (for well dear
brother I know,
If thou wast not granted to sing thou would'st
surely die.)

5

Over the breast of the spring, the land, amid
cities,
Amid lanes and through old woods, where lately
the violets peep'd from the ground, spot-
ting the gray debris,
Amid the grass in the fields each side of the
lanes, passing the endless grass,
Passing the yellow-spear'd wheat, every grain
from its shroud in the dark-brown fields
uprisen,
Passing the apple-tree blows of white and pink
in the orchards, 30
Carrying a corpse to where it shall rest in the
grave,
Night and day journeys a coffin.

6

Coffin that passes through lanes and streets,
Through day and night with the great cloud
darkening the land,
With the pomp of the inloop'd flags with the
cities draped in black,
With the show of the States themselves as of
crape-veil'd women standing,
With processions long and winding and the
flambeaus of the night,
With the countless torches lit, with the silent
sea of faces and the unbared heads,
With the waiting depot, the arriving coffin, and
the somber faces,
With dirges through the night, with the thou-
sand voices rising strong and solemn, 40
With all the mournful voices of the dirges
pour'd round the coffin,
The dim-lit churches and the shuddering or-
gans—where amid these you journey,
With the tolling tolling bells' perpetual clang,
Here, coffin that slowly passes,
I give you my sprig of lilac.

7

(Nor for you, for one alone,
Blossoms and branches green to coffins all I
bring,
For fresh as the morning, thus would I chant a
song for you O sane and sacred death.

All over bouquets of roses,
O death, I cover you over with roses and early
lilies, 50

But mostly and now the lilac that blooms the
    first,
Copious I break, I break the sprigs from the
    bushes,
With loaded arms I come, pouring for you,
For you and the coffins all of you O death.)

8

O western orb sailing the heaven,
Now I know what you must have meant as a
    month since I walk'd,
As I walk'd in silence the transparent shadowy
    night,
As I saw you had something to tell as you bent
    to me night after night,
As you droop'd from the sky low down as if
    to my side, (while the other stars all
    look'd on,)
As we wander'd together the solemn night, (for
    something I know not what kept me
    from sleep,)   60
As the night advanced, and I saw on the
    rim of the west how full you were of
    woe,
As I stood on the rising ground in the breeze
    in the cool transparent night,
As I watch'd where you pass'd and was lost in
    the netherward black of the night,
As my soul in its trouble dissatisfied sank, as
    where you sad orb,
Concluded, dropt in the night, and was gone.

9

Sing on there in the swamp,
O singer bashful and tender, I hear your notes,
    I hear your call,
I hear, I come presently, I understand you,
But a moment I linger, for the lustrous star has
    detain'd me,
The star my departing comrade holds and de-
    tains me.   70

10

O how shall I warble myself for the dead one
    there I loved?
And how shall I deck my song for the large
    sweet soul that has gone?
And what shall my perfume be for the grave
    of him I love?

Sea-winds blown from east and west,
Blown from the Eastern sea and blown from
    the Western sea, till there on the prairies
    meeting,
These and with these and the breath of my
    chant,
I'll perfume the grave of him I love.

11

O what shall I hang on the chamber walls?
And what shall the pictures be that I hang cn
    the walls,
To adorn the burial-house of him I love?   80

Pictures of growing spring and farms and
    homes,
With the Fourth-month eve at sundown, and
    the gray smoke lucid and bright,
With floods of the yellow gold of the gorgeous,
    indolent, sinking sun, burning, expand-
    ing the air,
With the fresh sweet herbage under foot, and
    the pale green leaves of the trees pro-
    lific,
In the distance the flowing glaze, the breast of
    the river, with a wind-dapple here and
    there,
With ranging hills on the banks, with many a
    line against the sky, and shadows,
And the city at hand with dwellings so dense,
    and stacks of chimneys,
And all the scenes of life and the workshops,
    and the workmen homeward returning.

12

Lo, body and soul—this land,
My own Manhattan with spires, and the spar-
    kling and hurrying tides, and the ships,
The varied and ample land, the South and the
    North in the light, Ohio's shores and
    flashing Missouri,   91
And ever the far-spreading prairies cover'd with
    grass and corn.

Lo, the most excellent sun so calm and haughty,
The violet and purple morn with just-felt
    breezes,
The gentle soft-born measureless light,
The miracle spreading bathing all, the fulfill'd
    noon,
The coming eve delicious, the welcome night
    and the stars,
Over my cities shining all, enveloping man and
    land.

13

Sing on, sing on you gray-brown bird,
Sing from the swamps, the recesses, pour your
    chant from the bushes,   100
Limitless out of the dusk, out of the cedars and
    pines.

Sing on dearest brother, warble your reedy song,
Loud human song, with voice of uttermost woe.

O liquid and free and tender!
O wild and loose to my soul—O wondrous
    singer!
You only I hear—yet the star holds me, (but
    will soon depart,)
Yet the lilac with mastering odor holds me.

14

Now while I sat in the day and look'd forth,
In the close of the day with its light and the
    fields of spring, and the farmers prepar-
    ing their crops,
In the large unconscious scenery of my land
    with its lakes and forests,   110
In the heavenly aerial beauty, (after the per-
    turb'd winds and the storms,)
Under the arching heavens of the afternoon
    swift passing, and the voices of children
    and women,
The many-moving sea-tides, and I saw the ships
    how they sail'd,
And the summer approaching with richness, and
    the fields all busy with labor,
And the infinite separate houses, how they all
    went on, each with its meals and minutia
    of daily usages,
And the streets how their throbbings throbb'd,
    and the cities pent—lo, then and there,
Falling upon them all and among them all, en-
    veloping me with the rest,
Appear'd the cloud, appear'd the long black
    trail,
And I knew death, its thought, and the sacred
    knowledge of death.

Then with the knowledge of death as walking
    one side of me,   120
And the thought of death close-walking the
    other side of me,
And I in the middle as with companions, and as
    holding the hands of companions,
I fled forth to the hiding receiving night that
    talks not,
Down to the shores of the water, the path by
    the swamp in the dimness,
To the solemn shadowy cedars and ghostly
    pines so still.

And the singer so shy to the rest receiv'd me,
The gray-brown bird I know receiv'd us com-
    rades three,
And he sang the carol of death, and a verse for
    him I love.

From deep secluded recesses,
From the fragrant cedars and the ghostly pines
    so still,   130

Came the carol of the bird.

And the charm of the carol rapt me,
As I held as if by their hands my comrades in
    the night,
And the voice of my spirit tallied the song of
    the bird.

Come lovely and soothing death, [1]
Undulate round the world, serenely arriving,
    arriving,
In the day, in the night, to all, to each,
Sooner or later delicate death.

Prais'd be the fathomless universe,
For life and joy, and for objects and knowledge
    curious,   140
And for love, sweet love—but praise! praise!
    praise!
For the sure-enwinding arms of cool-enfolding
    death.

Dark mother always gliding near with soft feet,
Have none chanted for thee a chant of fullest
    welcome?
Then I chant it for thee, I glorify thee above
    all,
I bring thee a song that when thou must indeed
    come, come unfalteringly.

Approach strong deliveress,
When it is so, when thou hast taken them I
    joyously sing the dead,
Lost in the loving floating ocean of thee,
Laved in the flood of thy bliss O death.   150

From me to thee glad serenades,
Dances for thee I propose saluting thee, adorn-
    ments and feastings for thee,
And the sights of the open landscape and the
    high-spread sky are fitting,
And life and the fields, and the huge and
    thoughtful night.

The night in silence under many a star,
The ocean shore and the husky whispering wave
    whose voice I know,
And the soul turning to thee O vast and well-
    veil'd death,
And the body gratefully nestling close to thee.

[1] Compare "O eloquent, just, and mighty Death!
Whom none could advise, thou hast persuaded;
what none hath dared, thou hast done; and whom
all the world hath flattered, thou only hast cast
out of the world and despised; thou hast called
together all the far-stretched greatness, all the
pride, cruelty, and ambition of man, and covered
it all over with these two narrow words, *Hic
jacet!*" Sir Walter Raleigh, *The History of the
World.*

Over the tree-tops I float thee a song,
Over the rising and sinking waves, over the
myriad fields and the prairies wide,
Over the dense-pack'd cities all and the teeming
wharves and ways, 161
I float this carol with joy, with joy to thee O
death.

15

To the tally of my soul,
Loud and strong kept up the gray-brown
bird,
With pure deliberate notes spreading filling the
night.

Loud in the pines and cedars dim,
Clear in the freshness moist and the swamp-
perfume,
And I with my comrades there in the night.

While my sight that was bound in my eyes unclosed,
As to long panoramas of visions. 170

And I saw askant the armies,
I saw as in noiseless dreams hundreds of battle-
flags,
Borne through the smoke of the battles and
pierc'd with missiles I saw them,
And carried hither and yon through the smoke,
and torn and bloody,
And at last but a few shreds left on the staffs,
(and all in silence,)
And the staffs all splinter'd and broken.

I saw battle-corpses, myriads of them,
And the white skeletons of young men, I saw
them,
I saw the debris and debris of all the slain
soldiers of the war, 179
But I saw they were not as was thought,
They themselves were fully at rest, they suffer'd
not,
The living remain'd and suffer'd, the mother
suffer'd,
And the wife and the child and the musing com-
rade suffer'd,
And the armies that remain'd suffer'd.

16

Passing the visions, passing the night,
Passing, unloosing the hold of my comrades'
hands,
Passing the song of the hermit bird and the
tallying song of my soul,
Victorious song, death's outlet song, yet varying ever-altering song,

As low and wailing, yet clear the notes, rising
and falling, flooding the night,
Sadly sinking and fainting, as warning and warning, and yet again bursting with joy, 190
Covering the earth and filling the spread of the
heaven,
As that powerful psalm in the night I heard
from recesses,
Passing, I leave thee lilac with heart-shaped
leaves,
I leave thee there in the door-yard, blooming,
returning with spring.

I cease from my song for thee,
From my gaze on thee in the west, fronting the
west, communing with thee,
O comrade lustrous with silver face in the night.

Yet each to keep and all, retrievements out of
the night,
The song, the wondrous chant of the gray-
brown bird,
And the tallying chant, the echo arous'd in my
soul, 200
With the lustrous and drooping star with the
countenance full of woe,
With the holders holding my hand nearing the
call of the bird,
Comrades mine and I in the midst, and their
memory ever to keep, for the dead I
loved so well,
For the sweetest, wisest soul of all my days
and lands—and this for his dear sake,
Lilac and star and bird twined with the chant
of my soul,
There in the fragrant pines and the cedars dusk
and dim.

1865

O CAPTAIN! MY CAPTAIN! [1]

O Captain! my Captain! our fearful trip is
done,
The ship has weather'd every rack, the prize
we sought is won,
The port is near, the bells I hear, the people
all exulting,
While follow eyes the steady keel, the vessel
grim and daring;
  But O heart! heart! heart!
    O the bleeding drops of red,
      Where on the deck my Captain lies,
        Fallen cold and dead.

[1] In this and a few other poems Whitman brings his
work more nearly into the conventional poetic
form. Does a study of them indicate that Whitman could or could not have written successfully
in the prevailing artistic forms?

O Captain! my Captain! rise up and hear the
    bells;
Rise up—for you the flag is flung—for you the
    bugle trills,   10
For you bouquets and ribbon'd wreaths—for
    you the shores•a-crowding,
For you they call, the swaying mass, their eager
    faces turning;
    Here Captain! dear father!
    This arm beneath your head!
    It is some dream that on the deck,
        You've fallen cold and dead.

My Captain does not answer, his lips are pale
    and still,
My father does not feel my arm, he has no
    pulse nor will,
The ship is anchor'd safe and sound, its voyage
    closed and done,
From fearful trip the victor ship comes in with
    object won;   20
    Exult O shores, and ring O bells!
    But I with mournful tread,
    Walk the deck my Captain lies,
        Fallen cold and dead.
                                              1865-6

AN ARMY CORPS ON THE MARCH

With its cloud of skirmishers in advance,
With now the sound of a single shot snapping
    like a whip, and now an irregular volley,
The swarming ranks press on and on, the dense
    brigades press on,
Glittering dimly, toiling under the sun—the
    dust-cover'd men,
In columns rise and fall to the undulations of
    the ground,
With artillery interspers'd—the wheels rumble,
    the horses sweat,
As the army corps advances.
                                              1865-6

ONE'S-SELF I SING [1]

ONE'S-SELF I sing, a simple separate person,
Yet utter the word Democratic, the word En-
    Masse.

Of physiology from top to toe I sing,
Not physiognomy alone nor brain alone is
    worthy for the Muse, I say the Form
    complete is worthier far,
The Female equally with the Male I sing.

[1] This poem Whitman placed at the beginning of his
final revised edition of his poems.

Of Life immense in passion, pulse, and power,
Cheerful, for freest action form'd under the
    laws divine,
The Modern Man I sing.
                                              1867

DAREST THOU NOW O SOUL

Darest thou now O soul,
Walk out with me toward the unknown region,
Where neither ground is for the feet nor any
    path to follow?

No map there, nor guide,
Nor voice sounding, nor touch of human hand,
Nor face with blooming flesh, nor lips, nor eyes,
    are in that land.

I know it not O soul,
Nor dost thou, all is a blank before us,
All waits undream'd of in that region, that in-
    accessible land.

Till when the ties loosen,   10
All but the ties eternal, Time and Space,
Nor darkness, gravitation, sense, nor any bounds
    bounding us.

Then we burst forth, we float,
In Time and Space O soul, prepared for them,
Equal, equipt at last, (O joy! O fruit of all!)
    them to fulfil O soul.
                                              1870

A NOISELESS PATIENT SPIDER

A noiseless patient spider,
I mark'd where on a little promontory it stood
    isolated,
Mark'd how to explore the vacant vast sur-
    rounding,
It launch'd forth filament, filament, filament,
    out of itself,
Ever unreeling them, ever tirelessly speeding
    them.

And you O my soul where you stand,
Surrounded, detached, in measureless oceans of
    space,
Ceaselessly musing, venturing, throwing, seek-
    ing the spheres to connect them,
Till the bridge you will need be form'd, till the
    ductile anchor hold,   9
Till the gossamer thread you fling catch some-
    where, O my soul.
                                              1870

THE LAST INVOCATION

At the last, tenderly,
From the walls of the powerful fortress'd
   house,
From the clasp of the knitted locks, from the
   keep of the well-closed doors,
Let me be wafted.

Let me glide noiselessly forth;
With the key of softness unlock the locks—with
   a whisper,
Set ope the doors O soul.

Tenderly—be not impatient,
(Strong is your hold O mortal flesh,   9
Strong is your hold O love.)
                                     1870

ETHIOPIA SALUTING THE COLORS

Who are you dusky woman, so ancient hardly
   human,
With your woolly-white and turban'd head, and
   bare bony feet?
Why rising by the roadside here, do you the
   colors greet?

('Tis while our army lines Carolina's sands and
   pines,
Forth from thy hovel door thou Ethiopia
   com'st to me,
As under doughty Sherman I march toward
   the sea.)

Me master years a hundred since from my par-
   ents sunder'd,
A little child, they caught me as the savage
   beast is caught,
Then hither me across the sea the cruel slaver
   brought.

No further does she say, but lingering all the
   day,   10
Her high-borne turban'd head she wags, and
   rolls her darkling eye,
And courtesies to the regiments, the guidons
   moving by.

What is it fateful woman, so blear, hardly
   human?
Why wag your head with turban bound yellow,
   red and green?
Are the things so strange and marvelous you
   see or have seen?
                                     1870

JOY, SHIPMATE, JOY!

Joy, shipmate, joy!
(Pleas'd to my soul at death I cry,)
Our life is closed, our life begins,
The long, long anchorage we leave,
The ship is clear at last, she leaps!
She swiftly courses from the shore,
Joy, shipmate, joy!

                                     1870

THE MYSTIC TRUMPETER

1

Hark, some wild trumpeter, some strange musician,
Hovering unseen in air, vibrates capricious
   tunes tonight.

I hear thee trumpeter, listening alert I catch
   thy notes,
Now pouring, whirling like a tempest round me,
Now low, subdued, now in the distance lost.

2

Come nearer bodiless one, haply in thee re-
   sounds
Some dead composer, haply thy pensive life
Was fill'd with aspirations high, unform'd ideals,
Waves, oceans musical, chaotically surging,
That now ecstatic ghost, close to me bending,
   thy cornet echoing, pealing,   10
Gives out to no one's ears but mine, but freely
   gives to mine,
That I may thee translate.

3

Blow trumpeter free and clear, I follow thee,
While at thy liquid prelude, glad, serene,
The fretting world, the streets, the noisy hours
   of day withdraw,
A holy calm descends like dew upon me,
I walk in cool refreshing night the walks of
   Paradise,
I scent the grass, the moist air and the roses;
Thy song expands my numb'd imbonded spirit,
   thou freest, launchest me,
Floating and basking upon heaven's lake.

4

Blow again trumpeter! and for my sensuous
   eyes,   21
Bring the old pageants, show the feudal world
What charm thy music works! thou makest
   pass before me,

Ladies and cavaliers long dead, barons are in
　　their castle halls, the troubadours are
　　singing,
Arm'd knights go forth to redress wrongs, some
　　in quest of the holy Graal; [1]
I see the tournament, I see the contestants in-
　　cased in heavy armor seated on stately
　　champing horses,
I hear the shouts, the sounds of blows and
　　smiting steel;
I see the Crusaders' tumultuous armies—hark,
　　how the cymbals clang,
Lo, where the monks walk in advance, bearing
　　the cross on high.

5

Blow again trumpeter! and for thy theme,
Take now the enclosing theme of all, the solvent
　　and the setting,　　　　　　　　　　31
Love, that is pulse of all, the sustenance and
　　the pang,
The heart of man and woman all for love,
No other theme but love—knitting, enclosing,
　　all-diffusing love.

O how the immortal phantoms crowd around
　　me!
I see the vast alembic [2] ever working, I see and
　　know the flames that heat the world,
The glow, the blush, the beating hearts of lovers,
So blissful happy some, and some so silent, dark,
　　and nigh to death;
Love, that is all the earth to lovers—love, that
　　mocks time and space,
Love, that is day and night—love, that is sun
　　and moon and stars,　　　　　　　40
Love, that is crimson, sumptuous, sick with
　　perfume,
No other words but words of love, no other
　　thought but love.

6

Blow again trumpeter—conjure war's alarums.

Swift to thy spell a shuddering hum like distant
　　thunder rolls,
Lo, where the arm'd men hasten—lo, mid the
　　clouds of dust the glint of bayonets,
I see the grime-faced cannoneers, I mark the
　　rosy flash amid the smoke, I hear the
　　cracking of the guns;
Nor war alone—thy fearful music-song, wild
　　player, brings every sight of fear,

[1] The cup from which it was believed Christ drank at
the last supper; legend represented it as having
vanished from earth, but as appearing at times
to the pure in heart. See note 1, p. 587.
[2] an old-time chemical vessel used for distillation;
hence a change-producing agent

The deeds of ruthless brigands, rapine, murder
　　—I hear the cries for help!
I see ships foundering at sea, I behold on deck
　　and below deck the terrible tableaus.

7

O trumpeter, methinks I am myself the instru-
　　ment thou playest,　　　　　　　　50
Thou melt'st my heart, my brain—thou movest,
　　drawest, changest them at will;
And now thy sullen notes send darkness through
　　me,
Thou takest away all cheering light, all hope,
I see the enslaved, the overthrown, the hurt,
　　the opprest of the whole earth,
I feel the measureless shame and humiliation
　　of my race, it becomes all mine,
Mine too the revenges of humanity, the wrongs
　　of ages, baffled feuds and hatreds,
Utter defeat upon me weighs—all lost—the foe
　　victorious,
(Yet 'mid the ruins Pride colossal stands un-
　　shaken to the last,
Endurance, resolution to the last.)

8

Now trumpeter for thy close,　　　　　60
Vouchsafe a higher strain than any yet,
Sing to my soul, renew its languishing faith
　　and hope,
Rouse up my slow belief, give me some vision
　　of the future,
Give me for once its prophecy and joy.

O glad, exulting, culminating song!
A vigor more than earth's is in thy notes,
Marches of victory—man disenthral'd—the
　　conqueror at last,
Hymns to the universal God from universal
　　man—all joy!
A reborn race appears—a perfect world, all joy!
Women and men in wisdom innocence and
　　health—all joy!　　　　　　　　70
Riotous laughing bacchanals fill'd with joy!
War, sorrow, suffering gone—the rank earth
　　purged—nothing but joy left!
The ocean fill'd with joy—the atmosphere all
　　joy!
Joy! joy! in freedom, worship, love! joy in the
　　ecstasy of life!
Enough to merely be! enough to breathe!
Joy! joy! all over joy!　　　　　　　1872

YOUTH, DAY, OLD AGE, AND NIGHT

Youth, large, lusty, loving—youth full of grace,
　　force, fascination,

Do you know that Old Age may come after you
　　with equal grace, force, fascination?
Day full-blown and splendid—day of the im-
　　mense sun, action, ambition, laughter,
The Night follows close with millions of suns,
　　and sleep and restoring darkness.

TO THE MAN-OF-WAR BIRD [1]

Thou who hast slept all night upon the storm,
Waking renew'd on thy prodigious pinions,
(Burst the wild storm? above it thou ascend-
　　ed'st,
And rested on the sky, thy slave that cradled
　　thee,)
Now a blue point, far, far in heaven floating,
As to the light emerging here on deck I watch
　　thee,
(Myself a speck, a point on the world's floating
　　vast.)

Far, far at sea,
After the night's fierce drifts have strewn the
　　shore with wrecks,
With re-appearing day as now so happy and
　　serene,　　　　　　　　　　　　　　10
The rosy and elastic dawn, the flashing sun,
The limpid spread of air cerulean,
Thou also re-appearest.

Thou born to match the gale, (thou art all
　　wings,)
To cope with heaven and earth and sea and hur-
　　ricane,
Thou ship of air that never furl'st thy sails,
Days, even weeks untired and onward, through
　　spaces, realms gyrating,
At dusk that look'st on Senegal, [2] at morn
　　America,
That sport'st amid the lightning-flash and thun-
　　der-cloud,
In them, in thy experiences, had'st thou my
　　soul,　　　　　　　　　　　　　　　20
What joys! what joys were thine!

　　　　　　　　　　　　　　　　　　1876

ITALIAN MUSIC IN DAKOTA

[*"The Seventeenth—the finest Regimental Band
　　　　I ever heard."*]

Through the soft evening air enwinding all,
Rocks, woods, fort, cannon, pacing sentries, end-
　　less wilds,
In dulcet streams, in flutes' and cornets' notes,

Electric, pensive, turbulent, artificial,
(Yet strangely fitting even here, meanings un-
　　known before,
Subtler than ever, more harmony, as if born
　　here, related here,
Not to the city's fresco'd rooms, not to the
　　audience of the opera house,
Sounds, echoes, wandering strains, as really
　　here at home,
Sonnambula's innocent love, trios with *Norma's*
　　anguish,
And thy ecstatic chorus *Poliuto*); [3]　　10
Ray'd in the limpid yellow slanting sundown,
Music, Italian music in Dakota.

While Nature, sovereign of this gnarl'd realm,
Lurking in hidden barbaric grim recesses,
Acknowledging rapport however far remov'd,
(As some old root or soil of earth its lastborn
　　flower or fruit,)
Listens well pleas'd.

WITH HUSKY-HAUGHTY LIPS, O SEA!

With husky-haughty lips, O sea!
Where day and night I wend thy surf-beat
　　shore,
Imaging to my sense thy varied strange sugges-
　　tions,
(I see and plainly list thy talk and conference
　　here),
Thy troops of white-maned racers racing to the
　　goal,
Thy ample, smiling face, dash'd with the spark-
　　ling dimples of the sun,
Thy brooding scowl and murk—thy unloos'd
　　hurricanes,
Thy unsubduedness, caprices, wilfulness;
Great as thou art above the rest, thy many
　　tears—a lack from all eternity in thy
　　content,
(Naught but the greatest struggles, wrongs, de-
　　feats, could make thee greatest—no less
　　could make thee,)　　　　　　　　10
Thy lonely state—something thou ever seek'st
　　and seek'st, yet never gain'st,
Surely some right withheld—some voice, in
　　huge monotonous rage, of freedom-lover
　　pent,
Some vast heart, like a planet's chain'd and
　　chafing in those breakers,
By lengthen'd swell, and spasm, and panting
　　breath,
And rhythmic rasping of thy sands and waves,

---

[1] Compare with Bryant's "To a Waterfowl," p. 249, and
　　with Shelley's "To a Skylark," noting the differ-
　　ence in the inner spirit of the three authors.
[2] a French colony in western Africa

[3] Italian operas by Bellini and by Donizetti, composers
　　of the nineteenth century

And serpent hiss, and savage peals of laughter,
And undertones of distant lion roar,
(Sounding, appealing to the sky's deaf ear—
        but now, rapport for once,
A phantom in the night thy confidant for once,)
The first and last confession of the globe,
Outsurging, muttering from thy soul's abysms,
The tale of cosmic elemental passion,   22
Thou tellest to a kindred soul.

                                        1884

SIDNEY LANIER 1842-1881

Lanier was born in Macon, Georgia; he graduated from Oglethorpe College, taught there for a year, at twenty entered the Confederate army, and served during most of the war. He was taken prisoner and came home with greatly impaired health. Forced by necessity, he took up law, but his passion for literature and music was too strong to be resisted. Though self-taught, he was an accomplished musician, and became well known professionally. After the publication of "Corn," 1875, he was commissioned to write the official ode for the Centennial Exposition, 1876. From 1879 he was a lecturer on phases of English literature at Johns Hopkins University. The last six years of his life were a fever of activity, constantly interrupted and frustrated by illness. A volume of his poems appeared in 1877, *The Science of English Verse* in 1880, *The English Novel* in 1883, *Shakespeare and his Forerunners* in 1902.

Though Lanier has been criticized as an "improvisatore," such an estimate is not only unsympathetic but narrow. His work, though not great in bulk, is strongly American in subject, original, and fertile in invention. Some of it is as rich in music as Swinburne's, and one of its strongest characteristics is a spontaneous enthusiasm rare in American poetry in his time. He is the foremost poet of the South after Poe.

Biography: E. Mims, (AML) 1905. Criticism: Bradford, (AP); same, *No. Am.* 211:805-17; Pattee; Burton; Chubb; Stedman; Macy; N. Foerster, "Lanier as a Poet of Nature," *Nation* 108: 981-3.

BARNACLES

I

My soul is sailing through the sea,
But the Past is heavy and hindereth me.
The Past hath crusted cumbrous shells
That hold the flesh of cold sea-mells
        About my soul.
The huge waves wash, the high waves roll,
Each barnacle clingeth and worketh dole
        And hindereth me from sailing!

II

Old Past let go, and drop i' the sea
Till fathomless waters cover thee!   10
For I am living but thou art dead;
Thou drawest back, I strive ahead
        The Day to find.
Thy shells unbind! Night comes behind,
I needs must hurry with the wind
        And trim me best for sailing!

1867   1867

CORN

Today the woods are trembling through and
        through
With shimmering forms, that flash before my
        view,
Then melt in green as dawn-stars melt in blue.
    The leaves that wave against my cheek caress
    Like women's hands; the embracing boughs
        express
        A subtlety of mighty tenderness;
    The copse-depths into little noises start,
    That sound anon like beatings of a heart,
    Anon like talk 'twixt lips not far apart.
    The beech dreams balm, as a dreamer hums a
        song;   10
    Through that vague wafture, expirations
        strong
    Throb from young hickories breathing deep
        and long
With stress and urgence bold of prisoned spring
        And ecstasy of burgeoning. [1]
    Now, since the dew-plashed road of morn is
        dry,
    Forth venture odors of more quality
    And heavenlier giving. Like Jove's locks
        awry,
        Long muscadines [2]
Rich-wreathe the spacious foreheads of great
        pines,   19
And breathe ambrosial passion from their vines.
    I pray with mosses, ferns and flowers shy
    That hide like gentle nuns from human eye
    To lift adoring perfumes to the sky.
    I hear faint bridal-sighs of brown and green
    Dying to silent hints of kisses keen
    As far lights fringe into a pleasant sheen.
        I start at fragmentary whispers, blown
        From undertalks of leafy souls unknown,
        Vague purports sweet, of inarticulate tone.

Dreaming of gods, men, nuns and brides, between   30
Old companies of oaks that inward lean

[1] bursting of buds
[2] vines of the Malaga grape

To join their radiant amplitudes of green
  I slowly move, with ranging looks that pass
  Up from the matted miracles of grass
Into yon veined complex of space,
Where sky and leafage interlace
  So close, the heaven of blue is seen
  Inwoven with a heaven of green.

I wander to the zigzag-cornered fence
Where sassafras, intrenched in brambles dense,
Contests with stolid vehemence   41
  The march of culture, setting limb and thorn
  As pikes against the army of the corn.

There, while I pause, my fieldward-faring eyes
Take harvests, where the stately corn-ranks rise
  Of inward dignities
And large benignities and insights wise,
  Graces and modest majesties.
Thus, without theft, I reap another's field;
Thus, without tilth, I house a wondrous yield,
And heap my heart with quintuple crops con-
  cealed.   51

Look, out of line one tall corn-captain stands
Advanced beyond the foremost of his bands,
  And waves his blades upon the very edge
  And hottest thicket of the battling hedge.
Thou lustrous stalk, that ne'er mayst walk nor
  talk,
  Still shalt thou type the poet-soul sublime
  That leads the vanward of his timid time
  And sings up cowards with commanding
  rime—
Soul calm, like thee, yet fain, like thee, to grow
By double increment, above, below;   61
  Soul homely, as thou art, yet rich in grace
  like thee,
  Teaching the yeomen selfless chivalry
  That moves in gentle curves of courtesy;
Soul filled like thy long veins with sweetness
  tense,
  By every godlike sense
Transmuted from the four wild elements.
  Drawn to high plans,
  Thou lift'st more stature than a mortal man's,
Yet ever piercest downward in the mold
  And keepest hold   70
  Upon the reverend and steadfast earth
  That gave thee birth;
  Yea, standest smiling in thy future grave,
  Serene and brave,
  With unremitting breath
  Inhaling life from death,
Thine epitaph writ fair in fruitage eloquent,
  Thyself thy monument.

As poets should   80
Thou hast built up thy hardihood
With universal food,
  Drawn in select proportion fair
  From honest mold and vagabond air;
From darkness of the dreadful night,
  And joyful light;
  From antique ashes, whose departed flame
  In thee has finer life and longer fame;
From wounds and balms,
From storms and calms,   90
  From potsherds and dry bones
  And ruin-stones.
Into thy vigorous substance thou hast wrought
Whate'er the hand of Circumstance hath
  brought;
  Yea, into cool solacing green hast spun
  White radiance hot from out the sun.
So thou dost mutually leaven
Strength of earth with grace of heaven;
  So thou dost marry new and old
  Into a one of higher mold;   100
  So thou dost reconcile the hot and cold,
  The dark and bright,
And many a heart-perplexing opposite:
  And so,
  Akin by blood to high and low,
Fitly thou playest out thy poet's part,
Richly expending thy much-bruisèd heart
  In equal care to nourish lord in hall
  Or beast in stall:
  Thou took'st from all that thou might'st give
  to all.   110

O steadfast dweller on the selfsame spot
Where thou wast born, that still repinest not—
Type of the home-fond heart, the happy lot!—
  Deeply thy mild content rebukes the land
  Whose flimsy homes, built on the shifting
  sand
Of trade, forever rise and fall
With alternation whimsical,
  Enduring scarce a day,
  Then swept away
By swift engulfments of incalculable tides
Whereon capricious Commerce rides.   121
Look, thou substantial spirit of content!
Across this little vale, thy continent,
  To where, beyond the moldering mill,
  Yon old deserted Georgian hill
Bares to the sun his piteous aged crest
  And seamy breast,
  By restless-hearted children left to lie
Untended there beneath the heedless sky,
  As barbarous folk expose their old to die.
Upon that generous-rounding side,   131
  With gullies scarified

Where keen Neglect his lash hath plied,
Dwelt one I knew of old, who played at toil,
And gave to coquette Cotton soul and soil.
  Scorning the slow reward of patient grain,
  He sowed his heart with hopes of swifter gain,
  Then sat him down and waited for the rain.
He sailed in borrowed ships of usury—
A foolish Jason on a treacherous sea,   140
Seeking the Fleece and finding misery.
  Lulled by smooth-rippling loans, in idle
    trance
  He lay, content that unthrift Circumstance
  Should plow for him the stony field of
    Chance.
Yea, gathering crops whose worth no man might
    tell,
He staked his life on games of Buy-and-Sell,
And turned each field into a gambler's hell.
  Aye, as each year began,
  My farmer to the neighboring city ran;
  Passed with a mournful anxious face   150
Into the banker's inner place;
Parleyed, excused, pleaded for longer grace;
  Railed at the drought, the worm, the rust, the
    grass;
  With many an *oh* and *if* and *but alas*
Parried or swallowed searching questions rude,
And kissed the dust to soften Dives's [1] mood.
At last, small loans by pledges great renewed,
  He issues smiling from the fatal door,   159
  And buys with lavish hand his yearly store
  Till his small borrowings will yield no more.
Aye, as each year declined,
With bitter heart and ever-brooding mind
He mourned his fate unkind.
  In dust, in rain, with might and main,
  He nursed his cotton, cursed his grain,
  Fretted for news that made him fret again,
Snatched at each telegram of Future Sale,
And thrilled with Bulls' or Bears' [2] alternate
    wail—
In hope or fear alike forever pale.   170
  And thus from year to year, through hope
    and fear,
  With many a curse and many a secret tear,
  Striving in vain his cloud of debt to clear,
    At last
He woke to find his foolish dreaming past,
  And all his best-of-life the easy prey
  Of squandering scamps and quacks that lined
    his way
    With vile array,
From rascal statesman down to petty knave;
Himself, at best, for all his bragging brave,   180

[1] "a rich man" (Lat.) See *Luke* xiv, 19.
[2] Stock exchange terms; the "bulls" benefit by a rise,
  the "bears" by a fall in the price of stocks.

A gamester's catspaw and a banker's slave.
  Then, worn and gray, and sick with deep
    unrest,
  He fled away into the oblivious West,
    Unmourned, unblest.

Old hill! old hill! thou gashed and hairy Lear [3]
Whom the divine Cordelia of the year,
E'en pitying Spring, will vainly strive to cheer—
  King, that no subject man nor beast may
    own,
  Discrowned, undaughtered and alone—
Yet shall the great God turn thy fate,   190
And bring thee back into thy monarch state
    And majesty immaculate.
  Lo, through hot waverings of the August
    morn,
  Thou givest from thy vasty sides forlorn
  Visions of golden treasuries of corn—
Ripe largesse lingering for some bolder heart
That manfully shall take thy part,
    And tend thee,
    And defend thee,   199
With antique sinew and with modern art.
1874   1875

A SONG OF THE FUTURE

  Sail fast, sail fast,
  Ark of my hopes, Ark of my dreams;
  Sweep lordly o'er the drowned Past,
  Fly glittering through the sun's strange
    beams;
  Sail fast, sail fast.
Breaths of new buds from off some drying lea
With news about the Future scent the sea:
My brain is beating like the heart of Haste:
I'll loose me a bird upon this Present waste;   10
  Go, trembling song,
  And stay not long; oh, stay not long:
  Thou'rt only a gray and sober dove,
  But thine eye is faith and thy wing is love.
1875   1876

EVENING SONG

Look off, dear Love, across the sallow sands,
  And mark yon meeting of the sun and sea,
How long they kiss in sight of all the lands.
  Ah! longer, longer, we.

Now in the sea's red vintage melts the sun,
  As Egypt's pearl dissolved in rosy wine,
And Cleopatra night drinks all. [4] 'Tis done,
  Love, lay thine hand in mine.

[3] See Shakespeare's *King Lear*.
[4] Pliny says that Cleopatra in a wager with Antony
  dissolved in wine and drank a priceless pearl.
  See also *Hamlet* V, ii, 283.

Come forth, sweet stars, and comfort heaven's
    heart;
  Glimmer, ye waves, round else-unlighted
    sands.   10
O night! divorce our sun and sky apart
    Never our lips, our hands.
1876   1877

THE STIRRUP-CUP

Death, thou'rt a cordial old and rare:
Look how compounded, with what care!
Time got his wrinkles reaping thee
Sweet herbs from all antiquity.

David to thy distillage went,
Keats, and Gotama [1] excellent,
Omar Khayyàm, [2] and Chaucer bright,
And Shakespeare for a king-delight.

These were to sweeten thee with song;
The blood of heroes made thee strong.   10
What heroes! Ah, for shame, for shame!
The worthiest died without a name.

Then, Time, let not a drop be spilt:
Hand me the cup whene'er thou wilt;
'Tis thy rich stirrup-cup to me;
I'll drink it down right smilingly.
1877   1877

FROM THE FLATS

What heartache—ne'er a hill!
Inexorable, vapid, vague and chill
The drear sand-levels drain my spirit low.
With one poor word they tell me all they know;
Whereat their stupid tongues, to tease my pain,
Do drawl it o'er again and o'er again.
They hurt my heart with griefs I cannot name:
  Always the same, the same.

Nature hath no surprise,   9
No ambuscade of beauty 'gainst mine eyes
From brake or lurking dell or deep defile;
No humors, frolic forms—this mile, that mile;
No rich reserves or happy-valley hopes
Beyond the bend of roads, the distant slopes.
Her fancy fails, her wild is all run tame:
  Ever the same, the same.

Oh might I through these tears
But glimpse some hill my Georgia high uprears,
Where white the quartz and pink the pebble
    shine,

The hickory heavenward strives, the musca-
    dine [3]   20
Swings o'er the slope, the oak's far-falling shade
Darkens the dogwood in the bottom-glade,
And down the hollow from a ferny nook
  Bright leaps a living brook!
1877   1877

SONG OF THE CHATTAHOOCHEE [4]

  Out of the hills of Habersham, [5]
    Down the valleys of Hall,
I hurry amain to reach the plain,
Run the rapid and leap the fall,
Split at the rock and together again,
Accept my bed, or narrow or wide,
And flee from folly on every side
With a lover's pain to attain the plain
    Far from the hills of Habersham,
    Far from the valleys of Hall.   10

  All down the hills of Habersham,
    All through the valleys of Hall,
The rushes cried *Abide, abide,*
The willful waterweeds held me thrall,
The laving laurel turned my tide,
The ferns and the fondling grass said *Stay,*
The dewberry dipped for to work delay,
And the little reeds sighed *Abide, abide,*
    Here in the hills of Habersham,
    Here in the valleys of Hall.   20

  High o'er the hills of Habersham,
    Veiling the valleys of Hall,
The hickory told me manifold
Fair tales of shade, the poplar tall
Wrought me her shadowy self to hold,
The chestnut, the oak, the walnut, the pine,
Overleaning, with flickering meaning and sign,
Said, *Pass not, so cold, these manifold*
    Deep shades of the hills of Habersham,
    These glades in the valleys of Hall.   30

  And oft in the hills of Habersham,
    And oft in the valleys of Hall,
The white quartz shone, and the smooth brook-
    stone
Did bar me of passage with friendly brawl,
And many a luminous jewel lone
—Crystals clear or a-cloud with mist,
Ruby, garnet, and amethyst—
Made lures with the lights of streaming stone
    In the clefts of the hills of Habersham,
    In the beds of the valleys of Hall.   40

[1] the family name of Buddha, the founder of Buddhism,
    who lived in the 6th century
[2] a Persian poet of the 11th and 12th centuries
[3] See note 2, p. 704.
[4] Cf. Tennyson's "The Brook."
[5] Habersham and Hall are counties in Georgia on the
    upper waters of the Chattahoochee.

But oh, not the hills of Habersham,
And oh, not the valleys of Hall
Avail: I am fain for to water the plain.
Downward the voices of Duty call—
Downward, to toil and be mixed with the main,
The dry fields burn, and the mills are to turn,
And a myriad flowers mortally yearn,
And the lordly main from beyond the plain
 Calls o'er the hills of Habersham, 49
 Calls through the valleys of Hall.

1877   1877

THE MOCKING BIRD

Superb and sole, upon a pluméd spray
 That o'er the general leafage boldly grew,
 He summ'd the woods in song; or typic
  drew [1].
The watch of hungry hawks, the lone dismay
Of languid doves when long their lovers stray,
 And all birds' passion-plays that sprinkle dew
 At morn in brake or bosky avenue.
Whate'er birds did or dreamed, this bird could
 say.
Then down he shot, bounced airily along
The sward, twitched-in a grasshopper, made
 song   10
 Midflight, perched, prinked, and to his art
  again.
 Sweet Science, this large riddle read me
  plain:
How may the death of that dull insect be
The life of yon trim Shakespeare on the tree?

             1877

THE HARLEQUIN OF DREAMS

Swift, through some trap mine eyes have never
 found,
 Dim-panel'd in the painted scene of Sleep,
 Thou, giant Harlequin of Dreams, dost leap
Upon my spirit's stage. Then Sight and Sound,
Then Space and Time, then Language, Mete
 and Bound,
 And all familiar Forms that firmly keep
 Man's reason in the road, change faces, peep
Betwixt the legs and mock the daily round.
Yet thou canst more than mock: sometimes my
 tears
 At midnight break through bounden lids—
  a sign   10
  Thou hast a heart: and oft thy little leaven
Of dream-taught wisdom works me bettered
 years.
 In one night witch, saint, trickster, fool
  divine,

[1] represented in his song

   I think thou'rt Jester at the Court of
   Heaven!

1878   1878

THE MARSHES OF GLYNN [2]

Glooms of the live-oaks, beautiful-braided and
 woven
With intricate shades of the vines that myriad-
 cloven
 Clamber the forks of the multiform
  boughs,—
   Emerald twilights,—
   Virginal shy lights,
Wrought of the leaves to allure to the whisper
 of vows,
When lovers pace timidly down through the
 green colonnades
 Of the dim sweet woods, of the dear dark
 woods,
 Of the heavenly woods and glades,
That run to the radiant marginal sand-beach
 within   10
 The wide sea-marshes of Glynn;—

Beautiful glooms, soft dusks in the noon-day
 fire,—
Wildwood privacies, closets of lone desire,
Chamber from chamber parted with wavering
 arras of leaves,—
Cells for the passionate pleasure of prayer to
 the soul that grieves,
Pure with a sense of the passing of saints
 through the wood,
Cool for the dutiful weighing of ill with good;—

O braided dusks of the oak and woven shades
 of the vine,
While the riotous noon-day sun of the June-day
 long did shine
Ye held me fast in your heart and I held you
 fast in mine;   20
But now when the noon is no more, and riot is
 rest,
And the sun is a-wait at the ponderous gate of
 the West,
And the slant yellow beam down the wood-aisle
 doth seem
Like a lane into heaven that leads from a
 dream,—
Ay, now, when my soul all day hath drunken
 the soul of the oak,
And my heart is at ease from men, and the
 wearisome sound of the stroke
 Of the scythe of time and the trowel of trade
 is low,

[2] the sea-coast marshes of Glynn County, Georgia

And belief overmasters doubt, and I know
   that I know,
And my spirit is grown to a lordly great
   compass within,
That the length and the breadth and the sweep
   of the marshes of Glynn   30
  Will work me no fear like the fear they have
   wrought me of yore
When length was fatigue, and when breadth was
   but bitterness sore,
And when terror and shrinking and dreary un-
   namable pain
Drew over me out of the merciless miles of the
   plain,—

  Oh, now, unafraid, I am fain to face
    The vast sweet visage of space.
  To the edge of the wood I am drawn, I am
   drawn,
Where the gray beach glimmering runs, as a
   belt of the dawn,
   For a mete and a mark
   To the forest-dark:—   40
      So:
Affable live-oak leaning low—
  Thus—with your favor—soft, with a reverent
   hand,
(Not lightly touching your person, Lord of the
   land!)
Bending your beauty aside, with a step I stand
  On the firm-packed sand,
   Free
By a world of marsh that borders a world of
   sea.

Sinuous southward and sinuous northward the
   shimmering band
  Of the sand-beach fastens the fringe of the
   marsh to the folds of the land.   50
Inward and outward to northward and southward the beach-lines linger and curl
As a silver-wrought garment that clings to and
   follows the firm sweet limbs of a girl.
  Vanishing, swerving, evermore curving again
   into sight,
  Softly the sand-beach wavers away to a dim
   gray looping of light.
  And what if behind me to westward the wall
   of the woods stands high?
  The world lies east: how ample, the marsh
   and the sea and the sky!
  A league and a league of marsh-grass waist-
   high, broad in the blade,
  Green, and all of a height, and unflecked with
   a light or a shade,
   Stretch leisurely off, in a pleasant plain,
   To the terminal blue of the main.   60

Oh, what is abroad in the marsh and the terminal sea?
  Somehow my soul seems suddenly free
  From the weighing of fate and the sad discussion of sin,
By the length and the breadth and the sweep
   of the marshes of Glynn.

Ye marshes, how candid and simple and nothing-
   withholding and free
Ye publish yourselves to the sky and offer yourselves to the sea!

Tolerant plains, that suffer the sea and the rains
   and the sun,
Ye spread and span like the catholic [1] man who
   hath mightily won
God out of knowledge and good out of infinite
   pain
And sight out of blindness and purity out of a
   stain.   70

As the marsh-hen secretly builds on the watery
   sod,
Behold I will build me a nest on the greatness
   of God:
I will fly in the greatness of God as the marsh-
   hen flies
In the freedom that fills all the space 'twixt
   the marsh and the skies:
By so many roots as the marsh-grass sends in
   the sod
I will heartily lay me a hold on the greatness of
   God:
Oh, like to the greatness of God is the greatness
   within
The range of the marshes, the liberal marshes of
   Glynn.

And the sea lends large, as the marsh: lo, out
   of his plenty the sea
Pours fast: full soon the time of the flood-tide
   must be: 80
Look how the grace of the sea doth go
About and about through the intricate channels
   that flow
   Here and there,
    Everywhere,
Till his waters have flooded the uttermost creeks
   and the low-lying lanes,
And the marsh is meshed with a million veins,
That like as with rosy and silvery essences flow
   In the rose-and-silver evening glow. Fare-
   well, my lord Sun!
The creeks overflow: a thousand rivulets run
'Twixt the roots of the sod; the blades of the
   marsh-grass stir;   91

[1] liberal, tolerant-minded

Passeth a hurrying sound of wings that westward whirr:
Passeth, and all is still; and the currents cease
to run;
And the sea and the marsh are one.

How still the plains of the waters be!
The tide is in his ecstasy.
The tide is at his highest height:
And it is night.

And now from the Vast of the Lord will the
waters of sleep
Roll in on the souls of men,   100
But who will reveal to our waking ken
The forms that swim and the shapes that creep
Under the waters of sleep?
And I would I could know what swimmeth
below when the tide comes in
On the length and the breadth of the marvelous
marshes of Glynn.

1878   1879?

THE REVENGE OF HAMISH

It was three slim does and a ten-tined [1] buck
in the bracken lay;
And all of a sudden the sinister smell of a
man,
Awaft on a wind-shift, wavered and ran
Down the hill-side, and sifted along through the
bracken and passed that way.

Then Nan got a-tremble at nostril; she was the
daintiest doe;
In the print of her velvet flank on the velvet
fern
She reared, and rounded her ears in turn.
Then the buck leaped up, and his head as a
king's to a crown did go
Full high in the breeze, and he stood as if Death
had the form of a deer;
And the two slim does long lazily stretching
arose,   10
For their day-dream slowlier came to a close,
Till they woke and were still, breath-bound with
waiting and wonder and fear.

Then Alan the huntsman sprang over the hillock,
the hounds shot by,
The does and the ten-tined buck made a marvelous bound,
The hounds swept after with never a sound,
But Alan loud winded his horn in sign that the
quarry was nigh.

[1] with ten points on the antlers

For at dawn of that day proud Maclean of
Lochbuy to the hunt had waxed wild,
And he cursed at old Alan till Alan fared off
with the hounds
For to drive him the deer to the lower glen-
grounds:
"I will kill a red deer," quoth Maclean, "in the
sight of the wife and the child."   20

So gayly he paced with the wife and the child
to his chosen stand;
But he hurried tall Hamish the henchman
ahead: "Go turn,"
Cried Maclean—"if the deer seek to cross to
the burn,
Do thou turn them to me: nor fail, lest thy back
be red as thy hand!"

Now hard-fortuned Hamish, half blown of his
breath with the height of the hill,
Was white in the face when the ten-tined buck
and the does
Drew leaping to burn-ward; huskily rose
His shouts, and his nether lip twitched, and his
legs were o'er-weak for his will.

So the deer darted lightly by Hamish and
bounded away to the burn.
But Maclean never bating his watch tarried
waiting below.   30
Still Hamish hung heavy with fear for to go
All the space of an hour; then he went, and his
face was greenish and stern,

And his eye sat back in the socket, and shrunken
the eyeballs shone,
As withdrawn from a vision of deeds it were
shame to see.
"Now, now, grim henchman, what is't with
thee?"
Brake Maclean, and his wrath rose red as a
beacon the wind hath upblown.

"Three does and a ten-tined buck made out,"
spoke Hamish, full mild,
"And I ran for to turn, but my breath it was
blown, and they passed;
I was weak, for ye called ere I broke me my
fast."
Cried Maclean: "Now a ten-tined buck in the
sight of the wife and the child   40

I had killed if the gluttonous kern had not
wrought me a snail's own wrong!"
Then he sounded, and down came kinsmen
and clansmen all:

"Ten blows, for ten tine, on his back let
    fall,
And reckon no stroke if the blood follow not at
    the bite of the thong!"

So Hamish made bare, and took him his strokes;
    at the last he smiled.
    "Now I'll to the burn," quoth Maclean, "for
      it still may be
    If a slimmer-paunched henchman will hurry
      with me,
I shall kill me the ten-tined buck for a gift to
    the wife and the child!"

Then the clansmen departed, by this path and
    that; and over the hill
    Sped Maclean with an outward wrath for an
      inward shame;   50
    And that place of the lashing full quiet be-
      came;
And the wife and the child stood sad; and
    bloody-backed Hamish sat still.

But look! red Hamish has risen; quick about
    and about turns he.
    "There is none betwixt me and the crag-top!"
      he screams under breath.
    Then, livid as Lazarus lately from death,
He snatches the child from the mother, and
    clambers the crag toward the sea.

Now the mother drops breath; she is dumb, and
    her heart goes dead for a space,
    Till the motherhood, mistress of death,
      shrieks, shrieks through the glen,
    And that place of the lashing is live with
      men,
And Maclean, and the gillie [1] that told him,
    dash up in a desperate race.   60

Not a breath's time for asking; an eye-glance
    reveals all the tale untold.
    They follow mad Hamish afar up the crag
      toward the sea,
    And the lady cries: "Clansmen, run for a
      fee!—
Yon castle and lands to the two first hands that
    shall hook him and hold

Fast Hamish back from the brink!"—and ever
    she flies up the steep,
    And the clansmen pant, and they sweat, and
      they jostle and strain.
    But, mother, 'tis vain; but, father, 'tis vain;
Stern Hamish stands bold on the brink, and
    dangles the child o'er the deep.

[1] man-servant

Now a faintness falls on the men that run, and
    they all stand still.
    And the wife prays Hamish as if he were
      God, on her knees,   70
    Crying: "Hamish! O Hamish! but please,
      but please
For to spare him!" and Hamish still dangles
    the child, with a wavering will.

On a sudden he turns; with a sea-hawk scream,
    and a gibe, and a song,
    Cries: "So; I will spare ye the child if, in
      sight of ye all,
Ten blows on Maclean's bare back shall fall,
And ye reckon no stroke if the blood follow
    not at the bite of the thong!"

Then Maclean he set hardly his tooth to his lip
    that his tooth was red,
    Breathed short for a space, said: "Nay, but
      it never shall be!
    Let me hurl off the damnable hound in the
      sea!"
But the wife: "Can Hamish go fish us the child
    from the sea, if dead?   80

Say yea!—Let them lash *me*, Hamish?"—
    "Nay!"—"Husband, the lashing will
      heal;
    But, oh, who will heal me the bonny sweet
      bairn in his grave?
    Could ye cure me my heart with the death of
      a knave?
Quick! Love! I will bare thee—so—kneel!"
    Then Maclean 'gan slowly to kneel

With never a word, till presently downward he
    jerked to the earth.
    Then the henchman—he that smote Hamish
      —would tremble and lag;
    "Strike, hard!" quoth Hamish, full stern,
      from the crag;
Then he struck him, and "One!" sang Hamish,
    and danced with the child in his mirth.

And no man spake beside Hamish; he counted
    each stroke with a song.
    When the last stroke fell, then he moved him
      a pace down the height,   90
    And he held forth the child in the heart-
      aching sight
Of the mother, and looked all pitiful grave, as
    repenting a wrong.

And there as the motherly arms stretched out
    with the thanksgiving prayer—

And there as the mother crept up with a
    fearful swift pace,
Till her finger nigh felt of the bairnie's face—
In a flash fierce Hamish turned round and lifted
    the child in the air,

And sprang with the child in his arms from the
    horrible height in the sea,
Shrill screeching, "Revenge!" in the wind-
    rush; and pallid Maclean,
Age-feeble with anger and impotent pain,
Crawled up on the crag, and lay flat, and locked
    hold of dead roots of a tree—   100

And gazed hungrily o'er, and the blood from his
    back drip-dripped in the brine,
And a sea-hawk flung down a skeleton fish as
    he flew,
And the mother stared white on the waste of
    blue,
And the wind drove a cloud to seaward, and the
    sun began to shine.

1878   1878

THE CRYSTAL

At midnight, death's and truth's unlocking-time,
When far within the spirit's hearing rolls
The great soft rumble of the course of things—
A bulk of silence in a mask of sound—
When darkness clears our vision that by day
Is sun-blind, and the soul's a ravening owl
For truth and flitteth here and there about
Low-lying woody tracts of time, and oft
Is minded for to sit upon a bough,
Dry-dead and sharp, of some long-stricken tree
And muse in that gaunt place—'twas then my
    heart,   11
Deep in the meditative dark, cried out:
    "Ye companies of governor-spirits grave,
Bards, and old bringers-down of flaming news
From steep-walled heavens, holy malcontents,
Sweet seers, and stellar visionaries, all
That brood about the skies of poesy,
Full bright ye shine, insuperable stars;
Yet, if a man look hard upon you, none
With total luster blazeth, no, not one   20
But hath some heinous freckle of the flesh
Upon his shining cheek, not one but winks
His ray, opaqued with intermittent mist
Of defect; yea, you masters all must ask
Some sweet forgiveness, which we leap to give,
We lovers of you, heavenly-glad to meet
Your largesse so with love, and interplight
Your geniuses with our mortalities.

Thus unto thee, O sweetest Shakespeare sole,
A hundred hurts a day I do forgive   30
('Tis little, but, enchantment! 'tis for thee):
Small curious quibble; [1] Juliet's prurient pun [2]
In the poor, pale face of Romeo's fancied death;
Cold rant of Richard; [3] Henry's fustian roar
Which frights away that sleep he invocates; [4]
Wronged Valentine's unnatural haste to yield; [5]
Too-silly shifts of maids that mask as men
In faint disguises that could ne'er disguise—
Viola, Julia, Portia, Rosalind; [6]
Fatigues most drear, and needless overtax   40
Of speech obscure that had as lief be plain;
Last I forgive (with more delight, because
'Tis more to do) the labored-lewd discourse
That e'en thy young invention's youngest heir [7]
Besmirched the world with.

                    Father Homer! thee,
Thee also I forgive thy sandy wastes
Of prose and catalogue, thy drear harangues
That tease the patience of the centuries;
Thy sleazy scrap of story—but a rogue's
Rape of a light-o'-love—too soiled a patch
To broider with the gods.

                    Thee, Socrates,   51
Thou dear and very strong one, I forgive
Thy year-worn cloak, [8] thine iron stringencies
That were but dandy upside-down, thy words
Of truth that, mildlier spoke had mainlier [9]
    wrought.

So, Buddha, beautiful! I pardon thee
That all the All thou hadst for needy man
Was Nothing, and thy Best of being was
But not to be. [10]

                  Worn Dante, I forgive
The implacable hates that in thy horrid hells   60

[1] Any cheap play on words; cf. *Julius Caesar*, I, i, 11-36; *Hamlet*, V, i, 1 ff. Or, possibly, the allusion is to *The Merchant of Venice*, with particular reference to the "pound of flesh" upon which rests the main plot.
[2] *Romeo and Juliet*, III, ii
[3] *Richard III*, I, i, 1 ff.
[4] *2 Henry IV*, III, i, 5-31
[5] *Two Gentlemen of Verona*, V, iv, 77-83
[6] in *Twelfth Night, Two Gentlemen of Verona, The Merchant of Venice*, and *As You Like It*, respectively
[7] *Venus and Adonis*
[8] Socrates seems to have taken pride in wearing shabby clothing.
[9] more effectively
[10] The highest spiritual state of the Buddhist is generally supposed to be absorption in the all-perfect, even as a drop of water is absorbed by the ocean. Buddha taught that perfection may be reached in this life when the cardinal sins die out in the heart. He did not himself teach the merging of the soul in God, or bliss in death. (See *Encyclopaedia Britannica*, IV, 744.)

Or burn or freeze thy fellows, never loosed
By death, nor time, nor love. [1]

                 And I forgive
Thee, Milton, those thy comic-dreadful wars
Where, armed with gross and inconclusive steel,
Immortals smite immortals mortalwise
And fill all heaven with folly. [2]

               Also thee,
Brave Aeschylus, thee I forgive, for that
Thine eye, by bare bright justice basilisked, [3]
Turned not, nor ever learned to look where
    Love   69
Stands shining.

         So, unto thee, Lucretius mine
(For oh! what heart hath loved thee like to
    this
That's now complaining?), freely I forgive
Thy logic poor, thine error rich, thine earth
Whose graves eat souls and all. [4]

            Yea, all you hearts
Of beauty, and sweet righteous lovers large:
Aurelius [5] fine, oft superfine; mild Saint
à Kempis, overmild; Epictetus,
Whiles low in thought, still with old slavery
    tinct;
Rapt Behmen, [6] rapt too far; high Swedenborg,
O'ertoppling; Langley, that with but a touch
Of art hadst sung Piers Plowman to the top   81
Of English songs, whereof 'tis dearest now
And most adorable; Caedmon, [7] in the morn
A-calling angels with the cow-herd's call
That late brought up the cattle; Emerson,

[1] Whatever Lanier's opinion, Dante was actuated not by hatred but by a stern sense of the unrelenting consequences of sin.
[2] *Paradise Lost*, Bk. VI
[3] Greek tragedy usually depicted the gods as avenging fates, influenced only by ideas of justice, not mercy. The basilisk, an imaginary monster of the ancients, struck mortals dead with the intensity of its glance.
[4] Lucretius, a Roman philosophical poet (96?-55 B.C.). author of *De Rerum Natura;* he did not believe in immortality.
[5] Marcus Aurelius (121-180), Roman Emperor and Stoic philosopher, wrote *Meditations.* Thomas à Kempis, 1380-1471, was author of *De Imitatione Christi.* Epictetus, born a slave, was a Greek Stoic philosopher of the first century.
[6] More correctly Jakob Böhme, or Böhm, 1575-1624, a German mystic; Swedenborg was a Swedish mystic, 1688-1772; and William Langland, 1330?-1400?, the supposed author of the *Vision of Piers the Plowman.*
[7] The first English Christian poet, who possibly lived in the 7th century. Both Bede and Alfred, the only early writers mentioning him, say that the care of the cattle was given "for that night" to Caedmon, a secular monk in the monastery. From this fact it has become usual to say that Caedmon was a cowherd.

Most wise, that yet, in finding Wisdom, lost
Thy Self, sometimes; tense Keats, with angel's
    nerves
Where men's were better; Tennyson, largest
    voice
Since Milton, yet some register [8] of wit
Wanting;—all, all, I pardon, ere 'tis asked,   90
Your more or less, your little mole that marks
You brother and your kinship seals to man.

    But Thee, but Thee, O sovereign Seer of
    time,
But Thee, O poet's Poet, Wisdom's Tongue,
But Thee, O man's best Man, O love's best
    Love,
O perfect life in perfect labor writ,
O all men's Comrade, Servant, King, or
    Priest,—
What *if* or *yet,* what mole, what flaw, what
    lapse,
What least defect or shadow of defect,
What rumor tattled by an enemy,   100
Of inference loose, what lack of grace,
Even in torture's grasp, or sleep's, or death's—
Oh, what amiss may I forgive in Thee,
Jesus, good Paragon, thou Crystal Christ?"
1880   1880

A BALLAD OF TREES AND THE MASTER

Into the woods my Master went, [9]
Clean forspent, forspent.
Into the woods my Master came,
Forspent with love and shame.
But the olives they were not blind to Him,
The little gray leaves were kind to Him:
The thorn-tree had a mind to Him
When into the woods He came.

Out of the woods my Master went,
And he was well content.   10
Out of the woods my Master came,
Content with death and shame.
When Death and Shame would woo Him last,
From under the trees they drew Him last:
'Twas on a tree they slew Him—last
When out of the woods He came.
1880   1880

SUNRISE—A HYMN OF THE MARSHES [10]

In my sleep I was fain of their fellowship, fain
Of the live-oak, the marsh, and the main.

[8] compass, range
[9] *Matthew* xxvi, 36, ff.
[10] This was the last poem completed by Lanier.

The little green leaves would not let me alone
    in my sleep;
Up-breathed from the marshes, a message of
    range and of sweep,
Interwoven with waftures of wild sea-liberties,
    drifting,
Came through the lapped leaves sifting, sifting,
    Came to the gates of sleep.
Then my thoughts, in the dark of the dungeon-
    keep
Of the Castle of Captives hid in the City of
    Sleep,
Upstarted, by twos and by threes assembling:
    The gates of sleep fell a-trembling   11
Like as the lips of a lady that forth falter *yes*,
    Shaken with happiness:
    The gates of sleep stood wide.

I have waked, I have come, my beloved! I
    might not abide:
I have come ere the dawn, O beloved, my live-
    oaks, to hide
    In your gospeling glooms,—to be
As a lover in heaven, the marsh, my marsh and
    the sea my sea.

Tell me, sweet burly-barked, man-bodied Tree
That mine arms in the dark are embracing, dost
    know   20
From what fount are these tears at thy feet
    which flow?
They rise not from reason, but deeper inconse-
    quent deeps.
    Reason's not one that weeps.
    What logic of greeting lies
Betwixt dear over-beautiful trees and the rain
    of the eyes?

O cunning green leaves, little masters! like as
    ye gloss
All the dull-tissued dark with your luminous
    darks that emboss
The vague blackness of night into pattern and
    plan,
        So
(But would I could know, but would I could
    know),   30
With your question embroid'ring the dark of
    the question of man,—
So, with your silences purfling [1] this silence of
    man
While his cry to the dead for some knowledge
    is under the ban,
    Under the ban,—
    So, ye have wrought me

[1] decorating, as the border of a violin may be decorated with inlaid work

Designs on the night of our knowledge—yea, ye
    have taught me,
        So,
That haply we know somewhat more than we
    know.

    Ye lispers, whisperers, singers in storms,
    Ye consciences murmuring faiths under
        forms,   40
    Ye ministers meet for each passion that
        grieves,
    Friendly, sisterly, sweetheart leaves,
Oh, rain me down from your darks that contain
    me
Wisdoms ye winnow from winds that pain
    me,—
Sift down tremors of sweet-within-sweet
That advise me of more than they bring,—
    repeat
Me the woods-smell that swiftly but now
    brought breath
From the heaven-side bank of the river of
    death,—
Teach me the terms of silence,—preach me
The passion of patience,—sift me,—impeach
    me,—   50
    And there, oh there
As ye hang with your myriad palms upturned
    in the air,
    Pray me a myriad prayer.

My gossip, the owl, is it thou
That out of the leaves of the low-hanging bough,
    As I pass to the beach, art stirred?
Dumb woods, have ye uttered a bird?
                    * * *
Reverend Marsh, low-couched along the sea,
Old chemist, rapt in alchemy,
    Distilling silence,—lo,   60
That which our father-age had died to know—
The menstruum [2] that dissolves all matter—
    thou
Hast found it: for this silence, filling now
The globéd charity of receiving space,
This solves us all: man, matter, doubt, dis-
    grace,
Death, love, sin, sanity,
Must in yon silence' clear solution lie.
Too clear! That crystal nothing who'll peruse?
The blackest night could bring us brighter news.
Yet precious qualities of silence haunt   70
Round these vast margins, ministrant.
Oh, if thy soul's at latter gasp for space,
With trying to breathe no bigger than thy race
Just to be fellow'd, when that thou hast found
No man with room, or grace enough of bound

[2] solvent

To entertain that New thou tell'st, thou art,—
'Tis here, 'tis here thou canst unhand thy heart
And breathe it free, and breathe it free,
By rangy marsh, in lone sea-liberty.

The tide's at full: the marsh with flooded streams   80
Glimmers, a limpid labyrinth of dreams.
Each winding creek in grave entrancement lies
A rhapsody of morning-stars. The skies
Shine scant with one forked galaxy,—
The marsh brags ten; looped on his breast they lie.
 Oh, what if a sound should be made!
 Oh, what if a bound should be laid
To this bow-and-string tension of beauty and silence a-spring,—
To the bend of beauty the bow, or the hold of silence the string!
I fear me, I fear me yon dome of diaphanous gleam   90
Will break as a bubble o'er-blown in a dream,—
Yon dome of too tenuous tissues of space and of night,
Overweighted with stars, overfreighted with light,
Oversated with beauty and silence, will seem
But a bubble that broke in a dream,
If a bound of degree to this grace be laid
Or a sound or a motion made.

But no: it is made: list! somewhere—mystery, where?
In the leaves? in the air?
In my heart? is a motion made: 100
'Tis a motion of dawn, like a flicker of shade on shade.
In the leaves 'tis palpable; low multitudinous stirring
Upwinds through the woods; the little ones, softly conferring,
Have settled my lord's to be looked for; so; they are still;
But the air and my heart and the earth are a-thrill,—
And look where the wild duck sails round the bend of the river,—
And look where a passionate shiver
Expectant is bending the blades
Of the marsh-grass in serial shimmers and shades,—
And invisible wings, fast fleeting, fast fleeting,
Are beating   111
The dark overhead as my heart beats,—and steady and free
Is the ebb-tide flowing from marsh to sea—
 (Run home, little streams,

With your lapfuls of stars and dreams),
And a sailor unseen is hoisting a-peek,
For list, down the inshore curve of the creek
 How merrily flutters the sail,—
And lo, in the East! Will the East unveil?
The East is unveiled, the East hath confessed
A flush: 'tis dead; 'tis alive: 'tis dead, ere the West   121
Was aware of it: nay, 'tis abiding, 'tis unwithdrawn:
Have a care, sweet Heaven! 'Tis Dawn.

Now a dream of a flame through that dream of a flush is uprolled:
To the zenith ascending, a dome of undazzling gold
Is builded, in shape as a bee-hive, from out of the sea:
The hive is of gold undazzling, but oh, the Bee,
 The star-fed Bee, the build-fire Bee,
Of dazzling gold is the great Sun-Bee
That shall flash from the hive-hole over the sea.   130

Yet now the dew-drop, now the morning gray,
Shall live their little lucid sober day
Ere with the sun their souls exhale away.
Now in each pettiest personal sphere of dew
The summ'd morn shines complete as in the blue
Big dew-drop of all heaven. With these lit shrines
O'er silvered to the farthest sea-confines,
The sacramental marsh one pious plain
Of worship lies. Peace to the ante-reign
Of Mary Morning, blissful mother mild,   140
Minded of naught but peace, and of a child.

Not slower than Majesty moves, for a mean and a measure
Of motion, not faster than dateless Olympian leisure
Might pace with unblown ample garments from pleasure to pleasure,—
The wave-serrate sea-rim sinks unjarring, unreeling,
Forever revealing, revealing, revealing,
Edgewise, bladewise, halfwise, wholewise,—'tis done!
        Good-morrow, lord Sun!
With several voice, with ascription [1] one,
The woods and the marsh and the sea and my soul   150

[1] homage, tribute

Unto thee, whence the glittering stream of all
    morrows doth roll,
Cry good and past-good, and most heavenly
    morrow, lord Sun.

O Artisan born in the purple,—Workman Heat,
Parter of passionate atoms that travail to meet
And be mixed in the death-cold oneness, inner-
    most Guest
At the marriage of elements,—Fellow of pub-
    licans,—blest
King in the blouse of flame, that loiterest o'er
The idle skies yet laborest fast evermore,—
Thou, in the fine forge-thunder, thou, in the
    beat
Of the heart of a man, thou Motive,—Laborer
    Heat: 160
Yea, Artist, thou, of whose art yon sea's all
    news,
With his inshore greens and manifold mid-sea
    blues,
Pearl-glint, shell-tint, ancientest perfectest hues
Ever shaming the maidens,—lily and rose
Confess thee, and each mild flame that glows
In the clarified virginal bosoms of stones that
    shine,
    It is thine, it is thine:

Thou chemist of storms, whether driving the
    winds a-swirl
Or a-flicker the subtiler essences polar that
    whirl
In the magnet earth,—yea, thou with a storm
    for a heart,   170
Rent with debate, many-spotted with question,
    part
From part oft sundered, yet ever a globèd light,
Yet ever the artist, ever more large and bright
Than the eye of a man may avail of :—manifold
    One,
I must pass from thy face, I must pass from the
    face of the Sun:
Old Want is awake and agog, every wrinkle
    a-frown;
The worker must pass to his work in the ter-
    rible town:
But I fear not, nay, and I fear not the thing
    to be done;
I am strong with the strength of my lord the
    Sun:
How dark, how dark soever the race that must
    needs be run,   180
    I am lit with the Sun.

Oh, never the mast-high run of the seas
    Of traffic shall hide thee,
Never the hell-colored smoke of the factories

Hide thee,
Never the reek of the time's fen-politics
    Hide thee,
And ever my heart through the night shall with
    knowledge abide thee,
And ever by day shall my spirit, as one that
    hath tried thee,
Labor, at leisure, in art,—till yonder beside
    thee   190
    My soul shall float, friend Sun,
    The day being done.
1880   *1882*

HELEN HUNT JACKSON
1831-1885

Helen Maria Fiske represented both the East and
the West of the United States. She took up literature at thirty-five, after the death of her first
husband, Captain Hunt, and their children. Her
early work included poetry (*Verses by H. H.*, 1870;
Sonnets and Lyrics, 1887), and novels of New England life. Later she went to Colorado for her
health, married Mr. Jackson, became interested in
the wrongs of the Indians, and wrote *A Century of
Dishonor*, 1881. As a result in 1883 she was appointed one of two commissioners to report on the
Mission Indians of California. Her desire further
to arouse public sympathy for the Indians gave us
Ramona, 1884, one of the most popular romances
of the period, and of permanent interest as a picture of old Spanish days.

Biography and criticism: T. W. Higginson, *Short
Studies of American Authors;* C. C. Davis and W.
A. Alderson, *The True Story of Ramona*, 1914;
D. A. Hufford, *The True Ramona*, 1900; G. W.
James, *Through Ramona's Country*, 1909; "How
Ramona Was Written," *Atlan.* 86 :712-14; T. W.
Higginson, *Nation* 41 :150-1, good sketch of life;
A. W. Tourgée, "A Study in Civilization," *No. Am.*
143 :246-61.

SPINNING [1]

Like a blind spinner in the sun,
    I tread my days;
I know that all the threads will run
    Appointed ways;
I know each day will bring its task,
And, being blind, no more I ask.

I do not know the use or name
    Of that I spin:
I only know that some one came,
    And laid within   10
My hand the thread, and said, "Since you
Are blind, but one thing you can do."

[1] Copyright, 1873, by Little, Brown and Company.

Sometimes the threads so rough and fast
  And tangled fly,
I know wild storms are sweeping past,
  And fear that I
Shall fall; but dare not try to find
A safer place, since I am blind.

I know not why, but I am sure
  That tint and place,   20
In some great fabric to endure
  Past time and race
My threads will have; so from the first,
Though blind, I never felt accurst.

I think, perhaps, this trust has sprung
  From one short word
Said over me when I was young,—
  So young, I heard
It, knowing not that God's name signed
My brow, and sealed me His, though blind.

But whether this be seal or sign   31
  Within, without,
It matters not. The bond divine
  I never doubt.
I know He set me here, and still,
And glad, and blind, I wait His will;

But listen, listen, day by day,
  To hear their tread
Who bear the finished web away,
  And cut the thread,   40
And bring God's message in the sun,
"Thou poor blind spinner, work is done."

1874

OCTOBER [1]

Bending above the spicy woods which blaze,
Arch skies so blue they flash, and hold the sun
Immeasurably far; the waters run
Too slow, so freighted are the river-ways
With gold of elms and birches from the maze
Of forests. Chestnuts, clicking one by one,
Escape from satin burs; her fringes done,
The gentian spreads them out in sunny days,
And, like late revelers at dawn, the chance
Of one sweet, mad, last hour, all things assail,
And conquering, flush and spin; while, to en-
  hance   11
The spell, by sunset door, wrapped in a veil
Of red and purple mists, the summer, pale,
Steals back alone for one more song and dance.

CORONATION [1]

At the king's gate the subtle noon
  Wove filmy yellow nets of sun;

[1] Copyright, 1873, by Little, Brown and Company.

Into the drowsy snare too soon
  The guards fell one by one.

Through the king's gate, unquestioned then,
  A beggar went, and laughed, "This brings
Me chance, at last, to see if men
  Fare better, being kings!"

The king sat bowed beneath his crown,
  Propping his face with listless hand;   10
Watching the hour-glass sifting down
  Too slow its shining sand.

"Poor man, what wouldst thou have of me?"
  The beggar turned, and, pitying,
Replied, like one in dream, "Of thee,
  Nothing. I want the king."

Uprose the king, and from his head
  Shook off the crown and threw it by.
"O man, thou must have known," he said,
  "A greater king than I."   20

Through all the gates, unquestioned then,
  Went king and beggar hand in hand.
Whispered the king, "Shall I know when
  Before *his* throne I stand?"

The beggar laughed. Free winds in haste
  Were wiping from the king's hot brow
The crimson lines the crown had traced.
  "This is his presence now."

At the king's gate, the crafty noon
  Unwove its yellow nets of sun;   30
Out of their sleep in terror soon
  The guards waked one by one.

"Ho here! Ho there! Has no man seen
  The king?" The cry ran to and fro;
Beggar and king, they laughed, I ween,
  The laugh that free men know.

On the king's gate the moss grew gray;
  The king came not. They called him dead;
And made his eldest son one day
  Slave in his father's stead.   40

EMILY DICKINSON
1830-1886

Though Miss Dickinson was contemporary with
Hawthorne, Emerson, Whitman, and Poe at the
flowering of their genius, and with one of the most
critical periods of American history, she was curiously untouched by outward influences. Her family helped to found Amherst, Massachusetts, where

she was born and where she spent practically all her life. She attended the public schools, later going to South Hadley Female Seminary and to Amherst Academy. In 1853 during a visit to Washington and Philadelphia she is said to have formed a violent but hopeless attachment. At any rate from that time on she led a life of absolute seclusion, seeing only a few intimate friends. During her life only one of her poems was published, and that without her knowledge; but since her death three series, beginning with 1890, have appeared.

James Muirhead in *America the Land of Contrasts,* calls Miss Dickinson an example of the American in literature, and thinks her "full as national a type as Mr. Howells." "The subjects of her poems are few, but the piercing delicacy and depth of vision with which she turned from death and eternity to nature and to love make us feel the presence of that rare thing, genius. Hers is a wonderful instance of the way in which genius can dispense with experience; she sees more by pure intuition than others distill from the serried facts of an eventful life."

The Complete Poems of Emily Dickinson, ed. by Martha D. Bianchi, 1925; *Further Poems,* 1929.

Biography and criticism: Bianchi, *The Life and Letters of Emily Dickinson,* 1924; G. Bradford, *Portraits of American Women;* same, *Atlan.* 124: 216-26; L. F. Abbott, "Emily Dickinson," *Outlook* 140:211-13; C. K. Trueblood, *Dial* 80:301-11; C. B. Green, "A Reminiscence of Emily Dickinson," *Bookm.* 60:291-3; M. Hartley, *Dial* 65:95-7; M. H. Shackford, "The Poetry of Emily Dickinson," *Atlan.* 111:93-7; C. Aiken, *Dial* 76:301-8.

—o—

This is my letter to the world,
That never wrote to me,—
The simple news that Nature told,
With tender majesty.

Her message is committed
To hands I cannot see;
For love of her, sweet countrymen,
Judge tenderly of me!

—o—

OUR SHARE OF NIGHT TO BEAR

Our share of night to bear,
Our share of morning,
Our blank in bliss to fill,
Our blank in scorning.

Here a star, and there a star,
Some lose their way.
Here a mist, and there a mist,
Afterwards—day!

I HAD NO TIME TO HATE

I had no time to hate, because
The grave would hinder me,
And life was not so ample I
Could finish enmity.

Nor had I time to love; but since
Some industry must be,
The little toil of love, I thought,
Was large enough for me.

ALTER? WHEN THE HILLS DO

Alter? When the hills do.
Falter? When the sun
Question if his glory
Be the perfect one.

Surfeit? When the daffodil
Doth of the dew:
Even as herself, O friend!
I will of you!

IN VAIN [1]

I cannot live with you,
It would be life,
And life is over there
Behind the shelf

The sexton keeps the key to,
Putting up
Our life, his porcelain,
Like a cup

Discarded of the housewife,
Quaint or broken;
A newer Sèvres pleases,
Old ones crack.

I could not die with you,
For one must wait
To shut the other's gaze down,—
You could not.

And I, could I stand by
And see you freeze,
Without my right of frost,
Death's privilege?

Nor could I rise with you,
Because your face
Would put out Jesus',
That new grace

[1] Cf. Christina Rossetti's sonnet: "Many in aftertimes will say of you—"

Glow plain and foreign
On my homesick eye,
Except that you, than he
Shone closer by.

They'd judge us—how?
For you served Heaven, you know, 30
Or sought to;
I could not,

Because you saturated sight,
And I had no more eyes
For sordid excellence
As Paradise.

And were you lost, I would be,
Though my name
Rang loudest
On the heavenly fame. 40

And were you saved,
And I condemned to be
Where you were not,
That self were hell to me.

So we must keep apart,
You there, I here,
With just the door ajar
That oceans are,
And prayer,
And that pale sustenance, 50
Despair!

RENUNCIATION

There came a day at summer's full
Entirely for me;
I thought that such were for the saints,
Where revelations be.

The sun, as common, went abroad,
The flowers, accustomed, blew,
As if no soul the solstice passed
That maketh all things new.

The time was scarce profaned by speech;
The symbol of a word 10
Was needless, as at sacrament
The wardrobe of our Lord.

Each was to each the sealed church,
Permitted to commune this time,
Lest we too awkward show
At supper of the Lamb.

The hours slid fast, as hours will,
Clutched tight by greedy hands;

So faces on two decks look back,
Bound to opposing lands. 20

And so, when all the time had failed,
Without external sound,
Each bound the other's crucifix,
We gave no other bond.

Sufficient troth that we shall rise—
Deposed, at length, the grave—
To that new marriage, justified
Through Calvaries of Love!

A SERVICE OF SONG

Some keep the Sabbath going to church;
I keep it staying at home,
With a bobolink for a chorister,
And an orchard for a dome.

Some keep the Sabbath in surplice;
I just wear my wings,
And instead of tolling the bell for church,
Our little sexton sings.

God preaches,—a noted clergyman,—
And the sermon is never long; 10
So instead of getting to heaven at last,
I'm going all along!

A DAY

I'll tell you how the sun rose,—
A ribbon at a time.
The steeples swam in amethyst,
The news like squirrels ran.

The hills untied their bonnets,
The bobolinks begun.
Then I said softly to myself,
"That must have been the sun!"

* * *

But how he set, I know not.
There seemed a purple stile 10
Which little yellow boys and girls
Were climbing all the while

Till when they reached the other side,
A dominie in gray
Put gently up the evening bars,
And led the flock away.

AUTUMN

The morns are meeker than they were,
The nuts are getting brown;
The berry's cheek is plumper,
The rose is out of town.

The maple wears a gayer scarf,
The field a scarlet gown.
Lest I should be old-fashioned,
I'll put a trinket on.

I NEVER SAW A MOOR

I never saw a moor,
I never saw the sea;
Yet know I how the heather looks,
And what a wave must be.

I never spoke with God,
Nor visited in heaven;
Yet certain am I of the spot
As if the chart were given.

I'M NOBODY! WHO ARE YOU?

I'm nobody! who are you?
Are you nobody, too?
Then there's a pair of us—don't tell!
They'd banish us, you know.

How dreary to be somebody!
How public, like a frog
To tell your name the livelong day
To an admiring bog!

WE PLAY AT PASTE

We play at paste,
Till qualified for pearl,
Then drop the paste,
And deem ourself a fool.
The shapes, though, were similar,
And our new hands
Learned gem-tactics
Practising sands.

THE TEST

I can wade grief,
Whole pools of it,—
I'm used to that.
But the least push of joy
Breaks up my feet,
And I tip—drunken.
Let no pebble smile,
'Twas the new liquor,—
That was all!
Power is only pain,   10
Stranded, through discipline,
Till weights will hang.
Give balm to giants,
And they'll wilt, like men.
Give Himmaleh, [1]
They'll carry him!

—another spelling of Himalaya

SURGEONS MUST BE VERY CAREFUL

Surgeons must be very careful
When they take the knife!
Underneath their fine incisions
Stirs the culprit,—Life!

THE SHOW

The show is not the show,
But they that go.
Menagerie to me
My neighbor be.
Fair play—
Both went to see.

SECRETS

The skies can't keep their secret!
They tell it to the hills—
The hills just tell the orchards—
And they the daffodils!

A bird, by chance, that goes that way
Soft overheard the whole.
If I should bribe the little bird,
Who knows but she would tell?

I think I won't, however,
It's finer not to know;   10
If summer were an axiom,
What sorcery had snow?

So keep your secret, Father!
I would not, if I could,
Know what the sapphire fellows do,
In your new-fashioned world!

THE SEA

An everywhere of silver,
With ropes of sand
To keep it from effacing
The track called land.

SIMPLICITY

How happy is the little stone
That rambles in the road alone,
And doesn't care about careers,
And exigencies never fears;
Whose coat of elemental brown
A passing universe put on;
And independent as the sun,
Associates or glows alone,
Fulfilling absolute decree
In casual simplicity.

I READ MY SENTENCE STEADILY

I read my sentence steadily,
Reviewed it with my eyes,
To see that I made no mistake
In its extremest clause,—

The date, and manner of the shame;
And then the pious form
That "God have mercy" on the soul
The jury voted him.

I made my soul familiar
With her extremity,   10
That at the last it should not be
A novel agony,

But she and Death, acquainted,
Meet tranquilly as friends,
Salute and pass without a hint—
And there the matter ends.

WHAT INN IS THIS?

What inn is this [1]
Where for the night
Peculiar traveler comes?
Who is the landlord?
Where the maids?
Behold, what curious rooms!
No ruddy fires on the hearth,
No brimming tankards flow.
Necromancer, landlord,
Who are these below?

FORBIDDEN FRUIT. I

Forbidden fruit a flavor has
That lawful orchards mocks;
How luscious lies the pea within
The pod that Duty locks!

FORBIDDEN FRUIT. II

Heaven is what I cannot reach!
The apple on the tree,
Provided it do hopeless hang,
That "heaven" is, to me.

The color on the cruising cloud,
The interdicted ground
Behind the hill, the house behind,—
There Paradise is found!

A WORD

A word is dead   I say it just
When it is said,   Begins to live
Some say.   That day.

[1] Cf. Christina Rossetti's "Uphill."

PARTING

My life closed twice before its close;
It yet remains to see
If Immortality unveil
A third event to me,

So huge, so hopeless to conceive,
As these that twice befell.
Parting is all we know of heaven,
And all we need of hell.

WHAT SOFT, CHERUBIC CREATURES

What soft, cherubic creatures
These gentlewomen are!
One would as soon assault a plush
Or violate a star.

Such dimity convictions,
A horror so refined
Of freckled human nature,
Of Deity ashamed,—

It's such a common glory,
A fisherman's degree!   10
Redemption, brittle lady,
Be so, ashamed of thee.

TO MAKE A PRAIRIE

To make a prairie it takes a clover
and one bee,—
One clover, and a bee,
And revery.
The revery alone will do
If bees are few.

WE NEVER KNOW WE GO

We never know we go,—when we are going
We jest and shut the door;
Fate following behind us bolts it,
And we accost no more.

ETERNITY

On this wondrous sea,
Sailing silently,
Ho! pilot, ho!
Knowest thou the shore
Where no breakers roar?
Where the storm is o'er?

In the silent west
Many sails at rest,
Their anchors fast;
Thither I pilot thee—   10
Land, ho! Eternity!
Ashore at last!

FRANK R. STOCKTON 1834-1902

The work of Frank Stockton abounds in a type of humor quite different from that of Mark Twain, though none the less American. Stockton entered literature as a vocation rather late in life. After an ordinary schooling in Philadelphia he supported himself for many years as a wood engraver. His skill brought him into contact with authors whose works he was illustrating and led him at length into journalism, and afterwards, in 1874, to the staff of *St. Nicholas*. Although he had practiced writing from his youth, his first notable piece of fiction was *Rudder Grange*, 1879. From this time forward his books appeared frequently, his most popular works being *The Casting Away of Mrs. Lecks and Mrs. Aleshine*, 1886; *Squirrel Inn*, 1890; and *The Adventures of Captain Horn*, 1890. His most notable short story is "The Lady or the Tiger?"

Stockton's humor is kindly, neither boisterous nor cynical. Its mock gravity, full of caprice and whim, forms a distinct contribution to American humor. His characters are typically rather stodgy middle-class people of limited experience, but are strongly and convincingly drawn. Their goodness of heart, fixedness of purpose and lack of humor often lead them into situations of the utmost absurdity.

Novels and Stories, 23 volumes, 1899-1904.

Biography and criticism: Marian E. Stockton, "A Memorial Sketch" (in *A Bicycle of Cathay*, 1904). J. H. Morse, "Frank R. Stockton at Home," *Critic* 32:259-61; E. W. Bowen, *Sewanee R.* 11:474-8; *Outlook* 70:1000-1; *R. of Rs.* 25: 698-9; *Ind.* 90:28.

THE LADY OR THE TIGER? [1]

In the very olden time, there lived a semi-barbaric king, whose ideas, though somewhat polished and sharpened by the progressiveness of distant Latin neighbors, were still large, florid, and untrammeled, as became the half of him which was barbaric. He was a man of exuberant fancy, and, withal, of an authority so irresistible that, at his will, he turned his varied fancies into facts. He was greatly given to self-communing, and when he and himself agreed upon anything, the thing was done. When every member of his domestic and political systems moved smoothly in its appointed course, his nature was bland and genial; but whenever there was a little hitch, and some of his orbs got out of their orbits, he was blander and more genial still, for nothing pleased him so much as to make the crooked straight, and crush down uneven places.

[1] From *Novels and Stories of Frank Stockton*. Copyright, Messrs. Charles Scribner's Sons, publishers. By permission.

Among the borrowed notions by which his barbarism had become semified [2] was that of the public arena, in which, by exhibitions of manly and beastly valor, the minds of his subjects were refined and cultured.

But even here the exuberant and barbaric fancy asserted itself. The arena of the king was built, not to give the people an opportunity of hearing the rhapsodies of dying gladiators, nor to enable them to view the inevitable conclusion of a conflict between religious opinions and hungry jaws, but for purposes far better adapted to widen and develop the mental energies of the people. This vast amphitheater, with its encircling galleries, its mysterious vaults, and its unseen passages, was an agent of poetic justice, in which crime was punished, or virtue rewarded, by the decrees of an impartial and incorruptible chance.

When a subject was accused of a crime of sufficient importance to interest the king, public notice was given that on an appointed day the fate of the accused person would be decided in the king's arena—a structure which well deserved its name; for, although its form and plan were borrowed from afar, its purpose emanated solely from the brain of this man, who, every barleycorn a king, knew no tradition to which he owed more allegiance than pleased his fancy, and who ingrafted on every adopted form of human thought and action the rich growth of his barbaric idealism.

When all the people had assembled in the galleries, and the king, surrounded by his court, sat high up on his throne of royal state on one side of the arena, he gave a signal, a door beneath him opened, and the accused subject stepped out into the amphitheater. Directly opposite him, on the other side of the enclosed space, were two doors, exactly alike and side by side. It was the duty and the privilege of the person on trial to walk directly to these doors and open one of them. He could open either door he pleased. He was subject to no guidance or influence but that of the aforementioned impartial and incorruptible chance. If he opened the one, there came out of it a hungry tiger, the fiercest and most cruel that could be procured, which immediately sprang upon him, and tore him to pieces, as a punishment for his guilt. The moment that the case of the criminal was thus decided, doleful iron bells were clanged, great wails went up from the hired mourners posted on the outer rim of the arena, and the vast audience, with bowed heads and downcast hearts, wended slowly their

[2] probably coined from semi, half; reduced by half

homeward way, mourning that one so young and fair, or so old and respected, should have merited so dire a fate.

But if the accused person opened the other door, there came forth from it a lady, the most suitable to his years and station that his Majesty could select among his fair subjects; and to this lady he was immediately married, as a reward of his innocence. It mattered not that he might already possess a wife and family, or that his affections might be engaged upon an object of his own selection. The king allowed no such subordinate arrangement to interfere with his great scheme of retribution and reward. The exercises, as in the other instance, took place immediately, and in the arena. Another door opened beneath the king, and a priest, followed by a band of choristers, and dancing maidens blowing joyous airs on golden horns and treading epithalamic [1] measure, advanced to where the pair stood side by side, and the wedding was promptly and cheerily solemnized. Then the gay brass bells rang forth their merry peals, the people shouted glad hurrahs, and the innocent man, preceded by children strewing flowers on his path, led his bride to his home.

This was the king's semi-barbaric method of administering justice. Its perfect fairness is obvious. The criminal could not know out of which door would come the lady. He opened either he pleased, without having the slightest idea whether, in the next instant, he was to be devoured or married. On some occasions the tiger came out of one door, and on some out of the other. The decisions of this tribunal were not only fair—they were positively determinate. The accused person was instantly punished if he found himself guilty, and if innocent he was rewarded on the spot, whether he liked it or not. There was no escaping from the judgments of the king's arena.

The institution was a very popular one. When the people gathered together on one of the great trial days, they never knew whether they were to witness a bloody slaughter or a hilarious wedding. This element of uncertainty lent an interest to the occasion which it could not otherwise have attained. Thus the masses were entertained and pleased, and the thinking part of the community could bring no charge of unfairness against this plan; for did not the accused person have the whole matter in his own hands?

The semi-barbaric king had a daughter as blooming as his most florid fancies, and with a soul as fervent and imperious as his own. As is usual in such cases, she was the apple of his eye, and was loved by him above all humanity. Among his courtiers was a young man of that fineness of blood and lowness of station common to the conventional heroes of romance who love royal maidens. This royal maiden was well satisfied with her lover, for he was handsome and brave to a degree unsurpassed in all this kingdom, and she loved him with an ardor that had enough of barbarism in it to make it exceedingly warm and strong. This love affair moved on happily for many months, until, one day, the king happened to discover its existence. He did not hesitate nor waver in regard to his duty in the premises. [2] The youth was immediately cast into prison, and a day was appointed for his trial in the king's arena. This, of course, was an especially important occasion, and his Majesty, as well as all the people, was greatly interested in the workings and development of this trial. Never before had such a case occurred—never before had a subject dared to love the daughter of a king. In after years such things became commonplace enough, but then they were, in no slight degree, novel and startling.

The tiger cages of the kingdom were searched for the most savage and relentless beasts, from which the fiercest monster might be selected for the arena, and the ranks of maiden youth and beauty throughout the land were carefully surveyed by competent judges, in order that the young man might have a fitting bride in case fate did not determine for him a different destiny. Of course, everybody knew that the deed with which the accused was charged had been done. He had loved the princess, and neither he, she, nor any one else thought of denying the fact. But the king would not think of allowing any fact of this kind to interfere with the workings of the tribunal, in which he took such great delight and satisfaction. No matter how the affair turned out, the youth would be disposed of, and the king would take an aesthetic pleasure in watching the course of events which would determine whether or not the young man had done wrong in allowing himself to love the princess.

The appointed day arrived. From far and near the people gathered, and thronged the great galleries of the arena, while crowds, unable to gain admittance, massed themselves against its outside walls. The king and his court were in their places, opposite the twin

---

[1] bridal

[2] that is, since this was the fact

doors—those fateful portals, so terrible in their similarity!

All was ready. The signal was given. A door beneath the royal party opened, and the lover of the princess walked into the arena. Tall, beautiful, fair, his appearance was greeted with a low hum of admiration and anxiety. Half the audience had not known so grand a youth had lived among them. No wonder the princess loved him! What a terrible thing for him to be there!

As the youth advanced into the arena, he turned, as the custom was, to bow to the king. But he did not think at all of that royal personage; his eyes were fixed upon the princess, who sat to the right of her father. Had it not been for the moiety of barbarism in her nature, it is probable the lady would not have been there. But her intense and fervid soul would not allow her to be absent on an occasion in which she was so terribly interested. From the moment that the decree had gone forth that her lover should decide his fate in the king's arena, she had thought of nothing, night or day, but this great event and the various subjects connected with it. Possessed of more power, influence, and force of character than any one who had ever before been interested in such a case, she had done what no other person had done—she had possessed herself of the secret of the doors. She knew in which of the two rooms behind those doors, stood the cage of the tiger, with its open front, and in which waited the lady. Through these thick doors, heavily curtained with skins on the inside, it was impossible that any noise or suggestion should come from within to the person who should approach to raise the latch of one of them. But gold, and the power of a woman's will, had brought the secret to the princess.

Not only did she know in which room stood the lady, ready to emerge, all blushing and radiant, should her door be opened, but she knew who the lady was. It was one of the fairest and loveliest of the damsels of the court who had been selected as the reward of the accused youth, should he be proved innocent of the crime of aspiring to one so far above him; and the princess hated her. Often had she seen, or imagined that she had seen, this fair creature throwing glances of admiration upon the person of her lover, and sometimes she thought these glances were perceived and even returned. Now and then she had seen them talking together. It was but for a moment or two, but much can be said in a brief space. It may have been on most unimportant topics, but how could she know that? The girl was lovely, but she had dared to raise her eyes to the loved one of the princess, and, with all the intensity of the savage blood transmitted to her through long lines of wholly barbaric ancestors, she hated the woman who blushed and trembled behind that silent door.

When her lover turned and looked at her, and his eyes met hers as she sat there paler and whiter than any one in the vast ocean of anxious faces about her, he saw, by that power of quick perception which is given to those whose souls are one, that she knew behind which door crouched the tiger, and behind which stood the lady. He had expected her to know it. He understood her nature, and his soul was assured that she would never rest until she had made plain to herself this thing, hidden to all other lookers-on, even to the king. The only hope for the youth in which there was any element of certainty was based upon the success of the princess in discovering this mystery, and the moment he looked upon her, he saw she had succeeded.

Then it was that his quick and anxious glance asked the question, "Which?" It was as plain to her as if he shouted it from where he stood. There was not an instant to be lost. The question was asked in a flash; it must be answered in another.

Her right arm lay on the cushioned parapet before her. She raised her hand and made a slight, quick movement toward the right. No one but her lover saw her. Every eye but his was fixed on the man in the arena.

He turned, and with a firm and rapid step he walked across the empty space. Every heart stopped beating, every breath was held, every eye was fixed immovably upon that man. Without the slightest hesitation, he went to the door on the right, and opened it.

Now the point of the story is this: Did the tiger come out of that door, or did the lady?

The more we reflect upon this question, the harder it is to answer. It involves a study of the human heart which leads us through devious mazes of passion, out of which it is difficult to find our way. Think of it, fair reader, not as if the decision of the question depended upon yourself, but upon that hot-blooded, semi-barbaric princess, her soul at a white heat beneath the combined fires of despair and jealousy. She had lost him, but who should have him?

How often, in her waking hours and in her dreams, had she started in wild horror and covered her face with her hands as she thought of her lover opening the door on the other side of which waited the cruel fangs of the tiger!

But how much oftener had she seen him at the other door! How in her grievous reveries had she gnashed her teeth and torn her hair when she saw his start of rapturous delight as he opened the door of the lady! How her soul had burned in agony when she had seen him rush to meet that woman, with her flushing cheek and sparkling eye of triumph; when she had seen him lead her forth, his whole frame kindled with the joy of recovered life; when she had heard the glad shouts from the multitude, and the wild ringing of the happy bells; when she had seen the priest, with his joyous followers, advance to the couple, and make them man and wife before her very eyes; and when she had seen them walk away together upon their path of flowers, followed by the tremendous shouts of the hilarious multitude, in which her one despairing shriek was lost and drowned?

Would it not be better for him to die at once, and go to wait for her in the blessed regions of semi-barbaric futurity?

And yet, that awful tiger, those shrieks, that blood!

Her decision had been indicated in an instant, but it had been made after days and nights of anguished deliberation. She had known she would be asked, she had decided what she would answer, and, without the slightest hesitation she had moved her hand to the right.

The question of her decision is one not to be lightly considered, and it is not for me to presume to set up myself as the one person able to answer it. So I leave it with all of you: Which came out of the opened door—the lady or the tiger?

1884

MARK TWAIN (SAMUEL LANGHORNE CLEMENS) 1835-1910

Of the major American writers of the nineteenth century, few were more strikingly American in experiences, material, and attitude, than Mark Twain. He was born in the teeming center of American life, on the Mississippi at Florida, Missouri. He was a local compositor, printer, and editor. He served an apprenticeship as a Mississippi River pilot. Soon after he received his license the Civil War came on. He enlisted in the Confederate forces, but deserted and made his way to Nevada where he became editor of a Virginia City newspaper. From San Francisco, where he was next engaged in newspaper work, he sailed to the Sandwich Islands and upon his return he gave his first public lecture upon his experiences there. This was the beginning of a long career as a lecturer. A tour of Europe and the Levant produced *Innocents Abroad*, 1870. This book, humorously satirical of some European pretentions, and of some European estimates of Americans, was one of the most popular books of the day.

Mark Twain wrote books of travel, essays, and history; but his treatment of American life centering upon the Mississippi River in *Life on the Mississippi*, 1883, and of American boyhood in *Tom Sawyer*, 1876, and *Huckleberry Finn*, 1884, form his greatest contribution to literature. The two latter books are marked by creative invention; their characters are realistic and natively American, developed with full realization of how an untamed, natural boy would think and act. Other well-known books of Mark Twain's are *Roughing It*, 1872; *A Connecticut Yankee in King Arthur's Court*, 1889; *Joan of Arc*, 1896. His collected works appeared in 25 volumes in 1910. Much of his humorous work is characterized by ridiculous situations and grotesque exaggerations; but it often expresses a forthright common sense that is frequently thought of as characteristically American. His strength lies in his humor and characterizations rather than philosophy and social criticism, and in his backgrounds sketched in a large, dashing manner but essentially true to American life.

Biography: *Mark Twain's Letters*, 2 vols., 1917; *Mark Twain's Autobiography*, 2 vols., 1924; Albert B. Paine, *Mark Twain: A Biography*, 3 vols., 1912; Mary Lawton, *A Lifetime with Mark Twain*, 1925. Criticism: W. D. Howells, *My Mark Twain*, 1910; Macy; Carl Van Doren (AN); Trent and Erskine; Phelps (EB); Chubb; C. Van Doren, "Mark Twain and Bernard Shaw," *Cent.* 109:705-10; (1) *Harper* 144:273-80, 455-60; 145:310-5; (2) *Lit. Digest* 85:36-40; 86:38-40; G. Bradford, "Mark Twain," *Atlan.* 125:462-73 (also in *American Portraits*); B. Matthews, "Mark Twain and the Art of Writing," *Harper* 141:635-43; V. W. Brooks, "Mark Twain's Humor," *Dial* 68:275-91; "Mark Twain's Satire," same, 424-43.

From LIFE ON THE MISSISSIPPI [1]

CHAPTER VII

A DARING DEED

When I returned to the pilot-house St. Louis was gone, and I was lost. Here was a piece of river which was all down in my book, but I could make neither head nor tail of it; you understand, it was turned around. I had seen it when coming up-stream, but I had never faced about to see how it looked when it was

[1] From *Life on the Mississippi* by Mark Twain. Copyright. By permission of Messrs. Harper and Brothers, publishers.

behind me. My heart broke again, for it was plain that I had got to learn this troublesome river *both ways*.

The pilot-house was full of pilots, going down to "look at the river." What is called the "upper river" (the two hundred miles between St. Louis and Cairo, where the Ohio comes in) was low; and the Mississippi changes its channel so constantly that the pilots used to always find it necessary to run down to Cairo to take a fresh look, when their boats were to lie in port a week; that is, when the water was at a low stage. A deal of this "looking at the river" was done by poor fellows who seldom had a berth, and whose only hope of getting one lay in their being always freshly posted and therefore ready to drop into the shoes of some reputable pilot, for a single trip, on account of such a pilot's sudden illness, or some other necessity. And a good many of them constantly ran up and down inspecting the river, not because they ever really hoped to get a berth, but because (they being guests of the boat) it was cheaper to "look at the river" than stay ashore and pay board. In time these fellows grew dainty in their tastes, and only infested boats that had an established reputation for setting good tables. All visiting pilots were useful, for they were always ready and willing, winter and summer, day or night, to go out in the yawl and help buoy the channel or assist the boat's pilots in any way they could. They were likewise welcome because all pilots are tireless talkers, when gathered together, and as they talk only about the river they are always understood and are always interesting. Your true pilot cares nothing about anything on earth but the river, and his pride in his occupation surpasses the pride of kings.

We had a fine company of these river inspectors along this trip. There were eight or ten, and there was abundance of room for them in our great pilot-house. Two or three of them wore polished silk hats, elaborate shirt-fronts, diamond breastpins, kid gloves, and patent-leather boots. They were choice in their English and bore themselves with a dignity proper to men of solid means and prodigious reputation as pilots. The others were more or less loosely clad, and wore upon their heads tall felt cones that were suggestive of the days of the Commonwealth. [1]

I was a cipher in this august company, and felt subdued, not to say torpid. I was not even of sufficient consequence to assist at the

[1] the government of England under Cromwell, 1653-58

wheel when it was necessary to put the tiller hard down in a hurry; the guest that stood nearest did that when occasion required—and this was pretty much all the time, because of the crookedness of the channel and the scant water. I stood in a corner; and the talk I listened to took the hope all out of me. One visitor said to another:

"Jim, how did you run Plum Point, coming up?"

"It was in the night, there, and I ran it the way one of the boys on the *Diana* told me; started out about fifty yards above the woodpile on the false point, and held on the cabin under Plum Point till I raised [2] the reef—quarter less twain [3]—then straightened up for the middle bar till I got well abreast the old one-limbed cottonwood in the bend, then got my stern on the cottonwood, and head on the low place above the point, and came through a-booming—nine and a half." [4]

"Pretty square crossing, an't it?"

"Yes, but the upper bar's working down fast."

Another pilot spoke up and said:

"I had better water than that, and ran it lower down; started out from the false point—mark twain [5]—raised the second reef abreast the big snag in the bend, and had quarter less twain."

One of the gorgeous ones remarked:

"I don't want to find fault with your leadsmen, but that's a good deal of water for Plum Point, it seems to me."

There was an approving nod all around as this quiet snub dropped on the boaster and "settled" him. And so they went on talk-talk-talking. Meantime, the thing that was running in my mind was, "Now, if my ears hear aright, I have not only to get the names of all the towns and islands and bends, and so on, by heart, but I must even get up a warm personal acquaintanceship with every old snag and one-limbed cottonwood and obscure wood-pile that ornaments the banks of this river for twelve hundred miles; and more than that, I must actually know where these things are in the dark, unless these guests are gifted with eyes that can pierce through two miles of solid blackness. I wish the piloting business was in Jericho and I had never thought of it."

[2] came within sight of
[3] terms used in taking soundings on the Mississippi; here, one quarter of a fathom less than two fathoms deep   [4] nine and a half feet
[5] With the water as deep as the "2" (twain) mark on the sounding line; the frequently repeated call of the leadsman, "Mark twain!," Clemens adopted as his pseudonym.

At dusk Mr. Bixby tapped the big bell three times (the signal to land), and the captain emerged from his drawing-room in the forward-end of the "texas,"[1] and looked up inquiringly. Mr. Bixby said:

"We will lay up here all night, captain."

"Very well, sir."

That was all. The boat came to shore and was tied up for the night. It seemed to me a fine thing that the pilot could do as he pleased, without asking so grand a captain's permission. I took my supper and went immediately to bed, discouraged by my day's observations and experiences. My late voyage's note-booking was but a confusion of meaningless names. It had tangled me all up in a knot every time I had looked at it in the daytime. I now hoped for respite in sleep; but no, it reveled all through my head till sunrise again, a frantic and tireless nightmare.

Next morning I felt pretty rusty and low-spirited. We went booming along, taking a good many chances, for we were anxious to "get out of the river" (as getting out to Cairo was called) before night should overtake us. But Mr. Bixby's partner, the other pilot, presently grounded the boat, and we lost so much time getting her off that it was plain the darkness would overtake us a good long way above the mouth. This was a great misfortune, especially to certain of our visiting pilots, whose boats would have to wait for their return, no matter how long that might be. It sobered the pilot-house talk a good deal. Coming upstream, pilots did not mind low water or any kind of darkness; nothing stopped them but fog. But down-stream work was different; a boat was too nearly helpless, with a stiff current pushing behind her; so it was not customary to run down-stream at night in low water.

There seemed to be one small hope, however; if we could get through the intricate and dangerous Hat Island crossing before night, we could venture the rest, for we would have plainer sailing and better water. But it would be insanity to attempt Hat Island at night. So there was a deal of looking at watches all the rest of the day, and a constant ciphering upon the speed we were making. Hat Island was the eternal subject; sometimes hope was high and sometimes we were delayed in a bad crossing, and down it went again. For hours all hands lay under the burden of this suppressed excitement; it was even communicated to me, and

[1] a structure on the hurricane deck of a steamer containing the officers' cabin and the pilot house

I got to feeling so solicitous about Hat Island, and under such an awful pressure of responsibility, that I wished I might have five minutes on shore to draw a good, full, relieving breath, and start over again. We were standing no regular watches. Each of our pilots ran such portions of the river as he had run when coming upstream, because of his greater familiarity with it; but both remained in the pilot-house constantly.

An hour before sunset Mr. Bixby took the wheel and Mr. W. stepped aside. For the next thirty minutes every man held his watch in his hand and was restless, silent, and uneasy. At last somebody said, with a doomful sigh:

"Well, yonder's Hat Island—and we can't make it."

All the watches closed with a snap, everybody sighed and muttered something about its being "too bad, too bad—ah, if we could *only* have got here half an hour sooner!" and the place was thick with the atmosphere of disappointment. Some started to go out, but loitered, hearing no bell-tap to land. The sun dipped behind the horizon, the boat went on. Inquiring looks passed from one guest to another; and one who had his hand on the door-knob and had turned it, waited, then presently took away his hand and let the knob turn back again. We bore steadily down the bend. More looks were exchanged, and nods of surprised admiration—but no words. Insensibly the men drew together behind Mr. Bixby, as the sky darkened and one or two dim stars came out. The dead silence and sense of waiting became oppressive. Mr. Bixby pulled the cord, and two deep, mellow notes from the big bell floated off on the night. Then a pause, and one more note was struck. The watchman's voice followed, from the hurricane deck:

"Labboard lead, there! Stabboard lead!"

The cries of the leadsmen began to rise out of the distance, and were gruffly repeated by the word-passers on the hurricane-deck.

"M-a-r-k three! M-a-r-k three! Quarter-less-three! Half twain! Quarter twain! M-a-r-k twain! Quarter-less——"

Mr. Bixby pulled two bell-ropes and was answered by faint jinglings far below in the engine-room, and our speed slackened. The steam began to whistle through the gauge-cocks. The cries of the leadsmen went on—and it is a weird sound, always, in the night. Every pilot in the lot was watching now, with fixed eyes, and talking under his breath. Nobody was calm and easy but Mr. Bixby. He would put his wheel down and stand on a spoke, and as the steamer swung into her (to me) utterly invisible marks—for we seemed to be in the midst of a wide and gloomy sea—he would meet and fasten her there. Out of the murmur of half-audible talk, one caught a coherent sentence now and then—such as:

"There; she's over the first reef all right!"

After a pause, another subdued voice:

"Her stern's coming down just *exactly* right, by *George!*"

"Now she's in the marks; over she goes!"

Somebody else muttered:

"Oh, it was done beautiful—*beautiful!*"

Now the engines were stopped altogether, and we drifted with the current. Not that I could see the boat drift, for I could not, the stars being all gone by this time. This drifting was the dismalest; it held one's heart still. Presently I discovered a blacker gloom than that which surrounded us. It was the head of the island. We were closing right down upon it. We entered its deeper shadow, and so imminent seemed the peril that I was likely to suffocate; and I had the strongest impulse to do *something*, anything, to save the vessel. But still Mr. Bixby stood by his wheel, silent, intent as a cat, and all the pilots stood shoulder to shoulder at his back.

"She'll not make it!" somebody whispered.

The water grew shoaler and shoaler, by the leadsman's cries, till it was down to:

"Eight-and-a-half! E-i-g-h-t feet! E-i-g-h-t feet! Seven-and—"

Mr. Bixby said warningly through his speaking tube to the engineer:

"Stand by, now!"

"Ay, ay, sir!"

"Seven-and-a-half! Seven feet! Six-and—"

We touched bottom! Instantly Mr. Bixby set a lot of bells ringing, shouted through the tube, "*Now*, let her have it—every ounce you've got!" then to his partner, "Put her hard down! snatch her! snatch her!" The boat rasped and ground her way through the sand, hung upon the apex of disaster a single tremendous instant, and then over she went! And such a shout as went up at Mr. Bixby's back never loosened the roof of a pilot-house before!

There was no more trouble after that. Mr. Bixby was a hero that night; and it was some little time, too, before his exploit ceased to be talked about by river men.

Fully to realize the marvelous precision required in laying the great steamer in her marks in that murky waste of water, one should know that not only must she pick her intricate way through snags and blind reefs, and then shave the head of the island so closely as to brush the overhanging foliage with her stern, but at one place she must pass almost within arm's reach of a sunken and invisible wreck that would snatch the hull timbers from under her if she should strike it, and destroy a quarter of a million dollars' worth of steamboat and cargo in five minutes, and maybe a hundred and fifty human lives into the bargain.

The last remark I heard that night was a compliment to Mr. Bixby, uttered in soliloquy and with unction by one of our guests. He said:

"By the Shadow of Death, but he's a lightning pilot!"

1879, 1883

From THE ADVENTURES OF TOM SAWYER [1]

THE CAT AND THE PAIN-KILLER

One of the reasons why Tom's mind had drifted away from its secret troubles was that it had found a new and weighty matter to interest itself about. Becky Thatcher had stopped coming to school. Tom had struggled with his pride a few days, and tried to "whistle her down the wind," but failed. He began to find himself hanging around her father's house, nights, and feeling very miserable. She was ill. What if she should die! There was distraction in the thought. He no longer took an interest in war, nor even in piracy. The charm of life was gone; there was nothing but dreariness left. He put his hoop away, and his bat; there was no joy in them any more. His aunt was concerned. She began to try all manner of remedies on him. She was one of those people who are infatuated with patent medicines and all new-fangled methods of producing health or mending it. She was an inveterate experimenter in these things. When something fresh in this line came out she was in a fever, right away, to try it; not on herself, for she was never ailing, but on anybody else that came handy. She was a subscriber for all the "Health" periodicals and phrenological frauds; and the solemn ignorance they were inflated with was breath to her nostrils. All the "rot" they contained about ventilation, and how to go to bed, and how to get up, and what to eat, and what to drink, and how much

---

[1] From *The Adventures of Tom Sawyer* by Mark Twain. Copyright. By permission of Messrs. Harper and Brothers, publishers.

exercise to take, and what frame of mind to keep one's self in, and what sort of clothing to wear, was all gospel to her, and she never observed that her health-journals of the current month customarily upset everything they had recommended the month before. She was as simple-hearted and honest as the day was long, and so she was an easy victim. She gathered together her quack periodicals and her quack medicines, and thus armed with death, went about on her pale horse, [1] metaphorically speaking, with "hell following after." But she never suspected that she was not an angel of healing and the balm of Gilead [2] in disguise, to the suffering neighbors.

The water treatment was new, now, and Tom's low condition was a windfall to her. She had him out at daylight every morning, stood him up in the woodshed and drowned him with a deluge of cold water; then she scrubbed him down with a towel like a file, and so brought him to; then she rolled him up in a wet sheet and put him away under blankets till she sweated his soul clean and "the yellow stains of it came through his pores"—as Tom said.

Yet notwithstanding all this, the poor boy grew more and more melancholy and pale and dejected. She added hot baths, sitz baths, shower baths, and plunges. The boy remained as dismal as a hearse. She began to assist the water with a slim oatmeal diet and blister-plasters. She calculated his capacity as she would a jug's, and filled him up every day with quack cure-alls.

Tom had become indifferent to persecution by this time. This phase filled the old lady's heart with consternation. This indifference must be broken up at any cost. Now she heard of Pain-killer for the first time. She ordered a lot at once. She tasted it and was filled with gratitude. It was simply fire in a liquid form. She dropped the water treatment and everything else, and pinned her faith to Pain-killer. She gave Tom a teaspoonful and watched with the deepest anxiety for the result. Her troubles were instantly at rest, her soul at peace again; for the "indifference" was broken up. The boy could not have shown a wilder, heartier interest if she had built a fire under him.

Tom felt that it was time to wake up; this sort of life might be romantic enough, in his blighted condition; but it was getting to have

too little sentiment and too much distracting variety about it. So he thought over various plans for relief, and finally hit upon that of professing to be fond of Pain-killer. He asked for it so often that he became a nuisance, and his aunt ended by telling him to help himself and quit bothering her. If it had been Sid, she would have had no misgivings to alloy her delight; but since it was Tom, she watched the bottle clandestinely. She found that the medicine did really diminish, but it did not occur to her that the boy was mending the health of a crack in the sitting-room floor with it.

One day Tom was in the act of dosing the crack when his aunt's yellow cat came along, purring, eying the teaspoon avariciously, and begging for a taste. Tom said:

"Don't ask for it unless you want it, Peter."

But Peter signified that he did want it.

"You better make sure."

Peter was sure.

"Now you've asked for it, and I'll give it to you, because there ain't anything mean about *me;* but if you find you don't like it, you mustn't blame anybody but your own self."

Peter was agreeable. So Tom pried his mouth open and poured down the Pain-killer. Peter sprang a couple of yards in the air, and then delivered a war-whoop and set off round and round the room, banging against furniture, upsetting flower-pots, and making general havoc. Next he rose on his hind feet and pranced around, in a frenzy of enjoyment, with his head over his shoulder and his voice proclaiming his unappeasable happiness. Then he went tearing around the house again spreading chaos and destruction in his path. Aunt Polly entered in time to see him throw a few double somersets, deliver a final mighty hurrah, and sail through the open window, carrying the rest of the flower-pots with him. The old lady stood petrified with astonishment, peering over her glasses; Tom lay on the floor expiring with laughter.

"Tom, what on earth ails that cat?"

"*I* don't know, aunt," gasped the boy.

"Why, I never see anything like it. What *did* make him act so?"

"'Deed I don't know, Aunt Polly; cats always act so when they're having a good time."

"They do, do they?" There was something in the tone that made Tom apprehensive.

"Yes'm. That is, I believe they do."

"You *do?*"

"Yes'm."

The old lady was bending down, Tom watching, with interest emphasized by anxiety. Too

[1] *Revelation* vi, 8
[2] a balsam from which a fragrant ointment is made; the reference is to *Jeremiah* viii, 22: "Is there no balm in Gilead?"

late he devined her "drift." The handle of the telltale teaspoon was visible under the bed-valance. Aunt Polly took it, held it up. Tom winced, and dropped his eyes. Aunt Polly raised him by the usual handle—his ear—and cracked his head soundly with her thimble.

"Now, sir, what did you want to treat that poor dumb beast so for?"

"I done it out of pity for him—because he hadn't any aunt."

"Hadn't any aunt!—you numbskull. What has that got to do with it?"

"Heaps. Because if he'd 'a' had one she'd 'a' burnt him out herself! She'd 'a' roasted his bowels out of him 'thout any more feeling than if he was a human!"

Aunt Polly felt a sudden pang of remorse. This was putting the thing in a new light; what was cruelty to a cat *might* be cruelty to a boy, too. She began to soften; she felt sorry. Her eyes watered a little, and she put her hand on Tom's head and said gently:

"I was meaning for the best, Tom. And, Tom, it *did* do you good."

Tom looked up in her face with just a perceptible twinkle peeping through his gravity.

"I know you was meaning for the best, auntie, and so was I with Peter. It done *him* good, too. I never see him get around so since—"

"Oh, go 'long with you, Tom, before you aggravate me again. And you try and see if you can't be a good boy, for once, and you needn't take any more medicine."

Tom reached school ahead of time. It was noticed that this strange thing had been occurring every day lately. And now, as usual of late, he hung about the gate of the schoolyard instead of playing with his comrades. He was sick, he said, and he looked it. He tried to seem to be looking everywhere but whither he really was looking—down the road. Presently Jeff Thatcher hove in sight, and Tom's face lighted; he gazed a moment, and then turned sorrowfully away. When Jeff arrived, Tom accosted him, and "led up" warily to opportunities for remark about Becky, but the giddy lad never could see the bait. Tom watched and watched, hoping whenever a frisking frock came in sight, and hating the owner of it as soon as he saw she was not the right one. At last frocks ceased to appear, and he dropped hopelessly into the dumps; he entered the empty school-house and sat down to suffer. Then one more frock passed in at the gate, and Tom's heart gave a great bound. The next instant he was out, and "going on" like an Indian; yelling, laughing, chasing boys, jumping over the fence at risk of life and limb, throwing hand-springs, standing on his head—doing all the heroic things he could conceive of, and keeping a furtive eye out, all the while, to see if Becky Thatcher was noticing. But she seemed to be unconscious of it all; she never looked. Could it be possible that she was not aware that he was there? He carried his exploits to her immediate vicinity; came war-whooping around, snatched a boy's cap, hurled it to the roof of the school-house, broke through a group of boys, tumbling them in every direction, and fell sprawling himself, under Becky's nose, almost upsetting her—and she turned, with her nose in the air, and he heard her say: "Mf! some people think they're mighty smart—always showing off!"

Tom's cheeks burned. He gathered himself up and sneaked off, crushed and crestfallen.

1876

FRANCIS BRET HARTE
1836-1902

Harte was born in Albany, New York, amid cultured surroundings. His father was a student of languages and a teacher, and the lad became well acquainted with good literature in his own home. After his father's death he came with his mother to California, and at the age of eighteen entered upon a life of adventure. He was a placer miner, a school teacher, a store clerk, and an express messenger. In the late '60's he began writing for San Francisco publications, and in 1868 published his most famous tales, including "The Luck of Roaring Camp," in the *Overland Monthly*, of which he was the first editor. Though little popular in California, where they were thought to reflect upon the moral status of the new community, these stories were eagerly received in the East.

Harte's contributions to American literature were the California background, and such a treatment of the transplanted Easterners and Southerners—combining the color and strong contrasts of romance with a fundamental realism—as to produce characters virtually new in American fiction of high grade. In technique he followed the strict unity developed by Poe. Unfortunately for his own artistic development, he left the West after he had gathered but a handful of its rich materials; and was apparently content to paint for years, with some shifting of figures, scenes from his youthful experiences. He was United States consul at Crefeld, Prussia, and later at Glasgow, and spent the latter part of his life in England.

Biography and criticism: Geoffrey Bret Harte, *The Letters of Bret Harte*, 1926; H. W. Boynton, *Bret Harte*, 1903; T. E. Pemberton, *Bret Harte*, 1903; H. C. Merwin, *The Life of Bret Harte*, 1911;

Pattee; Trent and Erskine; I. Jones, "The Bret Harte Country," *Am. Mercury* 7:147-53; J. P. Collins, "Bret Harte's Genius," *19th Cent.* 96: 537-43; *Liv. Age* 323:515-20; H. S. Canby, "The Luck of Bret Harte," *Sat. R. Lit.* 2:717-8; G. W. James, "Bret Harte," *Overland* ns 78:10-8 Dec. '21; "Bret Harte and Mark Twain in the 'Seventies," *Atlan.* 130:341-8; A. D. Robinson, "Footprints on Piety Hill," *Bookm.* 51:445-8.

THE OUTCASTS OF POKER FLAT [1]

As Mr. John Oakhurst, gambler, stepped into the main street of Poker Flat on the morning of the 23rd of November, 1850, he was conscious of a change in its moral atmosphere since the preceding night. Two or three men conversing earnestly together, ceased as he approached, and exchanged significant glances. There was a Sabbath lull in the air, which, in a settlement unused to Sabbath influences, looked ominous.

Mr. Oakhurst's calm, handsome face betrayed small concern in these indications. Whether he was conscious of any predisposing cause was another question. "I reckon they're after somebody," he reflected; "likely it's me." He returned to his pocket the handkerchief with which he had been whipping away the red dust of Poker Flat from his neat boots, and quietly discharged his mind of any further conjecture.

In point of fact, Poker Flat was "after somebody." It had lately suffered the loss of several thousand dollars, two valuable horses, and a prominent citizen. It was experiencing a spasm of virtuous reaction, quite as lawless and ungovernable as any of the acts that had provoked it. A secret committee had determined to rid the town of all improper persons. This was done permanently in regard of two men who were then hanging from the boughs of a sycamore in the gulch, and temporarily in the banishment of certain other objectionable characters. I regret to say that some of these were ladies. It is but due to the sex, however, to state that their impropriety was professional, and it was only in such easily established standards of evil that Poker Flat ventured to sit in judgment.

Mr. Oakhurst was right in supposing that he was included in this category. A few of the committee had urged hanging him as a possible example, and a sure method of reimbursing themselves from his pockets of the sums he had won from them. "It's agin justice," said Jim Wheeler, "to let this yer young man from Roaring Camp—an entire stranger—carry away

[1] By permission of Houghton Mifflin Company, authorized publishers.

our money." But a crude sentiment of equity residing in the breasts of those who had been fortunate enough to win from Mr. Oakhurst overruled this narrower local prejudice.

Mr. Oakhurst received his sentence with philosophic calmness, none the less coolly that he was aware of the hesitation of his judges. He was too much of a gambler not to accept fate. With him life was at best an uncertain game, and he recognized the usual percentage in favor of the dealer.

A body of armed men accompanied the deported wickedness of Poker Flat to the outskirts of the settlement. Besides Mr. Oakhurst, who was known to be a coolly desperate man, and for whose intimidation the armed escort was intended, the expatriated party consisted of a young woman familiarly known as the "Duchess"; another who had won the title of "Mother Shipton"; and "Uncle Billy," a suspected sluice-robber [2] and confirmed drunkard. The cavalcade provoked no comments from the spectators, nor was any word uttered by the escort. Only when the gulch which marked the uttermost limit of Poker Flat was reached, the leader spoke briefly and to the point. The exiles were forbidden to return at the peril of their lives.

As the escort disappeared, their pent-up feelings found vent in a few hysterical tears from the Duchess, some bad language from Mother Shipton, and a Parthian [3] volley of expletives from Uncle Billy. The philosophic Oakhurst alone remained silent. He listened calmly to Mother Shipton's desire to cut somebody's heart out, to the repeated statements of the Duchess that she would die in the road, and to the alarming oaths that seemed to be bumped out of Uncle Billy as he rode forward. With the easy good-humor characteristic of his class, he insisted upon exchanging his own riding horse, "Five Spot," for the sorry mule which the Duchess rode. But even this act did not draw the party into any closer sympathy. The young woman readjusted her somewhat draggled plumes with a feeble, faded coquetry; Mother Shipton eyed the possessor of "Five Spot" with malevolence, and Uncle Billy included the whole party in one sweeping anathema.

The road to Sandy Bar—a camp that, not having as yet experienced the regenerating influences of Poker Flat, consequently seemed to

[2] one who steals gold from the wooden flumes where gold-bearing gravel is washed
[3] The Parthians were an ancient race noted for fighting on horseback and shooting their arrows behind them as they pretended to flee.

offer some invitation to the emigrants—lay over a steep mountain range. It was distant a day's severe travel. In that advanced season, the party soon passed out of the moist, temperate regions of the foot-hills into the dry, cold, bracing air of the Sierras. The trail was narrow and difficult. At noon the Duchess, rolling out of her saddle upon the ground, declared her intention of going no farther, and the party halted.

The spot was singularly wild and impressive. A wooded amphitheater, surrounded on three sides by precipitous cliffs of naked granite, sloped gently toward the crest of another precipice that overlooked the valley. It was, undoubtedly, the most suitable spot for a camp, had camping been advisable. But Mr. Oakhurst knew that scarcely half the journey to Sandy Bar was accomplished, and the party were not equipped or provisioned for delay. This fact he pointed out to his companions curtly, with a philosophic commentary on the folly of "throwing up their hand before the game was played out." But they were furnished with liquor, which in this emergency stood them in place of food, fuel, rest, and prescience. In spite of his remonstrances, it was not long before they were more or less under its influence. Uncle Billy passed rapidly from a bellicose state into one of stupor, the Duchess became maudlin, and Mother Shipton snored. Mr. Oakhurst alone remained erect, leaning against a rock, calmly surveying them.

Mr. Oakhurst did not drink. It interfered with a profession which required coolness, impassiveness, and presence of mind, and, in his own language, he "couldn't afford it." As he gazed at his recumbent fellow-exiles, the loneliness begotten of his pariah-trade, his habits of life, his very vices, for the first time seriously oppressed him. He bestirred himself in dusting his black clothes, washing his hands and face, and other acts characteristic of his studiously neat habits, and for a moment forgot his annoyance. The thought of deserting his weaker and more pitiable companions never perhaps occurred to him. Yet he could not help feeling the want of that excitement which, singularly enough, was most conducive to that calm equanimity for which he was notorious. He looked at the gloomy walls that rose a thousand feet sheer above the circling pines around him; at the sky, ominously clouded; at the valley below, already deepening into shadow; and, doing so, suddenly he heard his own name called.

A horseman slowly ascended the trail. In the fresh, open face of the newcomer Mr. Oakhurst recognized Tom Simson, otherwise known as the "Innocent," of Sandy Bar. He had met him some months before over a "little game," and had, with perfect equanimity, won the entire fortune—amounting to some forty dollars—of that guileless youth. After the game was finished, Mr. Oakhurst drew the youthful speculator behind the door and thus addressed him: "Tommy, you're a good little man, but you can't gamble worth a cent. Don't try it over again." He then handed him his money back, pushed him gently from the room, and so made a devoted slave of Tom Simson.

There was a remembrance of this in his boyish and enthusiastic greeting of Mr. Oakhurst. He had started, he said, to go to Poker Flat to seek his fortune. "Alone?" No, not exactly alone; in fact (a giggle), he had run away with Piney Woods. Didn't Mr. Oakhurst remember Piney? She that used to wait on the table at the Temperance House? They had been engaged a long time, but old Jake Woods had objected, and so they had run away, and were going to Poker Flat to be married, and here they were. And they were tired out, and how lucky it was they had found a place to camp, and company. All this the Innocent delivered rapidly, while Piney, a stout, comely damsel of fifteen, emerged from behind the pine-tree where she had been blushing unseen, and rode to the side of her lover.

Mr. Oakhurst seldom troubled himself with sentiment, still less with propriety; but he had a vague idea that the situation was not fortunate. He retained, however, his presence of mind sufficiently to kick Uncle Billy, who was about to say something, and Uncle Billy was sober enough to recognize in Mr. Oakhurst's kick a superior power that would not bear trifling. He then endeavored to dissuade Tom Simson from delaying further, but in vain. He even pointed out the fact that there was no provisions, nor means of making a camp. But, unluckily, the Innocent met this objection by assuring the party that he was provided with an extra mule loaded with provisions, and by the discovery of a rude attempt at a log-house near the trail. "Piney can stay with Mrs. Oakhurst," said the Innocent, pointing to the Duchess, "and I can shift for myself."

Nothing but Mr. Oakhurst's admonishing foot saved Uncle Billy from bursting into a roar of laughter. As it was, he felt compelled to retire up the cañon until he could recover his gravity. There he confided the joke to the tall pine-trees, with many slaps of his leg, contortions of his face, and the usual profanity. But when he returned to the party, he found them seated by a fire—for the air had grown strangely chill and the sky overcast—in apparently amicable conversation. Piney was actually talking in an impulsive, girlish fashion to the Duchess, who was listening with an interest and animation she had not shown for many days. The Innocent was holding forth, apparently with equal effect, to Mr. Oakhurst and Mother Shipton, who was actually relaxing into amiability. "Is this yer a d—d picnic?" said Uncle Billy, with inward scorn, as he surveyed the sylvan group, the glancing fire, and the tethered animals in the foreground. Suddenly an idea mingled with the alcoholic fumes that disturbed his brain. It was apparently of a jocular nature, for he felt impelled to slap his leg again and cram his fist into his mouth.

As the shadows crept slowly up the mountain, a slight breeze rocked the tops of the pine-trees, and moaned through their long and gloomy aisles. The ruined cabin, patched and covered with pine-boughs, was set apart for the ladies. As the lovers parted they unaffectedly exchanged a kiss, so honest and sincere that it might have been heard above the swaying pines. The frail Duchess and the malevolent Mother Shipton were probably too stunned to remark upon this last evidence of simplicity, and so turned without a word to the hut. The fire was replenished, the men lay down before the door, and in a few minutes were asleep.

Mr. Oakhurst was a light sleeper. Toward morning he awoke benumbed and cold. As he stirred the dying fire, the wind, which was now blowing strongly, brought to his cheek that which caused the blood to leave it,—snow!

He started to his feet with the intention of awakening the sleepers, for there was no time to lose. But turning to where Uncle Billy had been lying, he found him gone. A suspicion leaped to his brain, and a curse to his lips. He ran to the spot where the mules had been tethered; they were no longer there. The tracks were already rapidly disappearing in the snow.

The momentary excitement brought Mr. Oakhurst back to the fire with his usual calm. He did not waken the sleepers. The Innocent slumbered peacefully, with a smile on his good-humored, freckled face; the virgin Piney slept beside her frailer sisters as sweetly as though attended by celestial guardians, and Mr. Oakhurst, drawing his blanket over his shoulders, stroked his mustaches and waited for the dawn. It came slowly in a whirling mist of snowflakes,

that dazzled and confused the eye. What could be seen of the landscape appeared magically changed. He looked over the valley, and summed up the present and future in two words,—"Snowed in!"

A careful inventory of the provisions, which, fortunately for the party, had been stored within the hut, and so escaped the felonious fingers of Uncle Billy, disclosed the fact that with care and prudence they might last ten days longer. "That is," said Mr. Oakhurst, *sotto voce* to the Innocent, "if you're willing to board us. If you ain't—and perhaps you'd better not—you can wait till Uncle Billy gets back with provisions." For some occult reason, Mr. Oakhurst could not bring himself to disclose Uncle Billy's rascality, and so offered the hypothesis that he had wandered from the camp and had accidentally stampeded the animals. He dropped a warning to the Duchess and Mother Shipton, who of course knew the facts of their associate's defection. "They'll find out the truth about us *all* when they find out anything," he added, significantly, "and there's no good frightening them now."

Tom Simson not only put all his worldly store at the disposal of Mr. Oakhurst, but seemed to enjoy the prospect of their enforced seclusion. "We'll have a good camp for a week, and then the snow'll melt, and we'll all go back together." The cheerful gayety of the young man and Mr. Oakhurst's calm infected the others. The Innocent, with the aid of pine-boughs, extemporized a thatch for the roofless cabin, and the Duchess directed Piney in the re-arrangement of the interior with a taste and tact that opened the blue eyes of that provincial maiden to their fullest extent. "I reckon now you're used to finer things at Poker Flat," said Piney. The Duchess turned away sharply to conceal something that reddened her cheeks through their professional tint, and Mother Shipton requested Piney not to "chatter." But when Mr. Oakhurst returned from a weary search for the trail, he heard the sound of happy laughter echoed from the rocks. He stopped in some alarm, and his first thoughts naturally reverted to the whiskey, which he had prudently cached. [1] "And yet it don't somehow sound like whiskey," said the gambler. It was not until he caught sight of the blazing fire through the still blinding storm and the group around it that he settled to the conviction that it was "square fun."

Whether Mr. Oakhurst had cached his cards with the whiskey as something debarred the

[1] hidden

free access of the community, I cannot say. It was certain that, in Mother Shipton's words, he "didn't say cards once" during that evening. Haply the time was beguiled by an accordion, produced somewhat ostentatiously by Tom Simson from his pack. Notwithstanding some difficulties attending the manipulation of this instrument, Piney Woods managed to pluck several reluctant melodies from its keys, to an accompaniment by the Innocent on a pair of bone castanets.[1] But the crowning festivity of the evening was reached in a rude camp-meeting hymn, which the lovers, joining hands, sang with great earnestness and vociferation. I fear that a certain defiant tone and Covenant-er's[2] swing to its chorus, rather than any devotional quality, caused it speedily to infect the others, who at last joined in the refrain:—

"I'm proud to live in the service of the Lord,
    And I'm bound to die in His army."

The pines rocked, the storm eddied and whirled above the miserable group, and the flames of their altar leaped heavenward, as if in token of the vow.

At midnight the storm abated, the rolling clouds parted, and the stars glittered keenly above the sleeping camp. Mr. Oakhurst, whose professional habits had enabled him to live on the smallest possible amount of sleep, in dividing the watch with Tom Simson, somehow managed to take upon himself the greater part of that duty. He excused himself to the Innocent by saying that he had "often been a week without sleep." "Doing what?" asked Tom. "Poker!" replied Oakhurst, sententiously; "when a man gets a streak of luck—nigger-luck, —he don't get tired. The luck gives in first. Luck," continued the gambler, reflectively, "is a mighty queer thing. All you know about it for certain is that it's bound to change. And it's finding out when it's going to change that makes you. We've had a streak of bad luck since we left Poker Flat,—you come along, and slap you get into it, too. If you can hold your cards right along, you're all right. For," added the gambler, with cheerful irrelevance,—

"I'm proud to live in the service of the Lord,
    And I'm bound to die in His army."

The third day came, and the sun, looking through the white-curtained valley, saw the outcasts divide their slowly decreasing store of provisions for the morning meal. It was one of the peculiarities of that mountain climate that its rays diffused a kindly warmth over the wintry landscape, as if in regretful commiseration of the past. But it revealed drift on drift of snow piled high around the hut,—a hopeless, uncharted, trackless sea of white lying below the rocky shores to which the castaways still clung. Through the marvelously clear air the smoke of the pastoral village of Poker Flat rose miles away. Mother Shipton saw it, and from a remote pinnacle of her rocky fastness hurled in that direction a final malediction. It was her last vituperative attempt, and perhaps for that reason was invested with a certain degree of sublimity. It did her good, she privately informed the Duchess. "Just you go out there and cuss, and see." She then set herself to the task of amusing "the child," as she and the Duchess were pleased to call Piney. Piney was no chicken, but it was a soothing and original theory of the pair thus to account for the fact that she didn't swear and wasn't improper.

When night crept up again through the gorges, the reedy notes of the accordion rose and fell in fitful spasms and long-drawn gasps by the flickering camp-fire. But music failed to fill entirely the aching void left by insufficient food, and a new diversion was proposed by Piney, story-telling. Neither Mr. Oakhurst nor his female companions caring to relate their personal experiences, this plan would have failed, too, but for the Innocent. Some months before he had chanced upon a stray copy of Mr. Pope's ingenious translation of the *Iliad*. He now proposed to narrate the principal incidents of that poem—having thoroughly mastered the argument and fairly forgotten the words—in the current vernacular of Sandy Bar. And so for the rest of that night the Homeric demigods again walked the earth. Trojan bully and wily Greek wrestled in the winds, and the great pines in the cañon seemed to bow to the wrath of the son of Peleus.[3] Mr. Oakhurst listened with quiet satisfaction. Most especially was he interested in the fate of "Ash-heels," as the Innocent persisted in denominating the "swift-footed Achilles."

So with small food and much of Homer and the accordion, a week passed over the heads of the outcasts. The sun again forsook them, and again from leaden skies the snowflakes were sifted over the land. Day by day closer around them drew the snowy circle, until at last they looked from their prison over drifted walls of dazzling white, that towered twenty feet above their heads. It became more and more difficult to replenish their fires, even from

[1] small clappers held in the hands
[2] A Scotch religious-political party of the 17th century; their hymns had very swinging melodies.
[3] Achilles

the fallen trees beside them, now half hidden in the drifts. And yet no one complained. The lovers turned from the dreary prospect and looked into each other's eyes, and were happy. Mr. Oakhurst settled himself coolly to the losing game before him. The Duchess, more cheerful than she had been, assumed the care of Piney. Only Mother Shipton—once the strongest of the party—seemed to sicken and fade. At midnight on the tenth day she called Oakhurst to her side. "I'm going," she said in a voice of querulous weakness, "but don't say anything about it. Don't waken the kids. Take the bundle from under my head and open it." Mr. Oakhurst did so. It contained Mother Shipton's rations for the last week, untouched. "Give 'em to the child," she said, pointing to the sleeping Piney. "You've starved yourself," said the gambler. "That's what they call it," said the woman, querulously, as she lay down again, and, turning her face to the wall, passed quietly away.

The accordion and the bones [1] were put aside that day, and Homer was forgotten. When the body of Mother Shipton had been committed to the snow, Mr. Oakhurst took the Innocent aside and showed him a pair of snow-shoes, which he had fashioned from the old pack-saddle. "There's one chance in a hundred to save her yet," he said, pointing to Piney; "but it's there," he added, pointing toward Poker Flat. "If you can reach there in two days, she's safe." "And you?" asked Tom Simson. "I'll stay here," was the curt reply.

The lovers parted with a long embrace. "You are not going, too?" said the Duchess, as she saw Mr. Oakhurst apparently waiting to accompany him. "As far as the cañon," he replied. He turned suddenly and kissed the Duchess, leaving her pallid face aflame and her trembling limbs rigid with amazement.

Night came, but not Mr. Oakhurst. It brought the storm again and the whirling snow. Then the Duchess, feeding the fire, found that some one had quietly piled beside the hut enough fuel to last a few days longer. The tears rose to her eyes, but she hid them from Piney. The women slept but little. In the morning, looking into each other's faces, they read their fate. Neither spoke; but Piney, accepting the position of the stronger, drew near and placed her arm around the Duchess's waist. They kept this attitude for the rest of the day. That night the storm reached its greatest fury, and, rending asunder the protecting pines, invaded the very hut.

[1] the castanets

Toward morning they found themselves unable to feed the fire, which gradually died away. As the embers slowly blackened, the Duchess crept closer to Piney, and broke the silence of many hours: "Piney, can you pray?" "No, dear," said Piney, simply. The Duchess, without knowing exactly why, felt relieved, and, putting her head upon Piney's shoulder, spoke no more. And so reclining, the younger and purer pillowing the head of her soiled sister upon her virgin breast, they fell asleep.

The wind lulled as if it feared to waken them. Feathery drifts of snow, shaken from the long pine-boughs, flew like white-winged birds, and settled about them as they slept. The moon through the rifted clouds looked down upon what had been the camp. But all human stain, all trace of earthly travail, was hidden beneath the spotless mantle mercifully flung from above.

They slept all that day and the next, nor did they waken when voices and footsteps broke the silence of the camp. And when pitying fingers brushed the snow from their wan faces, you could scarcely have told, from the equal peace that dwelt upon them, which was she that had sinned. Even the law of Poker Flat recognized this, and turned away, leaving them still locked in each other's arms.

But at the head of the gulch, on one of the largest pine-trees, they found the deuce of clubs pinned to the bark with a bowie-knife. It bore the following, written in pencil, in a firm hand:—

Beneath this tree
Lies the body
of
JOHN OAKHURST
Who struck a streak of bad luck
On the 23rd of November, 1850,
and
Handed in his checks
On the 7th of December, 1850.

And pulseless and cold, with a derringer by his side and a bullet in his heart, though still calm as in life, beneath the snow lay he who was at once the strongest and yet the weakest of the outcasts of Poker Flat.

1869

"JIM" [1]

Say there! P'r'aps
    Some on you chaps
        Might know Jim Wild?
Well,—no offense:
    Thar ain't no sense
        In gittin' riled!

Jim was my chum
    Up on the Bar:
That's why I come
    Down from up yar,   10
Lookin' for Jim.
Thank ye, sir! *You*
Ain't of that crew,—
    Blest if you are!

Money? Not much:
    That ain't my kind;
I ain't no such.
    Rum? I don't mind,
Seein' it's you.

Well, this yer Jim,—   20
    Did you know him?
Jes' 'bout your size;
    Same kind of eyes;—
Well, that is strange:
    Why, it's two year
Since he came here,
    Sick, for a change.

Well, here's to us:
    Eh?
The h—— you say!   30
    Dead?
That little cuss?

What makes you star',
    You over thar?
Can't a man drop
    's glass in yer shop
But you must r'ar?
    It wouldn't take
D——d much to break
    You and your bar.   40

    Dead!
Poor—little—Jim!
Why, thar was me,
    Jones, and Bob Lee,
Harry and Ben,—
    No-account men:
Then to take *him*!

Well, thar—Good-by,—
    No more, sir—I—

[1] By permission of Houghton Mifflin Company, authorized publishers.

Eh?   50
What's that you say?
    Why, dern it!—sho!—
No? Yes! By Joe!
    Sold!
Sold! Why, you limb,
    You ornery,
        Derned old
Long-legged Jim.

1870

DICKENS IN CAMP [1]

[1812-1870]

Above the pines the moon was slowly drifting,
    The river sang below;
The dim Sierras, far beyond, uplifting
    Their minarets of snow.

The roaring camp-fire, with rude humor, painted
    The ruddy tints of health
On haggard face and form that drooped and fainted
    In the fierce race for wealth;

Till one arose, and from his pack's scant treasure
    A hoarded volume drew,   10
And cards were dropped from hands of listless leisure
    To hear the tale anew.

And then, while round them shadows gathered faster,
    And as the firelight fell,
He read aloud the book wherein the Master
    Had writ of "Little Nell." [2]

Perhaps 'twas boyish fancy,—for the reader
    Was youngest of them all,—
But, as he read, from clustering pine and cedar
    A silence seemed to fall;   20

The fir-trees, gathering closer in the shadows,
    Listened in every spray,
While the whole camp with "Nell" on English meadows
    Wandered and lost their way.

And so in mountain solitudes—o'ertaken
    As by some spell divine—
Their cares dropped from them like the needles shaken
    From out the gusty pine.

[2] in Dickens's *Old Curiosity Shop*

Lost is that camp, and wasted all its fire;
  And he who wrought that spell?   30
Ah, towering pine and stately Kentish spire,
  Ye have one tale to tell!

Lost is that camp, but let its fragrant story
  Blend with the breath that thrills
With hop-vine's incense all the pensive glory
  That fills the Kentish hills.

And on that grave where English oak and holly
  And laurel wreaths entwine,
Deem it not all a too presumptuous folly,
  This spray of Western pine!   40
July, 1870

JOHN HAY 1838-1905

John Hay is better known as a statesman and diplomat than as a writer. He was born at Salem, Indiana, graduated from Brown University, studied law in Lincoln's office, was assistant private secretary to Lincoln as President, and saw active service in the Civil War. From 1865 to 1870 he was connected with the United States legations at Paris, Vienna, and Madrid. Returning to America, he became one of the most efficient editorial writers of the *New York Tribune*. Again he was called into government service as Secretary of State and as ambassador to England under McKinley. He wrote *Castilian Days*, 1871, sketches of Spain, and *Poems*, 1890. In collaboration with J. G. Nicolay he produced the authoritative *Life of Lincoln*, 10 volumes, 1890, and *Abraham Lincoln; Complete Works*, 2 volumes, 1894. Hay's poetry does not rise to great heights; generally it is conventional and is often courtly and tender. Its most distinctive form is that of the dialect ballad, written in the colloquial language of the Middle West.

Biography and criticism: Wm. R. Thayer, *Life and Letters of John Hay*, 2 vols., 1915; W. D. Howells, *Harper* 132:310-3; also *Dial* 59:411-5; *Nation* 101:570-2; *Outlook* 111:809-12; *Contemp.* 109:122-4; *No. Am.* 203:143-5.

JIM BLUDSO OF THE PRAIRIE BELLE [1]

Wall, no! I can't tell whar he lives,
  Becase he don't live, you see;
Leastways, he's got out of the habit
  Of livin' like you and me.
Whar have you been for the last three year
  That you haven't heard folks tell
How Jimmy Bludso passed in his checks
  The night of the Prairie Belle?

He weren't no saint,—them engineers
  Is all pretty much alike,—   10

[1] By permission of Houghton Mifflin Company, authorized publishers.

One wife in Natchez-under-the-Hill
  And another one here, in Pike;
A keerless man in his talk was Jim,
  And an awkward hand in a row,
But he never flunked, and he never lied,—
  I reckon he never knowed how.

And this was all the religion he had,—
  To treat his engine well;
Never be passed on the river;
  To mind the pilot's bell;   20
And if ever the Prairie Belle took fire,—
  A thousand times he swore,
He'd hold her nozzle agin the bank
  Till the last soul got ashore.

All boats has their day on the Mississip,
  And her day come at last,—
The Movastar was a better boat,
  But the Belle she *wouldn't* be passed.
And so she come tearin' along that night—
  The oldest craft on the line—   30
With a nigger squat on her safety-valve,
  And her furnace crammed, rosin and pine.

The fire bust out as she clared the bar,
  And burnt a hole in the night,
And quick as a flash she turned, and made
  For that willer-bank on the right.
There was runnin' and cursin', but Jim yelled out,
  Over all the infernal roar,
"I'll hold her nozzle agin the bank
  Till the last galoot's ashore."   40

Through the hot, black breath of the burnin' boat
  Jim Bludso's voice was heard,
And they all had trust in his cussedness,
  And knowed he would keep his word.
And, sure's you're born, they all got off
  Afore the smokestacks fell,—
And Bludso's ghost went up alone
  In the smoke of the Prairie Belle.

He weren't no saint,—but at jedgment
  I'd run my chance with Jim,   50
'Longside of some pious gentlemen
  That wouldn't shook hands with him.
He seen his duty, a dead-sure thing,—
  And went for it thar and then;
And Christ ain't a-going to be too hard
  On a man that died for men.

                             1871

JOAQUIN MILLER 1841-1913

Miller was born, so he says, in a covered wagon near the Indiana line. His father, who was a wandering pioneer school teacher in Indiana, set out, a few years after his son's birth, on the Oregon trail for the West. Into his four-score years Miller seems to have gathered most of the picturesque experiences of the American occupation of the Pacific coast. He was a miner, an express messenger, a lawyer, an editor, and a county judge. When merely a boy he was a filibuster with Walker in Nicaragua, and when an old man he was a newspaper reporter in the Klondyke rush.

His first success as a poet he gained in London with his *Songs of the Sierras,* published there in 1871 after he had failed to find an American publisher. In London he became something of a literary lion and was accepted there in his fringed buckskin coat and high boots as a genuinely typical product of the Pacific United States. During his last years his home was in the eucalyptus-clad hills above Oakland, facing the Golden Gate. Miller's best poetry, which is sometimes reminiscent of Whitman, is uneven in quality. It is full of the adventure of the Pacific West, sometimes cheaply romantic, sometimes revealing the rugged beauty of mountains and forests or touching with genuine feeling the realistic tragedy of the frontier; and through it runs a vein of mysticism.

Autobiographical material in introduction to *Joaquin Miller's Poems,* 6 vols., 1909-1917, and *Life Among the Modocs,* 1873. Criticism: H. C. Thompson, "A Sierra Poet in the Making," *Bookm.* 51:553-7; E. S. Mighels, "Justice to Joaquin Miller," *Overland* ns 84:216-7; G. Sterling, *Am. Mercury* 7:220-9; P. H. Boynton, *New Repub.* 10: 99-101; H. M. Bland, *Craftsman* 20:496-504; H. Garland, *Sunset* 30:765-70; A. J. Waterhouse, *Sunset* 30:393-6; *Dial* 54:165-7.

EXODUS FOR OREGON [1]

A tale half told and hardly understood;
The talk of bearded men that chanced to meet,
That lean'd on long quaint rifles in the wood,
That look'd in fellow faces, spoke discreet
And low, as half in doubt and in defeat
Of hope; a tale it was of lands of gold
That lay below the sun. Wild-wing'd and fleet
It spread among the swift Missouri's bold
Unbridled men, and reach'd to where Ohio
	roll'd.

Then long chain'd lines of yoked and patient
	steers;	10
Then long white trains that pointed to the west,

[1] Permission to use this poem granted by the Harr Wagner Publishing Company, publishers of Joaquin Miller's *Complete Poems.*

Beyond the savage west; the hopes and fears
Of blunt, untutor'd men, who hardly guess'd
Their course; the brave and silent women,
	dress'd
In homely spun attire, the boys in bands,
The cheery babes that laugh'd at all, and bless'd
The doubting hearts, with laughing lifted
	hands! . . . .
What exodus for far untraversed lands!

The Plains! The shouting drivers at the
	wheel;
The crash of leather whips; the crush and
	roll	20
Of wheels; the groan of yokes and grinding steel
And iron chain, and lo! at last the whole
Vast line, that reach'd as if to touch the goal,
Began to stretch and stream away and wind
Toward the west, as if with one control;
Then hope loom'd fair, and home lay far behind;
Before, the boundless plain, and fiercest of
	their kind.

At first the way lay green and fresh as seas,
And far away as any reach of wave;
The sunny stream went by in belt of trees;	30
And here and there the tassel'd tawny brave
Swept by on horse, look'd back, stretch'd forth
	and gave
A yell of warn, and then did wheel and rein
Awhile, and point away, dark-brow'd and grave
Into the far and dim and distant plain
With signs and prophecies, and then plunged on
	again.

Some hills at last began to lift and break;
Some streams began to fail of wood and tide,
The somber plain began betime to take
A hue of weary brown, and wild and wide	40
It stretch'd its naked breast on every side.
A babe was heard at last to cry for bread
Amid the deserts; cattle low'd and died,
And dying men went by with broken tread,
And left a long black serpent line of wreck and
	dead.

Strange hunger'd birds, black-wing'd and still
	as death,
And crown'd of red with hooked beaks, blew
	low
And close about, till we could touch their
	breath—
Strange unnamed birds, that seem'd to come
	and go
In circles now, and now direct and slow,	50

Continual, yet never touch the earth;
Slim foxes slid and shuttled to and fro
At times across the dusty weary dearth
Of life, look'd back, then sank like crickets in
    a hearth.

Then dust arose, a long dim line like smoke
From out of riven earth. The wheels went
    groaning by,
Ten thousand feet in harness and in yoke,
They tore the ways of ashen alkali,
And desert winds blew sudden, swift and dry.
The dust! it sat upon and fill'd the train!   60
It seem'd to fret and fill the very sky,
Lo! dust upon the beasts, the tent, the plain,
And dust, alas! on breasts that rose not up
    again.

They sat in desolation and in dust
By dried-up desert streams; the mother's hands
Hid all her bended face; the cattle thrust
Their tongues and faintly call'd across the lands.
The babes, that knew not what this way
    through sands
Could mean, did ask if it would end today . . .
The panting wolves slid by, red-eyed, in bands
To pools beyond. The men look'd far away,   71
And, silent, saw that all a boundless desert lay.

They rose by night; they struggled on and on
As thin and still as ghosts; then here and there
Beside the dusty way before the dawn,
Men silent laid them down in their despair,
And died. But woman! Woman, frail as fair!
May man have strength to give to you your
    due;
You falter'd not, nor murmur'd anywhere,
You held your babes, held to your course, and
    you   80
Bore on through burning hell your double bur-
    dens through.

Men stood at last, the decimated few,
Above a land of running streams, and they?
They push'd aside the boughs, and peering
    through
Beheld afar the cool, refreshing bay;
Then some did curse, and some bend hands to
    pray;
But some look'd back upon the desert, wide
And desolate with death, then all the day,
They mourned. But one, with nothing left be-
    side
His dog to love, crept down among the ferns
    and died.   90
              1873

THOMAS BAILEY ALDRICH
1836-1907

The Story of a Bad Boy, 1870, so well portrays
Aldrich's childhood in his birthplace, Portsmouth,
New Hampshire, that no other account of his early
years is necessary. It shows the life of an active,
fun-loving boy in a small New England city. The
death of his father brought an end to the lad's
academic training, threw him upon his own resources, but did not prevent his writing. He
worked his way upward into journalism and in
1891 followed William Dean Howells as editor of
the *Atlantic Monthly.* Aldrich's work includes
short stories ("Marjorie Daw," 1873, being the
most notable); novels (*Prudence Palfrey,* 1874,
The Stillwater Tragedy, 1880); and a book of
travel, *From Ponkapog to Pesth,* 1883; and several
volumes of verse from 1854 to 1898. Aldrich's
skill as a poet lies in expressing the mood of a
passing moment, the keenly felt, dramatic situation,
often tinged with humor, pathos, or gallantry; at
the same time he is held in check by a seriousness
that unites him with the poets of New England.

    Biography: Ferris Greenslet, *The Life of Thomas
Bailey Aldrich,* 1908; Mrs. T. B. Aldrich, *Crowd-
ing Memories,* rev. by C. N. Rourke, *New Repub.*
25:175-6. Criticism: More (Shel. 7); Bliss
Perry, *Park Street Papers,* 141-70; C. H. Gratton,
"Thomas Bailey Aldrich," *Am. Mercury* 5:41-5.

GUILIEMUS REX [1]

The folk who lived in Shakespeare's day
And saw that gentle figure pass
By London Bridge, his frequent way—
They little knew what man he was.

The pointed beard, the courteous mien,
The equal port [2] to high and low,
All this they saw or might have seen—
But not the light behind the brow!

The doublet's modest gray or brown,
The slender sword-hilt's plain device,   10
What sign had these for prince or clown?
Few turned, or none, to scan him twice.

Yet 'twas the king of England's kings!
The rest with all their pomps and trains
Are moldered, half-remembered things—
'Tis he alone that lives and reigns!
              1896

EUGENE FIELD 1850-1895

Although he was born in St. Louis, and spent
most of his life in the West, Field was brought up

[1] King William. By permission of Houghton Mifflin
    Company, authorized publishers.
[2] same manner

in his ancestral New England. He attended Williams College, and then Knox College and the University of Missouri. At the age of twenty-three he found his life-work, journalism, and for many years edited and in the main wrote the "Sharps and Flats" column of the Chicago *News*. In this column much of his poetry first appeared. *A Little Book of Profitable Tales,* and *A Little Book of Western Verse,* 1889, are characteristic of his best poetry. *With Trumpet and Drum,* 1892, and *Love Songs of Childhood,* 1894, are comparable in aim with Stevenson's *Child's Garden of Verses.* Children delight in their merry rhythms: their elders understand and appreciate their whimsy and caprice. Critics have termed Field "the Poet Laureate of childhood." His rimes and songs have entertained children for a generation or two, and it is likely that his verses will soothe babies to sleep for decades to come. Field's prose, consisting mostly of essays, has the same whimsical and endearing characteristics as these that fill his verse.

Biography and criticism: S. Thompson, *Eugene Field,* 2 vols., 1901; F. Wilson, *The Eugene Field I Knew,* 1898; also "Eugene Field the Humorist," *Cent.* 64:446-52; C. H. Dennis, *Eugene Field's Creative Years,* 1924; A. B. Maurice, "Yorick—with a Dash of Ariel," *Bookm.* 60:775-8; Chubb; see also *Poetry* 28:268-74; *Bookm.* 56:44-8; *Scrib. M.* 76:157-62; *Lit. Digest* 75:26-8, Oct. 28, '22.

LITTLE BOY BLUE [1]

The little toy dog is covered with dust,
  But sturdy and staunch he stands;
And the little toy soldier is red with rust,
  And his musket moulds in his hands.
Time was when the little toy dog was new
  And the soldier was passing fair,
And that was the time when our Little Boy
    Blue
  Kissed them and put them there.

"Now, don't you go till I come," he said,
  "And don't you make any noise!"   10
So toddling off to his trundle-bed
  He dreamt of the pretty toys;
And as he was dreaming, an angel song
  Awakened our Little Boy Blue—
Oh, the years are many, the years are long,
  But the little toy friends are true!

Ay, faithful to Little Boy Blue they stand,
  Each in the same old place—
Awaiting the touch of a little hand,
  The smile of a little face;   20
And they wonder, as waiting the long years
    through,

[1] Copyright. By permission of Messrs. Charles Scribner's Sons.

In the dust of that little chair,
What has become of our Little Boy Blue
  Since he kissed them and put them there.
                   1894

SEEIN' THINGS [1]

I ain't afeard uv snakes, or toads, or bugs, or
    worms, or mice,
An' things 'at girls are skeered uv I think are
    awful nice!
I'm pretty brave, I guess; an' yet I hate to go
    to bed,
For, when I'm tucked up warm an' snug an'
    when my prayers are said,
Mother tells me "Happy Dreams!" and takes
    away the light,
An' leaves me lyin' all alone an' seein' things at
    night!

Sometimes they're in the corner, sometimes
    they're by the door,
Sometimes they're all a-standin' in the middle
    uv the floor;
Sometimes they are a-sittin' down, sometimes
    they're walkin' round
So softly an' so creepylike they never make a
    sound!   10
Sometimes they are as black as ink, an' other
    times they're white—
But the color ain't no difference when you see
    things at night!

Once, when I licked a feller 'at had just moved
    on our street,
An' father sent me up to bed without a bite
    to eat,
I woke up in the dark an' saw things standin'
    in a row,
A-lookin' at me cross-eyed an' p'intin' at me—
    so!
Oh, my! I wuz so skeered that time I never
    slep' a mite—
It's almost alluz when I'm bad I see things at
    night!

Lucky thing I ain't a girl, or I'd be skeered to
    death!
Bein' I'm a boy, I duck my head an' hold my
    breath;   20
An' I am, oh! *so* sorry I'm a naughty boy, an'
    then
I promise to be better an' I say my prayers
    again!
Gran'ma tells me that's the only way to make
    it right
When a feller has been wicked an' sees things
    at night!

An' so, when other naughty boys would coax me
   into sin,
I try to skwush the Tempter's voice 'at urges
   me within;
An' when they's pie for supper, or cakes 'at's
   big and nice,
I want to—but I do not pass my plate f'r them
   things twice!
No, ruther let Starvation wipe me slowly out
   o' sight
Than I should keep a-livin' on an' seein' things
   at night!   30
                            1904

ALWAYS RIGHT [1]

Don't take on so, Hiram,
  But do what you're told to do;
It's fair to suppose that yer mother knows
  A heap sight more than you.
I'll allow that sometimes *her* way
  Don't seem the wisest, quite;
But the *easiest* way,
When she's had her say,
  Is to reckon yer mother is right.

Courted her ten long winters,   10
  Saw her to singin'-school;
When she went down one spell to town,
  I cried like a durned ol' fool;
Got mad at the boys for callin'
  When I sparked her Sunday night:
But she said she knew
A thing or two,—
  An' I reckoned yer mother wuz right.

I courted till I wuz aging,
  And she wuz past her prime,—   20
I'd have died, I guess, if she hadn't said yes
  When I popped f'r the hundredth time.
Said she'd never have took me
  If I hadn't stuck so tight;
Opined that we
Could never agree,—
  And I reckon yer mother wuz right!   1889

EDWARD ROWLAND SILL
1841-1887

Although Sill was born in Windsor, Connecticut, and was a graduate of Yale, he spent almost half his life in California where he went in search of health and where he engaged in various occupations. After a few years he came back to the East to study for the ministry at Harvard, but soon turned to literature and teaching. Again for several years he was in California, professor of English for almost eight years at the State University. Finally he devoted himself entirely to his writing until his death at Cuyahoga, Ohio. His poems, simple in diction, are often didactic in intent, though vigor and originality save them from being conventionally moralistic.

Biography and criticism: W. B. Parker, *Edward Rowland Sill,* 1915; E. L. Baker, "Edward Rowland Sill, Poet-Teacher," *Overland* ns 83 :154-5; *Nation* 101 :207-8; *Dial* 58 :143-5.

OPPORTUNITY [2]

This I beheld, or dreamed it in a dream:—
There spread a cloud of dust along a plain;
And underneath the cloud, or in it, raged
A furious battle, and men yelled, and swords
Shocked upon swords and shields. A prince's
  banner
Wavered, then staggered backward, hemmed by
  foes.
A craven hung along the battle's edge,
And thought, "Had I a sword of keener steel—
That blue blade that the king's son bears,—but
  this
Blunt thing—!" he snapped and flung it from
  his hand,   10
And lowering crept away, and left the field.
Then came the king's son, wounded, sore bestead,
And weaponless, and saw the broken sword,
Hilt-buried in the dry and trodden sand,
And ran and snatched it, and with battle-shout
Lifted afresh he hewed his enemy down,
And saved a great cause that heroic day.
1878-80   1887

THE FOOL'S PRAYER [2]

The royal feast was done; the King
  Sought some new sport to banish care,
And to his jester cried: "Sir Fool,
  Kneel now, and make for us a prayer!"

The jester doffed his cap and bells,
  And stood the mocking court before;
They could not see the bitter smile
  Behind the painted grin he wore.

He bowed his head, and bent his knee
  Upon the monarch's silken stool;   10
His pleading voice arose: "O Lord,
  Be merciful to me, a fool!

"No pity, Lord, could change the heart
  From red with wrong to white as wool;

[1] Copyright. By permission of Messrs. Charles Scribner's Sons.

[2] Copyright. By permission of Houghton Mifflin Company, authorized publishers.

The rod must heal the sin: but, Lord,
　Be merciful to me, a fool!

" 'Tis not by guilt the onward sweep
　Of truth and right, O Lord, we stay;
'Tis by our follies that so long
　We hold the earth from heaven away.　　20

"These clumsy feet, still in the mire,
　Go crushing blossoms without end;
These hard, well-meaning hands we thrust
　Among the heart-strings of a friend.

"The ill-timed truth we might have kept—
　Who knows how sharp it pierced and stung?
The word we had not sense to say—
　Who knows how grandly it had rung?

"Our faults no tenderness should ask,
　The chastening stripes must cleanse them all;
But for our blunders—oh, in shame　　31
　Before the eyes of heaven we fall.

"Earth bears no balsam for mistakes;
　Men crown the knave; and scourge the tool
That did his will; but Thou, O Lord,
　Be merciful to me, a fool!"

The room was hushed; in silence rose
　The King, and sought his gardens cool,
And walked apart, and murmured low,　　39
　"Be merciful to me, a fool!"
1873-80　　　　　　　　　　　　　1887

JOEL CHANDLER HARRIS
1848-1908

It was through journalism that Harris came into
authorship. He was born in Georgia, had a limited common-school education, but was apprenticed when a boy to a rather eccentric country
editor and newspaper publisher from whom he
received good training in the essentials of journalism. In 1876 he came to the staff of the *Atlanta
Constitution,* and was its editor in 1890. Pressed,
in an emergency to fill a column for that paper, he
wrote the first of the "Uncle Remus Stories" based
upon tales told him when a child by an old negro
plantation servant. These tales show the genuine
folk imagination of the Negro race, modified, perhaps, by two or three generations in America. They
are partly pagan, certainly naïve; they reflect the
kindliness, humor, and rich inventiveness of the
people from which they sprang. The first that were
published were almost verbatim narratives of the
old servant; how much of Harris's own invention is
found in the later tales is not known. Leading
titles among his collections are *Nights with Uncle
Remus,* 1883; *Mungo and Other Sketches,* 1884;

Balaam and his Master, 1891; *Told by Uncle
Remus—New Series,* 1905.

Biography and criticism: Julia C. Harris, *The
Life and Letters of Joel Chandler Harris,* 1918;
Harry A. Toulmin, *Social Historians,* 1911; H. E.
Harman, "Joel Chandler Harris," *Bookm.* 61:
433-6; E. C. Parsons, "Joel Chandler Harris and
Negro Folklore," *Dial* 66:491-3; see also: *Cur.
Opinion* 65:324-6; *Bookm.* 48:50-6.

From UNCLE REMUS [1]

IV

HOW MR. RABBIT WAS TOO SHARP FOR MR. FOX

"Uncle Remus," said the little boy one evening, when he had found the old man with
little or nothing to do, "did the fox kill and eat
the rabbit when he caught him with the Tar-
Baby?" [2]

"Law, honey, ain't I tell you 'bout dat?"
replied the old darkey, chuckling slyly. "I
'clar ter grashus I ought er tole you dat, but
old man Nod wuz ridin' on my eyeleds 'twel a
leetle mo'n I'd a dis'member'd my own name,
en den on to dat here come yo' mammy hol-
lerin' atter you.

"W'at I tell you w'en I fus' begin? I tole
you Brer Rabbit wuz a monstus soon creetur;
leas'ways dat's w'at I laid out fer ter tell you.
Well, den, honey, don't you go en make no
udder calkalashuns, kaze in dem days Brer
Rabbit en his fambly wuz at de head er de
gang w'en enny racket wuz on han', en dar dey
stayed. 'Fo' you begins fer ter wipe yo' eyes
'bout Brer Rabbit, you wait en see whar'bouts
Brer Rabbit gwineter fetch up at. But dat's
needer yer ner dar.

"W'en Brer Fox fine Brer Rabbit mixt up
wid de Tar-Baby, he feel mighty good, en he
roll on de groun' en laff. Bimeby he up'n say,
sezee:

" 'Well, I speck I got you dis time, Brer Rabbit,' sezee; 'maybe I ain't, but I speck I is. You
been runnin' roun' here sassin' atter me a
mighty long time, but I speck you done come
ter de een' er de row. You bin cuttin' up yo'
capers en bouncin' 'roun' in dis neighborhood
ontwel you come ter b'leeve yo'se'f de boss er
de whole gang. En den youer allers some'rs
whar you got no bizness,' sez Brer Fox, sezee.
'Who ax you fer ter come en strike up a 'quaint-
ance wid dish yer Tar-Baby? En who stuck

[1] From *Uncle Remus: His Songs and His Sayings* by
Joel Chandler Harris, by permission of Messrs. D.
Appleton and Company, publishers.
[2] The fox had caught the rabbit by setting up a tar
baby in the road, to which the rabbit had stuck
when he tried to beat it for refusing to speak.

you up dar whar you iz? Nobody in de roun' worril. You des tuck en jam yo'se'f on dat Tar-Baby widout waitin' fer enny invite,' sez Brer Fox, sezee, 'en dar you is, en dar you'll stay twel I fixes up a bresh-pile and fires her up, kaze I'm gwineter bobbyque you dis day, sho,' sez Brer Fox, sezee.

"Den Brer Rabbit talk mighty 'umble.

" 'I don't keer w'at you do wid me, Brer Fox,' sezee, 'so you don't fling me in dat brier-patch. Roas' me, Brer Fox,' sezee, 'but don't fling me in dat brier-patch,' sezee.

" 'Hit's so much trouble fer ter kindle a fier,' sez Brer Fox, sezee, 'dat I speck I'll hatter hang you,' sezee.

" 'Hang me des ez high as you please, Brer Fox,' sez Brer Rabbit, sezee, 'but do fer de Lord's sake don't fling me in dat brier-patch,' sezee.

" 'I ain't got no string,' sez Brer Fox, sezee, 'en now I speck I'll hatter drown you,' sezee.

" 'Drown me des ez deep ez you please, Brer Fox,' sez Brer Rabbit, sezee, 'but do don't fling me in dat brier-patch,' sezee.

" 'Dey ain't no water nigh,' sez Brer Fox, sezee, 'en now I speck I'll hatter skin you,' sezee.

" 'Skin me, Brer Fox,' sez Brer Rabbit, sezee, 'snatch out my eyeballs, t'ar out my years by de roots, en cut off my legs,' sezee, 'but do please, Brer Fox, don't fling me in dat brier-patch,' sezee.

"Co'se Brer Fox wanter hurt Brer Rabbit bad ez he kin, so he cotch 'im by de behime legs en slung 'im right in de middle er de brier-patch. Dar was a considerbul flutter whar Brer Rabbit struck de bushes, en Brer Fox sorter hang 'roun' fer ter see w'at wuz gwineter happen. Bimeby he hear somebody call 'im, en way up de hill he see Brer Rabbit settin' cross-legged on a chinkapin log koamin' de pitch outen his har wid a chip. Den Brer Fox know dat he bin swop off mighty bad. Brer Rabbit wuz bleedzed fer ter fling back some er his sass, en he holler out:

" 'Bred en bawn in a brier-patch, Brer Fox—bred en bawn in a brier-patch!' en wid dat he skip out des ez lively ez a cricket in de embers."

WHY MR. POSSUM LOVES PEACE

"One night," said Uncle Remus—taking Miss Sally's little boy on his knee, and stroking the child's hair thoughtfully and caressingly—"one night Brer Possum call by fer Brer Coon, 'cordin' ter 'greement, en atter gobblin' up a dish er fried greens en smokin' a seegyar, dey rambled fort' fer ter see how de ballunce er de settlement wuz gittin' 'long. Brer Coon, he wuz one er deze yer natchul pacers, en he racked 'long same ez Mars John's bay pony, en Brer Possum he went in a han'-gallup; en dey got over heap er groun', mon. Brer Possum, he got his belly full er 'simmons, en Brer Coon, he scoop up a 'bunnunce er frogs en tadpoles. Dey amble 'long, dey did, des ez sociable ez a basket er kittens, twel bimeby dey hear Mr. Dog talkin' ter hisse'f way off in de woods.

" 'Spozen he runs up on us, Brer Possum, w'at you gwineter do?' sez Brer Coon, sezee. Brer Possum sorter laff 'round de cornders un his mouf.

" 'Oh, ef he come, Brer Coon, I'm gwineter stan' by you,' sez Brer Possum. 'W'at you gwineter do?' sezee.

" 'Who? me?' sez Brer Coon. 'Ef he run up onter me, I lay I give 'im one twis',' sezee."

"Did the dog come?" asked the little boy.

"Go 'way, honey!" responded the old man, in an impressive tone. "Go way! Mr. Dog, he come en he come a zoonin'. En he ain't wait fer ter say howdy, nudder. He des sail inter de two un um. De ve'y fus pas he make Brer Possum fetch a grin fum year ter year, en keel over like he wuz dead. Den Mr. Dog, he sail inter Brer Coon, en right dar's whar he drap his money purse, kaze Brer Coon wuz cut out fer dat kinder bizness, en he fa'rly wipe up de face er de yeth wid 'im. You better b'leeve dat w'en Mr. Dog got a chance to make hisse'f skase he tuck it, en w'at der wuz lef' un him went skaddlin' thoo de woods like hit wuz shot outen a muskit. En Brer Coon, he sorter lick his cloze inter shape en rack off, en Brer Possum, he lay dar like he wuz dead, twel bimeby he raise up sorter keerful like, en w'en he fine de coas' cle'r he scramble up en scamper off like sumpin was atter 'im."

Here Uncle Remus paused long enough to pick up a live coal of fire in his fingers, transfer it to the palm of his hand, and thence to his clay pipe, which he had been filling—a proceeding that was viewed by the little boy with undisguised admiration. The old man then proceeded:

"Nex' time Brer Possum meet Brer Coon, Brer Coon 'fuse ter 'spon' ter his howdy, en dis make Brer Possum feel mighty bad, seein' ez how dey useter make so many 'scurshuns ter-gedder.

" 'W'at make you hol' yo' head so high, Brer Coon?' sez Brer Possum, sezee.

" 'I ain't runnin' wid cowerds deze days,' sez

Brer Coon. 'W'en I wants you I'll sen' fer you,' sezee.

"Den Brer Possum git mighty mad.

" 'Who's enny cowerd?' sezee.

" 'You is,' sez Brer Coon, 'dat's who. I ain't soshatin' wid dem w'at lies down on de groun' en plays dead w'en dar's a free fight gwine on,' sezee.

"Den Brer Possum grin en laugh fit to kill hisse'f.

" 'Lor', Brer Coon, you don't speck I done dat kaze I wuz 'feared, duz you?' sezee. 'W'y I want no mo' 'feared dan you is dis minnit. W'at wuz dey fer ter be skeered un?' sezee. 'I know'd you'd git away wid Mr. Dog ef I didn't, en I des lay dar watchin' you shake him, waitin' fer ter put in w'en de time come,' sezee.

"Brer Coon tu'n up his nose.

" 'Dat's a mighty likely tale,' sezee, 'w'en Mr. Dog ain't mo'n tech you 'fo' you keel over, en lay dar stiff,' sezee.

" 'Dat's des w'at I wuz gwineter tell you 'bout,' sez Brer Possum, sezee. 'I want no mo' skeer'd dan you is right now, en' I wuz fixin' fer ter give Mr. Dog a sample er my jaw,' sezee, 'but I'm de most ticklish chap w'at you ever laid eyes on, en no sooner did Mr. Dog put his nose down yer 'mong my ribs dan I got ter laughin', en I laughed twel I ain't had no use er my lim's' sezee, 'en it's a mussy unto Mr. Dog dat I wuz ticklish, kaze a little mo' en I'd e't 'im up,' sezee. 'I don't min' fighting', Brer Coon, no mo' dan you duz,' sezee, 'but I declar' ter grashus ef I kin stan' ticklin'. Git me in a row whar dey ain't no ticklin' 'lowed, en I'm your man,' sezee.

"En down ter dis day"—continued Uncle Remus, watching the smoke from his pipe curl upward over the little boy's head—"down ter dis day, Brer Possum's bound ter s'render w'en you tech him in de short ribs, en he'll laugh ef he knows he's gwineter be smashed fer it."

Here Uncle Remus paused long enough to

JOHN BURROUGHS 1837-1921

The early training of Burroughs, perhaps the best known American writer upon nature between Thoreau and Beebe, was that of the country home and the country school. He was born at Roxbury, southern New York State, and his father's farm and its surroundings were the lad's first laboratory and museum. After teaching school and working on a newspaper he became a guard, and later a clerk, in the United States Treasury at Washington. All his spare time he used in the out-door study of plants and animals. He spent his later life in his camp-like home, "Slabsides," not far from the Hudson. His best known books are *Wake*

Robin, 1870; *Locusts and Wild Honey,* 1879; *Fresh Fields,* 1884; *Literary Values,* 1902; *Time and Change,* 1912.

Burrough's particular subject-matter came from rather commonplace facts and experiences; his manner is one of pleasing directness. In his later years he became much interested in literature and philosophy, and produced some literary and philosophical criticism. Notable is his essay upon Whitman, of whom he was a friend and companion.

Autobiographical: *My Boyhood,* 1922; also *Harper* 144:137-51; 341-9; 515-24. Biography and criticism: C. Barrus, *Our Friend John Burroughs,* 1914; H. James, *View and Reviews,* 1906; R. J. H. De Loach, *Rambles with John Burroughs,* 1912; D. L. Sharp, *The Seer of Slabsides,* 1921; C. Barrus, "Whitman and Burroughs as Comrades," *Yale R.* ns 15:59-81; H. L. West, "John Burroughs," *Bookm.* 49:389-98; H. Garland, "My Friend John Burroughs," *Cent.* 102:731-42; S. Hartman, "A Visit to John Burroughs," *Cent.* 101:619-21; see also N. Foerster, *No. Am.* 214:177-82; W. M. Lodge, *Overland* ns 77:50-2, April, '21.

From MY BOYHOOD [1]

The old farm must have had at least ten miles of stone walls upon it, many of them built new by Father from stones picked up in the fields, and many of them relaid by him, or rather by his boys and hired men. Father was not skillful at any sort of craft work. He was a good plowman, a good mower and cradler, excellent with a team of oxen drawing rocks, and good at most general farm work, but not an adept at constructing anything. Hiram was the mechanical genius of the family. He was a good wall-layer, and skillful with edged tools. It fell to his lot to make the sleds, the stone-boats, [2] the hay-rigging, the ax helves, the flails, to mend the cradles and rakes, to build the haystacks, and once, I remember, he rebuilt the churning machine. He was slow but he hewed exactly to the line. Before and during my time on the farm Father used to count on building forty or fifty rods of stone wall each year, usually in the spring and early summer. These were the only lines of poetry and prose Father wrote. They are still very legible on the face of the landscape and cannot be easily erased from it. Gathered out of the confusion of nature, built up of fragments of the old Devonian [3] rock and shale, laid with due regard to the wear and tear of time, well-bottomed and

[1] From *My Boyhood* by John Burroughs, copyright 1922, Doubleday, Page and Company.
[2] flat, runnerless sleds for transporting stones
[3] rocks of the Paleozoic age; named from Devon, England

well-capped, establishing boundaries and defining possessions, etc., these lines of stone wall afford a good lesson in many things besides wall building. [1] They are good literature and good philosophy. They smack of the soil, they have local color, they are a bit of chaos brought into order. When you deal with nature only the square deal is worth while. How she searches for the vulnerable points in your structure, the weak places in your foundation, the defective material in your building!

The farmer's stone wall, when well built, stands about as long as he does. It begins to reel and look decrepit when he begins to do so. But it can be relaid and he cannot. One day I paused by the roadside to speak with an old man who was rebuilding a wall. "I laid this wall fifty years ago," he said. "When it is laid up again I shall not have the job." He had stood up longer than had his wall.

A stone wall is a friend of all the wild creatures. It is a safe line of communication with all parts of the landscape. What do the chipmunks, red squirrels, and weasels do in a country without stone fences? The woodchucks and the coons and foxes also use them.

It was my duty as a farm boy to help pick up the stone and pry up the rocks. I could put the bait [2] under the lever, even if my weight on top of it did not count for much. The slow, patient, hulky oxen, how they would kink their tails, hump their backs, and throw their weight into the bows when they felt a heavy rock behind them and Father lifted up his voice and laid on the "gad"! It was a good subject for a picture which, I think, no artist has ever painted. How many rocks we turned out of their beds, where they had slept since the great ice sheet tucked them up there, maybe a hundred thousand years ago—how wounded and torn the meadow or pasture looked, bleeding as it were, in a score of places, when the job was finished! But the further surgery of the plow and harrow, followed by the healing touch of the seasons, soon made all whole again.

The work on the farm in those days varied little from year to year. In winter the care of the cattle, the cutting of the wood, and the thrashing of the oats and rye filled the time. From the age of ten or twelve till we were grown up, we went to school only in winter, doing the chores morning and evening, and engaging in general work every other Saturday, which was a holiday. Often my older brothers would have to leave school by three o'clock to get home to put up the cows in my father's absence. Those school days, how they come back to me!—the long walk across lots, through snow-choked fields and woods, our narrow path so often obliterated by a fresh fall of snow; the cutting winds, the bitter cold, the snow squeaking beneath our frozen cowhide boots, our trousers' legs often tied down with tow strings to keep the snow from pushing them up above our boot tops; the wide-open white landscape with its faint black lines of stone wall when we had passed the woods and began to dip down into West Settlement Valley; the Smith boys and Bouton boys and Dart boys, afar off, threading the fields on their way to school, their forms etched on the white hillsides, one of the bigger boys, Ria Bouton, who had many chores to do, morning after morning running the whole distance so as not to be late; the red school house in the distance by the roadside with the dark spot in its center made by the open door of the entry way; the creek in the valley, often choked with anchor ice, [3] which our path crossed and into which I one morning slumped, reaching the school house with my clothes freezing upon me and the water gurgling in my boots; the boys and girls there, Jay Gould [4] among them, two thirds of them now dead and the living scattered from the Hudson to the Pacific; the teachers now all dead; the studies, the games, the wrestlings, the baseball—all these things and more pass before me as I recall those long-gone days.

.   .   .   .   .   .

The first considerable work in spring was sugar-making, always a happy time for me. Usually the last half of March, when rills from the melting snow began to come through the fields, the veins of the sugar maples began to thrill with the spring warmth. There was a general awakening about the farm at this time: the cackling of the hens, the bleating of young lambs and calves, and the wistful lowing of the cows. Earlier in the month the "sap spiles" had been overhauled, resharpened, and new ones made, usually from bass wood. In my time the sap gouge was used instead of the auger and the manner of tapping was crude and wasteful. A slanting gash three or four inches long and a half inch or more deep was cut, and an inch below the lower end of this the gouge was driven in to make the place for the spile, a piece of wood two inches wide, shaped to the

---

[1] See Frost's "Mending Wall," p. 819.
[2] a fulcrum, as for a crowbar

[3] ground ice, sometimes formed on the bottom of still or running water
[4] an American financier and millionaire, 1836-1892

gouge, and a foot or more in length. It gave the tree a double and unnecessary wound. The bigger the gash the more the sap, seemed to be the theory, as if the tree was a barrel filled with liquid, whereas a small wound made by a half-inch bit does the work just as well and is far less injurious to the tree.

When there came a bright morning, wind northwest and warm enough to begin to thaw by eight o'clock, the sugar-making utensils— pans, kettles, spiles, hogsheads—were loaded upon the sled and taken to the woods, and by ten o'clock the trees began to feel the cruel ax and gouge once more. It usually fell to my part to carry the pans and spiles for one of the tappers, Hiram or Father, and to arrange the pans on a level foundation of sticks or stones, in position. Father often used to haggle the tree a good deal in tapping. "By Fagus," he would say, "how awkward I am!" The rapid tinkle of those first drops of sap in the tin pan, how well I remember it! Probably the note of the first song sparrow or first bluebird, or the spring call of the nuthatch, sounded in unison. Usually only patches of snow lingered here and there in the woods and the earth-stained remnants of old drifts on the sides of the hills and along the stone walls. Those lucid warm March days in the naked maple woods under the blue sky, with the first drops of sap ringing in the pans, had a charm that does not fade from my mind. After the trees were all tapped, two hundred and fifty of them, the big kettles were again set up in the old stone arch, and the hogs-heads in which to store the sap placed in position. By four o'clock many of the pans—milk pans from the dairy—would be full, and the gathering with neck yoke and pails began. When I was fourteen or fifteen I took a hand in this part of the work. It used to tax my strength to carry the two twelve-quart pails full through the rough places and up the steep banks in the woods and then lift them up and alternately empty them into the hogsheads without displacing the neck yoke. But I could do it. Now all this work is done by the aid of a team and a pipe fastened on a sled. Before I was old enough to gather sap it fell to me to go to the barns and put in hay for the cows and help stable them. The next morning the boiling of the sap would begin, with Hiram in charge. The big deep iron kettles were slow evaporators compared with the broad shallow sheet-iron pans now in use. Profundity cannot keep up with shallowness in sugar-making, the more superficial your evaporator, within limits, the more rapid your progress. It took the

farmers nearly a hundred years to find this out, or at least to act upon it.

At the end of a couple of days of hard boiling Hiram would "syrup off," having reduced two hundred pails of sap to five or six of syrup. The syruping-off often occurred after dark. When the liquid dropped from a dipper which was dipped into it and, held up in the cool air, formed into stiff thin masses, it had reached the stage of syrup. How we minded our steps over the rough path, in the semi-darkness of the old tin lantern, in carrying those precious pails of syrup to the house, where the final process of "sugaring off" was to be completed by Mother and Jane!

The sap runs came at intervals of several days. Two or three days would usually end one run. A change in the weather to below freezing would stop the flow, and a change to much warmer would check it. The fountains of sap are let loose by frosty sunshine. Frost in the ground, or on it in the shape of snow and the air full of sunshine are the most favorable conditions. A certain chill and crispness, something crystalline, in the air are necessary. A touch of enervating warmth from the south or a frigidity from the north and the trees feel it through their thick bark coats very quickly. Between the temperatures of thirty-five to fifty degrees they get in their best work. After we have had one run ending in rain and warmth, a fresh fall of snow—"sap snow," the farmers call such—will give us another run. Three or four good runs make a long and successful season. My boyhood days in the spring sugar bush were my most enjoyable on the farm. How I came to know each of those two hundred and fifty trees—what a distinct sense of individuality seemed to adhere to most of them, as much so as to each cow in a dairy! I knew at which trees I would be pretty sure to find a full pan and at which ones a less amount. One huge tree always gave a cream-pan full—a double measure—while the others were filling an ordinary pan. This was known as "the old cream-pan tree." Its place has long been vacant; about half the others are still standing, but with the decrepitude of age appearing in their tops, a new generation of maples has taken the place of the vanished veterans.

While tending the kettles there beside the old arch in the bright, warm March or April days, with my brother, or while he had gone to dinner, looking down the long valley and off over the curving backs of the distant mountain ranges, what dreams I used to have, what vague longings, and, I may say, what happy anticipations! I am sure I gathered more than sap and sugar in those youthful days amid the maples. When I visit the old home now I have to walk up to the sugar bush and stand around the old "boiling place," trying to transport myself back into the magic atmosphere of that boyhood time. The man has his dreams, too, but to his eyes the world is not steeped in romance as it is to the eyes of youth.

.   .   .   .   .   .

About this time I heard another new word. We were working on the road, and I with my hoe was working beside an old Quaker farmer, David Corbin, who used to be a school teacher. A large flat stone was turned over, and beneath it in some orderly arrangement were some smaller stones. "Here are some antiquities," said Mr. Corbin, and my vocabulary received another addition. A new word or a new thing was very apt to make its mark upon my mind. I have told elsewhere what a revelation to me was my first glimpse of one of the warblers, the black-throated blue-black, indicating as it did a world of bird life of which I had never dreamed, the bird life in the inner heart of the woods. My brothers and other boys were with me but they did not see the new bird. The first time I saw the veery, or Wilson's thrush, also stands out in my memory. It alighted in the road before us on the edge of the woods. "A brown thrasher," said Bill Chase. It was not the thrasher but it was a new bird to me and the picture of it is in my mind as if made only yesterday. Natural History was a subject unknown to me in my boyhood, and such a thing as nature study in the schools was of course unheard of. Our natural history we got unconsciously in the sport at noon time, or on our way to and from school or in our Sunday excursions to the streams and woods. We learned much about the ways of foxes and woodchucks and coons and skunks and squirrels by hunting them. The partridge, too, and the crows, hawks, and owls, and the song birds of the field and orchard, all enter into the farm boy's life. I early became familiar with the songs and habits of all the common birds, and with field mice, and the frogs, toads, lizards, and snakes. Also with the wild bees and wasps. One season I made a collection of bumblebee honey, studying the habits of five or six different kinds, and rifling their nests. I kept my store of bumblebee honey in the attic where I had a small box full of the comb and a large phial filled with the honey. How well I came to know the different dispositions of the various kinds—the small red-vested that made its

nest in a hole in the ground; the small black-vested, the large black-vested, the yellow-necked, the black-banded, etc., that made their nests in old mice nests in the meadow or in the barn and other places. I used to watch and woo the little piping frogs in the spring marshes when I had driven the cows to pasture at night, till they would sit in my open hand and pipe. I used to creep on my hands and knees through the woods to see the partridge in the act of drumming.[1] I used to watch the mud wasps building their nests in the old attic and noted their complaining cry while in the act of pressing on the mud. I noted the same complaining cry from the bees when working on the flower of the purple-flowering raspberry, what we called "Scotch caps." I tried to trap foxes and soon learned how far the fox's cunning surpassed mine. My first lesson in animal psychology I got from old Nat Higby as he came riding by on horseback one winter day, his huge feet almost meeting under the horse, just as a hound was running a fox across our upper mountain lot. "My boy," he said, "that fox may be running as fast as he can, but if you stood behind that big rock beside his course, and as he came along should jump out and shout 'hello,' he would run faster." That was the winter when in fond imagination I saw a stream of silver dollars coming my way from the red foxes I was planning to deprive of their pelts when they needed them most. I have told elsewhere of my trapping experiences and how completely I failed.

.   .   .   .   .   .

1922

JOHN MUIR 1838-1914

From a childhood in Scotland, the most interesting hours of which included rambles in the fields and by the sea, Muir was transplanted with his parents into the midst of the Wisconsin forest and lake region. There he spent his youth, snatching what time he could from the almost ceaseless toil of a pioneer farm, for studying plants, animals, rocks, and reading such books as fell into his hands. When of age he began to make his way through the University of Wisconsin, supporting himself by manual labor. Soon after leaving the university he traveled afoot to Florida, studying botany and geology as he went, and made his way to California. For many years the formations of the valleys and contours of the Sierras and the life they sustained were the objects of his study. He was especially interested in the work of glaciers, past and present, pursuing his observations of them

[1] making a noise with the wings like the beating of a drum

into Alaska and other regions of active glaciation. On foot and alone, often in great bodily danger, he carried on this exploration, making himself familiar with the forces that molded the mountains. Muir looked upon nature not solely with the critical eye of the scientist, but also with the imagination of a poet. His books interest us through their enthusiasm, their individuality, the spirit of adventure that pervades them; and through the passionate fondness which they reflect for the titanic beauty of the mountains. Muir's chief books are *The Mountains of California*, 1894, 1911; *Stickeen*, 1909 (a charming dog story); *My First Summer in the Sierras*, 1911; *The Yosemite*, 1912.

Biography and criticism: Wm. Fred. Badè, *The Life and Letters of John Muir*, 2 vols., 1924; *The Story of My Boyhood and Youth*, 1913; T. Roosevelt, "John Muir: An Appreciation," *Outlook* 109: 27-8; S. H. Young, "Alaska Days with John Muir," *Outlook* 110:188-99; 430-42; 723-33; E. Wyatt, "Two Woodsmen," *No. Am.* 204:433-6; "How John Muir Inspired Roosevelt," *Cur. Opinion* 78: 337-8; see also: *Outlook* 139:32-3; *Bookm* 61: 88-90; *Poet Lore* 36:45-62.

From THE MOUNTAINS OF CALIFORNIA [1]

A WIND-STORM IN THE FORESTS

. . . . There is always something deeply exciting, not only in the sounds of winds in the woods, which exert more or less influence over every mind, but in their varied waterlike flow as manifested by the movements of the trees, especially those of the conifers. By no other trees are they rendered so extensively and impressively visible, not even by the lordly tropic palms or tree-ferns responsive to the gentlest breeze. The waving of a forest of the giant Sequoias is indescribably impressive and sublime, but the pines seem to me the best interpreters of winds. They are mighty waving goldenrods, ever in tune, singing and writing wind-music all their long century lives. Little, however, of this noble tree-waving and tree-music will you see or hear in the strictly alpine portion of the forests. The burly Juniper, whose girth sometimes more than equals its height, is about as rigid as the rocks on which it grows. The slender lash-like sprays of the Dwarf Pine stream out in wavering ripples, but the tallest and slenderest are far too unyielding to wave even in the heaviest gales. They only shake in quick, short vibrations. The Hemlock Spruce, however, and the Mountain Pine, and some of the tallest thickets of the Two-leaved species bow in storms with considerable scope

[1] From *The Mountains of California* by John Muir, by permission of The Century Company, publishers.

and gracefulness. But it is only in the lower and middle zones that the meeting of winds and woods is to be seen in all its grandeur.

One of the most beautiful and exhilarating storms I ever enjoyed in the Sierra occurred in December, 1874, when I happened to be exploring one of the tributary valleys of the Yuba River. The sky and the ground and the trees had been thoroughly rain-washed and were dry again. The day was intensely pure, one of those incomparable bits of California winter, warm and balmy and full of white sparkling sunshine, redolent of all the purest influences of the spring, and at the same time enlivened with one of the most bracing wind-storms conceivable. Instead of camping out, as I usually do, I then chanced to be stopping at the house of a friend. But when the storm began to sound, I lost no time in pushing out into the woods to enjoy it. For on such occasions Nature has always something rare to show us, and the danger to life and limb is hardly greater than one would experience crouching deprecatingly beneath a roof.

It was still early morning when I found myself fairly adrift. Delicious sunshine came pouring over the hills, lighting the tops of the pines, and setting free a steam of summery fragrance that contrasted strangely with the wild tones of the storm. The air was mottled with pine-tassels and bright green plumes, that went flashing past in the sunlight like birds pursued. But there was not the slightest dustiness, nothing less pure than leaves, and ripe pollen, and flecks of withered bracken and moss. I heard trees falling for hours at the rate of one every two or three minutes; some uprooted, partly on account of the loose, water-soaked condition of the ground; others broken straight across, where some weakness caused by fire had determined the spot. The gestures of the various trees made a delightful study. Young Sugar Pines, light and feathery as squirrel-tails, were bowing almost to the ground; while the grand old patriarchs, whose massive boles had been tried in a hundred storms, waved solemnly above them, their long, arching branches streaming fluently on the gale, and every needle thrilling and ringing and shedding off keen lances of light like a diamond. The Douglas Spruces, with long sprays drawn out in level tresses, and needles massed in a gray, shimmering glow, presented a most striking appearance, as they stood in bold relief along the hilltops. The madroños in the dells, with their red bark and large glossy leaves tilted every way, reflected the sunshine in throbbing spangles like those one so often sees on the rippled surface of a glacier lake. But the Silver Pines were now the most impressively beautiful of all. Colossal spires 200 feet in height waved like supple goldenrods chanting and bowing low as if in worship, while the whole mass of their long, tremulous foliage was kindled into one continuous blaze of white sun-fire. The force of the gale was such that the most steadfast monarch of them all rocked down to its roots with a motion plainly perceptible when one leaned against it. Nature was holding high festival, and every fiber of the most rigid giants thrilled with glad excitement.

I drifted on through the midst of this passionate music and motion, across many a glen, from ridge to ridge; often halting in the lee of a rock for shelter, or to gaze and listen. Even when the grand anthem had swelled to its highest pitch, I could distinctly hear the varying tones of individual tree—Spruce, and Fir, and Pine, and leafless Oak,—and even the infinitely gentle rustle of the withered grasses at my feet. Each was expressing itself in its own way—singing its own song, and making its own peculiar gestures,—manifesting a richness of variety to be found in no other forest I have yet seen. The coniferous woods of Canada, and the Carolinas, and Florida, are made up of trees that resemble one another about as nearly as blades of grass, and grow close together in much the same way. Coniferous trees, in general, seldom possess individual character, such as is manifest among Oaks and Elms. But the California forests are made up of a greater number of distinct species than any other in the world. And in them we find, not only a marked differentiation into special groups, but also a marked individuality in almost every tree, giving rise to storm effects indescribably glorious.

Toward midday, after a long, tingling scramble through copses of hazel and ceanothus, I gained the summit of the highest ridge in the neighborhood; and then it occurred to me that it would be a fine thing to climb one of the trees to obtain a wider outlook and get my ear close to the Aeolian music of its topmost needles. But under the circumstances the choice of a tree was a serious matter. One whose instep was not very strong seemed in danger of being blown down, or of being struck by others in case they should fall; another was branchless to a considerable height above the ground, and at the same time too large to be grasped with arms and legs in climbing; while others were not favorably situated for clear views. After cautiously casting about, I made choice of the tallest of a group of Douglas Spruces that were growing close together like a tuft of grass, no one of which seemed likely to fall unless all the rest fell with it. Though comparatively young, they were about 100 feet high, and their lithe, brushy tops were rocking and swirling in wild ecstasy. Being accustomed to climb trees in making botanical studies, I experienced no difficulty in reaching the top of this one, and never before did I enjoy so noble an exhilaration of motion. The slender tops fairly flapped and swished in the passionate torrent, bending and swirling backward and forward, round and round, tracing indescribable combinations of vertical and horizontal curves, while I clung with muscles firm braced, like a bobolink on a reed.

In its widest sweeps, my tree-top described an arc of from twenty to thirty degrees, but I felt sure of its elastic temper, having seen others of the same species still more severely tried—bent almost to the ground indeed, in heavy snows—without breaking a fiber. I was therefore safe, and free to take the wind into my pulses and enjoy the excited forest from my superb outlook. The view from here must be extremely beautiful in any weather. Now my eye roved over the piny hills and dales as over fields of waving grain, and felt the light running in ripples and broad swelling undulations across the valleys from ridge to ridge, as the shining foliage was stirred by corresponding waves of air. Oftentimes these waves of reflected light would break up suddenly into a kind of beaten foam, and again, after chasing one another in regular order, they would seem to bend forward in concentric curves, and disappear on some hillside, like sea-waves on a shelving shore. The quantity of light reflected from the bent needles was so great as to make whole groves appear as if covered with snow, while the black shadows beneath the trees greatly enhanced the effect of the silvery splendor.

Excepting only the shadows there was nothing somber in all this wild sea of pines. On the contrary, notwithstanding this was the winter season, the colors were remarkably beautiful. The shafts of the pine and libocedrus [1] were brown and purple, and most of the foliage was well tinged with yellow; the laurel groves, with the pale undersides of their leaves turned upward, made masses of gray; and then there was many a dash of chocolate color from clumps of manzanita, and jet of vivid crimson from the

[1] a Sierran genus of cedar trees

bark of the madroños, while the ground on the hillsides, appearing here and there through openings between the groves, displayed masses of pale purple and brown.

The sounds of the storm corresponded gloriously with this wild exuberance of light and motion. The profound bass of the naked branches and boles booming like waterfalls; the quick, tense vibrations of the pine-needles, now rising to a shrill, whistling hiss, now falling to a silky murmur; the rustling of laurel groves in the dells, and the keen metallic click of leaf on leaf—all this was heard in easy analysis when the attention was calmly bent.

The varied gestures of the multitude were seen to fine advantage, so that one could recognize the different species at a distance of several miles by this means alone, as well as by their forms and colors, and the way they reflected the light. All seemed strong and comfortable, as if really enjoying the storm, while responding to its most enthusiastic greetings. We hear much nowadays concerning the universal struggle for existence, but no struggle in the common meaning of the word was manifest here; no recognition of danger by any tree; no deprecation; but rather an invincible gladness as remote from exultation as from fear.

I kept my lofty perch for hours, frequently closing my eyes to enjoy the music by itself, or to feast quietly on the delicious fragrance that was streaming past. The fragrance of the woods was less marked than that produced during warm rain, when so many balsamic buds and leaves are steeped like tea; but, from the chafing of resiny branches against each other, and the incessant attrition of myriads of needles, the gale was spiced to a very tonic degree. And besides the fragrance from these local sources there were traces of scents brought from afar. For this wind came first from the sea, rubbing against its fresh, briny waves, then distilled through the redwoods, threading rich ferny gulches, and spreading itself in broad undulating currents over many a flower-enameled ridge of the coast mountains, then across the golden plains, up the purple foot-hills, and into these piny woods with the varied incense gathered by the way.

Winds are advertisements of all they touch, however much or little we may be able to read them; telling their wanderings even by their scents alone. Mariners detect the flowery perfume of land-winds far at sea, and sea-winds carry the fragrance of dulse and tangle far inland, where it is quickly recognized, though mingled with the scents of a thousand land-flowers. As an illustration of this, I may tell here that I breathed sea-air on the Firth of Forth, in Scotland, while a boy; then was taken to Wisconsin, where I remained nineteen years; then, without in all this time having breathed one breath of the sea, I walked quietly, alone, from the middle of the Mississippi Valley to the Gulf of Mexico, on a botanical excursion, and while in Florida, far from the coast, my attention wholly bent on the splendid tropical vegetation about me, I suddenly recognized a sea-breeze, as it came sifting through the palmettos and blooming vine-tangles, which at once awakened and set free a thousand dormant associations, and made me a boy again in Scotland, as if all the intervening years had been annihilated.

Most people like to look at mountain rivers, and bear them in mind; but few care to look at the winds, though far more beautiful and sublime, and though they become at times about as visible as flowing water. When the north winds in winter are making upward sweeps over the curving summits of the High Sierra, the fact is sometimes published with flying snow-banners a mile long. Those portions of the winds thus embodied can scarce be wholly invisible, even to the darkest imagination. And when we look around over an agitated forest, we may see something of the wind that stirs it, by its effects upon the trees. Yonder it descends in a rush of water-like ripples, and sweeps over the bending pines from hill to hill. Nearer, we see detached plumes and leaves, now speeding by on level currents, now whirling in eddies, or, escaping over the edges of the whirls, soaring aloft on grand, upswelling domes of air, or tossing on flame-like crests. Smooth, deep currents, cascades, falls, and swirling eddies, sing around every tree and leaf, and over all the varied topography of the region with telling changes of form, like mountain rivers conforming to the features of their channels.

After tracing the Sierra streams from their fountains to the plains, marking where they bloom white in falls, glide in crystal plumes, surge gray and foam-filled in boulder-choked gorges, and slip through the woods in long, tranquil reaches—after thus learning their language and forms in detail, we may at length hear them chanting all together in one grand anthem, and comprehend them all in clear inner vision, covering the range like lace. But even this spectacle is far less sublime and not a whit more substantial than what we may behold of these storm-streams of air in the mountain woods.

We all travel the milky way together, trees and men; but it never occurred to me until this storm-day, while swinging in the wind, that trees are travelers, in the ordinary sense. They make many journeys, not extensive ones, it is true; but our own little journeys, away and back again, are only little more than tree wavings—many of them not so much.

When the storm began to abate, I dismounted and sauntered down through the calming woods. The storm-tones died away, and, turning toward the east, I beheld the countless hosts of the forests hushed and tranquil, towering above one another on the slopes of the hills like a devout audience. The setting sun filled them with amber light, and seemed to say, while they listened, "My peace I give unto you."

As I gazed on the impressive scene, all the so-called ruin of the storm was forgotten, and never before did these noble woods appear so fresh, so joyous, so immortal.

1894, 1911

THEODORE ROOSEVELT
1858-1919

The ancestry of Roosevelt was Manhattan Dutch with strains of Huguenot and Scotch-Irish blood. He was born in New York City, spent his boyhood on Long Island, and graduated from Harvard, 1880. With persistent physical exercise and two years of cattle ranching in the Northwest he built up a frail constitution and returned home to enter politics. Although "irregular" in respect to party politics he rose in office, filled important posts on commissions of the New York police, and of the National Civil Service, and became assistant Secretary of the United States Navy, 1897. He served in the Spanish-American War as colonel of the "Rough Riders" regiment, was elected Governor of New York, 1898, Vice-President of the United States in 1900; and was President of the United States from the death of McKinley, 1901, until 1908. The remaining ten years of his life were marked by political activity relieved by hunting and scientific expeditions that took him into Africa and South America. President Roosevelt's uncompromising honesty, his zeal for reform and "a square deal," was made effective by a dynamic aggressiveness in speech, writing, and action. He was the most influential American of his day. His literary works consist of history, biography, adventure, and essays on a wide variety of social and didactic topics. Prominent are *The Naval Operations of the War .... 1812-1815*, 1882; *Winning of the West*, 1889-96; *American Ideals*, 1897; *The Rough Riders*, 1899; *Big Game Hunting*, 1899; *African Game Trails*, 1910; *The Strenuous Life*, 1910. His robust personality is expressed in a style of vigorous, enthusiastic narrative when his object is to entertain; or trenchant invective or exhortation when he would arouse the reader to action. To the end he maintained an eager, almost boyish attitude toward life.

Biography and criticism: W. R. Thayer, *Theodore Roosevelt*, 1919; Bradley Gilman, *Roosevelt the Happy Warrior*, 1921; J. B. Bishop, *Theodore Roosevelt and His Time*, 1920; Lord Charnwood, *Theodore Roosevelt*, 1923; J. Corbin, "Roosevelt in His Writings," *Sat. R. Lit.* 3:590-1; C. W. Ferguson, "Roosevelt, Man of Letters," *Bookm.* 64: 726-9; "Mr. Roosevelt in Literature," *Lit. Digest* 60:27-8, Jan. 25, '19.

From RANCH LIFE AND THE HUNTING TRAIL [1]
CHAPTER III.
THE HOME RANCH

A ranchman's work is, of course, free from much of the sameness attendant upon that of a mere cowboy. One day he will ride out with his men among the cattle, or after strayed horses; the next he may hunt, so as to keep the ranch in meat; then he can make the tour of his outlying camps; or, again, may join one of the round-ups for a week or two, perhaps keeping with it the entire time it is working. On occasions he will have a good deal of spare time on his hands, which, if he chooses, he can spend in reading or writing. If he cares for books, there will be many a worn volume in the primitive little sitting-room, with its log walls and huge fire-place; but after a hard day's work a man will not read much, but will rock to and fro in the flickering firelight, talking sleepily over his success in the day's chase and the difficulty he has had with the cattle; or else may simply lie stretched at full length on the elk-hides and wolf-skins in front of the hearth-stone, listening in drowsy silence to the roar and crackle of the blazing logs and to the moaning of the wind outside.

In the sharp fall weather the riding is delicious all day long; but even in the late spring, and all through the summer, we try, if we can, to do our work before the heat of the day, and if going on a long ride, whether to hunt or for other purposes, leave the ranch house by dawn.

The early rides in the spring mornings have a charm all their own, for they are taken when, for the one and only time during the year, the same brown landscape of these high plains turns to a vivid green, as the new grass sprouts and

---

[1] From *Ranch Life and the Hunting Trail* by Theodore Roosevelt, by permission of The Century Company, publishers.

the trees and bushes thrust forth the young leaves; and at dawn, with the dew glittering everywhere, all things show at their best and freshest. The flowers are out and a man may gallop for miles at a stretch with his horse's hoofs sinking at every stride into the carpet of prairie roses, whose short stalks lift the beautiful blossoms but a few inches from the ground. Even in the waste places the cactuses are blooming; and one kind in particular, a dwarfish, globular plant, with its mass of splendid crimson flowers glows against the sides of the gray buttes [1] like a splash of flame.

The ravines winding about and splitting into a labyrinth of coulées, [2] with chains of rounded hills to separate them, have groves of trees in their bottoms, along the sides of the water courses. In these are found the blacktail deer, and his cousin, the whitetail, too, with his flaunting flag; but in the spring-time, when we are after antelope only, we must go out farther to the flat prairie land on the divide. Here, in places, the level, grassy plains are strewn with mounds and hillocks of red or gray scoria, that stand singly or clustered into little groups, their tops crested, or their sides covered, by queer detached masses of volcanic rock, wrought into strange shapes by the dead forces whose blind, hidden strength long ago called them into being. The road our wagons take, when the water is too high for us to come down the river bottom, stretches far ahead—two dark, straight, parallel furrows which merge into one in the distance. Quaint little horned frogs crawl sluggishly along in the wheel tracks, and the sickle-billed curlews run over the ground or soar above and around the horsemen, uttering their mournful, never-ceasing clamor. The grassland stretches out in the sunlight like a sea, every wind bending the blades into a ripple, and flecking the prairie with shifting patches of a different green from that around, exactly as the touch of light squall or wind-gust will fleck the smooth surface of the ocean. Our Western plains differ widely in detail from those of Asia; yet they always call to mind

. . . . The Scythian

On the wide steppe, unharnessing
His wheel'd house at noon.
He tethers his beast down, and makes his meal—
Mares' milk, and bread
Baked on the embers;—all around
The boundless, waving grass-plains stretch. . . .

[1] (pronounced *bewt*) a conspicuously isolated steep hill or small mountain
[2] the beds of deep water courses having steep sides

. . . ; before him, for long miles,
Alive with bright green lizards
And the springing bustard fowl,
The track, a straight black line,
Furrows the rich soil; here and there
Clusters of lonely mounds
Topp'd with rough hewn,
Gray, rain-blear'd statues, overpeer
The sunny waste.

In the spring mornings the rider on the plains will hear bird songs unknown in the East. The Missouri skylark sings while soaring above the great plateaus so high in the air that it is impossible to see the bird; and this habit of singing while soaring it shares with some sparrow-like birds that are often found in company with it. The white-shouldered lark-bunting, in its livery of black, has rich, full notes, and as it sings on the wing it reminds one of the bobolink; and the sweet-voiced lark-finch also utters its song in the air. These birds, and most of the sparrows of the plains, are characteristic of this region.

But many of our birds, especially those found in the wooded river bottoms, answer to those of the East; only almost each one has some marked point of difference from its Eastern representative. The bluebird out West is very much of a blue bird indeed, for it has no "earth tinge" on its breast at all; while the indigo-bird, on the contrary, has gained the ruddy markings that the other has lost. The flicker has the shafts of its wing and tail quills colored orange instead of yellow. The towhee has lost all title to its name, for its only cry is a mew like that of a cat-bird; while, most wonderful of all, the meadow-lark has found a rich, strong voice, and is one of the sweetest and most incessant singers we have.

Throughout June the thickets and groves about the ranch house are loud with bird music from before dawn till long after sunrise. The thrashers have sung all the night through from among the thorn-bushes if there has been a moon, or even if there has been bright starlight; and before the first glimmer of gray the bell-like, silvery songs of the shy woodland thrushes chime in; while meadow-lark, robin, bluebird, and song sparrow, together with many rarer singers, like the grosbeak, join in swelling the chorus. There are some would-be singers whose intention is better than their execution. Blackbirds of several kinds are plenty round the house and stables, walking about with a knowing air, like so many dwarf crows; and now and then a flock of yellow-heads will mix for a few days with their purple or rusty-colored brethren. The males of these yellow-headed grackles are really handsome, their orange and yellow heads contrasting finely with the black of the rest of their plumage; but their voices are discordant to a degree. When a flock has done feeding it will often light in straggling order among the trees in front of the veranda, and then the males will begin to sing, or rather to utter the most extraordinary collection of broken sounds—creakings, gurglings, hisses, twitters, and every now and then a liquid note or two. It is like an accentuated representation of the noise made by a flock of common blackbirds. At nightfall the poor-wills begin to utter their boding call from the wooded ravines back in the hills; not "whip-poor-will," as in the East, but with two syllables only. They often come round the ranch house. Late one evening I had been sitting motionless on the veranda, looking out across the water and watching the green and brown of the hill-tops change to purple and umber and then fade off into shadowy gray as the somber darkness deepened. Suddenly a poor-will lit on the floor beside me and stayed some little time; now and then uttering its mournful cries, then ceasing for a few moments as it flitted round after insects, and again returning to the same place to begin anew. The little owls, too, call to each other with tremulous, quavering voices throughout the livelong night, as they sit in the creaking trees that overhang the roof. Now and then we hear the wilder voices of the wilderness, from animals that in the hour of darkness do not fear the neighborhood of man: the coyotes wail like dismal ventriloquists, or the silence may be broken by the strident challenge of a lynx, or by the snorting and stamping of a deer that has come to the edge of the open.

In the hot noontide hours of midsummer the broad ranch veranda, always in the shade, is almost the only spot where a man can be comfortable; but here he can sit for hours at a time, leaning back in his rocking chair, as he reads or smokes, or with half-closed, dreamy eyes gazes across the shallow, nearly dry river-bed to the wooded bottoms opposite, and to the plateaus lying back of them. Against the sheer white faces of the cliffs, that come down without a break, the dark green tree-tops stand out in bold relief. In the hot, lifeless air all objects that are not near by seem to sway and waver. There are few sounds to break the stillness. From the upper branches of the cot-tonwood trees overhead, whose shimmering, tremulous leaves are hardly ever quiet, but if the wind stirs at all, rustle and quiver and sigh all day long, comes every now and then the soft, melancholy cooing of the mourning dove, whose voice always seems far away and expresses more than any other sound in nature the sadness of gentle, hopeless, never-ending grief. The other birds are still; and very few animals move about. Now and then the black shadow of a wheeling vulture falls on the sun-scorched ground. The cattle, that have strung down in long files from the hills, lie quietly on the sand-bars, except that some of the bulls keep traveling up and down, bellowing and routing [1] or giving vent to long, surly grumblings as they paw the sand and toss it up with their horns. At times the horses, too, will come down to drink, and to splash and roll in the water.

In making a journey over ground we know, during the hot weather we often prefer to ride by moonlight. The moon shines very brightly through the dry, clear night air, turning the gray buttes into glimmering silver; and the horses travel far more readily and easily than under the glaring noonday sun. The road between my upper and lower ranch houses is about forty miles long, sometimes following the river-bed, and then again branching off inland, crossing the great plateaus and winding through the ravines of the broken country. It is a five-hours' fair ride; and so, in a hot spell, we like to take it during the cool of the night, starting at sunset. After nightfall the face of the country seems to alter marvelously, and the clear moonlight only intensifies the change. The river gleams like running quicksilver, and the moonbeams play over the grassy stretches of the plateaus and glance off the wind-rippled blades as they would from water. The Bad Lands [2] seem to be stranger and wilder than ever, the silvery rays turning the country into a kind of grim fairyland. The grotesque, fantastic outlines of the higher cliffs stand out with startling clearness, while the lower buttes have become formless, misshapen masses, and the deep gorges are in black shadow; in the darkness there will be no sound but the rhythmic echo of the hoof-beats of the horses, and the steady, metallic clank of the steel bridle-chains.

[1] lowing
[2] a rocky, unfertile, gullied region running through the West, called by early French explorers *les terres mauvaises*

From Chapter XI
THE BIG-HORN SHEEP

The day on which I was lucky enough to shoot my largest and finest ram was memorable in more ways than one. The shot was one of the best I ever made,—albeit the element of chance doubtless entered into it far more largely than the element of skill,—and on coming home from the hunt I got quite badly frozen.

The day before we had come back from a week's trip after deer; for we were laying in the winter stock of meat. We had been camped far down the river, and had intended to take two days on the return trip, as the wagon was rather heavily loaded, for we had killed eight deer. The morning we broke camp was so mild that I did not put on my heaviest winter clothing, starting off in the same that I had worn during the past few days' still-hunting among the hills. Before we had been gone an hour, however, the sky grew overcast and the wind began to blow from the north with constantly increasing vigor. The sky grew steadily more gloomy and lowering, the gusts came ever harder and harder, and by noon the winter day had darkened and a furious gale was driving against us. The blasts almost swept me from my saddle and the teamster from his seat, while we were glad to wrap ourselves in our huge fur coats to keep out the growing cold. Soon after midday the wagon suddenly broke down while we were yet in mid-prairie. It was evident that we were on the eve of a furious snow-blizzard, which might last a few hours, or else, perhaps, as many days. We were miles from any shelter that would permit us to light a fire in the face of such a storm; so we left the wagon as it was, hastily unharnessed the team horses, and, with the driver riding one and leading the other, struck off homeward at a steady gallop. Once fairly caught by the blizzard in a country that we only partly knew, it would have been hopeless to do more than to try for some ravine in which to cower till it was over; so we pushed our horses to their utmost pace. Our object was to reach the head coulées of a creek leading down to the river but a few miles from the ranch. Could we get into these before the snow struck us we felt we would be all right, for we could then find our way home, even in pitch-darkness, with the wind in the quarter from which it was coming. So, with the storm on our backs, we rode at full speed through the gathering gloom, across the desolate reaches of prairie. The tough little horses, instead of faltering, went stronger mile by mile. At last the weird rows of hills loomed vaguely up in our front, and we plunged into the deep ravines for which we had been heading just as the whirling white wreaths struck us—not the soft, feathery flakes of a sea-board snow-storm, but fine ice-dust, driven level by the wind, choking us, blinding our eyes, and cutting our face if we turned toward it. The roar of the blizzard drowned our voices when we were but six feet apart; had it not been on our backs we could not have gone a hundred yards, for we could no more face it than we could face a frozen sand-blast. In an instant the strange, wild outlines of the high buttes between which we were riding were shrouded from our sight. We had to grope our way through a kind of shimmering dusk; and when once or twice we were obliged by some impassable cliff or cañon to retrace our steps, it was all that we could do to urge the horses even a few paces against the wind-blown snow-grains which stung like steel filings. But this extreme violence only lasted about four hours. The moon was full, and its beams struggled through scudding clouds and snow-drift, so that we reached the ranch without difficulty, and when we got there the wind had already begun to lull. The snow still fell thick and fast; but before we went to bed this also showed signs of stopping. Accordingly we determined that we would leave the wagon where it was for a day or two, and start early next morning for a range of high hills some ten miles off, much haunted by sheep; for we did not wish to let pass the chance of tracking the game offered by the first good snow of the season.

Next morning we started by starlight. The snow lay several inches deep on the ground; the whole land was a dazzling white. It was very cold. Within the ranch everything was frozen solid in spite of the thick log walls; but the air was so still and clear that we did not realize how low the temperature was. Accordingly, as the fresh horse I had to take was young and wild, I did not attempt to wear my fur coat. I soon felt my mistake. The windless cold ate into my marrow; and when, shortly after the cloudless winter sunrise, we reached our hunting-grounds and picketed out the horses, I was already slightly frost-bitten. But the toil of hunting over the snow-covered crags soon made me warm.

All day we walked and climbed through a white wonderland. On every side the snowy hills, piled one on another, stretched away, chain after chain, as far as sight could reach. The stern and iron-bound land had been changed to a frozen sea of billowy, glittering peaks and ridges. At last, late in the afternoon, three great big-horn suddenly sprang up to our right and crossed the table-land in front of and below us at a strong, stretching gallop. The lengthening sunbeams glinted on their mighty horns; their great supple brown bodies were thrown out in bold relief against the white landscape; as they plowed with long strides through the powdery snow, their hoofs tossed it up in masses of white spray. On the left of the plateau was a ridge, and as they went up this I twice fired at the leading ram, my bullets striking under him. On the summit he stopped and stood for a moment looking back, three hundred and fifty yards off, [1] and my third shot went fairly through his lungs. He ran over the hill as if unharmed, but lay down a couple of hundred yards on, and was dead when we reached him.

It was after nightfall when we got back to the horses, and we rode home by moonlight. To gallop in such weather insures freezing; so the ponies shambled along at a single-foot trot, their dark bodies white with hoar-frost, and the long icicles hanging from their lips. The cold had increased steadily; the spirit thermometer at the ranch showed 26° Fahrenheit below zero. We had worked all day without food or rest, and were very tired. On the ride home I got benumbed before I knew it and froze my face, one foot, and both knees. Even my companion, who had a great-coat, froze his nose and cheeks. Never was a sight more welcome than the gleam of the fire-lit ranch windows to us that night. But the great ram's head was a trophy that paid for all.

1888

HENRY JAMES 1843-1916

Henry James, who was born in New York and died in London, was a cosmopolitan almost from childhood. His father was a well-known theological writer. The two sons, Henry, the novelist, and William, the famous psychologist, were fortunate in receiving a broad education through tutors. They shared in the best intellectual life of Boston and New York, and had the further advantage of long periods of residence and study in Europe. In 1860 Henry began to study law at Harvard, but he soon found literature to be his bent. After a few years he lived chiefly abroad, where he made the acquaintance of many celebrities in European literature and found an atmosphere stimulating to his literary work. He settled at length in England

and, sympathizing greatly with the English cause in the World War, became a naturalized British citizen. Shortly before his death, which was hastened by his philanthropic activities, he was given the Order of Merit.

James's books belong to two centuries. In their leisurely atmosphere his novels are reminiscent of the mid-Victorian: in their method, that of strict realism,—full of detail and of the analytical development of complex characters—they are of today. The greatest fault in James's style is involved sentence structure. Nevertheless, his work is full of wit, and of the wisdom of an incisive critic of society at large. His novels are very numerous; among them are The American, 1877, Daisy Miller, 1879, The Portrait of a Lady, 1881, The Wings of a Dove, 1902, The Ambassadors, 1903, The Golden Bowl, 1904. He also wrote stories, short and long, plays, and critical essays. His characters are typically people of his own social group who have the leisure, the intellect, and the disposition to make of living a fine art. The prefaces to his various novels are of value for their discussion of his own work and methods.

Autobiographical: A Small Boy and Others, 1913; Notes of a Son and Brother, 1914; The Middle Years, 1917; Letters of Henry James, 2 vols., 1920.

Biography: P. Edgar, Henry James, 1927; Rebecca West, Henry James, 1916.

Criticism: Introduction to Collected Novels and Tales, 26 vols., 1907-1917; Macy; Van Doren (AN); Phelps (EN); Follett (SMN), also Atlan. 117:801-11; Brownell; Elton; Sherman; Bradford, E. L. Cary, The Novels of Henry James, 1905; F. M. Ford, Henry James: a Critical Study, 1915; J. W. Beach, The Methods of Henry James, 1918; V. W. Brooks, "Henry James: the First Phase," Dial 74: 433-50; R. Herrick, "A Visit to Henry James," Yale R. ns 12:724-41; W. Randell, "The Art of Mr. Henry James," Fortn. 105:620-32; same, Liv. Age 290:281-90; W. de la Mare, "Henry James," Liv. Age 289:122-5; J. Conrad, "Henry James: An Appreciation," No. Am. 203:585-91; W. D. Howells, "Mr. Henry James's Later Work," No. Am. 203:572-84; E. Wyatt, "Henry James: an Impression," No. Am. 203: 592-9; T. Bosanquet, "Henry James," Fortn. 107:995-1009; same, Bookm. 45:571-81; same, Liv. Age 294:346-57.

MISS GUNTON OF POUGHKEEPSIE [2]

"It's astonishing what you take for granted!" Lady Champer had exclaimed to her young friend at an early stage; and this might have served as a sign that even then the little plot had begun to thicken. The reflection was uttered at the time the outlook of the charming American girl in whom she found herself so interested was still much in the rough. They had often met, with pleasure to each, during a winter spent in Rome; and Lily had come to her in London toward the end of May with further news of a situation the dawn of which, in March and April, by the Tiber, the Arno, and the Seine, had considerably engaged her attention. The Prince had followed Miss Gunton to Florence and then with almost equal promptitude to Paris, where it was both clear and comical for Lady Champer that the rigor of his uncertainty as to parental commands and remittances now detained him. This shrewd woman promised herself not a little amusement from her view of the possibilities of the case. Lily was on the whole showing a wonder; therefore the drama would lose nothing from her character, her temper, her tone. She was waiting—this was the truth she had imparted to her clever protectress —to see if her Roman captive would find himself drawn to London. Should he really turn up there she would the next thing start for America, putting him to the test of that wider range and declining to place her confidence till he should have arrived in New York at her heels. If he remained in Paris or returned to Rome she would stay in London and, as she phrased it, have a good time by herself. Did he expect her to go back to Paris for him? Why not in that case just as well go back to Rome at once? The first thing for her, Lily intimated to her London adviser, was to show what, in her position, *she* expected.

Her position meanwhile was one that Lady Champer, try as she would, had as yet succeeded neither in understanding nor in resigning herself not to understand. It was that of being extraordinarily pretty, amazingly free, and perplexingly good, and of presenting these advantages in a positively golden light. How was one to estimate a girl whose nearest approach to a drawback—that is to an incumbrance—appeared to be a grandfather carrying on business in an American city her ladyship had never otherwise heard of, with whom communication was all by cable and on the subject of "drawing"? Expression was on the old man's part moreover as concise as it was expensive, consisting as it inveterately did of but the single word "Draw." Lily drew, on every occasion in life, and it at least could not be said of the pair —when the "family idea," as embodied in America, was exposed to criticism—that they were not in touch. Mr. Gunton had given her further Mrs. Brine, to come out with her, and with this provision and the perpetual pecuniary he plainly figured—to Lily's own mind—as solicitous to the point of anxiety. Mrs. Brine's

scheme of relations seemed in truth to be simpler still. There was a transatlantic "Mr. Brine," of whom she often spoke—and never in any other way; but she wrote for newspapers; she prowled in catacombs, visiting more than once even those of Paris; she haunted hotels; she picked up compatriots; she spoke above all a language that often baffled comprehension. She mattered, however, but little; she was mainly so occupied in having what Lily had likewise independently glanced at—a good time by herself. It was difficult enough indeed to Lady Champer to see the wonderful girl reduced to that, yet she was a little person who kept one somehow in presence of the incalculable. Old measures and familiar rules were of no use at all with her—she had so broken the molds and so mixed the marks. What was commanding was her disparities—the juxtaposition in her of beautiful sunflushed heights and deep dark holes. She had none of the things that the other things implied. She dangled in the air in a manner that made one dizzy; though one took comfort, at the worst, in feeling that one was there to catch her if she fell. Falling, at the same time, appeared scarce one of her properties, and it was positive for Lady Champer at moments that if one held out one's arms one might be, after all, much more likely to be pulled up. That was really a part of the excitement of the acquaintance.

"Well," said this friend and critic on one of the first of the London days, "say he does, on your return to your own country, go after you: how do you read, on that occurrence, the course of events?"

"Why, if he comes after me I'll have him."

"And do you think it so easy to 'have' him?"

Lily appeared, lovely and candid,—and it was an air and a way she often had,—to wonder what she thought. "I don't know that I think it any easier than he seems to think it to have *me*. I know moreover that, though he wants awfully to see the country, he wouldn't just now come to America unless to marry me; and if I take him at all," she pursued, "I want first to be able to show him to the girls."

"Why 'first'?" Lady Champer asked. "Wouldn't it do as well last?"

"Oh, I should want them to see me in Rome, too," said Lily. "But, dear me, I'm afraid I want a good many things! What I most want of course is that he should show me unmistakably what *he* wants. Unless he wants me more than anything else in the world, I don't want him. Besides, I hope he doesn't think I'm going to be married anywhere but in my own place."

"I see," said Lady Champer. "It's for your wedding you want the girls. And it's for the girls you want the Prince."

"Well, we're all bound by that promise. And of course *you'll* come!"

"Ah, my dear child—!" Lady Champer gasped.

"You can come with the old Princess. You'll be just the right company for her."

The elder friend considered afresh, with depth, the younger's beauty and serenity. "You *are*, love, beyond everything!"

The beauty and serenity took on for a moment a graver cast. "Why do you so often say that to me?"

"Because you so often make it the only thing to say. But you'll some day find out why," Lady Champer added with an intention of encouragement.

Lily Gunton, however, was a young person to whom encouragement looked queer; she had grown up without need of it, and it seemed indeed scarce required in her situation. "Do you mean you believe his mother won't come?"

"Over mountains and seas to see you married?—and to be seen also of the girls? If she does, *I* will. But we had perhaps better," Lady Champer wound up, "not count our chickens before they're hatched." To which, with one of the easy returns of gaiety that were irresistible in her, Lily made answer that neither of the ladies in question struck her quite as chickens.

The Prince at all events presented himself in London with a promptitude that contributed to make the warning gratuitous. Nothing could have exceeded, by this time, Lady Champer's appreciation of her young friend, whose merits "town" at the beginning of June [1] threw into renewed relief; but she had the imagination of greatness, and, though she believed she tactfully kept it to herself, she thought what the young man had thus done a great deal for a Roman prince to do. Take him as he was, with the circumstances—and they were certainly peculiar, and he was charming—it was a far cry for him from Piazza Colonna to Clarges Street. If Lady Champer had the imagination of greatness, which the Prince in all sorts of ways gratified, Miss Gunton of Poughkeepsie—it was vain to pretend the contrary—was not great in any particular save one. She was great when she "drew." It was true that at the beginning of June she did draw with unprecedented energy and in a manner that, though Mrs. Brine's remarkable nerve apparently could stand it, fairly

made a **poor baronet's widow**, little as it was her business, hold her breath. It was none of her business at all, yet she talked of it even with the Prince himself—to whom it was indeed a favorite subject and whose greatness, oddly enough, never appeared to shrink in the effect it produced upon him. The line they took together was that of wondering if the scale of Lily's drafts made really most for the presumption that the capital at her disposal was rapidly dwindling, or for that of its being practically infinite. "Many a fellow," the young man smiled, "would marry her to pull her up." He was in any case of the opinion that it was an occasion for deciding—one way or the other—quickly. Well, he did decide—so quickly that, within the week, Lily communicated to her friend that he had offered her his hand, his heart, his fortune, and all his titles, grandeurs, and appurtenances. She had given him his answer, and he was in bliss; though nothing, as yet, was settled but that.

Tall, fair, active, educated, amiable, simple, carrying so naturally his great name and pronouncing so kindly Lily's small one, the happy youth, if he was one of the most ancient of princes, was one of the most modern of Romans. This second character it was his special aim and pride to cultivate. He would have been pained at feeling himself an hour behind his age; and he had a way—both touching and amusing to some observers—of constantly comparing his watch with the dial of the day's news. It was in fact easy to see that in deciding to ally himself with a young alien of vague origin, whose striking beauty was reinforced only by her presumptive money, he had even put forward a little the fine hands of his timepiece. No one else, however,—not even Lady Champer, and least of all Lily herself,—had quite taken the measure, in this connection, of his merit. The quick decision he had spoken of was really a flying leap. He desired incontestably to rescue Miss Gunton's remainder; but to rescue it he had to take it for granted, and taking it for granted was nothing less than—at whatever angle considered—a risk. He never, naturally, used the word to her, but he distinctly faced a peril. The sense of what he had staked on a vague return gave him, at the height of the London season, bad nights, or rather bad mornings—for he danced with his intended, as a usual thing, till dawn—besides obliging him to take, in the form of long, explanatory, argumentative, and persuasive letters to his mother and sisters, his uncles, aunts, cousins, and preferred confidants, large measures of justification at home. The family sense was strong in his huge old house, just as the family array was numerous; he was dutifully conscious of the trust reposed in him, and moved from morning till night, he knew perfectly, as the observed of a phalanx of observers; whereby he the more admired himself for his passion, precipitation, and courage. He had only a probability to go upon, but he was—and by the romantic tradition of his race—so in love that he should surely not be taken in.

His private agitation of course deepened when, to do honor to her engagement and as if she would have been ashamed to do less, Lily "drew" again most gloriously; but he managed to smile beautifully on her asking him if he didn't want her to be splendid, and at his worst hours he went no further than to wish that he might be married on the morrow. Unless it were the next day, or at most the next month, it really at moments seemed best that it should never be at all. On the most favorable view—with the solidity of the residuum [1] fully assumed—there were still minor questions and dangers. A vast America, arching over his nuptials, bristling with expectant bridesmaids and underlaying their feet with expensive flowers, stared him in the face and prompted him to the reflection that if she dipped so deep into the mere remote overflow her dive into the fount itself would verily be a header. If she drew at such a rate in London how wouldn't she draw at Poughkeepsie? he asked himself, and practically asked Lady Champer; yet bore the strain of the question, without an answer, so nobly that when, with small delay, Poughkeepsie seemed simply to heave with reassurances, he regarded the ground as firm and his tact as rewarded. "And now at last, dearest," he said, "since everything's so satisfactory, you *will* write?" He put it appealingly, endearingly, yet as if he could scarce doubt.

"Write, love? Why," she replied, "I've done nothing *but* write! I've written ninety letters."

"But not to mamma," he smiled.

"Mamma?"—she stared. "My dear boy, I've not at this time of day to remind you that I've the misfortune to have no mother. I lost mamma, you know, as you lost your father, in childhood. You may be sure," said Lily Gunton, "that I wouldn't otherwise have waited for you to prompt me."

There came into his face a kind of amiable convulsion. "Of course, darling, I remember—your beautiful mother (she *must* have been beautiful!) whom I should have been so glad to know. I was thinking of *my* mamma—who'll be so delighted to hear from you." The Prince

spoke English in perfection—had lived in it from the cradle and appeared, particularly when alluding to his home and family, to matters familiar and of fact, or to those of dress and sport, of general recreation, to draw such a comfort from it as made the girl think of him as scarce more a foreigner than a pleasant, auburn, slightly awkward, slightly slangy, and extremely well-tailored young Briton would have been. He sounded "mamma" like a rosy English schoolboy; yet just then, for the first time, the things with which he was connected struck her as in a manner strange and far-off. Everything in him, none the less—face and voice and tact, above all his deep desire—labored to bring them near and make them natural. This was intensely the case as he went on: "Such a little letter as you *might* send would really be awfully jolly."

"My dear child," Lily replied on quick reflection, "I'll write to her with joy the minute I hear from her. Won't she write to *me?*"

The Prince just visibly flushed. "In a moment if you'll only—"

"Write to her first?"

"Just to pay her a little—no matter how little—your respects."

His attenuation of the degree showed perhaps a sense of a weakness of position; yet it was no perception of this that made the girl immediately say: "Oh, *caro*, [2] I don't think I can begin. If you feel that *she* won't—as you evidently do—is it because you've asked her and she has refused?" The next moment, "I see you *have!*" she exclaimed. His rejoinder to this was to catch her in his arms, to press his cheek to hers, to murmur a flood of tender words in which contradiction, confession, supplication, and remonstrance were oddly confounded; but after he had sufficiently disengaged her to allow her to speak again, his effusion was checked by what came. "Do you really mean you can't induce her?" It renewed itself on the first return of ease; or it, more correctly perhaps, in order to renew itself, took this return—a trifle too soon for granted. Singular, for the hour, was the quickness with which ease could leave them—so blissfully at one as they were; and, to be brief, it had not come back even when Lily spoke of the matter to Lady Champer. It is true that she waited but little to do so. She then went straight to the point. "What would you do if his mother doesn't write?"

"The old Princess—to *you?*" Her ladyship had not had time to mount guard in advance over the tone of this, which was doubtless (as

---

[1] (of her fortune)

[2] dear

she instantly, for that matter, herself became aware) a little too much that of "Have you really expected she would?" What Lily expected found itself therefore not unassisted to come out—and came out indeed to such a tune that with all kindness, but with a melancholy deeper than any she had ever yet in the general connection used, Lady Champer was moved to remark that the situation might have been found more possible had a little more historic sense been brought to it. "You're the dearest thing in the world, and I can't imagine a girl's carrying herself in any way, in a difficult position, better than you do; only I'm bound to say I think you ought to remember that you're entering a very great house, of tremendous antiquity, fairly groaning under the weight of ancient honors, the heads of which—through the tradition of the great part they've played in the world—are accustomed to a great deal of deference. The old Princess, my dear, you see"—her ladyship gathered confidence a little as she went—"is a most prodigious personage."

"Why, Lady Champer, of course she is, and that's just what I like her for!" said Lily Gunton.

"She has never in her whole life made an advance, any more than any one has ever dreamed of expecting it of her. It's a pity that while you were there you didn't see her, for I think it would have helped you to understand. However, as you did see his sisters, the two Duchesses and dear little Donna Claudia, you know how charming they all *can* be. They only want to be nice, I know, and I dare say that on the smallest opportunity you'll hear from the Duchesses."

The plural had a sound of splendor, but Lily quite kept her head. "What do you call an opportunity? Am I not giving them, by accepting their son and brother, the best—and in fact the only—opportunity they could desire?"

"I like the way, darling," Lady Champer smiled, "you talk about 'accepting'!"

Lily thought of this—she thought of everything. "Well, say it would have been a better one still for them if I had refused him."

Her friend caught her up. "But you haven't."

"Then they must make the most of the occasion as it is." Lily was very sweet, but very lucid. "The Duchesses may write or not, as they like, but I'm afraid the Princess simply *must*." She hesitated, but after a moment went on. "He oughtn't to be willing moreover that I shouldn't expect to be welcomed."

"He isn't!" Lady Champer blurted out.

Lily jumped at it. "Then he has told you? It's her attitude?"

She had spoken without passion, but her friend was scarce the less frightened. "My poor child, what can he do?"

Lily saw perfectly. "He can make her."

Lady Champer turned it over, but her fears were what was clearest. "And if he doesn't?"

"If he 'doesn't'?" The girl ambiguously echoed it. I mean if he can't."

Well, Lily, more cheerfully, declined, for the hour, to consider this. He would certainly do for her what was right; so that after all, though she had herself put the question, she disclaimed the idea that an answer was urgent. There was time, she conveyed—which Lady Champer only desired to believe; a faith moreover somewhat shaken in the latter when the Prince entered her room the next day with the information that there was none—none at least to leave everything in the air. Lady Champer had not yet made up her mind as to which of these young persons she liked most to draw into confidence, nor as to whether she most inclined to take the Roman side with the American or the American side with the Roman. But now in truth she was settled; she gave proof of it in the increased lucidity with which she spoke for Lily.

"Wouldn't the Princess depart—a—from her usual attitude for such a great occasion?"

The difficulty was a little that the young man so well understood his mother. "The devil of it is, you see, that it's for Lily herself, so much more, she thinks the occasion great."

Lady Champer mused. "If you hadn't her consent I could understand it. But from the moment she thinks the girl good enough for you to marry—"

"Ah, she doesn't!" the Prince gloomily interposed. "However," he explained, "she accepts her because there are reasons—my own feeling, now so my very life, don't you see? But it isn't quite open arms. All the same, as I tell Lily, the arms *would* open."

"If she'd make the first step? Hum!" said Lady Champer, not without the note of grimness. "She'll be obstinate."

The young man, with a melancholy eye, quite coincided. "She'll be obstinate."

"So that I strongly recommend you to manage it," his friend went on after a pause. "It strikes me that if the Princess can't do it for Lily she might at least do it for you. Any girl you marry becomes thereby somebody."

"Of course—doesn't she? She certainly ought to do it for *me*. I'm after all the head of the house."

"Well, then, make her!" said Lady Champer a little impatiently.

"I will. Mamma adores me, and I adore *her*."

"And you adore Lily, and Lily adores you—therefore everybody adores everybody, especially as I adore you both. With so much adoration all round, therefore, things ought to march."

"They shall!" the young man declared with spirit. "I adore you, too—you don't mention that; for you help me immensely. But what do you suppose she'll do if she doesn't?"

The agitation already visible in him ministered a little to vagueness; but his friend after an instant disembroiled it. "What do I suppose Lily will do if your mother remains stiff?" Lady Champer faltered, but she let him have it. "She'll break."

His wondering eyes became strange. "Just for that?"

"You may certainly say it isn't much—when people love as you do."

"Ah, I'm afraid then Lily doesn't!"—and he turned away in his trouble.

She watched him while he moved, not speaking for a minute. "My dear young man, are you afraid of your mamma?"

He faced short about again. "I'm afraid of this—that if she does do it she won't forgive her. She *will* do it—yes. But Lily will be for her, in consequence, ever after, the person who has made her submit herself. She'll hate her for that—and then she'll hate me for being concerned in it." The Prince presented it all with clearness—almost with charm. "What do you say to that?"

His friend had to think. "Well, only, I fear, that we belong, Lily and I, to a race unaccustomed to counting with such passions. Let her hate!" she, however, a trifle inconsistently wound up.

"But I love her so!"

"Which?" Lady Champer asked it almost ungraciously; in such a tone at any rate that, seated on the sofa with his elbows on his knees, his much-ringed hands nervously locked together and his eyes of distress wide open, he met her with visible surprise. What she met *him* with is perhaps best noted by the fact that after a minute his hands covered his bent face and she became aware that she had drawn tears. This produced such regret in her that before they parted she did what she could to attenuate and explain—making a great point, at all events, of her rule, with Lily, of putting only his own side of the case. "I insist awfully, you know, on your greatness!"

He jumped up, wincing. "Oh, that's horrid."

"I don't know. Whose fault is it, then, at any rate, if trying to help you may have that side?" This was a question that, with the tangle he had already to unwind, only added a twist; yet she went on as if positively to add another. "Why on earth don't you, all of you, leave them alone?"

"Leave them—?"

"All your Americans."

"Don't you like them then—the women?"

She hesitated. "No. Yes. They're an interest. But they're a nuisance. It's a question, very certainly, if they're worth the trouble they give."

This at least it seemed he could take in. "You mean that one should be quite sure first what they *are* worth?"

He made her laugh now. "It would appear that you never *can* be. But also really that you can't keep your hands off."

He fixed the social scene an instant with his heavy eye. "Yes. Doesn't it?"

"However," she pursued as if he again a little irritated her. "Lily's position is quite simple."

"Quite. She just loves me."

"I mean simple for herself. She really makes no differences. It's only we—you and I—who make them all."

The Prince wondered. "But she tells me she delights in us; has, that is, such a sense of what we are supposed to 'represent.'"

"Oh, she *thinks* she has. Americans think they have all sorts of things; but they haven't. That's just *it*"—Lady Champer was philosophic. "Nothing but their Americanism. If you marry anything, you marry that; and if your mother accepts anything that's what she accepts." Then, though the young man followed the demonstration with an apprehension almost pathetic, she gave him without mercy the whole of it. "Lily's rigidly logical. A girl—as *she* knows girls—is 'welcomed,' on her engagement, before anything else can happen, by the family of her young man; and the motherless girl, alone in the world, more punctually than any other. His mother—if she's a 'lady'—takes it upon herself. Then the girl goes and stays with them. But she does nothing before. *Tirez-vous de là.*" [1]

The young man sought on the spot to obey this last injunction, and his effort presently produced a flash. "Oh, if she'll come and *stay* with us—all would, easily, be well!" The flash went out, however, when Lady Champer returned: "Then let the Princess invite her."

[1] "Make what you can of that."

Lily a fortnight later simply said to her, from one hour to the other, "I'm going home," and took her breath away by sailing on the morrow with the Bransbys. The tense cord had somehow snapped; the proof was in the fact that the Prince, dashing off to his good friend at this crisis an obscure, an ambiguous note, started the same night for Rome. Lady Champer, for the time, sat in darkness, but during the summer many things occurred; and one day in the autumn, quite unheralded and with the signs of some of them in his face, the Prince appeared again before her. He was not long in telling her his story, which was simply that he had come to her, all the way from Rome, for news of Lily and to talk of Lily. She was prepared, as it happened, to meet his impatience; yet her preparation was but little older than his arrival and was deficient moreover in an important particular. She was not prepared to knock him down, and she made him talk to gain time. She had, however, to understand, put a primary question: "She never wrote, then?"

"Mamma? Oh, yes—when she at last got frightened at Miss Gunton's having become so silent. She wrote in August; but Lily's own decisive letter—letter to me, I mean—crossed with it. It was too late—that put an end."

"A *real* end?"

Everything in the young man showed how real. "On the ground of her being willing no longer to keep up, by the stand she had taken, such a relation between mamma and *me*. But her rupture," he wailed, "keeps it up more than anything else."

"And is it very bad?"

"Awful, I assure you. I've become for my mother a person who has made her make, all for nothing, an unprecedented advance, a humble submission; and she's so disgusted, all round, that it's no longer the same old charming thing for us to be together. It makes it worse for her that I'm still madly in love."

"Well," said Lady Champer after a moment, if you're still madly in love I can only be sorry for you."

"You can *do* nothing for me?—don't advise me to go over?"

She had to take a longer pause. "You don't at all know then what has happened?—that old Mr. Gunton has died and left her everything?"

All his vacancy and curiosity came out in a wild echo. "Everything?"

"She writes me that it's a great deal of money."

"You've just heard from her, then?"

"This morning. I seem to make out," said Lady Champer, an extraordinary number of dollars."

"Oh, I was sure it was!" the young man moaned.

"And she's engaged," his friend went on, "to Mr. Bransby."

He bounded, rising before her. "Mr. Bransby?"

"'Adam P.'—the gentleman with whose mother and sisters she went home. *They*, she writes, have beautifully welcomed her."

"*Dio mio!*" [1] The Prince stared; he had flushed with the blow, and the tears had come into his eyes. "And I believed she loved me!"

"*I* didn't!" said Lady Champer with some curtness.

He gazed about; he almost rocked; and unconscious of her words, he appealed, inarticulate and stricken. At last, however, he found his voice. "What on earth then shall I do? I can less than ever go back to mamma!"

She got up for him, and thought for him, pushing a better chair into her circle. "Stay here with me, and I'll ring for tea. Sit there nearer the fire—you're cold."

"Awfully!" he confessed as he sank. "And I believed she loved me," he repeated as he stared at the fire.

"I didn't!" Lady Champer once more declared. This time, visibly, he heard her, and she immediately met his wonder. "No—it was all the rest; your great historic position, the glamour of your name, and your past. Otherwise what she stood out for wouldn't be excusable. But she has the sense of such things, and *they* were what she loved." So, by the fire, his hostess explained it, while he wondered the more.

"I thought that last summer you told me just the contrary."

It seemed, to do her justice, to strike her. "Did I? Oh, well, how does one know? With Americans one is lost!"

1900

EDITH WHARTON 1862-

Mrs. Wharton is probably the most distinguished among American women novelists. Much in her life and work reminds one of Henry James. In her youth she received every advantage in the way of social surroundings and educational advantages both in this country and Europe; and the atmosphere of most of her novels resembles that of James's, for in all of her books except one, her characters are persons of leisure and refinement

[1] Good Heavens!

whose lives are spent chiefly in society distinguished for its good breeding. In her most distinguished story, *Ethan Frome,* 1911, she departed from this stratum of society. In it a farmer, his "help," and his wife work out the tragedy of their lives with a relentlessness not equaled by Miss Jewett or Miss Wilkins. Her interest, like that of James's, lies in the analysis of motives. Outstanding among her works, besides *Ethan Frome,* are *The Valley of Decision,* 1902; *The House of Mirth,* 1907; *The Age of Innocence,* 1920, both of the latter two laid in New York; and *The Glimpses of the Moon,* 1922.

Biography and criticism: R. M. Lovett, *Edith Wharton,* 1925; Phelps (EN); Van Doren (CAN); Cooper; Boynton; Follett (SMN); E. Bjorkman, in *Voices of Tomorrow,* 1913; H. D. Sedgwick, in *The New American Type,* 1908; Underwood; C. K. Trueblood, "Edith Wharton," *Dial* 68:80-91; H. D. Sedgwick, "The Novels of Mrs. Wharton," *Atlan.* 98:217-28; F. Hackett, "Mrs. Wharton's Art," *New Repub.* 10:50-2; R. Herrick, "Mrs. Wharton's World," *New Repub.* 2:40-2; *Liv. Age* 284:604-16; "Edith Wharton: Two Conflicting Estimates of her Art," *Cur. Opinion* 58:272.

THE VERDICT [1]

I had always thought Jack Gisburn rather a cheap genius—though a good fellow enough— so it was no great surprise to me to hear that, in the height of his glory, he had dropped his painting, married a rich widow, and established himself in a villa on the Riviera. (Though I rather thought it would have been Rome or Florence.)

"The height of his glory"—that was what the women called it. I can hear Mrs. Gideon Thwing—his last Chicago sitter—deploring his unaccountable abdication. "Of course it's going to send the value of my picture 'way up; but I don't think of that, Mr. Rickham—the loss to Arrt is all I think of." The word, on Mrs. Thwing's lips, multiplied its *r*'s as though they were reflected in an endless vista of mirrors. And it was not only the Mrs. Thwings who mourned. Had not the exquisite Hermia Croft, at the last Grafton Gallery show, stopped me before Gisburn's "Moon-dancers" to say, with tears in her eyes: "We shall not look upon its like again"?

Well!—even through the prism of Hermia's tears I felt able to face the fact with equanimity. Poor Jack Gisburn! The women had made him—it was fitting that they should mourn him. Among his own sex fewer regrets were heard, and in his own trade hardly a murmur. Professional jealousy? Perhaps. If it

were, the honor of the craft was vindicated by little Claude Nutley, who, in all good faith, brought out in the *Burlington* [2] a very handsome "obituary" on Jack—one of those showy articles stocked with random technicalities that I have heard (I won't say by whom) compared to Gisburn's painting. And so—his resolve being apparently irrevocable—the discussion gradually died out, and, as Mrs. Thwing had predicted, the price of "Gisburns" went up.

It was not till three years later that, in the course of a few weeks' idling on the Riviera, it suddenly occurred to me to wonder why Gisburn had given up his painting. On reflection, it really was a tempting problem. To accuse his wife would have been too easy—his fair sitters had been denied the solace of saying that Mrs. Gisburn had "dragged him down." For Mrs. Gisburn—as such—had not existed till nearly a year after Jack's resolve had been taken. It might be that he had married her— since he liked his ease—because he didn't want to go on painting; but it would have been hard to prove that he had given up his painting because he had married her.

Of course, if she had not dragged him down, she had equally, as Miss Croft contended, failed to "lift him up"—she had not led him back to the easel. To put the brush into his hand again—what a vocation for a wife! But Mrs. Gisburn appeared to have disdained it—and I felt it might be interesting to find out why.

The desultory life of the Riviera lends itself to such purely academic speculations; and having, on my way to Monte Carlo, caught a glimpse of Jack's balustraded terraces between the pines, I had myself borne thither the next day.

I found the couple at tea beneath their palm-trees; and Mrs. Gisburn's welcome was so genial that, in the ensuing weeks, I claimed it frequently. It was not that my hostess was "interesting": on that point I could have given Miss Croft the fullest reassurance. It was just because she was *not* interesting—if I may be pardoned the bull—that I found her so. For Jack, all his life, had been surrounded by interesting women; they had fostered his art, it had been reared in the hothouse of their adulation. And it was therefore instructive to note what effect the "deadening atmosphere of mediocrity" (I quote Miss Croft) was having on him.

I have mentioned that Mrs. Gisburn was rich; and it was immediately perceptible that her husband was extracting from this circumstance a delicate but substantial satisfaction.

[2] a magazine devoted to art

It is, as a rule, the people who scorn money who get most out of it; and Jack's elegant disdain of his wife's big balance enabled him, with an appearance of perfect good-breeding, to transmute it into objects of art and luxury. To the latter, I must add, he remained relatively indifferent; but he was buying Renaissance [1] bronzes and eighteenth-century pictures with a discrimination that bespoke the amplest resources.

"Money's only excuse is to put beauty into circulation," was one of the axioms he laid down across the Sèvres [2] and silver of an exquisitely appointed luncheon-table, when, on a later day, I had again run over from Monte Carlo; and Mrs. Gisburn, beaming on him, added for my enlightenment: "Jack is so morbidly sensitive to every form of beauty."

Poor Jack! It had always been his fate to have women say such things of him: the fact should be set down in extenuation. What struck me now was that, for the first time, I resented the tone. I had seen him, so often, basking under similar tributes—was it the conjugal note that robbed them of their savor? No —for, oddly enough, it became apparent that he was fond of Mrs. Gisburn—fond enough not to see her absurdity. It was his own absurdity he seemed to be wincing under—his own attitude as an object for garlands and incense.

"My dear, since I've chucked painting people don't say that stuff about me—they say it about Victor Grindle," was his only protest, as he rose from the table and strolled out onto the sunlit terrace.

I glanced after him, struck by his last word. Victor Grindle was, in fact, becoming the man of the moment—as Jack himself, one might put it, had been the man of the hour. The younger artist was said to have formed himself at my friend's feet, and I wondered if a tinge of jealousy underlay the latter's mysterious abdication. But no—for it was not till after that event that the fashionable drawing-rooms had begun to display their "Grindles."

I turned to Mrs. Gisburn, who had lingered to give a lump of sugar to her spaniel in the dining-room.

"Why *has* he chucked painting?" I asked abruptly.

She raised her eyebrows with a hint of good-humored surprise.

"Oh, he doesn't *have* to now, you know; and I want him to enjoy himself," she said quite simply.

I looked about the spacious white-paneled room, with its *famille-verte*[3] vases, repeating the tones of the pale damask curtains, and its eighteenth-century pastels in delicate faded frames.

"Has he chucked his pictures, too? I haven't seen a single one in the house."

A slight look of constraint crossed Mrs. Gisburn's open countenance. "It's his ridiculous modesty, you know. He says they're not fit to have about; he's sent them all away except one—my portrait—and that I have to keep upstairs."

His ridiculous modesty—Jack's modesty about his pictures? My curiosity was growing like the bean-stalk. I said persuasively to my hostess: "I must really see your portrait, you know."

She glanced out almost timorously at the terrace where her husband, lounging in a hooded chair, had lit a cigar and drawn the Russian deer-hound's head between his knees.

"Well, come while he's not looking," she said, with a laugh that tried to hide her nervousness; and I followed her between the marble Emperors of the hall, and up the wide stairs with terra-cotta nymphs poised among flowers at each landing.

In the dimmest corner of her boudoir, amid a profusion of delicate and distinguished objects, hung one of the familiar oval canvases, in the inevitable garlanded frame. The mere outline of the frame called up all Gisburn's past!

Mrs. Gisburn drew back the window-curtains, moved aside a *jardiniere* full of pink azaleas, pushed an armchair away, and said: "If you stand here you can just manage to see it. I had it over the mantelpiece, but he wouldn't let it stay."

Yes—I could just manage to see it—the first portrait of Jack's I had ever had to strain my eyes over! Usually they had the place of honor—say the central panel in a pale yellow or *rose Dubarry*[4] drawing-room, or a monumental easel placed so that it took the light through curtains of old Venetian point. The more modest place became the picture better; yet, as my eyes grew accustomed to the half-light, all the characteristic qualities came out— all the hesitations disguised as audacities, the trick of prestidigitation by which, with such consummate skill, he managed to divert at-

[1] The Renaissance period produced ornate works of art.
[2] porcelain made at Sèvres near Paris
[3] the name given to a type of the 18th century Chinese porcelain in which a vivid green glaze predominates
[4] a delicate pink-crimson color named in honor of Madame du Barry of the court of Louis XV

tention from the real business of the picture to some pretty irrelevance of detail. Mrs. Gisburn, presenting a neutral surface to work on—forming, as it were, so inevitably the background to her own picture—had lent herself in an unusual degree to the display of this false virtuosity.[1] The picture was one of Jack's "strongest," as his admirers would have put it —it represented, on his part, a swelling of muscles, a congesting of veins, a balancing, straddling and straining, that reminded one of the circus-clown's ironic efforts to lift a feather. It met, in short, at every point the demand of lovely woman to be painted "strongly" because she was tired of being painted "sweetly"—and yet not to lose an atom of the sweetness.

"It's the last he painted, you know," Mrs. Gisburn said with pardonable pride. "The last but one," she corrected herself—"but the other doesn't count, because he destroyed it."

"Destroyed it?" I was about to follow up this clue when I heard a footstep and saw Jack himself on the threshold.

As he stood there, his hands in the pockets of his velveteen coat, the thin brown waves of hair pushed back from his white forehead, his lean sunburnt cheeks furrowed by a smile that lifted the tips of a self-confident moustache, I felt to what a degree he had the same quality as his pictures—the quality of looking cleverer than he was.

His wife glanced at him deprecatingly, but his eyes traveled past her to the portrait.

"Mr. Rickham wanted to see it," she began as if excusing herself. He shrugged his shoulders, still smiling.

"Oh, Rickham found me out long ago," he said lightly; then passing his arm through mine: "Come and see the rest of the house."

He showed it to me with a kind of naïve suburban pride: the bathrooms, the speaking-tubes, the dress-closets, the trouser-presses—all the complex simplifications of the millionaire's domestic economy. And whenever my wonder paid the expected tribute he said, throwing out his chest a little: "Yes, I really don't see how people manage to live without that."

Well—it was just the end one might have foreseen for him. Only he was, through it all and in spite of it all—as he had been through, and in spite of, his pictures—so handsome, so charming, so disarming, that one longed to cry out: "Be dissatisfied with your leisure!" as once one had longed to say: "Be dissatisfied with your work!"

[1] skill of a master in any art

But, with the cry on my lips, my diagnosis suffered an unexpected check.

"This is my own lair," he said, leading me into a dark plain room at the end of a florid vista. It was square and brown and leathery: no "effects," no bric-a-brac, none of the air of posing for reproduction in a picture weekly—above all, no least sign of ever having been used as a studio.

The fact brought home to me the absolute finality of Jack's break with his old life.

"Don't you ever dabble with paint any more?" I asked, still looking about for a trace of such activity.

"Never," he said briefly.

"Or water-color—or etching?"

His confident eyes grew vague, and his cheeks changed color a little under their handsome sunburn.

"Never think of it, my dear fellow—any more than if I'd never touched a brush."

And his tone told me in a flash that he never thought of anything else.

I moved away, instinctively embarrassed by my unexpected discovery; and as I turned, my eye fell on a small picture above the mantelpiece—the only object breaking the plain oak paneling of the room.

"Oh, by Jove!" I said.

It was a sketch of a donkey—an old tired donkey standing in the rain under a wall.

"By Jove—a Stroud!" I cried.

He was silent; but I felt him close behind me, breathing a little quickly.

"What a wonder! Made with a dozen lines —but on everlasting foundations. You lucky chap, where did you get it?"

He answered slowly: "Mrs. Stroud gave it to me."

"Ah—I didn't know you even knew the Strouds. He was such a hermit."

"I didn't—till after . . . She sent for me to paint him when he was dead."

"When he was dead? You?"

I must have let a little too much amazement escape through my surprise, for he answered with a deprecating laugh: "Yes—she's an awful simpleton, you know, Mrs. Stroud. Her only idea was to have him done by a fashionable painter—ah, poor Stroud! She thought it the surest way of proclaiming his greatness— of forcing it on a purblind public. And at the moment I was *the* fashionable painter.

"Ah, poor Stroud—as you say. Was *that* his history?"

"That was his history. She believed in him, gloried in him—or thought she did. But she couldn't bear not to have all the drawing-rooms with her. She couldn't bear the fact that, on varnishing [1] days, one could always get near enough to see his pictures. Poor woman! she's just a fragment groping for other fragments. Stroud is the only whole I ever knew."

"You ever knew? But you just said—"

Gisburn had a curious smile in his eyes.

"Oh, I knew him, and he knew me—only it happened after he was dead."

I dropped my voice instinctively. "When she sent for you?"

"Yes—quite insensible to the irony. She wanted him vindicated—and by me!"

He laughed again, and threw back his head to look up at the sketch of the donkey. "There were days when I couldn't look at that thing—couldn't face it. But I forced myself to put it here; and now it's cured me—cured me. That's the reason why I don't dabble any more, my dear Rickham; or rather Stroud himself is the reason."

For the first time my idle curiosity about my companion turned into a serious desire to understand him better.

"I wish you'd tell me how it happened," I said.

He stood looking up at the sketch, and twirling between his fingers a cigarette he had forgotten to light. Suddenly he turned toward me.

"I'd rather like to tell you—because I've always suspected you of loathing my work."

I made a deprecating gesture, which he negatived with a good-humored shrug.

"Oh, I didn't care a straw when I believed in myself—and now it's an added tie between us!"

He laughed slightly, without bitterness, and pushed one of the deep arm-chairs forward. "There: make yourself comfortable—and here are the cigars you like."

He placed them at my elbow and continued to wander up and down the room, stopping now and then beneath the picture.

"How it happened? I can tell you in five minutes—and it didn't take much longer to happen. . . . I can remember now how surprised and pleased I was when I got Mrs. Stroud's note. Of course, deep down, I had always *felt* there was no one like him—only I had gone with the stream, echoed the usual platitudes about him, till I half got to think he was a failure, one of the kind that are left

behind. By Jove, and he *was* left behind—because he had come to stay! The rest of us had to let ourselves be swept along or go under, but he was high above the current—on everlasting foundations, as you say.

"Well, I went off to the house in my most egregious mood—rather moved, Lord forgive me, at the pathos of poor Stroud's career of failure being crowned by the glory of my painting him! Of course I meant to do the picture for nothing—I told Mrs. Stroud so when she began to stammer something about her poverty. I remember getting off a prodigious phrase about the honor being *mine*—oh, I was princely, my dear Rickham! I was posing to myself like one of my own sitters.

"Then I was taken up and left alone with him. I had sent all my traps in advance, and I had only to set up the easel and get to work. He had been dead but twenty-four hours, and he died suddenly, of heart disease, so there had been no preliminary work of destruction—his face was clear and untouched. I had met him once or twice, years before, and thought him insignificant and dingy. Now I saw that he was superb.

"I was glad at first, with a merely aesthetic satisfaction: glad to have my hand on such a 'subject.' Then his strange life-likeness began to affect me queerly—as I blocked the head in I felt as if he were watching me do it. The sensation was followed by the thought: if he *were* watching me, what would he say to my way of working? My strokes began to go a little wild—I felt nervous and uncertain.

"Once, when I looked up, I seemed to see a smile behind his close grayish beard—as if he had the secret, and were amusing himself by holding it back from me. That exasperated me still more. The secret? Why, I had a secret worth twenty of his! I dashed at the canvas furiously, and tried some of my bravura [2] tricks! But they failed me, they crumbled. I saw he wasn't watching the showy bits—I couldn't distract his attention; he just kept his eyes on the hard passages between. Those were the ones I had always shirked, or covered up with some lying paint. And how he saw through my lies!

"I looked up again, and caught sight of that sketch of the donkey hanging on the wall near his bed. His wife told me afterward it was the last thing he had done—just a note taken with a shaking hand, when he was down in Devonshire recovering from a previous heart attack. Just a note! But it tells his whole

[1] the day previous to the opening of an exhibition of paintings when the artists varnish or retouch their pictures, and critics are admitted

[2] showy

history. There are years of patient scornful persistence in every line. A man who had swum with the current could never have learned that mighty up-stream stroke. . . .

"I turned back to my work, and went on groping and muddling; then I looked at the donkey again. I saw that when Stroud laid in the first stroke he knew just what the end would be. He had possessed his subject, absorbed it, recreated it. When had I done that with any of my things? They hadn't been born of me—I had just adopted them. . . .

"Hang it, Rickham, with that face watching me I couldn't do another stroke. The plain truth was, I didn't know where to put it—*I had never known*. Only, with my sitters and my public, a showy splash of color covered up the fact—I just threw the paint into their eyes. . . . Well, paint was one medium those dead eyes could see through—see straight to the tottering foundations underneath. Don't you know how, in talking a foreign language, even fluently, one says half the time, not what one wants to, but what one can? Well—that was the way I painted; and as he lay there and watched me the thing they called my 'technique' collapsed like a house of cards. He didn't sneer, you understand, poor Stroud—he just lay there quietly watching, and on his lips, through the gray beard, I seemed to hear the question: 'Are you sure you know where you're coming out?'

"If I could have painted that face, with that question on it, I should have done a great thing. The next greatest thing was to see that I couldn't—and that grace was given me. But, oh, at that minute, Rickham, was there anything on earth I wouldn't have given to have Stroud alive before me, and to hear him say: 'It's not too late—I'll show you how'?

"It *was* too late—it would have been, even if he'd been alive. I packed up my traps and went down and told Mrs. Stroud. Of course I didn't tell her *that*—it would have been Greek to her. I simply said I couldn't paint him, that I was too moved. She rather liked the idea—she's so romantic! It was that that made her give me the donkey. But she was terribly upset at not getting the portrait— she did so want him 'done' by some one showy! At first I was afraid she wouldn't let me off— and at my wits' end I suggested Grindle. Yes, it was I who started Grindle: I told Mrs. Stroud he was the 'coming' man, and she told somebody else, and so it got to be true. . . . And he painted Stroud without wincing; and she hung the picture among her husband's things. . . ."

He flung himself down in the arm-chair near mine, laid back his head, and clasping his arms beneath it, looked up at the picture above the chimney-piece.

"I like to fancy that Stroud himself would have given it to me, if he'd been able to say what he thought that day."

And, in answer to a question I put half-mechanically—"Begin again?" he flashed out. "When the one thing that brings me anywhere near him is that I knew enough to leave off?"

He stood up and laid his hand on my shoulder with a laugh. "Only the irony of it is that I *am* still painting—since Grindle's doing it for me! The Strouds stand alone, and happen once—but there's no exterminating our kind of art."

1908

MARY E. WILKINS FREEMAN
1862-

New England of the countryside in the sixth and seventh generations from the original planting, a region of small farms of decreasing fertility, and of gossiping villages; New England in decline, with its decaying families, unceasing toil, fixed habits, and all but conventionalized morality—this is the field of Mrs. Freeman. Family tradition and youthful experience bore their part in fitting Mrs. Freeman for her work, for, like Hawthorne, she had as one of her ancestors a member of the Salem witchcraft court and her youth was spent in Massachusetts and Vermont. She was educated at Mt. Holyoke Seminary. She became secretary to William Dean Howells, and early in her twenties was a contributor to *St. Nicholas* and *The Youth's Companion.* *A Humble Romance and Other Stories,* 1887, brought her prominently into notice, and *A New England Nun,* 1891, still further raised her reputation.

Although the sentiment of Mrs. Freeman's stories is sometimes romantic, her method is that of realism. Her characters are generally humble people bent with labor and sometimes distorted in spirit by the weight of a hidden burden often stubbornly self-imposed. They represent the stagnant waters of the vital tide of Puritanism that swept on into deeper channels.

Criticism: C. M. Thompson, "Miss Wilkins: an Idealist in Masquerade," *Atlan.* 83:665-75; M. Moss, "Some Representative American Storytellers: Mary E. Wilkins," *Bookm.* 24:20-9, both very helpful articles.

IN BUTTERFLY TIME [1]

"Seems to me the butterflies is dretful thick this season, Becca."

[1] Copyright. By permission of Messrs. Harper and Brothers, publishers.

"Yes, they do seem to be consider'ble thick, mother."

"I never see 'em so thick. Thar's hull swarms on 'em; lots of them common yaller ones, an' leetle rusty red ones; an' thar's some of them big spotted ones, ain't thar? Near's I kin see through my specs, thar's one now a-settin' on that head of clover."

"Yes, there is one, mother."

"Thar's lots of grasshoppers too. The grasshoppers air a-risin' up around my feet, an' the butterflies air flyin' up in my face out of the flowers. Law, hev we got to the bars a'ready? I hadn't no idee on 't. Bee keerful about lettin' on 'em down, Becca."

The younger of the two old women let down the bars which separated the blooming field which they had been traversing from the road, and they passed through.

"S'pose you'd better put 'em up agin, Becca, though thar ain't any need on 't, as I see. Thar ain't nothin' in the field to git out but the butterflies an' the grasshoppers, an' they'll git out if they want to, whether or no. Let me take holt."

"There ain't any need of it, mother."

"Yes, I will, too, Becca Wheat. I'm jest as strong in my arms as ever I was. You ain't no call to think I ain't."

"I don't think so, mother; I know you're real strong."

"I allers was pretty strong to lift—stronger'n you."

The bars up, the two women kept on down the road. It was bordered by stone walls and flowering bushes. Ahead, just as far as they could see, was one white house. They were going there to a woman's prayer-meeting.

The older of the two kept a little ahead of the younger, trotting weakly through the short, dusty grass. Her small, old head in a black straw bonnet bobbed in time to every step; her sharp, yellow little face peeped out of the bonnet, alert and half aggressive. She wore a short black shawl tightly drawn over her narrow, wiry back, and held her hands folded primly in front over the two ends.

The other woman, her daughter, pacing dreamily behind, was taller and slenderer. Her face was pale and full, but slightly wrinkled, with a sweet, wide mouth. The pleasant expression about it was so decided that it was almost a smile. Her dress was slightly younger, a hat instead of a bonnet, and no shawl over her black calico afternoon dress.

As they drew nearer to the house the old woman peered anxiously ahead through her spectacles.

"See any one thar, Becca?"

"I should think two women jest went in. I couldn't tell who they was."

"You'd orter wear your spectacles, Becca; your eyesight ain't so good as mine was at your age. She's got her front room open for the meetin'. I kin see the curtains flappin'."

Quite a strong soft wind was blowing. As they went up the front walk between the phlox bushes with their purplish-pink heads, the green curtains with a flowery border swung out of the windows of Mrs. Thomas's best room, the one on the right of the front door.

The door stood open, and a mildly curious face or two showed through the windows.

"Thar's old Mis' Wheat an' Becca," said some one in a whisper to Mrs. Thomas, and she came to the door.

There was a solemn composure on her large, comfortable face. "Good afternoon, Mis' Wheat," said she; "good afternoon, Becca. Walk in."

They walked in with staid demeanour, and took their seats. The chairs were set close to the walls around the room. There were nine or ten women there with good, grave faces. One old woman sat close to the mantel-shelf, and Mrs. Wheat took a vacant chair beside her.

"How d'ye do, Mis' Dill?" whispered she, reaching out her little skinny hand.

The other shook it stiffly. She was as small as Mrs. Wheat, but her little face was round, and her chin had a square decision in its cut, instead of a sharp one. She had a clean, nicely-folded white handkerchief in her lap, and she wiped her spectacles carefully with it and looked through them at Mrs. Wheat before replying.

"I'm enjoyin' pretty good health jest now, thankee, Mis' Wheat," whispered she.

Mrs. Wheat's eyes snapped. "You do seem to be lookin' pretty middlin' for one of your age," said she.

Mrs. Dill gave a stony look at her.

The meeting began then. The good woman read in the Bible and prayed, one after another, the others silent on their knees beside her. Their husbands and sons in the hay-fields, the children in the district school, the too light-minded though innocent village girls, the minister wrestling with his dull sermon faithfully in his shabby study, the whole world, were remembered in their homely petitions. The south wind sang in at the windows; a pine-tree around the corner of the house soughed; the locusts cried shrilly over in the blossoming fields; and their timid prayers went up.

Old Mrs. Wheat, in her corner, on her knees, listened with an outward show of reverence, but she was inwardly torn with jealousy. She was the last one called upon to take part; even old Mrs. Dill was preferred before her. But she had her revenge; when she did get her chance to speak, long and weary was the time she kept her devout sisters on their aching knees.

She had been storing up a good deal to say while the others were praying, and now she said it. For church and town and commonwealth, for missions at home and abroad, her shrill cry went up. Lastly she prayed, with emphatic quavers, for old Mrs. Dill. "O Lord," pleaded she, "remember, we pray thee, this aged handmaiden at my side. May she long enjoy what blessin's are left to her in her age and decrepitood. Sanctify her trials unto her, an' enable her to look away from the feebleness an' want of strength which is now her lot on this airth, to that better country where the wicked cease from troubling and the weary air at rest."

When the prayer was ended, Mrs. Dill rose softly from her knees and sat down. Her face was absolutely immovable as she met Mrs. Wheat's glance when the meeting dispersed.

The two old ladies were left alone in the best room for a little while. Mrs. Thomas, who was Mrs. Dill's daughter, wanted to see Becca about something, so she called her out into the sitting-room.

"You an' Mis' Wheat can visit a little while, while Becca an' I are out here," said she.

Mrs. Dill looked at her daughter when she said this, as if inclined to decline the proposal. Then an expression of stubborn fortitude came over her face, and she settled herself solidly in her chair.

The two looked primly at each other when they were left alone.

"How is Mis' Thomas?" said Mrs. Wheat; "and how is Adoniram?"

"They air both well, thank ye."

"I s'pose Adoniram is to work?"

"Hayin'."

"I thought I ketched a glimpse of him in the field over thar when I come in. Adoniram grows old, don't he?"

"I don't know."

"I sot lookin' at him in meetin' last Sabbath, an' thinkin' how dretfully he was altered. I hope he'll be spared to you as long as you live, Mis' Dill. It' consider'ble better on your account that he hain't never got married, ain't it?"

Mrs. Dill reddened, and stiffened her chin a little. "Thar's a good many folks don't git married, Mis' Wheat, men an' women too, sometimes."

"Becca could 'a got married dozens of times, if she'd wanted to, Mis' Dill."

"I s'pose so."

"See here, Mis' Dill, s'pose we come to the p'int. You're allers kinder flingin' at me, an' I know well enough what it means. You've allers blamed me 'cause you thought I come betwixt my Becca an' your Adoniram, an' I didn't as I knows on."

"Oh, no; course you didn't."

"I s'pose you don't believe it, Mis' Dill?"

"No; I ain't forgot how Adoniram come home from your house, jest about this time o' year, a matter o' forty year ago."

"I don't know what you mean."

Mrs. Dill sat up straight in her chair, and talked with slow emphasis. Her eyes never winked.

"Jest about this time in the afternoon, an' this time o' year, 'bout forty year ago, Adoniram come home from your house. They'd got the hay in the day before, so he had a leetle restin' spell, an' he went right over thar. I knowed where he'd gone well enough, though he made up an arrant after a rake to Deacon White's. I knowed he'd stop to Becca's before he got home. She'd been off visitin', an' he hadn't seen her for a week. She'd jest got home that mornin'. Well, Adoniram went, an' he come home. I was a-goin' through the front entry when he come in through the settin'-room. He was jest as pale as death. I asked him what the matter was, an' he wouldn't say nothin'. The door stood open in here, an' he come in an' dropped into a cheer by the table, an' put his head down on it. I coaxed an' coaxed, an' finally I got it out of him. He'd been over to Becca's, an' you'd treated him so he couldn't ever go agin. He said you didn't like him, an' that was the end on't. Becca couldn't go agin her mother's wishes, an' he wasn't ever goin' to ask her to. Adoniram had jest joined the church that spring, an' he'd jest as soon cut his hand off as to lead Becca to disobey her parents. He's allers had a strong feelin' that marriages made that way wa'n't blessed. I've heerd him say so a good many times. So—"

"I'd like to know what I ever did to mistreat Adoniram, Mis' Dill."

"He never told me the hull perticklars. Thar was somethin' 'bout a butterfly."

"Lor', I remember. 'Twa'n't nothin'—

nothin' at all. **Young** folks air so silly! I remember jest as well as ef 'twas yisterday. Adoniram an' Becca was out in the yard in front of the house. Becca had it all laid out in flowerbeds jest as it is now, an' thar was swarms of butterflies round 'em. They was out thar in the yard, an' I was in the settin'-room winder. They was kinder foolin', an' all of a sudden Adoniram he begun chasin' a butterfly. It was one of them great blue-spotted ones. He caught it mighty spry, an' was a givin' it to Becca, when I said somethin' out o' the winder. I don't jest know what it was. I thought 'twas dretful silly for him to waste his time ketchin' butterflies, an' Becca had some sewin' I wanted her to do. I s'pose 'twas somethin' 'bout that."

"You didn't think Adoniram was good enough for Becca; that was the hull on't."

"That wa'n't it, Mis' Dill. I don't see how you come to think such a thing."

"You'd jest set your heart on havin' her git that rich Arms feller; you know you had. But she didn't; she didn't git anybody."

Mrs. Dill's thin voice quavered and shook, and her little bony form trembled all over, but the spirit within her manifested itself bravely through shakes and quavers.

"You air misjudgin' of me, Mis' Dill, an' you ain't showin' a Christian spirit. You'll be sorry for it when you come to think it over. You'll see 'twas all jest the way I said 'twas, an' I didn't mean nothin'. Let alone anything else, it's awful cruel to ketch butterflies; you know that, Mis' Dill."

"You've done a crueller thing than ketchin' butterflies, Martha Wheat."

"Well, Mis' Dill, we'd better not talk 'bout this any longer. 'Tain't jest becomin' after the meetin' we've jest had to git to disputin'. Thar's Becca."

Going home along the green-bordered road and across the flowery field, Rebecca Wheat noticed that something seemed to have disturbed her mother. The nervous old woman fretted and fidgeted. In the middle of the field she stopped short, and almost danced up and down with feeble, childish wrath.

"Why, what is the matter, mother?"

"Them pesky butterflies!" ejaculated her mother, waving her trembling hands. "I'd like to poison their honey for 'em."

"Let me go on ahead, mother; then they won't bother you so much. I kin kinder brush them away."

"Well, you may, ef you're a mind ter. Say, Becca—speakin' of butterflies brings it to mind. You never thought I was ter blame 'bout separatin' you an' Adoniram Dill, did you?"

The old daughter looked pleasantly into her old mother's face. "I didn't blame anybody, mother. I didn't think you used to like Adoniram very well; but it's all over now."

"You didn't take it to heart much, did you, Becca?"

"Not enough to hurt me any, I guess. Do you mind the butterflies so much with me ahead?"

"No, I guess I don't. I've kinder been thinkin' on't over lately, an' ef I was kinder sharp 'bout that butterfly business, an' hinderin' you an' Adoniram's makin' a match on't, I ain't above sayin' I might hev been a leetle more keerful. Adoniram's turned out pretty well. Mis' Higgins told me yesterday that he'd jest bought that ten-acre lot of Deacon White's. I guess he must hev been layin' up money. Well, Becca, I dessay you air better off than you would be ef you'd been married. It's pretty resky."

Rebecca, plodding before her mother, looked ahead at the familiar landscape, with that expression of strong, pleasant patience which the years seemed to have brought out in relief on her face, like the chasing on silver. It made her more attractive than she had been in her youth, for she had never been pretty.

She and her mother reached the comfortable house, with three great elms in front of it, where they lived, two hours before sunset.

About an hour later Adoniram Dill also went home from his labor across the fields. He was a tall, muscular old man, with a strong-featured, beardless face. He was so straight and agile that he looked, the width of a field away, like a young man. When he came nearer, one saw his iron-gray hair, the deep seams, and the old brown tint of his face, with a start of surprise.

Supper was not quite ready, so after he had washed his face and hands at the kitchen sink he went into the sitting-room, and sat down in a calico-covered rocking-chair with a newspaper. His mother looked in presently, and saw him there.

She stood in the entry-door and beckoned him solemnly. "Come into the parlor a minute," she whispered; "I've got somethin' I want to tell you, an' the children will be racin' in here."

Adoniram rose and followed her in obediently.

She shut the parlor door and looked round at him. "Adoniram, what do you think? Mis' Wheat was over to the meetin' this afternoon, an' she an' me hed a little talk arter the others was gone, an' she brought up that old affair of you an' Becca agin."

"There ain't any use bringin' it up, mother."

"She says she didn't mean a thing when she talked to you so about that butterfly business. She jest thought you hadn't orter be wastin' your time doin' sech cruel things as ketchin' butterflies, an' she wanted Becca to come in an' do some sewin'. That's what she said. I let her know I didn't believe a word on't. I told her right to her face that she thought you wa'n't good enough for Becca, an' she wanted her to hev that rich Arms feller."

"Seems to me I'd have let it all gone, mother."

"I war'n't goin' to let it all go, Adoniram. I'm slow-spoken, an' I don't often speak, but once in a while I've got to. She's the most aggervatin'—I don't know what you would hev done with her ef you hed married Becca. You'd hed to hev her arter Mr. Wheat died. She 'ain't never liked me. She tried to be dretful nice to me to-day, 'cause she'd got an axe to grind; but she'd got so much spite in her she couldn't help it showin' out a leetle. Why she kerried it into the prayer-meetin', she did, Adoniram. She *prayed* for me, 'cause I was so old an' broken down, an' she's three years older'n me. I think it's awful to show out that way in a prayer-meetin'."

"P'rhaps she didn't mean anything."

"Yes, she did. I knew just what she meant by the hull on't, Adoniram Dill. She's got kinder sick livin' thar alone with Becca, without any man to split up kindlin'-wood an' bring in water, an' she's tryin' to git you back agin. She jest the same as said she hedn't no objections to it. I guess she thinks you've been doin' pretty well, too. She thinks it would be a mighty nice thing now to hev you step in thar with your money an' wait on 'em. I see through her."

"P'rhaps it ain't so, mother."

"Yes, 'tis. Adoniram Dill, you don't mean to say you'd hev any idee of marryin' Becca Wheat, arter you've been treated as you hev?"

"You 'ain't heard me say any such thing, mother."

"I thought you looked kinder queer. You wouldn't, would you, Adoniram?"

"Not if it didn't seem for—the best. I don't—know."

All of a sudden Adoniram Dill sat down beside the little parlor table and leaned his head on it as he had forty years ago.

"What's the matter?" his mother asked, with a scared start, looking at him with awed eyes.

It was almost like a coming back of the dead, this rising of her son's youth from its snowy and grassy grave in her sight. "O Adoniram, you poor boy, you ain't felt jest the same way about her all these years? It's awful. I hadn't any idee on't."

"Never mind, mother. Jane's callin' us to supper; you go right along, an' I'll come in a minute."

"Thar an't any need of your havin' any more frettin' about it, anyhow, Adoniram. Her mother's willin' an' I 'ain't a doubt but Becca is. I've seen her look kinder downhearted sometimes; for all she's so good and uncomplainin', I guess she's been worried as well as some other folks. You jest slick up arter supper, an' go right over an' ask her. Thar ain't no reason at all why you shouldn't. You ain't nuther of you so very old, not more'n sixty. An' I don't know as Mis' Wheat'll be so very bad to git along with. I dessay she's meant all right."

Adoniram said nothing. He rose with an effort, and went out to supper with his mother, who kept gazing at him with loving, questioning eyes.

"Ain't you goin'?" she whispered when they were in the sitting-room again.

"I guess not to-night, mother."

"Well, mebbe 'tis jest as well to wait till tomorrer. I don't want Mis' Wheat to think you was in too much of a rush."

After his mother had gone to bed, and out of doors the summer night was complete with all its stars, he sat down alone on the front doorstep, and thought. He felt like a wanderer returned to some beautiful, dear country, the true home of his heart, which he had thought to never see again. To-night the golden gates of youth swung open with sweet music for Adoniram Dill, with his gray locks and his hard, seamed face, and he entered in, never knowing he was any different.

The steadiness with which he had kept to his ideas of duty for the last forty years gave his happiness, now that the long strain was over, an almost unearthly, holy character. It was truly the reward of virtue. The faithful old man who had taken what he considered to be the right course for himself and the woman he loved, without question or appeal to that mandate of obedience which he read so literally, was capable at sixty of being as freely happy as a child.

The sordid motives which had possibly actuated Becca's mother to withdraw her opposition at last did not fret him at all. He was far above it. That hard, shrill voice which had rung out of that sitting-room window for him for the last forty years was still. The voice had truly said cruel things, more cruel than its owner would own to now. The poor, honest young man had gone away that day with the full and settled understanding that his sweetheart's mother was bitterly opposed to him, and that must be the end of it all. He never dreamed of such a thing as urging her to marry him without her mother's consent.

So he had never been since in that front yard, full of roses and pinks and butterflies.

He and Rebecca had met in the village society like kindly acquaintants for all these years.

Adoniram, looking across the little country church Sunday after Sunday as the years went on, might have seen the woman growing old who should have grown old by his side, with bitter regret, and Rebecca, with patient sadness, have marked his entrance among all the congregation; but no one had known.

The day after the meeting Adoniram had to drive over to the store on business. On his way back he passed a house where an aged sister of Mrs. Wheat's lived, and saw, with a start, the latter's thin face at a window. "I wonder if Becca's home?" said he. Then he drove on quicker, with a gathering resolution.

About four o'clock he was going across lots through the field toward the Wheats'. He had on his Sunday coat. When about half-way across he saw a woman's figure approaching. Soon he saw it was Rebecca. He stood in the narrow footpath, between the tall clover and daisies and herd's-grass which came up to his knees, and waited.

She greeted him, when she reached him, in her usual good, placid way. "How do you do, Mr. Dill?"

"I was comin' to see you, Becca."

She looked at him, and the calm lines in her face changed a little. "I'll go back. I was going after mother, that was all; but she won't be in any hurry."

"No, there ain't any need of your goin' back. I can say what I wanted to jest as well here, an' then you can keep right on after your mother. Becca, supposin' 'twas forty year ago, an' you an' me was here, an' your mother was willin'; what would you say ef I asked you to marry me?"

Great tears stood in her eyes. "Oh Adoniram, it wouldn't be fair!"

"Don't you think your mother would be willin'?"

"I don't think she's so set agin it as she was, but 'twouldn't be fair. I'm sixty year old, Adoniram."

"So 'm I, Becca."

She shook her head. "No, Adoniram, it ain't any use. It might have been different once. Now, after all this time, when I'm old an' broken down, an' the fault of all the trouble on my side of the house, I ain't goin' to be so mean as to let you marry me. It ain't fair."

Adoniram gave one step forward, and caught his old sweetheart in his arms. "I've been waitin' for you forty year, Becca, an' there ain't nothin' more comin' betwixt us. Don't you say anything more about its not bein' fair."

"You know mother'll hev to live with us."

"I'll try an' make her jest as happy as I can."

The clover and the grasses rustled in the wind, and the butterflies came flying around the old man and his old sweetheart standing there. It would have made no difference to them if they had been waiting in their little chrysalis coffins a hundred years or so, they were butterflies now. There were yellow ones and little rusty red ones, and now and then a gorgeous large one with blue spots on his black wings. Seeing one of these made Adoniram remember something swiftly.

"Want me to ketch a butterfly for you, Becca?"

"I've got one now you caught forty year ago."

1887

HAMLIN GARLAND 1860-

The country west of the Mississippi and north of the Missouri Mr. Garland may well claim as his own by right of having made it known through his realistic fiction. He was born in Wisconsin of parents whose lives were spent in the endless toil of pioneer farmers, always on the move westward in search of richer farm-sites. He was graduated from the Cedar Valley Seminary in Iowa, farmed and taught school, and until middle life was generally upon the frontier of the mountain and prairie states, and in Canada and the Klondyke. He was a social reformer and propagandist, a newspaper reporter and writer of special articles; throughout the wanderings that these occupations required, he was gathering material for his stories and novels.

Realism is Garland's method; what romance there is, is born of the frontier background, part of the dogged struggle for daily bread. His realism, untouched by bitterness or pessimism, is as wholesome as is Howells'. Prominent among Mr. Garland's works are *Main-Traveled Roads*, 1890-1898; *Rose of Dutcher's Coolly*, 1895-1898; *The Captain of the Gray-Horse Troop*, 1902; *A Son of the Middle Border,* 1917, and *A Daughter of the Middle Border,* 1921, both autobiographical, reminiscent, and descriptive of life in the northern prairie states when they were being settled; *The Trail Makers,* 1926.

Criticism: Chubb; "Limitations of Authorship in America," *Bookm.* 59:257-62; "Pioneers and City Dwellers," *Bookm.* 58:369-72; C. Van Doren, "Contemporary American Novelists: XI. Hamlin Garland," *Nation* 113:596-7; "The Evolution of a Literary Radical," *Cur. Opinion* 72:389-91; W. D. Howells, "Mr. Garland's Books," *No. Am.* 196:523-8.

From A SON OF THE MIDDLE BORDER [1]

CHAPTER I

HOME FROM THE WAR

All of this universe known to me in the year 1864 was bounded by the wooded hills of a little Wisconsin coulee, [2] and its center was the cottage in which my mother was living alone—my father was in the war. As I project myself back into that mystical age, half-lights cover most of the valley. The road before our doorstone begins and ends in vague obscurity—and Granma Green's house at the fork of the trail stands on the very edge of the world in a sinister region peopled with bears and other menacing creatures. Beyond this point all is darkness and terror.

It is Sunday afternoon and my mother and her three children, Frank, Harriet, and I (all in our best dresses) are visiting the Widow Green, our nearest neighbor, a plump, jolly woman whom we greatly love. The house swarms with stalwart men and buxom women and we are all sitting around the table heaped with the remains of a harvest feast. The women are "telling fortunes" by means of tea-grounds. Mrs. Green is the seeress. After shaking the cup with the grounds at the bottom, she turns it bottom side up in a saucer. Then whirling it three times to the right and three times to the left, she lifts it and silently studies the position of the leaves which cling to the sides of the cup, what time we all wait in breathless suspense for her first word.

"A soldier is coming to you!" she says to my mother. "See," and she points into the cup. We all crowd near, and I perceive a leaf with a stem sticking up from its body like a bayonet over a man's shoulder. "He is almost home," the widow goes on. Then with a sudden dramatic turn she waves her hand toward

[1] From *A Son of the Middle Border* by Hamlin Garland, by permission of The Macmillan Company, publishers.
[2] valley

the road. "Heavens and earth!" she cries. "There's Richard now!"

We all turn and look toward the road, and there, indeed, is a soldier with a musket on his back, wearily plodding his way up the low hill just north of the gate. He is too far away for mother to call, and besides I think she must have been a little uncertain, for he did not so much as turn his head toward the house. Trembling with excitement she hurries little Frank into his wagon and telling Hattie to bring me, sets off up the road as fast as she can draw the baby's cart. It all seems a dream to me and I move dumbly, almost stupidly like one in a mist. . . .

We did not overtake the soldier, that is evident, for my next vision is that of a blue-coated figure leaning upon the fence, studying with intent gaze our empty cottage. I cannot, even now, precisely divine why he stood thus, sadly contemplating his silent home—but so it was. His knapsack lay at his feet, his musket was propped against a post on whose top a cat was dreaming, unmindful of the warrior and his folded hands.

He did not hear us until we were close upon him, and even after he turned, my mother hesitated, so thin, so hollow-eyed, so changed was he. "Richard, is that you?" she quaveringly asked.

His worn face lighted up. His arms rose. "Yes, Belle! Here I am," he answered.

Nevertheless though he took my mother in his arms, I could not relate him to the father I had heard so much about. To me he was only a strange man with big eyes and care-worn face. I did not recognize in him anything I had ever known, but my sister, who was two years older than I, went to his bosom of her own motion. She knew him, whilst I submitted to his caresses rather for the reason that my mother urged me forward than because of any affection I felt for him. Frank, however, would not even permit a kiss. The gaunt and grizzled stranger terrified him.

"Come here, my little man," my father said. —*"My little man!"* Across the space of half-a-century I can still hear the sad reproach in his voice. "Won't you come and see your poor old father when he comes home from the war?"

"My little man!" How significant that phrase seems to me now! The war had in very truth come between this patriot and his sons. I had forgotten him—the baby had never known him.

Frank crept beneath the rail fence and stood there, well out of reach, like a cautious kitten warily surveying an alien dog. At last the soldier stooped and drawing from his knapsack a big red apple, held it toward the staring babe, confidently calling, "Now, I guess he'll come to his poor old pap home from the war."

The mother apologized. "He doesn't know you, Dick. How could he? He was only nine months old when you went away. He'll go to you by and by."

The babe crept slowly toward the shining lure. My father caught him despite his kicking, and hugged him close. "Now I've got you," he exulted.

Then we all went into the little front room and the soldier laid off his heavy army shoes. My mother brought a pillow to put under his head, and so at last he stretched out on the floor the better to rest his tired, aching bones, and there I joined him.

"Oh, Belle!" he said, in tones of utter content. "This is what I've dreamed about a million times."

Frank and I grew each moment more friendly and soon began to tumble over him while mother hastened to cook something for him to eat. He asked for "hot biscuits and honey and plenty of coffee."

That was a mystic hour—and yet how little I can recover of it! The afternoon glides into evening while the soldier talks, and at last we all go out to the barn to watch mother milk the cow. I hear him ask about the crops, the neighbors.—The sunlight passes. Mother leads the way back to the house. My father follows carrying little Frank in his arms.

He is a "strange man" no longer. Each moment his voice sinks deeper into my remembrance. He is my father—that I feel ringing through the dim halls of my consciousness. Harriet clings to his hand in perfect knowledge and confidence. We eat our bread and milk, the trundle-bed is pulled out, we children clamber in, and I go to sleep to the music of his resonant voice recounting the story of the battles he had seen, and the marches he had made.

The emergence of an individual consciousness from the void is, after all, the most amazing fact of human life and I should like to spend much of this first chapter in groping about in the luminous shadow of my infant world because, deeply considered, childish impressions are the fundamentals upon which an author's fictional out-put is based; but to linger might weary my reader at the outset, although I count myself most fortunate in the fact that my boyhood was spent in the midst

of a charming landscape and during a certain heroic era of western settlement.

The men and women of that far time loom large in my thinking for they possessed not only the spirit of adventurers but the courage of warriors. Aside from the natural distortion of a boy's imagination I am quite sure that the pioneers of 1860 still retained something broad and fine in their action, something a boy might honorably imitate.

. . . .

My father who had bought his farm "on time," just before the war, could not enlist among the first volunteers, though he was deeply moved to do so, till his land was paid for—but at last in 1863 on the very day that he made the last payment on the mortgage, he put his name down on the roll and went back to his wife, a soldier.

I have heard my mother say that this was one of the darkest moments of her life and if you think about it you will understand the reason why. My sister was only five years old, I was three and Frank was a babe in the cradle. Broken-hearted at the thought of the long separation and scared by visions of battle my mother begged the soldier not to go; but he was of the stern stuff which makes patriots—and besides his name was already on the roll, therefore he went away to join Grant's army at Vicksburg. "What sacrifice! What folly!" said his pacifist neighbors—"to leave your wife and children for an idea, a mere sentiment; to put your life in peril for a striped silken rag." But he went. For thirteen dollars a month he marched and fought while his plow rusted in the shed and his cattle called to him from their stalls.

My conscious memory holds nothing of my mother's agony of waiting, nothing of the dark days when the baby was ill and the doctor far away—but into my sub-conscious ear her voice sank, and the words *Grant, Lincoln, Sherman, "furlough," "mustered out,"* ring like bells, deep-toned and vibrant. I shared dimly in every emotional utterance of the neighbors who came to call and a large part of what I am is due to the impressions of these deeply passionate and poetic years.

Dim pictures come to me. I see my mother at the spinning wheel, I help her to fill the candle molds. I hold in my hands the queer carding combs with their crinkly teeth, but my first definite connected recollection is the scene of my father's return at the close of the war.

I was not quite five years old, and the events of that day are so commingled with later impressions,—experiences which came long after—that I cannot be quite sure which are true and which imagined, but the picture as a whole is very vivid and very complete.

Thus it happened that my first impressions of life were martial, and my training military, for my father brought back from his two years' campaigning under Sherman and Thomas the temper and the habit of a soldier.

He became naturally the dominant figure in my horizon, and his scheme of discipline impressed itself almost at once upon his children.

I suspect that we had fallen into rather free and easy habits under mother's government, for she was too jolly, too tender-hearted, to engender fear in us even when she threatened us with a switch or a shingle. We soon learned, however, that the soldier's promise of punishment was swift and precise in its fulfillment. We seldom presumed a second time on his forgetfulness or tolerance. We knew he loved us, for he often took us to his knees of an evening and told us stories of marches and battles, or chanted war-songs for us, but the moments of his tenderness were few and his fondling did not prevent him from almost instant use of the rod if he thought either of us needed it.

His own boyhood had been both hard and short. Born of farmer folk in Oxford County, Maine, his early life had been spent on the soil in and about Lock's Mills with small chance of schooling. Later, as a teamster, and finally as a shipping clerk for Amos Lawrence, [1] he had enjoyed three mightily improving years in Boston. He loved to tell of his life there, and it is indicative of his character to say that he dwelt with special joy and pride on the actors and orators he had heard. He could describe some of the great scenes and repeat a few of the heroic lines of Shakespeare, and the roll of his deep voice as he declaimed, "Now is the winter of our discontent made glorious summer by this son of York," [2] thrilled us—filled us with desire of something far off and wonderful. But best of all we loved to hear him tell of "Logan at Peach Tree Creek," and "Kilpatrick on the Granny White Turnpike."

He was a vivid and concise story-teller and his words brought to us (sometimes all too clearly), the tragic happenings of the battle-fields of Atlanta and Nashville. To him Grant, Lincoln, Sherman, and Sheridan were among the noblest men of the world, and he would not tolerate any criticism of them.

Next to his stories of the war I think we loved best to have him picture "the pineries" of Wisconsin, for during his first years in the State he had been both lumberman and raftsman, and his memory held delightful tales of wolves and bears and Indians.

He often imitated the howls and growls and actions of the wild animals with startling realism, and his river narratives were full of unforgettable phrases like "the Jinny Bull Falls," "Old Moosinee" and "running the rapids."

In addition to his military character, Dick Garland also carried with him the odor of the pine forest and exhibited the skill and training of a forester, for in those early days even at the time when I began to remember the neighborhood talk, nearly every young man who could get away from the farm or the village went north, in November, into the pine woods which covered the entire upper part of the State, and my father, who had been a raftsman and timber cruiser [3] and pilot ever since his coming west, was deeply skilled with axe and steering oars. The lumberman's life at that time was rough but not vicious, for the men were nearly all of native American stock, and my father was none the worse for his winters in camp.

His field of action as lumberman was for several years in and around Big Bull Falls (as it was then called), near the present town of Wausau, and during that time he had charge of a crew of loggers in winter and in summer piloted rafts of lumber down to Dubuque and other points where saw mills were located. He was called at this time, "Yankee Dick, the Pilot."

As a result of all these experiences in the woods, he was almost as much woodsman as soldier in his talk, and the heroic life he had led made him very wonderful in my eyes. According to his account (and I have no reason to doubt it) he had been exceedingly expert in running a raft and could ride a canoe like a Chippewa. I remember hearing him very forcefully remark, "God forgot to make the man I could not follow."

He was deft with an axe, keen of perception, sure of hand and foot, and entirely capable of holding his own with any man of his weight. Amid much drinking he remained temperate, and strange to say never used tobacco in any form. While not a large man he was nearly six feet in height, deep-chested and sinewy, and

[1] a Boston merchant and philanthropist, 1786-1852
[2] *Richard III*, I, i, i

[3] a woodsman who explores forests for tracts of valuable timber and reports to lumber companies

of dauntless courage. The quality which defended him from attack was the spirit which flamed from his eagle-gray eyes. Terrifying eyes they were, at times, as I had many occasions to note.

As he gathered us all around his knee at night before the fire, he loved to tell us of riding the whirlpools of Big Bull Falls, or of how he lived for weeks on a raft with the water up to his knees (sleeping at night in his wet working clothes), sustained by the blood of youth and the spirit of adventure. His endurance even after his return from the war, was marvelous, although he walked a little bent and with a peculiar measured swinging stride— the stride of Sherman's veterans.

As I was born in the first smoke of the great conflict, so all of my early memories of Green's coulee are permeated with the haze of the passing war-cloud. My soldier dad had taught me the manual of arms, and for a year Harriet and I carried broom-sticks, flourished lath sabers, and hammered on dishpans in imitation of officers and drummers. Canteens made excellent water-bottles for the men in the harvest fields, and the long blue overcoats which the soldiers brought back with them from the South lent many a vivid spot of color to that far-off landscape.

All the children of our valley inhaled with every breath this mingled air of romance and sorrow, history and song, and through those epic days runs a deep-laid consciousness of maternal pain. My mother's side of those long months of waiting was never fully delineated, for she was natively reticent and shy of expression. But piece by piece I drew from her the tale of her long vigil, and obtained some hint of the bitter anguish of her suspense after each great battle.

1917

O. HENRY (WILLIAM SYDNEY PORTER) 1852-1919

O. Henry, after a rather meager schooling, began life as a pharmacist and drug clerk in the town of Greensboro, North Carolina, his birthplace; threatened with consumption he went to the West where he worked on a cattle ranch; in Texas he was a newspaper reporter and journalist, and became a teller in a small bank. In this last position he was charged with embezzlement, a crime of which he was probably innocent. He fled to Honduras, but returned to serve a term in a Federal penitentiary. Especially through this time spent in an Ohio prison where, as pharmacist, he was brought into contact with men from all grades of society, he gained rich material for his stories. His work is therefore singular in the variety of characters and situations it includes. A leading characteristic of his stories is cleverness in the handling of plot which brings a sudden and wholly unexpected ending. He is most at home in those aspects of life in which whim, chance, and caprice play a part, rather than in those aspects that are deeply and typically significant.

Biography: C. A. Smith, *Biography of O. Henry*, 1916; also *World's Work* 33 :54-64. Criticism: Cooper; Stephen Leacock, "The Amazing Genius of O. Henry" in *Essays and Literary Studies*, 1916; A. S. J. Adcock, "O. Henry," *Liv. Age* 291: 482-8; for further interesting details see *Bookm.* 43 : 569-70; 44 :229-36; 50 :474-6; 52 :536-8; 56 :152-7, 61 :436-7; *Cur. Opinion* 72 :529-31; *Lit. Digest* 72 . 35-6, Mar. 25, '22.

THE HIDING OF BLACK BILL [1]

A lank, strong, red-faced man with a Wellington beak and small, fiery eyes tempered by flaxen lashes, sat on the station platform at Los Pinos swinging his legs to and fro. At his side sat another man, fat, melancholy, and seedy, who seemed to be his friend. They had the appearance of men to whom life had appeared as a reversible coat—seamy on both sides.

"Ain't seen you in about four years, Ham," said the seedy man. "Why way you been travelling?"

"Texas," said the red-faced man. "It was too cold in Alaska for me. And I found it warm in Texas. I'll tell you about one hot spell I went through there.

"One morning I steps off the International at a water-tank and lets it go on without me. 'Twas a ranch country, and fuller of spite-houses than New York City. Only out there they build 'em twenty miles away so you can't smell what they've got for dinner, instead of running 'em up two inches from their neighbors' windows.

"There wasn't any roads in sight, so I footed it 'cross country. The grass was shoe-top deep, and the mesquite timber looked just like a peach orchard. It was so much like a gentleman's private estate that every minute you expected a kennelful of bulldogs to run out and bite you. But I must have walked twenty miles before I came in sight of a ranch-house It was a little one, about as big as an elevated railroad station.

[1] From *Options* by O. Henry, copyright 1909 by Doubleday, Page and Company; and reprinted by permission of Doubleday, Doran and Company, Inc., publishers.

"There was a little man in a white shirt and brown overalls and a pink handkerchief around his neck rolling cigarettes under a tree in front of the door.

"'Greetings,' says I. 'Any refreshment, welcome, emoluments, or even work for a comparative stranger?'

"'Oh, come in,' says he, in a refined tone. 'Sit down on that stool, please. I didn't hear your horse coming.'

"'He isn't near enough yet,' says I. 'I walked. I don't want to be a burden, but I wonder if you have three or four gallons of water handy.'

"'You do look pretty dusty,' says he; 'but our bathing arrangements—'

"'It's a drink I want,' says I. 'Never mind the dust that's on the outside.'

"He gets me a dipper of water out of a red jar hanging up, and then goes on:

"'Do you want work?'

"'For a time,' says I. 'This is a rather quiet section of the country, isn't it?'

"'It is,' says he. 'Sometimes—so I have been told—one sees no human being pass for weeks at a time. I've been here only a month. I bought the ranch from an old settler who wanted to move farther west.'

"'It suits me,' says I. 'Quiet and retirement are good for a man sometimes. And I need a job. I can tend bar, salt mines,[1] lecture, float stock, do a little middle-weight slugging, and play the piano.'

"'Can you herd sheep?' asks the little ranchman.

"'Do you mean *have* I heard sheep?' says I.

"'Can you herd 'em—take charge of a flock of 'em?' says he.

"'Oh,' says I, 'now I understand. You mean chase 'em around and bark at 'em like collie dogs. Well, I might,' says I. 'I've never exactly done any sheep-herding, but I've often seen 'em from car windows masticating daisies, and they don't look dangerous.'

"'I'm short a herder,' says the ranchman. 'You never can depend on the Mexicans. I've only got two flocks. You may take out my bunch of muttons—there are only eight hundred of 'em—in the morning, if you like. The pay is twelve dollars a month and your rations furnished. You camp in a tent on the prairie with your sheep. You do your own cooking, but wood and water are brought to your camp. It's an easy job.'

"'I'm on,' says I. 'I'll take the job even if

[1] place rich ore in worthless mines in order to deceive a buyer

I have to garland my brow and hold on to a crook and wear a loose effect and play on a pipe like the shepherds do in pictures.'

"So the next morning the little ranchman helps me drive the flock of muttons from the corral to about two miles out and let 'em graze on a little hillside on the prairie. He gives me a lot of instructions about not letting bunches of them stray off from the herd, and driving 'em down to a water-hole to drink at noon.

"'I'll bring out your tent and camping outfit and rations in the buckboard before night,' says he.

"'Fine,' says I. 'And don't forget the rations. Nor the camping outfit. And be sure to bring the tent. Your name's Zollicoffer, ain't it?'

"'My name,' says he, 'is Henry Ogden.'

"'All right, Mr. Ogden,' says I. 'Mine is Mr. Percival Saint Clair.'

"I herded sheep for five days on the Rancho Chiquito; and then the wool entered my soul. That getting next to Nature certainly got next to me. I was lonesomer than Crusoe's goat. I've seen a lot of persons more entertaining as companions than those sheep were. I'd drive 'em to the corral and pen 'em every evening, and then cook my corn-bread and mutton and coffee, and lie down in a tent the size of a tablecloth, and listen to the coyotes and whippoor-wills singing around the camp.

"The fifth evening, after I had corralled my costly but uncongenial muttons, I walked over to the ranch-house and stepped in the door.

"'Mr. Ogden,' says I, 'you and me have got to get sociable. Sheep are all very well to dot the landscape and furnish eight-dollar cotton suitings for man, but for table-talk and fireside companions they rank along with five-o'clock teazers. If you've got a deck of cards, or a parcheesi outfit, or a game of authors, get 'em out, and let's get on a mental basis. I've got to do something in an intellectual line, if it's only to knock somebody's brains out.'

"This Henry Ogden was a peculiar kind of ranchman. He wore finger-rings and a big gold watch and careful neckties. And his face was calm, and his nose-spectacles was kept very shiny. I saw once, in Muscogee, an outlaw hung for murdering six men, who was a dead ringer for him. But I knew a preacher in Arkansas that you would have taken to be his brother. I didn't care much for him either way; what I wanted was some fellowship and communion with holy saints or lost sinners—anything sheepless would do.

"'Well, Saint Clair,' says he, laying down the book he was reading, 'I guess it must be pretty lonesome for you at first. And I don't deny that it's monotonous for me. Are you sure you corralled your sheep so they won't stray out?'

"'They're shut up as tight as the jury of a millionaire murderer,' says I. 'And I'll be back with them long before they'll need their trained nurse.'

"So Ogden digs up a deck of cards, and we play casino. After five days and nights of my sheep-camp it was like a toot on Broadway. When I caught big casino I felt as excited as if I had made a million in Trinity. And when H. O. loosened up a little and told the story about the lady in the Pullman car I laughed for five minutes.

"That showed what a comparative thing life is. A man may see so much that he'd be bored to turn his head to look at a $3,000,000 fire or Joe Weber or the Adriatic Sea. But let him herd sheep for a spell, and you'll see him splitting his ribs laughing at 'Curfew Shall Not Ring To-night,' or really enjoying himself playing cards with ladies.

"By-and-by Ogden gets out a decanter of Bourbon, and then there is a total eclipse of sheep.

"'Do you remember reading in the papers, about a month ago,' says he, 'about a train hold-up on the M. K. & T.? The express agent was shot through the shoulder and about $15,000 in currency taken. And it's said that only one man did the job.'

"'Seems to me I do,' says I. 'But such things happen so often they don't linger long in the human Texas mind. Did they overtake, overhaul, seize, or lay hands upon the despoiler?'

"'He escaped,' says Ogden. 'And I was just reading in a paper to-day that the officers have tracked him down into this part of the country. It seems the bills the robber got were all the first issue of currency to the Second National Bank of Espinosa City. And so they've followed the trail where they've been spent, and it leads this way.'

"Ogden pours out some more Bourbon, and shoves me the bottle.

"'I imagine,' says I, after ingurgitating another modicum of the royal booze, 'that it wouldn't be at all a disingenuous idea for a train-robber to run down into this part of the country to hide for a spell. A sheep-ranch, now,' says I, 'would be the finest kind of a place. Who'd ever expect to find such a desperate character among these song-birds and muttons and wild flowers? And, by the way,' says I, kind of looking H. Ogden over, 'was

there any description mentioned of this single-handed terror? Was his lineaments or height and thickness or teeth fillings or style of habiliments set forth in print?'

"'Why, no,' says Ogden; 'they say nobody got a good sight of him .because he wore a mask. But they know it was a train-robber called Black Bill, because he always works alone and because he dropped a handkerchief in the express-car that had his name on it.'

"'All right,' says I. 'I approve of Black Bill's retreat to the sheep-ranges. I guess they won't find him.'

"'There's one thousand dollars reward for his capture,' says Ogden.

"'I don't need that kind of money,' says I, looking Mr. Sheepman straight in the eye. 'The twelve dollars a month you pay me is enough. I need a rest, and I can save up until I get enough to pay my fare to Texarkana, where my widowed mother lives. If Black Bill,' I goes on, looking significantly at Ogden, 'was to have come down this way—say, a month ago—and bought a little sheep-ranch and—'

"'Stop,' says Ogden, getting out of his chair and looking pretty vicious. 'Do you mean to insinuate—'

"'Nothing,' says I; 'no insinuations. I'm stating a hypodermical case. I say, if Black Bill had come down here and bought a sheep-ranch and hired me to Little-Boy-Blue 'em and treated me square and friendly, as you've done, he'd never have anything to fear from me. A man is a man, regardless of any complications he may have with sheep or railroad trains. Now you know where I stand.'

"Ogden looks black as camp-coffee for nine seconds, and then he laughs, amused.

"'You'll do, Saint Clair,' says he. 'If I was Black Bill I wouldn't be afraid to trust you. Let's have a game or two of seven-up to-night. That is, if you don't mind playing with a train-robber.'

"'I've told you,' says I, 'my oral sentiments, and there's no strings to 'em.'

"While I was shuffling after the first hand, I asks Ogden, as if the idea was a kind of a casualty, where he was from.

"'Oh,' says he, 'from the Mississippi Valley.'

"'That's a nice little place,' says I. 'I've often stopped over there. But didn't you find the sheets a little damp and the food poor? Now, I hail,' says I, 'from the Pacific Slope. Ever put up there?'

"'Too draughty,' says Ogden. 'But if you're ever in the Middle West just mention my name, and you'll get foot-warmers and dripped coffee.'

" 'Well,' says I, 'I wasn't exactly fishing for your private telephone number and the middle name of your aunt that carried off the Cumberland Presbyterian minister. It don't matter. I just want you to know you are safe in the hands of your shepherd. Now don't play hearts on spades, and don't get nervous.'

" 'Still harping,' says Ogden, laughing again. 'Don't you suppose that if I was Black Bill and thought you suspected me, I'd put a Winchester bullet into you and stop my nervousness if I had any?'

" 'Not any,' says I. 'A man who's got the nerve to hold up a train single-handed wouldn't do a trick like that. I've knocked about enough to know that them are the kind of men who put a value on a friend. Not that I can claim being a friend of yours, Mr. Ogden,' says I, 'being only your sheep-herder; but under more expeditious circumstances we might have been.'

" 'Forget the sheep temporarily, I beg,' says Ogden, 'and cut for deal.'

"About four days afterward, while my muttons was mooning on the water-hole and I deep in the interstices of making a pot of coffee, up rides softly on the grass a mysterious person in the garb of the being he wished to represent. He was dressed somewhere between a Kansas City detective, Buffalo Bill, and the town dog-catcher of Baton Rouge. His chin and eye wasn't molded on fighting lines, so I knew he was only a scout.

" 'Herdin' sheep?' he asks me.

" 'Well,' says I, 'to a man of your evident gumptional endowments, I wouldn't have the nerve to state that I am engaged in decorating old bronzes or oiling bicycle sprockets.'

" 'You don't talk or look like a sheep-herder to me,' says he.

" 'But you talk like what you look like to me,' says I.

"And then he asks me who I was working for, and I shows him Rancho Chiquito, two miles away, in the shadow of a low hill, and he tells me he's a deputy sheriff.

" 'There's a train-robber called Black Bill supposed to be somewhere in these parts,' says the scout. 'He's been traced as far as San Antonio, and may be farther. Have you seen or heard of any strangers around here during the past month?'

" 'I have not,' says I, 'except a report of one over at the Mexican quarters of Loomis' ranch, on the Frio.'

" 'What do you know about him?' asks the deputy.

" 'He's three days old,' says I.

" 'What kind of a looking man is the man you work for?' he asks. 'Does old George Ramey own this place yet? He's run sheep here for the last ten years, but never had no success.'

" 'The old man has sold out and gone West,' I tells him. 'Another sheep-fancier bought him out about a month ago.'

" 'What kind of a looking man is he?' asks the deputy again.

" 'Oh,' says I, 'a big, fat kind of a Dutchman with long whiskers and blue specs. I don't think he knows a sheep from a ground-squirrel. I guess old George soaked him pretty well on the deal,' says I.

"After indulging himself in a lot more non-communicative information and two thirds of my dinner, the deputy rides away.

"That night I mentions the matter to Ogden.

" 'They're drawing the tendrils of the octopus around Black Bill,' says I. And then I told him about the deputy sheriff, and how I'd described him to the deputy, and what the deputy said about the matter.

" 'Oh, well,' says Ogden, 'let's don't borrow any of Black Bill's troubles. We've a few of our own. Get the Bourbon out of the cupboard and we'll drink to his health—unless,' says he, with his little cackling laugh, 'you're prejudiced against train-robbers.'

" 'I'll drink,' says I, 'to any man who's a friend to a friend. And I believe that Black Bill,' I goes on, 'would be that. So here's to Black Bill, and may he have good luck.'

"And both of us drank.

"About two weeks later comes shearing-time. The sheep had to be driven up to the ranch, and a lot of frowzy-headed Mexicans would snip the fur off of them with back-action scissors. So the afternoon before the barbers were to come I hustled my under-done muttons over the hill, across the dell, down by the winding brook, and up to the ranch-house, where I penned 'em in a corral and bade 'em my nightly adieus.

"I went from there to the ranch-house. I find H. Ogden, Esquire, lying asleep on his little cot bed. I guess he had been overcome by anti-insomnia or diswakefulness or some of the diseases peculiar to the sheep business. His mouth and vest were open, and he breathed like a second-hand bicycle pump. I looked at him and gave vent to just a few musings. 'Imperial Caesar,' says I, 'asleep in such a way, might shut his mouth and keep the wind away.'

"A man asleep is certainly a sight to make angels weep. What good is all his brain, muscle, backing, nerve, influence, and family connections? He's at the mercy of his enemies, and more so of his friends. And he's about as beautiful as a cab-horse leaning against the Metropolitan Opera House at 12:30 A.M. dreaming of the plains of Arabia. Now, a woman asleep you regard as different. No matter how she looks, you know it's better for all hands for her to be that way.

"Well, I took a drink of Bourbon and one for Ogden, and started in to be comfortable while he was taking his nap. He had some books on his table on indigenous subjects, such as Japan and drainage and physical culture—and some tobacco, which seemed more to the point.

"After I'd smoked a few, and listened to the sartorial breathing of H. O., I happened to look out the window toward the shearing-pens, where there was a kind of a road coming up from a kind of road across a kind of creek farther away.

"I saw five men riding up to the house. All of 'em carried guns across their saddles, and among 'em was the deputy that had talked to me at my camp.

"They rode up careful, in open formation, with their guns ready. I set apart with my eye the one I opinionated to be the boss muckraker of this law-and-order cavalry.

"'Good-evening, gents,' says I. 'Won't you 'light and tie your horses?'

"The boss rides up close, and swings his gun over till the opening in it seems to cover my whole front elevation.

"'Don't you move your hands none,' says he, 'till you and me indulge in a adequate amount of necessary conversation.'

"'I will not,' says I. 'I am no deaf-mute, and therefore will not have to disobey your injunctions in replying.'

"'We are on the lookout,' says he, 'for Black Bill, the man that held up the Katy for $15,000 in May. We are searching the ranches and everybody on 'em. What is your name, and what do you do on this ranch?'

"'Captain,' says I, 'Percival Saint Clair is my occupation, and my name is sheep-herder. I've got my flock of veals—no, muttons—penned here to-night. The searchers are coming tomorrow to give them a hair-cut—with baa-a-rum, I suppose.'

"'Where's the boss of this ranch?' the captain of the gang asks me.

"'Wait just a minute, cap'n,' says I. 'Wasn't there a kind of a reward offered for the capture of this desperate character you have referred to in your preamble?'

"'There's a thousand dollars reward offered,' says the captain, 'but it's for his capture and conviction. There don't seem to be no provision made for an informer.'

"'It looks like it might rain in a day or so,' says I, in a tired way, looking up at the cerulean blue sky.

"'If you know anything about the locality, disposition, or secretiveness of this here Black Bill,' says he, in a severe dialect, 'you are amiable to the law in not reporting it.'

"'I heard a fence-rider say,' says I, in a desultory kind of voice, 'that a Mexican told a cowboy named Jake over at Pidgin's store on the Nueces that he heard that Black Bill had been seen in Matamoras by a sheepman's cousin two weeks ago.'

"'Tell you what I'll do, Tight Mouth,' says the captain, after looking me over for bargains. 'If you put us on so we can scoop Black Bill, I'll pay you a hundred dollars out of my own— out of our own—pockets. That's liberal,' says he. 'You ain't entitled to anything. Now, what do you say?'

"'Cash down now?' I ask.

"The captain has a sort of discussion with his helpmates, and they all produce the contents of their pockets for analysis. Out of the general results they figured up $102.30 in cash and $31 worth of plug tobacco.

"'Come nearer, capitan meeo,' says I, 'and listen.' He so did.

"'I am mighty poor and low down in the world,' says I. 'I am working for twelve dollars a month trying to keep a lot of animals together whose only thought seems to be to get asunder. Although,' says I, 'I regard myself as some better than the State of South Dakota, it's a come-down to a man who has heretofore regarded sheep only in the form of chops. I'm pretty far reduced in the world on account of foiled ambitions and rum and a kind of cocktail they make along the P.R.R. all the way from Scranton to Cincinnati—dry gin, French vermouth, one squeeze of a lime, and a good dash of orange bitters. If you're ever up that way, don't fail to let one try you. And, again,' says I, 'I have never yet went back on a friend. I've stayed by 'em when they had plenty, and when adversity's overtaken me I've never forsook 'em.

"'But,' I goes on, 'this is not exactly the case of a friend. Twelve dollars a month is only bowing-acquaintance money. And I do not consider brown beans and corn-bread the food of friendship. I am a poor man,' says I, 'and I have a widowed mother in Texarkana. You will find Black Bill, says I, 'lying asleep in this house on a cot in the room to your right. He's the man you want, as I know from his words and conversation. He was in a way a friend,' I explains, 'and if I was the man I once was the entire product of the mines of Gondola would not have tempted me to betray him. But,' says I, 'every week half of the beans was wormy, and not nigh enough wood in camp.

" 'Better go in careful, gentlemen,' says I. 'He seems impatient at times, and when you think of his late professional pursuits one would look for abrupt actions if he was come upon sudden.'

"So the whole posse unmounts and ties their horses, and unlimbers their ammunition and equipments, and tiptoes into the house. And I follows, like Delilah when she set the Philip Steins on to Samson.

"The leader of the posse shakes Ogden and wakes him up. And then he jumps up, and two more of the reward-hunters grab him. Ogden was mighty tough with all his slimness, and he gives 'em as neat a single-footed tussle against odds as I ever see.

" 'What does this mean?' he says, after they had him down.

"You're scooped in, Mr. Black Bill,' says the captain. 'That's all.'

" 'It's an outrage,' says H. Ogden, madder yet.

" 'It was,' says the peace-and-good-will man. 'The Katy wasn't bothering you, and there's a law against monkeying with express packages.'

"And he sits on H. Ogden's stomach and goes through his pockets symptomatically and careful.

" 'I'll make you perspire for this,' says Ogden, perspiring some himself. 'I can prove who I am.'

" 'So can I,' says the captain, as he draws from H. Ogden's inside coat-pocket a handful of new bills of the Second National Bank of Espinosa City. 'Your regular engraved Tuesdays-and-Fridays visiting card wouldn't have a louder voice in proclaiming your indemnity than this here currency. You can get up now and prepare to go with us and expatriate your sins.'

"H. Ogden gets up and fixes his necktie. He says no more after they have taken the money off of him.

" 'A well-greased idea,' says the sheriff captain, admiring, 'to slip down here and buy a little sheep-ranch where the hand of man is seldom heard. It was the slickest hide-out I ever see,' says the captain.

"So one of the men goes to the shearing-pen and hunts up the other herder, a Mexican they call John Sallies, and he saddles Ogden's horse, and the sheriffs all ride up close around him with their guns in hand, ready to take their prisoner to town.

"Before starting, Ogden puts the ranch in John Sallies' hands and gives him orders about the shearing and where to graze the sheep, just as if he intended to be back in a few days. And a couple of hours afterward one Percival Saint Clair, an ex-sheep-herder of the Rancho Chiquito, might have been seen, with a hundred and nine dollars—wages and blood money—in his pocket, riding south on another horse belonging to said ranch."

The red-faced man paused and listened. The whistle of a coming freight-train sounded far away among the low hills.

The fat, seedy man at his side sniffed, and shook his frowzy head slowly and disparagingly.

"What is it, Snipy?" asked the other. "Got the blues again?"

"No, I ain't," said the seedy one, sniffing again. "But I don't like your talk. You and me have been friends, off and on, for fifteen year; and I never yet knew or heard of you giving anybody up to the law—not no one. And here was a man whose saleratus you had et and at whose table you had played games of cards—if casino can be so called. And yet you inform him to the law and take money for it. It never was like you, I say."

"This H. Ogden," resumed the red-faced man, "through a lawyer, proved himself free by alibis and other legal terminalities, as I so heard afterward. He never suffered no harm. He did me favors, and I hated to hand him over."

"How about the bills they found in his pocket?" asked the seedy man.

"I put 'em there," said the red-faced man, "while he was asleep, when I saw the posse riding up. I was Black Bill. Look out, Snipy, here she comes! We'll board her on the bumpers when she takes water."

1920

FINLEY PETER DUNNE (Mr. Dooley) 1867-

The satire of Mr. Dunne, good-humored, witty, and showing a penetrating estimate of passing events, grew out of the author's direct contact with men and public affairs in his newspaper work. Mr. Dunne was born in Chicago, was educated there in the public schools, at eighteen became a newspaper reporter, and advanced through all grades of journalism. Most of his essays appeared in newspapers, through which they reached a vast number of readers. In the character of Mr. Dooley, supposed to be a Chicago saloon-keeper, Mr. Dunne expressed in Irish-American dialect his views on well-known men and events, and on social and political problems of the moment. Mr. Dooley's shrewd observations based upon his own hard life, his conversation with his customers, and a little reading, are a mixture of good-natured wit and common sense. Keen as are his unexpected thrusts, they show a nature much more inclined to kindliness than to cynicism.

Mr. Dunne's essays are collected in *Mr. Dooley in Peace and War*, 1898; *Mr. Dooley in the Hearts of his Countrymen*, 1898; *Mr. Dooley's Philosophy*, 1900, and *Mr. Dooley Says*, 1910.

Criticism: "People in the Foreground," *Cur. Lit.* 38:29; F. G. Clark, *Bookm.* 12:321-3; W. D. Howells, *No. Am.* 176:743-6.

From MR. DOOLEY SAYS [1]

GLORY

"Hogan has been in here this afthernoon, an' I've heerd more scandal talked thin I iver thought was in the wurrld."

"Hogan had betther keep quiet," said Mr. Hennessy. "If he goes circulatin' anny stories about me I'll—"

"Ye needn't worry," said Mr. Dooley. "We didn't condiscend to talk about annywan iv ye'er infeeryor station. If ye want to be the subjick iv our scand'lous discoorse ye'd betther go out an' make a repytation. No, sir, our talk was entirely about th' gr-reat an' illusthrees an' it ran all th' way fr'm Julius Cayzar to Ulysses Grant.

"Dear, oh dear, but they were th' bad lot. Thank th' Lord nobody knows about me. Thank th' Lord I had th' good sinse to retire fr'm pollyticks whin me repytation had spread as far as Halsted Sthreet. If I'd let it go a block farther I'd've been sorry f'r it th' rest iv me life an' some years afther me death.

"I wanted to be famous in thim days, whin I was young an' foolish. 'Twas th' dhream iv me life to have people say as I wint by: 'There goes Dooley, th' gr-reatest statesman iv his age,' an' have thim name babies, sthreets, schools, canal boats, an' five-cent seegars afther me, an' whin I died to have it put in th' books that 'at this critical peeryod in th' history of America there was need iv a man who combined strenth iv charackter with love iv

counthry. Such a man was found in Martin Dooley, a prom'nent retail liquor dealer in Ar-rchey Road.'

"That's what I wanted, an' I'm glad I didn't get me wish. If I had, 'tis little attintion to me charackter that th' books iv what Hogan calls bi-ography wud pay, but a good deal to me debts. Though they mintioned th' fact that I resked death f'r me adopted fatherland, they'd make th' more intherestin' story about the time I almost met it be fallin' down stairs while runnin' away fr'm a polisman. F'r wan page they'd print about me love iv counthry, they'd print fifty about me love iv dhrink.

"Th' things thim gr-reat men done wud give thim a place in Byrnes's book. If Julius Caysar was alive to-day he'd be doin' a lock-step down in Joliet. He was a corner loafer in his youth an' a robber in his old age. He busted into churches, fooled ar-round with other men's wives, curled his hair with a poker an' smelled iv perfumery like a Saturday night car. An' his wife was a suspicyious charackter an' he turned her away.

"Napolyon Bonypart, impror iv the Fr-rinch, was far too gay aven f'r thim friv'lous people, an' had fits. His first wife was no betther than she shud be, an' his second wife didn't care f'r him. Willum Shakespeare is well known as an author of plays that no wan can play, but he was betther known as a two-handed dhrinker, a bad actor, an' a thief. His wife was a common scold an' led him th' life he desarved.

"They niver leave th' ladies out iv these stories iv th' gr-reat. A woman that marries a janius has a fine chance iv her false hair becomin' more immortal thin his gr-reatest deed. It don't make anny diff'rence if all she knew about her marital hero was that he was a consistent feeder, a sleepy husband, an' indulgent to his childher an' sometimes to himsilf, an' that she had to darn his socks. Nearly all th' gr-reat men had something th' matther with their wives. I always thought Mrs. Washington, who was th' wife iv the father iv our counthry, though childless hersilf, was about right. She looks good in th' pitchers, with a shawl ar-round her neck an' a frilled night-cap on her head. But Hogan says she had a tongue sharper thin George's soord, she insulted all his frinds, an' she was much older thin him. As f'r George, he was a case. I wish th' counthry had got itsilf a diff'rent father. A gr-reat moral rellijous counthry like this desarves a betther parent.

"They were all alike. I think iv Bobby Burns as a man that wrote good songs, aven if they were in a bar'brous accint, but Hogan thinks iv him as havin' a load all th' time an' bein' th' scandal iv his parish. I remimber Andhrew Jackson as th' man that licked th' British at Noo Orleans be throwin' cotton bales at thim, but Hogan remimbers him as a man that cudden't spell an' had a wife who smoked a corncob pipe. I remimber Abraham Lincoln f'r freein' the slaves, but Hogan remimbers how he used to cut loose yarns that made th' bartinder shake th' stove harder thin it needed. I remimber Grant f'r what he done ar-round Shiloh whin he was young, but Hogan remimbers him f'r what he done arr-round New York whin he was old.

"An' so it goes. Whin a lad with nawthin' else to do starts out to write a bi-ography about a gr-reat man, he don't go to th' war departmint or th' public library. No, sir, he begins to search th' bureau dhrawers, old pigeon-holes, th' records iv th' polis coort, an' th' recollections iv th' hired girl. He likes letters betther thin annything else. He don't care much f'r th' kind beginnin': 'Dear wife, I'm settin' in front iv th' camp fire wearin' th' flannel chest protector ye made me, an' dhreamin' iv ye,' but if he can find wan beginnin': 'Little Bright Eyes: Th' old woman has gone to th' counthry,' he's th' happiest bi-ographer ye cud see in a month's thraval.

"Hogan had wan iv thim books in here th' other day. 'Twas written by a frind, so ye can see it wasn't prejudiced wan way or another. 'At this time,' says the book, 'an ivint happened that was destined to change th' whole coorse iv our hero's life. Wan day, while in a sthreet car, where he lay dozin' fr'm dhrink, he awoke to see a beautiful woman thryin' to find a nickel in a powder puff. Th' brutal conductor towered over her, an' it was more thin th' Gin'ral cud bear. Risin' to his feet, with an oath, he pulled th' rope iv th' fare register an' fell off th' car.

" 'Th' incident made a deep impression on th' Gin'ral. I have no doubt he often thought iv his beautiful Madonna iv th' throlly, although he niver said so. But wan night as he staggered out iv th' dinin'-room at th' German Ambassadure's, who shud he run acrost but th' fair vision iv th' surface line. She curtsied low an' picked him up, an' there began a frindship so full iv sorrow an' happiness to both iv thim. He seldom mintioned her, but wan night he was heard to mutter: 'Her face is like wan iv Rembrand's saints.' A few historyans contind that what he said was: 'Her face looks like a remnant sale,' but I cannot believe this.

" 'They exchanged brilliant letters f'r manny years, in fact ontil th' enchanthress was locked up in an insane asylum. I have not been able to find anny iv his letters, but her's fell into th' hands iv wan iv his faithful servants, who presarved an' published thim. (Love an' Letters iv Gin'ral Dhreadnaught an' Alfaretta Agonized; Stolen, Collected an' Edited be James Snooper.') . . . Next year was mim'rable f'r his gloryous victhry at Punkheim, all th' more wondherful because at th' time our hero was sufferin' fr'm deleeryyum thremens.

" 'It shows th' fortitude iv th' Gin'ral an' that he was as gr-reat a liar as I have indicated in th' precedin' pages, that with th' cheers iv his sojers ringin' in his ears, he cud still write home to his wife: 'Ol' girl—I can't find annything fit to dhrink down here. Can't ye sind me some cider fr'm th' farm.' . . . In 1865 he was accused iv embezzlemint, but th' charges niver reached his ears or th' public's ontil eight years afther his death. . . . In '67 his foster brother, that he had neglected in Kansas City, slipped on his ballroom flure an' broke his leg. . . . In '70 his wife died afther torturin' him f'r fifty years. They were a singularly badly mated couple, with a fam'ly iv fourteen childher, but he did not live long to enjoy his happiness. F'r some reason he niver left his house, but passed away within a month, one of th' gr-reatest men th' cinchry has projooced. For further details iv th' wrong things he done see th' notes at th' end iv th' volume.'

"It seems to me, Hinnissy, that this here thing called bi-ography is a kind iv an offset f'r histhry. Histhry lies on wan side, an' bi-ography comes along an' makes it rowl over an' lie on th' other side. Th' historyan says, go up; th' bi-ographer says, come down among us. I don't believe ayether iv thim.

"I was talkin' with Father Kelly about it afther Hogan wint out. 'Were they all so bad, thim men that I've been brought up to think so gloryous?' says I. 'They were men,' says Father Kelly. 'Ye mustn't believe all ye hear about thim, no matther who says it,' says he. 'It's a thrait iv human nature to pull down th' gr-reat an strong. Th' hero sthruts through histhry with his chin up in th' air, his scipter in his hand an' his crown on his head. But behind him dances a boot-black imitatin' his walk an' makin' faces at him. Fame invites a man out iv his house to be crowned f'r his gloryous deeds, an' sarves him with a warrant f'r batin' his wife. 'Tis not in th' nature iv things that it shudden't be so. We'd all perish iv humilyation if th' gr-reat men iv th' wurruld didn't have nachral low-down thraits. If they don't happen to possess thim, we make some up f'r thim. We allow no man to tower over us. Wan way or another we level th' wurruld to our own height. If we can't reach th' hero's head we cut off his legs. It always makes me feel aisier about mesilf whin I r-read how bad Julius Cayzar was. An' it stimulates compytition. If gr-reatness an' goodness were hand in hand 'tis small chance anny iv us wud have iv seein' our pitchers in th' pa-apers.'

"An' so it is that the battles ye win, th' pitchers ye paint, th' people ye free, th' childher that disgrace ye, th' false step iv ye'er youth, all go thundherin' down to immortality together. An afther all, isn't it a good thing? Th' only bi-ography I care about is th' one Mulligan th' stone-cutter will chop out f'r me. I like Mulligan's style, f'r he's no flatthrer, an' he has wan model iv bi-ography that he uses f'r old an' young, rich an' poor. He merely writes something to th' gin'ral effect that th' deceased was a wondher, an' lets it go at that."

"Which wud ye rather be, famous or rich?" asked Mr. Hennessey.

"I'd like to be famous," said Mr. Dooley, "an' have money enough to buy off all threatenin' bi-ographers."

1910

OWEN WISTER 1860-

Owen Wister, despite his ability to interpret the Western mind, is no more of the West than of the East. In him two hundred years of Pennsylvania ancestry and three scholastic degrees at Harvard are pitted against numberless journeys through the desert states, whose romance drew him to them again and again. He has been an editor, a musician, a critic; he is a member of the American Academy of Arts and Letters, as well as of similar European learned societies. His life has been full and active but always dominated by his literary impulse. *Red Men and White,* in 1896, called attention to Mr. Wister as a short-story writer; *The Virginian,* 1902, of which the author says, "It pictures an era and personifies a type," and *Lady Baltimore,* 1906, his highest artistic success, have made him well known as a novelist. The romance in his work is firmly based in realism, for, like other chroniclers of the West, he has felt the desire to interpret truly the picturesque life of the plains and the mountains. He has grown increasingly able to mirror the inner life of the types with which he has come into contact, particularly the Indians. In *Lin McLean,* 1898, he cast a novel into the form of a series of short stories, thus interpreting "the nomadic West by a nomadic artform." Occasionally he depicts scenes from the romantic Spanish occupation of the Pacific coast. His work is clean and sure, and always full of life.

Criticism: H. W. Boynton, "A Word on 'The Genteel Critic,'" *Dial* 59:303-6; *Bookm.* 27: 458-66.

PADRE IGNACIO [1]

I

At Santa Ysabel del Mar the season was at one of those moments when the air rests quiet over land and sea. The old breezes were gone; the new ones were not yet risen. The flowers in the mission garden opened wide; no wind came by day or night to shake the loose petals from their stems. Along the basking, silent, many-colored shore gathered and lingered the crisp odors of the mountains. The dust hung golden and motionless long after the rider was behind the hill, and the Pacific lay like a floor of sapphire, whereon to walk beyond the setting sun into the East. One white sail shone there. Instead of an hour, it had been from dawn till afternoon in sight between the short headlands; and the Padre had hoped that it might be the ship his homesick heart awaited. But it had slowly passed. From an arch in his garden cloisters he was now watching the last of it. Presently it was gone, and the great ocean lay empty. The Padre put his glasses in his lap. For a while he read in his breviary, but soon forgot it again. He looked at the flowers and sunny ridges, then at the huge blue triangle of sea which the opening of the hills let into sight. "Paradise," he murmured, "need not hold more beauty and peace. But I think I would exchange all my remaining years of this for one sight again of Paris or Seville. May God forgive me such a thought!"

Across the unstirred fragrance of oleanders the bell for vespers began to ring. Its tones passed over the Padre as he watched the sea in his garden. They reached his parishioners in their adobe dwellings near by. The gentle circles of sound floated outward upon the smooth, immense silence—over the vines and pear-trees; down the avenues of the olives; into the planted fields, whence women and children began to return; then out of the lap of the valley along the yellow uplands, where the men that rode among the cattle paused, looking down like birds at the map of their home. Then the sound widened, faint, unbroken, until it met Temptation in the guise of a youth, riding toward the Padre from the South, and cheered the steps of Temptation's jaded horse.

"For a day, one single day of Paris!" repeated the Padre, gazing through his cloisters at the empty sea.

Once in the year, the mother-world remembered him. Once in the year, from Spain, tokens and home-tidings came to him, sent by certain beloved friends of his youth. A barkentine brought him these messages. Whenever thus the mother-world remembered him, it was like the touch of a warm hand, a dear and tender caress; a distant life, by him long left behind, seemed to be drawing the exile homeward from these alien shores. As the time for his letters and packets drew near, the eyes of Padre Ignacio would be often fixed wistfully upon the harbor, watching for the barkentine. Sometimes, as to-day, he mistook other sails for hers, but hers he mistook never. That Pacific Ocean, which, for all its hues and jeweled mists, he could not learn to love, had, since long before his day, been furrowed by the keels of Spain. Traders, and adventurers, the men of God had passed along this coast, planting their colonies and cloisters; but it was not his ocean. In the year that we, a thin strip of patriots away over on the Atlantic edge of the continent, declared ourselves an independent nation, a Spanish ship, in the name of Saint Francis, was unloading the centuries of her own civilization at the Golden Gate. San Diego had come earlier. Then, slowly, as mission after mission was built along the soft coast wilderness, new ports were established—at Santa Barbara, and by Point San Luis for San Luis Obispo, which lay inland a little way up the gorge where it opened among the hills. Thus the world reached these missions by water; while on land, through the mountains, a road led to them, and also to many more that were too distant behind the hills for ships to serve—a rough road, long and lonely, punctuated with church towers and gardens. For the Fathers gradually so stationed their settlements that the traveler might each morning ride out from one mission and by evening of a day's fair journey ride into the next. A lonely, rough, dangerous road, but lovely, too, with a name like music—El Camino Real. [1] Like music also were the names of the missions—San Juan Capistrano, San Luis Rey de Francis, San Miguel, Santa Ynez—their very list is a song.

So there, by-and-by, was our continent, with the locomotive whistling from Savannah to Boston along its eastern edge, and on the western the scattered chimes of Spain, ringing among the unpeopled mountains. Thus grew the two sorts of civilization—not equally. We know what has happened since. To-day the locomotive is whistling also from The Golden

Gate to San Diego; but still the old mission-road goes through the mountains, and along it the footsteps of vanished Spain are marked with roses, and broken cloisters, and the crucifix.

But this was 1855. Only the barkentine brought to Padre Ignacio the signs from the world that he once had known and loved so dearly. As for the new world making a rude noise to the northward, he trusted that it might keep away from Santa Ysabel, and he waited for the vessel that was overdue with its package containing his single worldly luxury.

As the little, ancient bronze bell continued swinging in the tower, its plaintive call reached something in the Padre's memory. Softly, absently, he began to sing. He took up the slow strain not quite correctly, and dropped it, and took it up again, always in cadence with the bell:

At length he heard himself, and, glancing at the belfry, smiled a little. "It is a pretty tune," he said, "and it always made me sorry for poor Fra Diavolo. [2] Auber himself confessed to me that he had made it sad and put the hermitage bell to go with it, because he too was grieved at having to kill his villain, and wanted him, if possible, to die in a religious frame of mind. And Auber touched glasses with me and said— how well I remember it!—'Is it the good Lord, or is it merely the devil, that makes me always have a weakness for rascals?' I told him it was the devil. I was not a priest then. I could not be so sure with my answer now." And then Padre Ignacio repeated Auber's remark in French: "'Est-ce le bon Dieu, ou est-ce bien le diable, qui veut toujours que j'aime les coquins?' I don't know! I don't know! I wonder if Auber has composed anything lately? I wonder who is singing 'Zerlina' [3] now?"

He cast a farewell look at the ocean, and took his steps between the monastic herbs, the jasmines and the oleanders to the sacristy. "At least," he said, "if we cannot carry with us into exile the friends and the places we have loved,

---

[1] the King's Highway, the original road from San Diego northward connecting all the coast missions of Spanish California

[2] a character in *Fra Diavolo*, an opera by Auber, a French composer, 1782-1871
[3] the leading soprano rôle in *Fra Diavolo*

music will go whither we go, even to an end of the world such as this.—Felipe!" he called to his organist. "Can they sing the music I taught them for the *Dixit Dominus* [1] to-night?"

"Yes, father, surely."

"Then we will have that. And, Felipe—" The Padre crossed the chancel to the small, shabby organ. "Rise, my child, and listen. Here is something you can learn. Why, see now if you cannot learn it from a single hearing."

The swarthy boy of sixteen stood watching his master's fingers, delicate and white, as they played. Thus, of his own accord, he had begun to watch them when a child of six; and the Padre had taken the wild, half-scared, spellbound creature and made a musician of him.

"There, Felipe!" he said now. "Can you do it? Slower, and more softly, muchacho mio. [2] It is about the death of a man, and it should go with our bell."

The boy listened. "Then the father has played it a tone too low," said he, "for our bell rings the note of *sol,* or something very near it, as the father must surely know." He placed the melody in the right key—an easy thing for him; and the Padre was delighted.

"Ah, my Felipe," he exclaimed, "what could you and I not do if we had a better organ! Only a little better! See! above this row of keys would be a second row, and many more stops. Then we would make such music as has never yet been heard in California. But my people are so poor and so few! And some day I shall have passed from them, and it will be too late."

"Perhaps," ventured Felipe, "the Americanos—"

"They care nothing for us, Felipe. They are not of our religion—or of any religion, from what I can hear. Don't forget my *Dixit Dominus.*"

The Padre retired once more to the sacristy, while the horse that brought Temptation came over the hill.

The hour of service drew near; and as the Padre waited he once again stepped out for a look at the ocean; but the blue triangle of water lay like a picture in its frame of land, bare as the sky. "I think, from the color, though," said he, "that a little more wind must have begun out there."

The bell rang a last short summons to prayer. Along the road from the south a young rider,

leading a pack-animal, ambled into the mission and dismounted. Church was not so much in his thoughts as food and, after due digestion, a bed; but the doors stood open, and, as everybody was passing within them, more variety was to be gained by joining this company than by waiting outside alone until they should return from their devotions. So he seated himself in a corner near the entrance, and after a brief, jaunty glance at the sunburned, shaggy congregation, made himself as comfortable as might be. He had not seen a face worth keeping his eyes open for. The simple choir and simple fold, gathered for even-song, paid him no attention—a rough American bound for the mines was but an object of aversion to them.

The Padre, of course, had been instantly aware of the stranger's presence. To be aware of unaccustomed presences is the sixth sense with vicars of every creed and heresy; and if the parish is lonely and the worshipers few and seldom varying, a newcomer will gleam out like a new book to be read. And a trained priest learns to read keenly the faces of those who assemble to worship under his guidance. But American vagrants, with no thoughts save of gold-digging, and an overweening illiterate jargon for speech, had long ceased to interest this priest, even in his starvation for company and talk from the outside world; and therefore after the intoning he sat with his homesick thoughts unchanged, to draw both pain and enjoyment from the music that he had set to the *Dixit Dominus.* He listened to the tender chorus that opens *William Tell;* [3] and, as the Latin psalm proceeded, pictures of the past rose between him and the altar. One after another came these strains he had taken from operas famous in their day, until at length the Padre was murmuring to some music seldom long out of his heart—not the Latin verse which the choir sang, but the original French words:

> "Ah, voilà mon envie,
> Voilà mon seul désir:
> Rendez moi ca patrie,
> Ou laissez moi mourir."

Which may be rendered:

> "But one wish I implore,
> One wish is all my cry:
> Give back my native land once more,
> Give back, or let me die."

Then it happened that his eye fell again upon the stranger near the door, and he straightway forgot his *Dixit Dominus.* The face of the

[1] an antiphon (*Psalm* 110) used in several liturgies at vespers and set to different musical arrangements
[2] my lad
[3] an opera by Rossini, an Italian composer, 1792-1868

young man was no longer hidden by the slouching position he had at first taken. "I only noticed his clothes at first," thought the Padre. Restlessness was plain upon the handsome brow, and violence was in the mouth; but Padre Ignacio liked the eyes. "He is not saying any prayers," he surmised, presently. "I doubt if he has said any for a long while. And he knows my music. He is of educated people. He cannot be American. And now—yes, he has taken —I think it must be a flower, from his pocket. I shall have him to dine with me." And vespers ended with rosy clouds of eagerness drifting across the Padre's brain.

II

But the stranger made his own beginning. As the priest came from the church, the rebellious young figure was waiting. "Your organist tells me," he said impetuously, "that it is you who—"

"May I ask with whom I have the great pleasure of speaking?" said the Padre, putting formality to the front and his pleasure out of sight.

The stranger's face reddened beneath its sunbeaten bronze, and he became aware of the Padre's pale features, molded by refinement and the world. "I beg your lenience," said he, with a graceful and confident utterance, as of equal to equal. "My name is Gaston Villeré, and it was time I should be reminded of my manners."

The Padre's hand waved a polite negative.

"Indeed, yes, Padre. But your music has amazed me. If you carried such associations as—Ah! the days and the nights!"—he broke off. "To come down a California mountain and find Paris at the bottom! *The Huguenots,* [1] Rossini, Hérold [2]—I was waiting for *Il Trovatore.*" [3]

"Is that something new?" inquired the Padre, eagerly.

The young man gave an exclamation. "The whole world is ringing with it!" he cried.

"But Santa Ysabel del Mar is a long way from the whole world," murmured Padre Ignacio.

"Indeed, it would not appear to be so," returned young Gaston. "I think the Comédie Française [4] must be round the corner."

A thrill went through the priest at the theater's name. "And have you been long in America?" he asked.

[1] an opera by Meyerbeer, a German composer, 1791-1864
[2] a French composer, 1791-1833
[3] an opera by Verdi, an Italian composer, 1813-1901
[4] the official name of the Théâtre Française

"Why, always—except two years of foreign travel after college."

"An American!" exclaimed the surprised Padre, with perhaps a tone of disappointment in his voice. "But no Americans who are yet come this way have been—have been"—he veiled the too-blunt expression of this thought —"have been familiar with *The Huguenots,*" he finished, making a slight bow.

Villeré took his under-meaning. "I come from New Orleans," he returned. "And in New Orleans there live many of us who can recognize a—who can recognize good music wherever we hear it." And he made a slight bow in his turn.

The Padre laughed outright with pleasure and laid his hand upon the young man's arm. "You have no intention of going away tomorrow, I trust?"

"With your leave," answered Gaston, "I will have such an intention no longer."

It was with the air and gait of mutual understanding that the two now walked on together toward the Padre's door. The guest was twenty-five, the host sixty.

"And have you been in America long?" inquired Gaston.

"Twenty years."

"And at Santa Ysabel how long?"

"Twenty years."

"I should have thought," said Gaston, looking lightly at the desert and unpeopled mountains, "that now and again you might have wished to travel."

"Were I your age," murmured Padre Ignacio, "it might be so."

The evening had now ripened to the long after-glow of sunset. The sea was the purple of grapes, and wine-colored hues flowed among the high shoulders of the mountains.

"I have seen a sight like this," said Gaston, "between Granada and Malaga."

"So you know Spain!" said the Padre.

Often he had thought of this resemblance, but never till now met any one to share his thought. The courtly proprietor of San Fernando and the other patriarchal rancheros with whom he occasionally exchanged visits across the wilderness knew hospitality and inherited gentle manners, sending to Europe for silks and laces to give their daughters; but their eyes had not looked upon Granada, and their ears had never listened to *William Tell.*

"It is quite singular," pursued Gaston, "how one nook in the world will suddenly remind you of another nook that may be thousands of miles away. One morning, behind the Quai

Voltaire, [1] an old, yellow house with rusty balconies made me almost homesick for New Orleans."

"The Quai Voltaire!" said the Padre.

"I heard Rachel [2] in *Valerie* [3] that night," the young man went on. "Did you know that she could sing, too? She sang several verses by an astonishing little Jew violin-cellist that is come up over there."

The Padre gazed down at his blithe guest. "To see somebody, somebody, once again, is very pleasant to a hermit!"

"It cannot be more pleasant than arriving at an oasis," returned Gaston.

They had delayed on the threshold to look at the beauty of the evening, and now the priest watched his parishioners come and go. "How can one make companions—" he began; then, checking himself, he said: "Their souls are as sacred and immortal as mine, and God helps me to help them. But in this world it is not immortal souls that we choose for companions; it is kindred tastes, intelligences, and —and so I and my books are growing old together, you see," he added, more lightly. "You will find my volumes as behind the times as myself."

He had fallen into talk more intimate than he wished; and while the guest was uttering something polite about the nobility of missionary work, he placed him in an easy-chair and sought *aguardiente* [4] for his immediate refreshment. Since the year's beginning there had been no guest for him to bring into his rooms, or to sit beside him in the high seats at table, set apart for the *gente fina*. [5]

Such another library was not then in California; and though Gaston Villeré, in leaving Harvard College, had shut *Horace* and *Sophocles* for ever at the earliest instant possible under academic requirements, he knew the Greek and Latin names that he now saw as well as he knew those of *Shakespeare, Dante, Molière,* and *Cervantes*. These were here also; but it could not be precisely said of them, either, that they made a part of the young man's daily reading. As he surveyed the Padre's august shelves, it was with a touch of the histrionic Southern gravity which his Northern education had not wholly schooled out of him that he said:

"I fear I am no scholar, sir. But I know

what writers every gentleman ought to respect." The polished Padre bowed gravely to this compliment.

It was when his eyes caught sight of the music that the young man felt again at ease, and his vivacity returned to him. Leaving his chair, he began enthusiastically to examine the tall piles that filled one side of the room. The volumes lay piled and scattered everywhere, making a pleasant disorder; and, as perfume comes from a flower, memories of singers and chandeliers rose bright from the printed names. *Norma,* [6] *Tancredi,* [7] *Don Pasquale,* [8] *La Vestale,* [9] dim lights in the fashions of to-day, sparkled upon the exploring Gaston, conjuring the radiant halls of Europe before him. *"The Barber of Seville!"* [10] he presently exclaimed. "And I happened to hear it in Seville."

But Seville's name brought over the Padre a new rush of home thoughts. "Is not Andalusia beautiful?" he said. "Did you see it in April, when the flowers come?"

"Yes," said Gaston, among the music. "I was at Cordova then."

"Ah, Cordova!" murmured the Padre.

"Semiramide!" [11] exclaimed Gaston, lighting upon that opera. "That *was* a week! I should like to live it over, every day and night of it!"

"Did you reach Malaga from Marseilles or Gibraltar?" asked the Padre, wistfully.

"From Marseilles. Down from Paris through the Rhone Valley, you know."

"Then you saw Provence! And did you go, perhaps, from Avignon to Nismes by the Pont du Gard? [12] There is a place I have made here —a little, little place—with olive-trees. And now they have grown, and it looks something like that country, if you stand in a particular position. I will take you there to-morrow. I think you will understand what I mean."

"Another resemblance!" said the volatile and happy Gaston. "We both seem to have an eye for them. But, believe me, Padre, I could never stay here planting olives. I should go back and see the original ones—and then I'd hasten on to Paris." And, with a volume of Meyerbeer open in his hand, Gaston hummed: "'Robert, Robert, toi que j'aime.' [13] Why, Padre, I think that your library contains none

[1] a street on the bank of the Seine bordering the Latin quarter
[2] Elisa Rachel, a French tragédienne, 1821-1858
[3] probably Feltre's opera
[4] a strong spirituous liquor
[5] those of higher social rank

[6] an opera by Bellini, an Italian composer, 1801-1835
[7] an opera by Rossini
[8] an opera by Donizetti, an Italian composer, 1797-1848
[9] an opera by Spontini, an Italian composer, 1774-1851
[10] a comic opera by Rossini
[11] an opera by Rossini
[12] all places in southern France, with a climate like that of the California coast
[13] "Robert, Robert, thee whom I love" from Meyerbeer's *Robert the Devil*

of the masses and all of the operas in the world!"

"I will make you a little confession," said Padre Ignacio, "and then you shall give me a little absolution."

"For a penance," said Gaston; "you must play over some of these things to me."

"I suppose I could not permit myself this luxury," began the Padre, pointing to his operas, "and teach these to my choir, if the people had any worldly associations with the music. But I have reasoned that the music cannot do them harm—"

The ringing of a bell here interrupted him. "In fifteen minutes," he said, "our poor meal will be ready for you." The good Padre was not quite sincere when he spoke of a "poor meal." While getting the *aguardiente* for his guest he had given orders, and he knew how well such orders would be carried out. He lived alone, and generally supped simply enough, but not even the ample table at San Fernando could surpass his own on occasions. And this was for him indeed an occasion!

"Your half-breeds will think I am one of themselves," said Gaston, showing his dusty clothes. "I am not fit to be seated with you." But he did not mean this any more than his host had meant his remark about the food. In his pack, which an Indian had brought from his horse, he carried some garments of civilization. And presently, after fresh water and not a little painstaking with brush and scarf, there came back to the Padre a young guest whose elegance and bearing and ease of the great world were to the exiled priest as sweet as was his traveled conversation.

They repaired to the hall and took their seats at the head of the long table. For the Spanish centuries of stately custom lived at Santa Ysabel del Mar, inviolate, feudal, remote.

They were the only persons of quality present; and between themselves and the *gente de razon* [1] a space intervened. Behind the Padre's chair stood an Indian to wait upon him, and another stood behind the chair of Gaston Villeré. Each of these servants wore one single white garment, and offered the many dishes to the *gente fina* and refilled their glasses. At the lower end of the table a general attendant waited upon *mesclados*—the half-breeds. There was meat with spices, and roasted quail, with various cakes and other preparations of grain; also the brown fresh olives and grapes, with several sorts of figs and plums, and preserved fruits, and white and red wine—the

[1] here, those of lower station

white fifty years old. Beneath the quiet shining of candles, fresh-cut flowers leaned from vessels of old Mexican and Spanish make.

There at one end of this feast sat the wild, pastoral, gaudy company, speaking little over their food; and there at the other the pale Padre, questioning his visitor about Rachel. The mere name of a street could bring memories crowding to his lips; and when his guest told him of a new play he was ready with old quotations from the same author. Alfred de Vigny they spoke of, and Victor Hugo, whom the Padre disliked. Long after the *dulce*, or sweet dish, when it was the custom for the *vaqueros* and the rest of the retainers to rise and leave the *gente fina* to themselves, the host sat on in the empty hall, fondly talking to his guest of his bygone Paris and fondly learning of the later Paris that the guest had seen. And thus the two lingered, exchanging their enthusiasms, while the candles waned, and the long-haired Indians stood silent behind the chairs.

"But we must go to my piano," the host exclaimed. For at length they had come to a lusty difference of opinion. The Padre, with ears critically deaf, and with smiling, unconvinced eyes, was shaking his head, while young Gaston sang *Trovatore* at him, and beat upon the table with a fork.

"Come and convert me, then," said Padre Ignacio, and he led the way. "Donizetti I have always admitted. There, at least, is refinement. If the world has taken to this Verdi, with his street-band music—But there, now! Sit down and convert me. Only don't crush my poor little Érard [2] with Verdi's hoofs. I brought it when I came. It is behind the times, too. And, oh, my dear boy, our organ is still worse. So old, so old! To get a proper one I would sacrifice even this piano of mine in a moment—only the tinkling thing is not worth a sou to anybody except its master. But there! Are you quite comfortable?" And having seen to his guest's needs, and placed spirits and cigars and an ash-tray within his reach, the Padre sat himself comfortably in his chair to hear and expose the false doctrine of *Il Trovatore*.

By midnight all of the opera that Gaston could recall had been played and sung twice. The convert sat in his chair no longer, but stood singing by the piano. The potent swing and flow of rhythms, the torrid, copious inspiration of the South, mastered him. "Verdi has grown," he cried. "Verdi is become a giant." And he swayed to the beat of the melodies, and

[2] Just before 1800 the elder Érard began piano making in Paris.

waved an enthusiastic arm. He demanded every note. Why did not Gaston remember it all? But if the barkentine would arrive and bring the whole music, then they would have it right! And he made Gaston teach him what words he knew. " 'Non ti scordar,' he sang— " 'non ti scordar di mi.' [1] That is genius. But one sees how the world moves when one is out of it. 'A nostri monti ritorneremo'; [2] home to our mountains. Ah, yes, there is genius again." And the exile sighed and his spirit voyaged to distant places, while Gaston continued brilliantly with the music of the final scene.

Then the host remembered his guest. "I am ashamed of my selfishness," he said. "It is already to-morrow."

"I have sat later in less good company," answered the pleasant Gaston. "And I shall sleep all the sounder for making a convert."

"You have dispensed roadside alms," said the Padre, smiling. "And that should win excellent dreams."

Thus, with courtesies more elaborate than the world has time for at the present day, they bade each other good-night and parted, bearing their late candles along the quiet halls of the mission. To young Gaston in his bed easy sleep came without waiting, and no dreams at all. Outside his open window was the quiet, serene darkness, where the stars shone clear, and tranquil perfumes hung in the cloisters. But while the guest lay sleeping all night in unchanged position like a child, up and down between the oleanders went Padre Ignacio, walking until dawn. Temptation indeed had come over the hill and entered the cloisters.

III

Day showed the ocean's surface no longer glassy, but lying like a mirror breathed upon; and there between the short headlands came a sail, gray and plain against the flat water. The priest watched through his glasses, and saw the gradual sun grow strong upon the canvas of the barkentine. The message from his world was at hand, yet to-day he scarcely cared so much. Sitting in his garden yesterday, he could never have imagined such a change. But his heart did not hail the barkentine as usual. Books, music, pale paper, and print—this was all that was coming to him, and some of its savor had gone; for the siren voice of Life had been speaking with him face to face, and

[1] "Forget me not," from *Il Trovatore*
[2] "Home to our mountains, Oh, let us return," from *Il Trovatore*

in his spirit, deep down, the love of the world was restlessly answering it. Young Gaston showed more eagerness than the Padre over this arrival of the vessel that might be bringing *Trovatore* in the nick of time. Now he would have the chance, before he took his leave, to help rehearse the new music with the choir. He would be a missionary, too: a perfectly new experience.

"And you still forgive Verdi the sins of his youth?" he said to his host. "I wonder if you could forgive mine?"

"Verdi has left his behind him," retorted the Padre.

"But I am only twenty-five!" exclaimed Gaston, pathetically.

"Ah, don't go away soon!" pleaded the exile. It was the first unconcealed complaint that had escaped him, and he felt instant shame.

But Gaston was too much elated with the enjoyment of each new day to comprehend the Padre's soul. The shafts of another's pain might hardly pierce the bright armor of his gaiety. He mistook the priest's entreaty, for anxiety about his own happy spirit.

"Stay here under your care?" he asked. "It would do me no good, Padre. Temptation sticks closer to me than a brother!" and he gave that laugh of his which had disarmed severer judges than his host. "By next week I should have introduced some sin or other into your beautiful Garden of Ignorance here. It will be much safer for your flock if I go and join the other serpents at San Francisco."

Soon after breakfast the Padre had his two mules saddled, and he and his guest set forth down the hills together to the shore. And, beneath the spell and confidence of pleasant, slow riding and the loveliness of everything, the young man talked freely of himself.

"And seriously," said he, "if I missed nothing else at Santa Ysabel, I should long for—how shall I say it?—for insecurity, for danger, and of all kinds—not merely danger to the body. Within these walls, beneath these sacred bells, you live too safe for a man like me."

"Too safe!" These echoed words upon the lips of the pale Padre were a whisper too light, too deep, for Gaston's heedless ear.

"Why," the young man pursued in a spirit that was but half levity, "though I yield often to temptation, at times I have resisted it, and here I should miss the very chance to resist. Your garden could never be Eden for me, because temptation is absent from it."

"Absent!" Still lighter, still deeper, was this whisper that the Padre breathed.

"I must find life!" exclaimed Gaston. "And my fortune at the mines, I hope. I am not a bad fellow, Father. You can easily guess all the things I do. I have never, to my knowledge, harmed any one. I didn't even try to kill my adversary in an affair of honor. I gave him a mere flesh-wound, and by this time he must be quite recovered. He was my friend. But as he came between me—"

Gaston stopped, and the Padre, looking keenly at him, saw the violence that he had noticed in church pass like a flame over the young man's handsome face.

"There's nothing dishonorable," said Gaston, answering the priest's look. And then, because this look made him not quite at his ease: "Perhaps a priest might feel obliged to say it was dishonorable. She and her father were— a man owes no fidelity before he is—but you might say that had been dishonorable."

"I have not said so, my son."

"I did what every gentleman would do," insisted Gaston.

"And that is often wrong!" said the Padre, gently and gravely. "But I'm not your confessor."

"No," said Gaston, looking down. "And it is all over. It will not begin again. Since leaving New Orleans I have traveled an innocent journey straight to you. And when I make my fortune I shall be in a position to return and—"

"Claim the pressed flower?" suggested the Padre. He did not smile.

"Ah, you remember how those things are!" said Gaston; and he laughed and blushed.

"Yes," said the Padre, looking at the anchored barkentine, "I remember how those things are."

For a while the vessel and its cargo and the landed men and various business and conversations occupied them. But the freight for the mission once seen to, there was not much else to detain them.

The barkentine was only a coaster like many others which had begun to fill the sea a little more of late years, and presently host and guest were riding homeward. Side by side they rode, companions to the eye, but wide apart in mood; within the turbulent young figure of Gaston dwelt a spirit that could not be more at ease, while revolt was steadily kindling beneath the schooled and placid mask of the Padre.

Yet still the strangeness of his situation in such a remote, resourceless place came back as a marvel into the young man's lively mind.

Twenty years in prison, he thought, and hardly aware of it! And he glanced at the silent priest. A man so evidently fond of music, of theaters, of the world, to whom pressed flowers had meant something once—and now contented to bleach upon these wastes! Not even desirous of a brief holiday, but finding an old organ and some old operas enough recreation! "It is his age, I suppose," thought Gaston. And then the notion of himself when he should be sixty occurred to him, and he spoke.

"Do you know, I do not believe," said he, "that I should ever reach such contentment as yours."

"Perhaps you will," said Padre Ignacio, in a low voice.

"Never!" declared the youth. "It comes only to the few, I am sure."

"Yes. Only to the few," murmured the Padre.

"I am certain that it must be a great possession," Gaston continued; "and yet—and yet —dear me! life is a splendid thing!"

"There are several ways to live it," said the Padre.

"Only one for me!" cried Gaston. "Action, men, women, things—to be there, to be known, to play a part, to sit in the front seats; to have people tell one another, 'There goes Gaston Villeré,' and to deserve one's prominence. Why, if I were Padre of Santa Ysabel del Mar for twenty years—no! for one year—do you know what I should have done? Some day it would have been too much for me. I should have left these savages to a pastor nearer their own level, and I should have ridden down this cañon upon my mule, and stepped on board the barkentine, and gone back to my proper sphere. You will understand, sir, that I am far from venturing to make any personal comment. I am only thinking what a world of difference lies between natures that can feel as alike as we do upon so many subjects. Why, not since leaving New Orleans have I met any one with whom I could talk, except of the weather and the brute interests common to us all. That such a one as you should be here is like a dream."

"But it is not a dream," said the Padre.

"And, sir—pardon me if I do say this—are you not wasted at Santa Ysabel del Mar? I have seen the priests at the other missions. They are—the sort of good men that I expected. But are you needed to save such souls as these?"

"There is no aristocracy of souls," said the Padre, again whispering.

"But the body and the mind!" cried Gaston. "My God, are they nothing? Do you think that they are given to us for nothing but a trap? You cannot teach such a doctrine with your library there. And how about all the cultivated men and women away from whose quickening society the brightest of us grow numb? You have held out. But will it be for long? Are you never to save any souls of your own kind? Are not twenty years of *mesclados* enough? No, no!" finished young Gaston, hot with his unforeseen eloquence; " I should ride down some morning and take the barkentine."

Padre Ignacio was silent for a space.

"I have not offended you?" asked the young man.

"No. Anything but that. You are surprised that I should—choose—to stay here. Perhaps you may have wondered how I came to be here at all?"

"I had not intended any impertinent—"

"Oh no. Put such an idea out of your head, my son. You may remember that I was going to make you a confession about my operas. Let us sit down in this shade."

So they picketed the mules near the stream and sat down.

IV

"You have seen," began Padre Ignacio, "what sort of a man I—was once. Indeed, it seems very strange to myself that you should have been here not twenty-four hours yet, and know so much of me. For there has come no one else at all"—the Padre paused a moment and mastered the unsteadiness that he had felt approaching in his voice—"there has been no one else to whom I have talked so freely. In my early days I had no thought of being a priest. My parents destined me for a diplomatic career. There was plenty of money and—and all the rest of it; for by inheritance came to me the acquaintance of many people whose names you would be likely to have heard of. Cities, people of fashion, artists—the whole of it was my element and my choice; and by-and-by I married, not only where it was desirable, but where I loved. Then for the first time Death laid his staff upon my enchantment, and I understood many things that had been only words to me hitherto. To have been a husband for a year, and a father for a moment, and in that moment to lose all—this unblinded me. Looking back, it seemed to me that I had never done anything except for myself all my days. I left the world. In due time I became a priest and lived in my own country. But my worldly experience and my secular education had given to my opinions a turn too liberal for the place where my work was laid. I was soon advised concerning this by those in authority over me. And since they could not change me and I could not change them, yet wished to work and to teach, the New World was suggested, and I volunteered to give the rest of my life to missions. It was soon found that some one was needed here, and for this little place I sailed, and to these humble people I have dedicated my service. They are pastoral creatures of the soil. Their vineyard and cattle days are apt to be like the sun and storm around them—strong alike in their evil and in their good. All their years they live as children—children with men's passions given to them like deadly weapons, unable to measure the harm their impulses may bring. Hence, even in their crimes, their hearts will generally open soon to the one great key of love, while civilization makes locks which that key cannot always fit at the first turn. And coming to know this," said Padre Ignacio, fixing his eyes steadily upon Gaston, "you will understand how great a privilege it is to help such people, and how the sense of something accomplished—under God—should bring Contentment with Renunciation."

"Yes," said Gaston Villeré. Then, thinking of himself, "I can understand it in a man like you."

"Do not speak of me at all!" exclaimed the Padre, almost passionately. "But pray Heaven that you may find the thing yourself some day —Contentment with Renunciation—and never let it go."

"Amen!" said Gaston, strangely moved.

"That is the whole of my story," the priest continued, with no more of the recent stress in his voice. "And now I have talked to you about myself quite enough. But you must have my confession." He had now resumed entirely his half-playful tone. "I was just a little mistaken, you see—too self-reliant, perhaps—when I supposed, in my first missionary ardor, that I could get on without any remembrance of the world at all. I found that I could not. And so I have taught the old operas to my choir—such parts of them as are within our compass and suitable for worship. And certain of my friends still alive at home are good enough to remember this taste of mine and to send me each year some of the new music that I should never hear of otherwise. Then we study these things also. And although our organ is a miserable affair, Felipe manages very cleverly to make it do. And while the voices are singing these operas, especially the old ones, what harm is there if sometimes the priest is thinking of something else? So there's my confession! And now, whether *Trovatore* is come or not, I shall not allow you to leave us until you have taught all you know of it to Felipe."

The new opera, however, had duly arrived. And as he turned its pages Padre Ignacio was quick to seize at once upon the music that could be taken into his church. Some of it was ready fitted. By that afternoon Felipe and his choir could have rendered "Ah! se l'error t'ingombra"[1] without slip or falter.

Those were strange rehearsals of *Il Trovatore* upon this California shore. For the Padre looked to Gaston to say when they went too fast or too slow, and to correct their emphasis. And since it was hot, the little Érard piano was carried each day out into the mission garden. There, in the cloisters among the jessamine, the orange blossoms, the oleanders, in the presence of the round yellow hills and the blue triangle of sea, the *Miserere*[2] was slowly learned. The Mexicans and Indians gathered, swarthy and black-haired, around the tinkling instrument that Felipe played; and presiding over them were young Gaston and the pale Padre, walking up and down the paths, beating time or singing now one part and now another. And so it was that the wild cattle on the uplands would hear *Trovatore* hummed by a passing *vaquero*, while the same melody was filling the streets of the far-off world.

For three days Gaston Villeré remained at Santa Ysabel del Mar; and though not a word of restlessness came from him, his host could read San Francisco and the gold-mines in his countenance. No, the young man could not have stayed here for twenty years! And the Padre forbore urging his guest to extend his visit.

"But the world is small," the guest declared at parting. "Some day it will not be able to spare you any longer. And then we are sure to meet. But you shall hear from me soon, at any rate."

Again, as upon the first evening, the two exchanged a few courtesies, more graceful and particular than we, who have not time, and fight no duels, find worth a man's while at the present day. For duels are gone, which is a very good thing, and with them a certain careful politeness, which is a pity; but that is the way in the eternal profit and loss. So young

Gaston rode northward out of the mission, back to the world and his fortune; and the Padre stood watching the dust after the rider had passed from sight. Then he went into his room with a drawn face. But appearances at least had been kept up to the end; the youth would never know of the elder man's unrest.

V

Temptation had arrived with Gaston, but was destined to make a longer stay at Santa Ysabel del Mar. Yet it was perhaps a week before the priest knew this guest was come to abide with him. The guest could be discreet, could withdraw, was not at first importunate.

Sail away on the barkentine? A wild notion, to be sure! although fit enough to enter the brain of such a young scapegrace. The Padre shook his head and smiled affectionately when he thought of Gaston Villeré. The youth's handsome, reckless countenance would shine out, smiling, in his memory, and he repeated Auber's old remark, "Is it the good Lord, or is it merely the devil, that always makes me have a weakness for rascals?"

Sail away on the barkentine! Imagine taking leave of the people here—of Felipe! In what words should he tell the boy to go on industriously with his music? No, this was not imaginable! The mere parting alone would make it for ever impossible to think of such a thing. "And then," he said to himself each new morning, when he looked out at the ocean, " I have given to them my life. One does not take back a gift."

Pictures of his departure began to shine and melt in his drifting fancy. He saw himself explaining to Felipe that now his presence was wanted elsewhere; that there would come a successor to take care of Santa Ysabel—a younger man, more useful, and able to visit sick people at a distance. "For I am old now. I should not be long here in any case." He stopped and pressed his hands together; he had caught his Temptation in the very act. Now he sat staring at his Temptation's face, close to him, while there in the triangle two ships went sailing by.

One morning Felipe told him that the barkentine was here on its return voyage south. "Indeed?" said the Padre, coldly. "The things are ready to go, I think." For the vessel called for mail and certain boxes that the mission sent away. Felipe left the room in wonder at the Padre's manner. But the priest was laughing secretly to see how little it was to him where the barkentine was, or whether it should be coming or going. But in the afternoon, at his piano, he found himself saying, "Other ships call here, at any rate." And then for the first time he prayed to be delivered from his thoughts. Yet presently he left his seat and looked out of the window for a sight of the barkentine; but it was gone.

The season of the wine-making passed, and the preserving of all the fruits that the mission fields grew. Lotions and medicines were distilled from garden herbs. Perfume was manufactured from the petals of flowers and certain spices, and presents of it despatched to San Fernando and Ventura, and to friends at other places; for the Padre had a special receipt. As the time ran on, two or three visitors passed a night with him; and presently there was a word at various missions that Padre Ignacio had begun to show his years. At Santa Ysabel del Mar they whispered, "The Padre is not well." Yet he rode a great deal over the hills by himself, and down the cañon very often, stopping where he had sat with Gaston, to sit alone and look up and down, now at the hills above, and now at the ocean below. Among his parishioners he had certain troubles to soothe, certain wounds to heal; a home from which he was able to drive jealousy; a girl whom he bade her lover set right. But all said, "The Padre is unwell." And Felipe told them that the music seemed nothing to him any more; he never asked for his *Dixit Dominus* nowadays. Then for a short time he was really in bed, feverish with the two voices that spoke to him without ceasing. "You have given your life," said one voice. "And, therefore," said the other, "have earned the right to go home and die." "You are winning better rewards in the service of God," said the first voice. "God can be better served in other places," answered the second. As he lay listening he saw Seville again, and the trees of Aranhal, where he had been born. The wind was blowing through them, and in their branches he could hear the nightingales. "Empty! Empty!" he said, aloud. And he lay for two days and nights hearing the wind and the nightingales in the far trees of Aranhal. But Felipe, watching, only heard the Padre crying through the hours, "Empty! Empty!"

Then the wind in the trees died down, and the Padre could get out of bed, and soon be in the garden. But the voices within him still talked all the while as he sat watching the sails when they passed between the headlands. Their words, falling for ever the same way, beat his spirit sore, like blows upon flesh

already bruised. If he could only change what they said, he would rest.

"Has the Padre any mail for Santa Barbara?" asked Felipe. "The ship bound southward should be here tomorrow."

"I will attend to it," said the priest, not moving. And Felipe stole away.

At Felipe's words the voices had stopped as a clock finishes striking. Silence, strained like expectation, filled the Padre's soul. But in place of the voices came old sights of home again, the waving trees at Aranhal; then it would be Rachel for a moment, declaiming tragedy while a houseful of faces that he knew by name watched her; and through all the panorama rang the pleasant laugh of Gaston. For a while in the evening the Padre sat at his Érard playing *Trovatore*. Later, in his sleepless bed he lay, saying now and then: "To die at home! Surely I may be granted at least this." And he listened for the inner voices. But they were not speaking any more, and the black hole of silence grew more dreadful to him than their arguments. Then the dawn came in at his window, and he lay watching its gray grow warm into color, until suddenly he sprang from his bed and looked at the sea. Blue it lay, sapphire-hued and dancing with points of gold, lovely and luring as a charm; and over its triangle the south-bound ship was approaching. People were on board who in a few weeks would be sailing the Atlantic, while he would stand here looking out of this same window. "Merciful God!" he cried, sinking on his knees. "Heavenly Father, Thou seest this evil in my heart! Thou knowest that my weak hand cannot pluck it out! My strength is breaking, and still Thou makest my burden heavier than I can bear." He stopped, breathless and trembling. The same visions were flitting across his closed eyes; the same silence gaped like a dry crater in his soul. "There is no help in earth or heaven," he said, very quietly; and he dressed himself.

VI

It was still so early that few of the Indians were stirring, and one of these saddled the Padre's mule. Felipe was not yet awake, and for a moment it came in the priest's mind to open the boy's door softly, look at him once more, and come away. But this he did not, nor even take a farewell glance at the church and organ. He bade nothing farewell, but, turning his back upon his room and his garden, rode down the cañon.

The vessel lay at anchor, and some one had landed from her and was talking with other men on the shore. Seeing the priest slowly coming, this stranger approached to meet him.

"You are connected with the mission here?" he inquired.

"I—am."

"Perhaps it is with you that Gaston Villeré stopped?"

"The young man from New Orleans? Yes. I am Padre Ignacio."

"Then you'll save me a journey. I promised him to deliver these into your own hands."

The stranger gave them to him.

"A bag of gold-dust," he explained, "and a letter. I wrote it at his dictation while he was dying. He lived hardly an hour afterward."

The stranger bowed his head at the stricken cry which his news elicited from the priest, who, after a few moments' vain effort to speak, opened the letter and read:

My dear Friend,—It is through no man's fault but mine that I have come to this. I have had plenty of luck, and lately have been counting the days until I should return home. But last night heavy news from New Orleans reached me, and I tore the pressed flower to pieces. Under the first smart and humiliation of broken faith I was rendered desperate, and picked a needless quarrel. Thank God, it is I who have the punishment. My dear friend, as I lie here, leaving a world that no man ever loved more, I have come to understand you. For you and your mission have been much in my thoughts. It is strange how good can be done, not at the time when it is intended, but afterward; and you have done this good to me. I say over your words, "Contentment with Renunciation," and believe that at this last hour I have gained something like what you would wish me to feel. For I do not think that I desire it otherwise now. My life would never have been of service, I am afraid. You are the last person in this world who has spoken serious words to me, and I want you to know that now at length I value the peace of Santa Ysabel as I could never have done but for seeing your wisdom and goodness. You spoke of a new organ for your church. Take the gold-dust that will reach you with this, and do what you will with it. Let me at least in dying have helped some one. And since there is no aristocracy in souls—you said that to me; do you remember?—perhaps you will say a mass for this departing soul of mine. I only wish, since my body must go under ground in

a strange country, that it might have been at Santa Ysabel del Mar, where your feet would often pass.

" 'At Santa Ysabel del Mar, where your feet would often pass.' " The priest repeated this final sentence aloud, without being aware of it.

"Those are the last words he ever spoke," said the stranger, "except bidding me good-by."

"You know him well, then?"

"No; not until after he was hurt. I'm the man he quarreled with."

The priest looked at the ship that would sail onward this afternoon.

Then a smile of great beauty passed over his face, and he addressed the stranger. "I thank you. You will never know what you have done for me."

"It is nothing," answered the stranger, awkwardly. "He told me you set great store on a new organ."

Padre Ignacio turned away from the ship and rode back through the gorge. When he had reached the shady place where once he had sat with Gaston Villeré, he dismounted and again sat there, alone by the stream, for many hours. Long rides and outings had been lately so much his custom that no one thought twice of his absence; and when he returned to the mission in the afternoon, the Indian took his mule, and he went to his seat in the garden. But it was with another look that he watched the sea; and presently the sail moved across the blue triangle, and soon it had rounded the headland.

With it departed Temptation for ever.

Gaston's first coming was in the Padre's mind; and, as the vespers bell began to ring in the cloistered silence, a fragment of Auber's plaintive tune passed like a sigh across his memory:

For the repose of Gaston's young, world-loving spirit, they sang all that he had taught them of *Il Trovatore*.

After this day, Felipe and all those who knew and loved the Padre best, saw serenity had returned to his features; but for some reason they began to watch those features with more care.

"Still," they said, "he is not old." And as the months went by they would repeat: "We shall have him yet for many years."

Thus the season rolled round, bringing the time for the expected messages from the world. Padre Ignacio was wont to sit in his garden, waiting for the ship, as of old.

"As of old," they said, cheerfully, who saw him. But Renunciation with Contentment they could not see; it was deep down in his silent and thankful heart.

One day Felipe went to call him from his garden seat, wondering why the ringing of the bell had not brought him to vespers. Breviary in lap, and hands folded upon it, the Padre sat among his flowers, looking at the sea. Out there amid the sapphire-blue, tranquil and white, gleamed the sails of the barkentine. It had brought him a new message, not from this world; and Padre Ignacio was slowly borne in from the garden, while the mission-bell tolled for the passing of a human soul.

1900

WILLIAM VAUGHAN MOODY
1869-1910

Although Moody was born in Indiana and spent the greater part of his active life in the Middle West, there is little in his poetry that reflects the spirit of that region. He attended a preparatory academy on the Hudson, was graduated from Harvard, and spent the brief remainder of his career as a teacher of English literature at Harvard and the University of Chicago. His vacations he usually spent on extended walking and bicycling tours in Europe, and he made one journey by wagon through Arizona. A notable career in American literature was cut short by his early death.

Moody's work reflects inner experience and culture more than contact with outer life; or, when based upon actual experience, it shows that fusion of fact with invention and reflection that constitutes the permanent in literature. There is a force in the sweep of his imagination that belongs to the great poets. His poetry is notable for its seriousness, its concern with the eternal and unsolvable questions of life and destiny, and also for its recognition of the graver social problems of today; for he feels that science has forced upon man a new assessment of himself. His lyrics are noteworthy for their manly sincerity, their strength, their tenderness, and their fineness of form. In seriousness, Moody stands with the New England poets of the nineteenth century, but goes beyond them in the variety and the breadth of his interests. He is, in fact, a transition poet, true to the past in form and in high purpose, but questioning, forward-looking. In addition to his poems, Moody produced plays, the most successful being *The Great Divide*, 1906.

Criticism: Boynton, *American Poetry*; K. W. Baker, "A Poet of the Lean Years," *Forum* 68: 843-50; W. Chislett, Jr., "William Vaughan Moody

and William Blake," *Dial* 59:142; H. Hagedorn, "William Vaughan Moody," *Ind.* 74:314-6; C. M. Lewis, "William Vaughan Moody," *Yale R.* ns 2:688-703; May Sinclair, "Three American Poets of Today," *Atlan.* 98:325-35.

Biography and criticism: E. H. Lewis, *William Vaughan Moody*, 1914; D. G. Mason, ed. *Some Letters of William Vaughan Moody*, 1913.

THE MENAGERIE [1]

Thank God my brain is not inclined to cut
Such capers every day! I'm just about
Mellow, but then—There goes the tent-flap shut.
Rain's in the wind. I thought so: every snout
Was twitching when the keeper turned me out.

That screaming parrot makes my blood run cold.
Gabriel's trump! the big bull elephant
Squeals "Rain!" to the parched herd. The monkeys scold,
And jabber that it's rain water they want.
(It makes me sick to see a monkey pant.)   10

I'll foot it home, to try and make believe
I'm sober. After this I stick to beer,
And drop the circus when the sane folks leave.
A man's a fool to look at things too near:
They look back, and begin to cut up queer.

Beasts do, at any rate; especially
Wild devils caged. They have the coolest way
Of being something else than what you see;
You pass a sleek young zebra nosing hay,
A nylghau looking bored and distingué,—   20

And think you've seen a donkey and a bird.
Not on your life! Just glance back, if you dare.
The zebra chews, the nylghau hasn't stirred;
But something's happened, Heaven knows what or where
To freeze your scalp and pompadour your hair.

I'm not precisely an aeolian lute
Hung in the wandering winds of sentiment,
But drown me if the ugliest, meanest brute
Grunting and fretting in that sultry tent
Didn't just floor me with embarrassment!   30

'Twas like a thunder-clap from out the clear,—
One minute they were circus beasts, some grand,
Some ugly, some amusing, and some queer;
Rival attractions to the hobo band,
The flying jenny, and the peanut stand.

Next minute they were old hearth-mates of
   mine!
Lost people, eyeing me with such a stare!
Patient, satiric, devilish, divine;
A gaze of hopeless envy, squalid care,
Hatred, and thwarted love, and dim despair. 40

Within my blood my ancient kindred spoke,—
Grotesque and monstrous voices, heard afar
Down ocean waves when behemoth awoke,
Or through fern forests roared the plesiosaur
Locked with the giant-bat in ghastly war.

And suddenly, as in a flash of light,
I saw great Nature working out her plan;
Through all her shapes from mastodon to mite
Forever groping, testing, passing on
To find at last the shape and soul of Man. 50

Till in the fullness of accomplished time,
Comes brother Forepaugh, [1] upon business bent,
Tracks her through frozen and through torrid
   clime,
And shows us, neatly labeled in a tent,
The stages of her huge experiment;

Blabbing aloud her shy and reticent hours;
Dragging to light her blinking, slothful moods;
Publishing fretful seasons when her powers
Worked wild and sullen in her solitudes,
Or when her mordant laughter shook the
   woods. 60

Here, round about me, were her vagrant births;
Sick dreams she had, fierce projects she es-
   sayed;
Her qualms, her fiery prides, her crazy mirths;
The troublings of her spirit as she strayed,
Cringed, gloated, mocked, was lordly, was
   afraid,

On that long road she went to seek mankind;
Here were the darkling coverts that she beat
To find the Hider she was sent to find;
Here the distracted footprints of her feet
Whereby her soul's Desire she came to greet. 70

But why should they, her botch-work, turn
   about
And stare disdain at me, her finished job?
Why was the place one vast suspended shout
Of laughter? Why did all the daylight throb
With soundless guffaw and dumb-stricken sob?

Helpless I stood among those awful cages;
The beasts were walking loose, and I was
   bagged!

[1] a famous circus owner

I, I, last product of the toiling ages,
Goal of heroic feet that never lagged,—
A little man in trousers, slightly jagged. 80

Deliver me from such another jury!
The Judgment-day will be a picnic to't.
Their satire was more dreadful than their fury,
And worst of all was just a kind of brute
Disgust, and giving up, and sinking mute.

Survival of the fittest, adaptation,
And all their other evolution terms,
Seem to omit one small consideration,
To wit, that tumblebugs and angle-worms
Have souls: there's soul in everything that
   squirms. 90

And souls are restless, plagued, impatient
   things,
All dream and unaccountable desire;
Crawling, but pestered with the thought of
   wings;
Spreading through every inch of earth's old
   mire,
Mystical hanker after something higher.

Wishes *are* horses, as I understand.
I guess a wistful polyp that has strokes
Of feeling faint to gallivant on land
Will come to be a scandal to his folks;
Legs he will sprout, in spite of threats and
   jokes. 100

And at the core of every life that crawls,
Or runs or flies or swims or vegetates—
Churning the mammoth's heart-blood, in the
   galls
Of shark and tiger planting gorgeous hates,
Lighting the love of eagles for their mates;

Yes, in the dim brain of the jellied fish
That is and is not living—moved and stirred
From the beginning a mysterious wish,
A vision, a command, a fatal Word:
The name of Man was uttered, and they
   heard. 110

Upward along the aeons of old war
They sought him: wing and shank-bone, claw
   and bill
Were fashioned and rejected; wide and far
They roamed the twilight jungles of their will;
But still they sought him, and desired him still.

Man they desired, but mind you, Perfect Man,
The radiant and the loving, yet to be!
I hardly wonder, when they came to scan

The upshot of their strenuosity,
They gazed with fixed emotions upon *me*.   120

Well, my advice to you is, Face the creatures,
Or spot them sideways with your weather eye,
Just to keep tab on their expansive features;
It isn't pleasant when you're stepping high
To catch a giraffe smiling on the sly.

If nature made you graceful, don't get gay
Back-to before a hippopotamus;
If meek and godly, find some place to play
Besides right where three mad hyenas fuss:
You may hear language that we won't dis-
  cuss.   130

If you're a sweet thing in a flower-bed hat,
Or her best fellow with your tie tucked in,
Don't squander love's bright springtime gird-
  ing at
An old chimpanzee with an Irish chin:
There may be hidden meaning in his grin.
1900

GOOD FRIDAY NIGHT [1]

At last the bird that sang so long
In twilight circles, hushed his song:
Above the ancient square
The stars came here and there.

Good Friday night! Some hearts were bowed,
But some amid the waiting crowd
Because of too much youth
Felt not that mystic ruth;

And of these hearts my heart was one:
Nor when beneath the arch of stone   10
With dirge and candle flame
The cross of passion came,

Did my glad spirit feel reproof,
Though on the awful tree aloof,
Unspiritual, dead,
Drooped the ensanguined Head.

To one who stood where myrtles made
A little space of deeper shade
(As if I could half descry,
A stranger, even as I),   20

I said, "These youths who bear along
The symbols of their Savior's wrong,
The spear, the garment torn,
The flaggel, [2] and the thorn,—

"Why do they make this mummery?
Would not a brave man gladly die
For a much smaller thing
Than to be Christ and King?"

He answered nothing, and I turned.
Throned in its hundred candles burned   30
The jeweled eidolon [3]
Of her who bore the Son.

The crowd was prostrate; still, I felt
No shame until the stranger knelt;
Then not to kneel, almost
Seemed like a vulgar boast.

I knelt. The doll-face, waxen white,
Flowered out a living dimness; bright
Dawned the dear mortal grace
Of my own mother's face.   40

When we were risen up, the street
Was vacant; all the air hung sweet
With lemon-flowers; and soon
The sky would hold the moon.

More silently than new-found friends
To whom much silence makes amends
For the much babble vain
While yet their lives were twain,

We walked along the odorous hill.
The light was little yet; his will   50
I could not see to trace
Upon his form or face.

So when aloft the gold moon broke,
I cried, heart-stung. As one who woke
He turned unto my cries
The anguish of his eyes.

"Friend! Master!" I cried falteringly,
"Thou seest the thing they make of thee.
Oh, by the light divine
My mother shares with thine,   60

"I beg that I may lay my head
Upon thy shoulder and be fed
With thoughts of brotherhood!"
So through the odorous wood,

More silently than friends new-found
We walked. At first meadow bound
His figure ashen-stoled
Sank in the moon's broad gold.
1897

[2] scourge

[3] image

(WILLIAM) BLISS CARMAN
1861-1929

Though born in Fredericton, New Brunswick, Carman ranks as an American poet by his descent from old Connecticut stock and by his residence in the United States since 1889. He was educated at the University of New Brunswick, at the University of Edinburgh, and at Harvard. He studied law, practiced engineering, taught school, edited *The Independent* and *Chap Book.* He produced a number of volumes of verse with a wide range of subjects. The first, *Low Tide at Grand Pré,* 1893, was inspired by the very picturesque "Evangeline" country; three volumes of *Songs from Vagabondia,* 1894, 1896, 1900, in which he collaborated with Richard Hovey, contain some of his best poems, songs of the "open road." Typically, Carman's material lies away from the beaten track of poetry followed when he began to write, and his style has the carefree swing of outdoor song; his verse is robust, full-throated, cheering. He is sometimes thought of with Moody as a transitional poet. He is free from the conventions of the nineteenth century, and free also from the iconoclastic, pessimistic attitude taken at times by poets of the twentieth century.

Biography and criticism: Odell Shepard, *Bliss Carman,* 1924; Rittenhouse; Untermeyer; R. H. Hathaway, "Bliss Carman: An Appreciation," *Canad. M.* 56:521-36; R. Duffy, "When They Were Twenty-One," *Bookm.* 38:521-4, recollections of Carman and Hovey.

A VAGABOND SONG [1]

There is something in the autumn that is native
    to my blood—
Touch of manner, hint of mood;
And my heart is like a rhyme,
With the yellow and the purple and the crimson
    keeping time.

The scarlet of the maples can shake me like a
    cry
Of bugles going by.
And my lonely spirit thrills
To see the frosty asters like a smoke upon the
    hills.

There is something in October sets the gypsy
    blood astir;
We must rise and follow her,   10
When from every hill of flame
She calls and calls each vagabond by name.
                1896

MOMENT MUSICALE [1]

The round moon hangs above the rim
  Of silent and blue-shadowed trees,

And all the earth is vague and dim
  In its blue veil of mysteries.

On such a night one must believe
  The Golden Age returns again
With lyric beauty, to retrieve
  The world from dreariness and pain.

And down the wooded aisles, behold
  What dancers through the dusk appear!   10
Piping their rapture as of old,
  They bring immortal freedom near.

A moment on the brink of night
  They tread their transport in the dew,
And to the rhythm of their delight,
  Behold, all things are made anew!

THE JOYS OF THE ROAD [1]

Now the joys of the road are chiefly these:
A crimson touch on the hard-wood trees;

A vagrant's morning wide and blue,
In early fall, when the wind walks, too;

A shadowy highway cool and brown
Alluring up and enticing down

From rippled water to dappled swamp,
From purple glory to scarlet pomp;

The outward eye, the quiet will,
And the striding heart from hill to hill;   10

The tempter apple over the fence;
The cobweb bloom on the yellow quince;

The palish asters along the wood,—
A lyric touch of the solitude;

An open hand, an easy shoe,
And a hope to make the day go through,—

Another to sleep with, and a third
To wake me up at the voice of a bird;

The resonant far-listening morn,
And the hoarse whisper of the corn;   20

The crickets mourning their comrades lost,
In the night's retreat from the gathering frost;

(Or is it their slogan, plaintive and shrill,
As they beat on their corselets, valiant still?)

[1] Copyright. Used by permission of Messrs. Dodd, Mead and Company, Inc.

A hunger fit for the kings of the sea,
And a loaf of bread for Dickon [1] and me;

A thirst like that of the Thirsty Sword,
And a jug of cider on the board;

An idle noon, a bubbling spring,
The sea in the pine-tops murmuring.   30

A scrap of gossip at the ferry;
A comrade neither glum nor merry,

Asking nothing, revealing naught,
But minting his words from a fund of thought,

A keeper of silence eloquent,
Needy, yet royally well-content,

Of the mettled breed, yet abhorring strife,
And full of the mellow juice of life,

A taster of wine, with an eye for a maid,
Never too bold, and never afraid,   40

Never heart-whole, never heart-sick,
(These are the things I worship in Dick),

No fidget and no reformer, just
A calm observer of ought and must,

A lover of books, but a reader of man,
No cynic and no charlatan,

Who never defers and never demands,
But, smiling, takes the world in his hands,—

Seeing it good as when God first saw
And gave it the weight of his will for law.   50

And O the joy that is never won,
But follows and follows the journeying sun,

By marsh and tide, by meadow and stream,
A will-o'-the-wind, a light-o'-dream,

Delusion afar, delight anear,
From morrow to morrow, from year to year,

A jack-o'-lantern, a fairy fire,
A dare, a bliss, and a desire!

The racy smell of the forest loam,
When the stealthy, sad-heart leaves go home;   60

(O leaves, O leaves, I am one with you,
Of the mould and the sun and the wind and the
     dew!)

[1] probably Richard Hovey

The broad gold wake of the afternoon;
The silent fleck of the cold new moon;

The sound of the hollow sea's release
From stormy tumult to starry peace.

With only another league to wend;
And two brown arms at the journey's end!

These are the joys of the open road—
For him who travels without a load.   70

RICHARD HOVEY 1864-1900

Though Hovey was born at Normal, Illinois,
and much of the spirit of the West appears in his
poems, he spent the greater part of his life in the
East. He lived for a while in Washington, D.C.;
after graduating from Dartmouth, he attended the
General Theological Seminary in New York City,
and became lay assistant in the Church of St. Mary
the Virgin. Shortly after, however, he took literature as his life work, and was journalist, dramatist,
and lecturer in English literature at Barnard College. For several years he lived abroad, becoming
familiar with the work of modern French poets
and translating some of the work of the Belgian
poet, Maeterlinck. Hovey is best known for *Songs
from Vagabondia,* 1894, 1896, 1900, in which he
collaborated with Bliss Carman. Unless the authors had designated which of the poems belonged
to each, it would have been difficult to separate the
work of the two in these books. The poems are
carefree and buoyant, reflecting the joy of the spirit
in a wholesome, robust contact with nature along
the open road. In the work of Hovey there is
something of Whitman, combined with a seriousness of emotion and an artistic purpose that promised much. Hovey planned a long series of poems
on the Arthurian theme, entitled *Launcelot and
Guenevere: a Poem in Dramas,* 1907, but finished
only five of the nine planned.

Criticism: Rittenhouse; Boynton, *American
Poetry;* B. Carman, "How Hovey Wrote Barney
McGee," *Bookm.* 42:561-3; A. von Ende, "The
Ethical Message of Richard Hovey's Poem in
Dramas," *Poet Lore* 20:69-76; C. H. Page, "Rich-
ard Hovey's *Taliesin*—A Poet's Poem," *Bookm.* 11:
125-31.

THE SEA GYPSY [2]

I am fevered with the sunset,
I am fretful with the bay,
For the wander-thirst is on me
And my soul is in Cathay.

There's a schooner in the offing,
With her topsails shot with fire,

[2] Used by permission of Dodd, Mead and Company, Inc.

And my heart has gone aboard her
For the Islands of Desire.

I must forth again tomorrow!
With the sunset I must be   10
Hull down on the trail of rapture
In the wonder of the sea.
                                   1896

THE WANDER-LOVERS [1]

Down the world with Marna!
That's the life for me!
Wandering with the wandering wind,
Vagabond and unconfined!
Roving with the roving rain
Its unboundaried domain!
Kith and kin of wander-kind,
Children of the sea!

Petrels of the sea-drift!
Swallows of the lea!   10
Arabs of the whole wide girth
Of the wind-encircled earth!
In all climes we pitch our tents,
Cronies of the elements,
With the secret lords of birth
Intimate and free.

All the seaboard knows us
From Fundy to the Keys; [2]
Every bend and every creek
Of abundant Chesapeake;   20
Ardise hills and Newport coves
And the far-off orange groves,
Where Floridian oceans break,
Tropic tiger seas.

Down the world with Marna,
Tarrying there and here!
Just as much at home in Spain
As in Tangier or Touraine!
Shakespeare's Avon knows us well,
And the crags of Neufchâtel;   30
And the ancient Nile is fain
Of our coming near.

Down the world with Marna,
Daughter of the air!
Marna of the subtle grace,
And the vision in her face!
Moving in the measures trod
By the angels before God!
With her sky-blue eyes amaze
And her sea-blue hair!   40

[1] Used by permission of Dodd, Mead and Company, Inc.
[2] islands off the coast of Florida

Marna with the trees' life
In her veins a-stir!
Marna of the aspen heart
Where the sudden quivers start!
Quick-responsive, subtle, wild!
Artless as an artless child,
Spite of all her reach of art!
Oh, to roam with her!

Marna with the wind's will,
Daughter of the sea!   50
Marna of the quick disdain,
Starting at the dream of stain!
At a smile with love aglow,
At a frown a statued woe,
Standing pinnacled in pain
Till a kiss sets free!

Down the world with Marna,
Daughter of the fire!
Marna of the deathless hope,
Still alert to win new scope   60
Where the wings of life may spread
For a flight unhazarded!
Dreaming of the speech to cope
With the heart's desire!

Marna of the far quest
After the divine!
Striving ever for some goal
Past the blunder-god's control!
Dreaming of potential years
When no day shall dawn in fears!   70
That's the Marna of my soul,
Wander-bride of mine!

                                    1893

EDWIN MARKHAM 1852-

Edwin Markham, born amidst the pioneer life of Oregon, came with his widowed mother to California where he spent his youth upon a hill ranch in the central part of the state. By plowing for neighbors he earned money to buy books, and Byron and Tennyson became the models for his youthful attempts at poetry. To give him school advantages, his mother moved to San José where at the State Normal School he fitted himself for teaching. He followed this occupation successfully, and became principal of the high school at Oakland. The immediate success of "The Man with the Hoe," published in a San Francisco newspaper, opened to him a literary career, and since 1899 he has lived in the vicinity of New York City. His poem "Lincoln, the Man of the People" was chosen to be read at the dedication of the Lincoln Memorial at Washington. Mr. Markham's volumes of poetry include *The Shoes of Happiness, and Other Poems*, 1915; and *Gates of Paradise*, 1920. "The

Man with the Hoe" grew out of Markham's experiences with toilers and was the work of many years of patient composition and revision. Whether or not it interprets exactly Millet's conception of the toiler, it is remarkable for its blunt presentation of the tragedy that binds millions of workers in hopeless poverty, and for its appeal to the generous-hearted to provide a way of escape from such a life.

Criticism: Wilkinson (NV); Stedman; Untermeyer; A. L. Morrison, "A Fresh Air School of Pioneer Days," *Overland* ns 83:167; B. Millard, "Edwin Markham and his Golden Shower," *Bookm.* 41:397-9; "The Launching of a Famous Poem," *Bookm.* 27:267-72; "When They Were Twenty-One," *Bookm.* 37:300-1; H. M. Bland, "Edwin Markham: The Boy, The Man, His Art," *Overland* ns 66:333-40.

THE MAN WITH THE HOE [1]

Written After Seeing the Painting by Millet

God made man in His own image, in the image
of God made He him.—*Genesis.*

Bowed by the weight of centuries he leans
Upon his hoe and gazes on the ground,
The emptiness of ages in his face,
And on his back the burden of the world.
Who made him dead to rapture and despair,
A thing that grieves not and that never hopes,
Stolid and stunned, a brother to the ox?
Who loosened and let down this brutal jaw?
Whose was the hand that slanted back this brow?
Whose breath blew out the light within this brain?   10

Is this the Thing the Lord God made and gave
To have dominion over sea and land;
To trace the stars and search the heavens for power;
To feel the passion of Eternity?
Is this the dream He dreamed who shaped the suns
And markt their ways upon the ancient deep?
Down all the caverns of Hell to their last gulf
There is no shape more terrible than this—
More tongued with censure of the world's blind greed—
More filled with signs and portents for the soul—   20
More packt with danger to the universe.

What gulfs between him and the seraphim!
Slave of the wheel of labor, what to him
Are Plato and the swing of Pleiades?

What the long reaches of the peaks of song,
The rift of dawn, the reddening of the rose?
Thru this dread shape the suffering ages look;
Time's tragedy is in that aching stoop;
Thru this dread shape humanity betrayed,
Plundered, profaned and disinherited,   30
Cries protest to the Powers behind the world,
A protest that is also prophecy.

O masters, lords and rulers in all lands,
Is this the handiwork you give to God,
This monstrous thing distorted and soul-quencht?
How will you ever straighten up this shape;
Touch it again with immortality;
Give back the upward looking and the light;
Rebuild in it the music and the dream;
Make right the immemorial infamies,   40
Perfidious wrongs, immedicable woes?

O masters, lords and rulers in all lands,
How will the future reckon with this Man?
How answer his brute question in that hour
When whirlwinds of rebellion shake all shores?
How will it be with kingdoms and with kings—
With those who shaped him to the thing he is—
When this dumb Terror shall rise to judge the world,
After the silence of the centuries?
1898   1899

LINCOLN, THE MAN OF THE PEOPLE [1]

When the Norn [2] Mother saw the Whirlwind Hour
Greatening and darkening as it hurried on,
She left the Heaven of Heroes and came down
To make a man to meet the mortal need.
She took the tried clay of the common road—
Clay warm yet with the genial heat of Earth,
Dasht through it all a strain of prophecy;
Tempered the heap with thrill of human tears;
Then mixt a laughter with the serious stuff.
Into the shape she breathed a flame to light   10
That tender, tragic, ever-changing face;
And laid on him a sense of the Mystic Powers,
Moving—all husht—behind the mortal vail.
Here was a man to hold against the world,
A man to match the mountains and the sea.

The color of the ground was in him, the red earth;
The smack and tang of elemental things;
The rectitude and patience of the cliff;
The good-will of the rain that loves all leaves;

[1] Copyright. From *Collected Poems* by Edwin Markham in preparation for 1930.

[2] one of the Scandinavian demi-goddesses presiding over the fates of men and gods

The friendly welcome of the wayside well;   20
The courage of the bird that dares the sea;
The gladness of the wind that shakes the corn;
The pity of the snow that hides all scars;
The secrecy of streams that make their way
Under the mountain to the rifted rock;
The tolerance and equity of light
That gives as freely to the shrinking flower
As to the great oak flaring to the wind—
To the grave's low hill as to the Matterhorn
That shoulders out the sky.   Sprung from the
        West,   30
He drank the valorous youth of a new world.
The strength of virgin forests braced his mind,
The hush of spacious prairies stilled his soul,
His words were oaks in acorns; and his thoughts
Were roots that firmly gript the granite truth.

Up from log cabin to the Capitol,
One fire was on his spirit, one resolve—
To send the keen ax to the root of wrong,
Clearing a free way for the feet of God,
The eyes of conscience testing every stroke,   40
To make his deed the measure of a man.
He built the rail-pile as he built the State,
Pouring his splendid strength through every
        blow;
The grip that swung the ax in Illinois
Was on the pen that set a people free.

So came the Captain with the mighty heart;
And when the judgment thunders split the
        house,
Wrenching the rafters from their ancient rest,
He held the ridgepole up, and spikt again
The rafters of the Home.   He held his place—
Held the long purpose like a growing tree—   51
Held on through blame and faltered not at
        praise.
And when he fell in whirlwind, he went down
As when a lordly cedar, green with boughs,
Goes down with a great shout upon the hills,
And leaves a lonesome place against the sky.
1900   1906

GEORGE STERLING 1869-1926

Although Sterling was born at Sag Harbor, New York, and was educated in the East, he ranks as a western poet, having moved about 1895 to California where he produced his poetry and where he died. Sterling was indifferent to criticism and to financial success; he refused to follow the new vogue in poetry, and belongs with the poets of the nineteenth century rather than with those of his own productive years.   His work, contained in several slim volumes, includes *The Testimony of the Suns*, 1903, *A Wine of Wizardry*, 1908, *The*

House of Orchids, 1911, and *Beyond the Breakers*, 1914.   A note of seriousness runs through his work, a sense of the relentlessness of time, of the futility of all that man has done when measured against the background of the ages.   Even his nature lyrics and his legends of the sea often express man's yearning for some spiritual height that it is impossible for him to reach.

Criticism: Untermeyer; H. M. Bland, "Sterling, the Poet of Seas and Stars," *Overland* ns 66 :474-8; H. Monroe, "The Poetry of George Sterling," *Poetry* 7 :307-13; M. Austin, "George Sterling at Carmel," *Am. Mercury* 11 :65-72; H. Monroe, "Two Poets Say Farewell," *Poetry* 29 :208-13; see also *Overland* ns 85, March, for appreciation and tributes.

THE BLACK VULTURE [1]

Aloof within the day's enormous dome,
    He holds unshared the silence of the sky.
    Far down his bleak, relentless eyes descry
The eagle's empire and the falcon's home—
Far down, the galleons of sunset roam;
    His hazards on the sea of morning lie;
    Serene, he hears the broken tempest sigh
Where cold sierras gleam like scattered foam.

And least of all he holds the human swarm—
    Unwitting now that envious men prepare   10
        To make their dream and its fulfilment one,
When, poised above the caldrons of the storm,
        Their hearts, contemptuous of death, shall
            dare
        His roads between the thunder and the sun.

THE LAST DAYS [1]

The russet leaves of the sycamore
Lie at last on the valley floor—
By the autumn wind swept to and fro
Like ghosts in a tale of long ago.
Shallow and clear the Carmel [2] glides
Where the willows droop on its vine-walled
        sides.

The bracken-rust is red on the hill;
The pines stand brooding, somber and still;
Gray are the cliffs, and the waters gray,
Where the seagulls dip to the sea-born spray.
Sad November, lady of rain,   11
Sends the goose-wedge over again.

Wilder now, for the verdure's birth,
Falls the sunlight over the earth;
Kildees call from the fields where now

[1] Copyright.   By permission of A. M. Robertson, publisher.
[2] a stream of central California

The banding blackbirds follow the plow;
Rustling poplar and brittle weed
Whisper low to the river-reed.

Days departing linger and sigh;
Stars come soon to the quiet sky; 20
Buried voices, intimate, strange,
Cry to body and soul of Change;
Beauty, eternal fugitive,
Seeks the home that we cannot give.

THE MASTER MARINER [1]

My grandsire sailed three years from home,
    And slew unmoved the sounding whale:
Here on a windless beach I roam
    And watch far out the hardy sail.

The lions of the surf [2] that cry
    Upon this lion-colored shore
On reefs of midnight met his eye:
    He knew their fangs as I their roar.

My grandsire sailed uncharted seas,
    And toll of all their leagues he took: 10
I scan the shallow bays at ease,
    And tell their colors in a book.

The anchor-chains his music made
    And wind in shrouds and running-gear:
The thrush at dawn beguiles my glade,
    And once, 'tis said, I woke to hear.

My grandsire in his ample fist
    The long harpoon upheld to men:
Behold obedient to my wrist
    A gray gull's-feather for my pen! 20

Upon my grandsire's leathern cheek
    Five zones their bitter bronze had set:
Some day their hazards I will seek,
    I promise me at times. Not yet.

I think my grandsire now would turn
    A mild but speculative eye
On me, my pen and its concern,
    Then gaze again to sea—and sigh.

LOUISE IMOGEN GUINEY
1861-1920

Miss Guiney was born at Roxbury, Massachusetts, of mingled Irish, Scotch, and French ancestry, and was educated at private schools in Providence. After the death of her father, a general in the

[1] Copyright. By permission of A. M. Robertson, publisher.
[2] sea lions of the Pacific coast

Union Army, she was for several years postmistress at Auburndale, Massachusetts, and then cataloguer in the Boston Public Library. From 1901 she lived in England, and is buried at Oxford.

From the age of twenty-three, literary editorship, the writing of essays and poetry, and a voluminous and vivacious correspondence filled Miss Guiney's life. She spent much time in investigating obscure men and events in past epochs of history and literature, especially the period of the seventeenth century; she rejoiced in bringing to light the story of some lost cause, or of some person who fell in gallant battle for an ideal. Her verse is spontaneous, full of courage; her vigorous imagination sometimes expresses itself with Celtic tenderness, sometimes with martial strength. Notable among her books are *The White Sail and Other Poems*, 1887, *A Roadside Harp*, 1893, which she thought her "best book," and *Patrins*, 1897, a collection of essays.

Biography and criticism: E. M. Tenison, *Louise Imogen Guiney: Her Life and Works*, 1923; Rittenhouse; Edmund L. Pearson, "An American Poet," *Outlook* 136:68-9; A. Brown, "An American Poet," *No. Am.* 213:502-17; "Louise Imogen Guiney," ed. by M. Earls, *Bookm.* 55:163-9, 591-6; *World* 121:596-603; "Letters of Louise Imogen Guiney: a Comment and Some Letters," *Cath.* 56:705-9.

THE WILD RIDE [3]

I hear in my heart, I hear in its ominous pulses
All day, on the road, the hoofs of invisible
    horses,
All night, from their stalls, the importunate
    pawing and neighing.

Let cowards and laggards fall back! but alert
    to the saddle
Weatherworn and abreast, go men of our galloping legion,
With a stirrup-cup each to the lily of women
    that loves him.

The trail is through dolor and dread, over crags
    and morasses;
There are shapes by the way, there are things
    that appal or entice us:
What odds? We are Knights of the Grail, we
    are vowed to the riding.

Thought's self is a vanishing wing, and joy is a
    cobweb, 10
And friendship a flower in the dust, and glory
    a sunbeam:
Not here is our prize, nor, alas! after these our
    pursuing.

[3] This poem, says Alice Brown,
    "first beat out its galloping measure in a dream."
Copyright. By permission of Houghton Mifflin Company, authorized publishers.

A dipping of plumes, a tear, a shake of the
bridle,
A passing salute to this world and her pitiful
beauty:
We hurry with never a word in the track of our
fathers.

*I hear in my heart, I hear in its ominous pulses,
All day, on the road, the hoofs of invisible
horses,
All night, from their stalls, the importunate
pawing and neighing.*

We spur to a land of no name, outracing the
storm-wind;
We leap to the infinite dark like sparks from the
anvil.   20
Thou leadest, O God! All's well with Thy
troopers that follow.

THEODOSIA GARRISON
FAULKS 1874-

Mrs. Faulks has lived all her life in New Jersey,
where she was born, educated, and now resides.
She contributes both prose and poetry to magazines, and has published three volumes of verse:
Joy o' Life and Other Poems, 1909; *Earth Cry
and Other Poems*, 1910; *The Dreamers*, 1917.
The appeal of Mrs. Faulks's verse lies in its honesty and optimism, and the fresh, concrete images
through which she expresses emotion. Both in
manner and form her work may naturally be
grouped with that of the nineteenth century.
Bookm. 16:16; 47:398.

STAINS [1]

The three ghosts on the lonesome road
Spake each to one another,
"Whence came that stain about your mouth
No lifted hand may cover?"
"From eating of forbidden fruit,
Brother, my brother."

The three ghosts on the sunless road
Spake each to one another,
"Whence came that red burn on your foot
No dust nor ash may cover?"   10
"I stamped a neighbor's hearth-flame out,
Brother, my brother."

The three ghosts on the windless road
Spake each to one another,
"Whence came that blood upon your hand
No other hand may cover?"

"From breaking of a woman's heart,
Brother, my brother."

"Yet on the earth clean men we walked,
Glutton and Thief and Lover;   20
White flesh and fair it hid our stains
That no man might discover."
"Naked the soul goes up to God,
Brother, my brother."

APRIL [2]

Something tapped at my window-pane,
Someone called me without my door,
Someone laughed like the tinkle o' rain,
The robin echoed it o'er and o'er.

I threw the door and the window wide;
Sun and the touch of the breeze and then—
"Ah, were you expecting me, dear?" she cried,
And here was April come back again.

THE DREAMERS [3]

The gypsies passed her little gate—
She stopped her wheel to see.—
A brown-faced pair who walked the road,
Free as the wind is free;
And suddenly her tidy room
A prison seemed to be.

Her shining plates against the walls,
Her sunlit, sanded floor,
The brass-bound wedding chest that held
Her linen's snowy store,   10
The very wheel whose humming died,—
Seemed only chains she bore.

She watched the foot-free gypsies pass;
She never knew or guessed
The wistful dream that drew them close—
The longing in each breast
Some day to know a home like hers,
Wherein their hearts might rest.

HENRY VAN DYKE 1852-

Henry van Dyke, besides following for years his
profession as a clergyman, has been a professor of
English literature at Princeton and was for four
years Minister of the United States to Holland and
Luxemburg. He was born at Germantown, Pennsylvania, was graduated from Princeton, and has
received honorary degrees from many universities,

[1] From *Scribner's* magazine, copyright, 1904, by
Charles Scribner's Sons; also from *The Joy of
Life*, copyright, 1909, by Mitchell Kennerley,
publisher.

[2] From *The Joy of Life*, copyright, 1909, by Mitchell
Kennerley, publisher.
[3] From *The Dreamer and Other Poems* by Theodosia
Garrison, copyright, 1917, by George H. Doran
Company and reprinted by special permission of
the publishers, Doubleday, Doran and Company,
Inc.

American and European. The range of his literary interests is wide; he has been a literary editor, a critic, and a writer of poems, stories, and essays upon a variety of subjects—nature, religion, travel. Among his books are *Little Rivers*, 1895, *Fisherman's Luck*, 1899, *The Blue Flower*, 1902, *Music and Other Poems*, 1904, *Le Génie de L'Amérique*, 1909. His works were collected in 1920. Among his more recent books are *Camp-Fires and Guide Posts*, 1921, *Half-Told Tales*, 1925. Doctor van Dyke's poetry is simple and luminous, serious but devoid of labored didacticism, and reflects a courageous and optimistic view of life.

H. W. Mabie, "Henry van Dyke," *Cent.* 67: 579-81; sketch, *Cur. Lit.* 28:282; *Nation* 104:54-5; H. W. Mabie, "Personal Portraits," *Bookm.* 38:20.

THE THREE BEST THINGS [1]

WORK

Let me but do my work from day to day,
  In field or forest, at the desk or loom,
  In roaring market-place or tranquil room;
Let me but find it in my heart to say,
  When vagrant wishes beckon me astray,
  "This is my work; my blessing, not my doom;
  "Of all who live, I am the one by whom
"This work can best be done in the right way."

Then shall I see it not too great, nor small,
  To suit my spirit and to prove my powers;
  Then shall I cheerful greet the labouring hours,
And cheerful turn, when the long shadows fall
At eventide, to play and love and rest,
Because I know for me my work is best.
April, 1902

LIFE

Let me but live my life from year to year,
  With forward face and unreluctant soul;
  Not hurrying to, nor turning from, the goal;
Not mourning for the things that disappear
In the dim past, nor holding back in fear
  From what the future veils; but with a whole
  And happy heart, that pays its toll
To Youth and Age, and travels on with cheer.

So let the way wind up the hill or down,
  O'er rough and smooth, the journey will be joy:
  Still seeking what I sought when but a boy,
New friendship, high adventure, and a crown,
My heart will keep the courage of the quest,
And hope the road's last turn will be the best.
May, 1892

LOVE

Let me but love my love without disguise,
  Nor wear a mask of fashion old or new,
  Not wait to speak till I can hear a clue,
Nor play a part to shine in others' eyes,
Nor bow my knees to what my heart denies;
  But what I am, to that let me be true,
  And let me worship where my love is due,
And so through love and worship let me rise.

For love is but the heart's immortal thirst
  To be completely known and all forgiven,
  Even as sinful souls that enter Heaven:
So take me, dear, and understand my worst,
  And freely pardon it, because confessed,
  And let me find in loving thee, my best.
May, 1902

LIZETTE WOODWORTH REESE
1856-

Miss Reese was born in Baltimore County, Maryland, and has spent her life in or near the city of Baltimore, where for many years she has been a teacher of English in the Western High School. Even the titles of her volumes are suggestive of delicacy and quietude, and a spirit that finds more than a passing refreshment in nature: *A Branch of May*, 1887; *A Handful of Lavender*, 1891; *A Quiet Road*, 1896; *A Wayside Lute*, 1909; *Spicewood*, 1920; *Wild Cherry*, 1923. Always her work has been notable for individuality and independence, firmness and directness of diction, and excellence of finish. Miss Reese seems to have been unmoved by current fashions in verse, for from the first her poetry anticipated in qualities of exactness and clarity the style of Sara Teasdale and Edna St. Vincent Millay; and at the same time in its joyousness or seriousness, seems to have much in common with the untrammeled spirit of the Elizabethans.

Criticism: Rittenhouse; Untermeyer; Mrs. L. H. Wrenshall in *Library of Southern Literature*, Vol. 10.

TEARS [2]

When I consider Life and its few years—
A wisp of fog betwixt us and the sun;
A call to battle, and the battle done
Ere the last echo dies within our ears;
A rose choked in the grass; an hour of fears;
The gusts that past a darkening shore do beat;
The burst of music down an unlistening street—
I wonder at the idleness of tears.
Ye old, old dead, and ye of yesternight,
Chieftains, and bards, and keepers of the sheep,

By every cup of sorrow that you had,
Loose me from tears, and make me see aright
How each hath back what once he stayed to
        weep:
Homer his sight, David his little lad!

1899

OLD SAUL [1]

I cannot think of any word
    To make it plain to you,
How white a thing the hawthorn bush
    That delicately blew

Within a crook of Tinges Lane;
    Each May Day there it stood;
And lit a flame of loveliness
    For the small neighborhood.

So fragile-white a thing it was,
    I cannot make it plain;   10
Or the sweet fumbling of the bees,
    Like the break in a rain.

Old Saul lived near. And this his life:—
    To cobble for his bread;
To mourn a tall son lost at sea;
    A daughter worse than dead.

And so, in place of all his lack,
    He set the hawthorn tree;
Made it his wealth, his mirth, his god,
    His Zion to touch and see.   20

Born English he. Down Tinges Lane
    His lad's years came and went;

[1] From the *Selected Poems* of Lizette Woodworth Reese,
    copyright, 1926, George H. Doran, publisher.

He saw out there behind his thorn,
    A hundred thorns of Kent.

At lovers slipping through the dusk
    He shook a lover's head;
Grudged them each flower. It was too white
    For any but the dead.

Once on a blurred, wet, silver day
    He said to two or three: 30
"Folks, when I go, pluck yonder bloom
    That I may take with me."

But it was winter when he went,
    The road wind-drenched and torn;
They laid upon his coffin lid
    A wreath made all of thorn.

THE LARK [2]

(SALISBURY, ENGLAND)

    A close, gray sky,
    And poplars gray and high,
    The country-side along;
    The steeple bold
    Across the acres old—
    And then a song!

    Oh, far, far, far,
    As any spire or star,
    Beyond the cloistered wall!
    Oh, high, high, high,   10
    A heart-throb in the sky—
    Then not at all.

1909

[2] From *A Wayside Lute,* copyright, 1909, by Thomas B.
    Mosher, publisher.

THE EARLY
TWENTIETH CENTURY

IN THE three centuries of American literature, great changes have taken place in its outlook and form. The first American immigrants left the England of Shakespeare with an attitude toward the world that was characteristic of the Elizabethans. During the three hundred years since, English literature has gone through change after change—puritanism, pseudo-classicism, romanticism, Victorianism. For two of these three centuries American literature, as literature, was virtually stagnant or dormant, and its development has taken place in a little more than a century. In that hundred and thirty years American literature has gone through cycles of change: imitation of foreign, especially English, literature; a growth into national individuality; and finally a development parallel with that of the world-current of thought and expression. The future can scarcely bring any marked impairment in our hard-won national distinctiveness. The Anglo-Saxon stream of blood has had too many additions from Celt, Italian, German, and Slav ever to re-emerge as a solely determining element; what American literature is and will be depends not so much upon blood and tradition as upon American democracy and social conditions. Nevertheless we have unavoidably approached the general European trend of thought since 1900. The Spanish-American War made us a world power; the Great War forced us into many new contacts; the break-down of the effects of distance due to airplanes, radio, and the wireless telegraph, while apparently only a physical break-down, marks an inevitable trend toward a world-wide commingling of ideas.

These years have tended also to reinforce the break with the old that science began. Forms long-cherished have been cast aside; free verse, with its abandonment of regular meter—the change, to use American names of the last thirty years, from Moody to Amy Lowell—indicates this departure from the past. And though free verse is already on the decline, its eager search for newness is deeply significant. We face "a brave new world." The nineteenth century broke new ground in half a hundred directions. In all these directions the twentieth century is going forward, uncertainly and capriciously it may be, but always intensely. It is yet far too early to pass on the permanent value of what is today being written. But this may confidently be said: its alert sincerity has high value for us; in its experimental complexity lies a seed of life.

STEPHEN CRANE 1870-1900

Stephen Crane attained distinction at the age of twenty-five through his novel *The Red Badge of Courage,* written before he had seen war. This is a realistic narrative of experiences in the Civil War, with all the interest centered upon a young country-bred soldier through whom one sees the whole drama of battle. Crane broke so sharply away from current literary conventions that H. G. Wells pronounced him "one of the most brilliant, most significant and most distinctly American of all English writers." He was an Imagist before Imagism was known. Crane's poetry, like his prose, is founded upon the use of exact, simple words, and a vigorous, homely phrasing of ideas. Since all his work is forward-looking in its style, it belongs to the twentieth century.

Crane's life was unfortunately shortened by early hardships and lack of recognition. His first novel, *Maggie, a Girl of the Streets,* 1891, was almost wholly neglected until *The Red Badge of Courage* appeared. His birthplace was Newark, New Jersey; he took up journalism at sixteen, and he was educated at Lafayette College and Syracuse University. During the Greco-Turkish and the Spanish-American wars he was correspondent for the *New York Journal.* In Cuba his health broke down; he settled in England, but was soon taken to Germany, where he died. In his short career he produced a variety of work: novels, historical essays, special articles, and poetry. Among his significant works are *The Black Riders,* 1895, and *War Is Kind,* 1899.

Biography and criticism: T. Beer, *Stephen Crane,* 1924; E. Garnett, *Friday Nights,* ser. 1, 1922; Van Doren (AN); Mrs. Joseph Conrad, "Recollections of Stephen Crane," *Bookm.* 63:134-7; F. Dell, "Stephen Crane and the Genius Myth," *Nation* 119:637-8; see also H. Wickham, *Am. Mercury* 7:291-7; J. Conrad, *Bookm.* 50:529-31; E. Wyatt, *New Repub.* 4:148-50; *Poetry* 14:148-52; *Cur. Opinion* 76:39-40; 68:537-8; 62:202-3.

I EXPLAIN [1]

I explain the silvered passing of a ship at night,
The sweep of each sad lost wave,
The dwindling boom of the steel thing's striving,
The little cry of a man to a man,
A shadow falling across the grayer night,
And the sinking of the small star;

Then the waste, the far waste of waters,
And the soft lashing of black waves
For long and in loneliness.

Remember, thou, O ship of love,   10
Thou leavest a far waste of waters,
And the soft lashing of black waves
For long and in loneliness.

THE BLACK RIDERS [1]

Black riders came from the sea.
There was clang and clang of spear and shield,
And clash and clash of hoof and heel,
Wild shouts and the wave of hair
In the rush upon the wind:
Thus the ride of sin.

THE BLADES OF GRASS [1]

In Heaven,
Some little blades of grass
Stood before God.
"What did you do?"
Then all save one of the little blades
Began eagerly to relate
The merits of their lives.
This one stayed a small way behind,
Ashamed.
Presently, God said,   10
"And what did you do?"
The little blade answered, "Oh, my Lord,
Memory is bitter to me,
For, if I did good deeds,
I know not of them."
Then God, in all his splendor,
Arose from his throne.
"Oh, best little blade of grass!" he said.

A NEWSPAPER [1]

A newspaper is a collection of half-injustices
Which, bawled by boys from mile to mile,
Spreads its curious opinion
To a million merciful and sneering men,
While families cuddle the joys of the fireside
When spurred by tale of dire love agony.
A newspaper is a court
Where everyone is kindly and unfairly tried
By a squalor of honest men.

A newspaper is a market   10
Where wisdom sells its freedom
And melons are crowned by the crowd.
A newspaper is a game
Where his error scores the player victory
While another's skill wins death.
A newspaper is a symbol;
It is fetless life's chronicle,
A collection of loud tales
Concentrating eternal stupidities,
That in remote ages lived unhaltered,   20
Roaming through a fenceless world.

THE PEAKS [1]

In the night
Gray, heavy clouds muffled the valleys,
And the peaks looked toward God alone.
"O Master, that movest the wind with a
finger,
Humble, idle, futile peaks are we.
Grant that we may run swiftly across the
world
To huddle in worship at Thy feet."

In the morning
A noise of men at work came the clear blue
miles,
And the little black cities were apparent. 10
"O Master, that knowest the meaning of
raindrops,
Humble, idle, futile peaks are we.
Give voice to us, we pray, O Lord,
That we may sing Thy goodness to the
sun."

In the evening
The far valleys were sprinkled with tiny lights.
"O Master,
Thou that knowest the value of kings and
birds,
Thou hast made us humble, idle, futile
peaks.
Thou only needest eternal patience; 20
We bow to Thy wisdom, O Lord—
Humble, idle, futile peaks."

In the night
Gray, heavy clouds muffled the valleys,
And the peaks looked toward God alone.

A SLANT OF SUN [1]

A slant of sun on dull brown walls,
A forgotten sky of bashful blue.

Toward God a mighty hymn,
A song of collisions and cries,
Rumbling wheels, hoof-beats, bells,
Welcomes, farewells, love-calls, final moans,
Voices of joy, idiocy, warning, despair,
The unknown appeals of brutes,
The chanting of flowers,
The screams of cut trees, 10
The senseless babble of hens and wise men—
A cluttered incoherency that says at the stars:
"O God, save us!"

1899

[1] Reprinted from *The Works of Stephen Crane* by permission of and special arrangement with Alfred
Knopf, Inc., authorized publishers.

AMY LOWELL 1874-1925

Miss Lowell was born in Brookline, Massachusetts, and died there. She was a member of the
family from which James Russell Lowell sprang,
and of her brothers one was the astronomer, Percival Lowell, and another is president of Harvard
University. She was educated at private schools.
She took literature for her vocation and worked at
it deliberately and conscientiously. Her first book
of poems, *A Dome of Many-Colored Glass*, 1912,
appeared only after she had spent ten painstaking
years in developing her style. *Sword Blades and
Poppy Seed* appeared in 1914; *Men, Women, and
Ghosts* in 1916; *What's O'clock,* just after her
death. Miss Lowell also produced *Can Grande's
Castle,* "polyphonic prose," [2] 1918; and in criticism
Six French Poets, 1915, and *Tendencies in Modern
American Poetry*, 1917. Her most scholarly work
is her biographical and critical study, *John Keats*,
1925.

Part of Miss Lowell's verse is in usual metrical
and stanzaic form, but her most characteristic pattern is "free verse," without regular stanzas, meter,
or rime. More important than the form of her
verse was her theory of what poetry should be.
In her mind poetry should be "hard and clear,
never blurred nor indefinite"; concentration should
be its "very essence." To this end words should
"render particulars exactly and not deal in vague
generalities, however magnificent and sonorous";
they should be "*exact*, not nearly-exact," not
"merely decorative." She does not insist upon the
necessity of free verse, but upon liberty to use it.
The group of poets who showed these tendencies
were known as Imagists. Among the Imagists
Miss Lowell has included the American poets
"H.D." (Hilda Doolittle), John Gould Fletcher,
and herself, and an equal number of contemporary
English poets. Whatever may be thought of her
theories concerning poetry, Miss Lowell has had a
decidedly constructive influence in the work of the
younger generation of writers, and her own poetry
is remarkable for its strength and for its penetrating views of life and of nature.

Biography and criticism: C. Wood, *Amy Lowell*;
R. Hunt and R. H. Snow, *Amy Lowell*, 1921;
Phelps (EP); also *Bookm.* 47:255-60; Untermeyer;
Boynton; Wilkinson (NV); E. S. Sergeant, "Amy
Lowell," *New Repub.* 44:322-6; A. MacLeish,
"Amy Lowell and the Art of Poetry," *No. Am.* 221:
508-21; H. Monroe, "Memories of Amy Lowell,"
Poetry 26:208-14; H. B. Kizer, "Amy Lowell, a
Personality," *No. Am.* 207:736-47; W. A. Bradley,
"Four American Poets," *Dial* 61:528-30; W. M.
Patterson, "New Verse and New Prose," *No. Am.*
207:257-67; C. Aiken, "The Technique of Poly-
phonic Prose," *Dial* 65:346-8.

[2] "'Polyphonic' means 'many-voiced' and the form is
so called because it makes use of all the 'voices' of
poetry, viz.: meter, *vers libre* [free verse], as-
sonance, alliteration, rime, and return." [Amy
Lowell, *Tendencies in Modern American Poetry*,
p. 321.]

MEETING-HOUSE HILL [1]

I must be mad, or very tired,
When the curve of a blue bay beyond a rail-
    road track
Is shrill and sweet to me like the sudden spring-
    ing of a tune,
And the sight of a white church above thin
    trees in a city square
Amazes my eyes as though it were the Par-
    thenon.
Close, reticent, superbly final,
With the pillars of its portico refined to a
    cautious elegance,
It dominates the weak trees,
And the shot of its spire
Is cool, and candid,   10
Rising into an unresisting sky.
Strange meeting-house
Pausing a moment upon a squalid hill-top.
I watch the spire sweeping the sky,
I am dizzy with the movement of the sky,
I might be watching a mast
With its royals set full
Straining before a two-reef breeze.
I might be sighting a tea-clipper, [2]
Tacking into the blue bay,   20
Just back from Canton
With her hold full of green and blue porcelain,
And a Chinese coolie leaning over the rail
Gazing at the white spire
With dull, sea-spent eyes.

                             1925

PATTERNS [1]

I walk down the garden paths,
And all the daffodils
Are blowing, and the bright blue squills.
I walk down the patterned garden-paths
In my stiff, brocaded gown.
With my powdered hair and jeweled fan,
I too am a rare
Pattern. As I wander down
The garden paths.

My dress is richly figured,   10
And the train
Makes a pink and silver stain
On the gravel, and the thrift [3]
Of the borders.
Just a plate of current fashion,
Tripping by in high-heeled, ribboned shoes.
Not a softness anywhere about me,

Only whalebone and brocade.
And I sink on a seat in the shade
Of a lime tree. For my passion   20
Wars against the stiff brocade.
The daffodils and squills
Flutter in the breeze
As they please.
And I weep;
For the lime tree is in blossom
And one small flower has dropped upon my
    bosom.

And the plashing of waterdrops
In the marble fountain
Comes down the garden-paths.   30
The dripping never stops.
Underneath my stiffened gown
Is the softness of a woman bathing in a marble
    basin,
A basin in the midst of hedges grown
So thick, she cannot see her lover hiding,
But she guesses he is near,
And the sliding of the water
Seems the stroking of a dear
Hand upon her.
What is Summer in a fine brocaded gown!   40
I should like to see it lying in a heap upon the
    ground.
All the pink and silver crumpled up on the
    ground.

I would be the pink and silver as I ran along
    the paths,
And he would stumble after,
Bewildered by my laughter.
I should see the sun flashing from his sword-
    hilt
And the buckles on his shoes.
I would choose
To lead him in a maze along the patterned
    paths,
A bright and laughing maze for my heavy-
    booted lover.   50
Till he caught me in the shade,
And the buttons of his waistcoat bruised my
    body as he clasped me,
Aching, melting, unafraid.
With the shadows of the leaves and the sun-
    drops,
And the plopping of the waterdrops,
All about us in the open afternoon—
I am very like to swoon
With the weight of this brocade,
For the sun sifts through the shade.

Underneath the fallen blossom   60
In my bosom,

---

[1] Copyright. By permission of Houghton Mifflin Company, authorized publishers.
[2] fast sailing vessel carrying tea
[3] a plant

Is a letter I have hid.
It was brought to me this morning by a rider
    from the Duke.
"Madam, we regret to inform you that Lord
    Hartwell
Died in action Thursday se'nnight."
As I read it in the white, morning sunlight,
The letters squirmed like snakes.
"Any answer, Madam," said my footman.
"No," I told him.
"See that the messenger takes some refresh-
    ment.   70
No, no answer."
And I walked into the garden,
Up and down the patterned paths,
In my stiff, correct brocade.
The blue and yellow flowers stood up proudly
    in the sun,
Each one.
I stood upright too,
Held rigid to the pattern
By the stiffness of my gown.
Up and down I walked,   80
Up and down.

In a month he would have been my husband.
In a month, here, underneath this lime,
We would have broke the pattern;
He for me, and I for him,
He as Colonel, I as Lady,
On this shady seat.
He had a whim
That sunlight carried blessing.
And I answered, "It shall be as you have
    said."   90
Now he is dead.

In Summer and in Winter I shall walk
Up and down
The patterned garden-paths
In my stiff, brocaded gown.
The squills and daffodils
Will give place to pillared roses, and to asters,
    and to snow.
I shall go
Up and down,
In my gown.   100
Gorgeously arrayed,
Boned and stayed.
And the softness of my body will be guarded
    from embrace
By each button, hook, and lace.
For the man who should loose me is dead,
Fighting with the Duke in Flanders,
In a pattern called a war.
Christ! What are patterns for?

       1915

JOHN GOULD FLETCHER 1886-

Amy Lowell assigns Mr. Fletcher a place of importance in modern American poetry as one of the
first definitely to adopt free verse, and also to
produce some noteworthy poems in "polyphonic
prose." He was born at Little Rock, Arkansas, of
good pioneer stock. In the course of his education
at Phillips Academy, Andover, and at Harvard, he
gained a thorough familiarity with languages and
literature, and on graduating he determined to be
a writer. After extensive travel he settled in England and, in 1912, moved by the Post-Impressionist
Exhibition in London, he became one of the leaders
of the Imagists. Mr. Fletcher's gift lies in the ability to phrase definite impressions in sensuous, startling words. *Breakers and Granite,* 1921, aims to
put part of the American scene into brilliant pictures. *Preludes and Symphonies,* 1922, contains
two earlier works, *Irradiations* and *Goblins and
Pagodas,* the latter showing the influence of oriental poetry.

Biography and criticism: Lowell; Wilkinson
(NV); Untermeyer; C. Aiken, "Possessor and Possessed," *Dial* 66:189-91; *Poetry* 7:44-7; 9:43-7;
13:340-1; 19:155-7; for a discussion of Imagism
see *New Repub.* 3:75; 154; 204.

DOWN THE MISSISSIPPI [1]

I

EMBARKATION

Dull masses of dense green,
The forests range their somber platforms;
Between them silently, like a spirit,
The river finds its own mysterious path.

Loosely the river sways out, backward, forward,
Always fretting the outer side;
Shunning the invisible focus of each crescent,
Seeking to spread into shining loops over fields.

Like an enormous serpent, dilating, uncoiling,
Displaying a broad scaly back of earth-smeared
    gold;   10
Swaying out sinuously between the dull motion-
    less forests,
As molten metal might glide down the lip of
    a vase of dark bronze;

It goes, while the steamboat drifting out upon
    it,
Seems now to be floating not only outwards but
    upwards;
In the flight of a petal detached and gradually
    moving skyward
Above the pink explosion of the calyx of the
    dawn.

[1] From *Breakers and Granite* by John Gould Fletcher,
  by permission of The Macmillan Company, publishers.

II

HEAT

As if the sun had trodden down the sky,
Until no more it holds living air, but only humid
    vapor,
Heat pressing upon earth with irresistible
    languor,
Turns all the solid forest into half-liquid
    smudge.

The heavy clouds like cargo-boats strain slowly
    against its current;
And the flickering of the haze is like the thunder
    of ten thousand paddles
Against the heavy wall of the horizon, pale blue
    and utterly windless,
Whereon the sun hangs motionless, a brassy
    disk of flame.

III

FULL MOON

Flinging its arc of silver bubbles, quickly shifts
    the moon
From side to side of us as we go down its path;
I sit on the deck at midnight and watch it
    slipping and sliding,
Under my tilted chair, like a thin film of spilt
    water.

It is weaving a river of light to take the place
    of this river;
A river where we shall drift all night, then
    come to rest in its shallows;
And then I shall wake from my drowsiness and
    look down from some dim tree-top
Over white lakes of cotton, like moon-fields on
    every side.

IV

THE MOON'S ORCHESTRA

When the moon lights up
Its dull red camp-fire through the trees;
And floats out, like a white balloon,
Into the blue cup of the night, borne by a
    casual breeze;
The moon-orchestra then begins to stir.
Jiggle of fiddles commence their crazy dance
    in the darkness.
Crickets churr
Against the stark reiteration of the rusty flutes
    which frogs
Puff at from rotted logs
In the swamp.   10

And then the moon begins her dance of frozen
    pomp
Over the lightly quivering floor of the flat and
    mournful river.
Her white feet lightly twist and swirl.
She is a mad girl
In an old unlit ball-room
Whose walls, half-guessed-at through the gloom,
Are hung with the rusty crape of stark black cy-
    press
Which show, through gaps and tatters, red
    stains half hidden away.

V

THE STEVEDORES

Frieze of warm bronze that glides with cat-like
    movements
Over the gangplank poised and yet awaiting,
The sinewy thudding rhythm of forty shuffling
    feet
Falling like muffled drum beats on the stillness.
Oh, roll the cotton down,
Roll, roll the cotton down,
From the further side of Jordan,
Oh roll the cotton down!

And the river waits,
The river listens,   10
Chuckling little banjo-notes that break with a
    flop on the stillness;
And by the low dark shed that holds the heavy
    freights,
Two lonely cypress trees stand up and point
    with stiffened fingers
Far southward where a single chimney stands
    out aloof in the sky.

VI

NIGHT LANDING

After the whistle's roar has bellowed and shud-
    dered,
Shaking the sleeping town and the somnolent
    river,
The deep-toned floating of the pilot's bell
Suddenly warns the engines.

They stop like heart-beats that abruptly stop,
The shore glides to us, in a wide low curve.

And then—supreme revelation of the river—
The tackle is loosed—the long gangplank
    swings outwards—
And poised at the end of it, half naked beneath
    the searchlight,
A blue-black negro with gleaming teeth waits
    for his chance to leap.   10

VII

THE SILENCE

There is a silence I carry about with me always;
A silence perpetual, for it is self-created;
A silence of heat, of water, of unchecked fruit-
fulness
Through which each year the heavy harvests
bloom, and burst and fall.

Deep, matted green silence of my South,
Often within the push and the scorn of great
cities,
I have seen that mile-wide waste of water swaying out to you,
And on its current glimmering, I am going to
the sea.

There is a silence I have achieved; I have
walked beyond its threshold;
I know it is without horizons, boundless, fathomless, perfect.   10
And some day maybe, far away,
I shall curl up in it at last and sleep an endless
sleep.

1915

THE WRECK [1]

Amid the immense broad brownness of the
sands
Where water, wind, and solitude join hands;
From a sunken pool, the blackened side
Of a buried ship sticks out at low tide.
The soaked and rotting curve of prow
Points seaward, and the old sea now
Growls still as harsh and hungrily
As when this derelict rode the sea.
Men in some century to come
May go a-grubbing in dry land   10
And find some bolts of iron; a hand
May hold them and a mouth be dumb.

1924

JOHN G. NEIHARDT 1881-

Mr. Neihardt has spent his life mostly in the
region that he celebrates in his poems, the valley of
the Missouri and its tributaries. During his youth
while at the Nebraska Normal College, and later,
he interested himself in stories and records of the
exploration and pioneer life of this region, especially
during the nineteenth century. He lived with the
Indians to find out their ways; he searched early
newspapers, diaries, personal records, the accounts
of trading companies, and legal archives that would
help him reconstruct the early days; and he
learned the stories of such survivors of the pioneer
life as he could find. His narratives, therefore, are
as far as possible the record of actual events and
persons.

Mr. Neihardt's work rises above local interest because he finds in these events the ending of the
great westward movement of the Indo-Aryan race,
in progress since the dawn of history, and the last
chapters of its ruthless dealings with races that
have stood across its path. He carries on the story
of this conflict between our own civilization and
that of Stone-Age nomads from the point where
Cooper leaves it in *The Prairie*. He has a keen realization of the epic features of the struggle and sees
in it the last phase of a spirit of adventure that
has swept on across more than two continents and
an intervening ocean to the lands beside the Pacific.
Its heroes he finds filled with the same impetus that
urged on Ulysses. He tells their story in iambic
measures of open couplets, well adapted to the
poetry of adventure. This form, together with the
style, reminds us of the heroic poetry of classic
times; we measure the heroism of the adventures
he relates by the spirit we find in ancient literature.

The outstanding work of Mr. Neihardt is found
in *The Song of Hugh Glass*, 1915; *The Song of
Three Friends*, 1919; and *The Song of the Indian
Wars*, 1925. His poems were collected in 1926.

Biography and criticism: J. T. House, *John G.
Neihardt: Man and Poet*, 1920; Phelps (EP), and
Bookm. 47:395; H. Monroe, "What of Mr. Nei-
hardt?" *Poetry* 30:99-104; "The Poet Laureate of
Nebraska," *Lit. Digest* 69:31, May 14, '21; see also
Bookm. 49:496-9; *Poetry* 7:264-9; 17:94-8; "Old
River Captain Rich in Experience," *Am. Mercury*
81:53-4.

From THE SONG OF THE INDIAN WARS [2]

I

From THE SOWING OF THE DRAGON [3]

At last the four year storm of fratricide
Had ceased at Appomattox, and the tide

[2] "The Song of the Indian Wars is a part of the Epic
Cycle of the West. . . . My purpose in writing
this cycle is to preserve the great race-mood of
courage that was developed west of the Missouri
River in the 19th century. The period . . . is beyond question the great American period, beginning in 1822 and ending in 1890. . . . In 1822 the
first Ashley-Henry band ascended the Missouri
and, after Lewis and Clark, the most important explorers of the West were Ashley-Henry men. . . .
The year 1890 marked the end of Indian resistance
on the Plains. . . . The Song of the Indian Wars
deals with the last great fight for the bison pastures of the Plains between the westering white
men and the prairie tribes—the struggle for the
right of way between the Missouri River and the
Pacific Ocean." [Neihardt's note]

From *The Song of the Indian Wars* by John G.
Neihardt, by permission of The Macmillan Company, publishers.

[3] a reference to the old myth of Cadmus, who slew a
dragon and sowed its teeth, from which sprang up
armed men who fought together till only five were
left

Of war-bit myriads, like a turning sea's,
Recoiled upon the deep realities
That yield no foam to any squall of change.

Now many a hearth of home had gotten strange
To eyes that knew sky-painting flares of war.
So much that once repaid the striving for
No longer mattered. Yonder road that ran
At hazard once beyond the ways of Man   10
By haunted vale and space-enchanted hill,
Had never dreamed of aught but Jones's Mill—
A dull pedestrian!   The spring, where erst
The peering plowboy sensed a larger thirst,
Had shoaled from awe, so long the man had
          drunk
At deeper floods. How yonder field had shrunk
That billowed once mysteriously far
To where the cow-lot nursed the evening star
And neighbored with the drowsing moon and
          sun!
For O what winds of wrath had boomed and
          run   20
Across what vaster fields of moaning grain—
Rich seedlings, nurtured by a ghastly rain
To woeful harvest!   So the world went small.
But 'mid the wreck of things remembered tall
An epidemic rumor murmured now.
Men leaned upon the handles of the plow
To hear and dream; and through the harrow-
          smoke
The weird voice muttered and the vision broke
Of distant, princely acres unpossessed.   30

Again the bugles of the Race blew west
That once the Tigris and Euphrates heard.
In unsuspected deeps of being stirred
The ancient and compelling Aryan [1] urge.
A homing of the homeless, surge on surge,
The valley roads ran wagons, and the hills
Through lane and by-way fed with trickling
          rills
The man-stream mighty with a mystic thaw.
All summer now the Mississippi saw
What long ago the Hellespont [2] beheld.   40
The shrewd, prophetic eyes that peered of eld
Across the Danube, visioned naked plains
Beyond the bleak Missouri, clad with grains,
Jeweled with orchard, grove and greening
          garth [3]—
Serene abundance centered in a hearth
To nurture lusty children.

                              On they swirled,
The driving breed, the takers of the world,
The makers and the bringers of the law.

[1] the parent race of all Indo-European peoples
[2] the Dardanelles   [3] garden

Now up along the bottoms of the Kaw [4]   50
The drifting reek of wheel and hoof arose.
The kiotes talked about it and the crows
Along the lone Republican; [5] and still
The bison saw it on the Smoky Hill
And Solomon; while yonder on the Platte
Ten thousand wagons scarred the sandy flat
Between the green grass season and the brown.

A name sufficed to make the camp a town,
A whim unmade. In spaces wide as air,
And late as empty, now the virile share [6]   60
Quickened the virgin meadow-lands of God;
And lo, begotten of the selfsame sod,
The house and harvest!

                              So the Cadmian breed, [7]
The wedders of the vision and the deed,
Went forth to sow the dragon-seed again.

But there were those—and they were also
          men—
Who saw the end of sacred things and dear
In all this wild beginning; saw with fear
Ancestral pastures gutted by the plow,   70
The bison harried ceaselessly, and how
They dwindled moon by moon; with pious
          dread
Beheld the holy places of their dead
The mock of aliens.

                              Sioux, Arapahoe,
Cheyenne, Comanche, Kiowa, and Crow
In many a council pondered what befell
The prairie world. Along the Musselshell,
The Tongue, the Niobrara, all they said
Upon the Platte, the Arkansaw, the Red   80
Was echoed word by peril-laden word.
Along Popo Agie [8] and the Horn they heard
The clank of hammers and the clang of rails
Where hordes of white men conjured iron trails
Now crawling past the Loup Fork and the Blue.
By desert-roaming Cimarron they knew,
And where La Poudre heads the tale was known,
How, snoring up beyond the Yellowstone,
The medicine-canoes breathed flame and steam
And, like weird monsters of an evil dream,   90
Spewed foes—a multitudinary spawn!

Were all the teeming regions of the dawn
Unpeopled now? What devastating need
Had set so many faces pale with greed
Against the sunset? Not as men who seek

[4] Kansas River
[5] A river in Nebraska; all the rivers mentioned in this
          passage lie in the vast region between Kansas
          and Canada, and almost all are tributary to
          the Missouri.
[6] plowshare   [8] pronounced po-po-a'ghee
[7] See note 3, page 813.

Some meed of kindness, suppliant and meek,
These hungry myriads came. They did but
      look,
And whatsoever pleased them, that they took.
Their faded eyes were icy, lacking ruth,
And all their tongues were forked to split the
      truth   100
That word and deed might take diverging ways.
Bewildered in the dusk of ancient days
The Red Men groped; and howsoever loud
The hopeful hotheads boasted in the crowd,
The wise one heard prophetic whisperings
Through aching hushes; felt the end of things
Inexorably shaping. What should be
Already was to them. And who can flee
His shadow or his doom? Though cowards
      stride
The wind-wild thunder-horses, Doom shall ride
The arrows of the lightning and prevail.   111
Ere long whole tribes must take the spirit trail
As once they traveled to the bison hunt.
Then let it be with many wounds—in front—
And many scalps, to show their ghostly kin
How well they fought the fight they could not
      win,
To perish facing what they could not kill.

So down upon the Platte and Smoky Hill
Swept war; and all their valleys were afraid.
The workers where the trails were being laid
To speed the iron horses, now must get   121
Their daily wage in blood as well as sweat
With gun and shovel. Often staring plains
Beheld at daybreak gutted wagon-trains
Set foursquare to the whirling night-attack,
With neither hoof nor hand to bring them back
To Omaha or Westport. Every week
The rolling coaches bound for Cherry Creek
Were scarred in running battle. Every day
Some ox-rig, creeping California way—   130
That paradise of every hope fulfilled—
Was plundered and the homesick driver killed,
Forlornly fighting for his little brood.
And often was the prairie solitude
Aware by night of burning ricks and roofs,
Stampeding cattle and the fleeing hoofs
Of wild marauders.
1924   1925

EDGAR LEE MASTERS 1869-

Mr. Masters was born in Kansas. After graduating from Knox College in Illinois he entered upon
the study of law and was called to the bar. He
began his literary work as early as 1898, and has
since produced books of drama, poetry, and essays.
The appearance of his *Spoon River Anthology*,
1915, brought him at once into prominence. The

theme was original, and treated in a manner entirely new. In its attitude, mood, and form it
represents a revolt against nineteenth century conventions. The dead, lying in the graveyard of
Spoon River, Illinois, tell the story of their lives
with startling frankness, and speak the truth that
was hidden or told only in whispers while they
lived. In these poems the constantly recurring
themes are the urge of passion and the irony of
fate that have tossed human beings hither and yon;
they stress the difference between reputations and
actualities. Frequently characters are made to explain each other; hidden motives and emotions
come to light when the reverse side of the picture
is shown. The social value of such poetry is its
arresting and stimulating quality when it is set
over against a view of life that has become sentimentally dishonest. The form of the poems, vigorous free verse, is well fitted to the subject-matter.

Mr. Masters' later work includes *Songs and
Satires* and *The Great Valley*, 1916; *Toward the
Gulf*, 1918; and *The New Spoon River Anthology*,
1924.

Criticism: Lowell; Boynton, *Some Contempo-
rary Americans;* Untermeyer; Phelps (EP); also
Bookm. 47:262-6; W. A. Bradley, "Four American
Poets," *Dial* 61:528-30; "Frost and Masters,"
Poetry 9:202-7; H. Monroe, "Edgar Lee Masters,"
Poetry 24:204-10; "What is Great Poetry," *Poetry*
26:349-51; *Bookm.* 55:514; see also: *Forum* 55:
109-23; *Bookm.* 41:355-7, 432-3.

ANNE RUTLEDGE [1]

Out of me unworthy and unknown
The vibrations of deathless music;
"With malice toward none, with charity for
      all."
Out of me the forgiveness of millions toward
      millions,
And the beneficent face of a nation
Shining with justice and truth.
I am Anne Rutledge who sleep beneath these
      weeds,
Beloved in life of Abraham Lincoln,
Wedded to him, not through union,
But through separation.   10
Bloom forever, O Republic,
From the dust of my bosom!
                                          1914, 1915

HENRY ZOLL, THE MILLER [2]

Have you ever noticed the mill pond in the
      dog days?
How it breeds wriggling life,
And seethes and crackles with poisonous froth,
Then lies as still as a snake gone blind?

[1] From *Spoon River Anthology* by Edgar Lee Masters,
      by permission of The Macmillan Company, pub-
      lishers.
[2] Copyright. From *New Spoon River Anthology*, by
      kind permission of the author.

And how can the mill pond know itself
When its water has caked to scum and worms?
And how can it know the world or the sky
When it has no mirror with which to see them?
But the river above the bend is wise:
Its waters are swift and cold and clear,   10
Always changing and always fresh,
And full of ripples and swirls and waves,
That image a thousand stars by night,
And a thousand phases of sun and clouds,
By a changing movie of forest and hills!
And down in its healthful depths the pickerel
Chase each other like silver shadows;
And the swift game fish swim up the stream.
Well, this is the soul of a man, my friend:
You brood at first, then froth with regret,   20
Then cake with hatred, and sink to dullness;
Or else you struggle and keep on the move,
Forget and solve and learn and emerge,
Full of sparkle and stars.
And down in your depths there's flashing laugh-
       ter,
Swimming against the current!

                                        1924

BENJAMIN FRANKLIN HAZARD [1]

You built the new Court House, Spoon River,
You laid one stone upon another—
But what made them stay? Was it the mortar
       only?
You put in arches, and groined ceilings—
What held them up? Was it the material,
Or the placing of material obedient to laws?
Who made those laws, who compelled you,
Even if you wanted neither air nor light,
Not to make vacuums of rooms, lest they col-
       lapse?
What do I mean, I who preach Americanism?
I am hinting at Americanism, laws, constitu-
       tions.   11
Can you make laws and constitutions the way
       you want to,
Against soul gravitations, arches without keys?
Rooms without air?
Or must you make them according to the laws
       of the soul?
What is The Law, the constitution, or the law of
       the soul?
What is Americanism? I tell you:
It is to be an Athenian, an Atlantian: [2]
Free, joyous, harmonious, balanced,
Simple, just tolerant, wise,   20

Peaceful, loving beauty,
Unprejudiced, seeking to learn,
Devoted to nature and to the happiness that
       comes from these,
And a maker of new gods in the image of per-
       fected hope,
And adoration!

                                        1924

HENRY COGDAL [1]

Bring from the Big Creek a huge boulder,
Put it at the head of me,
And bolt upon it a tablet of bronze
With these words:
Here was buried the body of Henry Cogdal,
A private who fell in the war for Wisdom,
And Beauty and Truth.
He strove to be a guide to the creative spirit,
And to uphold the singers and tellers of stories,
Who keep the vision of a nation   10
Upon the clear realities of life.
At the height of his power and work
He lost his place and means of support
Through a rich manufacturer who bought the
       newspaper,
And began to popularize it,
And to lower its criticisms
To the level of advertisers and optimists:—
There will come a time when crimes against
       culture
Will be punished the same as murder!

                                        1924

THE CLIPPER SHIPS [3]

New Bedford and Nantucket launched the
       traders and the whalers,
Launched the clipper ships whose wake fol-
       lowed Hawkins, followed Drake; [4]
Gave the ratlines and the brailers [5] to such
       sea hardened sailors
As had seen Hang Kow, Whampao, and Borneo,
Rio de Janeiro, and all the Canton trade,
Wherever there was barter that repaid any raid.

So anciently were schooners and brigs for these
       harpooners
When Sutter's [6] roused the cutters and Dana [7]
       sailed the seas,
When just to peddle notions was enough to sail
       the oceans,
And Emerson took a journey to Ferney [8] and
       was happy,   10

Nor missed the twenty knotters, nor the talk
  of globe trotters,
Nor the swimming pools, nor lifts, nor the state-
  room's ease.

But of all clipper builders whose shipmanship
  bewilders,
Over Jackson, over Briggs, over Hall was
  McKay.
Taking oak and southern pine he made harmony
  of line,
With no lack of hackmatack, 'mid the maul
  and hammer claque;
And with copper and with Taunton, and with
  truss and with stay
Did he build the *Flying Cloud* with its figure
  head so proud
Of an angel with a trumpet blowing to the sea
  exultant
Happiness for the wind's speed along the sea's
  way.   20

There was *Sovereign of the Seas* long of keel
  which could heel,
And shoot the waves which sought her with
  her sails and ropes tauter;
Which could righten like a racer, and leap forward like a pacer
With a stout heart and better start between the
  towering water.
There were *Red Jacket, Stag Hound,* swift ships
  and both renowned,
Trim as shiny mackerel, and sharpened like a
  pike.
And *Lightning* bound for Liverpool whose gun-
  wales passed the funnels,
Swifter than an eagle and as agile as a shrike.

But of all the clippers McKay builded in that
  wonder day,
None so great was or symbolic as the clipper
  Great Republic;   30
With her fifty feet of beam, and her strength
  and shapely length,
With her square masts and her spanker-masts
  and gaff-topsails,
And her acres of white canvas—how her pen-
  nants streamed the gales;
How they towed her from the slip [1] starting on
  her maiden trip;
But how fire ran up her ropes; how to ashes
  went her hopes;
How they scuttled her and diminished her pro-
  portions when re-finished;
How Australia never knew all the canvas that
  she flew.

[1] berthing-place

There was Portsmouth, there was Salem, there
  was Marblehead and Boston;
And Canton wharves and India wharves, and
  docks on the rocks.
And there you'd sit a-smoking while the sailors
  were a-joking;   40
And there you'd see the clipper ships by the
  rolling waters tossed on,
Dropping in from every shore, St. Petersburg
  and Singapore;
And never a roof to hide them like these sheds
  hide the piers.
New York enjoys no better luck than Omaha
  or Keokuk,
We never see a steamer dock, or see her when
  she clears.

1928

EDWIN ARLINGTON ROBINSON
1869-

Although Mr. Robinson is no longer a constant
resident of New England, his mind is of the serious
cast that we often associate with New England;
and the locality and people of his birthplace, Gar-
diner, Maine, have inspired some of his most
characteristic poems. His earlier poems, especially,
reflect a New England that is like Frost's in its
insistence upon secluded, out-of-the-way characters
and scenes. Unlike Frost's, Robinson's New England poetry is in shadow; a questioning, though
gentle irony pervades it, a searching for the deeper
values and the higher pleasures of life with no
certainty that they have been or can be found;
often the tragic note is dominant, not generally
harrowing, but thought-compelling.

Mr. Robinson's field is large, ranging from simple incidents to Arthurian legend. His verse is
"conventional" in form; its foremost characteristics
are severity and simplicity of diction, and a chaste-
ness and quietness that produce clear and exact
effects. His verse is close-knit; a swift ending,
which at first seems almost artificial, is found inevitably to result from the thought or material of
the poem. Notable among Mr. Robinson's books
of poems are *The Children of the Night,* 1897, *The
Man Against the Sky,* 1916, *Merlin,* 1917, *Tristram,*
1927. His poems were collected in 1921. In his
later romances especially, the verbal simplicity is
striking, for whole passages are prevailingly mono-
syllabic; yet the tales retain all the charm and
atmosphere of romance.

Biography and criticism: B. R. Redman, *Ed-
win Arlington Robinson,* 1926; M. Van Doren,
Edwin Arlington Robinson, 1927; *The Poetry
of Edwin Arlington Robinson,* Phelps (EP); Boyn-
ton, *Some Contemporary Americans;* Untermeyer;
Wilkinson (NV); Lowell; also *Dial* 72:130-42;
Y. Winters, "A Cool Master," *Poetry* 19:278-88;
A. W. Colton, *Lit. R.* 3:781-2; J. Drinkwater,
Fortn. 117:649-60; *Yale R.* ns 11:467-76; "An
Appreciation of the Poetry of Edwin Arlington

Robinson," *Scrib. M.* 66:763-4; S. Roth, "Edwin Arlington Robinson," *Bookm.* 50:507-11; L. MacVeagh, "Edwin Arlington Robinson," *New Repub.* 2:267-8.

REUBEN BRIGHT [1]

Because he was a butcher and thereby
Did earn an honest living (and did right),
I would not have you think that Reuben Bright
Was any more a brute than you or I;
For when they told him that his wife must die,
He stared at them, and shook with grief and
 fright,
And cried like a great baby half that night,
And made the women cry to see him cry.

And after she was dead, and he had paid
The singers and the sexton and the rest,   10
He packed a lot of things that she had made
Most mournfully away in an old chest
Of hers, and put some chopped-up cedar boughs
In with them, and tore down the slaughter-
 house.

1890-1897

THE HOUSE ON THE HILL [1]

They are all gone away,
 The House is shut and still,
There is nothing more to say.

Through broken walls and gray
 The winds blow bleak and shrill:
They are all gone away.

Nor is there one today
 To speak them good or ill:
There is nothing more to say.

Why is it then we stray   10
 Around the sunken sill?
They are all gone away,

And our poor fancy-play
 For them is wasted skill:
There is nothing more to say.

There is ruin and decay
 In the House on the Hill:
They are all gone away,
There is nothing more to say.

1890-1897

MINIVER CHEEVY [1]

Miniver Cheevy, child of scorn,
 Grew lean while he assailed the seasons;

[1] Copyright. Messrs. Charles Scribner's Sons, publishers.

He wept that he was ever born,
 And he had reasons.

Miniver loved the days of old
 When swords were bright and steeds were
 prancing;
The vision of a warrior bold
 Would set him dancing.

Miniver sighed for what was not,
 And dreamed, and rested from his labors;   10
He dreamed of Thebes and Camelot, [2]
 And Priam's neighbors. [3]

Miniver mourned the ripe renown
 That made so many a name so fragrant;
He mourned Romance, now on the town,
 And Art, a vagrant.

Miniver loved the Medici, [4]
 Albeit he had never seen one;
He would have sinned incessantly
 Could he have been one.   20

Miniver cursed the commonplace
 And eyed a khaki suit with loathing;
He missed the medieval grace
 Of iron clothing.

Miniver scorned the gold he sought,
 But sore annoyed was he without it;
Miniver thought, and thought, and thought,
 And thought about it.

Miniver Cheevy, born too late,
 Scratched his head and kept on thinking;   30
Miniver coughed and called it fate,
 And kept on drinking.

1910

STAFFORD'S CABIN [5]

Once there was a cabin here, and once there was
 a man;
And something happened here before my memory began.
Time has made the two of them the fuel of
 one flame
And all we have of them is now a legend and a
 name.

[2] Thebes, an ancient Egyptian city; Camelot, the residence of King Arthur, in Wales
[3] Priam was king of Troy when it was destroyed.
[4] noble Florentine family powerful during the Italian Renaissance, and notable for their patronage of art, their tyranny, and their crimes
[5] From *Collected Poems* of Edwin Arlington Robinson, by permission of The Macmillan Company, publishers.

All I have to say is what an old man said to me,
And that would seem to be as much as there
  will ever be.
"Fifty years ago it was we found it where it
  sat."—
And forty years ago it was old Archibald said
  that.

"An apple tree that's yet alive saw something,
  I suppose,
Of what it was that happened there, and what
  no mortal knows.   10
Some one on the mountain heard far off a mas-
  ter shriek,
And then there was a light that showed the way
  for men to seek.

"We found it in the morning with an iron bar
  behind,
And there were chains around it; but no search
  could ever find,
Either in the ashes that were left, or anywhere,
A sign to tell of who or what had been with
  Stafford there.

"Stafford was a likely man with ideas of his
  own—
Though I could never like the kind that likes
  to live alone;
And when you met, you found his eyes were
  always on your shoes,
As if they did the talking when he asked you
  for the news.   20

"That's all, my son. Were I to talk for half a
  hundred years
I'd never clear away from there the cloud that
  never clears.
We buried what was left of it,—the bar, too,
  and the chains;
And only for the apple tree there's nothing that
  remains."

Forty years ago it was I heard the old man say,
"That's all, my son."—And here again I find
  the place today,
Deserted and told only by the tree that knows
  the most,
And overgrown with golden-rod as if there were
  no ghost.

                                                  1916

ROBERT FROST 1875-

Although he was born in San Francisco, circumstances took Mr. Frost to his ancestral New England before his boyhood was past, and with New
England his life and work are essentially connected. He was for a while at Harvard, and
shortly afterwards spent some time in England
where he came into contact with some of the vigorous poets of the day. There his first books of
poems, *A Boy's Will*, 1913, and *North of Boston*,
1914, were published, and at once made him favorably known. Since returning to this country he has
passed much of his life upon farms in New Hampshire and Vermont, with some intervals spent in
teaching at Amherst; he has published *Mountain
Interval*, 1916, *New Hampshire*, 1923. At the University of Michigan he has spent two years as an
informal adviser to students of literary inclination
and ambition.

With few exceptions, Mr. Frost's work is the
product of New England in scene, characters, and
sentiment. It reflects the present spirit of the less
frequented localities now occupied by the less fortunate descendants of the old families, and by newcomers of foreign blood. It is the comedy or more
often the tragedy of the hill country and the remote
valleys that is notable in his books, the tragedy of
lives distorted or sometimes ennobled by the blind
following of the beaten path. However grim and
gnarled his characters may be, Frost himself is an
optimist; life, to him, is exceedingly worth living.

Criticism: Lowell; Untermeyer; Boynton, *Some
Contemporary Americans;* Wilkinson (NV); Phelps
(EP); Garnett; H. Monroe, "Robert Frost," *Poetry*
25 :146-53; E. S. Sergeant, "Robert Frost, a Good
Greek out of New England," *New Repub.* 44:
144-8; C. Van Doren, "The Soil of the Puritans,"
Cent. 105 :629-36; G. R. Elliott, "The Neighborliness of Robert Frost," *Nation* 109 :713-5; E. Garnett, "A New American Poet," *Atlan.* 116 :214-21;
S. Baxter, "New England's New Poet," *R. of Rs.*
51 :432-4; P. Colum, "The Poetry of Robert Frost,"
New Repub. 9 :219 ff.; S. H. Cox, "The Sincerity
of Robert Frost," *New Repub.* 12 :109-11.

MENDING WALL [1]

Something there is that doesn't love a wall,
That sends the frozen-ground-swell under it,
And spills the upper boulders in the sun;
And makes gaps even two can pass abreast.
The work of hunters is another thing:
I have come after them and made repair
Where they have left not one stone on a stone,
But they would have the rabbit out of hiding,
To please the yelping dogs. The gaps I mean,
No one has seen them made or heard them
  made,   10
But at spring mending-time we find them there.
I let my neighbor know beyond the hill;
And on a day we meet to walk the line
And set the wall between us once again.
We keep the wall between us as we go.
To each the boulders that have fallen to each.
And some are loaves and some so nearly balls

---

[1] Copyright. By permission of Messrs. Henry Holt and
    Company, publishers.

We have to use a spell to make them balance:
"Stay where you are until our backs are
    turned!"
We wear our fingers rough with handling them.
Oh, just another kind of outdoor game,   21
One on a side. It comes to little more:
There where it is we do not need the wall:
He is all pine and I am apple-orchard.
My apple trees will never get across
And eat the cones under his pines, I tell him.
He only says, "Good fences make good neigh-
    bors."
Spring is the mischief in me, and I wonder
If I could put a notion in his head: 29
"*Why* do they make good neighbors? Isn't it
Where there are cows? But here there are no
    cows.
Before I built a wall I'd ask to know
What I was walling in or walling out,
And to whom I was like to give offence.
Something there is that doesn't love a wall,
That wants it down." I could say "Elves" to
    him,
But it's not elves exactly, and I'd rather
He said it for himself. I see him there
Bringing a stone grasped firmly by the top
In each hand, like an old-stone savage armed.
He moves in darkness as it seems to me,   41
Not of woods only and the shade of trees.
He will not go behind his father's saying,
And he likes having thought of it so well
He says again, "Good fences make good
    neighbors."
1912   1914

THE DEATH OF THE HIRED MAN [1]

Mary sat musing on the lamp-flame at the table
Waiting for Warren. When she heard his step,
She ran on tip-toe down the darkened passage
To meet him in the doorway with the news
And put him on his guard. "Silas is back."
She pushed him outward with her through the
    door
And shut it after her. "Be kind," she said.
She took the market things from Warren's
    arms
And set them on the porch, then drew him
    down
To sit beside her on the wooden steps.   10

"When was I ever anything but kind to him?
But I'll not have the fellow back," he said.
"I told him so last haying, didn't I?
'If he left then,' I said, 'that ended it.'
What good is he? Who else will harbor him

[1] Copyright. By permission of Messrs. Henry Holt and
    Company, publishers.

At his age for the little he can do?
What help he is there's no depending on.
Off he goes always when I need him most.
'He thinks he ought to earn a little pay,
Enough at least to buy tobacco with,   20
So he won't have to beg and be beholden.'
'All right,' I say, 'I can't afford to pay
Any fixed wages, though I wish I could.'
'Someone else can.' 'Then someone else will
    have to.'
I shouldn't mind his bettering himself
If that was what it was. You can be certain,
When he begins like that, there's someone at
    him
Trying to coax him off with pocket-money,—
In haying time, when any help is scarce.
In winter he comes back to us. I'm done."   30

"Sh! not so loud: he'll hear you," Mary said.

"I want him to: he'll have to soon or late."

"He's worn out. He's asleep beside the stove.
When I came up from Rowe's I found him here,
Huddled against the barn-door fast asleep,
A miserable sight, and frightening, too—
You needn't smile—I didn't recognize him—
I wasn't looking for him—and he's changed.
Wait till you see."

    "Where did you say he'd been?"   40

"He didn't say. I dragged him to the house,
And gave him tea and tried to make him smoke.
I tried to make him talk about his travels.
Nothing would do: he just kept nodding off."

"What did he say? Did he say anything?"

"But little."

    "Anything? Mary, confess
He said he'd come to ditch the meadow for me."

"Warren!"

    "But did he? I just want to know."   50

"Of course he did. What would you have him
    say?
Surely you wouldn't begrudge the poor old man
Some humble way to save his self-respect.
He added, if you really care to know,
He meant to clear the upper pasture, too.
That sounds like something you have heard
    before?
Warren, I wish you could have heard the way
He jumbled everything. I stopped to look

Two or three times—he made me feel so
    queer—
To see if he was talking in his sleep.   60
He ran on Harold Wilson—you remember—
The boy you had in haying four years since.
He's finished school, and teaching in his college.
Silas declares you'll have to get him back.
He says they two will make a team for work:
Between them they will lay this farm as
    smooth!
The way he mixed that in with other things.
He thinks young Wilson a likely lad, though
    daft
On education—you know how they fought
All through July under the blazing sun,   70
Silas up on the cart to build the load,
Harold along beside to pitch it on."

"Yes, I took care to keep well out of earshot."

"Well, those days trouble Silas like a dream.
You wouldn't think they would.   How some
    things linger!
Harold's young college boy's assurance piqued
    him.
After so many years he still keeps finding
Good arguments he sees he might have used.
I sympathize.   I know just how it feels
To think of the right thing to say too late.   80
Harold's associated in his mind with Latin.
He asked me what I thought of Harold's saying
He studied Latin like the violin
Because he liked it—that an argument!
He said he couldn't make the boy believe
He could find water with a hazel prong—
Which showed how much good school had ever
    done him.
He wanted to go over that.   But most of all
He thinks if he could have another chance
To teach him how to build a load of hay—"   90

"I know, that's Silas' one accomplishment.
He bundles every forkful in its place,
And tags and numbers it for future reference,
So he can find and easily dislodge it
In the unloading.   Silas does that well.
He takes it out in bunches like big birds' nests.
You never see him standing on the hay
He's trying to lift, straining to lift himself."

"He thinks if he could teach him that, he'd be
Some good perhaps to someone in the world.
He hates to see a boy the fool of books.   101
Poor Silas, so concerned for other folk,
And nothing to look backward to with pride,
And nothing to look forward to with hope,
So now and never any different."

Part of a moon was falling down the west,
Dragging the whole sky with it to the hills.
Its light poured softly in her lap.   She saw
And spread her apron to it.   She put out her
    hand
Among the harp-like morning-glory strings,
Taut with the dew from garden bed to eaves,
As if she played unheard the tenderness   111
That wrought on him beside her in the night.
"Warren," she said, "he has come home to die;
You needn't be afraid he'll leave you this time."

"Home," he mocked gently.

        "Yes, what else but home?
It all depends on what you mean by home.
Of course he's nothing to us, any more
Than was the hound that came a stranger to us
Out of the woods, worn out upon the trail."

"Home is the place where, when you have to
    go there,   121
They have to take you in."

        "I should have called it
Something you somehow haven't to deserve."

Warren leaned out and took a step or two,
Picked up a little stick, and brought it back
And broke it in his hand and tossed it by.
"Silas has better claim on us you think
Than on his brother?   Thirteen little miles
As the road winds would bring him to his door.
Silas has walked that far no doubt today.   131
Why didn't he go there?   His brother's rich,
A somebody—director in the bank."

"He never told us that."

        "We know it though."

"I think his brother ought to help, of course.
I'll see to that if there is need.   He ought of
    right
To take him in, and might be willing to—
He may be better than appearances.
But have some pity on Silas.   Do you think
If he'd had any pride in claiming kin   141
Or anything he looked for from his brother,
He'd keep so still about him all this time?"

"I wonder what's between them."

        "I can tell you.
Silas is what he is—we wouldn't mind him—
But just the kind that kinsfolk can't abide.
He never did a thing so very bad.
He don't know why he isn't quite as good

As anyone. He won't be made ashamed 150
To please his brother, worthless though he is."

"*I* can't think Si ever hurt anyone."

"No, but he hurt my heart the way he lay
And rolled his old head on that sharp-edged
    chair-back.
He wouldn't let me put him on the lounge.
You must go in and see what you can do.
I made the bed up for him there tonight.
You'll be surprised at him—how much he's
    broken.
His working days are done; I'm sure of it."

"I'd not be in a hurry to say that." 160

"I haven't been. Go, look, see for yourself.
But, Warren, please remember how it is:
He's come to help you ditch the meadow.
He has a plan. You mustn't laugh at him.
He may not speak of it, and then he may.
I'll sit and see if that small sailing cloud
Will hit or miss the moon."

                It hit the moon.
Then there were three there, making a dim
    row,
The moon, the little silver cloud, and she. 170

Warren returned—too soon, it seemed to her,
Slipped to her side, caught up her hand and
    waited.

"Warren," she questioned.

           "Dead," was all he answered.
1905   1914

STORM FEAR [1]

When the wind works against us in the dark,
And pelts with snow
The lower chamber window on the east,
And whispers with a sort of stifled bark,
The beast,
"Come out! Come out!"—
It costs no inward struggle not to go,
Ah, no!
I count our strength,
Two and a child, 10
Those of us not asleep subdued to mark
How the cold creeps as the fire dies at length,
How drifts are piled,
Dooryard and road ungraded,

[1] Copyright. By permission of Messrs. Henry Holt and
    Company, publishers.

Till even the comforting barn grows far away;
And my heart owns a doubt
Whether 'tis in us to arise with day
And save ourselves unaided.
1910(?)   1913

NOT TO KEEP [1]

They sent him back to her. The letter came
Saying. . . . And she could have him. And
    before
She could be sure there was no hidden ill
Under the formal writing, he was in her sight,
Living. They gave him back to her alive—
How else? They are not known to send the
    dead—
And not disfigured visibly. His face?
His hands? She had to look, to ask,
"What is it, dear?" And she had given all 9
And still she had all—*they* had—they the lucky!
Wasn't she glad now? Everything seemed won,
And all the rest for them permissible ease.
She had to ask, "What was it, dear?"

                      "Enough,
Yet not enough. A bullet through and through,
High in the breast. Nothing but what good care
And medicine and rest, and you a week,
Can cure me of to go again." The same
Grim giving to do over for them both.
She dared no more than ask him with her eyes
How was it with him for a second trial. 21
And with his eyes he asked her not to ask.
They had given him back to her, but not to
    keep.
1915   1917

CARL SANDBURG 1878-

    Galesburg, Illinois, was the birthplace and early
home of Carl Sandburg, whose ancestors were
Swedish immigrants. After a boyhood spent in
the public schools, and a youth that included many
experiences as an itinerant laborer on farms and
railroads from Illinois to Colorado, and service in
the Spanish-American War, Sandburg came back
to Galesburg and worked his way through Lom-
bard College. For several years more he engaged in
various occupations, chiefly salesmanship, advertis-
ing, and newspaper work, and at length found a
place on the staff of the Chicago *Daily News*. His
poetry is found mainly in *Chicago Poems*, 1916;
Cornhuskers, 1916; *Smoke and Steel*, 1920; and
Slabs of the Sunburned West, 1923. His *Abraham
Lincoln, the Prairie Years*, 1926, is one of the most
popular lives of the president.
    The first impression of Sandburg's poetry is its
likeness to Whitman's; the two are strongly similar
in manner, subject matter, and in general outlook
upon society. Democracy with the laborer as the

central figure is a theme common to both, though Sandburg glorifies the ego less than Whitman. Sandburg's technique is his own; he chooses his words carefully for their individual, naked strength. The result is compression and sharp emphasis upon fact.

Criticism: R. West, Preface to Sandburg's *Selected Poems*, 1926; Lowell; Phelps (EP); Sherman, *Americans;* Untermeyer; also *Dial* 65:263-4; C. and M. Van Doren, *American and British Literature;* also *Cent.* 106:786-92; Boynton; H. Monroe, "Carl Sandburg," *Poetry* 24:320-6; S. Anderson, *Bookm.* 54:360-1; P. Rosenfeld, *Bookm.* 53:389-96; W. Yust, *Bookm.* 52:385-90; E. Carnevali, "Our Great Carl Sandburg," *Poetry* 17:266-72.

CLEAN CURTAINS [1]

New neighbors came to the corner house at Congress and Green Streets.

The look of their clean white curtains was the same as the rim of a nun's bonnet.

One way was an oyster pail factory, one way they made candy, one way paper boxes, strawboard cartons.

The warehouse trucks shook the dust of the ways loose and the wheels whirled dust —there was dust of hoof and wagon wheel and rubber tire—dust of police and fire wagons—dust of the winds that circled at midnight and noon listening to no prayers.

"O mother, I know the heart of you," I sang passing the rim of a nun's bonnet—O white curtains—and people clean as the prayers of Jesus here in the faded ramshackle at Congress and Green.

Dust and the thundering trucks won—the barrages of the street wheels and the lawless wind took their way—was it five weeks or six the little mother, the new neighbors, battled and then took away the white prayers in the windows?

A.E.F. [1]

There will be a rusty gun on the wall, sweetheart,
The rifle grooves curling with flakes of rust.
A spider will make a silver string nest in the darkest, warmest corner of it.
The trigger and the range-finder, they too will be rusty.

[1] From *Smoke and Steel* by Carl Sandburg, copyright, 1920, by Harcourt, Brace and Company, Inc.

And no hands will polish the gun, and it will hang on the wall.
Forefingers and thumbs will point absently and casually toward it.
It will be spoken about among half-forgotten, wished-to-be-forgotten things.
They will tell the spider: Go on, you're doing good work.

CHICAGO [2]

Hog Butcher for the World,
Tool Maker, Stacker of Wheat,
Player with Railroads and the Nation's Freight Handler;
Stormy, husky, brawling,
City of the Big Shoulders:

They tell me you are wicked, and I believe them; for I have seen your painted women under the gas lamps luring the farm boys.
And they tell me you are crooked, and I answer: Yes, it is true I have seen the gunman kill and go free to kill again.
And they tell me you are brutal, and my reply is: On the faces of women and children I have seen the marks of wanton hunger.
And having answered so I turn once more to those who sneer at this my city, and I give them back the sneer and say to them:
Come and show me another city with lifted head singing so proud to be alive and coarse and strong and cunning.
Flinging magnetic curses amid the toil of piling job on job, here is a tall bold slugger set vivid against the little soft cities;
Fierce as a dog with tongue lapping for action, cunning as a savage pitted against the wilderness,
Bareheaded,
Shoveling,
Wrecking,
Planning,
Building, breaking, rebuilding,
Under the smoke, dust all over his mouth, laughing with white teeth,
Under the terrible burden of destiny laughing as a young man laughs,
Laughing even as an ignorant fighter laughs who has never lost a battle,
Bragging and laughing that under his wrist is the pulse, and under his ribs the heart of the people,

[2] Copyright. By permission of Messrs. Henry Holt and Company, publishers.

Laughing!
Laughing the stormy, husky, brawling laughter
   of Youth, half-naked, sweating, proud to
   be Hog Butcher, Tool Maker, Stacker
   of Wheat, Player with Railroads and
   Freight Handler to the Nation.

1916

GRASS [1]

Pile the bodies high at Austerlitz and Waterloo. [2]
Shovel them under and let me work—
      I am the grass; I cover all.

And pile them high at Gettysburg
And pile them high at Ypres and Verdun. [3]
Shovel them under and let me work.
Two years, ten years, and passengers ask the
   conductor:

      What place is this?
      Where are we now?

      I am the grass.
      Let me work.

LOST [1]

Desolate and lone
All night long on the lake
Where fog trails and mist creeps,
The whistle of a boat
Calls and cries unendingly,
Like some lost child
In tears and trouble
Hunting the harbor's breast
And the harbor's eyes.

FOG [1]

The fog comes
on little cat feet.

It sits looking
over harbor and city
on silent haunches
and then moves on.

LAUGHING CORN [1]

There was a high majestic fooling
Day before yesterday in the yellow corn.

[1] Copyright. By permission of Messrs. Henry Holt and
   Company, publishers.
[2] Famous battlefields of the Napoleonic wars; Napoleon,
   victor at Austerlitz, 1805, was defeated at Waterloo, 1815.
[3] famous battlefields of the World War

And day after tomorrow in the yellow corn
There will be high majestic fooling.

The ears ripen in late summer
And come on with a conquering laughter,
Come on with a high and conquering laughter.

The long-tailed blackbirds are hoarse.
One of the smaller blackbirds chitters on a stalk
And a spot of red is on its shoulder   10
And I never heard its name in my life.

Some of the ears are bursting.
A white juice works inside.
Cornsilk creeps in the end and dangles in the
   wind.
Always—I never knew it any other way—
The wind and the corn talk things over together.
And the rain and the corn and the sun and the
   corn
Talk things over together.

Over the road is the farmhouse.
The siding is white and a green blind is slung
   loose.   20
It will not be fixed till the corn is husked.
The farmer and his wife talk things over to-
   gether.

NICHOLAS VACHEL LINDSAY
1879-

   Mr. Lindsay stands out among living American
poets for his highly individual theories of the
part poetry might play in the lives of the masses,
and of the methods he uses to bring his poetry before the public. After receiving a high school and
college education in Springfield, Illinois, his birthplace, he studied art in Chicago and New York
City, and for two years was a Young Men's Christian Association lecturer and settlement worker.
He then spent five years tramping through parts
of the Mississippi Valley preaching his "gospel of
beauty," the underlying idea of which was the enriching and beautifying of the life of the small
community. He worked his way by reciting, chanting, and distributing his own rimes and verses.
(See *Adventures While Preaching the Gospel of
Beauty*, 1914.) His chief books of poetry are *General William Booth Enters into Heaven*, 1913, *The
Congo and Other Poems*, 1914, *The Chinese Nightingale*, 1917, *Going to the Sun*, 1923, *Collected
Poems*, 1925. Like Whitman and Sandburg he
attempts to voice modern, democratic America. He
differs from them in the great importance he attaches to rhythm. He attempts to reproduce circus
music, the primitive tom-tom, and even "jazz." In
so doing he catches the popular ear, deaf to the
subtler melodies of poetry, and now and then he
reaches effects of unusual beauty.

Criticism: Untermeyer; Phelps (EP); also *Bookm.* 47:125-34; J. B. Rittenhouse, "Contemporary Poetry," *Bookm.* 46:575-7; E. L. Masters, "Vachel Lindsay," *Bookm.* 64: 156-60; C. Van Doren, "Salvation with Jazz," *Cent.* 105:951-6; F. Dell, "Two American Poets: A Study in Possibilities," *Nation* 118:439-40; H. S. Gorman, "Vachel Lindsay: Evangelist of Poetry," *No. Am.* 219: 123-8; G. Frank, "The Rodin of American Poetry," *Cent.* 102:638-40.

ABRAHAM LINCOLN WALKS AT MIDNIGHT [1]

(*In Springfield, Illinois*)

It is portentous, and a thing of state
That here at midnight, in our little town,
A mourning figure walks, and will not rest,
Near the old court-house pacing up and down,

Or by his homestead, or in shadowed yards
He lingers where his children used to play,
Or through the market, on the well-worn stones
He stalks until the dawn-stars burn away.

A bronzed, lank man! His suit of ancient black,
A famous high top-hat and plain worn shawl   10
Make him the quaint great figure that men love,
The prairie-lawyer, master of us all.

He cannot sleep upon his hillside now.
He is among us:—as in times before!
And we who toss and lie awake for long
Breathe deep, and start, to see him pass the door.

His head is bowed. He thinks on men and kings.
Yea, when the sick world cries, how can he sleep?
Too many peasants fight, they know not why,
Too many homesteads in black terror weep.   20

The sins of all the war-lords burn his heart.
He sees the dreadnaughts scouring every main.
He carries on his shawl-wrapped shoulders now
The bitterness, the folly and the pain.

He cannot rest until a spirit-dawn
Shall come;—the shining hope of Europe free:
The league of sober folk, the Workers' Earth,
Bringing long peace to Cornland, Alp, and Sea.

It breaks his heart that kings must murder still,
That all his hours of travail here for men   30

---

[1] From *Collected Poems* by Vachel Lindsay, by permission of The Macmillan Company, publishers.

Seem yet in vain. And who will bring white peace
That he may sleep upon his hill again?

1925

THESE ARE THE YOUNG [2]

Dedicated to the Reverend Charles Pease,
Minister of the Unitarian Society,
Spokane, Washington

I

"What new mob disturbs the days?
Who are these, with intrusive ways,
Who speak with an alien tongue?
Who are these Olympian-white
Butterflies of flame,
High upon Sun Mountain,
Invading now, every fountain,
Obeying their own captains
And to no men tame;
Whispering so low   10
We cannot hear at all,
Yet calling: 'Brother,' 'Sister'
Through the sun-mountain wall?
Who are these Olympian-white
Butterflies of flame,
Full of a holy grace?
Tell me their spiritual name."

The Answer

"This is a separate race,
Speaking an alien tongue—
These are the young!"   20

II

"Tell me of the Olympian-white
Aspen trees of flame,
And of the Olympian-white
Mariposa lilies,
Climbing great Sun Mountain,
Invading now, every fountain,
Tell me their spiritual name."

The Answer

"This is a chosen people,
This is a separate race
Speaking an alien tongue—   30
These are the young!"

III

"Tell me of the Olympian-white
Basket-flowers of flame,
The marching-plumes of flame,

---

[2] Copyright. By permission of Messrs. D. Appleton and Company, New York, publishers.

Climbing great Sun Mountain,
Invading now, every fountain,
While our hearts grow greater
And our climbing songs are sung;
While the days grow later,
While the sun still lingers,   40
Or great storm bells are rung,
And the lightning splits the hills,
And now, the falling fountain fills.
Tell me of these high-plumed tribes
Of Indian basket-flowers
That march up the Sun Mountain glacier,
Through the holy hours,
What is their spiritual name?"

The Answer

"This is a separate race,
Speaking an alien tongue—   50
These are the young!"

IV

"Who are these boys and girls on horseback
Who go by next day,
The horses loaded for camping,
No guides to lead the way?
Girls Olympian white
Or painted to the eyes,
Innocently wicked,
Innocently wise;
Innocently impudent,   60
Innocently gay—
Boys who are Young America,
Scholars, lean and white,
Or athletes red and gay,
Proud young man America,
Well on its way,
Girls most bewitching,
Boys most untamed,
Hotly praised and preached at; hotly, *very*
     hotly blamed.
Who are these? What is their aim?   70
What is now their game?
What is their spiritual name?"

The Answer

"This is a chosen people,
This is a separate race,
Speaking an alien tongue—
These are the darlings of my heart,
These are the young."

                     1926

THE ANGEL SONS [1]

We will have angels and men for sons,
For I have gone out to you

[1] Copyright. By permission of Messrs. D. Appleton and
Company, New York, publishers.

Wearing the wings of desire,
In the rain, in the storm, in the dew.

Strong men, stronger than any we see,
Strong angels, stronger than any we see,
Singing of love round the poppy bed,
For they have soft eyes, and they weary of
     waiting
For our souls to reach the ultimate mating,
Weary of waiting, worn with waiting,   10
Till half of their glory is dead.

My soul has gone out on their poppy song,
Wearing such wings of desire
That our angel sons will have strength to the
     uttermost,
Beauty and dreaming power to the uttermost,
Veins filled with snow and uttermost fire,
Snow from the top of the Great Sun Mountain,
Fire from these flowers of desire!

They will rule our sons who are merely men,
Enforcing our will on the earth again,   20
Beginning, beginning at Great Sun Mountain,
They will make over the land,
They will make over the age,
Granite each angel house,
Crimson each written page.

They will rule our sons who are merely men,
Earth sons with this elder brother start!
Born from beneath your earthly heart!
Born from your lily side,
Strong, with the sternest eyes,   30
They will conquer the land and its pride.

Dear girl, when these wild years die,
When other lovers go by,
Playing Sun Mountain games,
With faith that their love will also save,
Their pride of love from destruction's breath,
Their sun-born stock from uttermost death,
And their earth-born stock from uttermost
     death,
These lovers will say our names,
And, climbing Sun Mountain high,   40
Will stop where our bodies lie,
And leave as the sign of faith
A poppy upon your grave,
Yes—
A mountain poppy upon my grave!

                     1926

MARGARET WIDDEMER

Miss Widdemer, a native of Doylestown, Pennsylvania, was educated privately and later was graduated from the Drexel Institute Library School. She began writing during childhood, and since 1912 has contributed essays, reviews, poems, and short stories to various periodicals. In her first published poem, "The Factories," Miss Widdemer struck her most distinctive note, the dependence of those of one social level upon those of other levels. Such social sympathy has marked the work of many women poets, notably that of Mrs. Browning. Even in those of Miss Widdemer's lyrics that reflect no serious social purpose there is, characteristically, a poignant feminine quality. Besides her volumes of verse—*Factories*, 1915; *The Old Road to Paradise*, 1918, which divided the Pulitzer Prize for Poetry with Sandburg's *Cornhuskers; Cross-Currents,* 1921; *Poems, Ballads and Lyrics,* 1925—she has produced several light novels and popular stories for girls.

Criticism: *Bookm.* 42:458; 47:392-3; *Poetry* 7: 150; 14:273; Phelps (EP); Wilkinson (NV).

FACTORIES [1]

I have shut my little sister in from life and
    light
  (For a rose, for a ribbon, for a wreath across
    my hair),
I have made her restless feet still until the
    night,
  Locked from sweets of summer and from
    wild spring air;
I who ranged the meadowlands, free from sun
    to sun,
  Free to sing and pull the buds and watch the
    far wings fly,
I have bound my sister till her playing time
    was done—
  Oh, my little sister, was it I? Was it I?

I have robbed my sister of her day of maiden-
    hood
  (For a robe, for a feather, for a trinket's
    restless spark),   10
Shut from love till dusk shall fall, how shall
    she know good,
  How shall she go scatheless through the sun-
    lit dark?
I who could be innocent, I who could be gay,
  I who could have love and mirth before the
    light went by,
I have put my sister in her mating-time away—
  Sister, my young sister, was it I? Was it I?

I have robbed my sister of the lips against her
    breast
  (For a coin, for the weaving of my children's
    lace and lawn),

[1] From *Factories with Other Lyrics* by Margaret Widdemer. Copyright. By permission of Messrs. Henry
Holt and Company, publishers.

Feet that pace beside the loom, hands that can-
    not rest—
  How can she know motherhood, whose
    strength is gone?   20
I who took no heed of her, starved and labor-
    worn,
  I, against whose placid heart my sleepy gold-
    heads lie,
Round my path they cry to me, little souls
    unborn—
  God of Life! Creator! It was I! It was I!
    1915

THE WATCHER [2]

She always leaned to watch for us,
  Anxious if we were late,
In winter by the window,
  In summer by the gate;

And though we mocked her tenderly,
  Who had such foolish care,
The long way home would seem more safe
  Because she waited there.

Her thoughts were all so full of us,
  She never could forget!   10
And so I think that where she is
  She must be watching yet,

Waiting till we come home to her,
  Anxious if we are late—
Watching from Heaven's window,
  Leaning from Heaven's gate.
    1920

THE MODERN WOMAN TO HER LOVER [3]

I shall not lie to you any more,
  Flatter or fawn to attain my end—
I am what never has been before,
  Woman—and Friend.

I shall be strong as a man is strong,
  I shall be fair as a man is fair,
Hand in locked hand we shall pass along
  To a purer air:

I shall not drag at your bridle-rein,
  Knee pressed to knee we shall ride the hill; 10
I shall not lie to you ever again—
  Will you love me still?
    1914

[2] From *Cross Currents* by Margaret Widdemer, copyright, 1921, by Harcourt, Brace and Company, Inc.
[3] From *The Old Road to Paradise* by Margaret Widdemer. Copyright. By permission of Messrs. Henry
Holt and Company, publishers.

SARA TEASDALE 1884-

Of present-day American lyric poets, one of the most prominent is Sara Teasdale (Mrs. E. B. Filsinger). She is a native of St. Louis, Missouri, where she was educated in private schools. She has traveled much in America, Europe, and the Near East, and now lives in New York City. From her first volume of poems, *Sonnets to Duse, and Other Poems,* 1907, through *Helen of Troy and Other Poems,* 1911, *Rivers to the Sea,* 1915, *Flame and Shadow,* 1920, and *Dark of the Moon,* 1926, Miss Teasdale's work has steadily advanced both in workmanship and in lyric depth. Her poetry is spontaneous and direct, serious, sensuous yet delicate, and composed of the simplest of materials. In its poignancy and its revelation of woman's heart it is akin to Emily Dickinson's. In variety of forms and artistic technique it ranks notably high.

Criticism: Phelps (EP); also *Bookm.* 47:392; Untermeyer, Wilkinson (NV); also "Sara Teasdale's Poems," *Forum* 65:229-35; J. B. Rittenhouse, "Sara Teasdale," *Bookm.* 65:290-4; P. Colum, "Sara Teasdale's Poems," *New Repub.* 15:239-41; H. Monroe, "Sara Teasdale's Prize," *Poetry* 12: 264-9; see also *Bookm.* 42:365; 457-8; *Poetry* 7: 148-50; 17:272-5.

BLUE SQUILLS [1]

How many million Aprils came
  Before I ever knew
How white a cherry bough could be,
  A bed of squills, how blue!

And many a dancing April
  When life is done with me,
Will lift the blue flame of the flower
  And the white flame of the tree.

Oh burn me with your beauty, then,
  Oh, hurt me, tree and flower,   10
Lest in the end death try to take
  Even this glistening hour.

O shaken flowers, O shimmering trees,
  O sunlit white and blue,
Wound me, that I, through endless sleep,
  May bear the scar of you.

1920

AUGUST MOONRISE [1]

The sun was gone, and the moon was coming
Over the blue Connecticut hills;
The west was rosy, the east was flushed,
And over my head the swallows rushed
This way and that, with changeful wills.
I heard them twitter and watched them dart
Now together and now apart

[1] From *Flame and Shadow* by Sara Teasdale, by permission of The Macmillan Company, publishers.

Like dark petals blown from a tree;
The maples stamped against the west
Were black and stately and full of rest,   10
And the hazy orange moon grew up
And slowly changed to yellow gold
While the hills were darkened, fold on fold
To a deeper blue than a flower could hold.
Down the hill I went, and then
I forgot the ways of men,
For night-scents, heady, and damp and cool
Wakened ecstasy in me
On the brink of a shining pool.

O Beauty, out of many a cup   20
You have made me drunk and wild
Ever since I was a child,
But when have I been sure as now
That no bitterness can bend
And no sorrow wholly bow
One who loves you to the end?
And though I must give my breath
And my laughter all to death,
And my eyes through which joy came,
And my heart, a wavering flame;   30
If all must leave me and go back
Along a blind and fearful track
So that you can make anew,
Fusing with intenser fire,
Something nearer your desire;
If my soul must go alone
Through a cold infinity,
Or even if it vanish, too,
Beauty, I have worshiped you.

Let this single hour atone   40
For the theft of all of me.

1920

ON THE DUNES [1]

If there is any life when death is over,
  These tawny beaches will know much of me,
I shall come back, as constant and as changeful
  As the unchanging, many-colored sea.

If life was small, if it has made me scornful,
  Forgive me; I shall straighten like a flame
In the great calm of death, and if you want me
  Stand on the sea-ward dunes and call my
    name.

1920

THE UNSEEN [1]

Death went up the hall
  Unseen by every one,
Trailing twilight robes
  Past the nurse and the nun.

He paused at every door
  And listened to the breath
Of those who did not know
  How near they were to Death.

Death went up the hall
  Unseen by nurse and nun;   10
He passed by many a door—
  But he entered one.

                                    1920

A STAR MAP [1]

All of heaven in my hands—
  With one finger I can turn
Till I sink Orion's bands,
  And the Lyre begins to burn.

I can make a night of spring,
  Shivering Spica, white Altair,
And above me I can swing
  Slowly Berenice's Hair.

Winter evening, autumn dawn
  Man has charted; I can see   10
How Midsummer Night moves on
  Tranquilly and terribly;

Light lost in light, death lost in death,
  Time without end, Space without bound—
I, whose life is but a breath,
  Turn Infinity around.

                                    1926

ROBERT HAVEN SCHAUFFLER
1879-

Mr. Schauffler, born in Austria of American parents, received his education at Northwestern University, at Princeton, and at the University of Berlin. His activities and interests have lain in many fields: as an athlete and tennis champion he has taken part in the Olympic Games; he has been a musician and sculptor; he saw active service in the World War; he has edited many anthologies, notably the *Poetry Cure* (a "medicine-chest of verse, music, and pictures"), 1925; and he has contributed essays and poems to leading periodicals. His essays descriptive of travel and musical experiences (*Romantic Germany*, 1909; *The Musical Amateur*, 1911; *Fiddler's Luck*, 1920; *Peter Pantheism*, 1925) are in a light, familiar style, graced by spontaneous humor. His books of poetry are *Scum o' the Earth*, 1912; *The White Comrade*, 1920; *Magic Flame and Other Poems*, 1923; *Hobnails in Eden*, 1929.

[1] Copyright. By permission of the author and of *The Bookman*, New York.
[1] A globe of the heavens (an astronomical globe); the names are those of constellations.

Mr. Schauffler's poetry is wholesomely optimistic. It shows a keen sensitiveness to social injustice, yet faith that men will be able to solve their social problems, and, given time, work out their spiritual destiny. His out-of-door poems, unusually graphic in details, reveal a healthy body and vigorous mind reacting with enthusiasm to the experiences of primitive forests and lakes.

Criticism: *N. Y. Times Lit. Sup.* Apr. 22, '23; *Sat. R. Lit.* 2:451, Dec. 26, '25; *N. Y. Times* p. 7, Apr. 22, '23; *Outlook* 135:113.

"SCUM O' THE EARTH" [2]

I

At the gate of the West I stand,
On the isle where the nations throng.
We call them "scum o' the earth";

Stay, are we doing you wrong,
Young fellow from Socrates' land?—
You, like a Hermes so lissome and strong—
Fresh from the master Praxiteles' [3] hand?
So you're of Spartan birth?
Descended, perhaps, from one of the band—
Deathless in story and song—   10
Who combed their long hair at Thermopylae's [4]
    pass? . . .
Ah, I forget what straits, alas!
More tragic than theirs, more compassion-
    worth,
That have doomed you to march in our "immi-
    grant class"
Where you're nothing but "scum o' the earth."

II

You Pole with a child on your knee,
What dower bring you to the land of the free?
Hark! does she croon
That sad little tune
That Chopin [5] once found on his Polish lea   20
And mounted in gold for you and for me?
Now a ragged young fiddler answers
In wild Czeck melody
That Dvořák [6] took whole from the dancers.
And the heavy faces bloom
In the wonderful Slavic way;
The little, dull eyes, the brows a-gloom,
Suddenly dawn like the day.
While, watching these folks and their mystery,
I forget that we,   30
In our scornful mirth,
Brand them as "Polacks"—and "scum o' the
    earth."

[2] Copyright. By permission of Houghton Mifflin and Company, authorized publishers.
[3] famous Greek sculptor, fl. 340 B.C.
[4] a mountain pass in Greece, where the Greeks defeated the Persians 480 B.C.
[5] Polish-French pianist and composer, 1809-49
[6] [dvôr'zhäk] Bohemian composer, 1841-1904

III

Genoese boy of the level brow,
Lad of the lustrous, dreamy eyes
Astare at Manhattan's pinnacles now
In the first, sweet shock of a hushed surprise;
Within your far-rapt seer's eyes
I catch the glow of the wild surmise
That played on the *Santa Maria's* prow   40
In that still gray dawn,
Four centuries gone,
When a world from the wave began to rise.
Oh, it's hard to foretell what high emprise
Is the goal that gleams
When Italy's dreams
Spread wing and sweep into the skies.
Caesar dreamed him a world ruled well;
Dante [1] dreamed Heaven out of Hell;
Angelo [2] brought us there to dwell;   50
And you, are you of different birth?—
You're only a "dago,"—and "scum o' the
        earth"!

IV

Stay, are we doing you wrong
Calling you "scum o' the earth,"
Man of the sorrow-bowed head,
Of the features tender yet strong,—
Man of the eyes full of wisdom and mystery
Mingled with patience and dread?
Have I not known you in history,
Sorrow-bowed head?   60
Were you the poet-king, [3] worth
Treasures of Ophir [4] unpriced?
Were you the prophet, perchance, whose art
Foretold how the rabble would mock
That shepherd of spirits, erelong,
Who should carry the lambs on his heart
And tenderly feed his flock?
Man—lift that sorrow-bowed head. . .
Behold the face of the Christ!

The vision dies at its birth.   70
You're merely a butt for our mirth.
You're a "sheeny"—and therefore despised
And rejected as "scum o' the earth."

V

Countrymen, bend and invoke
Mercy for us blasphemers,
For that we spat on these marvelous folk,
Nations of darers and dreamers,

[1] great Italian poet, 1265-1321, author of the *Divine Comedy*
[2] Michael Angelo, 1475-1564, Italian painter, sculptor, architect
[3] David
[4] a country, possibly India or Arabia, frequently mentioned in the Bible as rich in gold, silver, jewels, ivory, and sandal wood

Scions of singers and seers,
Our peers, and more than our peers.
"Rabble and refuse" we name them,   80
And "scum o' the earth," to shame them.
Mercy for us of the few, young years,
Of the culture so callow and crude,
Of the hands so grasping and rude,
The lips so ready for sneers
At the sons of our ancient more-than-peers.
Mercy for us who dare despise
Men in whose loins our Homer lies;
Mothers of men who shall bring to us   89
The glory of Titian, [5] the grandeur of Huss; [6]
Children in whose frail arms shall rest
Prophets and singers and saints of the West.

Newcomers all from the eastern seas,
Help us incarnate dreams like these.
Forget, and forgive, that we did you wrong.
Help us to father a nation, strong
In the comradeship of an equal birth,
In the wealth of the richest bloods of earth.
1909   1911

HELEN OF LAUGHING LEDGE [7]

Young Helen's beauty has its source
Within the tumbling water course
Where leagues of ripple, race and pool
Have put this woman-child to school
With rainbow streamers in the mist
Where rapids grind their feathery grist;
Woods mirrored upside down and wet,
The current's velvet clairionet,
The sob and chuckle of the eddy,
Cool river gusts—high-spiced and heady   10
With incense of bruised bark and tones
Of fluent log-drive xylophones—
Bearing the cataracts organ-shout
With every single stop pulled out.

Poised for a dive, she can compare
With a young birch, and her crisp hair
Centers the sun, as birch-leaves hold
Something of all September's gold.

The blur of down upon her skin
Suggests a muted violin   20
That hums of melting frosts of dew
On iris leaves when dawn is new.

Prisoned in city walls, I think
Of her when thirsting for a drink
Poured by the loveliness of Maine.
Dreaming of her, I know again
Iced runnels from Katahdin slides,

[5] Italian painter, 1477-1576
[6] John Huss, Bohemian Protestant reformer, 1369-1415
[7] Copyright. By permission of the author.

Shelves where the broody partridge hides,
The hush of lappings in a cove
Where herons wade and otters rove,   30
The whole dear gamut of wild water
That knows young Helen for its daughter.

1929

GOD'S-EYE VIEW [1]

*"Let us imagine the whole gradual and laborious
attainments of mankind compressed into the compass of a single lifetime. Let us assume that a
single generation of men have in fifty years managed
to accumulate all that now passes for civilization.
They would have to start, as all individuals do, absolutely uncivilized, and their task would be to re-
capitulate what has occupied the race for, let us
guess, at least five hundred thousand years. Each
year in the life of a generation would therefore
correspond to ten thousand years in the progress of
the race."*

—JAMES HARVEY ROBINSON, *The Mind
in the Making*

I

Vexed by the distant,
Maddeningly persistent
Bangs of a little planetary war,
God said: "I'll stand no more!
This rascal Earth and his unruly child
Presume upon my fatherly predilection.
I've been too mild;
Now for correction!

"But there's one thing:
Before I swing   10
The sword I have in mind,
Perhaps I should endeavor to condone
These adolescent follies of mankind.
For one must own
That, on a model throne,
Calm study of each miscreant's way of life
Always precedes the knife.
So I'll review the human story
In every sorry category.

"But hold! I find   20
This vast historical agglomeration
Confusing to convenient contemplation."
Therefore, to make it bulk the less,
God placed all human history in a press
And diligently squeezed it to the span
Of the half-century life of mortal man.

II

After this condensation man appears,
For nine and forty of his fifty years,

Beneath God's altered sight,   29
A cave-brute, or a wandering savage bowman,
Before he starts to weave and till and sow.
Barely six moons ago
He learns to write—
Portentous omen!
Another three
Find poetry, sculpture and philosophy
Upon a height
Whose counterpart God vainly seeks
Through all of the remaining weeks.

For two months, now,   40
The Christian clan
Has decked its faith in creed and rite and vow
Fit to appal the simple Son of Man.

Li Po and Gutenberg are a fortnight old;
Watt is a week; Rodin and Brahms, [2] a day;
The wingèd man has hardly learned to play.
A dawn ago astonished humans rolled
Their words from land to land the ether way.
And now, this dark night past,
Dazed by the glory of his perfected toy,   50
Man, like a half-wit boy,
Set up war's cannon-cracker, red and vast,
And gaily lit the fuse that might destroy, [3]
In one magnificent blast,
All the creations of his year of joy.

III

God weighs the savage forty-nine
Against the single year of grace;
And a slow smile, half humorous, half divine,
Steals on the angry face.

1929

TRASH [1]

Three moons I trekked the woods without a
          trail
And found no sign of man upon the earth;
My zest in solitude began to fail;
I longed for human speech and song and mirth,
Until I chanced on rubbish in a pile,
And beamed at broken saws, charred rabbit
          skin,
Hobnails, a nine of hearts, a flask, a file,
And sweet lips on a crushed tobacco tin.
If I were driven from earth by a flaming lash,
To roam the flinty rocks of Capricorn,
I think no sorriest bit of human trash
Would be abject enough to win my scorn;

I'd find the sodden hobo sage and clean,
Own brother to the vagrant Nazarene.

1929

JOYCE KILMER 1886-1918

Kilmer was born in New Brunswick, New Jersey. After graduating from Rutgers College and Columbia University he became in turn teacher, editor, and writer. When the United States entered the World War he enlisted as a private and fell during the advance on the Marne. He had a love for homely, everyday things, and many of his poems show a simplicity that is both frank and penetrating. His books of verse include *Summer and Love,* 1911; *Trees and Other Poems,* 1914; *Main Street and Other Poems,* 1916.

Biography and criticism: *Poems, Essays and Letters,* 2 vols., 1915, memoir by R. C. Holliday; Wilkinson (NV); R. Le Gallienne, "Joyce Kilmer," *Bookm.* 48:133-9; K. Bregy, "Joyce Kilmer: Poet and Patriot," *Outlook* 122:467-9; see also *Poetry* 11:281-2; 13:149-54; *Lit. Digest* 58:32-3, 42-6, Sept. 7, '18; *R. of Rs.* 58:431-2.

TREES [1]

I think that I shall never see
A poem lovely as a tree.

A tree whose hungry mouth is prest
Against the earth's sweet flowing breast;

A tree that looks at God all day,
And lifts her leafy arms to pray;

A tree that may in Summer wear
A nest of robins in her hair;

Upon whose bosom snow has lain;
Who intimately lives with rain.

Poems are made by fools like me,
But only God can make a tree.

1914

ALAN SEEGER 1888-1916

Alan Seeger was one of many young men of his generation filled with a longing to express themselves in some artistic form, but whirled down in the maelstrom of the World War. He was born in New York City, passed some of his childhood in Mexico, spent a year in California, and was educated at various schools. After graduating from Harvard he lived for two years in New York unable to decide upon a profession. Then, feeling that Europe offered a more congenial atmosphere for artistic work, he went to Paris, where the opening of the war found him. He enlisted with the

Foreign Legion of France and was in almost continuous service until he fell. His work is small in bulk; most of it was written in Paris and at the front. In the circumstances it is not surprising that, as Mr. Untermeyer remarks, "his literary promise was far greater than his poetic accomplishment." Nevertheless, his best-known poem, quoted below, expresses in words that cannot be forgotten the spirit of millions of high-spirited men who fell in a struggle in which the individual was less than a pawn.

Poems, 1916, biographical and critical introduction by William Archer. Criticism: Phelps (EP); Wilkinson (NV); H. Reeves, "The Tragedy of Alan Seeger," *New Repub.* 10:160-2; W. A. Roberts, "The Alan Seeger I Knew," *Bookm.* 47:585-90; "Alan Seeger: America's Soldier Poet," *Liv. Age* 294:221-5; "Alan Seeger, Poet, Killed in France," *Scrib. M.* 61:123-5.

I HAVE A RENDEZVOUS WITH DEATH [2]

I have a rendezvous with Death
At some disputed barricade,
When Spring comes back with rustling shade
And apple-blossoms fill the air—
I have a rendezvous with Death
When Spring brings back blue days and fair.

It may be he shall take my hand
And lead me into his dark land
And close my eyes and quench my breath—
It may be I shall pass him still.   10
I have a rendezvous with Death
On some scarred slope of battered hill,
When Spring comes round again this year
And the first meadow-flowers appear.

God knows 'twere better to be deep
Pillowed in silk and scented down,
Where love throbs out in blissful sleep,
Pulse nigh to pulse, and breath to breath,
Where hushed awakenings are dear. . . .
But I've a rendezvous with Death   20
At midnight in some flaming town,
When Spring trips north again this year,
And I to my pledged word am true,
I shall not fail that rendezvous.

1916   1916

FRANKLIN PIERCE ADAMS 1881-

Mr. Adams is pre-eminent among contemporary humorous poets. He has the gift of condensing criticism into trenchant and witty verse. He was

[1] From *Trees and Other Poems* by Joyce Kilmer, copyright, 1914, George H. Doran Company, publishers.

[2] Copyright. By permission of Mr. Charles L. Seeger and Charles Scribner's Sons, publishers.

born in Chicago. After attending the University of Michigan for a short time he took up the insurance business, and then newspaper work upon the Chicago *Journal*. Later he was upon the staff of the New York *Mail*, the New York *Tribune*, and the New York *World*. He served in France during the World War as an officer in the service of Military Intelligence.

Thousands of readers of the *World* turn first to F.P.A.'s "Conning Tower Colyum," and the news of the day waits upon their enjoyment of his satire, his puns, his imitations of Horace. Many of his thrusts are directed against the extremes of social folly, and among his aversions are "jazz" music and slovenly English. Both in subject-matter and style he often resembles Eugene Field, but he excels Field in variety of rhythms, meters, and stanzaic forms.

His volumes of verse include *Tobogganing on Parnassus*, 1910, *Weights and Measures*, 1917, and *So There!*, 1922.

Criticism: Phelps (EP); also *Bookm.* 47:268-9; C. Van Doren, "Day In and Day Out," *Cent.* 107:308-15; "The Colyumists' Confessional (IV), F.P.A.," by Rupert Hughes, *Everybody's* 42: April, 52-53.

ERRING IN COMPANY [1]

"If I have erred, I err in company with Abraham Lincoln."—THEODORE ROOSEVELT

If e'er my riming be at fault,
    If e'er I chance to scribble dope,
If that my meter ever halt,
    I err in company with Pope.

An [2] that my grammar go awry,
    An that my English be askew,
Sooth, I can prove an alibi—
    The Bard of Avon did it, too.

If often toward the bottled grape
    My errant fancy fondly turns,   10
Remember, leering jackanape,
    I err in company with Burns.

If now and then I sigh "Mine own!"
    Unto another's wedded wife,
Remember, I am not alone—
    Hast ever read Lord Byron's LIFE?

If frequently I fret and fume,
    And absolutely will not smile,
I err in company with Hume,
    Old Socrates and T. Carlyle.   20

[1] From *Tobogganing on Parnassus* by Franklin Pierce Adams, copyright, 1911, by Doubleday, Page and Company, publishers.
[2] Elizabethan usage: if

If e'er I fail in etiquette,
    And foozle on The Proper Stuff
Regarding manners, don't forget
    A. Tennyson's were pretty tough. [3]

Eke if I err upon the side
    Of talking overmuch of Me,
I err, it cannot be denied,
    In most illustrious company.

                                        1910

DE SENECTUTE [4]

When as a young and budding pote
I gazed upon the stuff I wrote,
I knew that stuff so weak and poor
Would never rank as Literature.

And yet, I thought, what I have sung
Is not so bad for one so young;
When years and ripeness shall be mine,
I may achieve the Mighty Line. [5]

And in that withered yesteryear
I used to take unwonted cheer   10
In that De Morgan [6] was a man
Of seventy when he began.

But now that years have bowed my bean
And I am more than seventeen,
I tell myself the bitter truth
And know I was a lying youth.

Now of my verse so thin and cold
I say, Not bad for one so old;
When I was twenty-four or -five
Then, then my verses were alive.   20

Now I, as creeping age defeats
Me, think of Chatterton or Keats,
And say, Look at the stuff he did,
When he was nothing but a kid!

But Time has taught me this, to wit:
That Age has naught to do with it,
That plenty be the years or scant,
Some can be poets, and some can't.

                                        1922

[3] Tennyson's behavior toward unwelcome guests was sometimes boorish.
[4] From *So There!* by Franklin Pierce Adams, copyright, 1923, by Doubleday, Page and Company.
[5] a reference to Ben Jonson's famous saying: "Marlowe's mighty line"
[6] William De Morgan, 1839-1917, an English artist and novelist, wrote his first novel, *Joseph Vance*, when he was seventy.

EDNA ST. VINCENT MILLAY
1892-

Miss Millay, one of the foremost American lyric poets, was born at Rockland, Maine, and spent her early life along the Maine coast. Before entering college she had written, at the age of nineteen, her remarkable "Renascence." After graduating from Vassar she settled in "Greenwich Village" in New York City, and for a time wrote for and acted with the Provincetown Players, who first produced her *Aria da Capo*, 1917. Besides *Renascence and Other Poems*, 1917, she has produced *A Few Figs from Thistles*, 1920; *Second April*, 1921; *The Harp-Weaver and Other Poems*, 1923, which won the Pulitzer Prize for poetry; *The Buck in the Snow*, 1929. Miss Millay's work is marked by originality of conception, and a use of fresh, untrammeled words and phrases that bring a series of concrete images before the mind.

Criticism : W. Bynner, "Edna St. Vincent Millay," *New Repub.* 41: Dec. 10, '24, sup. 14-5; C. Van Doren, "Youth and Wings," *Cent.* 106:310-6; C. W. Ferguson, *Bookm.* 65:83-5, 56:272-8; *Poetry* 13:167-8; *Outlook* 145:268-70; *Nation* 124:263, 267-8; *New Repub.* 50:101-2; *R. of Rs.* 75:435-6; *Lit. Digest* 92:27-8, Mar. 19, '27.

GOD'S WORLD [1]

O World, I cannot hold thee close enough!
Thy winds, thy wide gray skies!
Thy mists, that roll and rise!
Thy woods, this autumn day, that ache and sag
And all but cry with color! That gaunt crag
To crush! To lift the lean of that black bluff!
World, World, I cannot get thee close enough!

Long have I known a glory in it all
But never knew I this.
Here such a passion is   10
As stretcheth me apart. Lord, I do fear
Thou'st made the world too beautiful this year.
My soul is all but out of me—let fall
No burning leaf; prithee, let no bird call.

1917

JOURNEY [2]

Ah, could I lay me down in this long grass
And close my eyes, and let the quiet wind
Blow over me—I am so tired, so tired
Of passing pleasant places! All my life,
Following Care along the dusty road,
Have I looked back at loveliness and sighed;
Yet at my hand an unrelenting hand
Tugged ever, and I passed. All my life long

Over my shoulder have I looked at peace;
And now I fain would lie in this long grass   10
And close my eyes.

Yet onward!

Cat-birds call
Through the long afternoon, and creeks at dusk
Are gutteral. Whip-poor-wills wake and cry,
Drawing the twilight close about their throats.
Only my heart makes answer. Eager vines
Go up the ricks and wait; flushed apple-trees
Pause in their dance and break the ring for me;
Dim, shady wood-roads, redolent of fern   20
And bayberry, that through sweet bevies thread
Of round-faced roses, pink and petulant,
Look back and beckon ere they disappear.
Only my heart, only my heart responds.
Yet, ah, my path is sweet on either side
All through the dragging day—sharp underfoot,
And hot, and like dead mist the dry dust hangs—
But far, oh, far as passionate eye can reach,
And long, ah, long as rapturous eye can cling,
The world is mine; blue hill, still silver lake, 30
Broad field, bright flower, and the long white road.
A gateless garden, and an open path:
My feet to follow, and my heart to hold.

1921

TRAVEL [2]

The railroad track is miles away,
    And the day is loud with voices speaking,
Yet there isn't a train goes by all day
    But I hear its whistle shrieking.

All night there isn't a train goes by,
    Though the night is still for sleep and dreaming,
But I see its cinders red on the sky,
    And hear its engine steaming.

My heart is warm with the friends I make,
    And better friends I'll not be knowing,
Yet there isn't a train I wouldn't take,
    No matter where it's going.

1921

WOODROW WILSON 1856-1924

Woodrow Wilson, twenty-eighth President of the United States, was born at Staunton, Virginia, of Scotch and English ancestry, 1856. He was graduated from Princeton in 1875, studied law at the University of Virginia, and politics and history at Johns Hopkins University. For eight years he was president of Princeton. He was elected governor

---

[1] From *Renascence*, published by Harper and Brothers, copyright, 1917, by Edna St. Vincent Millay.
[2] From *Second April*, published by Harper and Brothers, copyright, 1921, by Edna St. Vincent Millay.

of New Jersey in 1910 and President of the United States in 1913. He brought to the office a scholarly knowledge of statesmanship unequaled by any other President. His vigorous domestic administration was interrupted by the Great War, at the close of which, largely through his statesmanship, the League of Nations was formed. He died in Washington.

President Wilson's writings include *A History of the American People,* 1902; *Mere Literature,* 1893; *Constitutional Government in the United States,* 1908; *The New Freedom,* 1913. President Wilson's state papers and speeches are notable among public documents for the discrimination they show in wording and for their clearness of exposition. His style is based upon a comprehensive knowledge of the best in literature. Conciseness and accuracy are its fundamentals, and much of its force lies in its restrained emotion.

Biography and criticism: R. S. Baker, *Woodrow Wilson, Life and Letters,* [first] 2 vols., 1927; W. E. Dodd, *Woodrow Wilson and his Work,* 1920; D. Lawrence, *The True Story of Woodrow Wilson,* 1924; J. P. Tumulty, *Woodrow Wilson as I Know Him,* 1921; *Woodrow Wilson, the Man, his Times and his Task,* 1924; *Life and Letters of Walter Hines Page,* 3 vols., 1922-5; *The Intimate Papers of Colonel House,* 4 vols., 1926, 1929; W. A. White, "The End of an Epoch," *Scrib. M.* 79:561-70; see also *R. of Rs.* 75:371-5; *Atlan.* 133:815-23; *Liv. Age* 320:537-40; *Contemp.* 125:282-9; *Nation* 118: 156-8.

FIRST INAUGURAL ADDRESS [1]

There has been a change of government. It began two years ago, when the House of Representatives became Democratic by a decisive majority. It has now been completed. The Senate about to assemble will also be Democratic. The offices of President and Vice President have been put into the hands of Democrats. What does the change mean? That is the question uppermost in our minds to-day. That is the question I am going to try to answer, in order, if I may, to interpret the occasion.

It means much more than the mere success of a party. The success of a party means little except when the Nation is using that party for a large and definite purpose. No one can mistake the purpose for which the Nation now seeks to use the Democratic Party. It seeks to use it to interpret a change in its own plans and point of view. Some old things with which we had grown familiar, and which had begun to creep into the very habit of our thought and of our lives, have altered their aspect as we have

latterly looked critically upon them, with fresh, awakened eyes; have dropped their disguises and shown themselves alien and sinister. Some new things, as we look frankly upon them, willing to comprehend their real character, have come to assume the aspect of things long believed in and familiar, stuff of our own convictions. We have been refreshed by a new insight into our own life.

We see that in many things that life is very great. It is incomparably great in its material aspects, in its body of wealth, in the diversity and sweep of its energy, in the industries which have been conceived and built up by the genius of individual men and the limitless enterprise of groups of men. It is great, also, very great, in its moral force. Nowhere else in the world have noble men and women exhibited in more striking forms the beauty and the energy of sympathy and helpfulness and counsel in their efforts to rectify wrong, alleviate suffering, and set the weak in the way of strength and hope. We have built up, moreover, a great system of government, which has stood through a long age as in many respects a model for those who seek to set liberty upon foundations that will endure against fortuitous change, against storm and accident. Our life contains every great thing and contains it in rich abundance.

But the evil has come with the good, and much fine gold has been corroded. With riches has come inexcusable waste. We have squandered a great part of what we might have used, and have not stopped to conserve the exceeding bounty of nature, without which our genius for enterprise would have been worthless and impotent, scorning to be careful, shamefully prodigal as well as admirably efficient. We have been proud of our industrial achievements, but we have not hitherto stopped thoughtfully enough to count the human cost, the cost of lives snuffed out, of energies overtaxed and broken, the fearful physical and spiritual cost to the men and women and children upon whom the dead weight and burden of it all has fallen pitilessly the years through. The groans and agony of it all had not yet reached our ears, the solemn, moving undertone of our life, coming up out of the mines and factories and out of every home where the struggle had its intimate and familiar seat. With the great Government went many deep secret things which we too long delayed to look into and scrutinize with candid, fearless eyes. The great Government we loved has too often been made use of for private and selfish purposes, and those who used it had forgotten the people.

---

[1] This address was delivered by President Wilson at the Capitol, March 4, 1913.

At last a vision has been vouchsafed us of our life as a whole. We see the bad with the good, the debased and decadent with the sound and vital. With this vision we approach new affairs. Our duty is to cleanse, to reconsider, to restore, to correct the evil without impairing the good, to purify and humanize every process of our common life without weakening or sentimentalizing it. There has been something crude and heartless and unfeeling in our haste to succeed and be great. Our thought has been "Let every man look out for himself, let every generation look out for itself," while we reared giant machinery which made it impossible that any but those who stood at the levers of control should have a chance to look out for themselves. We had not forgotten our morals. We remembered well enough that we had set up a policy which was meant to serve the humblest as well as the most powerful, with an eye single to the standards of justice and fair play, and remembered it with pride. But we were very heedless and in a hurry to be great.

We have come now to the sober second thought. The scales of heedlessness have fallen from our eyes. We have made up our minds to square every process of our national life again with the standards we so proudly set up at the beginning and have always carried at our hearts. Our work is a work of restoration.

We have itemized with some degree of particularity the things that ought to be altered and here are some of the chief items: A tariff which cuts us off from our proper part in the commerce of the world, violates the just principles of taxation, and makes the Government a facile instrument in the hands of private interests; a banking and currency system based upon the necessity of the Government to sell its bonds fifty years ago and perfectly adapted to concentrating cash and restricting credits; an industrial system which, take it on all its sides, financial as well as administrative, holds capital in leading strings, restricts the liberties and limits the opportunities of labor, and exploits without renewing or conserving the natural resources of the country; a body of agricultural activities never yet given the efficiency of great business undertakings or served as it should be through the instrumentality of science taken directly to the farm, or afforded the facilities of credit best suited to its practical needs; watercourses undeveloped, waste places unreclaimed, forests untended, fast disappearing without plan or prospect of renewal, unregarded waste heaps at every mine. We have studied as perhaps no other nation has the most effective means of production, but we have not studied cost or economy as we should either as organizers of industry, as statesmen, or as individuals.

Nor have we studied and perfected the means by which government may be put at the services of humanity, in safeguarding the health of the Nation, the health of its men and its women and its children, as well as their rights in the struggle for existence. This is no sentimental duty. The firm basis of government is justice, not pity. These are matters of justice. There can be no equality of opportunity, the first essential of justice in the body politic, if men and women and children be not shielded in their lives, their very vitality, from the consequences of great industrial and social processes which they can not alter, control, or singly cope with. Society must see to it that it does not itself crush or weaken or damage its own constituent parts. The first duty of law is to keep sound the society it serves. Sanitary laws, pure food laws, and laws determining conditions of labor which individuals are powerless to determine for themselves are intimate parts of the very business of justice and legal efficiency.

These are some of the things we ought to do, and not leave the others undone, the old-fashioned, never-to-be-neglected, fundamental safeguarding of property and of individual right. This is the high enterprise of the new day: To lift everything that concerns our life as a Nation to the light that shines from the hearthfire of every man's conscience and vision of the right. It is inconceivable that we should do this as partisans; it is inconceivable we should do it in ignorance of the facts as they are or in blind haste. We shall restore, not destroy. We shall deal with our economic system as it is and as it may be modified, not as it might be if we had a clean sheet of paper to write upon; and step by step we shall make it what it should be, in the spirit of those who question their own wisdom and seek counsel and knowledge, not shallow self-satisfaction or the excitement of excursions whither they can not tell. Justice, and only justice, shall always be our motto.

And yet it will be no cool process of mere science. The Nation has been deeply stirred, stirred by a solemn passion, stirred by the knowledge of wrong, of ideals lost, of government too often debauched and made an instrument of evil. The feelings with which we face this new age of right and opportunity sweep across our heartstrings like some air out of God's own presence, where justice and mercy are reconciled and the judge and the brother are one. We know our task to be no mere task of politics but a task which shall search us through and through, whether we be able to understand our time and the need of our people, whether we be indeed their spokesmen and interpreters, whether we have the pure heart to comprehend and the rectified will to choose our high course of action.

This is not a day of triumph; it is a day of dedication. Here muster, not the forces of party, but the forces of humanity. Men's hearts wait upon us; men's lives hang in the balance; men's hopes call upon us to say what we will do. Who shall live up to the great trust? Who dares fail to try? I summon all honest men, all patriotic, all forward-looking men, to my side. God helping me, I will not fail them, if they will but counsel and sustain me!

ON ABRAHAM LINCOLN'S BIRTHPLACE [1]

No more significant memorial could have been presented to the nation than this. It expresses so much of what is singular and noteworthy in the history of the country; it suggests so many of the things that we prize most highly in our life and in our system of government. How eloquent this little house within this shrine is of the vigor of democracy! There is nowhere in the land any home so remote, so humble, that it may not contain the power of mind and heart and conscience to which nations yield and history submits its processes. Nature pays no tribute to aristocracy, subscribes to no creed of caste, renders fealty to no monarch or master of any name or kind. Genius is no snob. It does not run after titles or seek by preference the high circles of society. It affects humble company as well as great. It pays no special tribute to universities or learned societies or conventional standards of greatness, but serenely chooses its own comrades, its own haunts, its own cradle even, and its own life of adventure and of training. Here is proof of it. This little hut was the cradle of one of the great sons of men, a man of singular, delightful, vital genius who presently emerged upon the great stage of the nation's history, gaunt, shy, ungainly, but dominant and majestic, a natural ruler of men, himself inevitably the central figure of the great plot. No man can explain this, but every man can see how it demon-

[1] Mr. Wilson's address on the acceptance by the War Department of a Deed of Gift to the Nation of the Lincoln Farm at Hodgenville, Kentucky, September 4, 1916

strates the vigor of democracy, where every door is open, in every hamlet and countryside, in city and wilderness alike, for the ruler to emerge when he will and claim his leadership in the free life. Such are the authentic proofs of the validity and vitality of democracy.

Here, no less, hides the mystery of democracy. Who shall guess this secret of nature and providence and a free polity? Whatever the vigor and vitality of the stock from which he sprang, its mere vigor and soundness do not explain where this man got his great heart that seemed to comprehend all mankind in its catholic and benignant sympathy, the mind that sat enthroned behind those brooding, melancholy eyes, whose vision swept many an horizon which those about him dreamed not of— that mind comprehended what it had never seen, and understood the language of affairs with the ready ease of one to the manner born —or that nature which seemed in its varied richness to be the familiar of men of every way of life. This is the sacred mystery of democracy, that its richest fruits spring up out of soils which no man has prepared and in circumstances amidst which they are the least expected. This is a place alike of mystery and of reassurance.

It is likely that in a society ordered otherwise than our own, Lincoln could not have found himself or the path of fame and power upon which he walked serenely to his death. In this place it is right that we should remind ourselves of the solid and striking facts upon which our faith in democracy is founded. Many another man besides Lincoln has served the nation in its highest places of counsel and of action whose origins were as humble as his. Though the greatest example of the universal energy, richness, stimulation, and force of democracy, he is only one example among many. The permeating and all-pervasive virtue of the freedom which challenges us in America is to make the most of every gift and power we possess, every page of our history serves to emphasize and illustrate. Standing here in this place, it seems almost the whole of the stirring story.

Here Lincoln had his beginnings. Here the end and consummation of that great life seem remote and a bit incredible. And yet there was no break anywhere between beginning and end, no lack of natural sequence anywhere. Nothing really incredible happened. Lincoln was unaffectedly as much at home in the White House as he was here. Do you share with me the feeling, I wonder, that he was permanently at home nowhere? It seems to me that in the case of a man—I would rather say of a spirit—like Lincoln the question *where* he was is of little significance, that it is always *what* he was that really arrests our thought and takes hold of our imagination. It is the spirit always that is sovereign. Lincoln, like the rest of us, was put through the discipline of the world—a very rough and exacting discipline for him, an indispensable discipline for every man who would know what he is about in the midst of the world's affairs; but his spirit got only its schooling there. It did not derive its character or its vision from the experiences which brought it to its full revelation. The test of every American must always be, not where he is, but what he is. That, also, is of the essence of democracy, and is the moral of which this place is most gravely expressive.

We would like to think of men like Lincoln and Washington as typical Americans, but no man can be typical who is so unusual as these great men were. It was typical of American life that it should produce such men with supreme indifference as to the manner in which it produced them, and as readily here in this hut as amidst the little circle of cultivated gentlemen to whom Virginia owed so much in leadership and example. And Lincoln and Washingtons were typical Americans, in the use they made of their genius. But there will be few such men at best, and we will not look into the mystery of how and why they come. We will only keep the door open for them always, and a hearty welcome—after we have recognized them.

I have read many biographies of Lincoln; I have sought out with the greatest interest the many intimate stories that are told of him, the narratives of nearby friends, the sketches at close quarters, in which those who had the privilege of being associated with him have tried to depict for us the very man himself "in his habit as he lived"; but I have nowhere found a real intimate of Lincoln. I nowhere get the impression in any narrative or reminiscence that the writer had in fact penetrated to the heart of his mystery, or that any man could penetrate to the heart of it. That brooding spirit had no real familiars. I get the impressions that it never spoke out in complete self-revelation, and that it could not reveal itself completely to anyone. It was a very lonely spirit that looked out from underneath those shaggy brows and comprehended men without fully communing with them, as if, in spite of all its genial efforts at comradeship, it dwelt apart, saw its visions of duty where no man

looked on. There is a very holy and very terrible isolation for the conscience of every man who seeks to read the destiny in affairs for others as well as for himself, for a nation as well as for individuals. That privacy no man can intrude upon. That lonely search of the spirit for the right perhaps no man can assist. This strange child of the cabin kept company with invisible things, was born into no intimacy but that of its own silently assembling and deploying thoughts.

I have come here today, not to utter a eulogy on Lincoln; he stands in need of none, but to endeavor to interpret the meaning of this gift to the nation of the place of his birth and origin. Is not this an altar upon which we may forever keep alive the vestal fire of democracy as upon a shrine at which some of the deepest and most sacred hopes of mankind may from age to age be rekindled? For these hopes must constantly be rekindled, and only those who live can rekindle them. The only stuff that can retain the life-giving heat is the stuff of living hearts. And the hopes of mankind cannot be kept alive by words merely, by constitutions and doctrines of right and codes of liberty. The object of democracy is to transmute these into the life and action of society, the self-denial and self-sacrifice of heroic men and women willing to make their lives an embodiment of right and service and enlightened purpose. The commands of democracy are as imperative as its privileges and opportunities are wide and generous. Its compulsion is upon us. It will be great and lift a great light for the guidance of the nations only if we are great and carry that light high for the guidance of our own feet. We are not worthy to stand here unless we ourselves be in deed and in truth real democrats and servants of mankind, ready to give our very lives for the freedom and justice and spiritual exaltation of the great nation which shelters and nurtures us.

AGNES REPPLIER 1855-

Conservative attitudes toward modern social problems are dominant in the essays of Agnes Repplier whose work frequently appears in the best American magazines. Miss Repplier was born of French ancestry in Philadelphia and was educated at the Roman Catholic Convent of the Sacred Heart at Torresdale, Pennsylvania. The estimation in which her writing is held is shown by the honorary degrees she has received from the University of Pennsylvania and from Yale. She began writing early. Her first collection of essays, *Books and Men,* was published in 1888. Since then every few years has seen a new volume, including *In the Dozy Hours*, 1894; *Compromises*, 1904; *Counter-Currents*, 1915; and *Under Dispute*, 1924. Miss Repplier is clear-headed and analytical. She expresses her convictions urbanely yet strikingly and positively. Her common sense combined with her good humor keeps the spirit of her work in excellent balance.

Criticism: F. Hackett, "Standing Pat," *New Repub.* 7:20-1; "A Plea for Reticence," *Lit. Digest* 48:827-8; "Miss Repplier's Essays," *Spect.* 117:105-6.

THE CHILD [1]

"I was not initiated into any rudiments 'till near four years of age."—JOHN EVELYN[2]

The courage of mothers is proverbial. There is no danger which they will not brave in behalf of their offspring. But I have always thought, that, for sheer foolhardiness, no one ever approached the English lady who asked Dr. Johnson[3] to read her young daughter's translation from Horace. He did read it, because the gods provided no escape; and he told his experience to Miss Reynolds,[4] who said soothingly, "And how was it, Sir?" "Why, very well for a young Miss's verses," was the contemptuous reply. "That is to say, as compared with excellence, nothing; but very well for the person who wrote them. I am vexed at being shown verses in that manner."

The fashion of focussing attention upon children had not in Dr. Johnson's day assumed the fell proportions which, a few years later, practically extinguished childhood. It is true that he objected to Mr. Bennet Langton's[5] connubial felicity, because the children were "too much about"; and that he betrayed an unworthy impatience when the ten little Langtons recited fables, or said their alphabets in Hebrew for his delectation. It is true also that he answered with pardonable rudeness when asked what was the best way to begin a little boy's education. He said it mattered no more how it was begun, that is, what the child was taught first, than it mattered which of his little legs he first thrust into his breeches,—a callous speech, painful to parents' ears. Dr. Johnson had been dead five years when Mrs. Hartley, daughter of Dr. David Hartley[6] of Bath, wrote to Sir William Pepys:—[7]

"Education is the rage of the times. Everybody tries to make their children more wonderful than any children of their acquaintance. The poor little things are so crammed with knowledge that there is scant time for them to obtain by exercise, and play, and *vacancy of mind*, that strength of body which is much more necessary in childhood than learning."

I am glad this letter went to Sir William, who was himself determined that his children should not, at any rate, be less wonderful than other people's bantlings. When his eldest son had reached the mature age of six, we find him writing to Miss Hannah More[8] and Mrs. Chapone,[9] asking what books he shall give the poor infant to read, and explaining to these august ladies his own theories of education. Mrs. Chapone, with an enthusiasm worthy of Mrs. Blimber,[10] replies that she sympathizes with the rare delight it must be to him to teach little William Latin; and that she feels jealous for the younger children, who, being yet in the nursery, are denied their brother's privileges. When the boy is ten, Sir William reads to him "The Faerie Queene,"[11] and finds that he grasps "the beauty of the description and the force of the allegory." At eleven he has "an animated relish for Ovid and Vergil." And the more the happy father has to tell about the precocity of his child, the more Mrs. Chapone stimulates and confounds him with tales of other children's prowess. When she hears that the "sweet Boy" is to be introduced, at five, to the English classics, she writes at once about a little girl who, when "rather younger than he is" (the bitterness of that!), "had several parts of Milton by heart." These "she understood so well as to apply to her Mother the speech of the Elder Brother in 'Comus,' when she saw her uneasy for want of a letter from the Dean; and began of her own accord with

'Peace, Mother, be not over exquisite
To cast the fashion of uncertain evils' ";—

advice which would have exasperated a normal parent to the boxing point.

There were few normal parents left, however, at this period, to stem the tide of infantile precocity. Child study was dawning as a new and fascinating pursuit upon the English world; and the babes of Britain responded nobly to

[2] 1620-1707, English author and diarist
[3] Samuel Johnson, 1709-1784, a celebrated English author and critic, notorious for his gruff exterior
[4] 1723-1792, sister of the famous painter, Sir Joshua
[5] a member of Johnson's famous circle of friends called the Literary Club
[6] 1705-1757, English physician and philosopher
[7] 1775-1856, English chemist and philosopher

[8] 1745-1833, English didactic essayist
[9] 1727-1801, English authoress
[10] a character in Dickens's *Dombey and Son,* who made a pretense of learning
[11] a long allegorical poem by Edmund Spenser, 1552-1599

the demands made upon their incapacity. Miss Anne Seward [1] lisped Milton at three, "recited poetical passages, with eyes brimming with delight," at five, and versified her favorite psalms at nine. Her father, who viewed these alarming symptoms with delight, was so ill-advised as to offer her, when she was ten, a whole half-crown, if she would write a poem on Spring; whereupon she "swiftly penned" twenty-five lines, which have been preserved to an ungrateful world, and which shadow forth the painful prolixity of future days. At four years of age, little Hannah More was already composing verses with ominous ease. At five, she "struck mute" the respected clergyman of the parish by her exhaustive knowledge of the catechism. At eight, we are told her talents "were of such a manifestly superior order that her father did not scruple to combine with the study of Latin some elementary instruction in mathematics; a fact which her readers might very naturally infer from the clear and logical cast of her argumentative writings."

It is not altogether easy to trace the connection between Miss More's early sums and her argumentative writings; but, as an illustration of her logical mind, I may venture to quote a "characteristic" anecdote, reverently told by her biographer, Mr. Thompson. A young lady, whose sketches showed an unusual degree of talent, was visiting in Bristol; and her work was warmly admired by Miss Mary, Miss Sally, Miss Elizabeth, and Miss Patty More. Hannah alone withheld all word of commendation, sitting in stony silence whenever the drawings were produced; until one day she found the artist hard at work, putting a new binding on a petticoat. *Then,* "fixing her brilliant eyes with an expression of entire approbation upon the girl, she said: 'Now, my dear, that I find you can employ yourself usefully, I will no longer forbear to express my admiration of your drawings.'"

Only an early familiarity with the multiplication table could have made so ruthless a logician.

If Dr. Johnson, being childless, found other people's children in his way, how fared the bachelors and spinsters who, as time went on, were confronted by a host of infant prodigies; who heard little Anna Letitia Aikin—afterwards Mrs. Barbauld [2]—read "as well as most women" at two and a half years of age; and little Anna Maria Porter [2] declaim Shakespeare "with precision of emphasis and firmness of

voice" at five; and little Alphonso Hayley [3] recite a Greek ode at six. We wonder if anybody ever went twice to homes that harbored childhood; and we sympathize with Miss Ferrier's [4] bitterness of soul, when she describes a family dinner at which Eliza's sampler and Alexander's copy-book are handed round to the guests, and Anthony stands up and repeats "My name is Norval" from beginning to end, and William Pitt is prevailed upon to sing the whole of "God Save the King." It was also a pleasant fashion of the time to write eulogies on one's kith and kin. Sisters celebrated their brothers' talents in affectionate verse, and fathers confided to the world what marvelous children they had. Even Dr. Burney, [5] a man of sense, poetizes thus on his daughter Susan:—

> Nor did her intellectual powers require
> The usual aid of labor to inspire
> Her soul with prudence, wisdom, and a taste
> Unerring in refinement, sound and chaste.

This was fortunate for Susan, as most young people of the period were compelled to labor hard. There was a ghastly pretence on the part of parents that children loved their tasks, and that to keep them employed was to keep them happy. Sir William Pepys persuaded himself without much difficulty that little William, who had weak eyes and nervous headaches, relished Ovid and Virgil. A wonderful and terrible letter written in 1786 by the Baroness de Bode, an Englishwoman married to a German and living at Deux-Ponts, lays bare the process by which ordinary children were converted into the required miracle of precocity. Her eldest boys, aged eight and nine, appear to have been the principal victims. The business of their tutor was to see that they were "fully employed," and this is an account of their day.

"In their walks he [the tutor] teaches them natural history and botany, not dryly as a task, but practically, which amuses them very much. In their hours of study come drawing, writing, reading, and summing. Their lesson in writing consists of a theme which they are to translate into three languages, and sometimes into Latin, for they learn that a little also. The boys learn Latin as a recreation, and not as a task, as is the custom in England. Perhaps *one or two hours a day* is at most all that is given to that study. 'T is certainly not so dry a study, when learnt like modern languages. We have bought

[1] 1747-1809, English poet
[2] The first, 1743-1825, was an English poet; the second, c. 1780-1832, was an English novelist.
[3] 1780-1800, English sculptor
[4] c. 1782-1854, Scotch novelist
[5] 1726-1814, English musical composer, father of Fanny Burney (Madame D'Arblay), 1752-1840, celebrated novelist, author of *Evelina*

them the whole of the Classical Authors, so that they can instruct themselves if they will; between ninety and a hundred volumes in large octavo. You would be surprised,—even Charles Auguste, who is only five, reads German well, and French tolerably. They all write very good hands, both in Roman and German texts. Clem and Harry shall write you a letter in English, and send you a specimen of their drawing. Harry (the second) writes musick, too. He is a charming boy, improves very much in all his studies, plays very prettily indeed upon the harpsichord, and plays, too, all tunes by ear. Clem will, I think, play well upon the violin; but 't is more difficult in the beginning than the harpsichord. He is at this moment taking his lesson, the master accompanying him on the pianoforte; and when Henry plays that, the master accompanies on the violin, which forms them both, and pleases them at the same time. In the evening their tutor generally recounts to them very minutely some anecdote from history, which imprints it on the memory, amuses them, and hurts no eyes."

There is nothing like it on record except the rule of life which Frederick William the First [1] drew up for little Prince Fritz, when that unfortunate child was nine years old, and which disposed of his day, hour by hour, and minute by minute. But then Frederick William—a truth-teller if a tyrant—made no idle pretence of pleasing and amusing his son. The unpardonable thing about the Baroness de Bode is her smiling assurance that one or two hours of Latin a day afforded a pleasant pastime for children of eight and nine.

This was, however, the accepted theory of education. It is faithfully reflected in all the letters and literature of the time. When Miss More's redoubtable "Coelebs" [2] asks Lucilla Stanley's little sister why she is crowned with woodbine, the child replies: "Oh, sir, it is because it is my birthday. I am eight years old today. I gave up all my gilt books with pictures this day twelvemonth; and today I give up all my story-books, and I am now going to read such books as men and women read." Whereupon the little girl's father—that model father whose wisdom flowers into many chapters of counsel—explains that he makes the renouncing of baby books a kind of epoch in his daughters' lives; and that by thus distinctly marking the period, he wards off any return to the immature pleasures of childhood. "We have in our domestic plan several of these

artificial divisions of life. These little celebrations are eras that we use as marking-posts from which we set out on some new course."

Yet the "gilt books," so ruthlessly discarded at eight years of age, were not all of an infantile character. For half a century these famous little volumes, bound in Dutch gilt paper—whence their name—found their way into every English nursery, and provided amusement and instruction for every English child. They varied from the "histories" of Goody-Two-Shoes and Miss Sally Spellwell to the "histories" of Tom Jones [3] and Clarissa Harlowe, [4] "abridged for the amusement of youth"; and from "The Seven Champions of Christendom" to "The First Principles of Religion, and the Existence of a Deity; Explained in a Series of Conversations, Adapted to the Capacity of the Infant Mind." The capacity of the infant mind at the close of the eighteenth century must have been something very different from the capacity of the infant mind today. In a gilt-book dialogue (1792) I find a father asking his tiny son: "Dick, have you got ten lines of Ovid by heart?"

"Yes, Papa, and I've wrote my exercise."

"Very well, then you shall ride with me. The boy who does a little at seven years old, will do a great deal when he is fourteen."

This was poor encouragement for Dick, who had already tasted the sweets of application. It was better worth while for Miss Sally Spellwell to reach the perfection which her name implies, for *she* was adopted by a rich old lady with a marriageable son,—"a young Gentleman of such purity of Morals and good Understanding as is not everywhere to be found." In the breast of this paragon "strange emotions arise" at sight of the well-informed orphan; his mother, who sets a proper value on orthography, gives her full consent to their union; and we are swept from the contemplation of samplers and horn-books [5] to the triumphant conclusion: "Miss Sally Spellwell now rides in her coach and six." Then follows the unmistakable moral:—

If Virtue, Learning, Goodness are your Aim,
Each pretty Miss may hope to do the same;

an anticipation which must have spurred many a female child to diligence. There was no ill-advised questioning of values in our great-grandmothers' day to disturb this point of view.

---

[1] 1688-1740, King of Prussia
[2] the hero of a novel, *Coelebs in Search of a Wife*

[3] hero of a novel of the same name by Henry Fielding, 1707-1754
[4] heroine of a novel of the same name by Samuel Richardson, 1689-1761
[5] a frame holding transparent sheets of horn protecting a copy of the alphabet

As the excellent Mrs. West observed in her "Letters to a young Lady," a book sanctioned by bishops, and dedicated to the Queen: "We unquestionably were created to be the wedded mates of man. Nature intended that man should sue, and woman coyly yield."

The most appalling thing about the precocious young people of this period was the ease with which they slipped into print. Publishers were not then the adamantine race whose province it is now to blight the hopes of youth. They beamed with benevolence when the first fruits of genius were confided to their hands. Bishop Thirlwall's [1] first fruits, his "Primitiae," were published when he was eleven years old, with a preface telling the public what a wonderful little boy Connop was;—how he studied Latin at three, and read Greek with ease and fluency at four, and wrote with distinction at seven. It is true that the parent Thirlwall appears to have paid the costs, to have launched his son's "slender bark" upon seas which proved to be stormless. It is true also that the bishop suffered acutely in later years from this youthful production, and destroyed every copy he could find. But there was no proud and wealthy father to back young Richard Polwhele, [2] who managed when he was a schoolboy in Cornwall, to get his first volume of verse published anonymously. It was called "The Fate of Llewellyn," and was consistently bad, though no worse, on the whole, than his maturer efforts. The title-page stated modestly that the writer was "a young gentleman of Truro School"; whereupon an ill-disposed critic in the "Monthly Review" intimated that the master of Truro School would do well to keep his young gentlemen out of print. Dr. Cardew, the said master, retorted hotly that the book had been published without his knowledge, and evinced a lack of appreciation, which makes us fear that his talented pupil had a bad half-hour at his hands.

Miss Anna Maria Porter—she who delighted "critical audiences" by reciting Shakespeare at five—published her "Artless Tales" at fifteen; and Mrs. Hemans [3] was younger still when her "Blossoms of Spring" bloomed sweetly upon English soil. Some of the "Blossoms" had been written before she was ten. The volume was a "fashionable quarto," was dedicated to that hardy annual, The Prince Regent, [4] and appears

to have been read by adults. It is recorded that an unkind notice sent the little girl crying to bed; but as her "England and Spain; or Valor and Patriotism" was published nine months later, and as at eighteen she "beamed forth with a strength and brilliancy that must have shamed her reviewer," we cannot feel that her poetic development was very seriously retarded.

And what of the marvelous children whose subsequent histories have been lost to the world? What of the two young prodigies of Lichfield, "Aonian [5] flowers of early beauty and intelligence," who startled Miss Seward and her friends by their "shining poetic talents," and then lapsed into restful obscurity? What of the wonderful little girl (ten years old) whom Miss Burney saw at Tunbridge Wells; [6] who sang "like an angel," conversed like "an informed, cultivated, and sagacious woman," played, danced, acted with all the grace of comédienne, wept tears of emotion without disfiguring her pretty face, and, when asked if she read the novels of the day (what a question!), replied with a sigh: "But too often! I wish I did not." Miss Burney and Mrs. Thrale [7] were so impressed—as well they might be—by this little Selina Birch, that they speculated long and fondly upon the destiny reserved for one who so easily eclipsed the other miraculous children of this highly miraculous age.

"Doubtful as it is whether we shall ever see the sweet Syren again," writes Miss Burney, "nothing, as Mrs. Thrale said to her" (this, too, was well advised), "can be more certain than that we shall hear of her again, let her go whither she will. Charmed as we all were, we agreed that to have the care of her would be distraction. 'She seems the girl in the world,' Mrs. Thrale wisely said, 'to attain the highest reach of human perfection as a man's mistress. As such she would be a second Cleopatra, and have the world at her command.'

"Poor thing! I hope to Heaven she will escape such sovereignty and such honors!"

She did escape scot-free. Whoever married —let us hope he married—Miss Birch, was no Mark Antony to draw fame to her feet. His very name is unknown to the world. Perhaps, as "Mrs.—Something—Rogers," [8] she illustrated

---

[1] Connop Thirlwall, 1797-1875, English bishop and historian
[2] 1759?-1839, English antiquarian and poet
[3] 1794-1835, English poet
[4] later George IV

[5] from Aonia, an ancient name of Boeotia in Greece, the supposed home of the Muses
[6] a famous watering place in Kent
[7] (Mrs. Piozzi) 1739-1821, English authoress and friend of Dr. Johnson
[8] a phrase from "The Belle of the Ball Room," by Winthrop Mackworth Praed, 1802-1839

in her respectable middle age that beneficent process by which Nature frustrates the educator, and converts the infant Cleopatra or the infant Hypatia [1] into the rotund matron, of whom she stands permanently in need.

1908

(CHARLES) WILLIAM BEEBE
1877-

From the time that Mr. Beebe, a native of Brooklyn, was graduated from Columbia, 1898, he has been engaged in scientific research. He brought to a high degree of perfection the collection of living birds of the New York Zoölogical Society; he organized scientific expeditions to various parts of the globe; he secured many extraordinary specimens of marine fauna and flora; and he has extended man's knowledge of rare animal life in jungles and forests. *Two Bird-lovers in Mexico,* 1905; *Tropical Wild Life,* 1917; *Jungle Peace,* 1918; *Galapagos,* 1923; *Jungle Days,* 1925; *The Arcturus Adventure,* 1925; *Pheasant Jungles,* 1927, quite apart from their scientific value, are fascinating accounts of the work of an enthusiastic naturalist. According to Theodore Roosevelt, Mr. Beebe combines the true naturalist's essential qualifications: the ability to see, to understand what he sees, to interpret it in the light of wide knowledge, and to record it "with comprehensive vividness and charm no less than with accurate fidelity to fact." This last-mentioned gift makes Beebe known above most living writers upon nature. He imparts to his readers his own acute realization of what he sees, and the situations into which his work takes him, whether to the slopes of the Himalayas or to the floor of a shark-infested bay of the tropics. Coolly scientific though he is, he responds to each new experience with unflagging zest, for each arouses his emotions and his imagination.

Criticism: "Beebe's Strange Cargo of Self-Lighted Fishes," *Lit. Digest* 86:34-6, Aug. 15, '25; E. Wilson, "A Conversation in the Galapagos: Mr. William Beebe and a Marine Iguana," *Atlan.* 136: 577-87; T. Roosevelt, "A Naturalist's Tropical Laboratory," *Scrib. M.* 61:46-64.

From THE EDGE OF THE JUNGLE [2]

From A TROPIC GARDEN [3]

.   .   .   .

No month or day or hour fails to bring vital changes—tragedies and comedies—to the network of life of these tropical gardens; but as we drive along the broad paths of an afternoon,

[1] a celebrated female philosopher and mathematician of the 4th century

[2] From *The Edge of the Jungle* by William Beebe. Copyright. By permission of Messrs. Henry Holt and Company, publishers.

[3] The chapter refers to the Botanical Gardens of Georgetown, British Guiana.

the quiet vistas show only waving palms, weaving vultures, and swooping kiskadees, with bursts of color from bougainvillea, flamboyant, and queen of the flowers. At certain times, however, the tide of visible change swelled into a veritable bore of life, gently and gradually, as quiet waters become troubled and then pass into the seething uproar of rapids. In late afternoon, when the long shadows of palms stretched their blue-black bars across the terra-cotta roads, the foliage of the green bamboo islands was dotted here and there with a scattering of young herons, white and blue and parti-colored. Idly watching them through glasses, I saw them sleepily preening their sprouting feathers, making ineffectual attempts at pecking one another, or else hunched in silent heron-dream. They were scarcely more alive than the creeping, hour-hand tendrils about them, mere double-stemmed, fluffy petaled blossoms, no more strange than the nearest vegetable blooms —the cannon-ball mystery, the sand-box puzzle, sinister orchids, and the false color-alarms of the white-bracted silver-leaf. Compared with these, perching herons are right and seemly fruit.

As I watched them I suddenly stiffened in sympathy, as I saw all vegetable sloth drop away and each bird become a detached individual, plucked by an electric emotion from the appearance of a thing of sap and fiber to a vital being of tingling nerves. I followed their united glance, and overhead there vibrated, lightly as a thistledown, the first incoming adult heron, swinging in from a day's fishing along the coast. It went on and vanished among the fronds of a distant island; but the calm had been broken, and through all the stems there ran a restless sense of anticipation, a zeitgeist [4] of prophetic import. One felt that memory of past things was dimming, and content with present comfort was no longer dominant. It was the future to which both the baby herons and I were looking, and for them realization came quickly. The sun had sunk still lower, and great clouds had begun to spread their robes and choose their tints for the coming pageant.

And now the vanguard of the homing host appeared,—black dots against blue and white and salmon,—thin, gaunt forms with slow-moving wings which cut the air through half the sky. The little herons and I watched them come—first a single white egret, which spiralled down, just as I had many times seen the first

[4] literally, the spirit of the times

returning Spad eddy downward to a cluster of great hump-backed hangars; then a trio of tri-colored herons, and six little blues, and after that I lost count. It seemed as if these tiny islands were magnets drawing all the herons in the world.

Parrakeets whirl roostwards with machine-like synchronism of flight; geese wheel down in more or less regular formation; but these herons concentrated along straight lines, each describing its individual radius from the spot where it caught its last fish or shrimp to its nest or the particular branch on which it will spend the night. With a hemicircle of sufficient size, one might plot all of the hundreds upon hundreds of these radii, and each would represent a distinct line, if only a heron's width apart.

At the height of the evening's flight there were sometimes fifty herons in sight at once, beating steadily onward until almost overhead, when they put on brakes and dropped. Some, as the little egrets, were rather awkward; while the tricolors were the most skilful, sometimes nose-diving, with a sudden flattening out just in time to reach out and grasp a branch. Once or twice, when a fitful breeze blew at sunset, I had a magnificent exhibition of aeronautics. The birds came upwind slowly, beating their way obliquely but steadily, long legs stretched out far behind the tail and swinging pendulum-like whenever a shift of ballast was needed. They apparently did not realize the unevenness of the wind, for when they backed air, ready to descend, a sudden gust would often undercut them and over they would go, legs, wings, and neck sprawling in mid-air. After one or two somersaults or a short, swift dive, they would right themselves, feathers on end, and frantically grasp at the first leaf or twig within reach. Panting, they looked helplessly around, reorientation coming gradually.

At each arrival, a hoarse chorus went up from hungry throats, and every youngster within reach scrambled wildly forward, hopeful of a fish course. They received but scant courtesy and usually a vicious peck tumbled them off the branch. I saw a young bird fall to the water, and this mishap was from no attack, but due to his tripping over his own feet, the claws of one foot gripping those of the other in an insane clasp which overbalanced him. He fell through a thin screen of vines and splashed half onto a small Regia leaf. With neck and wings he struggled to pull himself up, and had almost succeeded when heron and leaf sank slowly, and only the bare stem swung up again. A few bubbles led off in a silvery path toward deeper water, showing where a crocodile swam slowly off with his prey.

For a time the birds remained still, and then crept within the tangles, to their mates or nests, or quieted the clamor of the young with warm-storage fish. How each one knew its own off-spring was beyond my ken, but on three separate evenings scattered through one week, I observed an individual, marked by a wing-gap of two lost feathers, come, within a quarter-hour of six o'clock, and feed a great awkward youngster which had lost a single feather from each wing. So there was no hit-or-miss method —no luck in the strongest birds taking toll from more than two of the returning parents.

Observing this vesper migration in different places, I began to see orderly segregation on a large scale. All the smaller herons dwelt to-gether on certain islands in more or less social tolerance; and on adjoining trees, separated by only a few yards, scores of hawks concentrated and roosted, content with their snail diet, and wholly ignoring their neighbors. On the other side of the gardens, in aristocratic isolation, was a colony of stately American egrets, dainty and graceful. Their circumference of radiation was almost or quite a circle, for they preferred the ricefields for their daily hunting. Here the great birds, snowy white, with flowing aigrettes, and long, curving necks, settled with dignity, and here they slept and sat on their rough nests of sticks.

When the height of homing flight of the host of herons had passed, I noticed a new element of restlessness, and here and there among the foliage appeared dull-brown figures. There occurred the comic explanation of white herons who had crept deep among the branches, again emerging in house coat of drab! These were not the same, however, and the first glance through binoculars showed the thick-set, humped figures and huge, staring eyes of night herons.

As the last rays of the sun left the summit of the royal palms, something like the shadow of a heron flashed out and away, and then the import of these facts was impressed upon me. The egret, the night heron, the vampire—here were three types of organisms, characterizing the actions and reactions in nature. The islands were receiving and giving up. Their heart was becoming filled with the many day-feeding birds, and now the night-shift was leaving, and the very branch on which a night-heron might have been dozing all day was now occupied, perhaps, by a sleeping egret. With eyes enlarged to gather together the scanty rays of light, the night herons were slipping away in the path of the vampires—both nocturnal, but unlike in all other ways. And I wondered if, in the very early morning, infant night herons would greet their returning parents; and if their callow young ever fell into the dark waters, what awful deathly alternates would night reveal; or were the slow-living crocodiles sleepless, with cruel eyes which never closed so soundly but that the splash of a young night heron brought instant response?

1920

"PAUL BUNYAN"

It is impossible to tell where the Paul Bunyan stories arose. Every locality in pioneer America had its athletic woodsmen whose prowess with axe and saw passed into local legend together with the stories of their scarcely less famous teams of oxen and horses. The Paul Bunyan tales were current fifty years ago among the lumbermen of the Great Lakes and St. Lawrence regions; as the timber cutters moved to the West the stories went with them, modified to suit the locality, and increasing in fabulous nature. They form a loose legend around the figure of Paul Bunyan, a Herculean logging contractor, and Babe, his gigantic ox with half-human intelligence. There are some evidences of Canadian French origin in the stories, though the humor is full of the exaggeration which is thought characteristic of the United States. As they have been recounted by countless story-tellers of crude but vigorous imagination to groups about the red-hot stoves of lumber camps, they have taken various forms, and the legend is still growing. The selection following is from a collection by Esther Shephard, Seattle, 1924; another collection is by James Stevens, New York, 1925. See K. B. Stewart and H. A. Watt, "Legends of Paul Bunyan," *Transactions of the Wisconsin Academy of Sciences* 18:639-51.

PAUL BUNYAN [1]

Collected by ESTHER SHEPHARD

From THE BUCKSKIN HARNESS

I suppose everybody's seen pictures of the big log loads we used to haul in the woods in the old times. Loads piled up, ten or twelve rows of logs on top of each other, and the teamster standin' alongside the load, and the top log way up in the air there above his head, and I can tell you them pictures ain't no exaggeration nor nothin' out of the ordinary. Three or four times as high as a man's head I've seen them loads many times. Naturally you had to have a good top-loader to get 'em that high, but that was the top-loader's business to be a good top-loader, and if he knowed what he was

[1] From *Paul Bunyan* by Esther Shephard, copyright, 1924, by Harcourt, Brace and Company.

about he knowed how to build 'em as high as you'd a mind to have 'em.

In Paul's camp, though, we had 'em higher'n any you could ever of seen in any of the pictures. They used to be so high we had to have a telephone to phone up to the loader, and noontime they always sent his dinner up to him in a balloon. Generally he used to write a letter before he went up in the mornin's to send to his mother in case he shouldn't never come down again.

Course they couldn't of drawed them big loads if it hadn't of been for the buckskin harness that was invented about that time. That come in just before Paul went into Minnesota to log in them big white pine woods there. He used to hitch up Babe by Lake Vermilion and then the logs would be drawed down to Duluth or Two Harbors in one pull.

Everybody knows how buckskin stretches when it gets wet, and then shrinks all up to nothin' almost when it gets dry and warm in the sun. Well, that's the principle the buckskin harness was invented on, and the same as with many inventions, I guess, it was invented practically by pure accident. Look at the way Watt invented the steam engine, just watchin' an old teakettle boil.

But I was goin' to tell about the buckskin harness, and the way that come to be invented was, one of the bull-cooks was goin' to haul the wood in for the cook-house stove. They'd used up all the wood that was nearby already, and so he had to go out a good ways out in the woods to get it. The cook was a pretty cranky feller and he' told him he'd better bring home something dry that would burn if he knowed what was good for him, and so the bull-cook took his ox and went away over to the south of the camp where the burnt-over land was. Figured some of them burnt trunks would be dry on the inside anyway. It was rainin' pitchforks that mornin' and nothin' couldn't happen to be dry on the outside by any way or chance.

The ox he had was a big one, though of course not big like Babe, and he had a bran new buckskin harness on him.

And so when he got there he cut down a couple of dozen burnt trees and put the logs on the sled and then he starts out for home with 'em, over the trail. First part of it was just kind of a narrow sled-track through the woods, but about half way that road turned out on one of the big main loggin' roads. He was glad he hit that part of the road and from there on he drove a little faster, walkin' along beside the ox and not botherin' to look back any. And course it was rainin' all the time hard as ever.

Well, when he got to camp it was about noon, and he drove his ox up right close to the door back of the cook-house, and then when he turned around he seen he didn't have no load at all, but the harness was stretched out all the way down the road to the big tree where the turn was, where the log trail went into the woods, and he knowed his load of stove wood must be somewheres down there behind the tree standin' there. He was just goin' to start back and get it when the dinnerhorn commenced to toot, and he calculated he might as well go in and eat his dinner and go and tend to his load afterwards.

"That'll be the best thing I can do," he says.

And then while he was eatin' his dinner and while all of the rest of us was eatin' dinner, the sun come out.

And so, in about fifteen minutes, when the bull-cook come back out again, there was his load of wood standin' there right in front of him, and pretty near climbin' up on the old ox's back, so he had to hurry and cut him loose before it went right up on top of him, and he had to holler for help and everythin'.

You know, what happened was, when the sun come out, that buckskin harness had begun to shrink. And that's how it had pulled the load up by itself, without the ox doin' no pullin' at all on his part.

One of the cookees called Paul to see it, and Paul took out a patent on the harness, and the buckskin harness was used for all long hauls in Paul's camp ever since. A fine invention, you see, that come about that way, only the sun hadn't dried out the wood enough, and the cook swore at the bull-cook just the same, like as if he hadn't tried to do his best.

Paul did some great loggin' in Minnesota. Them forests up there was sure fine forests—stretches of pine and spruce and hemlock, with sometimes some white birches in between. Get up on a rise and you could see them all below you like a great ocean, big dark waves where the spruce was, and light patches of jack pine climbin' up on the hills, and the red willows that used to grow along the cricks. Paul used to climb up on Jasper Point sometimes just to enjoy the sight of it, and at the same time to make sure that the three rivers that make their start there was doin' their job of keepin' his three loggin' operations apart—he'd put 'em in on purpose for that, so he wouldn't get 'em mixed up. They're the Nelson-Saskatchewan, you know, and the St. Lawrence and the Mississippi. Jasper Point is the height of land between 'em.

Paul always liked it in Minnesota, though. There was plenty of Swedes around all the time that he could get hold of to work for him whenever he wanted, and then the huntin' was good in them there woods too.

One time, I know, Paul went huntin' spruce patridges. And he hadn't got out in the woods very far yet and hadn't been lookin' around very long till all of a sudden he seen 540 of 'em sittin in a row on a spruce bough, and he begun figgurin' how was the best way to get 'em.

Course he had his shotgun along and his rifle too, and with his shotgun he could of got 'em all, because there was just enough shot in the load for one shot for each patridge, but he didn't like to get 'em that way if he could help, because he knowed they would be so much trouble to pick up afterwards each one by itself that way.

So what he done was, he took his rifle and went over to the end of the limb and fired and sent the bullet right through the length of the limb and split it open all the way to the tree, and then, just as he figgured, the patridges all got their toes caught in the rebound in the crack he'd made and stuck fast. And then he reloaded his rifle, leavin' the ramrod in, and shot that right through all the patridges. That way he got all but four that he didn't get quite big enough a hold on to make 'em stick on the rod.

He'd finished that shot, and had just turned round, when he seen a fine big buck standin' there not so very far away. He fired his shotgun at him quick and he seen the buck tumble over the ledge just as he fired.

It was such a fine carcass he couldn't hardly wait to get there to get hold of it, so he run as fast as he could to the place where the buck had been. Well, he run too fast. Result was, he run faster than the load, and got ahead of it, and got the whole charge of buckshot in his own back. For the buck'd got scared to death when he sees Paul, and hadn't waited for the shot to reach him.

Ole the Blacksmith come out and helped Paul back to camp and carried the patridges and the buck in for him. The buck when dressed weighed nine hundred seventy-five pounds.

There in Minnesota, the Minneapolis millmen used to want peeled logs, and Paul never liked that much. Oh, there was some sense to it, I spose—would keep the logs from rottin' if they had to lay in the water a long time—but not much—Paul always said it was nothin' but fol-de-rol, and I think he was about right. Anyway, it used to make him all-fired plaguey mad. The way he'd peel 'em when he got mad, he'd just hitch the Blue Ox to 'em and jerk 'em out whole. Even, he didn't bother to cut the trees down sometimes but just pulled 'em out from the top, so he got the heart out and left the limbs and bark standin'. That way a good deal was wasted, of course, and it was a lot of trouble, because he couldn't do but one at a time. I don't know how mad he would of got, but they quit askin' for 'em after awhile— maybe the sawmill men heard how Paul felt about it, and thought they'd better not ask to get peeled logs no more.

What Paul liked best to do was a whole lot of trees at a time. There in Minnesota he got himself a long fallin' saw that would reach across half a mile or more. Of course if the country was a little hilly or there was a hollow or rise of ground, it didn't work so good, because they'd just get the tops of the trees that growed down in the hollows and up on the hills the saw would hit in the ground and get dulled on the rocks. Paul had to keep a gang of two hundred filers to keep that saw filed. And that was the saw that Paul always pulled one end of himself. He didn't care who pulled the other end, and he didn't care if they'd ride the saw, he said, if they felt like it, but what he didn't want was for 'em to drag their feet— he drawed the line on that.

Paul always liked to do things on a big scale. One of his ways was just to hitch Babe onto a whole section of timber at a time and haul it into camp and clear it off. If he got one in about sundown, after the day's work was over, he'd generally get it all cleared before supper.

That was efficient so far as the time it took was concerned anyway. But he couldn't of done it without Babe to haul it in for him.

Like one of these here efficiency experts would say, the over-head cost and maintenance for Babe was high, but on account of low operatin' expense and great efficiency, he was pretty economical camp equipment. And Paul couldn't of done much without him, I know that.

Like the time when they drove the wrong logs down the river and over the St. Anthony Falls; Babe just drank the river dry above the falls and sucked 'em all back again.

. . . .

WILLIAM McFEE 1881-

William McFee, the son of a sea captain, spent his childhood in England and was educated there.

In 1905, after several years of engineering experience, he went to sea as a marine engineer. In this capacity he came to know and sympathize with working men, and to entertain socialistic ideas. He did an immense amount of reading as he traveled from port to port, and it was not long before he began to write, producing, in 1908, *An Ocean Tramp*. Three years later he came to America and settled here; he has since become a naturalized citizen. He writes both essays and novels; important titles are: *Aliens*, 1914; *Casuals of the Sea*, 1916; *Harbors of Memory*, 1921; *Command*, 1922.

McFee preaches the doctrine of self-realization and finds romance to be dependent on one's outlook. Believing that "what is one man's meat is another man's poison," he has a habit of contrasting two people's reactions to the same environment. Wilson Follett says of him that he "materializes the spiritual and gives the abstract a name," and this sums up admirably his ironic manner of uniting aesthetic sensations and concrete observations.

Criticism: Wilson Follett, "Casuals, Romance, and Little Brown Boxes," *Bookm.* 46:172-6; "The Marine Engineer Who Has Become a Novelist," *Cur. Opinion* 61:263; Arthur J. Elder, "William McFee—Engineer and Author," *Bookm.* 44:57-62.

THE MARKET [1]

There is a sharp, imperative rap on my outer door; a rap having within its insistent urgency a shadow of delicate diffidence, as though the person responsible were a trifle scared of the performance and on tiptoe to run away. I roll over and regard the clock. Four-forty. One of the dubious by-products of continuous service as a senior assistant at sea is the habit of waking automatically about 4 A.M. This gives one several hours, when ashore, to meditate upon one's sins, frailties, and (more rarely) triumphs and virtues. For a man who gets up at say, four-thirty, is regarded with aversion ashore. His family express themselves with superfluous vigor. He must lie still and meditate, or suffer the ignominy of being asked when he is going away again.

But this morning, in these old Chambers in an ancient Inn buried in the heart of London City, I have agreed to get up and go out. The reason for this momentous departure from a life of temporary but deliberate indolence is a lady. *"Cherchez la femme,"* [2] as the French say with the dry animosity of a logical race. Well, she is not far to seek, being on the outside of my heavy oak door, tapping, as already hinted, with a sharp insistent delicacy. To this romantic

[1] From *Harbours of Memory* by William McFee. Copyright, 1921, Doubleday, Page and Company. By permission of Messrs. Doubleday, Doran and Company.
[2] "Look for the woman."

summons I reply with an articulate growl of acquiescence, and proceed to get ready. To relieve the anxiety of any reader who imagines an impending elopement it may be stated in succinct truthfulness that we are bound on no such desperate venture. We are going round the corner a few blocks up the Strand,[1] to Covent Garden Market, to see the arrival of the metropolitan supply of produce.

Having accomplished a hasty toilet, almost as primitive as that favored by gentlemen aroused to go on watch, and placating an occasional repetition of the tapping by brief protests and reports of progress, I take hat and cane, and drawing the huge antique bolts of my door, discover a young woman standing by the window looking out upon the quadrangle of the old Inn. She is a very decided young woman, who is continually thinking out what she calls "stunts" for articles in the press. That is her profession, or one of her professions—writing articles for the press. The other profession is selling manuscripts, which constitutes the tender bond between us. For the usual agent's commissions she is selling one of my manuscripts. Being an unattached and, as it were, unprotected male, she plans little excursions about London to keep me instructed and entertained. Here she is attired in the flamboyant finery of a London flower-girl. She is about to get the necessary copy for a special article in a morning paper. With the exception of a certain expectant flash of her bright black Irish eyes, she is entirely businesslike. Commenting on the beauty of an early summer morning in town, we descend, and passing out under the ponderous ancient archway, we make our leisurely progress westward down the Strand.

London is always beautiful to those who love and understand that extraordinary microcosm; but at five of a summer morning there is about her an exquisite quality of youthful fragrance and debonair freshness which goes to the heart. The newly-hosed streets are shining in the sunlight as though paved with "patins of bright gold."[2] Early 'buses rumble by from neighboring barns where they have spent the night. And, as we near the new Gaiety Theater, thrusting forward into the great rivers of traffic soon to pour round its base like some bold Byzantine promontory, we see Waterloo Bridge thronged with wagons, piled high. From all quarters they are coming, past Charing Cross the great wains are arriving from Paddington Terminal, from the market-garden section of Middlesex

and Surrey. Down Wellington Street come carts laden with vegetables from Brentwood and Coggeshall; and neat vans packed with crates of watercress which grows in the lush lowlands of Suffolk and Cambridgeshire; and behind us are thundering huge four-horse vehicles from the docks, vehicles with peaches from South Africa, potatoes from the Canary Islands, onions from France, apples from California, oranges from the West Indies, pineapples from Central America, grapes from Spain, and bananas from Colombia.

We turn in under an archway behind a theater and adjacent to the stage-door of the Opera House. The booths are rapidly filling with produce. Gentlemen in long alpaca coats and carrying formidable marbled notebooks walk about with an important air. A mountain range of pumpkins rises behind a hill of cabbages. Festoons of onions are being suspended from rails. The heads of barrels are being knocked in, disclosing purple grapes buried in cork-dust. Pears and figs, grown under glass for wealthy patrons, repose in soft tissue-lined boxes. A broken crate of Tangerine oranges has spilled its contents in a splash of ruddy gold on the plank runway. A wagon is driven in, a heavy load of beets, and the broad wheels crush through the soft fruit so that the air is heavy with the acrid sweetness.

We pick our way among the booths and stalls until we find the flowers. Here is a crowd of ladies—young, so-so, and some quite matronly, and all dressed in this same flamboyant finery of which I have spoken. They are grouped about an almost overpowering mass of blooms. Roses just now predominate. There is a satisfying solidity about the bunches, a glorious abundance which, in a commodity so easily enjoyed without ownership, is scarcely credible. I feel no desire to own these huge aggregations of odorous beauty. It would be like owning a harem, one imagines. Violets, solid patches of vivid blue in round baskets, eglantine in dainty boxes, provide a foil to the majestic blazonry of the roses and the dew-spangled forest of maidenhair fern near by.

"And what are those things at all?" demands my companion, diverted for a moment from the flowers. She nods towards a mass of dull-green affairs piled on mats or being lifted from big vans. She is a cockney and displays surprise when she is told those things are bananas. She shrugs and turns again to the musk-roses, and forgets. But to me, as the harsh, penetrating odor of the green fruit cuts across the heavy perfume of the flowers, comes a picture of the farms in distant Colombia or perhaps Costa Rica. There is nothing like an odor to stir memories. I see the timber pier and the long line of rackety open-slatted cars jangling into the dark shed, pushed by a noisy, squealing locomotive. I see the boys lying asleep between shifts, their enormous straw hats covering their faces as they sprawl. In the distance rise the blue mountains; behind is the motionless blue sea. I hear the whine of the elevators, the monotonous click of the counters, the harsh cries of irresponsible and argumentative natives. I feel the heat of the tropic day, and see the gleam of the white waves breaking on yellow sands below tall palms. I recall the mysterious impenetrable solitude of the jungle, a solitude alive, if one is equipped with knowledge, with a ceaseless warfare of winged and crawling hosts. And while my companion is busily engaged in getting copy for a special article about the Market, I step nimbly out of the way of a swarthy gentleman from Calabria, [1] who with his two-wheeled barrow is the last link in the immense chain of transportation connecting the farmer in the distant tropics and the cockney pedestrian who halts on the sidewalk and purchases a banana for a couple of pennies.

1921

WILLA SIBERT CATHER 1876-

Though born in the Shenandoah Valley, Miss Cather has lived mostly in the North. After she received her education at the University of Nebraska she spent some years in editorial work in Pittsburgh and New York City. Miss Cather's notable work in fiction began with *O Pioneers,* 1913, a story of pioneer life in the Middle West; *My Antonia,* 1918, has also the Middle West as its background; and the story, *One of Ours,* 1922, which obtained the Pulitzer prize, begins in Nebraska and ends in France. Although her memories of the prairie states figure so largely in Miss Cather's novels, she has won notable success in one of her latest stories, *Death Comes for the Archbishop,* 1927, by a flight far beyond the range of her own experiences. Sympathetic, penetrating characterization by means of quiet, convincing scenes placed together almost without plot, is a distinctive feature of Miss Cather's work.

Criticism: Carl Van Doren, *Contemporary American Novelists;* "Willa Cather," *Nation* 113:92-3; Latrobe Carroll, "Willa Sibert Cather," *Bookm.* 53: 212-16; Lloyd Morris, "Willa Cather," *No. Am.* 219:641-52; E. S. Sergeant, "Willa Cather," *New Repub.* 43: 91-4; William Whitman, 3rd, "Eminence Comes for Miss Cather," *Ind.* 119:283; T. K. Whipple, "Willa Cather," *Literary Review* 4:331-2.

[1] a province of southern Italy

A WAGNER MATINÉE [2]

I received one morning a letter, written in pale ink on glassy, blue-lined note-paper, and bearing the postmark of a little Nebraska village. This communication, worn and rubbed, looking as if it had been carried for some days in a coat pocket that was none too clean, was from my uncle Howard, and informed me that his wife had been left a small legacy by a bachelor relative, and that it would be necessary for her to go to Boston to attend to the settling of the estate. He requested me to meet her at the station and render her whatever services might be necessary. On examining the date indicated as that of her arrival, I found it to be no later than tomorrow. He had characteristically delayed waiting until, had I been away from home for a day, I must have missed my aunt altogether.

The name of my Aunt Georgiana opened before me a gulf of recollection so wide and deep that, as the letter dropped from my hand, I felt suddenly a stranger to all the present conditions of my existence, wholly ill at ease and out of place amid the familiar surroundings of my study. I became, in short, the gangling farmerboy my aunt had known, scourged with chilblains and bashfulness, my hands cracked and sore from the corn husking. I sat again before her parlor organ, fumbling the scales with my stiff, red fingers, while she, beside me, made canvas mittens for the huskers.

The next morning, after preparing my landlady for a visitor, I set out for the station. When the train arrived I had some difficulty in finding my aunt. She was the last of the passengers to alight, and it was not until I got her into the carriage that she seemed really to recognize me. She had come all the way in a day coach; her linen duster had become black with soot and her black bonnet gray with dust during the journey. When we arrived at my boardinghouse the landlady put her to bed at once and I did not see her again until the next morning.

Whatever shock Mrs. Springer experienced at my aunt's appearance, she considerately concealed. As for myself, I saw my aunt's battered figure with that feeling of awe and respect with which we behold explorers who have left their ears and fingers north of Franz-Joseph-Land, or their health somewhere along the Upper Congo. My Aunt Georgiana had been a music teacher at the Boston Conservatory,

[2] Reprinted from *Youth and The Bright Medusa* by Willa Cather, by and with permission of and special arrangement with Alfred A. Knopf, Inc., authorized publishers.

somewhere back in the latter sixties. One summer, while visiting in the little village among the Green Mountains where her ancestors had dwelt for generations, she had kindled the callow fancy of my uncle, Howard Carpenter, then an idle, shiftless boy of twenty-one. When she returned to her duties in Boston, Howard followed her, and the upshot of this infatuation was that she eloped with him, eluding the reproaches of her family and the criticism of her friends by going with him to the Nebraska frontier. Carpenter, who, of course, had no money, took up a homestead in Red Willow County, fifty miles from the railroad. There they had measured off their land themselves, driving across the prairie in a wagon, to the wheel of which they had tied a red cotton handkerchief, and counting its revolutions. They built a dug-out in the red hillside, one of those cave dwellings whose inmates so often reverted to primitive conditions. Their water they took from the lagoons where the buffalo drank, and their slender stock of provisions was always at the mercy of bands of roving Indians. For thirty years my aunt had not been farther than fifty miles from the homestead.

I owed to this woman most of the good that ever came my way in boyhood, and had a reverential affection for her. During the years when I was riding herd for my uncle, my aunt, after cooking the three meals—the first of which was ready at six o'clock in the morning—and putting the six children to bed, would often stand until midnight at her ironing-board, with me at the kitchen table beside her, hearing me recite Latin declensions and conjugations, gently shaking me when my drowsy head sank down over a page of irregular verbs. It was to her, at her ironing or mending, that I read my first Shakespeare, and her old text-book on mythology was the first that ever came into my empty hands. She taught me my scales and exercises on the little parlor organ which her husband had bought her after fifteen years during which she had not so much as seen a musical instrument. She would sit beside me by the hour, darning and counting, while I struggled with the "Joyous Farmer." She seldom talked to me about music, and I understood why. Once when I had been doggedly beating out some easy passages from an old score of *Euryanthe* [1] I had found among her music books, she came up to me and, putting her hands over my eyes, gently drew my head back upon her shoulder, saying tremulously, "Don't love it so well, Clark, or it may be taken from you."

When my aunt appeared on the morning after her arrival in Boston, she was still in a semi-somnambulant state. She seemed not to realize that she was in the city where she had spent her youth, the place longed for hungrily half a lifetime. She had been so wretchedly train-sick throughout the journey that she had no recollection of anything but her discomfort, and, to all intents and purposes, there were but a few hours of nightmare between the farm in Red Willow County and my study on Newbury Street. I had planned a little pleasure for her that afternoon, to repay her for some of the glorious moments she had given me when we used to milk together in the straw-thatched cowshed and she, because I was more than usually tired, or because her husband had spoken sharply to me, would tell me of the splendid performance of the *Huguenots* [2] she had seen in Paris, in her youth.

At two o'clock the Symphony Orchestra was to give a Wagner program, and I intended to take my aunt; though, as I conversed with her, I grew doubtful about her enjoyment of it. I suggested our visiting the Conservatory and the Common before lunch, but she seemed altogether too timid to wish to venture out. She questioned me absently about various changes in the city, but she was chiefly concerned that she had forgotten to leave instructions about feeding half-skimmed milk to a certain weakling calf, "old Maggie's calf, you know, Clark," she explained, evidently having forgotten how long I had been away. She was further troubled because she had neglected to tell her daughter about the freshly-opened kit of mackerel in the cellar, which would spoil if it were not used directly.

I asked her whether she had ever heard any of the Wagnerian operas, and found that she had not, though she was perfectly familiar with their respective situations, and had once possessed the piano score of *The Flying Dutchman.* [3] I began to think it would be best to get her back to Red Willow County without waking her, and regretted having suggested the concert.

From the time we entered the concert hall, however, she was a trifle less passive and inert, and for the first time seemed to perceive her surroundings. I had felt some trepidation lest she might become aware of her queer, country clothes, or might experience some painful embarrassment at stepping suddenly into the world to which she had been dead for a quarter of a century. But, again, I found how superficially I had judged her. She sat looking about her

[1] an opera by Von Weber, first performed 1823

[2] an opera by Meyerbeer
[3] an opera by Wagner, 1843

with eyes as impersonal, almost as stony, as those with which the granite Rameses in a museum watches the froth and fret that ebbs and flows about his pedestal. I have seen this same aloofness in old miners who drift into the Brown hotel at Denver, their pockets full of bullion, their linen soiled, their haggard faces unshaven; standing in the thronged corridors as solitary as though they were still in a frozen camp on the Yukon.

The matinée audience was made up chiefly of women. One lost the contour of faces and figures, indeed any effect of line whatever, and there was only the color of bodices past counting, the shimmer of fabrics soft and firm, silky and sheer; red, mauve, pink, blue, lilac, purple, écru, rose, yellow, cream, and white, all the colors that an impressionist finds in a sunlit landscape, with here and there the dead shadow of a frock coat. My aunt Georgiana regarded them as though they had been so many daubs of tube-paint on a palette.

When the musicians came and took their places, she gave a little stir of anticipation, and looked with quickening interest down over the rail at that invariable grouping, perhaps the first wholly familiar thing that had greeted her eye since she had left old Maggie and her weakling calf. I could feel how all those details sank into her soul, for I had not forgotten how they had sunk into mine when I came fresh from plowing forever and forever between green aisles of corn, where, as in a treadmill, one might walk from daybreak to dusk without perceiving a shadow of change. The clean profiles of the musicians, the gloss of their linen, the dull black of their coats, the beloved shapes of the instruments, the patches of yellow light on the smooth, varnished bellies of the 'cellos and the bass viols in the rear, the restless, wind-tossed forest of fiddle necks and bows—I recalled how, in the first orchestra I ever heard, those long bow-strokes seemed to draw the heart out of me, as a conjurer's stick reels out yards of paper ribbon from a hat.

The first number was the *Tannhauser* [1] overture. When the horns drew out the first strain of the Pilgrims' Chorus, Aunt Georgiana clutched my coat sleeve. Then it was I first realized that for her this broke a silence of thirty years. With the battle between the two motives, with the frenzy of the Venusberg theme and its ripping of strings, there came to me an overwhelming sense of the waste and wear we are so powerless to combat; and I saw again the tall, naked house on the prairie, black and grim as a wooden fortress; the black

pond where I had learned to swim, its margin pitted with sun-dried cattle tracks; the rain gullied clay banks about the naked house, the four dwarf ash seedlings where the dish-cloths were always hung to dry before the kitchen door. The world there was the flat world of the ancients; to the east, a cornfield that stretched to daybreak; to the west, a corral that reached to sunset; between, the conquests of peace, dearer-bought than those of war.

The overture closed, my aunt released my coat sleeve, but she said nothing. She sat staring dully at the orchestra. What, I wondered, did she get from it? She had been a good pianist in her day, I knew, and her musical education had been broader than that of most music teachers of a quarter of a century ago. She had often told me of Mozart's operas and Meyerbeer's, and I could remember hearing her sing, years ago, certain melodies of Verdi. When I had fallen ill with a fever in her house she used to sit by my cot in the evening—when the cool, night wind blew in through the faded mosquito netting tacked over the window and I lay watching a certain bright star that burned red above the cornfield—and sing "Home to our mountains, O let us return!" in a way fit to break the heart of a Vermont boy near dead of homesickness already.

I watched her closely through the prelude to *Tristan and Isolde*, [2] trying vainly to conjecture what that seething turmoil of strings and winds might mean to her, but she sat mutely staring at the violin bows that drove obliquely downward, like the pelting streaks of rain in a summer shower. Had this music any message for her? Had she enough left to at all comprehend this power which had kindled the world since she had left it? I was in a fever of curiosity, but Aunt Georgiana sat silent upon her peak in Darien. [3] She preserved this utter immobility throughout the number from *The Flying Dutchman*, though her fingers worked mechanically upon her black dress, as if, of themselves, they were recalling the piano score they had once played. Poor hands! They had been stretched and twisted into mere tentacles to hold and lift and knead with;—on one of them a thin, worn band that had once been a wedding ring. As I pressed and gently quieted one of those groping hands, I remembered with quivering eyelids their services for me in other days.

Soon after the tenor began the "Prize Song," [4] I heard a quick drawn breath and

[1] a romantic opera by Wagner

[2] an opera by Wagner based upon an Arthurian legend
[3] See Keats's sonnet, "On First Looking into Chapman's Homer."
[4] from *Die Meistersinger*, a comic opera by Wagner

turned to my aunt. Her eyes were closed, but the tears were glistening on her cheeks, and I think, in a moment more, they were in my eyes as well. It never really died, then—the soul which can suffer so excruciatingly and so interminably; it withers to the outward eye only; like that strange moss which can lie on a dusty shelf half a century and yet, if placed in water grows green again. She wept so throughout the development and elaboration of the melody.

During the intermission before the second half, I questioned my aunt and found that the "Prize Song" was not new to her. Some years before there had drifted to the farm in Red Willow County a young German, a tramp cowpuncher, who had sung in the chorus at Bayreuth [1] where he was a boy, along with the other peasant boys and girls. Of a Sunday morning he used to sit on his gingham-sheeted bed in the hands' bedroom which opened off the kitchen, cleaning the leather of his boots and saddle, singing the "Prize Song," while my aunt went about her work in the kitchen. She had hovered over him until she had prevailed upon him to join the country church, though his sole fitness for this step, in so far as I could gather, lay in his boyish face and his possession of this divine melody. Shortly afterward, he had gone to town on the Fourth of July, been drunk for several days, lost his money at a faro table, ridden a saddled Texas steer on a bet, and disappeared with a fractured collar-bone. All this my aunt told me huskily, wanderingly, as though she were talking in the weak lapses of illness.

"Well, we have come to better things than the old *Trovatore* at any rate, Aunt Georgie?" I queried, with a well meant effort at jocularity.

Her lip quivered and she hastily put her handkerchief up to her mouth. From behind it she murmured, "And you have been hearing this ever since you left me, Clark?" Her question was the gentlest and saddest of reproaches.

The second half of the program consisted of four numbers from the *Ring,* [2] and closed with Siegfried's funeral march. [3] My aunt wept quietly, but almost continuously, as a shallow vessel overflows in a rain-storm. From time to time her dim eyes looked up at the lights, burning softly under their dull glass globes.

The deluge of sound poured on and on; I never knew what she found in the shining cur-rent of it; I never knew how far it bore her, or past what happy islands. From the trembling of her face I could well believe that before the last number she had been carried out where the myriad graves are, into the gray, nameless burying ground of the sea; or into some world of death vaster yet, where, from the beginning of the world, hope has lain down with hope and dream with dream and, renouncing, slept.

The concert was over; the people filed out of the hall chattering and laughing, glad to relax and find the living level again, but my kinswoman made no effort to rise. The harpist slipped the green felt cover on his instrument; the flute-players shook the water from their mouth-pieces; the men of the orchestra went out one by one, leaving the stage to the chairs and music stands, empty as a winter cornfield.

I spoke to my aunt. She burst into tears and sobbed pleadingly, "I don't want to go, Clark, I don't want to go!"

I understood. For her, just outside the concert hall, lay the black pond with the cattle-tracked bluffs; the tall, unpainted house, with weather-curled boards, naked as a tower; the crook-backed ash seedlings where the dish-cloths hung to dry; the gaunt, molting turkeys picking up refuse about the kitchen door.

1920

CHRISTOPHER (DARLINGTON) MORLEY 1890-

After graduating from Haverford College at his birthplace in Pennsylvania, Mr. Morley was a Rhodes Scholar at Oxford. Since his return to this country he has been in the service of a number of publishing houses and newspapers as a literary editor and journalist. He has also been a constant contributor to critical reviews. Among the books he has written are *Songs for a Little House,* 1917, *Mince Pie* (essays), 1920, *Travels in Philadelphia,* 1920, *Where the Blue Begins,* 1922, *Thunder on the Left* (novel), 1925. Mr. Morley's essays are typical of the day: light, yet with a sound basis in humanity and good sense; suggesting, not explaining; passing with the quickness of caprice from topic to topic. Paradoxical, whimsical, entertaining, they are worthy successors to the essays of Oliver Wendell Holmes.

Vincent O'Sullivan, "America and the English Literary Tradition," *Liv. Age* 303:170-76; *Ind.* 108:49; *Lit. Dig.* 80:31, Jan. 17, '24; Carl Van Doren, "Day In and Day Out," *Cent.* 107:308-15; H. S. Canby, "C. Morley," *Sat. R. Lit.* 4:625-6; T. S. Matthews, "Christopher Morley," *New Repub.* 54:167-9.

---

[1] Wagner's theater was at Bayreuth.
[2] *The Ring of the Nibelung,* a series of four musical dramas by Wagner, some of his most important
[3] from *The Twilight of the Gods,* one of the dramas of the *Ring*

NURSERY RHYMES FOR THE TENDER-HEARTED [1]

I

Scuttle, scuttle, little roach—
How you run when I approach:
Up above the pantry shelf,
Hastening to secrete yourself.

Most adventurous of vermin,
How I wish I could determine
How you spend your hours of ease,
Perhaps reclining on the cheese.

Cook has gone, and all is dark—
Then the kitchen is your park: 10
In the garbage heap that she leaves
Do you browse among the tea leaves?

How delightful to suspect
All the places you have trekked:
Does your long antenna whisk its
Gentle tip across the biscuits?

Do you linger, little soul,
Drowsing in our sugar bowl?
Or, abandonment must utter,
Shake a shimmy on the butter?   20

Do you chant your simple tunes
Swimming in the baby's prunes?
Then, when dawn comes, do you slink
Homeward to the kitchen sink?

Timid roach, why be so shy?
We are brothers, thou and I.
In the midnight, like yourself,
I explore the pantry shelf!

IV

I knew a black beetle, who lived down a drain,
And friendly he was, though his manners were
    plain;
When I took a bath he would come up the pipe,
And together we'd wash and together we'd
    wipe.

Though mother would sometimes protest with
    a sneer
That my choice of a tub-mate was wanton and
    queer,
A nicer companion I never have seen;
He bathed every night, so he must have been
    clean.

Whenever he heard the tap splash in the tub
He'd dash up the drain-pipe and wait for a
    scrub,   10
And often, so fond of ablution was he,
I'd find him there floating and waiting for me.

But nurse has done something that seems a
    great shame:
She saw him there, waiting, prepared for a
    game;
She turned on the hot and she scalded him sore
And he'll never come bathing with me any more.

TO THE LITTLE HOUSE [2]

Dear little house, dear shabby street,
Dear books and beds and food to eat!
How feeble words are to express
The facets of your tenderness.

How white the sun comes through the pane!
In tinkling music drips the rain!
How burning bright the furnace glows!
What paths to shovel when it snows!

O dearly loved Long Island trains!
O well remembered joys and pains.   10
How near the housetops Beauty leans
Along that little street in Queens!

Let these poor rhymes abide for proof
Joy dwells beneath a humble roof;
Heaven is not built of country seats
But little queer suburban streets!

WHAT MEN LIVE BY [3]

What a delicate and rare and gracious art is
the art of conversation! With what a dexterity and skill the bubble of speech must be
maneuvered if mind is to meet and mingle with
mind.

There is no sadder disappointment than to
realize that a conversation has been a complete
failure. By which we mean that it has failed
in blending or isolating for contrast the ideas,
opinions, and surmises of two eager minds. So
often a conversation is ship-wrecked by the
very eagerness of one member to contribute.
There must be give and take, parry and thrust,
patience to hear and judgment to utter. How
uneasy is the qualm as one looks back on an

hour's talk and sees that the opportunity was wasted; the precious instant of intercourse gone forever: the secrets of the heart still incommunicate! Perhaps we were too anxious to hurry the moment, to enforce our own theory, to adduce instance from our own experience. Perhaps we were not patient enough to wait until our friend could express himself with ease and happiness. Perhaps we squandered the dialogue in tangent topics, in a multitude of irrelevances.

How few, how few are those gifted for real talk! There are fine merry fellows, full of mirth and shrewdly minded observation, who will not abide by one topic, who must always be lashing out upon some new by-road, snatching at every bush they pass. They are too excitable, too ungoverned for the joys of patient intercourse. Talk is so solemn a rite it should be approached with prayer and must be conducted with nicety and forbearance. What steadiness and sympathy are needed if the thread of thought is to be unwound without tangles or snapping! What forbearance, while each of the pair, after tentative gropings here and yonder, feels his way toward truth as he sees it. So often two in talk are like men standing back to back, each trying to describe to the other what he sees and disputing because their visions do not tally. It takes a little time for minds to turn face to face.

Very often conversations are better among three than between two, for the reason that then one of the trio is always, unconsciously, acting as umpire, interposing fair play, recalling wandering wits to the nub of the argument, seeing that the aggressiveness of one does no foul to the reticence of another. Talk in twos may, alas! fall into speaker and listener: talk in threes rarely does so.

It is little realized how slowly, how painfully, we approach the expression of truth. We are so variable, so anxious to be polite, and alternately swayed by caution or anger. Our mind oscillates like a pendulum: it takes some time for it to come to rest. And then, the proper allowance and correction has to be made for our individual vibrations that prevent accuracy. Even the compass needle doesn't point the true north, but only the magnetic north. Similarly our minds at best can but indicate magnetic truth, and are distorted by many things that act as iron filings do on the compass. The necessity of holding one's job: what an iron filing that is on the compass card of a man's brain!

We are all afraid of truth: we keep a battalion of our pet prejudices and precautions ready to throw into the argument as shock troops, rather than let our fortress of Truth be stormed. We have smoke bombs and decoy ships and all manner of cunning colorizations by which we conceal our innards from our friends, and even from ourselves. How we fume and fidget, how we bustle and dodge rather than commit ourselves.

In days of hurry and complication, in the incessant pressure of human problems that thrust our days behind us, does one never dream of a way of life in which talk would be honored and exalted to its proper place in the sun? What a zest there is in that intimate unreserved exchange of thought, in the pursuit of the magical blue bird of joy and human satisfaction that may be seen flitting distantly through the branches of life. It was a sad thing for the world when it grew so busy that men had no time to talk. There are such treasures of knowledge and compassion in the minds of our friends, could we only have time to talk them out of their shy quarries. If we had our way, we would set aside one day a week for talking. In fact, we would reorganize the week altogether. We would have one day for Worship (let each man devote it to worship of whatever he holds dearest); one day for Work; one day for Play (probably fishing); one day for Talking; one day for Reading, and one day for Smoking and Thinking. That would leave one day for Resting, and (incidentally) interviewing employers.

The best week of our life was one in which we did nothing but talk. We spent it with a delightful gentleman who has a little bungalow on the shore of a lake in Pike County. He had a great many books and cigars, both of which are conversational stimulants. We used to lie out on the edge of the lake, in our oldest trousers, and talk. We discussed ever so many subjects; in all of them he knew immensely more than we did. We built up a complete philosophy of indolence and good will, according to Food and Sleep and Swimming their proper share of homage. We rose at 10 in the morning and began talking; we talked all day and until 3 o'clock at night. Then we went to bed and regained strength and combativeness for the coming day. Never was a week better spent. We committed no crimes, planned no secret treaties, devised no annexations or indemnities. We envied no one. We examined the entire world and found it worth while. Meanwhile our wives, who were watching (perhaps with a little quiet indignation) from the veranda, kept on asking us, "What on earth do you talk about?"

Bless their hearts, men don't have to have anything to talk *about*. They just talk.

And there is only one rule for being a good talker: learn how to listen.

1920

ON UNANSWERING LETTERS [1]

There are a great many people who really believe in answering letters the day they are received, just as there are people who go to the movies at 9 o'clock in the morning; but these people are stunted and queer.

It is a great mistake. Such crass and breathless promptness takes away a great deal of the pleasure of correspondence.

The psychological didoes involved in receiving letters and making up one's mind to answer them are very complex. If the tangled process could be clearly analyzed and its component involutions isolated for inspection we might reach a clearer comprehension of that curious bag of tricks, the efficient Masculine Mind.

Take Bill F., for instance, a man so delightful that even to contemplate his existence puts us in good humor and makes us think well of a world that can exhibit an individual equally comely in mind, body, and estate. Every now and then we get a letter from Bill, and immediately we pass into a kind of trance, in which our mind rapidly enunciates the ideas, thoughts, surmises, and contradictions that we would like to write to him in reply. We think what fun it would be to sit right down and churn the ink-well, spreading speculation and cynicism over a number of sheets of foolscap to be wafted Billward.

Sternly we repress the impulse for we know that the shock to Bill of getting so immediate a retort would surely unhinge the well-fitted panels of his intellect.

We add his letter to the large delta of unanswered mail on our desk, taking occasion to turn the mass over once or twice and run through it in a brisk, smiling mood, thinking of all the jolly letters we shall write some day.

After Bill's letter has lain on the pile for a fortnight or so it has been gently silted over by about twenty other pleasantly postponed manuscripts. Coming upon it by chance, we reflect that any specific problems raised by Bill in that manifesto will by this time have settled themselves. And his random speculations upon household management and human destiny will probably have taken a new slant by now, so that to answer his letter in its own tune will

not be congruent with his present fevers. We had better bide a wee until we really have something of circumstance to impart.

We wait a week.

By this time a certain sense of shame has begun to invade the privacy of our brain. We feel that to answer that letter now would be an indelicacy. Better to pretend that we never got it. By and by Bill will write again and then we will answer promptly. We put the letter back in the middle of the heap and think what a fine chap Bill is. But he knows we love him, so it doesn't really matter whether we write or not.

Another week passes by, and no further communication from Bill. We wonder whether he does love us as much as we thought. Still— we are too proud to write and ask.

A few days later a new thought strikes us. Perhaps Bill thinks we have died and he is annoyed because he wasn't invited to the funeral. Ought we to wire him? No, because after all we are not dead, and even if he thinks we are, his subsequent relief at hearing the good news of our survival will outweigh his bitterness during the interval. One of these days we will write him a letter that will really express our heart, filled with all the grindings and gearwork of our mind, rich in affection and fallacy. But we had better let it ripen and mellow for a while. Letters, like wines, accumulate bright fumes and bubblings if kept under cork.

Presently we turn over that pile of letters again. We find in the lees of the heap two or three that have gone for six months and can safely be destroyed. Bill is still on our mind, but in a pleasant, dreamy kind of way. He does not ache or twinge us as he did a month ago. It is fine to have old friends like that and keep in touch with them. We wonder how he is and whether he has two children or three. Splendid old Bill!

By this time we have written Bill several letters in imagination and enjoyed doing so, but the matter of sending him an actual letter has begun to pall. The thought no longer has the savor and vivid sparkle it had once. When one feels like that it is unwise to write. Letters should be spontaneous outpourings: they should never be undertaken merely from a sense of duty. We know that Bill wouldn't want to get a letter that was dictated by a feeling of obligation.

Another fortnight or so elapsing, it occurs to us that we have entirely forgotten what Bill said to us in that letter. We take it out and con it over. Delightful fellow! It is full of his own felicitous kinks of whim, though some

[1] From *Mince Pie* by Christopher Morley. Copyright, 1919, by Doubleday, Page and Company. By permission of Doubleday, Doran and Company.

of it sounds a little old-fashioned by now. It seems a bit stale, has lost some of its freshness and surprise. Better not answer it just yet, for Christmas will soon be here and we shall have to write then anyway. We wonder, can Bill hold out until Christmas without a letter?

We have been rereading some of those imaginary letters to Bill that have been dancing in our head. They are full of all sorts of fine stuff. If Bill ever gets them he will know how we love him. To use O. Henry's immortal joke, we have days of Damon and Knights of Pythias writing those uninked letters to Bill. A curious thought has come to us. Perhaps it would be better if we never saw Bill again. It is very difficult to talk to a man when you like him so much. It is much easier to write in the sweet fantastic strain. We are so inarticulate when face to face. If Bill comes to town we will leave word that we have gone away. Good old Bill! He will always be a precious memory.

A few days later a sudden frenzy sweeps over us, and though we have many pressing matters on hand, we mobilize pen and paper and literary shock troops and prepare to hurl several battalions at Bill. But, strangely enough, our utterance seems stilted and stiff. We have nothing to say. *My dear Bill,* we begin, *it seems a long time since we heard from you. Why don't you write? We still love you, in spite of all your shortcomings.*

That doesn't seem very cordial. We muse over the pen and nothing comes. Bursting with affection, we are unable to say a word.

Just then the phone rings. "Hello?" we say. It is Bill, come to town unexpectedly.

"Good old fish!" we cry, ecstatic. "Meet you at the corner of Tenth and Chestnut in five minutes."

We tear up the unfinished letter. Bill will never know how much we love him. Perhaps it is just as well. It is very embarrassing to have your friends know how you feel about them. When we meet him we will be a little bit on our guard. It would not be well to be betrayed into any extravagance of cordiality.

And perhaps a not altogether false little story could be written about a man who never visited those most dear to him, because it panged him so to say good-bye when he had to leave.

1920

WITTER BYNNER 1881-

Mr. Bynner has been engaged in literary work during all his active life. He was born in Brooklyn, graduated from Harvard, and was for twelve

years or more on the staff of New York publishing houses. His work includes the following plays: *Tiger,* 1913; *Iphigenia in Tauris,* 1915; *A. Book of Plays,* 1922. Among his volumes of verse are *The New World,* 1915; *A Canticle of Praise,* 1919; *The Beloved Stranger,* 1919; *Caravan,* 1925. Although much of Mr. Bynner's work is simple and direct, some of it is highly figurative. In such cases we must interpret it through the idea it suggests or the mood it arouses; especially since it is liable to be over-lavish in figure and in phrasing.

Criticism: William M. Reedy in preface to *The Beloved Stranger;* R. M. Alden, *Dial* 59:275; O. M. Firkins, *Nation* 101:406.

A FORTUNE-TELLER [1]

Turning the secrets from her pack of cards,
Warning of sickness, tracing out a theft,
Guarding from danger as an omen guards,
Her hand grew withered as it grew more deft. . . .

Till in the stuffy parlor where she lies,
Now to these clients, neighbors, debtors, friends,
Truest is proven of her prophecies,
"I shall be dead before December ends."

That old man, facing us, who many years   10
Carried the marvellous message of her art,
Now hear him how he tells us with his tears
The simpler larger wisdom of her heart.

For she was quick to share the good that came,
So that young mothers turned at last and slept
And loafers gruffly reverenced her name—
Yet more than all she gave away she kept,

Kept red geraniums on her window-sill
And a gay garden in that narrow plot
Fenced-in behind her house. You'll find there still
Her hoe, her rake, her rusty watering-pot.   20

Bright, in the midst of all these dingy yards,
Her roses, hollyhocks, and pansies grew;
As if some happy jester in the cards
Whispered the gayest secret that he knew.

1917

TRAIN-MATES [1]

Outside hove Shasta, snowy height on height,
A glory; but a negligible sight,
For you had often seen a mountain peak

[1] Reprinted from *Grenstone Poems* by Witter Bynner by and with permission of and special arrangement with Alfred A. Knopf, Inc., authorized publishers.

But not my paper. So we came to speak . . .
A smoke, a smile,—a good way to commence
The comfortable exchange of difference!
You a young engineer, five feet eleven,
Forty-five chest, with football in your heaven,
Liking a road-bed newly built and clean,
Your fingers hot to cut away the green   10
Of brush and flowers that bring beside a track
The kind of beauty steel lines ought to lack,—
And I a poet, wistful of my betters,
Reading George Meredith's [1] high-hearted let-
       ters,
Joining betweenwhile in the mingled speech
Of a drummer, circus-man, and parson, each
Absorbing to himself—as I to me
And you to you—a glad identity!

       .   .   .   .   .

After a time, when others went away,
A curious kinship made us choose to stay,   20
Which I could tell you now; but at the time
You thought of baseball teams and I of rhyme,
Until we found that we were college men
And smoked more easily and smiled again;
And I from Cambridge cried, the poet still:
"I know your fine Greek theater on the hill
At Berkeley!" With your happy Grecian head
Upraised, "I never saw the place," you said—
"Once I was free of class, I always went
Out to the field."

            Young Engineer, you meant   30
As fair a tribute to the better part
As ever I did. Beauty of the heart
Is evident in temples. But it breathes
Alive where athletes quicken curly wreaths,
Which are the lovelier because they die.
You are a poet quite as much as I,
Though differences appear in what we do,
And I an athlete quite as much as you.
Because you half-surmise my quarter-mile
And I your quatrain, we could greet and smile.
Who knows but we shall look again and find   41
The circus-man and drummer, not behind
But leading in our visible estate—
As discus-thrower and as laureate?

                              1917

ROOFS [2]

I don't know what it is
That sets me flying
Over the roofs this morning
Swift on tiptoe,

Touching the chimneys and railings.
Not even the middle of roofs,
Only the edges.
I don't know why it is
So many dancers
Dance in my dawn,   10
Hailing this hard city,
For most of the dancers that lead me
Point in directions daily
Of mountain and of sea,
Toward little villages
And houses nestling,
Rivers,
Hills.
I don't know what it is
That sets me flying   20
Over the roofs this early morning
Swift on tiptoe . . .

You!

                              1919

WILLIAM ROSE BENÉT 1886-

Mr. Benét was born at Fort Hamilton, New York Harbor. Though he comes of a military family, and was graduated from the Sheffield Scientific School, Yale, he turned to literature, beginning his career as a free lance writer in California. Then he was successively reader for the *Century Magazine,* second lieutenant in the U. S. Air Service, assistant editor of the New York *Evening Post,* and in 1924 co-founder and editor of *The Saturday Review of Literature.*

He has published several volumes of poems: *Merchants from Cathay,* 1913; *The Falconer of God,* 1914; *The Great White Wall,* 1917; *The Burglar of the Zodiac,* 1918; *Moons of Grandeur,* 1920; a finely drawn romance, *First Person Singular,* 1921; and many critical essays.

Mr. Benét's vigor in the conception and treatment of a poetic theme is a marked trait of his verse. A strong and sometimes fantastic imagination often develops his germ idea into a structure of original and unfamiliar beauty. Frequent use of allegory makes his work sometimes difficult to understand.

Criticism: M. Wilkinson (NV); also "Mirrors of the Renaissance," *Bookm.* 53:168-70; Phelps (EP); also *Bookm.* 47:557; W. M. Payne, "Recent Poetry," *Dial* 56:67-8; "The Literary Spotlight," *Bookm.* 58:135-9; *Poetry* 5:91; 9:322-4; 15:48-51.

THE FALCONER OF GOD [3]

I flung my soul to the air like a falcon flying.
I said: "Wait on, wait on, while I ride below!

[1] English novelist, 1828-1909
[2] Reprinted from *The Beloved Stranger* by Witter Bynner by and with permission of and special arrangement with Alfred A. Knopf, Inc., authorized publishers.

[3] Reprinted from *The Falconer of God and Other Poems* by William Rose Benét, published by the Yale University Press.

I shall start a heron soon
In the marsh beneath the moon—
A strange white heron rising with silver on its
    wings,
    Rising and crying
    Wordless, wondrous things;
The secret of the stars, of the world's
    heart-strings
    The answer to their woe.
Then stoop [1] thou upon him, and grip and hold
    him so!"   10

My wild soul waited on as falcons hover.
I beat the reedy fens as I trampled past.
    I heard the mournful loon
    In the marsh beneath the moon.
And then, with feathery thunder, the bird of my
    desire
    Broke from the cover
    Flashing silver fire.
High up among the stars I saw his pinions
    spire.
    The pale clouds gazed aghast
As my falcon stooped upon him, and gripped
    and held him fast.   20

My soul dropped through the air—with heav-
    enly plunder?—
Gripping the dazzling bird my dreaming knew?
    Nay! but a piteous freight,
    A dark and heavy weight
Despoiled of silver plumage, its voice forever
    stilled—
    All of the wonder
    Gone that ever filled
Its guise with glory. O bird that I have
    killed,
    How brilliantly you flew
Across my rapturous vision when first I
    dreamed of you!   30

Yet I fling my soul on high with new endeavor,
And I ride the world below with a joyful
    mind.

    I shall start a heron soon
    In the marsh beneath the moon—
A wondrous silver heron its inner darkness
    pledges!
    I beat forever
    The fens and the sedges.
The pledge is still the same—for all dis-
    astrous pledges,
    All hopes resigned!
My soul still flies above me for the quarry it
    shall find!   40
        1914

[1] a term used in falconry; to swoop down

THE HORSE THIEF [2]

There he moved, cropping the grass at the pur-
    ple canyon's lip.
His mane was mixed with the moonlight that
    silvered his snow-white side,
For the moon sailed out of a cloud with the
    wave of a spectral ship.
I crouched and I crawled on my belly, my lariat
    coil looped wide.

Dimly and darkly the mesas broke on the starry
    sky.
A pall covered every color of their gorgeous
    glory at noon.
I smelt the yucca and mesquite, and stifled my
    heart's quick cry,
And wormed and crawled on my belly to where
    he moved against the moon!

Some Moorish barb was that mustang's sire.
    His lines were beyond all wonder.
From the prick of his ears to the flow of his
    tail he ached in my throat and eyes.   10
Steel and velvet grace! As the prophet [3] says,
    God had "clothed his neck with thun-
    der."
Oh, marvelous with the drifting cloud he drifted
    across the skies!

And then I was near at hand—crouched, and
    balanced, and cast the coil;
And the moon was smothered in cloud, and the
    rope through my hands with a rip!
But somehow I gripped and clung, with the
    blood in my brain aboil—
With a turn round the rugged tree-stump there
    on the purple canyon's lip.

Right into the stars he reared aloft, his red eye
    rolling and raging.
He whirled and sunfished and lashed, and
    rocked the earth to thunder and flame.
He squealed like a regular devil horse. I was
    haggard and spent and aging—
Roped clean, but almost storming clear, his
    fury too fierce to tame.   20

And I cursed myself for a tenderfoot moon-
    dazzled to play the part;
But I was doubly desperate then, with the posse
    pulled out from the town,
Or I'd never have tried it. I only knew I must
    get a mount and a start.
The filly had snapped her foreleg short—I had
    had to shoot her down.

[2] Reprinted from *The Burglar of the Zodiac and Other Poems* by William Rose Benét, published by the Yale University Press.
[3] Job

So there he struggled and strangled, and I
    snubbed him around the tree.
Nearer, a little nearer—hoofs planted, and loll-
    ing tongue—
Till a sudden slack pitched me backward. He
    reared right on top of me.
Mother of God—that moment! He missed me
    . . . and up I swung.

Somehow, gone daft completely and clawing a
    bunch of his mane,
As he stumbled and tripped in the lariat, there
    I was—up and astride   30
And cursing for seven counties! And the mus-
    tang? *Just insane!*
Crack-bang! went the rope; we cannoned off
    the tree; then—gods, that ride!

A rocket—that's all, a rocket. I dug with my
    teeth and nails.
Why, we never hit even the high spots (though
    I hardly remember things);
But I heard a monstrous booming like a thunder
    of flapping sails
When he spread—well, *call* me a liar!—when he
    spread those wings, those wings!

So white that my eyes were blinded; thick
    feathered and wide unfurled,
They beat the air into billows. We sailed and
    the earth was gone.
Canyon and desert and mesa withered below,
    with the world.
And then I knew that mustang; for I was Bel-
    lerophon! [1]   40

Yes, glad as a Greek, and mounted on a horse
    of the elder gods,
With never a magic bridle or a fountain-mirror
    nigh!
*My chaps and spurs and holster must have
    looked it!* What's the odds?
I'd a leg over lightning and thunder, careening
    across the sky!

And forever streaming before me, fanning my
    forehead cool,
Flowed a mane of molten silver; and just before
    my thighs
(As I gripped his velvet-muscled ribs, while I
    cursed myself for a fool),
The steady pulse of those pinions—their won-
    derful fall and rise!

The bandanna I bought in Bowie blew loose
    and whipped from my neck.

My shirt was stuck to my shoulders, and rib-
    boning out behind.   50
The stars were dancing and wheeling and glanc-
    ing, dipping with smirk and beck.
The clouds were flowing, dusking and glowing.
    We rode a roaring wind.

We soared through the silver starlight to knock
    at the planets' gates.
New shimmering constellations came whirling
    into our ken.
Red stars and green and golden swung out of
    the void that waits
For man's great last adventure; the Signs [2]
    took shape—and then

I knew the lines of that Centaur the moment
    I saw him come!
The musical-box of the heavens all around us
    rolled to a tune
That tinkled and chimed and trilled with silver
    sounds that struck you dumb,
As if some archangel were grinding out the
    music of the moon.   60

Melody-drunk on the Milky Way, as we swept
    and soared hilarious,
Full in our pathway, sudden he stood—the Cen-
    taur of the Stars,
Flashing from head and hoof and breast! I
    knew him for Sagittarius. [3]
He reared, and bent and drew his bow. He
    crouched as a boxer spars.

Flung back on his haunches, weird he loomed;
    then leapt—and the dim void lightened.
Old White Wings shied and swerved aside, and
    fled from the splendor-shod.
Through a flashing welter of worlds we charged.
    I knew why my horse was frightened.
He *had* two faces,—a dog's and a man's—that
    Babylonian god!

Also, he followed us real as fear. Ping! went
    an arrow past.
My broncho buck-jumped, humping high. We
    plunged . . . I guess that's all!   70
I lay on the purple canyon's lip, when I opened
    my eyes at last—
Stiff and sore and my head like a drum, but I
    broke no bones in the fall.

So you know—and now you may string me up.
    Such was the way you caught me.
Thank you for letting me tell it straight, though
    you never could greatly care.

[1] a hero of Greek mythology who rode the winged horse,
    Pegasus

[2] of the Zodiac
[3] a southern constellation pictured as a centaur

For I took a horse that wasn't mine! . . . . But
    there's one the heavens brought me,
And I'll hang right happy because I know he is
    waiting for me up there.

From creamy muzzle to cannon-bone, by God,
    he's a peerless wonder!
He is steel and velvet and furnace-fire, and
    death's supremest prize;
And never again shall be roped on earth that
    neck that is "clothed with thunder" . . . .
String me up, Dave! Go dig my grave! *I rode
    him across the skies!*   80
                                              1916

STEPHEN VINCENT BENÉT
1898-

Stephen Benét, brother of William Benét, produced his first volume of verse, *Five Men and Pom-
pey,* in 1915 before he had entered college. He was
born at Bethlehem, Pennsylvania, received both his
bachelor's and master's degrees at Yale, and before
he graduated was given the first John Masefield
poetry prize. Since then he has continued to win
poetry prizes, and has published *Heavens and
Earth,* 1920, and *Tiger Joy,* 1925, in verse; and
The Beginning of Wisdom, 1921, and *The Spanish
Bayonet,* 1926, both novels. Mr. Benét's work is
full of vigorous realism, of clear sense impressions,
whether the record of his own experiences or of his
imagination. Much of it is inspired by American
life; his most ambitious poem, *John Brown's Body,*
1928, is a long narrative poem of the Civil War,
beginning with the remote causes of the conflict.
By many critics this poem is reckoned one of the
most notable of the decade.

Criticism: Untermeyer; Phelps; *Dial* 71:597-600;
Poetry 16:53-4; *Sat. R. Lit.* 2:903; *Lit. Digest* 98:
37, Sept. 29, '28; *Sat. R. Lit.* 5: Sept. 29, '28.

PORTRAIT OF A BOY [1]

After the whipping he crawled into bed,
Accepting the harsh fact with no great weeping.
How funny uncle's hat had looked striped red!
He chuckled silently. The moon came, sweep-
    ing
A black, frayed rag of tattered cloud before
In scorning; very pure and pale she seemed,
Flooding his bed with radiance. On the floor
Fat motes danced. He sobbed; closed his eyes
    and dreamed.
Warm sand flowed around him. Blurts of crim-
    son light
Splashed the white grains like blood. Past the
    cave's mouth   10

[1] Reprinted from *Young Adventure* by Stephen V.
Benét, published by the Yale University Press.

Shone with a large, fierce splendor, wildly
    bright,
The crooked constellations of the South;

Here the Cross [2] swung; and there, affronting
    Mars,
The Centaur [3] stormed aside a froth of stars.
Within, great casks like wattled aldermen
Sighed of enormous feasts, and cloth of gold
Glowed on the walls like hot desire. Again,
Beside webbed purples from some galleon's
    hold,
A black chest bore the skull and bones in white
Above a scrawled "Gunpowder!" By the
    flames,   20
Decked out in crimson, gemmed with syenite,
Hailing their fellows with outrageous names,
The pirates sat and diced. Their eyes were
    moons.
"Doubloons!" they said. The words crashed
    gold.
        "Doubloons!"
                                              1917

THE BALLAD OF WILLIAM SYCAMORE [4]
(1790-1880)

My father he was a mountaineer,
His fist was a knotty hammer;
He was quick on his feet as a running deer,
And he spoke with a Yankee stammer.

My mother she was merry and brave
And so she came to labor,
With a tall green fir for her doctor grave,
And a stream for her comforting neighbor.

And some are wrapped in the linen fine,
And some like a godling's scion;   10
But I was cradled on twigs of pine
In the skin of a mountain lion.

And some remember a white, starched lap
And a ewer with silver handles;
But I remember a coonskin cap
And the smell of bayberry candles!

The cabin logs with the bark still rough,
And my mother who laughed at trifles,
And the tall, lank visitors, brown as snuff,
With their long, straight squirrel-rifles.   20

[2] Southern Cross, a constellation in the southern hemi-
    sphere
[3] a southern constellation
[4] From *Tiger Joy* by Stephen Vincent Benét, copyright,
    1925, Doubleday, Doran and Company, Inc., pub-
    lishers.

I can hear them dance, like a foggy song,
Through the deepest one of my slumbers,
The fiddle squeaking the boots along
And my father calling the numbers.

The quick feet shaking the puncheon-floor, [1]
And the fiddle squeaking and squealing,
Till the dried herbs rattled above the door
And the dust went up to the ceiling.

There are children lucky from dawn till dusk,
But never a child so lucky!   30
For I cut my teeth on "Money Musk"
In the Bloody Ground of Kentucky!

When I grew tall as the Indian Corn,
My father had little to lend me,
But he gave me his great old powder-horn
And his woodsman's skill to befriend me.

With a leather shirt to cover my back,
And a redskin nose to unravel
Each forest sign, I carried my pack
As far as a scout could travel.   40

Till I lost my boyhood and found my wife,
A girl like a Salem clipper!
A woman straight as a hunting-knife
With eyes as bright as the Dipper!

We cleared our camp where the buffalo feed,
Unheard-of streams were our flagons,
And I sowed my sons like the apple-seed
On the trail of the Western wagons.

They were right, tight boys, never sulky or
        slow,
A fruitful, a goodly muster!   50
The eldest died at the Alamo. [2]
The youngest fell with Custer. [3]

The letter that told it burned my hand.
Yet we smiled and said, "So be it!"
But I could not live when they fenced the land,
For it broke my heart to see it.

I saddled a red, unbroken colt
And rode him into the day there,
And he threw me down like a thunderbolt
And rolled on me as I lay there.   60

The hunter's whistle hummed in my ear
As the city-men tried to move me,

[1] made from broad, flat pieces of rough timber
[2] a fortified mission at San Antonio, Texas, taken by
    Mexicans, 1836, after all the defenders were killed
[3] an American general, 1839-1876, killed in battle with
    the Sioux Indians

And I died in my boots like a pioneer
With the whole wide sky above me.

Now I lie in the heart of the fat, black soil
Like the seed of a prairie-thistle;
It has washed my bones with honey and oil
And picked them clean as a whistle.

And my youth returns, like the rains of Spring,
And my sons, like the wild geese flying,   70
And I lie and hear the meadow-lark sing
And have much content in my dying.

Go play with the towns you have built of blocks,
The towns where you would have bound me!
I sleep in my earth like a tired fox,
And my buffalo have found me.

                                                   1922

NATHALIA (RUTH CLARA) CRANE 1913-

Nathalia Crane was born in New York City,
but now lives in Brooklyn. She was brought up
in a home of good books and intelligent conversation, and began very early to write. Her books
thus far have been *The Janitor's Boy*, 1924; *Lava
Lane and Other Poems*, 1925; *The Singing Crow
and Other Poems*, 1926; *The Sunken Garden*
(prose romance), 1926; *Venus Invisible and Other
Poems*, 1928. Some of her poems show a maturity
of thought far beyond her years; others record in
simple, naïve verse what is generally a closed book,
the real, inner emotion aroused in children by ordinary experiences. A writer in *The Nation* sees her
as "a sort of double personality, one half of which
is a child quite frankly absorbed in childish things,
and the other half an adult who smiles at the immaturity of her twin." Her later work shows,
of course, an increasing maturity of thought.

Criticism: Untermeyer; "The Infant Muse," *Na-
tion* 121:589; W. R. Benét, "Nathalia Crane," *Sat.
R. Lit.* 2:350; L. Untermeyer, "The Mystery of a
Poet," *Sat. R. Lit.* 3:857-8; "A Poet at Twelve,"
Lit. Digest 87:29, Oct. 10, '25; "Who Wrote Nath-
alia's Verses?" *Lit. Digest* 87:29, Dec. 5, '25; G. S.
Hubbell, "A Little Girl's Utopia," *Bookm.* 64:
306-9.

THE FLATHOUSE ROOF [4]

I linger on the flathouse roof, the moonlight is
        divine.
But my heart is all a-flutter like the washing on
        the line.

I long to be a heroine, I long to be serene,

[4] From *The Janitor's Boy* by Nathalia Crane, copyright,
    1924, Thomas Seltzer, Inc., by permission of
    Messrs. Albert and Charles Boni, Inc.

But my feet, they dance in answer to a distant
tambourine.

And, oh! the dreams of ecstasy. Oh! Babylon
and Troy!
I've a hero in the basement, he's the janitor's
red-haired boy.

There's the music of his mallet and the jigging
of his saw;
I wonder what he's making on that lovely cellar
floor?

He loves me, for he said it when we met upon
the stair,
And that is why I'm on the roof to get a breath
of air.   10

He said it! Oh! He said it! And the only
thing I said
Was, "Roger Jones, I like you, for your hair
is very red."

We parted when intruders came a-tramping
through the hall;
He's got my pocket handkerchief, and I have
got his ball.

And so it is I'm on the roof. Oh! Babylon
and Troy!
I'm very sure that I'm in love with someone
else's boy.

Alone, upon the starry heights, I'm dancing on
a green,
To the jingling and the jangling of a distant
tambourine,

To the stamping of a hammer and the jigging
of a saw,
And the secret sort of feeling I'm in love forever more,   20

Do you think it's any wonder, with the moonlight so divine,
That my heart is all a-flutter, like the washing
on the line?
                                                   1924

THE POE COTTAGE [1]

There they dwelt in the wrennet's cot
    Just as it was to be;
Paced the halls of a miniature—
    Poe and Annabel Lee.

[1] From *Venus Invisible and Other Poems* by Nathalia
Crane, copyright, 1928, Coward-McCann, Inc.

He was garbed in a courtly suit,
    She in Colonial low;
Heads together they walked the halls—
    Annabel Lee and Poe.

These indeed were particular hours;
    No one tells of their glee,   10
How they laughed in the wrennet's cot—
    Poe and Annabel Lee.

What if all of the snow that fell
    Never was really snow;
What if all of their griefs were thus—
    Annabel Lee and Poe.

What if all of the shadows there
    Merely an imagery;
Nothing to do with the wrennet's cot—
    Poe and Annabel Lee.   20
                                                   1928

ARTHUR GUITERMAN 1871-

Mr. Guiterman seems to be notoriously free of
the affectations of the poet's trade. His fine sense
of humor is evidently a charm against the various
fopperies which he has cleverly brought together in
a set of "Don'ts for Poets." He was born of American parents in Vienna, but has lived the greater
part of his life in New York, where he has done
editorial work, given lectures on journalism, and
become a member of several societies for authors.
He has turned from the short story to verse exclusively, and has produced, among other volumes,
The Laughing Muse, 1915; *The Mirthful Lyre*,
1918; *Chips of Jade*, 1920; *The Light Guitar*, 1923;
I Sing the Pioneer, 1926. His rhymed reviews are
excellent.

Guiterman's work has steadily gained in meati-
ness. There is a solidity about his later verse that
gives his generous fun a philosophical foundation.
We find in him a practical and clever yet idealistic
American.

Criticism: Joyce Kilmer, "The Most American
of Poets," *Ind.* 88:312-13; Edmund Pearson, "I
Sing the Pioneer," *Outlook* 145:154-6.

AFTERNOON TEA [2]

A SONNET SEQUENCE

*As wildly raged the tea-imbibing throng
    About the urn, with measured step and slow,
The mighty spirits of the realm of song
    (At some weird séance on the floor below
Materialized), among them moved, amazed
    At what they heard. A teacup dropped and
        broke,*

[2] Copyright. By permission of Messrs. Harper and
Brothers, publishers.

All unregarded, when, with hand upraised,
Full solemnly the shade of Milton spoke:

I

RESIGNATION

When I consider how my time is spent
  At gatherings to meet some tender bride,
  Or "Just a few dear friends," or, woe betide!
Some foreign super-person, eloquent,
Whom women rave about, or, ill-content,
  Some bashful English poet, wistful-eyed,
  Who yearns, I know, to run away and hide—
Rebelliously I question, "Was I meant
To hear this talk that runs around in rings?
  And must I waste the blessèd afternoon?"
  Then, "Hush!" says Patience; "Think upon
      the fate
Of those who needs must pass the tea and
      things—
  Who may not say, 'Good-by,' as you shall
      soon—
    Who have to serve, and, likewise, stand
      and wait!"

Backed up against a shelf whereon reposed
  His works (with leaves uncut, I sadly fear),
Stood Wordsworth. Intermittently he dozed,
  The solitary bard of Windermere; [1]
Then, waking from a pleasant forty winks,
  He drew about his shape its cloak of gray,
And, borrowing a sonnet-form, methinks
  Employed by Shelley, thus he said his say:

II

SOME FOLKS ARE TOO MUCH WITH US

Some folks are too much with us—much too
      much.
  "Yes," sighed the lady with the gems galore,
"One's life in Europe puts one out of touch
  With matters here; but then, this dreadful
      war
Just fairly drove us back. And we had such
  A weary hunt to find a house before
We took that spacious, fine old Tudor place,
  Or mansion, rather. Then the coal, you
      know!
We burn twelve tons a week in any case;
  But no one would deliver it, and so
We had to send the touring-cars, with Brace,
Our second-man, the five chauffeurs, and Fred,
  To load and fetch it home and store it!" "Oh,
I'm glad you are so rich!" said I, and fled.

[1] a lake in Westmoreland, England

The ablest critics working at the trade,
  As poets know, are often much mistaken;
So was it Shakespeare's self that next essayed
  The lofty strain—or was it only Bacon?

III

SONNET XXX

When to these sessions, more of speech than
      thought,
  By custom urged, reluctantly I come,
I know that I converse not as I ought
  In courtesy. Yet, better far be dumb
Than prate like these, "Yes, Youth will have its
      fling!"
  Or, "Isn't it a small world, after all?"
Or, haply, "Money isn't everything."
  The sugar in my cup is turned to gall
When one declares, "I never bear a grudge,"
  Or lauds his "sense of humor," save the
      mark!
Or proses how, "It isn't right to judge
  By mere appearances." But hark! oh, hark!
What cultured wight is yon that says, "My
      friend,
All Art is but a Means to reach an End!"

"One lump, or two?" the hostess breathed
      again;
  Light laughter rippled up and down the scale;
The tea-urn bubbled musically, when
  The shade of Shelley told its wondrous tale:

IV

GARGANTUA OF GOTHAM

I met a traveler from an antique land,
  Who said: "The finest pilaf [2] ever known
I ate in Cairo at the Hotel Grand;
  The chef is excellent, though overprone
To use of garlic. But the ablest hand
  For flavoring a goulash [3] to a dot,
Is Samovarovitch of Budapest.
  Then, if you're fond of ices (I am not;
Those fancy dishes don't appeal to me),
  Remember, you will always get the best
At Andrea's in Rome. But, with your tea
  Or coffee, in the Kilmenoff Café
In Petrograd, they serve you pirozhki [4]
  That melt upon the tongue and die away!"

As gabbling tongues the deafened ear assailed
  With vapid eloquence in every key,
The gentle Keats inordinately railed—
  Intoxicated on a cup of tea:

[2] a dish of rice cooked with meat, dried fruits, or spices,
      much relished by Mohammedans
[3] a stew of meat and vegetables highly seasoned
[4] small pies filled with meat or vegetables

V

ON FIRST LOOKING IN ON A TEA RIOT

Much having travailed over weighty schemes,
　　To lighter chat I lend a ready ear;
　　Yet, even so, I would not choose to hear
Soft adolescents tell their silly dreams,
Nor would I give a brace of chocolate creams
　　To learn "what Willie said, the little dear!"
　　While operations, more or less severe,
Are palpably unpardonable themes.
I do not care about your family ties,
　　And "Fashion" is a word I fain would ban.
Oh, ye that chatter on, while Chronos flies,
　　Of babies, dress and servants, futile clan,
I stare upon ye all in pained surprise.
　　Silence!—I'd rather speak with Mary Ann!

Recovering a square of buttered toast
　From off the rug where, right side down, it
　　fell,
In kindly words the ever-gracious ghost
　Of Mrs. Browning sighed a sad farewell:

VI

SONNET FROM THE PORTUGUESE

I lift my brimming teacup solemnly
　　As once Electra her sepulchral urn,
　　For I do fear that it would overturn
If I should set it sudden on my knee
As skilful jugglers do. I like your tea;
　　It has a pleasant hint of wildwood fern;
　　Where do you get it? And I fain would learn
Just how you brown your toast so daintily.
A food on which a fairy might be fed,
　　Your angel-cake is soft and light as snow.　10
These cookies are delicious! Have you read
　　The "Bacchae" of Euripides? I know
You have! But, mercy! how the day has fled!
　　A lovely time! but I must really go!
1918

STRICTLY GERM-PROOF [1]

The Antiseptic Baby and the Prophylactic Pup
Were playing in the garden when the Bunny
　　gamboled up;
They looked upon the Creature with a loathing
　　undisguised;—
It wasn't Disinfected and it wasn't Sterilized.

They said it was a Microbe and a Hotbed of
　　Disease;
They steamed it in a vapor of a thousand-odd
　　degrees;

[1] Copyright. By permission of Messrs. Harper and
Brothers, publishers.

They froze it in a freezer that was cold as Ban-
　　ished Hope
And washed it in permanganate with carbolated
　　soap;

In sulphureted hydrogen they steeped its wiggly
　　ears;
They trimmed its frisky whiskers with a pair of
　　hard-boiled shears;　　　　　　10
They donned their rubber mitten and they took
　　it by the hand
And 'lected it a member of the Fumigated Band.

There's not a Micrococcus in the garden where
　　they play;
They bathe in pure iodoform a dozen times a
　　day;
And each imbibes his rations from a Hygienic
　　Cup—
The Bunny and the Baby and the Prophylactic
　　Pup.

1915

ELINOR WYLIE 1885-1928

Elinor Wylie was born in New Jersey of a family
who had long been residents of Pennsylvania. She
was educated at schools in Pennsylvania and in
Washington, D.C., and afterwards spent several
years in Europe. In 1923 she married William Rose
Benét. Mrs. Wylie's novels include *Jennifer Lorn,*
1923; *The Venetian Glass Nephew,* 1925; and *The
Orphan Angel,* 1927, which deals with Shelley,
whom she idealized. Her books of poems were
chiefly *Nets to Catch the Wind,* 1921; *Black Armour,* 1923; and *Trivial Breath,* 1928. Her distinction lies in her condensation and restraint; her
poetry seems to be the crystallized product of quiet
yet intense thought resulting from a complex personality. Her typical work is extremely figurative,
a pattern of simple, sharply-cut images forming a
highly-colored, symbolic picture.

Criticism: H. S. Gorman, "Daughter of Donne,"
No. Am. 219:679-86; E. S. Sergeant, "Elinor
Wylie," *New Repub.* 49:36-9; "Black Armour,"
Sat. R. Lit. 5, Dec. 29, '28; Harriet Monroe, *Poetry*
33:266-72; Rebecca West, *Bookm.* 69:55-6; W. R.
Benét, *Commonweal* 9:432; C. Van Doren, *Bookm.*
68:609-11.

ATAVISM [2]

I always was afraid of Somes's Pond:
Not the little pond, by which the willow stands,
Where laughing boys catch alewives in their
　　hands
In brown, bright shallows; but the one beyond.

[2] Reprinted from *Nets to Catch the Wind* by Elinor
Wylie, by and with permission of and special arrangement with Alfred A. Knopf, Inc., authorized
publishers; and by permission of *Poetry; a Magazine of Verse,* Chicago.

There, where the frost makes all the birches
    burn
Yellow as cow-lilies, and the pale sky shines
Like a polished shell between black spruce and
    pines,
Some strange thing tracks us, turning where we
    turn.
You'll say I dream it, being the true daughter
Of those who in old times endured this dread.
Look! Where the lily-stems are showing red
A silent paddle moves below the water.
A sliding shape has stirred them like a breath;
Tall plumes surmount a painted mask of Death.

CASTILIAN [1]

Velasquez took a pliant knife
And scraped his palette clean;
He said, "I lead a dog's own life
Painting a king and queen."

He cleaned his palette with oily rags
And oakum from Seville wharves;
"I am sick of painting painted hags
And bad ambiguous dwarves.

"The sky is silver, the clouds are pearl,
Their locks are looped with rain.   10
I will not paint Maria's girl
For all the money in Spain."

He washed his face in water cold,
His hands in turpentine;
He squeezed out color like coins of gold
And color like drops of wine.

Each color lay like a little pool
On the polished cedar wood;
Clear and pale and ivory-cool
Or dark as solitude.   20

He burnt the rags in the fireplace
And leaned from the window high;
He said, "I like that gentleman's face
Who wears his cap awry."

This is the gentleman, there he stands,
Castilian, sombre-caped,
With arrogant eyes, and narrow hands
Miraculously shaped.

DU BOSE HEYWARD 1885-

Mr. Heyward, lecturer and writer, comes of English and French Huguenot stock; he was born in
Charleston, South Carolina, where he now lives.
His first publication was *Carolina Chansons*, 1922,
in which he collaborated with Hervey Allen. In
1924 appeared *Skylines and Horizons,* a book of
verse; and in 1925 a novel, *Porgy,* a study of contemporary Negro life, which has been successfully
dramatized. In his poems Mr. Heyward reflects
the South of today somewhat as Frost represents
the New England of today. His virile treatment of
tragic themes growing out of local social conditions
is particularly noticeable.

Biography: H. Allen, *Du Bose Heyward.*

For selections from *Porgy,* see *Bookm.* 61:629-35;
62:165-71.

THE MOUNTAIN WOMAN [2]

Among the sullen peaks she stood at bay
And paid life's hard account from her small
    store.
Knowing the code of mountain wives, she bore
The burden of the days without a sigh;
And, sharp against the somber winter sky,
I saw her drive her steers afield each day.

Hers was the hand that sunk the furrows deep
Across the rocky, grudging southern slope.
At first youth left her face, and later, hope;
Yet through each mocking spring and barren
    fall   10
She reared her lusty brood, and gave them all
That gladder wives and mothers love to keep.

And when the sheriff shot her eldest son
Beside his still, so well she knew her part,
She gave no healing tears to ease her heart;
But took the blow upstanding, with her eyes
As drear and bitter as the winter skies.
Seeing her then, I thought that she had won.

But yesterday her man returned too soon   19
And found her tending, with a reverent touch,
One scarlet bloom; and having drunk too much,
He snatched its flame and quenched it in the
    dirt.
Then, like a creature with a mortal hurt,
She fell, and wept away the afternoon.
    1924

DUSK IN THE LOW COUNTRY [3]

A league of broomgrass, rose, and mauve, and
    umber,
Gashed by a road into the setting sun;
Three heavy laden carts that groan and lumber
Toward the woods, then vanish one by one.

A line of scarlet, and a blur of madder
Behind the trees. The resting earth exhales
Warm, humid dusk; and infinitely sadder
Than death or birth, a lone marsh creature
    wails.

Land of wide beauty, and eternal waiting,
You have made loveliness a thing to seek.   10
How small our loving seems, how little hating,
How less than breath the scattered words we
    speak.
Here where the aeons pass, and seasons flutter
Like sun and shade across your ample breast,
Your silence thunders down the songs I utter,
Who come to be your singer, and your guest.

                1925

PRODIGAL [1]

Some day, when the stern seeker in my brain
Has ceased to drive me stumbling through the
    dark,
Dropping dead cinders for each faint new spark,
Only to see the new one wax and wane;
When all my dreams are numbered with the
    slain;
And wisdom, that egregious patriarch,
Has told his last half truth, and left me stark;
I shall go home, I shall go home again.

Laughter will greet me, waiting in the hall;
And friendships will come trooping down the
    stairs,   10
Sweet as old rose leaves wrinkled in a jar.
Battles and loves will move me not at all.
There will be juleps, billiards, family prayers,
And a clean passport for another star.

                1925

THE HALF PINT FLASK [2]

I picked up the book and regarded it with
interest. Even its format suggested the author:
the practical linen covered boards, the compact
exact paragraphing. I opened the volume at
random. There he was again: "There can be no
doubt," "An undeniable fact," "I am prepared
to assert." A statement in the preface leaped
from the context and arrested my gaze:
"The primitive American Negro is of a
deeply religious nature, demonstrating in his
constant attendance at church, his fervent
prayers, his hymns, and his frequent mention of
the Deity that he has cast aside the last vestiges

of his pagan background, and has unreservedly
espoused the doctrine of Christianity."
I spun the pages through my fingers until a
paragraph in the last chapter brought me up
standing:
"I was hampered in my investigation by a
sickness contracted on the island that was accompanied by a distressing insomnia, and in its
final stages, extreme delirium. But I already
had sufficient evidence in hand to enable me to
prove—"
Yes, there it was, fact upon fact. I was overwhelmed by the permanence, the unanswerable
last word of the printed page. In the face of
it my own impressions became fantastic, dis-
credited even in my own mind. In an effort at
self justification I commenced to rehearse my
impressions of that preposterous month as opposed to Barksdale's *facts;* my feeling for effects and highly-developed fiction-writer's imagination on the one hand; and on the other, his
cold record of a tight, three dimensional world
as reported by his five good senses.
Sitting like a crystal gazer, with the book in
my hand, I sent my memory back to a late
afternoon in August, when, watching from the
shore near the landing on Ediwander Island, I
saw the "General Stonewall Jackson" slide past
a frieze of palmetto trees, shut off her steam,
and nose up to the tenuous little wharf against
the ebb.
Two barefooted Negroes removed a section
of the rail and prepared to run out the gang
plank. Behind them gathered the passengers
for Ediwander landing: ten or a dozen Negroes
back from town with the proceeds of a month's
labor transformed into flaming calico, amazing
bonnets, and new, flimsy, yellow luggage; and
trailing along behind them, the single white passenger.
I would have recognized my guest under
more difficult circumstances and I experienced
that inner satisfaction that comes from having
a new acquaintance fit neatly into a preconceived pattern. The obstinacy of which I had
been warned was evident in the thin immobile
line of the mouth over the prognathous jaw.
The eyes behind his thick glasses were a bright
hard blue and moved methodically from object
to object, allowing each its allotted time for
classification then passing unhurriedly on to
the next. He was so like the tabloid portrait in
the letter of the club member who had sent him
down that I drew the paper from my pocket
and refreshed my memory with a surreptitious
glance.

"He's the museum, or collector type," Spencer had written; "spends his time collecting facts—some he sells—some he keeps to play with. Incidentally his hobby is American glass, and he has the finest private collection in the state."

We stood eyeing each other over the heads of the noisy landing party without enthusiasm. Then when the last Negro had come ashore he picked up his bag with a meticulousness that vaguely exasperated me, and advanced up the gangplank.

Perfunctory introductions followed: "Mr. Courtney?" from him, with an unnecessarily rising inflection; and a conventional "Mr. Barksdale, I presume," from me in reply.

The buckboard had been jogging along for several minutes before he spoke.

"Very good of Mr. Spencer to give me this opportunity," he said in a close clipped speech. "I am doing a series of articles on Negroid Primates, and I fancy the chances for observation are excellent here."

"Negroid Primates!" The phrase annoyed me. Uttered in that dissecting voice, it seemed to strip the human from the hundred or more Negroes who were my only company except during the duck season when the club members dropped down for the shooting.

"There are lots of Negroes here," I told him a little stiffly. "Their ancestors were slaves when the island was the largest rice plantation in South Carolina, and isolation from modern life has kept them primitive enough, I guess."

"Good!" he exclaimed. "I will commence my studies at once. Simple souls, I fancy. I should have my data within a month."

We had been traveling slowly through deep sand ruts that tugged at the wheels like an undertow. On either side towered serried ranks of virgin long-leaf pine. Now we topped a gentle rise. Before us was the last outpost of the forest crowning a diminishing ridge. The straight columned trees were bars against a released splendor of sunset sky and sea.

Impulsively I called his attention to it:

"Rather splendid, don't you think?"

He raised his face, and I was immediately cognizant of the keen methodical scrutiny that passed from trees to sea, and from sea back to that last wooded ridge that fell away into the tumble of dunes.

Suddenly I felt his wire-tight grasp about my arm.

"What's that?" he asked, pointing with his free hand. Then with an air of authority, he snapped: "Stop the cart. I've got to have a look at it."

"That won't interest you. It's only a Negro burying ground. I'll take you to the quarters tomorrow, where you can study your 'live primates.'"

But he was over the wheel with surprising alacrity and striding up the slight ascent to the scattered mounds beneath the pines.

The sunset was going quickly, dragging its color from the sky and sea, rolling up leagues of delicately tinted gauze into tight little bales of primary color, then draping these with dark covers for the night. In sharp contrast against the light the burying ground presented its pitiful emblems of the departed. Under the pine needles, in common with all Negro graveyards of the region, the mounds were covered with a strange litter of half emptied medicine bottles, tin spoons, and other futile weapons that had failed in the final engagement with the last dark enemy.

Barksdale was puttering excitedly about among the graves, peering at the strange assortment of crockery and glass. The sight reminded me of what Spencer had said of the man's hobby and a chill foreboding assailed me. I jumped from the buckboard.

"Here," I called, "I wouldn't disturb those things if I were you."

But my words went unheeded. When I reached Barksdale's side, he was holding a small flat bottle, half filled with a sticky black fluid, and was rubbing the earth from it with his coat sleeve. The man was electric with excitement. He held the flask close to his glasses, then spun around upon me.

"Do you know what this is?" he demanded, then rushed on triumphantly with his answer: "It's a first issue, half pint flask of the old South Carolina state dispensary. It gives me the only complete set in existence. Not another one in America. I had hoped that I might get on the trail of one down here. But to fall upon it like this!"

The hand that held the flask was shaking so violently that the little palmetto tree and single X that marked it described small agitated circles. He drew out his handkerchief and wrapped it up tenderly, black contents and all.

"Come," he announced, "we'll go now."

"Not so fast," I cautioned him. "You can't carry that away. It simply isn't done down here. We may have moral lapses but there are certain things that—well—can't be thought of. The graveyard is one. We let it alone."

He placed the little linen covered package tenderly in his inside pocket and buttoned his coat with an air of finality; then he faced me truculently.

"I have been searching for this flask for ten years," he asserted. "If you can find the proper person to whom payment should be made I will give a good price. In the meantime I intend to keep it. It is certainly of no use to anyone, and I shan't hesitate for a silly superstition."

I could not thrash him for it and I saw that nothing short of physical violence would remove it from his person. For a second I was tempted to argue with him; tell him why he should not take the thing. Then I was frustrated by my own lack of a reason. I groped with my instinctive knowledge that it was not to be done, trying to embody the abstract into something sufficiently concrete to impress him. And all the while I felt his gaze upon me, hard, very blue, a little mocking, absolutely determined.

Behind the low crest of the ridge sounded a single burst of laughter, and the ring of a trace chain. A strange panic seized me. Taking him by the arm I rushed him across the short distance to the buckboard and into his seat; then leaped across him and took up the lines.

Night was upon us, crowding forward from the recesses of the forest, pushing out beyond us through the last scattered trees, flowing over the sea and lifting like level smoke into the void of sky. The horse started forward, wrenching the wheels from the clutching sand.

Before us, coming suddenly up in the dusk, a party of field Negroes filled the road. A second burst of laughter sounded, warm now, volatile and disarming. It made me ashamed of my panic. The party passed the vehicle, dividing and flowing by on both sides of the road. The last vestiges of day brought out high lights on their long earth-polished hoes. Teeth were a white accent here and there. Only eyes, and fallen sockets under the brows of the very old, seemed to defy the fading glimmer, bringing the night in them from the woods. Laughter and soft Gullah words [1] were warm in the air about us.

"Howdy Boss."

"Ebenin' Boss."

The women curtsied in their high tucked-up skirts; the men touched hat brims. Several mules followed, grotesque and incredible in the thickening dark, their trace chains dangling and chiming faintly.

[1] the dialect of the sea-island negroes of South Carolina and Georgia, descendants of "Gullah" slaves of unknown African origin

The party topped the rise, then dropped behind it.

Silence, immediate and profound, as though a curtain had been run down upon the wheels of the last.

"A simple folk," clipped out my companion. "I rather envy them starting out at zero, as it were, with everything to learn from our amazing civilization."

"Zero, hell!" I flung out. "They had created a Congo art before our ancestors drugged and robbed their first Indian."

Barksdale consigned me to limbo with his mocking, intolerable smile.

The first few days at the club were spent by my guest in going through the preliminary routine of the systematic writer. Books were unpacked and arranged in the order of study, looseleaf folders were laid out, and notes made for the background of his thesis. He was working at a table in his bedroom which adjoined my own, and as I also used my sleeping apartment as a study for the fabrication of the fiction which, with my salary as manager of the club, discharged my financial obligations, I could not help seeing something of him.

On the morning of the second day I glanced in as I passed his door, and surprised him gloating over his find. It was placed on the table before him, and he was gazing fixedly at it. Unfortunately, he looked up; our glances met and, with a self-consciousness that smote us simultaneously, remained locked. Each felt that the subject had better remain closed—yet there the flask stood evident and unavoidable.

After a strained space of time I managed to step into the room, pick up a book and say casually:

"I am rather interested in Negroes myself. Do you mind if I see what you have here?"

While I examined the volume he passed behind me and put the flask away, then came and looked at the book with me. *"African Religions and Superstitions,"* he said, reading the title aloud; then supplemented:

"An interesting mythology for the American Negro, little more. The African Gullah Negro, from whom these are descended, believed in a God you know, but he only created, then turned his people adrift to be preyed upon by malign spirits conjured up by their enemies. Really a religion, or rather a superstition, of senseless terror."

"I am not so sure of the complete obsoleteness of the old rites and superstitions," I told him, feeling as I proceeded that I was engaged in a useless mission. "I know these Negroes pretty well. For them, Plat-eye, for instance, is a very actual presence. If you will notice the cook you will see that she seems to get along without a prayer book, but when she goes home after dark she sticks a sulphur match in her hair. Sulphur is a charm against Plat-eye."

"Tell me," he asked with a bantering light in his hard eyes, "just what is Plat-eye?"

I felt that I was being laughed at and floundered ahead at the subject, anxious to be out of it as soon as possible.

"Plat-eye is a spirit which takes some form which will be particularly apt to lure its victims away. It is said to lead them into danger or lose them in the woods and, stealing their wits away, leave them to die alone."

He emitted a short acid laugh.

"What amusing rot. And I almost fancy you believe it."

"Of course I don't," I retorted but I experienced the feeling that my voice was overemphatic and failed to convince.

"Well, well," he said, "I am not doing folk lore but religion. So that is out of my province. But it is amusing and I'll make a note of it. Plat-eye, did you say?"

The next day was Thursday. I remember that distinctly because, although nearly a week's wages were due, the last servant failed to arrive for work in the morning. The club employed three of them: two women and a man. Even in the off season this was a justifiable expense, for a servant could be hired on Ediwander for four dollars a week. When I went to order breakfast the kitchen was closed, and the stove cold.

After a makeshift meal I went out to find the yard boy. There were only a few Negroes in the village and these were women hoeing in the small garden patches before the cabins. There were the usual swarms of lean mongrel hounds, and a big sow lay nourishing her young in the warm dust of the road. The women looked up as I passed. Their soft voices, as they raised their heads one after another to say "Mornin' Boss," seemed like emanations from the very soil, so much a part of the earth did they appear.

But the curs were truculent that morning: strange, canny, candid little mongrels. If you want to know how you stand with a Negro, don't ask him—pat his dog.

I found Thomas, the hired boy, sitting before his cabin watching a buzzard carve half circles in the blue.

"When are you coming to work?" I demanded. "The day's half done."

"I gots de toot' ache, Boss. I can't git ober 'fore termorrer." The boy knew that I did not

believe him. He also knew that I would not take issue with him on the point. No Negro on the island will say "no" to a white man. Call it "good form" if you will, but what Thomas had said to me was merely the code for "I'm through." I did not expect him and I was not disappointed.

Noon of the following day I took the buckboard, crossed the ferry to the mainland, and returned at dark with a cheerful, wholesome Negress, loaned me by a plantation owner, who answered for her faithfulness and promised that she would cook for us during the emergency. She got us a capital supper, retired to the room adjoining the kitchen that I had prepared for her, as I did not wish her to meet the Negroes in the village, and in the morning had vanished utterly. She must have left immediately after supper, for the bed was undisturbed.

I walked straight from her empty room to Barksdale's sanctum, entered, crossed to the closet where he had put the flask, and threw the door wide. The space was empty. I spun around and met his amused gaze.

"Thought I had better put it away carefully. It is too valuable to leave about."

Our glances crossed like the slide of steel on steel. Then suddenly my impotence to master the situation arose and overwhelmed me. I did not admit it even to myself, but that moment saw what amounted to my complete surrender.

We entered upon the haphazard existence inevitable with two preoccupied men unused to caring for their own comfort; impossible makeshift meals, got when we were hungry; beds made when we were ready to get into them; with me, hours put into work that had to be torn up and started over the next day; with Barksdale, regular tours of investigation about the island and two thousand words a day, no more, no less, written out in longhand, and methodically filed. We naturally saw less and less of each other—a fact which was evidently mutually agreeable.

It was therefore a surprise to me one night in the second week to leap from sleep into a condition of lucid consciousness and find myself staring at Barksdale who had opened the door between our rooms. There he stood like a bird of ill omen, tall and slightly stooping, with his ridiculous nightshirt and thin slightly bowed shanks.

"I'll leave this open if you don't mind," he said with a new note of apology in his voice. "Haven't been sleeping very well for a week or so, and thought the draft through the house might cool the air."

Immediately I knew that there was something behind the apparently casual action of the man. He was the type who could lie through conviction; adopt some expedient point of view, convince himself that it was the truth, then assert it as a fact; but he was not an instinctive liar, and that new apologetic note gave him away. For a while after he went back to bed, I lay wondering what was behind his request.

Then for the first time I felt it; but hemmed in by the appalling limitations of human speech, how am I to make the experience plain to others!

Once I was standing behind the organ of a great cathedral when a bass chord was pressed upon the keys; suddenly the air about me was all sound and movement. The demonstration that night was like this a little, except that the place of the sound was taken by an almost audible silence, and the vibrations were so violent as to seem almost a friction against the nerve terminals. The wave of movement lasted for several minutes, then it abated slowly. But this was the strange thing about it: the agitation was not dissipated into the air; rather it seemed to settle slowly, heavily, about my body, and to move upon my skin like the multitudinous crawling of invisible and indescribably loathsome vermin.

I got up and struck a light. The familiar disorder of the room sprang into high relief, reassuring me, telling me coolly not to be a fool. I took the lamp into Barksdale's room. There he lay, his eyes wide and fixed, braced in his bed with every muscle tense. He gave me the impression of wrenching himself out of invisible bonds as he turned and sat up on the edge of his bed.

"Just about to get up and work," he said in a voice that he could not manage to make casual. "Been suffering from insomnia for a week, and it's beginning to get on my nerves."

The strange sensation had passed from my body but the thought of sleep was intolerable. We went to our desks leaving the door ajar, and wrote away the four hours that remained until daylight.

And now a question arises of which due cognizance must be taken even though it may weaken my testimony. Is a man quite sane who has been without sleep for ten days and nights? Is he a competent witness? I do not know. And yet the phenomena that followed my first startled awakening entered into me and became part of my life experience. I live them over shudderingly when my resistance is

low and memory has its way with me. I know that they transpired with that instinctive certainty which lies back of human knowledge and is immune from the skepticism of the cynic.

After the first night the house was filled with the vibrations. I closed the door to Barksdale's room, hoping a superstitious hope that I would be immune. After an hour I opened it again, glad for even his companionship. Only while I was wide awake and driving my brain to its capacity did the agitation cease. At the first drowsiness it would commence faintly, then swell up and up, fighting sleep back from the tortured brain, working under leaden eyelids upon the tired eyes.

Ten days and nights of it! Terrible for me: devastating for Barksdale. It wasted him like a jungle fever.

Once when I went near him and his head had dropped forward on his desk in the vain hope of relief, I made a discovery. He was the *center*. The moment I bent over him my nerve terminals seemed to become living antennae held out to a force that frayed and wasted them away. In my own room it was better. I went there and sat where I could still see him for what small solace there was in that.

I entreated him to go away, but with his insane obstinacy he would not hear of it. Then I thought of leaving him, confessing myself a coward—bolting for it. But again, something deeper than logic, some obscure tribal loyalty, held me bound. Two members of the same race; and out there the palmetto jungle, the village with its fires bronze against the midnight trees, the malign, beleaguering presence. No, it could not be done.

But I did slip over to the mainland and arrange to send a wire to Spencer telling him to come and get Barksdale, that the man was ill.

During that interminable ten days and nights the fundamental difference between Barksdale and myself became increasingly evident. He would go to great pains to explain the natural causes of our malady.

"Simple enough," he would say, while his bloodshot eyes, fixed on me, shouted the lie to his words. "One of those damn swamp fevers. Livingstone complained of them you will remember, and so did Stanley. Here in this subtropical belt we are evidently subject to the plague. Doubtless there is a serum. I should have inquired before coming down."

To this I said nothing, but I confess now, at risk of being branded a coward, that I had become a victim of a superstitious terror. Frequently when Barksdale was out I searched for the flask without finding the least trace of it. Finally I capitulated utterly and took to carrying a piece of sulphur next to my skin. Nothing availed.

The strange commotion in the atmosphere became more and more persistent. It crowded over from the nights into the days. It came at noon; any time that drowsiness fell upon our exhausted bodies it was there, waging a battle with it behind the closed lids. Only with the muscles tense and the eyes wide could one inhabit a static world. After the first ten days I lost count of time. There was a nightmare quality to its unbreakable continuity.

I remember only the night when I saw *her* in Barksdale's doorway, and I think that it must have been in the third week. There was a full moon, I remember, and there had been unusual excitement in the village. I have always had a passion for moonlight and I stood long on the piazza watching the great disc change from its horizon copper to gold, then cool to silver as it swung up into the immeasurable tranquillity of the southern night. At first I thought that the Negroes must be having a dance, for I could hear the syncopation of sticks on a cabin floor, and the palmettos and moss-draped live oaks that grew about the buildings could be seen the full quarter of a mile away, a ruddy bronze against the sky from a brush fire. But the longer I waited listening the less sure I became about the nature of the celebration. The rhythm became strange, complicated; and the chanting that rose and fell with the drumming rang with a new, compelling quality, and lacked entirely the abandon of dancers.

Finally I went to my room, stretched myself fully dressed on the bed, and almost achieved oblivion. Then suddenly I was up again, my fists clenched, my body taught. The agitation exceeded anything that I had before experienced. Before me, across Barksdale's room, were wide open double doors letting on the piazza. They molded the moonlight into a square shaft that plunged through the darkness of the room, cold, white, and strangely substantial among the half obliterated familiar objects. I had the feeling that it could be touched. That hands could be slid along its bright surface. It possessed itself of the place. It was the one reality in a swimming nebulous cube. Then it commenced to tremble with the vibrations of the apartment.

And now the incredible thing happened. Incredible because belief arises in each of us out of the corroboration of our own life experience; and I have met no other white man who has beheld Plat-eye. I have no word, no symbol which can awaken recognition. But who has not seen heat shaking upward from hot asphalt, shaking upward until the things beyond it wavered and quaked? That is the nearest approach in the material world. Only the thing that I witnessed was colored a cold blue, and it was heavy with the perfume of crushed jasmine flowers.

I stood, muscle locked to muscle by terror.

The center of the shaft darkened; the air bore upon me as though some external force exerted a tremendous pressure in an effort to render an abstraction concrete: to mold moving unstable elements into something that could be seen—touched.

Suddenly it was done—accomplished. I looked—I saw *her*.

The shock released me, and I got a flare from several matches struck at once. Yellow light bloomed on familiar objects. I got the fire to a lamp wick, then looked again.

The shaft of moonlight was gone. The open doors showed only a deep blue vacant square. Beyond them something moved. The lamp light steadied, grew. It warmed the room like fire. It spread over the furniture, making it real again. It fell across Barksdale's bed, dragging my gaze with it. *The bed was empty.*

I got to the piazza just as he disappeared under a wide armed live oak. The Spanish moss fell behind him like a curtain. The place was a hundred yards away. When I reached it, all trace of him had vanished.

I went back to the house, built a rousing fire, lit all the lamps, and stretched myself in a deep chair to wait until morning.

Then! an automobile horn on Ediwander Island. Imagine that! I could not place it at first. It crashed through my sleep like the trump of judgment. It called me up from the abysses into which I had fallen. It infuriated me. It reduced me to tears. Finally it tore me from unutterable bliss, and held me blinking in the high noon, with my silly lamps still burning palely about me.

"You're a hell of a fellow," called Spencer. "Think I've got nothing to do but come to this jungle in summer to nurse you and Barksdale."

He got out of a big muddy machine and strode forward laughing. "Oh, well," he said, "I won't row with you. It gave me a chance to try out the new bus. That's why I'm late. Thought I'd motor down. Had a hell of a time getting over the old ferry; but it was worth it to see the negroes when I started upon

Ediwander. Some took to trees—one even jumped overboard."

He ended on a hearty burst of laughter. Then he looked at me and broke off short. I remember how his face looked then, close to mine, white and frightened.

"My God, man!" he exclaimed, "what's wrong? You aren't going to die on me, are you?"

"Not today," I told him. "We've got to find Barksdale first."

We could not get a Negro to help us. They greeted Spencer, who had always been popular with them, warmly. They laughed their deep laughter—were just as they had always been with him. Mingo, his old paddler, promised to meet us in half an hour with a gang. They never showed up; and later, when we went to the village to find them, there was not a human being on the premises. Only a pack of curs there that followed us as closely as they dared and hung just out of boot reach, snapping at our heels.

We had to go it alone: a stretch of jungle five miles square, a large part of it accessible only with bush hooks and machetes. We dared not take the time to go to the mainland and gather a party of whites. Barksdale had been gone over twelve hours when we started and he would not last long in his emaciated condition.

The chances were desperately against us. Spencer, though physically a giant, was soft from office life. I was hanging on to consciousness only by a tremendous and deliberate effort. We took food with us, which we ate on our feet during breathing spells, and we fell in our tracks for rest when we could go no farther.

At night, when we were eating under the high, white moon, he told me more of the man for whom we were searching.

"I ought to have written you more fully at the start. You'd have been more sorry for him then, not angry with him. He does not suggest Lothario now, but he was desperately in love once.

"She was the most fantastically imaginative creature, quick as light, and she played in circles around him. He was never dull' in those days. Rather handsome, in the lean Gibson manner; but he was always—well—matter-of-fact. She had all there was of him the first day, and it was hers to do as she pleased with. Then one morning she saw quite plainly that he would bore her. She had to have someone who

could play. Barksdale could have died for her, but he could not play. Like that," and Spencer gave a snap of his fingers, "she jugged him. It was at a house party. I was there and saw it. She was the sort of surgeon who believes in amputation and she gave it to Barksdale there without an anaesthetic and with the crowd looking on.

"He changed after that. Wouldn't have anything he couldn't see, feel, smell. He had been wounded by something elusive, intangible. He was still scarred; and he hid behind the defences of his five good senses. When I met him five years later he had gone in for facts and glass."

He stopped speaking for a moment. The August dark crowded closer, pressing its low, insistent nocturne against our ears. Then he resumed in a musing voice: "Strange the obsession that an imaginative woman can exercise over an unimaginative man. It is the sort of thing that can follow a chap to the grave. Celia's living in Europe now, married—children —but I believe that if she called him today he'd go. She was very beautiful, you know."

"Yes," I replied, "I know. Very tall, blonde, with hair fluffed and shining about her head like a madonna's halo. Odd way of standing, too, with head turned to one side so that she might look at one over her shoulder. Jasmine perfume, heavy, almost druggy."

Spencer was startled: "You've seen her!"

"Yes, here. She came for Barksdale last night. I saw her as plainly as I see you."

"But she's abroad, I tell you."

I turned to Spencer with a sudden resolve: "You've heard the Negroes here talk of Plateye?"

He nodded.

"Well, I've got to tell you something whether you believe it or not. Barksdale got in wrong down here. He stole a flask from the graveyard. There's been hell turned loose ever since: fires and singing every night in the village and a lot more. I am sure now what it all meant— conjuring, and Plat-eye, of course, to lead Barksdale away and do him in, at the same time emptying the house so that it could be searched for the flask."

"But Celia; how could they know about her?"

"They didn't. But Barksdale knew. They had only to break him down and let his old obsession call her up. I probably saw her on the reflex from him, but I'll swear she was there."

Spencer was leaning toward me, the moon shining full upon his face. I could see that he believed.

"Thank God you see it," I breathed. "Now you see why we've got to find him soon."

In the hour just before dawn we emerged from the forest at the far side of the island. The moon was low and reached long fingers of pale light through the trees. The east was a swinging nebula of half light and vapor. A flight of immense blue heron broke suddenly into the air before us, hurling the mist back into our faces from their beating wings. Spencer, who was ahead of me, gave a cry and darted forward, disappearing behind a palmetto thicket.

I grasped my machete and followed.

Our quest was ended. Barksdale lay face downward in the marsh with his head toward the east. His hands flung out before him were already awash in the rising tide.

We dragged him to high ground. He was breathing faintly in spasmodic gasps, and his pulse was a tiny thread of movement under our finger tips. Two saplings and our coats gave us a makeshift litter, and three hours of stumbling, agonizing labor brought us with our burden to the forest's edge.

I waited with him there, while Spencer went for his car and some wraps.

When he returned his face was a study.

"Had a devil of a time finding blankets," he told me, as we bundled Barksdale up for the race to town. "House looks as though a tornado had passed through it; everything out on the piazza, and in the front yard."

With what strength I had left I turned toward home. Behind me lay the forest, dark even in the summer noon; before me, the farthest hill, the sparse pines, and tumble of mounds in the graveyard.

I entered the clearing and looked at the mound from which Barksdale had taken the flask. There it was again. While it had been gone the cavity had filled with water; now this had flooded out when the bottle had been replaced and still glistened gray on the sand, black on the pine needles.

I regained the road and headed for the club.

Up from the fields came the hands, dinner bound; fifteen or twenty of them; the women taking the direct sun indifferently on their bare heads. Bright field hoes gleamed on shoulders. The hot noon stirred to deep laughter, soft Gullah accents:

"Mornin' Boss—howdy Boss."

They divided and flowed past me, women curtseying, men touching hat brims. On they went; topped the ridge; dropped from view.

Silence, immediate and profound.

1927

Spencer was leaning toward me, the moon shining full upon his face. I could see that he believed.

I grasped my machete and followed.

Our quest was ended. Barksdale lay face downward in the marsh with his head toward the east. His hands flung out before him were already awash in the rising tide.

We dragged him to high ground. He was breathing faintly in spasmodic gasps, and his pulse was a tiny thread of movement under our finger tips. Two saplings and our coats gave us a makeshift litter, and three hours of stumbling, agonizing labor brought us with our burden to the forest's edge.

I regained the road and headed for the club. Up from the fields came the bands, dinner bound; fifteen or twenty of them; the women taking the direct sun indifferently on their bare heads. Bright field hoes gleamed on shoulders. The hot noon stirred to deep laughter, soft Gullah accents:

"Mornin, Boss—howdy Boss."

APPENDIX

APPENDIX

KEY TO REFERENCES AND ABBREVIATIONS USED IN THE HEADNOTES THROUGHOUT THE TEXT OF THE VOLUME

Am. Mercury	American Mercury, New York	AP	American Portraits, Gamaliel Bradford
And. Rev.	Andover Review, Boston		
Atlan.	Atlantic Monthly, Boston	AS	American Statesmen [Series]
Blackw.	Blackwood's Magazine, Edinburgh	BB	Beacon Biographies [Series]
Bookm.	Bookman, New York	CAN	Contemporary American Novelists, Carl Van Doren
Canad. M.	Canadian Magazine, Toronto		
Cath. World	Catholic World, New York		
Cent.	Century, New York	EB	Essays on Books, W. L. Phelps
Commonweal	Commonweal, New York	EN	The Advance of the English Novel, W. L. Phelps
Contemp.	Contemporary Review, London		
Craftsman	Craftsman, New York		
Critic	Critic, New York	EP	The Advance of English Poetry, W. L. Phelps
Cur. Lit.	Current Literature, New York		
Cur. Opinion	Current Opinion, New York	GW	Great Writers [Series]
Dial	Dial, New York	HKA	How to Know the Authors [Series]
Everybody's	Everybody's Magazine, New York		
Fortn.	Fortnightly Review, London		
Forum	Forum, New York	HL	Hours in a Library, Sir Leslie Stephen
Harper	Harper's Magazine, New York		
Ind.	Independent, New York	LJ	Little Journeys to the Homes of American Authors [Series]
Lit. Digest	Literary Digest, New York		
Lit. Rev.	Literary Review New York Evening Post, New York	NV	New Voices, Marguerite Wilkinson
Liv. Age	Living Age, Boston	Shel.	Shelburne Essays [Numbered in series], P. E. More
Nation	Nation, New York		
New Eng. M. ns	New England Magazine, Boston	SMN	Some Modern Novelists, Helen Follett
New Repub.	New Republic, New York		
19th Cent.	Nineteenth Century, New York		
No. Am.	North American Review, New York		

1. The headnotes under each author throughout the volume contain references to books, magazine articles, and critical essays, or chapters in books.

Outlook	Outlook, New York
Overland ns	Overland Monthly, San Francisco
Poet Lore	Poet Lore, Boston
Poetry	Poetry, Chicago
R. of Rs.	Review of Reviews, New York
Sat. R. Lit.	Saturday Review of Literature, New York
Scrib. M.	Scribner's Magazine, New York
Sewanee R.	Sewanee Review, Sewanee, Tennessee
Spect.	Spectator, London
Sunset	Sunset Magazine, San Francisco
World's Work	World's Work, New York
Yale R. ns	Yale Review, New Haven, Connecticut

2. When, in the headnotes, a single critic is mentioned, e.g., Bradford, More, not followed by the title of a book, the student may locate the criticism desired by looking under the critic's name in the list of MISCELLANEOUS CRITICAL WORKS at the beginning of the Bibliography.

3. Additional references may be found under the title GENERAL HISTORY, and also in the bibliography of the period to which the author belongs.

The following abbreviations are used to identify more quickly certain volumes or series of volumes:

AML	American Men of Letters [Series]
AN	The American Novel, Carl Van Doren

4. Many references to books and bibliographical and critical articles concerning authors will be found in the bibliographical sections of The Cambridge History of American Literature. (See page 880.)

5. Special attention is called to articles in the Encyclopaedia Britannica and the Dictionary of American Biography (first volume, 1928).

KEY TO REFERENCES AND ABBREVIATIONS USED IN
THE HEADNOTES THROUGHOUT THE TEXT
OF THE VOLUME

Am Mercury	American Mercury, New York
And Rev	Andover Review, Boston
Atlan	Atlantic Monthly, Boston
Blackw	Blackwood's Magazine, Edinburgh
Bookm	Bookman, New York
Canad. M	Canadian Magazine, Toronto
Cath. World	Catholic World, New York
Cent.	Century, New York
Commonweal	Commonweal, New York
Contemp R	Contemporary Review, London
Craftsman	Craftsman, New York
Critic	Critic, New York
Cur Lit	Current Literature, New York
Cur Opinion	Current Opinion, New York
Dial	Dial, New York
Everybody's	Everybody's Magazine, New York
Fortn	Fortnightly Review, London
Forum	Forum, New York
Harper	Harper's Magazine, New York
Ind	Independent, New York
Lit Digest	Literary Digest, New York
Lit Rev	Literary Review, New York Evening Post, New York
Liv Age	Living Age, Boston
Nation	Nation, New York
New Eng M ns	New England Magazine, Boston
New Repub	New Republic, New York
No Am	North American Review, New York
Outlook	Outlook, New York
Overland ns	Overland Monthly, San Francisco
Poet Lore	Poet Lore, Boston
Poetry	Poetry, Chicago
R of R	Review of Reviews, New York
Sat R Lit	Saturday Review of Literature, New York
Scribner M	Scribner's Magazine, New York
Sewanee R	Sewanee Review, Sewanee, Tennessee
Spect	Spectator, London
Sunset	Sunset Magazine, San Francisco
World's Work	World's Work, New York
Yale R ns	Yale Review, New Haven, Connecticut

The following abbreviations are used to identify more quickly certain volumes or series of volumes:

AML	American Men of Letters [Series]
AN	The American Novel, Carl Van Doren
AP	American Portraits, Gamaliel Bradford
AS	American Statesmen [Series]
BB	Beacon Biographies [Series]
CAN	Contemporary American Novelists, Carl Van Doren
EB	Essays on Books, W. L. Phelps
EN	The Advance of the English Novel, W. L. Phelps
EP	The Advance of English Poetry, W. L. Phelps
GW	Great Writers [Series]
HKA	Help to Know the Authors [Series]
HL	Hours in a Library, Sir Leslie Stephen
LJ	Little Journeys to the Homes of American Authors [Series]
NV	New Voices, Marguerite Wilkinson
Shel	Shelburne Essays [Numbered in series], P. E. More
SMN	Some Modern Novelists, Helen Follet

1. The headnotes under each author throughout the volume contain references to books, magazine articles, and critical essays, or chapters in books.

2. When, in the headnotes, a single critic is mentioned, e.g., Bradford, More, not followed by the title of a book, the student may locate the criticism desired by looking under the critic's name in the list of Miscellaneous Critical Works at the beginning of the Bibliography.

3. Additional references may be found under the title General History, and also in the bibliography of the period to which the author belongs.

4. Many references to books and biographical and critical articles concerning authors will be found in the bibliographical sections of The Cambridge History of American Literature. (See page 880.)

5. Special attention is called to articles in the Encyclopaedia Britannica and the Dictionary of American Biography (first volume, 1928).

BIBLIOGRAPHY

MISCELLANEOUS CRITICAL WORKS

The Encyclopaedia Britannica, 12th ed.—London and New York, 1922

The New International Cyclopaedia, 2nd ed.—New York, Dodd Mead, 1925

The Dictionary of American Biography—New York, Scribner's, (first volume 1928)

BAKER, ERNEST A. *History of the English Novel. The age of romance; from the beginnings to the Renaissance*—London, Witherby, 1924

BRADFORD, GAMALIEL *American Portraits (1875-1900)*—Boston, Houghton Mifflin, 1922

BROWNELL, WM. C. *American Prose Masters*—New York, Scribner's, 1923

BRUCE, PHILIP A. *The Rise of the New South*—Philadelphia, Barrie, 1905

    The Social Life of Virginia in the 17th Century—Richmond, Va., Whittet and Shepperson, 1907

BURTON, RICHARD *Literary Leaders of America*—New York, Chautauqua Press, 1903

CHUBB, EDWIN WATTS *Stories of Authors, British and American*—New York, Macmillan, 1926

COX, JOHN H. *Folk Songs of the South*—Cambridge, Harvard University Press, 1925

CROSS, WILBUR LUCIUS *The Development of the English Novel*—New York, Macmillan, 1899

DICKINSON, THOS. H. *Playwrights of the New American Theatre*—New York, Macmillan, 1925

EASTMAN, MAX *Enjoyment of Poetry*—New York, Scribner's, 1914

ELTON, OLIVER *Modern Studies*—London, Arnold, 1907

ERSKINE, JOHN *Leading American Novelists*—New York, Holt, 1910

GARNETT, EDWARD *Friday Nights*—London, Cape, 1922

GRISWOLD, R. W. *The Poets and Poetry of America,* 9th ed.—Philadelphia, Carey & Hart, 1848

HARKINS, EDWARD F. *Famous Authors (Women)*—Boston, Page, 1906

HAZARD, LUCY L. *The Frontier in American Literature*—New York, Crowell, 1927

HIGGINSON, THOS. W. *Short Studies of American Authors,* enlarged edition—Boston, Lee and Shepard, 1888

LOWELL, AMY *Tendencies in Modern American Poetry*—New York, Macmillan, 1917

LOWES, JOHN L. *Convention and Revolt in Poetry*—Boston, Houghton Mifflin, 1919

MACY, JOHN A. *The Spirit of American Literature*—Garden City, Doubleday Page, 1913

MITCHELL, D. G. *American Lands and Letters* (first and second series)—New York, Scribner's, 1897 and 1899

MORE, PAUL ELMER *Shelburne Essays* (eleven series)—New York, Putnam's 1904-1921

MOSES, MONTROSE J. *The American Dramatist,* 2nd rev. ed.—Boston, Little Brown, 1917

NOYES, ALFRED *Some Aspects of Modern Poetry*—New York, Stokes, 1924

OVERTON, GRANT *American Nights Entertainment*—New York, Appleton, 1923

    Cargoes for Crusoes—New York, Appleton, 1924

    When Winter Comes to Main Street—New York, Doran, 1922

    The Women Who Make Our Novels—New York, Moffat Yard, 1918

    Authors of the Day—New York, Doran, 1924

PARRINGTON, VERNON L. *Main Currents in American Thought:* Vol. 1, The Colonial Mind; Vol. 2, The Romantic Revolution in America; Vol. 3, The Beginnings of Critical Realism in America (in preparation)—New York, Harcourt Brace, 1927

PATTEE, F. L. *The Development of the American Short Story,* 1st ed.—New York, Harper, 1923

PAYNE, W. M. *Leading American Essayists*—New York, Holt, 1910

PERRY, BLISS *The American Mind*—Boston, Houghton Mifflin, 1912

    The American Spirit in Letters—New Haven, Yale University Press, 1918

    A Study of Poetry—Boston, Houghton Mifflin, 1920.

PHELPS, W. L. *The Advance of the English Novel*—New York, Dodd Mead, 1916.

    Essays on Books—New York, Macmillan, 1914.

RITTENHOUSE, JESSIE B. *The Younger American Poets*—Boston, Little Brown, 1913

SHERMAN, STUART P. *Americans*—New York, Scribner's, 1922.

    On Contemporary Literature—New York, H. Holt, 1917

    Points of View—New York, Scribner's, 1924.

STEDMAN, EDMUND C. *Poets of America*—Boston, Houghton Mifflin, 1899

STEPHEN, SIR LESLIE *Hours in a Library,* 4 vols.—New York, Putnam's, 1904

    Studies of a Biographer, 4 vols.—New York, Putnam's, 1907

TRENT, W. P. and ERSKINE, J. *Great American Writers*—New York, Holt, 1912

UNDERWOOD, JOHN CURTIS *Literature and Insurgency*—New York, Kennerley, 1914

VAN DOREN, CARL *The American Novel*—New York, Macmillan, 1921

WALLINGTON, NELLIE U. *American History by American Poets,* 2 vols.—New York, Duffield, 1911

WHARTON, EDITH *The Writing of Fiction*—New York, Scribner's, 1925

WILSON, RUFUS R. *New England in Letters*—New York, Wessels, 1904

WOLFE, THEO. F. *Literary Shrines*—Philadelphia, Lippincott, 1895

WOOD, CLEMENT *Poets of America*—New York, Dutton, 1925

WOODBERRY, GEO. E. *Makers of Literature*—New York, Macmillan, 1900

GENERAL HISTORY

The Cambridge History of American Literature, edited by W. P. Trent, John Erskine, Stuart Sherman, and Carl Van Doren, 3 vols. in four. New York, Putnam's, 1917-1921

A Short History of American Literature, (based on the above) one vol. Putnam's, 1922

ADAMS, OSCAR FAY *A Dictionary of American Authors*—Boston, Houghton Mifflin, 1905

ALLIBONE, SAMUEL A. *A Critical Dictonary of English Literature and of British and American Authors*—Philadelphia, Lippincott, 1891

CAIRNS, W. B. *A History of American Literature*—New York, Oxford University Press, 1912

DUYCKINCK, EVERT A. *Cyclopaedia of American Literature*, revis. ed. in 2 vols.—Philadelphia, Zell, 1875

RICHARDSON, CHAS. F. *American Literature, 1607-1885*—New York, Putnam's, 1889

STANTON, THEODORE *A Manual of American Literature*—New York, Putnam's, 1909

TRENT, WILLIAM P. *A History of American Literature, 1607-1865*—New York, Appleton, 1903

WENDELL, BARRETT *A Literary History of America*, 7th ed.—New York, Scribner's, 1914

WHITCOMB, SELDEN L. *Chronological Outlines of American Literature*—New York, Macmillan, 1906

BIBLIOGRAPHY OF PERIODS

THE COLONIAL AND PROVINCIAL PERIODS

ADAMS, JAMES T. *The Founding of New England*—Boston, Atlantic Monthly Press, 1921

Revolutionary New England (1691-1776)—Boston, Atlantic Monthly Press, 1923

MARBLE, ANNIE R. *Heralds of American Literature*—Chicago, University of Chicago Press, 1907

MURDOCK, KENNETH B. *Increase Mather, the Foremost American Puritan*—Cambridge, Harvard University Press, 1925

TRENT, W. P. and WELLS, B. W. *Colonial Prose and Poetry, 1607-1775*, 3 vols.—New York, Crowell, 1901

TYLER, MOSES COIT, *A History of American Literature, 1607-1765*—New York, Putnam's, 1878

The Literary History of the American Revolution—New York, Putnam's, 1897

Three Men of Letters—New York, Putnam's, 1895

WINSOR, JUSTIN *The Memorial History of Boston (1630-1680)*, including Suffolk Co., Mass., (1630-1880), 4 vols.—Boston, Osgood, 1880-81

THE NINETEENTH CENTURY

ELLSWORTH, W. W. *A Golden Age of Authors*—Boston, Houghton Mifflin Co., 1919

Helen H. Jackson, W. D. Howells, B. Harte, W. Whitman, J. Burroughs, A. Lincoln, M. Wilkins, E. A. Poe, John Hay, R. H. Dana, S. Lanier, John Muir, Mark Twain

FOERSTER, NORMAN *Nature in American Literature*—New York, Macmillan, 1923

HOWELLS, W. D. *Literary Friends and Acquaintance*—New York, Harper, 1921

HUBBARD, ELBERT *Little Journeys to the Homes of American Authors*, 6th ed.—New York, Putnam's, 1896

PATTEE, FRED L. *A History of American Literature Since 1870*—New York, Century, 1915

QUINN, A. H. *A History of the American Drama from the Civil War to the Present*, 2 vols.—New York, Harper, 1927

RUSK, R. L. *The Literature of the Middle Western Frontier*, 2 vols.—New York, Columbia University, 1925

THE EARLY TWENTIETH CENTURY

BOYNTON, PERCY H. *Some Contemporary Americans*—Chicago, University of Chicago Press, 1924

COOPER, FRED. T. *Some American Story Tellers*—New York, Holt, 1911

FOLLETT, HELEN T. and FOLLETT, WILSON. *Some Modern Novelists*—New York, Holt, 1918

FOLLETT, WILSON *The Modern Novel*—New York, Knopf, 1918

LEISY, ERNEST E. *American Literature: An Interpretative Survey*—New York, Crowell, 1929

MANLY, J. M. and RICKERT, EDITH *Contemporary American Literature*—New York, Harcourt, Brace, 1922.

PHELPS, W. L. *The Advance of the English Novel*—New York, Dodd, Mead, 1916

The Advance of English Poetry in the Twentieth Century—New York, Dodd, Mead, 1919

Lindsay, Frost, Robinson, Lowell, Masters, Untermeyer, Teasdale, Widdemer, Sandburg, Neihardt, Bynner, Seeger, S. V. Benét, W. R. Benét

ROBERTS, CARL E. B. *The Literary Renaissance in America*—London, Heinemann, 1923

UNTERMEYER, LOUIS *American Poetry Since 1900*—New York, Holt, 1923

The New Era in American Poetry—New York, Holt, 1919.

Modern American Poetry—New York, Harcourt revised edition, 1925

VAN DOREN, CARL and VAN DOREN, MARK *American and British Literature Since 1890*—New York, Century, 1925

Contemporary American Novelists, 1900-1920—New York, Macmillan, 1922.
Many Minds—New York, Knopf, 1924
Frost, Sherman, Millay, Mencken, Sandburg, Lindsay
WEIRICK, BRUCE *From Whitman to Sandburg in American Poetry*—New York, Macmillan, 1924
WILKINSON, MARGUERITE *New Voices; an Introduction to Contemporary Poetry*—New York, Macmillan, 1919
Contemporary Poetry—New York, Macmillan, 1924

BIOGRAPHICAL SERIES

American Men of Letters Ed. by Charles Dudley Warner—Boston, Houghton Mifflin Co.

G. Ripley	(Frothingham, O. B.)
W. H. Prescott	(Ogden, Rollo)
Nath. P. Willis	(Beers, Henry A.)
Wm. C. Bryant	(Bigelow, John)
John G. Whittier	(Carpenter, G. R.)
G. W. Curtis	(Cary, Edward)
H. W. Longfellow	(Higginson, T. W.)
M. Fuller Ossoli	(Higginson, T. W.)
R. W. Emerson	(Holmes, O. W.)
H. D. Thoreau	(Sanborn, F. B.)
Noah Webster	(Scudder, H. E.)
Francis Parkman	(Sedgwick, H. D.
Bayard Taylor	(Smyth, Albert H.)
Wm. G. Simms	(Trent, W. P.)
W. Irving	(Warner, C. D.)
E. A. Poe	(Woodberry, G. E.)
N. Hawthorne	(Woodberry, G. E.)
J. F. Cooper	(Lounsbury, T. R.)
B. Franklin	(McMaster, J. B.)

American Statesmen Ed. by John T. Morse, Jr.—Boston, Houghton Mifflin Co.

Calhoun	(H. E. Von Holt)
Webster	(H. C. Lodge)
Washington	(H. C. Lodge)
Lincoln	(J. T. Morse, Jr.)
Franklin	(J. T. Morse, Jr.)
Jefferson	(J. T. Morse, Jr.)
Sumner	(M. Storey)
Henry	(M. C. Tyler)

English Men of Letters Ed. by John Morley—New York, The Macmillan Co.

Whitman	(G. R. Carpenter)
Whitman	(John Bailey)
Emerson	(G. E. Woodberry)
Melville	(John Freeman)
Bryant	(W. A. Bradley)
Whittier	(T. W. Higginson)
Prescott	(H. T. Peck)
Poe	(E. Shanks)

Great Writers Ed. by E. S. Robertson—London, W. Scott. Contains biographies of :

Whittier	(W. J. Linton)

Hawthorne	(M. D. Conway)
Emerson	(R. Garnett)
Longfellow	(E. S. Robertson)
Thoreau	(H. S. Salt)

How to Know the Authors Series Ed. by Will D. Howe—Indianapolis, Bobbs, Merrill Co.

Emerson	(Crothers, S.)
Poe	(Smith, C.)
Whitman	(Whitlock, B.)
Hawthorne	(Woodberry, G.)

Little Journeys to Homes of American Authors, 6th ed. Ed. by Elbert Hubbard—New York, Putnam's

Emerson	(G. W. Curtis)
Bryant	(C. H. Kirkland)
Prescott	(G. S. Hilliard)
Lowell	(C. F. Briggs)
Whitman	(E. Hubbard)
Hawthorne	(G. W. Curtis)
Irving	(H. T. Tuckerman)
Longfellow	(G. W. Curtis)
Everett	(G. S. Hilliard)
Bancroft	(G. W. Greene)
Simms	(W. C. Bryant)

National Studies in American Letters Ed. by George E. Woodberry—The Macmillan Co.

Old Cambridge	(T. W. Higginson)
Brook Farm	(L. Swift)
The Hoosiers	(M. Nicholson)
The Clergy in American Life and Letters	(D. D. Addison)

ANTHOLOGIES

ALDEN, RAYMOND MACDONALD *Poems of the English Race*—New York, Scribner's, 1921
BOYNTON, PERCY HOLMES *American Poetry*—New York, Scribner's, 1921
BRONSON, WALTER COCHRANE *American Poems (1625-1892)*—Chicago, University of Chicago Press, 1912
BROWN, SHARON *Poetry of Our Times*—Chicago, Scott, Foresman & Co., 1928
COOKE, GEORGE W. *The Poets of Transcendentalism*—Boston, Houghton Mifflin, 1903
FOERSTER, NORMAN *American Poetry and Prose (1607-1916)*—Boston, Houghton Mifflin, 1925
MONROE, HARRIET and HENDERSON, ALICE *The New Poetry*—New York, Macmillan, 1923
LE GALLIENNE, RICHARD *The Le Gallienne Book of American Verse*—New York, Boni & Liveright, 1925
LOUNSBURY, THOS. R. *The Yale Book of American Verse*—New Haven, Yale University Press, 1912
PAGE, CURTIS HIDDEN *The Chief American Poets*—Boston, Houghton Mifflin, 1905
STEDMAN, EDMUND C. *An American Anthology (1787-1900)*—Boston, Houghton Mifflin, 1900
STEVENSON, BURTON E. *The Home Book of Verse (1580-1920)*—New York, Holt, fifth ed., 1923

The Home Book of Modern Verse—New York, Holt, 1925
    Poems of American History—Boston, Houghton Mifflin, 1908

IMPORTANT PERIODICALS

Atlantic Monthly, Boston
Bookman, New York
Century, New York

Forum, New York
Harper's Magazine, New York
Independent, New York
Literary Digest, New York
New Republic, New York
Nineteenth Century, New York
North American Review, New York
Poetry, Chicago
Saturday Review of Literature, New York
Scribner's Magazine, New York
Yale Review ns, New Haven

CHRONOLOGY

CHRONOLOGY

CHRONOLOGY

From American literature, the works noted are chiefly those represented by selections in the book, and from English literature those especially interesting in relation to American writings. The dates are those of publication, unless otherwise noted. In the case of American poems especially, the titles of the works in which they appeared are usually given rather than the titles of the selections themselves.

AMERICAN	ENGLISH

1601-1610

	1602 Shakespeare: *Hamlet; Twelfth Night* (acted)
	1603 Jonson; *Sejanus*
	1603 Elizabeth died; James I
	1605 Bacon: *Advancement of Learning*
1607 Jamestown founded	
1608 J. Smith: *A True Relation*	
	1610 Beaumont and Fletcher: *Knight of the Burning Pestle*
	1610 Shakespeare: *Macbeth* (acted)

1611-1620

	1611 Shakespeare: *Winter's Tale* (acted)
	1611 Bible, Authorized Version, printed
	1612 Bacon: *Essays* (first edition, 1597)
	1614 Raleigh: *History of the World*
	1616 Shakespeare died
1620 Plymouth Colony founded	1620 Bacon: *Novum Organum*

1621-1630

	1623 Shakespeare: *Plays* (first folio edition)
1624 J. Smith: *The General History of Virginia*	1624 Webster: *Duchess of Malfi*
1625 Strachey: *A True Reportory of the Wrack*	1625 Purchas: *Hakluyt's Posthumus, or Purchas His Pilgrimes*
	1625 Charles I
	1627 Drayton: *Battle of Agincourt*
1630 Massachusetts Bay Colony founded	1630 Quarles: *Divine Poems*
1630 Bradford: *History of Plimoth Plantation* begun about this time	
1630 Winthrop: *Journal* begun, ended 1649	

1631-1640

	1633 Massinger: *New Way to Pay Old Debts*
	1634 Crashaw: *Epigrammata Sacra*
	1634 Milton: *Comus* (acted)
1636 Harvard College established	
1636 Providence founded	
1637 Anne Hutchinson banished	
1638 New Haven founded	1638 Trial of John Hampden
	1638 Milton: *Lycidas*
1639 Printing press established, Cambridge, Massachusetts	1639 Webster: *Appius and Virginia*
1640 *The Bay Psalm Book* [The first book printed in British North America]	

AMERICAN	ENGLISH

1641-1650

	1642 Browne: *Religio Medici*
1644 Williams: *The Bloudy Tenent*	1644 Milton: *Areopagitica*
[Liberal Puritanism]	1644 Battle of Marston Moor
	1645 Waller: *Poems*
1647 N. Ward: *The Simple Cobler*	1647 Taylor: *Liberty of Prophesying*
[Crabbed Puritanism]	1648 Herrick: *Hesperides*
	1649 Charles I executed; The Commonwealth
1650 A. Bradstreet: *Poems*	1650 Baxter: *The Saints' Everlasting Rest*

1651-1660

	1651 Taylor: *Holy Dying*
	1653 Walton: *The Complete Angler*
	1656 Davenant: *The Siege of Rhodes*
	1660 The monarchy restored; Charles II
	1660 Pepys: *Diary* begun, ended 1669
	1660 Dryden: *Astrea Redux*

1661-1670

1662 Wigglesworth: *The Day of Doom*	
[The most popular poem of the time; retained its vogue for a century]	
	1663 Butler: *Hudibras*, Pt. I
	1663 Dryden: *The Wild Gallant*
	1666 London Fire
	1667 Milton: *Paradise Lost*
	1667 Dryden: *Annus Mirabilis*

1671-1680

	1671 Milton: *Paradise Regained*
	1671 Milton: *Samson Agonistes*
	1672 Dryden: *Conquest of Granada*
1673 Sewall: *Diary* begun, ended 1729	
	1674 Milton died
1676 King Philip's War, New England, Indian Wars in Virginia: English supremacy in the colonies confirmed	
1676 Tompson: *New-Englands Crisis*	
[First book of poems published in the English colonies]	1678 Bunyan: *The Pilgrim's Progess*

1681-1690

1681 C. Mather: *Diary* begun	1681 Dryden: *Absalom and Achitophel*
1682 Philadelphia founded	1682 Dryden: *MacFlecknoe*
The New England Primer probably first published in this decade	1682 Otway: *Venice Preserved*
	1685 James II
	1687 Newton: *Principia*
	1688 The English Revolution; William and Mary
1689 King William's War	
	1690 Locke: *Essay Concerning the Human Understanding*

AMERICAN   **ENGLISH**

1691-1700

1692 Salem witchcraft trials

1697 Congreve: *The Mourning Bride*
1697 Dryden: *Alexander's Feast*
1698 Collier: *Short View of the Immorality and Prophaneness of the Stage*
1700 Congreve: *The Way of the World*

1701-1710

1701 Yale College established
1702-13 Queen Anne's War
1702 C. Mather: *Magnalia Christi Americana*
1704 *Boston News Letter* established
[First newspaper in America (weekly)]
1704-05 S. Knight: *Journal* (written)

1701 Defoe: *The True-Born Englishman*
1702-13 The War of the Spanish Succession

1704 Swift: *Tale of a Tub*
1704 Clarendon: *History of the Great Rebellion*

1709 Pope: *Pastorals*
1709 Steele and Addison: *The Tatler* begun

1711-1720

1711 Steele and Addison: *The Spectator* begun
1712 Pope: *The Rape of the Lock*
1713 Addison: *Cato*
1714 George I
1715 Gay: *Poems*
1715 Pope: *Translation of the Iliad*

1716 Church: *King Philip's War*

1718 Prior: *Poems*
1719 Defoe: *Robinson Crusoe*

1721-1730

1721 Ramsay: *Poems*
1722 Defoe: *Journal of the Plague Year*
1725 Pope: *Edition of Shakespeare*
1726 Swift: *Gulliver's Travels*
1726 Thomson: *Winter*
1727 George II

1722 Edwards: *Diary* begun

1728 Byrd: *History of the Dividing Line* (written)

1728 Gay: *Beggar's Opera*
1728 Pope: *Dunciad*

1731-1740

1732 Byrd: *Progress to the Mines* (written)
1733 Franklin: *Poor Richard's Almanac* (begun)

1732 Pope: *Essay on Man*

1737 Shenstone: *The Schoolmistress*
1738 Johnson: *London*
1740 Richardson: *Pamela*

1741-1750

1741 Edwards: *Sinners in the Hands of an Angry God*

1741 Hume: *Essays, Moral and Political*
1742 Fielding: *Joseph Andrews*
1742 Young: *Night Thoughts*
1743 Blair: *The Grave*
1744 Pope dies

AMERICAN

ENGLISH

1745 Swift dies
1747 Gray: *Ode on Eton College*
1748 Richardson: *Clarissa Harlowe*
1749 Fielding: *Tom Jones*
    [The beginning of the modern English novel]
1750 Johnson: *The Rambler* (begun)

1751-1760

1751 Gray: *Elegy . . Country Churchyard*
1753 Smollett: *Ferdinand, Count Fathom*
1753 Hume: *Essays and Treatises*
1755 Johnson: *English Dictionary*

1756 Woolman: *Journal* (begun)
1758 Franklin: *The Way to Wealth* in *Poor Richard's Almanac*

1759 Sterne: *Tristram Shandy*
1759 Johnson: *Rasselas*
1760 George III

1761-1770

1762 Macpherson: *The Poems of Ossian*

1763 End of the French and Indian War
    [British domain in America extended]

1764 Walpole: *The Castle of Otranto*
    [Gothic novel]
1765 Godfrey: *Juvenile Poems* (with the *Prince   1765 Percy: *Reliques of Ancient Poetry*
    of Parthia*, the first American drama)
1765 The Stamp Act   1765 Watt's steam engine begins the industrial revo-
                                                         lution
                                                    1766 Goldsmith: *The Vicar of Wakefield*
                                                    1768 Sterne: *Sentimental Journey*
                                                    1770 Goldsmith: *The Deserted Village*

1771-1780

1771 Franklin: *Autobiography*, first part, written   1771 *Encyclopaedia Britannica*, first edition
    [The first American book of wide European
    circulation]
1772 Trumbull: *Progress of Dulness*, part I
1773 P. Wheatley: *Poems*   1773 Goldsmith: *She Stoops to Conquer*
                                                    1774 Chesterfield: *Letters to his Son*
1775 Trumbull: *M'Fingal*   1775 Burke: *Speech on Conciliation*
1775 Henry: *Speech* in the Virginia Convention   1775 Sheridan: *The Rivals*
1775 The fight at Lexington and Concord   [Comedy of manners]
1776 The Declaration of Independence   1776 Gibbon: *History of the Decline and Fall of
1776 Paine: *Common Sense*   the Roman Empire*
1778 F. Hopkinson: *Battle of the Kegs*

                                                    1779 Johnson: *Lives of the Poets*
1780 Franklin: *Dialogue between Franklin and the
    Gout*

1781-1790

1783 The Treaty of Paris   1783 Crabbe: *The Village*
                                                    1784 Beckford: *Vathek*

AMERICAN

1785 Dwight: *The Conquest of Canaan*
1786 Freneau: *Poems*
1788 Dwight: *The Triumph of Infidelity*
1789 Franklin: *Autobiography*, second part, written.
1789 The Constitution established

1791-1800

1792 Whitney invents the cotton gin

1796 Barlow: *Hasty Pudding*
1796 Washington: *Farewell Address*
1798 Brown: *Wieland*
1798 J. Hopkinson: *Hail Columbia*

1801-1810

1801 Jefferson: *Inaugural Address*
1803 Louisiana purchased

1806 Franklin: *Works*

1809 Irving: *Knickerbocker's History of New York*

1811-1820

1812-1814 War with England
1814 Key: *Star-Spangled Banner*

1815 Freneau: *Poems*
1815 Wilde: *My Life is like the Summer Rose*

1817 Bryant: *Thanatopsis*
1819 Irving: *Sketch Book*
1819 Drake: *The American Flag*

1821-1830

1821 Bryant: *Poems*

1822 Irving: *Bracebridge Hall*
1823 Payne: *Home, Sweet Home*
1823 Cooper: *The Pilot*

ENGLISH

1785 Cowper: *The Task*
1786 Burns: *Poems*

1789 French Revolution
1789 Blake: *Songs of Innocence*

1790 Burke: *Thoughts on the Revolution in France*

1791 Boswell: *Life of Dr. Johnson*

1793 Godwin: *Inquiry concerning Political Justice*
1794 Radcliffe: *Mysteries of Udolpho*
1795 Lewis: *The Monk*

1798 Wordsworth and Coleridge: *Lyrical Ballads* [First important publication of the Romantic school]

1804 Napoleon Emperor
1805 Scott: *Lay of the Last Minstrel*

1808 Scott: *Marmion*
1809 Byron: *English Bards and Scotch Reviewers*
1809 Edgeworth: *Tales of Fashionable Life*
1810 Scott: *Lady of the Lake*

1811 Austen: *Sense and Sensibility*
1812 Byron: *Childe Harold*, I, II
1814 Scott: *Waverley* [Romantic fiction established]
1814 Wordsworth: *Excursion*
1815 Battle of Waterloo

1816 Coleridge: *Christabel*
1817 Moore: *Lalla Rookh*
1819 Byron: *Don Juan*, I, II

1820 Keats: *Poems*
1820 Shelley: *Prometheus Unbound*
1820 George IV

1821 De Quincey: *Confessions of an Opium Eater*
1821 Scott: *Kenilworth*
1821 Shelley: *Adonais*

1824 Lamb: *Essays of Elia*

AMERICAN

1825 Pinckney: *Rodolph and Other Poems*
1825 Erie Canal, unites the Great Lakes and the Atlantic
1826 Woodworth: *Old Oaken Bucket*
1827 Cooper: *The Prairie*
1827 Simms: *Lyrical and Other Poems*
1827 R. H. Dana: *Poems*
1827 Drake: *Alnwick Castle and Other Poems*
1829 Jefferson: *Correspondence and Miscellaneous*
1829 First steam railway in the United States

ENGLISH

1824 Landor: *Imaginary Conversations*
1825 Macaulay: *Essay on Milton*

1827 A. and C. Tennyson: *Poems by Two Brothers*

1830 Tennyson: *Poems Chiefly Lyrical*
1830 William IV

1831-1840

1831 Poe: *Poems*
1832 Irving: *The Alhambra*
1832 S. Smith: *America*

1834 McCormick's reaper
1834 Bancroft: *History of the United States*, Vol. I
1835 Drake: *The Culprit Fay and Other Poems*
1835 Simms: *The Yemassee*
1835 Willis: *Pencilings by the Way*
1836 Holmes: *Poems*
1836 Franklin: *Works*, Sparks ed.
1837 Hawthorne: *Twice-Told Tales*
1837 Whittier: *Poems*
1839 Poe: *Tales of the Grotesque and Arabesque*
1839 Longfellow: *Voices of the Night*
1839 Very: *Essays and Poems*
1840 R. H. Dana, Jr.: *Two Years Before the Mast*
1840 Furness: *Manual of Domestic Worship*

1832 Scott died; end of the romantic era
1833 Carlyle: *Sartor Resartus*
1833 Tennyson: *Poems*
1834 Bulwer-Lytton; *Last Days of Pompeii*

1835 Browning: *Paracelsus*

1836 Dickens: *Pickwick Papers*
1836 Marryat: *Mr. Midshipman Easy*
1837 Carlyle: *French Revolution*
1837 Queen Victoria

1840 Dickens: *Old Curiosity Shop*

1841-1850

1841 Cooper: *Deerslayer*
1841 Emerson: *Essays*, first series
1841 Longfellow: *Ballads and Other Poems*

1843 Willis: *Poems of Passion*
1843 Prescott: *Conquest of Mexico*
1844 Emerson: *Essays*, second series
1844 Lowell: *Poems*
1845 Sumner: *The True Grandeur of Nations*
1845 Poe: *The Raven and Other Poems*
1846 Hawthorne: *Mosses from an Old Manse*
1846-1848 The War with Mexico
1846 Taylor: *Views Afoot*
1846 Melville: *Typee*
1847 Emerson: *Poems*
1847 Longfellow: *Evangeline*
1847 O'Hara: *Bivouac of the Dead*
1848 Lowell: *Biglow Papers*, I
1848 Lowell: *Vision of Sir Launfal*
1848 Lowell: *A Fable for Critics*

1841 Carlyle: *Heroes and Hero-Worship*

1842 Browning: *Dramatic Lyrics*
1843 Macaulay: *Essays*
1843 Ruskin: *Modern Painters*, I
1844 E. B. Browning: *Poems*

1846 Dickens: *Dombey and Son*

1847 Tennyson: *The Princess*
1847 Thackeray: *Vanity Fair*
1847 C. Brontë: *Jane Eyre*
1848 Macaulay: *History of England*, I, II

AMERICAN

1849 G. Ticknor: *History of Spanish Literature*
1850 Whittier: *Songs of Labor*
1850 Longfellow: *The Seaside and the Fireside*
1850 Hawthorne: *The Scarlet Letter*

1851-1860

1851 Hawthorne: *The House of the Seven Gables*
1851 Parkman: *The Conspiracy of Pontiac*
1851 Taylor: *Romances, Lyrics and Songs*

1853 Calhoun: *Works*
1853 Thoreau: *Walden*

1855 Whitman: *Leaves of Grass*
1855 Longfellow: *Hiawatha*
1856 Story: *Poems*
1856 Stoddard: *Songs of Summer*
1856 Motley: *The Rise of the Dutch Republic*
1856 Curtis: *Prue and I*
1858 Holmes: *The Autocrat of the Breakfast Table*

1859 Everett: *Orations and Speeches*

1861-1870

1861 Holmes: *Songs in Many Keys*
1861-1865 The Civil War
1862-1866 Lowell: *Biglow Papers, II*
1862 Choate: *Works*
1863 Bryant: *Thirty Poems*
1863 Longfellow: *Tales of a Wayside Inn*
1863 Thompson: *Music in Camp*
1864 Boker: *Poems of the War*

1865 M. Preston: *Beechenbrook*
1865 Whitman: *Drum Taps*
1866 Read: *Poems*
1866 Whittier: *Snow-Bound*
1866 J. Howe: *Later Lyrics*
1867 Longfellow: *Divina Commedia* (translated)
1867 Parsons: *Inferno* (translated)
1868 Whittier: *Among the Hills*
1868 Hale: *The Man Without a Country and Other Tales*
1868 Harte: *The Luck of Roaring Camp*
1869 Transcontinental railroad joins Atlantic and Pacific

1871-1880

1871 Miller: *Songs of the Sierras*
1871 Lowell: *My Study Windows*

ENGLISH

1849 Thackeray: *Pendennis*
1850 Tennyson: *In Memoriam*

1851 E. B. Browning: *Casa Guidi Windows*

1852 Thackeray: *Henry Esmond*
1852 Wallace: *Travels on the Amazon*

1854 Thackeray: *The Newcomes*
1855 R. Browning: *Men and Women*
1855 Tennyson: *Maud*
1856 E. B. Browning: *Aurora Leigh*

1858 Carlyle: *History of Friedrich The Great*, I, II
1859 Darwin: *The Origin of Species*
1859 G. Eliot (M. Evans): *Adam Bede*
1860 Morris: *Poems*

1861 Reade: *The Cloister and the Hearth*

1863 G. Eliot (M. Evans): *Romola*

1864 R. Browning: *Dramatis Personæ*
1864 Newman: *Apologia pro Vita Sua*
1864 Swinburne: *Atalanta in Calydon*
1864 Tennyson: *Enoch Arden*

1866 Ruskin: *A Crown of Wild Olive*

1867 Arnold: *The Study of Celtic Literature*

1868 R. Browning: *The Ring and the Book*

1869 Arnold: *Culture and Anarchy*

1870 D. G. Rossetti: *Poems*

1871 Swinburne: *Songs before Sunrise*
1871 Tennyson: *The Last Tournament*

AMERICAN

1872 Hayne: *Legends and Lyrics*
1873 Timrod: *Poems*
1873 Pike: *Poems*

1875 Hope: *Elegiac Ode and Other Poems*

1876 Mark Twain: *Tom Sawyer*
1876 Bell's telephone
1877 James: *The American*
1877 Lanier: *Poems*
1879 F. Ticknor: *Poems*
1879 Stockton: *Rudder Grange*
1879 Burroughs: *Locusts and Wild Honey*
1880 Ryan: *Poems*

1881 Whittier: *The King's Missive*

1883 Harris: *Nights with Uncle Remus*
1883 Mark Twain: *Life on the Mississippi*
1884 Mark Twain: *Huckleberry Finn*
1884 Burroughs: *Fresh Fields*

1886 H. Jackson: *Sonnets and Lyrics*

1887 M. Wilkins: *A Humble Romance*
1887 L. Reese: *A Branch of May*
1888 A. Repplier: *Books and Men*
1889-1896 Roosevelt: *The Winning of the West*

1890 Hay: *Poems*
1890 E. Dickinson: *Poems*, first series
1890-1898 Garland: *Main Traveled Roads*

1891 Wilkins: *A New England Nun*
1891 Whitman: *Goodbye, My Fancy*

1893 Wilson: *Mere Literature*
1894 Field: *Songs of Childhood*
1894 Muir: *The Mountains of California*
1894-1896-1900 Carman and Hovey: *Songs from
　　　Vagabondia*
1895 van Dyke: *Little Rivers*
1895 Crane: *The Red Badge of Courage*
1896 Wister: *Red Men and White*
1897 Robinson: *The Children of the Night*
1898 Dunne: *Mr. Dooley in Peace and War*

ENGLISH

1873 Arnold: *Literature and Dogma*

1874 Green: *A Short History of the English People*
1875 R. Browning: *Aristophanes' Apology*
1875 Meredith: *Beauchamp's Career*
1876 Morris: *Sigurd the Volsung*
1876 Spencer: *Principles of Sociology*
1877 Tennyson: *Harold*

1879 Arnold: *Mixed Essays*
1879 R. Browning: *Dramatic Idyls*

1881-1890

1881 Rossetti: *Ballads and Sonnets*
1882 Swinburne: *Tristram of Lyonesse*
1883 Stevenson: *Treasure Island*

1885 Meredith: *Diana of the Crossways*
1886 Stevenson: *Kidnapped*
1886 Tennyson: *Locksley Hall Sixty Years After*
1887 Kipling: *Plain Tales from the Hills*

1889 Barrie: *A Window in Thrums*
1889 Pater: *Appreciations*
1889 Browning dies

1891-1900

1892 Hardy: *Tess of the D'Urbervilles*
1892 Tennyson: *The Death of Oenone*
1892 Tennyson died
1892 The Celtic revival in Ireland gains force

1894 Yeats: *The Land of Heart's Desire*
1894 Kipling: *The Jungle Book*

1895 Conrad: *Aylmer's Folly*

1896 Housman: *A Shropshire Lad*

1898 Wilde: *Ballad of Reading Gaol*

AMERICAN   ENGLISH

1898 Dunne: *Mr. Dooley in the Hearts of his
     Countrymen*
1899 van Dyke: *Fisherman's Luck*
1899 Markham: *The Man with the Hoe*

                                1900 Conrad: *Lord Jim*

1901-1910

1901 Moody: *Poems*
1902 James: *The Wings of a Dove*
1902 Wister: *The Virginian*
1902 Wilson: *A History of the American People*
1903 Wright Brothers airplane
1904 James: *The Golden Bowl*
1904 Moving pictures established
1904 Moody: *The Fire-Bringer*

1907 E. Wharton: *The House of Mirth*
1907 Wilson: *Constitutional Government*
1909 L. Reese: *A Wayside Lute*
1909 Peary reaches the North Pole
1910 Roosevelt: *African Game Trails*
1910 Dunne: *Mr. Dooley Says*
1910 The automobile in general use

1901 Kipling: *Kim*
1902 Masefield: *Salt-Water Ballads*

1903 Conrad: *Typhoon*
1904 Hardy: *The Dynasts*, I
1904 Barrie: *Peter Pan*

1905 Synge: *Riders to the Sea*
1906 Noyes: *Drake*

1909 Wells: *Tono Bungay*

1910 Galsworthy: *Justice*

1911-1920

1911 Sterling: *The House of Orchids*

1912, 1917 E. Millay: *Renascence*
1913 Lindsay: *General Booth Enters into Heaven*
1913 W. Cather: *O Pioneers*
1914 The World War begins
1914 Frost: *North of Boston*
1914 W. Benét: *The Falconer of God*
1914 A. Lowell: *Sword Blades and Poppy Seeds*
1915 Bynner: *The New World*
1915 Markham: *The Shoes of Happiness*
1915 Masters: *Spoon River Anthology*
1915 Teasdale: *Rivers to the Sea*
1916 Sandburg: *Chicago Poems*
1916 Robinson: *The Man Against the Sky*
1916 Frost: *Mountain Interval*
1917 Garland: *A Son of the Middle Border*
1917 A. Lowell: *Men, Women, and Ghosts*
1917 The United States enters the World War
1918 Beebe: *Jungle Peace*

1919 The Atlantic crossed by air
1919 Neihardt: *The Song of Three Friends*
1920 Sandburg: *Smoke and Steel*
1920 S. Teasdale: *Flame and Shadow*
1920 Morley: *Mince Pie*
1920 Eugene O'Neill: *Beyond the Horizon*

1911 Masefield: *The Everlasting Mercy*
1911 Noyes: *Robin Hood*

1912 de la Mare: *Collected Poems*
1913 Masefield: *Dauber*
1913 Bridges: *Poetical Works*
1914 "A.E.": *Collected Poems*

1915 Brooke: *Poems*

1916 Davies: *Collected Poems*
1916 Lawrence: *Amores*

1917 Hodgson: *New Poems*

1918 Drinkwater: *Abraham Lincoln*
1918 Stephens: *Reincarnations*
1918 Sassoon: *Counter-Attack*
1919 Masefield: *Reynard the Fox*

AMERICAN

ENGLISH

1921-1930

1921 Fletcher: *Breakers and Granite*
1922 E. Wharton: *Glimpses of the Moon*
1922 Morley: *Where the Blue Begins*
1923 Frost: *New Hampshire*
1924 Masters: *New Spoon River Anthology*
1924 Heyward: *Skylines and Horizons*
1925 Neihardt: *The Song of the Indian Wars*
1925 Beebe: *The Arcturus Adventure*
1926 S. Teasdale: *Dark of the Moon*
1927 Robinson: *Tristram*
1927 Beebe: *Pheasant Jungles*
1927 W. Cather: *Death Comes for the Archbishop*
1928 S. Benét, *John Brown's Body*
1928 The Pacific crossed by air
1929 Frost: *West-Flowing Brook*

1921 Chesterton: *The Uses of Diversity*
1922 "A.E." Russell: *The Interpreters*
1922 Galsworthy: *Loyalties*
1923 Stephen: *Deirdre*
1924 Galsworthy: *Old English*

1925 Drinkwater: *The Pilgrim of Eternity*

1926 Wells: *The World of William Clissold*
1927 Masefield: *The Midnight Folk*

1928 V. Woolf: *Orlando*

INDEX

INDEX TO AUTHORS, TITLES, AND FIRST LINES

5 6 7 8 9 10 11 12 13 14 15 16 17 18 19 20 21 22 23 24 25   55 54 53 52 51 50 49 48 47